BOOKS FOR COLLEGE LIBRARIES

BOOKS
FOR COLLEGE
LIBRARIES

A CORE COLLECTION OF 50,000 TITLES

Third edition

A project of the Association of College and Research Libraries

Volume 3
History

American Library Association
Chicago and London 1988

Preliminary pages composed by Impressions, Inc.,
    in Times Roman on a Penta-driven
    Autologic APS-μ5
    Phototypesetting system

Text pages composed by Logidec, Inc., in Times Roman on an
    APS-5 digital typesetter

Printed on 50 lb. Glatfelter B-16, a pH neutral stock,
    and bound in Roxite B-grade cloth by
    Edwards Brothers.

The paper used in this publication meets the minimum
requirements of American National Standard for Information
Sciences—Permanence of Paper for Printed Library Materials,
ANSI Z39.48-1984.

∞

Library of Congress Cataloging-in-Publication Data

Books for college libraries.

"A project of the Association of College and Research
Libraries."

Contents: v. 1. Humanities—v. 2. Language
and literature—v. 3. History—[etc.]
    1. Libraries, University and college—Book
lists. 2. Bibliography—Best books. I. Association of
College and Research Libraries.
Z1039.C65B67 1988   025.2′1877   88-16714
ISBN 0-8389-3357-2 (v. 1)
ISBN 0-8389-3356-4 (v. 2)
ISBN 0-8389-3355-6 (v. 3)
ISBN 0-8389-3354-8 (v. 4)
ISBN 0-8389-3358-0 (v. 5)
ISBN 0-8389-3359-9 (v. 6)

BOOKS FOR COLLEGE LIBRARIES

Volumes 1–6 Contents

Volume 3   Contents

Introduction

BOOKS FOR COLLEGE LIBRARIES (BCL3) presents a third recommended core collection for undergraduate libraries in full awareness of the tensions and paradoxes implicit in such list making. There is the pull between ideals of excellence and sufficient coverage of all subjects. There is the balance to be weighed among subjects. There are the rival temptations to identify the basic with the time tested and to equate the important with the new. There is the risk of ranking with the obsolete the merely temporary victims of scholarly fashion. There is the certainty that new definitive works will be published just as the selection closes.

That BCL3 exists supposes some resolution of these problems. A final paradox remains: BCL3 can fully succeed only by failing. It would be disastrous should the collection it suggests serve perfectly to ratify the finished work of the book selection in any library. Some inclusions and some omissions should displease everyone; for on-going professional questioning and the search for individual library answers remain as basic to collection development as basic book lists.

In overall plan and appearance, BCL3 is much the same as BCL2 (1975). The division into five volumes takes the same liberties with Library of Congress classification to provide coherent subject groups and volumes similar in size. Individual entries contain the same elements of full cataloging and classification information; and within volumes, entries are arranged in exact call number order.

BCL3 also exists as a database to allow further development of formats alternative to print. An electronic tape version will be made available. Since BCL2, online catalogs and reference databases have become familiar library tools. The provision of BCL3 in searchable form is thus important; and it may add possible uses of the list within larger libraries—easy identification of key titles in very large online catalogs, for instance.

HISTORY

The first bibliography to bear this title was published in 1967 as a replacement for Charles B. Shaw's *List of Books for College Libraries* (1931). The origin of BCL1 was in the University of California's New Campuses Program (1961–1964), which also made use of other compilations such as the published catalog of Harvard's Lamont Library (1953) and the shelflist of the undergraduate library of the University of Mich-

igan. The 1963 cut-off date for BCL1 titles deliberately coincided with the 1964 beginning of *Choice*, whose current reviews for academic libraries were foreseen as a complementary, on-going revision and supplement. Such a role proved impossible, however, even for so comprehensive a journal as *Choice* with its 6,600 reviews a year and its retrospective evaluation of perhaps another 1,000 titles in topical monthly bibliographic essays. Periodic reassessments that could include categories of material not usually reviewed by *Choice* (revisions, fiction, works published abroad, for instance) seemed still an essential aid in college library collection development. BCL2 appeared in 1975; work on BCL3 began in late 1985.

SIZE AND SCOPE: STANDARDS, LIBRARIES AND BOOK LISTS

The number of books of which college libraries need potentially to be aware continues its relentless growth. In the years from the Shaw list to BCL1, total annual United States book output averaged slightly more than 11,500 volumes. Between the cut-off dates for BCL1 and BCL2, that figure (revised to show titles, a lesser number) was just under 32,000. Since the 1973 BCL2 cut-off, the annual average has been 41,000.[1] Given such increase, the task of book selectors would be challenging enough, even had the growth of buildings and book budgets characteristic of the late 1960s and early 1970s continued. By the time BCL2 was published, however, the rate of academic library book acquisitions had begun to fall. This downward trend continues, and it makes careful title selection ever more vital, especially for the small library.[2]

When BCL1 was published, the already outdated 1959 standards for college libraries called for a minimum undergraduate collection of only 50,000 titles; BCL1 recommended 53,400. BCL2 and the 1975 revision of those standards appeared in the same year. The new standards set out a formula whose add-on stipulations plus a starting figure of 85,000 raised basic requirements for even very small institutions to 100,000. The 1970 proposal for BCL2 called for a list of 40,000 titles. The thinking behind this lower figure may be explained by a published study of 1977 library

[1]*Bowker Annual of Library & Book Trade Information.* New York: Bowker. 26th ed., 1981; 32nd ed., 1987.
[2]"Three Years of Change in College and University Libraries, Prepared by the National Center for Education Statistics, Washington, D.C." *College & Research Libraries News* 45 (July/August 1984): 359–361.

statistics against the 1975 standards. This analysis found that 52 percent of all undergraduate libraries still reported fewer than 100,000 volumes and that 55 percent of private undergraduate libraries held even fewer than the "starter" figure of 85,000.[3] A very brief basic list might thus serve rather than intimidate the many libraries still far below standard.

The college library standards were revised again in 1985, just as work on BCL3 began.[4] The same formula (Standard 2.2, Formula A) was recommended. Applying it to a very small hypothetical college of 100 faculty and 1,000 students pursuing majors in only 10 fields of study yields a basic book requirement of 104,000 volumes. BCL3 suggests about half that number, hoping again to pause somewhere between usefulness and utopia. Very recent figures show that the average book expenditures for academic libraries in 26 U.S. states fall below the figure that would be necessary to meet the median annual growth rate of our hypothetical library, also set by the 1985 standards.[5]

In scope, the focus of BCL3 remains the traditionally book-using disciplines. Contributors were asked to keep in mind an imaginary college or small university that concentrates on the customary liberal arts and sciences curriculum but also offers work at the undergraduate level in business, computer science, engineering, and the health sciences. The proportions of the broad subject groupings by volume have remained roughly constant through the three BCL editions. (See Table 1.) There have been steady decreases in the humanities and literature allocations, however, very slightly offset by increased use of single-entry "complete works" citations that include large numbers of titles.

These changes have come about despite editorial quotas candidly designed to minimize them. Sharp

[3]Ray L. Carpenter, "College Libraries: A Comparative Analysis in Terms of the ACRL Standards," *College and Research Libraries* 42 (January 1981): 7–18.

[4]"Standards for College Libraries, 1986, Prepared by the College Library Standards Committee, Jacquelyn M. Morris, chair," *College & Research Libraries News* 47 (March 1986): 189–200.

[5]*Bowker Annual of Library & Book Trade Information.* 32nd ed. New York: Bowker, 1987. The preceding calculation by the BCL editor is based on figures given in the *Bowker Annual* using the formula in the standards cited in note 4.

difficulties confront both BCL editors and librarians juggling hopes for lasting value, necessities for current coverage, and the certainties of obsolescence. Some of the growth in Volume 5 is attributable to a marked increase in its bibliography component, which serves all subjects; but it may be well to repeat, with reference both to Volume 4 and to Volume 5, a statement from my BCL2 introduction that "Perhaps only those works already sufficiently outdated to be ranked as history may safely be included in a 'basic' collection." Despite their increases, both volumes remain brief in comparison with the volume of publication.

As to those titles constituting the rest of the minimal 104,000 requirement but not named in BCL3, much of any collection must respond uniquely to the demands of individual and current curricula. But some, it is to be hoped, will continue to consist of those works, especially belles lettres, not subject to cumulation and replacement by current scholarship. These are often difficult to continue to justify in lists which though "basic" cannot remain immune to shifts in academic enthusiasms.

Across these proportionate subject representations, the focus remains the undergraduate user of the undergraduate library. Both are protean concepts, but they permit some limitation, for instance almost wholly to works in English except for dictionaries and editions chosen to support foreign-language study. With the exception of some of the more basic surveys among "annual reviews" and some serial reference works, the limitation is not only to print but, further, to monographs. There is a need for college-level model collections of periodicals and of nonprint material, but this project does not address it. Still further to define the print universe, BCL3 contributors were asked not to recommend classroom texts unless exceptional, especially for their bibliographies. Volumes of previously published works are seldom listed except for literary anthologies which, together with their indexes, received special consideration in this edition. In-print availability was not considered an important factor.

CONTRIBUTORS AND WORKING MATERIALS

BCL3 was from the beginning designed as a two-stage selection process and there were two distinct sets

Table 1. Distribution of Titles by Volume. (In percentages.)

Volumes & Subjects	BCL1	BCL2	BCL3
v. 1 (Humanities)	16.4	15.1	13.6
v. 2 (Language & Literature)	32.2	30.0	28.4
v. 3 (History)	18.7	19.7	18.8
v. 4 (Social Sciences)	20.8	21.2	22.2
v. 5 (Psychology, Science, Technology, Bibliography)	11.9	14.0	17.0

of contributors. The first-round team numbered more than 400 college faculty members and about 50 academic reference librarians who made the reference selections. The second group consisted of 64 academic librarian referees, picked for their combination of subject specialization and collection development skills. The librarian referees were asked to review broader subject areas than their faculty counterparts with the intent of adding a wider perspective to help assure the overall coverage and balance to the collection.

Virtually all of the first-round contributors and about half of the second-round referees are *Choice* reviewers. They were selected for excellence, needed subject coverage, altruism (all served unpaid), and availability at the crucial time. (A few sabbaticals were much regretted in the BCL office.) Contributors were not selected with statistical games in mind, but it is an interesting if incidental function of the nature of the *Choice* reviewer pool that they prove a nationally representative lot. They come from 265 institutions in 44 states. The 10 states with the most academic institutions provide 8 of the 10 largest contributor groups. Institutions are divided between public, including federal (145) and private (120), with a mix of small and large from each sector. There are 10 representatives of 2-year campuses. There are 134 women. There are 15 Canadian and 2 British contributors.

As working materials, the round-one contributors received pages from BCL2 (latest titles 1973) and selected *Choice* review cards (1972 through 1985). Approximately 60,000 of some 85,000 reviews published in those years were distributed. Contributors were asked to assign one of four rankings to each title; they were also urged to recommend any other titles they felt essential to undergraduate work in their fields. Many did so. Assignments, some of which overlapped, ranged from 25 to 600 titles.

Preparation of 450 packets of working lists involved the fascinating task of reconciling various assumptions about the organization of knowledge. It was necessary to "deconstruct" and rearrange the LC-classed BCL2 and the subject organization of *Choice* to match the convictions of academics as to just what constituted the definitions and boundaries of their subjects.

COMPILATION AND REVIEW

Working list packets came back displaying varying neatness, erudition, zeal, and attention to editorial instructions and deadlines. A very few were reassigned; most were extremely well done and miraculously on time. All titles rated "essential" (and some lesser ratings, depending on subject coverage and the rigor of contributor selectivity) were requested, by LC card number if possible, from the Utlas database. (Utlas, the Canadian bibliographic utility, had previously been

selected as the vendor to house the BCL3 database while the collection was being compiled.)

As lists came in and major blocks of LC classification were judged to be reasonably complete, Utlas was asked to produce provisional catalogs in LC class order, showing complete catalog records. These catalogs, after review by the editor, were divided among the second-round referees, whose assignments typically included the work of several first-round contributors. Referees were asked to assess overall quality and suitability of the selections, coverage of the various aspects of a field, and compliance with numerical quotas. The editor's review included the making and insertion of page headings and further observations of (and occasional interventions in) rival views of knowledge as the academic visions of round one were once more refracted through the prism, the worldview of LC classification. A second set of provisional catalogs, reviewed by the editor's assistant, incorporated referee suggestions and the page headings for a final check before typesetting.

PRESENTATION: HEADINGS, ENTRIES, AND ARRANGEMENT

Page headings are phrased to outline LC classification, to gloss the sometimes very miscellaneous contents of the sections they head, and to indicate the method of arrangement of some special sequences. The printed BCL3 entries contain conventionally complete cataloging and classification information, but not every element of a full LC MARC record. Among notes, only the general (MARC tag 500) are printed; cross-reference and authority information tagged in the 800s is omitted. Those entries for items retained from BCL2 in exactly the same version carry a special symbol, a heavy dot (.) preceding the item number. Entries are sequentially numbered within each volume. The cataloging in some of the entries made by contributors to the Utlas database is less full than the original LC cataloging; some entries vary in other ways.

Database response to titles requested for the collection displayed significant changes since the compilation of BCL2. During that project, both LC MARC and electronic cataloging and bibliographic utilities were new. Nearly two-thirds of BCL2 entries had to be converted especially for that project. BCL3 is in some ways the victim of the success of such cataloging enterprises. There are now many versions of catalog records, especially for pre-1968 titles. These offer varying degrees of adoption of AACR2 and equally various and often unsignalled states of adherence to LC classification, to say nothing of the range of simple cataloging and typing skills. It is therefore impossible to repeat here the certainties of the BCL2 Introduction about the use of LC cataloging and classification, although preference was certainly for LC records. Call numbers completed or assigned by BCL are identified with "x" as the final character, but there are numbers not so flagged that are not LC assignments. BCL3 is designed as a book selection guide, however, not as an exemplar of either cataloging or classification.

Arrangement has been stated to be by LC call number; but some catalog records carry more than one number, some sections of LC classification are being redeveloped, and some allow alternate treatments. BCL3's editor, therefore, had decisions to make. In all volumes, the existence of new LC sequences is signposted with cross-references. Individual subject classification of titles published in series was preferred to numerical gatherings within series. For Volume 2, alternate national literature numbers were selected or created in preference to PZ3 and PZ4 for fiction. Works by and about individual Canadian, Caribbean, African, South Asian, and Australasian authors writing in English have been pulled from the PR4000–6076 sequence and united with the general historical and critical material on those literatures in the PR9000s. Volume 5 displays the decision to keep most subject bibliography in class Z.

INDEXES

The computer-made Author Index lists personal and institutional names of writers, editors, compilers, translators, sponsoring bodies, and others identified in the numbered "tracings" that bear roman numerals at the ends of entries. The Title Index, also machine generated, lists both uniform and title page titles from the printed entries, including nondistinctive titles and adding variant titles if traced. Because of the use of many "complete works" entries, many famous and highly recommended titles, especially novels, are absent from this index though present by implication in the list. References in the Author and Title indexes are to the sequential numbers, within volume, assigned to each entry. The Subject Index is a handmade guide to classification. It has its own brief explanatory introduction.

LACUNAE, ERRORS AND REVISIONS

The virtual absence of serials and the exclusion of formats other than print have been noted under Size and Scope. Additionally, although undergraduate study ranges ever wider, student information needs outside fairly "academic" disciplines and some traditional sporting activities are not fulfilled here; users are referred to college bookstores and recommended lists for public libraries for titles in many craft, technical, and recreational subjects.

Errors of cataloging and questionable classifications will, as it has been stated, be noted. They are present in the database used and though many were corrected, others as surely remain. Reports of errors, expressions of opinion about favorite titles missing and abhorrences present, and general suggestions for future revisions are sincerely sought. They may be addressed to: Editor, Books for College Libraries, c/o *Choice*, 100 Riverview Center, Middletown, CT 06457–3467.

With the breakup of BCL1 into the individual volumes of BCL2, separate revision in an on-going project was predicted. That did not happen, and it would offer some difficulties in indexing and the handling of subjects split among volumes. It is a challenge to assemble the mix of organization to command the seemingly more and more specialized contributors required, the technology to facilitate presentation, and the finance to enable the whole. But it is to be hoped that the even greater challenges college libraries face in collection development will continue to find *Choice* and its reviewers, ACRL, and ALA ready with the help future circumstances require.

VIRGINIA CLARK, *Editor*

Acknowledgments

Without the contributors and referees of the many subject lists, BCL3 would not exist. They are named in the appropriate volumes and identified by academic or other professional institution and by subject field. To enable the calling together of this team, however, and the presentation of its work took vision, planning, determination, and much help from many groups and individuals.

Both the users and the editorial staff of BCL3 owe thanks to the staff and two successive Executive Directors of the Association of College and Research Libraries (ACRL). Julie Virgo and JoAn S. Segal convened a preliminary investigative committee and commissioned a request for proposal (RFP) that established the first outline of the project for the revised edition. Patricia Sabosik, newly appointed Editor and Publisher of *Choice*, encompassed in her initial plans for the magazine the BCL project. Her response to ACRL's RFP involved the *Choice* staff in the editorial work and the Canadian bibliographic utility Utlas in the technical construction of the database. The staffs of *Choice* and BCL3 are grateful to ACRL for accepting this proposal and to Publishing Services of the American Library Association for co-funding the project with ACRL. Patricia Sabosik served as Project Manager. Liaison with ALA Books was Managing Editor Helen Cline.

An editorial advisory committee, chaired by Richard D. Johnson, SUNY College at Oneonta, was selected to allow the BCL3 Editor to draw advice from representatives of academic libraries of different types, sizes, and locales. Stephen L. Gerhardt, Cerritos College; Michael Haeuser, Gustavus Adolphus College; Barbara M. Hirsh, formerly Marist College; Thomas Kirk, Berea College; Craig S. Likness, Trinity University; and Mary K. Sellen, Spring Valley College, served the project well. Special thanks are due Richard D. Johnson and Craig S. Likness, each of whom also contributed subject lists, and Michael Haeuser, who spent several days as a volunteer in the BCL office and served as committee secretary.

The BCL project was housed in space in the *Choice* office and enjoyed a unique member/guest relationship that involved virtually every member of the *Choice* staff in some work for BCL. The subject editors—Robert Balay, Claire C. Dudley, Ronald H. Epp, Francine Graf, Helen MacLam, and Kenneth McLintock—suggested from their reviewer lists most of the BCL contributors and several referees. Claire C. Dudley and Helen MacLam served as referees; Claire C. Dudley

and Francine Graf gave much other valuable help. Library Technical Assistant Nancy Sbona, Systems Manager Lisa Gross, Office Assistant Mary Brooks, and Administrative Assistant Lucille Calarco deserve special mention for extraordinary assistance.

In addition to using the bibliographic and personnel resources of *Choice*, the Editor of BCL relied for vital support on the collections, equipment, and staffs of five very gracious institutions. Particular thanks go to the libraries of Kenyon College, Wesleyan University, and the Library Association, London, for use of behind-the-scenes cataloging and classification tools in addition to reference sources publicly available; to Trinity University, San Antonio, for tapes of BCL2; and to Trinity College, Hartford, for outstanding help from George R. Graf on preliminary aspects of the project in addition to those for which he is named in the contributor lists.

For work without regard for office hours or job description the Editor would particularly like to thank Judith Douville. She edited the science sections of Volume 5 in addition to assisting the Editor with some parts of Volume 4. She coordinated the corrections to the BCL3 computer file and reviewed the final page proofs. Her enthusiasm and dedication were vital in bringing the project to completion.

BCL3 secretary Anna Barron worked throughout the project. Special thanks are also owed to short-term staff members Alison Johnson and Virginia Carrington.

CONTRIBUTORS

Title selection for BCL3 reflects three types of expert opinion: from scholars teaching in the field, from reference librarians, and from special referees chosen for their combination of subject and collection-development knowledge. Names appear in the approximate order of contributions in the volume, but Library of Congress classification will have scattered many titles selected by those named here into other sections of the list. The topical labels try to suggest both the depth of specialization required of some contributors and the broad knowledge and responsibility demanded of others; but no list such as this can do more than hint at the nature and amount of work for which these contributors are most gratefully thanked. The History consultants, in addition to the sections of this volume, participated also in selecting the titles listed under Economic and Social History and under Politics in Volume 4.

HISTORY: *General*: Richard Harvey, Ohio University; Douglas R. Skopp, SUNY College at Plattsburgh.

ARCHAEOLOGY: C. C. Lamberg-Karlovsky, Harvard University.

EUROPE: *Classical Antiquity*: Stanley Mayer Burstein, California State University, Los Angeles; Richard I. Frank, University of California, Irvine. *Medieval & Modern Europe*: Reed Browning, Kenyon College, and Edward J. Kealey, College of the Holy Cross (England); Charles L. Hamilton, Simon Fraser University (Scotland); R. Islwyn Pritchard, Cardiff (Wales); John W. Auld, California State University, Dominguez Hills (Ireland); Paul P. Bernard, University of Illinois at Urbana-Champaign (Central Europe); Robert O. Lindsay, University of Montana, and Barry Rothaus, University of Northern Colorado (France); Robert E. Neil, Oberlin College (Germany); Theodore Natsoulas, University of Toledo (Greece); Marion S. Miller, University of Illinois at Chicago (Italy); Gerlof D. Homan, Illinois State University (Netherlands); Sherman D. Spector, Russell Sage College (Soviet Union, Balkan Europe); Paul W. Knoll, University of Southern California (Poland); Kenneth Smemo, Moorhead State University (Scandinavia); Richard L. Kagan, Johns Hopkins University (Spain); Onesimo T. Almeida, Brown University (Portugal); Maria Otero-Boisvert, University of Nevada–Reno (Basques); Robert L. Baker, Kenyon College (Middle Ages). *Reference & Referees*: Carol A. Becker, U.S. Department of State; Thomas Izbicki, Wichita State University; Dennis Lambert, Johns Hopkins University; W. Daviess Menefee, Jr., Ohio State University; William S. Moran, Dartmouth College; Susanne Roberts, Yale University; James H. Spohrer, University of California, Berkeley; Marcella Stark, Syracuse University; Mariann E. Tiblin, University of Minnesota; Mark R. Yerburgh, Trinity College, Vt.

ASIA: L. Michael Lewis, Eastern Kentucky University (Arab Middle East); Steven Bowman, University of Cincinnati (Judaica); George L. Montagno, Mount Union College (South Asia); Helen R. Chauncey, Georgetown University (Southeast Asia); Edward H. Kaplan, Western Washington University (China); Mikiso Hane, Knox College (Japan); John H. Boyle, California State University, Chico (Korea). *Reference & Referees*: Lee S. Dutton, Northern Illinois University; M. Keith Ewing, St. Cloud State University; Hide Ikehara, Eastern Michigan University; David Kranzler, Queensborough Community College, CUNY; Om P. Sharma, University of Michigan; Dona S. Straley, Ohio State University; Karen Wei, University of Illinois at Urbana-Champaign.

AFRICA: Norman R. Bennett, Boston University; Leslie C. Duly, Bemidji State University; Phyllis Martin, Indiana University; Richard Pankhurst, Addis Ababa University. *Reference & Referee*: David L. Easterbrook, University of Illinois at Chicago.

AUSTRALASIA: Leslie C. Duly, Bemidji State University; Charles J. Weeks, Southern College of Technology. *Reference & Referee*: Murray S. Martin, Tufts University.

UNITED STATES: *By Period*: James H. O'Donnell III, Marietta College; Phyllis F. Field, Ohio University; James L. Jablonowski, Marquette University. *By Region*: Thomas F. Armstrong, Georgia College (South); Philip Brown, South Dakota State University (Middle West); G. Thomas Edwards, Whitman College (West). *Special Fields*: Milton Cantor, University of Massachusetts at Amherst (Social History); Shari T. Grove, Boston College (Indians of North America); Lorraine M. Lees, Old Dominion University (European Ethnic Groups); Barbara Roberts, formerly University of Connecticut (Diplomatic History); Paul D. Starr, Auburn University (Asian Ethnic Groups); John C. Walter, Smith College (Afro-American Studies); Jeffery C. Wanser, Hiram College (Archaeology, Indians of North America); Cary D. Wintz, Texas Southern University (Hispanic Ethnic Groups). *Reference & Referees*: John D. Haskell, Jr., College of William and Mary; Helen MacLam, *Choice Magazine* (Afro-American Studies).

CANADA: P. B. Waite, Dalhousie University. *Reference*: Liana Van der Bellen, National Library of Canada.

LATIN AMERICA: Mark A. Burkholder, University of Missouri–St. Louis; Keith A. Dixon, California State University, Long Beach (Archaeology; Indians of Southwestern North America and Latin America); C. E. Frazier, Jr., Sam Houston State University. *Reference*: Nadine George, Kenyon College. Referee: Ann Hartness, University of Texas at Austin.

SPECIAL FIELDS OF HISTORY: *Military & Naval*: Edward K. Eckert, St. Bonaventure University; Bertram H. Groene, Southeastern Louisiana University; Alan Gropman, National War College; Robert H. Larson, Lycoming College. *Reference & Referee*: Myron H. Smith, Jr., Salem College. *Women's History*: Naomi Rosenthal, SUNY College at Old Westbury; M. Jane Slaughter, University of New Mexico. *Reference & Referee*: see Women's Studies, v. 4.

CB HISTORY OF CIVILIZATION AND CULTURE

Columbia College (Columbia University)   • 3.1
Introduction to contemporary civilization in the West; a source book prepared by the Contemporary civilization staff of Columbia College, Columbia University. 3d ed. New York Columbia University Press 1960-61. v.; 24 cm. 1. Civilization — History — Sources I. T. II. Title: Contemporary civilization in the West
CB5 C574 1965   LC 60-16650

Mumford, Lewis, 1895-.   • 3.2
The human prospect. Edited by Harry T. Moore and Karl W. Deutsch. Boston, Beacon Press [1955] 319 p. 21 cm. (Beacon paperbacks, 13) 'Essays and other writings ... from ... [the author's] books and previously uncollected magazine articles.' 1. Civilization, Modern I. T.
CB7.M8   LC 55-10921

CB15–19 Historiography. Philosophy. Theory

Perry, Marvin.   3.3
Arnold Toynbee and the crisis of the West / Marvin Perry. — Washington, D.C.: University Press of America, c1982. xiii, 138 p.; 23 cm. Includes index. 1. Toynbee, Arnold Joseph, 1889-1975. 2. Civilization, Occidental 3. History — Philosophy 4. Historians — Great Britain — Biography. I. T.
CB18.T65 P47 1982   907/.2024 19   LC 81-40162   ISBN 0819120251

Abell, Walter.   • 3.4
Collective dream in art; a psycho–historical theory of culture based on relations between the arts, psychology, and the social sciences. Cambridge, Harvard U.P., 1957. 378 p., 39 p. of plates. ill. 25 cm. 1. Civilization — Philosophy 2. Civilization — History 3. Art — Psychology I. T.
CB19.A25   901   LC 57-9067

Adams, Robert Martin, 1915-.   3.5
Decadent societies / Robert M. Adams. — San Francisco: North Point Press, 1983. 196 p.; 21 cm. 1. Civilization — Philosophy 2. Civilization — History I. T.
CB19.A35 1983   901 19   LC 82-73710   ISBN 0865471037

Brown, Norman Oliver, 1913-.   3.6
Life against death: the psychoanalytical meaning of history / by Norman O. Brown. — 2nd ed. / with an introduction by Christopher Lasch. — Middletown, Conn.: Wesleyan University Press; Scranton, Pa.: Distributed by Harper & Row, 1985, c1959. xx, 366 p.; 23 cm. Includes index. 1. Civilization — Philosophy 2. Civilization — Psychological aspects. 3. Psychohistory 4. Psychoanalysis 5. Death instinct I. T.
CB19.B69 1985   150.19/52 19   LC 85-17928   ISBN 0819551481

Condorcet, Jean-Antoine-Nicolas de Caritat, marquis de,   3.7
1743-1794.
[Esquisse d'un tableau historique des progrès de l'esprit humain. English] Sketch for a historical picture of the progress of the human mind / Antoine–Nicolas de Condorcet; translated by June Barraclough; with an introd. by Stuart Hampshire. — Westport, Conn.: Hyperion Press, 1979, c1955. xvi, 202 p.; 22 cm. Translation of Esquisse d'un tableau historique des progrès de L'esprit humain. Reprint of the ed. published by Noonday Press, New York, in series: Library of Ideas. 1. Civilization — Philosophy 2. Civilization — History 3. Progress I. T. II. Title: The progress of the human mind.
CB19.C5613 1979b   190/.9   LC 78-20458   ISBN 0883558386

Eliot, T. S. (Thomas Stearns), 1888-1965.   • 3.8
Notes towards the definition of culture. [1st American ed.] New York, Harcourt, Brace [1949] 128 p. 22 cm. 1. Culture I. T.
CB19.E48 1949   901   LC 49-1605 *

Kroeber, A. L. (Alfred Louis), 1876-1960.   • 3.9
An anthropologist looks at history. With a foreword by Milton Singer. Edited by Theodora Kroeber. Berkeley, University of California Press, 1963. xix, 213 p. 20 cm. 1. Civilization — History — Addresses, essays, lectures. I. T.
CB19.K686 1963   901.9   LC 63-16250

Kroeber, A. L. (Alfred Louis), 1876-1960.   • 3.10
Style and civilizations. — Ithaca, N.Y.: Cornell University Press [1957] 191 p. 1. Civilization — Philosophy I. T.
CB19.K687   901   LC 57-4434

Kroeber, A. L. (Alfred Louis), 1876-1960.   • 3.11
Culture; a critical review of concepts and definitions, by A. L. Kroeber and Clyde Kluckhohn, with the assistance of Wayne Untereiner and appendices by Alfred G. Meyer. Cambridge, Mass., The Museum, 1952. viii, 223 p. 27 cm. (Papers of the Peabody Museum of American Archæology and Ethnology, Harvard University, v. 47, no. 1) 1. Culture. 2. Civilization. I. Kluckhohn, Clyde, 1905- joint author.
CB19.K7x   901   LC a 53-9890

Nef, John Ulric, 1899-.   • 3.12
A search for civilization. — Chicago, H. Regnery Co., 1962. 210 p. 21 cm. 1. Civilization — Philosophy I. T.
CB19.N42   901.9   LC 62-10716

Northrop, F. S. C. (Filmer Stuart Cuckow), 1893- ed.   • 3.13
Ideological differences and world order; studies in the philosophy and science of the world's cultures. Edited by F. S. C. Northrop. Westport, Conn., Greenwood Press [1971, c1949] xi, 486 p. 23 cm. 1. Civilization — Philosophy I. T.
CB19.N59 1971   901.9/4   LC 74-136078   ISBN 0837152283

Northrop, F. S. C. (Filmer Stuart Cuckow), 1893-.   • 3.14
The meeting of East and West, an inquiry concerning world understanding, by F. S. C. Northrop. — New York: The Macmillan company, 1946. xxii p., 1 l., 531 p.: col. front., xvi pl. (incl. plan) on 8 l., diagrs.; 22 cm. 1. Civilization — Philosophy I. T.
CB19.N6   901   LC 46-4813

Rougemont, Denis de, 1906-.   • 3.15
Man's Western quest: the principles of civilization / by Denis de Rougemont; translated from the French by Montgomery Belgion. — 1st ed. — New York: Harper, 1957. xxiv, 197 p. — (World perspectives,; v. 13) Translation of L'aventure occidentale de l'homme. 1. Civilization — Philosophy 2. Civilization, Occidental I. T.
CB19 R653   CB19 R673.   LC 57-6127

Schweitzer, Albert, 1875-1965.   • 3.16
The philosophy of civilization / Albert Schweitzer; translated by C.T. Campion. — New York: Macmillan, 1951. xvii, 347 p. — (Macmillan paperbacks; 12) 1. Civilization — Philosophy I. T.
CB19 S423   CB19 S3983 1960.

Spengler, Oswald, 1880-1936.   • 3.17
Man and technics; a contribution to a philosophy of life; translated from the German by Charles Francis Atkinson. New York, Knopf, 1932. 104 p. 21 cm. 1. Man 2. Civilization — History 3. Technology I. Atkinson, Charles Francis, 1880- tr. II. T.
CB19.S63   901   LC 32-5140

Toynbee, Arnold Joseph, 1889-1975.   • 3.18
Comparing notes: a dialogue across a generation [by] Arnold and Philip Toynbee. — London, Weidenfeld and Nicolson [1963] 155 p. 23 cm. 'Conversations between Arnold Toynbee and his son, Philip ... as they were recorded on tape.' I. Toynbee, Philip. II. T.
CB19.T62   192   LC 64-5454

White, Leslie A., 1900-1975.   • 3.19
The science of culture; a study of man and civilization, by Leslie A. White. — [2d ed.]. — New York: Farrar, Straus and Giroux, [1969] xl, 444 p.; 21 cm. 1. Culture 2. Civilization I. T.
CB19.W48 1969   301.2   LC 75-7130

Wilson, Colin, 1931-.   • 3.20
The outsider. — Boston: Houghton Mifflin, 1956. 288 p.; 22 cm. 1. Civilization — Philosophy I. T.
CB19.W53 1956a   901   LC 56-11983

Wilson, Colin, 1931-. • 3.21
Religion and the rebel. Boston, Houghton Mifflin, 1957. x, 338 p. 21 cm.
Bibliographical references included in 'Notes' (p. [323]-329) 1. Civilization —
Philosophy 2. Religious thought — 20th century I. T.
CB19.W533   901   *LC* 57-14602

CB51–113 General Works, 1801– , by Nationality

CB51–59 American, to 1973

Barnes, Harry Elmer, 1889-1968. • 3.22
An intellectual and cultural history of the Western World, by Harry Elmer
Barnes [and others]. — 3d rev. ed. — New York, Dover Publications [1965] 3 v.
(xii, 1381 p.) illus. 22 cm. Includes bibliographies. 1. Civilization — Hist.
2. Civilization, Occidental I. T.
CB53.B36 1965   914   *LC* 63-21675

Kroeber, Alfred Louis, 1876-. • 3.23
Configurations of culture growth. Berkeley Los Angeles, University of
California press, 1944. x, 882 p. illus. (map) diagrs. 24 cm. 1. Civilization —
History 2. Culture 3. Sociology I. T.
CB53.K7   *LC* a 45-694

Lovejoy, Arthur O. (Arthur Oncken), 1873-1962. • 3.24
Primitivism and related ideas in antiquity, by Arthur O. Lovejoy [and] George
Boas. With supplementary essays by W. F. Albright and P.–E. Dumont. —
New York, Octagon Books, 1965 [c1935] xv, 482 p. 25 cm. — (Contributions to
the history of primitivism) First published in 1935 as v. 1 of A documentary
history of primitivism and related ideas, edited by A. O. Lovejoy.
Bibliographical footnotes. 1. Primitivism 2. Progress 3. Civilization I. Boas,
George, 1891- joint author. II. T. III. Series.
CB53.L58 1965   901.901   *LC* 65-25872

Mumford, Lewis, 1895-. • 3.25
The condition of man [by] Lewis Mumford. — New York, Harcourt, Brace and
company [1944] x, 467 p. plates. 24 1/2 cm. 'First edition.' Bibliography: p.
425-447. 1. Civilization — Hist. I. T.
CB53.M8   901   *LC* 44-5038

Mumford, Lewis, 1895-. • 3.26
The transformations of man. [1st ed.] New York, Harper, [1956] 249 p. 20 cm.
(World perspectives, v. 7) 1. Civilization — History 2. Man I. T.
CB53.M82   *LC* 56-6030

Whitehead, Alfred North, 1861-1947. • 3.27
Adventures of ideas, by Alfred North Whitehead. — New York: The
Macmillan company, 1933. xii, 392 p.; 22 cm. 'The three books—science and
the modern world. Process and reality, Adventure of ideas— ... supplement
each other's omissions or compressions.'—Pref. 1. Civilization — History
2. Sociology — History 3. Cosmology — History. 4. Philosophy — History
5. History — Philosophy 6. Ideology I. T.
CB53.W5   901   *LC* 33-5611

Muller, Herbert Joseph, 1905-. • 3.28
The uses of the past; profiles of former societies. — New York: Oxford
University Press, 1952. xi, 394 p.; 22 cm. 1. Civilization — History I. T.
CB57.M9   901   *LC* 52-6168

Bowle, John. • 3.29
Man through the ages. [1st ed.] Boston, Little, Brown [1963, c1962-] v. illus. 24
cm. 1. Civilization — History I. T.
CB59.B63   *LC* 62-17032

Kroeber, Alfred Louis, 1876-1960. • 3.30
A roster of civilizations and culture / by A. L. Kroeber. — Chicago: Aldine
Pub. Co., 1962. 96 p.; 26 cm. — (Viking fund publications in anthropology; no.
33) 1. Civilization — History — Outlines, syllabi, etc. I. T. II. Series.
CB59.K7   *LC* 62-14933

McNeill, William Hardy, 1917-. • 3.31
The rise of the West; a history of the human community. Drawings by Béla
Petheö. — Chicago: University of Chicago Press, [1963] xvi, 828 p.: ill.
1. Civilization — History 2. Civilization, Occidental I. T.
CB59.M3   901.9   *LC* 63-13067

Parkinson, C. Northcote (Cyril Northcote), 1909-. • 3.32
East and West. Boston, Houghton Mifflin, 1963. xxii, 330 p. maps. 22 cm.
1. Civilization — History I. T.
CB59.P28   901.9   *LC* 63-17631

CB61–68 English, to 1973

Buckle, Henry Thomas. • 3.33
History of civilization in England / summarized and abridged by Clement
Wood; introd. by Hans Kohn. New York: Ungar, 1964. 137 p. (Milestones of
thought in the history of ideas) 1. Civilization — History I. T. II. Series.
CB63.B8   *LC* 64-15688

Toynbee, Arnold Joseph, 1889-1975. • 3.34
A study of history, by Arnold J. Toynbee. . — London: Oxford University
Press, 1934-. 10 v. tables (1 fold.) 23 cm. 1. Civilization 2. History —
Philosophy I. Royal Institute of International Affairs. II. T.
CB63.T6   901   *LC* 34-20998

Toynbee, Arnold Joseph, 1889-1975. 3.35
A study of history [by] Arnold Toynbee. — A new ed., rev. and abridged by the
author and Jane Caplan. — New York: Oxford University Press; distributed in
the United States by American Heritage Press, [1972] 576 p.: illus.; 30 cm.
1. Civilization 2. History — Philosophy I. Caplan, Jane. II. T.
CB63.T6433 1972   909   *LC* 72-2220   *ISBN* 0070651299

Gargan, Edward T., 1922-. • 3.36
The intent of Toynbee's History: a cooperative appraisal / edited by Edward T.
Gargan; pref. by Arnold J. Toynbee. — Chicago: Loyola University Press,
1961. viii, 224 p.; 24 cm. 1. Toynbee, Arnold Joseph, 1889-1975. Study of
history. I. T.
CB63.T68 G3   *LC* 61-10704

Barker, Ernest, Sir, 1874-1960. • 3.37
Traditions of civility; eight essays. — [Hamden, Conn.]: Archon Books, 1967.
viii, 369 p.: front.; 22 cm. Reprint of the 1948 ed. 1. Civilization — Addresses,
essays, lectures. I. T.
CB67.B3 1967   901.9   *LC* 67-28551

Bury, J. B. (John Bagnell), 1861-1927. • 3.38
The idea of progress; an inquiry into its origin and growth, by J. B.
Bury...introduction by Charles A. Beard. New York, The Macmillan company,
1932. xl, 357 p. 23 cm. 1. Progress 2. History — Philosophy I. Beard, Charles
Austin, 1874-1948. II. T.
CB67.B8 1932   *LC* 32-11686

Clark, Kenneth, 1903-. • 3.39
Civilisation: a personal view / [by] Kenneth Clark. — [1st U.S. ed.]. — New
York: Harper & Row, [1970, c1969]. –. xviii, 359 p.: ill. (part col.); 26 cm. —
1. Civilization — History 2. Art — History I. T.
CB68.C55 1970   901.9   *LC* 75-97174

CB69 American and English, 1974–

Boorstin, Daniel J. (Daniel Joseph), 1914-. 3.40
The discoverers / Daniel J. Boorstin. — 1st ed. — New York: Random House,
c1983. xvi, 745 p.; 24 cm. Includes index. 1. Civilization — History
2. Discoveries (in geography) 3. Science — History I. T.
CB69.B66 1983   909 19   *LC* 83-42766   *ISBN* 0394402294

McNeill, William Hardy, 1917-. 3.41
The human condition: an ecological and historical view / William H. McNeill.
— Princeton, N.J.: Princeton University Press, 1981. viii, 81 p.; 23 cm. —
(Bland-Lee lecture series delivered at Clark University, 1979) Includes index.
1. Civilization — Addresses, essays, lectures. 2. Human ecology — Addresses,
essays, lectures. I. T.
CB69.M33   304.2   *LC* 80-7547   *ISBN* 0691053170

CB71–113 Other

Grousset, René, 1885-1952. • 3.42
The sum of history. English version by A. and H. Temple Patterson. [Hadleigh,
Essex] Tower Bridge Publications [1951] 254 p. 22 cm. 1. Civilization —
History I. T.
CB77.G713   *LC* 52-1840

Chamberlain, Houston Stewart, 1855-1927. • 3.43
The foundations of the nineteenth century / by Houston Stewart Chamberlain;
a translation from the German by John Lees ... With an introduction by Lord
Redesdale ... — London: Lane, 1911. 2 v.: ill. (incl. maps) 22 cm. Translation of
Die grundlagen des neunzehnten jahrhunderts. 1. Nineteenth century
2. History — Philosophy I. T.
CB83.C45 1911   901   *LC* A 11-252

Elias, Norbert.   **3.44**
[Über den Prozess der Zivilisation. English (Oxford, Oxfordshire)] The civilizing process / Norbert Elias; translated by Edmund Jephcott with some notes and revisions by the author. — Oxford: B. Blackwell, 1982-. 3 v. Translation of: Über den Prozess der Zivilisation. 1. Civilization — History — Collected works. 2. Civilization — Philosophy — Collected works. I. T.
CB83.E413 1982b   909 19   *LC* 82-227377   *ISBN* 0631196803

Weber, Alfred, 1868-1958.   **• 3.45**
Farewell to European history: or, The conquest of nihilism / tr. from the German by R.F.C. Hull. New Haven: Yale Univ. Press, 1948. 204 p. 'Published on the Louis Stern Memorial Fund.' Translation of Abschied von der bisherigen Geschichte. 1. Civilization — History 2. Philosophy — History 3. Nihilism I. Hull, R. F. C. (Richard Francis Carrington), 1913-1974. II. T. III. Title: The conquest of nihilism.
CB83.W384 1948   *LC* 48-6494

Rüstow, Alexander, 1885-1963.   **3.46**
Freedom and domination: a historical critique of civilization / Alexander Rüstow; abbreviated translation from the German by Salvator Attanasio; edited, and with introd., by Dankwart A. Rustow. — Princeton, N.J.: Princeton University Press, c1980. xxix, 716 p.; 25 cm. 'Abridged translation of Ortsbestimmung der Gegenwart.' 1. Civilization — History I. Rustow, Dankwart A. II. T.
CB88.R84213   909   *LC* 80-10575   *ISBN* 0691053045

Ortega y Gasset, José, 1883-1955.   **• 3.47**
Man and crisis. Translated from the Spanish by Mildred Adams. — [1st ed.]. — New York, Norton [1958] 217 p. 22 cm. Translation of En torno a Galileo. 1. Civilization — Hist. I. T.
CB103.O683   901   *LC* 58-9282

Ortega y Gasset, José, 1883-1955.   **• 3.48**
The revolt of the masses / Jose Ortega y Gasset; authorized translation from the Spanish. — 25th anniversary ed. — New York: Norton, 1957, c1932. 190 p. 1. Civilization 2. Proletariat 3. Europe — Civilization I. T.
CB103.O72 1957

Birket-Smith, Kaj, 1893-.   **• 3.49**
The paths of culture; a general ethnology. Translated from the Danish by Karin Fennow. — Madison, University of Wisconsin Press, 1965. xi, 535 p. plates. 25 cm. Bibliography: p. 487-524. 1. Civilization — Hist. 2. Ethnology I. T.
CB113.D3B513   301.2   *LC* 64-8488

Polak, Frederik Lodewijk.   **• 3.50**
The image of the future; enlightening the past, orientating the present, forecasting the future. Leyden, A. W. Sythoff; New York, Oceana Publications, 1961. 2 v. 24 cm. (European aspects: a collection of studies relating to European integration. Series A: Culture, no. 1) Translation of De toekomst is verleden tijd. 1. Culture 2. Civilization — History 3. Utopias I. Polak, Fred. Toekomst is verleden tijd. English. II. T.
CB113.D8 P713   *LC* 61-8137

CB151–155 Special Aspects

Barzun, Jacques, 1907-.   **• 3.51**
Of human freedom, by Jacques Barzun. Boston, Little, Brown and company [c1939] 6 p. l., 334 p. 21 cm. 'An Atlantic monthly press book.' 'First edition.' 1. Culture 2. Democracy I. T.
CB151.B3   *LC* 39-27843

Bernal, J. D. (John Desmond), 1901-.   **• 3.52**
Science in history [by] J.D. Bernal. [3d ed.]. New York, Hawthorn Books [1965] xxviii, 1039 p. illus., maps. 23 cm. 1. Science and civilization 2. Civilization — History I. T.
CB151.B4 1965   901.9   *LC* 65-22660

Caillois, Roger, 1913-.   **• 3.53**
Man, play, and games / Roger Caillois; translated from the French by Meyer Barash. — New York: Free Press, 1961. ix, 208 p.; 22 cm. Translation of Les jeux et les hommes. 1. Play 2. Civilization — Philosophy I. T.
CB151.C273   790.13   *LC* 61-14109

Easlea, Brian.   **3.54**
Liberation and the aims of science; an essay on obstacles to the building of a beautiful world. — Totowa, N.J.: Rowman and Littlefield, 1974, c1973. xiv, 370 p.: illus.; 25 cm. 1. Science and civilization 2. Civilization, Modern I. T.
CB151.E27 1973b   901.94   *LC* 74-170436   *ISBN* 087471477X

Huizinga, Johan, 1872-1945.   **• 3.55**
[Homo ludens. English] Homo ludens; a study of the play–element in culture. Boston, Beacon Press [1955, c1950] 220 p. 21 cm. (Humanitas, Beacon reprints in humanities) Beacon paperbacks, 15. 1. Play 2. Civilization — Philosophy I. T.
CB151.H815x   901   *LC* 55-13793

Jacob, Heinrich Eduard, 1889-1967.   **• 3.56**
Six thousand years of bread; its holy and unholy history. Translated by Richard and Clara Winston. — Westport, Conn.: Greenwood Press, [1970, c1944] xiv, 399 p.: illus.; 24 cm. 1. Bread 2. Civilization — History I. T.
CB151.J34 1970   901.9   *LC* 75-110043   *ISBN* 0837144310

Laski, Harold Joseph, 1893-1950.   **• 3.57**
Faith, reason, and civilization; an essay in historical analysis. — Freeport, N.Y.: Books for Libraries Press, [1972, c1944] 187 p.; 23 cm. — (Essay index reprint series) 1. Civilization 2. Christianity 3. Socialism 4. Communism — Russia. I. T.
CB151.L36 1972   901.9   *LC* 74-167375   *ISBN* 0836926625

Lindsay, Robert Bruce.   **• 3.58**
Role of science in civilization. New York: Harper & Row, 1963. 318 p. 1. Science and civilization I. T.
CB151 L5   901.9   *LC* 63-10752

Redfield, Robert, 1897-.   **• 3.59**
The primitive world and its transformations. — Ithaca, N.Y.: Cornell University Press, [1953] 185 p.; 23 cm. 1. Social change 2. Cities and towns I. T.
CB151.R38   901   *LC* 53-8239

Taylor, Henry Osborn, 1856-1941.   **• 3.60**
Freedom of the mind in history. — Westport, Conn.: Greenwood Press, [1970] xii, 297 p.; 23 cm. Reprint of the 1923 ed. 1. Civilization 2. Progress 3. Learning and scholarship I. T.
CB151.T3 1970   901.9   *LC* 74-109861   *ISBN* 0837143527

Becker, Carl Lotus, 1873-1945.   **• 3.61**
Progress and power; introd. by Leo Gershoy. [1st Borzoi ed.] New York, A. A. Knopf, 1949. xli, 116 p. 20 cm. 'Lectures delivered at Stanford University, on the Raymond Fred West Memorial Foundation, in April 1935.' 1. Progress 2. Inventions 3. Civilization — Philosophy I. T.
CB155.B4 1949   *LC* 49-10663

Edelstein, Ludwig, 1902-1965.   **• 3.62**
The idea of progress in classical antiquity. — Baltimore, John Hopkins Press [1967] xxxiii, 211 p. 24 cm. Bibliography: p. 181-198. 1. Progress 2. Philosophy, Ancient I. T.
CB155.E26   901   *LC* 67-16483

Lynch, Kevin, 1918-.   **3.63**
What time is this place? Cambridge, MIT Press [1972] viii, 277 p. illus. 24 cm. 1. Progress — Addresses, essays, lectures. 2. Cycles — Addresses, essays, lectures. 3. Time perception — Addresses, essays, lectures. I. T.
CB155.L95   301.24   *LC* 72-7059   *ISBN* 0262120615

Murray, Gilbert, i.e. George Gilbert Aimé, 1866-1957.   **• 3.64**
Hellenism and the modern world. Boston, Beacon Press [1954] 60 p. 19 cm. 1. Hellenism 2. Civilization, Modern I. T.
CB155.M78 1954   913.38   *LC* 54-1637

Wagar, W. Warren.   **3.65**
Good tidings; the belief in progress from Darwin to Marcuse [by] W. Warren Wagar. — Bloomington: Indiana University Press, [1972] viii, 398 p.; 24 cm. 1. Progress I. T.
CB155.W28 1972   901.9   *LC* 73-180484   *ISBN* 0253325900

CB158–161 Forecasts

Cornish, Edward, 1927-.   **3.66**
The study of the future: an introduction to the art and science of understanding and shaping tomorrow's world / by Edward Cornish with members and staff of the World Future Society. — Washington, D.C.: The Society, c1977. x, 307 p.; 23 cm. Includes index. 1. Forecasting I. World Future Society. II. T.
CB158.C67   001.4/33 19   *LC* 77-75308   *ISBN* 0930242033

Helmer, Olaf, 1910-.   **3.67**
Looking forward: a guide to futures research / Olaf Helmer. — Beverly Hills, Calif.: Sage Publications, c1983. 376 p.: ill.; 23 cm. 1. Forecasting — Methodology. 2. Forecasting — Research. I. T.
CB158.H415 1983   003/.2 19   *LC* 83-4520   *ISBN* 0803920172

Polak, Fred.   **3.68**
[Toekomst is verleden tijd. English] The image of the future / [by] Fred Polak; translated from the Dutch and abridged by Elise Boulding. — Amsterdam; New York: Elsevier Scientific Pub. Co., 1973. x, 321 p.; 24 cm. Abridged translation of De toekomst is verleden tijd. 1. Forecasting — History. 2. Civilization — History 3. Eschatology — Comparative studies. 4. Utopias I. Boulding, Elise. ed. II. T.
CB158.P6213 1973   901.94   *LC* 72-83209

Tugwell, Franklin, 1942- comp.   **3.69**
Search for alternatives: public policy and the study of the future. — Cambridge, Mass.: Winthrop Publishers, [1973] xvi, 335 p.: illus.; 23 cm. 1. Forecasting — Addresses, essays, lectures. I. T.
CB158.T84   309.1   *LC* 72-13747   *ISBN* 0876268319

World Future Society.   **3.70**
The future: a guide to information sources. — 2d ed. — Washington: World Future Society, c1979. viii, 722 p.; 26 cm. Includes indexes. 1. Forecasting — Societies, etc. — Directories. 2. Forecasting — Bibliography. I. T.
CB158.W67 1979   309/.06/2   *LC* 79-19398   *ISBN* 0930242076

Darwin, Charles Galton, Sir, 1887-.   • **3.71**
The next million years. [1st American ed.] Garden City, N.Y., Doubleday, 1953 [c1952] 210 p. 21 cm. 1. Prophecies I. T.
CB160.D3 1953   *LC* 52-13372

Kahn, Herman, 1922-.   • **3.72**
The year 2000; a framework for speculation on the next thirty–three years, by Herman Kahn and Anthony J. Wiener, with contributions from other staff members of the Hudson Institute. Introd. by Daniel Bell. — New York: Macmillan, [1967] xxviii, 431 p.: illus.; 24 cm. 1. Twentieth century — Forecasts I. Wiener, Anthony J., joint author. II. Hudson Institute. III. T.
CB160.K3 1967   301.2   *LC* 67-29488

Beckwith, Burnham P. (Burnham Putnam), 1904-.   • **3.73**
The next 500 years: scientific predictions of major social trends / with a foreword by Daniel Bell. — [1st ed.] New York: Exposition Press [1967] xvi, 341 p.; 22 cm. (An Exposition-university book) 1. Twenty-fifth century — Forecasts I. T.
CB161.B4   901.9   *LC* 67-26389

Clarke, I. F. (Ignatius Frederick)   **3.74**
The pattern of expectation, 1644–2001 / I. F. Clarke. — New York: Basic Books, 1979. xi, 344 p., [16] leaves of plates: ill.; 23 cm. 1. Forecasting — History. 2. Twentieth century — Forecasts 3. Progress I. T.
CB161.C52 1979   909.08   *LC* 78-19669   *ISBN* 0465054579

McHale, John.   • **3.75**
The future of the future. — New York: G. Braziller, [1969] ix, 322 p.: illus.; 22 cm. 1. Technology and civilization 2. Twenty-first century — Forecasts I. T.
CB161.M3   301.3   *LC* 69-15827

Peccei, Aurelio.   **3.76**
One hundred pages for the future: reflections of the president of the Club of Rome / Aurelio Peccei. — New York: Pergamon Press, c1981. 191 p.: ill.; 21 cm. Ill. on lining paper. 1. Twenty-first century — Forecasts 2. Twentieth century — Forecasts 3. Civilization, Modern — 1950- I. T.
CB161.P35 1981   303.4/9 19   *LC* 82-133898   *ISBN* 0080281109

CB201–281 Special Civilizations

CB203–245 Western Civilization

Barker, Ernest, Sir, 1874-1960.   • **3.77**
National character and the factors in its formation. — [4th and rev. ed.]. — London, Methuen [1948] xix, 268 p. 23 cm. 1. National characteristics 2. National characteristics, English I. T.
CB203.B3 1948   901   *LC* 49-14737 *

Burke, Peter.   **3.78**
Popular culture in early modern Europe / Peter Burke. — New York: New York University Press, 1978. xi, 365 p., [8] leaves of plates: ill.; 22 cm. — 1. Europe — Popular culture. I. T.
CB203.B87 1978   940.2   *LC* 78-52051   *ISBN* 0814710115

The Enlightenment in national context / edited by Roy Porter and Mikuláš Teich.   **3.79**
Cambridge; New York: Cambridge University Press, 1981. xii, 275 p.; 24 cm. Includes index. 1. Enlightenment — Addresses, essays, lectures. 2. Europe — Intellectual life — Addresses, essays, lectures. 3. Europe — History — 18th century — Addresses, essays, lectures. I. Porter, Roy, 1946- II. Teich, Mikuláš.
CB203.E54   940.2/53 19   *LC* 80-41750   *ISBN* 0521237572

Gerhard, Dietrich, 1896-.   **3.80**
Old Europe: a study of continuity, 1000–1800 / Dietrich Gerhard. — New York: Academic Press, c1981. xii, 147 p.; 24 cm. — (Studies in social discontinuity.) 1. Europe — Civilization 2. Europe — Social conditions I. T. II. Series.
CB203.G47   940 19   *LC* 81-14872   *ISBN* 0122807200

Lach, Donald Frederick, 1917-.   • **3.81**
Asia in the making of Europe [by] Donald F. Lach. — Chicago: University of Chicago Press, [1965-. v.: illus., maps, ports.; 24 cm. 1. Europe — Civilization — Oriental influences 2. Asia — History 3. Asia — Discovery and exploration. I. T.
CB203.L32   *LC* 64-19848

The Legacy of Greece: a new appraisal / edited by M. I. Finley.   **3.82**
Oxford: Clarendon Press; New York: Oxford University Press, 1981. 479, [16] p. of plates: ill.; 22 cm. 1. Greece — Civilization — Addresses, essays, lectures. 2. Europe — Civilization — Greek influences — Addresses, essays, lectures. I. Finley, M. I. (Moses I.), 1912-
CB203.L38   940   *LC* 80-40188   *ISBN* 0198219156

Stone, Lawrence.   **3.83**
The past and the present / Lawrence Stone. — Boston: Routledge & K. Paul, 1981. xii, 274 p.; 23 cm. Chiefly reprints of previously published articles. 1. Historiography — Addresses, essays, lectures. 2. Europe — Civilization — Addresses, essays, lectures. I. T.
CB203.S76   940 19   *LC* 80-41657   *ISBN* 0710006284

Wohl, Robert.   **3.84**
The generation of 1914 / Robert Wohl. — Cambridge, Mass.: Harvard University Press, 1979. ix, 307 p., [14] leaves of plates: ill.; 24 cm. 1. Youth — Europe — History. 2. Conflict of generations 3. World War, 1914-1918 — Influence. 4. Youth in literature 5. Europe — Intellectual life — 20th century I. T.
CB203.W63   909.82/1   *LC* 78-21124   *ISBN* 0674344650

The Celtic consciousness / edited by Robert O'Driscoll.   **3.85**
New York: Braziller, 1982, c1981. xxxi, 642 p.: ill; 24 cm. Papers first presented at a symposium held in Toronto, February, 1978. Omits 'Section VII: Considerations in the transmission of Celtic culture: Canada and the Celtic consciousness' (ca. 54 p.) found in the edition published in 1981 by McClelland and Stewart and the Dolmen Press. 1. Civilization, Celtic — Congresses. I. O'Driscoll, Robert.
CB206.C44 1982   909/.0974916 19   *LC* 82-1269   *ISBN* 0807610410

Barker, Ernest, Sir, 1874-1960.   • **3.86**
The European inheritance / edited by Ernest Barker, George Clark, P. Vaucher. — Oxford: Clarendon Press, 1954. 3 v.: ill., maps (some fold.) Includes index. 1. Europe — Civilization I. T.
CB245.B35   *LC* 54-9923

Baumer, Franklin Le Van, ed.   • **3.87**
Main currents of Western thought; readings in Western European intellectual history from the Middle Ages to the present. — 2d ed., rev. [and enl.]. — New York: Knopf, 1964. xviii, 746 p.; 25 cm. 1. Europe — Intellectual life — Addresses, essays, lectures. I. T.
CB245.B37 1964   914   *LC* 64-14416

Bolgar, R. R.   • **3.88**
The classical heritage and its beneficiaries. — Cambridge [Eng.] University Press, 1954. vii, 591 p. 24 cm. Includes bibliographies. 1. Civilization, Occidental — Hist. I. T.
CB245.B63   901   *LC* 54-13284

Brinton, Crane, 1898-1968.   • **3.89**
Ideas and men; the story of Western thought. — 2d ed. — Englewood Cliffs, N.J.: Prentice-Hall, [1963] 484 p.; 24 cm. 1. Civilization — History 2. Civilization, Occidental I. T.
CB245.B73 1963   901   *LC* 63-13270

Columbia College (Columbia University)   • **3.90**
Chapters in Western civilization / edited by the Contemporary civilization staff of Columbia College, Columbia University. — 3d ed. New York: Columbia University Press, 1961-1962. 2 v. 1. Civilization, Occidental 2. Civilization — History I. T.
CB245.C362   *LC* 61-13862

Dawson, Christopher, 1889-1970. • 3.91
Understanding Europe. — New York, Sheed and Ward, 1952. 261 p. 22 cm.
1. Europe — Civilization 2. Civilization, Occidental I. T.
CB245.D37   901   LC 52-10609

Hayes, Carlton Joseph Huntley, 1882-1964. • 3.92
Christianity and Western civilization. Stanford, Stanford University Press
[1954] 63 p. 23 cm. (The Raymond Fred West memorial lectures at Stanford
University, 1954.) 1. Civilization, Occidental 2. Civilization, Christian I. T.
CB245.H35   LC 54-11786

Lopez, Robert Sabatino, 1910-. • 3.93
[Naissance de l'Europe. English] The birth of Europe / [by] Robert S. Lopez. —
New York: M. Evans; distributed in association with Lippincott, Philadelphia,
[1967] xxiii, 442 p.: ill. (part col.) maps (part col.), plans; 27 cm. Translation of
Naissance de l'Europe. 1. Civilization, Occidental I. T.
CB245.L613 1967b   910.09/18/21   LC 66-23414

Muller, Herbert Joseph, 1905-. • 3.94
Freedom in the Western World, from the Dark Ages to the rise of democracy.
— [1st ed.]. — New York, Harper & Row [1963] 428 p. illus. 25 cm.
1. Civilization, Occidental 2. Liberty. I. T.
CB245.M8   914   LC 63-8427

Rawson, Elizabeth. 3.95
The Spartan tradition in European thought. — Oxford: Oxford University
Press, 1969. ix, 390 p., 6 plates.: illus., ports.; 23 cm. 1. Spartanism 2. Europe
— Civilization I. T.
CB245.R28 1969   914/.03   LC 72-120555   ISBN 0198143508

Webb, Walter Prescott, 1888-1963. • 3.96
The Great Frontier. Introd. by Arnold J. Toynbee. Austin, University of Texas
Press [1964] xviii, 434 p. illus., maps. 24 cm. 1. Civilization, Occidental —
Philosophy. 2. Social history 3. Frontier and pioneer life I. T.
CB245.W4 1964   914   LC 64-10321

Weber, Eugen Joseph, 1925- ed. • 3.97
The Western tradition; from the ancient world to Louis XIV. [Compiled by]
Eugen Weber. — 3d ed. — Lexington, Mass.: Heath, [1972] xxxii, 500 p.; 24
cm. 1. Civilization, Occidental I. T.
CB245.W44 1972   910/.03/1812   LC 72-172911   ISBN
0669811661

CB251 EAST AND WEST

Baudet, E. H. P. (Ernest Henri Philippe), 1919-. • 3.98
Paradise on earth; some thoughts on European images of non–European man.
Translated by Elizabeth Wentholt. — New Haven, Yale University Press, 1965.
xii, 87 p. 23 cm. Bibliographical references included in 'Notes' (p. 77-87)
1. East and West I. T.
CB251.B3813   301.154   LC 65-11174

Grousset, René, 1885-1952. • 3.99
[Civilisations de l'Orient. English] The civilizations of the East. Translated
from the French by Catherine Alison Phillips. [New York] Cooper Square
Publishers [1967, c1931-34] 4 v. illus. 24 cm. Translation of Les civilisations de
l'Orient. 1. Civilization, Oriental 2. Art, Oriental I. T.
CB251.G72 1967   915/.03   LC 66-30807

Hudson, Geoffrey Francis, 1903-. • 3.100
Europe & China; a survey of their relations from the earliest times to 1800.
Boston Beacon Press [1961,c1931] 336p. 1. Europe — Civilization 2. China —
Civilization 3. Europe — Relations — China 4. China — Relations — Europe
I. T.
CB251 H78 1961

Ward, Barbara, 1914-. • 3.101
The interplay of East and West, points of conflict and cooperation. [1st ed.]
New York, Norton [1957] 152 p. 22 cm. (The Sir Edward Beatty memorial
lectures, ser. 2) 1. East and West I. T. II. Series.
CB251.J3   901   LC 57-8337

Malraux, André, 1901-1976. • 3.102
The temptation of the West / André Malraux; translated and with an introd. by
Robert Hollander. — New York: Vintage Books, [1961]. x, [7], 122 p.; 21 cm.
(A Vintage original; V-193.) I. T.
CB251.M313   909.82/2   LC 60-12160

Toynbee, Arnold Joseph, 1889-1975. • 3.103
Civilization on trial. New York, Meridian Books [1960] 348 p. 18 cm.
1. Civilization — Addresses, essays, lectures. 2. History — Philosophy 3. East

and West I. Somervell, D. C. (David Churchill), 1885-1965. II. T. III. Title:
The world and the west.
CB251.T69 1960   LC 58-8525

Unesco. • 3.104
Interrelations of cultures, their contribution to international understanding.
Westport, Conn., Greenwood Press [1971, c1953] 387 p. 23 cm. (Its Collection
of intercultural studies) 1. Acculturation I. T. II. Series.
CB251.U53 1971   301.2/41   LC 72-88956   ISBN 0837131537

Watt, W. Montgomery (William Montgomery) • 3.105
The influence of Islam on Medieval Europe [by] W. Montgomery Watt.
Edinburgh, University Press [1972] viii, 125 p. 21 cm. (Islamic surveys, 9)
1. Civilization, Occidental — Islamic influences 2. Europe — Relations —
Islamic Empire 3. Islamic Empire — Relations — Europe I. T. II. Series.
CB251.W3x   910/.031/17671 s 914/.03/1   LC 70-182902   ISBN
0852242182

Zinkin, Maurice. • 3.106
Asia and the West. — [Rev. ed.] — New York: International Secretariat,
Institute of Pacific Relations, 1953. 300 p.: maps. Original imprint covered by
label: London, Chatto and Windus. 'Issued under the auspices of the
International Secretariat, Institute of Pacific Relations.' 1. Civilization,
Oriental 2. Eastern question 3. Asia — Politics and government I. T.
CB251.Z5x

CB253 ORIENTAL CIVILIZATION

De Bary, William Theodore, 1918- ed. • 3.107
Approaches to Asian civilizations. Edited by Wm. Theodore de Bary and
Ainslie T. Embree. — New York, Columbia University Press, 1964. xxv, 293 p.
22 cm. Bibliographical footnotes. 1. Civilization, Oriental — Addresses, essays,
lectures. I. Embree, Ainslie Thomas. joint ed. II. T.
CB253.D39   915   LC 63-20226

Dean, Vera Micheles, 1903-1972. • 3.108
The nature of the non–Western World. — [New York] New American Library
[1957] 284 p. illus. 18 cm. — (A Mentor book, MD 190) 1. Civilization,
Oriental 2. Africa — Civilization 3. Latin America — Civilization. I. T.
CB253.D4   901   LC 57-8030

Nakamura, Hajime, 1912-. • 3.109
Ways of thinking of Eastern peoples: India, China, Tibet, Japan / Hajime
Nakamura. — Rev. English translation / edited by Philip P. Wiener. —
Honolulu: University Press of Hawaii, 1971, c1964. xx, 712 p.; 24 cm.
1. National characteristics, Oriental. 2. Philosophy, Oriental I. Wiener, Philip
P. II. T.
CB253.N313 1964   915   ISBN 0824800788

Reischauer, Edwin O. (Edwin Oldfather), 1910-. • 3.110
A history of East Asian civilization / Edwin O. Reischauer, John K. Fairbank.
— Boston: Houghton Mifflin, [1960-1965] 2 v.: ill., maps (part fold.), ports. Vol.
2 by John K. Fairbank, Edwin O. Reischauer, and Albert M. Craig.
1. Civilization, Oriental — History. I. Fairbank, John King, 1907- II. Craig,
Albert M. III. T. IV. Title: East Asian civilization.
CB253.R4   LC 60-4269//r65

Schwab, Raymond. 3.111
[Renaissance orientale. English] Oriental renaissance: Europe's rediscovery of
India and the East, 1680–1880 / Raymond Schwab; translated by Gene
Patterson–Black and Victor Reinking; foreword by Edward W. Said. — New
York: Columbia University Press, 1984. xx, 542 p.; 25 cm. Translation of:
Renaissance orientale. Includes index. 1. East and West 2. Europe —
Civilization — Indic influences 3. Europe — Intellectual life 4. Europe —
Civilization — Oriental influences I. T.
CB253.S3813 1984   909/.09811 19   LC 83-25279   ISBN
0231041381

CB301–428 Periods of Civilization

CB301–303 ORIGINS

Braidwood, Robert J. (Robert John), 1907-. • 3.112
The Near East and the foundations for civilization; an essay in appraisal of the
general evidence. Eugene, Oregon State System of Higher Education, 1952.

45 p. illus., maps. 26 cm. 1. Civilization, Ancient 2. Man, Prehistoric 3. Middle East — History I. T.
CB301.B63   LC 53-62030

Clark, Grahame, 1907-.   • 3.113
Aspects of prehistory [by] Grahame Clark. — Berkeley: University of California Press, 1970. xiii, 161 p.: illus., maps.; 23 cm. 1. Man, Prehistoric 2. Evolution I. T.
CB301.C57   913.03/1   LC 73-94989   ISBN 0520015843

Hawkes, Charles Francis Christopher, 1905-.   • 3.114
The prehistoric foundations of Europe to the Mycenean age / by C. F. C. Hawkes. — London: Methuen, 1940. xv, 414 p.: ill., 6 maps (part fold.) 1. Man, Prehistoric — Europe 2. Europe — Civilization — History 3. Europe — History I. T.
CB301.H3   LC 41-17904   ISBN 0416790208

Mellaart, James.   • 3.115
Earliest civilizations of the Near East. — New York: McGraw-Hill, [1965] 143 p.: illus. (part col.) maps.; 22 cm. — (The Library of early civilizations) 1. Stone age — Near East. 2. Civilization, Ancient I. T.
CB301.M38   913.35031   LC 65-19415

Piggott, Stuart. ed.   • 3.116
The dawn of civilization; the first world survey of human cultures in early times. Texts by Grahame Clark [and others] New York, McGraw-Hill [1961] 403 p. illus. (part col.) maps (part col.) diagrs. 36 cm. 1. Civilization, Ancient I. Clark, Grahame, 1907- II. T.
CB301.P5 1961   901.91   LC 61-11703

CB311–325 ANCIENT

Aymard, André.   • 3.117
L'Orient et la Grèce antique / par André Aymard et Jeannine Auboyer; préface générale par Maurice Crouzet. — 4e éd. rev. et corr. — Paris: Presses universitaires de France, 1961. xii, 701 p.: ill., maps. — (Histoire générale des civilisations. t.1) 1. Civilization, Ancient I. Auboyer, Jeannine. II. T. III. Series.
CB311.A9 1961   LC 62-1252

Childe, V. Gordon (Vere Gordon), 1892-1957.   • 3.118
Man makes himself. London Watts [1936] 275p. (Library of science and culture, v. 5) 1. Civilization, Ancient 2. Archaeology 3. Man, Prehistoric 4. Progress I. T.
CB311 C5

Childe, Vere Gordon.   • 3.119
What happened in history. London: Max Parrish, 1960 c1942. 250p.: maps. 1. Civilization, Ancient 2. History, Ancient 3. Man, Prehistoric I. T.
CB311.C56 1960

Hawkes, Jacquetta Hopkins, 1910-.   3.120
The atlas of early man / Jacquetta Hawkes, assisted by David Trump. New York: St. Martin's Press, 1976. 255 p.: ill. (some col.); 29 cm. Includes indexes. 1. Civilization, Ancient 2. Man, Prehistoric I. Trump, David H. joint author. II. T.
CB311.H35 1976   930   LC 75-43424

Peoples and places of the past: the National Geographic   3.121
illustrated cultural atlas of the ancient world.
[Washington, D.C.]: National Geographic Society, c1983. 424 p.: col. ill., maps; 48 cm. 'Milestones of world culture' and 'Life in the castle' ([2] folded p.) inserted. Includes index. 1. Civilization, Ancient 2. Civilization, Medieval I. National Geographic Society (U.S.)
CB311.P44 1983   909.07 19   LC 83-2208   ISBN 087044462X

Rostovzeff, Michael Ivanovitch, 1870-1952.   • 3.122
Out of the past of Greece & Rome. — New York: Biblo and Tannen, 1963. xvii, 129 p.: ill.; 24 cm. 1. Civilization, Ancient 2. Greece — Civilization 3. Cities and towns, Ancient I. T.
CB311.R6 1963   913.3   LC 63-18047

Symposium on Urbanization and Cultural Development in the   • 3.123
Ancient Near East, University of Chicago, 1958.
City invincible: a Symposium on Urbanization and Cultural Development in the Ancient Near East held at the Oriental Institute at the University of Chicago, December 4–7, 1958 / edited for the Planning Committee by Carl H. Kraeling and Robert M. Adams. — Chicago: University of Chicago Press, 1960. xiv, 447 p.: ill., maps (1 fold) (Oriental Institute special publication) 1. Cities and towns, Ancient 2. Civilization, Ancient I. Kraeling, Carl Hermann, 1897- II. Adams, Robert M., 1926- III. T.
CB311.S9 1958   LC 60-13791

CB351–355 MEDIEVAL

Artz, Frederick Binkerd, 1894-.   • 3.124
The mind of the Middle Ages, A.D. 200–1500; an historical survey. 3d ed., rev. New York, Knopf, 1958 [c1954] 566 p. illus. 24 cm. 1. Civilization, Medieval 2. Europe — Intellectual life I. T.
CB351.A56 1958   909.07   LC 58-11857

Cantor, Norman F.   3.125
The meaning of the Middle Ages; a sociological and cultural history [by] Norman F. Cantor. — Boston: Allyn and Bacon, [1973] viii, 321 p.; 22 cm. 1. Civilization, Medieval I. T.
CB351.C25   901/.93   LC 77-190550

Dahmus, Joseph Henry, 1909-.   3.126
Dictionary of medieval civilization / Joseph Dahmus. — New York: Macmillan, c1984. viii, 700 p.; 25 cm. 1. Civilization, Medieval — Dictionaries. I. T.
CB351.D24 1984   909.07/03/21 19   LC 83-25583   ISBN 0029078709

Dales, Richard C.   3.127
The intellectual life of western Europe in the middle ages / Richard C. Dales. — Washington: University Press of America, c1980. 313 p.; 23 cm. Includes index. 1. Civilization, Medieval 2. Europe — Intellectual life I. T.
CB351.D27   940.1   LC 79-5515   ISBN 0819109002

Erickson, Carolly, 1943-.   3.128
The medieval vision: essays in history and perception / Carolly Erickson. — New York: Oxford University Press, 1976. vii, 247 p.; 21 cm. Includes index. 1. Civilization, Medieval — Addresses, essays, lectures. 2. Religious thought — Middle Ages — Addresses, essays, lectures. I. T.
CB351.E76   940.1   LC 75-10179   ISBN 0195019644

Essays on medieval civilization / by Richard E. Sullivan ... [et   3.129
al.]; introd. by Bryce Lyon; edited by Bede Karl Lackner & Kenneth Roy Philp.
Austin: University of Texas Press, c1978. xxi, 178 p.; 23 cm. — (Walter Prescott Webb memorial lectures. 12 0083-713X) 1. Civilization, Medieval — Addresses, essays, lectures. I. Sullivan, Richard Eugene, 1921- II. Lackner, Bede K. III. Philp, Kenneth R., 1941- IV. Series.
CB351.E78   940.1/4   LC 77-17068   ISBN 0292720238

Evans, Joan, 1893- ed.   • 3.130
The flowering of the Middle Ages. Texts by Christopher Brooke [and others]. — New York: McGraw-Hill, [1966] 360 p.: illus., facsims. (part col.), maps, plans, plates (part col.), ports. (part col.); 36 cm. 1. Middle Ages I. Brooke, Christopher Nugent Lawrence. II. T.
CB351.E9 1966a   914.031708   LC 66-18208

Herlihy, David. comp.   • 3.131
Medieval culture and society. New York: Harper & Row [1968] xv, 410 p. 21 cm. (Documentary history of Western civilization) (Harper torchbooks, TB1340) 1. Civilization, Medieval I. T.
CB351.H4   914.03/1   LC 68-13326

Jarrett, Bede, 1881-1934.   • 3.132
Social theories of the Middle Ages 1200–1500. — 1st ed., new impression. — London: Cass, 1968. ix, 280 p.; 22 cm. First ed. originally published, London, Benn, 1926. 1. Civilization, Medieval 2. Social history — Medieval, 500-1500 I. T.
CB351.J3 1968   300/.9/02   LC 68-100853

Laistner, Max Ludwig Wolfram, 1890-.   • 3.133
Thought and letters in western Europe, A. D. 500 to 900 / M. L. W. Laistner. — Rev. ed. — Ithaca, N.Y.: Cornell University Press, [1957]. 416 p.; 22 cm. 1. Civilization, Medieval 2. Literature, Medieval — History and criticism 3. Learning and scholarship I. T.
CB351.L26 1957   CB351.L.   LC 57-5744

Painter, Sidney, 1902-1960.   • 3.134
Mediaeval society. — Ithaca: Cornell University Press, [1951] 109 p.; 22 cm. — (The Development of Western civilization) 1. Civilization, Medieval I. T.
CB351.P3   940.1 19   LC 51-7082

Rand, Edward Kennard, 1871-1945.   • 3.135
Founders of the Middle Ages. — New York: Dover Publications, [1957, c1928] 365 p.; 21 cm. 1. Civilization, Medieval 2. Literature, Medieval — History and criticism 3. Middle Ages I. T.
CB351.R3 1957   901   LC 57-59148

Southern, R. W. (Richard William), 1912-.   • 3.136
The Making of the Middle Ages. — New Haven: Yale University Press, 1953. 280 p.: illus., map; 24 cm. 1. Middle Ages I. T.
CB351.S6 1953a   LC 53-5280

Stephenson, Carl, 1886-.   • 3.137
Mediaeval institutions: selected essays / Carl Stephenson; edited by Bryce D.
Lyon. Ithaca, N.Y. . Cornell University Press, 1954. 289 p. (Cornell
paperbacks) 'Writings of Carl Stephenson': p. 285-289. 1. Middle Ages
2. Civilization, Medieval I. T.
CB351.S75   LC 54-4979

Taylor, Henry Osborn, 1856-1941.   • 3.138
The mediaeval mind: a history of the development of thought and emotion in
the Middle Ages / Henry O. Taylor. — 4th ed. Cambridge, Mass. Harvard
University Press, 1949. 2 v. 1. Middle Ages 2. Civilization, Medieval
3. Philosophy, Medieval I. T.
CB351T3x   901.92   LC 49-9872

Wolff, Philippe, 1913-.   • 3.139
[Éveil intellectuel de l'Europe. English] The cultural awakening. Translated
from the French by Anne Carter. [1st American ed.] New York, Pantheon
Books, [c1968] 314 p. maps. 22 cm. Translation of L'éveil intellectuel de
l'Europe. 1. Civilization, Medieval I. T.
CB351.W613 1968   914/.03/1   LC 68-13014

CB353 Special Aspects

Boas, George, 1891-.   • 3.140
Essays on primitivism and related ideas in the Middle Ages. — New York,
Octagon Books, 1966 [c1948] xii, 227 p. 26 cm. — (Contributions to the history
of primitivism) 1. Primitivism 2. Civilization, Medieval I. T. II. Series.
CB353.B6 1966   901.903   LC 66-17502

Daniel, Norman.   3.141
The Arabs and mediaeval Europe / Norman Daniel. — London: Longman,
1975. xiv, 378 p., [2] leaves of plates: ill.; 23 cm. (Arab background series)
Includes index. 1. Civilization, Medieval 2. Europe — Relations — Islamic
Empire 3. Islamic Empire — Relations — Europe I. T.
CB353.D26   301.29/4/0174927   LC 73-93276   ISBN 0582780454

Dawson, Christopher, 1889-1970.   • 3.142
The making of Europe; an introduction to the history of European unity. New
York: Meridian Books, 1956. 274 p.: ill.; 18 cm. (Meridian books, M35)
1. Church history — Middle Ages, 600-1500 2. Civilization, Medieval
3. Europe — Civilization I. T.
CB353.D3x   901   LC 56-10016

Graboïs, Aryeh, 1930-.   3.143
The illustrated encyclopedia of medieval civilization / Aryeh Graboïs. — New
York: Mayflower Books, 1980. 751 p.: ill.; 25 cm. Includes index.
1. Civilization, Medieval — Dictionaries. I. T.
CB353.G7 1980   909/.1/03   LC 79-13630   ISBN 070640856X

Southern, R. W. (Richard William), 1912-.   3.144
Medieval humanism, by R. W. Southern. New York, Harper & Row [1970] x,
261 p. facsims. 23 cm. (A Torchbook library edition) On spine: Medieval
humanism and other studies. 1. Middle Ages — Addresses, essays, lectures.
I. T. II. Title: Medieval humanism and other studies.
CB353.S65 1970   144   LC 70-129867

White, Lynn Townsend, 1907-.   • 3.145
Medieval technology and social change. — Oxford: Clarendon Press, 1962.
194 p.: illus.; 22 cm. 1. Civilization, Mediaeval. 2. Technology and civilization
I. T.
CB353.W5   901.92   LC 62-2973

University of Wisconsin. Division of Humanities.   • 3.146
Twelfth-century Europe and the foundations of modern society: proceedings of
a symposium sponsored by the Division of Humanities of the University of
Wisconsin and the Wisconsin Institute for Medieval and Renaissance Studies,
November 12–14, 1957. Edited by Marshall Clagett, Gaines Post and Robert
Reynolds. Madison: University of Wisconsin Press, 1961. xvi, 219 p. illus. 25
cm. Includes bibliographical references. 1. Twelfth century I. Clagett,
Marshall, 1916- ed. II. Wisconsin Institute for Medieval and Renaissance
Studies. III. T.
CB353.W65 1957   940.14   LC 60-5663

Packard, Sidney Raymond, 1893-.   3.147
12th century Europe; an interpretive essay, by Sidney R. Packard. — Amherst:
University of Massachusetts Press, 1973. ix, 362 p.; 23 cm. 1. Civilization,
Medieval 2. Europe — Civilization I. T.
CB354.6.P32   914/.03/17   LC 73-79507

The Year 1200: a symposium. Texts by: François Avril [and   3.148
others]. Introd. by Jeffrey Hoffeld.
[New York]: Metropolitan Museum of Art, [1975] 594 p.: illus.; 25 cm. English,
French, German and Italian. 1. Civilization, Medieval — Congresses.
2. Europe — Civilization — Congresses. I. Avril, François.
CB354.6.Y35   914/.03/17   LC 74-12418   ISBN 0870990926

CB357–427 MODERN

Friedell, Egon, 1878-1938.   • 3.149
A cultural history of the modern age; the crisis of the European soul from the
black death to the world war, by Egon Friedell: translated from the German by
Charles Francis Atkinson. — New York, A. A. Knopf, 1930-32. 3 v. 27 cm.
1. Europe — Civilization — History. I. Atkinson, Charles Francis, 1880- tr.
II. T.
CB357.F73   LC 30-1796

Smith, Preserved, 1880-1941.   • 3.150
A history of modern culture / Preserved Smith; new introd. by Crane Brinton.
— New York: Collier Books, 1962, c1934. 2 v. 1. Civilization — History I. T.
CB357.S6 1962   901.9   LC 62-20297

Barzun, Jacques, 1907-.   • 3.151
Science: the glorious entertainment. — [1st ed.]. — New York: Harper & Row,
[1964] x, 322 p.; 22 cm. 1. Science and civilization I. T.
CB358.B3   901.94   LC 62-14520

Plaine, Henry L.   • 3.152
Darwin, Marx, and Wagner; a symposium. [Columbus] Ohio State University
Press [1962] viii, 165 p. 22 cm. 'A group of faculty members at Ohio State
planned .. [the] conference for October 1959.' 1. Darwin, Charles, 1809-1882.
2. Marx, Karl, 1818-1883. 3. Wagner, Richard, 1813-1883. 4. Civilization,
Modern I. Ohio State University. II. T.
CB358.P53 1962   LC 61-12066

CB361–369 Renaissance

The Civilization of the Renaissance, by James Westfall   • 3.153
Thompson [and others].
New York: Ungar, [1959] 136 p.: illus.; 19 cm. 1. Renaissance 2. Art,
Renaissance I. Thompson, James Westfall, 1869-1941.
CB361.C5 1959   901.93   LC 58-59873

The Darker vision of the Renaissance: beyond the fields of   3.154
reason / edited, with introd., by Robert S. Kinsman.
Berkeley: University of California Press, 1974. 320 p.; 24 cm. — (Contributions
- UCLA Center for Medieval and Renaissance studies; 6) 1. Renaissance —
Addresses, essays, lectures. 2. Supernatural — History. I. Kinsman, Robert S.
CB361.D33   909.07   LC 72-78939   ISBN 0520022599

Ferguson, Wallace Klippert, 1902-.   • 3.155
The renaissance, by Wallace K. Ferguson. — New York: H. Holt and company,
[c1940] viii, 148 p.; 20 cm. — (The Berkshire studies in European history)
1. Renaissance I. T. II. Series.
CB361.F37   940.21   LC 40-5856

Ferguson, Wallace Klippert, 1902-.   • 3.156
The Renaissance in historical thought; five centuries of interpretation. —
Boston, Houghton Mifflin Co. [1948] xiii, 429 p. 22 cm. Bibliography: p.
398-407. Bibliographical footnotes. 1. Renaissance 2. Historiography I. T.
CB361.F373   940.21   LC 48-9685 *

Kristeller, Paul Oskar, 1905-.   • 3.157
Studies in Renaissance thought and letters. — Roma, Edizioni di storia e
letteratura, 1956. xvi, 680 p. facsims. 26 cm. — (Storia e letteratura, v. 54)
Italian or English. 'Bibliography and indices, by M. L. de
Nicola': p. [589]-680. 1. Ficino, Marsilio, 1433-1499. 2. Renaissance —
Addresses, essays, lectures. I. T. .
CB361.K7   901   LC A 58-2341

Kristeller, Paul Oskar, 1905-.   • 3.158
The classics and Renaissance thought / by Paul Oskar Kristeller. —
Cambridge, Mass.: Published for Oberlin College by Harvard University Press,
1955. 106 p. — (Martin classical lectures. v. 15) 1. Renaissance 2. Humanism
I. T. II. Series.
PA25 M3 v.15 CB361.K7x   LC 55-9440

Mazzeo, Joseph Anthony, 1923-.　　　　　　　　• 3.159
Renaissance and revolution; the remaking of European thought. — New York:
Pantheon Books, [1966, c1965] xi, 349 p.; 22 cm. 1. Renaissance 2. Humanism
I. T.
CB361.M39　　　914.0321　　　LC 65-25080

Metropolitan Museum of Art (New York, N.Y.)　　　• 3.160
The renaissance: six essays / by Wallace K. Ferguson [et al.]. — New York:
Harper and Row, 1962. viii, 184 p.: ill.; 19 cm. — (Harper torchbooks. The
Academy Library; TB1084) "Originally published by the Metropolitan
Museum of art in 1953 under the title: The Renaissance, a symposium."
1. Renaissance — Addresses, essays, lectures. I. T.
CB361.N412　　　940.921082　　　LC 63-1056　　　ISBN 0061310840

Patronage in the Renaissance / edited by Guy Fitch Lytle and　　3.161
Stephen Orgel.
Princeton, N.J.: Princeton University Press, 1982. xiv, 389 p.: ill.; 25 cm. —
(Folger Institute essays.) Includes index. 1. Renaissance — Congresses. 2. Art
patronage — Europe — History — Congresses. I. Lytle, Guy Fitch, 1944-
II. Orgel, Stephen. III. Series.
CB361.P27 1981　　　940.2/1 19　　　LC 81-47143　　　ISBN 0691053383

Renaissance letters: revelations of a world reborn / edited with　　3.162
introd., commentary, and translation by Robert J. Clements and
Lorna Levant.
[New York]: New York University Press, c1976. xxvi, 468 p.: ill.; 26 cm.
Includes index. 1. Renaissance — Sources I. Clements, Robert John, 1912-
II. Levant, Lorna.
CB361.R39　　　940.2/1　　　LC 75-21806　　　ISBN 0814713629

Symposium on the Renaissance (1959: University of　　　• 3.163
Wisconsin—Milwaukee)
The Renaissance: a reconsideration of the theories and interpretations of the
age. Edited by Tinsley Helton. Contributors: Garrett Mattingly [and others]. —
Madison, University of Wisconsin Press, 1961. xiii, 160 p. 22 cm. Includes
bibliographies. 1. Renaissance — Congresses. I. Helton, Tinsley. ed. II. T.
CB361.S93 1959　　　901.93　　　LC 61-5903

Trinkaus, Charles Edward, 1911-.　　　　　　　　3.164
The scope of Renaissance humanism / Charles Trinkaus. — Ann Arbor:
University of Michigan Press, c1983. xxvii, 479 p.; 24 cm. 1. Renaissance —
Addresses, essays, lectures. 2. Humanism — Addresses, essays, lectures. I. T.
CB361.T74 1983　　　001.3/09/024 19　　　LC 83-6650　　　ISBN
0472100319

Ullmann, Walter, 1910-.　　　　　　　　　　　3.165
Medieval foundations of renaissance humanism / Walter Ullmann. — Ithaca,
N.Y.: Cornell University Press, c1977. xii, 212 p.; 25 cm. 1. Humanism
2. Renaissance I. T.
CB361.U43　　　144/.094　　　LC 77-278　　　ISBN 0801411106

Utley, Francis Lee, 1907- ed.　　　　　　　　　• 3.166
The forward movement of the fourteenth century. Columbus, Ohio State
University Press [1961] 166 p. plates. 24 cm. 1. Fourteenth century. I. T.
CB365.U8　　　LC 60-14642

Allen, Percy Stafford, 1869-1933.　　　　　　　• 3.167
The age of Erasmus; lectures delivered in the universities of Oxford and
London. — New York, Russell & Russell, 1963. 303 p. 23 cm. 1. Erasmus,
Desiderius, d. 1536. 2. Renaissance I. T.
CB367.A5 1963　　　922.2492　　　LC 63-11026

Haydn, Hiram Collins, 1907-1973.　　　　　　　• 3.168
The counter-Renaissance. — New York, Scribner, 1950. xvii, 705 p. 24 cm.
Bibliography: p. 672-687. 1. Renaissance I. T.
CB369.H35　　　901　　　LC 50-7225

Taylor, Henry Osborn, 1856-1941.　　　　　　　• 3.169
Thought and expression in the sixteenth century. — 2d rev. ed. — New York:
Ungar, [1959] 2 v.; 22 cm. 1. Humanism 2. Sixteenth century 3. Europe —
Intellectual life I. T.
CB369.T3 1959　　　940.22　　　LC 59-11670

CB401–411 16th, 17th, 18th Centuries

Clark, G. N. (George Norman), Sir, 1890-.　　　• 3.170
War and society in the seventeenth century. — Cambridge [Eng.] University
Press, 1958. 156 p. 22 cm. — (The Wiles lectures, 1956) Includes bibliography.
1. War and society 2. Seventeenth century I. T.
CB401.C62　　　172.4　　　LC 58-1704

Clark, George Norman, 1890-.　　　　　　　　• 3.171
The seventeenth century. — 2d ed. — Oxford, Clarendon Press, 1947. xix,
378 p. fold. maps. 23 cm. 1. Europe — Civilization I. T.
CB401.C6x　　　LC A 48-3857 *

Elliott, John Huxtable.　　　　　　　　　　　3.172
The old world and the new 1492-1650, by J. H. Elliott. Cambridge [Eng.]:
University Press, 1970. x, 118 p.: front.; 22 cm. — (Wiles lectures. 1969)
(Cambridge studies in early modern history.) 1. Europe — Civilization —
Addresses, essays, lectures. 2. America — Discovery and exploration —
Addresses, essays, lectures. I. T. II. Series.
CB401.E43　　　914/.03　　　LC 73-121362　　　ISBN 0521079373

Friedrich, Carl J. (Carl Joachim), 1901-.　　　• 3.173
The age of power [by] Carl J. Friedrich and Charles Blitzer. Ithaca, N.Y.,
Cornell University Press [1957] 200 p. illus. 22 cm. (The Development of
Western civilization) 1. Europe — Civilization — 17th century. I. Blitzer,
Charles. joint author. II. T.
CB401.F7　　　909/.06 19　　　LC 57-4449

Hatton, Ragnhild Marie.　　　　　　　　　　• 3.174
Europe in the age of Louis XIV [by] Ragnhild Hatton. [New York] Harcourt,
Brace & World [1969] 263 p. illus. (part col.), geneal. table, maps, ports. 21 cm.
(History of European civilization library) 1. Europe — Civilization — 17th
century. I. T.
CB401.H3 1969b　　　914/.03/25　　　LC 70-78869

Mandrou, Robert.　　　　　　　　　　　　　3.175
[Des humanistes aux hommes de science (XVIe et XVIIe siècles). English]
From humanism to science, 1480-1700 / Robert Mandrou; translated by Brian
Pearce. — Atlantic Highlands, N.J.: Humanities Press, 1979. 329 p.: maps; 23
cm. Translation of Des humanistes aux hommes de science (XVIe et XVIIe
siècles). Includes index. 1. Civilization, Modern 2. Renaissance 3. Humanism
I. T.
CB401.M3613 1979　　　909/.08　　　LC 78-10510　　　ISBN 0391005413

Chaunu, Pierre.　　　　　　　　　　　　　• 3.176
La civilisation de l'Europe classique / Pierre Chaunu. — Paris: Arthaud, 1966.
705 p.: ill., facsims., maps (part fol. col.) plates (part col.) ports.; 23 cm.
(Collection Les Grandes civilisations. 5) 1. Civilization, Modern I. T.
II. Series.
CB411.C45　　　LC 66-99945

Cobban, Alfred.　　　　　　　　　　　　　• 3.177
The eighteenth century: Europe in the age of enlightenment. Texts by Alfred
Cobban [and others] Edited by Alfred Cobban. — New York: McGraw-Hill,
[1969] 360 p.: illus. (part col.), maps, ports.; 36 cm. 1. Europe — Civilization
— 18th century I. T.
CB411.C6 1969　　　914/.03/25　　　LC 78-75160

Hampson, Norman.　　　　　　　　　　　　• 3.178
A cultural history of the Enlightenment. — [1st American ed.]. — New York:
Pantheon Books, [c1968] 304 p.; 22 cm. 1. Enlightenment — History. I. T.
CB411.H38 1968　　　914/.03/253　　　LC 68-26043

Jacob, Margaret C., 1943-.　　　　　　　　　3.179
The Radical Enlightenment: Pantheists, Freemasons, and Republicans /
Margaret C. Jacob. — London; Boston: Allen & Unwin, 1981. xiii, 312 p., [1]
leaf of plates: ill.; 23 cm. — (Early modern Europe today. 3) 1. Freemasons —
History 2. Enlightenment 3. Pantheism — History. 4. Europe — Civilization
— 18th century 5. Europe — Civilization — 17th century. I. T. II. Series.
CB411.J33 1981　　　940.2/5 19　　　LC 80-41893　　　ISBN 0049010298

Kraus, Michael, 1901-.　　　　　　　　　　• 3.180
The Atlantic civilization: eighteenth-century origins. New York, Russell &
Russell, 1961 [c1949] 334 p. 22 cm. 1. Civilization, Modern — 18th century
2. United States — Relations — Europe 3. Europe — Relations — United
States I. T.
CB411.K7 1961　　　901.93　　　LC 61-12131

Mazzeo, Joseph Anthony, 1923- ed.　　　　　• 3.181
Reason and the imagination; studies in the history of ideas, 1600-1800. — New
York, Columbia University Press, 1962. viii, 321 p. plates. 23 cm. The studies
are in honor of Marjorie Hope Nicolson. Bibliographical footnotes.
1. Nicolson, Marjorie Hope, 1894- 2. Seventeenth century — Addresses,
essays, lectures. 3. Eighteenth century — Addresses, essays, lectures. I. T.
CB411.M3　　　901.93　　　LC 62-7773

Woloch, Isser, 1937-.　　　　　　　　　　　3.182
Eighteenth-century Europe, tradition and progress, 1715-1789 / Isser Woloch.
— 1st ed. — New York: Norton, c1982. xvii, 364 p.: ill.; 22 cm. — (Norton
history of modern Europe.) Includes index. 1. Europe — Civilization — 18th
century I. T. II. Series.
CB411.W64 1982　　　940.2/53 19　　　LC 81-11226　　　ISBN 0393015068

CB415–428 19th–20th Centuries

Biddiss, Michael Denis.   3.183
The age of the masses: ideas and society in Europe since 1870 / Michael D. Biddiss. — Atlantic Highlands, N.J.: Humanities Press, 1977. 379 p.; 23 cm. 1. Philosophy, Modern — 19th century 2. Philosophy, Modern — 20th century 3. Europe — Intellectual life — 20th century I. T.
CB417.B47 1977   190   *LC* 77-7542   *ISBN* 039100736X

Masur, Gerhard, 1901-.   • 3.184
Prophets of yesterday; studies in European culture, 1890–1914. — New York: Macmillan, 1961. 481 p.; 22 cm. 1. Civilization, Modern — 19th century 2. Europe — Intellectual life I. T.
CB417.M36   914   *LC* 61-9729

Regin, Deric.   • 3.185
Culture and the crowd; a cultural history of the proletarian era. — [1st ed.]. — Philadelphia: Chilton Book Co., [1968] xii, 512 p.; 24 cm. 1. Civilization, Modern — 19th century 2. Civilization, Modern — 20th century I. T.
CB417.R4   901.9/4   *LC* 68-19178

Berdiaev, Nikolaĭ, 1874-1948.   • 3.186
The fate of man in the modern world / [Translated by Donald A. Lowrie. — Ann Arbor]: University of Michigan Press, [1961, c1935] 131 p.; 21 cm. (Ann Arbor paperbacks, AA59) 1. Civilization — Philosophy 2. Collectivism 3. Nationalism 4. Sociology, Christian I. T.
CB425.B37 1961   901.94   *LC* 61-65396

Berman, M. (Marshall), 1939-.   3.187
All that is solid melts into air: the experience of modernity / Marshall Berman. — New York: Simon and Schuster, c1982. 383 p. 1. Civilization, Modern — 20th century 2. Civilization, Modern — 19th century I. T.
CB425.B458   CB425 B445.   909.82 19   *LC* 81-16640   *ISBN* 067124602X

Boulding, Kenneth Ewart, 1910-.   3.188
The meaning of the twentieth century; the great transition [by] Kenneth E. Boulding. [1st ed.] New York, Harper & Row [1964] xvi, 199 p. 20 cm. (World perspectives, v. 34) 1. Civilization, Modern — 1950- I. T. II. Title: Great transition.
CB425.B668   301.24   *LC* 64-20540

Crouzet, Maurice.   • 3.189
L'Époque contemporaine, à la recherche d'une civilisation nouvelle. 5e édition revue et augmentée. Paris, Presses Universitaires de France, 1969. 944p. illus.,maps,plates. 24cm. (Histoire générale des civilisations. t.7) 1. Twentieth century I. T. II. Series.
CB425.C77 1969   *LC* 70-410869

Harrington, Michael, 1928-.   • 3.190
The accidental century. New York, Macmillan [1965] 322 p. 22 cm. 1. Civilization, Modern — 20th century I. T.
CB425.H24   901.94   *LC* 65-16935

Jaspers, Karl, 1883-1969.   • 3.191
Man in the modern age / by K. Jaspers; translated by Eden and Cedar Paul. — London: G. Routledge & Sons, 1933. vii, 243 p. 1. Civilization I. T.
CB425 J342

Kohn, Hans, 1891-1971.   • 3.192
The twentieth century: the challenge to the West and its response / by Hans Kohn. — New and enl. ed. — New York: Macmillan, 1957. 300 p. 1. Twentieth century I. T.
CB425.K65 1957   *LC* 57-10778

Public opinion, 1935–1946. Under the editorial direction of   • 3.193
Hadley Cantril. Prepared by Mildred Strunk.
Princeton, Princeton University Press, 1951. lix, 1191 p. 30 cm. 'Opinion poll results ... collected from 23 organizations in 16 countries.' 1. Public opinion 2. Twentieth century I. Cantril, Hadley, 1906-1969. ed. II. Strunk, Mildred.
CB425.P79   301.154   *LC* 51-272

Romains, Jules, 1885-1972.   • 3.194
As it is on earth / Jules Romains; translated from the French by Richard Howard. — New York: Macmillan, 1962. 111 p. Translation of: Situation de la terre. 1. Civilization, Modern — 20th century I. T.
CB425.R7233   901.94   *LC* 62-10647

Chase, Stuart, 1888-.   • 3.195
The most probable world. — [1st ed.]. — New York: Harper & Row, [c1968] xii, 239 p.; 22 cm. 1. Civilization, Modern — 20th century — Addresses, essays, lectures. I. T.
CB427.C48   901.9/4   *LC* 67-28803

Fabun, Don.   • 3.196
The dynamics of change, by Don Fabun, assisted by Niels Sundermeyer. Art director: Bob Conover. — Englewood Cliffs, N.J.: Prentice-Hall, [1967] 1 v. (various pagings): illus. (part col.); 29 cm. 'Material ... originated in commemoration of the twentieth anniversary of Kaiser Aluminum & Chemical Corporation. It first appeared in a special series of six issues of Kaiser aluminum news.' 1. Civilization, Modern — 1950- I. Sundermeyer, Niels. II. T.
CB427.F25   901.94   *LC* 67-25569

Spengler, Oswald, 1880-1936.   • 3.197
The decline of the West / Oswald Spengler. — Special edition, October, 1939. — New York: Knopf, 1939. 2 v. in 1: tables(3 fold); 24 cm. Each volume has special t.p. 'Authorized translation with notes.' Complete in one volume. 1. Civilization — History I. Atkinson, Charles Francis, 1880- II. T.
CB427.F54

Sakharov, Andreĭ, 1921-.   • 3.198
Progress, coexistence, and intellectual freedom / by Andrei D. Sakharov; translated by the New York Times; with introd., afterword, and notes by Harrison E. Salisbury. — New York: Norton, 1968. 158 p. 1. Civilization, Modern — 1950 — Addresses, essays, lectures. I. Salisbury, Harrison Evans, 1908- II. T.
CB427.S2313   901.945   *LC* 68-57368

Bullock, Alan, 1914-.   3.199
The twentieth century; a Promethean age. Texts by Alan Bullock [and others] Edited by Alan Bullock. New York, McGraw-Hill [1971] 371 p. illus. (part col.) 36 cm. 1. Twentieth century — Addresses, essays, lectures. I. T.
CB428.B83 1971b   901.94   *LC* 75-159299   *ISBN* 0070088705

Hardison, O. B.   3.200
Entering the maze: identity and change in modern culture / O.B. Hardison, Jr. — New York: Oxford University Press, 1981. xiv, 304 p.; 22 cm. 1. Civilization, Modern — 20th century — Addresses, essays, lectures. 2. Arts and society — Addresses, essays, lectures. 3. Technology and civilization — Addresses, essays, lectures. 4. Popular culture — Addresses, essays, lectures. 5. Identity — Addresses, essays, lectures. 6. United States — Civilization — 1945- — Addresses, essays, lectures. 7. United States — Popular culture — Addresses, essays, lectures. I. T.
CB428.H37   303.4 19   *LC* 81-299   *ISBN* 0195029534

Heilbroner, Robert L.   3.201
An inquiry into the human prospect [by] Robert L. Heilbroner. — [1st ed.]. — New York: Norton, [1974] 150 p.; 21 cm. 1. Civilization, Modern — 1950- 2. Regression (Civilization) I. T.
CB428.H44 1974   909.82   *LC* 73-21879   *ISBN* 0393055140

Muller, Herbert Joseph, 1905-.   3.202
In pursuit of relevance [by] Herbert J. Muller. — Bloomington: Indiana University Press, [1971] xii, 306 p.; 25 cm. 1. Civilization, Modern — 1950- 2. Science and the humanities 3. U.S. — Civilization — 1945- I. T.
CB428.M85 1971   901.9/45   *LC* 70-163517   *ISBN* 0253141907

Muller, Herbert Joseph, 1905-.   3.203
Uses of the future [by] Herbert J. Muller. — Bloomington: Indiana University Press, [1974] xviii, 264 p.; 22 cm. 1. Civilization, Modern — 1950- 2. Twenty-first century — Forecasts 3. United States — Civilization — 1970- I. T.
CB428.M854   901.94   *LC* 73-15240   *ISBN* 0253362105

Pawley, Martin.   3.204
The private future: causes and consequences of community collapse in the West. — [1st American ed.]. — New York: Random House, [1974] 217 p.; 22 cm. 1. Civilization, Modern — 1950- 2. Regression (Civilization) I. T.
CB428.P4   901.94   *LC* 73-5044   *ISBN* 0394480724

Roszak, Theodore, 1933-.   3.205
Where the wasteland ends: politics and transcendence in postindustrial society. — [1st ed.]. — Garden City, N.Y.: Doubleday, 1972. xxxiv, 492 p.; 22 cm. 1. Civilization, Modern — 1950- I. T.
CB428.R67   910/.03/0904   *LC* 78-170179   *ISBN* 0385027281

Stavrianos, Leften Stavros.   3.206
The promise of the coming dark age / L. S. Stavrianos. — San Francisco: W. H. Freeman, c1976. x, 211 p.; 22 cm. 1. Civilization, Modern — 1950- 2. Civilization — History 3. Regression (Civilization) I. T.
CB428.S8   909.82   *LC* 76-8232   *ISBN* 0716704978

Toynbee, Arnold Joseph, 1889-1975.   3.207
Surviving the future [by] Arnold Toynbee. — London; New York: Oxford University Press, 1971. xii, 164 p.; 23 cm. Revision of a dialogue between Kei Wakaizumi and Arnold Toynbee, originally published, in Japanese, in installments, in the Mainichi Shimbun. 1. Civilization, Modern — 1950- — Addresses, essays, lectures. 2. Civilization — Philosophy I. Wakaizumi, Kei, 1930- II. T.
CB428.T69 1971   901.9   *LC* 77-167854   *ISBN* 0192152521

CB440–481 Special Topics

Clough, Shepard Bancroft, 1901-.   • 3.208
The rise and fall of civilization; an inquiry into the relationship between economic development and civilization. New York, McGraw-Hill [1951] xiii, 291 p. maps. 21 cm. 1. Civilization — History 2. Economic history I. T.
CB448.C57   901   LC 51-12730

Bronowski, Jacob, 1908-1974.   3.209
Magic, science, and civilization / J. Bronowski. — New York: Columbia University Press, 1978. 88 p.; 21 cm. — (Bampton lectures in America. no. 20) 1. Science and civilization — Addresses, essays, lectures. 2. Science — Europe — History — Addresses, essays, lectures. 3. Philosophy — Europe — History — Addresses, essays, lectures. 4. Magic — Europe — Addresses, essays, lectures. I. T. II. Series.
CB478.B73 1978   909.08   LC 78-1660   ISBN 0231044844

Foster, George McClelland, 1913-.   • 3.210
Traditional cultures, and the impact of technological change. — New York: Harper, [1962] 292 p.; 22 cm. Second ed. published in 1973 under title: Traditional societies and technological change. 1. Technology and civilization I. T.
CB478.F6   301.24   LC 62-10483

Mumford, Lewis, 1895-.   • 3.211
Myth of the machine. New York: Harcourt, Brace & World, 1967-70. 2 v.: ill. Vol. 2 has imprint: New York, Harcourt Brace Jovanovich. 1. Technology and civilization I. T.
CB478 M78   901.9   LC 67-16088   ISBN 0156716100

Myths of information: technology and postindustrial culture /   3.212
edited by Kathleen Woodward.
Madison, WI: Coda Press, 1980. 250 p.; cm. (Theories of contemporary culture; 2) 1. Technology and civilization — Addresses, essays, lectures. 2. Information theory — Addresses, essays, lectures. 3. Mass media — Addresses, essays, lectures. I. Woodward, Kathleen M.
CB478.M9   303.4/83   LC 80-23653   ISBN 0930956125

Nef, John Ulric, 1899-.   • 3.213
Cultural foundations of industrial civilization. Cambridge [Eng.] University Press, 1958. xiv, 163 p.; 22 cm. (The Wiles lectures, 1956) Erratum slip inserted. Bibliographical footnotes. 1. Technology and civilization 2. Civilization — History I. T. II. Series.
CB478.N4 1958   LC A 59-642

Peccei, Aurelio.   • 3.214
The chasm ahead. — [New York]: Macmillan, [1969] xvi, 297 p.: illus.; 22 cm. 1. Technology and civilization I. T.
CB478.P4   901.9   LC 69-11395

Taylor, Gordon Rattray.   • 3.215
The doomsday book; can the world survive?. — New York: World Pub. Co., [1970] 335 p.; 22 cm. 1. Technology and civilization 2. Human ecology I. T.
CB478.T38 1970b   301.31   LC 75-124280

Nef, John Ulric, 1899-.   • 3.216
War and human progress; an essay on the rise of industrial civilization, by John U. Nef. — New York: Russell & Russell, [1968, c1950] ix, 464 p.; 24 cm. 1. War and civilization I. T.
CB481.N4 1968   901.9   LC 68-10934

CC ARCHAEOLOGY

Binford, Sally R.   • 3.217
New perspectives in archeology. Edited by Sally R. Binford and Lewis R. Binford. — Chicago: Aldine Pub. Co., [1968] x, 373 p.: illus., maps, plans.; 25 cm. Includes 11 papers, (substantially rev.), presented at a symposium held during the 64th annual meeting of the American Anthropological Association, Denver, Nov. 1965. 1. Archeology — Addresses, essays, lectures. I. Binford, Lewis Roberts, 1930- joint author. II. American Anthropological Association. III. T.
CC65.B5   913.03/1   LC 67-27386

The Concise encyclopedia of archaeology, edited by Leonard   3.218
Cottrell.
3rd ed. [revised]. — London: Hutchinson, 1974. xxv, 430 p.: maps.; 23 cm. 1. Archaeology — Dictionaries. I. Cottrell, Leonard. ed.
CC70.C6 1974   913/.031/03   LC 74-174138   ISBN 0091184509

The Facts on File dictionary of archaeology / editor, Ruth D.   3.219
Whitehouse.
New York, N.Y.: Facts on File, 1984. 597 p.: ill. Originally published under title: The Macmillan dictionary of archaeology. Includes index. 1. Archaeology — Dictionaries. I. Whitehouse, Ruth. II. Facts on File, Inc.
CC70.F32 1984   930.1/03/21 19   LC 83-16396   ISBN 0871960486

Salmon, Merrilee H.   3.220
Philosophy and archaeology / Merrilee H. Salmon. — New York, N.Y.: Academic Press, 1982. 203 p.; 24 cm. — (Studies in archaeology.) Includes indexes. 1. Archaeology — Philosophy 2. Archaeology — Methodology I. T. II. Series.
CC72.S24 1982   930.1/01 19   LC 82-8828   ISBN 0126156506

Theory and explanation in archaeology: the Southampton   3.221
conference / edited by Colin Renfrew, Michael J. Rowlands,
Barbara Abbott Segraves.
New York: Academic Press, 1982. xxi, 480 p.: ill.; 24 cm. Papers presented at the 2nd open conference of the Theoretical Archaeology Group, held in Southampton, England, Dec. 14-16, 1980; sponsored by the Dept. of Archaeology, University of Southampton, and the Dept. of Prehistory and Archaeology, University of Sheffield. 1. Archaeology — Philosophy — Congresses. 2. Archaeology — Methodology — Congresses. I. Renfrew, Colin, 1937- II. Rowlands, M. J. III. Segraves, Barbara Abbott. IV. Theoretical Archaeology Group (England) V. University of Southampton. Dept. of Archaeology. VI. University of Sheffield. Dept. of Archaeology and Prehistory.
CC72.T47 1982   930.1/01 19   LC 81-17613   ISBN 0125869606

Watson, Patty Jo, 1932-.   3.222
Archeological explanation: the scientific method in archeology / Patty Jo Watson, Steven A. LeBlanc, Charles L. Redman. — New York: Columbia University Press, 1984. xi, 309 p.: ill.; 24 cm. Includes index. 1. Archaeology — Philosophy 2. Archaeology — Methodology I. LeBlanc, Steven A. II. Redman, Charles L. III. T.
CC72.W37 1984   930.1/01 19   LC 84-5014   ISBN 0231060289

Gibbon, Guy E., 1939-.   3.223
Anthropological archaeology / Guy Gibbon. — New York: Columbia University Press, 1984. xii, 455 p.: ill.; 25 cm. 1. Social archaeology 2. Ethnoarchaeology I. T.
CC72.4.G53 1984   930.1 19   LC 84-4321   ISBN 0231056621

Renfrew, Colin, 1937-.   3.224
Approaches to social archaeology / Colin Renfrew. — Cambridge, Mass.: Harvard University Press, 1984. viii, 430 p.: ill.; 23 cm. 1. Social archaeology — Addresses, essays, lectures. 2. Anthropology, Prehistoric — Addresses, essays, lectures. 3. Man, Prehistoric — Addresses, essays, lectures. I. T.
CC72.4.R46 1984   306/.093 19   LC 83-22548   ISBN 0674041658

CC73–81 Methodology. Environmental Archaeology

Noël Hume, Ivor.   • 3.225
Historical archaeology. — [1st ed.]. — New York: Knopf, 1969. xiii, 355, v p.: illus.; 24 cm. 1. Archaeology — Methodology 2. Archaeology and history I. T.
CC73.N6 1969   913.03/1028   LC 68-12662

Aitken, M. J. (Martin Jim)   3.226
Physics and archaeology / by M. J. Aitken. — 2d ed. — Oxford: Clarendon Press, 1974. viii, 291 p.: ill.; 23 cm. 1. Archaeology — Methodology I. T.
CC75.A3 1974   930/.1/028   LC 75-310409   ISBN 0198519222

Binford, Lewis Roberts, 1930-.   3.227
An archaeological perspective [by] Lewis R. Binford. With a contribution by George I. Quimby. — New York: Seminar Press, 1972. xii, 464 p.: illus.; 25 cm. — (Studies in archaeology) 1. Archaeology — Methodology — Addresses, essays, lectures. I. Quimby, George Irving, 1913- II. T.
CC75.B48   913/.031/0285   LC 77-183460   ISBN 0128077506

Brothwell, Don R. ed.   • 3.228
Science in archaeology; a survey of progress and research. Edited by Don Brothwell and Eric Higgs. With a foreword by Grahame Clark. — Rev. and enl.

ed. — New York: Praeger, [1970] 720 p.: illus., maps, plates.; 26 cm.
1. Archaeology — Methodology I. Higgs, Eric S. joint ed. II. T.
CC75.B73 1970   913.03/1/018   *LC* 76-92580

Clarke, David L.   **3.229**
Models in archaeology; edited by David L. Clarke. — London: Methuen, 1972.
xxiv, 1055, [2] p., [4] leaves.: illus., maps.; 24 cm. 'Distributed in the U.S.A. by
Harper & Row Publishers Inc., Barnes & Noble Import Division.'
1. Archaeology — Methodology I. T.
CC75.C48 1972   913/.031/0184   *LC* 73-152392   *ISBN* 0416165400

Clarke, David L.   **3.230**
Analytical archaeology / David L. Clarke. — 2d ed. / rev. by Bob Chapman. —
New York: Columbia University Press, 1978. xxi, 526 p.: ill.; 24 cm. Includes
index. 1. Archaeology — Methodology I. Chapman, Bob. II. T.
CC75.C535 1978   930/.1/028   *LC* 78-16957   *ISBN* 0231046308

Coles, J. M. (John M.)   **3.231**
Archaeology by experiment / John Coles. — New York: Scribner, [1974]
c1973. 182 p., [6] leaves of plates: ill.; 21 cm. Includes index. 1. Archaeology —
Methodology 2. Man, Prehistoric I. T.
CC75.C57 1974   913/.031/028   *LC* 74-3668   *ISBN* 0684138182

Coles, J. M. (John M.)   **3.232**
Field archaeology in Britain [by] John Coles. London, Methuen, 1972. ix, 267,
[4] p. illus., maps. 22 cm. Distributed in the USA by Harper & Row Publishers,
Inc., Barnes & Noble Import Division. 1. Archaeology — Methodology
2. Great Britain — Antiquities I. T.
CC75.C58 1972   913/.031/028   *LC* 73-152393   *ISBN* 0416760406
ISBN 0416765408

Doran, J. E.   **3.233**
Mathematics and computers in archaeology / J. E. Doran and F. R. Hodson. —
Cambridge, Mass.: Harvard University Press, 1975. xi, 381 p.: ill. Includes
index. 1. Archaeology — Methodology — Data processing. 2. Archaeology —
Classification — Data processing. I. Hodson, F. R. II. T.
CC75.D63   930/.1/0285   *ISBN* 0674554558

Laet, Sigfried J. de.   **3.234**
Archaeology and its problems / by Sigfried J. de Laet; translated by Ruth
Daniel; with a foreword by Glyn E. Danie. — New York: Macmillian, [1957].
136 p.: ill.; 22 cm. 1. Archaeology — Methodology I. T.
CC75.Lx   913.031028

Trigger, Bruce G.   **3.235**
Time and traditions: essays in archaeological interpretation / Bruce G. Trigger.
— New York: Columbia University Press, 1978. xii, 273 p.; 21 cm. Includes
index. 1. Archaeology — Methodology — Addresses, essays, lectures.
2. Archaeology — History — Addresses, essays, lectures. I. T.
CC75.T68 1978   930.1   *LC* 77-28524   *ISBN* 0231045484

Wheeler, Robert Eric Mortimer, Sir, 1890-.   • **3.236**
Archaeology from the earth. Oxford, Clarendon Press, 1954. xi, 221 p. illus.,
maps (1 fold.) 23 cm. 1. Archaeology — Methodology I. T.
CC75.W46   *LC* a 54-4655

Social archeology: beyond subsistence and dating / edited by   **3.237**
Charles L. Redman ... [et al.].
New York: Academic Press, c1978. xiv, 471 p.: ill.; 24 cm. — (Studies in
archeology) 1. Archaeology — Methodology — Addresses, essays, lectures.
2. Man, Prehistoric — Addresses, essays, lectures. I. Redman, Charles L.
CC75.7.S6   930/.1/028   *LC* 78-16390   *ISBN* 0125851502

Spatial archaeology / edited by David L. Clarke.   **3.238**
London; New York: Academic Press, 1977. xi, 386 p.: ill.; 24 cm.
1. Archaeology — Methodology — Addresses, essays, lectures. I. Clarke,
David L.
CC75.7.S68   930/.1/028   *LC* 76-55909   *ISBN* 0121757501

Joukowsky, Martha.   **3.239**
A complete manual of field archaeology: tools and techniques of field work for
archaeologists / Martha Joukowsky. — Englewood Cliffs, N.J.: Prentice-Hall,
c1980. x, 630 p.: ill.; 23 cm. — (A Spectrum book) Includes index.
1. Archaeology — Field work — Handbooks, manuals, etc. I. T. II. Title:
Field archaeology: tools and techniques of field work for archaeologists.
CC76.J68   930.1   *LC* 79-25847   *ISBN* 0131621645

Bass, George Fletcher.   • **3.240**
Archaeology under water [by] George F. Bass. — New York: Praeger, [1966]
224 p.: illus., maps (1 fold.), ports.; 21 cm. — (Ancient peoples and places, v.
48) 1. Underwater archaeology I. T.
CC77.B3   913.031028   *LC* 66-12992

Chang, Kwang-chih.   • **3.241**
Rethinking archaeology [by] K. C. Chang. — New York: Random House,
[1967] xiv, 172 p.: illus.; 19 cm. — (Studies in anthropology, AS6) Lectures

delivered at an anthropology seminar at Yale University in 1966.
1. Archaeology — Methodology I. T.
CC77.C48   913/.001/8   *LC* 67-10916

Archaeological geology / edited by George Rapp, Jr. and John   **3.242**
A. Gifford.
New Haven: Yale University Press, c1985. xvii, 435 p.: ill.; 25 cm. Includes
index. 1. Archaeological geology — Addresses, essays, lectures. I. Rapp,
George Robert, 1930- II. Gifford, John A., 1947-
CC77.5.A73 1985   930.1 19   *LC* 84-40201   *ISBN* 0300031424

Dunnell, Robert C., 1942-.   **3.243**
Systematics in prehistory [by] Robert C. Dunnell. — New York: Free Press,
[1971] x, 214 p.: illus.; 22 cm. 1. Archaeology — Classification.
2. Anthropology, Prehistoric I. T.
CC78.D85   913.03/1   *LC* 76-142359

Fleming, Stuart James.   **3.244**
Dating in archaeology: a guide to scientific techniques / Stuart Fleming. New
York: St. Martin's Press, 1977, c1976. 272 p.: ill.; 26 cm. Includes index.
1. Archaeological dating I. T.
CC78.F54 1977   930/.1/0285   *LC* 76-20199

Gould, Richard A.   **3.245**
Living archaeology / R. A. Gould. — Cambridge [Eng.]; New York:
Cambridge University Press, 1980. xv, 270 p.: ill.; 24 cm. — (New studies in
archaeology) Includes index. 1. Ethnoarchaeology 2. Australian aborigines —
Australia — Western Desert. 3. Australia — Antiquities I. T.
CC79.E85 G68   930/.1   *LC* 79-20788   *ISBN* 0521230934

Hodder, Ian.   **3.246**
The present past: an introduction to anthropology for archaeologists / Ian
Hodder. — New York: Pica Press: Distributed by Universe Books, 1983, c1982.
239 p.: ill.; 23 cm. Includes index. 1. Ethnoarchaeology I. T.
CC79.E85 H63 1983   930.1 19   *LC* 82-17437   *ISBN* 0876637365

Cornwall, Ian Wolfram.   **3.247**
Bones for the archaeologist / by I. W. Cornwall. — Rev. ed. — London: Dent,
1974. 259 p.: ill.; 24 cm. Includes index. 1. Animal remains (Archaeology)
2. Archaeology — Methodology 3. Bones 4. Mammals I. T.
CC79.5.A5 C67 1974   930.1   *LC* 75-308588   *ISBN* 0460042297

Rye, Owen S.   **3.248**
Pottery technology: principles and reconstruction / Owen S. Rye. —
Washington, D.C.: Taraxacum, 1981. ix, 150 p.: ill.; 29 cm. — (Manuals on
archeology. 4) Includes index. 1. Pottery — Analysis. 2. Archaeology —
Methodology I. T. II. Series.
CC79.5.P6 R93   738.1 19   *LC* 80-53439   *ISBN* 096028222X

Schiffer, Michael B.   **3.249**
Behavioral archeology / Michael B. Schiffer. — New York: Academic Press,
c1976. xviii, 222 p.: ill.; 24 cm. (Studies in archeology) Includes index.
1. Archaeology — Methodology 2. Pueblo Indians — Implements. 3. Indians
of North America — Arizona — Implements. 4. Joint site, Ariz. I. T.
CC80.S33   930/.1/028   *LC* 75-32035   *ISBN* 0126241503

Butzer, Karl W.   **3.250**
Archaeology as human ecology: method and theory for a contextual approach /
Karl W. Butzer. — Cambridge; New York: Cambridge University Press, 1982.
xiii, 364 p.; 24 cm. Includes index. 1. Environmental archaeology 2. Human
ecology I. T.
CC81.B87 1982   930.1 19   *LC* 81-21576   *ISBN* 0521246520

Evans, John G.   **3.251**
An introduction to environmental archaeology / John G. Evans. — Ithaca,
N.Y.: Cornell University Press, 1978. xii, 154 p.: ill.; 23 cm. — (Cornell
paperbacks) Includes index. 1. Environmental archaeology I. T.
CC81.E93 1978   930/.1   *LC* 77-90903   *ISBN* 0801411726

CC100–115 History. Biography

Daniel, Glyn Edmund.   **3.252**
A hundred and fifty years of archaeology / Glyn Daniel. — 2d ed. —
Cambridge, Mass.: Harvard University Press, 1976. 410 p.; 22 cm. First ed.
published in 1950 under title: A hundred years of archaeology. Includes index.
1. Archaeology — History. I. T.
CC100.D27 1976   930/.1   *LC* 76-7214   *ISBN* 0674426312

Daniel, Glyn Edmund.   3.253
A short history of archaeology / Glyn Daniel. — London: Thames & Hudson c1981. 232 p.: ill. (some col.); 25 cm. — (Ancient peoples and places; v. 100) Includes index. 1. Archaeology — History. I. T.
CC100.D278   *ISBN* 0500021015

Fagan, Brian M.   3.254
The adventure of archaeology / by Brian M. Fagan. — 1st ed. — Washington, DC: National Geographic Society, c1985. 368 p.: ill. (some col.); 29 cm. Includes index. 1. Archaeology — History. 2. Archaeologists — Biography. I. T.
CC100.F33 1985   930.1 19   *LC* 85-15275   *ISBN* 0870446037

Ceram, C. W., 1915-1972.   3.255
Gods, graves, and scholars; the story of archaeology, by C. W. Ceram. Translated from the German by E. B. Garside and Sophie Wilkins. — 2d, rev. and substantially enl. ed. — New York: Knopf, 1967. xvi, 441 p.: illus., maps, 32 plates, ports.; 22 cm. Translation of Götter, Gräber, und Gelehrte. 1. Archaeology — History. I. T.
CC100.M313 1967   913.03/1   *LC* 67-11119   *ISBN* 0394426614

Silberman, Neil Asher, 1950-.   3.256
Digging for God and country: exploration, archeology, and the secret struggle for the Holy Land, 1799–1917 / Neil Asher Silberman. — 1st ed. — New York: Knopf: Distributed by Random House, 1982. xv, 228 p., [24] p. of plates: ill.; 24 cm. Includes index. 1. Archaeology — Palestine — History. 2. Palestine — History — 1799-1917 I. T.
CC101.I75 S57 1982   956.94/03 19   *LC* 81-48104   *ISBN* 0394511395

Mongaït, Aleksandr L'vovich.   • 3.257
Archaeology in the USSR. / [Translated from the Russian by David Skvirsky]. — Moscow: Foreign Languages Pub. House, 1959. 428 p.: ill. (part col.), maps (part fold.); 27 cm. At head of title: Academy of Sciences of the U. S. S. R. Institute of the History of Material Culture. Errata slip inserted. 1. Archaeology — History. 2. Soviet Union — Antiquities I. T.
CC105.R9 M613   *LC* 60-37241

McNairn, Barbara.   3.258
The method and theory of V. Gordon Childe: economic, social, and cultural interpretations of prehistory / Barbara McNairn. — Edinburgh: Edinburgh University Press, c1980. vii, 184 p.; 18 cm. Includes index. 1. Childe, V. Gordon (Vere Gordon), 1892-1957. 2. Anthropology, Prehistoric 3. History — Philosophy 4. Culture I. T.
CC115.C45 M38   930.1/092/4 B 19   *LC* 81-145332   *ISBN* 0852243898

Trigger, Bruce G.   3.259
Gordon Childe, revolutions in archaeology / Bruce G. Trigger. — New York: Columbia University Press, c1980. 207, [8] leaves of plates: 33 ill.; 24 cm. 1. Childe, V. Gordon (Vere Gordon), 1892-1957. 2. Man, Prehistoric 3. Archaeologists — Great Britain — Biography. I. T.
CC115.C45 T74 1980   930/.1/0924 B 19   *LC* 79-26410   *ISBN* 0231050380

Wheeler, Robert Eric Mortimer, Sir, 1890-.   • 3.260
Still digging; interleaves from an antiquary's notebook. London, M. Joseph, c1955. 236 p., [9] leaves of plates. ill. 23 cm. 1. Wheeler, Robert Eric Mortimer, Sir, 1890- 2. Wheeler, Robert Eric Mortimer, Sir, 1890- 3. Archaeologists — Biography. I. T.
CC 115 W58 A4 1955   *LC* 55-22546

Hawkes, Jacquetta Hopkins, 1910-.   3.261
Adventurer in archaeology: the biography of Sir Mortimer Wheeler / Jacquetta Hawkes. — New York, N.Y.: St. Martin's Press, c1982. x, 387 p., [16] p. of plates: ill.; 24 cm. Includes index. 1. Wheeler, Robert Eric Mortimer, Sir, 1890- 2. Archaeologists — Great Britain — Biography. I. T.
CC115.W58 H38 1982   930.1/092/4 B 19   *LC* 81-21493   *ISBN* 0312006586

CC160–205 General Works

Binford, Lewis Roberts, 1930-.   3.262
In pursuit of the past: decoding the archaeological record / Lewis R. Binford; with the editorial collaboration of John F. Cherry, and Robin Torrence. — New York, N.Y. (500 5th Ave., New York, 10110): Thames and Hudson, 1983. 256 p.: ill.; 25 cm. Includes index. 1. Archaeology 2. Man, Prehistoric 3. Civilization, Ancient I. Cherry, John F. II. Torrence, Robin. III. T.
CC165.B48 1983   930.1 19   *LC* 82-50816

The Cambridge encyclopedia of archaeology / editor, Andrew   3.263
Sherratt; foreword by Grahame Clark.
New York: Crown Publishers, 1980. 495 p.: ill.; 27 cm. Includes index. 1. Archaeology 2. Man, Prehistoric 3. Civilization, Ancient I. Sherratt, Andrew. II. Clarke, Grahame, 1907-
CC165.C3 1980b   930/.1/03   *LC* 78-16232   *ISBN* 0517534975

Childe, Vere Gordon, 1882-.   • 3.264
A short introduction to archaeology. — London, F Muller [1956] 142 p. illus. 20 cm. (Man and society series) 1. Archaeology I. T.
CC165.C5   913   *LC* 57-212

Thomas, David Hurst.   3.265
Archaeology / David Hurst Thomas; ill. by Dennis O'Brien. — New York: Holt, Rinehart and Winston, c1979. xvii, 510 p.: ill.; 24 cm. Includes index. 1. Archaeology I. T.
CC165.T48   930/.1   *LC* 78-27568   *ISBN* 0030199263

Price, Percival, 1901-.   3.266
Bells and man / Percival Price. — Oxford; New York: Oxford University Press, 1983. xviii, 288 p.: ill.; 25 cm. 1. Bells — History. I. T.
CC205.P75 1983   789/.5/09 19   *LC* 83-215401   *ISBN* 0193181037

CD–CE Diplomatics. Archives. Chronology

Duckett, Kenneth W.   3.267
Modern manuscripts: a practical manual for their management, care, and use / Kenneth W. Duckett. — Nashville: American Association for State and Local History, [1975] xvi, 375 p.: ill.; 24 cm. Includes index. 1. Archives — Handbooks, manuals, etc. I. American Association for State and Local History. II. T.
CD950.D8   025.17/1   *LC* 75-5717   *ISBN* 0910050163

Posner, Ernst.   3.268
Archives in the ancient world. — Cambridge, Mass.: Harvard University Press, 1972. xvii, 283 p.: illus.; 24 cm. 1. Archives — History — To 500 2. Archives — History — 500-1500 I. T.
CD996.P67   930/.007/2   *LC* 79-158426   *ISBN* 0674044630

Thomas, Daniel H. ed.   3.269
The new guide to the diplomatic archives of Western Europe / edited by Daniel H. Thomas and Lynn M. Case. — [Philadelphia]: University of Pennsylvania Press, c1975. xi, 441 p.; 22 cm. Edition for 1959 published under title: Guide to the diplomatic archives of Western Europe. 1. Archives — Europe. I. Case, Lynn Marshall, 1903- joint ed. II. T.
CD1001.T4 1975   027.5/094   *LC* 75-10127   *ISBN* 0812276973

United States. National Historical Publications and Records   3.270
Commission.
Directory of archives and manuscript repositories in the United States. — Washington: National Historical Publications and Records Commission, 1978. 905 p.; 28 cm. Cover title. 1. Archives — United States — Directories. I. T.
CD3020.U54 1978   016.091/025/73   *LC* 78-23870

The Book of calendars / Frank Parise, editor.   3.271
New York: Facts on File, c1982. 387 p.; 24 cm. Includes index. 1. Calendars I. Parise, Frank.
CE11.B66 1982   529/.3 19   *LC* 80-19974

Freeman-Grenville, G. S. P. (Greville Stewart Parker)   3.272
The Muslim and Christian calendars: being tables for the conversion of Muslim and Christian dates from the Hijra to the year A.D. 2000 / G. S. P. Freeman-Grenville. — 2d ed. — London: R. Collings, 1977. vii, 87 p.; 22 cm. Distributed in the USA by Rowman and Littlefield, Totowa, N.J. 1. Calendar, Islamic 2. Church calendar I. T.
CE59.F7 1977   529/.32/7   *LC* 78-309244   *ISBN* 0860360598

CJ NUMISMATICS

Junge, Ewald.　　　　　　　　　　　　　　3.273
World coin encyclopedia / Ewald Junge. — 1st U.S. ed. — New York: W. Morrow, c1984. 297 p., [8] p. of plates: ill. (some col.); 26 cm. 1. Coins — Dictionaries. 2. Numismatics — Dictionaries. I. T.
CJ67.J86 1984　　　737.4/03 19　　　LC 84-60663　　　ISBN 0688040829

Kraay, Colin M.　　　　　　　　　　　　　• 3.274
Greek coins / by Colin M. Kraay; photos by Max Hirmer. — New York: Abrams, 1966. 396 p.: maps, plates (part mounted col.); 31 cm. I. Hirmer, Max. II. T.
CJ335.K7　　　737.49495　　　LC 66-13272

Seltman, Charles Theodore, 1886-1957.　　　　• 3.275
Greek coins; a history of metallic currency and coinage down to the fall of the Hellenistic kingdoms. — [2d ed.]. — London, Methuen [1955] xxvi, 311 p. illus., maps. 23 cm. — (Methuen's handbooks of archaeology) Bibliography: p. xv—xxvi. 1. Coinage — Greece — Hist. 2. Coins, Greek I. T.
CJ335.S4 1955　　　737.4　　　LC 55-2059

Kraay, Colin M.　　　　　　　　　　　　　3.276
Archaic and classical Greek coins / Colin M. Kraay. Berkeley: University of California Press, c1976. xxvi, 390 p., [32] leaves of plates: ill.; 26 cm. (Library of numismatics.) Includes indexes. 1. Numismatics, Greek I. T. II. Series.
CJ401.K72　　　737.4/9/38　　　LC 76-14303　　　ISBN 0520032543

Grant, Michael, 1914-.　　　　　　　　　　• 3.277
Roman history from coins; some uses of the imperial coinage to the historian. Cambridge Cambridge University Press 1958. 96p. 1. Coins, Roman 2. Rome — History I. T.
CJ833 G7 1958

Mattingly, Harold, 1884-1964.　　　　　　　• 3.278
Roman coins from the earliest times to the fall of the Western Empire: reprinted with further corrections and additional notes / by Harold Mattingly. — London: Methuen, 1967. xiv, 305 p.: 64 plates.; 22 cm. Distributed in the U.S.A. by Barnes & Noble. 1. Numismatics, Roman 2. Coinage — Rome — History. I. T.
CJ833.M3 1967　　　737.493　　　LC 67-98240

Sutherland, C. H. V. (Carol Humphrey Vivian), 1908-.　　3.279
Roman coins / by C. H. V. Sutherland. — New York: Putnam, 1974. 311 p.: ill. (some col.); 25 cm. (The World of numismatics) Includes index. 1. Coins, Roman I. T. II. Series.
CJ833.S9 1974　　　737.4/9/37　　　LC 73-81400　　　ISBN 0399112391

Dolley, Michael.　　　　　　　　　　　　3.280
The Norman conquest and the English coinage, by Michael Dolley. — London: Spink, [1966] 40 p.: illus., 2 maps, tables.; 22 cm. 1. Coins, British I. T.
CJ2491.D7　　　737.4942　　　LC 67-70404

Hill, George Francis, Sir, 1867-1948.　　　　　3.281
Medals of the Renaissance / George Hill. — Rev. and enl. ed. / by Graham Pollard. — London: British Museum Publications, 1978. 230 p., [16] leaves of plates: ill.; 28 cm. (A Colonnade book) 1. Medals, Renaissance I. Pollard, J. Graham (John Graham), 1929- II. T.
CJ5767.H5 1978　　　737/.2　　　LC 78-308866　　　ISBN 071410843X

CN INSCRIPTIONS

Woodhead, A. G. (Arthur Geoffrey)　　　　　• 3.282
The study of Greek inscriptions. Cambridge [Eng.] University Press, 1959. xi, 138 p. illus. 22 cm. 1. Inscriptions, Greek I. T.
CN350.W65　　　481.7　　　LC 59-16150/L

Meiggs, Russell.　　　　　　　　　　　　• 3.283
A selection of Greek historical inscriptions to the end of the fifth century B.C.; edited by Russell Meiggs and David Lewis. — Oxford: Clarendon P., 1969. xix, 308 p.; 23 cm. English and Greek. 1. Inscriptions, Greek I. Lewis, David Malcolm, joint author. II. T.
CN360.M4　　　LC 70-418962　　　ISBN 0198142668

Ventris, Michael, 1922-1956.　　　　　　　• 3.284
Documents in Mycenaean Greek: three hundred selected tablets from Knossos, Pylos and Mycenae with commentary and vocabulary / by Michael Ventris and John Chadwick; with a foreword by Alan J.B. Wace. — Cambridge, Eng.: Cambridge University Press, 1956. xxx, 452 p., 3 leaves of plates: ill.; 25 cm. Includes index. 1. Inscriptions, Mycenae. 2. Inscriptions, Linear B I. Chadwick, John, 1920- II. T.
CN362 V4　　　P1035.V4.　　　481.7　　　LC 57-404

CR HERALDRY

Franklyn, Julian.　　　　　　　　　　　　• 3.285
An encyclopaedic dictionary of heraldry / by Julian Franklyn and John Tanner; illustrated by Violetta Keeble. — [1st ed.]. — Oxford; New York: Pergamon Press, [1970] xiii, 367 p.: ill. (part col.); 26 cm. 1. Heraldry — Dictionaries. I. Tanner, John, 1927- joint author. II. T.
CR13.F7 1970　　　929.6/03　　　LC 79-15403　　　ISBN 0080132979

Campbell, Gordon, 1886-1953.　　　　　　　3.286
The book of flags / [by] Gordon Campbell, and I. O. Evans. — 7th ed. — London: Oxford University Press, 1974. xii, 120 p., xv leaves of plates: ill. (some col.); 23 cm. Includes index. 1. Flags I. Evans, Idrisyn Oliver, 1894- joint author. II. T.
CR101.C3 1974　　　929.9　　　LC 74-196829　　　ISBN 0192731327

Talocci, Mauro.　　　　　　　　　　　　3.287
[Guida alle bandiere di tutto il mondo. English] Guide to the flags of the world / Mauro Talocci; illustrations by Guido Canestrari, Carlo Giordana, Paolo Riccioni; translated from the Italian by Ronald Strom. — Rev. and updated / by Whitney Smith. — New York: Morrow, 1982. 271 p.: col. ill.; 20 cm. Translation of: Guida alle bandiere di tutto il mondo. 'First U.S. edition'—T.p. verso. Includes index. 1. Flags 2. Heraldry I. Canestrari, Guido. II. Giordana, Carlo. III. Riccioni, Paolo. IV. Smith, Whitney. V. T.
CR101.T3413 1982　　　929.9/2 19　　　LC 81-16890　　　ISBN 0688011039

Flags of the world / edited by E.M.C. Barraclough and W.G. Crampton.　　3.288
2nd ed., with revisions and suppl. — London; New York: F. Warne, 1981. 262 p.: ill. (some col.); 24 cm. Includes index. 1. Flags I. Barraclough, E. M. C. II. Crampton, W. G. (William G.)
CR109.F554 1981　　　929.9/2 19　　　LC 82-228603　　　ISBN 0723227977

Briggs, Geoffrey.　　　　　　　　　　　　3.289
National heraldry of the world / Geoffrey Briggs; illustrated by Glenn Steward, B. L. Ainsworth and Carol Kane. — New York: Viking Press, 1974. xxiii, 146 p.: col. coats of arms; 25 cm. (A Studio book) 1. Heraldry 2. Emblems, National I. T.
CR191.B74　　　929.8　　　LC 72-91830　　　ISBN 0670504521

CR4501–4595 Chivalry

Barber, Richard W.　　　　　　　　　　　3.290
The reign of chivalry / Richard Barber. — New York: St. Martin's Press, [c1980] 208 p.: ill.; 29 cm. 1. Chivalry — History. 2. Knights and knighthood 3. Middle Ages — History I. T.
CR4513.B33　　　394/.7/0902　　　LC 79-3747　　　ISBN 0312669941

Keen, Maurice Hugh.　　　　　　　　　　　3.291
Chivalry / Maurice Keen. — New Haven: Yale University Press, 1984. x, 303 p., [40] p. of plates: ill. (some col.); 24 cm. Includes index. 1. Chivalry 2. Knights and knighthood — Europe. 3. Heraldry — Europe. 4. Civilization, Medieval 5. Europe — Nobility — History. I. T.
CR4513.K44 1984　　　394/.7 19　　　LC 83-23282　　　ISBN 0300031505

Painter, Sidney, 1902-1960.　　　　　　　　• 3.292
French chivalry; chivalric ideas and practices in mediaeval France, by Sidney Painter. — Baltimore, The Johns Hopkins press, 1940. ix, 179 p. 22 cm. 1. Chivalry 2. France — Civilization — Hist. 3. Civilization, Medieval I. T. II. Title: Chivalric ideas and practices in mediaeval France.
CR4529.F8P3　　　914.4　　　LC 40-8951

CS Genealogy. Family Histories

Doane, Gilbert Harry, 1897-. • 3.293
Searching for your ancestors; the how and why of genealogy. [3d ed.] Minneapolis, University of Minnesota Press [1960] 198 p. illus. 23 cm. 1. Genealogy 2. United States — Genealogy — Handbooks, manuals, etc. 3. United States — Genealogy — Bibliography. I. T.
CS16.D6 1960   929.1   *LC* 60-12200

Blockson, Charles L. 3.294
Black genealogy / Charles L. Blockson with Ron Fry. Englewood Cliffs, N.J.: Prentice-Hall, c1977. 232 p.: facsims.; 22 cm. Includes index. 1. Afro-Americans — Genealogy — Handbooks, manuals, etc. I. Fry, Ron, joint author. II. T.
CS21.B55   929/.1/028   *LC* 77-3150   *ISBN* 0130776858

Greenwood, Val D. 3.295
The researcher's guide to American genealogy, by Val D. Greenwood. With an introd. by Milton Rubincam. — Baltimore: Genealogical Pub., 1973. xv, 535 p.: illus.; 24 cm. 1. Archives — United States 2. United States — Genealogy. 3. Canada — Genealogy. I. T.
CS47.G73   929/.1/072073   *LC* 73-6902   *ISBN* 0806305606

Whittemore, Henry, 1833-. • 3.296
Genealogical guide to the early settlers of America, with a brief history of those of the first generation and references to the various local histories, and other sources of information where additinal data may be found. Baltimore, Genealogical Pub. Co., 1967. 438 p. coats of arms. 26 cm. 'Excerpted and reprinted from the Spirit of '76, volumes 5-12, September, 1898-June, 1906.' 1. United States — Genealogy. I. Spirit of '76 (New York) II. T.
CS61.W5 1967   *LC* 67-23072

Burke's presidential families of the United States of America / 3.297
[edited by Hugh Montgomery–Massingberd].
London: Burke's Peerage, 1975. xix, 676 p.: col. ill., coat of arms, geneal. tables, ports.; 26 cm. (Burke's genealogical series) Distributed in the U.S. by Arco Pub. Co., New York. Includes index. 1. Presidents — United States — Genealogy. 2. United States — Genealogy. I. Title: Presidential families of the United States of America.
CS69.B82   973/.0992   *LC* 74-25177   *ISBN* 0850110173

Cowles, Virginia. 3.298
The Astors / Virginia Cowles. — 1st American ed. — New York: Knopf, 1979. 256 p.: ill.; 26 cm. Includes index. 1. Astor family 2. Great Britain — Genealogy. I. T.
CS71.A85 1979   929/.2/0941   *LC* 79-2219   *ISBN* 0394414780

Sanders, I. J. (Ivor John) 3.299
English baronies: a study of their origin and descent, 1086–1327. Oxford, Clarendon Press, 1963. 1. Great Britain — Peerage I. T.
CS429.S3   *LC* 60-52228

Forster, Robert, 1926-. 3.300
The house of Saulx–Tavanes; Versailles and Burgundy, 1700–1830. — Baltimore: Johns Hopkins Press, [1971] x, 277 p.: illus.; 24 cm. 1. Saulx-Tavannes family. I. T.
CS599.S484 1971   929.2/0944   *LC* 75-150041   *ISBN* 080181247X

Davies, John Kenyon. 3.301
Athenian propertied families, 600–300 B.C., by J. K. Davies. Oxford, Oxford University Press, 1971. xxxi, 655 p., 4 plates (2 fold.); geneal. tables. 24 cm. English or Greek. 1. Athens (Greece) — Genealogy. I. T.
CS738.A8 D38   301.44/1/09385

Arthur, William, 1796-1875. • 3.302
An etymological dictionary of family and Christian names; with an essay on their derivation and import. New York, Sheldon, Blakeman, 1857. Detroit, Gale Research Co., 1969. iv, 300 p. 22 cm. 1. Names, Personal 2. Onomastics I. T.
CS2309.A7 1969   929.4   *LC* 68-17911

Dunkling, Leslie, 1935-. 3.303
The Facts on file dictionary of first names / Leslie Dunkling and William Gosling. — New York, N.Y.: Facts on File Publications, 1984, c1983. xiv, 305 p.; 24 cm. Rev. ed. of: Everyman's dictionary of first names. 1983. 1. Names, Personal — English. 2. English language — Etymology — Names

I. Gosling, William. II. Dunkling, Leslie, 1935- Everyman's dictionary of first names. III. T.
CS2367.D83 1984   929.4/4/0321 19   *LC* 84-4175   *ISBN* 0871962748

Withycombe, Elizabeth Gidley, 1902-. • 3.304
The Oxford dictionary of English Christian names / by E.G. Withycombe. — Oxford: Clarendon Press, 1950. xlviii, 294 p.; 19 cm. 1. Names, Personal — English. I. T.
CS2375.G7 W5 1950   *LC* 51-5089

Smith, Elsdon Coles, 1903-. 3.305
New dictionary of American family names [by] Elsdon C. Smith. — [1st ed.]. — New York: Harper & Row, [1972, c1973] xxix, 570 p.; 24 cm. Published in 1956 under title: Dictionary of American family names. 1. Names, Personal — United States. I. T.
CS2481.S55 1973   929/.4/0973   *LC* 72-79693   *ISBN* 0060139331

Smith, Elsdon Coles, 1903-. • 3.306
American surnames / [by] Elsdon C. Smith. — [1st ed.]. — Philadelphia: Chilton Book Co., [1969] xx, 370 p.; 24 cm. 1. Names, Personal — U.S. I. T.
CS2485.S63   929.4   *LC* 71-85245

Hook, J. N. (Julius Nicholas), 1913-. 3.307
Family names: how our surnames came to America / J.N. Hook. — New York: Macmillan; London: Collier Macmillan, c1982. 388 p.; 22 cm. Includes index. 1. Names, Personal — United States. 2. Ethnology — United States I. T.
CS2487.H66 1982   929.4/2/0973 19   *LC* 81-18646   *ISBN* 0025521004

Cottle, Basil. • 3.308
The Penguin dictionary of surnames. Harmondsworth, Penguin, 1967. 334 p. 19 cm. (Penguin reference books, R32) 1. Names, Personal — Great Britain. I. T.
CS2505.C67   929.4/0941   *LC* 67-112240

Dolan, J. R. • 3.309
English ancestral names; the evolution of the surname from medieval occupations [by] J. R. Dolan. — [1st ed.]. — New York: C. N. Potter; distributed by Crown Publishers, [1972] xvi, 381 p.; 24 cm. 1. Names, Personal — English. 2. English language — Etymology — Names I. T.
CS2505.D65 1972   929.4   *LC* 73-139349

Reaney, Percy Hide. 3.310
A dictionary of British surnames / by P. H. Reaney. — 2d ed. with corrections and additions / by R. M. Wilson. — London; Boston: Routledge & K. Paul, 1976. lxiv, 398 p.; 25 cm. 1. Names, Personal — English. I. Wilson, Richard Middlewood. II. T.
CS2505.R39 1976   929.4/0941   *LC* 76-357472   *ISBN* 0710081065

CT Biography

CT21–25 Biography, Autobiography as Literary Forms

Bowen, Catherine Drinker, 1897-1973. • 3.311
Biography: the craft and the calling. [1st ed.] Boston, Little, Brown [1969] xvi, 174 p. 21 cm. 'An Atlantic Monthly Press book.' 1. Biography (as a literary form) I. T.
CT21.B564   808.06/6/92   *LC* 69-11259

Garraty, John Arthur, 1920-. 3.312
Nature of biography. New York: Knopf, [1957] [301] p. (A Caravelle edition; V-520) 1. Biography (as a literary form) I. T.
CT21.G3   920   808   *LC* 57-10559

Nadel, Ira Bruce. 3.313
Biography: fiction, fact, and form / Ira Bruce Nadel. — New York: St. Martin's Press, 1984. x, 248 p.; 23 cm. 1. Biography (as a literary form) I. T.
CT21.N3 1984   808/.06692 19   *LC* 83-21288   *ISBN* 0312078684

Novarr, David. 3.314
The lines of life: theories of biography, 1880–1970 / David Novarr. — West Lafayette, Ind.: Purdue University Press, 1986. xvii, 202 p.; 24 cm. Includes index. 1. Biography (as a literary form) I. T.
CT21.N68 1986   808/.06692 19   *LC* 85-24562   *ISBN* 0911198792

Telling lives, the biographer's art / by Leon Edel ... [et al.]; **3.315**
edited by Marc Pachter.
Washington: New Republic Books, 1979. 151 p.; 24 cm. 1. Biography (as a
literary form) I. Edel, Leon, 1907- II. Pachter, Marc.
CT21.T44   808/.066/92   *LC* 79-698   *ISBN* 0915220547

Autobiography, essays theoretical and critical / edited by James **3.316**
Olney.
Princeton, N.J.: Princeton University Press, c1980. viii, 360 p.: ill.; 24 cm.
Includes index. 1. Autobiography — Addresses, essays, lectures. I. Olney,
James.
CT25.A95   809   *LC* 79-17556   *ISBN* 0691064121

Olney, James. **3.317**
Metaphors of self: the meaning of autobiography. — [Princeton, N.J.]:
Princeton University Press, [1972] xi, 342 p.; 25 cm. 1. Autobiography I. T.
CT25.O44   920   *LC* 71-173758   *ISBN* 0691062218

Pascal, Roy, 1904-. **3.318**
Design and truth in autobiography / Roy Pascal. — Cambridge, Mass.:
Harvard University Press, 1960. 202 p.; 23 cm. 1. Autobiography I. T.
CT25 P37   *LC* 60-51956

Spengemann, William C. **3.319**
The forms of autobiography: episodes in the history of a literary genre /
William C. Spengemann. — New Haven: Yale University Press, 1980. xvii,
254 p.; 22 cm. Includes index. 1. Autobiography I. T.
CT25.S63 1980   808.8/0351   *LC* 79-22575   *ISBN* 0300024738

Weintraub, Karl Joachim, 1924-. **3.320**
The value of the individual: self and circumstance in autobiography / Karl
Joachim Weintraub. — Chicago: University of Chicago Press, 1978. xix, 439 p.:
ill.; 24 cm. Includes index. 1. Autobiography 2. Individuality I. T.
CT25.W37   128   *LC* 77-9435   *ISBN* 0226886212

Women's autobiography: essays in criticism / edited with an **3.321**
introd. by Estelle C. Jelinek.
1st Midland Book ed. — Bloomington: Indiana University Press, 1979. xii,
274 p.; 22 cm. 1. Autobiography — Women authors I. Jelinek, Estelle C.
CT25.W6   810/.9/9287   *LC* 79-2600   *ISBN* 0253191939

Altick, Richard Daniel, 1915-. • **3.322**
Lives and letters; a history of literary biography in England and America, by
Richard D. Altick. [1st ed.] New York, Knopf, 1965. xvii, 438 p. 25 cm.
1. Biography (as a literary form) I. T.
CT31.A4   *LC* 64-17699

Bayle, Pierre, 1647-1706. • **3.323**
Historical and critical dictionary; selections. Translated, with an introd. and
notes, by Richard H. Popkin, with the assistance of Craig Brush. Indianapolis,
Bobbs-Merrill [1965] xliv, 456 p. 21 cm. (The Library of liberal arts)
1. Biography — Dictionaries. I. T.
CT95.B333 1965   *LC* 64-16703

CT100–206 General Collective Biography

Current biography yearbook. • **3.324**
1940-. New York: H. W. Wilson. v. ports. 28 cm. Annual. Cumulated from
monthly numbers. Kept up to date by monthly issues entitled: Current
biography. 1. Biography — 20th century I. Block, Maxine, ed. II. Rothe,
Anna Herthe, ed. III. Candee, Marjorie Dent, 1904- ed. IV. H.W. Wilson
Company. V. Current biography.
CT100.C8   *LC* 40-27432

Webster's new biographical dictionary. **3.325**
Springfield, Mass.: Merriam-Webster, c1983. xvii, 1130 p.; 26 cm. Rev. ed. of:
Webster's biographical dictionary. c1980. Includes index. 1. Biography
I. Merriam-Webster, Inc. II. Title: New biographical dictionary.
CT103.W4 1983   920/.02 19   *LC* 83-933   *ISBN* 0877795436

Twentieth century American nicknames / edited by Laurence **3.326**
Urdang; compiled by Walter C. Kidney and George C. Kohn;
with a foreword by Leslie Alan Dunkling.
New York: H. W. Wilson, 1979. xi, 398 p.; 24 cm. 1. Nicknames — United
States. I. Urdang, Laurence. II. Kidney, Walter C. III. Kohn, George C.
CT108.T83   929.4/0973   *LC* 79-23390   *ISBN* 0824206428

Biography news. **3.327**
v. 1- Jan. 1974-. Detroit: Gale Research Co. v.: illus.; 28 cm. Monthly.
1. Biography — 20th century — Periodicals.
CT120.B53   920/.009/04   *LC* 74-642922

The International who's who. **3.328**
1st- ed. London, Europa Publications Ltd. [1935-. v. 26 x 20 cm. Annual.
1. Biography I. Europa Publications Limited.
CT120.I5   920.01   *LC* 35-10257

Obituaries from the Times, 1961–1970, including an index to all **3.329**
obituaries and tributes appearing in the Times during the years
1961–1970 / compiler, Frank C. Roberts.
Reading, Eng.: Newspaper Archive Developments, c1975. 952 p.; 31 cm.
1. Times (London, England) — Indexes. 2. Obituaries 3. Biography — 20th
century 4. Obituaries — Indexes I. Roberts, Frank C. II. Times (London,
England)
CT120.O17   920/.02   *ISBN* 0903713985

Who's who in the world. **3.330**
1st- ed.; 1971/72-. Chicago, Marquis Who's Who, inc. v. 31 cm. 1. Biography
— 20th century
CT120.W5   920.02   *LC* 79-139215

CT210–3090 National Biography

CT210–275 UNITED STATES

Garraty, John Arthur, 1920-. **3.331**
Encyclopedia of American biography. John A. Garraty, editor. Jerome L.
Sternstein, associate editor. — [1st ed.]. — New York: Harper & Row, [1974]
xiv, 1241 p.; 25 cm. 1. United States — Biography — Dictionaries.
I. Sternstein, Jerome L., joint author. II. T.
CT213.G37 1974   920/.073   *LC* 74-1807   *ISBN* 0060114384

The New York times obituaries index. **3.332**
New York: New York times, 1970-1980. 2 v.; 29 cm. 1. New York times —
Indexes 2. Obituaries — Indexes I. New York times
CT213.N47   920/.02 B 19   *LC* 72-113422   *ISBN* 0667005986

Terkel, Studs, 1912-. **3.333**
American dreams, lost and found / Studs Terkel. — 1st ed. — New York:
Pantheon Books, c1980. xxv, 470 p.; 25 cm. 1. Interviews 2. National
characteristics, American 3. United States — Biography I. T.
CT220.T42   920/.073   *LC* 80-7703   *ISBN* 0394507932

Baker, Lewis, 1953-. **3.334**
The Percys of Mississippi: politics and literature in the new South / Lewis
Baker. — Baton Rouge: Louisiana State University Press, c1983. 237 p.: ill.,
ports.; 24 cm. — (Southern biography series.) Includes index. 1. Percy family
I. T. II. Series.
CT274.P48 B34 1983   929/.2/0973 19   *LC* 83-7916   *ISBN*
0807111023

Muhlenfeld, Elisabeth, 1944-. **3.335**
Mary Boykin Chesnut: a biography / Elisabeth Muhlenfeld. — Baton Rouge:
Louisiana State University Press, c1981. xv, 271 p.: ill.; 23 cm. — (Southern
biography series.) Includes index. 1. Chesnut, Mary Boykin Miller, 1823-1886.
2. South Carolina — Biography. I. T. II. Series.
CT275.C548 M84   975.7/03/0924 B 19   *LC* 80-26610   *ISBN*
0807108529

Buel, Joy Day. **3.336**
The way of duty: a woman and her family in revolutionary America / Joy Day
Buel and Richard Buel, Jr. — 1st ed. — New York: Norton, c1984. xviii, 309 p.,
[4] p. of plates: ill.; 21 cm. Includes index. 1. Fish, Mary, 1736-1818.
2. Women — United States — History — 18th century. 3. Family — United
States — History — 18th century. 4. United States — History — Revolution,
1775-1783 — Women 5. United States — Biography I. Buel, Richard, 1933-
II. T.
CT275.F5586 B83 1984   973.3/092/4 B 19   *LC* 83-12176   *ISBN*
0393017672

James, Alice, 1848-1892. **3.337**
The death and letters of Alice James: selected correspondence / edited, with a
biographical essay, by Ruth Bernard Yeazell. — Berkeley: University of
California Press, c1981. viii, 214 p., [16] p. of plates: ill., ports.; 23 cm. Includes

index. 1. James, Alice, 1848-1892. 2. James family 3. United States —
Biography I. Yeazell, Ruth Bernard. II. T.
CT275.J29 A4 1981   973.8/092/2 B 19   *LC* 78-59454   *ISBN*
0520037456

Strouse, Jean.   **3.338**
Alice James, a biography / Jean Strouse. — Boston: Houghton Mifflin, c1980.
xv, 367 p., [8] leaves of plates: ill.; 24 cm. 1. James, Alice, 1848-1892. 2. James
family 3. United States — Biography I. T.
CT275.J29 S77   929/.2/0973 19   *LC* 80-22103   *ISBN* 0395277876

Mumford, Lewis, 1895-.   **3.339**
Sketches from life: the autobiography of Lewis Mumford: the early years. —
New York: Dial Press, c1982. x, 500 p., 16 leaves of plates: ill.; 24 cm. Includes
index. 1. Mumford, Lewis, 1895- 2. Social reformers — United States —
Biography. 3. City planners — United States — Biography. 4. Architects —
United States — Biography. I. T.
CT275.M734 A37 1982   973.9/092/4 B 19   *LC* 81-17508   *ISBN*
038527405X

Pirsig, Robert M.   **3.340**
Zen and the art of motorcycle maintenance: an inquiry into values, by Robert
M. Pirsig. — New York: Morrow, 1974. 412 p.; 21 cm. Autobiographical.
1. Pirsig, Robert M. I. T.
CT275.P648 A33   917.3/04/920924 B   *LC* 73-12275   *ISBN*
0688002307

The Macmillan dictionary of Canadian biography / edited by   **3.341**
W. Stewart Wallace.
4th ed., rev., enl., and updated / by W. A. McKay. — Toronto: Macmillan of
Canada, c1978. 914 p.; 25 cm. Previous editions published under title: The
Dictionary of Canadian biography. 'Canadians who died before 1976.'
1. Canada — Biography. I. Wallace, W. Stewart (William Stewart),
1884-1970. ed. II. McKay, William Angus.
CT283.D52 1978   920/.071   *LC* 79-308717   *ISBN* 0770514626

CT300-3090 OTHER COUNTRIES

Gray, James Henry, 1906-.   **3.342**
The boy from Winnipeg [by] James H. Gray. Illustrated by Myra Lowenthal. —
Toronto: Macmillan of Canada, [c1970] 204 p.: illus.; 24 cm. — 1. Gray, James
Henry, 1906- I. T.
CT310.G728 A3   917.127/4   *LC* 79-587925

The Pastons: a family in the Wars of the Roses / edited by   **3.343**
Richard Barber.
Harmondsworth: Penguin Books, 1984, c1981. 208 p.: ill., 1 geneal. table, 1
map. 1. Paston family 2. Great Britain — History — Wars of the Roses,
1455-1485 — Sources. I. Barber, Richard W.
CT787.P37 P37 1984   942.04/0922 19   *LC* 81-215117   *ISBN*
0140570020

Boylan, Henry.   **3.344**
A dictionary of Irish biography / Henry Boylan. — New York: Barnes & Noble
Books, 1978. xi, 385 p.; 23 cm. 1. Ireland — Biography. I. T.
CT862.B69   920/.0415   *LC* 79-102572   *ISBN* 0064906205

Forster, Robert, 1926-.   **3.345**
Merchants, landlords, magistrates: the Depont family in eighteenth-century
France / Robert Forster. — Baltimore: Johns Hopkins University Press, c1980.
xii, 275 p.: map; 24 cm. Includes index. 1. Depont family 2. Social mobility —
France — Case studies. I. T.
CT1017.D46 F67   305.5/0944   *LC* 80-14944   *ISBN* 0801824060

Wistrich, Robert S., 1945-.   **3.346**
Who's who in Nazi Germany / Robert Wistrich. — 1st American ed. — New
York: Macmillan, 1982. 359 p.; 25 cm. 1. National socialists — Biography —
Dictionaries. 2. Brain drain — Germany — History — 20th century —
Dictionaries. 3. Germany — Biography — Dictionaries. I. T.
CT1063.W48 1982   920/.043 19   *LC* 82-4704   *ISBN* 002630600X

Eminent Indians who was who, 1900-1980, also annual diary of   **3.347**
events.
1st ed. — New Delhi: Durga Das Pvt. Ltd., 1985. xv, 420 p.: ill.; 25 cm. Spine
title: Who was who, 1900-1980. 1. India — Biography — Dictionaries.

2. India — History — 20th century — Chronology. I. Durga Das Pvt. Ltd.
II. Title: Who was who, 1900-1980.
CT1502.E54 1985   920/.054 19   *LC* 85-905271

McClellan, Edwin, 1925-.   **3.348**
Woman in the crested kimono: the life of Shibue Io and her family / drawn from
Mori Ōgai's Shibue Chūsai [by] Edwin McClellan. — New Haven: Yale
University Press, c1985. xiii, 192 p.; 22 cm. Includes index. 1. Shibue, Io,
1816-1884. 2. Shibue, Chūsai, 1805-1858. 3. Shibue family 4. Wives — Japan
— Biography. 5. Mothers — Japan — Biography. 6. Physicians — Japan —
Biography. I. Mori, Ōgai, 1862-1922. Shibue Chūsai II. T.
CT1838.S517 M38 1985   952/.025/0922 B 19   *LC* 85-5359   *ISBN*
0300034849

Ongka.   **3.349**
Ongka: a self-account by a New Guinea big-man / translated by Andrew
Strathern. — New York: St. Martin's Press, c1979. xxii, 162 p., [6] leaves of
plates: ill.; 23 cm. 1. Ongka. 2. Papua New Guinea — Biography. I. Strathern,
Andrew. II. T.
CT2950.O36 A36 1979   995/.3 B   *LC* 79-3904   *ISBN* 0312585667

CT3200-3830 Women

The International dictionary of women's biography / compiler   **3.350**
and editor, Jennifer S. Uglow; assistant editor (for science,
mathematics and medicine) Frances Hinton.
New York: Continuum: Macmillan, 1982. xvi, 534 p.: ill.; 24 cm. Previously
published as: The Macmillan dictionary of women's biography. 1. Women —
Biography I. Uglow, Jennifer S. II. Hinton, Frances.
CT3202.I57 1982   920.72 B 19   *LC* 82-7417   *ISBN* 0826401929

The Women's book of world records and achievements / edited   **3.351**
by Lois Decker O'Neill.
1st ed. — Garden City, N.Y.: Anchor Press/Doubleday, 1979. xiii, 798 p., [36]
leaves of plates: ill.; 25 cm. 'An Information House book.' Includes index.
1. Women — Biography 2. Biography — 19th century 3. Biography — 20th
century I. O'Neill, Lois Decker.
CT3234.W65   920.72   *LC* 77-82961   *ISBN* 0385127324

Notable American women, 1607-1950: a biographical dictionary   • **3.352**
/ Edward T. James, editor; Janet Wilson James, associate
editor; Paul S. Boyer, assistant editor.
Cambridge, Mass.: Belknap Press of Harvard University Press, 1971. 3 v.; 27
cm. 'Prepared under the auspices of Radcliffe College.' 1. Women — United
States — Biography. I. James, Edward T. ed. II. James, Janet Wilson, 1918-
ed. III. Boyer, Paul S. ed. IV. Radcliffe College.
CT3260.N57   920.72/0973   *LC* 76-152274   *ISBN* 0674627318

Notable American women: the modern period: a biographical   **3.353**
dictionary / edited by Barbara Sicherman, Carol Hurd Green
with Ilene Kantrov, Harriette Walker.
Cambridge, Mass.: Belknap Press of Harvard University Press, 1980. xxii,
773 p.; 26 cm. 1. Women — United States — Biography. I. Sicherman,
Barbara. II. Green, Carol Hurd.
CT3260.N573   920.72/0973   *LC* 80-18402   *ISBN* 0674627326

Willard, Frances Elizabeth, 1839-1898. ed.   **3.354**
American women: fifteen hundred biographies with over 1,400 portraits; a
comprehensive encyclopedia of the lives and achievements of American women
during the nineteenth century. Edited by Frances E. Willard and Mary A.
Livermore. Newly rev. with the addition of a classified index. New York, Mast,
Crowell & Kirkpatrick. Detroit, Gale Research Co., 1973, [c1897] 2 v. ports. 23
cm. Reprint of the 1897 ed., which was first published in 1893 under title: A
woman of the century; another rev. ed. was published in 1901 under title:
Portraits and biographies of prominent American women. 1. Women —
United States — Biography. I. Livermore, Mary Ashton Rice, 1820-1905. joint
ed. II. T.
CT3260.W56 1973   920.72/0973   *LC* 73-7985

Fowler, Marian, 1929-.   **3.355**
The embroidered tent: five gentlewomen in early Canada: Elizabeth Simcoe,
Catharine Parr Traill, Susanna Moodie, Anna Jameson, Lady Dufferin /
Marian Fowler. — Toronto: Anansi, c1982. 239 p.: ill.; 22 cm. 1. Women —
Canada — Biography. 2. Pioneers — Canada — Biography. 3. Canada —
Biography. I. T.
CT3270.F68 1982   971/.009/92 B 19   *LC* 82-184489   *ISBN*
0887840914

D1-24 GENERAL WORKS. COLLECTIONS

The annual register of world events: a review of the year. • **3.356**
London: Longmans, Green, etc., 1758-. v. : maps; 21-23 cm. Vols. for 1784-85 issued in combined form; 1820, in 2 pts. Vols. for 1863-1946 called new ser. Vols. for 1920- called v. 162- Some vols. in rev. editions. Title varies: 1758-1953, The Annual register. Subtitle varies. Indexes: 1758-80, 1 v.; 1758-1819, 1 v.; 1781-1792, 1 v. 1. History — Yearbooks. I. Title: The annual register.
D2.A7   *LC* 04-17979

Centennial Symposium on the Future of History, Vanderbilt   **3.357**
University, 1975.
The future of history: essays in the Vanderbilt University Centennial Symposium / edited by Charles F. Delzell. — Nashville: Vanderbilt University Press, 1977. xi, 263 p.; 24 cm. 1. History — Congresses. I. Delzell, Charles F. II. Vanderbilt University. III. T.
D3.U6 C4 1975   900   *LC* 76-48199   *ISBN* 0826512054

Gay, Peter, 1923- comp.   **3.358**
Historians at work. Edited by Peter Gay and Gerald J. Cavanaugh. — [1st ed.]. — New York: Harper & Row, [1972-75] 4 v.; 25 cm. Vol. 2-3 edited by P. Gay and V. G. Wexler. 1. History — Addresses, essays, lectures. I. Cavanaugh, Gerald J., joint comp. II. Wexler, Victor G. joint comp. III. T.
D6.G35   908   *LC* 75-123930   *ISBN* 0060114738

Braudel, Fernand.   **3.359**
On history / Fernand Braudel; translated by Sarah Matthews. — Chicago: University of Chicago Press, c1980. ix, 226 p.; 24 cm. Translation of: Écrits sur l'histoire. 1. History — Collected works. I. T.
D7.B7513   901   *LC* 80-11201   *ISBN* 0226071502

Holborn, Hajo, 1902-1969.   **3.360**
History and the humanities. Introd. by Leonard Krieger. — [1st ed.]. — Garden City, N.Y.: Doubleday, 1972. 229 p.; 22 cm. 1. History — Addresses, essays, lectures. 2. History — Philosophy — Addresses, essays, lectures. I. T.
D7.H6 1972   901   *LC* 73-186027

Huizinga, Johan, 1872-1945.   • **3.361**
Men and ideas: history, the Middle Ages, the Renaissance; essays. Translated by James S. Holmes and Hans van Marle. New York, Meridian Books [1959] 378 p. 19 cm. (Meridian books, M61) 'Translated from texts in 'Verzamelde werken' (1948-53)' 1. History — Collected works. I. T.
D7.H823   *LC* 59-7177

Kohn, Hans, 1891-1971.   • **3.362**
Reflections on modern history; the historian and human responsibility. Princeton, N.J., D. Van Nostrand [1963] xvi, 360 p. 24 cm. 1. History, Modern I. T.
D7.K73   *LC* 63-6466

Mommsen, Theodor Ernst, 1905-1958.   • **3.363**
Medieval and Renaissance studies. Edited by Eugene F. Rice, Jr. — Ithaca, N.Y.: Cornell University Press, [1959] xiii, 353 p.: group port.; 24 cm. 1. Petrarca, Francesco, 1304-1374 — Addresses, essays, lectures. 2. Christian literature, Early — History and criticism — Addresses, essays, lectures. 3. Renaissance — Italy — Addresses, essays, lectures. 4. Italy — History — 1265-1492 — Addresses, essays, lectures. 5. Italy — History — 1492-1559 — Addresses, essays, lectures. I. T.
D7.M77   908.1   *LC* 60-125

Schmitt, Bernadotte Everly, 1886-1969.   • **3.364**
The fashion and future of history; historical studies and addresses. Cleveland, Press of Western Reserve University, 1960. 205 p. 24 cm. 1. History, Modern I. T.
D7.S323   *LC* 60-15088

Trevor-Roper, H. R. (Hugh Redwald), 1914-.   • **3.365**
Men and events: historical essays / by H. R. Trevor-Roper. — New York: Harper, 1957. viii, 324 p. 1. History — Addresses, essays, lectures. I. T. II. Title: Historical essays.
D7.T79 1957a   *LC* 58-6157

Wedgwood, C. V. (Cicely Veronica), 1910-.   • **3.366**
The sense of the past. [London] Cambridge University Press, 1957. 26 p. 19 cm. (The Leslie Stephen lecture, 1957) 1. James, Henry, 1843-1916. The sense of the past. 2. History — Addresses, essays, lectures. I. T.
D8.W4   *LC* 58-1771

Dictionary of world history; general editor G. M. D. Howat.   **3.367**
London: Nelson, 1973. xxvii, 1720 p.; 29 cm. 1. History — Dictionaries I. Howat, G. M. D. (Gerald Malcolm David), 1928- ed.
D9.D55   903   *LC* 74-174563   *ISBN* 0171440556

D11 Chronology

Freeman-Grenville, G. S. P. (Greville Stewart Parker)   **3.368**
Chronology of world history: a calendar of principal events from 3000 BC to AD 1976 / G. S. P. Freeman-Grenville. — 2d ed. — Totowa, N.J.: Rowman and Littlefield, 1978. 746 p.; 25 cm. Includes index. 1. Chronology, Historical — Tables. I. T.
D11.F75 1978   902/.02   *LC* 78-113042   *ISBN* 0847660400

Grun, Bernard, 1901-1972.   **3.369**
The timetables of history: a horizontal linkage of people and events, based on Werner Stein's Kulturfahrplan / Bernard Grun. — English language ed. — New York: Simon and Schuster, c1975. 661 p.; 29 cm. Includes index. 1. Chronology, Historical — Tables. I. Stein, Werner. Kulturfahrplan. II. T.
D11.G78   902/.02   *LC* 73-7704   *ISBN* 0671216821

Steinberg, S. H. (Sigfrid Henry), 1899-1969.   **3.370**
Historical tables, 58 BC-AD 1985 / S.H. Steinberg; foreword by G.P. Gooch. — 11th ed. / updated by John Paxton. — New York, NY: Garland Pub., 1986. p. cm. Rev. ed. of: Historical tables, 58 B.C.-A.D. 1978. 10th ed. 1979. 1. Chronology, Historical — Tables. I. Paxton, John. II. Steinberg, S. H. (Sigfrid Henry), 1899-1969. Historical tables, 58 B.C.-A.D. 1978. III. T.
D11.S83 1986   902/.02 19   *LC* 86-18326   *ISBN* 0824089510

World chronology series.   **3.371**
Dobbs Ferry, N.Y.: Oceana Publications. Began in 1973? 1. Chronology, Historical.
D11.W6x   909 11   *LC* sn 85-3090

Collison, Robert Lewis.   • **3.372**
Dictionary of dates, compiled by Robert Collison. — New York: Greenwood Press, [1969, c1961] 428 p.; 23 cm. Title on spine: Newnes dictionary of dates. London editions published 1962- under title: Newnes dictionary of dates. 1. Calendars 2. Anniversaries — Dictionaries. I. T. II. Title: Newnes dictionary of dates.
D11.5.C6 1969   902/.02   *LC* 77-95116   *ISBN* 0837124956

Ross, Martha.   **3.373**
Rulers and governments of the world. — London; New York: Bowker, 1977-78. 3 v.; 23 cm. Vols. 2 and 3 are translated with revisions from v. 3 and 4 of B. Spuler's Regenten und Regierungen der Welt. Includes indexes. 1. Kings and rulers — Chronology. 2. Heads of state — Chronology. 3. Cabinet officers — Chronology. I. Spuler, Bertold, 1911- joint author. II. T.
D11.5.R67 1977   920.02   *LC* 77-70294   *ISBN* 0859350517

Williams, Neville, 1924-.   **3.374**
Chronology of the expanding world, 1492–1762. — [1st American ed.]. — New York: McKay, [1969] x, 700 p.; 26 cm. 1. History, Modern — Chronology. I. T.
D11.5.W48 1969b   909.08/02/02   *LC* 79-83695

Williams, Neville, 1924-.   **3.375**
Chronology of the modern world: 1763 to the present time. — Rev. [American] ed. — New York: D. McKay Co., [1968] xiii, 923 p.; 26 cm. 1. History, Modern — Chronology. I. T.
D11.5.W5 1968   909.8/02/02   *LC* 75-11332

D13–15 Historiography

Barnes, Harry Elmer, 1889-1968.   • **3.376**
A history of historical writing. — 2d rev. ed. — New York: Dover Publications, [1962] 440 p.: illus.; 22 cm. 1. Historiography I. T.
D13.B32 1962   907.2   LC 62-53030

Barraclough, Geoffrey, 1908-.   • **3.377**
History in a changing world / Geoffrey Barraclough. — Oxford: Blackwell, 1955. viii, 246 p. 1. Historiography I. T.
D13.B33

Barzun, Jacques, 1907-.   • **3.378**
The modern researcher [by] Jacques Barzun & Henry F. Graff. — Rev. ed. — New York, Harcourt, Brace & World [1970] xvii, 430 p. 22 cm. 1. Historiography 2. Report writing I. Graff, Henry F. (Henry Franklin), 1921- joint author. II. T.
D13.B334 1970   907.2   LC 72-115861   ISBN 0151614822

Becker, Carl Lotus, 1873-1945.   • **3.379**
Detachment and the writing of history: essays and letters of Carl L. Becker. Edited by Phil L. Snyder. — Westport, Conn.: Greenwood Press, [1972, c1958] xvi, 240 p.; 22 cm. 1. Historiography — Addresses, essays, lectures. I. T.
D13.B38 1972   907/.2   LC 70-152590   ISBN 0837160235

Beales, Derek Edward Dawson.   **3.380**
History and biography: an inaugural lecture / Derek Beales. — Cambridge: Cambridge University Press, 1981. 36 p.; 19 cm. Cover title. 1. Historiography 2. Biography I. T.
D13.B4x   D13   907/.2 18   907/.2 19   ISBN 0521284740

Bloch, Marc Léopold Benjamin, 1886-1944.   • **3.381**
The historian's craft; introd. by Joseph R. Strayer. Translated from the French by Peter Putnam. — New York, Knopf, 1963 [c1953] 197 p. 20 cm. — (Borzoi book) Translation of Apologie pour l'histoire. 1. Historiography I. T.
D13.B5613   907   LC 52-12182

Breisach, Ernst.   **3.382**
Historiography: ancient, medieval, & modern / Ernst Breisach. — Chicago: University of Chicago Press, c1983. xii, 487 p.: ill.; 24 cm. Includes indexes. 1. Historiography — History. I. T.
D13.B686 1983   907/.2 19   LC 82-20246   ISBN 0226072746

Butterfield, Herbert, Sir, 1900-.   • **3.383**
Man on his past: the study of the history of historical scholarship. — London: Cambridge U.P., 1955. xvi, 237 p.; 22 cm. — (Wiles lectures. 1954) 1. Historiography I. T. II. Series.
D13.B79 1969   907/.2   LC 55-13806

Butterfield, Herbert, Sir, 1900-.   • **3.384**
The whig interpretation of history, by H. Butterfield ... London, G. Bell and Sons, 1931. vi p., 1 l., 132 p. 20 cm. 1. Historiography I. T.
D13.B8   907   LC 31-35009

Collingwood, R. G. (Robin George), 1889-1943.   • **3.385**
The idea of history, by R. G. Collingwood. — Oxford, Clarendon press, 1946. xxvi, 339, [1] p.; 23 cm. Based on lectures written in 1936 on the philosophy of history. cf. Editor's preface signed: T. M. Knox. 1. Historiography 2. History — Philosophy I. Knox, T. M. (Thomas Malcolm), 1900- ed. II. T.
D13.C6   907   LC 47-113

Croce, Benedetto, 1866-1952.   • **3.386**
[Storia come pensiero e come azione. English] History as the story of liberty. [Translated by Sylvia Sprigge] Chicago, Regnery [1970] 320 p. 21 cm. 'A Gateway edition.' Translation of La storia come pensiero e come azione. 1. Historiography 2. History — Philosophy 3. Historicism I. T.
D13.C682 1970   907/.2   LC 71-105123

Croce, Benedetto, 1866-1952.   • **3.387**
History; its theory and practice / Benedetto Croce; authorized translation by Douglas Ainslie. — New York: Russell & Russell, 1960. 317 p.; 22 cm. Translation of Teoria e storia della storiografia. First published in 1921. Title varies Theory and history of historiography: On history. 1. Historiography I. T. II. Title: Teoria e storia della storiografia. III. Title: Theory and history of historiography.
D13.C7 1960   LC 60-14177

Gooch, G. P. (George Peabody), 1873-1968.   • **3.388**
History and historians in the nineteenth century / by G. P. Gooch; with a new introd. by the author. — 2d ed. — Boston: Beacon Press, c1959. xli, 547 p. — (Beacon paperback; no. 76) 1. Historiography 2. Historians I. T.
D13.G7 1959   LC 59-6390

Gottschalk, Louis Reichenthal, 1899-1975.   • **3.389**
Understanding history; a primer of historical method [by] Louis Gottschalk. — 2d ed. — New York: Knopf, [1969] xix, 310, vi p.; 21 cm. 1. Historiography I. T.
D13.G75 1969   907.2   LC 69-10669

Hay, Denys.   **3.390**
Annalists and historians: Western historiography from the eighth to the eighteenth centuries / Denys Hay. — London: Methuen; [New York]: distributed by Harper & Row, Barnes & Noble Import Division, 1977. viii, 215 p.; 23 cm. 1. Historiography — History. I. T.
D13.H358   907/.20182/1   LC 78-305597   ISBN 0416811809

Heller, Agnes.   **3.391**
A theory of history / Agnes Heller. — London; Boston: Routledge & Kegan Paul, 1982. viii, 333 p.; 23 cm. 1. Historiography 2. History — Philosophy I. T.
D13.H4145 1982   907/.2 19   LC 81-12173   ISBN 0710090102

Hexter, J. H. (Jack H.), 1910-.   • **3.392**
Reappraisals in history. [Evanston, Ill.] Northwestern University Press, 1961. 214 p. 23 cm. 1. Historiography 2. Great Britain — History — Addresses, essays, lectures. I. T.
D13.H42 1961a   907.2   LC 61-17740

Higham, John.   • **3.393**
History [by] John Higham, with Leonard Krieger and Felix Gilbert. — Englewood Cliffs, N. J., Prentice-Hall [1965] xiv, 402 p. 22 cm. — (The Princeton studies: humanistic scholarship in America) Bibliographical footnotes. 1. Historiography I. Krieger, Leonard. II. Gilbert, Felix, 1905- III. T. IV. Series.
D13.H43   907.2   LC 64-23563

Iggers, Georg G.   **3.394**
New directions in European historiography / by Georg G. Iggers. — Rev. ed. — Middletown, Conn.: Wesleyan University Press; Scranton, Pa.: Distributed by Harper & Row, 1984. xii, 267 p.; 22 cm. Includes index. 1. Historiography — Europe — History — 20th century. 2. Historians — Europe. I. T.
D13.I35 1984   940/.07/2 19   LC 83-25975   ISBN 0819560715

Jaspers, Karl, 1883-1969.   • **3.395**
[Vom Ursprung und Ziel der Geschichte. English] The origin and goal of history. [Translated from the German by Michael Bullock] New Haven, Yale University Press, 1953. 294 p. 23 cm. 1. Historiography I. T.
D13.J314 1953a   907   LC 53-11595

LaCapra, Dominick, 1939-.   **3.396**
History & criticism / Dominick LaCapra. — Ithaca, N.Y.: Cornell University Press, 1985. 145 p.; 24 cm. 1. Historiography I. T.
D13.L26 1985   907/.2 19   LC 84-16990   ISBN 0801417880

Lewis, Bernard.   **3.397**
History—remembered, recovered, invented / Bernard Lewis. — Princeton: Princeton University Press, [1975] 111 p.; 21 cm. Originally presented as the Benjamin Gottesman Lectures, Yeshiva University, 1974. 1. Historiography — Addresses, essays, lectures. 2. History — Philosophy — Addresses, essays, lectures. 3. Middle East — Historiography — Addresses, essays, lectures. I. T.
D13.L46 1975   907/.2   LC 74-25607   ISBN 0691035474

McCullagh, C. Behan.   **3.398**
Justifying historical descriptions / C. Behan McCullagh. — Cambridge; New York: Cambridge University Press, 1984. x, 252 p.; 24 cm. Includes index. 1. Historiography I. T.
D13.M363 1984   907.2 19   LC 84-7028   ISBN 0521267226

Momigliano, Arnaldo.   **3.399**
Studies in historiography / Arnaldo Momigliano. — New York: Harper & Row, 1966. 263 p. (Harper torchbooks. The Academy library; TB1288) 1. Historians 2. Historiography — Addresses, essays, lectures I. T.
D13.M64   LC 66-27622

Momigliano, Arnaldo.   **3.400**
Essays in ancient and modern historiography / Arnaldo Momigliano. — Middletown: Wesleyan University Press, 1977. 387 p.: 23 cm. 1. Historians 2. Historiography — Addresses, essays, lectures. I. T.
D 13 M72 1977   LC 76-41484   ISBN 0819550108

Neff, Emery Edward, 1892-. • **3.401**
The poetry of history; the contribution of literature and literary scholarship to the writing of history since Voltaire. New York, Columbia Univ. Press, 1947. viii, 258 p. 22 cm. 1. Literature and history 2. Historiography I. T.
D13.N35   *LC* 47-30933

Nevins, Allan, 1890-1971. **3.402**
Allan Nevins on history / compiled and introduced by Ray Allen Billington. — New York: Scribner, [1975] xxvii, 420 p.; 24 cm. Includes index. 1. Historiography — Addresses, essays, lectures. 2. Historians — United States — Biography — Addresses, essays, lectures. I. T.
D13.N367 1975   907/.2   *LC* 75-4870   *ISBN* 0684143208

Ranke, Leopold von, 1795-1886. **3.403**
[Selections. English. 1973] The theory and practice of history / edited with an introd. by Georg G. Iggers and Konrad von Moltke; new translations by Wilma A. Iggers and Konrad von Moltke. — Indianapolis: Bobbs-Merrill [1973] lxx, 514 p.; 21 cm. (European historiography series.) 'Konrad von Moltke has revised and abridged the 1901 Fowler translation of the History of the popes and translated the last two sections which were not previously available in English.' 1. Historiography — Collected works. I. Humboldt, Wilhelm, Freiherr von, 1767-1835. II. Ranke, Leopold von, 1795-1886. Die römischen päpste. English. 1973. III. T. IV. Series.
D13.R32   901   *LC* 79-167691   *ISBN* 067251673X *ISBN* 0672609207

Ritter, Harry. **3.404**
Dictionary of concepts in history / Harry Ritter. — Westport, Conn.: Greenwood Press, 1986. xix, 490 p.; 25 cm. — (Reference sources for the social sciences and humanities, 0730-3335; no. 3) 1. Historiography — Dictionaries. I. T. II. Series.
D13.R49 1986   907/.2/0321 19   *LC* 85-27305   *ISBN* 0313227004

Salvemini, Gaetano, 1873-1957. • **3.405**
Historian and scientist; an essay on the nature of history and the social sciences, by Gaetano Salvemini. Cambridge, Mass., Harvard university press, 1939. viii, 203 p. 20 cm. 1. Historiography 2. Social sciences I. T.
D13.S35   *LC* 39-25859   *ISBN* 836910494

Thompson, James Westfall, 1869-1941. • **3.406**
A history of historical writing, by James Westfall Thompson with the collaboration of Bernard J. Holm. — Gloucester, Mass.: P. Smith, 1967 [c1942] 2 v.: illus.; 24 cm. 1. Historiography I. Holm, Bernard J., joint author. II. T.
D13.T5 1967   907/.2/01821   *LC* 67-8627

Tillinghast, Pardon E. **3.407**
The specious past: historians and others [by] Pardon E. Tillinghast. — Reading, Mass.: Addison-Wesley Pub. Co., [1972] vii, 198 p.; 21 cm. — (Addison-Wesley series in history) 1. Historiography 2. History I. T.
D13.T53   907/.2   *LC* 76-178269

Visions of history / by MARHO—the Radical Historians **3.408**
Organization; edited by Henry Abelove ... [et al.]; drawings by Josh Brown.
1st ed. — New York: Pantheon Books, c1983. xi, 323 p.: ill.; 24 cm. 'Interviews with E.P. Thompson, Eric Hobsbawm, Sheila Rowbotham, Linda Gordon, Natalie Zemon Davis, William Appleman Williams, Staughton Lynd, David Montgomery, Herbert Gutman, Vincent Harding, John Womack, C.L.R. James, Moshe Lewin.' 1. Historiography — Addresses, essays, lectures. 2. Historians — Interviews. I. Abelove, Henry. II. Thompson, E. P. (Edward Palmer), 1924- III. MARHO (Organization)
D13.V57 1983   907/.2 19   *LC* 83-47743   *ISBN* 0394722000

White, Hayden V., 1928-. **3.409**
Metahistory: the historical imagination in nineteenth–century Europe [by] Hayden White. — Baltimore: Johns Hopkins University Press, [1973] xii, 448 p.; 25 cm. 1. Historiography — History. 2. History — Philosophy I. T.
D13.W565   907/.2   *LC* 73-8110   *ISBN* 0801814693

Barzun, Jacques, 1907-. **3.410**
Clio and the doctors: psycho–history, quanto–history & history / Jacques Barzun. — Chicago: University of Chicago Press, 1974. xi, 173 p. 1. Historiography I. T.
D13.2 B37   *LC* 74-5723   *ISBN* 022603849X

Geyl, Pieter, 1887-. • **3.411**
Encounters in history. Cleveland, Meridian Books [1962, c1961] 405 p. 19 cm. (Meridian books, M114) 1. Historiography — Addresses, essays, lectures. I. T.
D13.2.G42   907.2   *LC* 61-11475

Hexter, J. H. (Jack H.), 1910-. **3.412**
On historians / J. H. Hexter. — Cambridge, Mass.: Harvard University Press, 1979. viii, 310 p.: ill.; 22cm. 1. Historiography — Addresses, essays, lectures. 2. Historians — Addresses, essays, lectures. I. T.
D13.2.H42   907/.2   *LC* 78-16635   *ISBN* 0674634268

The Writing of history: literary form and historical **3.413**
understanding / edited by Robert H. Canary and Henry Kozicki.
Madison: University of Wisconsin Press, 1978. xv, 165 p.; 24 cm. Includes index. 1. Historiography — Addresses, essays, lectures. 2. Prose literature — Technique — Addresses, essays, lectures. 3. Literature and history — Addresses, essays, lectures. I. Canary, Robert H. II. Kozicki, Henry, 1924-
D13.2.W74   907/.2   *LC* 78-4590   *ISBN* 0299075702

The Historian at work / edited by John Cannon. **3.414**
London; Boston: Allen & Unwin, 1980. xiv, 210 p.; 23 cm. 1. Historiography — Europe — Addresses, essays, lectures. 2. Historians — Europe — Biography — Addresses, essays, lectures. I. Cannon, John Ashton.
D13.5.E85 H57 1980   907/.204 19   *LC* 81-217031   *ISBN* 0049010255

Bann, Stephen. **3.415**
The clothing of Clio: a study of the representation of history in nineteenth–century Britain and France / Stephen Bann. — Cambridge [Cambridgeshire]; New York: Cambridge University Press, 1984. xii, 196 p.: ill.; 24 cm. Includes index. 1. Historiography — Great Britain — History — 19th century. 2. Historiography — France — History — 19th century. I. T.
D13.5.G7 B36 1984   907/.2041 19   *LC* 83-20909   *ISBN* 052125616X

Angus-Butterworth, L. M. (Lionel Milner). • **3.416**
Ten master historians. Freeport, N.Y., Books for Libraries Press [1969, c1961] x, 184 p. ports. 23 cm. (Essay index reprint series) 1. Historians, British. I. T.
D14.A6 1969   942/.0072/022   *LC* 69-18919   *ISBN* 0836900006

Fitzsimons, M. A. (Matthew Anthony), 1912-. **3.417**
The past recaptured: great historians and the history of history / M.A. Fitzsimons. — Notre Dame, Ind.: University of Notre Dame Press, c1983. ix, 230 p.; 23 cm. 1. Historians — Europe. 2. Historiography — History. I. T.
D14.F57 1983   907.2 19   *LC* 83-1168   *ISBN* 0268015503

Schmitt, Bernadotte Everly, 1886-1969. ed. • **3.418**
Some historians of modern Europe; essays in historiography, edited by Bernadotte E. Schmitt. — Port Washington, N.Y.: Kennikat Press, [1966, c1942] ix, 533 p.; 22 cm. 1. Historians I. T.
D14.S35 1966   940.0922   *LC* 66-25941

Beringause, Arthur F., 1919-. • **3.419**
Brooks Adams; a biography. [1st ed.] New York, Knopf, 1955. xiii, 404, x p. port. 25 cm. 1. Adams, Brooks, 1848-1927. I. T.
D15.A3 B4   *LC* 55-8357

Wilkins, Burleigh Taylor. • **3.420**
Carl Becker: a biographical study in American intellectual history / Burleigh Taylor Wilkins. — Cambridge M.I.T. Press 1961. 246p. 1. Becker, Carl Lotus, 1873-1945. I. T.
D15.B33 W5   *LC* 61-7870

Namier, Julia, Lady. • **3.421**
Lewis Namier: a biography by Julia Namier. — London; New York: Oxford University Press, 1971. xvii, 347 p., 12 plates:; illus., 2 maps, ports.; 23 cm. 1. Namier, Lewis Bernstein, Sir, 1888-1960. I. T.
D15.N3 N35 1971   907/.2/024 B   *LC* 76-852488   *ISBN* 0192117068

Krieger, Leonard. **3.422**
Ranke: the meaning of history / Leonard Krieger. Chicago: University of Chicago Press, 1977. xii, 402 p.; 24 cm. Includes index. 1. Ranke, Leopold von, 1795-1886. 2. History 3. Historicism 4. Historians — Germany — Biography. I. T.
D15.R3 K74   907/.2/024   *LC* 76-25633   *ISBN* 0226453499

Von Laue, Theodore H. (Theodore Hermann) • **3.423**
Leopold Ranke, the formative years. Princeton, Princeton University Press, 1950. ix, 230 p. port. 23 cm. (Princeton studies in history, v. 4) 1. Ranke, Leopold von, 1795-1886. I. T.
D15.R3 V6   928.3   *LC* 50-3230

Brumfitt, J. H. • **3.424**
Voltaire, historian. [London] Oxford University Press, 1958. 178 p. 22 cm. (Oxford modern languages and literature monographs) 'A shortened version of a doctoral thesis presented in the University of Oxford.' 1. Voltaire, 1694-1778. I. T.
D15.V6 B7   *LC* 58-923

D16 Methodology

Baum, Willa K.   3.425
Oral history for the local historical society / by Willa K. Baum. — 2d ed., rev. — Nashville, Tenn.: American Association for State and Local History, 1971. 63 p.: ill.; 22 cm. 1. Oral history I. American Association for State and Local History. II. T.
D16.B3   970/.2

Bodin, Jean, 1553-1596.   • 3.426
Method for the easy comprehension of history. Translated by Beatrice Reynolds. — New York, Octagon Books, 1966 [c1945] xxix, 402 p. 24 cm. — (Records of civilization, sources and studies. no. 37) Bibliography: p. [381]-388. 1. History — Study and teaching 2. History — Methodology I. Reynolds, Beatrice, 1891- ed. and tr. II. T. III. Series.
D16.B642 1966   901.8   LC 66-16000

Curtis, L. Perry (Lewis Perry), 1932-.   3.427
The historian's workshop; original essays by sixteen historians. Edited by L. P. Curtis, Jr. [1st ed.] New York, Knopf [1970] xxiv, 326 p. 24 cm. 1. History — Methodology — Addresses, lectures. 2. Historians — Biography. I. T.
D16.C85 1970   907.2 19   LC 70-107456   ISBN 0394307232

The Dimensions of quantitative research in history. Edited by   • 3.428
William O. Aydelotte, Allan G. Bogue [and] Robert William
Fogel. Contributors: William O. Aydelotte [and others].
Princeton, N.J.]: Princeton University Press, [1972] ix, 435 p.: illus.; 25 cm. — (Quantitative studies in history) 1. History — Statistical methods — Addresses, essays, lectures. 2. Social sciences — Statistical methods — Addresses, essays, lectures. I. Aydelotte, William Osgood. ed. II. Bogue, Allan G. ed. III. Fogel, Robert William. ed. IV. Series.
D16.D47   907/.2   LC 75-166370   ISBN 0691075441

The Dimensions of the past; materials, problems, and   • 3.429
opportunities for quantitative work in history. Edited by Val R.
Lorwin and Jacob M. Price.
New Haven, Yale University Press, 1972. vi, 568 p. 24 cm. 'Essays presented to the American Historical Association's Committee on Quantitative Data.' 1. History — Statistical methods — Addresses, essays, lectures. I. Lorwin, Val R. (Val Rogin), 1907- ed. II. Price, Jacob M. ed. III. American Historical Association. Committee on Quantitative Data.
D16.D48   907/.2073   LC 78-151587

Explorations in psychohistory; the Wellfleet papers. Edited by   3.430
Robert Jay Lifton, with Eric Olson.
Simon and Schuster [1975, c1974] 372 p. 1. Psychohistory — Addresses, essays, lectures. 2. History 3. Psychology I. Lifton, Robert Jay, 1926- ed. II. Olson, Eric, ed.
D16.E9   LC 74-13758   ISBN 0671218484

Fischer, David Hackett, 1935-.   • 3.431
Historians' fallacies; toward a logic of historical thought. — [1st ed.]. — New York: Harper & Row, [1970] xxii, 338 p.; 24 cm. (Colophon books (New York, N.Y.) 1. History — Methodology I. T.
D16.F53   901/.8   LC 69-15583

Frick, Elizabeth.   3.432
Library research guide to history: illustrated search strategy and sources / by Elizabeth Frick. — Ann Arbor, Mich.: Pierian Press, 1980. x, 86 p. (p. 82-86 blank): ill.; 28 cm. — (Library research guides series; no. 4) Includes index. 1. History — Research I. T.
D16.F87   907/.2 19   LC 80-83514   ISBN 0876501196

Garraghan, Gilbert J. (Gilbert Joseph), 1871-1942.   • 3.433
A guide to historical method ... by Gilbert J. Garraghan ... edited by Jean Delanglez ... — New York, Fordham university press, 1946. xv, 482 p. diagrs. 24 cm. With this is bound, as issued: Appel, L. Bibliographical citation in the social sciences ... Madison, 1946. Includes bibliographies. 1. History — Methodology I. Delanglez, Jean, 1896-1949. ed. II. T.
D16.G37   901.8   LC 46-8087

Hughes, H. Stuart (Henry Stuart), 1916-.   • 3.434
History as art and as science: twin vistas on the past. — [1st ed.] New York: Harper & Row, [1964] xix, 107 p.; 20 cm. (World perspectives, v. 32) 1. History — Methodology I. T.
D16.H775   901.8   LC 63-20291

The New psychohistory / Lloyd deMause, editor.   3.435
New York: Psychohistory Press, c1975. 313 p.: ill.; 24 cm. 1. Psychohistory — Addresses, essays, lectures. I. DeMause, Lloyd.
D16.N48   301.2   LC 75-14687   ISBN 0914434012

The Psychoanalytic interpretation of history, edited by   • 3.436
Benjamin B. Wolman. Foreword by William L. Langer.
New York, Basic Books [1971] x, 240 p. 25 cm. 1. Stalin, Joseph, 1879-1953. 2. Herzl, Theodor, 1860-1904. 3. Hitler, Adolf, 1889-1945. 4. Psychohistory — Addresses, essays, lectures. I. Wolman, Benjamin B. ed.
D16.P8   907.2/2   LC 71-135561   ISBN 0465065937

Teggart, Frederick John, 1870-1946.   • 3.437
Theory and processes of history. Berkeley, University of California Press, 1960. 323 p. 19 cm. A reprint of the edition published by the University of California Press in 1941, containing the author's Theory of history and The processes of history. 1. History — Methodology 2. Historiography I. T.
D16.T32 1960   907   LC 60-16196

Vansina, Jan.   3.438
Oral tradition; a study in historical methodology. Translated by H. M. Wright. — Chicago, Aldine Pub. Co. [1965] xiv, 226 p. illus. 23 cm. Revision of thesis, University of Louvain. Bibliography: p. 216-222. 1. Oral tradition 2. History — Methodology I. T.
D16.V2783   901.8   LC 64-11942

Varieties of psychohistory / edited by George M. Kren and   3.439
Leon H. Rappoport.
New York: Springer Pub. Co., c1976. 370 p.; 24 cm. 1. Psychohistory — Addresses, essays, lectures. I. Kren, George M., 1926- II. Rappoport, Leon.
D16.V282   155   LC 76-225   ISBN 0826119409

White, Morton Gabriel, 1917-.   • 3.440
Foundations of historical knowledge, by Morton White. — [1st ed.]. — New York: Harper & Row, [1965] 299 p.; 22 cm. 1. History — Methodology 2. History — Philosophy I. T.
D16.W59   901   LC 64-25124

Baum, Willa K.   3.441
Transcribing and editing oral history / by Willa K. Baum. — Nashville: American Association for State and Local History, c1977. 127 p.; 23 cm. 1. Oral history I. American Association for State and Local History. II. T.
D16.14.B38   907/.2   LC 77-3340   ISBN 0910050260

Henige, David P.   3.442
Oral historiography / David Henige. — London; New York: Longman, 1982. 150 p.; 24 cm. Includes index. 1. Oral history 2. Historiography I. T.
D16.14.H46 1982   907/.2 19   LC 82-168   ISBN 0582643643

Friedländer, Saul, 1932-.   3.443
History and psychoanalysis: an inquiry into the possibilities and limits of psychology / by Saul Friedländer; translated by Susan Suleiman. — New York: Holmes & Meier, 1978. 175 p.; 24 cm. Translation of Histoire et psychanalyse. 1. Psychohistory I. T.
D16.16.F7413 1978   155   LC 77-18524   ISBN 0841903395

Loewenberg, Peter.   3.444
Decoding the past: the psychohistorical approach / Peter Loewenberg. — 1st ed. — New York: Knopf, 1983, c1982. xiv, 300 p. 1. Psychohistory I. T.
D16.16.L68 1982   901/.9 19   LC 82-47796   ISBN 0394481526

Seton-Watson, R. W. (Robert William), 1879-1951.   3.445
The historian as a political force in central Europe: an inaugural lecture delivered on 2 November 1922 / by R.W. Seton–Watson. — London: School of Slavonic studies in the University of London, King's College, 1922. 36 p. 1. Historiography 2. Europe — History — Study and teaching I. T.
D16.2 S3   D16.2 S39.   LC 26-1663

Historical study in the west: France, Great Britain, Western   • 3.446
Germany, the United States [by] Michel François [and others]
With an introd. by Boyd C. Shafer.
New York: Appleton-Century-Crofts, [1968] viii, 239 p.; 22 cm. On cover and spine Shafer's name appears first. 1. History — Study and teaching I. François, Michel. II. Shafer, Boyd C.
D16.25.H46   907/.2   LC 68-19485

Steward, Julian Haynes, 1902-1972.   • 3.447
Area research, theory and practice. — New York: Social Science Research Council, 1950. xix, 164 p. , 23 cm. — (Canadian Social Science Research Council / Bulletin; 63) 1. Area studies I. Canadian Social Science Research Council. II. T.
D16.25.S8   LC 50-14624

Perkins, Dexter, 1889-.   • 3.448
The education of historians in the United States [by] Dexter Perkins, John L. Snell and Committee on Graduate Education of the American Historical Association. — New York, McGraw-Hill, 1962. xiii, 244 p. 22 cm. — (The Carnegie series in American education) This study was sponsored by the American Historical Association through its Committee on Graduate Education. Bibliographical footnotes. 1. History — Study and teaching —

United States. I. American Historical Association. Committee on Graduate Education. II. T. III. Series.
D16.3.P4   907   *LC* 61-16529

Fussner, F. Smith.   • **3.449**
The historical revolution; English historical writing and thought, 1580–1640. New York, Columbia University Press, 1962. 343 p. 23 cm. 1. Historiography 2. Historians, English. I. T.
D16.4.G7F8 1962a   907   *LC* 62-10147

Shteppa, Konstantin Feodos'evich, 1896-1958.   • **3.450**
Russian historians and the Soviet State. New Brunswick, N.J., Rutgers University Press [c1962] 437 p. 25 cm. 1. History — Study and teaching — Soviet Union 2. Historians — Soviet Union. I. T.
D16.4.R9 S45   907   *LC* 61-10266

D16.7–16.9 Philosophy of History

D16.7 To 1800

Ibn Khaldūn, 1332-1406.   **3.451**
The Muqaddimah; an introduction to history, translated from the Arabic by Franz Rosenthal. London Routledge & K. Paul [1958] 3 v. plates, col. maps (1 fold.) diagrs., facsims. (part col.) 1. History — Philosophy 2. Civilization I. Rosenthal, Franz, 1914- ed. and tr. II. T.
D16.7 I233 1958A

Ibn Khaldūn, 1332-1406.   • **3.452**
[Kitāb al-'ibar. Muqaddimah English] The Muqaddimah, an introduction to history. Translated from the Arabic by Franz Rosenthal. Abridged and edited by N. J. Dawood. [Princeton, N.J.] Princeton University Press [1969] xiv, 465 p. 21 cm. (Bollingen series. 160) Translation of the author's introduction to his Kitāb al-'ibar. 1. History — Philosophy — Early works to 1800. 2. Civilization — Early works to 1800. I. Rosenthal, Franz, 1914- ed. II. Dawood, N. J. ed. III. T. IV. Series.
D16.7.I2413 1969   901.9   *LC* 72-8164

D16.8 1801–

D16.8 A–B

Adams, Henry, 1838-1918.   • **3.453**
The degradation of the democratic dogma. With an introd. by Brooks Adams. — New York, P. Smith, 1949 [c1919] 317 p. 21 cm. 1. Adams, John Quincy, 1767-1848. 2. History — Philosophy 3. Science I. T. II. Title: Democratic dogma.
D16.8.A2x   *LC* A 50-9750

Arendt, Hannah.   • **3.454**
Between past and future, six exercises in political thought. — New York: Viking Press, 1961. 246 p.; 22 cm. 1. History — Philosophy I. T.
D16.8.A65   901   *LC* 61-7281

Aron, Raymond, 1905-.   • **3.455**
Introduction to the philosophy of history: an essay on the limits of historical objectivity / translated by George J. Irwin. — Boston: Beacon Press, [1961]. 351 p.; 21 cm. 1. History — Philosophy I. T.
D16.8.A723   901   *LC* 61-5882

Aron, Raymond, 1905-.   **3.456**
Politics and history: selected essays / by Raymond Aron; collected, translated, and edited by Miriam Bernheim Conant. — New York: Free Press, c1978. xxx, 274 p.; 24 cm. 1. History — Philosophy — Addresses, essays, lectures. 2. Political science — Addresses, essays, lectures. 3. Social sciences — Addresses, essays, lectures. I. Conant, Miriam Bernheim. II. T.
D16.8.A725   901   *LC* 78-54122   *ISBN* 0029010004

Atkinson, Ronald F., 1928-.   **3.457**
Knowledge and explanation in history: an introduction to the philosophy of history / R. F. Atkinson. — Ithaca, N.Y.: Cornell University Press, 1978. x, 229 p.; 22 cm. — (Cornell paperbacks) Includes index. 1. History — Philosophy I. T.
D16.8.A75   901   *LC* 77-90896   *ISBN* 0801411165

Bagby, Philip.   • **3.458**
Culture and history; prolegomena to the comparative study of civilizations. Berkeley, University of California Press, 1959. 244 p. illus. 23 cm. 1. History — Philosophy 2. Civilization 3. Culture I. T.
D16.8.B27 1959   901   *LC* 60-871

Becker, Carl Lotus, 1873-1945.   • **3.459**
Everyman his own historian; essays on history and politics, by Carl L. Becker. — Chicago: Quadrangle Books, [1966] 325 p.; 21 cm. — (Quadrangle paperbacks, 33) 1. History — Philosophy I. T.
D16.8.B318 1966   901   *LC* 67-1041

Berdiaev, Nikolaĭ, 1874-1948.   • **3.460**
The meaning of history / Translated from the Russian by George Reavey. — Cleveland: Meridian Books, [1962, c1936] 191 p.; 19 cm. — (Living age books, LA36) 1. History — Philosophy 2. Christianity — Philosophy I. T.
D16.8.B326 1962   901   *LC* 62-287

Burckhardt, Jacob, 1818-1897.   • **3.461**
Force and freedom: reflections on history [by] Jacob Burckhardt. Edited by James Hastings Nichols. [New ed.] New York, Pantheon Books [1964, c1943] vi, 382 p. 22 cm. Translation of Weltgeschichtliche Betrachtungen. Bibliographical footnotes. 1. History — Philosophy I. T.
D16.8.B812 1964   901   *LC* 64-5204

Burke, Kenneth, 1897-.   • **3.462**
Attitudes toward history / by Kenneth Burke. — 2d ed., rev. — Los Altos, Calif.: Hermes Publications, 1959. xvi, 375 p. 1. History — Philosophy I. T.
D16.8.B83 1959   *LC* 58-12006

D16.8 C–G

Carr, Edward Hallett, 1892-.   • **3.463**
What is history?. — [1st American ed.]. — New York: Knopf, 1962 [c1961] 209 p.; 20 cm. — (The George Macaulay Trevelyan lectures, 1961) 1. History — Philosophy I. T.
D16.8.C33 1962   901   *LC* 61-17812

Danto, Arthur Coleman, 1924-.   • **3.464**
Analytical philosophy of history, by Arthur C. Danto. Cambridge [Eng.] University Press, 1965. xi, 318 p. 24 cm. Bibliographical references included in 'Notes' (p. 285-313) 1. History — Philosophy I. T.
D16.8.D23   901   *LC* 65-11205

D'Arcy, Martin Cyril, 1888-1976.   • **3.465**
The sense of history: secular and sacred. — London, Faber and Faber [1959] 309 p. 23 cm. 1. History — Philosophy I. T.
D16.8.D25   901   *LC* 59-2975

Dawson, Christopher, 1889-1970.   **3.466**
The dynamics of world history / Edited by John J. Mulloy. — New York: Sheed and Ward [1956] 489 p.; 22 cm. 1. History — Philosophy I. T.
D16.8.D3   901   *LC* 56-7738

Dentan, Robert Claude, 1907- ed.   • **3.467**
The idea of history in the ancient Near East, by Roland H. Bainton [and others]. — New Haven, Yale University Press, 1955. ix, 376 p. 25 cm. — (American oriental series. v. 38) 'Lectures of the Department of Near Eastern Languages and Literatures at Yale University.' Includes bibliographical references. 1. History — Philosophy I. Bainton, Roland Herbert, 1894- II. T. III. Series.
D16.8.D37   901   *LC* 55-6144

Dilthey, Wilhelm, 1833-1911.   • **3.468**
Pattern & meaning in history: thoughts on history & society / edited & introduced by H.P. Rickman. New York: Harper, 1962, c1961. 170 p. (Harper torchbooks. TB1075. The Academy library) Translation of 'the texts ... taken from volume VII of Dilthey's works, published by the Teubner Verlag, Stuttgart.' 1. History — Philosophy I. T. II. Series.
D16.8.D49 1962   *LC* 62-5023   *ISBN* 0061384828

Dray, William H.   **3.469**
Perspectives on history / William Dray. — London; Boston: Routledge and K. Paul, 1980. ix, 142 p.; 22 cm. 1. History — Philosophy — Addresses, essays, lectures. I. T.
D16.8.D69   901 19   *LC* 79-42651   *ISBN* 0710005695

Dray, William H.   • **3.470**
Philosophy of history. — Englewood Cliffs, N.J.: Prentice-Hall, [1964] ix, 116 p.; 22 cm. — (Foundations of philosophy series) 1. History — Philosophy I. T.
D16.8.D7   901   *LC* 64-16442

Dray, William H. ed.   • **3.471**
Philosophical analysis and history, edited by William H. Dray. — [New York: Harper & Row, 1966] 390 p.; 21 cm. — (Sources in contemporary philosophy) 1. History — Philosophy — Collections. I. T.
D16.8.D72   901   *LC* 66-12554

Gallie, W. B., 1912-.   • **3.472**
Philosophy and the historical understanding [by] W. B. Gallie. — 2d ed. — New York: Schocken Books, [1968] xii, 236 p.; 21 cm. 1. History — Philosophy I. T.
D16.8.G27 1968   901   *LC* 68-16656

Gardiner, Patrick, ed.   • **3.473**
Theories of history; readings from classical and contemporary sources. Glencoe, Ill., Free Press [1959] 549 p. 25 cm. (The Free Press textbooks in philosophy) 1. History — Philosophy I. T.
D16.8.G33   901   *LC* 58-6481

Geyl, Pieter, 1887-.   • **3.474**
Debates with historians. New York: Meridian Books [1958] 287 p.; 18 cm. (Meridian books, M57) 1. History — Philosophy I. T.
D 16.8 G39 1958   *LC* 58-11924

Geyl, Pieter, 1887-1966.   • **3.475**
Use and abuse of history. — [Hamden, Conn.]: Archon Books, 1970 [c1955] vi, 97 p.; 19 cm. 1. History — Philosophy I. T.
D16.8.G44 1970   901   *LC* 77-113016   *ISBN* 0208008276

Goldstein, Leon J.   **3.476**
Historical knowing / by Leon J. Goldstein. — Austin: University of Texas Press, [1976] xxvii, 242 p.; 24 cm. Includes index. 1. History — Philosophy I. T.
D16.8.G64   901   *LC* 75-20137   *ISBN* 0292730020

D16.8 H–R

Hegel, Georg Wilhelm Friedrich, 1770-1831.   • **3.477**
The philosophy of history. With prefaces by Charles Hegel and the translator, J. Sibree, and a new introd. by C. J. Friedrich. New York, Dover Publications [1956] xvi, 457 p. 21 cm. 'An unabridged and unaltered republication of the last revision of the Sibree translation. [1944?]' Translation of Vorlesungen über die Philosophie der Geschichte. 1. History — Philosophy I. T.
D16.8.H46 1956   901   *LC* 57-401

Herder, Johann Gottfried, 1744-1803.   **3.478**
[Ideen zur Philosophie der Geschichte der Menschheit. English] Outlines of a philosophy of the history of man. Translated from the German Ideen zur Philosophie der Geschichte der Menschheit by T. Churchill. New York, Bergman Publishers [1966?] xvi, 632 p. 27 cm. First published in London in 1800. 1. Churchill, T. O. 2. History — Philosophy I. T.
D16.8.H495 1966   901   *LC* 66-26785

Klibansky, Raymond, 1905- ed.   • **3.479**
Philosophy & history; essays presented to Ernst Cassirer. Edited by Raymond Klibansky and H. J. Paton. New York, Harper & Row [1963] xii, 363 p. illus., port. 21 cm. (Harper Torchbooks. The Academy library) 'TB1115.' This book has been edited with the support of the Warburg Institute, London. 1. History — Philosophy 2. Philosophy — Addresses, essays, lectures. I. Paton, Herbert James, 1887- joint ed. II. Cassirer, Ernst, 1874-1945. III. Warburg Institute. IV. T.
D16.8.K52 1963   901   *LC* 64-2913

Mandelbaum, Maurice, 1908-.   • **3.480**
The problem of historical knowledge: an answer to relativism / by Maurice Mandelbaum; pref. by the author. — New York: Harper & Row [1967] x, 338, 4 p.; 21 cm. (Harper torchbooks, TB1338) Reissue of the 1938 ed. 1. History — Philosophy 2. History — Methodology I. T. II. Title: Historical knowledge.
D16.8.M26 1967   901   *LC* 68-172

Maritain, Jacques, 1882-1973.   **3.481**
On the philosophy of history / Jacques Maritain; Edited by Joseph W. Evans. — Clifton [N.J.]: A. M. Kelley, 1973 [c1957] xi, 180 p.; 22 cm. — (Scribner reprint editions) 1. History — Philosophy I. T.
D16.8.M286 1973   901   *LC* 73-128059   *ISBN* 0678027609

Federn, Karl, 1868-1942.   • **3.482**
The materialist conception of history; a critical analysis. — Westport, Conn.: Greenwood Press, [1971] xiv, 262 p.; 23 cm. Reprint of the 1939 ed. 1. Marx, Karl, 1818-1883. 2. History — Philosophy I. T.
D16.8.M294 F4 1971   901   *LC* 75-114523   *ISBN* 0837147891

Mazlish, Bruce, 1923-.   • **3.483**
The riddle of history: the great speculators from Vico to Freud / Bruce Mazlish. — New York: Harper & Row, 1966. viii, 484 p. 1. History — Philosophy I. T.
D16.8.M37   901   *LC* 66-12559

Meiland, Jack W.   • **3.484**
Scepticism and historical knowledge [by] Jack W. Meiland. — New York, Random House [1965] vii, 209 p. 19 cm. — (Random House studies in philosophy, SPH 5) Bibliography: p. [205]-206. 1. History — Philosophy I. T.
D16.8M43   901   *LC* 65-17445

Meinecke, Friedrich, 1862-1954.   • **3.485**
[Entstehung des Historismus. English] Historism; the rise of a new historical outlook. [Translated by J. E. Anderson. New York] Herder and Herder [1972] lxi, 524 p. 22 cm. Translation of Die Entstehung des Historismus. 1. History — Philosophy 2. Historiography — History. I. T.
D16.8.M4613 1972b   907/.2   *LC* 73-186993

Munz, Peter, 1921-.   **3.486**
The shapes of time: a new look at the philosophy of history / by Peter Munz. — 1st ed. — Middletown, Conn.: Wesleyan University Press, c1977. xi, 382 p.; 24 cm. Includes index. 1. History — Philosophy I. T.
D16.8.M867   901   *LC* 77-2459   *ISBN* 0819550175

New York University Institute of Philosophy. 5th, 1962.   • **3.487**
Philosophy and history, a symposium. Edited by Sidney Hook. — [New York]: New York University Press, 1963. x, 403 p.; 21 cm. 1. History — Philosophy — Congresses. I. Hook, Sidney, 1902- ed. II. New York University. III. T.
D16.8.N43 1962   901   *LC* 63-11298

Ortega y Gasset, José, 1883-1955.   • **3.488**
History as a system, and other essays toward a philosophy of history. With an afterword by John William Miller. — New York, Norton [1961] 269 p. 22 cm. — (The Norton library, N122.) These essays were originally published under the title: Toward a philosophy of history. 1. History — Philosophy I. T.
D16.8.O72 1961   901   *LC* 61-5613

Popper, Karl Raimund, Sir, 1902-.   • **3.489**
The poverty of historicism / by Karl R. Popper. — New York: Harper & Row, 1964. x, 166 p.; 21 cm. — (Harper torchbooks. The Academy library; TB 1126) 1. History — Philosophy I. T.
D16.8.P57 1964   901   *LC* 64-3717

Press, Gerald A. (Gerald Alan), 1945-.   **3.490**
The development of the idea of history in antiquity / Gerald A. Press. — Kingston: McGill-Queen's University Press, c1982. xii, 179 p.; 24 cm. (McGill-Queen's studies in the history of ideas, 0711-0995; 2) Includes indexes. 1. History — Philosophy 2. History, Ancient — Historiography. I. T.
D16.8.P735 1982   901 19   *LC* 84-239837   *ISBN* 0773510028

Ranke, Leopold von, 1795-1886.   **3.491**
The secret of world history: selected writings on the art and science of history / Leopold von Ranke; edited, with translations, by Roger Wines. — New York: Fordham University Press, 1981. x, 276 p., [2] p. of plates: ill.; 24 cm. Includes index. 1. History — Philosophy — Addresses, essays, lectures. 2. Historiography — Addresses, essays, lectures. I. Wines, Roger. II. T.
D16.8.R29 1981   901 19   *LC* 80-65600   *ISBN* 0823210502

Renier, Gustaaf Johannes, 1892-.   **3.492**
History, its purpose and method / by Gustaaf Johannes Renier. — Macon, Ga.: Mercer University Press, 1982, c1950. 272 p.; 24 cm. — (ROSE.) 1. History — Philosophy 2. History — Methodology I. T. II. Series.
D16.8.R38 1982   901 19   *LC* 82-3522   *ISBN* 0865540365

Ricoeur, Paul, 1913-.   **3.493**
The reality of the historical past / by Paul Ricoeur; under the auspices of the Wisconsin–Alpha Chapter of Phi Sigma Tau. — Milwaukee: Marquette University Press, 1984. 51 p.; 19 cm. — (Aquinas lecture. 1984) 1. History — Philosophy I. T. II. Series.
D16.8.R5 1984   *LC* 84-60012   *ISBN* 0874621526

Rossi, Paolo, 1923-.   **3.494**
[Segni del tempo. English] The dark abyss of time: the history of the earth & the history of nations from Hooke to Vico / Paolo Rossi; translated by Lydia G. Cochrane. — Chicago: University of Chicago Press, c1984. xvi, 338 p.; 24 cm. Translation of: I segni del tempo. Includes index. 1. Vico, Giambattista, 1668-1744. 2. History — Philosophy — History. 3. Science — Philosophy — History. I. T.
D16.8.R6813 1984   901 19   *LC* 84-8481   *ISBN* 0226728358

Rotenstreich, Nathan, 1914-.   **3.495**
Philosophy, history and politics: studies in contemporary English philosophy of history / by Nathan Rotenstreich. — The Hague: Martinus Nijhoff, 1976. 158 p.; 24 cm. (Melbourne international philosophy series; v. 1) Includes indexes. 1. History — Philosophy I. T. II. Series.
D16.8.R845   901   *LC* 76-365026   *ISBN* 9024717434

D16.8 S–Z

Sée, Henri Eugène, 1864-1936.   • **3.496**
[Matérialisme historique et interprétation économique de l'histoire. English]
The economic interpretation of history. Translation and introd. by Melvin M.
Knight. New York, A. M. Kelley, 1968. viii, 154 p. 21 cm. (Reprints of
economic classics) Translation of Matérialisme historique et interprétation
économique de l'histoire. Reprint of the 1929 ed. 1. Marx, Karl, 1818-1883.
2. History — Philosophy 3. Economics I. T.
D16.8.S4 1968   901   LC 67-30863

Strayer, Joseph Reese, 1904- ed.   • **3.497**
The interpretation of history, by Jacques Barzun, Hajo Holborn, Herbert
Heaton, Dumas Malone [and] George La Piana; edited with an introduction by
Joseph A. Strayer. Princeton, Princeton university press, 1943. 186 p. 23 cm.
([Princeton books in the humanities]) The Spencer Trask lectures for
1941-1942. 1. History — Philosophy I. Barzun, Jacques, 1907- II. Holborn,
Hajo, 1902-1969. III. Heaton, Herbert, 1890- IV. Malone, Dumas, 1892-
V. La Piana, George, 1879- VI. T.
D16.8.S7   901   LC a 43-1106

Taylor, Henry Osborn, 1856-1941.   • **3.498**
A layman's view of history, by Henry Osborn Taylor. New York, The
Macmillan Company, 1935. vii p. 1 l., 133 p. 21 cm. 1. History — Philosophy
2. World War, 1914-1918 — Addresses, essays, letcures. I. T.
D16.8.T1   904   LC 35-3699

Taylor, Henry Osborn, 1856-1941.   • **3.499**
A historian's creed. — Port Washington, N.Y.: Kennikat Press, [1969, c1939]
137 p.; 21 cm. — (Essay and general literature index reprint series) 1. History
— Philosophy 2. Man 3. Continuity I. T.
D16.8.T28 1969   901   LC 70-86065   ISBN 0804605904

Trompf, G. W.   **3.500**
The idea of historical recurrence in Western thought: from antiquity to the
Reformation / G. W. Trompf. — Berkeley: University of California Press,
c1979. x, 381 p.; 27 cm. Includes index. 1. History — Philosophy I. T.
II. Title: Historical recurrence in Western thought.
D16.8.T76   901   LC 77-76188   ISBN 0520034791

Walsh, W. H. (William Henry)   • **3.501**
An introduction to philosophy of history / William Henry Walsh. — London:
Hutchinson's University Library 1951. 173 p.; 19 cm. (Hutchinson's university
library: Philosophy) 1. History — Philosophy I. T.
D16.W28   LC 51-13553

Weiss, Paul, 1901-.   • **3.502**
History: written and lived / Paul Weiss. — Carbondale Southern Illinois
University Press [1962] 245p. 1. History — Philosophy I. T.
D16.8.W45   LC 62-15006

Wilkins, Burleigh Taylor.   **3.503**
Has history any meaning?: A critique of Popper's philosophy of history /
Burleigh Taylor Wilkins. — Ithaca, N.Y.: Cornell University Press, 1978.
251 p.; 21 cm. 1. Popper, Karl Raimund, Sir, 1902- 2. History — Philosophy
I. T.
D16.8.W597   901   LC 78-58054   ISBN 0801411874

D16.9 Special Topics

Adams, Brooks, 1848-1927.   • **3.504**
The law of civilization and decay; an essay on history. With an introd. by
Charles A. Beard. — New York: Books for Libraries Press, [1971, c1943] 349,
xi p.; 23 cm. — (Essay index reprint series) 1. History — Philosophy
2. Civilization — History 3. Degeneration I. T.
D16.9.A2 1971   901   LC 71-37125   ISBN 0836924789

Berlin, Isaiah.   • **3.505**
Historical inevitability. — London, New York, Oxford University Press [1955]
79 p. 23 cm. — (Auguste Comte memorial trust lecture, no. 1) 'Delivered on 12
May 1953 at the London School of Economics and Political Science.'
1. History — Philosophy I. T. II. Series.
D16.9.B4   901   LC 55-14152

Cohen, Gerald Allan, 1941-.   **3.506**
Karl Marx's theory of history: a defence / by G. A. Cohen. — Oxford:
Clarendon Press, 1978. xv, 369 p.; 22 cm. 1. Marx, Karl, 1818-1883.
2. Historical materialism I. T.
D16.9.C56   D16.9 C56.   901   LC 78-40242   ISBN 0198271964

Dray, William H.   • **3.507**
Laws and explanation in history. [London] Oxford University Press, 1957.
174 p. 22 cm. (Oxford classical & philosophical monographs) 1. History —
Philosophy I. T.
D 16.9 D76   LC 57-59125

Ferrero, Guglielmo, 1871-1942.   • **3.508**
The principles of power: the great political crises of history / by Guglielmo
Ferrero; translated by Theodore R. Jaeckel. — New York: Putnam, c1942. ix,
333 p.; 23 cm. — Translation of Potere. 'The third volume of a trilogy. The first
two volumes-The gamble and The reconstruction of Europe-were originally
published in Paris. The Principles of power is appearing in New York because it
could not be published in Europe on account of the greatly increased
censorship'.-Pref. 1. Revolutions 2. Europe — History — Philosophy. I. T.
D16.9.F452   940   LC 42-19725

Gardiner, Patrick L.   • **3.509**
The nature of historical explanation. London, Oxford University Press, 1952.
xii, 142 p. 23 cm. (Oxford classical & philosophical monographs) 1. History —
Philosophy I. T. II. Title: Historical explanation.
D16.9.G34 1961   LC 52-4279

Giddens, Anthony.   **3.510**
A contemporary critique of historical materialism / Anthony Giddens. —
Berkeley: University of California Press, c1981-< 1985 >. v. < 1-2 >: ill.; 23
cm. 1. Historical materialism I. T.
D16.9.G47   335.4/119 19   LC 81-43382   ISBN 0520045351

Hook, Sidney, 1902-.   • **3.511**
The hero in history, a study in limitation and possibility. New York,
Humanities Press [1950, c1943] xiv, 273 p. 21 cm. 1. History — Philosophy
2. Heroes I. T.
D16.9.H67 1950   901   LC A 52-5214

Löwith, Karl, 1897-1973.   • **3.512**
Meaning in history. [Chicago] University of Chicago Press [1957, c1949] 257 p.
21 cm. (Phoenix books, P16) 1. History — Philosophy I. T.
D16.9.L64 1957   LC 57-7900

Mandelbaum, Maurice, 1908-.   **3.513**
The anatomy of historical knowledge / Maurice Mandelbaum. — Baltimore:
Johns Hopkins University Press, c1977. viii, 230 p.; 24 cm. 1. History —
Philosophy 2. Causation I. T.
D16.9.M26   901   LC 76-46945   ISBN 0801819296

Martin, Rex.   **3.514**
Historical explanation: re–enactment and practical inference / Rex Martin. —
Ithaca, N.Y.: Cornell University Press, 1977. 267 p.; 22 cm. — (Contemporary
philosophy) Includes index. 1. History — Philosophy I. T. II. Series.
D16.9.M279   901   LC 77-3121   ISBN 0801410843

Niebuhr, Reinhold, 1892-1971.   • **3.515**
Faith and history: a comparison of Christian and modern views of history. —
New York: C. Scribner's Sons, 1949. viii, 257 p.; 22 cm. 1. History —
Philosophy 2. Christianity — Philosophy 3. Apologetics — 20th cent. I. T.
D16.9.N5   901   LC 49-8484 *

Plekhanov, Georgiĭ Valentinovich, 1856-1918.   • **3.516**
Essays in historical materialism: The materialist conception of history, The role
of the individual in history. New York International Publishers [c1940]
48,5-62p. 1. History — Philosophy 2. Materialism 3. Individualism
I. Plekhanov, Georgiĭ Valentinovich. The materialist conception of history
II. Plekhanov, Georgiĭ Valentinovich. The role of the individual in history
III. T.
D16.9 P46

D17–21.3 World Histories.
Outlines

Rashīd al-Dīn Ṭabīb, 1247?-1318.   **3.517**
[Jāmiʻ al-tavārīkh. English] The successors of Genghis Khan. Translated from
the Persian by John Andrew Boyle. New York, Columbia University Press,
1971. xi, 372 p. geneal. tables. 23 cm. (Persian heritage series ; no. 10)
Translation of v. 2 of the first section (commonly known as Tārīkh-i Ghāzānī)
of the author's Jāmiʻ al-tavārīkh. 1. Mongols — History I. T. II. Series.
D17.R26933 1971   950/.2   LC 70-135987   ISBN 0231033516

Theophanes, the Confessor, d. ca. 818.   **3.518**
[Chronographia. English] The chronicle of Theophanes: an English translation
of anni mundi 6095–6305 (A.D. 602–813) / with introduction and notes by
Harry Turtledove. — Philadelphia: University of Pennsylvania Press, 1982.
xxiv, 201 p.; 24 cm. — (Middle Ages.) Translation of: Chronographia. Includes
index. 1. World history — Early works to 1800 I. Turtledove, Harry. II. T.
III. Series.
D17.T513 1982   909/.1 19   LC 82-4861   ISBN 0812278429

International Commission for a History of the Scientific and Cultural Development of Mankind.   • 3.519
History of mankind: [cultural and scientific development. 1st ed.]. — New York: Harper & Row, [1963-. v.   : illus., plates, maps.; 25 cm. Errata slip inserted in v. 1. 1. World history I. T.
D20.I66   909   LC 62-15718   *ISBN* 0060146222

Peuples et civilisations, histoire générale.   • 3.520
Paris: Alcan: P.U.F., 1926-. I. Title: Peuples et civilisations
D20.P37   LC 52-25504

Pirenne, Jacques, 1891-.   • 3.521
The tides of history. Translated from the French by Lavett Edwards. [1st ed.] New York, Dutton, 1962-. v. maps (part fold.) 23 cm. 'Translated from Les grands courants de l'histoire universelle.' 1. World history I. T.
D20.P513   LC 62-7800

Propyläen Weltgeschichte; ein Universalgeschichte. Hrsg. von   • 3.522
Golo Mann und Alfred Heuss.
Berlin, Propyläen-Verlag [1960-   v. 1, 1961] v. illus. (part col.) ports. (part col.) maps (part fold., part col.) facsims. (part in pocket) 27 cm. Vol. 5-7 edited by G. Mann and A. Nitschke; v. 8-10 edited by G. Mann. 1. World history 2. Civilization — History 3. History — Bibliography. I. Mann, Golo, 1909- II. Heuss, Alfred, 1909- III. Nitschke, August, 1926-
D20.P946   LC 60-35516

Bossuet, Jacques Bénigne, 1627-1704.   3.523
[Discours sur l'histoire universelle. English] Discourse on universal history / Jacques–Bénigne Bossuet; translated by Elborg Forster; edited and with an introd. by Orest Ranum. — Chicago: University of Chicago Press, 1976. xlvi, 376 p.; 21 cm. — (Classic European historians) Translation of Discours sur l'histoire universelle. 1. World history — Early works to 1800 I. T. II. Series.
D21.B745513 1976   909   LC 75-9062   *ISBN* 0226067084

Burckhardt, Jacob, 1818-1897.   • 3.524
Judgments on history and historians / Jakob Christoph Burckhardt; translated by Harry Zohn, with an introd. by H. R. Trevor-Roper. — Boston Beacon Press [1958] 280p. Translation of Historische Fragmente. 1. World history I. T.
D21.B973   LC 58-6250

Garraty, John Arthur, 1920-.   3.525
The Columbia history of the world. Editors: John A. Garraty [and] Peter Gay. — [1st ed.]. — New York: Harper & Row, [1972] xx, 1237 p.: maps.; 25 cm. — (A Cass Canfield book) 1. World history I. Gay, Peter, 1923- joint author. II. Columbia University. III. T.
D21.G28   909   LC 76-181621   *ISBN* 0060114325

Langer, William L. (William Leonard), 1896-1977.   • 3.526
An encyclopedia of world history; ancient, medieval, and modern, chronologically arranged. Compiled and edited by William L. Langer. — 5th ed., rev. and enl. with maps and geneal. tables. — Boston: Houghton Mifflin, 1972. xxxix, 1569 p.: illus.; 25 cm. 1. History — Outlines, syllabi, etc. I. T.
D21.L27 1972   902/.02   LC 72-186219   *ISBN* 0395135923

Halecki, Oskar, 1891-1973.   • 3.527
The limits and divisions of European history. — London, New York, Sheed & Ward, 1950. xiii, 242 p. 21 cm. Bibliographical references included in 'Notes' (p. [203]-232) 1. Europe — Hist. — Outlines, syllabi, etc. I. T.
D21.3.H3 1950   940   LC 50-2807

McNeill, William Hardy, 1917-.   3.528
The shape of European history [by] William H. McNeill. — New York: Oxford University Press, 1974. vi, 181 p.; 22 cm. 1. Europe — History 2. Europe — Historiography. I. T.
D21.3.M3   940/.07/2   LC 73-90359   *ISBN* 0195018060

D21.5 Historical Geography

Pounds, Norman John Greville.   3.529
An historical geography of Europe; 450 B.C.–A.D. 1330 [by] Norman J. G. Pounds. — Cambridge [Eng.]: University Press, 1973. xiv, 475 p.: maps.; 24 cm. 1. Europe — Historical geography. I. T.
D21.5.P63   911/.4   LC 72-75299   *ISBN* 0521085632

Pounds, Norman John Greville.   3.530
An historical geography of Europe, 1500–1840 / N. J. G. Pounds. — Cambridge [Eng.]; New York: Cambridge University Press, 1980 (c1979). xvi, 438 p.: ill.; 24 cm. 1. Europe — Historical geography. I. T.
D21.5.P634   940.2   LC 79-11528   *ISBN* 0521223792

Raynal, abbé, 1713-1796.   • 3.531
[Histoire philosophique et politique des établissemens et du commerce des Européens dans les deux Indes English] Philosophical and political history of the settlements and trade of the Europeans in the East and West Indies. Newly translated from the French by J. O. Justamond, with a new set of maps. 2d ed. New York, Negro Universities Press [1969] 6 v. illus. 22 cm. Translation of Histoire philosophique et politique des établissemens et du commerce des Européens dans les deux Indes. Reprint of the 1798 ed. 1. Colonization — History. 2. Commerce — History 3. America — Discovery and exploration 4. East Indies I. T.
D22.R334   973.1   LC 69-18996

D25–27 Military and Naval History (General)

Dupuy, R. Ernest (Richard Ernest), 1887-1975.   3.532
The encyclopedia of military history from 3500 B.C. to the present / R. Ernest Dupuy and Trevor N. Dupuy. — 2nd rev. ed. — New York: Harper & Row, c1986. xv, 1524 p.: ill., maps; 25 cm. Includes indexes. 1. Military history — Dictionaries. 2. Military art and science — History — Dictionaries. I. Dupuy, Trevor Nevitt, 1916- II. T.
D25.A2 D8 1986   355/.009 19   LC 84-48158   *ISBN* 0061812358

Harbottle, Thomas Benfield, d. 1904.   3.533
[Dictionary of battles] Harbottle's Dictionary of battles. — 3rd ed. / revised by George Bruce. — New York: Van Nostrand Reinhold, 1981, c1979. 303 p.; 24 cm. Includes index. 1. Battles — Dictionaries. I. Bruce, George Ludgate, 1910- II. T. III. Title: Dictionary of battles.
D25.A2 H2 1981   904.7 19   LC 80-53498   *ISBN* 0442223366

Eggenberger, David.   • 3.534
A dictionary of battles. — New York: Crowell, [1967] x, 526 p.: plans (part col.); 26 cm. 'Covers ... the first battle of Megiddo in 1479 B.C. to the fighting in Vietnam during the 1960's.' 1. Battles — Dictionaries. I. T.
D25.E35   904/.7   LC 67-12400

Fuller, J. F. C. (John Frederick Charles), 1878-1966.   3.535
A military history of the Western World. — New York, Funk & Wagnalls, 1954-56. 3 v. illus., maps. 24 cm. London ed. (Eyre & Spottiswoode) has title: The decisive battles of the Western World and their influence upon history. Bibliographical footnotes. 1. Military history I. T.
D25.F935   909   LC 54-9733 rev2

Keegan, John, 1934-.   3.536
The face of battle / John Keegan. New York: Viking Press, 1976. 354 p., [4] leaves of plates: ill.; 22 cm. Includes index. 1. Battles 2. Military history I. T.
D25.K43 1976   355.4/8   LC 76-10611   *ISBN* 0670304328

Liddell Hart, Basil Henry, Sir, 1895-1970.   • 3.537
[Decisive wars of history] Strategy / [by] B. H. Liddell Hart. — 2d rev. ed. New York: Praeger [1967] 430 p.: maps; 21 cm. First published in 1929 under title: The decisive wars of history. 1. Military history 2. Strategy I. T.
D25.L45 1967   355.4/3   LC 67-23638

Preston, Richard Arthur.   3.538
Men in arms: a history of warfare and its interrelationships with Western society / Richard A. Preston, Sydney F. Wise. — 4th ed. — New York: Holt, Rinehart, and Winston, c1979. vii, 450 p.: ill.; 21 cm. Includes index. 1. Military history I. Wise, S. F. (Sydney F.), 1924- joint author. II. T.
D25.P7 1979   909   LC 78-21298   *ISBN* 0030456819

Bowen, E. G. (Emrys George), 1900-.   3.539
Britain and the Western seaways; a history of cultural interchange through Atlantic coastal waters [by] E. G. Bowen. New York, Praeger [1972] 196 p. illus. 22 cm. (Ancient peoples and places, v. 80) 1. Migrations of nations 2. Man — Migrations 3. Europe — History, Naval. 4. Europe — Antiquities I. T.
D27.B77 1972   936.1   LC 72-77070

Mahan, A. T. (Alfred Thayer), 1840-1914.   • 3.540
The influence of sea power upon history, 1660–1783; by Captain A. T. Mahan. 15th ed. Boston: Little, Brown and company, 1898. xxiv, 557 p. 4 maps (1 fold.) plans. 24 cm. 1. Naval history I. T.
D27.M21 D27.M215   LC 01-11051

Padfield, Peter.   3.541
Tide of empires: decisive naval campaigns in the rise of the west / Peter Padfield. — London: Routledge & Kegan Paul, 1982. 270 p.: ill., maps, ports.; 24 cm. 1. Naval history I. T.
D27.P14   359.4/09/03   LC 79-320645   *ISBN* 0710001509

Pemsel, Helmut, 1928-.   3.542
A history of war at sea: an atlas and chronology of conflict at sea from earliest times to the present / Helmut Pemsel; translated by Major i. G. D. G. Smith. — 1st English ed., fully rev. — Annapolis, Md.: Naval Institute Press, 1978 (c1977). 176 p.: ill., maps.; 26 cm. 1. Naval battles I. T.
D27.P448   359.48   LC 76-45237   ISBN 0870218034

Sea power: a naval history / editor, E.B. Potter; assistant   3.543
editors, Roger Fredland, Henry H. Adams; authors, Henry H. Adams ... [et al.].
2nd ed. — Annapolis, Md.: Naval Institute Press, c1981. vii, 419 p.: ill.; 26 cm. Includes index. 1. Naval history — Addresses, essays, lectures. 2. Sea-power — Addresses, essays, lectures. I. Potter, E. B. (Elmer Belmont), 1908- II. Fredland, Roger. III. Adams, Henry Hitch, 1917-
D27.S37 1981   359/.009 19   LC 81-81668   ISBN 0870216074

D31–34 POLITICAL AND DIPLOMATIC HISTORY (GENERAL)

Seton-Watson, Hugh.   3.544
Nations and states: an enquiry into the origins of nations and the politics of nationalism / Hugh Seton–Watson. — Boulder, Colo.: Westview Press, 1977. xv, 563 p.; 24 cm. Includes indexes. 1. Nationalism — History. I. T.
D32.S47   320.5/4   LC 77-4237   ISBN 0891582274

D51–95 ANCIENT HISTORY

Godolphin, Francis Richard Borroum, ed.   • 3.545
The Greek historians. The complete and unabridged historical works of Herodotus, translated by George Rawlinson; Thucydides, translated by Benjamin Jowett; Xenophon, translated by Henry G. Dakyns [and] Arrian, translated by Edward J. Chinnock. Edited, with an introduction, revisions and additional notes, by Francis R. B. Godolphin. New York, Random house [1942] 2 v. fold. map. 24 cm. 'First printing.' 1. History, Ancient — Collections. 2. Historians — Greece. I. Herodotus. II. Thucydides. III. Xenophon. IV. Arrian. V. Rawlinson, George, 1812-1902. tr. VI. Jowett, Benjamin, 1817-1893. tr. VII. Dakyns, Henry Graham, tr. VIII. Chinnock, Edward James, tr. IX. T.
D52.G6   938.0082   LC 42-11883

Ehrich, Robert W., ed.   • 3.546
Chronologies in Old World archaeology / edited by Robert W. Ehrich. — Chicago: University of Chicago Press, [1965] xii, 557 p.: ill., maps.; 23 cm. 'Supersedes the earlier Relative chronologies in Old World archaeology, published ... in 1954.' 1. History, Ancient — Chronology I. T.
D54.5.E4 1965   930.02   LC 65-17296

Waters, Kenneth H.   3.547
Herodotos, the historian: his problems, methods, and originality / K.H. Waters. — 1st ed. — Norman: University of Oklahoma Press, c1985. 194 p.; 23 cm. Includes index. 1. Herodotus. I. T.
D56.52.H45 W37 1985   938/.0072024 B 19   LC 84-19504   ISBN 0806119284

Hornblower, Jane.   3.548
Hieronymus of Cardia / Jane Hornblower. — Oxford; New York: Oxford University Press, 1981. xi, 301 p.; 23 cm. — (Oxford classical and philosophical monographs.) Includes indexes. 1. Hieronymus, of Cardia. I. T. II. Series.
D56.52.H53 H67 1981   930/.07/2024 19   LC 83-149861   ISBN 0198147171

The Cambridge ancient history.   • 3.549
3rd ed. London, Cambridge University Press, 1970- < 1984 > . < v. 1; v. 2, pt. 2; v. 3, pt. 1, 3; v. 7, pt. 1; in 5 > illus., maps (some col.) 24 cm. Individual chapters have already appeared as fascicles, 1961-1968. 1. History, Ancient
D57.C252   930   LC 75-85719   ISBN 0521070511

Raleigh, Walter, Sir, 1552?-1618.   3.550
The history of the world. Edited by C. A. Patrides. — Philadelphia: Temple University Press, [1972, c1971] xvi, 418 p.; 23 cm. Extracts reprinted from 1st ed., 1614. 1. History, Ancient I. T.
D57.R183 1972   930   LC 76-163312   ISBN 0877220115

Rostovzeff, Michael Ivanovitch, 1870-1952.   • 3.551
[Ocherk istorii drevniago mira. English] A history of the ancient world, by M. Rostovtzeff. Westport, Conn., Greenwood Press [1971] 2 v. illus., maps, plans, ports. 24 cm. Translation of Ocherk istorii drevniago mira. 1. History, Ancient I. T.
D57.R8 1971   930   LC 73-109834   ISBN 0837144167

Starr, Chester G., 1914-.   • 3.552
A history of the ancient world / Chester G. Starr. — 2d ed. — New York: Oxford University Press, 1974. xvii, 742 p., [16] leaves of plates: ill.; 24 cm. Includes index. 1. History, Ancient I. T.
D59.S75 1974   930   LC 74-79633   ISBN 0195018141

Ehrenberg, Victor, 1891-.   • 3.553
Aspects of the ancient world: essays and reviews / by Victor Ehrenberg. — New York: Salloch, 1946. ix, 256p. 1. History, Ancient — Addresses, essays, lectures I. T.
D60.E37

Childe, V. Gordon (Vere Gordon), 1892-1957.   • 3.554
The dawn of European civilization. 6th ed., rev. New York, Knopf, 1958 [c1957] xii, 367 p. illus., maps. 24 cm. (The History of civilization. [Pre-history and antiquity]) 1. Archaeology 2. Man, Prehistoric 3. Europe — Civilization I. T.
D65.C5 1958   901   LC 58-5914

Piggott, Stuart.   • 3.555
Ancient Europe from the beginnings of agriculture to classical antiquity; a survey. Chicago, Aldine Pub. Co. [1966, c1965] xiii, 340 p. illus., maps, plans. 26 cm. 1. Europe — Antiquities 2. Europe — History — To 476 I. T.
D65.P65 1966   913/.36/03   LC 64-21369

Powell, T. G. E. (Thomas George Eyre), 1916-.   • 3.556
The Celts. New York: F. A. Praeger [1958] 282 p.: ill., plates, maps; 21 cm. 1. Celts I. T.
D70.P6   LC 58-8173

Stipčević, Aleksandar.   3.557
[Iliri. English] The Illyrians: history and culture / by Aleksandar Stipčević; translated by Stojana Čulić Burton. — Park Ridge, N.J.: Noyes Press, c1977. vii, 291 p.: ill.; 25 cm. Translation of Iliri. 1. Illyrians I. T.
D90.I3 S7413   939/.8   LC 77-150   ISBN 0815550529

Casson, Lionel, 1914-.   • 3.558
The ancient mariners: seafarers and sea fighters of the Mediterranean in ancient times. — New York: Macmillan, 1959. 286 p.: ill.; 22 cm. 1. Naval history, Ancient I. T.
D95.C35   930   LC 58-12437

D101–847 MEDIEVAL AND MODERN HISTORY

Previté-Orton, Charles William, 1877-1947.   • 3.559
A history of Europe from 1198 to 1378. [3d ed.] New York, Barnes & Noble [1951] 464 p. illus. 23 cm. 1. Europe — History — 476-1492 I. T.
D102.M44 vol. 3   LC 52-9644

Hay, Denys.   • 3.560
Europe: the emergence of an idea. — Revised ed. — Edinburgh: Edinburgh U.P., 1968. xxiv, 151 p.: 9 plates, illus., facsims., geneal. table, maps.; 21 cm. — (Edinburgh University publications; history, philosophy and economics, no. 7) 1. Europe (The word) 2. Europe — Historical geography. I. T.
D104.H27 1968   911.4   LC 68-19886   ISBN 0852240112

Schuman, Frederick Lewis, 1904-.   • 3.561
International politics; anarchy and order in the world society [by] Frederick L. Schuman. Maps by George Brodsky. — 7th ed. — New York: McGraw-Hill, [1968, c1969] xx, 751 p.: maps.; 23 cm. — (McGraw-Hill series in political science) 1. World politics 2. International relations — History. 3. State, The 4. Nationalism 5. Imperialism I. T.
D105.S35 1969   327   LC 68-27512

Tapsell, R. F., 1936-.   3.562
Monarchs, rulers, dynasties, and kingdoms of the world / compiled by R.F. Tapsell. — New York: Facts on File Publications, 1983. 511 p.; 25 cm. Includes index. 1. Kings and rulers — Biography. 2. Kings and rulers — Genealogy 3. Royal houses — History. I. T.
D107.T36 1983   920/.02 19   LC 82-15726   ISBN 0871961210

Egan, E. W. **3.563**
Kings, rulers, and statesmen / compiled and edited by Edward W. Egan, Constance B. Hintz, and L. F. Wise. Rev. ed. — New York: Sterling Pub. Co., c1976. 512 p.: ill.; 25 cm. Previous ed. by L. F. Wise and E. W. Egan. 1. Kings and rulers 2. Statesmen I. Hintz, Constance B., joint author. II. Wise, Leonard F., joint author. III. T.
D107.W5 1976 909 B LC 76-151225 ISBN 0806900504

D111–203 Medieval History

Froissart, Jean, 1338?-1410? • **3.564**
Chronicles. Carbondale, Southern Illinois University Press [1963] 224 p. (Centaur classics) 1. Hundred Years' War, 1339-1453 2. France — History — House of Valois, 1328-1589 3. Great Britain — History — 14th century 4. Flanders — History. 5. Burgundy (France) — History 6. Europe — History — 476-1492 I. T.
D113.F77 1963 LC 63-14937

Froissart, Jean, 1338?-1410? • **3.565**
[Chroniques. English] Chronicles. Translated and edited by John Jolliffe. New York: Modern Library [1968, c1967] xxiii, 448 p. geneal. tables, maps. 19 cm. (The Modern library of the world's best books [ML387]) 1. Hundred Years' War, 1339-1453 2. France — History — 14th century 3. Great Britain — History. 5. Burgundy (France) — History 6. Europe — History — 476-1492 I. Jolliffe, John Edward Austin, 1891- ed. II. T.
D113.F77 1968 944/.025 LC 66-21508

Ordericus Vitalis, 1075-1143? **3.566**
[Historia ecclesiastica English] The ecclesiastical history of Orderic Vitalis; edited and translated with introduction and notes by Marjorie Chibnall. Oxford, Clarendon P., 1969-1980. 6 v. 23 cm. (Oxford medieval texts.) Translation of Historiae ecclesiasticae libri XIII. 1. Church history 2. Normans 3. Crusades 4. Normandy (France) — History — To 1515 5. Great Britain — History — To 1485 I. Chibnall, Marjorie, ed. II. T. III. Series.
D113.O7213 1969 270.4 LC 70-25316 ISBN 0198222041

Dictionary of the Middle Ages / Joseph R. Strayer, editor in chief. **3.567**
New York: Scribner, c1982- <c1986 >. v. < 1-4, 6-7 >: ill.; 29 cm. + interim index (ix, 190 p.; 28 cm.) 1. Middle Ages — Dictionaries. I. Strayer, Joseph Reese, 1904-
D114.D5 1982 909.07 19 LC 82-5904 ISBN 0684167603

Dahmus, Joseph Henry, 1909-. **3.568**
Seven medieval historians / Joseph Dahmus. — Chicago: Nelson-Hall, c1982. xvi, 323 p.; 23 cm. Includes index. 1. Middle Ages — Historiography 2. Medievalists 3. Medievalists — Biography. I. T.
D116.D29 940.1/072022 19 LC 81-11332 ISBN 0882297120

Medieval studies: an introduction / edited by James M. M. Powell. **3.569**
1st ed. — Syracuse, N.Y.: Syracuse University Press, 1976. x, 389 p.; 23 cm. 1. Middle Ages — Historiography — Addresses, essays, lectures. I. Powell, James M.
D116.M4 940.1/07/2 LC 76-8870 ISBN 0815621752

Smalley, Beryl. **3.570**
Historians in the Middle Ages / Beryl Smalley. — New York: Scribner, [1975] c1974. 202 p.: ill.; 25 cm. 1. Middle Ages — Historiography 2. Historiography — History. I. T.
D116.S6 1975 909.07/07/2 LC 74-14155 ISBN 0684141213

Mahdi, Muhsin. **3.571**
Ibn Khaldūn's philosophy of history: a study in the philosophic foundation of the science of culture. — [Chicago]: University of Chicago Press, [1964] 325 p.; 21 cm. — (Phoenix books) 1. Ibn Khaldūn, 1332-1406. I. T.
D116.7.I3 M3 1964 901 LC 64-23414

The Cambridge medieval history. • **3.572**
[2d ed.] — Cambridge [Eng.]: University Press, 1966-. v.: fold. col., maps.; 24 cm. Planned by J. B. Bury. Vol. 1-3, 5-9 reprints of 1st ed. (some with corrections) 1. Middle Ages — History I. Bury, J. B. (John Bagnell), 1861-1927.
D117.C32 909.07

Cheyney, Edward Potts, 1861-1947. • **3.573**
The dawn of a new era, 1250-1453, by Edward P. Cheyney. New York, London, Harper & Brothers, 1936. x p., 2 l., 389 p. illus. (2 maps), plates, ports.

23 cm. (Rise of modern Europe.) Maps on lining-papers. 'First edition.' 1. Europe — History — 476-1492 I. T. II. Series.
D117.C5 1936 940.18 LC 36-3968

Previté-Orton, Charles William, 1877-1947. **3.574**
The shorter Cambridge medieval history. — Cambridge [Eng.]: University Press, 1952. 2 v. (xxi, 1202 p.): illus., maps.; 22 cm. 'The author's concise version of the Cambridge medieval history, of which he had been one of the editors.' 1. Middle Ages — History I. The Cambridge medieval history. II. T.
D117.P75 940.1 LC 52-12272

Tierney, Brian. **3.575**
Western Europe in the Middle Ages, 300–1475: formerly entitled a History of the Middle Ages, 284–1500 / Brian Tierney, Sidney Painter. — 4th ed. — New York: Knopf, c1983. xiv, 633, xx p.: ill.; 26 cm. 1. Middle Ages — History I. Painter, Sidney, 1902-1960. II. T.
D117.T6 1983 940.1 19 LC 82-10034 ISBN 0394330609

Morrall, John B. • **3.576**
The medieval imprint: the founding of the Western European tradition [by] John B. Morrall. — New York: Basic Books, [1968, c1967] xi, 156 p.: illus.; 22 cm. 1. Middle Ages — History — Addresses, essays, lectures. I. T.
D119.M68 1968 914/.03/1 LC 68-20962

Dopsch, Alfons, 1896-1953. • **3.577**
[Wirtschaftliche und soziale Grundlagen der europäischen Kulturentwicklung. English] The economic and social foundations of European civilization. With an introd. by Robert Latouche. New York, H. Fertig, 1969. xvii, 404 p. 23 cm. Translation of Wirtschaftliche und soziale Grundlagen der europäischen Kulturentwicklung. 1. Civilization, Medieval 2. Germanic tribes 3. Europe — History — 392-814 I. T.
D121.D62 1969 901.92/1 LC 68-9591

Pirenne, Henri, 1862-1935. • **3.578**
[Mohomet et Charlemagne. English] Mohammed and Charlemagne; [translated from the French by Bernard Miall]. 1st ed., 5th impression. London: Allen & Unwin, 1968. 3-293 p. 22 cm. (Unwin university books, 61) Translation of Mohomet et Charlemagne. 1. Europe — History — 392-814 2. Islamic Empire — History I. T.
D121.P52 1968 940.1/1 LC 72-363566

Power, Eileen Edna, 1889-1940. • **3.579**
Medieval people. — [10th ed.]. — London: Methuen; New York: Barnes & Noble, [1963] xii, 210 p.: illus., fold. map.; 22 cm. 1. Civilization, Medieval I. T.
D127.P6 1963 901.92 LC 63-24493

Bloch, Marc Léopold Benjamin, 1886-1944. • **3.580**
Feudal society / translated from the French by L. A. Manyou; forword by M. M. Postan. — Chicago: University of Chicago P., 1961. xxi, 498 p.: ill., plates. — 1. Feudalism 2. Europe — History — 476-1496. I. T.
D131 B513 1961a 940.14

Stephenson, Carl, 1886-1954. • **3.581**
Mediaeval feudalism, by Carl Stephenson. — Ithaca, N.Y.: Cornell university press, 1942. ix, 116 p.: incl. front., illus.; 21 cm. 1. Feudalism I. T.
D131.S8 940.14 LC 42-8382

D135–148 Migrations

Bury, J. B. (John Bagnell), 1861-1927. • **3.582**
The invasion of Europe by the barbarians. — New York: Russell & Russell, 1963. 296 p.; 23 cm. 1. Migrations of nations 2. Rome — History — Germanic Invasions, 3d-6th centuries I. T.
D135.B8 1963 937.09 LC 63-8359

Musset, Lucien. **3.583**
[Invasions: les vagues germaniques. English] The Germanic invasions: the making of Europe, AD 400–600 / Lucien Musset; translated by Edward and Columba James. — University Park: Pennsylvania State University Press, c1975. xiii, 287 p.: maps; 23 cm. Translation of Les invasions: les vagues germaniques. Includes index. 1. Migrations of nations I. T.
D135.M8813 940.1/1 LC 75-14261 ISBN 027101198X

Mänchen-Helfen, Otto. **3.584**
The world of the Huns; studies in their history and culture, by Otto J. Maenchen-Helfen. Edited by Max Knight. Berkeley, University of California Press, 1973. xxix, 602 p. illus. 26 cm. 1. Attila, d. 453. 2. Huns I. T.
D141.M33 910/.039/42 LC 79-94985 ISBN 0520015967

Dvornik, Francis, 1893-.   • **3.585**
The Slavs in European history and civilization. — New Brunswick, N.J.:
Rutgers University Press, [1962] xxviii, 688 p.: maps.; 25 cm. 1. Slavs —
History. I. T.
D147.D84   947   *LC* 61-10259

D151–173 CRUSADES

Shaw, Margaret Renée Bryers, ed. and tr.   • **3.586**
Chronicles of the Crusades. — Baltimore: Penguin Books [1963] 362 p.: maps.;
18 cm. — (The Penguin classics, L124) 1. Crusades I. Villehardouin, Geoffroi
de, d. ca. 1212. The conquest of Constantinople. II. Joinville, Jean, sire de,
1224?-1317? The life of Saint Louis. III. T.
D151.S5   940.18   *LC* 63-5725

William, of Tyre, Archbishop of Tyre, ca. 1130-ca. 1190.   • **3.587**
A history of deeds done beyond the sea / by William, archbishop of Tyre;
translated and annotated by Emily Atwater Babcock and A.C. Krey. New
York: Columbia university press, 1943. 2 v.: maps (1 fold.); 23 1/2 cm. (Records
of civilization: sources and studies; A.P. Evans, editor. No. XXXV) Translation
of Historia rerum in partibus transmarinis gestarum. The edition of William's
history used as the basis of this translation is that prepared by A. Beugnot and
A. Le Prevost for the French academy ... The present translation has been done
by Mrs. Babcock.'- Introd., v.1, p. 44. 1. Crusades 2. Jerusalem — History —
Latin Kingdom, 1099-1244 I. Babcock, Emily Atwater. II. Krey, August C.
(August Charles), 1887-1961. III. T. IV. Series.
D152.G78   *LC* 44-583

Erdmann, Carl, 1898-1945.   **3.588**
[Entstehung des Kreuzzugsgedankens. English] The origin of the idea of
crusade / Carl Erdmann; translated from the German by Marshall W. Baldwin
and Walter Goffart; foreword and additional notes by Marshall W. Baldwin. —
Princeton, N.J.: Princeton University Press, 1977. xxxvi, 446 p.; 23 cm.
Translation of Die Entstehung des Kreuzzugsgedankens. Includes index.
1. Crusades I. T.
D157.E713   909.07   *LC* 77-71980   *ISBN* 0691052514

Runciman, Steven, Sir, 1903-.   • **3.589**
A history of the Crusades. — [1st ed.]. — Cambridge [Eng.] University Press,
1951-54. 3 v. illus., ports., maps, fold. geneal. table. 22 cm. Includes
bibliographies. 1. Crusades I. T.
D157.R8   940.18   *LC* 51-10801 rev

Setton, Kenneth Meyer, 1914-.   • **3.590**
A history of the Crusades. Kenneth M. Setton, general editor. [2d ed.] Madison,
University of Wisconsin Press, 1969-. v.: ill., col. maps. plates.; 26 cm.
1. Crusades I. T.
D157.S482   940.1/8   *LC* 68-9837   *ISBN* 0299066703

Smail, R. C.   • **3.591**
Crusading warfare (1097–1193) / by R.C. Smail. — Cambridge [England]:
University Press, c1956. xi, 272 p.: ill.; 22 cm. (Cambridge studies in medieval
life and thought, new ser.; v. 3) Includes index. 1. Crusades I. T.
D160.S55   940.18   *LC* 56-58455   *ISBN* 0521213156

Krey, August C. (August Charles), 1887-1961. ed. and tr.   • **3.592**
The first Crusade: the accounts of eye–witnesses and participants / by August
Krey. — Gloucester, Mass.: P. Smith, 1958. viii, 299 p.: maps (part. fold.); 21
cm. 1. Crusades — First, 1096-1099 I. T.
D161.1.A3 K7   *LC* 22-1292

Odo de Deuil, Abbot of Saint Denis, d.ca.1162.   • **3.593**
De profectione Ludovici VII in orientem = The journey of Louis VII to the
East / [by] Odo of Deuil; edited with an English translation, by Virginia
Gingerick Berry. — New York: Norton, [1965, c1948] xliv, 154 p.: facsim.,
maps.; 21 cm. (Records of civilization, sources and studies. no.42) 1. Louis VII,
le jeune, King of France, 1119-1180. 2. Crusades — Second, 1147-1149
I. Berry, Virginia (Gingerick) II. T. III. Series.
D162.1.O3 1965   940.18

Villehardouin, Geoffroi de, d. ca. 1212.   • **3.594**
Memoirs of the crusades, by Villehardouin & De Joinville. Tr. by Sir Frank
Marzials. — London, J. M. Dent & co.; New York, E. P. Dutton & co. [1908]
xli, [1], 340 p. 18 cm. — (Half-title: Everyman's library, ed. by Ernest Rhys.
History. [no. 333]) 1. Louis IX, King of France, 1214-1270. 2. Crusades —
Fourth, 1202-1204 3. Crusades — Seventh, 1248-1250 4. Constantinople —
History. 5. Latin Empire, 1204-1261 I. Joinville, Jean, sire de, 1224?-1317?
II. Marzials, Frank Thomas, Sir, 1840-1912, tr. III. T.
D164.A3Vx   *LC* A 10-2386

Atiya, Aziz Suryal, 1898-.   • **3.595**
The crusade in the later Middle Ages, by Aziz S. Atiya. — 2d ed. — New York:
Kraus Reprint Co., 1970. xvi, 604 p.: illus., maps.; 24 cm. Reprint of the 1965
ed. 1. Crusades — Later, 13th, 14th, and 15th centuries I. T.
D171.A88 1970   909.07   *LC* 78-126642

D175–195 LATIN KINGDOM OF JERUSALEM

Prawer, Joshua.   **3.596**
The Crusaders' kingdom; European colonialism in the Middle Ages. — New
York: Praeger, [1972] v, 587 p.: illus.; 22 cm. 1. Jerusalem — History — Latin
Kingdom, 1099-1244 I. T.
D182.P68   956.94/4/03   *LC* 72-77069

D198–199 ISLAMIC EMPIRE

Gibb, Hamilton Alexander Rosskeen, Sir.   **3.597**
Studies on the civilization of Islam. Boston: Beacon P., 1962. 369p. (Beacon
books on world affairs.) "Articles drawn from a wide variety of publications
over a span of nearly four decades." 1. Civilization, Islamic I. T. II. Series.
D199.3.G5   915.6   *LC* 62-7195

Goitein, S. D., 1900-.   **3.598**
A Mediterranean society; the Jewish communities of the Arab world as
portrayed in the documents of the Cairo Geniza [by] S. D. Goitein. Berkeley,
University of California Press, 1967- < 1983 >. v. < 1-2, 4 > illus., facsims.,
maps. 24 cm. 'Published under the auspices of the Near Eastern Center,
University of California, Los Angeles.' 1. Jews — Islamic Empire —
Civilization. 2. Cairo Genizah 3. Islamic Empire — Civilization. I. Gustave
E. von Grunebaum Center for Near Eastern Studies. II. T.
D199.3.G58   915.6/09/74924   *LC* 67-22430   *ISBN* 0520018672

Schroeder, Eric, 1904-.   **3.599**
Muhammad's people: a tale by anthology; the religion and politics, poetry and
violence, science, ribaldry, & finance of the Muslims, from the age of ignorance
before Islam and the mission of God's prophet to sophistication in the eleventh
century; a mosaic translation. — Portland, Me.: Bond Wheelwright Co.,
[c1955] xviii, 838 p.: map. Includes indexes. 1. Muslims — History. I. T.
D199.3.S42   *LC* 54-10621

Von Grunebaum, Gustave E. (Gustave Edmund), 1909-1972.   • **3.600**
Medieval Islam; a study in cultural orientation. 2d ed. Chicago, University of
Chicago Press [1953] vii, 378 p. maps (on lining papers) 24 cm. (An Oriental
Institute essay) 1. Civlization, Islamic. I. T.
D199.3.V64 1953   950   *LC* 53-9941

D200–203 LATER MIDDLE AGES (14TH–15TH CENTURIES)

Heer, Friedrich, 1916-.   • **3.601**
[Mittelalter. English] The medieval world: Europe, 1100–1350. Translated
from the German by Janet Sondheimer. [1st ed.] Cleveland: World Pub. Co.
[1962] 365 p.: illus. 25 cm. Translation of Mittelalter. 1. Civilization, Medieval
I. T.
D200.H413 1962   940.17   *LC* 61-12020

Brooke, Christopher Nugent Lawrence.   • **3.602**
Europe in the central Middle Ages, 962–1154, [by] Christopher Brooke. New
York, Holt, Rinehart and Winston [1964?] 403 p. geneal. tables, maps. 22 cm.
(A General history of Europe) 1. Europe — History — 476-1492 I. T.
D201.B7   901.92   *LC* 64-12616

Hay, Denys.   • **3.603**
Europe in the fourteenth and fifteenth centuries. New York, Holt, Rinehart and
Winston [c1966] x, 420 p. geneal. tables, maps. 22 cm. (A General history of
Europe) 1. Civilization, Medieval — 14th century 2. Fifteenth century I. T.
D202.8.H3   914/.03/17   *LC* 66-23561

Aston, Margaret.   • **3.604**
The fifteenth century; the prospect of Europe. — [1st American ed. — New
York]: Harcourt, Brace & World, [1968] 216 p.: illus. (part col.), facsims., maps
(part col.), ports.; 22 cm. — ([History of European civilization library])
1. Fifteenth century I. T.
D203.A8 1968b   940.2   *LC* 67-27968

D204–847 Modern History

Harper encyclopedia of the modern world; a concise reference • **3.605**
history from 1760 to the present. Edited by Richard B. Morris
and Graham W. Irwin.
[1st ed.]. — New York: Harper & Row, [1970] xxxii, 1271 p.: maps.; 24 cm.
1. History, Modern — Dictionaries. I. Morris, Richard Brandon, 1904- ed.
II. Irwin, Graham W., ed.
D205.H35 1970　　903　　*LC* 73-81879

The Making of the modern world; general editor Douglas • **3.606**
Johnson.
London: Benn; New York: Barnes & Noble, 1971-. v.　　: illus., facsims.,
maps, ports.; 23 cm. 1. History, Modern I. Johnson, Douglas W. J. ed.
D208.M33　　901.9/3　　*LC* 70-26009　　*ISBN* 0389041289

The New Cambridge modern history. • **3.607**
Cambridge [Eng.]: University Press, 1957-70. 14 v.; 24 cm. Includes also the 2d
ed. of v. 12, with title: The shifting balance of world forces, 1898-1945, edited by
C. L. Mowat. 1. History, Modern
D208.N4　　940.2　　*LC* 57-14935

Wolf, Eric Robert, 1923-. **3.608**
Europe and the people without history / Eric R. Wolf; cartographic
illustrations by Noël L. Diaz. — Berkeley: University of California Press,
c1982. xi, 503 p.: ill.; 25 cm. Includes index. 1. Social change 2. Europe —
Economic conditions 3. Europe — Social conditions 4. Europe — History —
1492- I. T.
D208.W64 1982　　940.2 19　　*LC* 81-24031　　*ISBN* 0520044592

Palmer, R. R. (Robert Roswell), 1909-. **3.609**
A history of the modern world / R.R. Palmer, Joel Colton. — 6th ed. — New
York: Knopf, c1984. xvi, 1106 p.: ill. (some col.); 26 cm. Includes index.
1. History, Modern 2. Europe — History I. Colton, Joel G., 1918- II. T.
D209.P26 1984　　909.08 19　　*LC* 83-47988　　*ISBN* 0394533968

Acton, John Emerich Edward Dalberg Acton, baron. • **3.610**
Lectures on modern history / Lord Acton; with an introd. by Hugh Trevor-
Roper. — New York: Meridian, 1961, c1960 printing. 319 p. 'Meridian
books,M109.' 1. History, Modern — Addresses, essays, lectures. I. T.
D210.A2 1961　　940.2　　*LC* 60-15294

Fagan, Brian M. **3.611**
Clash of cultures / Brian M. Fagan. — New York: W.H. Freeman, c1984.
318 p.: ill.; 24 cm. Includes index. 1. Culture conflict 2. Discoveries (in
geography) 3. Europe — History — 1492- 4. Europe — Territorial expansion.
I. T.
D210.F25 1984　　940.2 19　　*LC* 84-4053　　*ISBN* 0716716224

Namier, Lewis Bernstein, Sir, 1888-1960. • **3.612**
Personalities and powers. London, H. Hamilton [1955] 157 p. 23 cm.
1. History, Modern — Addresses, essays, lectures. I. T.
D210.N32　　*LC* 55-3092

The Responsibility of power; historical essays in honor of Hajo • **3.613**
Holborn. Edited by Leonard Krieger and Fritz Stern.
London, Melbourne, Macmillan, 1968. [1], xiv, 464 p. 23 cm. 1. History,
Modern — Addresses, essays, lectures. 2. Power (Philosophy) — Addresses,
essays, lectures. I. Holborn, Hajo, 1902-1969. II. Krieger, Leonard. ed.
III. Stern, Fritz Richard, 1926- ed.
D210.R43 1968　　320/.01　　*LC* 74-363904

Romein, Jan Marius, 1893-1962. **3.614**
[Op het breukvlak van twee eeuwen. English] The watershed of two eras:
Europe in 1900 / Jan Romein; translated by Arnold J. Pomerans. — 1st ed. —
Middletown, Conn.: Wesleyan University Press, c1978. xxxviii, 783 p.; 24 cm.
Translation of Op het breukvlak van twee eeuwen. Includes index. 1. History,
Modern — Addresses, essays, lectures. I. T.
D210.R6313　　909.82　　*LC* 77-14841　　*ISBN* 0819550264

Tuchman, Barbara Wertheim. **3.615**
The march of folly: from Troy to Vietnam / Barbara W. Tuchman. — 1st ed. —
New York: Knopf: Distributed by Random House, 1984. xiv, 447 p., [32] p. of
plates: ill. (some col.); 24 cm. 1. History, Modern 2. History — Errors,
inventions, etc. 3. Power (Social sciences) 4. Judgment I. T.
D210.T89 1984　　909.08 19　　*LC* 83-22206　　*ISBN* 0394527771

Zagorin, Perez. **3.616**
Rebels and rulers, 1500–1660 / Perez Zagorin. — Cambridge; New York:
Cambridge University Press, 1982. 2 v.; 24 cm. 1. Revolutions — Europe —

History — 16th century. 2. Revolutions — Europe — History — 17th century.
3. Europe — History — 1492-1648 4. Europe — History — 17th century I. T.
D210.Z33 1982　　940.2 19　　*LC* 81-17039　　*ISBN* 0521244722

National consciousness, history, and political culture in early– **3.617**
modern Europe. Edited by Orest Ranum.
Baltimore, Johns Hopkins University Press [1975] x, 177 p. illus. 23 cm. (Johns
Hopkins symposia in comparative history. 5th) Based on the 1973 Schouler
lectures, sponsored by the Dept. of History of the Johns Hopkins University.
1. Europe — Politics and government — 1492-1648 — Addresses, essays,
lectures. 2. Europe — Politics and government — 1648-1789 — Addresses,
essays, lectures. 3. Europe — Civilization — Addresses, essays, lectures.
I. Ranum, Orest A. ed. II. Series.
D217.N37 1975　　320.9/4/02　　*LC* 74-6837　　*ISBN* 080181619X

Petrie, Charles Alexander, bart., 1895-. • **3.618**
Earlier diplomatic history, 1492–1713. — New York: Macmillan, 1949. xii,
251 p.: maps. 1. World politics I. T.
D217.P42 1949

Petrie, Charles, Sir, 1895-. • **3.619**
Diplomatic history, 1713–1933 / by Sir Charles Petrie. — London: Hollis and
Carter, 1946. xii, 384 p.: maps.; 23 cm. 1. World politics I. T.
D217.P43　　*LC* 46-6073

D220–234 16TH CENTURY (1453-1648)

Klarwill, Victor, 1873- ed. **3.620**
[Fugger-Zeitungen. English] The Fugger news–letters, first series; being a
selection of unpublished letters from the correspondents of the House of Fugger
during the years 1568–1605. Edited by Victor von Klarwill. Authorized
translation by Pauline de Chary. Foreword by H. Gordon Selfridge. Freeport,
N.Y., Books for Libraries Press [1970] xlv, 284 p. illus., ports. 23 cm. Reprint of
the 1924 ed. 1. Fugger family 2. Europe — History — 1517-1648 I. T.
D220.F8 K413 1970　　940.2/3　　*LC* 79-140360　　*ISBN* 0836956036

Koenigsberger, H. G. (Helmut Georg) • **3.621**
Europe in the sixteenth century [by] H. G. Koenigsberger and George L.
Mosse. New York, Holt, Rinehart and Winston [1968] xiii, 399 p. illus., geneal.
tables, maps. 21 cm. (A General history of Europe) 1. Europe — History —
1492-1648 I. Mosse, George L. (George Lachmann), 1918- joint author. II. T.
D220.K6 1968b　　914/.03/23　　*LC* 68-17107　　*ISBN* 0030836344

Davis, James C. (James Cushman) comp. • **3.622**
Pursuit of power; Venetian ambassadors' reports on Spain, Turkey, and France
in the age of Philip II, 1560–1600. Edited and translated by James C. Davis. —
New York: Harper & Row, [1970] xi, 283 p.: illus., maps, ports.; 22 cm. — (A
Torchbook Library edition) 1. Europe — History — 1517-1648 — Sources.
I. T.
D221.V4 D3 1970　　940.2/32　　*LC* 70-134281

Chudoba, Bohdan. • **3.623**
Spain and the Empire, 1519–1643. — New York: Octagon Books, 1969. xi,
299 p.: geneal. tables, maps (on lining papers); 24 cm. Reprint of the 1952 ed.,
with a new pref. by the author. 1. Europe — History — 1517-1648 2. Spain —
History — House of Austria, 1516-1700 3. Holy Roman Empire — History —
1517-1648 I. T.
D228.C48 1969　　946/.04　　*LC* 71-84177

Cowie, Leonard W. **3.624**
Sixteenth–century Europe / Leonard W. Cowie. — Edinburgh: Oliver & Boyd;
New York: Longman, c1977. 340 p. Includes index. 1. Europe — History —
1492-1648 I. T.
D228.C68　　940.2/3　　*LC* 76-23419　　*ISBN* 0050028294

Dickens, A. G. (Arthur Geoffrey), 1910-. **3.625**
The age of humanism and reformation: Europe in the fourteenth, fifteenth, and
sixteenth centuries [by] A. G. Dickens. Englewood Cliffs, N.J., Prentice-Hall
[1972] ix, 290 p. illus. 24 cm. 1. Europe — History — 1492-1648 I. T.
D228.D52 1972　　914/.03/2　　*LC* 74-39361　　*ISBN* 0130186147
ISBN 0130186066

Elliott, John Huxtable. • **3.626**
Europe divided, 1559–1598 [by] J.H. Elliott. New York, Harper & Row [1969,
c1968] 432 p. illus., geneal. tables, maps. 21 cm. (The Fontana history of
Europe) (Harper Torchbooks TB1414.) 1. Europe — History — 1517-1648
I. T.
D228.E38 1969　　940.2/32　　*LC* 69-15491

Elton, G. R. (Geoffrey Rudolph) 3.627
Reformation Europe, 1517–1559. Cleveland, Meridian Books [1964, c1963] 349 p. maps. 21 cm. (Meridian histories of modern Europe) 'M174.' 1. Reformation 2. Europe — History — 1517-1648 I. T.
D228.E4 1964 940.23 *LC* 64-11049

Gilmore, Myron Piper, 1910-. ● 3.628
The world of humanism, 1453–1517. — [1st ed.]. — New York, Harper [1952] xv, 326 p. illus., ports., maps. 23 cm. — (Rise of modern Europe. [2]) Bibliography: p. 271-317. 1. Renaissance 2. Humanism I. T. II. Series.
D228.G5x 940.2 *LC* 52-11685

Hale, J. R. (John Rigby), 1923-. 3.629
Renaissance Europe: individual and society, 1480–1520 [by] J. R. Hale. [1st U.S. ed.] New York, Harper & Row [1972, c1971] 350 p. maps. 22 cm. (History of Europe) 1. Europe — History — 1492-1517 I. T.
D228.H23 1972 914/.03/21 *LC* 74-181626 *ISBN* 0060129042

O'Connell, Marvin Richard. 3.630
The Counter Reformation, 1559–1610, by Marvin R. O'Connell. [1st ed.] New York, Harper & Row [1974] xv, 390 p. illus. 21 cm. (Rise of modern Europe.) 1. Counter-Reformation 2. Europe — History — 1517-1648 I. T. II. Series.
D228.O26 1974 940/.08 s 270.6 *LC* 73-14278 *ISBN* 0060132337

Wilson, Charles, 1914-. 3.631
The transformation of Europe, 1558–1648 / Charles Wilson. — Berkeley: University of California Press, c1976. xi, 301 p., [9] leaves of plates: ill.; 25 cm. Includes index. 1. Europe — History — 1517-1648 I. T.
D228.W54 940.2/3 *LC* 75-17283 *ISBN* 0520030753

Marcu, Eva Dorothea, 1907-. 3.632
Sixteenth century nationalism / E. D. Marcu. New York: Abaris Books, c1976. 126 p.: ill.; 24 cm. Includes index. 1. Nationalism — Europe. 2. Europe — History — 1517-1648 I. T.
D231.M28 320.9/4/0232 *LC* 75-39172 *ISBN* 0913870080

D242–283 17TH CENTURY (1601-1715)

Friedrich, Carl J. (Carl Joachim), 1901-. ● 3.633
The age of the baroque, 1610–1660. — [1st ed.]. — New York, Harper [1952] xv, 367 p. illus., ports., maps (on lining paper) 22 cm. — (Rise of modern Europe. [5]) 'The learned ax, a bibliographical essay': p. 327-354. 1. Europe — History — 17th century I. T. II. Series.
D246.F7x 940.22 *LC* 52-5435

Maland, David. 3.634
Europe at war 1600–1650 / David Maland. — Totowa, N.J.: Rowman and Littlefield, 1980. viii, 219 p.: maps; 23 cm. Includes index. 1. Thirty Years' War, 1618-1648 2. Europe — History — 17th century 3. Netherlands — History — Wars of Independence, 1556-1648 I. T.
D247.M23 1979 940.2/4 *LC* 79-18053 *ISBN* 0847662136

Merriman, Roger Bigelow, 1876-1945. ● 3.635
Six contemporaneous revolutions. Hamden, Conn., Archon Books, 1963. viii, 230 p. An expansion of the David Murray lecture, University of Glasgow, 1937. 1. Revolutions — Europe. 2. Europe — History — 17th century I. T.
D247.M42 1963 *LC* 64-10706

Mousnier, Roland. ● 3.636
[Fureurs paysannes, les paysans dans les révoltes du XVIIe siècle (France, Russie, Chine) English] Peasant uprisings in seventeenth–century France, Russia, and China. Translated from the French by Brian Pearce. [1st U.S. ed.] New York, Harper & Row [1970] xx, 358 p. illus., maps. 22 cm. (Great revolutions) Translation of Fureurs paysannes, les paysans dans les révoltes du XVIIe siècle (France, Russie, Chine). 1. Peasant uprisings I. T.
D247.M6813 1970 322/.42 *LC* 72-95975

Pagès, Georges, 1867-1939. ● 3.637
[Guerre de trente ans, 1618-1648. English] The Thirty Years War, 1618–1648. Translated by David Maland and John Hooper. Foreword by Theodore K. Rabb. New York, Harper [1970] 269 p. map. 23 cm. (A Torchbook library edition) Translated from La guerre de trente ans, 1618-1648. 1. Thirty Years' War, 1618-1648 I. T.
D258.P313 940.2/4 *LC* 77-148426 *ISBN* 0061360341

Polišenský, Josef V. 3.638
[Třicetiletá válka a evropské krize 17. století. English] The thirty years war [by] J. V. Polišenský. Translated from the Czech by Robert Evans. Berkeley, University of California Press, 1971. 305 p. illus. 23 cm. Translation of Třicetiletá válka a evropské krize 17. století. 1. Thirty Years' War, 1618-1648 I. T.
D258.P6413 940.2/4 *LC* 77-89894 *ISBN* 0520018680

Wedgwood, C. V. (Cicely Veronica), 1910-. ● 3.639
The thirty years war / by C. V. Wedgwood. — New Haven: Yale University Press, 1956. 544 p.: ill., fold. map. 'Published on the Foundation established in memory of William McKean Brown. [Publication no. 11]' 1. Habsburg, House of 2. Thirty Years' War, 1618-1648 I. T.
D258.W4 1939

Symcox, Geoffrey. comp. 3.640
War, diplomacy, and imperialism, 1618–1763. — New York: Walker, [1974] viii, 338 p.; 24 cm. — (Documentary history of Western civilization) 1. Europe — History — 1648-1789 — Sources. I. T.
D273.A2 S92 1974 940.2/5 *LC* 73-83305 *ISBN* 0802720560

Dorn, Walter Louis. 3.641
Competition for empire, 1740–1763, by Walter L. Dorn. New York, London, Harper & Brothers, 1940. xii p., 1 l., 426 p. front., plates, ports., maps (1 fold.) 23 cm. (The Rise of modern Europe) 'The plates which preceded title-page have half-title: Seventy illustrations drawn from unusual sources and specially chosen by the author.' Map on lining-papers. 'First edition.' 1. Europe — History — 1648-1789. I. T. II. Series.
D273.D67 1940 940.22 *LC* 40-3701

Nussbaum, Frederick Louis, 1885-. ● 3.642
The triumph of science and reason, 1660–1685. — [1st ed.]. — New York, Harper [1953] xiv, 304 p. illus., ports., map (on lining papers) 22 cm. — (Rise of modern Europe. [6]) Bibliography: p. 261-290. 1. Europe — Hist. — 1648-1715. 2. Seventeenth century I. T. II. Series.
D273.N8x 940.22 *LC* 52-7295

Wolf, John Baptist, 1907-. ● 3.643
The emergence of the great powers, 1685–1715. — [1st ed.]. — New York, Harper [1951] xv, 336 p. illus., ports., map (on lining papers) 22 cm. — (Rise of modern Europe. [7]) 1. Europe — Politics and government — 1648-1715 2. Europe — Intellectual life I. T. II. Series.
D273.W6x 940.2 *LC* 51-12900

Hazard, Paul, 1878-1944. ● 3.644
The European mind, the critical years, 1680–1715. — New Haven, Yale University Press, 1953. 454 p. 23 cm. 'This translation from the original French, La crise de la conscience européenne... was made by J. Lewis May.' 1. Europe — Intellectual life 2. Eighteenth century 3. Seventeenth century 4. Philosophy, Modern — Hist. 5. Literature, Modern — 18th cent. — Hist. & crit. I. T.
D273.5.H32 1953a 914 *LC* 53-12258

McKay, Derek. 3.645
The rise of the great powers, 1648–1815 / Derek McKay and H.M. Scott. — London; New York: Longman, 1983. xi, 378 p.: maps; 21 cm. Includes index. 1. Great powers — History — 17th century. 2. Great powers — History — 18th century. 3. Great powers — History — 19th century. 4. Europe — History — 1789-1815 5. Europe — History — 1648-1789 I. Scott, H. M. (Hamish M.), 1946- II. T.
D273.5.M36 1983 940 19 *LC* 82-159 *ISBN* 0582485541

Powley, Edward Barzillai, 1887-1968. 3.646
The naval side of King William's war, 16th/26th November 1688–14th June 1690. Foreword [by] Sir Arthur Bryant. — [Hamden, Conn.]: Archon Books, 1972. 392 p.: illus.; 23 cm. 1. Grand Alliance, War of the, 1689-1697 2. Great Britain — History, Naval — Stuarts, 1603-1714 I. T.
D279.5.P69 1972 941.56 *LC* 72-178755 *ISBN* 020801084X

D284–297 18TH CENTURY (1715-1789)

Anderson, M. S. (Matthew Smith) ● 3.647
Europe in the eighteenth century, 1713–1783. New York, Holt, Rinehart and Winston [1961] 364 p. illus. 22 cm. (A General history of Europe) 1. Europe — History — 18th century I. T.
D286.A5 940.25 *LC* 61-12769

Roberts, J. M. (John Morris), 1928-. ● 3.648
Revolution and improvement: the Western World, 1775–1847 / John Roberts. — Berkeley: University of California Press, c1976. xii, 290 p., [8] leaves of plates: ill.; 25 cm. Includes index. 1. History, Modern — 18th century 2. History, Modern — 19th century 3. Revolutions — History. I. T.
D286.R63 909.7 *LC* 75-17288 *ISBN* 0520030761

Roberts, Penfield, 1892-1944. ● 3.649
The quest for security, 1715–1740 / by Penfield Roberts. — 1st ed. — New York; London: Harper, 1947. x, 300 p.: ill., map on lining papers. — (Rise of modern Europe. 8) 1. Europe — History — 18th century I. T. II. Series.
D286.R65x *LC* 47-3219

Devèze, Michel.   • **3.650**
L'Europe et le monde à fin du XVIIIe siècle / Michel Devèze. — Paris: A. Michel, 1971. 703 p.: ill., maps; 18 cm. — (L'Evolution de l'humanité , 27.) 1. Europe — History — 18th century 2. Colonization — History. I. T.
D288.D46   *LC* 70-23737

Gershoy, Leo, 1897-.   • **3.651**
From despotism to revolution, 1763–1789, by Leo Gershoy. New York, and London, Harper & Brothers, 1944. xvi p., 1 l., 355 p. fronts (incl. ports.) 23 cm. (Rise of modern Europe.) Maps on lining-papers. 'First edition.' 1. Europe — Politics and government — 1648-1789 I. T. II. Series.
D295.G47 1944   940.22   *LC* 44-5542

Palmer, R. R. (Robert Roswell), 1909-.   • **3.652**
The age of the democratic revolution; a political history of Europe and America, 1760–1800. — Princeton, N. J., Princeton University Press, 1959-64. 2 v. 25 cm. 1. Europe — Politics — 18th cent. 2. Constitutional history I. T. II. Title: The democratic revolution.
D295.P3   940.25   *LC* 59-10068 rev

D299 1789-

Best, Geoffrey Francis Andrew.   **3.653**
War and society in revolutionary Europe, 1770–1870 / Geoffrey Best. — New York: St. Martin's Press, 1982. 336 p.; 23 cm. Includes index. 1. Social classes — Europe — History — 18th century. 2. Social classes — Europe — History — 19th century. 3. Europe — History — 1789-1900 4. Europe — History, Military — 18th century 5. France — History — 1789-1900 6. Europe — History, Military — 19th century I. T.
D299.B484 1982   940.2/8 19   *LC* 82-3261   *ISBN* 0312855516

Hobsbawm, E. J. (Eric J.), 1917-.   • **3.654**
The age of revolution: Europe 1789–1848 [by] E. J. Hobsbawm. New York, Praeger Publishers [1969, c1962] xvi, 356 p. illus., maps, ports. 25 cm. (History of civilization) 1. Industry — History 2. Europe — History — 1789-1900 I. T.
D299.H6 1969   914/.03/28   *LC* 75-99597

McManners, John.   **3.655**
Lectures on European history, 1789–1914: men, machines and freedom by John McManners. New York: Harper & Row, 1967. viii, 420 p. 22 cm. Sequel to J. M. Thompson's Lectures on foreign history, 1494-1789. 1. Europe — History — 1789-1900 2. Europe — History — 1871-1918 I. Thompson, J. M. (James Matthew), 1878-1956. Lectures on foreign history, 1494-1789. II. T.
D299.M2 1967   *LC* 79-2711/r83

Palmer, Alan Warwick.   • **3.656**
A dictionary of modern history, 1789–1945, by A.W.Palmer. Philadelphia: Dufour Editions, 1964. vii, 314 p.; 22 cm. 1. History, Modern — Dictionaries. I. T.
D299.P32   909.03   *LC* 64-18500

Tholfsen, Trygve R.   **3.657**
Ideology and revolution in modern Europe: an essay on the role of ideas in history / Trygve R. Tholfsen. — New York: Columbia University Press, 1984. xv, 287 p.; 24 cm. 1. Revolutions — Europe — Philosophy. 2. Ideology — Political aspects — Europe. 3. Europe — History — 1789-1900 — Philosophy. 4. Europe — History — 20th century — Philosophy. 5. Europe — Intellectual life I. T.
D299.T49 1984   940/.01 19   *LC* 84-3178   *ISBN* 0231058861

Thomson, David, 1912-.   • **3.658**
Europe since Napoleon / David Thomson. — Rev. ed. — Harmondsworth: Penguin, 1966. 1004 p.: maps, diagrs.; 20 cm. — (A Pelican book) Includes index. 1. Europe — History — 1789-1900 2. Europe — History — 20th century I. T.
D299.T53 1966   940.28

D301–309 French Revolution (1789-1815)
(see also: DC139-249)

Brinton, Crane, 1898-1968.   • **3.659**
A decade of revolution, 1789–1799, by Crane Brinton. New York, London, Harper & Brothers, 1934. x p., 2 l., 330 p. plates, ports., maps. 23 cm. (Rise of modern Europe.) Maps on lining-papers. 'First edition.' 1. Europe — History — 1789-1815 2. France — History — Revolution, 1789-1799 3. France — History — Revolution, 1789-1799 — Influence I. T. II. Series.
D308.B8 1934   944.04   *LC* 34-33841

Bruun, Geoffrey, 1898-.   • **3.660**
Europe and the French imperium, 1799–1814, by Geoffrey Bruun. New York, London, Harper & Brothers, 1938. xiv, p., 1 l., 280 p. front., illus. (maps) plates, ports. 22 1/2 cm. (Rise of modern Europe.) The plates, which precede t.-p., have half-title: Sixty-two illustrations drawn from unusual sources and specially chosen by the author. 'First edition.' 1. Napoleon I, Emperor of the French, 1769-1821. 2. Europe — History — 1789-1815 3. France — History — Consulate and Empire, 1799-1815 I. T. II. Series.
D308.B86 1938   940.27   *LC* 38-12852

Ford, Franklin L. (Franklin Lewis), 1920-.   • **3.661**
Europe, 1780–1830 [by] Franklin L. Ford. New York, Holt, Rinehart and Winston [c1970] xvii, 423 p. maps. 21 cm. (A General history of Europe) 1. Europe — History — 1789-1815 2. Europe — History — 1815-1848 I. T.
D308.F65 1970   914/.03/27   *LC* 76-110097   *ISBN* 0030861470

Hampson, Norman.   • **3.662**
The first European revolution, 1776–1815. — [New York]: Harcourt, Brace & World, [1969] 215 p.: illus. (part col.), maps, ports. (part col.); 21 cm. — (History of European civilization library) 1. Europe — History — 1789-1815 2. France — History — Revolution, 1789-1799 3. Europe — Intellectual life I. T.
D308.H3 1969b   940.2/7   *LC* 77-78868

Palmer, R. R. (Robert Roswell), 1909-.   • **3.663**
The world of the French Revolution [by] R. R. Palmer. [1st U.S. ed.] New York, Harper & Row [1971] vi, 282 p. 22 cm. (Great revolutions) 1. Europe — History — 1789-1815 2. France — History — Revolution, 1789-1799 — Influence I. T.
D308.P26 1971   940.2/7   *LC* 78-81880

Rudé, George F. E.   • **3.664**
Revolutionary Europe, 1783–1815 / George Rudé. — Cleveland: Meridian Books, [1964] 350 p.: maps.; 21 cm. — (History of Europe) (Meridian histories of modern Europe) 1. Europe — History — 1789-1815 2. France — History — 1789-1815 I. T.
D308.R8   940.27   *LC* 64-23497

D351–400 19th Century

Postgate, Raymond William, 1896-1971. ed.   • **3.665**
Revolution from 1789 to 1906; documents selected and edited with notes and introductions by Raymond Postgate. — Gloucester, Mass.: P. Smith, 1969. xvi, 398 p.; 21 cm. Reprint of the 1962 ed. 1. Revolutions — Europe — History — Sources. 2. Europe — History — 1789-1900 — Sources. I. T.
D351.P86 1969   940.2/7   *LC* 70-10678

Woodward, E. L. (Ernest Llewellyn), Sir, 1890-.   • **3.666**
Three studies in European conservatism: Metternich, Guizot, the Catholic church in the nineteenth century. [Hamden, Conn.] Archon Books, 1963. viii, 350 p. 23 cm. 1. Metternich, Clemens Wenzel Lothar, Fürst von, 1773-1859. 2. Guizot, M. (François), 1787-1874. 3. Catholic Church — History 4. Europe — Politics and government — 1789-1900 I. T.
D355.W6 1963   *LC* 63-15493

Hobsbawm, E. J. (Eric J.), 1917-.   **3.667**
The age of capital, 1848–1875 / E. J. Hobsbawm. — New York: Scribner, c1975. xv, 354 p., [16] leaves of plates: ill.; 25 cm. — (History of civilization) 1. History, Modern — 19th century 2. Economic history — 1750-1918 I. T.
D358.H56 1975b   940.2/8   *LC* 75-29583   *ISBN* 0684144506

Carr, Edward Hallett, 1892-.   **3.668**
From Napoleon to Stalin, and other essays / by E.H. Carr. — New York: St. Martin's Press, c1980. ix, 277 p.; 23 cm. 1. Intellectuals — Addresses, essays, lectures. 2. Socialism — Addresses, essays, lectures. 3. Europe — History — 1789-1900 — Addresses, essays, lectures. 4. Europe — History — 20th century — Addresses, essays, lectures. 5. Russia — History — 20th century — Addresses, essays, lectures. I. T.
D359.C37 1980   940   *LC* 80-18439   *ISBN* 0312307748

Namier, Lewis Bernstein, Sir, 1888-1960.   • **3.669**
Vanished supremacies; essays on European history, 1812–1918 / Lewis Namier. — London: H. Hamilton, [1958] vi, 179 p.; 23 cm. — (His Collected essays, v.1) 1. Europe — History — 1789-1900 2. Europe — Politics and government — 1789-1900 3. Europe — History — 1871-1918 I. T.
D 359 N17

Palmer, Alan Warwick.   **3.670**
The chancelleries of Europe / Alan Palmer. — London; Boston: Allen & Unwin, 1983. xi, 275 p.; 25 cm. Maps on lining papers. 1. World politics — 19th century 2. World politics — 1900-1918 3. Diplomacy 4. Europe — Foreign relations — 1815-1871 5. Europe — Foreign relations — 1871-1918

6. Europe — Politics and government — 1815-1871 7. Europe — Politics and government — 1871-1918 I. T.
D359.P33 1983   327.4 19   *LC* 83-6442   *ISBN* 0049400711

Rich, Norman.   **3.671**
The age of nationalism and reform, 1850–1890 / Norman Rich; [cartography by Harold K. Faye, picture research by Liesel Bennett]. 2d ed. — New York: Norton, c1977. xv, 270 p.: ill.; 21 cm. (The Norton history of modern Europe) Includes index. 1. Europe — History — 1848-1871 2. Europe — History — 1871-1918 I. T.
D359.R48 1977   940.2/8   *LC* 76-21080   *ISBN* 0393056074

Smith, Woodruff D.   **3.672**
European imperialism in the nineteenth and twentieth centuries / Woodruff D. Smith. — Chicago: Nelson-Hall, c1982. vii, 273 p.: maps; 23 cm. Includes index. 1. Imperialism — History — 19th century. 2. Imperialism — History — 20th century. 3. Europe — Territorial expansion. 4. Europe — Colonies. 5. Europe — Politics and government — 1789-1900 6. Europe — Politics and government — 20th century I. T.
D359.S63 1982   940.2/8 19   *LC* 82-7859   *ISBN* 0882297066

Taylor, A. J. P. (Alan John Percivale), 1906-.   **• 3.673**
The struggle for mastery in Europe, 1848–1918. Oxford, Clarendon Press, 1954. xxxvi, 638 p. maps (3 fold.) 23 cm. (Oxford history of modern Europe.) 1. Europe — History — 1848-1871 2. Europe — History — 1871-1918 I. T. II. Series.
D359.T33   *LC* 54-13436

Woodward, E. L. (Ernest Llewellyn), Sir, 1890-.   **3.674**
Prelude to modern Europe, 1815–1914 [by] Llewellyn Woodward. London, Methuen [1972] viii, 309 p. 21 cm. 'Distributed in the U.S.A. by Harper & Row Publishers Inc., Barnes & Noble import division.' 1. Europe — Politics and government — 1815-1871 2. Europe — Politics and government — 1871-1918 I. T.
D359.W59 1972   914/.03/28   *LC* 72-188553   *ISBN* 0416201806

Anderson, Eugene Newton. ed.   **• 3.675**
Europe in the nineteenth century; a documentary analysis of change and conflict, by Eugene N. Anderson, Stanley J. Pincetl, Jr., [and] Donald J. Ziegler. — [1st ed.]. — Indianapolis, Bobbs-Merrill, 1961] 2 v. 21 cm. 1. Europe — History — 1815-1871 2. Europe — History — 1871-1918 3. Europe — Social conditions — Collections. I. T.
D360.A5   940.2082   *LC* 61-13154

Howard, Michael Eliot, 1922-.   **• 3.676**
Studies in war and peace [by] Michael Howard. — New York: Viking Press, [1971, c1970] 262 p.; 23 cm. 1. Military history, Modern — 19th century — Addresses, essays, lectures. 2. Military history, Modern — 20th century — Addresses, essays, lectures. 3. Disarmament — Addresses, essays, lectures. I. T.
D361.H75   341.3   *LC* 70-134325   *ISBN* 0670679747

Kiernan, V. G. (Victor Gordon), 1913-.   **3.677**
From conquest to collapse: European empires from 1815 to 1960 / V.G. Kiernan. — 1st American ed. — New York: Pantheon Books, c1982. 285 p.; 22 cm. Includes index. 1. Military history, Modern — 19th century 2. Military history, Modern — 20th century 3. Europe — Colonies — History — 19th century. 4. Europe — Colonies — History — 20th century. I. T.
D361.K52 1982   909.8 19   *LC* 82-47883   *ISBN* 0394509595

Albrecht-Carrié, René, 1904-.   **• 3.678**
A diplomatic history of Europe since the Congress of Vienna. — New York: Harper, [1958] 736 p.: illus.; 25 cm. — (Harper's historical series) 1. Europe — History — 1789-1900 2. Europe — History — 20th century I. T.
D363.A58   940.28   *LC* 58-6131

Bridge, F. R.   **3.679**
The great powers and the European states system, 1815–1914 / F. R. Bridge and Roger Bullen. — London; New York: Longman, 1980. 208 p.: maps; 23 cm. Includes indexes. 1. Europe — Foreign relations — 1815-1871 2. Europe — Politics and government — 1815-1871 3. Europe — Politics and government — 1871-1918 I. Bullen, R. J. joint author. II. T.
D363.B75   327.4   *LC* 79-41567   *ISBN* 0582491347

Marx, Karl, 1818-1883.   **3.680**
[Selected works. English. 1974] Political writings / Edited and with an introd. by David Fernbach. — [1st American ed.] New York: Random House, 1974. 417 p.; 21 cm. 1. World politics — 19th century — Collected works. 2. Socialism — Collected works. 3. Europe — History — 1848-1849 — Collected works. I. T.
D363.M37 1974b   320.9/4/028   *LC* 73-20559   *ISBN* 0394489381

Mosse, George L. (George Lachmann), 1918-.   **3.681**
Masses and man: nationalist and Fascist perceptions of reality / George L. Mosse. — 1st ed. — New York: H. Fertig, 1980. xii, 362 p.; 24 cm. 1. Nationalism — Europe — Addresses, essays, lectures. 2. Fascism — Europe

— Addresses, essays, lectures. 3. Jews — Germany — History — 20th century — Addresses, essays, lectures. 4. Europe — Politics and government — 1789-1900 — Addresses, essays, lectures. 5. Europe — Politics and government — 20th century — Addresses, essays, lectures. I. T.
D363.M65   320.5/4/094   *LC* 80-15399   *ISBN* 0865273340

D371–378 Eastern Question
(see also D461-472)

Anderson, M. S. (Matthew Smith)   **• 3.682**
The Eastern question, 1774–1923: a study in international relations [by] M. S. Anderson. — London; Melbourne [etc.]: Macmillan; New York: St. Martin's P., 1966. xxi, 436 p.: 10 maps.; 23 cm. 1. Eastern question 2. Eastern question (Balkan) 3. Turkey — Foreign relations I. T.
D371.A43 1966   949.6   *LC* 66-13896

Marriott, J. A. R. (John Arthur Ransome), Sir, 1859-1945.   **• 3.683**
The Eastern question: an historical study in European diplomacy / by J.A.R. Marriott. — 4th ed. — Oxford: Clarendon Press, 1940. xii, 602 p.: maps (2 fold. incl. front.); 20 cm. References at end of most of the chapters. 1. Eastern question (Balkan) 2. Eastern question I. T.
D371.M32 1940

Jelavich, Barbara, 1923-.   **3.684**
The Ottoman Empire, the great powers, and the straits question, 1870–1887 [by] Barbara Jelavich. Bloomington, Indiana University Press [1973] xi, 209 p. illus. 22 cm. 1. Eastern question (Balkan) 2. Straits question I. T.
D375.J44   949.6/1/01   *LC* 72-88631   *ISBN* 0253342767

Medlicott, W. N. (William Norton), 1900-.   **• 3.685**
The Congress of Berlin and after: a diplomatic history of the Near Eastern settlement 1878–1880. — 2d ed. — [Hamden, Conn.] Archon Books, 1963. 442 p. illus. 22 cm. 1. Congress of Berlin (1878) 2. Berlin, Treaty of, 1878 3. Eastern question (Balkan) 4. Balkan Peninsula — Politics. 5. Europe — Politics — 1871-1918. I. T.
D375.3.M4 1963   909.81   *LC* 63-3197

Gillard, David, 1929-.   **3.686**
The struggle for Asia, 1828–1914: a study in British and Russian imperialism / David Gillard. — New York: Holmes & Meier, c1977. 214 p.: maps; 24 cm. Includes index. Original imprint: London: Methuen, covered by label. 1. Eastern question 2. Great Britain — Foreign relations — Soviet Union. 3. Soviet Union — Foreign relations — Great Britain. I. T.
D376.G7 G54 1977   325/.35   *ISBN* 0416132502

Seton-Watson, R. W. (Robert William), 1879-1951.   **• 3.687**
Disraeli, Gladstone, and the Eastern question; a study in diplomacy and party politics. — London, F. Cass [1962] xiii, 590 p. 23 cm. Imprint covered by label: New York, Barnes & Noble. Bibliographical footnotes. 1. Eastern question 2. Great Britain — For. rel. — 1837-1901. 3. Great Britain — Pol. & govt. — 1837-1901. 4. Europe — Politics — 1871-1918. I. T.
D376.G7S4 1962   940.28   *LC* 63-2605

Temperley, Harold William Vazeille, 1879-1939.   **• 3.688**
England and the Near East: The Crimea. By Harold Temperley. [Hamden, Conn.] Archon Books, 1964. xxx, 548 p. 3 fold. maps. port. 22 cm. Vol. 1 of a planned 3 vol. work. No more published. 'Unaltered and unabridged edition.' Includes bibliographical references. 1. Eastern question 2. Crimean War, 1853-1856 3. Europe — Politics — 1848-1871. 4. Great Britain — Foreign relations — 1837-1901 5. Turkey — History — 1829-1878 I. T.
D376.G7T4 1964   949.6   *LC* 64-15911

Sumner, Benedict Humphrey, 1893-1951.   **• 3.689**
Russia and the Balkans 1870–1880. Hamden [Conn.] Archon Books, 1962. 724 p. illus. 22 cm. 1. Eastern question (Balkan) 2. Panslavism 3. Soviet Union — Foreign relations — 1855-1881 4. Balkan Peninsula — History 5. Europe — Politics and government — 1871-1918 I. T.
D376.R7 S8 1962   *LC* 62-51020

Kohn, Hans, 1891-1971.   **• 3.690**
Pan-Slavism: its history and ideology. — 2d ed., rev. — New York: Vintage Books, 1960. 468 p.; 19 cm. — (Vintage Russian library, V-710) 1. Panslavism I. T.
D377.3.K57 1960   327.47   *LC* 60-51957

Petrovich, Michael Boro.   **3.691**
The emergence of Russian Panslavism, 1856–1870 / by Michael Boro Petrovich. — Westport, Conn.: Greenwood Press, 1985. xiv, 312 p.; 23 cm. Reprint. Originally published: New York: Columbia University Press, 1956. Includes index. 1. Panslavism 2. Soviet Union — Intellectual life — 1801-1917 I. T.
D377.5.S65 P47 1985   320.5/4 19   *LC* 84-25242   *ISBN* 0313247420

D383 Holy Alliance. Quadruple Alliance (1815–1830)

Artz, Frederick Binkerd, 1894-. • **3.692**
Reaction and revolution, 1814–1832, by Frederick B. Artz. New York, London, Harper & brothers, 1934. viii p., 1 l., 317 p. plates, ports. 23 cm. (Rise of modern Europe.) Maps on lining-papers. 'First edition.' 1. Revolutions — Europe. 2. Europe — History — 1815-1848 I. T. II. Series.
D383.A7 1934   940.28   *LC* 34-33840

Droz, Jacques, 1909-. • **3.693**
[De la Restauration à la Révolution, 1815-1848. English] Europe between revolutions, 1815–1848. Translated by Robert Baldick. [1st U.S. ed.] New York, Harper & Row [1967] 286 p. maps. 22 cm. (History of Europe) Translation of De la Restauration à la Révolution, 1815-1848. 1. Europe — History — 1815-1848 I. T.
D383.D7   914/.03/282   *LC* 67-22496

Kissinger, Henry, 1923-. • **3.694**
A world restored; Metternich, Castlereagh and the problems of peace, 1812–22. Boston, Houghton Mifflin, 1957. 354 p. illus. 23 cm. 1. Metternich, Clemens Wenzel Lothar, Fürst von, 1773-1859. 2. Castlereagh, Robert Stewart, Viscount, 1769-1822. 3. Europe — Politics and government — 1815-1848 I. T.
D383.K5 1957a   940.27   *LC* 57-10969

May, Arthur James, 1899-1968. • **3.695**
The age of Metternich, 1814–1848. — Rev. ed. — New York: Holt, Rinehart and Winston, [c1963] viii, 152 p.; 19 cm. — (Berkshire studies in European history) 1. Metternich-Winneberg, Clemens Lothar Wenzel, Fürst von, 1773-1859. 2. Europe — History — 1815-1848 3. Europe — Politics and government — 1815-1848 I. T. II. Series.
D383.M3 1963   940.28   *LC* 63-22477

Temperley, Harold William Vazeille, 1879-1939. • **3.696**
The foreign policy of Canning, 1822–1827; England, the neo–holy alliance, and the New World. With a new introd. by Herbert Butterfield. — [2d ed.] — Hamden, Conn.] Archon Books, 1966. xlvi, 636 p. facsim., ports. 23 cm. Bibliographical references included in 'Notes to certain chapters' (p. 479-530) 1. Canning, George, 1770-1827. 2. Great Britain — Hist. — George IV, 1820-1830. 3. Europe — Hist. — 1815-1848. I. T.
D383.T4 1966a   327.42   *LC* 66-4116

Walker, Mack. comp. • **3.697**
Metternich's Europe. — New York: Walker, [1968] vi, 352 p.; 24 cm. — (The Documentary history of Western civilization) 1. Europe — History — 1815-1848 — Sources. I. T.
D383.W27 1968   940.2/82/08   *LC* 68-27383

Webster, Charles Kingsley, 1886-. • **3.698**
The foreign policy of Castlereagh, 1812–1815, Britain and the reconstruction of Europe, by C.K. Webster. London, G. Bell and sons, ltd., 1931. xv, 589 p. plates, 2 port. (incl. front.) 23 cm. 'Notes on the system of references: p. xiv-xv.' 1. Castlereagh, Robert Stewart, Viscount, 1769-1822. 2. Great Britain — Foreign relations — 1800-1837 3. Europe — Politics and government — 1789-1815 I. T.
D383.W38   *LC* 31-23150

Langer, William L. (William Leonard), 1896-1977. • **3.699**
Political and social upheaval, 1832–1852, by William L. Langer. [1st ed.] New York, Harper & Row [1969] xviii, 674 p. illus., maps, ports. 22 cm. (Rise of modern Europe.) 1. Europe — Politics and government — 1815-1848 2. Europe — Social conditions — 1789-1900 3. Europe — Economic conditions — 19th century I. T. II. Series.
D385.L36 1969   940.2/83   *LC* 69-17284

D387–393 1848–1870

Eyck, Frank. comp. **3.700**
The revolutions of 1848–49. — New York: Barnes & Noble Books, [1972] viii, 202 p.; 23 cm. — (Evidence and commentary) 1. Europe — History — 11848-1849 — Sources. I. T.
D387.E9 1972b   940.2/84/08   *LC* 73-163426   *ISBN* 0064920526

Fejtö, François, 1909- ed. • **3.701**
[Printemps des peuples, 1848 dans le monde. English] The opening of an era: 1848; an historical symposium. With an introd. by A. J. P. Taylor. New York, Grosset & Dunlap [1973, c1948] xxvii, 444 p. 21 cm. (The Universal library [267] 'The essays, with the exception of those on Great Britain and the U.S.A., were translated by Hugh Shelley.' Translation of Le printemps des peuples, 1848 dans le monde. 1. Europe — History — 1848-1849 I. T.
D387.F4213 1973   940.2/84   *LC* 73-158929   *ISBN* 0448002671

Herzen, Aleksandr, 1812-1870. • **3.702**
From the other shore, and The Russian people and socialism, an open letter to Jules Michelet. Introd. by Isaiah Berlin. — [1st American ed.] New York: G. Braziller, 1956. 208 p.; 19 cm. — (Library of ideas) 1. Europe — Hist. — 1848-1849. I. Herzen, Aleksandr, 1812-1870. The Russian people and socialism. II. T. III. Title: The Russian people and socialism.
D387.H413   940.28   *LC* 56-41455

Namier, Lewis Bernstein, Sir, 1888-1960. • **3.703**
1848; the revolution of the intellectuals / by Lewis Namier. — Garden City, N.Y.: Anchor Books, 1964. 153 p. — (Doubleday Anchor books; A385) 1. Europe — History — 1848-1849 I. T. II. Title: The revolution of the intellectuals.
D387.N3 1964   *LC* 64-3105

Robertson, Priscilla Smith. • **3.704**
Revolutions of 1848, a social history. — Princeton: Princeton University Press, 1952. xi, 464 p.: maps; 25 cm. 1. Revolutions — Europe. 2. Europe — History — 1848-1849 I. T.
D387.R6   940.28   *LC* 52-5838

Sigmann, Jean, 1912-. **3.705**
[1848 i.e. Dix-huit cent quarante-huit] 1848: the romantic and democratic revolutions in Europe. Translated from the French by Lovett F. Edwards. [1st U.S. ed.] New York, Harper & Row [1973] 352 p. 22 cm. (Great revolutions) 1. Europe — History — 1848-1849 I. T.
D387.S4713 1973   320.9/4/0284   *LC* 79-181646   *ISBN* 0060138718

Stearns, Peter N. **3.706**
1848: the revolutionary tide in Europe [by] Peter N. Stearns. — [1st ed.]. — New York: Norton, [1974] 278 p.: maps.; 21 cm. — (Revolutions in the modern world) 1. Europe — History — 1848-1849 I. T.
D387.S7 1974   940.2/84   *LC* 73-16474   *ISBN* 0393055108

Taylor, A. J. P. (Alan John Percivale), 1906-. • **3.707**
The Italian problem in European diplomacy, 1847–1849, by A. J. P. Taylor. [Manchester, Eng.] Manchester University Press; New York, Barnes & Noble [1970] viii, 252 p. 22 cm. 'First published 1934.' 1. Italian question, 1848-1870. 2. Europe — Politics and government — 1848-1871 3. Italy — History — Revolution of 1848 4. Italy — Foreign relations — 1849-1870 I. T.
D387.T3 1970   327.4/045   *LC* 73-21516   *ISBN* 0719003997

Whitridge, Arnold, 1891-. • **3.708**
Men in crisis; the revolutions of 1848. — [Hamden, Conn.]: Archon Books, 1967 [c1949] 364 p.: illus., port.; 23 cm. 1. Europe — History — 1848-1849 2. United States — Foreign relations — 1845-1849 I. T.
D387.W5 1967   940.2/84   *LC* 67-26662

Albrecht-Carrié, René, 1904- comp. • **3.709**
The Concert of Europe. — New York: Walker, [1968] 384 p.; 24 cm. — (Documentary history of Western civilization) 1. Concert of Europe I. T.
D388.A55   341.184   *LC* 68-13327

Binkley, Robert Cedric, 1897-1940. • **3.710**
Realism and nationalism, 1852–1871, by Robert C. Binkley. New York, London, Harper & Brothers, 1935. xx p., 1 l., 337 p. plates, ports., maps. 23 cm. (Rise of modern Europe.) Maps on lining-papers. 'First edition.' 1. Nationalism — Europe. 2. Europe — History — 1848-1871 I. T. II. Series.
D389.B56 1935   940.28   *LC* 36-11

Case, Lynn Marshall, 1903-. **3.711**
French opinion on war and diplomacy during the Second Empire, by Lynn M. Case. — New York: Octagon Books, 1972 [c1954] xii, 339 p.; 24 cm. 1. Public opinion — France. 2. Europe — History — 1848-1871 I. T.
D389.C3 1972   301.15/43/94407   *LC* 70-120242   *ISBN* 0374913021

D394–400 1870–

Hayes, Carlton Joseph Huntley, 1882-1964. • **3.712**
A generation of materialism, 1871–1900, by Carlton J.H. Hayes. New York, London, Harper & Brothers, 1941. xii p., 1 l., 390 p. illus. (maps), plates, ports. 23 cm. (Rise of modern Europe.) Maps on lining-papers. 'First edition.' 1. Europe — History — 1871-1918 2. Europe — History — Philosophy. I. T. II. Series.
D395.H284 1941   940.28   *LC* 41-22911

Stone, Norman. **3.713**
Europe transformed, 1878–1919 / Norman Stone. — Cambridge, Mass.: Harvard University Press, 1984, c1983. 447 p.; 22 cm. Includes index. 1. Europe — History — 1871-1918 I. T.
D395.S77 1984   940.2/8 19   *LC* 83-22830   *ISBN* 0674269225

Bond, Brian.   **3.714**
War and society in Europe, 1870–1970 / Brian Bond. — New York: St.
Martin's Press, 1983. 256 p.; 23 cm. Includes index. 1. Europe — History,
Military — 19th century 2. Europe — History, Military — 20th century
3. Europe — Social conditions — 19th century. 4. Europe — Social conditions
— 20th century I. T.
D396.B63 1983   940.2/8 19   *LC* 83-40281   *ISBN* 0312855478

Falls, Cyril Bentham, 1888-.   • **3.715**
A hundred years of war / Cyril Falls. — 2d ed. London: Duckworth, 1961.
421 p.,maps. (Hundred years series.) 1. Military history, Modern — 19th
century 2. Military history, Modern — 20th century I. T. II. Series.
D396.F3 1961   *LC* 66-35731

Baumont, Maurice, 1892-.   • **3.716**
L'essor industriel et l'impérialisme colonial (1878–1904) Paris: F. Alcan, 1937.
610 p.; 23 cm. — (Peuples et civilisations. 18) 1. Imperialism 2. Competition,
International 3. Europe — Politics 4. Europe — Civilization I. T. II. Series.
D397 B3

Gooch, G. P. (George Peabody), 1873-1968.   • **3.717**
Studies in diplomacy and statecraft. — New York: Russell & Russell, [1969] vii,
373 p.; 22 cm. Essays. Reprint of the 1942 ed. 1. Europe — History —
1871-1918 — Addresses, essays, lectures. I. T.
D397.G58 1969   327.2   *LC* 77-75464

Langer, William L. (William Leonard), 1896-1977.   • **3.718**
European alliances and alignments, 1871–1890 [by] William L. Langer. [1st ed.]
New York, A. A. Knopf, 1931. xiii, 509, xiv p. maps, diagrs. 25 cm. 1. Europe
— Politics and government — 1871-1918 I. T.
D397.L28   *LC* 31-23943

Langer, William L. (William Leonard), 1896-1977.   • **3.719**
The diplomacy of imperialism, 1890–1902. 2d ed., with supplementary
bibliographies. New York, Knopf, 1951 [c1950] xxii, 797, xxii p. maps., diagr.
25 cm. Half title: Bureau of International Research, Harvard University and
Radcliffe College. 1. World politics 2. History, Modern — 19th century
3. Colonies 4. Imperialism I. T.
D397.L282 1951   940.28   *LC* 51-343

Langer, William L. (William Leonard), 1896-1977.   • **3.720**
The Franco–Russian Alliance, 1890–1894. — New York: Octagon Books, 1967
[c1929] ix, 455 p.; 24 cm. — (Harvard historical studies. v. 30) 1. Franco-
Russian Alliance 2. Europe — Politics and government — 1871-1918 I. T.
II. Series.
D397.L3 1967   940.2/87   *LC* 67-18772

Medlicott, W. N. (William Norton), 1900-.   • **3.721**
Bismarck, Gladstone, and the Concert of Europe, by W. N. Medlicott. New
York, Greenwood Press [1969] xiv, 353 p. maps. 23 cm. 1. Bismarck, Otto,
Fürst von, 1815-1898. 2. Gladstone, W. E. (William Ewart), 1809-1898.
3. Concert of Europe 4. Europe — Politics and government — 1871-1918
I. T.
D397.M4 1969   320.9/4   *LC* 69-13994

Schmitt, Bernadotte Everly, 1886-1969.   • **3.722**
Triple alliance and triple entente. New York, H. Fertig, 1971 [c1961] viii, 131 p.
illus. 21 cm. 1. Triple Alliance, 1882 2. Triple Entente, 1907 3. World War,
1914-1918 — Causes. 4. Europe — Politics and government — 1871-1918
I. T.
D397.S26 1971   940.2/8   *LC* 70-80590

D410–847 20TH CENTURY

Facts on file yearbook.   • **3.723**
v. 1- 1941-. [New York, N.Y., Facts on File, Inc.] v. 28 cm. Annual. 1. History
— Yearbooks.
D410.F3   905   *LC* 42-24704

Keesing's contemporary archives.   **3.724**
v. 1- July 1, 1931-. Bath [etc.] Longman Group [etc.] v. ill., maps, facsims.,
plates, ports. 29 cm. Monthly. 'Record of national and international current
affairs with continually updated indexes.' Published also in French, German
and Dutch. Vol. 1 preceded by supplement: Synopsis of important events, 1918
(end of World War) - 1931 (June). 1. History — Periodicals
D410.K4   *LC* 38-14078

Cameron, James, 1911-.   • **3.725**
1914 / by James Cameron. — Westport, Conn.: Greenwood Press, 1975, c1959.
vi, 210 p.; 22 cm. Reprint of the ed. published by Cassell, London. Includes
index. 1. History — Yearbooks — 1914. 2. World War, 1914-1918 I. T.
D410.5 1914. C3 1975   940.3   *LC* 74-31338   *ISBN* 0837178614

Joll, James.   • **3.726**
Three intellectuals in politics. [New York] Pantheon Books [1961, c1960] xiv,
203 p. 23 cm. Published in 1960 under title: Intellectuals in politics. 1. Blum,
Léon, 1872-1950. 2. Rathenau, Walther, 1867-1922. 3. Marinetti, Filippo
Tommaso, 1876-1944. I. T.
D412.6.J64 1961   *LC* 61-10030

The history makers; leaders and statesmen of the 20th century.   **3.727**
Edited by Lord Longford & Sir John Wheeler–Bennett.
Chronologies and editorial assistance by Christine Nicholls.
New York: St. Martin's Press, [1973] 448 p.: illus.; 24 cm. 1. Heads of state —
Biography. 2. Statesmen — Biography. I. Wheeler-Bennett, John Wheeler,
Sir, 1902-1975. joint author. II. Longford, Frank Pakenham, Earl of, 1905-
D412.7.L66 1973b   920/.02   *LC* 73-79066

Taylor, Edmond, 1908-.   • **3.728**
The fall of the dynasties; the collapse of the old order, 1905–1922. — [1st ed.].
— Garden City, N.Y.: Doubleday, 1963. 421 p.: illus.; 25 cm. — (Mainstream
of the modern world series) 1. Europe — History — 1871-1918 2. Europe —
Kings and rulers I. T.
D412.7.T3   940.28   *LC* 63-10518

Fischer, Louis, 1896-1970.   • **3.729**
Men and politics: an autobiography. With an appendix of lectures from Eleanor
Roosevelt added to the reprint ed. — Westport, Conn.: Greenwood Press,
[1970, c1946] ix, 672 p.; 24 cm. 1. Fischer, Louis, 1896-1970. 2. Journalists —
Correspondence, reminiscences, etc. 3. Europe — Politics and government —
1918-1945 I. T.
D413.F5 A3 1970   940.5/0924   *LC* 73-111498   *ISBN* 0837146410

Lyons, Eugene, 1898-.   • **3.730**
Assignment in Utopia. — Westport, Conn.: Greenwood Press, [1971, c1937]
xiii, 658 p.; 23 cm. Autobiography. 1. Lyons, Eugene, 1898- 2. Journalists —
Correspondence, reminiscences, etc. 3. Communism — Russia. 4. Russia —
Description and travel — 1917- I. T.
D413.L9 A3 1971   914.7/03/842   *LC* 76-110271   *ISBN*
0837149973

Monnet, Jean, 1888-.   **3.731**
[Mémoires. English] Memoirs / Jean Monnet; introd. by George W. Ball;
translated from the French by Richard Mayne. — 1st ed. — Garden City, N.Y.:
Doubleday, 1978. 544 p., [8] leaves of plates: ill.; 22 cm. Translation of
Mémoires. 1. Monnet, Jean, 1888- 2. Statesmen — Europe — Biography.
3. Economists — Europe — Biography. I. T.
D413.M56 A3313 1978b   940.5/092/4 B   *LC* 76-56322   *ISBN*
0385125054

Barros, James.   **3.732**
Office without power: Secretary–General Sir Eric Drummond, 1919–1933 / by
James Barros. — Oxford: Clarendon Press; New York: Oxford University
Press, 1979. xii, 423 p.; 23 cm. 1. Perth, James Eric Drummond, 16th Earl of,
1876- 2. League of Nations. 3. League of Nations — Biography. 4. Diplomats
— Great Britain — Biography. 5. Europe — Politics and government —
1918-1945 I. T.
D413.P45 B37   341.22/092/4 B 19   *LC* 78-40312   *ISBN*
0198225512

Beloff, Max, 1913-.   • **3.733**
The great powers; essays in twentieth century politics. London Allen & Unwin
[1959] 240 p.; 23 cm. 1. World politics — Addresses, essays, lectures
2. Twentieth century — Addresses, essays, lectures I. T.
D415 B4   *LC* 62-53403

Laqueur, Walter, 1921-.   **3.734**
A dictionary of politics / edited by Walter Laqueur, with the assistance of
Evelyn Anderson ... [et al.]. — Rev. ed. — New York: Free Press, 1974, c1973.
565 p.; 25 cm. 1. World politics — 20th century — Dictionaries. I. T.
D419.L36 1974   320/.03   *LC* 74-9232

Palmer, Alan Warwick.   **3.735**
The Penguin dictionary of twentieth–century history / Alan Palmer. — 2nd ed.
— Harmondsworth, Middlesex, England; New York, N.Y., U.S.A.: Penguin
Books, 1983. 411 p.; 20 cm. (Penguin reference books.) 1. History, Modern —
20th century — Dictionaries. I. T. II. Series.
D419.P29 1983   909.82/03/21 19   *LC* 84-199758   *ISBN*
0140511318

Binion, Rudolph, 1927-.   **3.736**
Soundings: psychohistorical and psycholiterary / by Rudolph Binion. — New
York: Psychohistory Press, 1981. v, 164 p.; 23 cm. 1. Kafka, Franz, 1883-1924
Verwandlung — Addresses, essays, lectures. 2. Pirandello, Luigi, 1867-1936
Sei personaggi in cerca d'autore — Addresses, essays, lectures.
3. Psychohistory — Addresses, essays, lectures. 4. Europe — History — 20th
century — Addresses, essays, lectures. I. T.
D421.B49   940/.01/9 19   *LC* 81-5200   *ISBN* 0914434160

Grenville, J. A. S. (John Ashley Soames), 1928-. 3.737
A world history of the twentieth century / J.A.S. Grenville. — Hanover, N.H.:
Published for Brandeis University Press by University Press of New England,
1984- c1980-. v. < 1 > : maps; 20 cm. Includes indexes. 1. History, Modern —
20th century I. T.
D421.G65 1984   909.82 19   LC 84-40300   ISBN 0874513154

Johnson, Paul, 1928-. 3.738
Modern times: the world from the twenties to the eighties / Paul Johnson. —
1st U.S. ed. — New York: Harper & Row, c1983. ix, 817 p.; 25 cm. 1. History,
Modern — 20th century I. T.
D421.J64 1983   909.82 19   LC 82-48836   ISBN 0060151595

Renouvin, Pierre, 1893-1974. 3.739
[Crises du XXe siècle. 1. De 1914 à 1929. English] War and aftermath,
1914–1929. Translated by Rémy Inglis Hall. [1st ed.] New York, Harper &
Row [1968] xi, 369 p. 22 cm. Translation of Les crises du XXe siècle. 1. De 1914
à 1929. 1. History, Modern — 20th century I. T.
D421.R413   909.82   LC 68-11954

Renouvin, Pierre, 1893-1974. • 3.740
[Crises du XXe siècle. 2. De 1929 à 1945. English] World War II and its origins;
international relations, 1929–1945. Translated by Rémy Inglis Hall. [1st ed.]
New York, Harper & Row [1968, c1969] x, 402 p. 22 cm. Translation of Les
crises du XXe siècle. 2. De 1929 à 1945. 1. History, Modern — 20th century
I. T.
D421.R413 1969   940.53   LC 72-1076

Holborn, Hajo, 1902-1969. • 3.741
The political collapse of Europe. — [1st ed.]. — New York: Knopf, 1951. xi,
207 p.; 20 cm. 1. Europe — Politics and government — 20th century I. T.
D424.H6   940.5   LC 51-10940

Hughes, H. Stuart (Henry Stuart), 1916-. 3.742
Contemporary Europe: a history. — 6th ed. / H. Stuart Hughes, James
Wilkinson. — Englewood Cliffs, N.J.: Prentice-Hall, c1987. 582 p. 1. Europe
— History — 20th century I. Wilkinson, James D., 1947- II. T.
D424.H83 1987   940.5 19   LC 86-30434   ISBN 0131699474

Lichtheim, George, 1912-. 3.743
Europe in the twentieth century. — New York: Praeger Publishers, [1972] xiv,
409 p.: illus.; 25 cm. 1. Europe — History — 20th century I. T.
D424.L53   914/.03/2   LC 70-187278

Ross, Graham, 1933-. 3.744
The great powers and the decline of the European states system, 1914–1945 /
Graham Ross. — London; New York: Longman, 1983. vii, 181 p.: maps; 22 cm.
— (A Longman paperback) Includes index. 1. Europe — Foreign relations —
1871-1918 2. Europe — Foreign relations — 1918-1945 3. Europe — Politics
and government — 1871-1918 4. Europe — Politics and government —
1918-1945 I. T.
D424.R66 1983   327.4 19   LC 83-686   ISBN 0582491886

The Times in review; a New York times decade book. 3.745
New York: Arno Press, 1970-73 [v. 1, 1973; v. 5, 1970] 5 v.: illus.; 43 cm. Vol. 5
published by New York times, New York. 1. History, Modern — 20th century
— Chronology. I. New York times
D427.T5   909.82   LC 74-139439   ISBN 0405003757

Aron, Raymond, 1905-. • 3.746
The century of total war. — [1st ed.]. — Garden City, N.Y.: Doubleday, 1954.
379 p.; 22 cm. 1. Military history, Modern — 20th century 2. World politics
— 20th century I. T.
D431.A7   940.5 909.82*   LC 54-5714

D440–472 Political and Diplomatic History

Survey of international affairs, 1920–23 • 3.747
1920/23-1963. London: Oxford University Press [etc.] v. in   : maps (part
fold., part col.); 25 cm. Some vols. have also distinctive titles. Includes wartime
series for 1939/46, in 11 v. 1. World politics — Yearbooks. 2. History, Modern
— 20th century — Yearbooks. I. Toynbee, Arnold Joseph, 1889-1975.
II. Royal Institute of International Affairs.
D442.S8   LC 25-22280*

Documents on international affairs. 1928–. • 3.748
London: Oxford University Press, 1929-. v.; 25 cm. Some vols. issued in 2 parts.
1. International relations — Sources. 2. World politics I. Royal Institute of
International Affairs.
D442.S82   LC 30-10914

Craig, Gordon Alexander, 1913-. 3.749
Force and statecraft: diplomatic problems of our time / Gordon A. Craig,
Alexander L. George. — New York: Oxford University Press, 1983. xiv, 288 p.;
24 cm. 1. World politics — 20th century 2. World politics — 19th century
3. World politics — To 1900 4. International relations 5. Diplomacy
I. George, Alexander L. II. T.
D443.C73 1983   327/.09/04 19   LC 81-22304   ISBN 0195031156

Hale, Oron J. (Oron James) • 3.750
The great illusion, 1900–1914 / by Oron J. Hale. — 1st Torchbook ed. — New
York: Harper & Row, c1971. xv, 361 p. [32] p. of plates.: ill., maps, ports. —
(The Rise of modern Europe) Includes index. 1. Europe — History —
1871-1918 I. T.
D443.H3x   914/.03/288   LC 76-123933   ISBN 0061315788

Royal Institute of International Affairs. Information Dept. • 3.751
South–eastern Europe: a political and economic survey / prepared by the
Information Department of the Royal Institute of International Affairs in
collaboration with the London and Cambridge Economic Service. London: The
Royal Institute of International Affairs; New York: Oxford University Press,
[1939] xvi, 203 p.: ill.; 23 cm. 1. Europe — Politics and government —
1918-1945 2. Europe — Economic conditions — 1918-1945 3. Balkan
Peninsula I. London and Cambridge Economic Service. II. T.
D443.R69   LC 39-17709

Stillman, Edmund O. • 3.752
Politics of hysteria; the sources of twentieth–century conflict / by Edmund
Stillman and William Pfaff. New York: Harper & Row, 1965, c1964. 273 p.
(Harper Colophon books.) 1. World politics I. Pfaff, William, 1928- II. T.
D443.S77 1965   LC 62-20118

Wolfers, Arnold, 1892-. • 3.753
Britain and France between two wars; conflicting strategies of peace since
Versailles. — Hamden, Conn., Archon Books, 1963 [c1940] 467 p. 22 cm.
Bibliography: p. 417-451. 1. Peace 2. Great Britain — For. rel. — 20th cent.
3. France — For. rel. — 1914-1940. 4. Europe — Politics — 1918-1945. I. T.
D443.W63 1963   940.51   LC 63-16552

Yost, Charles Woodruff. • 3.754
The insecurity of nations; international relations in the twentieth century, by
Charles Yost. — New York: Published for the Council on Foreign Relations
[by] Praeger, [1968] x, 276 p.; 22 cm. 1. History, Modern — 20th century
I. Council on Foreign Relations. II. T.
D443.Y63   909.82   LC 68-11324

Grimal, Henri, 1910-. 3.755
Decolonization: the British, French, Dutch, and Belgian Empires, 1919–1963 /
Henri Grimal; translated by Stephan De Vos. — Boulder, Colo.: Westview
Press, 1978. xi, 443 p.: ill.; 23 cm. An updated translation of La décolonisation,
1919-1963. Includes index. 1. History, Modern — 20th century 2. States, New
3. Decolonization — History. 4. Great Britain — Colonies — History
5. France — Colonies — History. 6. Netherlands — Colonies — History.
7. Belgium — Colonies — History. I. T.
D445.G7313 1978   909.82   LC 77-922   ISBN 0891587322

Kohn, Hans, 1891-1971. • 3.756
The age of nationalism; the first era of global history. [1st ed.] New York,
Harper [1962] 172 p. 20 cm. (World perspectives, v. 28) 1. History, Modern —
20th century 2. Nationalism — History. I. T.
D445.K58   909.82   LC 62-11474

Snyder, Louis Leo, 1907-. • 3.757
The new nationalism, by Louis L. Snyder. — Ithaca, N.Y.: Cornell University
Press, [1968] xiv, 387 p.; 24 cm. 1. Nationalism 2. History, Modern — 20th
century I. T.
D445.S66   320.1/58   LC 68-16391

Weisberger, Bernard A., 1922-. 3.758
Cold War, cold peace: the United States and Russia since 1945 / Bernard A.
Weisberger; introduction by Harrison E. Salisbury. — New York: American
Heritage; Boston: Distributed by Houghton Mifflin, c1984. 341 p., [16] p. of
plates: ill.; 24 cm. Includes index. 1. World politics — 20th century 2. United
States — Foreign relations — Soviet Union 3. Soviet Union — Foreign
relations — United States I. T.
D445.W37 1984   327/.0904 19   LC 81-20495   ISBN 0828111634

Meyer, Henry Cord, 1913-. • 3.759
Mitteleuropa in German thought and action, 1815–1945 / by Henry Cord
Meyer. — The Hague: Nijhoff, 1955. xv, 378 p.; 25 cm. — (International
scholars forum. 4) 1. Pangermanism 2. Central Europe — Politics and
government. 3. Germany — History — Historiography. I. T. II. Series.
D447.M4   LC 56-2311

Namier, Lewis Bernstein, 1888-.   • **3.760**
Facing East. New York, Harper, 1948. 159 p. 19 cm. 1. Pangermanism
2. Europe — Politics — 20th century. I. T.
D447.N3 1948   *LC* 48-4739

Lee, Dwight Erwin, 1898-.   **3.761**
Europe's crucial years; the diplomatic background of World War I, 1902–1914,
by Dwight E. Lee. — Hanover, N.H.: Published for Clark University Press by
the University Press of New England, 1974. xiv, 482 p.: illus.; 24 cm. 1. World
War, 1914-1918 — Diplomatic history. 2. Europe — Politics and government
— 1871-1918 I. T.
D453.L43   940.3/112   *LC* 73-91315   *ISBN* 0874510945

D461–472 EASTERN QUESTION

(see also: D371-378)

Earle, Edward Mead, 1894-.   • **3.762**
Turkey, the great powers, and the Bagdad railway; a study in imperialism, by
Edward Mead Earle ... New York: The Macmillan Company, 1923. xiii, 364 p.:
maps.; 20 cm. Author's doctoral dissertation, Columbia University, 1923, but
not issued as a thesis. 1. Bagdad Railroad. 2. Eastern question 3. Turkey —
Economic conditions — 1918- I. T.
D463.E2   *LC* 23-11389

Kohn, Hans, 1891-1971.   • **3.763**
Nationalism and imperialism in the hither East. — New York: Harcourt, Brace,
1932. viii, 339 p.: ill. (maps); 24 cm. Tr. by M.M. Green. Includes index.
1. Eastern question 2. Nationalism 3. Imperialism 4. Muslims I. T.
D463.K6 1932   956

Stavrianos, Leften Stavros.   • **3.764**
Balkan federation; a history of the movement toward Balkan unity in modern
times [by] L. S. Stavrianos. Hamden, Conn.: Archon Books, 1964. x, 338 p. 24
cm. 'Originally published 1942, Smith College studies in history, vol. 27, nos.
1-4. Reprinted, 1964, unaltered and unabridged.' 1. Eastern question (Balkan)
2. Balkan Peninsula — Politics and government 3. Balkan Peninsula —
History I. T.
D463.S7 1964

The Great powers and the end of the Ottoman Empire / edited   **3.765**
by Marian Kent.
London; Boston: G. Allen & Unwin, 1984. x, 237 p., [2] leaves of plates: 2 maps;
25 cm. Includes index. 1. Eastern question (Balkan) 2. Great powers
3. Europe — Foreign relations — Turkey 4. Turkey — Foreign relations —
Europe 5. Europe — Foreign relations — 1871-1918 6. Europe — Foreign
relations — 1918-1945 I. Kent, Marian.
D465.G753 1984   327.5604 19   *LC* 83-15896   *ISBN* 0049560131

Schmitt, Bernadotte Everly, 1886-1969.   • **3.766**
The annexation of Bosnia, 1908–1909. — New York: H. Fertig, 1970. viii,
264 p.; 21 cm. Reprint of the 1937 ed. 1. Eastern question (Balkan) 2. Bosnia
and Herzegovina — Annexation to Austria. 3. Europe — Politics and
government — 1871-1918 I. T.
D465.S33 1970   949.7/42   *LC* 71-80588

D501–680 World War I (1914–1918)

Geiss, Imanuel. ed.   • **3.767**
[Julikrise und Kriegsausbruch 1914. English] July 1914; the outbreak of the
First World War; selected documents. New York, Scribner [1968, c1967] 400 p.
24 cm. Translation of Juli 1914, an abridged ed. of the compiler's 2 vol. work,
Julikrise und Kriegsausbruch 1914. 1. World War, 1914-1918 — Diplomatic
history. I. T.
D505.G2713 1968   940.3/112/08   *LC* 68-11752

Snyder, Louis Leo, 1907- ed.   • **3.768**
Historic documents of World War I. Princeton, N.J.: Van Nostrand [1958]
192 p.; 18 cm. (An Anvil original, no. 33) 1. World War, 1914-1918 — Sources.
I. T.
D505.S7   940.3082   *LC* 58-14438

Herwig, Holger H.   **3.769**
Biographical dictionary of World War I / Holger H. Herwig and Neil M.
Heyman. — Westport, Conn.: Greenwood Press, 1982. xiv, 424 p.: maps; 29
cm. Includes index. 1. World War, 1914-1918 — Biography — Dictionaries.
I. Heyman, Neil M. II. T.
D507.H47 1982   940.3/092/2 B 19   *LC* 81-4242   *ISBN*
0313213569

D511–520 CAUSES. AIMS

Albertini, Luigi, 1871-1941.   • **3.770**
The origins of the war of 1914. Translated and edited by Isabella M. Massey. —
London, New York, Oxford University Press, 1952-57. 3 v. fold. maps. 26 cm.
Bibliography: v. 1, p. [xxiii]—xxviii. 1. World War, 1914-1918 — Causes.
2. Europe — Politics — 1871-1918. 3. World War, 1914-1918 — Diplomatic
history. I. T.
D511.A574   940.311   *LC* 52-12126

Fay, Sidney Bradshaw, 1876-.   • **3.771**
The origins of the World War. 2d ed., rev. New York, Free Press [1966] 2 v.
facsim., maps. 21 cm. (A Free Press paperback) 1. World War, 1914-1918 —
Causes. 2. Europe — Politics and government — 1871-1918 I. T.
D511.F23 1966   940.3/11   *LC* 68-2275

Kennan, George Frost, 1904-.   **3.772**
The fateful alliance: France, Russia, and the coming of the First World War /
George F. Kennan. — 1st ed. — New York: Pantheon Books, c1984. xx, 300 p.,
[12] p. of plates: ill.; 24 cm. Includes index. 1. World War, 1914-1918 —
Causes. 2. Triple Alliance, 1882. 3. France — Foreign relations — Soviet
Union. 4. France — Foreign relations — 1870-1940 5. Russia — Foreign
relations — 1894-1917. 6. Soviet Union — Foreign relations — France. I. T.
D511.K34 1984   940.3/11 19   *LC* 84-42709   *ISBN* 0394534948

Lafore, Laurence Davis.   • **3.773**
The long fuse, an interpretation of the origins of World War I [by] Laurence
Lafore. [1st ed.] Philadelphia, Lippincott [1965] 282 p. maps. 21 cm. (Critical
periods of history) 1. World War, 1914-1918 — Causes. I. T.
D511.L19   940.3112   *LC* 65-15251

Military History Symposium (Canada) 3d, Royal Military   **3.774**
College, 1976.
War aims and strategic policy in the Great War, 1914–1918: [papers] / edited
by Barry Hunt and Adrian Preston. — London: Croom Helm; Totowa, N.J.:
Rowman and Littlefield, 1977. 131 p.; 23 cm. 1. World War, 1914-1918 —
Causes — Congresses. 2. Strategy — Congresses. I. Hunt, Barry D. (Barry
Dennis), 1937- II. Preston, Adrian W. III. T.
D511.M525 1976   940.4/01   *LC* 77-23577   *ISBN* 0874718724

Military strategy and the origins of the First World War: an   **3.775**
International security reader / edited by Steven E. Miller.
Princeton, N.J.: Princeton University Press, [1985] 186 p.: ill.; 25 cm. 1. World
War, 1914-1918 — Causes — Addresses, essays, lectures. 2. World War,
1914-1918 — Addresses, essays, lectures. 3. Strategy — Addresses, essays,
lectures. I. Miller, Steven E. II. International security.
D511.M53 1985   940.3/1 19   *LC* 84-61326   *ISBN* 0691076790

Schmitt, Bernadotte Everly, 1886-1969.   • **3.776**
The coming of the war, 1914, by Bernadotte E. Schmitt. New York, H. Fertig,
1966 [c1958] 2 v. 24 cm. 1. World War, 1914-1918 — Causes. 2. Europe —
Politics and government — 1871-1918 I. T.
D511.S275 1966   940.3112   *LC* 66-24353

Tuchman, Barbara Wertheim.   • **3.777**
The Zimmermann telegram [by] Barbara W. Tuchman. [New ed.] New York,
Macmillan [1966] xii, 244 p. facsim., ports. 22 cm. 1. Zimmermann, Arthur,
1864-1940. 2. World War, 1914-1918 — Causes. I. T.
D511.T77 1966   940.3112   *LC* 66-26604

Fischer, Fritz, 1908-.   • **3.778**
[Griff nach der Weltmacht. English] Germany's aims in the First World War.
With introd. by Hajo Holborn and James Joll. New York, W. W. Norton [1967]
xxviii, 652 p. illus., maps, ports. 25 cm. Translation of Griff nach der
Weltmacht. 1. World War, 1914-1918 — Causes. 2. World War, 1914-1918 —
Germany. 3. Germany — Foreign relations — 1888-1918 I. T.
D515.F2713 1967b   940.3/11   *LC* 64-23876

Rothwell, Victor.   **3.779**
British war aims and peace diplomacy, 1914–1918, [by] V. H. Rothwell.
Oxford, Clarendon Press, 1971. ix, 315 p. 23 cm. 1. World War, 1914-1918 —
Great Britain 2. World War, 1914-1918 — Diplomatic history. I. T.
D517.R73   940.3/22/42   *LC* 70-886729   *ISBN* 0198223498

Steiner, Zara S.   **3.780**
Britain and the origins of the First World War / Zara S. Steiner. — New York:
St. Martin's Press, 1977. 305 p.; 22 cm. — (The Making of the 20th century)
Includes index. 1. World War, 1914-1918 — Causes. 2. World War,
1914-1918 — Great Britain. 3. Great Britain — Foreign relations — 1901-1910
4. Great Britain — Foreign relations — 1910-1936 I. T.
D517.S816 1977   940.3/11   *LC* 76-55861   *ISBN* 0312098189

D521–523 GENERAL WORKS

Barnett, Correlli.   **3.781**
The Great War / Correlli Barnett. — 1st American ed. — New York: Putnam, 1980, c1979. 192 p.: ill.; 31 cm. Includes index. 1. World War, 1914-1918 I. T.
D521.B24 1980   940.3   LC 79-87446   *ISBN* 0399123865

Chambers, Frank Pentland, 1900-.   **3.782**
The war behind the war, 1914–1918; a history of the political and civilian fronts, by Frank P. Chambers. New York, Arno Press, 1972 [c1967] xv, 620 p. maps (1 fold.) 23 cm. (World affairs: national and international viewpoints) 1. World War, 1914-1918 I. T. II. Series.
D521.C47 1972   940.3   LC 72-4267   *ISBN* 0405045646

Churchill, Winston, Sir, 1874-1965.   • **3.783**
The world crisis / by Winston S. Churchill. — London: Butterworth, 1923-31. 6 v.: ill.; 25 cm. Includes index. 1. World War, 1914-1918 2. World War, 1914-1918 — Great Britain 3. Reconstruction (1914-1939) 4. World politics I. T.
D521.C513   LC 65-59059

Falls, Cyril Bentham, 1888-.   • **3.784**
The Great War. New York, Putnam [1959] 447 p. 22 cm. 1. World War, 1914-1918 I. T.
D521.F25   940.3   LC 59-7851

Ferro, Marc.   **3.785**
[Grande guerre, 1914-1918. English] The Great War, 1914–1918. Translated by Nicole Stone. London, Routledge & K. Paul [1973] xi, 239 p. illus. 23 cm. Translation of La Grande guerre, 1914-1918. 1. World War, 1914-1918 I. T.
D521.F313 1973   940.3/1   LC 73-174964   *ISBN* 071007574X
ISBN 0710075758

Liddell Hart, Basil Henry, Sir, 1895-1970.   **3.786**
[Real war, 1914-1918] History of the First World War. [Enlarged ed.] London, Cassell, 1970. 635 p. maps. 25 cm. First published in 1930 under title: The real war, 1914-1918. Enl. ed. published in 1934 under title: A history of the World War, 1914-1918. Companion vol. to his History of the Second World War. 1. World War, 1914-1918 I. T.
D521.L48 1970   940.4   LC 70-557411   *ISBN* 0304936537

Schmitt, Bernadotte Everly, 1886-1969.   **3.787**
The world in the crucible, 1914–1919 / by Bernadotte E. Schmitt and Harold C. Vedeler. — 1st ed. — New York: Harper & Row, c1984. xvii, 553 p.: ill., maps; 22 cm. — (Rise of modern Europe.) Includes index. 1. World War, 1914-1918 2. World War, 1914-1918 — Influence. 3. Revolutions — Europe — History — 20th century. 4. Europe — History — 1871-1918 5. Europe — History — 1918-1945 I. Vedeler, Harold C. II. T. III. Series.
D521.S367 1984   940.3 19   LC 83-48384   *ISBN* 0060152680

Taylor, A. J. P. (Alan John Percivale), 1906-.   • **3.788**
The First World War, an illustrated history / A.J.P. Taylor. — London: Hamish Hamilton, 1963. 224 p.: ill., ports., maps. 1. World War, 1914-1918 — Pictorial works. I. T.
D522.T3 1963   *ISBN* 0241901871

Ashworth, Tony.   **3.789**
Trench warfare, 1914–1918: the live and let live system / Tony Ashworth. — New York, N.Y.: Holmes & Meier, 1980. xi, 266 p., [8] leaves of plates: ill.; 23 cm. 1. World War, 1914-1918 — Trench Warfare. I. T.
D523.A756 1980   940.4/14   LC 80-13696   *ISBN* 0841906157

Leed, Eric J.   **3.790**
No man's land: combat & identity in World War I / Eric J. Leed. — Cambridge; New York: Cambridge University Press, 1977. xii, 257 p.; 24 cm. Includes index. 1. World War, 1914-1918 — Psychological aspects. 2. World War, 1914-1918 — Influence. 3. World War, 1914-1918 — Moral and ethical aspects. I. T.
D523.L443   940.3/14   LC 78-26396   *ISBN* 0521224713

D530–578 MILITARY OPERATIONS

D530–549 Western Europe

Barnett, Correlli.   • **3.791**
The swordbearers; supreme command in the First World War. New York, Morrow, 1964 [c1963] xv, 392 p. illus., ports., maps, diagrs. 25 cm. 1. World War, 1914-1918 — Campaigns 2. World War, 1914-1918 — Biography. I. T.
D530.B26 1964   940.414   LC 64-16445

Tuchman, Barbara Wertheim.   • **3.792**
The guns of August. New York, Macmillan, 1962. 511 p. illus. 24 cm. London ed. (Constable) has title: August 1914. 1. World War, 1914-1918 — Campaigns I. T.
D530.T8   940.421   LC 62-7515

Ludendorff, Erich, 1865-1937.   • **3.793**
[Meine Kriegserinnerungen. English] Ludendorff's own story, August 1914–November 1918; the Great War from the siege of Liège to the signing of the armistice as viewed from the grand headquarters of the German Army. Freeport, N.Y., Books for Libraries Press [1971, c1920] 2 v. illus., maps (part fold., mounted on lining papers) 23 cm. Translation of Meine Kriegserinnerungen, 1914-1918. 1. Ludendorff, Erich, 1865-1937. 2. World War, 1914-1918 — Germany. I. T.
D531.L7713 1971   940.4/09/43   LC 72-165647   *ISBN* 0836959566

Wolff, Leon.   • **3.794**
In Flanders fields; the 1917 campaign. New York, Viking Press, 1958. 308 p. illus. 22 cm. 1. World War, 1914-1918 — Campaigns — Belgium 2. Belgium — History — German occupation, 1914-1918 I. T.
D541.W7   940.4/33 19   LC 58-10607

Terraine, John.   **3.795**
To win a war: 1918, the year of victory / John Terraine. — Garden City, N.Y.: Doubleday, 1981. xvi, 268 p., [16] leaves of plates: ill.; 25 cm. Includes indexes. 1. World War, 1914-1918 — Campaigns — France. 2. France — History — German occupation, 1914-1918 I. T.
D544.T43 1981   940.4/35 19   LC 79-7119   *ISBN* 0385153163

Middlebrook, Martin, 1932-.   **3.796**
The first day on the Somme, 1 July 1916. — New York: Norton, [1972] xii, 346 p.: illus.; 24 cm. 1. Somme, Battle of the, 1916 I. T.
D545.S7 M53 1972   940.4/272   LC 71-159456   *ISBN* 039305442X

Horne, Alistair.   **3.797**
The price of glory; Verdun 1916. — New York: St. Martin's Press, [1963, c1962] 371 p.: illus.; 22 cm. Second vol. in a trilogy; the 1st of which is The fall of Paris; the siege and the Commune, 1870-71; and the 3d of which is To lose a battle; France 1940. 1. Verdun, Battle of, 1916 I. T.
D545.V3 H6   940.427   LC 62-19735

Alexander, Harold Rupert Leofric George Alexander, 1st Earl, 1891-1969.   • **3.798**
The Alexander memoirs, 1940–1945 / edited by John North. — New York: McGraw-Hill, [c1962] xiii, 209 p.: ill., group ports., maps (part fold.); 22 cm. 1. World War, 1939-1945 — Campaigns I. T.
D546.A58A3   940.542   LC 63-12437

Hankey, Maurice Pascal Alers Hankey, Baron, 1877-1963.   • **3.799**
The Supreme Command, 1914–1918. — London, Allen and Unwin [1961] 2 v. illus. 24 cm. 1. Great Britain. Committee of Imperial Defense. 2. Great Britain. War Cabinet. 3. World War, 1914-1918 — Gt. Brit. I. T.
D546.H43   940.40942   LC 61-3901

Lloyd George, David, 1863-1945.   • **3.800**
War memoirs of David Lloyd George ... — London, I. Nicholson & Watson [1933-36] 6 v. fronts., plates, ports., maps, facsims. (1 fold.) 23 cm. Paged continuously. 1. World War, 1914-1918 I. T.
D546.L5 1933   940.342   LC 33-28755

Williams, John, 1908-.   **3.801**
The other battleground: the home fronts: Britain, France and Germany, 1914–1918 / John Williams. — Chicago: H. Regnery, c1972. 325 p., [7] leaves of plates: ill., ports.; 23 cm. 1. World War, 1914-1918 — Great Britain 2. World War, 1914-1918 — France 3. World War, 1914-1918 — Germany I. T.
D546.W55   LC 77-183803

Woodward, E. L. (Ernest Llewellyn), Sir, 1890-.   • **3.802**
Great Britain and the War of 1914–1918 [by] Llewellyn Woodward. Boston, Beacon Press [1970] xxxix, 610 p. maps. 21 cm. (Europe in the twentieth century, BP 372) 1. World War, 1914-1918 — Great Britain I. T.
D546.W6 1970   940.3/42   LC 71-125402   *ISBN* 080705657X

Cassar, George H.   **3.803**
The tragedy of Sir John French / George H. Cassar. — Newark: University of Delaware Press; London: Associated University Presses, c1985. 324 p.: ill.; 25 cm. Includes index. 1. French, John Denton Pinkstone, Earl of Ypres, 1852-1925. 2. World War, 1914-1918 — Campaigns — France 3. France — History — German occupation, 1914-1918 I. T.
D548.C28 1985   940.54/21 19   LC 82-49302   *ISBN* 087413241X

Watt, Richard M., 1930-. • **3.804**
Dare call it treason. Introd. by Colonel John Elting. — New York, Simon and Schuster, 1963. 344 p. illus. 24 cm. 1. France. Armée — Hist. 2. World War, 1914-1918 — Campaigns — France. 3. Mutiny — France. I. T.
D548.W3   940.457   *LC* 62-17979

D550–569 Eastern Campaigns

Churchill, Winston, Sir, 1874-1965. • **3.805**
The unknown war; the eastern front. New York, C. Scribner's sons, 1931. xv, [1] p., 1 l., 396 p. incl. geneal. tab. front., ports., maps (1 fold.) 23 cm. 1. World War, 1914-1918 2. World War, 1914-1918 — Campaigns — Eastern I. T. II. Title: The eastern front.
D550.C4   *LC* 31-32920

Stone, Norman. **3.806**
The eastern front, 1914–1917 / by Norman Stone. — New York: Scribner, c1975. 348 p.: maps; 24 cm. 1. World War, 1914-1918 — Campaigns — Eastern 2. Soviet Union — History — Revolution, 1917-1921 — Causes. I. T.
D550.S76   940.4/147   *LC* 75-18914   *ISBN* 0684144921

Bush, Eric Wheler. **3.807**
Gallipoli / by Eric Wheler Bush. — New York: St. Martin's Press, 1975. 335 p., [8] leaves of plates: ill.; 25 cm. 1. World War, 1914-1918 — Campaigns — Turkey — Gallipoli Peninsula I. T.
D568.3.B87 1975b   940.4/143   *LC* 75-9470

Rhodes James, Robert, 1933-. • **3.808**
Gallipoli. New York, Macmillan, 1965. xi, 384 p. illus., maps, plans, ports. 24 cm. 1. World War, 1914-1918 — Campaigns — Turkey — Gallipoli Peninsula I. T.
D568.3.J3 1965a   940.425   *LC* 65-12661

Lawrence, T. E. (Thomas Edward), 1888-1935. • **3.809**
Seven pillars of wisdom; a triumph. Garden City, N.Y., Doubleday, 1966 [c1935] xiv, 622 p. maps. 22 cm. 1. World War, 1914-1918 — Campaigns — Turkey and the Near East. 2. Arabs 3. Bedouins 4. Wahhābīyah — Saudi Arabia 5. Arabian Peninsula — Social life and customs. I. T.
D568.4.L4 1966   940.415   *LC* 65-29663

Liddell Hart, Basil Henry, 1895-. • **3.810**
'T.E.Lawrence' in Arabia and after. London: Cape, 1936. 489 p.: ill. American edition (New York,Dodd,Mead and company) has title:Colonel Lawrence, the man behind the legend. 1. Lawrence, T. E. (Thomas Edward), 1888-1935. 2. World War, 1914-1918 — Turkey and the Near East. — Campaigns 3. World War, 1914-1918 — Arabia. I. T.
D568.4.L45 L52 1965

Mack, John E., 1929-. **3.811**
A prince of our disorder: the life of T. E. Lawrence / John E. Mack. — 1st ed. — Boston: Little, Brown, c1976. xviii, 561 p., [16] leaves of plates: ill.; 24 cm. Includes index. 1. Lawrence, T. E. (Thomas Edward), 1888-1935. I. T.
D568.4.L45 M28   941.083/092/4 B   *LC* 75-22481   *ISBN* 0316542326

Barker, A. J. • **3.812**
[Neglected war] The bastard war; the Mesopotamian campaign of 1914–1918 [by] A. J. Barker. New York, Dial Press, 1967. xiv, 449 p. illus., maps, ports. 24 cm. London ed. (Faber) has title: The neglected war. 1. World War, 1914-1918 — Campaigns — Iraq I. T.
D568.5.B33 1967b   940.4/15   *LC* 66-27391

D570 United States

Coffman, Edward M. • **3.813**
The war to end all wars; the American military experience in World War I [by] Edward M. Coffman. New York, Oxford University Press, 1968. xvi, 412 p. illus., plans, ports. 24 cm. 1. World War, 1914-1918 — United States. I. T.
D570.C6   940.4/12/73   *LC* 68-29715

Palmer, Frederick, 1873-1958. • **3.814**
Newton D. Baker; America at war, based on the personal papers of the secretary of war in the world war; his correspondence with the President and important leaders at home and abroad... New York, Dodd, Mead, 1931. 2 v. illus. 1. Baker, Newton Diehl, 1871-1937. 2. World War, 1914-1918 — United States I. T.
D570.P32   973.913   *LC* 31-28311

Pershing, John J. (John Joseph), 1860-1948. • **3.815**
My experiences in the world war. New York, Frederick A. Stokes company, 1931. 2 v. fronts., plates, ports. maps (part fold.) diagrs. 25 cm. 1. World War, 1914-1918 — United States. I. T.
D570.P44 1931   *LC* 31-10662

Kennedy, David M. **3.816**
Over here: the First World War and American society / David M. Kennedy. — New York: Oxford University Press, 1980. vii, 404 p.; 24 cm. Includes index. 1. World War, 1914-1918 — United States. 2. United States — History — 1913-1921 3. United States — Social conditions — 1865-1918 I. T.
D570.1.K43   940.3/73   *LC* 80-11753   *ISBN* 0195027299

Cummings, E. E. (Edward Estlin), 1894-1962. • **3.817**
The enormous room. [Introd. by Robert Graves] New York, Liveright [1970, c1922] xix, 9-271 p. 21 cm. (Liveright paperbound edition) 'Liveright L-1.' 1. Cummings, E. E. (Edward Estlin), 1894-1962 — Biography. 2. World War, 1914-1918 — Personal narratives, American. 3. World War, 1914-1918 — Prisoners and prisons, French. 4. Soldiers — United States — Biography. I. T.
D570.9.C82 1970   940.4/81/73   *LC* 77-114387

D580–595 Naval Operations

Hough, Richard Alexander, 1922-. **3.818**
The Great War at sea, 1914–1918 / Richard Hough. — Oxford; New York: Oxford University Press, 1983. xii, 353 p., [24] p. of plates: ill., maps, ports.; 25 cm. Includes index. 1. Great Britain. Royal Navy — History — World War, 1914-1918. 2. World War, 1914-1918 — Naval operations, British. I. T.
D581.H56 1983   940.4/5941 19   *LC* 84-106046   *ISBN* 0192158716

Costello, John. **3.819**
Jutland, 1916 / John Costello and Terry Hughes. New York: Holt, Rinehart and Winston, 1977, c1976. 230, [8] p.: ill.; 24 cm. Includes index. 1. Jutland, Battle of, 1916 I. Hughes, Terry. joint author. II. T.
D582.J8 C63 1977   940.4/56   *LC* 76-15599   *ISBN* 0030184665

Bailey, Thomas Andrew, 1902-. **3.820**
The Lusitania disaster: an episode in modern warfare and diplomacy / Thomas A. Bailey and Paul B. Ryan. — New York: Free Press, [1975] xv, 383 p., [8] leaves of plates: ill.; 24 cm. Includes index. 1. Lusitania (Steamship) 2. World War, 1914-1918 — Naval operations I. Ryan, Paul B. joint author. II. T.
D592.L8 B34   940.4/514   *LC* 75-2806   *ISBN* 0029012406

D600–607 Aerial Operations

Norman, Aaron. **3.821**
The great air war. New York, Macmillan [1968] xi, 558 p. illus. 24 cm. 1. World War, 1914-1918 — Aerial operations I. T.
D600.N6   940.4/4   *LC* 68-10180

Jones, Neville. **3.822**
The origins of strategic bombing; a study of the development of British air strategic thought and practice up to 1918. London, Kimber, 1973. 240, [8] p. illus., map, ports. 24 cm. Includes index. 1. World War, 1914-1918 — Aerial operations, British. 2. Bombing, Aerial — History. I. T.
D602.J66   940.4/49/42   *LC* 74-164725   *ISBN* 0718300939

Morrow, John Howard, 1944-. **3.823**
German air power in World War I / John H. Morrow, Jr. — Lincoln: University of Nebraska Press, c1982. xii, 267 p., [8] p. of plates: ill.; 24 cm. Includes index. 1. World War, 1914-1918 — Aerial operations, German. 2. Aeronautics, Military — Germany — History — 20th century. I. T.
D604.M64 1982   940.54/4943 19   *LC* 81-11588   *ISBN* 0803230761

D610–621 Diplomatic History

Gottlieb, Wolfram Wilhelm. • **3.824**
Studies in secret diplomacy during the first World War / W. W. Gottlieb. — London: George Allen & Unwin, 1957. 430 p.: map; 23 cm. 1. World War, 1914-1918 — Diplomatic History I. T.
D610.G62   940.32   *LC* 57-4503

Mayer, Arno J. • **3.825**
Political origins of the new diplomacy, 1917–1918 [by] Arno J. Mayer. New York, H. Fertig, 1969. xiv, 435 p. 23 cm. (Yale historical publications. [Studies, 18]) Reprint of the 1959 ed. 1. World War, 1914-1918 — Diplomatic history. I. T. II. Title: New diplomacy. III. Series.
D610.M33 1969   940.3/2   *LC* 68-9616

Zeman, Z. A. B. (Zbyněk A. B.), 1928-. **3.826**
[Gentlemen negotiators] A diplomatic history of the First World War [by] Z.A.B. Zeman. London, Weidenfeld and Nicolson, 1971. xi, 402 p. maps. 23 cm. American ed. (New York, Macmillan) has title: The gentlemen negotiators. 1. World War, 1914-1918 — Diplomatic history. I. T.
D610.Z44 1971b   940.3/2   *LC* 72-582020   *ISBN* 0297003003

Calder, Kenneth J. **3.827**
Britain and the origins of the new Europe, 1914–1918 / Kenneth J. Calder. — Cambridge [Eng.]; New York: Cambridge University Press, 1976. viii, 268 p.:

map; 23 cm. — (International studies) Includes index. 1. World War, 1914-1918 — Diplomatic history. 2. World War, 1914-1918 — Great Britain 3. Minorities — Europe, Eastern. 4. Self-determination, National 5. Great Britain — Foreign relations — 1910-1936 I. T.
D611.C35   940.3/22/41   LC 75-12161   ISBN 0521208971

Martin, Laurence W.   • 3.828
Peace without victory; Woodrow Wilson and the British liberals [by] Laurence W. Martin. Port Washington, N.Y., Kennikat Press [1973, c1958] xiv, 230 p. 22 cm. Original ed. issued in series: Yale historical publications. Miscellany 70. 1. Wilson, Woodrow, 1856-1924. 2. World War, 1914-1918 — Diplomatic history. 3. World War, 1914-1918 — Great Britain 4. World War, 1914-1918 — United States. I. T.
D611.M37 1973   940.3/22/73   LC 72-85282   ISBN 0804617015

Trask, David F.   3.829
Captains & cabinets: Anglo–American naval relations, 1917–1918 / [by] David F. Trask. — [Columbia, Mo.]: University of Missouri Press [1972] 396 p.: ill.; 25 cm. 1. World War, 1914-1918 — Diplomatic history. 2. World War, 1914-1918 — Naval operations 3. World War, 1914-1918 — United States. I. T.
D611.T73   940.4/5   LC 72-84202   ISBN 0826201296

Wheeler-Bennett, John Wheeler, 1902-.   • 3.830
The forgotten peace, Brest–Litovsk, March 1918. New York W. Morrow 1939. 478 p. pl., ports., fold. map; 23 cm. (Studies in modern history) 1. Brest-Litovsk, Treaty of, Mar. 3, 1918 (Russia) 2. Russia — History — Revolution, 1917-1921 3. World War, 1914-1918 — Russia I. T.
D614 B6 W45 1939

Gregory, Ross.   • 3.831
The origins of American intervention in the First World War. [1st ed.] New York, Norton [1971] xi, 162 p. 21 cm. (The Norton essays in American history) 1. World War, 1914-1918 — United States. I. T.
D619.G73 1971   940.531/2   LC 70-141588   ISBN 0393054381
ISBN 0393099806

Lansing, Robert, 1864-1928.   • 3.832
War memoirs of Robert Lansing, Secretary of State. Westport, Conn., Greenwood Press [1970] 383 p. port. 24 cm. Reprint of the 1935 ed. 1. World War, 1914-1918 — United States. 2. United States — Foreign relations — 1913-1921 3. United States — Neutrality I. T.
D619.L347 1970   940.3/22/73   LC 78-110853   ISBN 0837145201

May, Ernest R.   • 3.833
The World War and American isolation, 1914–1917. Cambridge, Harvard University Press, 1959. viii, 482 p. 22 cm. (Harvard historical studies. v. 71) 1. World War, 1914-1918 — Diplomatic history. 2. United States — Foreign relations — 1913-1921 I. T. II. Series.
D619.M383   940.32   LC 58-12971

Rochester, Stuart I., 1945-.   3.834
American liberal disillusionment: in the wake of World War I / Stuart I. Rochester. — University Park: Pennsylvania State University Press, c1977. 172 p.; 24 cm. 1. World War, 1914-1918 — United States. 2. Liberalism — United States. 3. United States — Politics and government — 1913-1921 I. T.
D619.R53   940.3   LC 76-49447   ISBN 0271012331

Seymour, Charles, 1885-1963.   3.835
American diplomacy during the world war / by Charles Seymour. — Baltimore: The Johns Hopkins press, 1934. xii, 417 p.; 20 cm. (The Albert Shaw lectures on diplomatic history, 1933. The Walter Hines Page school of international relations) 1. Wilson, Woodrow, 1856-1924. 2. World War, 1914-1918 — United States. 3. United States — Foreign relations — 1913-1921 I. T.
D619.S43   [940.37302] 940.32273   LC 34-11641

Seymour, Charles, 1885-1963.   • 3.836
American neutrality, 1914–1917: essays on the causes of American intervention in the World War. — [Hamden, Conn.]: Archon Books, 1967[c1935] vii, 187 p. 1. World War, 1914-1918 — United States. 2. United States — Neutrality 3. United States — Foreign relations — 1913-1921 I. T.
D619.S435 1967

Stevenson, D. (David), 1954-.   3.837
French war aims against Germany, 1914–1919 / D. Stevenson. — Oxford, 1982. xiv, 283 p.: maps; 22 cm. Includes index. 1. Treaty of Versailles (1919). 2. World War, 1914-1918 — Diplomatic history. 3. Germany — Foreign relations — France 4. France — Foreign relations — Germany I. T.
D621.F8 S75 1982   940.3/2 19   LC 82-1121   ISBN 0198225741

D622–640 Special Topics. Personal Narratives

Mock, James Robert.   • 3.838
Words that won the war; the story of the Committee on Public Information, 1917–1919, by James R. Mock and Cedric Larson. New York, Russell & Russell [1968] xvi, 372 p. illus., facsims., ports. 25 cm. Reprint of the 1939 ed. 1. Creel, George, 1876-1953. 2. United States. Committee on Public Information. 3. Propaganda, American 4. World War, 1914-1918 — Public opinion 5. World War, 1914-1918 — United States. I. Larson, Cedric, 1908- joint author. II. T.
D632.M64 1968   940.4/886/73   LC 68-25073

Burk, Kathleen.   3.839
Britain, America and the sinews of war, 1914–1918 / Kathleen Burk. — Boston; London: G. Allen & Unwin, 1985. x, 286 p.; 23 cm. Includes index. 1. World War, 1914-1918 — Economic aspects — United States. 2. World War, 1914-1918 — Economic aspects — Great Britain. 3. United States — Foreign economic relations — Great Britain. 4. Great Britain — Foreign economic relations — United States. I. T.
D635.B87 1985   940.3/1 19   LC 84-9262   ISBN 0049400762

Horn, Daniel.   • 3.840
The German naval mutinies of World War I. New Brunswick, N.J., Rutgers University Press [1969] xiii, 346 p. 22 cm. 1. Germany. Kriegsmarine. 2. Mutiny — Germany. 3. World War, 1914-1918 — Naval operations, German. I. T.
D639.M82 G45   940.4/59/43   LC 71-75677   ISBN 0813505984

Barbeau, Arthur E.   3.841
The unknown soldiers; Black American troops in World War I [by] Arthur E. Barbeau and Florette Henri. Foreword by Burghardt Turner. Philadelphia, Temple University Press [1974] xvii, 279 p. illus. 23 cm. 1. United States. Army — Afro-American troops 2. World War, 1914-1918 — Afro-American participation. I. Henri, Florette. joint author. II. T.
D639.N4 B37   940.4/03   LC 72-95880   ISBN 0877220638

Roetter, Charles.   3.842
The art of psychological warfare, 1914–1945 / Charles Roetter. — New York: Stein and Day, 1974. 199 p., [8] leaves of plates: ill.; 24 cm. Includes indexes. 1. World War, 1914-1918 — Propaganda. 2. World War, 1939-1945 — Propaganda I. T.
D639.P6 R63 1974   940.4/88   LC 74-80901   ISBN 0812817370

Sanders, Michael, 1945-.   3.843
British propaganda during the First World War, 1914–1918 / M.L. Sanders and Philip M. Taylor. — London: Macmillan, 1982. x, 320 p.: ill.; 23 cm. 1. Propaganda, British 2. World War, 1914-1918 — Propaganda I. Taylor, Philip M. II. T.
D639.P7 S35   ISBN 0333292758

Bloch, Marc Léopold Benjamin, 1886-1944.   3.844
[Souvenirs de guerre, 1914-1915. English] Memoirs of war, 1914–15 / Marc Bloch; translated and with an introd. by Carole Fink. — Ithaca, N.Y.: Cornell University Press, c1980. 177 p.: ill.; 25 cm. Translation of Souvenirs de guerre, 1914-15. 1. Bloch, Marc Léopold Benjamin, 1886-1944. 2. World War, 1914-1918 — Personal narratives, French. I. T.
D640.B581713   940.4/81/44 19   LC 79-6849   ISBN 080141220X

Sassoon, Siegfried, 1886-1967.   • 3.845
Memoirs of an infantry officer [by] Siegfried Sassoon. New York, Coward, McCann, 1930. 322 p. 20 cm. Sequel: Sherston's progress. 1. World War, 1914-1918 — Personal narratives, English. I. T.
D640.S3415   LC 30-25630

D641–651 Armistice. Peace

Bailey, Thomas Andrew, 1902-.   • 3.846
Wilson and the peacemakers: combining Woodrow Wilson and the lost peace and Woodrow Wilson and the great betrayal / by Thomas A. Bailey. — New York: Macmillan, 1947. 2 v. in 1 (xii, 381, xii, 429 p.): ill., maps; 22 cm. Each vol. has also special t.p. Includes indexes. 1. Wilson, Woodrow, 1856-1924. 2. Paris Peace Conference (1919-1920). 3. Treaty of Versailles (1919). 4. World War, 1914-1918 — United States. 5. United States — Politics and government — 1913-1921 I. T. II. Title: Woodrow Wilson and the lost peace. III. Title: Woodrow Wilson and the great betrayal.
D643.A7 B32   LC 48-5001

Mayer, Arno J.   3.847
Politics and diplomacy of peacemaking; containment and counterrevolution at Versailles, 1918–1919 [by] Arno J. Mayer. [1st ed.] New York, Knopf, 1967. viii, 918, xx p. map. 25 cm. Sequel to Political origins of the new diplomacy,

1917-1918. 1. Treaty of Versailles (1919). 2. History, Modern — 20th century I. T.
D643.A7 M3   940.3/141   *LC* 67-18598

Schwabe, Klaus.   **3.848**
[Deutsche Revolution und Wilson-Frieden. English] Woodrow Wilson, Revolutionary Germany, and peacemaking, 1918–1919: missionary diplomacy and the realities of power / by Klaus Schwabe; translated from German by Rita and Robert Kimber. — Chapel Hill: University of North Carolina Press, c1985. ix, 565 p.; 24 cm. (Supplementary volumes to The papers of Woodrow Wilson.) Abridged and updated translation of: Deutsche Revolution und Wilson-Frieden. Includes index. 1. Wilson, Woodrow, 1856-1924. 2. Treaty of Versailles (1919). 3. World War, 1914-1918 — Peace I. T. II. Series.
D643.A7 S34513 1985   940.3/141 19   *LC* 84-13073   *ISBN* 0807816183

United States. Dept. of State.   • **3.849**
The Treaty of Versailles and after; annotations of the text of the treaty. New York, Greenwood Press [1968] xiv, 1018 p. maps. 24 cm. Reprint of the 1944 ed. 'Annotations were prepared by Mr. Denys P. Myers.' 1. Treaty of Versailles (1919). 2. World War, 1914-1918 — Influence. I. Myers, Denys Peter, 1884- II. T.
D643.A7 U5 1968   940.3/141   *LC* 68-55121

Elcock, H. J. (Howard James)   **3.850**
Portrait of a decision: the Council of Four and the Treaty of Versailles [by] Howard Elcock. London, Eyre Methuen, 1972. xiii, 386 p. illus., map. 23 cm. 1. Paris Peace Conference (1919-1920). 2. Treaty of Versailles (1919). I. T.
D644.E5 1972   940.3/141   *LC* 73-156447   *ISBN* 0413283704

Marks, Sally.   **3.851**
The illusion of peace: international relations in Europe, 1918–1933 / Sally Marks. — New York: St. Martin's Press, 1976. 184 p.; 21 cm. — (The Making of the 20th century) Includes index. 1. League of Nations. 2. World War, 1914-1918 — Peace 3. World War, 1939-1945 — Causes I. T.
D644.M37 1976   327.4   *LC* 76-11281

Nicolson, Harold George, Sir, 1886-1968.   • **3.852**
Peacemaking, 1919, by Harold Nicolson. New York, Grosset & Dunlap [1965] vii, 378 p. front. 21 cm. (The Universal library, UL-178) First published in 1933. 1. Paris Peace Conference (1919-1920). 2. World War, 1914-1918 — Peace I. T.
D644.N36 1965   940.3141   *LC* 65-13213

Bonsal, Stephen, 1865-1951.   • **3.853**
Suitors and suppliants; the little nations at Versailles. Introd. by Arthur Krock. Port Washington, N.Y., Kennikat Press [1969, c1946] xiii, 301 p. 22 cm. (Essay and general literature index reprint series) 1. Paris Peace Conference (1919-1920). 2. World War, 1914-1918 — Peace 3. World War, 1914-1918 — Territorial questions I. T.
D645.B6 1969   940.3/141   *LC* 68-26226

Marston, F. S. (Frank Swain)   • **3.854**
The Peace Conference of 1919, organization and procedure / by F.S. Marston. — London: Oxford University Press, 1944. xi, 276 p.; 22 cm. Includes index. 1. Paris Peace Conference (1919-1920). I. Royal Institute of International Affairs. II. T.
D645.M387   940.3/141 19   *LC* 45-6755

Tillman, Seth P.   **3.855**
Anglo–American relations at the Paris Peace Conference of 1919. — Princeton, N. J., Princeton University Press, 1961. xiv, 442 p. 25 cm. Based on the author's doctoral dissertation. 1. Paris Peace Conference (1919-1920). 2. U.S. — For. rel. — Gt. Brit. 3. Gt. Brit. — For. rel. — U.S. I. T.
D645.T5   940.3141   *LC* 61-7426

Trachtenberg, Marc, 1946-.   **3.856**
Reparation in world politics: France and European economic diplomacy, 1916–1923 / Marc Trachtenberg. — New York: Columbia University Press, 1980. x, 423 p.; 24 cm. Includes index. 1. World War, 1914-1918 — Reparations. 2. World War, 1914-1918 — Germany. 3. France — Foreign economic relations. I. T.
D648.T72   940.3/1422   *LC* 79-26898   *ISBN* 023104786X

D650–651 Individual Countries

King, Jere Clemens.   • **3.857**
Foch versus Clemenceau; France and German dismemberment, 1918–1919. — Cambridge, Harvard University Press, 1960. vi, 137 p. 21 cm. — (Harvard historical monographs. 44) 'Bibliographical note': p. [129]-132. 1. Foch, Ferdinand, 1851-1929. 2. Clemenceau, Georges, 1841-1929. 3. World War, 1914-1918 — Territorial questions — Rhine River and Valley. I. T. II. Series.
D650.M5K5   944.08   *LC* 60-11557

Nelson, Keith L.   **3.858**
Victors divided: America and the Allies in Germany, 1918–1923 / Keith L. Nelson. — Berkeley: University of California Press, 1975. xiii, 441 p., [4] leaves of plates: ill.; 23 cm. Includes index. 1. World War, 1914-1918 — Territorial questions — Germany (West) — Rhineland. 2. Rhineland (Germany) — History — Separatist movement, 1918-1924 3. Germany — History — Allied occupation, 1918-1930 4. United States — Foreign relations — 1913-1921 I. T. II. Title: America and the Allies in Germany, 1918-1923.
D650.M5 N44   940.3/142   *LC* 72-87203   *ISBN* 0520023153

Albrecht-Carrié, René, 1904-.   • **3.859**
Italy at the Paris Peace Conference / René Albrecht–Carrié. — Hamden, Conn.: Archon Books, 1966. 575 p. — 1. Paris. Peace Conference, 1919. Italy. 2. European war, 1914-1918. I. T.
D651I7 A8 1966   940.3141   *LC* 66-13339

Thompson, John M.   • **3.860**
Russia, Bolshevism, and the Versailles peace [by] John M. Thompson. Princeton, N.J., Princeton University Press, 1966 [i.e. 1967] vii, 429 p. maps. 24 cm. (Studies of the Russian Institute, Columbia University) 1. World War, 1914-1918 — Soviet Union. 2. World War, 1914-1918 — Peace 3. Communism — Soviet Union I. T.
D651.R8 T5   940.3/141   *LC* 66-17712

Helmreich, Paul C.   **3.861**
From Paris to Sèvres: the partition of the Ottoman Empire at the Peace Conference of 1919–1920 [by] Paul C. Helmreich. Columbus, Ohio State University Press [1974] xiii, 376 p. maps. 23 cm. 1. Paris Peace Conference (1919-1920). Turkey. 2. World War, 1914-1918 — Territorial questions — Turkey. I. T.
D651.T9 H44   949.6   *LC* 73-12812   *ISBN* 0814201709

D652–728 1919–1939

Toynbee, Arnold Joseph, 1889-1975.   • **3.862**
The world after the Peace conference, being an epilogue to the 'History of the Peace conference of Paris' and a prologue to the 'Survey of international affairs, 1920–1923'. London, New York [etc.] H. Milford, Oxford university press, 1925. 91 p. fold. map. 25 cm. 'Issued under the auspices of the British institute of international affairs.' Originally written as an introduction to the author's Survey of international affairs in 1920-23 and intended for publication as part of the same volume. cf. Pref. 1. World War, 1914-1918 — Influence 2. World politics I. British Institute of International Affairs. II. T.
D653.T6   *LC* 25-19520

Angell, James W. (James Waterhouse), 1898-1986.   • **3.863**
The recovery of Germany, by James W. Angell. Enl. and rev. ed. Westport, Conn., Greenwood Press [1972, c1932] xix, 442 p. 22 cm. Original ed. issued in series: Publications of the Council on Foreign Relations. 1. Reconstruction (1914-1939) — Germany. 2. Germany — Economic conditions — 1918-1945 I. T.
D659.G3 A7 1972   330.943/08   *LC* 75-138197   *ISBN* 0837155509

Kohn, Hans, 1891-1971.   • **3.864**
Revolutions and dictatorships; essays in contemporary history. — Freeport, N.Y.: Books for Libraries Press, [1969, c1939] xii, 437 p.; 23 cm. — (Essay index reprint series) 1. Revolutions 2. Dictators 3. Nationalism 4. History, Modern — 20th century 5. World politics — 20th century I. T.
D720.K6 1969   909.82   *LC* 75-80388   *ISBN* 0836911458

Namier, Lewis Bernstein, Sir, 1888-1960.   • **3.865**
Europe in decay; a study in disintegration, 1936–1940. — Gloucester, Mass., P. Smith, 1963. 329 p. 21 cm. 1. Europe — Hist. — 1918-1945. 2. World War, 1939-1945 — Causes I. T.
D720.N3 1963   940.52   *LC* 63-4320

Sontag, Raymond James, 1897-1972.   • **3.866**
A broken world, 1919–1939, by Raymond J. Sontag. [1st ed.] New York, Harper & Row [1971] xviii, 415 p. illus., maps (on lining papers), ports. 23 cm. (Rise of modern Europe.) 1. Europe — History — 1918-1945 I. T. II. Series.
D720.S66 1971   940.5   *LC* 77-156572   *ISBN* 0060139544

Carsten, F. L. (Francis Ludwig)   **3.867**
The rise of fascism / F.L. Carsten. — 2d ed. — Berkeley: University of California Press, 1980, c1967. 279 p.; 23 cm. Includes index. 1. Fascism — Europe. 2. Europe — History — 20th century I. T.
D726.5.C35 1980   320.5/33/094 19   *LC* 80-51592   *ISBN* 0520043073

Fascism in Europe / edited by S.J. Woolf.   **3.868**
London; New York: Methuen, 1981. 408 p.; 23 cm. Rev. ed. of: European fascism. 1968. Includes index. 1. Fascism — Europe — History — Addresses, essays, lectures. I. Woolf, S. J. (Stuart Joseph) II. European fascism.
D726.5.F37 1981   335.6/094 19   *LC* 81-181035   *ISBN* 0416302300

Nolte, Ernst, 1923-.   • 3.869
[Faschismus in seiner Epoche. English] Three faces of fascism; Action Française Italian fascism, National Socialism. Translated from the German by Leila Vennewitz. [1st ed.] New York, Holt, Rinehart and Winston [1966, c1965] xi, 561 p. 24 cm. Translation of Der Faschismus in seiner Epoche. 1. Fascism — History. I. T.
D726.5.N613   320.533   LC 66-10262

Barros, James.   3.870
Betrayal from within: Joseph Avenol, Secretary–General of the League of Nations, 1933–1940. — New Haven: Yale University Press, 1969. xii, 289 p.: ports.; 25 cm. 1. Avenol, Joseph, 1879-1952. 2. League of Nations. 3. Europe — Politics and government — 1918-1945 I. T.
D727.B33   341.22/092/4 B   LC 75-81413

Chamberlain, Neville, 1869-1940.   • 3.871
In search of peace. — Freeport, N.Y.: Books for Libraries Press, [1971] viii, 309 p.: port.; 24 cm. — (Essay index reprint series) Reprint of the 1939 ed. 1. Peace — Addresses, essays, lectures. 2. Europe — Politics and government — 1918-1945 — Addresses, essays, lectures. 3. Great Britain — Foreign relations — 1936-1945 — Addresses, essays, lectures. I. T.
D727.C5 1971   942.084   LC 77-156627   ISBN 0836922743

Churchill, Winston, Sir, 1874-1965.   • 3.872
Step by step, 1936–1939. Freeport, N.Y., Books for Libraries Press [1971, c1939] xii, 323 p. port. 24 cm. (Essay index reprint series) 1. Europe — Politics and government — 1918-1945 — Addresses, essays, lectures. 2. Great Britain — Foreign relations — 1936-1945 — Addresses, essays, lectures. I. T.
D727.C54 1971   940.5/2   LC 72-156631   ISBN 0836923103

Craig, Gordon Alexander, 1913- ed.   • 3.873
The diplomats: 1919–1939. Princeton, Princeton University Press, 1953. x, 700 p. ports. 25 cm. 1. World politics I. Gilbert, Felix, 1905- joint ed. II. T.
D727.C7   LC 53-6378

Eubank, Keith.   • 3.874
Munich. [1st ed.] Norman, University of Oklahoma Press [1963] xiv, 322 p. illus., ports., maps. 24 cm. 1. Munich Four-Power Agreement (1938) 2. World War, 1939-1945 — Causes I. T.
D727.E9   LC 63-8987

Gatzke, Hans Wilhelm, 1915- comp.   3.875
European diplomacy between two wars, 1919–1939. Edited with an introd. by Hans W. Gatzke. — Chicago: Quadrangle Books, 1972. 277 p.; 22 cm. — (Modern scholarship on European history) 1. World War, 1939-1945 — Causes — Addresses, essays, lectures. 2. Europe — Politics and government — 1918-1945 — Addresses, essays, lectures. 3. Germany — Foreign relations — 1918-1933 — Addresses, essays, lectures. 4. Germany — Foreign relations — 1933-1945 — Addresses, essays, lectures. I. T.
D727.G38 1972   940.531/1   LC 71-158826   ISBN 0812901983

Maier, Charles S.   3.876
Recasting bourgeois Europe: stabilization in France, Germany, and Italy in the decade after World War I / Charles S. Maier. — Princeton, N.J.: Princeton University Press, [1975] xiv, 650 p.; 25 cm. Includes index. 1. Europe — Politics and government — 1918-1945 2. Europe — Economic conditions — 1918-1945 I. T.
D727.M236   320.9/4/051   LC 73-2488   ISBN 0691052204

Murray, Williamson.   3.877
The change in the European balance of power, 1938–1939: the path to ruin / Williamson Murray. — Princeton, N.J.: Princeton University Press, c1984. xix, 494 p.: ill.; 24 cm. Includes index. 1. Munich Four-Power Agreement (1938) 2. World War, 1939-1945 — Causes 3. Balance of power 4. Europe — Politics and government — 1918-1945 I. T.
D727.M87 1984   940.5/2 19   LC 83-43085   ISBN 0691054134

Robbins, Keith.   • 3.878
Munich 1938. London, Cassell, 1968. [10], 398 p. 16 plates, illus., 2 maps, ports. 22 cm. 1. Munich Four-Power Agreement (1938) 2. Czechoslovakia — History — 1918-1938 3. Germany — Foreign relations — 1933-1945 4. Europe — Politics and government — 1918-1945 I. T.
D727.R6   940.531/2   LC 68-108772   ISBN 0304931292

Salvemini, Gaetano, 1873-1957.   • 3.879
Prelude to World War II. London: Gollancz, 1953, c1951. 519 p.; 22 cm. Errata slip mounted on p. 15. 1. World politics 2. World War, 1939-1945 — Causes I. T.
D727.Sx   LC 54-1895

Taylor, Telford.   3.880
Munich: the price of peace / by Telford Taylor. — 1st ed. — Garden City, N.Y.: Doubleday, 1979. xvi, 1084 p., [16] leaves of plates: ill.; 24 cm. Includes index. 1. Munich Four-Power Agreement (1938) 2. World War, 1939-1945 — Causes I. T.
D727.T37 1979   940.53/12   LC 73-22794   ISBN 0385020538

D731–838 World War II (1939–1945)

United States. Department of State.   • 3.881
The Conferences at Malta and Yalta, 1945. Washington: U. S. Govt. Print. Off., 1955. lxxviii, 1032 p.: ill.; 24 cm. (Its Foreign relations of the United States: diplomatic papers) [U. S.] Dept. of State. Publication 6199. 'The compiling and professional editing of this volume were done by a special staff in the Historical Division of the Department of State, under the direction of the chief of the division. The technical editing was done by the Division of Publishing Services.' 1. Crimea Conference, Yalta, Russia, 1945. 2. World War, 1939-1945 — Documents, etc., sources. 3. Malta. Conference, 1945. I. T.
D734.A1 U555   LC 56-60328

Wilson, Theodore A., 1940-.   • 3.882
The first summit; Roosevelt and Churchill at Placentia Bay 1941 [by] Theodore A. Wilson. — Boston: Houghton Mifflin, 1969. xvi, 344 p.: illus., facsims., ports.; 22 cm. 1. Atlantic declaration, August 14, 1941. I. T.
D734.A8 W5   940.531/4   LC 69-15032

Feis, Herbert, 1893-1972.   • 3.883
Between war and peace; the Potsdam Conference. Princeton, N.J., Princeton University Press, 1960. viii, 367 p. maps. 24 cm. 'A continuation of the narrative in [the author's] Churchill-Roosevelt-Stalin.' 1. Potsdam Conference (1945) I. T.
D734.B4 1945ad   940.5314   LC 60-12230

Snell, John L. ed.   • 3.884
The meaning of Yalta; Big Three diplomacy and the new balance of power. With a foreword by Paul H. Clyde. — Baton Rouge, Louisiana State University Press [1956] xiii, 239 p. illus., maps. 23 cm. Bibliographical footnotes. 1. Crimea Conference, Yalta, Russia, 1945. 2. World War, 1939-1945 — Territorial questions 3. World politics — 1945- I. T.
D734.C7 1945j   940.531   LC 56-7960

Stettinius, Edward R. (Edward Reilly), 1900-1949.   • 3.885
Roosevelt and the Russians; the Yalta Conference. Edited by Walter Johnson. Westport, Conn., Greenwood Press [1970, c1949] xvi, 367 p. illus., facsims., group ports. 23 cm. 1. Roosevelt, Franklin D. (Franklin Delano), 1882-1945. 2. Yalta Conference (1945) I. T.
D734.C7 1970   940.531   LC 75-100179   ISBN 0837129761

Germany. Auswärtiges Amt.   • 3.886
Documents and materials relating to the eve of the Second World war. — New York: International Publishers [1948] 2 v.: facsims. Secret documents from the archives of the German Ministry of Foreign Affaires captured by the Soviet army in Berlin. 1. World War, 1939-1945 — Diplomatic history 2. Germany — Foreign relations — 1933-1945 I. Dirksen, Herbert von, 1882- II. T.
D735.G366 1948a   D735 G43 1978.   LC 49-7210   ISBN 0897120701

Soviet Union. Komissiia po izdaniiu diplomaticheskikh dokumentov.   • 3.887
Stalin's correspondence with Churchill, Attlee, Roosevelt, and Truman: 1941–45. New York, Dutton, 1958. 400, 301 p. 23 cm. Contains the 2 vols. as published in 1957 by the Foreign Languages Pub. House in Moscow under title: Correspondence between the Chairman of the Council of Ministers of the U.S.S.R. and the Presidents of the U.S.A. and the Prime Ministers of Great Britain during the Great Patriotic War of 1941-1945. Translated from Russian. (transliterated: PErepiska Predsedatelia Soveta Ministrov SSSR) 1. World War, 1939-1945 — Sources. I. Stalin, Joseph, 1879-1953. II. T.
D735.R87   940.532247   LC 63-1395

World War II, policy and strategy: selected documents with commentary / Hans–Adolf Jacobsen and Arthur L. Smith, Jr.   3.888
Santa Barbara, Calif.: Clio Books, c1979. xiii, 505 p.: ill.; 24 cm. 1. World War, 1939-1945 — Sources. I. Jacobsen, Hans Adolf. II. Smith, Arthur Lee, 1927-
D735.W65   940.53/1   LC 79-11507   ISBN 0874362911

Keegan, John, 1934-.   3.889
Who was who in World War II / edited by John Keegan. — New York: T. Y. Crowell, 1978. 224 p.: ill.; 31 cm. 'A Bison book.' 1. World War, 1939-1945 — Biography I. T.
D736.K43 1978   940.53/092/2   LC 77-95149   ISBN 0690017537

The Simon and Schuster encyclopedia of World War II / edited by Thomas Parrish, chief consultant editor, S. L. A. Marshall.   3.890
New York: Simon and Schuster, c1978. 767 p.: ill.; 29 cm. 'A Cord Communications book.' Includes index. 1. World War, 1939-1945 — Dictionaries. I. Parrish, Thomas (Thomas D.) II. Marshall, S. L. A. (Samuel Lyman Atwood), 1900-1977.
D740.S57   940.53/03   LC 78-9590   ISBN 0671242776

Snyder, Louis Leo, 1907-.   3.891
[Historical guide to World War II] Louis L. Snyder's Historical guide to World War II / Louis L. Snyder. — Westport, Conn.: Greenwood Press, 1982. xii, 838 p.; 24 cm. Includes index. 1. World War, 1939-1945 — Dictionaries. I. T.

II. Title: Historical guide to World War II. III. Title: Historical guide to World War Two.
D740.S65 1982   940.53/03/21 19   *LC* 81-13433   *ISBN* 0313232164

D741–742 CAUSES

Aster, Sidney, 1942-.   3.892
1939: the making of the Second World War. — New York: Simon and Schuster, [1974, c1973] 455 p.: illus.; 24 cm. 1. World War, 1939-1945 — Causes I. T.
D741.A75 1974   940.53/112   *LC* 73-13578   *ISBN* 0671216899

The Fascist challenge and the policy of appeasement / edited by   3.893
Wolfgang J. Mommsen and Lothar Kettenacker.
London; Boston: G. Allen & Unwin, 1983. xii, 436 p.; 25 cm. 1. World War, 1939-1945 — Causes — Addresses, essays, lectures. 2. Fascism — Addresses, essays, lectures. 3. World politics — 1933-1945 — Addresses, essays, lectures. 4. Europe — Foreign relations — 1918-1945 — Addresses, essays, lectures. 5. Europe — Politics and government — 1918-1945 — Addresses, essays, lectures. I. Mommsen, Wolfgang J., 1930- II. Kettenacker, Lothar.
D741.F37 1983   940.53/1 19   *LC* 83-3759   *ISBN* 0049400681

Taylor, A. J. P. (Alan John Percivale), 1906-.   • 3.894
The origins of the Second World War / A.J.P. Taylor. — London: Hamilton, 1962, [c1961] 296 p.: ill.; 22 cm. 1. World War, 1939-1945 — Causes I. T.
D741.T34 1962   *LC* 62-7543

Watt, Donald Cameron.   3.895
Too serious a business: European armed forces and the approach to the Second World War / Donald Cameron Watt. — Berkeley: University of California Press, 1975. 200 p.; 23 cm. Based on lectures delivered at Cambridge University, 1973. Includes index. 1. World War, 1939-1945 — Causes 2. Europe — Politics and government — 1918-1945 3. Europe — Armed Forces. I. T.
D741.W37   940.53/11   *LC* 74-82853   *ISBN* 0520028295

Churchill, Winston, Sir, 1874-1965.   • 3.896
War speeches. Compiled by Charles Eade. Boston: Houghton, Mifflin, 1953. 3 v. 26 cm. 1. World War, 1939-1945 — Addresses, sermons, etc. 2. World War, 1939-1945 — Great Britain. I. T.
D742.G7 C5594   940.5304   *LC* 53-553

Patton, George S. (George Smith), 1885-1945.   • 3.897
War as I knew it / George S. Patton, Jr.; annotated by Colonel Paul D. Harkins; edited by Beatrice Ayer Patton. — Boston: Houghton Mifflin, c1947. xix, 425 p.: ill., maps. 1. World War, 1939-1945 — Personal narratives, American. 2. World War, 1939-1945 — Campaigns — Africa, North 3. World War, 1939-1945 — Campaigns — Western I. Harkins, Paul Donal, 1904- II. T.
D742P3   940.542   *ISBN* 0395080746

Melosi, Martin V., 1947-.   3.898
The shadow of Pearl Harbor: political controversy over the surprise attack, 1941–1946 / by Martin V. Melosi. — 1st ed. — College Station: Texas A & M University Press, c1977. 183 p.; 24 cm. Includes index. 1. World War, 1939-1945 — Causes 2. World War, 1939-1945 — United States. 3. Pearl Harbor (Hawaii), Attack on, 1941 4. United States — Politics and government — 1933-1945 I. T.
D742.U5 M44   940.53/75   *LC* 77-23578   *ISBN* 0890960313

D743–745 GENERAL WORKS

Bryant, Arthur, Sir, 1899-.   • 3.899
Triumph in the west; a history of the war years based on the diaries of Field–Marshal Lord Alanbrooke, chief of the Imperial General Staff. [1st ed.] Garden City, N. Y.: Doubleday, 1959. xviii, 438 p.: maps.; 24 cm. 1. World War, 1939-1945 I. Alanbrooke, Alan Francis Brooke, Viscount, 1883- II. T.
D743.B73   *LC* 59-13960

Calvocoressi, Peter, 1921-.   3.900
Total war: causes and courses of the Second World War. — 2nd ed. / Peter Calvocoressi, Guy Wint, John Pritchard. — London: Viking, 1987. [264] p.: ill. 1. World War, 1939-1945 I. Wint, Guy. II. Pritchard, John, 19—— III. T.
D743.C24 1987   940.53 19   *ISBN* 0670807958

Churchill, Winston, Sir, 1874-1965.   • 3.901
The Second World War. Boston, Published in association with the Cooperation Pub. Co. [by] Houghton Mifflin, 1948-53. 6 v. illus., maps. 22 cm. 1. World War, 1939-1945 2. World War, 1939-1945 — Great Britain. I. T.
D743.C47   *LC* 48-2880

Eisenhower, Dwight D. (Dwight David), 1890-1969.   • 3.902
Crusade in Europe. Garden city, N.Y., Garden City Books [1952] 573 p. illus., maps.; 19 cm. I. T.
D743.E35 1952

Fuller, J. F. C. (John Frederick Charles), 1878-1966.   • 3.903
The Second World War, 1939–45: a strategical and tactical history, by J. F. C. Fuller. New York, Meredith Press [1968] 431 p. illus., maps, plans. 22 cm. First published 1948; 3d impression (with revisions) 1954; 3d printing, 1968. 1. World War, 1939-1945 — Campaigns I. T.
D743.F85 1968   940.541   *LC* 70-2043

Greenfield, Kent Roberts, 1893-1967.   • 3.904
American strategy in World War II: a reconsideration. Baltimore, Johns Hopkins Press, 1963. viii, 145 p. 22 cm. 'Based on the tenth series of J. P. Young lectures in American history ... at Memphis State University on October 28-30, 1962.' Bibliographical references included in 'Notes' (p. 122-137) 1. World War, 1939-1945 2. Strategy I. T.
D743.G666   940.54012   *LC* 63-19554

Jacobsen, Hans Adolf. ed.   • 3.905
[Entscheidungsschlachten des zweiten Weltkrieges. English] Decisive battles of World War II; the German view. Edited by H. A. Jacobsen and J. Rohwer. Introd. by Cyril Falls. Translated from the German by Edward Fitzgerald. [1st American ed.] New York, Putnam [1965] 509 p. illus., maps, group ports. 24 cm. 1. World War, 1939-1945 I. Rohwer, Jürgen. joint ed. II. T.
D743.J313 1965   940.54   *LC* 64-13541

Jones, James, 1921-1977.   3.906
WW II / James Jones; graphics direction Art Weithas. — New York: Grosset & Dunlap, c1975. 272 p.: ill.; 32 cm. Includes index. 1. Jones, James, 1921-1977. 2. World War, 1939-1945 3. World War, 1939-1945 — Art and the war 4. World War, 1939-1945 — Personal narratives, American. I. T.
D743.J65   940.53/73   *LC* 74-27944   *ISBN* 0448118963

Liddell Hart, Basil Henry, Sir, 1895-1970.   • 3.907
History of the Second World War. — [1st American ed.]. — New York: Putnam, [1971, c1970] xvi, 768 p.: maps.; 25 cm. 1. World War, 1939-1945 I. T.
D743.L514 1971   940.53   *LC* 79-136796

Michel, Henri, 1907-.   3.908
The second world war. Translated by Douglas Parmee. — New York: Praeger, [1975] xxii, 947 p.: ill., maps; 24 cm. — Translation of La seconde guerre mondiale. 1. World War, 1939-1945 I. T.
D743.M4913   940.53   *LC* 70-134534

Morison, Samuel Eliot, 1887-1976.   • 3.909
Strategy and compromise / Samuel Eliot Morison. — Boston: Little, Brown, 1958. 120 p. 1. World War, 1939-1945 — Campaigns I. T.
D743.M74   *LC* 58-6030

Command decisions / edited with introductory essay by Kent   3.910
Roberts Greenfield; the authors: Martin Blumenson [et al.]
Washington, D.C.: G.P.O., 1960. viii, 565 p. 20 maps (part fold., part col., 1 in pocket) 24 cm. Bibliographical references. 1. World War, 1939-1945 — Campaigns I. Greenfield, Kent Roberts, 1893-1967. ed. II. United States. Dept. of the Army. Office of Military History.
D743.U44 1960   940.542   *LC* 59-60007

United States. War Dept.   • 3.911
Prelude to invasion: an account based upon official reports / by Henry L. Stimson, Secretary of War; [M. B. Schnapper, editor]. — [Washington]: Public Affairs Press, [1944] iii, 332 p.: ill.; 22 cm. 1. World War, 1939-1945 — Chronology. 2. World War, 1939-1945 — United States. I. Stimson, Henry Lewis, 1867-1950. II. Schnapper, Morris Bartel, 1912- ed. III. American Council on Public Affairs. IV. T.
D743.U5   940.53/73   *LC* 74-15218   *ISBN* 0837178150

Wedemeyer, Albert C. (Albert Coady), 1896-.   • 3.912
Wedemeyer reports!. — [1st ed.]. — New York: Holt, [1958] 497 p.: illus.; 22 cm. 1. World War, 1939-1945 I. T.
D743.W4   940.53   *LC* 58-14458

Wright, Gordon, 1912-.   • 3.913
The ordeal of total war, 1939–1945. — [1st ed.]. — New York: Harper & Row, 1968. xv, 315 p.: ill., maps, ports.; 22 cm. — (Rise of modern Europe. 20) 1. World War, 1939-1945 2. Europe — History — 1918-1945 I. T. II. Series.
D743.W7x   940.53   *LC* 68-28221

Cruickshank, Charles Greig.   3.914
Deception in World War II / Charles Cruickshank. — Oxford; New York: Oxford University Press, 1979. 248 p., [8] leaves of plates: ill.; 22 cm. Includes index. 1. World War, 1939-1945 — Campaigns 2. Strategy 3. Deception I. T.
D744.C77   940.54/1   *LC* 79-40615   *ISBN* 019215849X

Higgins, Trumbull.   • 3.915
Winston Churchill and the second front, 1940–1943. New York, Oxford University Press, 1957. 281 p. 22 cm. 1. Churchill, Winston, Sir, 1874-1965.

2. World War, 1939-1945 — Campaigns 3. Strategy I. T. II. Title: Second front.
D744.H5 *LC* 57-10388

Mauldin, Bill, 1921-. • **3.916**
Up front. Text and pictures by Bill Mauldin. Foreword by David Halberstam. New York, Norton [1968] x, 228 p. illus. 25 cm. Reprint of the 1945 ed. with a new introduction. 1. World War, 1939-1945 — Caricatures and cartoons I. T.
D745.2.M34 1968   741.5973   *LC* 68-24264

D748–754 DIPLOMATIC HISTORY

Douglas, Roy, 1924-. **3.917**
From war to cold war, 1942–48 / Roy Douglas. — New York: St. Martin's Press, 1981. 224 p., [4] leaves of plates: ill.; 23 cm. Includes index. 1. World War, 1939-1945 — Diplomatic history 2. World politics — 1945-1955 3. United States — Foreign relations — Russia. 4. Russia — Foreign relations — United States. I. T.
D748.D68 1981   940.53/2 19   *LC* 80-27270   *ISBN* 0312308620

Douglas, Roy, 1924-. **3.918**
New alliances, 1940–41 / Roy Douglas. — New York: St. Martin's Press, 1982. 154 p., [8] p. of plates: ill.; 23 cm. Includes index. 1. World War, 1939-1945 — Diplomatic history I. T.
D748.D69 1982   940.53/2 19   *LC* 81-9283   *ISBN* 0312564813

Eisenhower, John S. D., 1922-. **3.919**
Allies, Pearl Harbor to D–Day / John S.D. Eisenhower. — 1st ed. — Garden City, N.Y.: Doubleday, 1982. xxv, 500 p., [32] p. of plates: ill.; 25 cm. Includes index. 1. World War, 1939-1945 — Diplomatic history I. T.
D748.E57 1982   940.53/2 19   *LC* 77-16914   *ISBN* 0385114796

Feis, Herbert, 1893-1972. • **3.920**
Churchill, Roosevelt, Stalin; the war they waged and the peace they sought. — Princeton, N.J.: Princeton University Press, 1957. xi, 692 p.: maps.; 24 cm. 1. World War, 1939-1945 — Diplomatic history I. T.
D748.F4   940.5322   *LC* 57-5470

Smith, Bradley F. **3.921**
Operation Sunrise: the secret surrender / by Bradley F. Smith and Elena Agarossi. — New York: Basic Books, c1979. 234 p., [4] leaves of plates: ill.; 24 cm. Includes index. 1. Operation Sunrise 2. World War, 1939-1945 — Diplomatic history I. Aga Rossi, Elena. joint author. II. T.
D748.S55   940.54/21   *LC* 78-73767   *ISBN* 0465052908

Wheeler-Bennett, John Wheeler, Sir, 1902-1975. **3.922**
The semblance of peace: the political settlement after the Second World War / by John Wheeler–Bennett and Anthony Nicholls. — [New York]: St. Martin's Press, [1972] xiv, 878 p.: ill.; 25 cm. 1. World War, 1939-1945 — Diplomatic history 2. World War, 1939-1945 — Peace I. Nicholls, Anthony James, 1934- joint author. II. T.
D748.W47 1972b   940.53/14   *LC* 72-79783   *ISBN* 0333043022

Eubank, Keith. **3.923**
Summit at Teheran / Keith Eubank. — 1st ed. — New York: W. Morrow, c1985. 528 p.: ill.; 24 cm. Includes index. 1. Teheran Conference (1943) 2. World War, 1939-1945 — Diplomatic history I. T.
D749.E82 1985   940.53/2 19   *LC* 84-25538   *ISBN* 0688043364

Sainsbury, Keith. **3.924**
The turning point: Roosevelt, Stalin, Churchill, and Chiang–Kai–Shek, 1943: the Moscow, Cairo, and Teheran conferences / Keith Sainsbury. — Oxford: Oxford University Press, 1985. 373 p.; 22 cm. Includes index. 1. Moscow Conference (1943) 2. Cairo Conference (1943) 3. Teheran Conference (1943) 4. World War, 1939-1945 — Diplomatic history I. T.
D749.S25 1985   940.53/2 19   *LC* 84-12237   *ISBN* 0192158589

D750–754 By Country

Henderson, Nevile, Sir, 1882-1942. • **3.925**
Failure of a mission; Berlin 1937–1939, by the Right Honorable Sir Nevile Henderson. New York, G. P. Putnam's sons [c1940] xi, 334 p. front. (port.) 22 cm. 1. Henderson, Nevile, Sir, 1882-1942. 2. World War, 1939-1945 — Diplomatic history 3. World War, 1939-1945 — Personal narratives, English. 4. World War, 1939-1945 — Germany. 5. Great Britain — Foreign relations — Germany 6. Germany — Foreign relations — Great Britain. I. T.
D750.H4   940.531   *LC* 40-27393

Kersaudy, François, 1948-. **3.926**
Churchill and De Gaulle / François Kersaudy. — 1st American ed. — New York: Atheneum, 1982, c1981. 476 p., [8] p. of plates: ill.; 24 cm. Includes index. 1. Churchill, Winston, Sir, 1874-1965. 2. Gaulle, Charles de, 1890-1970. 3. World War, 1939-1945 — Diplomatic history 4. Prime ministers — Great Britain — Biography. 5. France — Foreign relations —

Great Britain. 6. Great Britain — Foreign relations — France. 7. France — Presidents — Biography. I. T.
D750.K47 1982   940.53/22/41 19   *LC* 81-69154   *ISBN* 0689112653

Parkinson, Roger. **3.927**
Blood, toil, tears and sweat; the war history from Dunkirk to Alamein, based on the War Cabinet papers of 1940 to 1942. — [1st American ed.]. — New York: D. McKay Co., [1973] x, 538 p.: illus.; 22 cm. 1. World War, 1939-1945 — Diplomatic history 2. World War, 1939-1945 — Great Britain. 3. Great Britain — Foreign relations — 1936-1945 I. T.
D750.P36 1973   940.53/22/42   *LC* 73-77296

Parkinson, Roger. **3.928**
A day's march nearer home; the war history from Alamein to VE Day based on the War Cabinet papers of 1942 to 1945. — [1st American ed.]. — New York: D. McKay Co., [1974] xxiv, 551 p.: maps.; 22 cm. 1. World War, 1939-1945 — Diplomatic history 2. World War, 1939-1945 — Great Britain. 3. Great Britain — Foreign relations — 1936-1945 I. T.
D750.P364 1974b   940.53/2   *LC* 74-78663   *ISBN* 0679504710

Reynolds, David, 1952-. **3.929**
The creation of the Anglo–American alliance, 1937–41: a study in competitive co-operation / David Reynolds. — Chapel Hill: University of North Carolina Press, 1982, c1981. xiii, 397 p.; 25 cm. Based on the author's thesis (Ph.D.) Includes index. 1. World War, 1939-1945 — Diplomatic history 2. Great Britain — Foreign relations — United States. 3. United States — Foreign relations — Great Britain. 4. Great Britain — Foreign relations — 1936-1945 I. T.
D750.R48 1982   940.53/22/41 19   *LC* 81-16503   *ISBN* 0807815071

Woodward, E. L. (Ernest Llewellyn), Sir, 1890-. • **3.930**
British foreign policy in the Second World War, by Sir Llewellyn Woodward. London, H.M.S.O., 1970-. v. 26 cm. (History of the Second World War.) 1. World War, 1939-1945 — Diplomatic history 2. Great Britain — Foreign relations — 1936-1945 I. T. II. Series.
D750.W62   940.532/2/42   *LC* 70-143172   *ISBN* 0116300523

Divine, Robert A. comp. • **3.931**
Causes and consequences of World War II / edited with an introd. by Robert A. Divine. — Chicago: Quadrangle Books, 1969. 375 p.; 22 cm. 1. World War, 1939-1945 — Diplomatic history — Addresses, essays, lectures. 2. World War, 1939-1945 — U.S. — Addresses, essays, lectures. I. T.
D753.D56   940.532/2/73   *LC* 71-78305

Divine, Robert A. • **3.932**
The reluctant belligerent; American entry into World War II [by] Robert A. Divine. — New York: Wiley, [1965] xi, 172 p.: maps.; 22 cm. — (America in crisis.) 1. World War, 1939-1945 — Causes 2. World War, 1939-1945 — United States. 3. United States — Foreign relations — 1933-1945 I. T. II. Series.
D753.D57   940.5373   *LC* 65-14618

Feis, Herbert, 1893-1972. • **3.933**
The road to Pearl Harbor; the coming of the war between the United States and Japan. — Princeton: Princeton University Press, 1950. xii, 356 p.: fold. map.; 25 cm. 1. World War, 1939-1945 — United States. 2. World War, 1939-1945 — Japan. 3. United States — Foreign relations — Japan 4. Japan — Foreign relations — United States I. T.
D753.F4   940.532273   *LC* 50-9585

Harriman, W. Averell (William Averell), 1891-1986. **3.934**
Special envoy to Churchill and Stalin, 1941–1946 / by W. Averell Harriman and Elie Abel. — 1st ed. — New York: Random House, c1975. xii, 595 p., [8] leaves of plates: ill.; 24 cm. 1. Harriman, W. Averell (William Averell), 1891-1986. 2. World War, 1939-1945 — Diplomatic history 3. World War, 1939-1945 — United States. 4. Statesmen — United States — Biography. 5. United States — Foreign relations — 1933-1945 I. Abel, Elie. joint author. II. T.
D753.H28   940.53/2   *LC* 75-10275   *ISBN* 0394482964

Kimball, Warren F. • **3.935**
The most unsordid act; lend–lease, 1939–1941 [by] Warren F. Kimball. — Baltimore: Johns Hopkins Press, [1969] ix, 281 p.; 24 cm. 1. Lend-lease operations (1941-1945) 2. U.S. — Politics and government — 1933-1945. I. T.
D753.K5   320.9/73   *LC* 69-14712   *ISBN* 0801810175

Langer, William L. (William Leonard), 1896-1977. • **3.936**
Our Vichy gamble, by William L. Langer. Hamden, Conn., Archon Books, 1965, c1947. ix, 412, xi p. 22 cm. 'The Murphy-Weygand accord': p. 399-401. 'Text of the protocols signed at Paris May 27-28, 1941': p. 402-412. 1. World War, 1939-1945 — Diplomatic history 2. World War, 1939-1945 — United States. 3. United States — Foreign relations — France 4. France — Foreign relations — United States I. T.
D753.L25 1965   *LC* 65-15013

Lash, Joseph P., 1909-.   **3.937**
Roosevelt and Churchill, 1939–1941: the partnership that saved the West /
Joseph P. Lash. — 1st trade ed. — New York: Norton, c1976. 528 p., [8] leaves
of plates: ill.; 24 cm. Includes index. 1. Roosevelt, Franklin D. (Franklin
Delano), 1882-1945. 2. Churchill, Winston, Sir, 1874-1965. 3. World War,
1939-1945 — Diplomatic history 4. World War, 1939-1945 — United States.
5. World War, 1939-1945 — Great Britain. I. T.
D753.L27 1976   940.53/2   LC 76-18276   ISBN 0393055949

Sherwin, Martin J.   **3.938**
A world destroyed: the atomic bomb and the Grand Alliance / Martin J.
Sherwin. — 1st ed. — New York: Knopf: distributed by Random House, 1975.
xvi, 315, xi p.; 24 cm. Includes index. 1. World War, 1939-1945 — Diplomatic
history 2. World War, 1939-1945 — United States. 3. Atomic bomb —
History. 4. United States — Foreign relations — 1933-1945 I. T.
D753.S48 1975   940.53/2   LC 75-8213   ISBN 0394497945

Smith, Gaddis.   • **3.939**
American diplomacy during the second World War, 1941–1945. New York,
Wiley [1965] ix, 194 p. maps. 22 cm. (America in crisis.) 1. World War,
1939-1945 — Diplomatic history 2. United States — Foreign relations —
1933-1945 I. T. II. Series.
D753.S54   940.532 19   LC 64-8713

Steele, Richard W.   **3.940**
The first offensive 1942; Roosevelt, Marshall and the making of American
strategy [by] Richard W. Steele. — Bloomington: Indiana University Press,
[1973] ix, 239 p.; 24 cm. 1. World War, 1939-1945 — United States. I. T.
D753.S73   940.53/73   LC 73-75792   ISBN 0253322154

Stenehjem, Michele Flynn.   **3.941**
An American first: John T. Flynn and the America First Committee / Michele
Flynn Stenehjem. — New Rochelle, N.Y.: Arlington House Publishers, c1976.
250 p.; 24 cm. Includes index. 1. Flynn, John Thomas, 1883-1964. 2. America
First Committee. 3. World War, 1939-1945 — United States. 4. United States
— Neutrality I. T.
D753.S74   322.4   LC 75-37622   ISBN 0870003399

Martel, Leon.   **3.942**
Lend–lease, loans, and the coming of the Cold War: a study of the
implementation of foreign policy / Leon Martel. — Boulder, Colo.: Westview
Press, 1979. xix, 304 p.; 24 cm. — (Westview special studies in international
relations) Includes index. 1. Lend-lease operations (1941-1945) 2. World War,
1939-1945 — Influence 3. Russia — Foreign relations — United States.
4. United States — Foreign relations — Russia. I. T.
D753.2.R9 M37   327.73/047   LC 79-13678   ISBN 0891584536

McCann, Frank D.   **3.943**
The Brazilian–American alliance, 1937–1945 [by] Frank D. McCann, Jr. —
[Princeton, N.J.]: Princeton University Press, [1974, c1973] xiv, 527 p.: maps.;
23 cm. 1. World War, 1939-1945 — Diplomatic history 2. Brazil — Foreign
relations — United States. 3. United States — Foreign relations — Brazil.
4. Brazil — Politics and government — 1930-1954 I. T.
D754.B8 M3   327.73/081   LC 72-14030   ISBN 0691056552

Carroll, Joseph T.   **3.944**
Ireland in the war years / Joseph T. Carroll. — Newton Abbot: David and
Charles; New York: Crane, Russak & Co., 1975. 190 p., [8] p. of plates: ill.,
ports.; 23 cm. Includes index. 1. De Valera, Eamonn, 1882-1975. 2. World
War, 1939-1945 — Ireland. 3. Ireland — Neutrality. 4. Ireland — History —
1922- I. T.
D754.I5 C37 1975   940.53/417   LC 74-16547   ISBN 0844805653

Ike, Nobutaka. ed.   **3.945**
Japan's decision for war; records of the 1941 policy conferences. Translated,
edited, and with an introd. by Nobutaka Ike. — Stanford, Calif., Stanford
University Press, 1967. xxx, 306 p. map. 24 cm. 'Bibliographical note': p.
[297]-298. 1. World War, 1939-1945 — Japan. 2. Japan — Hist. — Showa
period — 1926- — Sources. I. T.
D754.J3I4   940.5352   LC 67-13659

Humphreys, R. A. (Robert Arthur), 1907-.   **3.946**
Latin America and the Second World War / by R.A. Humphreys. — London:
Published for the Institute of Latin American Studies, University of London
[by] Athlone; [Atlantic Highlands], N.J.: Distributor for U.S.A., Humanities
Press, 1982 (c1981). 232 p. (Institute of Latin American Studies monographs.
0776-0846; 10.) 1. World War, 1939-1945 — Latin America. 2. Latin America
— History — 1898-1948 I. University of London. Institute of Latin American
Studies. II. T. III. Series.
D754.L29 H85   980/.033 19   LC 81-166643   ISBN 0485177102

Weinberg, Gerhard L.   • **3.947**
Germany and the Soviet Union 1939–1941, by Gerhard L. Weinberg. Leiden,
E. J. Brill, 1972. vii, 218 p. 25 cm. (Studies in east European history, 1) Imprint
covered by label: Distributed in the U.S.A. by Humanities Press, New York.
Reprint of the 1954 edition. 1. World War, 1939-1945 — Diplomatic history

2. Soviet Union — Foreign relations — Germany. 3. Germany — Foreign
relations — Soviet Union. I. T. II. Series.
D754.R9 W4 1972   940.53/2   LC 72-196908

Scandinavia during the Second World War / edited by Henrik   **3.948**
S. Nissen; translated by Thomas Munch–Petersen.
Minneapolis: University of Minnesota Press; Oslo: Universitetsforlaget, c1983.
x, 407 p.: ill.; 24 cm. — (Nordic series. v. 9) Includes index. 1. World War,
1939-1945 — Scandinavia — Addresses, essays, lectures. 2. World War,
1939-1945 — Finland — Addresses, essays, lectures. 3. Scandinavia — History
— 20th century — Addresses, essays, lectures. 4. Finland — History —
1917-1945 — Addresses, essays, lectures. I. Nissen, Henrik S. II. Series.
D754.S29 S27 1983   940.53/48 19   LC 82-2779   ISBN 0816611106

Roberts, Walter R., 1916-.   **3.949**
Tito, Mihailović, and the Allies, 1941–1945 [by] Walter R. Roberts. New
Brunswick, N.J., Rutgers University Press [1973] xv, 406 p. illus. 26 cm.
1. Tito, Josip Broz, 1892-1980. 2. Mihailović, Draža, 1893-1946. 3. World
War, 1939-1945 — Yugoslavia. 4. World War, 1939-1945 — Diplomatic
history I. T.
D754.Y9 R6   940.53/497   LC 72-4197   ISBN 0813507405

Beaufre, André.   • **3.950**
[Drame de 1940. English] 1940; the fall of France. Translated from the French
by Desmond Flower. With a pref. by Sir Basil Liddell Hart. [1st American ed.]
New York, Knopf, 1968 [c1967] xxi, 215, xii p. maps. 22 cm. Translation of Le
drame de 1940. 1. World War, 1939-1945 — Personal narratives, French.
2. World War, 1939-1945 — France I. T.
D755.1.B813 1968   944.081/0924   LC 67-18628

Douglas, Roy, 1924-.   **3.951**
The advent of war, 1939–40 / Roy Douglas. — New York: St. Martin's Press,
1979, c1978. xiii, 167 p., [5] leaves of plates: ill.; 23 cm. Includes index.
1. World War, 1939-1945 I. T.
D755.1.D68 1979   940.53   LC 78-12266   ISBN 0312006500

D756–769 MILITARY OPERATIONS

D756–763 Western Europe

Bradley, Omar Nelson, 1893-1981.   • **3.952**
A soldier's story. — [1st ed.]. — New York: Holt, [1951] xix, 618 p.: illus.,
ports., maps.; 22 cm. 1. Bradley, Omar Nelson, 1893-1981. 2. World War,
1939-1945 — Campaigns — Western 3. World War, 1939-1945 — Personal
narratives, American. I. T.
D756.B7   940.542   LC 51-11294

Ellis, Lionel Frederic, 1885-.   • **3.953**
Victory in the West / by Major L.F. Ellis. — London: Her Majesty's Stationery
Office, 1962-68. 2v.: ill., maps (part fold., some col.) — (History of the Second
World War: United Kingdom Military Series) 1. World War, 1939-1945 —
Campaigns — Western 2. World War, 1939-1945 — Campaigns —
Normandy. I. T. II. Series.
D756.E39   LC 63-1156

Ellis, L.F. (Lionel Frederic), 1885-.   **3.954**
The war in France and Flanders, 1939–1940 / by L.F. Ellis. — London: H.M.
Stationery Off., 1953. — xviii, 425 p.: ill., maps, ports.; 25 cm. — (History of the
Second World War. United Kingdom military series) 1. World War,
1939-1945 — Campaigns — France 2. World War, 1939-1945 — Campaigns
— Belgium I. T. II. Series.
D756.E4   940.5421   940.95   LC 54-1808

MacDonald, Charles Brown, 1922-.   • **3.955**
The mighty endeavor; American armed forces in the European theater in World
War II [by] Charles B. MacDonald. New York, Oxford University Press, 1969.
564 p. illus., maps, ports. 24 cm. 1. World War, 1939-1945 — Campaigns —
Western 2. World War, 1939-1945 — United States. 3. United States —
History — 1933-1945 I. T.
D756.M27   940.542/1   LC 70-83047

Wilmot, Chester.   • **3.956**
The struggle for Europe. — Westport, Conn.: Greenwood Press, [1972, c1952]
766 p.: maps.; 23 cm. 1. World War, 1939-1945 — Campaigns — Western
I. T.
D756.W53 1972   940.53   LC 75-138138   ISBN 0837157110

Eisenhower, John S. D., 1922-.   • **3.957**
The bitter woods: the dramatic story, told at all echelons, from supreme
command to squad leader, of the crisis that shook the Western coalition:
Hitler's surprise Ardennes offensives / by John D. Eisenhower. — New York:
Putnam, [1969] 506 p.: illus., plans, ports.; 25 cm. 1. Ardennes, Battle of the,
1944-1945 I. T.
D756.5.A7 E4   940.542/1   LC 68-15504

Mason, Francis K. **3.958**
Battle over Britain; a history of the German air assaults on Great Britain, 1917–18 and July–December 1940, and of the development of Britain's air defences between the World Wars [by] Francis K. Mason. German research material edited by Martin Windrow. Colour and tone illus. by Michael P. Roffe. Garden City, N.Y., Doubleday [1970, c1969] 636 p. illus. (part col.), maps, ports. 25 cm. 1. Great Britain. Royal Air Force. 2. Britain, Battle of, 1940 3. World War, 1939–1945 — Aerial operations, German. 4. World War, 1914–1918 — Aerial operations, German. I. Windrow, Martin. ed. II. T.
D756.5.B7 M3 1970   940.54/21   LC 75-91103

Taylor, Telford. • **3.959**
The breaking wave; the Second World War in the summer of 1940. — New York: Simon and Schuster, [1967] ix, 378 p.: illus. (incl. ports.) maps (part fold.); 24 cm. 1. Germany. Wehrmacht. 2. Britain, Battle of, 1940 I. T.
D756.5.B7 T3   940.542/1   LC 66-20249

Bennett, Ralph Francis. **3.960**
Ultra in the West: the Normandy campaign, 1944–45 / Ralph Bennett. — 1st U.S. ed. — New York: Scribner, 1980, c1979. xvi, 336 p.: ill.; 22 cm. Includes index. 1. World War, 1939–1945 — Campaigns — France — Normandy 2. World War, 1939–1945 — Cryptography 3. World War, 1939–1945 — Secret service — Great Britain 4. Normandy (France) — History I. T.
D756.5.N6 B44 1980   940.54/21 19   LC 80-50912   ISBN 0684167042

Ryan, Cornelius. • **3.961**
The longest day: June 6, 1944. New York, Simon and Schuster, 1959. 350 p. illus., ports., col. maps (on lining papers) 24 cm. 1. World War, 1939–1945 — Campaigns — France — Normandy I. T.
D756.5.N6 R9   940.5421   LC 59-9499

Tute, Warren. **3.962**
D–day [by] Warren Tute, John Costello [and] Terry Hughes . — London: Sidgwick & Jackson, [1974] 256 p.: ill. 1. World War, 1939–1945 — Campaigns — Normandy. I. Hughes, Terry. joint author. II. Costello, John. joint author. III. T.
D756.5.N6 T84   D756.5 N6 T88.   940.54/21   LC 73-19973   ISBN 028398144X

D757 Germany

Germany. Wehrmacht. Oberkommando. • **3.963**
Hitler directs his war; the secret records of his daily military conferences, selected and annotated by Felix Gilbert, from the manuscript in the University of Pennsylvania Library. New York, Oxford University Press, 1950. xxxiii, 187 p. maps. 21 cm. Bibliography: p. [181] 1. World War, 1939–1945 — Germany. I. Hitler, Adolf, 1889–1945. II. Gilbert, Felix, 1905- ed. III. T.
D757.A5 1950   940.5401343   LC 50-10858

Cecil, Robert, 1913-. **3.964**
Hitler's decision to invade Russia, 1941 / [by] Robert Cecil. — 1st American ed. — New York: David McKay, 1976, c1975. 192 p.: map; 23 cm. — (The Politics and strategy of the Second World War) Includes index. 1. World War, 1939–1945 — Germany. 2. Strategy 3. World War, 1939–1945 — Campaigns — Russia. I. T. II. Series.
D757.C36 1976   940.53/47   LC 76-43120   ISBN 0679507159

Guderian, Heinz, 1888-1954. • **3.965**
Panzer leader. Foreword by B.H. Liddell Hart. Translated from the German by Constantine Fitzgibbon. New York, Dutton, 1952. 528 p. illus. 24 cm. Translation of Erinnerungen eines Soldaten. 1. World War, — 1939–1945 — Germany. 2. World War, — 1949–1945 — Personal narratives, — German. I. T.
D757.G813   940.5343 943.086*   LC 52-7787

Irving, David John Cawdell, 1938-. **3.966**
Hitler's war / David Irving. New York: Viking Press, 1977. xxxiii, 926 p.: maps (on lining papers); 25 cm. Includes index. 1. Hitler, Adolf, 1889–1945. 2. World War, 1939–1945 — Germany. 3. Heads of state — Germany — Biography. I. T.
D757.I69 1977   940.54/0943   LC 76-18195   ISBN 0670374121

Liddell Hart, Basil Henry, Sir, 1895-1970. • **3.967**
The German generals talk / B.H. Liddell Hart. — New York: W. Morrow, 1948. xi, 308 p.: maps.; 21 cm. — 1. World War, 1939–1945 — Campaigns 2. World War, 1939–1945 — Germany. 3. Generals — Germany. I. Liddell Hart, Basil Henry, Sir, 1895-1970. Other side of the hill. II. T. III. Title: The other side of the hill.
D757.L5 1948a   940.5343   LC 48-4499

Manstein, Erich von, 1887-1973. **3.968**
[Verlorene Siege. English] Lost victories / by Erich von Manstein; edited and translated by Anthony G. Powell; foreword by B.H. Liddell Hart; introduction to this edition by Martin Blumenson. — Novato, Calif.: Presidio, 1982, c1958.

574 p., [4] leaves of plates: ill.; 22 cm. Translation of: Verlorene Siege. Reprint. Originally published: Chicago: H. Regency Co., 1958. With new introd. Includes index. 1. Hitler, Adolf, 1889-1945. 2. Manstein, Erich von, 1887-1973. 3. World War, 1939–1945 — Germany. 4. World War, 1939–1945 — Campaigns 5. Strategy 6. World War, 1939–1945 — Personal narratives, German. 7. Germany — History — 1933-1945 I. T.
D757.M3213 1982   940.54/013 19   LC 82-3779   ISBN 0891411305

Mellenthin, F. W. von (Friedrich Wilhelm), 1904-. **3.969**
Panzer battles: a study of the employment of armor in the Second World War / F. W. von Mellenthin; translated by H. Betzler; edited by L. C. F. Turner. — Norman: University of Oklahoma Press, 1956. xx, 383 p., 26 p. of plates (some folded): ill., maps, ports.; 24 cm. Includes index. 1. Germany. Heer. Artillerie. 2. World War, 1939–1945 — Campaigns 3. Artillery — Germany. 4. Tank warfare 5. World War, 1939–1945 — Personal narratives, German. I. T.
D757.M372   940.542   LC 56-5997

Speidel, Hans, 1897-. • **3.970**
[Invasion 1944. English] Invasion 1944: Rommel and the Normandy campaign / introd. by Truman Smith. — Westport, Conn.: Greenwood Press [1971, c1950] xiii, 176 p.: ill.; 23 cm. 1. Rommel, Erwin, 1891-1944. 2. World War, 1939–1945 — Germany. 3. World War, 1939–1945 — Campaigns — France — Normandy 4. Germany — History — 1933-1945 5. Normandy (France) — History I. T.
D757.S7713 1971   940.542/1   LC 79-147223   ISBN 0837159881

Steinert, Marlis G. **3.971**
[Hitlers Krieg und die Deutschen. English] Hitler's war and the Germans: public mood and attitude during the Second World War / by Marlis G. Steinert; edited and translated by Thomas E. J. de Witt. — Athens: Ohio University Press, c1977. x, 387 p.; 24 cm. Translation of Hitlers Krieg und die Deutschen. Includes index. 1. World War, 1939–1945 — Germany. 2. Germany — History — 1933-1945 I. T.
D757.S8613   940.53/43 19   LC 76-25618   ISBN 0821401866

Stein, George H., 1934-. • **3.972**
The Waffen SS: Hitler's elite guard at war, 1939–1945 / by George H. Stein. — Ithaca, N.Y.: Cornell University Press, 1966. xxxiv, 330 p.: ill. 1. Waffen-SS. 2. World War, 1939–1945 — Germany. I. T.
D757.85.S8   LC 66-11049

Sydnor, Charles W. **3.973**
Soldiers of destruction: the SS Death's Head Division, 1933–1945 / Charles W. Sydnor, Jr. — Princeton, N.J.: Princeton University Press, c1977. xvi, 371 p.: ill.; 23 cm. Includes index. 1. Waffen-SS. Panzer-Division Totenkopf, 3. 2. World War, 1939–1945 — Regimental histories — Germany. 3. World War, 1939–1945 — Campaigns — France 4. World War, 1939–1945 — Campaigns — Soviet Union. 5. France — History — German occupation, 1940-1945 6. Russia — History — German occupation, 1941-1944. I. T.
D757.85.S95   940.54/13/43   LC 77-72138   ISBN 0691052557

Coffey, Thomas M. **3.974**
Decision over Schweinfurt: the U.S. 8th Air Force battle for daylight bombing / Thomas M. Coffey. — New York: D. Mckay Co., c1977. viii, 373 p., [4] leaves of plates: ill.; 24 cm. Includes index. 1. United States. Air Force. Air Force, 8th. 2. World War, 1939–1945 — Aerial operations, American. 3. Schweinfurt (Germany) — Bombardment, 1943. I. T.
D757.9.S35 C63   940.54/49/73   LC 77-1278   ISBN 0679507639

D759–761 Britain. France

Bryant, Arthur, Sir, 1899-. • **3.975**
The turn of the tide; a history of the war years based on the diaries of Field–Marshal Lord Alanbrooke, chief of the Imperial General Staff. [1st ed.] Garden City, N.Y.: Doubleday, 1957. 624 p.: ill.; 25 cm. 1. World War, 1939–1945 — Great Britain. I. Alanbrooke, Alan Francis Brooke, Viscount, 1883- II. T.
D759.B78 1957a   940.5342   LC 57-6705

Fraser, David, 1920-. **3.976**
And we shall shock them: the British Army in the Second World War / David Fraser. — London: Hodder and Stoughton, 1984. xiii, 429 p., [12] p. of plates: ill., maps, ports.; 24 cm. Includes index. 1. Great Britain. Army — History — World War, 1939–1945. 2. World War, 1939–1945 — Regimental histories — Great Britain. I. T.
D759.F7 1984   940.54/12/41 19   LC 83-106360   ISBN 0340270853

Bloch, Marc Léopold Benjamin, 1886-1944. • **3.977**
Strange defeat; a statement of evidence written in 1940. With an introd. by Sir Maurice Powicke and a foreword by Georges Altman. Translated from the French by Gerard Hopkins. — New York: Octagon Books, 1968. xxii, 178 p.; 21 cm. Reprint of the 1949 ed. 1. World War, 1939–1945 — France 2. World War, 1939–1945 — Personal narratives, French. I. T.
D761.B562 1968   940.5344   LC 68-15797

Gaulle, Charles de, 1890-1970.   • **3.978**
War memoirs. New York, Simon and Schuster, 1955-60. 5 v. illus. 22 cm.
1. World War, 1939-1945 — France I. T.
D761.G3733   940.5344   *LC* 55-8440

Gunsburg, Jeffery A.   **3.979**
Divided and conquered: the French high command and the defeat of the West,
1940 / Jeffery A. Gunsburg. — Westport, Conn.: Greenwood Press, 1979. xxiii,
303 p.: ill.; 25 cm. — (Contributions in military history. no. 18 0084-9251)
1. World War, 1939-1945 — France 2. France — History — 1914-1940 I. T.
II. Series.
D761.G85   940.54/0944   *LC* 78-22725   *ISBN* 0313210926

Horne, Alistair.   **3.980**
To lose a battle; France 1940. — [1st ed.]. — Boston: Little, Brown, [1969] xxiv,
647 p.: illus., maps, ports.; 24 cm. Third vol. in a trilogy; the 1st of which is The
fall of Paris; the siege and the Commune, 1870-71; and the 2d of which is The
price of glory; Verdun 1916. 1. World War, 1939-1945 — France 2. France —
History — 1914-1940 3. France — History, Military — 20th century I. T.
D761.H6   940.542/1   *LC* 69-15069

Weigley, Russell Frank.   **3.981**
Eisenhower's lieutenants: the campaign of France and Germany, 1944–1945 /
Russell F. Weigley. — Bloomington: Indiana University Press, c1981. xviii,
800 p.: ill.; 24 cm. 1. United States. Army — Biography 2. World War,
1939-1945 — Campaigns — Germany. 3. World War, 1939-1945 — United
States. 4. World War, 1939-1945 — Campaigns — France 5. Generals —
United States — Biography. 6. France — History — German occupation,
1940-1945 7. Germany — History — 1933-1945 I. T.
D761.W4   940.54/21 19   *LC* 80-8175   *ISBN* 0253133335

D763 Italy. Netherlands

Jackson, William Godfrey Fothergill, 1917-.   **3.982**
The battle for Italy [by] W. G. F. Jackson. — New York: Harper & Row, [1967]
372 p.: illus., maps, ports.; 25 cm. 1. World War, 1939-1945 — Campaigns —
Italy I. T.
D763.I8 J25 1967b   940.542/1   *LC* 67-21952

Ryan, Cornelius.   **3.983**
A bridge too far. — New York: Simon and Schuster, [1974] 670 p.: illus.; 23 cm.
1. Arnhem, Battle of, 1944 I. T.
D763.N4 R9   940.54/21   *LC* 74-3253   *ISBN* 0671217925

D764–766 Eastern Europe. Near East. Africa

Bialer, Seweryn. comp.   • **3.984**
Stalin and his generals; Soviet military memoirs of World War II. New York,
Pegasus [1969] x, 644 p. maps. 24 cm. 1. Stalin, Joseph, 1879-1953. 2. World
War, 1939-1945 — Soviet Union. 3. World War, 1939-1945 — Personal
narratives, Russian. 4. Generals — Soviet Union. I. T.
D764.B47   940.54/0947   *LC* 67-25506

Chuĭkov, V. I. (Vasiliĭ Ivanovich), 1900-.   • **3.985**
The battle for Stalingrad. Introd. by Hanson W. Baldwin. Translated from the
Russian by Harold Silver. — New York: Holt, Rinehart and Winston, [1964]
364 p.: illus., ports., maps.; 22 cm. 1. Stalingrad, Battle of, 1942-1943 I. T.
D764.C48513   940.5421   *LC* 64-11015

Chuĭkov, V. I. (Vasiliĭ Ivanovich), 1900-.   • **3.986**
The beginning of the road. Translated from the Russian by Harold Silver.
London, Macgibbon & Kee, 1963. 388 p. illus., ports., maps (1 fold.) 22 cm.
1. Stalingrad, Battle of, 1942-1943 I. T.
D764.C48513 1963   *LC* 64-36008

Erickson, John.   **3.987**
The road to Berlin: continuing the history of Stalin's war with Germany / John
Erickson. — Boulder, Colo.: Westview Press, 1984 (c1983). xiii, 877 p.: maps;
25 cm. Includes index. 1. Stalin, Joseph, 1879-1953. 2. World War, 1939-1945
— Campaigns — Eastern I. Erickson, John. Stalin's war with Germany. II. T.
D764.E737   940.54/21 19   *LC* 83-1123   *ISBN* 0891587950

Erickson, John.   **3.988**
The road to Stalingrad / John Erickson. — 1st U.S. ed. — New York: Harper &
Row, [1975] x, 594 p., [4] leaves of plates: ill.; 25 cm. (His Stalin's war with
Germany; v. 1) (A Cass Canfield book) Includes index. 1. Stalingrad, Battle of,
1942-1943 I. T.
D764.E74 1975b vol. 1 D764.3.S7   940.54/21 s 940.54/21   *LC*
74-24657   *ISBN* 0060111410

The Russian war, 1941–1945 / edited by Daniela Mrázková and   **3.989**
Vladimír Remeš; introd. by Harrison Salisbury; pref. and notes
by A. J. P. Taylor.
1st American ed. — New York: Dutton, 1977, c1975. vii, 152 p.: ill.; 24 x 29 cm.
Translation of Fotografovali válku. 1. World War, 1939-1945 — Campaigns —
Russia — Pictorial works. 2. News photographers 3. Russia — History —
German occupation, 1941-1944 — Pictorial works. I. Mrázková, Daniela.
II. Remeš, Vladimír.
D764.F6813 1977   940.54/21   *LC* 77-1970   *ISBN* 0525195602

Gouré, Leon.   • **3.990**
The siege of Leningrad. — Stanford, Calif., Stanford University Press, 1962. xii,
363 p. illus., maps. 24 cm. 'An earlier version of this study was submitted to
Georgetown University in February 1961 ... for the degree of Doctor of
Philosophy.' Bibliography: p. [343]-354. 1. Leningrad — Siege, 1941-1944.
I. T.
D764.G66 1962   940.5421   *LC* 62-8662

Carell, Paul.   • **3.991**
[Unternehmen Barbarossa. English] Hitler's war on Russia [by] Paul Carell;
translated from the German by Ewald Osers. London: Transworld, 1966. x,
691 p. plates (some col.), maps. 18 cm. (A Corgi book) Translation of
Unternehmen Barbarossa. 1. World War, 1939-1945 — Campaigns — Eastern
I. T.
D764.S3613 1966   940.542/1   *LC* 68-95227

Seaton, Albert, 1921-.   **3.992**
The Russo–German War, 1941–45. — New York: Praeger, [1971] xix, 628 p.:
illus., maps.; 25 cm. 1. World War, 1939-1945 — Campaigns — Eastern I. T.
D764.S377 1971   940.542/1   *LC* 70-130459

Stalin, Joseph, 1879-1953.   • **3.993**
The great patriotic war of the Soviet Union. New York: Greenwood Press
[1969, c1945] 167 p.; 23 cm. 1. World War, 1939-1945 — Addresses, essays,
lectures. 2. World War, 1939-1945 — Soviet Union. I. T.
D764.S825 1969   940.5347   *LC* 70-97320   *ISBN* 0837125596

Werth, Alexander, 1901-.   • **3.994**
Russia at war, 1941–1945. New York, Dutton, 1964. xxv, 1100 p. maps (part
fold.) 23 cm. 1. World War, 1939-1945 — Soviet Union. I. T.
D764.W48   940.5347   *LC* 64-19533

Salisbury, Harrison Evans, 1908-.   • **3.995**
The 900 days; the siege of Leningrad [by] Harrison E. Salisbury. [1st ed.] New
York, Harper & Row [1969] xi, 635 p. illus., maps (1 col.) 25 cm. 1. Leningrad
(R.S.F.S.R.) — History — Siege, 1941-1944. I. T.
D764.3.L4 S2   940.542/1   *LC* 68-28215

Craig, William, 1929-.   **3.996**
Enemy at the gates; the battle for Stalingrad. — [1st ed.]. — New York:
Reader's Digest Press, 1973. xvii, 457 p.: illus.; 25 cm. 1. Stalingrad, Battle of,
1942-1943 I. T.
D764.3.S7 C7 1973   940.54/21   *LC* 72-95037   *ISBN* 0883490005

Ciechanowski, Jan M.   **3.997**
The Warsaw Rising of 1944 / [by] Jan M. Ciechanowski. — [London; New
York]: Cambridge University Press, 1974. xi, 332 p.: map; 22 cm. (Soviet and
East European studies.) Rev. and abridged version of the author's thesis, The
political and ideological background of the Warsaw Rising, 1944, University of
London, 1968, and the Polish ed. published 1971 under title: Powstanie
Warszawskie. 1. Warsaw (Poland) — History — Uprising of 1944 I. T.
II. Series.
D765.2.W3 C48   940.53/438/4   *LC* 73-79315   *ISBN* 0521202035

Mark, Bernard, 1908-1966.   **3.998**
[Powstanie w getcie warszawskim. English] Uprising in the Warsaw ghetto /
Ber Mark; translated from Yiddish by Gershon Freidlin. — New York:
Schocken Books, 1975. xi, 209 p.: ill.; 21 cm. Translation from Yiddish ed. of
the work first published in Polish under title: Powstanie w getcie warszawskim.
Includes index. 1. Warsaw (Poland) — History — Uprising of 1943 I. T.
D765.2.W3 M293   943.8/4/05   *LC* 74-26913   *ISBN* 0805235787

Stroop, Jürgen, 1895-.   **3.999**
[Es gibt keinen jüdischen Wohnbezirk in Warscahu mehr. English] The Stroop
report: the Jewish quarter of Warsaw is no more! / Translated from the German
by Sybil Milton; introd. by Andrzej Wirth. — 1st American ed. — New York:
Pantheon Books, c1979. ca. [250] p.: ill.; 26 cm. Translation of Es gibt keinen
jüdischen Wohnbezirk in Warschau mehr. 1. Stroop, Jürgen, 1895- 2. Warsaw
(Poland) — History — Uprising of 1943 — Personal narratives. I. T.
D765.2.W3 S78613 1979   D765.2W3 S78613 1979.   940.53/438/4
LC 79-1900   *ISBN* 0394504437

Barnett, Correlli.   **3.1000**
The desert generals / Correlli Barnett. — 2nd ed. — Bloomington: Indiana
University Press, c1982. 352 p., [16] p. of plates: maps, ports.; 22 cm.
1. Cunningham, Alan, Sir. 2. Ritchie, Neil, Sir. 3. Auchinleck, Claude John

Eyre, Sir, 1884- 4. Montgomery of Alamein, Bernard Law Montgomery, Viscount, 1887-1976. 5. Great Britain. Army — Biography. 6. World War, 1939-1945 — Campaigns — Africa, North 7. Generals — Great Britain — Biography. I. T.
D766.82.B32 1982   940.54/23 19   *LC* 82-47957   *ISBN* 0253116007

Rommel, Erwin, 1891-1944.   • **3.1001**
The Rommel papers / edited by B.H. Liddell Hart; with the assistance of Lucie–Maria Rommel, Manfred Rommel, and Fritz Bayerlein; translated by Paul Findlay. — New York: Harcourt, Brace, 1953. xxx, 545 p.: ill.; 22 cm. 1. World War, 1939-1945 — Campaigns — Africa, North 2. World War, 1939-1945 — Campaigns — Italy I. Liddell Hart, Basil Henry, Sir, 1895-1970. II. T.
D766.82.R6 1953   *LC* 53-5656

Lucas, James Sidney.   **3.1002**
War in the desert: the Eighth Army at El Alamein / James Lucas. — 1st American ed. — New York: Beaufort Books, 1983. 284 p., [16] p. of plates: ill.; 24 cm. Includes index. 1. Great Britain. Army. Army, Eighth — History. 2. al 'Alamayn, Battle of, 1942. 3. World War, 1939-1945 — Regimental histories — Great Britain. 4. World War, 1939-1945 — Campaigns — Africa, North I. T.
D766.9.L83 1982b   940.54/23 19   *LC* 83-6015   *ISBN* 082530153X

Marder, Arthur Jacob.   **3.1003**
Operation Menace: the Dakar expedition and the Dudley North affair / Arthur Marder. — London; New York: Oxford University Press, 1976. xxv, 289 p., [5] leaves of plates: ill.; 23 cm. Includes index. 1. North, Dudley Burton Napier, Sir, 1881-1961. 2. Operation Menace I. T.
D766.99.S4 M37   940.54/23   *LC* 76-364807   *ISBN* 0192158112

D767 Far East

Belote, James H.   **3.1004**
Titans of the seas: the development and operations of Japanese and American carrier task forces during World War II / James H. Belote, William M. Belote. — 1st ed. — New York: Harper & Row, [1975] x, 336 p., [8] leaves of plates: ill.; 24 cm. Includes index. 1. World War, 1939-1945 — Pacific Ocean. 2. Aircraft carriers — United States. 3. Aircraft carriers — Japan. 4. World War, 1939-1945 — Naval operations 5. World War, 1939-1945 — Aerial operations I. Belote, William M., joint author. II. T.
D767.B47 1975   940.54/4   *LC* 74-1971   *ISBN* 0060102780

Cruickshank, Charles Greig.   **3.1005**
SOE in the Far East / Charles Cruickshank. — Oxford; New York: Oxford University Press, 1984 (c1983). xv, 285 p., [16] p. of plates: ill.; 23 cm. Includes index. 1. Great Britain. Special Operations Executive — History. 2. World War, 1939-1945 — Campaigns — Asia, Southeastern. 3. World War, 1939-1945 — Commando operations — Asia, Southeastern. 4. Asia, Southeastern — History I. T. II. Title: S.O.E. in the Far East.
D767.C75   940.54/25 19   *LC* 83-235317   *ISBN* 0192158732

Spector, Ronald H., 1943-.   **3.1006**
Eagle against the sun: the American war with Japan / Ronald H. Spector. — New York: Free Press, c1985. xvi, 589 p., [16] p. of plates: ill.; 24 cm. Map on lining papers. Includes index. 1. World War, 1939-1945 — Campaigns — Pacific Area. 2. World War, 1939-1945 — United States. 3. World War, 1939-1945 — Japan. 4. United States — History — 1933-1945 5. Japan — History — 1912-1945 I. T.
D767.S69 1985   940.54/26 19   *LC* 84-47888   *ISBN* 0029303605

U.S. Strategic Bombing Survey.   • **3.1007**
The campaigns of the Pacific war. — [Washington]: U.S. Strategic Bombing Survey (Pacific), Naval Analysis Division.; New York: Greenwood Press, [1969] xv, 389 p.: illus. (part fold.), maps (part fold.); 29 cm. Reprint of the 1946 ed. 1. World War, 1939-1945 — Pacific Ocean. 2. World War, 1939-1945 — Naval operations, Japanese. 3. World War, 1939-1945 — Naval operations, American 4. World War, 1939-1945 — Aerial operations I. T.
D767.U55 1969   940.542/6   *LC* 77-90739   *ISBN* 0837123135

Feis, Herbert, 1893-1972.   • **3.1008**
[Japan subdued] The atomic bomb and the end of World War II. [Rev. ed.] Princeton, N.J., Princeton University Press, 1966. vi, 213 p. 24 cm. 'Originally published in 1961 under the title: Japan subdued.' 1. United States. Army. Corps of Engineers. Manhattan District. 2. World War, 1939-1945 — Japan. I. T.
D767.2.F4 1966   940.5425   *LC* 66-13312

Havens, Thomas R. H.   **3.1009**
Valley of darkness: the Japanese people and World War Two / Thomas R. H. Havens. — 1st ed. — New York: Norton, c1978. xi, 280 p.: ill.; 22 cm. Includes index. 1. World War, 1939-1945 — Japan. 2. Japan — Social life and customs I. T.
D767.2.H29 1978   940.53/52 19   *LC* 77-11115   *ISBN* 0393056562

Willmott, H. P.   **3.1010**
The barrier and the javelin: Japanese and Allied Pacific strategies, February to June 1942 / H.P. Willmott. — Annapolis, Md.: Naval Institute Press, c1983. xvii, 596 p.: ill., maps; 24 cm. Second vol. of a trilogy that began with Empires in the balance. Includes indexes. 1. World War, 1939-1945 — Japan. 2. Coral Sea, Battle of the, 1942 3. Midway, Battle of, 1942 4. Japan — History — 1912-1945 I. T.
D767.2.W537 1983   940.54/26 19   *LC* 83-17218   *ISBN* 0870210920

Hersey, John, 1914-.   • **3.1011**
Hiroshima / [by] John Hersey. — New York: A. A. Knopf, 1946. 5 p., l., 3-117, [1] p., 1 l.; 20 cm. At head of title: John Hersey. 'A Borzoi book.' 'First edition.' 'Originally appeared in the New Yorker.' 1. World War, 1939-1945 — Japan — Hiroshima-shi. 2. Atomic bomb — Blast effect 3. Hiroshima-shi (Japan) — Bombardment, 1945. I. T.
D767.25.H6 H4 1946c   940.544   *LC* 46-11953

Hiroshima and Nagasaki, the physical, medical, and social   **3.1012**
effects of the atomic bombings / The Committee for the
Compilation of Materials on Damage Caused by the Atomic
Bombs in Hiroshima and Nagasaki; translated by Eisei Ishikawa
and David L. Swain.
New York: Basic Books, c1981. xlv, 706 p.: ill.; 25 cm. Translation of: Hiroshima Nagasaki no genbaku saigai. Includes index. 1. Atomic bomb — Physiological effect 2. Atomic bomb — Blast effect 3. Nagasaki-shi (Japan) — Bombardment, 1945. 4. Hiroshima-shi (Japan) — Bombardment, 1945. I. Hiroshima-shi Nagasaki-shi Genbaku Saigaishi Henshū Iinkai.
D767.25.H6 H6713 1981   940.54/26 19   *LC* 80-68179   *ISBN* 046502985X

Knebel, Fletcher.   • **3.1013**
No high ground / by Fletcher Knebel and Charles W. Bailey II. — 1st ed. — New York: Harper, 1960. 272 p.: ill. , 22 cm. 1. Atomic bomb 2. Hiroshima. I. Bailey, Charles W., joint author. II. T.
D767.25.H6 K55   940.5442   *LC* 60-7531

Lord, Walter, 1917-.   • **3.1014**
Day of infamy / illustrated with photos. — [1st ed.] New York: Holt [1957] 243 p.: ill.; 22 cm. 1. Pearl Harbor (Hawaii), Attack on, 1941 I. T.
D767.92.L6   940.542   *LC* 57-6189

Stephan, John J.   **3.1015**
Hawaii under the rising sun: Japan's plans for conquest after Pearl Harbor / John J. Stephan. — Honolulu: University of Hawaii Press, c1984. xii, 228 p.: maps; 24 cm. Includes index. 1. World War, 1939-1945 — Hawaii. 2. World War, 1939-1945 — Japan. 3. Japan — Military policy. 4. Hawaii — History — 1900-1959 I. T.
D767.92.S835 1984   940.54/0952 19   *LC* 83-9101   *ISBN* 082480872X

Trefousse, Hans Louis.   **3.1016**
Pearl Harbor, the continuing controversy / by Hans L. Trefousse. — Original ed. — Malabar, Fla.: Krieger, 1982. 215 p.; 19 cm. (Anvil series) 'An Anvil original.' Includes index. 1. Pearl Harbor (Hawaii), Attack on, 1941 I. T.
D767.92.T69 1982   940.54/26 19   *LC* 81-14237   *ISBN* 0898742617

Wohlstetter, Roberta.   • **3.1017**
Pearl Harbor; warning and decision. Stanford, Calif.: Stanford University Press, 1962. 426 p.: ill.; 25 cm. 1. Intelligence service — United States 2. Pearl Harbor (Hawaii), Attack on, 1941 I. T.
D767.92.W6   940.5426   *LC* 62-15966

Tregaskis, Richard, 1916-1973.   • **3.1018**
Guadalcanal diary / by Richard Tregaskis. — New York: Random House, 1955. 180 p.: ill. — (Landmark books; 55) 1. United States. Marine Corps. 2. World War, 1939-1945 — Biography, American. 3. World War, 1939-1945 — Campaigns — Solomon Islands. I. T.
D767.98.T7 1955   *LC* 55-5820   *ISBN* 0394903552

D768.15 Canada

Douglas, William A. B., 1929-.   **3.1019**
Out of the shadows: Canada in the Second World War / W. A. B. Douglas and Brereton Greenhous. — Toronto; New York: Oxford University Press, 1977. 288 p.: ill.; 25 cm. Includes index. 1. World War, 1939-1945 — Canada. 2. Canada — History — 1914-1945 I. Greenhous, Brereton, 1929- joint author. II. T.
D768.15.D65   940.53/71   *LC* 78-306661   *ISBN* 019540257X

D769 United States

United States. Dept. of the Army. Office of Military History.　3.1020
United States Army in World War II. Washington, 1947-. v. illus., ports., maps (part fold. col.) 26 cm. 1. United States. Army — History — World War, 1939-1945. 2. World War, 1939-1945 — United States. I. T.
D769.A533　　*LC* 47-46404

U.S. Dept. of the Army. Office of Military History.　• 3.1021
United States Army in World War II. Master index: reader's guide / compiled by the Chief Historian. — Washington, D.C.: Office of the Chief of Military History, 1955-. v.; 26 cm. Photocopy. 1. United States. Army — History 2. World War, 1939-1945 — United States I. The Chief Historian. II. T.
D769 A533 Index

Buchanan, Albert Russell, 1906-.　• 3.1022
The United States and World War II. [1st ed.] New York, Harper & Row, [1964] 2 v. (xvii, 635 p.) illus., ports., maps. 22 cm. (New American National series) 1. World War, 1939-1945 — United States. I. T.
D769.B8　　*LC* 63-20287

Pratt, Fletcher, 1897-1956.　• 3.1023
War for the world: a chronicle of our fighting forces in World War II. — New Haven: Yale University Press, 1950. xi, 364 p.: illus., maps.; 21 cm. — (Chronicles of America series. v. 54) 1. World War, 1939-1945 — United States. I. T. II. Series.
D769.P73 E173.C55 vol. 54　　940.5373　　*LC* 50-8830

United States. Marine Corps.　• 3.1024
History of U.S. Marine operations in World War II. — [Washington]: Historical Branch, G-3 Division, Headquarters, U.S. Marine Corps, [1958-71; v. 5, 1968] 5 v.: illus., maps (part fold. col.); 26 cm. Vol. 4 issued by Historical Division, Headquarters, U.S. Marine Corps. 1. United States. Marine Corps — History — World War, 1939-1945 I. T.
D769.369.U53　　940.54/12/73　　*LC* 58-60002

And justice for all: an oral history of the Japanese American　3.1025
detention camps / [compiled by] John Tateishi.
1st ed. — New York: Random House, c1984. xxvii, 259 p., [16] p. of plates: ill.; 25 cm. 1. Japanese Americans — Evacuation and relocation, 1942-1945 2. World War, 1939-1945 — Personal narratives, American. I. Tateishi, John, 1939-
D769.8.A6 A67 1984　　940.54/72/73 19　　*LC* 82-42823　　*ISBN* 0394539826

Daniels, Roger.　• 3.1026
Concentration camps USA: Japanese Americans and World War II. — New York: Holt, Rinehart and Winston, [1971] xiv, 188 p.: illus.; 23 cm. — (Berkshire studies in history. Berkshire studies in minority history) Edition of 1981 published under title: Concentration camps North America. 1. Japanese Americans — Evacuation and relocation, 1942-1945 I. T.
D769.8.A6 D35　　940.547/2/73　　*LC* 72-143320　　*ISBN* 0030818699

Weglyn, Michi, 1926-.　3.1027
Years of infamy: the untold story of America's concentration camps / by Michi Weglyn. New York: Morrow, 1976. 351 p.: ill.; 25 cm. Includes index. 1. Japanese Americans — Evacuation and relocation, 1942-1945 I. T.
D769.8.A6 W43　　940.54/72/73　　*LC* 75-34397　　*ISBN* 0688029965

D770–784 Naval Operations

Rohwer, Jürgen.　3.1028
Chronology of the war at sea, 1939–1945 / J. Rohwer and G. Hummelchen; translated from the German by Derek Masters. — New York: Arco Pub. Co., 1972-1974. 2 v. (xii, 650 p.): ill. Revised translation of Chronik des Seekrieges 1939-1945. 1. World War, 1939-1945 — Naval operations — Chronology. I. Hümmelchen, Gerhard, 1927- II. T.
D770.R5913 1972　　*LC* 73-78526　　*ISBN* 0668033088

Ruge, Friedrich.　• 3.1029
Der Seekrieg: the German Navy's story, 1939–1945 / translated by M. G. Saunders. — Annapolis: U.S. Naval Institute [1957] 440 p.: ill.; 24 cm. 1. World War, 1939-1945 — Naval operations I. T. II. Title: The German Navy's story.
D770.R833　　940.545　　*LC* 57-14768

Roskill, Stephen Wentworth.　• 3.1030
White ensign: the British Navy at war, 1939–1945. — Annapolis, Md.: U. S. Naval Institute, [1960] 480 p.: ill.; 24 cm. 1. World War, 1939-1945 — Naval operations, British. I. T.
D771.R69 1960　　940.545942　　*LC* 60-15791

Wheatley, Ronald.　• 3.1031
Operation Sea Lion: German plans for the invasion of England, 1939–1942. — Oxford: Clarendon Press, 1958. viii, 201 p.: ports., fold. maps; 22 cm. Thesis

(B. LITT.)—Oxford. Without thesis statement. Bibliography: p. 170-174. 1. Operation Sea Lion I. T.
D771.W38 1958　　940.542　　*LC* 58-2322

Morison, Samuel Eliot, 1887-1976.　• 3.1032
History of United States naval operations in World War II / by Samuel Eliot Morison. — Boston: Little, Brown and company, [1947-1962] 15 v.: ill., ports., maps (part fold., part col.); 23 cm. 'An Atlantic monthly press book.' 'First edition.' I. T.
D773.M6　　940.75　　*LC* 47-1571

Morison, Samuel Eliot, 1887-1976.　• 3.1033
The two ocean war: a short history of the United States Navy in the Second World War. — [1st ed.]. — Boston: Little, Brown, [1963] 611 p.: ill.; 24 cm. 1. World War, 1939-1945 — Naval operations, American I. T.
D773.M62　　940.545973　　*LC* 63-8307

Willoughby, Malcolm Francis.　• 3.1034
The U. S. Coast Guard in World War II / by Malcolm F. Willoughby. — Annapolis: United States Naval Institute, 1957. xvii, 347 p.: ill., ports., maps; 28 cm. 1. United States. Coast Guard. 2. World War, 1939-1945 — Naval operations I. T.
D 773 W73 1957　　*LC* 57-9314

Prange, Gordon William, 1910-.　3.1035
Miracle at Midway / Gordon W. Prange, Donald M. Goldstein and Katherine V. Dillon. — New York: McGraw-Hill, c1982. xvii, 469 p., [16] p. of plates: ill. maps; 24 cm. Includes index. 1. Midway, Battle of, 1942 I. Goldstein, Donald M. II. Dillon, Katherine V. III. T.
D774.M5 P7 1982　　940.54/26 19　　*LC* 82-4691　　*ISBN* 0070506728

Bragadin, Marc' Antonio, 1906-.　• 3.1036
The Italian navy in World War II / by Commander (R) Marc' Antonio Bragadin, Giuseppe Fioravanzo; translated by Gale Hoffman. — Annapolis, Md.: United States Naval Institute, 1957. xviii, 380 p.: ill., maps. 1. World War, 1939-1945 — Naval operations, Italian. I. T.
D775.B683　　*LC* 57-6515

Milner, Marc.　3.1037
North Atlantic run: the Royal Canadian Navy and the battle for the convoys / Marc Milner. — Annapolis, Md.: Naval Institute Press, c1985. xxiii, 326 p., [32] p. of plates: ill.; 24 cm. Includes index. 1. World War, 1939-1945 — Naval operations, Canadian. 2. Naval convoys — Canada — History — 20th century. 3. World War, 1939-1945 — Campaigns — Atlantic Ocean I. T.
D779.C2 M55 1985　　940.54/5971 19　　*LC* 85-60967　　*ISBN* 0870214500

Donitz, Karl, 1892-.　• 3.1038
Memoirs: ten years and twenty days / translated by R.H. Stevens, in collaboration with David Woodward. 1st ed. Cleveland: World Pub. Co., 1959. 500 p.: ill.; 23 cm. Translation of Zehn Jahre und zwanzig Tage. 1. World War, 1939-1945 — Naval operations — Submarine 2. World War, 1939-1945 — Naval operations, German 3. World War, 1939-1945 — Germany. I. T. II. Title: Ten years and twenty days.
D781.D613　　*LC* 59-11530

Hadley, Michael L.　3.1039
U–boats against Canada: German submarines in Canadian waters / Michael L. Hadley. — Kingston: McGill-Queen's University Press, c1985. xxii, 360 p., [24] p. of plates: ill.; 24 cm. Includes index. 1. World War, 1939-1945 — Naval operations — Submarine 2. World War, 1939-1945 — Naval operations, German 3. World War, 1939-1945 — Campaigns — Canada. I. T.
D781.H27 1985　　940.54/51 19　　*LC* 86-110765　　*ISBN* 0773505849

Blair, Clay, 1925-.　3.1040
Silent victory: the U.S. submarine war against Japan. — [1st ed.]. — Philadelphia: Lippincott, [1975] 1072 p.: illus.; 24 cm. 1. World War, 1939-1945 — Naval operations — Submarine 2. World War, 1939-1945 — Naval operations, American 3. World War, 1939-1945 — Pacific Ocean. I. T.
D783.B58 1975　　940.54/51　　*LC* 74-2005　　*ISBN* 0397007531

D785–792 Aerial Operations

Overy, R. J.　3.1041
The air war, 1939–1945 / R.J. Overy. — New York: Stein and Day, c1980. xii, 263 p., [6] p. of plates: ill.; 24 cm. Includes index. 1. World War, 1939-1945 — Aerial operations 2. Military history, Modern — 20th century I. T.
D785.O9　　940.54/4 19　　*LC* 80-6200　　*ISBN* 0812827929

Tedder, Arthur William Tedder, baron, 1890-.　• 3.1042
Air power in war / by the Lord Tedder. — London: Hodder and Stoughton, [1948] 124 p.: maps (on lining-papers) diagrs.; 23 cm. 1. World War, 1939-1945 — Aerial operations — Addresses, essays, lectures. I. T.
D785.T4　　940.54/4　　*LC* 75-7243　　*ISBN* 0837181038

United States Strategic Bombing Survey. • **3.1043**
The United States Strategic Bombing Survey: summary report (European War) [Washington, U.S. Govt. Print off.] 1945. 18 p.; 26 cm. 1. World War, 1939-1945 — Aerial operations 2. World War, 1939-1945 — Europe. I. T.
D785.U6 no.1 940.544 *LC* 45-37594 rev.

United States Strategic Bombing Survey. • **3.1044**
The effects of the atomic bomb on Hiroshima, Japan / [by] the U.S. Strategic Bombing Survey, Physical Damage Division. — [Washington], 1947. 3 v.: ill., maps (part fold., part col.); 27 cm. (Its Reports, Pacific war; 92.) 1. Atomic bomb — Japan. 2. Hiroshima-shi (Japan) — Bombardment, 1945. 3. Nagasaki-shi (Japan) — Bombardment, 1945. I. T.
D785.U63 no. 92 623.4/5 *LC* 55-57769

United States Strategic Bombing Survey. • **3.1045**
Effects of the atomic bomb on Nagasaki, Japan / [by] the U. S. Strategic Bombing Survey, Physical Damage Division. — [Washington], 1947. 3 v.: ill., maps (part fold., part col.); 27 cm. (Its Reports, Pacific war; 93.) 1. Atomic bomb — Japan. 2. Hiroshima-shi (Japan) — Bombardment, 1945. 3. Nagasaki-shi (Japan) — Bombardment, 1945. I. T.
D785.U63 no. 93 623.4/5 *LC* 55-57770

Verrier, Anthony. • **3.1046**
The bomber offensive. — [1st American ed. — New York]: Macmillan, [1969, c1968] x, 373 p.: illus., maps, ports.; 24 cm. 1. World War, 1939-1945 — Aerial operations 2. Bombardment I. T.
D785.V47 1968b 940.544/2 *LC* 76-75410

Webster, Charles Kingsley, Sir, 1886-1961. • **3.1047**
The strategic air offensive against Germany, 1939–1945, by Charles Webster and Noble Frankland. London, H. M. Stationery Off., 1961. 4 v. illus., ports., maps (part fold., part col.) 25 cm. (History of the Second World War; United Kingdom military series) 1. World War, 1939-1945 — Aerial operations I. Frankland, Noble, 1922- joint author. II. T. III. Series.
D785.W38 940.544 *LC* 61-65443

Wood, Derek, 1930-. • **3.1048**
The narrow margin: the Battle of Britain and the rise of air power 1930–40 / [by] Derek Wood & Derek Dempster. — 1st ed. New York: McGraw-Hill [1961] 536 p.: ill.; 22 cm. 1. Britain, Battle of, 1940 2. World War, 1939-1945 — Aerial operations I. Dempster, Derek D. joint author. II. T.
D785.W6 1961 *LC* 61-15451

Lyall, Gavin. • **3.1049**
The war in the air: the Royal Air Force in World War II / edited by Gavin Lyall. — New York: Morrow, [1969, c1968] xv, 422 p.: ill., ports.; 24 cm. Published in 1968 under title: The war in the air 1939-1945: an anthology of personal experience. 1. World War, 1939-1945 — Aerial operations, British I. T.
D786.L93 1969 940.544/9/42 *LC* 69-12310

Richards, Denis. **3.1050**
Royal Air Force, 1939–1945 / [by Denis Richards and Hilary St. George Saunders]. [Rev. ed.]. — London: H. M. S. O., 1974-1975. 3 v.: ill., maps (some col.), ports.; 22 cm. 1. Great Britain. Royal Air Force. 2. World War, 1939-1945 — Aerial operations, British I. Saunders, Hilary Aldan St. George, 1898-1951, joint author. II. T.
D786.R49 1974 940.54/49/41 *LC* 76-367101 *ISBN* 0117715921

Terraine, John. **3.1051**
A time for courage: the Royal Air Force in the European War, 1939–1945 / by John Terraine. — New York, N.Y.: Macmillan, c1985. xix, 828 p., [24] p. of plates: ill.; 24 cm. Includes index. 1. World War, 1939-1945 — Aerial operations, British 2. Great Britain — Royal Air Force — History — World War, 1939-1945. I. T.
D786.T44 1985 940.54/4941 19 *LC* 84-17098 *ISBN* 0026169703

Middleton, Drew, 1913-. • **3.1052**
The sky suspended: the Battle of Britain / Drew Middleton. — London: Secker & Warburg, [1960] 255 p.: ill.; 21 cm. 1. Britain, Battle of, 1940 I. T.
D787.M5 1960a *LC* 61-2011

Murray, Williamson. **3.1053**
Luftwaffe / Williamson Murray. — Baltimore, Md.: Nautical & Aviation Pub. Co. of America, c1985. xiv, 337 p.: ill.; 25 cm. Rev. ed. of: Strategy for defeat. 1983. Includes index. 1. Germany. Luftwaffe — History — World War, 1939-1945. 2. Germany. Luftwaffe — History — 20th century. 3. World War, 1939-1945 — Aerial operations, German. I. Murray, Williamson. Strategy for defeat. II. T.
D787.M84 1985 940.54/4943 19 *LC* 84-22735 *ISBN* 0933852452

United States. USAF Historical Division. • **3.1054**
The Army Air Forces in World War II. Prepared under the editorship of Wesley Frank Craven [and] James Lea Cate. [Chicago] University of Chicago Press [1948-58] 7 v. illus., ports., maps (part fold.) 25 cm. Vols. 1-2 prepared by the division under its earlier names: v. 1 by the Office of Air Force History and

v. 2 by the Air Historical Group. 1. United States. Army Air Forces — History. 2. World War, 1939-1945 — Aerial operations, American. I. Craven, Wesley Frank, 1905- ed. II. Cate, James Lea, 1899- ed. III. T.
D790.A47 940.544973 *LC* 48-3657

Inoguchi, Rikihei. • **3.1055**
[Kamikaze Tokubetsu Kōgekitai. English] The divine wind. Annapolis, United States Naval Institue [1958] 240 p. illus. 24 cm. 1. Japan, Kaigan. Kamikaze Tokubetsu Kōgekitai. 2. World War, 1939-1945 — Aerial operations, Japanese. I. Nakajima, Tadashi. joint author. II. T.
D792.J3 I513 *LC* 58-13974

Hardesty, Von, 1939-. **3.1056**
Red phoenix: the rise of Soviet air power, 1941–1945 / Von Hardesty. — 1st ed. — Washington, D.C.: Smithsonian Institution Press, c1982. 288 p.: ill., maps; 26 cm. Map on lining papers. Includes index. 1. Soviet Union. Raboche-Krest'ianskaia Krasnaia Armiia. Voenno-Vozdushnye Sily — History — World War, 1939-1945. 2. Germany. Luftwaffe — History — World War, 1939-1945. 3. World War, 1939-1945 — Aerial operations, Russian. 4. World War, 1939-1945 — Aerial operations, German. I. T.
D792.S65 H37 1982 940.54/4947 19 *LC* 82-600153 *ISBN* 0874745101

D802 OCCUPIED TERRITORY

Holborn, Hajo, 1902-1969. • **3.1057**
American military government: its organization and policies / by Hajo Holborn. Washington, D.C.: Infantry Journal Press, 1947. xiii, 243 p.; 24 cm. 1. Allied Military Government. 2. World War, 1939-1945 — Occupied territories 3. United States — Foreign relations — 1933-1945 I. T.
D802.A2 H6 940.5338 *LC* 47-3001

Petrow, Richard. **3.1058**
The bitter years; the invasion and occupation of Denmark and Norway, April 1940–May 1945. — New York: Morrow, 1974. viii, 403 p.: illus.; 24 cm. 1. World War, 1939-1945 — Campaigns — Denmark 2. World War, 1939-1945 — Campaigns — Norway 3. Denmark — History — German occupation, 1940-1945 4. Norway — History — German occupation, 1940-1945 I. T.
D802.D4 P45 940.54/21 *LC* 74-9576 *ISBN* 0688002757

Rings, Werner. **3.1059**
[Leben mit dem Feind. English] Life with the enemy: collaboration and resistance in Hitler's Europe, 1939–1945 / Werner Rings; translated from the German by J. Maxwell Brownjohn. — 1st ed. in the United States of America. — Garden City, N.Y.: Doubleday, 1982. vii, 351 p., [46] p. of plates.; 24 cm. Translation of: Leben mit dem Feind. Includes indexes. 1. World War, 1939-1945 — Underground movements — Europe. 2. Europe — History — 1918-1945 3. Germany — Foreign relations — 1933-1945 I. T.
D802.E9 R5613 940.53/4 19 *LC* 80-2980 *ISBN* 0385170823

Wilkinson, James D., 1943-. **3.1060**
The intellectual resistance in Europe / James D. Wilkinson. — Cambridge, Mass.: Harvard University Press, 1981. x, 358 p.: ill.; 25 cm. Includes index. 1. World War, 1939-1945 — Underground movements — Europe. 2. Intellectuals — Europe. 3. Europe — Intellectual life — 20th century I. T.
D802.E9 W54 940.53/4 19 *LC* 80-24469 *ISBN* 0674457757

Azéma, Jean-Pierre. **3.1061**
[De Munich à la libération, 1938-1944. English] From Munich to the Liberation, 1938–1944 / Jean-Pierre Azéma; translated by Janet Lloyd. — Cambridge [Cambridgeshire]; New York: Cambridge University Press, 1985 (c1984). xxxix, 294 p.; 24 cm. (Cambridge history of modern France. 6) Translation of: De Munich à la libération, 1938-1944. Includes index. 1. Munich Four-Power Agreement (1938) 2. World War, 1939-1945 — France 3. France — History — 1914-1940 4. France — German occupation, 1940-1945 I. T. II. Series.
D802.F8 A92313 940.53/44 19 *LC* 84-5828 *ISBN* 0521252377

Fourcade, Marie Madeleine. **3.1062**
[Arche de Noé. English] Noah's Ark. Translated from the French by Kenneth Morgan. Pref. by Kenneth Cohen. [1st ed.] New York, Dutton, 1974 [c1973] 377 p. illus. 24 cm. Translation of L'Arche de Noé. 1. World War, 1939-1945 — Underground movements — France. I. T.
D802.F8 F6313 1974 940.53/44 *LC* 78-95482 *ISBN* 0525168206

Gordon, Bertram M., 1945-. **3.1063**
Collaborationism in France during the Second World War / Bertram M. Gordon. — Ithaca, N.Y.: Cornell University Press, 1980. 393 p.; 24 cm. Includes indexes. 1. World War, 1939-1945 — Collaborationists — France. 2. France — History — German occupation, 1940-1945 I. T.
D802.F8 G67 940.53/24/44 *LC* 79-25281 *ISBN* 0801412633

Kedward, H. R. (Harry Roderick)   **3.1064**
Resistance in Vichy France: a study of ideas and motivation in the Southern Zone, 1940–1942 / by H. R. Kedward. — Oxford [Eng.]; New York: Oxford University Press, 1978. ix, 311 p.: maps; 23 cm. Includes index. 1. World War, 1939-1945 — Underground movements — France. 2. France — History — German occupation, 1940-1945 I. T.
D802.F8 K4   940.53/44   LC 77-30165   ISBN 0198225296

Sweets, John F., 1945-.   **3.1065**
The politics of resistance in France, 1940–1944: a history of the Mouvements unis de la Résistance / John F. Sweets. — Dekalb: Northern Illinois University Press, [1976] xii, 260 p.; 24 cm. Includes index. 1. Mouvements unis de la Résistance. 2. World War, 1939-1945 — Underground movements — France. 3. France — Politics and government — 1940-1945 I. T.
D802.F8 S88   940.53/44   LC 75-15014   ISBN 0875800610

Pryce-Jones, David, 1936-.   **3.1066**
Paris in the Third Reich: a history of the German occupation, 1940–1944 / by David Pryce–Jones; Michael Rand, picture editor. — 1st ed. — New York: Holt, Rinehart, and Winston, c1981. x, 294 p., [8] leaves of plates: ill.; 29 cm. 1. World War, 1939-1945 — France — Paris. 2. Paris (France) — History — 1940-1944 I. T.
D802.F82 P376   940.53/44 19   LC 80-21256   ISBN 0030456215

Eudes, Dominique.   **3.1067**
[Kapétanios. English] The kapetanios; partisans and civil war in Greece, 1943–1949. Translated from the French by John Howe. New York: Monthly Review Press, 1973. 381 p. illus. 21 cm. 1. World War, 1939-1945 — Underground movements — Greece. 2. Communists, Greek. 3. Greece — Politics and government — 1935- 4. Greece — History — Civil War, 1944-1949 I. T.
D802.G8 E913 1973   940.53/495   LC 72-92032   ISBN 085345275X

Hondros, John Louis.   **3.1068**
Occupation and resistance: the Greek agony, 1941–44 / John Louis Hondros. — New York, NY: Pella Pub. Co., 1983. 340 p.; 24 cm. Based on the author's thesis, Vanderbilt University. 1. World War, 1939-1945 — Underground movements — Greece. 2. Greece — History — Occupation, 1941-1944 I. T.
D802.G8 H66 1983   940.53/495 19   LC 83-62478   ISBN 0918618193

Gjelsvik, Tore, 1916-.   **3.1069**
[Hjemmefronten, den sivile motstand under okkupasjonen 1940-1945. English] Norwegian resistance, 1940–1945 / by Tore Gjelsvik; translated from the Norwegian by Thomas Kingston Derry. — London: C. Hurst, c1979. x, 224 p.: ill.; 22 cm. Translation of Hjemmefronten, den sivile motstand under okkupasjonen 1940-1945. Includes index. 1. Gjelsvik, Tore, 1916- 2. World War, 1939-1945 — Personal narratives, Norwegian. 3. World War, 1939-1945 — Underground movements — Norway — Biography. 4. Guerrillas — Norway — Biography. 5. Norway — History — German occupation, 1940-1945 I. T.
D802.N7 G5413 1979   940.53/481   LC 79-322482   0838905122

Reitlinger, Gerald, 1900-.   • **3.1070**
The House built on sand: the conflicts of German policy in Russia, 1939–1945 / Gerald Reitlinger. — New York: Viking Press, 1960. 459 p.: fold maps; 23 cm. 1. Russia — History — German occupation, 1941-1944 I. T.
D802.R8 R4 1960a   LC 60-9628

Dallin, Alexander.   **3.1071**
German rule in Russia, 1941–1945: a study of occupation policies / by Alexander Dallin. — 2nd, rev., ed. — Boulder, Colo.: Westview Press, 1981. xx, 707 p.: ill.; 25 cm. 1. World War, 1939-1945 — Soviet Union. 2. World War, 1939-1945 — Germany. 3. Soviet Union — History — German occupation, 1941-1944 I. T.
D802.S75 D34 1981   940.53/47 19   LC 80-52877   ISBN 0865311021

Deakin, F. W. (Frederick William), 1913-.   **3.1072**
The embattled mountain [by] F. W. D. Deakin. New York, Oxford University Press, 1971. xiii, 284 p. illus., maps, ports. 22 cm. 1. Deakin, F. W. (Frederick William), 1913- 2. World War, 1939-1945 — Underground movements — Yugoslavia. 3. World War, 1939-1945 — Personal narratives, English. I. T.
D802.Y8 D4   940.5342/0924   LC 74-169160

D804 WAR CRIMES
(see also: JX6731)

Göring, Hermann, 1893-1946. defendant.   • **3.1073**
Trial of the major war criminals before the International Military Tribunal, Nuremberg, 14 November 1945–1 October 1946. — Nuremberg, Ger., 1947-49. 42 v. 24 cm. Trial of Hermann Göring and 23 others. 1. International Military Tribunal. I. T.
D804.G42I55   341.4   LC 47-31575 *

Jackson, Robert Houghwout, 1892-1954.   • **3.1074**
The Nürnberg case / as presented by Robert H. Jackson, chief of counsel for the United States, together with other documents. — 1st ed. New York: A. A. Knopf, 1947. xviii, 268 p.: ill., plates, ports.; 22 cm. 'A Borzoi book.' 1. War crimes — Trials — Nuremberg, 1945-1946. I. International Military Tribunal. II. T.
D804.G42 J32   LC 47-1412

Smith, Bradley F.   **3.1075**
Reaching judgment at Nuremberg / Bradley F. Smith. — New York: Basic Books, c1977. xviii, 349 p.; 24 cm. Includes index. 1. Nuremberg Trial of Major German War Criminals, Nuremberg, Germany, 1945-1946 I. T.
D804.G42 S64   341.6/9   LC 76-26715   ISBN 0465068391

D805 PRISONERS. PRISONS

Reid, P. R. (Patrick Robert), 1910-.   • **3.1076**
The Colditz story. Philadelphia, Lippincott, 1953 [c1952] 288 p. illus. 22 cm. Sequel: Men of Colditz. 1. Reid, P. R. (Patrick Robert), 1910- 2. Schloss Colditz (Colditz, Germany) 3. World War, 1939-1945 — Prisoners and prisons, German 4. World War, 1939-1945 — Personal narratives, English. 5. Prisoners of war — Germany — Biography. I. T.
D805.G3 R35 1953   940.54/72/43094321   LC 52-13728

The Auschwitz album: a book based upon an album discovered   **3.1077**
by a concentration camp survivor, Lili Meier / text by Peter Hellman.
1st ed. — New York: Random House, c1981. xxxiii, 167 p.: ill.; 23 x 29 cm. 1. Auschwitz (Poland: Concentration camp) — Pictorial works. 2. Holocaust, Jewish (1939-1945) — Pictorial works. I. Meier, Lili, 1926- II. Hellman, Peter.
D805.P7 A93   943.086 19   LC 80-53907   ISBN 0394519329

The Death camp Treblinka: a documentary / edited by   **3.1078**
Alexander Donat; [cover design by Eric Gluckman].
New York: Holocaust Library: [distributed by Schocken Books], c1979. 320 p.: ill.; 22 cm. 1. Holocaust, Jewish (1939-1945) — Personal narratives 2. Treblinka (Poland: Concentration camp) — Addresses, essays, lectures. I. Donat, Alexander.
D805.P7 D37   940.53/1503/924   LC 79-53471   ISBN 0896040097

D810.C88 CRYPTOGRAPHY

Jones, R. V. (Reginald Victor), 1911-.   **3.1079**
The wizard war: British scientific intelligence, 1939–1945 / R. V. Jones. — 1st American ed. — New York: Coward, McCann & Geoghegan, 1978. xx, 556 p., [16] leaves of plates: ill.; 23 cm. 1. Jones, R. V. (Reginald Victor), 1911- 2. World War, 1939-1945 — Secret service — Great Britain 3. World War, 1939-1945 — Cryptography 4. World War, 1939-1945 — Personal narratives, English. I. T.
D810.C88 J66 1978   940.54/86/41   LC 77-17984   ISBN 0698108965

Lewin, Ronald.   **3.1080**
The American magic: codes, ciphers, and the defeat of Japan / Ronald Lewin. — New York: Farrar Straus Giroux, c1982. xv, 332 p., [16] p. of plates: ill., maps; 24 cm. Includes index. 1. World War, 1939-1945 — Cryptography 2. World War, 1939-1945 — Secret service — United States. 3. World War, 1939-1945 — Pacific Ocean. 4. World War, 1939-1945 — Japan. 5. Japan — History — 1912-1945 I. T.
D810.C88 L48   940.54/86/73 19   LC 81-15099   ISBN 0374104174

Montagu, Ewen, 1901-.   **3.1081**
[Beyond Top Secret U] Beyond Top Secret Ultra / Ewen Montagu. — 1st American ed. — New York: Coward, McCann & Geoghegan, 1978, c1977. 192 p.; 22 cm. First published in 1977 under title: Beyond Top Secret U. Includes index. 1. Montagu, Ewen, 1901- 2. World War, 1939-1945 — Secret service — Great Britain 3. World War, 1939-1945 — Personal narratives, English. 4. World War, 1939-1945 — Cryptography I. T.
D810.C88 M66 1978   940.54/86/41   LC 77-13469   ISBN 0698108825

D810.J4 JEWS. HOLOCAUST

Ainsztein, Reuben.   **3.1082**
Jewish resistance in Nazi–occupied Eastern Europe: with a historical survey of the Jew as fighter and soldier in the Diaspora / Reuben Ainsztein. — New York: Barnes & Noble Books, [1975] xxviii, 970 p.: ill.; 25 cm. Errata slip inserted. Includes indexes. 1. World War, 1939-1945 — Underground movements, Jewish 2. World War, 1939-1945 — Participation, Jewish 3. Warsaw (Poland) — History — Uprising of 1943 I. T.
D810.J4 A43   940.54/04   LC 74-1759   ISBN 0064900304

Bauer, Yehuda.   3.1083
The Holocaust in historical perspective / Yehuda Bauer. — Seattle: University
of Washington Press, c1978. ix, 181 p.; 21 cm. (Samuel and Althea Stroum
lectures in Jewish studies.) 1. Brand, Joel, 1906- — Addresses, essays, lectures.
2. Holocaust, Jewish (1939-1945) — Addresses, essays, lectures. 3. Holocaust,
Jewish (1939-1945) — Historiography — Addresses, essays, lectures. 4. Jews
— United States — Politics and government — Addresses, essays, lectures.
5. United States — Politics and government — 1933-1945 — Addresses,
essays, lectures. I. T. II. Series.
D810.J4 B315824   940.53/1503/924   *LC* 78-2988   *ISBN*
0295956062

Browning, Christopher R.   3.1084
The final solution and the German Foreign Office: a study of Referat D III of
Abteilung Deutschland, 1940–43 / by Christopher R. Browning. — New York:
Holmes & Meier, 1978. 276 p.: map; 24 cm. Includes index. 1. Germany.
Auswärtiges Amt. 2. Holocaust, Jewish (1939-1945) I. T.
D810.J4 B77   940.53/15/03924]   *LC* 78-8996   *ISBN* 0841904030

The Catastrophe of European Jewry: antecedents, history,   3.1085
reflection: selected papers / edited by Yisrael Gutman and Livia
Rothkirchen.
[S.l.]: KTAV, 1977,(c1976) 757 p.; 23 cm. Includes bibliographical references
and indexes. 1. Holocaust, Jewish (1939-1945) — Addresses, essays, lectures.
2. Antisemitism — Germany — Addresses, essays, lectures. 3. World War,
1939-1945 — Underground movements — Jews — Addresses, essays, lectures.
I. Gutman, Israel. II. Rotkirchen, Livia.
D 810 J4 C36 1976   *LC* 77-24217   *ISBN* 0870683365

Dawidowicz, Lucy S.   3.1086
The war against the Jews, 1933–1945 / Lucy S. Dawidowicz. — 1st ed. — New
York: Holt, Rinehart and Winston, [1975] xviii, 460 p.: maps; 24 cm. Includes
index. 1. Holocaust, Jewish (1939-1945) 2. Antisemitism — Germany. I. T.
D810.J4 D33   940.53/15/03924   *LC* 74-15470   *ISBN* 003013661X

Documents on the Holocaust: selected sources on the   3.1087
destruction of the Jews of Germany and Austria, Poland, and
the Soviet Union / edited by Yitzhak Arad, Yisrael Gutman,
Abraham Margaliot.
New York: Ktav Pub. House in association with Yad Vashem [and the] Anti
Defamation League, [1982] xvi, 504 p.: ill.; 23 cm. Includes indexes.
1. Holocaust, Jewish (1939-1945) — Sources. 2. Jews — Germany — History
— 1933-1945 — Sources. 3. Germany — Ethnic relations — Sources. I. Arad,
Yitzhak, 1926- II. Gutman, Israel. III. Margaliot, Abraham, 1920-
D810.J4 D63 1982   940.53/15/03924 19   *LC* 82-15324   *ISBN*
0870687549

Feig, Konnilyn G.   3.1088
Hitler's death camps: the sanity of madness / Konnilyn G. Feig. — New York:
Holmes & Meier Publishers, 1981, c1979. xxiv, 547 p.: ill.; 24 cm. Includes
index. 1. Holocaust, Jewish (1939-1945) 2. Concentration camps 3. World
War, 1939-1945 — Concentration camps I. T.
D810.J4 F36 1981   943.086 19   *LC* 81-140   *ISBN* 0841906750

Fein, Helen, 1934-.   3.1089
Accounting for genocide: national responses and Jewish victimization during
the Holocaust / Helen Fein. — New York: Free Press, c1979. xxi, 468 p.; 24
cm. Includes indexes. 1. Holocaust, Jewish (1939-1945) 2. Jews — Poland —
Warsaw — Persecutions. 3. Warsaw (Poland) — Ethnic relations. I. T.
D810.J4 F376   940.53/1503/924   *LC* 78-53085   *ISBN* 0029102200

Fleming, Gerald.   3.1090
[Hitler und die Endlösung. English] Hitler and the final solution / Gerald
Fleming; with an introduction by Saul Friedländer. — Berkeley: University of
California Press, c1984. xxxvi, 219 p., [16] p. of plates: ill.; 22 cm. Translation
of: Hitler und die Endlösung. Includes index. 1. Hitler, Adolf, 1889-1945 —
Views on Jews. 2. Holocaust, Jewish (1939-1945) 3. Germany — Ethnic
relations. I. T.
D810.J4 F5413 1984   940.53/15/03924 19   *LC* 83-24352   *ISBN*
0520051033

Frank, Anne, 1929-1945.   • 3.1091
[Achterhuis English] The diary of a young girl / translated from the Dutch by
B. M. Mooyaart–Doubleday; with an introd. by Eleanor Roosevelt. — [1st ed.]
Garden City, N.Y.: Doubleday, 1952. 285 p.: ill.; 20 cm. Translation of Het
achterhuis. 1. World War, 1939-1945 — Jews — Netherlands. 2. Jews —
Netherlands 3. Netherlands — History — German occupation, 1940-1945
I. T.
D810.J4 F715   940.53492 949.2   *LC* 52-6355

Friedman, Saul S., 1937-.   3.1092
No haven for the oppressed; United States policy toward Jewish refugees,
1938–1945, by Saul S. Friedman. Detroit, Wayne State University Press, 1973.
315 p. 24 cm. Originally presented as the author's thesis, Ohio State University.
1. Refugees, Jewish 2. Holocaust, Jewish (1939-1945) 3. Jews — United

States — Politics and government. 4. United States — Emigration and
immigration I. T.
D810.J4 F75 1973   940.53/159   *LC* 72-2271   *ISBN* 0814314740

Hilberg, Raul, 1926-.   3.1093
The destruction of the European Jews / Raul Hilberg. — Rev. and definitive ed.
— New York: Holmes & Meier, 1985. 3 v. (1,273 p.): ill., maps; 24 cm. Errata
slip inserted. 1. Holocaust, Jewish (1939-1945) 2. Germany — Politics and
government — 1933-1945 I. T.
D810.J4 H5 1985b   940.53/15/03924 19   *LC* 83-18369   *ISBN*
084190832X

Hilberg, Raul, 1926- comp.   • 3.1094
Documents of destruction: Germany and Jewry, 1933–1945 / edited with
commentary by Raul Hilberg. — Chicago: Quadrangle Books, 1971. xii, 242 p.;
22 cm. 1. Holocaust, Jewish (1939-1945) — Sources. I. T.
D810.J4 H52   940.54/05   *LC* 77-152092   *ISBN* 0812901924

A Holocaust reader / edited, with introductions and notes, by   3.1095
Lucy S. Dawidowicz.
New York: Behrman House, c1976. xiv, 397 p.; 24 cm. (Library of Jewish
studies) Includes index. 1. Holocaust, Jewish (1939-1945) — History —
Sources. I. Dawidowicz, Lucy S.
D810.J4 H65   940.53/1503/924   *LC* 75-33740   *ISBN* 0874412196

Legalizing the Holocaust: the early phase, 1933–1939 /   3.1096
introduction by John Mendelsohn.
New York: Garland, 1982. lii, 212 p.: ill.; 29 cm. — (Holocaust. 1) 1. Jews —
Legal status, laws, etc. — Germany — History — Sources. I. Mendelsohn,
John, 1928- II. Series.
D810.J4 H655 vol. 1 KK928   940.53/15/03924 s 342.43/0873
940.53/15/03924 s 344.302873 19   *LC* 81-80309   *ISBN* 082404875X

Legalizing the Holocaust, the later phase, 1939–1943 /   3.1097
introduction by John Mendelsohn.
New York: Garland Pub.,, 1982. 355 p.: ill.; 29 cm. — (Holocaust. 2) 1. Jews
— Germany — History — 1933-1945 — Sources. 2. Holocaust, Jewish
(1939-1945) — Sources. 3. Germany — Ethnic relations — Sources. I. Series.
D810.J4 H655 vol. 2 DS135.G33   940.53/15/03924 s 940.53/15/03924
19   *LC* 81-80310   *ISBN* 0824048768

The Crystal Night Pogrom / introduction by John Mendelsohn.   3.1098
New York: Garland, 1982. 402 p.; 29 cm. — (Holocaust. 3) 1. Crystal Night,
1938 — Sources. 2. Germany — Ethnic relations — Sources. I. Mendelsohn,
John, 1928- II. Series.
D810.J4 H655 vol. 3 DS135.G33   940.53/15/03924 s 940.53/15/03924
19   *LC* 81-80311   *ISBN* 0824048776

Propaganda and aryanization, 1938–1944 / introduction by John   3.1099
Mendelsohn.
New York: Garland, 1982. 288 p.: ill.; 29 cm. (Holocaust. 4) 1. Antisemitism
— Germany — History — Sources. 2. Jewish property — Europe — History
— Sources. 3. Confiscations — Europe — History — Sources. I. Series.
D810.J4 H655 vol. 4 DS146.G4   940.53/15/03924 19   *LC* 81-80312
ISBN 0824048784

Jewish emigration from 1933 to the Evian conference of 1938 /   3.1100
introduction by John Mendelsohn.
New York: Garland Pub., 1982. 282 p.: ill.; 29 cm. — (Holocaust. 5) 1. Jews —
Germany — Migrations — Sources. 2. Germany — Emigration and
immigration — History — 1933-1945 — Sources. I. Series.
D810.J4 H655 vol. 5 DS135.G33   940.53/15/03924 s 940.53/15/03924
19   *LC* 81-80313   *ISBN* 0824048792

Jewish emigration 1938–1940, Rublee negotiations, and   3.1101
Intergovernmental Committee / introduction by John
Mendelsohn.
New York: Garland Pub., 1982. 256 p.: ill.; 29 cm. — (Holocaust. 6) 1. Rublee,
George, 1868- 2. Jews — Germany — Migrations — Sources. 3. Germany —
Emigration and immigration — History — 1933-1945 — Sources.
I. Intergovernmental Committee on Refugees. II. Series.
D810.J4 H655 vol. 6 DS135.G33   940.53/15/03924 s 940.53/15/03924
19   *LC* 81-80314   *ISBN* 0824048806

Jewish emigration: the S.S. St. Louis affair and other cases /   3.1102
introduction by John Mendelsohn.
New York: Garland Pub., 1982. 270 p.: ill.; 29 cm. — (Holocaust. 7) English
and German. 1. St. Louis (Ship) 2. Jews — Germany — Migrations —
Sources. 3. Cuba — Emigration and immigration — Sources. 4. Germany —
Emigration and immigration — Sources. I. Mendelsohn, John, 1928-
II. Series.
D810.J4 H655 vol. 7 DS135.G33   940.53/15/03924 s 940.53/15/03924
19   *LC* 81-80315   *ISBN* 0824048814

Deportation of the Jews to the east: Stettin, 1940, to Hungary,   **3.1103**
1944 / introduction by John Mendelsohn.
New York: Garland, 1982. 254 p.: ill.; 29 cm. — (Holocaust. 8) 1. Holocaust, Jewish (1939-1945) — Sources. I. Mendelsohn, John, 1928- II. Series.
D810.J4 H655 vol. 8   940.53/15/03924 s 940.53/15/03924 19   *LC*
81-80316   *ISBN* 0824048822

Medical experiments on Jewish inmates of concentration camps   **3.1104**
/ introduction by John Mendelsohn.
New York: Garland Pub., 1982. 245 p.: ill.; 29 cm. — (Holocaust. 9)
1. Holocaust, Jewish (1939-1945) — Sources. 2. Human experimentation in medicine — Germany — Sources. I. Series.
D810.J4 H655 vol. 9   940.53/15/03924 s 940.53/15/03924 19   *LC*
81-80317   *ISBN* 0824048830

The Einsatzgruppen or murder commandos / introduction by   **3.1105**
Willard A. Fletcher.
New York: Garland, 1982. 250 p.: ill.; 29 cm. — (Holocaust. 10) 1. Jews — Soviet Union — Persecutions — Sources. 2. Holocaust, Jewish (1939-1945) — Soviet Union — Sources. 3. Soviet Union — Ethnic relations — Sources. I. Fletcher, Willard Allen. II. Series.
D810.J4 H655 vol. 10 DS135.R92   940.53/15/03924 s 947/.00492 19
   LC 81-80318   *ISBN* 0824048849

Wannsee-Konferenz (1942: Berlin, Germany)   **3.1106**
The Wannsee Protocol and a 1944 Report on Auschwitz by the Office of Strategic Services / introduction by Robert Wolfe. — New York: Garland Pub., 1982. 278 p.: port.; 29 cm. — (Holocaust. 11) English and German.
1. Holocaust, Jewish (1939-1945) — Sources. 2. Germany — Politics and government — 1933-1945 — Sources. I. Wolfe, Robert, 1921- II. United States. Office of Strategic Services. Report on Auschwitz. III. T. IV. Series.
D810.J4 H655 vol. 11   940.53/15/03924 s 940.53/15/03924 19   *LC*
81-80319   *ISBN* 0824048857

The 'Final solution' in the extermination camps and the   **3.1107**
aftermath / introduction by Henry Friedlander.
New York: Garland Pub., 1982. 240 p.: ill., map; 29 cm. — (Holocaust. 12)
1. Holocaust, Jewish (1939-1945) — Sources. I. Series.
D810.J4 H655 vol. 12   940.53/15/03924 s 940.53/15/03924 19   *LC*
81-80320   *ISBN* 0824048865

The Judicial system and the Jews in Nazi Germany /   **3.1108**
introduction by John Mendelsohn.
New York: Garland, 1982. 290 p.: ill.; 29 cm. — (Holocaust. 13) 1. Jews — Germany — History — 1933-1945 — Sources. 2. Holocaust, Jewish (1939-1945) — Germany — Sources. 3. Jews — Legal status, laws, etc. — Germany — Sources. 4. Justice, Administration of — Germany — Sources. 5. Germany — Ethnic relations — Sources. I. Mendelsohn, John, 1928- II. Series.
D810.J4 H655 vol. 13 DS135.G33   940.53/15/03924 s 943/.004924 19
   LC 81-80321   *ISBN* 0824048873

Relief and rescue of Jews from Nazi oppression, 1943–1945 /   **3.1109**
introduction by John Mendelsohn.
New York: Garland Pub., 1982. 242 p.: ill.; 29 cm. — (Holocaust. 14) 1. World War, 1939-1945 — Jews — Rescue — Sources. I. Series.
D810.J4 H655 vol. 14   940.53/15/03924 s 940.53/15/03924 19   *LC*
81-80322   *ISBN* 0824048881

Relief in Hungary and the failure of the Joel Brand mission /   **3.1110**
introduction by John Mendelsohn.
New York: Garland Pub., 1982. 249 p.: ill.; 29 cm. — (Holocaust. 15) 1. Brand, Joel, 1906- 2. Holocaust, Jewish (1939-1945) — Hungary — Sources. 3. World War, 1939-1945 — Jews — Rescue — Hungary — Sources. 4. Jews — Hungary — Persecutions — Sources. 5. Hungary — Ethnic relations — Sources. I. Series.
D810.J4 H655 vol. 15 DS135.H9   940.53/15/039240439 19   *LC*
81-80323   *ISBN* 082404889X

Rescue to Switzerland: the Musy and Saly Mayer affairs /   **3.1111**
introduction by Sybil Milton.
New York: Garland Pub., 1982. 219 p.; 29 cm. — (Holocaust. 16) 1. Mayer, Saly, 1882-1950. 2. Refugees, Jewish — Switzerland — Sources. 3. Jews — Switzerland — Politics and government — Sources. 4. World War, 1939-1945 — Jews — Rescue — Switzerland — Sources. 5. Switzerland — Ethnic relations — Sources. I. Series.
D810.J4 H655 vol. 16 DS135.S9   940.53/15/03924 s
940.53/15/039240494 19   *LC* 81-80324   *ISBN* 0824048903

Punishing the perpetrators of the Holocaust: the Brandt, Pohl,   **3.1112**
and Ohlendorf cases / introduction by John Mendelsohn.
New York: Garland, 1982. 266 p.: ports.; 29 cm. — (Holocaust. 17) 1. Holocaust, Jewish (1939-1945) — Sources. 2. Nuremberg War Crime Trials, Nuremberg, Germany, 1946-1949 I. Mendelsohn, John, 1928- II. Series.
D810.J4 H655 vol. 17   940.53/15/03924 s 364.1/38 19   *LC* 81-80325
   ISBN 0824048911

Punishing the perpetrators of the Holocaust: the Ohlendorf and   **3.1113**
von Weizsaecker cases / introduction by John Mendelsohn.
New York: Garland Pub., 1982. 259 p.: port.; 29 cm. (Holocaust. 18)
1. Ohlendorf, Otto, 1907-1951 — Trials, litigation, etc. 2. Weizsäcker, Ernst, Freiherr von, 1882-1951 — Trials, litigation, etc. 3. Nuremberg War Crime Trials, Nuremberg, Germany, 1946-1949 4. Holocaust, Jewish (1939-1945) I. Mendelsohn, John, 1928- II. Series.
D810.J4 H655 vol. 18 LAW   940.53/15/03924 s 345/.0238
940.53/15/03924 s 342.5238 19   *LC* 81-80326   *ISBN* 082404892X

Jewish leadership during the Nazi era: patterns of behavior in   **3.1114**
the Free World / edited by Randolph L. Braham.
New York: Social Science Monographs: Institute for Holocaust Studies of the City University of New York, 1985. xiv, 154 p.; 24 cm. (East European monographs. no. 175) (Holocaust studies series.) 1. Holocaust, Jewish (1939-1945) — Public opinion — Addresses, essays, lectures. 2. World War, 1939-1945 — Jews — Rescue — Addresses, essays, lectures. 3. Jews — Politics and government — Addresses, essays, lectures. 4. Public opinion — Jews — Addresses, essays, lectures. I. Braham, Randolph L. II. Series. III. Series: Holocaust studies series.
D810.J4 J346 1985   940.53/15/03924 19   *LC* 84-52081   *ISBN*
0880330678

Krakowski, Shmuel.   **3.1115**
[Lehimah Yehudit be-Polin neged ha-Natsim, 1942-1944. English] The war of the doomed: Jewish armed resistance in Poland, 1942–1944 / Shmuel Krakowski; foreword by Yehuda Bauer; translated from the Hebrew by Orah Blaustein. — New York: Holmes and Meier, 1984. xii, 340 p.: maps; 24 cm. Translation of: Lehimah Yehudit be-Polin neged ha-Natsim, 1942-1944. Includes index. 1. World War, 1939-1945 — Underground movements, Jewish — Poland. 2. Jews — Poland — Persecutions. 3. Holocaust, Jewish (1939-1945) — Poland 4. Poland — History — Occupation, 1939-1945 5. Poland — Ethnic relations. I. T.
D810.J4 K68413 1984   940.53/15/03924 19   *LC* 83-18537   *ISBN*
0841908516

Laqueur, Walter, 1921-.   **3.1116**
The terrible secret: suppression of the truth about Hitler's 'final solution' / Walter Laqueur. — Boston: Little, Brown, 1981 (c1980). 262 p.; 22 cm.
1. Holocaust, Jewish (1939-1945) — Censorship. I. T.
D810.J4 L278 1980b   943.086 19   *LC* 80-26613   *ISBN* 0316514748

Levin, Nora.   • **3.1117**
The holocaust: the destruction of European Jewry, 1933–1945. — New York: T. Y. Crowell Co., [1968] xvi, 768 p.: ill., facsims., maps, ports.; 24 cm.
1. World War, 1939-1945 — Jews — Europe. 2. Jews — Europe I. T.
D810.J4 L455   940.531/5   *LC* 67-23676

Minco, Marga.   **3.1118**
Bitter herbs; a little chronicle. [Translated from the Dutch by Roy Edwards. — Oxford; New York]: Pergamon Press, [1969, c1960] vii, 78 p.; 20 cm. — (Athena books) (The Pergamon English library.) Translation of Het bittere kruid. 1. World War, 1939-1945 — Personal narratives, Dutch. 2. World War, 1939-1945 — Jews — Netherlands. 3. Jews — Netherlands I. T.
D810.J4M5x   940.548/1/492   *LC* 77-3677

Perl, William R.   **3.1119**
The four-front war: from the Holocaust to the Promised Land / by William R. Perl. — New York: Crown Publishers, c1979. viii, 376 p., [4] leaves of plates: ill.; 24 cm. Rev. ed. published as: Operation action. 1983. 1. Perl, William R. 2. Holocaust, Jewish (1939-1945) — Personal narratives 3. World War, 1939-1945 — Jews — Rescue 4. Palestine — Emigration and immigration I. T.
D810.J4 P477 1979   940.53/1503/924   *LC* 79-16255   *ISBN*
0517538377

Survivors, victims, and perpetrators: essays on the Nazi   **3.1120**
Holocaust / edited by Joel E. Dimsdale.
Washington: Hemisphere Pub. Corp., c1980. xxii, 474 p.; 24 cm. 1. Holocaust, Jewish (1939-1945) — Psychological aspects — Addresses, essays, lectures. 2. Refugees, Jewish — Psychology — Addresses, essays, lectures. 3. National socialism — Psychological aspects — Addresses, essays, lectures. 4. Persecution — Psychological aspects — Addresses, essays, lectures. I. Dimsdale, Joel E., 1947-
D810.J4 S87   940.53/1503/924   *LC* 79-24834   *ISBN* 0891161457

Trunk, Isaiah.   **3.1121**
Jewish responses to Nazi persecution: collective and individual behavior in extremis / Isaiah Trunk. — New York: Stein and Day, c1979. xii, 371 p.: ill.; 25 cm. 1. Holocaust, Jewish (1939-1945) 2. World War, 1939-1945 — Personal narratives, Jewish I. T.
D810.J4 T7   940.53/1503/924   *LC* 78-6378   *ISBN* 0812825004

Trunk, Isaiah.   **3.1122**
Judenrat; the Jewish councils in Eastern Europe under Nazi occupation. Introd. by Jacob Robinson. New York, Macmillan [1972] xxxv, 664 p. illus. 24 cm.

1. Jews — Europe, Eastern — Politics and government. 2. Holocaust, Jewish (1939-1945) I. T.
D810.J4 T72   940.53/15/03924   *LC* 70-173692

Wyman, David S.   **3.1123**
The abandonment of the Jews: America and the Holocaust, 1941–1945 / David S. Wyman. — 1st ed. — New York: Pantheon Books, c1984. xv, 444 p.; 25 cm. Includes index. 1. United States. War Refugee Board. 2. Holocaust, Jewish (1939-1945) 3. World War, 1939-1945 — United States. 4. World War, 1939-1945 — Jews — Rescue — United States. 5. United States — Emigration and immigration I. T.
D810.J4 W95 1984   940.53/15/03924 19   *LC* 84-42711   *ISBN* 0394428137

Yad Vashem International Historical Conference. (4th: 1980: Jerusalem)   **3.1124**
[Mahanot ha-rikuz ha-Natsiyim. English] The Nazi concentration camps: structure and aims, the image of the prisoner, the Jews in the camps: proceedings of the fourth Yad Vashem International Historical Conference, Jerusalem, January 1980 / editors, Yisrael Gutman, Avital Saf; translations, Dina Cohen ... et al.]. — Jerusalem: Yad Vashem, 1984. 746 p., [6] leaves of plates (some folded): ill., facsims., map, plans; 23 cm. Translation of: Mahanot ha-rikuz ha-Natsiyim. 1. Holocaust, Jewish (1939-1945) — Congresses. 2. World War, 1939-1945 — Concentration camps — Congresses. I. Gutman, Israel. II. Saf, Avital. III. Yad va-shem, rashut ha-zikaron la-Sho'ah vela-gevurah. IV. T.
D810.J4 Y29 1980a   940.53/15/03924 19   *LC* 85-178402

Zimmels, Hirsch Jakob.   **3.1125**
The echo of the Nazi holocaust in rabbinic literature / by H. J. Zimmels. [New York]: Ktav Pub. House, 1977, c1975. xxiii, 372 p. on cm. On spine: The Nazi holocaust. 1. Holocaust and Jewish law 2. Holocaust, Jewish (1939-1945) 3. Responsa — 1800- I. T. II. Title: The Nazi holocaust.
D810.J4 Z55 1977   296.1/8   *LC* 76-56778   *ISBN* 0870684272

D810.N4 Afro–Americans

Buchanan, Albert Russell, 1906-.   **3.1126**
Black Americans in World War II / A. Russell Buchanan. Santa Barbara, Calif.: Clio Books, c1977. ix, 148 p.; 24 cm. Includes index. 1. World War, 1939-1945 — Afro-Americans 2. United States — Race relations I. T.
D810.N4 B82   940.54/03   *LC* 76-53577   *ISBN* 0874362276

The Invisible soldier: the experience of the Black soldier, World War II / compiled and edited by Mary Penick Motley; with a foreword by Howard Donovan Queen.   **3.1127**
Detroit: Wayne State University Press, 1975. 364 p.: ill.; 24 cm. Includes index. 1. World War, 1939-1945 — Participation, Afro-American — History — Sources. 2. Afro-Americans — Interviews. 3. Afro-Americans — History — 1877-1964 — Sources. 4. United States — Race relations I. Motley, Mary Penick, 1920-
D810.N4 I58   940.54/03   *LC* 75-29420   *ISBN* 081431550X

McGuire, Phillip, 1944-.   **3.1128**
Taps for a Jim Crow army: letters from black soldiers in World War II / Phillip McGuire; with a foreword by Benjamin Quarles. — Santa Barbara, Calif.: ABC-Clio, c1983. li, 278 p.: ill.; 24 cm. Includes index. 1. World War, 1939-1945 — Participation, Afro-American. 2. World War, 1939-1945 — Personal narratives, American. 3. Afro-American soldiers — Correspondence. 4. United States — Armed Forces — Afro-Americans 5. United States — Armed Forces — Military life I. T.
D810.N4 M38 1983   940.54/03 19   *LC* 82-22689   *ISBN* 0874360242

Osur, Alan M., 1941-.   **3.1129**
Blacks in the Army Air Forces during World War II: the problem of race relations / by Alan M. Osur. — Washington: Office of Air Force History: for sale by the Supt. of Docs., U.S. Govt. Print. Off., foreword 1977. 227 p., [4] leaves of plates: ill.; 24 cm. Includes index. 1. United States. Army Air Forces — Afro-American troops. 2. World War, 1939-1945 — Participation, Afro-American. 3. Afro-Americans — Segregation I. T.
D810.N4 O76   940.54/03   *LC* 76-20772

Wynn, Neil A.   **3.1130**
The Afro–American and the Second World War / Neil A. Wynn. New York: Holmes & Meier Publishers, 1976, c1975. viii, 183 p.; 24 cm. Includes index. 1. World War, 1939-1945 — Afro-Americans 2. Afro-Americans — Civil rights 3. United States — Race question. 4. United States — Armed Forces — Afro-Americans I. T.
D810.N4 W93 1976   940.53/1503/96073   *LC* 76-3767   *ISBN* 0841902313

D810.P6–.P7 Propaganda

Film & radio propaganda in World War II / edited by K.R.M. Short.   **3.1131**
1st ed. — Knoxville: University of Tennessee Press, 1983. 341 p.; 23 cm. 1. World War, 1939-1945 — Propaganda — Addresses, essays, lectures. 2. Radio in propaganda — Addresses, essays, lectures. 3. Motion pictures in propaganda — Addresses, essays, lectures. I. Short, K. R. M. (Kenneth R. M.) II. Title: Film and radio propaganda in World War II.
D810.P6 F5 1983   940.54/88 19   *LC* 82-23838   *ISBN* 0870493868

Balfour, Michael Leonard Graham, 1908-.   **3.1132**
Propaganda in war, 1939–1945: organisations, policies, and publics, in Britain and Germany / Michael Balfour. — London; Boston: Routledge & Kegan Paul, 1979. xvii, 520 p.; 25 cm. Includes index. 1. World War, 1939-1945 — Propaganda 2. Propaganda, British — History. 3. Propaganda, German — History. I. T.
D810.P7 G7216   940.54/88   *LC* 79-40304   *ISBN* 0710001932

D810.S7 Secret Service

Brown, Anthony Cave.   **3.1133**
Bodyguard of lies / Anthony Cave Brown. — 1st ed. — New York: Harper & Ron, c1975. x, 947 p., [8] leaves of plates: ill.; 24 cm. Includes index. 1. World War, 1939-1945 — Secret service I. T.
D810.S7 C36 1975   D810S7 C36 1975.   940.54/85   *LC* 72-9749   *ISBN* 0060105518

Hinsley, F. H. (Francis Harry), 1918-.   **3.1134**
British intelligence in the Second World War: its influence on strategy and operations / by F. H. Hinsley; with E. E. Thomas, C. F. G. Ranson, R. C. Knight. — London: H.M. Stationery Off., 1979- < 1981 >. v. < 1-2 >: maps; 26 cm. — (History of the Second World War.) 1. World War, 1939-1945 — Secret service — Great Britain 2. Great Britain — History — George VI, 1936-1952 I. Thomas, E. E. (Edward Eastaway) II. T. III. Series.
D810.S7 H49 1979b   940.54/86/41   *LC* 79-322049   *ISBN* 0116309334

Kahn, David, 1930-.   **3.1135**
Hitler's spies: German military intelligence in World War II / David Kahn. — New York: Macmillan, c1978. xiii, 671 p., [20] leaves of plates: ill.; 24 cm. Includes index. 1. World War, 1939-1945 — Secret service — Germany. 2. Military intelligence — Germany — History — 20th century. 3. Germany — History — 1933-1945 I. T.
D810.S7 K25   940.54/87/43   *LC* 77-25271   *ISBN* 0025606107

Stafford, David.   **3.1136**
Britain and European resistance, 1940–1945: a survey of the Special Operations Executive, with documents / David Stafford. — Toronto: University of Toronto Press, 1980. xiii, 295 p.; 22 cm. Includes index. 1. Great Britain. Special Operations Executive — History. 2. World War, 1939-1945 — Secret service — Great Britain 3. World War, 1939-1945 — Underground movements — Europe. I. T.
D810.S7 S76 1980   940.54/86/41   *LC* 79-19224   *ISBN* 0802023614

D810.W7 Women

Rupp, Leila J., 1950-.   **3.1137**
Mobilizing women for war: German and American propaganda, 1939–1945 / Leila J. Rupp. — Princeton, N.J.: Princeton University Press, c1978. xii, 243 p.: ill.; 23 cm. Includes index. 1. World War, 1939-1945 — Women — United States. 2. World War, 1939-1945 — Propaganda 3. Women — United States — Social conditions. 4. Women — Germany — Social conditions. 5. Propaganda, German 6. Propaganda, American 7. World War, 1939-1945 — Women — Germany. I. T.
D810.W7 R8   940.54/88   *LC* 77-85562   *ISBN* 0691046492

Summerfield, Penny.   **3.1138**
Women workers in the Second World War: production and patriarchy in conflict / Penny Summerfield. — London; Dover, N.H.: Croom Helm, c1984. 214 p.: ill.; 23 cm. Includes index. 1. World War, 1939-1945 — Women 2. Women — Employment — Great Britain — History — 20th century. I. T.
D810.W7 S79 1984   331.4/0941 19   *LC* 85-127263   *ISBN* 0709923171

D811 Personal Narratives

Stilwell, Joseph Warren, 1883-1946.   **• 3.1139**
The Stilwell papers, arr. and ed. by Theodore H. White. — New York: W. Sloane Associates, [1948] xvi, 357 p.: illus., ports., maps, facsims.; 22 cm. 1. World War, 1939-1945 — Campaigns — Burma 2. World War, 1939-1945

— China. 3. World War, 1939-1945 — Personal narratives, American. I. White, Theodore Harold, 1915- ed. II. T.
D811.S83   940.54   *LC* 48-6966

Shirer, William L. (William Lawrence), 1904-.   • **3.1140**
Berlin diary; the journal of a foreign correspondent, 1934–1941 [by] William L. Shirer. New York, A. A. Knopf, 1941. 3. p. 1., [v]-vi p., 2 l., [3]-605, xxi, [1] p. 22 cm. 'First edition.' Sequel: End of a Berlin diary. 1. Hitler, Adolf, 1889-1945. 2. Shirer, William L. (William Lawrence), 1904- 3. Shirer, William L. (William Lawrence), 1904- 4. World War, 1939-1945 — Personal narratives, American. 5. World War, 1939-1945 — Germany. 6. Europe — Politics and government — 1918-1945 7. Germany — Politics and government — 1933-1945 I. T.
D811.5.S5 1941   940.5343   *LC* 41-9746

D812–829 PEACE. RECONSTRUCTION

Dunn, Frederick Sherwood, 1893-1962.   • **3.1141**
Peace-making and the settlement with Japan. Principal collaborators: Annemarie Shimony, Percy E. Corbett [and] Bernard C. Cohen. Princeton, N.J., Princeton University Press, 1963. 210 p. 23 cm. 1. World War, 1939-1945 — Peace 2. World War, 1939-1945 — Japan. 3. United States — Foreign relations administration I. T.
D814.8.D84   940.5314   *LC* 63-7155

Armstrong, Anne, 1924-.   • **3.1142**
Unconditional surrender; the impact of the Casablanca policy upon World War II. — New Brunswick, N.J.: Rutgers University Press, [1961] 304 p.; 22 cm. 1. World War, 1939-1945 — Peace 2. Anti-Nazi movement 3. Capitulations, Military I. T.
D815.A7   940.54/012 19   *LC* 61-10253

Byrnes, James Francis, 1879-1972.   • **3.1143**
Speaking frankly. — [1st ed.]. — New York: Harper, [1947] xii, 324 p.: illus., ports., map (on lining-papers); 22 cm. 1. World War, 1939-1945 — Peace 2. World politics — 1945- 3. World War, 1939-1945 — Diplomatic history I. T.
D815.B9   940.531   *LC* 47-11175

O'Connor, Raymond Gish.   • **3.1144**
Diplomacy for victory; FDR and unconditional surrender [by] Raymond G. O'Connor. — [1st ed.]. — New York: Norton, [1971] xiii, 143 p.: maps.; 21 cm. — (The Norton essays in American history) 1. World War, 1939-1945 — Peace 2. World War, 1939-1945 — Diplomatic history 3. U.S. — Foreign relations — 1933-1945. I. T.
D816.O24 1971   940.532/2/73   *LC* 70-155986   *ISBN* 0393054411

Backer, John H., 1902-.   **3.1145**
The decision to divide Germany: American foreign policy in transition / John H. Backer. — Durham, N.C.: Duke University Press, 1978. x, 212 p.; 25 cm. Includes index. 1. World War, 1939-1945 — Peace 2. World War, 1939-1945 — Germany. 3. World War, 1939-1945 — Reparations 4. World War, 1939-1945 — Diplomatic history 5. United States — Foreign relations — Germany. 6. Germany — Foreign relations — United States. I. T.
D821.G4 B3   940.53/14   *LC* 77-84614   *ISBN* 0822303914

Butow, Robert Joseph Charles, 1924-.   **3.1146**
Japan's decision to surrender. Foreword by Edwin O. Reischauer. Stanford, Stanford University Press, 1954. xi, 259 p. 25 cm. (The Hoover Library on War, Revolution, and Peace. Publication no. 24) Issued also as thesis, Stanford University, in microfilm form. Bibliography: p. 234-240. 1. World War, 1939-1945 — Japan. I. T.
D821.J3B8 1954   940.5314   *LC* 54-8145

D839–888 Post–War History, 1945–

Conference of Heads of State or Government of Non-aligned Countries.   3.1147
Neither East nor West: the basic documents of non–alignment / edited by Henry M. Christman. — New York: Sheed & Ward, [1973] ix, 206 p.; 21 cm. Selected addresses and documents from the 1st-3d Conferences, held in 1961, 1964, and 1970. 1. World politics — 1945- — Congresses. I. Christman, Henry M. ed. II. T.
D839.2.C65 1970   327   *LC* 72-6689   *ISBN* 0836205006

Hammarskjöld, Dag, 1905-1961.   • **3.1148**
Markings / Dag Hammarskjöld; translated from the Swedish by Leif Sjöberg & W.H. Auden; with a foreword by W.H. Auden. — New York: Knopf, 1964. xxiii, 221 p. Translation of Vägmärken. Verse and prose. I. T.
D839.7.H3 A313   *LC* 64-19087

Stolpe, Sven, 1905-.   • **3.1149**
Dag Hammarskjöld: a spiritual portrait / by Sven Stolpe, English translation by Naomi Walford. — New York: Scribner, c1966. 127 p.: port.; 22 cm. (The Scribner library; 138) Translation of Dag Hammarskjöld's andliga väg. 1. Hammarskjöld, Dag, 1905-1961. I. T.
D839.7.H3S753   D839.7H3 S753 1966.   248.2   *LC* 66-12027

Urquhart, Brian.   **3.1150**
Hammarskjold. [1st ed.] New York, Knopf, 1972. xv, 630, xxv p. illus. 25 cm. 1. Hammarskjold, Dag, 1905-1961. 2. United Nations — Biography. 3. World politics — 1945-1955 4. World politics — 1955-1965 5. Statesmen — Sweden — Biography. I. T.
D839.7.H3 U7   341.23/24 B 19   *LC* 72-2255   *ISBN* 0394479602

Thant, U, 1909-1974.   **3.1151**
View from the UN / U Thant. — 1st ed. — Garden City, N.Y.: Doubleday, 1978. xix, 508 p.; 22 cm. 1. Thant, U, 1909-1974. 2. United Nations — Biography. 3. Statesmen — Biography. I. T.
D839.7.T5 A35   341.23/3/0924 B   *LC* 76-57517   *ISBN* 0385115415

Kennan, George Frost, 1904-.   • **3.1152**
Russia, the atom and the West. [1st ed.] New York, Harper [1958] 116 p. 22 cm. 1. World politics — 1955- I. T.
D 840 K34   *LC* 58-8078L

Seton-Watson, Hugh.   • **3.1153**
Neither war nor peace: the struggle for power in the postwar world. — New York: Praeger, [1960] 504 p.; 23 cm. — (Books that matter) 1. World politics — 1945- 2. International relations I. T.
D840.S4   909.82   *LC* 60-6992

American Universities Field Staff.   • **3.1154**
Expectant peoples; nationalism and development. Under the editorship of K. H. Silvert. With a pref. by Kenneth W. Thompson. — New York, Random House [c1963] xxi, 489 p. 22 cm. Bibliography: p. [451]-468. 1. Nationalism 2. History, Modern — 1945- 3. Community development I. Silvert, Kalman H. ed. II. T.
D842.A765   909.82   *LC* 63-19716

The New history, the 1980s and beyond: studies in   3.1155
interdisciplinary history / edited by Theodore K. Rabb and
Robert I. Rotberg; contributors, Peter H. Smith ... [et al.].
Princeton, N.J.: Princeton University Press, c1982. 332 p.; 25 cm. 1. History, Modern — 1945- — Historiography. 2. Historiography I. Rabb, Theodore K. II. Rotberg, Robert I. III. Smith, Peter H.
D842.N38 1982   909.82/8/072 19   *LC* 82-47634   *ISBN* 0691053707

Pearcy, George Etzel, 1905-.   • **3.1156**
A handbook of new nations / [by] G. Etzel Pearcy & Elvyn A. Stoneman; cartography by Frank J. Ford & Clare Ford. — New York: Crowell, [1968] xx, 327 p.: maps.; 24 cm. 1. States, New — Handbooks, manuals, etc. I. Stoneman, Elvyn A. joint author. II. T. III. Title: New nations.
D842.P4   910   *LC* 68-11070

D843–847 POLITICAL AND DIPLOMATIC HISTORY

Angell, Robert Cooley, 1899-.   3.1157
The quest for world order / Robert Cooley Angell. — Ann Arbor: University of Michigan Press, c1979. 186 p.; 23 cm. — (Michigan faculty series) 1. United Nations. 2. World politics — 1945- I. T.
D843.A523 1979   327/.09/04   *LC* 78-14248   *ISBN* 0472063049

Aron, Raymond, 1905-.   • **3.1158**
[Espoir et peur du siècle. De la guerre. English] On war / translated from the French by Terence Kilmartin. — New York: W. W. Norton [1968] ix, 143 p.; 20 cm. (The Norton library, 107) Translation of De la guerre, an essay in a book entitled Espoir et peur du siècle originally published in 1957. 1. World politics — 1955-1965 2. War I. T.
D843.A683 1968   909.82   *LC* 68-2039

Balfour, Michael Leonard Graham, 1908-.   3.1159
The adversaries: America, Russia, and the open world, 1941–62 / Michael Balfour. — London; Boston: Routledge & Kegan Paul, 1981. xv, 259 p.; 23 cm. Includes index. 1. World politics — 1945- 2. World politics — 1933-1945 3. United States — Relations — Soviet Union 4. Soviet Union — Relations — United States I. T.
D843.B247   909.82 19   *LC* 80-41559   *ISBN* 071000687X

Ball, George W.   • **3.1160**
The discipline of power; essentials of a modern world structure, by George W. Ball. — [1st ed.]. — Boston: Little, Brown, [1968] 363 p.; 22 cm. 'An Atlantic

Monthly Press book.' 1. World politics — 1945- — Addresses, essays, lectures. I. T.
D843.B25   327   LC 67-28228

Churchill, Winston Leonard Spencer, 1874-1965.   • **3.1161**
The sinews of peace, post–war speeches / ed. by Randolph S. Churchill. — Boston: Houghton Mifflin Co. [1949] 256 p.; 22 cm. 'Covers the ... period from ... June, 1945, to the close of ... 1946.' 1. World politics — 1945- 2. Gt. Brit. — Pol. & govt. — 1945- I. T.
D843.C53   940.55   LC 49-9229 *

Crozier, Brian.   • **3.1162**
The rebels: a study of post–war insurrections / Brian Crozier. — Boston: Beacon Press, 1960. 256 P. — 1. Revolutions 2. World politics — 1945- I. T.
D843.C73 1960   LC 60-11735

Feis, Herbert, 1893-1972.   • **3.1163**
From trust to terror; the onset of the cold war, 1945–1950. — [1st ed.]. — New York: Norton, [1970] xx, 428 p.: illus., map, ports.; 25 cm. 1. World politics — 1945-1955 I. T.
D843.F387 1970   327/.1   LC 70-116122   ISBN 039305425X

Gaulle, Charles de, 1890-1970.   • **3.1164**
Memoirs of hope: renewal and endeavor / translated by Terence Kilmartin. — New York: Simon and Schuster [1971] 392 p.; 23 cm. Translation of Mémoires d'espoir. 1. World politics — 1945- I. T.
D843.G2813 1971b   944.083/0924   LC 76-163103   ISBN 0671211188

Halle, Louis Joseph, 1910-.   • **3.1165**
The cold war as history, by Louis J. Halle. — [1st U.S. ed.]. — New York: Harper & Row, [1967] xiv, 434 p.; 22 cm. 1. History, Modern — 1945- I. T.
D843.H26 1967a   909.825   LC 67-21259

Herken, Gregg, 1947-.   **3.1166**
The winning weapon: the atomic bomb in the cold war, 1945–1950 / Gregg Herken. — 1st ed. — New York: Knopf: distributed by Random House, 1981 (c1980). x, 425 p.; 25 cm. Includes index. 1. World politics — 1945-1955 2. Atomic bomb 3. World War, 1939-1945 — Diplomatic history 4. United States — Foreign relations — 1933-1945 5. United States — Foreign relations — 1945-1953 I. T.
D843.H438   327/.09044 19   LC 80-7643   ISBN 0394503945

Holsti, K. J. (Kalevi Jaakko), 1935-.   **3.1167**
Why nations realign: foreign policy restructuring in the postwar world / K.J. Holsti; with Miguel Monterichard ... [et al.]. — London; Boston: Allen & Unwin, 1982. xi, 225 p.; 24 cm. 1. World politics — 1955-1965 — Addresses, essays, lectures. 2. World politics — 1965-1975 — Addresses, essays, lectures. 3. World politics — 1975-1985 — Addresses, essays, lectures. 4. International relations — Addresses, essays, lectures. I. T.
D843.H654 1982   327/.0904 19   LC 81-22843   ISBN 0043510620

Ward, Barbara, 1914-.   • **3.1168**
Policy for the West / by Barbara Ward. — Westport, Conn.: Greenwood Press, [1970, c1951] viii, 317 p.; 23 cm. 1. International organization 2. World politics — 1945- I. T.
D843.J3 1970   327/.11/09044   LC 73-100236   ISBN 0837134285

Jaspers, Karl, 1883-1969.   **3.1169**
[Atombombe und die Zukunft des Menschen. English] The future of mankind. Translated by E. B. Ashton. [Chicago] University of Chicago Press [1961] 342 p. 24 cm. Translation of Die Atombombe und die Zukunft des Menschen. 1. World politics — 1955-1965 2. Atomic bomb I. T.
D843.J3714   909.82   LC 60-7237

Liska, George.   **3.1170**
Russia & world order: strategic choices and the laws of power in history / George Liska. — Baltimore: Johns Hopkins University Press, c1980. xii, 194 p.; 24 cm. 1. World politics — 1945- 2. Russia — Foreign relations — 1945- I. T.
D843.L53   327/.09/04   LC 79-22872   ISBN 0801823145

Sigmund, Paul E. ed.   • **3.1171**
The ideologies of the developing nations / edited by Paul E. Sigmund. — 2d rev. ed. New York: Praeger [1972] viii, 483 p.; 21 cm. 1. World politics — 1945- 2. Developing countries — Politics and government. I. T.
D843.S52 1972   320.9/172/4   LC 71-150706

Thant, U, 1909-.   • **3.1172**
Toward world peace: addresses and public statements, 1957–1963 / U. Thant; selected by Jacob Baal-Teshuva; Foreword by Adlai E. Stevenson.— New York: T. Yoseloff, 1964. 404 p.: ill., ports. 1. World politics — Addresses, essays, lectures. I. Baal-Teshuva, Jacob. II. T.
D843 T418 1964   341.13081   LC 64-21343

Thompson, Kenneth W., 1921-.   **3.1173**
Cold war theories / Kenneth W. Thompson. — Baton Rouge: Louisiana State University Press, c1981. 216 p. 1. World politics — 1945- 2. Balance of power I. T.
D843.T423   327.1/12 19   LC 81-6001   ISBN 0807108766

Zacharias, Ellis M., 1890-.   • **3.1174**
Behind closed doors: the secret history of the cold war / by Ellis M. Zacharias in collaboration with Ladislas Farago. — New York: Putnam [1950] viii, 367 p.; 22 cm. Bibliographical references: p. 333-357. 1. World politics — 1945- 2. Russia — Foreign relations — 1945- I. T.
D843.Z2 1950   940.55   LC 50-8878

Russell, Bertrand, 1872-1970.   • **3.1175**
Unarmed victory. New York: Simon and Shuster, 1963. 155 p.; 21 cm. 1. Sino-Indian Border Dispute, 1957- 2. World politics — 1955- 3. Military bases, Russian — Cuba. I. T.
D844.R89   LC 63-16994

D845 NATO
(see also: UA646.3)

Kissinger, Henry, 1923-.   • **3.1176**
The troubled partnership: a re–appraisal of the Atlantic alliance / by Henry A. Kissinger. — [1st ed.] New York: Published for the Council on Foreign Relations by McGraw-Hill [1965] xiv, 266 p.; 22 cm. (Atlantic policy studies.) Based on 3 lectures delivered at the Council on Foreign Relations in March 1964. 1. North Atlantic Treaty Organization. I. T. II. Series.
D845.K5   327.4073 19   LC 65-17493

D847 Communist Countries. Warsaw Pact

Brzezinski, Zbigniew K., 1928-.   • **3.1177**
The Soviet bloc, unity and conflict, by Zbigniew K. Brzezinski. — Rev. and enl. ed. — Cambridge: Harvard University Press, 1967. xviii, 599 p.; 24 cm. — (Russian Research Center studies, 37) 1. Communist countries I. T.
D847.B7 1967   909.82   LC 67-12531

Change in Communist systems. Contributors: Jeremy R. Azrael   • **3.1178**
[and others] Edited by Chalmers Johnson.
Stanford: Stanford University Press, 1970. xiii, 368 p.; 24 cm. Based on discussions of the Workshop on the Comparative Study of Communism held at the Center for Advanced Study in the Bahavioral Sciences in 1968. 1. Communist countries — Politics and government. 2. Communist countries — Economic policy. I. Azrael, Jeremy R., 1935- II. Johnson, Chalmers A. ed. III. Workshop on the Comparative Study of Communism, Center for Advanced Study in the Behavioral Sciences, 1968.
D847.C45   320.9/171/7   LC 77-97914   ISBN 0804707235

Remington, Robin Alison.   **3.1179**
The Warsaw pact; case studies in Communist conflict resolution. — Cambridge, Mass.: MIT Press, [1971] xix, 268 p.: illus.; 24 cm. — (Studies in communism, revisionism, and revolution) 1. Warsaw pact, 1955. I. T. II. Series.
D847.2.R45 1971   355.03/1   LC 76-148971   ISBN 0262180502

D848–888 History, 1965-

CBS News.   **3.1180**
60 Minutes verbatim: who said what to whom: the complete text of 114 stories with Mike Wallace, Morley Safer, Dan Rather, Harry Reasoner, and Andy Rooney / introd. by William A. Leonard. — New York: Arno Press: CBS News, c1980. xiii, 651 p.: ill.; 24 cm. At head of title: Season XII. '[Transcripts of] stories aired during the 1979-80 television season.' 1. History, Modern — 1945- — Sources. 2. United States — History — 1945- — Sources. I. 60 minutes (Television program) II. T.
D848.C23 1980   791.45/72 19   LC 80-23836   ISBN 0405137230

Miller, Lynn H.   **3.1181**
Global order: values and power in international politics / Lynn H. Miller. — Boulder: Westview Press, 1985. xii, 226 p.; 23 cm. 1. World politics — 1975-1985 2. International relations I. T.
D849.M542 1985   327/.09/047 19   LC 84-17203   ISBN 081330069X

Morris, Jan, 1926-.   **3.1182**
Destinations: essays from Rolling stone / by Jan Morris. — New York: Oxford University Press, 1980. 242 p.: ill.; 24 cm. 1. Morris, Jan, 1926- — Addresses, essays, lectures. 2. Voyages and travels — 1951- — Addresses, essays, lectures. 3. World politics — 1975-1985 — Addresses, essays, lectures. I. Rolling stone. II. T.
D849.M72   320.9/047   LC 79-28492   ISBN 0195027086

Garvey, Terence.   3.1183
Bones of contention: an enquiry into East–West relations / Terence Garvey. —
New York: St. Martin's Press, 1980 (c1978). 203 p.; 22 cm. Includes index.
1. World politics — 1965-1975 2. World politics — 1975-1985 3. Communist
countries I. T.
D850.G37 1978b   327/.09/047 19   *LC* 79-21623   *ISBN*
0312087721

Gurtov, Melvin.   3.1184
The roots of failure: United States policy in the Third World / Melvin Gurtov,
Ray Maghroori. — Westport, Conn.: Greenwood Press, 1984. viii, 224 p.; 22
cm. (Contributions in political science. 0147-1066; no. 108) Includes index.
1. Developing countries — Foreign relations — United States. 2. United States
— Foreign relations — Developing countries. 3. United States — Foreign
relations — 1945- I. Maghroori, Ray. II. T. III. Series.
D888.U6 G87 1984   327.73 19   *LC* 84-10718   *ISBN* 0313245614

D901–980 DESCRIPTION. TRAVEL

Gottmann, Jean.   3.1185
A geography of Europe. — 4th ed. — New York: Holt, Rinehart and Winston, [1969] xii, 866 p.: illus., maps (part col.); 24 cm. 1. Europe — Description and travel I. T.
D907.G6 1969   914   LC 69-20455   ISBN 0030808154

Wilson, Edmund, 1895-1972.   • 3.1186
Europe without Baedeker; sketches among the ruins of Italy, Greece, and England, together with notes from a European diary, 1963–1964. [2d ed.] New York, Farrar, Straus and Giroux [1966] xi, 467 p. 20 cm. 1. Europe — Description and travel — 1945- I. T.
D921.W525 1966   LC 66-14040

A Geography of Europe: problems and prospects / edited by   3.1187
George W. Hoffman; contributors, Christopher Shane Davies ... [et al.].
5th ed. — New York: Wiley, c1983. xv, 647 p.: ill., maps; 24 cm. 1. Europe — Description and travel — 1971- I. Hoffman, George Walter. II. Davies, Christopher S. (Christopher Shane)
D923.G46 1983   914 19   LC 83-6964   ISBN 0471897086

Monkhouse, Francis John, 1914-   .   3.1188
A regional geography of Western Europe / [by] F. J. Monkhouse. — 4th ed. — [Harlow]: Longmans, 1974. –. iii-xxi, 704 p.: ill., maps.; 25 cm. — Includes index. - 1. Europe — Description and travel — 1945- I. T.
D967.M693 1974   914.4   LC 74-165365   ISBN 0582484243

D972–973 Mediterranean Region

Semple, Ellen Churchill, 1863-1932.   • 3.1189
The geography of the Mediterranean region; its relation to ancient history. New York, H. Holt [c1931] viii, 737 p. illus., maps. 23 cm. 1. Physical geography — Mediterranean sea. 2. History, Ancient 3. Mediterranean Region — Historical geography. I. T.
D973.S45   LC 31-33866

Walker, Donald Smith.   • 3.1190
The Mediterranean lands. London, Methuen; New York, Wiley [1960] xxiii, 524 p. illus., maps. 21 cm. 1. Mediterranean Region I. T.
D973.W18   LC 61-850

D1050–1065 HISTORY

Lichtheim, George, 1912-.   • 3.1191
The new Europe: today, and tomorrow. New York, Praeger [1963] 232 p. 21 cm. (Praeger paperbacks) Books that matter. 1. Europe — History — 1945- I. T.
D1051.L5   940.8   LC 63-11152

Mayne, Richard J.   3.1192
Postwar, the dawn of today's Europe / Richard Mayne. — 1st American ed. — New York: Schocken Books, 1983. 336 p.; 24 cm. Includes index. 1. Europe — History — 1945- I. T.
D1051.M39 1983   940.5 19   LC 83-42720   ISBN 0805238646

The Successor generation: international perspectives of postwar   3.1193
Europeans / edited by Stephen F. Szabo.
London: Butterworths, 1983. viii, 183. p. 1. Europe — History — 1945- I. Szabo, Stephen F.
D1051   D1051 S8.   940.55 19   ISBN 0408108177

White, Theodore Harold, 1915-.   • 3.1194
Fire in the ashes: Europe in mid–century. — New York: Sloane, 1953. 405 p.; 22 cm. 1. Europe — Politics and government — 1945- 2. United States — Foreign relations — 1945-1953 I. T.
D1051.W4   940.55   LC 53-10166

Beloff, Max, 1913-.   • 3.1195
Europe and the Europeans, an international discussion. With an introd. by Denis de Rougemont. A report prepared at the request of the Council of Europe. London, Chatto & Windus, 1957. xix, 288 p. 23 cm. 1. European federation 2. Europe — Civilization I. Council of Europe. II. T.
D1055.B4   LC a 58-2321

Lukacs, John A.   • 3.1196
Decline and rise of Europe; a study in recent history, with particular emphasis on the development of a European consciousness, by John Lukacs. [1st ed.] Garden City, N.Y., Doubleday, 1965. xii, 295 p. 22 cm. 1. European federation 2. Europe — Civilization I. T.
D1055.L8   LC 65-10638

Rougemont, Denis de, 1906-.   • 3.1197
The meaning of Europe. Translated from the French by Alan Braley. New York, Stein and Day [1965, c1963] 126 p. 22 cm. 1. Europe — Civilization I. T.
D1055.R633   LC 65-22272

Nations without a State: ethnic minorities in Western Europe /   3.1198
edited by Charles R. Foster.
New York, N.Y.: Praeger, 1980. ix, 215 p.; 24 cm. 1. Minorities — Europe. 2. Nationalism — Europe. 3. Europe — Ethnic relations. I. Foster, Charles Robert, 1927-
D1056.N37   323.1/4 19   LC 80-20900   ISBN 0030568072

Fry, Earl H.   3.1199
The other Western Europe: a political analysis of the smaller democracies / Earl H. Fry and Gregory A. Raymond, in collaboration with David Bohn and James L. Waite. — Santa Barbara, Calif.: ABC-Clio, c1980. ix, 251 p.; 24 cm. — (Studies in international and comparative politics. 14) 1. Europe — Politics and government — 1945- I. Raymond, Gregory A. joint author. II. T. III. Series.
D1058.F79   320.9/4/055   LC 79-24252   ISBN 0874362679

Laqueur, Walter, 1921-.   3.1200
A continent astray: Europe, 1970–1978 / Walter Laqueur. — New York: Oxford University Press, 1979. vii, 293 p.; 24 cm. 1. Europe — Politics and government — 1945- 2. Europe — Economic conditions — 1945- I. T.
D1058.L25   309.1/4/055   LC 78-12021   ISBN 0195025105

Hallstein, Walter, 1901-.   • 3.1201
United Europe; challenge and opportunity. — Cambridge, Harvard University Press, 1962. 109 p. 22 cm. — (The William L. Clayton lectures on international economic affairs and foreign policy, 1961-1962) 1. European federation I. T.
D1060.H3   940.55   LC 62-19216

Zurcher, Arnold John, 1902-.   • 3.1202
The struggle to unite Europe, 1940–1958; an historical account of the development of the contemporary European Movement from its origin in the Pan–European Union to the drafting of the treaties for Euratom and the European Common Market / by Arnold J. Zurcher. — New York: New York University Press, 1958. xix, 254 p. 1. European federation I. T.
D1060.Z8   LC 58-6825

Soviet strategy toward Western Europe / edited by Edwina   3.1203
Moreton, Gerald Segal.
London; Boston: Allen & Unwin, 1984. 296 p.; 23 cm. 1. Europe — Foreign relations — Soviet Union — Addresses, essays, lectures. 2. Soviet Union — Foreign relations — Europe — Addresses, essays, lectures. 3. Europe — Foreign relations — 1945- — Addresses, essays, lectures. I. Moreton, N. Edwina. II. Segal, Gerald, 1953-
D1065.S65 S694 1984   327.4704 19   LC 83-15895   ISBN 0043303374

Barnet, Richard J.   3.1204
The alliance—America, Europe, Japan: makers of the postwar world / Richard J. Barnet. — New York: Simon and Schuster, c1983. 511 p.: ill.; 24 cm. Includes index. 1. Europe — Relations — United States 2. United States — Relations — Europe 3. United States — Relations — Japan 4. Japan — Relations —

United States 5. Europe — History — 1945- 6. Japan — History — 1945-
I. T.
D1065.U5 B273 1983   327.7304 19   *LC* 83-14870   *ISBN*
0671425021

Beloff, Max, 1913-.   • **3.1205**
The United States and the unity of Europe. — Washington, Brookings
Institution [1963] 124 p. 24 cm. Includes bibliography. 1. U.S. — For. rel. —
Europe. 2. European federation I. T.
D1065.U5B4   327.7304   *LC* 63-15630

Servan-Schreiber, Jean Jacques.   • **3.1206**
[Défi américain] The American challenge [by] J. J. Servan–Schreiber. With a
foreword by Arthur Schlesinger, Jr. Translated from the French by Ronald
Steel. [1st ed.] New York, Atheneum, 1968. xviii, 291 p. 22 cm. Translation of
Le Défi américain. 1. Investments, American — Europe. 2. Industrial
management — United States. 3. Industrial management — Europe. I. T.
D1065.U5 S413   332.67/373/04   *LC* 68-19793

DA1-890 Britain

DA1–3 HISTORIOGRAPHY

Butterfield, Herbert, Sir, 1900-. • **3.1207**
The Englishman and his history, by H. Butterfield. With a new pref. by the author. — [Hamden, Conn.]: Archon Books, 1970. x, 142 p.; 18 cm. Reprint of the 1944 ed. 1. Gt. Brit. — Historiography — Addresses, essays, lectures. 2. Gt. Brit. — Politics and government — Addresses, essays, lectures. I. T.
DA1.B875 1970   942/.0072/042   LC 76-121754   *ISBN* 0208009930

Gransden, Antonia. **3.1208**
Historical writing in England. — Ithaca, N.Y.: Cornell University Press, 1974-1982. 2 v.; 24 cm. 1. Great Britain — Historiography. I. T.
DA1.G75x   942/.007/2 19   *LC* 74-23267   *ISBN* 0801407702

The historiography of the British Empire–Commonwealth: • **3.1209**
trends, interpretations and resources / edited by Robin W.
Winks.
Durham, N.C.: Duke University Press, 1966. 596 p. 1. Great Britain — Colonies — History — Historiography. 2. Great Britain — Colonies — History — Bibliography. 3. Commonwealth of Nations — History — Historiography. 4. Commonwealth of Nations — History — Bibliography. I. Winks, Robin W.
DA1.W55   *LC* 66-15555

Douglas, David Charles, 1898-. • **3.1210**
English scholars, 1660–1730. — [2d rev. ed.]. — London, Eyre & Spottiswoode [1951] 291 p. ports. 23 cm. Bibliographical footnotes. 1. Scholars, British. 2. Learning and scholarship — England. 3. Historians, British. 4. Gt. Brit. — Hist. — 1660-1714. I. T.
DA3.A1D6 1951   942.007   *LC* 52-1346

Macaulay, Thomas Babington Macaulay, Baron, 1800-1859. **3.1211**
The letters of Thomas Babington Macaulay, edited by Thomas Pinney. — [London]: Cambridge University Press, 1974-1981. 6 v.; 24 cm. On spine: The letters of Macaulay. Vols. 5-6 have imprint: Cambridge; New York: Cambridge University Press. Includes index. 1. Macaulay, Thomas Babington Macaulay, Baron, 1800-1859. I. Pinney, Thomas. ed. II. T. III. Title: The letters of Macaulay.
DA3.M3 A4 1974   828/.8/09 B   *LC* 73-75860   *ISBN* 0521211263

Clive, John Leonard, 1924-. **3.1212**
Macaulay: the shaping of the historian. — [1st ed.]. — New York: Knopf, 1973. xiv, 499, xxxvi p.: illus.; 25 cm. 1. Macaulay, Thomas Babington Macaulay, Baron, 1800-1859. I. T.
DA3.M3 C5   907/.2024 B 19   *LC* 72-8727   *ISBN* 0394472780

Hamburger, Joseph, 1922-. **3.1213**
Macaulay and the Whig tradition / Joseph Hamburger. Chicago: University of Chicago Press, 1976. 274 p.; 21 cm. 1. Macaulay, Thomas Babington Macaulay, Baron, 1800-1859. 2. Historians — Great Britain — Biography. 3. Statesmen — Great Britain — Biography. 4. Great Britain — Politics and government — 19th century I. T.
DA3.M3 H27   941.081/092/4 B   *LC* 75-27892   *ISBN* 0226314723

Taylor, A. J. P. (Alan John Percivale), 1906-. **3.1214**
A personal history / A.J.P. Taylor. — 1st American ed. — New York: Atheneum, 1983. 278 p., [8] p. of plates: ill.; 25 cm. Includes index. 1. Taylor, A. J. P. (Alan John Percivale), 1906- 2. University of Oxford — Faculty — Biography. 3. Historians — Great Britain — Biography. I. T.
DA3.T36 A37 1983   907/.2024 B 19   *LC* 83-45086   *ISBN* 0689114125

DA10–18 BRITISH EMPIRE. COMMONWEALTH OF NATIONS

Bowle, John. **3.1215**
The imperial achievement: the rise and transformation of the British Empire / John Bowle. — 1st American ed. — Boston: Little, Brown, 1975, c1974. xi, 484 p., [16] leaves of plates: ill.; 24 cm. 1. Great Britain — Colonies — History 2. Great Britain — History — Modern period, 1485- I. T.
DA16.B63 1975   909/.09/71/241   *LC* 75-8594   *ISBN* 0316104094

Calder, Angus. **3.1216**
Revolutionary empire: the rise of the English–speaking empires from the fifteenth century to the 1780s / Angus Calder. — 1st American ed. — New York: E.P. Dutton, 1981. xxiii, 916 p., [30] p. of plates: ill., ports.; 25 cm. Includes index. 1. Imperialism 2. Great Britain — History — Modern period, 1485- 3. Great Britain — Colonies — History I. T.
DA16.C24 1981   941 19   *LC* 80-70170   *ISBN* 0525190805

The Cambridge history of the British Empire. • **3.1217**
[2d ed.] Cambridge [Eng.] University Press, 1963-. v. 24 cm. Bibliography: v. 8, p. [917]-1017. 1. Great Britain — History 2. Great Britain — Colonies — History I. Walker, Eric A. (Eric Anderson), 1886- ed.
DA16.C252   942   *LC* 63-24285

Carrington, Charles Edmund, 1897-. • **3.1218**
The British overseas: exploits of a nation of shopkeepers, by C. E. Carrington. — 2nd ed. — London: Cambridge U.P., 1968-. v.   : plates, illus., maps, ports.; 21 cm. 1. Gr. Brit. — Colonies — History. I. T.
DA16.C32   325.3/42   *LC* 68-23176   *ISBN* 052109514X

Churchill, Winston, Sir, 1874-1965. • **3.1219**
A history of the English–speaking peoples. [1st ed.] New York, Dodd, Mead, 1956-58. 4 v. maps. 22 cm. 1. Great Britain — History I. T.
DA16.C47   942   *LC* 56-6868

Gallagher, John, 1919-. **3.1220**
The decline, revival, and fall of the British Empire: the Ford lectures and other essays / by John Gallagher; edited by Anil Seal. -- Cambridge [Cambridgeshire]; New York: Cambridge University Press, 1982. xxvii, 211 p.; 24 cm. Consists of a lecture delivered by J. Gallagher in the series of Ford lectures in the University of Oxford in 1974 and reprints of 3 articles published between 1953-1973. 1. Great Britain — Colonies — History — Addresses, essays, lectures. 2. Great Britain — History — Addresses, essays, lectures. I. Seal, Anil. II. Robinson, Ronald Edward, 1920- III. T.
DA16.G34 1982   909/.0971241 19   *LC* 82-4291   *ISBN* 0521246423

Grierson, Edward, 1914-1975. **3.1221**
The death of the imperial dream: the British Commonwealth & Empire, 1775–1969. — [1st ed. in U.S.]. — Garden City, N.Y.: Doubleday, 1972. 348 p.; 22 cm. 1. Commonwealth of Nations — History. 2. Great Britain — Colonies I. T.
DA16.G736 1972b   910/.09/171242   *LC* 72-186024

Hyam, Ronald. **3.1222**
Reappraisals in British imperial history / Ronald Hyam and Ged Martin. — Toronto: Macmillan of Canada, 1976 (c1975). viii, 234 p.; 22 cm. 1. Great Britain — Colonies — History — Addresses, essays, lectures. 2. Great Britain — History — Modern period, 1485- — Addresses, essays, lectures. I. Martin, Ged. joint author. II. T.
DA16.H94   941   *LC* 76-375045   *ISBN* 0770513611

Knaplund, Paul, 1885-1964. • **3.1223**
The British empire, 1815–1939. — New York: H. Fertig, 1969. xx, 850 p.: maps.; 23 cm. 1. Imperial federation 2. Gt. Brit. — Colonies — History. I. T.
DA16.K65 1969   325.3/42   *LC* 68-9617

McIntyre, W. David (William David), 1932-. • **3.1224**
The Commonwealth of nations: origins and impact, 1869–1971 / by W. David McIntyre. — Minneapolis: University of Minnesota Press, c1977. xvii, 596 p., [6] leaves of plates: ill.; 24 cm. (Europe and the world in the Age of Expansion. v. 9) Includes index. 1. Commonwealth of Nations — History. I. T. II. Series.
DA16.M234   909/.09/71241   *LC* 76-19602   *ISBN* 0816607923

Mansergh, Nicholas.   3.1225
The Commonwealth experience / Nicholas Mansergh. — Rev. ed. — Toronto;
Buffalo: University of Toronto Press, 1983 (c1982). 2 v.; 24 cm.
1. Commonwealth of Nations — History. I. T.
DA16.M248 1983   909/.0971/241 19   *LC* 83-112050   *ISBN*
0802024912

Mansergh, Nicholas. ed.   • 3.1226
Documents and speeches on British Commonwealth affairs, 1931–1952. —
London, New York, Oxford University Press, 1953. 2 v. (xli, 1308 p.) 24 cm.
Bibliography: v. 1, p. xxxiii—xxxv. 1. Commonwealth of Nations — Hist. —
Sources. I. T. II. Title: British Commonwealth affairs, 1931-1952.
DA16.M25   942.084   *LC* 53-4142

Porter, Bernard.   3.1227
The lion's share: a short history of British imperialism, 1850–1970 / Bernard
Porter. — London; New York: Longman, 1975. xiii, 408 p.; 22 cm. (A
Longman paperback) Includes index. 1. Great Britain — History — Victoria,
1837-1901 2. Great Britain — History — 20th century 3. Great Britain —
Colonies — History 4. Great Britain — Foreign relations — 1837-1901
5. Great Britain — Foreign relations — 20th century I. T.
DA16.P67   941.08   *LC* 75-16224   *ISBN* 0582481031

Seeley, John Robert, Sir, 1834-1895.   • 3.1228
The expansion of England. Edited and with an introd. by John Gross. —
Chicago: University of Chicago Press, [1971] xxvii, 248 p.; 23 cm. — (Classics
of British historical literature) 'Consists of two sets of lectures which were
originally delivered to Cambridge undergraduates in the autumn of 1881 and
the spring of 1882.' 1. Great Britain — Colonies — Addresses, essays, lectures.
2. Great Britain — History — 18th century — Addresses, essays, lectures.
3. India — Politics and government — 1765-1947 — Addresses, essays,
lectures. I. T.
DA16.S45 1971   909/.09/71242   *LC* 73-152225   *ISBN* 0226744280

Hancock, W. K. (William Keith), 1898-.   • 3.1229
Survey of British commonwealth affairs / by W.K. Hancock; with a
supplementary legal chapter by R.T.E. Latham — London: Oxford University
Press, 1937-1942. 2 v. in 3: maps. 'Issued under the auspices of the Royal
Institute of International Affairs.' 1. Imperial federation 2. Great Britain —
Foreign relations — 20th century 3. Great Britain — Colonies — History
4. Commonwealth of Nations — History I. Latham, Richard Thomas Edwin
II. T.
DA18.H26   *LC* 37-23223

Keith, Arthur Berriedale, 1879-1944. ed.   • 3.1230
Speeches and documents on the British dominions, 1918–1931; from self-
government to national sovereignty; edited with an introduction and notes by
Arthur Berriedale Keith ... — London, Oxford University Press, [1932] xlvii,
[1], 501, [1] p. 16 cm. — (Half-title: The world's classics. CDIII) 'Sources': p.
[xiii]-xiv. 1. Gt. Brit. — Pol. & govt. — 1910-1936. 2. Gt. Brit. — Colonies.
3. Gt. Brit. — For. rel. — 1910-1936. 4. Imperial federation I. T.
DA18.K4   942   *LC* 33-4173

Mansergh, Nicholas.   • 3.1231
Survey of British Commonwealth affairs / by Nicholas Mansergh. — London;
Toronto: Oxford University Press, 1952-1958. 2 v.; 25 cm. 'Issued under the
auspices of the Royal Institute of International Affairs.' 1. Imperial federation
2. Nationalism 3. Great Britain — Foreign relations — 20th century 4. Great
Britain — Colonies I. T.
DA18.M328   *LC* 52-3954

DA20–690 ENGLAND

English historical documents / general editor: David C. Douglas.   • 3.1232
New York: Oxford University Press, 1953-. v.: ill., maps; 25 cm. 1. Great
Britain — History — Sources. I. Douglas, David Charles, 1898-
DA26.E55   *LC* 53-1506//r

Bolingbroke, Henry St. John, Viscount, 1678-1751.   3.1233
Historical writings. Edited and with an introd. by Isaac Kramnick. Chicago,
University of Chicago Press [1972] liii, 343 p. 23 cm. (Classics of British
historical literature) 1. History — Collected works. 2. Great Britain —
History — Collected works. I. T.
DA27.B73   942   *LC* 72-75608   *ISBN* 0226063453

Maitland, Frederic William, 1850-1906.   • 3.1234
Selected historical essays. Chosen and introduced by Helen M. Cam.
Cambridge [Eng.] Published in association with the Selden Society at the
University Press, 1957. xxix, 277 p.; 23 cm. 'Bibliographical note': p. viii.

Bibliographical footnotes. 1. Law — Great Britain — History and criticism
2. Great Britain — History — Addresses, essays, lectures. I. T.
DA27.M26   942.004   *LC* 57-14461

DA28 Biography

The dictionary of national biography: founded in 1882 by   • 3.1235
George Smith / edited by Sir Leslie Stephen and Sir Sidney
Lee; from the earliest times to 1900 ...
London: Oxford University Press, [1921-1927]. 22 v.: front (port); 24 cm. Vol.
23 (3 v. in 1) has title: The dictionary of national biography...Supplement,
January 1901-December 1911, edited by Sir Sidney Lee. Vol. 24 has title: The
dictionary of national biography ... 1912-1921, edited by H. W. C. Davis and J.
R H. Weaver; with an index covering the years 1901-1921 in one alphabetical
series. 1. Great Britain — Biography 2. Great Britian — Bio-bibliography.
3. Great Britain — Biography — Dictionaries. I. Stephen, Leslie, Sir,
1832-1904. ed. II. Lee, (Sir) Sidney, 1859-1926, ed. III. Smith, George,
1824-1901.
DA28.D4 1921   920   *LC* 30-29308

Who's who: an annual biographical dictionary, with which is   3.1236
incorporated 'Men and women of the time:.
London: Baily Brothers, 18— v.; 19 cm. Subtitle varies.
DA28.W6   *LC* 04-16933

Who was who: a companion to Who's who, containing the   • 3.1237
biographies of those who died.
Vol 1 is 4th rev. ed., publ. 1953. London: A. & C. Black, 1897/1915-. 5 v.; 22
cm. Subtitle varies. 1. Biography — Dictionaries. 2. Great Britain —
Biography — Dictionaries.
DA28.W65   920   *LC* 20-14622

Robinson, John Martin.   3.1238
The Dukes of Norfolk: a quincentennial history / John Martin Robinson. —
Oxford [Oxfordshire]; New York: Oxford University Press, 1983. xiii, 264 p.,
[8] leaves of plates: ill. (some col.); 26 cm. Includes index. 1. Norfolk, Dukes of
2. Howard family I. T.
DA28.35.N67 R63 1983   942/.009/92 19   *LC* 82-8002   *ISBN*
0192158694

Van Thal, Herbert Maurice, 1904-.   3.1239
The Prime Ministers / edited by Herbert Van Thal; with an introduction by G.
W. Jones. — London: Allen and Unwin, 1974-1975. 2 v.: 47 ports.; 23 cm. Vol.
2 introd. by Robert Blake. 1. Prime ministers — Great Britain — Biography.
I. T.
DA28.4.V36 1974   941/.00992 B   *LC* 76-361099   *ISBN*
004942131X

DA30–35 History: General Works

Clark, G. N. (George Norman), Sir, 1890-.   • 3.1240
English history: a survey, George Clark. Oxford, Clarendon Press, 1971. xix,
567 p.; maps. 21 cm. 1. Great Britain — History I. T.
DA30.C6   942   *LC* 70-595865   *ISBN* 0198223390

Hume, David, 1711-1776.   3.1241
The history of England: from the invasion of Julius Caesar to the Revolution in
1688 / David Hume; abridged and with an introd. by Rodney W. Kilcup. —
Chicago: University of Chicago Press, 1975. lvi, 392 p.; 23 cm. (Classics of
British historical literature) Reprint of the selections from the 1879 ed.
published in 6 volumes by Harper, New York. Includes index. 1. Great Britain
— History I. Kilcup, Rodney W. II. T.
DA30.H92 1975   942   *LC* 74-16685   *ISBN* 0226360652

The Political history of England / Edited by William Hunt   3.1242
[and] Reginald L. Poole.
[New York: AMS Press, 1969] 12 v.: maps (part col.); 23 cm. Half-title. Reprint
of the 1905-14 ed. 1. Gt. Brit. — History. I. Hunt, William, 1842-1931. ed.
II. Poole, Reginald Lane, 1857-1939. ed.
DA30.P7622   942   *LC* 68-59462

Trevelyan, George Macaulay, 1876-1962.   • 3.1243
[English social history] Illustrated English social history. Illus. selected by Ruth
C. Wright. London; New York: Longmans, Green, [1949-1952] 4 v.: ill. (part

col.) map.; 23 cm. First ed. published in 1942 under title: English social history. 1. Great Britain — History 2. Great Britain — Social conditions I. T.
DA32.T74873   942   *LC* 50-5891

The Cambridge historical encyclopedia of Great Britain and   **3.1244**
Ireland / editor, Christopher Haigh.
Cambridge [Cambridgeshire]; New York: Cambridge University Press, 1985. 392 p.: ill. (some col.); 27 cm. Includes index. 1. Great Britain — History — Dictionaries. 2. Ireland — History — Dictionaries. I. Haigh, Christopher.
DA34.C28 1985   941/.003/21 19   *LC* 85-47568   *ISBN* 0521255597

Powicke, F. M. (Frederick Maurice), 1879-1963.   • **3.1245**
Handbook of British chronology, edited by F. Maurice Powicke and E.B. Fryde. 2d ed. London, Offices of the Royal Historical Society, 1961. xxxviii, 565 p. 25 cm. (Guides and handbooks. no. 2) 1. Great Britain — History — Chronology. I. Fryde, E. B. II. T. III. Series.
DA34.P6 1961   942.002   *LC* 62-3079

DA40–48 Political and Diplomatic History

Cobban, Alfred. ed.   • **3.1246**
The debate on the French Revolution, 1789–1800. 2d ed. London: A. and C. Black [1963, 1960] xx, 495 p. 23 cm. (The British political tradition; book 2.) Imprint covered by label: New York, Barnes & Noble. 1. Political science — History — Great Britain. 2. France — History — Revolution — Foreign public opinion. 3. Great Britain — Politics and government — 1789-1820 I. T. II. Series.
DA42.C6x   *LC* 61-17763

Strang, William Strang, Baron, 1893-.   • **3.1247**
Britain in world affairs: the fluctuation in power and influence from Henry VIII to Elizabeth II / by Lord William Strang. — New York: Praeger, c1961. 426 p.; 21 cm. 1. Great Britain — Foreign relations I. T.
DA 42 S89   327.42   *LC* 61-10747

Hechter, Michael.   **3.1248**
Internal colonialism: the Celtic fringe in British national development, 1536–1966 / Michael Hechter. — Berkeley: University of California Press, 1975. xviii, 361 p.: ill.; 23 cm. 1. Celts — British Isles. 2. British Isles — Politics and government. I. T.
DA44.H4   320.9/41   *LC* 73-84392   *ISBN* 0520025598

Taylor, A. J. P. (Alan John Percivale), 1906-.   • **3.1249**
The trouble makers: dissent over foreign policy, 1729–1939 / by A.J.P. Taylor. Bloomington: Indiana University Press, 1958. 207 p.; 23 cm. (Ford lectures; 1956) 1. Great Britain — Foreign relations — 19th century 2. Great Britain — Foreign relations — 20th century I. T.
DA45.T3   *LC* 58-9370

Ward, Adolphus William, Sir, 1837-1924. ed.   • **3.1250**
The Cambridge history of British foreign policy, 1783–1919. Edited by A. W. Ward and G. P. Gooch. — New York: Octagon Books, 1970. 3 v.; 24 cm. Reprint of the 1922-23 ed. 1. World politics 2. Gt. Brit. — Foreign relations. I. Gooch, G. P. (George Peabody), 1873-1968. joint ed. II. T.
DA45.W35 1970   327.42   *LC* 70-119436

Wiener, Joel H. comp.   **3.1251**
Great Britain: foreign policy and the span of empire, 1689–1971; a documentary history. Edited with commentaries by Joel H. Wiener. Introd.: J. H. Plumb. — New York: Chelsea House Publishers, [1972] 4 v. (liii, 3423 p.); 24 cm. 1. Great Britain — Foreign relations — Sources. 2. Great Britain — Colonies — History — Sources. 3. Commonwealth of Nations — History — Sources. I. T.
DA45.W53   327.42   *LC* 78-179375   *ISBN* 0070797307

Horn, David Bayne, 1901-1969.   • **3.1252**
Great Britain and Europe in the eighteenth century. — Oxford: Clarendon P., 1967. xi, 411 p.: plate (map).; 22 1/2 cm. 1. Great Britain — Foreign relations — Europe. 2. Europe — Foreign relations — Great Britain. 3. Great Britain — Foreign relations — 18th century I. T.
DA47.H6   327.4/042   *LC* 67-88613

Korr, Charles P.   **3.1253**
Cromwell and the new model foreign policy: England's policy toward France, 1649–1658 / Charles P. Korr. — Berkeley: University of California Press, c1975. x, 268 p.; 24 cm. Includes index. 1. Cromwell, Oliver, 1599-1658. 2. Great Britain — Foreign relations — France. 3. France — Foreign relations — Great Britain. 4. Great Britain — Foreign relations — 1649-1660 I. T.
DA47.1.K67   327.41/044   *LC* 72-82231   *ISBN* 0520022815

Gilbert, Martin, 1936-.   **3.1254**
The roots of appeasement / Martin Gilbert. — New York; Toronto: New American Library, [1967, c1966] xvi, 254 p.: cartes. — (A Plume book) 1. Great Britain — Foreign relations — Germany 2. Germany — Foreign relations — Great Britain 3. Great Britain — Foreign relations — 1910-1936 4. Great Britain — Foreign relations — 1936-1945 I. T.
DA47.2.G53 1967   327.42043   *LC* 67-14724

Kennedy, Paul M., 1945-.   **3.1255**
The rise of the Anglo–German antagonism, 1860–1914 / Paul M. Kennedy. — London; Boston: Allen & Unwin, 1980. xiv, 604 p.; 24 cm. Includes index. 1. Great Britain — Foreign relations — Germany 2. Germany — Foreign relations — Great Britain. I. T.
DA47.2.K44   327.41043 19   *LC* 80-40461   *ISBN* 0049400606

Rock, William R.   **3.1256**
British appeasement in the 1930s / William R. Rock. — 1st ed. — New York: Norton, 1978 (c1977). viii, 111 p.; 21 cm. — (Foundations of modern history) Includes index. 1. Chamberlain, Neville, 1869-1940. 2. Great Britain — Foreign relations — Germany 3. Germany — Foreign relations — Great Britain. 4. Great Britain — Foreign relations — 1936-1945 5. Great Britain — Politics and government — 1936-1945 I. T.
DA47.2.R63   327.41/043   *LC* 77-17549   *ISBN* 0393056686

Wilson, Charles, 1914-.   • **3.1257**
Queen Elizabeth and the revolt of the Netherlands [by] Charles Wilson. Berkeley, University of California Press, 1970. xiv, 168 p.: map, plates.; 23 cm. 1. Great Britain — Foreign relations — Netherlands. 2. Netherlands — Foreign relations — Great Britain. 3. Netherlands — History — Wars of Independence, 1556-1648 I. T.
DA47.3.W52 1970b   949/.203   *LC* 76-119009   *ISBN* 0520017447

Rothwell, Victor.   **3.1258**
Britain and the Cold War, 1941–1947 / Victor Rothwell. — London: Cape, 1982. vii, 551 p.; 23 cm. 1. World War, 1939-1945 — Diplomatic history 2. World politics — 1945-1955 3. Great Britain — Foreign relations — 1936-1945 4. Great Britain — Foreign relations — 1945- 5. Great Britain — Foreign relations — Soviet Union. 6. Soviet Union — Foreign relations — Great Britain. I. T.
DA47.65.R58 1982   327.41047 19   *LC* 81-208119   *ISBN* 0224014781

Wigley, Philip G.   **3.1259**
Canada and the transition to Commonwealth: British–Canadian relations, 1917–1926 / Philip G. Wigley. Cambridge; New York: Cambridge University Press, 1977. x, 294 p.; 24 cm. (Cambridge Commonwealth series) Includes index. 1. Great Britain — Foreign relations — Canada. 2. Canada — Foreign relations — Great Britain. 3. Great Britain — Foreign relations — 1910-1936 4. Commonwealth of Nations — Foreign relations. I. T.
DA47.9.C2 W53   327.41/071   *LC* 76-48989   *ISBN* 0521211573

Endicott, Stephen Lyon, 1928-.   **3.1260**
Diplomacy and enterprise: British China policy, 1933–1937 / Stephen Lyon Endicott. — [Vancouver]: University of British Columbia Press, 1975. xv, 209 p.: ill.; 24 cm. Includes index. 1. Great Britain — Foreign relations — China. 2. China — Foreign relations — Great Britain. 3. Great Britain — Foreign relations — 1910-1936 4. Great Britain — Foreign economic relations — China. 5. China — Foreign economic relations — Great Britain. I. T.
DA47.9.C5 E52   327.41/051   *LC* 75-324980   *ISBN* 0774800364

Boardman, Robert, 1945-.   **3.1261**
Britain and the People's Republic of China, 1949–74 / Robert Boardman. — New York: Barnes & Noble Books, 1976. xi, 210 p.; 23 cm. Includes index. 1. Great Britain — Foreign relations — China. 2. China — Foreign relations — Great Britain. 3. Great Britain — Foreign relations — 1945- I. T.
DA47.9.C6 B6 1976   327.41/051   *LC* 75-30214   *ISBN* 0064905144

Knox, D. Edward, 1940-.   **3.1262**
The making of a new Eastern Question: British Palestine policy and the origins of Israel, 1917–1925 / by D. Edward Knox. — Washington, D.C.: Catholic University of America Press, c1981. vi, 219 p.; 24 cm. 1. Great Britain — Foreign relations — Palestine. 2. Palestine — Foreign relations — Great Britain. 3. Great Britain — Foreign relations — 1910-1936 4. Palestine — History — 1917-1948 5. Israel — History I. T.
DA47.9.I77 K58   327.4105694 19   *LC* 80-21879   *ISBN* 0813205557

DA49–69 Military History

Beeler, John.   **3.1263**
Warfare in England, 1066–1189 / [by] John Beeler. Ithaca, N.Y., Cornell University Press, 1966. xiii, 493 p. illus., maps. (part fold.) 25 cm. 1. Battles — Great Britain. 2. Great Britain — History, MilitarV — Medieval period. I. T.
DA60.B4   942/.02   *LC* 66-16896

Barnett, Correlli.   ● **3.1264**
Britain and her army, 1509–1970; a military, political, and social survey. — New York: W. Morrow, 1970. xx, 529 p.: illus., facsims., maps, ports.; 25 cm. 1. Gt. Brit. — History, Military. I. T.
DA65.B283 1970   355/.00942   *LC* 74-116805

Longford, Elizabeth Harman Pakenham, Countess of, 1906-.   ● **3.1265**
Wellington [by] Elizabeth Longford. [1st U.S. ed.] New York, Harper & Row [1970-73, c1969-72] 2 v. illus., facsims., maps, ports. 25 cm. 1. Wellington, Arthur Wellesley, Duke of, 1769-1852. I. T.
DA68.12.W4 L62   942.07/092/4 B   *LC* 75-95973   *ISBN* 0060126698

Chenevix Trench, Charles, 1914-.   **3.1266**
The road to Khartoum: a life of General Charles Gordon / Charles Chenevix Trench. — 1st American ed. — New York: Norton, 1979, c1978. 320 p., [6] leaves of plates: ill.; 24 cm. 1. Gordon, Charles George, 1833-1885. 2. Great Britain. Army — Biography. 3. Generals — Great Britain — Biography. 4. Colonial administrators — Africa — Biography. 5. Egypt — History — British occupation, 1882-1936 6. Sudan — History — 1862-1899 I. T.
DA68.32.G6 C46 1979   962.4/03/0924 B   *LC* 78-21043   *ISBN* 0393012379

Magnus, Philip Montefiore, Sir, Bart., 1906-.   ● **3.1267**
Kitchener: portrait of an imperialist [by] Philip Magnus. — Harmondsworth: Penguin, 1968. 485 p.: 16 plates, illus., 2 maps, ports.; 18 cm. 1. Kitchener, Horatio Herbert Kitchener, 1st Earl, 1850-1916. I. T.
DA68.32.K6 M3 1968   942.08/0924 B   *LC* 72-366576

Fraser, David, 1920-.   **3.1268**
Alanbrooke / David Fraser; with a prologue and epilogue by Arthur Bryant. — 1st ed. — New York: Atheneum, 1982. 604 p., [8] p. of plates: ill.; 24 cm. Includes index. 1. Alanbrooke, Alan Francis Brooke, Viscount, 1883- 2. Great Britain. Army — Biography. 3. Generals — Great Britain — Biography. I. T.
DA69.3.A55 F7   941.085/092/4 B 19   *LC* 81-69156   *ISBN* 068911267X

Williams, Jeffery.   **3.1269**
Byng of Vimy: general and governor general / Jeffery Williams. — London: Leo Cooper in association with Secker & Warburg, 1984 (c1983). xvi, 398 p., [24] p. of plates: ill., maps, ports.; 24 cm. Maps on lining papers. Includes indexes. 1. Byng, Julian Hedworth George Byng, viscount, 1862-1935. 2. Marshals — Great Britain — Biography. 3. Statesmen — Canada — Biography. I. T.
DA69.3.B9   941.082/092/4 19   *ISBN* 0436571102

Terraine, John.   **3.1270**
Douglas Haig, the educated soldier. — London, Hutchinson [1963] xviii, 508 p. illus., facsim., maps, ports. 24 cm. 1. Haig, Douglas, Sir, 1861-1928. I. T.
DA69.3.H3T4 1963a   923.542   *LC* 64-56201

Hamilton, Nigel.   **3.1271**
Monty: the making of a general, 1887–1942 / Nigel Hamilton. — New York: McGraw-Hill, c1981. xix, 871 p., [32] p. of plates: ill.; 25 cm. Includes index. 1. Montgomery of Alamein, Bernard Law Montgomery, Viscount, 1887-1976. 2. Great Britain. Army — Biography. 3. Generals — Great Britain — Biography. I. T.
DA69.3.M56 H35   941.082/092/4 B 19   *LC* 81-8327   *ISBN* 0070258058

Hamilton, Nigel.   **3.1272**
Master of the battlefield: Monty's war years, 1942–1944 / Nigel Hamilton. — New York: McGraw-Hill, c1983. xxxi, 863 p., [72] p. of plates: ill.; 24 cm. Includes index. 1. Montgomery of Alamein, Bernard Law Montgomery, Viscount, 1887-1976. 2. Great Britain. Army — Biography. 3. Generals — Great Britain — Biography. I. T.
DA69.3.M56 H355 1983   941.082/092/4 B 19   *LC* 83-11262
ISBN 0070258066

Lewin, Ronald.   **3.1273**
Slim, the standardbearer: a biography of Field–Marshal the Viscount Slim, KG, GCB, GCMG, GCVO, GBE, DSO, MC / by Ronald Lewin. Hamden, Conn.: Archon Books, c1976. xv, 350 p., [8] leaves of plates: ill.; 24 cm. Includes index.

1. Slim, William Slim, 1st viscount, 1891-1970. 2. Great Britain. Army — Biography. 3. Generals — Great Britain — Biography. I. T.
DA69.3.S55 L48 1976   940.54/25/0924 B   *LC* 77-353858   *ISBN* 0208016376

DA70–89 Naval History

Andrews, Kenneth R.   ● **3.1274**
Drake's voyages: a re-assessment of their place in Elizabethan maritime expansion [by] Kenneth R. Andrews. — New York: Scribner, [1968, c1967] 190 p.: 7 maps.; 22 cm. 1. Drake, Francis, Sir, 1540?-1596. 2. Great Britain — History, Naval — Tudors, 1485-1603 I. T.
DA86.A7 1968   942.05/5/0924   *LC* 68-12504

Corbett, Julian Stafford, Sir, 1854-1922.   ● **3.1275**
Sir Francis Drake. — New York: AMS Press, [1969] vi, 209 p.: port.; 23 cm. Reprint of the 1890 ed. 1. Drake, Francis, Sir, 1540?-1596. I. T.
DA86.22.D7 C8 1969   942.055/0924   *LC* 77-105513

Williamson, James Alexander, 1886-.   ● **3.1276**
Hawkins of Plymouth; a new history of Sir John Hawkins and of the other members of his family prominent in Tudor England, by James A. Williamson. — 2d ed. — New York: Barnes & Noble, [1969] xi, 348 p.: illus., facsims., maps, ports.; 23 cm. 1. Hawkins, John, Sir, 1532-1595. I. T.
DA86.22.H3 W49 1969b   942.05/5/0924 B   *LC* 72-7944   *ISBN* 0389012033

Lacey, Robert.   **3.1277**
Sir Walter Ralegh. — [1st American ed.]. — New York: Atheneum, 1974 [c1973] 415 p.: illus.; 25 cm. 1. Raleigh, Walter, Sir, 1552?-1618. I. T.
DA86.22.R2 L3 1974   942.05/5/0924 B   *LC* 73-80750   *ISBN* 0689105703

Magnus, Philip Montefiore, Sir, bart., 1906-.   ● **3.1278**
Sir Walter Raleigh, by Philip Magnus. Hamden, Conn., Archon Books [1968] 158 p. maps, ports. 21 cm. (Makers of history) 1. Raleigh, Walter, Sir, 1552?-1618. I. T.
DA86.22.R2 M17 1968   942.05/5/0924 B   *LC* 68-3593

Corbett, Julian Stafford, Sir, 1854-1922.   **3.1279**
England in the Seven Years' War; a study in combined strategy. — 2d ed. London, Longmans, Green, 1918. — [New York: AMS Press, 1973] 2 v.: illus.; 22 cm. 1. Anglo-French War, 1755-1763 2. Strategy I. T.
DA87.C7 1973   940.2/534   *LC* 76-154130   *ISBN* 0404092241

Bennett, Geoffrey Martin.   ● **3.1280**
Nelson, the commander / [by] Geoffrey Bennett. — New York: Scribner, [1972] xii, 322 p.: ill.; 23 cm. 1. Nelson, Horatio Nelson, Viscount, 1758-1805. I. T.
DA87.1.N4 B37 1972b   359.3/3/10924 B   *LC* 71-38567   *ISBN* 0684128861

Lloyd, Christopher, 1906-.   **3.1281**
Nelson and sea power. — London: English Universities Press, 1973. 156, [8] p.: illus., maps, ports.; 23 cm. — (Men and their times) 1. Nelson, Horatio Nelson, Viscount, 1758-1805. I. T.
DA87.1.N4 L53   359.3/3/10924 B   *LC* 73-161901   *ISBN* 034012413X

Mahan, A. T. (Alfred Thayer), 1840-1914.   ● **3.1282**
The life of Nelson, the embodiment of the sea power of Great Britain. 2d ed., rev. New York, Haskell House, 1969. xvi, 764 p. illus., maps, plans, ports. 23 cm. This ed. was first published in 1899. 1. Nelson, Horatio Nelson, Viscount, 1758-1805. I. T.
DA87.1.N4 M3 1969   942.07/3/0924 B   *LC* 68-26361   *ISBN* 0838301827

Thomas, Donald.   **3.1283**
Cochrane: Britannia's last sea–king / Donald Thomas. — New York: Viking Press, 1978. 383 p., [4] leaves of plates: ill.; 24 cm. Includes index. 1. Dundonald, Thomas Cochrane, Earl of, 1775-1860. 2. Admirals — Great Britain — Biography. 3. Great Britain — History, Naval — 19th century I. T.
DA88.1.D9 T44 1978   359.3/31/0924 B   *LC* 78-6940   *ISBN* 0670226440

Terraine, John.   **3.1284**
Trafalgar / John Terraine; eye–witness accounts compiled by John Westwood. — New York: Mason/Charter, 1976. 205 p.: ill. (some col.); 26 cm. 1. Trafalgar (Cape), Battle of, 1805 — Personal narratives. 2. Seamen — Great Britain — Biography. I. T.
DA88.5 1805.T47 1976b   940.2/7   *LC* 76-11423   *ISBN* 0884053873

Roskill, Stephen Wentworth.   3.1285
Admiral of the Fleet Earl Beatty: the last naval hero: an intimate biography / Stephen Roskill. — 1st American ed. — New York: Atheneum, 1981, c1980. 430 p., [8] leaves of plates: ill.; 24 cm. Includes index. 1. Beatty, David Beatty, Earl, 1871-1936. 2. Great Britain. Royal Navy — Biography. 3. World War, 1914-1918 — Naval operations, British. 4. Admirals — Great Britain — Biography. I. T.
DA89.1.B4 R6 1981   940.4/5941/0924 B 19   *LC* 80-19778   *ISBN* 0689111193

Mackay, Ruddock F.   3.1286
Fisher of Kilverstone / by Ruddock F. Mackay. — Oxford: Clarendon Press, 1974 (c1973) xvi, 539 p.: ill.; 23 cm. 1. Fisher, John Arbuthnot Fisher, Baron, 1841-1920. I. T.
DA89.1.F5 M3   359.3/2/20924 B   *LC* 74-158694   *ISBN* 0198224095

Hough, Richard Alexander, 1922-.   3.1287
Mountbatten / Richard Hough. — 1st ed. — New York: Random House, c1981. xv, 302 p., [16] leaves of plates: ill.; 25 cm. 1. Mountbatten of Burma, Louis Mountbatten, Earl, 1900-1979. 2. Great Britain. Royal Navy — Biography. 3. Admirals — Great Britain — Biography. 4. Viceroys — India — Biography. I. T.
DA89.1.M59 H68   941.082/092/4 B 19   *LC* 80-6023   *ISBN* 039451162X

DA110–125 Civilization. Intellectual Life. Ethnography

Barker, Ernest, Sir, 1874-1960. ed.   • 3.1288
The character of England. — Oxford, Clarendon Press, 1947. xii, 595 p. illus., ports., facsims. 25 cm. Collection of articles describing 'what is characteristically English in each field, and ... the characteristic English contribution in that field.' 1. Great Britain. 2. Gt. Brit. — Civilization. 3. National characteristics, English I. T.
DA110.B36   914.2   *LC* A 48-17 *

Heineman, Benjamin W.   3.1289
The politics of the powerless; a study of the Campaign Against Racial Discrimination [by] Benjamin W. Heineman, Jr. — London: published for the Institute of Race Relations by Oxford University Press, 1972. xvi, 244 p.; 23 cm. 1. Campaign Against Racial Discrimination. 2. Great Britain — Race relations. I. T.
DA125.A1 H4   301.45/1/0420942   *LC* 73-150590   *ISBN* 0192181785

Hiro, Dilip.   3.1290
Black British, white British. Rev. ed. New York: Monthly Review Press [1973] xxii, 346 p.; 21 cm. 1. Race discrimination — England. 2. England — Foreign population. 3. England — Race relations. I. T.
DA125.A1 H53 1973   301.45/1/0942   *LC* 72-92026   *ISBN* 0853452709

Kerridge, Roy.   3.1291
Real wicked, guy: a view of Black Britain / Roy Kerridge. — Oxford, England: B. Blackwell, 1983. 210 p.; 23 cm. 1. Minorities — Great Britain. 2. Great Britain — Foreign population. 3. Great Britain — Race relations. I. T.
DA125.A1 K44 1983   305.8/00941 19   *LC* 83-184760   *ISBN* 0631132392

Layton-Henry, Zig.   3.1292
The politics of race in Britain / Zig Layton-Henry. — London; Boston: Allen & Unwin, 1984. xvi, 191 p.; 23 cm. Includes index. 1. Racism — Great Britain. 2. Blacks — Great Britain. 3. Great Britain — Politics and government — 1945- 4. Great Britain — Race relations. I. T.
DA125.A1 L39 1984   323.1/1/0941 19   *LC* 84-6265   *ISBN* 0043230261

Blackett, R. J. M., 1943-.   3.1293
Building an antislavery wall: Black Americans in the Atlantic abolitionist movement, 1830–1860 / R.J.M. Blackett. — Baton Rouge: Louisiana State University Press, c1983. xii, 237 p.; 24 cm. Includes index. 1. Afro-Americans — Great Britain — History — 19th century. 2. Abolitionists — Great Britain. 3. Slavery — United States — Anti-slavery movements. 4. Slavery — United States — Public opinion. 5. Public opinion — Great Britain. I. T.
DA125.N4 B54 1983   941/.00496073 19   *LC* 82-21724   *ISBN* 0807110825

Lorimer, Douglas A.   3.1294
Colour class, and the Victorians: English attitudes to the Negro in the mid-nineteenth century / Douglas A. Lorimer. — [Leicester, Eng.]: Leicester

University Press; New York: Holmes & Meier, 1978. 300 p.; 23 cm. Includes index. 1. Blacks — England — Public opinion. 2. Public opinion — England. 3. Social classes — England. 4. England — Race relations. I. T.
DA125.N4 L67 1978   DA125N4 L67 1978.   301.15/43/30145196
LC 78-6396   *ISBN* 0841903921

Scobie, Edward.   3.1295
Black Britannia; a history of Blacks in Britain. Chicago, Johnson Pub. Co., 1972. ix, 316 p. illus. 24 cm. 1. Blacks — England — History. 2. England — Race relations. I. T.
DA125.N4 S36   301.45/19/6042   *LC* 72-82184   *ISBN* 0874850568

Walvin, James.   3.1296
The Black presence; a documentary history of the Negro in England, 1555–1860. New York, Schocken Books [1972, c1971] 222 p. 23 cm. (Sourcebooks in Negro history) 1. Blacks — England — History — Sources. I. T. II. Series.
DA125.N4 W35   301.45/1/96042   *LC* 75-169829

DA130–592 English History, by Period

DA130–260 EARLY. MEDIEVAL, TO 1485

Partner, Nancy F.   3.1297
Serious entertainments: the writing of history in twelfth–century England / Nancy F. Partner. — Chicago: University of Chicago Press, 1977. 289 p.; 23 cm. Includes index. 1. Henry of Huntingdon, 1084?-1155. The chronicle of Henry of Huntingdon. 2. William of Newburgh, 1136-1198? Historia rerum anglicarum Wilhelmi Parvi. 3. Richard of Devizes, fl, 1191. Chronicon Ricardi Divisiensis de rebus gestis Ricardi Primi regis Angliae. 4. Great Britain — History — To 1066 5. Great Britain — History — Norman period, 1066-1154 6. Great Britain — History — Richard I, 1189-1199 7. Great Britain — History — To 1485 — Historiography I. T.
DA130.H413 P37   942/.007/2   *LC* 77-4402   *ISBN* 0226647633

Myers, A. R. (Alec Reginald), 1912-1980.   • 3.1298
England in the late Middle Ages. — Harmondsworth, Mddx.: Penguin Books, 1952. xv, 263 p.: maps; 18 cm. — (Pelican history of England. v.4) 1. Great Britain — History — To 1485 I. T. II. Series.
DA130.M8   *LC* 67-4045

Poole, Austin Lane, 1889-1963. ed.   • 3.1299
Medieval England. A new ed. rewritten and rev. Oxford, Clarendon Press, 1958. 2 v. (xxviii, 661 p.) illus., plates, maps, coats of arms. 24 cm. Includes bibliographies. 1. Great Britain — History — Anglo Saxon period, 449-1066 2. Great Britain — History — Medieval period, 1066-1485 3. Great Britain — Civilization. I. T.
DA130.P65 1958   942   *LC* 58-4429

Sayles, G. O. (George Osborne), 1901-.   • 3.1300
The medieval foundations of England. [2d ed., rev. and with new introductory chapter] London, Methuen [1950] xxv, 482p. 23cm. 1. Great Britain — History — To 1485 I. T.
DA130.S39 1950a   942.01   *LC* 50-58227

DA135–62 To 1066

MacDougall, Hugh A.   3.1301
Racial myth in English history: Trojans, Teutons, and Anglo–Saxons / Hugh A. MacDougall. — Montreal: Harvest House; Hanover, N.H.: University Press of New England, 1982. ix, 146 p.; 21 cm. 1. Geoffrey, of Monmouth, Bishop of St. Asaph, 1100?-1154. 2. British — Origin. 3. Anglo-Saxon race 4. Mythology, British 5. Great Britain — History — To 1066 — Historiography I. T.
DA135.M15 1982   942.01 19   *LC* 81-69941   *ISBN* 087451228X

Geoffrey, of Monmouth, Bishop of St. Asaph, 1100?-1154.   • 3.1302
History of the Kings of Britain / Geoffrey of Monmouth; translated by Sebastian Evans; rev. by Charles W. Dunn; introd. by Gwyn Jones. — London: Dent, 1963, c1958. xxii, 281 p.; 19 cm. — (Everyman's library; 577) Includes indexes. 1. Arthur, King. 2. Merlin (Prose romance) 3. Celts — Folklore 4. Great Britain — History — To 449 I. Evans, Sebastian, 1830-1909. II. T.
DA140.G353   *LC* 65-1872

Tatlock, John S. P. (John Strong Perry), 1876-1948.   • **3.1303**
The legendary history of Britain. Berkeley, University of California Press, 1950. xi, 545 p. 25 cm. 1. Geoffrey, of Monmouth, Bishop of St. Asaph, 1100?-1154. Historia Britonum I. T.
DA140.G37 T3 1950   *LC* 50-7428

Laing, Lloyd Robert.   **3.1304**
Celtic Britain / Lloyd Laing. — New York: Scribner, c1979. xi, 190 p.: ill.; 24 cm. — (Britain before the Conquest) Includes index. 1. Celts — Great Britain. 2. Great Britain — Antiquities, Celtic. I. T. II. Series.
DA140.L33 1979b   936.1   *LC* 78-66127   *ISBN* 0684162253

DA145–147 ROMANS

Collingwood, R. G. (Robin George), 1889-1943.   • **3.1305**
The archaeology of Roman Britain [by] R. G. Collingwood and Ian Richmond; with a chapter by B. R. Hartley on Samian ware. [New] ed., entirely revised. London, Methuen, 1969. xxv, 350 p. 27 plates, illus., plans. 25 cm. (Methuen's handbooks of archaeology) Distributed in the U.S.A. by Barnes & Noble, New York. 1. Romans — Great Britain. 2. Great Britain — Antiquities, Roman I. Richmond, Ian Archibald, Sir, 1902-1965. II. T.
DA145.C57 1969   913.3/6   *LC* 79-407851   *ISBN* 041627580X

Salway, Peter.   **3.1306**
Roman Britain / by Peter Salway. — Oxford: Clarendon Press; New York: Oxford University Press, 1981. xviii, 824 p.: ill.; 22 cm. — (Oxford history of England. 1A) Includes index. 1. Great Britain — History — Roman period, 55 B.C.-449 A.D. I. T. II. Series.
DA145.S26   936.1/04 19   *LC* 80-41811   *ISBN* 019821717X

Wacher, J. S.   **3.1307**
The towns of Roman Britain / John Wacher. — Berkeley: University of California Press, 1975, c1974. 460 p.: ill.; 26 cm. 1. Romans — Great Britain. 2. Cities and towns, Ancient — Great Britain. 3. Great Britain — Antiquities, Roman I. T.
DA145.W13 1975   936.1   *LC* 73-91663   *ISBN* 0520026691

DA150–155 SAXONS

Anglo-Saxon chronicle.   • **3.1308**
The Anglo–Saxon chronicle / translated and edited by G. N. Garmonsway. — London: Dent, 1953. xlix, 295 p.: facsim. (Everyman's University Library; no. 1624) 1. Great Britain — History — Anglo-Saxon period, 449-1066 — Sources. I. Garmonsway, George Norman. II. T.
DA150.A58 1953   942.01   *LC* 53-13456   *ISBN* 0460016245

Anglo-Saxon chronicle.   • **3.1309**
The Anglo–Saxon chronicle. A revised translation / edited by Dorothy Whitelock, with David C. Douglas and Susiel. Tucker. Introd. by Dorothy Whitelock. — New Brunswick, N.J.: Rutgers University Press, 1962, c1961. xxxii, 240 p.: geneal. tables; 26 cm. 1. Great Britain — History — Anglo-Saxon period, 449-1066 — Sources. I. Whitelock, Dorothy. ed. II. T.
DA 150.A6 1962   *LC* 61-17284

Anglo-Saxon chronicle.   **3.1310**
The Anglo–Saxon chronicle: a collaborative edition / general editors, David Dumville & Simon Keynes. — Cambridge [Cambridgeshire]: D.S. Brewer; Totowa, NJ: Biblio Distribution Services, 1983-. v. < 4, 17 >; 25 cm. Text of chronicle in Anglo-Saxon; explanatory material in English; editions of Latin texts. 1. Great Britain — History — To 1066 I. Dumville, D. N. II. Keynes, Simon. III. Taylor, Simon. IV. T.
DA150.A6 1983b   942.01 19   *LC* 83-17130   *ISBN* 0859911047

Anglo-Saxon chronicle.   **3.1311**
Two of the Saxon chronicles parallel: with supplementary extracts from the others; a revised text edited with introd. notes, appendices, and glossary by Charles Plummer, on the basis of an edition by John Earle; with a bibliographical note by Dorothy Whitelock. — Oxford: Clarendon Press, 1892-1899, 1972 printing. 2 v. The Parker MSS. (Corpus Christi College, Cambridge, no. 173) and the Laud MSS. (Bodleian Laud 636) Reissued in 1952 with a bibliographical note by Dorothy Whitelock 1. Great Britain — History — Anglo-Saxon period, 499-1066 — Sources I. Earle, John, 1824-1903. II. Plummer, Charles, 1851-1927. III. Whitelock, Dorothy. IV. Cambridge, Eng. University. Corpus Christi College. Library. MSS. 173 V. Oxford, Eng. University. Bodleian Library. MSS. (Laud misc. 636) VI. T.
DA150 A68 1972

Ethelwerd, d. 998.   • **3.1312**
The chronicle of Aethelweard / Edited by A. Campbell. — London; New York: Nelson, [1962] lxiii, 56, 57-68 p. 23 cm. — (Medieval texts) Added t.p.: Chronicon Aethelweardi. Latin and English on opposite pages numbered in duplicate. 1. Great Britain — History — Anglo Saxon period, 449-1066 I. Campbell, A. (Alistair), 1907- II. T. III. Title: Chronicon Aethelweardi.
DA150.E8 1962   PR1539.A3 C3.   942.01   *LC* 64-5203

Alcock, Leslie.   **3.1313**
Arthur's Britain; history and archaeology, AD 367–634. — New York: St. Martin's Press, [1972, c1971] xvii, 415 p.: illus.; 25 cm. 1. Arthur, King. 2. Great Britain — History — Anglo Saxon period, 449-1066 3. Great Britain — History — Roman period, 55 B.C.-449 A.D. 4. Great Britain — Antiquities I. T.
DA152.A7 1972   914.2/03/1   *LC* 72-185252

Campbell, James, 1935-.   **3.1314**
The Anglo–Saxons / James Campbell, Eric John, Patrick Wormald; general editor, James Campbell; with contributions from P.V. Addyman ... [et al]. — Ithaca, N.Y.: Cornell University Press, 1982. 272 p.: ill. (some col.); 29 cm. 'Cornell/Phaidon books.' Includes index. 1. Great Britain — History — Anglo Saxon period, 449-1066 I. John, Eric. II. Wormald, Patrick. III. T.
DA152.C28 1982   942.01 19   *LC* 81-70710   *ISBN* 0801414822

Hollister, C. Warren (Charles Warren), 1930-.   • **3.1315**
Anglo–Saxon military institutions on the eve of the Norman Conquest. — Oxford, Clarendon Press, 1962. 170 p. 23 cm. 1. Anglo-Saxons 2. Gt. Brit. — History, Military. I. T.
DA152.H66   942.01   *LC* 63-158

Myres, J. N. L. (John Nowell Linton)   **3.1316**
The English settlements / by J.N.L. Myres. — Oxford [Oxfordshire]: Clarendon Press; New York: Oxford University Press, 1986. xxviii, 248 p.: ill., maps; 22 cm. (Oxford history of England. 1B) Includes index. 1. Great Britain — History — Anglo Saxon period, 449-1066 I. T. II. Series.
DA152.M97 1986   942.01 19   *LC* 85-15538   *ISBN* 0198217196

Stenton, F. M. (Frank Merry), 1880-1967.   • **3.1317**
Anglo–Saxon England, by F. M. Stenton. 3d ed. Oxford [Eng.] Clarendon Press, 1971. xli, 765 p. maps (1 fold.) 22 cm. (Oxford history of England. 2) 1. Anglo-Saxons — England. 2. Great Britain — History — Anglo Saxon period, 449-1066 I. T. II. Series.
DA152.S74 1971   942.01   *LC* 71-22751   *ISBN* 0198217161

Whitelock, Dorothy.   • **3.1318**
The beginnings of English society, by D. Whitelock. Harmondsworth [Eng.] Penguin Books [1952] 256 p. 18 cm. (Pelican history of England. 2) Pelican books, A245. Bibliography: p. [244]-248. 1. Great Britain — Civilization — To 1066 I. T. II. Series.
DA152.W4x   *LC* 66-46212

Hunter Blair, Peter, 1912-1982.   **3.1319**
An introduction to Anglo–Saxon England / Peter Hunter Blair. — 2d ed. — Cambridge [Eng.]; New York: Cambridge University Press, 1977. xv, 379 p., [8] leaves of plates: ill.; 23 cm. Includes index. 1. England — Civilization — To 1066 I. T.
DA152.2.H86 1977   942.01   *LC* 77-71404   *ISBN* 0521216508.
ISBN 0521292190 pbk

Asser, John, d. ca. 909.   **3.1320**
[De Rebus gestis Aelfredi. English] Alfred the Great, Asser's Life of King Alfred and other contemporary sources / translated with an introduction and notes by Simon Keynes and Michael Lapidge. — Harmondsworth, Middlesex, England; New York, N.Y., U.S.A.: Penguin Books, 1983. 368 p.: ill.; 20 cm. — (Penguin classics.) Translation of: De rebus gestis Aelfredi. 1. Alfred, King of England, 849-899. 2. Great Britain — Kings and rulers — Biography 3. Great Britain — History — To 1241 — Sources. I. Keynes, Simon. II. Lapidge, Michael. III. T. IV. Series.
DA153.A8213 1983   942.01/64/0924 B 19   *LC* 84-119802   *ISBN* 0140444092

Barlow, Frank.   **3.1321**
Edward the Confessor. Berkeley, University of California Press, 1970. xxviii, 375 p. fold. geneal. table, maps, plates. 25 cm. 1. Edward, King of England, ca. 1003-1066. I. T.
DA154.8.B297   942.02/0924   *LC* 70-104107   *ISBN* 0520016718

The life of King Edward, who rests at Westminster. Attributed   • **3.1322**
to a monk of St. Bertin. Edited and translated with introd. and notes by Frank Barlow.
London, Nelson [1962] lxxxii, 81, 81, 85-145 p. illus., geneal. table. 23 cm. — (Medieval texts) English and Latin on opposite pages numbered in duplicate. Bibliographical footnotes. 1. Edward, King of England, ca. 1003-1066. I. Barlow, Frank. ed. and tr. II. A monk of St. Bertin.
DA154.8.V5   923.142   *LC* 62-6101

Wilson, David Mackenzie., ed.   **3.1323**
The Archaeology of Anglo–Saxon England / edited by David M. Wilson. London: Methuen, 1976. xvi, 532 p., [12] leaves of plates: ill.; 26 cm. Includes index. 1. Anglo-Saxons — Addresses, essays, lectures. 2. England — Antiquities, Saxon — Addresses, essays, lectures. 3. England — Civilization — To 1066 — Addresses, essays, lectures. I. Wilson, David McKenzie. II. T.
DA155.A7   942.01   *LC* 77-351019   *ISBN* 041615090X

Loyn, H. R. (Henry Royston)   **3.1324**
The Vikings in Britain / H. R. Loyn. — New York: St. Martin's Press, 1977.
175 p., [4] leaves of plates: ill.; 24 cm. Includes index. 1. Northmen in Great
Britain — History. 2. Great Britain — History — Invasions 3. Scandinavia —
History I. T.
DA158.L68 1977b   942.01   LC 77-73918   ISBN 0312846711

DA170–260 Medieval (1066–1485)

Poole, Austin Lane, 1889-1963.   **• 3.1325**
From Domesday book to Magna Carta, 1087–1216. — 2d ed. — Oxford,
Clarendon Press, 1955. xv, 541 p. maps. 23 cm. — (Oxford history of England.
[v. 3]) Bibliography: p. [487]-512. 1. Gt. Brit. — Hist. — Medieval period,
1066-1485. I. T. II. Series.
DA175.P6 1955   942.02   LC 56-13761

Beresford, M. W. (Maurice Warwick), 1920-.   **• 3.1326**
Deserted medieval villages: studies. Edited by Maurice Beresford and John G.
Hurst. — New York: St. Martin's Press, [1972, c1971] xviii, 340 p.: illus.; 26
cm. 1. Cities and towns, Ruined, extinct, etc — Great Britain. 2. Excavations
(Archaeology) — Great Britain. I. Hurst, John G., 1927- joint author. II. T.
DA176.B44 1972   914.2/03   LC 75-190102

Cam, Helen Maud, 1885-1968.   **• 3.1327**
Liberties & communities in medieval England: collected studies in local
administration and topography. — New York: Barnes & Noble [1963] xiv,
267 p.: maps. 1. Local government — Great Britain 2. Great Britain —
History, Local I. T.
DA176.C3 1963   LC 64-3937

Barnie, John.   **3.1328**
War in medieval English society; social values in the Hundred Years War,
1337–99. — Ithaca, N.Y.: Cornell University Press, [1974] xiii, 204 p.; 23 cm.
1. Hundred Years' War, 1339-1453 — Public opinion. 2. England —
Civilization — Medieval period, 1066-1485 I. T.
DA185.B27 1974   914.2/03/37   LC 74-2687   ISBN 0801408652

Coulton, G. G. (George Gordon), 1858-1947.   **• 3.1329**
Medieval panorama: the English scene from conquest to Reformation. New
York: Noonday Press, c1955, 1964 printing. 801p.,illus. 'Meridian
books;MG2.' 1. Civilization, Medieval 2. Catholic Church in England.
3. Great Britain — History — Medieval period, 1066-1485 4. Great Britain —
Civilization — History. I. T.
DA185 C865 1955   942   LC 55-7582

Historical Association (Great Britain)   **• 3.1330**
Social life in early England; Historical Association essays. New York, Barnes &
Noble [1960] xi, 264 p.: maps (1 fold.) plans (part fold.) 23 cm. 1. Arms
and armor 2. Trade routes 3. Great Britain — Social life and customs
I. Barraclough, Geoffrey, 1908- ed. II. T.
DA185.H58   LC 59-15211

Homans, George Caspar, 1910-.   **• 3.1331**
English villagers of the thirteenth century / George Caspar Homans. — New
York: Russell & Russell, Inc, [c1941]. xiv, 478 p.: ill. 1. Village communities
— Great Britain. 2. Agriculture — England. 3. Peasantry — England.
4. England — Social life and customs I. T.
DA185.H685 1960   DA185.H68.   LC 60-8200

Jusserand, J. J. (Jean Jules), 1855-1932.   **• 3.1332**
English wayfaring life in the Middle Ages / Jean A.A.J. Jusserand; translated
from the French by Lucy Toulmin Smith. 4th ed. New York: Putnam, 1950.
315 p. Translation of Les Anglais au Moyen Age. 1. Wayfaring life — Great
Britain. 2. Travel, Medieval 3. Pilgrims and pilgrimages — England.
4. England — Social life & customs. I. T.
DA185.J8x   LC 51-4881

Stenton, Doris Mary Parsons, Lady.   **• 3.1333**
English society in the early middle ages, (1066–1307) [by] Doris Mary Stenton.
— 4th ed. — Harmondsworth: Penguin, 1965. 320 p.; 19 cm. — (Pelican
history of England. 3) Pelican books, A 252. 1. Great Britain — History —
Medieval period, 1066-1454. I. T. II. Series.
DA185.S7x   914.2/03/2   LC 67-96327

Stenton, F. M. (Frank Merry), 1880-1967.   **• 3.1334**
The first century of English feudalism, 1066–1166. — 2d ed. — Oxford,
Clarendon Press, 1961. 312 p. 22 cm. — (The Ford lectures, 1929)
1. Feudalism — Gt. Brit. I. T.
DA185.S8 1961   942.02   LC 61-19123

Young, Charles R.   **3.1335**
The royal forests of medieval England / Charles R. Young. — Philadelphia:
University of Pennsylvania Press, 1979. ix, 220 p.; 24 cm. — (Middle Ages.)

Includes index. 1. Royal forests — England — History. 2. Great Britain —
Politics and government — 1066-1485 I. T. II. Series.
DA188.Y68   333.7/5   LC 78-65109   ISBN 0812277600

DA190–199 NORMANS

Domesday book.   **3.1336**
Domesday book: a survey of the counties of England / text and translation
edited by John Morris. — Chichester: Phillimore, 1975-. v.: maps; 22 cm. —
(History from the sources) Latin and English. 1. Real property — England —
Sources. 2. England — Antiquities I. Morris, John. II. T. III. Series.
DA190.D513x   ISBN 0850331455

Sawyer, P. H.   **3.1337**
Domesday book: a reassessment / edited by Peter Sawyer. — London;
Baltimore, Md., USA: E. Arnold, 1985. x, 182 p.: ill.; 25 cm. 1. Domesday
book. 2. Real property — England — History. 3. Land tenure — England —
History. 4. Great Britain — History — Norman period, 1066-1154 5. England
— Economic conditions — Medieval period, 1066-1485 I. T.
DA190.D7 D656 1985   333.3/22/0942 19   LC 86-103554   ISBN
0713164409

Finn, R. Welldon (Rex Welldon)   **3.1338**
Domesday Book: a guide / R. Welldon Finn. — London: Phillimore, 1975
(c1973). xiv, 109 p.; 22 cm. Includes index. 1. Domesday book. I. T.
DA190.D7 F48   333.3/22/0942   LC 75-308919   ISBN 0850331013

Galbraith, V. H. (Vivian Hunter), 1889-.   **3.1339**
Domesday book: its place in administrative history / by V. H. Galbraith. —
[S.l.]: Oxford, 1975 (c1974) xxxv, 193 p., [1] fold. leaf of plates; 23 cm. Includes
index. 1. Domesday book. 2. Land tenure — England. 3. England — Rural
conditions. I. T.
DA190.D7 G28   333.3/22/0942   LC 75-308915   ISBN
0198224249

Chibnall, Marjorie.   **3.1340**
Anglo–Norman England, 1066–1166 / Marjorie Chibnall. — New York: Basil
Blackwell, 1986. 1 v. Includes index. 1. Great Britain — History — Norman
period, 1066-1154 I. T.
DA195.C47 1986   942.02 19   LC 85-11255   ISBN 0631132341

Round, John Horace, 1854-1928.   **• 3.1341**
Feudal England; historical studies on the eleventh and twelfth centuries, by J.
H. Round. Foreword by F. M. Stenton. New York, Barnes & Noble [1964]
444 p. geneal. tables. (part fold.) 23 cm. 'First published 1895 ... Reset with new
foreword 1964.' 1. Domesday book. 2. Great Britain — History — Norman
period, 1066-1154 I. T.
DA195.R86 1964a   942.02   LC 65-1163

Douglas, David Charles, 1898-.   **3.1342**
William the Conqueror; the Norman impact upon England [by] David C.
Douglas. Berkeley, University of California Press, 1964. xii, 476 p. geneal.
tables, maps, port. 24 cm. 1. William I, King of England, 1027 or 8-1087.
2. Normans — England. 3. Normandy (France) — History — To 1515 I. T.
DA197.D6   942.021   LC 64-5124

Barlow, Frank.   **3.1343**
William Rufus / Frank Barlow. — Berkeley: University of California Press,
1984 (c1983). xix, 484 p., 16 p. of plates: ill.; 24 cm. Includes index. 1. William
II, King of England, 1056?-1100. 2. Great Britain — History — William II,
Rufus, 1087-1100 3. Great Britain — Kings and rulers — Biography I. T.
DA197.5.B37   942.02/2/0924 B 19   LC 82-45902   ISBN
0520049365

Gesta Stephani, Regis Anglorum. English & Latin.   **3.1344**
Gesta Stephani / edited and translated by K. R. Potter; with new introd. and
notes by R. H. C. Davis. — Oxford: Clarendon Press, 1976. xl, 249 p.: map.; 23
cm. (Oxford medieval texts.) English and Latin. Includes index. 1. Stephen,
King of England, 1097?-1154. I. Potter, Kenneth Reginald. II. Davis, R. H. C.
(Ralph Henry Carless), 1918- III. T. IV. Series.
DA198.5.G42 1976   942.02/4/0924 B   LC 76-364954   ISBN
0198222343

William, of Malmesbury, ca. 1090-1143.   **• 3.1345**
The Historia novella. Translated from the Latin with introd. and notes by K. R.
Potter. — London, New York, T. Nelson [1955] xliii, 77, 77, [78]-84 map. 23
cm. — (Medieval texts) Latin and English on opposite pages numbered in
duplicate. 1. Gt. Brit. — Hist. — Stephen, 1135-1154. I. T.
DA198.5.W52   942.024   LC 55-3699

Kealey, Edward J.   **3.1346**
Roger of Salisbury, viceroy of England, by Edward J. Kealey. — Berkeley:
University of California Press, 1972. xvi, 312 p.; 25 cm. 1. Roger of Salisbury,

Bp. of Salisbury, 1065?-1139. 2. Great Britain — Politics and government — 1066-1154 I. T.
DA199.R6 K4   942.02/092/4 B   *LC* 78-92681   *ISBN* 0520019857

DA200–209 ANGEVINS (1154–1216)

Warren, Wilfred Lewis.   **3.1347**
Henry II [by] W. L. Warren. — Berkeley: University of California Press, 1973. 693 p.: illus.; 25 cm. 1. Henry II, King of England, 1133-1189. 2. Great Britain — Politics and government — 1154-1189 I. T.
DA206.W37 1973   942.03/1/0924 B   *LC* 72-82220   *ISBN* 0520022823

Gillingham, John.   **3.1348**
Richard the Lionheart / John Gillingham. — New York: Times Books, [1979] c1978. 318 p.: ill.; 22 cm. Includes index. 1. Richard I, King of England, 1157-1199. 2. Great Britain — Kings and rulers — Biography I. T.
DA207.G48 1979   942.03/2/0924 B   *LC* 78-63599   *ISBN* 0812908023

Holt, James Clarke.   • **3.1349**
The northerners, a study in the reign of King John. Oxford, Clarendon Press 1961. 272 p. illus. 23 cm. 1. Great Britain — History — John, 1199-1216 I. T.
DA208.H6   942.033   *LC* 61-65767

Painter, Sidney, 1902-1960.   • **3.1350**
The reign of King John. Baltimore, John Hopkins Press, 1949. viii, 397 p. 24 cm. 1. John, King of England, 1167-1216. 2. Magna Carta. 3. Great Britain — History — John, 1199-1216 4. Great Britain — Kings and rulers — Biography I. T.
DA208.P3   942.033   *LC* 49-49221

Warren, Wilfred Lewis.   **3.1351**
King John / W. L. Warren. — Berkeley: University of California Press, c1978. xi, 350 p., [5] leaves of plates: ill.; 22 cm. — (Campus; 209) Includes index. 1. John, King of England, 1167-1216. 2. Great Britain — History — John, 1199-1216 3. Great Britain — Kings and rulers — Biography I. T.
DA208.W33 1978b   942.03/3/0924 B   *LC* 77-20332   *ISBN* 0520036107

Kelly, Amy Ruth, 1878-.   • **3.1352**
Eleanor of Aquitaine and the four kings. Cambridge, Harvard University Press, 1950. xii, 431 p. illus., map (on lining papers) 24 cm. 1. Eleanor, Queen, consort of Henry II, King of England, 1122?-1204. 2. Great Britain — History — Plantagenets, 1154-1399 I. T.
DA209.E6 K45 1950   923.142   *LC* 50-6545

Bartlett, Robert.   **3.1353**
Gerald of Wales, 1146–1223 / Robert Bartlett. — Oxford: Clarendon Press; New York; Oxford University Press, 1982. 246 p.; 23 cm. (Oxford historical monographs) Includes index. 1. Giraldus, Cambrensis, 1146?-1223? I. T.
DA209.G5 B37 1982   942.9/007/2024 19   *LC* 82-145750   *ISBN* 0198218923

Duby, Georges.   **3.1354**
[Guillaume le Maréchal. English] William Marshal: the flower of chivalry / Georges Duby; translated from the French by Richard Howard. — 1st American ed. — New York: Pantheon Books, [1986], c1985. 155 p.; 22 cm. Translation of: Guillaume le Marechal. 1. Pembroke, William Marshal, Earl of, 1144?-1219. 2. Regents — Great Britain — Biography. 3. Knights and knighthood — Great Britain — History. 4. Chivalry 5. Great Britain — History — Angevin period, 1154-1216 I. T.
DA209.P4 D8313 1986   942.03/4/0924 B 19   *LC* 85-42837   *ISBN* 0394543092

Painter, Sidney, 1902-1960.   • **3.1355**
William Marshal, knight-errant, baron, and regent of England, by Sidney Painter ... — Baltimore, The Johns Hopkins press, 1933. xi, 305 p. 23.5 cm. — (Half-title: The Johns Hopkins historical publications) 'This biography was originally written as a dissertation for the degree of doctor of philosophy in Yale university [1930]'—Pref. 1. Pembroke, William Marshal, Earl of, 1144?-1219. 2. Gt. Brit. — Hist. — Angevin period, 1154-1216. I. T.
DA209.P4P3   923.242   *LC* 33-8958

Smalley, Beryl.   **3.1356**
The Becket conflict and the schools; a study of intellectuals in politics. Totowa, N.J., Rowman and Littlefield [1973] xiv, 257 p. 23 cm. 1. Thomas, à Becket, Saint, 1118?-1170. 2. Scholasticism 3. England — Intellectual life — Medieval period, 1066-1485 I. T.
DA209.T4 S6 1973   942.03/1/0924 B   *LC* 72-14254   *ISBN* 087471172X

DA220–237 PLANTAGENETS (1216–1399)

Green, Vivian Hubert Howard.   • **3.1357**
The later Plantagenets; a survey of English history between 1307 and 1485. London, E. Arnold [1955] 438 p. maps, diagr., geneal. tables. 23 cm. 1. Great Britain — History — 14th century 2. Great Britain — History — Lancaster and York, 1399-1485 I. T.
DA225.G7   *LC* 55-4313

Keen, Maurice Hugh.   **3.1358**
England in the later Middle Ages: a political history [by] M. H. Keen. — London: Methuen, 1973. xii, 581 p.: geneal. tables, maps.; 23 cm. 'Distributed in the USA by Harper & Row Publishers Inc., Barnes & Noble Import Division.' 1. Great Britain — Politics and government — 1066-1485 I. T.
DA225.K4 1973   942.03   *LC* 73-153838   *ISBN* 0416759904

Powicke, Maurice, Sir.   • **3.1359**
The thirteenth century, 1216–1307 / Sir Frederick Maurice Powicke. 2d ed. Oxford: Clarendon Press, 1962. xiv, 829 p.: (fold.)geneal. table, maps. (Oxford history of England. 4) 1. Great Britain — History — 13th century I. T. II. Series.
DA225.P65 1962   942.034   *LC* 62-6745   *ISBN* 0198217080

Powicke, Frederick Maurice, 1879-.   • **3.1360**
King Henry III and the Lord Edward; the community of the realm in the thirteenth century, by F. M. Powicke ... — Oxford, The Clarendon press, 1947. 2 v. maps (part fold.) 24.5 cm. 1. Henry III, King of England, 1207-1272. 2. Edward I, King of England, 1239-1307. 3. Gt. Brit. — Hist. — Henry III, 1216-1272. I. T.
DA227.P6   942.034   *LC* 47-4620

Treharne, R. F. (Reginald Francis), 1901-1967.   **3.1361**
The baronial plan of reform, 1258–1263, by R. F. Treharne. Including the Raleigh lecture on history delivered to the British Academy, 1954. [Reprinted with additional material] [Manchester, Eng.] Manchester University Press; New York, Barnes & Noble 1972 (c1971) 478 p. (Publications of the University of Manchester, no. 221) (Historical series, no. 62) (The Ward bequest, v. 6) 1. Montfort, Simon de, Earl of Leicester, 1208?-1265. 2. Great Britain — History — Barons' War, 1263-1267 3. Great Britain — Politics and government — 1216-1272 I. T.
DA227.5.T72   942.03/4   *LC* 72-182919   *ISBN* 0389041165

Labarge, Margaret Wade.   • **3.1362**
Simon de Montfort / by Margaret Wade Labarge. — New York: Norton, 1962. xi, 312 p.: ill.; 22 cm. Includes index. 1. Montfort, Simon de, Earl of Leicester, 1208?-1265. I. T.
DA228.M7 L3   942.03/4/0924 B   *LC* 63-6618

Prestwich, Michael.   **3.1363**
The three Edwards: war and state in England, 1272–1377 / Michael Prestwich. — New York: St. Martin's Press, 1980. 336 p., [8] leaves of plates: ill.; 22 cm. Includes index. 1. Edward I, King of England, 1239-1307. 2. Edward II, King of England, 1284-1327. 3. Edward III, King of England, 1312-1377. 4. Great Britain — History — Edward I-III, 1272-1377 I. T.
DA229.P73 1980   942.03   *LC* 80-5095   *ISBN* 031280251X

The life of Edward the Second, by the so–called Monk of   • **3.1364**
Malmesbury. Translated from the Latin with introd. and notes by N. Denholm–Young.
London, New York, T. Nelson [1957] xxviii, 145, 145, [146]-150 23 cm. — (Medieval texts) Added t.-p.: Vita Edwardi Secundi. Latin and English on opposite pages, numbered in duplicate. 'Thomas Hearne's original transcript ... survives in the Bodleian Library, Oxford ... and is the source of this new edition.' 1. Edward II, King of England, 1284-1327. I. Denholm-Young, Noël, ed. and tr. II. Monk of Malmesbury.
DA230.L5   923.142   *LC* 57-4170

McKisack, May.   • **3.1365**
The fourteenth century, 1307–1399. Oxford, Clarendon Press, 1959. xix, 598 p. maps, geneal. tables. 23 cm. (Oxford history of England. 5) Bibliography: p. [533]-566. 1. Great Britain — History — 14th century I. T. II. Series.
DA230.M25   942.037   *LC* 59-16710

Tout, Thomas Frederick, 1855-1929.   • **3.1366**
The place of the reign of Edward 2 in English history; based upon the Ford lectures delivered in the University of Oxford in 1913. 2d ed., rev. Manchester University Press 1936. 375p. (Publications of the University of Manchester: Historical series, no. 21) 1. Edward II, King of England, 1284-1327. 2. Great Britain — History — Edward II, 1307-1327. I. T.
DA230 T6 1936

Barber, Richard W.   **3.1367**
Edward, Prince of Wales and Aquitaine: a biography of the Black Prince / Richard Barber. — New York: Scribner, c1978. 298 p., [8]leaves of plates: ill.; 23 cm. Includes index. 1. Edward, Prince of Wales, 1330-1376. 2. Great

Britain — History — Edward III, 1327-1377 3. Great Britain — Princes and princesses — Biography. I. T.
DA234.B37   942.03/7/0924 B   *LC* 78-54019   *ISBN* 0684158647

Holinshed, Raphael, d. 1580?   • 3.1368
Richard II, 1398–1400 and Henry V, edited by R.S. Wallace and Alma Hansen. Oxford Clarendon Press 1917. 136p. (Holinshed's chronicles) 1. Richard II, King of England, 1367-1400. 2. Henry V, King of England, 1387-1422. I. Wallace, Robert Strachan, 1882-, ed. II. Hansen, Alma, jt. ed. III. T.
DA235 H65

The Reign of Richard II: essays in honour of May McKisack,   3.1369
edited by F. R. H. Du Boulay and Caroline M. Barron.
[London]: University of London, Athlone Press, 1972. xvi, 335 p.: illus.; 23 cm. 1. Gt. Brit. — Politics and government — 1377-1399 — Addresses, essays, lectures. I. McKisack, May. II. Du Boulay, F. R. H. ed. III. Barron, Caroline M. ed.
DA235.R4   320.9/42/038   *LC* 70-886835   *ISBN* 0485111306

Steel, Anthony Bedford, 1900-.   • 3.1370
Richard II / by Anthony Steel; with a foreword by G.M. Trevelyan. — Cambridge: University Press, 1941. x, 320 p.: facsim. 22 cm. 1. Richard II, King of England, 1367-1400. 2. Great Britain — History — Richard II, 1377-1399 I. T.
DA235 S7   *LC* A 42-750

Trevelyan, George Macaulay, 1876-1962.   • 3.1371
England in the age of Wycliffe; by George Macaulay Trevelyan ... — New ed. — London, New York and Bombay, Longmans, Green, and co., 1904. xiv, 380 p. 3 fold. maps. 23 cm. 'Originally composed as a dissertation sent in to compete for a fellowship at Trinity college, Cambridge.'—Pref. Supplemented by 'The peasants' uprising and the Lollards; a collection of unpublished documents forming an appendix to 'England in the age of Wycliffe,' edited by Edgar Powell and G. M. Trevelyan. London, 1899.' I. Wycliffe, John, d. 1384. 2. Tyler's Insurrection, 1381 3. Gt. Brit. — Hist. — Richard II, 1377-1399. 4. Gt. Brit. — Church history — Medieval period. I. T.
DA235.T83   942.02   *LC* 05-41997

The Westminster Chronicle, 1381–1394 / edited and translated   3.1372
by L.C. Hector and Barbara F. Harvey.
Oxford: Clarendon Press; New York: Oxford University Press, 1982. lxxvii, 563 p.; 22 cm. — (Oxford medieval texts.) Manuscript part of Corpus Christi College, Cambridge, MS. 197A. 1. Great Britain — History — Richard II, 1377-1399 — Sources. I. Hector, L. C. (Leonard Charles) II. Harvey, Barbara F. III. Corpus Christi College (University of Cambridge) IV. Series.
DA235.W37 1982   942.03/8 19   *LC* 82-173289   *ISBN* 0198222556

DA240–260 Lancaster. York (1399-1485)

Bennett, H. S. (Henry Stanley), 1889-.   • 3.1373
The Pastons and their England: studies in an age of transition, by H. S. Bennett. — 2nd ed. reprinted. — London: Cambridge U.P., 1968. xvi, 271 p.; 21 cm. 1. Paston letters. 2. Great Britain — Social life and customs — Medieval period, 1066-1485 I. T.
DA240.B4 1968   914.2/03/4   *LC* 68-23175   *ISBN* 0521095131

Paston letters.   • 3.1374
The Paston letters. 'Edited by John Fenn and re-edited by Mrs. Archer-Hind.' London: Dent; New York: Dutton,[1935?] 2 v.: double geneal. tab.; 18 cm. (Everyman's library, 752-753. History) I. Archer-Hind, Laura, ed. II. Fenn, John, Sir, 1739-1794 III. T.
DA240.P3x

Jacob, Ernest Fraser, 1894-.   • 3.1375
The fifteenth century, 1399–1485. — Oxford, Clarendon Press, 1961. xvi, 775 p. maps (part fold.) 23 cm. — (Oxford history of England. v. 6) Errata slip inserted. Bibliography: p. [688]-721. 1. Gt. Brit. — Hist. — Lancaster and York, 1399-1485. I. T. II. Series.
DA245.J3   942.04   *LC* 61-66708

Gillingham, John.   3.1376
The Wars of the Roses: peace and conflict in fifteenth–century England / John Gillingham. — Baton Rouge: Louisiana State University Press, 1982 (c1981). xv, 274 p., [16] p. of plates: ill.; 24 cm. Includes index. 1. Great Britain — History — Wars of the Roses, 1455-1485 I. T.
DA250.G54   942.04 19   *LC* 81-83851   *ISBN* 0807110051

Lander, J. R. (Jack Robert), 1921-.   3.1377
Government and community, England, 1450-1509 / J. R. Lander. — Cambridge, Mass.: Harvard University Press, 1980. vii, 406 p.: geneal. table; 24 cm. (The New history of England) Includes index. 1. Great Britain — History — Wars of the Roses, 1455-1485 2. Great Britain — History — Henry VII, 1485-1509 I. T.
DA250.L29   942.04/4   *LC* 80-15   *ISBN* 0674357930

Ross, Charles Derek.   3.1378
The Wars of the Roses: a concise history / Charles Ross. London: Thames and Hudson, 1977 (c1976). 190 p.: ill.; 25 cm. Includes index. 1. Great Britain — History — Wars of the Roses, 1455-1485 I. T.
DA250.R76   942.04   *LC* 76-374627   *ISBN* 0500250499

Allmand, C. T.   3.1379
Lancastrian Normandy, 1415–1450: the history of a medieval occupation / C.T. Allmand. — Oxford [Oxfordshire]: Clarendon Press; New York: Oxford University Press, 1983. xiii, 349 p.; 22 cm. Includes index. 1. Great Britain — History — Henry V, 1413-1422 2. Great Britain — History — Henry VI, 1422-1461 3. Normandy (France) — History — To 1515 I. T.
DA256.A42 1983   942.04/3 19   *LC* 83-3958   *ISBN* 019822642X

Gesta Henrici Quinti = The deeds of Henry the Fifth /   3.1380
translated from the Latin, with introd. and notes by Frank Taylor and John S. Roskell.
Oxford [Eng.]: Clarendon Press, 1975. xlix, 206 p., [1] leaf of plates: ill.; 23 cm. (Oxford medieval texts.) The text of the Gesta is contained in 2 anonymous 15th cent. mss. in the British Museum: Cotton Ms. Julius E IV, article 4, and Sloane Ms. 1776. Includes index. 1. Henry V, King of England, 1387-1422. 2. Great Britain — History — Henry V, 1413-1422 3. Normandy (France) — History I. Taylor, Frank, 1910- II. Roskell, John Smith. III. Title: The deeds of Henry the Fifth. IV. Series.
DA256.G4   942.04/2/0924 B   *LC* 76-350978   *ISBN* 0198222319

Ross, Charles Derek.   3.1381
Edward IV / Charles Ross. — Berkeley: University of California Press, 1975 (c1974). xvi, 479 p., [12] leaves of plates: ill. (1 col.); 25 cm. Includes index. 1. Great Britain — Politics and government — 1461-1483 I. T.
DA258.R67   942.04/4/0924 B   *LC* 74-79771   *ISBN* 0520027817

Ross, Charles Derek.   3.1382
Richard III / Charles Ross. — Berkeley: University of California Press, 1982 (c1981). liii, 265 p., [25] p. of plates: ill.; 24 cm. On jacket: English monarchs. Includes index. 1. Richard III, King of England, 1452-1485. 2. Great Britain — History — Richard III, 1483-1485 3. Great Britain — Kings and rulers — Biography I. T. II. Title: English monarchs.
DA260.R67   942.04/6/0924 B 19   *LC* 81-43381   *ISBN* 0520045890

DA300–592 Modern (1485-

Lloyd, Trevor Owen.   3.1383
The British Empire, 1558–1983 / T.O. Lloyd. — New York: Oxford University Press, 1984. xvi, 430 p.: maps; 24 cm. — (Short Oxford history of the modern world.) Includes index. 1. Great Britain — History — Modern period, 1485- 2. Great Britain — Colonies — History 3. Great Britain — Colonies — Administration 4. Great Britain — Territorial expansion. I. T. II. Series.
DA300.L58 1984   909/.0971241 19   *LC* 83-19481   *ISBN* 0198730241

Routh, C. R. N. (Charles Richard Nairne)   • 3.1384
They saw it happen: an anthology of eye–witnesses' accounts of events in British history, 1485–1688 / compiled by C.R.N. Routh; with a foreword by R. Birley. — Oxford: Blackwell, 1956. 220 p.; 23 cm. 1. Great Britain — History — 1500-1800 — Sources. I. T.
DA300.R6   *LC* 57-763

DA310–360 Tudors (1485–1603)

Ferguson, Arthur B.   3.1385
Clio unbound: perception of the social and cultural past in Renaissance England / Arthur B. Ferguson. — Durham, N.C.: Duke University Press, 1979. xv, 443 p.; 25 cm. — (Duke monographs in medieval and Renaissance studies. no. 2) 1. Renaissance — England — Historiography. 2. Great Britain — History — Tudors, 1485-1603 — Historiography. 3. Great Britain — History — Early Stuarts, 1603-1649 — Historiography. 4. England — Civilization — 16th century 5. England — Civilization — 17th century I. T. II. Series.
DA314.F47   907/.2042   *LC* 78-67198   *ISBN* 0822304171

Bindoff, S. T. (Stanley Thomas), 1908-.   3.1386
Tudor England [by] S. T. Bindoff. — Harmondsworth, Middlesex: Penguin Books, [1950] 319 p.; 19 cm. — (Pelican history of England. 5) (Pelican books, A212.) 1. Great Britain — History — Tudors, 1485-1603 I. T. II. Series.
DA315.B5x   *LC* 67-35446

Crowson, P. S. (Paul Spiller)   3.1387
Tudor foreign policy [by] P. S. Crowson. New York, St. Martin's Press [1973]
xiii, 288 p. illus. 22 cm. (Modern British foreign policy) 1. Great Britain —
Foreign relations — 1485-1603 I. T.
DA315.C76 1973   327.42   *LC* 73-81733

Elton, G. R. (Geoffrey Rudolph)   • 3.1388
England under the Tudors / by G. R. Elton. — New York: Putnam, [1955 or 6]
xi, 504 p., fold. leaf: geneal. table, maps; 22 cm. — (A History of England; 4)
Distributed in the USA by Harper and Row Publishers, Barnes & Noble Import
Division. Includes index. 1. Great Britain — History — Tudors, 1485-1603
I. T.
DA315.E6   942.05   *LC* 74-185525   *ISBN* 0416787207

Jones, Whitney R. D. (Whitney Richard David), 1924-.   3.1389
The mid–Tudor crisis, 1539–1563 / Whitney R. D. Jones. — New York, N.Y.:
Barnes & Noble, 1973. 226 p.; 23 cm. 1. Great Britain — History — Tudors,
1485-1603 I. T.
DA315.J66   *ISBN* 064933903

Levine, Mortimer.   3.1390
Tudor dynastic problems, 1460–1571. — London: Allen and Unwin; New
York: Barnes and Noble, 1973. 191 p., geneal. tables.; 23 cm. — (Historical
problems; studies and documents, 21) 1. Great Britain — Politics and
government — 1485-1603 2. Great Britain — Kings and rulers — Succession
I. T. II. Series.
DA315.L46   942.04   *LC* 74-153265

Russell, Conrad.   3.1391
The crisis of Parliaments: English history 1509–1660. — London: Oxford
University Press, 1971. xvi, 434 p.: geneal. tables.; 24 cm. — (Short Oxford
history of the modern world.) 1. Gt. Brit. — Politics and government —
1485-1603. 2. Gt. Brit. — Politics and government — 1603-1649. 3. Gt. Brit.
— Politics and government — 1649-1660. I. T. II. Series.
DA315.R87   914.2/03/5   *LC* 72-580803   *ISBN* 0199130337

Slavin, Arthur Joseph.   3.1392
The precarious balance: English government and society, 1450–1640. — [1st
ed.]. — New York: Knopf; [distributed by Random House, 1973] xiv, 397 p.:
illus.; 25 cm. — (The Borzoi history of England, v. 3) 1. Great Britain —
Politics and government — 1485-1603 2. Great Britain — Politics and
government — 1603-1649 3. Great Britain — Economic conditions 4. Great
Britain — Social conditions I. T. II. Series.
DA315.S5x DA26B65 Vol. 3   942 s 942   *LC* 72-11840   *ISBN*
0394479513

Wernham, R. B. (Richard Bruce), 1906-.   • 3.1393
Before the Armada: the emergence of the English Nation, 1485–1588 [by] R. B.
Wernham. [1st American ed.] New York, Harcourt, Brace & World [1966]
447 p. maps. 22 cm. 1. Great Britain — Foreign relations — 16th century I. T.
DA315.W4 1966a   327.42   *LC* 66-23809

Ridley, Jasper Godwin.   • 3.1394
Thomas Cranmer. — Oxford, Clarendon Press, 1962. 450 p. illus. 23 cm.
Includes bibliography. 1. Cranmer, Thomas, 1489-1556. I. T.
DA317.8.C8R5   922.342   *LC* 62-2124

Stone, Lawrence.   3.1395
Family and fortune: studies in aristocratic finance in the sixteenth and
seventeenth centuries. Oxford: Clarendon Press, 1973. xviii, 315, [7] p., 4 fold.
leaves.: illus., geneal. tables, plans.; 24 cm. 1. Upper classes — England.
2. England — Civilization — 16th century 3. England — Civilization — 17th
century I. T.
DA320.S874   332/.024   *LC* 73-175161   *ISBN* 019822401X

Mackie, John Duncan, 1887- .   • 3.1396
The earlier Tudors, 1485–1558 / by J. D. Mackie. — Oxford, Eng.: Clarendon
Press, 1952. xxi, 699 p.: maps, geneal. tables; 23 cm. — (Oxford history of
England. v07) 1. Great Britain — History — Tudors, 1485-1603 I. T.
II. Series.
DA325.M3   942.05   *LC* 52-4641

DA330 Henry VII, 1485–1509

Alexander, Michael Van Cleave, 1937-.   3.1397
The first of the Tudors: a study of Henry VII and his reign / by Michael Van
Cleave Alexander. — Totowa, N.J.: Rowman and Littlefield, c1980. x, 280 p.,
[1] leaf of plates: port.; 25 cm. Includes index. 1. Henry VII, King of England,
1457-1509. 2. Great Britain — History — Henry VII, 1485-1509 3. Great
Britain — Kings and rulers — Biography I. T.
DA330.A43 1980   942.05/1/0924 B   *LC* 79-28135   *ISBN*
0847662594

Bacon, Francis, 1561-1626.   3.1398
[Historie of the raigne of King Henry the Seventh] The history of the reign of
King Henry the Seventh. Edited by F. J. Levy. New York, Bobbs-Merrill Co.
[1972] xi, 319 p. 21 cm. (European historiography series.) 1. Great Britain —
History — Henry VII, 1485-1509 I. Levy, Fred Jacob, ed. II. T. III. Series.
DA330.B12 1972   942.05/1   *LC* 70-177471

DA331–339 Henry VIII, 1509–1547

Elton, G. R. (Geoffrey Rudolph)   • 3.1399
Policy and police; the enforcement of the Reformation in the age of Thomas
Cromwell [by] G. R. Elton. Cambridge [Eng.] University Press, 1972. xi, 446 p.
24 cm. 1. Reformation — England 2. Treason — England. 3. Great Britain —
Politics and government — 1509-1547 I. T.
DA332.E496   942.05/2   *LC* 79-172831   *ISBN* 0521083834

Elton, G. R. (Geoffrey Rudolph)   3.1400
Reform and Reformation—England, 1509–1558 / G. R. Elton. — Cambridge,
Mass.: Harvard University Press, 1978 (c1977). vi, 423 p.; 24 cm. (New history
of England.) Includes index. 1. Reformation — England 2. Great Britain —
History — Henry VIII, 1509-1547 3. Great Britain — History — Edward VI
and Mary, 1547-1558 I. T. II. Series.
DA332.E497   941.05/092/2   *LC* 77-6464   *ISBN* 0674752457

Pollard, A. F. (Albert Frederick), 1869-1948.   • 3.1401
Henry VIII. — Introd. to the Torchbook ed. by A. G. Dickens. — New York,
Harper & Row [1966] xxx, 385 p. ports. 21 cm. — (Harper torchbooks. The
Academy library, TB1249Q) 'Originally published in 1902.' Bibliography: p.
xxiv-xxv. 1. Henry VIII, King of England, 1491-1547. I. T.
DA332.P78 1966   942.0520924 (B)   *LC* 66-4649

Scarisbrick, J. J.   • 3.1402
Henry VIII, by J. J. Scarisbrick. — Berkeley: University of California Press,
1968. xiv, 561 p.: illus., ports. (1 col.); 24 cm. 1. Henry VIII, King of England,
1491-1547. I. T.
DA332.S25 1968b   942.05/2/0924 B   *LC* 68-10995

Smith, Lacey Baldwin, 1922-.   • 3.1403
Henry VIII: the mask of royalty. — [1st American ed.]. — Boston: Houghton
Mifflin Co., 1971. xii, 335 p.: illus.; 24 cm. 1. Henry VIII, King of England,
1491-1547. I. T.
DA332.S63 1971b   942.05/2/0924 B   *LC* 70-162004   *ISBN*
0395127238

Mattingly, Garrett, 1900-1962.   • 3.1404
Catherine of Aragon, by Garrett Mattingly. — London: J. Cape, [1942] 343 p.:
incl. geneal. tables. front. (port.); 23 cm. 'First published 1942.' 1. Catharine of
Aragon, consort of Henry VIII, King of England, 1485-1536. I. T.
DA333.A6 M3 1942   923.142   *LC* 42-20687

Ridley, Jasper Godwin.   3.1405
Statesman and saint: Cardinal Wolsey, Sir Thomas More, and the politics of
Henry VIII / Jasper Ridley. — New York: Viking Press, 1983, c1982. 338 p.,
[16] p. of plates: ill., ports.; 25 cm. Includes index. 1. Wolsey, Thomas,
1475?-1530. 2. More, Thomas, Sir, Saint, 1478-1535. 3. Statesmen — Great
Britain — Biography. 4. Cardinals — England — Biography. 5. Christian
saints — England — Biography. 6. Great Britain — History — Henry VIII,
1509-1547 7. Great Britain — Church history — 16th century I. T.
DA334.A1 R52 1983   942.05/2/0922 B 19   *LC* 82-70122   *ISBN*
0670489050

Beckingsale, B. W.   3.1406
Thomas Cromwell, Tudor minister / by B. W. Beckingsale. — Totowa, N.J.:
Rowman and Littlefield, 1978. 181 p. Includes index. 1. Cromwell, Thomas,
Earl of Essex, 1485?-1540. 2. Statesmen — Great Britain — Biography.
3. Great Britain — History — Henry VIII, 1509-1547 I. T.
DA334.C9 B42 1978   942.05/2/0924 B   *LC* 77-29057   *ISBN*
0847660532

Elton, G. R. (Geoffrey Rudolph)   3.1407
Reform and renewal; Thomas Cromwell and the common weal [by] G. R.
Elton. Cambridge [Eng.] University Press, 1973. x, 175 p. 23 cm. (Wiles
lectures. 1972) 1. Cromwell, Thomas, Earl of Essex, 1485?-1540. I. T.
II. Series.
DA334.C9 E47   942.05/2/0924 B   *LC* 72-87180   *ISBN*
0521200547 *ISBN* 0521098092

Essential articles for the study of Thomas More / edited with   3.1408
an introd. and bibliography by R. S. Sylvester and G. P.
Marc'hadour.
Hamden, Conn.: Archon Books, 1977. xxiii, 676 p.; 23 cm. — (The Essential
articles series) 1. More, Thomas, Sir, Saint, 1478-1535 — Addresses, essays,
lectures. 2. More, Thomas, Sir, Saint, 1478-1535. Utopia 3. Statesmen —
Great Britain — Biography — Addresses, essays, lectures. 4. Christian saints
— Great Britain — Biography — Addresses, essays, lectures. 5. Utopias

6. Consolation — Early works to 1800. I. Sylvester, Richard Standish.
II. Marc'hadour, Germain.
DA334.M8 E85   942.05/2/0924 B 19   *LC* 76-42303   *ISBN*
020801554X

Kenny, Anthony John Patrick.   **3.1409**
Thomas More / Anthony Kenny. — Oxford [Oxfordshire]; New York: Oxford
University Press, 1983. 111 p.; 18 cm. — (Past masters.) Includes index.
1. More, Thomas, Sir, Saint, 1478-1535. 2. Statesmen — Great Britain —
Biography. 3. Christian saints — England — Biography. 4. Great Britain —
History — Henry VIII, 1509-1547 I. T. II. Series.
DA334.M8 K46 1983   942.05/2/0924 B 19   *LC* 83-4209   *ISBN*
0192875736

Marius, Richard.   **3.1410**
Thomas More: a biography / Richard Marius. — New York: Knopf:
Distributed by Random House, 1984. xxiv, 562 p.; 25 cm. Includes index.
1. More, Thomas, Sir, Saint, 1478-1535. 2. Statesmen — Great Britain —
Biography. 3. Christian saints — England — Biography. 4. Great Britain —
History — Henry VIII, 1509-1547 I. T.
DA334.M8 M275 1984   942.05/2/0924 B 19   *LC* 84-47645   *ISBN*
0394459822

Ferguson, Charles Wright, 1901-.   • **3.1411**
Naked to mine enemies; the life of Cardinal Wolsey. [1st ed.] Boston, Little,
Brown [1958] 543 p. illus. 22 cm. 1. Wolsey, Thomas, 1475?-1530. 2. Great
Britain — Politics and government — 1509-1547 I. T.
DA334.W8 F38   923.242 922.242   *LC* 57-9320

Pollard, A. F. (Albert Frederick), 1869-1948.   • **3.1412**
Wolsey: church and state in sixteenth–Century England / introd. to the
Torchbook ed. by A.G. Dickens. — New York: Harper & Row, [1966] xxxv,
393 p.; 21 cm. — (Harper torchbooks; TB1248Q.) 1. Wolsey, Thomas,
1475?-1530. I. T.
DA30.P7622 vol. 6   DA334.W8 P6 1966.   942.05   *LC* 66-4726

Sylvester, Richard Standish. ed.   • **3.1413**
Two early Tudor lives: the life and death of Cardinal Wolsey, by George
Cavendish [and] The life of Sir Thomas More, by William Roper / edited by
Richard S. Sylvester and Davis P. Harding. — New Haven: Yale University
Press, 1962. xxi, 260 p.; 21 cm. 1. Wolsey, Thomas, 1475?-1530. 2. More,
Thomas, Sir, Saint, 1478-1535. I. Harding, Davis Philoon, 1914- joint editor.
II. Cavendish, George, 1500-1561? The life and death of Cardinal Wolsey.
III. Roper, William, 1496-1578. The life of Sir Thomas More. IV. T.
DA334.W8S85   923.242   *LC* 62-8232

The Lisle letters: an abridgement / edited by Muriel St. Clare   **3.1414**
Byrne; selected and arranged by Bridget Boland; foreword by
Hugh Trevor–Roper.
Chicago: University of Chicago Press, 1983. xxvi, 436 p.: ill.; 24 cm. Includes
index. 1. Lisle, Arthur Plantagenet, Viscount, 1480?-1542. 2. Statesmen —
Great Britain — Correspondence. 3. England — Social life and customs —
16th century — Sources. I. Byrne, M. St. Clare (Muriel St. Clare), 1895-
II. Boland, Bridget.
DA335.L5 L572 1983   942.05 19   *LC* 82-15914   *ISBN* 0226088006

DA345 Edward VI, 1547–1553

Bush, M. L.   **3.1415**
The government policy of Protector Somerset / M. L. Bush. Montreal: McGill-
Queen's University Press, 1975. x, 182 p.: ports. (on lining paper); 24 cm.
1. Somerset, Edward Seymour, 1st Duke of, 1506?-1552. 2. Great Britain —
Politics and government — 1547-1553 I. T.
DA345.B8 1975b   942.05/3   *LC* 76-366433   *ISBN* 0773502602

Jordan, Wilbur Kitchener, 1902-.   • **3.1416**
Edward VI: the threshold of power; the dominance of the Duke of
Northumberland, by W. K. Jordan. London, Allen & Unwin [1970] 565 p. 23
cm. 1. Somerset, Edward Seymour, 1st Duke of, 1506?-1552.
2. Northumberland, John Dudley, Duke of, 1502-1553. 3. Great Britain —
History — Edward VI, 1547-1553 I. T.
DA345.J59   942.05/3   *LC* 78-556152   *ISBN* 0049420836

Jordan, Wilbur Kitchener, 1902-.   • **3.1417**
Edward VI: the young King; the protectorship of the Duke of Somerset, by W.
K. Jordan. London, Allen & Unwin, 1968. 3-544 p. 23 cm. 1. Somerset,
Edward Seymour, 1st Duke of, 1506?-1552. 2. Great Britain — History —
Edward VI, 1547-1553 I. T.
DA345.J6   942.05/3   *ISBN* 0049420720

Land, Stephen K.   **3.1418**
Kett's rebellion: the Norfolk rising of 1549 / Stephen K. Land. — Ipswich
[Eng.]: Boydell Press; Totowa, N.J.: Rowman and Littlefield, 1978 (c1977).
165 p.; 22 cm. Includes index. 1. Kett's Rebellion, 1549 I. T.
DA345.L36   942.05/3   *LC* 78-307172   *ISBN* 087471995X

DA347 Mary I, 1553–1558

Loades, D. M.   **3.1419**
The reign of Mary Tudor: politics, government, and religion in England,
1553–1558 / D. M. Loades. — New York: St. Martin's Press, c1979. xii, 516 p.,
[8] leaves of plates: ill.; 22 cm. Includes index. 1. Mary I, Queen of England,
1516-1558. 2. Great Britain — Politics and government — 1553-1558
3. England — Church history — 16th century I. T.
DA347.L58 1979   942.05/4/0924   *LC* 79-16479   *ISBN*
031267029X

DA350–360 Elizabeth I, 1558–1603

Ashton, Robert.   **3.1420**
Reformation and revolution, 1558–1660 / Robert Ashton. — London; New
York: Granada, 1984. xx, 503 p.; 24 cm. — (The Paladin history of England;
[4]) Includes index. 1. Great Britain — History — Elizabeth, 1558-1603
2. Great Britain — History — Stuarts, 1603-1714 I. T.
DA355.A84 1984   942.05/5 19   *LC* 83-197192   *ISBN* 0246106662

Black, John Bennett, 1883-1964.   • **3.1421**
The reign of Elizabeth, 1558–1603. 2d ed. Oxford, Clarendon Press, 1959. xxvi,
539 p. maps, fold. geneal. tables. 23 cm. (Oxford history of England. 8)
1. Church and state in England. 2. Great Britain — Civilization I. T.
II. Series.
DA355.B65 1959   942.055   *LC* 59-3629

MacCaffrey, Wallace T.   **3.1422**
Queen Elizabeth and the making of policy, 1572–1588 / by Wallace T.
MacCaffrey. — Princeton, N.J.: Princeton University Press, 1981. 530 p.; 23
cm. Includes index. 1. Elizabeth I, Queen of England, 1533-1603. 2. Great
Britain — Politics and government — 1558-1603 I. T.
DA355.M26   942.05/5 19   *LC* 80-8564   *ISBN* 0691053243

MacCaffrey, Wallace T.   • **3.1423**
The shaping of the Elizabethan regime, by Wallace MacCaffrey. — Princeton,
N.J.: Princeton University Press, 1968. xiv, 501 p.: ports.; 23 cm. 1. Great
Britain — History — Elizabeth, 1558-1603 I. T.
DA355.M27   942.05/5   *LC* 68-27409

Neale, John Ernest, Sir, 1890-.   • **3.1424**
Queen Elizabeth I. London: J. Cape, [1959] 402 p. illus. 23 cm. (The Bedford
historical series) First published in 1934 under title: Queen Elizabeth.
1. Elizabeth I, Queen of England, 1533-1603. I. T.
DA355.N4   923.142   *LC* 59-16032

Rowse, A. L. (Alfred Leslie), 1903-.   • **3.1425**
The expansion of Elizabethan England. London, Macmillan; New York, St.
Martin's Press, 1955. xiii, 449 p. illus., ports., maps, facsim. 23 cm. (His The
Elizabethan age [2]) 1. Great Britain — Foreign relations — 1558-1603
2. Great Britain — Politics and government — 1558-1603 I. T.
DA355.R67 1955a   942.055   *LC* 56-171

Smith, Lacey Baldwin, 1922-.   **3.1426**
Elizabeth Tudor: portrait of a queen / Lacey Baldwin Smith. — 1st ed. —
Boston: Little, Brown, [1975] xi, 234 p.: port.; 21 cm. — (The Library of world
biography) Includes index. 1. Elizabeth I, Queen of England, 1533-1603. I. T.
DA355.S59   942.05/5/0924 B   *LC* 75-19170   *ISBN* 0316801526

Wernham, R. B. (Richard Bruce), 1906-.   **3.1427**
The making of Elizabethan foreign policy, 1558–1603 / R. B. Wernham. —
Berkeley: University of California Press, 1981 (c1980). vii, 109 p.: maps; 22 cm.
(Una's lectures. 3) Includes index. 1. Great Britain — Foreign relations —
1485-1603 I. T. II. Series.
DA355.W39   327.42   *LC* 80-10425   *ISBN* 0520039661

Williamson, James Alexander, 1886-.   • **3.1428**
The age of Drake. 4th ed. London, A. & C. Black [1960] viii, 399 p. maps (1
fold. col.) 23 cm. (The Pioneer histories) Imprint covered by label: New York,
Barnes & Noble. 1. Drake, Francis, Sir, 1540?-1596. 2. Great Britain —
History, Naval — Tudors, 1485-1603 3. Great Britain — History — Elizabeth,
1558-1603 I. T.
DA355.W484 1960   942.055   *LC* 63-4459

Collinson, Patrick.   **3.1429**
The Elizabethan puritan movement. — Berkeley: University of California
Press, [1967] 527 p.: map (on lining papers); 23 cm. 1. Puritans — England.
2. Great Britain — Politics and government — 1558-1603 3. England —
Church history — 16th century I. T.
DA356.C58   285/.9/0942 19   *LC* 67-12298

McGrath, Patrick.   • **3.1430**
Papists and Puritans under Elizabeth I. — New York: Walker, [1967] x, 434 p.:
illus., facsims., maps, ports.; 21 cm. — (Blandford history series) 1. Great

Britain — History — Elizabeth, 1558-1603 2. Great Britain — Church history
— Modern period, 1485- I. T.
DA356.M25 1967b   942.05/5   *LC* 67-23085

Neale, John Ernest, Sir, 1890-.   • 3.1431
Elizabeth I and her Parliaments / by J.E. Neale. — New York: St. Martin's
Press, 1958. 2 v.: ill., ports. 1. Elizabeth I, Queen of England, 1533-1603.
2. Great Britain — Politics and government — 1558-1603 I. T.
DA356.N42   942.055   *LC* 58-319

Stone, Lawrence.   • 3.1432
The crisis of the aristocracy, 1558–1641. — Oxford, Clarendon Press, 1965.
xxiv, 841 p. illus. 24 cm. Bibliographical footnotes. 1. Upper classes — Great
Britain 2. Great Britain — Nobility 3. Great Britain — Civilization — 16th
cent. I. T.
DA356.S8   914.2   *LC* 65-3206

Wernham, R. B. (Richard Bruce), 1906-.   3.1433
After the Armada: Elizabethan England and the struggle for Western Europe,
1588–1595 / R.B. Wernham. — Oxford [Oxfordshire]: Clarendon Press; New
York: Oxford University Press, 1984. xxi, 613 p.: maps; 23 cm. 1. Armada,
1588 2. Great Britain — Politics and government — 1558-1603 3. Great
Britain — Foreign relations — Europe. 4. Europe — Foreign relations —
Great Britain. 5. Europe — History — 1517-1648 6. Great Britain — Foreign
relations — 1558-1603 I. T.
DA356.W47 1984   940.2/32 19   *LC* 83-8281   *ISBN* 0198227531

DA358 Biography of Contemporaries

Beckingsale, B. W.   • 3.1434
Burghley: Tudor statesman, 1520–1598 [by] B. W. Beckingsale. — London;
Melbourne [etc.]: Macmillan; New York: St. Martin's P., 1967. x, 340 p.: front.,
16 plates (incl. ports., facsims.).; 22 1/2 cm. 1. Burghley, William Cecil, Baron,
1520-1598. I. T.
DA358.B9 B4   942.05/0924 B   *LC* 67-19278

Read, Conyers, 1881-1959.   • 3.1435
Lord Burghley and Queen Elizabeth. New York, Knopf, 1960. 603 p. ports.,
facsim. 26 cm. Sequel to Mr. Secretary Cecil and Queen Elizabeth.
Bibliographical references included in 'Notes' (p. 549-590) 1. Burghley,
William Cecil, Baron, 1520-1598. 2. Elizabeth I, Queen of England, 1533-1603.
I. T.
DA358.B9R38   923.242   *LC* 60-1682

Read, Conyers, 1881-1959.   • 3.1436
Mr. Secretary Cecil and Queen Elizabeth. New York, Knopf, 1955. 510 p. illus.,
ports. 26 cm. Erratum slip inserted. Bibliographical references included in
'Notes' (p. 469-495). 1. Burghley, William Cecil, 1st baron, 1520-1598.
2. Elizabeth I, Queen of England, 1533-1603. I. T.
DA358.B9 R4   923.242   *LC* 54-7211

Wallace, Malcolm William, 1873-1960.   3.1437
The life of Sir Philip Sidney. — New York, Octagon Books, 1967. 428 p.
facsim., geneal. table. 24 cm. Reprint of the 1915 ed. 1. Sidney, Philip, Sir,
1554-1586. I. T.
DA358.S5.W3 1967   828/.3/09 (B)   *LC* 67-18790

Read, Conyers, 1881-.   • 3.1438
Mr. Secretary Walsingham and the policy of Queen Elizabeth, by Conyers Read
... — Oxford, The Clarendon press, 1925. 3 v. front., ports., 3 facsim. (2 fold.) 24
cm. 1. Walsingham, Francis, Sir, 1530?-1590. 2. Elizabeth I, Queen of
England, 1533-1603. 3. Gt. Brit. — Hist. — Elizabeth, 1558-1603. 4. Gt. Brit.
— Pol. & govt. — 1558-1603. I. T.
DA358.W2R4   *LC* 26-932

DA360 Armada

Martin, Colin.   3.1439
Full fathom five: wrecks of the Spanish Armada / Colin Martin; with
appendices by Sydney Wignall. — New York: Viking Press, 1975. 288 p., [10]
leaves of plates: ill.; 22 cm. Includes index. 1. Armada, 1588 2. Shipwrecks —
Ireland. 3. Shipwrecks — Scotland. 4. Underwater archaeology I. T.
DA360.M27 1975   942.05/5   *LC* 75-1420   *ISBN* 0670331937

Mattingly, Garrett, 1900-1962.   • 3.1440
The Armada. — Boston: Houghton Mifflin, 1959. 443 p.: illus.; 22 cm.
1. Armada, 1588 I. T.
DA360.M3   942.055   *LC* 59-8861

DA375–462 17th Century

Coward, Barry.   3.1441
The Stuart age: a history of England 1603–1714 / Barry Coward. — London;
New York: Longman, 1980. xii, 493 p.: geneal. tables, maps; 22 cm. — (A
History of England) Includes index. 1. Great Britain — History — Stuarts,
1603-1714 I. T.
DA375.C74 1980   941.06 19   *LC* 79-42887   *ISBN* 0582482798

Hill, Christopher, 1912-.   • 3.1442
The century of revolution, 1603–1714. Edinburgh, T. Nelson [1961] 340 p. illus.
23 cm. (A History of England, v. 5) 1. Great Britain — History — Stuarts,
1603-1714 I. T.
DA375.H5   942.06   *LC* 61-66046

Hill, Christopher, 1912-.   3.1443
[Essays] The collected essays of Christopher Hill / Christopher Hill. —
Amherst: University of Massachusetts Press, 1985- < 1986 >. v. < 1-2 >; 23
cm. 1. English literature — 17th century — History and criticism —
Addresses, essays, lectures. 2. Literature and society — Great Britain —
Addresses, essays, lectures. 3. Great Britain — History — Stuarts, 1603-1714
— Addresses, essays, lectures. 4. Great Britain — Intellectual life — 17th
century — Addresses, essays, lectures. I. T.
DA375.H54 1985   082 19   *LC* 84-16446   *ISBN* 0870234676

Howat, G. M. D. (Gerald Malcolm David), 1928-.   3.1444
Stuart and Cromwellian foreign policy / [by] G. M. D. Howat. — New York:
St. Martin's Press, c1974. viii, 191 p.: maps; 23 cm. — (Modern British foreign
policy) 1. Great Britain — Foreign relations — 1603-1688 I. T.
DA375.H68   327.42   *LC* 73-91111

Jones, J. R. (James Rees), 1925-.   • 3.1445
Britain and Europe in the seventeenth century, by J. R. Jones. New York,
Norton [c1967] vi, 119 p. 21 cm. (Foundations of modern history) Copyright
date cancelled by a stamp. 1. Great Britain — History — Stuarts, 1603-1714
2. Great Britain — Relations — Europe 3. Europe — Relations — Great
Britain I. T.
DA375.J62 1967   942.06   *LC* 66-28650

Roberts, Clayton.   • 3.1446
The growth of responsible government in Stuart England / by Clayton Roberts.
— Cambridge: Cambridge University Press, 1966. xii, 467 p.; 24 cm.
1. Ministerial responsibility — Great Britain. 2. Great Britain — Politics and
government — 1603-1714 3. Great Britain — Constitutional history I. T.
DA375. R6   320/.941   *LC* 66-11033

Trevelyan, George Macaulay, 1876-1962.   • 3.1447
England under the Stuarts / by George Macaulay Trevelyan. — New York:
G.P. Putnam's Sons, 1949. xiii, 466 p.: maps (some col.); 23 cm. 1. Great
Britain — History — Stuarts, 1603-1714 I. T.
DA375.T7 1949   *LC* 50-14448

DA377 COLLECTIVE BIOGRAPHY

Walton, Izaak, 1593-1683.   • 3.1448
The lives of Dr. John Donne, Sir Henry Wotton, Mr. Richard Hooker, Mr.
George Herbert, 1670. — Menston, (Yorks.): Scolar P., 1969. [431] p.: 2 ports.;
24 cm. 'A Scolar Press facsimile.' Facsimile reprint of 1st ed., London, printed
by Tho. Newcomb for Richard Marriott, 1670. Wing W671. 1. Donne, John,
1572-1631. 2. Wotton, Henry, Sir, 1568-1639. 3. Hooker, Richard, 1553 or
4-1600. 4. Herbert, George, 1593-1633. I. T.
DA377.W2 1670a   914.2/03/610922   *LC* 75-473305   *ISBN*
0854171657

DA380 CIVILIZATION

Hill, John Edward Christopher, 1912-.   • 3.1449
Intellectual origins of the English revolution. — Oxford, Clarendon Press,
1965. ix, 333 p. 23 cm. Bibliographical footnotes. 1. Gt. Brit. — Intellectual life
— 17th cent. 2. Gt. Brit. — Hist. — Puritan Revolution, 1642-1660. I. T.
DA380.H48   942.06   *LC* 65-3182

Hill, John Edward Christopher, 1912-.   • 3.1450
Puritanism and revolution: studies in interpretation of the English revolution in
the 17th century / by Christopher Hill. — New York: Schocken books, 1964,
c1958. xii, 402 p.; 21 cm. — (Schocken paperbacks; SB74) 1. Great Britain —
History — Puritan Revolution, 1642-1660 2. Great Britain — Social
conditions I. T.
DA380.H495 1964   *LC* 64-15220

Hill, John Edward Christopher, 1912-.   • 3.1451
Society and Puritanism in pre-Revolutionary England / Christopher Hill. —
New York: Schocken Books, 1964. 520 p.; 22 cm. 1. Puritans 2. Great Britain

— History — Civil War, 1642-1649 — Causes 3. Great Britain — Social
conditions I. T.
DA380.H52 1964   *LC* 64-13350

Hill, Christopher, 1912-.   **3.1452**
The world turned upside down; radical ideas during the English Revolution
[by] Christopher Hill. New York, Viking Press [1972] 351 p. 24 cm. 1. Great
Britain — Intellectual life — 17th century 2. Great Britain — History —
Puritan Revolution, 1642-1660 3. England — Religion — 17th century I. T.
DA380.H53 1972b   914.2/03/62   *LC* 72-78983   *ISBN* 0670789755

Hill, John Edward Christopher, 1912-.   **3.1453**
Change and continuity in seventeenth–century England / Christopher Hill. —
Cambridge, Mass.: Harvard University Press, 1975. xiv, 370 p.; 22 cm.
1. England — Civilization — 17th century I. T.
DA380.H645 1975   941.06   *LC* 74-12878   *ISBN* 0674107659

Notestein, Wallace, 1878-1969.   • **3.1454**
The English people on the eve of colonization, 1603–1630. — [1st ed.]. — New
York: Harper, [1954] xvii, 302 p.: illus., ports., maps.; 22 cm. — (The New
American nation series) 1. Great Britain — History — Early Stuarts,
1603-1649 2. England — Civilization — 17th century I. T.
DA380.N6   942.061   *LC* 54-8978

Shapiro, Barbara J.   **3.1455**
Probability and certainty in seventeenth–century England: a study of the
relationships between natural science, religion, history, law, and literature /
Barbara J. Shapiro. — Princeton, N.J.: Princeton University Press, c1983. x,
347 p.; 24 cm. 1. Knowledge, Theory of — History — 17th century.
2. England — Intellectual life — 17th century I. T. II. Title: Probability and
certainty in 17th-century England.
DA380.S53 1983   001.2 19   *LC* 82-61385   *ISBN* 0691053790

DA390 EARLY STUARTS (1603–1642)

Bridenbaugh, Carl.   • **3.1456**
Vexed and troubled Englishmen, 1590–1642. — New York: Oxford University
Press, 1968 [c1967] xix, 487 p.; 24 cm. — (The Beginnings of the American
people, 1) 1. Great Britain — History — Early Stuarts, 1603-1649 2. Great
Britain — Emigration and immigration. I. T.
DA390.B7   942.06   *LC* 68-17604

Davies, Godfrey, 1892-1957.   • **3.1457**
The early Stuarts, 1603–1660. 2d ed. Oxford, Clarendon Press, 1959. xxiii,
458 p. maps. 23 cm. (The Oxford history of England, 9) 1. Great Britain —
History — Early Stuarts, 1603-1649 2. Great Britain — History —
Commonwealth and Protectorate, 1649-1660 I. T.
DA 390 D25 1959   *LC* 59-1862

Gardiner, Samuel Rawson, 1829-1902.   • **3.1458**
History of England from the accession of James I. to the outbreak of the civil
war 1603–1642, by Samuel R. Gardiner ... — London, Longmans, Green, and
co., 1884-86. 10 v.: fronts. (v.6, 10) maps.; 20 cm. 1. Gt. Brit. — Hist. — James
I, 1603-1625. 2. Gt. Brit. — Hist. — Charles I, 1625-1649. I. T.
DA390.G121 1884   *LC* 16-2846

Gardiner, Samuel Rawson, 1829-1902.   • **3.1459**
History of the Commonwealth and Protectorate, 1649–1656. — New ed. —
London, Longmans, Green, 1903. 4 v. maps.; 20 cm. I. T.
DA390.G123

Gardiner, Samuel Rawson, 1829-1902.   • **3.1460**
History of the great civil war, 1642–1649 / by Samuel R. Gardiner ... —
London; New York: Longmans, Green, 1898-1901. 4 v.: maps (part fold.); 20
cm. 1. Great Britain — History — Civil War, 1642-1649 I. T.
DA390.G312 1898   *LC* 02-21027

Hirst, Derek.   **3.1461**
Authority and conflict: England, 1603–1658 / Derek Hirst. — Cambridge,
Mass.: Harvard University Press, 1986. viii, 390 p.; 24 cm. (New history of
England.) Includes index. 1. Great Britain — History — Early Stuarts,
1603-1649 2. Great Britain — History — Commonwealth and Protectorate,
1649-1660 I. T. II. Series.
DA390.H57 1986   941.06 19   *LC* 85-24957   *ISBN* 0674052900

Stone, Lawrence.   **3.1462**
The causes of the English Revolution, 1529–1642. — New York: Harper &
Row, [1972] xiv, 168 p.; 22 cm. — (Torchbook library editions) 1. Great
Britain — History — Civil War, 1642-1649 — Causes 2. Great Britain —
Politics and government — 1558-1603 3. Great Britain — Politics and
government — 1603-1649 I. T.
DA390.S85 1972b   942.06/2   *LC* 72-83621   *ISBN* 0061360961

DA391–394 James I, 1603–1625

Akrigg, G. P. V.   • **3.1463**
Jacobean pageant; or, The court of King James I. Cambridge, Harvard
University Press, 1962. xi, 431 p. illus., ports., plan. 26 cm. 1. James I, King of
England, 1566-1625. 2. Great Britain — Court and courtiers. I. T.
DA391.A4   942.061   *LC* 62-5508

James I, King of England, 1566-1625.   **3.1464**
[Correspondence. Selections] Letters of King James VI & I / edited, with an
introduction, by G.P.V. Akrigg. — Berkeley: University of California Press,
c1984. xxii, 546 p., [1] leaf of plates: col. ill.; 22 cm. Includes index. 1. James I,
King of England, 1566-1625. 2. Great Britain — History — James I,
1603-1625 — Sources. 3. Scotland — History — James VI, 1567-1625 —
Sources. 4. Great Britain — Kings and rulers — Correspondence. 5. Scotland
— Kings and rulers — Correspondence. I. Akrigg, G. P. V. II. T.
DA391.J35 1984   941.06/1/0924 19   *LC* 82-20135   *ISBN*
0520047079

Willson, David Harris, 1901-.   • **3.1465**
King James VI and I. New York: Holt, [1956] 480 p.: ill.; 22 cm. 1. James I,
King of England, 1566-1625. I. T.
DA391.W47   *LC* 56-2623

Lockyer, Roger.   **3.1466**
Buckingham, the life and political career of George Villiers, first Duke of
Buckingham, 1592–1628 / by Roger Lockyer. — London; New York:
Longman, 1981. xix, 506 p., [16] p. of plates: ill.; 24 cm. Includes index.
1. Buckingham, George Villiers, Duke of, 1592-1628. 2. Politicians — Great
Britain — Biography. 3. Great Britain — Politics and government —
1603-1649 4. Great Britain — Court and courtiers — Biography. I. T.
DA391.1.B9 L63 1981   942.06/2/0924 B 19   *LC* 80-40578   *ISBN*
0582502969

DA395–398 Charles I, 1625–1649

Zagorin, Perez.   • **3.1467**
The court and the country; the beginning of the English Revolution. [1st
American ed.]. — New York: Atheneum, 1970 [c1969] xiv, 366 p.; 25 cm.
1. Great Britain — History — Charles I, 1625-1649 2. Great Britain — Social
conditions — 17th century I. T.
DA395.Z3 1970   320.9/42   *LC* 72-104129

Wingfield-Stratford, Esmé Cecil, 1882-.   • **3.1468**
King Charles the martyr, 1643–1649. — London, Hollis & Carter, 1950. xi,
385 p. plates, ports., maps. 22 cm. 1. Charles I, King of Great Britain,
1600-1649. 2. Gt. Brit. — Hist. — Civil War, 1642-1649. I. T.
DA396.A2W52   923.142   *LC* 50-14449

Hexter, J. H. (Jack H.), 1910-.   • **3.1469**
The reign of King Pym, by J. H. Hexter ... Cambridge: Harvard University
Press, 1941. 245 p.; 23 cm. (Half-title: Harvard historical studies ... vol.
XLVIII) Bibliography: p. [217]-223. 1. Pym, John, 1584-1643. 2. Great
Britain — History — Early Stuarts, 1603-1649 3. Great Britain — Politics and
government — 1603-1649 I. T.
DA396.P9H4   923.242   *LC* A 41-4164

Wedgwood, C. V. (Cicely Veronica), 1910-.   • **3.1470**
Strafford, 1593–1641, by C. V. Wedgwood. Westport, Conn., Greenwood Press
[1970] 366 p. ports. 23 cm. Reprint of the 1935 ed. 1. Strafford, Thomas
Wentworth, Earl of, 1593-1641. 2. Great Britain — History — Charles I,
1625-1649 I. T.
DA396.S8 W4 1970   942.06/2/0924 B   *LC* 76-110882   *ISBN*
083714566X

D'Ewes, Simonds, Sir, 1602-1650.   • **3.1471**
The journal of Sir Simonds D'Ewes; from the first recess of the Long Parliament
to the withdrawal of King Charles from London. Edited by Willson Havelock
Coates. [Hamden, Conn.] Archon Books, 1970 [c1942] xliv, 459 p. 23 cm.
1. Great Britain. Parliament, 1640-1648. 2. Great Britain — Politics and
government — 1625-1649 I. Coates, Willson Havelock. ed. II. T.
DA397.D43 1970   942.06/2/0924   *LC* 71-122400   *ISBN*
0208009485

DA400–419 Civil War, 1642–1649

Clarendon, Edward Hyde, Earl of, 1609-1674.   • **3.1472**
The history of the rebellion and civil wars in England begun in the year 1641, by
Edward, earl of Clarendon. Re–edited from a fresh collation of the original ms.
in the Bodleian library, with marginal dates and occasional notes, by W. Dunn
Macray ... — Oxford, Clarendon press, [1888] 6 v. 20 cm. 1. Gt. Brit. — Hist.
— Stuarts, 1603-1714. I. Macray, William Dunn, 1826-1916. ed. II. T.
DA400.C6 1888   *LC* 01-3232

Gardiner, Samuel Rawson, 1829-1902. ed. • **3.1473**
The constitutional documents of the Puritan revolution 1625–1660, selected and edited by Samuel Rawson Gardiner ... — 2d ed., rev. and enl. — Oxford, Clarendon press, 1899. lxviii, 476 p. 20 cm. 1. Great Britain — Constitutional history 2. Great Britain — Hist. — Puritan revolution, 1642-1660. I. Great Britain. Parliament. II. T.
DA400.G22   *LC* 03-26688

Haller, William, 1885- ed. • **3.1474**
The Leveller tracts, 1647–1653. Edited by William Haller and Godfrey Davies. — Gloucester, Mass., P. Smith, 1964 [c1944] vi, 481 p. illus. 21 cm. 1. Lilburne, John, 1614?-1657. 2. Levellers 3. Gt. Brit. — Hist. — Puritan Revolution, 1642-1660 — Sources. 4. Gt. Brit. — Pol. & govt. — 1642-1660. I. Davies, Godfrey, 1892-1957. joint ed. II. T.
DA400.H3 1964   942.063   *LC* 64-4072

Hobbes, Thomas, 1588-1679. • **3.1475**
Behemoth: the history of the causes of the civil wars of England, and of the counsels and artifices by which they were carried on from the year 1640 to the year 1660. Edited by William Molesworth. New York, B. Franklin [1963] 256 p. 24 cm. (Burt Franklin research and source works series, no. 38) 1. Great Britain — History — Puritan Revolution, 1640-1660. I. T.
DA400.H6 1963   942.062   *LC* 63-14025

Richardson, R. C. **3.1476**
The debate on the English Revolution / R. C. Richardson. — New York: St. Martin's Press, 1977. xi, 195 p.; 23 cm. Includes index. 1. Great Britain — History — Puritan Revolution, 1642-1660 — Historiography. I. T.
DA403.R53 1977b   941.06/07/2   *LC* 77-73803   *ISBN* 0312188900

Hill, Christopher, 1912-. **3.1477**
The experience of defeat: Milton and some contemporaries / Christopher Hill. — 1st American ed. — N.Y., N.Y.: Viking, 1984. 342 p.; 24 cm. 'Elisabeth Sifton books.' 1. Milton, John, 1608-1674 — Political and social views. 2. Religious thought — England. 3. Religious thought — 17th century 4. England — Intellectual life — 17th century 5. Great Britain — History — Puritan Revolution, 1642-1660 — Influence. I. T.
DA405.H49 1984   941.06 19   *LC* 83-40211   *ISBN* 0670302082

Wedgwood, C. V. (Cicely Veronica), 1910-. • **3.1478**
The King's peace, 1637–1641. New York, Macmillan, 1955. 510 p. illus., ports. 22 cm. (Her The Great rebellion [1]) Includes bibliographies. 1. Great Britain — History — Charles I, 1625-1649 I. T.
DA405.W42 vol.1   942.062   *LC* 55-3603

Wedgwood, C. V. (Cicely Veronica), 1910-. • **3.1479**
The King's war, 1641–1647. New York, Macmillan, 1959 [c1958] 702 p. ports., maps. 22 cm. (Her The great rebellion [2]) 'Bibliographical note': p. 627-629. Bibliography: p. 633-[681] 1. Great Britain — History — Civil War, 1642-1649 I. T.
DA405.W42 vol. 2   942.062   *LC* 59-7446

Ashley, Maurice, 1907-. • **3.1480**
Cromwell's generals. — New York: St. Martin's Press, 1955. 256 p.: ill.; 23 cm. 1. Cromwell, Oliver, 1599-1658. 2. Gt. Brit. — Hist. — Commonwealth and Protectorate, 1649-1660. 3. Generals — Gt. Brit. I. T.
DA407A1 A8x   942.063   *LC* 55-9052

Gregg, Pauline. • **3.1481**
Free-born John: a biography of John Lilburne / Pauline Gregg. — London: Harrap, 1961. 424 p.: ill.; 22 cm. 1. Lilburne, John, 1614?-1657. I. T.
DA407.L65 G7 1961   *LC* 62-5784

Holmes, Clive. **3.1482**
The Eastern Association in the English Civil War / Clive Holmes. — London: Cambridge University Press, 1974. x, 322 p.; 23 cm. Includes index. 1. Eastern Association. 2. Great Britain — History — Civil War, 1642-1649 I. T.
DA415.H75   942.6/06/2   *LC* 73-91616

Manning, Brian Stuart. **3.1483**
The English people and the English revolution, 1640–1649 / Brian Manning. — London: Heinemann, 1976. x, 390 p.; 23 cm. 1. Great Britain — History — Civil War, 1642-1649 2. Great Britain — Social conditions — 17th century I. T.
DA415.M36   941.06/2   *LC* 76-370634   *ISBN* 0435325655

Reactions to the English Civil War, 1642–1649 / edited by John Morrill. **3.1484**
New York: St. Martin's Press, 1984 (c1983). 257 p.; 23 cm. Includes index. 1. Public opinion — England — History — 17th century. 2. Great Britain — History — Civil War, 1642-1649 — Public opinion. 3. Great Britain — Politics and government — 1642-1649 I. Morrill, J. S. (John Stephen)
DA415.R38   941.06/2 19   *LC* 82-25538   *ISBN* 0312664435

Russell, Conrad. **3.1485**
The origins of the English Civil War. Edited by Conrad Russell. — New York: Barnes & Noble Books, [1973] x, 286 p.; 23 cm. 1. Great Britain — History — Civil War, 1642-1649 — Causes I. T.
DA415.R8 1973b   942.0/62   *LC* 73-169818   *ISBN* 0064960250

Solt, Leo Frank, 1921-. • **3.1486**
Saints in arms; Puritanism and democracy in Cromwell's army [by] Leo F. Solt. Stanford, Calif., Stanford University Press, 1959. — [New York: AMS Press, 1971] 150 p.; 23 cm. — (Stanford University publications. University series. History, economics, and political science, v. 18) 1. Chaplains, Military — Gt. Brit. 2. Puritans — Gt. Brit. 3. Christianity and politics 4. Gt. Brit. — History — Civil War, 1642-1649. I. T.
DA415.S65 1971   320.9/42/062   *LC* 74-153355   *ISBN* 0404509762

Underdown, David. **3.1487**
Pride's Purge: politics in the Puritan revolution. Oxford, Clarendon Press, 1971. xi, 424 p. 23 cm. 1. Great Britain — Politics and government — 1642-1649 I. T.
DA415.U5   941.06/2 19   *LC* 78-853456   *ISBN* 0198223420

DA420–429 COMMONWEALTH, 1649–1660.
CROMWELL

Brailsford, Henry Noel, 1873-1958. • **3.1488**
The Levellers and the English revolution. Edited and prepared for publication by Christopher Hill. [Stanford, Calif.] Stanford University Press, 1961. xvi, 715 p. 23 cm. Includes bibliographical references. 1. Levellers 2. Great Britain — Politics and government — 1642-1660 I. T.
DA425.B7   942.062   *LC* 61-11501

Capp, B. S. **3.1489**
The fifth monarchy men; a study in seventeenth–century English millenarianism, [by] B. S. Capp. — Totowa, N.J.: Rowman and Littlefield, 1972. 315 p.; 22 cm. 1. Fifth Monarchy Men 2. Millennialism — England. 3. Great Britain — Politics and government — 1649-1660 I. T.
DA425.C25   914.2/03/63   *ISBN* 0874711150

Woolrych, Austin H. **3.1490**
Commonwealth to protectorate / by Austin Woolrych. — Oxford: Clarendon Press; New York: Oxford University Press, 1982. xii, 446 p.; 22 cm. Includes index. 1. Great Britain — Politics and government — 1649-1660 I. T.
DA425.W59 1982   941.06/3 19   *LC* 82-167677   *ISBN* 0198226594

Fraser, Antonia, 1932-. **3.1491**
Cromwell, the Lord Protector [by] Antonia Fraser. [1st American ed.] New York, Knopf, 1973. xx, 774 p. illus. 25 cm. 1. Cromwell, Oliver, 1599-1658. I. T.
DA426.F7 1973   942.06/4/0924 B   *LC* 73-7270   *ISBN* 0394470346

Hill, Christopher, 1912-. • **3.1492**
God's Englishman; Oliver Cromwell and the English Revolution [by] Christopher Hill. New York, Dial Press, 1970. 324 p. illus., ports. 22 cm. (Crosscurrents in world history) 1. Cromwell, Oliver, 1599-1658. 2. Great Britain — History — Puritan Revolution, 1642-1660 I. T.
DA426.H49 1970b   942.06/4/0924 B   *LC* 75-111450

DA430–462 LATER STUARTS (1660–1714)

Clark, G. N. (George Norman), Sir, 1890-. • **3.1493**
The later Stuarts, 1660–1714, by Sir George Clark. 2d ed. [reprinted with corrections] Oxford, Clarendon Press [1961] xxiii, 479 p. geneal. tables, maps. 23 cm. (Oxford history of England. 10) 1. Great Britain — History — Stuarts, 1603-1714 I. T. II. Series.
DA435.C55 1961   *LC* 68-105542

Jones, J. R. (James Rees), 1925-. • **3.1494**
Country and court: England, 1658-1714 / J. R. Jones. — Cambridge, Mass.: Harvard University Press, 1978. 377 p.; 24 cm. — (New history of England.) Includes index. 1. Great Britain — History — Commonwealth and Protectorate, 1649-1660 2. Great Britain — History — 1660-1714 I. T. II. Series.
DA435.J66   942.06   *LC* 78-5362   *ISBN* 0674175255

Macaulay, Thomas Babington Macaulay, Baron, 1800-1859. • **3.1495**
History of England from the accession of James II. Introd. by Douglas Jerrold. London, Dent; New York, Dutton [1953] 4 v.; 19 cm. (Everyman's library, 34-37. History) 1. Great Britain — History — James II, 1685-1688 2. Great Britain — History — William and Mary, 1689-1702 I. T.
DA435.M14 1953   942.067   *LC* 53-11664

Prall, Stuart E.   **3.1496**
The bloodless revolution; England, 1688. — Garden City, N.Y., Doubleday, 1972. xv, 343 p. ports.; 19 cm. (Anchor books, A842) Bibliography: p. [327]-330. I. T.
DA435.P7

DA445–448 Charles II, 1660–1685

Lee, Maurice.   • **3.1497**
The Cabal. — Urbana: University of Illinois Press, 1965. 275 p.: ports.; 24 cm. Bibliographical footnotes. 1. Gt. Brit. — Hist. — Restoration, 1660-1688. I. T.
DA445.L4   942.066   *LC* 65-11735

Ogg, David, 1887-1965.   • **3.1498**
England in the reign of Charles II. — 2d ed. — Oxford, Clarendon Press, 1955. 2 v. 23 cm. Includes bibliographies. 1. Great Britain — Hist. — Charles II, 1660-1685. I. T.
DA445.O5x   *LC* A 57-8602

DA447 Biography. Memoirs

The Memoirs of Anne, Lady Halkett and Ann, Lady Fanshawe   **3.1499**
/ edited with an introd. by John Loftis.
Oxford [Eng.]: Clarendon Press; New York: Oxford University Press, 1979. xxi, 272 p.; 23 cm. Original ms. of A. M. Halkett's memoirs edited by J. G. Nichols and published in 1875 under the title: The autobiography of Anne, Lady Halkett. Includes index. 1. Halkett, Anne Murray, Lady, 1622-1699. 2. Fanshawe, Anne Harrison, Lady, 1625-1680. 3. Great Britain — History — Charles II, 1660-1685 — Sources. 4. Great Britain — Nobility — Biography. I. Loftis, John Clyde, 1919- II. Nichols, John Gough, 1806-1873. III. Gardiner, Samuel Rawson, 1829-1902. IV. Halkett, Anne Murray, Lady, 1622-1699. Autobiography of Anne, Lady Halkett. 1979. V. Fanshawe, Anne Harrison, Lady, 1625-1680. Memoirs of Lady Fanshawe. 1979.
DA447.A3 M45   942.06/092/2   *LC* 78-40238   *ISBN* 0198120877

Harris, R. W. (Ronald Walter)   **3.1500**
Clarendon and the English Revolution / R.W. Harris. — Stanford, Calif.: Stanford University Press, 1983. 456 p., [1] leaf of plates.: ill.; 24 cm. 1. Clarendon, Edward Hyde, Earl of, 1609-1674. 2. Statesmen — Great Britain — Biography. 3. Historians — Great Britain — Biography. 4. Great Britain — Politics and government — 1660-1688 5. Great Britain — Politics and government — 1625-1649 6. Great Britain — Politics and government — 1649-1660 I. T.
DA447.C6 H37 1983   941.06/092/4 B 19   *LC* 83-40092   *ISBN* 0804712166

Wormald, B.H.G.   • **3.1501**
Clarendon: politics, historiography and religion, 1640–1660 / by B.H.G. Wormald. — Cambridge: University Press, 1964. x, 330 p.; 23 cm. 1. Clarendon, Edward Hyde, Earl of, 1609-1674. I. T.
DA447 C6W6 1964

Evelyn, John, 1620-1706.   • **3.1502**
Diary. Now first printed in full from the mss. belonging to John Evelyn, and edited by E. S. de Beer. — Oxford, Clarendon Press, 1955. 6 v. illus., ports., fold. map, facsims., geneal. tables. 23 cm. Includes bibliographies. 1. Gt. Brit. — Hist. — Stuarts, 1603-1714. 2. Gt. Brit. — Court and courtiers. I. T.
DA447.E9A44   928.2   *LC* 56-13545

Pepys, Samuel, 1633-1703.   • **3.1503**
The diary of Samuel Pepys. A new and complete transcription edited by Robert Latham and William Matthews. Contributing editors: William A. Armstrong [and others] Berkeley: University of California Press, [1970]-. v.: ill., facsims., maps, ports.; 23 cm. 1. Pepys, Samuel, 1633-1703. 2. Statesmen — Great Britain — Diaries. 3. Authors, English — Early modern, 1500-1700 — Diaries. 4. Great Britain — Social life and customs — 17th century I. Latham, Robert, 1912- ed. II. Matthews, William, 1905- ed. III. T.
DA447.P4 A4 1970   914.2/03/6   *LC* 70-96950   *ISBN* 0520015754

Pepys, Samuel, 1633-1703.   **3.1504**
[Diary. Selections] The shorter Pepys / selected and edited by Robert Latham from The diary of Samuel Pepys, a new and complete transcription, edited by Robert Latham and William Matthews. — Berkeley: University of California Press, 1985. l, 1096, [16] p. of plates: ill.; 24 cm. Includes index. 1. Pepys, Samuel, 1633-1703. 2. Statesmen — Great Britain — Diaries. 3. Authors, English — Early modern, 1500-1700 — Diaries. 4. Great Britain — Social life and customs — 17th century. I. Latham, Robert, 1912- II. Pepys, Samuel, 1633-1703. Diary. III. T.
DA447.P4 A425 1985   941.06/6/0924 B 19   *LC* 85-40210   *ISBN* 0520034260

DA448 Special Topics

Jones, J. R. (James Rees), 1925-.   • **3.1505**
The first Whigs; the politics of the Exclusion Crisis, 1678–1683. — London, New York, Oxford University Press, 1961. 224 p. 23 cm. — (University of Durham publications) 1. Gt. Brit. — Pol. & govt. — 1660-1688. 2. Whig Party (Gt. Brit.) I. T. II. Title: Exclusion Crisis.
DA448.J6   942.066   *LC* 61-66249

Kenyon, J.P. (John Philipps), 1927-.   • **3.1506**
The Popish Plot [by] John Kenyon. New York: St. Martin's Press, [1972] 300 p.: ill.; 23 cm. 1. Popish Plot, 1678 I. T.
DA448.K45 1972   942.06/6   *LC* 72-76795

Miller, John (John Leslie)   **3.1507**
Popery and politics in England 1660–1688 [by] John Miller. Cambridge [Eng.], University Press, 1973. xiii, 288 p. 23 cm. 1. Catholic Church — England. 2. Popish Plot, 1678 3. Great Britain — Politics and government — 1660-1688 I. T.
DA448.M54   322/.1/0942   *LC* 73-79306   *ISBN* 0521202361

Earle, Peter, 1937-.   **3.1508**
Monmouth's rebels: the road to Sedgemoor 1685 / Peter Earle. — New York: St. Martin's Press, 1977. xi, 236 p., [4] leaves of plates: ill.; 23 cm. 1. Monmouth's Rebellion, 1685 I. T.
DA448.9.E17   942.06/7   *LC* 77-84928   *ISBN* 0312545126

DA450–452 James II, 1685–1688

Ashley, Maurice, 1907-.   **3.1509**
James II / Maurice Ashley. — Minneapolis: University of Minnesota Press, 1978 (c1977). 342 p., [8] leaves of plates: ill.; 24 cm. Includes index. 1. James II, King of England, 1633-1701. 2. Great Britain — History — James II, 1685-1688 3. Great Britain — Kings and rulers — Biography I. T.
DA450.A83   942.06/7/0924 B   *LC* 78-103953   *ISBN* 0816608261

Hosford, David H.   **3.1510**
Nottingham, nobles, and the North: aspects of the revolution of 1688 / by David H. Hosford. — Hamden, Conn.: Published for the Conference on British Studies and Wittenberg University by Archon Books, 1976. xvi, 182 p.; 23 cm. (Studies in British history and culture; v. 4) Includes index. 1. Great Britain — History — Revolution of 1688 I. T. II. Series.
DA452.H7   941.06/7   *LC* 75-19458   *ISBN* 0208015655

Jones, J. R. (James Rees), 1925-.   **3.1511**
The Revolution of 1688 in England [by] J. R. Jones. New York, Norton [1973, c1972] xx, 345 p. map. 21 cm. (Revolutions in the modern world) 1. Great Britain — History — Revolution of 1688 I. T.
DA452.J63 1973   942.06/7   *LC* 73-4726   *ISBN* 0393054594 *ISBN* 0393099989

Schwoerer, Lois G.   **3.1512**
The Declaration of Rights, 1689 / Lois G. Schwoerer. — Baltimore: Johns Hopkins University Press, c1981. xvi, 391 p.: ill.; 24 cm. Includes index. 1. Great Britain. Parliament. Declaration of Rights 2. Great Britain. Bill of Rights 3. Great Britain — Politics and government — Revolution of 1688 I. T.
DA452.S3   342.41/085 344.10285 19   *LC* 81-2942   *ISBN* 0801824303

Trevelyan, George Macaulay, 1876-1962.   • **3.1513**
The English revolution, 1688–1689, by George Macaulay Trevelyan. London: T. Butterworth, ltd. [1939] 255, 1 p.: ill.; 17 cm. (The home university library of modern knowledge.) 1. Great Britain — History — Revolution of 1688 I. T.
DA452.T7 1939a   *LC* 40-6687

DA460–462 William and Mary, 1689–1702

Baxter, Stephen Bartow, 1929-.   • **3.1514**
William III and the defense of European liberty, 1650–1702. — 1st American ed. — New York: Harcourt, Brace, & World, 1966. xi, 462 p. ,[4] leaves of plates: ill.,diagrs., geneal. tables, maps, ports.; 22cm. I. T.
DA460.B3 1966a   *LC* 66-19482

Churchill, Winston, Sir, 1874-1965.   • **3.1515**
Marlborough, his life and times. — London, G.G. Harrap [1947] 2 v. illus., ports., maps (part fold., part col.) 23 cm. Bibliography at end of each vol. 1. Marlborough, John Churchill, Duke of, 1650-1722. 2. Gt. Brit. — Hist. — 1660-1714. I. T.
DA462.M3C45 1947   923.542   *LC* 48-19354 *

DA470–522 18th Century

Charles-Edwards, Thomas Charles comp.   • **3.1516**
They saw it happen: an anthology of eyewitnesses' accounts of events in British history, 1689–1897, by T. Charles Edwards and B. Richardson; with a foreword by David Mathew. — Oxford: Blackwell, 1958. xix, 311 p.: coats of arms (on lining papers); 22 cm. 1. Great Britain — History — 18th century — Sources 2. Great Britain — History — 19th century — Sources I. Richardson, Brian. jt. comp. II. T.
DA470 C35

Cole, G. D. H. (George Douglas Howard), 1889-1959.   • **3.1517**
The common people, 1746–1946, by G. D. H. Cole and Raymond Postgate. [2d ed., reprinted with minor corrections] London, Methuen [1956] 742 p. illus. 19 cm. 1. Labor and laboring classes — Great Britain — History 2. Middle classes — Great Britain — History. 3. Great Britain — Economic conditions 4. Great Britain — History 5. Great Britain — Social conditions I. Postgate, Raymond William, 1896-1971. joint author. II. T.
DA470.C6 1956   330.942   *LC* 56-4032

Wiener, Joel H. comp.   **3.1518**
Great Britain: the lion at home; a documentary history of domestic policy, 1689–1973. Editor: Joel H. Wiener. — New York: Chelsea House Publishers, 1974. 4 v. (xlvi, 3971 p.); 24 cm. 1. Great Britain — History — 18th century — Sources. 2. Great Britain — History — 19th century — Sources. 3. Great Britain — History — 20th century — Sources. I. T.
DA470.W48   942   *LC* 74-7447   *ISBN* 0835207765

Maccoby, Simon.   • **3.1519**
The English radical tradition, 1763–1914. [1st U.S. ed.] New York, New York University Press [1957] 236 p. 21 cm. 1. Great Britain — Politics and government 2. Great Britain — Social conditions I. T.
DA472.M3 1957   942.07   *LC* 57-6377

Foord, Archibald S.   • **3.1520**
His Majesty's Opposition, 1714–1830. — Oxford, Clarendon Press, 1964. xi, 494 p. 22 cm. 'Bibliographical note': p. [471]-424. 1. Gt. Brit. — Pol. & govt. — 1714-1837. 2. Political parties — Gt. Brit. 3. Gt. Brit. — Constitutional history. I. T.
DA480.F6 1964   942.07   *LC* 64-4287

Marshall, Dorothy.   • **3.1521**
Eighteenth century England. New York, D. McKay Co. [1962] 537 p. illus. 23 cm. (A History of England in ten volumes) Includes bibliography. 1. Great Britain — History — 18th century I. T.
DA480.M37   942.07   *LC* 62-52772

Michael, Wolfgang, 1862-1945.   • **3.1522**
[Englische geschichte im achtsehnten jahrhundevt. English.] England under George I: the beginnings of the Hanoverian dynasty / Wolfgang Michael; translated and adapted from the German. — London: Macmillan, 1936. viii, 406 p.; 23 cm. — (Studies in modern history) Errata slip inserted. Translation of: Englische geschichte im achtsehnten jahrhundevt (v.1, books 2-3). Translated and adapted unter the supervision of Professor L. B. Namier. 1. Great Britain — History — 18th century I. T. II. Title: The beginnings of the Hanoverian dynasty
DA480 M513   DA480 M62.   942/.071   *LC* 36-16361

Namier, Lewis Bernstein, Sir, 1888-1960.   • **3.1523**
Crossroads of power; essays on eighteenth–century England. — Freeport, N.Y.: Books for Libraries Press, [1970, c1962] viii, 234 p.; 23 cm. — (His Collected essays, v. 2.) (Essay index reprint series.) 1. Gt. Brit. — History — 18th century — Addresses, essays, lectures. I. T.
DA480.N3 1970   942.07/08   *LC* 77-119604   *ISBN* 0836916905

Plumb, J. H. (John Harold), 1911-.   **3.1524**
The first four Georges / J. H. Plumb. Boston: Little, Brown, 1975, c1956. 208 p.: ill. (some col.); 31 cm. Includes index. 1. Great Britain — History — 1714-1837 2. Great Britain — Kings and rulers — Biography I. T.
DA480.P55 1975   942.07/092/2 B   *LC* 74-12150

DA483 BIOGRAPHY. MEMOIRS

Sherrard, Owen Aubrey, 1887-1962.   • **3.1525**
Lord Chatham: a war minister in the making / O. A. Sherrard. — London: Bodley Head, 1952. 323 p., [7] leaves of plates: ill.; 23 cm. 1. Pitt, William, Earl of Chatham, 1708-1778. I. T.
DA483.P6 S5   354/.41/0610924 B   *LC* 52-4029

Sherrard, Owen Aubrey, 1887-1962.   • **3.1526**
Lord Chatham and America. — London, Bodley Head [1958] 395 p. 22 cm. 1. Pitt, William, Earl of Chatham, 1708-1778. I. T.
DA483.P6S52   923.242   *LC* 58-1749

Williams, Basil, 1867-1950.   • **3.1527**
The life of William Pitt, earl of Chatham. New York, Octagon Books, 1966. 2 v. illus., port. 23 cm. 1. Pitt, William, Earl of Chatham, 1708-1778. 2. Great Britain — Politics and government — 18th century I. T.
DA483.P6 W5 1966a   942.07/3/0924 B   *LC* 66-30301

Walpole, Horace, 1717-1797.   • **3.1528**
[Correspondence (Yale edition of Horace Walpole's correspondence)] The Yale edition of Horace Walpole's correspondence / edited by W.S. Lewis. — [New Haven: Yale University Press, 1937]-. v. in : ill.; 27 cm. Index: v. 44-48. 1. Walpole, Horace, 1717-1797. 2. Authors, English — 18th century — Correspondence. 3. Great Britain — Nobility — Correspondence. I. Lewis, W. S. (Wilmarth Sheldon), 1895-1979. II. T.
DA483.W2 A12   828/.609 B 19   *LC* 52-4945

Ketton-Cremer, Robert Wyndham, 1906-.   • **3.1529**
Horace Walpole; a biography, by R. W. Ketton-Cremer. [3d ed.] Ithaca, N. Y., Cornell University Press [1966, c1964] xv, 317 p. geneal. table, plates, ports. 23 cm. 1. Walpole, Horace, 1717-1797. I. T.
DA483.W2 K4 1966   *LC* 66-11431

DA485–486 CIVILIZATION

Humphreys, A. R. (Arthur Raleigh), 1911-.   • **3.1530**
The Augustan world; life and letters in eighteenth–century England. — London, Methuen [1954] x, 283 p. 21 cm. Bibliography: p. 261-269. 1. Great Britain — Hist. — 18th cent. 2. English literature — 18th cent. — Hist. & crit. 3. Great Britain — Intellectual life I. T.
DA485.H85   942.07   *LC* A 55-1694

Jarrett, Derek.   **3.1531**
England in the age of Hogarth / Derek Jarrett. — New York: Viking Press, 1975 (c1974). 256 p.: ill.; 26 cm. Includes index. 1. Hogarth, William, 1697-1764. 2. England — Civilization — 18th century I. T.
DA485.J37   942.07   *LC* 74-5538   *ISBN* 0670296244

Malcolmson, Robert W.   **3.1532**
Popular recreations in English society, 1700–1850 [by] Robert W. Malcolmson. — Cambridge [Eng.]: University Press, 1973. x, 188 p.: illus.; 24 cm. Originally presented as the author's thesis, University of Warwick. 1. Recreation — England. 2. England — Social life and customs — 18th century 3. England — Social life and customs — 19th century I. T.
DA485.M217 1973   301.5/7/0942   *LC* 72-91958   *ISBN* 0521201470

Turberville, Arthur Stanley, 1888-1945.   • **3.1533**
English men and manners in the eighteenth century: an illustrated narrative. — 1st Galaxy ed. — New York: Oxford University Press, 1957. xxiii, 539 p.: ill., maps, ports., facsims.; 20 cm. — (A Galaxy book; GB10) 1. Eighteenth century 2. Great Britain — Social life and customs 3. Great Britain — History — 18th century I. T.
DA485.T75 1957   *LC* 57-14002

Woodforde, James, 1740-1803.   • **3.1534**
The diary of a country parson, 1758–1802. Passages selected and edited by John Beresford. — London, New York, Oxford University Press [1949] xviii, 622 p. geneal. table. 16 cm. — (The World's classics, 514) The present selection was published in 1935 under title: Woodforde; passages from the five volumes of The diary of a country parson, 1758-1802. 1. England — Soc. life & cust. I. T.
DA485.W62 1949   914.2   *LC* 50-14450

Reed, Michael A.   **3.1535**
The Georgian triumph, 1700–1830 / Michael Reed. — London; Boston: Routledge & Kegan Paul, 1983. xvi, 240 p.: ill., maps; 25 cm. — (Making of Britain, 1066-1939.) Includes index. 1. Landscape — Great Britain — History — 18th century. 2. Landscape — Great Britain — History — 19th century. 3. Great Britain — Historical geography. 4. Great Britain — Social conditions — 18th century 5. Great Britain — Social conditions — 19th century 6. Great Britain — History — 18th century 7. Great Britain — History — 1800-1837 I. T. II. Series.
DA486.R43 1983   941.07 19   *LC* 82-16640   *ISBN* 0710094140

DA490–497 Anne, 1702–1714

Gregg, Edward.   **3.1536**
Queen Anne / Edward Gregg. — London; Boston: Routledge & Kegan Paul, 1980. xii, 483 p., [7] leaves of plates: ports.; 24 cm. Includes index. 1. Anne, Queen of Great Britain, 1665-1714. 2. Great Britain — History — 1660-1714 3. Great Britain — Kings and rulers — Biography I. T.
DA495.G73   941.06/9/0924 B   *LC* 79-41312   *ISBN* 0710004001

Trevelyan, George Macaulay, 1876-1962.   • **3.1537**
England under Queen Anne ... by George Macaulay Trevelyan ... London, New York [etc.] Longmans, Green and co., 1930-34. 3 v. front. (v. 3, port.) maps

(part fold.) 23 cm. Bibliography: vol. I, p. [434]-435; vol. II, p. [419]-422; vol. III, p. [341]-343. 1. Spanish Succession, War of, 1701-1714 2. Great Britain — History — Anne, 1702-1714 I. T. II. Title: Blenheim. III. Title: Ramillies and the union with Scotland.
DA495.T7   942.069   *LC* 30-23326

DA498–503 George I, 1714–1727. George II, 1727–1760

Addison, Joseph, 1672-1719.   **3.1538**
The freeholder / Joseph Addison; edited with an introd. and notes by James Leheny. — Oxford: Clarendon Press; New York: Oxford University Press, 1979. xi, 283 p., [1] leaf of plates: ill.; 23 cm. 1. Whig Party (Great Britain) — Collected works. 2. Great Britain — Politics and government — 1714-1727 — Collected works. I. Leheny, James. II. T.
DA498.A3 1979   320.9/41/071 19   *LC* 78-41130   *ISBN* 0198124945

Black, Jeremy.   **3.1539**
British foreign policy in the age of Walpole / Jeremy Black. — Edinburgh: J. Donald; Atlantic Highlands, NJ, USA: Exclusive distribution in the U.S.A. and Canada by Humanities Press, c1985. xi, 202 p.; 24 cm. Includes index. 1. Walpole, Robert, Earl of Orford, 1676-1745. 2. Great Britain — Foreign relations — 1714-1727 3. Great Britain — Foreign relations — 1727-1760 I. T.
DA498.B53 1985   941.07/1 19   *LC* 85-213381   *ISBN* 0859761266

Speck, W. A. (William Arthur), 1938-.   **3.1540**
Stability and strife: England, 1714–1760 / W. A. Speck. — Cambridge, Mass.: Harvard University Press, 1977. 311 p.; 25 cm. (New history of England.) Includes index. 1. Great Britain — Politics and government — 1714-1760 I. T. II. Series.
DA498.S68   942.07/2   *LC* 77-22773   *ISBN* 0674833473

Williams, Basil, 1867-1950.   • **3.1541**
The Whig supremacy, 1714–1760. 2d ed. rev. by C. H. Stuart. Oxford, Clarendon Press, 1962. xix, 504 p. maps, plan. 23 cm. (Oxford history of England. 11) Bibliography: p. [434]-468. 1. Great Britain — Politics and government — 1714-1760 2. Great Britain — History — George I, II, 1714-1760 3. Great Britain — Social conditions I. T. II. Series.
DA498.W5 1962   942.071   *LC* 62-2655

Gipson, Lawrence Henry, 1880-.   • **3.1542**
The British Empire before the American Revolution. — [Completely rev.]. — New York, Knopf, 1958-. v. maps. 25 cm. Bibliographical footnotes. 1. Gt. Brit. — Hist. — 18th cent. 2. Ireland — Hist. — 18th cent. 3. Gt. Brit. — Colonies — America. 4. U.S. — Hist. — Colonial period. I. T.
DA500.G52   942.072   *LC* 58-9670

Owen, John Beresford.   • **3.1543**
The rise of the Pelhams, by John B. Owen. — New York: Barnes & Noble, [1971] x, 357 p.; 23 cm. Reprint of the 1957 ed. 1. Pelham, Henry, 1695?-1754. 2. Gt. Brit. — Politics and government — 1727-1760. I. T.
DA500.O85 1971   942.07/2   *LC* 76-24488   *ISBN* 0389041459

Hatton, Ragnhild Marie.   **3.1544**
George I, elector and king / Ragnhild Hatton. — Cambridge, Mass.: Harvard University Press, 1979 (c1978). 416 p., [8] leaves of plates: ill.; 24 cm. Includes index. 1. George I, King of Great Britain, 1660-1727. 2. Great Britain — Kings and rulers — Biography 3. Great Britain — History — George I, 1714-1727 I. T.
DA501.A2 H4   941.07/1/0924 B   *LC* 77-15058   *ISBN* 0674349350

Hervey of Ickworth, John Hervey, Baron, 1696-1743.   • **3.1545**
[Memoirs] Some materials towards memoirs of the reign of King George II. Edited by Romney Sedgwick. New York, AMS Press [1970] 3 v. (lx, 1003 p.) ports. 23 cm. Title on spine: Memoirs. Originally published in 1848 under title: Memoirs of the reign of George the Second. Reprint of the 1931 ed. 1. George II, King of Great Britain, 1683-1760. 2. Great Britain — History — George II, 1727-1760 I. Sedgwick, Romney, 1894- ed. II. T.
DA501.A3 H47 1970   942.07/2   *LC* 79-119102   *ISBN* 0404033008

Kramnick, Isaac.   • **3.1546**
Bolingbroke and his circle; the politics of nostalgia in the age of Walpole. Cambridge, Mass., Harvard University Press, 1968. xiii, 321 p. port. 24 cm. (Harvard political studies) 1. Bolingbroke, Henry St. John, Viscount, 1678-1751. I. T. II. Series.
DA501.B6 K7 1968   942.07/1   *LC* 68-15639

Varey, Simon, 1951-.   **3.1547**
Henry St. John, Viscount Bolingbroke / by Simon Varey. — Boston: Twayne Publishers, c1984. 139 p.: port.; 22 cm. — (Twayne's English authors series. TEAS 362) Includes index. 1. Bolingbroke, Henry St. John, Viscount,

1678-1751. 2. Politicians — Great Britain — Biography. I. T. II. Title: Henry Saint John, Viscount Bolingbroke. III. Series.
DA501.B6 V37 1984   941.07/092/4 B 19   *LC* 83-22831   *ISBN* 0805768483

Chesterfield, Philip Dormer Stanhope, Earl of, 1694-1773.   • **3.1548**
The letters of Philip Dormer Stanhope, 4th Earl of Chesterfield. Edited, with an introd. by Bonamy Dobrée. London: Eyre & Spottiswoode; New York: Viking Press, 1932. 6 v.: front. (port.) fold. geneal. tab.; 23 cm. 1. Chesterfield, Philip Dormer Stanhope, Earl of, 1694-1773. I. Dobrée, Bonamy, 1891- ed. II. T.
DA501.C5 A32   942.07/092/4   *LC* 68-59007

Shellabarger, Samuel, 1888-1954.   • **3.1549**
Lord Chesterfield and his world. New York, Biblo and Tannen, 1971 [c1951] 456 p. port. 23 cm. 1. Chesterfield, Philip Dormer Stanhope, Earl of, 1694-1773. I. T.
DA501.C5 S52 1971   942.07/1/0924   *LC* 72-156737   *ISBN* 0819602728

Halsband, Robert, 1914-.   **3.1550**
Lord Hervey; eighteenth–century courtier. New York, Oxford University Press, 1974 [c1973] xiv, 380 p. illus. 22 cm. 1. Hervey of Ickworth, John Hervey, Baron, 1696-1743. I. T.
DA501.H47 H34 1974   942.07/2/0924 B   *LC* 73-87774   *ISBN* 0195017315

Montagu, Lady Mary (Pierrepont) Wortley, 1689-1762.   • **3.1551**
The complete letters of Lady Mary Wortley Montagu / edited by Robert Halsband. — Oxford: Clarendon Press, 1965-1967. 3 v.; illus., facsims., ports. 23 cm. I. Halsband, Robert, 1914- II. T.
DA501.M7 A48

Halsband, Robert, 1914-.   • **3.1552**
The life of Lady Mary Wortley Montagu. — Oxford, Clarendon Press, 1956 [i. e. 1957] 313 p. illus. 23 cm. 1. Montagu, Mary (Pierrepont) Wortley, Lady, 1639-1762. I. T.
DA501.M7H3   928.2   *LC* 56-14373

Plumb, J. H. (John Harold), 1911-.   • **3.1553**
Sir Robert Walpole [by] J. H. Plumb. Clifton [N.J.] A. M. Kelley, 1973-. v. illus. 23 cm. (Houghton Mifflin reprint editions) Reprint of the 1956-61 ed. 1. Walpole, Robert, Earl of Orford, 1676-1745. I. T.
DA501.W2 P522   942.06/9/0924 B   *LC* 72-128080   *ISBN* 0678035512

DA505–522 George III, 1760–1820

Butterfield, Herbert, Sir, 1900-.   • **3.1554**
George III and the historians. Rev. ed. New York, Macmillan, 1959. 304 p. 22 cm. Includes bibliographical references. 1. George III, King of Great Britain, 1738-1820. 2. Great Britain — History — George III, 1760-1820 — Historiography. I. T.
DA505.B974 1959   942.073   *LC* 59-7967

Christie, Ian R.   **3.1555**
Wars and revolutions: Britain 1760–1815 / Ian R. Christie. — Cambridge, Mass.: Harvard University Press, 1982. 359 p.; 25 cm. — (New history of England.) Includes index. 1. Great Britain — Politics and government — 1760-1820 2. Great Britain — Foreign relations — France. 3. France — Foreign relations — Great Britain. I. T. II. Series.
DA505.C48 1982   941.07/3 19   *LC* 82-3009   *ISBN* 0674947606

Harlow, Vincent Todd, 1898-1961.   • **3.1556**
The founding of the Second British Empire, 1763–1793 / by Vincent T. Harlow. — London: Longmans, 1952-1964. v.: maps; 25 cm. 1. Great Britain — Colonies — History 2. Great Britain — History — George III, 1760-1820 I. T. II. Title: British Empire, 1763-1793.
DA505.H37   *LC* 52-11742

Namier, Lewis Bernstein, Sir, 1888-1960.   • **3.1557**
England in the age of the American Revolution. — 2d ed. — New York, St. Martin's Press, 1961 [i. e. 1962] 450 p. 23 cm. 1. Gt. Brit. — Hist. — George II, 1727-1760. 2. Gt. Brit. — Hist. — 1760-1789. 3. U.S. — Hist. — Revolution — Causes. I. T.
DA505.N25 1962   942.072   *LC* 62-2311

Pares, Richard, 1902-1958.   • **3.1558**
King George III and the politicians; the Ford lectures delivered in the University of Oxford, 1951–2. London, New York [etc.] Oxford U.P., 1967. [7], 214 p. 21 cm. (Ford lectures, 1951-2) (Oxford paperback no. 130.) 1. George III, King of Great Britain, 1738-1820. 2. Great Britain — Politics and government — 1760-1820 I. T.
DA505.P3 1967   320.9/42   *LC* 68-93556   *ISBN* 0198950131

Watson, John Steven.   • **3.1559**
The reign of George III, 1760–1815 / by J. Steven Watson. — Oxford: Clarendon Press, c1960. xviii, 637 p.: fold. maps.; 23 cm. (Oxford history of England. 12) 1. Great Britain — History — George III, 1760-1820 I. T. II. Series.
DA505.W38   *LC* 60-50916

DA506 Biography. Memoirs

Brooke, John, 1920-.   • **3.1560**
King George III. With a foreword by H. R. H. the Prince of Wales. New York, McGraw-Hill [1972] xix, 411 p. col. front., illus. 26 cm. (American Revolution bicentennial program) 1. George III, King of Great Britain, 1738-1820. I. T. II. Series.
DA506.A2 B75   942.07/3/0924 B   *LC* 72-2011   *ISBN* 0070080593

Cone, Carl B.   • **3.1561**
Burke and the nature of politics. [Lexington]: University of Kentucky Press [1957-1964] 2 v.: ill., port.; 25 cm. Bibliographical footnotes. 1. Burke, Edmund, 1729-1797. 2. Great Britain — Politics and government — 1700-1820. I. T.
DA506.B9C54   923.242   *LC* 57-11380

Magnus, Philip Montefiore, Sir, bart., 1906-.   • **3.1562**
Edmund Burke: a life / by Philip Magnus. — 1st ed. — London: J. Murray, 1939. 367 p., [8] leaves of plates: ill., ports.; 23 cm. 1. Burke, Edmund, 1729-1797. I. T.
DA506.B9 M3

Derry, John Wesley.   **3.1563**
Charles James Fox [by] John W. Derry. — New York: St. Martin's Press, [1972] 454 p.: illus.; 23 cm. 1. Fox, Charles James, 1749-1806. I. T.
DA506.F7 D47 1972b   942.07/3/0924 B   *LC* 73-176065

Thomas, Peter David Garner.   **3.1564**
Lord North / Peter D. G. Thomas. — New York: St. Martin's Press, 1976. viii, 176 p.; 23 cm. — (British political biography) Includes index. 1. North, Frederick, Lord, 1732-1792. I. T.
DA506.N7 T48 1976   941.07/3/0924 B   *LC* 75-29819

Walpole, Horace, 1717-1797.   **3.1565**
[Correspondence. 1973] Selected letters of Horace Walpole. Edited by W. S. Lewis. New Haven, Yale University Press, 1973. xix, 323 p. illus. 22 cm. 1. Walpole, Horace, 1717-1797. I. Lewis, W. S. (Wilmarth Sheldon), 1895-1979, ed. II. T.
DA506.W2 A4 1973   826/.6   *LC* 72-91300   *ISBN* 0300016433
ISBN 0300016697

DA510–512 1760–1789

Brewer, John, 1947-.   **3.1566**
Party ideology and popular politics at the accession of George III / John Brewer. — Cambridge; New York: Cambridge University Press, 1976. ix, 382 p.; 24 cm. Includes index. 1. Political parties — Great Britain 2. Great Britain — Politics and government — 1760-1789 I. T.
DA510.B67   320.9/41/073   *LC* 76-14773   *ISBN* 0521210496

Brooke, John.   • **3.1567**
The Chatham administration, 1766-1768. — London, Macmillan; New York, St. Martin's Press, 1956. 400 p. 23 cm. — (England in the age of the American Revolution) 1. Pitt, William, Earl of Chatham, 1708-1778. 2. Gt. Brit. — Pol. & govt. — 1760-1820. I. T.
DA510.B7   942.073   *LC* 56-14302

Christie, Ian R.   • **3.1568**
The end of North's ministry, 1780–1782. London, Macmillan; New York: St. Martin's Press, 1958. xiii, 428 p. (England in the age of the American revolution) 1. North, Frederick North, Baron, 1732-1792. 2. Great Britain — Politics and government — 1714-1830. I. T.
DA510.C45   942.073   *LC* 58-4847

Ritcheson, Charles R.   • **3.1569**
British politics and the American Revolution. [1st ed.] Norman, University of Oklahoma Press [1954] xv, 320 p.: ports.; 22 cm. 1. Great Britain — Politics and government — 1760-1789 2. United States — History — Revolution — Causes. I. T.
DA510.R5   *LC* 54-5933

Kronenberger, Louis, 1904-.   **3.1570**
The extraordinary Mr. Wilkes: his life and times. — [1st ed.]. — Garden City, N.Y.: Doubleday, 1974. xv, 269 p.: illus.; 22 cm. 1. Wilkes, John, 1727-1797. 2. Great Britain — Politics and government — 1760-1789 I. T.
DA512.W6 K76   328.42/092/4 B   *LC* 73-79686   *ISBN* 038505131X

Rudé, George F. E.   • **3.1571**
Wilkes and liberty; a social study of 1763 to 1774. Oxford, Clarendon Press, 1962. xvi, 240 p.: front.; 23 cm. Bibliography: p. 224-228. 1. Wilkes, John, 1727-1797. 2. Great Britain — Politics and government — 1760-1789 I. T.
DA512.W6R8   923.242   *LC* 62-1596

DA520–522 1789–1820. The Regency

Dozier, Robert R., 1932-.   **3.1572**
For king, constitution, and country: the English Loyalists and the French Revolution / Robert R. Dozier. — Lexington, Ky.: University Press of Kentucky, c1983. xi, 213 p.; 23 cm. On spine: For king, constitution & country. Includes index. 1. Great Britain — History — 1789-1820 2. France — History — Revolution, 1789-1793 — Influence. I. T. II. Title: English Loyalists and the French Revolution. III. Title: For king, constitution & country.
DA520.D69 1983   941.07/3 19   *LC* 83-1221   *ISBN* 081311490X

Goodwin, Albert.   **3.1573**
The friends of liberty: the English democratic movement in the age of the French revolution / Albert Goodwin. — Cambridge, Mass.: Harvard University Press, 1979. 594 p., [2] leaves of plates: ill., ports.; 22 cm. Includes index. 1. Radicalism — Great Britain. 2. Great Britain — Politics and government — 1789-1820 I. T.
DA520.G6 1979   320.9/41/073   *LC* 78-15673   *ISBN* 0674323394

Dixon, Peter, 1932-.   **3.1574**
George Canning, politician and statesman / Peter Dixon. — New York: Mason/Charter, 1976. 355 p.; 24 cm. Includes index. 1. Canning, George, 1770-1827. 2. Great Britain — Politics and government — 1789-1820 I. T.
DA522.C2 D59 1976   941.07/3/0924 B   *LC* 75-43867   *ISBN* 0884053520

Spater, George.   **3.1575**
William Cobbett, the poor man's friend / George Spater. — Cambridge; New York: Cambridge University Press, 1982. 2 v. (xv, 653 p.): ill.; 24 cm. Maps on lining papers. Includes indexes. 1. Cobbett, William, 1763-1835. 2. Politicians — Great Britain — Biography. 3. Authors, English — 19th century — Biography. 4. Great Britain — Politics and government — 1789-1820 I. T.
DA522.C5 S66   941.07/3/0924 B 19   *LC* 81-3859   *ISBN* 0521222168

Gash, Norman.   **3.1576**
Lord Liverpool: the life and political career of Robert Banks Jenkinson, Second Earl of Liverpool, 1770–1828 / Norman Gash. — Cambridge, Mass.: Harvard University Press, 1985 (c1984). xvii, 265 p., [8] p. of plates: ill.; 25 cm. 1. Liverpool, Robert Banks Jenkinson, Earl of, 1770-1828. 2. Prime ministers — Great Britain — Biography. 3. Great Britain — Politics and government — 1800-1837 I. T.
DA522.L7 G37   942.07/4/0924 B 19   *LC* 84-12842   *ISBN* 0674539109

Derry, John Wesley.   **3.1577**
Castlereagh / John W. Derry. — New York: St. Martin's Press, 1976. viii, 247 p.; 23 cm. (British political biography) Includes index. 1. Castlereagh, Robert Stewart, Viscount, 1769-1822. 2. Great Britain — Politics and government — 1789-1820 3. Ireland — Politics and government — 1760-1820 I. T.
DA522.L8 D47 1976   941.07/3/0924 B   *LC* 75-29820

Ehrman, John.   • **3.1578**
The younger Pitt. New York, Dutton [1969-. v. illus., ports. (1 col.) 26 cm. 1. Pitt, William, 1759-1806. I. T.
DA522.P6 E36   941.07/3/0924 B 19   *LC* 78-87178

Mackesy, Piers.   **3.1579**
War without victory: the downfall of Pitt, 1799–1802 / Piers Mackesy. — Oxford: Clarendon Press; New York: Oxford University Press, 1984. xi, 248 p.: maps; 23 cm. Includes index. 1. Pitt, William, 1759-1806. 2. Melville, Henry Dundas, Viscount, 1742-1811. 3. Second Coalition, War of the, 1798-1801 4. Great Britain — Politics and government — 1789-1820 I. T.
DA522.P6 M33 1984   941.07/3 19   *LC* 84-232979   *ISBN* 0198224958

Pollock, John Charles.   • **3.1580**
Wilberforce / John Pollock. — New York: St. Martin's Press, 1978, c1977. xvi, 368 p., [6] leaves of plates (1 fold.): ill.; 24 cm. Includes index. 1. Wilberforce, William, 1759-1833. 2. Politicians — Great Britain — Biography. 3. Great Britain — Politics and government — 1760-1820 4. Great Britain — Politics and government — 1820-1830 I. T.
DA522.W6 P64 1978   326/.092/4   *LC* 77-86525   *ISBN* 0312879423

DA530–565 19th Century

Briggs, Asa, 1921-.   • **3.1581**
The age of improvement. London, New York, Longmans, Green [1959] 547 p.
23 cm. (A History of England) 1. Great Britain — History — George III,
1760-1820 2. Great Britain — History — 19th century I. T.
DA530.B68   *LC* 59-816

Halévy, Elie, 1870-1937.   • **3.1582**
A history of the English people in the nineteenth century / by Elie Halevy;
translated from the French by E.I. Watkin and D.A. Barber. — 2d rev. ed. —
London: E. Benn, 1949-1952. 6 v. in 7: ill.; 23 cm. 1. Great Britain — History
— 19th century 2. Great Britain — Civilization 3. Great Britain — Economic
conditions 4. Great Britain — History — 20th century I. T.
DA530.H443   *LC* 52-9366 rev

Harrison, Brian Howard.   **3.1583**
Peaceable kingdom: stability and change in modern Britain / by Brian
Harrison. — Oxford: Clarendon Press; New York: Oxford University Press,
1982. 493 p.; 23 cm. 1. Great Britain — Politics and government — 19th
century — Addresses, essays, lectures. 2. Great Britain — Politics and
government — 20th century — Addresses, essays, lectures. 3. Great Britain —
Politics and government — 1760-1820 — Addresses, essays, lectures.
4. England — Social conditions — 19th century — Addresses, essays, lectures.
5. England — Social conditions — 20th century — Addresses, essays, lectures.
6. England — Social conditions — 18th century — Addresses, essays, lectures.
I. T.
DA530.H446 1982   306/.0941 19   *LC* 82-6400   *ISBN* 0198226039

Hayes, Paul M.   **3.1584**
The nineteenth century, 1814–80 / Paul Hayes. New York: St. Martin's Press,
1975. xi, 334 p.: maps; 23 cm. (Modern British foreign policy) Includes index.
1. Great Britain — Foreign relations — 19th century I. T.
DA530.H447 1975b   327.41   *LC* 75-10760

Seton-Watson, R. W. (Robert William), 1879-1951.   • **3.1585**
Britain in Europe, 1789–1914; a survey of foreign policy. New York, H. Fertig,
1968. ix, 716 p. 24 cm. Reprint of the 1937 ed. 1. Great Britain — Foreign
relations — 19th century 2. Europe — Politics and government — 1789-1900
3. Great Britain — Foreign relations — 20th century 4. Europe — Politics and
government — 20th century I. T.
DA530.S4 1968   327.42   *LC* 68-9599

Trevelyan, George Macaulay, 1876-1962.   • **3.1586**
British history in the nineteenth century and after, 1782–1919. New York,
Harper & Row, 1966. xvi, 512 p. maps. 21 cm. (Harper Torchbooks. Academy
library; TB1251Q.) 1. Great Britain — History — 19th century 2. Great
Britain — History — 20th century I. T.
DA530.T7 1966   *LC* 66-1980

Woodward, E. L. (Ernest Llewellyn), Sir, 1890-.   • **3.1587**
The age of reform, 1815–1870 / Sir Ernest L. Woodward. — 2d ed. — Oxford:
Clarendon Press, 1962. xix, 681 p.: maps; 23 cm. — (Oxford history of England.
13) 1. Great Britain — Politics and government — 19th century 2. Great
Britain — History — 19th century 3. Great Britain — Social conditions I. T.
II. Series.
DA530.W6 1962b   *LC* 62-4675

Altick, Richard Daniel, 1915-.   **3.1588**
Victorian people and ideas; a companion for the modern reader of Victorian
literature [by] Richard D. Altick. — [1st ed.]. — New York: Norton, [1973] xii,
338 p.: illus.; 22 cm. 1. English literature — 19th century — History and
criticism. 2. England — Civilization — 19th century I. T.
DA533.A55 1973   914.2/03/81   *LC* 72-10138   *ISBN* 039304260X

Drabble, Margaret, 1939-.   **3.1589**
For Queen and country: Britain in the Victorian age / Margaret Drabble. — 1st
American ed. — New York: Seabury Press, 1979, c1978. 144 p., [4] leaves of
plates: ill.; 25 cm. 'A Clarion book.' Includes index. 1. Victoria, Queen of Great
Britain, 1819-1901. 2. England — Civilization — 19th century I. T.
DA533.D7 1979   941.081   *LC* 78-9682   *ISBN* 0816432228

Heyck, Thomas William, 1938-.   **3.1590**
The transformation of intellectual life in Victorian England / T.W. Heyck. —
New York: St. Martin's Press, 1982. 262 p.; 22 cm. Includes index. 1. England
— Intellectual life — 19th century I. T.
DA533.H48 1982   305.5/52/0942 19   *LC* 82-840   *ISBN*
0312814275

Himmelfarb, Gertrude.   • **3.1591**
Victorian minds. — [1st ed.]. — New York: Knopf, 1968. xiii, 392, v p.; 22 cm.
Essays. 1. Great Britain — Intellectual life — 19th century I. T.
DA533.H55   942.081   *LC* 67-18617

Houghton, Walter Edwards, 1904-.   • **3.1592**
The Victorian frame of mind, 1830–1870. — New Haven: Published for
Wellesley College by Yale University Press, 1957. 467 p.; 24 cm. 1. Great
Britain — Civilization — 19th century I. T.
DA533.H85   942.081   *LC* 57-6339

Kitson Clark, G. S. R. (George Sidney Roberts), 1900-1975.   • **3.1593**
The making of Victorian England. Cambridge, Harvard University Press, 1962.
xiii, 312 p. 23 cm. (Ford lectures, 1960) 1. Great Britain — Civilization I. T.
DA533.K55   914.2   *LC* 62-51827

Read, Donald.   **3.1594**
England, 1868-1914: the age of urban democracy / by Donald Read. —
London; New York: Longman, 1979. xiv, 530 p.: ill.; 22 cm. (A History of
England) (Longman paperback) 1. England — Civilization — 19th century
2. England — Civilization — 20th century I. T.
DA533.R37   942.081   *LC* 78-41034   *ISBN* 058248278X

Somervell, D. C. (David Churchill), 1885-1965.   • **3.1595**
English thought in the nineteenth century. 5th ed. London: Methuen [1947] x,
241 p.; 20 cm. 1. Nineteenth century 2. Great Britain — Intellectual life I. T.
DA533.S65x   *LC* 50-7103

Wiener, Martin J.   **3.1596**
English culture and the decline of the industrial spirit, 1850–1980 / Martin J.
Wiener. — Cambridge; New York: Cambridge University Press, 1981. xi,
217 p.; 24 cm. 1. Industry — Social aspects — England. 2. England —
Civilization — 19th century 3. England — Civilization — 20th century I. T.
DA533.W59   942.08 19   *LC* 80-22684   *ISBN* 0521234182

Williams, Raymond.   • **3.1597**
Culture and society, 1780–1950. — New York, Columbia University Press,
1958. 363 p.; 23 cm. 1. Great Britain — Intellectual life I. T.
DA533.W6 1958   914.2   *LC* 58-4388

DA535–542 1801–1837

Gash, Norman.   **3.1598**
Aristocracy and people: Britain, 1815–1865 / Norman Gash. — Cambridge,
Mass.: Harvard University Press, 1980 (c1979). 375 p.: map; 24 cm. — (The
New history of England, v. 8) Includes index. 1. Upper classes — Great Britain
— History. 2. Great Britain — Politics and government — 1800-1837 3. Great
Britain — Politics and government — 1837-1901 4. Great Britain — Nobility
— History. 5. Great Britain — Economic conditions — 1760-1860 I. T.
DA535.G37   309.1/41/07   *LC* 79-13638   *ISBN* 0674044908

Webster, Charles Kingsley, Sir, 1886-1961.   • **3.1599**
The foreign policy of Palmerston, 1830–1841; Britain, the liberal movement,
and the Eastern question. New York, Humanities Press, 1969. 2 v. (xi, 914 p.)
port. 22 cm. 1. Palmerston, Henry John Temple, Viscount, 1784-1865.
2. Great Britain — Foreign relations — 19th century 3. Europe — Politics and
government — 1815-1871 I. T.
DA535.W4 1969   327.42   *LC* 72-10921

Woodham Smith, Cecil Blanche (FitzGerald) 1896-.   • **3.1600**
The reason why, by Cecil Woodham–Smith. [2d ed.] New York, McGraw-Hill
[1971, c1953] 287 p. illus., maps, ports. 24 cm. 1. Cardigan, James Thomas
Brudenell, Earl of, 1797-1868. 2. Lucan, George Charles Bingham, Earl of,
1800-1888. 3. Balaklava, Battle of, 1854 I. T.
DA536.C3 W6 1971   942.081/0924   *LC* 72-155886   *ISBN*
0070716706

Read, Donald.   • **3.1601**
Cobden and Bright: a Victorian political partnership. New York, St. Martin's
Press, 1968 [c1967] ix, 275 p. ill., ports. 23 cm. 1. Cobden, Richard, 1804-1865.
2. Bright, John, 1811-1889. I. T.
DA536.C6 R4 1968   *LC* 68-15436   *ISBN* 0713153067

Greville, Charles, 1794-1865.   • **3.1602**
The great world: portraits and scenes from Greville's memoirs [1814–1860] /
edited with an introd. by Louis Kronenberger. — 1st ed. — Garden City, N. Y.:
Doubleday, 1963. 354 p.; 22 cm. 1. Great Britain — History — 19th century
I. T.
DA536.G8A423   *LC* 63-7703

Cecil, David, Lord, 1902-.   • **3.1603**
Melbourne. — [Indianapolis, Bobbs-Merrill, c1954] 450 p.: ports.; 22 cm.
(Charter books, 101) 'Parts I and II were published in 1939 under the title of
The young Melbourne.' 1. Melbourne, William Lamb, Viscount, 1779-1848.
2. Lamb, Caroline, Lady, 1785-1828. 3. Victoria, Queen of Great Britain,
1819-1901. I. T.
DA536.M5C5   923.242   *LC* 54-9486

Bourne, Kenneth.   3.1604
Palmerston, the early years, 1784–1841 / by Kenneth Bourne. — New York: Macmillan, c1982. xiv, 749 p., [16] p. of plates: ill.; 25 cm. Includes index. 1. Palmerston, Henry John Temple, Viscount, 1784-1865. 2. Prime ministers — Great Britain — Biography. 3. Great Britain — Foreign relations — 1837-1901 4. Great Britain — Politics and government — 1837-1901 I. T.
DA536.P2 B68 1982   941.081/092/4 B 19   LC 81-18582   ISBN 0029037409

Gash, Norman.   ● 3.1605
Mr. Secretary Peel; the life of Sir Robert Peel to 1830. — Cambridge, Harvard University Press, 1961. xiv, 693 p. ports. 23 cm. Bibliography: p. 675-681. 1. Peel, Robert, Sir, 1788-1850. I. T.
DA536.P3G3   923.242   LC 61-9686

Gash, Norman.   3.1606
Sir Robert Peel; the life of Sir Robert Peel after 1830. Totowa, N.J., Rowman and Littlefield [1972] xx, 743 p. illus. 23 cm. 1. Peel, Robert, Sir, 1788-1850. I. T.
DA536.P3 G32 1972b   942.081/092/4   LC 72-171399   ISBN 0874711320

Ziegler, Philip.   3.1607
King William IV. — [1st U.S. ed.]. — New York: Harper & Row, [1973] x, 372 p.: illus.; 22 cm. 1. William IV, King of Great Britain, 1765-1837. 2. Great Britain — History — William IV, 1830-1837 I. T.
DA539.Z5 1973   942.07/5/0924 B   LC 71-181652   ISBN 0060147881

DA550–565 Victorian Era (1837–1901)

Bourne, Kenneth.   ● 3.1608
The foreign policy of Victorian England, 1830–1902. — Oxford: Clarendon P., 1970. xii, 531 p.; 23 cm. 1. Gt. Brit. — Foreign relations — 1837-1901. 2. Gt. Brit. — History — Victoria, 1837-1901 — Sources. I. T.
DA550.B68 1970   327.42   LC 75-543411   ISBN 0198730071

Burn, William Laurence.   ● 3.1609
The age of equipoise; a study of the mid–Victorian generation. — New York: Norton, [1964] 340 p.; 24 cm. 1. Great Britain — History — Victoria, 1837-1901 2. Great Britain — Civilization I. T.
DA550.B8   914.2   LC 64-2007

Jones, Wilbur Devereux.   3.1610
The Peelites, 1846–1857, by Wilbur Devereux Jones [and] Arvel B. Erickson. [Columbus] Ohio State University Press [1972] xii, 259 p. 24 cm. 1. Peel, Robert, Sir, 1788-1850. 2. Conservative Party (Great Britain) 3. Great Britain — Politics and government — 1837-1901 I. Erickson, Arvel B. joint author. II. T.
DA550.J65   942.081   LC 79-157717   ISBN 0814201628

Southgate, Donald.   ● 3.1611
The passing of the Whigs, 1832–1886. — London: Macmillan; New York: St. Martin's Press, 1962. xvi, 488 p.: ill.; 23 cm. 1. Gt. Brit. — Pol. & govt. — 1837-1901. I. T.
DA550.S65 1962   942.08   LC 62-51525

Young, G. M. (George Malcolm), 1882-1959.   ● 3.1612
Victorian England; portrait of an age. 2d ed. London, Oxford University Press [1960] 219 p.; 20 cm. (Oxford paperbacks, no. 12) 1. Great Britain — History — Victoria, 1837-1901 I. T.
DA550.Y6 1960   942.08   LC 60-51632

Victoria, Queen of Great Britain, 1819-1901.   3.1613
Dear and honoured lady; the correspondence between Queen Victoria and Alfred Tennyson. Edited by Hope Dyson and Charles Tennyson. — [1st American ed.]. — Rutherford [N.J.]: Fairleigh Dickinson University Press, [1971, c1969] 152 p.: illus., facsims., ports.; 22 cm. I. Tennyson, Alfred Tennyson, Baron, 1809-1892. II. Dyson, Hope. ed. III. Tennyson, Charles, Sir, 1879- ed. IV. T.
DA552.D38 1971   942.081/0924 B   LC 72-151284   ISBN 0838679226

Longford, Elizabeth Harman Pakenham, Countess of, 1906-.   ● 3.1614
[Victoria R.I.] Queen Victoria: born to succeed, by Elizabeth Longford. [1st ed.] New York, Harper & Row [1965, c1964] 635 p. illus., fold. geneal. table, ports. 25 cm. First published in London in 1964 under title: Victoria R.I. 1. Victoria, Queen of Great Britain, 1819-1901. 2. Great Britain — Kings and rulers — Biography 3. Great Britain — History — 1837-1901. I. T.
DA554.L6 1965   923.142   LC 64-25117

Strachey, Lytton, 1880-1932.   ● 3.1615
Queen Victoria, by Lytton Strachey. London, Chatto & Windus, 1969. [6], 257 p. 23 cm. 1. Victoria, Queen of Great Britain, 1819-1901. 2. Great Britain

— Kings and rulers — Biography 3. Great Britain — History — Victoria, 1837-1901 I. T.
DA554.S7 1969   942.081/0924 B   LC 72-435370   ISBN 0701111313

Woodham Smith, Cecil Blanche Fitz Gerald, 1896-.   3.1616
Queen Victoria, from her birth to the death of the Prince Consort [by] Cecil Woodham–Smith. — [1st American ed.]. — New York: Knopf; [distributed by Random House], 1972. xii, 486 p.: illus.; 25 cm. 1. Victoria, Queen of Great Britain, 1819-1901. 2. Great Britain — History — Victoria, 1837-1901 I. T.
DA554.W8 1972   942.081/092/4 B   LC 72-2235   ISBN 039448245X

Gash, Norman.   ● 3.1617
Reaction and reconstruction in English politics, 1832–1852. Oxford, Clarendon Press, 1965. 227 p. 22 cm. (The Ford lectures, 1964) Bibliography: p. [219] Bibliographical footnotes. 1. Great Britain — Politics and government — 1830-1837 2. Great Britain — Politics and government — 1837-1901 I. T.
DA559.7.G35   LC 66-609

Briggs, Asa, 1921-.   ● 3.1618
Victorian people; a reassessment of persons and themes, 1851–67. — Rev. ed. — [Chicago]: University of Chicago Press, [1970] ix, 312 p.: illus.; 21 cm. 1. Gt. Brit. — History — Victoria, 1837-1901. 2. Gt. Brit. — Biography. I. T.
DA560.B84 1970   914.2/03/810922 B   LC 71-16973   ISBN 0226074900

Ensor, Robert Charles Kirkwood, 1877-.   ● 3.1619
England, 1870–1914, by R. C. K. Ensor. — Oxford: The Clarendon press, 1936. xxiii, 634 p., 1 l.: 7 fold. maps.; 23 cm. — (Oxford history of England. 14) 1. Great Britain — History — Victoria, 1867-1901. 2. Great Britain — History — 20th century I. T. II. Series.
DA560.E6   942.08   LC 36-10581

Feuchtwanger, E. J.   3.1620
Democracy and empire: Britain, 1865–1914 / E.J. Feuchtwanger. — London: E. Arnold, 1985. 408 p.: ports.; 25 cm. (The New history of England; 9) Ports. on lining papers. Includes index. 1. Great Britain — Politics and government — 1837-1901 2. Great Britain — Politics and government — 1901-1936 I. T.
DA560.F48 1985   941.081 19   LC 85-173115   ISBN 0713161612

Howard, Christopher H. D. (Christopher Henry Durham), 1913-. ● 3.1621
Splendid isolation: a study of ideas concerning Britain's international and foreign policy during the later years of the third Marquis of Salisbury. London, Melbourne [etc.] Macmillan; New York, St. Martin's P., 1967. xv, 120 p. 23 cm. 1. Great Britain — Foreign relations — 1837-1901 I. T.
DA560.H59   327.42   LC 67-19736

Kennedy, Paul M., 1945-.   3.1622
The realities behind diplomacy: background influences on British external policy, 1865–1980 / Paul Kennedy. — London; Boston: Allen & Unwin in association with Fontana Books, 1981. 416 p.; 18 cm. 1. Great Britain — Foreign relations — 1837-1901 2. Great Britain — Foreign relations — 20th century 3. Great Britain — Politics and government — 1837-1901 4. Great Britain — Politics and government — 20th century 5. Great Britain — Economic conditions — 19th century 6. Great Britain — Economic conditions — 20th century I. T.
DA560.K43   327.41 19   LC 81-161801   ISBN 0049020056

Pugh, Martin.   3.1623
The making of modern British politics, 1867–1939 / Martin Pugh. — New York: St. Martin's Press, 1982. xi, 337 p.: ill.; 24 cm. Includes index. 1. Political parties — Great Britain — History. 2. Great Britain — Politics and government — 1901-1936 3. Great Britain — Politics and government — 1936-1945 4. Great Britain — Politics and government — 1837-1901 I. T.
DA560.P79 1982   941.08 19   LC 81-23292   ISBN 0312507011

DA562–565 Biography. Memoirs

Strachey, Lytton, 1880-1932.   3.1624
Eminent Victorians, by Lytton Strachey. With four portraits. Garden City, N.Y., Garden City publishing co., inc. [1918? ix, 351 p. 4 port. (incl. front.) 21 cm. At head of title: Cardinal Manning—Florence Nightingale—Dr. Arnold—General Gordon. Bibliography at end of each biography. 1. Manning, Henry Edward, 1808-1892. 2. Nightingale, Florence, 1820-1910. 3. Arnold, Thomas, 1795-1842. 4. Gordon, Charles George, 1833-1885. I. T.
DA562.S8 1918b   920.042   LC 30-30967

DA563–564 Prime Ministers

Feuchtwanger, E. J.   3.1625
Gladstone / E. J. Feuchtwanger. — New York: St. Martin's Press, 1975. x, 315 p.; 23 cm. (British political biography) Includes index. 1. Gladstone,

William Ewart, 1809-1898. 2. Great Britain — Politics and government —
1837-1901 I. T.
DA563.4.F48 1975b   941.081/092/4 B   *LC* 75-7712

Morley, John, 1838-1923.   • **3.1626**
The life of William Ewart Gladstone. New York, Greenwood Press [1968,
c1903] 3 v. illus. 24 cm. 1. Gladstone, W. E. (William Ewart), 1809-1898.
2. Great Britain — Politics and government — 1837-1901 I. T.
DA563.4.M8 1968   942.081/092/4 B   *LC* 68-57630

Shannon, Richard.   **3.1627**
Gladstone / Richard Shannon. — Chapel Hill: University of North Carolina
Press, 1984. 580 p.: ill. Originally published: London: Hamilton, 1982.
1. Gladstone, W. E. (William Ewart), 1809-1898. 2. Prime ministers — Great
Britain — Biography. 3. Great Britain — Politics and government —
1837-1901 I. T.
DA563.4.S5 1984   941.081/092/4 B 19   *LC* 83-19860   *ISBN*
0807815918

Hammond, John Lawrence Le Breton, 1872-1949.   • **3.1628**
Gladstone and liberalism, by J. L. Hammond and M. R. D. Foot. New York,
Collier Books [1966] 180 p. 18 cm. 'Note on books': p. 167-168. 1. Gladstone,
W. E. (William Ewart), 1809-1898. 2. Liberal Party (Great Britain) 3. Great
Britain — Politics and government — 1837-1901 I. Foot, M. R. D. (Michael
Richard Daniel), 1919- joint author. II. T.
DA563.5.H28 1966   942.0810924 B   *LC* 66-27708

Blake, Robert, 1916-.   • **3.1629**
Disraeli. New York, St. Martin's Press [1967, c1966] xxiv, 819 p. illus., ports.
24 cm. 1. Disraeli, Benjamin, Earl of Beaconsfield, 1804-1881. I. T.
DA564.B3 B6 1967   942.081/0924 B   *LC* 67-11837

Hibbert, Christopher, 1924-.   **3.1630**
Disraeli and his world / Christopher Hibbert. — New York: Scribner, c1978.
128 p.: ill.; 24 cm. Includes index. 1. Disraeli, Benjamin, Earl of Beaconsfield,
1804-1881. 2. Prime ministers — Great Britain — Biography. 3. Great Britain
— Politics and government — 1837-1901 I. T.
DA564.B3 H52 1978b   941.081/092/4 B   *LC* 78-59111   *ISBN*
0684159155

Rhodes James, Robert, 1933-.   • **3.1631**
Rosebery, a biography of Archibald Philip, fifth earl of Rosebery. [Reprinted,
with some amendments]. — London, Weidenfeld and Nicolson [1963] xiv,
534 p. illus., ports, map. 23 cm. 'Notes on sources': p. [513]-516.
Bibliography: p. [517]-521. 1. Rosebery, Archibald Philip Primrose, Earl of,
1847-1929. I. T.
DA564.R7J3 1963   *LC* 63-24262

Prest, John M.   **3.1632**
Lord John Russell [by] John Prest. Columbia, University of South Carolina
Press [1972] xvi, 558 p. illus. 24 cm. 1. Russell, John Russell, Earl, 1792-1878.
I. T.
DA564.R8 P73 1972b   942.081/092/4 B   *LC* 72-5340   *ISBN*
0872492699

DA565 Other Contemporaries

Robbins, Keith.   **3.1633**
John Bright / Keith Robbins. — London; Boston: Routledge & K. Paul, 1979.
xvi, 288 p., [8] leaves of plates: ill.; 23 cm. Includes index. 1. Bright, John,
1811-1889. 2. Statesmen — Great Britain — Biography. 3. Great Britain —
Politics and government — 1837-1901 I. T.
DA565.B8 R59   942.081/092/4 B   *LC* 79-309083   *ISBN*
0710089929

Trevelyan, George Macaulay, 1876-1962.   • **3.1634**
The life of John Bright. — Westport, Conn.: Greenwood Press, [1971] x, [1],
480 p.: illus.; 23 cm. Reprint of the 1913 ed. 1. Bright, John, 1811-1889. 2. Gt.
Brit. — Politics and government — 19th century. I. T.
DA565.B8 T8 1971   942.081/0924 B   *LC* 72-110873   *ISBN*
083714552X

Wilson, John, 1924-.   **3.1635**
CB: a life of Sir Henry Campbell-Bannerman. — New York: St. Martin's Press,
[1974, c1973] 717 p.: illus.; 25 cm. 1. Campbell-Bannerman, Henry, Sir,
1836-1908. I. T.
DA565.C15 W54 1974   942.082/092/4 B   *LC* 73-85379

Jay, Richard.   **3.1636**
Joseph Chamberlain, a political study / Richard Jay. — Oxford: Clarendon
Press; New York: Oxford University Press, 1981. ix, 383 p., [1] leaf of plates:
port.; 23 cm. Includes index. 1. Chamberlain, Joseph, 1836-1914. 2. Statesmen

— Great Britain — Biography. 3. Great Britain — Politics and government —
1901-1910 4. Great Britain — Politics and government — 1837-1901 I. T.
DA565.C4 J39   941.081/092/4 19   *LC* 80-40812   *ISBN*
0198226233

Churchill, Winston, Sir, 1874-1965.   • **3.1637**
Lord Randolph Churchill / by Winston S. Churchill. — London: Odhams
Press, [1952]. — 840 p.: ill., ports.; 22 cm. Includes index. 1. Churchill,
Randolph Henry Spencer, Lord, 1849-1895. 2. Statesmen — Great Britain —
Biography 3. Great Britain — Politics and government — 1837-1901 I. T.
DA565.C6 C6 1952   941.0810924

Pottinger, George.   **3.1638**
The Afghan connection: the extraordinary Adventures of Major Eldred
Pottinger / George Pottinger. — Edinburgh: Scottish Academic Press, c1983.
xix, 239 p.: ill., ports. Includes index. 1. Pottinger, Eldred, 1811-1843.
2. Afghan Wars — Sources I. T.
DA565.P874 P7   *ISBN* 0707302862

DA566–592 20th Century

Pelling, Henry.   • **3.1639**
Modern Britain, 1885–1955 / Henry Pelling. — Edinburgh: T. Nelson, 1960.
xii, 212 p.: ill., maps, plates, ports.; 23 cm. — (History of England ; v. 8.)
1. Great Britain — History — Victoria, 1837-1901 2. Great Britain — History
— 20th century I. T. II. Series.
DA566.P4 1960   *LC* 61-3048

Seaman, L. C. B. (Lewis Charles Bernard)   • **3.1640**
Post–Victorian Britain: 1902–1951 [by] L. C. B. Seaman. — London, Methuen,
1966. xi, 531 p. illus., 16 plates (incl. ports) maps, tables. 22 cm.
Bibliography: p. [503]-504. 1. Gt. Brit. — Hist. — 20th cent. I. T.
DA566.S4   942.082   *LC* 66-71853

Taylor, A. J. P. (Alan John Percivale), 1906-.   • **3.1641**
English history, 1914–1945 [by] A. J. P. Taylor. — New York, Oxford
University Press, 1965. xxvii, 708 p. maps. 23 cm. — (Oxford history of
England. 15) Bibliography: p. [602]-639. 1. Gt. Brit. — Hist. — 20th cent.
I. T. II. Series.
DA566.T38   942.083   *LC* 65-27513

Barnett, Correlli.   **3.1642**
The collapse of British power. — New York: Morrow, 1972. xii, 643 p.; 24 cm.
1. National characteristics, English 2. Great Britain — Foreign relations —
20th century 3. Great Britain — Politics and government — 20th century
4. Commonwealth of Nations — History. I. T.
DA566.2.B37   327.42   *LC* 71-182972   *ISBN* 0688000010

Graves, Robert, 1895-.   **3.1643**
The long week end: a social history of Great Britain, 1918–1939 / by Robert
Graves and Alan Hodge. — 1st print. — New York: Macmillan Co., 1941. x,
[1], 455 p. First American edition. Higginson A52b. 1. Great Britain —
History — 20th century 2. Great Britain — Social life and customs — 20th
century I. Hodge, Alan, 1915- (joint author) II. T.
DA566.4.G7x 1941   *LC* 41-8248

Marwick, Arthur, 1936-.   • **3.1644**
Britain in the century of total war; war, peace, and social change, 1900–1967. —
[1st American ed.]. — Boston: Little, Brown, [1968] 511 p.; 22 cm. 'An Atlantic
Monthly Press book.' 1. History, Modern — 20th century 2. Great Britain —
Civilization — 20th century I. T.
DA566.4.M357 1968   942.082   *LC* 68-17276

Williams, Raymond.   • **3.1645**
The long revolution. New York, Columbia University Press, 1961. 369 p. 23
cm. 1. Great Britain — Intellectual life I. T.
DA566.4.W48   914.2   *LC* 61-6336

DA566.7 POLITICAL AND DIPLOMATIC HISTORY

Barber, James.   **3.1646**
Who makes British foreign policy? / James Barber. — Milton Keynes: Open
University Press, 1976. 132 p.: diagr.; 21 cm. 1. Great Britain — Foreign
relations I. T.
DA566.7.B37   *ISBN* 0335019625

Beer, Samuel Hutchison, 1911-.   **3.1647**
British politics in the collectivist age, by Samuel H. Beer. — [1st ed.]. — New
York, Knopf, 1965. xii, 390, xiii p. 22 cm. Bibliographical footnotes. 1. Gt.
Brit. — Pol. & govt. — 20th cent. 2. Political parties — Gt. Brit. I. T.
DA566.7.B4   320.942   *LC* 65-11116 rev

Beloff, Max, 1913-.   • **3.1648**
Imperial sunset. — [1st American ed.]. — New York: Knopf, 1970- [c1969-.
v.   : illus., maps.; 25 cm. 1. Gt. Brit. — Foreign relations — 20th century.
I. T.
DA566.7.B442   327.42   *LC* 69-11480

Beloff, Max, 1913-.   **3.1649**
Wars and welfare: Britain, 1914–1945 / Max Beloff. — London; Baltimore,
Md., USA: E. Arnold, 1984. vi, 281 p.; 25 cm. (The New history of England; 10)
Includes index. 1. Great Britain — Politics and government — 20th century
I. T.
DA566.7.B446 1984   941.083 19   *LC* 84-116530   *ISBN*
0713161639

Lloyd, Trevor Owen.   • **3.1650**
Empire to welfare state; English history 1906–1967 [by] T. O. Lloyd. —
[London]: Oxford University Press, 1970. xv, 465 p.: illus., maps.; 24 cm. —
(Short Oxford history of the modern world.) 1. Great Britain — Politics and
government — 20th century 2. Great Britain — Economic conditions — 20th
century 3. Great Britain — Social conditions — 20th century I. T. II. Series.
DA566.7.L56   942.082   *LC* 78-134634

Medlicott, W. N. (William Norton), 1900-.   • **3.1651**
British foreign policy since Versailles, 1919–1963 [by] W. N. Medlicott. 2nd ed.
revised & enlarged. London, Methuen, 1968. xxi, 362 p. 22 cm. 'Distributed in
the U.S.A. by Barnes & Noble.' 1. World politics — 20th century 2. Great
Britain — Foreign relations — 20th century 3. Europe — Politics and
government — 1918-1945 I. T.
DA566.7.M4 1968   327.42   *LC* 73-363297   *ISBN* 0416107702

DA566.9 BIOGRAPHY. MEMOIRS

DA566.9 A–J

Young, G. M. (George Malcolm), 1882-1959.   • **3.1652**
Stanley Baldwin. London, R. Hart-Davis, 1952. 266 p. illus. 23 cm. 1. Baldwin,
Stanley Baldwin, Earl, 1867-1947. 2. Great Britain — Politics and government
— 1910- I. T.
DA566.9.B15Y6 1952   923.242   *LC* 52-14968

Zebel, Sydney Henry, 1914-.   **3.1653**
Balfour; a political biography [by] Sydney H. Zebel. — Cambridge [Eng.]:
University Press, 1973. viii, 312 p.; 23 cm. — (Conference on British Studies.
Biographical series) 1. Balfour, Arthur James Balfour, 1st Earl of, 1848-1930.
I. T. II. Series.
DA566.9.B2 Z42 1973   942.08/092/4   *LC* 70-190421   *ISBN*
0521085365

Taylor, A. J. P. (Alan John Percivale), 1906-.   **3.1654**
Beaverbrook [by] A. J. P. Taylor. New York, Simon and Schuster [1972] xvii,
712 p. illus. 25 cm. 1. Beaverbrook, Max Aitken, Baron, 1879-1964. I. T.
DA566.9.B37 T39 1972b   070.5/092/4 B   *LC* 72-80688   *ISBN*
0671213768

Churchill, Winston, Sir, 1874-1965.   • **3.1655**
The unwritten alliance: speeches 1953 to 1959. Edited by Randolph S.
Churchill. London, Cassell [1961] xi, 332 p. 23 cm. 1. Great Britain — Politics
and government — 1945-   - Addresses, essays, lectures. 2. Great Britain —
Relations — United States 3. United States — Relations — Great Britain I. T.
DA566.9.C5 A375 1961   *LC* 63-6468

Gilbert, Martin, 1936-.   **3.1656**
Winston Churchill, the wilderness years / Martin Gilbert. — 1st American ed.
— Boston: Houghton Mifflin, 1982. 279 p.: ill.; 24 cm. Includes index.
1. Churchill, Winston, Sir, 1874-1965. 2. Prime ministers — Great Britain —
Biography. 3. Great Britain — Politics and government — 1936-1945 4. Great
Britain — Politics and government — 1910-1936 I. T.
DA566.9.C5 G463 1982   941.082/092/4 B 19   *LC* 82-9279   *ISBN*
0395318696

Manchester, William Raymond, 1922-.   **3.1657**
The last lion, Winston Spencer Churchill: visions of glory, 1874–1932 / William
Manchester. — 1st ed. — Boston: Little, Brown, c1983. xv, 973 p.: ill., maps,
ports. Includes index. 1. Churchill, Winston, Sir, 1874-1965. 2. Prime
ministers — Great Britain — Biography. 3. Great Britain — Foreign relations
— 1901-1910 4. Great Britain — Foreign relations — 1910-1936 5. Great
Britain — Politics and government — 1901-1936 I. T.
DA566.9.C5 M26 1983   DA566.9C5 M26 1983.   941.084/092/4 B 19
LC 82-24972   *ISBN* 0316545031

Pelling, Henry.   **3.1658**
Winston Churchill / Henry Pelling. — 1st ed. — New York: Dutton, [1974]
724 p., [8] leaves of plates: ill.; 23 cm. Includes index. 1. Churchill, Winston,
Sir, 1874-1965. I. T.
DA566.9.C5 P38 1974b   942.082/092/4 B   *LC* 73-21276   *ISBN*
0525235108

Schoenfeld, Maxwell Philip, 1936-.   • **3.1659**
The war ministry of Winston Churchill. [1st ed.] Ames, Iowa State University
Press [1972] xix, 283 p. illus. 23 cm. 1. Churchill, Winston, Sir, 1874-1965.
2. World War, 1939-1945 — Great Britain. 3. Great Britain — Foreign
relations — 1936-1945 I. T.
DA566.9.C5 S36   942.084   *LC* 72-153159   *ISBN* 0813802601

Thompson, Kenneth W., 1921-.   **3.1660**
Winston Churchill's world view: statesmanship and power / Kenneth W.
Thompson. — Baton Rouge: Louisiana State University Press, c1983. viii,
364 p.; 24 cm. 1. Churchill, Winston, Sir, 1874-1965 — Views on international
relations. 2. International relations I. T.
DA566.9.C5 T39 1983   327.1/01 19   *LC* 82-4699   *ISBN*
0807110450

Citrine, Walter McLennan Citrine, baron, 1887-.   • **3.1661**
Men and work: an autobiography / [by] Lord Citrine. — London: Hutchinson
[1964] 384 p.: ports.; 24 cm. 1. Trades Union Congress. 2. Great Britain —
Politics and government — 20th century 3. Labor and laboring classes — Gt.
Brit. I. T.
DA566.9 C515 A3

Eden, Anthony, Earl of Avon, 1897-.   • **3.1662**
Facing the dictators; the memoirs of Anthony Eden, earl of Avon. — Boston:
Houghton Mifflin, 1962. 746 p.: illus.; 23 cm. Sequel: The reckoning. 1. Great
Britain — Foreign relations — 1910-1936 2. Great Britain — Foreign relations
— 1936-1945 I. T.
DA566.9.E28 A36   941.085/5/0924 B   *LC* 62-18265

Eden, Anthony, Earl of Avon, 1897-.   • **3.1663**
Full circle; the memoirs of Anthony Eden. — Boston: Houghton Mifflin, 1960.
676 p.: illus.; 22 cm. Sequel to The reckoning. 1. Great Britain — Politics and
government — 1945-1964 I. T.
DA566.9.E28 A363 1960   923.242   *LC* 59-8856

Eden, Anthony, Earl of Avon, 1897-.   **3.1664**
The reckoning; the memoirs of Anthony Eden, Earl of Avon. — Boston:
Houghton Mifflin Co., 1965. x, 716 p.: maps (part fold.); 22 cm. Sequel to
Facing the dictators. Sequel: Full circle. 1. World War, 1939-1945 —
Diplomatic history I. T.
DA566.9.E28 A37 1965b   940.532242   *LC* 65-15163

Carlton, David, 1938-.   **3.1665**
Anthony Eden: a biography / David Carlton. — London: A. Lane, 1981.
528 p., [8] p. of plates: ill., ports. 1. Eden, Anthony, Earl of Avon, 1897-
2. Prime ministers — Great Britain — Biography. I. T.
DA566.9.E28 C36   DA566.9E28 C36.   *ISBN* 0713918297

Williams, Philip Maynard.   **3.1666**
Hugh Gaitskell: a political biography / Philip M. Williams. — London: J. Cape,
1980 (c1979). xx, 1007 p.; [16] leaves of plates: ill.; 24 cm. Includes index.
1. Gaitskell, Hugh, 1906-1963. 2. Politicians — Great Britain — Biography.
3. Great Britain — Politics and government — 1945-1964 4. Great Britain —
Politics and government — 1936-1945 I. T.
DA566.9.G3 W54   941.0855/092/4 B   *LC* 79-322770   *ISBN*
022401451X

Koss, Stephen E.   • **3.1667**
Lord Haldane; scapegoat for liberalism [by] Stephen E. Koss. — New York:
Columbia University Press, 1969. ix, 263 p.: facsims., ports.; 24 cm.
1. Haldane, R. B. Haldane (Richard Burdon Haldane), Viscount, 1856-1928.
I. T.
DA566.9.H27 K6   942.083/0924   *LC* 69-19460

DA566.9 L–Z

Grigg, John, 1924-.   **3.1668**
Lloyd George, from peace to war, 1912–1916 / John Grigg. — Berkeley:
University of California Press, 1985. 527 p., [16] p. of plates: ill.; 24 cm.
Continues: Lloyd George, the people's champion, 1902-1911. 1. Lloyd George,
David, 1863-1945 — Political career before 1917. 2. Statesmen — Great
Britain — Biography. 3. Great Britain — Politics and government —
1901-1936 I. T.
DA566.9.L5 G777 1985   941.083/092/4 B 19   *LC* 84-16150
ISBN 0520054172

Grigg, John, 1924-.   3.1669
Lloyd George, the people's champion, 1902–1911 / John Grigg. — Berkeley: University of California Press, c1978. 391 p., [5] leaves of plates: ill.; 24 cm. Continues The young Lloyd George. Sequel: Lloyd George, from peace to war, 1912-1916. Includes index. 1. Lloyd George, David, 1863-1945. 2. Statesmen — Great Britain — Biography. 3. Great Britain — Politics and government — 1901-1936 I. T.
DA566.9.L5 G78 1978b   941.083/092/4 B   *LC* 77-91762   *ISBN* 0520036344

Grigg, John, 1924-.   3.1670
The young Lloyd George. Berkeley, University of California Press [1974, c1973] 320 p. illus. 24 cm. Continued by Lloyd George, the people's champion, 1902-1911. 1. Lloyd George, David, 1863-1945. I. T.
DA566.9.L5 G8 1974   942.081/092/4 B   *LC* 73-91067   *ISBN* 0520026772

Perham, Margery Freda, Dame, 1895-.   • 3.1671
Lugard, by Margery Perham. — Hamden, Conn.: Archon Books, 1968. 2 v.: illus., maps, ports.; 23 cm. Reprint of the 1956 ed. 1. Lugard, Frederick John Dealtry, Baron, 1858-1945. I. T.
DA566.9.L82 P42   966.9/03/0924 B   *LC* 68-6290

Marquand, David.   3.1672
Ramsay MacDonald / David Marquand. London: J. Cape, 1977. xvi, 903 p., [20] leaves of plates: ill.; 24 cm. Includes index. 1. MacDonald, James Ramsay, 1866-1937. 2. Prime ministers — Great Britain — Biography. 3. Great Britain — Politics and government — 1910-1936 I. T.
DA566.9.M25 M37   942.083/092/4 B   *LC* 77-358953   *ISBN* 0224012959

Macmillan, Harold, 1894-.   • 3.1673
Tides of fortune, 1945–1955. — [1st U.S. ed.]. — New York: Harper & Row, [1969] xxii, 729 p.: ports.; 24 cm. Autobiographical. 1. Gt. Brit. — Politics and government — 20th century. 2. Gt. Brit. — Foreign relations — 20th century. I. T.
DA566.9.M33 A28 1969   942.085/0924   *LC* 78-83609

Fisher, Nigel, Sir.   3.1674
Harold Macmillan: a biography / by Nigel Fisher. — New York, N.Y.: St. Martin's Press, c1982. xi, 404 p., [8] p. of plates: ports.; 24 cm. dIncludes index. 1. Macmillan, Harold, 1894-. 2. Prime ministers — Great Britain — Biography 3. Great Britain — Politics and government — 1945-1964 I. T.
DA566.9.M33 F57 1982   941.085/5/0924 B 19   *LC* 81-48509   *ISBN* 0312363222

Gollin, A. M. (Alfred M.)   • 3.1675
Proconsul in politics; a study of Lord Milner in opposition and in power, by A.M. Gollin. With an introductory section, 1854–1905. New York: Macmillan, 1964. xi, 627 p.: ill., ports;23 cm. I. T.
DA566.9.M5 G6 1964a   *LC* 64-13121

Darroch, Sandra Jobson.   3.1676
Ottoline: the life of Lady Ottoline Morrell / Sandra Jobson Darroch. — 1st American ed. — New York: Coward, McCann & Geoghegan, 1975. 317 p., [16] leaves of plates: ill.; 24 cm. Includes index. 1. Morrell, Ottoline Violet Anne Cavendish-Bentinck, Lady, 1873-1938. 2. England — Intellectual life — 20th century I. T.
DA566.9.M63 D37 1975   941.083/0924 B   *LC* 74-16641   *ISBN* 0698106342

Koss, Stephen E.   3.1677
Asquith / Stephen Koss. — New York: St. Martin's Press, 1976. x, 310 p.; 23 cm. (British political biography) Includes index. 1. Asquith, H. H. (Herbert Henry), 1852-1928. 2. Prime ministers — Great Britain — Biography. 3. Great Britain — Politics and government — 1901-1936 4. Great Britain — Politics and government — 1837-1901 I. T.
DA566.9.O7 K67 1976b   941.083/092/4 B   *LC* 76-20200

Vernon, Betty.   3.1678
Ellen Wilkinson, 1891–1947 / Betty D. Vernon. — London: Croom Helm, 1982. 254 p.; 23 cm. Includes index. 1. Wilkinson, Ellen Cicely, 1891-1947. 2. Statesmen — Great Britain — Biography. 3. Great Britain — Politics and government — 20th century I. T.
DA566.9.W459 V47 1982   941.082/092/4 B 19   *LC* 81-208231   *ISBN* 0856649848

DA567–570 Edward VII, 1901–1910

Magnus, Philip Montefiore, Sir, bart., 1906-.   • 3.1679
King Edward the Seventh [by] Philip Magnus. [1st ed.] New York, Dutton, 1964. xv, 528 p. illus., geneal. tables, ports. (part col.) 24 cm. 1. Edward VII, King of Great Britain, 1841-1910. I. T.
DA567.M26 1964   923.142   *LC* 64-11062

St. Aubyn, Giles.   3.1680
Edward VII, Prince and King / Giles St. Aubyn. — New York: Atheneum, 1979. 555 p., [16] leaves of plates: ill.; 24 cm. Includes index. 1. Edward VII, King of Great Britain, 1841-1910. 2. Great Britain — History — Victoria, 1837-1901 3. Great Britain — History — Edward VII, 1901-1910 4. Great Britain — Kings and rulers — Biography I. T.
DA567.S24   DA567 S134 1979a.   941.082/3/0924 B   *LC* 78-63294   *ISBN* 0689109377

Cross, Colin.   • 3.1681
The Liberals in power, 1905–1914. — London, Barrie and Rockliff [1963] x, 198 p. ports. 22 cm. Bibliography: p. 190-192. 1. Gt. Brit. — Pol. & govt. — 1901-1936. 2. Liberal Party (Gt. Brit.) I. T.
DA570.C7   *LC* 64-9229

Hynes, Samuel Lynn.   3.1682
The Edwardian turn of mind / by Samuel Hynes. — Princeton, N.J.: Princeton University Press, 1971 (c1968). xiv, 427 p.: ill., geneal. table, ports.; 23 cm. 1. Great Britain — Civilization — 19th century I. T.
DA570.H9   914.2/03/82   *LC* 68-12929

Searle, G. R. (Geoffrey Russell)   3.1683
The quest for national efficiency: a study in British politics and political thought, 1899–1914 [by] G. R. Searle. — Berkeley: University of California Press, 1971. x, 286 p.; 23 cm. 1. Great Britain — Politics and government — 1901-1936 2. Great Britain — Politics and government — 1837-1901 I. T.
DA570.S4 1971b   320.9/42/082   *LC* 75-126758   *ISBN* 0520017943

DA573–580 George V, 1910–1936. Edward VIII, 1936

Nicolson, Harold George, Sir, 1886-1968.   • 3.1684
King George the Fifth: his life and reign / Hon. Harold George Nicolson. — London: Constable, 1952. xxiii, 570 p.: plates, ports; 24 cm. 'Reference notes': p. 535-539. 1. George V, King of Britain, 1865-1936. I. T.
DA573.N5   *LC* 52-10694

Keynes, John Maynard, 1883-1946.   • 3.1685
Essays in biography: new edition with three additional essays ed. by Geoffrey Keynes. New York: Horizon Press, 1951. 354 p.: port.; 20 cm. 1. Statesmen 2. Statesmen, British. 3. Economists, British. 4. Economists — History — Great Britain 5. Europe — Politics — 1914- I. Keynes,Geoffrey Langdon, 1887- ed II. T.
DA574 .A1 K4   *LC* 51-7759

Skidelsky, Robert Jacob Alexander, 1939-.   3.1686
Oswald Mosley [by] Robert Skidelsky. New York, Holt, Rinehart and Winston [c1975] 578 p. illus. 23 cm. 1. Mosley, Oswald, Sir, 1896- 2. Statesmen — Great Britain — Biography. I. T.
DA574.M6 S55   942.084/092/4 B   *LC* 74-6941   *ISBN* 0030865808

Blake, Robert, 1916-.   3.1687
The decline of power, 1915–1964 / Robert Blake. — New York: Oxford University Press, 1985. x, 462 p., [6] p. of plates: maps; 24 cm. (Paladin history of England.) Includes index. 1. Great Britain — Politics and government — 1910-1936 2. Great Britain — Politics and government — 1936-1945 3. Great Britain — Politics and government — 1945-1964 I. T. II. Series.
DA576.B53 1985   941.082 19   *LC* 85-4909   *ISBN* 0195204808

Dangerfield, George, 1904-1986.   • 3.1688
The strange death of Liberal England. — New York, Capricorn Books [1961, c1935] 449 p. 19 cm. — (A Capricorn book, CAP50) 1. Gt. Brit. — Pol. & govt. — 1910-1936. 2. Liberalism 3. Liberal Party (Gt. Brit.) I. T. II. Title: Liberal England.
DA576.D3 1961   942.083   *LC* 61-2982

Morgan, Kenneth O.   3.1689
Consensus and disunity: the Lloyd George Coalition government, 1918–1922 / Kenneth O. Morgan. — Oxford: Clarendon Press; New York: Oxford University Press, 1979. ix, 436 p.: graphs; 23 cm. Includes index. 1. Lloyd George, David, 1863-1945. 2. Labor policy — Great Britain. 3. Great Britain — Politics and government — 1910-1936 4. Great Britain — Social policy. 5. Great Britain — Foreign relations — 1910-1936 I. T.
DA576.M67   320.9/41/083   *LC* 79-40263   *ISBN* 0198224974

Northedge, F. S.   • 3.1690
The troubled giant; Britain among the great powers, 1916–1939, by F. S. Northedge. — New York: Published for the London School of Economics and Political Science [by] Praeger, [1966, i.e. 1967] xi, 657 p.: maps; 23 cm. 1. World politics — 1900-1945 2. Great Britain — Foreign relations — 1910-1936 3. Great Britain — Foreign relations — 1936-1945 I. London School of Economics and Political Science. II. T.
DA576.N6 1967   327.42   *LC* 66-26556

Wilson, Trevor, 1928-.   • 3.1691
The downfall of the Liberal Party, 1914–1935 [by] Trevor Wilson. Ithaca, N.Y., Cornell University Press [1966] 415 p. illus., ports. 22 cm. 1. Liberal Party (Great Britain) 2. Great Britain — Politics and government — 1910-1936 I. T.
DA576.W55 1966a   329.942   LC 66-27932

Beaverbrook, Max Aitken, Baron, 1879-1964.   • 3.1692
Men and power, 1917–1918. [Hamden, Conn.] Archon Books, 1968 [c1956] 447 p. illus., facsims., ports. 23 cm. 1. World War, 1914-1918 — Great Britain 2. Great Britain — Politics and government — 1910-1936 I. T.
DA577.B34 1968   320.9/42   LC 68-7599

Marwick, Arthur, 1936-.   • 3.1693
The deluge; British society and the First World War. [1st American ed.] Boston, Little, Brown [1966, c1965] 336 p. illus. 22 cm. 1. World War, 1914-1918 — Great Britain 2. Reconstruction (1914-1939) — Great Britain. 3. Great Britain — Social conditions — 20th century I. T.
DA577.M37   914.20383   LC 66-10818

Woodward, David R., 1939-.   3.1694
Lloyd George and the generals / David R. Woodward. — Newark: University of Delaware Press; London: Associated University Presses, c1983. 367 p.: ill.; 25 cm. Includes index. 1. Lloyd George, David, 1863-1945. 2. World War, 1914-1918 — Great Britain 3. Great Britain — Politics and government — 1910-1936 I. T.
DA577.W66 1983   941.083 19   LC 81-52983   ISBN 0874132118

Churchill, Winston, Sir, 1874-1965.   • 3.1695
While England slept; a survey of world affairs, 1932–1938. With a pref. and notes by Randolph S. Churchill. Freeport, N.Y., Books for Libraries Press [1971] xii, 404 p. port. 24 cm. Speeches. Reprint of the 1938 ed. 1. Disarmament 2. Security, International 3. Germany — Politics and government — 1933-1945 4. Great Britain — Foreign relations — 20th century 5. Europe — Politics and government — 1918-1945 I. T.
DA578.C48 1971   327.42   LC 76-165621   ISBN 0836959280

George, Margaret.   • 3.1696
The warped vision; British foreign policy, 1933–1939. [Pittsburgh] University of Pittsburgh Press [1965] xxiii, 238 p. 23 cm. Bibliography: p. 227-232. 1. Great Britain — Foreign relations — 1910-1936 2. Great Britain — Foreign relations — 1936-1945 I. T.
DA578.G39   327.42   LC 65-14623

Donaldson, Frances Lonsdale, Lady.   3.1697
Edward VIII / by Frances Donaldson. — Philadelphia: Lippincott, [1975] 477 p. [8] leaves of plates: ill.; 25 cm. 1. Windsor, Edward, Duke of, 1894-1972. 2. Great Britain — Kings and rulers — Biography 3. Great Britain — History — Edward VIII, 1936 I. T.
DA580.D64 1975   942.084/092/4 B   LC 74-31274   ISBN 0397007655

DA584–592 George VI, 1937–1952. Elizabeth II, 1952–

Wheeler-Bennett, John Wheeler, 1902-.   • 3.1698
King George VI, his life and reign. — New York, St. Martin's Press [1958] xii, 891 p. illus., ports. (part col.) geneal. table. 24 cm. Bibliography: p. 830-834. 1. George VI, King of Great Britain, 1895-1952. I. T.
DA584.W45   923.142   LC 58-13050

Foot, Michael, 1913-.   • 3.1699
Aneurin Bevan, a biography. [1st American ed.] New York: Atheneum, 1963-   [c1962. v.: ill.; 22 cm. 1. Bevan, Aneurin, 1897-1960. I. T.
DA585.B38 F62   942/.084/092/4   LC 63-17846   ISBN 0689105878

Bullock, Alan Louis Charles, 1914-.   3.1700
Ernest Bevin: foreign secretary, 1945–1951 / Alan Bullock. — New York: Norton, 1984 (c1983). xvi, 896 p., [16] p. of plates: ill., ports; 24 cm. 1. Bevin, Ernest, 1881-1951. 2. Great Britain — Politics and government — 1945-1964 3. Great Britain — Foreign relations — 1945- I. T.
DA585.B4 B79   ISBN 0393018253

Feiling, Keith Grahame, Sir, 1884-.   • 3.1701
The life of Neville Chamberlain, by Keith Feiling. — Hamden, Conn.: Archon Books, 1970. xi, 477 p.: facsim., ports.; 23 cm. Reprint of the 1946 ed. with a new pref. and bibliography (p. 467-468) 1. Chamberlain, Neville, 1869-1940. I. T.
DA585.C5 F4 1970   942.084/0924 B   LC 75-95598

Douglas, Roy, 1924-.   3.1702
In the year of Munich / Roy Douglas. — New York: St. Martin's Press, 1978 (c1977). viii, 155 p., [4] leaves of plates: ill.; 23 cm. Includes index. 1. Munich Four-Power Agreement (1938) 2. World War, 1939-1945 — Causes 3. Great

Britain — Foreign relations — 1936-1945 4. Europe — Politics and government — 1918-1945 I. T.
DA586.D6   940.53/112   LC 77-82823   ISBN 0312411790

Calder, Angus.   • 3.1703
The people's war; Britain, 1939–1945. — [1st American ed.]. — New York: Pantheon Books, [1969] 656 p.: illus., ports.; 24 cm. 1. World War, 1939-1945 — Gt. Brit. I. T.
DA587.C28 1969b   940.5342   LC 67-19178

Bartlett, C. J. (Christopher John), 1931-.   3.1704
A history of postwar Britain, 1945–1974 / C. J. Bartlett. — London; New York: Longman, 1977. viii, 360 p.; 23 cm. Includes index. 1. Great Britain — History — 20th century I. T.
DA588.B28   941.085   LC 77-3000   ISBN 0582483190

Britain and West Germany: changing societies and the future of • 3.1705
foreign policy; edited by Karl Kaiser and Roger Morgan.
London, Oxford University Press for the Royal Institute of International Affairs, 1971. x, 294 p. 23 cm. The chapters which make up this volume were presented ... to a conference convened by the Royal Institute of International Affairs in consultation with the Deutsche Gesellschaft für Answärtige Politik, and held at Chatham House in April 1969. 1. Great Britain — Foreign relations — 1945- 2. Germany (West) — Foreign relations. 3. Great Britain — Foreign relations — Germany (West) 4. Germany (West) — Foreign relations — Great Britain. I. Kaiser, Karl, 1934- ed. II. Morgan, Roger, 1932- III. Royal Institute of International Affairs. IV. Deutsche Gesellschaft für Answärtige Politik.
DA588.B63 1971   327.42/043   LC 72-869395   ISBN 0192149873

Frankel, Joseph.   3.1706
British foreign policy 1945–1973 / Joseph Frankel. — London; New York: Published for the Royal Institute of International Affairs by Oxford University Press, 1975. 356 p.; 23 cm. Includes index. 1. Great Britain — Foreign relations — 1945- 2. Great Britain — Foreign relations administration. I. T.
DA588.F697   327.41   LC 75-320212   ISBN 0192183060

Morgan, Kenneth O.   3.1707
Labour in power, 1945–1951 / by Kenneth O. Morgan. — Oxford: Clarendon Press, 1984. xviii, 546 p.; 23 cm. Includes index. 1. Attlee, C. R. (Clement Richard), 1883-1967. 2. Labour Party (Great Britain) — History. 3. Great Britain — Social policy. 4. Great Britain — Foreign relations — 1945- 5. Great Britain — Politics and government — 1945-1964 6. Great Britain — Economic policy — 1945- I. T.
DA588.M637 1984   941.085/4 19   LC 83-19290   ISBN 0192158651

Pelling, Henry.   3.1708
The labour governments, 1945–51 / Henry Pelling. — New York: St. Martin's Press, 1984. vii, 313 p., [8] leaves of plates: ill.; 23 cm. Includes index. 1. Labour Party (Great Britain) 2. Great Britain — Politics and government — 1945-1964 I. T.
DA588.P44 1984   941.0854 19   LC 83-22977   ISBN 0312462883

Sked, Alan, 1947-.   3.1709
Post–war Britain: a political history / Alan Sked and Chris Cook. — 2nd ed. — Harmondsworth, Middlesex, England; New York, N.Y., U.S.A.: Penguin, 1984. 478 p.; 20 cm. (Pelican books) (A Pelican book) Includes index. 1. Great Britain — Politics and government — 1945- I. Cook, Chris, 1945- II. T.
DA588.S53 1984   941.085 19   LC 85-130319   ISBN 0140225943

Bruce-Gardyne, Jock.   3.1710
Mrs. Thatcher's first administration: the prophets confounded / Jock Bruce–Gardyne. — New York: St. Martin's Press, 1984. xi, 199 p.; 23 cm. Includes index. 1. Thatcher, Margaret. 2. Great Britain — Politics and government — 1979- I. T.
DA589.7.B78 1984   941.085/7 19   LC 84-11528   ISBN 0312551401

Sampson, Anthony.   3.1711
The changing anatomy of Britain / Anthony Sampson. — 1st ed. — New York: Random House, c1982. xv, 476 p.; 25 cm. 1. Elite (Social sciences) — Great Britain. 2. Great Britain — Politics and government — 1979- 3. Great Britain — Economic conditions — 1945- I. T.
DA589.7.S25 1982   941.085 19   LC 82-42811   ISBN 0394531434

Longford, Elizabeth Harman Pakenham, Countess of, 1906-.   3.1712
The Queen: the life of Elizabeth II / Elizabeth Longford. — 1st American ed. — New York: Knopf: Distributed by Random House, 1983. xi, 415 p., [44] p. of plates: ill.; 25 cm. Includes index. 1. Elizabeth II, Queen of Great Britain, 1926- 2. Great Britain — Kings and rulers — Biography 3. Great Britain — History — Elizabeth II, 1952- I. T.
DA590.L64 1983   941.085/092/4 B 19   LC 83-48115   ISBN 0394523288

Castle, Barbara, 1911-.   **3.1713**
The Castle diaries, 1964–70 / Barbara Castle. — London: Weidenfeld and Nicolson, c1984. xvi, 858 p.; 26 cm. Includes index. 1. Castle, Barbara, 1911- 2. Cabinet officers — Great Britain — Biography. 3. Great Britain — Politics and government — 1964-1979 I. T.
DA591.C37 A326 1984   941.085/6/0924 B 19   LC 84-252672
    ISBN 0297783742

Crossman, R. H. S. (Richard Howard Stafford), 1907-1974.   **3.1714**
The diaries of a Cabinet Minister / [by] Richard Crossman. — New York: Holt, Rinehart & Winston, 1975. 688 p.: ill. 1. Crossman, R. H. S. (Richard Howard Stafford), 1907-1974. 2. Statesmen — Great Britain — Biography. 3. Great Britain — Politics and government — 1964-1979 I. T.
DA591.C76 A34 1975   940.085/092/4 B 19   LC 76-367071   ISBN 0241891108

Husbands, Christopher T.   **3.1715**
Racial exclusionism and the city: the urban support of the National Front / Christopher T. Husbands. — London; Boston: Allen & Unwin, 1983. xii, 191 p.: ill.; 23 cm. Includes index. 1. National Front (Great Britain) 2. Racism — Great Britain — History — 20th century. 3. Great Britain — Politics and government — 1964-1979 4. Great Britain — Race relations. 5. Great Britain — Politics and government — 1979- I. T.
DA592.H79 1983   305.8/00941 19   LC 83-7084   ISBN 0043290450

Is Britain dying?: Perspectives on the current crisis / edited by Isaac Kramnick.   **3.1716**
Ithaca, N.Y.: Cornell University Press, 1979. 286 p.; 23 cm. Essays originally presented at a conference held at Cornell University, Apr. 13-15, 1978, and sponsored by the Western Societies Program of the Center for International Studies. 1. Great Britain — Politics and government — 1964-1979 — Addresses, essays, lectures. 2. Great Britain — Economic policy — 1945- — Addresses, essays, lectures. I. Kramnick, Isaac. II. Cornell University. Western Societies Program.
DA592.I8   320.9/41/0857   LC 79-12895   ISBN 080141234X

Rhodes James, Robert, 1933-.   **3.1717**
Ambitions and realities: British politics, 1964–70. — [1st U.S. ed.] New York: Harper & Row [1972] 311 p.; 23 cm. (A Cass Canfield book) 1. Great Britain — Politics and government — 1964-1979 I. T.
DA592.J34 1972b   320.9/42/085   LC 72-79898   ISBN 0060121640

Wilson, Harold, Sir, 1916-.   **3.1718**
[Labour Government, 1964-1970] A personal record: the Labour Government, 1964–1970. — [1st American ed.] Boston: Little, Brown [1971] 386 p.: ill.; 25 cm. 'An Atlantic Monthly Press book.' First published under title: The Labour Government, 1964-1970; a personal record. 1. Wilson, Harold, Sir, 1916- 2. Great Britain — Politics and government — 1964-1979 I. T. II. Title: Labour Government, 1964-1970.
DA592.W49 1971b   942.085/0924 B   LC 70-170166

DA600–690 Description. Local History

Darby, H. C. (Henry Clifford), 1909-.   **3.1719**
A new historical geography of England, edited by H. C. Darby. Cambridge [Eng.] University Press, 1973. xiv, 767 p. illus. 24 cm. 1. England — Historical geography. I. T.
DA600.D35   942   LC 72-93145   ISBN 0521201160

Hoskins, W. G. (William George), 1908-.   **3.1720**
The making of the English landscape [by] W. G. Hoskins. [Harmondsworth, Eng.] Penguin Books [1970] 325 p. illus., maps. 18 cm. (Pelican books) 1. England — Historical geography. I. T.
DA600.H6 1970   911/.42   LC 77-21107   ISBN 0140210350

Beresford, M. W. (Maurice Warwick), 1920-.   • **3.1721**
Medieval England, an aerial survey, by M. W. Beresford & J. K. S. St. Joseph. — Cambridge [Eng.] University Press, 1958. xiii, 274 p. illus., maps. 29 cm. — (Cambridge air surveys. 2) Includes bibliographies. 1. England — Historical geography. I. St. Joseph, John Kenneth Sinclair, joint author. II. T. III. Series.
DA610.B4   942   LC 58-1947

Darby, H. C. (Henry Clifford), 1909-.   **3.1722**
Domesday England / by H. C. Darby. — Cambridge [Eng.]; New York: Cambridge University Press, 1977. xiii, 416 p., [1] leaf of plates: ill.; 24 cm. (The Domesday geography of England) 1. Domesday book. 2. England — Historical geography. I. T. II. Series.
DA610.D23   911/.42   LC 76-11485   ISBN 052121307X

Darby, H. C. (Henry Clifford), 1909-.   • **3.1723**
The Domesday geography of eastern England, by H. C. Darby. [3d ed.] Cambridge [Eng.] University Press, 1971. xiv, 400 p. illus. 24 cm. 1. Domesday book. 2. England — Historical geography. I. T.
DA610.D24 1971   911/.425   LC 70-108106   ISBN 0521080223

Darby, H. C. (Henry Clifford), 1909- ed.   • **3.1724**
The Domesday geography of midland England, edited by H. C. Darby and I. B. Terrett. 2d ed. Cambridge, University Press, 1971. xvii, 490 p. maps, facsim. 24 cm. 1. Domesday book. 2. England — Historical geography. I. Terrett, I. B., joint ed. II. T.
DA610.D25 1971   911/.426   LC 78-134626   ISBN 0521080789

Darby, H. C. (Henry Clifford), 1909-.   • **3.1725**
The Domesday geography of northern England, edited by H. C. Darby and I. S. Maxwell. Cambridge [Eng.] University Press, 1962. xv, 540 p. maps (part col.) col. facsim. 24 cm. (The Domesday geography of England, 4) 1. Domesday book. 2. England — Historical geography. I. Maxwell, Ian Stanley. II. T.
DA610.D255   LC 62-53452

Darby, H. C. (Henry Clifford), 1909- ed.   • **3.1726**
The Domesday geography of south–east England, edited by H.C. Darby and Eila M.J. Campbell. Cambridge [Eng.] University Press, 1962. xvi, 658 p. maps, facsim. 24 cm. 1. Domesday book. 2. England — Historical geography. I. Campbell, Eila M. J., joint ed. II. T.
DA610.D26   914.22   LC 62-6262

Darby, H. C. (Henry Clifford), 1909-.   • **3.1727**
The Domesday geography of South–west England, edited by H. C. Darby and R. Welldon Finn. London, Cambridge U.P., 1967. xiv, 469 p. front. (facsim.), maps (some col.), tables. 24 cm. ([The Domesday geography of England]) 1. Domesday book. 2. England — Historical geography. I. Finn, R. Welldon (Rex Welldon) II. T. III. Series.
DA610.D27   LC 67-11519

Defoe, Daniel, 1661?-1731.   • **3.1728**
A tour through England and Wales: divided into circuits or journies / by Daniel Defoe. — London: J.M. Dent; New York: E.P. Dutton, 1928. 2 v.; 18 cm. — (Everyman's library. Travel and topography; 820-821) 1. England — Description and travel 2. Wales — Description and travel I. T.
DA620.D31 1928   LC 29-103

Cobbett, William, 1763-1835.   • **3.1729**
Rural rides / by William Cobbett. — London: J.M. Dent; New York: E.P. Dutton, [1932, '30]. 2 v.: ill.; 18 cm. — (Everyman's library: Travel and topography; no. 638) 1. England — Description and travel — 1801-1900 I. T.
DA625.C654 1932   914.2

Great Britain. Central Office of Information.   • **3.1730**
Britain; an official handbook. — Annual. London: Reference Division, Central Office of Information,1949/50-. v. maps.; 22-24 cm. Annual. 1. Great Britain. 2. Great Britain — Statistics. I. T.
DA630.A17   DA632.B7.   LC 50-14073rev

Priestley, J. B. (John Boynton), 1894-.   **3.1731**
English journey / J.B. Priestley. — Jubilee ed. — Chicago: University of Chicago Press, c1984. 320 p.: ill.; 24 cm. Includes index. 1. Priestley, J. B. (John Boynton), 1894- — Journeys — England. 2. Priestley, J. B. (John Boynton), 1894- — Biography. 3. England — Description and travel — 1901-1945 I. T.
DA630.P7 1984   914.2/0483 19   LC 83-40619   ISBN 0226682129

Dury, G. H. (George Harry), 1916-.   **3.1732**
The British Isles / [by] G.H. Dury. — 5th ed. — New York: Barnes & Noble, 1973. –. xiv, 365 p.: ill., maps; 26 cm. — Includes index. - 1. Great Britain — Description and travel I. T.
DA631.D8 1973   ISBN 06491836X

Darby, H. C. (Henry Clifford), 1909-.   • **3.1733**
Domesday gazetteer / by H. C. Darby and G. R. Versey. — Cambridge [Eng.]; New York: Cambridge University Press, 1975. viii, 544 p., 65 p.: col. maps; 24 cm. 1. Domesday book. 2. England — Gazetteers. I. Versey, G. R., joint author. II. T.
DA640.D27   914.2/003   LC 75-19532   ISBN 0521206669

Ekwall, Eilert, 1877-1964.   • **3.1734**
The concise Oxford dictionary of English place–names / by Eilert Ekwall. — 4th ed. — Oxford: Clarendon Press, 1960. l, 546 p.; 24 cm. 1. Names, Geographical — England. 2. English language — Etymology — Names I. T. II. Title: English place-names.
DA645.E38 1960   LC 60-2031

DA670–690 COUNTIES. CITIES

Rowse, A. L. (Alfred Leslie), 1903-.   • **3.1735**
Tudor Cornwall; portrait of a society, by A. L. Rowse. [New ed.] New York, C. Scribner [1969] 462 p. illus., maps., port. 22 cm. 1. Cornwall (County) — History. I. T.
DA670.C8 R6 1969b   914.23/7/035   *LC* 69-17046

Hunt, William, 1944-.   **3.1736**
The Puritan moment: the coming of revolution in an English county / William Hunt. — Cambridge, Mass.: Harvard University Press, 1983. xiii, 365 p.: map; 25 cm. — (Harvard historical studies. v. 102) 1. Puritans — England — Essex — History. 2. Essex — History. 3. Essex — Economic conditions. 4. Great Britain — History — Civil War, 1642-1649 — Causes I. T. II. Series.
DA670.E7 H8 1983   942.6/7062 19   *LC* 82-11992   *ISBN* 0674739035

Clark, Peter, 1944-.   **3.1737**
English provincial society from the Reformation to the Revolution: religion, politics, and society in Kent, 1500–1640 / Peter Clark. — 1st American ed. — Rutherford [N.J.]: Fairleigh Dickinson University Press, 1978 (c1977). xiii, 504 p.: maps; 25 cm. 1. Reformation — England — Kent. 2. Kent — Politics and government. 3. Kent — Church history. I. T.
DA670.K3 C494   942.2/3/05   *LC* 76-53900   *ISBN* 0838620752

Wordsworth, William, 1770-1850.   • **3.1738**
A guide through the district of the lakes in the north of England, with a description of the scenery, &c., for the use of tourists and residents. With illus. by John Piper, and an introd. by W. M. Merchant. New York, Greenwood Press, 1968. 174 p. illus., map. 23 cm. Reprint of the 1952 ed. 1. Lake District (England) — Description and travel — Guide-books. I. T.
DA670.L1 W67 1968   914.28   *LC* 68-55639

Thompson, Flora.   **3.1739**
Lark Rise to Candleford, a trilogy. London, New York [etc.] Oxford University Press, 1945. xv p., 3 l., [3]-556 p. illus. 21 cm. 1. Oxfordshire — Social life and customs. I. T. II. Title: Over to Candleford. III. Title: Candleford Green.
DA670.O9 T52   *LC* 45-8104

Fletcher, Anthony.   **3.1740**
A county community in peace and war: Sussex 1600–1660. — London; New York: Longman, 1976 (c1975). xi, 445 p., fold. plate: maps; 24 cm. Includes index. 1. Sussex — History. I. T.
DA670.S98 F63   309.1/422/506   *LC* 76-367711   *ISBN* 0582500249

Rasmussen, Steen Eiler, 1898-.   **3.1741**
[London. English] London, the unique city / by Steen Eiler Rasmussen; with an introduction by James Bone. — Rev. ed. — Cambridge, Mass.: M.I.T. Press, c1982. 468 p.: ill.; 23 cm. Translation of: London. Includes index. 1. City planning — England — London. 2. London (England) — City planning. 3. Architecture — England — London. 4. London (England) — History I. T.
DA677.R273 1982   942.1/2 19   *LC* 82-132   *ISBN* 0262680270

Merrifield, Ralph.   **3.1742**
London, city of the Romans / Ralph Merrifield. — Berkeley: University of California Press, 1984 (c1983). xi, 288 p.: ill.; 26 cm. Bibliography: p. 270-272. Includes index. 1. Romans — England — London. 2. London (England) — History — To 1500 3. England — Antiquities, Roman 4. London (England) — Antiquities, Roman. I. T.
DA677.1.M46   936.2/1203 19   *LC* 82-40412   *ISBN* 0520049225

Myers, A. R. (Alec Reginald), 1912-1980.   **3.1743**
London in the age of Chaucer, by A. R. Myers. [1st ed.] Norman, University of Oklahoma Press [1972] xi, 236 p. 20 cm. (Centers of civilization series. v. 31) 1. London (England) — History — To 1500 I. T. II. Series.
DA680.M9   914.21/03/3   *LC* 73-177342   *ISBN* 0806109971

Stow, John, 1525?-1605.   **3.1744**
Survey of London. Introduction by H. B. Wheatley. [Rev. ed.] London: Dent; New York: Dutton [1965] xxiv, 533 p.: map.; 19 cm. (Everyman's library, no.589) 1. London (England) — History — To 1600. 2. London (England) — Description — To 1800. I. T.
DA680.S87x

Rudé, George F. E.   • **3.1745**
Hanoverian London, 1714–1808 [by] George Rudé. Berkeley, University of California, 1971. xvi, 271 p. illus., plans. 25 cm. (The History of London) 1. London (England) — History — 18th century I. T.
DA682.R8   914.21/03/7   *LC* 69-10590   *ISBN* 0520017781

Schwartz, Richard B.   **3.1746**
Daily life in Johnson's London / Richard B. Schwartz. — Madison, Wis.: University of Wisconsin Press, 1984, (c1983). xix, 196 p.: ill.; 21 cm. Includes index. 1. Johnson, Samuel, 1709-1784 — Homes and haunts — England —

London. 2. London (England) — Description — To 1800 3. London (England) — Social life and customs — 18th century I. T.
DA682.S38   942.107 19   *LC* 83-50080   *ISBN* 0299094944

The Bloomsbury group: a collection of memoirs, commentary,   **3.1747**
and criticism / edited by S. P. Rosenbaum.
Toronto; Buffalo: University of Toronto Press, c1975. xxi, 444 p., [4] leaves of plates: ill.; 23 cm. 1. Bloomsbury group 2. London (England) — Biography. I. Rosenbaum, S. P. (Stanford Patrick), 1929-
DA688.B65 1975b   942.1/082   *LC* 75-331714   *ISBN* 0802021824. *ISBN* 0802062687 pbk

Gadd, David.   **3.1748**
The loving friends: a portrait of Bloomsbury / David Gadd. — New York: Harcourt Brace Jovanovich, [1975] c1974. xii, 210 p., [8] leaves of plates: ill.; 21 cm. Includes index. 1. Authors, English — 20th century — Biography. 2. London (England) — Intellectual life I. T.
DA688.G23 1975   914.21/03/820922   *LC* 74-26596   *ISBN* 0151547408. *ISBN* 0156543001 pbk

Walmsley, Robert, 1905-.   • **3.1749**
Peterloo: the case reopened. New York, A. M. Kelley, 1969. xx, 585 p. illus. 25 cm. 1. Peterloo Massacre, Manchester, Greater Manchester, 1819 I. T.
DA690.M4 W3 1969b   942.7/2   *LC* 73-81146

Anglo-Saxon chronicle.   • **3.1750**
The Peterborough chronicle, 1070–1154. Edited from Ms. Bodley Laud misc. 636, with introd., commentary, and an appendix containing the interpolations by Cecily Clark. — [London] Oxford University Press, 1958. lxx, 120 p. 23 cm. — (Oxford English monographs) Bibliographical footnotes. 1. Peterborough Cathedral. 2. Gt. Brit. — Hist. — To 1485 — Sources. I. Clark, Cecily. ed. II. T.
DA690.P47A49 1969   942.55   *LC* 58-1160 A

DA700–745 WALES

The Dictionary of Welsh biography down to 1940. Under the   **3.1751**
auspices of the Honourable Society of Cymmrodorion. [Editors:
John Edward Lloyd, R. T. Jenkins]
London, 1959. lvii, 1157 p. map. 25 cm. Translation of Y Bywgraffiadur Cymreig hyd 1940. 1. Wales — Biography — Dictionaries. I. Honourable Society of Cymmrodorion (London, England)
DA710.A1 B913   920.0429   *LC* 59-4309

Morgan, Prys.   **3.1752**
The eighteenth century renaissance / Prys Morgan. — Llandybïe, Dyfed: C. Davies, 1981. 174 p., [8] leaves of plates: ill., facsims., ports. — (New history of Wales). 1. Wales — Social life and customs I. T. II. Series.
DA711.5 M67   *ISBN* 071540603

Peate, Iorwerth Cyfeiliog, 1901-.   **3.1753**
Tradition and folk life: a Welsh view, by Iorwerth C. Peate. — London: Faber and Faber Ltd, 1972. 3-147, [24] p.: illus., facsim.; 23 cm. 1. Wales — Social life and customs. I. T.
DA711.5.P4   914.29/03   *LC* 72-190275   *ISBN* 0571098045

Williams, Glanmor.   **3.1754**
Religion, language and nationality in Wales: historical essays by Glanmor Williams. — Cardiff: University of Wales Press, 1979. xi, 252 p., [5] leaves of plates: ill.; 22 cm. Includes index. 1. Wales — Civilization — Collected works. I. T.
DA711.5.W54   942.9   *LC* 79-305219   *ISBN* 0708307027

Jones, Gareth Elwyn.   **3.1755**
Modern Wales: a concise history, c. 1485–1979 / Gareth Elwyn Jones. — Cambridge [Cambridgeshire]; New York: Cambridge University Press, 1984. xii, 364 p.: maps; 23 cm. Includes index. 1. Wales — History 2. Wales — Economic conditions. 3. Wales — Social conditions. I. T.
DA714.J585 1984   942.9 19   *LC* 84-9590   *ISBN* 0521242320

Morgan, Prys.   **3.1756**
Wales: the shaping of a nation / Prys Morgan and David Thomas. — Newton Abbot; North Pomfret, Vt.: David & Charles, c1984. 272 p.: ill.; 23 cm. Includes index. 1. Wales — History I. Thomas, David, 1931- II. T.
DA714.M67 1984   942.9 19   *LC* 86-109841   *ISBN* 071538418X

Roderick, Arthur James, ed.   • **3.1757**
Wales through the ages / edited by A.J. Roderick. — Swansea: C. Davies, c[1959-60] 2 v.: ill.; 22 cm. 1. Wales — History I. T.
DA714.R6   942.9   *LC* 61-2284

Welsh society and nationhood: historical essays presented to   **3.1758**
Glanmor Williams / edited by R.R. Davies ... [et al.].
Cardiff: University of Wales Press, 1984. 274 p.: ill.; 26 cm. Includes index.
1. Williams, Glanmor. 2. Wales — History — Addresses, essays, lectures.
I. Williams, Glanmor. II. Davies, R. R.
DA714.W44 1984   942.9 19   *LC* 83-231233   *ISBN* 0708308600

Williams, Gwyn A.   **3.1759**
The Welsh in their history / Gwyn A. Williams. — London: Croom Helm,
1982. 206 p., ill., map; 23 cm. 1. Wales — History — Addresses, essays,
lectures. I. T.
DA714.W54 1982   942.9 19   *LC* 82-165180   *ISBN* 0709927118

Davies, R. R.   **3.1760**
Conquest, coexistence, and change: Wales, 1063–1415 / by R.R. Davies. —
Oxford; New York: Oxford University Press, 1987. xv, 530 p.: geneal. tables,
maps; 25 cm. — (History of Wales. 2) Includes index. 1. Wales — History —
To 1536 I. T. II. Series.
DA715.D37 1987   942 19   *LC* 86-31066   *ISBN* 0198217323

Davies, Wendy.   **3.1761**
Wales in the early Middle Ages / Wendy Davies. — [Leicester]: Leicester
University Press; Atlantic Highlands, NJ: Distributed in North America by
Humanities Press, 1982. xii, 263 p.: ill.; 24 cm. — (Studies in the early history of
Britain.) Includes index. 1. Wales — History — To 1536 I. T. II. Series.
DA715.D38 1982   942.9 19   *LC* 83-203157   *ISBN* 0718512359

Lloyd, John Edward, Sir, 1861-1947.   **3.1762**
A history of Wales: from the earliest times to the Edwardian conquest. 3d ed.
London: Longmans, 1939. 2 v. 1. Wales — History — To 1536 I. T.
DA715.L4 1939   *LC* 40-3123

Walker, David, 1923-.   **3.1763**
The Norman conquerors / David Walker. — Swansea: C. Davies, 1977. 109 p.,
[2] leaves of plates: ill.; 22 cm. — (New history of Wales.) Includes index.
1. Normans — Wales. 2. Wales — History — To 1536 I. T. II. Series.
DA715.W26   942.9/01   *LC* 77-368499   *ISBN* 0715403028

Evans, Evan David.   **3.1764**
A history of Wales, 1660–1815 / [by] E. D. Evans. — Cardiff: University of
Wales Press, 1976. x, 267 p.: maps; 23 cm. — (Welsh history text books; v. 2)
1. Wales — History I. T. II. Series.
DA720.E79   942.9/06   *LC* 77-378785   *ISBN* 0708306241

A People and a proletariat: essays in the history of Wales,   **3.1765**
1780–1980 / edited by David Smith.
London: Pluto Press in association with Llafur, the Society for the Study of
Welsh Labour History, 1980. 239 p.; 21 cm. 1. Wales — History — Addresses,
essays, lectures. I. Smith, David, 1945- II. Society for the Study of Welsh
Labour History.
DA720.P46 1980   942.9 19   *LC* 81-136466   *ISBN* 0861043227

Thomas, Hugh, 1923-.   **3.1766**
A history of Wales, 1485–1660. — Cardiff: University of Wales Press, 1972. viii,
246 p.: illus., maps, plans.; 23 cm. — (Welsh history text books, v. 1) 1. Wales
— History I. T. II. Series.
DA720.T48   942.905   *LC* 72-187417   *ISBN* 0708304664

Williams, Gwyn A.   **3.1767**
The search for Beulah Land: the Welsh and the Atlantic Revolution / Gwyn A.
Williams. — London: C. Helm, c1980. 190 p.: ill.; 23 cm. 1. Nationalism —
Wales. 2. Wales — Politics and government 3. Wales — Civilization —
American influences 4. United States — History — Revolution, 1775-1783 —
Influence I. T.
DA720.W496 1980   DA720 W56 1980.   942.9/07/3   *ISBN*
0709901763

Morgan, Kenneth O.   **3.1768**
Rebirth of a nation: Wales, 1880–1980 / by Kenneth O. Morgan. — New York:
Oxford University Press, 1981. xi, 463 p.: maps; 24 cm. — (History of Wales.)
Includes index. 1. Wales — History I. T. II. Series.
DA722.M62   942.9   *LC* 80-40337   *ISBN* 0198217366

Philip, Alan Butt.   **3.1769**
The Welsh question: nationalism in Welsh politics, 1945–1970 / Alan Butt
Philip. — Cardiff: University of Wales Press, 1975. xv, 367 p.: ill., map; 23 cm.
Includes index. 1. Plaid Cymru. 2. Nationalism — Wales. 3. Wales — Politics
and government — 20th century I. T.
DA722.P47   320.9/429/085   *LC* 75-316747   *ISBN* 0708305377

Williams, David, 1900-.   **3.1770**
The Rebecca Riots, a study in agrarian discontent. Cardiff, University of Wales
Press, 1955. 377 p. illus. 23 cm. 1. Rebecca Riots, 1839-1844 I. T.
DA722.W5   942.9   *LC* 56-32132

Rees, Alwyn D.   **3.1771**
Life in a Welsh countryside; a social study of Llanfihangel yng Ngwynfa.
Cardiff: University of Wales Press, 1975. 1 v. 1. Llanfihangel yng Ngwynfa,
Wales (Parish) 2. Country life — Wales I. T.
DA745 L74 R44

Williams, Gwyn A.   **3.1772**
The Merthyr rising / Gwyn A. Williams. — London: Croom Helm, c1978.
237 p., [2] leaves of plates: ill.; 23 cm. (Croom Helm social history series)
1. Lewis, Richard, called Dic Penderyn, 1808-1831. 2. Riots — Wales —
Merthyr Tydfil (Mid Glamorgan) 3. Merthyr Tydfil (Mid Glamorgan) —
History. I. T.
DA745.M47 W54   942.9/75   *LC* 78-315066   *ISBN* 0856644935

DA750–890 S<small>COTLAND</small>

Dickinson, William Croft, 1897- ed.   • **3.1773**
A source book of Scottish history, edited by William Croft Dickinson, Gordon
Donaldson [and] Isabel A. Milne. London Nelson [1952-54] 1. Scotland —
History — Sources I. Donaldson, Gordon. jt. ed. II. Milne, Isabel A, jt. ed.
III. T.
DA755 D53

Donaldson, Gordon. comp.   • **3.1774**
Scottish historical documents [compiled by] Gordon Donaldson. — New York:
Barnes & Noble, [1970] xi, 287 p.; 23 cm. 1. Scotland — History — Sources.
I. T.
DA755.D57   941   *LC* 71-21537   *ISBN* 0389040479

Kellas, James G.   **3.1775**
Modern Scotland / James G. Kellas. — 2d ed. — London; Boston: G. Allen &
Unwin, 1980. 193 p.; 23 cm. Includes index. 1. Scotland. I. T.
DA757.5.K44 1980   941.108   *LC* 79-41693   *ISBN* 0049410083

Donaldson, Gordon.   **3.1776**
Who's who in Scottish history [by] Gordon Donaldson and Robert S. Morpeth.
— New York: Barnes & Noble Books, [1973] xx, 254 p.: illus.; 23 cm.
1. Scotland — Biography. 2. Scotland — History I. Morpeth, Robert S., joint
author. II. T.
DA758.D66 1973b   941/.00992   *LC* 74-180274   *ISBN* 0064917398

Duncan, A. A. M. (Archibald Alexander McBeth)   **3.1777**
Scotland, the making of the kingdom / Archibald A. M. Duncan. — New York:
Barnes & Noble, 1975. xii, 705 p.: ill.; 24 cm. — (The Edinburgh history of
Scotland; v. 1) Includes index. 1. Scotland — History — To 1603 I. T.
DA760.E3 vol. 1 DA775   941.1 s 941.1   *LC* 75-5386   *ISBN*
0064918300

Nicholson, Ranald.   **3.1778**
Scotland: the later Middle Ages / Ranald Nicholson. — New York: Barnes &
Noble, 1974. xvi, 695 p.: ill.; 23 cm. (The Edinburgh history of Scotland; v. 2)
Includes index. 1. Scotland — History — 1057-1603 I. T.
DA760.E3 vol. 2 DA783   941 s 941.03   *LC* 74-190410   *ISBN*
0064951472

Donaldson, Gordon.   • **3.1779**
Scotland, James V to James VII / Gordon Donaldson. — New York: Praeger,
1966, c1965. x, 449 p.: maps. — (The Edinburgh history of Scotland; v. 3)
1. Scotland — History — 16th century 2. Scotland — History — 17th century
I. T. II. Series.
DA760.E3 vol.3   941   *LC* 66-11446

Ferguson, William, 1924-.   • **3.1780**
Scotland: 1689 to the present. New York, Praeger [1968] ix, 464 p.: map.; 23
cm. (The Edinburgh history of Scotland, v. 4) Bibliography: p. 416-438.
Bibliographical footnotes. 1. Scotland — History I. T.
DA760.E3 vol. 4   941   *LC* 67-26473

Mitchison, Rosalind.   • **3.1781**
A history of Scotland; illustrated by George Mackie. — London: Methuen,
1970. x, 468 p.: illus., geneal. table, maps, music.; 22 cm. 'Distributed in the
U.S.A. by Barnes & Noble, inc.' 1. Scotland — History I. T.
DA760.M58 1970   941   *LC* 75-476603   *ISBN* 0416144500

Harvie, Christopher T.   **3.1782**
Scotland and nationalism: Scottish society and politics, 1707–1977 /
Christopher Harvie. — London: Allen & Unwin, 1977. 318 p.: maps; 23 cm.
Includes index. 1. Nationalism — Scotland — History. 2. Scotland — Politics
and government I. T.
DA765.H37   320.9/411   *LC* 77-368131   *ISBN* 0049410067

Smout, T. C. (T. Christopher)   • **3.1783**
A history of the Scottish people, 1560–1830, by T. C. Smout. — New York: Scribner, [1970, c1969] 576 p.: illus., maps.; 24 cm. 1. Scotland — Civilization 2. Scotland — Economic conditions I. T.
DA772.S63 1970   914.1/03   *LC* 75-92624

Donaldson, Gordon.   • **3.1784**
The Scots overseas. London, R. Hale [1966] 232 p. plates (incl. ports.) 23 cm. 1. Scotch in foreign countries. 2. Scotland — Emigration and immigration. I. T.
DA774.5.D6 1966   *LC* 66-68133

Webster, Bruce.   **3.1785**
Scotland from the eleventh century to 1603 / by Bruce Webster. — Ithaca, N.Y.: Cornell University Press, 1975. 239 p.; 23 cm. (The Sources of history: Studies in the uses of historical evidence) 1. Scotland — History — To 1603 — Historiography. I. T.
DA774.8.W4   941.1/007/2   *LC* 74-19416   *ISBN* 080140942X

DA775–826 By Period

Dickinson, William Croft, 1897-.   **3.1786**
Scotland from the earliest times to 1603 / W. Croft Dickinson. — 3d ed. rev. and edited / by Archibald A. M. Duncan. — Oxford [Eng.]: Clarendon Press, 1977. x, 442 p.: ill.; 23 cm. Includes index. 1. Scotland — History — To 1603 I. Duncan, A. A. M. (Archibald Alexander McBeth) II. T.
DA775.D5 1977   941.1   *LC* 77-5540   *ISBN* 0198224532. *ISBN* 0198224656 pbk

Smyth, Alfred P.   **3.1787**
Warlords and holy men: Scotland, AD 80–1000 / Alfred P. Smyth. — London; Baltimore, Md., USA: E. Arnold, 1984. viii, 279 p.: ill.; 20 cm. (New history of Scotland. 1) Includes index. 1. Scotland — History — To 1057 I. T. II. Series.
DA777.S68 1984   941.101 19   *LC* 84-120168   *ISBN* 0713163054

Barrow, G. W. S.   **3.1788**
Kingship and unity: Scotland, 1000–1306 / G.W.S. Barrow. — Toronto; Buffalo: University of Toronto Press, 1981. 185 p.; 21 cm. — (New history of Scotland. 2) Includes index. 1. Scotland — History — 1057-1603 2. Scotland — History — To 1057 I. T. II. Series.
DA780.B37   941.102 19   *LC* 81-182606   0802023486

Ritchie, Robert Lindsay Graeme, 1880-.   **3.1789**
The Normans in Scotland. Edinburgh: University Press, 1954. 466p. (Edinburgh University publications; history, philosophy, and economics, no. 4) 1. Normans in Scotland I. T.
DA780 R55

Grant, Alexander.   **3.1790**
Independence and nationhood: Scotland, 1306–1469 / Alexander Grant. — London; Baltimore, Md., USA: E. Arnold, 1984. 248 p.: ill.; 20 cm. (New history of Scotland. 3) 1. Scotland — History — 1057-1603 2. Scotland — History — Autonomy and independence movements. I. T. II. Series.
DA783.G72 1984   941.1 19   *LC* 84-71796   *ISBN* 0713163097

Barrow, G. W. S.   **3.1791**
Robert Bruce and the community of the realm of Scotland / G. W. S. Barrow. 2d ed. — Edinburgh: Edinburgh University Press, 1976. xx, 502 p., [8] leaves of plates: ill.; 18 cm. Includes index. 1. Robert I, King of Scotland, 1274-1329. 2. Scotland — Kings and rulers — Biography. 3. Scotland — History — War of Independence, 1285-1371 I. T.
DA783.4.B34 1976   941.1/02/0924   *LC* 77-358763   *ISBN* 0852243073

Wormald, Jenny, 1942-.   **3.1792**
Court, kirk, and community: Scotland 1470–1625 / Jenny Wormald. — Toronto: University of Toronto Press, 1981. viii, 216 p.; 21 cm. — (The New history of Scotland; 4) 1. Scotland — History — 15th century 2. Scotland — History — 16th century I. T.
DA784.W67   941.104 19   *ISBN* 0802064507 pbk

Donaldson, Gordon.   **3.1793**
All the Queen's men: power and politics in Mary Stewart's Scotland / Gordon Donaldson. — New York: St. Martin's Press, 1983. 193 p., [8] p. of plates: ill.; 25 cm. 1. Mary, Queen of Scots, 1542-1587. 2. Scotland — Politics and government — 16th century I. T.
DA786.D66 1983   941.05 19   *LC* 83-653   *ISBN* 0312020090

Donaldson, Gordon.   **3.1794**
Mary, Queen of Scots / [by] Gordon Donaldson; with a foreword by A. L. Rowse. — London: English Universities Press, 1974. 200 p., [8] p. of plates: ill.,

ports.; 23 cm. (Men and their times) Includes index. 1. Mary, Queen of Scots, 1542-1587. I. T.
DA787.A1 D59   941.05/092/4 B   *LC* 74-186753   *ISBN* 0340123834

Fraser, Antonia, 1932-.   **3.1795**
Mary Queen of Scots / Antonia Fraser. — Illustrated abridged ed. — New York: Delacorte Press, c1978. 208 p.: ill.; 28 cm. Includes index. 1. Mary, Queen of Scots, 1542-1587. 2. Scotland — History — Mary Stuart, 1542-1567 3. Scotland — History — James VI, 1567-1625 4. Great Britain — History — Elizabeth, 1558-1603 5. Scotland — Kings and rulers — Biography. I. T.
DA787.A1 F742 1978   941.105/092/4 B   *LC* 78-703   *ISBN* 0440052610

Lee, Maurice.   • **3.1796**
James Stewart, Earl of Moray; a political study of the Reformation in Scotland. — Westport, Conn.: Greenwood Press, [1971, c1953] ix, 320 p.; 23 cm. 1. Moray, James Stewart, 1st Earl of, 1531?-1570. 2. Reformation — Scotland. I. T.
DA787.M6 L4 1971   942.05   *LC* 73-104251   *ISBN* 0837139759

Hewitt, George R.   **3.1797**
Scotland under Morton, 1572–80 / George R. Hewitt. — Edinburgh: J. Donald, c1982. vii, 232 p.; 25 cm. Includes index. 1. Douglas, James, Earl of Morton, d. 1581. 2. Scotland — History — James VI, 1567-1625 3. Scotland — Politics and government — 1371-1707 I. T.
DA788.H4   *ISBN* 0859760774

Lee, Maurice.   • **3.1798**
John Maitland of Thirlestane and the foundation of the Stewart despotism in Scotland. Princeton, N. J., Princeton University Press, 1959. 314 p. illus. (Princeton studies in history, 11) 1. Maitland, John, baron of Thirlestane, 1543-1595 2. Scotland — History — To 1603 I. T.
DA788.L4   914.105   *LC* 59-9097

Mitchison, Rosalind.   **3.1799**
Lordship to patronage: Scotland, 1603–1745 / Rosalind Mitchison. — London; Baltimore, Md., U.S.A.: E. Arnold, 1983. 198 p.; 20 cm. (New history of Scotland. 5) Includes index. 1. Scotland — History — 17th century 2. Scotland — History — 1689-1745 I. T. II. Series.
DA800.M56 1983   941.106 19   *LC* 83-217946   *ISBN* 0713163135

Lee, Maurice.   **3.1800**
Government by pen: Scotland under James VI and I / Maurice Lee, Jr. — Urbana: University of Illinois Press, c1980. xiv, 232 p., [4] leaves of plates: ports.; 24 cm. 1. James I, King of England, 1566-1625. 2. Scotland — Politics and government — 1371-1707 I. T.
DA803.15.L43   941.1/04   *LC* 79-16830   *ISBN* 0252007654

Cowan, Edward J.   **3.1801**
Montrose: for covenant and king / Edward J. Cowan. — London: Weidenfeld and Nicolson, c1977. vii, 326 p.: map; 23 cm. 1. Montrose, James Graham, Marquis of, 1612-1650. 2. Generals — Scotland — Biography. 3. Scotland — History — Charles I, 1625-1650. I. T.
DA803.7.A3 C68   941.062/092/4 B   *LC* 77-365889   *ISBN* 0297772090

Lenman, Bruce.   **3.1802**
Integration, enlightenment, and industrialization: Scotland 1746–1832 / Bruce Lenman. — Buffalo: University of Toronto Press, 1981. vi, 186 p.; 21 cm. — (New history of Scotland. 6) Includes index. 1. Scotland — History — 18th century 2. Scotland — History — 19th century I. T. II. Series.
DA809.L46 1981   941.107 19   *LC* 81-193623   *ISBN* 0713163143

Daiches, David, 1912-.   **3.1803**
The paradox of Scottish culture: the eighteenth–century experience. — London, New York, Oxford University Press, 1964. vii, 97 p. 19 cm. — (Whidden lectures. 1964) Bibliographical footnotes. 1. Scotland — Civilization 2. Scottish literature — 18th cent. — Hist. & crit. I. T. II. Series.
DA812.D3   914.1   *LC* 64-56259

Lenman, Bruce.   **3.1804**
The Jacobite risings in Britain, 1689–1746 / Bruce Lenman. — New York: Holmes & Meir, 1980. 320 p.; 24 cm. 1. Jacobites 2. Great Britain — History — 1689-1714 3. Great Britain — History — George I, II, 1714-1760 I. T.
DA813.L4   941.07 19   *LC* 80-496548   *ISBN* 0413396509

Speck, W. A. (William Arthur), 1938-.   **3.1805**
The Butcher: the Duke of Cumberland and the suppression of the 45 / W.A. Speck. — Oxford: Blackwell, 1982 (c1981). x, 230 p.: ill.; 25 cm. 1. William Augustus, Duke of Cumberland, 1721-1765. 2. Jacobite Rebellion, 1745-1746 3. Culloden, Battle of, 1746 I. T.
DA814.5.S64   941.07/2 19   *LC* 81-169642   *ISBN* 0631105018

Checkland, S. G.   **3.1806**
Industry and ethos: Scotland, 1832–1914 / Sydney and Olive Checkland. — London; Baltimore, Md., U.S.A.: E. Arnold, 1984. 218 p.; 20 cm. — (New history of Scotland. 7) Includes index. 1. National characteristics, Scottish 2. Scotland — History — 19th century 3. Scotland — History — 20th century 4. Scotland — Industries — History. I. Checkland, Olive. II. T. III. Series.
DA815.C44 1984   941.1081 19   *LC* 84-246669   *ISBN* 0713163178

Hanham, H. J.   • **3.1807**
Scottish nationalism [by] H. J. Hanham. — London: Faber, 1969. 3-250 p.; 23 cm. 1. Nationalism — Scotland. I. T.
DA821.H3   320.158/0941   *LC* 79-407512   *ISBN* 057109080X

Harvie, Christopher, 1944-.   **3.1808**
No gods and precious few heroes: Scotland 1914–1980 / Christopher Harvie. — Toronto: University of Toronto Press, 1981. ix, 182 p.; 21 cm. — (The New history of Scotland; 8) 1. Scotland — History — 20th century. I. T.
DA821.H37   941.1083 19   *ISBN* 0802024505

DA850–890 Description. Local History

Johnson, Samuel, 1709-1784.   • **3.1809**
[Journey to the western islands of Scotland] Johnson's Journey to the western islands of Scotland; and Boswell's Journal of a tour to the Hebrides with Samuel Johnson, LL.D; edited by R. W. Chapman. London, New York, Oxford U.P., 1970. xix, 475 p., fold. plate. facsims., map. 21 cm. (Oxford paperbacks, 205) 1. Hebrides (Scotland) — Description and travel. 2. Scotland — Description and travel — To 1800 I. Boswell, James, 1740-1795. Journal of a tour to the Hebrides. 1970. II. Chapman, R. W. (Robert William), 1881-1960. ed. III. T. IV. Title: Journey to the western islands of Scotland. V. Title: Journal of a tour to the Hebrides with Samuel Johnson, LL.D.
DA880.H4 J6 1970   914.11/7/047   *LC* 75-507901   *ISBN* 0192810723

Mackenzie, W. C. (William Cook), 1862-1952.   • **3.1810**
The Highlands and isles of Scotland: a historical survey / by W.C. Mackenzie. — Edinburgh [Scotland]: Moray Press, 1937. 326 p., plates: ill., maps, ports. Map on lining papers. 1. Highlands of Scotland — History 2. Scotland — History I. T.
DA880H6 M247   DA880H6 M247.   941.1   *LC* 38-21682

Gaskell, Philip.   • **3.1811**
Morvern transformed: a Highland parish in the nineteenth century. — London: Cambridge U.P., 1968. xix, 273 p.: 17 plates, illus., tables, maps, ports.; 24 cm. 1. Morvern — History. I. T.
DA890.M87 G3   941.3/8   *LC* 67-24944

DA900–990 IRELAND

Hughes, Kathleen. 3.1812
Early Christian Ireland: introduction to the sources. — Ithaca, N.Y.: Cornell University Press, 1973 (c1972) 320 p.; 23 cm. — (The Sources of history: studies in the uses of historical evidence) 1. Ireland — Historiography. 2. Ireland — Church history — Historiography. I. T.
DA908.H83   914.15/03/1   *LC* 72-1498   *ISBN* 0801407214

Bottigheimer, Karl S. 3.1813
Ireland and the Irish: a short history / Karl S. Bottigheimer. — New York: Columbia University Press, 1982. ix, 301 p.: ill.; 24 cm. Includes index. 1. Ireland — History 2. Ireland — Civilization I. T.
DA910.B67 1982   941.5 19   *LC* 82-4160   *ISBN* 0231046103

Beckett, J. C. (James Camlin), 1912-. 3.1814
A short history of Ireland: from earliest times to the present day / [by] J. C. Beckett. — 6th ed. — London: Hutchinson, 1979. 191 p.: 2 maps; 23 cm. Includes index. 1. Ireland — History I. T.
DA912.B4 1979   941.5   *LC* 80-470098   *ISBN* 0091398401

A New history of Ireland / edited by T. W. Moody, F. X. 3.1815
Martin, F. J. Byrne.
Oxford [Eng.]: Clarendon Press, < 1976-1986 >. v. < 3-4, 8-9 >: ill.; 24 cm. 1. Ireland — History — Collected works. I. Moody, T. W. (Theodore William), 1907- II. Martin, F. X. (Francis X.) III. Byrne, F. J. (Francis John), 1934-
DA912.N48   941.5   *LC* 76-376168   *ISBN* 0198217390

The Course of Irish History / edited by T.W. Moody and F.X. 3.1816
Martin.
Rev. and enl. ed. — Cork: Published in association with Radio Telefís Éireann by The Mercier Press, 1984. 479 p.: ill.; 21 cm. Includes index. 1. Ireland — History — Addresses, essays, lectures. I. Moody, T. W. (Theodore William), 1907- II. Martin, F. X. (Francis X.) III. Radio Telefís Éireann.
DA913.C66 1984   941.5 19   *LC* 84-237579   *ISBN* 0853427100

The Gill history of Ireland / General editors; James Dydon 3.1817
[and] Margaret MacCurtain.
[Dublin: Gill and MacMillan, c1972] 11 v.: maps. 1. Ireland — History. I. MacCurtain, Margaret, ed. II. Dydon, James, ed.
DA914.G4x

DA930–965 By Period

Giraldus, Cambrensis, 1146?-1223? 3.1818
[Topographia Hiberniae. English] The history and topography of Ireland = (Topographia Hiberniae) / Giraldus Cambrensis (Gerald of Wales); here translated from the Latin by John J. O'Meara; with a map & drawings from a contemporary copy c1200 A.D. — Rev. ed. — North America: Humanities; Portlaoise: Dolmen, 1982. 136 p.: ill., 1 map; 23 cm. — (Dolmen text; 4) 1. Ireland — History — To 1172 I. Giraldus, Cambrensis, 1146?-1223? First version of the Topography of Ireland. II. O'Meara, John J. (John Joseph), 1919- III. T. IV. Title: Topographia Hiberniae. English
DA930G5x   941.5 19   *ISBN* 0851053114

Ó Corráin, Donnchadh. 3.1819
Ireland before the Normans / Donncha Ó Corráin. — Dublin: Gill and Macmillan, 1972. 210 p.: ill., geneal. tables, maps. — (The Gill history of Ireland; 2) 1. Ireland — History — To 1172 I. T. II. Series.
DA930.O36   *ISBN* 0717105598

O'Curry, Eugene, 1796-1862. 3.1820
On the manners and customs of the ancient Irish. Edited with an introd., appendixes, etc., by W. K. Sullivan. New York, Lemma Pub. Corp., 1971. 3 v. illus. 24 cm. Reprint of the 1873 ed. Appendix in v. 3 in English and Irish. 1. Music — Ireland — History and criticism. 2. Musical instruments —

Ireland 3. Ireland — Social life and customs — To 1500 4. Ireland — History — To 1172 I. T.
DA930.5.O2 1971   914.15   *LC* 77-110290   *ISBN* 0876960107

MacNiocaill, G. 3.1821
Ireland before the Vikings [by] Gearóid MacNiocaill. — [Dublin]: Gill and Macmillan, [1972] 172 p.: illus.; 19 cm. — (The Gill history of Ireland, 1) 1. Ireland — Politics and government — To 1172 I. T. II. Series.
DA932.4.M33   941.5/1   *LC* 73-171184   *ISBN* 071710558X

Dolley, Michael. 3.1822
Anglo–Norman Ireland, c1100–1318 [by] Michael Dolley. — [Dublin]: Gill and MacMillan, [c1972] 210 p.: maps.; 19 cm. — (The Gill history of Ireland, 3) 1. Ireland — History — 1172-1603 2. Ireland — History — To 1172 I. T. II. Series.
DA933.D64   941.503   *LC* 75-303840   *ISBN* 071710560X

Lydon, James F. 3.1823
Ireland in the later Middle Ages / James Lydon. Dublin: Gill and Macmillan, c1973. 193 p.: maps; 19 cm. (The Gill history of Ireland; 6) Includes index. 1. Ireland — History — 1172-1603 I. T. II. Series.
DA933.L89   941.5   *LC* 77-356009   *ISBN* 0717105636

Nicholls, K. W. (Kenneth W.) 3.1824
Gaelic and Gaelicised Ireland in the Middle Ages. [Dublin] Gill and Macmillan [1972] 197 p. maps. 19 cm. (The Gill history of Ireland, 4) 1. Ireland — History — 1172-1603 2. Ireland — Economic conditions 3. Ireland — Social conditions. I. T. II. Series.
DA933.N5   309.1/415   *LC* 72-171463   *ISBN* 071710561X

Orpen, Goddard Henry, 1852-1932. 3.1825
Ireland under the Normans 1196–1333 / by Goddard Henry Orpen. — Oxford, Clarendon Press, 1911-20. 4 v. fold. maps 24 cm. 1. Ireland — History — To 1603 I. T.
DA933.O7   *LC* 11-27534

Frame, Robin. 3.1826
English lordship in Ireland, 1318–1361 / Robin Frame. — Oxford: Clarendon Press; New York: Oxford University Press, 1982. xiv, 381 p.: map; 22 cm. Includes index. 1. Ireland — Politics and government — 1172-1603 I. T.
DA934.F73 1982   941.503 19   *LC* 82-177820   *ISBN* 019822673X

Otway-Ruthven, Annette Jocelyn, 1909-. 3.1827
A history of medieval Ireland / A. J. Otway–Ruthven; with an introd. by Kathleen Hughes. — 2d ed. — New York: St. Martin's Press, 1980. xv, 454 p.: ill.; 23 cm. Includes index. 1. Ireland — History — 1172-1603 I. T.
DA934.O8 1980   941.5 19   *LC* 79-18849   *ISBN* 0312381395

Ellis, Steven G., 1950-. 3.1828
Tudor Ireland: crown, community, and the conflict of cultures, 1470–1603 / Steven G. Ellis. — London; New York: Longman, 1985. x, 388 p.: maps; 22 cm. Includes index. 1. Ireland — History — 1172-1603 2. Great Britain — Politics and government — 1485-1603 I. T.
DA935.E58 1985   941.505 19   *LC* 84-27874   *ISBN* 0582493412

MacCurtain, Margaret. 3.1829
Tudor and Stuart Ireland [by] Margaret MacCurtain. — [Dublin]: Gill and Macmillan, [c1972] 211 p.: illus.; 19 cm. — (The Gill history of Ireland, 7) 1. Ireland — History — 16th century 2. Ireland — History — 17th century I. T. II. Series.
DA935.M22   941.55   *LC* 74-173300

Canny, Nicholas P. 3.1830
The Elizabethan conquest of Ireland: a pattern established, 1565–76 / Nicholas P. Canny. — New York: Barnes & Noble Books, 1976. xi, 205 p.; 23 cm. Based on the author's thesis, University of Pennsylvania. Includes index. 1. Ireland — History — 1558-1603 I. T.
DA937.C36 1976   941.505   *LC* 75-10019   *ISBN* 0064909549

Beckett, J. C. (James Camlin), 1912-. 3.1831
The making of modern Ireland, 1603–1923 [by] J. C. Beckett. [1st ed.] New York, Knopf, 1966. 496 p. maps. 22 cm. 1. Ireland — History — 17th century 2. Ireland — History — 1691- I. T.
DA938.B37 1966a   941.5   *LC* 66-14919

O'Farrell, Patrick James.   3.1832
Ireland's English question; Anglo–Irish relations 1534–1970 [by] Patrick O'Farrell. — New York: Schocken Books, [1971] 336 p.; 23 cm. — ([Fabric of British history]) 1. Irish question 2. Ireland — Politics and government I. T.
DA938.O37 1971   327.415/042   *LC* 75-159481

Canny, Nicholas P.   3.1833
The upstart earl: a study of the social and mental world of Richard Boyle, first Earl of Cork, 1566–1643 / Nicholas Canny. — Cambridge [Cambridgeshire]; New York: Cambridge University Press, 1982. xii, 211 p.; 22 cm. 1. Cork, Richard Boyle, Earl of, 1566-1643. 2. Statesmen — Ireland — Biography. 3. Statesmen — Great Britain — Biography. 4. Ireland — Social life and customs — 16th century 5. Ireland — Social life and customs — 17th century I. T.
DA940.5.C7 C36 1982   941.506/092/4 B 19   *LC* 81-21687   *ISBN* 0521244161

Barnard, T. C. (Toby Christopher)   3.1834
Cromwellian Ireland: English government and reform in Ireland 1649–1660 / by T. C. Barnard. — London: Oxford University Press, 1975. ix, 349 p.; 23 cm. (Oxford historical monographs) Includes index. 1. Ireland — History — 1649-1660 I. T.
DA944.4.B37   941.5/06   *LC* 75-317054   *ISBN* 0198218583

Beckett, J. C. (James Camlin), 1912-.   3.1835
The Anglo–Irish tradition / J. C. Beckett. — Ithaca, N.Y.: Cornell University Press, 1977 (c1976). 158 p.; 23 cm. Includes index. 1. British — Ireland — History. 2. Irish question I. T.
DA947.B4   941.5/004/21   *LC* 76-20093   *ISBN* 0801410568

James, Mr. Francis Godwin.   3.1836
Ireland in the Empire, 1688–1770; a history of Ireland from the Williamite Wars to the eve of the American Revolution. — Cambridge, Mass.: Harvard University Press, 1973. 356 p.: illus.; 21 cm. — (Harvard historical monographs. 68) 1. Ireland — Politics and government — 18th century I. T. II. Series.
DA947.J35   320.9/415/07   *LC* 72-87772   *ISBN* 0674466268

Johnston, Edith Mary.   3.1837
Ireland in the eighteenth century / Edith Mary Johnston. — Dublin: Gill and Macmillan, c1974. 212 p.: graphs, maps; 19 cm. (The Gill history of Ireland; 8) Includes index. 1. Ireland — History — 18th century I. T. II. Series.
DA947.J63   941.5   *LC* 75-333220   *ISBN* 0717105652

McDowell, R. B. (Robert Brendan), 1913-.   • 3.1838
Ireland in the age of imperialism and revolution, 1760–1801 / by R. B. McDowell. — Oxford: Clarendon Press; New York: Oxford University Press, 1979. 740 p.; 23 cm. Includes index. 1. Ireland — History — 1760-1820 I. T.
DA947.M198   941.507   *LC* 79-40413   *ISBN* 019822480X

Pakenham, Thomas, 1933-.   • 3.1839
The year of liberty; the story of the great Irish rebellion of 1798. [1st American ed.] Englewood Cliffs, N.J., Prentice-Hall [1970, c1969] 416 p. illus., facsims., maps, ports. 25 cm. 1. Ireland — History — Rebellion of 1798 I. T.
DA949.P3 1970   941.5/7   *LC* 79-96825   *ISBN* 0139718958

DA950–958 19TH CENTURY

Boyce, David George, 1942-.   3.1840
Nationalism in Ireland / D. George Boyce. — Baltimore, Md.: Johns Hopkins University Press, 1982. 441 p.: maps; 22 cm. Includes index. 1. Nationalism — Ireland. 2. Ireland — Politics and government — 19th century 3. Ireland — Politics and government — 20th century I. T.
DA950.B68 1982   320.5/4/09415 19   *LC* 81-13731   *ISBN* 0801827361

Brown, Malcolm Johnston, 1910-.   3.1841
The politics of Irish literature: from Thomas Davis to W. B. Yeats / by Malcolm Brown. — Seattle: University of Washington Press, [1972] xii, 431 p.; 24 cm. 1. English literature — Irish authors — History and criticism. 2. Ireland — Politics and government — 19th century I. T.
DA950.B76 1972b   941.58   *LC* 72-152328   *ISBN* 0295951702

Hoppen, K. Theodore, 1941-.   3.1842
Elections, politics, and society in Ireland, 1832–1885 / K. Theodore Hoppen. — Oxford [Oxfordshire]: Clarendon Press; New York: Oxford University Press, 1984. xix, 569 p.: maps; 24 cm. Includes index. 1. Elections — Ireland — History — 19th century. 2. Ireland — Politics and government — 1837-1901 3. Ireland — Social conditions. I. T.
DA950.H68 1984   324.9415/081 19   *LC* 84-4347   *ISBN* 0198226306

Ireland under the Union: varieties of tension: essays in honour   3.1843
of T. W. Moody / edited by F. S. L. Lyons & R. A. J. Hawkins.
Oxford: Clarendon Press; New York: Oxford University Press, 1980. x, 337 p., [1] leaf of plates: port.; 23 cm. 1. Moody, T. W. (Theodore William), 1907- — Addresses, essays, lectures. 2. Ireland — History — 19th century — Addresses, essays, lectures. I. Moody, T. W. (Theodore William), 1907- II. Lyons, F. S. L. (Francis Steward Leland), 1923- III. Hawkins, R. A. J.
DA950.I68   941.5081   *LC* 79-40386   *ISBN* 0198224699

MacDonagh, Oliver.   3.1844
Ireland: the Union and its aftermath / Oliver MacDonagh. — Rev. and enl. ed. — London: G. Allen & Unwin, 1977. 176 p.; 22 cm. Includes index. 1. Ireland — History — 19th century 2. Ireland — History — 20th century I. T.
DA950.M18 1977   941.508   *LC* 77-372393   *ISBN* 0049410040

MacDonagh, Oliver.   3.1845
States of mind: a study of Anglo–Irish conflict, 1780–1980 / Oliver MacDonagh. — London; Boston: Allen & Unwin, 1983. viii, 151 p.; 23 cm. 1. Irish question 2. Ireland — Politics and government — 20th century 3. Great Britain — Foreign relations — Ireland. 4. Ireland — Foreign relations — Great Britain. 5. Ireland — Politics and government — 19th century I. T.
DA950.M184 1983   941.508 19   *LC* 83-6427   *ISBN* 0049410121

O'Farrell, Patrick James.   3.1846
England and Ireland since 1800 / Patrick O'Farrell. — London; New York: Oxford University Press, 1975. 193 p.; 21 cm. Includes index. 1. Irish question 2. Ireland — Politics and government — 19th century 3. Ireland — Politics and government — 20th century I. T.
DA950.O37   327.42/0415   *LC* 76-351038   *ISBN* 0192158147

Ó Tuathaigh, Gearóid.   3.1847
Ireland before the famine, 1798–1848. — [Dublin]: Gill and Macmillan, [1972] 237 p.: maps.; 19 cm. — (The Gill history of Ireland, 9) 1. Ireland — Politics and government — 19th century 2. Ireland — Economic conditions I. T. II. Series.
DA950.2.O88   309.1/415/058   *LC* 72-171913   *ISBN* 0717105660

Gwynn, Denis Rolleston, 1893-.   • 3.1848
Daniel O'Connell. — Rev. centenary ed. — [Cork] Cork Univ. Press, 1947. 262 p. 22 cm. 'Bibliography': p. 262. 1. O'Connell, Daniel, 1775-1847. 2. Ireland — Pol. & govt. — 19th cent. I. T.
DA950.22.G85x   *LC* A 48-8203 *

Edwards, R. Dudley (Robert Dudley), 1909- ed.   • 3.1849
The great famine; studies in Irish history 1845–52. Editors, R. Dudley Edwards [and] T. Desmond Williams. — [1st U.S. ed. New York]. — New York: New York University Press, 1957. xvi, 517 p. illus., maps. 22 cm. Bibliographical references included in 'Notes' (p. 437-498) 'Select bibliography': p. 499-509. 1. Ireland — Famines. 2. Ireland — Hist. — 1837-1901. I. Williams, Thomas Desmond. joint ed. II. T.
DA950.7.E3   941.58   *LC* 57-8843

Woodham Smith, Cecil Blanche Fitz Gerald, 1896-.   3.1850
The great hunger: Ireland 1845–1849. [1st ed.] New York, Harper & Row 1982. 510 p. illus. 22 cm. 1. Famines — Ireland 2. Ireland — Emigration and immigration. I. T.
DA950.7.W6 1962a   338.15   *LC* 62-11223

Lyons, F. S. L. (Francis Stewart Lelend), 1923-.   3.1851
Ireland since the famine [by] F. S. L. Lyons. New York, Scribner [1971] xiii, 852 p. 25 cm. 1. Ireland — Politics and government — 1837-1901 2. Ireland — Politics and government — 20th century 3. Northern Ireland — Politics and government I. T.
DA951.L94 1971b   309.1/415/08   *LC* 78-141708   *ISBN* 0684103699

Mansergh, Nicholas.   3.1852
The Irish question, 1840–1921: a commentary on Anglo–Irish relations and on social and political forces in Ireland in the age of reform and revolution / by Nicholas Mansergh. — 3d ed. — Toronto: University of Toronto Press, 1976 (c1975). 341 p. 'First published in 1940 under title: Ireland in the age of reform and revolution.' 1. Irish question 2. Ireland — Politics and government I. T.
DA951.M3 1975   DA951 M3 1975.   *ISBN* 0802022278

Norman, Edward R.   • 3.1853
The Catholic Church and Ireland in the age of rebellion, 1859–1873 / [by] E. R. Norman. — Ithaca, N. Y.: Cornell University Press [1965] xi, 485 p.: ill., ports.; 23 cm. Bibliography: p. 463-[476] 1. Ireland — Pol. & govt. — 1837-1901. 2. Catholic Church in Ireland. I. T.
DA955.N6 1965   941.58   *LC* 64-25406

Moody, T. W. (Theodore William), 1907-.   3.1854
Davitt and Irish revolution, 1846–82 / by T.W. Moody. — Oxford: Clarendon Press; New York: Oxford University Press, 1982 (c1981). xxiv, 674 p., [12] p. of

plates: ill.; 24 cm. Includes index. 1. Davitt, Michael, 1846-1906. 2. Land League (Ireland) — History. 3. Fenians — History. 4. Revolutionists — Ireland — Biography. 5. Ireland — Politics and government — 1837-1901 I. T.
DA958.D2 M66 1981　　941.5081/092/4 19　　LC 82-124277　　ISBN 019822382X

Lyons, Francis Stewart Leland, 1923-. 　　　　　　　3.1855
Charles Stewart Parnell / F. S. L. Lyons. — New York: Oxford University Press, 1977. 704 p.; 24 cm. 1. Parnell, Charles Stewart, 1846-1891. 2. Home rule (Ireland) 3. Politicians — Ireland — Biography. 4. Ireland — Politics and government — 1837-1901 I. T.
DA958.P2 L89　　941.5081/092/4 B　　LC 77-367920　　ISBN 0195199499

O'Brien, Conor Cruise, 1917-. 　　　　　　　• 3.1856
Parnell and his party, 1880–90. — Oxford, Clarendon Press, 1957. xii, 373 p. port., diagr., tables. 23 cm. '[Originated] as a thesis for the degree of doctor of philosophy in the University of Dublin.' Bibliography: p. [357]-365. 1. Parnell, Charles Stewart, 1846-1891. 2. Irish question I. T.
DA958.P2O16　　941.58　　LC 57-3208 rev

DA959–965 20TH CENTURY

Bell, J. Bowyer, 1931-. 　　　　　　　3.1857
The secret army: the IRA, 1916–1979 / J. Bowyer Bell. — MIT Press ed. — Cambridge, Mass.: MIT Press, 1980, c1979. xiv, 481 p., [8] leaves of plates: ill.; 24 cm. Includes index. 1. Irish Republican Army — History. 2. Ireland — History — 20th century 3. Northern Ireland — History I. T.
DA959.B43 1980　　941.508　　LC 79-90067　　ISBN 0262021455

Murphy, John A. 　　　　　　　3.1858
Ireland in the twentieth century / John A. Murphy. — Dublin: Gill and Macmillan, 1975. 180 p.; 19 cm. — (The Gill history of Ireland; 11) Includes index. 1. Ireland — Politics and government — 20th century 2. Northern Ireland — Politics and government I. T. II. Series.
DA959.M87　　941.508/2　　LC 75-320167　　ISBN 0717105687

O'Brien, Conor Cruise, 1917-. 　　　　　　　3.1859
States of Ireland. — [1st American ed.]. — New York: Pantheon Books, [c1972] 336 p.; 22 cm. 1. Ireland — History — 20th century 2. Northern Ireland — History I. T.
DA959.O19 1972　　941.59　　LC 72-3415　　ISBN 0394471172

O'Malley, Padraig. 　　　　　　　3.1860
The uncivil wars: Ireland today / Padraig O'Malley. — Boston: Houghton Mifflin, 1983. xvii, 481 p.; 22 cm. Includes index. 1. Irish question 2. Home rule (Ireland) 3. Ireland — Politics and government — 20th century 4. Northern Ireland — Politics and government — 1969- I. T.
DA959.O5 1983　　941.50824 19　　LC 83-10677　　ISBN 039534414X

Curran, Joseph Maroney, 1932-. 　　　　　　　3.1861
The birth of the Irish Free State, 1921–1923 / by Joseph M. Curran. — University: University of Alabama Press, c1980. vi, 356 p. Includes index. 1. Ireland — History — 1910-1921 2. Ireland — History — Civil War, 1922-1923 I. T.
DA960.C87　　DA960 C87.　　941.5082/2　　LC 79-4088　　ISBN 0817300139

Dangerfield, George, 1904-1986. 　　　　　　　3.1862
The damnable question: a study in Anglo–Irish relations / by George Dangerfield. — 1st ed. — Boston: Little, Brown, c1976. xiv, 400 p.: map.; 24 cm. 'An Atlantic Monthly Press book.' Includes index. 1. Irish question 2. Ireland — History — Sinn Fein Rebellion, 1916 — Causes. I. T.
DA962.D27　　941.5082/1　　LC 76-5456　　ISBN 0316172006

Lawlor, Sheila. 　　　　　　　3.1863
Britain and Ireland 1914–23 / Sheila Lawlor. — Dublin: Gill and Macmillan; Totowa, N.J.: Barnes & Noble Books, 1983. xii, 291 p.; 23 cm. Spine title: Britain & Ireland 1914-23. Includes index. 1. Ireland 2. Ireland — History — 1910-1921 3. Ireland — History — Sinn Fein Rebellion, 1916 — Causes. 4. Great Britain — Foreign relations — Ireland. 5. Ireland — Foreign relations — Great Britain. 6. Great Britain — Foreign relations — 1910-1936 I. T. Title: Britain & Ireland 1914-23.
DA962.L34 1983　　941.5082/1 19　　LC 83-10015　　ISBN 0389204099

Ward, Alan J. 　　　　　　　3.1864
The Easter Rising: revolution and Irish nationalism / Alan J. Ward. — Arlington Heights, Ill.: AHM Pub. Corp., c1980. vi, 184 p.: maps; 21 cm. —

(AHM Europe since 1500 series.) Includes index. 1. Nationalism — Ireland — History — 20th century. 2. Ireland — Politics and government — 1910-1921 I. T. II. Series.
DA962.W33　　941.5082/1 19　　LC 79-55729　　ISBN 0882958038

Younger, Calton. 　　　　　　　• 3.1865
Ireland's civil war. — London: Muller, 1968. [1], viii, 534 p.: 12 plates, illus., ports.; 23 cm. 1. Ireland — History — Civil War, 1922-1923 I. T.
DA962.Y6　　941.5/9　　LC 70-367247

Greaves, C. Desmond. 　　　　　　　• 3.1866
The life and times of James Connolly / by C. Desmond Greaves. — New York: International Publishers, [1971, c1961] 448 p.; 20 cm. — (New World paperbacks, NW-S-14) 1. Connolly, James, 1868-1916. I. T.
DA965.C7 G7 1971　　335.4/092/4 B　　LC 78-188758

Longford, Frank Pakenham, Earl of, 1905-. 　　　　　　　• 3.1867
Eamon de Valera [by] the Earl of Longford & Thomas P. O'Neill. [1st American ed.] Boston, Houghton Mifflin, 1971, [c1970] xix, 499 p. illus., maps, ports. 24 cm. 1. De Valera, Eamonn, 1882-1975. I. O'Neill, Thomas P., joint author. II. T.
DA965.D4 L6 1971　　941.5/9/0924 B　　LC 77-144076　　ISBN 0395121019

DA969–990 Description

Young, Arthur, 1741-1820. 　　　　　　　• 3.1868
A tour in Ireland, with general observations on the present state of that kingdom made in the years 1776, 1777 and 1778. Selected & edited by Constantia Maxwell. Cambridge University Press 1925. 244p. 1. Ireland — Description and travel I. Maxwell, Constantia Elizabeth, 1885-, ed. II. T.
DA972 Y68　　LC 26-22239

Freeman, Thomas Walter. 　　　　　　　• 3.1869
Ireland, a general and regional geography / by T. W. Freeman. — [3d ed.]. — London: Methuen; New York: Dutton, [1965] xix, 560 p.: ill., maps, plates.; 23 cm. — ([Methuen's advanced geographies]) First published in 1950 under title: Ireland, its physical, historical, social, and economic geography. 1. Ireland — Description and travel — 1901-1950 I. T.
DA977.F72 1965　　LC 68-569

Encyclopaedia of Ireland. 　　　　　　　• 3.1870
Dublin: A. Figgis; New York: McGraw-Hill, 1968. 463 p.: illus., maps.; 29 cm. 1. Ireland.
DA979.E5　　914.15　　LC 68-54316

DA990–995 NORTHERN IRELAND

Smyth, Alfred P. 　　　　　　　3.1871
Celtic Leinster: towards an historical geography of early Irish civilization, A.D. 500–1600 / Alfred P. Smyth. — Blackrock, County Dublin: Irish Academic Press, 1983 (c1982). xvi, 197 p., [6] p. of plates: ill. (some col.); 30 cm. 1. Celts — Ireland — Leinster. 2. Leinster (Ireland) — Historical geography. 3. Ireland — Civilization I. T.
DA990.L5 S63　　941.8 19　　LC 83-100005　　ISBN 0716500973

Bew, Paul. 　　　　　　　3.1872
The state in Northern Ireland, 1921–72: political forces and social classes / Paul Bew, Peter Gibbon and Henry Patterson. — New York: St. Martin's Press, 1979. viii, 231 p.; 23 cm. 1. Ulster Unionist Party. 2. Social classes — Northern Ireland. 3. Northern Ireland — Politics and government I. Gibbon, Peter. joint author. II. Patterson, Henry, 1947- joint author. III. T.
DA990.U46 B36 1979　　320.9/416/082　　LC 79-13020　　ISBN 0312756089

Stewart, Anthony Terence Quincey. 　　　　　　　3.1873
The Ulster crisis / [by] A. T. Q. Stewart. — London: Faber, 1967. 3-284 p.: 12 plates (incl. ports.), 2 maps, tables.; 22 1/2 cm. 1. Carson, Edward Henry Carson, Baron, 1854-1935. 2. Home rule (Ireland) 3. Ulster (Northern Ireland and Ireland) — Politics and government. I. T.
DA990.U46 S78　　941.6　　LC 67-84876

DB1–99 Austria.
Austro-Hungarian Empire

Johnston, William M., 1936-.   **3.1874**
The Austrian mind; an intellectual and social history, 1848–1938 [by] William
M. Johnston. — Berkeley: University of California Press, 1972. xv, 515 p.:
illus.; 25 cm. 1. Austria — Intellectual life — History. 2. Austria — Social
conditions. I. T.
DB30.J64   914.36/03/4   *LC* 75-111418   *ISBN* 0520017013

Kann, Robert A., 1906-.   • **3.1875**
A study in Austrian intellectual history; from late baroque to romanticism. —
New York, Praeger [1960] 367 p. illus. 22 cm. — (Books that matter)
1. Abraham a Sancta Clara, 1644-1709. 2. Sonnenfels, Joseph von, 1733-1817.
3. Austria — Civilization I. T. II. Title: Austrian intellectual history.
DB30.K3   914.36   *LC* 60-9207

Crankshaw, Edward.   • **3.1876**
The Habsburgs: portrait of a dynasty. — New York: Viking Press, [1971]
272 p.: illus.; 27 cm. — (A Studio book) 1. Habsburg, House of — History.
2. Austria — Politics and government I. T.
DB36.1.C7   943.6   *LC* 72-156753   *ISBN* 0670361348

Tapié, Victor Lucien, 1900-1974.   • **3.1877**
[Monarchie et peuples du Danube. English] The rise and fall of the Habsburg
monarchy [by] Victor–L. Tapié. Translated by Stephen Hardman. New York,
Praeger [1971] viii, 430 p. 25 cm. Translation of: Monarchie et peuples du
Danube. 1. Habsburg, House of 2. Hungary — Politics and government
3. Bohemia (Czechoslovakia) — Politics and government 4. Austria —
Politics and government I. T.
DB47.T313   943.6/03   *LC* 77-137893

Gehl, Jürgen.   • **3.1878**
Austria, Germany, and the Anschluss, 1931–1938. Foreword by Alan Bullock.
— London, New York, Oxford University Press, 1963. x, 212 p. maps. 23 cm.
Based on thesis, St. Antony's College, Oxford. Bibliography: p. [196]-203.
1. Anschluss movement, 1918-1938 2. Austria — For. rel. — Germany.
3. Germany — For. rel. — Austria. I. T.
DB48.G4 1963   943.605   *LC* 63-25360

Leeper, Alexander Wigram Allen, 1887-1935.   • **3.1879**
A history of medieval Austria / by A. W. A. Leeper; edited by R. W. Seton-
Watson & C. A. Macartney. — London: Oxford University Press, 1941. vi,
420 p.; 23 cm. 1. Austria — History — To 1273 I. Seton-Watson, R. W.
(Robert William), 1879-1951. II. Macartney, Carlile Aylmer, 1895- III. T.
DB51.L4 1978   943.6/02

Evans, Robert John Weston.   **3.1880**
The making of the Habsburg monarchy, 1550–1700: an interpretation / R. J.
W. Evans. — Oxford: Clarendon Press; New York: Oxford University Press,
1979. xxiii, 531 p.; 23 cm. Includes index. 1. Austria — History — 1519-1740
I. T.
DB65.E9   943.6/03   *LC* 79-40616   *ISBN* 0198225601

Kann, Robert A., 1906-.   **3.1881**
A history of the Habsburg Empire, 1526–1918 / Robert A. Kann. — Berkeley:
University of California Press, [1974] xiv, 646 p.: maps; 24 cm. Includes index.
1. Habsburg, House of — History. 2. Austria — History 3. Hungary —
History I. T.
DB65.K36   943.6/03   *LC* 72-97733   *ISBN* 0520024087

Fichtner, Paula S.   **3.1882**
Ferdinand I of Austria: the politics of dynasticism in the age of the Reformation
/ Paula Sutter Fichtner. — Boulder [Colo.]: East European Monographs; New
York: Distributed by Columbia University Press, 1982. 362 p.; 23 cm. — (East
European monographs. no. 100) Includes index. 1. Ferdinand I, Holy Roman
Emperor, 1503-1564. 2. Austria — History — Ferdinand I, 1521-1564
3. Austria — Kings and rulers — Biography. I. T. II. Series.
DB65.3.F48   943.6/032/0924 19   *LC* 82-126190   *ISBN*
0914710958

Roider, Karl A.   **3.1883**
Austria's eastern question, 1700–1790 / Karl A. Roider, Jr. — Princeton, N.J.:
Princeton University Press, c1982. 256 p.: maps; 23 cm. Includes index.
1. Austria — Foreign relations — 18th century 2. Austria — Foreign relations
— Turkey. 3. Turkey — Foreign relations — Austria. 4. Austria — Foreign
relations — Soviet Union. 5. Soviet Union — Foreign relations — Austria.
I. T.
DB66.5.R64 1982   327.436 19   *LC* 81-48141   *ISBN* 0691053553

Crankshaw, Edward.   • **3.1884**
Maria Theresa. — New York: Viking Press, [1970, c1969] 366 p.: illus., geneal.
table, fold. map, ports.; 22 cm. 1. Maria Theresa, Empress of Austria,
1717-1780. 2. Austria — History — Maria Theresa, 1740-1780 I. T.
DB71.C7 1970   943/.053/0924 B   *LC* 70-94850   *ISBN* 0670456314

Bernard, Paul P.   • **3.1885**
Joseph II, by Paul P. Bernard. New York, Twayne Publishers [1968] 215 p. 21
cm. (Twayne's rulers and statesmen of the world series, 5) 1. Joseph II, Holy
Roman Emperor, 1741-1790. I. T.
DB74.B43   943/.057/0924 B   *LC* 67-25205

Bernard, Paul P.   • **3.1886**
Jesuits and Jacobins; enlightenment and enlightened despotism in Austria [by]
Paul P. Bernard. — Urbana: University of Illinois Press, [1971] ix, 198 p.; 24
cm. 1. Enlightenment 2. Jesuits — Austria 3. Josephinism 4. Austria —
History — Joseph II, 1780-1790 5. Austria — Intellectual life I. T.
DB74.3.B397 1971   914.36/03/3   *LC* 78-151997   *ISBN*
025200180X

Wangermann, Ernst.   • **3.1887**
From Joseph II to the Jacobin trials: government policy and public opinion in
the Habsburg dominions in the period of the French Revolution. 2nd ed.
London, Oxford U.P., 1969. xiii, 218 p. 23 cm. (Oxford Historical monographs)
1. Joseph II, Holy Roman Emperor, 1741-1790. 2. Leopold II, Holy Roman
Emperor, 1747-1792. 3. Austria — Politics and government — 18th century
I. T.
DB74.3.W3 1969   943.6/03   *LC* 74-444349   *ISBN* 019821832X

DB80–99 19th–20th Centuries

Macartney, C. A. (Carlile Aylmer), 1895-1978.   • **3.1888**
The Habsburg Empire, 1790–1918 [by] C. A. Macartney. — [1st American ed.].
— New York: Macmillan, [1969] xiv, 886 p.; 24 cm. 1. Austria — History —
1789-1900 2. Austria — History — 1867-1918 I. T.
DB80.M3 1969   943.6/04   *LC* 69-12834

Taylor, A. J. P. (Alan John Percivale), 1906-.   • **3.1889**
The Habsburg monarchy, 1809–1918; a history of the Austrian Empire and
Austria–Hungary. New ed. London, H. Hamilton [1948] 279 p. ports., maps
(on lining-papers) 22 cm. 'An entirely rewritten version of an earlier work with
the same title ... published in 1941.' 1. Austria — History — 1789-1900
2. Austria — History — 20th century I. T.
DB80.T382   943.6   *LC* 49-19763

Bertier de Sauvigny, Guillaume de, 1912-.   • **3.1890**
Metternich and his times, by G. de Bertier de Sauvigny. Translated by Peter
Ryde. — London, Darton, Longman & Todd [1962] xviii, 315 p. illus., maps,
ports. 23 cm. Bibliography: p. [307]-312 1. Metternich, Clemens Wenzel
Lothar, Fürst von, 1773-1859. I. T.
DB80.8.M57B43   *LC* 65-32777

Kraehe, Enno E.   • **3.1891**
Metternich's German policy / by Enno E. Kraehe. — Princeton, N. J.,
Princeton University Press, 1963-1983. 2 v. : ill., maps. ; 24 cm. 1. Metternich,
Clemens Wenzel Lothar, Fürst von, 1773-1859. 2. Austria — Foreign relations
— 1789-1900 I. T.
DB80.8.M57K7   943.603   *LC* 63-9994   *ISBN* 0691051860

Schroeder, Paul W.   • **3.1892**
Metternich's diplomacy at its zenith, 1820–1823, by Paul W. Schroeder. New
York, Greenwood Press [1969, c1962] xii, 292 p. maps, port. 23 cm.
1. Metternich, Clemens Wenzel Lothar, Fürst von, 1773-1859. 2. Europe —
Politics and government — 1815-1848 I. T.
DB80.8.M57 S33 1969   943.6/04   *LC* 78-95135   *ISBN* 0837124719

Rath, Reuben John, 1910-.   • **3.1893**
The Viennese Revolution of 1848 [by] R. John Rath. New York, Greenwood Press [1969, c1957] ix, 424 p. maps. 23 cm. 1. Vienna (Austria) — History — Revolution, 1848-1849. I. T.
DB83.R3 1969   943.6/04   *LC* 70-94617   *ISBN* 0837124654

Crankshaw, Edward.   **3.1894**
The fall of the House of Habsburg / by Edward Crankshaw. — New York: Penguin, 1983. 459 p.: map; 20 cm. Reprint. Originally published: New York: Viking Press, 1963. 1. Franz Joseph I, Emperor of Austria, 1830-1916. 2. Habsburg, House of. 3. Austria — History — Francis Joseph, 1848-1916 I. T.
DB85.C7 1983   943.6/04 19   *LC* 82-18071   *ISBN* 0140064591

Carsten, F. L. (Francis Ludwig)   **3.1895**
Fascist movements in Austria: from Schönerer to Hitler / F. L. Carsten. — London; Beverly Hills: Sage Publications, 1977. 356 p.; 23 cm. — (Sage studies in 20th century history; v. 7) Includes index. 1. Fascism — Austria. 2. Austria — Politics and government — 1918-1938 3. Austria — Politics and government — 1848-1918 I. T.
DB86.C39   320.5/33/09436   *LC* 76-22935   *ISBN* 0803999925

Kann, Robert A., 1906-.   • **3.1896**
The multinational empire; nationalism and national reform in the Habsburg monarchy, 1848–1918. — New York, Octagon Books, 1964 [c1950] 2 v. maps. 24 cm. Vol. 2 issued also as thesis, Columbia University. 1. Austria — Pol. & govt. 1848-1918. 2. Austria — Hist. — 1848-1867. 3. Austria — Hist. — 1867-1918. 4. Nationalism — Austria. 5. Minorities — Austria. I. T.
DB86.K3   943.6   *LC* 64-16383

Brook-Shepherd, Gordon, 1918-.   **3.1897**
Archduke of Sarajevo: the romance and tragedy of Franz Ferdinand of Austria / Gordon Brook–Shepherd; [maps by Brian Elkins]. — 1st American ed. — Boston: Little, Brown, c1984. xv, 301 p., [12] p. of plates: ill.; 24 cm. Includes index. 1. Franz Ferdinand, Archduke of Austria, 1863-1914. 2. Austria — Princes and princesses — Biography. 3. Austria — History — 1867-1918 I. T.
DB89.F7 B76 1984   943.6/04/0924 B 19   *LC* 84-81201   *ISBN* 0316109517

Dedijer, Vladimir.   • **3.1898**
The road to Sarajevo. — New York: Simon and Schuster, [1966] 550 p. : ill., col. map, ports. Map on lining papers. 1. Franz Ferdinand, Archduke of Austria, 1863-1914 — Assassination. 2. Austria — Politics and government — 1867-1918 I. T.
DB89.F7D4   943.604   *LC* 65-24282

Remak, Joachim, 1920-.   • **3.1899**
Sarajevo: the story of a political murder. New York: Criterion Books, c1959. 301 p.: ill.; 22 cm. 1. Franz Ferdinand, Archduke of Austria — Assasination I. T.
DB89.F7 R4   943.604   *LC* 59-6557   *ISBN*

Zeman, Z. A. B.   • **3.1900**
The break–up of the Habsburg Empire, 1914–1918; a study in national and social revolution. — London, New York, Oxford University Press, 1961. 274 p. illus. 22 cm. Includes bibliography. 1. Austria — Hist. — 20th cent. 2. Nationalism — Austria. I. T.
DB91.Z4   943.604   *LC* 61-66610

Carsten, F. L. (Francis Ludwig)   **3.1901**
The first Austrian Republic, 1918–1938: a study based on British and Austrian documents / F.L. Carsten. — Aldershot, Hants, England; Brookfield, Vermont, USA: Gower, c1986. 309 p.: map; 23 cm. Includes index. 1. Austria — Politics and government — 1918-1938 I. T.
DB96.C37 1986   943.6/051 19   *LC* 86-219029   *ISBN* 0566051621

Low, Alfred D.   **3.1902**
The Anschluss movement, 1931–1938, and the great powers / by Alfred D. Low. — Boulder: East European Monographs; New York: Distributed by Columbia University Press, 1985. xv, 507 p., [1] p. of plates: map; 23 cm. — (East European monographs; no. 185) Includes index. 1. Anschluss movement, 1918-1938 2. Austria — Foreign relations — 1918-1938 I. T. II. Series.
DB97.L68 1985   943.6/051 19   *LC* 85-70774   *ISBN* 0880330783

Luža, Radomír.   **3.1903**
Austro–German relations in the Anschluss era / Radomír Luža. — Princeton, N.J.: Princeton University Press, [1975] xvi, 438 p.: map; 24 cm. Includes index. 1. Schirach, Baldur von, 1907- 2. Anschluss movement, 1918-1938 3. Nationalism — Germany. 4. Austria — History — 1938-1945 5. Austria — Politics and government — 1918-1938 I. T.
DB99.L89   943.6/05   *LC* 74-25619   *ISBN* 0691075689

Whitnah, Donald Robert, 1925-.   **3.1904**
The American occupation of Austria: planning and early years / Donald R. Whitnah and Edgar L. Erickson. — Westport, Conn.: Greenwood Press, 1985. xiv, 352 p., [12] p. of plates: ill.; 22 cm. (Contributions in military studies;

0883-6884; no. 46) Includes index. 1. Austria — History — Allied occupation, 1945-1955 2. United States — History, Military — 20th century I. Erickson, Edgar L. II. T. III. Series.
DB99.1.W48 1985   355.4/9/09436 19   *LC* 85-5428   *ISBN* 031324894X

DB191–217 CZECHOSLOVAKIA

Czechoslovakia, a country study / Foreign Area Studies, the   **3.1905**
American University; edited by Richard F. Nyrop.
2nd ed. — Washington: The Studies: For sale by the Supt. of Docs., U.S. G.P.O., 1982. xxv, 356 p.: ill.; 24 cm. — (Area handbook series.) (DA pam. 550-158) 'Research completed April 1981.' Rev. ed. of: Area handbook for Czechoslovakia / Eugene K. Keefe. 1972. Includes index. 1. Czechoslovakia. I. Nyrop, Richard F. II. Keefe, Eugene K. Area handbook for Czechoslovakia. III. American University (Washington, D.C.). Foreign Area Studies. IV. Series. V. Series: DA pam. 550-158
DB196.C9x DB2011.C93 1982   943.7 19   *LC* 82-1716

Wallace, William V.   **3.1906**
Czechoslovakia / by William V. Wallace. — Boulder, Colo.: Westview Press, 1977 (c1976). xv, 374 p., [8] leaves of plates: ill.; 23 cm. — (Nations of the modern world.) 1. Czechoslovakia — History I. T. II. Series.
DB196.W28   943.7   *LC* 76-4494   *ISBN* 0891580271

Wiskemann, Elizabeth.   • **3.1907**
Czechs & Germans: a study of the struggle in the historic provinces of Bohemia and Moravia. 2nd ed. London, Melbourne [etc.] issued under the auspices of the Royal Institute of International Affairs [by] Macmillan; New York, St. Martin's P., 1967. xiv, 299 p. 4 maps (1 col.), tables. 22 1/2 cm. 1. Germans in Bohemia. 2. Germans in Moravia. 3. Czechoslovakia — Politics and government I. Royal Institute of International Affairs. II. T.
DB200.7.W5 1967   943.7   *LC* 67-10945

Bradley, J. F. N. (John Francis Nejez), 1930-.   **3.1908**
Czechoslovakia: a short history, by J. F. N. Bradley. Edinburgh, Edinburgh University Press, 1971. iii-xii, 212 p., 33 plates. illus., maps, ports. 23 cm. (Short histories of Europe, 2) 1. Czechoslovakia — History I. T.
DB205.B68 1971   943.7   *LC* 78-159593   *ISBN* 0852241933

Thomson, Samuel Harrison, 1895-1975.   • **3.1909**
Czechoslovakia in European history / S. Harrison Thomson. — 2d ed. enlarged. — Princeton, N.J.: Princeton Univesity Press, 1953. 485 p.: ill.; 23 cm. 1. Bohemia — History. 2. Czechs 3. Slovaks 4. Czechoslovakia — History I. T.
DB205.1.T48 1953   DB2062.T48 1953.   *LC* 52-8780

Heymann, Frederick Gotthold, 1900-.   • **3.1910**
Poland & Czechoslovakia [by] Frederick G. Heymann. Englewood Cliffs, N.J., Prentice-Hall [1966] viii, 181 p. maps. 21 cm. (Modern nations in historical perspective) (A Spectrum book.) 1. Czechoslovakia — History 2. Poland — History I. T.
DB205.3.H4   943.7   *LC* 66-22803

Heymann, Frederick Gotthold, 1900-.   • **3.1911**
John Žižka and the Hussite revolution, by Frederick G. Heymann. — New York: Russell & Russell, [1969, c1955] 521 p.: illus., maps.; 25 cm. 1. Žižka, Jan, 1360 (ca.)-1424. I. T.
DB208.H4 1969   943.7/02/0924 B   *LC* 71-77671

Kaminsky, Howard, 1924-.   • **3.1912**
A history of the Hussite revolution. — Berkeley: University of California Press, 1967. xv, 580 p.: illus., maps.; 25 cm. 1. Hussites I. T. II. Title: The Hussite revolution.
DB208.K3   943.7/02   *LC* 67-12608

Heymann, Frederick Gotthold, 1900-.   • **3.1913**
George of Bohemia, King of Heretics / by Frederick G. Heymann. — Princeton, N.J.: Princeton University Press, 1965. xvi, 671 p.: ill., maps, ports.; 24 cm. 1. Jiří, z Poděbrad, King of Bohemia, 1420-1471. 2. Bohemia — History — 1403-1526. I. T.
DB209.H4   DB2126.H49.   *LC* 64-19821

Odložilík, Otakar, 1899-.   • **3.1914**
The Hussite King: Bohemia in European affairs, 1440–1471. — New Brunswick, N. J., Rutgers University Press [1965] ix, 337 p. illus., maps (1 fold.) ports. 25 cm. Bibliography: p. 315-321. 1. Jiří, z Poděbrad, King of Bohemia, 1420-1471. 2. Europe — Hist. — 476-1492. I. T.
DB209.O3   943.702   *LC* 65-19406

Kerner, Robert Joseph, 1887-1956.   • **3.1915**
Bohemia in the eighteenth century; a study in political, economic, and social history, with special reference to the reign of Leopold II, 1790–1792. New York, AMS Press [1969] xii, 412 p. 24 cm. Reprint of the 1932 ed. 1. Leopold II, Holy Roman Emperor, 1747-1792. 2. Bohemia (Czechoslovakia) — Politics and government 3. Bohemia (Czechoslovakia) — Constitutional history. 4. Bohemia (Czechoslovakia) — Economic conditions. 5. Bohemia (Czechoslovakia) — History — 1618-1848 I. T.
DB212.K4 1969b   943.7/02   LC 79-94315

DB214–217 19th–20th Centuries

Beneš, Edvard, 1884-1948.   • **3.1916**
Memoirs: from Munich to new war and new victory / trans. [from the Czech original] by Godfrey Lias. — London: Allen, 1954. 346 p. 1. World War, 1939-1945 — Czechoslovakia. 2. Czechoslovakia — Politics and government I. Lias, Godfrey. II. T.
DB215.B4144 1954a

A History of the Czechoslovak Republic, 1918–1948. Edited by   **3.1917**
Victor S. Mamatey and Radomír Luža.
Princeton, N.J.: Princeton University Press, [1973] xi, 534 p.: illus.; 25 cm. 1. Czechoslovakia — History — 1918- — Addresses, essays, lectures. I. Mamatey, Victor S. ed. II. Luža, Radomír. ed.
DB215.H54   943.7/03   LC 79-39791   ISBN 0691052050

Procházka, Theodor.   **3.1918**
The Second Republic: the disintegration of post–Munich Czechoslovakia, October 1938–March 1939 / Theodore Procházka, Sr. — Boulder: East European Monographs; New York: Distributed by Columbia University Press, 1981. vii, 231 p. of plates: maps; 23 cm. (East European monographs. no. 90) Based on the author's thesis (doctoral—University of Paris, l954) presented under the title: La Tchécoslovaquie de Munich à Mars 1939. Includes index. 1. Munich Four-Power Agreement (1938) 2. Czechoslovakia — History — 1938-1945 I. T. II. Series.
DB215.P7x   943.7/03 19   LC 81-65161   ISBN 0914710842

Vondracek, Felix John, 1901-.   • **3.1919**
The foreign policy of Czechoslovakia, 1918–1935. New York Columbia University 1937. 2,7-451p. 1. Czechoslovak Republic — Foreign relations I. T.
DB215 V65 1937

Wheeler-Bennett, John Wheeler, Sir, 1902-1975.   • **3.1920**
Munich: prologue to tragedy. New York, Duell, Sloan and Pearce [1948] xiii, 507 p. illus., maps. 22 cm. Bibliography: p. 489-493. 1. Munich Four-Power Agreement (1938) 2. Europe — Politics — 1918-1945. I. T.
DB215.W45   940.52   LC 48-8501 *

Zinner, Paul E.   • **3.1921**
Communist strategy and tactics in Czechoslovakia, 1918–48 / Paul E. Zinner. — New York: Praeger, 1963. xi, 264 p.; 22 cm. (Praeger publications in Russian history and world communism; no. 129) 1. Komunistická strana Československa. 2. Czechoslovakia — Politics and government 3. Czechoslovakia — History — Coup d'état, 1948 I. T.
DB215.2.Z55   943.7/03   LC 63-10829

Mastny, Vojtech, 1936-.   • **3.1922**
The Czechs under Nazi rule; the failure of national resistance, 1939–1942. New York, Columbia University Press, 1971. xiii, 274 p. 24 cm. (East Central European studies of Columbia University) 1. Czechoslovakia — History — 1938-1945 2. Bohemia and Moravia (Protectorate, 1939-1945) — Politics and government. I. T.
DB215.3.M38   943.7/03   LC 72-132065   ISBN 0231033036

Golan, Galia.   **3.1923**
The Czechoslovak reform movement: communism in crisis, 1962–1968. — Cambridge [Eng.]: University Press, 1972 (c1971). viii, 349 p.; 23 cm. — (Soviet and East European studies.) 1. Czechoslovakia — Politics and government — 1945- 2. Czechoslovakia — Intellectual life — 1945- I. T. II. Series.
DB215.5.G5   309.1/437/04   LC 76-163059

Komunistická strana Československa. Ústřední výbor. Komise   • **3.1924**
pro vyřizování stranických rehabilitací.
The Czechoslovak political trials, 1950–1954; the suppressed report of the Dubček Government's commission of inquiry. Edited with a pref. and a postscript by Jiří Pelikán. Stanford, Calif., Stanford University Press, 1971. 360 p. 23 cm. German translation has title: Das unterdrückte Dossier.

1. Political purges — Czechoslovakia. 2. Czechoslovakia — Politics and government — 1945- I. T.
DB215.5.K633 1971   320.9/437/04   LC 70-150328   ISBN 0804707693

Kusin, Vladimir V.   • **3.1925**
The intellectual origins of the Prague spring; the development of reformist ideas in Czechoslovakia, 1956–1967, by Vladimir V. Kusin. Cambridge [Eng.] University Press, 1971. v, 153 p. 23 cm. (Soviet and East European studies.) 1. Czechoslovakia — Politics and government — 1945-1968. 2. Czechoslovakia — History — Intervention, 1968- I. T. II. Series.
DB215.5.K87   320.9/437/04   LC 73-155582   ISBN 0521081246

Myant, M. R. (Martin R.)   **3.1926**
Socialism and democracy in Czechoslovakia, 1945–1948 / M.R. Myant. — Cambridge; New York: Cambridge University Press, 1981. ix, 302 p.; 23 cm. — (Soviet and East European studies.) Includes index. 1. Czechoslovakia — Politics and government — 1945- I. T. II. Series.
DB215.5.M9x   943.7/042 19   LC 80-41951   ISBN 0521236681

Ripka, Hubert, 1895-.   • **3.1927**
Czechoslovakia enslaved; the story of the communist coup d'état. London, Gollancz, 1950. 339 p. 23 cm. 1. Czechoslovak Republic — Politics and government — 1945- I. T.
DB215.5.R52   943.7   LC 50-2995

Dawisha, Karen.   **3.1928**
The Kremlin and the Prague spring / Karen Dawisha. — Berkeley: University of California Press, c1984. xiv, 426 p.: map; 24 cm. (International crisis behavior series. v. 4) Includes index. 1. Czechoslovakia — History — Intervention, 1968- 2. Czechoslovakia — Foreign relations — Soviet Union. 3. Soviet Union — Foreign relations — Czechoslovakia. I. T. II. Series.
DB215.6.D3x   327.470437 19   LC 83-21351   ISBN 0520049713

Golan, Galia.   **3.1929**
Reform rule in Czechoslovakia: the Dubček era, 1968–1969. — Cambridge [Eng.]: University Press, 1973. vii, 326 p.; 23 cm. 1. Czechoslovakia — Politics and government — 1968- I. T.
DB215.6.G578 1973   320.9/437/04   LC 72-83587   ISBN 0521085861

Schwartz, Harry, 1919-.   • **3.1930**
Prague's 200 days; the struggle for democracy in Czechoslovakia. New York, Praeger [1969] x, 274 p. map. 22 cm. 1. Komunisticka strana Ceskoslovenika. 2. Czechoslovakia — Politics and government — 1968- 3. Czechoslovakia — History — Intervention, 1968- I. T.
DB215.6.S33   943.7/04   LC 69-19700

Beneš, Edvard, Pres. Czechoslovak Republic, 1884-1948.   • **3.1931**
My war memoirs, by Eduard Beneš. Translated from the Czech by Paul Selver. Westport, Conn., Greenwood Press [1971] 512 p. port. 23 cm. Reprint of the 1928 ed. 1. Beneš, Edvard, Pres. Czechoslovak Republic, 1884-1948. 2. World War, 1914-1918 — Czechoslovakia. I. T.
DB217.B3 A4 1971   943.7/03/0924   LC 70-114467   ISBN 0837147638

DB231–851 Special Provinces, Regions, and Cities of Central Europe

Eterovich, Francis H. ed.   • **3.1932**
Croatia: land, people, culture. Francis H. Eterovich, editor; Christopher Spalatin, associate editor. Foreword by Ivan Meštrović. — [Toronto] Published for the Editorial Board by University of Toronto Press [1964-. v. illus., 10 fold. maps, ports. 24 cm. Includes bibliographies. 1. Croatia. 2. Croats I. T.
DB366.E8   914.394   LC 65-2286

Hitchins, Keith.   • **3.1933**
The Rumanian national movement in Transylvania, 1780–1849. Cambridge, Harvard University Press, 1969. xi, 316 p. 21 cm. (Harvard historical monographs. 61) Based on the author's thesis, Harvard, 1964. 1. Transylvania (Romania) — Politics and government. I. T. II. Series.
DB739.H57   320.1/58/094984   LC 69-12724

Schorske, Carl E.   **3.1934**
Fin–de–siècle Vienna: politics and culture / Carl E. Schorske. — 1st ed. — New York: Knopf: distributed by Random House, 1980 (c1979). xxx, 378 p., [8] leaves of plates: ill.; 25 cm. 1. Vienna (Austria) — Intellectual life —

Addresses, essays, lectures. 2. Austria — Politics and government — 1867-1918 — Addresses, essays, lectures. I. T.
DB851.S42   943.6/1304 19   *LC* 79-2155   *ISBN* 0394505964

DB901–975 HUNGARY

Helmreich, Ernst Christian. ed.   • **3.1935**
Hungary. New York, Published for the Mid-European Studies Center of the Free Europe Committee by Praeger [1957] xiv, 466 p. maps, tables. 24 cm. (East-Central Europe under the Communists) (Praeger publications in Russian history and world communism, v. no. 49) (Books that matter) 1. Communism — Hungary. 2. Hungary. 3. Hungary — History — Revolution, 1956 I. Free Europe Committee. Mid-European Studies Center. II. T.
DB906.H4   *LC* 57-9334

Keefe, Eugene K.   **3.1936**
Area handbook for Hungary. Coauthors: Eugene K. Keefe [and others] Rev. ed. [Washington, For sale by the Supt. of Docs., U.S. Govt. Print. Off.] 1983. xiv, 339 p. illus. 24 cm. 'DA Pam 550-165.' 'One of a series of handbooks prepared by Foreign Area Studies (FAS) of The American University.' 1. Hungary. I. American University (Washington, D.C.). Foreign Area Studies. II. T.
DB906.K36   914.39   *LC* 73-600190

Macartney, C. A. (Carlile Aylmer), 1895-1978.   • **3.1937**
Hungary, a short history. — Chicago, Aldine Pub. Co. [1962] 262 p. illus. 22 cm. 1. Hungary — Hist. I. T.
DB925.M16   943.9   *LC* 62-19084

Sinor, Denis.   • **3.1938**
History of Hungary / Denis Sinor. — New York: Praeger, [1959] 310 p.; 23 cm. — (Books that matter) 1. Hungary — History I. T.
DB925.1.S5   943.91   *LC* 59-15752

Janos, Andrew C.   **3.1939**
The politics of backwardness in Hungary, 1825–1945 / Andrew C. Janos. — Princeton, N.J.: Princeton University Press, c1982. xxxvi, 370 p.: maps; 24 cm. Includes index. 1. Hungary — Politics and government — 19th century 2. Hungary — Politics and government — 20th century I. T.
DB933.J36 1982   943.9/04 19   *LC* 81-47137   *ISBN* 0691076332

Barany, George, 1922-.   • **3.1940**
Stephen Széchenyi and the awakening of Hungarian nationalism, 1791–1841. — Princeton, N.J.: Princeton University Press, 1968. xviii, 487 p.: illus., facsims., ports.; 25 cm. A revision of the author's thesis, University of Colorado. 1. Széchenyi, István, gróf, 1791-1860. 2. Nationalism — Hungary. I. T.
DB933.3.S8 B3 1968   943.9/1/040924 B   *LC* 68-20865

Deák, István.   **3.1941**
The lawful revolution: Louis Kossuth and the Hungarians, 1848–1849 / István Deák. — New York: Columbia University Press, 1979. xxi, 415 p., [8] leaves of plates: ill.; 24 cm. Includes index. 1. Kossuth, Lajos, 1802-1894. 2. Statesmen — Hungary — Biography. 3. Hungary — History — Uprising of 1848-1849 I. T.
DB937.D42   943.9/04/0924 B   *LC* 78-22063   *ISBN* 0231046022

DB947–957 20th Century

Horthy, Miklós, nagybányai, 1868-1957.   • **3.1942**
Memoirs / Nicholas Horthy; with an introd. by Nicholas Roosevelt. — New York: R. Speller, 1957. 268 p., [23] leaves of plates: ill., ports.; 22 cm.

Translation of Ein Leben für Ungarn. 1. Horthy, Miklós, nagybányai, 1868-1957. 2. Statesmen — Hungary — Biography. 3. Hungary — History — 20th century I. T.
DB950.H6 A33   943.91   *LC* 57-2991

Macartney, Carlile Aylmer, 1895-.   • **3.1943**
October fifteenth; a history of modern Hungary, 1929–1945. 2d ed. Edimburg: University Press, [c1961, 1956]. 2v. I. T.
DB955.M223

Nagy-Talavera, Nicholas M., 1929-.   • **3.1944**
The Green Shirts and the others; a history of Fascism in Hungary and Rumania, by Nicholas M. Nagy–Talavera. Stanford, Calif., Hoover Institution Press, Stanford University [1970] xii, 427 p. maps (on lining papers) 23 cm. (Hoover Institution publications, 85) Based on the author's thesis, University of California. 1. Szálasi, Ferenc, 1897-1946. 2. Codreanu, Corneliu Zelea, 1899-1938. 3. Hungary — Politics and government — 1918-1945 4. Romania — Politics and government — 1914-1944 I. T.
DB955.N37   943.9/05   *LC* 74-98136   *ISBN* 0817918515

Toma, Peter A.   **3.1945**
Politics in Hungary / Peter A. Toma and Ivan Volgyes. — San Francisco: W. H. Freeman, c1977. x, 188 p.; 24 cm. Includes index. 1. Hungary — Politics and government — 1945- I. Völgyes, Iván, 1936- joint author. II. T.
DB956.T63   320.9/439/05   *LC* 76-29613   *ISBN* 0716705575

Váli, Ferenc A. (Ferenc Albert), 1905-.   • **3.1946**
Rift and revolt in Hungary; nationalism versus communism. — Cambridge, Harvard University Press, 1961. xvii, 590 p. fold. map, diagrs. 25 cm. Bibliography: p. [515]-520. 1. Hungary — Pol. & govt. — 1945- 2. Communism — Hungary. I. T.
DB956.V3   943.9105   *LC* 61-13745

Zinner, Paul E.   • **3.1947**
Revolution in Hungary / by Paul E. Zinner. — New York: Columbia University Press, 1962. xi, 380 p. 1. Communism — Hungary. 2. Hungary — Politics and government — 1945- 3. Hungary — History — Revolution, 1956 I. T.
DB956.Z5   *LC* 62-17062

Lasky, Melvin J., ed.   • **3.1948**
The Hungarian revolution; a white book. The story of the October uprising as recorded in documents, dispatches, eye–witness accounts, and world–wide reactions. Edited by Melvin J. Lasky. — Freeport, N.Y.: Books for Libraries Press, [1970, c1957] 318 p.: illus., maps, ports.; 27 cm. 1. Hungary — History — Revolution, 1956 I. T.
DB957.L3 1970   943.9/105   *LC* 70-119936   *ISBN* 0836953797

Lettis, Richard.   • **3.1949**
The Hungarian revolt: October 23–November 4, 1956 / Richard Lettis and William E. Morris. — New York: Scribner, 1961. 219 p.: ill. — (A Scribner research anthology) 1. Hungary — History — Revolution, 1956 I. Morris, William E. II. T.
DB957 L48   DB957 L48.   *LC* 61-19091

Lomax, William.   **3.1950**
Hungary 1956 / [by] Bill Lomax. — New York: St. Martin's Press, 1976. 222 p.; 23 cm. 1. Hungary — History — Revolution, 1956 I. T.
DB957.L6/1976   943.9/05   *LC* 76-41633

DB2000–3150 CZECHOSLOVAKIA
(Works classified after ca. 1980: this sequence not used; see DB191-217)

DC   France

DC20–29 DESCRIPTION

Adams, Henry, 1838-1918.   • **3.1951**
Mont–Saint–Michel and Chartres [by] Henry Adams. With an introduction by Ralph Adams Cram. Boston, New York, Houghton Mifflin company, 1936. xiv p., 1 l., 397 p. front., illus., plates. 22 cm. 1. Cathédrale de Chartres. 2. Middle Ages 3. Le Mont-Saint-Michel (France) I. Cram, Ralph Adams, 1863-1942. ed. II. T.
DC20.A2 1936   914.4   *LC* 36-27246

Young, Arthur, 1741-1820.   • **3.1952**
Travels in France during the years 1787, 1788 & 1789, by Arthur Young, Edited by Constantia Maxwell ... Cambridge [Eng.] The University press, 1929. lvi, 428 p. front. (port.) fold. map. 21 cm. 'Principal works referred to by the editor': p. [408]-412. 1. Agriculture — France. 2. France — Description and travel I. Maxwell, Constantia Elizabeth, ed. II. T.
DC25.Y68 1950

DC30–34 CIVILIZATION

Davis, Natalie Zemon, 1928-.   **3.1953**
Society and culture in early modern France: eight essays / by Natalie Zemon Davis. — Stanford, Calif.: Stanford University Press, 1975. xviii, 362 p., [4] leaves of plates: ill.; 23 cm. 1. France — Civilization — Collected works. I. T.
DC33.D33   944/.027   *LC* 74-82777   *ISBN* 0804708681

Padover, Saul Kussiel, 1905-.   • **3.1954**
French institutions: values and politics, by Saul K. Padover with the collaboration of François Goguel, Louis Rosenstock–Franck [and] Eric Weil. [Stanford] Stanford University Press, 1954. vi, 102 p. diagr. 23 cm. (Hoover Institute studies. Series E: Institutions, no. 2) Bibliography: p. 89. Bibliographical references included in 'Notes' (p. 95-102) 1. France — Civilization 2. France — Politics and government — 1945- I. T.
DC33.P25   914.4   *LC* 53-11875

Huizinga, Johan, 1872-1945.   **3.1955**
[Herfsttij der Middeleeuwen. English] The waning of the Middle Ages: a study of the forms of life, thought, and art in France and the Netherlands in the XIVth and XVth centuries / by J. Huizinga. — New York: St. Martin's Press, [1985], c1924. viii, 328 p., [14] p. of plates: ill.; 23 cm. Reprint. Originally published: London: E. Arnold, 1924. Translation of: Herfsttij der Middeleeuwen. Includes index. 1. Civilization, Medieval 2. France — Civilization — 1328-1600 3. Netherlands — Civilization I. T.
DC33.2.H83 1985   944 19   *LC* 84-9980   *ISBN* 0312855400

Riché, Pierre.   **3.1956**
[Vie quotidienne dans l'Empire carolingien. English] Daily life in the world of Charlemagne / Pierre Riché; translated by Jo Ann McNamara. — [Philadelphia]: University of Pennsylvania Press, 1978. xvi, 336 p.: ill.; 24 cm. — (Middle Ages.) Translation of La vie quotidienne dans l'Empire carolingien. 1. France — Civilization — 700-1000 I. T. II. Series.
DC33.2.R5413   944/.01   *LC* 78-53330   *ISBN* 0812277511. *ISBN* 0812210964 pbk

Febvre, Lucien Paul Victor, 1878-1956.   **3.1957**
Life in Renaissance France / Lucien Febvre; edited and translated by Marian Rothstein. — Cambridge, Mass.: Harvard University Press, 1977. xx, 163 p.; 24 cm. Translation of 5 essays first published in Revue des cours et conférences and later reprinted in the author's Pour une histoire à part entière. 1. France — Civilization — 1328-1600 I. Rothstein, Marian, 1944- II. T.
DC33.3.F4 1977   944/.02   *LC* 77-7454   *ISBN* 0674531752

Kelley, Donald R.   **3.1958**
The beginning of ideology: consciousness and society in the French Reformation / Donald R. Kelley. — Cambridge [Eng.]; New York: Cambridge University Press, 1981. xv, 351 p.; 24 cm. 1. France — Civilization — 1328-1600 2. France — History — 16th century I. T.
DC33.3.K44   944/.028 19   *LC* 80-41237   *ISBN* 0521235049

Mandrou, Robert.   **3.1959**
[Introduction à la France moderne, 1500-1640. English] Introduction to modern France, 1500–1640: an essay in historical psychology / Robert Mandrou; translated by R. E. Hallmark. — New York: Holmes & Meier, 1976, c1975. xiii, 285 p., [6] leaves of plates: ill.; 24 cm. Translation of Introduction à la France moderne, 1500-1640. Includes index. 1. France — Civilization — 1328-1600 2. France — Social life and customs I. T.
DC33.3.M3513 1976   944/.028   *LC* 75-28239   *ISBN* 0841902453

Stone, Donald.   • **3.1960**
France in the sixteenth century; a medieval society transformed, by Donald Stone, Jr. — Englewood Cliffs, N.J.: Prentice-Hall, [1969] x, 180 p.; 21 cm. — (French literary backgrounds series) 1. French literature — 16th century — History and criticism. 2. France — Civilization — 1328-1600 3. France — History — 16th century I. T.
DC33.3.S75   914.4/03/28   *LC* 69-11352

Wiley, William Leon.   • **3.1961**
The gentleman of Renaissance France, by W. L. Wiley. — Westport, Conn.: Greenwood Press, [1971, c1954] xii, 303 p.: illus.; 23 cm. 1. France — Court and courtiers I. T.
DC33.3.W5 1971   914.4/03/2   *LC* 75-152622   *ISBN* 083716169X

Ford, Franklin L. (Franklin Lewis), 1920-.   • **3.1962**
Robe and sword; the regrouping of the French aristocracy after Louis XIV. — Cambridge: Harvard University Press, 1953. xii, 280 p.: illus.; 22 cm. — (Harvard historical studies. v. 64.) 'An essay on bibliography':p. 253-272. 1. France — Court & courtiers. 2. France — Nobility 3. France — History — Bourbons, 1589-1789 I. T. II. Series.
DC33.4.F7   944.034   *LC* 52-12261

Havens, George Remington, 1890-.   • **3.1963**
The age of ideas; from reaction to revolution in eighteenth–century France. New York, Holt [1955] 474 p. illus. 25 cm. 1. Eighteenth century 2. France — Civilization I. T.
DC33.4.H35   944.03   *LC* 55-6056

Mandrou, Robert.   **3.1964**
La France au 17 et 18 siècles / par Robert Mandrou. — 3. ed. rev. et corr. Paris Presses universitaires de France 1974, c1967. 357 p.: ill., maps. — (Nouvelle Clio; l'histoire et ses problèmes; 33) 1. France — Civilization — History 2. France — History — Bourbons, 1589-1789 I. T.
DC33.4 M28x 1974

The French romantics / edited by D.G. Charlton.   **3.1965**
Cambridge [Cambridgeshire]; New York; Cambridge University Press, 1984. 2 v.: ill.; 24 cm. Includes index. 1. Romanticism — France — History — Addresses, essays, lectures. 2. Arts — France — History — 19th century — Addresses, essays, lectures. 3. France — Civilization — 1789-1830 — Addresses, essays, lectures. 4. France — Civilization — 1830-1900 — Addresses, essays, lectures. I. Charlton, D. G. (Donald Geoffrey)
DC33.5.F73 1984   944.06 19   *LC* 83-21010   *ISBN* 0521244137

Reardon, Bernard M. G.   **3.1966**
Liberalism and tradition: aspects of Catholic thought in nineteenth–century France / Bernard Reardon. — Cambridge; New York: Cambridge University Press, 1975. viii, 308 p.; 24 cm. 1. Theology, Catholic — France. 2. Religious thought — 19th century — France. 3. France — Intellectual life — 19th century I. T.
DC33.6.R4 1975   230/.2/44   *LC* 75-7214   *ISBN* 0521207762

Weber, Eugen Joseph, 1925-.   **3.1967**
France, fin de siècle / Eugen Weber. — Cambridge, Mass.: Belknap Press, 1986. x, 294 p.: ill.; 25 cm. Includes index. 1. France — Civilization — 1830-1900 I. T.
DC33.6.W43 1986   944.06 19   *LC* 85-30569   *ISBN* 0674318129

Weber, Eugen Joseph, 1925-.   • **3.1968**
The nationalist revival in France, 1905–1914. Berkeley University of California Press 1959. viii, 237 p. (University of California publications in history, v. 60) 1. Nationalism — France 2. France — Politics and government — 1879-1940 I. T.
DC34 W43

Zeldin, Theodore, 1933-.   • **3.1969**
The French / Theodore Zeldin. — 1st American ed. — New York: Pantheon Books, c1982. 538 p.: ill.; 25 cm. Includes index. 1. National characteristics, French I. T.
DC34.Z45 1982   306/.08941 19   *LC* 82-19113   *ISBN* 0394529472

DC35–412 History

Denieul-Cormier, Anne.   **3.1970**
[Rois fous et sages de la première maison de Valois. English] Wise and foolish kings: the first house of Valois, 1328–1498 / Anne Denieul–Cormier. — 1st ed. — Garden City, N.Y.: Doubleday, 1980. viii, 398 p., [8] leaves of plates: ill.; 22 cm. Translation of Rois fous et sages de la première maison de Valois. Includes index. 1. France — Kings and rulers — Biography. 2. France — History — House of Valois, 1328-1589 I. T.
DC36.6.D4613   944/.025   *LC* 77-175365   *ISBN* 038504903X

Seward, Desmond, 1935-.   **3.1971**
The Bourbon kings of France / Desmond Seward. New York: Barnes & Noble Books, 1976. xiv, 331 p., [7] leaves of plates: ill.; 23 cm. 1. Bourbon, House of 2. France — Kings and rulers — Biography. I. T.
DC36.8.B7 S48   944/.03/0922 B   *LC* 75-40528   *ISBN* 0064961850

Le Roy Ladurie, Emmanuel.   **3.1972**
[Territoire de l'historien. v. 1. English] The territory of the historian / Emmanuel Le Roy Ladurie; translated from the French by Ben and Siân Reynolds. — Chicago: University of Chicago Press, 1979. viii, 345 p.; 23 cm. Translation of Le territoire de l'historien, v. 1. 1. France — Historiography. I. T.
DC36.9.L37213 1979   944/.0072 19   *LC* 78-31362   *ISBN* 0226473279

Le Roy Ladurie, Emmanuel.   **3.1973**
[Territoire de l'historien. v. 2. English. Selections] The mind and method of the historian / Emmanuel Le Roy Ladurie; translated by Siân Reynolds and Ben Reynolds. — Chicago: University of Chicago Press, c1981. v, 310 p.; 22 cm. Translation of Le territoire de l'historien, v. 2. Translated from a selection of 9 of the 15 essays. 1. France — Historiography. I. T.
DC36.9.L37213 1981   944/.0072 19   *LC* 81-449   *ISBN* 0226473260

Stoianovich, Traian.   **3.1974**
French historical method: the Annales paradigm / by Traian Stoianovich; with a foreword by Fernand Braudel. — Ithaca, N.Y.: Cornell University Press, 1976. 260 p.; 23 cm. 1. France — Historiography. I. T.
DC36.9.S76   907/.2   *LC* 75-36996   *ISBN* 080140861X

Lavisse, Ernest, 1842-1922. ed.   • **3.1975**
Histoire de France depuis les origines jusqu'à la révolution; publiée avec la collaboration de mm. Bayet, Bloch [e.a.] Paris: Hachette et cie, 1900-[1911?] 9 v.: ill., maps (1 fold.) 1. France — History I. T.
DC38 L42

DC55–59 Political and Diplomatic History

Carroll, Eber Malcolm, 1893-1959.   • **3.1976**
French public opinion and foreign affairs, 1870–1914, by E. Malcolm Carroll. New York, London, The Century co. [c1931] viii, 348 p. 23 cm. At head of title: The American historical association. 1. Public opinion — France. 2. Press — France. 3. France — Foreign relations — 1870-1940 4. Europe — Politics — 1871-1918. I. American Historical Association. II. T.
DC58.C3   *LC* 31-12228

Wakefield, Walter Leggett.   **3.1977**
Heresy, crusade, and inquisition in southern France, 1100–1250 [by] Walter L. Wakefield. — Berkeley: University of California Press, 1974. 288 p.: maps.; 23 cm. 1. Albigenses 2. Waldenses — France. 3. Inquisition — France. 4. France — Church history — Middle Ages, 987-1515 I. T.
DC59.5.W34 1974b   274.4   *LC* 72-93524   *ISBN* 0520023803

Barker, Nancy Nichols.   **3.1978**
The French experience in Mexico, 1821–1861: a history of constant misunderstanding / by Nancy Nichols Barker. — Chapel Hill: University of North Carolina Press, c1979. xv, 264 p.: ill.; 24 cm. Includes index. 1. France — Foreign relations — Mexico. 2. Mexico — Foreign relations — France. 3. France — Foreign relations — 19th century I. T.
DC59.8.M6 B37   327/.44/072   *LC* 78-12935   *ISBN* 0807813397

DC60–412 By Period

DC60–109 Early. Medieval to 1515

Drinkwater, J. F.   **3.1979**
Roman Gaul: the three provinces, 58 BC – AD 260 / J.F. Drinkwater. — Ithaca, N.Y.: Cornell University Press, c1983. x, 256 p. Includes index. 1. Gaul — History — 58 B.C.-511 A.D. I. T.
DC62.D69 1983   936.4 19   *LC* 83-45143

James, Edward, 1947-.   **3.1980**
The origins of France: from Clovis to the Capetians, 500–1000 / Edward James. — New York: St. Martin's Press, 1982. xxiii, 253 p.: ill., maps; 23 cm. 1. France — History — To 987 I. T.
DC65.J35 1982   944/.01 19   *LC* 82-10691   *ISBN* 0312588623

Wallace-Hadrill, J. M. (John Michael)   • **3.1981**
The long-haired kings, and other studies in Frankish history. — New York: Barnes & Noble, [1962] 261 p.: ill.; 23 cm. 1. Merovingians 2. France — Hist. — Carlovingian and early period to 987. 3. France — Kings and rulers I. T.
DC65.W3   944.01   *LC* 63-1094

Fichtenau, Heinrich.   • **3.1982**
The Carolingian empire; the age of Charlemagne. Translated by Peter Munz. — New York: Barnes & Noble, 1963 [i.e. 1965] xxiv, 196 p. 23 cm. — (Studies in mediaeval history, 9.) 1. Carolingians I. T.
DC70.F513 1963   944.01   *LC* 65-2046

Halphen, Louis, 1880-1950.   • **3.1983**
[Charlemagne et l'empire carolingien. English] Charlemagne and the Carolingian Empire / by Louis Halphen; translated by Giselle de Nie. — Amsterdam; New York: North-Holland Pub. Co., 1977. xx, 366 p.: ill.; 24 cm. — (Europe in the Middle Ages. v. 3) Translation of Charlemagne et l'empire carolingien. Includes index. 1. Carolingians 2. France — History — To 987 I. T. II. Series.
DC70.H313   944/.01   *LC* 76-3514   *ISBN* 0720490073

Loyn, H. R. (Henry Royston)   **3.1984**
The Reign of Charlemagne: documents on Carolingian government and administration / [compiled by] H. R. Loyn and John Percival. — New York: St. Martin's Press, 1976, c1975. ix, 164 p.; 25 cm. (Documents of medieval history; 2) Includes index. 1. Charlemagne, Emperor, 742-814. 2. France — History — To 987 — Sources. I. Percival, John, 1937- II. T. III. Series.
DC73.A2 R39 1976   944/.01   *LC* 75-32935

Cabaniss, Allen, 1911-.   **3.1985**
Charlemagne, by Allen Cabaniss. New York, Twayne Publishers [1972] 176 p. 21 cm. (Twayne's rulers and statesmen of the world series, TROW 15) 1. Charlemagne, Emperor, 742-814. I. T.
DC73.C15   944/.01/0924 B   *LC* 79-181717

Calmette, Joseph, 1873-1952.   **3.1986**
Charlemagne / Joseph Calmette. — [1 éd.] Paris: Presses Universitaires de France, 1951. 127 p.: map; 18 cm. (Que sais-je? 471.) 1. Charlemagne, Emperor, 742-814. I. T. II. Series.
DC73.C212

Folz, Robert.   **3.1987**
[Couronnement impérial de Charlemagne. English] The coronation of Charlemagne, 25 December 800 / Robert Folz; translated by J. E. Anderson. — London: Routledge & K. Paul, 1975 (c1974). xii, 266 p., [12] leaves of plates: ill.; 22 cm. Translation of Le couronnement impérial de Charlemagne, 25 décembre 800. Includes index. 1. Charlemagne, Emperor, 742-814. I. T.
DC73.F613   944/.01/0924 B   *LC* 75-300794   *ISBN* 0710078471

Ganshof, François Louis, 1895-.   • **3.1988**
The Carolingians and the Frankish monarchy; studies in Carolingian history [by] F. L. Ganshof. Translated by Janet Sondheimer. Ithaca, N.Y., Cornell University Press [1971] ix, 314 p. 25 cm. A collection of articles originally in French or German. 1. Charlemagne, Emperor, 742-814. 2. France — History — Carlovingian and early period to 987. I. T.
DC73.G34   944/.01   *LC* 72-147074   *ISBN* 0801406358

Einhard, 770(ca.)-840.   **3.1989**
[Vita Karoli Magni imperatoris. English] The life of Charlemagne. The Latin text with a new English translation, introd. and notes by Evelyn Scherabon Firchow and Edwin H. Zeydel. Coral Gables, Fla., University of Miami Press,

[1972] 144 p. illus. 22 cm. 1. Charlemagne, Emperor, 742-814. I. Firchow, Evelyn Scherabon. ed. II. Zeydel, Edwin H., ed. III. T.
DC73.3 1972   944.01/092/4 B   LC 71-163840   ISBN 0870242121

Fawtier, Robert, 1885-. • 3.1990
[Capétieus et la France. English] The Capetian kings of France; monarchy & nation, 987–1328. Translated into English by Lionel Butler and R. J. Adam. London, Macmillan; New York, St. Martin's Press, 1960. 242 p. illus. 23 cm. Translation of Les Capétiens et la France. 1. France — History — Capetians, 987-1328 I. T.
DC82.F313   944.021   LC 60-1438

Perit-Dutaillis, Charles Edmond 1868-1947. • 3.1991
The feudal monarchy in France and England, from the tenth to the thirteenth century. [Translated from the French by E.D.Hunt] New York, Barnes & Noble [1964] xx, 420 p. geneal. tables, maps. 25 cm. 1. Monarchy 2. Feudalism — France 3. Feudalism — Great Britain. 4. France — History — Capetians, 987-1328 5. Great Britain — History — Medieval period, 1066-1485 I. T.
DC83.P42 1964   944.021   LC 64-3684

Strayer, Joseph Reese, 1904-. • 3.1992
The Albigensian Crusades [by] Joseph R. Strayer. — New York: Dial Press, 1971. 201 p.: map (on lining papers); 22 cm. — (Crosscurrents in world history) 1. Albigenses I. T.
DC83.3.S87   944/.023   LC 70-150404

Sumption, Jonathan. 3.1993
The Albigensian Crusade / Jonathan Sumption. — London; Boston: Faber, 1978. 269 p.: maps; 23 cm. Includes index. 1. Albigenses 2. Languedoc (France) — History. I. T.
DC83.3.S93   272/.3   LC 78-318324   ISBN 0571110649

Joinville, Jean, sire de, 1224?-1317? • 3.1994
The life of St. Louis; translated by René Hague from the text edited by Natalis de Wailly. — New York, Sheed and Ward, 1955. 306 p. illus. 22 cm. — (The Makers of Christendom) Translation of L'histoire et chronique du ... roy S. Loys. 1. Louis IX, King of France, 1214-1270. 2. Crusades — Seventh, 1248-1250 I. T.
DC91.J7 1955   923.144   LC 55-10924

Jordan, William C., 1948-. 3.1995
Louis IX and the challenge of the Crusade: a study in rulership / William Chester Jordan. — Princeton, N.J.: Princeton University Press, 1980 (c1979). xv, 291 p.: ill.; 25 cm. A revision of the author's thesis, Princeton, 1973, entitled: Saint Louis' influence on French Society and life in the thirteenth century. Includes index. 1. Louis IX, King of France, 1214-1270. 2. Crusades — Seventh, 1248-1250 3. Crusades — Eighth, 1270 4. France — History — Louis IX, 1226-1270 I. T.
DC91.J75   944/.023   LC 79-83996   ISBN 0691052859

Pernoud, Régine, 1909-. 3.1996
[Reine Blanche. English] Blanche of Castile / Régine Pernoud; translated by Henry Noel. — 1st American ed. — New York: Coward, McCann & Geoghegan, 1975. 319 p.: [8] leaves of plates: ill., geneal. table (on lining paper); 22 cm. Translation of La reine Blanche. Includes index. 1. Blanche, of Castile, Queen, consort of Louis VIII, King of France, 1188-1252. I. T.
DC91.6.B5 P4713 1975   944/.023/0924 B   LC 74-79678   ISBN 0698105958

Strayer, Joseph Reese, 1904-. 3.1997
The reign of Philip the Fair / by Joseph R. Strayer. — Princeton, N.J.: Princeton University Press, c1980. xvi, 450 p.; [2] leaves of plates: ill.; 24 cm. Includes index. 1. Philip IV, King of France, 1268-1314. 2. France — History — Philip IV, 1285-1314 3. France — Kings and rulers — Biography. I. T.
DC92.S83   944/.024/0924 B   LC 79-3232   ISBN 0691053022

DC96–106 Hundred Years' War. Joan of Arc. Louis XI

Fowler, Kenneth Alan. • 3.1998
The Hundred Years War; edited by Kenneth Fowler. — London: Macmillan; [New York]: St. Martin's Press, 1971. ix, 229 p.; 23 cm. — (Problems in focus series) 1. Hundred Years' War, 1339-1453 I. T.
DC96.F7 1971   944/.025   LC 71-156288   ISBN 0333100115

Perroy, Édouard. • 3.1999
The Hundred Years War / by Edouard Perroy; translated by W.B. Wells; with an introd. to the English edition by David C. Douglas. — Bloomington: Indiana University Press, 1959. 376 p.: maps; 23 cm. 1. Hundred Years' War, 1339-1453 I. T.
DC96.Px   ISBN 039950110X

Seward, Desmond, 1935-. 3.2000
The Hundred Years War: the English in France, 1337–1453 / Desmond Seward. — 1st American ed. — New York: Atheneum, 1978. 296 p., [7] leaves of plates: ill.; 24 cm. Includes index. 1. Hundred Years' War, 1339-1453 I. T.
DC96.S48 1978   944/.025   LC 78-55424   ISBN 0689109199

Gies, Frances. 3.2001
Joan of Arc: the legend and the reality / Frances Gies. — 1st ed. — New York: Harper & Row, c1981. 306 p.: ill.; 22 cm. Includes index. 1. Joan, of Arc, Saint, 1412-1431. 2. Christian saints — France — Biography. I. T.
DC103.G47 1981   944/.026/0924 B 19   LC 80-7900   ISBN 0690019424

Guillemin, Henri, 1903-. 3.2002
[Jeanne dite Jeanne d'Arc. English] Joan, Maid of Orleans. Translated by Harold J. Salemson. [1st American ed.] New York, Saturday Review Press [1973, c1970] 280 p. illus. 22 cm. Translation of Jeanne dite Jeanne d'Arc. 1. Joan, of Arc, Saint, 1412-1431. I. T.
DC103.G86713 1973   944/.026/0924 B   LC 72-88652   ISBN 0841502277

Lucie-Smith, Edward. 3.2003
Joan of Arc / Edward Lucie-Smith. — 1st American ed. — New York: Norton, 1977, c1976. xiv, 326 p., [10] leaves of plates: ill.; 24 cm. Includes index. 1. Joan, of Arc, Saint, 1412-1431. 2. Christian saints — France — Biography. I. T.
DC103.L96 1977   944/.026/0924 B   LC 77-9509   ISBN 0393075206

Warner, Marina, 1946-. 3.2004
Joan of Arc: the image of female heroism / Marina Warner. — 1st American ed. — New York: Knopf, 1981. 349 p.: ill. 1. Joan, of Arc, Saint, 1412-1431. 2. Christian saints — France — Biography. I. T.
DC103.W27 1981   944/.026/0924 B 19   LC 80-2720   ISBN 0394411455

Tyrrell, Joseph M. 3.2005
Louis XI / by Joseph M. Tyrrell. — Boston: Twayne, 1980. 201 p.: ill.; 21 cm. (Twayne's world leaders series; TWLS 82) Includes index. 1. Louis XI, King of France, 1423-1483. 2. France — Kings and rulers — Biography. I. T.
DC106.T9   944/.027/0924 B   LC 79-20907   ISBN 0805777288

DC110–412 MODERN (1515-

Briggs, Robin. 3.2006
Early modern France 1560–1715 / Robin Briggs. — Oxford; New York: Oxford University Press, 1977. xi, 242 p.: ill.; 21 cm. Includes index. 1. France — History — 16th century 2. France — History — 17th century I. T.
DC110.B723   944/.03   LC 77-375942   ISBN 0192158155

Cobban, Alfred. • 3.2007
A history of modern France / Alfred Cobban. — New ed. rev. and enl. — New York: Braziller, 1965. 3 v. in 1.: maps. 1. France — History 2. France — History — Revolution, 1789 I. T.
DC110.C57 1965   LC 65-14605

Guérard, Albert Léon, 1880-1959. • 3.2008
The life and death of an ideal: France in the classical age / Albert Guérard. — New York: G. Braziller, 1956, c1928. x, 391 p.; 21 cm. 1. France — History — 16th century 2. France — History — Bourbons, 1589-1789 3. France — History — 18th century 4. France — History — 17th century I. T. II. Title: France in the classical age.
DC110.G8 1956   944/.03   LC 56-2497

Wright, Gordon, 1912-. • 3.2009
France in modern times: 1760 to the present. — Chicago: Rand McNally, [c1960] 621 p.: illus.; 24 cm. — (Rand McNally history series) 1. France — History I. T.
DC110.W7   944   LC 60-12278

DC111–120 16th Century (1515–1589)

Kingdon, Robert McCune, 1927-. • 3.2010
Geneva and the coming of the wars of religion in France, 1555-1563. — Genève: E. Droz, 1956. 163 p.; 26 cm. — (Travaux d'humanisme et renaissance; 22) Abstracted in Dissertation abstracts, v.15 (1955) no. 5, p. 809-810. 1. Compagnie des pasteurs et professeurs de Genève. 2. France — History — Wars of the Huguenots, 1562-1598 I. T.
DC111.K5

Neale, John Ernest, Sir, 1890-.   • **3.2011**
The age of Catherine de Medici. New York, Barnes & Noble [1959, c1958]
111 p. 21 cm. 1. Catherine de Médicis, consort of Henry II, King of France,
1519-1589. 2. France — History — Wars of the Huguenots, 1562-1598 I. T.
DC111.3.N4   *LC* a 59-8073

Kelley, Donald R.   **3.2012**
François Hotman; a revolutionary's ordeal, by Donald R. Kelley. —
[Princeton, N.J.]: Princeton University Press, [1973] xvi, 370 p.: illus.; 23 cm.
1. Hotman, François, sieur de Villiers Saint Paul, 1524-1590. 2. France —
Politics and government — 16th century I. T.
DC112.H67 K44   284/.5/0924 B   *LC* 72-735

Knecht, R. J. (Robert Jean)   **3.2013**
Francis I / R.J. Knecht. — Cambridge; New York: Cambridge University
Press, 1982. xv, 480 p., [8] leaves of plates: ill.; 24 cm. Includes index.
1. Francis I, King of France, 1494-1547. 2. France — History — Francis I,
1515-1547 3. France — Kings and rulers — Biography. I. T.
DC113.K58   944/.028/0924 19   *LC* 81-12197   *ISBN* 0521243440

Salmon, J. H. M. (John Hearsey McMillan), 1925-.   **3.2014**
Society in crisis: France in the sixteenth century / J. H. M. Salmon. New York:
St. Martin's Press, 1975. 383 p., [6] leaves of plates: ill.; 25 cm. Includes index.
1. Church and state in France. 2. France — History — Wars of the
Huguenots, 1562-1598 3. France — Social conditions I. T.
DC116.5.S25 1975b   944/.028   *LC* 75-5141

Héritier, Jean, 1892-.   • **3.2015**
Catherine de Médicis. Nouv. éd. entièrement refondue. — Paris, A. Fayard
[c1959] 626 p. 19 cm. 1. Catherine de Médicis, Queen, consort of Henry II,
King of France, 1519-1589. I. T.
DC119.8.H44 1959   *LC* 60-33887

DC121–130 17th Century (1589–1715)

Esmonin, Edmond, 1877-.   • **3.2016**
Études sur la France des XVIIe et XVIIIe siècles. Paris, Presses universitaires
de France, 1964. 538 p.; 25 cm. (Grenoble. Université. Faculté des lettres.
Publications, 32) Bibliographical footnotes. I. T. II. Title: Etudes sur la
France des dix-septième et dix-huitième siècles
DC121.E8

Stankiewicz, W. J.   • **3.2017**
Politics & religion in seventeenth–century France; a study of political ideas
from the monarchomachs to Bayle, as reflected in the toleration controversy. —
Berkeley, University of California Press, 1960. x, 269 p. 25 cm. Bibliography: p.
[246]-257. 1. France — Pol. & govt. — 17th cent. 2. Edict of Nantes.
3. Freedom of religion — France. I. T.
DC121.3.S8   944.03   *LC* 60-10648

Lough, John.   • **3.2018**
An introduction to seventeenth century France. — [U.S.A. ed. — New York]:
McKay, [1969] xxi, 296 p.: illus., maps, ports.; 22 cm. 1. France — Civilization
— 17th-18th centuries 2. France — History — 17th century I. T.
DC121.7.L6 1969   914.4/03/32   *LC* 79-8758

Buisseret, David.   **3.2019**
Henry IV / David Buisseret. — London; Boston: G. Allen & Unwin, 1984. xiv,
235 p., [12] p. of plates: ill.; 24 cm. Includes index. 1. Henry IV, King of
France, 1553-1610. 2. France — History — Henry IV, 1589-1610 3. France —
Kings and rulers — Biography. I. T.
DC122.B88 1984   944/.031/0924 19   *LC* 83-22464   *ISBN*
0049440128

Mousnier, Roland.   **3.2020**
[Assassinat d'Henri IV. English] The assassination of Henry IV; the tyrannicide
problem and the consolidation of the French absolute monarchy in the early
seventeenth century. Translated by Joan Spencer. New York, Scribner [1973]
428 p. illus. 23 cm. Translation of L'assassinat d'Henri IV. 1. Henry IV, King
of France, 1553-1610. 2. France — History — Henri IV, 1589-1610. 3. France
— Church history — 16th century I. T.
DC122.3.M613   944/.031/0924   *LC* 72-11214   *ISBN* 0684133571

Liublinskaia, Aleksandra Dmitrievna.   • **3.2021**
[Frantsuzskiĭ absoliutizm. English] French absolutism: the crucial phase
1620-1629 [by] A. D. Lublinskaya; translated [from the Russian] by Brian
Pearce, with a foreword by J. H. Elliot. London, Cambridge U.P., 1968. xvi,
350 p. map. 24 cm. Translation of Frantsuzskiĭ absoliutizm v pervoĭ treti
semnadtsatogo v. (romanized form) 1. France — History — Louis XIII,
1610-1643 2. France — Economic conditions I. T.
DC123.L5813   944/.032   *LC* 68-21395   *ISBN* 0521071178

Tapié, Victor Lucien, 1900-1974.   **3.2022**
[France de Louis XIII et de Richelieu. English] France in the age of Louis XIII
and Richelieu [by] Victor-L. Tapié. Translated and edited by D. McN. Lockie.
With a foreword by A. G. Dickens. New York, Praeger [1975] xix, 622 p. illus.
22 cm. Translation of La France de Louis XIII et de Richelieu. 1. Louis XIII,
King of France, 1601-1643. 2. Richelieu, Armand Jean du Plessis, duc de,
1585-1642. 3. France — History — Louis XIII, 1610-1643 I. T.
DC123.T313 1975   944/.032   *LC* 74-8919   *ISBN* 0275525309

Ranum, Orest A.   • **3.2023**
Richelieu and the councillors of Louis XIII: a study of the secretaries of state
and superintendents of finance in the ministry of Richelieu, 1635–1642. —
Oxford [Eng.] Clarendon Press, 1963. vi, 211 p. ports. 23 cm. Bibliography: p.
[199]-205. 1. Richelieu, Armand Jean du Plessis, duc de, 1585-1642. 2. France
— Pol. & govt. — 1610-1643. I. T.
DC123.3.R3 1963   944.032   *LC* 63-3603

Church, William Farr, 1912-.   • **3.2024**
Richelieu and reason of state, by William F. Church. — Princeton, N.J.:
Princeton University Press, [1973, c1972] 554 p.; 25 cm. 1. Richelieu, Armand
Jean du Plessis, duc de, 1585-1642. 2. France — Politics and government —
1610-1643 I. T.
DC123.9.R5 C5   944/.032/0924   *LC* 76-181518   *ISBN*
0691051992

Marvick, Elizabeth Wirth.   **3.2025**
The young Richelieu: a psychoanalytic approach to leadership / Elizabeth
Wirth Marvick. — Chicago: University of Chicago Press, c1983. x, 276 p.; 23
cm. (Chicago original paperbacks) Includes index. 1. Richelieu, Armand Jean
du Plessis, duc de, 1585-1642 — Psychology. 2. Statesmen — France —
Biography. 3. France — History — Louis XIII, 1610-1643 I. T.
DC123.9.R5 M38 1983   944/.032/0924 B 19   *LC* 82-24754   *ISBN*
0226509052

Treasure, G. R. R. (Geoffrey Russell Richards)   **3.2026**
Cardinal Richelieu and the development of absolutism [by] G. R. R. Treasure.
— New York: St. Martin's Press, [1972] 316 p.: map.; 23 cm. 1. Richelieu,
Armand Jean du Plessis, duc de, 1585-1642. I. T.
DC123.9.R5 T7   944/.032/0924 B   *LC* 76-183397

Wedgwood, C. V. (Cicely Veronica), 1910-.   • **3.2027**
Richelieu and the French monarchy. New, rev. ed. New York, Collier Books
[1962] 155 p. 18 cm. (Men and history, BS130V) 1. Richelieu, Armand Jean du
Plessis, duc de, 1585-1642. I. T.
DC123.9.R5 W4 1962   923.244   *LC* 62-19197

Kossmann, E. H. (Ernst Heinrich), 1922-.   • **3.2028**
La Fronde. Leiden, Universitaire Pers Leiden, 1954. 275 p. 25 cm. (Leidse
historische reeks, deel 3) 1. Fronde I. T.
DC 124.4 K86   *LC* 55-21638

Moote, Alanson Lloyd.   **3.2029**
The revolt of the judges; the Parlement of Paris and the Fronde, 1643–1652, by
A. Lloyd Moote. — Princeton, N.J.: Princeton University Press, [1972, c1971]
xiv, 407 p.; 25 cm. 1. France. Parlement (Paris) 2. Fronde I. T.
DC124.4.M66   944/.03   *LC* 78-155003   *ISBN* 0691051917

DC125–130 Louis XIV, 1638–1715

Voltaire, 1694-1778.   • **3.2030**
The age of Louis XIV / Translated by Martyn P. Pollack. London: Dent; New
York: Dutton, [1926] xiv, 475 p.; 18 cm. 1. France — History — Louis XIV,
1643-1715 I. T.
DC125.V6x   *LC* a 26-193

Mongrédien, Georges, 1901-.   • **3.2031**
La vie quotidienne sous Louis XIV. [Paris] Hachette [1948] 250 p. 20 cm.
1. France — Social life and customs I. T.
DC126.M54   944.033   *LC* 49-24648

André, Louis, 1867-1948.   **3.2032**
Louis XIV et l'Europe. Paris, Michel, 1950. xxix, 395 p. ports., fold. maps.
(L'Évolution de l'humanité, synthèse collective, 3. sect., 64) 1. Louis XIV,
King of France, 1638-1715. I. T.
DC127.3 A6

Louis XIV and Europe / edited by Ragnhild Hatton.   **3.2033**
Columbus: Ohio State University Press, 1976. xiii, 311 p.: maps; 23 cm.
1. France — Foreign relations — 1643-1715 — Addresses, essays, lectures.
2. France — Politics and government — 1643-1715 — Addresses, essays,
lectures. I. Hatton, Ragnhild Marie.
DC127.3.L68 1976   320.9/44/033   *LC* 75-45334   *ISBN*
0814202543

Lewis, W. H. (Warren Hamilton), 1895-.   • **3.2034**
The splendid century; life in the France of Louis XIV. Garden City, N.Y.,
Doubleday, 1957 [c1953] 304 p. illus. 19 cm. (Doubleday anchor books, A122)
1. France — Social life and customs I. T.
DC128 L4x   944.033   LC 57-3377

Klaits, Joseph.   **3.2035**
Printed propaganda under Louis XIV: absolute monarchy and public opinion /
by Joseph Klaits. — Princeton, N.J.: Princeton University Press, 1977 (c1976).
xiii, 341 p.; 23 cm. Includes index. 1. Public opinion — France.
2. Propaganda, French 3. France — Politics and government — 1643-1715
I. T.
DC128.5.K58   354.44/0075   LC 76-3268   ISBN 0691052387

Goubert, Pierre.   • **3.2036**
Louis XIV and twenty million Frenchmen; translated [from the French] by
Anne Carter. — London: Allen Lane, 1970. 350 p.; 23 cm. Translation of Louis
XIV et vingt millions de Français. 1. Louis XIV, King of France, 1638-1715.
2. France — History — Louis XIV, 1643-1715 I. T.
DC129.G613 1970b   944/.033   LC 76-498058   ISBN 0713901039

Louis XIV and the craft of kingship, edited by John C. Rule.   • **3.2037**
[Columbus]: Ohio State University Press, [1970, c1969] x, 478 p.: illus., port.;
24 cm. Includes chiefly papers originally presented at a conference held at Ohio
State University, Dec., 1964. 1. Louis XIV, King of France, 1638-1715.
I. Rule, John C. ed.
DC129.L68   944/.033/0924   LC 72-79845

Wolf, John Baptist, 1907-.   • **3.2038**
Louis XIV, by John B. Wolf. — [1st ed.]. — New York: Norton, [1968] xix,
678 p.: illus., coat of arms, maps, port.; 25 cm. 1. Louis XIV, King of France,
1638-1715. I. T.
DC129.W6 1968   944/.033/0924 B   LC 67-20618

Orléans, Charlotte-Elisabeth, duchesse d', 1652-1722.   **3.2039**
[Selections. English. 1984] A woman's life in the court of the Sun King: letters
of Liselotte von der Pfalz, Elisabeth Charlotte, Duchesse d'Orléans, 1652–1722
/ translated and introduced by Elborg Forster. — Baltimore: Johns Hopkins
University Press, 1984. lx, 287 p.; 26 cm. 'Based on a text originally published in
German in 1958 by Langwiesche Verlag, Ebenhausen, as Liselotte von der
Pfalz, Elisabeth Charlotte von der Pfalz, Duchesse d'Orléans, Madame,
Briefe'—Verso t.p. Includes index. 1. Orléans, Charlotte-Elisabeth, duchesse
d', 1652-1722. 2. France — History — Louis XIV, 1643-1715 3. France —
Court and courtiers 4. France — Princes and princesses — Correspondence.
I. Forster, Elborg, 1931- II. T.
DC130.O7 A4 1984   944/.033/0924 19   LC 84-5718   ISBN
0801831598

Saint-Simon, Louis de Rouvroy, duc de, 1675-1755.   • **3.2040**
Historical memoirs of the duc de Saint-Simon; a shortened version. Edited and
translated by Lucy Norton, with an introd. by D. W. Brogan. New York:
McGraw-Hill, [1968-72. v. 1, c. 1967] 3 v.: illus., maps.; 24 cm. 1. Saint-Simon,
Louis de Rouvroy, duc de, 1675-1755. 2. Saint-Simon, Louis de Rouvroy, duc
de, 1675-1755. 3. France — History — Louis XIV, 1643-1715 4. France —
History — Regency, 1715-1723 5. France — Court and courtiers I. Norton,
Lucy. ed. II. T.
DC130.S2 A1992   944/.033/0924   LC 67-24825   ISBN
007054459X

DC131–138 18th Century (1715–1789)

Behrens, Catherine Betty Abigail.   • **3.2041**
The ancien régime [by] C. B. A. Behrens. — [1st American ed. — New York]:
Harcourt, Brace & World, [1967] 215 p.: illus. (part col.), maps, ports.; 21 cm.
1. France — History — Louis XV, 1715-1774 2. France — History — Louis
XVI, 1774-1793 3. Europe — History — 18th century I. T.
DC131.B4 1967   944/.034   LC 67-11707

Gottschalk, Louis Reichenthal, 1899-.   • **3.2042**
The era of the French revolution (1715–1815). Boston: Houghton Mifflin,
[c1929]. 509 p. 1. Napoleon I, Emperor of the French, 1769-1821. 2. France —
Politics and government 3. France — History — Revolution, 1789-1799
4. France — History — Consulate and Empire, 1799-1815 I. T.
DC131.G6   LC 29-9131

Du Pont de Nemours, Pierre Samuel, 1739-1817.   **3.2043**
[Enfance et la jeunesse de Du Pont de Nemours racontées par lui-même.
English] The autobiography of Du Pont de Nemours / translated, and with an
introduction by Elizabeth Fox-Genovese. — Wilmington, Del.: Scholarly
Resources, c1984. xviii, 298 p.: ill.; 24 cm. Translation of the manuscript in the
Eleutherian Mills Historical Library: Mémoires de Pierre Samuel Du Pont
adressés à ses enfans; first published as: L'enfance et la jeunesse de Du Pont de
Nemours, racontées par lui-même. Paris, 1906. 1. Du Pont de Nemours, Pierre

Samuel, 1739-1817. 2. Du Pont family 3. Intellectuals — France —
Biography. 4. France — History — 18th century I. T.
DC131.9.D85 A3413 1984   944.04/092/4 B 19   LC 84-10645

Murphy, Orville Theodore.   **3.2044**
Charles Gravier, Comte de Vergennes: French diplomacy in the age of
revolution, 1719–1787 / by Orville T. Murphy. — Albany: State University of
New York Press, c1982. xi, 607 p.; 24 cm. Includes index. 1. Vergennes,
Charles Gravier, comte de, 1719-1787. 2. Diplomats — France — Biography.
3. France — Foreign relations — 1715-1793 I. T.
DC131.9.V3 M84 1982   327.2/092/ B 19   LC 81-2281   ISBN
0873954823

Gaxotte, Pierre.   • **3.2045**
Le siècle de Louis XV. Nouv. éd., rev. et augm. Paris A. Fayard [1958] 492p.
(Les Grandes études historiques) 1. France — History — Louis XV, 1715-1774
I. T.
DC133 G3 1958

Darnton, Robert.   **3.2046**
The literary underground of the Old Regime / Robert Darnton. — Cambridge,
Mass.: Harvard University Press, 1982. ix, 258 p.; 24 cm. 1. Underground
literature — France. 2. France — History — Revolution, 1789-1799 — Causes
I. T.
DC133.3.D37 1982   944.04/2 19   LC 82-2918   ISBN 0674536568

Gooch, G. P. (George Peabody), 1873-1968.   • **3.2047**
Louis XV; the monarchy in decline. — London, New York, Longmans, Green
[1956] 285 p. illus. 23 cm. 1. Louis XV, King of France, 1710-1774. I. T.
DC133.3.G6   923.144   LC 56-59058

Lough, John.   • **3.2048**
An introduction to eighteenth century France / by John Lough. — London:
Longmans, c1960. 349 p.: ill.; 22 cm. 1. France — Civilization 2. France —
History — Bourbons, 1589-1789 I. T.
DC133.8.L6   944.034   LC 60-2946

Butler, Rohan d'Olier.   **3.2049**
Choiseul, Vol.1: Father and son, 1719–1754. — Oxford: Clarendon Press, Apr.
1980. [1350] p. 1. Statesmen — France — Biography. I. T.
DC135.C5   944/.034/0924   LC 79-41033   ISBN 0198225091

Cronin, Vincent.   **3.2050**
Louis and Antoinette / by Vincent Cronin. — New York: Morrow, 1975,
c1974. 445 p., [9] leaves of plates: ill.; 24 cm. 1. Louis XVI, King of France,
1754-1793. 2. Marie Antoinette, Queen, consort of Louis XVI, King of France,
1755-1793. I. T.
DC137.C76 1975   944/.035/0924 B   LC 74-15762   ISBN
0688003311

Jordan, David P., 1939-.   **3.2051**
The king's trial: the French Revolution vs. Louis XVI / David P. Jordan. —
Berkeley: University of California Press, c1979. xx, 275 p., [7] leaves of plates:
ports.; 24 cm. Includes index. 1. Louis XVI, King of France, 1754-1793.
2. France — History — Revolution, 1792-1793 3. France — Kings and rulers
— Biography. I. T.
DC137.08.J68   944/.035/0924 B   LC 78-54797   ISBN 0520036840

Walzer, Michael. comp.   **3.2052**
Regicide and revolution; speeches at the trial of Louis XVI. Edited with an
introd. by Michael Walzer. Translated by Marian Rothstein. — [London; New
York]: Cambridge University Press, [1974] vii, 219 p.; 22 cm. — (Cambridge
studies in the history and theory of politics) 1. Louis XVI, King of France,
1754-1793. 2. Monarchy — France 3. Regicides 4. France — History —
Revolution, 1792-1793 I. T.
DC137.08.W34   944/.035/0924   LC 73-94370   ISBN 0521203708

Huisman, Philippe.   **3.2053**
[Marie-Antoinette. English] Marie Antoinette [by] Philippe Huisman and
Marguerite Jallut. New York, Viking Press [1971] 249 p. illus. (part col.),
facsims., maps, ports. (part col.) 27 cm. (A Studio book) 1. Marie Antoinette,
Queen, consort of Louis XVI, King of France, 1755-1793. I. Jallut, Marguerite,
joint author. II. T.
DC137.1.H8413   944/.035/0924 B   LC 70-162666   ISBN
0670456977

Seward, Desmond, 1935-.   **3.2054**
Marie Antoinette / Desmond Seward. — New York: St. Martin's Press, c1981.
297 p.: ports.; 22 cm. Includes index. 1. Marie Antoinette, Queen, consort of
Louis XVI, King of France, 1755-1793. 2. France — Queens — Biography.
I. T.
DC137.1.S47 1981   944/.035/0924 B 19   LC 81-21442   ISBN
0312514670

Loomis, Stanley.   3.2055
The fatal friendship: Marie Antoinette, Count Fersen and the flight to Varennes / Stanley Loomis. — New York: Doubleday, 1972. 341 p.: ill.; 25 cm. 1. Marie Antoinette, Queen, consort of Louis XVI, King of France, 1755-1793. 2. Fersen, Hans Axel von, greve, 1755-1810. 3. France — History — Revolution, 1789-1799 I. T.
DC137.19.L66   *LC* 72-175388

Dakin, Douglas.   • 3.2056
Turgot and the ancien régime in France. New York, Octagon Books, 1965. xi, 361 p. map, port. 24 cm. 'Originally published 1939 ... reprinted 1965.' 1. Turgot, Anne-Robert-Jacques, baron de l'Aulne, 1727-1781. 2. Finance, Public — France — To 1789 3. Taxation — France — History. 4. France — Politics and government — 1774-1793 I. T.
DC137.5.T9 D3 1965   *LC* 65-16771

Egret, Jean.   3.2057
[Pré-révolution française, 1787-1788. English] The French prerevolution, 1787–1788 / Jean Egret; translated by Wesley D. Camp; introd. by J. F. Bosher. — Chicago: University of Chicago Press, 1978 (c1977). xxii, 314 p.; 24 cm. Translation of La pré-révolution française, 1787-1788. Includes indexes. 1. France — History — Revolution, 1789-1799 — Causes 2. France — History — Louis XVI, 1774-1793 I. T.
DC138.E3613   944/.035   *LC* 77-78776   *ISBN* 0226191427

Furet, François, 1927-.   3.2058
[Penser la Révolution française. English] Interpreting the French Revolution / François Furet; translated by Elborg Forster. — Cambridge; New York: Cambridge University Press; Paris: Editions de la Maison des sciences de l'homme, 1981. x, 204 p.; 24 cm. Translation of: Penser la Révolution française. 1. Cochin, Augustin, 1876-1916. 2. Tocqueville, Alexis de, 1805-1859. 3. France — History — Revolution, 1789-1799 — Causes 4. France — History — Revolution, 1789-1799 — Historiography. I. T.
DC138.F813   944.04 19   *LC* 80-42290   *ISBN* 052123574X

Godechot, Jacques Léon, 1907-.   • 3.2059
France and the Atlantic revolution of the eighteenth century, 1770–1799 [by] Jacques Godechot. Translated by Herbert H. Rowen. — New York, Free Press [1965] vii, 279 p. 22 cm. Translation of Les révolutions, 1770-1799. Bibliography: p. 249-274. 1. France — Hist. — Revolution — Causes and character. 2. History, Modern — 18th cent. 3. Europe — Hist. — 1789-1815. I. T.
DC138.G543   940.27   *LC* 65-16268

Mornet, Daniel, 1878-1954.   • 3.2060
Les Origines intellectuelles de la Révolution française, 1715–1787. Préface de René Pomeau ... — 6e édition. — Paris, A. Colin, 1967. xii, 552 p. 24 cm. Bibliography: p. [505]-548. 1. France — Hist. — Revolution — Causes and characters. 2. France — Intellectual life I. T.
DC138.M56 1967   *LC* 68-86443

Herr, Richard.   • 3.2061
Tocqueville and the old regime. — Princeton, N. J., Princeton University Press, 1962. 146 p. 23 cm. Bibliographical footnotes. 1. Tocqueville, Alexis de, 1805-1859. L'ancien régime et la révolution. I. T.
DC138.T6344H4   944.04   *LC* 62-7404

DC139–249 Revolution. Napoleonic Period (1789–1815)

Roberts, J. M. (John Morris), 1928- ed.   • 3.2062
French Revolution documents. Editors: J. M. Roberts and R. C. Cobb. — New York, Barnes & Noble, 1966-1973. 2 v. 23 cm. 1. France — History — Revolution — Sources. I. Cobb, Richard, 1917- joint ed. II. T.
DC141.F7x   944.04

Gilchrist, John Thomas.   3.2063
The press in the French Revolution; a selection of documents taken from the press of the Revolution for the years 1789–1794 [compiled by] J. Gilchrist [and] W. J. Murray. — [New York]: St. Martin's Press, [1971] xvi, 335 p.; 24 cm. 1. France — History — Revolution, 1789-1794 — Sources. I. Murray, W. J. (William J.) joint comp. II. T.
DC141.G5 1971   944.04   *LC* 77-150256

Stewart, John Hall, 1904-.   • 3.2064
A documentary survey of the French Revolution. — New York, Macmillan [1951] xxviii, 818 p. facsims. (on lining papers) 22 cm. Includes bibliographies. 1. France — Hist. — Revolution — Sources. I. T.
DC141.7.S8   944.04   *LC* 51-10629

DC146 Biography

Gershoy, Leo, 1897-.   • 3.2065
Bertrand Barere; a reluctant terrorist. — Princeton, N. J., Princeton University Press, 1962. 459 p. illus. 23 cm. 1. Barère, B. (Bertrand), 1755-1841. I. T.
DC146.B2G43   923.244   *LC* 61-11848

Hampson, Norman.   3.2066
Danton / Norman Hampson. — New York: Holmes & Meier Publishers, 1978. x, 182 p.: port.; 23 cm. Includes index. 1. Danton, Georges Jacques, 1759-1794. 2. Revolutionists — France — Biography. 3. France — History — Revolution, 1789-1794 I. T.
DC146.D2 H35 1978   944.04/092/4 B   *LC* 78-9817   *ISBN* 0841904081

Necheles, Ruth F., 1936-.   3.2067
The abbé Grégoire, 1787–1831; the odyssey of an egalitarian [by] Ruth F. Necheles. Westport, Conn., Greenwood Pub. Corp. [1971] xviii, 333 p. port. 22 cm. (Contributions in Afro-American and African studies. no. 9) 'A Negro Universities Press publication.' 1. Grégoire, Henri, 1750-1831. I. T. II. Series.
DC146.G84 N4   282.0924 B   *LC* 75-105987   *ISBN* 0837133122

Gottschalk, Louis Reichenthal, 1899-1975.   3.2068
Lafayette in the French revolution; from the October days through the federation. By Louis Gottschalk and Margaret Maddox. Chicago, University of Chicago Press, 1973. 586 p. 24 cm. 1. Lafayette, Marie Joseph Paul Yves Roch Gilbert Du Motier, marquis de, 1757-1834. 2. France — History — Revolution, 1789-1793 I. Maddox, Margaret. joint author. II. T.
DC 146 L2 G683 1973   *LC* 72-94731   *ISBN* 0226305473

Acomb, Frances Dorothy, 1907-.   3.2069
Mallet du Pan (1749–1800); a career in political journalism [by] Frances Acomb. Durham, N.C., Duke University Press, 1973. xii, 304 p. 25 cm. 1. Mallet du Pan, M. (Jacques), 1749-1800. I. T.
DC146.M25 A64   070/.92/4 B   *LC* 72-96985   *ISBN* 0822302950

Carr, John Laurence.   3.2070
Robespierre; the force of circumstance. New York, St. Martin's Press [1973, c1972] xiii, 240 p. illus. 23 cm. 1. Robespierre, Maximilien, 1758-1794. I. T.
DC146.R6 C27 1973   944.04/092/4 B   *LC* 72-90765

Jordan, David P., 1939-.   3.2071
The revolutionary career of Maximilien Robespierre / David P. Jordan. — New York: Free Press, c1985. xii, 308 p.: ports.; 25 cm. Includes index. 1. Robespierre, Maximilien, 1758-1794. 2. France — History — Revolution, 1789-1794 I. T.
DC146.R6 J67 1985   944.04 19   *LC* 85-1871   *ISBN* 002916530X

Rudé, George F. E.   3.2072
Robespierre: portrait of a Revolutionary Democrat / George Rudé. — New York: Viking Press, 1976, c1975. 254 p., [6] leaves of plates: ill.; 25 cm. Includes index. 1. Robespierre, Maximilien, 1758-1794. I. T.
DC146.R6 R83 1976   944.04/1/0924 B   *LC* 75-2448   *ISBN* 0670601284

Bruun, Geoffrey, 1898-.   • 3.2073
Saint–Just, apostle of the terror. Hamden, Conn., Archon Books, 1966 [c1932] 168 p. 21 cm. 1. Saint-Just, 1767-1794. 2. France — History — Revolution, 1793-1794 I. T.
DC146.S135 B7 1966   944.0440924   *LC* 66-16083

Van Deusen, Glyndon G. (Glyndon Garlock), 1897-.   • 3.2074
Sieyes: his life and his nationalism, by Glyndon G. Van Deusen. New York, AMS Press [1970] 170 p. 23 cm. (Studies in history, economics, and public law, no. 362) Reprint of the 1932 ed. 1. Sieyès, Emanuel Joseph, comte, 1748-1836. 2. Nationalism — France 3. France — Politics and government — 1774-1793 4. France — Politics and government — 1789-1815 I. T.
DC146.S5 V3 1970   944.04/0924   *LC* 68-58632   *ISBN* 040451362X

Herold, J. Christopher.   • 3.2075
Mistress to an age; a life of Madame de Staël. [1st ed.] Indianapolis, Bobbs-Merrill Co. [1958] 500 p. illus. 22 cm. 1. Staël, Madame de (Anne-Louise-Germaine), 1766-1817. I. T.
DC146.S7 H44   928.4   *LC* 58-12385

DC147–150 General Works

Doyle, William, 1942-.   3.2076
Origins of the French revolution / by William Doyle. — Oxford; New York: Oxford University Press, 1981 (c1980). 247 p.; 21 cm. 1. France — History — Revolution, 1789-1799 — Historiography. 2. France — History — Revolution, 1789-1799 — Causes I. T.
DC147.8.D69   944.04/072 19   *LC* 80-40740   *ISBN* 0198730209

Farmer, Paul, 1918-. • 3.2077
France reviews its revolutionary origins: social politics and historical opinion in the Third Republic / by Paul Farmer. — New York: Octagon Books, 1963. vi, 145 p. 1. Historians, French. 2. France — History — Revolution, 1789-1799 3. France — History — Historiography. 4. France — Politics and government — 1870-1940 I. T.
DC147.8.F3 1963 944 LC 63-20890 ISBN 0374926980

Bouloiseau, Marc. 3.2078
[République jacobine. English] The Jacobin Republic, 1792–1794 / Marc Bouloiseau; translated by Jonathan Mandelbaum. — Cambridge [Cambridgeshire]; New York: Cambridge University Press; Paris: Editions de la Maison des sciences de l'homme, 1984 (c1983). xvi, 251 p.: ill.; 22 cm. — (French Revolution. 2) Translation of: La République jacobine. 1. France — History — Revolution, 1792-1794 I. T. II. Series.
DC148.F7 944.04 s 944.04/3 19 LC 83-5293 ISBN 0521247268

Vovelle, Michel. 3.2079
[Chute de la monarchie, 1787-1792. English] The fall of the French monarchy, 1787–1792 / Michel Vovelle; translated by Susan Burke. — Cambridge [Cambridgeshire]; New York: Cambridge University Press; Paris: Editions de la Maison des sciences de l'homme, c1984. xv, 247 p.: ill.; 22 cm. (French Revolution. 1) Translation of: La chute de la monarchie, 1787-1792. Includes index. 1. France — History — Revolution, 1789-1799 — Causes 2. France — History — Revolution, 1789-1793 I. T. II. Series.
DC148.F7 1983 vol. 1 DC138 944/.035 19 LC 83-7800 ISBN 0521247233

Godechot, Jacques Léon, 1907-. 3.2080
[Contre-révolution: doctrine et action, 1789-1804. English] The counter-revolution: doctrine and action, 1789–1804 [by] Jacques Godechot. Translated from the French by Salvator Attanasio. [1st American ed.] New York, H. Fertig, 1971. x, 405 p. 24 cm. Translation of La contre-révolution: doctrine et action, 1789-1804. 1. France — History — 1789-1815 2. France — History — Revolution, 1789-1799 — Foreign public opinion. I. T.
DC148.G5513 1971 320.9/44/04 LC 70-159820

Godechot, Jacques Léon, 1907-. • 3.2081
La grande nation; l'expansion révolutionnaire de la France dans le monde de 1789 à 1799. Paris: Aubier, 1956. 2 v. (758 p.); 20 cm. (Collection historique) 1. France — History — Revolution I. T.
DC148 G56 1956

Hampson, Norman. • 3.2082
A social history of the French Revolution. — London: Routledge and K. Paul, [1963] viii, 278 p.; 22 cm. — (Studies in social history) Bibliography: p. 266-271. 1. France — Hist. — Revolution. 2. Social classes — France. I. T.
DC148.H26 LC 64-1533

Kropotkin, Petr Alekseevich, kniaz', 1842-1921. 3.2083
[Grande Révolution. English] The great French Revolution, 1789–1793. Translated from the French by N. F. Dryhurst. Foreword by George Woodcock and Ivan Avakumović. New York, Schocken Books [1971] xix, 610 p. 22 cm. (Studies in the libertarian and Utopian tradition) Reprint of the 1909 ed. Translation of La grande révolution. 1. France — History — Revolution, 1789-1793 2. France — History — Revolution, 1789-1799 — Causes I. T.
DC148.K8 1971 944.04 LC 75-163336

Lefebvre, Georges, 1874-1959. • 3.2084
[Revolution française. English] The French Revolution. Translated from the French by Elizabeth Moss Evanson. London, Routledge & K. Paul; New York, Columbia University Press, 1962-64. 2 v. 23 cm. Vol. 2 translated by John Hall Stewart and James Friguglietti. 1. France — History — Revolution, 1789-1799 I. T.
DC148.L413 944.04 LC 64-11939

Soboul, Albert. 3.2085
[Précis d'histoire de la Révolution française. English] The French Revolution, 1787–1799; from the storming of the Bastille to Napoleon. Translated from the French by Alan Forrest & Colin Jones. [1st American ed.] New York: Random House, 1975. 638 p. 22 cm. Translation of Précis d'histoire de la Révolution française. 1. France — History — Revolution, 1789-1799 I. T.
DC148.S5613 1975 944.04 LC 74-8159 ISBN 0394473922

Soboul, Albert. 3.2086
A short history of the French Revolution, 1789–1799 / Albert Soboul; translated by Geoffrey Symcox. — Berkeley: University of California Press, 1977. xxvi, 171 p. 1. France — History — Revolution, 1789-1799 I. T.
DC148.S6213 LC 74-16717 ISBN 0520028554

Sydenham, M. J. 3.2087
The first French republic, 1792–1804 [by] M. J. Sydenham. — Berkeley: University of California Press, 1974. xi, 360 p.: illus.; 23 cm. 1. France — History — Revolution, 1789-1799 2. France — History — Consulate and Empire, 1799-1815 I. T.
DC148.S985 1974b 944.04 LC 73-85796 ISBN 0520025776

Tocqueville, Alexis de, 1805-1859. • 3.2088
The European revolution & correspondence with Gobineau. Introduced, edited, and translated by John Lukacs. — Garden City, N. Y., Doubleday, 1959. xi, 340 p. 18 cm. — (Doubleday anchor books, A163) 1. France — Hist. — Revolution. 2. Europe — Hist. — 1789-1900. I. Gobineau, Arthur, comte de, 1816-1882. II. T.
DC148.T683 LC 59-6275

Mathiez, Albert, 1874-1932. • 3.2089
The French Revolution. Translated from the French by Catherine Alison Phillips. New York, Russell & Russell, 1962 [c1956] 509 p. 25 cm. 1. France — History — Revolution. I. T.
DC149.M26 1962 LC 62-13841

Burke, Edmund, 1729-1797. • 3.2090
Reflections on the revolution in France / Edmund Burke; edited with an introd. by Thomas Mahoney, with an analysis by Oskar Peist. — New York:Liberal Arts Press, [c1955] xliv,307p. (Library of liberal arts. no.46) 1. France — History — Revolution, 1789-1799 — Causes I. T. II. Series.
DC150.B852 944.04 LC 56-491

DC151–159 SPECIAL ASPECTS

Chandler, David G. • 3.2091
The campaigns of Napoleon [by] David G. Chandler. — New York: Macmillan, [1966] xliii, 1172 p.: illus., facsims., maps (part col.), ports.; 24 cm. 1. Napoleon I, Emperor of the French, 1769-1821. 2. Europe — History — 1789-1815 3. France — History, Military — 1789-1815 I. T.
DC151.C48 940.270924 LC 66-12970

Phipps, Ramsay Weston, 1838-1923. • 3.2092
The armies of the first French Republic and the rise of the marshals of Napoleon I ... by the late Colonel Ramsay Weston Phipps ... — London: Oxford University Press, 1926-. v.: fold. maps.; 24 cm. 1. France. Armée — History. 2. Marshals — France. 3. France — History, Military — 1789-1815 4. France — History — Revolution, 1791-1797 5. France — History — Revolution, 1797-1799 I. T.
DC151.P46 1926 LC 27-14675

Mahan, A. T. (Alfred Thayer), 1840-1914. • 3.2093
The influence of sea power upon the French Revolution and Empire, 1793-1812. New York, Greenwood Press [1968, c1892] 2 v. illus. 23 cm. 'Originally published in 1898.' 1. Sea-power 2. France — History — Revolution, 1793-1799 3. France — History — Consulate and Empire, 1799-1815 4. France — History, Naval I. T.
DC153.M216 1968 944.04 LC 69-10127

Aulard, F.-A. (François-Alphonse) 1849-1928. • 3.2094
The French Revolution; a political history, 1789–1804, by A. Aulard. Translated from the French of the 3d ed., with a pref., notes, and historical summary, by Bernard Miall. New York, Russell & Russell, 1965. 4 v. 21 cm. Translation of Histoire politique de la révolution française. 1. Republicanism in France. 2. Political parties — France. 3. France — History — 1789-1815 4. France — Politics and government — 1789-1815 I. Miall, Bernard, 1876- ed. and tr. II. T.
DC155.A92 1965 LC 65-13947

McManners, John. • 3.2095
The French Revolution and the Church. — London: S.P.C.K. for the Church Historical Society, 1969. xiv, 161 p.; 19 cm. — (Church history outlines, 4) 1. France — History — Revolution, 1789-1799 — Religious history I. Church Historical Society (Great Britain) II. T.
DC158.2.M3 322/.1/0944 LC 70-465912 ISBN 0281023352

Cobban, Alfred. • 3.2096
The social interpretation of the French Revolution. — London: Cambridge U.P., 1968. xii, 178 p.; 20cm. — (Wiles lectures. 1962) 1. France — History — Revolution, 1789-1799 2. France — Social conditions — 18th century I. T. II. Series.
DC158.8.C6 1968 944.04 LC 71-474746 ISBN 0521095484

Hunt, Lynn Avery. 3.2097
Politics, culture, and class in the French Revolution / Lynn Hunt. — Berkeley: University of California Press, c1984. xv, 251 p.: ill.; 22 cm. (Studies on the history of society and culture.) 1. Politics and culture — France — History — 18th century. 2. Social classes — France — History — 18th century. 3. France — History — Revolution, 1789-1799 — Social aspects. I. T. II. Series.
DC158.8.H86 1984 306/.2/0944 19 LC 83-27528 ISBN 0520052048

Kates, Gary, 1952-.   3.2098
The Cercle social, the Girondins, and the French Revolution / Gary Kates. —
Princeton, N.J.: Princeton University Press, c1985. xiv, 325 p.: ill.; 22 cm.
Revision of thesis (Ph. D.)—University of Chicago, 1978. Includes index.
1. Cercle social (Paris, France) 2. Girondists 3. France — History —
Revolution, 1789-1799 I. T.
DC158.8.K38 1985   944/.3604 19   *LC* 84-42890   *ISBN*
0691054401

Roberts, J. M. (John Morris), 1928-.   3.2099
The French Revolution / J. M. Roberts. — Oxford [Eng.]; New York: Oxford
University Press, 1978. ix, 176 p.; 20 cm. (opus) Includes index. 1. France —
History — Revolution, 1789-1799 — Causes I. T.
DC158.8.R62   944.04   *LC* 78-40193   *ISBN* 0192890697

Rudé, George F. E.   • 3.2100
The crowd in the French Revolution. Oxford, Clarendon Press, 1959. viii,
267 p. fold. map, tables. 23 cm. 1. Crowds — France. 2. France — History —
Revolution, 1789-1799 — Economic aspects I. T.
DC158.8.R8   944.04   *LC* 59-1108

Soboul, Albert.   • 3.2101
The Parisian sans–culottes and the French Revolution, 1793–4 / English
translation by Gwynne Lewis. Oxford: Clarendon Press, 1964. 280 p.
1. Sansculottes 2. France — History — Revolution, 1793-1794 I. T.
DC158.8.S613   *LC* 64-5298

DC161–249 By Period

DC161–190 Assemblies. Directory
(1787/1789–1799)

Michelet, Jules, 1798-1874.   3.2102
[Histoire de la Révolution française. English] History of the French Revolution.
Histoire de la Révolution française. Translated by Keith Botsford. Text and
notes by Gérald Walter. Wynnewood, Pa.: Livingston Pub. Co., 1972-73. v.
illus. 24 cm. 'A Kolokol Press book.' 1. France — History — Revolution,
1789-1799 2. France — History — Revolution, 1789-1799 — Causes I. T.
DC161.M51532   944.04   *LC* 78-178737   *ISBN* 0870980386

Thompson, J. M. (James Matthew), 1878-1956.   • 3.2103
The French Revolution / by J. M. Thompson. — 5th ed. — Oxford: B.
Blackwell, 1955. xvi, 544 p.: ill., ports., maps. — 'The fifty best books on the
Revolution':p. iii-v. 1. France — History — Revolution, 1789-1794 I. T.
DC161.T47 1955   *LC* 56-3363

Lefebvre, Georges, 1874-1959.   • 3.2104
Coming of the French Revolution, 1789 / G. Lefebvre; tr. from the French by
R. Palmer. — New York: Vintage Books, 1957. 191 p. (Vintage book, K-43.)
"First published in French, under the title Quatre-vingt-neuf, in 1939." —
1. France — History — Revolution — Causes and character. I. T.
DC163.L4 1957   944.04   *LC* 57-1034

Lefebvre, Georges, 1874-1959.   • 3.2105
[Grande peur de 1789. English] The Great Fear of 1789; rural panic in
revolutionary France. Introd. by George Rudé. Translated from the French by
Joan White. [1st American ed.] New York, Pantheon Books [1973] xvi, 234 p.
maps. 22 cm. Translation of La grande peur de 1789. 1. Peasantry — France
2. Depressions 3. France — Economic conditions 4. France — History —
Revolution, 1789 5. France — History — Revolution, 1789-1799 — Causes
I. T.
DC163.L413 1973   944.04/1   *LC* 72-12379   *ISBN* 0394484944

Guérin, Daniel, 1904-.   3.2106
[Lutte de classes, sous la Première République. English] Class struggle in the
first French republic: bourgeois and bras nus 1793–1795 / Daniel Guérin;
translated from the French by Ian Patterson. — London: Pluto, 1978 (c1977).
xv, 295 p.; 21 cm. Translation of La Lutte de classes, sous la Première
République. Includes index. 1. France — Politics and government —
Revolution, 1789-1799 2. France — History — Revolution, 1793-1795 I. T.
DC176.G8313   944.04/3   *LC* 78-326072   *ISBN* 090438330X

Patrick, Alison.   3.2107
The men of the First French Republic; political alignments in the National
Convention of 1792. Baltimore, Johns Hopkins University Press [1972] xviii,
407 p. 23 cm. 1. France. Convention nationale. 2. France — History —
Revolution, 1792-1795 — Biography. I. T.
DC176.P37   944.04/2   *LC* 72-4018   *ISBN* 0801813050

Palmer, R. R. (Robert Roswell), 1909-.   • 3.2108
Twelve who ruled; the year of the terror in the French Revolution. Princeton
Princeton University Press [1958] 417p. 1. France. Convention nationale.

Comité de salut public. 2. France — History — Revolution, 1793-1794
3. France — History — Revolution — Biography I. T.
DC177 P3 1958

Brinton, Crane, 1898-1968.   • 3.2109
The Jacobins; an essay in the new history. — New York, Russell & Russell,
1961 [c1957] 319 p. 22 cm. Includes bibliography. 1. Jacobins I. T.
DC178.B8 1961   944.04   *LC* 61-13765

Kennedy, Michael L.   3.2110
The Jacobin clubs in the French Revolution: the first years / Michael L.
Kennedy. — Princeton, N.J.: Princeton University Press, c1982. xii, 381 p.:
map; 22 cm. Includes index. 1. Jacobins 2. France — History — Revolution,
1789-1799 — Clubs I. T.
DC178.K45   944.04/06 19   *LC* 81-47138   *ISBN* 0691053375

Sydenham, M. J.   • 3.2111
The Girondins. — [London] University of London, Athlone Press, 1961. viii,
252 p. ports., map. 23 cm. — (University of London historical studies, 8) 'An
abridgement of work approved by the University of London for the award of the
degree of doctor of philosophy.' Bibliography: p. [232]-240. 1. France.
Convention nationale. 2. Girondists 3. France — Hist. — Revolution,
1789-1793. I. T.
DC179.S92   944.041   *LC* 61-19510

Sirich, John Black, 1910-.   • 3.2112
The revolutionary committees in the departments of France, 1793–1794. —
New York: H. Fertig, 1971 [c1943] xii, 238 p.; 23 cm. 1. France — Politics and
government — Revolution, 1789-1799 2. France — History — Revolution,
1793-1794 I. T.
DC183.5.S57 1971   944.04   *LC* 73-85082

Lyons, Martyn.   3.2113
France under the directory / Martyn Lyons. — Cambridge [Eng.]; New York:
Cambridge University Press, 1975. x, 259 p.: ill.; 22 cm. Includes index.
1. France — History — Revolution, 1795-1799 I. T.
DC186.L9   944.04/5   *LC* 76-351309   *ISBN* 0521207851

Rose, R. B.   3.2114
Gracchus Babeuf: the first revolutionary Communist / R. B. Rose. — Stanford,
Calif.: Stanford University Press, 1978. viii, 434 p.: ill.; 24 cm. Includes index.
1. Babeuf, Gracchus, 1760-1797. 2. Revolutionists — France — Biography.
I. T.
DC187.8.R67 1978   944.04/092/4 B   *LC* 76-54099   *ISBN*
0804709491

Thomson, David, 1912-.   • 3.2115
The Babeuf plot; the making of a Republican legend. London K. Paul, Trench,
Trubner [1947] xi, 112 p. ports. 1. Babeuf, Gracchus, 1760-1797. 2. Socialism
— France I. T.
DC187.8 T5

DC191–219 Consulate (1799–1804). First
Empire (1804–1815). Napoleon

Slavin, Morris, 1913-.   3.2116
The French Revolution in miniature: section Droits–de–l'Homme, 1789–1795 /
Morris Slavin. — Princeton, N.J.: Princeton University Press, c1984. xvii,
449 p.: ill.; 24 cm. Includes index. 1. Droits-de-l'Homme (Paris, France) —
History. 2. Paris (France) — History — Revolution, 1789-1799 I. T.
DC194.S57 1984   944.04 19   *LC* 83-16034   *ISBN* 0691054150

Forrest, Alan I.   3.2117
Society and politics in revolutionary Bordeaux / by Alan Forrest. — London;
New York: Oxford University Press, 1975. 300 p.: maps; 23 cm. — (Oxford
historical monographs) Includes index. 1. Bordeaux (France) — Politics and
government. 2. Bordeaux (France) — Social conditions. 3. France — History
— Revolution, 1789-1799 I. T.
DC195.B6 F67   944/.71   *LC* 75-322598   *ISBN* 0198218591

Lucas, Colin.   3.2118
The structure of the Terror; the example of Javogues and the Loire. [London]
Oxford University Press, 1973. xv, 411 p. maps. 23 cm. (Oxford historical
monographs) 1. Javogues, Claude, 1759-1796. 2. Loire (France: Dept.) —
History. 3. France — History — Revolution, 1789-1799 I. T.
DC195.L7 L8   944/.581/0440924   *LC* 73-164199   *ISBN*
0198218435

Scott, William, 1940-.   3.2119
Terror and repression in revolutionary Marseilles. New York, Barnes & Noble
Books [1973] xii, 385 p. illus. 23 cm. 1. France — History — Revolution,
1789-1799 2. Marseille (France) — History. I. T.
DC195.M33 S36 1973b   944/.91   *LC* 73-169429   *ISBN*
0064961346

Hunt, Lynn Avery.   **3.2120**
Revolution and urban politics in Provincial France: Troyes and Reims, 1786–1790 / Lynn Avery Hunt. — Stanford, Calif.: Stanford University Press, 1978. viii, 187 p.; 22 cm. Includes index. 1. France — History — Revolution, 1789-1790 2. Troyes (France) — Politics and government. 3. Reims (France) — Politics and government. I. T.
DC195.T8 H86   944.04/1   *LC* 76-48016   *ISBN* 0804709408

Bergeron, Louis, 1929-.   **3.2121**
[Episode napoléonien, aspects intérieurs, 1799-1815. English] France under Napoleon / by Louis Bergeron; translated by R.R. Palmer. — Princeton, N.J.: Princeton University Press, c1981. xiv, 230 p.; 23 cm. Translation of: L'épisode napoléonien, aspects intérieurs, 1799-1815. 1. France — History — Consulate and Empire, 1799-1815 I. T.
DC201.B4713   944.05 19   *LC* 81-4549   *ISBN* 0691053332

Deutsch, Harold C. (Harold Charles)   **3.2122**
The genesis of Napoleonic imperialism. Cambridge: Harvard University Press; London: H. Milford, Oxford University Press, 1938. xxi, 460 p.; 23 cm. — (Harvard historical studice, No. 41) 1. France — History — 1804-1815 — Empire I. T. II. Series.
DC201.D4

Lefebvre, Georges, 1874-1959.   • **3.2123**
[Napoléon. English. Selections] Napoleon, from 18 Brumaire to Tilsit, 1799–1807. Translated from the French by Henry F. Stockhold. New York, Columbia University Press, 1969. x, 337 p. 22 cm. 'Translation of the first three parts of Napoléon ... published in 1936 ... this translation is based on the fifth (1965) edition.' 1. Napoleon I, Emperor of the French, 1769-1821. 2. France — History — Consulate and Empire, 1799-1815 3. France — History, Military — 1789-1815 I. T.
DC201.L3413 1969   944.05   *LC* 68-29160

Lefebvre, Georges, 1874-1959.   • **3.2124**
Napoleon; from Tilsit to Waterloo, 1807–1815. Translated from the French by J. E. Anderson. New York, Columbia University Press, 1969 [c1936] viii, 414 p. 22 cm. 'Translation of the second three parts of Napoléon ... published in 1936 ... this translation is based on the fifth (1965) edition.' 1. Napoleon I, Emperor of the French, 1769-1821. 2. France — History — Consulate and Empire, 1799-1815 3. France — History, Military — 1789-1815 I. T.
DC201.L3513   944.05   *LC* 74-79193

Glover, Michael, 1922-.   **3.2125**
The Peninsular War, 1807–1814; a concise military history. — Newton Abbot [Eng.]: David & Charles; Hamden, Conn.: Archon Books, 1974. 431 p.: illus.; 23 cm. 1. Peninsular War, 1807-1814 2. France — History, Military — 1789-1815 I. T.
DC202.1.G55 1974   940.2/7   *LC* 74-166379   *ISBN* 0208014268

Holtman, Robert B.   • **3.2126**
Napoleonic propaganda, by Robert B. Holtman. — New York: Greenwood Press, [1969, c1950] xv, 272 p.; 23 cm. 1. Napoleon I, Emperor of the French, 1769-1821. 2. Propaganda, French 3. France — History — Consulate and Empire, 1799-1815 I. T.
DC202.5.H65 1969   944/.04/6   *LC* 78-90530   *ISBN* 083712140X

Mowat, Robert Balmain, 1883-1941.   **3.2127**
The diplomacy of Napoleon. New York, Russell & Russell [1971] 307 p. 23 cm. Reprint of the 1924 ed. 1. Napoleon I, Emperor of the French, 1769-1821. 2. France — History — 1789-1815 3. Europe — History — 1789-1815 I. T.
DC202.7.M6 1971   940.27/0924   *LC* 76-139931

Castelot, André.   **3.2128**
[Bonaparte. English] Napoleon. Translated from the French by Guy Daniels. [1st ed.] New York, Harper & Row [1971] vii, 627 p. illus. 25 cm. 1. Napoleon I, Emperor of the French, 1769-1821. I. T.
DC203.C2713 1971   944.05/0924 B   *LC* 70-83587   *ISBN* 0060106786

Cronin, Vincent.   **3.2129**
Napoleon Bonaparte; an intimate biography. New York, Morrow, 1972 [c1971] 480 p. illus. 25 cm. 1. Napoleon I, Emperor of the French, 1769-1821. I. T.
DC203.C9 1972   944.05/092/4 B   *LC* 72-166356

Thompson, J. M. (James Matthew), 1878-1956.   • **3.2130**
Napoleon Bonaparte / J.M. Thompson. — New York: Oxford University Press, 1952. ix, 463 p., [3] leaves of plates: facsims., maps on lining paper), ports.; 25 cm. 1. Napoleon I, Emperor of the French, 1769-1821. 2. France — Kings and rulers — Biography. I. T.
DC203.T53 1952a   *LC* 52-9576

Geyl, Pieter, 1887-1966.   • **3.2131**
Napoleon, for and against, translated from the Dutch by Olive Renier. — New Haven, Yale University Press, 1949. 477 p. fold. col. maps. 23 cm. Bibliographical footnotes. 1. Napoleon I, Emperor of the French, 1769-1821.

2. France — Hist. — 1789-1815. 3. Historians, French. 4. France — Hist. — Historiography. I. T.
DC203.8.G42   923.144   *LC* A 49-9829 *

Napoleon I, Emperor of the French, 1769-1821.   • **3.2132**
The mind of Napoleon; a selection from his written and spoken words, edited and translated by J. Christopher Herold. — New York, Columbia University Press, 1955. 322 p. 23 cm. I. T.
DC214.H4   308.1   *LC* 55-9068

DC220–249 Napoleonic Wars. Congress of Vienna

Mackesy, Piers.   **3.2133**
Statesmen at war: the strategy of overthrow, 1798–1799. — [London; New York]: Longman, [1974] x, 340 p.: maps; 24 cm. Label mounted on t.p.: Distributed in the U.S.A. by Longman Inc., New York. 1. Second Coalition, War of the, 1798-1801 I. T. II. Title: The strategy of overthrow, 1798-1799.
DC221.M32   940.2/7   *LC* 73-86128   *ISBN* 0582120772

Lloyd, Christopher, 1906-.   **3.2134**
The Nile Campaign: Nelson and Napoleon in Egypt. Newton Abbot, David and Charles; New York, Barnes and Noble, 1973. 120 p. illus., facsims., maps, ports. 26 cm. (Illustrated sources in history) 1. Nelson, Horatio Nelson, Viscount, 1758-1805. 2. Napoleonic Wars, 1800-1814 — Campaigns — Egypt. 3. Egypt — History — French occupation, 1798-1801 I. T.
DC225.L55 1973   940.2/7   *LC* 73-159590   *ISBN* 0064843372

Butterfield, Herbert, 1900-.   **3.2135**
The peace tactics of Napoleon, 1806–1808. Cambridge [Eng.] University Press 1929. 395p. 1. Napoleon I, Emperor of the French, 1769-1821 — Empire, 1804-1814 2. Tilsit, Treaty of, 1807- 3. France — Foreign relations — 1789-1815 4. Europe — Politics — 1789-1815 I. T.
DC230 T5 B8

Tarle, Evgenïĭ Viktorovich, 1874-1955.   • **3.2136**
[Nashestvie Napoleona na Rossiiu. English] Napoleon's invasion of Russia, 1812 [by] Eugene Tarle. New York, Octagon Books, 1971 [c1942] 422 p. plans (on lining paper) 23 cm. Translation of Nashestvie Napoleona na Rossiiu (romanized form) 1. Napoleon I, Emperor of the French, 1769-1821 — Invasion of Russia, 1812. I. T.
DC235.T32 1971   940.2/7   *LC* 77-120670

Duffy, Christopher, 1936-.   **3.2137**
Borodino and the War of 1812. — New York: Scribner, [1973] 208 p.: illus.; 23 cm. 1. Borodino, Battle of, 1812 I. T.
DC235.5.B7 D8 1973   940.2/7   *LC* 72-5758   *ISBN* 0684131730

MacKenzie, Norman Ian.   **3.2138**
The escape from Elba: the fall and flight of Napoleon, 1814–1815 / Norman MacKenzie. — New York: Oxford University Press, 1982. xv, 299 p., [8] p. of plates: ill.; 25 cm. Includes index. 1. Napoleon I, Emperor of the French, 1769-1821 — Elba and the Hundred Days, 1814-1815 I. T.
DC238.M32 1982   944.05 19   *LC* 81-18672   *ISBN* 0192158635

Nicolson, Harold George, Hon., 1886-.   • **3.2139**
The Congress of Vienna, a study in allied unity: 1812–1822, by Harold Nicolson ... — London, Constable & co. ltd. [1946] xiii, 312 p. front., ports. 22.5 cm. Maps on lining-papers. 'First published 1946.' 'List of books consulted': p. 300-302. 1. Congress of Vienna (1814-1815) 2. Europe — Politics — 1789-1815. I. T.
DC249.N5 1946   940.27   *LC* 46-21112

Webster, Charles Kingsley, Sir, 1886-1961.   • **3.2140**
The Congress of Vienna, 1814–1815. New York: Barnes & Noble, 1963. 213 p. 1. Congress of Vienna (1814-1815) I. T.
DC249.W4 1963a   940.27   *LC* 63-4077

DC251–326 19th Century

Taine, Hippolyte, 1828-1893.   **3.2141**
[Origines de la France contemporaine. Selections. English] The origins of contemporary France: the ancient regime, the Revolution, the modern regime: selected chapters / Hippolyte Adolphe Taine; edited and with an introd. by Edward T. Gargan. — Chicago: University of Chicago Press, 1974. xlv, 446 p.; 21 cm. (Classic European historians) Translation of Les origines de la France contemporaine. 1. France — Civilization. 2. France — Politics and government 3. France — Social life and customs 4. France — History — Revolution, 1789-1799 — Causes I. T. II. Series.
DC251.T143 1974   944   *LC* 73-87311   *ISBN* 0226789349

Bertocci, Philip A., 1940-. 3.2142
Jules Simon: Republican anticlericalism and cultural politics in France, 1848–1886 / Philip A. Bertocci. — Columbia: University of Missouri Press, 1978. vi, 247 p.; 21 cm. Includes index. 1. Simon, Jules, 1814-1896. 2. Anticlericalism — France. 3. France — Politics and government — 19th century I. T.
DC255.S5 B47 320.5 *LC* 77-14668 *ISBN* 082620239X

DC256–274 1815-1851

Bertier de Sauvigny, Guillaume de, 1912-. • 3.2143
La Restauration / G. de Bertier de Sauvigny. — Paris: Flammarion, c1955. 652 p.; 20 cm. (L'Histoire) Includes indexes. 1. France — History — Restoration, 1814-1830 I. T.
DC256.B46 1974 944.06 *LC* 56-17916

Jardin, André, 1912-. 3.2144
[France des notables. English] Restoration and reaction, 1815–1848 / André Jardin, André–Jean Tudesq; translated by Elborg Forster. — Cambridge; New York: Cambridge University Press; Paris: Editions de la Maison des sciences de l'homme, 1984 (c1983). xviii, 409 p.; ill., maps; 24 cm. — (Cambridge history of modern France. 1) Translation of: La France des notables. Includes index. 1. France — History — Restoration, 1814-1830 2. France — History — Louis Philip, 1830-1848 3. France — History, Local. I. Tudesq, André Jean. II. T. III. Series.
DC256.J314 944.06 19 *LC* 83-5240 *ISBN* 0521252415

Spitzer, Alan B. (Alan Barrie), 1925-. 3.2145
Old hatreds and young hopes; the French Carbonari against the Bourbon Restoration [by] Alan B. Spitzer. — Cambridge, Mass.: Harvard University Press, 1971. 334 p.; 21 cm. — (Harvard historical monographs. 63) 1. Carbonari — France. 2. France — Politics and government — 1814-1830 I. T. II. Series.
DC256.8.S67 322/.42/0944 *LC* 76-139722 *ISBN* 0674632206

Pinkney, David H. • 3.2146
The French revolution of 1830, by David H. Pinkney. — [Princeton] N.J.: Princeton University Press, [1972] ix, 397 p.; 23 cm. 1. France — History — July Revolution, 1830 I. T.
DC261.P56 944.07 *LC* 72-39051 *ISBN* 0691052026

1830 in France / edited with an introd. by John M. Merriman. 3.2147
New York: New Viewpoints, 1975. 231 p.; 21 cm. (Modern scholarship on European history) Includes index. 1. France — History — July Revolution, 1830 — Addresses, essays, lectures. I. Merriman, John M.
DC262.E35 944.06/3 *LC* 75-15796 *ISBN* 0531053733

Tocqueville, Alexis de, 1805-1859. • 3.2148
[Souvenirs. English] Recollections. Translated by Alexander Teixeira de Mattos. Edited with many additions from the original text and an introd. by J. P. Mayer. New York, Columbia University Press, 1949. xxvi, 331 p. 23 cm. 1. Tocqueville, Alexis de, 1805-1859. 2. Historians — France — Biography. 3. France — History — February Revolution, 1848 I. T.
DC270.T652 1949 944.07 *LC* 49-50219

Stewart-McDougall, Mary Lynn. 3.2149
The artisan republic: revolution, reaction, and resistance in Lyon, 1848–1851 / Mary Lynn Stewart–McDougall. — Kingston: McGill-Queen's University Press, 1984. xix, 211 p.: ill.; 24 cm. Includes index. 1. Lyon (France) — History 2. France — History — Revolution, 1848. 3. France — History — Second Republic, 1848-1852 I. T.
DC271.L9 S74 1984 944/.582307 19 *LC* 85-167713 *ISBN* 0773504265

Agulhon, Maurice. 3.2150
[1848, ou, L'apprentissage de le République, 1848-1852. English] The Republican experiment, 1848–1852 / Maurice Agulhon; translated by Janet Lloyd. — Cambridge [Cambridgeshire]; New York: Cambridge University Press; Paris: Editions de la Maison des sciences de l'homme, 1983. xiv, 211 p.: ill., maps; 24 cm. — (Cambridge history of modern France. 2) Translation of: 1848, ou, L'apprentissage de la République, 1848-1852. Includes index. 1. France — History — Second Republic, 1848-1852 I. T. II. Series.
DC272.A3513 1983 944.07 19 *LC* 82-23461 *ISBN* 0521248299

Price, Roger. 3.2151
The French Second Republic; a social history. — Ithaca, N.Y.: Cornell University Press, [1972] vii, 386 p.; 23 cm. 1. France — Politics and government — 1848-1852 2. France — Social conditions I. T.
DC272.P7 320.9/44/07 *LC* 70-173282 *ISBN* 0801406862

Merriman, John M. 3.2152
The agony of the Republic: the repression of the left in revolutionary France, 1848–1851 / John M. Merriman. — New Haven: Yale University Press, 1978.

xxxvi, 298 p.: ill.; 22 cm. Includes index. 1. Radicalism — France — History. 2. France — Politics and government — 1848-1852 I. T.
DC272.5.M42 320.9/44/07 *LC* 77-10434 *ISBN* 0300021518

Jennings, Lawrence C. 3.2153
France and Europe in 1848: a study of French foreign affairs in time of crisis, [by] Lawrence C. Jennings. — Oxford, 1973. ix, 280 p.; 23 cm. Includes index. 1. France — History — Second Republic, 1848-1852 2. France — Foreign relations — Europe. 3. Europe — Foreign relations — France. I. T.
DC273.6.J46 327.44/04 *LC* 73-173775 *ISBN* 0198225148

DC275–326 SECOND EMPIRE. FRANCO–GERMAN WAR (1852–1871)

Napoleon III, Emperor of the French, 1808-1873. 3.2154
The political and historical works of Louis Napoleon Bonaparte, President of the French Republic. Now first collected with an original memoir of his life, brought down to the promulgation of the constitution of 1852; and occasional notes. New York, H. Fertig, 1972. 2 v. port. 23 cm. Reprint of the 1852 ed. 1. France — Politics and government — Second Republic, 1848-1852 — Sources. I. T.
DC275.2.N4 1972 944.07/092/4 B *LC* 71-144132

Campbell, Stuart L., 1938-. 3.2155
The Second Empire revisited: a study in French historiography / Stuart L. Campbell. — New Brunswick, N.J.: Rutgers University Press, c1978. xv, 231 p.; 24 cm. Based on the author's thesis, University of Rochester, 1969. Includes index. 1. France — History — Second Empire, 1852-1870 — Historiography. I. T.
DC276.5.C35 944.07/07/2 *LC* 77-20247 *ISBN* 0813508568

Echard, William E., 1931-. 3.2156
Napoleon III and the Concert of Europe / William E. Echard. — Baton Rouge: Louisiana State University Press, c1983. xiv, 327 p.; 24 cm. Includes index. 1. Napoleon III, Emperor of the French, 1808-1873. 2. Concert of Europe 3. France — Foreign relations — 1848-1870 I. T.
DC277.E27 1983 944.07 19 *LC* 82-12660 *ISBN* 0807110566

Zeldin, Theodore, 1933-. • 3.2157
The political system of Napoleon III. — London, Macmillan; New York, St. Martin's Press, 1958. 195 p. illus. 23 cm. Includes bibliography. 1. Napoleon III, Emperor of the French, 1808-1873. 2. France — Pol. & govt. — 1852-1870. I. T.
DC277.1.Z4 944.07 *LC* 58-3067

Corley, T. A. B. (Thomas Anthony Buchanan), 1923-. • 3.2158
Democratic despot; a life of Napoleon III. — London, Barrie and Rockliff [1961] 402 p. illus. 23 cm. Includes bibliography. 1. Napoléon III Emperor of the French, 1808-1873. I. T.
DC280.C6 *LC* 61-66635

Smith, W. H. C. (William Herbert Cecil), 1925-. 3.2159
Napoleon III [by] W. H. C. Smith. — New York: St. Martin's Press, [1973, c1972] 296 p.; 25 cm. 1. Napoleon III, Emperor of the French, 1808-1873. I. T.
DC280.S67 1973 944/.07/0924 B *LC* 72-88872

Thompson, J. M. (James Matthew), 1878-1956. • 3.2160
Louis Napoleon and the Second Empire. — Oxford, Blackwell, 1954. 342 p. illus. 23 cm. 1. Napoleon III, Emperor of the French, 1808-1873. 2. France — Hist. — Second Empire, 1852-1870. I. T.
DC280.T5 944.07 *LC* 54-4946

Steefel, Lawrence Dinkelspiel, 1894-. • 3.2161
Bismarck, the Hohenzollern candidacy, and the origins of the Franco–German War of 1870. — Cambridge, Harvard University Press, 1962. xi, 281 p. 22 cm. Bibliography: p. 259-270. 1. Bismarck, Otto, Fürst von, 1815-1898. 2. Franco-German War, 1870-1871 — Causes I. T.
DC292.S7 943.082 *LC* 62-13271

Howard, Michael Eliot, 1922-. • 3.2162
The Franco–Prussian War; the German invasion of France, 1870–1871. — New York: Macmillan, 1961. 512 p.: illus.; 23 cm. 1. Franco-German War, 1870-1871 I. T.
DC293.H6 943.082 *LC* 61-65482

Horne, Alistair. 3.2163
The fall of Paris; the siege and the Commune, 1870–71. New York, St. Martin's Press [1966, c1965] xiv, 458 p. illus., facsims., maps, ports. 22 cm. First vol. in a trilogy; the 2d of which is The price of glory; Verdun 1916; and the 3d of which is To lose a battle; France 1940. 1. Paris (France) — History — Siege, 1870-1871. 2. Paris (France) — History — Commune, 1871. I. T.
DC311.H68 944.081 *LC* 65-24584

Kranzberg, Melvin.   • 3.2164
The siege of Paris, 1870–1871; a political and social history. Westport, Conn., Greenwood Press [1971, c1950] xi, 213 p. 23 cm. A revision of the author's thesis, Harvard University. 1. Paris (France) — History — Siege, 1870-1871. I. T.
DC312.K7 1971   944.08   *LC* 78-112326   *ISBN* 083714714X

Edwards, Stewart, 1937- comp.   3.2165
The communards of Paris, 1871. [Documents translated by Jean McNeil] Ithaca, N.Y., Cornell University Press [1973] 180 p. illus. 22 cm. (Documents of revolution) 1. Paris (France) — History — Commune, 1871 I. T. II. Series.
DC316.E29   944/.36/081   *LC* 72-13387   *ISBN* 0801407796

Edwards, Stewart, 1937-.   3.2166
The Paris Commune, 1871. [1st American ed.] Chicago: Quadrangle Books, 1973. viii, 417 p. illus. 23 cm. 1. Paris (France) — History — Commune, 1871 I. T.
DC316.E3 1973   *LC* 72-80213   *ISBN* 0812902599

Mason, Edward Sagendorph, 1899-.   • 3.2167
The Paris Commune; an episode in the history of the Socialist movement. New York, H. Fertig, 1967 [i.e.1968] xiv,386p. 24cm. Reprint of the 1930 ed. 1. Socialism — France 2. Paris (France) — History — Commune, 1871 I. T.
DC316.M34 1968   *LC* 67-24588

Greenberg, Louis M., 1933-.   • 3.2168
Sisters of liberty; Marseille, Lyon, Paris, and the reaction to a centralized state, 1868–1871, by Louis M. Greenberg. Cambridge, Mass., Harvard University Press, 1971. 391 p. 21 cm. (Harvard historical monographs. 62) 1. Paris (France) — History — Commune, 1871 2. Marseille (France) — History. 3. Lyon (France) — History I. T. II. Series.
DC317.G74   944.07   *LC* 70-134952   *ISBN* 0674810007

Tombs, Robert.   3.2169
The war against Paris, 1871 / Robert Tombs. — Cambridge; New York: Cambridge University Press, 1981. xii, 256 p.: ill.; 24 cm. Includes index. 1. France. Armée — History — 19th century. 2. Paris (France) — History — Commune, 1871 3. France — History, Military — 19th century I. T.
DC317.T66 1981   944/.36081 19   *LC* 80-42024   *ISBN* 0521235510

DC330–412 19th–20th Centuries

Zeldin, Theodore, 1933-.   3.2170
France, 1848–1945, by Theodore Zeldin. — Oxford, 1977. 2 v.; 22 cm. — (Oxford history of modern Europe) Includes indexes. 1. France — Civilization — 1830-1900 2. France — Civilization — 1901-1945 I. T.
DC330.Z44   944.081   *LC* 73-180595   *ISBN* 0198221045

Brabant, Frank Herbert, 1892-.   3.2171
The beginning of the third republic in France; a history of the National assembly (February–September 1871) London: Macmillan and Co., Ltd., 1940. 555p. (Studies in modern history. General editor: L.B. Namier) 1. Thiers, Adolphe, 1797-1877. 2. France. Assemblée nationale (1871-1942) — History 3. France — Politics and government — 1870-1940 I. T.
DC331 B73

Brogan, D. W. (Denis William), 1900-1974.   • 3.2172
The development of modern France, 1870–1939 [by] D. W. Brogan. Rev. ed. New York, Harper & Row [1966] 2 v. 21 cm. (Harper torchbooks. The Academy library, TB1184-TB1185) 1. France — History — Third Republic, 1870-1940 2. France — Politics and government — 1870-1940 I. T.
DC335.B75 1966   *LC* 66-2183

Chapman, Guy.   • 3.2173
The Third Republic of France: the first phase 1871–1894. — [New York]: St Martin's Press, 1962 [i.e. 1963] 433 p. illus. 23 cm. Includes bibliography. 1. France — History — Third Republic, 1870-1940 I. T.
DC335.C48 1962b   944.08   *LC* 62-21077

Shattuck, Roger.   • 3.2174
The banquet years; the origins of the avant garde in France, 1885 to World War I: Alfred Jarry, Henri Rousseau, Erik Satie [and] Guillaume Apollinaire. — Rev. ed. — New York: Vintage Books, [1968] xiv, 397 p.: illus., facsims., music, ports.; 19 cm. First ed. published in 1958 under title: The banquet years, the arts in France, 1885-1918. 1. Jarry, Alfred, 1873-1907. 2. Rousseau, Henri Julien Félix, 1844-1910. 3. Satie, Erik, 1866-1925. 4. Apollinaire, Guillaume, 1880-1918. 5. France — Intellectual life I. T.
DC338.S48 1968   914.4/03/810922   *LC* 68-12411

Curtis, Michael, 1923-.   • 3.2175
Three against the Third Republic: Sorel, Barrès, and Maurras. — Princeton, Princeton University Press, 1959. 313 p. 23 cm. Bibliography: p. 275-307.

1. Barrès, Maurice, 1862-1923. 2. Maurras, Charles, 1868-1952. 3. Sorel, Georges, 1847-1922. 4. France — Hist. — Third Republic, 1870-1940. I. T.
DC340.C8   944.08   *LC* 59-11075

Halévy, Daniel, 1872-1962.   3.2176
[Fin des notables. English] The end of the notables. Edited, with introd. and notes, by Alain Silvera. Translated by Alain Silvera and June Guicharnaud. [1st English ed.] Middletown, Conn., Wesleyan University Press [1974] xxi, 225 p. 22 cm. Translation of La fin des notables. 1. France — Politics and government — 1870-1940 I. T.
DC340.H313   320.9/44/08   *LC* 73-6009   *ISBN* 0819540668 *ISBN* 0819560308

Locke, Robert R., 1932-.   3.2177
French legitimists and the politics of moral order in the early Third Republic [by] Robert R. Locke. — Princeton, N.J.: Princeton University Press, [1974] x, 321 p.; 25 cm. 1. Right and left (Political science) 2. France — Politics and government — 1870-1940 I. T.
DC340.L6   320.9/44/081   *LC* 73-17404   *ISBN* 0691052158

Mitchell, Allan.   3.2178
The German influence in France after 1870: the formation of the French Republic / by Allan Mitchell. — Chapel Hill: University of North Carolina Press, c1979. xviii, 279 p.; 24 cm. Includes index. 1. France — Politics and government — 1870-1940 2. France — Relations — Germany 3. Germany — Relations — France I. T.
DC340.M64   320.9/44/081   *LC* 78-31677   *ISBN* 0807813575

Schuman, Frederick Lewis, 1904-.   • 3.2179
War and diplomacy in the French Republic; an inquiry into political motivations and the control of foreign policy [by] Frederick L. Schuman. With an introd. by Quincy Wright. — New York: H. Fertig, 1969. xvii, 452 p.; 24 cm. Reprint of the 1931 ed. 1. Diplomacy 2. France — Foreign relations — 1870-1940 3. France — Politics and government — 1870-1940 4. Europe — Politics and government — 1871-1918 I. T.
DC340.S35 1969   327.44   *LC* 68-9635

Keiger, John F. V.   3.2180
France and the origins of the first World War / John F.V. Keiger. — New York: St. Martin's Press, 1983. vii, 201 p.; 23 cm. — (Making of the 20th century.) Includes index. 1. World War, 1914-1918 — Causes. 2. France — Foreign relations — 1870-1940 I. T. II. Series.
DC341.K44 1983   327.73 19   *LC* 83-8660   *ISBN* 0312302924

DC342–354 BIOGRAPHY. DREYFUS CASE

Seager, Frederic H.   • 3.2181
The Boulanger affair; political crossroad of France, 1886–1889 [by] Frederic H. Seager. Ithaca, N.Y., Cornell University Press [1969] xiv, 276 p. 22 cm. 1. Boulanger, Georges-Ernest-Jean-Marie, 1837-1891. 2. France — Politics and government — 1870-1940 I. T.
DC342.8.B7 S4   944.081/0924   *LC* 68-9753

Ellis, Jack D.   3.2182
The early life of Georges Clemenceau, 1841–1893 / Jack D. Ellis. — Lawrence: Regents Press of Kansas, c1980. xix, 272 p.; 23 cm. Includes index. 1. Clemenceau, Georges, 1841-1929 — Childhood and youth. 2. Clemenceau, Georges, 1841-1929 — Political career before 1893. 3. Statesmen — France — Biography. I. T.
DC342.8.C6 E45   944.081/092/4 B 19   *LC* 79-19118   *ISBN* 0700601961

Watson, David Robin.   3.2183
Georges Clemenceau: a political biography. New York: David McKay, 1976. 463 p.: illus.; 24 cm. 1. Clemenceau, Georges, 1841-1929. I. T.
DC342.8.C6 W34 1976   944.081/092/4 B   *LC* 76-28607   *ISBN* 0679507035

Bury, J. P. T. (John Patrick Tuer), 1908-.   3.2184
Gambetta and the making of the Third Republic [by] J. P. T. Bury. London, Longman 1974 (c1973). xi, 499 p. illus. 23 cm. 1. Gambetta, Léon, 1838-1882. 2. France — Politics and government — 1870-1940 I. T.
DC342.8.G3 B79   944.081/092/4 B   *LC* 73-180812   *ISBN* 0582500524

Bury, J. P. T. (John Patrick Tuer), 1908-.   • 3.2185
Gambetta and the national defence; a republican dictatorship in France, by J. P. T. Bury. Westport, Conn., Greenwood Press [1971] xxiv, 341 p. illus., map, ports. 23 cm. Reprint of the 1936 ed. 1. Gambetta, Léon, 1838-1882. 2. Franco-German War, 1870-1871 3. France — Politics and government — 1870-1940 4. France — Defenses. I. T.
DC342.8.G3 B8 1971   944.81/0924   *LC* 77-114490   *ISBN* 0837148189

Goldberg, Harvey, 1923-.   • **3.2186**
The life of Jean Jaurès. Madison, University of Wisconsin Press, 1962. 590 p. illus. 25 cm. Includes bibliography. 1. Jaurès, Jean, 1859-1914. 2. Socialism — France I. T.
DC342.8.J4G63   923.244   *LC* 62-7216

Martin, Benjamin F., 1947-.   **3.2187**
Count Albert de Mun, paladin of the Third Republic / Benjamin F. Martin. — Chapel Hill: University of North Carolina Press, c1978. xix, 367 p.; 23 cm. Includes index. 1. Mun, Albert, comte de, 1841-1914. 2. Politicians — France — Biography. 3. Church and social problems — France 4. France — Politics and government — 1870-1940 I. T.
DC342.8.M8 M34   320.9/44/081 B   *LC* 78-1739   *ISBN* 0807813257

Griffiths, Richard M.   **3.2188**
[Marshal Pétain] Pétain; a biography of Marshal Philippe Pétain of Vichy [by] Richard Griffiths. [1st ed. in the U.S.] Garden City, N.Y., Doubleday, 1972 [c1970] xix, 379 p. illus. 25 cm. First published in London under title: Marshal Pétain. 1. Pétain, Philippe, 1856-1951. I. T.
DC342.8.P4 G7 1972   944.081/092/4 B   *LC* 73-157595

Lottman, Herbert R.   **3.2189**
Pétain, hero or traitor: the untold story / Herbert R. Lottman. — 1st ed. — New York: W. Morrow, c1985. 444 p.; 25 cm. Includes index. 1. Pétain, Philippe, 1856-1951. 2. France. Armée — Biography. 3. Heads of state — France — Biography. 4. Marshals — France — Biography 5. France — Politics and government — 1914-1940 6. France — Politics and government — 1940-1945 I. T.
DC342.8.P4 L67 1985   944.081/092/4 B 19   *LC* 84-221511   *ISBN* 0688037569

Chapman, Guy.   • **3.2190**
The Dreyfus case, a reassessment. New York, Reynal [1956, c1955] 400 p. illus. 22 cm. 1. Dreyfus, Alfred, 1859-1935. I. T.
DC354.C47 1956   923.544   *LC* 56-5250

Halasz, Nicholas, 1895-.   • **3.2191**
Captain Dreyfus; the story of a mass hysteria. — New York: Simon and Schuster, 1955. 274 p.; 22 cm. 1. Dreyfus, Alfred, 1859-1935. I. T.
DC354.H15   944.08   *LC* 55-8810

Hoffman, Robert Louis, 1937-.   **3.2192**
More than a trial: the struggle over Captain Dreyfus / Robert L. Hoffman. — New York: Free Press , c1980. viii, 247 p., [7] leaves of plates: ill.; 25 cm. Includes index. 1. Dreyfus, Alfred, 1859-1935. I. T.
DC354.H63   944.081/092/4 B   *LC* 80-642   *ISBN* 0029147700

Snyder, Louis Leo, 1907-.   **3.2193**
The Dreyfus case: a documentary history [by] Louis L. Snyder. — New Brunswick, N.J.: Rutgers University Press, [1973] xxiii, 414 p.: illus.; 24 cm. 1. Dreyfus, Alfred, 1859-1935. I. T.
DC354.S6   944.081/092/4 B   *LC* 72-4200   *ISBN* 0813507413

DC361–423 20TH CENTURY

Andrew, Christopher M.   **3.2194**
The climax of French imperial expansion, 1914–1924 / Christopher M. Andrew and A.S. Kanya–Forstner. — Stanford, Calif.: Stanford University Press, 1981. 302 p.: maps. Published in Great Britain under title: France overseas: the Great War and the climax of French imperial expansion. 1. France — History — 1914-1940 2. France — Colonies 3. France — Politics and government — 1914-1940 I. Kanya-Forstner, A. S. II. T. III. Title: France overseas: the Great War and the climax of French imperial expansion.
DC361.A5   *LC* 80-53435   *ISBN* 0804711011

Contemporary France: illusion, conflict, and regeneration /   **3.2195**
edited, with an introd., by John C. Cairns.
New York: New Viewpoints, 1978. xii, 270 p.; 21 cm. — (Modern scholarship on European history) Includes index. 1. France — History — 20th century — Addresses, essays, lectures. I. Cairns, John Campbell, 1924-
DC361.C66   944.081   *LC* 77-16101   *ISBN* 0531053989. *ISBN* 0531056082 pbk

In search of France [by] Stanley Hoffmann [and others].   • **3.2196**
Cambridge, Harvard University Press, 1963. xiii, 443 p. 24 cm. 'Prepared under the auspices of the Center for International Affairs, Harvard University.' Bibliographical references included in 'Notes' (p. 409-428) 1. France — Pol. & govt. — 1945- 2. France — Soc. condit. 3. National characteristics, French I. Hoffmann, Stanley. II. Harvard University. Center for International Affairs.
DC361.I5   944.082   *LC* 63-9549

Hoffmann, Stanley.   **3.2197**
Decline or renewal? France since the 1930s. New York, Viking Press [1974] xiii, 529 p. 24 cm. 1. Gaulle, Charles de, 1890-1970. 2. France — Politics and government — 1945-. I. T.
DC369.H58 1974   320.9/44/08   *LC* 73-7086   *ISBN* 0670262358

McDougall, Walter A., 1946-.   **3.2198**
France's Rhineland diplomacy, 1914–1924: the last bid for a balance of power in Europe / Walter A. McDougall. — Princeton, N.J.: Princeton University Press, c1978. xiii, 420 p.: ill.; 25 cm. Includes index. 1. France — Foreign relations — Germany 2. Germany — Foreign relations — France 3. France — Politics and government — 1914-1940 I. T.
DC369.M2   327.44/043   *LC* 77-85550   *ISBN* 0691052689

Weber, Eugen Joseph, 1925-.   • **3.2199**
Action française; royalism and reaction in twentieth–century France. — Stanford, Calif., Stanford University Press, 1962. 594 p. 25 cm. Includes bibliography. 1. L'Action française. 2. France — Pol. & govt. — 1870-1940. I. T.
DC369.W36   *LC* 62-15267

Binion, Rudolph, 1927-.   • **3.2200**
Defeated leaders; the political fate of Caillaux, Jouvenel, and Tardieu. — Morningside Heights, N. Y., Columbia University Press, 1960. 425 p. 24 cm. Includes bibliography. 1. Caillaux, Joseph, 1863-1944. 2. Jouvenel, Henry de, 1876-1935. 3. Tardieu, André Pierre Gabriel Amédée, 1876-1945. I. T.
DC371.B5 1960   923.244   *LC* 59-14524

Colton, Joel G., 1918-.   • **3.2201**
Léon Blum, humanist in politics [by] Joel Colton. — [1st ed.]. — New York, Knopf, 1966. xiv, 512, xiv p. illus., ports. 25 cm. Bibliography: p. 495-512. 1. Blum, Léon, 1872-1950. I. T.
DC373.B5C6   944.08150924 (B)   *LC* 65-18764 rev

Lacouture, Jean.   **3.2202**
[Léon Blum. English] Léon Blum / by Jean Lacouture; translated by George Holoch. — New York, N.Y.: Holmes & Meier, 1982. xii, 571 p., [8] p. of plates: ill.; 23 cm. Translation of: Léon Blum. Includes index. 1. Blum, Léon, 1872-1950. 2. Statesmen — France — Biography. 3. France — Politics and government — 20th century I. T.
DC373.B5 L3313 1982   944.081/5/0924 B 19   *LC* 81-20083   *ISBN* 0841907765

Logue, William, 1934-.   **3.2203**
Léon Blum: the formative years, 1872–1914. — DeKalb: Northern Illinois University Press, [1973] 344 p.: port.; 24 cm. 1. Blum, Léon, 1872-1950. I. T.
DC373.B5 L64   944.081/5/0924 B   *LC* 72-7515   *ISBN* 0875800300

Crozier, Brian.   **3.2204**
De Gaulle. New York, Scribner 1974 (c1973). ix, 726 p. 25 cm. 1. Gaulle, Charles de, 1890-1970. I. T.
DC373.G3 C762   944.083/092/4 B   *LC* 72-1190   *ISBN* 0684129965

Lacouture, Jean.   • **3.2205**
[De Gaulle. English] De Gaulle. Translated by Francis K. Price. [New York] New American Library [1966] 215 p. 22 cm. 1. Gaulle, Charles de, 1890-1970. I. T.
DC373.G3 L2513   944.080924 B   *LC* 66-24425

King, Jere Clemens.   • **3.2206**
Generals & politicians; conflict between France's high command, Parliament, and Government, 1914–1918. Westport, Conn., Greenwood Press [1971, c1951] 294 p. 23 cm. 1. World War, 1914-1918 — France 2. France — Politics and government — 1914-1940 I. T.
DC387.K38 1971   944.08   *LC* 74-112325   *ISBN* 0837147131

Werth, Alexander, 1901-.   • **3.2207**
The twilight of France, 1933–1940. Edited with an introd. by D. W. Brogan. — New York: H. Fertig, 1966 [c1942] xxii, 368 p.; 24 cm. 1. World War, 1939-1945 — France 2. France — Politics and government — 1914-1940 3. France — Foreign relations — 1914-1940 I. Brogan, Denis William, 1900- ed. II. T.
DC396.W42 1966   944.0815   *LC* 66-24358

Paxton, Robert O.   • **3.2208**
Parades and politics at Vichy; the French officer corps under Marshal Pétain, by Robert O. Paxton. — Princeton, N. J., Princeton University Press, 1966. xi, 472 p. ports. 21 cm. Includes bibliographical references. 1. France. Armée — Officers. 2. France — Hist. — German occupation, 1940-1945. 3. France — Pol. & govt. — 1940-1945. I. T.
DC397.P36   944.0816   *LC* 66-10557

Paxton, Robert O. 3.2209
Vichy France: old guard and new order, 1940–1944 [by] Robert O. Paxton. — [1st ed.]. — New York: Knopf; distributed by Random House, 1972. 399, xix p.: illus.; 25 cm. 1. France — Politics and government — 1940-1945 2. France — History — German occupation, 1940-1945 I. T.
DC397.P37   320.9/44/0816   *LC* 74-171140   *ISBN* 0394473604

DC398–423 1947–

Smith, Tony, 1942-. 3.2210
The French stake in Algeria, 1945–1962 / Tony Smith. — Ithaca, N.Y.: Cornell University Press, 1978. 199 p.: map; 23 cm. Includes index. 1. France — Politics and government — 1945-1958 2. France — Politics and government — 1958- 3. France — Colonies 4. Algeria — History — Revolution, 1954-1962 I. T.
DC401.S6   944.082   *LC* 78-7713   *ISBN* 0801411254

Lacouture, Jean. 3.2211
[Pierre Mendès France. English] Pierre Mendès France / Jean Lacouture; translated by George Holoch. — New York: Holmes & Meier, 1985 (c1984). viii, 486 p.; 24 cm. Translation of: Pierre Mendès France. 1. Mendès-France, Pierre, 1907- 2. Statesmen — France — Biography. 3. Prime ministers — France — Biography. 4. France — Politics and government — 1945-1958 5. France — Politics and government — 1958- I. T.
DC407.M4 L3213   944.082/092/4 B 19   *LC* 84-10912   *ISBN* 0841908567

MacShane, Denis. 3.2212
François Mitterrand, a political odyssey / Denis MacShane. — New York: Universe Books, 1983, c1982. x, 278 p.: port.; 22 cm. Includes index. 1. Mitterrand, François, 1916- 2. France — Politics and government — 20th century 3. France — Presidents — Biography. I. T.
DC407.M5 M32 1983   944.083/8/0924 B 19   *LC* 82-23793   *ISBN* 0876634188

Aron, Raymond, 1905-. 3.2213
The elusive revolution; anatomy of a student revolt. Translated by Gordon Clough. — New York: Praeger Publishers, [1969] xix, 200 p.; 22 cm. Translation of La Révolution introuvable. 1. France — Politics and government — 1958- 2. Paris (France) — Riot, 1968. I. T.
DC412.A863 1969   944.083   *LC* 72-90262

Charlot, Jean. 3.2214
[Phénomène gaulliste. English] The Gaullist phenomenon: the Gaullist movement in the Fifth Republic. Translated by Monica Charlot and Marianne Neighbour. New York, Praeger 1972 (c1971). 205 p. illus. 23 cm. (Studies in political science, 6) Translation of Le phénomène gaulliste. 1. France — Politics and government — 1958- I. T.
DC412.C51413   320.9/44/083   *LC* 70-165527

Cohn-Bendit, Daniel. 3.2215
[Linksradikalismus. English] Obsolete Communism; the Left–Wing alternative [by] Daniel Cohn–Bendit and Gabriel Cohn–Bendit. Translated by Arnold Pomerans. [1st ed.] New York, McGraw-Hill [1968] 255 p. 21 cm. Translation of Linksradikalismus; Gewaltkur gegen die Alterskrankheit des Kommunismus. 1. Riots — France — Paris. 2. Communism — France. 3. France — Politics and government — 1958- 4. Paris (France) — History I. Cohn-Bendit, Gabriel. joint author. II. T.
DC412.C573 1968   944.083   *LC* 69-18158

Williams, Philip Maynard. 3.2216
Politics and society in de Gaulle's republic [by] Philip M. Williams and Martin Harrison. — [1st ed. in the U.S.]. — Garden City, N.Y.: Doubleday, 1973 [c1971] 468 p. 1. France — Politics and government — 1958- I. Harrison, Martin, 1930- joint author. II. T.
DC412.W54   944.083   *LC* 71-180115

Ledwidge, Bernard, 1915-. 3.2217
DeGaulle / Bernard Ledwidge. — 1st U.S. ed. — New York: St. Martin's Press, c1982. xiii, 418 p., [16] p. of plates: ill.; 24 cm. Includes index. 1. Gaulle, Charles de, 1890-1970. 2. World War, 1939-1945 — France 3. France — History — German occupation, 1940-1945 4. France — Politics and government — 1958- 5. France — Presidents — Biography. I. T.
DC420.L4 1982   944.083/6/0924 B 19   *LC* 82-61701   *ISBN* 0312191278

DC600–989 LOCAL HISTORY

Gallop, Rodney, 1901-1948. 3.2218
A book of the Basques. Illustrated with a map and drawings by Marjorie Gallop. — Reno: University of Nevada Press, 1970. xv, 298 p.: illus. (1 col.), map (on lining papers), music.; 23 cm. — (The Basque series) 1. Basques I. T.
DC611.B313 G3 1970   914.66/03   *LC* 76-137133   *ISBN* 087417029X

Cartellieri, Otto, 1872-1930. • 3.2219
[Am Hofe der Herzöge von Burgund. English] The Court of Burgundy. [Translated by Malcolm Letts] New York, Barnes & Noble [1972] xv, 282 p. illus. 24 cm. Translation of Am Hofe der Herzöge von Burgund. Reprint of the 1929 ed., issued in series: The History of civilization. 1. Civilization, Medieval 2. Burgundy (France) — Court and courtiers. 3. Burgundy (France) — Civilization I. T.
DC611.B78 C2813 1972   914.4/4/032   *LC* 72-186144   *ISBN* 0389044563

Vaughan, Richard, 1927-. 3.2220
Valois Burgundy / Richard Vaughan. — Hamden, Conn.: Archon Books, 1975. vii, 254 p.: maps; 23 cm. Includes index. 1. Burgundy (France) — History — House of Valois, 1363-1477 I. T.
DC611.B78 V357 1975   944/.4   *LC* 74-34019   *ISBN* 0208015116

Vaughan, Richard, 1927-. 3.2221
Charles the Bold; the last Valois Duke of Burgundy. New York, Barnes & Noble Books [1974, c1973] xvi, 491 p. illus. 23 cm. 1. Charles, Duke of Burgundy, 1433-1477. 2. Burgundy (France) — History — House of Valois, 1363-1477 3. Europe — History — 476-1492 I. T.
DC611.B781 V38 1974   944/.025/0924 B   *LC* 74-166215   *ISBN* 0064971716

Hélias, Pierre Jakez. 3.2222
[Cheval d'orgueil. English] The horse of pride: life in a Breton village / Pierre–Jakez Hélias; translated and abridged by June Guicharnaud; foreword by Laurence Wylie. — New Haven: Yale University Press, 1978. xvii, 351 p., [4] leaves of plates: ill.; 24 cm. Translation of Le cheval d'orgueil. 1. Hélias, Pierre Jakez. 2. Brittany (France) — Social life and customs. 3. Brittany (France) — Biography. I. Guicharnaud, June. II. T.
DC611.B9173 H4413   944/.11   *LC* 78-6929   *ISBN* 0300020368

Labarge, Margaret Wade. 3.2223
Gascony, England's first colony, 1204–1453 / [by] Margaret Wade Labarge. — London: H. Hamilton, 1980. xii, 276 p., [8] p. of plates: ill., maps, ports.; 23 cm. Includes index. 1. Gascony (France) — History. I. T.
DC611.G25 L24 1980   944/.7702 19   *LC* 81-452313   *ISBN* 0241103096

Bates, David, 1945-. 3.2224
Normandy before 1066 / David Bates. — London; New York: Longman, 1982. xx, 287 p.: maps.; 22 cm. 1. Normandy (France) — History I. T.
DC611.N856 B37 1982   944/.2 19   *LC* 81-17154   *ISBN* 0582484928

Le Patourel, John. 3.2225
The Norman empire / John Le Patourel. — [S.l.]: Oxford, 1976. vii, 416 p.: ill.; 23 cm. 1. Normandy (France) — Politics and government. I. T.
DC611.N862 L46   940/.04/41   *LC* 77-367215   *ISBN* 0198225253

Strayer, Joseph Reese, 1904-. • 3.2226
The administration of Normandy under Saint Louis. Cambridge, Mass., Mediaeval Academy of America, 1932. [New York, AMS Press, 1971] x, 133 p. 24 cm. 1. Normandy (France) — Politics and government — Medieval. 2. France — Politics and government — 1226-1270 I. T. II. Title: Normandy under Saint Louis.
DC611.N88 S7 1971   354.44/2   *LC* 72-171362   *ISBN* 0404062970

Wylie, Laurence William, 1909-. • 3.2227
Village in the Vaucluse / Laurence Wylie. — 2d ed., enlarged. — Cambridge, Mass.: Harvard University Press, c1964. xvii, 377 p., [8] lavs of plates: ill.; 22 Cm. 1. Vaucluse (France: Dept.) — Social life and customs. I. T.
DC611.V357 W9 1964   914.4/92   *LC* 64-23470

Ford, Hugh D., 1925- comp. 3.2228
The Left Bank revisited; selections from the Paris Tribune, 1917-1934. Edited with an introd. by Hugh Ford. Foreword by Matthew Josephson. University Park: Pennsylvania State University Press [1972] xxiv, 334 p.: ill.; 24 cm.

1. Americans — France — Paris 2. Paris (France) — Intellectual life — 20th century I. The Chicago tribune. European ed. II. T.
DC715.F67   301.45/11/13044361   *LC* 76-136964   *ISBN* 0271011440

Isherwood, Robert M., 1935-.   **3.2229**
Farce and fantasy: popular entertainment in eighteenth–century Paris / Robert M. Isherwood. — New York: Oxford University Press, 1986. ix, 324 p.: ill.; 25 cm. Includes index. 1. Performing arts — France — Paris — History — 18th century. 2. Music-halls (Variety-theaters, cabarets, etc.) — France — Paris — History — 18th century. 3. Paris (France) — Social life and customs — 18th century I. T.
DC729.I84 1986   790/.0944/36 19   *LC* 85-3072   *ISBN* 0195036484

Bezucha, Robert J.   **3.2230**
The Lyon uprising of 1834: social and political conflict in the early July monarchy / Robert J. Bezucha. — Cambridge, Mass.: Harvard University Press, 1974. xv, 271 p.: ill.; 24 cm. (Harvard studies in urban history.) Based on the author's thesis, University of Michigan, 1968. Includes index. 1. Lyon (France) — History — Insurrection, 1834 I. T. II. Series.
DC733.B45 1974   944.06/3   *LC* 74-75780   *ISBN* 0674539656

Pinkney, David H.   • **3.2231**
Napoleon III and the rebuilding of Paris. — Princeton, N. J., Princeton University Press, 1958. xi, 245 p. illus., maps, plans. 25 cm. Bibliography: p. 223-231. 1. Napoleon III, Emperor of the French, 1808-1873. 2. Cities and towns — Planning — Paris. 3. Paris — Public works. I. T.
DC733.P59   944.07   *LC* 58-6108

Flanner, Janet, 1892-.   • **3.2232**
Paris journal [by] Janet Flanner (Genêt) Edited by William Shawn. — [1st ed.]. — New York, Atheneum, 1965-71. 2 v. 25 cm. Selected from her series of letters first published in the New Yorker magazine. 1. Paris — History — 1944-2. France — Politics and government — 1945- 3. Paris — Intellectual life. I. Shawn, William, ed. II. The New Yorker (1925-) III. T.
DC737.F55 1965   944.082   *LC* 65-25903 rev

Lottman, Herbert R.   **3.2233**
The Left Bank: writers, artists, and politics from the Popular Front to the Cold War / Herbert R. Lottman. — Boston: Houghton Mifflin, 1982. xvi, 319 p.; 24 cm. 1. Left Bank (Paris, France) — Intellectual life. I. T.
DC752.L43 L67   944/.36 19   *LC* 81-13276   *ISBN* 0395313228

Ackerman, Evelyn Bernette.   **3.2234**
Village on the Seine: tradition and change in Bonnières, 1815–1914 / Evelyn Bernette Ackerman. — Ithaca, N.Y.: Cornell University Press, 1978. 185 p.:

ill.; 23 cm. Includes index. 1. Bonnières-sur-Seine, France — History. 2. Bonnières-sur-Seine, France — Social conditions. 3. Bonnières-sur-Seine, France — Economic conditions. I. T.
DC801.B693 A34   944/.36   *LC* 78-58071   *ISBN* 0801411785

Kaplow, Jeffry.   • **3.2235**
Elbeuf during the revolutionary period, history and social structure. — Baltimore, Johns Hopkins Press, 1964. 278, x p. tables. 24 cm. — (Johns Hopkins University studies in historical and political science. Series 81, no. 2) Bibliography: p. 265-275. 1. Elbeuf (France) — Hist. 2. Elbeuf (France) — Soc. condit. I. T. II. Series.
H31.J6 ser. 81, no. 2 DC801.E4 K3   309.14425   *LC* 64-15091

Le Roy Ladurie, Emmanuel.   **3.2236**
[Montaillou, village occitan de 1294 à 1324. English] Montaillou: the promised land of error / Emmanuel Le Roy Ladurie; translated by Barbara Bray. — 1st ed. — New York: G. Braziller, 1978. xvii, 383 p.: maps; 24 cm. Translation of Montaillou, village occitan de 1294 à 1324. 1. Montaillou (France) — History. 2. Montaillou (France) — Social life and customs. 3. Montaillou (France) — Religious life and customs. I. T.
DC801.M753 L4713 1978b   944/.88   *LC* 77-6124   *ISBN* 0807608750

Le Roy Ladurie, Emmanuel.   **3.2237**
Carnival in Romans / Emmanuel LeRoy Ladurie; translated from the French by Mary Feeney. — New York: G. Braziller, 1979. xvi, 426 p.: ill., maps; 24 cm. Translation of Le carnaval de Romans. 1. Romans-sur-Isère (France) — History. 2. France — History — Wars of the Huguenots, 1562-1598 I. T.
DC801.R75 L4713   944/.98   *LC* 79-52163   *ISBN* 0807609285

Ott, Sandra.   **3.2238**
The circle of mountains: a Basque shepherding community / Sandra Ott. — Oxford [Eng.]: Clarendon Press; New York: Oxford University Press, c1981. xv, 238 p., [5] leaves of plates: ill.; 23 cm. Includes index. 1. Basques — Social life and customs. 2. Sainte-Engrâce (France) — Social life and customs. I. T. II. Title: A Basque shepherding community.
DC801.S3636 O87   944/.79 19   *LC* 80-40976   *ISBN* 0198231997

Chrisman, Miriam Usher.   **3.2239**
Lay culture, learned culture: books and social change in Strasbourg, 1480–1599 / Miriam Usher Chrisman. — New Haven: Yale University Press, c1982. xxx, 401 p.: ill.; 25 cm. Includes index. 1. Printing — France — Strasbourg — History. 2. Strasbourg (France) — Intellectual life. 3. Strasbourg (France) — Imprints. I. T.
DC801.S577 C47 1982   001.1/0944/3835 19   *LC* 82-2771   *ISBN* 0300025300

DD   Germany

DD1–78 General Works. Civilization

Snyder, Louis Leo, 1907- ed. • 3.2240
Documents of German history. New Brunswick, N. J., Rutgers University Press, 1958. xxiii, 619 p. fold. maps. 24 cm. Bibliography: p. [583]-587. 1. Germany — History — Sources. I. T.
DD3.S55   943.0082   LC 57-10968

Staël, Madame de (Anne-Louise-Germaine), 1766-1817. • 3.2241
De l'Allemagne: nouvelle édition, publiée d'après les mauscrits et les éditions originales. Avec des variantes, une introduction, des notices et des notes par la comtesse Jean de Pange, avec le concours de Simone Balayé. Paris: Hachette, c1958. 2 v.; 23 cm. 1. Germany. 2. Germany — Intellectual life I. Pange, Pauline Laure Marie de Broglie, comtesse de, 1888- II. T.
DD35 S75 1958   LC 59-3495

Dickinson, Robert Eric, 1905-. • 3.2242
Germany; a general and regional geography, by Robert E. Dickinson. — [2d ed.]. — London, Methuen [1964] xxiii, 716 p. illus., maps. 24 cm. On label on t.p.: Distributed in the United States by Barnes & Noble, Inc. Bibliography: p. 683-702. 1. Germany — Descr. & trav. — 1945- 2. Physical geography — Germany. I. T.
DD43.D5 1964   LC 67-59646

Wells, C. M. (Colin Michael) 3.2243
The German policy of Augustus: an examination of the archaeological evidence / [by] C. M. Wells. — Oxford: Clarendon Press, 1972. xxiv, 337 p., [fold leaf]: ill., maps, plans; 22 cm. Based on author's thesis, Oxford. 1. Romans — Germany. 2. Germany — Antiquities, Roman 3. Rome — History — Augustus, 30 B.C.-14 A.D. I. T.
DD53.W43   913.363   LC 72-170074   ISBN 0198131623

Epstein, Klaus, • 3.2244
The genesis of German conservatism. — Princeton, N.J.: Princeton University Press, 1966. xii, 733 p.; 25 cm. 1. Conservatism — Germany. 2. Germany — Intellectual life I. T.
DD65.E6   320.50943   LC 66-11970

Veblen, Thorstein, 1857-1929. • 3.2245
Imperial Germany and the industrial revolution, by Thorstein Veblen; with an introduction by Dr. Joseph Dorfman. — New York, The Viking press, 1939. xxi, 343 p. 20 cm. 'New edition.' 1. Germany — Civilization 2. Germany — Economic policy I. T.
DD67.V4 1939   943.08   LC 39-27516

Ergang, Robert Reinhold, 1898-. • 3.2246
Herder and the foundations of German nationalism. New York, Octagon Books, 1966 [c1931] 288 p. 24 cm. (Studies in history, economics, and public law, no. 341) Reprint of the author's thesis, Columbia University. 1. Herder, Johann Gottfried, 1744-1803. 2. Nationalism — Germany. I. T.
DD76.E7 1966   193   LC 66-19732

Stern, Fritz Richard, 1926-. • 3.2247
The politics of cultural despair; a study in the rise of the Germanic ideology. Berkeley, University of California Press, 1961. 367 p. 24 cm. Revision of the author's thesis, Columbia University, issued in microfilm form in 1954 under title: Cultural despair and the politics of discontent. 1. Lagarde, Paul de, 1827-1891. 2. Langbehn, Julius, 1851-1907. 3. Moeller van den Bruck, Arthur, 1876-1925. 4. Nationalism — Germany. 5. National socialism I. T.
DD76.S72 1961   943   LC 61-7517

DD84–261 History

Iggers, Georg G. • 3.2248
The German conception of history; the national tradition of historical thought from Herder to the present, by Georg G. Iggers. [1st ed.] Middletown, Conn.,

Wesleyan University Press [1968] xii, 363 p. 24 cm. 1. Germany — Historiography. I. T.
DD86.I34   914.3/0072   LC 68-17147

Barraclough, Geoffrey, 1908-. • 3.2249
The origins of modern Germany, by G. Barraclough. — Oxford: B. Blackwell, 1966. xi, 481 p.: maps.; 22 cm. Reprint of the 2d rev. ed., 1947. 1. Germany — History I. T.
DD89.B27 1966   943   LC 68-7947

Handbuch der deutschen Geschichte, begründet von Otto • 3.2250
Brandt, fortgeführt bon Arnold Oskar Meyer. Neu hrsg. von
Leo Just unter Mitwirkung von Walter Bussmann [et al.]
Konstanz, Akademische Verlagsgesellschaft Athenaion [c1956- v. 1, c1957] v.   : fold. col. map (in pocket); 27 cm. Each vol. has also special t.p. Vol. <4, pt. 1 > published in Frankfurt am M. Vol. <3, pt. 1b > published in Wiesbaden. Vol. <6 > published in Essen. Issued also in parts. 1. Germany — History I. Brandt, Otto, 1892-1935. II. Meyer, Arnold Oskar, 1877-1944. ed. III. Just, Leo, 1901-1964. ed.
DD89.H313   LC 64-50340   ISBN 3799708073

Heer, Friedrich, 1916-. • 3.2251
[Heilige Römische Reich. English] The Holy Roman Empire. Translated by Janet Sondheimer. New York, Praeger [1968] xiv, 309 p. plates (part col.) 26 cm. Translation of Das Heilige Römische Reich. 1. Germany — History 2. Austria — History 3. Holy Roman Empire — History I. T.
DD89.H3513 1968   943   LC 68-30935

Bryce, James Bryce, Viscount, 1838-1922. • 3.2252
The Holy Roman empire, by James Bryce ... — A new ed., enl. and rev. throughout, with a chronological table of events and three maps. — New York, The Macmillan company; London, Macmillan & co., ltd., 1904. lii p., 1 l., 575 p. 3 double maps. 21 cm. 'List of books on the history of the empire which may be consulted by the student': p. 543-544. 1. Holy Roman Empire — Hist. I. T.
DD90.B952   LC 04-34916

Gebhardt, Bruno, 1858-1905. • 3.2253
Handbuch der deutschen Geschichte. 9., neu bearb. Aufl. hrsg. von Herbert Grundmann. Stuttgart, Union Verlag, 1970-. v.; 25 cm. Vol. 4 pt. 2 published by E. Klett, Stuttgart. 1. Germany — History I. Grundmann, Herbert, 1902-1970. II. T.
DD90.G32 1970   943 19   LC 78-533119   ISBN 3800210118

Görlitz, Walter, 1913-. • 3.2254
[Deutsche Generalstab. English] History of the German General Staff, 1657–1945. Translated by Brian Battershaw. Introd. by Walter Millis. New York, Praeger [1953] xviii, 508 p. ports. 22 cm. 1. Germany. Heer. Generalstab. 2. World War, 1939-1945 — Germany. 3. Germany — History, Military 4. Germany — History — 1871- I. T.
DD101.G614 1953   943   LC 52-13106

Kitchen, Martin. 3.2255
A military history of Germany: from the eighteenth century to the present day / Martin Kitchen. — Bloomington: Indiana University Press, [1975] 384 p.: maps; 22 cm. Includes index. 1. Germany — History, Military I. T.
DD101.K57 1975   355/.00943   LC 74-17022   ISBN 0253338387

Kehr, Eckart, 1902-1933. 3.2256
[Primat der Innenpolitik. English. Selections] Economic interest, militarism, and foreign policy: essays on German history / Eckart Kehr; edited and with an introd. by Gordon A. Craig; translated by Grete Heinz. — Berkeley: University of California Press, c1977. xxi, 209 p.; 23 cm. Translation of 10 of the 16 essays collected as Der Primat der Innenpolitik. 1. Germany — History, Military — Addresses, essays, lectures. 2. Prussia (Germany) — History, Military — Addresses, essays, lectures. 3. Prussia (Germany) — Social conditions — Addresses, essays, lectures. 4. Germany — Historiography — Addresses, essays, lectures. I. T.
DD101.5.K4213 1977   943.08   LC 74-22964   ISBN 0520028805

Showalter, Dennis E. 3.2257
Railroads and rifles: soldiers, technology, and the unification of Germany / Dennis E. Showalter. — Hamden, Conn.: Archon Books, 1975. 267 p.: maps; 23 cm. Includes index. 1. Krupp, Alfred, 1812-1887. 2. Railroads — Germany. 3. Germany — History, Military — 19th century 4. Prussia (Germany) — History, Military. 5. Germany — Defenses — History. I. T.
DD103.S54   DD103 S54.   355/.00943   LC 75-17710   ISBN 0208015051

Herwig, Holger H.   3.2258
Luxury fleet: the Imperial Germany Navy, 1888–1918 / Holger H. Herwig. —
London; Boston: Allen & Unwin, 1980. 314 p., [6] leaves of plates: ill.; 23 cm.
Includes index. 1. Germany. Kriegsmarine — History. 2. Germany —
History, Naval I. T.
DD106.H47   359/.00943 19   *LC* 80-482767   *ISBN* 0049430238

DD110–120 Political and Diplomatic History

Krieger, Leonard.   • 3.2259
German idea of freedom: history of a political tradition / L. Krieger. — Boston:
Beacon Press [1957] xii, 540 p.; 22 cm. 1. Nationalism — Germany.
2. Liberalism 3. Germany — Politics and government I. T.
DD112.K82   943   *LC* 57-9088

Ritter, Gerhard, 1888-1967.   • 3.2260
[Staatskunst und Kriegshandwerk. English] The sword and the scepter; the
problem of militarism in Germany. Translated from the German by Heinz
Norden. Coral Gables, Fla., University of Miami Press [1969-. v. 25 cm.
Translation of Staatskunst und Kriegshandwerk. 1. Militarism — Germany.
2. Politics and war 3. Germany — Politics and government 4. Germany —
History, Military I. T.
DD112.R5213   320.9/43   *LC* 68-31041   *ISBN* 0870241273

Wertheimer, Mildred Salz, 1896-.   • 3.2261
The Pan–German League, 1890–1914, by Mildred S. Wertheimer. — New
York: Octagon Books, 1971 [c1924] 256 p.; 24 cm. — (Studies in history,
economics, and public law, no. 251) Originally presented as the author's thesis,
Columbia University, 1924. 1. Alldeutscher Verband. 2. Pangermanism I. T.
DD119.W4 1971   320.5/4/0943   *LC* 79-159257   *ISBN* 0374983526

Sontag, Raymond James, 1897-1972.   • 3.2262
Germany and England: background of conflict, 1848–1894. — New York,
Russell & Russell, 1964 [c1938] xvii, 362 p. 23 cm. Bibliography: p. 343-355.
1. Germany — For. rel. — Gt. Brit. 2. Gt. Brit. — For. rel. — Germany.
3. Germany — Pol. & govt. — 1848-1870. 4. Germany — Pol. & govt. —
1871-1918. 5. Gt. Brit. — Pol. & govt. — 1837-1901. I. T.
DD120.G7S6 1964   327.420943   *LC* 64-15034

DD121–261 History, by Period

DD121–174 MEDIEVAL, TO 1519. HOLY ROMAN EMPIRE

Barraclough, Geoffrey, 1908- tr.   • 3.2263
Mediaeval Germany, 911–1250; essays by German historians, translated with
an introduction by Geoffrey Barraclough. — Oxford: B. Blackwell, 1938. 2 v.:
illus. (map); 23 cm. — (Studies in mediaeval history, edited by Geoffrey
Barraclough [1-2]) 1. Investiture 2. Church and state in Germany.
3. Germany — Constitutional history 4. Germany — History — 843-1273
I. T.
DD126.B35   943.02   *LC* 39-18883

Fleckenstein, Josef.   3.2264
[Grundlagen und Beginn der deutschen Geschichte. English] Early medieval
Germany / Josef Fleckenstein; translated by Bernard S. Smith. — Amsterdam;
New York: North-Holland Pub. Co.; New York: distributors for the U.S.A. and
Canada, Elsevier North-Holland, 1978. xv, 212 p.; 23 cm. — (Europe in the
Middle Ages. 16) Translation of Grundlagen und Beginn der deutschen
Geschichte. Includes index. 1. Germany — History — To 843 2. Germany —
History — 843-1273 I. T. II. Series.
DD126.F5513   943/.01   *LC* 78-890   *ISBN* 0444851348

Hampe, Karl, 1869-1936.   3.2265
[Deutsche Kaisergeschichte in der Zeit der Salier und Staufer. English]
Germany under the Salian and Hohenstaufen emperors. Translated with an
introd. by Ralph Bennett. Totowa, N.J., Rowman and Littlefield, 1973 [i.e.
1974] ix, 315 p. map. 22 cm. Translation of the 11th ed. of Deutsche
Kaisergeschichte in der Zeit der Salier und Staufer. 1. Germany — History —
843-1273 2. Holy Roman Empire — History — 843-1273 I. T.
DD126.H313 1973   943/.02   *LC* 71-185304   *ISBN* 0874711738

Leyser, Karl.   3.2266
Medieval Germany and its neighbours, 900–1250 / K.J. Leyser. — London:
Hambledon Press, c1982. xii, 288 p., [2] leaves of plates: ill.; 24 cm. — (History
series; v. 12) 1. Germany — History — 843-1273 2. Europe — Relations —
Germany 3. Germany — Relations — Europe I. T.
DD126.L49 1982   943/.02 19   *LC* 82-199757   *ISBN* 0907628087

Thompson, James Westfall, 1869-1941.   • 3.2267
Feudal Germany. — New York, F. Ungar Pub. Co. [1962] 2 v. illus. 22 cm.
1. Germany — Hist. — 843-1273. 2. Holy Roman Empire — Hist. —
843-1273. I. T.
DD126.T5 1962   943.02   *LC* 62-17093

Duckett, Eleanor Shipley.   • 3.2268
Carolingian portraits; a study in the ninth century. — Ann Arbor: University of
Michigan Press, [1962] 311 p.: illus.; 24 cm. 1. Carlovingians 2. Germany —
History — 843-918 I. T.
DD131.D8   943.021   *LC* 62-18441

Fuhrmann, Horst.   3.2269
[Deutsche Geschichte im hohen Mittelalter. English] Germany in the High
Middle Ages, c. 1050–1200 / Horst Fuhrmann; translated by Timothy Reuter.
— Cambridge [Cambridgeshire]; New York: Cambridge University Press,
1986. vii, 209 p.; 23 cm. — (Cambridge medieval textbooks.) Translation of:
Deutsche Geschichte im hohen Mittelalter. Includes index. 1. Germany —
History — 843-1273 I. T. II. Series.
DD141.F8313 1986   943/.023 19   *LC* 85-29988   *ISBN* 0521266386

Otto I, Bishop of Freising, d. 1158.   • 3.2270
The deeds of Frederick Barbarossa, by Otto of Freising and his continuator,
Rahewin. Translated and annotated with an introd. by Charles Christopher
Mierow, with the collaboration of Richard Emery. New York, Columbia
University Press, 1953. x, 366 p.: front.; 24 cm. (Records of civilization, sources
and studies. no. 49) 1. Frederick I, Barbarossa, Emperor of Germany,
1121-1190. 2. Germany — History — Frederick I, 1152-1190 — Sources.
I. Rahewin, d. 1177. II. Mierow, Charles Christopher, 1883- III. T.
IV. Series.
DD149.O784   943.024

Kantorowicz, Ernst Hartwig, 1895-1963.   • 3.2271
Frederick the Second, 1194–1250. Authorized English version by E. O.
Lorimer. — New York, F. Ungar Pub. Co. [1957] xxvii, 724 p. (part fold.)
22 cm. Bibliography: p. xxv—xxvii. 1. Frederick II, Holy Roman Emperor,
1194-1250. 2. Germany — Hist. — Frederick II, 1215-1250. 3. Holy Roman
Empire — Hist. — Frederick II, 1215-1250. I. T.
DD151.K33 1957   923.143   *LC* 57-9408

Van Cleve, Thomas Curtis, 1888-.   3.2272
The Emperor Frederick II of Hohenstaufen, immutator mundi. Oxford,
Clarendon Press, 1972. xx, 607 p. illus. 24 cm. 1. Frederick II, Holy Roman
Emperor, 1194-1250. I. T.
DD151.V34   943/.025/0924 B   *LC* 73-150754   *ISBN* 019822513X

Du Boulay, F. R. H.   3.2273
Germany in the later Middle Ages / by F.R.H. Du Boulay. — London: Athlone
Press, 1983. xii, 260 p., [4] p. of plates: ill.; 23 cm. Includes index. 1. Germany
— History — 1273-1517 I. T.
DD156.D83x 1983b   *LC* 84-672301   *ISBN* 0485112205

Benecke, Gerhard.   3.2274
Maximilian I (1459-1519): an analytical biography / Gerhard Benecke. —
London; Boston: Routledge & Kegan Paul, 1982. xiii, 205 p., [16] p. of plates:
ill.; 23 cm. 1. Maximilian I, Holy Roman Emperor, 1459-1519. 2. Holy
Roman Empire — Kings and rulers — Biography. 3. Germany — History —
Maximilian I, 1493-1519 I. T.
DD174.B46 1982   943/.029/0924 B 19   *LC* 82-608   *ISBN*
0710090234

Strauss, Gerald, 1922- comp.   3.2275
Manifestations of discontent in Germany on the eve of the Reformation; a
collection of documents selected, translated, and introduced, by Gerald Strauss.
Bloomington, Indiana University Press [1971] xxiii, 247 p. 24 cm.
1. Reformation — Germany 2. Germany — History — Frederick III,
1440-1493 — Sources. 3. Germany — History — Maximilian I, 1493-1519 —
Sources. 4. Germany — Church history — 16th century — Sources. I. T.
DD174.S87   943/.03   *LC* 75-135014   *ISBN* 0253336708

DD175–261 1519-

Holborn, Hajo, 1902-1969.   • 3.2276
A history of modern Germany. — [1st ed.]. — New York: A. A. Knopf,
1959-69. 3 v.: illus., maps (part fold.); 24 cm. 1. Germany — History I. T.
DD175.H62   943   *LC* 59-5991

Lau, Franz.   3.2277
[Reformationsgeschichte bis 1532. English] A history of the Reformation in
Germany to 1555, by Franz Lau and Ernst Bizer; translated [from the German]
by Brian A. Hardy. London, Black, 1969. xii, 249 p. 24 cm. (A History of the
Christian Church) Translation of Reformationsgeschichte bis 1532, by Franz
Lau, and Reformationsgeschichte 1532 bis 1555, by Ernst Bizer.
1. Reformation — Germany 2. Germany — History — 1517-1648
3. Germany — Church history — 16th century I. Bizer, Ernst. II. Bizer,
Ernst. Reformationsgeschichte 1532 bis 1555. English. 1969. III. T.
DD176.L313   943/.03   LC 72-415895   ISBN 0713609052

Blickle, Peter.   3.2278
[Revolution von 1525. English] The Revolution of 1525: the German Peasants'
War from a new perspective / Peter Blickle; translated by Thomas A. Brady,
Jr., and H.C. Erik Midelfort. — Baltimore: Johns Hopkins University Press,
c1981. xxvi, 246 p.: ill.; 24 cm. Translation of: Die Revolution von 1525.
Includes indexes. 1. Peasants' War, 1524-1525 I. T.
DD182.B613   943/.031 19   LC 81-47603   ISBN 0801824729

Bireley, Robert.   3.2279
Religion and politics in the age of the counterreformation: Emperor Ferdinand
II, William Lamormaini, S.J., and the formation of imperial policy / Robert
Bireley. — Chapel Hill: University of North Carolina Press, c1981. xiii, 311 p.:
ill.; 24 cm. Includes index. 1. Ferdinand II, Holy Roman Emperor, 1578-1637.
2. Lamormaini, William. 3. Thirty Years' War, 1618-1648 4. Counter-
Reformation — Germany. 5. Germany — History — 1618-1648 I. T.
DD189.B54   943/.042 19   LC 80-27334   ISBN 0807814709

Germany in the Thirty Years War / [edited by] Gerhard   3.2280
Benecke.
New York: St. Martin's Press, 1979. xii, 108 p., [1] leaf of plates: maps; 21 cm.
— (Documents of modern history) 1. Thirty Years' War, 1618-1648
2. Germany — History — 1618-1648 I. Benecke, Gerhard.
DD189.G47 1979   943/.041   LC 78-21443   ISBN 0312326262

Bruford, Walter Horace.   • 3.2281
Germany in the eighteenth century: the social background of the literary
revival, by W. H. Bruford ... — Cambridge [Eng.] The University press, 1965. x,
354 p. front. (ports.) fold. map. 23 cm. Bibliography: p. [337]-346. 1. Germany
— Soc. life & cust. 2. Germany — Pol. & govt. — 18th cent. 3. Germany —
Econ. condit. 4. German literature — 18th cent. — Hist. & crit. I. T.
DD193.B7   914.3   LC 35-7429

Meinecke, Friedrich, 1862-1954.   3.2282
[Zeitalter der deutschen Erhebung. English] The age of German liberation,
1795–1815 / Friedrich Meinecke; edited with an introd. by Peter Paret;
[translated by Peter Paret and Helmuth Fischer]. — Berkeley: University of
California Press, c1977. xxiii, 131 p.; 23 cm. Translation of Das Zeitalter der
deutschen Erhebung. Includes index. 1. Germany — History — 1789-1900
2. Prussia (Germany) — History — 1740-1815. I. T.
DD197.M413   943/.06   LC 74-79767   ISBN 0520027922

Fichte, Johann Gottlieb, 1762-1814.   • 3.2283
[Reden an die deutsche Nation. English] Addresses to the German nation.
Edited with an introd. by George Armstrong Kelly. New York, Harper & Row
[1968] xxxv, 228 p. 21 cm. (European perspectives) (Harper torchbooks,
TB1366.) Translation of Reden an die deutsche Nation. 1. Education and state
— Germany — Addresses, essays, lectures. 2. National characteristics,
German — Addresses, essays, lectures. 3. Germany — Politics and
government — 1806-1815 — Addresses, essays, lectures. I. T.
DD199.F413 1968   914.3/03/6   LC 68-5895

DD201–261 19th–20th Centuries

Brandenburg, Erich, 1868-1946.   • 3.2284
Die reichsgründung / von Erich Brandenburg. — Leipzig: Quelle & Mayer,
1916. 2 v.; 24 cm. 1. Germany — History — 1815-1866 2. Germany —
History — 1866-1871 3. Germany — Politics and government I. T.
DD203.B7   LC 20-22140

Carr, William, 1921-.   3.2285
A history of Germany, 1815–1985 / William Carr. — 3rd ed. — London:
Edward Arnold, 1987. ix, 419 p.: maps; 24 cm. Includes index. 1. Germany —
History — 1789-1900 2. Germany — History — 20th century I. Carr,
William, 1921- History of Germany, 1815-1945. II. T.
DD203.C3 1987   943/.07 19   ISBN 0713164956

Fest, Wilfried, 1943-.   3.2286
Dictionary of German history, 1806–1945 / Wilfried Fest. — New York: St.
Martin's Press, c1978. 189 p.; 24 cm. 1. Germany — History — 1789-1900 —
Dictionaries. 2. Germany — History — 20th century — Dictionaries. I. T.
DD203.F47 1978   943/.07/03   LC 79-100882   ISBN 0860431088

Mann, Golo, 1909-.   • 3.2287
[Deutsche Geschichte des 19. und 20. Jahrhunderts. English] The history of
Germany since 1789. Translated from the German by Marian Jackson. New
York, Praeger [1968] xii, 547 p. 25 cm. Translation of Deutsche Geschichte des
19. und 20. Jahrhunderts. 1. Germany — History — 1789-1900 2. Germany
— History — 20th century I. T.
DD203.M2713   943   LC 67-24685

Nipperdey, Thomas.   3.2288
Deutsche Geschichte 1800–1866: Bürgerwelt und starker Staat / Thomas
Nipperdey. — München: C.H. Beck, c1983. 838 p.; 23 cm. Includes index.
1. Germany — History — 1789-1900 I. T.
DD203.N55 1983   943/.07 19   LC 83-227261   ISBN 340609354X

Pinson, Koppel Shub, 1904-1961.   • 3.2289
Modern Germany: its history and civilization / Koppel S. Pinson, chapter 23 by
Klaus Epstein. — 2d ed. — New York: Macmillan, c1966. xv, 682 p.: map (on
lining papers); 25 cm. 1. Germany — History — 1789-1900 2. Germany —
History — 20th century I. T.
DD203.P5 1966   943/.08   LC 66-16925

Schnabel, Franz, 1887-.   • 3.2290
Deutsche Geschichte im neunzehnten jahrhundert, von Franz Schnabel ... —
Freiburg im Breisgau, Herder 1929-. v. 24 cm. Bibliographical references in
'Anmerkungen' (v. 1, p. [569]-619) 'Ich habe mich bemüht, die innige
verflochtenheit aller lebensgebiete zu untersuchen und darzustellen, um so in
grossen zügen eine biographie des europäischen und des deutschen menschen
zu geben und die gegenwärtige lage der europäischen kultur und im besondern
des deutschen volkes historisch zu deuten.'—Vorwort. 1. Germany — Hist. —
1789-1900. 2. Germany — Civilization I. T.
DD203.S33   LC 30-3083

Snell, John L.   3.2291
The democratic movement in Germany, 1789–1914 / by John L. Snell; edited
and completed by Hans A. Schmitt. Chapel Hill: University of North Carolina
Press, c1976. x, 501 p.; 22 cm. (James Sprunt studies in history and political
science. v. 55) Includes index. 1. Democracy — History. 2. Germany —
Politics and government — 1789-1900 3. Germany — Politics and government
— 1888-1918 I. Schmitt, Hans A. joint author. II. T. III. Series.
DD203.S63   320.9/43   LC 76-10254   ISBN 0807812838

Taylor, A. J. P. (Alan John Percivale), 1906-.   • 3.2292
The course of German history, a survey of the development of Germany since
1815, by A. J. P. Taylor ... London, H. Hamilton [1945] 229 p. maps. 21.5 cm.
'First published 1945.' 1. Germany — History — 1789-1900 2. Germany —
History — 20th century I. T.
DD203.T3   943.07   LC 45-8396

Treitschke, Heinrich Gotthard von, 1834-1896.   3.2293
[Deutsche Geschichte im neunzehnten Jahrhundert. English. Selections]
History of Germany in the nineteenth century: selections from the translation of
Eden and Cedar Paul / Heinrich von Treitschke; edited and with an introd. by
Gordon A. Craig. — Chicago: University of Chicago Press, 1975. xxix, 411 p.;
21 cm. (Classic European historians) Selections from the translation of the
author's work first published under title: Deutsche Geschichte im neunzehnten
Jahrhundert. 1. German literature — History and criticism. 2. Germany —
History — 1789-1900 3. Germany — Intellectual life — 19th century I. Craig,
Gordon Alexander, 1913- II. T. III. Series.
DD203.T78213   943/.07   LC 75-5072   ISBN 0226812782

Treitschke, Heinrich Gotthard von, 1834-1896.   • 3.2294
Treitschke's history of Germany in the nineteenth century, tr. by Eden & Cedar
Paul, with an introduction by William Harbutt Dawson. London, Jarrold &
sons [etc.] 1915-19. 7 v.; 23 cm. 1. German literature — History and criticism.
2. Germany — History — 1789-1900 3. Germany — Intellectual life I. Paul,
Eden, tr. II. Paul, Cedar. tr. III. T.
DD203.T8 1915a   LC 16-16685

Ward, Adolphus William, Sir, 1837-1924.   • 3.2295
Germany, 1815–1890. Cambridge, The University press, 1916-18. 3 v. 20 cm.
(Cambridge historical series [8]) 1. Germany — History — 1789-1900
I. Wilkinson, Spenser, 1853-1937. II. T.
DD203.W3   LC 16-17397

Blackbourn, David, 1949-.   3.2296
[Mythen deutscher Geschichtsschreibung. English] The peculiarities of
German history: bourgeois society and politics in nineteenth–century Germany
/ David Blackbourn and Geoff Eley. — Oxford [Oxfordshire]; New York:
Oxford University Press, 1984. viii, 300 p.; 23 cm. Rev. and expanded
translation of the authors' Mythen deutscher Geschichtsschreibung. Includes
index. 1. Germany — History — 1789-1900 — Historiography. I. Eley, Geoff,
1949- II. T.
DD204.B5213 1984   943/.07 19   LC 84-10051   ISBN 0198730586

Mosse, Werner Eugen. • **3.2297**
The European powers and the German question, 1848–71, with special reference to England and Russia, by W. E. Mosse. — New York: Octagon Books, 1969. ix, 409 p.; 24 cm. Reprint of the 1958 ed. 1. Nationalism — Germany. 2. Germany — Politics and government — 1848-1870 3. Germany — Foreign relations 4. Europe — Politics and government — 1815-1871 I. T.
DD204.M6 1969   943/.07   *LC* 74-76002

Sheehan, James J. **3.2298**
German liberalism in the nineteenth century / James J. Sheehan. — Chicago: University of Chicago Press, 1978. 411 p.; 24 cm. Includes index. 1. Liberalism — Germany. 2. Germany — Politics and government — 19th century I. T.
DD204.S53   320.5/12/0943   *LC* 77-25971   *ISBN* 0226752070

Anderson, Margaret Lavinia. **3.2299**
Windthorst: a political biography / by Margaret Lavinia Anderson. — Oxford: Clarendon Press; New York: Oxford University Press, 1981. xi, 522 p.; 22 cm. Includes index. 1. Windthorst, Ludwig Josef Ferdinand Gustav, 1812-1891. 2. Statesmen — Germany — Biography. 3. Kulturkampf — Germany. 4. Germany — Politics and government — 1871-1918 5. Germany — Politics and government — 1848-1870 6. Prussia (Germany) — Politics and government — 1815-1870 I. T.
DD205.W4 A83   943.08/092/4 B 19   *LC* 80-41313   *ISBN* 0198225784

DD207 1848–1849

Valentin, Veit, 1885-1947. • **3.2300**
1848; chapters of German history. Translated by Ethel Talbot Scheffauer. Hamden, Conn., Archon Books, 1965. 480 p. 21 cm. 'First published in 1940; reprinted 1965 in an unaltered and unabridged edition.' An abridged translation of Geschichte der deutschen Revolution von 1848-49. 1. Germany — History — Revolution, 1848-1849 I. T.
DD207.V352   943.07   *LC* 65-16974

Eyck, Frank. • **3.2301**
The Frankfurt Parliament 1848–1849. London, Melbourne [etc.] Macmillan, New York, St. Martin's P., 1968. xiv, 425 p. 8 plates, 1 illus., map, ports. 23 cm. 1. Deutsche Nationalversammlung (1848-1849: Frankfurt am Main, Germany) 2. Germany — History — Revolution, 1848-1849 3. Germany — Politics and government — 1848-1849 I. T.
DD207.5.E87   328.43/09   *LC* 68-14232

Legge, James Granville, 1861-1940. • **3.2302**
Rhyme and revolution in Germany; a study in German history, life, literature, and character, 1813–1850. — [1st AMS ed.]. — New York: AMS Press, [1970] xxiv, 584 p.; 23 cm. Reprint of the 1918 ed. 1. Political poetry, German 2. German poetry — Translation into English. 3. English poetry — Translations from German. 4. Germany — History — 1815-1866 5. Germany — History — Revolution, 1848-1849 I. T.
DD207.5.L4 1970   914.3/03/7   *LC* 72-126646   *ISBN* 0404039472

Stadelmann, Rudolf, 1902-1949. • **3.2303**
Soziale und politische Geschichte der Revolution von 1848. [München] Münchner Verlag 1948. 216 p.; 23 cm. 1. Germany — History — Revolution, 1848-1849 I. T.
DD207.5 S7

DD210 1850–1871

Böhme, Helmut, 1936- comp. **3.2304**
[Reichsgründung. English] The foundation of the German Empire: select documents; edited by Helmut Böhme; translated [from the German] by Agatha Ramm. London, Oxford University Press, 1971. xxi, 271 p. 23 cm. Translation of Die Reichsgründung. 1. Germany — History — 1848-1870 — Sources. I. T.
DD210.B613   943/.07   *LC* 79-30796   *ISBN* 0198730128

Eley, Geoff, 1949-. **3.2305**
From unification to Nazism: reinterpreting the German past / Geoff Eley. — Boston: Allen & Unwin, 1986. 290 p.; 24 cm. 1. Germany — History — 1848-1870 2. Germany — History — 1871- I. T.
DD210.E48 1986   943.08 19   *LC* 85-11183   *ISBN* 0049430386

Hamerow, Theodore S. • **3.2306**
The social foundations of German unification, 1858–1871 [by] Theodore S. Hamerow. — Princeton, N.J.: Princeton University Press, 1969-72. 2 v.; 23 cm. 1. Bismarck, Otto, Fürst von, 1815-1898. 2. Germany — Politics and government — 1848-1870 3. Germany — Economic conditions — 19th century 4. Germany — Social conditions I. T.
DD210.H25   320.9/43/07   *LC* 75-75241   *ISBN* 0691051747

Sybel, Heinrich von, 1817-1895. • **3.2307**
[Begründung des Deutschen Reiches durch Wilhelm I. English] The founding of the German Empire by William I; based chiefly upon Prussian state

documents. Translated by Marshall Livingston Perrin, assisted by Gamaliel Bradford, Jr. New York, Greenwood Press [1968] 7 v. maps, ports. 23 cm. Reprint of the 1890-97 ed. Translation of Die Begründung des Deutschen Reiches durch Wilhelm I. Vols. 6 and 7 translated by Helene Schimmelfennig White. 1. Germany — History — 1815-1866 2. Germany — History — 1866-1871 3. Germany — Politics and government — 1815-1866 4. Germany — Politics and government — 1866-1871 I. T.
DD210.S7132   943.08   *LC* 68-31005

DD217–231 NEW EMPIRE (1871–1918)

DD218 Bismarck

Bismarck, Otto, Fürst von, 1815-1898. • **3.2308**
The memoirs, being the reflections and reminiscences of Otto, Prince von Bismarck, written and dictated by himself after his retirement from office. Translated from the German under the supervision of A. J. Butler. New York, H. Fertig, 1966. 2 v. illus., ports. 24 cm. Translation of Gedanken und Erinnerungen. Bibliographical footnotes. 1. Germany — History — 1789-1900 2. Germany — Politics and government — 1789-1900 3. Europe — Politics — 1789-1900. 4. Prussia (Germany) — Politics and government — 1815-1870 I. T.
DD218.A2 1966   943.080924   *LC* 66-24343

Becker, Otto, 1885-1955. • **3.2309**
Bismarcks Ringen um Deutschlands Gestaltung: hrsg. und ergänzt / von Alexander Scharff. — Heidelberg: Quelle & Meyer [1958] 963 p.: ill.; 23 cm. I. Bismarck, Otto, Fürst von, 1815-1898. II. T.
DD218B4   DD218.B4.   *LC* 59-28340

Busch, Moritz, 1821-1899. • **3.2310**
Bismarck; some secret pages of his history, being a diary kept by Moritz Busch during twenty–five years' official and private intercourse with the great chancellor. New York, Macmillan, 1898. — St. Clair Shores, Mich.: Scholarly Press, [1971] 2 v.: illus.; 21 cm. 1. Bismarck, Otto, Fürst von, 1815-1898. I. T.
DD218.B98 1971   943.08/0924   *LC* 70-144925   *ISBN* 0403008158

Crankshaw, Edward. **3.2311**
Bismarck / Edward Crankshaw. — New York: Viking Press, 1981. x, 451 p., [8] leaves of plates: ill.; 24 cm. Includes index. 1. Bismarck, Otto, Fürst von, 1815-1898. 2. Statesmen — Germany — Biography. 3. Germany — Politics and government — 1871-1888 4. Prussia (Germany) — Politics and government — 1815-1870. I. T.
DD218.C7   943.08/092/4 B 19   *LC* 80-29171   *ISBN* 067016982X

Eyck, Erich, 1878-. • **3.2312**
Bismarck and the German Empire. — London, Allen & Unwin [1950] 327 p. port. 22 cm. 'A summary of [the author's] ... three-volume Bismarck, published in German.' 1. Bismarck, Otto, Fürst von, 1815-1898. I. T.
DD218.E92   923.243   *LC* 50-9287

Mitchell, Ian R. **3.2313**
Bismarck and the development of Germany / Ian R. Mitchell. — Edinburgh: Holmes McDougall, 1980. v, 142 p.: ill., maps, ports.; 19 x 25 cm. Includes index. 1. Bismarck, Otto, Fürst von, 1815-1898. 2. Germany — History — 1848-1870 — Study and teaching (Secondary) 3. Germany — History — 1871-1918 — Study and teaching (Secondary) 4. Germany — Politics and government — 1848-1870 — Study and teaching (Secondary) 5. Germany — Economic conditions — 19th century — Study and teaching (Secondary) I. T.
DD218.M58   943/.08   *ISBN* 0715717936

Pflanze, Otto. • **3.2314**
Bismarck and the development of Germany; the period of unification, 1815–1871. — Princeton, N.J.: Princeton University Press, 1963. 510 p.: illus.; 25 cm. 1. Bismarck, Otto, Fürst von, 1815-1898. 2. Germany — History — 1815-1866 3. Germany — History — 1866-1871 I. T.
DD218.P44   943.604   *LC* 63-7159

Richter, Werner, 1888-1969. • **3.2315**
Bismarck. Translated from the German by Brian Battershaw. Foreword by F. H. Hinsley. — [1st American ed.]. — New York, Putnam [1965, c1964] 420 p. illus., ports. 22 cm. Bibliography: p. 413-414. 1. Bismarck, Otto, Fürst von, 1815-1898. I. T.
DD218.R513 1965   923.243   *LC* 64-23090

Taylor, A. J. P. (Alan John Percivale), 1906-. • **3.2316**
Bismarck, the man and the statesman. [1st American ed.] New York, Knopf, 1955. 286 p. illus. 22 cm. 1. Bismarck, Otto, Fürst von, 1815-1898. 2. Statesmen — Germany — Biography. I. T.
DD218.T33 1955a   923.243   *LC* 55-10649

DD219 Other Biography

Holstein, Friedrich von, 1837-1909.   • **3.2317**
The Holstein papers, edited by Norman Rich & M. H. Fisher. — Cambridge [Eng.] University Press, 1955-63. 4 v. ports., facsim. 26 cm. Bibliographical footnotes. 1. Germany — Pol. & govt. — 1871-1918. 2. Germany — For. rel. — 1871-1918. I. Rich, Norman. ed. II. Fisher, M. H., ed. III. T.
DD219.H6A3   *LC* 55-3247 rev

Rich, Norman.   • **3.2318**
Friedrich von Holstein, politics and diplomacy in the era of Bismarck and Wilhelm II. — Cambridge [Eng.] University Press, 1965. 2 v. (870 p.) illus., ports. 26 cm. 1. Holstein, Friedrich von, 1837-1909. 2. Germany — Pol. & govt. — 1871-1918. 3. Germany — For. rel. — 1871-1918. I. T.
DD219.H6R5   943.08   *LC* 64-21565

Stadelmann, Rudolf, 1902-1949.   • **3.2319**
Moltke und der staat / Rudolf Stadelmann. — Krefeld: Scherpe-Verlag, 1950. 566 p.: ports., facsims.; 23 cm. 1. Moltke, Helmuth, Graf von, 1800-1891. 2. Germany — History — 1848-1870 3. Germany — History — 1871-1918 4. Prussai — History — 1789-1900 I. T.
DD219.M7 S7   *LC* 51-22891

Dorpalen, Andreas.   • **3.2320**
Heinrich von Treitschke. New Haven, Yale University Press, 1957. ix, 345 p. port., map. 23 cm. 1. Treitschke, Heinrich Gotthard von, 1834-1896. I. T.
DD219.T7 D6   *LC* 57-6337   *ISBN* 0804616930

DD220–229 1878–1918

Calleo, David P., 1934-.   **3.2321**
The German problem reconsidered: Germany and the world order, 1870 to the present / David Calleo. — Cambridge; New York: Cambridge University Press, 1978. xi, 239 p.; 24 cm. Includes index. 1. World politics — 19th century 2. World politics — 20th century 3. Germany — History — 1871-1918 4. Germany — History — 20th century 5. Germany — History — Philosophy. I. T.
DD220.C34   943.08   *LC* 78-9683   *ISBN* 0521223091

Craig, Gordon Alexander, 1913-.   **3.2322**
Germany, 1866–1945 / by Gordon A. Craig. — New York: Oxford University Press, 1978. xv, 825 p.; 22 cm. — (Oxford history of modern Europe.) Includes index. 1. Germany — History — 1866-1871 2. Germany — History — 1871-1918 3. Germany — History — 1918-1933 4. Germany — History — 1933-1945 I. T. II. Series.
DD220.C72 1978b   943.08   *LC* 78-58471   *ISBN* 0198221134

Imperial Germany: essays / edited by Volker Dürr, Kathy   **3.2323**
Harms, Peter Hayes.
Madison, Wis.: Published for Monatshefte [by] University of Wisconsin Press, 1985. vii, 196 p.; 24 cm. — (Monatshefte occasional volumes. no. 3) 'Papers read at the seminar series on Imperial Germany held at Northwestern University in the fall of 1980'—P. vii. 1. Germany — History — 1870-1918 — Congresses. 2. Prussia (Germany) — History — 1870- — Congresses. I. Dürr, Volker. II. Harms, Kathy. III. Hayes, Peter, 1946- IV. Northwestern University (Evanston, Ill.) V. Series.
DD220.I64 1985   943.08 19   *LC* 84-40571   *ISBN* 0299970167

Wehler, Hans Ulrich.   **3.2324**
[Deutsche Kaiserreich, 1871-1918. English] The German Empire, 1871–1918 / Hans–Ulrich Wehler; translated from the German by Kim Traynor. — Leamington Spa, Warwickshire, UK; Dover, N.H.: Berg Publishers, 1985. 293 p.; 23 cm. Translation of: Das Deutsche Kaiserreich, 1871-1918. Includes index. 1. Germany — History — 1871-1918 I. T.
DD220.W413 1985   943.08/3 19   *LC* 84-73484   *ISBN* 0907582222

Williamson, D. G.   **3.2325**
Bismarck and Germany, 1862–1890 / D.G. Williamson. — London; New York: Longman, 1986. v, 138 p.: ill.; 20 cm. — D.G. Williamson. — (Seminar studies in history.) Includes index. 1. Bismarck, Otto, Fürst von, 1815-1898. 2. Germany — History — 1871-1918 3. Germany — History — 1848-1870 I. T. II. Series.
DD220.W48 1986   943.08 19   *LC* 85-19714   *ISBN* 0582354137

Craig, Gordon Alexander, 1913-.   • **3.2326**
The politics of the Prussian Army 1640–1945. New York, Oxford University Press, 1956 [c1955] xx, 536 p. 22 cm. 1. Germany. Heer. 2. Prussia (Kingdom). Armee. 3. Germany — Politics and government — 1871- 4. Prussia (Germany) — Politics and government. I. T.
DD221.C7 1956   943.08   *LC* 56-8006

Ziekursch, Johannes, 1876-.   • **3.2327**
Politische Geschichte des neuen deutschen Kaiserreiches, von Johannes Ziekursch ... Frankfurt am Main, Frankfurter Societäts-Druckerei, 1925-30. 3 v.; 24 cm. 1. Germany — History — 1806-1918 I. T.
DD221.Z5

Geiss, Imanuel.   **3.2328**
German foreign policy, 1871–1914 / [by] Imanuel Geiss. — London; Boston: Routledge and Kegan Paul, 1976. x, 259 p.; 24 cm. (Routledge direct editions) Includes index. 1. Germany — Foreign relations — 1871-1918 I. T.
DD221.5.G42   327.43   *LC* 76-365027   *ISBN* 0710083033

Nichols, J. Alden, 1919-.   **3.2329**
The year of the three kaisers: Bismarck and the German succession, 1887–88 / J. Alden Nichols. — Urbana: University of Illinois Press, c1987. xii, 413 p.: ill.; 24 cm. Includes index. 1. Bismarck, Otto, Fürst von, 1815-1898. 2. Germany — History — 1871-1918 3. Germany — Kings and rulers — Succession. I. T. II. Title: Year of the 3 kaisers.
DD223.9.N53 1987   943.08 19   *LC* 86-7028   *ISBN* 0252013077

Bennett, Daphne.   • **3.2330**
Vicky: Princess Royal of England and German Empress. — [New York]: St. Martin's Press, [1972] 382 p.: illus.; 24 cm. 1. Victoria, consort of Frederick III, German Emperor, 1840-1901. I. T.
DD224.9.B45 1972   943.08/4/0924 B   *LC* 74-145442

Pachter, Henry Maximilian, 1907-.   **3.2331**
Modern Germany: a social, cultural, and political history / Henry M. Pachter. — Boulder, Colo.: Westview Press, 1978. xi, 415 p.: maps; 24 cm. Includes indexes. 1. Germany — History — William II, 1888-1918 2. Germany — History — 20th century I. T.
DD228.P33   943.08/4 19   *LC* 78-2030   *ISBN* 0891581669

Eley, Geoff, 1949-.   **3.2332**
Reshaping the German right: radical nationalism and political change after Bismarck / Geoff Eley. — New Haven: Yale University Press, 1980. xii, 387 p.: ill.; 24 cm. Includes index. 1. Nationalism — Germany — History. 2. Germany — Politics and government — 1888-1918 I. T.
DD228.5.E45   320.9/43/084   *LC* 79-20711   *ISBN* 0300023863

Eyck, Erich, 1878-1964.   • **3.2333**
Das persönliche Regiment Wilhelm II: politische Geschichte des deutschen Kaiserreiches von 1890 bis 1914 / Erich Eyck. — Erlenbach-Zürich: E. Rentsch, 1948. 814 p.; 23 cm. 1. William II, German Emperor, 1859-1941. 2. Germany — Politics and government — 1888-1918 I. T.
DD228.5.E9   *LC* 48-25609

Fischer, Fritz, 1908-.   **3.2334**
[Krieg der Illusionen. English] War of illusions: German policies from 1911 to 1914 / by Fritz Fischer; with a foreword by Sir Alan Bullock; translated from the German by Marian Jackson. — New York: Norton, [1975] xiii, 578 p.; 24 cm. Translation of Krieg der Illusionen. Includes index. 1. World War, 1914-1918 — Causes. 2. Germany — Foreign relations — 1888-1918 3. Germany — Politics and government — 1888-1918 I. T.
DD228.5.F5513   327.43   *LC* 74-34142   *ISBN* 0393054802

Nichols, John Alden, 1919-.   • **3.2335**
Germany after Bismarck, the Caprivi era, 1890–1894. Cambridge: Harvard University Press, 1958. xii, 404 p. illus., port. 25 cm. 1. Caprivi de Caprara de Montecuculi, Georg Leo, Grafvon, 1831-1899. 2. Germany — History — 1871-1918 I. T.
DD228.5.N5 1958   943.084

Röhl, John C. G.   • **3.2336**
Germany without Bismarck; the crisis of government in the Second Reich, 1890–1900 [by] J. C. G. Röhl. — Berkeley: University of California Press, 1967. 304 p.; 23 cm. 1. Bismarck, Otto, Fürst von, 1815-1898. 2. Germany — History — William II, 1888-1918 3. Germany — Politics and government — 1888-1918 I. T.
DD228.5.R6 1967   943.08/4   *LC* 67-26960

Brandenburg, Erich, 1868-1946.   • **3.2337**
From Bismarck to the world war: a history of German foreign policy 1870–1914 / by Erich Brandenburg; translated by Annie Elizabeth Adams. — London Oxford University Press 1927. xiii, 542 p.; 23 cm. 1. Germany — Foreign relations — 1871- 2. Germany — Politics and government — 1871- 3. World War, 1914-1918 — Causes I. Adams, Annie Elizabeth, d. 1926, tr. II. Germany. Auswärtiges Amt. III. T.
DD228.6 B72

Berghahn, Volker Rolf.   **3.2338**
Germany and the approach of war in 1914 [by] V. R. Berghahn. New York, St. Martin's Press [1973] 260 p. maps. 21 cm. (The Making of the 20th century) 1. Bethmann Hollweg, Theobald von, 1856-1921. 2. World War, 1914-1918 — Germany. 3. Germany — Politics and government — 1888-1918 I. T.
DD228.8.B38 1973b   940.3/112   *LC* 73-86664

Gatzke, Hans Wilhelm, 1915-.   • **3.2339**
Germany's drive to the west (Drang nach Westen) A study of Germany's western war aims during the First World War. Baltimore, Johns Hopkins Press, 1950. x, 316 p. 24 cm. A revision of the author's thesis—Harvard University. 'Bibliographical note': p. 295-300. 1. World War, 1914-1918 — Germany. 2. Germany — Politics and government — 1888-1918 I. T.
DD228.8.G3 1950   940.343   *LC* 50-7516

Kitchen, Martin.   **3.2340**
The silent dictatorship: the politics of the German high command under Hindenburg and Ludendorff, 1916–1918 / Martin Kitchen. — New York: Holmes & Meier Publishers, 1976. 301 p.; 23 cm. Includes index. 1. Hindenburg, Paul von, 1847-1934. 2. Ludendorff, Erich, 1865-1937. 3. Germany. Heer. Oberkommando. 4. World War, 1914-1918 — Germany. 5. Germany — Politics and government — 1888-1918 I. T.
DD228.8.K5 1976   940.3/43   *LC* 76-16055   *ISBN* 0841902771

Lutz, Ralph Haswell, 1886-1968. ed.   • **3.2341**
Fall of the German Empire, 1914–1918. Translations by David G. Rempel and Gertrude Rendtorff. New York, Octagon Books, 1969 [c1932] 2 v. 24 cm. (Hoover War Library publications, no. 1-2) 1. World War, 1914-1918 — Germany. 2. World War, 1914-1918 — Sources. 3. World War, 1914-1918 — Diplomatic history. 4. Germany — History — William II, 1888-1918 — Sources. 5. Germany — History — Revolution, 1918 — Sources. 6. Germany — Politics and government — 1888-1918 I. T.
DD228.8.L8 1969   943.08/4   *LC* 71-89977

Mendelssohn-Bartholdy, Albrecht, 1874-1936.   • **3.2342**
The war and German society; the testament of a liberal. New York, H. Fertig, 1971. xiv, 299 p. 24 cm. (Economic and social history of the World War. German series) Reprint of the 1937 ed. 1. World War, 1914-1918 — Germany. 2. World War, 1914-1918 — Economic aspects — Germany. 3. Germany — Politics and government — 1888-1918 I. T.
DD228.8.M43 1971   943.08/4   *LC* 70-114589

William II, German Emperor, 1859-1941.   • **3.2343**
The Kaiser's memoirs, Wilhelm II, emperor of Germany, 1888–1918; English translation by Thomas R. Ybarra. New York, Harper, 1922. 4 p. l., 365 [1] p.: front. (port.); 22 1/2 cm. 1. World War, 1914-1918 2. Germany — Politics and government — 1888-1918 I. Ybarra, Thomas Russell, 1880- II. T.
DD229.A45   943.084   *LC* 22-21224

Balfour, Michael Leonard Graham, 1908-.   • **3.2344**
The Kaiser and his times, by Michael Balfour. — Boston, Houghton Mifflin, 1964. xi, 524 p. illus., geneal. table, ports. 22 cm. 'Notes on sources': p. [448]-487. 1. William II, German Emperor, 1859-1941. I. T.
DD229.B26 1964a   923.143   *LC* 64-22678

Viktoria Luise, Herzogin zu Braunschweig und Lüneburg, 1892-.   **3.2345**
[Selected works. English. 1977] The Kaiser's daughter: memoirs of H. R. H. Viktoria Luise, Duchess of Brunswick and Lüneburg, Princess of Prussia / translated and edited by Robert Vacha. — 1st U.S. ed. — Englewood Cliffs, N.J.: Prentice-Hall, c1977. xii, 276 p., [12] leaves of plates: ill.; 25 cm. Translated, compiled, and edited from the author's Ein Leben als Tochter des Kaisers, Im Glanz der Krone, and Im Strom der Zeit. Includes index. 1. Viktoria Luise, Herzogin zu Braunschweig und Lüneburg, 1892- 2. Germany — Princes and princesses — Biography. 3. Germany — History — 20th century — Sources. I. Vacha, Robert. II. T.
DD229.8.V5 A2513 1977b   943.08/092/4 B   *LC* 77-79339   *ISBN* 0135146534

DD231 Biography. Memoirs

Jarausch, Konrad Hugo.   **3.2346**
The enigmatic chancellor; Bethmann Hollweg and the hubris of Imperial Germany, by Konrad H. Jarausch. — New Haven, Yale University Press, 1973 [c1972] xiv, 560 p. port. 25 cm. 1. Bethmann Hollweg, Theobald von, 1856-1921. I. T.
DD231.B5 J37   943.08/4/0924 B   *LC* 72-89101   *ISBN* 0300012950

Bülow, Bernhard Heinrich Martin Karl, Fürst von, 1849-1929.   • **3.2347**
[Denkwürdigkeiten. English] Memoirs of Prince von Bülow. [Translated from the German by F. A. Voigt] New York, AMS Press [1972] 4 v. illus. 24 cm. Translation of Denkwürdigkeiten. Reprint of the 1931-32 ed. 1. Bülow, Bernhard Heinrich Martin Karl, Fürst von, 1849-1929. 2. Germany — Politics and government — 1871-1918 3. Germany — Foreign relations — 1871-1918 I. T.
DD231.B8 A17 1972   943.08/4/0924 B   *LC* 77-127900   *ISBN* 0404012302

Field, Geoffrey G.   **3.2348**
Evangelist of race: the Germanic vision of Houston Stewart Chamberlain / Geoffrey G. Field. — New York: Columbia University Press, 1981. x, 565 p.: ill.

; 24 cm. Includes index. 1. Chamberlain, Houston Stewart, 1855-1927. 2. National socialists — Biography. 3. Racism — History. I. T.
DD231.C4 F53   943.08/4/0924 B 19   *LC* 80-21000   *ISBN* 0231048602

Epstein, Klaus.   • **3.2349**
Matthias Erzberger and the dilemma of German democracy. — New York: H. Fertig, 1971 [c1959] xiii, 473 p.: port.; 24 cm. 1. Erzberger, Matthias, 1875-1921. I. T.
DD231.E7 E6 1971   943.08/4/0924 B   *LC* 75-80546

Wheeler-Bennett, John Wheeler, Sir, 1902-1975.   • **3.2350**
Hindenburg:the wooden Titan. London, Melbourne; Macmillan: New York; St. Martin's Press, 1967. xviii, 507 p.: front., 8 plates (incl. ports.); 22 1/2 cm. Original American ed.(New York, Morrow, 1936) has title:Wooden titan,Hindenburg in twenty years of German History. 1. Hindenburg, Paul von, 1847-1934. 2. Germany — History — 20th century I. T. II. Title: Wooden titan.
DD231.H5 W5 1967

Maximilian, prince of Baden, 1867-.   • **3.2351**
The memoirs of Prince Max of Baden / authorised translation by W. M. Calder and C. W. H. Sutton. — London: Constable & Co., 1928. 2 v.: front. (port.) fold. map.; 23 cm. 1. World War, 1914-1918 I. Calder, William Moir, 1881- II. Sutton, C W H III. T.
DD231.M3 A4   *LC* 29-83

Raeder, Erich, 1876-1960.   • **3.2352**
My life; translated from the German by Henry W. Drexel. Annapolis, United States Naval Institute, 1960. 430 p. illus. 24 cm. 1. Germany — History, Naval — 20th century I. T.
DD231.R17 A313   *LC* 60-9236

Kessler, Harry, Graf, 1868-1937.   • **3.2353**
[Walther Rathenau; sein Leben und sein Werk. English] Walther Rathenau; his life and work. [Translated by W. D. Robson-Scott and Lawrence Hyde, and rev. by the author, with notes and additions for English readers] New York, H. Fertig, 1969 [c1928] 400 p. facsim., ports. 23 cm. 1. Rathenau, Walther, 1867-1922. 2. Germany — History — 20th century I. T.
DD231.R3 K43 1969   943.085/0924 B   *LC* 68-9663

Scheidemann, Philipp, 1865-1939.   • **3.2354**
[Memoiren eines Sozialdemokraten. English] The making of new Germany: memoirs of a Social Democrat, by Philip Scheidemann. Translated by J. E. Michell. Freeport, N.Y., Books for Libraries Press [1970, c1929] 2 v. (x, 688 p.) 23 cm. Translation of Memoiren eines Sozialdemokraten. 1. Scheidemann, Philipp, 1865-1939. 2. Sozialdemokratische Partei Deutschlands. 3. Germany — Politics and government — 20th century I. T. II. Title: Memoirs of a Social Democrat.
DD231.S35 A33 1970   320.9/43/084   *LC* 73-140372   *ISBN* 083695615X

Stresemann, Gustav, 1878-1929.   • **3.2355**
Gustav Stresemann: his diaries, letters, and papers / edited and translated by Erie Sutton. — London: Macmillan, 1935-40. 3 v.: ill. (v.1-2) plates, ports; 23 cm. — The original,'Gustav Stresemann, Vermächtnis,' was published in 3 v., 1932-33, under the general editorship of Henry Bernhard. The English edition has been slightly condensed. cf. Editor's note. - 1. Germany — Politics and government — 20th century 2. Germany — Foreign relations — 20th century I. Bernhard, Henry, ed. II. T.
DD231.S83 A332   *LC* 35-30709 Revised

Gatzke, Hans Wilhelm, 1915-.   • **3.2356**
Stresemann and the rearmament of Germany. Baltimore, Johns Hopkins Press [1954] 132 p. port. 23 cm. 1. Stresemann, Gustav, 1878-1929. 2. German History, Military. I. T.
DD231.S83 G3   *LC* 54-11254

Tirpitz, Alfred von, 1849-1930.   • **3.2357**
My memoirs. New York, AMS Press [1970] 2 v. 23 cm. Reprint of the 1919 ed. 1. Tirpitz, Alfred von, 1849-1930. 2. Germany — History — Naval operations, German. 5. Admirals — Germany — Biography. 6. World War, 1914-1918 — Germany. I. T.
DD231.T5 A3513 1970   940.4/512/0924   *LC* 77-111779   *ISBN* 0404064647

DD232–251 20TH CENTURY (1918–1934)

Mosse, George L. (George Lachmann), 1918-.   • **3.2358**
The crisis of German ideology; intellectual origins of the Third Reich, by George L. Mosse. [1st ed.] New York, Grosset & Dunlap [1964] vi, 373 p. 21 cm. 1. Nationalism — Germany — History. 2. National socialism — History. 3. Ideology — History. 4. Germany — Intellectual life — 20th century I. T.
DD232.M6   320.943   *LC* 64-21950

Ryder, A. J.   3.2359
Twentieth–century Germany: from Bismarck to Brandt [by] A. J. Ryder. — New York: Columbia University Press, 1973. xviii, 656 p.: illus.; 25 cm. 1. Germany — History — 20th century 2. Germany — History — William II, 1888-1918 I. T.
DD232.R9   943.08   LC 72-3650   ISBN 0231036922

Horkenbach, Cuno, ed.   • 3.2360
Das Deutsche Reich von 1918 bis heute / hrsg. von Cuno Horkenbach mit sachlicher Unterstützung der Reichsbehörden, von Parlamentariern und Journalisten, Parteien, Körperschaften und Verbänden. — Berlin: Verlag für Presse, Wirtschaft und Politik [1931-1935] 4 v.: tables (part fold.); 26 cm. 1. Germany — History — Revolution, 1918 2. Germany — Politics and government — 1918- 3. Germany — Statistics 4. Germany — Biography 5. Germany — History — 1933-6 6. Germany — Politics and government — 1933- I. T.
DD233.H6   LC 38-22973

Brecht, Arnold, 1884-.   • 3.2361
Prelude to silence; the end of the German Republic. — New York: H. Fertig, 1968. xxi, 160 p.; 21 cm. Reprint of the 1944 ed., with a new preface by the author. 1. Germany — History — 1918-1933 2. Germany — History — 1933-1945 I. T.
DD237.B7 1968   943.085   LC 67-24580

Eyck, Erich, 1878-1964.   • 3.2362
[Geschichte der Weimarer Republik. English] A History of the Weimar Republic. Translated by Harlan P. Hanson and Robert G. L. Waite. Cambridge, Harvard University Press, 1962-1963. 2 v. 24 cm. 1. Germany — History — 1918-1933 I. T. II. Title: Weimar Republic.
DD237.E913   9453.085   LC 62-17219

Halperin, Samuel William.   • 3.2363
Germany tried democracy, a political history of the Reich from 1918 to 1933. Hamden, Conn., Archon Books [1963, c1946] 567 p.; 22 cm. 1. Germany — History — 1918-1933 I. T.
DD237.H3 1963   943.085   LC 63-11731

Hiden, John W.   3.2364
The Weimar Republic / J. W. Hiden. — London: Longman, 1974. viii, 114 p. — (Seminar studies in history.) 1. Germany — History — 1918-1933 I. T.
DD237.H48   DD237 H48.   ISBN 0582352169

Rosenberg, Arthur, 1889-1943.   3.2365
A history of the German Republic. Translated by Ian F.D. Morrow and L. Marie Sieveking. New York, Russell & Russell, 1965. xi, 350 p. 23 cm. 1. Germany — History — 1918-1933 I. T.
DD237.R68 1965   943.085   LC 65-18829

Carsten, F. L. (Francis Ludwig)   • 3.2366
The Reichswehr and politics: 1918–1933 [by] F. L. Carsten. — Oxford, Clarendon P., 1966. viii, 427 p. 22 1/2 cm. Originally published as Reichswehr und Politik. Cologne, Kipenheuer & Witsch. Bibliography: p. [406]-411. 1. Germany. Reichswehr. 2. Germany — Politics and government — 1918-1933 I. T.
DD238.C313   943.085   LC 66-74192

Herf, Jeffrey, 1947-.   3.2367
Reactionary modernism: technology, culture, and politics in Weimar and the Third Reich / Jeffrey Herf. — Cambridge [Cambridgeshire]; New York: Cambridge University Press, 1984. xii, 251 p.; 24 cm. Revision of the author's thesis (Brandeis University) 1. Enlightenment — Influence. 2. Germany — History — 1918-1933 3. Germany — Intellectual life — 20th century I. T.
DD238.H45 1984   943.086 19   LC 84-3227   ISBN 0521265665

Lebovics, Herman.   • 3.2368
Social conservatism and the middle classes in Germany, 1914–1933. — Princeton, N.J.: Princeton University Press, 1969. xi, 248 p.; 23 cm. 1. Conservatism — Germany. 2. Middle classes — Germany. 3. Germany — Politics and government — 1888-1918 4. Germany — Politics and government — 1918-1933 I. T.
DD238.L43   320.5/2   LC 68-56316

Waite, Robert George Leeson, 1919-.   • 3.2369
Vanguard of nazism: the Free Corps movement in post-war Germany, 1918–1923 / by Robert G.L. Waite. — Cambridge, Mass.: Harvard University Press, 1952. xii, 344 p.; 22 cm. — (Harvard historical studies. 60.) 'Extensive revision of the author's thesis submitted to Harvard University.' 1. Germany. Heer. Freikorps. 2. Germany — History — 1918-1933 I. T. II. Series.
DD238 W34 /   943.085

Laqueur, Walter, 1921-.   3.2370
Weimar: a cultural history, 1918–1933 / Walter Laqueur. — 1st American ed. — New York: Putnam, 1974. 308 p., [16] leaves of plates: ill.; 22 cm. Includes

index. 1. Germany — Politics and government — 1918-1933 2. Germany — Intellectual life — 20th century I. T.
DD239.L3 1974b   943.085   LC 74-16605   ISBN 0399114491

DD240–241 Political and Diplomatic History

Bracher, Karl Dietrich, 1922-.   • 3.2371
Die Auflösung der Weimarer Republik; eine Studie zum Problem des Machtverfalls in der Demokratie. — Villingen/Schwarzwald: Ring-Verlag, 1960. xxiii, 809 p.: tables.; 23 cm. — (Schriften des Institutes fur Politische Wissenschaft, Bd. 4) Bibliography: p. [650]-693. 1. Germany — Pol. & govt. — 1918-1933. I. T.
DD240.B67   LC 62-46211

Gordon, Harold J.   • 3.2372
The Reichswehr and the German Republic, 1919–1926, by Harold J. Gordon, Jr. — Port Washington, N.Y.: Kennikat Press, [1972, c1957] xvi, 478 p.; 23 cm. 1. Germany. Heer. 2. Germany — Military policy. 3. Germany — Politics and government — 1918-1933 I. T.
DD240.G66 1972   943.085   LC 74-159087   ISBN 0804616299

Heiden, Konrad.   • 3.2373
A history of national socialism, by Konrad Heiden, translated from the German. — 1st American ed. New York, A. A. Knopf, 1935. xvi, 430, ix, [1] p. 25 cm. 'This translation has been made from Herr Heiden's two books, geschichte des nationalozialismus (1932) and Geburt des dritten reiches (1934).'—Translator's note. 'First American edition.' Bibliography: p. [429]-430. 1. Hitler, Adolf, 1889-1945. 2. Nationalsozialistische deutsche arbeiter-partel. 3. Germany — Pol. & govt. — 1918- I. T. II. Title: National socialsim, A history of.
DD240.H373 1965   943.065   LC 35-2984

Kaufmann, Walter H.   • 3.2374
Monarchism in the Weimar Republic / Walter H. Kaufmann. — New York: Bookman Associates, c1953. 305 p.; 23 cm. Includes index. 1. Germany — Politics and government — 1918-1933 I. T.
DD240.K34   LC 53-8591

Stampfer, Friedrich, 1874-.   • 3.2375
Die vierzehn Jahre der ersten deutschen Republik. Karlsbad, 'Graphia,' 1936. 636 p. 23 cm. 1. Germany (East) — Politics and government — 1918-1933. 2. Germany (East) — History — 1918-1933. I. T.
DD240.S75   LC af 47-6801

Taylor, Simon.   3.2376
Germany, 1918–1933: revolution, counter–revolution and the rise of Hitler / Simon Taylor. — London: Duckworth, 1983. 131 p., [4] p. of plates: ill.; 25 cm. Includes index. 1. Germany — Politics and government — 1918-1933 I. T.
DD240.T36 1983   943.085 19   LC 82-237174   ISBN 0715616897

Turner, Henry Ashby.   • 3.2377
Stresemann and the politics of the Weimar Republic. — Princeton, N. J., Princeton University Press, 1963. v, 287 p. 23 cm. 1. Stresemann, Gustav, 1879-1929. 2. Germany — Pol. & govt. — 1918-1933. I. T.
DD240.T8   943.085   LC 63-10002

Von Klemperer, Klemens, 1916-.   • 3.2378
Germany's new conservatism, its history and dilemma in the twentieth century. Foreword by Sigmond Neumann. Princeton, Princeton University Press, 1957. xxvi, 250 p. 23 cm. 1. Conservatism — Case studies. 2. Germany — Politics and government — 1918-1933 3. Germany — Politics and government — 20th century I. T.
DD240.V6   943.085   LC 57-5462

Wheeler-Bennett, John Wheeler, Sir, 1902-1975.   • 3.2379
The nemesis of power; the German Army in politics, 1918–1945 [by] John W. Wheeler–Bennett. — 2d ed. — London: Macmillan; New York: St. Martin's Press, 1964. xxii, 831 p.: illus., ports.; 23 cm. 1. Germany. Heer. 2. World War, 1939-1945 — Germany. 3. Germany — Politics and government — 1918-1933 4. Germany — Politics and government — 1933-1945 I. T.
DD240.W5 1964   943.085   LC 64-55914

DD247 Biography

DD247 A–H

Arendt, Hannah.   • 3.2380
Eichmann in Jerusalem; a report on the banality of evil. New York, Viking Press [1963] 275 p. 22 cm. Includes bibliography. 1. Eichmann, Adolf, 1906-1962. 2. Jews — Europe — Persecutions. I. T.
DD247.E5A7   923.543   LC 63-12361

Goebbels, Joseph, 1897-1945.   • 3.2381
The early Goebbels diaries, 1925–1926. With a pref. by Alan Bullock. Edited by Helmut Heiber. Translated from the German by Oliver Watson. New York, Praeger [1963,c1962] 156 p. 23 cm. (Books that matter) Translation of Das Tagebuch von Joseph Goebbels, 1925/26; mit weiteren Dokumenten hrsg. von Helmut Heiber. I. Heiber, Helmut, 1924- II. T.
DD247.G6 A223 1963   923.234   *LC* 63-7570

Goebbels, Joseph, 1897-1945.   • 3.2382
[Goebbels Tagebücher. English] The Goebbels diaries, 1942–1943. Edited, translated, and with an introd. by Louis P. Lochner. Westport, Conn., Greenwood Press [1970, c1948] ix, 566 p. group port. 23 cm. Translation of Goebbels Tagebücher. 1. Goebbels, Joseph, 1897-1945. I. Lochner, Louis Paul, 1887-1975. ed. and tr. II. T.
DD247.G6 A25 1970   943.086/0924   *LC* 74-108391   *ISBN* 0837138159

Goebbels, Joseph, 1897-1945.   3.2383
[Tagebücher 1924-1945. Tagebücher 1945. English] Final entries, 1945: the diaries of Joseph Goebbels; edited, introduced, and annotated by Hugh Trevor-Roper; translated from the German by Richard Barry. — New York: Putnam, c1978. xli, 368 p., [17] leaves of plates: ill.; 24 cm. Translation of a part of Tagebücher 1924-1945 entitled: Tagebücher 1945. Includes index. 1. Goebbels, Joseph, 1897-1945. 2. Statesmen — Germany — Biography. 3. World War, 1939-1945 — Germany. 4. Propaganda, German 5. Germany — Politics and government — 1933-1945 I. Trevor-Roper, H. R. (Hugh Redwald), 1914- II. T.
DD247.G6 A2913 1978   940.54/82/43   *LC* 78-6707   *ISBN* 0399121161

Goebbels, Joseph, 1897-1945.   3.2384
[Tagebücher 1924-1945. Tagebücher 1939-1941. English] The Goebbels diaries, 1939–1941 / translated and edited by Fred Taylor. — 1st American ed. — New York: Putnam, 1983, c1982. xiii, 490 p., [16] p. of plates: ill.; 24 cm. Translation of a part of Tagebücher 1924-1945 entitled: Tagebücher 1939-1941. Includes index. 1. Goebbels, Joseph, 1897-1945. 2. Statesmen — Germany — Biography. 3. World War, 1939-1945 — Germany. 4. Propaganda, German. 5. Germany — Politics and government — 1933-1945 I. Taylor, Fred. II. T.
DD247.G6 A2913 1983   943.086 19   *LC* 82-18574   *ISBN* 0399127631

Manvell, Roger, 1909-.   • 3.2385
Dr. Goebbels, his life and death. New York: Simon and Schuster, 1960. 306 p.: ill.; 23 cm. 1. Goebbels, Joseph, 1897-1945. I. Fraenkel, Heinrich, 1897- II. T.
DD247.G6 M33   *LC* 59-13878

Ritter, Gerhard, 1888-1967.   • 3.2386
The German resistance; Carl Goerdeler's struggle against tyranny. Translated by R. T. Clark. — New York, Praeger [1958] 330 p. 23 cm. 1. Goerdeler, Carl Friedrich, 1884-1944. 2. Germany — Pol. & govt. — 1933-1945. 3. Anti-Nazi movement I. T.
DD247.G63R513   943.086   *LC* 58-8190

Mosley, Leonard, 1913-.   3.2387
The Reich Marshal; a biography of Hermann Goering. — [1st ed.]. — Garden City, N.Y.: Doubleday, 1974. xi, 394 p.: illus.; 25 cm. 1. Göring, Hermann, 1893-1946. I. T.
DD247.G67 M67   943.086/092/4 B   *LC* 73-20825   *ISBN* 0385049617

Hassell, Ulrich von, 1881-1944.   • 3.2388
The Von Hassell diaries, 1938–1944; the story of the forces against Hitler inside Germany, as recorded by Ambassador Ulrich von Hassell, a leader of the movement. With an introd. by Allen Welsh Dulles. — [1st ed.]. — Garden City, N. Y., Doubleday, 1947. xiv, 400 p. 24 cm. Translation of Vom andern Deutschland. 1. Germany — Pol. & govt. — 1933-1945. 2. World War, 1939-1945 — Germany. I. T.
DD247.H33A315   943.086   *LC* 47-11273 *

Manvell, Roger, 1909-.   • 3.2389
[Heinrich Himmler] Himmler [by] Roger Manvell and Heinrich Fraenkel. [1st American ed.] New York, Putnam [1965] xvii, 285 p. illus., ports. 23 cm. First published in London under title: Heinrich Himmler. 1. Himmler, Heinrich, 1900-1945. I. Fraenkel, Heinrich, 1897- joint author. II. T.
DD247.H46 M3 1965a   923.243   *LC* 64-18020

DD247 Hitler

Hitler, Adolf, 1889-1945.   • 3.2390
[Mein kampf] English] Mein kampf, by Adolf Hitler, translated by Ralph Manheim. Boston, Houghton Mifflin company, 1943. xxi, 694 p. 21 cm. 1. Nationalsozialistische Deutsche Arbeiter-Partei. 2. Germany — Politics and government — 20th century I. Manheim, Ralph, 1907- tr. II. T.
DD247.H5 A322   923.143   *LC* 43-14343

Hitler, Adolf, 1889-1945.   • 3.2391
The testament of Adolf Hitler; the Hitler–Bormann documents, February–April 1945, edited by François Genoud. Translated from the German by R. H. Stevens. With an introd. by H. R. Trevor-Roper. — [2d ed.]. — London, Cassell [1961, c1960] 115 p. port. 19 cm. 'First published in France under the title: Le testament politique de Hitler.' 1. Germany — Pol. & govt. — 1933-1945. 2. National socialism 3. World War, 1939-1945 — Germany. I. Bormann, Martin, 1900-1945. II. Genoud, François, ed. III. T.
DD247.H5A664553 1961   940.53   *LC* 65-7281

Hitler, Adolf, 1889-1945.   • 3.2392
Secret conversations, 1941–1944 [translated by Norman Cameron and R.H. Stevens] With an introductory essay on The mind of Adolf Hitler, by H.R. Trevor-Roper. New York, Farrar, Straus and Young [1953] 597 p.; 22 cm. London ed. (Weidenfeld and Nicolson) has title: Table talk, 1941-1944. I. T. II. Title: Table talk, 1941-1944.
DD247.H5 A685 1953a   943.085   *LC* 53-9116

Hitler, Adolf, 1889-1945.   • 3.2393
The speeches of Adolf Hitler, April 1922–August 1939; An English translation of representative passages arranged under subjects and edited by Norman H. Baynes. — New York: H. Fertig, 1969. 2 v. (xii, 1980 p.); 23 cm. Reprint of the 1942 ed. 1. National socialism 2. Germany — Politics and government — 1933-1945 3. Germany — Foreign relations — 1933-1945 I. Baynes, Norman Hepburn, 1877-1961. ed. II. T.
DD247.H5 A73 1969   943.085/0924   *LC* 68-57828

Binion, Rudolph, 1927-.   3.2394
Hitler among the Germans / Rudolph Binion. — DeKalb, Ill.: Northern Illinois University Press, [1984] xviii, 207 p.; 23 cm. Reprint. Originally published: New York: Elsevier, 1976. Includes index. 1. Hitler, Adolf, 1889-1945. 2. Heads of state — Germany — Biography. I. T.
DD247.H5 B54 1984   943.086/092/4 B 19   *LC* 84-1198   *ISBN* 0875805310

Bullock, Alan, 1914-.   • 3.2395
Hitler, a study in tyranny. Completely rev. ed. New York, Harper & Row [c1962] 848 p. illus., ports., maps, geneal. table. 22 cm. 1. Hitler, Adolf, 1889-1945. I. T. II. Title: A study in tyranny.
DD247.H5 B85 1962a   923.143   *LC* 63-21045

Carr, William, 1921-.   3.2396
Hitler: a study in personality and politics / William Carr. — London: Edward Arnold, 1978. x, 200 p.; 24 cm. Includes index. 1. Hitler, Adolf, 1889-1945. 2. Heads of state — Germany — Biography. 3. Germany — History — 1933-1945 I. T.
DD247.H5 C325 1978   943.086/092/4 B   *LC* 80-465328   *ISBN* 0713161418

Deutsch, Harold C. (Harold Charles)   3.2397
Hitler and his generals; the hidden crisis, January–June 1938, by Harold C. Deutsch. — Minneapolis: University of Minnesota Press, [1974] xxv, 452 p.: illus.; 24 cm. 1. Hitler, Adolf, 1889-1945. 2. Generals — Germany. I. T.
DD247.H5 D477 1974   943.086/092/4 B   *LC* 73-86627   *ISBN* 0816606498

Fest, Joachim C., 1926-.   3.2398
[Hitler. English] Hitler [by] Joachim C. Fest. Translated from the German by Richard and Clara Winston. [1st ed.] New York, Harcourt Brace Jovanovich [1974] xiii, 844 p. illus. 24 cm. 'A Helen and Kurt Wolff book.' 1. Hitler, Adolf, 1889-1945. I. T.
DD247.H5 F4713   943.086/092/4 B   *LC* 73-18154   *ISBN* 0151416508

Gordon, Harold J.   3.2399
Hitler and the Beer Hall Putsch [by] Harold J. Gordon, Jr. — Princeton, N.J.: Princeton University Press, 1972. xii, 666 p.: illus.; 24 cm. 1. Hitler, Adolf, 1889-1945. 2. Germany — History — Beer Hall Putsch, 1923 I. T.
DD247.H5 G637   943.085   *LC* 70-154997   *ISBN* 0691051895

Haffner, Sebastian.   3.2400
The meaning of Hitler / Sebastian Haffner; translated by Ewald Osers. — 1st American ed. — New York: Macmillian Pub., c1979. 165 p.; 22 cm. Translation of Anmerkungen zu Hitler. 1. Hitler, Adolf, 1889-1945. 2. Heads of state — Germany — Biography. I. T.
DD247.H5 H26513   943.086/092/4   *LC* 79-89431   *ISBN* 0025472909

Heiden, Konrad, 1901-1966.   • 3.2401
[Fuehrer. English] Der Fuehrer; Hitler's rise to power. Translated by Ralph Manheim. Boston, Beacon Press [1969, c1944] x, 788 p. 21 cm. (Europe in the twentieth century) (A Beacon paperback no. 336.) 1. Hitler, Adolf, 1889-1945. 2. Nationalsozialistische Deutsche Arbeiter-Partei. I. T.
DD247.H5 H344 1969   943.085/0924   *LC* 79-89960

Jenks, William Alexander, 1918-.   • **3.2402**
Vienna and the young Hitler. New York: Columbia University Press, 1960.
252 p.; 24 cm. Includes bibliographies. 1. Hitler, Adolf, 1889-1945. 2. Vienna
(Austria) — Social conditions. 3. Vienna (Austria) — Intellectual life. I. T.
DD247.H5J38   923.143   *LC* 60-5285

Jetzinger, Franz.   • **3.2403**
Hitler's youth. Translated from the German by Lawrence Wilson. Foreword by
Alan Bullock. London, Hutchinson [1958] 200 p.; ill.; 22 cm. 1. Hitler, Adolf,
1889-1945. I. T.
DD247.H5 J453   943.085   *LC* 59-960

Kubizek, August.   • **3.2404**
The young Hitler I knew. Translated from the German by E.V. Anderson; with
a introd. by H.R. Trevor–Roper. Boston, Houghton Mifflin, 1955 (c1954).
298 p.: ill.; 22 cm. 1. Hitler, Adolf, 1889-1945. I. T.
DD247.H5 K813 1955   943.085   *LC* 55-5301

Maser, Werner, 1922-.   **3.2405**
[Hitlers Briefe und Notizen. English] Hitler's letters and notes / Werner Maser;
translated from the German by Arnold Pomerans. — 1st U.S. ed. — New York:
Harper & Row, c1974. 390 p.: ill.; 24 cm. Translation of Hitlers Briefe und
Notizen. Includes index. 1. Hitler, Adolf, 1889-1945. 2. Hitler, Adolf,
1889-1945 — Manuscripts — Facsimiles. I. Hitler, Adolf, 1889-1945. II. T.
DD247.H5 M284513 1974b   943.086/092/4 B   *LC* 73-10677
     ISBN 0060128321

Peterson, Edward Norman.   • **3.2406**
The limits of Hitler's power [by] Edward N. Peterson. — Princeton, N.J.:
Princeton University Press, 1969. xxiii, 472 p.; 23 cm. 1. Hitler, Adolf,
1889-1945. 2. Germany — Politics and government — 1933-1945 I. T.
DD247.H5 P39   320.9/43   *LC* 69-18066   *ISBN* 0691051755

Trevor-Roper, H. R. (Hugh Redwald), 1914-.   • **3.2407**
The last days of Hitler [by] H. R. Trevor-Roper. 4th ed. London, Macmillan,
1971. lxiii, 286 p., 5 plates. facsim., map, plan, port. 21 cm. 1. Hitler, Adolf,
1889-1945. I. T.
DD247.H5 T7 1971   943.086/092/4 B   *LC* 72-176406   *ISBN*
0333075277

Waite, Robert George Leeson, 1919-.   **3.2408**
The psychopathic god: Adolf Hitler / Robert G. L. Waite. — New York: Basic
Books, c1977. xx, 482 p., [4] leaves of plates: ill.; 24 cm. 1. Hitler, Adolf,
1889-1945. 2. Heads of state — Germany — Biography. I. T.
DD247.H5 W23   943.086/092/4 B   *LC* 76-43484   *ISBN*
0465067433

DD247 K–Z

Krebs, Albert, 1899-.   **3.2409**
[Tendenzen und Gestalten der NSDAP. English] The infancy of Nazism: the
memoirs of ex–Gauleiter Albert Krebs, 1923–1933 / edited and translated by
William Sheridan Allen. — New York: New Viewpoints, 1976. xiii, 328 p.; 21
cm. Translation of Tendenzen und Gestalten der NSDAP. Includes index.
1. Krebs, Albert, 1899- 2. Nationalsozialistische Deutsche Arbeiter-Partei.
3. Germany — Politics and government — 1918-1933 I. Allen, William
Sheridan. II. T.
DD247.K73 A3713   943.085/092/4   *LC* 75-29153   *ISBN*
0531053768. *ISBN* 0531055833 pbk

Balfour, Michael Leonard Graham, 1908-.   **3.2410**
Helmuth von Moltke; a leader against Hitler, by Michael Balfour and Julian
Frisby. [London] St. Martin's Press [1972] x, 388 p. illus. 22 cm. 1. Moltke,
Helmuth James, Graf von, 1906-1945. 2. Anti-Nazi movement I. Frisby,
Julian, joint author. II. T.
DD247.M6 B34   943.086/092/4 B   *LC* 72-86789   *ISBN*
0333140303

Papen, Franz von, 1879-1969.   • **3.2411**
Memoirs / Franz von Papen; translated by Brian Connell. — London: A.
Deutsch, 1952. 630 p., [8] leaves of plates: ill., ports.; 22 cm. 1. Papen, Franz
von, 1879-1969. 2. Statesmen — Germany — Biography I. T.
DD247.P3 A33   *LC* 52-4947

Salomon, Ernst von, 1902-1972.   **3.2412**
The outlaws / by Ernst von Salomon; translated from the German by Ian F.D.
Morrow. — Millwood, N.Y.: Kraus Reprint, 1983. xiii, 432 p. 1. Salomon,
Ernst von, 1902-1972. 2. World War, 1914-1918 — Germany. 3. Germany —
History — Revolution, 1918 I. T.
DD247.S3 A3   *LC* 31-24181

Schacht, Hjalmar Horace Greeley, 1877-1970.   • **3.2413**
Confessions of 'the Old Wizard': autobiography. Translated by Diane Pyke.
Boston, Houghton Mifflin, 1956. xx, 484 p. illus. 22 cm. Translation of 76 [i. e.

Sechsundsiebzig] Jahre meines Lebens. 1. Finance — Germany. 2. Germany
(East) — Economic conditions — 1918-1945. I. T.
DD247.S335 A352   *LC* 55-11550

Speer, Albert, 1905-.   • **3.2414**
[Erinnerungen. English] Inside the Third Reich: memoirs, Translated from the
German by Richard and Clara Winston. Introd. by Eugene Davidson. [New
York] Macmillan [1970] xviii, 596 p. illus., facsims., plans, ports. 24 cm.
Translation of Erinnerungen. 1. Speer, Albert, 1905- 2. Hitler, Adolf,
1889-1945. 3. Architects — Germany — Biography. 4. National socialists —
Biography. 5. Germany — Politics and government — 1933-1945 I. T.
DD247.S63 A313 1970   943.086/0924 B   *LC* 70-119132

Sykes, Christopher, 1907-.   • **3.2415**
[Troubled loyalty] Tormented loyalty; the story of a German aristocrat who
defied Hitler. [1st U.S. ed.] New York, Harper & Row [1969] 477 p. illus., ports.
22 cm. First published in London in 1968 under title: Troubled loyalty. 1. Trott
zu Solz, Adam von, 1909-1944. 2. Hitler, Adolf, 1889-1945 — Assassination
attempt, 1944 (July 20) 3. Anti-Nazi movement I. T.
DD247.T7 S95 1969   943.086/0924 B   *LC* 69-15266

DD248–251 Special Topics, 1918–1934

Haffner, Sebastian.   **3.2416**
Failure of a revolution: Germany 1918–19; translated [from the German] by
Georg Rapp. New York, Library Press, 1972 [i.e. 1973] 205 p. illus., facsims.,
ports. 23 cm. index. Translation of Die verratene Revolution. 1. Germany —
History — Revolution, 1918 I. T.
DD248.H2713 1972   DD248.H2713 1973.   943.085   *LC* 73-155723

Lutz, Ralph Haswell, 1886-1968.   • **3.2417**
The German Revolution, 1918–1919. New York, AMS Press [1968] 186 p. 22
cm. (Stanford University publications. University series: history, economics,
and political science, v. 1, no. 1) Reprint of the 1922 ed. 1. Germany — History
— Revolution, 1918 I. T.
DD248.L8 1968   943.085   *LC* 68-54283

Angress, Werner T.   • **3.2418**
Stillborn revolution; the Communist bid for power in Germany, 1921–1923, by
Werner T. Angress. — Port Washington, N.Y.: Kennikat Press, [1972, c1963] 2
v. (xv, 513 p.): map.; 23 cm. 1. Communism — Germany 2. Germany —
Politics and government — 1918-1933 I. T.
DD249.A78 1972   943.085   *LC* 79-159080   *ISBN* 0804616221

Cornebise, Alfred E.   **3.2419**
The Weimar in crisis: Cunós Germany and the Ruhr occupation / Alfred E.
Cornebise. — Washington, D.C.: University Press of America, c1977. v, 419 p.:
ports.; 22 cm. 1. Germany — Politics and government — 1918-1933 I. T.
DD249.C6   *ISBN* 0819102377

Matthias, Erich, ed.   • **3.2420**
Das Ende der Parteien, 1933 / hrsg. von Eirch Matthias und Rudolf Morsey. —
Düsseldorf: Droste Verlag, 1960. xv, 816 p.: ill., ports., maps (1 col. on lining
paper); 26 cm. (Veröffentlichung der Kommission für Geschichte des
Parlamentarismus und der Politischen Parteien) 1. Political parties —
Germany 2. Germany — Politics and government — 1918-1933 I. Morsey,
Rudolf. jt. ed. II. T.
DD251 M36   *LC* A 61-219

DD253–256 1933-1945 NATIONAL SOCIALISM. THIRD REICH

Neumann, Franz L. (Franz Leopold), 1900-1954.   • **3.2421**
Behemoth; the structure and practice of national socialism 1933–1944. — [2d
ed. with new appendix]. — New York, Octagon Books, 1963 [c1944] 649 p. 24
cm. 1. National socialism I. T.
DD253.N43 1963   943.086   *LC* 63-14347

Rauschning, Hermann, 1887-.   • **3.2422**
The revolution of nihilism; warning to the West, by Hermann Rauschning. —
New York, Alliance book corporation, Longmans, Green & co. [c1939] xvii,
300 p. 24 cm. 'Translated from German by E. W. Dickes.'
1. Nationalsozialistische Deutsche Arbeiter-Partei. 2. Germany — Pol. &
govt. — 1933-1945. I. Dickes, E. W. (Ernest Walter), b. 1876. tr. II. T.
DD253.R38   943.085   *LC* 39-21141

Thyssen, Fritz, 1873-1951.   • **3.2423**
I paid Hitler. [Translated from the original by Cesar Saerchinger. — Port
Washington, N.Y.: Kennikat Press, [1972, c1941] xxix, 281 p.; 22 cm. Dictated
to Emery Reves and, in part, revised, corrected and approved by the author.
1. Hitler, Adolf, 1889-1945. 2. Nationalsozialistische Deutsche Arbeiter-
Partei. 3. Germany — Politics and government — 1918-1933 4. Germany —

Politics and government — 1933-1945 I. Saerchinger, César, 1889- tr. II. Reves, Emery, 1904- III. T.
DD253.T55 1972   943.086/0924 B   *LC* 71-153243   *ISBN* 0804615535

Kele, Max H.   3.2424
Nazis and workers: National Socialist appeals to German labor, 1919–1933, by Max H. Kele. — Chapel Hill: University of North Carolina Press, [1972] ix, 243 p.; 22 cm. 1. Nationalsozialistische Deutsche Arbeiter-Partei — History. 2. Labor and laboring classes — Germany. I. T.
DD253.25.K44   301.44/42/0943   *LC* 77-174786   *ISBN* 080781184X

Orlow, Dietrich.   • 3.2425
The history of the Nazi Party. — [Pittsburgh]: University of Pittsburgh Press, [1969-73] 2 v.; 24 cm. 1. Nationalsozialistische Deutsche Arbeiter-Partei — History. I. T.
DD253.25.O7   329.9/43   *LC* 69-20026   *ISBN* 0822931834

Burden, Hamilton Twombly, 1937-.   • 3.2426
The Nuremberg Party rallies: 1923–39 [by] Hamilton T. Burden. Foreword by Adolf A. Berle. — New York: Praeger, [1967] xv, 206 p.: illus., maps, ports.; 25 cm. 1. Nationalsozialistische Deutsche Arbeiter-Partei. Reichsparteitag. I. T.
DD253.27.B8   943.086   *LC* 67-20473

Höhne, Heinz, 1926-.   • 3.2427
[Orden unter dem Totenkopf. English] The Order of the Death's Head; the story of Hitler's S.S. Translated from the German by Richard Barry. [1st American ed.] New York, Coward-McCann [1970, c1969] xii, 690 p. illus., maps, ports. 25 cm. Translation of Der Orden unter dem Totenkopf. 1. Nationalsozialistische Deutsche Arbeiter-Partei. Schutzstaffel. I. T.
DD253.6.H613 1970   943.086   *LC* 69-19032

Koehl, Robert Lewis, 1922-.   3.2428
The Black Corps: the structure and power struggles of the Nazi SS / Robert Lewis Koehl. — Madison, Wis.: University of Wisconsin Press, 1983. xxxi, 437 p.: ill.; 24 cm. Includes index. 1. Nationalsozialistische Deutsche Arbeiter-Partei. Schutzstaffel. I. T.
DD253.6.K63 1983   943.08 19   *LC* 81-69824   *ISBN* 0299091902

Deutsch, Harold C. (Harold Charles)   • 3.2429
The conspiracy against Hitler in the twilight war, by Harold C. Deutsch. — Minneapolis: University of Minnesota Press, [1968] x, 394 p.; 24 cm. 1. Hitler, Adolf, 1889-1945. 2. Pius XII, Pope, 1876-1958. 3. Anti-Nazi movement I. T.
DD256.3.D43 1968   364.13/1   *LC* 68-22365

Dulles, Allen Welsh, 1893-1969.   • 3.2430
Germany's underground. [1st ed.] New York: Macmillan, 1947. xiii, 207 p.; 21 cm. 1. Hitler, Adolf, 1889-1945. 2. Anti-Nazi movement I. T.
DD256.3 D8

Hoffmann, Peter, 1930-.   3.2431
[Widerstand, Staatsstreich, Attentat. English] The history of the German resistance, 1933–1945 / Peter Hoffmann; translated from the German by Richard Barry. — 1st MIT Press ed. — Cambridge, Mass.: MIT Press, 1977. xii, 847 p.: ill.; 24 cm. Translation of Widerstand, Staatsstreich, Attentat. Includes index. 1. Hitler, Adolf, 1889-1945 — Assassination attempt, July 20, 1944. 2. Anti-Nazi movement I. T.
DD256.3.H613   DD256.3 H613 1977.   943.086   *LC* 76-151691   *ISBN* 0262080885

Rothfels, Hans, 1891-1976.   • 3.2432
The German opposition to Hitler: an appraisal. — Hinsdale, Ill., H. Regnery Co., 1948. 172 p. 20 cm. 1. Germany — Politics and government — 1933-1945 I. T.
DD256.3.R6   *LC* 48-3753

Allen, William Sheridan.   • 3.2433
The Nazi seizure of power; the experience of a single German town, 1930–1935. — Chicago: Quadrangle Books, 1965. xi, 345 p.: illus., map.; 22 cm. 1. Local government — Germany — Case studies. 2. National socialism 3. Germany — Politics and government — 1918-1933 I. T.
DD256.5.A58   943.086   *LC* 65-10378

Bracher, Karl Dietrich, 1922-.   • 3.2434
[Deutsche Diktatur; Entstehung, Struktur, Folgen des Nationalsozialismus. English] The German dictatorship; the origins, structure, and effects of national socialism. Translated from the German by Jean Steinberg. With an introd. by Peter Gay. New York, Praeger Publishers [1970] xv, 553 p. 25 cm. Translation of Die deutsche Diktatur; Entstehung, Struktur, Folgen des Nationalsozialismus. 1. National socialism — History. 2. Anti-Nazi movement — Germany 3. Germany — Politics and government — 1933-1945 I. T.
DD256.5.B66313 1970   329.943   *LC* 70-95662

Bracher, Karl Dietrich, 1922-.   • 3.2435
Die nationalsozialistische Machtergreifung; Studien zur Errichtung des totalitären Herrschaftssystems in Deutschland 1933/34 [von] Karl Dietrich Bracher, Wolfgang Sauer [und] Gerhard Schulz. — Köln, Westdeutscher Verlag, 1960. xx, 1034 p. 25 cm. — (Schriften des Instituts für Politische Wissenschaft, Bd. 14) Bibliogr.: p. [973]-1010. 1. Germany — Pol. & govt. — 1933-1945. I. T.
DD256.5.B665   *LC* 61-35850

Bramsted, Ernest Kohn.   • 3.2436
Goebbels and National Socialist propaganda, 1925–1945, by Ernest K. Bramsted. — [East Lansing]: Michigan State University Press, 1965. xxxvii, 488 p.; 24 cm. 1. Goebbels, Joseph, 1897-1945. 2. Germany. Reichsministerium für Volksaufklärung und Propaganda. 3. Propaganda, German 4. World War, 1939-1945 — Propaganda I. T.
DD256.5.B674   301.15230943   *LC* 64-19392

François-Poncet, André, 1887-.   • 3.2437
[Souvenirs d'une ambassade à Berlin, septembre 1931-octobre 1938. English] The fateful years; memoirs of a French ambassador in Berlin, 1931–1938. Translated from the French by Jacques LeClercq. New York, H. Fertig, 1972 [c1946] xiii, 295 p. 21 cm. Translation of Souvenirs d'une ambassade à Berlin, septembre 1931-octobre 1938. 1. Hitler, Adolf, 1889-1945. 2. National socialism 3. Germany — Politics and government — 1933-1945 I. T.
DD256.5.F71513 1972   943.086   *LC* 76-80549

Gisevius, Hans Bernd, 1904-.   • 3.2438
To the bitter end. Tr. from the German by Richard and Clara Winston. Boston, Houghton Mifflin Co., 1947. xv, 632 p. 22 cm. 1. Nationalsozialistische deutsche Arbeiter-Partel. 2. Germany — Politics and government — 1933-1945 I. Winston, Richard. tr. II. T.
DD256.5.G52   943.086   *LC* 47-5861 *

Grunberger, Richard.   3.2439
The 12–year Reich; a social history of Nazi Germany, 1933–1945. [1st ed.] New York, Holt, Rinehart and Winston [1971] vi, 535 p. illus., ports. 24 cm. London ed. (Weidenfeld and Nicolson) has title: A social history of the Third Reich. 1. Germany — Politics and government — 1933-1945 2. Germany — Social conditions — 1933-1945 3. Germany — Intellectual life I. T.
DD256.5.G78 1971b   914.3/03/86   *LC* 69-16189   *ISBN* 0030764351

Haigh, R. H.   3.2440
The years of triumph?: German diplomatic and military policy, 1933–41 / R.H. Haigh, D.S. Morris, A.R. Peters. — Aldershot: Gower, c1986. 325 p.; 23 cm. 1. Germany — History — 1933-1945 2. Germany — Foreign relations — 1933-1945 3. Germany — History, Military — 20th century I. Morris, D. S. II. Peters, A. R. III. T.
DD256.5.H27 1986   943.086 19   *LC* 85-1343   *ISBN* 0566008459

Kershaw, Ian.   3.2441
The Nazi dictatorship: problems and perspectives of interpretation / Ian Kershaw. — London; Baltimore, Md., USA: E. Arnold, 1985. viii, 164 p.; 24 cm. Includes index. 1. National socialism — History. 2. Germany — Politics and government — 1933-1945 I. T.
DD256.5.K47 1985   321.9/4/0943 19   *LC* 85-175474   *ISBN* 0713164085

Kogon, Eugen, 1903-.   • 3.2442
The theory and practice of hell: the German concentration camps and the system behind them / by Eugen Kogon; translated by Heinz Norden. — New York: Farrar, Straus, [1950?] 307 p.: ill.; 22 cm. Translation of Der SS-Staat, das System der deutschen Konzentrationslager. 1. Nationalsozialistische Deutsche Arbeiter-Partei. Schutzstaffel. 2. Concentration camps — Germany I. T.
DD256.5.K614   *LC* 50-10716

Mau, Hermann.   3.2443
German history, 1933–45: an assessment by German historians / by Hermann Mau and Helmut Krausnick; translated from the German by Andrew and Eva Wilson. — 1st American ed. — New York: F. Ungar Pub. Co., 1963. 157 p.; 21 cm. 1. Germany — History — 1933-1945 I. Krausnick, Helmut. II. T.
DD256.5.M383 1963   943.086   *LC* 63-21989

Meinecke, Friedrich, 1862-1954.   3.2444
The German catastrophe: reflections and recollections / by Friedrich Meinecke; translated by Sidney B. Fay. — Cambridge: Harvard University Press, 1950. xiii, 121 p. 1. Hitler, Adolf, 1889-1945. 2. National socialism 3. Germany — History — 1933-1945 I. T.
DD256.5.M42   943.086   *LC* 50-5221

Noakes, Jeremy.   3.2445
Documents on Nazism, 1919–1945 / introduced and edited by Jeremy Noakes and Geoffrey Pridham. — New York: Viking Press, 1975, c1974. 704 p.; 25 cm. Includes index. 1. Nationalsozialistische Deutsche Arbeiter-Partei — History — Sources. 2. National socialism — History — Sources. 3. Germany —

History — 1933-1945 — Sources. I. Pridham, Geoffrey, 1942- joint author. II. T.
DD256.5.N59 1975   943.086   *LC* 74-5514   *ISBN* 0670275840

Reitlinger, Gerald, 1900-.   • 3.2446
The SS, alibi of a nation, 1922–1945. — New York: Viking Press, 1957. xi, 502 p.: ill., ports., maps.; 23 cm. 1. Nationalsozialistische Deutsche Arbeiter-Partei. Schutzstaffel. 2. Germany — Politics and government — 1933-1945 I. T.
DD256.5.R42x

Rich, Norman.   3.2447
Hitler's war aims. — [1st ed.]. — New York: Norton, [1973-. v.   : illus.; 25 cm. 1. Hitler, Adolf, 1889-1945. 2. World War, 1939-1945 — Occupied territories 3. National socialism 4. World War, 1939-1945 — Germany. 5. Germany — Foreign relations — 1933-1945 I. T.
DD256.5.R473   943.086/092/4 B   *LC* 78-116108   *ISBN* 0393054543

Schoenbaum, David.   • 3.2448
Hitler's social revolution; class and status in Nazi Germany, 1933–1939. [1st ed.] Garden City, N.Y., Doubleday, 1966. xxiii, 336 p. 22 cm. Based on thesis, Oxford University. 1. Germany — History — 1933-1945 2. Germany — Social conditions — 1933-1945 I. T.
DD256.5.S336   943.086   *LC* 66-17420

Shirer, William L. (William Lawrence), 1904-.   3.2449
The rise and fall of the Third Reich: a history of Nazi Germany / by William L. Shirer. — New York: Simon and Schuster, 1960. 1245 p. 1. Germany — History — 1933-1945 I. T.
DD256.5.S48   943.086   *LC* 60-6729

Vogt, Hannah.   3.2450
[Schuld oder Verhängnis? English] The burden of guilt, a short history of Germany, 1914–1945. Translated by Herbert Strauss. With an introd. by Gordon A. Craig. New York, Oxford University Press, 1964. xviii, 318 p. illus., maps, ports. 22 cm. Translation of Schuld oder Verhängnis? 1. Germany — History — 1933-1945 2. Germany — History — 20th century I. T.
DD256.5.V5713   943.085   *LC* 64-20266

Weinberg, Gerhard L.   • 3.2451
The foreign policy of Hitler's Germany; diplomatic revolution in Europe, 1933–36 [by] Gerhard L. Weinberg. — Chicago: University of Chicago Press, [1970] xi, 397 p.: map (on lining papers); 24 cm. 1. Germany — Foreign relations — 1933-1945 I. T.
DD256.5.W417   327.43   *LC* 70-124733   *ISBN* 0226885097

Weinberg, Gerhard L.   3.2452
The foreign policy of Hitler's Germany: starting World War II, 1937–1939 / Gerhard L. Weinberg. — Chicago: University of Chicago Press, 1980. xii, 728 p.: map (on lining papers); 24 cm. Includes index. 1. World War, 1939-1945 — Causes 2. Germany — Foreign relations — 1933-1945 I. T.
DD256.5.W418   327.43   *LC* 79-26406   *ISBN* 0226885119

Williamson, D. G.   3.2453
The Third Reich / D.G. Williamson. — Harlow, Essex, UK: Longman, 1982. iv, 108 p.; 20 cm. — (Seminar studies in history.) Includes index. 1. Germany — History — 1933-1945 I. T. II. Series.
DD256.5.W49 1982   943.086 19   *LC* 82-237970   *ISBN* 0582353068

DD257 ALLIED OCCUPATION, 1945–

Clay, Lucius D. (Lucius DuBignon), 1897-1978.   • 3.2454
Decision in Germany. — [1st ed.]. — Garden City, N. Y., Doubleday, 1950. xiv, 522 p. illus., ports., maps (on lining papers) 22 cm. 1. Germany — Hist. — 1945- I. T.
DD257.C55   943.086   *LC* 50-5813

Clay, Lucius D. (Lucius DuBignon), 1897-1978.   3.2455
The papers of General Lucius D. Clay: Germany, 1945–1949. Edited by Jean Edward Smith. Bloomington, Indiana University Press [1974] 2 v. (xli, 1210 p.) ports. 25 cm. (A Publication of the Institute of German Studies at Indiana University) 1. Germany — History — Allied occupation, 1945- — Sources. 2. Germany (Territory under Allied occupation, 1945-1955: U.S. Zone) — History — Sources. 3. Berlin (Germany) — Blockade, 1948-1949 — History — Sources. 4. Germany (West) — History — Sources. I. Smith, Jean Edward, ed. II. T.
DD257.C58 1974   943.087   *LC* 73-16536   *ISBN* 0253342880

U.S. occupation in Europe after World War II: papers and reminiscences from the April 23–24, 1976 conference held at the George C. Marshall Research Foundation, Lexington, Virginia / edited with an introd. by Hans A. Schmitt.   3.2456
Lawrence: Regents Press of Kansas, c1978. viii, 172 p.: maps; 24 cm. 'A George C. Marshall Research Foundation publication.' 1. Clay, Lucius D. (Lucius DuBignon), 1897-1978 — Congresses. 2. Germany (West) — Politics and government — Congresses. 3. Austria — History — Allied occupation, 1945-1955 — Congresses. 4. Germany — History — Allied occupation, 1945- — Congresses. I. Schmitt, Hans A. II. George C. Marshall Research Foundation.
DD257.U54   355.4/9   *LC* 78-51611   *ISBN* 0700601783

Gimbel, John.   • 3.2457
The American occupation of Germany; politics and the military, 1945–1949. Stanford, Calif., Stanford University Press, 1968. xiv, 335 p. map. 24 cm. 1. Economic assistance, American — History. 2. Berlin (Germany) — Blockade, 1948-1949 3. Germany (Territory under Allied occupation, 1945-1955: U.S. Zone) I. T.
DD257.2.G5   355.02/8/0943   *LC* 68-26778

Binder, Gerhart.   3.2458
Deutschland seit 1945; eine dokumentierte gesamtdeutsche Geschichte in der Zeit der Teilung. [Stuttgart-Degerloch] Seewald [1969] 608p. 1. Germany — Politics and government — 1945- 2. German reunification question (1949-) I. T.
DD257.4 B53

Grosser, Alfred, 1925-.   3.2459
[Allemagne de notre temps. English] Germany in our time; a political history of the postwar years. Translated by Paul Stephenson. New York, Praeger [1971] 378 p. map. 25 cm. Translation of L'Allemagne de notre temps. 1. Germany — Politics and government — 1945- I. T.
DD257.4.G77913   320.9/43/087   *LC* 77-130529

Peterson, Edward Norman.   3.2460
The American occupation of Germany: retreat to victory / Edward N. Peterson. — Detroit: Wayne State University Press, 1977, c1978. 376 p.; 24 cm. Includes index. 1. Berlin question (1945-) 2. Germany (Territory under Allied occupation, 1945-1955: U.S. Zone) I. T.
DD257.4.P43   940.53/144/0943   *LC* 77-28965   *ISBN* 0814315887

Balfour, Michael Leonard Graham, 1908-.   3.2461
West Germany: a contemporary history / Michael Balfour. — New York: St. Martin's Press, 1982. 307 p.: map; 22 cm. Includes index. 1. Germany (West) — History. 2. Germany (West) — Politics and government I. T.
DD258.7.B35 1982   943.087 19   *LC* 81-21293   *ISBN* 0312862970

Feldman, Lily Gardner.   3.2462
The special relationship between West Germany and Israel / Lily Gardner Feldman. — Boston: Allen & Unwin, 1984. xix, 330 p.; 24 cm. Includes index. 1. Germany (West) — Relations — Israel 2. Israel — Relations — Germany (West) 3. Middle East — History — 20th century. 4. Israel — Politics and government — 1948- I. T.
DD258.85.I75 F45 1984   303.4/8243/05694 19   *LC* 84-6168   *ISBN* 0043270689

DD259 FEDERAL REPUBLIC, 1949–

Craig, Gordon Alexander, 1913-.   3.2463
The Germans / Gordon A. Craig. — New York: Putnam, c1982. 350 p.: maps; 24 cm. Includes index. 1. Germany (West) — History. I. T.
DD259.C7 1982   943 19   *LC* 81-8650   *ISBN* 0399124365

Federal Republic of Germany: a country study / Foreign Area Studies, the American University; edited by Richard F. Nyrop.   3.2464
2nd ed. — [Washington, D.C.: American University, Foreign Area Studies]: For sale by the Supt. of Docs., U.S. G.P.O., 1982. xxxii, 454 p.: ill.; 23 cm. — (Area handbook series.) (DA pam. 550-173) Rev. ed. of: Area handbook for the Federal Republic of Germany. 1975. Includes index. 1. Germany (West) I. Nyrop, Richard F. II. American University (Washington, D.C.). Foreign Area Studies. III. Area handbook for the Federal Republic of Germany. IV. Series. V. Series: DA pam. 550-173
DD259.F43   943 19   *LC* 83-2515

Prittie, Terence, 1913-.   3.2465
The velvet chancellors: a history of post-war Germany / Terence Prittie. — London: Muller, 1979. xii, 286 p., [4] leaves of plates: ill.; 24 cm. Includes index. 1. Germany (West) — History. 2. Germany — History — Allied occupation, 1945- I. T.
DD259.P74 1979   943.087   *LC* 80-464210   *ISBN* 0584104618

Germany and Eastern Europe since 1945: from the Potsdam   3.2466
Agreement to Chancellor Brandt's 'Ostpolitik'.
New York: Scribner [1973] xi, 322 p.: maps; 21 cm. (Keesing's research report)
'Based on information contained in Keesing's contemporary archives.'
1. Berlin question (1945-) 2. Germany (West) — Foreign relations — Europe,
Eastern. 3. Europe, Eastern — Foreign relations — Germany (West)
4. Germany — History — Allied occupation, 1945- I. Keesing's
contemporary archives.
DD259.4.G38   943.087   *LC* 72-7729   *ISBN* 0684131900 *ISBN*
0684131919

Grosser, Alfred, 1925-.   3.2467
[République fédérale d'Allemagne. English] The Federal Republic of Germany;
a concise history. Translated by Nelson Aldrich. New York, Praeger [1964]
150 p. 21 cm. 1. Germany (West) — History. I. T.
DD259.4.G763   309.143   *LC* 64-16677

Hanrieder, Wolfram F.   3.2468
The foreign policies of West Germany, France, and Britain / Wolfram F.
Hanrieder, Graeme P. Auton. — Englewood Cliffs, N.J.: Prentice-Hall, c1980.
xviii, 314 p.; 23 cm. Includes index. 1. North Atlantic Treaty Organization.
2. France — Foreign relations — 1945- 3. Great Britain — Foreign relations
— 1945- 4. Germany (West) — Foreign relations. 5. Germany (West) —
Politics and government 6. France — Politics and government — 1945-
7. Great Britain — Politics and government — 1945- I. Auton, Graeme P.
joint author. II. T.
DD259.4.H238   320.9/4/055   *LC* 79-14688   *ISBN* 0133263975

The West German model: perspectives on a stable state / edited   3.2469
by William E. Paterson and Gordon Smith.
London: F. Cass; Totowa, N.J.: Biblio Distribution Centre [distributor], 1982
(c1981). v, 176 p.: ill.; 23 cm. 1. Germany (West) — Politics and government
— Addresses, essays, lectures. I. Paterson, William E. II. Smith, Gordon R.
DD259.4.W4264 1981   943.087 19   *LC* 81-167994   *ISBN*
0714631809

Who's who in German politics; a biographical guide to 4,500   3.2470
politicians in the Federal Republic of Germany / edited by
Karl–Otto Saur.
New York, R. R. Bowker Co., 1971. x, 342 p. 22 cm. In German; preface also in
English. 1. Statesmen, German — Biography. 2. Germany (West) —
Biography. I. Saur, Karl Otto.
DD259.63.S28   *LC* 72-204749

Adenauer, Konrad, 1876-1967.   • 3.2471
Memoirs / Konrad Adenauer; Translated by Beate Ruhm von Oppen. —
Chicago: H. Regnery Co., c1966-. v. : illus., ports.; 25 cm. 1. World politics —
1945- 2. Germany (West) — Politics and government. 3. Germany — Politics
and government — 1945- I. T.
DD259.7.A3A333   943.0870924   *LC* 65-26906

Hiscocks, Richard.   • 3.2472
The Adenauer era. Philadelphia, Lippincott [1966] x, 312 p. 22 cm.
1. Adenauer, Konrad, 1876-1967. 2. Germany (West) — Politics and
government 3. Germany (West) — Social conditions. I. T.
DD259.7.A3 H5   943.0870924   *LC* 66-23243

Prittie, Terence, 1913-.   3.2473
Konrad Adenauer, 1876–1967 [by] Terence Prittie. [Chicago] Cowles Book Co.
[c1971] xvi, 334 p. illus. 25 cm. On spine: Adenauer. 1. Adenauer, Konrad,
1876-1967. I. T.
DD259.7.A3 P75 1971   943.087/092/4 B   *LC* 70-163245

Prittie, Terence, 1913-.   3.2474
Willy Brandt; portrait of a statesman [by] Terence Prittie. New York, Schocken
Books [1974] 356 p. illus. 24 cm. 1. Brandt, Willy, 1913- I. T.
DD259.7.B7 P74 1974b   943.087/092/4 B   *LC* 74-9229   *ISBN*
0805235612

DD261 DEMOCRATIC REPUBLIC, 1949-

East Germany: a country study / Foreign Area Studies, the   3.2475
American University; edited by Eugene K. Keefe.
2nd ed. — Washington, D.C.: American University, Foreign Area Studies: For
sale by the Supt. of Docs., U.S. G.P.O., 1982. xxxi, 348 p. ill.; 24 cm. — (Area
handbook series.) (DA pam. 550-155) 'Research completed July 1981.' Includes
index. 1. Germany (East) I. Keefe, Eugene K. II. American University
(Washington, D.C.). Foreign Area Studies. III. Series. IV. Series: DA pam.
550-155
DD261.E27 1982   943.1 19   *LC* 82-8696

The German Democratic Republic: a developed Socialist society   3.2476
/ edited by Lyman H. Legters.
Boulder, Colo.: Westview Press, 1978, c1977. xiv, 285 p. — (Westview special
studies on the Soviet Union and Eastern Europe.) 1. Germany (East) —
Addresses, essays, lectures. I. Legters, Lyman Howard, 1928- II. Series.
DD261.G415   DD261 G335.   943/.1087   *LC* 77-578   *ISBN*
0891581421

McCauley, Martin.   3.2477
The German Democratic Republic since 1945 / Martin McCauley. — New
York: St. Martin's Press, 1984 (c1983). xiv, 282 p.: maps; 23 cm. Includes index.
1. Germany (East) — History I. T.
DD261.M36 1983   943.1087 19   *LC* 83-3410   *ISBN* 0312325533

Smith, Jean Edward.   • 3.2478
Germany beyond the wall; people, politics ... and prosperity. [1st ed.] Boston,
Little, Brown [1969] xiv, 338 p. 25 cm. 1. Germany (East) I. T.
DD261.S53   309.1/431   *LC* 69-12636

DD301–901 Local History

DD301–454 PRUSSIA

Anderson, Eugene Newton.   • 3.2479
Nationalism and the cultural crisis in Prussia, 1806–1815; [essays]. — New
York: Octagon Books, 1966 [c1939] ix, 303 p.; 21 cm. 1. Nationalism —
Prussia. I. T.
DD331.A6 1966   943/.1   *LC* 66-29328

Hintze, Otto, 1861-1940.   • 3.2480
Die Hohenzollern und ihr Werk; fünfhundert Jahre vaterländischer
Geschichte, von Otto Hintze. — 1. zehntausend. — Berlin: P. Parey, 1915. xvi,
704 p.; 26 cm. 1. Hohenzollern, House of 2. Prussia (Germany) — History.
3. Germany — History I. T.
DD347.H55 1915   *LC* 16-4403

Marriott, J. A. R. (John Arthur Ransome), Sir, 1859-1945.   • 3.2481
The Evolution of Prussia: the making of an empire / by Sir J. A. R.
Marriott...and Sir Charles Grant Robertson. — Rev ed. — Oxford: The
Clarendon press, 1946. 499, 1 p. . illus. (maps); 19 cm. 1. Prussia — History.
I. Robertson, Charles Grant, Sir, 1869-1948. II. T.
DD347.M28   *LC* 47-5661

Carsten, F. L. (Francis Ludwig)   • 3.2482
The origins of Prussia / Francis Carsten. — Oxford: Clarendon P., 1954. 309 p.:
fold. map.; 23 cm. 1. Prussia (Germany) — History. I. T.
DD378.C3   *LC* 54-4860

Schevill, Ferdinand, 1868-1954.   • 3.2483
The Great Elector. — [Reprinted in an unaltered and unabridged ed.]. —
Hamden, Conn., Archon Books, 1965 [c1947] ix, 442 p. illus., maps, ports. 23
cm. Bibliographical footnotes. 1. Friedrich Wilhelm, Elector of Brandenburg,
1620-1688. I. T.
DD394.S4 1965   923.143   *LC* 65-16972

Ergang, Robert Reinhold, 1898-.   • 3.2484
The Potsdam führer, Frederick William I, father of Prussian militarism, by
Robert Ergang. New York, Columbia university press, 1941. 290 p. 23 cm.
1. Frederick William I, King of Prussia, 1688-1740. I. T.
DD399.E7   *LC* 41-19534   *ISBN* 0374926239

Easum, Chester Verne.   • 3.2485
Prince Henry of Prussia, brother of Frederick the Great, by Chester V. Easum.
— Westport, Conn.: Greenwood Press, [1971, c1942] 403 p.: illus., facsims.,
geneal. table, fold. map, ports.; 23 cm. 1. Heinrich, Prince of Prussia,
1726-1802. I. T.
DD402.H4 E2 1971   943/.053/0924   *LC* 75-113061   *ISBN*
0837146976

Gooch, G. P. (George Peabody), 1873-1968.   • 3.2486
Frederick the Great, the ruler, the writer, the man. Hamden, Conn., Archon
Books [1962] 363 p.: ill.; 22 cm. I. Frederick II, King of Prussia, 1712-1786.
II. T.
DD403.G6 1962   923.143   *LC* 62-16045

Koser, Reinhold, 1852-1914.   **3.2487**
Geschichte Friedrichs des Grossen. Ed. 6 [and] 7. Stuttgart: Cotta, 1921-. v.: maps (part fold. col.); 24 cm. Vol. 4 is Ed. 4 [and] 5, rev. 1. Frederick II, the Great, King of Prussia, 1712-1786 2. Germany — History — 1556-1806 I. T.
DD404.K82

Lavisse, Ernest, 1842-1922.   • **3.2488**
[Jeunesse du Grand Frédéric. English] The youth of Frederick the Great. Translated from the French by Mary Bushnell Coleman. Chicago, S. C. Griggs, 1892. [New York, AMS Press, 1972] xv, 445 p. front. 19 cm. Translation of La jeunesse du Grand Frédéric. 1. Frederick II, King of Prussia, 1712-1786. I. T.
DD404.L413 1972   943/.053/0924 B   LC 71-172308   *ISBN* 0404038913

Ritter, Gerhard, 1888-1967.   • **3.2489**
Frederick the Great; a historical profile. Translated, with an introd., by Peter Paret. Berkeley: University of California Press, 1968. xiv, 207 p.: port.; 23 cm. 1. Frederick II, King of Prussia, 1712-1786. I. T.
DD404.R513   943/.053/0924 B   LC 68-15815

Schieder, Theodor.   **3.2490**
Friedrich der Grosse: ein Königtum der Widersprüche / Theodor Schieder. — Berlin: Propyläen Verlag, 1983. 538 p., [16] p. of plates: ill.; 23 cm. Includes index. 1. Frederick II, King of Prussia, 1712-1786. 2. Prussia (Germany) — Kings and rulers — Biography. 3. Prussia (Germany) — History — Frederick II, the Great, 1740-1786 I. T.
DD404.S28 1983   943/.053/0924 B 19   LC 84-103994   *ISBN* 354907638X

Ford, Guy Stanton, 1873-1962.   • **3.2491**
Stein and the era of reform in Prussia, 1807–1815. — Gloucester, Mass., P. Smith, 1965 [c1922] vii, 336 p. 21 cm. Bibliographical footnotes. 1. Stein, Karl, Freiherr vom und zum, 1757-1831. 2. Prussia — Pol. & govt. — 1806-1848. I. T.
DD416.S8F6 1965   943.060924 (B)   LC 65-9668

Ritter, Gerhard, 1888-1967.   • **3.2492**
Stein; eine politische Biographie. Neugestaltete [3.] Aufl. Stuttgart, Deutsche Verlags-Anstalt [1958] 656 p.: port.; 24 cm. 1. Stein, Karl, Freiherr vom und zum, 1757-1831. I. T.
DD416.S8 R5 1958   943.06

Paret, Peter.   **3.2493**
Yorck and the era of the Prussian reform, 1807–1815. — Princeton, N.J.: Princeton University Press, 1966. vii, 309 p.: plans, port.; 25 cm. 1. Yorck von Wartenburg, Hans David Ludwig, Graf, 1759-1830. 2. Prussia (Germany) — History, Military. I. T.
DD418.6.Y7 P3   943.060924   LC 66-17706

Paret, Peter.   **3.2494**
Clausewitz and the state / Peter Paret. — New York: Oxford University Press, 1976. viii, 467 p.: ill.; 24 cm. Includes indexes. 1. Clausewitz, Carl von, 1780-1831. 2. Intellectuals — Germany — Biography. 3. State, The 4. War 5. Germany — Nobility — Biography. I. T.
DD422.C5 P33   943/.06/0924 B 19   LC 75-16901   *ISBN* 0195019881

Sweet, Paul Robinson, 1907-.   **3.2495**
Wilhelm von Humboldt: a biography / by Paul R. Sweet. — Columbus: Ohio State University Press, c1978-c1980. 2 v.: port.; 25 cm. Includes index. 1. Humboldt, Wilhelm, Freiherr von, 1767-1835. 2. Statesmen — Germany — Biography. I. T.
DD422.H8 S93   943/.06/0924 B 19   LC 77-26654   *ISBN* 0814202748

Friedjung, Heinrich, 1851-1920.   • **3.2496**
The struggle for supremacy in Germany, 1859–1866. Translated by A. J. P. Taylor and W. L. McElwee. — New York, Russell & Russell, 1966. xxxi, 339 p. map. 23 cm. Reprint of the 1935 abridged translation of the 10th German ed. of 1916-17. Bibliographical footnotes. 1. Austro-Prussian War, 1866 2. Austro-Italian War, 1866 I. Taylor, A. J. P. (Alan John Percivale), 1906- tr. II. McElwee, William Lloyd, 1907- tr. III. T.
DD438.F92 1966   943.07   LC 66-13169

DD491–901 OTHER REGIONS

Fay, Sidney Bradshaw, 1876-.   • **3.2497**
The rise of Brandenburg–Prussia to 1786 / by Sidney Bradshaw Fay. New York, H. Holt [c1937] viii, 155 p.: front. (map) double diagr.; 20 cm. (The Berkshire studies in European history) 1. Brandenburg — History I. T. II. Series.
DD491.B85 F28   943.05   LC 37-12570

Droz, Jacques.   • **3.2498**
Le libéralisme rhénan, 1815–1848: contribution à l'histoire du libéralisme allemand ... / par Jacques Droz. — Paris: F. Sorlot, 1940. xviii, 463 p.; 23 cm. 1. Liberalism 2. Rhine Province (Germany) — History 3. Germany — Politics and government — 1815-1866 I. T.
DD491.R48 D7   LC 46-42542

Steefel, Lawrence Dinkelspiel, 1894-.   • **3.2499**
The Schleswig-Holstein question, by Lawrence D. Steefel. Cambridge: Harvard University Press, 1932. xii, 400 p. incl. geneal. tab. fold. mounted maps. 23 cm. (Harvard historical studies, v. 32) 'This monograph has grown out of a thesis presented in 1923 in partial fulfilment of the requirements for the degree of doctor of philosophy at Harvard University.' — Pref. 1. Schleswig-Holstein question I. T.
DD491.S68 S8   LC 32-9250

Blanning, T. C. W.   **3.2500**
The French Revolution in Germany: occupation and resistance in the Rhineland, 1792–1802 / T.C.W. Blanning. — Oxford [Oxfordshire]: Clarendon Press; New York: Oxford University Press, 1983. vi, 353 p., [1] p. of plates: map; 23 cm. Includes index. 1. Rhineland (Germany) — History — French occupation, 1792-1801 2. France — History — Revolution, 1789-1799 — Occupied territories. 3. France — History — Revolution, 1789-1799 — Influence I. T.
DD747.B53 1983   944.04 19   LC 83-3960   *ISBN* 0198225644

Friedrich, Otto, 1929-.   **3.2501**
Before the deluge; a portrait of Berlin in the 1920's. [1st ed.] New York, Harper & Row [1972] xi, 418 p. illus. 25 cm. 1. Berlin (Germany) — History — 1918-1945 2. Berlin (Germany) — Intellectual life. I. T.
DD880.F75 1972   914.3/155/0385   LC 70-156522   *ISBN* 0060113723

Shlaim, Avi.   **3.2502**
The United States and the Berlin Blockade, 1948–1949: a study in crisis decision–making / Avi Shlaim. — Berkeley: University of California Press, c1983. xiii, 463 p.; 25 cm. 'International Crisis Behavior Project.' Includes index. 1. Berlin (Germany) — History — Blockade, 1948-1949 2. United States — Foreign relations — Soviet Union — Decision making. 3. Soviet Union — Foreign relations — United States — Decision making. I. International Crisis Behavior Project. II. T.
DD881.S46 1983   943.1/550874 19   LC 81-19636   *ISBN* 0520043855

Smith, Jean Edward.   **3.2503**
The defense of Berlin. — Baltimore, Johns Hopkins Press, 1963. ix, 431 p. fold. maps. 24 cm. Bibliographical references included in 'Notes' (p. 343-355) Bibliography: p. 388-406. 1. Berlin — Hist. — Allied occupation, 1945- I. T.
DD881.S54   943.155   LC 63-17670

Gimbel, John.   • **3.2504**
A German community under American occupation: Marburg, 1945–52. Stanford, Calif., Stanford University Press, 1961. vi, 259 p. 23 cm. (Stanford studies in history, economics, and political science, 21) Bibliographical references included in 'Notes' (p. [215]-242) 'Bibliographical note': p. [243]-249. 1. Marburg (Germany) — Politics and government. 2. Germany — History — Allied occupation, 1945- — Case studies. I. T. II. Series.
DD901.M275G5   943.087   LC 61-7798

Ford, Franklin L. (Franklin Lewis), 1920-.   • **3.2505**
Strasbourg in transition, 1648–1789. Cambridge, Harvard University Press, 1958. xvii, 321 p. illus., ports., maps. 22 cm. Bibliographical references included in 'Notes' (p. [267]-306) 1. Strassburg (Germany) — History. I. T.
DD901.S87F6   943.445   LC 58-7247

Bruford, Walter Horace, 1894-.   • **3.2506**
Culture and society in classical Weimar, 1775–1806. — [London] Cambridge University Press, 1962. 465 p. illus. 23 cm. Includes bibliography. 1. Goethe, Johann Wolfgang von, 1749-1832. 2. Weimar — Intellectual life. I. T.
DD901.W4B7   943.23   LC 62-6747

Alexander, Edgar.   **3.2507**
Adenauer and the new Germany, the chancellor of the vanquished. Pref. by Alvin Johnson, epilogue by Konrad Adenauer. [Translated from the German by Thomas E. Goldstein]. — New York, Farrar, Straus and Cudahy [1957] 300 p. 22 cm. 1. Adenauer, Konrad, 1876-1967. 2. German reunification question (1949-) I. T.
DD259.7.A3A72   *943.087   LC 57-12507

DE MEDITERRANEAN REGION. GRECO-ROMAN WORLD

Harvey, Paul, Sir, 1869-1948.   • **3.2508**
The Oxford companion to classical literature, compiled and edited by Sir Paul Harvey. — Oxford: The Clarendon press, 1937. xi, [1] 468 p.: plates, maps, plans.; 19 cm. 1. Classical dictionaries I. T.
DE5.H3   913.38   *LC* 38-1064

The New Century classical handbook / Edited by Catherine B.   • **3.2509**
Avery; editorial consultant, Jotham Johnson.
New York: Appleton-Century-Crofts, c1962. xiii, 1162 p.: ill., maps (on lining papers) 1. Classical dictionaries I. Avery, Catherine B. II. Title: Classical handbook.
DE5.N4   913.38   *LC* 62-10069

The Oxford classical dictionary, edited by N. G. L. Hammond   • **3.2510**
and H. H. Scullard.
2d ed. Oxford [Eng.] Clarendon Press, 1970. xxii, 1176 p. 26 cm. 1. Classical dictionaries I. Hammond, N. G. L. (Nicholas Geoffrey Lemprière), 1907- ed. II. Scullard, H. H. (Howard Hayes), 1903- ed.
DE5.O9 1970   913.38003   *LC* 73-18819

Avi-Yonah, Michael, 1904-1974.   **3.2511**
Illustrated encyclopaedia of the classical world / Michael Avi Yonah and Israel Shatzman; foreword by F. W. Walbank. — New York: Harper & Row, [c1975] 509 p.: ill., (part. col.) maps; 25 cm. 1. Classical dictionaries 2. Greece — Antiquities 3. Rome — Antiquities I. Shatzman, Israel. joint author II. T.
DE5.Y65   939.03   *LC* 73-14245   *ISBN* 0060101784

Plutarch.   • **3.2512**
[Vitae parallelae. English. Dryden-Clough. 1932] The lives of the noble Grecians and Romans, translated by John Dryden and revised by Arthur Hugh Clough. New York, The Modern library [1932] xxiv, 1309 p. 21 cm. (The Modern library of the world's best books. [Modern library giants]) At head of title: Plutarch. 1. Greece — Biography 2. Rome — Biography I. Dryden, John, 1631-1700. II. Clough, Arthur Hugh, 1819-1861. ed. III. T. IV. Series.
DE7.P5 1932   920.03 888.8   *LC* 32-17475

Finley, M. I. (Moses I.), 1912-.   **3.2513**
Ancient history: evidence and models / M.I. Finley. — 1st American ed. — New York, N.Y., U.S.A.: Viking, 1986, c1985. 131 p.; 23 cm. 'Elisabeth Sifton books.' Includes index. 1. History — Research 2. Greece — Historiography. 3. Rome — Historiography. I. T.
DE8.F55 1986   938/.0072 19   *LC* 85-40616   *ISBN* 0670809705

Fornara, Charles W.   **3.2514**
The nature of history in ancient Greece and Rome / Charles William Fornara. — Berkeley: University of California Press, 1984 (c1983). xiv, 215 p.; 23 cm. — (Eidos) 1. Historiography — Greece. 2. Historiography — Rome. 3. Greece — Historiography. 4. Rome — Historiography. I. T.
DE8.F67 1983   949.5/0072 19   *LC* 82-21888   *ISBN* 0520049101

Grant, Michael, 1914-.   • **3.2515**
The ancient historians. — New York: Scribner, [1970] xviii, 486 p.: illus., facsims., maps, ports.; 24 cm. 1. Historians — Greece. 2. Historians — Rome I. T.
DE8.G7   938/.0072/022   *LC* 70-106551

Sources for ancient history / edited by Michael Crawford; with   **3.2516**
contributions from Emilio Gabba, Fergus Millar, Anthony
Snodgrass.
Cambridge [Cambridgeshire]; New York: Cambridge University Press, 1983. xi, 238 p.: ill.; 23 cm. — (Sources of history, studies in the uses of historical evidence.) 1. Greece — Historiography — Addresses, essays, lectures. 2. Rome — Historiography — Addresses, essays, lectures. I. Crawford, Michael H. (Michael Hewson), 1939- II. Gabba, Emilio. III. Millar, Fergus. IV. Snodgrass, Anthony M. V. Series.
DE8.S67 1983   938/.0072 19   *LC* 82-23656   *ISBN* 0521247829

Cary, M. (Max), 1881-1958.   • **3.2517**
The geographic background of Greek & Roman history.— Oxford: Clarendon Press, 1949. 331 p.: maps. 1. Classical geography I. T.
DE29.C35   *LC* 49-3013

Heyden, A. A. M. van der. ed.   • **3.2518**
Atlas of the classical world. Edited by A. A. M. van der Heyden and H. H. Scullard. [London, New York] Nelson 1959 [i.e. 1960] 221 p. illus., col. maps (1 fold.) 36 cm. 1. Greece — Civilization — Pictorial works. 2. Classical geography — Maps 3. Rome — Civilization — Pictorial works. I. Scullard, H. H. (Howard Hayes), 1903- joint ed. II. T.
DE29.H463   911.38   *LC* 60-1130

The Oxford history of the classical world / edited by John   **3.2519**
Boardman, Jasper Griffin, Oswyn Murray.
Oxford [Oxfordshire]; New York: Oxford UNiversity Press, 1986. vii, 872 p., [14] p. of plates: ill., maps (some col.); 26 cm. 1. Civilization, Classical I. Boardman, John, 1927- II. Griffin, Jasper. III. Murray, Oswyn.
DE59.O94 1986   938 19   *LC* 85-21774   *ISBN* 0198721129

The Princeton encyclopedia of classical sites / Richard Stillwell,   **3.2520**
editor, William L. MacDonald, associate editor, Marian Holland
McAllister, assistant editor.
Princeton, N.J.: Princeton University Press, 1976. xxii, 1019 p., [12] leaves of plates: maps; 29 cm. Includes index. 1. Classical antiquities 2. Excavations (Archaeology) I. Stillwell, Richard, 1899- II. MacDonald, William Lloyd. III. McAllister, Marian Holland.
DE59.P7   938/.003   *LC* 75-30210   *ISBN* 0691035423

Cary, M. (Max), 1881-1958.   • **3.2521**
Life and thought in the Greek and Roman world / by M. J. Cary and T. J. Haarhoff. — London: Methuen, 1961. x, 355 p. — (University paperbacks; UP 27) 1. Civilization, Greco-Roman I. Haarhoff, T. J. (Theodore Johannes), 1892- II. T.
DE71.C27   *LC* 41-3107   *ISBN* 0416677703

Haarhoff, T. J. (Theodore Johannes), 1892-.   • **3.2522**
The stranger at the gate: aspects of exclusiveness and co-operation in ancient Greece and Rome, with some reference to modern times. — Oxford: Blackwell, 1948. 354 p.; 22 cm. 1. Greece — Civilization 2. Hellenism 3. Nationalism 4. Rome — Civilization I. T.
DE71.Hx   913.38

Toynbee, Arnold Joseph, 1889-1975.   • **3.2523**
Hellenism: the history of a civilization. — New York: Oxford University Press, 1959. 272p.: ill.; 21 cm. 1. Hellenism — History. I. T.
DE71.T6   901.91   *LC* 59-7810

Sandars, N. K. (Nancy K.)   **3.2524**
The sea peoples: warriors of the ancient Mediterranean, 1250–1150 B.C. / N. K. Sandars. — London: Thames and Hudson, c1978. 224 p.: ill.; 25 cm. (Ancient peoples and places; v. 89) Includes index. 1. Sea Peoples 2. Mediterranean Region — History. I. T.
DE73.2.S4 S26   939.1   *LC* 77-83798   *ISBN* 050002085X

Braudel, Fernand.   **3.2525**
The Mediterranean and the Mediterranean World in the age of Philip II / Fernand Braudel; translated from the French by Sian Reynolds. — New York: Harper & Row, 1972-1973. 2 v. (1375 p., [35] p. of plates): ill., maps. 1. Physical geography — Mediterranean region 2. Mediterranean Region — History I. T.
DE80.B7713   *LC* 72-138708   *ISBN* 006010452X

Levi, Mario Attilio, 1902-.   • **3.2526**
[Lotta politica nel mondo antico. English] Political power in the ancient world / Translation by Jane Costello. [New York]: New American Library [1966, c1965] 194 p.; 22 cm. Translation of La lotta politica nel mondo antico. 1. Civilization, Greco-Roman 2. Rome — Politics and government 3. Greece — Politics and government I. T.
DE83.L413 1966   320.5093   *LC* 65-24023

Grant, Michael, 1914-.   **3.2527**
From Alexander to Cleopatra: the Hellenistic world / Michael Grant. — New York: Scribner, 1983 (c1982). xv, 319 p., [16] p. of plates: ill.; 24 cm. Includes index. 1. Hellenism 2. Mediterranean Region — History. I. T.
DE86.G73 1982   909/.09822 19   *LC* 82-10802   *ISBN* 0684177803

Rose, J. Holland (John Holland), 1855-1942.   • 3.2528
The Mediterranean in the ancient world. — 2nd ed. — Cambridge, [Eng]:
University Press, 1934. xi, 184 p.: illus.; 23 cm. 1. History, Ancient
2. Mediterranean Region — History. I. T.
DE86.R67   930/.096/38   LC 36-10977

Translated documents of Greece and Rome.   3.2529
[Cambridge: The University Press, 1983-] v.; 24 cm.
DE86.Tx

DF GREECE

DF10–289 Ancient Greece

Cary, M. (Max), 1881-1958.   • 3.2530
The documentary sources of Greek history. New York, Greenwood Press
[1969] xi, 140 p. 23 cm. Reprint of the 1927 ed. 1. Greece — History —
Sources. I. T.
DF12.C3 1969   938   LC 78-90478   ISBN 0837122155

Crawford, Michael H. (Michael Hewson), 1939-.   3.2531
Archaic and Classical Greece: a selection of ancient sources in translation /
Michael Crawford, David Whitehead. — Cambridge [Cambridgeshire,
England]; New York: Cambridge University Press, 1983. xxiii, 634 p.: ill.,
maps; 24 cm. 1. Greece — History — To 146 B.C. — Sources. I. Whitehead,
David, Ph. D. II. T.
DF12.C7 1983   938 19   LC 82-4355   ISBN 0521227755

Myres, John Linton, Sir, 1869-1954.   • 3.2532
Geographical history in Greek lands / by John L. Myres. — Oxford: Clarendon
Press, 1953. ix, 381 p., [12] leaves of plates: ill., maps. 'A select list of the works
of John Linton Myres': p. [351]-381. 1. Greece — Descriptive geography I. T.
DF30 M79   LC 53-1115

DF75–135 ANTIQUITIES. CIVILIZATION. CULTURE

Ehrenberg, Victor, 1891-.   3.2533
From Solon to Socrates: Greek history and civilization during the sixth and fifth
centuries B.C. — 2d ed. London: Methuen [distributed by Barnes & Noble,
New York] 1973 xvii, 505 p.: maps; 21 cm. 1. Greece — Civilization — To 146
B.C. 2. Greece — History — To 146 B.C. I. T.
DF77.E35 1973   913.38/03   LC 73-180774   ISBN 0416776108
ISBN 0416777600

Finley, M. I. (Moses I.), 1912-.   • 3.2534
The ancient Greeks, an introduction to their life and thought. New York,
Viking Press [1963] 177 p. illus. 22 cm. 1. Greece — Civilization — To 146
B.C. I. T.
DF77.F5   913.38   LC 63-8453

Finley, M. I. (Moses I.), 1912-.   • 3.2535
Early Greece: the Bronze and archaic ages / [by] M. I. Finley. — New York:
Norton [1970] 155 p.: ill., maps, plan.; 21 cm. (Ancient culture and society)
1. Bronze age — Greece. 2. Civilization, Homeric 3. Greece — History —
Geometric period, ca. 900-700 B.C. 4. Greece — History — Age of Tyrants,
7th-6th centuries, B.C. 5. Greece — Antiquities I. T.
DF77.F53 1970   913.38/03/11   LC 78-95884   ISBN 0393054101

Frost, Frank J., 1929-.   3.2536
Greek society / Frank J. Frost. — 2nd ennd. — Lexington, Mass.; Toronto:
Heath, c1980. xv, 215 p.: ill.; 24 cm. 1. Greece — Civilization — To 146 B.C.
I. T.
DF77.F75 1980   938   LC 79-89480   ISBN 066902452X

Hadas, Moses, 1900-1966.   • 3.2537
Hellenistic culture: fusion and diffusion / by Moses Hadas. — New York:
Columbia U.P., 1959. vi, 324 p. 1. Hellenism 2. Greece — Civilization I. T.
DF77.H3   913.38   LC 59-13777

Jaeger, Werner Wilhelm, 1888-1961.   • 3.2538
Paideia: the ideals of Greek culture, by Werner Jaeger, translated ... by Gilbert
Highet ... 2d ed. New York, Oxford University Press, 1945-. 3 v. 23 cm.

1. Education, Greek 2. Greece — Civilization 3. Greek literature — History
and criticism. I. Highet, Gilbert, 1906-1978. tr. II. T.
DF77.J274   LC 45-9752

Levi, Peter.   3.2539
Atlas of the Greek world / by Peter Levi. — New York, N.Y.: Facts on File,
c1980. 239 p.: ill. (some col.), maps; 31 cm. Includes index. 1. Greece —
Civilization — To 146 B.C. 2. Mediterranean Region — Description and travel
3. Mediterranean Region — Historical geography — Maps. I. T.
DF77.L43   938 19   LC 81-122477   ISBN 0871964481

MacKendrick, Paul Lachlan, 1914-.   • 3.2540
The Greek stones speak: the story of archaeology in Greek lands. — New York:
St. Martin's Press [1962] 470 p.: ill.; 22 cm. 1. Excavations (Archaeology) —
Greece, Modern. 2. Greece, Modern — Antiquities. I. T.
DF77.M18   938   LC 62-10902

Murray, Oswyn.   3.2541
Early Greece / Oswyn Murray. — Brighton, Sussex: Harvester Press; Atlantic
Highlands, N.J.: Humanities Press, 1980. 319 p.: ill.; 23 cm. — (Fontana
history of the ancient world.) Includes indexes. 1. Greece — Civilization — To
146 B.C. I. T. II. Series.
DF77.M82 1980   938/.02 19   LC 81-151908   ISBN 039100767X

Starr, Chester G.   • 3.2542
The origins of Greek civilization, 1100–650 B.C. / by Chester G. Starr. — New
York: Knopf, 1961. 385 p.: ill., maps. 1. Greece — Civilization 2. Greece —
History I. T.
DF77 S62   913.38   LC 60-53446

Tarn, W. W. (William Woodthorpe), 1869-1957.   • 3.2543
Hellenistic civilisation. — 3d ed., rev. by the author and G. T. Griffith. —
London, E. Arnold [1952] xi, 372 p. maps. 22 cm. 'List of general works': p.
361. Bibliographical footnotes. 1. Hellenism 2. Greece — Civilization I. T.
DF77.T3 1952   913.38   LC 52-8411

Andrewes, Antony, 1910-.   3.2544
The Greeks. [1st American ed.] New York: Knopf, 1967. xxiii, 294 p.: maps, 32
plates (incl. ports.); 22 cm. (The History of human society) 1. Greece —
Civilization — To 146 B.C. I. T.
DF78.A5 1967b   913.3/8/03   LC 66-19367

Detienne, Marcel.   3.2545
[Ruses d'intelligence. English] Cunning intelligence in Greek culture and
society / Marcel Detienne and Jean–Pierre Vernant; translated from the French
by Janet Lloyd. — Hassocks [Eng.]: Harvester Press; Atlantic Highlands, N.J.:
Humanities Press, c1978. 337 p.; 24 cm. — (European philosophy and the
human sciences.) Translation of: Les ruses d'intelligence. Includes index.
1. Philosophy, Ancient 2. Reasoning 3. Greece — Intellectual life I. Vernant,
Jean Pierre. II. T. III. Series.
DF78.D4613   938 19   LC 80-154770   ISBN 0391007408

Donlan, Walter.   3.2546
The aristocratic ideal in ancient Greece: attitudes of superiority from Homer to
the end of the fifth century B.C. / by Walter Donlan. — Lawrence, Kan.:
Coronado Press, 1980. xiv, 222 p.; 22 cm. 1. Attitude (Psychology) — Greece.
2. Aristocracy 3. Greece — Civilization — To 146 B.C. I. T.
DF78.D66   938 19   LC 81-167664   ISBN 0872911403

Ehrenberg, Victor, 1891-.   • 3.2547
Society and civilization in Greece and Rome. — Cambridge: Published for
Oberlin College by Harvard University Press, 1965 [c1964] xiv, 106 p.: ill. —
(Martin classical lectures. v.18) 1. Greece — Social life and customs 2. Rome
— Social life and customs. I. T. II. Series.
DF78.E35   LC 64-19580

Flacelière, Robert, 1904-.   • 3.2548
[Vie quotidienne en Grece au siecle de Pericles. English] Daily life in Greece at
the time of Pericles / Translated from the French by Peter Green. [1st
American ed.] New York: Macmillan, 1965. xvi, 310 p.: ill., maps; 22 cm.
(Daily life series) 1. Greece — Social life and customs I. T.
DF78.F5513 1965   913.8   LC 65-13591

Fuks, Alexander, 1917-.   3.2549
Social conflict in ancient Greece / by Alexander Fuks. — Jerusalem: Magness
Press, the Hebrew University; Leiden: E.J. Brill, 1984. 363 p.; 25 cm. Includes
index. 1. Greece — Social conditions — To 146 B.C. 2. Greece — Economic
conditions — To 146 B.C. I. T.
DF78.F84 1984   303.6/0938 19   LC 84-239502   ISBN 9652234664

Gernet, Louis, 1882-.   3.2550
[Anthropologie de la Grèce antique. English] The anthropology of ancient
Greece / Louis Gernet; translated by John Hamilton and Blaise Nagy. —
Baltimore: Johns Hopkins University Press, c1981. xiii, 378 p.; 24 cm.
Translation of: Anthropologie de la Grèce antique. 1. Mythology, Greek —
Addresses, essays, lectures. 2. Philosophy, Ancient — Addresses, essays,

lectures. 3. Greece — Civilization — To 146 B.C. — Addresses, essays, lectures. 4. Greece — Religion — Addresses, essays, lectures. I. T.
DF78.G5313   938 19   *LC* 81-47598   *ISBN* 0801821126

Momigliano, Arnaldo.   3.2551
Alien wisdom: the limits of Hellenization / Arnaldo Momigliano. — Cambridge; New York: Cambridge University Press, 1975. 174 p.; 23 cm. 1. Greece — Civilization — To 146 B.C. — Addresses, essays, lectures. I. T.
DF78.M6   938   *LC* 75-10237   *ISBN* 0521208769

Vernant, Jean Pierre.   3.2552
Myth and society in ancient Greece / Jean-Pierre Vernant; translated from the French by Janet Lloyd. Sussex: Harvester Press; Atlantic Highlands, N.J.: Humanities Press, 1980. x, 242 p.; 23 cm. (European philosophy and the human sciences) 'First published in France as Mythe et société en Grèce ancienne, Editions Maspero, 1974.' 1. Mythology, Greek 2. Greece — Social life and customs 3. Greece — Social conditions I. T.
DF78.V4713x   *ISBN* 0855279834

Vernant, Jean Pierre.   3.2553
[Origines de la pensée grecque. English] The origins of Greek thought / Jean-Pierre Vernant. — Ithaca, N.Y.: Cornell University Press, 1982. 144 p.; 23 cm. Translation of: Les origines de la pensée grecque. Includes index. 1. Philosophy, Ancient 2. Greece — Civilization — To 146 B.C. I. T.
DF78.V4813 1982   938 19   *LC* 81-15247   *ISBN* 0801410045

DF81-90 Politics

Adcock, Frank Ezra, Sir, 1886-1968.   3.2554
Diplomacy in ancient Greece / Sir Frank Adcock, D. J. Mosley. — New York: St. Martin's Press, 1975. 287 p.: maps; 23 cm. — (Aspects of Greek and Roman life) 1. Greece — Politics and government — To 146 B.C. 2. Greece — Foreign relations — To 146 B.C. I. Mosley, Derek J., joint author. II. T. III. Series.
DF81.A3 1975b   327.38   *LC* 74-30066

Whitehead, David, Ph. D.   3.2555
The demes of Attica, 508/7–ca. 250 B.C.: a political and social study / by David Whitehead. — Princeton, N.J.: Princeton University Press, c1986. xxvii, 485 p.: map; 25 cm. Includes indexes. 1. Local government — Attikē. 2. Greece — Politics and government — To 146 B.C. 3. Attikē (Greece) — Politics and government. 4. Attikē (Greece) — Social conditions. I. T.
DF82.W47 1986   938 19   *LC* 85-42709   *ISBN* 0691094128

Meritt, Benjamin Dean, 1899-.   • 3.2556
The Athenian tribute lists / by Benjamin Dean Meritt, H.T. Wade-Gery [and] Malcolm Francis McGregor. — Cambridge, Mass.: Harvard University Press, [1939-. v.: ill., plates; 30-36 cm. 'Published for the American School of Classical Studies at Athens.' Imprint varies: v.2-4 published at Princeton, N. J. for the American School of Classical Studies at Athens. 1. Taxation — Greece — Athens. 2. Inscriptions, Greek — Greece — Athens. I. Wade-Gery, Henry Theodore. II. McGregor, Malcolm Francis, 1910- III. American School of Classical Studies at Athens. IV. T.
DF83.M415   *LC* 39-6671

Jones, A. H. M. (Arnold Hugh Martin), 1904-1970.   • 3.2557
The cities of the eastern Roman provinces. Rev. by Michael Avi-Yonah [and others] 2d ed. Oxford [Eng.] Clarendon Press, 1971. xvii, 595 p. fold. maps. 25 cm. 1. Cities and towns, Ancient 2. Hellenism 3. Rome — Provinces — Administration. 4. Greece — Colonies I. T.
DF85.J6 1971   938/.009/732   *LC* 74-25037

Jones, A. H. M. (Arnold Hugh Martin), 1904-1970.   • 3.2558
The Greek city from Alexander to Justinian, by A. H. M. Jones ... Oxford, The Clarendon press, 1940. x, 393, [1] p. 26 cm. 'By the 'Greek city' I mean not only cities Greek by origin and blood, but any community organized on the Greek model and using Greek for its official language.'—Pref. 1. Cities and towns, Ancient 2. Cities and towns — Greece. 3. Municipal government — Greece. 4. Municipal government — Rome I. T.
DF85.J615   352.038   *LC* 40-29459

Griffith, Guy Thompson.   • 3.2559
The mercenaries of the Hellenistic world / by G. T. Griffith. — Cambridge: University Press, 1935. x, 340 p.; 22 cm. ERIN, cop. 1, has imprint: Groningen, Bouma's Boekhuis N.V. Publishers, 1968. Microfilm-xerography reprint. Includes bibliography. I. T.
DF89 G7

DF91-129 Social Life. Customs

De Ste. Croix, G. E. M. (Geoffrey Ernest Maurice)   3.2560
The class struggle in the ancient Greek world: from the archaic age to the Arab conquests / G.E.M. de Ste. Croix. — Ithaca, N.Y.: Cornell University Press, 1981. xi, 732 p., [1] leaf of plates: col. ill.; 26 cm. Includes indexes. 1. Social classes — Greece — History. 2. Slavery — Greece — History. 3. Greece — Social life and customs 4. Greece — Social conditions I. T.
DF91.D4   305.5/09495 19   *LC* 81-66650   *ISBN* 0801414423

Kurtz, Donna C.   • 3.2561
Greek burial customs [by] Donna C. Kurtz and John Boardman. — Ithaca, N.Y.: Cornell University Press, [1971] 384 p.: illus., maps, plans.; 23 cm. — (Aspects of Greek and Roman life) 1. Funeral rites and ceremonies — Greece. I. Boardman, John, 1927- joint author. II. T. III. Series.
DF101.K87 1971   393   *LC* 74-150980   *ISBN* 0801406439

Parke, H. W. (Herbert William), 1903-.   3.2562
Festivals of the Athenians / H. W. Parke. — Ithaca, N.Y.: Cornell University Press, 1977. 208 p., [16] leaves of plates: ill.; 23 cm. (Aspects of Greek and Roman life) Includes index. 1. Festivals — Greece. 2. Festivals — Greece — Athens. 3. Athens (Greece) — Social life and customs. 4. Greece — Religious life and customs. 5. Greece — Social life and customs I. T. II. Series.
DF123.P37   394.2/0938/5   *LC* 76-12819   *ISBN* 0801410541

DF207-241 HISTORY

DF209-212 Sources. Historiography

Brown, Truesdell Sparhawk, 1906- ed.   • 3.2563
Ancient Greece, edited by Truesdell S. Brown. [New York] Free Press of Glencoe [c1965] viii, 262 p. 21 cm. (Sources in Western civilization, 2) 1. Greece — History — Sources. 2. Greece — Civilization — To 146 B.C. I. T. II. Series.
DF209.5.B7   913.38   *LC* 65-11889

Hill, George Francis, Sir, 1867-1948. comp.   • 3.2564
Sources for Greek history between the Persian and Peloponnesian wars. New ed. by R. Meiggs and A. Andrewes. Oxford: Clarendon Press, 1951. xx, 426 p.; 23 cm. 1. Greece — History — Sources. I. T.
DF209.5.H65 1951   938.04   *LC* 52-6068

Tod, Marcus Niebuhr, 1878- ed.   • 3.2565
A selection of Greek historical inscriptions. — Oxford, Clarendon Press, 1933-48. 2 v. 23 cm. Bibliography: v. 1, p. [xiii]—xviii; v. 2, p. [ix]—xi. 1. Inscriptions, Greek 2. Greece — Hist. — Sources. I. T.
DF209.5.T5   938   *LC* 33-15667

Brown, Truesdell Sparhawk, 1906-.   3.2566
The Greek historians / [by] Truesdell S. Brown. — Lexington, Mass.: Heath, [1973] 208 p.: ill.; 23 cm. — (Civilization and society) 1. Historians — Greece. 2. History, Ancient — Historiography. 3. Greece — Historiography. I. T.
DF211.B7   938/.007/2022   *LC* 72-13903   *ISBN* 0669838810

Bury, J. B. (John Bagnell), 1861-1927.   • 3.2567
The ancient Greek historians. New York, Dover Publications [1958] 281 p. 21 cm. 1. Greece — Historiography. I. T.
DF211.B8 1958   938.007   *LC* 58-11272

Gomme, A. W. (Arnold Wycombe)   • 3.2568
The Greek attitude to poetry and history. Berkeley, University of California Press, 1954. vi, [2], 190 p. front. 24 cm. (Sather classical lectures. v. 27) 1. Greece — History — Historiography. I. T. II. Series.
DF211.G65   *LC* 54-6471

Jacoby, Felix, 1876-.   • 3.2569
Atthis: the local chronicles of ancient Athens. — Oxford: Clarendon Press, 1949. vi, 431 p.; 25 cm. Bibliographical references included in 'Notes' (p. [227]-398). 1. Greece — Hist. — Historiography. I. T.
DF211.J3   938.007   *LC* 50-722

Pearson, Lionel Ignacius Cusack.   • 3.2570
The local historians of Attica, by Lionel Pearson. — Westport, Conn.: Greenwood Press, [1972] xii, 167 p.; 22 cm. Reprint of the 1942 ed., which was issued as no. 11 of Philological monographs. A revision of the author's thesis, Yale, 1939. 1. Historians — Greece. 2. Greece — Historiography. I. T.
DF211.P4 1972   938/.5/0072   *LC* 71-152621   *ISBN* 0837160200

Starr, Chester G., 1914-.   3.2571
The awakening of the Greek historical spirit, by Chester G. Starr. [1st ed.] New York, Knopf, 1968. xii, 157, iii p. illus. 22 cm. 1. Greece — Historiography. 2. Greece — Civilization — To 146 B.C. I. T.
DF211.S7   938/.02/072   LC 68-12679

Pearson, Lionel Ignacius Cusack.   • 3.2572
Early Ionian historians. Oxford Clarendon Press 1939. 240p. 1. Greek historians I. T.
DF212 A2 P4

DF213–217 General Works

Davies, John Kenyon.   3.2573
Democracy and classical Greece / J. K. Davies. — Hassocks [Eng.]: Harvester Press; Atlantic Highlands, N. J.: Humanities Press, 1978. 284 p., [4] leaves of plates: ill.; 23 cm. — (Fontana history of the ancient world) Includes index. 1. Greece — History — To 146 B.C. I. T.
DF214.D37 1978   938   LC 79-302314   ISBN 0391007661

Bury, John Bagnell.   • 3.2574
A history of Greece to the death of Alexander the Great / J. B. Bury. — 3d ed. / rev. by Russell Meiggs. — London: Macmillan, 1959. 925 p.: ill., maps; 26 cm. Includes index. 1. Greece — History — To 146 B.C. I. Meiggs, Russell. II. T.
DF214   DF214 D4 1963.   938

Forrest, William George Grieve.   3.2575
The emergence of Greek democracy, 800–400 B.C. [by] W. G. Forrest. — New York: McGraw-Hill, [1966] 254 p.: ill., maps (part col.); 19 cm. — (World university library) 1. Greece — History I. T.
DF214.F6   938   LC 65-23825

Grote, George, 1794-1871.   • 3.2576
A history of Greece: from the earliest period to the close of the generation contemporary with Alexander the Great / by George Grote. London: Dent, [1906]. 12 v.: ill.; 19 cm. 1. Greece — History — To 146 B.C. I. T.
DF214.G9 1971   938   LC 75-137236   ISBN 0404029507

Hammond, N. G. L. (Nicholas Geoffrey Lemprière), 1907-.   3.2577
A history of Greece to 322 B.C. / by N.G.L. Hammond. — 3rd ed. — Oxford [Oxfordshire]: Clarendon Press; New York: Oxford University Press, 1986. xxi, 691 p., [13] p. of plates: ill., maps; 22 cm. Includes index. 1. Greece — History — To 146 B.C. I. T.
DF214.H28 1986   938 19   LC 86-5222   ISBN 0198730969

Sealey, Raphael.   3.2578
A history of the Greek city states, ca. 700–338 B.C. / Raphael Sealey. — Berkeley: University of California Press, c1976. xxi, 516 p.: ill.; 24 cm. — (Campus; 165) 1. City-states — Greece — History. 2. Greece — History — To 146 B.C. I. T.
DF214.S45   938   LC 75-27934

DF220–241 By Period

DF220–221 Mythical, Minoan, Mycenaean Ages

Chadwick, John, 1920-.   3.2579
The Mycenaean world / John Chadwick. Cambridge [Eng.]; New York: Cambridge University Press, 1976. xvii, 201 p.: ill.; 25 cm. Includes index. 1. Civilization, Mycenaean I. T.
DF220.C43   938/.01   LC 75-36021   ISBN 0521210771

Coldstream, J. N. (John Nicolas), 1927-.   3.2580
Geometric Greece / J. N. Coldstream; [maps by Kenneth Clarke]. — New York: St. Martin's Press, 1977. 405 p.: ill.; 25 cm. 1. Greece — Civilization 2. Civilization, Homeric 3. Greece, Modern — Antiquities. I. T.
DF220.C58 1977   938   LC 77-78085   ISBN 0312323654

Desborough, Vincent Robin d'Arba.   3.2581
The Greek dark ages / [by] V. R. d'A. Desborough. — New York: St. Martin's Press, [1972] 388 p.: ill.; 25 cm. 1. Civilization, Aegean I. T.
DF220.D44 1972   913.38/03/1   LC 79-180736

Desborough, Vincent Robin d'Arba.   • 3.2582
The last Mycenaeans and their successors: an archaeological survey, c. 1200–c. 1000 B.C. / by V.R. d'A. Desborough. — Oxford: Clarendon, 1964. xviii, 288 p.: ill., maps. 1. Civilization, Mycenaean 2. Mycenae (Ancient city) I. T.
DF220.D45   913.391   LC 64-1295

Dunbabin, Thomas James.   • 3.2583
The Greeks and their eastern neighbours: studies in the relations between Greece and the countries of the near east in the eighth and seventh centuries B.C. / by T. J. Dunbabin; with a foreword by Sir John Beazley , edited by John Boardman. — London: Society for the Promotion of Hellenic Studies, 1957. 96 p.: ill., map, port. (Society for the Promotion of Hellenic Studies, London. Supplementary paper; no. 8) Correction slip mounted on t.p. List of the published works of T. J. Dunbabin: p.[88]-91. 1. Greece — Relations — Middle East 2. Middle East — Relations — Greece I. T.
DF220 D77 1957

Hooker, J. T.   3.2584
Mycenaean Greece / J. T. Hooker. — London; Boston: Routledge & K. Paul, 1977 (c1976). xiii, 316 p.: ill.; 22 cm. — (States and cities of ancient Greece) Includes index. 1. Civilization, Mycenaean I. T.
DF220.H65   938/.01   LC 77-353999   ISBN 0710083793

McDonald, William A. (William Andrew), 1913-.   • 3.2585
Progress into the past; the rediscovery of Mycenaean civilization [by] William A. McDonald. New York, Macmillan [1967] xx, 476 p. illus., maps, plans, ports. 24 cm. 1. Civilization, Mycenaean 2. Greece — Antiquities I. T.
DF220.M23   913.38/8/03   LC 67-19952

Palmer, Leonard Robert, 1906-.   • 3.2586
Mycenaeans and Minoans: Aegean prehistory in the light of the Linear B tablets / by Leonard R. Palmer. — 2d ed., substantially rev. and enl. — New York: Knopf, 1965. 369 p.: ill.; 22 cm. 1. Civilization, Mycenaean 2. Crete — Antiquities I. T.
DF220.P3 1965   LC 64-19093

Taylour, William, Lord, 1904-.   3.2587
The Mycenaeans / Lord William Taylour. — Rev. ed. — New York, N.Y.: Thames and Hudson, 1983. 180 p.: ill.; 25 cm. — (Ancient peoples and places) Includes index. 1. Civilization, Mycenaean I. T.
DF220.T39 1983   LC 82-50813

Vermeule, Emily.   • 3.2588
Greece in the bronze age. — Chicago: University of Chicago Press, [1964] xix, 406 p.: illus., maps, 48 plates.; 25 cm. 1. Bronze age — Greece. 2. Civilization, Mycenaean I. T.
DF220.V4   913.38   LC 64-23427

DF221 Special Localities

Kelly, Thomas, 1929-.   3.2589
A history of Argos to 500 B.C. / Thomas Kelly. — Minneapolis: University of Minnesota Press, 1977 (c1976). viii, 214 p., [1] leaf of plates: maps; 23 cm. — (Minnesota monographs in the humanities; v. 9) Includes index. 1. Civilization, Mycenaean — Greece — Argos. 2. Argos (Greece) — History. I. T. II. Series.
DF221.A8 K44 1976   938/.8   LC 76-11500   ISBN 0816607907

Betancourt, Philip P., 1936-.   3.2590
The history of Minoan pottery / by Philip P. Betancourt. — Princeton, N.J.: Princeton University Press, c1985. xxi, 226 p., [32] p. of plates: ill.; 27 cm. Includes indexes. 1. Pottery, Minoan 2. Pottery — Expertising 3. Pottery dating 4. Crete — Antiquities 5. Greece — Antiquities I. T.
DF221.C8 B564 1985   738.3/0939/18 19   LC 84-22305   ISBN 0691035792

Evans, Arthur, Sir, 1851-1941.   • 3.2591
The Palace of Minos: a comparative account of the successive stages of the early Cretan civilization as illustrated by the discoveries at Knossos / [Sir Arthur Evans]. — New York: Biblo and Tannen, 1964. 4 v. in 6.: illus. (part col.) 2 fold. col. maps, plans.; 27 cm. Part of illustrative matter folded in pocket, v.3-6. 1. Greece — Civilization 2. Minoans 3. Art, Cretan 4. Crete — Antiquities I. T.
DF221.C8 E75 1964   913.3918

Hutchinson, Richard Wyatt, 1894-.   • 3.2592
Prehistoric Crete. — [Harmondsworth]: Penguin Books [1962] 373 p.: ill.; 18 cm. — (Pelican books, A501) 1. Crete — Antiq. I. T.
DF221.C8H8   913.3918   LC 62-6461

Willetts, R. F., 1915-.   3.2593
The civilization of ancient Crete / R. F. Willetts. — Berkeley: University of California Press, 1978, c1977. 279 p., [8] leaves of plates: ill.; 24 cm. Includes indexes. 1. Crete — Civilization I. T.
DF221.C8 W54 1977b   939.1/8   LC 76-55575   ISBN 0520034066

Doumas, Christos.   3.2594
Thera, Pompeii of the ancient Aegean: excavations at Akrotiri, 1967–79 / Christos G. Doumas. — New York, N.Y.: Thames and Hudson, 1983. 168 p.: 123 ill. (some col.); 26 cm. (New aspects of antiquity) Includes index. 1. Excavations (Archaeology) — Greece — Thera Island. 2. Excavations (Archaeology) — Greece — Akrōtērion. 3. Thera Island (Greece) —

Antiquities. 4. Akrŏtĕrion (Greece) — Antiquities. 5. Greece — Antiquities
I. T. II. Series.
DF221.T38 D68 1983   939/.15 19   *LC* 81-86685   *ISBN*
0500390169

Blegen, Carl William, 1887-.   • 3.2595
Troy and the Trojans. New York, Praeger [1963] 240 p. illus., map, plans. 21
cm. (Ancient peoples and places, v. 33) (Books that matter) 1. Troy (Ancient
city) I. T.
DF221.T8 B55   939.21   *LC* 63-8040

DF222–228 775–431 B.C

Andrewes, A.   • 3.2596
The Greek tyrants. — London: Hutchinson's University Library, 1956. 167 p.:
map on lining papers; 20 cm. — (Hutchinson's University library: Classical
historyand literature.) 1. Dictators 2. Greece — History I. T. II. Series.
DF222.A6   *LC* 56-8629   *ISBN* 0090295633

Burn, A. R. (Andrew Robert), 1902-.   • 3.2597
The lyric age of Greece / by Andrew Robert Burn. — New York: St. Martin's
Press, 1960. xvi, 422 p.: maps.; 21 cm. 1. Greece — Civilization I. T.
DF222.B85 1960   913.3/8/03   *LC* 60-13276

Snodgrass, Anthony M.   3.2598
Archaic Greece: the age of experiment / Anthony Snodgrass. — London: J.M.
Dent, 1980. 236 p. [12] leaves of plates: ill.; 24 cm. Includes index. 1. Greece —
History — To 146 B.C. I. T.
DF222.S66   938/.01 19   *LC* 82-464126   *ISBN* 0460043382

Jeffery, Lilian Hamilton.   3.2599
Archaic Greece: the city–states, c. 700–500 B.C. / L. H. Jeffery. — New York:
St. Martin's Press, 1976. 272 p., [16] leaves of plates: ill.; 25 cm. 1. City-states
— Greece. 2. Greece — Politics and government — To 146 B.C. I. T.
DF222.2.J44 1976   320.9/38/02   *LC* 75-10758

Woodhouse, William John, 1866-1937.   • 3.2600
Solon the liberator: a study of the agrarian problem in Attika in the seventh
century / by W.J. Woodhouse. — New York: Octagon Books, 1965. xvi, 218 p.;
21 cm. 1. Solon. 2. Land tenure — Greece. 3. Peasantry — Greece. 4. Attika
— History. I. T.
DF224.S7 W6 1965   *LC* 65-16783

Burn, A. R. (Andrew Robert), 1902-.   • 3.2601
Persia and the Greeks: the defence of the West, c. 546–478 B.C. New York, St.
Martin's Press, 1962 [i.e. 1963] xvi, 586 p. maps. 23 cm. 1. Greece — History
— Persian Wars, 500-449 B.C. I. T.
DF225.B8   938.03   *LC* 62-21076

Hignett, Charles.   • 3.2602
Xerxes' invasion of Greece. — Oxford: Clarendon Press, 1963. xii, 496 p.: 8
maps; 23 cm. Bibliography: p. [469]-472. 1. Greece — Hist. — Persian Wars,
500-449 B.C. I. T.
DF225.H5   938.03   *LC* 63-2777

Burn, A. R. (Andrew Robert), 1902-.   • 3.2603
Pericles and Athens. New York, Macmillan, 1949. xxv, 253 p. front., maps
(part col.) 18 cm. 1. Pericles, 499-429 B. C. 2. Athens (Greece) — History
I. T.
DF227.B8   *LC* 49-10369

Hornblower, Simon.   3.2604
The Greek world, 479–323 BC / Simon Hornblower. — London; New York:
Methuen, 1983. xi, 354 p.: maps; 23 cm. (Classical civilizations.) Includes
index. 1. Greece — History — Athenian supremacy, 479-431 B.C. 2. Greece
— History — Peloponnesian War, 431-404 B.C. 3. Greece — History —
Spartan and Theban Supremacies, 404-362 B.C. 4. Greece — History —
Macedonian Expansion, 359-323 B.C. I. T. II. Title: Greek world, 479-323
B.C. III. Series.
DF227.H67 1983   938 19   *LC* 83-13062   *ISBN* 0416749909

Meiggs, Russell.   3.2605
The Athenian empire / Russell Meiggs. — Oxford: Clarendon Press; New
York: Oxford University Press, c1972. xvi, 620 p.: maps; 22 cm. Includes
indexes. 1. Greece — History — Athenian supremacy, 479-431 B.C. 2. Athens
(Greece) — History 3. Greece — History — Peloponnesian War, 431-404 B.C.
I. T.
DF227.M44 1979   938/.04   *LC* 80-456017   *ISBN* 0198148437

Podlecki, Anthony J.   3.2606
The life of Themistocles: a critical survey of the literary and archaeological
evidence / A. J. Podlecki. — Montreal: McGill-Queen's University Press, 1975.
xiii, 250 p., [4] leaves of plates: ill.; 26 cm. Includes indexes. 1. Themistocles,
ca. 524-ca. 459 B.C. I. T.
DF228.T4 P6   938/.03/0924 B   *LC* 73-93001   *ISBN* 0773501851

DF229–232 431–362 B.C. PELOPONNESIAN WAR

Thucydides.   3.2607
[History of the Peloponnesian War. English] The Peloponnesian War /
Thucydides; the Crawley translation revised, with an introduction, by T.E.
Wick. — 1st ed. — New York: Modern Library, c1982. xxxi, 574 p.: maps; 19
cm. (Modern Library college editions) Translation of: History of the
Peloponnesian War. Includes index. 1. Greece — History — Peloponnesian
War, 431-404 B.C. I. Crawley, Richard, 1840-1893. II. Wick, T. E. III. T.
DF229.T55 C7 1982   938/.05 19   *LC* 82-2294   *ISBN* 0394329783

Thucydides.   3.2608
[History of the Peloponnesian War Selections. English. 1974] The speeches and
the military harangues, by H. F. Harding. [Lawrence, Kan.] Coronado Press,
1973. vi, 373 p. maps. 22 cm. Selections from the author's De bello
peloponnesiaco. I. Harding, Harold Friend, 1903- ed. II. T.
DF229.T55 H37   938/.007/2024   *LC* 73-85648   *ISBN* 0872910601

Edmunds, Lowell.   3.2609
Chance and intelligence in Thucydides / Lowell Edmunds. — Cambridge,
Mass.: Harvard University Press, 1975. 243 p.; 22 cm. — (Loeb classical
monographs) A rewriting of the author's thesis. Includes index. 1. Thucydides.
2. Pericles, 499-429 B.C. 3. Fortune 4. Intellect 5. History — Philosophy
6. Greece — History — Athenian supremacy, 479-431 B.C. I. T. II. Series.
DF229.T6 E35 1975   938/.007/2024   *LC* 74-75311   *ISBN*
0674107403

Finley, John Huston, 1904-.   • 3.2610
Thucydides. — Ann Arbor, Michigan: Univ. of Michigan Press, [1963,c1942].
344 p. (Ann Arbor paperbacks) 1. Thucydides. I. T.
DF229.T6 F5x   888

Pouncey, Peter R.   3.2611
The necessities of war: a study of Thucydides' pessimism / Peter R. Pouncey. —
New York: Columbia University Press, 1980. xv, 195 p.; 24 cm. Includes index.
1. Thucydides. History of the Peloponnesian War 2. Greece — History —
Peloponnesian War, 431-404 B.C. I. T.
DF229.T6 P68   938/.0072024   *LC* 80-16887   *ISBN* 0231049943

De Ste. Croix, G. E. M. (Geoffrey Ernest Maurice)   3.2612
The origins of the Peloponnesian War / [by] G. E. M. de Ste. Croix. — Ithaca,
N.Y.: Cornell University Press [1972] xii, 444 p.: front.; 26 cm. 1. Greece —
History — Peloponnesian War, 431-404 B.C. 2. Greece — Historiography.
I. T.
DF229.2.D46 1972   938/.05   *LC* 72-627   *ISBN* 0801407192

Kagan, Donald.   • 3.2613
The outbreak of the Peloponnesian War. — Ithaca [N.Y.]: Cornell University
Press, [1969] xvi, 420 p.; 24 cm. 1. Greece — History — Peloponnesian War,
431-404 B.C. I. T.
DF229.2.K3   938/.05   *LC* 69-18212   *ISBN* 0801405017

Kagan, Donald.   3.2614
The Archidamian War / Donald Kagan. — Ithaca: Cornell University Press,
1974. 392 p.: maps; 24 cm. Includes index. 1. Thucydides. History of the
Peloponnesian War 2. Greece — History — Peloponnesian War, 431-404 B.C.
I. T.
DF229.3.K33   938/.05   *LC* 74-4901   *ISBN* 080140889X

Kagan, Donald.   3.2615
The Peace of Nicias and the Sicilian Expedition / Donald Kagan. — Ithaca:
Cornell University Press, 1981. 393 p.: maps; 24 cm. Includes indexes.
1. Nicias. 2. Sicilian Expedition, 415-413 B.C. 3. Greece — History —
Peloponnesian War, 431-404 B.C. I. T.
DF229.57.K33   938/.05 19   *LC* 81-3150   *ISBN* 0801413672

Buckler, John.   3.2616
The Theban hegemony, 371–362 BC / John Buckler. — Cambridge, Mass.:
Harvard University Press, 1980. x, 339 p.: ill.; 24 cm. (Harvard historical
studies. v. 98) Includes index. 1. Greece — History — Spartan and Theban
Supremacies, 404-362 B.C. 2. Thebes (Greece) — History. I. T. II. Series.
DF231.2.B8   938/.06   *LC* 79-24928   *ISBN* 0674876458

Cargill, Jack.   3.2617
The Second Athenian League: empire or free alliance? / Jack Cargill. —
Berkeley: University of California Press, c1981. xvii, 215 p.; 24 cm. 1. Delian
League, Second, 4th cent. B.C. 2. Greece — History — Spartan and Theban
Supremacies, 404-362 B.C. 3. Greece — History — Macedonian Expansion,
359-323 B.C. I. T.
DF231.2.C37 1981   938/.06 19   *LC* 80-22532   *ISBN* 0520040694

Hamilton, Charles Daniel, 1940-.   3.2618
Sparta's bitter victories: politics and diplomacy in the Corinthian War / Charles
D. Hamilton. — Ithaca, N.Y.: Cornell University Press, 1979. 346 p.; 24 cm.
Includes index. 1. Greece — History — Corinthian War, 395-386 B.C.

2. Greece — History — Peloponnesian War, 431-404 B.C. — Influence.
3. Sparta (Ancient city) — History I. T.
DF231.4.H35   938/.06   *LC* 78-58045   *ISBN* 0801411580

Heisserer, A. J.   **3.2619**
Alexander the Great and the Greeks: the epigraphic evidence / by A. J. Heisserer. — 1st ed. — Norman: University of Oklahoma Press, c1980. xxvii, 252 p.: ill.; 26 cm. Includes index. 1. Alexander, the Great, 356-323 B.C. 2. Inscriptions, Greek 3. Greece — History — Macedonian expansion, 359-323 B.C. — Sources. 4. Greece — History — Macedonian expansion, 359-323 B.C. — Historiography. I. T.
DF232.5.H44   938/.07   *LC* 79-6712   *ISBN* 0806116129

DF233–241 339 B.C.–476 A.D

Cawkwell, George.   **3.2620**
Philip of Macedon / George Cawkwell. — London; Boston: Faber & Faber, 1978. 215 p.: maps; 23 cm. Includes index. 1. Philip II, King of Macedonia, 382-336 B.C. 2. Macedonia — Kings and rulers — Biography. 3. Greece — Kings and rulers — Biography. I. T.
DF233.C38   938/.1/070924 B   *LC* 78-316519   *ISBN* 0571109586

Ellis, John R.   **3.2621**
Philip II and Macedonian imperialism / [by] J. R. Ellis. London: Thames and Hudson, 1976. 312 p.: geneal. table, maps; 23 cm. (Aspects of Greek and Roman life) Includes index. 1. Philip II, King of Macedonia, 382-336 B.C. 2. Greece — History — To 146 B.C. 3. Macedonia — History 4. Greece — Kings and rulers — Biography. I. T. II. Series.
DF233.E4   938/.1/070924   *LC* 76-380632   *ISBN* 0500400288

Jaeger, Werner Wilhelm, 1888-1961.   • **3.2622**
Demosthenes: the origin and growth of his policy. — New York, Octagon Books, 1963 [c1938] x, 273 p. 24 cm. — (Sather classical lectures. v. 13) 'The translation of this book from the German manuscript has been made by Edward Schouten Robinson.' Bibliographical references included in 'Notes' (p. 207-260) 1. Demosthenes. I. T. II. Series.
DF.J313 1963   928.8   *LC* 63-20891

Philip of Macedon / edited by Miltiades B. Hatzopoulos,   **3.2623**
Louisa D. Loukopoulos.
Athens: Ekdotike Athenon, 1980. 254 p.: ill. (some col.); 29 cm. Includes index. 1. Philip II, King of Macedonia, 382-336 B.C. 2. Macedonia — Kings and rulers — Biography. 3. Greece — Kings and rulers — Biography. I. Chatzopoulos, Miltiadēs V. II. Loukopoulou, Louiza D.
DF233.P48   938/.07/0924 B 19   *LC* 81-203694

Bosworth, A. B.   **3.2624**
A historical commentary on Arrian's History of Alexander / by A. B. Bosworth. — Oxford: Clarendon Press; New York: Oxford University Press, 1980-. v. <1>; 22 cm. Includes indexes. 1. Arrian. Anabasis. 2. Alexander, the Great, 356-323 B.C — Campaigns. I. T.
DF234.A773 B67   938/.07   *LC* 79-40885   *ISBN* 0198148283

Green, Peter, 1924-.   **3.2625**
Alexander of Macedon, 356–323 B.C.: a historical biography. — Revised and enlarged [ed.] Harmondsworth: Penguin, 1974. xxxi, 617 p.: ill.; geneal. table, maps, plans.; 19 cm. (Pelican biographies) Earlier ed. published in 1970 under title: Alexander the Great. Includes index. 1. Alexander, the Great, 356-323 B.C. I. T.
DF234.G68 1974   938/.07/0924 B   *LC* 74-166969   *ISBN* 0140216901

Hamilton, J. R.   **3.2626**
Alexander the Great / J. R. Hamilton. — Pittsburgh: University of Pittsburgh Press, 1974. 196 p.: maps (1 fold.) 1. Alexander, the Great, 356-323 B.C. I. T.
DF234.H3 1974   *LC* 73-19953   *ISBN* 0822960842

Robinson, Charles Alexander, 1900-1965.   • **3.2627**
The history of Alexander the Great. Providence, R.I., Brown University, 1953–63. Millwood, N.Y., Kraus Reprint Co., 1967-72. 2 v. 26 cm. Vol. 2 originally published by Brown University Press. Original ed. issued as v. 16 and 26 of Brown University studies. 1. Alexander, the Great, 356-323 B.C. I. T.
DF234.R663   938/.07/0924 B   *LC* 72-5737

Tarn, William Woodthorpe, Sir, 1869-1957.   **3.2628**
Alexander the Great. Cambridge [Eng.] University Press, 1948. 2 v. fold. map. 23 cm. 'Vol. I consists in the main of ... chapters XII and XIII in volume VI of the Cambridge ancient history ... carefully corrected and brought up to date.' 1. Alexander, the Great, 356-323 B.C. I. T.
DF234.T3   938.07   *LC* 48-10280

Wilcken, Ulrich.   • **3.2629**
Alexander the Great / by Ulrich Wilcken; translated by G.C. Richards; with pref., an introd. to Alexander studies, notes, and bibliography by Eugene N.

Borza. — New York: W. W. Norton, 1967. xxxi, 365 p.: map; 20 cm. 1. Macedonia — History — To 168 B.C. I. Borza, Eugene N. II. T.
DF234.W713 1967   938/.07   *LC* 67-15823   *ISBN* 0393003817

Alexander the Great: the main problems / edited by G. T.   • **3.2630**
Griffith.
Cambridge: Heffer, 1966. xii, 382 p. — (Views and controversies about classical antiquity) 1. Alexander, the Great, 356-323 B.C. I. Griffith, Guy Thompson II. Series.
DF234.2.G7 1966   DF234.2.A4 1966.   930.40924   *LC* 66-72639

Pearson, Lionel Ignacius Cusack.   **3.2631**
The lost histories of Alexander the Great / by Lionel Pearson. — [Chico, Calif.: Scholars Press], 1983. p. cm. Reprint. Originally published: Philadelphia, Pa.: American Philological Association, 1960. (Philological monographs; nr. 20) Includes index. 1. Alexander, the Great, 356-323 B.C. 2. Greece — History — Macedonian Expansion, 359-322 B.C. — Historiography. I. T.
DF234.2.P4 1983   938/.07/0924 19   *LC* 83-11709   *ISBN* 0891306412

Wheeler, Robert Eric Mortimer, Sir, 1890-.   • **3.2632**
Flames over Persepolis, turning–point in history [by] Mortimer Wheeler. New York, Reynal in association with W. Morrow [1968] 180 p. illus. (part col.), maps, plans. 26 cm. 1. Alexander, the Great, 356-323 B.C — Campaigns — Iran. 2. Alexander, the Great, 356-323 B.C — Campaigns — India. 3. Persepolis (Iran) — Destruction, 331 or 330 B.C. 4. India — Civilization — Greek influences 5. Iran — History — Macedonian Conquest, 334-325 B.C. I. T.
DF234.55.W5 1968b   935/.06   *LC* 68-25488

The Hellenistic world from Alexander to the Roman conquest: a   **3.2633**
selection of ancient sources in translation / M.M. Austin.
Cambridge; New York: Cambridge University Press, 1981. xv, 488 p.: maps; 24 cm. Includes index. 1. Greece — History — Macedonian Hegemony, 323-281 B.C. — Sources. 2. Greece — History — 281-146 B.C. — Sources. I. Austin, M. M.
DF235.A1 H44 1981   938/.08 19   *LC* 81-6136   *ISBN* 0521228298

Walbank, F. W. (Frank William), 1909-.   **3.2634**
The Hellenistic world / F.W. Walbank. — Cambridge, Mass.: Harvard University Press, 1982, c1981. 287 p., [10] p. of plates: ill.; 21 cm. Reprint. Originally published: [London]: Fontana, 1981 (Fontana history of the ancient world) 1. Hellenism 2. Greece — History — Macedonian Hegemony, 323-281 B.C. 3. Greece — History — 281-146 B.C. I. T.
DF235.W3 1982   938/.08 19   *LC* 81-20050   *ISBN* 0674387252

Macurdy, Grace Harriet, d. 1946.   • **3.2635**
Hellenistic queens: a study of woman–power in Macedonia, Seleucid Syria, and Ptolemaic Egypt / by Grace Harriet Macurdy. — Baltimore: Johns Hopkins Press, 1932. xv, 250 p. pl. (Johns Hopkins University. Studies in archaeology; ed. by David M. Robinson, No. 14) 1. Queens and Empresses 2. Seleucid dynasty 3. Egypt — History, Ancient 4. Macedonia — History I. T. II. Series.
DF235.3 M3

Rostovzeff, Michael Ivanovitch, 1870-1952.   • **3.2636**
The social & economic history of the Hellenistic world / by M. Rostovtzeff. — Oxford: Clarendon Press, 1941. 3 v.: ill., plans, ports. — 1. Greece — History 2. Greece — Social conditions 3. Greece — Economic conditions I. T.
DF235.3.R6   *LC* 41-4669

Tarn, W. W. (William Woodthorpe), 1869-1957.   **3.2637**
Antigonos Gonatas / by William Woodthorpe Tarn. — New York: Oxford University Press, 1913. xi, [1], 501 p. [1] p.: ill., incl. geneal. tables, front.; 24 cm. 1. Antigonus Gonatas, king of Macedonia, B. C. 319?-239. 2. Macedonia — History 3. Greece — History I. T.
DF237.A6 T3   *LC* a 14-3069

Walbank, F. W. (Frank William), 1909-.   • **3.2638**
Philip V of Macedon, by F. W. Walbank. [Hamden, Conn.] Archon Books, 1967. xii, 387 p. maps, 2 plates. 22 cm. First published 1940. 1. Philip V, King of Macedonia, B.C. 237-179. 2. Macedonia — History — To 168 B.C. 3. Rome — History — Republic, 265-30 B.C. I. T.
DF238.9.P5 W3 1967   938.108   *LC* 67-12981

DF251–289 LOCAL HISTORY

Boardman, John, 1927-.   **3.2639**
The Greeks overseas: their early colonies and trade / John Boardman. — New and enl. ed. — New York: Thames and Hudson, 1980. 288 p.: ill.; 25 cm. 1. Greece — Colonies — History. I. T.
DF251.B6 1980   938/.02 19   *LC* 79-66132   *ISBN* 0500250693

Cook, J. M. (John Manuel) • 3.2640
The Greeks in Ionia and the East. — New York: Praeger, [1963] 268 p.: ill.; 21 cm. — (Ancient peoples and places, v. 31) Books that matter. 1. Greeks in Asia. I. T.
DF251.C6　　　913.392　　　*LC* 63-8041

Salmon, J. B. 3.2641
Wealthy Corinth: a history of the city to 338 BC / J.B. Salmon. — Oxford: Clarendon Press; New York: Oxford University Press, 1984. xviii, 464 p., [24] p. of plates: ill.; 24 cm. Includes indexes. 1. Corinth (Greece) — History. I. T.
DF261.C65 S24 1984　　　938/.7 19　　　*LC* 83-4138　　　*ISBN* 019814833X

Willetts, R. F., 1915-. • 3.2642
Aristocratic society in ancient Crete. London, Routledge and Paul [1955] xv, 280 p. 22 cm. 1. Domestic relations — Greece — Crete. 2. Law — Greece — Crete. 3. Crete — Social life and customs. I. T.
DF261.C8 W5 1955　　　939.18　　　*LC* 56-168

Fontenrose, Joseph Eddy, 1903-. 3.2643
The Delphic oracle: its responses and operations, with a catalogue of responses / Joseph Fontenrose. — Berkeley: University of California Press, c1978. xviii, 476 p.: ill., plan; 25 cm. Errata slip inserted. Includes indexes. 1. Delphian oracle 2. Oracles I. T.
DF261.D35 F6　　　DF261D35 F58.　　　292/.3/2　　　*LC* 76-47969
　ISBN 0520033604

Parke, H. W. (Herbert William), 1903-. • 3.2644
The Delphic oracle / by H. W. Parke, D. E. W. Wormell. — Oxford: Blackwell, 1956. 2 v.; 23 cm. Revised and enlarged edition of Parke's A history of the Delphic oracle. 1. Delphian oracle I. Wormell, Donald Ernest Wilson. II. T.
DF261.D35P3 1956　　　938.3　　　*LC* A 57-3245

Mylonas, George E. (George Emmanuel), 1898-. • 3.2645
Eleusis and the Eleusinian mysteries. — Princeton N.J.: Princeton University Press, 1961. xx, 346 p.: ill., map. 1. Eleusis. 2. Eleusinian mysteries I. T.
DF261.E4 M88　　　*LC* 61-7421

Legon, Ronald P., 1941-. 3.2646
Megara, the political history of a Greek city–state to 336 B.C. / Ronald P. Legon. — Ithaca, N.Y.: Cornell University Press, 1981. 324 p.: ill.; 24 cm. Includes indexes. 1. Megara (Greece) — Politics and government. I. T.
DF261.M43 L43　　　938/.4 19　　　*LC* 80-25668　　　*ISBN* 0801413702

Cartledge, Paul. 3.2647
Sparta and Lakonia: a regional history, 1300–362 BC / Paul Cartledge. — London; Boston: Routledge & Kegan Paul, 1979. xv, 410 p.: maps; 23 cm. — (States and cities of ancient Greece) Includes index. 1. Sparta (Ancient city) — History 2. Lakōnia (Greece) — History. I. T.
DF261.S8 C37 1979　　　938.9 19　　　*LC* 79-40977　　　*ISBN* 0710003773

Forrest, William George Grieve. 3.2648
A history of Sparta, 950–192 B.C. / W. G. Forrest. — 2d ed. — London: Norton, 1980. 160 p.: maps; 23 cm. 1. Sparta (Ancient city) — History I. T.
DF261.S8 F67 1980　　　938/.9 19

Michell, H. (Humfrey), 1883-. • 3.2649
Sparta / by H. Michell. — Cambridge: University Press, 1952. 348 p. 1. Sparta (Greece) I. T.
DF261S8 M55　　　*LC* 52-8225

Tigerstedt, Eugène Napoleon, 1907-. 3.2650
The legend of Sparta in classical antiquity. Stockholm, Almqvist & Wiksell, [1965-74] 2 v. 25 cm. (Acta Universitatis Stockholmiensis. Stockholm studies in history of literature. 9, 15) 1. Sparta in literature. 2. Sparta (Greece) — History. I. T. II. Series.
DF261.S8 T5　　　*LC* a 66-352

Roberts, J. W. 3.2651
City of Sokrates: an introduction to classical Athens / J.W. Roberts. — London; Boston: Routledge & K. Paul, 1984. xi, 265 p.: ill.; 24 cm. Includes index. 1. Athens (Greece) — Social life and customs. 2. Athens (Greece) — Social conditions. 3. Greece — Civilization — To 146 B.C. I. T.
DF275.R62 1984　　　938/.5 19　　　*LC* 83-19142　　　*ISBN* 0710098057

Mossé, Claude, docteur ès lettres. 3.2652
Athens in decline, 404–86 B.C. / translated from the French by Jean Stewart. — London; Boston: Routledge & K. Paul, [1973] 181 p.: ill.; 22 cm. 1. Athens (Greece) — Politics and government. I. T.
DF277.M713　　　913.3/85　　　*LC* 73-81598　　　*ISBN* 0710076495

Connor, W. Robert (Walter Robert), 1934-. 3.2653
The new politicians of fifth–century Athens [by] W. Robert Connor. Princeton, N.J., Princeton University Press, 1971. xii, 218 p. 23 cm. 1. Athens (Greece) — Politics and government. I. T.
DF285.C67　　　320.9/38/04　　　*LC* 70-141502　　　*ISBN* 0691035393

Ferguson, William Scott, 1875-1954. • 3.2654
Hellenistic Athens; an historical essay. New York, H. Fertig, 1969. xviii, 487 p. 24 cm. Reprint of the 1911 ed. 1. Athens (Greece) — History I. T.
DF285.F4 1969　　　938　　　*LC* 68-9652

DF501–649 Medieval Greece. Byzantine Empire (323–1453)

Byzantium: church, society, and civilization seen through 3.2655
contemporary eyes / [compiled by] Deno John Geanakoplos.
Chicago: University of Chicago Press, 1984. xxxix, 485 p.: ill.; 25 cm. Includes index. 1. Byzantine Empire — History — Sources. I. Geanakoplos, Deno John.
DF503.B983 1984　　　949.5 19　　　*LC* 83-4806　　　*ISBN* 0226284603

Cameron, Averil. 3.2656
Procopius and the sixth century / Averil Cameron. — Berkeley: University of California Press, c1985. xiii, 297 p.: ill.; 24 cm. (Transformation of the classical heritage. 10) Includes indexes. 1. Procopius. 2. Byzantine Empire — Intellectual life. 3. Byzantine Empire — History — Justinian I, 527-565 — Historiography. I. T. II. Series.
DF505.7.P7 C35　　　907/.2024 19　　　*LC* 84-28020　　　*ISBN* 0520055179

Diehl, Charles, 1859-1944. • 3.2657
Byzantine portraits / translated by Harold Bell. — New York: Knopf, 1927. vii, 342 p.; 23 cm. Plan in pocket at end of vol. 1. Byzantine Empire — Civilization 2. Byzantine Empire — Court and courtiers 3. Women in the Byzantine empire I. T.
DF506.D52

Mango, Cyril A. 3.2658
Byzantium, the empire of New Rome / Cyril Mango. — New York: Scribner, 1981 (c1980). xiii, 334 p., [12] leaves of plates: ill.; 24 cm. — (History of civilization) Includes index. 1. Byzantine Empire — Civilization I. T.
DF521.M36　　　949.5 19　　　*LC* 80-5870　　　*ISBN* 0684167689

Diehl, Charles, 1859-1944. • 3.2659
[Byzance: grandeur et décadence. English] Byzantium: greatness and decline. Translated from the French by Naomi Walford. With introd. and bibliography by Peter Charanis. New Brunswick, N.J., Rutgers University Press, 1957. xviii, 366 p. illus., facsims. 25 cm. (Rutgers Byzantine series) 1. Byzantine Empire — History 2. Byzantine Empire — Civilization I. T.
DF531.D42　　　949.5　　　*LC* 57-6223

Nicol, Donald MacGillivray. 3.2660
Church and society in the last centuries of Byzantium / Donald M. Nicol. — Cambridge [Eng.]; New York: Cambridge University Press, 1979. 162 p.; 22 cm. (The Birkbeck lectures; 1977) Includes index. 1. Byzantine Empire — Civilization — 1081-1453 2. Byzantine Empire — History — 1081-1453 I. T. II. Series.
DF531.N5　　　949.5/04　　　*LC* 78-72092　　　*ISBN* 0521224381

Vryonis, Speros, 1928-. 3.2661
The decline of medieval Hellenism in Asia Minor and the process of Islamization from the eleventh through the fifteenth century [by] Speros Vryonis, Jr. Berkeley, University of California Press, 1971. xvii, 532 p. illus. 24 cm. (Publications of the Center for Medieval and Renaissance Studies, UCLA, 4) 1. Hellenism 2. Byzantine Empire — Civilization — 1081-1453 3. Byzantine Empire — History — 1081-1453 4. Turkey — History. I. T.
DF545.V78　　　913.3/95/03　　　*LC* 75-94984　　　*ISBN* 0520015975

Browning, Robert, 1914-. 3.2662
Byzantium and Bulgaria: a comparative study across the early medieval frontier / Robert Browning. — Berkeley: University of California Press, [1975] 232 p.: maps; 23 cm. Includes index. 1. Byzantine Empire — Relations — Bulgaria 2. Bulgaria — Relations — Byzantine Empire I. T.
DF552.B75 1975　　　309.1/495/02　　　*LC* 73-91665　　　*ISBN* 0520026705

Cheetham, Nicolas, Sir, 1910-. 3.2663
Mediaeval Greece / Nicolas Cheetham. — New Haven: Yale University Press, 1981. viii, 341 p., [1] leaf of plates: maps; 22 cm. Includes index. 1. Greece, Medieval — History. I. T.
DF552.C48　　　949.5　　　*LC* 80-13559　　　*ISBN* 0300024215

Obolensky, Dimitri, 1918-. • 3.2664
The Byzantine commonwealth; Eastern Europe, 500–1453. New York, Praeger Publishers [1971] xiv, 445 p. illus. 25 cm. (History of civilization) 1. Byzantine Empire. 2. Byzantine Empire — Civilization 3. Balkan Peninsula —

Civilization — Byzantine influences 4. Europe, Eastern — Civilization — Byzantine influences I. T.
DF552.O25 1971b   914.95/03   *LC* 73-137892

Vasiliev, Alexander Alexandrovich, 1867-1953.   • **3.2665**
History of the Byzantine Empire, 324–1453 / A.A. Vasiliev. — 2nd English ed. rev. — Madison, Wi.: University of Wisconsin Press, 1952. — xi, 846 p.: maps, geneal tables; 26cm. Includes index. 1. Byzantine Empire — History I. T.
DF552.V3 1952   949.5   *LC* 52-13951

Ostrogorski, Georgije.   • **3.2666**
[Geschichte des byzantinischen Staates. English] History of the Byzantine state [by] George Ostrogorsky. Translated from the German by Joan Hussey. With a foreword by Peter Charanis. Rev. ed. New Brunswick, N.J., Rutgers University Press, 1969. xl, 624 p. illus., col. maps. 25 cm. (Rutgers Byzantine series) Translation of Geschichte des byzantinischen Staates. 1. Byzantine Empire — History I. T.
DF552.5.O8153 1969   949.5   *LC* 71-83571   *ISBN* 0813505992

DF553–599 Eastern Empire (323/476-1057

Procopius.   • **3.2667**
History of the wars; Secret history; and Buildings / Newly tr. edition, abridged, and with an introduction by Averil Cameron. — New York: Washington Square Press, [1967] xlii, 351 p.: maps.; 18 cm. (The Great histories series.) 1. Byzantine Empire — History — Justinian I, 525-565. I. Cameron, Averil. ed. II. T. III. Series.
DF572.P999 1967   949.501   *LC* 67-28144

Diehl, Charles, 1859-1944.   **3.2668**
[Théodora, impératrice de Byzance. English] Theodora, Empress of Byzantium. Translated by Samuel R. Rosenbaum. New York, F. Ungar Pub. Co. 1973 (c1972) xi, 204 p. illus. 22 cm. 1. Theodora, Empress, consort of Justinian I, Emperor of the East, d. 548. I. T.
DF572.5.D513   949.5/01/0924 B   *LC* 75-189879   *ISBN* 0804412308

Bury, J. B. (John Bagnell), 1861-1927.   • **3.2669**
A history of the Eastern Roman Empire from the fall of Irene to the accession of Basil I, 802–867. New York: Russell & Russell, 1965. xv, 530 p.; 23 cm. 1. Byzantine Empire — History I. T.
DF581.B8 1965   *LC* 65-18794

Toynbee, Arnold Joseph, 1889-1975.   **3.2670**
Constantine Porphyrogenitus and his world [by] Arnold Toynbee. London, New York, Oxford University Press, 1973. xix, 768, [5] p., fold. leaf. illus., 5 maps (4 col.) 25 cm. 1. Constantine VII Porphyrogenitus, Emperor of the East, 905-959. 2. Byzantine Empire — Foreign relations 3. Byzantine Empire — Economic conditions. 4. Byzantine Empire — Civilization — 527-1081 I. T.
DF591.T69 1973   914.95/03/2   *LC* 73-162209   *ISBN* 019215253X

DF600–649 1057-1453

Comnena, Anna, b. 1083.   • **3.2671**
[Alexiad. English.] The Alexiad of the Princess Anna Comnena, being the history of the reign of her father, Alexius I, Emperor of the Romans, 1081–1118 A.D. Translated by Elizabeth A. S. Dawes. New York, Barnes & Noble [1967] vii, 439 p.; 23 cm. Reprint of the 1928 ed. Translation of Alexias. 1. Alexius I Comnenus, Emperor of the East, 1048-1118. 2. Byzantine Empire — History — Alexius I Comnenus, 1081-1118 I. T.
DF605.C6 1967a   949.5/03/0924 B   *LC* 67-5910

Chronicle of Morea.   • **3.2672**
Crusaders as conquerors: the Chronicle of Morea. Translated from the Greek, with notes and introd., by Harold E. Lurier. New York: Columbia University Press, 1964. 346 p.: ill., map.; 23 cm. (Records of civilization, sources and studies. no. 69) 1. Achaea (Principality) I. Lurier, Harold E., tr. II. T. III. Series.
DF623.C563   949.52   *LC* 62-9367

Ducas, fl. 1455.   **3.2673**
[Historia Byzantina. English] Decline and fall of Byzantium to the Ottoman Turks / by Doukas; an annotated translation of 'Historia Turco-Byzantina' by Harry J. Magoulias. — Detroit: Wayne State University Press, 1975. 346 p.: ill.; 24 cm. First ed. published under title: Historia Byzantina. Includes index. 1. Byzantine Empire — History — 1081-1453 2. Turkey — History — 1288-1453 I. Magoulias, Harry J. II. T.
DF631.A2 D813   949.5   *LC* 75-9949   *ISBN* 0814315402

Vakaloupoulos, Apostolos E. (Apostolos Euangelou), 1909-.   • **3.2674**
[Historia tou neou Hellēnismou. v. 1. English] Origins of the Greek nation; the Byzantine period, 1204–1461, by Apostolos E. Vacalopoulos. New Brunswick, N.J., Rutgers University Press [1970] xxviii, 401 p.: ill., maps.; 25 cm. (Rutgers Byzantine series) Revised translation of v. 1 of Historia tou neou Hellēnismou. 1. Byzantine Empire — History — 1081-1453 2. Greece — History — 323-1453 3. Greece — Civilization I. T.
DF631.B313 1970   949.5/04   *LC* 75-119511   *ISBN* 081350659X

Nicol, Donald MacGillivray.   **3.2675**
The end of the Byzantine Empire / D.M. Nicol. — New York: Holmes & Meier Publishers, 1980 (c1979). 109 p.: map; 22 cm. (Foundations of medieval history.) Imprint under label reads: Edward Arnold. Includes index. 1. Byzantine Empire — History — 1081-1453 I. T. II. Series.
DF631.N49   949.5/04 19   *LC* 80-19902   *ISBN* 0841906440

Nicol, Donald MacGillivray.   **3.2676**
The last centuries of Byzantium, 1261–1453 [by] Donald M. Nicol. New York, St. Martin's Press [1972] xii, 481 p. illus. 23 cm. 1. Byzantine Empire — History — 1081-1453 I. T.
DF631.N5 1972b   949.5/04   *LC* 72-85195

Geanakoplos, Deno John.   • **3.2677**
Emperor Michael Palaeologus and the West, 1258–1282; a study in Byzantine-Latin relations. — Cambridge: Harvard University Press, 1959. xii, 434 p.: ill., ports., maps facsims.; 24 cm. Bibliography: p. 387-417. 1. Michael VIII Palaeologus, Emperor of the East, 1234-1282. 2. Byzantine Empire — For. rel. I. T.
DF635.G4   949.504   *LC* 59-7652

Phrantzēs, Geōrgios, b. 1401.   **3.2678**
[Chronikon Geōrgiou Phrantzē. English] The fall of the Byzantine Empire: a chronicle / by George Sphrantzes, 1401–1477; translated by Marios Philippides. — Amherst: University of Massachusetts Press, 1980. 174 p.; 24 cm. Translation of Chronikon Geōrgiou Phrantzē. Includes indexes. 1. Byzantine Empire — History — 1081-1453 2. Istanbul (Turkey) — History — Siege, 1453. I. Philippides, Marios, 1950- II. T.
DF645.P4813   949.5/04   *LC* 79-5498   *ISBN* 0870232908

DF701–951 Modern Greece

Greece: a country study / Foreign Area Studies, The American University; edited by Rinn S. Shinn.   **3.2679**
3rd ed. — Washington, D.C.: For sale by the Supt. of Docs., U.S. G.P.O., 1986. xxx, 408 p.: ill., maps; 24 cm. — (DA pam; 550-87) Rev. ed. of: Area handbook for Greece / Eugene K. Keefe. 2nd ed. 1977. Includes index. 1. Greece. I. Shinn, Rinn-Sup. II. Keefe, Eugene K. Area handbook for Greece. III. American University (Washington, D.C.). Foreign Area Studies. IV. Series.
DF717.G78 1986   949.5 19   *LC* 86-1231

The Greek world: classical, Byzantine, and modern / texts by Robert Browning ... et al.; edited by Robert Browning.   **3.2680**
London: Thames and Hudson, c1985. 328 p.: ill.; 31 cm. Includes index. 1. Greece — Civilization I. Browning, Robert, 1914-
DF741.G73 1985   949.5 19   *LC* 86-158583   *ISBN* 0500250928

Clogg, Richard, 1939-.   **3.2681**
A short history of modern Greece / Richard Clogg. — Cambridge: Cambridge University Press, 1979. viii, 241 p.: map; 23 cm. Includes index. 1. Greece — History — 1453- I. T.
DF757.C56   949.5   *LC* 78-72083   *ISBN* 0521224799

Toynbee, Arnold Joseph, 1889-1975.   **3.2682**
The Greeks and their heritages / Arnold Toynbee. — Oxford; New York: Oxford University Press, 1981. x, 334 p.; 24 cm. Includes index. 1. Hellenism 2. Greece — History 3. Greece — Civilization — To 146 B.C. I. T.
DF757.T68 1981   949.5 19   *LC* 81-198525   *ISBN* 0192152564

Woodhouse, C. M. (Christopher Montague), 1917-.   **3.2683**
Modern Greece: a short history / C. M. Woodhouse. — London: Faber, 1977. 332 p.: map; 20 cm. (Faber paperbacks) First published in 1968 under title: The story of modern Greece. Includes index. 1. Greece — History — 1453-1821 2. Greece — History — 1821- 3. Byzantine Empire — History I. T.
DF757.W6 1977   949.5   *LC* 78-310161   *ISBN* 0571049362

Holden, David.   **3.2684**
Greece without columns: the making of the modern Greeks. — Philadelphia: Lippincott, [1972] 336 p.; 22 cm. 1. National characteristics, Greek (Modern) 2. Greece, Modern — History. I. T.
DF759.H64 1972   949.5/07   *LC* 79-38333   *ISBN* 0397007795

Barros, James.   **3.2685**
Britain, Greece, and the politics of sanctions: Ethiopia, 1935–1936 / James Barros. — London: Royal Historical Society; Atlantic Highland, NJ: Humanities Press, 1983 (c1982). x, 248 p.; 23 cm. (Royal Historical Society studies in history series. no. 33) 1. Sanctions (International law) 2. Italo-Ethiopian War, 1935-1936 — Diplomatic history 3. Greece — Foreign relations — Great Britain. 4. Great Britain — Foreign relations — Greece. 5. Greece — Foreign relations — Italy. 6. Italy — Foreign relations — Greece. 7. Greece — Foreign relations — 1935-1967 8. Great Britain — Foreign relations — 1910-1936 9. Italy — Foreign relations — 1914-1945 I. T. II. Series.
DF787.G7 B3   963/.056 19   LC 83-208315   ISBN 0901050865

Koliopoulos, Giannēs.   **3.2686**
Greece and the British connection, 1935–1941 / John S. Koliopoulos. — Oxford, 1978 (c1977). xvii, 315 p.: ill.; 24 cm. Includes index. 1. Greece — Foreign relations — Great Britain. 2. Great Britain — Foreign relations — Greece. 3. Greece — Foreign relations — 1935-1967 I. T.
DF787.G7 K64   327.495/041   LC 77-6672   ISBN 0198225237

Borowiec, Andrew.   **3.2687**
The Mediterranean feud / Andrew Borowiec. — New York, N.Y.: Praeger Publishers, 1983. xii, 190 p.; 25 cm. Includes index. 1. Greece — Foreign relations — Turkey. 2. Turkey — Foreign relations — Greece. 3. Cyprus — History — Cyprus Crisis, 1974- 4. United States — Foreign relations — Greece. 5. Greece — Foreign relations — United States. 6. United States — Foreign relations — Turkey. 7. Turkey — Foreign relations — United States. I. T.
DF787.T8 B67 1983   327.4950561 19   LC 82-16624   ISBN 0030618479

Vakalopoulos, Apostolos E. (Apostolos Euangelou), 1909-.   **3.2688**
[Historia tou neou Hellēnismou. v. 2. English] The Greek nation, 1453–1669: the cultural and economic background of modern Greek society / by Apostolos E. Vacalopoulos; translated from the Greek by Ian and Phania Moles. — New Brunswick, N.J.: Rutgers University Press, c1976. xiv, 457 p.: ill.; 24 cm. Translation of v. 2 of Historia tou neou Hellēnismou. Includes index. 1. Greece — History — 1453-1821 I. T.
DF801.B3313   949.5/05   LC 75-23273   ISBN 081350810X

Braddock, Joseph, 1902-.   **3.2689**
The Greek phoenix. [1st American ed.] New York, Coward, McCann & Geoghegan [1973, c1972] xii, 233 p. illus. 22 cm. 1. Greece — History — 1453-1821 2. Greece — History — War of Independence, 1821-1829 I. T.
DF801.B73 1973   949.5   LC 75-146091   ISBN 0698104870

Dakin, Douglas.   **3.2690**
The unification of Greece, 1770–1923. — New York: St. Martin's Press, [1972] xiv, 344 p.: maps.; 25 cm. 1. Greece, Modern — History. I. T.
DF801.D3   949.5/06   LC 76-187329

The Movement for Greek independence, 1770–1821: a collection   **3.2691**
of documents / edited and translated and with an introd. by
Richard Clogg.
New York: Barnes & Noble, 1976. xxiii, 232 p., [1] leaf of plates; 23 cm. — (Studies in Russian and East European history) Includes index. 1. Greece — History — 1453-1821 — Sources. I. Clogg, Richard, 1939-
DF801.M68 1976b   949.5/05   LC 75-44747   ISBN 0064912167

Zakythēnos, Dionysios A., 1905-.   **3.2692**
The making of modern Greece: from Byzantium to independence / D. A. Zakythinos; translated with an introd. by K. R. Johnstone. — Totowa, N. J.: Rowman and Littlefield, 1976. 235 p.; 23 cm. Based on a series of lectures delivered to the School of Political Sciences in the University of Athens and published under title: Hē Tourkokratia in 1957; and containing passages from Hē politikē historia tēs Neōteras Hellados, published in 1965. Includes index. 1. Greece — History — 1453-1821 I. T.
DF801.Z34 1976   949.5   LC 76-366696   ISBN 0874717965

Kousoulas, D. George (Dimitrios George), 1923-.   **3.2693**
Modern Greece; profile of a nation [by] D. George Kousoulas. New York, Scribner [1974] xvi, 300 p. illus. 24 cm. 1. Greece — History — 1821- I. T.
DF802.K69   949.5/06   LC 73-1319   ISBN 0684137321 ISBN 0684137313

Makrygiannēs, Iōoannēs, 1797-1864.   • **3.2694**
The memoirs of General Makriyannis, 1797–1864; edited and translated [from the Greek] by H.A. Lidderdale; foreword by C.M. Woodhouse. London, Oxford U.P., 1966. 234 p. ill. 1. Greece — History — War of Independence, 1821-1829 2. Greece — History — Otho I, 1832-1862 I. T.
DF803.9.M3 A313   949.5061

Dakin, Douglas.   **3.2695**
The Greek struggle for independence, 1821–1833. Berkeley, University of California Press [1973] viii, 344 p. illus. 22 cm. 1. Greece — History — War of Independence, 1821-1829 I. T.
DF805.D24 1973   949.5/06   LC 72-89798   ISBN 0520023420

Pappas, Paul Constantine.   **3.2696**
The United States and the Greek War for Independence, 1821–1828 / Paul Constantine Pappas. — Boulder: East European Monographs; New York: Distributed by Columbia University Press, 1985. xvi, 190 p.; 23 cm. (East European monographs. no. 173) Includes index. 1. Greece — History — War of Independence, 1821-1829 2. Greece — Foreign relations — 1821-1862 3. Greece — Foreign relations — United States. 4. United States — Foreign relations — Greece. 5. United States — Foreign relations — 1817-1825 6. United States — Foreign relations — 1825-1829 I. T. II. Series.
DF807.P29 1985   949.5/06 19   LC 84-80971   ISBN 0880330651

Woodhouse, C. M. (Christopher Montague), 1917-.   **3.2697**
The Philhellenes, by C. M. Woodhouse. [1st American ed.] Rutherford [N.J.]: Fairleigh Dickinson University Press, 1971. 192 p. ports. 22 cm. 1. Byron, George Gordon Byron, Baron, 1788-1824. 2. Philhellenism — Great Britain. 3. Greece — History — War of Independence, 1821-1829 I. T.
DF807.W64 1971   949.5/06   LC 78-149828   ISBN 0838679129

Woodhouse, C. M. (Christopher Montague), 1917-.   **3.2698**
Capodistria: the founder of Greek independence [by] C. M. Woodhouse. London, New York, Oxford University Press, 1973. xi, 544 p., leaf. map, port. 25 cm. 1. Kapodistrias, Iōannēs Antōniou, 1776-1831. I. T.
DF815.K3 W66 1973   949.5/05/0924 B   LC 73-162273   ISBN 0192111965

Petropulos, John Anthony.   • **3.2699**
Politics and statecraft in the kingdom of Greece, 1833–1843. Princeton, N.J., Princeton University Press, 1968. xix, 646 p. 24 cm. 1. Greece — Politics and government — 19th century I. T.
DF823.P4   329.9/495   LC 66-21837

Papacosma, S. Victor, 1942-.   **3.2700**
The military in Greek politics: the 1909 coup d'état / S. Victor Papacosma. — Kent, Ohio: Kent State University Press, 1978 (c1977). xi, 254 p.; 24 cm. Includes index. 1. Greece — History — George I, 1863-1913 I. T.
DF831.P36   949.5/07   LC 77-22391   ISBN 0873382080

Woodhouse, C. M. (Christopher Montague), 1917-.   **3.2701**
Karamanlis, the restorer of Greek democracy / C.M. Woodhouse. — Oxford: Clarendon Press; New York: Oxford University Press, c1982. vi, 297 p.: ill.; 23 cm. 1. Karamanlis, Konstantinos, 1907- 2. Statesmen — Greece — Biography. 3. Greece — Presidents — Biography. 4. Greece — History — 1950-1967 5. Greece — History — 1974- I. T.
DF836.K37 W66 1982   949.5/07/0924 B 19   LC 82-6393   ISBN 0198225849

Smith, Michael Llewellyn, 1939-.   **3.2702**
Ionian vision; Greece in Asia Minor, 1919–1922. New York, St. Martin's Press [1973] 401 p. illus. 23 cm. 1. Greco-Turkish War, 1921-1922 2. Greeks — Asia Minor. 3. Greece — Politics and government — 1917-1935 I. T.
DF845.S4 1973   949.5/06   LC 73-80083

Iatrides, John O.   **3.2703**
Revolt in Athens; the Greek Communist 'Second Round,' 1944–1945, by John O. Iatrides. With a foreword by William Hardy McNeill. Princeton, N.J., Princeton University Press [1972] xiv, 340 p. 23 cm. 1. Kommounistikon Komma tēs Hellados. 2. World War, 1939-1945 — Underground movements — Greece. 3. Greece — Politics and government — 1935-1967 I. T.
DF849.I2   320.9/495/07   LC 76-39052   ISBN 0691052034

Xydēs, Stephanos G., 1913-1975.   • **3.2704**
Greece and the Great Powers, 1944–1947: prelude to the 'Truman doctrine' / by Stephen G. Xydis. — Thessaloniki: Institute for Balkan Studies, 1963. xxi, 758 p., [8] leaves of plates: maps, ports.; 25 cm. — (Hidryma Meletōn Chersonēsou tou Haimou (Series) 60) Errata slip inserted. 1. Greece, Modern — Foreign relations. I. T. II. Series.
DF849.X9   LC 65-83320

Averoff-Tossizza, Evangelos, 1910-.   **3.2705**
[Feu et la hache. English] By fire and axe: the Communist Party and the civil war in Greece, 1944–1949 / Evangelos Averoff-Tossizza; translated by Sarah Arnold Rigos. — 1st English language ed. — New Rochelle, N.Y.: Caratzas Brothers, 1978. xi, 438 p.: ill.; 23 cm. Translation of Le feu et la hache. 1. Kommounistikon Komma tēs Hellados. 2. Greece — History — Civil War, 1944-1949 I. T.
DF850.A9213   949.5/07   LC 77-91603   ISBN 0892410787

Clogg, Richard, 1939-.   • **3.2706**
Greece under military rule; edited by Richard Clogg and George Yannopoulos. London, Secker & Warburg [1972] xxii, 272 p. 24 cm. 1. Greece — Politics and

government — 1967-1974 I. Yannopoulos, George N., 1936- joint author. II. T.

DF852.C56   309.1/495/07   *LC* 73-150404   *ISBN* 0436102552

Katrēs, Giannēs.   3.2707
Eyewitness in Greece; the colonels come to power [by] John A. Katris. [1st ed.] St. Louis, New Critics Press, 1971. 317 p. 22 cm. Rev. ed. published in 1974 in Greek under title: He gennēsē tou neophasismou. 1. Greece — History — Coup d'état, 1967 (April 21) 2. Greece — Politics and government — 1967- I. T.

DF852.K38   320.9/495/07   *LC* 72-165332   *ISBN* 0878530029

Papandreou, Andreas George.   • 3.2708
Democracy at gunpoint: the Greek front [by] Andreas Papandreou. [1st ed.] Garden City, N.Y., Doubleday, 1970. xv, 365 p. 25 cm. 1. Greece — Politics and government — 1935- I. T.

DF852.P34   949.5/07   *LC* 73-101714

Danopoulos, Constantine P. (Constantine Panos)   3.2709
Warriors and politicians in modern Greece / by Constantine P. Danopoulos. — Chapel Hill, N.C., U.S.A.: Documentary Publications, 1985. x, 225 p., [7] p. of plates: ill.; 23 cm. (Excellence in doctoral dissertations. v. 1) Includes index. 1. Greece. Stratos — Political activity. 2. Greece — Politics and government — 1967-1974 3. Greece — Politics and government — 1974- 4. Greece — History — Coup d'état, 1967 (April 21) I. T. II. Series.

DF853.D36 1984   949.5/07 19   *LC* 82-72804   *ISBN* 0897121449

Barros, James.   3.2710
The Corfu incident of 1923; Mussolini and the League of Nations. — Princeton, N. J., Princeton University Press, 1965. xxi, 339 p. maps. 21 cm. Bibliography: p. 323-329. 1. Corfu — Hist. — Italian occupation, 1923. 2. League of Nations. I. T.

DF901.C7B35   327.45   *LC* 65-14305

DG ITALY

DG11–265 Ancient Italy. Rome to 476

Lewis, Naphtali. ed.   • 3.2711
Roman civilization: selected readings / edited with an introd. and notes, by Naphtali Lewis & Meyer Reinhold. — New York: Columbia University Press, 1951-. v.; 24 cm. — (Records of civilization, sources and studies. no. 45) 1. Rome — Civilization 2. Rome — History — Sources. I. Reinhold, Meyer, 1909- joint author. II. T. III. Series.

DG13.L4   937   *LC* 51-14589

Thompson, David, 1938- comp.   3.2712
The idea of Rome; from antiquity to the Renaissance. — [1st ed.] — Albuquerque: University of New Mexico Press, [1971] xviii, 211 p.; 22 cm. 1. Rome. I. T.

DG13.T46   914.56/32   *LC* 75-138469   *ISBN* 0826302017

Chevallier, Raymond, 1929-.   3.2713
[Voies romaines. English] Roman roads / Raymond Chevallier; translated by N. H. Field. — Berkeley: University of California Press, 1976. 272 p.: ill.; 26 cm. Translation of Les voies romaines. Includes index. 1. Roads, Roman I. T.

DG28.C4613   388.1/0937   *LC* 74-82845   *ISBN* 0520028341

Chilver, Guy Edward Farquhar.   • 3.2714
Cisalpine Gaul; social and economic history from 49 B.C. to the death of Trajan. Oxford The Clarendon Press 1941. 2,235,1p. 1. Gaul, Cisalpine I. T.

DG51 G2 C5

Dunbabin, Thomas James.   • 3.2715
The western Greeks; the history of Sicily and South Italy from the foundation of the Greek colonies to 480 B.C., by T. J. Dunbabin. — Oxford: Clarendon P., 1968. ix, 504 p.; 25 cm. 'An early version of this book was in 1937 submitted to All Souls College for examination for fellowship by thesis.' 1. Greece — Colonies — Sicily. 2. Magna Grecia — History. I. T.

DG55.M3 D8 1968   913.3/7/8031   *LC* 77-353250

Dyson, Stephen L.   3.2716
The creation of the Roman frontier / Stephen L. Dyson. — Princeton, N.J.: Princeton University Press, c1985. xii, 324 p.; 25 cm. Includes index. 1. Rome

— Provinces — History. 2. Rome — Colonies — History. 3. Rome — Boundaries — History. 4. Rome — Frontier troubles. I. T.

DG59.A2 D97 1985   937 19   *LC* 84-42881   *ISBN* 0691035776

Mócsy, András.   3.2717
Pannonia and Upper Moesia: a history of the middle Danube provinces of the Roman Empire / András Mócsy; translation edited by Sheppard Frere. — London; Boston: Routledge & K. Paul, 1974. xxi, 453 p., [2] fold. leaves, [24] leaves of plates: ill.; 26 cm. (The Provinces of the Roman Empire) Includes indexes. 1. Pannonia — History. 2. Moesia Superior — History. 3. Rome — History — Empire, 30 B.C.-476 A.D. 4. Danube Valley — Antiquities, Roman. I. T. II. Series.

DG59.D43 M613   939/.8   *LC* 75-306910   *ISBN* 0710077149

Gjerstad, Einar, 1897-.   • 3.2718
Early Rome. Lund: C. W. K. Gleerup, 1953-. 6 v.: ill. (part col.) diagrs., plans; 30 cm. (Skrifter utg. av Svenska institutet i Rom. Acta Instituti Romani Regni Sueciae. 4§S XVII: 1-6) 1. Rome (Italy) — Antiquities 2. Italy — Antiquities I. T.

DG12.S8 vol. 17 DG63.Gx   *LC* 55-18753

Krautheimer, Richard, 1897-.   3.2719
Three Christian capitals: topography and politics / Richard Krautheimer. — Berkeley: University of California Press, c1983. xiv, 167 p.: ill.; 27 cm. (Una's lectures. 4) Four rev. and enl. lectures originally given at the University of Calif., Berkeley, in May 1979. 1. Christian antiquities — Italy — Rome — Addresses, essays, lectures. 2. Christian antiquities — Turkey — Istanbul — Addresses, essays, lectures. 3. Christian antiquities — Italy — Milan — Addresses, essays, lectures. 4. Church history — Primitive and early church, ca. 30-600 — Addresses, essays, lectures. 5. Church and state — Rome — Addresses, essays, lectures. 6. Rome (Italy) — Description — Addresses, essays, lectures. 7. Istanbul (Turkey) — Description — Addresses, essays, lectures. 8. Milan (Italy) — Description — Addresses, essays, lectures. I. T. II. Series.

DG63.K7 1983   937/.08 19   *LC* 81-13148   *ISBN* 0520045416

Todd, Malcom, FSA.   3.2720
The walls of Rome / Malcolm Todd. — Totowa, N.J.: Rowman and Littlefield, 1978. 91 p.: ill.; 24 cm. Includes index. 1. Rome (City). Wall of Aurelian. I. T.

DG67.T63 1978   937/.6   *LC* 78-103960   *ISBN* 0847660370

Brown, Frank Edward, 1908-.   3.2721
Cosa, the making of a Roman town / Frank E. Brown. — Ann Arbor: University of Michigan Press, c1980. 76 p., [32] leaves of plates (1 fold.): ill.; 27 cm. — (Jerome lectures. 13th ser.) 1. Excavations (Archaeology) — Italy — Ansedonia. 2. Romans — Italy — Ansedonia. 3. Ansedonia (Italy) — Antiquities, Roman. 4. Italy — Antiquities, Roman I. T. II. Series.

DG70.A587 B76 1980   937/.5   *LC* 79-23668   *ISBN* 0472041002

Meiggs, Russell.   3.2722
Roman Ostia / by Russell Meiggs. — 2d ed. — Oxford [Eng.]: Clarendon Press, 1974 (c1973). xix, 622 p., [41] leaves of plates: ill. (1 fold.); 24 cm. Includes indexes. 1. Ostia (Ancient city) I. T.

DG70.O8 M4 1973   913.37/6   *LC* 74-182367   *ISBN* 0198148100

Jashemski, Wilhelmina Mary Feemster, 1910-.   3.2723
The gardens of Pompeii: Herculaneum and the villas destroyed by Vesuvius / Wilhelmina F. Jashemski; photos., drawings, and plans, Stanley A. Jashemski. — New Rochelle, N.Y.: Caratzas Bros., 1979. x, 372 p., [2] fold. leaves: ill. (some col.); 32 cm. Includes index. 1. Gardens — Italy — Pompeii (Ancient city) 2. Horticulture — Italy — Pompeii (Ancient city) 3. Gardens in art 4. Art, Greco-Roman — Italy — Pompeii (Ancient city) 5. Animal remains (Archaeology) — Italy — Pompeii (Ancient city) 6. Plant remains (Archaeology) — Italy — Pompeii (Ancient city) 7. Pompeii (Ancient city) I. T.

DG70.P7 J29   937/.7 19   *LC* 79-51383   *ISBN* 0892410965

Ward-Perkins, J. B. (John Bryan), 1912-.   3.2724
Pompeii A.D. 79: essay and catalogue / by John Ward-Perkins and Amanda Claridge; with additions by the Department of Classical Art, Museum of Fine Arts, Boston. — New York: Knopf, 1978, c1976. 215 p.: ill. (some col.); 30 cm. 1. Pompeii (Ancient city) — Exhibitions. 2. Italy — Antiquities — Exhibitions. I. Claridge, Amanda. joint author. II. T.

DG70.P7 W34 1978   937/.7   *LC* 78-13870   *ISBN* 0394504917

DG75–109 ANTIQUITIES. CIVILIZATION

Cornell, Tim.   3.2725
Atlas of the Roman world / by Tim Cornell and John Matthews. — New York: Facts on File, c1982. 240 p.: ill. (some col.); 31 cm. Includes index. 1. Rome — Civilization 2. Rome — Maps. I. Matthews, John Frederick. II. T.

DG77.C597 1982   937/.02 19   *LC* 81-19591   *ISBN* 0871966522

Grimal, Pierre. • 3.2726
The civilization of Rome / Translated by W. S. Maguinness. — New York:
Simon and Schuster, 1963. 531 p.: ill., maps, facsims.; 22 cm. Bibliography: p.
[519]-531. 1. Rome — Civilization I. T.
DG77.G733   913.37   *LC* 63-11905

Mattingly, Harold, 1884-1964. • 3.2727
Roman imperial civilisation. New York, St. Martin's Press, 1957 [i.e. 1958]
312 p. illus. 23 cm. 1. Rome — Civilization I. T.
DG77.M38   *LC* 58-14525

Sandys, John Edwin, Sir, 1844-1922. ed. • 3.2728
A companion to Latin studies; ed. for the syndics of the University press. 3d ed.
— Cambridge University Press 1938. 891p. 'First edition 1910 ... third edition
1921, reprinted 1925 ... 1938.' 1. Latin philology 2. Rome — Antiquities
3. Rome — Description, geography 4. Art — Rome 5. Latin literature —
History and criticism I. T.
DG77 S3 1938   937 913.37   *LC* 39-21366

Carcopino, Jérôme, 1881-1970. 3.2729
[Vie quotidienne à Rome à l'apogée de l'empire] Daily life in ancient Rome; the
people and the city at the height of the empire, by Jérôme Carcopino, edited
with bibliography and notes by Henry T. Rowell. Translated from the French
by E. O. Lorimer. New Haven, Yale university press, 1940. xv, 342 p. front.,
plates, plan 25 cm. 'Published on the foundation established in memory of
Oliver Baty Cunningham of the class of 1917, Yale college.' 1. Rome — Social
life and customs. 2. Rome (Italy) — History — To 476 I. Rowell, Henry T.,
ed. II. Lorimer, Emily (Overend) tr. III. T.
DG78.C32   937.6   *LC* 40-34290

Dill, Samuel, Sir, 1844-. • 3.2730
Roman society from Nero to Marcus Aurelius / by Samuel Dill. — [2d ed.]
London: Macmillan and co., ltd.; New York: The Macmillan company, 1905.
xxii p., 1 l., 639 p.; 24 cm. 1. Rome — Social life and customs. 2. Rome —
Religion. I. T.
DG78.D58   *LC* 09-14379

Earl, Donald C. • 3.2731
The moral and political tradition of Rome, [by] Donald Earl. Ithaca, N.Y.:
Cornell University Press, [1967] 167 p.; 23 cm. — (Aspects of Greek and
Roman life) 1. Rome — Politics and government 2. Rome — Moral
conditions. I. T. II. Series.
DG78.E217   172/.0937   *LC* 67-20630

Friedlaender, Ludwig, 1824-1909. • 3.2732
[Darstellungen aus der Sittengeschichte Roms in der Zeit von August bis zum
Ausgang der Antonine. Band 1-3 English] Roman life and manners under the
early empire ... / authorized translation of the seventh enlarged and revised
edition of the Sittengeshichte Roms by Leonard A. Magnus. — London:
Routledge [1908]-1913. 4 v.; 21 cm. Translation of: Sittengeschichte Roms.
1. Rome — Social life and customs. I. T. II. Title: Darstellungen aus der
Sittengeschichte Roms in der Zeit von August bis zum Ausgang der Antonine.
Band 1-3 English
DG 78 F92 E5 1908

Toynbee, Arnold Joseph, 1889-1975. • 3.2733
Hannibal's legacy: the Hannibalic War's effects on Roman life / by Arnold J.
Toynbee. — London: Oxford University Press, 1965. 2 v.: 8 col. maps (fold in
pockets); 25 cm. 1. Rome — Civilization I. T. II. Title: The Hannibalic War's
effects on Roman life.
DG78.T67   DG78.T6.   913.3703   *LC* 65-29826

DG81–89 Politics

Frank, Tenney, 1876-1939. • 3.2734
Roman imperialism. New York, The Macmilan company, 1914. xiii, 365 p. 23
cm. 1. Imperialism 2. Rome — History 3. Rome — Politics and government
I. T.
DG81.F7   *LC* 14-6613

Taylor, Lily Ross, 1886-. • 3.2735
Party politics in the age of Caesar. — Berkeley: University of Calif. Press, 1949.
viii, 255 p.; 24 cm. — (Sather classical lectures. v.22) 1. Political parties —
Rome. 2. Rome — Politics and government — 265-30 B.C. I. T. II. Series.
DG81.T38   937.05   *LC* 49-2564

Badian, E. • 3.2736
Foreign clientelae, 264–70 B. C. — Oxford, Clarendon Press, 1958. x, 342 p. 25
cm. 'This study was ... submitted for the degree of doctor of philosophy.'
Bibliography: p. [322]-328. 1. Patron and client I. T.
DG83.3.B3   937.04   *LC* 58-2626

Gelzer, Matthias, 1886-1974. • 3.2737
[Nobilität der römischen Republik. English] The Roman nobility. Translated
with an introd. by Robin Seager. New York, Barnes & Noble, 1969. xiv, 164 p.
24 cm. Contains the author's The Nobility of the Roman Republic, a translation
of Die Nobilität der römischen Republik and his The nobility of the principate,
a translation of Die Nobilität der Kaiserzeit. 1. Rome — Nobility. I. Gelzer,
Matthias, 1886-1974. The nobility of the principate. Die Nobilität der
Kaiserzeit. 1969. II. T.
DG83.3.G413 1969b   929.7/5   *LC* 68-59641

Hill, Herbert. • 3.2738
The Roman middle class in the Republican period. Oxford: Blackwell, 1952. xi,
226 p.; 22 cm. 1. Equestrian order (Rome) I. T.
DG83.3 H5

DG90–109 Social Life. Customs

Balsdon, J. P. V. D. (John Percy Vyvian Dacre), 1901-. • 3.2739
Roman women: their history and habits / J.P.V.D. Balsdon. — [1st American
ed.] — New York: John Day Co., 1963. 351 p.: ill. 23 cm. Includes index.
1. Women — Rome. I. T.
DG91.B3 1963   HQ1136.B34 1963.   *LC* 63-10219

Toynbee, J. M. C. (Jocelyn M. C.), d. 1985. • 3.2740
Death and burial in the Roman world [by] J. M. C. Toynbee. Ithaca, N.Y.,
Cornell University Press [1971] 336 p. illus., plans. 23 cm. (Aspects of Greek
and Roman life) 1. Funeral rites and ceremonies — Rome 2. Tombs — Italy
— Rome. 3. Rome — Social life and customs. I. T. II. Series.
DG103.T69   393/.0937   *LC* 77-120603   *ISBN* 0801405939

MacCormack, Sabine. 3.2741
Art and ceremony in late antiquity / Sabine G. MacCormack. — Berkeley:
University of California Press, c1981. xvi, 417 p., [16] leaves of plates: ill.; 25
cm. — (The Transformation of the classical heritage; 1) Includes index.
1. Emperor worship, Roman 2. Rites and ceremonies — Rome. 3. Roman
emperors — Succession 4. Laudatory poetry, Latin — History and criticism.
5. Rome — History — Empire, 284-476 I. T.
DG124.M33   937/.06 19   *LC* 78-62864   *ISBN* 0520037790

Price, S. R. F. 3.2742
Rituals and power: the Roman imperial cult in Asia Minor / S.R.F. Price. —
Cambridge [Cambridgeshire]; New York: Cambridge University Press, 1984.
xxvi, 289 p., [4] p. of plates: ill.; 24 cm. Includes indexes. 1. Emperor worship,
Roman I. T.
DG124.P74 1984   939/.2 19   *LC* 83-18901   *ISBN* 0521259037

DG201–365 History

Laistner, Max Ludwig Wolfram, 1890-. • 3.2743
The greater Roman historians. Berkley: Univ. of California Press, 1947. viii,
196 p.; 24 cm. (Sather classical lectures. v. 21, 1947) 1. Historians — Rome
2. Rome — History — Historiography. I. T. II. Series.
DG206.A2 L3   937.007   *LC* 48-5105

Craddock, Patricia B. 3.2744
Young Edward Gibbon, gentleman of letters / Patricia B. Craddock. —
Baltimore: Johns Hopkins University Press, c1982. xvi, 380 p.: port.; 24 cm.
1. Gibbon, Edward, 1737-1794. 2. Historians — England — Biography. I. T.
DG206.G5 C73 1982   937/.06/0924 B 19   *LC* 81-13726   *ISBN*
0801827140

Parkinson, Richard N. 3.2745
Edward Gibbon, by R. N. Parkinson. — New York: Twayne Publishers, 1974,
(c1973) 158 p.; 21 cm. — (Twayne's English authors series, TEAS 159)
1. Gibbon, Edward, 1737-1794. I. T.
DG206.G5 P37   937/.06/072024 B   *LC* 72-13382   *ISBN*
0805712186

Walbank, F. W. (Frank William), 1909-. 3.2746
Polybius, by F. W. Walbank. Berkeley, University of California Press [1972] ix,
201 p. 24 cm. (Sather classical lectures. v. 42) 1. Polybius. I. T. II. Series.
DG206.P65 W34   907/.2/024 B   *LC* 72-189219   *ISBN*
0520021908

Hadas, Moses, 1900-1966. ed. and tr. • 3.2747
A history of Rome, from its origins to 529 A.D., as told by the Roman
historians. — [1st ed.] — Garden City, N.Y.: Doubleday, 1956. 305 p.: illus.;
18 cm. — (Doubleday anchor books, A78) 1. Rome — History I. T.
DG207.A1 H3   937   *LC* 56-7540

Luce, T. James (Torrey James), 1932-.   **3.2748**
Livy: the composition of his history / by T. J. Luce. — Princeton, N.J.:
Princeton University Press, c1977. xxvii, 322 p.; 23 cm. Includes index. 1. Livy.
Historiae Romanae decades 2. Rome — History I. T.
DG207.L583 L83   937   LC 77-72126   ISBN 0691035520

Sallust, 86-34 B.C.   **3.2749**
The Jugurthine War [and] The conspiracy of Catiline. Translated, with an
introd. by S. A. Handford. Baltimore, Penguin Books [1963] 240 p. maps. 19
cm. (Penguin classics, L132) 1. Catiline, ca. 108-62 B.C. 2. Jugurthine War,
111-105 B.C. 3. Rome — History — Conspiracy of Catilina, 65-62 B. C.
I. Handford, Stanley Alexander, 1898- tr. II. T. III. Title: Conspiracy of
Catilina.
DG207.S4 H3   937.05   LC 64-1293

Jones, A. H. M. (Arnold Hugh Martin), 1904-1970. comp.   • **3.2750**
A history of Rome through the fifth century, edited by A. H. M. Jones. New
York, Walker [1968-. v. 24 cm. (Documentary history of Western civilization)
1. Rome — History I. T.
DG209.J652   937   LC 68-13332

Mommsen, Theodore, 1817-1903.   • **3.2751**
The history of Rome: [Translation] Glencoe, Ill.: Free Press [1957] 5 v.: map; 20
cm. 1. Rome — History I. T.
DG209.M7444   937   LC 57-7123

Rostovtsev, M. I. (Mikhail Ivanovich)   • **3.2752**
Rome / M. Rostovtzeff; translated from the Russian by J.D. Duff; Elias J.
Bickerman, editor. — London: Oxford University Press, 1960. xiii, 347 p.: ill.,
maps.; 21 cm. — (A Galaxy book; GB42) Translation of v. 2 of Ocherk istorīī
drevniago mīra (romanized). Includes index. 1. Rome — History I. T.
DG209.R653   937   LC 60-15102   ISBN 0195002245 Pbk

Syme, Ronald, Sir, 1903-.   **3.2753**
Roman papers / Ronald Syme; edited by E. Badian. — Oxford: Clarendon
Press; New York: Oxford University Press, 1979. 2 v.: ill.; 24 cm. 1. Rome —
History — Collected works. I. Badian, E. II. T.
DG209.S95 1979   937/.06   LC 79-40437   ISBN 0198143672

Cary, M. (Max), 1881-1958.   **3.2754**
A history of Rome down to the reign of Constantine / M. Cary. and H. H.
Scullard. — 3d ed. — New York: St. Martin's Press, 1975. xxvii, 694 p.: ill.; 26
cm. 1. Rome — History I. Scullard, H. H. (Howard Hayes), 1903- joint
author. II. T.
DG210.C3 1975   937   LC 74-24818

DG221–365 By Period

DG221–225 Pre-Roman Italy. Etruscans

Salmon, Edward Togo.   **3.2755**
The making of Roman Italy / E.T. Salmon. — Ithaca, N.Y.: Cornell University
Press, 1982. xi, 212 p.: ill.; 23 cm. — (Aspects of Greek and Roman life)
1. Italic peoples — History. 2. Italic peoples — Cultural assimilation 3. Italy
— History — To 476 4. Rome — History — Republic, 510-30 B.C. I. T.
DG221.5.S24 1982   937 19   LC 81-68745   ISBN 0801414385

Banti, Luisa, 1894-.   **3.2756**
[Mondo degli Etruschi. English] Etruscan cities and their culture / Translated
by Erika Bizzarri. Berkeley: University of California Press, 1974. vi, 322 p.: ill.,
96 plates; 23 cm. Translation of Il mondo degli Etruschi. 1. Art, Etruscan
2. Etruria — Antiquities I. T.
DG223.B313 1974   913.37/5   LC 74-145781

Pallottino, Massimo.   **3.2757**
[Etruscologia. English] The Etruscans / translated by J. Cremona; edited by
David Ridgway. — Rev. and enl. Bloomington: Indiana University Press [1975]
316 p.: ill.; 25 cm. Translation of Etruscologia. 1. Etruscans I. T.
DG223.P283 1975   913.37/5/03   LC 74-6082   ISBN 0253320801

Richardson, Emeline Hill.   **3.2758**
The Etruscans, their art and civilization, by Emeline Richardson. — Chicago:
University of Chicago Press, [1964] xvii, 285 p.: illus.; 25 cm. 1. Etruscans
2. Art, Etruscan I. T.
DG223.R5   913.375   LC 64-15817

DG231–233 753–510 B.C

Alföldi, Andreas, 1895-1981.   **3.2759**
Early Rome and the Latins / by A. Alföldi. — Ann Arbor: University of
Michigan Press [1965] xxi, 433, 25 p.: ill., maps (1 fold.); 24 cm. — (Jerome
lectures, 7th series) Bibliographical footnotes. 1. Rome — Hist. — Aboriginal

and early period. 2. Rome — Hist. — Kings, 753-510 B.C. 3. Rome — Hist. —
Republic, 510-265 B.C. I. T. II. Series.
DG231.A7   937   LC 63-8076

Cowell, Frank Richard, 1897-.   **3.2760**
Cicero and the Roman Republic [by] F. R. Cowell. 5th ed. — Harmondsworth:
Penguin, 1973 [i.e. 1972] xvii, 398, [32] p.: illus., maps.; 18 cm. — (Pelican
books) 1. Cicero, Marius Tullius — Contemporary Rome. 2. Rome — History
— Republic, 510-30 B.C. 3. Rome — Civilization I. T.
DG231.C69 1972   913.37   LC 73-154909   ISBN 0140203206

Heitland, William Emerton, 1847-1935.   • **3.2761**
The Roman Republic. — New York: Greenwood Press, [1969] 3 v.: maps.; 24
cm. 'First published in 1909.' 1. Rome — History — Republic, 510-30 B.C.
I. T.
DG231.H4 1969   937/.02   LC 69-13930   ISBN 0837120772

Heurgon, Jacques.   **3.2762**
[Rome et la Méditerranée occidentale jusqu'aux guerres puniques. English] The
rise of Rome to 264 B.C. Translated by James Willis. Berkeley, University of
California Press, 1973. 344 p. maps. 23 cm. Translation of Rome et la
Méditerranée occidentale jusqu'aux guerres puniques. 1. Rome — History —
To 510 B.C. 2. Rome — History — Republic, 510-265 B.C. 3. Mediterranean
Region — History. I. T.
DG231.H4613 1973   913.37/6   LC 70-126762   ISBN 0520017951

Scullard, H. H. (Howard Hayes), 1903-.   • **3.2763**
A history of the Roman world from 753 to 146 B.C. / by Howard H. Scullard.
London: Methuen, 1969. xiv, 480 p.: maps; 22 cm. (Methuen's history of the
Greek and Roman world, 4) (University paperbacks, UP301.) 'Distributed in
the U.S.A. by Barnes & Noble.' 1. Rome — History — To 510 B.C. 2. Rome
— History — Republic, 510-30 B.C. I. T.
DG231.S35 1969   913.3/7/031   LC 70-384646   ISBN 0416436609

Harris, William Vernon.   **3.2764**
War and imperialism in Republican Rome, 327–70 B.C. / by William V. Harris.
— Oxford: Clarendon Press; New York: Oxford University Press, 1979. 293 p.;
23 cm. Includes index. 1. War 2. Imperialism 3. Rome — History —
Republic, 510-30 B.C. 4. Rome — Foreign relations — 510-30 B.C. I. T.
DG231.3.H3   937/.02   LC 78-40490   ISBN 0198148275

Ogilvie, R. M. (Robert Maxwell), 1932-.   **3.2765**
Early Rome and the Etruscans / R. M. Ogilvie. — Atlantic Highlands, N.J.:
Humanities Press, 1976. 189 p. — (Fontana history of the ancient world)
Includes index. 1. Etruscans 2. Rome — History — To 510 B.C. 3. Rome —
History — Republic, 510-265 B.C. I. T.
DG233.O44   937/.01   LC 76-18964   ISBN 0391006444

DG235–269 Republic (509–27 B.C.)

Gruen, Erich S.   **3.2766**
The Hellenistic world and the coming of Rome / Erich S. Gruen. — Berkeley:
University of California Press, c1984. 2 v. (x, 862 p.); 24 cm. Includes indexes.
1. Hellenism 2. Imperialism 3. Rome — History — Republic, 265-30 B.C.
4. Greece — History — 281-146 B.C. I. T.
DG241.2.G78 1984   937/.02 19   LC 82-8581   ISBN 0520045696

Dorey, T. A. (Thomas Alan)   **3.2767**
Rome against Carthage [by] T. A. Dorey and D. R. Dudley. [1st ed. in the
U.S.A.] Garden City, N.Y., Doubleday, 1972 [c1971] xviii, 205 p. illus. 22 cm.
1. Punic wars 2. Rome — History — Republic, 265-30 B.C. 3. Carthage
(Ancient city) — History. I. Dudley, Donald Reynolds. joint author. II. T.
DG242.D67   937/.04   LC 76-157585

Livy.   **3.2768**
[Ab urbe condita. Books 31-45. English] Rome and the Mediterranean: books
XXXI–XLV of The history of Rome from its foundation / [by] Livy; translated
[from the Latin] by Henry Bettenson; with an introduction by A. H. McDonald.
— Harmondsworth: Penguin, 1976. 699 p.: maps; 18 cm. — (The Penguin
classics) Includes indexes. 1. Bettenson, Henry Scowcroft. 2. Rome — History
— Republic, 265-30 B.C. I. T.
DG250.L58213   937/.02   LC 76-378574   ISBN 0140443185

Scullard, H. H. (Howard Hayes), 1903-.   • **3.2769**
Roman politics, 220–150 B.C. Oxford: Clarendon Press 1951. xvi, 325 p.: front.;
24 cm. 1. Rome — Politics and government — 265-30 B.C. I. T.
DG250 S3

Astin, A. E.   **3.2770**
Cato the censor / by Alan E. Astin. — Oxford [Eng.]: Clarendon Press; New
York: Oxford University Press, 1978. x, 371 p.; 24 cm. Includes indexes.
1. Cato, Marcus Porcius, 234-149 B.C. 2. Statesmen — Rome — Biography.
3. Orators — Rome — Biography. I. T.
DG253.C3 A87   937.04/0924 B   LC 77-30281   ISBN 0198148097

Astin, A. E. • 3.2771
Scipio Aemilianus, by A. E. Astin. — Oxford: Clarendon P., 1967. xiii, 374 p.: diagr.; 24 1/2 cm. 1. Scipio Aemilianus Africanus minor, Publius Cornelius. I. T.
DG253.S4 A8 937/.05/0924 B *LC* 67-82263

Gabba, Emilio. 3.2772
[Esercito e società nella tarda Republica romana. English. Selections] Republican Rome, the army, and the allies / Emilio Gabba; translated by P. J. Cuff. — Berkeley: University of California Press, 1977 (c1976). ix, 272 p.; 25 cm. Translation of selections from Esercito e società nella tarda Repubblica romana. 1. Rome — Politics and government — 265-30 B.C. 2. Rome — Army — History. I. T.
DG254.G3132 937/.05 *LC* 76-14307 *ISBN* 0520032594

Marsh, Frank Burr, 1880-1940. • 3.2773
The founding of the Roman Empire, by Frank Burr Marsh. Austin, The University of Texas, 1922. vii, [3]-329 p. 23 cm. 1. Rome — History — Republic, 265-30 B.C. 2. Rome — History — Augustus, 30 B.C.-14 A.D. I. T.
DG254.M3 *LC* 22-23925

Marsh, Frank Burr, 1880-1940. • 3.2774
A history of the Roman world from 146 to 30 B.C. / rev. with additional notes by H. H. Scullard. — [3d ed.] London: Methuen; New York: Barnes & Noble, [1963] 472 p.: ill.; 23 cm. (Methuen's history of the Greek and Roman world, 5) 1. Rome — History — Republic, 265-30 B.C. I. T.
DG254.M34 1963 937.05 *LC* 63-3016

Scullard, H. H. (Howard Hayes), 1903-. • 3.2775
From the Gracchi to Nero: a history of Rome from 133 B.C. to A.D. 68, by H. H. Scullard. 3rd ed. London, Methuen, 1970. xv, 484 p. map. 22 cm. 'Distributed in the U.S.A. by Barnes and Noble.' 1. Rome — History — Republic, 265-30 B.C. 2. Rome — History — The five Julii, 30 B.C.-68 A.D. I. T.
DG254.S35 1970 937/.05 *LC* 71-560931 *ISBN* 0416077501

Syme, Ronald, Sir, 1903-. • 3.2776
The Roman revolution / by Ronald Syme. — London: Oxford University Press, 1960. xi, 568 p.: geneal. tables. — (Oxford paperbacks; no. 1) 1. Rome — Politics and government — 265-30 B.C. 2. Rome — Politics and government — 30 B.C.-68 A.D. I. T.
DG254.S9 1960 937.05 *LC* 60-51198 *ISBN* 0198810016

Badian, E. • 3.2777
Roman imperialism in the late republic / by E. Badian. — [2d ed.]. — Ithaca, N.Y.: Cornell University Press, [1968] xii, 117 p.; 22 cm. 1. Imperialism 2. Rome — Politics and government — 265-30 B.C. I. T.
DG254.2.B3 1968b 937/.6/04 *LC* 68-8998

Seager, Robin. comp. • 3.2778
The crisis of the Roman republic: studies in political and social history; selected and introduced by Robin Seager. — Cambridge: Heffer; New York: Barnes & Noble, 1969. xiii, 218 p.: fold. plate.; 23 cm. — (Views and controversies about classical antiquity) Includes the pagination of the original articles. 1. Rome — Politics and government — 265-30 B.C. I. T. II. Series.
DG254.2.S4 309.1/37 *LC* 73-427018 *ISBN* 0852700245

Rawson, Beryl. 3.2779
The politics of friendship: Pompey and Cicero / [by] Beryl Rawson. — Sydney: Sydney University Press, 1978 (c1977). vi, 217 p.; 22 cm. (Sources in ancient history.) Stamped on t.p.: Exclusive distributor: ISBS, Inc., Forest Grove, Or. Includes index. 1. Pompey, the Great, 106-48 B.C. 2. Cicero, Marcus Tullius. 3. Statesmen — Rome — Biography. 4. Rome — History — 265-30 B.C. I. T. II. Series.
DG258.R38 937/.05/0924 B 19 *LC* 78-320651 *ISBN* 0424068001

Hardy, E.G. (Ernest George), 1852-1925. • 3.2780
The Catilinarian conspiracy in its context: a re-study of the evidence / by E. G. Hardy. Oxford: B. Blackwell, 1924. 115 p.; 19 cm. Includes index. 1. Rome — History — Conspiracy of Catiline, 65-62 B.C. I. T.
DG259.H3 1924 937/.05 *LC* 75-41128 *ISBN* 0404145493

Boissier, Gaston, 1823-1908. 3.2781
[Cicéron et ses amis. English] Cicero and his friends; a study of Roman society in the time of Caesar. Translated, with an index and table of contents, by Adnah David Jones. New York, Cooper Square Publishers, 1970. vii, 399 p. 23 cm. 'A Marandell book.' Reprint of the 1897 ed. Translation of Cicéron et ses amis. 1. Cicero, Marcus Tullius — Contemporary Rome. 2. Rome — History — Republic, 265-30 B.C. I. T.
DG260.A1 B62 1970 937.05/0924 *LC* 75-114085 *ISBN* 0815403186

Bailey, D. R. Shackleton (David Roy Shackleton), 1917-. 3.2782
Cicero [by] D. R. Shackleton Bailey. New York, Scribner [1972, c1971] xii, 290 p. front. 23 cm. (Classical life and letters) 1. Cicero, Marcus Tullius. I. T.
DG260.C5 B27 1972 937/.05/0924 B *LC* 78-176156 *ISBN* 0684126834

Lacey, W. K. (Walter Kirkpatrick) 3.2783
Cicero and the end of the Roman Republic / W. K. Lacey. — New York: Barnes & Noble, 1978. vi, 184 p.: maps; 22 cm. Includes index. 1. Cicero, Marcus Tullius. 2. Statesmen — Rome — Biography. 3. Orators — Rome — Biography. 4. Rome — History — Republic, 265-30 B.C. I. T.
DG260.C5 L25 937/.05/0924 B *LC* 78-1101 *ISBN* 0064940136

Rawson, Elizabeth. 3.2784
Cicero: a portrait / Elizabeth Rawson. — Rev. ed. — Ithaca, N.Y.: Cornell University Press, 1983, c1975. xvi, 341 p., [8] p. of plates: ill.; 23 cm. Includes indexes. 1. Cicero, Marcus Tullius. 2. Statesmen — Rome — Biography. 3. Orators — Rome — Biography. 4. Rome — History — Republic, 265-30 B.C. I. T.
DG260.C5 R38 1983 937/.05/0924 B 19 *LC* 83-70178 *ISBN* 0801416280

Mitchell, Thomas N., 1939-. 3.2785
Cicero, the ascending years / Thomas N. Mitchell. — New Haven: Yale University Press, 1979. xii, 259 p.; 22 cm. Includes indexes. 1. Cicero, Marcus Tullius. 2. Statesmen — Rome — Biography. 3. Orators — Rome — Biography. I. T.
DG260.C53 M57 937/.05/0924 B *LC* 78-31188 *ISBN* 0300022778

Ward, Allen Mason, 1942-. 3.2786
Marcus Crassus and the late Roman Republic / Allen Mason Ward. — Columbia: University of Missouri Press, c1977. vii, 323 p.; 24 cm. Includes index. 1. Crassus, Marcus Licinius. 2. Consuls, Roman — Biography. 3. Businessmen — Rome — Biography. 4. Generals — Rome — Biography. I. T.
DG260.C73 W37 937/.05/0924 B *LC* 76-56794 *ISBN* 0826202160

Gelzer, Matthias, 1886-1974. • 3.2787
[Caesar. English] Caesar: politician and statesman. Translated by Peter Needham. Cambridge, Harvard University Press, 1968. viii, 359 p. map, ports. 23 cm. 1. Caesar, Julius. 2. Rome — History — Republic, 265-30 B.C. I. T.
DG261.G414 1968 937/.05/0924 B *LC* 68-4657

Yavetz, Zvi, 1925-. 3.2788
[Caesar in der öffentlichen Meinung. English] Julius Caesar and his public image / Zwi Yavetz. — Ithaca, N.Y.: Cornell University Press, 1983. 286 p.; 23 cm. (Aspects of Greek and Roman life) Translation of: Caesar in der Öffentlichen Meinung. 1. Caesar, Julius — Psychology. 2. Public opinion — Rome. 3. Rome — Historiography. I. T.
DG262.Y3813 1983 937/.05/0924 19 *LC* 82-71588 *ISBN* 0801414407

DG270–365 EMPIRE (27 B.C.–476 A.D.)

Rostovzeff, Michael Ivanovitch, 1870-1952. • 3.2789
The social and economic history of the Roman Empire. — 2d ed. rev. by P. M. Fraser. — Oxford, Clarendon Press, 1957. 2 v. (xxxi, 847 p.) illus., ports. 25 cm. Bibliographical references included in 'Notes' (v. 2, p. [543]-751) 1. Rome — Hist. — Empire, 30 B. C. — 476 A. D. 2. Rome — Soc. condit. 3. Rome — Econ. condit. I. T.
DG271.R6 1957 937.06 *LC* 58-362

Starr, Chester G., 1914-. • 3.2790
Civilization and the Caesars: the intellectual revolution in the Roman Empire / Chester G. Starr. — Ithaca, N.Y.: Cornell University Press, 1954. xiv, 413 p.: ill. — 1. Rome — Civilization I. T.
DG272.S8 *LC* 54-13378

Scriptores historiae Augustae. 3.2791
Lives of the later Caesars: the first part of the Augustan history: with newly compiled Lives of Nerva and Trajan / translated and introduced by Anthony Birley. — Harmondsworth, Eng.; Baltimore [etc.]: Penguin Books, 1976. 336 p.: ill.; 18 cm. (Penguin classics) Includes index. 1. Roman emperors — Biography. 2. Rome — History — 30 B.C.-284 A.D. I. Birley, Anthony Richard. II. T.
DG274.S32 1976 937/.07/0922 B *LC* 76-373411 *ISBN* 0140443088

Salmon, Edward Togo. • 3.2792
A history of the Roman world from 30 B.C. to A.D. 138, by Edward T. Salmon. — 6th ed. — London: Methuen, 1968. xv, 367 p.: table, 5 maps; 23 cm. —

(Methuen's history of the Greek and Roman world, 6) 1. Rome — History — Empire, 30 B.C.-284 A.D. I. T.
DG276.S26 1968   937/.07   LC 73-355498   ISBN 0416107109

Campbell, J. B.   **3.2793**
The Emperor and the Roman Army, 31 BC–AD 235 / J.B. Campbell. — Oxford [Oxfordshire]: Clarendon Press; New York: Oxford University Press, 1984. xix, 468 p.; 23 cm. Includes indexes. 1. Rome. Army — Political activity. 2. Rome. Army — Organization. 3. Roman emperors — Duties 4. Rome — Politics and government — 30 B.C.-284 A.D. I. T.
DG276.5.C26 1984   322/.5/0937 19   LC 83-19353   ISBN 0198148348

Petit, Paul.   **3.2794**
[Paix romaine. English] Pax Romana / Paul Petit; translated by James Willis. — 1st English language ed. — Berkeley: University of California Press, 1976. 368 p.: maps; 23 cm. Translation of La Paix romaine. Includes index. 1. Rome — History — Empire, 30 B.C.-284 A.D. 2. Rome — Civilization I. T.
DG276.5.P413 1976b   937/.07   LC 76-379352   ISBN 0520021711

Bowersock, G. W. (Glen Warren), 1936-.   • **3.2795**
Augustus and the Greek world [by] G. W. Bowersock. — Oxford [Eng.] Clarendon Press, 1965. xii, 176 p. 23 cm. Bibliography: p. [162]-168. 1. Rome — Hist. — Augustus, 30 B.C.-14 A.D. 2. Rome — Relations (general) with Greece. 3. Greece — Relations (general) with Rome. I. T.
DG279.B68   LC 65-6502

Charles-Picard, Gilbert.   **3.2796**
[Auguste et Néron. English] Augustus and Nero / Translated from the French by Len Ortzen. — New York: T. Y. Crowell Co. [1968] xxviii, 190 p.; 19 cm. (Apollo editions A-183) 1. Augustus, Emperor of Rome, 63 B.C.-14 A.D. 2. Nero, Emperor of Rome, 37-68. I. T.
DG279.C483 1968   937/.06/0922   LC 68-19788

Rowell, Henry Thompson, 1904-.   • **3.2797**
Rome in the Augustan age . — Norman: University of Oklahoma Press, [1963, c1962] xv, 242 p.: map. — (Centers of civilization series; 5) 1. Rome (Italy) — History. 2. Rome — History — Augustus, 30 B.C.-14 A.D. 3. Rome — Civilization I. T.
DG279.R63   LC 62-11277   ISBN 0806109564

Marsh, Frank Burr, 1880-1940.   • **3.2798**
The reign of Tiberius. — New York, Barnes & Noble [1959] vi, 335 p. 22 cm. Bibliography: p. [311]-315. 1. Tiberius, Emperor of Rome, 42 B. C. — 37 A. D. 2. Rome — Hist. — Tiberius, 14 — 379 3. Rome — Hist. — Augustus, 30 B. C. — 14 A. D. I. T.
DG282.Mx   937.07   LC 61-19842

Balsdon, J. P. V. D. (John Percy Vyvian Dacre), 1901-.   • **3.2799**
The Emperor Gaius (Caligula) / by J. P. V. D. Balsdon ... — Oxford: The Clarendon press, 1934. xxix, 243, [1] p.: fold. geneal. tab.; 19.5 cm. 'Bibliography of modern works on Gaius': p. [xii]-xiv. 1. Caligula, emperor of Rome, 12 — 41. I. T.
DG283.B3   937.07   LC 35-1068

MacMullen, Ramsay, 1928-.   **3.2800**
Roman government's response to crisis, A.D. 235–337 / Ramsay MacMullen. New Haven: Yale University Press, 1976. ix, 308 p., [1] leaf of plates: ports.; 22 cm. 1. Rome — History — Maximinus, 235-238 2. Rome — Politics and government — 30 A.D.-284 A.D. I. T.
DG306.M3   937/.07   LC 75-43324   ISBN 0300020082

DG311–365 Decline and Fall (284–476)

Bury, J. B., 1861-1927.   • **3.2801**
History of the later Roman Empire from the Death of Theodosius I. to the Death of Justinian / by J. B. Bury. — New York: Dover Publications, 1958. 2v.(471,494p.): ill. 1. Rome — History — Empire, 284-476 2. Byzantine Empire — History I. T.
DG311.B98 1958   937.08   LC 58-11273

Gibbon, Edward, 1737-1794.   • **3.2802**
The history of the decline & fall of the Roman empire, by Edward Gibbon, illustrated from the etchings by Gian Battista Piranesi. The text edited by J. B. Bury, with the notes by Mr. Gibbon, and the introduction and the index as prepared by Professor Bury; also with a letter to the reader from Philip Guedalla. New York, The Heritage press, f[1946] 3 v. front., plates, maps. 24 cm. Paged continuously. Part of the illustrative matter is folded. 1. Rome — History — Empire, B.C. 30-A.D. 476. 2. Byzantine empire — History. I. Bury, John Bagnell, 1861-1927, ed. II. Piranesi, Giovanni Battista, 1720-1778, illus. III. T.
DG311.G56   LC 46-6725

Bond, Harold L.   • **3.2803**
The literary art of Edward Gibbon. — Oxford, Clarendon Press, 1960. 167 p. 22 cm. 'This study was originally prepared as a dissertation for the Ph. D. degree at Harvard ... [and] has been extensively revised.' Bibliographical footnotes. 1. Gibbon, Edward, 1787-1794. The history of the decline and fall of the Roman Empire. I. T.
DG311.G6B6   937   LC 60-2049

Grant, Michael, 1914-.   **3.2804**
The fall of the Roman Empire: a reappraisal / by Michael Grant. — [Radnor, Pa.]: Annenberg School Press; [New York]: distributed by C. N. Potter, c1976. 336 p., [1] leaf of plates: ill.; 27 cm. Includes index. 1. Rome — History — Empire, 30 B.C.-476 A.D. 2. Byzantine Empire — History — To 527 I. T.
DG311.G75   937/.09   LC 75-24826   ISBN 0517524481

Jones, A. H. M. (Arnold Hugh Martin), 1904-1970.   • **3.2805**
The later Roman Empire, 284–602: a social economic and administrative survey / by A.H.M. Jones. — 1st ed. — Norman: University of Oklahoma Press, 1964. — 2 v. (xv, 1518 p.) : ill. + atlas of 7 folded maps. 1. Rome — History — Empire, 284-476 2. Byzantine Empire — History I. T.
DG311.J6 1964a   LC 64-20762

Jones, A. H. M. (Arnold Hugh Martin), 1904-1970.   • **3.2806**
The decline of the ancient world [by] A. H. M. Jones. New York, Holt, Rinehart and Winston [1966] viii, 414 p. 3 fold. maps. 22 cm. (A General history of Europe) 1. Rome — History — Empire, 284-476 2. Byzantine Empire — History — To 527 I. T.
DG311.J62 1966a   937.08   LC 66-15446

Jones, Tom Bard, 1909-.   **3.2807**
In the twilight of antiquity: the R. S. Hoyt memorial lectures (1973) / by Tom B. Jones. — Minneapolis: University of Minnesota Press, c1978. ix, 146 p.: ill.; 23 cm. Includes index. 1. Church history — Primitive and early church, ca. 30-600 — Addresses, essays, lectures. 2. Rome — History — Empire, 284-476 — Addresses, essays, lectures. I. Hoyt, Robert S. (Robert Stuart) II. T.
DG311.J63 1978   937/.06   LC 77-83502   ISBN 0816608326

Lot, Ferdinand, 1866-1952.   • **3.2808**
[La fin du monde antique et le debut du moyen age. English] The end of the ancient world and the beginnings of the Middle Ages. New York, Barnes & Noble [1966] xxvi, 454 p. plates, 3 fold. maps. 25 cm. 1. Civilization, Medieval 2. Europe — History — 392-814 I. T.
DG311.L65 1966   LC 66-5248

Boak, Arthur Edward Romilly, 1888-1962.   • **3.2809**
Manpower shortage and the fall of the Roman Empire in the West. Ann Arbor: U. of Michigan P., 1955. 169 p.: map (on lining papers) bibl. (Jerome lectures. 3d ser.) 1. Rome — Population. 2. Rome — History — Empire, 284-476 I. T. II. Series.
DG312.B58   937.08   LC 55-14610

Williams, Stephen, 1942-.   **3.2810**
Diocletian and the Roman recovery / Stephen Williams. — New York: Methuen, 1985. 264 p., [8] p. of plates: ill.; 25 cm. Includes index. 1. Diocletian, Emperor of Rome, 245-313. 2. Rome — History — Diocletian, 284-305 3. Rome — History — Constantines, 306-363 I. T.
DG313.W54 1985   937/.06/0924 19   LC 85-3013   ISBN 0416011519

Barnes, Timothy David.   **3.2811**
Constantine and Eusebius / Timothy D. Barnes. — Cambridge, Mass.: Harvard University Press, 1981. vi, 458 p.: map; 24 cm. Includes indexes. 1. Constantine I, Emperor of Rome, d. 337. 2. Eusebius, of Caesarea, Bishop of Caesarea, ca. 260-ca. 340. 3. Church history — Primitive and early church, ca. 30-600 4. Rome — History — Constantine I, the Great, 306-337 I. T.
DG315.B35   937/.08/0922 19   LC 81-4248   ISBN 0674165306

Bowder, Diana.   **3.2812**
The age of Constantine and Julian / Diana Bowder. — New York: Barnes & Noble Books, 1978. xiii, 230 p., [16] leaves of plates: ill.; 25 cm. Includes index. 1. Church history — Primitive and early church, ca. 30-600 2. Rome — History — Empire, 284-476 I. T.
DG315.B68 1978   937/.08   LC 79-112742   ISBN 0064906019

Burckhardt, Jacob, 1818-1897.   • **3.2813**
The age of Constantine the Great; tr. by Moses Hadas. New York, Pantheon Books [1949] 400 p. map (on lining-paper) geneal. table. 22 cm. 'On the ancient sources': p. [377]-379. 1. Rome — Civilization 2. Rome — History — Constantines, 306-363 I. T.
DG315.B923   937.08   LC 49-8918

Dörries, Hermann, 1895-1977.   **3.2814**
[Konstantin der Grosse. English] Constantine the Great. Translated by Roland H. Bainton. New York, Harper & Row [1972] xi, 250 p. 21 cm. (Harper

torchbooks, HR 1567) 1. Constantine I, Emperor of Rome, d. 337. 2. Church history — Primitive and early church, ca. 30-600 I. T.
DG315.D613 1972   270.1/0924   *LC* 72-179281   *ISBN* 0061384957

Browning, Robert, 1914-.   3.2815
The Emperor Julian / Robert Browning. — Berkeley: University of California Press, c1976. xii, 256 p., [4] leaves of plates: ill.; 25 cm. Includes index. 1. Julian, Emperor of Rome, 331-363. I. T.
DG317.B76 1976   937/.08/0924 B   *LC* 75-13159   *ISBN* 0520030346

Alföldi, Andreas, 1895-1981.   • 3.2816
A conflict of ideas in the late Roman Empire: theclash between the Senate and Valentinian I ' translated by Harold Mattingly. Oxford: Clarendon Press, 1952. vi, 151 p. 1. Valentinian I, Emperor of Rome, 321-375. 2. Rome. Senate. 3. Rome — Civilization I. T.
DG319.A6   *LC* 52-7543

Goffart, Walter A.   3.2817
Barbarians and Romans, A.D. 418–584: the techniques of accommodation / by Walter Goffart. — Princeton, N.J.: Princeton University Press, c1980. xv, 278 p.; 23 cm. 1. Acculturation — Rome. 2. Rome — Foreign population. 3. Rome — History — Germanic Invasions, 3d-6th centuries I. T.
DG319.G63   940.1/2   *LC* 80-7522   *ISBN* 0691053030

Kaegi, Walter Emil.   • 3.2818
Byzantium and the decline of Rome. Princeton, N.J.: Princeton University Press, 1968. xi, 289 p.: ill.; 23 cm. A revision of the author's thesis, Harvard. 1. Rome — History — Empire, 284-476 2. Byzantine Empire — Relations — Rome. 3. Rome — Relations — Byzantine Empire. I. T.
DG319.K3   937/.09   *LC* 67-21026

Matthews, John Frederick.   3.2819
Western aristocracies and imperial court, A.D. 364–425 / by John Matthews. — Oxford: Clarendon Press, 1975. xiv, 427 p.; 23 cm. Includes index. 1. Church history — Primitive and early church, ca. 30-600 2. Rome — History — Empire, 284-476 3. Rome — Court and courtiers. I. T.
DG319.M37   322.4/3/0937   *LC* 75-309538   *ISBN* 0198148178

Holum, Kenneth G.   3.2820
Theodosian empresses: women and imperial dominion in late antiquity / Kenneth G. Holum. — Berkeley: University of California Press, c1982. xiv, 258 p.: ill.; 25 cm. — (Transformation of the classical heritage. 3) Originally presented as the author's thesis (Ph.D.)—University of Chicago. Includes index. 1. Roman empresses — Biography. 2. Rome — Nobility — Biography. 3. Rome — History — Theodosians, 379-455 I. T. II. Series.
DG322.H64 1982   937/.02 19   *LC* 81-43690   *ISBN* 0520041623

DG401–999 Medieval and Modern Italy (476–

Italy, a country study / Foreign Area Studies, the American University; edited by Rinn S. Shinn.   3.2821
2nd ed. — Washington, D.C.: Headquarters, Dept. of the Army: For sale by the Supt. of Docs., U.S. G.P.O., 1985. p. cm. (Area handbook series.) (DA pam. 550-182) 'Research completed September 1985.' Includes index. 1. Italy. I. Shinn, Rinn-Sup. II. American University (Washington, D.C.). Foreign Area Studies. III. Series. IV. Series: DA pam. 550-182
DG417.I887   945 19   *LC* 86-3392

Waley, Daniel Philip.   3.2822
The Italian city–republics [by] Daniel Waley. New York, McGraw-Hill [1969] 254 p. illus. (part col.), col. maps. 20 cm. (World university library) 1. Cities and towns, Medieval — Italy — History. 2. City-states — Italy — History. 3. Italy — History — 1268-1492 I. T.
DG417.W28   914.5/09/732   *LC* 68-25149

Dickens, Charles, 1812-1870.   3.2823
Pictures from Italy. With an introd. and notes by David Paroissien. [1st American ed.] New York, Coward, McCann & Geoghegan [1974] 270 p. illus. 22 cm. 1. Dickens, Charles, 1812-1870 — Journeys — Italy. 2. Italy — Description and travel — 1801-1860 I. Paroissien, David. ed. II. T.
DG426.D5 1974   914.5/04/8   *LC* 73-85661   *ISBN* 0698105680

Béthemont, Jacques.   3.2824
[Italie. English] Italy: a geographical introduction / Jacques Béthemont and Jean Pelletier; translated by Eleonore Kofman; edited by Russell King. — London; New York: Longman, 1983. 222 p.: ill.; 24 cm. Translation of: L'Italie.

1. Italy — Description and travel — 1975- I. Pelletier, Jean, 1926- II. King, Russell. III. T.
DG430.2.B4713 1983   945 19   *LC* 81-15661   *ISBN* 0582300738

Olschki, Leonardo, 1885-.   • 3.2825
The genius of Italy. Ithaca, N.Y. Cornell University Press [1954] 481p. 1. Italy — Civilization — History I. T.
DG441 O55 1954

Sforza, Carlo, conte, 1872-1952.   • 3.2826
Italy and Italians; translated by Edward Hutton. — New York: Dutton, 1949. 165 p. 1. Italy — Civilization I. T.
DG441.S428 1949   945

Becker, Marvin B.   3.2827
Medieval Italy: constraints and creativity / Marvin B. Becker. — Bloomington: Indiana University Press, c1981. 242 p. Includes index. 1. Italy — Civilization — 476-1268 2. Italy — Religious life and customs. I. T.
DG443.B42   945 19   *LC* 80-8376   *ISBN* 0253152941

A Concise encyclopaedia of the Italian Renaissance / edited by J.R. Hale.   3.2828
New York: Oxford University Press, 1981. 360 p.: ill.; 22 cm. 1. Renaissance — Italy — Dictionaries. 2. Italy — Civilization — 1268-1559 — Dictionaries. 3. Italy — Civilization — 1559-1789 — Dictionaries. I. Hale, J. R. (John Rigby), 1923-
DG445.C66   945/.05/0321 19   *LC* 81-81905   *ISBN* 0195202848

Rinascimento. English.   3.2829
The Renaissance: essays in interpretation / André Chastel ... [et al.]. — London; New York: Methuen, 1982. 336 p.; 24 cm. Translation of: Il Rinascimento. 1979. 1. Renaissance — Italy — Addresses, essays, lectures. 2. Renaissance — Europe — Addresses, essays, lectures. 3. Italy — Civilization — 1268-1559 — Addresses, essays, lectures. 4. Europe — Civilization — 16th century — Addresses, essays, lectures. 5. Europe — Civilization — 17th century — Addresses, essays, lectures. I. Chastel, André, 1912- II. T.
DG445.R5613 1982   945/.05 19   *LC* 83-9363   *ISBN* 041631130X

Venturi, Franco.   3.2830
Italy and the enlightenment: studies in a cosmopolitan century / Franco Venturi; edited with an introduction by Stuart Woolf; translated by Susan Corsi. — New York: New York University Press, 1973 (c1972). xxi, 302 p.; 22 cm. 1. Enlightenment 2. Italy — Intellectual life I. Woolf, S. J. II. T.
DG447.V38   B802.V4.   914.5/03/7   *LC* 72-77153   *ISBN* 0814787525

Tannenbaum, Edward R.   3.2831
The Fascist experience: Italian society and culture, 1922–1945 / Edward R. Tannenbaum. — New York: Basic Books, 1972. vi, 357 p.: ill. 1. Fascism — Italy 2. Italy — Social conditions I. T.
DG450.T36   *LC* 73-174813   *ISBN* 0465068774

DG461–579 HISTORY

Cochrane, Eric W.   3.2832
Historians and historiography in the Italian Renaissance / Eric Cochrane. — Chicago: University of Chicago Press, 1981. xx, 649 p.; 25 cm. 1. Historiography — History. 2. Humanism 3. Italy — Historiography. 4. Italy — History — 1492-1559 5. Italy — History — 1559-1789 6. Italy — History, Local. I. T.
DG465.C62   945/.0072   *LC* 80-16097   *ISBN* 0226111520

Phillips, Mark, 1946-.   3.2833
Francesco Guicciardini: the historian's craft / Mark Phillips. — Toronto; Buffalo: University of Toronto Press, c1977. x, 195 p.; 24 cm. — (University of Toronto romance series. 33) Includes index. 1. Guicciardini, Francesco, 1483-1540. 2. Italy — Historiography. I. T. II. Series.
DG465.7.G84 P48   945/.06/0924   *LC* 76-56341   *ISBN* 0802053718

Hearder, Harry.   3.2834
Italy in the age of the Risorgimento, 1790–1870 / Harry Hearder. — London; New York: Longman, 1983. x, 325 p.: maps; 24 cm. — (Longman history of Italy. v. 6) 1. Italy — History — 1789-1870 I. T. II. Series.
DG467.L67 1980 vol. 6 DG551   945/.08 19   *LC* 82-23974   *ISBN* 0582491460

Mack Smith, Denis, 1920-.   • 3.2835
Italy; a modern history. — New ed. rev. and enl. — Ann Arbor: University of Michigan Press, [1969] xi, 542, xxx p.: maps.; 25 cm. — (The University of Michigan history of the modern world) 1. Italy — History I. T.
DG467.M3 1969   945   *LC* 69-15851

Salvatorelli, Luigi, 1886-1974. • **3.2836**
A concise history of Italy from prehistoric times to our own day. London Allen & Unwin [1940] 688p. 1. Italy — History I. T.
DG467 S323 1940A

Trevelyan, Janet Penrose (Ward), 1879-. • **3.2837**
A short history of the Italian people, from the barbarian invasions to the present day. rev. [i.e. 4th] ed. London Allen & Unwin [1956] 425p. 1. Italy — History I. T.
DG468 T7 1956

Martines, Lauro. **3.2838**
Power and imagination: city–states in Renaissance Italy / by Lauro Martines. — 1st ed. — New York: Knopf, 1979. ix, 368 p., [8] leaves of plates: ill.; 24 cm. Includes index. 1. Cities and towns — Italy — History. 2. City-states — Italy — History. 3. Italy — Politics and government — 476-1268 4. Italy — Politics and government — 1268-1559 5. Italy — Civilization — 476-1268 6. Italy — Civilization — 1268-1559 I. T.
DG494.M37 1979   945   LC 78-11666   ISBN 0394501128

Cassels, Alan, 1929-. • **3.2839**
Mussolini's early diplomacy. — Princeton, N.J.: Princeton University Press, 1970. xvii, 425 p.: map.; 23 cm. 1. Italy — Politics and government — 1922-1945 2. Italy — Foreign relations — 1922-1945 I. T.
DG498.C27   327.45   LC 72-90944   ISBN 0691051798

Kogan, Norman. • **3.2840**
Italy and the Allies. Cambridge Harvard University Press 1956. 246p. 1. Italy — Foreign relations — 20th century 2. World War, 1939-1945 — Italy I. T.
DG498 K6

Diggins, John P. • **3.2841**
Mussolini and fascism; the view from America [by] John P. Diggins. — Princeton, N.J.: Princeton University Press, [1972] xx, 524 p.: illus.; 25 cm. 1. Mussolini, Benito, 1883-1945. 2. Fascism — Italy 3. Italian Americans 4. Italy — Foreign opinion, American. I. T.
DG499.U5 D5   914.5/03/91   LC 78-153845   ISBN 0691046042

DG500–579 By Period

DG500–549 MEDIEVAL TO 1815

Thompson, E. A. **3.2842**
Romans and barbarians: the decline of the western empire / E.A. Thompson. — Madison: University of Wisconsin Press, 1982. ix, 329 p.: maps; 24 cm. — (Wisconsin studies in classics.) 1. Rome — History — Germanic Invasions, 3d-6th centuries I. T. II. Series.
DG504.T46 1982   945/.01 19   LC 81-50828   ISBN 029908700X

Hyde, John Kenneth. **3.2843**
Society and politics in medieval Italy; the evolution of the civil life, 1000–1350 [by] J. K. Hyde. — New York: St. Martin's Press, [1973] xv, 229 p.: illus.; 23 cm. — (New studies in medieval history) 1. Italy — Politics and government — 476-1268 2. Italy — Social conditions I. T.
DG523.H9 1973   309.1/45   LC 73-80085

Pullan, Brian S. **3.2844**
A history of early Renaissance Italy: from the mid–thirteenth to the mid–fifteenth century [by] Brian Pullan. — New York: St. Martin's Press, [1973, c1972] 386 p.: maps; 23 cm. 1. Italy — History — 1268-1492 2. Italy — Civilization — 1268-1559 I. T.
DG530.P84 1973b   914.5/03/5   LC 72-93030

Burckhardt, Jacob, 1818-1897. • **3.2845**
The civilization of the Renaissance in Italy / Jacob Burckhardt; translation by S.G.C. Middlemore; introd. by Benjamin Nelson and Charles Trinkaus. — New York: Harper & Row, 1958. 2 v.: ill. — (Harper Colophon books; CN 459-460.) 'This translation is made from the 15th ed. of the German original.' 1. Renaissance — Italy. 2. Italy — Civilization I. T.
DG533.B94 1958a   ISBN 0060904593

Garin, Eugenio, 1909-. **3.2846**
[Umanesimo italiano. English] Italian humanism: philosophy and civic life in the Renaissance / Eugenio Garin; translated by Peter Munz. — Westport, Conn.: Greenwood Press, 1975, c1965. xxiv, 227 p.; 23 cm. Translation of L'umanesimo italiano, which was originally published in German under title: Der italienische Humanismus. Reprint of the ed. published by Harper and Row, New York. 1. Renaissance — Italy. I. T.
DG533.G323 1975   945/.05   LC 75-35025   ISBN 0837185785

Hay, Denys. **3.2847**
The Italian Renaissance in its historical background / by Denys Hay. 2d ed. — Cambridge, [Eng.]; New York: Cambridge University Press, 1977, c1976. xvi,

228 p., [12] leaves of plates: ill.; 22 cm. Includes index. 1. Renaissance — Italy. I. T.
DG533.H39 1977   945/.05   LC 76-8293   ISBN 0521213215

Lopez, Robert Sabatino, 1910-. **3.2848**
The three ages of the Italian Renaissance, by Robert S. Lopez. Charlottesville, University Press of Virginia [1970] vi, 103 p. illus. 25 cm. (Richard lectures for 1968-1969, University of Virginia) 1. Renaissance — Italy — Addresses, essays, lectures. I. T.
DG533.L65   914.5/03/5   LC 75-94759   ISBN 0813902703

Symonds, John Addington, 1840-1893. • **3.2849**
Renaissance in Italy. — New York, The Modern library [1935] 2 v. 21 cm. — (The modern library of the world's best books) 1. Renaissance — Italy. 2. Italy — History 3. Humanism 4. Art, Italian 5. Italian literature — History and criticism 6. Catholic Church — History I. T.
DG533.S945 1935   LC 35-27141

Bowsky, William M. • **3.2850**
Henry VII in Italy; the conflict of empire and city–state, 1310–1313. — Lincoln: University of Nebraska Press, 1960. xii, 301 p.: plates, map (on lining papers); 24 cm. 1. Heinrich VII, Emperor of Germany, 1269?-1313. 2. City-states — Italy — History. 3. Italy — History — 1268-1492 I. T.
DG535.B6   945.05   LC 60-7325

Baron, Hans, 1900-. • **3.2851**
The crisis of the early Italian Renaissance; civic humanism and republican liberty in an age of classicism and tyranny. — Rev. 1 vol. ed. with an epilogue. — Princeton, N. J., Princeton University Press, 1966. xviii, 584 p. illus. 21 cm. Bibliographical references included in 'Notes': (p. 465-564) 1. Italy — Pol. & govt. — 1268-1559. 2. Humanism 3. Renaissance — Italy. I. T.
DG537.B37 1966   945.05   LC 66-10549

Mallett, Michael Edward. **3.2852**
Mercenaries and their masters; warfare in renaissance Italy [by] Michael Mallett. — Totowa, N.J.: Rowman and Littlefield, [1974] 284 p.: illus.; 23 cm. 1. Condottieri 2. Italy — History, Military. 3. Italy — History — 1268-1492 I. T.
DG537.M34 1974   355.3/1   LC 74-154444   ISBN 0874714478

Guicciardini, Francesco, 1483-1540. **3.2853**
[Historia d'Italia. English] The history of Italy / by Francesco Guicciardini; translated, edited, with notes and an introduction by Sidney Alexander. — Princeton, N.J.: Princeton University Press, 1984, c1969. xxvii, 457 p.: ill.; 23 cm. Translation and abridgement of: Historia d'Italia. Previously published: New York: Macmillan, [1968, c1969] 1. Italy — History — 1492-1559 I. Alexander, Sidney, 1912- II. T.
DG539.G813 1984   945/.06 19   LC 83-43221   ISBN 0691054177

Dictionary of modern Italian history / Frank J. Coppa, editor–in–chief. **3.2854**
Westport, Conn.: Greenwood Press, 1985. xxvi, 496 p.; 24 cm. 1. Italy — History — 18th century — Dictionaries. 2. Italy — History — 19th century — Dictionaries. 3. Italy — History — 20th century — Dictionaries. I. Coppa, Frank J.
DG545.D53 1985   945/.003/21 19   LC 84-6704   ISBN 031322983X

Noether, Emiliana Pasca. • **3.2855**
Seeds of Italian nationalism, 1700–1815. — New York: AMS Press, [1969] 202 p.; 23 cm. — (Columbia University studies in the social sciences, 570) Reprint of the 1951 ed., issued also as thesis, Columbia University. 1. Nationalism — Italy. 2. Italy — Politics and government I. T.
DG545.N6 1969   320.1/58/0945   LC 79-94926

DG551–759 1815-

Albrecht-Carrié, René, 1904-. • **3.2856**
Italy from Napoleon to Mussolini. — New York: Columbia University Press, 1950. xiii, 314 p.; 24 cm. 1. Italy — History — 1815-1870 2. Italy — History — 1870-1915 3. Italy — History — 1914-1945 I. T.
DG551.A6   945.08   LC 49-50178

Berkeley, George Fitz-Hardinge, 1870-. • **3.2857**
Italy in the making. By G. F.–H. Berkeley. — Cambridge [Eng.]: The University press, 1932-[40] 3 v.: fronts. (ports.) maps (part fold.); 22 cm. Vol. 2-3: By G. F.–H. & J. Berkeley. 1. Italy — History — 1815-1870 I. Berkeley, Joan (Weld) Mrs. II. T.
DG551.B4   945.08   LC 33-7256

Tannenbaum, Edward R. **3.2858**
Modern Italy; a topical history since 1861. Edited by Edward R. Tannenbaum and Emiliana P. Noether. — New York: New York University Press, 1974.

xxix, 395 p.; 24 cm. 1. Italy — History — 19th century 2. Italy — History — 20th century I. Noether, Emiliana Pasca, joint author. II. T.
DG551.T36　　309.1/45/09　　LC 73-20031　　ISBN 081478156X

DG552–554 Risorgimento (1848–1871)

King, Bolton, 1860-.　　　　　　　　　　　　　　　• 3.2859
A history of Italian unity, being a political history of Italy from 1814 to 1871. — New York, Russell & Russell [1967] 2 v. maps. 23 cm. Reprint of the rev. ed. of 1924. Bibliography: v. 2, p. 399-424. 1. Italy — Hist. — 1815-1870. I. T.
DG552.K52 1967　　945/.08　　LC 66-24716

Mack Smith, Denis, 1920- comp.　　　　　　　　　• 3.2860
The making of Italy, 1796–1870. — New York: Walker, [1968] viii, 428 p.: maps.; 24 cm. — (Documentary history of Western civilization) 1. Italy — History — 19th century — Sources. I. T.
DG552.M26　　945/.08/08　　LC 68-13331

Lovett, Clara Maria, 1939-.　　　　　　　　　　　3.2861
The democratic movement in Italy, 1830–1876 / Clara M. Lovett. — Cambridge, Mass.: Harvard University Press, 1982. x, 285 p.; 25 cm. Includes index. 1. Liberalism — Italy — History — 19th century. 2. Revolutionists — Italy — Biography. 3. Italy — Politics and government — 1815-1870 I. T.
DG552.5.L68　　945/.08 19　　LC 81-6403　　ISBN 0674196457

Mack Smith, Denis, 1920-.　　　　　　　　　　　3.2862
Victor Emanuel, Cavour and the Risorgimento. London, New York, Oxford University Press, 1971. xviii, 381 p. 1 illus., maps, ports. 25 cm. 1. Cavour, Camillo Benso, conte di, 1810-1861. 2. Victor Emmanuel II, King of Italy, 1820-1878. 3. Italy — History — 1849-1870 I. T.
DG552.5.M3　　945/.08/0922　　LC 74-31860　　ISBN 0192125508

Grew, Raymond.　　　　　　　　　　　　　　　• 3.2863
A sterner plan for Italian unity; the Italian National Society in the Risorgimento. — Princeton, N. J., Princeton University Press, 1963. xiii, 500 p. fold. map. 25 cm. Bibliographical footnotes. 1. Società Nazionale Italiana. 2. Italy — Hist. — 1849-1870. I. T.
DG552.6.G7　　945.08　　LC 63-7068

Rudman, Harry William, 1908-.　　　　　　　　　3.2864
Italian nationalism and English letters; figures of the risorgimento and Vatican men of letters. New York Columbia University Press 1940. 444p. (Columbia University studies in English and comparative literature, no. 146) 1. Italians in London 2. Authors, English 3. English literature — 19th century — History and criticism I. T. II. Series.
DG552.7 R8

Lovett, Clara Maria, 1939-.　　　　　　　　　　　3.2865
Carlo Cattaneo and the politics of the Risorgimento, 1820–1860. — The Hague: Nijhoff, 1972 [1973] x, 138 p.; 24 cm. 1. Cattaneo, Carlo, 1801-1869. 2. Italy — Politics and government — 1815-1870 I. T.
DG552.8.C25 L68　　320.9/45/08　　LC 73-164298　　ISBN 9024712831

Mack Smith, Denis, 1920-.　　　　　　　　　　　3.2866
Cavour / Denis Mack-Smith. — New York: Knopf, 1985. xiii, 294 p.: maps; 24 cm. Includes index. 1. Cavour, Camillo Benso, conte di, 1810-1861. 2. Statesmen — Italy — Biography. 3. Italy — History — 1849-1870 I. T.
DG552.8.C3 M17 1985　　945/.08/0924 B 19　　LC 84-48815　　ISBN 0394538854

Thayer, William Roscoe, 1859-1923.　　　　　　　• 3.2867
The life and times of Cavour. — New York: H. Fertig, 1971 [c1911] 2 v.: geneal. tables, maps, ports.; 23 cm. 1. Cavour, Camillo Benso, conte di, 1810-1861. 2. Italy — History — 1849-1870 I. T.
DG552.8.C3 T5 1971　　945/.08/0924 B　　LC 68-9634

Whyte, Arthur James Beresford.　　　　　　　　　3.2868
The early life and letters of Cavour, 1810–1848. Oxford, Univ. Press, 1925. xix, 384 p. pl., port., facs. 1. Cavour, Camillo Benso, conte di, 1810-1861. I. T.
DG552.8.C3 W5

Whyte, Arthur James Beresford.　　　　　　　　　• 3.2869
The political life and letters of Cavour, 1848–1861 / by A. J. Whyte. — London: Oxford university press, H. Milford, 1930. xv, 478 p.: port.; 22 cm. 1. Cavour, Camillo Benso, conte di, 1810-1861. I. T.
DG552.8.C3 W52 1975　　945/.08/0924 B　　LC 31-7360

Lovett, Clara Maria, 1939-.　　　　　　　　　　　3.2870
Giuseppe Ferrari and the Italian Revolution / by Clara M. Lovett. — Chapel Hill: University of North Carolina Press, c1979. xiii, 278 p.: port.; 22 cm. Includes index. 1. Ferrari, Giuseppe, 1811-1876. 2. Statesmen — Italy — Biography. 3. Intellectuals — Italy — Biography. 4. Italy — Politics and government — 19th century. 5. France — Intellectual life I. T.
DG552.8.F46 L68　　945/.08/0924　　LC 78-24099　　ISBN 0807813540

Mack Smith, Denis, 1920-.　　　　　　　　　　　• 3.2871
Garibaldi, a great life in brief. — [1st ed.]. — New York: Knopf, 1956. 207 p.: illus.; 19 cm. — (Great lives in brief; a new series of biographies) 1. Garibaldi, Giuseppe, 1807-1882. I. T.
DG552.8.G2 M24　　923.245　　LC 56-5804

Trevelyan, George Macaulay, 1876-1962.　　　　　• 3.2872
Garibaldi and the making of Italy, by George Macaulay Trevelyan ... with four maps and numerous illustrations. — New York [etc.] Longmans, Green and co., 1911. xix, [1], 390 p. front., plates, ports., 4 fold. maps. 23.5 cm. Bibliography: p. 351-374. 1. Garibaldi, Giuseppe, 1807-1882. 2. Italy — Hist. — War of 1860-1861. I. T.
DG552.8.G2T7　　LC 11-35882

Trevelyan, George Macaulay, 1876-1962.　　　　　• 3.2873
Garibaldi and the Thousand / by George Macaulay Trevelyan. — London: Longmans, Green, 1909. xv, 395 p., [25] leaves of plates: ill., maps. 1. Garibaldi, Giuseppe, 1807-1882. 2. Expedition of the Thousand, 1860 3. Italy — History — War of 1860-1861 I. T.
DG552.8.G2 T75　　945/.08　　LC 10-1700

Mazzini, Giuseppe, 1805-1872.　　　　　　　　　• 3.2874
The living thoughts of Mazzini, presented by Ignazio Silone. — Westport, Conn.: Greenwood Press, [1972, c1939] 130 p.: front.; 22 cm. Original ed. issued in series: The living thoughts library. 'The selections are from Life and writings of Joseph Mazzini, published by Smith & Elder, 1864-1870.' 1. Mazzini, Giuseppe, 1805-1872. I. T.
DG552.8.M2918 1972　　320.5　　LC 79-138163　　ISBN 0837156203

Hales, Edward Elton Young, 1908-.　　　　　　　• 3.2875
Mazzini and the secret societies; the making of a myth. — New York, P. J. Kenedy [1956] 226 p. illus. 23 cm. 1. Mazzini, Giuseppe, 1805-1872. I. T.
DG552.8.M3H3　　923.245　　LC 56-9830

Salvemini, Gaetano, 1873-1957.　　　　　　　　　• 3.2876
Mazzini. Translated from the Italian by I.M. Rawson. Stanford, Stanford University Press [1957] 192 p. 23 cm. 1. Mazzini, Giuseppe, 1805-1872. I. T.
DG552.8.M3 S253　　LC 57-7972

Mack Smith, Denis, 1920-.　　　　　　　　　　　• 3.2877
Cavour and Garibaldi, 1860; a study in political conflict. — Cambridge [Eng.] University Press, 1954. xii, 458 p. ports., map (on lining-papers) 24 cm. Bibliographical footnotes. 1. Cavour, Camillo Benso, conte di, 1810-1861. 2. Garibaldi, Ginseppe, 1807-1882. 3. Italy — Hist. — War of 1860-1861. I. T.
DG554.M3　　945.08　　LC 54-3061

DG555–575 Monarchy. Fascism (1871–1947)

Croce, Benedetto, 1866-1952.　　　　　　　　　　• 3.2878
A history of Italy, 1871–1915/ Benedetto Croce; Translated by Cecilia M. Ady. — New York: Russell & Russell, 1963. 333 p. 1. Italy — History — 1870-1915 I. T.
DG555.C7713 1963　　LC 63-15154/ L

Lowe, C. J. (Cedric James), 1930-1975.　　　　　3.2879
Italian foreign policy, 1870–1940 / C. J. Lowe and F. Marzari. — London: Routledge & Paul, 1975. xi, 476 p.; 23 cm. (Foreign policies of the great powers) Includes index. 1. Italy — Foreign relations — 1870-1915 2. Italy — Foreign relations — 1914-1945 3. Italy — Politics and government — 1870-1915 4. Italy — Politics and government — 1914-1945 I. Marzari, F., 1938-1971, joint author. II. T.
DG555.L66　　327.45　　LC 75-310627　　ISBN 0710079877

Seton-Watson, Christopher.　　　　　　　　　　　• 3.2880
Italy from liberalism to fascism, 1870–1925. — [London]: Methuen, [1967] x, 772 p.: maps. 1. Italy — History — 1870-1915 2. Italy — History — 1914-1945 I. T.
DG555.S4 1967　　LC 67-114393

Salomone, A. William (Arcangelo William), 1915-.　• 3.2881
Italy in the Giolittian era; Italian democracy in the making, 1900–1914. Introductory essay by Gaetano Salvemini. — Philadelphia, University of Pennsylvania Press [1960] xxiv, 206 p. illus., ports. 24 cm. 'Section one, entitled 'Italian democracy in the making' ... appeared as a separate volume under that title in 1945 ... Section two will serve ... to bring up to date ... the materials.' Bibliography: p. 175-198. 1. Giolitti, Giovanni, 1842-1928. 2. Italy — Pol. & govt. — 20th cent. I. T.
DG566.S3 1960　　945.09　　LC 59-13438

Bosworth, R. J. B.　　　　　　　　　　　　　　　3.2882
Italy and the approach of the First World War / Richard Bosworth. — New York: St. Martin's Press, 1983. viii, 174 p.; 23 cm. — (Making of the 20th century.) 1. World War, 1914-1918 — Italy. 2. World War, 1914-1918 —

Causes. 3. Italy — Politics and government — 1870-1915 4. Italy — Foreign relations — 1870-1915 I. T. II. Series.
DG568.5.B66 1983   945.08 19   *LC* 82-16841   *ISBN* 0312439245

De Grand, Alexander J., 1938-.   **3.2883**
The Italian Nationalist Association and the rise of fascism in Italy / Alexander J. De Grand. — Lincoln: University of Nebraska Press, c1978. x, 238 p.; 23 cm. A revision of the author's thesis, University of Chicago. Includes index. 1. Associazione nazionalista italiana. 2. Fascism — Italy 3. Italy — Politics and government — 1915-1922 4. Italy — Politics and government — 1922-1945 I. T.
DG568.5.D48 1978   320.9/45/091   *LC* 77-24633   *ISBN* 0803209495

Historical dictionary of Fascist Italy / Philip V. Cannistraro, editor–in–chief.   **3.2884**
Westport, Conn.: Greenwood Press, 1982. xxix, 657 p.; 24 cm. 1. Fascism — Italy — Dictionaries. 2. Italy — Politics and government — 1922-1945 — Dictionaries. I. Cannistraro, Philip V., 1942-
DG571.A1 H57 1982   945.091/0321 19   *LC* 81-4493   *ISBN* 0313213178

Chabod, Federico.   • **3.2885**
A history of Italian fascism / Federico Chabod; translated from the Italian by Muriel Grindrod. — London: Weidenfeld and Nicolson, 1963. 192 p.; 22 cm. Translation of: L'Italia contemporanea. Includes index. 1. Fascism — Italy 2. Italy — History — 1914-1945 I. T.
DG571 C4443   *LC* 66-80589

Ledeen, Michael Arthur, 1941-.   **3.2886**
Universal fascism; the theory and practice of the fascist international, 1928–1936. — [1st ed.]. — New York: H. Fertig, 1972. xxi, 200 p.; 22 cm. 1. Fascism — Italy 2. Youth movement — Italy. 3. Fascism I. T.
DG571.L39   320.5/33/0945   *LC* 70-185794

Lyttelton, Adrian, 1937-.   **3.2887**
The seizure of power; Fascism in Italy, 1919–1929. — New York: Scribner, [1973] 544 p.; 25 cm. 1. Fascism — Italy 2. Italy — Politics and government — 1922-1945 I. T.
DG571.L95 1973b   321.9/4/0945   *LC* 73-3005   *ISBN* 0684134020

Mack Smith, Denis, 1920-.   **3.2888**
Mussolini's Roman Empire / Denis Mack Smith. — New York: Viking Press, 1976. xii, 322 p.: maps; 24 cm. Includes index. 1. Mussolini, Benito, 1883-1945. 2. Italy — Politics and government — 1922-1945 I. T.
DG571.M22   945.091/092/4   *LC* 75-46618   *ISBN* 0670496529

Molony, John N. (John Neylon), 1927-.   **3.2889**
The emergence of political catholicism in Italy: Partito popolare 1919–1926 / John N. Molony. — London: C. Helm; Totowa, N.J.: Rowman and Littlefield, 1977. 225 p.; 23 cm. Includes index. 1. Sturzo, Luigi, 1871-1959. 2. Partito popolare italiano. 3. Catholic Church in Italy. 4. Fascism — Italy 5. Italy — Politics and government — 1914-1945 I. T.
DG571.M57 1977   320.9/45/091   *LC* 76-54279   *ISBN* 0874719437

Mussolini, Benito, 1883-1945.   • **3.2890**
Fascism; doctrine and institutions. New York, H. Fertig, 1968. 313 p. 21 cm. Reprint of the 1935 ed. 'The doctrine of fascism' (p. [5]-42) is a translation of an article originally published in v. 14 (1932), p. 847-851, of the Enciclopedia italiana. 1. Partito nazionale fascista (Italy) 2. Fascism — Italy I. Italy. Laws, statutes, etc. II. T.
DG571.M764 1968   321.9/4/0945   *LC* 68-9636

Salvemini, Gaetano, 1873-1957.   • **3.2891**
The fascist dictatorship in Italy. New York, H. Fertig, 1967. ix, 319 p. ill., ports. 21 cm. 1. Fascism — Italy 2. Italy — Politics and government — 1922-1945 I. T.
DG571.S2 1967   *LC* 66-24352

Sarti, Roland, 1937- comp.   **3.2892**
The ax within: Italian fascism in action, edited with an introd. by Roland Sarti. — New York: New Viewpoints, 1974. xiv, 278 p.; 22 cm. — (Modern scholarship on European history) 1. Fascism — Italy 2. Italy — Politics and government — 1922-1945 I. T.
DG571.S276   320.9/45/091   *LC* 73-9559   *ISBN* 0531063674

Villari, Luigi, 1876-.   • **3.2893**
Italian foreign policy under Mussolini. New York, Devin-Adair Co., 1956. xii, 396 p. illus., ports. 22 cm. Includes bibliographical references. 1. Mussolini, Benito, 1883-1945. 2. Italy — Foreign relations — 1922-1945 I. T.
DG571.V535   327.45   *LC* 56-5712

Deakin, Frederick William, 1913-.   • **3.2894**
The brutal friendship: Mussolini, Hitler, and the fall of Italian fascism. — [1st American ed.]. — New York, Harper & Row [c1962] 896 p. 25 cm. Includes bibliography. 1. Mussolini, Benito, 1883-1945. 2. Hitler, Adolf, 1889-1945.

3. World War, 1939-1945 — Italy. 4. Germany — For. rel. — Italy. 5. Italy — For. rel. — Germany. I. T.
DG572.D38 1962a   945.091   *LC* 62-14527

Ciano, Edda Mussolini, Contessa.   **3.2895**
[Témoignage pour un homme. English] My truth / by Edda Mussolini Ciano as told to Albert Zarca; translated from the French by Eileen Finletter. — New York: Morrow, 1977. 256 p.: ill.; 22 cm. Translation of Témoignage pour un homme. Includes index. 1. Ciano, Edda Mussolini, Contessa. 2. Ciano, Galeazzo, conte, 1903-1944. 3. Mussolini, Benito, 1883-1945. 4. Statesmen — Italy — Biography. 5. Statesmen's wives — Italy — Biography. 6. Italy — Politics and government — 1922-1945 I. Zarca, Albert. II. T.
DG575.C516 A3513 1977   945.091/092/4 B 19   *LC* 76-26503   *ISBN* 0688030998

Ciano, Galeazzo, conte.   • **3.2896**
Ciano's diary, 1939–1943. Edited, with an introd. by Malcolm Muggeridge. Heinemann, 1947. xxii, 575 p., ports. 1. World War, 1939-1945 — Italy. 2. Italy — Foreign relations — 1922-1945 I. Muggeridge, Malcolm, ed. II. T.
DG575.C52 A32   940.5345   *LC* 47-28173

Ciano, Galeazzo, conte, 1903-1944.   • **3.2897**
Ciano's diplomatic papers: being a record of nearly 200 conversations held during the years 1936–42 with Hitler, Mussolini, Franco, Goering, Ribbentrop, Chamberlain, Eden, Sumner Welles, Schuschnigg, Lord Perth, Francois-Poncet, and many other world diplomatic and political figures, together with important memoranda, letters, telegrams, etc. / Ed by Malcolm Muggeridge; Tr. by Stuart Hood. — London: Odhams Press, 1948. xxii, 490 p.; 22 cm. 1. Europe — Politics — 1918-1945. 2. Italy — Foreign relations — 1922-1945 I. Muggeridge, Malcolm, 1903- II. Hood, Stuart. III. T.
DG575.C52 A413   *LC* 49-19765

Carrillo, Elisa A.   • **3.2898**
Alcide de Gasperi; the long apprenticeship, by Elisa A. Carrillo. [Notre Dame, Ind.] University of Notre Dame Press [1965] vii, 185 p. 25 cm. (Studies in Christian democracy) Bibliography: p. 173-178. 1. De Gasperi, Alcide, 1881-1954. I. T. II. Series.
DG575.G3C27   945.0920924 (B)   *LC* 65-23517

Fiori, Giuseppe, 1923-.   **3.2899**
[Vita di Antonio Gramsci. English] Antonio Gramsci: life of a revolutionary / [translated by Tom Nairn. — 1st ed.] New York: Dutton, 1971 [c1970] 304 p.; 24 cm. Translation of Vita di Antonio Gramsci. 1. Gramsci, Antonio, 1891-1937. I. T.
DG575.G69 F513 1971   335.43/0924 B   *LC* 70-148475   *ISBN* 0525056254

Mussolini, Benito, 1883-1945.   • **3.2900**
The fall of Mussolini: his own story / by Benito Mussolini; translated from the Italian by Frances Frenaye; edited and with a preface by Max Ascoli. New York: Farrar, Straus, 1948. 212 p.: map; 22 cm. Translation of Il tempo del bastone e della carota. 1. Mussolini, Benito, 1883-1945. 2. World War, 1939-1945 — Italy. 3. Italy — History — 1922-1945 — Sources. I. Ascoli, Max, 1888-. II. Frenaye, Frances. III. T.
DG 575 M8 A4 1948   *LC* 48-10400

Fermi, Laura.   • **3.2901**
Mussolini. — [Chicago]: University of Chicago Press, [1961] 477 p.: illus.; 23 cm. 1. Mussolini, Benito, 1883-1945. I. T.
DG575.M8 F42   923.245   *LC* 61-17075

Kirkpatrick, Ivone, Sir.   • **3.2902**
Mussolini: a study in power / by Ivone Kirkpatrick. — New York: Hawthorn Books, 1964. 726 p.: ill., geneal., table., maps, ports. 1. Mussolini, Benito, 1883-1945. 2. Italy — Politics and government — 1922-1945 I. T.
DG575M8 K5 1964   DG575M8 K5 1964.   923.245   *LC* 64-13278

Mack Smith, Denis, 1920-.   **3.2903**
Mussolini / Denis Mack Smith. — 1st American ed. — New York: Knopf, 1982. xiv, 429 p., [16] p. of plates: ill.; 24 cm. Includes index. 1. Mussolini, Benito, 1883-1945. 2. Fascism — Italy — History. 3. Heads of state — Italy — Biography. 4. Italy — Politics and government — 1922-1945 I. T.
DG575.M8 M223 1982   945.091/092/4 B 19   *LC* 81-48127   *ISBN* 0394506944

Mussolini, Rachele Guidi, 1892-.   **3.2904**
Mussolini: an intimate biography by his widow, Rachele Mussolini, as told to Albert Zarca. Morrow, 1974 (c1973). 291 p.: ill., ports. French ed. has title: Mussolini sans masque. 1. Mussolini, Benito, 1883-1945. I. Zarca, Albert. II. T.
DG575.M8 M8352   *LC* 74-1129   *ISBN* 0688002668

DG576–579 1948–

Grindrod, Muriel.   **3.2905**
The rebuilding of Italy: politics and economics, 1945–1955 / by Muriel Grindrod. — London; New York: Royal Institute of International Affairs, 1955. vii, 269 p.; 23 cm. Includes index. 1. Italy — Politics and government — 1945- 2. Italy — Economic conditions — 1945- I. Royal Institute of International Affairs. II. T.
DG577.G7   945.092   *LC* 56-13528

Woolf, S. J. (Stuart Joseph) ed.   **3.2906**
The rebirth of Italy, 1943–50. Edited by S.J. Woolf. New York, Humanities Press, 1972. 264 p. At head of title: Centre for the Advanced Study of Italian Society, University of Reading. 1. Italy — History — 1945- I. Reading, England. University. Centre for the Advanced Study of Italian Society. II. T.
DG577.W6   *ISBN* 039100249X

Hughes, H. Stuart (Henry Stuart), 1916-.   **3.2907**
The United States and Italy / H. Stuart Hughes. — 3d ed., enl. — Cambridge, Mass.: Harvard University Press, 1979. xiii, 324 p.: map; 22 cm. (The American foreign policy library) Includes index. 1. Italy — Politics and government — 1945-1976 2. Italy — Politics and government — 1976- 3. Italy — Economic conditions — 1945- 4. Italy — Relations — United States 5. United States — Relations — Italy I. T.
DG577.5.H83 1979   945.092   *LC* 79-63706   *ISBN* 0674925459

Kogan, Norman.   **3.2908**
A political history of Italy: the postwar years / Norman Kogan. — New York, NY: Praeger, 1983. xviii, 365 p.: map; 25 cm. Originally published as 2 separate works: A political history of postwar Italy, 1966 and A political history of postwar Italy: from the old to the new center-left, 1981. Includes index. 1. Italy — Politics and government — 1945- 2. Italy — Economic conditions — 1945-1976 3. Italy — Economic conditions — 1976- I. Kogan, Norman. Political history of postwar Italy. II. T.
DG577.5.K62 1983   945.092 19   *LC* 83-3963   *ISBN* 0030629594

DG600–999 Local History

Symcox, Geoffrey.   **3.2909**
Victor Amadeus II: absolutism in the Savoyard State, 1675–1730 / Geoffrey Symcox. — Berkeley: University of California Press, c1983. 272 p., [16] p. of plates: ill.; 23 cm. (Men in office.) 1. Victor Amadeus I, King of Sardinia, 1666-1732. 2. Savoy (France and Italy) — History 3. Sardinia — History 4. Piedmont (Principality) — History. 5. Savoy (France and Italy) — Kings and rulers — Biography. 6. Sardinia — Kings and rulers — Biography. 7. Piedmont (Principality) — Kings and rulers — Biography. I. T. II. Series.
DG618.53.S95 1983   945/.907/0924 19   *LC* 82-45904   *ISBN* 0520049748

DG651–679 Lombardy. Venice

Greenfield, Kent Roberts, 1893-1967.   **3.2910**
Economics and liberalism in the Risorgimento; a study of nationalism in Lombardy, 1814–1848. Introductory essay by Rosario Romeo. Rev. ed. Baltimore, Johns Hopkins Press, 1965. xxiii, 303 p. 24 cm. 1. Journalism — Lombardy. 2. Lombardy (Italy) — Economic conditions. 3. Italy — History — 1815-1870 I. T.
DG658.5.G7 1965   *LC* 65-27721

McNeill, William Hardy, 1917-.   **3.2911**
Venice: the hinge of Europe, 1081–1797 / William H. McNeill. — Chicago: University of Chicago Press, 1974. xvii, 334 p.: ill.; 23 cm. 1. Venice (Italy) — Civilization — To 1797 2. Europe — Civilization — Venetian influences 3. Venice (Italy) — History — 697-1508 4. Venice (Italy) — History — 1508-1797 I. T.
DG675.6.M23   945/.31   *LC* 73-84192   *ISBN* 0226561488

Lane, Frederic Chapin, 1900-.   **3.2912**
Venice, a maritime republic [by] Frederic C. Lane. Baltimore, Johns Hopkins University Press [1973] xiii, 505 p. illus. 27 cm. 1. Venice (Italy) — History 2. Venice (Italy) — Commerce — History. I. T.
DG676.L28   945/.31   *LC* 72-12342   *ISBN* 0801814456 *ISBN* 080181460X

Davis, James C. (James Cushman)   • **3.2913**
The decline of the Venetian nobility as a ruling class. — Baltimore, Johns Hopkins Press, 1962. 155 p. illus. 24 cm. — (Johns Hopkins University studies in historical and political science. ser. 80, no. 2) Bibliography: p. 144-148.

1. Venice — Nobility. 2. Venice — Hist. — 1508-1797. 3. Venice — Soc. condit. I. T. II. Series.
DG678.D3   945.31   *LC* 62-20558

Finlay, Robert, 1940-.   **3.2914**
Politics in Renaissance Venice / Robert Finlay. — New Brunswick, N.J.: Rutgers University Press, c1980. xvii, 308 p.; 24 cm. Includes index. 1. Venice (Italy) — Politics and government I. T.
DG678.235.F56   320.9/45/3105   *LC* 79-20012   *ISBN* 0813508886

Hale, J. R. (John Rigby), 1923-.   **3.2915**
Renaissance Venice. Edited by J. R. Hale. Totowa, N.J., Rowman and Littlefield [1973] 483 p. illus. 25 cm. 1. Venice (Italy) — Politics and government — 1508-1797 — Addresses, essays, lectures. 2. Venice (Italy) — Politics and government — 697-1508 — Addresses, essays, lectures. 3. Venice (Italy) — Civilization — To 1797 — Addresses, essays, lectures. I. T.
DG678.235.H34   914.5/31/035   *LC* 72-12940   *ISBN* 0874711665

Gilbert, Felix, 1905-.   **3.2916**
The Pope, his banker, and Venice / Felix Gilbert. — Cambridge, Mass.: Harvard University Press, 1980. vi, 157 p., [2] leaves of plates: ill.; 22 cm. 1. Julius II, Pope, 1443-1513. 2. Chigi, Agostino, 1466-1520. 3. Cambrai, League of, 1508 4. Catholic Church — Relations (diplomatic) — Italy — Venice 5. Papacy — History — 1447-1565 6. Venice (Italy) — History — 1508-1797 7. Venice (Italy) — Foreign relations — Catholic Church. I. T.
DG678.25.G54   945/.31   *LC* 80-13062   *ISBN* 0674689755

Ginsborg, Paul.   **3.2917**
Daniele Manin and the Venetian revolution of 1848–49 / Paul Ginsborg. — Cambridge; New York: Cambridge University Press, 1979. xiv, 417 p., [2] leaves of plates: maps; 24 cm. Includes index. 1. Manin, Daniele, 1804-1857. 2. Venice (Italy) — History — 1848-1849 I. T.
DG678.55.G56   945/.31   *LC* 78-56180   *ISBN* 0521220777

DG731–760 Florence

Cochrane, Eric W.   **3.2918**
Florence in the forgotten centuries, 1527–1800; a history of Florence and the Florentines in the age of the grand dukes [by] Eric Cochrane. Chicago, University of Chicago Press [1973] xiv, 593 p. illus. 25 cm. 1. Florence (Italy) — History I. T.
DG736.C55   945/.51/07   *LC* 72-90628   *ISBN* 0266111504

Schevill, Ferdinand, 1868-1954.   • **3.2919**
History of Florence, from the founding of the city through the Renaissance. — New York, F. Ungar Pub. Co. [1961] 536 p. illus. 24 cm. 1. Florence — Hist. 2. Renaissance — Italy. I. T.
DG736.S3 1961   945.51   *LC* 60-8571

Machiavelli, Niccolò, 1469-1527.   • **3.2920**
History of Florence and of the affairs of Italy, from the earliest times to the death of Lorenzo the Magnificent. — Introd. to the Torchbook ed. by Felix Gilbert. — New York, Harper [1960] xxv, 417 p. 21 cm. — (Harper torchbooks, TB1027. The Academy library) 1. Florence (Italy) — History. I. T.
DG737.A2M4 1960   945.51   *LC* 60-51391

Brucker, Gene A.   • **3.2921**
Renaissance Florence [by] Gene Brucker. New York, Wiley [1969] xiii, 306 p. illus., maps. 22 cm. (New dimensions in history. Historical cities.) 1. Renaissance — Italy — Florence. 2. Florence (Italy) — History — To 1421 3. Florence (Italy) — History — 1421-1737 I. T. II. Series.
DG737.B74   914.5/5   *LC* 77-82972   *ISBN* 0471113700

Brucker, Gene A.   **3.2922**
The civic world of early Renaissance Florence / by Gene Brucker. — Princeton, N.J.: Princeton University Press, c1977. xii, 526 p.; 25 cm. 1. Florence (Italy) — History — To 1421 2. Florence (Italy) — Politics and government — To 1421 3. Florence (Italy) — Social conditions. I. T.
DG737.26.B69   945/.51   *LC* 76-45891   *ISBN* 0691052441

Brucker, Gene A.   • **3.2923**
Florentine politics and society, 1343–1378. — Princeton, N. J., Princeton University Press, 1962. xiii, 431 p. map. 25 cm. — (Princeton studies in history, 12) 'Originated as a doctoral dissertation at Princeton University ... thoroughly revised.' Bibliography: p. 397-412. 1. Florence — Pol. & govt. I. T.
DG737.26.B7 1962   945.41   *LC* 62-7035

Trexler, Richard C., 1932-.   **3.2924**
Public life in Renaissance Florence / Richard C. Trexler. — New York: Academic Press, c1980. xxvi, 591 p.: ill.; 24 cm. — (Studies in social discontinuity.) Includes index. 1. Church and state — Italy — Florence

2. Florence (Italy) — History — 1421-1737 3. Florence (Italy) — Social conditions. I. T. II. Series.
DG737.4.T66   945/.5105 19   *LC* 80-22061   *ISBN* 0126995508

Hale, J. R. (John Rigby), 1923-. 3.2925
Florence and the Medici: the pattern of control / J. R. Hale. — [London]: Thames and Hudson, 1978 (c1977). 208 p., [8] leaves of plates: ill.; 24 cm. Includes index. 1. Medici, House of 2. Florence (Italy) — History — 1421-1737 3. Florence (Italy) — Kings and rulers — Biography. I. T.
DG737.42.H34   945/.51 19   *LC* 78-306330   *ISBN* 0500250596

Guicciardini, Francesco, 1483-1540. 3.2926
[Storie fiorentine dal 1378 al 1509. English] The history of Florence. Translation, introd., and notes, by Mario Domandi. [1st ed.] New York, Harper & Row [1970] xlvii, 327 p. map. 21 cm. (Harper torchbooks, TB 1470) Translation of Storie fiorentine dal 1378 al 1509. 1. Florence (Italy) — History — 1421-1737 I. T.
DG737.5.G813 1970   945/.51   *LC* 79-104704

Kent, D. V. (Dale V.) 3.2927
The rise of the Medici: faction in Florence, 1426–1434 / Dale Kent. — Oxford [Eng.]; New York: Oxford University Press, 1978. viii, 389 p., [2] fold. leaves of plates: ill.; 22 cm. Includes index. 1. Medici, House of 2. Medici, Cosimo di', 1389-1464. 3. Florence (Italy) — History — 1421-1737 I. T.
DG737.55.K46   945/.51   *LC* 77-30201   *ISBN* 0198225202

Martines, Lauro. • 3.2928
The social world of the Florentine humanists, 1390–1460. — Princeton, N. J., Princeton University Press, 1963. x, 419 p. 25 cm. Bibliography: p. 381-397. 1. Florence — Intellectual life. 2. Florence — Soc. life & cust. 3. Humanists I. T.
DG737.55.M3   914.551   *LC* 63-7073

Brown, Alison, 1934-. 3.2929
Bartolomeo Scala, 1430–1497, Chancellor of Florence: the humanist as bureaucrat / Alison Brown. — Princeton, N.J.: Princeton University Press, c1979. xi, 366 p.: port.; 25 cm. Includes index. 1. Scala, Bartolomeo, 1430-1497. 2. Statesmen — Italy — Florence — Biography. 3. Florence (Italy) — History — 1421-1737 4. Florence (Italy) — Biography. I. T.
DG737.58.S28 B76   445/.51/050924 B   *LC* 78-70280   *ISBN* 0691052700

Gilbert, Felix, 1905-. 3.2930
Machiavelli and Guicciardini; politics and history in sixteenth–century Florence. — Princeton, N. J., Princeton University Press, 1965. x, 349 p. 21 cm. 'Bibliographical essays': p. 305-337. 1. Machiavelli, Niccolò, 1469-1527. 2. Guicciardini, Francesco, 1483-1540. 3. Florence (Italy) — Hist. — Historiography. 4. Florence (Italy) — Pol. & govt. I. T.
DG738.13.G5   320.94551   *LC* 63-23405

Bondanella, Peter E., 1943-. 3.2931
Machiavelli and the art of Renaissance history [by] Peter E. Bondanella. — Detroit: Wayne State University Press, 1973 [i.e. 1974] 186 p.: port.; 24 cm. 1. Machiavelli, Niccolò, 1469-1527. I. T.
DG738.14.M2 B66 1974   914.5/03/60924 B   *LC* 73-9729   *ISBN* 0814314996

Ridolfi, Roberto, 1895-. • 3.2932
The life of Niccolò Machiavelli. Translated from the Italian by Cecil Grayson. — [Chicago] University of Chicago Press [1963] 337 p. illus. 25 cm. Includes bibliography. 1. Machiavelli, Niccolò, 1469-1527. I. T.
DG738.14.M2R513   923.245   *LC* 62-15048

DG797–799 Papal States

Partner, Peter. 3.2933
The lands of St. Peter; the Papal State in the Middle Ages and the early Renaissance. Berkeley, University of California Press, 1972. xvii, 471 p. illus. 24 cm. 1. Papal States — History — To 962 I. T.
DG797.P37 1972b   945/.6   *LC* 73-182793   *ISBN* 0520021819

Gregorovius, Ferdinand, 1821-1891. • 3.2934
Lucretia Borgia, according to original documents and correspondence of her day. Translated from the 3d German ed., by John Leslie Garner. — New York: B. Blom, [1968] xxiii, 378 p.: illus.; 20 cm. Reprint of 1903 ed. 1. Borgia, Lucrezia, 1480-1519. 2. Renaissance — Italy. 3. Italy — History — 1492-1559 I. Garner, John Leslie. tr. II. T.
DG797.83.G71 1968   945/.06/0924 B   *LC* 68-20226

Trevelyan, George Macaulay, 1876-1962. • 3.2935
Garibaldi's defence of the Roman Republic, 1848-9. Westport, Conn., Greenwood Press [1971] xv, 387 p. illus. 23 cm. Reprint of the 1912 ed.

1. Garibaldi, Giuseppe, 1807-1882. 2. Rome (Italy) — History — Revolution of 1848-1849 I. T.
DG798.5.T8 1971   945/.08/0924 B   *LC* 76-156214   *ISBN* 0837161657

Halperin, Samuel William. • 3.2936
Italy and the Vatican at war; a study of their relations from the outbreak of the Franco–Prussian War to the death of Pius IX, by S. William Halperin. — New York: Greenwood Press, [1968, c1939] xvii, 483 p.; 23 cm. 1. Roman question 2. Church and state — Italy I. T.
DG799.H3 1968   322/.1/0945   *LC* 68-57606

DG803–817 Rome (Modern City)

Brentano, Robert, 1926-. 3.2937
Rome before Avignon; a social history of thirteenth–century Rome. New York, Basic Books [1974] xiv, 340 p. illus. 24 cm. 1. Rome (Italy) — History — 476-1420 2. Rome (Italy) — Social conditions. I. T.
DG811.B73   914.5/632/03   *LC* 75-75306   *ISBN* 0465071252

Krautheimer, Richard, 1897-. 3.2938
Rome, profile of a city, 312–1308 / by Richard Krautheimer. — Princeton, N.J.: Princeton University Press, 1980. xvi, 389 p.: ill.; 29 cm. Includes index. 1. Church history — Primitive and early church, ca. 30-600 2. Church history — Middle Ages, 600-1500 3. Historic buildings — Rome. 4. Rome (Italy) — History — 476-1420 5. Rome (Italy) — History — To 476 6. Rome (Italy) — Buildings, structures, etc. I. T.
DG811.K7   945/.632 19   *LC* 78-70304   *ISBN* 069103947X

Partner, Peter. 3.2939
Renaissance Rome, 1500–1559: a portrait of a society / Peter Partner. — Berkeley: University of California Press, 1977 (c1976). 241 p., [16] leaves of plates: ill.; 24 cm. Includes index. 1. Papacy — History — 1447-1565 2. Rome (Italy) — History — 1420-1798 3. Rome (Italy) — Social life and customs 4. Rome (Italy) — Economic conditions. I. T.
DG812.P37   945/.632/06   *LC* 75-13154   *ISBN* 0520030265

Stinger, Charles L., 1944-. 3.2940
The Renaissance in Rome / Charles L. Stinger. — Bloomington: Indiana University Press, c1985. xv, 444 p.: ill., maps; 24 cm. Includes index. 1. Renaissance — Italy — Rome. 2. Papacy — History — 1447-1565 3. Rome (Italy) — Civilization — 15th century 4. Rome (Italy) — Civilization — 16th century I. T.
DG812.1.S75 1985   945/.63205 19   *LC* 83-49337   *ISBN* 0253350026

DG840–875 Naples. Sicily

Ryder, Alan Frederick Charles. 3.2941
The kingdom of Naples under Alfonso the Magnanimous: the making of a modern state / by Alan Ryder. — Oxford: Clarendon Press, 1976. viii, 409 p., [1] leaf of plates; 23 cm. Includes index. 1. Alfonso V, King of Aragon, 1396-1458. 2. Naples (Kingdom) — History — Spanish rule, 1442-1707 I. T.
DG848.115.R9   945./73/05   *LC* 77-356783   *ISBN* 0198225350

Romani, George T. • 3.2942
The Neapolitan revolution of 1820–1821. Evanston, Northwestern University Press, 1950. 190 p. ill. (Northwestern University studies. Social studies series, no.6) 1. Naples (Kingdom) — History — Revolution, 1820-1821 I. T.
DG848.51.R6   945.7308   *LC* 50-10812

Finley, M. I. (Moses I.), 1912-. • 3.2943
A history of Sicily. New York, Viking Press [1968] 3 v. illus., maps. 23 cm. 1. Sicily — History I. Mack Smith, Denis, 1920- II. T. III. Title: Ancient Sicily, to the Arab conquest. IV. Title: Medieval Sicily, 800-1713. V. Title: Modern Sicily, after 1713.
DG866.F5   937/.8   *LC* 68-31396   *ISBN* 0670122726

Runciman, Steven, Sir, 1903-. • 3.2944
The Sicilian Vespers: a history of the Mediterranean world in the later thirteenth century / by Steven Runciman. — Cambridge: University Press, 1958. xiii, 338 p.: ill., maps, ports., geneal. tables; 22 cm. 1. Sicily — History — 1189-1282. 2. Mediterranean Region — History. I. T.
DG867.28 R8   945.8   *LC* 58-2158

DG975 OTHER CITIES, A–Z

Douglass, William A.   3.2945
Emigration in a south Italian town: an anthropological history / William A. Douglass. — New Brunswick, N.J.: Rutgers University Press, c1984. xvi, 283 p.; 24 cm. Includes index. 1. Italians — Foreign countries — Migration and immigration. 2. Italy — Emigration and immigration. 3. Agnone (Italy) — History. 4. Agnone (Italy) — Economic conditions. 5. Agnone (Italy) — Social conditions. I. T.
DG975.A2229 D68 1984   945/.719 19   *LC* 82-21626   *ISBN* 081350984X

Levi, Carlo, 1902-1975.   3.2946
Christ stopped at Eboli: the story of a year / by Carlo Levi; translated from the Italian by Frances Frenaye; [with new introd. by author]. — New York: Farrar, Straus and Giroux, c1963. xii, 268 p.: map; 21 cm. 1. Basilicata (Italy) — Social life and customs. I. T.
DG975.L78 L43 1963   DG975B3 L43 1963.   914.577   *LC* 63-24529   *ISBN* 0374503168 Pbk

Cardoza, Anthony L., 1947-.   3.2947
Agrarian elites and Italian fascism: the Province of Bologna, 1901–1926 / Anthony L. Cardoza. — Princeton, N.J.: Princeton University Press, c1982. xvi, 477 p.: maps; 22 cm. Includes index. 1. Fascism — Italy — Bologna (Province) — History — 20th century. 2. Elite (Social sciences) — Italy — Bologna (Province) — History — 20th century. 3. Bologna (Italy: Province) — Politics and government. 4. Bologna (Italy: Province) — Rural conditions. I. T.
DG975.B64 C37 1982   945/.41 19   *LC* 82-47585   *ISBN* 069105360X

Gundersheimer, Werner L.   3.2948
Ferrara; the style of a Renaissance despotism [by] Werner L. Gundersheimer. Princeton, N.J., Princeton University Press, 1973. xii, 313 p. illus. 23 cm. 1. Este family 2. Ferrara (Italy) — Civilization. 3. Ferrara (Italy) — Politics and government. I. T.
DG975.F42 G86   914.5/45/035   *LC* 72-6518   *ISBN* 0691052107

Corner, Paul.   3.2949
Fascism in Ferrara, 1915–1925 / by Paul Corner. — London; New York: Oxford University Press, 1975. xii, 300 p.: map; 22 cm. — (Oxford historical monographs) A revision of the author's thesis, Oxford, 1971. Includes index. 1. Fascism — Italy — Ferrara. 2. Ferrara (Italy) — Politics and government. 3. Italy — Politics and government — 1915-1922 I. T.

DG975.F44 C67 1975   320.9/45/45091   *LC* 76-376589   *ISBN* 0198218575

Waley, Daniel Philip.   • 3.2950
Mediaeval Orvieto; the political history of an Italian city–state, 1157–1334. — Cambridge [Eng.] University Press, 1952. xxv, 170 p. plates, fold. map, geneal. tables. 23 cm. Bibliography: p. 159-164. 1. Orvieto — Hist. I. T.
DG975.O7W34   945.6   *LC* 52-8823

Herlihy, David.   • 3.2951
Pisa in the early Renaissance; a study of urban growth. — New Haven, Yale University Press, 1958. xx, 229 p. map. 23 cm. — (Yale historical publications. Miscellany. 68) 'This book grew of a dissertation written at Yale University.' 'Notes on the sources': p. 215-221. Bibliographical footnotes. 1. Pisa — Hist. I. T. II. Series.
DG975.P615H4   945.5   *LC* 58-6933

Herlihy, David.   • 3.2952
Medieval and Renaissance Pistoia; the social history of an Italian town, 1200–1430. — New Haven, Yale University Press, 1967. xviii, 297 p. maps. 24 cm. Bibliographical footnotes. 1. Pistoia (Italy) — Hist. 2. Pistoia (Italy) — Soc. condit. I. T.
DG975.P65H4   914.5/52/03   *LC* 67-13437

Bowsky, William M.   3.2953
A medieval Italian commune: Siena under the Nine, 1287–1355 / William M. Bowsky. — Berkeley: University of California Press, c1981. xxii, 327 p., [8] leaves of plates: ill.; 25 cm. 1. Siena (Italy) — History — Rule of the Nine, 1287-1355 I. T.
DG975.S5 B68 1981   945/.5804 19   *LC* 80-21234   *ISBN* 0520042565

Hook, Judith.   3.2954
Siena, a city and its history / Judith Hook. — London: H. Hamilton, 1980 (c1979). xii, 258 p., [8] leaves of plates: ill.; 23 cm. Includes index. 1. Siena (Italy) — History I. T.
DG975.S5 H66   945/.58   *LC* 80-481728   *ISBN* 0241102979

Schevill, Ferdinand, 1868-1954.   • 3.2955
Siena, the history of a mediaeval commune. — New York, Harper & Row [1964] xlii, 433 p. illus., maps. 21 cm. — (Harper torchbooks. The Academy library) 'TB 1164.' 'Originally published in 1909.' Bibliography: p. 423-426. 1. Siena — Hist. I. T.
DG975.S5S35 1964   914.558   *LC* 64-56203

DH1–207 GENERAL WORKS

Eyck, F. Gunther.   3.2956
The Benelux countries: an historical survey. — Princeton, N.J.: Van Nostrand, [1959] 192 p.: illus.; 18 cm. — (An Anvil original, no. 44) 1. Benelux countries — History. I. T.
DH107.E9   949.2   *LC* 59-15097

Rowen, Herbert Harvey. comp.   3.2957
The Low Countries in early modern times. Edited by Herbert H. Rowen. — New York: Walker, [1972] xxviii, 291 p.; 24 cm. — (Documentary history of Western civilization) 1. Benelux countries — History — Sources. I. T.
DH131.R68 1972b   949.2   *LC* 72-80544   *ISBN* 0802720358

Prevenier, Walter.   3.2958
[Les Pays-Bas bourguignons. English] The Burgundian Netherlands / Walter Prevenier and Wim Blockmans; picture research by An Blockmans–Delva, foreword by Richard Vaughan. Cambridge: Cambridge University Press, 1986. 403 p.: ill. (some col.), geneal. tables, maps (some col.), ports. (some col.); 33 cm. Includes index. Translation of: Les Pays-Bas bourguignons. 1. Netherlands — History — House of Burgundy, 1384-1477 2. Netherlands — History — House of Habsburg, 1477-1556 I. Blockmans, Willem Pieter. II. T.
DH175.P75 1986   *LC* gb85-45246   *ISBN* 0521306116

Haley, Kenneth Harold Dobson.   • 3.2959
The Dutch in the seventeenth century [by] K. H. D. Haley. — [1st American ed. — New York]: Harcourt Brace Jovanovich, [1972] 216 p.: illus. (part col.); 22 cm. 1. Netherlands — History — Wars of Independence, 1556-1648 2. Netherlands — History — 1648-1795 I. T.
DH186.5.H33 1972   914.92/03/4   *LC* 72-157880   *ISBN* 015126855X

Israel, Jonathan Irvine.   3.2960
The Dutch Republic and the Hispanic world, 1606–1661 / Jonathan I. Israel. — Oxford [Oxfordshire]: Clarendon Press; New York: Oxford University Press, 1982. xvi, 478 p.: ill.; 23 cm. Includes index. 1. Netherlands — History — Wars of Independence, 1556-1648 2. Netherlands — History — 1648-1714 3. Netherlands — Relations — Spain. 4. Spain — Relations — Netherlands. 5. Spain — History — House of Austria, 1516-1700 I. T.
DH186.5.I85 1982   949.2/03 19   *LC* 81-22571   *ISBN* 0198265344

Motley, John Lothrop, 1814-1877.   • 3.2961
The rise of the Dutch republic; a history / by John Lothrop Motley. — London: Dent; New York: Dutton [1928-30] 3 v.; 18 cm. 1. Netherlands — History — Wars of Independence, 1556-1648 I. T.
DH186.5.M6 1973 vol. 1-5   DH186.5.M7x.   949.2/008 s 949.2/03
    LC 73-8880   *ISBN* 0404045219

Parker, Geoffrey, 1943-.   • 3.2962
The Army of Flanders and the Spanish road, 1567–1659; the logistics of Spanish victory and defeat in the Low Countries' Wars. Cambridge [Eng.] University Press, 1972. xviii, 309 p. illus. 24 cm. (Cambridge studies in early modern history) 1. Netherlands — History — Wars of Independence, 1556-1648 I. T.
DH186.5.P28   949.2/03   *LC* 76-180021   *ISBN* 0521084628

Parker, Geoffrey, 1943-.   3.2963
The Dutch revolt / Geoffrey Parker. — Ithaca, N.Y.: Cornell University Press, 1977. 327 p.: ill.; 24 cm. 1. Netherlands — History — Wars of Independence, 1556-1648 I. T.
DH186.5.P283   949.2/03   *LC* 77-77553   *ISBN* 080141136X

Wedgwood, C. V. (Cicely Veronica), 1910-.   • 3.2964
William the Silent, William of Nassau, prince of Orange, 1533–1584, by C. V. Wedgwood. — London, J. Cape [1944] 256 p. 2 port. (incl. front.) fold. map. 22.5 cm. 'First published 1944.' 'Note on sources': p. 7-8. 1. William I, Prince of Orange, 1533-1584. 2. Netherlands — Hist. — Wars of independence, 1556-1648. I. T.
DH188.W7W4   923.1492   *LC* 44-7864

DH401–811 BELGIUM

Belgium, a country study / Foreign Area Studies, the American   3.2965
University; edited by Stephen B. Wickman.
2nd ed. — Washington, D.C.: The Studies: For sale by the Supt. of Docs., U.S. G.P.O., [1985], c1984. xxxix, 364 p.: ill.; 24 cm. (Area handbook series.) (DA pam. 550-170) 'Research completed November 1984.' Includes index. 1. Belgium. I. Wickman, Stephen B., 1953- II. American University (Washington, D.C.). Foreign Area Studies. III. Series. IV. Series: DA pam. 550-170
DH418.B44 1985   949.3 19   *LC* 85-15773

Mallinson, Vernon.   • 3.2966
Belgium. — New York: Praeger, [1970] 240 p.: illus., geneal. table, 2 maps (1 fold.), ports.; 23 cm. — (Nations of the modern world.) 1. Belgium. I. T. II. Series.
DH418.M25 1970   949.3   *LC* 72-104772

Kalken, Frans van, 1881-.   3.2967
Histoire de la Belgique et de son expansion coloniale / Frans van Kalken. — Bruxelles: Office de publicité, 1954. 869 p.: ill., ports., maps.; 20 cm. 1. Belgium — History I. T.
DH521.K278   *LC* 54-24324

Meeüs, Adrien de, 1900-.   • 3.2968
History of the Belgians / by Adrien de Meeüs; translated from the French by G. Gordon. — New York: Praeger, 1962. 378 p. — (Books that matter) 1. Belgium — History I. T.
DH521.M423   *LC* 62-13755

Pirenne, Henri, 1862-1935.   • 3.2969
Histoire de Belgique des origines à nos jours / Henri Pirenne; [rassemblée et commentée par Franz Schauwers et Jacques Paquet]. — [Bruxelles]: La Renaissance du livre, [1948-52]. 4 v.: ill., col. plates, ports. (part col.) maps, facsims. (part col.); 32 cm. 1. Belgium — History I. T.
DH521.P58   949.3

Helmreich, Jonathan E.   3.2970
Belgium and Europe: a study in small power diplomacy / Jonathan E. Helmreich. — The Hague: Mouton, 1976. xiii, 451 p.; 24 cm. (Issues in contemporary politics, historical and theoretical perspectives; 3) Includes index. 1. Belgium — Foreign relations I. T.
DH566.H4   327.493 19   *LC* 76-360519   *ISBN* 9027975612

Thomas, Daniel H.   3.2971
The guarantee of Belgian independence and neutrality in European diplomacy, 1830's–1930's / Daniel H. Thomas. — Kingston, R.I.: D.H. Thomas Pub., 1984 (c1983). xii, 789 p.: ill.; 24 cm. Includes index. 1. Belgium — Neutrality 2. Europe — Foreign relations — 1815-1871 3. Europe — Foreign relations — 1871-1918 4. Europe — Foreign relations — 1918-1945 I. T.
DH566.T47 1983   327.4 19   *LC* 82-99990

Kossmann, E. H. (Ernst Heinrich), 1922-.   3.2972
The low countries, 1780–1940 / by E. H. Kossmann. — Oxford [Eng.]: Clarendon Press; New York: Oxford University Press, 1978. ix, 784 p.: maps; 23 cm. (Oxford history of modern Europe.) Includes indexes. 1. Belgium — History 2. Netherlands — History — 1789-1900 3. Netherlands — History — Wilhelmina, 1898-1948 I. T. II. Series.
DH620.K67   949.3   *LC* 77-30291   *ISBN* 0198221088

Rooney, John W.   3.2973
Revolt in the Netherlands: Brussels, 1830 / by John W. Rooney, Jr. Lawrence, Kan.: Coronado Press, 1982. — vii, 250 p.: map; 22 cm. Includes index. 1. Belgium — History — Revolution, 1830-1839 I. T.
DH 651.R66   *ISBN* 087291156X

Emerson, Barbara.   3.2974
Leopold II of the Belgians: king of colonialism / Barbara Emerson. — New York: St. Martin's Press, 1979. xii, 324 p., [4] leaves of plates: ill.; 24 cm. Includes index. 1. Léopold II, King of the Belgians, 1835-1909. 2. Belgium — Kings and rulers — Biography. 3. Belgium — History — Leopold II, 1865-1909 I. T.
DH671.E47 1979   949.3/03/0924 B   *LC* 79-9397   *ISBN* 0312480121

Miller, Jane Kathryn.   • **3.2975**
Belgian foreign policy between two wars, 1919–1940. New York, Bookman
Associates [1951] 337 p. 23 cm. Bibliography: p. 301-315. 1. Belgium —
Foreign relations — 1914- 2. Belgium — History — 1914- I. T.
DH677.M5   327.493   *LC* 51-4901

Arango, E. Ramón (Ergasto Ramón)   • **3.2976**
Leopold III and the Belgian royal question. Baltimore, Johns Hopkins Press
[1963, c1961] xiv, 234 p. 22 cm. 1. Léopold III, King of the Belgians, 1901-
I. T.
DH687.A82   *LC* 63-19557

Keyes, Roger, 1919-.   **3.2977**
Outrageous fortune: the tragedy of Leopold III of the Belgians, 1901–1941 /
Roger Keyes. — London: Secker & Warburg, 1984. xv, 521 p., [16] p. of plates:
ill.; 24 cm. Includes index. 1. Léopold III, King of the Belgians, 1901-
2. Belgium — Kings and rulers — Biography. 3. Belgium — History — 1914-
I. T.
DH687.K48 1984   949.3/042/0924 B 19   *LC* 84-159598   *ISBN*
0436233207

Kieft, David Owen.   ◦ **3.2978**
Belgium's return to neutrality; an essay in the frustration of small power
diplomacy. — Oxford: Clarendon Press, 1972. xv, 201 p.; 22 cm. 1. Belgium —
Politics and government — 1914-1951 2. Belgium — Foreign relations —
1951- I. T.
DH687.K53   327.493   *LC* 72-183279   *ISBN* 0198214979

Voet, Léon, 1919-.   **3.2979**
[Gouden eeuw van Antwerpen. English] Antwerp, the golden age. The rise and
glory of the metropolis in the sixteenth century. Antwerp, Mercatorfonds, 1974
(c1973). 487 p. illus. (part col.) 34 cm. Part of illustrative matter in pockets.
Translation of De gouden eeuw van Antwerpen. 1. Antwerp (Belgium) —
Intellectual life. I. T.
DH811.A58 V613   914.93/2   *LC* 74-170991

Steen, Charlie R.   **3.2980**
A chronicle of conflict: Tournai, 1559–1567 / Charlie R. Steen. — Utrecht:
HES Publishers, 1985. v, 190 p., [1] leaf of plates: ill.; 23 cm. (HES studia
historica. 12) 1. Tournai (Belgium) — History. 2. Netherlands — History —
Wars of Independence, 1556-1648 I. T. II. Series.
DH811.T76 S74 1985   949.3/4 19   *LC* 85-116152   *ISBN*
9061944740

Newcomer, James.   **3.2981**
The Grand Duchy of Luxembourg: the evolution of nationhood, 963 A.D. to
1983 / by James Newcomer. — Lanham, MD: University Press of America;
Fort Worth, Tex.: Texas Christian University, c1984. xiii, 343 p.: [3] maps; 23
cm. Includes index. 1. Luxembourg — History. I. T.
DH908.N48 1984   949.3/5 19   *LC* 84-2236   *ISBN* 0819138452

DJ1–411 HOLLAND

Landheer, Bartholomeus, 1904- ed.   • **3.2982**
The Netherlands; chapters by Johan Willem Albarda, Adriaan Jacob Barnouw,
Hendrik Nicolaas Boon [and others]. Edited by Bartholomew Landheer. —
Berkeley; Los Angeles: University of California press, 1943. 5 p. l., ix-xviii p., 3
l., 3-464 p. incl. illus. (maps) tables.: front., plates, ports.; 23 cm. — (United
Nations series.) 1. Netherlands — History 2. Netherlands — Civilization I. T.
II. Series.
DJ5.L3   949.2   *LC* a 44-255

Bailey, Anthony.   **3.2983**
The light in Holland. — [1st ed.]. — New York: Knopf, 1970. viii, 263, vii p.:

illus., map.; 22 cm. 1. National characteristics, Dutch. 2. Netherlands —
Civilization I. T.
DJ71.B26   914.92/03/7   *LC* 78-118705

Huizinga, Johan, 1872-1945.   • **3.2984**
[Essays. English. Selections] Dutch civilisation in the seventeenth century, and
other essays [by] J.H. Huizinga. Selected by Pieter Geyl and F.W.N.
Hugenholtz. Translated by Arnold J. Pomerans. New York, F. Ungar Pub. Co.
[1968] 288 p. 21 cm. 1. History — Philosophy 2. Netherlands — Civilization
I. Geyl, Pieter, 1887-1966, comp. II. Hugenholtz, F. W. N. comp. III. T.
DJ71.H92 1968b   914.92/03   *LC* 68-22778

Newton, Gerald.   **3.2985**
The Netherlands: an historical and cultural survey, 1795–1977 / Gerald
Newton. — London: E. Benn; Boulder, Colo.: Westview Press, 1978. xii, 300 p.,
[8] leaves of plates: ill.; 23 cm. — (Nations of the modern world.) Includes
index. 1. Netherlands — Civilization I. T. II. Series.
DJ71.N48   949.2   *LC* 77-16100   *ISBN* 0891588027

Shetter, William Z.   **3.2986**
The pillars of society; six centuries of civilization in the Netherlands. [By]
William Z. Shetter. — The Hague: Nijhoff, 1971. 199 p.; 22 cm. 1. Netherlands
— Civilization I. T.
DJ71.S5   914.92/03   *LC* 79-851978

Barnouw, Adriaan Jacob, 1877-1968.   **3.2987**
The making of modern Holland, a short history. London: G. Allen & Unwin
[1948] 224 p.: maps (part fold.); 20 cm. 1. Netherlands — History I. T.
DJ111.B32 1948

Vandenbosch, Amry, 1894-.   • **3.2988**
Dutch foreign policy since 1815. The Hague, M. Nijhoff, 1959. 318 p. 25 cm.
1. Netherlands — Foreign relations I. T.
DJ147.V3   *LC* 59-2211

Geyl, Pieter, 1887-.   • **3.2989**
The revolt of the Netherlands (1555–1609) [2d ed.] New York, Barnes & Noble
[c1958] 310 p. maps. 22 cm. 'Sources': p. [295]-297. 1. Netherlands — History
— Wars of Independence, 1556-1648 I. T.
DJ156.G4 1958   *LC* A 59-3543

Geyl, Pieter, 1887-.   • **3.2990**
The Netherlands in the seventeenth century. Rev. and enl. ed. New York,
Barnes & Noble [1961-. v. illus. 23 cm. First published in 1936 under title: The
Netherlands divided (1609-1648) 'Sources of the quotations': v. 1, p. 263-267.
'Notes on sources and secondary works': p. 269-271. 1. Netherlands — History
— Wars of Independence, 1556-1648 2. Netherlands — History — 1648-1714
3. Netherlands — Civilization I. T.
DJ156.G482   949.203   *LC* 61-66073

Wilson, Charles, 1914-.   • **3.2991**
The Dutch Republic and the civilisation of the seventeenth century [by] Charles
Wilson. New York, McGraw-Hill [1968] 255 p. illus., facsims., maps, ports, (all
part col.) 20 cm. (World university library) 1. Netherlands — History — Wars
of Independence, 1556-1648 2. Netherlands — History — 1648-1714
3. Netherlands — Civilization I. T.
DJ156.W55   914.92/03/4   *LC* 68-14342

Warmbrunn, Werner.   • **3.2992**
The Dutch under German occupation, 1940–1945. — Stanford, Calif., Stanford
University Press, 1963. xiii, 338 p. 24 cm. 'Bibliographical notes for English
readers': p. [316]-318. Bibliography: p. [319]-331. 1. Netherlands — Hist. —
German occupation, 1940-1945. I. T.
DJ287.W3   940.5337   *LC* 63-10738

Zee, Henri A. van der.   **3.2993**
The hunger winter: occupied Holland 1944–5 / Henri A. van der Zee. —
London: J. Norman & Hobhouse, 1982. 330 p., [16] p. of plates: ill.; 23 cm.
Includes index. 1. World War, 1939-1945 — Netherlands. 2. Netherlands —
History — German occupation, 1940-1945 I. T.
DJ287.Z39 1982   940.53/37/09492 19   *LC* 82-128093   *ISBN*
090690871X

Kann, Robert A., 1906-.   3.2994
The peoples of the Eastern Habsburg lands, 1526–1918 / by Robert A. Kann and Zdeněk V. David. — Seattle: University of Washington Press, 1985 (c1984). xvi, 543 p.: maps; 25 cm. — (History of East Central Europe. v. 6) Maps on lining papers. Includes index. 1. Europe, Eastern — History 2. Central Europe — History. 3. Austria — History I. David, Zdeněk V. II. T. III. Series.
DJK4.S93 vol. 6 DJK38.K3x   943 s 943 19   LC 83-21629   ISBN 0295960957

Jones, Christopher D.   3.2995
Soviet influence in Eastern Europe: political autonomy and the Warsaw Pact / Christopher D. Jones. — Brooklyn, N.Y.: Praeger, 1981. x, 322 p.; 25 cm. — (Studies of influence in international relations.) 1. Warsaw Treaty Organization. 2. Europe, Eastern — Foreign relations — Soviet Union. 3. Soviet Union — Foreign relations — Europe, Eastern. 4. Europe, Eastern — Military relations — Soviet Union. 5. Soviet Union — Military relations — Europe, Eastern. I. T. II. Series.
DJK45.S65 J66   327/.0947 19   LC 81-5848   ISBN 0030490766

Soviet policy in Eastern Europe / edited by Sarah Meiklejohn   3.2996
Terry.
New Haven: Yale University Press, c1984. xv, 375 p.; 25 cm. 'A Council on Foreign Relations book.' 1. Europe, Eastern — Foreign relations — Soviet Union — Addresses, essays, lectures. 2. Soviet Union — Foreign relations — Europe, Eastern — Addresses, essays, lectures. 3. Soviet Union — Foreign relations — 1975- — Addresses, essays, lectures. I. Terry, Sarah Meiklejohn, 1937-
DJK45.S65 S68 1984   327.47 19   LC 83-21889   ISBN 0300031319

Rothschild, Joseph.   3.2997
East Central Europe between the two World Wars. Seattle, University of Washington Press [1974] xvii, 420 p. maps. 25 cm. (History of East Central Europe. v. 9) 1. Europe, Eastern — History I. T. II. Series.
DJK4.S93 vol. 9 DJK49.R6x   949 s 949 19   LC 74-8327   ISBN 0295953500 ISBN 0295953378

Staar, Richard Felix, 1923-.   3.2998
Communist regimes in Eastern Europe / Richard F. Staar. — 4th ed. — Stanford, Calif.: Hoover Institution Press, 1982. xiv, 375 p.; 23 cm. — (Hoover Press publication; 269) Includes index. 1. Communism — Europe, Eastern. 2. Europe, Eastern — Politics and government I. T.
DJK50.S7 1982   320.9171/7 19   LC 81-84232   ISBN 0817976922

Summerscale, Peter.   3.2999
The East European predicament: changing patterns in Poland, Czechoslovakia, and Romania / Peter Summerscale. — New York: St. Martin's Press, 1982. vii, 147 p.; 23 cm. 1. Europe, Eastern — Politics and government — 1945- 2. Europe, Eastern — Foreign relations — 1945- I. T.
DJK50.S95 1982   320.947 19   LC 81-9400   ISBN 0312224745

DK1–276 Soviet Union

Dmytryshyn, Basil, 1925- comp.   3.3000
Imperial Russia; a source book, 1700–1917. 2d ed. Hinsdale, Ill., Dryden Press [1974] xi, 497 p. maps. 23 cm. Companion volume: Medieval Russia. 1. Soviet Union — History — Sources. I. T.
DK3.D55 1974   947   *LC* 73-4179   *ISBN* 0030892376

Medieval Russia; a source book, 900–1700. Edited by Basil   3.3001
Dmytryshyn.
2d ed. New York: Holt, Rinehart and Winston, c1973. x, 357 p.: maps; 22 cm. 1. Russia — History — Sources. I. Dmytryshyn, Basil, 1925-
DK3.D57 1973   947   *LC* 70-182141   *ISBN* 0030864410

A Source book for Russian history from early times to 1917.   3.3002
George Vernadsky, senior editor. Ralph T. Fisher, Jr., managing editor. Alan D. Ferguson, Andrew Lossky. Sergei Pushkarev, compiler.
New Haven [Conn.] Yale University Press, 1972. 3 v. (884 p.) 27 cm. 1. Soviet Union — History — Sources. I. Vernadsky, George, 1887-1973. ed. II. Pushkarev, Sergeĭ Germanovich, 1888- comp.
DK3.S67 1972   947   *LC* 70-115369   *ISBN* 0300016255

Riha, Thomas, ed.   3.3003
Readings in Russian civilization, edited, with introductory notes, by Thomas Riha. 2d ed., rev. Chicago, University of Chicago Press [1969-. v. 24 cm. 1. Soviet Union — History — Collected works. I. T.
DK4.R52   914.7/03   *LC* 69-14825

Pokrovskiĭ, M. N. (Mikhail Nikolaevich), 1868-1932.   • 3.3004
Russia in world history; selected essays. Edited, with an introd. by Roman Szporluk. Translated by Roman and Mary Ann Szporluk. Ann Arbor, University of Michigan Press [c1970] 241 p. 22 cm. 1. Russia — History — Addresses, essays, lectures. 2. Russia — History — Revolution, 1917-1921 — Addresses, essays, lectures. I. T.
DK5.P653 1970   947.084/1   *LC* 75-107981   *ISBN* 0472087371

The Cambridge encyclopedia of Russia and the Soviet Union /   3.3005
general editors, Archie Brown ... [et al.].
Cambridge [Cambridgeshire]; New York: Cambridge University Press, 1982. 492 p.: ill. (some col.); 26 cm. Includes index. 1. Soviet Union — Dictionaries and encyclopedias. I. Brown, Archie, 1938- II. Title: Russia and the Soviet Union.
DK14.C35 1982   947/.00321 19   *LC* 81-9965   *ISBN* 0521231698

Maxwell, Robert, 1923-.   • 3.3006
Information U.S.S.R.: an authoritative encyclopaedia about the Union of Soviet Socialist Republics / edited and compiled by Robert Maxwell. — Oxford: Pergamon Press, 1962. xii, 982 p.: ill., maps (some fold., 1 fold. col.), ports.; 27 cm. — (Countries of the world: information series; v.01) Includes index. 1. Russia — Dictionaries and encyclopedias. I. T.
DK14.M38 1962   947   *LC* 62-9879

Gregory, James Stothert, 1912-.   • 3.3007
Russian land, Soviet people: a geographical approach to the U.S.S.R., by James S. Gregory. London, Harrap, 1968. 947 p. 26 fold. plates, illus., maps. 24 cm. 1. Soviet Union. 2. Soviet Union — History I. T.
DK17.G75   914.7   *LC* 68-122679

The Soviet Union and Eastern Europe / edited by George   3.3008
Schöpflin.
Rev. and updated ed. — New York, N.Y.: Facts on File, c1986. xvii, 637 p.: ill., maps; 24 cm. (Handbooks to the modern world.) 'First published in Great Britain in 1970 by Anthony Blond Ltd.'-T.p. verso. 1. Soviet Union — Handbooks, manuals, etc. 2. Europe, Eastern — Handbooks, manuals, etc. I. Schöpflin, George. II. Series.
DK17.S64 1986   947 19   *LC* 85-25403   *ISBN* 0816012601

The Soviet Union since Stalin / edited by Stephen F. Cohen,   3.3009
Alexander Rabinowitch and Robert Sharlet.
Bloomington: Indiana University Press, c1980. viii, 342 p.; 24 cm. Based on papers presented at a conference organized by the Indiana University Russian and East European Institute in 1978. 1. Russia — Congresses. I. Cohen, Stephen F. II. Rabinowitch, Alexander. III. Sharlet, Robert S.
DK17.S655   947.084/2   *LC* 79-3092   *ISBN* 0253322723

Keefe, Eugene K.   • 3.3010
Area handbook for the Soviet Union. Co–authors: Eugene K. Keefe [and others. Washington; For sale by the Supt. of Docs., U.S. Govt. Print. Off.] 1971. xviii, 827 p. illus., maps. 24 cm. 'DA pam 550-95.' 'One of a series of handbooks prepared by Foreign Area Studies (FAS) of the American University.' 1. Soviet Union. I. American University (Washington, D.C.). Foreign Area Studies. II. T.
DK18.K43   914.7/03/85   *LC* 71-609246

DK19–29 Description

Haxthausen, August, Freiherr von, 1792-1866.   3.3011
[Studien über die innern Zustände, das Volksleben und insbesondere die ländlichen Einrichtungen Russlands. English] Studies on the interior of Russia. Edited and with an introd. by S. Frederick Starr. Translated by Eleanore L. M. Schmidt. Chicago, University of Chicago Press [1972] xlv, 328 p. illus. 24 cm. Translation of Studien über die innern Zustände, das Volksleben und insbesondere die ländlichen Einrichtungen Russlands. 1. Soviet Union — Description and travel 2. Soviet Union — Politics and government — 1825-1855 I. T.
DK25.H213 1972   914.7/04/7   *LC* 71-190692   *ISBN* 0226320227

Wallace, Donald Mackenzie, Sir, 1841-1919.   • 3.3012
Russia; on the eve of war and revolution. Edited and introduced by Cyril E. Black. — New York, Vintage Books [1961] xiv, 528 p. 19 cm. — (Vintage Russian library, V724) 1. Russia. I. T.
DK26.W2 1961   947.08   *LC* 62-810

Utechin, Sergej, 1921-.   • 3.3013
A concise encyclopaedia of Russia / by S.V. Utechin. — New York: Dutton, 1964, c1961. –. xxvi, 623 p.: ill., ports., fold. map.; 19 cm. — First published in 1961 under title: Everyman's concise encyclopaedia of Russia. - 1. Russia — Dictionaries & encyclopedias I. T.
DK28.U83 1964   914.7   *LC* 64-55967

Kaiser, Robert G., 1943-.   3.3014
Russia: the people & the power / by Robert G. Kaiser. — 1st ed. — New York: Atheneum, 1976. xiii, 499 p.; 25 cm. 1. Russia — Description and travel — 1970- I. T.
DK29.K25 1976   947.085   *LC* 75-34069   *ISBN* 0689106963

Lydolph, Paul E.   3.3015
Geography of the U.S.S.R. / Paul E. Lydolph; cartographers, Don and Denise Temple. 3d ed. — New York: Wiley, c1977. xi, 495 p.: ill.; 26 cm. 1. Russia — Description and travel — 1970- I. T.
DK29.L9 1977   914.7   *LC* 76-26657   *ISBN* 0471557242

Shipler, David K., 1942-.   3.3016
Russia: broken idols, solemn dreams / David K. Shipler. — New York, N.Y.: Times Books, c1983. xii, 404 p.; 25 cm. Includes index. 1. Shipler, David K., 1942- 2. Soviet Union — Description and travel — 1970- 3. Soviet Union — Social conditions — 1970- 4. Soviet Union — Civilization — 1917- I. T.
DK29.S524 1983   947/.08 19   *LC* 83-45042   *ISBN* 081291080X

The Soviet Union, a systematic geography / Leslie Symons ...   3.3017
[et al.].
Totowa, N.J.: Barnes & Noble, 1983. xi, 266 p.: ill.; 26 cm. 1. Soviet Union — Description and travel — 1970- I. Symons, Leslie.
DK29.S725 1983   947.085 19   *LC* 82-6683   *ISBN* 0389203092

DK30–35 Civilization. Ethnography

Blinoff, Marthe.   • **3.3018**
Life and thought in old Russia. [University Park] Pennsylvania State University Press [1961] 222 p. illus. 25 cm. 1. Soviet Union — Civilization I. T.
DK32.B67   914.7   LC 61-11415

Masaryk, T. G. (Tomáš Garrigue), 1850-1937.   • **3.3019**
[Russland und Europa. English] The spirit of Russia; studies in history, literature and philosophy. Translated from the German original by Eden and Cedar Paul, with additional chapters and bibliographies by Jan Slavík; the former translated and the latter condensed and translated by W. R. & Z. Lee. [2d ed., 3d impression] London, Allen & Unwin; New York, Macmillan [1961-67] 3 v. 22 cm. Imprint covered by label: Barnes & Noble, New York; v. 3 has imprint: New York, Barnes & Noble, issued without edition statement. Vol. 3 edited by George Gibian and translated by Robert Bass. Translation of Russland und Europa. 1. Philosophy, Russian 2. Russian literature — History and criticism. 3. Soviet Union — Civilization 4. Soviet Union — History I. Gibian, George. ed. II. T.
DK32.M412   914.7/03/8   LC 68-31931

Miliukov, P. N. (Pavel Nikolaevich), 1859-1943.   • **3.3020**
Outlines of Russian culture, by Paul Miliukov, edited by Michael Karpovich; translated by Valentine Ughet and Eleanor Davis. Philadelphia, University of Pennsylvania Press, c1942. 3 v. ill. 23 cm. Abridged translation of Ocherki po istorii russkoĭ kul'tury. On spine: Russian culture. 'An authorized abridged version of the original, specially prepared for the American edition.'—Editor's foreword. 1. Soviet Union — Civilization I. T. II. Title: Ocherki polstorii russkoĭ kul'tury. III. Title: Russian culture.
DK 32 M6392 E5 1942   LC 42-6909

Strakhovsky, Leonid Ivan, 1898-1963. ed.   • **3.3021**
A handbook of Slavic studies. — Cambridge: Harvard Univ. Press, 1949. xxi, 753 p.; 24 cm. Includes bibliographies. 1. Slavic studies. I. T.
DK32.S86   936.7   LC 49-3015 *

Billington, James H.   • **3.3022**
The icon and the axe; an interpretive history of Russian culture, by James H. Billington. [1st ed.] New York, Knopf, 1966. xviii, 786, xxxiii p. illus., map, ports. 25 cm. 1. Soviet Union — Intellectual life I. T.
DK32.7.B5   914.703   LC 66-18687

Raeff, Marc. ed.   **3.3023**
Russian intellectual history; an anthology. With an introd. by Isaiah Berlin. New York, Harcourt, Brace & World [1966] x, 404 p. 23 cm. (The Harbrace series in Russian area studies) 1. Soviet Union — Intellectual life — Collections. I. T.
DK32.7.R3   914.703   LC 66-17350

Handbook of major Soviet nationalities / Zev Katz, editor;   **3.3024**
Rosemarie Rogers, associate editor; Frederic Harned, assistant editor.
New York: Free Press, [1975] xiv, 481 p.; 26 cm. 1. Ethnology — Soviet Union 2. Soviet Union. I. Katz, Zev, ed. II. Rogers, Rosemarie, 1936- ed. III. Harned, Frederic T., ed. IV. Title: Major Soviet nationalities.
DK33.H35 1975   914.7/06   LC 74-10458   ISBN 0029170907

Soviet nationality problems. Authors: Edward Allworth [and   • **3.3025**
others] Editor: Edward Allworth.
New York: Columbia University Press, 1971. xiv, 296 p.: illus., facsims., maps.; 24 cm. Based on papers from a research seminar on Soviet nationality problems, given at Columbia University in 1968-69 school year. 1. Minorities — Russia. I. Allworth, Edward.
DK33.S67 1971   301.45/0947   LC 77-166211   ISBN 0231034938

Wixman, Ronald, 1947-.   **3.3026**
The peoples of the USSR: an ethnographic handbook / Ronald Wixman. — Armonk, N.Y.: M.E. Sharpe, c1984. xviii, 246 p.: 15 maps; 24 cm. Map index. 1. Ethnology — Soviet Union — Handbooks, manuals, etc. I. T. II. Title: Peoples of the U.S.S.R.
DK33.W59 1984   947/.004 19   LC 83-18433   ISBN 0873322037

Akiner, Shirin.   **3.3027**
Islamic peoples of the Soviet Union: (with an appendix on the non–Muslim Turkic peoples of the Soviet Union) / Shirin Akiner. — London; Boston: Kegan Paul International, 1983. xiii, 462 p.: maps; 24 cm. Includes index. 1. Muslims — Soviet Union I. T.
DK34.M8 A35 1983   947/.00882971 19   LC 82-140   ISBN 0710300255

Bennigsen, Alexandre.   **3.3028**
Muslims of the Soviet empire: a guide / Alexandre Bennigsen, S. Enders Wimbush. — Bloomington: Indianna University Press, c1986. xvi, 294 p.: maps; 23 cm. Includes index. 1. Muslims — Soviet Union 2. Islam — Soviet Union. I. Wimbush, S. Enders. II. T.
DK34.M8 B46 1986   947/.00882971 19   LC 86-15343   ISBN 0253339588

DK36–276 History

The Modern encyclopedia of Russian and Soviet history / edited   **3.3029**
by Joseph L. Wieczynski.
Gulf Breeze, Fl: Academic International Press, 1976. 246 p.; 25 cm. (Academic International reference series) v. 1. 1. Soviet Union — History — Dictionaries. I. Wieczynski, Joseph L., 1934-
DK36.M55 1976   947/.003   LC 75-11091   ISBN 0875690645

Pushkarev, Sergeĭ Germanovich, 1888-.   **3.3030**
Dictionary of Russian historical terms from the eleventh century to 1917 / compiled by Sergei G. Pushkarev; edited by George Vernadsky and Ralph T. Fisher, Jr. — New Haven: Yale University Press, 1970. xi, 199 p.; 26 cm. 1. Russian language — Dictionaries — English. 2. Soviet Union — History — Dictionaries. I. T.
DK36.P78 1970   947/.003   LC 73-81426   ISBN 0300011369

Aksakov, S. T. (Sergeĭ Timofeevich), 1791-1859.   • **3.3031**
[Semeĭnaia khronika. English] The family chronicle. Translated by M. C. Beverley. Introd. by Ralph E. Matlaw. New York, Dutton, 1961. 227 p. 19 cm. (A Dutton paperback, D86) 1. Aksakov family. 2. Soviet Union — Social life and customs I. T.
DK37.8.A3 A3 1961   891.783   LC 61-65198

Tolstoy, Nikolai.   **3.3032**
The Tolstoys, twenty–four generations of Russian history, 1353–1983 / Nikolai Tolstoy. — 1st U.S. ed. — New York: W. Morrow, 1983. 368 p.: ill.; 26 cm. 1. Tolstoy family I. T.
DK37.8.T64 T65 1983b   947/.009/92 B 19   LC 83-61738   ISBN 068802341X

Black, Cyril Edwin, 1915- ed.   • **3.3033**
Rewriting Russian history; Soviet interpretations of Russia's past. — 2d ed., rev. — New York, Vintage Books [1962] xv, 431 p. 19 cm. — (Vintage Russian library, v738) 1. Russia — Hist. — Historiography. I. T.
DK38.B5 1962   947   LC 63-1520

Mazour, Anatole Gregory, 1900-.   **3.3034**
Modern Russian historiography. 2d ed. Princeton, N. J., Van Nostrand [1958] 260 p. illus. 22 cm. First ed. published in 1939 under title: An outline of modern Russian historiography. 1. Soviet Union. — Historiography. I. T.
DK38.M3 1958   LC 58-13572

Mazour, Anatole Gregory, 1900-.   • **3.3035**
The writing of history in the Soviet Union, by Anatole G. Mazour. Stanford, Calif., c1971. Hoover Institution Press [1971] xvi, 383 p. 24 cm. (Hoover Institution publications; 87) 1. Russia — Historiography. I. T.
DK38.M325   947/.0072/047   LC 76-99084   ISBN 081791871X

Vernadsky, George, 1887-1973.   **3.3036**
Russian historiography: a history / by George Vernadsky; edited by Sergei Pushkarev; translated by Nickolas Lupinin. — Belmont, Mass.: Nordland Pub. Co., c1978. iv, 575 p.; 23 cm. Includes index. 1. Russia — Historiography. I. Pushkarev, Sergeĭ Germanovich, 1888- II. T.
DK38.V4413   947/.007/2   LC 77-95207   ISBN 0913124257

Daniels, Robert Vincent.   **3.3037**
Russia, the roots of confrontation / Robert V. Daniels. — Cambridge, Mass.: Harvard University Press, 1985. xiii, 411 p.: ill.; 25 cm. (American foreign policy library.) Includes index. 1. Soviet Union — History I. T. II. Series.
DK40.D28 1985   947 19   LC 84-19152   ISBN 0674779657

Dukes, Paul, 1934-.   **3.3038**
A history of Russia: medieval, modern, and contemporary. New York, McGraw-Hill [1974] xi, 361 p. 23 cm. 1. Soviet Union — History I. T.
DK40.D84   947   LC 74-1154   ISBN 0070180326

Florinsky, Michael T., 1894-.   • **3.3039**
Russia: a history and an interpretation. New York, Macmillan, 1953. 2 v. maps. 22 cm. 1. Soviet Union — History I. T.
DK40.F6 1953   947   LC 53-11899

An Introduction to Russian history / edited by Robert Auty and   **3.3040**
Dimitri Obolensky, with the editorial assistance of Anthony
Kingsford.
Cambridge [Eng.]; New York: Cambridge University Press, 1976. xiii, 403 p.:
ill.; 24 cm. (Companion to Russian studies; 1) 1. Russia — History. I. Auty,
Robert. II. Obolensky, Dimitri, 1918- III. Series.
DK40.I57   947   LC 75-10688

Kliuchevskiĭ, V. O. (Vasiliĭ Osipovich), 1841-1911.   **3.3041**
A history of Russia, by V. O. Kluchevsky. Translated by C. J. Hogarth. — New
York, Russell & Russell, 1960. 5 v. 23 cm. 1. Russia — Hist. I. T.
DK40.K613   947   LC 60-6033 rev

Pares, Bernard, Sir, 1867-1949.   **3.3042**
A history of Russia. Definitive ed., with a new introd. by Richard Pares. New
York, Knopf, 1953. xxxvii, 611, xxxi p. maps. 25 cm. 1. Soviet Union —
History I. T.
DK40.P3 1953   947   LC 52-5077

Pipes, Richard.   **3.3043**
Russia under the old regime / Richard Pipes. — New York: Scribner, c1974.
xxii, 360 p., [24] leaves of plates: ill.; 24 cm. (History of civilisation) 1. Russia
— History. I. T.
DK40.P47 1974b   947   LC 74-32567   ISBN 0684140411

Pokrovskiĭ, M. N. (Mikhail Nikolaevich), 1868-1932.   • **3.3044**
History of Russia: from the earliest times to the rise of commercial capitalism /
by Professor M. N. Pokrovsky; translated and edited by J. D. Clarkson and M.
R. M. Griffiths. New York: Russell & Russell, 1966. xvi, 383 p.: maps; 24 cm.
Includes index. 1. Soviet Union — History I. Clarkson, Jesse Dunsmore,
1897- II. Griffiths, Mary Rose Millie, 1898- III. T.
DK40.P612 1966a   947   LC 66-24751

Riasanovsky, Nicholas Valentine, 1923-.   **3.3045**
A history of Russia / Nicholas V. Riasanovsky. — 4th ed. — New York:
Oxford University Press, 1984. xx, 695 p., [32] p. of plates: ill., maps; 24 cm.
Includes index. 1. Soviet Union — History I. T.
DK40.R5 1984   947 19   LC 83-4116   ISBN 0195033612

Solov'ev, Sergeĭ Mikhaĭlovich, 1820-1879.   **3.3046**
[Istoriia Rossii s drevneĭshikh vremen. English] History of Russia / Sergei M.
Soloviev; edited, translated and with an introd. by Hugh F. Graham. — Gulf
Breeze, FL: Academic International Press, 1976-<1984 > v. <7-9, 24, 29,
34-35 >: ill.; 23 cm. Translation of Istoriia Rossii s drevneĭshikh vremen.
1. Russia — History. I. T.
DK40.S6213   947   LC 75-11085   ISBN 0875690661

Vernadsky, George, 1887-1973.   • **3.3047**
A history of Russia, by George Vernadsky and Michael Karpovich ... [New
Haven, Yale university press; London, H. Milford, Oxford university press,
1943-. v. maps (part fold.) 25 cm. Half-title; each volume has special t.-p.
Includes bibliographies. 1. Soviet Union — History I. Karpovich, Michael,
1888-1959. II. T.
DK40.V44   947   LC A 43-1903 rev 3

Platonov, S. F. (Sergeĭ Fedorovich), 1860-1933.   • **3.3048**
History of Russia, by S. F. Platonov, translated by E. Aronsberg, edited by F.
A. Golder ... — New York, The Macmillan company, 1925. vii p., 3 l., 435 p.
maps (part double) geneal. tables. 21 cm. Bibliography: p. 417-420. 1. Russia
— Hist. I. Aronsberg, Emanuel, tr. II. Golder, Frank Alfred, 1877-1929. ed.
III. T.
DK41.P6   LC 25-24285

Sumner, Benedict Humphrey, 1893-.   **3.3049**
A short history of Russia. New York, Reynal & Hitchcock [1943] 5 p.l., 469 p.
illus. (maps) plates, ports. 22 cm. 1. Russia — History. I. T.
DK41.S8   LC 43-17185

Avrich, Paul.   **3.3050**
Russian rebels, 1600–1800. New York, Schocken Books [1972] 309 p. illus. 21
cm. 1. Revolutions — Soviet Union. I. T.
DK43.A95   947 B   LC 72-79444   ISBN 0805234586

Kerner, Robert Joseph, 1887-1956.   • **3.3051**
The urge to the sea; the course of Russian history. The role of rivers, portages,
ostrogs, monasteries, and furs, by Robert J. Kerner ... — Berkeley and Los
Angeles, University of California press, 1942. xvii, 212 p.: ill., maps (part fold.);
24 cm. — ([Publications of the Northeastern Asia seminar of the University of
California]) 1. Russia — Hist. I. T.
DK43.K47   947   LC 42-36949

Wesson, Robert G.   **3.3052**
The Russian dilemma; a political and geopolitical view [by] Robert G. Wesson.
New Brunswick, N.J., Rutgers University Press [1974] x, 228 p. 24 cm.

1. Geopolitics — Soviet Union. 2. Eurasianism 3. Soviet Union — History
I. T.
DK43.W4   327/.1/0110947   LC 74-1412   ISBN 081350774X

Duffy, Christopher, 1936-.   **3.3053**
Russia's military way to the West: origins and nature of Russian military power,
1700–1800 / Christopher Duffy. — London: Boston: Routledge & Kegan Paul,
1981. xiii, 256 p.: ill.; 26 cm. Includes index. 1. Soviet Union — History,
Military — To 1801 I. T.
DK52.5.D83   947 19   LC 82-100403   ISBN 0710007973

Curtiss, John Shelton.   • **3.3054**
Russian Army under Nicholas I, 1825–1855. Durham, N.C.: Duke University
Press, 1965. x, 386 p.: maps; 24 cm. 1. Russia. Armiia — History. 2. Russia —
History, Military — 1801-1917. I. T.
DK53.C85   355.0330947   LC 65-24927

Mitchell, Donald W. (Donald William), 1911-.   **3.3055**
A history of Russian and Soviet sea power [by] Donald W. Mitchell. New York,
Macmillan [1974] xxviii, 657 p. illus. 25 cm. 1. Soviet Union — History, Naval.
I. T.
DK56.M48   359/.00947   LC 72-93629

DK60–69 POLITICAL AND DIPLOMATIC HISTORY

Conference on a Century of Russian Foreign Policy, Yale   • **3.3056**
University, 1961.
Russian foreign policy; essays in historical perspective. Edited by Ivo J.
Lederer. New Haven, Yale University Press, 1962. xxiii, 620 p. 24 cm. 1. Soviet
Union — Foreign relations — Congresses. I. Lederer, Ivo J. ed. II. Yale
University. III. T.
DK61.C65   327.47   LC 62-8251

Beloff, Max, 1913-.   • **3.3057**
The foreign policy of Soviet Russia, 1929–1941. Issued under the auspices of the
Royal Institute of International Affairs. London, New York, Oxford University
Press, 1947-49. 2 v. maps (1 fold.) 23 cm. 1. Soviet Union — Foreign relations
— 1917-1945 I. T.
DK63.B4   327.47   LC 48-478

Eudin, Xenia Joukoff.   • **3.3058**
Soviet foreign policy, 1928–1934; documents and materials, by Xenia Joukoff
Eudin and Robert M. Slusser. University Park, Pennsylvania State University
Press [1967, c1966-. v. 25 cm. (Hoover Institution publications) 'A continuation
of the two Hoover Institution collections published in 1957; Soviet Russia and
the West, 1920-1927; a documentary survey, by X. J. Eudin and H. H. Fisher,
and Soviet Russia and the East, 1920-1927; a documentary survey, by X. J.
Eudin and R. C. North.' 1. Soviet Union — Foreign relations — 1917-1945
I. Slusser, Robert M. joint author. II. T.
DK63.E8   327.47   LC 66-25465

Kennan, George Frost, 1904-.   • **3.3059**
Soviet foreign policy, 1917–1941. Princeton, N.J., Van Nostrand [1960] 192 p.
19 cm. (Van Nostrand anvil books, no. 47) 1. Soviet Union — Foreign relations
— 1917-1945 I. T.
DK63.K4   327.47   LC 60-13459

Fleming, Denna Frank, 1893-.   • **3.3060**
The cold war and its origins, 1917–1960. Garden City, N.Y., Doubleday [1961]
2 v. (xx, 1158 p.) 25 cm. 1. Soviet Union — Foreign relations — 1917- I. T.
DK63.3.F55   327.47   LC 61-9193

Kennan, George Frost, 1904-.   • **3.3061**
Russia and the West under Lenin and Stalin. [1st ed.] Boston, Little, Brown
[1961] 411 p. 22 cm. 1. Soviet Union — Foreign relations — 1917-1945 I. T.
DK63.3.K38   327.47   LC 61-9292

Rubinstein, Alvin Z. ed.   • **3.3062**
The foreign policy of the Soviet Union / edited, with introductory essays, by
Alvin Z. Rubinstein. — 3d ed. New York: Random House [1972] xviii, 474 p.;
24 cm. 1. Soviet Union — Foreign relations — 1917- I. T.
DK63.3.R8 1972   327.47   LC 71-38820   ISBN 0394316991

Shulman, Marshall Darrow.   • **3.3063**
Stalin's foreign policy reappraised / Marshall D. Shulman. — Cambridge:
Harvard University Press, 1963. vi, 320 p. 22 cm. — (Russian Research Center
studies; 48) Bibliography: p. [275]-282. 1. Soviet Union — Foreign relations —
1945- I. T.
DK63.3.S368   327.47   LC 63-13816

Jelavich, Barbara, 1923-.   3.3064
St. Petersburg and Moscow: tsarist and Soviet foreign policy, 1814–1974 [by] Barbara Jelavich. Bloomington, Indiana University Press [1974] xii, 480 p. illus. 22 cm. 1. Soviet Union — Foreign relations — History. I. T.
DK66.J4 1974   327.47   *LC* 73-16537   *ISBN* 0253350506 *ISBN* 0253350514

Blackstock, Paul W., ed.   • 3.3065
The Russian menace to Europe; a collection of articles, speeches, letters, and news dispatches, by Karl Marx and Friedrich Engels. Selected and edited by Paul W. Blackstock and Bert F. Hoselitz. — Glencoe, Ill., Free Press [1952] 288 p. 22 cm. 'Bibliographical notes and editors' comments': p. 242-284. 1. Europe — Politics — 1789-1900. 2. Russia — For. rel. — Europe. I. Hoselitz, Berthold Frank, 1913- joint editor. II. Marx, Karl, 1818-1883. III. Engels, Friedrich, 1820-1895. IV. T.
DK67.B5   947.07   *LC* 52-13423

Eudin, Xenia Joukoff.   • 3.3066
Soviet Russia and the West, 1920–1927: a documentary survey / by Xenia Joukoff Eudin and Harold H. Fisher in collaboration with Rosemary Brown Jones. Stanford: Stanford University Press, 1957. xxxvii, 450 p.: ill.; 25 cm. — (Hoover Institution Publications; no. 26) Includes index. 1. Russia — Foreign relations — Europe. 2. Europe — Politics and government — 1918-1945 I. Fisher, Harold Henry, 1890- II. T.
DK67.E85   *LC* 57-6013

Platonov, S. F. (Sergeĭ Fedorovich), 1860-1933.   3.3067
Moscow and the West [by] S. F. Platonov. Translated and edited by Joseph L. Wieczyński. Introd. by Serge A. Zenkovsky. [Hattiesburg, Miss.] Academic International, 1972. xx, 171 p. map. 22 cm. (Russian series, v. 9) Translation of Moskva i Zapad. Includes bibliographical references. 1. Russia — Civilization — Occidental influences. I. T.
DK67.P5513   301.29/47/01821   *LC* 72-142000   *ISBN* 087569019X

Treadgold, Donald W., 1922-.   3.3068
The West in Russia and China; religious and secular thought in modern times [by] Donald W. Treadgold. Cambridge [Eng.] University Press, 1973. 2 v. 24 cm. 1. Soviet Union — Civilization — Occidental influences. 2. China — Civilization — Occidental influences I. T.
DK67.T7 1973   914.7/03   *LC* 72-78886   *ISBN* 0521085527

Jelavich, Charles.   • 3.3069
Tsarist Russia and Balkan nationalism; Russian influence in the internal affairs of Bulgaria and Serbia, 1879–1886. Berkeley, University of California Press, 1958. x, 304 p.: map.; 25 cm. (Russian and East European studies.) Bibliography: p. 287-294. Bibliographical footnotes. 1. Russia — Foreign relations — Bulgaria. 2. Bulgaria — Foreign relations — Russia. 3. Russia — Foreign relations — Serbia. 4. Serbia — Foreign relations — Russia. I. T. II. Series.
DK67.4.J4   327.4709497   *LC* 58-12830

Kennan, George Frost, 1904-.   3.3070
The decline of Bismarck's European order: Franco–Russian relations, 1875–1890 / by George F. Kennan. — Princeton, N.J.: Princeton University Press, c1979. xii, 466 p., [8] leaves of plates: ill.; 24 cm. Includes index. 1. Russia — Foreign relations — France. 2. France — Foreign relations — Russia. I. T.
DK67.5.F8 K36   327.47/044   *LC* 79-83997   *ISBN* 0691052824

Eudin, Xenia Joukoff.   • 3.3071
Soviet Russia and the East, 1920–1927: a documentary survey / by Xenia Joukoff Eudin and Robert C. North. — Stanford, Calif.: Stanford University Press, 1957. xviii, 478 p.: ill.; 25 cm. — (Hoover Library on War, Revolution, and Peace - Stanford University; no. 25) 1. Russia — Foreign relations — Asia. 2. Asia — Politics. I. North, Robert Carver. II. T.
DK68.E85   *LC* 56-8690

McLane, Charles B.   • 3.3072
Soviet policy and the Chinese Communists, 1931–1946. New York, Columbia University Press, 1958. viii, 310 p. 24 cm. (Studies of the Russian Institute, Columbia University) 1. Communism — China. 2. Soviet Union — Foreign relations — China. 3. China — Foreign relations — Soviet Union. I. T.
DK68.7.C5 M27   327.470951   *LC* 58-11903

Zagoria, Donald S.   • 3.3073
The Sino–Soviet Conflict, 1956–1961. Princeton, N.J., Princeton University Press, 1962. 484 p.; 25 cm. 1. Communism — History 2. Soviet Union — Foreign relations — China — History. 3. China. I. T.
DK68.7.C5 Z3   327.47051   *LC* 62-10890

Donaldson, Robert H.   3.3074
Soviet policy toward India: ideology and strategy / Robert H. Donaldson. — Cambridge, Mass.: Harvard University Press, 1974. x, 338 p.; 24 cm. (Russian Research Center studies; 74) Includes index. 1. Soviet Union — Foreign relations — India. 2. India — Foreign relations — Soviet Union. I. T.
DK68.7.I5 D66   327.47/054   *LC* 73-89708   *ISBN* 0674827767

Krammer, Arnold, 1941-.   3.3075
The forgotten friendship: Israel and the Soviet Bloc, 1947–53. Urbana: University of Illinois Press [1974] x, 224 p.: ill.; 24 cm. 1. Soviet Union — Foreign relations — Israel. 2. Israel — Foreign relations — Soviet Union. I. T.
DK68.7.I8 K72   327.47/05694   *LC* 74-7121   *ISBN* 0252003969

Ro'i, Yaacov.   3.3076
Soviet decision making in practice: the USSR and Israel, 1947–1954 / Yaacov Ro'i. — New Brunswick, N.J.: Transaction Books, c1980. 540 p.; 24 cm. (The monograph series - Shiloah Center for Middle Eastern and African Studies) Based on the author's thesis, Jerusalem, 1972. Includes indexes. 1. Antisemitism — Soviet Union. 2. Jews — Soviet Union — Politics and government — 1917- 3. Soviet Union — Foreign relations — Israel. 4. Israel — Foreign relations — Soviet Union. I. T.
DK68.7.I8 R64   327.47/05694   *LC* 79-64857   *ISBN* 0878552677

Rubinstein, Alvin Z.   3.3077
Soviet policy toward Turkey, Iran, and Afghanistan: the dynamics of influence / Alvin Z. Rubinstein. — New York, N.Y.: Praeger, 1982. xiii, 200 p.; 24 cm. — (Studies of influence in international relations.) Includes index. 1. Soviet Union — Foreign relations — Turkey. 2. Turkey — Foreign relations — Soviet Union. 3. Soviet Union — Foreign relations — Iran. 4. Iran — Foreign relations — Soviet Union. 5. Soviet Union — Foreign relations — Afghanistan. 6. Afghanistan — Foreign relations — Soviet Union. I. T. II. Series.
DK68.7.T9 R83 1982   327.4705 19   *LC* 82-7513   *ISBN* 0030525063

DK70–276 HISTORY, BY PERIOD

DK70–112 Early. Medieval, to 1613

Chadwick, Nora K. (Nora Kershaw), 1891-1972.   • 3.3078
The beginnings of Russian history: an enquiry into sources, by N. K. Chadwick ... — Cambridge [Eng.] The University press, 1946. xi, 180 p.: front.; 20 cm. Bibliographical foot-notes. 1. Nestor, annalist, d. 1115? 2. Russia — Hist. — To 1533 — Sources. I. T.
DK70.A2C5   947.02   *LC* 46-6223

The Nikonian chronicle / edited, introduced and annotated by Serge A. Zenkovsky; translated by Serge A. and Betty Jean Zenkovsky.   3.3079
Princeton, N.J.: Kingston Press, 1984-. v.: ill., genealogical tables. Errata inserted in v. 2. 1. Nikonovskiĭ svod 2. Russia — History — To 1533. 3. Russian S.F.S.R — History — Sources. 4. Russia — History — Kievan period, 862-1237 — Sources. 5. Ukraine — History — 862-1240 — Sources. I. Zenskovsky, Serge Alexander, 1907-. II. Zenkovsky, Betty Jean. III. Nikonovskiĭ svod.
DK70 N5413 1984   947   *ISBN* 0940670011

Povest'vremennykh let. English.   • 3.3080
The Russian primary chronicle: Laurentian text / translated and edited by Samuel Hazzard Cross and Olgerd P. Sherbowitz-Wetzor. — Cambridge, Mass.: Mediaeval Academy of America, 1953. 313 p.: maps, geneal. table.; 24 cm. (Mediaeval Academy of America.Publication; no. 60) 1. Russia — History — To 1533. I. Nestor, annalist, d. 1115? II. Cross, Samuel Hazzard, 1891-1946. III. Sherbowitz-Wetzor, Olgerd P. IV. T.
DK70.P612   *LC* 53-10264 rev

Karamzin, Nikolaĭ Mikhaĭlovich, 1766-1826.   • 3.3081
Memoir on ancient and modern Russia. A translation and analysis [by] Richard Pipes. — Cambridge, Harvard University Press, 1959. xiv, 266 p. port. 22 cm. — (Russian Research Center studies, 33) Bibliography: p. [255]-259. Translated from Russian. (transliterated: O drevneĭ i novoĭ Rossii) 1. Russia — Hist. I. Pipes, Richard. ed. and tr. II. T.
DK71.K343   947   *LC* 59-6162 rev

Vernadsky, George, 1887-1973.   • 3.3082
The origins of Russia. Oxford: Clarendon Press, 1959. x, 354 p.: ill.; 22 cm. 1. Soviet Union — History — To 1533 I. T.
DK72.V4   947   *LC* 59-1228

Halperin, Charles J.   3.3083
Russia and the Golden Horde: the Mongol impact on medieval Russian history / Charles J. Halperin. — Bloomington: Indiana University Press, c1985. ix, 180 p.: ill., 2 maps; 24 cm. Includes index. 1. Golden Horde 2. Soviet Union — History — 1237-1480 I. T.
DK90.H28 1985   947/.03 19   *LC* 84-48254   *ISBN* 0253350336

Presniakov, A. E. (Aleksandr Evgen'evich), 1870-1929.   • 3.3084
[Obrazovanie Velikorusskago gosudarstva. English] The formation of the great Russian state; a study of Russian history in the thirteenth to fifteenth centuries. Translated from the Russian by A. E. Moorhouse. Introd. by Alfred J. Rieber.

Chicago, Quadrangle Books [c1970] xlii, 414 p. 22 cm. (The Quadrangle series in Russian history) Translation of Obrazovanie Velikorusskago gosudarstva (romanized form) 1. Russia — History — 1237-1480. I. T.
DK90.P713   947/.03   *LC* 75-78314

Kurbskiĭ, Andreĭ Mikhaĭlovich, kniaz', d. 1583.   • **3.3085**
The correspondence between Prince A. M. Kurbsky and Tsar Ivan IV of Russia, 1564–1579 / edited with a translation and notes by J. L. I. Fennell ... — Cambridge: University Press, 1955. xi, 275 p.; 22 cm. 1. Soviet Union — History — Ivan IV, 1533-1584 — Sources. I. Ivan IV, Czar of Russia, 1530-1584. II. T.
DK106.A25   *LC* 56-4698

Fennell, John Lister Illingworth.   • **3.3086**
Ivan the Great of Moscow. London: Macmillan; New York: St. Martin's Press, 1961 [i.e. 1962] 386 p.: ill.; 23 cm. 1. Soviet Union — History — Ivan III, 1462-1505 I. T.
DK106.F4   947.04   *LC* 62-1391

Platonov, S. F. (Sergeĭ Fedorovich), 1860-1933.   **3.3087**
[Ivan Groznyĭ. English] Ivan the Terrible [by] S. F. Platonov. Edited and translated by Joseph L. Wieczynski. With In search of Ivan the Terrible, by Richard Hellie. [Gulf Breeze, Fla.] Academic International Press, 1974. xxxviii, 166 p. illus. 23 cm. (The Russian series, v. 28) Translation of Ivan Groznyi. 1. Ivan IV, Czar of Russia, 1530-1584. 2. Russia — History — Ivan IV, 1533-1584. I. Hellie, Richard. In search of Ivan the Terrible. 1974. II. T.
DK106.P5513   947/.04/0924 B   *LC* 77-176468   *ISBN* 0875690548

Grey, Ian, 1918-.   **3.3088**
Boris Godunov; the tragic Tsar. New York, Scribner [1973] 188 p. illus. 24 cm. 1. Boris Fyodorovich Godunov, Czar of Russia, 1551 or 2-1605. 2. Soviet Union — History — 1553-1613. I. T.
DK109.G73   947/.04/0924 B   *LC* 72-11119   *ISBN* 0684133393

Platonov, S. F. (Sergeĭ Fedorovich), 1860-1933.   **3.3089**
[Boris Godunov. English] Boris Godunov, Tsar of Russia. Translated from the Russian by L. Rex Pyles. With an introductory essay S. F. Platonov: Eminence and obscurity, by John T. Alexander. [Gulf Breeze, Fla.] Academic International Press, 1973. xlii, 230 p. port., map. 23 cm. (Russian series, v. 10) Translation of Boris Godunov. 1. Boris Fyodorovich Godunov, Czar of Russia, 1551 or 2-1605. 2. Soviet Union — History — Boris Godunov, 1598-1605 I. Alexander, John T. S. F. Platonov: Eminence and obscurity. 1973. II. T.
DK109.P513   947/.04/0924 B   *LC* 73-176467   *ISBN* 0875690246

Platonov, S. F. (Sergeĭ Fedorovich), 1860-1933.   • **3.3090**
[Smutnoe vremia. English] The time of troubles; a historical study of the internal crises and social struggle in sixteenth– and seventeenth–century Muscovy [by] S. F. Platonov. Translated by John T. Alexander. Lawrence, University Press of Kansas [c1970] xvii, 197 p. maps. 22 cm. (Kansas paperback, KP-8) Translation of Smutnoe vremia (romanized form) 1. Russia — History — Epoch of confusion, 1605-1613. I. T.
DK111.P5813   947/.04   *LC* 79-97029   *ISBN* 0700600620

DK113–187 17th–18th Centuries

Raeff, Marc.   **3.3091**
[Comprendre l'ancien régime russe. English] Understanding imperial Russia: state and society in the old regime / Marc Raeff; translated by Arthur Goldhammer; foreword by John Keep. — New York: Columbia University Press, 1984. xix, 248 p.: ill.; 24 cm. Translation of: Comprendre l'ancien régime russe. Includes index. 1. Soviet Union — History — 1613-1689 2. Soviet Union — History — 1689-1800 3. Soviet Union — History — 19th century I. T.
DK113.R3413 1984   947 19   *LC* 83-26241   *ISBN* 023105842X

Dukes, Paul, 1934-.   **3.3092**
The making of Russian absolutism, 1613–1801 / Paul Dukes. — London; New York: Longman, 1982. 197 p.: maps; 24 cm. — (Longman history of Russia.) Includes index. 1. Soviet Union — Politics and government — 1613-1689 2. Soviet Union — Politics and government — 1689-1800 I. T. II. Title: Absolutism, 1613-1801. III. Series.
DK113.2.D84   947 19   *LC* 81-8333   *ISBN* 058248684X

Bain, R. Nisbet (Robert Nisbet), 1854-1909.   • **3.3093**
The first Romanovs, 1613–1725; a history of Moscovite civilization and the rise of modern Russia under Peter the Great and his forerunners. New York, Russell & Russell [1967] xii, 413 p. fold. illus., ports. 22 cm. Reprint of ed. first published in 1905. 1. Romanov, House of 2. Soviet Union — History — 1613-1689 3. Soviet Union — History — Peter I, 1689-1725 I. T.
DK114.B2 1967   947/.04   *LC* 66-24666

Kliuchevskiĭ, V. O. (Vasiliĭ Osipovich), 1841-1911.   • **3.3094**
[Kurs russkoĭ istorii, v. 3. English] A course in Russian history: the seventeenth century, by V.O. Kliuchevsky. Translated from the Russian by Natalie

Duddington. Introd. by Alfred J. Rieber. Chicago, Quadrangle Books [1968] xl, 400 p. 22 cm. (Quadrangle series in Russian history) Translation of v. 3 of Kurs russkoĭ istorii (romanized form) 1. Soviet Union — History — 1613-1689 2. Soviet Union — History — Epoch of confusion, 1605-1613 I. T.
DK114.K573   947/.04   *LC* 68-26442

Longworth, Philip, 1933-.   **3.3095**
Alexis, tsar of all the Russias / Philip Longworth. — New York: F. Watts, 1984. xiii, 305 p., [8] p. of plates: ill.; 24 cm. Includes index. 1. Alekseĭ Mikhaĭlovich, Czar of Russia, 1629-1676. 2. Soviet Union — Kings and rulers — Biography. I. T.
DK118.L66 1984   947/.048/0924 B 19   *LC* 84-50633   *ISBN* 0531097706

Garrard, John Gordon.   **3.3096**
The eighteenth century in Russia; edited by J. G. Garrard. — Oxford: Clarendon Press, 1973. xiii, 356 p.: illus.; 23 cm. 1. Russia — History — 1689-1800. I. T.
DK127.G33   914.7/03/6   *LC* 74-150462   *ISBN* 0198156383

Rogger, Hans.   • **3.3097**
National consciousness in eighteenth–century Russia. Cambridge, Harvard University Press, 1960. viii, 319 p. 22 cm. (Russian Research Center studies, 38) Bibliography: p. [285]-295. 1. Nationalism — Russia. 2. Russia — History — 1689-1800. I. T.
DK127.R6   947.06   *LC* 60-8450

Anderson, M. S. (Matthew Smith)   **3.3098**
Peter the Great / M. S. Anderson. — London: Thames and Hudson, c1978. 207 p., [8] leaves of plates: ill.; 23 cm. (Men in office) Includes index. 1. Peter I, Emperor of Russia, 1672-1725. 2. Russia — History — Peter I, 1689-1725. 3. Russia — Kings and rulers — Biography. I. T.
DK131.A49 1978   947/.05/0924 B   *LC* 78-53047   *ISBN* 050087008X

Massie, Robert K., 1929-.   **3.3099**
Peter the Great, his life and world / Robert K. Massie. — 1st ed. — New York: Knopf, 1980. xii, 909 p., [12] leaves of plates: ill.; 25 cm. Includes index. 1. Peter I, Emperor of Russia, 1672-1725. 2. Russia — History — Peter I, 1689-1725. 3. Russia — Kings and rulers — Biography. I. T.
DK131.M28   947.05/092/4 B 19   *LC* 80-7635   *ISBN* 0394500326

Sumner, Benedict Humphrey, 1893-.   • **3.3100**
Peter the Great and the emergence of Russia. New York: Macmillan, 1951. vii, 216 p. port., maps (on lining papers) geneal. table. 18 cm. (Teach yourself history library) Addendum slip mounted on p. 211. 'Note on books': p. 210-211. 1. Peter I, Emperor of Russia, 1672-1725. 2. Russia — History — Peter I, 1689-1725. I. T. II. Series.
DK131.S88   947.05   *LC* A 52-973

Riasanovsky, Nicholas Valentine, 1923-.   **3.3101**
The image of Peter the Great in Russian history and thought / Nicholas V. Riasanovsky. — New York: Oxford University Press, 1985. ix, 331 p.: ill.; 25 cm. Includes index. 1. Peter I, Emperor of Russia, 1672-1725 — Influence. 2. Peter I, Emperor of Russia, 1672-1725. in fiction, drama, poetry, etc. 3. Peter I, Emperor of Russia, 1672-1725 — Psychology. 4. Soviet Union — Intellectual life I. T.
DK132.R53 1985   947/.05/0924 19   *LC* 83-25157   *ISBN* 0195034562

DK170–183 Catharine II, 1762–1796

Catherine II, Empress of Russia, 1729-1796.   • **3.3102**
The memoirs of Catherine the Great. Edited by Dominique Maroger, with an introd. by G. P. Gooch; translated from the French by Moura Budberg. — New York: Macmillan [1955] 400 p.: ports.; 23 cm. I. Maroger, Dominique, ed. II. T.
DK170.A262   923.147   *LC* 55-1967

Catherine the Great; a profile. Edited by Marc Raeff.   **3.3103**
[1st ed.] New York, Hill and Wang [1972] xiii, 331 p. 21 cm. (World profiles) 1. Catherine II, Empress of Russia, 1729-1796. I. Raeff, Marc. ed.
DK170.C35 1972   947/.06/0924 B   *LC* 77-163575   *ISBN* 0809033674 *ISBN* 0809014009

Gooch, G. P. (George Peabody), 1873-1968.   • **3.3104**
Catherine the Great, and other studies [by] G. P. Gooch. — Hamden, Conn., Archon Books, 1966. xi, 292 p. ports. 22 cm. First published in 1954. 1. Catherine II, Empress of Russia, 1729-1796. 2. Voltaire, 1694-1778. 3. Bismarck, Otto, Fürst von, 1815-1898. 4. France — Intellectual life I. T.
DK170.G65 1966   920.02   *LC* 66-18227

Thomson, Gladys Scott.   • **3.3105**
Catherine the Great and the expansion of Russia. — New York: Macmillan, 1950. x, 294 p.: port., col. map, geneal. table.; 19 cm. — (Teach yourself library) 1. Catherine II, Empress of Russia, 1729-1796. I. T.
DK170.T5 1950   *LC* 50-6988

De Madariaga, Isabel, 1919-.   **3.3106**
Russia in the age of Catherine the Great / Isabel de Madariaga. — New Haven: Yale University Press, c1981. xii, 698 p.: maps; 24 cm. Includes index. 1. Catherine II, Empress of Russia, 1729-1796. 2. Soviet Union — History — Catherine II, 1762-1796 I. T.
DK171.D45   947/.063 19   *LC* 80-21993   *ISBN* 0300025157

DK188–243 19th Century

Crankshaw, Edward.   **3.3107**
The shadow of the winter palace: Russia's drift to revolution, 1825–1917 / Edward Crankshaw. — New York: Viking Press, 1976. 429 p., [4] leaves of plates: ill.; 25 cm. Includes index. 1. Romanov, House of 2. Russia — History — 19th century. 3. Russia — History — Nicholas II, 1894-1917. I. T.
DK189.C66 1976   947/.07   *LC* 76-10636   *ISBN* 0670637823

Harcave, Sidney Samuel, 1916-.   **3.3108**
Years of the golden cockerel: the last Romanov tsars, 1814–1917, by Sidney Harcave. New York, Macmillan [1968] x, 515 p. geneal. table. 24 cm. 1. Romanov, House of 2. Soviet Union — Politics and government — 19th century 3. Soviet Union — Politics and government — 1894-1917 I. T.
DK189.H34   947/.07   *LC* 68-23633

Kornilov, A. A. (Aleksandr Aleksandrovich), 1862-1925.   • **3.3109**
[Kurs istorii Rossii XIX vieka. English] Modern Russian history; from the age of Catherine the Great to the end of the nineteenth century, Translated from the Russian by Alexander S. Kaun. With a bibliography by John S. Curtiss. New York, Russell & Russell [1970, c1944] 310, 284, x p. illus. 22 cm. Translation of Kurs istorii Rossii XIX vieka. 'Reproduced from the revised one-volume edition of 1943.' 1. Russia — History — 19th century. I. T.
DK189.K7 1970   947/.07   *LC* 74-102513

Seton-Watson, Hugh.   **3.3110**
The Russian empire, 1801–1917. Oxford, Clarendon P., 1967. xx, 813 p. maps. 22 1/2 cm. (Oxford history of modern Europe.) 1. Soviet Union — History — 19th century 2. Soviet Union — History — Nicholas II, 1894-1917 I. T. II. Series.
DK189.S44   947/.08   *LC* 67-93682

Ulam, Adam Bruno, 1922-.   **3.3111**
Russia's failed revolutions: from the Decembrists to the dissidents / Adam B. Ulam. — New York: Basic Books, c1981. vii, 453 p.; 24 cm. 1. Revolutions — Soviet Union. 2. Dissenters — Soviet Union. 3. Soviet Union — Politics and government — 19th century 4. Soviet Union — Politics and government — 20th century I. T.
DK189.U43   947.08 19   *LC* 80-50534   *ISBN* 046507152X

Venturi, Franco.   • **3.3112**
Roots of revolution; a history of the populist and socialist movements in nineteenth century Russia. Translated from the Italian by Francis Haskell. With an introd. by Isaiah Berlin. — New York, Knopf, 1960. 850 p. 25 cm. Translation of Il populismo russo. 1. Populism in Russia (Narodnichestvo) I. T.
DK189.V413   947.08   *LC* 59-5423

Yarmolinsky, Avrahm, 1890-.   • **3.3113**
Road to revolution: a century of Russian radicalism. — London: Cassell [1957] 369 p.: ill.; 22 cm. 1. Russia — Pol. & govt. — 19th cent. I. T.
DK189.Y3   947.07   *LC* 59-11042

Berdiaev, Nikolaĭ, 1874-1948.   **3.3114**
[Russkaia ideia. English] The Russian idea / Nicolas Berdyaev. — Westport, Conn.: Greenwood Press, 1979. 255 p.; 23 cm. Translation of Russkaia ideia. Reprint of the 1948 ed. published by McMillan Co., New York. 1. Russia — Intellectual life — 1801-1917. I. T.
DK189.2.B4613 1979   947/.07   *LC* 78-32021   *ISBN* 0313209685

Palmer, Alan Warwick.   **3.3115**
Alexander I: Tsar of war and peace [by] Alan Palmer. [1st U.S. ed.] New York, Harper & Row [1974] xviii, 487 p. illus. 24 cm. 1. Alexander I, Emperor of Russia, 1777-1825. 2. Soviet Union — History — Alexander I, 1801-1825 I. T.
DK191.P348   947/.07/0924 B   *LC* 74-1844   *ISBN* 0060132647

Strakhovsky, Leonid Ivan, 1898-1963.   • **3.3116**
Alexander I of Russia; the man who defeated Napoleon. — Westport, Conn.: Greenwood Press, [1970, c1947] 302 p.: illus., ports.; 23 cm. 1. Alexander I, Emperor of Russia, 1777-1825. I. T.
DK191.S75 1970   947/.07/0924 B   *LC* 77-100245   *ISBN* 083714034X

Grimsted, Patricia Kennedy.   • **3.3117**
The foreign ministers of Alexander I; political attitudes and the conduct of Russian diplomacy, 1801–1825. Berkeley, University of California Press, 1969. xxvi, 367 p. ports. 24 cm. (Russian and East European studies.) 1. Alexander I, Emperor of Russia, 1777-1825. 2. Statesmen — Soviet Union. 3. Soviet Union — Foreign relations — 1801-1825 I. T. II. Series.
DK197.G7 1969   327.47   *LC* 69-11615   *ISBN* 0520013875

Herzen, Aleksandr, 1812-1870.   • **3.3118**
My past and thoughts: the memoirs of Alexander Herzen / translated from the Russian by Constance Garnett. — London, Chatto & Windus, 1924-27. 6 v.; 16 cm. I. Garnett, Constance Black, 1862-1946. tr. II. T.
DK209.6.H4 A33   *LC* 24-17707

Herzen, Aleksandr, 1812-1870.   **3.3119**
[Byloe i dumy. English. Selections] My past and thoughts: the memoirs of Alexander Herzen. Translated by Constance Garnett; rev. by Humphrey Higgens. Introd. by Isaiah Berlin. Abridged, with a pref. and notes by Dwight Macdonald. [1st ed.] New York, Knopf; [distributed by Random House] 1973. xlix, 684, xi p. 22 cm. Translation of Byloe i dumy. 1. Herzen, Aleksandr, 1812-1870 — Biography. I. Macdonald, Dwight. II. T.
DK209.6.H4 A353   947/.07/0924 B   *LC* 72-11034   *ISBN* 0394483081

Lincoln, W. Bruce.   **3.3120**
Nicholas I, emperor and autocrat of all the Russias / W. Bruce Lincoln. — Bloomington: Indiana University Press, c1978. 424 p.; 24 cm. Includes index. 1. Nicholas I, Emperor of Russia, 1796-1855. 2. Russia — Kings and rulers — Biography. 3. Russia — History — Nicholas I, 1825-1855. I. T.
DK210.L56   947/.073/0924 B 19   *LC* 77-15764   *ISBN* 0253340594

Presniakov, A. E. (Aleksandr Evgen'evich), 1870-1929.   **3.3121**
[Apogeĭ samoderzhaviia—Nikolaĭ I. English] Emperor Nicholas I of Russia, the apogee of autocracy, 1825–1855 [by] A. E. Presniakov. Edited and translated by Judith C. Zacek. With Nicholas I and the course of Russian history, by Nicholas V. Riasanovsky. — [Gulf Breeze, Fla.]: Academic International Press, 1974. xl, 102 p.: illus.; 23 cm. — (The Russian series, v. 23) Translation of Apogeĭ samoderzhaviia—Nikolaĭ I. 1. Nicholas I, Emperor of Russia, 1796-1855. 2. Russia — History — Nicholas I, 1825-1855. I. Riasanovsky, Nicholas Valentine, 1923- Nicholas I and the course of Russian history. 1974. II. T.
DK210.P713   DK210 P713.   320.9/47/07   *LC* 74-176053   *ISBN* 087569053X

Riasanovsky, Nicholas Valentine, 1923-.   • **3.3122**
Nicholas I and official nationality in Russia, 1825–1855. Berkeley, University of California Press, 1959. viii, 296 p. 24 cm. (Russian and East European studies.) 1. Nicholas I, Emperor of Russia, 1796-1855. 2. Nationalism — Soviet Union I. T. II. Series.
DK210.R5   947.07   *LC* 59-11316

Mazour, Anatole Gregory, 1900-.   • **3.3123**
The first Russian revolution, 1825; the Decembrist movement, its origins, development, and significance. — Stanford, Calif., Stanford University Press [1961, c1937] 328 p. illus. 23 cm. 1. Russia — Hist. — Conspiracy of December, 1825. I. T.
DK212.M3 1961   947.07   *LC* 61-11048

Rich, Norman.   **3.3124**
Why the Crimean War?: a cautionary tale / Norman Rich. — Hanover [N.H.]: Published for Brown University by University Press of New England, 1985. xix, 258 p.: maps; 23 cm. Includes index. 1. Crimean War, 1853-1856 — Diplomatic history 2. Crimean War, 1853-1856 — Causes I. T.
DK215.R53 1985   947/.073 19   *LC* 84-40593   *ISBN* 0874513286

Schroeder, Paul W.   **3.3125**
Austria, Great Britain, and the Crimean War; the destruction of the European concert [by] Paul W. Schroeder. — Ithaca [N.Y.]: Cornell University Press, [1972] xx, 544 p.; 24 cm. 1. Crimean War, 1853-1856 — Diplomatic history 2. Europe — Politics and government — 1848-1871 I. T.
DK215.S35   947/.07   *LC* 72-3451   *ISBN* 0801407427

Pomper, Philip.   **3.3126**
Sergei Nechaev / Philip Pomper. — New Brunswick, N.J.: Rutgers University Press, c1979. x, 273 p., [1] leaf of plates: port.; 24 cm. Includes index.

1. Nechaev, Sergeĭ Gennadievich, 1847-1882. 2. Revolutionists — Russia — Biography. 3. Anarchism and anarchists — Russia — Biography. I. T. DK219.6.N4 P65   322.4/2/0924 B   *LC* 79-9983   *ISBN* 0813508673

Mosse, Werner Eugen.   • 3.3127
Alexander II and the modernization of Russia. New,rev.ed. New York: Collier Books, 1962. 159 p.; 18 cm. (Men and history, AS443V) 1. Alexander II,Emperor of Russia,1818-1881. I. T. II. Series.
DK220.M6 1962   923.147   *LC* 62-19202

Ulam, Adam Bruno, 1922-.   3.3128
In the name of the people: prophets and conspirators in prerevolutionary Russia / Adam B. Ulam. New York: Viking Press, 1977. xii, 418 p., [8] leaves of plates: ill.; 24 cm. 1. Revolutionists — Russia — Biography. 2. Russia — Politics and government — 1855-1881. 3. Russia — Intellectual life — 1801-1917. I. T.
DK221.U38 1977   947.08   *LC* 76-42221   *ISBN* 0670396915

Wortman, Richard.   • 3.3129
The crisis of Russian populism. London, Cambridge U.P., 1967. xii, 211 p. front. (ports.). 22 1/2 cm. 1. Populism — Soviet Union I. T.
DK221.W66   320.9/47   *LC* 67-12849

Zaĭonchkovskiĭ, Petr Andreevich.   3.3130
[Krizis samoderzhaviia na rubezhe 1870-1880-kh godov. English] The Russian autocracy in crisis, 1878–1882 / Peter A. Zaionchkovsky; edited, translated, and with a new introd. by Gary M. Hamburg. — Gulf Breeze, FL: Academic International Press, 1979. xiii, 375 p.; 23 cm. — (The Russian series; v. 33) 1. Russia — Politics and government — 1855-1881. I. Hamburg, Gary M. II. T.
DK221.Z313   320.9/47/08   *LC* 79-110846   *ISBN* 0875690319

Seton-Watson, Hugh.   • 3.3131
The decline of imperial Russia, 1855–1914. With 8 maps. New York, F. A. Praeger [1952] 406 p. illus. 22 cm. (Books that matter) 1. Soviet Union — History — 19th century 2. Soviet Union — History — 1904-1914 I. T.
DK223.S4   947.08   *LC* 52-7488

Byrnes, Robert Francis.   • 3.3132
Pobedonostsev, his life and thought [by] Robert F. Byrnes. — Bloomington: Indiana University Press, [1968] xiii, 495 p.: ports.; 25 cm. — (Indiana University international studies) 1. Pobedonostsev, Konstantine Petrovich, 1827-1907. I. T.
DK236.P6 B8   947.08/0924 B   *LC* 68-14598

Lincoln, W. Bruce.   3.3133
In war's dark shadow: the Russians before the Great War / W. Bruce Lincoln. — New York: Dial Press, c1983. xvi, 557 p., [16] p. of plates: ill., ports.; 25 cm. Includes index. 1. Soviet Union — History — Alexander III, 1881-1894 2. Soviet Union — History — Nicholas II, 1894-1917 3. Soviet Union — History — Revolution, 1917-1921 — Causes. I. T.
DK240.L56 1983   947.08 19   *LC* 82-22152   *ISBN* 0385274092

Rogger, Hans.   3.3134
Russia in the age of modernisation and revolution, 1881–1917 / Hans Rogger. — London; New York: Longman, 1983. viii, 323 p.: maps; 24 cm. — (Longman history of Russia.) Includes index. 1. Soviet Union — History — Alexander III, 1881-1894 2. Soviet Union — History — Nicholas II, 1894-1917 3. Soviet Union — History — Revolution, 1917-1921 — Causes. I. T. II. Series.
DK241.R63 1983   947.08/2 19   *LC* 83-714   *ISBN* 0582489113

DK246–276 20th Century

Kort, Michael.   3.3135
The Soviet colossus: a history of the USSR / Michael Kort. — New York: Scribner, c1985. xiii, 318 p.: ill.; 24 cm. Includes index. 1. Soviet Union — History — 20th century I. T.
DK246.K64 1985   947/.08 19   *LC* 84-20253   *ISBN* 0684181789

Pares, Bernard, Sir, 1867-1949.   • 3.3136
My Russian memoirs. [1st AMS ed.] New York, AMS Press [1969] 623 p. ports. 23 cm. Reprint of the 1931 ed. 1. World War, 1914-1918 — Soviet Union. 2. Soviet Union — History — Nicholas II, 1894-1917 3. Soviet Union — History — Revolution, 1917-1921 I. T.
DK246.P3 1969   947.08   *LC* 78-96471

Revolution and politics in Russia; essays in memory of B. I.   3.3137
Nicolaevsky. Edited by Alexander and Janet Rabinowitch, with Ladis K. D. Kristof.
Bloomington, Indiana University Press [1973, c1972] xii, 416 p. illus. 26 cm. (Russian and East European series, v. 41) 1. Nicolaevsky, Boris I., 1887-1966. 2. Russia — History — 19th century — Addresses, essays, lectures. 3. Russia — History — 20th century — Addresses, essays, lectures. I. Nicolaevsky, Boris

I., 1887-1966. II. Rabinowitch, Alexander. ed. III. Rabinowitch, Janet, ed. IV. Kristof, Ladis K. D., ed.
DK246.R47   947.08   *LC* 79-183608   *ISBN* 0253390419

Treadgold, Donald W., 1922-.   3.3138
Twentieth century Russia / Donald W. Treadgold. — 5th ed. — Boston: Houghton Mifflin, c1981. xiii, 555 p.: maps; 23 cm. Includes index. 1. Soviet Union — History — 20th century I. T.
DK246.T65 1981   947.08 19   *LC* 80-50983   *ISBN* 0395307589

Ulam, Adam Bruno, 1922-.   • 3.3139
The Bolsheviks; the intellectual and political history of the triumph of communism in Russia [by] Adam B. Ulam. New York, Macmillan [1965] ix, 598 p. ports. 24 cm. 1. Lenin, Vladimir Il'ich, 1870-1924. 2. Communism — Soviet Union — History. I. T.
DK246.U4   335.430947   *LC* 65-18463

Von Laue, Theodore H. (Theodore Hermann)   3.3140
Why Lenin? Why Stalin? A reappraisal of the Russian Revolution, 1900–1930 [by] Theodore H. Von Laue. 2d ed. Philadelphia, Lippincott [c1971] ix, 227 p. 21 cm. (Critical periods of history) 1. Russia — History — 20th century. I. T.
DK246.V58 1971   947.084   *LC* 79-152063

DK251–264 Nicholas II, 1894–1917

Golder, Frank Alfred, 1877-1929. ed.   • 3.3141
Documents of Russian history, 1914–1917, by Frank Alfred Golder, translated by Emanuel Aronsberg. New York, London, The Century co. [c1927] xvi, 663 p. 23 cm. (The Century historical series) 'The material for this book is taken from various places, but largely from two newspapers, the 'Reich' and the 'Izvestiia'.'—Pref. 1. World War, 1914-1918 — Russia. 2. Soviet Union — History — Revolution, 1917-1921 — Sources. 3. Soviet Union — Politics and government — 1917-1936 I. T.
DK251.G6   *LC* 28-1054

DK253–254 Biography. Memoirs

McNeal, Robert Hatch, 1930-.   3.3142
Bride of the revolution; Krupskaya and Lenin, by Robert H. McNeal. Ann Arbor, University of Michigan Press [1972] 326 p. illus. 24 cm. 1. Krupskaya, Nadezhda Konstantinovna, 1869-1939. 2. Lenin, Vladimir Il'ich, 1870-1924. 3. Communism — Russia. I. T.
DK254.K77 M3 1972   947.084/1/0924 B   *LC* 75-185155   *ISBN* 0472616005

Lenin, Vladimir Il'ich, 1870-1924.   • 3.3143
[Selections. English] The essentials of Lenin. London: Lawrence & Wishart, 1947. 2 v.: ill.; 23 cm. Vol. 2 has added half t.p.: V. I. Lenin. Selected works in two volumes. 1. Socialism — Collected works. 2. Soviet Union — Politics and government — 1917-1936 — Collected works. I. T.
DK254.L3 A254   335.43/092/4   *LC* 73-847   *ISBN* 0883550431

Lenin, Vladimir Il'ich, 1870-1924.   • 3.3144
[Selections. English. 1971] Selected works [of] V. I. Lenin; one–volume edition. [1st ed.] New York, International Publishers [1971] 798 p. 22 cm. (New World paperbacks, NW-133) Reprint of the 1968 ed. I. T.
DK254.L3 A254 1971   335.4/08   *LC* 75-175177   *ISBN* 0717803007

Lenin, Vladimir Il'ich, 1870-1924.   • 3.3145
Collected works of V.I. Lenin. Completely revised, edited and annotated. The only edition authorized by the V.I. Lenin institute, Moscow. [New York, International publishers, c1927-. v.; 23 cm. 'This is the only authorized English translation of Lenin's writings from 1893 to 1924.'—Editor's note, v. 13. I. Institut Lenina. II. T.
DK254.L3 A5   *LC* 28-6510

Fischer, Louis, 1896-1970.   • 3.3146
The life of Lenin. — [1st ed.]. — New York: Harper & Row, [1964] viii, 703 p.: ports.; 24 cm. 1. Lenin, Vladimir Il'ich, 1870-1924. I. T.
DK254.L4 F53   923.247   *LC* 64-14385

Shub, David, 1887-.   3.3147
Lenin, a biography. [1st ed.] Garden City, N.Y., Doubleday, 1948. viii, 438 p. ports. (on lining-papers) 22 cm. 1. Lenin, Vladimir Il'ich, 1870-1924. I. T.
DK254.L4 S48   *LC* 48-6641

Stalin, Joseph, 1879-1953.   • 3.3148
Leninism; selected writings by Joseph Stalin. — New York, International publishers [1942] 479 p. 22 cm. Reissue, with some omissions, of the author's Problems of Leninism, published in Moscow, 1940, as a translation of the 11th Russian edition. 1. Lenin, Vladimir Il'ich, 1870-1924. 2. Russia — Pol. & govt.

— 1917- 3. Communism — Russia. 4. Vsesoiuznaia kommunisticheskaia partiia (bol'shevikov) 5. Proletariat I. T.
DK254.L4S75 1942   947.084   LC 42-24314

Trotsky, Leon, 1879-1940.   • 3.3149
[Lenine. English] Lenin; notes for a biographer [by] Leon Trotsky. With an introd. by Bertram D. Wolfe. Translated from the Russian and annotated by Tamara Deutscher. New York, G. P. Putnam's Sons [c1971] 224 p. 22 cm. Translation of O Lenine (romanized form) 1. Lenin, Vladimir Il'ich, 1870-1924. I. T.
DK254.L4 T7 1971   947.084/1/0924   LC 75-136807

Warth, Robert D.   3.3150
Lenin, by Robert D. Warth. New York, Twayne Publishers [c1973] 198 p. 21 cm. (Twayne's rulers and statesmen of the world series, TROW 21) 1. Lenin, Vladimir Il'ich, 1870-1924. I. T.
DK254.L4 W27   947.08/0924 B   LC 73-1760   ISBN 0805730559

Wolfe, Bertram David, 1896-1977.   • 3.3151
Three who made a revolution; a biographical history. [4th rev. ed.] New York, Dial Press, 1964. viii, 659 p. ports. 22 cm. 1. Lenin, Vladimir Il'ich, 1870-1924. 2. Trotsky, Leon, 1879-1940. 3. Stalin, Joseph, 1879-1953. I. T.
DK254.L4 W6 1964   947.08   LC 64-3227

Tumarkin, Nina.   3.3152
Lenin lives!: the Lenin cult in Soviet Russia / Nina Tumarkin. — Cambridge, Mass.: Harvard University Press, 1983. xiii, 315 p. [of plates: ill.; 24 cm. Includes index. 1. Lenin, Vladimir Il'ich, 1870-1924 — Influence. 2. Statesmen — Soviet Union — Biography. 3. Soviet Union — History — 1917- I. T.
DK254.L46 T85 1983   947.084/1/0924 B 19   LC 82-15665   ISBN 0674524306

Pipes, Richard.   • 3.3153
Struve, liberal on the left. — Cambridge, Mass.: Harvard University Press, 1970-. v.   : ports.; 24 cm. — (Russian Research Center studies, 64) 1. Struve, Petr Berngardovich, 1870-1944. I. T.
DK254.S597 P5   947.08 B   LC 77-131463   ISBN 0674845951

Trotsky, Leon, 1879-1940.   • 3.3154
[Selected works. English. 1963] Basic writings. Edited and introduced by Irving Howe. New York, Random House [c1963] 427 p. 22 cm. 1. Communism 2. Soviet Union — Politics and government — 1917- I. Howe, Irving. ed. II. T.
DK254.T6 A25 1963   LC 63-16157

Deutscher, Isaac, 1907-1967.   • 3.3155
The prophet armed: Trotsky, 1879–1921. — New York: Oxford University Press, 1954. viii, 540 p.: fold. map.; 23 cm. The 1st vol. of the author's trilogy, the 2d of which is The prophet unarmed: Trotsky, 1921-1929, the 3d of which is The prophet outcast: Trotsky, 1929-1940. 1. Trotsky, Leon, 1879-1940. I. T.
DK254.T6 D4   947.083*   LC 54-5291

Deutscher, Isaac, 1907-1967.   • 3.3156
The prophet outcast: Trotsky, 1929–1940. — London; New York: Oxford University Press, 1963. xv, 543 p.: illus., ports., facsim.; 23 cm. The 3d vol. of the author's trilogy, the 1st of which is The prophet armed: Trotsky, 1879-1921, the 2d of which is The prophet unarmed: Trotsky, 1921-1929. 1. Trotsky, Leon, 1879-1940. I. T.
DK254.T6 D415   923.247   LC 63-24133

Deutscher, Isaac, 1907-1967.   • 3.3157
The prophet unarmed: Trotsky, 1921–1929. — London; New York: Oxford University Press, 1959. 490 p.: illus.; 23 cm. The 2d vol. of the author's trilogy, the 1st of which is The prophet armed: Trotsky, 1879-1921, the 3d of which is The prophet outcast: Trotsky, 1929-1940. 1. Trotsky, Leon, 1879-1940. I. T.
DK254.T6 D42   923.247   LC 59-3695

Witte, Sergeĭ IUl'evich, graf., 1849-1915.   • 3.3158
The memoirs of Count Witte. Translated from the original Russian manuscript and edited by Abraham Yarmolinsky. — New York, H. Fertig, 1967 [1921] xi, 445 p. port. 24 cm. Selections translated from Vospominaniia (romanized form) 1. Soviet Union — Politics and government — 1894-1917 I. Yarmolinsky, Avrahm, 1890- ed. and tr. II. T.
DK254.W5A5 1967   947.08/0924 (B)   LC 67-24601

Mehlinger, Howard D.   • 3.3159
Count Witte and the Tsarist government in the 1905 revolution [by] Howard D. Mehlinger and John M. Thompson. — Bloomington: Indiana University Press, [1972] xiv, 434 p.; 25 cm. — (Indiana University international studies) 1. Witte, Sergeĭ IUl'evich, graf, 1849-1915. 2. Russia — Politics and government — 1904-1914. 3. Russia — History — Revolution of 1905. I. Thompson, John M. joint author. II. T.
DK254.W5 M44 1972   947.08/092/4 B   LC 77-165048   ISBN .0253314704

DK258–260 Nicholas II: Life and Reign

Massie, Robert K., 1929-.   3.3160
Nicholas and Alexandra [by] Robert K. Massie. [1st ed.] New York, Atheneum, 1967. xvii, 584 p. illus., geneal. tables. maps (on lining papers), ports. 25 cm. 1. Nicholas II, Emperor of Russia, 1868-1918. 2. Alexandra, Empress, consort of Nicholas II, Emperor of Russia, 1872-1918. 3. Soviet Union — Politics and government — 1894-1917 I. T.
DK258.M3   947.08/0924 B   LC 67-24627

Gurko, Vladimir Iosifovich, 1863-1927.   • 3.3161
Features and figures of the past; government and opinion in the reign of Nicholas II, by V. I. Gurko. Edited by J. E. Wallace Sterling, Xenia Joukoff Eudin [and] H. H. Fisher. Translated by Laura Matveev. New York, Russell & Russell [1970, c1967] xix, 760 p. port. 23 cm. (The Hoover Library on War, Revolution, and Peace. Publication no. 14) 1. Agriculture — Soviet Union. 2. Soviet Union — Politics and government — 1894-1917 I. T.
DK260.G82 1970   320.9/47   LC 70-102501

Pares, Bernard, Sir, 1867-1949.   • 3.3162
The fall of the Russian monarchy; a study of evidence, by Bernard Pares. London, J. Cape [1939] 510 p. pl., ports., VI plans (part fold.) 23 cm. Erratum slip inserted. 'First published 1939.' 1. Rasputin, Grigori Efimovich, ca. 1870-1916. 2. World War, 1914-1918 — Soviet Union. 3. Soviet Union — History — Nicholas II, 1894-1917 4. Soviet Union — Politics and government — 1894-1917 5. Soviet Union — History — Revolution, 1917-1921 — Causes. I. T.
DK260.P3 1939   947.08   LC 39-19181

DK262–264 General Works. Revolution of 1905

Lieven, D. C. B.   3.3163
Russia and the origins of the First World War / D.C.B. Lieven. — New York: St. Martin's Press, 1983. 213 p.; 23 cm. — (Making of the 20th century.) Includes index. 1. World War, 1914-1918 — Causes. 2. Soviet Union — History — 1904-1914 I. T. II. Series.
DK262.L48 1983   947/.08/3 19   LC 82-24095   ISBN 0312696086

Lincoln, W. Bruce.   3.3164
Passage through Armageddon: the Russians in war and revolution, 1914–1918 / W. Bruce Lincoln. — New York: Simon and Schuster, c1986. 637 p., [16] p. of plates: ill., maps; 24 cm. Includes index. 1. World War, 1914-1918 — Soviet Union. 2. Soviet Union — History — Nicholas II, 1894-1917 3. Soviet Union — History — Revolution, 1917-1921 — Causes. 4. Soviet Union — History — Revolution, 1917-1921 I. T.
DK262.L53 1986   947.08/3 19   LC 86-3696   ISBN 0671557092

Maynard, John, Sir, 1865-1943.   • 3.3165
Russia in flux. Ed. and abridged by S. Haden Guest, from 'Russia in flux' and 'The Russian peasant and other studies.' With a foreword by Sir Bernard Pares. — New York, Macmillan Co., 1948. xviii, 564 p. 22 cm. 1. Russia — Hist. 2. Peasantry — Russia. I. Maynard, John, Sir, 1865-1943. The Russian peasant and other studies. II. Guest, Stephen Haden 1902- III. T.
DK262.M37   947.08   LC 48-5810 *

Miliukov, P. N. (Pavel Nikolaevich), 1859-1943.   • 3.3166
Russia and its crisis. With a new foreword by Donald W. Treadgold. — New York, Collier Books [1962] 416 p. 18 cm. — (Collier books, BS88) 'Based on ... lectures [given] in America in 1903 and 1904.' 1. Russia. 2. Russia — Pol. & govt. I. T.
DK262.M66 1962   947   LC 62-16982

Ol'denburg, S. S. (Sergeĭ Sergeevich)   3.3167
[TSarstvovanie Imperatora Nikolaia II. English] Last tsar: Nicholas II, his reign & his Russia / S. S. Oldenburg; translated by Leonid I. Mihalap and Patrick J. Rollins; edited by Patrick J. Rollins; with Searching for the last tsar by Patrick J. Rollins. — Gulf Breeze, Fla.: Academic International Press, 1975-1978. 4 v.: ill.; 23 cm. (The Russian series; v. 25) Translation of TSarstvovanie Imperatora Nikolaia II. 1. Nicholas II, Emperor of Russia, 1868-1918. 2. Russia — History — Nicholas II, 1894-1917. I. T.
DK262.O413   947.08/092/4 B   LC 76-351188   ISBN 0875690637

Pares, Bernard, Sir, 1867-1949.   • 3.3168
Russia: between reform and Revolution. Edited and with an introd. by Francis B. Randall. — New York, Schocken Books [1962] 425 p. 21 cm. — (Schocken paperbacks, SB34) First published in 1907 under title: Russia and reform. 1. Russia — Pol. & govt. 2. Russia — Social condit. I. T.
DK262.P26 1962   947   LC 62-19395

Robinson, Geroid Tanquary, 1892-.   • 3.3169
Rural Russia under the old régime: a history of the landlord–peasant world and a prologue to the peasant revolution of 1917 / Geroid Tanquary Robinson. — New York: Macmillan, 1949[c1932] xi, 342 p.: maps.; 22 cm. 1. Land tenure —

Russia. 2. Peasantry — Russia. 3. Serfdom — Russia. 4. Soviet Union — Social conditions 5. Soviet Union — History — Revolution of 1905 I. T.
DK263.R6 1949   *LC* 49-5682

Treadgold, Donald W., 1922-.   • **3.3170**
Lenin and his rivals; the struggle for Russia's future, 1898–1906 [by] Donald W. Treadgold. New York, Praeger, 1955. 291 p. 24 cm. (Praeger publications in Russian history and world communism, no. 33) 1. Lenin, Vladimir Il'ich, 1870-1924. 2. Soviet Union — Politics and government — 1894-1917 I. T.
DK263.T74   947.08   *LC* 54-13231

Trotsky, Leon, 1879-1940.   **3.3171**
[Tysiacha deviat'sot piatyĭ. English] 1905 / [by] Leon Trotsky; translated by Anya Bostock. — [1st ed.] New York: Random House, 1972 (c1971) xxi, 488 p. 25 cm. Translation of Tysiacha deviat'sot piatyĭ. 1. Soviet Union — History — Revolution of 1905 I. T.
DK263.T83   947/.08   *LC* 70-159382   *ISBN* 0394471776

Smith, Clarence Jay.   • **3.3172**
The Russian struggle for power, 1914–1917; a study of Russian foreign policy during the First World War, by C. Jay Smith, Jr. New York, Greenwood Press [1969, c1956] xv, 553 p. 23 cm. 1. World War, 1914-1918 — Soviet Union. 2. Soviet Union — Foreign relations — 1894-1917 I. T.
DK264.8.S5 1969   327.47   *LC* 75-90709   *ISBN* 0837122821

DK265 Revolution (1917–1921)

Conference on the Russian Revolution, Harvard University, 1967.   • **3.3173**
Revolutionary Russia [by] Oskar Anweiler [and others] Edited by Richard Pipes. Cambridge, Mass., Harvard University Press, 1968. x, 365 p. 25 cm. (Russian Research Center studies, 55) Cosponsored by the Joint Committee for Slavic Studies of the American Council of Learned Societies and the Russian Research Center of Harvard University. 1. Soviet Union — History — Revolution, 1917-1921 2. Soviet Union — History — Congresses. I. Anweiler, Oskar. II. Pipes, Richard. ed. III. Harvard University. Russian Research Center. IV. Joint Committee on Slavic Studies. V. T.
DK265.A135 1967aa   947.084/1   *LC* 68-15641

The Russian Revolution and the Soviet State, 1917–1921: documents / selected and edited by Martin McCauley.   **3.3174**
New York: Barnes & Noble, 1975. xiv, 315 p.: maps; 23 cm. 1. Russia — History — Revolution, 1917-1921 — Sources. I. McCauley, Martin.
DK265.A538 1975   947.084/1   *LC* 75-322340   *ISBN* 0064946789

Bunyan, James, 1898- comp.   • **3.3175**
The Bolshevik revolution, 1917–1918; documents and materials, by James Bunyan and H. H. Fisher. — Stanford University, Calif.: Stanford University Press, 1934. xii, 735 p. 23 cm. — (Hoover war library publications. no. 3) 'This volume follows chronologically the Documents of Russian history, 1914-1917, published by the late Professor Frank A. Golder ... A considerable number of the documents of the present volume were selected and translated by Mr. Golder.'—Pref. 1. Russia — Hist. — Revolution, 1917- — Sources. 2. Russia — Pol. & govt. — 1917- 3. World War, 1914-1918 — Documents, etc., sources. I. Fisher, Harold Henry, 1890- joint comp. II. Golder, Frank Alfred, 1877-1929. III. T.
DK265.B93   947.084   *LC* 34-35285

Bunyan, James, 1898-.   • **3.3176**
Intervention, civil war, and communism in Russia, April–December 1918: documents and materials / by James Bunyan. Baltimore: The Johns Hopkins Press, 1936. xv, 594 p.: double map.; 24 cm. At head of title: The Walter Hines Page school of international relations, the Johns Hopkins university. 'Follows chronologically The Bolshevik revolution 1917-1918.'-Foreword. 1. Russia — History — Revolution, 1917-1921 — Sources. 2. Russia — Politics and government — 1917-1936. 3. Russia — Foreign relations — 1917-1945. I. Walter Hines Page School of International Relations. II. T.
DK265.B94   947.0841   *LC* 37-51

Chamberlin, William Henry, 1897-.   • **3.3177**
The Russian revolution, 1917–1921 / William Henry Chamberlin. — New York: Macmillan, 1935. 2 v.; 24 cm. — 1. Russia — History — Revolution, 1917-1921. I. T.
DK265.C43   *LC* 35-7577

Chernov, V. M. (Viktor Mikhaĭlovich), 1873-1952.   • **3.3178**
The great Russian revolution, by Victor Chernov. Translated and abridged by Philip E. Mosely. — New York, Russell & Russell, 1966 [c1936] viii, 466 p. illus., ports. 23 cm. Bibliographical references in 'Notes' (p. [448]-454) 1. Russia — Hist. — Revolution, 1917-1921. I. Mosely Philip Edward, 1905- ed. and tr. II. T.
DK265.C48 1966   947.0841   *LC* 66-13165

Daniels, Robert Vincent.   • **3.3179**
Red October; the Bolshevik Revolution of 1917 [by] Robert V. Daniels. New York, Scribner [1967] xiv, 269 p. illus., maps (on lining papers), ports. 24 cm. 1. Soviet Union — History — Revolution, 1917-1921 I. T.
DK265.D27   947.084/1   *LC* 67-24060

Debo, Richard K., 1938-.   **3.3180**
Revolution and survival: the foreign policy of Soviet Russia, 1917–18 / Richard K. Debo. — Toronto; Buffalo: University of Toronto Press. xiii, 462 p.; 24 cm. Includes index. 1. Russia — Foreign relations — 1917-1945. I. T.
DK265.D35   327.47   *LC* 78-9671   *ISBN* 0802054110

Ferro, Marc.   **3.3181**
[Octobre, naissance d'une société. English] October 1917: a social history of the Russian revolution / Marc Ferro; translated by Norman Stone. — London; Boston: Routledge & Kegan Paul, 1980. xiv, 345 p.; 24 cm. Translation of: Octobre, naissance d'une société, v. 2 of the author's La Révolution de 1917. Includes index. 1. Soviet Union — History — Revolution, 1917-1921 I. T.
DK265.F46413 1980   947.084/1 19   *LC* 79-41592   *ISBN* 0710005342

Fitzpatrick, Sheila.   **3.3182**
The Russian Revolution / Sheila Fitzpatrick. — Oxford [Oxfordshire]; New York: Oxford University Press, 1982. vi, 181 p.: 23 cm. — (OPUS) Includes index. 1. Soviet Union — History — Revolution, 1917-1921 I. T. II. Series.
DK265.F48 1982   947.084/1 19   *LC* 82-3611   *ISBN* 0192191624

Florinsky, Michael T., 1894-.   • **3.3183**
The end of the Russian Empire. New York, Collier Books [1961] 254 p. 18 cm. (Collier books, BS3) 1. World War, 1914-1918 — Soviet Union. 2. Soviet Union — History — Nicholas II, 1894-1917 3. Soviet Union — Social conditions — 1801-1917 4. Soviet Union — Economic conditions I. T.
DK265.F5 1961   947.08   *LC* 61-17492

Footman, David, 1895-.   • **3.3184**
Civil War in Russia. New York: Praeger, c1961, 1962 printing. 328 p.: ill.; 23 cm. (Praeger publications in Russian history and world communism; no.114) (Books that matter.) 1. Russia — History — Revolution,1917-1921. I. T. II. Series.
DK265.F578 1962   *LC* 62-17560

Kerensky, Aleksandr Fyodorovich, 1881-1970.   • **3.3185**
The catastrophe; Kerensky's own story of the Russian revolution, by Alexander F. Kerensky. — New York: Appleton, 1927. xi, 376 p.: front. (port.); 23 cm. 1. Russia — Hist. — Revolution, 1917-1921. I. T.
DK265.K393   *LC* 27-23536

Luxemburg, Rosa, 1871-1919.   • **3.3186**
[Russische Revolution. English] The Russian Revolution, and Leninism or Marxism? / new introd. by Bertram D. Wolfe. — [Ann Arbor]: University of Michigan Press, [1961] 109 p.; 21 cm. (Ann Arbor paperbacks, AA57) 1. Communism — Soviet Union 2. Soviet Union — History — Revolution, 1917-1921 I. T. II. Title: Leninism or Marxism?
DK265.L882 1961   947.0841   *LC* 61-44218

Medvedev, Roy Aleksandrovich, 1925-.   **3.3187**
The October Revolution / Roy A. Medvedev; translated by George Saunders; foreword by Harrison E. Salisbury. — New York: Columbia University Press, 1979. xix, 240 p., [6] leaves of plates: ill.; 24 cm. 1. Russia — History — Revolution, 1917-1921. I. T.
DK265.M375   947.084   *LC* 79-9854   *ISBN* 0231045905

Miliukov, P. N. (Pavel Nikolaevich), 1859-1943.   **3.3188**
[Istoriia vtoroĭ russkoĭ revoliutsii. English] The Russian Revolution / Paul N. Miliukov; edited by Richard Stites; translated by Tatyana & Richard Stites. — Gulf Breeze, FL: Academic International Press, 1978-< 1984 >. v. <1-2 >: ports.; 23 cm. — (The Russian series; v. 44/1-< 2 >) Translation of Istoriia vtoroĭ russkoĭ revoliutsii. 1. Russia — History — Revolution, 1917-1921. I. Stites, Richard. II. T.
DK265.M49313   947.084/1   *LC* 78-111088   *ISBN* 0875690270

Paléologue, Maurice, 1859-1944.   • **3.3189**
[Russie des tsars pendant la grande guerre. English] An ambassador's memoirs. Translated by F. A. Holt. New York, Octagon Books, 1972. 3 v. illus. 24 cm. Translation of La Russie des tsars pendant la grande guerre. 1. World War — 1914-1918 — Soviet Union. 2. Soviet Union — History — Nicholas II, 1894-1917 3. Soviet Union — Social conditions — 1801-1917 I. T.
DK265.P255 1972   320.9/47/08   *LC* 77-159219   *ISBN* 0374961859

Radkey, Oliver Henry.   • **3.3190**
The sickle under the hammer: the Russian Socialist Revolutionaries in the early months of Soviet rule / by Oliver Henry Radkey. — New York: Columbia University Press, 1963. xiii, 525 p. — (Studies of the Russian Institute,

Columbia University) 1. Partiia sotsialistov-revoliutsionerov. 2. Soviet Union — History — Revolution, 1917-1921 I. T.
DK265.R228   LC 62-18252

Reed, John, 1887-1920.   • **3.3191**
Ten days that shook the world / by John Reed: with a foreword by V. I. Lenin, a preface by N. K. Krupskaya, and a new introd. by John Howard Lawson. — [New ed.]. — New York: International Publishers, c1967. l, 395 p.: ill.; 21 cm. 'NW-79.' 1. Soviet Union — History — Revolution, 1917-1921 I. T.
DK265.R38 1967   947.084/1   LC 67-27252   *ISBN* 0717802000

Rosenberg, Arthur, 1889-1943.   • **3.3192**
A history of bolshevism from Marx to the first Five years' plan. Translated from the German by Ian F. D. Morrow. — New York, Russell & Russell, 1965. viii, 250 p. 23 cm. A reprint of the 1934 ed. Translation of Geschichte des Bolshewismus von Marx bis zur Gegenwart. Bibliography: p. [241]-246. 1. Communism — Hist. 2. Communism — Russia. I. T.
DK265.R69 1965   335.43   LC 65-17919

Schapiro, Leonard Bertram, 1908-.   **3.3193**
The Russian revolutions of 1917: the origins of modern Communism / Leonard Schapiro. — New York: Basic Books, c1984. xi, 239 p.: map; 24 cm. Includes index. 1. Soviet Union — History — Revolution, 1917-1921 I. T.
DK265.S354 1984   947.084/1 19   LC 83-45262   *ISBN* 0465071546

Stalin, Joseph, 1879-1953.   • **3.3194**
The October revolution: a collection of articles and speeches / by Joseph Stalin. — New York: International Publishers, c1934. 168 p.; 22 cm. (Marxist library: Works of Marxism-Leninism; v. 21) 1. Communism — Soviet Union 2. Soviet Union — History — Revolution, 1917-1921 I. T. II. Series.
DK265.S668

Sukhanov, N. N. (Nikolaĭ Nikolaevich), 1882-1940.   • **3.3195**
The Russian Revolution, 1917: a personal record / by N.N. Sukhanov; edited, abridged and translated by Joel Carmichael from Zapiski o revoliutsii. — London, New York: Oxford University Press, 1955. 691 p.: ill.; 23 cm. 1. Russia — History — Revolution, 1917-1921. I. Carmichael, Joel. II. T.
DK265.S8475   LC 55-14322

Thompson, John M.   **3.3196**
Revolutionary Russia, 1917 / John M. Thompson. — New York: Scribner, c1981. xvi, 206 p.: ill.; 22 cm. Includes index. 1. Soviet Union — History — Revolution, 1917-1921 I. T.
DK265.T54   947.084/1 19   LC 81-8783   *ISBN* 068417278X

Trotsky, Leon, 1879-1940.   • **3.3197**
The history of the Russian Revolution. Translated from the Russian by Max Eastman. — Ann Arbor, University of Michigan Press [1957, c1932] 3 v. in 1. 25 cm. 1. Russia — Hist. — Revolution, 1917-1921. I. T.
DK265.T773 1957   947.084   LC 57-13948

DK265.19–265.9 Special Topics

Katkov, George.   • **3.3198**
Russia, 1917; the February revolution. [1st U.S. ed.] New York, Harper & Row [1967] xxviii, 489 p. illus., facsim., maps, ports. 22 cm. 1. Soviet Union — History — February Revolution, 1917 I. T.
DK265.19.K3 1967   947.084/1   LC 66-20739

Kenez, Peter.   **3.3199**
Civil War in South Russia, 1919–1920: the defeat of the Whites / Peter Kenez. — Berkeley: Published for the Hoover Institution on War, Revolution, and Peace [by] University of California Press, c1977. xviii, 378 p., [2] leaves of plates: ill.; 24 cm. Includes index. 1. Soviet Union — History — Revolution, 1917-1921 2. Soviet Union, Southern — History I. T.
DK265.2.K453   947.084/1   LC 76-47998   *ISBN* 0520033469

Bradley, J. F. N. (John Francis Nejez), 1930-.   • **3.3200**
Allied intervention in Russia. New York, Basic Books [1968] xix, 251 p. maps. 22 cm. 1. Soviet Union — History — Allied intervention, 1918-1920 I. T.
DK265.4.B67 1968b   940.4/147   LC 68-19845

Unterberger, Betty Miller.   • **3.3201**
America's Siberian expedition, 1918–1920; a study of national policy. New York, Greenwood Press [1969, c1956] 271 p. maps. 24 cm. 1. Soviet Union — History — Allied intervention, 1918-1920 2. United States — Foreign relations — Soviet Union 3. Soviet Union — Foreign relations — United States I. T.
DK265.42.U5 U52 1969   947.084/1   LC 69-14128

Rabinowitch, Alexander.   **3.3202**
The Bolsheviks come to power: the revolution of 1917 in Petrograd / Alexander Rabinowitch. — 1st ed. — New York: W. W. Norton, c1976. xxxiii, 393 p.: ill.; 25 cm. Includes index. 1. Lenin, Vladimir Il'ich, 1870-1924. 2. Kommunisticheskaia partiia Sovetskogo Soiuza — History. 3. Leningrad

(R.S.F.S.R.) — History — Revolution, 1917-1921 4. Russia — History — Revolution, 1917-1921. I. T.
DK265.8.L4 R27 1976   947/.45/0841   LC 76-20756   *ISBN* 0393055868

Kettle, Michael.   **3.3203**
The Allies and the Russian collapse, March 1917–March 1918 / Michael Kettle. — Minneapolis: University of Minnesota Press, c1981. 287 p., [4] leaves of plates: ill.; 25 cm. — (Russia and the Allies, 1917-1920; v. 1) 1. Russia — History — Revolution, 1917-1921. 2. Russia — Foreign economic relations. 3. Russia — Foreign relations — 1917-1945. I. T. II. Series.
DK265.9.E2 K43   947.084/1   LC 80-275   *ISBN* 0816609810

DK266 Soviet Regime, 1918–1924

Cohen, Stephen F.   **3.3204**
Rethinking the Soviet experience: politics and history since 1917 / Stephen F. Cohen. — New York: Oxford University Press, 1985. xiii, 222 p.; 22 cm. 1. Soviet Union — Historiography. 2. Soviet Union — Study and teaching — History. I. T.
DK266.A33 C64 1985   947/.0072 19   LC 84-749   *ISBN* 0195034686

Bauer, Raymond Augustine, 1916-.   • **3.3205**
How the Soviet system works: cultural, psychological, and social themes [by] Raymond A. Bauer, Alex Inkeles, and Clyde Kluckhohn. Cambridge, Harvard University Press, 1956. xiv, 274 p. 22 cm. (Russian Research Center studies, 24) 'Final report [of the] ... Harvard Project on the Soviet Social System.' 'Reports and publications of the Harvard Project on the Soviet Social System': p. [252]-258. 'References': p. [259]-265. 1. Communism — Russia. 2. Russia — Economic policy. I. T.
DK266.B26   *947.085   LC 56-8549

Carr, Edward Hallett, 1892-.   **3.3206**
A history of Soviet Russia. — London: Macmillan, 1951 [c1950]-[78] 14 v.; 23 cm. 1. Soviet Union — History — 1917- — Collected works. I. T.
DK266.C26   947.084   LC 51-232   *ISBN* 0333242165

Geller, Mikhail, 1922-.   **3.3207**
[Utopiia u vlasti. English] Utopia in power: the history of the Soviet Union from 1917 to the present / by Mikhail Heller and Aleksandr Nekrich; translated from the Russian by Phyllis B. Carlos. — New York: Summit Books, c1986. 877 p.; 25 cm. Translation of: Utopiia u vlasti / Mikhail Geller, Aleksandr Nekrich. 1. Soviet Union — History — 1917- I. Nekrich, A. M. (Aleksandr Moiseevich) II. T.
DK266.G3713 1986   947.084 19   LC 86-5792   *ISBN* 0671462423

McCauley, Martin.   **3.3208**
The Soviet Union since 1917 / Martin McCauley. — London; New York: Longman, 1981. xiv, 290 p.: maps; 25 cm. — (Longman history of Russia.) 1. Soviet Union — History — 1917- I. T. II. Series.
DK266.M354   947.084 19   LC 80-41827   *ISBN* 0582489792

Pipes, Richard.   • **3.3209**
The formation of the Soviet Union; Communism and nationalism, 1917–1923. — Rev. ed. — Cambridge, Harvard University Press, 1964. xii, 365 p. illus., maps, ports. 25 cm. — (Russian Research Center studies, 13) Bibliography: p. [305]-328. 1. Russia — Hist. — 1917- I. T.
DK266.P53 1964   947.0841   LC 64-21284

Ulam, Adam Bruno, 1922-.   **3.3210**
Expansion and coexistence: Soviet foreign policy, 1917–73 / [by] Adam B. Ulam. — 2d ed. New York: Praeger [1974] viii, 797 p.; 24 cm. 1. Soviet Union — Foreign relations — 1917- I. T.
DK266.U49 1974   327.47   LC 73-8181

Cultural revolution in Russia, 1928–1931 / edited by Sheila Fitzpatrick.   **3.3211**
Bloomington: Indiana University Press, c1978. vi, 309 p.: ill.; 22 cm. (Studies of the Russian Institute, Columbia University) 'The conference at which these papers were originally presented was jointly sponsored by the Research and Development Committee of the American Association for the Advancement of Slavic Studies and the Russian Institute, Columbia University.' 1. Russia — Intellectual life — 1917- — Congresses. I. Fitzpatrick, Sheila. II. American Association for the Advancement of Slavic Studies. Research and Development Committee. III. Columbia University. Russian Institute.
DK266.4.C86 1978   306/.2/0947 19   LC 77-74439   *ISBN* 0253315913

Schapiro, Leonard Bertram, 1908-.   • **3.3212**
The origin of the communist autocracy: political opposition in the Soviet State, first phase, 1917–1922 / by Leonard Schapiro. — Cambridge, Mass.: Harvard University Press, [c1955] xvii, 397 p.; 22 cm. 1. Russia — Politics and

government — 1917-1936. 2. Russia — History — Revolution, 1917-1921. I. T.
DK266.5.S3　　*LC 55-8644*　　*ISBN* 0674644514

DK267–273 Stalin, 1925–1953

Brzezinski, Zbigniew K., 1928-.　　　　　　　　• **3.3213**
The permanent purge; politics in Soviet totalitarianism. — Cambridge, Harvard University Press, 1956. 256 p. 22 cm. — (Russian Research Center studies, 20) Bibliography: p. [191]-199. 1. Political purges. I. T.
DK267.B76　　947.084　　*LC 56-5342 rev*

Conquest, Robert.　　　　　　　　　　　**3.3214**
The great terror; Stalin's purge of the thirties. [1st American ed.] New York, Macmillan [1968] xiv, 633 p. illus., ports. 24 cm. 1. Stalin, Joseph, 1879-1953. 2. Kommunisticheskaia partiia Sovetskogo Soiuza — Purges 3. Terrorism — Soviet Union. 4. Soviet Union — Politics and government — 1936-1953 I. T.
DK267.C65 1968　　947.084/2　　*LC 68-17513*

Hochman, Jiří.　　　　　　　　　　　**3.3215**
The Soviet Union and the failure of collective security, 1934–1938 / Jiri Hochman. — Ithaca: Cornell University Press, 1984. 253 p.; 25 cm. (Cornell studies in security affairs.) Includes index. 1. Security, International 2. World politics — 1933-1945 3. Soviet Union — Foreign relations — 1917-1945 I. T. II. Series.
DK267.H596 1984　　327.47 19　　*LC 84-45149*　　*ISBN* 0801416558

Kohn, Hans, 1891-1971.　　　　　　　　　**3.3216**
Nationalism in the Soviet Union; [tr. by E.W. Dickes] London: Routledge, 1933. xi, 164 p.; 19 cm. 1. Nationalism 2. Soviet 3. Nationalism and nationality 4. Russia — Politics and government 5. Russia — Nationality I. Dickes, E. W. (Ernest Walter), b. 1876. tr. II. T.
DK267.K62

Leites, Nathan Constantin, 1912-.　　　　　• **3.3217**
A study of bolshevism. — Glencoe, Ill.: Free Press [1953] 639 p.; 25 cm. Bibliography: p. 630-634. 1. Communism — Russia. I. T.
DK267.L415　　335.4　　*LC 53-7396 rev*

Lewytzkyj, Borys. comp.　　　　　　　　　**3.3218**
The Stalinist terror in the thirties; documentation from the Soviet press. Compiled with pref. and introd. by Borys Levytsky. Stanford, Calif., Hoover Institution Press [c1974] xxvii, 521 p. ports. 24 cm. (Hoover Institution publications, 126) 1. Kommunisticheskaia partiia Sovetskogo Soiuza — Purges 2. Terrorism — Soviet Union. 3. Soviet Union — Politics and government — 1936-1953 4. Soviet Union — Biography. I. T.
DK267.L425　　947.084/2　　*LC 72-137404*　　*ISBN* 0817912614

Medvedev, Roy Aleksandrovich, 1925-.　　• **3.3219**
[K sudu istorii. English] Let history judge: the origins and consequences of Stalinism [by] Roy A. Medvedev. Translated by Colleen Taylor. Edited by David Joravsky and by Georges Haupt. [1st ed.] New York, Knopf, 1971. xxxiv, 566, xviii p. 25 cm. Translation of K sudu istorii. 1. Stalin, Joseph, 1879-1953. 2. Russia — Politics and government — 1917-1936. 3. Russia — Politics and government — 1936-1953. I. T.
DK267.M41413　　947.084/2　　*LC 70-31702*　　*ISBN* 0394446453

Medvedev, Roy Aleksandrovich, 1925-.　　　**3.3220**
On Stalin and Stalinism / Roy A. Medvedev; translated by Ellen de Kadt. — Oxford; New York: Oxford University Press, 1979. vi, 205 p.; 23 cm. 1. Stalin, Joseph, 1879-1953. 2. Russia — Politics and government — 1917-1936. 3. Russia — Politics and government — 1936-1953. I. T.
DK267.M416　　947.084　　*LC 79-40170*　　*ISBN* 0192158422

Rubinstein, Alvin Z.　　　　　　　　　　**3.3221**
Soviet foreign policy since World War II: imperial and global / Alvin Z. Rubinstein. — Cambridge, Mass.: Winthrop Publishers, c1981. viii, 295 p.: maps; 23 cm. 1. Russia — Foreign relations — 1945- I. T.
DK267.R76　　327.47 19　　*LC 80-23072*　　*ISBN* 0876268092

Werth, Alexander, 1901-.　　　　　　　　• **3.3222**
Russia; the post–war years. Epilogue by Harrison E. Salisbury. — New York: Taplinger Pub. Co., [1971] xvii, 446 p.; 23 cm. Continuation of the author's Russia at war, 1941-1945. 1. Russia — History — 1925-1953. I. T.
DK267.W414 1971　　914.7/03/842　　*LC 75-143223*　　*ISBN* 0800869303

DK268 Biography. Memoirs

McNeal, Robert Hatch, 1930-.　　　　　　　**3.3223**
The Bolshevik tradition: Lenin, Stalin, Khrushchev, Brezhnev / Robert H. McNeal. — 2d ed. — Englewood Cliffs, N.J.: Prentice-Hall, [1975] xi, 210 p.; 21 cm. (A Spectrum book) First ed. published in 1963 under title: The Bolshevik tradition: Lenin, Stalin, Khrushchev. Includes index. 1. Lenin,

Vladimir Il'ich, 1870-1924. 2. Stalin, Joseph, 1879-1953. 3. Khrushchev, Nikita Sergeevich, 1894-1971. 4. Brezhnev, Leonid Il'ich, 1906-5. Communism — Soviet Union 6. Soviet Union — Politics and government — 1917- I. T.
DK268.A1 M3 1975　　335.43/0947　　*LC 74-20922*　　*ISBN* 0130797723. *ISBN* 0130797642 pbk

Medvedev, Roy Aleksandrovich, 1925-.　　　**3.3224**
[Oni okruzhali Stalina. English] All Stalin's men / Roy Medvedev; translated by Harold Shukman. — Garden City, N.Y.: Anchor Press/Doubleday, 1984, c1983. x, 184 p., [16] p. of plates: ill.; 22 cm. 1. Stalin, Joseph, 1879-1953 — Friends and associates. 2. Statesmen — Soviet Union — Biography. 3. Soviet Union — History — 1917- I. T.
DK268.A1 M4413 1984　　947.084/2/0924 19　　*LC 83-15843*　　*ISBN* 0385183887

Cohen, Stephen F.　　　　　　　　　　　**3.3225**
Bukharin and the Bolshevik Revolution; a political biography, 1888–1938 [by] Stephen F. Cohen. [1st ed.] New York, A. A. Knopf; [distributed by Random House] 1973. xix, 495, xvii p. 25 cm. 1. Bukharin, Nikolaĭ Ivanovich, 1888-1938. 2. Soviet Union — Politics and government — 1917-1936 3. Soviet Union — Economic policy — 1917-1928 I. T.
DK268.B76 C63 1973　　947.084/092/4 B　　*LC 73-7288*　　*ISBN* 0394460146

Medvedev, Roy Aleksandrovich, 1925-.　　　**3.3226**
Nikolai Bukharin: the last years / Roy A. Medvedev; translated by A. D. P. Briggs. — 1st ed. — New York: Norton, c1980. 176 p.; 22 cm. 1. Bukharin, Nikolaĭ Ivanovich, 1888-1938. 2. Statesmen — Russia — Biography. 3. Revolutionists — Russia — Biography. I. T.
DK268.B76 M42 1980　　947.084/092/4 B　　*LC 80-14287*　　*ISBN* 039301357X

Ginzburg, Evgeniia Semenovna.　　　　　　**3.3227**
[Krutoĭ marshrut. Tom 2. English] Within the whirlwind / Eugenia Ginzburg; translated by Ian Boland; introduction by Heinrich Böll. — 1st ed. — New York: Harcourt Brace Jovanovich, c1981. xix, 423 p.; 25 cm. 'A Helen and Kurt Wolff book.' Translation of: Krutoĭ marshrut. 1. Ginzburg, Evgeniia Semenovna. 2. Political prisoners — Russia — Biography. 3. Russia — Social conditions — 1917- I. T.
DK268.G47 A3413 1981　　365.6/092/4 B 19　　*LC 80-8748*　　*ISBN* 0151975175

Grigorenko, P. G. (Petr Grigor'evich), 1907-.　　**3.3228**
Memoirs / Petro G. Grigorenko; translated by Thomas P. Whitney. — 1st ed. — New York: Norton, c1982. x, 462 p., [8] p. of plates: ill.; 24 cm. Includes index. 1. Grigorenko, P. G. (Petr Grigor'evich), 1907- 2. Soviet Union. Armiia — Biography. 3. Generals — Soviet Union — Biography. 4. Dissenters — Soviet Union — Biography. 5. Political prisoners — Soviet Union — Biography. I. T.
DK268.G75 A36 1982　　361.230924 B 19　　*LC 82-7852*　　*ISBN* 039301570X

Farnsworth, Beatrice.　　　　　　　　　　**3.3229**
Aleksandra Kollontai: socialism, feminism, and the Bolshevik Revolution / Beatrice Farnsworth. — Stanford, Calif.: Stanford University Press, 1980. xiv, 432 p., [12] pages of plates: ill.; 25 cm. Includes index. 1. Kollontay, Aleksandra Mikhaylvna, 1872-1952. 2. Revolutionists — Soviet Union — Biography. 3. Communists — Soviet Union — Biography. 4. Feminists — Soviet Union — Biography. I. T. II. Title: Feminism and the Bolshevik Revolution.
DK268.K56 F37　　947.084/1/0924 B 19　　*LC 79-67775*　　*ISBN* 0804710732

Stalin, Joseph, 1879-1953.　　　　　　　　• **3.3230**
Works / J. V. Stalin. — Moscow: Foreign Languages Pub. House, 1952-. v. Added t. p. in Russian. I. T.
DK268.S75 A2513 1952

Stalin, Joseph, 1879-1953.　　　　　　　　• **3.3231**
[Selected works. English] Selected writings. Westport, Conn., Greenwood Press [1970] 479 p. 23 cm. Includes addresses, articles, and reports on the Communist program in Russia. 'Reprinted from an edition published ... in 1942.' 1. Communism — Russia — Addresses, essays, lectures. 2. Russia — Politics and government — 1917- — Addresses, essays, lectures. I. T.
DK268.S75 A34 1970　　335.43　　*LC 78-109976*　　*ISBN* 0837144825

Stalin, Joseph, 1879-1953.　　　　　　　　**3.3232**
The essential Stalin; major theoretical writings, 1905-52. Edited and with an introd. by Bruce Franklin. Garden City, N.Y., Anchor Books, 1972. viii, 511 p. 18 cm. I. Franklin, H. Bruce (Howard Bruce), 1934- ed. II. T.
DK268.S75 A38 1972　　335.43　　*LC 72-79434*　　*ISBN* 0385091923

Deutscher, Isaac, 1907-1967.   • 3.3233
Stalin; a political biography. 2d ed. New York, Oxford University Press, 1967,
[c1966] xvi, 661 p. illus., ports. 22 cm. 1. Stalin, Joseph, 1879-1953. I. T.
DK268.S8 D48 1967   947.084/2/0924   *LC* 67-4373

Khrushchev, Nikita Sergeevich, 1894-1971.   • 3.3234
[Rech' na zakrytom zasedanii dvadtsatogo s'ezda KPSS. English] The anatomy
of terror: Khrushchev's revelations about Stalin's regime / introd. by Nathaniel
Weyl. — Washington: Public Affairs Press [1956] 73 p.; 24 cm. Translation of
Rech' na zakrytom zasedanii dvadtsatogo s'ezda KPSS. 1. Stalin, Joseph,
1879-1953 — Addresses, essays, lectures. 2. Soviet Union — Politics and
government — 1936-1953 — Addresses, essays, lectures. I. T.
DK268.S8 K453   947.084/2/0924   *LC* 78-23884   *ISBN*
031321218X

Trotsky, Leon, 1879-1940.   • 3.3235
Stalin: an appraisal of the man and his influence / by Leon Trotsky; edited and
translated from the Russian by Charles Malamuth. — New ed. London:
MacGibbon & Kee, 1968. xv, 516 p.: 16 plates, ill., ports.; 25 cm. 1. Stalin,
Joseph, 1879-1953. I. T.
DK268.S8 T7 1968   947.084/2/0924 B   *LC* 77-386055   *ISBN*
0261620762

Tucker, Robert C.   3.3236
Stalin as revolutionary, 1879–1929; a study in history and personality [by]
Robert C. Tucker. [1st ed.] New York, Norton [1973] xx, 519 p. illus. 24 cm.
1. Stalin, Joseph, 1879-1953. I. T.
DK268.S8 T85 1973   947.084/2/0924 B   *LC* 73-6541   *ISBN*
039305487X

Ulam, Adam Bruno, 1922-.   3.3237
Stalin; the man and his era [by] Adam B. Ulam. New York, Viking Press [1973]
760 p. 24 cm. 1. Stalin, Joseph, 1879-1953. 2. Soviet Union — History —
1925-1953 I. T.
DK268.S8 U4 1973   947.084/2/0924 B   *LC* 73-6226   *ISBN*
0670666831

Wolfe, Bertram David, 1896-1977.   • 3.3238
Khrushchev and Stalin's ghost; text, background, and meaning of
Khrushchev's secret report to the Twentieth Congress on the night of February
24–25, 1956. New York: Praeger [c1957] 322 p. 22 cm. (Books that matter)
1. Stalin, Joseph, 1879-1953. 2. Russia — Politics and government — 1936-
I. Khrushchev, Nikita Sergeevich, 1894-1971. II. T.
DK268.S8W6   *947.085   *LC* 56-12224

Zhukov, Georgiĭ Konstantinovich, 1896-1974.   • 3.3239
[Vospominaniia i razmyshleniia. English] The memoirs of Marshal Zhukov.
[1st American ed.] New York, Delacorte Press [1971] 703, viii p. illus., plans
(part col.), ports. 23 cm. Translation of Vospominaniia i razmyshleniia. 'A
Seymour Lawrence book.' 1. Zhukov, Georgiĭ Konstantinovich, 1896-1974.
2. World War, 1939-1945 — Soviet Union. I. T.
DK268.Z52 A313 1971   940.542/1/0924   *LC* 73-120846

DK268.3 Social Life. Customs

Barghoorn, Frederick Charles, 1911-.   • 3.3240
Soviet Russian nationalism. — New York, Oxford University Press, 1956. ix,
330 p. 22 cm. Bibliographical references included in 'Notes' (p. 279-324).
1. Nationalism — Russia. I. T.
DK268.3.B32   *947.085   *LC* 56-7176

Bauer, Raymond Augustine, 1916-.   • 3.3241
Nine soviet portraits [by] Raymond A. Bauer with the assistance of Edward
Wasiolek. — [Cambridge] Published jointly by the Technology Press of
Massachusetts Institute of Technology, and Wiley, New York [1955] 190 p.
illus. 24 cm. — (Technology Press books in the social sciences) 1. Russia —
Soc. condit. — 1945- I. T.
DK268.3.B35   914.7   *LC* 55-14307

Ginzburg, Evgeniia Semenovna.   • 3.3242
[Krutoĭ marshrut. Tom 1. English] Journey into the whirlwind. Translated by
Paul Stevenson and Max Hayward. [1st ed.] New York, Harcourt, Brace &
World [1967] 418 p. map. 22 cm. 'A Helen and Kurt Wolff book.' Translation
of Krutoĭ marshrut. 1. Political prisoners — Soviet Union — Biography.
2. Soviet Union — Social conditions — 1917- I. T.
DK268.3.G513   947.084/2/0924   *LC* 67-26000

Swayze, Harold.   • 3.3243
Political control of literature in the USSR, 1946–1959. Cambridge, Harvard
University Press, 1962. ix, 301 p. 25 cm. (Russian Research Center studies, 44)
Bibliographical references included in 'Notes' (p. [269]-291) 1. Russian
literature — 20th century — History and criticism 2. Censorship — Russia.
3. Communism and literature I. T.
DK268.3.S95   891.70904   *LC* 62-9432

DK273 1939–1945

Gallagher, Matthew P.   • 3.3244
The Soviet history of World War II: myths, memories, and realities / Matthew
P. Gallagher. — New York: Praeger, 1963. 205 p.; 21 cm. — (Praeger
publications in Russian history and world communism; no. 121) 1. World War,
1939-1945 — Russia I. T. II. Series.
DK273.G3   *LC* 63-9908

Moore, Barrington, 1913-.   • 3.3245
Terror and progress USSR: some sources of change and stability in the Soviet
dictatorship. — Cambridge, Harvard University Press, 1954. xvii, 261 p. 22 cm.
— (Russian Research Center Studies, 12) Bibliographical references included in
'Notes' (p. [233]-250) 1. Communism — Russia. I. T.
DK273.M68   *947.085   *LC* 54-5995

DK274–276 1953–

Brumberg, Abraham. comp.   • 3.3246
In quest of justice; protest and dissent in the Soviet Union today. New York,
Praeger [1970] xiv, 477 p. 25 cm. 1. Soviet Union — Politics and government
— 1953- 2. Soviet Union — Social conditions — 1945- I. T.
DK274.B78 1970   914.7/03/85   *LC* 69-12700

Conquest, Robert.   • 3.3247
Power and policy in the U.S.S.R.; the study of Soviet dynastics. New York, St.
Martin's Press, 1961. x, 485 p. 23 cm. 1. Kommunisticheskaia partiia
Sovetskogo Soiuza. 2. Soviet Union — Politics and government — 1945- I. T.
DK274.C62   947.0842   *LC* 61-15941

The Domestic context of Soviet foreign policy / edited by   3.3248
Seweryn Bialer.
Boulder, Colo.: Westview Press, 1981. xviii, 441 p.; 24 cm. — (Studies of the
Research Institute on International Change, Columbia University) 1. Russia
— Foreign relations — 1975- — Addresses, essays, lectures. 2. Russia —
Politics and government — 1953- — Addresses, essays, lectures. 3. Russia —
Foreign relations administration — Addresses, essays, lectures. I. Bialer,
Seweryn.
DK274.D65   327.47   *LC* 80-11877   *ISBN* 0891587837

Edmonds, Robin.   3.3249
Soviet foreign policy—the Brezhnev years / Robin Edmonds. — Oxford
[Oxfordshire]; New York: Oxford University Press, 1983. xvii, 285 p.: maps; 20
cm. (A Galaxy book) Includes index. 1. Brezhnev, Leonid Il'ich, 1906-
2. Detente 3. Soviet Union — Foreign relations — 1953-1975 4. Soviet Union
— Foreign relations — 1975- I. T.
DK274.E3 1983   327.47 19   *LC* 83-4225   *ISBN* 019285125X

Grigorenko, P. G. (Petr Grigor'evich), 1907-.   3.3250
[Mysli sumasshedshego. English] The Grigorenko papers / writings by P. G.
Grigorenko and documents on his case; introd. by Edward Crankshaw. —
Boulder, Colo.: Westview Press, 1976. vi, 187 p.: ill.; 23 cm. Translation of
Mysli sumasshedshego. Includes index. 1. Grigorenko, P. G. (Petr
Grigor'evich), 1907- 2. Soviet Union. Raboche-Krest'ianskaia Krasnaia
Armiia — Biography. 3. Generals — Russia — Biography. 4. Political
prisoners — Russia — Biography. 5. Russia — Politics and government —
1917- — Addresses, essays, lectures. I. T.
DK274.G7313 1976   320.9/47/084   *LC* 76-5912   *ISBN*
0891586032

Haselkorn, Avigdor.   3.3251
The evolution of Soviet security strategy, 1965–1975 / Avigdor Haselkorn. —
New York: Crane, Russak, c1978. xiv, 139 p.: graphs; 24 cm. (Strategy paper;
no. 31) 1. Strategy 2. Russia — Foreign relations — 1953-1975. 3. Russia —
Defenses. I. T.
DK274.H33   355.03/3047   *LC* 77-85316   *ISBN* 0844812730

Hough, Jerry F., 1935-.   3.3252
Soviet leadership in transition / Jerry F. Hough. — Washington, D.C.:
Brookings Institution, c1980. xi, 175 p.: ill.; 24 cm. 1. Russia — Politics and
government — 1953- I. T.
DK274.H68   947.085 19   *LC* 80-67873   *ISBN* 0815737424

Leonhard, Wolfgang.   • 3.3253
The Kremlin since Stalin / Translated from the German by Elizabeth
Wiskemann and Marian Jackson. — New York: Praeger [1962] 403 p.; 21 cm.
— (Books that matter) Translation of Kremi ohne Stalin. 1. Russia — Pol. &
govt. — 1953- I. T.
DK274.L413 1962   947.085   *LC* 62-14888

Medvedev, Roy Aleksandrovich, 1925-.   3.3254
[Intervista sul dissenso in URSS. English.] On Soviet dissent / Roy Medvedev;
interviews with Piero Ostellino; translated from the Italian by William A.
Packer; edited by George Saunders. — New York: Columbia University Press,
1980. 158 p.; 24 cm. Translation of Intervista sul dissenso in URSS.

1. Medvedev, Roy Aleksandrovich, 1925- 2. Dissenters — Russia. 3. Russia — Politics and government — 1953- I. Ostellino, Piero. II. Saunders, George, 1936- III. T.
DK274.M3513   323.1/47   *LC* 79-27877   *ISBN* 0231048122

Mosely, Philip Edward, 1905-.   • **3.3255**
The Kremlin and world politics: studies in Soviet policy and action. — [1st ed.]. — New York: Vintage Books, 1960. viii, 557, x p.; 19 cm. — (Vintage Russian library; R-1002) Bibliographical footnotes. 1. World politics — 1955- 2. Russia — Foreign relations — 1945- I. T.
DK274.M59   327.47   *LC* 60-9146

Pipes, Richard.   **3.3256**
Survival is not enough: Soviet realities and America's future / Richard Pipes. — New York: Simon and Schuster, c1984. 302 p.; 23 cm. Includes index. 1. Communism — Soviet Union 2. Peace 3. Soviet Union — Politics and government — 1953- 4. Soviet Union — Economic conditions — 1976- 5. Soviet Union — Foreign relations — United States 6. United States — Foreign relations — Soviet Union I. T.
DK274.P53 1984   327.73047 19   *LC* 84-13848   *ISBN* 0671495356

Problems of communism.   • **3.3257**
Russia under Khrushchev; an anthology from Problems of communism, edited by Abraham Brumberg. New York, Praeger [1962] ix, 660 p.; 21 cm. (Books that matter) (Praeger publications in Russian history and world communism, no. 105.) 1. Soviet Union. I. Brumberg, Abraham. ed. II. T.
DK274.P7   *LC* 62-13165

Reddaway, Peter. comp.   **3.3258**
Uncensored Russia: protest and dissent in the Soviet Union; the unofficial Moscow journal, a Chronicle of current events. Edited, translated, and with a commentary by Peter Reddaway. With a foreword by Julius Telesin. New York, American Heritage Press [c1972] 499 p. illus. 23 cm. 1. Dissenters — Soviet Union. 2. Soviet Union — Politics and government — 1953- I. Khronika tekushchikh sobytiĭ. II. T.
DK274.R35   320.9/47/085   *LC* 71-37760   *ISBN* 0070513546

Reve, Karel van het. comp.   • **3.3259**
[Letters and telegrams to Pavel Litvinov] Dear comrade; Pavel Litvinov and the voices of Soviet citizens in dissent. Edited and annotated by Karel van het Reve. New York, Pitman Pub. Corp. [1969] xvii, 199 p. 25 cm. 'Originally published in the Netherlands ... under title: Letters and telegrams to Pavel Litvinov December 1967-May 1968.' Parallel text in English and Russian. 1. Litvinov, Pavel Mikhaĭlovich, 1940- 2. Public opinion — Soviet Union. 3. Censorship — Soviet Union. 4. Dissenters — Soviet Union. I. Litvinov, Pavel Mikhaĭlovich, 1940- II. T.
DK274.R38 1969   323.1/47   *LC* 71-79049

Rubinstein, Alvin Z.   **3.3260**
Soviet and Chinese influence in the Third World / edited by Alvin Z. Rubinstein. — New York: Praeger, 1975. ix, 231 p.; 25 cm. (Praeger special studies in international politics and government) Includes index. 1. Soviet Union — Foreign relations — 1953-1975 2. China — Foreign relations — 1949- 3. Developing countries — Foreign relations. I. T.
DK274.R8   327/.09172/4   *LC* 74-11604   *ISBN* 0275096408

Sakharov, Andreĭ, 1921-.   **3.3261**
[O strane i mire. English] My country and the world / Andrei D. Sakharov; translated by Guy V. Daniels. — 1st ed. — New York: Knopf: distributed by Random House, 1975. xvi, 109 p.; 22 cm. Translation of O strane i mire. 1. Disarmament 2. World politics — 1975-1985 3. Russia — Politics and government — 1953- 4. Russia — Foreign relations — 1975- 5. United States — Foreign relations — 1974-1977 I. T.
DK274.S276 1975   320.9/47/085   *LC* 75-24963   *ISBN* 039440226X

Sakharov, Andreĭ, 1921-.   **3.3262**
Sakharov speaks / [by] Andrei D. Sakharov; edited and with a foreword by Harrison E. Salisbury. — [1st ed.] New York: A. A. Knopf, 1974. vi, 245 p. 22 cm. 1. Sakharov, Andreĭ, 1921- 2. Civilization, Modern — 1950- — Addresses, essays, lectures. 3. Soviet Union — Politics and government — 1953- — Addresses, essays, lectures. I. T.
DK274.S277 1974   323.4/0947 B   *LC* 73-21154   *ISBN* 0394492090

The Samizdat register / edited by Roy Medvedev.   **3.3263**
New York: Norton, c1977. vi, 314 p.; 22 cm. Translations of eight essays which originally appeared in the first three issues of 'XX Century,' a journal published in Moscow. 1. Underground literature — Russia — Addresses, essays, lectures. 2. Dissenters — Russia — Addresses, essays, lectures. 3. Political prisoners — Russia — Biography — Addresses, essays, lectures. 4. Russia — Politics and government — 1917- — Addresses, essays, lectures. I. Medvedev, Roy Aleksandrovich, 1925-
DK274.S288 1977   320.9/47/085   *LC* 77-24984   *ISBN* 039305652X

The Samizdat register 2 / edited by Roy Medvedev.   **3.3264**
New York: W.W. Norton, c1981. xi, 323 p.; 22 cm. 1. Underground literature — Soviet Union — Addresses, essays, lectures 2. Dissenters — Soviet Union — Addresses, essays, lectures 3. Political prisoners — Soviet Union — Biography — Addresses, essays, lectures 4. Soviet Union — Politics and government — 1917- - Addresses, essays, lectures I. Medvedev, Roy Aleksandrovich, 1925- II. Onabe, Teruhiko, 1908- Nijisseiki
DK274 S2882   *ISBN* 0393014193

Solzhenitsyn, Aleksandr Isaevich, 1918-.   **3.3265**
Détente: prospects for democracy and dictatorship / Aleksandr Solzhenitsyn; with commentary by Alex Simirenko ... [et al.]. New Brunswick, N.J.: Transaction Books, c1976. 112 p.; 22 cm. (Issues in contemporary civilization) Based on the author's addresses delivered in Washington, D.C. and New York in 1975. 1. Solzhenitsyn, Aleksandr Isaevich, 1918- 2. Civilization, Modern — 1950- 3. Russia — Foreign relations — 1953-1975. 4. Russia — Foreign relations — United States. 5. United States — Foreign relations — Russia. 6. Russia — Politics and government — 1953- I. Simirenko, Alex. II. T.
DK274.S613   327.47/073   *LC* 76-15233   *ISBN* 0878551778

Tatu, Michel, 1933-.   • **3.3266**
[Pouvoir en U.R.S.S. English] Power in the Kremlin: from Krushchev to Kosygin. Translated by Helen Katel. New York, Viking Press [1969, c1968] 570 p. 24 cm. Translation of Le pouvoir en U.R.S.S. 1. Soviet Union — Politics and government — 1953- I. T.
DK274.T3613 1969b   320.9/47   *LC* 67-10216   *ISBN* 0670570281

Ulam, Adam Bruno, 1922-.   **3.3267**
Dangerous relations: the Soviet Union in world politics, 1970–1982 / Adam B. Ulam. — New York: Oxford University Press, 1983. vi, 325 p.; 22 cm. Includes index. 1. Detente 2. World politics — 1965-1975 3. World politics — 1975-1985 4. Soviet Union — Foreign relations — 1953-1975 5. Soviet Union — Foreign relations — 1975- I. T.
DK274.U4 1983   327.47 19   *LC* 82-14261   *ISBN* 0195032373

Werth, Alexander, 1901-.   • **3.3268**
Russia under Khrushchev / by Alexander Werth. — First American edition. — New York: Hill and Wang, [1962, c1961]. 352 p.; 21 cm. 1. Khrushchev, Nikita Sergeevich, 1894-1971. 2. Russia — Politics and government — 1953- 3. Russia — Foreign relations — 1953- I. T.
DK274.W4 1962   *LC* 62-11998

Khrushchev, Nikita Sergeevich, 1894-1971.   **3.3269**
[Memoirs. English. Selections] Khrushchev remembers; the last testament. Translated and edited by Strobe Talbott. With a foreword by Edward Crankshaw and an introd. by Jerrold L. Schecter. [1st ed.] Boston, Little, Brown [1974] xxxi, 602 p. illus. 24 cm. The second and concluding volume of the author's oral memoirs, begun in Khrushchev remembers, 1970. 1. Khrushchev, Nikita Sergeevich, 1894-1971. 2. Soviet Union — Politics and government — 1953- I. Talbott, Strobe. ed. II. T.
DK275.K5 A326   947.085/092/4 B   *LC* 74-4095

Crankshaw, Edward.   • **3.3270**
Khrushchev; a career. — New York: Viking Press, [1966] 311 p.: ports.; 24 cm. 1. Khrushchev, Nikita Sergeevich, 1894-1971. I. T.
DK275.K5 C7   947.085 B   *LC* 66-15880

Linden, Carl A.   • **3.3271**
Khrushchev and the Soviet leadership, 1957–1964 / [by] Carl A. Linden. — Baltimore: Johns Hopkins Press [1966] x, 270 p.; 22 cm. 'Published in co-operation with the Institute for Sino-Soviet Studies, George Washington University.' 1. Khrushchev, Nikita Sergeevich, 1894-1971. 2. Soviet Union — Politics and government — 1953- I. George Washington University. Institute for Sino-Soviet Studies. II. T.
DK275.K5 L5   320.924   *LC* 66-16035

Medvedev, Roy Aleksandrovich, 1925-.   **3.3272**
Khrushchev: the years in power / by Roy A. Medvedev, Zhores A. Medvedev. — New York: Columbia University Press, 1976. xi, 198 p., [4] leaves of plates: ill.; 22 cm. Translation of N. S. Khrushchev, gody u vlasti. 1. Khrushchev, Nikita Sergeevich, 1894-1971. 2. Russia — Politics and government — 1953- I. Medvedev, Zhores A., 1925- joint author. II. T.
DK275.K5 M413 1976   947.085/092/4 B   *LC* 76-19104   *ISBN* 0231039395

Conquest, Robert.   • **3.3273**
The politics of ideas in the U.S.S.R. New York, Praeger [1967] 175, [1] p. 23 cm. (Contemporary Soviet Union series: institutions and policies) (Praeger publications in Russian history and world communism, no. 197.) 1. Propaganda, Communist 2. Mass media — Soviet Union. 3. Kommunisticheskaia partiia Sovetskogo Soiuza. 4. Soviet Union — Intellectual life I. T. II. Series.
DK276.C6 1967   327.1/4   *LC* 67-27314

Miller, Wright Watts.   • 3.3274
Russians as people. With a pref. by Alexander Dallin. [1st ed.] New York, Dutton, 1961 [c1960] 205 p. illus. 21 cm. 1. Soviet Union — Social life and customs I. T.
DK276.M5 1961   914.7   LC 61-10642

Smith, Hedrick.   3.3275
The Russians / Hedrick Smith. — [Updated ed.]. — New York, N.Y.: Times Books, c1983. xi, 578 p., [16] p. of plates: ill.; 24 cm. 1. Soviet Union — Social life and customs — 1970- 2. Soviet Union — Social conditions — 1970- I. T.
DK276.S53 1983   306/.0947 19   LC 83-9289   ISBN 0812910869

DK400–443 POLAND

(Works classified before ca. 1980; see also: DK4010-4800)

The Cambridge history of Poland. Edited by W. F. Reddaway   • 3.3276
[and others].
New York: Octagon Books, 1971-. v.   : illus., maps (part col.), ports.; 25 cm. Vol. 1 first published 1950; v. 2, 1941. 1. Poland — History I. Reddaway, William Fiddian, 1872-1949. ed.
DK414.C32   943.8   LC 73-119437

Bromke, Adam.   3.3277
Poland's politics: idealism vs. realism. — Cambridge: Harvard University Press, 1967. x, 316 p.; 25 cm. — (Russian Research Center studies, 51) 1. Communism — Poland. 2. Poland — Politics and government I. T.
DK418.B7   320.9438   LC 66-21331

Wandycz, Piotr Stefan.   3.3278
Soviet–Polish relations, 1917–1921 / [by] Piotr S. Wandycz. — Cambridge: Harvard University Press, 1969. ix, 403 p.: maps; 24 cm. (Russian Research Center studies, 59) 1. Poland — Foreign relations — Soviet Union. 2. Soviet Union — Foreign relations — Poland. I. T.
DK418.5.R9 W29   327.438/047   LC 69-18047   ISBN 0674827805

Knoll, Paul W.   3.3279
The rise of the Polish monarchy; Piast Poland in East Central Europe, 1320–1370 [by] Paul W. Knoll. — Chicago: University of Chicago Press, [1972] x, 276 p.; 24 cm. 1. Poland — History — Vladislaus I, 1305-1333 2. Poland — History — Casimir III, 1333-1370 I. T.
DK424.7.K59   943.8/02   LC 77-187155   ISBN 0226448266

Kaplan, Herbert H.   • 3.3280
The first partition of Poland [by] Herbert H. Kaplan. New York, Columbia University Press, 1962. — [New York: AMS Press, 1972] xvi, 215 p.; 23 cm. Original ed. issued in series: East Central European studies of Columbia University. 1. Poland — History — First partition, 1772 I. T.
DK434.K33 1972   943.8/02   LC 76-171548   ISBN 0404036368

Lord, Robert Howard, 1885-1954.   • 3.3281
The second partition of Poland; a study in diplomatic history. — New York: AMS Press, [1969] xxx, 586 p.; 23 cm. Reprint of the 1915 ed. 1. Poland — History — Second partition, 1793 I. T.
DK434.L7 1969   943.8/02   LC 73-101268

Wandycz, Piotr Stefan.   3.3282
The lands of partitioned Poland, 1795–1918, by Piotr S. Wandycz. — Seattle: University of Washington Press, [1974] xvii, 431 p.: maps; 24 cm. — (A history of East Central Europe. Editors: Peter F. Sugar [and] Donald W. Treadgold) 1. Poland — History — 1795-1864 2. Poland — History — 1864-1918 I. T.
DR36.S88 vol. 7 DK434.9   DK434.9 W25.   914.9 s 914.38/03/3
     LC 74-8312   ISBN 0295953519

Leslie, R. F.   • 3.3283
Polish politics and the Revolution of November 1830, by R. F. Leslie. Westport, Conn., Greenwood Press [1969] xii, 307 p. geneal. table, maps. 23 cm. (University of London historical studies, 3) Reprint of the 1956 ed. 'Represents in part the work done for a Ph.D. thesis of the University of London.' 1. Poland — History — Revolution, 1830-1832 I. T.
DK436.L545 1969   943.8/03   LC 79-91766   ISBN 0837124166

Leslie, R. F.   • 3.3284
Reform and insurrection in Russian Poland, 1856–1865. — Westport, Conn.: Greenwood Press, [1969, c1963] ix, 272 p.; 23 cm. 1. Poland — History — 1830-1864 I. T.
DK437.L48 1969   943.8/03   LC 72-91767   ISBN 0837124158

Cienciala, Anna M.   3.3285
Poland and the Western powers 1938–1939: a study in the interdependence of Eastern and Western Europe, by Anna M. Cienciala. — London: Routledge & K. Paul; Toronto: University of Toronto P., 1968. x, 310 p.: plate, 2 maps, port.; 23 cm. — (Studies in political history) 1. Poland — Foreign relations — 1918-1945 2. Europe — Politics and government — 1918-1945 I. T.
DK440.C516   327.438   LC 68-111458   ISBN 0710050216

Polonsky, Antony.   3.3286
Politics in independent Poland 1921–1939: the crisis of constitutional government. — Oxford: Clarendon Press, 1972. xvi, 572 p.: maps; 23 cm. 1. Poland — Politics and government — 1918-1945 2. Poland — Foreign relations I. T.
DK440.P583   320.9/438/04   LC 72-188451   ISBN 0198271824

Piłsudski, Józef, 1867-1935.   • 3.3287
Joseph Pilsudski, the memories of a Polish revolutionary and soldier / translated and edited by D.R. Gillie. — London: Faber & Faber, 1931. x, 377 p.: plates, ports., maps; 23 cm. 1. Socialism — Poland 2. World War, 1914-1918 — Poland. 3. Poland — Politics and government I. Gillie, Darsie Rutherford. II. T.
DK440.5.P5 A42   LC 31-15807

DK445–465 FINLAND

Area handbook for Finland. Coauthors: Theodore L. Stoddard   3.3288
[and others] Prepared for the American University by the Institute for Cross–Cultural Research.
1st ed., 4th printing. [Washington; For sale by the Supt. of Docs., U.S. Govt. Print. Off.] 1985. xiv, 259 p. illus. 24 cm. 'One of a series of handbooks prepared under the auspices of Foreign Area Studies (FAS) of the American University.' 'DA pam 550-167.' 1. Finland. I. Stoddard, Theodore L. (Theodore Lothrop), 1926- II. Institute for Cross-Cultural Research (U.S.) III. American University (Washington, D.C.). Foreign Area Studies.
DK449.S83   948.97 19   LC 73-600338

Jutikkala, Eino, 1907-.   3.3289
[Suomen historia. English] A history of Finland [by] Eino Jutikkala and Kauko Pirinen. Translated by Paul Sjöblom. Rev. ed. New York, Praeger Publishers [1974] x, 293 p. 25 cm. Translation of Suomen historia. 1. Finland — History I. Pirinen, Kauko. joint author. II. T.
DK451.J78613 1974   947.1   LC 72-94339

Mazour, Anatole Gregory, 1900-.   • 3.3290
Finland between East and West. — Princeton, N.J.: Van Nostrand, 1956. xiv, 298 p.: ill., ports., maps (some col.) 1. Finland — History I. T.
DK451.M33   LC 56-8220

Wuorinen, John H. (John Henry), 1897-.   • 3.3291
A history of Finland, by John H. Wuorinen. — New York: Published for American-Scandinavian Foundation by Columbia University Press, 1965. xv, 548 p.: illus., maps, ports.; 24 cm. 1. Finland — History I. T.
DK451.W8   947.1   LC 65-13618

Jakobson, Max.   • 3.3292
Finnish neutrality; a study of Finnish foreign policy since the Second World War. — New York: Praeger, [1969, c1968] 116 p.: illus., map. Includes a chapter on the period 1917-1944. 1. Finland — Foreign relations — 1945- 2. Finland — Neutrality. I. T.
DK451.7.J3 1969   327.471   LC 69-16085

Allison, Roy.   3.3293
Finland's relations with the Soviet Union, 1944–84 / Roy Allison. — New York: St. Martin's Press, 1985. ix, 211 p.: map; 23 cm. Includes index. 1. Finland — Foreign relations — Soviet Union. 2. Soviet Union — Foreign relations — Finland. 3. Finland — Foreign relations — 1945- I. T.
DK451.8.S6x   327.4897047 19   LC 84-17694   ISBN 0312290667

Kirby, D. G.   3.3294
Finland in the twentieth century / by D.G. Kirby. — Minneapolis: University of Minnesota Press, 1980 (c1979). x, 253 p.: map; 23 cm. Includes index. 1. Finland — Politics and government — 20th century I. T.
DK459.K57   948.97/03 19   LC 79-11651   ISBN 0816608954

Upton, Anthony F.   3.3295
The Finnish Revolution, 1917–1918 / Anthony F. Upton. — Minneapolis: University of Minnesota Press, 1981 (c1980). 608 p.: maps; 24 cm. — (Nordic series. v. 3) Includes index. 1. Finland — History — Revolution, 1917-1918 I. T. II. Series.
DK459.U67   948.97/031   LC 80-477   0816609155

Chew, Allen F. • **3.3296**
The white death: the epic of the Soviet–Finnish Winter War, by Allen F. Chew. — [East Lansing]: Michigan State University Press, [1971] x, 313 p.: plans.; 24 cm. 1. Russo-Finnish War, 1939-1940 I. T.
DK459.5.C48   947/.103   LC 76-169986   ISBN 0870131672

Nevakivi, Jukka. **3.3297**
The appeal that was never made: the Allies, Scandinavia, and the Finnish Winter War, 1939–1940 / by Jukka Nevakivi. — Montreal: McGill-Queen's University Press, 1977 (c1976). x, 225 p.; 23 cm. Revised translation of Apu jota ei pyydetty; revised by the author, translated by his wife. Includes index. 1. Russo-Finnish War, 1939-1940 2. Finland — Foreign relations — 1917-1945 I. T.
DK459.5.N3513   947.1/03   LC 79-303609   ISBN 0773502629

Tanner, Väinö, 1881-1966. • **3.3298**
The winter war: Finland against Russia, 1939–1940. Stanford, Calif., Stanford University Press [1957] 274 p. illus. 25 cm. 1. Russo-Finnish War, 1939-1940 I. T.
DK459.5.T312   LC 57-5904

Mannerheim, Carl Gustaf Emil, friherre, 1867-1951. • **3.3299**
The memoirs of Marshal Mannerheim / translated by Eric Lewenhaupt. — 1st ed. New York Dutton 1954. 540p.: ill. — I. T.
DK461.M32 A33   LC 54-5060

DK501–973 SOVIET LOCAL HISTORY

DK507 Belorussia

Vakar, Nicholas P. • **3.3300**
Belorussia: the making of a nation, a case study. — Cambridge, Harvard University Press, 1956. xii, 297 p. ports., maps. 25 cm. — (Russian Research Center studies, 21) Bibliographical references included in 'Notes' (p. [229]-281) 1. White Russia — Hist. I. T.
DK507.V3   947.6   LC 54-8634

DK508 Ukraine

Allen, W. E. D. (William Edward David), 1901-. • **3.3301**
The Ukraine: a history / W.E.D. Allen. — New York: Russell & Russell, 1963. 404 p.: ill.; 23 cm. 1. Ukraine — History I. T.
DK508.5.A79 1963   LC 63-8355

Hrushevs'kyĭ, Mykhaĭlo, 1866-1934. • **3.3302**
[Istoriia Ukraïny-Rusy. English] A history of Ukraine, by Michael Hrushevsky. Edited by O. J. Frederiksen. Pref. by George Vernadsky. Published for the Ukrainian National Association. [Hamden, Conn.] Archon Books, 1970 [c1941] xviii, 629 p. maps. 23 cm. Translation of Istoriia Ukraïny-Rusy (romanized form) 1. Ukraine — History I. T.
DK508.5.H683 1970   947.7/1   LC 72-120370   ISBN 0208009671

Armstrong, John Alexander, 1922-. • **3.3303**
Ukrainian nationalism. 2d ed. New York, Columbia University Press, 1963. 361 p. illus. 25 cm. (Studies of the Russian Institute, Columbia University) 1. Nationalism — Ukraine. 2. World War, 1939-1945 — Ukraine. I. T.
DK508.8.A78 1963   947.71   LC 62-18367 rev

Sullivant, Robert S., 1925-. • **3.3304**
Soviet politics and the Ukraine, 1917–1957. New York, Columbia University Press, 1962. 438 p. illus. 24 cm. Issued, with variations, in microfilm form in 1958 as thesis, University of Chicago, under title: Soviet politics in the Ukraine, 1917-1957. 1. Nationalism — Ukraine. 2. Ukraine — Politics and government — 1917- I. T.
DK508.8.S75   320.158   LC 62-10455

DK511 Baltic States. Georgia (Transcaucasia)

Misiunas, Romuald J. **3.3305**
The Baltic States, years of dependence, 1940–1980 / by Romuald J. Misiunas and Rein Taagepera. — Berkeley: University of California Press, c1983. xvi, 333 p., 16 p. of plates: ill.; 23 cm. 'Sequel to Georg von Rauch's The Baltic States: the years of independence, 1917-1940 (1974)'—Pref. Includes index. 1. Baltic States — History I. Taagepera, Rein. II. Rauch, Georg von. Geschichte der baltischen Staaten. English III. T.
DK511.B3 M57 1983   947/.40842 19   LC 82-4727   ISBN 0520046250

Page, Stanley W. • **3.3306**
The formation of the Baltic States; a study of the effects of great power politics upon the emergence of Lithuania, Latvia, and Estonia, by Stanley W. Page. — New York: H. Fertig, 1970 [c1959] ix, 193 p.; 21 cm. — (Harvard historical monographs. [39]) 1. Baltic States — History I. T. II. Series.
DK511.B3 P28 1970   947.4   LC 74-80578

Pick, F.W. (Frederick Walter) 1912-. • **3.3307**
The Baltic nations: Estonia, Latvia and Lithuania / by F.W. Pick. — London: Boreas Pub. Co., 1945. — 172 p.: maps; 19 cm. 1. Baltic States — History I. T.
DK511.B3 P5 1945   LC 45-7863

Rauch, Georg von. **3.3308**
[Geschichte der baltischen Staaten. English] The Baltic States: the years of independence; Estonia, Latvia, Lithuania, 1917–1940, by Georg von Rauch. Translated from the German by Gerald Onn. Berkeley, University of California Press [1974] xv, 265 p. 23 cm. Translation of Geschichte der baltischen Staaten. 1. Baltic States — History I. T.
DK511.B3 R3413   947/.4/084   LC 73-86849   ISBN 0520026004

Reddaway, William Fiddian, 1872-1949. • **3.3309**
Problems of the Baltic / by W. F. Reddaway. — Cambridge [Eng.] The University Press 1940. 120 p.: ill. (map); 18 cm. (Current problems) 1. Baltic States — History I. T.
DK511 B3 R37

Royal Institute of International Affairs. Information Dept. • **3.3310**
The Baltic states: a survey of the political and economic structure and the foreign relations of Estonia, Latvia, and Lithuania / prepared by the Information department of the Royal institute of international affairs. — London, New York [etc.] Oxford University Press, 1938. 194 p.: fold. map.; 22 cm. 1. Baltic States
DK511.B3 R6   LC 39-8235

Jackson, J. Hampden (John Hampden), 1907-. • **3.3311**
Estonia / by J. Hampden Jackson. — 2d ed. with a postscript on the years 1940-1947. — London: Allen & Unwin, 1948. 272 p.: maps, diagrs.; 22 cm. 1. Estonia. I. T.
DK511.E5 J2 1948   947/.4   LC 49-1421

Lang, David Marshall. • **3.3312**
A modern history of Soviet Georgia / David Lang. — New York: Grove Press, [1962] 298 p.: ill.; 23 cm. 1. Georgian S.S.R — History. I. T.
DK511.G4 L3 1962   LC 62-13057

Bilmanis, Alfreds, 1887-1948. • **3.3313**
A history of Latvia. — Westport, Conn.: Greenwood Press, [1970, c1951] x, 441 p.: maps, port.; 24 cm. 1. Latvia — History I. T.
DK511.L17 B48 1970   947/.43   LC 69-13827   ISBN 0837114462

Gerutis, Albertas, 1905-. • **3.3314**
Lithuania 700 years. Edited by Dr. Albertas Gerutis. Translated by Algirdas Budreckis. Introd. by Raphael Sealey. — New York: Manyland Books, [1969] xii, 474 p.: illus., map, ports.; 24 cm. 1. Lithuania — History — Addresses, essays, lectures. I. T.
DK511.L2 G5   947/.5   LC 75-80057

Sabaliūnas, Leonas, 1934-. **3.3315**
Lithuania in crisis; nationalism to communism, 1939–1940. — Bloomington: Indiana University Press, [c1972] xxi, 293 p.; 22 cm. — (Indiana University international studies) 1. Smetona, Antanas, Pres. Lithuania, 1874-1944. 2. Nationalism — Lithuania. 3. Lithuania — History — 1918-1945 I. T.
DK511.L27 S2   947/.5/0842   LC 74-143247   ISBN 0253336007

Senn, Alfred Erich.   • 3.3316
The emergence of modern Lithuania / Alfred Erich Senn. — New York:
Columbia University Press, 1959. 272 p.: ill.; 24 cm. — (Studies of the Russian
institute, Columbia university) 1. Lithuania — History I. T.
DK511.L27 S4   947/.5/084   *LC* 59-6606

DK750–973 Russia in Asia. Siberia

Jukes, Geoffrey.   3.3317
The Soviet Union in Asia. — Berkeley: University of California Press, [1973]
304 p.: maps.; 23 cm. 1. Russia, Asiatic. I. T.
DK750.J83   301.29/47/05   *LC* 72-95303   *ISBN* 0520023935

Golder, Frank Alfred, 1877-1929.   • 3.3318
Russian expansion on the Pacific, 1641–1850; an account of the earliest and
later expeditions made by the Russians along the Pacific coast of Asia and
North America; including some related expeditions to the Arctic regions.
Gloucester, Mass., P. Smith, 1960 [c1914] 368 p. illus. 21 cm. 1. Discoveries (in
geography) — Russian. 2. Northeast Passage 3. Siberia (R.S.F.S.R. and
Kazakh S.S.R.) — Discovery and exploration. 4. Soviet Union — Colonies —
North America. I. T.
DK753.G7 1960   957   *LC* 60-52264

Kennan, George, 1845-1924.   • 3.3319
Siberia and the exile system. — New York: Russell & Russell, [1970] 2 v.: illus.,
maps, ports.; 25 cm. 'First published in 1891.' 1. Siberia — Description and
travel. 2. Siberia — Exiles. I. T.
DK755.K34122   915.7   *LC* 76-77675

Kolarz, Walter.   • 3.3320
The peoples of the Soviet Far East. [Hamden, Conn.] Archon Books, 1969. xii,
193 p. illus., maps. 23 cm. Reprint of the 1954 ed. 1. Ethnology — Russian
S.F.S.R. — Soviet Far East. I. T.
DK758.K6 1969   323.1/57   *LC* 69-12416   *ISBN* 0208007016

Allworth, Edward. ed.   • 3.3321
Central Asia; a century of Russian rule, edited by Edward Allworth.
Contributors: Edward Allworth [and others] New York, Columbia University
Press, 1967. xiv, 552 p. illus., maps, music, ports. 25 cm. Bibliographical
footnotes. 1. Soviet Central Asia I. Carrère d'Encausse, Hélène. II. T.
DK851.A4   958   *LC* 66-16288

Allworth, Edward.   3.3322
The nationality question in Soviet Central Asia. Edited by Edward Allworth. —
New York: Praeger, [1973] xiv, 217 p.; 25 cm. — (Praeger special studies in
international politics and government) 1. Minorities — Soviet Central Asia —
Addresses, essays, lectures. 2. Ethnology — Soviet Central Asia — Addresses,
essays, lectures. I. T.
DK855.4.A63 1973   301.45/1/0420957   *LC* 72-85986

Krader, Lawrence.   • 3.3323
Peoples of Central Asia / by Lawrence Krader. — Bloomington: Indiana
University, 1963. xvi, 319 p.: 2 fold. maps (in pocket); 26 cm. — (Uralic and
Altaic series Indiana University Publications. v. 26) (Research and studies in
Uralic and Altaic Languages. Project no. 12 and 62.) 1. Ethnology — Soviet
Central Asia I. Indiana University, Bloomington. II. T.
DK855.4.K7   915.8/4   *LC* 63-63330

The USSR and the Muslim world: issues in domestic and   3.3324
foreign policy / edited by Yaacov Ro'i.
London; Boston: Allen & Unwin, 1984. xv, 298 p.; 25 cm. 'Based on papers
given at a conference held by the Russian and East European Research Center
at Tel Aviv University in December 1980'—Acknowledgments. 1. Muslims —
Soviet Central Asia — Congresses. 2. Middle East — Foreign relations —
Soviet Union — Congresses. 3. Soviet Union — Foreign relations — Middle
East — Congresses. 4. Afghanistan — History — Soviet Occupation, 1979- —
Congresses. I. Ro'i, Yaacov. II. Universitat Tel-Aviv. Makhon le-heker Berit
ha-Mo'atsot u-Mizrah Eropah. III. Title: U.S.S.R. and the Muslim world.
DK855.5.M8 U85 1984   327.56047 19   *LC* 83-25709   *ISBN*
0043011713

Wheeler, Geoffrey.   • 3.3325
The modern history of Soviet Central Asia. — New York: Praeger [1964] xi,
272 p. illus., maps, ports. 23 cm. — (Asia-Africa series of modern histories)
Includes bibliographical references. 1. Soviet Central Asia — Hist. I. T.
DK856.W5 1964   958.4   *LC* 64-19966

Rywkin, Michael.   3.3326
Moscow's Muslim challenge: Soviet Central Asia / Michael Rywkin. —
Armonk, N.Y.: M.E. Sharpe, c1982. x, 186 p.: ill.; 24 cm. Includes index.
1. Soviet Central Asia — Politics and government. I. T.
DK859.R98   957/.08 19   *LC* 81-14414   *ISBN* 0873321960

Becker, Seymour.   • 3.3327
Russia's protectorates in Central Asia: Bukhara and Khiva, 1865–1924.
Cambridge, Harvard University Press, 1968. xiv, 416 p. illus., maps, ports. 25
cm. (Russian Research Center studies, 54) 1. Bukhara — Politics and
government. 2. Khiva — Politics and government. I. T.
DK879.B4   325.3/47/0958   *LC* 67-30825

DK4010–4800 POLAND
(Works classified after ca. 1980; see also:
DK400-443)

Poland, a country study / Foreign Area Studies, the American   3.3328
University; edited by Harold D. Nelson.
2nd ed. — Washington, D.C.: For sale by the Supt. of Docs., U.S. G.P.O., 1983.
xxxi, 483 p.: ill.; 24 cm. — (Area handbook series.) 'Research completed
January 1983.' 'DA Pam 550-162'—Verso t.p. Includes index. 1. Poland.
I. Nelson, Harold D. II. American University (Washington, D.C.). Foreign
Area Studies. III. Series.
DK4040.P57 1983   943.8 19   *LC* 83-22431

Davies, Norman.   3.3329
God's playground, a history of Poland / by Norman Davies. — New York:
Columbia University Press, 1982. 2 v.: ill.; 22 cm. Includes index. 1. Poland —
History I. T. II. Title: God's playground.
DK4140.D38 1982   943.8 19   *LC* 81-10241   *ISBN* 0231043260

Davies, Norman.   3.3330
Heart of Europe: a short history of Poland / by Norman Davies. — Oxford
[Oxfordshire]: Clarendon Press; New York: Oxford University Press, 1984. xxi,
511 p., 8 p. of plates: ill.; 23 cm. 1. Poland — History I. T.
DK4140.D385 1984   943.8 19   *LC* 83-22003   *ISBN* 0198730608

Halecki, Oskar, 1891-1973.   3.3331
A history of Poland / O. Halecki; with additional material by A. Polonsky. —
London: Kegan Paul, 1978, c1976. xii, 407 p.: maps; 23 cm. Translation with
additions of La Pologne de 963 à 1914. Includes index. 1. Poland — History
I. Polonsky, Antony. II. T.
DK4140.H3413 1978   943.8   *LC* 77-30740   *ISBN* 0710086474

History of Poland / by Aleksander Gieysztor ... [et al.;   3.3332
translation from the Polish manuscript, Krystyna Cekalska ... et
al.].
2d ed. — Warszawa: PWN, Polish Scientific Publishers, 1979. 668 p., 10 fold.
leaves of plates: ill., col. maps; 24 cm. Errata slip inserted. Includes index.
1. Poland — History I. Gieysztor, Aleksander.
DK4140.H58 1979   943.8   *LC* 79-322250   *ISBN* 8301003928

Fedorowicz, J. K., 1949-.   3.3333
A Republic of nobles: studies in Polish history to 1864 / edited and translated
by J.K. Fedorowicz, co–editors, Maria Bogucka, Henryk Samsonowicz. —
Cambridge [Cambridgeshire]; New York: Cambridge University Press, 1982.
xvi, 293 p.: ill.; 24 cm. Includes index. 1. Poland — History — To 1795 —
Addresses, essays, lectures. 2. Poland — History — 1795-1864 — Addresses,
essays, lectures. I. Bogucka, Maria. II. Samsonowicz, Henryk. III. T.
DK4188.R46 1982   943.8/02 19   *LC* 81-12284   *ISBN* 052124093X

Pasek, Jan Chryzostom.   3.3334
[Pamietniki. English] Memoirs of the Polish Baroque: the writings of Jan
Chryzostom Pasek, a squire of the Commonwealth of Poland and Lithuania /
edited, translated, with an introduction and notes by Catherine S. Leach;
foreword by Wiktor Weintraub. — Berkeley: University of California Press,
c1976. lxiv, 327 p., [10] leaves of plates: ill.; 25 cm. Translation of Pamietniki.
Includes index. 1. Pasek, Jan Chryzostom. 2. Poland — History — 17th
century 3. Poland — Gentry — Biography. I. T.
DK4312.P3 A3513   943.8/02/0924 B   *LC* 74-77731   *ISBN*
0520027523

Czartoryski and European unity, 1770–1861 / by M. Kukiel.   • 3.3335
Princeton: Princeton University Press, 1955. 354 p.: maps, ports. (Poland's
millennium series of the Kościuszko Foundation.) 1. Czartoryski, Adam Jerzy,
ksiaże, 1770-1861. 2. Poland — Politics and government — 1796-1918
3. Europe — Politics and government — 1789-1900
DK4355.C9 K85   *LC* 54-6076

Dziewanowski, M. K.　　　　　　　　　　3.3336
Poland in the twentieth century / M. K. Dziewanowski. New York: Columbia University Press, 1977. xiii, 309 p.; 24 cm. Includes index. 1. Poland — History — 20th century I. T.
DK4382.D9　　943.8　　*LC* 76-51216　　*ISBN* 0231035772

The History of Poland since 1863 / R. F. Leslie ... [et al.];　　　　　　　　　　3.3337
edited by R. F. Leslie.
Cambridge [Eng.]; New York: Cambridge University Press, 1980. xii, 494 p.: maps; 24 cm. — (Soviet and East European studies.) Includes index. 1. Poland — History — 20th century 2. Poland — History — 1864-1918 I. Leslie, R. F. II. Series.
DK4382.H57　　943.8　　*LC* 78-73246　　*ISBN* 0521226457

Watt, Richard M.　　　　　　　　　　3.3338
Bitter glory: Poland and its fate, 1918 to 1939 / Richard M. Watt. — New York: Simon and Schuster, c1982. 511 p., [32] p. of plates: ill.; 25 cm. Includes index. 'A Touchstone book.' 1. Poland — History — 1918-1945 I. T.
DK4400.W37　　943.8/04　　*LC* 79-12958　　*ISBN* 0671453785

Karski, Jan, 1914-.　　　　　　　　　　3.3339
The Great Powers & Poland, 1919–1945: from Versailles to Yalta / Jan Karski. — Lanham, MD: University Press of America, c1985. xvi, 697 p.; 24 cm. Includes index. 1. Paris Peace Conference (1919-1920). 2. Yalta Conference (1945) 3. Poland — Foreign relations — 1918-1945 4. Europe — Politics and government — 1918-1945 5. United States — Foreign relations — Poland. 6. Poland — Foreign relations — United States. I. T. II. Title: Great powers and Poland, 1919-1945.
DK4402.K37 1985　　943.8/04 19　　*LC* 84-22000　　*ISBN* 0819143987

Gross, Jan Tomasz.　　　　　　　　　　3.3340
Polish society under German occupation: the Generalgouvernement, 1939–1944 / Jan Tomasz Gross. — Princeton, N.J.: Princeton University Press, c1979. xviii, 343 p.; 23 cm. Includes index. 1. Poland — History — Occupation, 1939-1945 I. T.
DK4410.G76　　943.8/05　　*LC* 78-70298　　*ISBN* 0691093814

Ascherson, Neal.　　　　　　　　　　3.3341
The Polish August: the self–limiting revolution / Neal Ascherson. — New York: Viking Press, 1982. 320 p.; 24 cm. Includes index. 1. Poland — History — 1980- I. T.
DK4430.A83 1982　　943.8/05 19　　*LC* 81-52150　　*ISBN* 0670563056

Steven, Stewart, 1937-.　　　　　　　　　　3.3342
The Poles / Stewart Steven. — New York: Macmillan, c1982. xx, 427 p.; 25 cm. Includes index. 1. Poland — History — 1945- I. T.
DK4430.S74 1982　　943.8/05 19　　*LC* 82-9924　　*ISBN* 0026144603

Weschler, Lawrence.　　　　　　　　　　3.3343
Solidarity, Poland in the season of its passion / Lawrence Weschler; foreword by William W. Winpisinger. — New York: Simon and Schuster, c1982. xvii, 221 p., [16] p. of plates: ill., map; 25 cm. 'A Fireside book.' Includes index. 1. Weschler, Lawrence. 2. NSZZ 'Solidarność' (Labor organization) 3. Poland — History — 1945- I. T.
DK4430.W47 1982　　943.8/05 19　　*LC* 82-671　　*ISBN* 0671451901

Goldfarb, Jeffrey C.　　　　　　　　　　3.3344
On cultural freedom: an exploration of public life in Poland and America / Jeffrey C. Goldfarb. — Chicago: University of Chicago Press, 1982. x, 173 p.; 24 cm. 1. Politics and culture — Poland. 2. Politics and culture — United States. 3. Poland — Intellectual life — 1945- 4. United States — Intellectual life — 20th century I. T.
DK4440.G64 1982　　303.4/82438/073 19　　*LC* 82-8325　　*ISBN* 0226300994

Poland, genesis of a revolution / edited by Abraham Brumberg.　　　　　　　　　　3.3345
1st ed. — New York: Random House, c1983. xii, 322 p.; 25 cm. 1. Poland — History — 1980- — Addresses, essays, lectures. 2. Poland — History — 1945-1980 — Addresses, essays, lectures. I. Brumberg, Abraham.
DK4440.P58 1983　　943.8/056 19　　*LC* 82-40137　　*ISBN* 0394523237

De Weydenthal, Jan B.　　　　　　　　　　3.3346
The Polish drama, 1980–1982 / Jan B. de Weydenthal, Bruce D. Porter, Kevin Devlin. — Lexington, Mass.: Lexington Books, c1983. viii, 351 p.; 24 cm. 1. Communism — Europe. 2. Poland — History — 1980- I. Porter, Bruce D. II. Devlin, Kevin. III. T.
DK4442.D4 1983　　943.8 19　　*LC* 82-48527　　*ISBN* 0669062146

Raina, Peter K., 1935-.　　　　　　　　　　3.3347
Poland 1981: towards social renewal / Peter Raina. — London; Boston: G. Allen & Unwin, 1985. viii, 472 p.; 24 cm. Includes index. 1. NSZZ 'Solidarność' (Labor organization) 2. Poland — Politics and government — 1980- 3. Poland — Social conditions — 1980- I. T.
DK4442.R35 1985　　943.8/056 19　　*LC* 84-21590　　*ISBN* 0043350526

Staniszkis, Jadwiga.　　　　　　　　　　3.3348
Poland's self–limiting revolution / by Jadwiga Staniszkis; edited by Jan T. Gross. — Princeton, N.J.: Princeton University Press, c1984. xii, 352 p.; 22 cm. Includes index. 1. NSZZ 'Solidarność' (Labor organization) 2. Poland — Politics and government — 1980- 3. Poland — Politics and government — 1945-1980 4. Poland — Social conditions — 1980- I. Gross, Jan Tomasz. II. T.
DK4442.S72 1984　　943.8/055 19　　*LC* 82-61387　　*ISBN* 0691094039

DL1–42 GENERAL WORKS

Scott, Franklin Daniel, 1901-.   **3.3349**
Scandinavia / Franklin D. Scott. — Rev. & enl. ed. — Cambridge: Harvard University Press, 1975. x, 330 p.: map (on lining papers); 25 cm. (American foreign policy library.) First published in 1950 under title: The United States and Scandinavia. Includes index. 1. Scandinavia I. T. II. Series.
DL5.S44   948   *LC* 75-2818   *ISBN* 0674790006

Sømme, Axel Christian Zetlitz, 1899- ed.   • **3.3350**
A geography of Norden: Denmark, Finland, Iceland, Norway, Sweden. Editor: Axel Sømme. — New ed. — London; Melbourne [etc.]: Heinemann; New York: Wiley, 1968. 359 p.: 40 plates, illus., maps (some col.); 27 cm. 1. Scandinavia 2. Finland. I. T.
DL5.S6 1968b   914.8   *LC* 71-409716   *ISBN* 0435348205

Fullerton, Brian.   **3.3351**
Scandinavia; an introductory geography [by] Brian Fullerton and Alan F. Williams. — New York: Praeger Publishers, [1972] xiv, 374 p.: illus.; 23 cm. — (Praeger introductory geographies) 1. Scandinavia — Description and travel — 1945-1980 I. Williams, Alan F., joint author. II. T.
DL11.F84   914.8   *LC* 79-186468

Klindt-Jensen, Ole.   **3.3352**
A history of Scandinavian archaeology / Ole Klindt-Jensen; [translated from the Danish by G. Russell Poole]. — London: Thames and Hudson, [1975] 144 p.: ill., map; 24 cm. Includes index. 1. Scandinavia — Antiquities. I. T.
DL21.K5613   948   *LC* 75-328626   *ISBN* 050079006X

Shetelig, Haakon, 1877-1955.   • **3.3353**
Scandinavian archaeology / by Haakon Shetelig and Hjalmar Falk; translated by E.V. Gordon. — Oxford: Clarendon Press, 1937. xix, 458 p., [38] leaves of plates: ill.; 23 cm. 1. Archaeology 2. Scandinavia — Antiquities. I. Falk, Hjalmar, 1859-1928. II. T.
DL21.S57   *LC* 38-8139

Jones, Gwyn, 1907-.   • **3.3354**
A history of the Vikings. — London; New York [etc.]: Oxford U.P., 1968. xvi, 504 p.: illus., maps, plates.; 23 cm. 1. Civilization, Scandinavian. 2. Vikings I. T.
DL31.J6   914.8/03/2   *LC* 68-124332

Olrik, Axel, 1864-1917.   • **3.3355**
Viking civilization / by Axel Olrik; revised after the author's death by Hans Ellekilde; [translation by Jacob Wittmer Hartmann and Hanna Astry Larsen]. — New York: American-Scandinavian Foundation, 1930. 246 p., [10] leaves of plates; 21 cm. — ([Scandinavian classics; 34]) Translation of Nordisk aandsliv i vikingetid og tidlig middelalder. 1. Civilization, Scandinavian. 2. Civilization, Medieval 3. Vikings I. Ellekilde, Hans Lavrida, 1891- II. T.
DL31.O53   *LC* 30-30010

DL43–85 HISTORY

Derry, T. K. (Thomas Kingston), 1905-.   **3.3356**
A history of Scandinavia: Norway, Sweden, Denmark, Finland, and Iceland / by T. K. Derry. — Minneapolis: University of Minnesota Press, 1979 (c1978). x, 447 p.: map; 25 cm. Includes index. 1. Scandinavia — History I. T.
DL46.D43   948   *LC* 78-14284   *ISBN* 0816608350

Kirchner, Walther.   • **3.3357**
The rise of the Baltic question. Westport, Conn., Greenwood Press [1970, c1954] xi, 283 p. 23 cm. 1. Baltic States — Politics and government. 2. Europe — Politics and government 3. Livonia — History I. T.
DL59.K5 1970   947.4   *LC* 77-100237   *ISBN* 0837130093

Brøndsted, Johannes, 1890-1965.   **3.3358**
The Vikings / Johannes Brøndsted; translated by Kalle Skov. — Harmondsworth: Penguin Books, c1965. 347 p., [24] p. of plates: ill.; 18 cm. — (Pelican books: A459) Pelican original. 1. Vikings I. T.
DL65 B7   *LC* 65-2868

Davidson, Hilda Roderick Ellis.   **3.3359**
The Viking road to Byzantium / H. R. Ellis Davidson. — London: G. Allen & Unwin, 1976. 341 p., [2] leaves of plates: ill.; 23 cm. Includes index. 1. Vikings 2. Byzantine Empire — History — 527-1081 I. T.
DL65.D35   948/.02   *LC* 76-363365   *ISBN* 0049400495

Foote, Peter Godfrey.   • **3.3360**
The Viking achievement; a survey of the society and culture of early medieval Scandinavia [by] Peter G. Foote [and] David M. Wilson. — New York, Praeger [1970] xxv, 473 p. illus. 25 cm. 1. Northmen I. Wilson, David McKenzie. joint author. II. T.
DL65.F6 1970   914.8/03/2   *LC* 75-108560

Ingstad, Helge, 1899-.   • **3.3361**
[Vesterveg til Vinland. English] Westward to Vinland; the discovery of pre-Columbian Norse house-sites in North America [by] Helge Ingstad. Translated from the Norwegian by Erik J. Friis. [1st American ed.] New York, St. Martin's Press [1969] 249 p. illus. 24 cm. Translation of Vesterveg til Vinland. 1. Vikings 2. America — Discovery and exploration — Norse I. T.
DL65.I513 1969   973.1/3   *LC* 67-10089

Klindt-Jensen, Ole.   • **3.3362**
[Vikingernes verden. English] The world of the Vikings. Illustrated by Svenolov Ehrén. Washington, R. B. Luce [1970] 238 p. illus. (part col.), maps (part col.) 28 cm. Translation of Vikingernes verden. 1. Vikings I. T.
DL65.K513   948/.03/1   *LC* 73-119528

Logan, F. Donald.   **3.3363**
The Vikings in history / F. Donald Logan. — Totowa, N.J.: Barnes & Noble Books, 1983. 224 p., [4] p. of plates: ill., maps; 23 cm. 1. Vikings I. T.
DL65.L63 1983   940/.04395 19   *LC* 82-25533   *ISBN* 038920384X

Sawyer, P. H.   • **3.3364**
The age of the Vikings [by] P. H. Sawyer. — 2d ed. — New York: St. Martin's Press, [1972, c1971] vi, 275 p.: illus.; 23 cm. 1. Vikings I. T.
DL65.S25 1972   948/.02   *LC* 79-185487

Sawyer, P. H.   **3.3365**
Kings and Vikings: Scandinavia and Europe, A.D. 700–1100 / P.H. Sawyer. — London; New York: Methuen, 1983 (c1982). x, 182 p., [16] p. of plates: ill.; 22 cm. Includes index. 1. Vikings 2. Christianity — Scandinavia. 3. Scandinavia — Civilization 4. Europe — History — 476-1492 I. T.
DL65.S254   940/.04395 19   *LC* 82-12539   *ISBN* 0416741800

DL101–291 DENMARK

Jones, W. Glyn.   • **3.3366**
Denmark, by W. Glyn Jones. — New York: Praeger, [1970] 256 p.: illus., facsims., fold. map, plates, ports.; 23 cm. — (Nations of the modern world.) 1. Denmark. I. T. II. Series.
DL109.J6 1970   948/.9   *LC* 77-109476

Lauring, Palle.   • **3.3367**
Land of the Tollund man; the prehistory and archaeology of Denmark. [1st English ed.] London, Lutterworth Press [1957] 160 p. illus., maps. 26 cm. 1. Denmark — Antiquities I. T.
DL121.L313   *LC* a 58-3946

Lauring, Palle.   • **3.3368**
A history of the kingdom of Denmark. Translated from the Danish by David Hohnen. Drawings by Vibeke Lind. — 3rd. ed. — Copenhagen: Høst, 1968. 274 p.: illus., 16 plates.; 24 cm. 1. Denmark — History I. T.
DL148.L353 1968   948/.9   *LC* 68-118267

Oakley, Stewart.   **3.3369**
A short history of Denmark. — New York: Praeger Publishers, [1972] 269 p.: illus.; 23 cm. 1. Denmark — History I. T.
DL148.O2 1972   948.9   *LC* 72-78337

Randsborg, Klavs.   **3.3370**
The Viking age in Denmark: the formation of a State / Klavs Randsborg. — New York: St. Martin's Press, 1980. vi, 206 p.: ill.; 26 cm. Includes indexes. 1. Northmen — Denmark. 2. Denmark — History — To 1241 I. T.
DL162.R36 1980   948.9/01   *LC* 80-12248   *ISBN* 0312846509

Larson, Laurence Marcellus, 1868-1938.   • **3.3371**
Canute the Great, 995 (circ)–1035, and the rise of Danish imperialism during the Viking Age. New York, AMS Press [1970] xviii, 375 p. illus., facsim., maps. 23 cm. (Heroes of the nations) Reprint of the 1912 ed. 1. Canute I, King of England, 995?-1035. I. T. II. Series.
DL165.L3 1970   948/.901/0924   *LC* 71-111764   *ISBN* 0404038794

West, John F. (John Frederick)   **3.3372**
Faroe: the emergence of a nation, by John F. West. — London: C. Hurst; New York: P. S. Eriksson, 1973 [c1972] viii, 312 p.: map.; 22 cm. 1. Faroe Islands. I. T.
DL271.F2 W43 1972   914.91/5/03   *LC* 77-151438   *ISBN* 0839720637

DL301–398 Iceland

Malmström, Vincent Herschel, 1926-.   • **3.3373**
A regional geography of Iceland / by Vincent H. Malmström. — Washington, D.C.: National Academy of Sciences - National Research Council, 1958. 255 p.: ill., cartes. (Publication - National Academy of Sciences-National Research Council; 584) (Report - Foreign Field Research Program; no.1) I. T.
DL305 M27   *LC* 58-60026

Gjerset, Knut, 1865-1936.   • **3.3374**
History of Iceland / by Knut Gjerset. — New York: Macmillan, 1924. v, 482 p.: col. ill.; 23 cm. 1. Iceland — History 2. Iceland — Civilization. I. T.
DL338.G5   *LC* 24-2336

Sigurður A. Magnússon.   **3.3375**
Northern sphinx: Iceland and the Icelanders from the settlement to the present / by Sigurdur A. Magnússon. — Montreal: McGill-Queen's University Press, 1977. viii, 261 p.; 23 cm. Includes index. 1. Iceland — History I. T.
DL338.S53   949.1/2   *LC* 77-370324   *ISBN* 0773502777

DL401–596 Norway

Popperwell, Ronald G.   • **3.3376**
Norway, by Ronald G. Popperwell. — New York: Praeger, [1972] 335 p.: illus.; 23 cm. — (Nations of the modern world.) 1. Norway — Civilization I. T. II. Series.
DL431.P66   914.81/03   *LC* 72-154357

Falnes, Oscar Julius, 1898-.   • **3.3377**
National romanticism in Norway, by Oscar J. Falnes. New York, AMS Press [1968] 398 p. 22 cm. (Studies in history, economics, and public law, no. 386) Reprint of the 1933 ed., which was issued also as thesis, Columbia, 1933. 1. Romanticism — Norway. 2. Historians — Norway. 3. Folk literature — Norway — History and criticism. 4. Norwegian language 5. Norway — Nationality. 6. Norway — Historiography. I. T.
DL441.F3 1968   320.1/58/09481   *LC* 68-54263

Derry, T. K. (Thomas Kingston), 1905-.   • **3.3378**
A short history of Norway / by T. K. Derry. — London: Allen & Unwin, 1957. 281 p.: maps (on lining papers).; 23 cm. 1. Norway — History I. T.
DL448.D4   948.1   *LC* 57-3947

Gjerset, Knut, 1865-1936.   • **3.3379**
History of the Norwegian people. — [1st AMS ed.]. — New York: AMS Press, [1969] 2 v. in 1.: illus., maps, ports.; 23 cm. Reprint of the 1932 ed. 1. Norway — History I. T.
DL449.G5 1969   914.81/03   *LC* 79-101272   *ISBN* 0404028187

Eckstein, Harry.   • **3.3380**
Division and cohesion in democracy; a study of Norway. Princeton, N.J., Princeton University Press, 1966. xvii, 293 p. 23 cm. 'Published for the Center of International Studies, Princeton University.' 1. Norway — Politics and government I. Woodrow Wilson School of Public and International Affairs. Center of International Studies. II. T.
DL458.E25   320.9481   *LC* 66-17700

Derry, T. K. (Thomas Kingston), 1905-.   **3.3381**
A history of modern Norway, 1814–1972 [by] T. K. Derry. [S.l.]: Oxford, 1973. 503 p.: ill., map. Includes index. 1. Norway — History — 1814-1905 2. Norway — History — 1905-. I. T.
DL506.D47   948.1/03   *LC* 73-168733   *ISBN* 0198225032

Hayes, Paul M.   **3.3382**
Quisling: the career and political ideas of Vidkun Quisling, 1887–1945 [by] Paul M. Hayes. — Bloomington: Indiana University Press, 1972. 368 p.: port.; 25 cm. 1. Quisling, Vidkun, 1887-1945. I. T.
DL529.Q5 H38 1972   948.1/04/0924 B   *LC* 78-184523   *ISBN* 0253347602

Greve, Tim, 1926-.   **3.3383**
Haakon VII of Norway: the man and the monarch / translated from the Norwegian and edited by Thomas Kingston Derry. — New York: Hippocrene Books, 1983. — x, 212 p.: ports. (The Library of Nordic literature; v 1) Translation of: Haakon VII: menneske og monark. Includes index. 1. Haakon VII, King of Norway, 1872-1957. 2. Norway — History — 1905- 3. Norway — Kings and rulers — Biography. I. Derry, T. K. (Thomas Kingston), 1905- II. T. III. Title: Haakon 7 of Norway.
DL530.G7313 1983   948.1/041/0924 B 19   *ISBN* 0882548123

DL601–876 Sweden

Roberts, Michael, 1908-.   • **3.3384**
Sweden as a great power, 1611–1697: government, society, foreign policy. Edited by Michael Roberts. New York, St. Martin's Press, 1968. vi, 182, [1] p. 21 cm. (Documents of modern history) 1. Sweden — History — 1523-1718 — Sources. I. T.
DL603.R6 1968b   948.5/02   *LC* 68-29381

Scobbie, Irene.   • **3.3385**
Sweden. — New York: Praeger, [1972] 254 p.: illus.; 23 cm. — (Nations of the modern world.) 1. Sweden. I. T. II. Series.
DL609.S37 1972   948.5   *LC* 72-78336

Moberg, Vilhelm, 1898-1973.   • **3.3386**
A history of the Swedish people. Translated from the Swedish by Paul Britten Austin. [1st American ed.] Pantheon [c1972-. v. map. Translation of Min svenska historia. 1. Sweden — History I. T.
DL648.M613   *LC* 72-3411   *ISBN* 0394481925

Roberts, Michael, 1908-.   • **3.3387**
Essays in Swedish history. Minneapolis, University of Minnesota Press [1967, c1966] ix, 358 p. 22 cm. 1. Sweden — History — Addresses, essays, lectures. I. T.
DL648.R6 1967b   948.5   *LC* 68-4928

Scott, Franklin Daniel, 1901-.   **3.3388**
Sweden: the nation's history / Franklin D. Scott. — Minneapolis: University of Minnesota Press, c1977. xviii, 654 p., [18] leaves of plates: ill.; 24 cm. 'Published in association with the American-Scandinavian Foundation.' 1. Sweden — History I. American-Scandinavian Foundation. II. T.
DL648.S36 1977   948.5   *LC* 76-51154   *ISBN* 0816608040

Roberts, Michael, 1908-.   • **3.3389**
The early Vasas: a history of Sweden 1523–1611. — Cambridge; London: Cambridge U.P., 1968. xiv, 509 p.: 5 plates, table, 3 maps, 5 ports.; 24 cm. 1. Vasa, House of. 2. Sweden — History — 1523-1654 I. T.
DL701.R6   948.5/02   *LC* 68-10332   *ISBN* 0521069300

Roberts, Michael, 1908-.   **3.3390**
The Swedish imperial experience, 1560–1718 / Michael Roberts. — Cambridge; New York: Cambridge University Press, 1979. x, 156 p.: maps; 24 cm. (Wiles lectures.) 1. Sweden — History — 1523-1718 — Addresses, essays, lectures. I. T. II. Series.
DL701.R63   948.5/02   *LC* 78-58799   *ISBN* 0521225027

Ahnlund, Nils, 1889-1957.   • **3.3391**
Gustav Adolf the great / by Nils Ahnlund; translated from the Swedish by Michael Roberts. — Princeton: Princeton University Press; New York:

American-Scandinavian Foundation, 1940. ix, 314 p.: ill., maps, ports.; 23 cm. 1. Gustaf II Adolf, King of Sweden, 1594-1632. 2. Sweden — History — 1523-1654 I. T.
DL706.A34   948.502

Roberts, Michael.   • 3.3392
Gustavus Adolphus: a history of Sweden, 1611–1632. London: Longmans, Green, 1953-58. 2 v.: ill. , 23 cm. 1. Sweden — History — Gustavus II Adolphus, 1611-1632 I. T.
DL706.R75   LC 53-2040

Roberts, Michael, 1908-.   3.3393
Gustavus Adolphus and the rise of Sweden. — London: English Universities Press, 1973. 207, [8] p.: illus., facsims., maps (on lining papers), ports.; 23 cm. Includes index. 1. Gustaf II Adolf, King of Sweden, 1594-1632. 2. Sweden — History — Gustavus II Adolphus, 1611-1632 I. T.
DL706.R76   948.5/02/0924   LC 73-174479   ISBN 0340124148

Hatton, Ragnhild Marie.   • 3.3394
Charles XII of Sweden [by] R. M. Hatton. New York, Weybright and Talley [1969, c1968] xvii, 656 p. illus., maps, plan, ports. 25 cm. 1. Charles XII, King of Sweden, 1682-1718. I. T.
DL732.H35 1969   948.5/03/0924 B   LC 69-10605

Carlgren, W. M.   3.3395
[Svensk utrikespolitik 1939-1945. English] Swedish foreign policy during the Second World War / W. M. Carlgren; translated by Arthur Spencer. — New

York: St. Martin's Press, 1977. ix, 257 p.: ill.; 23 cm. Translation of Svensk utrikespolitik 1939-1945. Includes index. 1. Sweden — Foreign relations — 1905-1950 I. T.
DL868.5.C2813 1977   327.485   LC 77-78681   ISBN 0312780583

DL971 Lapland

Bosi, Roberto, 1924-.   • 3.3396
The Lapps. [Translated by James Cadell] New York, Praeger [1960] 220 p. illus. 21 cm. (Ancient peoples and places, v. 17) Books that matter. Includes bibliography. 1. Lapps I. T.
DL971.L2B673   947.17   LC 60-15600

Collinder, Björn, 1894-.   • 3.3397
The Lapps. — New York: Greenwood Press, [1969, c1949] 252 p.: illus.; 23 cm. 1. Lapps I. T.
DL971.L2 C6 1969   914.71/7/03   LC 73-90490   ISBN 0837122139

DP1–402 SPAIN

Keefe, Eugene K. 3.3398
Area handbook for Spain / co–authors, Eugene K. Keefe ... [et al.]. — 1st ed. — Washington: For sale by the Supt. of Docs., U.S. Govt. Print. Off., 1976. xviii, 424 p.: ill.; 24 cm. 'DA Pam 550-179.' 'One of a series of handbooks prepared by Foreign Area Studies (FAS) of the American University.' Includes index. 1. Spain. I. American University (Washington, D.C.). Foreign Area Studies. II. T.
DP17.K35   946   *LC* 76-9820

Madariaga, Salvador de, 1886-. • 3.3399
Spain, a modern history. — New York: Praeger, [1958] 736 p.; 25 cm. — (Books that matter) 1. Spain. 2. Spain — History I. T.
DP26.M3 1958   946   *LC* 58-9695

Borrow, George Henry, 1803-1881. • 3.3400
The Bible in Spain; or, The journeys, adventures, and imprisonments of an Englishman, in an attempt to circulate the Scriptures in the peninsula, by George Borrow; edited, with an introduction and notes, by Peter Quennell. London, Macdonald [c1959] L, 586 p.: plates, ports.; 19 cm. First published in 1843. 1. Spain — Description & travel. I. T.
DP41.B7 1959

Brenan, Gerald. • 3.3401
The face of Spain. — New York, Grove Press [1957, c1956] 310 p. illus. 21 cm. — (An Evergreen book, E-51) 1. Spain — Descr. & trav. — 1951- I. T.
DP42.B7x   914.6   *LC* 57-5548

DP44–53 Civilization

Bennassar, Bartolomé. 3.3402
[Homme espagnol. English] The Spanish character: attitudes and mentalities from the sixteenth to the nineteenth century / by Bartolomé Bennassar; translated & with a pref. by Benjamin Keen. — Berkeley: University of California Press, 1979. xiii, 325 p.; 23 cm. Translation of L'homme espagnol. Includes index. 1. National characteristics, Spanish 2. Spain — Social life and customs I. T.
DP48.B4913   946   *LC* 76-55563

Castro, Américo, 1885-1972. 3.3403
The Spaniards; an introduction to their history. Translated by Willard F. King and Selma Margaretten. Berkeley, University of California Press, 1971. xii, 628 p. 24 cm. Based on the author's The structure of Spanish history, which was a rev. translation of España en su historia. 1. Spain — Civilization I. T.
DP48.C365 1971   914.6/03   *LC* 67-14000   *ISBN* 0520016173

Crow, John Armstrong. 3.3404
Spain: the root and the flower: a history of the civilization of Spain and of the Spanish people / by John A. Crow. — Rev. ed. — New York: Harper & Row, 1975. xii, 475 p., [8] leaves of plates: ill.; 22 cm. 1. National characteristics, Spanish 2. Spain — Civilization I. T.
DP48.C8 1975   946   *LC* 74-1802   *ISBN* 006010919X

Defourneaux, Marcelin. 3.3405
[Vie quotidienne en Espagne au siècle d'or. English] Daily life in Spain in the golden age. Translated by Newton Branch. New York, Praeger Publishers [1971, c1970] 256 p. illus. 23 cm. (Daily life series) Translation of La vie quotidienne en Espagne au siècle d'or. 1. Spain — Civilization — 1516-1700 2. Spain — Social life and customs I. T.
DP48.D3813 1971   914.6/03/5   *LC* 79-134523

Vicens Vives, Jaime. ed. • 3.3406
Historia social y económica de España y América. Barcelona, Editorial Teide [1957-59] 4 v. in 5. illus. (part col.) ports., maps, diagrs., facsims. 26 cm. 1. Spain — Civilization — History. 2. Latin America — Civilization — History. I. T.
DP48.V45   *LC* 58-19380

Díaz-Plaja, Fernando. • 3.3407
The Spaniard and the seven deadly sins. Translated from the Spanish by John Inderwick Palmer. New York, Scribner [1967] 223 p. map (on lining papers) 21 cm. Translation of El español y los siete pecados capitales. 1. Deadly sins. 2. National characteristics, Spanish I. T.
DP52.D513   *LC* 67-21337

Menéndez Pidal, Ramón, 1869-1968. • 3.3408
The Spaniards in their history. Translated and with an introduction. by Walter Starkie. New York, Norton, c1950. 251 p. ill. (The Norton library, N353) Translated from the introd. to the author's Historia de España. 1. National characteristics, Spanish 2. Spain — Civilization I. Starkie, Walter, 1894- II. T.
DP52.M4 1950a   946

DP56–271 History

Diccionario de historia de España / dirigido por Germán • 3.3409
Bleiberg.
2. ed., corr. y aum. Madrid: Ediciones de la Revista de Occidente, 1968-69. 3 v.: col. maps. 1. Spain — History — Dictionaries. I. Bleiberg, Germán, 1915- ed.
DP56.D5 1968   *LC* 73-367315

Nader, Helen, 1936-. 3.3410
The Mendoza family in the Spanish Renaissance, 1350 to 1550 / Helen Nader. — New Brunswick, N.J.: Rutgers University Press, c1979. xiv, 275 p.: genealogical table; 24 cm. Includes index. 1. Mendoza family 2. Renaissance — Spain. 3. Spain — Civilization — 711-1516 I. T.
DP60.M4 N3   946/.02/0922   *LC* 79-9945   *ISBN* 0813508762

Kamen, Henry Arthur Francis. 3.3411
A concise history of Spain [by] Henry Kamen. — New York: Scribner, [c1973] 191 p.: illus.; 25 cm. 1. Spain — History I. T.
DP66.K3 1973b   946   *LC* 74-982   *ISBN* 0684138506

Merriman, Roger Bigelow, 1876-1945. • 3.3412
The rise of the Spanish Empire in the Old World and in the New. — New York, Cooper Square Publishers, 1962 [c1918] 4 v. maps, facsim., geneal. tables (part fold.) 24 cm. Includes bibliographical references. 1. Spain — Hist. I. T.
DP66.M42   946   *LC* 61-13267

Payne, Stanley G. 3.3413
A history of Spain and Portugal [by] Stanley G. Payne. — [Madison]: University of Wisconsin Press, [1973] 2 v.: illus.; 23 cm. 1. Spain — History 2. Portugal — History I. T.
DP66.P382   946   *LC* 72-7992   *ISBN* 0299062708

Vicens Vives, Jaime. • 3.3414
[Aproximación a la historia de España. English] Approaches to the history of Spain. Translated and edited by Joan Connelly Ullman. Berkeley, University of California Press, 1967. xxviii, 189 p. illus., maps. 21 cm. Translation of Aproximación a la historia de España. 1. Spain — History I. T.
DP66.V513   946   *LC* 67-27127

Vilar, Pierre, 1906-. • 3.3415
[Histoire de l'Espagne. English] Spain; a brief history. Translated by Brian Tate. [1st ed.] Oxford, New York, Pergamon Press [1967] vii, 140 p. map. 20 cm. (Pergamon Oxford Spanish series) Commonwealth and international library. Translation of Histoire de l'Espagne. 1. Spain — History I. T.
DP68.V5513 1967   946   *LC* 67-26694

Ortega y Gasset, José, 1883-1955. • 3.3416
Invertebrate Spain, by José Ortega y Gasset; translation and foreword by Mildred Adams. New York, W. W. Norton & company, inc. [c1937] 212 p. 'The first three essays ... were taken from the volume whose Spanish title, España invertebrada, provided the subject as well as the title for this book. The others were chosen from other volumes of Señor Ortega's work because they shed added light on problems which he indicated in that famous analysis, or because they were pertinent to aspects of the present struggle.'—Foreword. 'First edition.' 1. Spain — Politics and government 2. Spain — Civilization I. Fenton, Mildred Adams, 1899- II. T.
DP84.O7   946   *LC* 37-27312

DP91–271 By Period

DP91–96 To 711

Livermore, H. V., 1914-.   3.3417
The origins of Spain and Portugal, by H. V. Livermore. — [S.l.]: Humanities, 1973 (c1971) 3-438, [13] p.: illus., maps.; 23 cm. 1. Spain — History — To 711 2. Portugal — History — To 1385 I. T.
DP91.L58   946/.01   LC 72-176308   ISBN 0049460036

O'Callaghan, Joseph F.   3.3418
A history of medieval Spain / Joseph F. O'Callaghan. — Ithaca: Cornell University Press, 1975. 729 p., [4] leaves of plates: ill.; 24 cm. Includes index. 1. Spain — History — Gothic period, 414-711 2. Spain — History — 711-1516 3. Portugal — History — To 1385 4. Portugal — History — Period of discoveries, 1385-1580 I. T.
DP96.O25   946/.02   LC 74-7698   ISBN 0801408806

Thompson, E. A.   • 3.3419
The Goths in Spain, by E. A. Thompson. — Oxford: Clarendon P., 1969. xiv, 358 p.; 23 cm. 1. Visigoths — Spain 2. Spain — History — Gothic period, 414-711 I. T.
DP96.T48   946/.01   LC 78-399622   ISBN 0198142714

Visigothic Spain: new approaches / edited by Edward James.   3.3420
Oxford: Clarendon Press; New York: Oxford University Press, 1980. xiii, 303 p. [1] leaf of plates: facsims.; 23 cm. 1. Spain — History — Gothic period, 414-711 — Addresses, essays, lectures. I. James, Edward, 1947-
DP96.V57   946/.01   LC 79-40337   ISBN 0198225431

DP98–160 Moorish Domination. Reconquest (711–1516)

Glick, Thomas F.   3.3421
Islamic and Christian Spain in the early Middle Ages / by Thomas F. Glick. — Princeton, N.J.: Princeton University Press, c1979. xi, 376 p.: ill.; 25 cm. Includes index. 1. Spain — Civilization — 711-1492. I. T.
DP99.G47   946   LC 78-70296   ISBN 0691052743

Hillgarth, J. N.   3.3422
The Spanish kingdoms, 1250–1516 / by J. N. Hillgarth. — Oxford: Clarendon Press, 1976-1978. 2 v.: maps; 23 cm. Includes index. 1. Spain — History — 711-1516. I. T.
DP99.H54   946/.02   LC 76-364728   ISBN 019822530X

Jackson, Gabriel.   • 3.3423
The making of Medieval Spain. — [1st American ed. — New York]: Harcourt Brace Jovanovich, [1972] 216 p.: illus. (part col.); 21 cm. — (History of European civilization library) 1. Spain — History — 711-1516 I. T.
DP99.J32 1972b   946/.02   LC 73-151307   ISBN 0151559759

Lévi-Provençal, Évariste, 1894-1956.   • 3.3424
Histoire de l'Espagne musulmane / [a]E. Levi–Provençal. — Nouvelle éd. rev. et augm. — Paris: G.-P. Maisonneuve, 1950-. v.: ill., maps, geneal. tables; 24 cm. Tome 3 has imprint: Paris: G.-P. Maisonneuve & Larose, 1967. 1. Arabs in Spain. 2. Spain — History — 711-1516 I. T.
DP99.L55   LC a51-4381

Lomax, Derek W.   3.3425
The reconquest of Spain / Derek W. Lomax. — London; New York: Longman, 1978. xii, 212 p.: ill.; 23 cm. 1. Spain — History — 711-1516 I. T.
DP99.L69   946/.02   LC 77-3030   ISBN 0582502098

MacKay, Angus, 1939-.   3.3426
Spain in the Middle Ages: from frontier to empire, 1000–1500 / Angus MacKay. — New York: St. Martin's Press, 1977. xii, 245 p., [3] leaves of plates: ill.; 23 cm. — (New studies in medieval history) Includes index. 1. Spain — History — 711-1516 I. T.
DP99.M23 1977   946/.02   LC 76-52257   ISBN 0312749783

Menéndez Pidal, Ramón, 1869-1968.   3.3427
[España del Cid. English] The Cid and his Spain. Translated by Harold Sunderland. With a foreword by the Duke of Berwick and Alba. [London] F. Cass [1971] xiv, 474 p. illus. 23 cm. Distributed in the U.S. by International Book Services, Inc., Beaverton, Or. Reprint of the 1934 ed. Translation of La España del Cid. 1. El Cid Campeador. 2. Spain — History — 711-1516 I. T.
DP99.M43 1971   946/.02/0924 B   LC 75-171817   ISBN 0714615080

Watt, W. Montgomery (William Montgomery)   • 3.3428
A history of Islamic Spain [by] W. Montgomery Watt, with additional sections on literature by Pierre Cachia. — Edinburgh, Edinburgh U. P. [1965] xi, 210 p. 16 plates, 2 maps. 21 cm. — (Islamic surveys, 4) I. T.
DP99.W2x   946.02   LC 66-2646

The Worlds of Alfonso the Learned and James the Conqueror: 3.3429
intellect & force in the Middle Ages / Robert I. Burns, editor.
Princeton, N.J.: Princeton University Press, c1985. xxv, 232 p.: ill.; 22 cm. 'Published under the auspices of the Center for Medieval and Renaissance Studies, University of California, Los Angeles.' Includes index. 1. Alfonso X, King of Castile and Leon, 1221-1284. 2. James I, King of Aragon, 1208-1276. 3. Spain — History — 711-1516 I. Burns, Robert Ignatius. II. University of California, Los Angeles. Center for Medieval and Renaissance Studies.
DP99.W67 1985   946/.02/0922 19   LC 85-42678   ISBN 0691054517

Lane-Poole, Stanley, 1854-1931.   • 3.3430
[Story of the Moors in Spain] The Moors in Spain. With the collaboration of Arthur Gilman. Beirut, Khayats, 1967. xx, 285 p. illus., maps. 20 cm. (Khayats oriental reprint no. 23) Previous ed., 1886, has title: The story of the Moors in Spain. 1. Muslims — Spain — History — 711-1516. 2. Spain — History — 711-1516 I. Gilman, Arthur, 1837-1909. II. T.
DP102.L3 1967   914.6/03/2   LC 67-9727

Read, Jan.   3.3431
The Moors in Spain and Portugal / Jan Read. — Totowa, N.J.: Rowman and Littlefield, 1975. 268 p., [8] leaves of plates: ill.; 23 cm. Includes index. 1. Muslims — Spain — History — 711-1492. 2. Spain — History — 711-1516 3. Portugal — History — To 1385 I. T.
DP102.R4 1975   946/.02   LC 75-312213   ISBN 0874716446

Chejne, Anwar G.   3.3432
Muslim Spain, its history and culture [by] Anwar G. Chejne. Minneapolis, University of Minnesota Press [1974] xvi, 559 p. illus. 24 cm. 1. Muslims — Spain — History — 711-1492. 2. Spain — Civilization — 711-1516 I. T.
DP103.C46   946/.02   LC 73-87254   ISBN 0816606889

Procter, Evelyn Emma Stefanos, 1897-.   • 3.3433
Alfonso X of Castile; patron of literature and learning; being the Norman Maccoll Lectures delivered in the University of Cambridge in Lent term, 1949. Oxford, Clarendon Press, 1951. vi, 149 p. 1. Alfonso X, King of Castile, 1221-1284 2. Learning and scholarship I. T.
DP140.3.Px

DP161–232 Modern, 1459/1516–1885

Kagan, Richard L., 1943-.   3.3434
Lawsuits and litigants in Castile, 1500–1700 / Richard L. Kagan. — Chapel Hill: University of North Carolina Press, c1981. xxiv, 274 p.: ill.; 24 cm. Includes index. 1. Law — Spain — Castile — History and criticism. 2. Justice, Administration of — Spain — Castile — History. I. T.
DP161.K2x   347.46/3   LC 80-17565   ISBN 0807814571

Kamen, Henry Arthur Francis.   3.3435
Spain, 1469–1714: a society of conflict / Henry Kamen. — London; New York: Longman, 1983. xiv, 305 p.: ill., maps; 22 cm. Includes index. 1. Spain — History — Ferdinand and Isabella, 1479-1516 2. Spain — History — House of Austria, 1516-1700 3. Spain — History — Philip V, 1700-1746 I. T.
DP161.K35 1983   946 19   LC 82-23978   ISBN 0582492262

Prescott, William Hickling, 1796-1859.   • 3.3436
History of the reign of Ferdinand and Isabella, the Catholic / Abridged and edited by C. Harvey Gardiner. Carbondale, Ill.: Southern Illinois University Press, 1962. 303 p.: illus.; 23 cm. 1. Ferdinand V, King of Spain, 1452-1516. 2. Isabella I, Queen of Spain, 1451-1504. 3. Spain — History — Ferdinand and Isabella, 1479-1516 I. T.
DP162.P8 1962a   LC 62-16246

Domínguez Ortiz, Antonio.   • 3.3437
The golden age of Spain, 1516-1659. Translated by James Casey. — New York: Basic Books, [1971] 361 p.: map; 22 cm. — (The History of Spain) 1. Spain — History — House of Austria, 1516-1700 2. Spain — Civilization — 1516-1700 I. T.
DP171.D6513   914.6/03/4   LC 70-167765

Elliott, John Huxtable.   • 3.3438
Imperial Spain, 1469–1716. — New York: St. Martin's Press, [1964, c1963] 411 p.: 22 plates (incl. ports., facsims.) maps, diagrs., geneal. tables.; 22 cm. 1. Spain — History — House of Austria, 1516-1700 2. Spain — History — Ferdinand and Isabella, 1479-1516 I. T.
DP171.E4 1964   946.04   LC 64-13365

Lynch, John, 1927-.   3.3439
Spain under the Habsburgs / John Lynch. — 2nd ed. — New York: New York University Press, 1981. 2 v.: ill.; 22 cm. 1. Spain — History — House of Austria, 1516-1700 I. T.
DP171.L92 1981   946/.04 19   *LC* 81-11064   *ISBN* 0814750028

Stradling, R. A.   3.3440
Europe and the decline of Spain: a study of the Spanish system, 1580–1720 / R.A. Stradling. — London; Boston: Allen & Unwin, 1981. 222 p.; 23 cm. — (Early modern Europe today.) 1. Spain — History — House of Austria, 1516-1700 I. T. II. Series.
DP171.S7   946/.05 19   *LC* 81-189695   *ISBN* 0049400614

Haliczer, Stephen, 1942-.   3.3441
The Comuneros of Castile: the forging of a revolution, 1475–1521 / Stephen Haliczer. — Madison, Wis.: University of Wisconsin Press, 1981. ix, 305 p.: map; 24 cm. Includes index. 1. Spain — History — Charles I, 1516-1556 2. Spain — History — Ferdinand and Isabella, 1479-1516 3. Castile (Spain) — History — Uprising, 1520-1521 I. T.
DP174.H34   946/.04 19   *LC* 80-52294   *ISBN* 0299085007

Parker, Geoffrey, 1943-.   3.3442
Philip II / by Geoffrey Parker. — 1st ed. — Boston: Little, Brown, c1978. xix, 234 p.: ill.; 21 cm. (The Library of world biography) 1. Philip II, King of Spain, 1527-1598 2. Spain — History — Philip II, 1556-1598 3. Spain — Kings and rulers — Biography. I. T.
DP178.P37   946/.04/0924 B 19   *LC* 78-17122   *ISBN* 0316690805

Pierson, Peter.   3.3443
Philip II of Spain / Peter Pierson. — London: Thames and Hudson, 1975. 240 p., [8] leaves of plates; 23 cm. — (Men in office) 1. Philip II, King of Spain, 1527-1598 2. Spain — History — Philip II, 1556-1598 I. T.
DP178.P64   946/.04/0924 B   *LC* 76-351952   *ISBN* 0500870039

Maltby, William S., 1940-.   3.3444
Alba: a biography of Fernando Alvarez de Toledo, third duke of Alba, 1507–1582 / William S. Maltby. — Berkeley: University of California Press, c1983. xvii, 377 p., [8] leaves of plates: ill.; 24 cm. 1. Alba, Fernando Alvarez de Toledo, duque de, 1507-1582. 2. Statesmen — Spain — Biography. 3. Spain — Nobility — Biography. I. T.
DP181.A6 M34 1983   946/.04/0924 B 19   *LC* 82-8537   *ISBN* 0520046943

Brown, Jonathan.   3.3445
A palace for a king: the Buen Retiro and the court of Philip IV / Jonathan Brown and John H. Elliott. — New Haven: Yale University Press, 1980. 296 p. Includes index. 1. Philip IV, King of Spain, 1605-1665 — Art patronage. 2. Olivares, Gaspar de Guzmén, conde-duque de, 1587-1645. 3. Madrid. Buen Retiro. I. Elliott, John Huxtable. joint author. II. T.
DP185.B76   946/.052/0924   *LC* 80-13659   *ISBN* 0300025076

Kamen, Henry Arthur Francis.   3.3446
Spain in the later seventeenth century, 1665–1700 / Henry Kamen. — London; New York: Longman, 1980. xiii, 418 p.: ill.; 24 cm. Includes index. 1. Spain — History — Charles II, 1665-1700 I. T.
DP186.K35   946/.053   *LC* 79-42884   *ISBN* 0582490367

Herr, Richard.   • 3.3447
The eighteenth-century revolution in Spain. — Princeton, N.J.: Princeton University Press, 1958. 484 p.: illus.; 22 cm. 1. Enlightenment 2. Spain — History — Bourbons, 1700- 3. Spain — Intellectual life — 18th century I. T.
DP192.H4   946.054   *LC* 58-7126

Carr, Raymond.   • 3.3448
Spain, 1808–1939 / by Raymond Carr. — Oxford: Clarendon Press, 1966. xxix, 766 p., [4] leaves of plates: ill., maps. — (Oxford history of modern Europe.) 1. Spain — Politics and government — 19th century 2. Spain — Politics and government — 20th century 3. Spain — Social conditions I. T. II. Series.
DP203.C3   *LC* 66-72222   *ISBN* 0198221029

Marx, Karl, 1818-1883.   • 3.3449
Revolution in Spain, by Karl Marx and Frederick Engels. New York, International Publishers [c1939] 255 p. 22 cm. (Marxist Library; works of Marxism-Leninism, v. 12) 1. Revolutions 2. Spain — History — 19th century 3. Spain — History, Military 4. Spain — Social conditions I. Engels, Friedrich, 1820-1895. II. T.
DP203.M35   946.07   *LC* 39-12572

Lovett, Gabriel H.   • 3.3450
Napoleon and the birth of modern Spain, by Gabriel H. Lovett. — [New York]: New York University Press, 1965. 2 v. (vii, 884 p.): map; 25 cm. 1. Spain — History — Napoleonic Conquest, 1808-1813 I. T.
DP205.L65   946.06   *LC* 65-11764

Coverdale, John F., 1940-.   3.3451
The Basque phase of Spain's first Carlist war / John F. Coverdale. — Princeton, N.J.: Princeton University Press, c1984. ix, 332 p.: ill.; 25 cm. Includes index. 1. Carlists 2. Spain — History — Carlist War, 1833-1840 3. País Vasco (Spain) — History I. T.
DP219.2.C68 1984   946/.07 19   *LC* 83-43068   *ISBN* 0691054118

DP233–271 20th Century

Brenan, Gerald.   • 3.3452
The Spanish labyrinth; an account of the social and political background of the Civil War. [2d ed.] Cambridge [Eng.] University Press, 1950. xx, 384 p. maps. 23 cm. 1. Spain — Politics and government — 1886-1931 2. Spain — Politics and government — 1931-1939 3. Spain — Social conditions — 1886-1939 I. T.
DP233.B7 1950   946.08   *LC* 51-3672

Carr, Raymond.   3.3453
Modern Spain, 1875–1980 / Raymond Carr. — Oxford; New York: Oxford University Press, 1981 (c1980). xvii, 201 p., [1] leaf of plates: 1 map; 21 cm. — (OPUS) Includes index. 1. Spain — Politics and government — 20th century 2. Spain — Politics and government — 19th century I. T. II. Series.
DP233.C37   946.08 19   *LC* 80-40638   0192191578

Spain in the twentieth–century world: essays on Spanish   3.3454
diplomacy, 1898–1978 / edited by James W. Cortada.
Westport, Conn.: Greenwood Press, 1980, c1979. xiii, 294 p.; 23 cm. — (Contributions in political science. no. 30 0147-1066) Includes index. 1. Spain — Foreign relations — 20th century — Addresses, essays, lectures. I. Cortada, James W. II. Series.
DP233.8.S65 1980   327.46   *LC* 78-75257   *ISBN* 0313213267

Barea, Arturo, 1897-1957.   3.3455
The forging of a rebel. Translated by Ilsa Barea. — New York: Viking Press, 1974. xiv, 751 p.; 25 cm. 'A Richard Seaver book.' 1. Barea, Arturo, 1897-1957. 2. Rif Revolt, 1921-1926 3. Spain — Social life and customs 4. Spain — History — Civil War, 1936-1939 — Personal narratives I. T.
DP236.B3 A213 1972b   914.6/03/80924 B   *LC* 73-17675

Ben-Ami, Shlomo.   3.3456
Fascism from above: the dictatorship of Primo de Rivera in Spain, 1923–1930 / Shlomo Ben–Ami. — Oxford: Clarendon Press; New York: Oxford University Press, 1983. xiv, 454 p.; 23 cm. Includes index. 1. Primo de Rivera, Miguel, 1870-1930. 2. Spain — Politics and government — 1886-1931 I. T.
DP247.B38 1983   946.08 19   *LC* 84-127660   *ISBN* 0198225962

Ben-Ami, Shlomo.   3.3457
The origins of the Second Republic in Spain / by Shlomo Ben–Ami. — Oxford; New York: Oxford University Press, 1978. xii, 356 p.; 23 cm. — (Oxford historical monographs) Includes index. 1. Republicanism in Spain. 2. Spain — Politics and government — 1923-1930 3. Spain — Politics and government — 1931-1939 I. T.
DP247.B39   320.9/46/08   *LC* 78-40079   *ISBN* 0198218710

Jackson, Gabriel.   • 3.3458
The Spanish Republic and the Civil War, 1931–1939. — Princeton, N.J.: Princeton University Press, 1965. xiii, 578 p.: illus., maps; 22 cm. 1. Spain — History — Republic, 1931-1939 I. T.
DP254.J3   946.081   *LC* 65-10826

Preston, Paul, 1946-.   3.3459
The coming of the Spanish Civil War: reform, reaction, and revolution in the Second Republic, 1931–1936 / Paul Preston. — New York: Barnes & Noble Books, 1978. xiv, 264 p.; 22 cm. Based on the author's doctoral thesis. Includes index. 1. Socialism — Spain — History — 20th century. 2. Right and left (Political science) 3. Spain — Politics and government — 1931-1939 4. Spain — Social conditions — 1886-1939 5. Spain — History — Civil War, 1936-1939 — Causes I. T.
DP255.P73 1978   946.081   *LC* 78-6002   *ISBN* 0064957128

Carr, Raymond.   • 3.3460
The Republic and the Civil War in Spain; edited by Raymond Carr. — London: Macmillan; New York: St. Martin's Press, 1971. x, 275 p.; 23 cm. — (Problems in focus series) 1. Spain — Politics and government — 1931-1939 2. Spain — History — Civil War, 1936-1939 I. T.
DP257.C295 1971   946.081   *LC* 79-148464   *ISBN* 0333006321

Payne, Stanley G.   • 3.3461
Falange; a history of Spanish fascism. — Stanford, Calif., Stanford University Press, 1961. ix, 316 p. 23 cm. — (Stanford studies in history, economics, and political science, 22) Bibliography: p. [299]-307. 1. Fascism — Spain. 2. Spain — Pol. & govt. — 1931-1939. 3. Spain — Pol. & govt. — 1939- I. T. II. Series.
DP257.P34   946.081   *LC* 61-12391

Payne, Stanley G.   • 3.3462
The Spanish Revolution [by] Stanley G. Payne. — [1st ed.]. — New York:
Norton, [1970] xvi, 398 p.: maps.; 21 cm. — (Revolutions in the modern world)
1. Spain — History — 20th century 2. Spain — History — Civil War,
1936-1939 — Causes I. T.
DP257.P35 1970   946.081   LC 73-78891

Revolution and war in Spain, 1931–1939 / edited by Paul   3.3463
Preston.
London; New York: Methuen, 1985 (c1984). xi, 299 p., [1] leaf of plates: map;
23 cm. 1. Spain — History — Civil War, 1936-1939 — Causes — Addresses,
essays, lectures. 2. Spain — Politics and government — 1931-1939 —
Addresses, essays, lectures. I. Preston, Paul, 1946-
DP257.R38   946.081 19   LC 84-1070   ISBN 0416349609

DP269 CIVIL WAR (1936–1939)

Borkenau, Franz, 1900-1957.   • 3.3464
The Spanish cockpit; an eyewitness account of the political and social conflicts
of the Spanish Civil War. Foreword by Gerald Brenan. — [Ann Arbor]
University of Michigan Press [1963,c1937] xi, 303 p. 21 cm. 1. Spain — Hist.
— Civil War, 1936-1939. 2. Spain — Pol. & govt. — 1931-1939. I. T.
DP269.B66 1963   946.081   LC 63-23723

Fraser, Ronald, 1930-.   3.3465
Blood of Spain: an oral history of the Spanish Civil War / Ronald Fraser. — 1st
American ed. — New York: Pantheon Books, 1980 (c1979). 628 p.: maps; 24
cm. Includes indexes. 1. Oral history 2. Spain — History — Civil War,
1936-1939 — Personal narratives I. T.
DP269.F73   946.081   LC 78-20416   ISBN 0394489829

Historical dictionary of the Spanish Civil War, 1936–1939 /   3.3466
edited by James W. Cortada.
Westport, Conn.: Greenwood Press, 1982. xxviii, 571 p.: maps; 29 cm. Includes
index. 1. Spain — History — Civil War, 1936-1939 — Dictionaries.
I. Cortada, James W.
DP269.H54 1982   946.081/03/21 19   LC 81-13424   ISBN
0313220549

Jackson, Gabriel.   3.3467
A concise history of the Spanish Civil War. [1st American ed.] New York, John
Day Co. [1974] 192 p. illus. 25 cm. 1. Spain — History — Civil War, 1936-1939
I. T. II. Title: Spanish Civil War.
DP269.J16 1974   946.081   LC 73-16599   ISBN 0381982610

Jackson, Gabriel. comp.   3.3468
The Spanish Civil War. Edited with an introd. by Gabriel Jackson. — Chicago:
Quadrangle Books, [1972] vii, 212 p.; 22 cm. Articles and news reports from the
New York Times. 'A New York Times book.' 1. Spain — History — Civil War,
1936-1939 I. T.
DP269.J17   946.081   LC 78-182510   ISBN 0812902475

Thomas, Hugh, 1931-.   3.3469
The Spanish Civil War / Hugh Thomas. Rev. and enl. ed. — New York: Harper
& Row, c1977. xx, 1115 p., [8] leaves of plates: ill.; 25 cm. Includes index.
1. Spain — History — Civil War, 1936-1939 I. T.
DP269.T46 1977   946.081   LC 76-5531   ISBN 0060142782

Southworth, Herbert Rutledge.   3.3470
Guernica! Guernica!: A study of journalism, diplomacy, propaganda, and
history / Herbert Rutledge Southworth. — Berkeley: University of California
Press, c1977. xxvi, 537 p.; 25 cm. Includes index. 1. Guernica (Spain) —
Bombardment, 1937. 2. Spain — History — Civil War, 1936-1939 —
Journalism, Military. 3. Spain — History — Civil War, 1936-1939 —
Diplomatic history. 4. Spain — History — Civil War, 1936-1939 —
Propaganda.
DP269.27.G8 S69   946.081   LC 74-82850   ISBN 0520028309

Legarreta, Dorothy, 1926-.   3.3471
The Guernica generation: Basque refugee children of the Spanish Civil War /
Dorothy Legarreta. — Reno, Nev.: University of Nevada Press, 1984. xiv,
396 p., [17] p. of plates: ill.; 23 cm. (Basque series.) Includes index. 1. Children
— Spain — País Vasco — History — 20th century. 2. Spain — History — Civil
War, 1936-1939 — Children — Spain — País Vasco. 3. Spain — History —
Civil War, 1936-1939 — Evacuation of civilians — Spain — País Vasco. 4. País
Vasco (Spain) — History I. T. II. Series.
DP269.8.C4 L44 1984   946.081 19   LC 84-13136   ISBN
0874170885

Orwell, George, 1903-1950.   • 3.3472
Homage to Catalonia. — [1st American ed.]. — New York: Harcourt, Brace,
[1952] xxiii, 232 p.; 21 cm. — (A harvest book) 1. Spain — History — Civil
War, 1936-1939 — Personal narratives 2. Spain — Politics and government —
1931-1939 I. T.
DP269.9.O7 1952   946.081*   LC 52-6442

DP270 1939–

Carr, Raymond.   3.3473
Spain, dictatorship to democracy / Raymond Carr and Juan Pablo Fusi
Aizpurua. — London; Boston: G. Allen & Unwin, 1979. xxi, 282 p.; 23 cm.
1. Spain — History — 1939-1975 2. Spain — History — 1975- I. Fusi
Aizpurúa, Juan Pablo, 1945- joint author. II. T.
DP270.C258   946.082   LC 78-41081   ISBN 0049460129

Preston, Paul, 1946-.   3.3474
Spain in crisis: the evolution and decline of the Franco régime / editor Paul
Preston. New York: Barnes & Noble Books, c1976. 341 p.; 23 cm. 1. Spain —
History — 1939-1975 I. T.
DP270.S624 1976b   946.082   LC 76-375103   ISBN 006495711X

Gilmour, David, 1952-.   3.3475
The transformation of Spain: from Franco to the constitutional monarchy /
David Gilmour. — London; New York: Quartet Books, 1985. xi, 322 p.; 24 cm.
Includes index. 1. Spain — History — 1975- 2. Spain — History — 1939-1975
I. T.
DP272.G545 1985   946.083 19   LC 85-118311   ISBN 070432461X

The New Mediterranean democracies: regime transition in   3.3476
Spain, Greece, and Portugal / edited by Geoffrey Pridham.
London; Totowa, NJ: Frank Cass, 1984. viii, 193 p.: ill.; 23 cm. 'First appeared
in a special issue ... of West European politics, vol. 7, no. 2'—Verso of t.p.
1. Spain — Politics and government — 1975- — Addresses, essays, lectures.
2. Greece — Politics and government — 1974- — Addresses, essays, lectures.
3. Portugal — Politics and government — 1974- — Addresses, essays, lectures.
I. Pridham, Geoffrey, 1942-
DP272.N48 1984   946.083 19   LC 85-115098   ISBN 0714632449

Politics and change in Spain / edited by Thomas D. Lancaster,   3.3477
Gary Prevost.
New York: Praeger, 1985. xiv, 224 p.: ill. Includes index. 1. Political
participation — Spain — Addresses, essays, lectures. 2. Spain — Politics and
government — 1975- — Addresses, essays, lectures. I. Lancaster, Thomas D.
II. Prevost, Gary.
DP272.P65 1985   320.946 19   LC 84-18107   ISBN 0030009375

DP285–402 Local History

Laxalt, Robert, 1923-.   3.3478
In a hundred graves; a Basque portrait. Reno, University of Nevada Press,
1972. 146 p. 23 cm. (The Basque series) Autobiographical. 1. Laxalt, Robert,
1923- 2. País Vasco (Spain) — Social life and customs. I. T.
DP302.B467 L38   914.6/6   LC 72-86404   ISBN 0874170354

Basque politics: a case study in ethnic nationalism / edited by   3.3479
William A. Douglass.
[Tarrytown, N.Y.]: Associated Faculty Press; Reno, Nev.: Basque Studies
Program, University of Nevada, c1985. 334 p.; 23 cm. (Basque Studies Program
occasional papers series. no. 2) 1. Nationalism — Spain — País Vasco —
Addresses, essays, lectures. 2. Nationalism — France — Pays Basque —
Addresses, essays, lectures. 3. País Vasco (Spain) — Politics and government
— Addresses, essays, lectures. 4. Pays Basque (France) — Politics and
government — Addresses, essays, lectures. I. Douglass, William A. II. Series.
DP302.B47 B37 1985   320.946/6 19   LC 85-8596   ISBN
0804693986

Collins, Roger.   3.3480
The Basques / Roger Collins. — Oxford, UK; New York, NY, USA: Blackwell,
1986. xiii, 272 p.: ill.; 24 cm. — (Peoples of Europe.) 1. Basques — History.
2. País Vasco (Spain) — History 3. Pays Basque (France) — History. I. T.
II. Series.
DP302.B49 C65 1986   946/.6 19   LC 86-8285   ISBN 0631134786

Clark, Robert P.   3.3481
The Basque insurgents: ETA, 1952–1980 / Robert P. Clark. — Madison, Wis.:
University of Wisconsin Press, 1984. xx, 328 p.: ill.; 24 cm. 1. ETA
(Organization) — History. 2. Insurgency — Spain — History — 20th century.
3. País Vasco (Spain) — Politics and government — 20th century I. T.
DP302.B53 C54 1984   946/.6 19   LC 83-40259   ISBN 0299096505

Clark, Robert P.   3.3482
The Basques, the Franco years and beyond / Robert P. Clark. — Reno, Nev.:
University of Nevada Press, 1980 (c1979). xvii, 434 p.: maps; 23 cm. — (Basque
series) 1. Nationalism — Spain — País Vasco. 2. País Vasco (Spain) — History
— Autonomy and independence movements. I. T.
DP302.B53 C55   946/.004/9992   LC 79-24926   ISBN 0874170575

Payne, Stanley G.   **3.3483**
Basque nationalism / Stanley G. Payne. — Reno: University of Nevada Press, 1975. xii, 291 p., [8] leaves of plates: ill.; 22 cm. — (The Basque series) Includes index. 1. National liberation movements — Spain — País Vasco. 2. País Vasco (Spain) — History — Autonomy and independence movements. I. T.
DP302.B53 P38   946/.6   *LC* 75-15698   *ISBN* 0874170427

Fernández-Armesto, Felipe.   **3.3484**
The Canary Islands after the conquest: the making of a colonial society in the early sixteenth century / Felipe Fernández-Armesto. — Oxford: Clarendon Press; New York: Oxford University Press, 1982. ix, 244 p.: maps; 22 cm. — (Oxford historical monographs.) Includes index. 1. Canary Islands — History. I. T.
DP302.C42 F47 1982   964/.907 19   *LC* 81-14204   *ISBN* 0198218885

Read, Jan.   **3.3485**
The Catalans / Jan Read. — London: Faber and Faber, 1979 (c1978). 223 p.: ill.; 23 cm. 1. Catalonia (Spain) — History. I. T.
DP302.C62 R42   *ISBN* 0571109691

Elliott, John Huxtable.   • **3.3486**
The revolt of the Catalans, a study in the decline of Spain, 1598–1640. — Cambridge [Eng.] University Press, 1963. xvi, 623 p. illus., ports., fold. maps. 24 cm. 'Sources': p. 579-594. 1. Olivares, Gaspar de Guzmán, conde-duque de, 1587-1645. 2. Catalonia — Hist. 3. Spain — Hist. — Philip IV, 1621-1665. 4. Spain — Hist. — Philip III, 1598-1621. I. T.
DP302.C66E4   946.7   *LC* 63-3426

Bard, Rachel, 1921-.   **3.3487**
Navarra, the durable kingdom / Rachel Bard. — Reno, Nev.: University of Nevada Press, 1982. xiii, 254 p.: ill.; 23 cm. — (Basque series.) Includes index. 1. Navarre (Spain) — History. I. T. II. Series.
DP302.N27 B37 1982   946/.52 19   *LC* 82-8660   *ISBN* 0874170737

Burns, Robert Ignatius.   • **3.3488**
The crusader kingdom of Valencia; reconstruction on a thirteenth-century frontier. Cambridge, Harvard University Press, 1967. 2 v. (xviii, 561 p.) illus., maps. 24 cm. 1. Valencia (Kingdom) — History. 2. Valencia (Kingdom) — Church history. I. T.
DP302.V205 B8   946/.76/02   *LC* 67-10902

Burns, Robert Ignatius.   **3.3489**
Islam under the crusaders, colonial survival in the thirteenth-century Kingdom of Valencia by Robert I. Burns. — Princeton, N.J., Princeton University Press 1974 (c1973). xxxi, 475 p. illus. 25 cm. 1. James I, King of Aragon, 1208-1276. 2. Pedro III, King of Aragon, 1239-1285. 3. Mudéjares 4. Crusades 5. Valencia (Kingdom) — History. I. T.
DP302.V205 B83   946/.76   *LC* 72-4039   *ISBN* 0691052077

Burns, Robert Ignatius.   **3.3490**
Muslims, Christians, and Jews in the crusader kingdom of Valencia: societies in symbiosis / Robert I. Burns. — Cambridge [Cambridgeshire]; New York: Cambridge University Press, 1984. xx, 363 p.: ill.; 24 cm. — (Cambridge Iberian and Latin American studies.) Includes index. 1. Muslims — Spain — Valencia (Region) — Addresses, essays, lectures. 2. Christians — Spain — Valencia (Region) — Addresses, essays, lectures. 3. Jews — Spain — Valencia (Region) — Addresses, essays, lectures. 4. Acculturation — Spain — Valencia (Region) — History. 5. Valencia (Spain: Region) — Civilization — Addresses, essays, lectures. I. T. II. Series.
DP302.V205 B85 1984   946/.76 19   *LC* 83-2007   *ISBN* 0521243742

Pitt-Rivers, Julian Alfred.   • **3.3491**
The people of the Sierra / introd. by E. E. Evans-Pritchard. New York: Criterion Books, c1954. 232 p.: ill.; 23 cm. 1. Cities and towns — Spain — Andalusia — Case studies. 2. Spain — Social life and customs I. T.
DP402.A33 P5 1954a   *LC* 55-2571

DP501–776 PORTUGAL

Keefe, Eugene K.   **3.3492**
Area handbook for Portugal / coauthors, Eugene K. Keefe ... [et al.]. — 1st ed. — Washington: For sale by the Supt. of Docs., U.S. Govt. Print. Off., 1977. xiv, 456 p.: ill.; 24 cm. 'DA Pam 550-181.' 'One of a series of handbooks prepared by Foreign Area Studies (FAS) of American University.' Includes index. 1. Portugal. I. American University (Washington, D.C.). Foreign Area Studies. II. T.
DP517.K43   946.9   *LC* 76-608385

Marques, António Henrique R. de Oliveira.   **3.3493**
[Sociedade medieval portuguesa. English] Daily life in Portugal in the late Middle Ages [by] A. H. de Oliveira Marques. Translated by S. S. Wyatt. Drawings by Vítor André. Madison, University of Wisconsin Press, 1971. xvi, 355 p. illus., geneal. tables, maps, plan, ports. 25 cm. Translation of A sociedade medieval portuguesa. 1. Portugal — Social life and customs I. T.
DP532.3.M3413   914.69/03/2   *LC* 78-106040   *ISBN* 0299055809

Boxer, C. R. (Charles Ralph), 1904-.   **3.3494**
The Portuguese seaborne empire, 1415–1825, by C. R. Boxer. [1st American ed.] New York, A. A. Knopf, 1969. xxvi, 415, xiv p. illus., maps (1 fold.), ports. 22 cm. (The History of human society) 1. Portugal — History 2. Portugal — Colonies. I. T.
DP538.B68   946/.902   *LC* 75-79346

Livermore, H. V., 1914-.   • **3.3495**
A new history of Portugal [by] H. V. Livermore. — Cambridge: Cambridge U.P., 1966. xi, 365 p.: front., 13 plates, maps, table.; 24 cm. 1. Portugal — History I. T.
DP538.L72   946.9   *LC* 65-19147

Livermore, H. V., 1914-.   **3.3496**
Portugal; a short history [by] H. V. Livermore. — [Edinburgh]: Edinburgh University Press, [1973] 213 p.: illus.; 23 cm. — (Short histories of Europe, 3) 1. Portugal — History I. T.
DP538.L73   946.9   *LC* 71-159594   *ISBN* 0852242077

Marques, António Henrique R. de Oliveira.   • **3.3497**
History of Portugal [by] A. H. de Oliveira Marques. — New York: Columbia University Press, 1972. 2 v.: illus.; 23 cm. A completely rewritten and enlarged version in Portuguese was published in 1972- under title História de Portugal. 1. Portugal — History I. T.
DP538.M37   946.9   *LC* 77-184748   *ISBN* 0231031599

Nowell, Charles E.   • **3.3498**
A history of Portugal. New York, Van Nostrand [1952] xii, 259 p. illus., ports., maps. 24 cm. 1. Portugal — History I. T.
DP538.N68   946.9   *LC* 52-6387

Nowell, Charles E.   **3.3499**
Portugal [by] Charles E. Nowell. — Englewood Cliffs, N.J.: Prentice-Hall, [1973] xii, 178 p.: maps.; 22 cm. — (The Modern nations in historical perspective) (A Spectrum book) 1. Portugal — History I. T.
DP539.N68   946.9   *LC* 73-178768   *ISBN* 0136869157

Gallagher, Tom, 1954-.   **3.3500**
Portugal: a twentieth-century interpretation / Tom Gallagher. — Manchester: Manchester University Press, c1983. xii, 278 p.: maps; 24 cm. Includes index. 1. Portugal — Politics and government — 1910-1974 2. Portugal — Politics and government — 1974- I. T.
DP675.G34 1983   946.9/04 19   *LC* 82-20379   *ISBN* 071900876X

Robinson, Richard Alan Hodgson.   **3.3501**
Contemporary Portugal: a history / R. A. H. Robinson. — London; Boston: Allen & Unwin, 1979. 297 p.: ill.; 23 cm. Includes index. 1. Portugal — History — 1910-1974 2. Portugal — History — 1974- I. T.
DP675.R58   946.9/04 19   *LC* 79-40004   *ISBN* 0049460137

Wheeler, Douglas L.   **3.3502**
Republican Portugal: a political history, 1910–1926 / Douglas L. Wheeler. — Madison: University of Wisconsin Press, 1978. xii, 340 p.: ill.; 24 cm. Includes index. 1. Portugal — Politics and government — 1910-1926 I. T.
DP675.W47   946.9/04   *LC* 77-15059   *ISBN* 0299074501

Contemporary Portugal: the revolution and its antecedents /   **3.3503**
edited by Lawrence S. Graham and Harry M. Makler; foreword
by Juan J. Linz.
Austin: University of Texas Press, c1979. xliii, 357 p.: ill.; 24 cm. 1. Portugal — History — 1910-1974 2. Portugal — History — 1974- I. Graham, Lawrence S. II. Makler, Harry M., 1935-
DP680.C594   946.9/04   *LC* 78-11213   *ISBN* 029271047X

Figueiredo, Antonio de, 1929-.   **3.3504**
Portugal: fifty years of dictatorship / Antonio de Figueiredo. — New York: Holmes & Meier, 1976, c1975. vi, 260, [1] p.; 23 cm. 1. Portugal — History — 1910-1974 I. T.
DP680.F53 1976   946.9/042   *LC* 75-33644   *ISBN* 0841902372

In search of modern Portugal: the revolution & its consequences   **3.3505**
/ edited by Lawrence S. Graham & Douglas L. Wheeler.
Madison, Wis.: University of Wisconsin Press, 1983. xv, 380 p.; 24 cm. Papers presented at the June 1979 meeting of the International Conference Group on Modern Portugal. 1. Portugal — Politics and government — 1974- — Congresses. 2. Portugal — History — Revolution, 1974 — Influence —

Congresses. I. Graham, Lawrence S. II. Wheeler, Douglas L. III. International Conference Group on Modern Portugal.
DP680.I53 1983   946.9/044 19   *LC* 81-69819   *ISBN* 0299089908

Bruneau, Thomas C.   **3.3506**
Politics and nationhood: post–revolutionary Portugal / Thomas C. Bruneau. — New York, NY: Praeger, 1984. xiv, 175 p.; 25 cm. Includes index. 1. Portugal — Politics and government — 1974- I. T.
DP681.B78 1984   946.9/044 19   *LC* 83-17784   *ISBN* 0030694647

DQ Switzerland

Hughes, Christopher.   **3.3507**
Switzerland / Christopher Hughes. — New York: Praeger, 1975, c1974. 303 p., [8] leaves of plates: ill.; 23 cm. (Nations of the modern world.) Includes index.

1. Switzerland. I. T. II. Series.
DQ17.H8 1975   914.94/03/7   *LC* 73-15169   *ISBN* 0275333205

Lunn, Arnold Henry Moore, Sir, 1888-1974.   • **3.3508**
The Swiss and their mountains; a study of the influence of mountains on man. Chicago, Rand McNally [1963] 167 p. plates (part col.) ports. 23 cm.
1. Switzerland. I. T.
DQ17.L86   301.30914   *LC* 63-20089

Steinberg, Jonathan.   **3.3509**
Why Switzerland? / By Jonathan Steinberg. — Cambridge; New York: Cambridge University Press, 1976. 214 p. Includes index. 1. Switzerland. I. T.
DQ17.S7   949.4   *LC* 75-36024   *ISBN* 0521211395

Bonjour, Edgar, 1898-.   • **3.3510**
A short history of Switzerland, by E. Bonjour, H. S. Offler, and G. R. Potter. Oxford, Clarendon Press, 1952. 388 p. ill. 1. Switzerland — History I. Offler, H. S. II. T.
DQ54.B65   949.4   *LC* 52-12224

DR1–48 GENERAL WORKS

Fischer-Galati, Stephen A. comp.   • **3.3511**
Man, state, and society in East European history. Edited by Stephen Fischer–Galati. — New York: Praeger, [1970] xiii, 343 p.; 24 cm. — (Man, state, and society) 1. Europe, Eastern — History — Collections. I. T.
DR1.F56   309.1/47   LC 69-10516

Osborne, Richard Horsley.   • **3.3512**
East–Central Europe; an introductory geography [by] R. H. Osborne. — New York: Praeger, [1967] 384 p.: maps.; 21 cm. — (Praeger introductory geographies) 1. Europe, Eastern I. T.
DR10.O75 1967   914   LC 67-21456

Stoianovich, Traian.   • **3.3513**
A study in Balkan civilization. New York, Knopf [1967] vi, 215, vi p. maps. 21 cm. (Borzoi studies in history, BH3) 1. Balkan Peninsula — Civilization 2. Balkan Peninsula — Social life and customs. I. T.
DR22.S75   914.96/03   LC 67-10715

Portal, Roger.   • **3.3514**
[Slaves. English] The Slavs; a cultural and historical survey of the Slavonic peoples. Translated from the French by Patrick Evans. [1st U.S. ed.] New York, Harper & Row [c1969] xvii, 508 p. illus., maps, ports. 25 cm. (Studies in world history) 1. Slavs I. T.
DR25.P613 1969b   910.09/175/918   LC 72-93911

Hösch, Edgar, 1935-.   **3.3515**
[Geschichte der Balkanländer. English] The Balkans; a short history from Greek times to the present day. Translated by Tania Alexander. New York, Crane, Russak [1972] 213 p. maps. 23 cm. Translation of Geschichte der Balkanländer. 1. Balkan Peninsula — History I. T.
DR36.H613 1972b   949.6   LC 72-85180   ISBN 0844800724

Jelavich, Barbara, 1923-.   **3.3516**
History of the Balkans / Barbara Jelavich. — Cambridge; New York: Cambridge University Press, 1983. 2 v.: ill.; 25 cm. — (Joint Committee on Eastern Europe publication series. no. 12) 1. Balkan Peninsula — History I. T. II. Series.
DR36.J37 1983   949.6 19   LC 82-22093   ISBN 0521252490

Jelavich, Charles.   • **3.3517**
The Balkans [by] Charles and Barbara Jelavich. Englewood Cliffs, N.J., Prentice-Hall [1965] xi, 148 p. maps. 21 cm. (The Modern nations in historical perspective) (A Spectrum book.) 1. Balkan Peninsula — History I. Jelavich, Barbara, 1923- joint author. II. T.
DR36.J38   949.6   LC 65-14999

Jelavich, Charles. ed.   • **3.3518**
The Balkans in transition; essays on the development of Balkan life and politics since the eighteenth century. Edited by Charles and Barbara Jelavich. Berkeley: University of California Press, 1963. xvii, 451 p.: maps. diagrs., tables.; 25 cm. (Russian and East European studies.) Papers presented at a conference held at the University of California, Berkeley, June 13-15, 1960 and sponsored by the Center for Slavic and East European Studies. Includes bibliographical references. 1. Balkan Peninsula — History I. Jelavich, Barbara, 1923- joint ed. II. California. University. Center for Slavic and East European Studies. III. T. IV. Series.
DR36.J4   949.6   LC 63-19230

Palmer, Alan Warwick.   • **3.3519**
The lands between; a history of East–Central Europe since the Congress of Vienna [by] Alan Palmer. — [1st American ed. — New York]: Macmillan, [1970] ix, 405 p.: illus., maps, ports.; 25 cm. 1. Europe, Eastern — History 2. Central Europe — History. I. T.
DR36.P3 1970b   943   LC 74-83064

Stavrianos, Leften Stavros.   • **3.3520**
The Balkans since 1453. — New York, Rinehart [1958] xxi, 970 p. illus., ports., maps, facsims. 24 cm. — (Rinehart books in European history) Bibliography: p. 873-946. Bibliographical references included in 'Notes' (p. 847-871) 1. Balkan Peninsula — Hist. I. T.
DR36.S83   949.6   LC 58-7242

Sugar, Peter F.   **3.3521**
Southeastern Europe under Ottoman rule, 1354–1804 / by Peter F. Sugar. — Seattle: University of Washington Press, c1977. xvii, 365 p.: ill.; 24 cm. (History of East Central Europe. v. 5) Includes index. 1. Turks in the Balkan Peninsula. 2. Balkan Peninsula — History I. T. II. Series.
DJK4.S93 vol. 5 DR36.S8x   949 s 949.6   LC 76-7799   ISBN 0295954434

Sugar, Peter F.   • **3.3522**
Nationalism in Eastern Europe / edited by Peter F. Sugar and Ivo J. Lederer. — Seattle: University of Washington Press, [1969] ix, 465 p.; 25 cm. — (University of Washington. Far Eastern and Russian Institute. Publications on Russia and Eastern Europe, no. 1) 1. Nationalism — Europe, Eastern. I. Lederer, Ivo J. joint author. II. T. III. Series.
DR37.S94   320.1/58/0947   LC 74-93026

Seton-Watson, Hugh.   **3.3523**
The 'sick heart' of modern Europe: the problem of the Danubian lands / Hugh Seton–Watson. — Seattle: University of Washington Press, [1975] xi, 76 p.; 22 cm. Three Walker-Ames lectures given at the University of Washington. 1. Minorities — Central Europe — Addresses, essays, lectures. 2. Minorities — Europe, Eastern — Addresses, essays, lectures. 3. Central Europe — Politics and government — Addresses, essays, lectures. 4. Europe, Eastern — Politics and government — Addresses, essays, lectures. I. T.
DR38.2.S47   320.9/43   LC 74-30170   ISBN 0295953608

DR39–48 By Period

McNeill, William Hardy, 1917-.   • **3.3524**
Europe's steppe frontier, 1500–1800 [by] William H. McNeill. — Chicago, University of Chicago Press [1964] 252 p.: maps.; 23 cm. 'End-paper map errata': fold. leaf inserted. 'Bibliographical essay': p. 223-235. 1. Europe, Eastern — Hist. 2. Central Europe — Hist. 3. Turkey — Hist. I. T.
DR41.M3 1964   943   LC 64-22248

Jelavich, Charles.   **3.3525**
The establishment of the Balkan national states, 1804–1920 / Charles and Barbara Jelavich. — Seattle: University of Washington Press, c1977. xv, 358 p.: maps; 24 cm. — (History of East Central Europe. v. 8) Includes index. 1. Eastern question (Balkan) 2. Balkan Peninsula — Politics and government I. Jelavich, Barbara, 1923- joint author. II. T. III. Series.
DJK4.S93 vol. 8 DR43.J4x   949 s 949.6 19   LC 76-49162   ISBN 0295954442

Ristelhueber, René, 1881-1960.   • **3.3526**
[Histoire des peuples balkaniques. English] A history of the Balkan peoples. Edited and translated by Sherman David Spector. New York, Twayne Publishers [1971] 470 p. maps. 21 cm. Translation of Histoire des peuples balkaniques. 1. Ethnology — Balkan Peninsula 2. Balkan Peninsula — History — 19th century I. T.
DR43.R513 1971   949.6   LC 78-147184

Helmreich, Ernst Christian.   • **3.3527**
The diplomacy of the Balkan wars, 1912–1913. — New York: Russell & Russell, [1969, c1938] xiv, 523 p.; 23 cm. — (Harvard historical studies. v. 42) 'Study originated in a doctoral dissertation on The diplomacy of the first Balkan war, 1912-1913, which was presented at Harvard in 1932.' 1. Balkan Peninsula — History — War of 1912-1913 I. T. II. Series.
DR46.3.H4 1969   949.6   LC 68-27063

Lukacs, John, 1924-.   • **3.3528**
The great powers and Eastern Europe / John A. Lukacs. — New York: American Book Co., 1953. xii, 878 p.: maps.; 23 cm. 1. Europe, Eastern — History I. T.
DR47.L8   LC 53-13369

Macartney, C. A. (Carlile Aylmer), 1895-1978.   • **3.3529**
Independent Eastern Europe, a history, by C. A. Macartney and A. W. Palmer. — London: Macmillan; New York: St Martin's Press, 1962. 499 p.: illus.; 23 cm. 1. Europe, Eastern — History I. Palmer, Alan Warwick. joint author. II. T.
DR48.M25 1962   947   LC 62-3631

Seton-Watson, Hugh. • **3.3530**
Eastern Europe between the wars, 1918–1941. With a new pref. written for this ed. — [3d ed. — Hamden, Conn.]: Archon Books, 1962. 425 p. illus. 23 cm. 1. Europe, Eastern — Hist. I. T.
DR48.S38 1962   914.7   LC 62-53112

DR48.5 1945-

Braun, Aurel. **3.3531**
Small–state security in the Balkans / Aurel Braun. — Totowa, N.J.: Barnes & Noble Books, 1983. xi, 334 p.; 23 cm. (Studies in Russian and East European history) Includes index. 1. International economic relations 2. Balkan Peninsula — Foreign relations — 20th century 3. Balkan Peninsula — Politics and government — 20th century I. T.
DR48.5.B69 1983   327/.09496 19   LC 82-6639   ISBN 0389202886

Fejtö, François, 1909-. **3.3532**
[Histoire des démocraties populaires: Après Staline, 1953-1968. English] A history of the people's democracies: Eastern Europe since Stalin. Translated by Daniel Weissbort. New York, Praeger [1971] 374 p. map (on lining papers). 25 cm. Translation of Histoire des démocraties populaires: Après Staline, 1953-1968. 1. Central Europe — Politics and government. 2. Soviet Union — Foreign relations — 1945- I. T.
DR48.5.F413 1971   320.9/47   LC 73-95671

Ionescu, Ghiţa. • **3.3533**
The break–up of the Soviet Empire in Eastern Europe / Ghita Ionescu. — Baltimore: Penguin Books, 1965. 168 [1] p.; 19 cm. (Penguin special.) 1. Communism — Europe, Eastern. 2. Europe, Eastern — Politics. I. T.
DR48.5.I6   320.947   LC 65-6872

Lendvai, Paul, 1929-. • **3.3534**
Eagles in cobwebs: nationalism and communism in the Balkans. — [1st ed.]. — Garden City, N.Y.: Doubleday, 1969. xii, 396 p.: map (on lining papers); 22 cm. 1. Europe, Eastern — Politics and government — 1945- I. T. II. Title: Nationalism and communism in the Balkans.
DR48.5.L43   320.9/496   LC 69-10952

Pethybridge, Roger William, 1934- ed. • **3.3535**
The development of the Communist bloc. Edited with an introd. by Roger Pethybridge. — Boston: Heath, [1965] xii, 244 p.; 24 cm. — (Studies in history and politics) 1. Communist countries — History. I. T.
DR48.5.P45   909.097170825   LC 65-25436

Seton-Watson, Hugh. • **3.3536**
The East European revolution / Hugh Seton–Watson. — 3d ed. — London: Methuen, c1956. 435 p.: ill.; 23 cm. 1. Europe, Eastern — Politics. 2. Europe, Eastern — History I. T.
DR48.5.S4 1956   LC 57-1670

Steele, Jonathan. comp. **3.3537**
Eastern Europe since Stalin. — New York: Crane, Russak, [1974] 215 p.; 23 cm. 1. Europe, Eastern — Politics and government — 1945- — Addresses, essays, lectures. I. T.
DR48.5.S75 1974   320.9/47/085   LC 73-91603   ISBN 0844802735

Wolff, Robert Lee. **3.3538**
The Balkans in our time / by Robert Lee Wolff. — Rev. ed. — Cambridge, Mass.: Harvard University Press, 1974. xxi, 647 p.: maps; 22 cm. (American foreign policy library.) (Russian Research Center studies; [23]) 1. Communism — Balkan Peninsula. 2. Balkan Peninsula — History I. T. II. Series.
DR48.5.W6 1974   949.6   LC 73-92497   ISBN 0674060512

DR49–50 Local History. Ethnography

Hoddinott, R. F. (Ralph F.), 1913-. **3.3539**
The Thracians / R.F. Hoddinott. — New York: Thames and Hudson, 1981. 192 p.: ill.; 25 cm. — (Ancient peoples and places) 1. Thracians 2. Europe, Eastern — Antiquities I. T.
DR50.46.H625 1981b   939/.8 19   LC 80-51906   ISBN 050002099X

DR51–98 Bulgaria

Kosev, Dimitŭr Konstantinov, 1903-. • **3.3540**
A short history of Bulgaria. Sofia, Foreign Languages Press; [1963] 461 p. illus., ports., fold. maps, facsims. 21 cm. 1. Bulgaria — History I. Kristov, Khristo Angelov. II. Angelov, Dimitŭr Simeonov. III. T.
DR67.K5813   LC 64-705

Macdermott, Mercia. • **3.3541**
A history of Bulgaria, 1393–1885. New York, Praeger [1962] 354 p. illus. 23 cm. 1. Bulgaria — History — 1393-1878 I. T.
DR82.M3 1962a   LC 62-10304

Crampton, R. J. **3.3542**
Bulgaria 1878–1918: a history / Richard J. Crampton. — Boulder, Colo.: East European Monographs; New York: Distributed by Columbia University Press, 1983. x, 580 p.: ill.; 23 cm. — (East European monographs. no. 138) Includes index. 1. Bulgaria — History — Alexander, 1879-1886 2. Bulgaria — History — Interregnum, 1886-1887 3. Bulgaria — History — Ferdinand I, 1887-1918 I. T. II. Series.
DR86.C72 1983   949.7/702 19   LC 83-80483   ISBN 0880330295

Oren, Nissan. • **3.3543**
Revolution administered: Agrarianism and communism in Bulgaria. — Baltimore: Johns Hopkins University Press, [1973] xv, 204 p.; 24 cm. — (Integration and community building in Eastern Europe, EE8) 1. Communism — Bulgaria. 2. Bulgaria — Politics and government — 1878-1944 3. Bulgaria — Politics and government — 1944- I. T. II. Series.
DR89.O68   320.9/4977/03   LC 72-8831   ISBN 0801812097

Brown, J. F. (James F.), 1928-. • **3.3544**
Bulgaria under Communist rule [by] J. F. Brown. — New York: Praeger, [1970] ix, 339 p.; 22 cm. 1. Communism — Bulgaria. 2. Bulgaria — History — 1944- 3. Bulgaria — Economic policy — 1944- I. T.
DR90.B7   320.9/497/7   LC 78-83329

Keefe, Eugene K. **3.3545**
Area handbook for Bulgaria. Co–authors: Eugene K. Keefe [and others] 1st ed. [Washington; For sale by the Supt. of Docs., U.S. Govt. Print. Off.] 1974. xiv, 330 p. illus. 24 cm. 'DA pam 550-168.' 'One of a series of handbooks prepared by Foreign Area Studies (FAS) of the American University.' 1. Bulgaria. I. American University (Washington, D.C.). Foreign Area Studies. II. T.
DR90.K4   914.977/03/3   LC 74-600028

Sanders, Irwin Taylor, 1909-. • **3.3546**
Balkan village. Lexington: Univ. of Kentucky Press, 1949. xiii, 291 p.: ill., maps.; 25 cm. 1. Dragalevtsi, Bulgaria I. T.
DR98.D7 S3   914.97   LC 49-9009

DR201–298 Romania

Keefe, Eugene K. **3.3547**
Romania, a country study / Foreign Area Studies, the American University; coauthors, Eugene K. Keefe ... [et al.]. — 1st ed. — [Washington]: FAS:for sale by the Supt. of Docs., U.S. Govt. Print. Off., c1979. xiv, 320 p.: maps; 24 cm. — (Area handbook series.) Published in 1972 under title: Area handbook for Romania. 'DA pam 550-160.' Includes index. 1. Romania. I. American University (Washington, D.C.). Foreign Area Studies. II. T. III. Series.
DR205.K43 1979   949.8   LC 79-128956

Bobango, Gerald J. **3.3548**
The emergence of the Romanian national State / by Gerald J. Bobango. — Boulder [Colo.]: East European Quarterly; New York: distributed by Columbia University Press, 1979. xiii, 307 p., [4] leaves of plates: ports.; 23 cm. — (East European monographs. no. 58) Includes index. 1. Alexandru Ioan I Cuza, Prince of Romania, 1820-1873. 2. Romania — Politics and government — 1821-1866 I. T. II. Series.
DR244.B59   320.9/498/01   LC 79-50734   ISBN 0914710516

Fischer-Galaţi, Stephen A. • **3.3549**
Twentieth century Rumania / [by] Stephen Fischer–Galaţi. — New York: Columbia University Press, 1970. ix, 248 p.: ill., map.; 24 cm. 1. Romania — Politics and government — 20th century I. T.
DR250.F5   320.9/498   LC 77-108838   ISBN 0231028482

Fischer-Galat̡i, Stephen A.   • 3.3550
The new Rumania: from people's democracy to socialist republic. Cambridge, Mass., M. I. T. Press [1967] xi, 126 p. 24 cm. 1. Romania — History — 1944-2. Romania — Politics and government — 1945- I. T.
DR267.F5   LC 67-15603

Ionescu, Ghiț̤a.   • 3.3551
Communism in Rumania, 1944–1962. — London, New York, Oxford University Press, 1964. xvi, 378 p.; 23 cm. Bibliography: p. [358]-367. 1. Communism — Rumania. 2. Romania — History — 1944- I. T.
DR267.I65   949.803   LC 64-55367

Romania in the 1980s / edited by Daniel N. Nelson.   3.3552
Boulder, Colo.: Westview Press, 1981. xiii, 313 p. — (Westview special studies on the Soviet Union and Eastern Europe.) 1. Romania — Politics and government — 1944- 2. Romania — Economic conditions — 1945- 3. Romania — Social conditions — 1945- I. Nelson, Daniel N., 1948- II. Series.
DR267.R65   DR267 R65.   949.8/03 19   LC 81-3412   ISBN 0865310270

DR301–396 Yugoslavia

(Works classified before ca. 1980; see also: DR1202-2285)

History of Yugoslavia, by Vladimir Dedijer [and others. Translator: Kordija Kveder].   3.3553
New York: McGraw-Hill Book Co., [1974] ix, 752 p.: illus.; 24 cm. Translation of Istorija Jugoslavije. 1. Yugoslavia — History I. Dedijer, Vladimir.
DR317.I8613   949.7   LC 74-6164   ISBN 0070162352

Palmer, Alan Warwick.   • 3.3554
Yugoslavia / A.W. Palmer. — [London]: Oxford University Press, 1964. 127 p.: ill., maps (on lining papers) ports.; 19 cm. (Modern World, 6) 1. Yugoslavia — History I. T. II. Series.
DR318.P3   LC 64-4724

Clissold, Stephen.   3.3555
Yugoslavia and the Soviet Union, 1939–1973: a documentary survey / edited by Stephen Clissold. — London; New York: Published for the Royal Institute of International Affairs by Oxford University Press, 1975. xxiii, 318 p.; 25 cm. 1. Yugoslavia — Foreign relations — Russia — Sources. 2. Russia — Foreign relations — Yugoslavia — Sources. I. T.
DR327.R9 C55   327.497/4/047   LC 75-331958   ISBN 019218315X

Djilas, Milovan, 1911-.   • 3.3556
Memoir of a revolutionary [by] Milovan Djilas. Translated by Drenka Willen. [1st ed.] New York, Harcourt Brace Jovanovich [c1973] 402 p. 24 cm. 1. Djilas, Milovan, 1911- 2. Communism — Yugoslavia. I. T.
DR359.D5 A33   322.4/2/0924 B   LC 72-91835   ISBN 0151588503

Djilas, Milovan, 1911-.   • 3.3557
[Susreti sa Staljinom. English] Conversations with Stalin / translated from the SerboCroat by Michael B. Petrovich. — [1st ed.] New York: Harcourt, Brace & World [1962] 211 p.; 21 cm. Translation of Susreti sa Staljinom. 1. Communist countries — Politics and government. I. Stalin, Joseph, 1879-1953. II. T.
DR359.D513   949.702   LC 62-14470

Auty, Phyllis.   • 3.3558
Tito; a biography. New York, McGraw-Hill [1970] xiv, 343 p. illus., maps, ports. 23 cm. 1. Tito, Josip Broz, 1892-1980. I. T.
DR359.T5 A9 1970b   949/.702/0924 B   LC 75-107283

Dedijer, Valdimir.   • 3.3559
Tito. New York: Simon and Schuster, 1953 [i. e. 1952] 443 p.; 22 cm. 1. Tito, Josip Broz, 1892-1980. I. T.
DR359.T5D4   923.5497   LC 53-6161

Kerner, Robert Joseph, 1887-1956. ed.   • 3.3560
Yugoslavia; chapters by Griffith Taylor [and others] Berkeley: Univ. of California Press, 1949. xxi, 558 p.: ill., ports., maps.; 23 cm. (United Nations series.) 'Notes and referneces': p. [513]-528. 'A selected bibliogrpahy': p. [529]-544. 1. Yugoslavia. I. T. II. Series.
DR366.K47   949.7   LC 49-1741

West, Rebecca, Dame, 1892-.   • 3.3561
Black lamb and grey falcon; a journey through Yugoslavia, by Rebecca West. New York: Viking Press, 1943. 1181 p.: plates, ports.; 24 cm. 1. Yugoslavia — Description and travel 2. Yugoslavia — History 3. Serbia — History I. T.
DR366.W48 1943   LC 41-51964

Rubinstein, Alvin Z.   • 3.3562
Yugoslavia and the nonaligned world, by Alvin Z. Rubinstein. — Princeton, N.J.: Princeton University Press, 1970. xv, 353 p.; 23 cm. 1. Yugoslavia — Foreign relations — 1945- 2. Yugoslavia — Politics and government — 1945- I. T.
DR367.A1 R8   327.497   LC 78-90959   ISBN 0691051801

Campbell, John Coert, 1911-.   • 3.3563
Tito's separate road; America and Yugoslavia in world politics, by John C. Campbell. — [1st ed.]. — New York: Published for the Council on Foreign Relations by Harper & Row, [1967] viii, 180 p.; 21 cm. — (Policy book series of the Council on Foreign Relations) 1. Yugoslavia — Politics and government — 1945- 2. Yugoslavia — Foreign relations — 1945- I. Council on Foreign Relations. II. T.
DR370.C33   949.7/02   LC 67-15967

Doder, Dusko.   3.3564
The Yugoslavs / Dusko Doder. — 1st ed. — New York: Random House, c1978. xiv, 256 p.; 25 cm. Includes index. 1. Yugloslavia — Politics and government — 1945- 2. Yugoslavia — Social conditions. I. T.
DR370.D62   309/.1/49702   LC 77-90287   ISBN 0394425383

Hoffman, George Walter, 1914-.   • 3.3565
Yugoslavia and the new communism / [by] George W. Hoffman [and] Fred Warner Neal. — New York: Twentieth Century Fund, 1962. xvi, 546 p.: maps, diagrs., tables.; 24 cm. 1. Communism — Yugoslavia. 2. Yugoslavia — Economic conditions — 1945- I. Neal, Fred Warner. joint author. II. T.
DR370.H58   949.702   LC 62-13485

Ulam, Adam Bruno, 1922-.   • 3.3566
Titoism and the Cominform [by] Adam B. Ulam. — Westport, Conn.: Greenwood Press, [1971, c1952] viii, 243 p.; 23 cm. 1. Communism — Yugoslavia. 2. Communism — History I. T.
DR370.U4 1971   321.9/2   LC 70-100246   ISBN 0837134048

Vucinich, Wayne S.   • 3.3567
Contemporary Yugoslavia; twenty years of Socialist experiment [by] Jozo Tomasevich [and others] Edited by Wayne S. Vucinich. — Berkeley: University of California Press, 1969. xiii, 441 p.: maps.; 24 cm. Based on a conference on contemporary Yugoslavia, held at Stanford University, Dec. 4-5, 1965. 1. Yugoslavia — Politics and government — 1945- — Addresses, essays, lectures. I. Tomasevich, Jozo, 1908- II. Stanford University. III. T.
DR370.V8   320.9/497   LC 69-16512

DR401–593 Turkey

Dewdney, John C.   • 3.3568
Turkey: an introductory geography [by] J. C. Dewdney. — New York: Praeger, [1971] x, 214 p.: maps.; 23 cm. — (Praeger introductory geographies) 1. Turkey. I. T.
DR417.D48 1971   915.61   LC 79-101658

Nyrop, Richard F.   3.3569
Turkey, a country study / Richard F. Nyrop. — 3d ed. — Washington, D.C.: Foreign Area Studies, American University: for sale by the Supt. of Docs., U.S. Govt. Print. Off., 1980. xxvii, 370 p.: ill.; 24 cm. — (Area handbook series.) Published in 1973 under title: Area handbook for the Republic of Turkey. 'DA pam 550-80.' Includes index. 1. Turkey. I. American University (Washington, D.C.). Foreign Area Studies. II. T. III. Series.
DR417.R54 1980   956.1   LC 80-607042

Gökalp, Ziya, 1876-1924.   • 3.3570
[Selected works. English] Turkish nationalism and Western civilization; selected essays. Translated and edited with an introd. by Niyazi Berkes. New York, Columbia University Press, 1959. 336 p. 23 cm. 1. Nationalism — Turkey. 2. Turkey — Civilization — Occidental influences I. T.
DR432.G59213 1959   915.61   LC 59-65081

Creasy, Sir Edward Shepherd, 1812-1878.   • 3.3571
History of the Ottoman Turks / by Edward S. Creasy. With a new introd. by Zeine. — Beirut: Khayats, 1961. xix, 560 p.: facsim.; 20 cm. (Oriental reprints, no. 1.) Reprint of 2d ed. published in 1878. 1. Eastern question (Balkan) 2. Turkey — History I. T.
DR440.C91x   949.6

Shaw, Stanford Jay.   3.3572
History of the Ottoman Empire and modern Turkey / Stanford Shaw. — Cambridge; New York: Cambridge University Press, 1976-1977. 2 v.: maps; 25 cm. Vol. 2 by S. J. Shaw and E. K. Shaw. Includes indexes. 1. Turkey — History — Ottoman Empire, 1288-1918 2. Turkey — History — 1918-1960 3. Turkey — History — 1960- I. Shaw, Ezel Kural, joint author. II. T.
DR440.S5   956.1   *LC* 76-9179   *ISBN* 0521212804

Eliot, Charles Norton Edgecumbe, Sir, 1862-1931.   • 3.3573
Turkey in Europe / Sir Charles Eliot. — London: Barnes & Noble, 1965. 459 p.: 2 fold. col. maps; 23 cm. 1. Islam 2. Christians — Turkey 3. Eastern question (Balkan) 4. Turkey — History I. T.
DR441.E5 1965a   914.96

Lewis, Geoffrey L.   3.3574
Modern Turkey, by Geoffrey Lewis. — [4th ed.]. — New York: Praeger, [1974] 255 p.: illus.; 23 cm. — (Nations of the modern world.) First-3d ed. published under title: Turkey. 1. Turkey — History I. T. II. Series.
DR441.L45 1974   956.1   *LC* 73-15170   *ISBN* 0275334007

Itzkowitz, Norman.   3.3575
Ottoman Empire and Islamic tradition. — [1st ed.]. — New York: Knopf; [distributed by Random House, 1972] xiv, 117, vii p.; 21 cm. — (Studies in world civilization) 1. Islam — Turkey. 2. Turkey — History — Ottoman Empire, 1288-1918 I. T. II. Series.
DR445.I8   949.6   *LC* 72-1914   *ISBN* 0394317181

Dodd, C. H. (Clement Henry)   3.3576
Democracy and development in Turkey / C. H. Dodd. — Walkington, Eng.: Eothen Press, c1979. 231 p.: ill., map. Icludes index. 1. Turkey — Politics and government I. T.
DR471.D6   DR471 D6.   *ISBN* 0906719003(pa.)

Cahen, Claude.   • 3.3577
Pre-Ottoman Turkey; a general survey of the material and spiritual culture and history, c. 1071–1330. Translated from the French by J. Jones–Williams. — New York: Taplinger Pub. Co., [1968] xx, 458 p.: illus., maps.; 24 cm. 1. Turkey — History — To 1453 I. T.
DR481.C3313 1968b   915.61/03/1   *LC* 68-24744

Wittek, Paul, 1894-.   • 3.3578
The rise of the Ottoman Empire. — New York: B. Franklin, [1971] vii, 54 p.; 23 cm. (Burt Franklin research and source works series, 769. Byzantine series, 30) Reprint of the 1938 ed. which was issued as v. 23 of Royal Asiatic Society monographs. Lectures delivered at the University of London, May 4-6, 1937. 1. Turkey — History — 1288-1453 I. T.
DR481.W5 1971   956.1/01   *LC* 70-153023   *ISBN* 0833738550

İnalc8k, Halil, 1916-.   3.3579
The Ottoman Empire; the classical age, 1300–1600. Translated by Norman Itzkowitz and Colin Imber. New York, Praeger Publishers [1973] xii, 257 p. illus. 26 cm. (Praeger history of civilisation) 1. Turkey — History — 1288-1453 2. Turkey — History — 1453-1683 I. T.
DR486.I5 1973b   914.96/1/031   *LC* 76-187274

Kinross, Patrick Balfour, Baron, 1904-.   3.3580
The Ottoman centuries: the rise and fall of the Turkish empire / Lord Kinross. — New York: Morrow, 1977. 638 p.: ill.; 25 cm. Includes index. 1. Turkey — History — Ottoman Empire, 1288-1918 I. T.
DR486.K56   949.6   *LC* 76-28498   *ISBN* 0688030939

Babinger, Franz, 1891-1967.   3.3581
[Mehmed der Eroberer und seine Zeit. English] Mehmed the Conqueror and his time / Franz Babinger; translated from the German by Ralph Manheim; edited, with a pref., by William C. Hickman. — Princeton, N.J.: Princeton University Press, c1978. xx, 549 p., [23] leaves of plates: ill.; 24 cm. (Bollingen series. 96) Translation of Mehmed der Eroberer und seine Zeit. 1. Mehmed II, Sultan of the Turks, 1432-1481. 2. Turkey — History — Mehmet II, 1451-1481 I. T. II. Series.
DR501.B313   956.1/01/0924 B   *LC* 77-71972   *ISBN* 0691099006

Merriman, Roger Bigelow, 1876-.   • 3.3582
Suleiman the Magnificent, 1520–1566 / by Roger Bigelow Merriman. — Cambridge, Mass.: Harvard University Press, 1944. viii, 325 p.: double pl., ports.; 22 cm. Map on lining-papers. I. Coolidge, Archibald Cary, 1866-1928. II. T.
DR506.M4   *LC* 44-5977

Lybyer, Albert Howe, 1876-.   • 3.3583
The government of the Ottoman empire in the time of Suleiman, the Magnificent. Cambridge: Harvard university press, 1913. x, 349 p.; 23 cm. (Harvard historical studies, v.18) 1. Turkey — Politics and government I. T.
DR507.L8   949.6

DR556–592 19th–20th Centuries

Miller, William, 1864-1945.   • 3.3584
The Ottoman Empire and its successors, 1801–1927. — New York: Octagon Books, 1966. xv, 616 p.: fold. maps.; 23 cm. Reprint of the 3d edition, first published in 1927. 1. Turkey — History — 1909- 2. Eastern question (Balkan) 3. Turkey — History — 19th century I. T.
DR557.M6 1966a   956.101   *LC* 66-26861

Pushkin, Aleksandr Sergeevich, 1799-1837.   3.3585
[Puteshestvīe v Arzrum. English] A journey to Arzrum / Alexander Pushkin; translated by Birgitta Ingemanson. — 1st ed. — Ann Arbor, Mich.: Ardis, 1974. 111 p.: ports.; 23 cm. Translation of Puteshestvie v Arzrum. 1. Pushkin, Aleksandr Sergeevich, 1799-1837. 2. Russo-Turkish War, 1828-1829 3. Caucasus — Description and travel. 4. Erzurum (Turkey) — Description. I. T.
DR564.P8713   947.08   *LC* 74-14069   *ISBN* 0882330675

Davison, Roderic H.   • 3.3586
Reform in the Ottoman Empire, 1856–1876. — Princeton, N. J., Princeton University Press, 1963. xiii, 479 p. 25 cm. Bibliography: p. 425-463. 1. Turkey — Pol. & govt. — 1829-1878. I. T.
DR569.D3   956.101   *LC* 63-12669

Ramsaur, Ernest Edmondson.   • 3.3587
The Young Turks; prelude to the revolution of 1908. — New York: Russell & Russell, [1970, c1957] xii, 180 p.; 23 cm. 1. İttihad ve Terakki Cemiyeti. 2. Turkey — Politics and government — 1878-1909 I. T.
DR572.R3 1970   956.1/01   *LC* 79-81465

Lewis, Bernard.   • 3.3588
The emergence of modern Turkey. — 2nd ed. — London; New York [etc.]: issued under the auspices of the Royal Institute of International Affairs [by] Oxford U.P., 1968. xi, 530 p.: maps.; 21 cm. — (Oxford paperbacks no. 135) 1. Turkey — History — 1909- I. Royal Institute of International Affairs. II. T.
DR583.L48 1968   956.1   *LC* 68-139021

Ahmad, Feroz.   3.3589
The Young Turks; the Committee of Union and Progress in Turkish politics, 1908–1914. — Oxford: Clarendon Press, 1969. viii, 205 p.; 22 cm. Based on author's Ph.D. dissertation, London University. 1. İttihad ve Terakki Cemiyeti. 2. Turkey — Politics and government — 1909-1918 I. T.
DR584.A6   956.1/01   *LC* 70-436940   *ISBN* 0198214758

Howard, Harry N. (Harry Nicholas), 1902-1987.   • 3.3590
The partition of Turkey; a diplomatic history, 1913–1923, by Harry N. Howard. Norman: University of Oklahoma Press, 1931. 486 p.: maps (part fold.); 24 cm. 1. World War, 1914-1918 — Territorial questions — Turkey. 2. Eastern question (Balkan) 3. World War, 1914-1918 — Turkey. I. T.
DR584.H6   956.101   *LC* 66-24347

Kedourie, Elie.   • 3.3591
England and the Middle East: the destruction of the Ottoman Empire, 1914–1921 / Elie Kedourie. — [London]: Bowes & Bowes [1956] 236 p.; 23 cm. 1. Great Britain — Foreign relations — Near East. 2. Middle East — Politics and government. 3. Turkey — History — 1909- I. T.
DR588.K4   *ISBN* 0855278498

Ahmad, Feroz.   3.3592
The Turkish experiment in democracy, 1950–1975 / Feroz Ahmad. Boulder, Colo.: Westview Press, for the Royal Institute of International Affairs, London, 1977. xii, 474 p.; 22 cm. Includes index. 1. Political parties — Turkey. 2. Turkey — Politics and government — 1918-1960 3. Turkey — Politics and government — 1960- I. Royal Institute of International Affairs. II. T.
DR590.A694   320.9/561/03   *LC* 76-25499   *ISBN* 0891586296

Pevsner, Lucille W.   3.3593
Turkey's political crisis: background, perspectives, prospects / Lucille W. Pevsner; foreword by James W. Spain. — New York, N.Y.: Praeger, 1984. ix, 140 p.; 22 cm. (The Washington papers, 0278-937X; vol. XII, 110) 'Published with the Center for Strategic and International Studies, Georgetown University, Washington, D.C.' 1. Turkey — Politics and government — 1918-1960 2. Turkey — Politics and government — 1960- I. T.
DR590.P47 1984   956.1/02 19   *LC* 84-15185   *ISBN* 0030016479

Robinson, Richard D., 1921-.   • 3.3594
The First Turkish Republic; a case study in national development. — Cambridge, Harvard University Press, 1963. xii, 367 p. illus., ports. 22 cm. — (Harvard Middle Eastern studies. 9) Bibliographical references included in 'Notes' (p. [325]-346) 1. Turkey — Hist. — 1918-1960. I. T. II. Series.
DR590.R62   956.102   *LC* 63-17210

Atatürk, founder of a modern state / Ali Kazancigil and Ergun   3.3595
Özbudun, editors.
Hamden, Conn.: Archon Books, 1981. vi, 243 p.: port.; 22 cm. 1. Atatürk,
Kemal, 1881-1938 — Addresses, essays, lectures. 2. Turkey — Politics and
government — 1918-1960 — Addresses, essays, lectures. I. Özbudun, Ergun.
II. Kazancigil, Ali.
DR592.K4 A855 1981   956.1/024/0924 19   *LC* 81-19094   *ISBN*
0208019685

Kinross, Patrick Balfour, Baron, 1904-.   3.3596
Ataturk: the rebirth of a nation / Lord Kinross. — [S.l.]: Morrow, 1965. xviii,
542 p.: ill., maps. Also published under the title: Ataturk: a biography of
Mustafa Kemal, father of modern Turkey. 1. Atatürk, Kemal, 1881-1938.
2. Turkey — History — 1918- I. T.
DR589.B25   DR592.K4 K5.   956.102   *LC* 65-1608

Dodd, C. H. (Clement Henry)   3.3597
The crisis of Turkish democracy / C.H. Dodd. — [Beverley, North
Humberside]: Eothen Press, [c1983] viii, 136 p.; 21 cm. Includes index.
1. Turkey — Politics and government — 1960- I. T.
DR593.D63 1983   956.1/03 19   *LC* 83-181470   *ISBN* 0906719062

DR701–741 Local History and Description

Hammond, N. G. L. (Nicholas Geoffrey Lemprière), 1907-.   3.3598
A history of Macedonia. Oxford: Clarendon Press, 1972-. 2 v. 1. Macedonia —
History I. T.
DR701 M2 H35

Barker, Elisabeth.   • 3.3599
Macedonia: its place in Balkan power politics / by Elisabeth Barker. —
London: Royal Institute of International Affairs, 1950. 129 p.; 22 cm.
1. Macedonian question I. T.
DR701.M4 B28   *LC* 50-6759

DR701S5 Albania

Keefe, Eugene K.   3.3600
Area handbook for Albania. Co–authors: Eugene K. Keefe [and others.
Washington; For sale by the Supt. of Docs., U.S. Govt. Print. Off.] 1982. xiv,
223 p. map. 24 cm. 'DA pam 550-98.' 'One of a series of handbooks prepared by
Foreign Area Studies (FAS) of the American University.' 1. Albania.
I. American University (Washington, D.C.). Foreign Area Studies. II. T.
DR701.S5 K36   914.96/5   *LC* 73-609651

Marmullaku, Ramadan, 1939-.   3.3601
Albania and the Albanians / by Ramadan Marmullaku; translated from the
Serbo–Croatian by Margot and Boško Milosavljević. — Hamden, Conn.:
Archon Books,/Shoe String Press 1975. x, 178 p.: map; 23 cm. Includes index.
1. Albania. I. T.
DR701.S5 M3213 1975   949.65   *LC* 76-350538   *ISBN* 0208015582

Skendi, Stavro.   • 3.3602
The Albanian national awakening, 1878–1912. — Princeton, N.J.: Princeton
University Press, 1967. xvi, 498 p.; 23 cm. 1. Nationalism — Albania.
2. Albania — History — 1501-1912 I. T.
DR701.S5 S66   949.6/501   *LC* 66-17710

Swire, Joseph, 1903-.   • 3.3603
Albania; the rise of a kingdom [by] J. Swire. — New York: Arno Press, 1971.
xxiv, 560 p.: illus., maps, ports.; 24 cm. — (The Eastern Europe collection)
Reprint of the 1929 ed. 1. Albania — History I. T.
DR701.S5 S83 1971   949.6/501   *LC* 79-135835   *ISBN*
040502777X

DR1202–2285 Yugoslavia

(Works classified after ca. 1980; see also:
DR301-396)

Yugoslavia, a country study / Foreign Area Studies, The   3.3604
American University; edited by Richard F. Nyrop.
2nd ed. — Washington, D.C.: For sale by the Supt. of Docs., U.S. G.P.O.,
c1982. xxvii, 336 p.: ill.; 24 cm. — (Area handbook series.) (DA pam. 550-99)
Rev. ed. of: Area handbook for Yugoslavia. 1973. Includes index.
1. Yugoslavia. I. Nyrop, Richard F. II. American University (Washington,
D.C.). Foreign Area Studies. III. Area handbook for Yugoslavia. IV. Series.
V. Series: DA pam. 550-99
DR1214.Y83 1982   949.7 19   *LC* 82-11632

Singleton, Frederick Bernard.   3.3605
A short history of the Yugoslav peoples / Fred Singleton. — Cambridge
[Cambridgeshire]; New York: Cambridge University Press, 1985. xiii, 309 p.:
map; 23 cm. Includes index. 1. Yugoslavia — History I. T.
DR1246.S56 1985   949.7 19   *LC* 84-17625   *ISBN* 0521254787

Djilas, Milovan, 1911-.   3.3606
[Vlast. English] Rise and fall / Milovan Djilas. — 1st ed. — San Diego:
Harcourt Brace Jovanovich, c1985. vii, 424 p.; 24 cm. Translation of: Vlast.
Includes index. 1. Djilas, Milovan, 1911- 2. Statesmen — Yugoslavia —
Biography. 3. Yugoslavia — History — 1945- I. T.
DR1305.D56 A3813 1985   949.7/023/0924 19   *LC* 84-12972
ISBN 0151775729

Clissold, Stephen.   3.3607
Djilas, the progress of a revolutionary / Stephen Clissold; introduction by Hugh
Seton-Watson. — New York: Universe Books, 1983. 342 p.: ill.; 24 cm. Map on
lining papers. 1. Djilas, Milovan, 1911- 2. Statesmen — Yugoslavia —
Biography. 3. Authors, Serbian — 20th century — Biography. 4. Yugoslavia
— History — 1918-1945 5. Yugoslavia — History — 1945- I. T.
DR1305.D56 C57 1983   949.7/023/0924 B 19   *LC* 83-4906   *ISBN*
0876634315

DS   Asia

DS1–11 General Works. Description

The Far East and Australasia. • 3.3608
1969- . — London: Europa Publications, c1969-. v.: ill. maps (some col.); 26 cm. Annual. 1. Asia — Periodicals. 2. Oceania — Periodicals. I. Europa Publications Limited.
DS1.F3   950/.05 19   LC 74-417170

Cressey, George Babcock, 1896-1963. • 3.3609
Asia's lands and peoples, a geography of one–third of the earth and two–thirds of its people. — 3d ed. — New York: McGraw-Hill, [1963] 663 p.: illus.; 26 cm. — (McGraw-Hill series in geography) 1. Asia I. T.
DS5.C7 1963   915   LC 62-22087

Wint, Guy, 1910-1969. ed. • 3.3610
Asia; a handbook. New York, Praeger [1966] xiii, 856 p. maps (part fold.) 24 cm. Appendix (p. [737]-802): Post-war treaties and agreements. Includes bibliographies. 1. Automotive Service Industry Association. I. T.
DS5.W5   915   LC 65-13263

The Mongol mission: narratives and letters of the Franciscan missionaries in Mongolia and China in the thirteenth and fourteenth centuries / edited and with an introduction by Christopher Dawson; translated by a nun of Stanbrook Abbey. • 3.3611
New York: Sheed and Ward, 1955. xxxix, 246 p.: geneal. tables, fold. map. — (The Makers of Christendom) 1. Mongols — History 2. Asia — Description and travel I. Giovanni, da Pian del Carpine, Archbishop of Antivari, d. 1252. History of the Mongols. II. Ruysbroek, Willem von, 13th century. Journey of William of Rubruck. III. Dawson, Christopher, 1889-1970. IV. Series.
DS6.D313   LC 55-10925

Fa-hsien, ca. 337-ca. 422. • 3.3612
The travels of Fa–hsien (399–414 A. D.): or, Record of the Buddhistic kingdoms / re–translated by H. A. Giles. — London: Routledge and Paul, 1956. xx, 96 p.: ill., fold. map. Translation of Fo kuo chi. 1. Buddhism 2. Asia — Description and travel I. Fa-hsien, ca. 337-ca. 422. Fo kuo chi. English II. T. III. Title: Record of the Buddhistic kingdoms
DS6.F35 1956   LC 59-42037

Olschki, Leonardo, 1885-. • 3.3613
Marco Polo's Asia: an introduction to his 'Description of the world called 'Il milione' / by Leonardo Olschki; translated from the Italian by John A. Scott, and rev. by the author. — Berkeley: University of California Press, 1960. x, 459 p., [5] leaves of plates (1 fold.): ill., fold. map; 24 cm. Translation of L'Asia di Marco Polo. 1. Polo, Marco, 1254-1323? 2. Asia — Description and travel I. T.
DS6.O373   LC 60-8315

Dobby, Ernest Henry George. • 3.3614
Monsoon Asia / [by] E.H.G. Dobby. — 3rd ed. — London: University of London P., c1966. –. 381 p.: plates, maps, tables; 22 cm. — (A Systematic regional geography, v. 5) 1. Asia — Description and travel I. T.
DS10.D59 1966   915   LC 67-111124

Childe, V. Gordon (Vere Gordon), 1892-1957. • 3.3615
[Most ancient East] New light on the most ancient East. [4th ed.] New York, F. A. Praeger [1953] xiii, 255 p. illus., maps. 23 cm. (Books that matter) First published 1928 under title: The most ancient East. 1. Oriental antiquities 2. Man, Prehistoric 3. Civilization, Ancient I. T.
DS11.C52 1953   913.3   LC 52-13107

Russia and Asia; essays on the influence of Russia on the Asian peoples. Edited by Wayne S. Vucinich. 3.3616
Stanford, Calif., Hoover Institution Press, Stanford University [c1972] xiv, 521 p. map. 24 cm. (Hoover Institution publications, 107 [i.e. 109]) Papers originally presented at a conference held at Stanford University, Nov. 30-Dec. 2, 1967. 1. Asia — Civilization — Russian influences. I. Vucinich, Wayne S. ed. II. Stanford University.
DS12.R8   301.29/47/05   LC 79-152430   ISBN 0817910718

Said, Edward W. 3.3617
Orientalism / Edward W. Said. — 1st ed. — New York: Pantheon Books, c1978. xi, 368 p.; 25 cm. 1. Imperialism 2. East and West 3. Asia — Foreign opinion, Occidental. 4. Middle East — Foreign opinion, Occidental. 5. Asia — Study and teaching 6. Middle East — Study and teaching. I. T.
DS12.S24 1978   950/.07/2   LC 78-51803   ISBN 0394428145

DS17–27 Ethnography. Mongols

Permanent International Altaistic Conference. 5th, Bloomington, Ind., 1962. • 3.3618
Aspects of Altaic civilization; proceedings of the Fifth Meeting of the Permanent International Altaistic Conference held at Indiana University, June 4–9, 1962. Edited by Denis Sinor, assisted by David Francis. Bloomington Indiana University [1963] 263p. (Indiana University publications. Uralic and Altaic series, v. 23) 1. Ural-Altaic tribes I. Sinor, Denis. ed. II. Indiana University. III. T.
DS17 P4 1962

Prawdin, Michael, 1894-. • 3.3619
The Mongol Empire; its rise and legacy, by Michael Prawdin. Translated by Eden and Cedar Paul. [Rev. 4th impression] London, G. Allen and Unwin [1961] 581 p. maps, port. 23 cm. Translation of Tschingis-Chan und sein Erbe. 1. Genghis Khan, 1162-1227. 2. Mongols — History I. T.
DS19.C522 1961   LC 64-7297

Haydar Mīrzā, 1499 or 1500-1551. 3.3620
[Tarikh-i-Rashidi. English] A history of the Moghuls of central Asia; being the Tarikh–i–Rashidi of Mirza Muhammad Haidar, Dughlát. An English version edited, with commentary, notes and map by N. Elias. The translation by E. Denison Ross. London, Curzon Press; New York, Barnes and Noble 1973, (c1972) xxv, 535 p. fold. map. 23 cm. (Records in Asian history) Reprint of the 1898 ed. 1. Mongols — History 2. Asia, Central — History. I. T.
DS19.H3613   958   LC 73-158183   ISBN 0389016647

Howorth, Henry Hoyle, Sir, 1842-1923. • 3.3621
History of the Mongols, from the 9th to the 19th century. — New York: B. Franklin, [1965] 4 v. in 5.: maps.; 24 cm. — (Burt Franklin research and source work series, #85) L.C. set imperfect: maps in v. 1 wanting. Reprint of the 1876-1927 ed. 'Sources from which the history of the Mongols ... has been collected': pt. 1, p. xvi-xxviii. 1. Mongols — History 2. Asia — History I. T.
DS19.H862   909/.09/74942   LC 70-6598

Saunders, J. J. (John Joseph), 1910-1972. • 3.3622
The history of the Mongol conquests [by] J. J. Saunders. — New York: Barnes & Noble, [1971] xix, 275 p.: illus.; 22 cm. 1. Mongols — History, Military. I. T.
DS19.S27 1971   950/.2   LC 72-193146   ISBN 0389044512

Spuler, Bertold, 1911- comp. • 3.3623
[Geschichte der Mongolen, nach östlichen und europäischen Zeugnissen des 13. und 14. Jahrhunderts. English] History of the Mongols, based on Eastern and Western accounts of the thirteenth and fourteenth centuries. Translated from the German by Helga and Stuart Drummond. Berkeley, University of California Press, 1972. x, 221 p. maps. 23 cm. (The Islamic world series) Translation of Geschichte der Mongolen, nach östlichen und europäischen Zeugnissen des 13. und 14. Jahrhunderts. 1. Mongols — History I. T. II. Series.
DS19.S5613 1972   950/.2   LC 68-8720   ISBN 0520019601

Martin, Henry Desmond, 1908-. • 3.3624
The rise of Chingis Khan and his conquest of North China, by H. Desmond Martin. Introd. by Owen Lattimore. Edited by Eleanor Lattimore. New York, Octagon Books, 1971 [c1950] xvii, 360 p. 3 maps (fold. in pocket), plans, port. 24 cm. 1. Genghis Khan, 1162-1227. 2. China — History — Yüan dynasty, 1260-1368 I. T.
DS22.M3 1971   951/.025/0924   LC 70-120647

DS31–35 History and Politics (General)

Ziring, Lawrence, 1928-.   3.3625
The Asian political dictionary / Lawrence Ziring, C.I. Eugene Kim. — Santa Barbara, Calif.: ABC-Clio, c1985. xx, 438 p.: maps; 24 cm. (Clio dictionaries in political science. # 10) Includes index. 1. Asia — Politics and government — Dictionaries. I. Kim, C. I. Eugene (Chong Ik Eugene), 1930- II. T. III. Series.
DS31.Z57 1985   950/.03/21 19   *LC* 85-5994   *ISBN* 0874363683

University of London. School of Oriental and African Studies. • 3.3626
Historical writing on the peoples of Asia. London, New York, Oxford University Press, 1961-62. 4 v. 25 cm. Bibliographical footnotes. 1. Asia — History — Historiography. I. T.
DS32.5.L6   950.072   *LC* 61-4093 rev

Kim, C. I. Eugene (Chong Ik Eugene), 1930-.   3.3627
An introduction to Asian politics / by C. I. Eugene Kim, Lawrence Ziring. — Englewood Cliffs, N.J.: Prentice-Hall, c1977. x, 400 p.: ill.; 24 cm. 1. Asia — Politics and government I. Ziring, Lawrence, 1928- joint author. II. T.
DS33.K55   320.9/5/042   *LC* 76-28342   *ISBN* 0134780817

Kirk, George Eden, 1911-.   • 3.3628
A short history of the Middle East, from the rise of Islam to modern times, by George E. Kirk. — 7th rev. ed. — New York: Praeger, [1964] 340 p.: maps.; 21 cm. 1. Middle East — History I. T.
DS33.K57 1964   309.156   *LC* 64-25427

Lamb, Alastair, 1930-.   • 3.3629
Asian frontiers; studies in a continuing problem. — New York: Praeger, [1968] ix, 246 p.: maps.; 22 cm. 1. Asia — Boundaries. 2. Asia — Politics and government I. T.
DS33.3.L3 1968b   327.5   *LC* 68-18543

Scalapino, Robert A.   3.3630
Asia and the major powers; implications for the international order [by Robert A. Scalapino. — Washington: American Enterprise Institute for Public Policy Research, [1972] 117 p.: map.; 23 cm. — (AEI-Hoover policy studies, 3) (Hoover Institution studies, 37) 1. Asia — Foreign relations. 2. Asia — Politics and government I. T. II. Series. III. Series: Hoover Institution studies, 37
DS33.3.S3   327.5/0181/2   *LC* 72-93977

Asia and U.S. foreign policy / James C. Hsiung, Winberg Chai,   3.3631
editors.
New York: Praeger, 1981. 263 p.; 25 cm. Based on papers presented at the Annual Meeting of the International Studies Association, Los Angeles, Calif., March 1980. Includes index. 1. Asia — Foreign relations — United States — Addresses, essays, lectures. 2. United States — Foreign relations — Asia — Addresses, essays, lectures. I. Hsiung, James Chieh, 1935- II. Chai, Winberg. III. International Studies Association. Meeting. (1980: Los Angeles, Calif.)
DS33.4.U6 A84   327.5073 19   *LC* 81-12096   *ISBN* 0030590124

Clough, Ralph N., 1916-.   3.3632
East Asia and U.S. security / Ralph N. Clough. — Washington: Brookings Institution, 1975 (c1974) 248 p.; 24 cm. 1. Asia — Foreign relations — United States. 2. United States — Foreign relations — Asia. 3. United States — National security 4. Asia — Politics and government I. T.
DS33.4.U6 C56   327.73/05   *LC* 74-274   *ISBN* 0815714807

Harrison, Selig S.   3.3633
The widening gulf: Asian nationalism and American policy / Selig S. Harrison. — New York: Free Press, c1978. xi, 468 p.: map; 24 cm. Includes index. 1. Nationalism — Asia. 2. Asia — Foreign relations — United States. 3. United States — Foreign relations — Asia. I. T.
DS33.4.U6 H35   327.73/05   *LC* 76-57881   *ISBN* 0029140803

U.S. foreign policy and Asian–Pacific security: a transregional   3.3634
approach / edited by William T. Tow and William R. Feeney.
Boulder, Colo.: Westview Press, 1982. xiv, 264 p.: ill.; 24 cm. (Westview special studies in national security and defense policy.) 1. Asia — Foreign relations — United States — Addresses, essays, lectures. 2. United States — Foreign relations — Asia — Addresses, essays, lectures. 3. Pacific Area — Strategic aspects — Addresses, essays, lectures. I. Tow, William T. II. Feeney, William R. III. Title: US foreign policy and Asian-Pacific security. IV. Title: United States foreign policy and Asian-Pacific security. V. Series.
DS33.4.U6 U38 1982   327.7305 19   *LC* 82-50179   *ISBN* 0865313873

Albertini, Rudolf von.   3.3635
[Europäische Kolonialherrschaft, 1880-1940. English] European colonial rule, 1880–1940: the impact of the West on India, Southeast Asia, and Africa / Rudolf von Albertini with Albert Wirz; translated by John G. Williamson. — Westport, Conn.: Greenwood Press, c1982. xxix, 581 p.: maps; 24 cm. — (Contributions in comparative colonial studies. 0163-3813; no. 10) Translation of: Europäische Kolonialherrschaft, 1880-1940. Includes index. 1. Colonies 2. Africa — History — 1884-1960 3. Asia — History I. Wirz, Albert. II. T. III. Series.
DS33.7.A4313 1982   909/.09719 19   *LC* 81-4264   *ISBN* 0313212759

Asia and the western Pacific: towards a new international order   3.3636
/ edited by Hedley Bull.
Sydney: Nelson in association with the Australian Institute of International Affairs, 1975. xxviii, 387 p.; 23 cm. 'Papers presented to the international conference organised by the Australian Institute of International Affairs at the Australian National University, Canberra, from 14 to 17 April 1973.' 1. Asia — Politics and government — Congresses. 2. Asia — Economic conditions — Congresses. 3. Pacific Area — Politics and government — Congresses. 4. Pacific Area — Economic conditions — Congresses. I. Bull, Hedley. II. Australian Institute of International Affairs.
DS35.A75   320.9/5/042   *LC* 76-355738   *ISBN* 0170050467

Asia's nuclear future / William H. Overholt, editor;   3.3637
contributors, Lewis A. Dunn ... [et al.].
Boulder, Colo.: Westview Press, 1978 (c1977). xvi, 285 p.; 24 cm. — (Studies of the Research Institute on International Change, Columbia University) (A Westview special study) 1. Nuclear weapons 2. Asia — Politics and government 3. Asia — Defenses I. Overholt, William H.
DS35.A87   327/.174/095   *LC* 77-778   *ISBN* 0891582177

Barnett, A. D., ed.   • 3.3638
Communist strategies in Asia; a comparative analysis of governments and parties. — New York, Praeger [1963] x, 293 p. 21 cm. — (Praeger publications in Russian history and world communism, no. 132) 'Originally presented, in briefer form, as papers for a symposium on 'Communism in Asia' held during the 1962 Annual Meeting of the Association for Asian Studies.' Includes bibliographies. 1. Communism — Asia. 2. Asia — Politics. I. T.
DS35.B3   950   *LC* 63-10823

Changing patterns of security and stability in Asia / edited by   3.3639
Sudershan Chawla, D. R. SarDesai.
New York: Praeger Publishers, 1980. xi, 257 p.; 25 cm. 1. Asia — Politics and government 2. Asia — Foreign relations. 3. Asia — Defenses I. Chawla, Sudershan, 1924- II. SarDesai, D. R.
DS35.C43   320.9/5/042   *LC* 79-22977   *ISBN* 0030524164

Intra–Asian international relations / edited by George T. Yu.   3.3640
Boulder, Colo.: Westview Press, 1977. xi, 172 p.; 24 cm. — (Westview special studies on China and East Asia) (Westview special studies on South and Southeast Asia) 'This book originated from a panel organized for the 1976 annual conference of the Association for Asian Studies.' 1. Asia — Politics and government I. Yu, George T., 1931- II. Association for Asian Studies.
DS35.I57   327/.095   *LC* 77-24382   *ISBN* 0891581251

Romein, Jan Marius, 1893-.   • 3.3641
The Asian century; a history of modern nationalism in Asia, by Jan Romein in collaboration with Jan Erik Romein. Translated by R. T. Clark. With a foreword by K. M. Panikkar. — Berkeley, University of California Press, 1962. 448 p. 25 cm. 'First published in Dutch ... This edition translated from the German and with an additional section ('Last period') first published 1962.' 1. Asia — Hist. I. T.
DS35.R583   950.4   *LC* 62-51755

Scalapino, Robert A.   3.3642
Asia and the road ahead: issues for the major powers / by Robert A. Scalapino. — Berkeley: University of California Press, c1975. x, 337 p.: map; 23 cm. Includes index. 1. Asia — Politics and government 2. Asia — Foreign relations. 3. United States — Foreign relations — Asia. 4. Asia — Foreign relations — United States. I. T.
DS35.S347   320.9/5/042   *LC* 75-15219   *ISBN* 0520030664

Wilcox, Wayne Ayres.   3.3643
Asia and the international system / edited by Wayne Wilcox, Leo E. Rose [and] Gavin Boyd. — Cambridge, Mass.: Winthrop, [1972] x, 383 p.: map.; 24 cm. 1. Asia — Foreign relations. 2. Asia — Politics and government I. Rose, Leo E. joint author. II. Boyd, Gavin. joint author. III. T.
DS35.W547   327.5   *LC* 77-181336   *ISBN* 0876260466

DS35.3–49 Middle East. Islamic and Arab Countries (General)

The Cambridge history of Islam; edited by P. M. Holt, Ann K. • **3.3644**
S. Lambton [and] Bernard Lewis.
Cambridge [Eng.]: University Press, 1970. 2 v.: illus., maps.; 24 cm.
1. Civilization, Islamic 2. Islamic countries — History. I. Holt, P. M. (Peter Malcolm) ed. II. Lambton, Ann Katharine Swynford. ed. III. Lewis, Bernard. ed.
DS35.6.C3   910.03/176/7   LC 73-77291   ISBN 52107567X

Robinson, Francis.   **3.3645**
Atlas of the Islamic World since 1500 / by Francis Robinson. — New York, N.Y.: Facts On File, [c1982] 238 p.: ill. (some col.), col. maps; 31 cm. Includes index. 1. Islamic countries I. T.
DS35.6.R6 1982   911/.17671 19   LC 82-675002   ISBN 0871966298

Muslim peoples: a world ethnographic survey / edited by   **3.3646**
Richard V. Weekes; maps by John E. Coffman; Paul Ramier
Stewart, consultant.
2nd ed., rev. and expanded. — Westport, Conn.: Greenwood Press, 1984. 2 v. (xl, 953 p.): maps; 25 cm. 1. Muslims 2. Ethnology — Islamic countries. 3. Islamic countries — Social life and customs. I. Weekes, Richard V., 1924-
DS35.625.A1 M87 1984   305.6/971 19   LC 83-18494   ISBN 0313233926

Khalil, Muhammad, ed.   • **3.3647**
The Arab States and the Arab League; a documentary record. Beirut: Khayats [1962] 2 v.; 25 cm. 1. Arab countries — History — 20th century — Sources. I. League of Arab States. II. T.
DS36.2.K45   LC ne 63-705

Dempsey, Michael W.   **3.3648**
Atlas of the Arab world: a concise introduction to the economic, social, political, and military status of the Arab World / by Michael Dempsey and Norman Barrett. — New York, NY: Facts on File, 1983. 1 v. Includes index. 1. Arab countries I. Barrett, Norman S. II. T.
DS36.7.D45 1983   909/.0974927 19   LC 83-1725   ISBN 0871961385

Rodinson, Maxime.   **3.3649**
[Arabes. English] The Arabs / Maxime Rodinson; translated by Arthur Goldhammer. — Chicago: University of Chicago Press, c1981. xvi, 188 p.; 21 cm. Translation of Les Arabes. Includes index. 1. Arabs I. T.
DS36.7.R6213   909/.04927 19   LC 80-25916   ISBN 0226723550

Hodgson, Marshall G. S.   **3.3650**
The venture of Islam: conscience and history in a world civilization / Marshall G. S. Hodgson. — Chicago: University of Chicago Press, 1974. 3 v.: ill.; 24 cm. 1. Civilization, Islamic 2. Islamic Empire — History 3. Middle East — History — 1517- I. T.
DS36.85.H63   909/.09/7671   LC 73-87243   ISBN 0226346773

Bell, Richard, 1876-.   **3.3651**
[Introduction to the Qur'ān] Bell's introduction to the Qur'ān. [New ed.]; revised and enlarged by W. Montgomery Watt. Edinburgh, Edinburgh U.P., 1970. xi, 258 p. 21 cm. (Islamic surveys, 8) Earlier ed. published under title: Introduction to the Qur'ān. 1. Koran — Introductions. I. Watt, W. Montgomery (William Montgomery) II. T. III. Title: Introduction to the Qur'ān. IV. Series.
DS36.85.I8 no. 8   297/.122   LC 77-106474

Khalidi, Tarif, 1938-.   **3.3652**
Classical Arab Islam: the culture and heritage of the Golden Age / Tarif Khalidi. — Princeton, NJ, USA: Darwin Press, c1985. 158 p.; 25 cm. Includes index. 1. Civilization, Islamic I. T.
DS36.85.K4 1985   909/.097671 19   LC 84-70416   ISBN 0878500472

Schacht, Joseph, 1902-1969.   **3.3653**
The legacy of Islam / edited by Joseph Schacht, with C. E. Bosworth. — 2d ed. — Oxford: Clarendon Press, 1974. xiv, 530 p., [20] leaves of plates: ill.; 19 cm. First ed. (1931) edited by T. Arnold and A. Guillaume. 1. Civilization, Islamic 2. Islam — Addresses, essays, lectures. I. Bosworth, Clifford Edmund. joint author. II. Arnold, Thomas Walker, Sir, 1864-1930, ed. The legacy of Islam. III. T.
DS36.85.S3   909   LC 74-195528   ISBN 019821913X

Watt, W. Montgomery (William Montgomery)   **3.3654**
The majesty that was Islam; the Islamic world, 661–1100 [by] W. Montgomery Watt. New York, Praeger [1974] 276 p. illus. 24 cm. (Great civilizations series) 1. Civilization, Islamic 2. Islamic Empire — History I. T.
DS36.85.W37   910/.031/7671   LC 74-331   ISBN 0275518701

Lewis, Bernard. comp.   **3.3655**
Islam, from the Prophet Muhammad to the capture of Constantinople / edited and translated by Bernard Lewis. — New York: Walker, 1974. 2 v.; 21 cm. — (Documentary history of Western civilization) Includes indexes. 1. Civilization, Islamic — Sources. I. T.
DS36.855.L48 1974   DS36.855 L48 1974.   910/.031/7671   LC 72-7229   ISBN 0802720234

Rogers, Michael, 1935-.   **3.3656**
The spread of Islam / by Michael Rogers. — Oxford: Elsevier-Phaidon, 1976. 152 p.: ill. (chiefly col.), facsims. (chiefly col.), col. maps, plans (chiefly col.); 29 cm. (The Making of the past) Includes index. 1. Islamic Empire I. T.
DS36.855.R63   909/.097/671   LC 76-367216   ISBN 0729000168

Bat Ye'or.   **3.3657**
[Dhimmi. English] The Dhimmi: Jews and Christians under Islam / Bat Ye'or; with a preface by Jacques Ellul; translated from the French by David Maisel (author's text), Paul Fenton (document section), and David Littman. — Rev. and enl. English ed. — Rutherford, [N.J.]: Fairleigh Dickinson University Press; London: Associated University Presses, c1985. 444 p.: ill.; 24 cm. Translation of: Le dhimmi. Includes indexes. 1. Dhimmis 2. Islamic Empire — Ethnic relations. 3. Arab countries — Ethnic relations. I. T.
DS36.9.D47 B3813 1985   909/.097671 19   LC 84-47749   ISBN 0838632335

Shorter encyclopaedia of Islam / edited on behalf of the Royal • **3.3658**
Netherlands Academy by H.A.R. Gibb and J.H. Kramers.
Ithaca, N.Y.: Cornell University Press, 1953. viii, 671 p.: ill.; 27 cm. 'Includes all the articles contained in the first edition and supplement of the Encyclopaedia of Isalm which relate particularly to the religion and law of Islam.' 1. Islam — Dictionaries. I. Gibb, Hamilton Alexander Rosskeen, Sir, 1895-1971. II. Kramers, Johannes Hendrik, 1891-1951. III. Koninklijke Nederlandse Akademie van Wetenschappen.
DS37.E52 1953a   LC 57-59109

The Encyclopaedia of Islam.   • **3.3659**
New ed., prepared by a number of leading orientalists. Edited by an editorial commmittee consisting of H. A. R. Gibb ... [et al.]. — Leiden: Brill, 1960-. v.: ill., fold. maps (some col.) plans.; 26 cm. Issued in parts. Index to v. 1-3 compiled by H. & J.D. Pearson; edited by E. van Donzel. — 1. Islam — Dictionaries. 2. Islamic countries — Dictionaries and encyclopedias. I. Gibb, Hamilton Alexander Rosskeen, Sir, 1895-1971. II. Van Donzel, E. III. Pearson, H. IV. Pearson, J.D.
DS37.E523   956.003   LC 61-4395

Encyclopaedia of Islam.   **3.3660**
E.J. Brill's first encyclopaedia of Islam, 1913–1936 / edited by M.Th. Houtsma ... [et al.]. — Leiden; New York: E.J. Brill, 1987. p. cm. Reprint. Originally published: The Encyclopaedia of Islam. Leiden: E.J. Brill, 1913-1938. 1. Islam — Dictionaries. 2. Islamic countries — Dictionaries and encyclopaedias. I. Houtsma, M. Th. (Martijn Theodoor), 1851-1943. II. T. III. Title: First encyclopaedia of Islam.
DS37.E523x 1987   909/.097671 19   LC 87-10319   ISBN 9004082654

Hitti, Philip Khuri, 1886-.   • **3.3661**
History of the Arabs from the earliest times to the present [by] Philip K. Hitti. 10th ed. [London] Macmillan; [New York] St Martin's Press [1970] xxiv, 822 p. illus., geneal. tables, maps. 23 cm. 1. Arabs — History 2. Civilization, Arab 3. Islamic Empire — History I. T.
DS37.7.H58 1970   953   LC 74-102765

Issawi, Charles Philip.   **3.3662**
The Arab world's legacy: essays / by Charles Issawi. — Princeton, N.J.: Darwin Press, c1981. 378 p.; 24 cm. 1. Civilization, Arab — Addresses, lectures. 2. Arab countries — History — Addresses, essays, lectures. 3. Middle East — Addresses, essays, lectures. I. T.
DS37.7.I87   909/.04927 19   LC 81-3279   ISBN 0878500391

Mansfield, Peter, 1928-.   **3.3663**
The Arab world: a comprehensive history / Peter Mansfield. New York: Crowell, c1976. 572 p.: map; 24 cm. Includes index. 1. Arab countries — History I. T.
DS37.7.M33 1976   909/.04/927   LC 76-45442   ISBN 0690011709

Gaudefroy-Demombynes, Maurice, 1862-1957.   • **3.3664**
[Institutions musulmanes. English] Muslim institutions, translated from the French by John P. MacGregor. London, Allen & Unwin [1950] 216 p. 23 cm. 1. Islam I. T.
DS38.G314   297   LC 50-11430

Gibb, Hamilton Alexander Rosskeen, Sir, 1895-1971.   • **3.3665**
Islamic society and the West; a study of the impact of western civilization on Moslem culture in the Near East, by H. A. R. Gibb and Harold Bowen. — London; New York: Oxford University Press, 1950-. v. in   23 cm. 'Issued under the auspices of the Royal Institute of International Affairs.' Bibliography: v. 1, pt. 2, p. [263]-271. 1. Civilization, Mohammedan — Occidental influences. I. Bowen, Harold, joint author. II. T.
DS38.G485   949.6   LC 50-9162 rev

Smith, Wilfred Cantwell, 1916-.   • **3.3666**
Islam in modern history. Princeton: Princeton University Press, 1957. 317 p.; 25 cm. 1. Islam — History. 2. Civilization, Islamic 3. Islam — 20th century I. T.
DS38.S56   297   LC 57-5458

Donner, Fred McGraw, 1945-.   **3.3667**
The early Islamic conquests / by Fred McGraw Donner. — Princeton, N.J.: Princeton University Press, c1981. xviii, 489 p.; 24 cm. Includes indexes. 1. Islamic Empire — History — 622-661 I. T.
DS38.1.D66   909/.09767101 19   LC 80-8544   ISBN 0691053278

Bulliet, Richard W.   **3.3668**
Conversion to Islam in the medieval period: an essay in quantitative history / Richard W. Bulliet. — Cambridge: Harvard University Press, 1979. 158 p.: ill.; 24 cm. 1. Muslim converts — Islamic Empire. 2. Islam — History. 3. Islamic Empire — History 4. Islamic Empire — Social conditions. I. T.
DS38.3.B84   909/.09/7671   LC 79-14411   ISBN 0674170350

Hitti, Philip Khuri, 1886-.   **3.3669**
Capital cities of Arab Islam, by Philip K. Hitti. — Minneapolis: University of Minnesota Press, [1973] v, 176 p.: illus.; 24 cm. 1. Cities and towns — Islamic Empire. I. T.
DS38.3.H58 1973   910/.031/7671   LC 72-92335   ISBN 0816606633

Von Grunebaum, Gustave E. (Gustave Edmund), 1909-1972.   • **3.3670**
[Islam. English] Classical Islam; a history, 600–1258, by G. E. Von Grunebaum. Translated by Katherine Watson. [1st U.S. ed.] Chicago, Aldine Pub. Co. [1970] 243 p. illus., maps. 22 cm. Translation of Der Islam first published in Propyläen Weltgeschichte in 1963. 1. Islamic Empire I. T.
DS38.3.V6413 1970b   909.09/767   LC 78-75049   ISBN 020215016X

Shaban, M. A.   **3.3671**
Islamic history, a new interpretation [by] M. A. Shaban. Cambridge [Eng.]: University Press, 1971-. 2 v. : maps.; 23 cm. 1. Islamic Empire — History I. T.
DS38.5.S5   909/.09/767101   LC 79-145604   ISBN 0521081378

Wellhausen, Julius, 1844-1918.   • **3.3672**
[Arabische Reich und sein Sturz. English] The Arab kingdom and its fall. [Translated by Margaret Graham Weir. Edited and indexed by A. H. Harley] London, Curzon Press; Totowa, N.J., Rowman & Littlefield [1973] xvii, 591 p. 23 cm. Translation of Das arabische Reich und sein Sturz. Reprint of the 1927 ed. 1. Islamic Empire — History — 661-750 2. Islamic Empire — History — 622-661 I. T.
DS38.5.W4513 1973   953/.02   LC 73-764   ISBN 0874711746

Kennedy, Hugh (Hugh N.)   **3.3673**
The early Abbasid Caliphate: a political history / Hugh Kennedy. — London: Croom Helm; Totowa, N.J.: Barnes & Noble, c1981. 238 p.: maps; 23 cm. Includes index. 1. Islamic Empire — History — 750-1258 I. T.
DS38.6.K46   909/.09767101 19   LC 81-124084   ISBN 0389200182

Polk, William Roe, 1929-.   **3.3674**
The Arab world / William R. Polk. — 4th ed. — Cambridge, Mass.: Harvard University Press, 1980. xxix, 456 p.: maps; 25 cm. — (The American foreign policy library) Previous editions published under title: The United States and the Arab world. Includes index. 1. Arab countries — History 2. United States — Foreign relations — Arab countries. 3. Arab countries — Foreign relations — United States. I. T.
DS39.P64 1980   327.73017/4927   LC 80-16995   ISBN 0674043162

The Middle East, abstracts and index.   **3.3675**
v. 1- Mar. 1978-. Pittsburgh, Northumberland Press [etc.] v. 28 cm. Quarterly. 1. Middle East — Abstracts — Periodicals. I. Library Information and Research Service.
DS41.M44   016.956/005   LC 78-645468

Hurewitz, J. C., 1914- ed.   **3.3676**
The Middle East and North Africa in world politics: a documentary record / compiled, translated, and edited by J. C. Hurewitz. — 2d ed., rev. and enl. — New Haven: Yale University Press, 1975-. v.   ; 26 cm. First ed. originally published in 1956 under title: Diplomacy in the Near and Middle East. 1. Middle East — History — 1517- Sources. 2. Africa, North — History — 1882- Sources. 3. Middle East — Foreign relations — Sources. 4. Africa,

North — Foreign relations — Sources. 5. Africa, North — History — 1517-1882 — Sources. I. T.
DS42.H87 1975   909/.09/7671   LC 74-83525   ISBN 0300012942

Mideast file / Shiloah Center for Middle Eastern and African   **3.3677**
Studies, Tel–Aviv University.
Vol. 1, no. 1 (Mar. 1982)-   . — Oxford; Medford, N.Y.: Learned Information, c1982-. v.; 28 cm. Quarterly. Issued also on microfiche and in machine-readable form. 1. Middle East — Abstracts — Periodicals. I. Mekhon Shiloah le-heker ha-Mizrah ha-tikhon ve-Afrikah.
DS42.4.M53   956/.005 19   LC 82-645511

Brice, William Charles.   • **3.3678**
South–west Asia [by] William C. Brice. London, University of London P. [1967] 448 p. 16 plates, maps, tables, diagrs. 22 cm. (A Systematic regional geography, v. 8) Maps on endpapers. 1. Middle East — Description and travel. I. T.
DS44.B7x   915.6   LC 67-75420

The Cambridge atlas of the Middle East and North Africa /   **3.3679**
[edited by] Gerald Blake, John Dewdney, Jonathan Mitchell.
Cambridge [Cambridgeshire]; New York: Cambridge University Press, 1987. 1 v. 1. Middle East 2. Middle East — Maps. I. Blake, Gerald Henry. II. Dewdney, John C. III. Mitchell, Jonathan, 1959-
DS44.C36 1987   912/.56 19   LC 87-6548   ISBN 0521242436

Coon, Carleton Stevens, 1904-.   • **3.3680**
Caravan: the story of the Middle East. — Rev. ed. — New York: Holt, [1958] vi, 386 p.: ill., maps. 1. Middle East 2. Middle East — Civilization. I. T.
DS44.C6 1958   LC 58-13740

McClintock, Marsha Hamilton.   **3.3681**
The Middle East and North Africa on film: an annotated filmography / Marsha Hamilton McClintock. — New York: Garland Pub., 1982. xxiii, 542 p.; 23 cm. — (Garland reference library of the humanities. v. 159) Includes indexes. 1. Middle East — Film catalogs. 2. Africa, North — Film catalogs. I. T. II. Series.
DS44.M43 1982   011/.37 19   LC 82-12114   ISBN 0824092600

The Middle East: a political and economic survey / edited by   **3.3682**
Peter Mansfield.
5th ed. — Oxford; New York: Oxford University Press, 1980. ix, 579 p.: map; 23 cm. Includes index. 1. Middle East I. Mansfield, Peter, 1928-
DS44.M5 1980   956 19   LC 79-23699   ISBN 0192158511

Le Strange, G. (Guy), 1854-1933.   • **3.3683**
The lands of the Eastern Caliphate: Mesopotamia, Persia, and Central Asia from the Moslem conquest to the time of Timur. New York, Barnes & Noble [1966] xvii, 536 p. 19 maps. 23 cm. 1. Iraq — Historical geography. 2. Iran — Historical geography. 3. Asia, Central — Historical geography. 4. Turkey — Historical geography. I. T.
DS44.9.L6 1966   LC 66-1733

Fisher, W. B. (William Bayne)   **3.3684**
The Middle East: a physical, social, and regional geography / W. B. Fisher. — 7th ed., completely rev. and reset. — London: Methuen, 1978. xiv, 615 p.: ill.; 24 cm. Includes index. 1. Middle East — Description and travel. I. T.
DS49.F56 1978   956   LC 79-301895   ISBN 0416715109

The Middle East and North Africa.   **3.3685**
1948-. London: Europa Publications, 1948-. v. Annual. 1. Middle East 2. Africa, North I. Europa Publications Limited.
DS49.M5   LC 48-3250

Rostovzeff, Michael Ivanovitch, 1870-1952.   • **3.3686**
Caravan cities, by M. Rostovtzeff. Translated by D. and T. Talbot Rice. New York, AMS Press [1971] xiv, 232 p. map, plans, plates. 19 cm. 'Reprinted from the edition of 1932.' 1. Palmyra (Ancient city) 2. Gerasa. 3. Petra (Ancient city) 4. Dura-Europos (Ancient city) I. T.
DS49.R83 1971   915.6   LC 75-137287   ISBN 0404054455

Beaumont, Peter.   **3.3687**
The Middle East: a geographical study / Peter Beaumont, Gerald H. Blake, J. Malcolm Wagstaff. — London; New York: Wiley, c1976. xvii, 572 p.: ill.; 24 cm. Includes index. 1. Middle East — Description and travel. I. Blake, Gerald Henry. joint author. II. Wagstaff, J. Malcolm (John Malcolm), 1940- joint author. III. T.
DS49.7.B36   330.9/56/04   LC 74-28284   ISBN 0471061174. ISBN 0471061190 pbk

DS51 Special Cities, Peoples, Regions, A–Z

Le Strange, G. (Guy), 1854-1933.   **3.3688**
Baghdad during the Abbasid caliphate from contemporary Arabic and Persian sources. — London, Oxford university press, H. Milford [1942] xxxi, 381 p. fold. map, plans (part fold.) 23 cm. Part of the plans accompanied by a leaf containing descriptive letterpress, not included in the collation. 'Impression of 1924. First edition 1900. This impression has been produced photographically ... from sheets of the first edition.' 1. Baghdad (Iraq) I. T.
DS51.B3 L4 1942   LC 26-2950

Wiet, Gaston, 1887-1971.   • **3.3689**
Baghdad: metropolis of the Abbasid caliphate / translated by Seymour Feiler. — [1st ed.] Norman: University of Oklahoma Press [1971] vii, 184 p.: map; 20 cm. (Centers of civilization series.) 1. Baghdad (Iraq) — History. I. T. II. Series.
DS51.B3 W5   956.7   LC 72-123348   ISBN 080610922X

People without a country: the Kurds and Kurdistan / [by] A.R.   **3.3690**
Ghassemlou ... [et al.]; edited by Gerard Chaliand; translated
[from the French] by Michael Pallis.
London: Zed Press, 1980. [10], 246 p.: maps; 23 cm. — (Middle East series) Translation of: Les Kurdes et le Kurdistan. Includes index. 1. Kurds I. Ghassemlou, Abdul Rahman. II. Chaliand, Gérard, 1934-
DS51.K7 K86313   959.6/7 19   LC 81-103595   ISBN 090576269X

Magnarella, Paul J.   **3.3691**
Tradition and change in a Turkish town / [by] Paul J. Magnarella. — [Cambridge, Mass.]: Schenkman Pub. Co.; [distributed by Halsted Press, New York, 1974] xiii, 199 p.: ill.; 24 cm. 'A Halsted Press book.' 1. Susurluk (Turkey) I. T.
DS51.S94 M3   309.1/562   LC 74-14927   ISBN 0470563389 ISBN 0470563397

DS54–54.9 CYPRUS

American University (Washington, D.C.). Foreign Area Studies.   **3.3692**
Cyprus, a country study / edited by Frederica M. Bunge ... [et al.]. — 3d ed. — Washington, D.C.: Foreign Area Studies, American University: for sale by the Supt. of Docs., U.S. Govt. Print. Off., c1980. xxx, 306 p.: ill.; 24 cm. — (Area handbook series.) Supersedes the 1971 ed., by E. K. Keefe, and others, and issued under title: Area handbook for Cyprus. 'DA Pam 550-22.' Includes index. 1. Cyprus. I. Bunge, Frederica M. II. Keefe, Eugene K. Area handbook for Cyprus. III. T. IV. Series.
DS54.A3 K43 1980   956.45   LC 80-607041

Hill, George Francis, Sir, 1867-1948.   **3.3693**
A history of Cyprus, by Sir George Hill. — Cambridge [Eng.]: University Press, 1972. 4 v. illus. Includes bibliographical references. 1. Cyprus — Hist. 2. Cyprus — Antiq. I. T.
DS54.5.H5

Salih, Halil Ibrahim.   **3.3694**
Cyprus, the impact of diverse nationalism on a state / Halil Ibrahim Salih. — University: University of Alabama Press, c1978. x, 203 p.: ill.; 24 cm. Includes index. 1. Cyprus — History I. T.
DS54.5.S24   956.4/5   LC 76-21743   ISBN 0817357068

Crawshaw, Nancy.   **3.3695**
The Cyprus revolt: an account of the struggle for union with Greece / Nancy Crawshaw. — London: Boston: G. Allen & Unwin, 1978. 447 p.: map (on lining paper); 24 cm. Includes index. 1. Cyprus — History — 20th century I. T.
DS54.8.C66   956.4/5/03   LC 79-300300   ISBN 0049400533

Durrell, Lawrence.   • **3.3696**
Bitter lemons. — [1st American ed.]. — New York: Dutton, [c1957] 256 p.: illus.; 22 cm. 1. Cyprus — Social life and customs. 2. Cyprus — Politics and government. I. T.
DS54.8.D8 1957a   915.64   LC 58-5225

Markides, Kyriacos C.   **3.3697**
The rise and fall of the Cyprus Republic / Kyriacos C. Markides. New Haven: Yale University Press, 1977. xvii, 200 p.; 22 cm. 1. Cyprus — Politics and government. 2. Cyprus — Social conditions. I. T.
DS54.9.M37   320.9/564/504   LC 76-49767   ISBN 0300020899

Polyviou, Polyvios G., 1949-.   **3.3698**
Cyprus, conflict and negotiation, 1960–1980 / Polyvios G. Polyviou. — New York: Holmes & Meier Publishers, 1981 (c1980). 246 p. 1. Cyprus — Politics and government. I. T.
DS54.9.P638   956.45/04 19   LC 80-25942   ISBN 0841906831

DS56–63.1 History and Politics (General)

King, Philip J.   **3.3699**
American archaeology in the mideast: a history of the American schools of oriental research / Philip J. King. — Philadelphia: American Schools of Oriental Research, c1983. xiv, 291 p.; ill.; 24 cm. 1. American Schools of Oriental Research — History. 2. Archaeologists — United States. 3. Middle East — Antiquities. I. T.
DS56.K52 1983   956/.0072073 19   LC 82-24337   ISBN 0897575083

Moscati, Sabatino.   • **3.3700**
The face of the ancient Orient: a panorama of Near Eastern civilizations in pre-classical times. — Chicago: Quadrangle, 1960. xvi, 328 p.: ill.; 23 cm. 1. Civilization, Ancient 2. Middle East — Antiquities I. T.
DS56.M68 1960   901.91   935   LC 59-15207

Bates, Daniel G.   **3.3701**
Peoples and cultures of the Middle East / Daniel G. Bates, Amal Rassam. — Englewood Cliffs, NJ: Prentice-Hall, c1983. xiv, 289 p.: ill.; 23 cm. 1. Middle East — Social life and customs. I. Rassam, Amal. II. T.
DS57.B34 1983   956 19   LC 82-21547   ISBN 0136567932

The Central Middle East; a handbook of anthropology and   **3.3702**
published research on the Nile Valley, the Arab Levant,
southern Mesopotamia, the Arabian Peninsula, and Israel.
Louise E. Sweet, editor. With a foreword by William D.
Schorger and chapters by Harold B. Barclay [and others]
New Haven, HRAF Press, 1971. xi, 323 p. 22 cm. 1. Middle East — Social life and customs. 2. Middle East — Social life and customs — Bibliography. I. Sweet, Louise Elizabeth, 1916- ed. II. Barclay, Harold B.
DS57.C44   915.6/03/4   LC 70-148033   ISBN 0875361080

Gulick, John, 1924-.   **3.3703**
The Middle East: an anthropological perspective / John Gulick. — Pacific Palisades, Calif.: Goodyear Pub. Co., c1976. xvii, 244 p.; 24 cm. — (Goodyear regional anthropology series) 1. Ethnology — Middle East 2. Middle East — Social life and customs. I. T.
DS57.G84   956   LC 75-26052   ISBN 0876205783. ISBN 0876205775 pbk

Hawkes, Jacquetta Hopkins, 1910-.   **3.3704**
The first great civilizations; life in Mesopotamia, the Indus Valley, and Egypt [by] Jacquetta Hawkes. [1st ed.] New York, Knopf; [distributed by Random House] 1973. xxvi, 465, xvii p. illus. 25 cm. (The History of human society) 1. Indus civilization 2. Middle East — Civilization — To 622 I. T.
DS57.H37   913.35/03   LC 74-154939   ISBN 0394461614

Peoples of Old Testament times, edited by D. J. Wiseman for   **3.3705**
the Society for Old Testament Study.
Oxford, Clarendon Press, 1973. xxi, 402 p. illus. 22 cm. 1. Middle East — Civilization — To 622. 2. Middle East — History — To 622. I. Wiseman, D. J. (Donald John) ed. II. Society for Old Testament Study.
DS57.P44   221.9/1   LC 73-179589   ISBN 0198263163

Peters, F. E. (Francis E.)   **3.3706**
The harvest of Hellenism; a history of the Near East from Alexander the Great to the triumph of Christianity [by] F. E. Peters. New York, Simon and Schuster 1971. 800 p. maps. 23 cm. 1. Hellenism 2. Middle East — Civilization — To 622. I. T.
DS57.P46   939   LC 74-116509   ISBN 0671206583

Redman, Charles L.   **3.3707**
The rise of civilization: from early farmers to urban society in the ancient Near East / Charles L. Redman. — San Francisco: W. H. Freeman, c1978. viii, 367 p.: ill.; 24 cm. Includes index. 1. Middle East — Civilization. I. T.
DS57.R4   939   LC 78-1493   ISBN 0716700565

Von Grunebaum, Gustave E. (Gustave Edmund), 1909-1972.   • **3.3708**
Modern Islam: the search for cultural identity. Berkeley: University of California Press, 1962. vii, 303 p.; 24 cm. Articles by the author, which have

appeared previously in various collections. 1. Civilization, Islamic 2. Nationalism — Arabic countries I. T.
DS57.V6   915.6   *LC* 62-17178

Christians and Jews in the Ottoman empire: the functioning of a   **3.3709**
plural society / edited by Benjamin Braude and Bernard Lewis.
New York: Holmes & Meier Publishers, 1982. 2 v.; 24 cm. Essays that grew out of a research seminar and conference on the history and legacy of the Millet system, at Princeton University, the spring and summer of 1978. Includes index. 1. Christians — Near East — Congresses. 2. Jews — Near East — Congresses. 3. Christians — Turkey — Congresses. 4. Jews — Turkey — Congresses. 5. Minorities — Near East — Congresses. 6. Minorities — Turkey — Congresses. 7. Turkey — History — Ottoman Empire, 1288-1918 — Congresses. I. Braude, Benjamin. II. Lewis, Bernard.
DS58.C48 1982   956/.01 19   *LC* 80-11337   *ISBN* 0841905193

Bacharach, Jere L., 1938-.   **3.3710**
A Middle East studies handbook / Jere L. Bacharach. — Seattle: University of Washington Press, c1984. x, 160 p.: ill.; 29 cm. Rev. ed. of: A Near East studies handbook. Rev. ed. c1976. 1. Islamic Empire — History — Handbooks, manuals, etc. 2. Middle East — History — 1517- — Handbooks, manuals, etc. I. Bacharach, Jere L., 1938- Near East studies handbook. II. T.
DS61.B3 1984   956 19   *LC* 84-2225   *ISBN* 0295961384

Ziring, Lawrence, 1928-.   **3.3711**
The Middle East political dictionary / Lawrence Ziring. — Santa Barbara, Calif.: ABC-Clio Information Services, c1984. xviii, 452 p.; 24 cm. — (Clio dictionaries in political science. #5) Includes index. 1. Middle East — Politics and government — Dictionaries. 2. Middle East — Dictionaries and encyclopedias. I. T. II. Series.
DS61.Z58 1984   956/.003/21 19   *LC* 82-22673   *ISBN* 0874360447

Cleveland, William L.   • **3.3712**
The making of an Arab nationalist; Ottomanism and Arabism in the life and thought of Sati' al-Husri, by William L. Cleveland. Princeton, N.J., Princeton University Press, 1971 [i.e. 1972] xvi, 211 p. port. 23 cm. (Princeton studies on the Near East.) 1. Husrī, Abū Khaldūn Sāti', 1881-1968. I. T. II. Series.
DS61.52.H87 C55   320.5/4/0924 B   *LC* 78-155961   *ISBN* 069103088X

Drews, Robert.   **3.3713**
The Greek accounts of Eastern history. Washington, Center for Hellenic Studies; distributed by Harvard University Press, Cambridge, Mass., 1973. 220 p. 22 cm. (Publications of the Center for Hellenic Studies) 1. Herodotus. History. 2. Historians — Greece. 3. Middle East — Historiography. I. T.
DS61.6.D73   913.392/03/072038   *LC* 72-87771   *ISBN* 0674350152

Eddy, Samuel Kennedy, 1926-.   **3.3714**
The king is dead: studies in the Near Eastern resistance to Hellenism, 334–31 B. C. — Lincoln: University of Nebraska Press, 1961. x, 390 p.: plates, fold. map; 24 cm. Bibliography: p. 350-365. 1. Hellenism 2. History, Ancient 3. Near East — Hist. 4. Near East — Religion. I. T.
DS62.E3   935   *LC* 61-10151

Fisher, Sydney Nettleton, 1906-.   **3.3715**
The Middle East: a history / Sydney Nettleton Fisher. — 3d ed. — New York: Knopf, c1979. xix, 811 p.; 24 cm. 1. Middle East — History 2. Middle East — History — 20th century. I. T.
DS62.F5 1979   956   *LC* 78-17852   *ISBN* 0394320980

Goldschmidt, Arthur, 1938-.   **3.3716**
A concise history of the Middle East / Arthur Goldschmidt, Jr. — 2nd ed., rev. and updated. — Boulder, Colo.: Westview Press; Cairo, Egypt: American University in Cairo Press, 1983. xvi, 416 p.: ill., maps; 25 cm. Includes index. 1. Middle East — History I. T.
DS62.G64 1983   956 19   *LC* 83-50061   *ISBN* 0865315981

Hitti, Philip Khuri, 1886-.   • **3.3717**
The Near East in history, a 5000 year story. Princeton, N.J., Van Nostrand [1961] 574 p. illus. 24 cm. 1. Middle East — History I. T.
DS62.H68   956   *LC* 61-1098

Hottinger, Arnold.   • **3.3718**
The Arabs: their history, culture and place in the modern world. Berkeley, University of California Press, 1963. 344 p. illus., maps, facsims. 25 cm. 'For the English language edition, the original book has been revised and brought up to date.' 1. Nationalism — Arab countries. 2. Arab countries I. T.
DS62.H8233   953   *LC* 64-1108

Hallo, William W.   **3.3719**
The ancient Near East; a history [by] William W. Hallo [and] William Kelly Simpson. Under the general editorship of John Morton Blum. New York, Harcourt Brace Jovanovich [1971] x, 319 p. illus. 24 cm. 1. Middle East — History — To 622 I. Simpson, William Kelly. joint author. II. T.
DS62.2.H3   913.3/39/03   *LC* 71-155560   *ISBN* 0155027557

Van Seters, John.   **3.3720**
In search of history: historiography in the ancient world and the origins of Biblical history / John Van Seters. — New Haven: Yale University Press, c1983. xiii, 399 p.; 24 cm. Includes indexes. 1. Bible. O.T. Historical Books — Criticism, interpretation, etc. 2. Middle East — History — To 622 — Historiography. I. T.
DS62.2.V35 1983   939/.4 19   *LC* 82-48912   *ISBN* 0300028776

Hourani, Albert Habib.   **3.3721**
The emergence of the modern Middle East / Albert Hourani. — Berkeley: University of California Press, c1981. xx, 243 p. 1. Middle East — History I. T.
DS62.4.H678   *LC* 78-66071   *ISBN* 0520038626

Hudson, Michael C.   **3.3722**
Arab politics: the search for legitimacy / Michael C. Hudson. — New Haven: Yale University Press, 1977. xi, 434 p.; 24 cm. 1. Arab countries — Politics and government I. T.
DS62.4.H82   320.9/17/4927   *LC* 77-75379   *ISBN* 0300020430

Brown, L. Carl (Leon Carl), 1928-.   **3.3723**
International politics and the Middle East: old rules, dangerous game / L. Carl Brown. — Princeton, N.J.: Princeton University Press, c1984. xii, 363 p.: ill.; 23 cm. — (Princeton studies on the Near East.) Includes index. 1. Middle East — Politics and government. I. T. II. Series.
DS62.8.B76 1984   956 19   *LC* 83-43063   *ISBN* 069105410X

Drysdale, Alasdair.   **3.3724**
The Middle East and North Africa: a political geography / Alasdair Drysdale, Gerald H. Blake. — New York: Oxford University Press, 1985. xiii, 367 p.: ill., maps; 24 cm. 1. Geography, Political 2. Middle East — Politics and government. 3. Africa, North — Politics and government. 4. Middle East — Administrative and political divisions. 5. Africa, North — Administrative and political divisions. I. Blake, Gerald Henry. II. T.
DS62.8.D79 1985   956 19   *LC* 84-1095   *ISBN* 0195035372

The Government and politics of the Middle East and North   **3.3725**
Africa / edited by David E. Long and Bernard Reich.
2nd ed., rev. and updated. — Boulder: Westview Press, 1986. xii, 479 p.: maps; 24 cm. 1. Middle East — Politics and government — 1945- 2. Africa, North — Politics and government. I. Long, David E. II. Reich, Bernard.
DS62.8.G68 1986   320.956 19   *LC* 86-4102   *ISBN* 0813303362

Hurewitz, J. C., 1914-.   **3.3726**
Middle East politics: the military dimension [by] J. C. Hurewitz. — New York: Published for the Council on Foreign Relations, by Praeger, [1969] xviii, 553 p.: maps.; 22 cm. Pages 552-553, advertising matter. 1. Middle East — Armed forces — Political activity. 2. Middle East — Politics and government — 1945- I. Council on Foreign Relations. II. T.
DS62.8.H8 1969   320.9/56/04   *LC* 70-5881

Lenczowski, George.   **3.3727**
The Middle East in world affairs / George Lenczowski. — 4th ed. — Ithaca: Cornell University Press, 1980. 863 p.: map; 25 cm. Includes index. 1. Middle East — History — 20th century. 2. Middle East — Politics and government. I. T.
DS62.8.L46 1980   956 19   *LC* 79-17059   *ISBN* 0801412730

Mansfield, Peter, 1928-.   **3.3728**
The Ottoman Empire and its successors. — New York: St. Martin's Press, [1973] 210 p.: maps.; 21 cm. — (The Making of the 20th century) 1. Middle East — History — 20th century. I. T.
DS62.8.M348 1973b   949.6   *LC* 73-86362

Peretz, Don, 1922-.   **3.3729**
The Middle East today / Don Peretz. — 4th ed. — New York, NY: Praeger, 1983. xiii, 577 p.: maps; 24 cm. Includes index. 1. Middle East — Politics and government. I. T.
DS62.8.P45 1983   956 19   *LC* 83-10887   *ISBN* 0030633478

Antonius, George.   • **3.3730**
The Arab awakening: the story of the Arab national movement / by George Antonius. — London: Hamish Hamilton, [1945] 470 p.: fold. col. maps; 22 cm. 1. Arabs 2. World War, 1914-1918 — Arabia 3. Arabian Peninsula — History I. T.
DS63.A68   953

Daniel, Norman.   **3.3731**
Islam, Europe and Empire. — Edinburgh, Edinburgh U. P. [1966] xx, 619 p. illus., 34 plates (incl. facsims., ports.) 23 cm. — ([Edinburgh University publications; language and literature series, no. 15]) I. T.
DS63.D3   301.29/1767/04   *LC* 65-22498

Frye, Richard Nelson, 1920- ed.   • **3.3732**
The Near East and the Great Powers. With an introd. by Ralph Bunche. Edited by Richard N. Frye. Port Washington, N.Y., Kennikat Press [1969, c1951] viii,

214 p. 21 cm. 'The substance of the book was first presented in the form of papers ... in a conference entitled The Great Powers and the Near East, held at Harvard University ... August 7, 8 and 9 of 1950.' 1. Middle East — Politics and government I. T.
DS63.F7 1969   956   *LC* 77-79309   *ISBN* 0804605300

Haim, Sylvia G. ed.   **3.3733**
Arab nationalism, an anthology, selected and edited, with an introd., by Sylvia G. Haim. — Berkeley: University of California Press, 1962. 255 p.; 23 cm. 1. Nationalism — Arab countries — Addresses, essays, lectures. 2. Arab countries — Politics and government — Addresses, essays, lectures. I. T.
DS63.H27   956   *LC* 62-11492

Holt, P. M. (Peter Malcolm)   • **3.3734**
Egypt and the Fertile Crescent, 1516–1922; a political history [by] P. M. Holt. — Ithaca, N.Y.: Cornell University Press, [1966] xii, 337 p.: illus., geneal. tables, maps.; 23 cm. 1. Turkey — History 2. Egypt — Relations — Middle East 3. Middle East — Relations — Egypt I. T.
DS63.H62 1966a   956   *LC* 66-18429

Kuniholm, Bruce Robellet, 1942-.   **3.3735**
The origins of the cold war in the Near East: great power conflict and diplomacy in Iran, Turkey, and Greece / Bruce Robellet Kuniholm. — Princeton, N.J.: Princeton University Press, c1980. xxiii, 485 p.: maps; 24 cm. Includes index. 1. Middle East — Politics and government — 1945- 2. United States — Foreign relations — Russia. 3. Russia — Foreign relations — United States. 4. United States — Foreign relations — 1945-1953 I. T.
DS63.K86   327/.09/045   *LC* 79-83999   *ISBN* 0691046654

Lewis, Bernard.   **3.3736**
The Middle East and the West. — Bloomington: Indiana University Press, 1964. 160 p.; 23 cm. 'Published in cooperation with the Department of Government and the Asian Studies Program of Indiana University.' 1. Middle East — Politics and government. I. T.
DS63.L44   956   *LC* 64-10830

Ajami, Fouad.   **3.3737**
The Arab predicament: Arab political thought and practice since 1967 / Fouad Ajami. — Cambridge; New York: Cambridge University Press, 1981. xvi, 220 p.; 24 cm. 1. Arab countries — Politics and government — 1945- I. T.
DS63.1.A35   320.917/4927 19   *LC* 80-27457   *ISBN* 0521239141

Dawisha, A. I.   **3.3738**
The Arab radicals / Adeed Dawisha. — New York: Council on Foreign Relations, c1986. xv, 171 p.; 23 cm. Includes index. 1. Arab countries — Politics and government — 1945- I. T.
DS63.1.D39 1986   909/.09749270828 19   *LC* 86-19733   *ISBN* 087609020X

The Middle East / by Congressional Quarterly, Inc.   **3.3739**
6th ed. — Washington, D.C.: Congressional Quarterly, Inc., 1986. p. cm. Includes index. 1. Jewish-Arab relations — 1973- 2. Middle East — Politics and government — 1945- I. Congressional Quarterly, inc.
DS63.1.M484 1986   956/.04 19   *LC* 85-30875   *ISBN* 0871873613

Taylor, Alan R.   **3.3740**
The Arab balance of power / Alan R. Taylor. — 1st ed. — Syracuse, N.Y.: Syracuse University Press, 1982. xii, 165 p.: map; 23 cm. — (Contemporary issues in the Middle East.) 1. Arab countries — Politics and government — 1945- I. T. II. Series.
DS63.1.T39 1982   909/.0974927 19   *LC* 82-3394   *ISBN* 0815622678

Wright, Robin B., 1948-.   **3.3741**
Sacred rage: the crusade of modern Islam / Robin Wright. — New York: Linden Press/Simon and Schuster, 1985. p. cm. Includes index. 1. Islam and politics — Near East. 2. Terrorism — Near East. 3. Violence — Religious aspects — Islam 4. Islam — 20th century 5. Middle East — Politics and government — 1945- 6. Lebanon — History — 1974- I. T.
DS63.1.W75 1985   956.04 19   *LC* 85-18126   *ISBN* 067160113X

DS63.2–63.6 FOREIGN RELATIONS, BY COUNTRY, A–Z

Le Vine, Victor T.   **3.3742**
The Arab–African connection: political and economic realities / Victor T. Le Vine and Timothy W. Luke. — Boulder, Colo.: Westview Press, 1979. xvii, 155 p.; 24 cm. — (Westview special studies on Africa/the Middle East) Includes index. 1. Arab countries — Foreign relations — Africa. 2. Africa — Foreign relations — Arab countries. 3. Arab countries — Foreign economic relations — Africa. 4. Africa — Foreign economic relations — Arab countries. I. Luke, Timothy W. joint author. II. T.
DS63.2.A4 L48   327.6/017/4927   *LC* 78-27362   *ISBN* 089158398X

Lewis, Bernard.   **3.3743**
The Muslim discovery of Europe / by Bernard Lewis. — 1st ed. — New York: W.W. Norton, c1982. 350 p.: ill.; 24 cm. 1. Middle East — Relations — Europe 2. Europe — Relations — Middle East I. T.
DS63.2.E8 L48 1982   303.4/82 19   *LC* 81-19009   *ISBN* 0393015297

Abadi, Jacob.   **3.3744**
Britain's withdrawal from the Middle East, 1947–1971: the economic and strategic imperatives / Jacob Abadi. — Princeton, N.J.: Kingston Press, 1982, c1983. xvii, 283 p.: ill.; 24 cm. — (Kingston Press series. Leaders, politics, and social change in the Islamic world.) Includes index. 1. Middle East — Foreign relations — Great Britain. 2. Great Britain — Foreign relations — Middle East. I. T. II. Series.
DS63.2.G7 A22 1983   327.41056 19   *LC* 83-157159   *ISBN* 0940670194

Glubb, John Bagot, Sir, 1897-.   • **3.3745**
Britain and the Arabs: a study of fifty years, 1908 to 1958 / Lieutenant-General Sir John Bagot Glubb. — London: Hodder and Stoughton, 1959. 496 p.: maps (part fold.); 23 cm. 1. Great Britain — Foreign relations — Near East. 2. Middle East — Politics and government I. T.
DS63.2.G7 G5 1959   327.42056   *LC* 59-1659

Monroe, Elizabeth.   **3.3746**
Britain's moment in the Middle East, 1914–1971 / Elizabeth Monroe. — New and rev. ed., 2nd ed. / with a foreword by Peter Mansfield. — Baltimore, Md.: Johns Hopkins University Press, 1981. 254 p.: geneal. table, 2 maps; 23 cm. Previously published as: Britain's moment in the Middle East, 1914-1956. Includes index. 1. Middle East — Foreign relations — Great Britain. 2. Great Britain — Foreign relations — Near East. 3. Middle East — Politics and government — 1914-1945. I. T.
DS63.2.G7 M6 1981   327.41056 19   *LC* 80-8869   0801826260

Ramazani, Rouhollan K., 1928-.   **3.3747**
Revolutionary Iran: challenge and response in the Middle East / R.K. Ramazani. — Baltimore: Johns Hopkins University Press, c1986. xv, 311 p.: maps; 24 cm. Includes index. 1. Middle East — Foreign relations — Iran. 2. Iran — Foreign relations — Middle East. 3. Middle East — Politics and government — 1945- 4. Iran — Foreign relations — 1979- I. T.
DS63.2.I68 R36 1986   327.56055 19   *LC* 86-45440   *ISBN* 0801833779

Freedman, Robert Owen.   **3.3748**
Soviet policy toward the Middle East since 1970 / Robert O. Freedman. — Rev. ed. — New York: Praeger, 1978. viii, 373 p.; 24 cm. Includes index. 1. Middle East — Foreign relations — Russia. 2. Russia — Foreign relations — Middle East. I. T.
DS63.2.R9 F7 1978   327.47/056   *LC* 78-19457   *ISBN* 0030466016

Rubinstein, Alvin Z.   **3.3749**
Red star on the Nile: the Soviet–Egyptian influence relationship since the June war / by Alvin Z. Rubinstein. — Princeton, N.J.: Princeton University Press, c1977. xxiv, 383 p. — (A Foreign Policy Research Institute book) Includes index. 1. Egypt — Foreign relations — Russia. 2. Russia — Foreign relations — Egypt. I. T.
DS63.2.R9 R8   DS63.2R9 R8.   327.62/047   *LC* 76-3021   *ISBN* 0691075816

Sella, Amnon.   **3.3750**
Soviet political and military conduct in the Middle East / Amnon Sella. — New York: St. Martin's Press, c1981. xiii, 211 p.; 23 cm. Includes index. 1. Middle East — Foreign relations — Russia. 2. Russia — Foreign relations — Near East. I. T.
DS63.2.R9 S376 1981   327.47056   *LC* 80-13526   *ISBN* 0312748450

Smolansky, Oles M.   **3.3751**
The Soviet Union and the Arab East under Khrushchev [by] Oles M. Smolansky. Lewisburg [Pa.] Bucknell University Press [1974] 326 p. 21 cm. (The Modern Middle East series, v. 6) 1. Soviet Union — Foreign relations — Arab countries. 2. Arab countries — Foreign relations — Soviet Union. I. T.
DS63.2.R9 S55   327.47/017/4927   *LC* 73-2890   *ISBN* 0838713386

The Soviet Union in the Middle East: policies and perspectives   **3.3752**
/ edited by Adeed Dawisha and Karen Dawisha.
New York, N.Y.: Published by Holmes & Meier Publishers for the Royal Institute of International Affairs, 1982. 172 p.: map; 22 cm. 1. Middle East — Foreign relations — Soviet Union — Addresses, essays, lectures. 2. Soviet Union — Foreign relations — Near East — Addresses, essays, lectures.

I. Dawisha, A. I. II. Dawisha, Karen. III. Royal Institute of International Affairs.
DS63.2.S65 S67 1982   327.47056 19   *LC* 82-953   *ISBN* 084190796X

Bryson, Thomas A., 1931-.   3.3753
American diplomatic relations with the Middle East, 1784–1975: a survey / by Thomas A. Bryson. Metuchen, N.J.: Scarecrow Press, c1977. viii, 431 p.; 23 cm. Includes index. 1. Middle East — Foreign relations — United States. 2. United States — Foreign relations — Near East. I. T.
DS63.2.U5 B79   327.56/073   *LC* 76-44344   *ISBN* 0810809885

DeNovo, John A.   • 3.3754
American interests and policies in the Middle East, 1900–1939. Minneapolis, University of Minnesota Press [1963] xii, 447 p. maps. 24 cm. Bibliography: p. 397-410. 1. United States — Relations — Middle East 2. Middle East — Relations — United States I. T.
DS63.2.U5D4   327.73056   *LC* 63-21129

Eveland, Wilbur.   3.3755
Ropes of sand: America's failure in the Middle East / Wilbur Crane Eveland. — 1st ed. — London; New York: W. W. Norton, 1980. 382 p.: map; 24 cm. 1. Eveland, Wilbur. 2. United States. Central Intelligence Agency — Biography. 3. Diplomats — United States — Biography. 4. Spies — United States — Biography. 5. Middle East — Foreign relations — United States. 6. United States — Foreign relations — Middle East. I. T.
DS63.2.U5 E9 1980   327.73056   *LC* 79-27867   *ISBN* 0393013367

Field, James A.   • 3.3756
America and the Mediterranean world, 1776–1882, by James A. Field, Jr. . — Princeton, N.J.: Princeton University Press, 1969. xv, 485 p.: maps.; 25 cm. 1. Middle East — Foreign relations — U.S. 2. Mediterranean Region — Foreign relations — U.S. 3. U.S. — Foreign relations — Near East. 4. U.S. — Foreign relations — Mediterranean region. I. T.
DS63.2.U5 F47   327.56/073   *LC* 68-11440

Spiegel, Steven L.   3.3757
The other Arab–Israeli conflict: making America's Middle East policy, from Truman to Reagan / Steven L. Spiegel. — Chicago: University of Chicago Press, c1985. xvi, 522 p.; 24 cm. (Middle Eastern studies. monograph 1) Includes index. 1. Jewish-Arab relations — 1949- 2. Middle East — Foreign relations — United States. 3. United States — Foreign relations — Near East. 4. United States — Foreign relations — 1945- I. T. II. Series.
DS63.2.U5 S62 1985   327.73056 19   *LC* 84-16253   *ISBN* 0226769615

Tillman, Seth P.   3.3758
The United States in the Middle East, interests and obstacles / Seth P. Tillman. — Bloomington: Indiana University Press, c1982. xi, 333 p.; 24 cm. 1. Jewish-Arab relations — 1949- 2. Middle East — Foreign relations — United States. 3. United States — Foreign relations — Middle East. 4. Middle East — Politics and government — 1945- I. T.
DS63.2.U5 T54 1982   327.73056 19   *LC* 81-47777   *ISBN* 0253361729

Zeine, Zeine N.   3.3759
[Arab-Turkish relations and the emergence of Arab nationalism] The emergence of Arab nationalism; with a background study of Arab–Turkish relations in the Near East [by] Zeine N. Zeine. [3d ed.] Delmar, N.Y., Caravan Books [1973] viii, 192 p. illus. 23 cm. First ed. published in 1958 under title: Arab-Turkish relations and the emergence of Arab nationalism. 1. Nationalism — Arab countries. 2. Turkey — Foreign relations — Arab countries. 3. Arab countries — Foreign relations — Turkey. I. T.
DS63.6.Z44 1973   327.496/1/056   *LC* 76-39576   *ISBN* 0882060007

DS66 Hittites

Gurney, O. R. (Oliver Robert), 1911-.   • 3.3760
The Hittites. — London, Baltimore, Penguin Books [1952] 239 p. illus. 19 cm. (Pelican books, A259) 1. Hittites I. T.
DS66.G8   939   *LC* 52-14552

Macqueen, J. G. (James G.)   3.3761
The Hittites and their contemporaries in Asia Minor / J. G. Macqueen. — Boulder, Colo.: Westview Press, 1975. 206 p.: ill.; 21 cm. (Ancient peoples and places; v. 83) Includes index. 1. Hittites 2. Asia Minor — Civilization. I. T.
DS66.M23 1975   939.2   *LC* 75-26838   *ISBN* 0891585206

DS67–79 Iraq (Assyria. Babylonia)

Lloyd, Seton.   3.3762
The archaeology of Mesopotamia: from the Old Stone Age to the Persian conquest / Seton Lloyd. — London: Thames and Hudson, c1978. 252 p.; 25 cm. Includes index. 1. Iraq — Antiquities I. T.
DS68.L57   935   *LC* 78-52961   *ISBN* 0500780072

Luckenbill, Daniel David, 1881-1927.   • 3.3763
Ancient records of Assyria and Babylonia. — New York: Greenwood Press, [1968, c1926] 2 v.; 22 cm. 1. Assyria — History — Sources. I. T.
DS68.L8 1968   935/.03/08   *LC* 68-57626

Chiera, Edward, 1885-1933.   • 3.3764
They wrote on clay; the Babylonian tablets speak today, by Edward Chiera, edited by George G. Cameron. Chicago, Ill., The University of Chicago press [c1938] xv, 234, [1] p. front., illus. 20 cm. Map on lining-papers. 1. Excavations (Archaeology) — Iraq 2. Akkadian language — Texts. 3. Iraq — Antiquities I. Cameron, George Glenn, 1905- ed. II. T.
DS69.5.C5   913.358   *LC* 38-27631

Oppenheim, A. Leo, 1904-1974.   3.3765
Ancient Mesopotamia: portrait of a dead civilization / by A. Leo Oppenheim. — Rev. ed. / completed by Erica Reiner. — Chicago: University of Chicago Press, 1977. xvi, 445 p., [16] leaves of plates: ill.; 21 cm. 1. Civilization, Assyro-Babylonian 2. Iraq — Civilization — To 634 I. Reiner, Erica, 1926- II. T.
DS69.5.O6 1977   935   *LC* 76-28340   *ISBN* 0226631869

Adams, Robert McCormick, 1926-.   3.3766
Heartland of cities: surveys of ancient settlement and land use on the central floodplain of the Euphrates / Robert McC. Adams. — Chicago: University of Chicago Press, 1981. xx, 362 p.: ill., map (1 fold.); 29 cm. Includes index. 1. Cities and towns, Ancient — Iraq — Babylonia. 2. Land use — Iraq — Babylonia. 3. Irrigation — Iraq — Babylonia. 4. Babylonia — Antiquities. 5. Babylonia — Civilization. I. T.
DS70.A32   935   *LC* 80-13995   *ISBN* 0226005445

Lloyd, Seton.   3.3767
Foundations in the dust: the story of Mesopotamian exploration / Seton Lloyd. — Rev. and enl. ed. — London: Thames and Hudson, c1980. 216 p.: ill.; 24 cm. Includes index. 1. Excavations (Archaeology) — Iraq 2. Assyriologists 3. Archaeologists — Iraq. 4. Iraq — Antiquities I. T.
DS70.L48 1980b   935 19   *LC* 81-170132   *ISBN* 0500050384

Harris, George Lawrence, 1910-.   • 3.3768
Iraq: its people, its society, its culture. In collaboration with Moukhtar Ani [and others]. — New Haven: HRAF Press, [1958] 350 p.: maps, tables.; 22 cm. — (Survey of world cultures [3]) 1. Iraq. I. T. II. Series.
DS70.6.H3   915.67   *LC* 58-14179

American University (Washington, D.C.). Foreign Area Studies.   3.3769
Iraq, a country study / Foreign Area Studies, the American University; edited by Richard F. Nyrop. — 3d ed. — Washington, D.C.: The University: for sale by the Supt. of Docs., U.S. Govt. Print. Off., c1979. xxi, 320 p.: ill.; 24 cm. — (Area handbook series.) Supersedes the 1971 ed. prepared by H. H. Smith and others, and issued under title: Area handbook for Iraq. 'Research completed February 1979.' 'DA Pam 550-31.' Includes index. 1. Iraq. I. Nyrop, Richard F. II. Smith, Harvey Henry. Area handbook for Iraq. III. T. IV. Series.
DS70.6.S6 1979   956.7   *LC* 79-24184

Olmstead, Albert Ten Eyck, 1880-1945.   • 3.3770
History of Assyria. — [Chicago] University of Chicago Press [1960] 695 p. illus. 23 cm. — (Chicago reprint series) 1. Assyria — History 2. Civilization, Assyro-Babylonian I. T.
DS71.O6 1960   935   *LC* 60-51197

Oppenheim, A. Leo, 1904-1974. comp.   • 3.3771
Letters from Mesopotamia: official business, and private letters on clay tablets from two millennia. Translated and with an introd. by A. Leo Oppenheim. Chicago, University of Chicago Press [1967] xi, 217 p. illus., map, 24 cm. 1. Iraq — Civilization I. T.
DS71.O7   913.3/5/03   *LC* 67-20576

Kramer, Samuel Noah, 1897-.   3.3772
[From the tablets of Sumer] History begins at Sumer: thirty–nine firsts in man's recorded history / Samuel Noah Kramer. — 3rd rev. ed. — Philadelphia: University of Pennsylvania Press, 1981. xxvii, 388 p.: ill.; 24 cm. Originally published under title: From the tablets of Sumer: Indian Hills, Colo.: Falcon's Wing Press, 1956. 1. Sumerians I. T.
DS72.K7 1981   935/.01 19   *LC* 81-51144   *ISBN* 0812278127

Kramer, Samuel Noah, 1897-.   • **3.3773**
The Sumerians: their history, culture, and character. — [Chicago]: University of Chicago Press, [1963] xiv, 355 p.: illus., plates.; 25 cm. 1. Sumerians I. T.
DS72.K73   913.35   *LC* 63-11398

Contenau, G. (Georges), b. 1877.   • **3.3774**
[La vie quotidienne à Babylone et en Assyrie. English] Everyday life in Babylon and Assyria. New York, St. Martin's Press, 1954. xv, 324 p. illus., 24 plates, maps. 22 cm. 1. Babylonia — Social life and customs. 2. Assyria — Social life and customs. I. T.
DS75.S6 C62 1954   *LC* 54-10269

Morony, Michael G., 1939-.   **3.3775**
Iraq after the Muslim conquest / Michael G. Morony. — Princeton, N.J.: Princeton University Press, c1984. ix, 689 p.: ill.; 25 cm. — (Princeton studies on the Near East.) Includes index. 1. Ethnology — Iraq 2. Iraq — Social conditions. 3. Iraq — History — 634-1534 I. T. II. Series.
DS76.M67 1984   955/.02 19   *LC* 83-42569   *ISBN* 0691053952

Khadduri, Majid, 1909-.   • **3.3776**
Independent Iraq, 1932–1958; a study in Iraqi politics. 2d ed. London; New York: Oxford University Press, 1960. viii, 388 p.: fold. map; 23 cm. 1. Iraq — Politics and government I. T.
DS79 K43 1960

Simon, Reeva S.   **3.3777**
Iraq between the two world wars: the creation and implementation of a nationalist ideology / Reeva S. Simon. — New York: Columbia University Press, 1986. xv, 233 p.; 24 cm. Includes index. 1. Nationalism — Iraq — History. 2. Iraq — History — Hashemite Kingdom, 1921-1958 3. Iraq — Armed Forces — Political activity. I. T.
DS79.S57 1986   956.7/04 19   *LC* 85-29893   *ISBN* 0231060742

Helms, Christine Moss.   **3.3778**
Iraq: eastern flank of the Arab world / Christine Moss Helms. — Washington, D.C.: Brookings Institution, c1984. x, 215 p., [1] leaf of plates: ill.; 24 cm. 1. Iraq — Politics and government. I. T.
DS79.65.H45 1984   956.7/043 19   *LC* 84-14934   *ISBN* 0815735561

Khadduri, Majid, 1908-.   **3.3779**
Republican 'Iraq; a study in 'Iraqi politics since the revolution of 1958. London, New York, Oxford University Press, 1969. xii, 318 p. fold. map. 23 cm. 1. Iraq — Politics and government. I. T.
DS79.65.K48   320.9/55   *LC* 75-447193

Khadduri, Majid, 1908-.   **3.3780**
Socialist Iraq: a study in Iraqi politics since 1968 / Majid Khadduri. — Washington: Middle East Institute, 1978. 265 p.; 24 cm. Continues: Independent Iraq and Republican 'Iraq. Appendices (p. 183-260): A. The Interim Constitution.—B. The National Action Charter.—C. March 11 Manifesto on the Peaceful Settlement of the Kurdish Issue in Iraq.—D. The Iraqi-Soviet Treaty of Friendship and Cooperation.—E. Iran-Iraq Treaty on International Borders and Good Neighbourly Relations, done at Baghdad, June 13, 1975. 1. Iraq — Politics and government. I. T.
DS79.65.K49   320.9/567/04   *LC* 78-51916   *ISBN* 0916808165

Marr, Phebe.   **3.3781**
The modern history of Iraq / Phebe Marr. — Boulder, Colo.: Westview; London: Longman, 1985. xvii, 382 p.: ill.; 24 cm. Includes indexes. 1. Iraq — History — 1921- I. T.
DS79.65.M33 1985   956.7/04 19   *LC* 83-51519   *ISBN* 0865311196

DS80–89 Lebanon (Phoenicia)

Gordon, David C.   **3.3782**
The Republic of Lebanon: nation in jeopardy / David C. Gordon. — Boulder, Colo.: Westview Press; London: Croom Helm, 1983. xiv, 171 p.: ill.; 24 cm. — (Profiles. Nations of the contemporary Middle East) Includes index. 1. Lebanon. I. T. II. Series.
DS80.G67 1983   956.92 19   *LC* 82-20108   *ISBN* 0865314500

Smith, Harvey Henry, 1892-.   **3.3783**
Area handbook for Lebanon. 1st ed. coauthors: Harvey H. Smith [and others] 2d ed. [Washington, For sale by the Supt. of Docs., U.S. Govt. Print. Off.] 1974. xlvi, 354 p. illus. 24 cm. 'DA Pam 550-24.' 'One of a series of handbooks prepared under the auspices of Foreign Area Studies (FAS) of the American University.' 'Supersedes DA Pam 550-24, July 1969.' Consists of the 1969 handbook with a Summary of events: December 1968-December 1973.

1. Lebanon. I. American University (Washington, D.C.). Foreign Area Studies. II. T.
DS80.S63 1974   915.692/03/4   *LC* 74-13241

Cobban, Helena.   **3.3784**
The making of modern Lebanon / Helena Cobban. — Boulder, Colo.: Westview Press, 1985. 248 p.: ill., 2 maps; 22 cm. (Making of the Middle East.) 1. Lebanon — History — 1946- I. T. II. Series.
DS80.9   DS80.9.C63 1985b.   956.92 19   *LC* 85-51254   *ISBN* 0813303079

Hitti, Philip Khuri, 1886-.   • **3.3785**
Lebanon in history: from the earliest times to the present [by] Philip K. Hitti. — 3rd ed. — London; Melbourne [etc.]: Macmillan; New York: St. Martin's P., 1967. xx, 550 p.: front., illus. (incl. ports.) col. plate, maps, tables.; 22 1/2 cm. 1. Lebanon — History I. T.
DS80.9.H5 1967   956.92   *LC* 67-21542

Moscati, Sabatino.   • **3.3786**
[Mondo dei Fenici. English] The world of the Phoenicians. Translated from the Italian by Alastair Hamilton. New York, Praeger [1968] xxii, 281 p. illus., maps, plans. 26 cm. (Praeger history of civilization) Translation of Il mondo dei Fenici. 1. Phoenicians I. T.
DS81.M613 1968b   913.3/9/4403   *LC* 68-27432

Hudson, Michael C.   **3.3787**
The precarious republic: political modernization in Lebanon / Michael C. Hudson; consulting editor, Leonard Binder; written under the auspices of the Center for International Affairs, Harvard University. — Boulder, Colo.: Westview Press, 1985. xx, 364 p.: ill.; 23 cm. Originally published: New York: Random House, c1968. 'A Westview encore edition'—Cover. Includes index. 1. Lebanon — Politics and government I. Binder, Leonard. II. Harvard University. Center for International Affairs. III. T.
DS87.H8 1985   320.95692 19   *LC* 85-40311   *ISBN* 081330105X

Khalidi, Walid.   **3.3788**
Conflict and violence in Lebanon: confrontation in the Middle East / by Walid Khalidi. — Cambridge, MA: Center for International Affairs, Harvard University, 1979. 216 p.: ill.; 23 cm. (Harvard studies in international affairs. no. 38) 1. Lebanon — Politics and government — 1975- I. T. II. Series.
DS87.K397   956.92/044 19   *LC* 77-89806   *ISBN* 0876740387

Rabinovich, Itamar, 1942-.   **3.3789**
The war for Lebanon, 1970–1985 / Itamar Rabinovich. — Rev. ed. — Ithaca: Cornell University Press, 1985. 262 p.: ill.; 23 cm. (Cornell paperbacks) Rev. ed. of: The war for Lebanon, 1970-1983. 1984. Includes index. 1. Lebanon — History — 1946-1975 2. Lebanon — History — 1975- I. Rabinovich, Itamar, 1942- War for Lebanon, 1970-1983. II. T.
DS87.R332 1985   956.92/04 19   *LC* 85-14891   *ISBN* 0801493137

Israel. Va'adah la-hakirat ha-eru'im be-mahanot ha-pelitim be-Beirut.   **3.3790**
[Din ve-heshbon ha-Va'adah la-kakirat ha-eru'im be-mahanot ha-pelitim be-Beirut. English] The Beirut massacre: the complete Kahan Commission report / with an introduction by Abba Eban. — 1st ed. — Princeton: Karz-Cohl, c1983. xix, 136 p.; 23 cm. Translation of: Din ve-heshbon ha-Va'adah la-hakirat ha-eru'im be-mahanot ha-pelitim be-Beirut. 1. Palestinian Arabs — Lebanon — Beirut. 2. Massacres — Lebanon — Beirut. 3. Beirut (Lebanon) — History. 4. Lebanon — History — Israeli intervention, 1982- I. T.
DS87.53.I85 1983   956.92/044 19   *LC* 83-8385   *ISBN* 0943828554

Dothan, Trude Krakauer.   **3.3791**
The Philistines and their material culture / Trude Dothan. — New Haven: Yale University Press, c1982. xxii, 310 p.: ill.; 29 cm. Revised translation of ha-Pelishtim ve-tarbutam ve-homrit. Includes index. 1. Philistines — Material culture. 2. Palestine — Antiquities I. T.
DS90.D613 1982   933 19   *LC* 80-22060   *ISBN* 0300022581

DS92–99 Syria

American University (Washington, D.C.). Foreign Area Studies.   **3.3792**
Syria, a country study / Foreign Area Studies, the American University; edited by Richard F. Nyrop. — 3rd ed. — Washington: For sale by the Supt. of Docs., U.S. Govt. Print., Off., c1979. xix, 268 p.: ill.; 24 cm. — (Area handbook series.) Supersedes the 1971 ed. by R. F. Nyrop, published under title: Area handbook for Syria. 'DA pam 550-47.' Includes index. 1. Syria. I. Nyrop, Richard F. II. T. III. Series.
DS93.A65 1979   956.91/04   *LC* 79-607771

Devlin, John F., 1926-.   3.3793
Syria: modern state in an ancient land / John F. Devlin. — Boulder, Colo.:
Westview Press; London: C. Helm, 1983. xi, 140 p.: ill., map; 24 cm. —
(Profiles. Nations of the contemporary Middle East) Includes index. 1. Syria.
I. T. II. Series.
DS93.D48 1983   956.91 19   *LC* 82-15909   *ISBN* 0865311854

Abu Izzeddin, Nejla M.   3.3794
The Druzes: a new study of their history, faith, and society / by Nejla M. Abu–
Izzeddin. — Leiden: E.J. Brill, 1984. 259 p.: ill.; 25 cm. Includes index.
1. Druzes I. T.
DS94.8.D8 A24 1984   956.92/009/7671 19   *LC* 84-226664   *ISBN*
9004069755

Hitti, Philip Khûri, 1886-.   • 3.3795
History of Syria: including Lebanon and Palestine / by Philip K. Hitti. —
London: Macmillan; New York: St. Martin's Press, 1957. xxv, 750 p.: ill. (some
col.), maps (some fold.) 1. Syria — History I. T.
DS95.H5   915.691/04/3   *LC* 51-10100

Salibi, Kamal S. (Kamal Suleiman), 1929-.   3.3796
Syria under Islam: empire on trial, 634–1097 / by Kamal S. Salibi. — Delmar,
N.Y.: Caravan Books, 1977. 193 p.: ill.; 23 cm. Includes index. 1. Syria —
History I. T.
DS95.S24   956.91   *LC* 77-24197   *ISBN* 0882060139

Bevan, Edwyn Robert, 1870-1943.   • 3.3797
The house of Seleucus. New York: Barnes & Noble, [1966] 2 v.: ill., 3 fold. col.
maps, ports.; 23 cm. 1. History, Ancient 2. Seleucids I. T.
DS96.B57 1966   *LC* 66-782

Hourani, Albert Habib.   • 3.3798
Syria and Lebanon, a political essay. — London: Oxford University Press, 1946.
x, 402 p., [1] fold. leaf of plates: maps. 1. Syria — Politics and government
2. Lebanon — Politics and government I. T.
DS98.H65   *LC* 47-3024

Khoury, Philip S. (Philip Shukry), 1949-.   3.3799
Syria and the French mandate: the politics of Arab nationalism, 1920–1945 /
Philip S. Khoury. — Princeton, N.J.: Princeton University Press, c1986. 1 v.
Includes index. 1. Nationalism — Syria — History. 2. Nationalism — Arab
countries — History. 3. Syria — History — 20th century I. T.
DS98.K46 1986   946.08 19   *LC* 86-42859   *ISBN* 069105486X

Zeine, Zeine N.   3.3800
The struggle for Arab independence: Western diplomacy and the rise and fall of
Faisal's kingdom in Syria / by Zeine N. Zeine. — 2d ed. — Delmar, N.Y.:
Caravan Books, 1977. x, 257 p., [8] leaves of plates: ill.; 23 cm. Includes index.
1. Syria — History — 20th century 2. Great Britain — Foreign relations —
Near East. 3. Middle East — Foreign relations — Great Britain. 4. France —
Foreign relations — Near East. 5. Middle East — Foreign relations — France.
6. Middle East — History — 20th century. I. T.
DS98.Z4 1977   956.91/04   *LC* 77-5149   *ISBN* 0882060023

Dam, Nikolaos van.   3.3801
The struggle for power in Syria: sectarianism, regionalism, and tribalism in
politics, 1961–1978 / Nikolaos van Dam. — New York: St. Martin's Press,
1979. 147 p.: map; 23 cm. Rev. and updated version of the author's thesis,
University of Amsterdam, 1977. Includes index. 1. Minorities — Syria.
2. Syria — Politics and government. I. T.
DS98.2.D35 1979   320.9/5691/04   *LC* 78-11626   *ISBN*
0312768710

Seale, Patrick.   3.3802
The struggle for Syria: a study of post–war Arab politics, 1945–1958 / by
Patrick Seale; with a foreword by Albert Hourani. — New Haven: Yale
University Press, 1987, c1986. p. cm. Includes index. 1. Syria — Politics and
government. 2. Arab countries — Politics and government — 1945- I. T.
DS98.2.S4 1987   956.91/042 19   *LC* 87-8265   *ISBN* 0300039441

Downey, Glanville, 1908-.   • 3.3803
A history of Antioch in Syria: from Seleucus to the Arab conquest. —
Princeton, N.J.: Princeton University Press, 1961. xvii, 752 p.: ill., maps.
1. Antioch (Turkey) — History. 2. Antioch (Turkey) — Antiquities. I. T.
DS99.A6 D6   *LC* 61-6288

Rostovzeff, Michael Ivanovitch, 1870-1952.   3.3804
Dura–Europos and its art, by M. Rostovtzeff ... Oxford, Clarendon press, 1938.
xiv, 162 p., 1 l. front., ill., plates, fold. map, fold. plan. 1. Dura, Syria 2. Mural
painting and decoration 3. Decoration and ornament I. T.
DS99.D8 R7   *LC* 39-8531

DS101–151 Palestine. Israel. Jews

The Jew in the modern world: a documentary history / edited   3.3805
by Paul R. Mendes–Flohr, Jehuda Reinharz.
New York: Oxford University Press, 1980. xix, 556 p.: map; 24 cm. 1. Jews —
History — 17th century — Sources. 2. Jews — History — 18th century —
Sources. 3. Jews — History — 1789-1945 — Sources. 4. Judaism — History —
Modern period, 1750- — Sources. I. Mendes-Flohr, Paul R. II. Reinharz,
Jehuda.
DS102.J43   909/.04/924   *LC* 79-15050   *ISBN* 0195026314

Finkelstein, Louis, 1895- ed.   • 3.3806
The Jews: their history, culture, and religion. 3d ed. New York: Harper [1960] 2
v. (xxxvi, 1859 p.): ill., ports., maps (part col.), Facsims., music; 24 cm. Fourth
ed. (1970-71) published as a 3 v. work. Vol. 1 has title: The Jews: their history; v.
2: The Jews: their religion and culture; v. 3: The Jews: their role in civilization.
1. Jews — History 2. Judaism — History 3. Jewish literature — History and
criticism. 4. Civilization — Jewish influences. I. T.
DS102.4.F5 1960   956.93   *LC* 60-7383

Leftwich, Joseph, 1892- comp.   3.3807
The way we think; a collection of essays from the Yiddish. Compiled and
translated by Joseph Leftwich. South Brunswick, [N.J.] T. Yoseloff [1969] 2 v.
(841 p.) 25 cm. 1. Jews — Addresses, essays, lectures. I. T.
DS102.4.L4 1969   301.451/924   *LC* 68-27188   *ISBN* 0498064840

Encyclopaedia Judaica.   • 3.3808
Jerusalem, Encyclopaedia Judaica; [New York] Macmillan [c1971-72, v. 1,
c1972] 16 v. illus. (part col.) 32 cm. Part of illustrative matter in pocket. 1. Jews
— Dictionaries and encyclopedias
DS102.8.E496   909/.04924 19   *LC* 72-177492

Everyman's Judaica: an encyclopedic dictionary / edited by   3.3809
Geoffrey Wigoder.
Jerusalem: Keter Pub. House Jerusalem, [1975] xi, 673 p., [16] leaves of plates:
ill.; 29 cm. 1. Jews — Dictionaries and encyclopedias 2. Jews — Biography
I. Wigoder, Geoffrey, 1922- II. Title: Judaica.
DS102.8.E68 1975b   909/.04/924   *LC* 75-318522   *ISBN*
0706514122

The Jewish encyclopedia; a descriptive record of the history,   3.3810
religion, literature, and customs of the Jewish people from the
earliest times. Prepared under the direction of Cyrus Adler [and
others] Isidore Singer, projector and managing editor, assisted
by American and foreign boards of consulting editors.
[New York] Ktav Pub. House [1964?] 12 v. 1. Jews — Dictionaries and
encyclopedias I. Singer, Isidore, 1859-1939. ed. II. Adler, Cyrus, 1863-1940.
ed.
DS102.8.Jx   *LC* 64-9604

The Universal Jewish encyclopedia an authoritative and popular   • 3.3811
presentation of Jews and Judaism since the earliest times; edited
by Isaac Landman.
New York: The Universal Jewish encyclopedia, inc.; [c1939-43] 10 v.: fronts.,
illus., plates.; 28 cm. The illustrative material is partly colored and partly
folded. 1. Jews — Dictionaries and encyclopedias I. Landman, Isaac, 1880-
II. Cohen, Simon, 1894-
DS102.8.U5   *LC* 40-5070 Revised 2

DS103–113 DESCRIPTION. ANTIQUITIES.
CIVILIZATION

Harman, Avraham. ed.   • 3.3812
Israel / editors: Abe Harman [and] Yigael Yadin; pref.: David Ben–Gurion. —
Garden City, N. Y.: Doubleday [1958] 1 v. (chiefly ill., part col.); 30 cm.
1. Israel — History I. Yadin, Yigael, 1917-1984. joint ed. II. T.
DS108.5.H28   *915.694   *LC* 58-2753

Kenyon, Kathleen Mary.   3.3813
Digging up Jerusalem, by Kathleen M. Kenyon. — New York: Praeger, [1974]
xxxi, 288 p.: illus.; 23 cm. 1. Jerusalem — Antiquities. 2. Jerusalem — History
I. T.
DS109.K39   913.33   *LC* 73-10948   *ISBN* 0275466008

Cattan, Henry.   3.3814
Jerusalem / Henry Cattan. — New York: St. Martin's Press, 1981. 229 p.: ill.;
22 cm. 1. Jerusalem — History 2. Jerusalem — Politics and government. I. T.
DS109.9.C37 1981   956.94/4 19   *LC* 80-21235   *ISBN* 0312441827

Smith, George Adam, Sir, 1856-1942.   **3.3815**
Jerusalem; the topography, economics, and history from the earliest times to A.D. 70. Prolegomenon by Samuel Yeivin. 2 v. in 1. [New York] Ktav Pub. House, 1972. xciv, 498, xvi, 631 p. illus. 24 cm. (Library of Biblical studies.) Reprint of the 1907-08 ed., with a new prolegomenon by S. Yeivin. 1. Jews — History — To A.D. 70. 2. Jerusalem — History 3. Jerusalem — Description. I. T. II. Series.
DS109.912.S633   913.33   *LC* 68-19734   *ISBN* 0870681052

Cohen, Amnon, 1936-.   **3.3816**
[Yehudim be-shilton ha-Islam. English] Jewish life under Islam: Jerusalem in the sixteenth century / Amnon Cohen. — Cambridge, Mass.: Harvard University Press, 1984. xii, 267 p.: 1 map; 24 cm. Translation of: Yehudim be-shilton ha-Islam. 1. Jews — Jerusalem — History — 16th century. 2. Jerusalem — History 3. Jerusalem — Ethnic relations. I. T.
DS109.92.C6313 1984   956.94/4004924 19   *LC* 83-13025   *ISBN* 0674474368

Bovis, H. Eugene, 1928-.   **3.3817**
The Jerusalem question, 1917–1968 / [by] H. Eugene Bovis. — Stanford, Calif.: Hoover Institution Press [1971] xiii, 175 p.; 23 cm. (Hoover Institution studies, 29. Policy 1) Originally presented as the author's thesis, American University, 1968. 1. Jerusalem — Politics and government. I. T.
DS109.93.B68 1971   320.9/5694/4   *LC* 73-149796   *ISBN* 0817932917

Benvenisti, Meron, 1934-.   **3.3818**
Jerusalem, the torn city / Meron Benvenisti. — Minneapolis: University of Minnesota Press, c1976. xv, 407 p., [8] leaves of plates: ill.; 23 cm. Translation of Mul ha-homah ha-segurah. 1. Jerusalem — Politics and government. I. T. II. Title: Mul ha-homah ha-segurah.
DS 109.94 B47 E5 1976   *LC* 76-12226   *ISBN* 0816607958

Goodman, Martin, 1953-.   **3.3819**
State and society in Roman Galilee, A.D. 132–212 / Martin Goodman. — Totowa, NJ: Rowman & Allanheld, 1983. x, 305 p.; 24 cm. At head of title: Oxford Centre for Postgraduate Hebrew Studies. Includes index. 1. Jews — History — 70-638 2. Tannaim 3. Galilee (Israel) — History. 4. Rome — History — Empire, 30 B.C.-284 A.D. I. Oxford Centre for Postgraduate Hebrew Studies. II. T.
DS110.G2 G66 1983   956.94/5 19   *LC* 82-24281   *ISBN* 0865980896

Yadin, Yigael, 1917-1984.   **3.3820**
Hazor; the rediscovery of a great citadel of the Bible. — [1st American ed.]. — New York: Random House, [1975] 280 p.: illus.; 26 cm. 1. Hazor — Antiquities. 2. Gezer, Israel — Antiquities. 3. Megiddo. I. T.
DS110.H38 Y28 1975   220.9/3   *LC* 74-5406   *ISBN* 0394494547

Yadin, Yigael, 1917-1984.   **3.3821**
[Metsadah. English] Masada; Herod's fortress and the Zealot's last stand. [Translated from the Hebrew by Moshe Pearlman] New York, Random House [1966] 272 p. illus. (part col.) map, plans (part col.) 26 cm. 1. Masada Site (Israel) I. T.
DS110.M33 Y33   913.031028   *LC* 66-23094

Vaux, Roland de, 1903-1971.   **3.3822**
Archaeology and the Dead Sea scrolls. London, published for the British Academy by the Oxford University Press, 1973. xv, 142 p. illus., fold maps. 26 cm. (The Schweich lectures of the British Academy, 1959) Revised ed. in an English translation of L'archéologie et les manuscrits de la mer Morte. 1. Qumran Site. 2. Dead Sea scrolls. I. British Academy. II. T.
DS110.Q8 V313 1973   221/.44   *LC* 73-174845   *ISBN* 0197259316

Occupation, Israel over Palestine / edited by Naseer H. Aruri.   **3.3823**
Belmont, Mass.: Association of Arab-American University Graduates, 1983. xvii, 467 p., [2] p. of plates: ill.; 23 cm. (AAUG monograph; no. 18) Includes index. 1. Palestinian Arabs — Politics and government — Addresses, essays, lectures. 2. West Bank — Politics and government — Addresses, essays, lectures. 3. Gaza Strip — Politics and government — Addresses, essays, lectures. I. Aruri, Naseer Hasan, 1934-
DS110.W47 O23 1983   956.95 19   *LC* 84-141451   *ISBN* 0937694649

Dayan, Moshe, 1915-1981.   ● **3.3824**
[Yoman ma'arekhet Sinai. English] Diary of the Sinai Campaign. [1st ed.] New York, Harper & Row [1966] 236 p. illus., maps, ports. 22 cm. 1. Dayan, Moshe, 1915-1981. 2. Sinai Campaign, 1956 — Personal narratives, Israeli. 3. Israel — Armed Forces — Biography. I. T.
DS110.5.D313 1966a   956/.044   *LC* 66-15731

Glueck, Nelson, 1900-.   ● **3.3825**
Deities and dolphins; the story of the Nabataeans. New York, Farrar, Straus and Giroux [1965] xii, 650 p. illus., maps, plans. 27 cm. 1. Nabataeans 2. Dolphins 3. Petra (Ancient city) 4. Jordan — Antiquities I. T.
DS110.5.G55   913.39403   *LC* 64-19808

Browning, Iain.   **3.3826**
Petra. [Park Ridge, N.J.] Noyes Press [1973] 256 p. illus. 26 cm. 1. Petra (Ancient city) I. T.
DS110.7.B76 1973b   915.695/7 19   *LC* 73-78777   *ISBN* 0815550235

Encyclopedia of archaeological excavations in the Holy Land.   **3.3827**
Editor, English ed., Michael Avi–Yonah.
Englewood Cliffs, N.J., Prentice-Hall c1975- < 1978 >. v. < 1-2, 4 > illus. 28 cm. Rev. translation of Entsiklopedyah la-hafirot arkhe'ologiyot be-Erets Yiśra'el. Vol. 2-4 edited by Michael Avi-Yonah and Ephraim Stern. 1. Bible — Antiquities — Dictionaries. 2. Excavations (Archaeology) — Palestine — Dictionaries. 3. Palestine — Antiquities — Dictionaries. I. Avi-Yonah, Michael, 1904-1974. ed. II. Stern, Ephraim, 1934- ed.
DS111.A2 E5313 1975   220.9/3   *LC* 73-14997   *ISBN* 0132751151

Aharoni, Yohanan, 1919-1976.   **3.3828**
[Arkhe'ologyah shel Erets Yiśra'el. English] The archaeology of the land of Israel: from the prehistoric beginnings to the end of the First Temple period / by Yohanan Aharoni; edited by Miriam Aharoni; translated by Anson F. Rainey. — Philadelphia: Westminster Press, c1982. xvii, 344 p.: ill.; 23 cm. Translation of: Arkhe'ologyah shel Erets Yiśrael. Includes index. 1. Excavations (Archaeology) — Palestine 2. Palestine — Antiquities I. Aharoni, Miriam. II. T.
DS111.A3913 1982   933 19   *LC* 81-14742   *ISBN* 0664213847

Kenyon, Kathleen Mary, Dame.   **3.3829**
Archaeology in the Holy Land / Kathleen M. Kenyon. — 5th [i.e. 4th] ed. — Nashville: Nelson, 1985, c1979. xxi, 359 p., [B2] leaves of plates: ill.; 22 cm. Reprint. Originally published: London: E. Benn, 1979. Includes index. 1. Excavations (Archaeology) — Palestine 2. Palestine — Antiquities I. T.
DS111.K4 1985   933 19   *LC* 85-13733   *ISBN* 0840775210

Kenyon, Kathleen Mary.   ● **3.3830**
Royal cities of the Old Testament [by] Kathleen Kenyon. — New York: Schocken Books, [1971, i.e. 1972, c1971] xi, 164 p.: illus.; 25 cm. 1. Cities and towns, Ancient 2. Palestine — Antiquities I. T.
DS111.1.K46 1972   913.3   *LC* 79-159482   *ISBN* 0805234128

Moorey, P. R. S. (Peter Roger Stuart), 1937-.   **3.3831**
Excavation in Palestine / Roger Moorey. — 1st American ed. — Grand Rapids, Mich.: Eerdmans Pub. Co., 1983, c1981. 128 p.: ill.; 21 cm. — (Cities of the Biblical World.) 1. Excavations (Archaeology) — Palestine 2. Palestine — Antiquities I. T. II. Series.
DS111.1.M66 1983   933 19   *LC* 83-5707   *ISBN* 0802810357

Baron, Salo Wittmayer, 1895-.   ● **3.3832**
A social and religious history of the Jews. 2d ed., rev. and enl. New York: Columbia University Press, 1952-. v. ; 24 cm. 1. Jews — History 2. Judaism — History I. T.
DS112.B3152   909/.04924 19   *LC* 52-404   *ISBN* 0231088507

Cohn, Haim Hermann, 1911- comp.   **3.3833**
Jewish law in ancient and modern Israel; selected essays, with an introd. [New York] Ktav Pub. House, 1971. xxxiv, 259 p. 24 cm. 1. Jewish law I. T.
DS 112 C67 1971   *LC* 72-149604   *ISBN* 0870681370

Katz, Jacob, 1904-.   ● **3.3834**
Tradition and crisis; Jewish society at the end of the Middle Ages. — [New York] Free Press of Glencoe [1961] 280 p. 22 cm. Includes bibliography. 1. Jews — Soc. life & cust. 2. Jews — Hist. — 70-1789. I. T.
DS112.K373   915.693   *LC* 61-9168

Liebman, Charles S.   **3.3835**
Civil religion in Israel: traditional Judaism and political culture in the Jewish state / Charles S. Liebman, Eliezer Don–Yehiya. — Berkeley: University of California Press, c1983. 305 p.; 24 cm. Includes index. 1. Civil religion — Israel. 2. Zionism — Israel. 3. Israel — Civilization 4. Israel — Politics and government. I. Don-Yihya, Eli'ezer. II. T.
DS112.L65 1983   306/.2/095694 19   *LC* 82-17427   *ISBN* 0520048172

Vaux, Roland de, 1903-1971.   ● **3.3836**
Ancient Israel: its life and institutions. New York, McGraw-Hill [1961] 592 p. 1. Jews — Social life and customs I. T.
DS112.V313   *LC* 61-12360

Ginzberg, Louis, 1873-1953.   ● **3.3837**
Students, scholars and saints / by Louis Ginzberg. — New York: Meridian Books; Philadelphia: The Jewish Publication Society of America, 1958. xiii, 291 p. 1. Jews — Education 2. Jews — Biography I. Jewish Publication Society of America. II. T.
DS113 G7   *LC* 58-8532

Schwarz, Leo Walder, 1906-.   ● **3.3838**
Great ages and ideas of the Jewish people / by Salo W. Baron... [et al.]; edited, with an introd. by Leo W. Schwarz. — -. New York: Modern Library, 1956. — xxvii, 515 p.; 21 cm. — 1. Judaism — History I. Baron, Salo Wittmayer, 1895-II. T.
DS113.S38   LC 62-4323

Shulvass, Moses A. (Moses Avigdor), 1909-.   **3.3839**
Jewish culture in Eastern Europe: the classical period / by Moses A. Shulvass. — New York: Ktav Pub. House, 1975. viii, 180 p.; 24 cm. Includes index. 1. Talmud Torah (Judaism) 2. Jews — Europe, Eastern — Intellectual life. I. T.
DS113.S48   943.8/004/924   LC 74-34140   ISBN 0870682733

The Changing Bedouin / edited by Emanuel Marx, Avshalom   **3.3840**
Shmueli.
New Brunswick, USA: Transaction Books, c1984. xi, 197 p.: map; 24 cm. — (Collected papers series / Shiloah Center for Middle Eastern and African Studies) 1. Bedouins — Israel — Addresses, essays, lectures. 2. Israel — Social life and customs — Addresses, essays, lectures. I. Marx, Emanuel. II. Shemu'eli, Avshalom.
DS113.7.C52 1984   305 19   LC 83-17936   ISBN 0878554920

Lustick, Ian, 1949-.   **3.3841**
Arabs in the Jewish State: Israel's control of a national minority / by Ian Lustick. — Austin: University of Texas Press, c1980. xii, 385 p.: ill.; 24 cm. — (Modern Middle East series ; no. 6) Based on the author's thesis, University of California, Berkeley. Includes index. 1. Palestinian Arabs — Israel 2. Minorities — Israel. 3. Israel — Politics and government I. T.
DS113.7.L87 1980   323.1/19/2705694   LC 79-22311   0292703473

Deshen, Shlomo A.   **3.3842**
The predicament of homecoming: cultural and social life of North African immigrants in Israel / Shlomo Deshen and Moshe Shokeid. — Ithaca, N.Y.: Cornell University Press, 1974. 251 p.: ill.; 22 cm. — (Symbol, myth, and ritual) Includes index. 1. Jews, North African — Israel 2. Israel — Emigration and immigration. I. Shokeid, Moshe. joint author. II. T.
DS113.8.N6 D47   301.29/5694   LC 74-4902   ISBN 0801408857

Shokeid, Moshe.   **3.3843**
The dual heritage: immigrants from the Atlas mountains in an Israeli village / Moshe Shokeid; foreword by Max Gluckman. — Augm. ed. — New Brunswick, U.S.A.: Transaction Books, c1985. xxxiv, 253 p.; 23 cm. (Judaica series) Includes index. 1. Jews, Moroccan — Israel — Negev — Case studies. 2. Villages — Israel — Negev — Case studies. 3. Israel — Ethnic relations — Case studies. I. T.
DS113.8.N6 S474 1985   306/.095694/9 19   LC 84-24129   ISBN 088738028X

DS114–127 HISTORY

Bloch, Abraham P.   **3.3844**
Day by day in Jewish history: a chronology and calendar of historic events / by Abraham P. Bloch. — New York: Ktav Pub. House, c1983. xii, 336 p.; 24 cm. Includes index. 1. Jews — History — Miscellanea. 2. Jews — Biography — Anniversaries, etc. I. T.
DS114.B55 1983   909/.04924 19   LC 82-7769   ISBN 0870687360

Kochan, Lionel.   **3.3845**
The Jew and his history / Lionel Kochan. — New York: Schocken Books, 1977. x, 164 p.; 22 cm. Includes index. 1. Jews — History — Philosophy. 2. Historians, Jewish I. T.
DS115.5.K62   909/.04/924   LC 76-56105

Meyer, Michael A. comp.   **3.3846**
Ideas of Jewish history. Edited, with introductions and notes, by Michael A. Meyer. New York, Behrman House [1974] xiv, 360 p. 24 cm. (Library of Jewish studies) 1. Jews — History — Philosophy — Addresses, essays, lectures. 2. Jews — Historiography — Addresses, essays, lectures. I. T.
DS115.5.M48   909/.04/924   LC 73-19960   ISBN 0874412021

Whittaker, Molly.   **3.3847**
Jews and Christians: Graeco–Roman views / Molly Whittaker. — Cambridge [Cambridgeshire]; New York: Cambridge University Press, 1984. xii, 286 p.: maps; 23 cm. (Cambridge commentaries on writings of the Jewish and Christian world, 200 BC to AD 200; v. 6) Includes index. 1. Jews — History — To 70 A.D. — Historiography. 2. Judaism — History — To 70 A.D. — Historiography. 3. Church history — Primitive and early church, ca. 30-600 — Historiography. 4. Classical literature — History and criticism. 5. Greece — Religion 6. Rome — Religion. I. T.
DS115.5.W48 1984   930/.04924 19   LC 84-1880   ISBN 0521242517

Yerushalmi, Yosef Hayim, 1932-.   **3.3848**
Zakhor, Jewish history and Jewish memory / Yosef Hayim Yerushalmi. — Seattle: University of Washington Press, c1982. xvii, 144 p.; 23 cm. — (Samuel and Althea Stroum lectures in Jewish studies.) 1. Jews — Historiography. I. T. II. Series.
DS115.5.Y47 1982   909/.04924/0072 19   LC 82-15989   ISBN 0295959398

Dubnow, Simon, 1860-1941.   ● **3.3849**
[Istoriia evreiskogo naroda na Vostoka. English] History of the Jews. Translated from the Russian 4th definitive rev. ed. by Moshe Spiegel. South Brunswick [N.J.] T. Yoseloff [1967-73] 5 v. 24 cm. Translation of Istoriia evreĭskogo naroda na Vostoke (romanized form). 1. Jews — History I. T.
DS117.D7213   910/.03/924   LC 66-14785   ISBN 0498075370

Ben-Sasson, Haim Hillel, 1914-1977.   **3.3850**
[Toldot 'am Yiśra'el. English] A History of the Jewish people / A. Malamat ... [et al.]; edited by H. H. Ben–Sasson. — Cambridge, Mass.: Harvard University Press, 1976. xii, 1170 p., [24] leaves of plates: ill.; 25 cm. Translation of Toldot 'am Yiśra'el. Includes index. 1. Jews — History I. Malamat, Abraham. II. T.
DS117.T613 1976   909/.04/924   LC 75-29879   ISBN 0674397304

Avi-Yonah, Michael, 1904-1974.   **3.3851**
The Herodian period / editor, Michael Avi-Yonah; assistant editor, Zvi Baras. — [Tel-Aviv?]: Jewish History Publications Ltd.; New Brunswick: Rutgers University Press, 1975. xxii, 402 p., [12] leaves of plates: ill., maps; 27 cm. — (The World history of the Jewish People: Ancient times; 1st ser., v. 7) Includes index. 1. Herod, House of. 2. Jews — History — 168 B.C.-135 A.D. 3. Palestine — History — To 70 A.D. I. Baras, Zvi. II. T.
DS117.W6 vol. 7 DS122   933   LC 75-318967   ISBN 0813508061

Encyclopedia of Jewish history: events and eras of the Jewish   **3.3852**
people / [editor of the English edition Joseph Alpher].
New York, N.Y.: Facts on File Publications, c1986. 287 p.: ill. (some col.); 30 cm. Includes index. 1. Jews — History 2. Israel — History I. Alpher, Joseph.
DS118.E465 1986b   909/.04924/0321 909/.04924 19   LC 85-23941
     ISBN 0816012202

Noth, Martin, 1902-1968.   ● **3.3853**
The history of Israel. — 2d ed. [Translation rev. by P. R. Ackroyd]. — London, A. & C. Black [1960] 487 p. 24 cm. Includes bibliography. 1. Jews — Hist. I. T.
DS118.N553 1960   933   LC 60-50534

DS119–119.7 Jewish–Arab Relations. Palestinian Arabs

Goitein, S. D., 1900-.   ● **3.3854**
Jews and Arabs, their contacts through the ages. New York, Schocken Books [1955] 257 p. 22 cm. 1. Jews — Islamic countries 2. Jewish-Arab relations — History. I. T.
DS119.G58   956.94*   LC 55-7968

Kobler, Franz, 1882-1965. ed.   ● **3.3855**
A treasury of Jewish letters: letters from the famous and the humble. — [New York]: Publication of the East and West Library issued by Farrar [1953] 2 v. (lxxix, 672 p.): ill., ports.; 22 cm. 'Second edition.' I. Jewish letters II. T.
DS119.K58 1953   LC 53-8849

Herzog, Chaim, 1918-.   **3.3856**
The Arab–Israeli wars: war and peace in the Middle East / Chaim Herzog. — 1st ed. — New York: Random House, c1982. 392 p., [32] leaves of plates: ill.; 24 cm. Includes index. 1. Jewish-Arab relations — 1949- 2. Israel — History, Military. I. T.
DS119.2.H47 1982   956/.04 19   LC 80-5291   ISBN 0394503791

Brecher, Michael.   **3.3857**
Decisions in Israel's foreign policy / Michael Brecher. — New Haven: Yale University Press, 1975. xiv, 639 p., [1] fold. leaf: ill., maps; 23 cm. Includes indexes. 1. Israel — Foreign relations 2. Israel — Politics and government I. T.
DS119.6.B73 1975   327.5694   LC 73-77143   ISBN 0300016603

Israel in the Third World / edited by Michael Curtis and Susan   **3.3858**
Aurelia Gitelson.
New Brunswick, N.J.: Transaction Books, c1976. 410 p.; 24 cm. 1. Technical assistance, Israeli — Developing countries — Addresses, essays, lectures. 2. Developing countries — Foreign relations — Israel — Addresses, essays, lectures. 3. Israel — Foreign relations — Developing countries — Addresses, essays, lectures. I. Curtis, Michael, 1923- II. Gitelson, Susan Aurelia.
DS119.6.I77   327.5694/0172/4   LC 75-44817   ISBN 0878551301

Allen, Richard, 1903-.   **3.3859**
Imperialism and nationalism in the Fertile Crescent; sources and prospects of the Arab–Israeli conflict [by] Richard Allen. New York, Oxford University Press, 1974. x, 686 p. maps. 21 cm. 1. Jewish-Arab relations — History. 2. Middle East — Politics and government. I. T.
DS119.7.A6437   956 19   *LC* 73-90373   *ISBN* 019501782X

The Arab–Israeli conflict: readings and documents / edited by   **3.3860**
John Norton Moore; sponsored by the American Society of
International Law.
Abridged and rev. ed. — Princeton, N.J.: Princeton University Press, 1977. xxxvi, 1285 p.: maps; 25 cm. 1. Jewish-Arab relations — 1917- — Addresses, essays, lectures. 2. Jewish-Arab relations — 1917- — Sources. I. Moore, John Norton, 1937- II. American Society of International Law.
DS119.7.A6718 1977   956/.04   *LC* 76-45905   *ISBN* 0691010668

Bell, J. Bowyer, 1931-.   **3.3861**
Terror out of Zion: Irgun Zvai Leumi, LEHI, and the Palestine Underground, 1929–1949 / J. Bowyer Bell. — New York: St. Martin's Press, 1977. xi, 374 p. [17] leaves of plates: ill., facsims., ports. Includes index. 1. Irgun tseva'i le'umi. 2. Lohame herut Yiśra'el. 3. Jewish-Arab relations — 1917-1949 4. Israel-Arab War, 1948-1949 I. T.
DS119.7.B382   DS119.7 B382.   956.94/04   *LC* 75-26172   *ISBN* 0312792050

Caplan, Neil.   **3.3862**
Futile diplomacy / Neil Caplan. — London: F. Cass, 1983-1986. 2 v.: facsims., ports.; 22 cm. Includes indexes. 1. Jewish-Arab relations I. T. II. Title: Early Arab-Zionist negotiation attempts, 1913-1931. III. Title: Arab-Zionist negotiations and the end of mandate.
DS119.7.C275   *ISBN* 0714632147

Cobban, Helena.   **3.3863**
The Palestinian Liberation Organisation: people, power, and politics / Helena Cobban. — Cambridge [Cambridgeshire]; New York: Cambridge University Press, 1984. xii, 305 p.: ill.; 24 cm. — (Cambridge Middle East library.) 1. Munazzamat al-Tahrīr al-Filastīnīyah. 2. Jewish-Arab relations — 1949- 3. Middle East — Politics and government — 1945- I. T. II. Series.
DS119.7.C58 1984   322.4/2/095694 19   *LC* 83-18915   *ISBN* 0521251281

Dimbleby, Jonathan.   **3.3864**
The Palestinians / Jonathan Dimbleby; photos. by Donald McCullin. — [New York]: Quartet Books, 1980, c1979. 256 p.: ill. 1. Palestinian Arabs 2. Jewish-Arab relations — 1949- 3. Fedayeen 4. Palestine — Politics and government — 1949- I. McCullin, Don, 1935- II. T.
DS119.7.D56   956.94   *LC* 79-48038   *ISBN* 0704322560

Flapan, Simha.   **3.3865**
Zionism and the Palestinians / Simha Flapan. — London: Croom Helm; New York: Barnes & Noble Books, 1979. 361 p.; 23 cm. 1. Jewish-Arab relations — 1917-1949 2. Zionism — History. I. T.
DS119.7.F6 1979   956.94/001   *LC* 78-26044   *ISBN* 0064921042

Golan, Galia.   **3.3866**
The Soviet Union and the Palestine Liberation Organization: an uneasy alliance / Galia Golan. — New York, N.Y.: Praeger, 1980. vii, 289 p.; 24 cm. Includes index. 1. Munazzamat al-Tahrīr al-Filastīnīyah. 2. Middle East — Foreign relations — Russia. 3. Russia — Foreign relations — Middle East. I. T.
DS119.7.G623   327.47056   *LC* 80-18760   *ISBN* 003057319X

Harkabi, Yehoshafat, 1921-.   **3.3867**
Arab strategies and Israel's response / Yehoshafat Harkabi. New York: Free Press, c1977. xiii, 194 p.; 22 cm. 1. Jewish-Arab relations — 1949- 2. Israel — Foreign opinion, Arab. 3. Arab countries — Foreign opinion, Israeli. I. T.
DS119.7.H3686   327.5694/017/4927   *LC* 77-70273   *ISBN* 0029137608

Harkabi, Yehoshafat, 1921-.   **3.3868**
[ha-'Emdah ha-'aravit ba-konflikt ha-'aravi-yisre'eli. English] Arab attitudes to Israel [by] Y. Harkabi. Translated by Misha Louvish. New York, Hart Pub. Co. [1972, c1971] xxiii, 527 p. 24 cm. Translation of ha-'Emdah ha-'aravit ba-konflikt ha-'aravi-yisre'eli. 1. Jewish-Arab relations 2. Israel — Foreign opinion, Arab. I. T.
DS119.7.H37213 1972   327.5694/017/4927   *LC* 72-171897   *ISBN* 0805510273

Harkabi, Yehoshafat, 1921-.   **3.3869**
The Palestinian covenant and its meaning / Y. Harkabi. — London: Vallentine, Mitchell; Totowa, N.J.: Biblio Distribution Centre, 1979. 159 p.; 23 cm. 1. Munazzamat al-Tahrīr al-Filastīnīyah. 2. Mīthāq al-watanī al-Filastīnī. 3. Jewish-Arab relations — 1949- I. T.
DS119.7.H37543   322.4/2/095694   *LC* 80-457472   *ISBN* 0853032009

Heller, Mark.   **3.3870**
A Palestinian state: the implications for Israel / Mark A. Heller. — Cambridge, Mass.: Harvard University Press, 1983. x, 190 p.: maps; 24 cm. Includes index. 1. Jewish-Arab relations — 1973- 2. Palestine — Politics and government — 1948- I. T.
DS119.7.H3855 1983   956/.04 19   *LC* 82-15698   *ISBN* 0674652215

The Israel–Arab reader: a documentary history of the Middle   **3.3871**
East conflict.
Rev. and updated / Walter Laqueur and Barry Rubin, editors. — New York, N.Y.: Penguin Books, 1984. xi, 704 p., [1] leaf of plates: map; 20 cm. (Pelican books) 'Fourth revised and updated edition'—T.p. verso. 1. Jewish-Arab relations — 1917- — Sources. I. Laqueur, Walter, 1921- II. Rubin, Barry M.
DS119.7.I8256 1984b   956 19   *LC* 84-10992   *ISBN* 0140225889

Khouri, Fred J. (Fred John)   **3.3872**
The Arab–Israeli dilemma / Fred J. Khouri. — 3rd ed. — Syracuse, N.Y.: Syracuse University Press, 1985. x, 605 p.: map; 24 cm. (Contemporary issues in the Middle East.) Includes index. 1. Jewish-Arab relations — 1917- — History. I. T. II. Series.
DS119.7.K48 1985   956 19   *LC* 85-214257   *ISBN* 0815623399

Kuniholm, Bruce Robellet, 1942-.   **3.3873**
The Palestinian problem and United States policy: a guide to issues and references / text by Bruce R. Kuniholm; bibliographical essay by Michael Rubner. — Claremont, Calif.: Regina Books, c1986. ix, 157 p.: map; 23 cm. (Guides to contemporary issues. 5) Includes index. 1. Jewish-Arab relations — 1973- 2. Palestinian Arabs — Politics and government. 3. Jewish-Arab relations — 1973- — Bibliography. 4. West Bank — International status. 5. Gaza Strip — International status. 6. United States — Foreign relations — Israel — Bibliography. 7. Israel — Foreign relations — United States — Bibliography. I. Rubner, Michael. II. T. III. Series.
DS119.7.K86 1986   016.3277305694 19   *LC* 85-25687   *ISBN* 0941690180

Levins, Hoag.   **3.3874**
Arab reach: the secret war against Israel / Hoag Levins. — 1st ed. — Garden City, N.Y.: Doubleday, 1983. x, 324 p.; 22 cm. Includes index. 1. Jewish-Arab relations — 1973- 2. Arab countries — Foreign relations. I. T.
DS119.7.L475 1983   956/.048 19   *LC* 82-45255   *ISBN* 0385180578

Mandel, Neville J.   **3.3875**
The Arabs and Zionism before World War I / by Neville J. Mandel. Berkeley: University of California Press, c1976. xxiv, 258 p.: ill.; 25 cm. Based on the author's thesis, Oxford, 1965. Includes index. 1. Jewish-Arab relations — To 1917 I. T.
DS119.7.M263   327.5694/017/4927   *LC* 73-78545   *ISBN* 0520024664

National Lawyers Guild. 1977 Middle East Delegation.   **3.3876**
Treatment of Palestinians in Israeli–occupied West Bank and Gaza: report of the National Lawyers Guild 1977 Middle East Delegation. — New York: The Guild, 1978. xvi, 143 p.; 23 cm. 1. Palestinian Arabs — Legal status, laws, etc. — Israel 2. Israel-Arab War, 1967 — Occupied territories I. T.
DS 119.7 N27 1978   *LC* 78-21553   *ISBN* 0960218815

O'Neill, Bard E.   **3.3877**
Armed struggle in Palestine: a political–military analysis / Bard E. O'Neill. — Boulder, Colo.: Westview Press, 1979 (c1978). xiii, 320 p.: maps; 24 cm. — (Westview special studies on the Middle East) 1. Fedayeen 2. Jewish-Arab relations I. T.
DS119.7.O5   956.94/05   *LC* 78-2285   *ISBN* 0891583335

Ott, David H.   **3.3878**
Palestine in perspective: politics, human rights & the West Bank / David H. Ott. — London; New York: Quartet Books, 1980. 157 p.; 24 cm. 1. Jewish-Arab relations — 1973- 2. West Bank — Politics and government. I. T.
DS119.7.O88 1980   956.95/044 19   *LC* 81-17686   *ISBN* 0704322633

The Palestinians and the Middle East conflict: an international   **3.3879**
conference held at the Institute of Middle Eastern Studies,
University of Haifa, April 1976 / editor, Gabriel Ben–Dor.
Ramat Gan, Israel: Turtledove Pub., 1979 (c1978). 575 p.; 25 cm. 1. Jewish-Arab relations — 1917- — Congresses. 2. Palestinian Arabs — Congresses. I. Ben-Dor, Gabriel. II. Universitat Hefah. Makhon le-heker ve-limud ha-Mizrah ha-tikhon.
DS119.7.P28836   327.5694/017/4927   *LC* 79-111028   *ISBN* 9652000019

Peace–making in the Middle East: problems and prospects /   3.3880
edited by Paul Marantz & Janice Gross Stein.
Totowa, N.J.: Barnes & Noble Books, 1985. 244 p.; 22 cm. 1. Jewish-Arab relations — 1973- — Addresses, essays, lectures. I. Marantz, Paul. II. Stein, Janice Gross.
DS119.7.P38 1985   956 19   *LC* 84-21682   *ISBN* 0389205435

Rubin, Barry M.   3.3881
The Arab states and the Palestine conflict / Barry Rubin. — 1st ed. — Syracuse, N.Y.: Syracuse University Press, 1981. xvii, 298 p.; 24 cm. — (Contemporary issues in the Middle East.) Includes index. 1. Jewish-Arab relations — 1917- 2. Arab countries — Politics and government I. T. II. Series.
DS119.7.R75   327.5694017/4927 19   *LC* 81-5829   *ISBN* 0815622538

Safran, Nadav.   • 3.3882
From war to war: the Arab–Israeli confrontation, 1948–1967; a study of the conflict from the perspective of coercion in the context of inter–Arab and big power relations. New York, Pegasus [1969] 464 p. illus., maps. 22 cm. 1. Jewish-Arab relations — 1949-1967 2. Israel-Arab War, 1967 3. Middle East — Politics and government — 1945- I. T.
DS119.7.S32   956   *LC* 68-27991

Sandler, Shmuel.   3.3883
Israel, the Palestinians, and the West Bank: a study in intercommunal conflict / Shmuel Sandler, Hillel Frisch. — Lexington, Mass.: LexingtonBooks, c1984. xvi, 190 p.: map; 24 cm. Includes index. 1. Jewish-Arab relations 2. Palestinian Arabs — Politics and government. 3. West Bank — Politics and government. I. Frisch, Hillel. II. T.
DS119.7.S3386 1984   323.1/19275694 19   *LC* 82-49204   *ISBN* 0669064351

Touval, Saadia.   3.3884
The peace brokers: mediators in the Arab–Israeli conflict, 1948–1979 / Saadia Touval. — Princeton, N.J.: Princeton University Press, c1982. xiv, 377 p.: maps; 23 cm. 1. Jewish-Arab relations — 1949- 2. Mediation, International I. T.
DS119.7.T667 1982   DS119.7 T667 1982.   341.5/2/0956 19   *LC* 81-47955   *ISBN* 0691076383

DS121–127 By Period

DS121–122 To 70 A.D

Bright, John, 1908-.   3.3885
A history of Israel / John Bright. — 3d ed. — Philadelphia: Westminster Press, c1981. 511 p., 16 leaves of plates: maps; 25 cm. (Westminster aids to the study of the Scriptures) 1. Jews — History — To 70 A.D. I. T. II. Series.
DS121.B72 1981   933 19   *LC* 80-22774   *ISBN* 0664213812

Wellhausen, Julius, 1844-1918.   • 3.3886
Prolegomena to the history of ancient Israel. With a reprint of the article, Israel, from the Encyclopedia Britannica. Pref. by W. Robertson Smith. — New York, Meridian Books, 1957. 552 p. 21 cm. — (Meridian library, ML6) 1. Bible. O.T. — Criticism, interpretation, etc. 2. Jews — Hist. — To 953 B.C. 3. Judaism — Hist. — Ancient period. I. T.
DS121.W48 1957   932   *LC* 57-10843

Pearlman, Moshe, 1911-.   3.3887
The Maccabees. — [1st American ed.]. — New York: Macmillan, [1973] 272 p.: ill.; 26 cm. 1. Maccabees I. T.
DS121.7.P42 1973   933   *LC* 72-11280

Grant, Michael, 1914-.   3.3888
The Jews in the Roman world. New York: Scribner [1973] xv, 347 p.: maps; 24 cm. 1. Jews — Rome 2. Jews — History — 168 B.C.-135 A.D. I. T.
DS122.G73 1973   301.45/19/24037   *LC* 72-11118   *ISBN* 0684133407

Safrai, Shemuel, 1919- ed.   3.3889
The Jewish people in the first century: historical geography, political history, social, cultural and religious life and institutions / ed. by S. Safrai and M. Stern in co-operation with D. Flusser and W. C. van Unnik. — Philadelphia: Fortress Press, 1974-1976. 2 v. — (Compendia rerum Iudaicarum ad Novum Testamentum: section 1; v. 1-2) 1. Jews — History — 168 B. C.-135 A. D. — Addresses, essays, lectures 2. Jews — Political and social conditions — To 70 A. D. — Addresses, essays, lectures I. Stern, M., ed. II. T. III. Series.
DS122.J48   910/.03/924   *LC* 75-75908

The Jewish people in the first century: Historical geography,   3.3890
political history, social, cultural and religious life and
institutions / ed. by S. Safrai and M. Stern in co–operation
with D. Flusser and W. C. van Unnik.
Philadelphia: Fortress, 1974-1976. 2 v.: ill., maps; 25 cm. — (Compendia rerum Iudaicarum ad Novum Testamentum. section 1, v. 1-2) 1. Jews — History — 168 B.C.-135 A.D. — Addresses, essays, lectures. 2. Jews — Politics and government — To 70 A.D. I. Safrai, Shemuel, 1919- II. Stern, M. III. Series.
DS122.J48 1974   910/.03/924   *LC* 74-75908   *ISBN* 0800606027

Schürer, Emil, 1844-1910.   3.3891
A history of the Jewish people in the age of Jesus Christ (175 B.C. – A.D. 135) / by Emil Schürer. A new English version rev. and edited by Geza Vermes & Fergus Millar. Literary editor: Pamela Vermes. Organizing editor: Matthew Black. Edinburgh: T. & T. Clark, [1973-. v. 1. Jews — History — 586 B.C.-70 A.D. 2. Bible N.T. — History of contemporary events, etc. 3. Jews — Politics and government 4. Greek literature — Jewish authors — History and criticism 5. Bible. O.T. Apocrypha — Criticism, interpretation. etc. 6. Judaism I. Vermès, Géza, 1924- II. Millar, Fergus. III. T.
DS122 S42 1973   *ISBN* 0567022420

Smallwood, E. Mary.   3.3892
The Jews under Roman rule: from Pompey to Diocletian / by E. Mary Smallwood. — Leiden: Brill, 1976. xiv, 595 p.: ill.; 25 cm. (Studies in Judaism in late antiquity. v. 20) 1. Jews — History — 168 B.C.-135 A.D. 2. Rome — History — Empire, 30 B.C.-284 A.D. I. T. II. Series.
DS122.S62   *LC* 76-371075   *ISBN* 9004044914

Tcherikover, Avigdor, 1895-.   • 3.3893
Hellenistic civilization and the Jews. 1st ed. Philadelphia, Jewish Publication Society of America, 1959. vii, 566 p. 2 maps (on lining papers) 22 cm. 1. Jews — History — 586 B. C.-70. 2. Hellenism 3. Greece — History I. T.
DS122.T313   *LC* 59-8518

Zeitlin, Solomon, 1886-1976.   • 3.3894
The rise and fall of the Judaean state: a political, social and religious history of the Second Commonwealth. — [1st ed.] Philadelphia: Jewish Publication Society of America, 1962-1978. 3 v.: ill.; 22 cm. 1. Jews — History — 586 B.C.-70 A.D. I. T.
DS122.Z43   933   *LC* 61-11708

Israël, Gérard, 1928-.   3.3895
[Quand Jérusalem brûlait. English] When Jerusalem burned [by] Gérard Israël and Jacques Lebar. Translated from the French by Alan Kendall. New York, Morrow, 1973. xii, 177 p. illus. 22 cm. Translation of Quand Jérusalem brûlait. 1. Jews — History — Rebellion, 66-73 I. Lebar, Jacques, 1911- joint author. II. T.
DS122.8.I8713 1973   933   *LC* 73-4228

Josephus, Flavius.   • 3.3896
[De bello Judaico. English] The great Roman-Jewish war: A.D. 66-70 (De bello Judaico) The William Whiston translation as rev. by D. S. Margoliouth. Edited with an introd. by William R. Farmer. Including The life of Josephus. Gloucester, Mass., Peter Smith, 1970. xv, 332 p. geneal. tables, maps, port. 22 cm. The texts used in this ed. were first published in The works of Flavius Josephus in 1906. Translation of De bello Judaico. 1. Jews — History — Rebellion, 66-73 I. Whiston, William, 1667-1752. tr. II. Farmer, William Reuben. ed. III. Josephus, Flavius. Life of Flavius Josephus. 1970. IV. T. V. Title: Life of Flavius Josephus.
DS122.8.J73 1970   933   *LC* 70-23319

Josephus, the Jewish war; newly translated with extensive   3.3897
commentary and archaeological background illustrations /
Gaalya Cornfeld, general editor; Benjamin Mazar, Paul L.
Maier, consulting editors.
Grand Rapids, Mich.: Zondervan Pub. House, c1982. 526 p., [30] p. of plates: col. ill.; 31 cm. Includes indexes. 1. Josephus, Flavius. De bello Judaico. 2. Jews — History — Rebellion, 66-73 3. Jews — History — 168 B.C.-135 A.D. I. Josephus, Flavius. De bello Judaico. English. 1982. II. Mazar, Benjamin, 1906- III. Maier, Paul L.
DS122.8.J83 J67 1982   933 19   *LC* 82-1946   *ISBN* 0310392101

Yadin, Yigael, 1917-1984.   3.3898
Bar–Kokhba; the rediscovery of the legendary hero of the second Jewish revolt against Rome. New York, Random House [c1971] 271 p. ill. 1. Bar Kokhba, d. 135. 2. Mezada (Fortress), Israel. 3. Palestine — Antiquities I. T.
DS122.9.Y3   933   *LC* 76-152554   *ISBN* 0394471849

DS123–126.4 70-1948

Parkes, James William, 1896-.   • 3.3899
Whose land? A history of the peoples of Palestine. — New York: Taplinger, [1971, c1970] 333 p.: maps.; 22 cm. 'Based on A History of Palestine from 135 A.D. to modern times, 1949.' 1. Palestine — History I. T.
DS123.P36 1971   956.94   *LC* 70-148829   *ISBN* 0800882601

Wirth, Louis, 1897-1952. • 3.3900
The ghetto / by Louis Wirth; illustrations from woodcuts by Todros Geller. — Chicago, Ill.: The University of Chicago Press [1928] xvi, 306 p.: ill.; 20 cm. (The University of Chicago sociological series.) 1. Jews 2. Jews — Political and social conditions. 3. Jews — Illinois — Chicago I. T.
DS123.W5   LC 29-2559

Avi-Yonah, Michael, 1904-1974. 3.3901
[Bi-yeme Roma u-Bizantyon. English] The Jews of Palestine: a political history from the Bar Kokhba War to the Arab conquest / Michael Avi-Yonah. — New York: Schocken Books, 1976. xviii, 286 p.: ill.; 24 cm. Translation of author's Bi-yeme Roma u-Bizantyon. 1. Jews — Palestine — History. 2. Jews — History — 70-638 3. Palestine — History — 70-638 I. T.
DS123.5.A943   956.94/02   LC 74-26912   ISBN 0805235809

Baron, Salo Wittmayer, 1895-. • 3.3902
The Jewish community: its history and structure to the American Revolution. Westport, Conn., Greenwood Press [1972, c1942] 3 v. 23 cm. Original ed. issued in series: The Morris Loeb series. 1. Jews — Politics and government 2. Jews — Bibliography. I. T.
DS124.B29 1972   917.3/06/924   LC 74-97269   ISBN 0837132746

Marcus, Jacob Rader, 1896-. 3.3903
The Jew in the medieval world, a source book, 315–1791, by Jacob R. Marcus. Cincinnati, The Sinai press. 1938. xxiv, 504 p. 24 cm. (Jewish history source books) 'The publication of this volume was made possible by the establishment of a fund for the publication of Jewish religious school literature by the National federation of temple sisterhoods.' 1. Jews — History — Sources. 2. Jews — Political and social conditions. I. T.
DS124.M34   LC 38-14638

Roth, Cecil, 1899-1970. 3.3904
A history of the Marranos / Cecil Roth. — 4th ed. / with a new introd. by Herman P. Salomon. — New York: Hermon Press, 1974. xxiv, 424 p.: ill.; 24 cm. Includes index. 1. Marranos 2. Inquisition — Spain I. T.
DS124.R625 1974   296.8/2   LC 73-93367   ISBN 0872030407

Sharf, Andrew. • 3.3905
Byzantine Jewry from Justinian to the Fourth Crusade. New York, Schocken Books [1971] xiv, 239 p. maps. 23 cm. (The Littman Library of Jewish civilization) 1. Jews — Byzantine Empire — History. I. T.
DS124.S45 1971   914.95/06/924   LC 74-135519   ISBN 0805233873

Frangi, Abdallah. 3.3906
[PLO und Palästina. English] The PLO and Palestine / Abdallah Frangi; translated by Paul Knight. — London: Zed Books; Totowa, N.J.: U.S. distributor, Biblio Distribution Center, 1983. iii, 256 p.: ill.; maps; 22 cm. — (Third World studies.) Translation of: PLO und Palästina. 1. Munazzamat al-Tahrīr al-Filastīnīyah. 2. Jewish-Arab relations 3. Zionism — Controversial literature. 4. Palestine — History I. T. II. Title: P.L.O. and Palestine. III. Series.
DS125.F7613 1983   956.94/05 19   LC 83-222880   ISBN 0862321956

Mahler, Raphael, 1899-. • 3.3907
[Divre yeme Yiśra'el, dorot aharonim. English] A history of modern Jewry. New York, Schocken Books [1971-. v. 25 cm. Abridged translation of Divre yeme Yiśra'el, dorot aharonim. 1. Jews — History — 1789-1945 I. T.
DS125.M322132   909.04/924/07   LC 74-148838   ISBN 0805233989

Sachar, Howard Morley, 1928-. • 3.3908
The course of modern Jewish history. [1st ed.] Cleveland: World Pub. Co. [1958] 617 p.: maps; 24 cm. 1. Jews — History — 1789-1945 2. Jews — History — 1945- I. T.
DS125.S28   LC 58-6757

Sykes, Christopher, 1907-. • 3.3909
Crossroads to Israel. Cleveland, World Pub. Co. [1965] xii, 404 p. illus., maps. 22 cm. Bibliography: p. [381]-385. 1. Zionism 2. Israel — History 3. Palestine — History — 1917-1948 I. T.
DS125.S86   956.9404   LC 65-23372

Bar-Zohar, Michael, 1938-. • 3.3910
[Ben–Guryon. English] Ben–Gurion: a biography / Michael Bar–Zohar; translated by Peretz Kidron. — New York: Delacorte Press, [1979] c1978. xvii, 334 p., [8] leaves of plates: ill.; 24 cm. Condensation and translation of Ben-Guryon. Includes index. 1. Ben-Gurion, David, 1886-1973. 2. Prime ministers — Israel — Biography. 3. Zionists — Palestine — Biography. I. T.
DS125.3.B37 B285513 1979   956.94/05/0924 B   LC 78-11055   ISBN 0440009871

Teveth, Shabtai, 1925-. 3.3911
Ben–Gurion and the Palestinian Arabs: from peace to war / Shabtai Teveth. — Oxford [Oxfordshire]; New York: Oxford University Press, 1985. x, 234 p.

Includes index. 1. Ben-Gurion, David, 1886-1973 — Views on Jewish-Arab relations. 2. Jewish-Arab relations — 1917- I. T.
DS125.3.B37 T47 1985   956.94/05/0924 19   LC 84-29618   ISBN 0195035623

Eli'av, Ya'akov, 1917-. 3.3912
[Mevukash. English] Wanted / by Yaacov Eliav; translated and adapted from the Hebrew by Mordecai Schreiber. — New York: Shengold Publishers, c1984. 272 p.: ill., ports.; 25 cm. Translation of: Mevukash. Includes index. 1. Eli'av, Ya'akov, 1917- 2. Irgun tseva'i le'umi. 3. Lohame herut Yiśra'el. 4. Terrorists — Palestine — Biography. 5. Jews — Palestine — Politics and government. 6. Palestine — Ethnic relations. I. Schreiber, Mordecai. II. T.
DS125.3.E44 A3613 1984   956.94/04 19   LC 84-50676   ISBN 0884001075

Reinharz, Jehuda. 3.3913
Chaim Weizmann: the making of a Zionist leader / Jehuda Reinharz. — New York: Oxford University Press, 1985. x, 566 p.: ill.; 25 cm. Includes index. 1. Weizmann, Chaim, 1874-1952 — Political career before 1914. 2. Zionists — Great Britain — Biography. 3. Israel — Presidents — Biography. I. T.
DS125.3.W45 R45 1985   956.94/05/0924 B 19   LC 84-7898   ISBN 0195034465

Friedman, Isaiah. 3.3914
The question of Palestine, 1914–1918: British–Jewish–Arab relations. — New York: Schocken Books [1973] xiii, 433 p.; 23 cm. 1. Balfour Declaration. 2. Zionism — Great Britain. 3. Great Britain — Foreign relations — Middle East. 4. Middle East — Foreign relations — Great Britain. I. T.
DS125.5.F73 1973b   956.94/001   LC 73-80510   ISBN 0805235248

Begin, Menachem, 1913-. 3.3915
[Mered. English] The revolt / Menachem Begin. — Rev. ed. — New York: Nash Pub. Co., c1977. xxvii, 386 p., [18] leaves of plates: ill.; 24 cm. Translation of ha-Mered. Includes index. 1. Begin, Menachem, 1913- 2. Irgun tseva'i le'umi. 3. Prime ministers — Israel — Biography. 4. Palestine — History — 1929-1948 I. T.
DS126.B375 1977   956.94/04/0924 B 19   LC 77-10806   ISBN 0840213700

Hurewitz, J. C., 1914-. • 3.3916
The struggle for Palestine. — [1st ed.]. — New York, Norton [1950] 404 p. maps. 24 cm. Issued also as thesis, Columbia University, under title: The road to partition. Bibliography: p. 363-388. 1. Palestine — Hist. — 1929-1948. I. T.
DS126.H87   956.9   LC 50-9773 rev 2

Ingrams, Doreen. 3.3917
Palestine papers, 1917–1922: seeds of conflict / compiled and annotated by Doreen Ingrams. — London: J. Murray, 1972. iii-xii, 198, [8] p.: 2 leaves, ill., map, ports.; 23 cm. 1. Palestine — History — 1917-1948 — Sources. I. T.
DS126.I45   956.94/04/08   LC 72-189481   ISBN 0719526388

Lesch, Ann Mosely. 3.3918
Arab politics in Palestine, 1917–1939: the frustration of a nationalist movement / Ann Mosely Lesch. — Ithaca, N.Y.: Cornell University Press, c1979. 257 p.: map; 23 cm. — (The Modern Middle East series; v. 11) Includes index. 1. Palestinian Arabs — Politics and government. 2. Palestine — Politics and government I. T.
DS126.L37   956.94/04 19   LC 78-32059   ISBN 0801412374

Porath, Yehoshua. 3.3919
[Tsemihat ha-tenu'ah ha-le'umit ha-'Arvit-ha-Palestina'it, 1918-1929. English] The emergence of the Palestinian–Arab national movement, 1918–1929 [by] Y. Porath. London, Cass [1974] vi, 406 p. 22 cm. Continued by the author's The Palestinian Arab national movement, 1929-1939. Translation of Tsemihat ha-tenu'ah ha-le'umit ha-'Arvit-ha-Palestina'it, 1918-1929. A translation of the author's thesis, Hebrew University, 1971. 1. Palestinian Arabs 2. Palestine — History — 1917-1948 I. T.
DS126.P6313 1974   956.94/04   LC 72-92976   ISBN 0714629391

Porath, Yehoshua. 3.3920
[Mi-mehumot li-meridah. English] The Palestinian Arab national movement: from riots to rebellion / Y. Porath. Volume two, 1929–1939. — London: Totowa, N.J.: F. Cass, 1977. xii, 414 p.; 23 cm. Comprises v. 2 of the author's The emergence of the Palestinian-Arab national movement, 1918-1929. Translation of Mi-mehumot li-meridah. Includes index. 1. Palestinian Arabs 2. Palestine — History — 1929-1948 I. T.
DS126.P636 1977   956.94/04   LC 78-322346   ISBN 0714630705

Rose. N. A. 3.3921
The Gentile Zionists; a study in Anglo–Zionist diplomacy, 1929–1939 [by] N. A. Rose. — London: Cass, [1973] xiii, 242 p.: illus.; 22 cm. 1. Mandates — Palestine. 2. Zionism — Great Britain. 3. Palestine — History — 1929-1948 I. T.
DS126.R65 1973   956.94/001   LC 72-92977   ISBN 0714629405

Cohen, Michael Joseph, 1940-.   3.3922
Palestine and the Great Powers, 1945–1948 / Michael J. Cohen. — Princeton: Princeton University Press, c1982. viii, 417 p.: maps; 24 cm. Includes index. 1. Palestine — History — Partition, 1947 I. T.
DS126.4.C645 1982   956.94/04 19   *LC* 82-3858   *ISBN* 0691053715

Sherf, Zeev.   • 3.3923
Three days / Zeev Sharef; translated by Julian Louis Meltzer from the Hebrew. — Garden City, N.Y.: Doubleday, 1962. — 298 p. 1. Mandates — Palestine 2. Palestine — History — 1929-1948 I. T.
DS126.4 S48153 1962   956.9   *LC* 62-8911

DS126.5–128 1948-

American University (Washington, D.C.). Foreign Area Studies.   3.3924
Israel, a country study / Foreign Area Studies, the American University; edited by Richard F. Nyrop. — 2d ed. — Washington: The University: for sale by the Supt. of Docs., U.S. Govt. Print. Off., c1979. xxviii, 414 p.: ill.; 24 cm. — (Area handbook series.) First ed., by H. H. Smith, published in 1970 under title: Area handbook for Israel. 'DA pam 550-25, supersedes 1970 edition.' 1. Israel. I. Nyrop, Richard F. II. Smith, Harvey Henry, 1892- Area handbook for Israel. III. T. IV. Series.
DS126.5.A695 1979   956.94/05   *LC* 79-13733

Segre, Dan V.   3.3925
A crisis of identity: Israel and Zionism / Dan V. Segre. — Oxford; New York: Oxford University Press, 1980. x, 182 p.; 22 cm. 1. Zionism 2. Jews — Identity 3. Judaism and state 4. Israel — Politics and government I. T.
DS126.5.A919   956.94/001   *LC* 79-41789   *ISBN* 0192158627

Ben-Gurion, David, 1886-1973.   • 3.3926
Israel: years of challenge. — [1st ed.]. — New York: Holt, Rinehart and Winston, [1963] vi, 240 p.: illus., ports., maps.; 22 cm. 1. Israel — History 2. Israel — Social policy. I. T.
DS126.5.B44   956.94   *LC* 63-18431

Elon, Amos.   • 3.3927
The Israelis: founders and sons. [1st ed.] New York, Holt, Rinehart and Winston [1971] 359 p. 24 cm. 1. National characteristics, Israeli 2. Zionism 3. Israelis — Psychology. 4. Jewish-Arab relations 5. Israel — Politics and government I. T.
DS126.5.E4195   956.94   *LC* 75-138887   *ISBN* 0030859670

Isaac, Rael Jean.   3.3928
Israel divided: idealogical politics in the Jewish State / Rael Jean Isaac. — Baltimore: Johns Hopkins University Press, c1976. ix, 227 p.: maps; 24 cm. Errata sheet inserted. Includes index. 1. Jewish-Arab relations — 1967-1973 2. Israel — Politics and government I. T.
DS126.5.I68   320.9/5694/05   *LC* 75-36944   *ISBN* 0801817374

Lucas, Noah.   3.3929
The modern history of Israel. — New York: Praeger, [1975] 500 p.: maps.; 22 cm. 1. Israel — History 2. Palestine — History — 1917-1948 I. T.
DS126.5.L82 1975   956.94   *LC* 74-16411   *ISBN* 0275334503

Naamani, Israel T. comp.   3.3930
[Israel through the eyes of its leaders] Israel: its politics and philosophy; an annotated reader. Edited by Israel T. Naamani, David Rudavsky [and] Abraham I. Katsh. [Rev. ed.] New York, Behrman House [1974] xiii, 434 p. 22 cm. Published in 1971 in Tel Aviv under title: Israel through the eyes of its leaders. 1. Israel — Addresses, essays, lectures. I. Rudavsky, David. joint comp. II. Katsh, Abraham Isaac, 1908- joint comp. III. T.
DS126.5.N22 1974   915.694/05/08   *LC* 73-15645   *ISBN* 0874412498

Perlmutter, Amos.   3.3931
Politics and the military in Israel 1967–1977 / Amos Perlmutter. — London; Totowa, N.J.: F. Cass, 1978. xiv, 222 p.: maps; 23 cm. Sequel to Military and politics in Israel 1948-1967. 1. Israel-Arab War, 1973 — Influence 2. Israel — Politics and government 3. Israel — Armed Forces — Political activity. I. T.
DS126.5.P45 1978   322/.5/095694   *LC* 78-312288   *ISBN* 0714630799

Safran, Nadav.   3.3932
Israel, the embattled ally / Nadav Safran. — Cambridge, Mass.: Belknap Press, 1978. ix, 633 p.: maps; 25 cm. Includes index. 1. Israel. 2. Israel — Foreign relations — United States. 3. United States — Foreign relations — Israel. I. T.
DS126.5.S158   956.94/05   *LC* 77-22357   *ISBN* 0674468813

Dayan, Moshe, 1915-1981.   3.3933
[Story of my life] Moshe Dayan: story of my life / by Moshe Dayan. — New York: Morrow, 1976. 640 p.: ill.; 24 cm. Originally published under title: Story

of my life. Includes index. 1. Dayan, Moshe, 1915-1981. 2. Israel — History, Military. I. T.
DS126.6.D3 A35   956.94/05/0924 B   *LC* 76-18144   *ISBN* 0688030769

Eban, Abba Solomon, 1915-.   3.3934
Abba Eban: an autobiography. — 1st ed. — New York: Random House, c1977. xii, 628 p., [8] leaves of plates: ill.; 25 cm. Includes index. 1. Eban, Abba Solomon, 1915- 2. Statesmen — Israel — Biography. 3. Israel — Foreign relations I. T.
DS126.6.E2 A32   DS126.6E2 A32.   956.94/05/0924 B   *LC* 77-6003   *ISBN* 0394493028

Collins, Larry.   3.3935
O Jerusalem / [by] Larry Collins and Dominique Lapierre. — New York: Simon and Schuster [1972] 637 p.: ill.; 24 cm. 1. Israel-Arab War, 1948-1949 — Jerusalem. 2. Jerusalem — History — Siege, 1948. I. Lapierre, Dominique. joint author. II. T.
DS126.99.J4 C63   956.94/405   *LC* 77-185063   *ISBN* 0671211633

O'Ballance, Edgar.   • 3.3936
The third Arab–Israeli war. — Hamden, Conn.: Archon Books, 1972. 288 p.: maps.; 23 cm. 1. Israel-Arab War, 1967 I. T.
DS127.O23   956/.046   *LC* 72-1059   *ISBN* 0208012923

al-Badrī, Hasan.   3.3937
The Ramadan war, 1973 / Hassan el Badri, Taha el Magdoub, Mohammed Dia el Din Zohdy; foreword by Trevor N. Dupuy. — Dunn Loring, Va.: T.N. Dupuy Associates, 1978. ix, 239 p.: ill., maps; 24 cm. Translation of Harb Ramadan. 1. Israel-Arab War, 1973 I. al-Majdūb, Tāhā. II. Zuhdī, Diyā' al-Dīn. III. T.
DS128.1.B313 1978   956/.048   *LC* 77-24376   *ISBN* 088244608

Herzog, Chaim, 1918-.   3.3938
The War of Atonement, October, 1973 / Chaim Herzog. — 1st American ed. — Boston: Little, Brown, [1975] viii, 300 p., [4] leaves of plates: ill.; 24 cm. Includes index. 1. Israel-Arab War, 1973 I. T.
DS128.1.H467 1975   956/.048   *LC* 75-16118   *ISBN* 0316359009

Quandt, William B.   3.3939
Camp David: peacemaking and politics / William B. Quandt. — Washington, D.C.: Brookings Institution, c1986. xvi, 426 p.; 24 cm. Map on lining papers. Includes index. 1. Egypt. Treaties, etc. Israel, 1979 Mar. 26 2. Israel-Arab War, 1973 — Peace. 3. United States — Foreign relations — Near East. 4. Middle East — Foreign relations — United States. 5. United States — Foreign relations — 1977-1981 I. T.
DS128.183.Q36 1986   327.73056 19   *LC* 85-48174   *ISBN* 0815772904

DS133–135 JEWS OUTSIDE ISRAEL, BY PLACE, A–Z

DS135.A–E

Rozenblit, Marsha L., 1950-.   3.3940
The Jews of Vienna, 1867–1914: assimilation and identity / Marsha L. Rozenblit. — Albany, N.Y.: State University of New York Press, 1984. xvii, 284 p.: ill.; 24 cm. — (SUNY series in modern Jewish history.) Includes index. 1. Jews — Austria — Vienna — Social conditions. 2. Jews — Austria — Vienna — Cultural assimilation. 3. Vienna (Austria) — Social conditions. 4. Vienna (Austria) — Ethnic relations. I. T. II. Series.
DS135.A92 V559 1983   305.8/924/043613 19   *LC* 83-17885   *ISBN* 0873958446

Neusner, Jacob, 1932-.   • 3.3941
A history of the Jews in Babylonia. 2nd printing revised. Leiden, E. J. Brill, 1969-. v. 24 1/2 cm. (Studia post-Biblica. v. 9) Continued by the author's Talmudic Judaism in Sasanian Babylonia. 1. Jews — Iraq — Babylonia — History. 2. Judaism — History — Talmudic period, 10-425 3. Babylonia — Ethnic relations — Parthians — History. I. T. II. Series.
DS135.B2 N42   935/.004924 19   *LC* 70-468047

Kranzler, David, 1930-.   3.3942
Japanese, Nazis & Jews: the Jewish refugee community of Shanghai, 1938–1945 / David Kranzler; foreword by Abraham G. Duker. — New York: Yeshiva University Press: distributed by Sifria Distributors, 1976. 644 p., [14] leaves of plates: ill.; 24 cm. Rev. version of the author's thesis, Yeshiva University, 1971. Includes index. 1. Jews — China — Shanghai — History. 2. World War, 1939-1945 — Jews — China — Shanghai. 3. Shanghai (China) — History I. T.
DS135.C5 K7 1976   951/.132/004924   *LC* 76-20771   *ISBN* 0893620009

Leslie, Donald, 1922-.   **3.3943**
The survival of the Chinese Jews: the Jewish community of Kaifeng / by Donald Daniel Leslie. — Leiden: Brill, 1973 (c1972) xiv, 270 p.: ill.; 26 cm. (T'oung pao. Archives concernant l'histoire, les langues, la geographie, l'ethnographie et les arts de l'Asie orientale. Monographie, 10) 1. Jews — China — K'ai-feng hsien I. T. II. Series.
DS135.C5 L47   915.1/06/924   *LC* 72-169783   *ISBN* 9004034137

Pollak, Michael, 1918-.   **3.3944**
Mandarins, Jews, and missionaries: the Jewish experience in the Chinese Empire / Michael Pollak. — 1st ed. — Philadelphia: Jewish Publication Society of America, 1980. xviii, 436 p.: ill.; 25 cm. Includes index. 1. Jews — China — History. 2. Missions — China 3. China — History I. T.
DS135.C5 P6   951/.004/924   *LC* 79-84732   *ISBN* 0827601204

The Jews of Czechoslovakia: historical studies and surveys, vol 3 / ed. by Avigdor Dagan.   **3.3945**
[1st ed.] Philadelphia: Jewish Publication Society of America, 1984. 700 p.: ill., maps. Sponsored by the Society for the History of Czechoslovak Jews. 1. Jews in the Czechoslovak Republic 2. Czechoslovak Republic — Civilization — Jewish influences I. Society for the History of Czechoslovak Jews
DS135 C95 J45

Alderman, Geoffrey.   **3.3946**
The Jewish community in British politics / Geoffrey Alderman. — Oxford: Clarendon Press; New York: Oxford University Press, 1983. ix, 218 p.; 23 cm. 1. Jews — Great Britain — Politics and government. 2. Elections — Great Britain — History. 3. Great Britain — Ethnic relations. I. T.
DS135.E5 A58 1983   323.1/1924/041 19   *LC* 83-4115   *ISBN* 019827436X

Endelman, Todd M.   **3.3947**
The Jews of Georgian England, 1714–1830: tradition and change in a liberal society / Todd M. Endelman. — 1st ed. — Philadelphia: Jewish Publication Society of America, c1979. xiv, 370 p., [8] leaves of plates: ill.; 24 cm. Includes index. 1. Jews — Great Britain — History — 18th century. 2. Great Britain — History — 1714-1837 I. T.
DS135.E5 E48   941/.004/924   *LC* 78-78390

Fishman, William J.   **3.3948**
Jewish radicals: from Czarist stetl to London ghetto / by William J. Freeman. — 1st American ed. — New York: Pantheon Books, [1975] c1974. xvi, 336 p., [8] leaves of plates: ill.; 22 cm. Includes index. 1. Liebermann, Aaron Samuel, 1844-1880. 2. Rocker, Rudolf, 1873-1958. 3. Jews — England — London 4. Jewish radicals — England — London. 5. East End (London, England) I. T.
DS135.E5 F5 1975   914.21/06/924   *LC* 74-26194   *ISBN* 0394497643

Richardson, H. G. (Henry Gerald), 1884-.   ● **3.3949**
The English Jewry under Angevin kings. — London, Methuen [1960] 313 p. 22 cm. 1. Jews in Gt. Brit. — Hist. 2. Gt. Brit. — Hist. — Angevin period, 1154-1216. I. T.
DS135.E5R5   942.031   *LC* 61-286

Roth, Cecil, 1899-1970.   **3.3950**
A history of the Jews in England. — 3d ed. — Oxford, Clarendon Press, 1964. xiii, 311 p. 23 cm. 'Bibliographical note': p. [xi]—xii. Bibliographical footnotes. 1. Jews — Great Britain I. T.
DS135.E5R62 1964   301.451   *LC* 64-6814

Salbstein, M. C. N.   **3.3951**
The emancipation of the Jews in Britain: the question of the admission of the Jews to Parliament, 1828–1860 / M.C.N. Salbstein. — Rutherford, [N.J.]: Fairleigh Dickinson University Press, c1982. 266 p.; 24 cm. — (Littman library of Jewish civilization.) Includes index. 1. Jews — Great Britain — Emancipation. 2. Great Britain — Politics and government — 19th century 3. Great Britain — Ethnic relations. I. T. II. Series.
DS135.E5 S23 1982   941/.004924 19   *LC* 80-70901   *ISBN* 083863110X

Dawidowicz, Lucy S.   ● **3.3952**
The golden tradition: Jewish life and thought in Eastern Europe / [edited by] Lucy S. Dawidowicz. — [1st ed.] New York: Holt, Rinehart and Winston [1967] 502 p.: maps; 22 cm. 1. Jews — Europe, Eastern — Addresses, essays, lectures. 2. Europe, Eastern — Ethnic relations — Addresses, essays, lectures. I. T.
DS135.E8 D3   305.8/924/047 19   *LC* 66-13203

Mendelsohn, Ezra.   **3.3953**
The Jews of East Central Europe between the world wars / Ezra Mendelsohn. — Bloomington: Indiana University Press, c1983. xi, 300: maps; 24 cm. Includes index. 1. Jews — Europe, Eastern — History — 20th century. 2. Europe, Eastern — Ethnic relations. I. T.
DS135.E83 M37 1983   947/.0004924 19   *LC* 81-48676   *ISBN* 0253331609

Reitlinger, Gerald, 1900-.   **3.3954**
The final solution: the attempt to exterminate the Jews of Europe, 1939–1945. — 2d rev. and augm. ed. South Brunswick [N.J.]: T. Yoseloff [1968, c1961] xii, 667 p.: maps; 24 cm. 1. Holocaust, Jewish (1939-1945) I. T.
DS135.E83 R4 1968b   940.531/5   *LC* 68-15921

Yad Washem studies on the European Jewish catastrophe and resistance.   **3.3955**
[New York]: Ktav Pub. House., 1957-1974. 10v.; 23 cm. 1. Jews — Historiography — Periodicals. 2. Jews — Europe — History — 20th century — Periodicals. 3. Holocaust, Jewish (1939-1945) — Periodicals. 4. Europe — Ethnic relations — History — 20th century — Periodicals. I. Yad va-shem, rashut ha-zikaron la-Sho'ah vela-gevurah.
DS135.E83 Y32   940.53/1503/924   *LC* 75-648904

DS135.F–G

Chazan, Robert.   **3.3956**
Medieval Jewry in Northern France; a political and social history. Baltimore, Johns Hopkins University Press [1973] xi, 238 p. maps. 23 cm. (The Johns Hopkins University studies in historical and political science, 91st ser., 2) 1. Jews — France — History. I. T.
DS135.F81 C48   914.4/06/924   *LC* 73-8129   *ISBN* 0801815037

Hertzberg, Arthur.   ● **3.3957**
The French Enlightenment and the Jews. — New York: Columbia University Press, 1968. viii, 420 p.; 24 cm. 1. Jews — France — Political and social conditions — History. 2. Enlightenment I. T.
DS135.F82 H4   301.45/296/044   *LC* 68-18996

Schwarzfuchs, Simon.   **3.3958**
Napoleon, the Jews, and the Sanhedrin / Simon Schwarzfuchs. — London; Boston: Routledge & Kegan Paul, 1979. xii, 218 p.; 23 cm. (The Littman library of Jewish civilization) 1. Napoleon I, Emperor of the French, 1769-1821 — Relations with Jews. 2. Assemblée des Israélites de France et du royaume d'Italie (1806-1807: Paris, France) 3. Sanhédrin (1807: Paris, France) 4. Jews — France — Emancipation. 5. France — History — 1789-1815 I. T.
DS135.F82 S38   323.1/19/24044   *LC* 78-40812   *ISBN* 0710089554

Albert, Phyllis Cohen.   **3.3959**
The modernization of French Jewry: consistory and community in the nineteenth century / Phyllis Cohen Albert. — [s.l.]: Brandeis University Press; Hanover, N.H.: distributed by University Press of New England, 1978 (c1977). xxii, 450 p.: maps; 26 cm. Includes index. 1. Jews — France — Politics and government. 2. Judaism — France — History. 3. France — Politics and government — 19th century I. T.
DS135.F83 A43   944/.004/924   *LC* 76-50680   *ISBN* 0874511399

Byrnes, Robert Francis.   ● **3.3960**
Antisemitism in modern France, by Robert F. Byrnes. — New York: H. Fertig, 1969- [c1950-. v.   ; 24 cm. 1. Dreyfus, Alfred, 1859-1935. 2. Antisemitism — France. I. T.
DS135.F83 B93   301.451/924/044   *LC* 68-9613

Hyman, Paula, 1946-.   **3.3961**
From Dreyfus to Vichy: the remaking of French Jewry, 1906–1939 / Paula Hyman. — New York: Columbia University Press, 1979. xii, 338 p., [4] leaves of plates: ill.; 24 cm. Includes index. 1. Jews — France — History — 20th century. 2. France — History — 20th century I. T.
DS135.F83 H95   944/.004/924   *LC* 79-14401   *ISBN* 0231047223

Marrus, Michael Robert.   **3.3962**
[Vichy et les juifs. English] Vichy France and the Jews / Michael R. Marrus and Robert O. Paxton. — New York: Basic Books, c1981. xvi, 432 p.; 24 cm. Translation of: Vichy et les juifs. 1. Jews — France — Persecutions. 2. Holocaust, Jewish (1939-1945) — France. 3. World War, 1939-1945 — Deportations from France 4. France — Politics and government — 1940-1945 5. France — Ethnic relations. I. Paxton, Robert O. II. T.
DS135.F83 M3813   940.53/15039240944 19   *LC* 80-70307   *ISBN* 0465090052

Malino, Frances.   **3.3963**
The Sephardic Jews of Bordeaux: assimilation and emancipation in Revolutionary and Napoleonic France / Frances Malino. — University: University of Alabama Press, c1978. viii, 166 p.; 24 cm. (Judaic studies; 7) Includes index. 1. Assemblée des Israélites de France et du royaume d'Italie (1806-1807: Paris, France) 2. Sanhédrin (1807: Paris, France) 3. Jews — France — Bordeaux — History. 4. Sephardim — France — Bordeaux — History. 5. Bordeaux (France) — History I. T.
DS135.F85 B65   323.1/19/2404471   *LC* 77-22659   *ISBN* 0817369031

Kisch, Guido, 1889-.   ● **3.3964**
The Jews in medieval Germany; a study of their legal and social status. 2d ed. New York, Ktav Pub. House, 1970. xxviii, 655 p. 24 cm. 1. Jews — Legal

status, laws, etc. — Germany 2. Jews — Germany — History — 1096-1800
I. T.
DS135.G31 K58x   LC 74-86311   ISBN 087068017X

Schorsch, Ismar.   • 3.3965
Jewish reactions to German anti–Semitism, 1870–1914. New York: Columbia
University Press, 1972. vii, 291 p.; 23 cm. (Columbia University studies in
Jewish history, culture, and institutions, no. 3) Revision of the author's thesis,
Columbia. 1. Jews — Germany — History — 1800-1933 2. Antisemitism —
Germany. I. T.
DS102.C56 no. 3 DS135.G33   915.694/008 s 323.1/1924/043   LC
74-190193   ISBN 0231036434

Bach, Hans I. (Hans Israel), 1902-.   3.3966
The German Jew: a synthesis of Judaism and Western civilization, 1730–1930 /
by H.I. Bach. — Oxford [Oxfordshire]; New York: Published for the Littman
Library by Oxford University Press, 1984. 255 p.; 24 cm. (Littman library of
Jewish civilization.) Includes index. 1. Jews — Germany — Intellectual life.
2. Judaism — Germany 3. Germany — Civilization — Jewish influences
4. Germany — Ethnic relations. I. T. II. Series.
DS135.G33 B29 1984   943/.004924 19   LC 84-1004   ISBN
0197100333

Engelmann, Bernt, 1921-.   3.3967
[Deutschland ohne Juden. English] Germany without Jews / Bernt Engelmann;
translated by D.J. Beer. — Toronto; New York: Bantam Books, c1984. 380 p.;
18 cm. Translation of: Deutschland ohne Juden. 1. Jews — Germany —
Intellectual life. 2. Jews in public life — Germany. 3. Holocaust, Jewish
(1939-1945) — Germany. 4. Germany — Civilization — Jewish influences
I. T.
DS135.G33 E5413 1984   943/.004924 19   LC 85-107925   ISBN
0553244450

Grunfeld, Frederic V.   3.3968
Prophets without honour: a background to Freud, Kafka, Einstein, and their
world / Frederic V.Grunfeld. — 1st ed. — New York: Holt, Rinehart and
Winston, c1979. xiii, 349 p., [6] leaves of plates: ill.; 24 cm. Includes index.
1. Jews — Germany — Intellectual life. 2. Jews — Austria — Intellectual life.
3. Jews — Biography 4. Germany — Civilization — Jewish influences
5. Austria — Civilization — Jewish influences. I. T.
DS135.G33 G8   943/.004/924 B   LC 78-31645   ISBN 0030178711

Low, Alfred D.   3.3969
Jews in the eyes of the Germans: from the Enlightenment to Imperial Germany
/ Alfred D. Low. — Philadelphia: Institute for the Study of Human Issues,
c1979. x, 509 p., [8] leaves of plates: ill.; 24 cm. Includes index. 1. Jews —
Germany — Public opinion. 2. Public opinion — Germany. 3. Jews in
literature 4. Antisemitism — Germany. 5. Germany — Intellectual life I. T.
DS135.G33 L67   301.45/19/24043   LC 79-334   ISBN 091598086X

Scholem, Gershom Gerhard, 1897-.   3.3970
On Jews and Judaism in crisis: selected essays / Gershom Scholem; edited by
Werner J. Dannhauser. — New York: Schocken Books, [1977] xiii, 306 p.; 24
cm. 1. Scholem, Gershom Gerhard, 1897- 2. Buber, Martin, 1878-1965.
3. Benjamin, Walter, 1892-1940. 4. Jews — Germany — History — 1800-1933
— Addresses, essays, lectures. 5. Germany — History — 20th century —
Addresses, essays, lectures. I. T.
DS135.G33 S297   943/.004/924   LC 75-37010   ISBN 0805236139

Angel, Marc.   3.3971
The Jews of Rhodes: the history of a Sephardic community / by Marc D. Angel;
foreword by Solomon Gaon. — New York: Sepher-Hermon Press, 1978. 199 p.:
ill.; 24 cm. Includes index. 1. Jews in Rhodes — History. 2. Sephardim —
Greece — Rhodes — History. 3. Rhodes — History. I. T.
DS135.G72 R482   949.9/6   LC 77-93661   ISBN 0872030725

DS135.H–P

Braham, Randolph L.   3.3972
The politics of genocide: the Holocaust in Hungary / Randolph L. Braham. —
New York: Columbia University Press, 1981. 2 v. (xlii, 1269 p.): ill.; 24 cm.
1. Jews — Hungary — Persecutions. 2. Holocaust, Jewish (1939-1945) —
Hungary. 3. Hungary — Ethnic relations. I. T.
DS135.H9 B74   323.1/1924/0439   LC 80-11096   ISBN
0231044968

Loeb, Laurence D., 1942-.   3.3973
Outcaste: Jewish life in Southern Iran / Laurence D. Loeb. — New York:
Gordon and Breach, c1977. xxv, 328 p., [1] fold. leaf of plates: ill.; 24 cm.
(Library of anthropology) Includes indexes. 1. Jews — Iran — Shīrāz — Social
life and customs. 2. Shīrāz (Iran) — Social life and customs. I. T.
DS135.I65 L6   301.45/19/240557   LC 76-53663   ISBN
0677045301

Hyman, Louis, 1912-.   3.3974
The Jews of Ireland; from earliest times to the year 1910. Jerusalem, Published
jointly by the Jewish Historical Society of England, London and Israel
Universities Press, 1972. xix, 403 p. illus. 22 cm. 1. Jews — Ireland — History.
I. T.
DS135.I72 H88   914.15/06/924   LC 72-950265

Michaelis, Meir.   3.3975
Mussolini and the Jews: German–Italian relations and the Jewish question in
Italy, 1922–1945 / Meir Michaelis. — Oxford: Published for the Institute of
Jewish Affairs, London, by the Clarendon Press; New York: Oxford University
Press, 1979 (c1978). xii, 472 p.; 22 cm. Includes index. 1. Mussolini, Benito,
1883-1945 — Relations with Jews. 2. Jews — Italy — History — 20th century.
3. Antisemitism — Italy. 4. Italy — Foreign relations — Germany.
5. Germany — Foreign relations — Italy. I. T.
DS135.I8 M4   323.1/19/24045   LC 78-40260   ISBN 0198225423

Roth, Cecil, 1899-1970.   • 3.3976
The history of the Jews of Italy, by Cecil Roth. Philadelphia, The Jewish
publication society of America, 5706-1946. 575 p. ill. Map on lining-papers.
1. Jews — Italy — History. I. T.
DS135.I8 R6   296   LC 46-6577

Léon. Harry Joshua.   • 3.3977
Jews of ancient Rome. Philadelphia: Jewish Publication Society of America,
1960. 378 p.: ill. (Morris Loeb series.) 1. Jews — Rome — History.
2. Inscriptions, Jewish 3. Inscriptions, Greek 4. Inscriptions, Latin I. T.
DS135I85 R64   937   LC 60-9793

Pullan, Brian S.   3.3978
The Jews of Europe and the Inquisition of Venice, 1550–1670 / Brian Pullan. —
Totowa, N.J.: Barnes & Noble, 1983. xv, 348 p.; 24 cm. Includes index. 1. Jews
— Italy — Venice — History. 2. Marranos — Italy — Venice — History.
3. Inquisition — Italy — Venice — History. 4. Venice (Italy) — Ethnic
relations. I. T.
DS135.I85 V4256 1983   945/.31 19   LC 83-7147   ISBN
0389204145

Yerushalmi, Yosef Hayim, 1932-.   • 3.3979
From Spanish court to Italian ghetto; Isaac Cardoso: a study in seventeenth–
century marranism and Jewish apologetics. — New York: Columbia University
Press, 1971. xx, 524 p.: facsims.; 24 cm. — (Columbia University studies in
Jewish history, culture, and institutions, no. 1) Based on the author's thesis,
Columbia University, 1966. 1. Cardoso, Isaac, 1603 or 4-1683. 2. Jews — Italy
— Biography. 3. Marranos — Biography. 4. Judaism — Apologetic works —
History and criticism. 5. Physicians — Jewish — Italy — Biography. I. T.
DS102.C56 no. 1 DS135.I9C28x   914.6/06/9240924 B   LC 76-109544
     ISBN 0231032862

De Felice, Renzo, 1929-.   3.3980
[Ebrei in un paese arabo. English] Jews in an Arab land: Libya, 1835–1970 / by
Renzo De Felice; translated by Judith Roumani. — 1st ed. — Austin:
University of Texas Press, 1985. x, 406 p., [16] p. of plates: ill.; 24 cm.
Translation of: Ebrei in un paese arabo. Includes index. 1. Jews — Libya —
History. 2. Libya — Ethnic relations. I. T.
DS135.L44 D413 1985   961/.2004924 19   LC 84-11851   ISBN
0292740166

Gans, M. H. (Mozes Heiman)   3.3981
[Memorboek. English] Memorbook: history of Dutch Jewry from the
Renaissance to 1940 / text by Mozes Heiman Gans; [English translation
Arnold J. Pomerans]. — Baarn: Bosch & Keuning, 1978 (c1977) 851 p.: ill.,
facsims.; 32 cm. Translation of Memorboek. Includes indexes. 1. Jews —
Netherlands — History. 2. Netherlands — History I. T.
DS135.N4 G313   949.2/004/924   LC 77-373259   ISBN
9024642507

Hillesum, Etty, 1914-1943.   3.3982
[Verstoorde leven. English] An interrupted life: the diaries of Etty Hillesum,
1941–1943 / introduced by J.G. Gaarlandt; translated from the Dutch by Arno
Pomerans. — 1st American ed. — New York: Pantheon Books, c1984. xiv,
226 p.; 22 cm. Translation of: Het verstoorde leven. 1. Hillesum, Etty,
1914-1943. 2. Jews — Netherlands — Biography. 3. Holocaust, Jewish
(1939-1945) — Netherlands — Personal narratives. I. T.
DS135.N6 H54813   940.53/15/03924 B 19   LC 83-47750   ISBN
0394532171

Dobroszycki, Lucjan.   3.3983
Image before my eyes: a photographic history of Jewish life in Poland,
1864–1939 / Lucjan Dobroszycki and Barbara Kirshenblatt–Gimblett. — New
York: Schocken Books, 1977. xviii, 269 p.: ill.; 32 cm. 'Published in cooperation
with YIVO Institute for Jewish Research.' An exhibition of the photographs
was held at the Jewish Museum in 1976. Includes indexes. 1. Jews — Poland —
History. 2. Jews — Poland — Pictorial works. 3. Poland — History 4. Poland
— Description and travel — Views. I. Kirshenblatt-Gimblett, Barbara, joint

author. II. Yivo Institute for Jewish Research. III. Jewish Museum (New York, N.Y.) IV. T.
DS135.P6 D62   943.8/004/924   *LC* 75-35448   *ISBN* 0805236074

Heller, Celia Stopnicka.   **3.3984**
On the edge of destruction: Jews of Poland between the two World Wars / Celia S. Heller. — New York: Columbia University Press, 1977. xi, 369 p.: ill.; 24 cm. 1. Jews — Poland — History. 2. Antisemitism — Poland. 3. Poland — History — 1918-1945 4. Poland — Social conditions — 1945- I. T.
DS135.P6 H396   301.45/19/240438   *LC* 76-22646   *ISBN* 0231038194

Abramsky, Chimen, 1916-.   **3.3985**
The Jews in Poland / edited by Chimen Abramsky, Maciej Jachimczyk, and Antony Polansky. — Oxford [Oxfordshire]; New York, NY, USA: B. Blackwell, 1986. p. cm. Papers presented at the International Conference on Polish-Jewish Studies, held in Oxford, in Sept. 1984. Includes index. 1. Jews — Poland — History — Congresses. 2. Holocaust, Jewish (1939-1945) — Poland — Congresses. 3. Poland — Ethnic relations — Congresses. I. Jachimczyk, Maciej. II. Polonsky, Antony. III. International Conference on Polish-Jewish Studies (1984: Oxford, Oxfordshire) IV. T.
DS135.P6 J46 1986   943.8/004924 19   *LC* 86-3336   *ISBN* 0631148574

Litman, Jacob, 1920-.   **3.3986**
The economic role of Jews in Medieval Poland: the contribution of Yitzhak Schipper / Jacob Litman. — Lanham: University Press of America, c1984. xiii, 306 p.: map; 24 cm. Includes index. 1. Schiper, Ignacy, 1884-1943. 2. Jews — Poland — Economic conditions. 3. Poland — Economic conditions I. T.
DS135.P6 L57 1984   330.9438/0089924 19   *LC* 84-15305   *ISBN* 0819142441

Ringelblum, Emanuel, 1900-1944.   **3.3987**
Polish–Jewish relations during the Second World War / Emmanuel Ringelblum; edited and with footnotes by Joseph Kermish, Shmuel Krakowski; trans. from the Polish by Dafna Allon, Danuta Dabrowska, and Dana Keren. — 1st American ed. — New York: Fertig, 1976, c1974. xxxix, 330 p.: ill; 22 cm. 1. Ringelblum, Emanuel, 1900-1944. 2. Jews — Poland — Politics and government. 3. Holocaust, Jewish (1939-1945) — Poland 4. Poland — Politics and government — 1918-1945 I. T.
DS135.P6 R495 1976   943.8/004/924   *LC* 76-1394

Weinryb, Bernard Dov, 1900-.   **3.3988**
The Jews of Poland: a social and economic history of the Jewish community in Poland from 1100 to 1800 / by Bernard D. Weinryb. — [1st ed.] Philadelphia: Jewish Publication Society of America, 1973. xvi, 424 p.; 25 cm. 1. Jews — Poland — History. I. T.
DS135.P6 W38   914.38/06/924   *LC* 72-12178   *ISBN* 082760016X

The Chronicle of the Łódź ghetto, 1941–1944 / edited by   **3.3989**
Lucjan Dobroszycki; translated by Richard Lourie, Joachim
Neugroschel, and others.
English ed. — New Haven: Yale University Press, c1984. lxviii, 551 p., [58] p. of plates: ill.; 26 cm. Includes index. 1. Jews — Poland — Łódź — Persecutions. 2. Holocaust, Jewish (1939-1945) — Poland — Łódź — Personal narratives. 3. Łódź (Poland) — Ethnic relations. I. Dobroszycki, Lucjan.
DS135.P62 L627 1984   943.8/4 19   *LC* 84-3614   *ISBN* 0300032080

Czerniaków, Adam, 1880-1942.   **3.3990**
[Dziennik getta warszawskiego English] The Warsaw diary of Adam Czerniakow: prelude to doom / edited by Raul Hilberg, Stanislaw Staron, and Josef Kermisz; translated by Staron and the staff of Yad Vashem. — New York: Stein and Day, 1979. viii, 420 p., [97] leaves of plates: ill.; 24 cm. Translation of Dziennik getta warszawskiego. Includes index. 1. Czerniaków, Adam, 1880-1942. 2. Jews — Poland — Warsaw — Persecutions. 3. Holocaust, Jewish (1939-1945) — Poland — Warsaw. 4. Jews — Poland — Warsaw — Biography. 5. Warsaw (Poland) — History I. Hilberg, Raul, 1926- II. Staron, Stanislaw. III. Kermish, Joseph. IV. T.
DS135.P62 W2613   943.8/4   *LC* 78-9272   *ISBN* 0812825233

Gutman, Israel.   **3.3991**
[Yehude Varshah, 1939-1943. English] The Jews of Warsaw, 1939–1943: ghetto, underground, revolt / by Yisrael Gutman; translated from the Hebrew by Ina Friedman. — Bloomington: Indiana University Press, c1982. xviii, 487 p., [2] p. of plates: ill.; 25 cm. Translation of: Yehude Varshah, 1939-1943. Includes index. 1. Jews — Poland — Warsaw — Persecutions. 2. Holocaust, Jewish (1939-1945) — Poland — Warsaw. 3. Warsaw (Poland) — History — Uprising of 1943 4. Warsaw (Poland) — Ethnic relations. I. T.
DS135.P62 W27313 1982   940.53/15/03924 19   *LC* 81-47570
     ISBN 0253331749

DS135.R–Z

Baron, Salo Wittmayer, 1895-.   **3.3992**
The Russian Jew under tsars and Soviets / Salo W. Baron. — 2d ed., rev. and enl. — New York: Macmillan, c1976. xvii, 468 p.; 24 cm. 1. Jews — Soviet Union — History 2. Soviet Union — History I. T.
DS135.R9 B28 1976   323.1/19/24047   *LC* 75-19161   *ISBN* 0025073001

Dubnow, Simon, 1860-1941.   • **3.3993**
History of the Jews in Russia and Poland, from the earliest times until the present day, by S. M. Dubnow; tr. from the Russian by I. Friedlaender ... — Philadelphia, The Jewish publication society of America, 1916-20. 3 v. 20 cm. Bibliography: v. 3, p. 171-203. 1. Jews in Russia. 2. Jews in Poland. I. Friedlaender, Israel, 1876-1920. tr. II. T.
DS135.R9D8   *LC* 16-16352

The Jews in Soviet Russia since 1917 / edited by Lionel   • **3.3994**
Kochan.
London; New York: Published for the Institute of Jewish Affairs / [by] Oxford University Press, 1970. ix, 357 p.; 23 cm. 1. Jews — Russia — History — 1917- — Collections. I. Kochan, Lionel. ed. II. Institute of Jewish Affairs.
DS135.R9 J47 1970   914.7/09/74924   *LC* 71-490841   *ISBN* 0192151738

Stanislawski, Michael, 1952-.   **3.3995**
Tsar Nicholas I and the Jews: the transformation of Jewish society in Russia, 1825–1855 / Michael Stanislawski. — 1st ed. — Philadelphia: Jewish Publication Society of America, 1983. xvi, 246 p., [4] leaves of plates: ill.; 24 cm. Includes index. 1. Nicholas I, Emperor of Russia, 1796-1855 — Relations with Jews. 2. Jews — Soviet Union — History — 19th century. 3. Soviet Union — Ethnic relations. I. T.
DS135.R9 S77 1983   947/.004924 19   *LC* 82-16199   *ISBN* 0827602162

The Black book: the ruthless murder of Jews by German–   **3.3996**
Fascist invaders throughout the temporarily–occupied regions of
the Soviet Union and in the death camps of Poland during the
war of 1941–1945 / prepared under the editorship of Ilya
Ehrenburg & Vasily Grossman; translated from the Russian by
John Glad and James S. Levine.
New York: Holocaust Publications: Distributed by Schocken Books, c1981. xliv, 595 p.: ill.; 22 cm. 'Holocaust library.' Includes indexes. 1. Jews — Soviet Union — Persecutions — Addresses, essays, lectures. 2. Holocaust, Jewish (1939-1945) — Soviet Union — Addresses, essays, lectures. 3. Soviet Union — Ethnic relations — Addresses, essays, lectures. I. Ėrenburg, Il'ia, 1891-1967. II. Grossman, Vasiliĭ Semenovich.
DS135.R92 B53   DS135R92 B53.   940.53/15/03924047 19   *LC* 81-81517   *ISBN* 0896040321

Gilboa, Jehoshua A.   • **3.3997**
The black years of Soviet Jewry, 1939–1953 [by] Yehoshua A. Gilboa. Translated from the Hebrew by Yosef Shachter and Dov Ben-Abba. [1st ed.] Boston, Little, Brown [1971] x, 418 p. 25 cm. 1. Jews — Soviet Union — History — 1917- I. T.
DS135.R92 G5413   914.7/06/924   *LC* 70-143716

Pinkus, Benjamin, 1933-.   **3.3998**
The Soviet government and the Jews, 1948–1967: a documented study / Benjamin Pinkus; general editor, Jonathan Frankel. — Cambridge [Cambridgeshire]; New York: Cambridge University Press, 1984. xvi, 612 p.; 24 cm. 'Published in association with the Hebrew University of Jerusalem, Institute of Contemporary Jewry and the Israel Academy of Sciences and Humanities.' Includes index. 1. Jews — Soviet Union — History — 1917- 2. Antisemitism — Soviet Union. 3. Soviet Union — Ethnic relations. I. Frankel, Jonathan. II. T.
DS135.R92 P56 1984   323.1/1924/047 19   *LC* 83-18900   *ISBN* 0521247136

Sawyer, Thomas E.   **3.3999**
The Jewish minority in the Soviet Union / Thomas E. Sawyer. — Boulder, Colo.: Westview Press, 1979. xxii, 353 p.; 24 cm. (Westview's special studies on the Soviet Union and Eastern Europe) Includes index. 1. Jews — Soviet Union — Politics and government — 1917- 2. Soviet Union — Politics and government — 1917- I. T.
DS135.R92 S28   323.1/1924/047 19   *LC* 78-20724   *ISBN* 0891584803

Schroeter, Leonard.   **3.4000**
The last exodus. New York: Universe Books [1974] 432 p.; 22 cm. 1. Jews — Soviet Union — Politics and government. 2. Jews — Soviet Union — Persecutions 3. Israel — Emigration and immigration. 4. Soviet Union — Politics and government — 1953- I. T.
DS135.R92 S37   323.1/19/24047   *LC* 73-88461   *ISBN* 0876632045

DS145–151 ANTISEMITISM. ZIONISM

Aronson, Chaim, 1825-1888.   **3.4001**
A Jewish life under the tsars: the autobiography of Chaim Aronson, 1825–1888 / translated from the original Hebrew and edited by Norman Marsden. — Totowa, N.J.: Allanheld, Osmun, 1983. xvi, 352 p.; 24 cm. At head of title: Oxford Centre for Postgraduate Hebrew Studies. 1. Jews — Soviet Union — Biography. 2. Inventors — Soviet Union — Biography. I. Marsden, Norman. II. Oxford Centre for Postgraduate Hebrew Studies. III. T.
DS135.R95 A684 1983   947/.004924/0924 B 19   *LC* 81-10963
  ISBN 0865980667

Ashtor, Eliyahu, 1914-.   **3.4002**
[Korot ha-Yehudim bi-Sefarad ha-Muslemit. English] The Jews of Moslem Spain: v. l / by Eliyahu Ashtor; translated from the Hebrew by Aaron Klein and Jenny Machlowitz Klein. — Philadelphia: Jewish Publication Society of America, 1974 (c1973). 469 p. Translation of: Korot ha-Yehudim bi-Sefarad ha-Muslemit. 1. Jews — Spain — History. 2. Spain — Ethnic relations. I. T.
DS135.S7 A8313   946/.004924 19   *LC* 73-14081

Baer, Yitzhak, 1888-.   • **3.4003**
A history of the Jews in Christian Spain. Translated from the Hebrew by Louis Schoffman. [1st ed.] Philadelphia, Jewish Publication Society of America, 1961-66. 2 v. map (on lining papers of v. 2) 22 cm. 'May be regarded as a translation of the second [Hebrew] edition. Here and there ... the text has been slightly abridged ... Elsewhere, ... principally in the notes, the translation contains material not found in either of the Hebrew editions.' 1. Jews — Spain — History. I. T.
DS135.S7 B343   946.009174924   *LC* 61-16852

Neuman, Abraham A. (Abraham Aaron), 1890-.   • **3.4004**
The Jews in Spain, their social, political and cultural life during the Middle Ages, by Abraham A. Neuman ... Philadelphia, The Jewish publication society of America, 1942-5702. 2 v. fronts., plates, maps, facsims. 23 cm. (The Morris Loeb series) Bibliography: v. 2, [351]-370. 1. Jews — Spain I. Jewish Publication Society of America. II. T.
DS135.S7N4   296.0946   *LC* 42-21783

Raphael, Chaim.   **3.4005**
The road from Babylon: the story of Sephardi and Oriental Jews / Chaim Raphael. — 1st U.S. ed. — New York: Harper & Row, c1985. xiii, 294 p., [32] p. of plates: ill.; 24 cm. 'A Cornelia & Michael Bessie book.' Includes index. 1. Jews — Spain — History. 2. Sephardim — History. 3. Sephardim — Israel — History. 4. Jews, Oriental — Israel — History. 5. Spain — Ethnic relations. I. T.
DS135.S7 R36 1985   909/.04924 19   *LC* 85-42587   *ISBN* 0060390484

Barnett, Richard David, 1909- comp.   **3.4006**
The Sephardi heritage: essays on the history and cultural contribution of the Jews of Spain and Portugal / edited by R. D. Barnett. — New York: Ktav Pub. House, 1972 (c1971) 640 p.: ill.; 26 cm. English, Spanish, French, or Hebrew. 1. Jews — Spain — Addresses, essays, lectures. 2. Jews — Portugal — Addresses, essays, lectures. 3. Sephardim — Addresses, essays, lectures. 4. Marranos — Addresses, essays, lectures. I. T.
DS135.S7 S45   914.6/06/924   *LC* 70-165054   *ISBN* 0870681702

Moore, Kenneth, 1930-.   **3.4007**
Those of the street: the Catholic-Jews of Mallorca: a study in urban cultural change / Kenneth Moore. — Notre Dame, Ind.: University of Notre Dame Press, 1977 (c1976). viii, 218 p., [2] leaves of plates: ill.; 24 cm. Includes index. 1. Chuetas 2. Majorca (Spain) — Social conditions. I. T.
DS135.S75 M35   946/.75/004924   *LC* 76-636   *ISBN* 0268018308

Goitein, S. D., 1900-.   **3.4008**
Jews and Arabs: their contacts through the ages / S. D. Goitein. — 3d rev. ed. — New York: Schocken Books, [1974] viii, 263 p.; 21 cm. (Schocken paperbacks on Judaica) Includes index. 1. Jews — Islamic Empire 2. Jewish-Arab relations — History. I. T.
DS135.T8 G57 1974   301.29/17/671   *LC* 74-9141   *ISBN* 0805204644 pbk

Studies in Jewish demography survey for 1972–1980 / edited by   **3.4009**
U.O. Schmelz, P. Glikson, and S.J. Gould.
New York: Published for the Institute of Contemporary Jewry, the Hebrew University, Jerusalem and the Institute of Jewish Affairs, London by Ktav Pub. House, 1983. xi, 303 p.; 25 cm. 1. Jews — Statistics — Addresses, essays, lectures. 2. Jews — Statistics — Bibliography. I. Schmelz, U. O. (Usiel Oskar) II. Glikson, Paul. III. Gould, S. J. (Samuel Julius) IV. Universitah ha-'Ivrit bi-Yerushalayim. Makhon le-Yahadut zemanenu. V. Institute of Jewish Affairs.
DS143.S77 1983   304.6/089924 19   *LC* 83-4339   *ISBN* 0881250139

Katz, Jacob, 1904-.   **3.4010**
From prejudice to destruction: anti-Semitism, 1700–1933 / Jacob Katz. — Cambridge, MA: Harvard University Press, 1980. viii, 392 p.; 24 cm. 1. Antisemitism — History. I. T.
DS145.K354   305.8/924   *LC* 80-14404   *ISBN* 0674325052

Poliakov, Léon, 1910-.   • **3.4011**
[Histoire de l'antisémitisme. English] The history of anti-Semitism. Translated from the French by Richard Howard. New York, Vanguard Press [1965]- <c1985 >. v. <1-2, 4 > 24 cm. Translation of Histoire de l'antisémitisme. Vol. 2 translated by N. Gerardi. Vol. 4 translated by George Klim. 1. Antisemitism — History. I. T.
DS145.P4613   305.8/924 19   *LC* 65-10228   *ISBN* 0814901867

Prager, Dennis, 1948-.   **3.4012**
Why the Jews?: the reason for antisemitism / Dennis Prager and Joseph Telushkin. — New York: Simon and Schuster, c1983. 238 p.; 23 cm. Includes index. 1. Antisemitism — History. I. Telushkin, Joseph, 1948- II. T.
DS145.P484 1983   305.8/924 19   *LC* 83-4723   *ISBN* 0671452703

Wilson, Stephen, 1941-.   **3.4013**
Ideology and experience: antisemitism in France at the time of the Dreyfus affair / Stephen Wilson. — Rutherford, [N.J.]: Fairleigh Dickinson University Press; London: Associated University Presses, c1982. xviii, 812 p.: maps; 25 cm. — (The Littman library of Jewish civilization) Includes index. 1. Dreyfus, Alfred, 1859-1935. 2. Antisemitism — France. 3. Jews — France — Politics and government. 4. France — Ethnic relations. I. T.
DS146.F8 W54 1982   305.8/924/044 19   *LC* 81-65467   *ISBN* 0838630375

Mosse, George L.   • **3.4014**
Germans and Jews: the Right, the Left, and the search for a 'Third Force' in pre-Nazi Germany / George L. Mosse. — [1st ed.]. — New York: Grosset and Dunlap, 1970. 260 p.; 21 cm. 1. Antisemitism — Germany. 2. Jews in Germany — Intellectual life. 3. Germany — Politics and government — 20th century I. T.
DS146.G4 M66   305.8924043   *LC* 68-9631

Pulzer, Peter G. J.   • **3.4015**
The rise of political anti-Semitism in Germany and Austria [by] P. G. J. Pulzer. — New York: Wiley, [1964] xiv, 364 p.: illus., ports.; 21 cm. — (New dimensions in history: essays in comparative history) Based on the author's thesis, Cambridge, 1960. 1. Antisemitism — Germany. 2. Antisemitism — Austria. I. T. II. Series.
DS146.G4 P8   323.143   *LC* 64-23858

Dobkowski, Michael N.   **3.4016**
The tarnished dream: the basis of American anti-Semitism / Michael N. Dobkowski. — Westport, Conn.: Greenwood Press, 1979. x, 291 p.: ill.; 22 cm. (Contributions in American history; no. 81 0084-9219) Includes index. 1. Antisemitism — United States. 2. Jews — United States — Public opinion. 3. Public opinion — United States. 4. United States — Politics and government I. T.
DS146.U6 D6   301.45/19/24073   *LC* 78-67655   *ISBN* 0313206414

Avineri, Shlomo.   **3.4017**
The making of modern Zionism: intellectual origins of the Jewish state / Shlomo Avineri. — New York: Basic Books, c1981. x, 244 p.; 24 cm. 1. Zionism — History — Addresses, essays, lectures. 2. Zionists — Addresses, essays, lectures. I. T.
DS149.A874   956.94/001 19   *LC* 81-66102   *ISBN* 0465043283

Ganin, Zvi.   **3.4018**
Truman, American Jewry, and Israel, 1945–1948 / by Zvi Ganin. — New York: Holmes & Meier Publishers, 1979. xvi, 238 p., [6] leaves of plates: ill.; 24 cm. Includes index. 1. Truman, Harry S., 1884-1972 — Relations with Zionists. 2. Silver, Abba Hillel, 1893-1963. 3. Zionism — United States — History. 4. Palestine — History — Partition, 1947 5. United States — Foreign relations — Palestine. 6. Palestine — Foreign relations — United States. I. T.
DS149.G25 1979   DS149 G25 1979.   956.94/001   *LC* 78-10221   *ISBN* 0841904014

Gonen, Jay Y., 1934-.   **3.4019**
A psychohistory of Zionism / Jay Y. Gonen. — New York: Mason/Charter, 1975. x, 374 p.; 24 cm. Includes index. 1. Zionism — History. 2. Jews — Psychology 3. National characteristics, Israeli I. T.
DS149.G5493   956.94/001   *LC* 74-32355   *ISBN* 088405098X

Halperin, Samuel, 1930-.   **3.4020**
The political world of American Zionism. Detroit, Wayne State University Press, 1961. ix, 431 p. tables. 24 cm. 1. Zionism — History. I. T.
DS149.H337   *LC* 61-10126

Laqueur, Walter, 1921-. 3.4021
A history of Zionism [by] Walter Laqueur. New York, Holt, Rinehart and Winston [1972] xvi, 639 p. illus. 25 cm. 1. Zionism — History. I. T.
DS149.L256 1972   956.94/001   LC 72-78096   ISBN 0030916143

Urofsky, Melvin I. 3.4022
American Zionism from Herzl to the holocaust / Melvin I. Urofsky. — 1st ed. — Garden City, N.Y.: Anchor Press, 1975. ix, 538 p.; 22 cm. Includes index. 1. Zionism — United States. I. T.
DS149.U76   956.94/001   LC 74-19757   ISBN 0385036396

Urofsky, Melvin I. 3.4023
We are one!: American Jewry and Israel / Melvin I. Urofsky. — 1st ed. — Garden City, N.Y.: Anchor Press, 1978. xv, 536 p., [8] leaves of plates: ill.; 22 cm. 1. Zionism — United States. 2. Jews — United States — Politics and government. 3. Israel and the Diaspora 4. United States — Politics and government — 1945- I. T.
DS149.U77   956.94/001/06273   LC 77-12878   ISBN 0385075804

Vital, David. 3.4024
Zionism, the formative years / David Vital. — Oxford: Clarendon Press; New York: Oxford University Press, 1982. xviii, 514 p.; 23 cm. Includes index. 1. Zionism — History. I. T.
DS149.V52 1982   956.94/001 19   LC 82-147153   ISBN 0198274432

Elath, Eliahu, 1903-. 3.4025
[Yoman San-Frantsisko. English] Zionism at the UN: a diary of the first days / Eliahu Elath; translated from Hebrew by Michael Ben-Yitzhak; foreword by Howard M. Sachar. — Philadelphia: Jewish Publication Society of America, 1976. xix, 331 p., [8] leaves of plates: ill.; 22 cm. Translation of Yoman San-Frantsisko. 1. Elath, Eliahu, 1903- 2. United Nations Conference on International Organization (1945: San Francisco, Calif.) 3. Zionists — Biography 4. Palestine — History — 1929-1948 — Sources. I. T.
DS151.E366 A3913   956.94/001/0924   LC 77-371315   ISBN 0827600836

Elon, Amos. 3.4026
Herzl. [1st ed.] New York, Holt, Rinehart and Winston [1975] viii, 448 p. illus. 24 cm. 1. Herzl, Theodor, 1860-1904. 2. Zionists — Austria — Biography. I. T.
DS151.H4 E57   956.94/001/0924 B   LC 74-5128   ISBN 003013126X

Shapira, Anita. 3.4027
[Berl. English. Selections] Berl: the biography of a socialist Zionist, Berl Katznelson, 1887–1944 / Anita Shapira; [translated by Haya Galai]. — Cambridge [Cambridgeshire]; New York: Cambridge University Press, c1984. ix, 400 p., [12] p. of plates: ill., map, ports.; 24 cm. Translation of selections from: Berl. Includes index. 1. Katznelson, Berl, 1887-1944. 2. Labor Zionists — Palestine — Biography. I. T.
DS151.K327 S52513 1984   956.94/001/0924 B 19   LC 84-7008   ISBN 0521256186

Samuel, Maurice, 1895-1972. 3.4028
The worlds of Maurice Samuel: selected writings / edited, and with an introd. by Milton Hindus; foreword by Cynthia Ozick. — 1st ed. — Philadelphia: Jewish Publication Society of America, 1977. xxxii, 445 p.; 25 cm. 1. Samuel, Maurice, 1895-1972 — Addresses, essays, lectures. 2. Zionists — United States — Biography — Addresses, essays, lectures. 3. Jews — United States — Biography — Addresses, essays, lectures. 4. Judaism — Addresses, essays, lectures. 5. Yiddish literature — History and criticism — Addresses, essays, lectures. 6. Jews in literature — Addresses, essays, lectures. I. T.
DS151.S32 A25 1977   081   LC 76-52669   ISBN 0827600917

DS153–154 Jordan

American University (Washington, D.C.). Foreign Area Studies. 3.4029
Jordan, a country study / Foreign Area Studies, the American University; edited by Richard F. Nyrop. — 3d ed. — Washington, D.C.: The University, Foreign Area Studies; for sale by the Supt. of Docs., U.S. Govt. Print. Off., c1980. xxiv, 310 p., [1] fold. leaf of plates: ill.; 24 cm. — (Area handbook series.) Second ed., by R. F. Nyrop and others, issued under title: Area handbook for the Hashemite Kingdom of Jordan. 'DA Pam 550-34.' Includes index. 1. Jordan. I. Nyrop, Richard F. Area handbook for the Hashemite Kingdom of Jordan. II. T. III. Series.
DS153.A67 1980   956.95/04   LC 80-607127

Gubser, Peter. 3.4030
Jordan: crossroads of Middle Eastern events / Peter Gubser. — Boulder, Colo.: Westview Press; London, England: Croom Helm, 1983. xi, 139 p.: ill.; 24 cm. —

(Profiles. Nations of the contemporary Middle East) Includes index. 1. Jordan. I. T. II. Series.
DS153.G8 1983   956.95/04 19   LC 82-8361   ISBN 0891589864

Mishal, Shaul, 1945-. 3.4031
West Bank/East Bank: the Palestinians in Jordan, 1949–1967 / Shaul Mishal. — New Haven: Yale University Press, 1978. xiii, 129 p.: ill.; 21 cm.. 1. Palestinian Arabs — Jordan — Politics and government. 2. Jordan — Politics and government. I. T.
DS153.55.P34 M57   323.1/19/27569405695   LC 77-20692   ISBN 0300021917

Plascov, Avi. 3.4032
The Palestinian refugees in Jordan 1948–1957 / Avi Plascov. — London; Totowa, N.J.: F. Cass, c1981. xviii, 268 p., 8 p. of plates: ill., maps; 24 cm. Eight folded maps in pocket. Includes index. 1. Palestinian Arabs — Jordan. 2. Refugees, Arab — Jordan. 3. Jordan — Politics and government. I. T.
DS153.55.P34 P4 1981   323.1/19275694/05695 19   LC 81-157213   ISBN 0714631205

Bowersock, G. W. (Glen Warren), 1936-. 3.4033
Roman Arabia / G.W. Bowersock. — Cambridge, Mass.: Harvard University Press, 1983. xiv, 224 p., [17] p. of plates: ill., map; 22 cm. Includes index. 1. Nabateans — History. 2. Arabia, Roman — History. 3. Rome — History — Empire, 30 B.C.-476 A.D. I. T.
DS154.22.B68 1983   939 19   LC 82-23274   ISBN 0674777557

Vatikiotis, P. J. (Panayiotis J.), 1928-. 3.4034
Politics and the military in Jordan; a study of the Arab Legion, 1921–1957 [by] P. J. Vatikiotis. New York, Praeger [1967] xvi, 169 p. map. 23 cm. 1. Jordan. al-Jaysh al-'Arabi. I. T.
DS154.5.V3 1967b   956.95/04   LC 67-28182

Abdullah I, King of Jordan, 1882-1951. ● 3.4035
Memoirs of King Abdullah of Transjordan; edited by Philip P. Graves, with an introduction by R.J.C. Broadhurst. [translated by G. Khuri]. [New York]: Philosophical library, [1950] 278 p. ports. 1. Abdullah I, King of Jordan, 1882-1951. I. Graves, Philip Perceval, 1876-, ed. II. T.
DS154.52.A3 A27 1950

Jureidini, Paul A. 3.4036
Jordan: the impact of social change on the role of the tribes / Paul A. Jureidini, R.D. McLaurin; foreword by Robert G. Neumann. — New York, N.Y., U.S.A.: Praeger, 1984. xi, 98 p.; 22 cm. (The Washington papers, 0278-937X; 108, v. 12) 'Published with the Center for Strategic and International Studies, Georgetown University, Washington, D.C.' 1. Tribes — Jordan. 2. Bedouins — Jordan — Politics and government. 3. Jordan — Politics and government. I. McLaurin, R. D. (Ronald De), 1944- II. Georgetown University. Center for Strategic and International Studies. III. T.
DS154.55.J87 1984   305.8/0095695 19   LC 84-6931   ISBN 0030718538

Browning, Iain. 3.4037
Petra / by Iain Browning. — New and rev. ed. — London: Chatto & Windus, 1982. 255 p., [6] leaves of plates: ill. (some col.); 26 cm. Includes index. 1. Petra (Ancient city) I. T.
DS154.9.P48 B76 1982   915.695/7 19   LC 82-132760   ISBN 0701126221

DS155–199 Asia Minor. Armenia

Mellaart, James. 3.4038
The archaeology of ancient Turkey / James Mellaart; drawings by Shirley Felts; maps by Edgar Holloway. — Totowa, N.J.: Rowman and Littlefield, 1978. 111 p., [4] leaves of plates: ill. (some col.); 26 cm. Includes index. 1. Asia Minor — Antiquities. 2. Asia Minor — Civilization. 3. Turkey — Antiquities. I. T.
DS155.M44 1978b   939.2   LC 78-105011   ISBN 084766046X

Emlyn-Jones, C. J. 3.4039
The Ionians and Hellenism: a study of the cultural achievement of early Greek inhabitants of Asia Minor / by C.J. Emlyn-Jones. — London; Boston: Routledge & Kegan Paul, 1980. 237 p., [16] p. of plates: ill.; 23 cm. — (States and cities of ancient Greece.) Includes index. 1. Ionians 2. Hellenism 3. Ionia — Civilization. I. T. II. Series.
DS156.I6 E48 1980   939/.23 19   LC 80-41143   ISBN 0710004702

Hansen, Esther Violet, 1898-. 3.4040
The Attalids of Pergamon [by] Esther V. Hansen. 2d ed., rev., and expanded. Ithaca, Cornell University Press [1971] xx, 531 p. illus. 24 cm. (Cornell studies

in classical philology, v. 36) 1. Pergamum — Kings and rulers. 2. Pergamum — Civilization. I. T.
PA25.C7 vol. 36 DS156.P4 H3 1971   480 s 913.392/1   *LC* 71-142284
ISBN 0801406153

Lang, David Marshall.   **3.4041**
Armenia, cradle of civilization / David Marshall Lang. — 3rd ed. corr. — London; Boston: Allen & Unwin, 1980. 320 p., [8] p. of plates: ill. (some col.); 25 cm. Includes index. 1. Armenia — History I. T.
DS175.L35 1980   956.6/2 19   *LC* 81-154775   *ISBN* 0049560093

Burney, Charles Allen.   **3.4042**
The peoples of the hills; ancient Ararat and Caucasus [by] Charles Burney [and] David Marshall Lang. New York, Praeger [1972, c1971] xv, 323 p. illus. 25 cm. (History of civilisation) 1. Armenia — History — To 428 2. Georgian S.S.R. — History — To 1801 I. Lang, David Marshall. joint author. II. T.
DS181.B87 1972   913.39/55   *LC* 76-77301

Walker, Christopher J., 1942-.   **3.4043**
Armenia, the survival of a nation / Christopher J. Walker. — New York: St. Martin's Press, 1980. 446 p.: ill.; 24 cm. Includes index. 1. Armenia — History — 1801-1900 2. Armenia — History — 1901-. I. T.
DS194.W34 1980   956.6/201   *LC* 80-10461   *ISBN* 0312049477

Chaliand, Gérard, 1934-.   **3.4044**
[Génocide des Arméniens. English] The Armenians, from genocide to resistance / Gerard Chaliand, Yves Ternon; translated by Tony Berrett. — London: Zed Press; Totowa, N.J.: U.S. distributor, Biblio Distribution Center, 1983. 125 p.: ill.; 23 cm. Translation of: Le génocide des Arméniens. 1. Armenian massacres, 1915-1923 2. Genocide — Turkey. I. Ternon, Yves. II. T.
DS195.5.C4613 1983   956.6/2 19   *LC* 84-125014

Hovannisian, Richard G.   • **3.4045**
The Republic of Armenia [by] Richard G. Hovannisian. Berkeley: University of California Press, 1971-. v.: ill.; 25 cm. 1. Armenia — History — 1917-1921 I. T.
DS195.5.H56   956.6/2   *LC* 72-129613   *ISBN* 0520018052

DS201–248 Arabian Peninsula. Saudi Arabia

Saudi Arabia, a country study / edited by Richard F. Nyrop.   **3.4046**
4th ed. — Washington, D.C.: Foreign Area Studies, American University: For sale by the Supt. of Docs., U.S. G.P.O., 1984. xxxiii, 410 p.: ill.; 24 cm. (Area handbook series.) (DA pam. 550-51) Updated ed. of: Area handbook for Saudi Arabia / Richard F. Nyrop. 3rd ed. 1977. 'Research completed March 1984.' Includes index. 1. Saudi Arabia. I. Nyrop, Richard F. II. Nyrop, Richard F. Area handbook for Saudi Arabia. III. American University (Washington, D.C.). Foreign Area Studies. IV. Series. V. Series: DA pam. 550-51
DS204.S3115 1984   953/.8 19   *LC* 84-28460

Freeth, Zahra Dickson.   **3.4047**
Explorers of Arabia from the Renaissance to the end of the Victorian Era / Zahra Freeth and H. V. F. Winstone. — New York: Holmes & Meier, c1978. 308 p.: ill.; 24 cm. Includes index. 1. Arabian Peninsula — Discovery and exploration. I. Winstone, H. V. F. (Harry Victor Frederick) joint author. II. T.
DS204.5.F73 1978   953/.04   *LC* 77-15632   *ISBN* 0841903549

Burton, Richard Francis, Sir, 1821-1890.   • **3.4048**
[Personal narrative of a pilgrimage to El-Medinah and Meccah] Narrative of a pilgrimage to El–Medinah and Meccah. Introduction by J. M. Scott. [London] Distributed by Heron Books [1969?] 517 p. illus., plates, port. 21 cm. First published in 1854 under title: Personal narrative of a pilgrimage to El-Medinah and Meccah. 1. Burton, Richard Francis, Sir, 1821-1890. 2. Muslim pilgrims and pilgrimages — Saudi Arabia — Mecca — Personal narratives. 3. Arabian Peninsula — Description and travel. 4. Mecca (Saudi Arabia) — Description. 5. Medina (Saudi Arabia) — Description. I. T.
DS207.B964 1969   915.3/8   *LC* 77-518026

Doughty, Charles Montagu, 1843-1926.   • **3.4049**
Travels in Arabia Deserta / by Charles M. Doughty; with an introd. by T. E. Lawrence. — New York: Dover Publications, 1979. 2 v.: ill., maps (1 fold.); 24 cm. Reprint of the new and definitive ed. published in 1936 by J. Cape, London. 1. Doughty, Charles Montagu, 1843-1926. 2. Arabian Peninsula — Description and travel. 3. Arabian Peninsula — Social life and customs. I. T.
DS207.D73 1979   915.3/044 19   *LC* 79-52396   *ISBN* 0486238253

Cole, Donald Powell.   **3.4050**
Nomads of the nomads: the Āl Murrah Bedouin of the Empty Quarter / Donald Powell Cole. — Chicago: Aldine Pub. Co., 1975. 179 p.: ill.; 22 cm. (Worlds of man) 1. Bedouins — Saudi Arabia I. T.
DS219.B4 C67   301.45/19/35   *LC* 74-18211   *ISBN* 0202011178

Lancaster, William, 1938-.   **3.4051**
The Rwala Bedouin today / William Lancaster. -- Cambridge, [Cambridgeshire]; New York: Cambridge University Press, c1981. x, 179 p.: ill., map; 23 cm. (Changing cultures.) Includes index. 1. Bedouins — Saudi Arabia 2. Saudi Arabia — Social life and customs. I. T. II. Series.
DS219.B4 L36   305.8/927/09538 19   *LC* 80-41547   *ISBN* 0521238773

DS221–248 HISTORY

Hitti, Philip Khuri, 1886-.   • **3.4052**
The Arabs: a short history [by] Philip K. Hitti. 5th ed. London, Melbourne,[etc.] Macmillan, 1968. viii, 212 p. 8 maps. 21 cm. (Papermac 234) 1. Arabs — History 2. Civilization, Islamic I. T.
DS223.H48 1968b   910.09/174/927   *LC* 70-401353

Lewis, Bernard.   **3.4053**
The Arabs in history / Bernard Lewis. — Rev. ed. — New York: Harper & Row, 1967. 200 p.: maps; 21 cm. — (Harper Colophon books; CN 491) Includes index. 1. Arabs 2. Arabian Peninsula — History. I. T.
DS223.L4 1967   909.04927   *ISBN* 0061310298

Helms, Christine Moss.   **3.4054**
The cohesion of Saudi Arabia: evolution of political identity / Christine Moss Helms. — Baltimore: Johns Hopkins University Press, 1981. 313 p.: maps; 23 cm. Includes index. 1. Saudi Arabia — Politics and government. I. T.
DS244.H44 1981b   953/.8   *LC* 80-8026   *ISBN* 0801824753

Troeller, Gary.   **3.4055**
The birth of Saudi Arabia: Britain and the rise of the House of Sa'ud / Gary Troeller. London: F. Cass, 1976. xxii, 287 p.: ill.; 23 cm. Label mounted on verso of t. p.: Exclusive distributor: ISBS, Inc., Forest Grove, Or. Includes index. 1. Saudi Arabia — History 2. Saudi Arabia — Foreign relations — Great Britain. 3. Great Britain — Foreign relations — Saudi Arabia. I. T.
DS244.T73 1976   953/.8/04   *LC* 76-383635   *ISBN* 0714630624

Holden, David.   **3.4056**
The house of Saud: the rise and rule of the most powerful dynasty in the Arab world / by David Holden, Richard Johns. — 1st American ed. — New York: Holt, Rinehart, and Winston, 1982, c1981. xiv, 569 p., [20] p. of plates: ill., maps, ports.,; 25 cm. Includes index. 1. Saudi Arabia — History I. Johns, Richard. II. T.
DS244.52.H64 1982   953/.805 19   *LC* 81-47474   *ISBN* 0030437318

Persian Gulf states: country studies / Foreign Area Studies, the   **3.4057**
American University; edited by Richard F. Nyrop.
2nd ed. — Washington, D.C.: For sale by the Supt. of Docs., U.S. G.P.O., 1985. xxii, 542 p.: ill.; 24 cm. (Area handbook series.) (DA pam. 550-185) Rev. ed. of: Area handbook for the Persian Gulf states. 1st ed. 1977. 'Research completed August 1984.' Includes index. 1. Persian Gulf States I. Nyrop, Richard F. II. American University. Foreign Area Studies. III. Area handbook for the Persian Gulf states. IV. Series. V. Series: DA pam. 550-185
DS247.A13 P47 1985   953/.6 19   *LC* 85-6089

Peterson, John, 1947-.   **3.4058**
Oman in the twentieth century: political foundation of an emerging state / J. E. Peterson. — London: Croom Helm; New York: Barnes & Noble Books, 1978. 286 p.: maps; 23 cm. Includes index. 1. Oman — Politics and government. I. T.
DS247.O68 P47 1978   320.9/53/5   *LC* 78-761   *ISBN* 0064955222

Heard-Bey, Frauke, 1941-.   **3.4059**
From trucial states to United Arab Emirates: a society in transition / Frauke Heard–Bey. — London; New York: Longman, 1982. xxvi, 522 p.: maps; 22 cm. Maps on lining papers. Includes indexes. 1. United Arab Emirates — History. 2. United Arab Emirates — Social conditions. 3. United Arab Emirates — Economic conditions. I. T.
DS247.T88 H4 1982   953/.57 19   *LC* 82-16212   *ISBN* 0582780322

Zahlan, Rosemarie Said.   **3.4060**
The origins of the United Arab Emirates: a political and social history of the Trucial States / Rosemarie Said Zahlan. — New York: St. Martin's Press, c1978. xix, 278 p., [4] leaves of plates: ill.; 23 cm. Includes index. 1. United Arab Emirates — History. I. T.
DS247.T88 Z34 1978   953/.5   *LC* 78-6964   *ISBN* 0312588828

The Yemens: country studies / Foreign Area Studies, the   3.4061
American University; edited by Richard F. Nyrop.
2nd ed. — Washington, D.C.: American University, Foreign Area Studies,
1986. p. cm. (DA pam. 550-183) Rev. ed. of: Area handbook for the Yemens /
coauthors, Richard F. Nyrop ... [et al.]. 1977. 'Research completed June 1985.'
Includes index. 1. Yemen. 2. Yemen (People's Democratic Republic)
I. Nyrop, Richard F. II. American University (Washington, D.C.). Foreign
Area Studies. III. Area handbook for the Yemens. IV. Series.
DS247.Y4 Y46   953/.32 19   LC 86-1164

Bidwell, Robin Leonard.   3.4062
The two Yemens / Robin Bidwell. — Harlow, Essex: Longman; Boulder, Colo.:
Westview Press, 1983. xvii, 350 p.: maps; 22 cm. Includes index. 1. Yemen —
History 2. Yemen (People's Democratic Republic) — History. I. T.
DS247.Y45 B53 1983   953/.3 19   LC 82-15352   ISBN 0582783216

Contemporary Yemen: politics and historical background /   3.4063
edited by B.R. Pridham.
New York: St. Martin's Press, 1984. xi, 276 p.: ill.; 23 cm. Papers from a
symposium held in July 1983 by Exeter University's Centre for Arab Gulf
Studies. 1. Yemen — History — Congresses. 2. Yemen (People's Democratic
Republic) — History — Congresses. I. Pridham, B. R., 1934- II. University of
Exeter. Centre for Arab Gulf Studies.
DS247.Y48 C66 1984   953/.3205 19   LC 84-17693   ISBN
0312168578

Barth, Fredrik, 1928-.   3.4064
Sohar, culture and society in an Omani town / Fredrik Barth. — Baltimore:
Johns Hopkins University Press, c1983. viii, 264 p.: ill.; 24 cm. Includes index.
1. Suḥār (Oman) I. T.
DS248.S93 B37 1983   306/.095353 19   LC 82-9925   ISBN
0801828406

DS251–326 Iran (Persia). Persian Gulf

Encyclopædia Iranica / edited by Ehsan Yarshater.   3.4065
London; Boston: Routledge & Kegan Paul, 1985-. <v. 1; v. 2, fasc. 3; in 2 >:
ill.; 29 cm. 1. Iran — Dictionaries and encyclopedias. I. Yar-Shater, Ehsan.
DS253.E53 1985   955/.003/21 19   LC 86-193296   ISBN
0710090994

American University (Washington, D.C.). Foreign Area Studies.   3.4066
Iran, a country study / Foreign Area Studies, The American University; edited
by Richard F. Nyrop. — 3d ed. — Washington: For sale by the Supt. of Docs.,
U.S. Govt. Print. Off., c1978. xxviii, 492 p. (p. 491-492 publisher's list): ill.; 24
cm. — (Area handbook series.) Supersedes the 1971 ed. prepared by H. H.
Smith and others, and issued under title: Area handbook for Iran. 'Research
completed January 1978.' 'DA pam 550-68.' Includes index. 1. Iran. I. Nyrop,
Richard F. II. Smith, Harvey Henry, 1892- Area handbook for Iran. III. T.
IV. Series.
DS254.5.A63 1978   955   LC 78-11871

Bartol'd, V. V. (Vasiliĭ Vladimirovich), 1869-1930.   3.4067
[Istoriko-geograficheskiĭ obzor Irana. English] An historical geography of Iran
/ W. Barthold; translated by Svat Soucek; edited with an introduction by C.E.
Bosworth. — Princeton, N.J.: Princeton University Press, c1984. xv, 285 p.; 25
cm. — (Modern classics in Near Eastern studies.) Translation of: Istoriko-
geograficheskiĭ obzor Irana. Includes index. 1. Iran — Historical geography.
2. Soviet Central Asia — Historical geography. 3. Afghanistan — Historical
geography. I. Bosworth, Clifford Edmund. II. T. III. Series.
DS254.8.B3713 1984   911/.55 19   LC 83-24548   ISBN 0691054185

British Institute of Persian Studies.   3.4068
Pasargadae: a report on the excavations conducted by the British Institute of
Persian Studies from 1961 to 1963 / David Stronach. — Oxford [Eng.]; New
York: Clarendon Press, 1978. xii, 326 p., [96] leaves of plates: ill.; 32 cm.
1. Pasārgadae, Iran. I. Stronach, David. II. T.
DS262.P35 S77   935   LC 78-316368   ISBN 0198131909

Arberry, A. J. (Arthur John), 1905-1969. ed.   • 3.4069
The legacy of Persia. — Oxford: Clarendon Press, 1953. xvi, 421 p.: ill.; 19 cm.
— ([The Legacy series]) Bibliography: p. [388] 1. Iran — Civilization I. T.
DS266.A7   915.5   LC 53-2314

The Cambridge history of Iran.   • 3.4070
Cambridge: University Press, 1968-. v.: ill., maps, plates.; 24 cm. 1. Iran —
History I. Fisher, W. B. (William Bayne)
DS272.C34   955   LC 67-12845   ISBN 0521060351

Sykes, Percy Molesworth, Sir, 1867-1945.   3.4071
A history of Persia / by Brigadier–General Sir Percy Sykes. — 3d ed. with
supplementary essay. London: Macmillan, 1930. 2 v.: fronts., ill. (incl. facsims.)
plates, ports., fold. maps (1 in pocket); 23 cm. 1. Iran — History I. T.
DS272 S8 1930

Wilber, Donald Newton.   3.4072
Iran, past and present: from monarchy to Islamic republic / by Donald N.
Wilber. — 9th ed. — Princeton, N.J.: Princeton University Press, 1981. ix,
375 p., [12] p. of plates: ill.; 23 cm. Includes index. 1. Iran. I. T.
DS272.W49 1981   955 19   LC 82-192936   ISBN 0691031304

Ismael, Tareq Y.   3.4073
Iraq and Iran: roots of conflict / Tareq Y. Ismael. — 1st ed. — Syracuse, N.Y.:
Syracuse University Press, 1982. xii, 226 p.: ill.; 23 cm. — (Contemporary issues
in the Middle East.) 1. Iran — Foreign relations — Iraq. 2. Iraq — Foreign
relations — Iran. I. T. II. Series.
DS274.2.I57 I85 1982   327.550567 19   LC 82-10562   ISBN
0815622805

Frye, Richard Nelson, 1920-.   • 3.4074
The heritage of Persia. — [1st ed.]. — Cleveland: World Pub. Co., [1963] 301 p.:
illus.; 25 cm. — (The World histories of civilization) 1. Iran — History — To
640 A.D. I. T.
DS275.F7   935   LC 62-15708

Cook, J. M. (John Manuel)   3.4075
The Persian Empire / J.M. Cook. — 1st American ed. — New York: Schocken
Books, 1983. vii, 275 p., [24] p. of plates: ill.; 25 cm. 1. Achaemenid dynasty,
559-330 B.C. 2. Iran — History — To 640 A.D. I. T.
DS281.C66 1983   935/.05 19   LC 82-10382   ISBN 0805238468

Olmstead, Albert Ten Eyck, 1880-1945.   • 3.4076
History of the Persian Empire, Achaemenid period. Chicago, Univ. of Chicago
Press [1948] xix, 576 p. plates, maps. plan. 25 cm. 1. Iran — History —
Ancient to 640. I. T.
DS281.O4   LC 48-7317

Frye, Richard Nelson, 1920-.   3.4077
The golden age of Persia: the Arabs in the East / Richard N. Frye. — New
York: Barnes & Noble Books, 1975. xiii, 289 p., [8] leaves of plates: ill.; 25 cm.
— (History of civilisation) Includes index. 1. Arabs — Iran — History. 2. Iran
— Civilization 3. Iran — History — 640-1500 I. T.
DS288.F79   955/.02   LC 75-316890   ISBN 006492288X

Bosworth, Clifford Edmund.   3.4078
The Ghaznavids; their empire in Afghanistan and eastern Iran, 994–1040. —
2nd ed. — Beirut: Librairie du Liban, 1973. xi, 331 p. fold. maps, geneal. tables.
23 cm. '[Based on the author's] thesis, The transition from Ghaznavid to Seljuq
power in the Islamic East, submitted to Edinburgh University in 1961.'
1. Ghaznevids I. T.
DS288.7.B6 1963

Arjomand, Said Amir.   3.4079
The shadow of God and the Hidden Imam: religion, political order, and societal
change in Shi'ite Iran from the beginning to 1890 / Said Amir Arjomand. —
Chicago: University of Chicago Press, 1984. xii, 356 p.: ill.; 24 cm. (Publications
of the Center for Middle Eastern Studies. no. 17) Includes index. 1. Shī'ah —
Iran — History. 2. Islam and politics — Iran. 3. Iran — Politics and
government I. T. II. Series.
DS292.A75 1984   955 19   LC 83-27196   ISBN 0226027821

Savory, Roger.   3.4080
Iran under the Safavids / Roger Savory. — Cambridge; New York: Cambridge
University Press, 1980. x, 277 p.: ill.; 23 cm. 1. Safavids. 2. Iran — History —
16th-18th centuries I. T.
DS292.S26 1980   955/.03   LC 78-73817   ISBN 0521224837

Perry, John R.   3.4081
Karīm Khān Zand: a history of Iran, 1747–1779 / John R. Perry. — Chicago:
University of Chicago Press, 1979. xi, 340 p.: ill.; 24 cm. (Publications of the
Center for Middle Eastern Studies; no. 12) Includes index. 1. Karīm Khān
Zand, Shah of Iran, d. 1779. 2. Iran — History — 16th-18th centuries I. T.
DS295.P47   955/.03   LC 78-26553   ISBN 0226660982

Algar, Hamid.   3.4082
Religion and state in Iran, 1785–1906; the role of the ulama in the Qajar period.
Berkeley, University of California Press, 1969. xviii, 286 p. 24 cm. Revised
version of the author's thesis, University of Cambridge, 1965. 'Published under
the auspices of the Near Eastern Center, University of California, Los Angeles.'
1. Clergy — Iran — Political activity. 2. Iran — History — Qajar dynasty,
1779-1925 I. Gustave E. von Grunebaum Center for Near Eastern Studies.
II. T.
DS299.A45 1969   297/.197/7   LC 72-79959   ISBN 0520013867

Iran under the Pahlavis / George Lenczowski, editor. 3.4083
Stanford, Calif.: Hoover Institution Press, c1978. xxii, 550 p., [10] leaves of plates: ill. (some col.); 24 cm. (Hoover Institution publication; 164) Includes index. 1. Iran — History — 1909- I. Lenczowski, George.
DS316.3.I7   955/.05   LC 76-26773   ISBN 0817966412

Keddie, Nikki R. 3.4084
Roots of revolution: an interpretive history of modern Iran / Nikki R. Keddie; with a section by Yann Richard. — New Haven: Yale University Press, c1981. xii, 321 p., [8] p. of plates: map, plates; 22 cm. Includes index. 1. Iran — History — 20th century I. Richard, Yann. II. T.
DS316.3.K42   955/.05 19   LC 81-40438   ISBN 0300026064

Abrahamian, Ervand, 1940-. 3.4085
Iran between two revolutions / Ervand Abrahamian. — Princeton, N.J.: Princeton University Press, c1982. xiii, 561 p.: map; 24 cm. — (Princeton studies on the Near East.) Includes index. 1. Iran — Politics and government — 20th century 2. Iran — Social conditions. I. T. II. Series.
DS316.6.A27 1982   955/.05 19   LC 81-47905   ISBN 0691053421

Kapuściński, Ryszard. 3.4086
[Szachinszach. English] Shah of shahs / Ryszard Kapuściński; translated from the Polish by William R. Brand and Katarzyna Mroczkowska-Brand. — San Diego: Harcourt Brace, Jovanovich, c1985. 152 p.; 22 cm. Translation of: Szachinszach. 'A Helen and Kurt Wolff book.' 1. Iran — Politics and government — 1941-1979 I. T.
DS318.K31513 1985   955/.053 19   LC 84-10838   ISBN 015181483X

Khomeini, Ruhollah. 3.4087
Islam and revolution: writings and declarations of Imam Khomeini / translated and annotated by Hamid Algar. — Berkeley, [Calif.]: Mizan Press, c1981. 460 p.; 23 cm. 1. Islam and state — Iran — Addresses, essays, lectures. 2. Shiites 3. Iran — Politics and government — 1941-1979 — Addresses, essays, lectures. I. Algar, Hamid. II. T.
DS318.K394 1981   297/.1978 19   LC 80-24032   ISBN 0933782047

Laing, Margaret Irene. 3.4088
The Shah / Margaret Laing. London: Sidgwick & Jackson, 1977. 263 p., [6] leaves of plates: ports.; 24 cm. Includes index. 1. Mohammed Reza Pahlavi, Shah of Iran, 1919- 2. Iran — Kings and rulers — Biography. I. T.
DS318.L34 1977   955/.05/0924 B   LC 77-361185   ISBN 0283983361

Mohammed Reza Pahlavi, Shah of Iran, 1919-. 3.4089
[Réponse à l'histoire. English] Answer to history / Mohammad Reza Pahlavi; [translation, Michael Joseph Ltd.]. — New York: Stein and Day, 1980. 204 p.; 24 cm. Translation of Réponse à l'histoire. Includes index. 1. Mohammed Reza Pahlavi, Shah of Iran, 1919- 2. Iran — Kings and rulers — Biography. I. T.
DS318.M58413   955/.053/0924 B 19   LC 80-52039   ISBN 0812827554

Mohammed Reza Pahlavi, Shah of Iran, 1919-. 3.4090
Mission for my country. [1st ed.] New York, McGraw-Hill [1961, c1960] 336 p. illus. 24 cm. 1. Iran — Politics and government — 1945- I. T.
DS318.M6 1961   955.05   LC 61-7241

Bakhash, Shaul. 3.4091
The reign of the ayatollahs: Iran and the Islamic revolution / Shaul Bakhash. — New York: Basic Books, c1984. x, 276 p.; 24 cm. Includes index. 1. Iran — History — 1979- I. T.
DS318.8.B34 1984   955/.054 19   LC 83-46078   ISBN 0465068871

Kuniholm, Bruce Robellet, 1942-. 3.4092
The Persian Gulf and United States policy: a guide to issues and references / Bruce R. Kuniholm. — Claremont, Calif.: Regina Books, c1984. vii, 220 p.: maps; 23 cm. — (Guides to contemporary issues. #3) Includes index. 1. Persian Gulf Region — Politics and government. 2. Persian Gulf Region — Politics and government — Bibliography. 3. Persian Gulf Region — Foreign relations — United States. 4. Persian Gulf Region — Foreign relations — United States — Bibliography. 5. United States — Foreign relations — Persian Gulf Region. 6. United States — Foreign relations — Persian Gulf Region — Bibliography. I. T. II. Series.
DS326.K83 1984   327.73053 19   LC 84-9853   ISBN 0941690121

Rossabi, Morris. 3.4093
China and Inner Asia: from 1368 to the present day / Morris Rossabi. — New York: Pica Press: distributed by Universe Books, 1975. 320 p.: 4 maps; 23 cm. Includes index. 1. China — Relations — Asia, Central 2. Asia, Central — Relations — China I. T.
DS327.R67 1975b   327.51/058   LC 74-33174   ISBN 0876637160

DS335–499 SOUTH ASIA

Palmer, Norman Dunbar. • 3.4094
South Asia and United States policy [by] Norman D. Palmer. — Boston: Houghton Mifflin, [1966] x, 332 p.: map.; 24 cm. 1. South Asia — Foreign relations — United States. 2. United States — Foreign relations — South Asia. I. T.
DS335.P28   327.54073   LC 66-3463

Weiner, Myron. 3.4095
Political change in South Asia. — [1st ed.] Calcutta: K. L. Mukhopadhyay, 1963. viii, 285 p.; 23 cm. Bibliographical footnotes. I. T.
DS335.W4

Naik, J. A. 3.4096
India, Russia, China, and Bangla Desh, by J. A. Naik. — New Delhi: S. Chand, 1972. viii, 163 p.; 23 cm. 1. South Asia — Foreign relations — Russia. 2. Russia — Foreign relations — South Asia. 3. South Asia — Foreign relations — China. 4. China — Foreign relations — South Asia. I. T.
DS336.N35   LC 72-901925

Wilcox, Wayne Ayres. 3.4097
The emergence of Bangladesh; problems and opportunities for a redefined American policy in South Asia [by] Wayne Wilcox. — Washington: American Enterprise Institute for Public Policy Research, [1973] 79 p.; 23 cm. — (Foreign affairs study, 7) 1. South Asia — Foreign relations — United States. 2. United States — Foreign relations — South Asia. 3. South Asia — Politics and government. 4. Bangladesh — History — Revolution, 1971 I. T. II. Series.
DS336.3.U6 W54   327.73/054   LC 73-87975   ISBN 0844731129

Wolpert, Stanley A., 1927-. 3.4098
Roots of confrontation in South Asia: Afghanistan, Pakistan, India, and the superpowers / Stanley Wolpert. — New York: Oxford University Press, 1982. 222 p.: map; 22 cm. Includes index. 1. South Asia — History. 2. South Asia — Foreign relations. I. T.
DS340.W64 1982   954 19   LC 81-9454   ISBN 0195029941

Braun, Dieter. 3.4099
[Indische Ozean. English] The Indian Ocean: region of conflict or 'peace zone'? / by Dieter Braun; translated from the German by Carol Geldart and Kathleen Llanwarne. — New York: St. Martin's Press, 1983. xii, 228 p.: ill.; 23 cm. Translation of: Der Indische Ozean. Includes indexes. 1. Indian Ocean Region — Politics and government. 2. Indian Ocean Region — Strategic aspects. I. T.
DS341.B7313 1983   327/.09182/4 19   LC 83-9680   ISBN 0312413963

Choudhury, G. W. (Golam Wahed), 1926-. 3.4100
India, Pakistan, Bangladesh, and the major powers: politics of a divided subcontinent / G. W. Choudhury. — New York: Free Press, [1975] xii, 276 p.; 24 cm. (Institute book series of the Foreign Policy Research Institute) Includes index. 1. South Asia — Foreign relations. I. T.
DS341.C48   327.54   LC 74-34553   ISBN 0029053900

The States of South Asia: problems of national integration: essays in honour of W.H. Morris-Jones / A. Jeyaratnam Wilson, Dennis Dalton, editors. 3.4101
Honolulu: University Press of Hawaii, c1982. xviii, 343 p.: ill.; 23 cm. 1. Morris-Jones, W. H. (Wyndraeth Humphreys) — Addresses, essays, lectures. 2. South Asia — Politics and government — Addresses, essays, lectures. I. Morris-Jones, W. H. (Wyndraeth Humphreys) II. Wilson, A. Jeyaratnam. III. Dalton, Dennis.
DS341.S73 1982b   954.04 19   LC 84-126291   ISBN 0824808231

The Subcontinent in world politics: India, its neighbors and the great powers / edited by Lawrence Ziring. 3.4102
New York: Praeger, 1978. xiii, 238 p.; 24 cm. 1. South Asia — Politics and government. 2. South Asia — Foreign relations. I. Ziring, Lawrence, 1928-
DS341.S9   327/.0954   LC 78-19468   ISBN 0030429218

China South Asian relations, 1947–1980 / edited by R.K. Jain. 3.4103
Atlantic Highlands, N.J.: Humanities, 1981. 2 v., 1289 p. Chiefly documents. 1. South Asia — Relations — China — Sources. 2. China — Relations — South Asia — Sources. I. Jain, Rajendra Kumar.
DS341.3.C5 C48 1981b   327.51054 19   ISBN 0391022512

Soviet South Asian relations, 1947–1978 / [edited by] R. K.   3.4104
Jain.
Atlantic Highlands, N.J.: Humanities Press, 1979. 2 v.; 23 cm. 1. South Asia —
Relations — Soviet Union — Sources. 2. Soviet Union — Relations — South
Asia — Sources. I. Jain, Rajendra Kumar.
DS341.3.R9 S68 1979   301.29/47/059   LC 78-31667   ISBN
0391009745

Rudolph, Lloyd I.   3.4105
The regional imperative: the administration of U.S. foreign policy towards
South Asian states under Presidents Johnson and Nixon / Lloyd I. Rudolph,
Susanne Hoeber Rudolph, and others; with an epilogue by Christopher Van
Hollen. — Atlantic Highlands, N.J.: Humanities Press, 1980. xiv, 465 p., [2]
fold. leaves of plates: ill.; 23 cm. Originally published in 1975 as appendix 5 of v.
7 of the U.S. Commission on the Organization of the Government for the
Conduct of Foreign Policy's Report. 1. Johnson, Lyndon B. (Lyndon Baines),
1908-1973. 2. Nixon, Richard M. (Richard Milhous), 1913- 3. South Asia —
Relations — United States 4. United States — Relations — South Asia
I. Rudolph, Susanne Hoeber. joint author. II. T.
DS341.3.U6 R83 1980   327.73054 19   LC 80-21815   ISBN
0391021788

US–South Asian relations, 1947–1982 / edited by Rajendra K.   3.4106
Jain.
Atlantic Highlands, N.J.: Humanities Press, 1983. 3 v.; 23 cm. 1. South Asia —
Relations — United States — Sources. 2. United States — Relations — South
Asia — Sources. I. Jain, Rajendra Kumar.
DS341.3.U6 U75 1983   303.4/8254/073 19   LC 83-902383

Indian Ocean, five island countries / Foreign Area Studies, The   3.4107
American University; edited by Frederica M. Bunge.
2nd ed. — Washington, D.C.: The Studies: For sale by the Supt. of Docs., U.S.
G.P.O., c1982. xxvii, 346 p.: ill.; 24 cm. — (DA pam. 550-154) (Area handbook
series.) 'Research completed May 1982.' 'Supersedes DA Pam 550-154, 1971
edition and DA Pam 550-163, 1973 edition.'—T.p. verso. Includes index.
1. Islands of the Indian Ocean I. Bunge, Frederica M. II. American
University (Washington, D.C.). Foreign Area Studies. III. Series. IV. Series:
Area handbook series.
DS349.8.I5   969 19   LC 83-6395

DS350–375 Afghanistan

Afghanistan: a country study / Foreign Area Studies, the   3.4108
American University; edited by Richard F. Nyrop and Donald
M. Seekins.
5th ed. — Washington, D.C.: The Studies: For sale by the Supt. of Docs., U.S.
G.P.O., 1986. p. cm. (Area handbook series.) (DA pam. 550-65) 'Research
completed January 1986.' Includes index. 1. Afghanistan. I. Nyrop, Richard
F. II. Seekins, Donald M. III. American University (Washington, D.C.).
Foreign Area Studies. IV. Series. V. Series: DA pam. 550-65
DS351.5.A34 1986   958/.1 19   LC 86-3359

Dupree, Louis, 1925-.   3.4109
Afghanistan. — Princeton, N.J.: Princeton University Press, [c1973] xxiv,
760 p.: illus.; 25 cm. 1. Afghanistan. 2. Afghanistan — History I. T.
DS351.5.D86   915.81/03   LC 76-154993   ISBN 0691030065

Dupree, Louis, 1925-.   3.4110
Afghanistan in the 1970s. Edited by Louis Dupree [and] Linette Albert.
Foreword by Phillips Talbot. — New York: Praeger, [1974] xi, 266 p.: illus.; 25
cm. — (Praeger special studies in international economics and development)
1. Afghanistan — Addresses, essays, lectures. I. Albert. Linette, joint author.
II. T.
DS351.5.D87   915.8/1/034   LC 73-9059   ISBN 0275287459

Griffiths, John Charles.   3.4111
Afghanistan: key to a continent / John C. Griffiths. — Boulder, Colo.:
Westview Press, 1981. 255 p., [8] p. of plates: ill.; 23 cm. 1. Afghanistan. I. T.
DS351.5.G74 1981   958/.1042 19   LC 80-71079   ISBN
0865310807

Fraser-Tytler, William Kerr, Sir, 1886-.   • 3.4112
Afghanistan: a study of political developments in central and southern Asia, by
W. K. Fraser–Tytler. — 3rd ed., revised by M. C. Gillett. — London; New
York [etc.]: Oxford U.P., 1967. xvi, 362 p.: front., plates, maps, diagrs.; 22 1/2
cm. 1. Eastern question (Central Asia) 2. Afghanistan — History I. Gillett,
Michael Cavenagh, Sir, 1907- II. T.
DS356.F7 1967   958.1   LC 67-88066

Wilber, Donald Newton.   • 3.4113
Afghanistan: its people, its society, its culture. In collaboration with Elizabeth
E. Bacon [and others] New Haven, HRAF Press [1962] 320 p. illus. 22 cm.
(Survey of world cultures [11]) 1. Afghanistan. I. T.
DS356.W5 1962   LC 62-18167

Adamec, Ludwig W.   3.4114
Afghanistan's foreign affairs to the mid–twentieth century: relations with the
USSR, Germany, and Britain [by] Ludwig W. Adamec. Tucson, University of
Arizona Press [1974] ix, 324 p. illus. 23 cm. 1. Afghanistan — Foreign
relations — Soviet Union. 2. Soviet Union — Foreign relations — Afghanistan.
3. Afghanistan — Foreign relations — Great Britain. 4. Great Britain —
Foreign relations — Afghanistan. 5. Afghanistan — Foreign relations —
Germany. 6. Germany — Foreign relations — Afghanistan. I. T.
DS357.5.A63   327.581   LC 73-86450   ISBN 0816503885 ISBN
0816504598

Bosworth, Clifford Edmund.   3.4115
The later Ghaznavids: splendour and decay: the dynasty in Afghanistan and
northern India, 1040–1186 / Clifford Edmund Bosworth. — New York:
Columbia University Press, 1977. vi, 196 p.: ill.; 23 cm. — (Persian studies
series; no. 7) Continues the author's The Ghaznavids. Includes index.
1. Ghaznevids 2. Afghanistan — History 3. India — History — 1000-1526
I. T.
DS358.B63 1977   955/.02   LC 77-7879   ISBN 0231044283

Gregorian, Vartan.   • 3.4116
The emergence of modern Afghanistan; politics of reform and modernization,
1880–1946. — Stanford, Calif.: Stanford University Press, 1969. viii, 586 p.:
illus., maps, ports.; 25 cm. 1. Afghanistan — History I. T.
DS361.G68   958.1   LC 69-13178   ISBN 0804707065

Poullada, Leon B., 1913-.   3.4117
Reform and rebellion in Afghanistan, 1919–1929: King Amanullah's failure to
modernize a tribal society / [by] Leon B. Poullada. — Ithaca [N.Y.]: Cornell
University Press, [1973] xvii, 318 p.: ill.; 24 cm. 1. Amanullah Khan, Amir of
Afghanistan, 1892-1960. 2. Afghanistan — Politics and government I. T.
DS369.P68 1973   958.1/04   LC 72-12291   ISBN 0801407729

Newell, Richard S., 1933-.   • 3.4118
The politics of Afghanistan [by] Richard S. Newell. — Ithaca [N.Y.]: Cornell
University Press, [1972] xiv, 236 p.; 21 cm. — (South Asian political systems)
1. Afghanistan — Politics and government 2. Afghanistan — Economic
conditions. I. T. II. Series.
DS369.4.N44   320.9/581/04   LC 78-176487   ISBN 0801406889

Hammond, Thomas Taylor.   3.4119
Red flag over Afghanistan: the Communist coup, the Soviet invasion, and the
consequences / Thomas T. Hammond. — Boulder, Colo.: Westview Press,
1984. xvii, 262 p.; 24 cm. Includes index. 1. Afghanistan — History — Soviet
Occupation, 1979- I. T.
DS371.2.H35 1984   958/.1044 19   LC 83-10370   ISBN
0865314446

Robertson, George Scott, Sir, 1852-1916.   3.4120
The Kafirs of the Hindu–Kush / by Sir George Scott Robertson; illustrated by
A.D. McCormick. [1st ed. reprinted; with an introduction by Louis Dupree.
Karachi; London [etc.]: Oxford University Press, 1974. xxviii, vii-xx, 667 p., [2]
fold leaves of plate: ill., 2maps (1 col.), ports.; 24 cm. (Oxford in Asia historical
reprints from Pakistan.) 1. Nuristan — Description and travel. I. McCormick,
Arthur David. II. T. III. Series.
DS374.Nx   915.81   ISBN 0195771273

DS376–392 Pakistan

Pakistan, a country study / Foreign Area Studies, the American   3.4121
University; edited by Richard F. Nyrop.
5th ed. — Washington, D.C.: For sale by the Supt. of Docs., U.S. G.P.O.,
c1984. xxix, 372 p.: ill.; 24 cm. (Area handbook series.) (DA pam. 550-48) Rev.
ed. of: Area handbook for Pakistan / co-authors, Richard F. Nyrop et al. 4th
ed. 1975. 'Research completed October 1983.' Includes index. 1. Pakistan.
I. Nyrop, Richard F. II. American University (Washington, D.C.). Foreign
Area Studies. III. Area handbook for Pakistan. IV. Series. V. Series: DA pam.
550-48
DS376.9.P376 1984   954.9/104 19   LC 84-11101

Pakistan: past & present: a comprehensive study published in   **3.4122**
commemoration of the centenary of the birth of the founder of
Pakistan.
London: Stacey International, [c1977] 288 p.: ill.; 31 cm. Includes index.
1. Jinnah, Mohamed Ali, 1876-1948. 2. Pakistan.
DS376.9.P38   954.9   LC 77-376634   *ISBN* 0950330493

Ikram, Sheikh Mohamad, 1908- ed.   • **3.4123**
The cultural heritage of Pakistan, edited by S. M. Ikram and Percival Spear. —
[Karachi, New York] Oxford University Press [1955] 204 p. illus. 21 cm.
1. Pakistan — Civilization I. Spear, Thomas George Percival. joint ed. II. T.
DS379.I39   LC 56-13679

Wilber, Donald Newton.   • **3.4124**
Pakistan, its people, its society, its culture [by] Donald N. Wilber, in
collaboration with Donald Atwell [and others]. — New Haven: HRAF Press,
[1964] 487 p.: illus., maps.; 22 cm. — (Survey of world cultures [13])
1. Pakistan. I. Atwell, Donald. II. T. III. Series.
DS379.W5   915.491   LC 64-8647

Burke, S. M.   **3.4125**
Pakistan's foreign policy: an historical analysis. — London: Oxford University
Press, 1973. ix, 432 p.; 22 cm. 1. Pakistan — Foreign relations. I. T.
DS383.5.A2 B87 1973   327.549   LC 73-163550   *ISBN* 0192151797

Burki, Shahid Javed.   **3.4126**
Pakistan under Bhutto, 1971–1977 / Shahid Javed Burki. — New York: St.
Martin's Press, c1980. xii, 245 p.; 23 cm. Includes indexes. 1. Bhutto, Zulfikar
Ali. 2. Pakistan — Politics and government — 1971- I. T.
DS384.B88 1980b   954.9/1/050924   LC 78-31358   *ISBN*
0312594712

Choudhury, G. W. (Golam Wahed), 1926-.   **3.4127**
The last days of united Pakistan, [by] G. W. Choudhury. Bloomington, Indiana
University Press 1975 (c1974) xiv, 239 p. 23 cm. 1. Pakistan — Politics and
government 2. Bangladesh — Politics and government I. T.
DS384.C446   954.9/04   LC 74-8977   *ISBN* 0253332605

Feldman, Herbert.   • **3.4128**
From crisis to crisis: Pakistan 1962–1969. — London: Oxford University Press,
1972. xvi, 340 p.; 23 cm. Sequel to the author's Revolution in Pakistan.
1. Pakistan — Politics and government I. T.
DS384.F36   320.9/549/04   LC 72-189488   *ISBN* 0192151924

Feldman, Herbert.   **3.4129**
The end and the beginning: Pakistan, 1969–1971 / Herbert Feldman. —
London: Oxford University Press, 1978(c1975). 210 p.; 23 cm. 1. Pakistan —
Politics and government 2. Pakistan — History I. T.
DS384.F362   *ISBN* 0192158090

Jahan, Rounaq.   **3.4130**
Pakistan: failure in national integration. — New York: Columbia University
Press, [1972] ix, 248 p.: illus.; 23 cm. 1. Pakistan — Politics and government
2. Pakistan — Social conditions. 3. Pakistan — Economic conditions. I. T.
DS384.J34   320.9/549   LC 72-3771   *ISBN* 0231036256

Pakistan: the long view / William J. Barnds ... [et al.]; edited   **3.4131**
by Lawrence Ziring, Ralph Braibanti, and W. Howard Wriggins.
Durham, N.C.: Duke University Press, 1977. xviii, 485 p.; 24 cm. (Publication -
Duke University Center for Commonwealth and Comparative Studies; no. 43)
1. Pakistan — History I. Barnds, William J. II. Ziring, Lawrence, 1928-
III. Braibanti, Ralph J. D. IV. Wriggins, W. Howard (William Howard),
1918-
DS384.P36   954.9/04   LC 76-4320   *ISBN* 0822303639

Sayeed, Khalid B.   **3.4132**
Politics in Pakistan: the nature and direction of change / Khalid B. Sayeed. —
New York: Praeger, 1980. 194 p.: maps. Includes index. 1. Pakistan — Politics
and government I. T.
DS384.S29   954.9/1   LC 80-13625   *ISBN* 0030418119

Symonds, Richard, 1918-.   **3.4133**
The making of Pakistan / by Richard Symonds. — Islamabad: National
Committee for Birth Centenary Celebrations of Quaid-i-Azam Mohammad Ali
Jinnah, Ministry of Education, Govt. of Pakistan, 1977. 231 p., [1] leaf of plates:
maps; 23 cm. Reprint of the 1950 ed. published by Faber & Faber, London. On
verso of t.p.: National Book Foundation edition, 1976. 'The culture of Pakistan,
by Ahmed Ali': p. 195-216. Includes index. 1. Pakistan movement 2. Pakistan
— History I. T.
DS384.S95 1976   954.9/1/04   LC 77-930477

Wilcox, Wayne Ayres.   • **3.4134**
Pakistan; the consolidation of a nation. — New York, Columbia University
Press, 1963. 276 p. illus. 23 cm. 1. Pakistan — Pol. & govt. I. T.
DS384.W5   954.7   LC 63-9873

Ziring, Lawrence, 1928-.   **3.4135**
The Ayub Khan era; politics in Pakistan, 1958–1969. [1st ed. Syracuse, N.Y.]
Syracuse University Press [1971] x, 234 p. 2 maps. 24 cm. 1. Ayub Khan,
Mohammad, 1907-1974. 2. Pakistan — Politics and government I. T.
DS384.Z57   320.9/549/04   LC 78-135394   *ISBN* 0815600755

Ayub Khan, Mohammad, 1907-1974.   • **3.4136**
Friends not masters, a political autobiography. New York, Oxford University
Press, 1967. xiv, 275 p. illus., maps, ports. 24 cm. 1. Pakistan — Politics and
government I. T.
DS385.A9 A3   954.9/04/0924 B   LC 67-25583

Wolpert, Stanley A., 1927-.   **3.4137**
Jinnah of Pakistan / Stanley Wolpert. — New York: Oxford University Press,
1984. xii, 421 p., [12] p. of plates: ill.; 24 cm. Includes index. 1. Jinnah,
Mahomed Ali, 1876-1948. 2. Statesmen — Pakistan — Biography. I. T.
DS385.J5 W64 1984   954.9/042/0924 B 19   LC 83-13318   *ISBN*
0195034120

Jackson, Robert Victor.   **3.4138**
South Asian crisis: India, Pakistan, and Bangla Desh; a political and historical
analysis of the 1971 war [by] Robert Jackson. — New York: Praeger; Published
for the International Institute for Strategic Studies, [1975] 240 p.; 23 cm. —
(Praeger special studies in international politics and government) 1. India-
Pakistan Conflict, 1971 2. South Asia — Politics and government.
I. International Institute for Strategic Studies. II. T.
DS388.J3 1974   954.9/205   LC 74-8921   *ISBN* 0275095606

Burton, Richard Francis, Sir, 1821-1890.   **3.4139**
Sindh and the races that inhabit the Valley of the Indus. With an introd. by H.
T. Lambrick. — Karachi; New York: Oxford University Press, 1974 (c1973).
xxiv, 427 p.: map.; 23 cm. — (Oxford in Asia historical reprints) Reprint of the
1851 ed. published by W. H. Allen, London. 1. Ethnology — Pakistan — Sind.
2. Sind (Pakistan) — Social life and customs. I. T.
DS392.S56 B87   915.49/18/0331   LC 74-161754   *ISBN*
019636101X

DS393–395 Bangladesh

Bangla Desh: documents.   **3.4140**
[New Delhi: Ministry of External Affairs] 1. Bangladesh — Politics and
government — Sources. 2. Pakistan — Politics and government — Sources.
DS393.4.B3x   954.9/2   LC 78-926706

Baxter, Craig.   **3.4141**
Bangladesh: a new nation in an old setting / Craig Baxter. — Boulder:
Westview Press, 1985 (c1984). xii, 130 p.: ill.; 24 cm. — (Westview profiles.
Nations of contemporary Asia.) Includes index. 1. Bangladesh. I. T.
II. Series.
DS393.4.B4   954.9/2 19   LC 84-7383   *ISBN* 0865316309

Nicholas, Marta R.   • **3.4142**
Bangladesh: the birth of a nation; a handbook of background information and
documentary sources / compiled by Marta Nicholas and Philip Oldenburg;
(with contributions from Shamsul Bari [and others]. — Madras: M.
Seshachalam, 1972. xii, 156 p.: ill.; 22 cm. 1. Bangladesh. I. Oldenburg, Philip,
joint author. II. Bari, Shamsul. III. T.
DS393.4.N52   915.49/2/034   LC 73-929521   *ISBN* 0882532014

Nyrop, Richard F.   **3.4143**
Area handbook for Bangladesh / coauthors, Richard F. Nyrop ... [et al.]. — 1st
ed. — Washington: For sale by the Supt. of Docs., U.S. Govt. Print. Off., 1975.
xviii, 346 p.: ill.; 24 cm. 'One of a series of handbooks prepared by Foreign Area
Studies (FAS) of the American University.' 'DA Pam 550-175.' Includes index.
1. Bangladesh. I. American University (Washington, D.C.). Foreign Area
Studies. II. T.
DS393.4.N97   954.9/2   LC 75-619340

Johnson, B. L. C. (Basil Leonard Clyde), 1919-.   **3.4144**
Bangladesh / by B. L. C. Johnson. — New York: Barnes & Noble Books, 1975.
104 p.: ill.; 26 cm. Includes indexes. 1. Bangladesh — Description and travel.
2. Bangladesh — Economic conditions. I. T.
DS393.5.J64 1975   954.9/205   LC 75-319220   *ISBN* 0064933431

er-Rashid, Haroun.   **3.4145**
Geography of Bangladesh / Haroun Er Rashid. — Boulder, Colo.: Westview
Press, 1979, c1977. xvi, 579 p.: maps; 24 cm. Includes index. 1. Bangladesh —
Description and travel. I. T.
DS393.5.R37   954.9/205   LC 78-19679   *ISBN* 0891583564

O'Donnell, Charles Peter, 1904-.   **3.4146**
Bangladesh: biography of a Muslim nation / Charles Peter O'Donnell. —
Boulder, Colo.: Westview, 1985 (c1984). xiv, 322 p.: ill.; 24 cm. Includes index.
1. Bangladesh — Politics and government 2. Bangladesh — Economic
conditions. I. T.
DS394.7.O36   954.9/2 19   *LC* 83-23491   *ISBN* 0865316821

Sen Gupta, Jyoti, 1915-.   **3.4147**
History of freedom movement in Bangladesh, 1943–1973; some involvement. —
[1st ed.]. — Calcutta: Naya Prokash, [1974] xxiv, 506 p.; 23 cm. 1. Bangladesh
— Politics and government I. T.
DS395.S46   320.9/549/204   *LC* 74-901242

Franda, Marcus F.   **3.4148**
Bangladesh, the first decade / Marcus Franda. — New Delhi: South Asian
Publishers (dist. by South Asia Books), 1982. 351 p. Includes indexes.
1. Bangladesh — Politics and government — 1971- I. T.
DS395.5.F69   954.9/205 19   *LC* 81-19639   *ISBN* 0883330067

Islam, M. Rafiqul.   **3.4149**
A tale of millions: Bangladesh Liberation War, 1971 / Rafiq–ul–Islam. — 2nd
ed., rev. and enl. — Dacca: Bangladesh Books International, 1981. xv, 319, iii,
vii p., [31] p. of plates: ill., facsims., col. maps; 22 cm. Maps on lining papers.
1. Bangladesh — History — Revolution, 1971 I. T.
DS395.5.I855 1981   954.9/205 19   *LC* 81-905814

Rahman, Mizanur.   **3.4150**
Emergence of a new nation in a multi–polar world: Bangladesh / by Mizanur
Rahman. — Washington, D.C.: University Press of America, c1978. 189 p.; 23
cm. — (International studies series.) 1. Bangladesh — Politics and government
— 1971- I. T. II. Series.
DS395.5.R34   *LC* 78-59858   *ISBN* 0819105589

Roy Chowdhury, Subrata.   **3.4151**
The genesis of Bangladesh: a study in international legal norms and permissive
conscience. — London: Asia Publishing House, 1972. xii, 345 p.: map (on lining
papers).; 25 cm. 1. Self-determination, National 2. Crimes against humanity
3. Bangladesh — History — Revolution, 1971 4. Pakistan — Politics and
government I. T.
DS395.5.R69 1972   954.9/2/05   *LC* 73-165855   *ISBN* 021040504X

DS401–488 India

Balfour, Edward, 1813-1889.   **3.4152**
The cyclopaedia of India and of eastern and southern Asia. Graz: Akademische
Druck- u. Verlagsanstalt, 1967-68. 3 v.; 28 cm. 1. India — Dictionaries and
encyclopedias. I. T.
DS405.B182   *LC* 67-107209

Dey, Nundo Lal.   **3.4153**
The geographical dictionary of ancient and mediaeval India. — [3d ed.]. —
New Delhi: Oriental Books Reprint Corp.; exclusively distributed by
Munshiram Manoharlal, [1971] ix, 262 p.: fold. map.; 29 cm. First published in
1899. 1. India — Gazetteers. I. T.
DS405.D4 1971   915.4/003   *LC* 76-925971

Garrett, John, fl. 1845-1873.   **• 3.4154**
A classical dictionary of India. — Graz: Akademische Druck- u. Verlags-
anstalt, 1971. x, 793, 160 p.; 20 cm. Reprint of the Madras, 1871 ed. Includes
reprint of the supplement, published in Madras, 1873. 1. Mythology, Indic —
Dictionaries. 2. India — Dictionaries and encyclopedias. I. T.
DS405.G3 1971   913.3/4/003   *LC* 72-176849

India: a reference annual, 1953– / compiled by The Research   **3.4155**
and Reference Division, Ministry of Information and
Broadcasting, Government of India.
Delhi: Ministry of Information and Broadcasting, 1954. v.: ill., map. 1. India.
I. India. Ministry of Information and Broadcasting.
DS405.I64

The Gazetteer of India: Indian Union / issued on behalf of the   **3.4156**
Gazetteers Unit, Ministry of Education and Social Welfare,
Government of India.
[Delhi]: Publications Division, Ministry of Information and Broadcasting,
1965-1973. 2 v.: maps (some fold., some col.); 25 cm. — v.2 edited by P. N.
Chopra. 1. India — Gazetteers. I. India (Republic). Central Gazetteers Unit.
DS407.G337

India: a country study / Foreign Area Studies, the American   **3.4157**
University; edited by Richard F. Nyrop.
4th ed. — Washington, D.C.: For sale by the Supt. of Docs., U.S. G.P.O., 1985.
p. cm. (Area handbook series.) (DA pam / Headquarters, Department of the
Army; 550-21) Rev ed. of: Area handbook for India / coauthors, Richard F.
Nyrop ... [et al.]. 3rd ed. 1975. 'Research completed January 1985.' Includes
index. 1. India. I. Nyrop, Richard F. II. Nyrop, Richard F. Area handbook
for India. III. American University (Washington, D.C.). Foreign Area Studies.
IV. Series.
DS407.I5132   954 19   *LC* 85-18698

Lamb, Beatrice (Pitney), 1904-.   **• 3.4158**
India; a world in transition. — Rev. ed. — New York, F. A. Praeger [1966] xi,
382 p. fold. map. 21 cm. (Praeger paperbacks, P116) Bibliography: p. 361-374.
1. India. I. T.
DS407.L28 1966   915.4   *LC* 66-14163

Mehta, Ved, 1934-.   **• 3.4159**
Portrait of India, by Ved Mehta. New York, Farrar, Straus and Giroux [1970]
xi, 544 p. map (on lining paper) 24 cm. 1. India. I. T.
DS407.M4 1970   915.4/03   *LC* 76-97615

Moreland, W. H. (William Harrison), 1868-1938.   **• 3.4160**
A short history of India, by W. H. Moreland and Atul Chandra Chatterjee. 4th
ed. New York: Longmans, Green, [1957] xii, 594 p. maps (1 col.) 22 cm.
1. India — History I. Chatterjee, Atul Chandra, Sir 1874-1955, joint author.
II. T.
DS407.M7 1957   *LC* a 59-5016

Spate, O. H. K. (Oskar Hermann Khristian), 1911-.   **3.4161**
India and Pakistan: land, people and economy [by] O. H. K. Spate & A. T. A.
Learmonth with the collaboration of A. M. Learmonth and a chapter on Ceylon
by B. H. Farmer. — 3rd ed. revised and completely reset. — London: Methuen,
1972, c1967. 439 p.: ill. (University paperbacks, UP421) 1. India. 2. Pakistan.
3. Ceylon. I. Learmonth, A. T. A., joint author. II. T.
DS407.S67 1967   915.4

Majumdar, Ramesh Chandra. ed.   **• 3.4162**
The classical accounts of India: being a compilation of the English translations
of the accounts left by Herodotus, Megasthenes, Arrian, Strabo, Quintus,
Diodorus Siculus, Justin, Plutarch, Frontinus, Nearchus, Appollonius, Pliny,
Ptolemy, Aelian and others / with maps, editorial notes, comments, analysis
and introd. by R. C. Chandra. — Calcutta: Firma K. L. Mukhopadhyay, 1960.
xxvi, 492 p.; 23 cm. 1. Classical geography 2. India — Description and travel
— To 1000 I. T.
DS409.M3   *LC* 62-30287

Heber, Reginald, 1783-1826.   **• 3.4163**
[Narrative of a journey through the upper provinces of India. Selections] Bishop
Heber in northern India; selections from Heber's journal, edited by M. A.
Laird. London, Cambridge U.P., 1971. x, 324 p., plate; illus, maps, ports. 23
cm. (The European understanding of India) 1. India — Description and travel
— 1762-1858 2. India — Social life and customs I. T.
DS412.H443 1971   915/.4   *LC* 70-123673   *ISBN* 0521078733

Fairservis, Walter Ashlin, 1921-.   **• 3.4164**
The roots of ancient India; the archaeology of early Indian civilization [by]
Walter A. Fairservis, Jr. Drawings by Jan Fairservis. — New York: Macmillan,
[1971] xxv, 482 p.: illus., maps.; 24 cm. 1. India — Antiquities 2. India —
Civilization — To 1200 I. T.
DS418.F24   913.34/03   *LC* 69-10610

DS421–422 SOCIAL LIFE. CUSTOMS.
CASTE

Carstairs, G. M. (G. Morris)   **3.4165**
The twice–born; a study of a community of high–caste Hindus. With a pref. by
Margaret Mead. Bloomington, Indiana University Press, 1958. 343 p. 23 cm.
1. National characteristics, East Indian 2. Caste — India I. T.
DS421.C29   301.440954   *LC* 58-9003

Chaudhuri, Nirad C., 1897-.   **• 3.4166**
The autobiography of an unknown Indian, by Nirad C. Chaudhuri. —
Berkeley: University of California Press, 1968 [c1951] xii, 506 p.; 21 cm.
1. India — Social life and customs I. T.
DS421.C47 1968   915.4/03/350924   *LC* 68-25418

Dubois, Jean Antoine, 1765-1848.   **• 3.4167**
Hindu manners, customs and ceremonies, by the Abbé J. A. Dubois, translated
from the author's later French ms. and edited with notes, corrections, and
biography by Henry K. Beauchamp ... With a prefatory note by the Right Hon.
F. Max Müller, and a portrait. — 3d ed. — Oxford, The Clarendon press [1924]
2 p. l., [iii]-xxxiv, 741 p. front. (port.) 18.5 cm. 'Impression of 1924. First

edition, 1897.' 1. India — Soc. life & cust. 2. India — Civilization 3. India — Religion I. Beauchamp, Henry King, 1866-1907, ed. and tr. II. T.
DS421.D825 1924   LC 45-41402

Rai, Sudha.   **3.4168**
V.S. Naipaul: a study in expatriate sensibility / Sudha Rai. — New Jersey: Humantities, 1982. 136 p.; 22 cm. 1. Naipaul, Vidiadhar Surajprasad, 1932- . Area of darkness 2. Naipaul, Vidiadhar Surajprasad, 1932- . Overcrowded barracoon 3. Naipaul, Vidiadhar Surajprasad, 1932- . India: a wounded civilization I. T.
DS421 N327 1982   ISBN 0391026968

Rawlinson, H. G. (Hugh George), 1880-.   **• 3.4169**
India, a short cultural history. — New York: F. A. Praeger, [1952] xiv, 454 p.: illus., maps.; 26 cm. — (The Cresset historical series) 1. India — Civilization 2. India — History I. T.
DS421.R35 1952   934   LC 52-11243

Sen, Gertrude (Emerson)   **• 3.4170**
Voiceless India [by] Gertrude Emerson (Gertrude Sen). — Westport, Conn.: Greenwood Press, [1971] 458 p.: illus., map.; 23 cm. Reprint of the 1930 ed. 1. India — Social life and customs 2. India — Social conditions 3. Pachperwa, India. I. T.
DS421.S47 1971   915.4/2/035   LC 74-109975   ISBN 0837144817

Wiser, Charlotte Melina (Viall)   **• 3.4171**
Behind mud walls, 1930–1960, by William H. Wiser and Charlotte Viall Wiser. With a foreword by David G. Mandelbaum. — [Rev. and enl.]. — Berkeley: University of California Press, 1963. xv, 249 p.; 21 cm. Authors' names in reverse order in previous editions. 1. Villages — India. 2. India — Social life and customs I. Wiser, William Henricks, 1890-1961. joint author. II. T.
DS421.W73 1963   915.4   LC 63-19178

Béteille, André.   **• 3.4172**
Caste, class, and power: changing patterns of stratification in a Tanjore village. — Berkeley: University of California Press, c1965, 1969. 238 p. 1. Caste — India — Tanjore (District) I. T.
DS422.C3 B4 1965   LC 65-25628

Bouglé, Célestin Charles Alfred, 1870-1940.   **• 3.4173**
[Essais sur le régime des castes. English] Essays on the caste system. Translated with an introd. by D. F. Pocock. Cambridge [Eng.] University Press, 1971. xiv, 228 p. 23 cm. (European understanding of India) Translation of Essais sur le régime des castes. 1. Caste — India 2. India — Social conditions I. T.
DS422.C3 B6513 1971   301.44/0954   LC 79-154506   ISBN 0521080932

Ghurye, G. S. (Govind Sadashiv), 1893-.   **• 3.4174**
Caste and race in India [by] G. S. Ghurye. [5th ed.] Bombay, Popular Prakashan [1969] vi, 504 p. 23 cm. (Popular library of Indian sociology and social thought) Second and 3d editions (1950, 1956) have title: Caste and class in India; 4th ed., 1961, has title: Caste, class, and occupation. 1. Caste — India 2. Ethnology — India 3. Hindus I. T.
DS422.C3 G5 1969   301.44/0954   LC 71-905700

Hutton, J. H. (John Henry), 1885-1968.   **• 3.4175**
Caste in India, its nature, function and origins [by] J. H. Hutton. 4th ed. Indian Branch, Oxford University Press, [London] 1963. xiv, 324 p. illus., fold. maps. 25 cm. Bibliography: p. [263]-275. 1. Caste — India I. T.
DS422.C3H8 1963   301.440954   LC 64-5242

Isaacs, Harold R.   **• 3.4176**
India's ex–untouchables / Harold R. Isaacs. — New York: J. Day Co., 1965. 188 p. 'A study from the Center for International Studies, Massachusetts Institute of Technology.' 1. Caste — India 2. Untouchables 3. Social mobility I. Massachusetts Institute of Technology. Center for International Studies. II. T.
DS422.C3I8   305.560954   LC 65-10790

Mayer, Adrian C.   **3.4177**
Caste and kinship in central India: a village and its region. — Berkeley: University of California Press, 1960. 295 p.; ill.; 23 cm. Includes bibliographies. 1. Caste — India I. T.
DS422.C3M3   301.44   LC 60-2076

The Untouchables in contemporary India. J. Michael Mahar,   **3.4178**
editor. Contributors: S. Chandrasekhar [and others]
Tucson, University of Arizona Press [1972] xxxii, 496 p. illus. 23 cm. Contains mainly revised papers from a conference at the University of Arizona, sponsored by the Association for Asian Studies in Nov. 1967. 1. Untouchables — Addresses, essays, lectures. I. Mahar, J. Michael, ed. II. Chandrasekhar, S. (Sripati), 1918- ed.
DS422.C3 U57   301.44/94/0954   LC 79-152039   ISBN 0816502072

DS423-428 CIVILIZATION

A Cultural history of India / edited by A. L. Basham.   **3.4179**
Oxford, 1975. xx, 585 p. [18] leaves of plates: ill.; 24 cm. Includes index. 1. India — Civilization — History. I. Basham, A. L. (Arthur Llewellyn)
DS423.C86   954   LC 75-332022   ISBN 0198219148

De Bary, William Theodore, 1918- ed.   **• 3.4180**
Sources of Indian tradition. Compiled by Wm. Theodore De Bary [and others]. — New York: Columbia University Press, 1958. xxvii, 961 p.: maps.; 24 cm. — (Records of civilization: sources and studies, 56. Introduction to oriental civilizations) Translations from various sources and by various individuals. 1. India — Religion 2. India — Civilization 3. Pakistan — Civilization I. T.
DS423.D33   915.4   LC 58-4146

Elder, Joseph Walter.   **3.4181**
Civilization of India syllabus [by] Joseph W. Elder, editor, Willard L. Johnson [and] Christopher R. King. Madison, Dept. of Indian Studies, University of Wisconsin, 1965. unpaged. illus. 1. India — Civilization I. Wisconsin. University. Dept. of Indian Studies. II. T.
DS423.E5x

Gordon, Leonard A.   **• 3.4182**
A syllabus of Indian civilization, by Leonard A. Gordon and Barbara Stoler Miller. — New York: Columbia University Press, 1971. viii, 182 p.: maps.; 24 cm. 1. India — Civilization — History — Outlines, syllabi, etc. I. Miller, Barbara Stoler. joint author. II. T.
DS423.G68   915.4/03/0202   LC 70-168868   ISBN 0231035608

Lannoy, Richard.   **3.4183**
The speaking tree: a study of Indian culture and society. — London; New York: Oxford University Press, 1971. xxvii, 466 p., 25 plates; illus. (incl. 1 col.); 24 cm. 1. Religion and state — India. 2. India — Civilization I. T.
DS423.L27 1971   915.4/03   LC 74-158205   ISBN 0192151770

Saletore, Rajaram Narayan.   **3.4184**
Encyclopaedia of Indian culture / R.N. Saletore. — Atlantic Highlands, N.J.: Sole distributors, USA & Canada, Humanities Press; New Delhi: Sterling Publishers, 1981-1985. 5 v.: ill.; 25 cm. Includes index in v. 5. 1. India — Civilization — Dictionaries. I. T.
DS423.S218 1981   954/.003/21 19   LC 82-145096   ISBN 0391022822

Singer, Milton B. ed.   **• 3.4185**
Traditional India: structure and change. Philadelphia, American Folklore Society, 1959. xxviii, 332 p. illus. 26 cm. (American Folklore Society. Bibliographical and special series, v. 10) 1. Social change 2. India — Civilization I. T.
DS423.S57   LC 58-59652

Taylor, Edmond, 1908-.   **• 3.4186**
Richer by Asia. — 2d ed. — Boston: Houghton Mifflin, 1964. xvi, 420 p.; 22 cm. 1. India — Civilization I. T.
DS423.T3 1964   915.4   LC 64-57023

Tyler, Stephen A., 1932-.   **3.4187**
India: an anthropological perspective [by] Stephen A. Tyler. — Pacific Palisades, Calif.: Goodyear Pub. Co., [1973] 224 p.: ill.; 24 cm. — (Goodyear regional anthropology series) 1. Ethnology — India 2. India — Civilization I. T.
DS423.T93   301.29/54   LC 72-76937   ISBN 0876200757

Allchin, Bridget.   **• 3.4188**
The birth of Indian civilization; India and Pakistan before 500 B.C. [by] Bridget and Raymond Allchin. Baltimore, Penguin Books [1968] 365 p. illus. 18 cm. (Pelican books, A950) 1. India — Civilization — To 1200 I. Allchin, Frank Raymond, 1923- joint author. II. T.
DS425.A65 1968b   913.3/4/03   LC 79-1722

Allchin, Bridget.   **3.4189**
The rise of civilization in India and Pakistan / Bridget and Raymond Allchin. — Cambridge; New York: Cambridge University Press, 1982. xiv, 379 p.: ill.; 25 cm. — (Cambridge world archaeology.) Includes index. 1. India — Civilization — To 1200 2. Pakistan — Civilization I. Allchin, Frank Raymond, 1923- II. T. III. Series.
DS425.A66 1982   954.02 19   LC 82-1262   ISBN 0521242444

Auboyer, Jeannine.   **• 3.4190**
Daily life in ancient India: from approximately 200 B.C. to 700 A.D. New York: Macmillan, 1965. xv, 344 p., [12] leaves of plates: ill.; 22 cm. (The daily life series) 1. India — Civilization I. T. II. Series.
DS425.A953 1965a   915.49103   LC 65-17835

Basham, A. L. (Arthur Llewellyn) • **3.4191**
The wonder that was India; a survey of the history and culture of the Indian sub-continent before the coming of the Muslims [by] A. L. Basham. 3d rev. ed. New York, Taplinger Pub. Co. [1968] xxiii, 572 p. illus. (part col.), maps. 24 cm. 1. India — Civilization — To 1200 2. India — History — To 324 B.C. 3. India — History — 324 B.C.-1000 A.D. I. T.
DS425.B33 1968   913.34/03   LC 68-10737

Bīrūnī, Muhammad ibn Ahmad, 973?-1048. • **3.4192**
[Tārīkh al-Hind. English] Alberuni's India. Translated by Edward C. Sachau. Abridged ed. edited with introd. and notes by Ainslie T. Embree. New York, Norton [1971] xix, 246 p. illus. 20 cm. (The Norton library, N568) Translation of Tārīkh al-hind. 1. Civilization, Hindu I. Embree, Ainslie Thomas. ed. II. T.
DS425.B5713 1971   915.4/03/22   LC 79-29490   ISBN 0393005682

Davids, T. W. Rhys (Thomas William Rhys), 1843-1922. • **3.4193**
Buddhist India. Freeport, N.Y., Books for Libraries Press [1972] xv, 332 p. illus. 23 cm. Reprint of the 1903 ed. issued in series: The story of the nations. 1. Buddhism — India. 2. India — History — 324 B.C. to 1000 A.D. 3. India — Civilization — To 1200 4. India — History — To 324 B.C. I. T.
DS425.D37 1972   915.4/03   LC 78-38349   ISBN 0836967666

Drekmeier, Charles. • **3.4194**
Kingship and community in early India. Stanford, Calif. Stanford University Press 1962. 369p. 1. India — Civilization 2. India — Religion I. T.
DS425 D7

Renou, Louis, 1896-1966. • **3.4195**
The civilization of ancient India. [2d ed.] Calcutta Susil Gupta [India] Private Ltd. [1959] 189p. 1. India — Civilization 2. Civilization, Hindu I. T.
DS425 R433 1959

Ikram, Sheikh Mohamad, 1908-. • **3.4196**
Muslim civilization in India, by S. M. Ikram. Edited by Ainslie T. Embree. — New York: Columbia University Press, 1964. x, 325 p.: maps.; 25 cm. 'An abridgment of the author's fuller History of Muslim civilization in India and Pakistan (712-1858), published in Lahore in 1962.' 1. Civilization, Islamic I. T.
DS427.I42   915.4   LC 64-14656

Qureshi, Ishtiaq Husain. • **3.4197**
The Muslim community of the Indo–Pakistan sub–continent, 610–1947; a brief historical analysis. 's-Gravenhage, Mouton, 1962. 334 p. 25 cm. 1. Muslims — India I. T.
DS427.Q8   LC 63-2042

Kopf, David. **3.4198**
The Brahmo Samaj and the shaping of the modern Indian mind / David Kopf. — Princeton, N.J.: Princeton Univerity Press, c1979. xxiii, 399 p.; 25 cm. Includes index. 1. Intellectuals — Bengal. 2. Brahma-samaj 3. Bengal (India) — Intellectual life. 4. India — Intellectual life. I. T.
DS428.K66   LC 78-70303   ISBN 0691031258

Plain tales from the Raj: images of British India in the **3.4199**
twentieth century / edited by Charles Allen, in association with Michael Mason; introd. by Philip Mason.
New York: St. Martin's Press, 1976. 240 p., [8] leaves of plates: ill.; 25 cm. 1. British in India. 2. India — Description and travel — 1901-1946 I. Allen, Charles, 1940- II. Mason, Michael, 1924-
DS428.P55 1976   954/.004/21   LC 76-8693

Spear, Thomas George Percival. • **3.4200**
The nabobs; a study of the social life of the English in eighteenth century India, by Percival Spear. — Gloucester, Mass.: P. Smith, 1971 [c1963] xxi, 213 p.: illus.; 21 cm. 1. British in India. 2. India — Social life and customs 3. India — Politics and government — 1765-1947 I. T.
DS428.S6 1971   915.4/06/2   LC 71-22849

DS430–432 ETHNOGRAPHY

Anthropological Survey of India. • **3.4201**
Peasant life in India: a study in Indian unity & diversity / edited by Kirmal Kumar Bose. — Calcutta: [s.n.], 1961. [15] leaves of plates: ill., maps, plans. — (Memoir (Anthropological Survey of India) no. 8) 1. Ethnology — India 2. Peasantry — India I. T. II. Series.
DS430 A5   DS430 A5.   LC SA 66-5983

Majumdar, Dhirendra Nath. **3.4202**
Races and cultures of India. [4th rev. and enl. ed.] New York, Asia Pub. House [1961] 483 p. illus. 23 cm. 1. Ethnology — India 2. India — Social life and customs I. T.
DS430.M3 1961   LC 61-65566

Schermerhorn, R. A. (Richard Alonzo), 1903-. **3.4203**
Ethnic plurality in India / R. A. Schermerhorn. — Tucson: University of Arizona Press, c1978. xii, 369 p.: ill.; 24 cm. 1. Ethnology — India 2. Minorities — India. 3. India — Social life and customs I. T.
DS430.S28   301.45/0954   LC 77-75662   ISBN 0816506124. ISBN 0816505780 pbk

Fürer-Haimendorf, Christoph von, 1909-. **3.4204**
A Himalayan tribe: from cattle to cash / Christoph von Fürer–Haimendorf. — Berkeley: University of California Press, c1980. xi, 224 p., [8] leaves of plates: ill.; 23 cm. Includes index. 1. Apa Tanis I. T.
DS432.A6 F79   305.8/00954/163   LC 80-10732   ISBN 0520040740

Mines, Mattison, 1941-. **3.4205**
The warrior merchants: textiles, trade, and territory in South India / Mattison Mines. — Cambridge [Cambridgeshire]; New York: Cambridge University Press, 1985 (c1984). xiii, 178 p.: maps; 24 cm. Includes index. 1. Kaikōlar 2. India, South — Economic conditions. 3. India, South — Social conditions. I. T.
DS432.K17 M56 1984   306/.09548 19   LC 84-5899   ISBN 0521267145

Gorer, Geoffrey, 1905-. • **3.4206**
Himalayan village; an account of the Lepchas of Sikkim. With a new foreword by the author. — 2d ed. — New York: Basic Books, [1967] 488 p.: illus., map, ports.; 24 cm. 1. Lepchas I. T.
DS432.L4 G6 1967   390   LC 67-22188

Fuller, C. J. (Christopher John), 1949-. **3.4207**
The Nayars today / by C. J. Fuller. — Cambridge; New York: Cambridge University Press, 1977 (c1976). xi, 173 p.: ill.; 23 cm. (Changing cultures) Based, in part, on the author's thesis, University of Manchester, 1974. Includes index. 1. Nairs — Social life and customs. 2. Kinship — India — Kerala (State) I. T.
DS432.N324 F84   301.45/19/48/05483   LC 76-11078   ISBN 0521213010

Orans, Martin. • **3.4208**
The Santals. : Wayne State University Press, 1965. xiv, 154 p. 1. Santals — Social life and customs. I. T.
DS432.S2 O7   305.895   LC 65-12595

Leaf, Murray J. **3.4209**
Information and behavior in a Sikh village: social organization reconsidered / [by] Murray J. Leaf. — Berkeley: University of California Press, [1972] xi, 296 p.: ill.; 24 cm. 1. Sikhs 2. Villages — India — Punjab — Case studies. I. T.
DS432.S5 L43   301.29/54/552   LC 78-172390   ISBN 0520021150

McLeod, W. H. **3.4210**
The evolution of the Sikh community: five essays / W. H. McLeod. Oxford: Clarendon Press, 1976. viii, 119 p.; 23 cm. Includes index. 1. Sikhs — Addresses, essays, lectures. 2. Sikhism — Addresses, essays, lectures. I. T.
DS432.S5 M25   294.6/0954/552   LC 76-369262   ISBN 0198265298

Daniel, E. Valentine. **3.4211**
Fluid signs: being a person the Tamil way / E. Valentine Daniel. — Berkeley: University of California Press, 1985 (c1984). xiv, 320 p.; 22 cm. Includes index. 1. Tamils 2. Semiotics I. T.
DS432.T3 D3 1984   306/.089948 19   LC 84-163   ISBN 0520047257

DS433–485 HISTORY

Bhattacharya, Sachchidananda. • **3.4212**
A dictionary of Indian history. — [1st American ed.]. — New York: G. Braziller, [c1967] xii, 888 p.; 22 cm. 1. India — History — Dictionaries. I. T.
DS433.B48 1967b   954/.003   LC 68-19984

Mehra, Parshotam. **3.4213**
A dictionary of modern Indian history, 1707–1947 / Parshotam Mehra. — Delhi; New York: Oxford University Press, 1985. xv, 823 p.: maps; 25 cm. Maps on lining papers. Includes index. 1. India — History — British occupation, 1765-1947 — Dictionaries. 2. India — History — 1500-1765 — Dictionaries. I. T.
DS433.M43 1985   954.03/03/21 19   LC 85-904016

Philips, Cyril Henry, 1912- ed. **3.4214**
Historians of India, Pakistan and Ceylon. London, Oxford University Press, 1961. 504 p. (School of Oriental and African Studies, University of London. Historical writing on the peoples of Asia [1]) 1. Ceylon — History —

Historiography. 2. India — History — Historiography. 3. Pakistan — History
— Historiography. I. T.
DS435.Px

Warder, Anthony Kennedy.   • 3.4215
An introduction to Indian historiography [by] A. K. Warder. Bombay, Popular
Prakashan [1972] xii, 196 p. 22 cm. (Monographs of the Department of Sanskrit
and Indian Studies, University of Toronto, 1) 1. India — Historiography. I. T.
DS435.W37   954/.007/2   LC 72-904916

Hardy, Peter.   • 3.4216
Historians of medieval India; studies in Indo–Muslim historical writing.
London Luzac 1960. 146p. 1. Historians, Indic I. T.
DS435.5 H3

Crane. Robert I.   • 3.4217
The history of India: its study and interpretation. — Washington: Service
Center for Teachers of History, [1958] 46 p.; 23 cm. — (Service Center for
Teachers of History. Publication; no. 17) 1. India — History — Bibliography.
I. T. II. Series.
DS435.8.C7   Z3206.C7.   LC 58-59932

Singer, Milton B.   • 3.4218
Introducing India in liberal education. Chicago, University of Chicago [1957]
xiii, 287 p. 23 cm. 1. India — Civilization — Study and teaching. I. University
of Chicago. II. T.
DS435.8.S5   LC 57-4500

Nilakanta Sastri, K. A. (Kallidaikurichi Aiyah), 1892-1975.   • 3.4219
A history of South India from prehistoric times to the fall of Vijayanagar. 3d ed.
[Madras] Indian Branch, Oxford University Press 1966. 520p. 1. South India
— History I. T.
DS436 A1 N53 1966

Allan, John, 1884-1955.   • 3.4220
The Cambridge shorter history of India, by J. Allan, Sir T. Wolseley Haig [and]
H.H. Dodwell. [2d ed.] Edited by H.H. Dodwell. With additional chapters on
The last phase, 1919-1947 by R.R. Sethi. [2d ed.] Delhi: S. Chand, 1964. xxi,
784, xxxxvii p.: maps; 23 cm. Includes bibliography. I. Haig, Sir Wolseley,
1865-1938, jt. author II. Dodwell, Henry, 1879-1946. III. T.
DS436.A36 1964

The Cambridge history of India.   3.4221
Cambridge: University Press, 1922-. v.: ill., maps; 24 cm. — 1. India — History
I. Rapson, E. J. (Edward James), 1861-1937.
DS436.C22   LC 22-11272

Wheeler, Robert Eric Mortimer, Sir, 1890-.   • 3.4222
The Indus civilization: supplementary volume to the Cambridge history of
India / by Mortimer Wheeler. — 3d ed. — Cambridge: University Press, 1968.
xi, 143 p., [34] leaves of plates: ill., plans (1 fold.); 24 cm. 1. Mohenjo-daro
2. Harappa, Pakistan 3. India — History — To 324 B.C. I. T.
DS436.C22 Suppl. 1968   ISBN 0521069580

Griffiths, Percival Joseph, Sir, 1899-.   • 3.4223
Modern India, by Sir Percival Griffiths. — 4th ed. — New York: F. A. Praeger,
[1965] 311 p.: maps (1 fold.); 23 cm. — (Nations of the modern world.) 1. India
— History 2. India — Politics and government — 1947- 3. India — Economic
conditions — 1947- I. T. II. Series.
DS436.G7 1965   320.954   LC 65-14181

Smith, Vincent Arthur, 1848-1920.   3.4224
The Oxford history of India / by Vincent A. Smith. — 4th ed. / edited by
Percival Spear. — Delhi; New York: Oxford University Press, 1981. xv, 945 p.,
40, [1] p. of plates (some folded): ill., maps; 18 cm. 1. India — History I. Spear,
Thomas George Percival. II. T.
DS436.S55 1981   954 19   LC 81-181065   ISBN 0195612973

Spear, Thomas George Percival.   3.4225
India: a modern history / by Percival Spear. — New ed., rev. and enl. — Ann
Arbor: University of Michigan Press, [1972] x, 511, xix p.: illus.; 25 cm. —
(University of Michigan history of the modern world) 1. India — History I. T.
DS436.S68 1972   954   LC 72-81334   ISBN 0472071408

Thapar, Romila.   • 3.4226
A history of India. Baltimore, Penguin Books [1965-66, v. 2, 1965] 2 v. maps,
plans. 19 cm. (Pelican books, A769-A770) Vol. 2 by Percival Spear. 1. India —
History I. Spear, Thomas George Percival. II. T.
DS436.T37   954   LC 66-31497

Wolpert, Stanley A., 1927-.   3.4227
A new history of India / Stanley Wolpert. — New York: Oxford University
Press, 1977. xiii, 471 p.: maps. 1. India — History I. T.
DS436.W66   954   LC 76-42678   ISBN 0195021541

DS444–450 Political and Diplomatic History

Keith, Arthur Berriedale, 1879-1944. ed.   • 3.4228
Speeches & documents on Indian policy, 1750–1921. London Oxford
University Press [1922] (The World's classics, 231-232) 1. East India
Company (English) 2. India — Politics and government — 1765-1947 I. T.
DS446.3 K4

Bandyopadhyaya, Jayantanuja.   3.4229
The making of India's foreign policy: determinants, institutions, processes, and
personalities / Jayantanuja Bandyopadhyaya. — Rev. ed. — Bombay: Allied
Publishers, 1980. xiii, 361 p. 1. India — Foreign relations I. T.
DS448 B34 1980

Lajpat Rai, Lala, 1865-1928.   • 3.4230
Young India; an interpretation and a history of the nationalist movement from
within. — New York: Howard Fertig, 1968. xxvi, 257 p.: ports.; 21 cm. Reprint
of the 1916 ed. 1. India — Politics and government — 1765-1947 I. T.
DS448.L35 1968   320.9/54   LC 67-24593

Lovett, Harrington Verney, Sir, 1864-1945.   • 3.4231
A history of the Indian nationalist movement. — [3d ed.]. — New York: A. M.
Kelley, 1969. 303 p.; 23 cm. — (Reprints of economic classics) Reprint of the
1921 ed. 1. India — Politics and government — 1765-1947 I. T.
DS448.L7 1969   954.035   LC 79-94540   ISBN 0678051003

Rana, A. P.   3.4232
The imperatives of nonalignment: a conceptual study of India's foreign policy
strategy in the Nehru period / A. P. Rana. — Delhi: Macmillan Co. of India,
1976. xiii, 322 p.; 23 cm. Includes index. 1. Nehru, Jawaharlal, 1889-1964.
2. India — Foreign relations I. T.
DS448.R29   327.54   LC 76-902128

Labh, Kapileshwar, 1938-.   3.4233
India and Bhutan. [1st ed. New Delhi] Sindhu Publications [1974] vi, 275 p. 22
cm. (Studies in Asian history and politics, 1) 'Revised and enlarged version of
[the author's] thesis, 'India and Bhutan: 1858-1910,' approved for the Ph.D.
degree of the Indian School of International Studies ...' 1. India — Relations —
Bhutan 2. Bhutan — Relations — India I. T. II. Series.
DS450.B48 L3 1974   327.54/05498   LC 74-901370

Mehra, Parshotam.   3.4234
The McMahon Line and after: a study of the triangular contest on India's
north–eastern frontier between Britain, China, and Tibet, 1904–47 / Parshotam
Mehra. — Columbia, Mo.: South Asia Books, 1975 (c1974). xxx, 497 p.: maps;
25 cm. Includes index. 1. India — Boundaries — China. 2. China —
Boundaries — India. 3. Tibet (China) — Boundaries — India. 4. India —
Boundaries — Tibet (China). I. T.
DS450.C5 M4   327/.1011   ISBN 0883866161

Mohan Ram, 1933-.   3.4235
Politics of Sino–Indian confrontation. — Delhi: Vikas Pub. House, [1973] vi,
241 p.; 22 cm. 1. India — Foreign relations — China. 2. China — Foreign
relations — India. I. T.
DS450.C5 M64   327.54/051   LC 73-905939

Woodman, Dorothy.   • 3.4236
Himalayan frontiers: a political review of British, Chinese, Indian and Russian
rivalries. London, Barrie & Rockliff the Cresset P., 1969. xv, 423 p., 3 fold.
plates. facsim., maps. 23 cm. 1. Himalaya Mountains Region — Politics and
government. 2. India — Boundaries — China. 3. China — Boundaries —
India. I. T.
DS450.C5 W6   327.54   LC 76-464891   ISBN 0248997270

Banerji, Arun Kumar, 1944-.   3.4237
India and Britain, 1947–1968: the evolution of post–colonial relations / Arun
Kumar Banerji. — Columbia, Mo. South Asia Books 1978,c1977. viii, 341 p.;
22 cm. A revision of the author's thesis, University of London, 1972. Includes
index. 1. India — Foreign relations — Great Britain. 2. Great Britain —
Foreign relations — India. I. T.
DS450.G7 B36 1978   327.54/041   ISBN 0883869039

Ghosh, Sucheta, 1949-.   3.4238
The role of India in the emergence of Bangladesh / Sucheta Ghosh. — Calcutta:
Minerva Associates (Publications), 1983. 273 p.; 22 cm. Revision of the
author's thesis (Ph. D.—Jadavpur University, 1979) Includes index. 1. India
— Foreign relations — Pakistan. 2. Pakistan — Foreign relations — India.
3. Bangladesh — History — Revolution, 1971 I. T.
DS450.P18 G48 1983   327.5405492 19   LC 83-906917   ISBN
0836407806

DS451–481 History, by Period

DS451 To 997

Essays on Gupta culture / edited by Bardwell L. Smith.   **3.4239**
1st ed. — Columbia, Mo.: South Asia Books, 1983. xvii, 360 p., [72] p. of plates: ill.; 23 cm. 1. Gupta dynasty — Addresses, essays, lectures. 2. India — Civilization — To 1200 — Addresses, essays, lectures. 3. India — History — 324 B.C.-1000 A.D. I. Smith, Bardwell L., 1925-
DS451.E84 1983b   934/.06 19   *LC* 83-905898   *ISBN* 0836408713

Majumdar, Ramesh Chandra.   **3.4240**
Ancient India / R. C. Majumdar. — [Rev. i.e. 2d ed.] Delhi: Motilal Banarsidass, 1964. xvi, 538 p.: plates.; 23 cm. 1. India — History I. T.
DS451.M25

Mookerji, Radhakumud, 1884-1964.   • **3.4241**
The Gupta Empire. — [4th ed.]. — Delhi: Motilal Banarsidass, [1969] viii, 174 p.: illus., geneal. tables.; 25 cm. Label mounted on t.p.: Distributed by Lawrence Verry, Mystic, Conn. 1. Gupta dynasty. I. T.
DS451.M66 1969   934/.06   *LC* 74-17404

Narain, A. K.   • **3.4242**
The Indo–Greeks. Oxford Clarendon Press [1962] 201p. 1. Greeks in India 2. Bactria — History 3. Numismatics — India I. T.
DS451 N37 1962

Piggott, Stuart.   • **3.4243**
Prehistoric India to 1000 B. C. Harmondsworth, Middlesex Penguin Books [1950] 293 p. illus., maps. 19 cm. (Pelican books, A205) 1. India — Antiquities 2. India — History — To 324 B.C. I. T.
DS451.P46   *LC* 51-3580

Rawlinson, H. G. (Hugh George), 1880-.   • **3.4244**
Intercourse between India and the Western World; from the earliest times to the fall of Rome, by H. G. Rawlinson. 2d ed. New York, Octagon Books, 1971. vi, 196 p. illus. 24 cm. Reprint of the 1926 ed. 1. India — History — To 324 B.C. 2. India — History — 324 B.C.-1000 A.D. 3. India — Relations — Foreign countries 4. India — Commerce — History. 5. India — Civilization — Occidental influences. I. T.
DS451.R3 1971   301.29/34/01821   *LC* 75-159221   *ISBN* 0374967210

Tarn, W. W. (William Woodthorpe), 1869-1957.   **3.4245**
The Greeks in Bactria & India / by W.W. Tarn. — 3rd ed. / updated with a preface and new bibliography by Frank Lee Holt. — Chicago: Ares Publishers, 1985. — lix, 561 p.; 21 cm. Includes bibliographical references and index. Recent research on ancient Bactria: p. xix-xlii. 1. Greeks — India — History 2. Hellenism 3. India — History — 324 B.C.-1000 A.D. 4. Bactria — History I. T. II. Title: The Greeks in Bactria and India
DS451.T3 1985   *ISBN* 0890055246

Wheeler, Robert Eric Mortimer, Sir, 1890-.   • **3.4246**
Early India and Pakistan: to Ashoka [by] Sir Mortimer Wheeler. — Rev. ed. — New York: Praeger, [1968, c1959] 241 p.: illus., maps, plans.; 21 cm. — (Ancient peoples and places, v. 12) 1. India — Antiquities 2. Pakistan — Antiquities 3. India — History — To 324 B.C. I. T.
DS451.W48 1968   934   *LC* 68-28335

Mookerji, Radhakumud, 1884-1964.   • **3.4247**
Asoka / by Radhakumud Mookerji. — [3d, rev. ed.]. — Delhi: Motilal Banarsidass, 1962. xii, 289 p.: ill. 'Translation and annotation of the inscriptions', 'Text of the inscriptions': p. 107-254. 1. Aśoka, King of Magadha, fl. 259 B.C. 2. Inscriptions, Prakrit I. T.
DS451.5.M6 1962

Thapar, Romila.   • **3.4248**
Aśoka and the decline of the Mauryas / by Romila Thapar. — Delhi: Oxford University Press, [c1961]. viii, 283 p.: ill., map, facsims.; 19 cm. 1. Aśoka, King of Magadha, fl. 259 B.C. 2. Maurya dynasty I. T.
DS451.5 T5 1973   934.04   *ISBN* 0195603796

Mookerji, Radhakumud, 1884-1964.   • **3.4249**
Chandragupta Maurya and his times / by Radha Kumud Mookerji. — 4th ed. — Delhi: Motilal Banarsidass, 1966. xvi, 263 p. — (Sir William Meyer lectures. 1940-41) 1. Chandragupta Maurya, Emperor of Northern India. 2. India — History — To 324 B.C. 3. India — Politics and government — To 997 I. T. II. Series.
DS451.9.C5 M6 1966   *LC* 67-3518

DS452–462 MOSLEM RULE (997–1761). MOGUL EMPIRE (1526–1761)

Kulkarni, V. B.   **3.4250**
India and Pakistan; a historical survey of Hindu–Muslim relations, by V. B. Kulkarni. — Bombay: Jaico Pub. House, 1974 (c1973). vi, 528 p.; 22 cm. 1. Muslims — India 2. Hindus 3. India — Foreign relations — Pakistan. 4. Pakistan — Foreign relations — India. I. T.
DS452.K84   915.4   *LC* 74-900211

Elliot, Henry Miers, Sir, 1808-1853.   • **3.4251**
The history of India, as told by its own historians: the Muhammadan period: the posthumous papers of the late Sir H. M. Elliot, K.C.B. / edited and continued by John Dowson. — 1st Indian ed. — Allahabad: Kitab Mahal, [1963-1964] 8 v.; 23 cm. 1. India — History — 1000-1526 2. India — History — 1500-1765 I. Dowson, John, 1820-1881. II. T. III. Title: The posthumous papers of the late Sir H. M. Elliot, K.C.B.
DS457.E552   954.02   *LC* 64-4320

Edwardes, S. M. (Stephen Meredyth), 1873-1927.   • **3.4252**
Mughal rule in India, by S.M. Edwardes and H.L.O. Garrett. London, Oxford University Press, 1930. 374 p. illus. 1. Mogul Empire 2. India — History — 1500-1765 I. Garrett, H. L. O. (Herbert Leonard Offley), 1881-1941. II. T.
DS461.E4   954.025

Gascoigne, Bamber.   **3.4253**
The great Moghuls [by] Bamber Gascoigne. Photos. by Christina Gascoigne. — [1st U.S. ed.]. — New York: Harper & Row, [1971] 264 p.: illus., col. plates.; 26 cm. 1. Mogul Empire 2. India — History — 1500-1765 I. Gascoigne, Christina, 1938 or 9- illus. II. T.
DS461.G3 1971   954/.025   *LC* 77-152348   *ISBN* 0060114673

Spear, Thomas George Percival.   • **3.4254**
Twilight of the Mughuls; studies in late Mughul Delhi. Cambridge, [Eng.] University Press, 1951. x, 269 p. plates, fold. map. 23 cm. Photocopy. Ann Arbor, Mich., University Microfilms, 1978. 1. Mogul Empire 2. Delhi (India) — History. I. T.
DS 461 S74 1951   *LC* 51-7304

Smith, Vincent Arthur, 1848-1920.   • **3.4255**
Akbar, the Great Mogul, 1542–1605. 2d ed., rev. Delhi S. Chand 1966. 379p. 1. Akbar, Emperor of Hindustan, 1542-1605. 2. Mogul Empire I. T.
DS461.3 S5 1966

Bernier, François, 1620-1688.   • **3.4256**
Travels in the Mogul empire, A. D. 1656–1668. A rev. and improved [2d] ed. based upon Irving Brock's translation, by Archibald Constable. Rev. and improved [2] ed. Delhi S. Chand [1968] 497p. 1. Mogul Empire 2. India — History — 1500-1765 3. India — Description and travel — 1498-1761 4. India — Social life and customs I. Brock, Irving, tr. II. Constable, Archibald, ed. III. T.
DS461.7 B513 1968

Sarkar, Sir Jadunath, 1870-1958.   • **3.4257**
A short history of Aurangzib: 1618-1707 / Sir Jadunath Sarkar ... (Abridged from the larger work in five volumes). — 3rd ed. — Calcutta: M.C. Sarkar, 1962. 478 p. 1. Aurangzeb, Emperor of Hindustan, 1618-1707. 2. Mogul Empire 3. India — History — 1500-1765 I. T.
DS461.7 S32   DS461.7 S32 1962.

Irvine, William, 1840-1911.   • **3.4258**
Later Mughals. Edited and augmented with the History of Nadir Shah's invasion, by Jadunath Sarkar. — New Delhi: Oriental Books Reprint Corp.; [exclusively distributed by Munshiram Manoharlal, Delhi, 1971] 2 v. in 1. (xxxi, 432, 392 p.): port.; 23 cm. First published in 1921-22 in 2 v. 1. Mogul Empire 2. India — History — 18th century I. Sarkar, Jadunath, Sir, 1870-1958. ed. II. T.
DS461.8.I72   *LC* 73-919253

Hutchinson, Lester, 1904-.   • **3.4259**
European freebooters in Moghul India. New York, Asia Pub. House [c1964] vii, 192 p. map, ports. 23 cm. 1. India — History — 18th century I. T.
DS462.H87   954.029   *LC* 65-16107

DS463–480.83 ENGLISH RULE (1761–1947)

Bearce, George Donham, 1922-.   • **3.4260**
British attitudes towards India, 1784–1858. — [London, New York] Oxford University Press, 1961. 315 p. 23 cm. 1. Gt. Brit. — Relations (general) with India. 2. India — Relations (general) with Great Britain. I. T.
DS463.B35   327.42054   *LC* 61-66608

Guha, Ranajit. 3.4261
Elementary aspects of peasant insurgency in colonial India / Ranajit Guha. — Delhi: Oxford, 1983. viii, 361 p.; 23 cm. Includes index. 1. Peasant uprisings — India. 2. India — Politics and government — 1765-1947 I. T.
DS463.G84 1983　　　954.03 19　　　*LC* 83-904630　　　*ISBN* 0195615174

Hardy, Peter. 3.4262
The Muslims of British India [by] P. Hardy. — [London]: Cambridge University Press, 1973 (c1972). ix, 306 p.: maps.; 22 cm. — (Cambridge South Asian studies, no. 13) 1. Muslims — India 2. India — Politics and government — 1765-1947 I. T.
DS463.H37　　　320.9/54/03　　　*LC* 77-184772　　　*ISBN* 0521084881

Hutchins, Francis G. 3.4263
The illusion of permanence: British imperialism in India / by Francis G. Hutchins. — Princeton, N.J.: Princeton University Press, 1967. xv, 217 p.; 23 cm. 1. Great Britain — History — British occupation, 1765-1947. 2. Great Britain — Foreign relations — India. 3. India — Foreign relations — Great Britain. 4. India — History — British occupation, 1765-1947 I. T.
DS463 H85　　　327.42/054　　　*LC* 67-15828

Low, D. A. (Donald Anthony), 1927-. 3.4264
Soundings in modern South Asian history / edited by D. A. Low. — Berkeley: University of California Press, 1968. viii, 391 p.: fold. map.; 22 cm. 1. India — History — British occupation, 1765-1947 — Addresses, essays, lectures. I. T.
DS463.L68　　　954.03　　　*LC* 68-20442

Mason, Philip. • 3.4265
The men who ruled India / by Philip Woodruff [pseud.] — New York: Schocken Books, 1964. 2 v.: maps. — (Shocken books; SB69) 1. India — History — 1500-1765 2. India — History — British occupation, 1765-1947 I. T.
DS463.M263　　　*LC* 64-13320

Moorhouse, Geoffrey, 1931-. 3.4266
India Britannica / Geoffrey Moorhouse. — 1st U.S. ed. — New York: Harper & Row, c1983. 288 p.: ill. (some col.); 25 cm. Maps on lining papers. Includes index. 1. India — Politics and government — 1765-1947 I. T.
DS463.M73 1983　　　954 19　　　*LC* 82-48127　　　*ISBN* 0060151153

Murphey, Rhoads, 1919-. 3.4267
The outsiders: the Western experience in India and China / Rhoads Murphey. — Ann Arbor: University of Michigan Press, c1977. ix, 299 p., [4] leaves of plates: ill.; 24 cm. — (Michigan studies on China.) Includes index. 1. India — History — British occupation, 1765-1947 2. India — History — 1500-1765 3. India — Relations — Europe 4. Europe — Relations — India 5. China — Relations — Europe 6. Europe — Relations — China 7. East and West I. T. II. Series.
DS463.M84 1977　　　DS463 M845 1977.　　　954.03　　　*LC* 76-27279
　　　ISBN 0472086790

Thompson, Edward John, 1886-1946. 3.4268
The other side of the medal. 2nd ed. — London, Hogarth Press, 1926. 143 p. 1. India — History I. T.
DS463.T5 1926a

Thompson, Edward John, 1886-1946. • 3.4269
Rise and fulfilment of British rule in India / by Edward Thompson and G. T. Garrat. — London: Macmillan, 1934. 690 p.: maps, tables; 23 cm. 1. India — History — 1500-1765 2. India — History — British occupation, 1765-1947 3. India — Politics and government I. Garratt, Geoffrey Theodore, 1888-1942, jt. author II. T.
DS463 T516 1934

Moon, Penderel, 1905-. • 3.4270
Warren Hastings and British India. New York, Macmillan, 1949. ix, 361 p. port., maps (on lining papers) 18 cm. (Teach yourself history library) 'Note on books': p. 355-356. 1. Hastings, Warren, 1732-1818. I. T.
DS473.M82 1949　　　923.254　　　*LC* 49-10373 *

British imperial policy in India and Sri Lanka, 1858–1912: a 3.4271
reassessment / editors, Robert I. Crane and N. Gerald Barrier.
New Delhi: Heritage Publishers, [1981] 237 p.; 23 cm. Includes index. 1. India — Politics and government — 1857-1919 2. Sri Lanka — Politics and government I. Crane. Robert I. II. Barrier, N. Gerald (Norman Gerald)
DS475.B78　　　320.954 19　　　*LC* 81-901189

Brown, Judith M. (Judith Margaret), 1944-. 3.4272
Modern India: the origins of an Asian democracy / Judith M. Brown. — Delhi; New York: Oxford University Press, 1985. xvi, 429 p., [2] p. of plates: maps; 24 cm. — (Short Oxford history of the modern world.) Includes index. 1. India — History — 19th century 2. India — History — 20th century I. T. II. Series.
DS475.B79 1985　　　954 19　　　*LC* 83-11465　　　*ISBN* 0199131244

People, princes, and paramount power: society and politics in 3.4273
the Indian princely states / edited by Robin Jeffrey.
Delhi: Oxford University Press, 1979 (c1978). xii, 396 p.; 23 cm. 1. India — Politics and government — 1765-1947 2. India — History, Local. 3. India — Kings and rulers I. Jeffrey, Robin.
DS475.P4　　　320.9/54/03　　　*LC* 79-111136　　　*ISBN* 0195608860

Seal, Anil. • 3.4274
The emergence of Indian nationalism: competition and collaboration in the later nineteenth century. — London: Cambridge U.P., 1968. xvi, 416 p.: maps.; 23 cm. — (Political change in modern South Asia) 1. Nationalism — India. 2. India — Politics and government — 19th century I. T. II. Series.
DS475.S4　　　320.9/54　　　*LC* 68-18344　　　*ISBN* 0521062748

Lethbridge, Roper, Sir, 1840-1919. 3.4275
[Golden book of India] Prominent Indians of Victorian age: a biographical dictionary / by Sir Robert Lethbridge; preface by Shiv Lal. — New Delhi: Archives Rare Prints: Distributors, Archives Publishers Distributors, 1985. 584 p.: ill.; 25 cm. Reprint. The golden book of India, 1893. 1. India — History — 19th century — Biography — Dictionaries. 2. India — Biography — Dictionaries. I. T.
DS475.2.A2 L47 1985　　　920/.054 19　　　*LC* 85-904169

Embree, Ainslie Thomas. • 3.4276
Charles Grant and British rule in India. New York, Columbia University Press, 1962. 320 p. 23 cm. (Columbia studies in the social sciences, no. 606) 1. Grant, Charles, 1746-1823. 2. East India Company. 3. India — History — British occupation, 1765-1947 I. T.
DS475.2.G7 E4 1962a　　　*LC* 62-7591

Hibbert, Christopher, 1924-. 3.4277
The Great Mutiny: India, 1857 / Christopher Hibbert. — New York: Viking Press, 1978. 472 p., [12] leaves of plates: ill.; 25 cm. Includes index. 1. India — History — Sepoy Rebellion, 1857-1858 I. T.
DS478.H488 1978　　　954.03/17　　　*LC* 78-15825　　　*ISBN* 0670349836

The Last Empire: photography in British India, 1855–1911 / 3.4278
pref. by the Earl Mountbatten of Burma; with texts by Clark
Worswick and Ainslie Embree.
Millerton, N.Y.: Aperture, c1976. 146, [2] p.: ill.; 26 x 30 cm. 'Accompanies an exhibition organized by the Asia House Gallery of the Asia Society for the summer of 1976.' 1. India — History — British occupation, 1765-1947 — Pictorial works. I. Worswick, Clark. II. Embree, Ainslie Thomas. III. Asia House Gallery.
DS479.L28 1976　　　779/.9/954035　　　*LC* 76-21208　　　*ISBN* 091233486X

Metcalf, Thomas R., 1934-. • 3.4279
The aftermath of revolt: India, 1857–1870, by Thomas R. Metcalf. Princeton, N. J., Princeton University Press, 1964. xi, 352 p. maps (1 fold.) 21 cm. Bibliography: p. 329-337. 1. India — Politics and government — 1765-1947 I. T.
DS479.M46　　　954.035　　　*LC* 63-23412

Philips, Cyril Henry, 1912- ed. • 3.4280
The evolution of India and Pakistan, 1858 to 1947; select documents. With the co-operation of H. L. Singh and B. N. Pandey. — London, New York, Oxford University Press, 1962. xxi, 786 p. 25 cm. — (Select documents on the history of India and Pakistan, v. 4) Bibliographical footnotes. 1. India — Hist. — 1765-1947 — Sources. I. T. II. Series.
DS479.P5　　　954.03　　　*LC* 62-52888

Dayal, Deen. 3.4281
Princely India: photographs by Raja Deen Dayal, 1884–1910 / edited and with text by Clark Worswick; foreword by John Kenneth Galbraith. — 1st ed. — New York: Knopf, 1980. 151 p.: chiefly ill.; 24 x 29 cm. 1. Khan, Mahboob Ali, Sir, Nizam of Hyderabad, 1866-1911 — Iconography. 2. Hyderabad (India: State) — Court and courtiers — Pictorial works. 3. Hyderabad (India: State) — Kings and rulers — Iconography. I. Worswick, Clark. II. T.
DS479.1.K57 D38 1980　　　779/.9/95484035　　　*LC* 79-3506　　　*ISBN* 039450772X

Ahmad, Jamil-ud-Din. comp. 3.4282
Historic documents of the Muslim freedom movement. Compiled by Jamil-ud-Din Ahmad. — Lahore: Publishers United, 1972 (c1970) xvi, 575 p.; 23 cm. 1. Muslims — India — History — Sources. 2. Pakistan movement — Sources. 3. India — History — 20th century — Sources. I. T.
DS480.45.A64　　　954.9/008　　　*LC* 74-931588

Āzād, Abūlkalām, 1888-1958. • 3.4283
India wins freedom; an autobiographical narrative. With introd. and explanatory notes by Louis Fischer. — [1st American ed.]. — New York, Longmans, Green, 1960. 293 p. illus. 22 cm. 1. India — Hist. — 20th cent. I. T.
DS480.45.A9 1960　　　954.03　　　*LC* 60-10882

Bose, Subhas Chandra, 1897-1945.   • **3.4284**
The Indian struggle, 1920–1942. Compiled by the Netaji Research Bureau, Calcutta. Bombay Asia Pub. House [1964] 476p. 1. India — Politics and government — 1919-1947 I. Netaji Research Bureau. II. T.
DS480.45 B6 1964

Dixit, Prabha.   **3.4285**
Communalism: a struggle for power / Prabha Dixit. — New Delhi: Orient Longman, 1974. xi, 236 p.; 23 cm. Includes index. 1. Muslims — India 2. Hindus 3. India — Politics and government I. T.
DS480.45.D57   322/.1/0954   LC 74-903679

Iqbal, Muhammad, Sir, 1877-1938.   **3.4286**
Speeches and statements of Iqbal. Compiled by A. R. Tariq. — [1st ed.]. — Lahore: Sh. Ghulam Ali, [1973] xxix, 246 p.; 23 cm. 1. Muslims — India — Addresses, essays, lectures. 2. India — Politics and government — 1919-1947 — Addresses, essays, lectures. I. Tariq, Abdur-Rahman, 1915- comp. II. T.
DS480.45.I6 1973   LC 73-930419

The Partition of India: policies and perspectives, 1935–1947.   • **3.4287**
Edited by C. H. Philips and Mary Doreen Wainwright.
Cambridge: M.I.T. Press, [1970, c1969] 607 p.; 25 cm. Proceedings of a conference held in London in 1967. 1. Muslims — India 2. India — Politics and government — 1919-1947 — Addresses, essays, lectures. I. Philips, Cyril Henry, 1912- ed. II. Wainwright, Mary Doreen.
DS480.45.P33 1970b   320.9/54   LC 77-118351   ISBN 0262160439

Ramusack, Barbara N.   **3.4288**
The princes of India in the twilight of Empire: dissolution of a patron–client system, 1914–1939 / Barbara N. Ramusack. — Columbus: Published for the University of Cincinnati by the Ohio State University Press, c1978. xxii, 322 p.: ill.; 24 cm. Includes index. 1. India — Politics and government — 20th century 2. India — Kings and rulers I. T.
DS480.45.R294   320.9/54/035   LC 78-18161   ISBN 0814202721

The Transfer of power 1942–7; editor–in–chief Nicholas   • **3.4289**
Mansergh, assistant editor E. W. R. Lumby.
London, H.M.S.O., 1970-1983. 12 v. facsims., col. maps. 28 cm. At head of title: Constitutional relations between Britain and India. On spine: India; the transfer of power 1942-7. Unpublished documents drawn either from the official archives of the India Office in the custody of the India Office Records or from the private collections of the Viceregal papers in the India Office Library. Beginning with v. 5, assistant editor P. Moon. 1. India — Politics and government — 1919-1947 — Sources. 2. India — History — British occupation, 1765-1947 — Sources. I. Mansergh, Nicholas. ed. II. Lumby, Esmond Walter Rawson. ed. III. Moon, Penderel, 1905- IV. India Office Records. V. India Office Library. VI. Title: Constitutional relations between Britain and India. VII. Title: India; the transfer of power 1942-7.
DS480.83.T7   327.42/054   LC 72-129254   ISBN 0115800166

DS480.84–481 1947-

Brown, W. Norman (William Norman), 1892-1975.   • **3.4290**
The United States and India, Pakistan, Bangladesh, by W. Norman Brown. — [3d ed.]. — Cambridge: Harvard University Press, 1972. ix, 462 p.: map.; 25 cm. — (American foreign policy library.) Previous editions published under title: The United States and India and Pakistan. 1. India — History — 1947- 2. Pakistan — History 3. Bangladesh — History I. T. II. Series.
DS480.84.B73 1972   954./4   LC 72-81270   ISBN 0674924460

Collins, Larry.   **3.4291**
Freedom at midnight / Larry Collins and Dominique Lapierre. — New York: Simon and Schuster, [1975] 572 p.: ill.; 24 cm. Includes index. 1. India — History — 1947- I. Lapierre, Dominique. joint author. II. T.
DS480.84.C75   954.04   LC 75-16123   ISBN 0671220888

Dean, Vera Micheles, 1903-1972.   • **3.4292**
New patterns of democracy in India. — 2d ed. — Cambridge, Mass.: Harvard University Press, 1969. xii, 255 p.: illus., map.; 22 cm. 1. India — Politics and government — 1947- 2. India — Economic conditions — 1947- I. T.
DS480.84.D38 1969   954.04   LC 79-78516

Gauba, Khalid Latif, 1899-.   **3.4293**
Passive voices: a penetrating study of Muslims in India / [by] K. L. Gauba. — [1st ed.]. — New Delhi: Sterling Publishers, [1973] ix, 396 p.; 22 cm. 1. Muslims — India 2. India — Politics and government — 1947- I. T.
DS480.84.G36   323.1/54   LC 73-907280

Morris-Jones, W. H. (Wyndraeth Humphreys)   • **3.4294**
The government and politics of India, [by] W. H. Morris–Jones. — London: Hutchinson University Library, 1964. 236 p.: maps.; 20 cm. — (Hutchinson university library: Politics) 1. India — Politics and government — 1947- I. T.
DS480.84.M59 1967   320.954   LC 65-3425   ISBN

Appadorai, A. (Angadipuram), 1902- India's foreign policy and   **3.4295**
relations 1947-72.
Select documents on India's foreign policy and relations, 1947–1972 / [edited by] A. Appadorai. — Delhi: Oxford University Press, 1983 (c1982) 751 p.; 23 cm. Running title: Documents on India's foreign policy, 1947-72. Companion volume to: India's foreign policy and relations 1947-72 / by A. Appadorai and M.S. Rajan. 1. India — Foreign relations — Sources. I. T. II. Title: Documents in India's foreign policy, 1947-72.
DS480.84.S3853 1982   327.54 19   LC 83-122485   ISBN 0195613090

Suri, Surindar.   **3.4296**
Politics and society in India / Surindar Suri. — 1st ed. — Calcutta: Naya Prokash, 1974. xii, 338 p.: map (on lining papers); 22 cm. 1. India — Politics and government — 1947- 2. India — Social conditions — 1947- I. T.
DS480.84.S867   320.9/54/05   LC 75-902444

Tinker, Hugh.   • **3.4297**
India and Pakistan; a political analysis. Rev. ed. New York: F. A. Praeger [1968, c1967] 248 p.: maps; 21 cm. (Praeger university series, U-526) 1. India — Politics and government — 1947- 2. Pakistan — Politics and government I. T.
DS480.84.T5 1968   320.9/54   LC 68-16097

Maxwell, Neville George Anthony.   • **3.4298**
India's China war [by] Neville Maxwell. — London: Cape, 1970. 475 p., 6 fold. plates.: 6 maps.; 23 cm. Maps on lining papers. 1. Sino-Indian Border Dispute, 1957- I. T.
DS480.85.M38   954/.04   LC 77-536579   ISBN 0224618873

Keer, Dhananjay.   • **3.4299**
Dr. Ambedkar; life and mission. [2d ed.] Bombay Popular Prakashan [1962] 528p. 1. Ambedkar, Bhimrao Ramji, 1892-1956. I. T.
DS481 A6 K4 1962

Brown, Emily Clara.   **3.4300**
Har Dayal, Hindu revolutionary and rationalist / Emily C. Brown. — Tucson: University of Arizona Press, [1975] xiv, 321 p.; 23 cm. Includes index. 1. Dayal, Har, 1884-1939. I. T.
DS481.D365 B76   954.03/5/0924 B   LC 74-16895   ISBN 0816504229

Carras, Mary C.   **3.4301**
Indira Gandhi: in the crucible of leadership: a political biography / Mary C. Carras. — Boston: Beacon Press, c1979. xvi, 289 p.; 21 cm. 1. Gandhi, Indira, 1917-1984. 2. Prime ministers — India — Biography. 3. India — Politics and government — 1947- I. T.
DS481.G23 C37 1979   954.04/092/4 B   LC 78-19598   ISBN 0807002429

Moraes, Dom F., 1938-.   **3.4302**
Indira Gandhi / Dom Moraes. — 1st American ed. — Boston: Little, Brown, c1980. xvi, 336 p., [8] leaves of plates: ill.; 24 cm. Includes index. 1. Gandhi, Indira, 1917-1984. 2. Prime ministers — India — Biography. I. T.
DS481.G23 M67 1980   954.04/5/0924 B 19   LC 80-21167   ISBN 0316581917

Sahgal, Nayantara, 1927-.   **3.4303**
Indira Gandhi's emergence and style / Nayantara Sahgal. — Durham, N.C.: Carolina Academic Press, c1978. ix, 215 p.; 22 cm. 1. Gandhi, Indira, 1917-1984. 2. Prime ministers — India — Biography. 3. India — Politics and government — 1947- I. T.
DS481.G23 S19 1978b   954.04/092/4 B   LC 78-54439   ISBN 0890890900

Gandhi, Mahatma, 1869-1948.   • **3.4304**
The essential Gandhi, an anthology. Edited by Louis Fischer. New York, Random House [1962] 369 p. 21 cm. I. Fischer, Louis, 1896-1970. ed. II. T.
DS481.G3 A17 1962   923.254   LC 62-8458

Gandhi, Mahatma, 1869-1948.   **3.4305**
Selected writings of Mahatma Gandhi; selected and introduced by Ronald Duncan. London, Fontana, 1971. 288 p. 18 cm. I. Duncan, Ronald Frederick Henry, 1914- ed. II. T.
DS481.G3 A17 1971   301.6/32/08   LC 73-156439   ISBN 000632620X

Gandhi, Mahatma, 1869-1948.   **3.4306**
[Selections. 1985] The encyclopaedia of Gandhian thoughts / [compiled by] Ananda T. Hingorani, Ganga A. Hingorani. — 1st ed. — New Delhi: All India Congress Committee (I), 1985. xxii, 399 p.; 24 cm. 1. Gandhi, Mahatma, 1869-1948 — Dictionaries, indexes, etc. I. Hingorani, Anand T. II. Hingorani, Ganga A. (Ganga Anand), 1917- III. T. IV. Title: Gandhian thoughts.
DS481.G3 A25 1985b   954.0350924   LC 86-901305   Rs100.00

Brown, Judith M. (Judith Margaret), 1944-.   **3.4307**
Gandhi and civil disobedience: the Mahatma in Indian politics, 1928–34 / Judith M. Brown. — Cambridge: Cambridge University Press, 1977. xix, 414 p.: ill.; 23 cm. Includes index. 1. Gandhi, Mahatma, 1869-1948. 2. Passive resistance — India. 3. India — Politics and government — 1919-1947 I. T.
DS481.G3 B73   954.03/5/0924 B   LC 76-10407   ISBN 0521212790

Fischer, Louis, 1896-1970.   • **3.4308**
The life of Mahatma Gandhi. [1st ed.] New York, Harper [1950] ix, 558 p. illus., ports., map (on lining papers) 22 cm. 1. Gandhi, Mahatma, 1869-1948. I. T.
DS481.G3 F44   923.254   LC 50-9391

The Meanings of Gandhi. Edited by Paul F. Power.   • **3.4309**
[1st ed. Honolulu] University Press of Hawaii [c1971] 199 p. port. 23 cm. 'An East-West Center book.' 1. Gandhi, Mahatma, 1869-1948 — Addresses, essays, lectures. 2. Passive resistance — Addresses, essays, lectures. I. Power, Paul F., ed.
DS481.G3 M387   954.03/5/0924   LC 72-170180   ISBN 0824801040

Mehta, Ved, 1934-.   **3.4310**
Mahatma Gandhi and his apostles / Ved Mehta. — New York: Viking Press, 1977, c1976. xi, 260 p.; 24 cm. Includes index. 1. Gandhi, Mahatma, 1869-1948. 2. Statesmen — India — Biography. I. T.
DS481.G3 M43   954.03/5/0924 B   LC 76-27736   ISBN 0670450871

Rolland, Romain, 1866-1944.   • **3.4311**
Mahatma Gandhi; the man who became one with the universal being, by Romain Rolland, translated by Catherine D. Groth. New York, The Century Co. [c1924] 250 p. front. (port.) 19 cm. 1. Gandhi, Mahatma, 1869-1948. 2. India — Politics and government — 1919- I. Groth, Catherine Daae, 1888- II. T.
DS481.G3 R6   LC 24-4346

Bolitho, Hector, 1898-.   • **3.4312**
Jinnah, creator of Pakistan. [1st ed.] London, J. Murray [1954] 244 p. illus. 23 cm. 1. Jinnah, Mahomed Ali, 1876-1948. I. T.
DS481.J5B6 1954   LC 54-14996

Menon, Kumara Padmanabha Sivasankara, 1898-.   • **3.4313**
Many worlds: an autobiography. London: Oxford U.P., 1965. 324 p.: ill., ports.; 23 cm. 1. Menon, Kumara Padmanabha Sivasankara, 1898- 2. World politics — 1945- 3. India — Politics and government — 20th century I. T.
DS481M4 A3   320.954   B   LC 66-1547

Bhattacharjea, Ajit.   **3.4314**
Jayaprakash Narayan: a political biography. — Delhi: Vikas Pub. House, [1975] viii, 186 p., [8] leaves of plates: ill.; 22 cm. Includes index. 1. Narain, Jai Prakash. 2. India — Politics and government — 20th century I. T.
DS481.N3 B45   954.03/5/0924 B   LC 75-902443

Lal, Lakshmi Narain, 1925-.   **3.4315**
Jayaprakash: rebel extraordinary / Lakshmi Narain Lal. — New Delhi: Indian Book Company, 1975. 179 p.; 22 cm. 1. Narain, Jai Prakash. I. T.
DS481.N3 L35   954.03/5/0924 B   LC 75-902427

Nehru, Jawaharlal, 1889-1964.   **3.4316**
Jawaharlal Nehru, an anthology / edited by Sarvepalli Gopal. — Delhi: Oxford University Press, 1981 (c1980). xxi, 662 p., [1] leaf of plates: ports.; 23 cm. Includes index. 1. India — Addresses, essays, lectures. I. Gopal, Sarvepalli. II. T.
DS481.N35 A25   954 19   LC 81-129624   ISBN 0195612205

Nehru, Jawaharlal, 1889-1964.   **3.4317**
[Selections. 1984] Selected works of Jawaharlal Nehru. Second series. — New Delhi: Jawaharlal Nehru Memorial Fund: Distributed by Oxford, c1984-. v. <1-2 >: ill.; 25 cm. Includes index. I. T.
DS481.N35 A25 1984   954.04/2/0924 19   LC 84-900583   ISBN 0195616367

Nehru, Jawaharlal, 1889-1964.   • **3.4318**
Jawaharlal Nehru, an autobiography: with musings on recent events in India / Jawaharlal Nehru. — Bombay: Allied Publishers, 1962. xiii, 623 p. 1. Gandhi, Mahatma, 1869-1948. 2. Nehru, Jawaharlal, 1889-1964. 3. India — Politics and government — 1919-1947 I. T.
DS481.N35 A3 1962   LC 64-1400

Nehru, Jawaharlal, 1889-1964.   • **3.4319**
Nehru, the first sixty years; presenting in his own words the development of the political thought of Jawaharlal Nehru and the background against which it evolved ... Selected and edited, with introductory, historical and other interpretative commentary by Dorothy Norman, with a foreword by Jawaharlal Nehru. — New York: John Day Co., [1965] 2 v.: ports.; 23 cm. 1. Nehru,

Jawaharlal, 1889-1964. 2. India — Politics and government I. Norman, Dorothy, 1905- ed. II. T.
DS481.N35 A3 1965   320.954   LC 64-14203

Gopal, Sarvepalli.   **3.4320**
Jawaharlal Nehru: a biography / Sarvepalli Gopal. — Cambridge, Mass.: Harvard University Press, 1976-1984. 3 v.: ill.; 24 cm. 1. Nehru, Jawaharlal, 1889-1964. 2. Prime ministers — India — Biography. 3. India — Politics and government — 20th century I. T.
DS481.N35 G66 1976   954.04/2/0924 B   LC 75-33411   ISBN 0674473108

Pandey, B. N. (Bishwa Nath), 1929-.   **3.4321**
Nehru / by B. N. Pandey. — New York: Stein and Day, [1976] 499 p. ill. 1. Nehru, Jawaharlal, 1889-1964. I. T.
DS481.N35 P29   954.04/092/4 B   LC 75-37858

Sultan Muhammad Shah, Sir, agha khan, 1877-1957.   • **3.4322**
The memoirs of Aga Khan; world enough and time / by His Highness, The Aga Khan. —. New York, Simon and Schuster, 1954. xiv, 367 p., [8] p. of plates: ill., ports.; 24 cm. 1. Sultan Muhammad Shah, Sir, agha khan, 1877-1957. I. T.
DS481.S8A3   923.254 B   LC 54-8644

Tandon, Prakash.   **3.4323**
Beyond Punjab, 1937–1960. — Berkeley: University of California Press, 1972 (c1971). 222 p.; 23 cm. Sequel to Punjabi century, 1857-1947. 1. Tandon, Prakash. 2. India — Social life and customs I. T.
DS481.T24 A3   309.1/545/05   LC 73-123620   ISBN 0520017595

DS484–490 Local History

DS484 SOUTH INDIA

Irschick, Eugene F.   • **3.4324**
Politics and social conflict in South India; the non–Brahman movement and Tamil separatism, 1916–1929 [by] Eugene F. Irschick. Berkeley, University of California Press, 1969. 414 p. maps. 24 cm. Sponsored by the Center for South and Southeast Asia Studies, University of California, Berkeley. 1. Tamils 2. India, South — Politics and government. I. University of California, Berkeley. Center for South and Southeast Asia Studies. II. T.
DS484.I7   320.9/54/8   LC 68-31595

Moffatt, Michael, 1944-.   **3.4325**
An Untouchable community in South India, structure and consensus / Michael Moffatt. — Princeton, N.J.: Princeton University Press, c1979. xliii, 323 p.: ill.; 23 cm. Includes index. 1. Caste — India, South. 2. Untouchables 3. India, South — Social conditions. I. T.
DS484.M64   301.44/94/09548   LC 78-51183   ISBN 0691093776

DS485 ASSAM

Gupta, Shekhar.   **3.4326**
Assam, a valley divided / Shekhar Gupta. — New Delhi: Vikas, c1984. x, 218 p.; 23 cm. Includes index. 1. Assam (India) — Politics and government. 2. Assam (India) — Ethnic relations. I. T.
DS485.A88 G87 1984   954/.162 19   LC 84-901125   ISBN 0706925378

DS485 BENGAL

Chattopadhyaya, Gautam, 1924- comp.   • **3.4327**
Awakening in Bengal in early nineteenth century; selected documents. Edited by Goutam Chattopadhyay. Calcutta Progressive Publishers 1965. 1. Bengal — Intellectual life I. T.
DS485 B44 C53

Inden, Ronald B.   **3.4328**
Marriage and rank in Bengali culture: a history of caste and clan in middle period Bengal / Ronald B. Inden. — Berkeley: University of California Press, c1976. x, 161 p.; 25 cm. A revision of the author's thesis, University of Chicago, 1972. Includes index. 1. Caste — Bengal. 2. Clans — Bengal. 3. Marriage — Bengal. 4. Bengal (India) — Civilization. I. T.
DS485.B44 I5 1976   301.44/0954/14   LC 73-85789   ISBN 0520025695

Kopf, David.   • **3.4329**
British Orientalism and the Bengal renaissance; the dynamics of Indian modernization, 1773–1835. Berkeley, University of California Press, 1969. xii, 324 p. 25 cm. Bibliography: p. 295-316. 1. Bengal — Intellectual life. I. T.
DS485.B44K6   915.4/14/0331   LC 69-13135

Broomfield, J. H.   • 3.4330
Elite conflict in a plural society; twentieth–century Bengal [by] J. H. Broomfield. Berkeley, University of California Press, 1968. xv, 349 p. maps. 25 cm. 1. Hindus 2. Muslims — India — Bengal 3. Bengal (India) — Politics and government. I. T.
DS485.B49 B76   320.9/54/14   LC 68-13822

DS485 BHUTAN

Karan, Pradyumna P. (Pradyumna Prasad)   • 3.4331
The Himalayan kingdoms: Bhutan, Sikkim, and Nepal, by Pradyumna P. Karan and William M. Jenkins, Jr. — Princeton, N. J., Van Nostrand [1963] 144 p. illus. 21 cm. — (Van Nostrand searchlight book no.13) 1. Bhutan. 2. Nepal. 3. Sikkim (India) I. Jenkins, William M., joint author. II. T.
DS485.B503K3   915.696   LC 63-4420

Rahul, Ram.   3.4332
Modern Bhutan [by] Ram Rahul. — New York: Barnes & Noble, 1972, c1971. vii, 173 p.: illus. map (on lining paper); 22 cm. 1. Bhutan. I. T.
DS485.B503 R28   915.49/8/03

Rustomji, Nari, 1919-.   3.4333
Bhutan: the dragon kingdom in crisis / Nari Rustomji. — Delhi; New York: Oxford University Press, 1978. 150 p., [7] leaves of plates: ill., map (on lining paper); 23 cm. Includes index. 1. Rustomji, Nari, 1919- 2. Bhutan — Politics and government. 3. India — Officials and employees — Biography. I. T.
DS485.B503 R8   954.9/8   LC 78-106625

Singh, Nagendra.   3.4334
Bhutan: a kingdom in the Himalayas; a study of the land, its people, and their government. — New Delhi: Thomson Press (India), Publication Division, [1972] xv, 202 p.: illus. (part col.), col. maps.; 24 cm. 'Issued under the auspices of Jawaharlal Nehru University.' 1. Bhutan. I. T.
DS485.B503 S56   954.9/8   LC 72-907431

DS485 BURMA
(see also: DS527-530)

Bixler, Norma.   • 3.4335
Burma, a profile. — New York: Praeger Publishers, [1971] xii, 244 p.: illus., maps.; 22 cm. — (Praeger country profiles) 1. Burma. I. T.
DS485.B81 B55   915.91/03/5   LC 77-118047

Scott, James George, Sir, 1851-1935.   • 3.4336
The Burman: his life and notions / by Shway Yoe [pseud.]. — New York: Norton, [1963]. 609 p.: ill.; 20 cm. (The Norton library; N212) 1. Burma — Social life and customs. I. T.
DS485.B81 S4 1963   915.91   LC 63-5970   ISBN 0393002128

Nash, Manning.   • 3.4337
The golden road to modernity; village life in contemporary Burma. — New York, Wiley [1965] viii, 333 p. illus., maps. 24 cm. Bibliography: p. 325-326. 1. Burma — Soc. life & cust. I. T.
DS485.B84N3   390.09591   LC 65-21437

Cady, John Frank, 1901-.   • 3.4338
A history of modern Burma. — Ithaca, N. Y., Cornell University Press [1958] 682 p. illus. 24 cm. 1. Burma — Hist. I. T.
DS485.B86C2   959.1   LC 58-1545

Harvey, Godfrey Eric, 1889-.   3.4339
History of Burma: from the earliest times to 10 March, 1824, the beginning of the English conquest. — [1st ed.]. — New York: Octagon Books, 1967. xxxi, 415 p. illus., maps.; 23 cm. Bibliography: p. 373-390. Reprint of the 1925 ed. I. T.
DS485.B86 H3x

Furnivall, J. S. (John Sydenham)   • 3.4340
Colonial policy and practice; a comparative study of Burma and Netherlands India. — New York, New York University Press [1956] xii, [1], 568 p. map. 24 cm. Bibliography: p. [xiii], [556]-558. 1. Burma — Pol. & govt. 2. Indonesia — Pol. & govt. 3. Colonies — Administration I. T.
DS485.B89F8 1956   959.1   LC 56-10677

Butwell, Richard A., 1929-.   • 3.4341
U Nu of Burma [by] Richard Butwell. — Stanford, Calif., Stanford University Press [1969] viii, 327 p., illus., ports. 23 cm. 1. Nu, U. I. T.
DS485.B892 B8 1969   959.1/05/0924 B   LC 76-97911   ISBN 804701555 10.00

Johnstone, William Crane, 1901-.   • 3.4342
Burma's foreign policy; a study in neutralism. Cambridge Harvard University Press 1963. 339p. 1. Burma — Foreign relations I. T.
DS485 B892 J6

DS485 HIMALAYAS

Rahul, Ram.   3.4343
The Himalaya borderland. — Delhi: Vikas Publications, [1970] vi, 157 p.; 23 cm. 1. Himalaya Mountains region. I. T.
DS485.H6 R24   LC 70-915718

Shirakawa, Yoshikazu, 1935-.   3.4344
[Himaraya. English] Himalayas. Photos. and text by Yoshikazu Shirakawa. Testimonial by Mahendra Bir Bikram Shah Deva. Pref. by Arnold Toynbee. Introd. by Sir Edmund Hillary. Essay, 'The great Himalayas,' by Kyuya Fukada. New York, H. N. Abrams [1973, c1971] 1 v. (unpaged) illus. (part col.) 43 cm. Original Japanese ed. published under title: Himaraya. 1. Himalaya Mountains — Description and travel. I. T.
DS485.H6 S42713   954   LC 72-4401   ISBN 0810901625

DS485 KASHMIR

Lamb, Alastair, 1930-.   • 3.4345
[Crisis in Kashmir, 1947-1966] The Kashmir problem; a historical survey. New York, Praeger [1967] 163 p. 4 maps (1 fold.) 23 cm. First published in 1966 under title: Crisis in Kashmir, 1947-1966. 1. Kashmir — History. I. T.
DS485.K2 L33 1967   954.6   LC 67-11660

DS485 MAHARASHTRA

Shivaji and facets of Maratha culture / edited by Saryu Doshi.   3.4346
Bombay: Marg Publications, 1983 (c1982). viii, 202 p., [2] p. of plates: ill. (some col.), maps; 34 cm. 1. Shivaji, Raja, 1627-1680. 2. Marathas 3. Maharashtra (India) — Civilization. I. Doshi, Saryu.
DS485.M346 S48   954/.792 19   LC 82-904269

DS485 NEPAL
(see also: DS493.4-495)

Fürer-Haimendorf, Christoph von, 1909-.   • 3.4347
The Sherpas of Nepal, Buddhist highlanders. — Berkeley: University of California Press, 1964. xix, 298 p.: ill., fold. map, ports; 23 cm. 1. Sherpas 2. Nepal — Social life and customs. I. T.
DS485.N4 F8 1964   309.15496   LC 64-25908

Hagen, Toni, 1917-.   • 3.4348
[Nepal; Königreich am Himalaya. English] Nepal; the kingdom in the Himalayas [by] Toni Hagen, Friedrich Traugott Wahlen [and] Walter Robert Corti. [Translated by Britta M. Charleston and Toni Hagen; rev. by Ewald Osers. 3d ed.] Chicago, Distributed in the U.S.A. by Rand McNally [1971] 180 p. 84 illus. (part col.) maps. 31 cm. Translation of Nepal; Königreich am Himalaya. 1. Nepal — Description and travel. I. T.
DS485.N4 H283 1971   915.49/6/03   LC 79-28765

Karan, Pradyumna P. (Pradyumna Prasad)   • 3.4349
Nepal, a cultural and physical geography. With the collaboration of William M. Jenkins. Lexington, University of Kentucky Press, 1960. 100 p. illus., ports., 36 maps (1 col., 1 fold. col. in pocket) 1. Nepal — Description and travel. I. T.
DS485.N4 K3   915.426   LC 60-8518

Bista, Dor Bahadur.   3.4350
People of Nepal. — [2d ed.]. — Kathmandu: Ratna Pustak Bhandar, [1972] xvi, 210 p.: illus. (part col.), fold. col. map.; 25 cm. 1. Ethnology — Nepal I. T.
DS485.N442 B57 1972   915.49/603   LC 72-901318

DS485 ORISSA

Bailey, F. G. (Frederick George)   3.4351
Tribe, caste, and nation: a study of political activity and political change in highland Orissa / by F.G. Bailey. — Manchester: Manchester University Press, 1960. xii, 279 p.: ill. 1. Social change 2. Orissa (India) — Social life and customs. 3. Orissa (India) — Politics and government. I. T.
DS485.O6 B27   LC 61-3845   ISBN 719002508

DS485 PUNJAB

Tandon, Prakash.   • 3.4352
Punjabi century, 1857–1947. With a foreword by Maurice Zinkin. Berkeley, University of California Press, 1968. 274 p. map. 20 cm. Sequel: Beyond Punjab, 1937-1960. 1. Punjab — Social life and customs. I. T.
DS485.P19 T3 1968   309.1/54/5   LC 68-25959

The Punjab crisis: challenge and response / edited by Abida   3.4353
Samiuddin.
Delhi, India: Mittal Publications: Distributed by Mittal Publishers'
Distributors, 1985. xxviii, 714 p.: ill.; 25 cm. 59-9 1. Punjab (India) — Politics
and government — Addresses, essays, lectures. I. Samiuddin, Abida.
DS485.P2 P7585 1985   954/.552 19   LC 85-903277

Singh, Khushwant.   • 3.4354
A history of the Sikhs. — Princeton, N. J., Princeton University Press, 1963-66.
2 v. illus., geneal. tables, maps (part fold.) ports. 23 cm. Bibliography: v. 1, p.
385-397; v. 2, p. 341-368. 1. Sikhs — Hist. 2. Punjab — Hist. I. T.
DS485.P3S493   954.97   LC 63-7550 rev

DS485 SIKKIM

Coelho, V. H., 1917-.   3.4355
Sikkim and Bhutan [by] V. H. Coelho. Vikas (dist by Lawrence Verry), 1971. x,
138 p. illus., map. 24 cm. 1. Sikkim (India) 2. Bhutan. I. T.
DS485.S5 C6   LC 78-907999

Raghunadha Rao, P.   3.4356
India and Sikkim, 1814–1970 [by] P. R. Rao. xvi, 227 p. map. 22 cm. 'Revised
and enlarged version of the thesis submitted by [the author] to the Indian
School of International Studies, New Delhi in July 1968 ...' 1. Sikkim (India)
— Relations — India. 2. India — Relations — Sikkim. 3. Sikkim (India) —
History. I. T.
DS485.S5 R34   301.29/54/05497   LC 72-905562

DS485 UTTAR PRADESH

Brass, Paul R.   • 3.4357
Factional politics in an Indian state; the Congress Party in Uttar Pradesh [by]
Paul R. Brass. — Berkeley, University of California Press, 1965. xiv, 262 p.
illus., maps. 24 cm. Bibliography: p. 249-253. 1. Uttar Pradesh (India) — Pol.
& govt. I. T.
DS485.U6B7   329.9542   LC 65-23109

DS486 CITIES, A–Z

Moorhouse, Geoffrey, 1931-.   3.4358
Calcutta. [1st American ed.] New York, Harcourt Brace Jovanovich [1972,
c1971] xv, 376 p. illus. 22 cm. 1. Calcutta (India) I. T.
DS486.C2 M63 1972   915.4/14   LC 75-174512   ISBN 0151153698

Oldenburg, Veena Talwar.   3.4359
The making of colonial Lucknow, 1856–1877 / Veena Talwar Oldenburg. —
Princeton, N.J.: Princeton University Press, c1984. xxv, 287 p.: 2 maps; 22 cm.
Revision of thesis (doctoral)—University of Illinois at Urbana-Champaign.
Includes index. 1. Urbanization — India — Lucknow. 2. Lucknow (India) —
History. I. T. II. Title: Colonial Lucknow, 1856-1877.
DS486.L9 O42 1984   954/.2 19   LC 83-16008   ISBN 069106590X

Berreman, Gerald Duane, 1930-.   • 3.4360
Hindus of the Himalayas; ethnography and change, by Gerald D. Berreman. —
[2d ed., rev. and enlarged]. — Berkeley: University of California Press, 1972.
lvii, 440 p.: illus.; 23 cm. Based on the author's thesis, Cornell University, 1959.
1. Ethnology — India — Uttar Pradesh. 2. Villages — India — Uttar Pradesh.
3. Sirkanda, India. I. T.
DS486.S56 B4 1972   301.29/54/2   LC 73-156468   ISBN
0520014235

DS488–490 Sri Lanka (Ceylon)

Modern Sri Lanka: a society in transition / edited by Tissa   3.4361
Fernando and Robert N. Kearney; contributors, N. Balakrishnan
... [et al.].
Syracuse, N.Y.: Maxwell School of Citizenship and Public Affairs, Syracuse
University, 1979. viii, 297 p.: ill.; 23 cm. — (Foreign and comparative studies.
South Asian series. no. 4) 1. Sri Lanka. I. Fernando, Tissa. II. Kearney,
Robert N. III. Balakrishnan, Nagalingam. IV. Series.
DS489.M56   954.9/3/03   LC 79-13077   ISBN 0915984806

Nyrop, Richard F.   3.4362
Area handbook for Ceylon. Co-authors: Richard F. Nyrop [and others.
Washington; For sale by the Supt. of Docs., U.S. Govt. Print. Off.] 1985, c1970..
xvi, 525 p. maps. 25 cm. 'DA pam 550-96.' 'One of a series of handbooks
prepared by the Foreign Area Studies (FAS) of the American University.'

1. Sri Lanka. I. American University (Washington, D.C.). Foreign Area
Studies. II. T.
DS489.N9   915.493/03/3   LC 71-609526

Sri Lanka: a survey / edited by K. M. De Silva.   3.4363
Honolulu: University Press of Hawaii, c1977. xvi, 496 p.: maps; 22 cm. Includes
bibliographical references and index. 1. Sri Lanka. I. De Silva, K. M.
DS 489 S77 1977a   LC 77-73917   ISBN 0824805682

Sri Lanka, the ethnic conflict: myths, realities & perspectives /   3.4364
Committee for Rational Development.
New Delhi: Navrang, 1984. 277 p.; 23 cm. Spine title: The ethnic conflict. 1. Sri
Lanka — Ethnic relations — Addresses, essays, lectures. I. Committee for
Rational Development (Sri Lanka) II. Title: Ethnic conflict.
DS489.2.S75 1984   305.8/0095493 19   LC 84-903506

Yalman, Nur.   3.4365
Under the bo tree: studies in caste, kinship, and marriage in the interior of
Ceylon. — Berkeley: University of California Press, 1967. xii, 406 p.: ill., maps.;
25 cm. 1. Ethnology — Sri Lanka I. T.
DS489.2.Y3 1967   392/.095493   LC 67-11939

Arasaratnam, Sinnappah.   • 3.4366
Ceylon [by] S. Arasaratnam. Englewood Cliffs, N.J.: Prentice-Hall [1964] vi,
182 p.: maps; 21 cm. (The Modern nations in historical perspective) (A
Spectrum book.) 1. Sri Lanka — History I. T.
DS489.5.A778   954.89   LC 64-20750

Pakeman, Sidney Arnold, 1891-.   • 3.4367
Ceylon. — New York, Praeger [1964] 256 p. 1 fold. map. 23 cm. — (Nations of
the modern world.) Includes bibliographical references. 1. Ceylon — Hist.
I. T. II. Series.
DS489.5.P3   954.89   LC 64-16684

Phadnis, Urmila, 1931-.   3.4368
Religion and politics in Sri Lanka / Urmila Phadnis. — Columbia, Mo.: South
Asia Books, 1976. xiv, 376 p.; 22 cm. 1. Sri Lanka — Politics and government
2. Sri Lanka — Religion. I. T.
DS489.5.P45

Winius, George D. (George Davison)   3.4369
The fatal history of Portuguese Ceylon; transition to Dutch rule. Cambridge,
Harvard University Press, 1971. xxi, 215 p. illus. 24 cm. 1. Portuguese — Sri
Lanka — History. 2. Dutch — Sri Lanka — History. 3. Portuguese — India
— History. I. T.
DS489.5.W55   954/.9301   LC 75-152271   ISBN 0674295102

Prasad, Dhirendra Mohan, 1935-.   3.4370
Ceylon's foreign policy under the Bandaranaikes (1956–65); a political analysis.
New Delhi: S. Chand, [1973] xv, 465 p.; 23 cm. 'Based on the thesis approved by
the Bhagalpur University for the degree of Doctor of Philosophy.' 1. Sri Lanka
— Foreign relations. I. T.
DS489.57.P7   327.549/3   LC 73-905760

Jacob, Lucy M., 1925-.   3.4371
Sri Lanka from dominion to republic; a study of the changing relations with the
United Kingdom [by] Lucy M. Jacob. Delhi, National [Pub. House; overseas
distributors: Books from India, London, 1973] ix, 247 p. 22 cm. 'Substantially
based on a doctoral thesis ... submitted to the University of Rajasthan in 1970
...' 1. Sri Lanka — Relations — Great Britain 2. Great Britain — Relations —
Sri Lanka I. T.
DS489.59.G7 J3   301.29/549/3041   LC 73-906251

De Silva, K. M.   3.4372
Managing ethnic tensions in multi–ethnic societies: Sri Lanka, 1880–1985 /
K.M. de Silva. — Lanham, MD: University Press of America, c1986. xix,
429 p.: ill.; 23 cm. Includes index. 1. Sri Lanka — Politics and government
2. Sri Lanka — Ethnic relations. I. T.
DS489.7.D475 1986   305.8/0095493 19   LC 86-9116   ISBN
0819153974

Wilson, A. Jeyaratnam.   3.4373
Politics in Sri Lanka, 1947–1973 [by] A. Jeyaratnam Wilson. — New York: St.
Martin's Press, [1974] xiv, 347 p.: map.; 23 cm. 1. Sri Lanka — Politics and
government I. T.
DS489.8.W54 1974b   320.9/549/303   LC 73-90319

Sri Lanka in change and crisis / edited by James Manor.   3.4374
New York: St. Martin's Press, 1984. 240 p.: maps; 23 cm. 1. Sri Lanka —
Politics and government — 1978- I. Manor, James.
DS489.84.S69 1984   954.9/303 19   LC 84-15921   ISBN
0312754523

DS493.4–495 Nepal

(see also: DS485.N4)

Harris, George Lawrence, 1910-.   3.4375
Area handbook for Nepal, Bhutan, and Sikkim. Co–authors: George L. Harris [and others] 2d ed. [Washington; for sale by the Supt. of Docs., U.S. Govt. Print. Off.] 1973. lxxx, 431 p. maps 25 cm. 'DA Pam 550-35.' First ed., by Foreign Area Studies Division, American University, Washington, D.C., published in 1964 under title: Area handbook for Nepal (with Sikkim and Bhutan) 1. Nepal. 2. Sikkim (India) 3. Bhutan. I. American University (Washington, D.C.). Foreign Areas Studies Division. Area Handbook for Nepal (with Sikkim and Bhutan) II. T.
DS493.4.H37 1973   915.49/6/035   LC 73-600139

Rana, Pashupati Shumshere J. B., 1941-.   3.4376
Nepal in perspective. Edited by Pashupati Shumshere J. B. Rana and Kamal P. Malla; contributors: Dor Bahadur Bista [and others]. — Kathmandu: Centre for Economic Development and Administration, 1973. xiii, 310 p.: maps.; 28 cm. 1. Nepal. I. Malla, Kamal Prakash, 1936- ed. II. Bista, Dor Bahadur. III. T.
DS493.4.R36   915.49/6/03   LC 73-906643

Rose, Leo E.   3.4377
Nepal: profile of a Himalayan kingdom / Leo E. Rose & John T. Scholz. — Boulder, Colo.: Westview Press, 1980. ix, 144 p., [1] leaf of plates: map; 24 cm. (Nations of contemporary Asia) Includes index. 1. Nepal. I. Scholz, John T. joint author. II. T.
DS493.4.R67   954.9/6 19   LC 79-17857   ISBN 0891586512

Rose, Leo E.   3.4378
Nepal; strategy for survival [by] Leo E. Rose. Berkeley, University of California Press, 1971. xiii, 310 p. 24 cm. 'Sponsored by the Center for South and Southeast Asia Studies, University of California, Berkeley.' 1. Nepal — Foreign relations. I. University of California, Berkeley. Center for South and Southeast Asia Studies. II. T.
DS494.7.R67   327.549/6   LC 75-100022   ISBN 0520016432

Gaige, Frederick H.   3.4379
Regionalism and national unity in Nepal / Frederick H. Gaige. — Berkeley: University of California Press, c1975. xvii, 234 p.: maps; 25 cm. Includes index. 1. Regionalism — Nepal. 2. Tarai (Nepal) 3. Nepal — Politics and government. I. T.
DS495.8.T37 G34   301.5/92/095496   LC 74-76385   ISBN 0520027280

DS501–689 EAST ASIA (GENERAL). SOUTHEAST ASIA (GENERAL)

DS501–527 General Works. History

Northeast Asian security after Vietnam / edited by Martin E. Weinstein.   3.4380
Urbana: University of Illinois Press, c1982. xii, 182 p.; 24 cm. 1. East Asia — Politics and government — Addresses, essays, lectures. 2. East Asia — National security — Addresses, essays, lectures. I. Weinstein, Martin E., 1934-
DS504.5.N67 1982   327/.095 19   LC 82-1909   ISBN 0252009665

Dobby, Ernest Henry George.   3.4381
Southeast Asia / [by] E. H. G. Dobby. — 11th ed. — London: University of London Press, 1973. [2], 429 p.: ill., maps; 22 cm. Maps on lining papers. Includes index. 1. Asia, Southeastern — Description and travel. I. T.
DS508.2.D6 1973   915.9   LC 75-300405   ISBN 0340173858

Fisher, Charles Alfred.   • 3.4382
South–east Asia: a social, economic and political geography / Charles A. Fisher. — 2d ed. — London: Methuen; New York: E.P. Dutton, 1966. xix, 831 p.: ill., maps; 24 cm. 1. Asia, Southeastern — Description and travel. I. T.
DS508.2.F5 1966   LC 66-72859

Colloquy on Early South East Asia (1973: London, England)   3.4383
Early South East Asia: essays in archaeology, history, and historical geography / edited by R. B. Smith and W. Watson. — New York: Oxford University Press, 1979. xv, 561 p., [11] leaves of plates: ill.; 25 cm. 'The papers are, for the most part, those submitted to a Colloquy on Early South East Asia held at the School of Oriental and African Studies, London, in September 1973.' Includes index. 1. Excavations (Archaeology) — Asia, Southeastern — Congresses. 2. Asia, Southeastern — History — Congresses. 3. Asia, Southeastern — Antiquities — Congresses. I. Smith, R. B. (Ralph Bernard), 1939- II. Watson, William, 1917- III. T.
DS509.C64 1973   959   LC 79-112301   ISBN 0197135870

Kolb, Albert, 1906-.   3.4384
[Ostasien. English] East Asia: China, Japan, Korea, Vietnam: geography of a cultural region / by Albert Kolb; translated [from the German] by C. A. M. Sym. — London: Methuen, 1977. xvi, 591 p., [24] leaves of plates (16 fold.): charts, maps (some col.); 25 cm. — (University paperback; 628) Translation of Ostasien. Distributed in the U.S.A. by Harper & Row, Barnes & Noble Import Division, New York. Fold. col. map inserted in pocket. Includes index. 1. East Asia — Civilization 2. Vietnam — Civilization I. T.
DS509.3.K6313 1977   950 19   LC 78-323679   ISBN 0416084206. ISBN 0416707807 pbk

Provencher, Ronald.   3.4385
Mainland Southeast Asia: an anthropological perspective / Ronald Provencher. — Pacific Palisades, Calif.: Goodyear Pub. Co., 1975. viii, 216 p.: maps; 24 cm. (Goodyear regional anthropology series) 1. Ethnology — Asia, Southeastern 2. Asia, Southeastern — Civilization I. T.
DS509.5.A1 P76   959   LC 74-19947   ISBN 0876205384

Burling, Robbins, 1926-.   • 3.4386
Hill farms and padi fields: life in mainland Southeast Asia / Robbins Burling. — Englewood Cliffs, N. J.: Prentice-Hall, 1965. viii, 180 p.: maps; 21 cm. — (A Spectrum book; S-110) 1. Ethnology — Asia, Southeastern I. T.
DS509.5.B8   LC 65-13575

LeBar, Frank M.   • 3.4387
Ethnic groups of mainland Southeast Asia / Frank M. LeBar, Gerald C. Hickey, John K. Musgrave; contributing authors: Robbins Burling [et al.]. — New Haven: Human Relations Area Files Press, [1964] x, 288 p.: 2 fold. col. maps (in pocket); 30 cm. Published as a result of a grant to the Human Relations Area Files from the National Science Foundation. 1. Ethnology — Asia, Southeastern — Dictionaries. I. Hickey, Gerald Cannon, 1925- II. Musgrave, John K III. Human Relations Area Files, inc. IV. T.
DS509.5.L4   LC 64-25414

Murdock, George Peter, 1897- ed.   • 3.4388
Social structure in Southeast Asia. Chicago: Quadrangle Books, 1960. 182 p.: maps, diagrs., tables. (Viking Fund publications in anthropology. no.29.) Papers presented at a symposium on social structure in Southeast Asia, held at the 9th Pacific Science Congress, Bangkok, Thailand, 1957. 1. Ethnology — Asia, Southeastern I. T. II. Series.
DS509.5.M8   GN4.V5 no. 19.   LC 61-981

Purcell, Victor, 1896-1965.   • 3.4389
The Chinese in Southeast Asia. 2d ed. London, Oxford University Press, 1965. xvi, 623 p. maps (1 fold.) 25 cm. 'Issued under the auspices of the Royal Institute of International Affairs.' Bibliography: p. [574]-610. Bibliographical footnotes. 1. Chinese in Southeastern Asia. I. Royal Institute of International Affairs. II. T.
DS509.5.P8 1965   301.451   LC 65-4234

Southeast Asian tribes, minorities, and nations / edited by Peter Kunstadter.   • 3.4390
Princeton, N.J.: Princeton University Press, 1967. 2 v. (xiii, 902 p.): ill., maps; 24 cm. Consists of papers from a conference held at Princeton University under the auspices of the Center of International Studies, May 10-15, 1965; papers from a panel session held at the annual convention of the American Anthropological Association, Denver, Nov. 1965; and 3 other papers. 1. Minorities — Asia, Southeastern — Addresses, essays, lectures. 2. Minorities — China. 3. Minorities — India. I. Kunstadter, Peter, ed. II. Woodrow Wilson School of Public and International Affairs. Center of International Studies. III. American Anthropological Association.
DS509.5.S63   301.3/5/0954   LC 66-17703

DS511–517 HISTORY

Buchanan, Keith M.   • 3.4391
The Southeast Asian world; an introductory essay [by] Keith Buchanan. — New York: Taplinger, [1967] 176 p.: illus., maps; 23 cm. 1. Asia, Southeastern I. T.
DS511.B8   309.1/59   LC 67-20243

Cady, John Frank, 1901-.   • 3.4392
Southeast Asia: its historical development. — New York: McGraw-Hill,
[c1964] xvii, 657 p.: maps.; 24 cm. 1. Asia, Southeastern — History I. T.
DS511.C26   959   *LC 63-15888*

Cœdès, George.   • 3.4393
[Histoire ancienne des états hindouisés d'Extrême Orient. English] The
Indianized states of Southeast Asia, by G. Coedès. Edited by Walter F. Vella.
Translated by Susan Brown Cowing. Honolulu, East-West Center Press [1968]
xxi, 403 p. maps. 24 cm. Translation of Les états hindouisés d'Indochine et
d'Indonésie, which was first published under title: Histoire ancienne des états
hindouisés d'Extrême Orient. 1. East Indians in Southeastern Asia. 2. Asia,
Southeastern — History I. T.
DS511.C7713 1968   959   *LC 67-29224*

Hall, D. G. E. (Daniel George Edward), 1891-.   3.4394
A history of South-East Asia / D.G.E. Hall. — 4th ed. — New York: St.
Martin's Press, 1981. xxx, 1070 p., [1] leaf of plates: ill.; 22 cm. Includes index.
1. Asia, Southeastern — History I. T.
DS511.H15 1981   959   *LC 78-13972*   *ISBN 0312386419*

Harrison, Brian.   • 3.4395
South-East Asia: a short history. — 3rd ed. — London: Macmillan; New York:
St. Martin's Press, [c1966] xi, 278 p.: plates, maps; 22 1/2 cm. 1. Asia,
Southeastern — History I. T.
DS511.H3 1966   959   *LC 66-13529*

In search of Southeast Asia; a modern history [by] David Joel   • 3.4396
Steinberg [and others] Edited by David Joel Steinberg.
New York: Praeger Publishers, [1971] xii, 522 p.: illus., maps.; 24 cm. —
(Praeger paperbound texts) 1. Asia, Southeastern — History I. Steinberg,
David Joel. ed.
DS511.I5 1971   915.9/03   *LC 70-121850*

Lower, J. Arthur, 1907-.   3.4397
Ocean of destiny: a concise history of the North Pacific, 1500-1978 / J. Arthur
Lower. — Vancouver: University of British Columbia Press, c1978. xiv, 242 p.,
[4] leaves of plates: ill.; 24 cm. Includes index. 1. North Pacific region —
History. 2. Canada — Relations (general) with the North Pacific region.
3. North Pacific region — Relations (general) with Canada. I. T.
DS511.L68   909/.09644 19   *LC 81-472415*   *ISBN 0774801018*

Williams, Lea E.   3.4398
Southeast Asia: a history / Lea E. Williams. New York: Oxford University
Press, 1976. xiii, 299 p.: ill.; 24 cm. 1. Asia, Southeastern — History I. T.
DS511.W66   959   *LC 75-32358*   *ISBN 0195019997*

Walder, David.   3.4399
The short victorious war; the Russo-Japanese conflict, 1904-5. — [1st U.S. ed.].
— New York: Harper & Row, [1974, c1973] 321 p.: illus.; 22 cm. 1. Russo-
Japanese War, 1904-1905 I. T.
DS517.W34 1974   952.03/1   *LC 74-801*   *ISBN 0060145161*

Warner, Denis Ashton, 1917-.   3.4400
The tide at sunrise; a history of the Russo-Japanese War, 1904-1905, by Denis
and Peggy Warner. [Maps by Don Coutts. — New York: Charterhouse, [1974]
xi, 627 p.: illus.; 22 cm. 1. Russo-Japanese War, 1904-1905 I. Warner, Peggy.
joint author. II. T.
DS517.W37   952.03/1   *LC 74-175084*   *ISBN 0883270315*

Okamoto, Shumpei.   3.4401
The Japanese oligarchy and the Russo-Japanese War. — New York: Columbia
University Press, 1970. x, 358 p.; 24 cm. 1. Russo-Japanese War, 1904-1905
2. Japan — Politics and government — 1868-1912 I. T.
DS517.13.O37   952.03/1   *LC 74-114259*   *ISBN 0231034040*

DS518 POLITICS. FOREIGN RELATIONS

Iriye, Akira.   • 3.4402
After imperialism; the search for a new order in the Far East, 1921-1931. —
Cambridge, Harvard University Press, 1965. viii, 375 p. map. 24 cm. —
(Harvard East Asian series. 22) Bibliography: p. 337-358. 1. East (Far East) —
Hist. I. T. II. Series.
DS518.I75   327.5   *LC 65-22052*

Japan's Greater East Asia Co-prosperity Sphere in World War   3.4403
II: selected readings and documents / edited and introduced by
Joyce C. Lebra.
Kuala Lumpur; New York: Oxford University Press, 1975. xxi, 212 p.; 23 cm.
Includes index. 1. Greater East Asia co-prosperity sphere — Addresses, essays,
lectures. 2. Greater East Asia co-prosperity sphere — History — Sources.
I. Lebra-Chapman, Joyce, 1925-
DS518.J38   327.52/05   *LC 75-319240*   *ISBN 0196382653*

Pluvier, Jan M.   3.4404
South-East Asia from colonialism to independence / Jan Pluvier. — Kuala
Lumpur; New York: Oxford University Press, 1974. xxii, 571 p.: maps; 26 cm.
Includes index. 1. Asia, Southeastern — History I. T.
DS518.P55   959   *LC 74-941414*   *ISBN 0196382637*

Cady, John Frank, 1901-.   3.4405
The history of post-war Southeast Asia / John F. Cady. — Athens: Ohio
University Press, c1974. xxii, 720 p.: maps; 23 cm. On spine: Post-war
Southeast Asia. Includes index. 1. Asia, Southeastern — History I. T.
DS518.1.C23   959   *LC 74-82497*   *ISBN 0821401602*

Colbert, Evelyn Speyer, 1918-.   3.4406
Southeast Asia in international politics, 1941-1956 / Evelyn Colbert. — Ithaca,
N.Y.: Cornell University Press, 1977. 372 p.: map; 24 cm. Includes index.
1. World politics — 20th century 2. Asia, Southeastern — Foreign relations.
I. T.
DS518.1.C587   327/.0959   *LC 76-28008*   *ISBN 0801409713*

Hudson, Geoffrey Francis, 1903-.   3.4407
Reform and revolution in Asia. Edited by G. F. Hudson. — New York: St.
Martin's Press, 1973. 318 p.; 23 cm. 1. Asia — Politics and government I. T.
DS518.1.H85 1973   950/.42   *LC 72-85550*

Trager, Frank N. ed.   • 3.4408
Marxism in Southeast Asia; a study of four countries. Edited, with an introd.
and conclusion. With contributions by Jeanne S. Mintz [and others]. —
Stanford, Calif., Stanford University Press, 1959. 381 p. 24 cm. Bibliography: p.
[357]-369. 1. Communism — Asia, Southeastern. 2. Asia, Southeastern —
Politics. I. T.
DS518.1.T7   335.40959   *LC 59-12469*

Taylor, Jay, 1931-.   3.4409
China and Southeast Asia; Peking's relations with revolutionary movements. —
New York: Praeger, [1974] xx, 384 p.: map.; 25 cm. (Praeger special studies
in international politics and government) 1. Communism — Asia. 2. Asia,
Southeastern — Foreign relations — China. 3. China — Foreign relations —
Asia, Southeastern. 4. Asia, Southeastern — Politics and government I. T.
DS518.15.T38   327.51/059   *LC 74-3511*   *ISBN 027508910X*

Cady, John Frank, 1901-.   • 3.4410
The roots of French imperialism in Eastern Asia. Ithaca, N.Y. Published for the
American Historical Association [by] Cornell University Press [1954] xii,
322 p.: maps.; 24 cm. 1. French in the East 2. France — Colonies — East (Far
East) I. T.
DS518.2 C3

Lowe, Peter.   3.4411
Britain in the Far East: a survey from 1819 to the present / Peter Lowe. —
London; New York: Longman, 1981. 264 p.: maps; 22 cm. Includes index.
1. East Asia — Foreign relations — Great Britain. 2. Great Britain — Foreign
relations — East Asia. I. T.
DS518.4.L675 1981   950/.3   *LC 79-42619*   *ISBN 0582487307*

Tarling, Nicholas.   3.4412
Imperial Britain in South-East Asia / Nicholas Tarling. — Kuala Lumpur;
New York: Oxford University Press, 1975. viii, 273 p., [7] leaves of plates:
ports.; 23 cm. 1. British — Asia, Southeastern — History. 2. Asia,
Southeastern — Foreign relations — Great Britain. 3. Great Britain — Foreign
relations — Asia, Southeastern. I. T.
DS518.4.T37   327.41/059   *LC 75-940341*   *ISBN 0196382629*

Hellmann, Donald C., 1933-.   3.4413
Japan and East Asia: the new international order / [by] Donald C. Hellmann.
— New York: Praeger [1972] xii, 243 p.: map; 22 cm. 1. East Asia — Foreign
relations — Japan. 2. Japan — Foreign relations — East Asia. I. T.
DS518.45.H44   327.52/05   *LC 78-101663*

Soviet policy in East Asia / edited by Donald S. Zagoria.   3.4414
New Haven: Yale University Press, c1982. xiii, 360 p.: ill.; 25 cm. 'A Council on
Foreign Relations book'—Half title. 1. East Asia — Foreign relations — Soviet
Union. 2. Soviet Union — Foreign relations — East Asia. I. Zagoria, Donald
S. II. Council on Foreign Relations.
DS518.7.S68 1982   327.4705 19   *LC 82-50445*   *ISBN 0300027389*

Blum, Robert M.   3.4415
Drawing the line: the origin of the American containment policy in East Asia /
Robert M. Blum. — New York: Norton, c1982. xii, 273 p.; 24 cm. 1. East Asia
— Foreign relations — United States. 2. United States — Foreign relations —
East Asia. I. T.
DS518.8.B58 1982   327.7305 19   *LC 82-2187*   *ISBN 0393015653*

Dennett, Tyler, 1883-.   3.4416
Americans in eastern Asia: a critical study of the policy of the United States
with reference to China, Japan and Korea in the 19th century. — New York:
The Macmillan company, 1922. 1 v. 1. Eastern question (Far East) 2. United

States — Foreign relations 3. East Asia — Commerce — United States. 4. United States — Commercest (Far East) I. T.
DS518.8.D55   LC 22-25822

Griswold, Alfred Whitney, 1906-1963.   **3.4417**
The Far Eastern policy of the United States / by A. Whitney Griswold. — New York: Harcourt, Brace and company [c1938] 6 p. l., 3-530 p.: double map; 24 cm. At head of half-title: Institute of international studies. Maps on lining-papers. 'First edition.' 1. Eastern question (Far East) 2. United States — Foreign relations I. Yale University. Institute of International Studies. II. T.
DS518.8.G75   327.73095   LC 38-29014

DS520–527 SOUTHEASTERN ASIA

Perceptions of the past in Southeast Asia / edited by Anthony Reid and David Marr.   **3.4418**
Singapore: Published for the Asian Studies Association of Australia by Heinemann Educational Books (Asia), 1979. xvi, 436 p.: maps; 23 cm. (Asian Studies Association of Australia Southeast Asia publications series; no. 4) Includes index. 1. Asia, Southeastern — Historiography. 2. Asia, Southeastern — Intellectual life. I. Reid, Anthony. II. Marr, David G. III. Asian Studies Association of Australia.
DS524.4.P47 1979   959/.0072059 19   LC 80-942017   ISBN 0708117597

Osborne, Milton E.   **3.4419**
Southeast Asia: an introductory history / Milton Osborne. — 2nd ed. — Sydney; Boston: Allen & Unwin, 1983. 208 p.: map; 22 cm. Map on lining paper. Includes index. 1. Asia, Southeastern — History I. T.
DS525.O8x 1983   LC 84-673487   ISBN 0868612693

DS527.4–530 Burma

(see also: DS485.B8)

Cœdès, George.   **• 3.4420**
[Peuples de la péninsule indochinoise. English] The making of South East Asia, by G. Cœdès. Translated by H. M. Wright. Berkeley, University of California Press, 1966. xvi, 268 p. illus. 23 cm. Translation of Les peuples de la péninsule indochinoise. 1. Asia, Southeastern — History I. T.
DS527.C613   959   LC 66-4402

Burma, a country study / Foreign Area Studies, the American University; edited by Frederica M. Bunge.   **3.4421**
3rd ed. — Washington, D.C.: For sale by the Supt. of Docs., U.S. G.P.O., 1983. xxix, 326 p.: ill.; 24 cm. — (Area handbook series.) (DA pam. 550-61) Rev. ed. of: Area handbook for Burma. 1971. 'Research completed March 1983.' Includes index. 1. Burma. I. Bunge, Frederica M. II. American University (Washington, D.C.). Foreign Area Studies. III. Area handbook for Burma. IV. Series. V. Series: DA pam. 550-61
DS527.4.B88 1983   959.1/05 19   LC 83-25871

Steinberg, David I.   **3.4422**
Burma, a socialist nation of Southeast Asia / David I. Steinberg. — Boulder, Colo.: Westview Press, 1982. xiv, 150 p.: ill., maps; 24 cm. (Westview profiles. Nations of contemporary Asia.) 1. Burma. I. T. II. Series.
DS527.4.S8 1982   959.1 19   LC 82-2590   ISBN 0865311757

Krishna Murari, 1944-.   **3.4423**
Cultural heritage of Burma / Krishna Murari. — New Delhi: Inter-India Publications, 1985, c1983. xvi, 312 p., [24] p. of plates: ill., map, port.; 25 cm. Includes index. 1. Burma — Civilization. I. T.
DS527.9.K74 1983   959.1 19   LC 85-903003

Mi Mi Khaing, 1916-.   **• 3.4424**
Burmese family / Mi Mi Khaing; illustrated by E. G. N. Kinch. — Bloomington: Indiana University Press, 1962. 200 p.: ill.; 23 cm. 1. Women in Burma. 2. Burma — Social life and customs. I. T.
DS527.9.M5 1962   959.1   LC 62-8981   ISBN 0404152910

Aung-Thwin, Michael.   **3.4425**
Pagan: the origins of modern Burma / Michael Aung-Thwin. — Honolulu: University of Hawaii Press, c1985. xii, 264 p.: ill.; 24 cm. Includes index. 1. Burma — History — To 1824 2. Pagan (Burma) — History. I. T.
DS529.2.A86 1985   959.1/02 19   LC 85-14862   ISBN 0824809602

Hmannān maha yazawintawkyī. English.   **3.4426**
The Glass Palace chronicle of the kings of Burma / translated by Pe Maung Tin and G. H. Luce. London: Oxford University Press, 1923. xxiii, 179 p.: map; 23 cm. 'Issued by the Text Publication Fund of the Burma Research Society.' Reprint of the 1923 ed. published by Oxford University Press, H. Milford, London. 'Issued by the Text Publication Fund of the Burma Research Society.' 1. Burma — History — To 1824 2. Burma — Kings and rulers. I. Burma Research Society. Text Publication Fund. II. T.
DS529.2.H5613 1976   959.1/02   LC 75-41137   ISBN 0404145558

Moscotti, Albert D.   **3.4427**
British policy and the nationalist movement in Burma, 1917–1937 [by] Albert D. Moscotti. — [Honolulu]: University Press of Hawaii, 1974. xv, 264 p.; 23 cm. — (Asian studies at Hawaii. no. 11) Revision of the author's thesis, Yale University, 1950. 1. Nationalism — Burma. 2. Burma — Politics and government 3. Burma — History — 1824-1948 I. T. II. Series.
DS530.M67 1974   320.9/591/04   LC 73-86163   ISBN 0824802799

Silverstein, Josef.   **3.4428**
Burma: military rule and the politics of stagnation / Josef Silverstein. — Ithaca, N.Y.: Cornell University Press, 1977. xiii, 224 p.: ill.; 21 cm. — (Politics and international relations of Southeast Asia) An expansion of the author's sections on Burma originally published, 1959 and 1964, in Governments and politics of Southeast Asia, edited by G. M. Kahin. Includes index. 1. Burma — Politics and government I. T. II. Series.
DS530.4.S55   320.9/591/05   LC 77-3127   ISBN 080140911X

Silverstein, Josef.   **3.4429**
Burmese politics: the dilemma of national unity / Josef Silverstein. — New Brunswick, N.J.: Rutgers University Press, c1980. xi, 263 p.: maps; 24 cm. Includes index. 1. Burma — Politics and government 2. Burma — Ethnic relations. I. T.
DS530.4.S56   959.1/04   LC 80-200   ISBN 0813509009

DS531–553 French Indochina (to 1954)

Condominas, Georges.   **3.4430**
[Nous avons mangé la forêt de la pierre-génie Gôo. English] We have eaten the forest: the story of a Montagnard village in the central highlands of Vietnam / Georges Condominas; translated from the French by Adrienne Foulke; photos., maps, and diagrs. by the author. — 1st American ed. — New York: Hill and Wang, 1977. xxii, 423 p.: ill.; 25 cm. Translation of Nous avons mangé la forêt de la pierre-génie Gôo. Includes indexes. 1. Mnong (Indochinese people) 2. Sar Luk, Vietnam — Social life and customs. I. T.
DS539.M58 C63 1977   309.1/597/03   LC 77-887   ISBN 0809096722

Lancaster, Donald.   **• 3.4431**
The emancipation of French Indochina. — London; New York: Oxford University Press, 1961. xii, 445 p. fold. map. 23 cm. 'Issued under the auspices of the Royal Institute of International Affairs.' Bibliography: p. [434]-436. 1. Indochina, French — History. I. T.
DS541.L28   959.7   LC 61-1998

Thompson, Virginia McLean, 1903-.   **• 3.4432**
French Indo–China, by Virginia Thompson. — New York: Octagon Books, 1968. 516 p.: map; 24 cm. Reprint of the 1937 ed. 1. French in Indochina. 2. Indochina — History I. T.
DS541.T5 1968   959   LC 68-17756

Eastman, Lloyd E.   **• 3.4433**
Throne and mandarins: China's search for a policy during the Sino–French controversy, 1880–1885 [by] Lloyd E. Eastman. Cambridge, Harvard University Press, 1967. xiii, 254 p. map. 22 cm. (Harvard historical studies. v. 79) 1. Chinese-French War, 1884-1885 2. China — Foreign relations — 1644-1912 I. T. II. Series.
DS549.E2   951/.03   LC 67-12098

Evans, Grant, 1948-.   **3.4434**
Red brotherhood at war: Indochina since the fall of Saigon / Grant Evans, Kelvin Rowley. — London: Verso, 1985 (c1984). 312 p.: maps; 21 cm. Includes index. 1. Indochina — Politics and government. I. Rowley, Kelvin, 1948- II. T.
DS550.E93   959 19   LC 85-133343   ISBN 0860910903

Fall, Bernard B., 1926-1967.   **3.4435**
Street without joy: Indochina at war, 1946–54 / by Bernard B. Fall. — [4th ed.]. — Harrisburg, Pa.: Stackpole Co., [1964] 408 p.: ill., maps; 23 cm. 1. Indochina — History — 1945- I. T.
DS550.F3 1964   959.7   LC 64-23038

Hammer, Ellen J. (Ellen Joy), 1921-. • 3.4436
The Struggle for Indochina, 1940–1955. — Stanford: Stanford University Press, [1966, c1955] ix, 373 p.: map.; 24 cm. 1. French Indochina — History. I. T. DS550.H353   959.703   *LC* 66-24065

Randle, Robert F. • 3.4437
Geneva 1954; the settlement of the Indochinese War, by Robert F. Randle. — Princeton, N.J.: Princeton University Press, 1969. xviii, 639 p.: map, ports.; 24 cm. 1. Geneva Conference (1954) 2. Indochinese War, 1946-1954 — Peace. I. Geneva Conference (1954) II. T.
DS550.R3   327/.09597   *LC* 69-18069   *ISBN* 0691075298

Tran, Van Tra. 3.4438
Vietnam, history of the bulwark B2 theatre / by Tran Van Tra. — [U.S.]: Foreign Broadcast Information Service, 1983. v.: ill., maps, ports.; 28 cm. — (Southeast Asia report; no. 1247) 1. Vietnamese Conflict, 1961-1975 2. Vietnam — History — 1945-1975 3. Vietnam — History, Military I. T. DS552.3.B2T7x

Võ, Nguyên Giáp, 1912-. 3.4439
People's war, People's Army; the Viet Công insurrection manual for underdeveloped countries. Foreword by Roger Hilsman. Profile of Giap by Bernard B. Fall. New York, Praeger [1962] 217 p. illus. 21 cm. (Praeger publications in Russian history and world communism, no. 119) (Books that matter) 1. Indochinese War, 1946-1954 2. Vietnam (Democratic Republic) — History. I. T.
DS553.1.V62   959.704/1   *LC* 62-19110

DS554 Kampuchea. Cambodia

Osborne, Milton E. • 3.4440
The French presence in Cochinchina and Cambodia; rule and response (1859–1905), by Milton E. Osborne. Ithaca [N.Y.] Cornell University Press [1969] xvi, 379 p. illus., maps, ports. 22 cm. 1. French in Cochin China. 2. French in Cambodia. 3. Cochin China — Politics and government. 4. Cambodia — Politics and government I. T.
DS554.O7x   325.3/44/09597   *LC* 78-87021   *ISBN* 0801405122

Whitaker, Donald P. 3.4441
Area handbook for the Khmer Republic (Cambodia) / co–authors, Donald P. Whitaker ... [et al.]. — 2d ed. Washington: For sale by the Supt. of Docs., U.S. Govt. Print. Off., 1979. xiv, 389 p.: ill.; 25 cm. 'DA Pam 550-50.' 'Supersedes DA Pam 550-50, October 1968.' 'One of a series of handbooks prepared by Foreign Area Studies (FAS) of the American University.' First issued in 1956 by the Foreign Areas Studies Division of the American University, Washington, D.C. under title: U.S. Army area handbook for Cambodia. Includes index. 1. Cambodia. I. American University (Washington, D.C.). Foreign Areas Studies Division. U.S. Army area handbook for Cambodia. II. American University (Washington, D.C.). Foreign Area Studies. III. T.
DS554.3.W46   915.96/03/4   *LC* 72-600290

Vickery, Michael. 3.4442
Cambodia, 1975–1982 / Michael Vickery. — Boston, MA: South End Press, c1984. xiii, 361 p.: maps; 22 cm. Includes index. 1. Cambodia — History — 1975- I. T.
DS554.382.V53 1984   959.6/04 19   *LC* 83-61478   *ISBN* 0896081893

Briggs, Lawrence Palmer. • 3.4443
The ancient Khmer Empire. Philadelphia, American Philosophical Society, 1951. 295 p. illus., maps. 30 cm. (Transactions of the American Philosophical Society, new ser., v. 41, pt. 1) 1. Khmers — Antiquities. 2. Cambodia — History — 800-1444 — History — 800-1444. I. T.
DS554.5.B7x Q11.P6 n.s., vol.41, pt.1   959.6   *LC* 51-2328

Chandler, David P. 3.4444
A history of Cambodia / David P. Chandler. — Boulder, Colo.: Westview Press, 1983. xvi, 237 p.: ill.; 24 cm. Includes index. 1. Cambodia — History I. T.
DS554.5.C46 1983   959.6 19   *LC* 83-1391   *ISBN* 0865315787

Groslier, Bernard Philippe. • 3.4445
Angkor: art and civilization [by] Bernard Groslier [and] Jacques Arthaud. [Translated from the French by Eric Ernshaw Smith. Rev. ed.] New York, Praeger [1966] 236 p. illus., fold. maps, plans, col. plates. 28 cm. Translation of Angkor: hommes et pierres. Bibliography: p. 221-222. 1. Angkor (City) I. Arthaud, Jacques, joint author. II. T.
DS554.5.G7x 1966   913.59603   *LC* 66-20910

Etcheson, Craig, 1955-. 3.4446
The rise and demise of Democratic Kampuchea / Craig Etcheson. — Boulder, Colo.: Westview, 1984. xvi, 284 p.: ill.; 24 cm. (Westview special studies on South and Southeast Asia.) Includes index. 1. Communism — Cambodia — History. 2. Cambodia — History — 20th century I. T. II. Series.
DS554.7.E85 1984   959.6/04 19   *LC* 83-14781   *ISBN* 0865316503

Kiernan, Ben. 3.4447
How Pol Pot came to power: a history of communism in Kampuchea, 1930–1975 / Ben Kiernan. — London: Verso, 1985. xvii, 430 p., [8] p. of plates: ill.; 21 cm. 1. Communism — Cambodia — History. 2. Cambodia — Politics and government I. T.
DS554.7.K54 1985   959.6/04 19   *LC* 85-117036   *ISBN* 0860910970

Osborne, Milton E. 3.4448
Before Kampuchea: preludes to tragedy / Milton Osborne. — Sydney; Boston: G. Allen & Unwin, 1980 (c1979). 197 p.; 23 cm. Includes index. 1. Osborne, Milton E. 2. Cambodia. 3. Cambodia — History — 1953-1975 4. Cambodia — Description and travel I. T.
DS554.8.O82   959.6/04   *LC* 79-5307   *ISBN* 0868612499

Ponchaud, François, 1939-. 3.4449
[Cambodge année zéro. English] Cambodia: year zero / François Ponchaud; translated from the French by Nancy Amphoux. — New York: Holt, Rinehart and Winston, c1978. xvi, 212 p.: maps; 24 cm. Translation of Cambodge année zéro. 1. Cambodia — History — 1975- I. T.
DS554.8.P6613 1978   959.6/04   *LC* 77-15204   *ISBN* 0030403065

Smith, Roger M., 1930-. • 3.4450
Cambodia's foreign policy / by Roger M. Smith. Ithaca, N.Y.: Cornell University Press [1965] x, 273 p.: fold. map; 23 cm. 1. Cambodia — Foreign relations. I. T.
DS554.8.S63   327.596   *LC* 65-15375

The Third Indochina conflict / edited by David W.P. Elliott. 3.4451
Boulder, Colo.: Westview Press, 1981. xii, 247 p.; 24 cm. (A Westview replica edition) Based on a panel discussion at the annual meeting of the Association for Asian Studies, held Mar. 1979. 1. Cambodian-Vietnamese Conflict, 1977- — Congresses. 2. Indochina — History — 1945- — Congresses. I. Elliott, David W. P. II. Association for Asian Studies.
DS554.842.T47   959.704/4 19   *LC* 81-2736   *ISBN* 089158739X

DS555 Laos

Berval, René de. • 3.4452
Kingdom of Laos: the land of the million elephants and of the white parasol / by René de Berval in collaboration with Their Highnesses Princes Phetsarath and Souvanna Phouma [and others. English translation by Mrs. Teissier du Cros and others. — [1st ed.] Saigon, Viêt-Nam: France-Asie [1959] 506 p.: ill., ports., maps; 24 cm. 1. Laos. I. T.
DS555.B4x

Dommen, Arthur J. • 3.4453
Conflict in Laos; the politics of neutralization [by] Arthur J. Dommen. — Rev. ed. — New York: Praeger, [1971] xvi, 454 p.: maps.; 22 cm. 1. Laos — Politics and government. 2. Laos — Foreign relations. I. T.
DS555.D6x   959.4   *LC* 76-145945

Human Relations Area Files, Inc. 3.4454
Laos; its people, its society, its culture, by the staff and associates of the Human Relations Area Files. Editors: Frank M. LeBar [and] Adrienne Suddard. — New Haven: HRAF Press, [1960] 294 p.: illus.; 22 cm. — (Survey of world cultures, 8) 1. Laos. I. LeBar, Frank M. ed. II. Suddard, Adrienne, ed. III. T.
DS555.H8x   959.4   *LC* 60-7381

Langer, Paul Fritz, 1915-. • 3.4455
North Vietnam and the Pathet Lao; partners in the struggle for Laos [by] Paul F. Langer and Joseph J. Zasloff. Cambridge, Harvard University Press, 1970. xiv, 262 p. illus., maps. 22 cm. 1. Laos — Politics and government. 2. Vietnam (Democratic Republic) — Foreign relations — Laos. 3. Laos — Foreign relations — Vietnam (Democratic Republic, 1946-) I. Zasloff, Joseph Jermiah. joint author. II. T.
DS555.L27x   959.7/04   *LC* 73-134326   *ISBN* 0674626753

Laos: war and revolution. Edited by Nina S. Adams and Alfred W. McCoy. • 3.4456
[1st ed.]. — New York: Harper & Row, [c1970] xxiii, 482 p.: maps.; 21 cm. — (Harper colophon books, CN 221) 'A publication of the Committee of Concerned Asian Scholars.' 1. Laos — History — Addresses, essays, lectures.

I. Adams, Nina S. ed. II. McCoy, Alfred W. ed. III. Committee of Concerned Asian Scholars.
DS555.L3x   959.4/04   LC 76-140188   ISBN 0060902213

Toye, Hugh.   • 3.4457
Laos: buffer state or battleground. — London; New York [etc.]: Oxford U.P., 1968. xvii, 245 p.: 8 plates, illus., tables, 8 maps, ports.; 23 cm. 1. Laos — Politics and government. 2. Laos — History I. T.
DS555.T6x   959.4/04   LC 68-115716   ISBN 0192151584

Whitaker, Donald P.   3.4458
Area handbook for Laos. Co-authors: Donald P. Whitaker [and others. 2d ed., 5th printing. Washington, For sale by the Supt. of Docs., U.S. Govt. Print. Off.] 1985, c1971.. xiv, 337 p. maps. 25 cm. Edition of 1967 by T. D. Roberts; 2d ed. published in 1979 under title: Laos, a country study. 'One of a series of handbooks prepared by Foreign Area Studies (FAS) of the American University.' 'Research and writing were completed June 1971.' 'DA pam 550-58.' 1. Laos. I. Roberts, Thomas Duval, 1903- Area Handbook for Laos. II. American University (Washington, D.C.). Foreign Area Studies. III. T.
DS555.W5x   915.94/03/4   LC 72-600173

Contemporary Laos: studies in the politics and society of the   3.4459
Lao People's Democratic Republic / edited by Martin Stuart-Fox.
New York: St. Martin's Press, 1982. xxi, 345 p.: ill.; 23 cm. 1. Laos — History — 1975- I. Stuart-Fox, Martin, 1939-
DS555.84.C66 1982   959.4/04 19   LC 82-1974   ISBN 0312166761

DS556–560 Vietnam

Hickey, Gerald Cannon, 1925-.   3.4460
Free in the forest: ethnohistory of the Vietnamese central highlands, 1954–1976 / Gerald Cannon Hickey. — New Haven: Yale University Press, c1982. xxi, 350 p.: ill.; 24 cm. Includes indexes. 1. Montagnards (Vietnamese people) — History. 2. Insurgency — Vietnam — Central Highlands. 3. Ethnicity — Vietnam — Central Highlands. 4. Central Highlands (Vietnam) — History. I. T.
DS556.45.M6 H52 1982   959.7 19   LC 81-11595   ISBN 0300024371

Hickey, Gerald Cannon, 1925-.   3.4461
Sons of the mountains: ethnohistory of the Vietnamese central highlands to 1954 / Gerald Cannon Hickey. — New Haven: Yale University Press, c1982. xxi, 488 p.: ill.; 24 cm. Includes index. 1. Montagnards (Vietnamese people) — History. 2. Central Highlands (Vietnam) — History. I. T.
DS556.45.M6 H53 1982   959.7/004992 19   LC 80-21819   ISBN 0300024533

Duiker, William J., 1932-.   3.4462
Vietnam: nation in revolution / William J. Duiker. — Boulder, Colo.: Westview Press, 1983. xi, 171 p.: ill.; 24 cm. — (Westview profiles. Nations of contemporary Asia.) Includes index. 1. Vietnam — History I. T. II. Series.
DS556.5.D84 1983   959.7 19   LC 82-21946   ISBN 0865313369

Hodgkin, Thomas Lionel, 1910-.   3.4463
Vietnam: the revolutionary path / Thomas Hodgkin. — New York: St. Martin's Press, 1981. x, 433 p.: maps; 24 cm. Includes index. 1. Revolutions — Vietnam. 2. Vietnam — Politics and government I. T.
DS556.5.H62 1981   959.704   LC 79-21983   ISBN 031284588X

Taylor, Keith Weller.   3.4464
The birth of Vietnam / Keith Weller Taylor. — Berkeley: University of California Press, c1983. xxi, 397 p.: ill.; 24 cm. Includes index. 1. Vietnam — History — To 939 I. T.
DS556.6.T39 1983   959.7/03 19   LC 81-11590   ISBN 0520044282

Duiker, William J., 1932-.   3.4465
The Communist road to power in Vietnam / William J. Duiker. — Boulder, Colo.: Westview Press, 1981. xvi, 393 p.: maps; 24 cm. (Westview special studies on South and Southeast Asia) Includes index. 1. Communism — Vietnam — History. 2. Vietnam — History — 20th century I. T.
DS556.8.D83   959.704 19   LC 80-22098   ISBN 0891587942

Duiker, William J., 1932-.   3.4466
The rise of nationalism in Vietnam, 1900–1941 / William J. Duiker. — Ithaca: Cornell University Press, 1976. 313 p.: maps; 23 cm. Includes index. 1. Nationalism — Vietnam. 2. Vietnam — History — 1858-1945 I. T.
DS556.8.D84   320.9/597/03   LC 75-18723   ISBN 0801409519

Marr, David G.   3.4467
Vietnamese tradition on trial, 1920–1945 / David G. Marr. — Berkeley: University of California Press, c1981. xi, 468 p.: ill.; 24 cm. Includes index. 1. Intellectuals — Vietnam. 2. Nationalism — Vietnam. 3. Vietnam — Intellectual life. 4. Vietnam — History — 1858-1945 I. T.
DS556.8.M37   959.7/03   LC 80-15802   ISBN 0520041801

Spector, Ronald H., 1943-.   3.4468
United States Army in Vietnam. Advice and support: the early years, 1941–1960 / by Ronald H. Spector. — Washington, D.C.: Center of Military History: For sale by the Supt. of Docs., 1983. xviii, 391 p.: ill.; 26 cm. Title on spine: U.S. Army in Vietnam. 1. United States. Army — History 2. Vietnam — History, Military. 3. Vietnam — History — 20th century 4. United States — Foreign relations — Vietnam. 5. Vietnam — Foreign relations — United States. I. Center of Military History. II. T. III. Title: U.S. Army in Vietnam.
DS556.8.S67 1983   959.704 19   LC 83-600103

Chu Văn Tân.   3.4469
[Kỷ niệm Cú u quốc quân. English] Reminiscences on the army for National Salvation: memoir of General Chu Van Tan / translated by Mai Elliott. — Ithaca, N. Y.: Cornell University, 1974. vi, 217 p. (p. 208-217 advertisements): ill.; 28 cm. (Data paper - Southeast Asia program, Cornell University; no. 97) Translation of Ky niêm Cú u quôc quân. 1. Chu Văn Tân. 2. Cú'u quôc quân. I. T.
DS556.83.C48 A3513   959.704/092/4 B   LC 75-307246   ISBN 087727097X

Truong, Nhu Tang.   3.4470
A Vietcong memoir: an inside account of the Vietnam war and its aftermath / Truong Nhu Tang, with David Chanoff and Doan Van Toai. — 1st ed. — San Diego: Harcourt Brace Jovanovich, c1985. xiv, 350 p.: ill.; 24 cm. 1. TruËng, Nhu Tang. 2. Mặt trận dân tộc giải phóng miền nam Việt Nam — Biography. 3. Vietnamese Conflict, 1961-1975 — Personal narratives, Viet Cong. 4. Revolutionists — Vietnam — Biography. 5. Vietnam — Politics and government — 1945-1975 6. Vietnam — Politics and government — 1975- I. Chanoff, David. II. Doan, Van Toai, 1946- III. T. IV. Title: Viet Cong memoir.
DS556.93.T78 A38 1985   959.704/38 19   LC 84-25132   ISBN 0151936366

DS557–559 VIETNAMESE CONFLICT

Buttinger, Joseph.   3.4471
A dragon defiant; a short history of Vietnam. New York, Praeger [1972] xi, 147 p. map. 21 cm. (Praeger university series, U-742) 1. Vietnam — History I. T.
DS557.A5 B787   959.7   LC 73-189297

Buttinger, Joseph.   • 3.4472
Vietnam; a political history. — New York: Praeger, [1968] viii, 565 p.: maps.; 22 cm. A combined and abridged ed. of the author's The smaller dragon (1958) and Vietnam: a dragon embattled (1967) 1. Vietnam — History I. T.
DS557.A5 B84   959.7   LC 68-23351

Fall, Bernard B., 1926-1967.   • 3.4473
The two Viet–Nams; a political and military analysis [by] Bernard B. Fall. — 2d rev. ed. — New York: Praeger, [1967] xii, 507 p.: maps.; 22 cm. 1. Vietnam — History I. T.
DS557.A5 F34 1967   959.7   LC 66-14505

Gurtov, Melvin.   • 3.4474
The first Vietnam crisis; Chinese Communist strategy and United States involvement, 1953–1954. New York, Columbia University Press, 1967. xxiv, 228 p. 23 cm. (Studies of the East Asian Institute, Columbia University) 1. China — Foreign relations — Vietnam. 2. Vietnam — Foreign relations — China. 3. United States — Foreign relations — Vietnam. 4. Vietnam — Foreign relations — United States. I. T.
DS557.A5 G8   327.510597   LC 67-12207

Hickey, Gerald Cannon, 1925-.   • 3.4475
Village in Vietnam. — New Haven: Yale University Press, 1964. 314 [i.e. xxviii], 325 p.: illus., geneal. tables, maps, plans, ports.; 27 cm. 1. Ethnology — Vietnam 2. Khanh Hau, Vietnam. I. T.
DS557.A5 H5   309.1597   LC 64-20923

Lamb, Helen Boyden.   3.4476
Vietnam's will to live; resistance to foreign aggression from early times through the nineteenth century, by Helen B. Lamb. — New York: Monthly Review Press, 1973 (c1972) viii, 344 p.: maps.; 22 cm. 1. Vietnam — History I. T.
DS557.A5 L293   959.7   LC 72-81760   ISBN 0853452393

McAlister, John T., 1936-.   • **3.4477**
Viet Nam; the origins of revolution [by] John T. McAlister, Jr. [1st ed. Princeton, N.J.] Published for the Center of International Studies, Princeton University [by] Knopf, New York, 1969. xix, 377, xii p. maps. 22 cm. 1. Vietnam — Politics and government I. Woodrow Wilson School of Public and International Affairs. Center of International Studies. II. T.
DS557.A5 M17 1969   959.7   *LC* 69-10690

Smith, Harvey Henry, 1892-.   **3.4478**
Area handbook for South Vietnam. Co–authors: Harvey H. Smith [and others] Washington; For sale by the Supt. of Docs., U.S. Govt. Print. Off., 1967. xiv, 510 p. maps. 24 cm. 'DA pam no. 550-55.' 'One of a series of handbooks prepared by Foreign Area Studies (FAS) of the American University.' 1957, 1962, and 1964 editions issued by Foreign Areas Studies Division, American University, Washington, D.C., under title: Area handbook for Vietnam. The present revision is in two separate studies, South Vietnam and North Vietnam. 1. Vietnam. I. American University (Washington, D.C.). Foreign Area Studies. II. American University (Washington, D.C.). Foreign Areas Studies Division. Area handbook for Vietnam. III. T.
DS557.A5 S575 1967   915.97/03/4   *LC* 67-62089

Smith, R. B. (Ralph Bernard), 1939-.   • **3.4479**
Viet–Nam and the West [by] Ralph Smith. Ithaca, N.Y., Cornell University Press [1971] ix, 206 p. maps. 22 cm. 1. Vietnam — History I. T.
DS557.A5 S58 1971   915.97/03   *LC* 78-148717   *ISBN* 0801406366

FitzGerald, Frances, 1940-.   • **3.4480**
Fire in the lake; the Vietnamese and the Americans in Vietnam. — [1st ed.]. — Boston: Little, Brown, [1972] xiv, 491 p.: maps.; 24 cm. 'An Atlantic Monthly Press book.' 'Portions ... appeared originally in the New Yorker, in slightly different form.' 1. Vietnamese Conflict, 1961-1975 — United States 2. Vietnam — Politics and government — 1945-1975 I. T.
DS557.A6 F53   320.9/597/043   *LC* 72-186966

Nhât Hanh, Thích.   • **3.4481**
Vietnam: the lotus in the sea of fire. — London: S.C.M. Press, 1967. 128 p.; 18 cm. 1. Religion and state — Vietnam. 2. Vietnam — Politics and government I. T.
DS557.A6 N495 1967   959.7/04   *LC* 67-81292

Pike, Douglas Eugene, 1924-.   • **3.4482**
Viet Cong; the organization and techniques of the National Liberation Front of South Vietnam. Cambridge, Mass., M.I.T. Press [1966] xx, 490 p. illus., maps (on lining papers) ports. 24 cm. (Massachusetts Institute of Technology. Center for International Studies. Studies in international communism no. 7) 1. Mặt trận dân tộc giải phóng miền nam Việt Nam. 2. Vietnamese Conflict, 1961-1975 I. T.
DS557.A6 P54   959.704   *LC* 66-28896

Pike, Douglas Eugene, 1924-.   • **3.4483**
War, peace, and the Viet Cong. — Cambridge, Mass.: M.I.T. Press, [1969] xii, 186 p.; 22 cm. 1. Mặt trận dân tộc giải phóng miền nam Việt Nam. 2. Vietnamese Conflict, 1961-1975 I. T.
DS557.A6 P553   959.7/04   *LC* 70-83403

Cooper, Chester L.   • **3.4484**
The lost crusade; America in Vietnam, by Chester L. Cooper. With a foreword by W. Averell Harriman. — New York: Dodd, Mead, [1970] xi, 559 p.; 24 cm. 1. Vietnamese Conflict, 1961-1975 — United States 2. United States — Foreign relations — Vietnam. 3. Vietnam — Foreign relations — United States. I. T.
DS557.A63 C66   959.7/04   *LC* 79-135539   *ISBN* 0396062415

Draper, Theodore, 1912-.   • **3.4485**
Abuse of power. — New York: Viking Press, [1967] ix, 244 p.; 21 cm. 1. Vietnamese Conflict, 1961-1975 — United States I. T.
DS557.A63 D7   959.7/04   *LC* 66-18668

Hoopes, Townsend, 1922-.   • **3.4486**
The limits of intervention; an inside account of how the Johnson policy of escalation in Vietnam was reversed. New York, D. McKay Co. [1969] ix, 245 p. 21 cm. 1. Vietnamese Conflict, 1961-1975 — United States 2. Escalation (Military science) I. T.
DS557.A63 H6   959.7/04   *LC* 78-94505

Caldwell, Malcolm.   **3.4487**
Cambodia in the Southeast Asian war, by Malcolm Caldwell and Lek Tan. Pref. by Noam Chomsky. New York, Monthly Review Press [1973] xiii, 446 p. maps. 21 cm. 1. Vietnamese Conflict, 1961-1975 — Cambodia 2. Cambodia — History — Civil War, 1970-1975 I. Tan, Lek, joint author. II. T.
DS557.A64 C23   959.704/33596   *LC* 79-147877   *ISBN* 0853451710

Schell, Jonathan, 1943-.   • **3.4488**
The village of Ben Suc. — [1st ed.]. — New York: Knopf, 1967. 132 p.: map.; 22 cm. 1. Vietnamese Conflict, 1961-1975 — Destruction and pillage — Ben Suc. I. T.
DS557.A68 S33   959.7/04   *LC* 67-29479

Hồ, Chí Minh, 1890-1969.   • **3.4489**
[Selections. English. 1967] On revolution; selected writings, 1920–66. Edited and with an introd. by Bernard B. Fall. New York, Praeger [1967] xix, 389 p. 22 cm. (Praeger publications in Russian history and world communism, no. 190) I. Fall, Bernard B., 1926-1967. II. T.
DS557.A7 H533   959.7008   *LC* 67-20481

Smith, Harvey Henry, 1892-.   **3.4490**
Area handbook for North Vietnam. Co–authors: Harvey H. Smith [and others] Washington, For sale by the Supt. of Docs., U.S. Govt. Print. Off., 1967. xii, 494 p. illus., maps. 24 cm. 'DA pam no. 550-57.' Earlier editions, published under title, Area handbook for Vietnam, are entered under American University, Washington, D.C. Foreign Areas Studies Division. The present revision is published as two separate studies, South Vietnam and North Vietnam. 1. Vietnam (Democratic Republic) I. American University (Washington, D.C.). Foreign Areas Studies Division. Area handbook for Vietnam. II. T.
DS557.A7 S57   915.97   *LC* 68-60367

Race, Jeffrey.   • **3.4491**
War comes to Long An; revolutionary conflict in a Vietnamese Province. — Berkeley: University of California Press, 1972. xxiii, 299 p.: illus.; 24 cm. 1. Vietnamese Conflict, 1961-1975 2. Long An, Vietnam — History. I. T.
DS557.A8 L657 1972   959.704/31   *LC* 79-145793   *ISBN* 0520019148

Gourou, Pierre, 1900-.   **3.4492**
The peasants of the Tonkin Delta: a study of human geography; [translated by Richard R. Miller] / Pierre Gourou. — New Haven: Human Relations Area Files, 1955. 2 v. (xiii, 889 p.): ill., maps, diagrs., profiles.; 21 cm. — (Behavior science translations.) I. T.
DS557.T7 G62 1955   *LC* 56-1826

Isaacs, Arnold R.   **3.4493**
Without honor: defeat in Vietnam and Cambodia / Arnold R. Isaacs. — Baltimore: Johns Hopkins University Press, c1983. xv, 559 p.: ill.; 24 cm. Includes index. 1. Vietnamese Conflict, 1961-1975 2. Indochina — History — 1945- I. T.
DS557.7.I82 1983   959.704/3 19   *LC* 83-48054   *ISBN* 0801830605

Pentagon Papers. Negotiating volumes.   **3.4494**
The secret diplomacy of the Vietnam War: the Negotiating volumes of the Pentagon Papers / edited by George C. Herring. — 1st ed. — Austin: University of Texas Press, 1983. xl, 873 p.; 24 cm. 1. Vietnamese Conflict, 1961-1975 — Diplomatic history. 2. Vietnamese Conflict, 1961-1975 — Peace. I. Herring, George C., 1936- II. T.
DS557.7.P43 1983   959.704/32 19   *LC* 82-21960   *ISBN* 0292775733

Văn, Tiến Dũng.   **3.4495**
[—ại thắng mùa xuân. English] Our great spring victory: an account of the liberation of South Vietnam / by Văn Tiến Dũng; translated by John Spragens, Jr.; afterword by Cora Weiss and Don Luce. — New York: Monthly Review Press, c1977. x, 275 p., [8] leaves of plates: ill.; 21 cm. Translation of —ại thắng mùa xuân. 1. Văn, Tiến Dũng. 2. Vietnamese Conflict, 1961-1975 — Campaigns 3. Vietnamese Conflict, 1961-1975 — Personal narratives, North Vietnamese. I. T.
DS557.7.V3513   959.704/34   *LC* 76-58106   *ISBN* 0853454094

Shawcross, William.   **3.4496**
Sideshow: Kissinger, Nixon, and the destruction of Cambodia / William Shawcross. — New York: Simon and Schuster, c1979. 467 p., [8] leaves of plates: ill.; 25 cm. Includes index. 1. Kissinger, Henry, 1923- 2. Nixon, Richard M. (Richard Milhous), 1913- 3. Vietnamese Conflict, 1961-1975 — Campaigns — Cambodia 4. Cabinet officers — United States — Biography. 5. Cambodia — History — Civil War, 1970-1975 6. United States — Politics and government — 1969-1974 I. T.
DS557.8.C3 S5   959.704/342/09596   *LC* 78-31826   *ISBN* 0671230700

United States. Dept. of the Army.   **3.4497**
[Report of the Department of the Army review of the preliminary investigations into the My Lai incident] The My Lai Massacre and its cover–up: beyond the reach of law?: The Peers Commission report / Joseph Goldstein, Burke Marshall, Jack Schwartz. — New York: Free Press, c1976. xi, 586 p.: maps; 24 cm. W. R. Peers, chairman of the inquiry. Consists of the report first issued in 1974 under title: Report of the Department of the Army review of the preliminary investigations into the My Lai incident: volume I, The report of the investigation. Vols. 2 and 4 of the original report were not released and v. 3 was not reproduced. Includes texts of documents from World War II and

Nuremberg and from the Vietnam War. 1. Mỹ Lai 4 (Vietnam) — Massacre, 1968. I. Peers, William R. (William Raymond), 1914- II. Goldstein, Joseph. III. Marshall, Burke, 1922- IV. Schwartz, Jack, 1946- V. T.
DS557.8.M9 U54 1976   355.1/334   LC 75-38298   *ISBN* 0029122309

Baritz, Loren, 1928-.   **3.4498**
Backfire: a history of how American culture led us into Vietnam and made us fight the way we did / Loren Baritz. — 1st ed. — New York: W. Morrow, c1985. 393 p.; 25 cm. 1. Vietnamese Conflict, 1961-1975 — United States 2. United States — Civilization — 1945- I. T.
DS558.B37 1985   959.704/33/73 19   LC 84-22655   *ISBN* 068804185X

Berman, Larry.   **3.4499**
Planning a tragedy: the Americanization of the war in Vietnam / Larry Berman. — 1st ed. — New York: Norton, c1982. xvi, 203 p.; Includes index. 1. Vietnamese Conflict, 1961-1975 — United States 2. Political science — Decision making 3. United States — Politics and government — 1963-1969 I. T.
DS558.B47 1982   959.704/3 19   LC 81-22570   *ISBN* 0393016021

Herring, George C., 1936-.   **3.4500**
America's longest war: the United States and Vietnam, 1950–1975 / George C. Herring. — New York: Wiley, c1979. xiii, 298 p.: map; 22 cm. — (America in crisis.) Includes index. 1. Vietnamese Conflict, 1961-1975 — United States 2. Vietnam — History — 1945-1975 3. United States — History — 1945- 4. United States — Foreign relations — Vietnam. 5. Vietnam — Foreign relations — United States. I. T. II. Series.
DS558.H45   959.704   LC 79-16408   *ISBN* 0471015466

Karnow, Stanley.   **3.4501**
Vietnam, a history / Stanley Karnow. — New York: Viking Press, 1983. xiii, 750 p.: ill.; 25 cm. Published in conjunction with a proposed 1983 PBS program: Vietnam, a television history. Includes index. 1. Vietnamese Conflict, 1961-1975 — United States 2. United States — History — 1945- 3. Vietnam — History I. Vietnam, a television history (Television program) II. T.
DS558.K37 1983   959.704/33/73 19   LC 83-47905   *ISBN* 0670746045

Palmer, Bruce, 1913-.   **3.4502**
The 25-year war: America's military role in Vietnam / Bruce Palmer, Jr. — Lexington, Ky.: University Press of Kentucky, c1984. ix, 236 p., [16] p. of plates: ill., maps; 24 cm. Maps on lining papers. Includes index. 1. Vietnamese Conflict, 1961-1975 — United States I. T. II. Title: Twenty-five-year war.
DS558.P337 1984   959.704/33/73 19   LC 84-5091   *ISBN* 0813115132

Schandler, Herbert Y., 1928-.   **3.4503**
The unmaking of a president: Lyndon Johnson and Vietnam / Herbert Y. Schandler. — Princeton, N.J.: Princeton University Press, c1977. xx, 419 p.; ill.; 23 cm. Includes index. 1. Johnson, Lyndon B. (Lyndon Baines), 1908-1973. 2. Vietnamese Conflict, 1961-1975 — United States 3. United States — Politics and government — 1963-1969 I. T.
DS558.S33   959.704/3373   LC 76-24297   *ISBN* 0691075867

Snepp, Frank.   **3.4504**
Decent interval: an insider's account of Saigon's indecent end / told by the CIA's Chief Strategy Analyst in Vietnam, Frank Snepp. — 1st ed. — New York: Random House, c1977. xii, 590 p., [8] leaves of plates: ill.; 25 cm. Includes index. 1. United States. Central Intelligence Agency. 2. Vietnamese Conflict, 1961-1975 3. Vietnamese Conflict, 1961-1975 — Secret Service — United States. I. T.
DS558.S58   959.704/38   LC 77-155034   *ISBN* 0394407431

Stanton, Shelby L., 1948-.   **3.4505**
The rise and fall of an American army: U.S. ground forces in Vietnam, 1965–1973 / Shelby L. Stanton. — Novato, CA: Presidio, c1985. xvii, 411 p., [37] p. of plates: ill.; 24 cm. Includes index. 1. United States. Army — History — Vietnamese Conflict, 1961-1975. 2. Vietnamese Conflict, 1961-1975 — United States I. T.
DS558.S73 1985   959.704/342 19   LC 84-26616   *ISBN* 0891412328

Summers, Harry G.   **3.4506**
On strategy: a critical analysis of the Vietnam War / Harry G. Summers, Jr. — Novato, CA: Presidio Press, c1982. xiv, 225 p.: 1 map; 22 cm. Includes index. 1. Vietnamese Conflict, 1961-1975 — United States 2. Strategy I. T.
DS558.2.S95 1982   959.704/33/73 19   LC 82-7498   *ISBN* 0891411569

Hooper, Edwin Bickford.   **3.4507**
The United States Navy and the Vietnam conflict / by Edwin Bickford Hooper, Dean C. Allard, Oscar P. Fitzgerald. Washington: Naval History Division, Dept. of the Navy: for sale by the Supt. of Docs., U.S. Govt. Print. Off., 1976. 419 p.: ill.; 26 cm. Includes index. 1. United States. Navy — History —

Vietnamese Conflict, 1961-1975 2. Vietnamese Conflict, 1961-1975 — Naval operations, American. I. Allard, Dean C., 1933- joint author. II. Fitzgerald, Oscar P. joint author. III. T.
DS558.7.H66   959.704/345   LC 76-600006

Bloods, an oral history of the Vietnam War / by Black   **3.4508**
veterans; [edited by] Wallace Terry.
1st ed. — New York: Random House, c1984. xviii, 311 p., [8] p. of plates: ill.; 25 cm. 1. Vietnamese Conflict, 1961-1975 — Personal narratives, American. 2. Vietnamese Conflict, 1961-1975 — Afro-Americans. 3. Afro-American soldiers — Biography. I. Terry, Wallace.
DS559.5.B56 1984   959.704/3 19   LC 83-42775   *ISBN* 0394530284

Bryan, C. D. B. (Courtlandt Dixon Barnes)   **3.4509**
Friendly fire / C. D. B. Bryan. — New York: Putnam, c1976. 380 p.: ill.; 24 cm. 1. Mullen, Michael Eugene, 1944-1970. 2. Vietnamese Conflict, 1961-1975 — Casualties (Statistics, etc.) 3. Vietnamese Conflict, 1961-1975 — Protest movements — United States. I. T.
DS559.5.B79 1976   322.4/4/0973   LC 76-1335   *ISBN* 0399116885

Kovic, Ron.   **3.4510**
Born on the Fourth of July / Ron Kovic. — New York: McGraw-Hill, c1976. 208 p.; 22 cm. 1. Kovic, Ron. 2. Vietnamese Conflict, 1961-1975 — Personal narratives, American. I. T.
DS559.5.K68   959.704/38   LC 76-7508   *ISBN* 007035359X

Westmoreland, William C. (William Childs), 1914-.   **3.4511**
A soldier reports / William C. Westmoreland. — 1st ed. — Garden City, N.Y.: Doubleday, 1976. x, 446 p., [16] leaves of plates: ill.; 25 cm. Includes index. 1. Westmoreland, William C. (William Childs), 1914- 2. Vietnamese Conflict, 1961-1975 — Personal narratives, American. 3. Vietnamese Conflict, 1961-1975 4. Generals — United States — Biography. I. T.
DS559.5.W47   959.704/34/0924   LC 74-27593   *ISBN* 0385004346

Kelly, Gail Paradise.   **3.4512**
From Vietnam to America: a chronicle of the Vietnamese immigration to the United States / Gail Paradise Kelly. — Boulder, Colo.: Westview Press, 1978 (c1977). x, 254 p.: ill.; 24 cm. 1. Vietnamese Conflict, 1961-1975 — Refugees. 2. Refugees — Vietnam. 3. Refugees — United States. I. T.
DS559.63.K44   361.5/3/0973   LC 77-6383   *ISBN* 0891583262

Trullinger, James Walker.   **3.4513**
Village at war: an account of revolution in Vietnam / James Walker Trullinger, Jr. — New York: Longman, c1980. xix, 235 p., [6] leaves of plates: ill.; 24 cm. Includes index. 1. Vietnamese Conflict, 1961-1975 — Vietnam — Thôn Mỹ Thuy. 2. Thôn Mỹ Thuy (Vietnam) — History. I. T.
DS559.9.T48 T78   959.704/31 19   LC 79-25406   *ISBN* 0582281814

Duiker, William J., 1932-.   **3.4514**
Vietnam since the fall of Saigon / William J. Duiker. — Athens, Ohio: Ohio University, Center for International Studies, 1981 (c1980). ix, 77 p.: maps; 28 cm. — (Papers in international studies. Southeast Asia series. no. 56.) 1. Vietnam — History — 1975- I. T. II. Series.
DS559.912.D84   959.704/4 19   LC 80-21166   *ISBN* 0896801063

Nguyễn, Ngoc Ngan.   **3.4515**
The will of heaven: a story of one Vietnamese and the end of his world / Nguyễn Ngoc Ngan with E.E. Richey. — 1st ed. — New York: Dutton, c1980. 341 p.; 22 cm. 1. Nguyễn, Ngoc Ngan. 2. Refugees, Political — Vietnam — Biography. 3. Vietnam — Politics and government — 1975- I. Richey, E. E. II. T.
DS559.912.N37   959.704/4/0924 B 19   LC 81-7773   *ISBN* 0525030611

Nguyễn, Khac Vîen.   **3.4516**
Tradition and revolution in Vietnam / Nguyen Khac Vien; foreword by George McT. Kahin; edited, with a pref. by David Marr and Jayne Werner; translation by Linda Yarr, Jayne Werner, and Tran Tuong Nhu. — Berkeley, Calif.: Indochina Resource Center, 1974. xx, 169 p.: ill. 1. Vietnam (Democratic Republic) — Addresses, essays, lectures I. T.
DS560.3.N4513   959.704   LC 74-194705

DS563–589 Thailand (Siam)

Donner, Wolf.   **3.4517**
The five faces of Thailand: an economic geography / by Wolf Donner. — London: C. Hurst, c1978. xxii, 930 p.: ill.; 23 cm. 'A publication of the Institute

of Asian Affairs, Hamburg.' Includes index. 1. Thailand — Economic conditions. I. Institut für Asienkunde. II. T.
DS563.5.D65 1978b   330.9593/044 19   *LC* 78-325645   *ISBN* 0903983532

Bunge, Frederica M.   **3.4518**
Thailand: a country study / edited by Frederica M. Bunge ... [et al.]. — 5th ed. — Washington, D.C.: American University, Foreign Area Studies: for sale by the Supt. of Docs., U.S. Govt. Print. Off., 1981. xxvii, 354 p.: ill.; 24 cm. 'DA Pam 550-53.' 'Supersedes 1971 edition.' Edition for 1971 by J. W. Henderson, published under title: Area handbook for Thailand. Includes index. 1. Thailand. I. Henderson, John William, 1910- Area handbook for Thailand. II. American University (Washington, D.C.). Foreign Area Studies. III. T.
DS563.5.H46 1981   959.3 19   *LC* 80-23075

Moore, Frank J. (Frank John), 1922-.   **3.4519**
Thailand—its people, its society, its culture / Frank J. Moore, with chapters by Clark D. Neher. — New Haven: HRAF Press, c1974. 607 p.: map; 22 cm. (Survey of world cultures; [15]) Based on Handbook on Thailand, prepared by the Southeast Asia Program, Cornell University, which was published in 1956. Includes index. 1. Thailand. I. Neher, Clark D. joint author. II. Cornell University. Southeast Asia Program. Handbook on Thailand. III. T. IV. Series.
DS563.5.M66   959.3   *LC* 74-79218   *ISBN* 0875369294

Anuman Rajadhon, Phrayā, 1888-1969.   • **3.4520**
Life and ritual in old Siam: three studies of Thai life and customs / translated and edited by William J. Gedney. — New Haven: HRAF Press, [1961] 191 p.: ill., plates.; 23 cm. 1. Farm life — Thailand. 2. Buddha and Buddhism — Thailand. 3. Birth customs — Thailand. 4. Thailand — Social life and customs. I. Gedney, William J. ed. and tr. II. T.
DS568.A7   959.3   *LC* 61-13465

Skinner, G. William (George William), 1925-.   • **3.4521**
Chinese society in Thailand: an analytical history. Ithaca, N.Y., Cornell University Press [1957] xvii, 459 p.: maps (part fold.) diagrs., tables.; 24 cm. 1. Chinese — Thailand. I. T.
DS570.C5 S54   325.251   *LC* 57-3051

Geddes, W. R. (William Robert)   **3.4522**
Migrants of the mountains: the cultural ecology of the Blue Miao (Hmong Njua) of Thailand / by William Robert Geddes. — Oxford: Clarendon Press, 1976. xviii, 274 p., [9] leaves of plates: ill.; 24 cm. Includes index. 1. Hmong (Asian people) — Thailand. I. T.
DS570.M5 G4   301.29/593   *LC* 76-364261   *ISBN* 0198231873

Wyatt, David K.   **3.4523**
Thailand: a short history / David K. Wyatt. — New Haven [Conn.]: Yale University Press, c1984. xviii, 351 p., [1] leaf of plates: ill.; 24 cm. Includes index. 1. Thailand — History I. T.
DS571.W92 1984   959.3 19   *LC* 83-25953   *ISBN* 0300030541

Terwiel, B. J. (Barend Jan), 1941-.   **3.4524**
A history of modern Thailand, 1767–1942 / B.J. Terwiel. — St. Lucia; New York: University of Queensland Press, c1983. x, 379 p.: maps; 22 cm. — (University of Queensland Press' histories of Southeast Asia series. 0729-3887) Includes index. 1. Thailand — History — To 1782 2. Thailand — History — 1782-1945 I. T. II. Series.
DS577.T47 1983   959.3 19   *LC* 83-4089   *ISBN* 0702218928

Wood, William Alfred Rae, 1878-.   • **3.4525**
A history of Siam, from the earliest times to the year A.D. 1781, with a supplement dealing with more recent events / by W. A. R. Wood. — Rev. ed. — Bangkok: The Siam Barnakich Press, [1933] 300 p.: illus.; 23 cm. 1. Thailand — History — To 1782 I. T.
DS577.W66 1933   959.3/02   *LC* 71-179254   *ISBN* 0404548806

Chula, Prince, 1908-.   • **3.4526**
Lords of life: the paternal monarchy of Bangkok, 1782–1932, with the earlier and more recent history of Thailand / by His Royal Highness Prince Chula Chakrabongse of Thailand. New York: Taplinger, 1960. 352 p., [18] p. of plates (one col., one folded): ill., geneal. table, maps, ports.; 22 cm. Includes index. Map on folded leaf attached to lining papers. 1. Thailand — History I. T.
DS578.C48   959.3   *LC* 60-11970

Vella, Walter Francis, 1924-.   **3.4527**
Siam under Rama III, 1824–1851. Locust Valley, N.Y., Published for the Association for Asian Studies by J. J. Augustin [1957] ix, 180 p. illus., port., maps. 24 cm. 1. Phra Nang Klao, King of Thailand, d 1851. 2. Thailand — History I. T.
DS580.V4   *LC* 58-4430

Moffat, Abbot Low, 1901-.   • **3.4528**
Mongkut, the King of Siam / Abbot Low Moffat. — Ithaca, N.Y.: Cornell University Press, 1961. xvii, 254 p.: ill. 1. Mongkut, King of Siam, 1804-1868 2. Thailand — Kings and rulers — Biography I. T.
DS581 M6   *LC* 61-16666

Vella, Walter Francis, 1924-.   **3.4529**
Chaiyo!, King Vajiravudh and the development of Thai nationalism / Walter F. Vella. assisted by Dorothy B. Vella. — Honolulu: University Press of Hawaii, c1978. xvi, 347 p.: ill.; 24 cm. Includes index. 1. Vajiravudh, King of Siam, 1881-1925. 2. Nationalism — Thailand — History. 3. Thailand — History I. Vella, Dorothy B. joint author. II. T.
DS583.V44   959.3/04/0924 B   *LC* 78-1060   *ISBN* 0824804937

Batson, Benjamin A. (Benjamin Arthur), 1942-.   **3.4530**
The end of the absolute monarchy in Siam / Benjamin A. Batson. — Singapore; New York: Oxford University Press, 1984. xviii, 349 p., [4] p. of plates: ill., ports.; 22 cm. — (Southeast Asia publications series. no. 10) Includes index. 1. Prajadhipok, King of Siam, 1893-1941. 2. Monarchy — Thailand 3. Thailand — Politics and government I. T. II. Series.
DS584.B36 1984   959.3/042 19   *LC* 84-942085   *ISBN* 0195826124

Landon, Kenneth Perry, 1903-.   • **3.4531**
Siam in transition; a brief survey of cultural trends in the five years since the revolution of 1932. — New York: Greenwood Press, [1968] ix, 328 p.: fold. map.; 24 cm. Reprint of the 1939 ed. 1. Thailand. I. T.
DS584.L3 1968   915.93/03/4   *LC* 68-57615

Girling, J. L. S.   **3.4532**
Thailand, society and politics / John L. S. Girling. — Ithaca: Cornell University Press, 1981. 306 p.: maps; 22 cm. — (Politics and international relations of Southeast Asia) Includes index. 1. Thailand — Politics and government I. T. II. Series.
DS586.G57   959.3/044 19   *LC* 80-69822   *ISBN* 0801411300

DS591–605 Malaysia. Singapore

Malaysia: a country study / Foreign Area Studies, the   **3.4533**
American University; edited by Frederica M. Bunge.
4th ed. — Washington, D.C.: The Studies: For sale by the Supt. of Docs., U.S. G.P.O., 1985. xxxii, 366 p.: ill.; 24 cm. (Area handbook series.) (DA pam. 550-45) Rev. ed. of: Area handbook for Malaysia / coauthors, Nena Vreeland .. [et al.]. 3rd ed. 1977. 'Research completed January 1984.' Includes index. 1. Malaysia. I. Bunge, Frederica M. II. Vreeland, Nena, 1934- Area handbook for Malaysia. III. American University (Washington, D.C.). Foreign Area Studies. IV. Series. V. Series: DA pam. 550-45
DS592.M345 1985   959.5/053 19   *LC* 84-16790

Ooi, Jin-Bee.   **3.4534**
Peninsular Malaysia / Ooi Jin-Bee. — New ed. — London; New York: Longman, 1976. xvi, 437 p.: ill.; 24 cm. (Geographies for advanced study) Published in 1963 under title: Land, people, and economy in Malaya. Includes index. 1. Malaya. I. T.
DS592.O5 1976   959.5   *LC* 75-42166   *ISBN* 0582481856

Blythe, Wilfred.   • **3.4535**
The impact of Chinese secret societies in Malaya: a historical study. — London; Kuala Lumpur [etc.]: Issued under the auspices of the Royal Institute of International Affairs [by] Oxford U.P., 1969. xiv, 570 p.: 9 plates, illus., facsims., maps.; 25 cm. 1. Hung men. 2. Chinese in Malaya. I. Royal Institute of International Affairs. II. T.
DS595.B54   364.14/06   *LC* 71-396881   *ISBN* 0192149747

Newell, William Hare.   • **3.4536**
Treacherous river: a study of rural Chinese in North Malaya. Kuala Lumpur: University of Malaya P., c1962. xxv, 233 p.: ill., maps. bibl. 1. Chinese in Malaya. I. T.
DS595 N45   301.45   *LC* 63-2972

Andaya, Barbara Watson.   **3.4537**
A history of Malaysia / Barbara Watson Andaya and Leonard Y. Andaya. — New York: St. Martin's Press, 1982. xxi, 350 p.: maps; 25 cm. Includes index. 1. Malaysia — History. I. Andaya, Leonard Y. II. T.
DS596.A76 1982   959.5 19   *LC* 82-42612   *ISBN* 0312381204

Bastin, John Sturgus, 1927- comp.   **3.4538**
Malaysia: selected historical readings / compiled by John Bastin and Robin W. Winks. — 2d ed. with appendix. — Nendeln, Liechtenstein: KTO Press, 1979. xvi, 526 p.: maps; 24 cm. Includes index. 1. Malaysia — History — Addresses, essays, lectures. I. Winks, Robin W. joint comp. II. T.
DS596.B33 1979   959.5   *LC* 79-310363   *ISBN* 3262012165

Gullick, J. M.   • **3.4539**
Malaysia, by J. M. Gullick. — New York: Praeger, [1969] 304 p.: illus., fold. map, ports.; 23 cm. — (Nations of the modern world.) 1963-1964 editions published under title: Malaya. 1. Malaysia — History. 2. Malaysia — Politics and government. I. T. II. Series.
DS596.G83 1969b   991.1/52   *LC* 69-11867

Pye, Lucian W., 1921-.   • **3.4540**
Guerrilla communism in Malaya: its social and political meaning / by Lucian W. Pye. — Princeton, N.J.: Princeton University Press, c1956. xvi, 369 p.; 22 cm. 1. Communism — Malay Peninsula I. T.
DS596 P9   *LC* 56-10827

Abdullah, Munshi, 1796-1854.   **3.4541**
[Hikayat Abd Allah. English] The Hikayat Abdullah. An annotated translation by A. H. Hill. Kuala Lumpur, New York, Oxford University Press, 1970. viii, 353 p. illus., geneal. table, maps, plans. 23 cm. (Oxford in Asia historical reprints) This translation was originally published in the Journal of the Malayan Branch of the Royal Asiatic Society, 1955. 1. Raffles, Thomas Stamford, Sir, 1781-1826. 2. Malacca (State) — History. 3. Singapore — History. I. T.
DS596.5.A6313   959.5/1   *LC* 75-24371

Roff, William R.   **3.4542**
The origins of Malay nationalism / by William R. Roff. — New Haven: Yale University Press, 1967. xx, 297 p.: ill., ports. — (Yale Southeast Asia studies; 2) Includes index. 1. Nationalism — Malay Peninsula. 2. Elite (Social sciences) 3. Malay Peninsula — History. I. T. II. Series.
DS596.5.R6   DS596.6.R6.   *LC* 67-13447

Bedlington, Stanley S., 1928-.   **3.4543**
Malaysia and Singapore: the building of new states / Stanley S. Bedlington. — Ithaca, N.Y.: Cornell University Press, 1978. 285 p.: map; 22 cm. — (Politics and international relations of Southeast Asia) Includes index. 1. Malaysia — Politics and government. 2. Singapore — Politics and government. I. T. II. Series.
DS597.B42   320.9/595   *LC* 77-3114   *ISBN* 0801409101

Means, Gordon Paul.   **3.4544**
Malaysian politics / [by] Gordon P. Means. 2nd ed. — London: Hodder and Stoughton, 1976. 483 p.; 22 cm. Includes index. 1. Malaysia — Politics and government. I. T.
DS597.M4 1976   320.9/595/04   *LC* 76-376033   *ISBN* 0340181869

Ongkili, James P.   **3.4545**
Nation-building in Malaysia, 1946–1974 / James P. Ongkili. — Singapore; New York: Oxford University Press, 1985. xii, 275 p.; 23 cm. Revision of the author's thesis (Ph. D.—University of Malaya) Includes index. 1. Malaysia — Politics and government. I. T.
DS597.O54 1985   959.5 19   *LC* 85-941303   *ISBN* 0195825748

Short, Anthony.   **3.4546**
The Communist insurrection in Malaya, 1948–1960 / Anthony Short. — New York: Crane, Russak, [1975] 547 p.: map; 22 cm. Includes index. 1. Malaya — History — Malayan Emergency, 1948-1960 I. T.
DS597.S47   959.5/04   *LC* 73-93384   *ISBN* 0844803065

Vasil, R. K.   **3.4547**
Ethnic politics in Malaysia / R. K. Vasil. — New Delhi: Radiant, 1980. xii, 234 p.; 23 cm. Includes index. 1. Malaysia — Politics and government. 2. Malaysia — Ethnic relations. I. T.
DS597.2.V37   320.9595 19   *LC* 80-900166

Wang, Gungwu.   • **3.4548**
Malaysia: a survey / edited by Wang Gungwu. — New York: Praeger, 1964. 466 p.: maps; 26 cm. 1. Maylaysia — History. I. Wang, Gungwu. II. T.
DS597.2 W3 1964   959.5   *LC* 64-24586

Leigh, Michael B.   **3.4549**
The rising moon: political change in Sarawak / Michael B. Leigh; foreword by Datuk Haji Abdul Rahman Ya'kub. — [Sydney]: Sydney University Press; Portland, Or.: International Scholarly Book Services, 1974. xv, 232 p.; 23 cm. 1. Sarawak — Politics and government. I. T.
DS597.37.L44   320.9/595/405   *LC* 72-76423   *ISBN* 0424065800

Andaya, Leonard Y.   **3.4550**
The Kingdom of Johor, 1641–1728 / Leonard Y. Andaya. — Kuala Lumpur; New York: Oxford University Press, 1975. xvii, 394 p.: maps; 23 cm. (East Asian historical monographs) Includes index. 1. Johor — History. I. T.
DS598.J7 A5   959.5/1   *LC* 76-355729   *ISBN* 0195802624

Roff, William R.   **3.4551**
Kelantan; religion, society, and politics in a Malay state, edited by William R. Roff. — Kuala Lumpur: Oxford University Press, 1974. xvii, 371 p.: illus.; 26 cm. 1. Kelantan — Addresses, essays, lectures. I. T.
DS598.K3 R63   915.95/1   *LC* 74-182309   *ISBN* 0196382394

Vreeland, Nena, 1934-.   **3.4552**
Area handbook for Singapore / coauthors, Nena Vreeland ... [et al.]. — 1st ed. — Washington: For sale by the Supt. of Docs., U.S. Govt. Print. Off., 1977. xiv, 216 p.: maps; 24 cm. 'DA pam 550-184.' 'One of a series of handbooks prepared by Foreign Area Studies (FAS) of the American University.' Issued in 1965 under title: Area handbook for Malaysia and Singapore, by B. C. Maday, et al. 1. Singapore. I. Maday (Bela C. Area handbook for Malaysia and Singapore. II. American University (Washington, D.C.). Foreign Area Studies. III. T.
DS598.S7 V73   959.5/2/05   *LC* 77-608111

Crawfurd, John, 1783-1868.   **3.4553**
A descriptive dictionary of the Indian islands & adjacent countries. With an introd. by M. C. Ricklefs. Kuala Lumpur, New York, Oxford University Press, 1971. vii, 459 p. map. 26 cm. (Oxford in Asia historical reprints) Reprint of the 1856 ed. 1. Asia, Southeastern — Dictionaries and encyclopedias. I. T.
DS600.C7 1971   915.4/04/03   *LC* 70-943342

Cole, Fay Cooper, 1881-.   • **3.4554**
The peoples of Malaysia / Fay-Cooper Cole. — New York: D. Van Nostrand, 1945. xiv, 354 p.: ill., maps. 1. Malay race 2. Ethnology — Malay Archipelago 3. Malay Archipelago — Social life and customs I. T.
DS601.C63   *LC* 45-5386

Robequain, Charles, 1897-.   • **3.4555**
[Monde malais. English] Malaya, Indonesia, Borneo, and the Philippines; a geographical, economic, and political description of Malaya, the East Indies, and the Philip[p]ines. Translated by E. D. Laborde. Issued in co-operation with the International Secretariat, Institute of Pacific Relations. [2d ed.] London, New York, Longmans, Green [1958] xi, 466 p. illus., maps, diagrs. 23 cm. Translation of Le monde malais. 1. Malay Archipelago I. T.
DS601.R752 1958   991   *LC* 58-4431

DS611–649 Indonesia

Alisjahbana, S. Takdir (Sutan Takdir), 1908-.   • **3.4556**
Indonesia: social and cultural revolution. [Translated from the Indonesian by Benedict R. Anderson. 2d ed.] Kuala Lumpur, Oxford University Press, 1966. ix, 206 p.: map (on lining papers); 23 cm. First published in 1961 under title: Indonesia in the modern world. 1. Indonesia. I. T.
DS615.A68 1966   *LC* 66-7740

Indonesia: a country study / Foreign Area Studies, the   **3.4557**
American University; edited by Frederica M. Bunge.
4th ed. — Washington, D.C.: For sale by the Supt. of Docs., U.S. G.P.O., 1983. xxx, 343 p.: ill., maps (1 folded); 24 cm. — (Area handbook series.) (DA pam / Headquarters, Department of the Army; 550-39) Rev. ed. of: Area handbook for Indonesia / co-authors, Nena Vreeland ... [et al.] 3rd ed. 1975. 'Research completed October 1982.' Includes index. 1. Indonesia. I. Bunge, Frederica M. II. Vreeland, Nena, 1934- Area handbook for Indonesia. III. American University (Washington, D.C.). Foreign Area Studies. IV. Series.
DS615.I518 1983   959.8/03 19   *LC* 83-15446

McVey, Ruth Thomas. ed.   • **3.4558**
Indonesia [by] Herbert Feith [and others] New Haven, Southeast Asia studies, Yale University, by arrangement with HRAF Press [1963] 600 p. maps (2 fold. col.) tables. 22 cm. (Survey of world cultures; [12]) 1. Indonesia. I. T. II. Series.
DS615.M3   *LC* 62-21842

Hicks, David, 1939-.   **3.4559**
Tetum ghosts and Kin: fieldwork in an Indonesian community / David Hicks. — 1st ed. — Palo Alto, Calif.: Mayfield, 1976. ix, 143 p.: ill. — (Explorations in world ethnology) 1. Tetum (Indonesian people) I. T. II. Series.
DS632.T4 H5   301.45/19/922   *LC* 76-28114   *ISBN* 0874843685

The Chinese in Indonesia: five essays / edited by J. A. C.   **3.4560**
Mackie.
Honolulu: University Press of Hawaii in association with Australian Institute of International Affairs, c1976. x, 282 p.; 22 cm. Includes index. 1. Chinese in Indonesia — Addresses, essays, lectures. 2. Indonesia — Politics and government — 20th century — Addresses, essays, lectures. I. Mackie, J. A. C.
DS632.3.C5 C45   301.45/19/510598   *LC* 76-139   *ISBN* 082480449X

The Development of Indonesia society: from the coming of   **3.4561**
Islam to the present day / Harry Aveling, editor; [contributors]
Peter Carey ... [et al.].
New York: St. Martin's Press, 1980 (c1979). xii, 242 p., [10] leaves of plates: ill.; 22 cm. Includes index. 1. Indonesia — History 2. Indonesia — Civilization I. Aveling, Harry. II. Carey, P. B. R.
DS634.D47 1980   959.8/022   *LC* 79-11459   *ISBN* 031219661X

Furnivall, J. S. (John Sydenham) • **3.4562**
Netherlands India: a study of plural economy, by J. S. Furnivall; with an introduction by A. C. D. De Graeff. [1st ed.] reprinted. London, Cambridge U.P., 1967. xxiv, 502 p. maps. 22 cm. (Cambridge University Press. Library editions) First published 1939. 1. Indonesia — History 2. Indonesia — Politics and government 3. Indonesia — Economic conditions I. T.
DS634.F8 1967   309.1/91   LC 68-88337

Ricklefs, M. C. (Merle Calvin) **3.4563**
A history of modern Indonesia, c. 1300 to the present / M.C. Ricklefs. — Bloomington: Indiana University Press, c1981. 335 p.: maps. Includes index. 1. Indonesia — History I. T.
DS634.R52 1981   959.8 19   LC 81-47063   ISBN 0253195934

Sievers, Allen Morris, 1918-. **3.4564**
The mystical world of Indonesia: culture & economic development in conflict [by] Allen M. Sievers. — Baltimore: Johns Hopkins University Press, [1974] xix, 425 p.: illus.; 23 cm. 1. Indonesia — History 2. Indonesia — Economic conditions 3. Indonesia — Social conditions. I. T.
DS634.S52   915.98/03   LC 74-6838   ISBN 0801815916

Vlekke, Bernard Hubertus Maria, 1899-. • **3.4565**
Nusantara, a history of Indonesia. Rev. ed. Chicago, Quadrangle Books, 1960[c1959] 479 p. illus. 22 cm. 1. Indonesia — History I. T.
DS634.V55 1960   LC 62-58200

Mackie, J. A. C. **3.4566**
Konfrontasi: the Indonesia–Malaysia dispute, 1963–1966 / J. A. C. Mackie. — Kuala Lumpur; New York: Published for the Australian Institute of International Affairs [by] Oxford University Press, 1975 (c1974). xiv, 368 p.: maps; 26 cm. Includes index. 1. Indonesia — Foreign relations — Malaysia. 2. Malaysia — Foreign relations — Indonesia. 3. Indonesia — Politics and government — 1950-1966 I. Australian Institute of International Affairs. II. T.
DS640.M34 M3   327.598/0595   LC 75-312660   ISBN 0196382475

Indonesia: selected documents on colonialism and nationalism, 1830–1942 / edited and translated by Chr. L. M. Penders. **3.4567**
St. Lucia: University of Queensland Press, 1977. xi, 367 p.; 23 cm. Distributed in the United Kingdom by Prentice-Hall International, Hemel Hempstead, Eng. 1. Nationalism — Indonesia — History — Sources. 2. Indonesia — History — 1798-1942 — Sources. I. Penders, C. L. M. (Christian Lambert Maria), 1928-
DS643.I53   325/.3492/09598   LC 77-371030   ISBN 0702213241. ISBN 0702210293 pbk

Ingleson, John. **3.4568**
Road to exile: the Indonesian nationalist movement, 1927–1934 / John Ingleson. — Singapore: Published for the Asian Studies Association of Australia by Heinemann Educational Books (Asia), 1979. xii, 254 p.; 24 cm. — (Southeast Asia publications series. no. 1) Includes index. 1. Nationalism — Indonesia. 2. Indonesia — Politics and government — 1798-1942 I. Asian Studies Association of Australia. II. T. III. Series.
DS643.I543   320.9598   LC 79-941196   ISBN 070810309X

Anderson, Benedict R. O'G. (Benedict Richard O'Gorman), 1936-. **3.4569**
Java in a time of revolution; occupation and resistance, 1944–1946 [by] Benedict O'G. Anderson. Ithaca, Cornell University Press [1972] xv, 494 p. map. 24 cm. 'Prepared under the auspices of the Cornell Modern Indonesia Project.' 1. National liberation movements — Indonesia. 2. Indonesia — Politics and government — 1942-1949 I. Cornell University. Modern Indonesia Project. II. T.
DS644.A6936   959.8/022   LC 74-174891   ISBN 0801406870

Kahin, George McTurnan. • **3.4570**
Nationalism and revolution in Indonesia. Ithaca, Cornell University Press [1952] xii, 490 p. maps. 25 cm. 'Published under the auspices of the International Secretariat of the Institute of Pacific Relations and the Southeast Asia Program, Cornell University.' Bibliographical footnotes. 1. Nationalism — Indonesia. 2. Indonesia — Politics and government I. T.
DS644.K32   991   LC 52-4383

Leifer, Michael. **3.4571**
Indonesia's foreign policy / Michael Leifer. — London; Boston: Published for the Royal Institute of International Affairs by Allen & Unwin, 1983. xvii, 198 p.; 23 cm. 1. Indonesia — Foreign relations. I. T.
DS644.L364 1983   327.598 19   LC 82-24420   ISBN 0043270697

Reid, Anthony, 1939-. **3.4572**
The Indonesian national revolution, 1945–1950 / [by] Anthony Reid. — Hawthorn, Vic.: Longman, 1975 (c1974). xi, 193 p.: maps; 23 cm. (Studies in contemporary Southeast Asia) Includes index. 1. Indonesia — History — Revolution, 1945-1949 I. T.
DS644.R37   959.8/03   LC 75-318070   ISBN 0582710464

Penders, C. L. M. (Christian Lambert Maria), 1928-. **3.4573**
The life and times of Sukarno [by] C. L. M. Penders. London, Sidgwick & Jackson [1974] xi, 224 p. illus. 24 cm. 1. Soekarno, 1901-1970. 2. Indonesia — Politics and government — 20th century 3. Indonesia — Residents — Biography. I. T.
DS644.1.S8 P43 1974   959.8/03/0924 B   LC 74-165579   ISBN 0283484144

Hughes, John, 1930-. • **3.4574**
Indonesian upheaval. — New York: D. McKay Co., [1967] ix, 304 p.; 21 cm. 1. Indonesia — Politics and government — 1966- I. T.
DS644.4.H8   991/.03   LC 67-26500

May, Brian. **3.4575**
The Indonesian tragedy / Brian May. — London; Boston: Routledge & K. Paul, 1978. xvii, 438 p., [8] leaves of plates: ill.; 22 cm. 1. Indonesia — History — 1966- I. T.
DS644.4.M39   959.8/02   LC 78-40050   ISBN 0710088345

Trends in Indonesia, II: proceedings and background paper / edited by Leo Suryadinata and Sharon Siddique. **3.4576**
Singapore: Singapore University Press, 1982 (c1981) 165 p.; 22 cm. 'Issued under the auspices of the Institute of Southeast Asian Studies.' 1. Indonesia — Politics and government — 1966- — Congresses. 2. Indonesia — Economic conditions — 1945- — Congresses. I. Suryadinata, Leo. II. Siddique, Sharon. III. Institute of Southeast Asian Studies.
DS644.4.T734   959.8/03 19   LC 81-941973   ISBN 997169039X

DS646 Islands

Loeb, Edwin Meyer, 1894-. **3.4577**
Sumatra, its history and people [by] Edwin M. Loeb. With an additional chapter, by Robert Heine–Geldern. Kuala Lumpur, Oxford University Press, 1972. vi, 350 p. 22 cm. (Oxford in Asia paperbacks) Reprint of the original ed. published by Institut für Völkerkunde der Universität Wien in 1935, except the supplement of plates. 1. Ethnology — Indonesia — Sumatra 2. Sumatra (Indonesia) I. Heine-Geldern, Robert, 1885-1968. II. T.
DS646.1.L63 1972   915.98/1/033   LC 73-940081

Raffles, Thomas Stamford, Sir, 1781-1826. **3.4578**
The history of Java. With an introd. by John Bastin. Kuala Lumpur, New York, Oxford University Press, 1965. 2 v. illus. (part col.) maps (1 fold. col. in pocket of v. 1) 28 cm. (Oxford in Asia. Historical reprints) First published in London in 1817. 1. Malayan languages 2. Java (Indonesia) — Description & travel. 3. Java (Indonesia) — History. I. T.
DS646.2.R13 1965   LC 66-3056

Kartini, Raden Adjeng, 1879-1904. • **3.4579**
Letters of a Javanese princess / Raden Adjeng Kartini; translated from the Dutch by Agnes Louise Symmers; edited and with an introd. by Hildred Geertz; pref. by Eleanor Roosevelt. — New York: W. W. Norton, 1964. 246 p.; 20 cm. — (UNESCO collection of representative works: Indonesian series) (The Norton library) 1. Women — Java I. T. II. Series.
DS646.23.K3 1964   LC 64-5470   ISBN 0393002071

Day, Clive, 1871-1951. • **3.4580**
[Policy and administration of the Dutch in Java] The Dutch in Java. [1st ed. reprinted] with an introduction by John Bastin. Kuala Lumpur, New York [etc.] Oxford U.P. 1966. xxii, 434 p. front. (facsim.), tables. 21 1/2 cm. (Oxford in Asia. Historical reprints) 1st ed. published as The policy and administration of the Dutch in Java. 1. Netherlands — Colonies — Administration. 2. Java (Indonesia) — Politics and government. I. T.
DS646.27.D27 1966   325.349209922   LC 66-67566

Ricklefs, M. C. **3.4581**
Jogjakarta under Sultan Mangkubumi, 1749–1792: a history of the division of Java / by M. C. Ricklefs. — London; New York: Oxford University Press, 1974. xxv, 463 p.: maps; 23 cm. (London oriental series. v. 30) Includes index. 1. Hamengku Buwono I, Sultan of Yogyakarta, ca. 1712-1792. 2. Yogyakarta (Indonesia) — History. 3. Java (Indonesia) — History. I. T. II. Series.
DS646.29.Y63 R52   959.8/2   LC 74-186963   ISBN 0197135781

Tregonning, K. G. • **3.4582**
A history of modern Sabah (North Borneo, 1881–1963) 2d ed. [Singapore] Published for the University of Singapore by the University of Malaya Press, 1965. 275 p. illus., maps, ports. 22 cm. 1. British North Borheo Company. 2. Sabah — History. I. T.
DS646.33.T7 1965   LC 66-1275

Runciman, Steven, Sir, 1903-. • **3.4583**
The white rajahs; a history of Sarawak from 1841 to 1946. — Cambridge, University Press, 1960. 319 p. illus. 24 cm. 1. Sarawak — Hist. I. T.
DS646.36.R9   991.15   LC 60-50589

Budiardjo, Carmel.   **3.4584**
The war against East Timor / Carmel Budiardjo and Liem Soei Liong. —
London: Zed Books; Totowa, N.J.: US distributor, Biblio Distributor Center,
1985 (c1984). xviii, 253 p.: ill.; 23 cm. Includes index. 1. Timor Timur
(Indonesia) — History. I. Liem, Soei Liong. II. T.
DS646.57.B83   959.8/6 19   LC 84-152514   ISBN 0862322286

Belo, Jane, comp.   • **3.4585**
Traditional Balinese culture: essays. — New York: Columbia University Press,
1970. xxvii, 421 p.: ill., map, music; 28 cm. 1. Bali Island (Indonesia) —
Civilization — Addresses, essays, lectures. I. T.
DS647.B2 B4   919.2/3   LC 68-54454   ISBN 0231030843

Lansing, John Stephen.   **3.4586**
The three worlds of Bali / J. Stephen Lansing. — New York: Praeger, 1983. xii,
170 p.: ill., maps; 24 cm. Includes index. Maps on lining papers. 1. Arts,
Balinese — Indonesia — Bali (Province) 2. Bali (Indonesia: Province) —
Civilization. I. T.
DS647.B2 L26 1983   959.8/6 19   LC 83-4117   ISBN 003063816X

DS651–689 Philippine Islands

Philippines, a country study / Foreign Area Studies, the   **3.4587**
American University; edited by Frederica M. Bunge.
3rd ed. — Washington, D.C.: Foreign Area Studies, American University: For
sale by the Supt. of Docs., U.S. G.P.O., 1984. xxxiii, 368 p.: ill.; 24 cm. (Area
handbook series.) (DA pam / Headquarters, Department of the Army; 550-72)
'Research completed August 1983.' Rev. ed. of: Area handbook for the
Philippines / coauthors, Nena Vreeland ... [et al.] 2nd ed. 1976. Includes index.
1. Philippines. I. Bunge, Frederica M. II. Vreeland, Nena, 1934- Area
handbook for the Philippines. III. American University (Washington, D.C.).
Foreign Area Studies. IV. Series.
DS655.P598 1984   959.9 19   LC 84-6382

Peterson, Jean Treloggen, 1942-.   **3.4588**
The ecology of social boundaries: Agta foragers of the Philippines / Jean
Treloggen Peterson. — Urbana: University of Illinois Press, c1978. ix, 141 p.,
[5] leaves of plates: ill.; 24 cm. — (Illinois studies in anthropology. no. 11)
Includes index. 1. Aeta (Philippine people) I. T. II. Series.
DS666.A3 P4   959.9/1   LC 77-27467   ISBN 0252006082

Wickberg, Edgar.   • **3.4589**
The Chinese in Philippine life, 1850–1898. New Haven, Yale University Press,
1965. x, 280 p. illus., maps, port. 24 cm. (Yale Southeast Asia studies, 1)
1. Chinese in the Philippine Islands. I. T. II. Series.
DS666.C5 W5   301.451510914   LC 65-22475

Barton, Roy Franklin, 1883-1947.   • **3.4590**
The religion of the Ifugaos. — [Menasha, Wis.] American Anthropological
Assn. [1946-. v. 25 cm. (Memoir series of the American Anthropological
Association, no.65) American anthropologist, New ser., v.48, pt.2, October
1946. 1. Ifugaos — Religion. I. American anthropologist. II. T.
DS666.I15 B3x   299.921   LC 48-3664

Jocano, F. Landa.   **3.4591**
The Ilocanos: an ethnography of family and community life in the Ilocos region
/ F. Landa Jocano; with the special assistance of Arnora Edrozo ... [et al.]. —
Diliman, Quezon City: Asian Center, University of the Philippines, 1982. x,
264 p., [12] leaves of plates: ill.; 23 cm. Includes index. 1. Ilokanos — Social life
and customs. I. Edrozo, Arnora. II. University of the Philippines. Asian
Center. III. T.
DS666.I37 J63 1982   306/.09599/1 19   LC 83-235607

Rosaldo, Renato.   **3.4592**
Ilongot headhunting, 1883–1974: a study in society and history / Renato
Rosaldo. — Stanford, Calif.: Stanford University Press, 1980. vi, 313 p.: ill.; 24
cm. Includes indexes. 1. Ilongot (Philippine tribe) 2. Head-hunters —
Philippines — Luzon — History. I. T.
DS666.I4 R68   959.9/1 19   LC 79-64218   ISBN 0804710465

The Muslim Filipinos / editors, Peter G. Gowing and Robert D.   **3.4593**
McAmis.
Manila: Solidaridad Pub. House., c1974. xi, 311 p.: map; 26 cm. 1. Muslims —
Philippine Islands. 2. Philippines — Social life and customs. I. Gowing, Peter
G. II. McAmis, Robert D.
DS666.M8 M87   301.45/29/710599   LC 77-374889

Casino, Eric.   **3.4594**
The Jama Mapun: a changing Samal society in the southern Philippines / Eric
S. Casino. — Quezon City: Ateneo de Manila University Press, 1976. xiv,

159 p., [4] leaves of plates: ill. (some col.); 25 cm. Includes index. 1. Samals
(Philippine people) I. T.
DS666.S3 C37   306/.0899921 19   LC 82-463209

Nimmo, Harry.   **3.4595**
The sea people of Sulu: a study of social change in the Philippines / [by] H. Arlo
Nimmo. — San Francisco: Chandler Pub. Co. [1972] xi, 104 p.: ill.; 23 cm.
(Studies in social and economic change) 1. Bajau (Southeast Asian people)
2. Sulu Archipelago (Philippines) — Social conditions. I. T.
DS666.S3 N54   301.29/599/9   LC 70-179034   ISBN 0810204533

Philippine studies: history, sociology, mass media, and   **3.4596**
bibliography / Bruce Cruikshank ... [et al.]; Donn V. Hart,
editor.
[De Kalb]: Northern Illinois University, Center for Southeast Asian Studies;
Detroit: exclusive distribution by Cellar Book Shop, 1979 (c1978). xi, 402 p.; 23
cm. (Occasional paper - Northern Illinois University, Center for Southeast
Asian Studies; no. 6) Based on papers presented at the 26th Midwest
Conference on Asian Affairs held at Northern Illinois University, October
1977. 1. Philippines — Study and teaching. 2. Philippines — Bibliography.
I. Cruikshank, Bruce. II. Hart, Donn Vorhis, 1918- III. Midwest Conference
on Asian Affairs. 26th, Northern Illinois University, 1977.
DS667.28.P485   959.9   LC 79-123115

Phelan, John Leddy, 1924-.   **3.4597**
The Hispanization of the Philippines: Spanish aims and Filipino responses,
1565–1700. Madison, University of Wisconsin Press, 1967. xiv, 218 p. illus.,
maps. 22 cm. 1. Catholic Church — Philippines 2. Spaniards in the Philippine
Islands. 3. Philippines — History — 1521-1812. 4. Philippines — Civilization
— Spanish influences. I. T.
DS674.P5   LC a 59-8602

Schumacher, John N.   **3.4598**
The Propaganda Movement, 1880–1895: the creators of a Filipino
consciousness, the makers of revolution / John N. Schumacher. — Manila:
Solidaridad Pub. House, c1973. xii, 302 p.; 23 cm. Includes index.
1. Nationalism — Philippine Islands. 2. Filipinos in Europe — Politics and
government. 3. Philippines — Politics and government I. T.
DS675.S33   959.9/02   LC 79-320844

Bain, David Haward.   **3.4599**
Sitting in darkness: Americans in the Philippines / David Haward Bain. —
Boston: Houghton Mifflin, 1984. 464 p., [40] p. of plates: ill. (some col.); 24 cm.
Includes index. 1. Funston, Frederick, 1865-1917. 2. Aguinaldo, Emilio,
1869-1964. 3. Bain, David Haward. 4. Philippines — History — Insurrection,
1899-1901 5. Luzon (Philippines) — Description and travel. I. T.
DS679.B34 1984   959.9/027 19   LC 84-8945   ISBN 0395352851

Miller, Stuart Creighton, 1927-.   **3.4600**
'Benevolent assimilation': the American conquest of the Philippines, 1899–1903
/ Stuart Creighton Miller. — New Haven: Yale University Press, c1982. xii,
340 p., [10] p. of plates: ill.; 25 cm. Includes index. 1. Philippines — History —
Insurrection, 1899-1901 2. Philippines — History — 1898-1946 I. T.
DS679.M59 1982   959.9/03 19   LC 82-1957   ISBN 0300026978

Elliott, Charles Burke, 1861-1935.   • **3.4601**
The Philippines to the end of the commission government; a study in tropical
democracy. New York, Greenwood Press, 1968 [c1917] 541 p. ports. 24 cm.
1. Philippines — Politics and government I. T.
DS685.E4 1968   991.4/032   LC 69-10088

Friend, Theodore.   • **3.4602**
Between two empires; the ordeal of the Philippines, 1929–1946. New Haven,
Yale University Press, 1965. xviii, 312 p. illus., maps, ports. 25 cm. (Yale
historical publications. Studies, 22) Bibliography: p. [276]-293. 1. Nationalism
— Philippine Islands. 2. Philippines — History — 1898- I. T. II. Series.
DS685.F7   991.403   LC 65-12541

May, Glenn Anthony.   **3.4603**
Social engineering in the Philippines: the aims, execution, and impact of
American colonial policy, 1900–1913 / Glenn Anthony May. — Westport,
Conn.: Greenwood Press, 1980. xxvii, 268 p.: ill.; 22 cm. — (Contributions in
comparative colonial studies. no. 2 0163-3813) Includes index. 1. Education —
United States — Colonies. 2. Education — Philippines. 3. Philippines —
Politics and government — 1898-1935 4. Philippines — Economic conditions
5. United States — Colonies. I. T. II. Series.
DS685.M28   309.1/599/032   LC 79-7467   ISBN 0313209782

Roosevelt, Nicholas, 1893-.   • **3.4604**
The Philippines: a treasure and a problem. — New York: AMS Press [1970] xii,
315 p.; 23 cm. Reprint of the 1926 ed. 1. Philippines. 2. Philippines — Politics
and government — 1898-1935 I. T.
DS685.R7 1970   309.1/914   LC 71-100510   ISBN 0404006183

Stanley, Peter W.   **3.4605**
A Nation in the making: the Philippines and the United States, 1899–1921 [by] Peter W. Stanley. Cambridge, Mass., Harvard University Press, 1974. ix, 340 p. 25 cm. (Harvard studies in American-East Asian relations. 4) 1. Philippines — History — 1898-1946 2. Philippines — Foreign relations — United States. 3. United States — Foreign relations — Philippines. I. T. II. Series.
DS686.S75   959.9/03   *LC* 73-82342   *ISBN* 0674601254

Taruc, Luis, 1913-.   **3.4606**
Born of the people. With a foreword by Paul Robeson. — Westport, Conn.: Greenwood Press, [1973, c1953] 286 p.: maps.; 22 cm. 1. Taruc, Luis, 1913- 2. Hukbong Mapagpalaya ng Bayan (Philippine Islands) I. T.
DS686.2.T3 A3 1973   959.9   *LC* 72-11483   *ISBN* 0837166691

Kerkvliet, Benedict J.   **3.4607**
The Huk rebellion: a study of peasant revolt in the Philippines / by Benedict J. Kerkvliet. — Berkeley: University of California Press, c1977. xvii, 305 p.: maps; 25 cm. Includes index. 1. Hukbong Mapagpalaya ng Bayan (Philippines) 2. Philippines — Politics and government — 1935-1946 3. Philippines — History — 1946-1973. 4. Philippines — Politics and government — 1973- I. T.
DS686.5.K44   322.4/2/09599   *LC* 75-22656   *ISBN* 0520031067

Lachica, Eduardo.   **3.4608**
The Huks: Philippine agrarian society in revolt. — New York: Praeger, [1971] viii, 331 p.: illus.; 25 cm. — (Praeger special studies in international politics and public affairs) Philippine ed. (Manila, Solidaridad) has title: Huk: Philippine agrarian society in revolt. 1. Hukbong Mapagpalaya ng Bayan (Philippine Islands) I. T.
DS686.5.L23 1971b   320.9/599/04   *LC* 77-171236

Ravenholt, Albert.   • **3.4609**
The Philippines: a young Republic on the move / drawings by Manuel Rey Isip; map by Dorothy deFontaine. — Princeton, N. J.: Van Nostrand, 1962. 204 p.: ill.; 21 cm. (The Asia library.) 1. Philippines. I. T.
DS686.5.R3   991.4   *LC* 62-51874

DS701–798 China

De Bary, William Theodore, 1918- ed.   • **3.4610**
Sources of Chinese tradition, compiled by Wm. Theodore de Bary, Wing–tsit Chan [and] Burton Watson. With contributions by Yi–pao Mei [and others]. — New York: Columbia University Press, 1960. xxiv, 976 p.: illus., maps.; 24 cm. — (Records of civilization; sources and studies, 55. Introduction to oriental civilizations) Translations from various sources and by various individuals. 1. China — History — Sources. 2. China — Civilization I. T.
DS703.D4   951.0082   *LC* 60-9911

Harvard University. East Asian Research Center.   • **3.4611**
Papers on China. v.1-24; 1947-Dec. 1971. Cambridge, Mass., Harvard University, East Asian Research Center. v.; 28 cm. Annual. Title varies slightly. 1. China — Periodicals. I. Harvard University. East Asian Research Center. II. Harvard University. Committee on Regional Studies. III. T.
DS703.4.H3

The Cambridge encyclopedia of China / general editor, Brian **3.4612**
Hook.
Cambridge [Cambridgeshire]; New York: Cambridge University Press, 1982. 492 p.: ill. (some col.); 26 cm. 1. China — Dictionaries and encyclopedias. I. Hook, Brian.
DS705.C35   951/.003/21 19   *LC* 81-9927   *ISBN* 0521230993

China, a country study / Foreign Area Studies, the American **3.4613**
University; edited by Frederica M. Bunge and Rinn–Sup Shinn.
3rd ed. — Washington, D.C.: For sale by the Supt. of Docs., U.S. G.P.O., 1981. xxxi, 590 p.: ill.; 24 cm. — (Area handbook series.) (DA pam. 550-60) 'Research completed September 1980'—T.p. Rev. ed. of: Area handbook for the People's Republic of China / Donald P. Whitaker, Rinn-Sup Shinn ... [et al.]. 2nd ed. 1972. Includes index. 1. China. I. Bunge, Frederica M. II. Shinn, Rinn-Sup. III. Whitaker, Donald P. Area handbook for the People's Republic of China. IV. American University (Washington, D.C.). Foreign Area Studies. V. Series. VI. Series: DA pam. 550-60
DS706.C489 1981   951 19   *LC* 81-12878

The People's Republic of China: a handbook / edited by Harold **3.4614**
C. Hinton.
Boulder, Colo.: Westview Press, 1979 (c1978). xvii, 443 p.: ill.; 24 cm. 1. China. I. Hinton, Harold C.
DS706.P38 1979   951.05   *LC* 78-10306   *ISBN* 0891584196

Lattimore, Owen, 1900-.   • **3.4615**
Inner Asian frontiers of China. [2d ed.] Irvington-On-Hudson, N.Y. Capitol Pub. Co., and American Geographical Society, New York 1951. 585p. (American Geographical Society of New York. Research series, no. 21) 1. China — Historical geography 2. China — Boundaries I. T. II. Series.
DS706.5 L3 1951

Ennin, 794-864.   • **3.4616**
[Nittō guhō junrei gyōki English] Diary; the record of a pilgrimage to China in search of the law; translated from the Chinese by Edwin O. Reischauer. New York, Ronald Press Co. [1955] xvi, 454 p. col. port., maps (on lining papers) 25 cm. Translation of Nittō guhō junrei gyōki. 1. Buddha and Buddhism — China. 2. China — Description and travel 3. China — History — T'ang dynasty, 618-907 — Sources. I. Reischauer, Edwin O. (Edwin Oldfather), 1910- tr. II. T. III. Title: Pilgrimage to China in search of the law.
DS707.E512   951.016   *LC* 55-5553

Li Chih-ch'ang.   • **3.4617**
The travels of an alchemist; the journey of the Taoist Ch'ang–ch'un, from China to the Hindukush at the summons of Chingiz Khan, recorded by his disciple, Li Chih–ch'ang. Translated, with an introduction, by Arthur Waley. London, G. Routledge & sons, ltd. [1931] xi, 166 p.: double front. (map); 23 cm. (The Broadway travellers, edited by Sir E. Denison Ross and Eileen Power) Translation of Hsi yu chi (Se yew ke) 1. Ch'iu, Ch'ang-ch'un, 1148-1227. 2. Mongolia — Description and travel. 3. Asia, Central — Description and travel. 4. China — Description and travel I. Waley, Arthur. II. T.
DS707.L5   915.1   *LC* 31-31754

Reischauer, Edwin O. (Edwin Oldfather), 1910-.   • **3.4618**
Ennin's travels in T'ang China. — New York, Ronald Press Company [1955] xii, 341 p. 24 cm. 1. Ennin, 793 — 864. 2. China — Descr. & trav. I. T.
DS707.R45   951.016   *LC* 55-6273

Macartney, George Macartney, Earl, 1737-1806.   • **3.4619**
An embassy to China; being the journal kept by Lord Macartney during his embassy to the Emperor Ch'ien–lung, 1793–1794. Edited with an introd. and notes by J. L. Cranmer–Byng. — Hamden, Conn., Archon Books, 1963. 421 p. illus. 23 cm. 1. China — Descr. & trav. I. T.
DS708.M14   915.1   *LC* 63-6504

Thomson, J. (John), 1837-1921.   **3.4620**
China, the land and its people: early photographs / rev. and ed. by John Thomson. — 2d ed. — Hong Kong: J. Warner Publications, 1980, (c1979). 160 p.: ill.; 26 cm. First ed. published in 1873 under title: Illustrations of China and its people. 1. China — Description and travel — To 1900 — Views. I. T.
DS709.T475   951/.03 19   *LC* 80-133003   *ISBN* 9627015024

Cressey, George Babcock, 1896-1963.   • **3.4621**
Land of the 500 million; a geography of China. New York, McGraw-Hill, 1955. xv, 387 p. illus., maps, tables. 26 cm. (McGraw-Hill series in geography) 1. China — Description and travel — 1949-1975 I. T.
DS710.C73   915.1   *LC* 55-8895

Schell, Orville.   **3.4622**
In the People's Republic: an American's first–hand view of living and working in China / Orville Schell. — 1st ed. — New York: Random House, c1977. ix, 271 p., [12] leaves of plates: ill.; 22 cm. 1. Schell, Orville. 2. China — Description and travel — 1949- I. T.
DS711.S288   951.05   *LC* 76-53458   *ISBN* 0394499050

Tregear, T. R. (Thomas R.)   **3.4623**
China, a geographical survey / T. R. Tregear. — New York: Halsted Press, 1980. x, 372 p.: ill.; 26 cm. 1. China — Description and travel — 1976- I. T.
DS712.T73 1980   915.10457   *ISBN* 0470269251

Andersson, Johan Gunnar, 1874-1960.   **3.4624**
Children of the yellow earth: studies in prehistoric China / by J. Gunnar Andersson; [translated from the Swedish by E. Classen]. — New York: Macmillan, 1934. xxi, 345 p.: ill., 32 pl. double map; 22 cm. Translation of Den gula jordens barn. 1. Man, Prehistoric — China. 2. Excavations (Archaeology) — China 3. China — Antiquities I. T.
DS715.A52   *LC* 35-298

Chang, Kwang-chih.   **3.4625**
The archaeology of ancient China / Kwang–chih Chang. — 4th ed., rev. and enl. — New Haven, Conn.: Yale University Press, c1986. p. cm. Includes index. 1. Man, Prehistoric — China. 2. China — Antiquities 3. China — Civilization I. T.
DS715.C38 1983   931 19   *LC* 86-9186   *ISBN* 0300037821

Elisseeff, Danielle.   **3.4626**
[Nouvelles découvertes en Chine. English] New discoveries in China: encountering history through archeology / Danielle and Vadime Elisseeff; translated by Larry Lockwood, typography by Arts & Letters, Inc. — Secaucus, N.J.: Chartwell Books, c1983. 248 p.: ill. (some col.), maps; 31 cm. Includes index. Translation of: Nouvelles découvertes en Chine. 1. Paleolithic

period — China. 2. China — Antiquities 3. China — Civilization I. Elisseeff, Vadime. II. T. III. Title: Nouvelles découvertes en Chine. English
DS 715 E43 E5 1983   *ISBN* 0890098409

Qian, Hao.   3.4627
Out of China's earth: archeological discoveries in the People's Republic of China / Qian Hao, Chen Heyi, Ru Suichu. — New York: H.N. Abrams; Beijing: China Pictorial, 1981. 206 p.: ill. (some col.); 34 cm. Includes index. 1. China — Antiquities — Addresses, essays, lectures. I. Chen, Heyi. II. Ru, Suichu. III. T.
DS715.Q513   931 19   *LC* 81-2058   *ISBN* 0810907666

Granet, Marcel, 1884-1940.   • 3.4628
Festivals and songs of ancient China / by Marcel Granet; translated from the French by E. D. Edwards. — New York, E. P. Dutton & company, 1932. ix, 281 p. 22 cm. (The Broadway oriental library.) 1. Shih ching. 2. Chinese poetry — History and criticism. 3. Festivals — China. I. Edwards, Evangeline Dora, tr. II. T. III. Series.
DS719.G72   915.1   *LC* 33-4631

DS721–730 CIVILIZATION.
ETHNOGRAPHY

Balazs, Etienne, 1905-1963.   • 3.4629
Chinese civilization and bureaucracy: variations on a theme / by Étienne Balazs; translated by H. M. Wright; edited by Arthur F. Wright. — New Haven: Yale U.P., 1964. xix, 309 p. "Sponsored by the East Asian Research Center, Harvard University, and the Council on East Asian Studies, Yale University." Essays. 1. China — Civilization I. T.
DS721.B213   915.1   *LC* 64-20909   *ISBN* 030000138

Blunden, Caroline.   3.4630
Cultural atlas of China / Caroline Blunden and Mark Elvin. — New York, N.Y.: Facts on File Inc., c1983. 237 p.: col. ill.; 31 cm. Includes index. 1. China — Civilization I. Elvin, Mark. II. T.
DS721.B56 1983   951 19   *LC* 82-675304   *ISBN* 0871961326

Fairbank, John King, 1907- ed.   • 3.4631
Chinese thought and institutions. With contributions by T'ung-tsu Ch'ü [and others]. Chicago] University of Chicago Press [1957] xiii, 438 p. map, diagrs., tables. 25 cm. (Comparative studies of cultures and civilizations) 1. China — Intellectual life I. T.
DS721.F26   915.1   *LC* 57-5272

Fitzgerald, C. P. (Charles Patrick), 1902-.   • 3.4632
China: a short cultural history. [4th rev. ed.] New York, Praeger [1954] xviii, 621 p. illus., maps (1 fold.) 26 cm. 1. Art, Chinese 2. China — History 3. China — Civilization — History. 4. China — Religion I. T.
DS721.F55 1954   915.1   *LC* 54-6804

Gernet, Jacques.   • 3.4633
[Vie quotidienne en Chine. English] Daily life in China, on the eve of the Mongol invasion, 1250–1276. Translated from the French by H. M. Wright. Stanford, Calif., Stanford University Press [1962] 254 p. illus., maps. 22 cm. Translation of La vie quotidienne en Chine, à la veille de l'invasion mongole, 1250-1276. 1. China — Social life and customs — 960-1644 2. China — History — Sung dynasty, 960-1279 I. T.
DS721.G413 1962b   915.1/03/2   *LC* 73-110281   *ISBN* 0804707200

Granet, Marcel, 1884-1940.   • 3.4634
Chinese civilization. Translated by Kathleen E. Innes and Mabel R. Brailsford. New York Meridian Books [1958] 444p. 1. China — Social life and customs 2. China — History — Early to 1643 I. T.
DS721 G783 1958

Hsu, Francis L. K., 1909-.   • 3.4635
Americans and Chinese: purpose and fulfillment in great civilizations. — Garden City, N.Y.: Published for the American Museum of Natural History [by] the Natural History Press, [1970] xxviii, 493 p.; 25 cm. Revision of the 1953 ed., published under title: Americans and Chinese: two ways of life. 1. China — Civilization 2. U.S. — Civilization — 20th century. I. T.
DS721.H685 1970   915.1   *LC* 72-116215

Hucker, Charles O.   3.4636
China's imperial past: an introduction to Chinese history and culture / Charles O. Hucker. — Stanford, Calif.: Stanford University Press, 1975. xii, 474 p.: ill.; 25 cm. Includes index. 1. China — Civilization 2. China — History I. T.
DS721.H724   951   *LC* 74-25929   *ISBN* 0804708878

Isaacs, Harold Robert, 1910-.   • 3.4637
Images of Asia; American views of China and India [by] Harold R. Isaacs. New York, Capricorn Books [1962, c1958] 416 p. illus. 21 cm. (Cap giant 223)

'Published originally as Scratches on our minds. 1958.' Bibliographical footnotes. I. T.
DS721.I7   301.154   *LC* 64-7499

Levenson, Joseph Richmond, 1920-1969.   • 3.4638
Confucian China and its modern fate: the problem of intellectual continuity. Berkeley, University of California Press, 1958. 223 p. 23 cm. 1. Communism — China. 2. China — Intellectual life 3. China — Civilization — History. I. T.
DS721.L538   915.1   *LC* 58-2791

Liang, Ch'i-ch'ao, 1873-1929.   • 3.4639
Intellectual trends in the Ch'ing period: Ch'ing-tai hsüeh-shu kai-lun / by Liang Ch'i-ch'ao; translated with introd. and notes by Immanuel C. Y. Hsü; foreword by Benjamin I. Schwartz. — Cambridge, Mass.: Harvard University Press, 1959. xxii, 147, lii p. — (Harvard East Asian studies; 2) 1. China — Intellectual life I. T. II. Series.
DS721.L5483   915.1   *LC* 59-6158

Lin, Yü-sheng, 1934-.   3.4640
The crisis of Chinese consciousness: radical antitraditionalism in the May Fourth era / Lin Yü-sheng. — Madison: University of Wisconsin Press, 1979. xiv, 201 p.; 24 cm. Added Chinese title romanized: Chung-kuo i shih ti wei chi. Includes index. 1. May fourth movement. 2. China — Intellectual life I. T.
DS721.L567   951.05   *LC* 77-91057   *ISBN* 0299074102

Lin, Yutang, 1895-1976.   • 3.4641
My country and my people. Rev. illustrated ed. New York: J. Day Co., c1939. xxvi, 440 p. ill. 1. National characteristics, Chinese 2. China — Civilization I. T.
DS721.L58 1939   951   *LC* 39-7059

Needham, Joseph, 1900-.   • 3.4642
Science and civilisation in China, by Joseph Needham. Cambridge [Eng.] University Press, 1954- < 1985 >. < v. 1-6; in 13 > illus., maps (part fold.) 26 cm. 1. Science — China — History — Collected works. 2. Technology — China — History — Collected works. 3. Science and civilization — Collected works. 4. China — Civilization — Collected works. I. Wang, Ling. II. T.
DS721.N39   509.51 19   *LC* 54-4723

Needham, Joseph, 1900-.   3.4643
The shorter Science and civilisation in China: an abridgement of Joseph Needham's original text / Colin A. Ronan. — Cambridge; New York: Cambridge University Press, 1978-1981. 2 v.: ill.; 24 cm. Volume 2 contains Volume III and a section of Volume IV, Part 1 of the major series. Includes indexes. 1. Science — China — History. 2. China — Intellectual life 3. China — Civilization I. Ronan, Colin A. II. T.
DS721.N392   509/.51   *LC* 77-82513   *ISBN* 0521218217

Scott, A. C. (Adolphe Clarence), 1909-.   • 3.4644
Literature and the arts in twentieth century China. [1st ed.] Garden City, N. Y.: Doubleday, [1963] 212 p.: ill.; 18 cm. (Anchor books) 1. China — Intellectual life I. T.
DS721.S37   915.1   *LC* 63-8760

Self and society in Ming thought, by Wm. Theodore de Bary   3.4645
and the Conference on Ming Thought.
New York: Columbia University Press, 1970. xii, 550 p.; 24 cm. — (Studies in Oriental culture. no. 4) 'Most of the papers appearing herein were presented at [the Conference on Ming Thought] and subsequently revised for publication.' 1. China — Civilization — 960-1644 — Addresses, essays, lectures. 2. China — History — Ming dynasty, 1368-1644 I. De Bary, William Theodore, 1918- ed. II. Conference on Ming Thought, Champaign, Ill., 1966. III. Series.
DS721.S39   915.1/03/2   *LC* 78-101229   *ISBN* 0231032714

Toynbee, Arnold Joseph, 1889-1975.   3.4646
Half the world: the history and culture of China and Japan. Texts E. Glahn [and others] Edited by Arnold Toynbee. — New York: Holt, Rinehart and Winston, [1973] 368 p.: illus.; 31 cm. 1. China — Civilization — Addresses, essays, lectures. 2. Japan — Civilization — Addresses, essays, lectures. I. Glahn, Elsé. II. T.
DS721.T67 1973   915.1/03   *LC* 73-4198   *ISBN* 0030107164

Wang, Y. C. (Yi Chu), 1916-.   • 3.4647
Chinese intellectuals and the West, 1872–1949, by Y. C. Wang. — Chapel Hill, University of North Carolina Press [1966] xiv, 557 p. 24 cm. Bibliography: p. [519]-538. 1. China — Civilization — Occidental influences 2. Intercultural education 3. Returned students — China. I. T.
DS721.W334   915.1033   *LC* 66-10207

Chang, Kwang-chih.   3.4648
Early Chinese civilization: anthropological perspectives / K. C. Chang. — Cambridge, Mass.: Harvard University Press, 1976. xv, 229 p.; 24 cm. (Harvard-Yenching Institute monograph series; v. 23) Includes index. 1. China — Civilization — To 221 B.C. I. T.
DS723.C38   931   *LC* 75-14094   *ISBN* 0674219996

Creel, Herrlee Glessner, 1905-.   • **3.4649**
The birth of China; a study of the formative period of Chinese civilization. New York, F. Ungar Pub. Co. [1954, c1937] 402 p. illus., map (on lining papers) 24 cm. 1. Excavations (Archaeology) — China 2. Bronze age — China. 3. China — Civilization 4. China — Antiquities I. T.
DS723.C7x   913.31   *LC* 54-5633

Li, Chi, 1896-.   • **3.4650**
The beginnings of Chinese civilization; three lectures illustrated with finds at Anyang. Seattle, University of Washington Press, 1957. xvii, 123 p. illus., plates, map. 25 cm. 1. China — Antiquities I. T.
DS723.L5   *LC* 57-5285

Croizier, Ralph C. comp.   • **3.4651**
China's cultural legacy and communism. Edited by Ralph C. Croizier. — New York: Praeger Publishers, [1970] xiii, 313 p.: illus., ports.; 21 cm. — (Praeger library of Chinese affairs) (Praeger university series.) 1. China — Civilization — 1949- — Addresses, essays, lectures. I. T.
DS724.C7 1970   915.1/03/5   *LC* 77-83334

Dreyer, June Teufel, 1939-.   **3.4652**
China's forty millions: minority nationalities and national integration in the People's Republic of China / June Teufel Dreyer. Cambridge, Mass.: Harvard University Press, 1976. 333 p.: ill.; 24 cm. (Harvard East Asian series. 87) Includes index. 1. Minorities — China. I. T. II. Series.
DS730.D73   323.1/51   *LC* 76-19032   *ISBN* 0674119649

Eberhard, Wolfram, 1909-.   **3.4653**
China's minorities: yesterday and today / Wolfram Eberhard. — Belmont, Calif.: Wadsworth, c1982. xi, 176 p.: maps; 24 cm. — (Wadsworth civilization in Asia series.) Includes index. 1. Ethnology — China 2. China — Race relations. I. T. II. Series.
DS730.E17 1982   305.8/00951 19   *LC* 82-2629   *ISBN* 0534010806

Li, Chi, 1896-.   • **3.4654**
The formation of the Chinese people; an anthropological inquiry. — New York, Russell & Russell [1967] 283 p. illus., geneal. table, maps. 24 cm. Reprint of the 1928 ed. 1. Ethnology — China I. T.
DS730.L5 1967   572.9/51   *LC* 66-27117

DS731–798 HISTORY

Mackerras, Colin.   **3.4655**
The Uighur Empire according to the T'ang dynastic histories: a study in Sino–Uighur relations, 744–840. Colin Mackerras, editor and translator. [2d ed.] Columbia, University of South Carolina Press [1973, c1972] viii, 226 p. illus. 24 cm. (Asian publications series no. 2) First published in 1968 under title: The Uighur Empire (744-840) according to the T'ang dynastic histories. 1. Uighurs 2. China — History — T'ang dynasty, 618-907 I. T.
DS731.U4 M33 1973   951/.01   *LC* 73-1708   *ISBN* 0872492796

Fitzgerald, Stephen.   **3.4656**
China and the overseas Chinese; a study of Peking's changing policy, 1949–1970. Cambridge [Eng.] University Press, 1972. xii, 268 p. 24 cm. (Cambridge studies in Chinese history, literature and institutions) 1. Chinese — Foreign countries 2. China — Foreign relations — 1949- I. T.
DS732.F56   301.29/51   *LC* 77-177938   *ISBN* 0521084105

Library of Congress. Orientalia Division.   • **3.4657**
Eminent Chinese of the Ch'ing period (1644–1912) Edited by Arthur W. Hummel ... Washington, U.S. Govt. Print. Off., 1943-44. 2 v. 28 cm. At head of title: The Library of Congress. Paged continuously. Prepared by the Asiatic Division of the Library of Congress. cf. v. 1, p. viii. 1. China — Biography. I. Hummel, Arthur William, 1884- II. T.
DS734.U65   920.051   *LC* 43-53640

Gardner, Charles Sidney, 1900-.   • **3.4658**
Chinese traditional historiography. Cambridge: Harvard University Press, 1938. xi, 120 p.; 21 cm. (Harvard historical monographs, 11) 1. China — Historiography I. T.
DS734.7 G3

History in communist China, edited by Albert Feuerwerker. • **3.4659**
Cambridge: M.I.T. Press, [1968] xiv, 382 p.; 21 cm. 'In their original drafts most of ... [the essays] were prepared for ... a conference on Chinese communist historiography ... and held at Ditchley Manor, Oxfordshire, September 6-12, 1964.' 1. China — Historiography — Addresses, essays, lectures. I. Feuerwerker, Albert. ed.
DS734.7.H56   951/.0072   *LC* 68-18238

Fairbank, John King, 1907-.   **3.4660**
Chinabound: a fifty-year memoir / John King Fairbank. — 1st ed. — New York: Harper & Row, 1982. xiv, 480 p., [16] p. of plates: ill.; 24 cm. 'A

Cornelia & Michael Bessie book.' Maps on lining paper. Includes index. 1. Fairbank, John King, 1907- 2. Sinologists — United States — Biography. 3. United States — Relations — China 4. China — Relations — United States I. T.
DS734.9.F3 A33 1982   951/.04 19   *LC* 81-47656   *ISBN* 0060390050

Watson, Burton, 1925-.   • **3.4661**
Ssu–ma Ch'ien, grand historian of China. — New York, Columbia University Press, 1958. xi, 276 p. 24 cm. Bibliography: p. [241]-246. 1. Ssu-ma, Ch'ien, ca. 145-ca. 86 B.C. 2. China — Hist. — Historiography. I. T.
DS734.9.S8W3   951.007   *LC* 57-13030

Meskill, John Thomas, ed.   • **3.4662**
The pattern of Chinese history: cycles, development, or stagnation? Edited with an introd. by John Meskill. — Boston: Heath, [1965] xx, 108 p.; 24 cm. — (Problems in Asian civilizations) 1. China — History — Philosophy. I. T. II. Series.
DS734.95.M4   951.001   *LC* 65-17466

The Cambridge history of China / general editors, Denis   **3.4663**
Twitchett and John K. Fairbank.
Cambridge [Eng.]; New York: Cambridge University Press, 1978-1983. 1002 p. Includes indexes. 1. China — History I. Twitchett, Denis Crispin. II. Fairbank, John King, 1907-
DS735.C3145   951/.03   *LC* 76-29852   *ISBN* 0521214475

Eberhard, Wolfram, 1909-.   • **3.4664**
A history of China / Wolfram Eberhard. — 4th rev. ed. — Berkeley: University of California Press, 1977. xix, 388 p.: ill. Translation of Chinas Geschichte. 1. China — History I. T.
DS735.E214 1977   *ISBN* 0710083572

Elvin, Mark.   **3.4665**
The pattern of the Chinese past. — Stanford: Stanford University Press, 1973. 346 p.: illus.; 23 cm. 1. China — History 2. China — Economic conditions I. T.
DS735.E48 1973   915.1/03   *LC* 72-78869   *ISBN* 0804708266

Fairbank, John King, 1907-.   • **3.4666**
The United States and China. — 3d ed. — Cambridge, Mass.: Harvard University Press, 1971. xvi, 500 p.: maps.; 22 cm. — (The American foreign policy library) 1. China — History 2. U.S. — Foreign relations — China. 3. China — Foreign relations — U.S. I. T. II. Series.
DS735.F3 1971   327.51/073   *LC* 71-152270   *ISBN* 0674924010

Goodrich, L. Carrington (Luther Carrington), 1894-.   • **3.4667**
A short history of the Chinese people [by] L. Carrington Goodrich. 3rd ed., with a final chapter by W. A. C. Adie. London, Allen & Unwin, 1969. xv, 295 p. 17 maps. 23 cm. 1. China — History I. Adie, W. A. C. II. T.
DS735.G58 1969   951   *LC* 73-454308   *ISBN* 0049510150

Grousset, René, 1885-1952.   • **3.4668**
The rise and splendour of the Chinese Empire. [Translated by Anthony Watson–Gandy and Terence Gordon. 1st American ed.] Berkeley, University of California Press, 1953. 312 p. illus., port., maps. 23 cm. Translation of Histoire de la Chine. 1. China — History I. T.
DS735.G76   *LC* A 53-9939

Chesneaux, Jean.   **3.4669**
[Mouvement paysan chinois. English] Peasant revolts in China, 1840–1949. Translated by C. A. Curwen. [1st American ed. New York] Norton [1973] 180 p. illus. 22 cm. French ed. published in Paris, 1976 under title: Le mouvement paysan chinois. 1. Peasant uprisings — China. I. T.
DS736.C5123   951/.03   *LC* 72-13015   *ISBN* 0393054853 *ISBN* 0393093441

Liu, Chih-pu.   • **3.4670**
A military history of modern China, 1924–1949, by F. F. Liu. — Princeton, Princeton University Press, 1956. 312 p. illus. 25 cm. 1. China — History, Military I. T.
DS738.L5   951.04   *LC* 56-8386

DS740 POLITICAL AND DIPLOMATIC HISTORY

Chiang, Kai-shek, 1887-1975.   • **3.4671**
China's destiny, by Chiang Kai–shek; authorized translation by Wang Chung–hui, with an introduction by Lin Yutang. New York, Macmillan, 1947. xi, 260 p.: 21 cm. 'First edition (in Chinese), Chungking, March 1943. First English edition, New York, 1947. 'The translation was prepared by a group of Chinese scholars under the supervision of Dr. Wang Chung-hui.'—Introd., p.

ix. 1. Reconstruction (1939-1951) — China. 2. China — Foreign relations 3. China — Politics & government — 1912- I. Wang, Ch'ung-hui, 1881-1958. tr. II. T.
DS740.C5   *LC* 47-30071

China and Malaysia, 1949–1983 / edited by R.K. Jain.   3.4672
Atlantic Highlands, N.J.: Humanities Press, 1984. lx, 364 p.; 23 cm. — (China and Southeast Asia since 1949. 2) Includes index. 1. China — Foreign relations — Malaysia. 2. Malaysia — Foreign relations — China. I. Jain, Rajendra Kumar. II. Series.
DS740.C56 1984   *ISBN* 0391025988

Israel, John.   • 3.4673
Student nationalism in China, 1927–1937. — Stanford, Calif., Published for the Hoover Institution on War, Revolution, and Peace by Stanford University Press, 1966. ix, 253 p. illus., maps. 24 cm. — (Hoover Institution publications) Bibliography: p. [231]-244. 1. China — Pol. & govt. — 1912-1949. 2. Students — China. I. Hoover Institution on War, Revolution, and Peace. II. T.
DS740.2.I8   951.042   *LC* 66-15300

Perry, Elizabeth J.   3.4674
Rebels and revolutionaries in north China, 1845–1945 / Elizabeth J. Perry. — Stanford, Calif.: Stanford University Press, 1980. xiii, 324 p.: maps; 23 cm. Includes index. 1. Peasant uprisings — China. 2. Revolutions — China. 3. China — Politics and government — 19th century 4. China — Politics and government — 20th century I. T.
DS740.2.P47   951/.03 19   *LC* 79-65179   *ISBN* 0804710554

Teng, Ssu-yü, 1906-.   • 3.4675
China's response to the West; a documentary survey, 1839–1923 [by] Ssu-yü Teng [and] John. K. Fairbank, with E–tu Zen Sun, Chaoying Fang, and others. [Prepared in Coöperation with the International Secretariat of the Institute of Pacific Relations] Cambridge, Harvard University Press, 1954. vi, 296 p. 25 cm. 1. China — Relations — Foreign countries I. Fairbank, John King, 1907- joint author. II. T.
DS740.2.T4   303.4/82/0951 19   *LC* 53-5061

Frodsham, J. D. comp.   3.4676
The first Chinese embassy to the West; the journals of Kuo–Sung–T'ao, Liu Hsi–Hung and Chang Te–yi; translated and annotated by J. D. Frodsham. Oxford, Clarendon Press, 1974. lxv, 222 p. illus. 22 cm. 1. China — Relations — Europe 2. Europe — Relations — China I. Kuo, Sung-t'ao, 1818-1891. Shih hsi chi ch'eng. II. Liu, Hsi-hung. Ying yao jih chi. English. Selections. 1974. III. Chang, Te-i, 1847-1918. Sui shih jih chi. English. Selections. 1974. IV. T.
DS740.4.F7185   301.29/51/04   *LC* 74-180206   *ISBN* 019821555X

Hinton, Harold C.   3.4677
China's turbulent quest; an analysis of China's foreign relations since 1949 [by] Harold C. Hinton. — New and enl. ed. — Bloomington: Indiana University Press, [1972] xi, 352 p.; 20 cm. — (A Midland book, MB-157) 1. China — Foreign relations — 1949- I. T.
DS740.4.H5 1972   327.51   *LC* 72-83700   *ISBN* 0253201578

Morse, Hosea Ballou, 1855-1934.   • 3.4678
The international relations of the Chinese Empire. London; New York [etc.]: Longmans, Green, 1910-18. 3 v.: fronts., plates, ports. (1 col.) fold. maps, diagrs. (part fold.); 23 cm. 1. China — Foreign relations 2. China — Politics and government 3. China — History 4. Opium trade — China I. T.
DS740.4 M6

Barnett, A. Doak.   3.4679
China and the major powers in East Asia / A. Doak Barnett. — Washington: Brookings Institution, c1977. xii, 416 p.; 24 cm. 1. China — Foreign relations — Russia. 2. Russia — Foreign relations — China. 3. China — Foreign relations — Japan. 4. Japan — Foreign relations — China. 5. China — Foreign relations — United States. 6. United States — Foreign relations — China. I. T.
DS740.5.R8 B37   327.51   *LC* 77-21981   *ISBN* 0815708246

Brandt, Conrad.   • 3.4680
Stalin's failure in China, 1924–1927. Cambridge, Harvard University Press, 1958. xv, 226 p. 22 cm. (Russian Research Center studies, 31) 1. Stalin, Joseph, 1879-1953. 2. China — Foreign relations — Soviet Union. 3. Soviet Union — Foreign relations — China. I. T.
DS740.5.R8 B7   951.042   *LC* 58-12963

Clubb, O. Edmund (Oliver Edmund), 1901-.   • 3.4681
China & Russia; the 'great game' [by] O. Edmund Clubb. New York, Columbia University Press, 1971. xii, 578 p. illus., maps, ports. 24 cm. (Studies of the East Asian Institute, Columbia University) 1. Soviet Union — Foreign relations — China. 2. China — Foreign relations — Soviet Union. I. T.
DS740.5.R8 C63   327.47/051   *LC* 72-155362   *ISBN* 0231027400

Gittings, John.   • 3.4682
Survey of the Sino–Soviet dispute: a commentary and extracts from the recent polemics 1963–1967. — London; New York [etc.]: issued under the auspices of the Royal Institute of International Affairs [by] Oxford U.P., 1968. xix, 410 p.; 25 cm. 1. China — Foreign relations — Russia. 2. Russia — Foreign relations — China. I. Royal Institute of International Affairs. II. T.
DS740.5.R8 G5   327.51/047   *LC* 75-356659

North, Robert Carver.   • 3.4683
Moscow and Chinese Communists. — 2d ed. — Stanford, Calif., Stanford University Press [1963] viii, 310 p. 24 cm. Includes index. 1. Communism — China. 2. China — For. rel. — Russia. 3. Russia — For. rel. — China. I. T.
DS740.5.R8N6 1963   951.04   *LC* 62-18742

Whiting, Allen Suess, 1926-.   • 3.4684
Soviet policies in China, 1917–1924, by Allen S. Whiting. Stanford, Calif., Stanford University Press [1968, c1953] viii, 350 p. 24 cm. 1. China — Foreign relations — Soviet Union. 2. Soviet Union — Foreign relations — China. I. T.
DS740.5.R8 W5 1968   327.47/051   *LC* 68-12335

The Sino–Soviet conflict: a global perspective / edited by   3.4685
Herbert J. Ellison.
Seattle: University of Washington Press, c1982. xxii, 408 p.; 25 cm. 1. World politics — 1975-1985 — Congresses. 2. China — Foreign relations — Soviet Union — Congresses. 3. Soviet Union — Foreign relations — China — Congresses. I. Ellison, Herbert J. II. University of Washington. Center for Contemporary Chinese and Soviet Studies.
DS740.5.S65 S56 1982   327.51047 19   *LC* 81-51279   *ISBN* 0295958545

Fitzgerald, C. P. (Charles Patrick), 1902-.   • 3.4686
The southern expansion of the Chinese people, by C. P. FitzGerald. New York, Praeger [1972] xxi, 230 p. illus. 23 cm. 1. China — Relations — Asia, Southeastern 2. Asia, Southeastern — Relations — China I. T.
DS740.6.F58   301.29/51/059   *LC* 73-185594

DS741–778 History, by Period

DS741–753 Early to 1644

Chang, K. C. (Kwang-chih)   3.4687
The archaeology of ancient China / Kwang–Chih Chang. — 4th ed., rev. and enl. — New Haven; London: Yale University Press, 1987, c1986. [544] p.: ill.; 24 cm. 1. China — Civilization — To 221 B.C. I. T.
DS741.65.C4x   931 19

Chang, Kwang-chih.   3.4688
Art, myth, and ritual: the path to political authority in ancient China / K.C. Chang. — Cambridge, Mass.: Harvard University Press, 1983. x, 142 p.: ill.; 24 cm. 1. Political science — China — History. 2. China — Civilization — To 221 B.C. I. T.
DS741.65.C53 1983   931 19   *LC* 83-214   *ISBN* 0674048075

The Origins of Chinese civilization / edited by David N.   3.4689
Keightley; with contributions by Noel Barnard ... [et al.].
Berkeley: University of California Press, c1983. xxix, 617 p.: ill.; 24 cm. — (Studies on China. 1) 1. China — Civilization — To 221 B.C. I. Keightley, David N. II. Barnard, Noel. III. Series.
DS741.65.O74 1983   931 19   *LC* 81-4595   *ISBN* 0520042298

Chang, Kwang-chih.   3.4690
Shang civilization / Kwang–chih Chang. — New Haven: Yale University Press, 1980. xvii, 417 p.: ill.; 24 cm. Includes index. 1. China — History — Shang dynasty, 1766-1122 B.C. 2. China — Antiquities I. T.
DS744.C383   931   *LC* 79-19107   *ISBN* 0300024282

Keightley, David N.   3.4691
Sources of Shang history: the oracle–bone inscriptions of bronze age China / David N. Keightley. — Berkeley: University of California Press, 1979 (c1978). xvii, 281 p., [15] leaves of plates: ill.; 32 cm. Includes index. 1. Inscriptions, Chinese 2. Oracle bones — China. 3. China — History — Shang dynasty, 1766-1122 B.C. — Sources. I. T.
DS744.K44   931   *LC* 74-29806   *ISBN* 0520029690

Bodde, Derk, 1909-.   • 3.4692
China's first unifier: a study of the Ch'in dynasty as seen in the life of Li Ssŭ, 280?–208 B.C. — Hong Kong: Hong Kong U. P.; London: Oxford U.P., 1967. xii,270 p.: front.; 25 cm. (Sinica Leidensia. v 3.) 1. Li Ssŭ, 280?-208 B.C. 2. Ch'in Shih-huang, Emperor of China, 259-210 B.C. I. T. II. Series.
DS747.5.B6 1967b   931   *LC* 67-108881

Li, Yu-ning, ed.   3.4693
The First Emperor of China: the politics of historiography / edited by Li Yu-ning. — White Plains, N.Y.: International Arts and Sciences Press, [1975] lxxiii, 357 p.: ill.; 24 cm. — (The Politics of historiography) 1. Ch'in Shih-huang, Emperor of China, 259-210 B.C. I. Li, Yu-ning. II. T.
DS747.5.F57   931/.00994 B   *LC* 74-15390   *ISBN* 0873320670

**Ch'in Shih-huang ling ping ma yung / Shan-hsi Shih-huang ling   3.4694
Ch'in yung k'eng k'ao ku fa chüeh tui, Ch'in Shih-huang ping
ma yung po wu kuan pien; [she ying Lo Chung-min].**
Ti 1 pan. — Pei-ching: Wen wu ch'u pan she: Hsin hua shu tien Pei-ching fa hsing so fa hsing, 1983. 22, 20 p., [121] p. of plates: chiefly ill. (some col.); 27 cm. Chinese and English. Cover title also in English: Terra-cotta warriors & horses at the tomb of Qin Shi Huang. 1. Ch'in Shih-huang, Emperor of China, 259-210 B.C — Tomb. 2. Terra-cotta sculpture, Chinese — Ch'in-Han dynasties, 221 B.C.-220 A.D. I. Lo, Chung-min. II. Shan-hsi Shih-huang ling Ch'in yung k'eng k'ao ku fa chüeh tui. III. Ch'in Shih-huang ping ma yung po wu kuan. IV. Title: Terra-cotta warriors & horses at the tomb of Qin Shi Huang. V. Title: Terra-cotta warriors and horses at the tomb of Qin Shi Huang.
DS747.9.C47 C45 1983   931/.04 19   *LC* 84-114552

Loewe, Michael.   3.4695
Crisis and conflict in Han China, 104 BC to AD 9 / Michael Loewe. — London: Allen & Unwin, 1975 (c1974). 340 p., [3] leaves of plates (1 fold.): ill., geneal. tables, maps; 23 cm. 1. China — History — Han dynasty, 202 B.C.-220 A.D. I. T.
DS748.L577   931   *LC* 75-308728   *ISBN* 0049510215

Pan, Ku, 32-92.   3.4696
[Han shu. English. Selections] Courtier and commoner in ancient China; selections from the History of the former Han. Translated by Burton Watson. New York, Columbia University Press, 1974. 282 p. 23 cm. 'Translations from the Oriental classics.' Translation of selections from Han shu. 1. China — History — Han dynasty, 202 B.C.-220 A.D. I. T.
DS748.P3 1974   931   *LC* 73-18003   *ISBN* 0231037651

Pirazzoli-t'Serstevens, Michèle.   3.4697
[Chine des Han. English] The Han Dynasty / Michèle Pirazzoli-t'Serstevens; translated by Janet Seligman. — New York: Rizzoli, c1982. 240 p.: ill. (some col.); 30 cm. Translation of: La Chine des Han. Includes index. 1. China — History — Han dynasty, 202 B.C.-220 A.D. I. T.
DS748.P5713 1982   931/.04 19   *LC* 82-50109   *ISBN* 0847804380

Ssu-ma, Ch'ien, ca. 145-ca. 86 B.C.   • 3.4698
Records of the grand historian of China. Translated from the Shih chi of Ssu-ma Ch'ien by Burton Watson. New York, Columbia University Press, 1961. 2 v. maps. 24 cm. (Records of civilization, sources and studies. no. 65) UNESCO collection of representative works: Chinese series. 1. China — History — 1766 B.C.-220 A.D. I. Watson, Burton, 1925- tr. II. T. III. Series.
DS748.S7453   931   *LC* 60-13348

Wright, Arthur F., 1913-1976.   3.4699
The Sui dynasty / Arthur F. Wright. — 1st ed. — New York: Knopf, 1978. 237 p.: maps; 24 cm. Includes index. 1. China — History — Sui dynasty, 581-618 I. T.
DS749.2.W74 1978   951/.01   *LC* 78-54898   *ISBN* 0394492765

Fitzgerald, C. P. (Charles Patrick), 1902-.   • 3.4700
Son of heaven [a biography of Li Shih-Min, founder of the T'ang dynasty, by C. P. Fitzgerald] New York, AMS Press [1971] ix, 232 p. illus., geneal. table, maps, plans, port. 23 cm. Reprint of the 1933 ed. 1. T'ang T'ai-tsung, Emperor of China, 597-649. I. T.
DS749.3.F5 1971   951/.01/0924 B   *LC* 74-136382   *ISBN* 0404024041

Pulleyblank, Edwin G. (Edwin George), 1922-.   • 3.4701
The background of the rebellion of An Lu-shan. — London, Oxford University Press [1966, 1955] x, 264 p. 2 folded maps. folded tables. 23 cm. — (London oriental series, v. 4) Bibliography: p. [209]-221. 1. An, Lu-shan, 703-757. 2. China — Hist. — Early to 1643. I. T.
DS749.3.P8   *LC* A 58-1352

Schafer, Edward H.   • 3.4702
The vermilion bird; T'ang images of the South [by] Edward H. Schafer. Berkeley, University of California Press, 1967. viii, 380 p. illus., maps. 27 cm. 1. Natural history — China. 2. China — Description and travel 3. China — History — T'ang dynasty, 618-907 I. T.
DS749.3.S3   915.1   *LC* 67-10463

Wechsler, Howard J.   3.4703
Mirror to the Son of Heaven: Wei Cheng at the court of T'ang T'ai-tsung / Howard J. Wechsler. — New Haven: Yale University Press, 1974 [i.e. 1975] xi, 259 p.: map; 25 cm. (Yale historical publications: Miscellany; 105) Includes index. 1. Wei, Cheng, 580-643. 2. China — History — T'ang dynasty, 618-907 I. T.
DS749.3.W36 W42   951/.01/0924 B   *LC* 74-76649   *ISBN* 0300017154

Wang, Gungwu.   • 3.4704
The structure of power in North China during the five dynasties. Kuala Lumpur University of Malaya Press 1963. 257p. 1. China — Politics and government — Early to 1643 I. T.
DS749.5 W3

Sung biographies / ed. by Herbert Franke.   3.4705
1. Aufl. — Wiesbaden: Steiner, 1976. 4 v.; 24 cm. — (Münchener ostasiatische Studien. Bd. 16, 17) English, French, or German. 1. China — History — Sung dynasty, 960-1279 — Biography. 2. China — Biography. I. Franke, Herbert, 1914- II. Series.
DS751.5.S96   *LC* 77-462858   *ISBN* 3515024123

**From Ming to Ch'ing: conquest, region, and continuity in   3.4706
seventeenth-century China / edited by Jonathan D. Spence and
John E. Wills. Jr.**
New Haven: Yale University Press, 1979. xxiv, 413 p.: maps; 25 cm. Includes index. 1. China — History — Ming dynasty, 1368-1644 — Addresses, essays, lectures. 2. China — History — Ch'ing dynasty, 1644-1912 — Addresses, essays, lectures. I. Spence, Jonathan D. II. Wills, John E. (John Elliot), 1936-
DS753.F74   951   *LC* 78-15560   *ISBN* 0300022182

Hucker, Charles O.   3.4707
The Ming dynasty, its origins and evolving institutions / by Charles O. Hucker. — Ann Arbor: Center for Chinese Studies, University of Michigan, 1978. viii, 105 p.; 23 cm. — (Michigan papers in Chinese studies. 34) 1. China — History — Ming dynasty, 1368-1644 I. T. II. Series.
DS753.H829   951/.026   *LC* 78-17354   *ISBN* 0892640340

Hucker, Charles O.   • 3.4708
The traditional Chinese state in Ming times (1368-1644). — Tucson, University of Arizona Press, 1961. 85 p. 16 cm. 'In ... slightly different form this essay was prepared as a contribution to a conference on political power in traditional China ... held at Laconia, New Hampshire, in September, 1959.' 1. China — Pol. & govt. — Early to 1643. I. T.
DS753.H83   951.026   *LC* 61-15391

Michael, Franz H.   • 3.4709
The origin of Manchu rule in China; frontier and bureaucracy as interacting forces in the Chinese Empire. — New York, Octagon Books, 1965 [c1942] viii, 127 p. fold. map. 24 cm. Bibliography: p. 125-127. 1. Manchus. 2. China — Hist. — Early to 1643. 3. China — Hist. — Tatar Conquest, 1643-1644. I. T.
DS753.M5 1965   320.951   *LC* 65-25880

**Association for Asian Studies. Ming Biographical History   3.4710
Project Committee.**
Dictionary of Ming biography, 1368-1644 / the Ming Biographical History Project of the Association for Asian Studies; L. Carrington Goodrich, editor, Chaoying Fang, associate editor. — New York: Columbia University Press, 1976. 2 v. (xxi, 1751 p.), [6] leaves of plates: ill.; 27 cm. Added title: Ming tai ming jen chuan. Includes index. 1. China — History — Ming dynasty, 1368-1644 — Biography. 2. China — Biography. I. Goodrich, L. Carrington (Luther Carrington), 1894- II. Fang, Chao-ying, 1908- III. T.
DS753.5.A84 1976   951/.026/0922 B   *LC* 75-26938   *ISBN* 0231038011

DS754–773 Manchu Dynasty (1644–1912)

Hsü, Immanuel Chung-yueh, 1923-.   3.4711
The rise of modern China / Immanuel C. Y. Hsü. — 2d ed. — New York: Oxford University Press, 1975. xxii, 1002 p., [24] leaves of plates: ill.; 24 cm. 1. China — History — Ch'ing dynasty, 1644-1912 2. China — History — 20th century I. T.
DS754.H74 1975   951/.03   *LC* 75-7354

Marsh, Robert Mortimer.   • 3.4712
The mandarins; the circulation of elites in China, 1600-1900. Glencoe [Ill.] Free Press of Glencoe [1961] 300p. 1. Bureaucracy 2. Social mobility — China I. T.
DS754 M37

Grieder, Jerome B.   3.4713
Intellectuals and the state in modern China: a narrative history / Jerome B. Grieder. — New York: Free Press; London: Collier Macmillan, c1981. xix, 395 p.; 25 cm. — (Transformation of modern China series.) Includes index.

1. China — Intellectual life — 1644-1912 2. China — Intellectual life — 1912-1949 I. T. II. Series.
DS754.14.G74   951 19   LC 81-66436   ISBN 0029128102

Mancall, Mark.   3.4714
China at the center: 300 years of foreign policy / Mark Mancall. — New York: Free Press; London: Collier Macmillan, c1984. xviii, 540 p.; 25 cm. — (Transformation of modern China series.) Includes index. 1. China — Foreign relations — 1644-1912 2. China — Foreign relations — 1912-1949 3. China — Foreign relations — 1949- I. T. II. Series.
DS754.18.M36 1984   327.51 19   LC 83-47981   ISBN 0029198100

Fu, Lo-shu, 1920- ed.   • 3.4715
A documentary chronicle of Sino–Western relations, 1644-1820, compiled, translated, and annotated by Lo-shu Fu. Tucson, Published for the Association for Asian Studies by the University of Arizona Press [1966] 2 v. (xviii, 792 p.) 24 cm. (Association for Asian Studies. Monographs and papers no. 22) 1. China — History — Ch'ing dynasty, 1644-1912 — Sources. 2. China — Relations — Foreign countries — Sources. I. T. II. Series.
DS754.2.F8   951.03   LC 66-18529

Kahn, Harold L.   • 3.4716
Monarchy in the emperor's eyes; image and reality in the Ch'ien–lung reign [by] Harold L. Kahn. Cambridge, Mass., Harvard University Press, 1971. ix, 314 p. illus. 25 cm. (Harvard East Asian series. 59) 1. Ch'ien-lung, Emperor of China, 1711-1799. 2. China — History — Ch'ien lung, 1736-1795 I. T. II. Series.
DS754.4.C5 K3   951/.03/0924   LC 75-135546   ISBN 0674582306

K'ang-hsi, Emperor of China, 1654-1722.   3.4717
Emperor of China; self portrait of K'ang Hsi, by Jonathan D. Spence. [1st ed.] New York, Knopf; [distributed by Random House] 1974. xxv, 217, [1], viii p. illus. 22 cm. 1. K'ang-hsi, Emperor of China, 1654-1722. I. Spence, Jonathan D. II. T.
DS754.4.C53 A33 1974   951/.03/0924 B   LC 73-20743   ISBN 0394488350

Kessler, Lawrence D.   3.4718
K'ang-hsi and the consolidation of Ch'ing rule, 1661–1684 / Lawrence D. Kessler. — Chicago: University of Chicago Press, 1976. xi, 251 p.; 23 cm. Includes index. 1. K'ang-hsi, Emperor of China, 1654-1722. 2. China — History — K'ang hsi, 1662-1722 I. T.
DS754.4.C53 K47   951/.03/0924 B   LC 75-20897   ISBN 0226423033

Wu, Silas H. L., 1929-.   3.4719
Passage to power: K'ang-hsi and his heir apparent, 1661–1722 / Silas H. L. Wu. — Cambridge: Harvard University Press, 1979. xv, 252 p.: maps; 24 cm. — (Harvard East Asian series. 91) Includes index. 1. K'ang-hsi, Emperor of China, 1654-1722. 2. China — History — K'ang hsi, 1662-1722 I. T. II. Series.
DS754.4.C53 W8   951/.03/0924 B   LC 79-4191   ISBN 0674656253

Spence, Jonathan D.   • 3.4720
Ts'ao Yin and the K'ang-hsi Emperor; bondservant and master, by Jonathan D. Spence. New Haven, Yale University Press, 1966. xiv, 329 p. map. 24 cm. (Yale historical publications. Miscellany. 85) 1. Ts'ao, Yin, 1658-1712. 2. K'ang-hsi, Emperor of China, 1654-1722. I. T. II. Series.
DS754.4.T72 S66   951.030924   LC 66-21537

Kuhn, Philip A.   • 3.4721
Rebellion and its enemies in late imperial China, militarization and social structure, 1796–1864 [by] Philip A. Kuhn. — Cambridge, Mass.: Harvard University Press, 1970. 254 p.: illus., maps.; 25 cm. — (Harvard East Asian series. 49) 1. China — History — 19th century I. T. II. Series.
DS755.K77   951/.03   LC 75-115476   ISBN 0674749510

Li, Chien-nung.   • 3.4722
[Chung kuo chin pai nien cheng chih shih. English] The political history of China, 1840–1928. Translated and edited by Ssu-yu Teng and Jeremy Ingalls. Princeton, N.J., D. Van Nostrand Co. [1956] 545 p. illus. 24 cm. 1. China — Politics and government — 19th century 2. China — Politics and government — 1900-1949. 3. China — Foreign relations I. Teng, Ssu-yü, 1906- ed. and tr. II. Ingalls, Jeremy, 1911- ed. and tr. III. T.
DS755.L4313 1956   951.03   LC 56-12095

Chang, Hsin-pao, 1922-.   • 3.4723
Commissioner Lin and the Opium War. — Cambridge, Harvard University Press, 1964. xiv, 319 p. illus., maps, port. 24 cm. — (Harvard East Asian series. 18) Bibliography: p. [273]-301. 1. Lin, Tse-hsü, 1785-1850. 2. China — Hist. — War of 1840-1842. I. T. II. Series.
DS757.5.C45   951.03   LC 64-21786

Fay, Peter Ward, 1924-.   3.4724
The Opium War, 1840–1842: barbarians in the Celestial Empire in the early part of the nineteenth century and the war by which they forced her gates ajar /

by Peter Ward Fay. — Chapel Hill: University of North Carolina Press, [1975] xxi, 406 p.: ill.; 23 cm. Includes index. 1. China — History — War of 1840-1842. I. T.
DS757.5.F39   951/.03   LC 74-30200   ISBN 0807812439

Tan, Chung, 1929-.   3.4725
China and the brave new world: a study of the origins of the Opium War (1840–42) / Tan Chung. — Durham, N.C.: Carolina Academic Press, c1978. viii, 271 p.; 22 cm. Includes index. 1. Opium trade — China. 2. China — History — War of 1840-1842. I. T.
DS757.5.T28   951/.03   LC 78-50590   ISBN 9890890862

Waley, Arthur.   • 3.4726
The Opium War through Chinese eyes. Stanford, Calif., Stanford University Press [1968, c1958] 256 p. 22 cm. 1. China — History — War of 1840-1842. I. T.
DS757.5.W3 1968   951/.03   LC 68-12334

Boardman, Eugene Powers.   • 3.4727
Christian influence upon the ideology of the Taiping Rebellion, 1851–1864. — New York: Octagon Books, 1972 [c1952] xi, 188 p.: facsim.; 23 cm. 1. Christians — China 2. China — History — Taiping Rebellion, 1850-1864 I. T.
DS759.B6 1972   951/.03   LC 71-159168   ISBN 0374906971

Chien, Yu-wen, 1896-.   3.4728
The Taiping revolutionary movement, by Jen Yu–wen, with the editorial assistance of Adrienne Suddard. — New Haven: Yale University Press, 1973. xxiii, 616 p.: illus.; 25 cm. 1. Taiping Rebellion, 1850-1864. I. T.
DS759.C4148   951/.03   LC 72-91299   ISBN 0300015429

Clarke, Prescott.   3.4729
Western reports on the Taiping: a selection of documents / Prescott Clarke and J. S. Gregory. — Honolulu: University Press of Hawaii, 1982. xxx, 454 p.: maps; 22 cm. Includes indexes. 1. Taiping Rebellion, 1850-1864 — Sources. 2. China — Foreign population — History — Sources. I. Gregory, James Stothert, 1912- II. T.
DS759.C59   LC 81-68942   ISBN 082480807X

Meadows, Thomas Taylor.   • 3.4730
The Chinese and their rebellions, viewed in connection with their national philosophy, ethics, legislation, and administration. To which is added, an essay on civilization and its present state in the East and West. Stanford, Calif. Academic Reprints [1953] 656p. 1. Taiping Rebellion, 1850-1864 2. China — Civilization 3. China — Civilization I. T.
DS759 M48 1953

Michael, Franz H.   • 3.4731
The Taiping Rebellion: history and documents / by Franz Michael, in collaboration with Chung–li Chang. [Translations by Margery Anneberg ... [et al.]. — Seattle: University of Washington Press, 1966-71. –. 3 v.: maps; 25 cm. — (University of Washington publications on Asia) (v.2-3: Far Eastern and Russian Institute publications on Asia; no.14) 'A product of the Modern Chinese History Project carried on by the Far Eastern and Russian Institute of the University of Washington.'. - 1. Taiping Rebellion, 1850-1864. I. University of Washington. Far Eastern and Russian Institute. II. T.
DS759.M57   951.03   LC 66-13538

Shih, Yu-chung, 1902-.   • 3.4732
The Taiping ideology; its sources, interpretations, and influences, by Vincent Y. C. Shih. Seattle, University of Washington Press [1967] xix, 553 p. 24 cm. (Far Eastern and Russian Institute. Publications on Asia, no. 15) 1. Taiping Rebellion, 1850-1864. I. T.
DS759.S48   951/.03   LC 66-19571

Chiang, Siang-tseh.   • 3.4733
The Nien Rebellion. Seattle: University of Washington Press, 1954. xvi, 159 p.: maps,; 23 cm. (University of Washington publications on Asia) 1. Nien Rebellion, 1853-1868. I. T.
DS759.5.C5   LC 54-3971

Teng, Ssu-yü, 1906-.   • 3.4734
The Nien army and their guerrilla warfare, 1851–1868 [by] S. Y. Teng. Paris, Mouton, 1961. 254 p. illus., maps, plans. 24 cm. (Monde d'outre-mer, passé et présent. Etudes. 13) 1. China — History — Nien Rebellion, 1853-1868 I. T. II. Series.
DS759.5.T43   951/.03   LC 73-249839

Banno, Masataka.   • 3.4735
China and the West, 1858–1861: the origins of the Tsungli yamen. — Cambridge: Harvard University Press, 1964. x, 367, xiv p.; 22 cm. (Harvard East Asian series. 15) Bibliography: p. [i]–xxxiii. 1. China. Tsung li ko kuo shih wu ya men. 2. China — Hist. — Foreign intervention, 1857-1861. I. T. II. Series.
DS760.B3   327.51   LC 64-13419

DS761–773 1861–1912

Cameron, Meribeth Elliott, 1905-. • 3.4736
The reform movement in China, 1898–1912. Stanford University, Calif. Stanford University Press 1931. 223p. (Stanford University publications.University series. History, economics, and political science. v. 3, no. 1) 1. Tz'u-hsi, Empress dowager of China, 1835-1908. 2. China — Politics and government — 1900-1949 I. T. II. Series.
DS761 C3 1931

Powell, Ralph L. • 3.4737
The rise of Chinese military power, 1895–1912, by Ralph L. Powell. — Port Washington, N.Y.: Kennikat Press, [1972, c1955] x, 383 p.: map.; 23 cm. 1. China — History, Military I. T.
DS761.P69 1972   355/.00951   LC 76-159102   ISBN 0804616450

Purcell, Victor, 1896-1965. • 3.4738
The Boxer Uprising, a background study / by Victor Purcell. — Cambridge: University Press, 1963. xiv, 348 p.: maps; 24 cm. 1. China — History — 1861-1912 2. China — History — Boxer Rebellion, 1899-1901 I. T.
DS761.P8   951/.03   LC 63-26

Cohen, Paul A. • 3.4739
China and Christianity; the missionary movement and the growth of Chinese antiforeignism, 1860–1870. Cambridge, Harvard University Press, 1963. xiv, 392 p. illus., port. 22 cm. (Harvard East Asian series. 11) Based on thesis, Harvard University. 1. Missions — China 2. China — Foreign relations — 1644-1912 I. T. II. Series.
DS762.C6   LC 63-19135

Wright, Mary (Clabaugh) • 3.4740
The last stand of Chinese conservatism; the T'ung–chih restoration, 1862–1874. Stanford, Stanford University Press [1957] x, 426 p.; 25 cm. (Stanford studies in history, economics, and political science, v.13) 1. China — History — T'ung chih, 1861-1875 I. T.
DS762.W7   LC 57-5946

Hsiao, Kung-ch'üan, 1897-. 3.4741
A modern China and a new world: K'ang Yu–wei, reformer and utopian, 1858–1927 / Kung-chuan Hsiao. — Seattle: University of Washington Press, [1975] vii, 669 p.; 25 cm. (Publications on Asia of the Institute for Comparative and Foreign Area Studies; no. 25) Includes index. 1. K'ang, Yu-wei, 1858-1927. 2. China — History — Reform movement, 1898 I. T.
DS763.K3 H75   951/.03/0924 B   LC 74-28166   ISBN 0295953853

Huang, Philip C., 1940-. 3.4742
Liang Ch'i–ch'ao and modern Chinese liberalism, by Philip C. Huang. — Seattle: University of Washington Press, [1972] ix, 231 p.: illus.; 23 cm. — (Publications on Asia of the Institute for Comparative and Foreign Area Studies, no. 22) 1. Liang, Ch'i-ch'ao, 1873-1929. 2. China — Politics and government — 20th century I. T.
DS763.L67 H8   320.5/1/0924   LC 71-178703   ISBN 0295951753

Tan, Chester C. • 3.4743
The Boxer catastrophe, by Chester C. Tan. New York, Octagon Books, 1967. ix, 276 p. 24 cm. (Columbia studies in the social sciences no. 583) Reprint of the 1955 ed. 1. Boxers. 2. Manchoukuo — History. 3. China — Foreign relations — Soviet Union 4. Soviet Union — Foreign relations — China. I. T. II. Series.
DS771.T3 1967   951/.03   LC 66-18057   ISBN 0374977526

China in revolution: the first phase, 1900–1913. Edited and with • 3.4744
an introd. by Mary Clabaugh Wright.
New Haven: Yale University Press, 1968. xiii, 505 p.; 24 cm. Papers from a research conference held at Wentworth-by-the-Sea, Portsmouth, New Hampshire, Aug. 1965. 1. China — History — Revolution, 1911-1912 I. Wright. Mary (Clabaugh) ed.
DS773.C5145   951/.03   LC 68-27770

Gasster, Michael, 1930-. • 3.4745
Chinese intellectuals and the revolution of 1911; the birth of modern Chinese radicalism. — Seattle: University of Washington Press, [1969] xxix, 288 p.; 24 cm. — (Far Eastern and Russian Institute. Publications on Asia, no. 19) 1. China — History — Revolution, 1911-1912 I. T.
DS773.G35   915.1/03   LC 66-19568

Price, Don C. 3.4746
Russia and the roots of the Chinese revolution, 1896–1911 / Don C. Price. — Cambridge, Mass.: Harvard University Press, 1974. 303 p.; 25 cm. (Harvard East Asian series. 79) Includes index. 1. China — History — Revolution, 1911-1912 2. Soviet Union — Relations — China 3. China — Relations — Soviet Union I. T. II. Series.
DS773.P7   951/.03   LC 74-80443   ISBN 0674783204

DS774–778 1912–

Isaacs, Harold Robert, 1910-. • 3.4747
The tragedy of the Chinese revolution. — 2d rev. ed. — Stanford, Calif., Stanford University Press [1961] 392 p. 24 cm. 1. China — Hist. — 1912-1937. 2. Communism — China. I. T.
DS774.I7 1961   951.042   LC 61-11101

Schwartz, Benjamin Isadore, 1916-. • 3.4748
Chinese communism and the rise of Mao. Cambridge, Harvard University Press, 1951. 258 p. 22 cm. (Russian Research Center studies, 4) 1. Mao, Tse-tung, 1893-1976. 2. Communism — China. 3. China — History — 1900- I. T.
DS774.S37   951.04   LC 51-12067

Sheridan, James E. 3.4749
China in disintegration: the Republican era in Chinese history, 1912–1949 / James E. Sheridan. — New York: Free Press, [1975] xii, 338 p.: maps; 25 cm. (The Transformation of modern China series) Includes index. 1. China — History — Republic, 1912-1949 I. T.
DS774.S54   951.04   LC 74-28940   ISBN 0029286107

Spence, Jonathan D. 3.4750
The Gate of Heavenly Peace: the Chinese and their revolution, 1895–1980 / Jonathan D. Spence. — New York: Viking Press, 1981. xxii, 465 p.: ill., ports.; 25 cm. Map on lining papers. Includes index. 1. China — History — 20th century 2. China — History — 1861-1912 I. T.
DS774.S59 1981   951 19   LC 81-65264   ISBN 0670292478

Bianco, Lucien. • 3.4751
Origins of the Chinese revolution, 1915–1949. Translated from the French by Muriel Bell. — Stanford, Calif.: Stanford University Press, [1971] xiii, 223 p.: maps.; 23 cm. Translation of Les origines de la révolution chinoise, 1915-1949, revised by the author. 1. China — Politics and government — 1912-1949 I. T.
DS775.B513   951.04   LC 75-150321   ISBN 0804707464

Chou, Ts'ê-tsung, 1916-. • 3.4752
The May fourth movement: intellectual revolution in modern China. Cambridge, Harvard University Press, 1960. xv, 486 p. tables. 25 cm. (Harvard East Asian studies, 6) Added t.p. in Chinese. 1. May fourth movement. I. T.
DS775.C5386 1960   LC 60-10034

Chou, Ts'ê-tsung, 1916-. • 3.4753
Research guide to The May fourth movement; intellectual revolution in modern China, 1915–1924. — Cambridge, Harvard University Press, 1963. xi, 297 p. 24 cm. — (Harvard East Asian series. 13) 1. May fourth movement. I. Chou, Ts'ê-tsung, 1916- The May fourth movement. II. T. III. Series.
DS775.C53862   951.041   LC 63-22745

Pye, Lucian W., 1921-. 3.4754
Warlord politics; conflict and coalition in the modernization of Republican China [by] Lucian W. Pye. New York, Praeger [1971] ix, 212 p. illus. 24 cm. (Praeger library of Chinese affairs) 1. China — History — Warlord period, 1916-1928 I. T.
DS775.P9   320.9/51/04   LC 70-153394

Snow, Edgar, 1905-1972. • 3.4755
Red star over China. 1st rev. and enl. ed. New York, Grove Press [1968] 543 p. illus., col. maps (on lining papers), ports. 24 cm. 1. Communism — China. 2. China — History — Republic, 1912-1949 I. T.
DS775.S72 1968   951.04   LC 68-17724

Stuart, John Leighton. • 3.4756
Fifty years in China; the memoirs of John Leighton Stuart, missionary and ambassador. New York: Random House, 1954. 346 p.: illus. 1. Stuart, John Leighton. 2. Missionaries — Correspondence, reminiscences, etc. 3. China — History 4. China — History — Republic, 1912-1949 I. T.
DS775.S84   951   B   LC 54-7808

Trotsky, Leon, 1879-1940. • 3.4757
Problems of the Chinese revolution / with appendices by Zinoviev, Vuyovitch, Nassunov & others; translated with an introd. by Max Shachtman. 3d ed. New York: Paragon Book Reprint Corp., 1966. vi, 432 p.; 21 cm. 1. Chung-kuo kuo min tang. 2. Communism — China 3. China — Politics and government — 1912-1949 I. T.
DS775 T7 1966

Chung-kuo ti i jih. English. 3.4758
One day in China, May 21, 1936 / translated, edited, and introduced by Sherman Cochran and Andrew C. K. Hsieh with Janis Cochran. — New Haven: Yale University Press, c1983. xxvi, 290 p.: ill., maps. Translation of: Chung-kuo ti i jih. Includes index. 1. China — Social life and customs — 1912-1949 I. Cochran, Sherman, 1940- II. Hsieh, Andrew C. K., 1941- III. Cochran, Janis, 1947- IV. T.
DS775.2.C4813 1983   DS775.2 C4813 1983.   951.04/2 19   LC 82-48901   ISBN 0300028342

Sun, Yat-sen, 1866-1925. • **3.4759**
Memoirs of a Chinese revolutionary; a programme of national reconstruction for China. — New York: AMS Press, [1970] 254 p.: port.; 23 cm. Reprint of the 1927 ed. 1. Sun, Yat-sen, 1866-1925. 2. China — History — Revolution, 1911-1912 I. T.
DS777.A32 1970   951.04/1/0924   *LC* 73-111786   *ISBN* 0404063055

Sun, Yat-sen, 1866-1925. **3.4760**
[San min chu i. English] The triple demism of Sun Yat-sen. Translated from the Chinese, annotated and appraised by Paschal M. d'Elia. With introd. and index. English ed. Wuchang, The Franciscan Press, 1931. [New York, AMS Press, 1974] xxxvii, 747 p. illus. 23 cm. Translation of San min chu i, from the French ed. published in 1929 under title: Le triple démisme. I. Elia, Pasquale M. d', 1890- tr. II. T.
DS777.A55 1974   320.5/092/4   *LC* 78-38069   *ISBN* 0404569293

Wilbur, C. Martin (Clarence Martin), 1908-. **3.4761**
Sun Yat-sen, frustrated patriot / C. Martin Wilbur. — New York: Columbia University Press, 1976. x, 413 p., [4] leaves of plates: ill.; 24 cm. (Studies of the East Asian Institute, Columbia University) Includes index. 1. Sun, Yat-sen, 1866-1925. I. T.
DS777.A595 W55   951.04/1/0924 B   *LC* 76-18200   *ISBN* 0231040369

Jansen, Marius B. • **3.4762**
The Japanese and Sun Yat-sen. — Cambridge, Harvard University Press, 1954. viii, 274 p. group port., facsims. 21 cm. — (Harvard historical monographs. 27) 'A note on sources': p. [223]-231. Bibliographical references included in 'Notes' (p. [232]-264) 1. Sun, Yat-sen, 1866-1925. 2. China — For. rel. — Japan. 3. Japan — For. rel. — China. I. T. II. Series.
DS777.J3   951.041   *LC* 53-8021

Leng, Shao Chuan, 1921-. • **3.4763**
Sun Yat-sen and communism, by Shao Chuan Leng and Norman D. Palmer. — New York, F. A. Praeger [1961, c1960] viii, 234 p. 22 cm. — (The Foreign Policy Research Institute series, no. 10) Praeger publications in Russian history and world communism, no. 91. Books that matter. Bibliographical references included in 'Notes' (p. 183-217) Bibliography: p. 219-227. 1. Sun, Yat-sen, 1866-1925. 2. Communism — China. I. Palmer, Norman Dunbar. joint author. II. T. III. Series.
DS777.L4 1961   951.041   *LC* 60-16426

Schiffrin, Harold Z. **3.4764**
Sun Yat-sen, reluctant revolutionary / by Harold Z. Schiffrin. — 1st ed. — Boston: Little, Brown, c1980. viii, 290 p.; 21 cm. — (The Library of world biography) 1. Sun, Yat-sen, 1866-1925. 2. China — Presidents — Biography. I. T.
DS777.S33   951.04/1/0924 B   *LC* 80-16100   *ISBN* 0316773395

Sharman, Lyon, 1872-1957. • **3.4765**
Sun Yat-sen; his life and its meaning; a critical biography. — Stanford, Calif.: Stanford University Press, [1968, c1934] xxi, 420 p.; 23 cm. 1. Sun, Yat-sen, 1866-1925. 2. Chung-kuo kuo min tang. 3. China — History — Revolution, 1911-1912 4. China — History — Republic, 1912-1949 I. T.
DS777.S5 1968   951.04/1/0924 B   *LC* 68-17141

Feigon, Lee, 1945-. **3.4766**
Chen Duxiu, founder of the Chinese Communist Party / by Lee Feigon. — Princeton, N.J.: Princeton University Press, c1983. xv, 279 p.: ill.; 23 cm. Includes index. 1. Ch'en, Tu-hsiu, 1879-1942. 2. Chung-kuo kung ch'an tang — Biography. 3. Politicians — China — Biography. 4. Communists — China — Biography. I. T.
DS777.15.C5 F44 1983   324.251/075/0924 B 19   *LC* 83-42556   *ISBN* 0691053936

Ch'ên, Jerome, 1919-. • **3.4767**
Yuan Shih-k'ai. — 2d ed. — Stanford, Calif.: Stanford University Press, 1972. 258 p.: map.; 23 cm. 1. Yüan, Shih-k'ai, 1859-1916. I. T.
DS777.2.C48 1972   951/.03/0924 B   *LC* 76-153815   *ISBN* 0804707899

Young, Ernest P. **3.4768**
The presidency of Yuan Shih-k'ai: liberalism and dictatorship in early republican China / Ernest P. Young. Ann Arbor: University of Michigan Press, c1977. viii, 347 p., [4] leaves of plates: ill.; 24 cm. (Michigan studies on China.) Includes index. 1. Yüan, Shih-k'ai, 1859-1916. 2. China — History — 1912-1937. I. T. II. Series.
DS777.2.Y68 1977   951/.03/0924   *LC* 75-31057   *ISBN* 0472089951

Ch'en, Kung-po, 1892-1946. • **3.4769**
The Communist movement in China; an essay written in 1924. Edited with an introd. by C. Martin Wilbur. New York, Octagon Books, 1966 [c1960] vi, 138 p. 24 cm. 'Issued under the auspices of the East Asian Institute, Columbia University.' Thesis (M.A.)—Columbia University. 1. Communism — China.

I. Wilbur, C. Martin (Clarence Martin), 1908- II. Columbia University. East Asian Institute. III. Chung-kuo kung ch'an tang. IV. T.
DS777.44.C5 1966   *LC* 65-28873

Chi, Hsi-sheng. **3.4770**
Warlord politics in China, 1916-1928 / Hsi-sheng Ch'i. — Stanford, Calif.: Stanford University Press, 1976. 282 p., [1] leaf of plates: ill.; 23 cm. Includes index. 1. China — Politics and government — 1912-1928 I. T.
DS777.45.C54   320.9/51/041   *LC* 75-7482   *ISBN* 0804708940

Eastman, Lloyd E. **3.4771**
The abortive revolution: China under Nationalist rule, 1927-1937 / Lloyd E. Eastman. — Cambridge, Mass.: Harvard University Press, 1974. xvii, 398 p.; 25 cm. — (Harvard East Asian series. 78) Includes index. 1. China — Politics and government — 1928-1937 I. T. II. Series.
DS777.47.E24   320.9/51/042   *LC* 74-75639   *ISBN* 0674001753

White, Theodore Harold, 1915-. • **3.4772**
Thunder out of China [by] Theodore H. White and Annalee Jacoby. — [1st ed.]. — New York: William Sloane Associates, [1946] xvi, 331 p.: maps.; 22 cm. 1. World War, 1939-1945 — China. 2. Reconstruction (1939-1951) — China. 3. China — History — 1937-1945 I. Jacoby, Annalee, 1916- joint author. II. T.
DS777.47.W5   951.042   *LC* 46-11919

Eastman, Lloyd E. **3.4773**
Seeds of destruction: Nationalist China in war and revolution, 1937–1949 / Lloyd E. Eastman. — Stanford, Calif.: Stanford University Press, 1984. ix, 311 p.; 23 cm. Includes index. 1. China — History — 1937-1945 2. China — History — Civil War, 1945-1949 I. T.
DS777.518.E17 1984   951.04/2 19   *LC* 82-42861   *ISBN* 0804711917

DS777.53 Sino–Japanese Conflict, 1937–1945

Barnett, A. Doak. • **3.4774**
China on the eve of Communist takeover. — New York, Praeger [1963] 371 p. illus. 22 cm. — (Praeger publications in Russian history and world communism, no. 130) 1. China — Pol. & govt. — 1937-1949. 2. China — Soc. condit. 3. China — Econ. condit. — 1912-1949. I. T.
DS777.53.B32 1963   354.51   *LC* 63-10824

Belden, Jack, 1910-. • **3.4775**
China shakes the world. — New York: [Monthly Review Press, 1970] xvii, 524 p.; 21 cm. Reprint of the 1949 ed., with an introd. by Owen Lattimore. 1. Communism — China. 2. China — Politics and government — 1945-1949 I. T.
DS777.53.B38 1970   951.04/2   *LC* 77-105312

Johnson, Chalmers A. • **3.4776**
Peasant nationalism and communist power: the emergence of revolutionary China / Chalmers A. Johnson. — Stanford, Calif.: Stanford University Press, 1962. xii, 256 p.: maps. Includes index. 1. Communism — China. 2. Nationalism — China. 3. Peasantry — China. 4. World War, 1939-1945 — Yugoslavia. I. T.
DS777.53.J58   *LC* 62-16949

Li, Lincoln. **3.4777**
The Japanese Army in North China, July, 1937 – December, 1941: problems of political and economic control / Lincoln Li. — London: Oxford University Press, 1975. 278 p.: ill.; 23 cm. (East Asian historical monographs) Includes index. 1. Sino-Japanese Conflict, 1937-1945 2. China — History — 1937-1945 I. T.
DS777.53.L4634   951.04/2   *LC* 76-366647   *ISBN* 0195802691

Lindsay, Michael, 1909-. **3.4778**
The unknown war: North China 1937-1945 / Michael Lindsay. — London: Bergstrom & Boyle Books, 1977 (c1975). [112] p.: ill.; 26 cm. 1. Sino-Japanese Conflict, 1937-1945 — Underground movements 2. Sino-Japanese Conflict, 1937-1945 — China, Northwest. I. T.
DS777.53.L573   951.04/2   *LC* 76-367218   *ISBN* 0903767058

Snow, Edgar, 1905-1972. • **3.4779**
Random notes on Red China (1936–1945). Cambridge, Chinese Economic and Political Studies, Harvard University; distributed by Harvard University Press, 1957. 148 p. 28 cm. (Harvard University. Chinese Economic and Political Studies. Special series.) 1. Communism — China. 2. China — History — 1937-1949. I. T. II. Series.
DS777.53.S562   *LC* 58-146

Tsou, Tang, 1918-. • **3.4780**
America's failure in China, 1941-50. [Chicago] University of Chicago Press [1963] 614 p. 25 cm. 1. China — Politics and government — 1937-1945

2. China — Politics and government — 1945-1949 3. United States — Foreign relations — China. 4. China — Foreign relations — United States. I. T.
DS777.53.T866   327.73051   *LC* 63-13072

Young, Arthur N. (Arthur Nichols), 1890-.   • **3.4781**
China's wartime finance and inflation, 1937–1945 [by] Arthur N. Young. — Cambridge, Harvard University Press, 1965. xviii, 421 p. illus. 25 cm. — (Harvard East Asian series. 20) 'Bibliographic note': p. [385]-386. 1. Sino-Japanese Conflict, 1937-1945 2. Inflation (Finance) — China. I. T. II. Series.
DS777.53.Y62   336.51   *LC* 65-22049

Pepper, Suzanne.   **3.4782**
Civil War in China: the political struggle, 1945–1949 / by Suzanne Pepper. — Berkeley: University of California Press, c1978. xxi, 472 p.: map; 25 cm. Includes index. 1. China — History — Civil War, 1945-1949 I. T.
DS777.54.P44   951.04/2   *LC* 73-76103   *ISBN* 0520024400

DS777.55–778 PEOPLE'S REPUBLIC OF CHINA (1949-

Barnett, A. Doak.   • **3.4783**
Communist China: the early years, 1949–55 [by] A. Doak Barnett. New York, F. A. Praeger [1964] xiv, 336 p. 21 cm. (Praeger publications in Russian history and world communism, no. 152) 1. China — History — 1949-1976 I. T.
DS777.55.B322   951.05   *LC* 64-22487

Bodde, Derk.   • **3.4784**
Peking diary: a year of revolution. New York: Schuman, 1950. xxi, 292 p.: ill., ports. 1. Communism — China. 2. Peking — History. 3. China — Description and travel I. T.
DS777.55 B6   951.156   *LC* 50-10426

Brugger, Bill.   **3.4785**
China, liberation and transformation, 1942–1962 / Bill Brugger. — London: Croom Helm; Totowa, N.J.: Barnes & Noble Books, c1981. 288 p.; 23 cm. Includes index. 1. Communism — China. 2. China — History — 1949-1976 3. China — History — Civil War, 1945-1949 I. T.
DS777.55.B715 1981   951.05 19   *LC* 81-105026   *ISBN* 0389200867

China in crisis. Edited by Ping–ti Ho and Tang Tsou. With a   • **3.4786**
foreword by Charles U. Daly.
[Chicago] University of Chicago Press [1968-. v. 23 cm. Contains papers presented at two five-day conferences held at the University of Chicago, Center for Policy Study, Feb. 1967. 1. Ho, Ping-ti, ed. II. Tsou, Tang, 1918- ed. III. University of Chicago. Center for Policy Study.
DS777.55.C44684   915.1/03   *LC* 68-20981

Dietrich, Craig.   **3.4787**
People's China: a brief history / Craig Dietrich. — New York: Oxford University Press, 1986. xv, 327 p., [2] p. of plates: ill.; 23 cm. Includes index. 1. China — History — 1949- I. T.
DS777.55.D52 1986   951.05 19   *LC* 85-15217   *ISBN* 0195036883

Esmein, Jean, 1923-.   **3.4788**
[Révolution culturelle chinoise. English] The Chinese cultural revolution. Translated from the French by W. J. F. Jenner. [1st ed.] Garden City, N.Y., Anchor Press, 1973. xiv, 346 p. 18 cm. Translation of La révolution culturelle chinoise. 1. China — Politics and government — 1949- I. T.
DS777.55.E813   320.9/51/05   *LC* 73-79206   *ISBN* 0385050984

Goldman, Merle.   • **3.4789**
Literary dissent in Communist China / Merle Goldman. — Cambridge: Harvard University Press, 1967. xvii, 343 p.; 24 cm. — (Harvard East Asian series. 29) 1. China (People's Republic of China, — 1949-   ) — Intellectual life. I. T. II. Series.
DS777.55.G67   895/.109005   *LC* 67-17311

Hinton, Harold C.   **3.4790**
An introduction to Chinese politics [by] Harold C. Hinton. New York, Praeger [1973] xii, 323 p. maps. 21 cm. 1. China — Politics and government — 1949- 2. Taiwan — Politics and government — 1945-1975 I. T.
DS777.55.H5514   320.9/51/05   *LC* 72-75682

Hinton, William.   **3.4791**
Turning point in China: an essay on the cultural revolution. — New York: [Monthly Review Press, 1972] 112 p.; 21 cm. 1. China — Politics and government — 1949-1976 I. T.
DS777.55.H553   320.9/51/05   *LC* 76-178715   *ISBN* 0853452091

Ideology and politics in contemporary China. Edited by   **3.4792**
Chalmers Johnson. Contributors: John Israel [and others].
Seattle: University of Washington Press, [1973] xii, 390 p.; 25 cm. — (Studies in Chinese government and politics, 4) Based on papers from the 5th conference sponsored by the Subcommittee on Chinese Government and Politics of the

Joint Committe on Contemporary China of the American Council of Learned Societies and the Social Science Research Council, held at Santa Fe, N.M., Aug. 2-6, 1971. 1. Communism — China — Addresses, essays, lectures. 2. China — Politics and government — 1949-1976 — Addresses, essays, lectures. I. Israel, John, 1935- II. Johnson, Chalmers A. ed. III. Joint Committee on Contemporary China. Subcommittee on Chinese Government and Politics. IV. Series.
DS777.55.I3   320.9/51/05   *LC* 72-11514   *ISBN* 0295952474

Karol, K. S.   **3.4793**
[Deuxième révolution chinoise. English] The second Chinese revolution [by] K. S. Karol. Translated from the French by Mervyn Jones. New York, Hill and Wang [1974] 472 p. 21 cm. Translation of La deuxième révolution chinoise. 1. China — Politics and government — 1949-1976 I. T.
DS777.55.K32413 1974   320.9/51/05   *LC* 73-91174   *ISBN* 080908516X

Lifton, Robert Jay, 1926-.   • **3.4794**
Revolutionary immortality; Mao Tse–tung and the Chinese cultural revolution. — New York: Random House, [1968] xviii, 178 p.; 22 cm. 1. Mao, Tse-tung, 1893-1976. 2. China — Politics and government — 1949- I. T.
DS777.55.L457   320.9/51   *LC* 68-28545

Mao, Tse-tung, 1893-1976.   • **3.4795**
On the correct handling of contradictions among the people / Mao Tse–tung. — [Peking?: Foreign Languages Press?, 1957?] 26 p.; 26 cm. 'Text of a speech made on February 27, 1957 at the eleventh session (enlarged) of the Supreme State Conference.' 1. Communism — China. I. T.
DS777.55.M285 1957

Meisner, Maurice J., 1931-.   **3.4796**
Mao's China and after: a history of the People's Republic / Maurice Meisner. — New York: Free Press; London: Collier Macmillan, c1986. xx, 534 p.: map; 25 cm. — (Transformation of modern China series.) Rev. ed. of: Mao's China. c1977. Includes index. 1. China — History — 1949- I. Meisner, Maurice J., 1931- Mao's China. II. T. III. Series.
DS777.55.M455 1986   951.05 19   *LC* 86-4480   *ISBN* 002920870X

Myrdal, Jan.   • **3.4797**
[Rapport från kinesisk by. English] Report from a Chinese village. Illustrated and with photos. by Gun Kessle. Translated from the Swedish by Maurice Michael. New York, Pantheon Books [1965] xxxiv, 373 p. illus., ports. 22 cm. Translation of Rapport från kinesisk by. Sequel: China: the revolution continued. 1. China — Social life and customs 2. Liu-lin (China) I. T.
DS777.55.M913   309.151   *LC* 64-18346

The People's Republic of China, 1949–1979: a documentary   **3.4798**
survey / Harold C. Hinton, editor.
Wilmington, Del.: Scholarly Resources, 1980. 5 v. (xv, 2994 p.); 29 cm. Includes index. 1. China — History — 1949-1976 — Sources. 2. China — History — 1976- — Sources. I. Hinton, Harold C.
DS777.55.P4243   951.05 19   *LC* 80-5228   *ISBN* 0842021663

Rice, Edward E. (Edward Earl), 1909-.   **3.4799**
Mao's way / by Edward E. Rice. Berkeley, University of California Press [1972] ix, 596 p. map (on lining papers) 24 cm. 'Sponsored by the Center for Chinese Studies, University of California, Berkeley.' 1. Mao, Tse-tung, 1893-1976. 2. China — Politics and government — 1949-1976 I. University of California, Berkeley. Center for Chinese Studies. II. T.
DS777.55.R48   951.04/092/4   *LC* 70-186116   *ISBN* 0520021991

Schurmann, Franz, 1924-.   • **3.4800**
Ideology and organization in Communist China [by] Franz Schurmann. — 2d ed., enl. — Berkeley: University of California Press, 1968. lii, 642 p.: illus.; 25 cm. 1. Chung-kuo kung ch'an tang — Party work. 2. China — Politics and government — 1949-1976 I. T.
DS777.55.S35 1968   335.43/4/0951   *LC* 68-26124

Shabad, Theodore.   • **3.4801**
China's changing map; national and regional development, 1949–71. — Completely rev. ed. — New York: Praeger, [1972] xiii, 370 p.: maps.; 23 cm. — (Praeger library of Chinese affairs) 1. Physical geography — China. 2. China — Economic conditions — 1949-1976 3. China — Politics and government — 1949-1976 I. T.
DS777.55.S455 1972   330.951/05   *LC* 71-178868

Van Slyke, Lyman P.   • **3.4802**
Enemies and friends; the united front in Chinese Communist history [by] Lyman P. Van Slyke. — Stanford, Calif.: Stanford University Press, 1967. viii, 330 p.; 24 cm. 1. Communism — China. 2. China. I. T.
DS777.55.V36   951.05   *LC* 67-26531

MacFarquhar, Roderick. • 3.4803
The hundred flowers campaign and the Chinese intellectuals. With an epilogue by G. F. Hudson. New York, Praeger [1960] 324 p. 25 cm. 1. Communist self-criticism 2. China — Politics and government — 1949- I. T.
DS777.57.M3   951.05   LC 60-10877

Yu, Frederick T. C., 1921-. • 3.4804
Mass persuasion in Communist China [by] Frederick T. C. Yu. New York, Praeger [1964] viii, 186 p. 22 cm. (Praeger publications in Russian history and world communism, no. 145) Bibliographical references included in 'Notes' (p. 171-182) 1. Propaganda, Chinese 2. Public opinion — China I. T.
DS777.57.Y78   301.15230951   LC 64-13389

Goldman, Merle. 3.4805
China's intellectuals: advise and dissent / Merle Goldman. — Cambridge, Mass.: Harvard University Press, 1981. 276 p.; 24 cm. 1. China — Intellectual life — 1949- I. T.
DS777.6.G64   951.05 19   LC 81-2945   ISBN 0674119703

Brugger, Bill. 3.4806
China, radicalism to revisionism, 1962–1979 / Bill Brugger. — London: Croom Helm; Totowa, N.J.: Barnes & Noble, 1981. 275 p.: 1 map; 22 cm. Includes index. 1. China — Politics and government — 1949- I. T.
DS777.75.B78 1981   951.05/6 19   LC 81-102749   ISBN 0389200875

Domes, Jürgen. 3.4807
The government and politics of the PRC: a time of transition / Jürgen Domes. — Boulder: Westview Press, 1985. xv, 316 p.: ill.; 23 cm. Includes index. 1. China — Politics and government — 1949- I. T.
DS777.75.D66 1985   951.05 19   LC 84-29939   ISBN 0865315655

MacFarquhar, Roderick. 3.4808
The origins of the cultural revolution. New York: Published for the Royal Institute of International Affairs, the East Asian Institute of Columbia University, and the Research Institute on Communist Affairs of Columbia University by Columbia University Press, 1974-1983. 2 v.: ports.; 23 cm. (Studies of the East Asian Institute.) Vol. 1 lacks series statement. 1. China — Politics and government — 1949- I. The Royal Institute of International Affairs. II. Columbia University. East Asian Institute. III. Columbia University. Research Institute on Communist Affairs. IV. T. V. Series.
DS777.75.M32 1974   951.05   LC 73-15794   ISBN 0231038410

DS778 Biography. Memoirs

Bartke, Wolfgang. 3.4809
Who's who in the People's Republic of China / by Wolfgang Bartke; [English translation by Franciscus Verellen]. — Armonk, N.Y.: M. E. Sharpe, c1981. xii, 729 p.: ports.; 32 cm. Title also in Chinese: Chung-hua jen min kung ho kuo jen ming lu. 'A Publication of the Institute of Asian Affairs, Hamburg.' 1. China — History — 1949-1976 — Biography. 2. China — History — 1976- — Biography. 3. China — Biography. I. T. II. Title: Chung-hua jen min kung ho kuo jen ming lu.
DS778.A1 B33   920/.051 19   LC 80-27599   ISBN 0873321839

Biographical dictionary of Republican China. Howard L. • 3.4810
Boorman, editor; Richard C. Howard, associate editor.
New York: Columbia University Press, 1967-79. 5 v.: map.; 28 cm. Vol. 5: 'A personal name index, by Janet Krompart.' 1. China — History — Republic, 1912-1949 — Biography. 2. China — Biography. I. Boorman, Howard L., ed. II. Howard, Richard C. ed. III. Cheng, Joseph K. H.
DS778.A1 B5   920/.051   LC 67-12006   ISBN 0231089589

Klein, Donald W. • 3.4811
Biographic dictionary of Chinese communism, 1921–1965 [by] Donald W. Klein [and] Anne B. Clark. — Cambridge, Mass.: Harvard University Press, 1971. 2 v. (1194 p.): maps.; 27 cm. — (Harvard East Asian series. 57) 1. Communists — China — Biography. 2. China — Biography. I. Clark, Anne B., joint author. II. T. III. Series.
DS778.A1 K55 1971   951.04/922 B   LC 69-12725   ISBN 0674074106

Wales, Nym, 1907-. • 3.4812
The Chinese Communists: sketches and autobiographies of the Old Guard. Book 1: Red dust. Book 2: Autobiographical profiles and biographical sketches. Introd. to book 1 by Robert Carver North. — Westport, Conn.: Greenwood Pub. Co., [1972] xxi, 398 p.: illus.; 24 cm. First published in 1952 under title: Red Dust. 1. Communists — China. 2. China — Biography. I. Snow, Helen (Foster) 1907- Red dust. 1972. II. T.
DS778.A1 S499   335.43/4 B   LC 77-104236   ISBN 0837163218

McCormack, Gavan. 3.4813
Chang Tso–lin in northeast China, 1911–1928: China, Japan, and the Manchurian idea / Gavan McCormack. — Stanford, Calif.: Stanford University Press, 1977. vi, 334 p.: ill.; 24 cm. Includes index. 1. Chang, Tso-lin,

1875-1928. 2. Generals — China — Biography. 3. Japanese in Manchuria. 4. Manchoukuo — History. I. T.
DS778.C5 M3   951.04/1/0924   LC 76-48028   ISBN 0804709459

Witke, Roxane. 3.4814
Comrade Chiang Ch'ing / Roxane Witke. — 1st ed. — Boston: Little, Brown, c1977. xxvi, 549 p., [17] leaves of plates: ill.; 24 cm. 1. Chiang, Ch'ing, 1910- 2. Statesmen — China — Biography. 3. Women — China — Biography. 4. China — Biography. 5. China — History — 1900- I. T.
DS778.C5374 W57   951.05/092/4 B   LC 77-935   ISBN 0316949000

Crozier, Brian. 3.4815
The man who lost China: the first full biography of Chiang Kai–shek / by Brian Crozier, with the collaboration of Eric Chou. New York: Scribner, c1976. xv, 430 p., [8] leaves of plates: ill.; 25 cm. 1. Chiang, Kai-shek, 1887-1975. I. Chou, Eric, 1915- joint author. II. T.
DS778.C55 C7   951.04/2/0924 B   LC 76-10246   ISBN 068414686X

Hsu, Kai-yu, 1922-. • 3.4816
Chou En–lai: China's gray eminence. — [1st ed.]. — Garden City, N.Y.: Doubleday, 1968. xviii, 294 p.: illus., maps (part col.), ports.; 22 cm. 1. Chou, En-lai, 1898-1976. I. T.
DS778.C593 H8   951.04/0924 B   LC 68-10566

Wilson, Dick, 1928-. 3.4817
[Chou, the story of Zhou Enlai 1898-1976] Zhou Enlai: a biography / Dick Wilson. — 1st American ed. — New York, N.Y.: Viking, 1984. 349 p., [8] p. of plates: ill., ports.; 24 cm. 'Originally published in Great Britain under the title: Chou, the story of Zhou Enlai 1898-1976'—T.p. verso. Includes index. 1. Chou, En-lai, 1898-1976. 2. Prime ministers — China — Biography. I. T.
DS778.C593 W54 1984   951.05/092/4 B 19   LC 83-47928   ISBN 0670220116

Smedley, Agnes, 1890-1950. • 3.4818
The great road; the life and times of Chu Teh. New York, Monthly Review Press, 1956. 461 p. illus. 22 cm. 1. Chu, Te, 1886-1976. 2. Communism — China. I. T.
DS778.C6S5   923.551   LC 56-11272

Sheridan, James E. • 3.4819
Chinese warlord; the career of Feng Yü–hsiang [by] James E. Sheridan. — Stanford, Calif.: Stanford University Press, 1966. x, 386 p.: maps.; 24 cm. 1. Feng, Yü-hsiang, 1882-1948. I. T.
DS778.F45 S45   951.040924 B   LC 65-18978

Hsüeh, Chün-tu, 1922-. • 3.4820
Huang Hsing and the Chinese revolution. Stanford, Calif., Stanford University Press, 1961. 260 p. 23 cm. (Stanford studies in history, economics, and political science, 20) 1. Huang, Hsing, 1874-1916. 2. China — History — Revolution, 1911-1912 I. T.
DS778.H85 H7   LC 61-6531

Levenson, Joseph Richmond, 1920-1969. • 3.4821
Liang Ch'i–ch'ao and the mind of modern China. — Cambridge, Harvard University Press, 1959. 256 p. 21 cm. 1. Liang, Ch'i-ch'ao, 1873-1929. 2. China — Civilization I. T.
DS778.L45L4 1959   923.251   LC 59-16503 rev

Kau, Michael Y. M., ed. 3.4822
The Lin Piao affair: power politics and military coup / edited by Michael Y. M. Kau. — White Plains, N.Y.: International Arts and Sciences Press, [1975] lxxvii, 591 p.; 24 cm. 1. Lin, Piao, 1908-1971. 2. China — Politics and government — 1949-1976 — Sources. I. Kau, Michael Y. M., 1934- II. T.
DS778.L4725 L49   951.05/092/4   LC 73-92807

Dittmer, Lowell. 3.4823
Liu Shao–ch'i and the Chinese cultural revolution: the politics of mass criticism / Lowell Dittmer. — Berkeley: University of California Press, [1974] xiv, 386 p.: graphs; 24 cm. Includes index. 1. Liu, Shao-ch'i, 1898-1969. 2. Communist self-criticism 3. China — History — Cultural Revolution, 1966-1969 I. T.
DS778.L49 D57   951.05/092/4   LC 73-85786   ISBN 0520025741

DS778 Mao Tse–tung

Mao, Tse-tung, 1893-1976. 3.4824
Quotations from Chairman Mao Tse–tung. Edited and with an introductory essay and notes by Stuart R. Schram. Foreword by A. Doak Barnett. New York: Praeger, [c1967] xxxiv, 182 p.; 22 cm. Translated from the Chinese: (romanized: Mao chu hsi yü lu). I. T.
DS778.M3 A31353 1967b   951/.05/0924   LC 68-20400

Mao, Tse-tung, 1893-1976.   • **3.4825**
Mao papers, anthology and bibliography edited by Jerome Ch'en. — London;
New York: Oxford University Press, 1970. xxxiii, 221 p.: ports.; 23 cm. 1. Mao,
Tsê-tung, 1893- — Bibliography. I. Ch'ên, Jerome, 1919- ed. II. T.
DS778.M3 A4295   016.95105/0924   LC 76-147091   ISBN
0192151886

Mao, Tse-tung, 1893-1976.   • **3.4826**
Selected military writings. — [1st ed.]. — Peking: Foreign languages press,
1963. 408 p.: port. 1. Guerrilla warfare 2. China — Politics and government —
1912-1949 I. T.
DS778.M3 A515   LC 65-1840

Mao, Tse-tung, 1893-1976.   • **3.4827**
Selected works. — New York: International Publishers, [1954-62] 5 v.; 23 cm.
1. Communism — China. 2. China — Politics and government — Addresses,
essays, lectures. I. T.
DS778.M3 A52   951.05*   LC 54-9751

Mao, Tse-tung, 1893-1976.   • **3.4828**
Maoism, a sourcebook: selections from the writings of Mao Tse-tung /
introduced and edited by H. Arthur Steiner. — [Los Angeles] University of
California at Los Angeles 1952. 142 p.; 29 cm. 1. Communism — China
I. Steiner, H. Arthur, 1905-, ed. II. T.
DS778 M3 A53 1952

Mao, Tse-tung, 1893-1976.   • **3.4829**
The political thought of Mao Tse-tung [by] Stuart R. Schram. — Rev. and enl.
ed. — New York: Praeger, [1969] 479 p.; 22 cm. 1. Communism — China.
I. Schram, Stuart R. ed. II. T.
DS778.M3 A538 1969   320.9/51   LC 68-16093

Ch'ên, Jerome, 1919- comp.   • **3.4830**
Mao. — Englewood Cliffs, N.J.: Prentice-Hall, [1969] x, 176 p.; 22 cm. —
(Great lives observed) 1. Mao, Tse-tung, 1893-1976. I. T.
DS778.M3 C473   951.05/0924 B   LC 69-15346   ISBN
013555912X

Ch'ên, Jerome, 1919-.   • **3.4831**
Mao and the Chinese revolution. With thirty-seven poems by Mao Tse-tung
translated from the Chinese by Michael Bullock and Jerome Ch'en. — London;
New York: Oxford University Press, 1965. ix, 419 p.: maps, port.; 23 cm.
1. Mao, Tse-tung, 1893-1976. 2. Communism — China. I. Mao, Tse-tung,
1893-1976. II. T.
DS778.M3 C474   923.151   LC 65-2375

Hsiao, Yü, 1894-.   • **3.4832**
Mao Tse-tung and I were beggars. Illustrated by the author, Siao-yu. With a
foreword by Lin Yutang, pref. by Raymond F. Piper, and historical
commentary and notes by Robert C. North. [Syracuse, N. Y.] Syracuse
University Press [1959] 266 p. illus. 24 cm. 1. Mao, Tse-tung, 1893-1976. I. T.
DS778.M3H75   923.551   LC 59-15411

Pye, Lucian W., 1921-.   **3.4833**
Mao Tse-tung: the man in the leader / Lucian W. Pye. — New York: Basic
Books, c1976. xviii, 346 p., [7] leaves of plates: ill.; 22 cm. 1. Mao, Tse-tung,
1893-1976. I. T.
DS778.M3 P93   951.05/092/4 B   LC 75-31832   ISBN 0465043968

Rue, John E.   • **3.4834**
Mao Tse-tung in opposition, 1927-1935 [by] John E. Rue, with the assistance
of S. R. Rue. Stanford, Calif., Published for the Hoover Institution on War,
Revolution, and Peace by Stanford University Press, 1966. viii, 387 p. maps. 24
cm. 1. Mao, Tse-tung, 1893-1976. 2. Chung-kuo kung ch'an tang. 3. China —
Politics and government — 1928-1937 I. Hoover Institution on War,
Revolution, and Peace. II. T.
DS778.M3 R8   951.90430924   LC 66-15302

Schram, Stuart R.   • **3.4835**
Mao Tsê-tung [by] Stuart Schram. — New York: Simon and Schuster, [1967,
c1966] 351 p.: illus., ports.; 22 cm. 1. Mao, Tse-tung, 1893-1976. I. T.
DS778.M3 S3 1967   951/.05/0924 B   LC 67-12918

Schram, Stuart R.   **3.4836**
Mao Zedong, a preliminary reassessment / Stuart R. Schram. — Hong Kong:
The Chinese University Press; New York: St. Martin's Press, 1984 (c1983). xiii,
104 p., [8] p. of plates: ill., ports. 1. Mao, Tse-tung, 1893-1976. 2. Heads of
state — China — Biography. I. T.
DS778,M3 S33 1983b   951.05/092/4 B 19

Starr, John Bryan.   **3.4837**
Continuing the revolution: the political thought of Mao / John Bryan Starr. —
Princeton, N.J.: Princeton University Press, c1979. xv, 366 p.; 24 cm. Includes
index. 1. Mao, Tse-tung, 1893-1976 — Political and social views.
2. Dictatorship of the proletariat I. T.
DS778.M3 S76   320.5/323/0924   LC 78-63597   ISBN 0691075964

DS778 N–Z

Liew, K. S.   • **3.4838**
Struggle for democracy; Sung Chiao-jen and the 1911 Chinese revolution [by]
K. S. Liew. — Berkeley: University of California Press, 1971. ix, 260 p.: illus.;
23 cm. 1. Sung, Chiao-jen, 1882-1913. 2. China — History — Revolution,
1911-1912 I. T.
DS778.S8 L5 1971b   951/.03/0924 B   LC 74-123623   ISBN
0520017609

Bunker, Gerald E.   • **3.4839**
The peace conspiracy; Wang Ching-wei and the China war, 1937-1941 [by]
Gerald E. Bunker. — Cambridge, Mass.: Harvard University Press, 1972.
327 p.: illus.; 25 cm. — (Harvard East Asian series. 67) 1. Wang, Ching-wei,
1883-1944. 2. Sino-Japanese Conflict, 1937-1945 I. T. II. Series.
DS778.W3 B85   940.53/12/0924   LC 78-180149   ISBN
0674659155

Gillin, Donald G.   • **3.4840**
Warlord: Yen Hsi-shan in Shansi Province, 1911-1949, by Donald G. Gillin.
— Princeton, N.J.: Princeton University Press, 1967. xiv, 334 p.: maps, ports.;
22 cm. 1. Yen, Hsi-shan, 1883-1960. I. T.
DS778.Y4 G6   951.040924 B   LC 66-14308

DS779 Politics. Foreign Relations

China facts & figures annual.   **3.4841**
v. 1- 1978-. [Gulf Breeze, Fla.] Academic International Press. v. ill. 24 cm.
(Academic International reference series) Annual. 1. China — History —
1976- — Yearbooks. I. Scherer, John L. ed.
DS779.15.C48   951/.005   LC 79-640300

Moody, Peter R.   **3.4842**
Chinese politics after Mao: development and liberalization, 1976 to 1983 / Peter
R. Moody, Jr. — New York, N.Y., U.S.A.: Praeger, 1983. v, 210 p.; 25 cm.
Includes index. 1. China — Politics and government — 1976- I. T.
DS779.26.M66 1983   320.951 19   LC 83-13925   ISBN 0030635276

Pye, Lucian W., 1921-.   **3.4843**
The dynamics of Chinese politics / Lucian Pye. — Cambridge, Mass.:
Oelgeschlager, Gunn & Hain, c1981. xxv, 307 p.; 24 cm. Includes index.
1. China — Politics and government — 1976- I. T.
DS779.26.P93 1981   951 19   LC 81-14228   ISBN 0899461328

China and the world: Chinese foreign policy in the post-Mao   **3.4844**
era / edited by Samuel S. Kim.
Boulder: Westview Press, c1984. xi, 354 p.; 23 cm. Includes index. 1. China —
Foreign relations — 1976- — Addresses, essays, lectures. I. Kim, Samuel S.,
1935-
DS779.27.C4873 1984   327.51 19   LC 84-11852   ISBN 0865315574

China's foreign relations in the 1980s / edited by Harry   **3.4845**
Harding.
New Haven: Yale University Press, c1984. xv, 240 p.; 22 cm. 'Published in
cooperation with the Asia Society, New York'—Added t.p. 1. China —
Foreign relations — 1976- — Addresses, essays, lectures. I. Harding, Harry,
1946- II. Asia Society.
DS779.27.C5 1984   327.51 19   LC 84-3677   ISBN 0300032072

DS781–798 LOCAL HISTORY

Lattimore, Owen, 1900-.   • **3.4846**
The Mongols of Manchuria; their tribal divisions, geographical distribution,
historical relations with Manchus and Chinese, and present political problems.
New York, H. Fertig, 1969 [c1934] 311 p. map. 21 cm. 1. Mongols — History
2. Mongols — China — Manchuria 3. Eastern question (Far East)
4. Mongolia — History. I. T.
DS783.7.L3 1969   951/.7   LC 68-9626

Ogata, Sadako N.   **3.4847**
Defiance in Manchuria: the making of Japanese foreign policy, 1931-1932 / by
Sadako N. Ogata. — Westport, Conn.: Greenwood Press, 1984, c1964. p. cm.
Reprint. Originally published: Berkeley: University of California Press, 1964.
Includes index. 1. Japan. Rikugun. Kantōgun. 2. Manchuria (China) —
History — 1931-1945 3. Japan — Foreign relations — China — Manchuria.
4. Manchuria (China) — Foreign relations — Japan. I. T.
DS783.7.O4 1984   327.51/8/052 19   LC 84-543   ISBN
0313244286

Willoughby, Westel Woodbury, 1867-1945.   • **3.4848**
The Sino-Japanese controversy and the League of Nations. New York,
Greenwood Press, 1968 [c1935] xxv, 733 p. 22 cm. 1. League of Nations —

China. 2. League of Nations — Japan. 3. League of Nations. Council. 4. League of Nations. Special Assembly, 1932- 5. Japanese in Manchuria. 6. Manchoukuo. 7. Japan — Foreign relations — China. 8. China — Foreign relations — Japan. I. T.
DS783.7.W5 1968   951/.8   LC 68-54995

Yoshihashi, Takehiko, 1912-.   • 3.4849
Conspiracy at Mukden; the rise of the Japanese military. — New Haven: Yale University Press, 1963. xvi, 274 p.: maps; 23 cm. — (Yale studies in political science. 9) 1. Mukden Incident, 1931 2. Japan — Foreign relations — China. 3. China — Foreign relations — Japan. I. T. II. Series.
DS783.8.Y67 1963   952.033 19   LC 63-17025

Borg, Dorothy, 1902-.   • 3.4850
The United States and the Far Eastern crisis of 1933–1938; from the Manchurian incident through the initial stage of the undeclared Sino–Japanese war. — Cambridge, Harvard University Press, 1964. x, 674 p. 25 cm. — (Harvard East Asian series. 14) Bibliography: p. [547]-561. 1. Manchuria — Hist. — 1931-1945. 2. China — For. rel. — Japan. 3. Japan — For. rel. — China. 4. U.S. — For. rel. — 1933-1945. I. T. II. Series.
DS784.B65 1964   LC 64-13421

DS785–786 Tibet. Central Asia

Grousset, René, 1885-1952.   • 3.4851
[Empire des steppes. English] The empire of the steppes; a history of central Asia. Translated from the French by Naomi Walford. New Brunswick, N.J., Rutgers University Press [1970] xxx, 687 p. maps. 25 cm. 1. Asia, Central — History. I. T.
DS785.G8313   958   LC 77-108759   ISBN 0813506271

Lamb, Alastair, 1930-.   • 3.4852
Britain and Chinese Central Asia; the road to Lhasa, 1767 to 1905. London, Routledge and Paul [1960] 387 p. illus. 1. Great Britain — Foreign relations — Tibet. 2. Tibet — Foreign relations — Great Britain I. T.
DS785.L17   LC 61-1070

Rayfield, Donald, 1942-.   3.4853
The dream of Lhasa: the life of Nikolay Przhevalsky (1839–88) explorer of Central Asia / Donald Rayfield. [Athens]: Ohio University Press, 1976. xii, 221 p., [4] leaves of plates: ill.; 23 cm. Includes index. 1. Przheval'skiǐ, Nikolaǐ Mikhaǐlovich, 1839-1888. 2. Explorers — Asia, Central — Biography. 3. Asia, Central — Description and travel. I. T.
DS785.P93 R38 1976b   915.8/04 B   LC 76-20326   ISBN 0821403699

Kwanten, Luc.   3.4854
Imperial nomads: a history of central Asia, 500–1500 / Luc Kwanten. — [Philadelphia]: University of Pennsylvania Press, 1979. xv, 352 p.: ill.; 26 cm. Includes index. 1. Mongols — History 2. Asia, Central — History. I. T.
DS786.K93   958   LC 78-53339   ISBN 0812277503

Richardson, Hugh Edward, 1905-.   • 3.4855
A short history of Tibet. [1st American ed.] New York: Dutton, 1962. 308 p.: ill.; 22 cm. 'Published in England under the title of Tibet and its history.' 1. Tibet (China) — History I. T.
DS786.R5 1962   LC 61-6023

Stein, Rolf Alfred, 1911-.   • 3.4856
Tibetan civilization [by] R. A. Stein. Translated by J. E. Stapleton Driver. With original drawings by Lobsang Tendzin. Stanford, Calif., Stanford University Press, 1972. 333 p. illus. 23 cm. 'With minor revisions [of the original French ed.] by the author.' 1. Tibet (China) — Civilization I. T.
DS786.S7713 1972b   915.1/5/03   LC 72-183893   ISBN 0804708061

Tucci, Giuseppe, 1894-.   3.4857
[Tibet. English] Transhimalaya. Translated from the French by James Hogarth. Geneva, Nagel Publishers [1973] 239 p. illus. (part col.), maps (on lining papers). 24 cm. (Archaeologia mundi) Translation of Tibet. 1. Archaeology 2. Tibet (China) — Antiquities. I. T.
DS786.T7713   951/.5   LC 74-186286   ISBN 2826305751

DS793–796 Provinces, A–Z

Schafer, Edward H.   3.4858
Shore of pearls: Hainan Island in early times / by Edward H. Schafter. — Berkeley: University of California Press, 1970 [c1969] ix, 173 p.: maps (on lining papers); 23 cm. 1. Chinese literature — Hainan. 2. Hainan — History. I. T.
DS793.H3 S3 1970   915.1/27   LC 78-94990   ISBN 0520015924

Wakeman, Frederic E.   • 3.4859
Strangers at the gate; social disorder in South China, 1839–1861 [by] Frederic Wakeman, Jr. Berkeley, University of California Press [c1966] 276 p. maps. 24 cm. (Center for Chinese Studies. Publications) 1. Kwangtung Province (China) — History. 2. China — History — War of 1840-1842. I. T.
DS793.K7 W3   951.512703   LC 66-25349

Jagchid, Sechin, 1914-.   3.4860
Mongolia's culture and society / Sechin Jagchid and Paul Hyer; with a foreword by Joseph Fletcher. — Boulder, Colo.: Westview Press, c1979. xvi, 461 p.: ill.; 23 cm. Includes index. 1. Inner Mongolia (China) — Social life and customs. I. Hyer, Paul. joint author. II. T.
DS793.M7 J32   951/.77   LC 79-1438   ISBN 0891583904

McMillen, Donald H.   3.4861
Chinese Communist power and policy in Xinjiang, 1949–1977 / Donald H. McMillen. — Boulder, Colo.: Westview Press, 1979. xix, 373 p.; 23 cm. (A Westview/Dawson replica edition) Includes index. 1. Sinkiang Province (China) — Politics and government. I. T.
DS793.S62 M24 1979   320.9/51/605   LC 78-24645   ISBN 0891584528

Li, Chi, 1896-.   3.4862
Anyang / by Li Chi. — Seattle: University of Washington Press, c1977. xviii, 304 p., [10] leaves of plates: ill.; 25 cm. Includes index. 1. Excavations (Archaeology) — China — An-yang. 2. An-yang, China — Antiquities. I. T.
DS796.A55 L5   951/.18   LC 75-40873   ISBN 0295954905

Endacott, G. B.   • 3.4863
A history of Hong Kong. London: Oxford University Press, 1958. 322 p.: ill.; 23 cm. 1. Hong Kong — Hist. I. T.
DS796.H7 E5   LC 58-4392

Buck, David D., 1936-.   3.4864
Urban change in China: politics and development in Tsinan, Shantung, 1890–1949 / David D. Buck. — Madison: University of Wisconsin Press, 1978. xvi, 296 p.: ill.; 24 cm. Includes index. 1. Tsinan (China) — History. I. T.
DS796.T68 B8   309.1/51/14   LC 76-11309   ISBN 0299071103

DS798 Mongolia

Bawden, Charles R.   3.4865
The modern history of Mongolia [by] C. R. Bawden. New York, Praeger [1968] xvii, 460 p. illus., maps, ports. 23 cm. (The Praeger Asia-Africa series) 1. Mongolia — History. I. T.
DS798.B53 1968   951.7/3   LC 68-9814

Historical Evaluation and Research Organization.   3.4866
Area handbook for Mongolia. Co-authors: Trevor N. Dupuy [and others] Prepared for the American University by Historical Evaluation and Research Organization. Washington, For sale by the Supt. of Docs., U.S. Govt. Print. Off., 1970. xiv, 500 p. maps 24 cm. 'DA pam. no. 550-76.' 'One of a series of handbooks prepared by Foreign Area Studies (FAS) of the American University.' 1. Mongolia. I. Dupuy, Trevor Nevitt, 1916- II. American University (Washington, D.C.). Foreign Area Studies. III. T.
DS798.H57 1970   309.1/51/73   LC 74-607921

History of the Mongolian People's Republic: the contemporary   3.4867
period / translated from the Mongolian and annotated by
William A. Brown and Urgunge Onon.
Cambridge: East Asian Research Center, Harvard University: distributed by Harvard University Press, 1976. xv, 897 p.: ill.; 26 cm. (Harvard East Asian monographs. 65) Translation of the original work edited by Bagaryn Shirendyb et al., and published under title: Bŭgd Naǐramdakh Mongol Ard Ulsyn Tŭúkh. 3. Nén shiné ùe. 1. Mongolia — History. I. Brown, William A., 1930- II. Onon, Urgungge. III. Shirêndêv, B., 1912- IV. Series.
DS798.5.B813 1976   951/.73   LC 75-37731   ISBN 0674398629

Hsieh, Chiao-min.   3.4868
Taiwan–ilha formosa: a geography in perspective. -- Washington: Butterworths, 1964. viii, 372 p.: ill., maps.; 26 cm. 1. Formosa — Description and travel. 2. Formosa — History. I. T.
DS895.F7 H68   DS799.8.H8x.   LC 64-22305

The Taiwan experience, 1950–1980: contemporary Republic of   3.4869
China / edited by James C. Hsiung and others.
1st pbk. ed. — NY [i.e. New York]: American Association for Chinese Studies, 1981. xxi, 518 p.: ill.; 24 cm. 1. Taiwan — History — 1945- — Addresses, essays, lectures. I. Hsiung, James Chieh, 1935- II. American Association for Chinese Studies. III. Title: Contemporary Republic of China.
DS799.8.T3377 1981   951/.24905 19   LC 81-68480   ISBN 0960659404

DS801–897 Japan

Asakawa, Kanichi, 1874-1945, ed.   • **3.4870**
The documents of Iriki, illustrative of the development of the feudal institutions of Japan. Edited by K. Asakawa. New Haven, Yale University Press, 1929. 134 p. 26 cm. Cover title. Text in Japanese. 1. Feudalism — Japan 2. Land tenure — Kyushu, Japan. 3. Shimadzu family. 4. Iriki, Kyushu, Japan. I. T.
DS 803 A79 1929

Kodansha encyclopedia of Japan.   **3.4871**
1st ed. — Tokyo; New York, N.Y.: Kodansha, 1983. 9 v.: ill.; 29 cm. Includes index. 1. Japan — Dictionaries and encyclopedias. I. Kōdansha. II. Title: Encyclopedia of Japan.
DS805.K633 1983   952/.003/.21 19   *LC* 83-80778   *ISBN* 0870116207

Burks, Ardath W.   **3.4872**
Japan: profile of a postindustrial power / Ardath W. Burks. — Boulder, Colo.: Westview Press, 1981. xii, 260 p.: ill.; 24 cm. (Westview profiles. Nations of contemporary Asia.) Includes index. 1. Japan. I. T. II. Series.
DS806.B85   952   *LC* 80-14183   *ISBN* 0891587861

Hall, John Whitney, 1916-.   • **3.4873**
Twelve doors to Japan, by John Whitney Hall and Richard K. Beardsley. With chapters by Joseph K. Yamagiwa [and] B. James George, Jr. — New York, McGraw-Hill [1965] xxi, 649 p. maps. 24 cm. Bibliography: p. 587-623. 1. Japan. I. Beardsley, Richard King, 1918- joint author. II. T.
DS806.H25   915.203   *LC* 64-66015

Japan. Mombushō. Nihon Yunesuko Kokunai Iinkai.   **3.4874**
Japan; its land, people and culture, compiled by Japanese National Commission for UNESCO. — 3d ed. — [Tokyo]: University of Tokyo Press, [1973] xlviii, 702 p.: illus., fold. col. maps.; 26 cm. 1. Japan. I. T.
DS806.J199 1973   915.2/03   *LC* 73-174711

Japan: a country study / Foreign Area Studies, the American   • **3.4875**
University; edited by Frederica M. Bunge.
4th ed. — Washington, D.C.: The Studies: For sale by the Supt. of Docs., U.S. G.P.O., 1983, c1982. xxvii, 494 p.: ill.; 24 cm. — (Area handbook series.) Rev. ed. of: Area handbook for Japan / coauthors, Donald P. Whitaker and others. 3rd ed. 1974. 'DA pam 550-30.' 'Supersedes 1974 edition.' Includes index. 1. Japan — Handbooks, manuals, etc. I. Bunge, Frederica M. II. Whitaker, Donald P. Area handbook for Japan. III. American University (Washington, D.C.). Foreign Area Studies. IV. Series.
DS806.J223 1983   952 19   *LC* 82-22835

Reischauer, Edwin O. (Edwin Oldfather), 1910-.   **3.4876**
The Japanese / Edwin O. Reischauer. — Cambridge, Mass.: Belknap Press, 1977. 443 p.: ill.; 24 cm. Includes index. 1. Japan. I. T.
DS806.R35   952   *LC* 76-30708   *ISBN* 0674471768

Seidensticker, Edward, 1921-.   **3.4877**
This country, Japan / Edward Seidensticker. — 1st ed. — Tokyo; New York: Kodansha International, 1979. x, 332 p.; 22 cm. 1. Seidensticker, Edward, 1921- — Addresses, essays, lectures. 2. National characteristics, Japanese — Addresses, essays, lectures. 3. Japanese literature — History and criticism — Addresses, essays, lectures. 4. Translators — United States — Biography — Addresses, essays, lectures. 5. Japan — Addresses, essays, lectures. I. T.
DS806.S43   952 19   *LC* 74-77958

Cooper, Michael, 1930- ed.   **3.4878**
They came to Japan; an anthology of European reports on Japan, 1543–1640. — Berkeley: University of California Press, 1965. xviii, 439 p.: map (on lining papers); 24 cm. — (Publications of the Center for Japanese and Korean Studies) 1. Japan — Description and travel — To 1800 I. T.
DS808.C6   915.20325   *LC* 65-19250

Alcock, Rutherford, Sir, 1809-1897.   • **3.4879**
The capital of the tycoon: a narrative of a three years' residence in Japan. London, Longman, Green, Longman, Roberts, & Green, 1863. — St. Clair Shores, Mich.: Scholarly Press, [1969] 2 v.: illus.; 23 cm. 1. Japan — Description and travel — 1801-1900 2. Japan — Foreign relations — To 1868 I. T.
DS809.A35 1969   915.2   *LC* 73-8881

Perry, Matthew Calbraith, 1794-1858.   **3.4880**
Narrative of the expedition of an American squadron to the China Seas and Japan, performed in the years 1852, 1853, and 1854, under the command of Commodore M. C. Perry, United States Navy, by order of the Government of the United States. Compiled from the original notes and journals of Commodore Perry and his officers, at his request, and under his supervision, by Francis L. Hawks. Washington, B. Tucker, 1856. New York, AMS Press, 1967.

3 v. illus., charts, facsims., maps, plates and portfolio (15 fold. charts, maps) 29 cm. (33d Cong., 2d sess. Senate. Ex. doc. no. 79) On spine: United States Japan Expedition. "List of charts of the United States Japan Expedition" (15 fold sheets) issued in portfolio, to accompany v.2. Vol.2 (Natural history reports) by D. S. Green and others; v.3 has title: Observation on the zodiacal light, from April 2, 1853 to April 22, 1855, made chiefly on board the United States Steam-Frigate Mississippi ... with conclusions from the data thus obtained, by George Jones. 1. Unites States Naval Expedition to Japan, 1852-1854. 2. Japan — Description and travel — 1801-1900 I. Jones, George, 1800-1870. II. Hawks, Francis L. (Francis Lister), 1798-1866. comp. III. T. IV. Title: United States Japan Expedition.
DS809.P456 1967   952.02/5

Hearn, Lafcadio, 1850-1904.   • **3.4881**
Japan; an attempt at interpretation. Tokyo, Rutland, Vt., C.E. Tuttle Co. [1955, c1904] 498 p. 19 cm. 1. Japan — Civilization I. T.
DS810.H43 1955   *LC* 56-249

Trewartha, Glenn Thomas, 1896-.   • **3.4882**
Japan: a geography / Glenn T. Trewartha. — Madison: University of Wisconsin Press, 1965. x, 652 p.: ill., maps. 1. Japan — Description and travel — 1945- I. T.
DS811.T72   *LC* 65-11200   *ISBN* 0299034402 1732

DS815–832 CIVILIZATION

Japan. Monbushō.   • **3.4883**
Kokutai no hongi. Cardinal principles of the national entity of Japan. — Tr. by John Owen Gauntlett and ed. with an introd. by Robert King Hall. — Cambridge, Harvard University Press, 1949. viii, 200 p. 22 cm. 1. Japan — Civilization 2. National characteristics, Japanese I. T. II. Title: Cardinal principles of the national entity of Japan.
DS821.A16 1949   915.2   *LC* 49-9335 rev 2*

Benedict, Ruth, 1887-1948.   • **3.4884**
The chrysanthemum and the sword; patterns of Japanese culture, by Ruth Benedict. Boston, Houghton Mifflin company, 1946. 4 p., l., 324 p. 22 cm. 1. Japan — Social life and customs 2. Japan — Civilization I. T.
DS821.B46   915.2   *LC* 46-11843

Buruma, Ian.   **3.4885**
[Japanese mirror] Behind the mask: on sexual demons, sacred mothers, transvestites, gangsters, drifters and other Japanese cultural heroes / Ian Buruma. — 1st American ed. — New York: Pantheon Books, c1984. xiii, 242 p., [16] p. of plates: ill.; 22 cm. Previously published as: A Japanese mirror. London: Jonathan Cape, 1983. 1. National characteristics, Japanese 2. Japan — Popular culture I. T.
DS821.B796 1984   306/.0952 19   *LC* 83-25027   *ISBN* 0394537750

Chamberlain, Basil Hall, 1850-1935.   • **3.4886**
[Things Japanese] Japanese things; being notes on various subjects connected with Japan, for the use of travelers and others. Rutland, Vt., Tuttle [c1971] x, 568 p. fold. col. map (in pocket) 19 cm. Previous editions have title: Things Japanese. 1. Japan. I. T.
DS821.C43 1971   915.2/03/3103   *LC* 76-87791   *ISBN* 0804807132

Christopher, Robert C., 1924-.   **3.4887**
The Japanese mind: the Goliath explained / Robert C. Christopher. — New York: Linden Press/Simon & Schuster, 1983. 352 p.; 24 cm. Includes index. 1. National characteristics, Japanese 2. Japan — Civilization I. T.
DS821.C587 1983   952.04 19   *LC* 82-25896   *ISBN* 0671449478

Gibney, Frank, 1924-.   **3.4888**
Japan, the fragile superpower / by Frank Gibney. — 1st ed. — New York: Norton, [1975] 347 p.; 20 cm. 1. National characteristics, Japanese 2. Japan — Civilization 3. Japan — History — 1945- I. T.
DS821.G513 1975   952.04   *LC* 74-20833   *ISBN* 0393055302

Changing Japanese attitudes toward modernization / Edited by   • **3.4889**
Marius B. Jansen. Contributors: Robert N. Bellah ... [et al.].
Princeton, N.J.: Princeton U.P., 1965. x, 546 p.: ill. Papers prepared for a seminar held in Bermuda under the auspices of the Conference on Modern Japan of the Association for Asian Studies in Jan. 1962. 1. Japan — Civilization — Addresses, essays, lectures. I. Bellah, Robert Neelly, 1927- II. Jansen, Marius B. III. Conference on Modern Japan.
DS821 J334   915.2   *LC* 63-23406   *ISBN* 0691030073

Lebra, Takie Sugiyama, 1930-.   **3.4890**
Japanese patterns of behavior / Takie Sugiyama Lebra. Honolulu: University of Hawaii Press, 1976. xviii, 295 p.; 21 cm. 'An East-West Center book.' Includes index. 1. National characteristics, Japanese 2. Japan — Social life and customs I. T.
DS821.L346   301.29/52   *LC* 76-10392   *ISBN* 0824803965

Louis-Frédéric, 1923-.   **3.4891**
[Japon, art et civilisation. English] Japan, art and civilisation. New York, Abrams [1971, c1969] 503 p. illus. 32 cm. 1. Art — Japan — History. 2. Japan — Civilization I. T.
DS821.L6613 1971b   915.2/03   LC 77-125780   ISBN 0810902095

Sansom, George Bailey, Sir, 1883-1965.   • **3.4892**
Japan, a short cultural history. — Rev. ed. — New York: Appleton-Century-Crofts, [1962] 558 p.: illus.; 24 cm. 1. Japan — Civilization 2. Japan — History I. T.
DS821.S3 1962   952   LC 62-2310

Sansom, George Bailey, Sir, 1883-1965.   • **3.4893**
The Western World and Japan, a study in the interaction of European and Asiatic cultures. [1st ed.] New York, Knopf, 1950 [i.e. 1949] xvi, 504, xi p. illus., ports., maps. 25 cm. 1. Japan — Relations — Europe 2. Europe — Relations — Japan 3. Japan — Civilization — Occidental influences I. T.
DS821.S313   LC 50-5199

Taylor, Jared.   **3.4894**
Shadows of the Rising Sun: a critical view of the 'Japanese miracle' / Jared Taylor. — 1st ed. — New York: Morrow, 1983. 336 p.; 25 cm. 1. National characteristics, Japanese 2. Social values 3. Japan — Civilization I. T.
DS821.T275 1983   952 19   LC 83-9915   ISBN 0688024556

Tsunoda, Ryūsaku, ed.   • **3.4895**
Sources of the Japanese tradition, compiled by Ryūsaku Tsunoda, Wm. Theodore de Bary [and] Donald Keene. — New York: Columbia University Press, 1958. xxvi, 928 p.: maps.; 24 cm. — (Records of civilization: sources and studies, 54. Introduction to oriental civilizations) Translation from various sources and by various individuals. 1. Japan — Civilization 2. Japan — History — Sources. I. T.
DS821.T76   952.0082   LC 58-7167

Tradition and modernization in Japanese culture, edited by   **3.4896**
Donald H. Shively. Contributors: Carmen Blacker [and others].
Princeton, N.J.: Princeton University Press, 1971. xvii, 689 p.: illus.; 22 cm. — ([Studies in the modernization of Japan] 5) Papers from the fifth seminar of the Conference on Modern Japan, held in Puerto Rico, January, 1966. 1. Japan — Civilization — 1868- — Collections. 2. Japan — Civilization — Occidental influences — Collections. I. Shively, Donald Howard, 1921- ed. II. Blacker, Carmen. III. Conference on Modern Japan. IV. Series.
DS822.25.T7   915.2/03/3   LC 69-18071   ISBN 0691030723

Irokawa, Daikichi, 1925-.   **3.4897**
[Meiji no bunka. English] The culture of the Meiji period / Irokawa Daikichi; translation edited by Marius B. Jansen. — Princeton, N.J.: Princeton University Press, 1985. xvi, 320 p.; 23 cm. (Princeton library of Asian translations.) Translation of: Meiji no bunka. 1. Japan — Civilization — 1868-1912 I. T. II. Series.
DS822.3.I7613 1985   952.03/1 19   LC 84-42889   ISBN 0691066345

Pyle, Kenneth B.   **3.4898**
The new generation in Meiji Japan; problems of cultural identity, 1885–1895 [by] Kenneth B. Pyle. — Stanford, Calif.: Stanford University Press, 1969. viii, 240 p.; 24 cm. A revision of the author's thesis, Johns Hopkins University, 1966. 1. Japan — Intellectual life — Occidental influences. 2. Japan — Civilization — 1868-1945 I. T.
DS822.3.P9 1969   915.2/03/31   LC 69-13183

Arima, Tatsuo.   • **3.4899**
The failure of freedom; a portrait of modern Japanese intellectuals. — Cambridge: Harvard University Press, 1969. xiii, 296 p.; 22 cm. — (Harvard East Asian series. 39) 1. Intellectuals — Japan. 2. Liberalism — Japan. I. T. II. Series.
DS822.4.A7   915.2/03/320922   LC 74-82292   ISBN 0674291301

Katō, Shizue, 1897-.   **3.4900**
Facing two ways: the story of my life / Baroness Shidzué Ishimoto; with an introduction and an afterword by Barbara Molony. — Stanford, Calif.: Stanford University Press, 1984, c1935. 373, xxix p., [10] p. of plates: ill.; 23 cm. 1. Katō, Shizue, 1897- 2. Women's rights — Japan. 3. Feminists — Japan — Biography. 4. Japan — Social life and customs — 1912-1945 I. T.
DS822.4.K37 1984   952.03/092/4 B 19   LC 83-40621   ISBN 0804712395

Bell, Ronald, 1931-.   **3.4901**
The Japan experience, edited, with an introd., by Ronald Bell. — [1st ed.]. — New York: Weatherhill, [1973] xiv, 240 p.; 22 cm. 1. Japan — Foreign opinion. I. T.
DS822.5.B44   301.15/43/9152034   LC 73-9657   ISBN 0834800845

Morris, Ivan I.   **3.4902**
The world of the shining prince; court life in ancient Japan [by] Ivan Morris. [1st American ed.] New York, Knopf, 1964. xv, 336 p. illus. 22 cm. Bibliography: p. [321]-324. 1. Japan — Court and courtiers I. T.
DS824.M6 1964   915.2   LC 64-12310

DS833–897 HISTORY

Goedertier, Joseph M.   • **3.4903**
A dictionary of Japanese history [by] Joseph M. Goedertier. — [1st ed.]. — New York: Walker/Weatherhill [i.e. J. Weatherhill; distributed by Walker, 1968] 415 p.; 24 cm. 'Compiled under the auspices of the Oriens Institute for Religious Research.' 1. Japanese language — Dictionaries — English. 2. Japan — History — Dictionaries. I. Oriensu Shūkyō Kenkyūjo. II. T.
DS833.G63   952/.003   LC 68-15703

Varley, H. Paul.   **3.4904**
A syllabus of Japanese civilization, by H. Paul Varley. — 2d ed. — New York: Columbia University Press, 1972. ix, 98 p.: maps.; 23 cm. — (Companions to Asian studies.) 1. Japan — History — Outlines, syllabi, etc. 2. Japan — Civilization — History — Outlines, syllabi, etc. I. T. II. Series.
DS833.V3 1972   915.2/03/0202   LC 72-195883   ISBN 0231036779

Biographical dictionary of Japanese history / supervising editor,   **3.4905**
Seiichi Iwao; translator, Burton Watson.
1st ed. — Tokyo: International Society for Educational Information, 1978. 655 p.: ill.; 22 cm. Includes index. 1. Japan — Biography. I. Iwao, Seiichi, 1900-
DS834.B56   920/.052   LC 78-323261   ISBN 0870112740

The Japan biographical encyclopedia & who's who.   **3.4906**
1st-   ed.; 1958-. Tokyo, Japan Biographical Research Dept., Rengo Press. 1. Japan — Biography — Dictionaries.
DS834.J7

Morris, Ivan I.   **3.4907**
The nobility of failure: tragic heroes in the history of Japan / Ivan Morris. — 1st ed. — New York: Holt, Rinehart and Winston, [1975] xxiii, 500 p., [16] leaves of plates: ill.; 24 cm. Includes index. 1. Heroes — Japan. 2. Japan — Biography. I. T.
DS834.M64   952/.00992 B   LC 73-3750   ISBN 003010811X

Hane, Mikiso.   **3.4908**
Japan; a historical survey. — [New York]: Scribner, [1972] xiv, 650 p.: illus.; 24 cm. 1. Japan — History I. T.
DS835.H266   915.2/03   LC 79-37178   ISBN 0684127075

Kaempfer, Engelbert, 1651-1716.   **3.4909**
The history of Japan, together with a description of the Kingdom of Siam, 1690–92. Translated by J. G. Scheuchzer. — [1st AMS ed.] Glasgow, J. MacLehose, 1906. — [New York: AMS Press, 1971] 3 v.: illus., fold. maps, port.; 23 cm. 1. Thailand — Description and travel 2. Japan — History — To 1868 3. Japan — Description and travel — To 1800 I. Scheuchzer, John Gaspar, 1702-1729, tr. II. T.
DS835.K2 1971   915.2/03/25   LC 78-137313   ISBN 0404036309

Murdoch, James, 1856-1921.   • **3.4910**
A history of Japan. Foreword and selected bibliography by John L. Mish. F. Ungar Pub. Co. [c1964] 3v. in 6. illus. CONTENTS.-v.1. From the origins to the arrival of the Portuguese in 1542 A.D.-v.2. During the century of early foreign intercourse (1542-1651)-v.3. The Tokugawa epoch, 1652-1868. 1. Japan — History — To 1868 I. T.
DS835.M82 1964   LC 64-15695

Reischauer, Edwin O. (Edwin Oldfather), 1910-.   • **3.4911**
Japan; the story of a nation [by] Edwin O. Reischauer. [1st ed.] New York, Knopf [1970] xv, 345, xx p. maps. 21 cm. 1. Japan — History I. T.
DS835.R38 1970   952   LC 77-108925

Sansom, George Bailey, Sir, 1883-1965.   • **3.4912**
A history of Japan. — Stanford, Calif.: Stanford University Press, 1958-63. 3 v.: ill., maps, facsims.; 26 cm. — (Stanford studies in the civilizations of eastern Asia) 'Bibliographical note': v. 1, p. [485]-487; v. 2, p. [419]-426; v. 3, p. [249] 1. Japan — Hist. I. T. II. Series.
DS835.S27   952   LC 58-11694 rev

Totman, Conrad D.   **3.4913**
Japan before Perry: a short history / Conrad Totman. — Berkeley: University of California Press, c1981. xv, 246 p.: ill.; 22 cm. Includes index. 1. Japan — History — To 1868 I. T.
DS835.T58   952   LC 80-14708   ISBN 0520041321

Mitchell, Richard H.   • 3.4914
The Korean minority in Japan [by] Richard H. Mitchell. Berkeley, University
of California Press, 1967. 186 p. 1. Koreans in Japan I. T.
DS836 M5   *LC* 67-18074

DS840–849 POLITICAL AND DIPLOMATIC HISTORY

Beasley, W. G. (William G.), 1919- ed. and tr.   • 3.4915
Select documents on Japanese foreign policy, 1853–1868, translated and edited
by W. G. Beasley. — London, New York, Oxford University Press, 1955. xi,
359 p. 25 cm. Bibliography: p. [343]-348. Bibliographical footnotes. 1. Japan
— For. rel. — To 1867. I. T. II. Title: Japanese foreign policy, 1853-1868.
DS840.B4   *LC* 55-4067

Brown, Delmer Myers, 1909-.   • 3.4916
Nationalism in Japan; an introductory historical analysis [by] Delmer M.
Brown. — New York: Russell & Russell, 1971, c1955. viii, 336 p.; 24 cm.
Includes index. 1. Nationalism — Japan — History. I. T.
DS843.B76 1971   DS821.B69 1971.   952   *LC* 79-143555   *ISBN*
0846215748

The Fateful choice: Japan's advance into Southeast Asia,   3.4917
1939–1941: selected translations from Taiheiyō Sensō e no
michi, kaisen gaikō shi / edited by James William Morley.
New York: Columbia University Press, 1980. xi, 366 p.: map; 24 cm. —
(Japan's road to the Pacific war.) Includes index. 1. World War, 1939-1945 —
Diplomatic history 2. Japan — Foreign relations — 1912-1945. 3. Japan —
Foreign relations — Asia, Southeastern. 4. Asia, Southeastern — Foreign
relations — Japan. 5. Japan — Military policy. I. Morley, James William,
1921- II. Nihon Kokusai Seiji Gakkai. Taiheiyō Sensō Gen'in Kenkyūbu.
Taiheiyō Sensō e no michi. III. Series.
DS845.F37   327.52   *LC* 79-23486   *ISBN* 0231048041

Takeuchi, Tatsuji, 1904-.   • 3.4918
War and diplomacy in the Japanese empire / By Tatsuji Takeuchi; Introd. by
Quincy Wright. — Garden City, N. Y.: Doubleday, Doran & Company, 1935.
xix, 505 p.; 24 cm. Expansion of the author's thesis, University of Chicago,
issued under title: The control of foreign relations in Japan. 'The Constitution of
the Empire of Japan': p. 477-484. 1. Japan — Politics and government —
1912-1945 2. Japan — Foreign relations — 1912-1945 3. Japan — Foreign
relations — Treaties. I. Japan. Constitution. II. T.
DS845.T3   327.52   *LC* 36-10

The China quagmire: Japan's expansion on the Asian continent,   3.4919
1933–1941: selected translations from Taiheiyō Sensō e no
michi, kaisen gaikō shi / edited by James William Morley.
1st ed. — New York: Columbia University Press, 1983. xiii, 503 p.: maps; 24
cm. (Japan's road to the Pacific war.) (Studies of the East Asian Institute.)
Includes index. 1. Sino-Japanese Conflict, 1937-1945 2. Japan — Foreign
relations — China. 3. China — Foreign relations — Japan. 4. Japan —
Military policy. 5. China — Politics and government — 1928-1937 I. Morley,
James William, 1921- II. Taiheiyō Sensō e no michi. III. Series. IV. Series:
Studies of the East Asian Institute.
DS849.C6 C49 1983   327.52051 19   *LC* 82-12891   *ISBN*
0231055226

Lee, Chae-Jin, 1936-.   3.4920
Japan faces China: political and economic relations in the postwar era / Chae-
Jin Lee. — Baltimore: Johns Hopkins University Press, c1976. xiii, 242 p.: ill.;
24 cm. 1. Japan — Foreign relations — China. 2. China — Foreign relations
— Japan. 3. Japan — Foreign economic relations — China. 4. China —
Foreign economic relations — Japan. I. T.
DS849.C6 L33   327.52/051   *LC* 75-40408   *ISBN* 0801817382

Morton, William Fitch.   3.4921
Tanaka Giichi and Japan's China policy / William Fitch Morton. — New
York: St. Martin's Press, 1980. 329 p., [1] leaf of plates: ill.; 23 cm. Includes
index. 1. Tanaka, Giichi, 1863-1929. 2. Japan — Foreign relations — China.
3. China — Foreign relations — Japan. I. T.
DS849.C6 M64 1980   327.51052   *LC* 79-27570   *ISBN* 0312785003

Deterrent diplomacy: Japan, Germany, and the USSR,   3.4922
1935–1940: selected translations from Taiheiyō Sensō e no
michi, kaisen gaikō shi / edited by James William Morley.
New York: Columbia University Press, 1976. xii, 363 p.; 24 cm. (Japan's road to
the Pacific war.) (Studies of the East Asian Institute, Columbia University)
Translation of 3 essays from Taiheiyō Sensō e no michi: kaisen gaikō shi (The
road to the Pacific War: a diplomatic history of the origins of the war) which
was prepared by the Japan Association of International Relations and published
in 1962-1963. Includes index. 1. World War, 1939-1945 — Diplomatic history
— Addresses, essays, lectures. 2. Japan — Foreign relations — Germany —
Addresses, essays, lectures. 3. Germany — Foreign relations — Japan —

Addresses, essays, lectures. 4. Japan — Foreign relations — Russia —
Addresses, essays, lectures. 5. Russia — Foreign relations — Japan —
Addresses, essays, lectures. I. Morley, James William, 1921- II. Nihon
Kokusai Seiji Gakkai. Taiheiyō Sensō Gen'in Kenkyūbu. Taiheiyō Sensō e no
michi. III. Series.
DS849.G4 D47   327.52   *LC* 75-25524   *ISBN* 0231089694

Dennis, Alfred Lewis Pinneo, 1874- .   • 3.4923
The Anglo–Japanese alliance / by Alfred L. P. Dennis. — California:
University of California Press, 1923. 111 p.; 25 cm. — (University of California
publications, Bureau of International Relations; Vol. 1, no. 1) Contains
Appendix entitled: 'Anglo-Japanese treaties'. 1. Great Britain — Foreign
relations — Japan. 2. Japan — Foreign relations — Great Britain. 3. Great
Britain — Treaties — Japan. 4. Japan — Treaties — Great Britain. I. T.
II. Series.
DS849.G7 D4   *LC* a 23-1030

Saniel, Josefa M.   3.4924
Japan and the Philippines, 1868–1898 [by] Josefa M. Saniel. — New York:
Russell & Russell, [1973, c1969] xvi, 409 p.; 23 cm. Reprint of the ed. published
by the University of the Philippines, Quezon City. Originally presented as the
author's thesis, University of Michigan. 1. Japan — Relations — Philippines
2. Philippines — Relations — Japan I. T.
DS849.P5 S26 1973   301.29/52/0599   *LC* 72-94983   *ISBN*
0846217244

Lensen, George Alexander, 1923-.   • 3.4925
The Russian push toward Japan; Russo–Japanese relations, 1697–1875. New
York, Octagon Books, 1971 [c1959] xv, 553 p. illus. 25 cm. 1. Russia —
Foreign relations — Japan. 2. Japan — Foreign relations — Russia. 3. Siberia,
Eastern (R.S.F.S.R.) — History. I. T.
DS849.R7 L39 1971   327.47/052   *LC* 75-120640   *ISBN*
0374949360

Lensen, George Alexander, 1923-.   3.4926
The strange neutrality; Soviet–Japanese relations during the Second World
War, 1941–1945. Tallahassee, Diplomatic Press [1972] x, 332 p. illus. 24 cm.
1. World War, 1939-1945 — Diplomatic history 2. Japan — Foreign relations
— Soviet Union. 3. Soviet Union — Foreign relations — Japan. I. T.
DS849.R7 L42   940.53/2   *LC* 72-178091   *ISBN* 0910512140

Grew, Joseph C. (Joseph Clark), 1880-1965.   • 3.4927
Ten years in Japan, a contemporary record drawn from the diaries and private
and official papers of Joseph C. Grew, United States ambassador to Japan,
1932–1942. — New York, Simon and Schuster, 1944. xii, 554 p., 1 l. front,
plates, ports. 22 cm. 1. World war, 1939- — Causes. 2. U.S. — For. rel. —
Japan. 3. Japan — For. rel. — U.S. 4. Japan — Pol. & govt. I. T.
DS849.U6G7   327.730952   *LC* 44-40123

Moore, Frederick, 1877-.   • 3.4928
With Japan's leaders; an intimate record of fourteen years as counsellor to the
Japanese Government, ending December 7, 1941. New York Scribner 1942.
365p. 1. Japan — Foreign relations — U. S. 2. United States — Foreign
relations — Japan I. T.
DS849 U6 M68

DS851–890 BY PERIOD

DS851–871 Early to 1868

Kojiki. English.   • 3.4929
Kojiki / Translated with an introduction and notes by Donald L. Philippi. —
[Princeton, N.J.]: Princeton University Press, 1969, c1968. v, 655 p.; 24 cm.
Includes index. 1. Mythology, Japanese 2. Shinto 3. Japan — History — To
645 — Sources. I. Philippi, Donald L. II. T.
DS851.A2 K643 1969   915.2/03/1   *LC* 69-17446

Nihon shoki. English.   • 3.4930
Nihongi; chronicles of Japan from the earliest times to A.D. 697. Translated
from the original Chinese and Japanese by W. G. Aston. With an introd. to the
new ed. by Terence Barrow. — [1st Tuttle ed.]. — Rutland, Vt.: C. E. Tuttle
Co., [1972] 2 v. in 1.: illus.; 19 cm. — (Tut books. H) 1. Mythology, Japanese
2. Japan — History — To 645 I. Aston, William George, 1841- tr. II. T.
DS851.A2 N53 1972   915.2/03/1   *LC* 70-152110   *ISBN*
0804809844

Tsunoda, Ryusaku.   • 3.4931
Japan in the Chinese dynastic histories: Later Han through Ming dynasties.
South Pasadena [Calif.] P.D. and I. Perkins 1951. [187 leaves] (Perkins Asiatic
monographs, no. 2) 1. Japan — History — To 1867 — Sources I. Goodrich, L.
Carrington (Luther Carrington), 1894- ed. II. T. III. Series.
DS851 A2 T7

Kidder, J. Edward (Jonathan Edward) 3.4932
Early Buddhist Japan [by] J. Edward Kidder. New York, Praeger [1972] 212 p. illus. 21 cm. (Ancient peoples and places, v. 78) 1. Japan — History — To 794 2. Japan — Antiquities, Buddhist. I. T.
DS851.K48 1972 915.2/03/1 *LC* 70-189060

Kidder, J. Edward (Jonathan Edward) • 3.4933
Japan before Buddhism [by] J. E. Kidder, Jr. [Rev. ed.] New York, F. A. Praeger [1966] 284 p. illus., maps. 22 cm. (Ancient peoples and places, 10) 1. Japan — History — To 645 2. Japan — Antiquities I. T.
DS851.K5 1966 915.2031 *LC* 66-12521

Ōkagami. English. 3.4934
Okagami, the Great mirror: Fujiwara Michinaga (966–1027) and his times: a study and translation / by Helen Craig McCullough. — Princeton: Princeton University Press, c1980. x, 381 p.: ill.; 24 cm. — (Princeton library of Asian translations.) Translation of Ōkagami, 'Nihon koten bungaku taikei text, based on the Tomatsubon.' Variously ascribed to Fujiwara Tamenari, Fujiwara Yoshinobu, and others. Cf. Fujimura's Nihon bungaku daijiten; Kyōto Daigaku's Nihon shi jiten. 1. Japan — History — Heian period, 794-1185 I. Fujiwara, Tamenari, 12th cent. Ōkagami. II. Fujiwara, Yoshinobu, 995-1065. Ōkagami. III. McCullough, Helen Craig. IV. T. V. Series.
DS856.O3813 952/.01 *LC* 79-3222 *ISBN* 0691064199

Mass, Jeffrey P. 3.4935
Warrior government in early medieval Japan: a study of the Kamakura Bakufu, shugo and jitō / Jeffrey P. Mass. — New Haven: Yale University Press, 1974. x, 257 p., [1] leaf of plates: map; 23 cm. (Yale historical publications. Miscellany. 103) Includes index. 1. Local officials and employees — Japan — History. 2. Japan — Politics and government — 1185-1333 I. T. II. Series.
DS859.M25 320.9/52/02 *LC* 74-75875 *ISBN* 0300017561

Shinoda, Minoru. • 3.4936
The founding of the Kamakura shogunate, 1180–1185: with selected translations from the Azuma kagami / by Minoru Shinoda. — New York: Columbia University Press, c1960. xii, 385 p.: geneal. tables, maps. — (Records of civilization, sources and studies. no. 57) 'Substantial revision of the dissertation submitted in January, 1957 ... Columbia University.' 1. Japan — History — Kamakura period, 1185-1333 I. T. II. Title: Azumakagami. III. Series.
DS859.S48 1960a

Taiheiki. • 3.4937
The Taiheiki: a chronicle of medieval Japan. Translated, with an introd. and notes, by Helen Craig McCullough. New York, Columbia University Press, 1959. xlix, 401 p. illus. 24 cm. (Records of civilization: sources and studies, no.59.) 'As regards the Taiheiki's authorship, enough is known...to show fairly clearly that it has passed through many hands...[Ascribed] in the diary of Tōin Kansada (1340-1399)...[to] the monk Kojima.' 1. Godaigo, Emperor of Japan, 1288-1338. 2. Japan — History — To 1867. I. Kojima Hōshi, d. 1374. supposed author. II. McCullough, Helen Craig. ed. and tr. III. T.
DS861.T313 *LC* 59-6662

Perrin, Noel. 3.4938
Giving up the gun: Japan's reversion to the sword, 1543-1879 / Noel Perrin. — Boston: D. R. Godine, c1979. xii, 122 p.: ill.; 22 cm. 1. Firearms — Japan — History. 2. Swordplay — Japan — History. 3. Japan — History — Period of civil wars, 1480-1603 4. Japan — History — Tokugawa period, 1600-1868 I. T.
DS868.2.P47 952/.02 *LC* 78-74252 *ISBN* 0879232781

Berry, Mary Elizabeth, 1947-. 3.4939
Hideyoshi / Mary Elizabeth Berry. — Cambridge, Mass.: Harvard University Press, 1982. xiv, 293 p.: ill.; 25 cm. — (Harvard East Asian series. 97) 1. Toyotomi, Hideyoshi, 1536?-1598. 2. Generals — Japan — Biography. 3. Japan — History — Period of civil wars, 1480-1603 4. Japan — History — Azuchi Momoyama period, 1568-1603 I. T. II. Series.
DS869.T6 B47 1982 952/.023/0924 B 19 *LC* 82-1056 *ISBN* 0674390253

Earl, David Magarey, 1911-. • 3.4940
Emperor and nation in Japan; political thinkers of the Tokugawa period. Seattle, University of Washington Press [1964] x, 270 p. 22 cm. 'In its original form ... submitted as a doctoral dissertation to the Faculty of Political science of Columbia University.' Bibliography: p. 240-250. 1. Yoshida, Shōin, 1830-1859. 2. Patriotism — Japan. 3. Japan — History — Tokugawa period, 1600-1867. I. T.
DS871.E3 320.952 *LC* 63-20539 rev

Hall, John Whitney, 1916- comp. 3.4941
Studies in the institutional history of early modern Japan, edited by John W. Hall and Marius B. Jansen. With an introd. by Joseph R. Strayer. Contributors: Harumi Befu [and others]. — Princeton, N.J.: Princeton University Press, 1968. x, 396 p.: illus.; map.; 24 cm. 1. Japan — History — Tokugawa period, 1600-1868 — Addresses, essays, lectures. I. Jansen, Marius B. joint comp. II. T.
DS871.H29 952.02/5/08 *LC* 68-15766

Norman, E. Herbert, 1909-1957. • 3.4942
Andō Shōeki and the anatomy of Japanese feudalism / by E. Herbert Norman. — Tokyo: The Asiatic Society of Japan, 1949. 2 v.; 21 cm. — (The Transactions of the Asiatic Society of Japan; Third Ser., vol. 2, Dec. 1949) Supplementary volume contains the original text of passages quoted in Volume I from the Shizen Shineidō and the Tōdō Shinden. 1. Andō, Shōeki, 18th c. 2. Feudalism — Japan 3. Japanese literature I. Asiatic Society of Japan. II. T. III. Series.
DS871.N6x *LC* 51-2181

Totman, Conrad D. • 3.4943
Politics in the Tokugawa bakufu, 1600–1843 [by] Conrad D. Totman. — Cambridge: Harvard University Press, 1967. 346 p.: illus., maps.; 24 cm. — (Harvard East Asian series. 30) 1. Tokugawa family 2. Japan — Politics and government — 1600-1868 I. T. II. Series.
DS871.T6 952.02/5 *LC* 67-22873

Totman, Conrad D. 3.4944
Tokugawa Ieyasu, shogun: a biography / by Conrad Totman. San Francisco, Calif.: Heian, 1983. — xvi, 205 p.: ill.; maps; 22 cm. Includes index. 1. Tokugawa, Ieyasu, 1543-1616. 2. Japan — History — Tokugawa period, 1600-1868 3. Japan — Politics and government — 1600-1868 I. T.
DS871.T62 1983 *ISBN* 0893462101

Webb, Herschel. • 3.4945
The Japanese imperial institution in the Tokugawa period. New York, Columbia University Press, 1968. xi, 296 p. 22 cm. (Studies of the East Asian Institute, Columbia University) 1. Japan — Emperors 2. Japan — Politics and government — 1600-1868 I. T.
DS871.W3 320.9/52 *LC* 68-11912

Bolitho, Harold. 3.4946
Treasures among men; the fudai daimyo in Tokugawa Japan. — New Haven: Yale University Press, 1974. xiii, 278 p.; 23 cm. 1. Daimyo 2. Japan — Politics and government — 1600-1868 I. T.
DS871.5.B66 320.9/52/025 *LC* 73-86885 *ISBN* 0300016557

Ooms, Herman. 3.4947
Charismatic bureaucrat; a political biography of Matsudaira Sadanobu, 1758–1829. — Chicago: The University of Chicago Press, 1975. xiii, 225 p.; 24 cm. 1. Matsudaira, Sadanobu, 1759-1829. I. T.
DS872.M32 O65 952/.025/0924 B *LC* 74-10342 *ISBN* 0226630315

DS881–884 19th Century

Black, John Reddie, 1827-1880. • 3.4948
Young Japan: Yokohama and Yedo, 1858–79, by John R. Black. With an introduction by Grace Fox. — Tokyo; New York: Oxford Univ. P., 1968. 2 v.: col. front.; 23 cm. — (Oxford in Asia. Historical reprints) Reprint of 1883 ed. 1. Japan — History — Meiji period, 1868-1912 I. T.
DS881.B62 1968 952.031 *LC* 77-437868

Norman, E. Herbert, 1909-1957. • 3.4949
Japan's emergence as a modern state; political and economic problems of the Meiji period, by E. Herbert Norman. New York, International secretariat, Institute of Pacific relations, 1940. xvi 254 p., 24 cm. (I.P.R. inquiry series.) 'Selected bibliography on Meiji Japan': p. 211-222;'Works in western languages':p. 223-234. 1. Japan — Politics and government 2. Japan — Economic conditions 3. Japan — Economic policy I. Institute of Pacific Relations. American Council. II. T.
DS881.N6 *LC* 40-8128

Beasley, W. G. (William G.), 1919-. 3.4950
The Meiji restoration [by] W. G. Beasley. — Stanford, Calif.: Stanford University Press, 1972. vi, 513 p.: map.; 24 cm. 1. Japan — History — Restoration, 1853-1870 I. T.
DS881.3.B4 952.03/1 *LC* 72-78868 *ISBN* 0804708150

Harootunian, Harry D., 1929-. • 3.4951
Toward restoration; the growth of political consciousness in Tokugawa Japan [by] H. D. Harootunian. — Berkeley: University of California Press, 1970. xviii, 421 p.; 24 cm. — (Publications of the Center for Japanese and Korean studies) 1. Japan — History — Restoration, 1853-1870 2. Japan — Politics and government — 1600-1868 I. T.
DS881.3.H28 1970 915.2/03/25 *LC* 79-94993 *ISBN* 0520015665

Jansen, Marius B. • 3.4952
Sakamoto Ryōma and the Meiji Restoration. Princeton, N. J., Princeton University Press, 1961. xii, 423 p. ports., fold. map. 25 cm. Bibliography: p.

382-388. 1. Sakamoto, Ryōma, 1836-1867. 2. Japan — History — Restoration, 1853-1870 I. T.
DS881.3.J28   952.031   *LC 61-6909*

Satow, Ernest Mason, Sir, 1843-1929.   • 3.4953
A diplomat in Japan, by Sir Ernest Satow; with an introduction by Gordon Daniels. Tokyo, New York, Oxford U.P., 1968. xii, 427 p. illus., maps, ports. 23 cm. (Oxford in Asia. Historical reprints) Reprint of 1921 ed. 1. Japan — History — Restoration, 1853-1870 2. Japan — Foreign relations — To 1868 I. T.
DS881.3.S3 1968   952/.025/0924 19   *LC 72-430540*

Totman, Conrad D.   3.4954
The collapse of the Tokugawa bakufu, 1862–1868 / Conrad Totman. — Honolulu: University Press of Hawaii, c1980. xxiv, 588 p.: map; 24 cm. Includes index. 1. Japan — History — Restoration, 1853-1870 2. Japan — Politics and government — 1600-1868 I. T.
DS881.3.T63   952/.025   *LC 79-22094*

Straelen, H. J. J. M. van (Henricus Johannes Josephus Maria   • 3.4955
van), 1903-.
Yoshida Shōin, forerunner of the Meiji restoration; a biographical study. — Leiden, E. J. Brill, 1952. 149 p. 25 cm. — (T'oung pao; archives concernant l'histoire, les langues, la géographie, l'ethnographie et les arts de l'Asie orientale. Monographie 2) Bibliography: p. [137]-139. 1. Yoshida, Shōin, 1830-1859. I. T. II. Series.
DS881.5.Y6S7   923.252   *LC 52-12675*

Hunter, Janet.   3.4956
Concise dictionary of modern Japanese history / compiled by Janet Hunter. — Berkeley: University of California Press, c1984. xiv, 347 p.: maps; 24 cm. 1. Japan — History — 1868- — Dictionaries. I. T.
DS881.9.H86 1984   952.03 19   *LC 82-17456*   *ISBN 0520043901*

Japan examined: perspectives on modern Japanese history /   3.4957
edited by Harry Wray and Hilary Conroy.
Honolulu: University of Hawaii Press, c1983. x, 411 p.; 24 cm. 1. Japan — History — 1868- 2. Japan — History — 1868- — Historiography. I. Wray, Harry, 1931- II. Conroy, Hilary, 1919-
DS881.9.J29 1983   952.03 19   *LC 82-15926*   *ISBN 0824808061*

Nish, Ian Hill.   3.4958
Japanese foreign policy, 1869–1942: Kasumigaseki to Miyakezaka / Ian Nish. London; Boston: Routledge & K. Paul, 1977. x, 346 p.; 23 cm. (Foreign policies of the great powers) Includes index 1. Japan — Foreign relations — 1868-1912 2. Japan — Foreign relations — 1912-1945 I. T.
DS881.95.N57   327.52   *LC 77-358855*   *ISBN 0710084218*

Bowen, Roger W., 1947-.   3.4959
Rebellion and democracy in Meiji Japan: a study of commoners in the popular rights movement / Roger W. Bowen. — Berkeley: University of California Press, c1980. xv, 340 p.: map; 25 cm. Includes index. 1. Civil rights — Japan — History. 2. Peasant uprisings — Japan 3. Japan — Politics and government — 1868-1912 I. T.
DS882.5.B68   320.9/52/031   *LC 78-51755*   *ISBN 0520036654*

Najita, Tetsuo.   3.4960
Hara Kei in the politics of compromise, 1905–1915. — Cambridge, Mass.: Harvard University Press, 1967. xvii, 314 p.: port.; 22 cm. — (Harvard East Asian series. 31) Based on the author's thesis, Harvard University. 1. Hara, Takashi, 1856-1921. 2. Japan — Politics and government I. T. II. Series.
DS884.H28 N34   952.03/2/0924   *LC 67-27090*

Notehelfer, F. G.   3.4961
Kōtoku Shūsui, portrait of a Japanese radical [by] F. G. Notehelfer. Cambridge [Eng.] University Press, 1971. x, 227 p. ports. 24 cm. Based on the author's thesis, Princeton, 1968. 1. Kōtoku, Shūsui, 1871-1911. I. T.
DS884.K65 N68   952/.03/10924   *LC 76-134620*   *ISBN 0521079896*

Harada, Kumao, 1888-1946.   • 3.4962
[Saionji Kō to seikyoku. English] Fragile victory; Prince Saionji and the 1930 London treaty issue, from the memoirs of Baron Harada Kumao. Translated with an introd. and annotations by Thomas Francis Mayer–Oakes. Detroit, Wayne State University Press, 1968. 330 p. illus., map (on lining-papers), ports. 26 cm. At head of title: Saionji-Harada memoirs. Translation of v. 1 of Saionji Kō to seikyoku (romanized form) Originally published as the translator's thesis, University of Chicago, 1955, under title: Prince Saionji and the London Naval Conference. 1. Saionji, Kinmochi, 1849-1940. 2. London Naval Conference. 3. Japan — Politics and government — 1912-1945 4. Japan — Politics and government — 1868-1912 I. Mayer-Oakes, Thomas Francis, 1912- ed. II. T. III. Title: Prince Saionji and the 1930 London treaty issue. IV. Title: Saionji-Harada memoirs.
DS884.S3 H333 1968   327.52/042   *LC 66-22988*

Hackett, Roger F.   3.4963
Yamagata Aritomo in the rise of modern Japan, 1838–1922 [by] Roger F. Hackett. — Cambridge: Harvard University Press, 1971. ix, 377 p.: port.; 25 cm. — (Harvard East Asian series. 60) 1. Yamagata, Aritomo, 1838-1922. I. T. II. Series.
DS884.Y3 H3   952.03/1/0924   *LC 74-139719*   *ISBN 0674963016*

DS885–890 20th Century

Storry, Richard, 1913-.   3.4964
Japan and the decline of the West in Asia, 1894–1943 / Richard Storry. — New York: St. Martin's Press, 1979. viii, 186 p.; 23 cm. (The Making of the 20th century) Includes index. 1. World politics — 1900-1945 2. Japan — Foreign relations — 1912-1945 I. T.
DS885.S84 1979   327.52   *LC 78-31872*   *ISBN 0312440502*

Japan erupts: the London Naval Conference and the   3.4965
Manchurian Incident, 1928–1932: selected translations from
Taiheiyō Sensō e no michi, kaisen gaikō shi / edited by James
William Morley.
New York: Columbia University Press, 1984. xi, 410 p.: map; 24 cm. (Japan's road to the Pacific war.) (Studies of the East Asian Institute—Columbia University) Includes index. 1. London Naval Treaty (1930) 2. Mukden Incident, 1931 3. Japan — Foreign relations — 1912-1945 4. Manchuria (China) — History — 1931-1945 5. China — Foreign relations — Japan. 6. Japan — Foreign relations — China. I. Morley, James William, 1921- II. Taiheiyō Sensō e no michi. III. Series.
DS885.48.J36 1984   327.52 19   *LC 83-27320*   *ISBN 0231057822*

Peattie, Mark R., 1930-.   3.4966
Ishiwara Kanji and Japan's confrontation with the West / by Mark R. Peattie. — Princeton, N.J.: Princeton University Press, 1975. xix, 430 p., [2] leaves of plates: ill.; 23 cm. Based on the author's thesis, Princeton University. Includes index. 1. Ishihara, Kanji, 1889-1949. I. T.
DS885.5.I77 P4   952.03/3/0924 B   *LC 73-2489*   *ISBN 0691030995*

Wilson, George M. (George M.), 1937-.   • 3.4967
Radical nationalist in Japan: Kita Ikki, 1883–1937, [by] George M. Wilson. Cambridge, Mass., Harvard University Press, 1969. xii, 230 p. port. 22 cm. (Harvard East Asian series. 37) Developed from author's thesis, Harvard University. 1. Kita, Ikki, 1883-1937. I. T. II. Series.
DS885.5.K52 W5   322/.4 B   *LC 69-12740*

Oka, Yoshitake, 1902-.   3.4968
[Konoe Fumimaro] Konoe Fumimaro: a political biography / Yoshitake Oka; translated by Shumpei Okamoto and Patricia Murray. — [Tokyo]: University of Tokyo Press, c1983. viii, 214 p.; 24 cm. Translation of: Konoe Fumimaro. Includes index. 1. Konoye, Fumimaro, 1891-1945. 2. Prime ministers — Japan — Biography. 3. Japan — Politics and government — 1926-1945 I. T.
DS885.5.K6 O3813 1983   952.03/3/0924 B 19   *LC 83-165058*
    ISBN 0860083047

Duus, Peter, 1933-.   • 3.4969
Party rivalry and political change in Taishō Japan. — Cambridge, Mass.: Harvard University Press, 1968. viii, 317 p.; 25 cm. — (Harvard East Asian series. 35) Based on thesis, Harvard University. 1. Political parties — Japan. 2. Japan — Politics and government — 1912-1945 I. T. II. Series.
DS886.D88   329.9/51   *LC 68-21972*

Crowley, James B.   • 3.4970
Japan's quest for autonomy; national security and foreign policy, 1930–1938, by James B. Crowley. — Princeton, N.J.: Princeton University Press, 1966. xviii, 428 p.; 21 cm. Elaboration of a doctoral thesis, Yale University. 1. Eastern question (Far East) 2. Japan — Foreign relations — 1912-1945 I. T.
DS888.5.C7   327.52   *LC 66-10552*

Dilemmas of growth in prewar Japan. Edited by James William   3.4971
Morley. Contributors: George M. Beckmann [and others].
Princeton, N.J.: Princeton University Press, 1972 (c1971). ix, 527 p.; 21 cm. — (Studies in the modernization of Japan, 6) Papers from the 6th and final seminar of the Conference on Modern Japan, held in Puerto Rico, Jan. 1968. 1. Japan — Politics and government — 1912-1945 — Addresses, essays, lectures. 2. Japan — Economic conditions — 1918-1945 — Addresses, essays, lectures. I. Morley, James William, 1921- ed. II. Beckmann, George M. III. Conference on Modern Japan. IV. Series.
DS888.5.D54   309.1/52/033   *LC 79-155964*   *ISBN 069103074X*

Honjō, Shigeru, 1876-1945.   3.4972
[Honjō nikki. English] Emperor Hirohito and his chief aide–de–camp: the Honjō diary, 1933–36 / translation and introduction by Mikiso Hane. — [Tokyo]: University of Tokyo Press, 1983 (c1982). ix, 263 p.; 24 cm. 'Translated from Honjō nikki, published by Hara Shobō in 1967'-T.p. verso. Includes index. 1. Honjō, Shigeru, 1876-1945. 2. Hirohito, Emperor of Japan, 1901-3. Japan. Rikugun — Biography. 4. Japan. Rikugun — Political activity.

5. Generals — Japan — Biography. 6. Japan — History — 1926-1945 7. Japan — Emperors — Biography. I. Hane, Mikiso. II. T.
DS888.5.H5813　　952.03/3/0924 B 19　　*LC* 83-145006　　*ISBN* 0860083195

Maxon, Yale Candee, 1906-.　　　　　　　　　　• **3.4973**
Control of Japanese foreign policy; a study of civil–military rivalry, 1930–1945. — Berkeley: University of California Press, 1957. vi, 286 p.; 24 cm. — (University of California publications in political science, v. 5.) 1. Militarism — Japan. 2. Japan — Foreign relations — 1912-1945 3. Japan — Politics and government — 1912-1945 I. T.
DS888.5.M39　　327.52　　*LC* 72-12330　　*ISBN* 0837167280

Shillony, Ben-Ami.　　　　　　　　　　　　　　**3.4974**
Revolt in Japan; the young officers and the February 26, 1936 incident. — Princeton, N.J.: Princeton University Press, [1973] xiii, 263 p.; 23 cm. — (Studies in the modernization of Japan) 1. Japan — History — February Incident, 1936 (February 26) I. T. II. Series.
DS888.5.S487　　952.03/3　　*LC* 76-39793　　*ISBN* 0691075484

Storry, Richard, 1913-.　　　　　　　　　　• **3.4975**
The double patriots; a study of Japanese nationalism [by] Richard Storry. Westport, Conn., Greenwood Press [1973] 335 p. 22 cm. Reprint of the 1957 ed. 1. Japan — Foreign relations — 1912-1945 2. Japan — Politics and government — 1926-1945 I. T.
DS888.5.S7 1973　　952.03/3　　*LC* 72-10982　　*ISBN* 0837166438

DS889 1926–

Baerwald, Hans H.　　　　　　　　　　　　• **3.4976**
The purge of Japanese leaders under the occupation. Berkeley University of California Press 1959. 111p. (University of California publications in political science, v. 8) 1. Japan — History — Allied occupation, 1945-1952 I. T.
DS889 B2

Buckley, Roger, 1944-.　　　　　　　　　　　**3.4977**
Japan today / Roger Buckley. — Cambridge [Cambridgeshire]; New York: Cambridge University Press, 1985. xii, 139 p.: map; 23 cm. Includes index. 1. Japan — History — 1945- I. T.
DS889.B765 1985　　952.04 19　　*LC* 84-14300　　*ISBN* 0521260892

Kawai, Kazuo, 1904-.　　　　　　　　　　　• **3.4978**
Japan's American interlude. — [Chicago] University of Chicago Press [1960] 257 p. 22 cm. 1. Japan — Hist.— Allied occupation, 1945-1952. I. T.
DS889.K38　　952.04　　*LC* 59-14111

Martin, Edwin M.　　　　　　　　　　　　• **3.4979**
The Allied occupation of Japan [by] Edwin M. Martin. — Westport, Conn.: Greenwood Press, [1972, c1948] xiv, 155 p.; 22 cm. 1. Japan — History — Allied occupation, 1945-1952 I. T.
DS889.M29 1972　　952.04　　*LC* 76-169848　　*ISBN* 0837162483

Maruyama, Masao, 1914-.　　　　　　　　　• **3.4980**
Thought and behavior in modern Japanese politics. Expanded ed. Edited by Ivan Morris. London, New York, Oxford University Press [1969] xvii, 407 p. 21 cm. (A Galaxy book, 291) 1. Nationalism — Japan. 2. National characteristics, Japanese I. Morris, Ivan I. ed. II. T.
DS889.M34 1969　　320.9/52　　*LC* 74-90162

Morley, James William, 1921-.　　　　　　　**3.4981**
Forecast for Japan: security in the 1970's / edited by James William Morley; contributors: Donald C. Hellmann [and others]. — Princeton, N.J.: Princeton University Press, [1972] 249 p.; 23 cm. 1. Japan — Politics and government — 1945- 2. Japan — Defenses. I. Hellmann, Donald C., 1933-. II. T.
DS889.M58727　　355.03/35/52　　*LC* 71-37578　　*ISBN* 069103091X

Yoshida, Shigeru, 1878-1967.　　　　　　　• **3.4982**
The Yoshida memoirs; the story of Japan in crisis. Translated by Kenichi Yoshida. [1st American ed.] Boston, Houghton Mifflin, 1962 [c1961] 305 p. 23 cm. 1. Japan — History — Allied occupation, 1945-1952. I. T.
DS889.Y583 1962　　952.04　　*LC* 61-10350

Kataoka, Tetsuya.　　　　　　　　　　　　　**3.4983**
Waiting for a 'Pearl Harbor': Japan debates defense / Tetsuya Kataoka. — Stanford, Calif.: Hoover Institution Press, Stanford University, 1981 (c1980). xvi, 79 p.: ill.; 23 cm. — (Hoover international studies.) (Hoover Institution publication. 232) 1. Japan — Politics and government — 1945- 2. Japan — Defenses. 3. Japan — Military policy. 4. Japan — Armed Forces. I. T. II. Series. III. Series: Hoover Institution publication. 232
DS889.15.K34　　355/.033052 19　　*LC* 80-8326　　*ISBN* 0817973222

Langdon, Frank, 1919-.　　　　　　　　　　**3.4984**
Japan's foreign policy [by] F. C. Langdon. Vancouver, B.C., University of British Columbia Press [c1973] xiv, 231 p. maps. 24 cm. 1. Japan — Foreign relations — 1945- I. T.
DS889.15.L36　　327.52　　*LC* 73-78894　　*ISBN* 0774800151

DS890 Biography. Memoirs

Shigemitsu, Mamoru, 1887-1957.　　　　　　• **3.4985**
Japan and her destiny; my struggle for peace. Edited by F. S. G. Piggott. Translated by Oswald White. New York, Dutton, 1958. 392 p. port. 24 cm. 1. Japan — History — 1912-1945 2. Japan — Foreign relations — 1912-1945 I. T.
DS890.S513 A23　　*LC* 57-5005

Butow, Robert Joseph Charles, 1924-.　　　　• **3.4986**
Tojo and the coming of the war [by] Robert J. C. Butow. — Stanford, Calif.: Stanford University Press, [1969, c1961] 584 p.: illus., ports.; 25 cm. 1. Tōjō, Hideki, 1884-1948. 2. World War, 1939-1945 — Japan. I. T.
DS890.T57 B8 1969　　952.03/0924 B　　*LC* 73-93492

Dower, John W.　　　　　　　　　　　　　　**3.4987**
Empire and aftermath: Yoshida Shigeru and the Japanese experience, 1878–1954 / J. W. Dower. — Cambridge, Mass.: Council on East Asian Studies, Harvard University: distributed by Harvard University Press, 1979. xiii, 618 p., [1] leaf of plates: port.; 24 cm. — (Harvard East Asian monographs. 84) Includes index. 1. Yoshida, Shigeru, 1878-1967. 2. Prime ministers — Japan — Biography. 3. Japan — Foreign relations — 20th century 4. Japan — Politics and government — 20th century I. Harvard University. Council on East Asian Studies. II. T. III. Series.
DS890.Y6 D68　　952.03/3/0924 B　　*LC* 79-17810　　*ISBN* 0674251253

DS894–897 Local History

Huber, Thomas M.　　　　　　　　　　　　　**3.4988**
The revolutionary origins of modern Japan / Thomas M. Huber. — Stanford, Calif.: Stanford University Press, 1981. 260 p.: ill.; 23 cm. Includes index. 1. Chōshū-han (Japan) — Politics and government. 2. Chōshū-han (Japan) — Biography. 3. Japan — History — Restoration, 1853-1870 4. Japan — Biography. I. T.
DS894.79.Y349 C4637　　952.03/1/0922 B 19　　*LC* 79-64214　　*ISBN* 0804710481

Craig, Albert M.　　　　　　　　　　　　　• **3.4989**
Chōshū in the Meiji Restoration / Albert M. Craig. — Cambridge, Mass.: Harvard University Press, c1961. 385, xxxix p.: ill.; 21 cm. — (Harvard historical monographs. 47) 1. Chōshū-han (Japan) — History. 2. Japan — History — Restoration, 1853-1870 I. T. II. Series.
DS895.C5 C7　　*LC* 61-8839

DS901–925 Korea

McCune, Shannon Boyd-Bailey, 1913-.　　　　• **3.4990**
Korea: land of broken calm / Shannon McCune; drawings by Kim Foon. — Princeton, N. J.: Van Nostrand, [1966] ix, 221 p.: ill., maps; 21 cm. (The Asia library) 1. Korea I. T.
DS902.M22 1966　　915.19　　*LC* 66-16903

McCune, Shannon Boyd-Bailey, 1913-.　　　　• **3.4991**
Korea's heritage; a regional & social geography. [1st ed.] Tokyo, Rutland, Vt., C. E. Tuttle Co. [1956] xiii, 250 p. illus., maps, diagrs., tables. 22 cm. 'Bibliographical references and notes': p. 195-211. 1. Korea — Description and travel I. T.
DS902.M23　　915.19　　*LC* 56-6807

South Korea, a country study / Foreign Area Studies, the　　　**3.4992**
American University; edited by Frederica M. Bunge.
3rd ed. — Washington, D.C.: Headquarters, Dept. of the Army: For sale by the Supt. of Docs., U.S. G.P.O., c1982. xxv, 306 p.: ill.; 24 cm. — (Area handbook series.) (DA pam. 550-41) 'Research completed July 1981.' Rev. ed. of: Area handbook for South Korea / coauthors, Nena Vreeland and others. 2nd. 1975. Includes index. 1. Korea (South) I. Bunge, Frederica M. II. American University (Washington, D.C.). Foreign Area Studies. III. Title: Area handbook for South Korea. 2nd ed. 1975. IV. Series. V. Series: DA pam. 550-41
DS902.S68 1982　　951.9/5 19　　*LC* 82-11385

Jo, Yung-hwan, 1932- comp.   • 3.4993
Korea's response to the West. Kalamazoo, Mich., Korea Research and
Publications; [distributed by Cellar Book Shop, Detroit, 1971] xi, 254 p. 28 cm.
(Series on contemporary Korean problems, 6) 1. Korea — Civilization —
Occidental influences — Addresses, essays, lectures. 2. Korea — Relations —
Foreign countries — Addresses, essays, lectures. I. T. II. Series.
DS904.J57   327.519/018/21   LC 73-28403

Choy, Bong Youn, 1914-.   • 3.4994
Korea: a history. Foreword by Younghill Kang. — Rutland, Vt.: C. E. Tuttle
Co., [1971] 474 p.: maps.; 22 cm. 1. Korea — History I. T.
DS907.C62   915.19/03   LC 73-147180   ISBN 0804802491

Griffis, William Elliot, 1843-1928.   • 3.4995
Corea, the hermit nation. — 9th ed., rev. and enl. [1st AMS ed.]. — New York:
AMS Press, [1971] xxvii, 526 p.: illus., maps.; 23 cm. Reprint of the 1911 ed.
1. Korea — History 2. Korea — Social life and customs. I. T.
DS907.G8 1971   951.9/01   LC 74-158615   ISBN 0404029167

Han, U-gŭn.   • 3.4996
[Han'guk t'ongsa. English] The history of Korea, by Han Woo–keun.
Translated by Lee Kyung–shik. Edited by Grafton K. Mintz. Seoul, Eul-Yoo
Pub. Co. [1970] xii, 548 p. illus. (part col.), maps (part col.), ports. 23 cm.
Translation of Han'guk t'ongsa. 1. Korea — History I. T.
DS907.H299813   LC 71-275357

Henthorn, William E.   • 3.4997
A history of Korea [by] William E. Henthorn. — New York: Free Press, [1971]
xiv, 256 p.: illus.; 24 cm. 1. Korea — History I. T.
DS907.H45 1971   915.19/03   LC 75-143511

Hulbert, Homer Bezaleel, 1863-1949.   • 3.4998
History of Korea. Edited by Clarence Norwood Weems. — New York: Hillary
House Publishers, 1962. 2 v.: illus.; 24 cm. 1. Korea — History I. Weems,
Clarence Norwood, 1907- ed. II. T.
DS907.H8 1962   951.9   LC 62-9992

Yi, Ki-baek.   3.4999
[Han'guksa sillon. English] A new history of Korea / Ki–Baik Lee; translated
by Edward W. Wagner, with Edward J. Shultz. — Cambridge, Mass.:
Published for the Harvard-Yenching Institute by Harvard University Press,
1985 (c1984). xxii, 474 p., [13] p. of plates: ill. (some col.); 25 cm. Translation
of: Han'guksa sillon. Includes index. 1. Korea — History I. T.
DS907.16.Y5313   951.9 19   LC 83-246   ISBN 0674615751

Henderson, Gregory.   • 3.5000
Korea, the politics of the vortex. — Cambridge: Harvard University Press,
1968. xvi, 479 p.: illus., col. maps (on lining papers), ports.; 25 cm. 'Written
under the auspices of the Center for International Affairs, Harvard University.'
1. Korea — Politics and government I. Harvard University. Center for
International Affairs. II. T.
DS910.H4   320.9/519   LC 68-25611

McCune, George McAfee, 1908-1948. ed.   • 3.5001
Korean–American relations; documents pertaining to the Far Eastern
diplomacy of the United States. Edited, with an introd., by George M. McCune
and John A. Harrison. Berkeley, University of California Press, 1951-. v. 24 cm.
1. Korea — Foreign relations — United States. 2. United States — Foreign
relations — Korea. I. Harrison, John A., joint ed. II. T.
DS910.M3   327.7309519   LC 51-1111

DS915–922 19TH–20TH CENTURIES

Conroy, Hilary, 1919-.   • 3.5002
The Japanese seizure of Korea, 1868-1910; a study of realism and idealism in
international relations. — Philadelphia, University of Pennsylvania Press
[1960] 544 p. illus., ports., map (on lining papers) 22 cm. Bibliography,
including Japanese works in transliteration and in Japanese characters: p.
[508]-535. 1. Korea — Hist. — 1868-1910. I. T.
DS915.C6 1960   951.902   LC 60-6936

Deuchler, Martina, 1935-.   3.5003
Confucian gentlemen and barbarian envoys: the opening of Korea, 1875–1885 /
Martina Deuchler. — Seattle: University of Washington Press, 1978 (c1977).
xiv, 310 p., [2] leaves of plates: ill.; 24 cm. 'Published for the Royal Asiatic
Society, Korea Branch.' Rev. and expanded version of the author's thesis,
Harvard. Includes index. 1. Korea — History — 1864-1910 2. Korea —
Foreign relations I. T.
DS915.D48   951.9/02   LC 76-57228   ISBN 029595552X

Lensen, George Alexander, 1923-.   3.5004
Balance of intrigue: international rivalry in Korea & Manchuria, 1884–1899 /
George Alexander Lensen; foreword by John J. Stephan. — Tallahassee:

University Presses of Florida, c1982. 2 v. (xviii, 984 p.); 24 cm. 'A Florida State
University book.' 1. Korea — Foreign relations — 1864-1910 2. Soviet Union
— Foreign relations — East Asia. 3. East Asia — Foreign relations — Soviet
Union. 4. East Asia — Politics and government. I. T.
DS915.37.L46 1982   327.4705 19   LC 81-16287   ISBN 0813007224

Lee, Chong-Sik, 1931-.   • 3.5005
The politics of Korean nationalism. — Berkeley: University of California Press,
1963. xiv, 342 p.; 24 cm. Based on the author's doctoral dissertation, Korean
nationalist movement, 1905-1945, submitted to the University of California,
Berkeley, in 1961. 1. Nationalism — Korea. I. T.
DS916.L4   951.9   LC 63-19029

McCune, George McAfee, 1908-1948.   • 3.5006
Korea today, by George M. McCune with the collaboration of Arthur L. Grey,
Jr. — Cambridge, Harvard University Press, 1950. xxi, 372 p. map (on lining
papers) 21 cm. 'Issued under the auspices of the International Secretariat,
Institute of Pacific Relations.' A revision and expansion of the author's Korea's
postwar political problems, submitted as a document for the Tenth Conference
of the Institute of Pacific Relations in 1947. Bibliography: p. 349-366. 1. Korea
— Pol. & govt. I. Institute of Pacific Relations. II. T.
DS916.M13 1950   951.9   LC 50-8875

Allen, Richard C.   • 3.5007
Korea's Syngman Rhee: an unauthorized portrait / by Richard C. Allen. —
Rutland, Vermont: C. E. Tuttle, 1960. 259 p.: ill. 1. Rhee, Syngman, 1875-1965.
2. Statesmen — Korea (South) — Biography. I. T.
DS916.5.R5A65   951.904   B   LC 60-15606

Chǔng, Kyǔng Cho.   • 3.5008
New Korea; new land of the morning calm. New York: Macmillan, 1962. 274 p.
illus. 1. Korea — Politics and government — 1948- . I. T.
DS917.C482   LC 62-15611

Korean politics in transition / edited by Edward Reynolds   3.5009
Wright; contributors, Suk–choon Cho ... [et al.].
Seattle: Published for the Royal Asiatic Society, Korea Branch, by the
University of Washington Press, 1976 (c1975). xii, 399 p.: 1 map. (on lining
paper); 24 cm. 'Constitution of the Republic of Korea': p. 357-383. Includes
index. 1. Korea (South) — Politics and government — 1948-1960 I. Wright,
Edward Reynolds. ed. II. Cho, Suk-choon, 1929-
DS917.K667   320.9/519/5043   LC 74-34070   ISBN 0295954221

Oh, John Kie-chiang, 1930-.   • 3.5010
Korea; democracy on trial. — Ithaca, N.Y.: Cornell University Press, [1968]
xiv, 240 p.: map.; 23 cm. 1. Korea — Politics and government — 1948- I. T.
DS917.O28   320.9/519/5   LC 68-26693

The Two Koreas in East Asian affairs / edited by William J.   3.5011
Barnds.
New York: New York University Press, 1976. vii, 216 p.; 22 cm. 'Grew out of a
series of discussions held at the Council on Foreign Relations during the first
half of 1975.' 1. Korean reunification question (1945-) 2. Korea — Foreign
relations — 1945- 3. Korea (North) — Foreign relations. 4. East Asia —
Politics and government. I. Barnds, William J.
DS917.T86   327.519/3/05195   LC 75-27374   ISBN 0814709885

Korean reunification: new perspectives and approaches / edited   3.5012
by Tae–Hwan Kwak, Chonghan Kim, Hong Nack Kim.
Seoul, Korea: Kyungnam University Press, 1984. xix, 525 p.: ill.; 24 cm. (IFES
research series. no. 24) 'An outgrowth of panel presentations at the Symposium
on the problems of Korean Unification held in Washington, D.C. on January
14-16, 1982'—p. xiii. Includes index. 1. Korean reunification question (1945-)
— Addresses, essays, lectures. I. Kwak, Tae-Hwan, 1938- II. Kim, Chonghan.
III. Kim, Hong Nack. IV. Symposium on the Problems of Korean Unification
(1982: Washington, D.C.) V. Series.
DS917.25.K69 1984   951.9/04 19   LC 84-62862

Kihl, Young W., 1932-.   3.5013
Politics and policies in divided Korea: regimes in contest / Young Whan Kihl.
— Boulder: Westview Press, 1984. xvi, 307 p.: ill.; 24 cm. — (Westview special
studies on East Asia.) Includes index. 1. Korea — Politics and government —
1945-1948 2. Korea (South) — Politics and government 3. Korea (North) —
Politics and government. I. T. II. Series.
DS917.35.K5 1984   320.9519 19   LC 83-19711   ISBN 0865317003

Cumings, Bruce, 1943-.   3.5014
The origins of the Korean War: liberation and the emergence of separate
regimes, 1945–1947 / Bruce Cumings. — Princeton, N.J.: Princeton University
Press, c1981. xxxi, 606 p.: ill.; 25 cm. (Studies of the East Asian Institute,
Columbia University) 'The first of a planned two-volume study.' Includes
indexes. 1. Korean War, 1950-1953 — Causes 2. Korea — History — Allied
occupation, 1945-1948 I. T.
DS917.55.C85   951.9/042 19   LC 80-8543   ISBN 0691093830

Reeve, W. D.   • 3.5015
The Republic of Korea; a political and economic study. — London; New York:
Oxford University Press, 1963. ix, 197 p.; 22 cm. 'Law concerning
extraordinary measures for national reconstruction (promulgated on 6 June
1961)': p. [179]-185. 'Law no. 643, Anti-communist law (promulgated on 3 July
1961)': p. [186]-189. 1. Korea (South) — History — 1948-1960 2. Korea
(South) — Economic conditions I. Korea (South) Laws, statutes, etc. II. T.
DS917.7.R43 1963   951.9/04   LC 63-25579

DS918–921 Korean War, 1950–1953

Collins, J. Lawton (Joseph Lawton).   • 3.5016
War in peacetime: the history and lessons of Korea / by J. Lawton Collins. —
Boston: Houghton Mifflin, 1969. xiii, 416 p.: ill., maps, ports.; 24 cm.
1. Korean War, 1950-1953 I. T.
DS918.C62   951.9/042   LC 69-15008

Fehrenbach, T. R.   • 3.5017
This kind of war; a study in unpreparedness. New York, Macmillan [1963] xii,
688 p. illus., ports., maps. 25 cm. 1. Korean War, 1950-1953 I. T.
DS918.F37   951.9042   LC 63-9972

Goulden, Joseph C.   3.5018
Korea, the untold story of the war / Joseph C. Goulden. — New York, N.Y.:
Times Books, c1982. xxvi, 690 p., [16] p. of plates: ill.; 24 cm. 1. Korean War,
1950-1953 I. T.
DS918.G69 1982   951.9/042 19   LC 81-21262   ISBN 0812909852

Kahn, E. J. (Ely Jacques), 1916-.   • 3.5019
The peculiar war: impressions of a reporter in Korea / by E. J. Kahn. — New
York: Random House, 1952. 211 p. 1. Korean War, 1950-53 I. T.
DS918.K3   LC 52-5554

Leckie, Robert.   • 3.5020
Conflict; the history of the Korean War, 1950–53. — New York: Putnam,
[1962] 448 p.; illus.; 22 cm. 1. Korean War, 1950-1953 I. T.
DS918.L36   951.9042   LC 62-10975

Ridgway, Matthew B. (Matthew Bunker), 1895-.   • 3.5021
The Korean war: How we met the challenge: How all-out Asian war was
averted: Why MacArthur was dismissed: Why today's war objectives must be
limited [by] Matthew B. Ridgway. [1st ed.] Garden City, N.Y., Doubleday,
1967. xvii, 291 p. illus., maps, plans, ports. 24 cm. 1. Korean War, 1950-1953
I. T.
DS918.R49   951.9/042   LC 67-11172

Stone, I. F. (Isidor F.), 1907-.   • 3.5022
The hidden history of the Korean War [by] I. F. Stone. — New York: Monthly
Review Press, [1969, c1952] xvi, 368 p.: map.; 21 cm. Includes new appendix (p.
349-352) 1. Korean War, 1950-1953 2. U.S. — Foreign relations —
1945-1953. I. T.
DS918.S8 1969   951.9/042   LC 79-81788

U.S. Congress. Senate. Committee on Armed Services.   3.5023
Inquiry into the military situation on the Far East and the facts surrounding the
relief of General of the Army Douglas MacArthur from his assignment in that
area: report of proceedings. — Washington: Ward & Paul, official reporters
[1951] 43 v.; 29 cm. 1. U.S. Congress. Senate. Committee on Armed Services.
2. MacArthur, Douglas 1880- 3. Korean War, 1950- I. T.
DS918.U5 1951d   LC 51-6188

United States Army in the Korean War   • 3.5024
Washington, Office of the Chief of Military History, Dept. of the Army, 1961-.
v. ill. I. United States. Dept. of the Army. Office of Military History.
DS918.U5246

Marshall, S. L. A. (Samuel Lyman Atwood), 1900-1977.   • 3.5025
The river and the gauntlet; defeat of the Eighth Army by the Chinese
Communist forces, November, 1950, in the Battle of the Chongchon River,
Korea, by S. L. A. Marshall. Westport, Conn., Greenwood Press [1970, c1953]
x, 385 p. illus., maps. 23 cm. 1. United States. Army. Army, Eighth.
2. Ch'ŏngch'ŏn-gang, Battle of, 1950 3. Korean War, 1950-1953 —
Regimental histories — United States. I. T.
DS918.2.C4 M3 1970   951.9/042   LC 74-100239   ISBN
0837130115

United States. Marine Corps.   • 3.5026
U.S. Marine operations in Korea, 1950–1953. Washington, Historical Branch,
G–3, Headquarters, U.S. Marine Corps, 1954– . — Grosse Pointe, Mich.:
Scholarly Press, [1969?-. v.   : illus., maps, ports.; 23 cm. 1. United States.
Marine Corps — History — Korean War, 1950-1953 I. Montross, Lynn,
1895-1961. II. Canzona, Nicholas A. III. T.
DS919.A517   951.9   LC 77-8614

Donovan, Robert J.   3.5027
Nemesis: Truman and Johnson in the coils of war in Asia / by Robert J.
Donovan. — 1st ed. — New York: St. Martin's-Marek, c1984. 216 p., [8] p. of
plates: ill.; 25 cm. 1. Truman, Harry S., 1884-1972. 2. Johnson, Lyndon B.
(Lyndon Baines), 1908-1973. 3. Vietnamese Conflict, 1961-1975 — United
States 4. Korean War, 1950-1953 — United States. I. T.
DS919.D66 1984   951.9/042 19   LC 84-15967   ISBN 0312563701

The Korean War: a 25–year perspective / edited for the Harry   3.5028
S. Truman Library Institute for National and International
Affairs by Francis H. Heller.
Lawrence: Regents Press of Kansas, c1977. xxii, 251 p.: ill.; 24 cm. 1. Truman,
Harry S., 1884-1972 — Addresses, essays, lectures. 2. Korean War, 1950-1953
— United States — Addresses, essays, lectures. I. Heller, Francis Howard.
II. Harry S. Truman Library. Institute for National and International Affairs.
DS919.K67   951.9/042   LC 77-4003   ISBN 0700601570

Noble, Harold Joyce, 1903-1953.   3.5029
Embassy at war / Harold Joyce Noble; edited with an introd. by Frank
Baldwin. — Seattle: University of Washington Press, 1975. xxiv, 328 p., [2]
leaves of plates: ill.; 25 cm. (Studies of the East Asian Institute) 1. Korean War,
1950-1953 — United States. 2. United States — Foreign relations — Korea.
3. Korea — Foreign relations — United States. I. Baldwin, Frank. ed. II. T.
DS919.N6 1975   951.9/042   LC 74-23645   ISBN 0295953411

Paige, Glenn D.   • 3.5030
The Korean decision, June 24–30, 1950 [by] Glenn D. Paige. — New York:
Free Press, [1968] xxv, 394 p.; 22 cm. 1. Korean War, 1950-1953 — United
States. I. T.
DS919.P33   951.9/042   LC 68-10794

Spanier, John W.   • 3.5031
The Truman–MacArthur controversy and the Korean War. — Cambridge,
Mass.: Belknap Press, 1959. xii, 311 p.: illus.; 24 cm. 1. Korean War,
1950-1953 2. Civil supremacy over the military — United States. I. T.
DS919.S62   951.9042   LC 59-12976

Whiting, Allen Suess, 1926-.   • 3.5032
China crosses the Yalu; the decision to enter the Korean War [by] Allen S.
Whiting. — Stanford, Calif.: Stanford University Press, [1968, c1960] x, 219 p.:
maps.; 24 cm. 1. Korean War, 1950-1953 — China. I. T.
DS919.5.W5 1968   951.9/042   LC 68-13744

Kinkead, Eugene, 1906-.   • 3.5033
In every war but one. — [1st ed.]. — New York: Norton, [1959] 219 p.; 22 cm.
Expanded from an article published in the New Yorker magazine, Oct. 26,
1957, under title: The study of something new in history. 1. Korean War,
1950-1953 — Prisoners and prisons 2. Defectors I. T.
DS921.K46   951.9042   LC 58-11107

Geneva Conference (1954)   • 3.5034
The 1954 Geneva Conference; Indo–China and Korea. With a new introd.
written especially for the Greenwood reprint by Kenneth T. Young. — New
York: Greenwood Press, [1968] vi, 168, 42 p.; 26 cm. 'Combining Documents
relating to the discussion of Korea and Indo-China at the Geneva Conference,
April 27-June 15, 1954, and Further documents relating to the discussion of
Indo-China at the Geneva Conference, June 16-July 21, 1954.' Each reprint
includes facsim. of the original t.p. 1. Korean War, 1950-1953 — Peace.
2. Indochina — History — 1945- — Sources. I. Geneva. Conference, 1954.
Documents relating to the discussion of Korea and Indo-China at the Geneva
Conference. II. Geneva. Conference, 1954. Further documents relating to the
discussion of Indo-China at the Geneva Conference. III. T.
DS921.7.G4 1954ab   951.9/042   LC 68-57791

Vatcher, William H.   • 3.5035
Panmunjom; the story of the Korean military armistice negotiations. — New
York, Praeger [1958] ix, 322 p. illus., ports., map. 22 cm. — (Books that matter)
'Text of Armistice agreement': p. 281-312. 1. Korean War, 1950-1953 —
Armistices I. T.
DS921.7.V3   951.9   LC 58-7887

DS922 1960-

Chung, Kyung Cho.   • 3.5036
Korea; the third Republic. — New York: Macmillan, [1971] xii, 269 p.: illus.,
map, port.; 21 cm. 'The Constitution of the Republic of Korea': p. 231-256.
1. Korea (South) — Politics and government — 1960- I. Korea (South)
Constitution. English. 1971. II. T.
DS922.C69   320.9/519/04   LC 74-165110

Hinton, Harold C.   3.5037
Korea under new leadership: the Fifth Republic / Harold C. Hinton. — New
York, NY: Praeger, 1983. xi, 282 p.; 25 cm. 1. Korea (South) — Politics and
government — 1960- I. T.
DS922.35.H56 1983   951.9/053 19   *LC* 83-2238   *ISBN*
0030632846

DS930–935 Korea (Democratic People's Republic)

An, Tai Sung, 1931-.   3.5038
North Korea: a political handbook / by Tai Sung An. — Wilmington, Del.:
Scholarly Resources Inc., 1983. xvi, 294 p.: map; 24 cm. 1. Korea (North) —
Handbooks, manuals, etc. I. T.
DS932.A76 1983   951.9/3 19   *LC* 83-16307   *ISBN* 0842022058

North Korea: a country study / Foreign Area Studies, The   3.5039
American University; edited by Frederica M. Bunge.
3rd ed. — Washington, D.C.: [American University, Foreign Area Studies]: for
sale by the Supt. of Docs., U.S. G.P.O., 1981. xxv, 308 p.: ill.; 24 cm. — (Area
handbook series.) Includes index. 1. Korea (North) I. Bunge, Frederica M.
II. American University (Washington, D.C.). Foreign Area Studies.
III. Series.
DS932.N66 1981   951.9/3 19   *LC* 81-22915

An, Tai Sung, 1931-.   3.5040
North Korea in transition: from dictatorship to dynasty / Tai Sung An. —
Westport, Conn.: Greenwood Press, 1983. 212 p.; 22 cm. — (Contributions in
political science. 0147-1066; no. 95) Includes index. 1. Kim, Il-sŏng, 1912- —
Philosophy. 2. Korea (North) — Politics and government. I. T. II. Series.
DS934.6.K5 A75 1983   320.9/519/3 19   *LC* 82-15866   *ISBN*
0313236380

Scalapino, Robert A. ed.   • 3.5041
North Korea today. — New York, Praeger [1963] 141 p. diagr. 22 cm. —
(Praeger publications in Russian history and world communizm, no. 135) First
published in Great Britain in 1963 as a special issue of the China quarterly.
Bibliographical footnotes. 1. Korea (Democratic People's Republic) I. T.
DS935.S25   951.904   *LC* 63-20152

Koh, Byung Chul.   • 3.5042
The foreign policy of North Korea. — New York: F. A. Praeger, [1969] xxi,
237 p.; 24 cm. — (Praeger special studies in international politics and public
affairs) 1. Korea (Democratic People's Republic) — Foreign relations. I. T.
DS935.5.K6   327.519/3   *LC* 68-55009

Nam, Koon Woo.   3.5043
The North Korean Communist leadership, 1945–1965; a study of factionalism
and political consolidation. — University, Ala.: University of Alabama Press,
[1974] x, 214 p.; 22 cm. 1. Communism — Korea (Democratic People's
Republic) 2. Korea (North) — Politics and government. I. T.
DS935.5.N35   320.9/519/3043   *LC* 73-13433   *ISBN* 0817347232

DT   Africa

DT1–6 General Works

Africa / edited by Phyllis M. Martin and Patrick O'Meara; maps and charts by Cathryn L. Lombardi; picture selection by Mary Joy Pigozzi and the editors.   3.5044
2nd ed. — Bloomington: Indiana University Press, c1986. xxi, 456 p.: ill.; 24 cm. Includes index. 1. Africa I. Martin, Phyllis. II. O'Meara, Patrick.
DT3.A23 1986   960 19   LC 85-45413   ISBN 0253302110

The Cambridge encyclopedia of Africa / general editors, Roland Oliver, Michael Crowder.   3.5045
Cambridge [Eng.]; New York: Cambridge University Press, 1981. 492 p.: ill. (some col.); 27 cm. Includes index. 1. Africa — Dictionaries and encyclopedias. I. Oliver, Roland Anthony. II. Crowder, Michael, 1934-
DT3.C35 1981   960/.03/21   LC 79-42627   ISBN 0521230969

Hailey, William Malcolm Hailey, Baron, 1872-1969.   • 3.5046
An African survey: a study of problems arising in Africa South of the Sahara / by Lord Hailey. — Rev. 1956. — London: Oxford University Press, 1957. xxvi, 1676 p.: maps (part fold.) 'Issued under the auspices of the Royal Institute of International Affairs.' 1. Colonies — Administration 2. Africa, Sub-Saharan I. T.
DT3.H3 1957   LC 57-14073

Hallett, Robin.   • 3.5047
Penetration of Africa; European exploration in North and West Africa to 1815. New York: Praeger, 1965. 458p.,illus.,maps,ports. 1. Africa, North — Discovery and exploration. 2. Africa, West — Discovery and exploration. I. T.
DT3.H33   916   LC 65-25279

Mountfield, David, 1938-.   3.5048
A history of African exploration / David Mountfield. — Northbrook, Ill.: Domus Books, 1976. 160 p.: ill. (some col.), maps, plan, ports.; 31 cm. Maps on lining papers. Includes index. 1. Africa — Discovery and exploration. I. T.
DT3.M63   916/.04   LC 76-7331   ISBN 0891960031

Perham, Margery Freda, 1895- ed.   • 3.5049
African discovery; an anthology of exploration / by Margery Perham and J. Simmons. Evanston: Northwestern University Press 1963. 280 p.: illus.,ports., maps.; 23 cm. 'From the works of the British explorers of Africa, covering the period from 1769 to 1873.' 1. Africa — Discovery and exploration. I. Simmons, Jack, 1915- II. T.
DT3.P4 1963   960   LC 63-13480

DT7–16 Description. Ethnography

Oliver, Roland Anthony. ed.   • 3.5050
Africa in the days of exploration. Edited by Roland Oliver and Caroline Oliver. Englewood Cliffs, N.J., Prentice-Hall [1965] vi, 152 p. map. 21 cm. (Global history series.) (A Spectrum book, S-123.) 1. Africa — History — Sources. 2. Africa — Description and travel I. Oliver, Caroline. joint ed. II. T. III. Series.
DT7.O4   916.097496   LC 65-23297

Africa and the islands / by R. J. Harrison Church ... [et al.].   3.5051
4th ed. — London; New York: Longman, 1977. xvii, 542 p.: ill.; 22 cm. (Geographies, an intermediate series) 1. Africa — Description and travel — 1951- 2. Africa — History I. Church, R. J. Harrison (Ronald James Harrison)
DT12.2.A55 1977b   960   LC 78-304729   ISBN 0582351979

Best, Alan C. G.   3.5052
African survey / Alan C. G. Best, Harm J. de Blij. New York: Wiley, c1977. xi, 626 p.: ill.; 26 cm. 1. Africa — Description and travel — 1951- 2. Africa — Politics and government — 1960- I. De Blij, Harm J. joint author. II. T.
DT12.2.B44   960/.3   LC 76-44520   ISBN 0471200638

Hance, William Adams, 1916-.   3.5053
The geography of modern Africa / by William A. Hance. — 2d ed. — New York: Columbia University Press, 1975. xviii, 657 p.: ill.; 26 cm. Includes indexes. 1. Africa — Description and travel — 1951-1976 I. T.
DT12.2.H28 1975   916   LC 75-2329   ISBN 0231038690

Stamp, L. Dudley (Laurence Dudley), 1898-1966.   3.5054
Africa: a study in tropical development [by] Sir L. Dudley Stamp [and] W. T. W. Morgan. 3rd ed. New York, Wiley [1972] xi, 520 p. illus. 26 cm. 1. Africa — Description and travel — 1951-1976 I. Morgan, W. T. W. (William Thomas Wilson), 1927- joint author. II. T.
DT12.2.S66 1972   916   LC 75-178152   ISBN 0471820083

The African experience. Edited by John N. Paden and Edward W. Soja.   • 3.5055
Evanston, Northwestern University Press, 1970-. v. maps (part col.) 26 cm. Prepared at Northwestern University with the support of the U.S. Office of Education. 1. Africa — Civilization — Addresses, essays, lectures. 2. Africa — Civilization — Study and teaching. I. Paden, John N. ed. II. Soja, Edward W. ed. III. Northwestern University (Evanston, Ill.)
DT14.A37   916/.03/3   LC 70-98466   ISBN 0810102935

Murdock, George Peter, 1897-.   • 3.5056
Africa: its peoples and their culture history. — New York: McGraw-Hill, 1959. xiii, 456 p.: illus., maps (1 fold. in pocket); 24 cm. 1. Africa — Civilization I. T.
DT14.M8   572.96   LC 59-8552

Murray, Jocelyn.   3.5057
Cultural atlas of Africa / edited by Jocelyn Murray. — New York: Facts on File, 1981. 240 p.: col. ill.; 31 cm. Includes index. 1. Africa — Civilization I. T.
DT14.M84   960 19   LC 80-27762   ISBN 0871965585

Gibbs, James L., ed.   • 3.5058
Peoples of Africa. Edited by James L. Gibbs, Jr. — New York: Holt, Rinehart and Winston, [1965] xiv, 594 p.: illus., maps.; 24 cm. 1. Ethnology — Africa, Sub-Saharan. 2. Ethnology — South Africa I. T.
DT15.G53   309.16   LC 65-10276

International African Institute.   • 3.5059
African worlds; studies in the cosmological ideas and social values of African peoples. — London, New York, Oxford University Press, 1954. xvii, 243 p. diagrs., tables. 26 cm. On slip mounted on t.p.: Edited with an introduction by Daryll Forde. 1. Ethnology — Africa I. Forde, Cyril Daryll, 1902- ed. II. T.
DT15.I614 1954   LC A 54-5828

DT17–38 History

Henige, David P.   3.5060
The chronology of oral tradition; quest for a chimera, by David P. Henige. — Oxford: Clarendon Press, 1974. 265 p.; 22 cm. — (Oxford studies in African affairs.) 1. Oral tradition — Africa. 2. Africa — Historiography. I. T. II. Series.
DT19.H46   907/.2   LC 74-171156   ISBN 0198216947

Neale, Caroline.   3.5061
Writing 'independent' history: African historiography, 1960–1980 / Caroline Neale. — Westport, Conn.: Greenwood Press, 1985. 208 p.; 22 cm. (Contributions in Afro-American and African studies. 0069-9624; no. 85) Includes index. 1. Africa — Historiography. I. T. II. Series.
DT19.N43 1985   960/.072 19   LC 84-15756   ISBN 0313246521

Lystad, Robert A., ed.   • 3.5062
The African world: a survey of social research / edited for the African Studies Association by Robert A. Lystad. — New York: Praeger, [1965] xvi, 575 p.; 26 cm. 1. African studies. 2. Africa — Bibliography I. African Studies Association. II. T.
DT19.8.L9   916   LC 65-10753

Wiley, David, 1935-.   3.5063
Africa on film and videotape, 1960–1981: a compendium of reviews / written, compiled, and edited by David S. Wiley with Robert Cancel ... [et al.]. — East Lansing, Mich.: African Studies Center, Michigan State University, 1982. xxii, 551 p.; 28 cm. Includes index. 1. Motion pictures — Reviews 2. Africa —

Video tape catalogs. 3. Africa — Film catalogs. I. Michigan State University. African Studies Center. II. T.
DT19.8.Z9 W54 1982   016.96 19   *LC* 83-620777

African history / Philip Curtin ... [et al.].   **3.5064**
Boston: Little, Brown, c1978. xv, 612 p.: ill.; 23 cm. 1. Africa — History I. Curtin, Philip D.
DT20.A619   960   *LC* 77-79607

Bennett, Norman Robert, 1932-.   **3.5065**
Africa and Europe: from Roman times to national independence / Norman R. Bennett. — 2nd ed. — New York: Africana Pub. Co., 1984. xi, 196 p.: maps; 23 cm. Rev. ed. of: Africa and Europe from Roman times to the present. 1975. Includes index. 1. Africa — History 2. Africa — Colonization 3. Africa — Colonial influence. I. Bennett, Norman Robert, 1932- Africa and Europe from Roman times to the present. II. T.
DT20.B46   960 19   *LC* 83-12867   *ISBN* 0841909008

Bohannan, Paul.   • **3.5066**
Africa and Africans [by] Paul Bohannan & Philip Curtin. — Rev. ed. — Garden City, N.Y.: Published for the American Museum of Natural History [by] Natural History Press, [1971] vi, 391 p.: maps.; 22 cm. 1. Africa — History 2. Africa — Civilization I. Curtin, Philip D. joint author. II. T.
DT20.B6 1971   916/.03   *LC* 79-139006

The Cambridge history of Africa / general editors, J. D. Fage   **3.5067**
and Roland Oliver.
Cambridge; New York: Cambridge University Press, 1975- < 1986 > . v. < 1-8 > : ill.; 24 cm. 1. Africa — History — Collected works. I. Fage, J. D. II. Oliver, Roland Anthony.
DT20.C28   960   *LC* 76-2261   *ISBN* 0521209811

Davidson, Basil, 1914-.   • **3.5068**
Africa in history; themes and outlines. — [1st American ed. — New York]: Macmillan, [1969, c1968] 318 p.: illus., maps.; 22 cm. 1. Africa — History I. T.
DT20.D28 1969   960   *LC* 69-16910

Davidson, Basil, 1914- ed.   • **3.5069**
The African past; chronicles from antiquity to modern times. — [1st ed.]. — Boston: Little, Brown, [1964] xix, 392 p.: illus.; 22 cm. 1. Africa — History I. T.
DT20.D3   916   *LC* 64-13182

Fage, J. D.   **3.5070**
A history of Africa / J. D. Fage. — 1st American ed. — New York: Knopf: distributed by Random House, c1978. x, 534 p., [4] leaves of plates: ill.; 22 cm. — (The History of human society) Includes index. 1. Africa — History I. T.
DT20.F33 1978   960   *LC* 78-54921   *ISBN* 0394474902

The General history of Africa: studies and documents.   **3.5071**
1-. Paris, Unesco, 1978-. v. ill. 24 cm. 1. Africa — History — Collected works. I. Unesco.
DT20.G45 1978   *LC* sn 82-20096

General history of Africa / UNESCO International Scientific   **3.5072**
Committee for the Drafting of a General History of Africa.
London: Heinemann Educational Books; Berkeley: University of California Press, 1981- < 1985 > . v. < 1-2, 4, 7 > : ill., maps. 1. Africa — History — Collected works. I. Unesco. International Scientific Committee for the Drafting of a General History of Africa.
DT20.G45 1981   960 19   *LC* 78-57321   *ISBN* 0435948075

July, Robert William.   **3.5073**
A history of the African people / Robert W. July. — 3d ed. — New York: Scribner, c1980. xxii, 794 p.: ill.; 24 cm. 1. Africa — History I. T.
DT20.J8 1980   960   *LC* 79-18115   *ISBN* 0684162911

Murphy, E. Jefferson.   **3.5074**
History of African civilization, by E. Jefferson Murphy. Foreword by Hollis R. Lynch. — New York: Crowell, [1972] xxiv, 430 p.: illus.; 24 cm. 1. Africa — History I. T.
DT20.M87   916/.03   *LC* 72-78274   *ISBN* 0690381948

Oliver, Roland Anthony.   • **3.5075**
Africa since 1800, by Roland Oliver and Anthony Atmore. — London: Cambridge U.P., 1967. ix, 304 p.: maps.; 22 cm. 1. Africa — History I. Atmore, Anthony. joint author. II. T.
DT20.O38   960   *LC* 67-11527

Oliver, Roland Anthony.   **3.5076**
A short history of Africa / [by] Roland Oliver and J. D. Fage. — 5th ed. — Harmondsworth: Penguin, 1975. 304 p.: maps; 18 cm. (Penguin African library) Includes index. 1. Africa — History I. Fage, J. D. joint author. II. T.
DT20.O4 1975   960   *LC* 76-359942   *ISBN* 0140410023

Wauthier, Claude, 1923-.   • **3.5077**
The literature and thought of modern Africa; a survey [by] Claude Wauthier. Translated by Shirley Kay. — New York: F. A. Praeger, [1967, c1966] 323 p.; 23 cm. — (Praeger library of African affairs) Revised version of work first published under title: L'Afrique des africains, inventaire de la négritude. 1. Blacks — Race identity 2. Politics and literature — Africa. 3. Africa in literature. 4. Africa — Intellectual life. I. T.
DT21.W313 1967   320.5/4/096   *LC* 67-11467

The Warrior tradition in modern Africa / edited by Ali A.   **3.5078**
Mazrui.
Leiden: Brill, 1979 (c1977). 268 p.; 25 cm. — (International studies in sociology and social anthropology; v. 23) 1. War and society — Africa — Addresses, essays, lectures. 2. Warfare, Primitive — Addresses, essays, lectures. 3. Violence — Africa — Addresses, essays, lectures. 4. Africa — History, Military — Addresses, essays, lectures. I. Mazrui, Ali Al'Amin.
DT21.5.W37   355.02/2/096   *LC* 78-367672   *ISBN* 9004056467

Oliver, Roland Anthony.   **3.5079**
The African middle ages, 1400–1800 / Roland Oliver, Anthony Atmore. — Cambridge [Eng.]; New York: Cambridge University Press, 1981. viii, 216 p.: ill., maps; 22 cm. Includes index. 1. Africa — History — To 1884 I. Atmore, Anthony. joint author. II. T.
DT25.O39   960/.2 19   *LC* 80-40308   *ISBN* 0521233011

Shinnie, Margaret.   • **3.5080**
Ancient African kingdoms. — New York: St. Martin's Press, 1965. 160 p.: ill., maps. 1. Africa — History 2. Africa — Civilization I. T.
DT25.S5   *LC* 65-18634

Freund, Bill.   **3.5081**
The making of contemporary Africa: the development of African Society since 1800 / Bill Freund. — Bloomington: Indiana University Press, c1984. xv, 357 p., [8] p. of plates: ill.; 23 cm. Includes index. 1. Africa — History — 19th century 2. Africa — History — 1884-1960 3. Africa — History — 1960- 4. Africa — Economic conditions 5. Africa — Social conditions I. T.
DT28.F73 1984   960/.23 19   *LC* 83-48116   *ISBN* 0253336600

Leadership in 19th century Africa: essays from Tarikh / editor,   **3.5082**
Obaro Ikime; with a foreword by J. F. Ade Ajayi; and a preface
by J. B. Webster.
London: published for the Historical Society of Nigeria by Longman; Atlantic Highlands, N.J.: distributed by Humanities Press, 1975 (c1974). xvi, 179 p.: ill.; 22 cm. 1. Africa — History — 19th century — Addresses, essays, lectures. 2. Africa — Biography — Addresses, essays, lectures. I. Ikime, Obaro. II. Tarikh.
DT28.L4   960/.0992 B   *LC* 75-332971   *ISBN* 0391003577

Oliver, Roland Anthony.   **3.5083**
Africa since 1800 / Roland Oliver, Anthony Atmore. — 3d ed. — Cambridge [Eng.]; New York: Cambridge University Press, 1981. xii, 372 p.: maps; 23 cm. Includes index. 1. Africa — History — 19th century 2. Africa — History — 1884-1960 3. Africa — History — 1960- I. Atmore, Anthony. joint author. II. T.
DT28.O4 1981   960/.23 19   *LC* 80-49957   *ISBN* 0521234859

Robinson, David, 1938-.   **3.5084**
Sources of the African past: case studies of five nineteenth–century African societies / David Robinson and Douglas Smith. — New York: Africana Pub. Co., 1979. xiv, 203 p.: ill.; 24 cm. 1. Africa — History — To 1884 I. Smith, Douglas, 1949 May 27- II. T.
DT28.R6 1979   967   *LC* 78-5399   *ISBN* 0841903379. *ISBN* 0841903387 pbk

Davidson, Basil, 1914-.   **3.5085**
Let freedom come: Africa in modern history / by Basil Davidson. — 1st American ed. — Boston: Little, Brown, c1978. 431 p.: maps; 22 cm. 'An Atlantic Monthly Press book.' 1. Africa — History — 1884-1960 2. Africa — History — 1960- I. T.
DT29.D38 1978   967   *LC* 78-5924   *ISBN* 0316174351

DT30 1945–

Communism in Africa / edited by David E. Albright.   **3.5086**
Bloomington: Indiana University Press, c1980. viii, 277 p.; 24 cm. 1. Communism — Africa. 2. Africa — Foreign relations — 1960- I. Albright, David E.
DT30.C57   327/.096   *LC* 78-13813   *ISBN* 0253128145

Emerson, Rupert, 1899- ed.   • **3.5087**
The political awakening of Africa, edited by Rupert Emerson and Martin Kilson. Englewood Cliffs, N.J., Prentice-Hall [1965] x, 175 p. maps. 21 cm. (Global history series.) (A Spectrum book.) 1. Africa — Politics and government — 1960- I. Kilson, Martin. joint ed. II. T. III. Series.
DT30.E46   320.96   LC 65-20605

Gutteridge, William Frank, 1919-.   **3.5088**
Military regimes in Africa / W. F. Gutteridge. — London: Methuen; [New York]: distributed in the USA by Harper & Row Publishers, Barnes and Noble Import Division, 1975. 195 p.: map; 18 cm. (Studies in African history; 11) Includes index. 1. Africa — Politics and government — 1960- 2. Africa — Armed Forces — Political activity. I. T.
DT30.G85 1975   960/.3   LC 75-320783   ISBN 0416782302

Hatch, John Charles.   • **3.5089**
A history of postwar Africa [by] John Hatch. — New York: Praeger, [1965] 432 p.: maps.; 21 cm. 1. Africa — Politics and government — 1960- I. T.
DT30.H313   960.3   LC 65-18078

Lewis, William Hubert, 1928- ed.   • **3.5090**
French–speaking Africa; the search for identity. Edited by William H. Lewis. New York, Walker [1965] 256 p. map. 24 cm. Papers presented at a colloquium held in Washington, D.C., Aug. 17-21, 1964, sponsored by the U.S. Dept. of State and others. 1. France — Colonies — Africa. 2. Africa — Politics and government — 1960- 3. States, New — Politics and government 4. Africa — Colonial influence. I. United States. Dept. of State. II. T.
DT30.L46   309.16   LC 65-15988

Mazrui, Ali Al'Amin.   **3.5091**
Nationalism and new states in Africa from about 1935 to the present / Ali A. Mazrui and Michael Tidy. — Nairobi: Heinemann, 1984. xxix, 402 p.: ill.; 24 cm. Includes index. 1. Nationalism — Africa. 2. National liberation movements — Africa. 3. Decolonization — Africa. 4. States, New 5. Africa — Politics and government — 1945-1960 6. Africa — Politics and government — 1960- I. Tidy, Michael. II. T.
DT30.M339 1984   960/.32 19   LC 84-107948   ISBN 0435941461

Meredith, Martin.   **3.5092**
The first dance of freedom: Black Africa in the postwar era / Martin Meredith. — 1st U.S. ed. — New York: Harper & Row, c1985 (c1984). xiv, 412 p.: maps; 24 cm. Includes index. 1. Nationalism — Africa — History — 20th century. 2. National liberation movements — Africa. 3. Africa — Politics and government — 1945-1960 4. Africa — Politics and government — 1960- I. T.
DT30.M46   960/.32 19   LC 84-48181   ISBN 0064356582

Nkrumah, Kwame, 1909-1972.   • **3.5093**
Africa must unite. [New ed.] New York, International Publishers [1970] xvii, 229 p. 21 cm. 1. Pan-Africanism 2. Africa — History — 1960- 3. Ghana — History — 1957- I. T.
DT30.N45 1970   960   LC 70-140209   ISBN 0717802957

The Transfer of power in Africa: decolonization, 1940–1960 /   **3.5094**
edited by Prosser Gifford and Wm. Roger Louis.
New Haven: Yale University Press, c1982. xi, 654 p.: map; 25 cm. Based on a conference held at the Villa Serbelloni, Bellagio, Italy, Sept.-Oct. 1977, sponsored by the Rockefeller Foundation. Includes index. 1. Decolonization — Africa — History — Congresses. 2. Africa — Politics and government — 1945-1960 — Congresses. I. Gifford, Prosser. II. Louis, William Roger, 1936- III. Rockefeller Foundation.
DT30.T73 1982   960/.32 19   LC 82-1931   ISBN 0300025688

Wallerstein, Immanuel Maurice, 1930-.   • **3.5095**
Africa: the politics of unity; an analysis of a contemporary social movement [by] Immanuel Wallerstein. — New York: Random House, [1967] xi, 274 p.: map.; 22 cm. 1. Pan-Africanism I. T.
DT30.W34   320.1/59/6   LC 66-22247

African independence: the first twenty–five years / edited by   **3.5096**
Gwendolen M. Carter and Patrick O'Meara.
Bloomington: Indiana University Press; London: Hutchinson, 1985. xiii, 364 p.; 25 cm. Includes index. 1. Africa — Politics and government — 1960- — Addresses, essays, lectures. 2. Africa — Economic conditions — 1960- — Addresses, essays, lectures. 3. Africa — Social conditions — 1960- — Addresses, essays, lectures. I. Carter, Gwendolen Margaret, 1906-
DT30.5.A356 1985   960/.32 19   LC 84-48457   ISBN 0253302552

Jackson, Robert H.   **3.5097**
Personal rule in Black Africa: prince, autocrat, prophet, tyrant / Robert H. Jackson and Carl G. Rosberg. — Berkeley: University of California Press, c1982. xi, 316 p.: map; 24 cm. 1. Authoritarianism — Africa — Case studies. 2. Despotism — Case studies. 3. Oligarchy — Case studies. 4. Africa — Politics and government — 1960- I. Rosberg, Carl Gustav. joint author. II. T.
DT30.5.J32   320.96 19   LC 80-25439   ISBN 0520041852

The Political economy of African foreign policy: comparative   **3.5098**
analysis / edited by Timothy M. Shaw and Olajide Aluko.
New York: St. Martin's Press, 1984. xiii, 397 p.: map; 23 cm. Includes index. 1. Africa — Foreign relations — 1960- 2. Africa — Foreign economic relations. 3. Africa — Economic conditions — 1960- 4. Africa — Dependency on foreign countries. I. Shaw, Timothy M. II. Aluko, Olajide.
DT30.5.P66 1984   327.6 19   LC 83-13966   ISBN 0312622538

Young, Crawford, 1931-.   **3.5099**
Ideology and development in Africa / Crawford Young. — New Haven: Yale University Press, c1982. xvii, 376 p.: map.; 22 cm. 'Council on Foreign Relations books.' 1. Africa — Politics and government — 1960- 2. Africa — Economic conditions — 1960- 3. Africa — Social conditions — 1960- I. Council on Foreign Relations. II. T.
DT30.5.Y68 1982   960/.32 19   LC 81-15987   ISBN 0300027443

DT31–38 Political and Diplomatic History (General)

Azikiwe, Nnamdi, 1904-.   • **3.5100**
Renascent Africa. — New York: Negro Universities Press, [1969] 313 p.: port.; 23 cm. 'Originally published in 1937 by the author, Nigeria.' 1. Nationalism — Africa. I. T.
DT31.A95 1969   320.1/58/096   LC 79-94488   ISBN 0837123658

Boateng, E. A.   **3.5101**
A political geography of Africa / E. A. Boateng. — Cambridge; New York: Cambridge University Press, 1978. xix, 292 p.: maps; 24 cm. Includes index. 1. Geography, Political 2. Africa — Politics and government I. T.
DT31.B57   320.9/6   LC 77-80828   ISBN 0521217644

Buell, Raymond Leslie, 1896-1946.   • **3.5102**
The native problem in Africa / Raymond Leslie Buell. — [Hamden, Conn.]: Archon Books, 1965. 2 v.: maps; 25 cm. 1. Africa — Politics. 2. Africa — Native races. 3. Africa — Economic conditions — 1918- I. T.
DT31.B8 1965b   301.4519606

Christopher, A. J.   **3.5103**
Colonial Africa / A.J. Christopher. — London: Croom Helm; Totowa, N.J.: Barnes & Noble, 1984. 232 p.: ill., maps; 23 cm. — (Croom Helm historical geography series.) Includes index. 1. Africa — Colonization — History. 2. Africa — Historical geography. 3. Africa — History — 1884-1960 I. T. II. Series.
DT31.C52 1984   960/.3 19   LC 84-673289   ISBN 0389204528

Gann, Lewis H., 1924-.   • **3.5104**
Burden of empire; an appraisal of Western colonialism in Africa south of the Sahara, by L. H. Gann and Peter Duignan. New York, F. A. Praeger [1967] xii, 435 p. maps. 22 cm. (Hoover Institution publications) 1. Africa, Sub-Saharan — Politics and government — 1884-1960 I. Duignan, Peter. joint author. II. T.
DT31.G345   967   LC 67-26216

Gann, Lewis H., 1924- comp.   • **3.5105**
Colonialism in Africa, 1870–1960: edited by L. H. Gann & Peter Duignan. London, Cambridge U.P., 1969-1975. 5 v. maps. 24 cm. (Hoover Institution publications) vol. 4: Hoover Institution Publication 127. 1. Africa — Colonization — Addresses, essays, lectures. 2. Africa — Politics and government — Addresses, essays, lectures. I. Duignan, Peter. joint comp. II. T. III. Title: The history and politics of colonialism 1870-1914.
DT31.G35   960   LC 75-77289   ISBN 0521073731

Geiss, Imanuel.   **3.5106**
[Panafrikanismus. English] The pan–African movement: a history of pan-Africanism in America, Europe, and Africa / by Imanuel Geiss; translated by Ann Keep. — New York: Africana Pub. Co. [1974] xiv, 575 p.: maps; 25 cm. Translation of Panafrikanismus. 1. Pan-Africanism — History. I. T.
DT31.G5513   320.5/4/096   LC 74-6107   ISBN 0841901619

Hodgkin, Thomas Lionel, 1910-.   • **3.5107**
Nationalism in colonial Africa. — [1st U.S. ed. — New York]: New York University Press, [1957] 216 p.: illus.; 21 cm. 1. Nationalism — Africa. I. T.
DT31.H56 1957   323.16   LC 57-8133

Markovitz, Irving Leonard, 1934-.   **3.5108**
Power and class in Africa: an introduction to change and conflict in African politics / Irving L. Markovitz. Englewood Cliffs, N.J.: Prentice-Hall, c1977. xii, 398 p.: map; 23 cm. Includes index. 1. Social classes — Africa. 2. Elite (Social sciences) — Africa. 3. Africa — Politics and government I. T.
DT31.M34   301.5/92/096   LC 76-49660   ISBN 0136866913

Mathurin, Owen Charles.   3.5109
Henry Sylvester Williams and the origins of the pan–African movement, 1869–1911 / Owen Charles Mathurin. — Westport, Conn.: Greenwood Press, 1976. xvi, 183 p.; 22 cm. (Contributions in Afro-American and African studies. no. 21) Includes index. 1. Williams, Henry Sylvester, 1869-1911. 2. Pan-Africanism I. T. II. Series.
DT31.M36   320.5/4/0924 B   *LC* 75-35348   *ISBN* 0837185947

Mazrui, Ali Al'Amin.   3.5110
Africa's international relations: the diplomacy of dependency and change / Ali A. Mazrui. — London: Heinemann; Boulder, Colo.: Westview Press, 1977. 310 p.; 22 cm. 1. Africa — Foreign relations 2. Africa — Politics and government — 1960- I. T.
DT31.M375   327.6   *LC* 77-595   *ISBN* 0891587330

Padmore, George, 1903-1959.   3.5111
Pan–Africanism or communism. Foreword by Richard Wright. Introd. by Azinna Nwafor. — Garden City, N.Y.: Doubleday, 1971. xlii, 439 p.; 22 cm. 1. Nationalism — Africa. 2. Communism — Africa. 3. Africa — History 4. Africa — Native races. I. T.
DT31.P3 1971   320.5/4/096   *LC* 71-164438

Perham, Margery Freda, 1895-.   • 3.5112
The colonial reckoning; the end of imperial rule in Africa in the light of British experience. [1st ed.] New York, Knopf, 1962. 203 p. 20 cm. 1. Nationalism — Africa. I. T.
DT31.P37 1962   *LC* 62-11049

Sithole, Ndabaningi, 1920-.   • 3.5113
African nationalism. — 2nd ed. — London; New York [etc.]: Oxford U.P., 1968. vi, 196 p.: plate, port.; 21 cm. 1. Nationalism — Africa. I. T.
DT31.S55 1968   320.1/58/096   *LC* 68-133467

DT32–38 RELATIONS WITH PARTICULAR COUNTRIES

Britain and Germany in Africa: imperial rivalry and colonial rule. Edited by Prosser Gifford and Wm. Roger Louis. With the assistance of Alison Smith.   • 3.5114
New Haven: Yale University Press, 1967. xvii, 825 p.: maps.; 24 cm. 'Essays presented at a conference on imperial rivalry and colonial rule held at Yale University in the spring of 1965.' The conference was sponsored by the university's Concilium on International Studies. A related work, France and Britain in Africa: imperial rivalry and colonial rule, was published in 1971, containing papers of a second conference. 1. Great Britain — Colonies — Africa — Congresses. 2. Germany — Colonies — Africa — Congresses. I. Gifford, Prosser. ed. II. Louis, William Roger, 1936- ed. III. Smith, Alison. IV. Yale University. Concilium on International Studies.
DT32.B73   325.6   *LC* 67-24500

Robinson, Ronald.   • 3.5115
Africa and the Victorians; the climax of imperialism in the Dark Continent, by Ronald Robinson and John Gallagher, with Alice Denny. — New York, St. Martins Press, 1961. xii, 491 p. maps (part fold.) 22 cm. Bibliographical footnotes. 1. Gt. Brit. — Colonies — Africa. 2. British in Africa. 3. Imperialism I. Gallagher, John, 1919- joint author. II. T.
DT32.R55   325.342096   *LC* 61-18110

Lugard, Frederick John Dealtry, Baron, 1858-1945.   • 3.5116
The dual mandate in British tropical Africa [by] Lord Lugard. With a new introd. by Margery Perham. — [5th ed. — Hamden, Conn.] Archon Books, 1965. xlix, 643 p. 23 cm. 1. Great Britain — Colonies — Africa. 2. Great Britain — Colonies — Administration 3. Africa — Econ. condit. — 1918- 4. Africa, Sub-Saharan — Native races. 5. World War, 1914-1918 — Territorial questions — Africa. I. T. II. Title: Mandate in British tropical Africa. III. Title: British tropical Africa.
DT32.5.L8 1965   309.16   *LC* 65-15494 rev

Cooke, James J.   3.5117
New French imperialism, 1880–1910: the Third Republic and colonial expansion [by] James J. Cooke. — Newton Abbot: David & Charles; Hamden, Conn.: Archon Books, 1973. 223 p.; 23 cm. — (Library of politics and society) 1. France — Colonies — Africa. I. T.
DT33.C66 1973   325/.344/096   *LC* 73-163961   *ISBN* 0208013202

Fanon, Frantz, 1925-1961.   • 3.5118
[Damnés de la terre. English] The wretched of the earth. Pref. by Jean–Paul Sartre. Translated from the French by Constance Farrington. New York, Grove Press [1965, c1963] 255 p. 21 cm. 1. Offenses against the person 2. France — Colonies — Africa. 3. Algeria — History — 1945-1962 I. T.
DT33.F313 1965   306/.096 19   *LC* 65-14196

France and Britain in Africa: imperial rivalry and colonial rule.   3.5119
Edited by Prosser Gifford and Wm. Roger Louis.
New Haven: Yale University Press, 1972 (c1971). xix, 989 p.: maps.; 25 cm. Rev. papers of a conference held by the Concilium on International Studies in March 1968. A related work, Britain and Germany in Africa: imperial rivalry and colonial rule, contains the papers of the 1965 conference. 1. France — Colonies — Africa — Congresses. 2. Great Britain — Colonies — Africa — Congresses. 3. Great Britain — Foreign relations — France — Congresses. 4. France — Foreign relations — Great Britain — Congresses. I. Gifford, Prosser. ed. II. Louis, William Roger, 1936- ed. III. Yale University. Concilium on International Studies.
DT33.F7   325.6   *LC* 70-151574   *ISBN* 0300012896

Suret-Canale, Jean.   3.5120
[Afrique noire: occidentale et centrale. 2: L'ère coloniale (1900-1945) English] French colonialism in tropical Africa, 1900–1945. Translated from the French by Till Gottheiner. New York, Pica Press [1971] xvii, 521 p. illus., maps. 23 cm. Translation of Afrique noire: occidentale et centrale, v. 2: L'ère coloniale (1900-1945) 1. France — Colonies — Africa. I. T.
DT33.S9533   325.3/1   *LC* 75-95756   *ISBN* 0876637020

Cohen, William B., 1941-.   3.5121
The French encounter with Africans: white response to Blacks, 1530–1880 / William B. Cohen. — Bloomington: Indiana University Press, c1980. xix, 360 p.: ill.; 24 cm. 1. France — Colonies — Africa — History. 2. Africa — Colonization 3. Africa — History — To 1884 4. Africa — Race relations. 5. France — Race relations. I. T.
DT33.3.C63   325/.344/096   *LC* 79-84260   *ISBN* 0253349222

Chilcote, Ronald H.   • 3.5122
Portuguese Africa [by] Ronald H. Chilcote. — Englewood Cliffs, N. J., Prentice-Hall [1967] x, 149 p. maps. 21 cm. — (A Spectrum book: The modern nations in historical perspective) Bibliography: p. 129-141. 1. Portugal — Colonies — Africa. I. T.
DT36.C45   325.3/469/096   *LC* 67-14849

Duffy, James, 1923-.   • 3.5123
Portugal in Africa. — [Cambridge] Harvard University Press, 1962. 239 p. maps. 21 cm. Bibliography: p. 230-[232] 1. Portugal — Colonies — Africa. I. T.
DT36.D79 1962   325.3469   *LC* 62-6988

Ferreira, Eduardo de Sousa, 1936-.   3.5124
Portuguese colonialism in Africa: the end of an era: the effects of Portuguese colonialism on education, science, culture and information / by Eduardo de Sousa Ferreira; with an introd. by Basil Davidson. — Paris: Unesco Press, 1974. 170 p.; 21 cm. 1. Portugal — Colonies — Africa. I. T.
DT36.F43   325/.31   *LC* 75-305256   *ISBN* 9231011634

Hammond, Richard James, 1911-.   • 3.5125
Portugal and Africa, 1815–1910; a study in uneconomic imperialism [by] R. J. Hammond. — Stanford, Calif., Stanford University Press, 1966. xv, 384 p. illus., maps. 24 cm. — (A Publication of the Food Research Institute, Stanford University. Studies in tropical development) Bibliographical references included in 'Notes' (p. [343]-375) 1. Portugal — Colonies — Africa. 2. British in Africa. I. T.
DT36.H3   325.3469096   *LC* 66-17561

Newitt, M. D. D.   3.5126
Portugal in Africa: the last hundred years / by Malyn Newitt. — London: Longman, 1981. viii, 278 p.: ill.; 22 cm. Includes index. 1. Portugal — Colonies — Africa — History — 19th century. 2. Portugal — Colonies — Africa — History — 20th century. 3. Africa, Portuguese-speaking — History. I. T.
DT36.5.N48   325/.3469/096 19   *LC* 81-150129   *ISBN* 0582643791

McKinley, Edward H.   3.5127
The lure of Africa: American interests in tropical Africa, 1919–1939 [by] Edward H. McKinley. Indianapolis, Bobbs-Merrill [1974] x, 293 p. map. 24 cm. 1. Americans — Africa, Sub-Saharan 2. United States — Relations — Africa, Sub-Saharan 3. Africa, Sub-Saharan — Relations — United States I. T.
DT38.M33   301.29/73/067   *LC* 73-1789   *ISBN* 0672517361

Filesi, Teobaldo.   3.5128
[Relazioni della Cina con l'Africa nel Medio-Evo. English] China and Africa in the Middle Ages. Translated [from the Italian] by David L. Morison. London, F. Cass in association with the Central Asian Research Centre [1972] 101 p. illus. 22 cm. (Cass library of African studies. General studies, no. 144) Translation of Le relazioni della Cina con l'Africa nel Medio-Evo. 1. China — Relations — Africa 2. Africa — Relations — China I. T. II. Series.
DT38.9.C5 F513   301.29/6/051   *LC* 73-150979   *ISBN* 071462604X

Wilson, Edward Thomas.   3.5129
Russia and Black Africa before World War II. New York: Holmes & Meier [1974] xvi, 397 p.; 24 cm. 'Slightly edited version of a dissertation accepted by the Johns Hopkins University in May, 1972.' 1. Africa, Sub-Saharan —

Foreign relations — Soviet Union. 2. Soviet Union — Foreign relations — Africa, Sub-Saharan. I. T.
DT38.9.R8 W54 1974   327.47/067   *LC* 73-84939   *ISBN* 0841901090

DT43–154 EGYPT. SUDAN

DT43–107 Egypt

Conference on the Modern History of Egypt, University of London, 1965.   • **3.5130**
Political and social change in modern Egypt: historical studies from the Ottoman conquest to the United Arab Republic; edited by P. M. Holt. London, New York [etc.] Oxford U.P., 1968. xx, 400 p. 3 plates, 1 illus., facsims., map. 25 cm. English or French. 'The essays printed in this volume represent, in revised form, papers contributed to a Conference on the Modern History of Egypt, held in April 1965 at the School of Oriental and African Studies in the University of London.' 1. Egypt — History — 1517-1882 — Congresses. 2. Egypt — History — 1798- — Congresses. I. Holt, P. M. (Peter Malcolm) ed. II. University of London. School of Oriental and African Studies. III. T.
DT43.C63 1965a   962   *LC* 68-121481

Egypt, a country study / Foreign Area Studies, the American University; edited by Richard F. Nyrop.   **3.5131**
4th ed. — Washington, D.C.: For sale by the Supt. of Docs., U.S. G.P.O., 1983. xxxvi, 362 p.: ill.; 24 cm. — (Area handbook series.) (DA pam. 550-43) 'Research completed July 1982.' Rev. ed. of: Area handbook for Egypt / coauthors, Richard F. Nyrop ... [et al.]. 3rd ed. 1976. Includes index. 1. Egypt. I. Nyrop, Richard F. II. Nyrop, Richard F. Area handbook for Egypt. III. American University (Washington, D.C.). Foreign Area Studies. IV. Series. V. Series: DA pam. 550-43
DT46.E32 1983   962/.05 19   *LC* 83-600110

Golding, William, 1911-.   **3.5132**
An Egyptian journal / William Golding. — London; Boston: Faber and Faber, 1985. 207 p., [32] p. of plates: ill. (some col.); 24 cm. 1. Golding, William, 1911- — Journeys — Egypt. 2. Novelists, English — 20th century — Biography. 3. Egypt — 1945- — Description and travel. 4. Nile River Valley — Description and travel. I. T.
DT56.G54 1985   916.2 19   *LC* 85-6777   *ISBN* 0571135935

Excavating in Egypt: the Egypt Exploration Society, 1882–1982 / edited by T.G.H. James.   **3.5133**
Chicago: University of Chicago Press, 1982. 192 p.: ill., map; 25 cm. 1. Egypt Exploration Society — Addresses, essays, lectures. 2. Excavations (Archaeology) — Egypt — Addresses, essays, lectures. 3. Egypt — Antiquities — Addresses, essays, lectures. I. James, T. G. H. (Thomas Garnet Henry)
DT56.9.E96 1982   932 19   *LC* 81-21947   *ISBN* 0226391914

Ruffle, John.   **3.5134**
The Egyptians: an introduction to Egyptian archaeology / John Ruffle. — Ithaca, N.Y.: Cornell University Press, 1977. 224 p.: ill.; 26 cm. Includes index. 1. Egypt — Antiquities 2. Egypt — Civilization — To 332 B.C. 3. Egypt — Civilization — 332 B.C.-638 A.D. I. T.
DT56.9.R83 1977   932   *LC* 75-39567   *ISBN* 0801410037

Breasted, James Henry, 1865-1935. ed. and tr.   • **3.5135**
Ancient records of Egypt; historical documents from the earliest times to the Persian conquest, collected, edited, and translated with commentary. — New York, Russell & Russell, 1962. 5 v. 23 cm. 1. Egypt — Hist. — Sources. I. T.
DT57.B76 1962   932   *LC* 62-13827

Wilson, John Albert, 1899-.   • **3.5136**
Signs & wonders upon Pharaoh; a history of American Egyptology [by] John A. Wilson. — Chicago: University of Chicago Press, [1964] xxv, 243 p.: illus. ports.; 24 cm. 1. Egyptology I. T.
DT60.W65   913.32   *LC* 64-23535

Baumgartel, Elise J., 1892-.   • **3.5137**
The cultures of prehistoric Egypt / by Elise J. Baumgartel.–. London: Published on behalf of the Griffith Institute, Ashmolean Museum, Oxford University Press, 1947-1960. 2 v.: ill., plates, maps. 1. Egypt — Antiquities 2. Egypt — Civilization I. T.
DT 61.B35   *LC* 48-13407

Harris, John Richard.   **3.5138**
The legacy of Egypt; edited by J. R. Harris. — 2d ed. — Oxford [Eng.]: Clarendon Press, 1971. 510 p.: 24 plates.; 19 cm. First ed. by S. R. K. Glanville.

1. Egypt — Civilization. I. Glanville, Stephen Ranulph Kingdon, 1900-1956, ed. The legacy of Egypt. II. T.
DT61.H28 1971   913.32/03   *LC* 72-179507   *ISBN* 0198219121

James, T. G. H. (Thomas Garnet Henry)   **3.5139**
Pharaoh's people: scenes from life in Imperial Egypt / T.G.H. James. — Chicago: University of Chicago Press, 1984. 282 p., [16] p. of plates: ill.; 23 cm. Includes index. 1. Egypt — Social life and customs — To 332 B.C. 2. Egypt — History — Eighteenth dynasty, ca. 1570-1320 B.C. I. T.
DT61.J35 1984   932/.014 19   *LC* 84-2482   *ISBN* 0226391930

Michaels, Barbara, 1927-.   **3.5140**
Red land, black land: daily life in ancient Egypt / Barbara Mertz. — Rev. ed. — New York: Dodd, Mead, c1978. xiii, 385 p.: ill.; 24 cm. Includes index. 1. Egypt — Civilization — To 332 B.C. I. T.
DT61.M53 1978   932/.01   *LC* 78-9552   *ISBN* 0396075754

Romer, John.   **3.5141**
Ancient lives: daily life in Egypt of the pharaohs / John Romer. — 1st American ed. — New York, N.Y.: Holt, Rinehart, and Winston, c1984. xii, 235 p.: ill. (some col.); 24 cm. Includes index. 1. Egypt — Social life and customs — To 332 B.C. I. T.
DT61.R54 1984   932/.01 19   *LC* 84-12908   *ISBN* 003000733X

Romer, John.   **3.5142**
People of the Nile: everyday life in ancient Egypt / John Romer. — 1st American ed. — New York: Crown, 1982. 224 p.: ill. (some col.), map; 26 cm. Includes index. 1. Egypt — Civilization — To 332 B.C. 2. Egypt — Antiquities I. T.
DT61.R56 1982   932/.01 19   *LC* 82-7410   *ISBN* 0517548569

Wilson, John Albert, 1899-.   • **3.5143**
The burden of Egypt; an interpretation of ancient Egyptian culture. — [Chicago]: University of Chicago Press, [1951] xix, 332 p.: illus., ports., map (on lining papers); 25 cm. — (An Oriental Institute essay) 1. Egypt — Civilization — To 332 B.C. I. T.
DT61.W56   913.32   *LC* 51-9735

Harris, James E.   **3.5144**
X–raying the pharaohs [by] James E. Harris and Kent R. Weeks. New York, Scribner [1973] 195 p. illus. 26 cm. Report of an expedition conducted at the Egyptian Museum, Cairo, under the direction of the School of Dentistry, University of Michigan, with the cooperation of the School of Dentistry, University of Alexandria, and the Egyptian Antiquities Dept. of the Egyptian Museum. 1. Mummies — Egypt — Radiography. 2. Egypt — Antiquities I. Weeks, Kent R. joint author. II. Mathaf al-Misrī. III. University of Michigan. School of Dentistry. IV. T.
DT62.M7 H37   913/.031/0285   *LC* 72-1180   *ISBN* 0684130165

Leca, Ange Pierre.   **3.5145**
[Momies. English] The Egyptian way of death: mummies and the cult of the immortal / by Ange–Pierre Leca; translated by Louise Asmal. — Garden City, N.Y.: Doubleday, 1981, c1979. xviii, 292 p., [4] leaves of plates: ill.; 22 cm. Translation of Les momies. Includes index. 1. Mummies — Egypt. I. T.
DT62.M7 L413 1981   393/.3/0932 19   *LC* 78-68362   *ISBN* 0385146094

Edwards, I. E. S. (Iorwerth Eiddon Stephen), 1909-.   **3.5146**
The pyramids of Egypt [by] I. E. S. Edwards. — 3rd ed. — London: Penguin, 1972. 240 p.: illus.; 25 cm. — 1. Pyramids — Egypt I. T.
DT63.E3 1972   913.32   *LC* 73-186741   *ISBN* 0670583618

Fakhry, Ahmed.   • **3.5147**
The pyramids. — [Chicago]: University of Chicago Press, [1961] 260 p.: illus., maps, plans.; 24 cm. 1. Pyramids I. T.
DT63.F3   913.32   *LC* 61-8645

Mendelssohn, K. (Kurt), 1906-.   **3.5148**
The riddle of the pyramids. — New York, Praeger [1974] 224 p. illus. 25 cm. 1. Pyramids — Egypt 2. Pyramids — Design and construction 3. Indians of Mexico — Pyramids 4. State, The — History. I. T.
DT63.M43   913.32   *LC* 73-18485

Lane, Edward William, 1801-1876.   • **3.5149**
The manners and customs of the modern Egyptians, by Edward William Lane. [3d ed.] London, J. M. Dent & co.; New York, E. P. Dutton & co. [1908] xxix, [1], 630 p. illus. 18 cm. (Everyman's library, ed. by Ernest Rhys.) Ornamental lining-papers. Complete list of published works: p. ix. (Hunter Library copy missing p. 628-630.) 1. Egypt — Social life and customs I. T.
DT70.L27 1908   *LC* w 08-104

Fraser, P. M. (Peter Marshall)   **3.5150**
Ptolemaic Alexandria / [by] P. M. Fraser. — Oxford: Clarendon Press, 1972. 3 v. (xvi, 812 p.), 4 leaves (1 fold.); xii, 1116 p.: ill., maps; 25 cm. 1. Alexandria (Egypt) — Civilization. I. T.
DT73.A4 F7   932   *LC* 73-157923   *ISBN* 0198142781

DT74–107 History

Ancient Egypt: a social history / B.G. Trigger ... [et al.].   3.5151
Cambridge [Cambridgeshire]; New York: Cambridge University Press, 1983.
xiii, 450 p.: ill.; 24 cm. 'Chapters 1, 2, and 3 ... were previously published in The
Cambridge history of Africa, volume 1'—Verso t.p. Includes index. 1. Egypt —
History — To 332 B.C. 2. Egypt — Civilization — To 332 B.C. I. Trigger,
Bruce G. II. Cambridge history of Africa.
DT83.A656 1983   932/.01 19   LC 82-22196   ISBN 0521240808

Breasted, James Henry, 1865-1935.   • 3.5152
A history of Egypt: from the earliest times to the Persian conquest / by James
Henry Breasted. With two hundred illustrations and maps. — 2nd ed. New
York: C. Scribner's sons, 1909. xxix p., 2 l., 3-634 p.: col. front., illus., plates,
maps (1 fold.); 25 cm. 'Published ... 1905. New edition ... 1909. Reprinted ...
1929.' 1. Egypt — History — Ancient to 640 A.D. I. T.
DT83.B782 1912c   932   LC 30-25560

Gardiner, Alan Henderson, Sir, 1879-1963.   • 3.5153
Egypt of the Pharaohs, an introduction. — Oxford, Clarendon Press, 1961.
461 p. ill. 25 cm. 1. Egypt — History — To 332 B.C. I. T.
DT 83 G22   LC 61-1371

Carter, Howard, 1873-1939.   3.5154
The tomb of Tutankhamen. With 17 color plates and 65 monochrome illus. and
2 appendices. — New York: Dutton, [1972, c1954] 236 p.: illus.; 26 cm. A
shortened version of the 3-v. work entitled: The tomb of Tut-ankh-Amen,
originally published 1923-33. 1. Tutankhamen, King of Egypt. I. T.
DT87.5.C4 1972c   913.32/03/10924   LC 72-77218   ISBN
0525220801

Bell, Harold Idris, Sir, 1879-.   3.5155
Egypt, from Alexander the Great to the Arab conquest; a study in the diffusion
and decay of Hellenism. Oxford, Clarendon Press [1948] 168 p. (Gregynog
lectures, 1946) 1. Egypt — History — Greco Roman period, 332 B.C.-640
A.D. I. T.
DT92.B46   LC 49-9355

Bevan, Edwyn Robert, 1870-1943.   3.5156
The house of Ptolemy: a history of Egypt under the Ptolemaic dynasty. — [1st
American ed.] Chicago: Argonaut 1968. 409p. 1. Ptolemies, Kings of Egypt
2. Egypt — History — 332-30 B.C. I. Mahaffy, John Pentland, Sir, 1839-1919.
A history of Egypt under the Ptolemaic dynasty II. T. III. Title: A history of
Egypt under the Ptolomaic dynasty
DT92 B5 1968

Glubb, John Bagot, Sir, 1897-.   3.5157
Soldiers of fortune; the story of the Mamlukes [by] Sir John Glubb. — New
York: Stein and Day, [1973] 480 p.: illus.; 24 cm. 1. Mamelukes I. T.
DT96.G57 1973   962/.02   LC 73-80841   ISBN 0812816110

Crabbs, Jack A., 1938-.   3.5158
The writing of history in nineteenth-century Egypt: a study in national
transformation / Jack A. Crabbs, Jr. — Detroit: Wayne State University Press;
Cairo: American University in Cairo Press, 1984. 227 p.; 23 cm. Includes index.
1. History — Study and teaching — Egypt. 2. Egypt — History — 19th
century — Historiography. 3. Egypt — Intellectual life. I. T.
DT100.C73 1984   962/.03 19   LC 84-2176   ISBN 0814317618

Sayyid-Marsot, Afaf Lutfi.   3.5159
Egypt in the reign of Muhammad Ali / Afaf Lutfi al-Sayyid Marsot. —
Cambridge [Cambridgeshire]; New York: Cambridge University Press, 1984. x,
300 p.; 24 cm. — (Cambridge Middle East library.) Includes index.
1. Muhammad 'Alī, Wali of Egypt, 1769-1849. 2. Egypt — History —
Mohammed Ali, 1805-1849 I. T. II. Series.
DT104.S38 1984   962/.03 19   LC 83-5241   ISBN 0521247950

Safran, Nadav.   • 3.5160
Egypt in search of political community; an analysis of the intellectual and
political evolution of Egypt, 1804-1952. — Cambridge, Harvard University
Press, 1961. 298 p. 24 cm. — (Harvard Middle Eastern studies. 5) Harvard
political studies. Bibliography: p. [261]-266. 1. Egypt — Pol. & govt. I. T.
II. Series.
DT107.S2   962   LC 61-13742

Vatikiotis, P. J. (Panayiotis J.), 1928-.   3.5161
The history of Egypt / P.J. Vatikiotis. — 3rd ed. — Baltimore, Md.: Johns
Hopkins University Press, 1986. p. cm. Includes index. 1. Egypt — History —
1798- I. T.
DT107.V38 1986   962 19   LC 85-24200   ISBN 0801833256

Sayyid-Marsot, Afaf Lutfi.   3.5162
Egypt's liberal experiment, 1922-1936 / Afaf Lutfi al-Sayyid-Marsot. —
Berkeley: University of California Press, c1977. xii, 276 p.: ill.; 24 cm. Includes
index. 1. Egypt — History — Fuad, 1917-1936 I. T.
DT107.8.S39   962/.05   LC 75-22659   ISBN 0520031091

Haykal, Muhammad Hasanayn.   3.5163
The road to Ramadan / Mohamed Heikal. — New York: Quadrangle/New
York Times Book Co., 1975. 285 p., [6] leaves of plates: ill.; 22 cm. Includes
index. 1. Jewish-Arab relations — 1967-1973 2. Israel-Arab War, 1973
3. Egypt — Politics and government — 1952- I. T.
DT107.83.H375 1975   320.9/56/04   LC 75-8287   ISBN
0812905679

Neff, Donald, 1930-.   3.5164
Warriors at Suez: Eisenhower takes America into the Middle East / Donald
Neff. — New York: Linden Press/Simon and Schuster, 1981. 479 p., 32 leaves
of plates: ill.; 25 cm. Includes index. 1. Egypt — History — Intervention, 1956
I. T.
DT107.83.N436   962/.053 19   LC 81-8465   ISBN 0671410105

DT108 Sudan

(see also: DT154.1)

Fabunmi, L. A.   • 3.5165
The Sudan in Anglo-Egyptian relations; a case study in power politics,
1800-1956. — [London] Longmans [1960] xx, 466 p. illus. 23 cm. 'This
book has evolved from work done for the degree of doctor of philosophy ...
University of London.' Bibliography: p. 443-451. 1. Sudan — Hist. 2. Egypt
— For. rel. — Gt. Brit. 3. Gt. Brit. — For. rel. — Egypt. I. T.
DT108.F3   962.403   LC 61-19917

Gray, Richard, 1929-.   • 3.5166
A history of the Southern Sudan, 1839-1889. — [London] Oxford University
Press, 1961. viii, 219 p.: maps; 23 cm. 1. Sudan — Hist. I. T.
DT108.G7 1961   962.403   LC 61-66800

Holt, P. M. (Peter Malcolm)   3.5167
The history of the Sudan from the coming of Islan to the present day / P.M.
Holt, M.W. Daly. — 3rd ed. — Boulder, Colo.: Westview Press, 1979. xiii,
250 p., [24] p. of plates: ill., ports.; 23 cm. Includes index. 1. Sudan — History
I. Daly, M. W. II. T.
DT108.H72 1979   962.4 19   LC 79-3886   ISBN 0891589333

O'Fahey, R. S. (Rex S.)   3.5168
Kingdoms of the Sudan / R. S. O'Fahey and J. L. Spaulding. — London:
Methuen; [New York]: distributed by Harper & Row, Barnes & Noble Import
Division, 1975 (c1974). ix, 235 p.: maps; 19 cm. (Studies in African history; no.
9) Includes index. 1. Sudan — History — To 1820 2. Sennar (Kingdom)
3. Darfur (Sudan) — History. I. Spaulding, J. L. (Jay L.) joint author. II. T.
DT108.1.O33 1974   962.4/04   LC 75-311365   ISBN 0416774504

Beshir, Mohamed Omer, 1926-.   3.5169
Revolution and nationalism in the Sudan / Mohamed Omer Beshir. — New
York: Barnes & Noble Books, 1974. xii, 314 p.: map; 23 cm. Includes index.
1. Sudan — Politics and government. I. T.
DT108.6.B47 1974   320.9/624/03   LC 74-194650   ISBN
0064903788

Sudan, a country study / Foreign Area Studies, The American   3.5170
University; edited by Harold D. Nelson.
3rd ed. — Washington, D.C.: For sale by the Supt. of Docs., U.S. Govt. Print.
Off., 1982. xxvii, 365 p.: ill.; 24 cm. — (Area handbook series) (DA pam.
550-27) 'Research completed March 1982.' Rev. ed. of: Area handbook for
Sudan, 1972. Includes index. 1. Sudan. I. Nelson, Harold D. II. American
University (Washington, D.C.). Foreign Area Studies. III. Series. IV. Series:
DA pam. 550-27
DT108.7.A6x   962.4 19   LC 83-2718

DT115–154 Nile River. Local History of Egypt

Moorehead, Alan, 1910-. • 3.5171
The Blue Nile. — [Rev. ed.]. — New York: Harper & Row, [1972] 336 p.: illus.; 27 cm. 1. Nile Valley — History. 2. Blue Nile River. I. T.
DT115.M6 1972   962   *LC* 73-186776   *ISBN* 0060130113

Burton, Richard Francis, Sir, 1821-1890. • 3.5172
The Nile basin [by] Richard F. Burton and Captain Speke's discovery of the source of the Nile, by James MacQueen. New introd. by Robert O. Collins. — New York: Da Capo Press, 1967. xxxvii, 195 p.: maps.; 22 cm. Reprint of the 1864 ed. 1. Speke, John Hanning, 1827-1864. Journal of the discovery of the source of the Nile. 2. Nile River 3. Africa, Central — Description and travel I. MacQueen, James, 1778-1870. II. T.
DT117.B97 1967   916.7/04   *LC* 65-23403

Moorehead, Alan, 1910-. • 3.5173
The White Nile. — [Rev. ed.]. — New York: Harper & Row, [1971] 368 p.: illus., maps, ports.; 26 cm. Part of the illustrative matter is colored. 1. Nile Valley — History. I. T.
DT117.M6 1971   962.9/3   *LC* 78-160663   *ISBN* 0060130490

Barbour, Kenneth Michael. • 3.5174
The Republic of the Sudan; a regional geography. — London, University of London Press [1961] 292 p. illus., maps. 26 cm. Bibliographical footnotes. 1. Sudan — Descr. & trav. I. T.
DT124.B28   916.24   *LC* 61-65685

Evans-Pritchard, E. E. (Edward Evan), 1902-1973. 3.5175
The Azande: history and political institutions [by] E. E. Evans–Pritchard. — Oxford: Clarendon Press, 1971. xviii, 444 p., 6 plates:; ill., geneal. tables, maps, ports.; 23 cm. 1. Zande (African people) I. T.
DT132.E78   916.7   *LC* 70-889223   *ISBN* 0198231709

Evans-Pritchard, E. E. (Edward Evan), 1902-1973. 3.5176
Man and woman among the Azande. Edited by E. E. Evans–Pritchard. New York, Free Press [1974] 197 p. illus. 22 cm. 1. Zande (African people) 2. Marriage customs and rites, Zande. 3. Sex customs — Sudan. I. T.
DT132.E79 1974b   301.41/09629/5   *LC* 73-22630

Evans-Pritchard, E. E. (Edward Evan), 1902-1973. • 3.5177
The Nuer: a description of the modes of livelihood and political institution of a Nilotic people / by E. E. Evans–Pritchard. — Oxford: Clarendon Press, 1940. viii, 271 p.: ill., maps; 23 cm. 'A considerable part of the facts related ... have been previously recorded, chiefly in Sudan notes and records, and Africa.'— Pref. 1. Nuer (African tribe) I. T.
DT132.E91   DT132.N8 E82.   *LC* a 40-3181

Fahim, Hussein M., 1934-. 3.5178
Egyptian Nubians: resettlement and years of coping / Hussein M. Fahim. — Salt Lake City: University of Utah Press, c1983. xii, 195 p.: ill.; 25 cm. Includes index. 1. Nubians — Egypt. 2. Land settlement — Egypt. 3. Social change — Case studies. 4. Aswan High Dam (Egypt) I. T.
DT133.N79 F33 1983   305.8/931 19   *LC* 82-24723   *ISBN* 0874802156

Fernea, Robert A. (Robert Alan), 1932-. 3.5179
Nubians in Egypt: peaceful people / ethnographic essay by Robert A. Fernea; photos. by Georg Gerster; notes on Nubian architecture and architectural drawings by Horst Jaritz; foreword by Laila Shukry El Hamamsy; captions by Hamza El Din and Elizabeth Warnock Fernea; additional photos. by Abdul Fattah Eid. — Austin: University of Texas Press, 1974 (c1973) xiii, 146 p.: ill.; 29 cm. 1. Ethnology — Egypt — Nubia. 2. Nubians in Egypt. 3. Nubia — Social life and customs. I. Gerster, Georg, 1928- illus. II. T.
DT135.N8 F47   916.25/03   *LC* 73-3078   *ISBN* 029275504X

Trigger, Bruce G. 3.5180
Nubia under the pharaohs / Bruce G. Trigger. Boulder, Colo.: Westview Press, 1976. 216 p.: ill.; 21 cm. (Ancient peoples and places; v. 85) Includes index. 1. Nubia — History. I. T.
DT135.N8 T74 1976   939/.78   *LC* 76-168   *ISBN* 0891585443

Abu-Lughod, Janet L. • 3.5181
Cairo: 1001 years of the city victorious [by] Janet L. Abu–Lughod. Princeton, N.J., Princeton University Press, 1971. xiv, 284 p. illus., maps, 29 cm. (Princeton studies on the Near East.) 1. Cairo (Egypt) I. T. II. Series.
DT143.A26   962/.16   *LC* 73-112992   *ISBN* 0691030855

Wiet, Gaston, 1887-1971. • 3.5182
Cairo, city of art and commerce. Translated by Seymour Feiler. [1st ed.] Norman, University of Oklahoma Press [1964] xiii, 170 p. map. 19 cm. (Centers of civilization series.) 1. Cairo (Egypt) — History. 2. Cairo (Egypt) — Social life and customs. I. T. II. Series.
DT146.W513   916.216   *LC* 64-20764

DT154.1–159 Sudan. Anglo–Egyptian Sudan

(see also: DT108)

Evans-Pritchard, E. E. (Edward Evan), 1902-1973. 3.5183
Witchcraft, oracles, and magic among the Azande / E. E. Evans–Pritchard. — Abridged with an introd. by Eva Gillies. — Oxford: Clarendon Press, 1976. xxxiii, 265 p.; 22 cm. Includes index. 1. Zande (African people) 2. Witchcraft — Africa, Central. 3. Magic — Africa, Central. I. Gillies, Eva. II. T.
DT155.2.A93 E92 1976   133.4/0967   *LC* 76-375196   *ISBN* 0198740298

Wai, Dunstan M. 3.5184
The African–Arab conflict in the Sudan / Dunstan M. Wai. — New York: Africana Pub. Co., 1981. xxvi, 234 p: map; 24 cm. Includes index. 1. Sudan — History — Civil War, 1955-1972 I. T.
DT157.67.W34 1981   962.4/04   *LC* 80-15410   *ISBN* 0841906319

Adams, William Yewdale, 1927-. 3.5185
Nubia: corridor to Africa / William Y. Adams. — Princeton, N.J.: Princeton University Press, c1977. xxiv, 797 p., [12] leaves of plates: ill.; 25 cm. 1. Nubia — History. I. T.
DT159.6.N83 A32   962.4   *LC* 76-9394   *ISBN* 0691093709

Nubian ceremonial life: studies in Islamic syncretism and cultural change / edited by John G. Kennedy. 3.5186
Berkeley: University of California Press, 1981 (c1978). xxix, 257 p., [9] leaves of plates: ill.; 24 cm. Includes index. 1. Nubians — Egypt — Religion. 2. Islam — Egypt — Nubia. I. Kennedy, John G.
DT159.6.N83 N82   301.29/62/3   *LC* 74-77726   *ISBN* 0520027485

DT160–346 NORTH AFRICA

Charles-Picard, Gilbert. • 3.5187
The life and death of Carthage; a survey of Punic history and culture from its birth to the final tragedy, by Gilbert Charles Picard and Colette Picard. Translated from the French by Dominique Collon. New York, Taplinger Pub. Co. [1969, c1968] vi, 362 p. illus., maps. 24 cm. 1. Carthage (Ancient city) — History. I. Charles-Picard, Colette. joint author. II. T.
DT168.C4823 1969   939/.73   *LC* 69-12303

Ronart, Stephan. • 3.5188
Concise encyclopaedia of Arabic civilization: the Arab West [by] Stephan and Nandy Ronart. New York, Praeger [1966] vii, 410 p. maps. 22 cm. A revised German translation of this work and its companion volume, Concise encyclopaedia of Arabic civilization; the Arab East, published in 1972 with title: Lexikon der arabischen Welt. 1. Muslims — Spain — History — 711-1492 — Dictionaries. 2. Africa, North — Dictionaries and encyclopedias. I. Ronart, Nandy, joint author. II. T.
DT173.R6   910.03174927   *LC* 66-13401

Political elites in Arab North Africa: Morocco, Algeria, Tunisia, Libya, and Egypt / I. William Zartman ... [et al.]. 3.5189
New York: Longman, c1982. xii, 273 p.; 24 cm. 1. Elite (Social sciences) — Africa, North. 2. Africa, North — Politics and government. I. Zartman, I. William.
DT176.P6   306/.2/096 19   *LC* 81-145   *ISBN* 0582282519

Contemporary North Africa: issues of development and integration / Halim Barakat, editor. 3.5190
Washington, D.C.: Center for Contemporary Arab Studies, 1985. 271 p.; 22 cm. 1. Africa, North — Congresses. I. Barakat, Halim Isber. II. Georgetown University. Center for Contemporary Arab Studies.
DT181.5.C66 1985   961 19   *LC* 84-23312   *ISBN* 0932568114

Amin, Samir.   **3.5191**
The Maghreb in the modern world: Algeria, Tunisia, Morocco; translated [from the French] by Michael Perl. — Harmondsworth: Penguin, 1970. 256 p.: maps.; 18 cm. — (Penguin African library, AP 29) 1. Africa, North I. T.
DT185.A6313   309.1/61   *LC* 71-25840   *ISBN* 0140410295

Gellner, Ernest.   **3.5192**
Saints of the Atlas / Ernest Gellner. — Chicago: University of Chicago Press, 1969. xxiii, 317 p., [6] leaves of plates: ill. — (The nature of human society series) 1. Berbers I. T.
DT193 G44 1969b   *LC* 78-89515   *ISBN* 0226286991

Abun-Nasr, Jamil M.   **3.5193**
A history of the Maghrib / Jamil M. Abun-Nasr. — 2d ed. — Cambridge [Eng.]; New York: Cambridge University Press, 1975. ix, 422 p.: ill.; 23 cm. Includes index. 1. Africa, North — History I. T.
DT194.A23 1975   960   *LC* 74-25653   *ISBN* 0521207037

Julien, Charles André, 1891-.   **• 3.5194**
[Histoire de l'Afrique du Nord. 2 De la conquête arabe à 1830. English] History of North Africa: Tunisia, Algeria, Morocco. From the Arab Conquest to 1830, edited and rev. by R. Le Tourneau. Translated by John Petrie. Edited by C. C. Stewart. New York, Praeger [1970] xvi, 446 p. illus., maps. 23 cm. Translation of v. 2 of Histoire de l'Afrique du Nord: De la conquête arabe à 1830. 1. Africa, North — History I. T.
DT194.J82213   961   *LC* 79-104771

Hess, Andrew C.   **3.5195**
The forgotten frontier: a history of the sixteenth century Ibero–African frontier / Andrew C. Hess. — Chicago: University of Chicago Press, 1978. xiv, 278 p.: ill.; 23 cm. (Publications of the Center for Middle Eastern Studies. no. 10) Includes index. 1. Africa, North — Relations — Spain 2. Spain — Relations — North Africa. 3. Africa, North — History — 1517-1882 4. Spain — History — House of Austria, 1516-1700 5. Western Mediterranean — History. I. T. II. Series.
DT197.5.S7 H47   961 19   *LC* 77-25517   *ISBN* 0226330281

Fisher, Godfrey (Sir) 1885-.   **• 3.5196**
Barbary legend; war, trade and piracy in North Africa, 1415–1830. Oxford Clarendon Press 1957. 349p. 1. Barbary States — History — 1516-1830 2. Algeria — History — 1516-1830 3. Pirates I. T.
DT201 F5

Fāsī, 'Allāl, 1910-1974.   **• 3.5197**
[Harakāt al-istiqlālīyah fī al-Maghrib al-'Arabī. English] The independence movements in Arab North Africa [by] Alāl al-Fāsī. Translated from the Arabic by Hazem Zaki Nuseibeh. New York, Octagon Books, 1970 [c1954] xi, 414 p. 22 cm. (American Council of Learned Societies. Near Eastern Translation Program. [Publication] no. 8) Translation of al-Harakāt al-istiqlālīyah fī al-Maghrib al-'Arabī. 1. National liberation movements — Africa, North. 2. Morocco — Politics and government. 3. Africa, North — Politics and government. I. T.
DT204.F323 1970   320.1/59/61   *LC* 70-96201

Parker, Richard Bordeaux, 1923-.   **3.5198**
North Africa: regional tensions and strategic concerns / by Richard B. Parker. — New York: Praeger, 1984. xi, 194 p.: maps; 25 cm. 'Council on Foreign Relations books'—P. ii. Includes index. 1. Africa, North — Politics and government. 2. Africa, North — Strategic aspects. I. T.
DT204.P34 1984   961 19   *LC* 84-8298   *ISBN* 0030718465

DT211–239 Libya

American University (Washington, D.C.). Foreign Area Studies.   **3.5199**
Libya, a country study / Foreign Area Studies, the American University; edited by Harold D. Nelson. — 3d ed. — Washington: The University: for sale by the Supt. of Docs., U.S. Govt. Print. Off., 1979. xxviii, 350 p.: ill.; 24 cm. — (Area handbook series.) 'DA pam 550-85.' Second ed., by R. F. Nyrop and others, published in 1973 under title: Area handbook for Libya. Includes index. 1. Libya. I. Nelson, Harold D. II. Nyrop, Richard F. Area handbook for Libya. III. T. IV. Series.
DT215.A46 1979   961/.2   *LC* 79-24183

Segrè, Claudio G.   **3.5200**
Fourth shore: the Italian colonization of Libya / Claudio G. Segrè. — Chicago: University of Chicago Press, 1975 (c1974). xix, 237 p., [2] leaves of plates: ill.; 23 cm. (Studies in imperialism) Includes index. 1. Italians in Libya. 2. Libya — History. I. T.
DT235.S43   961/.203   *LC* 74-5734   *ISBN* 0226744744

Wright, John L.   **3.5201**
Libya, a modern history / John Wright. — Baltimore, Md.: Johns Hopkins University Press, 1982. 306 p.; 23 cm. Includes index. 1. Libya — Politics and government — 1969- I. T.
DT236.W74 1982   961/.2 19   *LC* 81-48183   *ISBN* 0801827671

Evans-Pritchard, E. E. (Edward Evan), 1902-1973.   **3.5202**
The Sanusi of Cyrenaica / by E. E. Evans–Pritchard. London; Toronto: Oxford University Press, 1949. v, 240 p., 5 leaves of plates: ill.; 23 cm. Includes index. 1. Bedouins in Cyrenaica — History. 2. Cyrenaica — History. I. T.
DT238.C8 E85

DT241–269 Tunisia

Tunisia: a country study / Foreign Area Studies, the American   **3.5203**
University; edited by Harold D. Nelson.
3rd ed. — Washington, D.C.: The Studies: For sale by the Supt. of Docs., U.S. G.P.O., 1986. p. cm. (Area handbook series.) (DA pam; 550-89) 'Research completed January 1986.' Includes index. 1. Tunisia. I. Nelson, Harold D. II. American University (Washington, D.C.). Foreign Area Studies. III. Series.
DT245.T7955 1986   961/.1 19   *LC* 86-3351

DT271–299 Algeria

Algeria, a country study / Foreign Area Studies, the American   **3.5204**
University; edited by Harold D. Nelson.
4th ed. — Washington, D.C.: For sale by the Supt. of Docs., U.S. G.P.O., 1985. p. cm. (Area handbook series.) (DA Pam; 550-44) 'Research completed July 1985.' Includes index. 1. Algeria. I. Nelson, Harold D. II. American University (Washington, D.C.). Foreign Area Studies. III. Series.
DT275.A5772   965/.05 19   *LC* 86-3583

Keenan, Jeremy, 1945-.   **3.5205**
The Tuareg: people of Ahaggar / Jeremy Keenan. — New York: St. Martin's Press, 1978 (c1977). xi, 385 p., [9] leaves of plates: ill.; 24 cm. Includes indexes. 1. Tuaregs — Algeria — Ahaggar Mountains. 2. Ahaggar Mountains (Algeria) — Social life and customs. I. T.
DT283.6.T83 K43 1977b   301.29/65/7   *LC* 77-77139   *ISBN* 0312822006

Wolf, John Baptist, 1907-.   **3.5206**
The Barbary Coast: Algiers under the Turks, 1500 to 1830 / John B. Wolf. — 1st ed. — New York: Norton, c1979. xii, 364 p.: ill.; 22 cm. Includes index. 1. Algeria — History — 1516-1830 I. T.
DT291.W64 1979   965/.02 19   *LC* 79-11044   *ISBN* 0393012050

Horne, Alistair.   **3.5207**
A savage war of peace: Algeria, 1954–1962 / Alistair Horne. — New York: Viking Press, 1978, c1977. 604 p., [8] leaves of plates: ill.; 24 cm. Includes index. 1. Algeria — History — Revolution, 1954-1962 I. T.
DT295.H64 1978   965/.04   *LC* 77-21518   *ISBN* 0670619647

Talbott, John E.   **3.5208**
The war without a name: France in Algeria, 1954–1962 / John Talbott. — 1st ed. — New York: Knopf: distributed by Random House, 1980. xii, 305 p.; 22 cm. Includes index. 1. Algeria — History — Revolution, 1954-1962 2. France — Politics and government — 1945- I. T.
DT295.T25 1980   965/.04   *LC* 80-344   *ISBN* 0394509099

DT301–330 Morocco

Morocco, a country study / Foreign Area Studies, the American   **3.5209**
University; edited by Harold D. Nelson.
5th ed. — Washington, D.C.: The University: For sale by the Supt. of Docs., U.S. G.P.O., 1985. p. cm. (DA pam. 550-49) (Area handbook series.) 'Research completed February 1985.' Includes index. 1. Morocco. I. Nelson, Harold D. II. American University (Washington, D.C.). Foreign Area Studies. III. Series. IV. Series: Area handbook series.
DT305.M64 1985   964 19   *LC* 85-600265

Arabs and Berbers: from tribe to nation in North Africa /   **3.5210**
edited by Ernest Gellner and Charles Micaud.
Lexington, Mass.: D. C. Heath, 1972. 448 p.: ill., maps; 24 cm. — 1. Berbers — Addresses, essays, lectures. 2. Morocco — Politics and government — Addresses, essays, lectures. 3. Algeria — Politics and government — Addresses, essays, lectures. I. Gellner, Ernest. ed. II. Micaud, Charles Antoine, 1910- ed.
DT313.2.A7 1972   *LC* 79-151780   *ISBN* 0669838659

Montagne, Robert, 1893-1954.   **3.5211**
[Vie sociale et la vie politique des Berberes. English] The Berbers; their social and political organisation; translated [from the French] and with an introduction by David Seddon; with a preface by Ernest Gellner. London, Cass, 1973. xliv, 93 p. maps. 23 cm. Translation of La vie sociale et la vie politique des Berbères, 1931. 1. Berbers I. T.
DT313.2.M6613 1973   309.1/64   *LC* 72-92972   *ISBN* 0714629685

Ling, Dwight L.   **3.5212**
Morocco and Tunisia, a comparative history / Dwight L. Ling. — Washington: University Press of America, c1979. iii, 204 p.: ill.; 21 cm. Includes index. 1. Morocco — History 2. Tunisia — History I. T.
DT315.L47   961   *LC* 79-5364   *ISBN* 0819108731

Hoisington, William A., 1941-.   **3.5213**
The Casablanca connection: French colonial policy, 1936–1943 / William A. Hoisington, Jr. — Chapel Hill: University of North Carolina Press, c1984. xiv, 320 p.: ill.; 24 cm. Includes index. 1. Morocco — History — 20th century I. T.
DT324.H54 1984   964/.04 19   *LC* 83-5902   *ISBN* 0807815748

Miller, James Andrew.   **3.5214**
Imlil, a Moroccan mountain community in change / James A. Miller. — Boulder, Colo.: Westview Press, 1984. xxvii, 285 p.: ill.; 23 cm. (A Westview replica edition) Includes index. 1. Berbers — Morocco — Imlil. 2. Imlil (Morocco) — Social life and customs. I. T.
DT329.I56 M54 1984   306/.0964/4 19   *LC* 83-14742   *ISBN* 0865319804

Fernea, Elizabeth Warnock.   **3.5215**
A street in Marrakech / Elizabeth Warnock Fernea. — 1st ed. — Garden City, N.Y.: Doubleday, 1975. 382 p.: map; 22 cm. 1. Fernea, Elizabeth Warnock. 2. Marrakech (Morocco) — Description. I. T.
DT329.M3 F47   916.4/6   *LC* 74-12686   *ISBN* 0385000960

Rosen, Lawrence, 1941-.   **3.5216**
Bargaining for reality: the construction of social relations in a Muslim community / Lawrence Rosen. — Chicago: University of Chicago Press, c1984. xii, 210 p.; 24 cm. Includes index. 1. Sefrou (Morocco) — Social life and customs. I. T.
DT329.S44 R67 1984   306/.0964/3 19   *LC* 84-2501   *ISBN* 0226726096

DT331–346 Sahara

Gautier, Émile Felix, 1864-.   • **3.5217**
Sahara, the great desert. New York, Columbia university press, 1935. xvii, 264 p. fron., illus., plates, maps (1 fold.) 25 cm. 1. Sahara I. Mayhew, Dorothy Ford, tr. II. T.
DT333.G32   *LC* 35-17669

Damis, John James.   **3.5218**
Conflict in northwest Africa: the western Sahara dispute / John Damis. — Stanford, Calif.: Hoover Institution Press, c1983. xvii, 196 p.: ill.; 24 cm. — (Hoover international studies.) (Hoover Press publication; 278) Includes index. 1. Western Sahara — Politics and government I. T. II. Series.
DT346.S7 D44 1983   964/.8 19   *LC* 82-21168   *ISBN* 0817977813

Clarke, Thurston.   **3.5219**
The last caravan / Thurston Clarke. — New York: Putnam, c1978. 286 p., [8] leaves of plates: ill.; 22 cm. Includes index. 1. Tuaregs 2. Sahara — Social conditions. I. T.
DT346.T7 C55 1978   966/.004/933   *LC* 77-9533   *ISBN* 0399119000

DT351–364 CENTRAL AFRICA. SUB-SAHARAN AFRICA

Africa South of the Sahara 1972.   **3.5220**
1971-. London: Europa Publications Ltd., 1972. 1050 p.: ill., map. Annual. 1. Africa, Sub-Saharan I. Europa Publications Limited. II. Who's who in Africa South of the Sahara.
DT351.A37   916.7   *LC* 78-112271

Stanley, Henry M. (Henry Morton), 1841-1904.   • **3.5221**
The exploration diaries of H. M. Stanley, now first published from the original manuscripts. Edited by Richard Stanley and Alan Neame. — New York, Vanguard Press [c1961] 208 p. illus., ports., maps. 25 cm. I. T.
DT351.S73 1961a   916.7   *LC* 62-11208

Hall, Richard Seymour, 1925-.   **3.5222**
Stanley: an adventurer explored / Richard Hall. — 1st American ed. — Boston: Houghton Mifflin, 1975, c1974. 400 p.: ill.; 24 cm. Includes indexes. 1. Stanley, Henry M. (Henry Morton), 1844-1904. I. T.
DT351.S9 H27 1975   916.7/04/0924 B   *LC* 74-30393   *ISBN* 0395194261

Vansina, Jan.   • **3.5223**
Kingdoms of the savanna. — Madison: University of Wisconsin Press, 1966. ix, 364 p.: maps (part fold.); 22 cm. 1. Africa, Central — History — To 1884 I. T.
DT351.V36   967   *LC* 65-16367

Balandier, Georges.   • **3.5224**
[Afrique ambiguë. English] Ambiguous Africa; cultures in collision. Translated from the French by Helen Weaver. New York, Pantheon Books [1966] ix, 276 p. illus., maps, plans. 22 cm. 1. Africa, Sub-Saharan — Civilization I. T.
DT352.B313 1966a   916.033   *LC* 65-10211

Contemporary Africa: geography and change / edited by C.   **3.5225**
Gregory Knight, James L. Newman.
Englewood Cliffs, N.J.: Prentice-Hall, c1976. xiv, 546 p.: ill.; 24 cm. Includes indexes. 1. Urbanization — Africa, Sub-Saharan — Addresses, essays, lectures. 2. Africa, Sub-Saharan — Description and travel — Addresses, essays, lectures. 3. Africa, Sub-Saharan — Economic conditions — Addresses, essays, lectures. 4. Africa, Sub-Saharan — Rural conditions — Addresses, essays, lectures. I. Knight, C. Gregory. II. Newman, James L.
DT352.C595   916.7   *LC* 76-4902   *ISBN* 0131700359

Davidson, Basil, 1914-.   • **3.5226**
Black mother; the years of the African slave trade. — [1st American ed.]. — Boston: Little, Brown, [1961] 311 p.: illus.; 22 cm. 1. Slave-trade — Africa, West — History. 2. Slave-trade — Africa, Eastern — History. 3. Africa, West — History — To 1884 4. Africa, Eastern — History I. T.
DT352.D33 1961a   967   *LC* 61-13894

Kimble, George Herbert Tinley, 1908-.   • **3.5227**
Tropical Africa / by George H. T. Kimble. — New York: Twentieth Century Fund, 1960. 2 v.: ill., port., maps (1 fold. col.); 25 cm. 1. Africa, Sub-Saharan I. T.
DT352.K48   *LC* 60-15160

Davidson, Basil, 1914-.   • **3.5228**
The lost cities of Africa. — Rev. ed. — Boston: Little, Brown, [1970] xxiii, 366 p.: illus., maps.; 22 cm. 1. Africa, Sub-Saharan — Civilization — History. I. T.
DT352.4.D3 1970   916/.03   *LC* 70-126061

Hull, Richard W., 1940-.   **3.5229**
Munyakare: African civilization before the batuuree [by] Richard W. Hull. New York, J. Wiley [1972] x, 232 p. maps. 23 cm. 1. Africa, Sub-Saharan — Civilization I. T.
DT352.4.H85   916.7/03   *LC* 72-37850   *ISBN* 0471420654

Stevenson, Robert F.   • **3.5230**
Population and political systems in tropical Africa [by] Robert F. Stevenson. — New York: Columbia University Press, 1968. xii, 306 p.: maps.; 24 cm. 1. Fortes, Meyer, ed. African political systems. 2. Ethnology — Africa, Sub-Saharan. 3. Africa, Sub-Saharan — Population. I. T.
DT352.42.S72   320.1/55/0967   *LC* 68-11435

African kingships in perspective: political change and   **3.5231**
modernization in monarchical settings / edited by Rene Lemarchand.
London: Cass, 1977. xiv, 325 p.; 24 cm. — (Cass library of African studies: General studies; no. 155) Includes index. 1. Africa, Sub-Saharan — Politics

and government — Addresses, essays, lectures. 2. Africa, Sub-Saharan — Kings and rulers — Addresses, essays, lectures. 3. Africa, Sub-Saharan — Social conditions — Addresses, essays, lectures. I. Lemarchand, René. II. Series.
DT352.5.A35 1977   301.5/92/0967   LC 73-84017   ISBN 0714630276

History of Central Africa / edited by David Birmingham and   3.5232
Phyllis M. Martin.
London; New York: Longman, 1983. 2 v.: maps; 24 cm. Includes indexes. 1. Africa, Central — History I. Birmingham, David. II. Martin, Phyllis.
DT352.5.H58 1983   967 19   LC 83-745   ISBN 0582646731

Lipschutz, Mark R.   3.5233
Dictionary of African historical biography / Mark R. Lipschutz & R. Kent Rasmussen. — 2nd ed., expanded and updated. — Berkeley: University of California Press, c1986. xiii, 328 p.; 25 cm. Includes indexes. 1. Africa, Sub-Saharan — Biography. 2. Africa, Sub-Saharan — History I. Rasmussen, R. Kent. II. T.
DT352.6.L56 1987   967/.009/92 19   LC 86-19157   ISBN 0520051793

Rotberg, Robert I.   • 3.5234
Protest and power in black Africa. Edited by Robert I. Rothberg and Ali A. Mazrui. New York, Oxford University Press, 1970. xxx, 1274 p. maps. 24 cm. 1. Nationalism — Africa, Sub-Saharan — Addresses, essays, lectures. 2. Africa, Sub-Saharan — History — Addresses, essays, lectures. I. Mazrui, Ali Al'Amin. joint author. II. T.
DT353.R6   967   LC 76-83051

Boahen, A. Adu.   • 3.5235
Britain, the Sahara, and the western Sudan, 1788–1861, by A. Adu Boahen. — Oxford, Clarendon Press, 1964. ix, 268 p. maps (part fold.) 23 cm. — (Oxford studies in African affairs.) Based on thesis, University of London, 1959. Bibliography: p. [253]-257. 1. Sahara — Hist. 2. British in the Sahara. 3. British in West Africa. I. T. II. Series.
DT356.B57   327.420661   LC 64-54602

Smith, Iain R.   3.5236
The Emin Pasha Relief Expedition, 1886–1890, by Iain R. Smith. Oxford, Clarendon Press, 1972. xx, 335 p., 6 leaves. illus., maps, ports. 23 cm. (Oxford studies in African affairs.) 1. Emin Pasha, 1840-1892. 2. Emin Pasha Relief Expedition (1887-1889) I. T. II. Series.
DT363.S64   962.4/03   LC 73-150747   ISBN 0198216793

DT365–469 EAST AFRICA

Freeman-Grenville, G. S. P. (Greville Stewart Parker) comp.   3.5237
The East African coast: select documents from the first to the earlier nineteenth century / [edited by] G. S. P. Freeman-Grenville. — 2nd ed. — London: Collings, 1975. [15], 314 p., fold. plate: maps; 23 cm. 1. Africa, Eastern — History — Sources. I. T.
DT365.A3 F73 1975   967   LC 76-365649   ISBN 0901720852

Ranger, T. O. (Terence O.)   3.5238
Dance and society in Eastern Africa, 1890–1970: the Beni ngoma / T. O. Ranger. — Berkeley: University of California Press, 1975. xiii, 176 p.: maps; 23 cm. 1. Beni (Dance) 2. Ethnology — Africa, Eastern. 3. Africa, Eastern — Social life and customs. I. T.
DT365.4.R36   967   LC 74-76389   ISBN 0520027299

DT371–398 Ethiopia

Ethiopia, a country study / Foreign Area Studies, the American   3.5239
University.
3rd ed. / edited by Harold D. Nelson and Irving Kaplan. — Washington, D.C.: For sale by the Supt. of Docs., U.S. G.P.O., 1981. xxix, 366 p.; 24 cm. — (DA pam. 550-28) Revision of: Area handbook for Ethiopia / Irving Kaplan, et al. 1971. 'Research completed August 1980.' Includes index. 1. Ethiopia. I. Nelson, Harold D. II. Kaplan, Irving, 1923- III. Kaplan, Irving, 1923- Area handbook for Ethiopia. IV. American University (Washington, D.C.). Foreign Area Studies. V. Series.
DT378.E73 1981   963/.06 19   LC 81-7928

Ullendorff, Edward.   • 3.5240
The Ethiopians; an introduction to country and people. — 3d ed. — London; New York: Oxford University Press, 1973. xiv, 239 p.: illus.; 21 cm. 1. Ethiopia — Civilization. I. T.
DT379.5.U4 1973   916.3/03/6   LC 73-174844   ISBN 019285061X

Budge, Sir Ernest Alfred Wallis, 1857-1934.   3.5241
A history of Ethiopia, Nubia [and] Abyssinia (according to the hieroglyphic inscriptions of Egypt and Nubia, and the Ethiopian chronicles) London, Methuen [1928] 2 vol. illus., pl., port., map, plan, facs. Paged continuously. 1. Ethiopia — Antiquities 2. Ethiopia — History 3. Ethiopia — History and antiquities I. T.
DT381. B8

Jones, A. H. M. (Arnold Hugh Martin), 1904-1970.   • 3.5242
A history of Ethiopia, by A. H. M. Jones and Elizabeth Monroe. — Oxford, Clarendon Press [1955] 196 p. illus. 19 cm. First published in 1935 under title: A history of Abyssinia. 1. Ethiopia — Hist. 2. Ethiopia — Religion. I. Monroe, Elizabeth. joint author. II. T.
DT381.J6 1955   963   LC 55-13861

Pankhurst, E. Sylvia (Estelle Sylvia), 1882-1960.   • 3.5243
Ethiopia, a cultural history. Witha foreword by Canon John A. Douglas. — Essex [Eng.] Lalibela House [1955] xxxviii, 747 p. illus. (part col.) ports., facsims., music, plans. 23 cm. 1. Ethiopia — Hist. I. T.
DT381.P35   963   LC 56-22371

Zewde Gabre-Sellassie.   3.5244
Yohannes IV of Ethiopia: a political biography / by Zewde Gabre-Sellassie. — Oxford, 1975. xiii, 334 p.: ill.; 22 cm. (Oxford studies in African affairs.) Includes index. 1. John IV, King of Ethiopia, 1839-1889. 2. Ethiopia — History — 1490-1889 3. Ethiopia — Foreign relations — To 1889 I. T. II. Series.
DT386.7.Z48   963/.04/0924   LC 76-359007   ISBN 0198216955

Marcus, Harold G.   3.5245
The life and times of Menelik II: Ethiopia 1844–1913 / by Harold G. Marcus. — Oxford: Clarendon Press, 1975. viii, 298 p.: 2 maps; 23 cm. — (Oxford studies in African affairs.) Includes index. 1. Menelik II, Negus of Ethiopia, 1844-1913. 2. Ethiopia — History — 1889-1974 I. T. II. Series.
DT387.M37   963/.04/0924 B   LC 75-308576   ISBN 0198216742

Gilkes, Patrick.   3.5246
The dying Lion: feudalism and modernization in Ethiopia / Patrick Gilkes. — New York: St. Martin's Press, 1975. xix, 307 p.: ill.; 23 cm. Includes indexes. 1. Land tenure — Ethiopia. 2. Ethiopia — Politics and government 3. Ethiopia — Economic conditions I. T.
DT387.7.G48 1975b   963/.06   LC 75-9388

Haile Selassie I, Emperor of Ethiopia, 1892-1975.   3.5247
My life and Ethiopia's progress, 1892–1937: the autobiography of Emperor Haile Sellassie I / translated and annotated by Edward Ullendorff. — Oxford [Eng.]: Oxford University Press, 1976. xxxii, 335 p., [5] leaves of plates: ill.; 23 cm. Spine title: The autobiography of Emperor Haile Sellassie I, 1832-1937. Translation of Heyewaténã Ya'Ityoṗyā 'ermejã. Includes index. 1. Haile Selassie I, Emperor of Ethiopia, 1892-1975. 2. Ethiopia — History — 1889-1974 I. Ullendorff, Edward. II. T. III. Title: The autobiography of Emperor Haile Sellassie I.
DT387.7.H2513 1976   963/.05/0924 B   LC 76-366562   ISBN 0197135897

Spencer, John H. (John Hathaway), 1907-.   3.5248
Ethiopia at bay: a personal account of the Haile Sellassie years / John H. Spencer. — Algonac, Mich.: Reference Publications, 1984. xiv, 397 p.: ill.; 24 cm. Includes index. 1. Spencer, John H. (John Hathaway), 1907- 2. Italo-Ethiopian War, 1935-1936 3. Diplomats — Ethiopia — Biography. 4. Diplomats — United States — Biography. 5. Ethiopia — History — 1889-1974 I. T.
DT387.7.S66 1984   963/.06 19   LC 83-43050   ISBN 0917256255

Baer, George W.   3.5249
Test case: Italy, Ethiopia, and the League of Nations / George W. Baer. — Stanford, Calif.: Hoover Institution Press, 1977 (c1976). xiv, 367 p.: map; 24 cm. (Hoover Institution publication; 159) Includes index. 1. League of Nations. 2. Italo-Ethiopian War, 1935-1936 — Influence. 3. World politics — 1933-1945 4. Italy — Politics and government — 1922-1945 I. T.
DT387.8.B335   963/.056   LC 76-20293   ISBN 0817965912

Marcus, Harold G.   3.5250
Ethiopia, Great Britain, and the United States, 1941–1974: the politics of empire / Harold G. Marcus. — Berkeley: University of California Press, c1983. xii, 205 p.: maps; 23 cm. Includes index. 1. Ethiopia — Politics and government — 1889-1974 2. Ethiopia — Foreign relations — 1889-1974 3. Ethiopia — Relations — United States. 4. United States — Relations —

Ethiopia. 5. Ethiopia — Relations — Great Britain. 6. Great Britain — Relations — Ethiopia. 7. Ethiopia — History — Coup d'état, 1960 I. T.
DT387.9.M37 1983   327.63 19   *LC* 82-8522   *ISBN* 0520046137

Halliday, Fred.   **3.5251**
The Ethiopian revolution / Fred Halliday, Maxine Molyneux. — London: NLB, 1981. 304 p.: maps; 22 cm. Includes index. 1. Ethiopia — History — Revolution, 1974 — Influence. 2. Ethiopia — Politics and government — 1974- I. Molyneux, Maxine. II. T.
DT387.95.H34 1981   963/.06 19   *LC* 81-193631   *ISBN* 0860910431

Lefort, René.   **3.5252**
[Éthiopie, la révolution hérétique. English] Ethiopia, an heretical revolution? / Rene Lefort; translated by A.M. Berrett. — London: Zed Press; Totowa, N.J., U.S.A.: U.S. distributor, Biblio Distribution Center, 1983. xii, 301 p.; 23 cm. — (Third World studies.) Translation of: Éthiopie, la révolution hérétique. Includes index. 1. Ethiopia — History — Revolution, 1974 2. Ethiopia — Politics and government — 1974- I. T. II. Series.
DT387.95.L4313 1983   963/.06 19   *LC* 84-149769   *ISBN* 0862321530

Schwab, Peter, 1940-.   **3.5253**
Ethiopia, politics, economics, and society / Peter Schwab. — Boulder, Colo.: Lynne Rienner Publishers, 1985. xx, 134 p.: ill., maps; 23 cm. (Marxist regimes series.) Includes index. 1. Ethiopia — Politics and government — 1974- 2. Ethiopia — Economic conditions — 1974- 3. Ethiopia — Social conditions — 1974- 4. Ethiopia — History — Revolution, 1974 — Causes. I. T. II. Series.
DT387.95.S39 1985   963/.07 19   *LC* 84-62184   *ISBN* 093147700X

Erlikh, Hagai.   **3.5254**
The struggle over Eritrea, 1962–1978: war and revolution in the Horn of Africa / Haggai Erlich. — Stanford, Calif.: Hoover Institution Press, c1983. xiv, 155 p.: map; 23 cm. (Hoover international studies.) Includes index. 1. National liberation movements — Ethiopia — Eritrea. 2. Eritrea (Ethiopia) — History — Revolution, 1962- 3. Ethiopia — Politics and government — 1889-1974 4. Ethiopia — Politics and government — 1974- I. T. II. Series.
DT397.E75 1983   963/.06 19   *LC* 81-81169   *ISBN* 0817976027

DT401–420 Somalia

Somalia, a country study / Foreign Area Studies, The American   **3.5255**
University; edited by Harold D. Nelson.
3rd ed. — Washington, D.C.: For sale by the Supt. of Docs., U.S. G.P.O., 1982. xxvii, 346 p.: ill.; 24 cm. — (Area handbook series.) (DA pam. 550-86) 'Research completed October 1981.' 'Supersedes 1977 edition'—T.p. verso. Includes index. 1. Somalia. I. Nelson, Harold D. II. American University (Washington, D.C.). Foreign Area Studies. III. Series. IV. Series: DA pam. 550-86
DT401.5.S68 1982   967/.73 19   *LC* 82-16401

Cassanelli, Lee V., 1946-.   **3.5256**
The shaping of Somali society: reconstructing the history of a pastoral people, 1600–1900 / Lee V. Cassanelli. — Philadelphia: University of Pennsylvania Press, 1982. xvi, 311 p.: ill.; 24 cm. — (Ethnohistory) Includes index. 1. Somalis — History. I. T.
DT402.3.C37 1982   967/.7301 19   *LC* 81-43520   *ISBN* 0812278321

Lewis, I. M.   **3.5257**
A modern history of Somalia: nation and state in the horn of Africa / I. M. Lewis. — [Rev. ed.]. — London; New York: Longman, 1981 (c1979). ix, 279 p.: maps. 1. Somalia — History I. T. II. Title: The modern history of Somaliland.
DT403.L395 1981   967/.73   *LC* 79-40569   *ISBN* 058264657X

DT421–433 East Africa (General)

Morgan, W. T. W. (William Thomas Wilson), 1927-.   **3.5258**
East Africa [by] W. T. W. Morgan. [London] Longman 1974 (c1973) xx, 410 p. illus. 24 cm. (Geographies for advanced study) Label mounted on t.p.: Distributed in the U.S.A. by Longman, New York. 1. Africa, East — Description and travel — 1951- I. T.
DT426.M6   916.7/02   *LC* 74-161775   *ISBN* 0582484650

Mangat, J. S.   • **3.5259**
A history of the Asians in East Africa, c.1886 to 1945, by J. S. Mangat. — Oxford: Clarendon P., 1969. xviii, 216 p.: 2 maps.; 23 cm. — (Oxford studies in African affairs.) 1. East Indians in East Africa. I. T. II. Series.
DT429.M3   967.6/09/74914   *LC* 70-390011   *ISBN* 0198216475

History of East Africa, edited by Roland Oliver and [others].   • **3.5260**
Oxford: Clarendon Press, 1963-1976. 3 v.: maps.; 22 cm. Errata slip mounted on p. 178 of v. 1. 1. Africa, East — History I. Oliver, Roland Anthony. ed.
DT431.H53   967   *LC* 63-4375

Ogot, Bethwell A.   • **3.5261**
Zamani; a survey of East African history, edited by B. A. Ogot and J. A. Kieran. — [Nairobi]: EAPH, [1968] 407 p.: maps.; 22 cm. 'Published for the Historical Association of Kenya.' 1. Africa, East — History I. Kieran, J. A., joint author. II. Historical Association of Kenya. III. T.
DT431.O37   967.6   *LC* 78-385251

Nicholls, C. S. (Christine Stephanie)   **3.5262**
The Swahili coast; politics, diplomacy and trade on the East African littoral, 1798–1856, by C. S. Nicholls. New York, Africana Pub. Corp. 1972 (c1971) 419 p. illus. 23 cm. 1. Sa'īd bin Sultān, Sultan of Zanzibar, 1791-1856. 2. Africa, East — History — To 1886 3. Africa, East — Commerce. 4. Oman — History I. T.
DT432.N5   967   *LC* 78-180670   *ISBN* 084190099X

Lamphear, John.   **3.5263**
The traditional history of the Jie of Uganda / by John Lamphear. Oxford [Eng.]: Clarendon Press, 1976. x, 281 p.: ill.; 23 cm. (Oxford studies in African affairs.) Revision of the author's thesis—London, 1972. Includes index. 1. Jie (African people) — History. I. T. II. Series.
DT433.242.L35 1976   967.6/1   *LC* 76-367064   *ISBN* 0198216920

Kavuma, Paulo, 1901-.   **3.5264**
Crisis in Buganda, 1953–55: the story of the exile and return of the Kabaka, Mutesa II / by Paulo Kavuma. — London: Collings, 1980 (c1979). viii, 112 p., plate: port.; 23 cm. Includes index. 1. Mutesa II, King of Buganda. 2. Kavuma, Paulo, 1901- 3. Buganda — History. 4. Uganda — History — 1890-1962 I. T.
DT433.27.K38   967.6/103 19   *LC* 81-457671   *ISBN* 0860360989

Melady, Thomas Patrick.   • **3.5265**
Idi Amin Dada: Hitler in Africa / Thomas and Margaret Melady. — Kansas City: Sheed Andrews and McMeel, c1977. vii, 184 p.: ill.; 21 cm. 1. Amin, Idi, 1925- 2. Melady, Thomas Patrick. 3. Melady, Margaret Badum. 4. Uganda — Presidents — Biography. 5. Uganda — Politics and government — 1971-1979 I. Melady, Margaret Badum. joint author. II. T.
DT433.282.A55 M44   967.6/104/0924 B   *LC* 77-11706   *ISBN* 0836207831

Wright. Michael A.   **3.5266**
Buganda in the heroic age [by] Michael Wright. — Nairobi; New York: Oxford University Press, 1971 [i.e. 1972] xvi, 244 p.: illus.; 22 cm. 1. Buganda — History. I. T.
DT433.29.B8 W73 1972   320.9/676/1   *LC* 72-188711

Tosh, John.   **3.5267**
Clan leaders and colonial chiefs in Lango: the political history of an East African stateless society c. 1800–1939 / by John Tosh. — Oxford [Eng.]: Clarendon Press; New York: Oxford University Press, 1979 (c1978). xi, 293 p.: maps; 23 cm. — (Oxford studies in African affairs.) Includes index. 1. Lango (African tribe) — Politics and government. 2. Lango, Uganda — Politics and government. I. T. II. Series.
DT433.29.L36 T67   301.5/92/096761   *LC* 78-40243   *ISBN* 0198227116

DT433.5 Kenya

Kenya, a country study / Foreign Area Studies, the American   **3.5268**
University; edited by Harold D. Nelson.
3rd ed. — Washington, D.C.: Foreign Area Studies, American University: For sale by the Supt. of Docs., U.S. G.P.O., 1983. xxix, 334 p.: ill.; 24 cm. (Area handbook series.) (DA pam / Headquarters, Department of the Army; 550-56) 'Research completed June 1983.' Rev. ed. of: Area handbook for Kenya / coauthors, Irving Kaplan [with] Margarita K. Dobert ... [et al.]. 2nd ed. 1976. Includes index. 1. Kenya. I. Nelson, Harold D. II. Kaplan, Irving, 1923- Area handbook for Kenya. III. American University (Washington, D.C.). Foreign Area Studies. IV. Series.
DT433.522.K46   967.6/2 19   *LC* 84-6420

Dinesen, Isak, 1885-1962.   3.5269
Out of Africa / Isak Dinesen. — 2nd Modern Library ed. — New York: Modern Library, 1983, c1938. ix, 389 p.; 19 cm. 1. Dinesen, Isak, 1885-1962. 2. Country life — Kenya. 3. Kenya — Social life and customs — 1895-1963 I. T.
DT433.54.D56 1983   967.6/2 19   LC 83-42696   ISBN 0394604989

Frost, Richard Aylmer, 1905-.   3.5270
Race against time: human relations and politics in Kenya before Independence / [by] Richard Frost. — London: Collings [etc.], 1979 (c1978). xvii, 292 p., fold. plate: map; 22 cm. A revision of the author's thesis, Oxford, 1973. Includes index. 1. Kenya — Race relations. 2. Kenya — Politics and government — To 1963 I. T.
DT433.542.F77   305.8/009676/2   LC 80-450071   ISBN 0860360814

Karp, Ivan.   3.5271
Fields of change among the Iteso of Kenya / Ivan Karp. — London; Boston: Routledge and Kegan Paul, 1978. x, 186 p.: ill.; 22 cm. — (International library of anthropology.) Includes index. 1. Teso tribe — Politics and government. 2. Teso tribe — Social life and customs. 3. Kinship — Kenya. I. T. II. Series.
DT433.542.K37   301.29/676/27   LC 78-40170   ISBN 0710088639

Munro, J. Forbes.   3.5272
Colonial rule and the Kamba: social change in the Kenya highlands, 1889–1939 / by J. Forbes Munro. — Oxford [Eng.]: Clarendon Press, 1975. vi, 276 p., [1] leaf of plates: ill.; 23 cm. — (Oxford studies in African affairs.) Originally presented as the author's thesis, University of Wisconsin, 1968. Includes index. 1. Kamba (African people) 2. Kenya — Native races. 3. Machakos (Kenya) — Social conditions. I. T. II. Series.
DT433.542.M83 1975   301.24/1/0967626   LC 76-352691   ISBN 0198216998

Muriuki, Godfrey.   3.5273
A history of the Kikuyu, 1500–1900. — Nairobi: Oxford University Press, 1974. viii, 190 p.; 22 cm. 1. Kikuyu tribe — History. I. T.
DT433.542.M85   916.76/2/06963   LC 74-186971   ISBN 0195723147

Tignor, Robert L.   3.5274
The colonial transformation of Kenya: the Kamba, Kikuyu, and Maasai from 1900 to 1939 / Robert L. Tignor. — Princeton, N.J.: Princeton University Press, c1976. 372 p.; 25 cm. Includes index. 1. Kamba (African people) 2. Kikuyu tribe. 3. Masai (African people) 4. Kenya — Native races. I. T.
DT433.542.T53   967.6/203   LC 75-3479   ISBN 0691031037

Oboler, Regina Smith, 1947-.   3.5275
Women, power, and economic change: the Nandi of Kenya / Regina Smith Oboler. — Stanford, Calif.: Stanford University Press, 1985. xiv, 348 p.: ill.; 23 cm. Includes index. 1. Nandi (African people) — Economic conditions. 2. Sex role — Kenya. I. T.
DT433.545.N34 O26 1985   305.4/8893 19   LC 83-45345   ISBN 0804712247

Spear, Thomas George Percival.   3.5276
Kenya's past: an introduction to historical method in Africa / Thomas Spear. — Harlow, Essex [England]: Longman, 1981. xxiv, 155 p.: ill.; 24 cm. 1. Kenya — History. I. T.
DT433.565.S65   967/.6/201   ISBN 0582646960

Murray-Brown, Jeremy, 1932-.   3.5277
Kenyatta. — [1st ed.]. — New York: E. P. Dutton, 1973. 445 p.: ill.; 25 cm. 1. Kenyatta, Jomo. I. T.
DT433.576.K46 M87 1972   967.6/2/030924 B   LC 72-94703   ISBN 0525138552

Miller, Norman N., 1933-.   3.5278
Kenya: the quest for prosperity / Norman N. Miller. — Boulder, Colo.: Westview Press, 1984. x, 180 p.: ill., map; 23 cm. — (Profiles. Nations of contemporary Africa.) Includes index. 1. Kenya — Politics and government — 1963-1978 2. Kenya — Politics and government — 1978- 3. Kenya — Economic conditions — 1963- 4. Kenya — Social conditions — 1963- 5. Kenya — Foreign relations. I. T. II. Series.
DT433.58.M55 1984   967.6/2 19   LC 84-5164   ISBN 0865310963

Kiwanuka, M. S. M. Semakula.   3.5279
A history of Buganda from the foundation of the kingdom to 1900 [by] M. S. M. Semakula Kiwanuka. — New York: Africana Pub. Corp., [1972] xv, 322 p.: illus.; 23 cm. 1. Buganda — History. I. T.
DT434.B8 K49 1972   967.6/1   LC 75-180672   ISBN 0841901147

Kenyatta, Jomo.   • 3.5280
Facing Mount Kenya; the tribal life of Gikuyu, by Jomo Kenyatta, with an introduction by B. Malinowski. — London: Secker and Warburg, [1938] xxv,

[1], 339 p.: illus. (incl. map) VIII pl. (incl. front. (port.)); 23 cm. 'First published in 1938.' 'Glossary': p.319-329. 1. Kikuyu tribe. I. T.
DT434.E2 K45   572.96765   LC 39-3764

Kenyatta, Jomo.   • 3.5281
Harambee! The Prime Minister of Kenya's speeches 1963–1964, from the attainment of internal self–government to the threshold of the Kenya Republic. Foreword by Malcolm MacDonald. The text edited and arr. by Anthony Cullen on instructions of the Permanent Secretary, Prime Minister's Office. — Nairobi, New York, Oxford University Press, 1964 [i. e. 1965] xi, 114 p. illus., ports. 22 cm. 1. Kenya — Pol. & govt. — Addresses, essays, lectures. I. T. II. Title: The Prime Minister of Kenya's speeches, 1963-1964.
DT434.E26K4   354.6762035   LC 65-4596

Mboya, Tom.   • 3.5282
Freedom and after. — [1st ed.]. — Boston: Little, Brown, [1963] x, 288 p.: illus., ports., map (on lining papers); 22 cm. Autobiographical. 1. Mboya, Tom. 2. Pan-Africanism 3. Kenya. 4. Africa — Politics and government — 1960- I. T.
DT434.E27 M35   967.62   LC 63-20102

Rosberg, Carl Gustav.   • 3.5283
The myth of 'Mau Mau'; nationalism in Kenya, by Carl G. Rosberg, Jr. and John Nottingham. — Stanford, Calif.: Published for the Hoover Institution on War, Revolution, and Peace by Praeger, New York, [1966] xviii, 427 p.: illus., maps (2 fold, in pocket), ports.; 23 cm. — (Hoover Institution publications) Errata slip inserted. 1. Nationalism — Kenya. I. Nottingham, John Cato, 1928- joint author. II. T.
DT434.E27 R6   967.6203   LC 66-21793

DT434 Uganda

Beattie, John.   • 3.5284
Bunyoro, an African kingdom. — New York: Holt, [1960] ix, 86 p.: illus., port., map.; 24 cm. — (Case studies in cultural anthropology.) 1. Ethnology — Uganda 2. Bunyoro-Kitara. I. T. II. Series.
DT434.U2 B4   572.8963   LC 60-7331

Herrick, Allison Butler.   3.5285
Area handbook for Uganda. Co–authors: Allison Butler Herrick [and others] Washington, For sale by the Supt. of Docs., U.S. Govt. Print. Off., 1980. xvi, 456 p. maps 24 cm. 'DA pam no. 550-74.' 'One of a series of handbooks prepared by Foreign Area Studies (FAS) of the American University.' 1. Uganda. I. American University (Washington, D.C.). Foreign Area Studies. II. T.
DT434.U2 H4   916.76/1/03   LC 73-601330

Karugire, Samwiri Rubaraza.   3.5286
A history of the kingdom of Nkore in Western Uganda to 1896. — Oxford: Clarendon Press, 1972 (c1971). xii, 291 p.: maps.; 23 cm. — (Oxford studies in African affairs.) 1. Ankole — History. I. T. II. Series.
DT434.U29 A844   967.6/1   LC 72-177878   ISBN 019821670X

DT435–446 Tanzania

Gray, John Milner, Sir, 1889-.   • 3.5287
History of Zanzibar, from the Middle Ages to 1856. London: Oxford University Press, 1962. 314 p.: ill.; 23 cm. 1. Sa'īd bin Sultān, Sultan of Zanzibar, 1791-1856. 2. Zanzibar — History I. T.
DT435.G7   967.81   LC 62-52499

Middleton, John, 1921-.   • 3.5288
Zanzibar: its society and its politics / John Middleton & Jane Campbell. London; New York: Oxford University Press, 1965. 71 p.: maps; 19 cm. 'Issued under the auspices of the Institute of Race Relations, London.' 1. Zanzibar — Description and travel. 2. Zanzibar — Politics and government I. Campbell, Jane, 1934- II. Institute of Race Relations. III. T. IV. Title: Zanzibar, its society and its politics.
DT435.M5   309.16781   LC 65-21925

Bennett, Norman Robert, 1932-.   3.5289
A history of the Arab State of Zanzibar / [by] Norman R. Bennett. — London: Methuen; distributed by Harper & Row Publishers, 1978. viii, 304 p.; 19 cm. (Studies in African history; 16) Includes index. 1. Arabs — Zanzibar — History. 2. Zanzibar — History — To 1890 I. T.
DT435.5.B46   967.8/1   LC 78-326151   ISBN 0416550800

Clayton, Anthony, 1928-. 3.5290
The Zanzibar, revolution and its aftermath / by Anthony Clayton. — Hamden, Conn.: Archon Books, 1981. xvi, 166 p.: ill.; 23 cm. 1. Karume, Abeid Amani, 1905-1971. 2. Zanzibar — History — Revolution, 1964 3. Zanzibar — History I. T.
DT435.75.C58 1981   967.8/104 19   LC 81-3486   ISBN 0208019251

Martin, Esmond Bradley. 3.5291
Zanzibar: tradition and revolution / Esmond Bradley Martin. — London: Hamilton, 1979 (c1978). x, 149 p., [16] leaves of plates: ill.; 24 cm. Includes index. 1. Zanzibar — History 2. Zanzibar — Social conditions — 1964- 3. Zanzibar — Economic conditions — 1964- 4. Pemba — History. I. T.
DT435.8.M37   967.8/1/04   LC 78-321704   ISBN 0241899370

American University (Washington, D.C.). Foreign Area Studies. 3.5292
Tanzania, a country study / Foreign Area Studies, the American University; edited by Irving Kaplan. — 2d ed. — Washington: Foreign Area Studies, American University: for sale by the Supt. of Docs., U.S. Govt. Print. Off., 1978. xix, 344 p.: ill.; 24 cm. — (Area handbook series.) Supersedes the 1968 ed. by A. B. Herrick and others, published under title: Area handbook for Tanzania. 'DA pam 550-62.' Includes index. 1. Tanzania. I. Kaplan, Irving, 1923- II. Herrick, Allison Butler. Area handbook for Tanzania. III. T. IV. Series.
DT438.A46 1978   967.8/04   LC 78-10304

Yeager, Rodger. 3.5293
Tanzania, an African experiment / Rodger Yeager. — Boulder, Colo.: Westview Press; Hampshire, England: Gower, 1982. xii, 136 p.: ill.; 24 cm. — (Profiles. Nations of contemporary Africa.) Includes index. 1. Tanzania. I. T. II. Series.
DT438.Y4 1982   967.8 19   LC 82-1965   ISBN 0891589236

Feierman, Steven, 1940-. 3.5294
The Shambaa kingdom; a history. — [Madison]: University of Wisconsin Press, [1974] xii, 235 p.: maps; 23 cm. 1. Shambala (African people) I. T.
DT443.F44 1974   916.78/22   LC 73-2044   ISBN 0299063607

Schmidt, Peter R. (Peter Ridgway), 1942-. 3.5295
Historical archaeology: a structural approach in an African culture / Peter R. Schmidt. — Westport, Conn.: Greenwood Press, 1978. xi, 363 p.: ill.; 25 cm. (Contributions in intercultural and comparative studies; no. 3 0147-1031) Includes index. 1. Haya (African tribe) — History. 2. Archaeology and history — Tanzania. 3. Oral history 4. Rugomora Katuruka site, Tanzania. I. T.
DT443.S29   967.8/27   LC 77-84758   ISBN 0837198496

Willis, Roy G. 3.5296
A state in the making: myth, history, and social transformation in pre–colonial Ufipa / Roy Willis. — Bloomington: Indiana University Press, c1981. xxv, 322 p.: ill.; 25 cm. — (African systems of thought.) Includes index. 1. Fipa (African people) — History. 2. Oral tradition — Tanzania. I. T. II. Series.
DT443.W49   967.8/28 19   LC 80-8155   ISBN 0253195373

Wilson, Monica Hunter. 3.5297
For men and elders: change in the relations of generations and of men and women among the Nyakyusa–Ngonde people, 1875–1971 / by Monica Wilson. — New York: Africana Pub. Co. for the International African Institute, 1978 (c1977). 209 p.: maps; 22 cm. Includes index. 1. Nyakyusa (African people) — Social life and customs. 2. Ngonde (African people) — Social life and customs. 3. Acculturation I. T.
DT443.W52 1977   301.29/678/28   LC 77-4203   ISBN 0841903131

Nyerere, Julius K. (Julius Kambarage), 1922-. • 3.5298
Freedom and unity: Uhuru na umoja; a selection from writings and speeches, 1952–65 [by] Julius K. Nyerere. London, Nairobi [etc.] Oxford U.P., 1967. xiii, 366 p. front., 8 plates (incl. ports.) 22 1/2 cm. 1. Africa — Politics and government — Addresses, essays, lectures. 2. Tanzania. I. T. II. Title: Uhuru na umoja.
DT446.N9 A5   320.9/6   LC 67-77497

Smith, William Edgett. 3.5299
We must run while they walk; a portrait of Africa's Julius Nyerere. [1st ed.] New York: Random House 1971. 296 p. 22 cm. 1. Nyerere, Julius K. (Julius Kambarage), 1922- I. T.
DT446.N9 S57   967/.804/0924 B   LC 78-159376   ISBN 0394467523

Iliffe, John. 3.5300
A modern history of Tanganyika / John Iliffe. — Cambridge; New York: Cambridge University Press, 1979. xvi, 616 p.; 24 cm. — (African studies series. [25]) Includes index. 1. Tanganyika — History I. T. II. Series.
DT447.I39   967.8/2   LC 77-95445   ISBN 0521220246

DT449–469 Other East African Countries

McDonald, Gordon C. 3.5301
Area handbook for Burundi. Co–authors: Gordon C. McDonald [and others] Washington, For sale by the Supt. of Docs., U.S. Govt. Print. Off., 1969. xiv, 203 p. maps. 24 cm. 'DA pam no. 550-83.' 'Prepared by Foreign Area Studies (FAS) of The American University.' 1. Burundi. I. American University (Washington, D.C.). Foreign Area Studies. II. T.
DT449.B8 M3   916.7/572   LC 70-605915

Arens, W., 1940-. 3.5302
On the frontier of change Mto Wa Mbu, Tanzania / William Arens. — Ann Arbor: University of Michigan Press: produced and distributed by University Microfilms International, c1979. xii, 150 p.: ill.; 23 cm. (Monograph publishing. Imprint series.) (Anthropology series) A revision of the author's thesis, University of Virginia, 1970. 1. Social change — Case studies. 2. Mto Wa Mbu (Tanzania) — History. 3. Mto Wa Mbu (Tanzania) — Social conditions. 4. Mto Wa Mbu (Tanzania) — Social life and customs. I. T. II. Series.
DT449.M7 A73 1979   967.8   LC 79-18843   ISBN 047202714X

Louis, William Roger. • 3.5303
Ruanda–Urundi, 1884–1919 / by Wm. Roger Louis. — Oxford: Clarendon Press, c1963. xvii, 290 p.: map; 23 cm. Includes index. 1. Ruanda-Urundi — History I. T.
DT449.R8 L6   967/.57   LC 78-27637   ISBN 0313209057

Nyrop, Richard F. 3.5304
Area handbook for Rwanda. Co–authors: Richard F. Nyrop [and others] Washington, For sale by the Supt. of Docs., U.S. Govt. Print. Off., 1985, c1974.. xiv, 212 p. maps. 25 cm. 'DA pam 550-84.' 'Prepared by Foreign Area Studies (FAS) of The American University.' 1. Rwanda. I. American University (Washington, D.C.). Foreign Area Studies. II. T.
DT449.R9 N9   916.7/571   LC 72-606089

Mozambique: a country study / Foreign Area Studies, the American University; edited by Harold D. Nelson. 3.5305
3rd ed. — Washington, D.C.: Foreign Area Studies, American University: For sale by the Supt. of Docs., U.S. G.P.O., 1985. xxxiii, 342 p.: ill.; 24 cm. (Area handbook series.) (DA pam / Headquarters, Department of the Army; 550-64) 'Research completed April 1984.' Includes index. 1. Mozambique. I. Nelson, Harold D. II. American University (Washington, D.C.). Foreign Area Studies. III. Series.
DT453.M64 1985   967/.9 19   LC 85-6027

Henriksen, Thomas H. 3.5306
Mozambique: a history / [by] Thomas H. Henriksen. — London: Collings [etc.], 1979 (c1978). xi, 276 p.: maps; 24 cm. 1. Mozambique — History I. T.
DT459.H46   967/.9   LC 79-309991   ISBN 0860360172

Henriksen, Thomas H. 3.5307
Revolution and counterrevolution: Mozambique's war of independence, 1964–1974 / Thomas H. Henriksen. — Westport, Conn.: Greenwood Press, 1983. xii, 289 p.: map; 24 cm. (Contributions in intercultural and comparative studies. 0147-1031; no. 6) Includes index. 1. National liberation movements — Mozambique. 2. Guerrillas — Mozambique. 3. Mozambique — Politics and government — To 1975 4. Mozambique — History — Revolution, 1964-1975 I. T. II. Series.
DT463.H46 1983   967/.903 19   LC 82-6132   ISBN 0313236054

Newitt, M. D. D. 3.5308
Portuguese settlement on the Zambesi; exploration, land tenure, and colonial rule in East Africa [by] M. D. D. Newitt. — New York: Africana Pub. Co., [1973] 434 p.: illus.; 23 cm. 1. Land tenure — Mozambique. 2. Mozambique — History I. T.
DT463.N49 1973   967/.9   LC 72-86888   ISBN 0841901325

Isaacman, Allen F. 3.5309
The tradition of resistance in Mozambique: the Zambesi Valley, 1850–1921 / Allen F. Isaacman in collaboration with Barbara Isaacman. — Berkeley: University of California Press, 1977 (c1976). xxiv, 232 p.: maps; 23 cm. (Perspectives on Southern Africa. 18) Includes index. 1. Insurgency — Mozambique — Zambézia. 2. Insurgency — Zambesi Valley. 3. Zambézia (Mozambique) — History. 4. Zambesi Valley — History. I. Isaacman, Barbara. joint author. II. T. III. Series.
DT465.Z2 I8   967/.9   LC 75-17292   ISBN 0520030656

Heseltine, Nigel. 3.5310
Madagascar. — New York: Praeger, [1971] x, 334 p.: illus.; 23 cm. — (Praeger library of African affairs) 1. Madagascar. I. T.
DT469.M26 H47 1971   309.1/69/1   LC 70-79070

Nelson, Harold D.   3.5311
Area handbook for the Malagasy Republic. Co–authors: Harold D. Nelson
[and others] 1st ed. [Washington, For sale by the Supt. of Docs., U.S. Govt.
Print. Off.] 1973. xiv, 327 p. illus. 24 cm. 'One of a series of handbooks prepared
by Foreign Area Studies (FAS) of The American University.' 'DA Pam
550-163.' 1. Madagascar. I. American University (Washington, D.C.).
Foreign Area Studies. II. T.
DT469.M26 N4   916.9/1/035   LC 73-600012

Kottak, Conrad Phillip.   3.5312
The past in the present: history, ecology, and cultural variation in highland
Madagascar / Conrad Phillip Kottak; foreword by Roy A. Rappaport. — Ann
Arbor: University of Michigan Press, c1980. xiv, 339 p., [3] leaves of plates: ill.;
24 cm. Includes index. 1. Betsileos 2. Madagascar — Social conditions.
3. Madagascar — History I. T.
DT469.M264 K67 1980   969.1/00499   LC 80-14575   ISBN
0472093231

Brown, Mervyn.   3.5313
Madagascar rediscovered: a history from early times to independence / Mervyn
Brown. — Hamden, Conn.: Archon Books, 1979. vii, 310 p., [4] leaves of plates:
ill.; 23 cm. Includes index. 1. Madagascar — History I. T.
DT469.M27 B77 1979   969/.101   LC 79-13593   ISBN
020801828X

Kent, Raymond K.   • 3.5314
From Madagascar to the Malagasy Republic. — New York: Praeger, [1962]
182 p.: illus.; 22 cm. — (Books that matter.) 1. Ethnology — Madagascar
2. Madagascar — History I. T.
DT469.M34 K4   969.1   LC 62-11772

Mutibwa, Phares M.   3.5315
The Malagasy and the Europeans: Madagascar's foreign relations, 1861–1895 /
Phares M. Mutibwa. — Atlantic Highlands, N.J.: Humanities Press, 1975
(c1974). xvi, 411 p.: ill., maps; 23 cm. — (Ibadan history series) Includes index.
1. Madagascar — History I. T. II. Series.
DT469.M34 M8   ISBN 0391003488

DT471–507 West Africa (Former British Areas, General)

Hargreaves, John D.   • 3.5316
Prelude to the partition of West Africa. — London, Macmillan; New York, St
Martin's Press, 1963. xi, 383 p. maps (1 fold.) 22 cm. Bibliography: p.
[350]-368. 1. Africa, West — Colonization. 2. Africa, West — Comm. — Hist.
3. Europeans — Africa, West I. T.
DT471.H29   966   LC 63-22836

July, Robert William.   • 3.5317
The origins of modern African thought; its development in West Africa during
the nineteenth and twentieth centuries. — New York: F. A. Praeger, [1968,
c1967] 512 p.: illus., map, ports.; 22 cm. 1. Nationalism — Africa, West.
2. Africa, West — Biography. I. T.
DT471.J84   916.6/03   LC 67-24684

Newbury, C. W. (Colin Walter), 1929-.   • 3.5318
The western slave coast and its rulers: European trade and administration
among the Yoruba and Adja–speaking peoples of South–western Nigeria,
southern Dahomey and Togo. — Oxford, Clarendon Press, 1961. ix, 234 p.
maps (part fold.) tables. 22 cm. — (Oxford studies in African affairs.)
Bibliography: p. [214]-226. 1. Slave coast — Hist. 2. Europeans — Africa,
West I. T. II. Series.
DT471.N38   966.8   LC 62-180

Welch, Claude Emerson.   • 3.5319
Dream of unity; Pan–Africanism and political unification in West Africa, by
Claude E. Welch, Jr. — Ithaca, N. Y., Cornell University Press [1966] xv,
396 p. maps. 22 cm. Bibliography: p. 362-385. 1. Africa, West — Politics.
2. Pan-Africanism 3. Regionalism — Africa, West. I. T.
DT471.W38   320.1596   LC 66-16290

Zolberg, Aristide R.   • 3.5320
Creating political order: the party–states of West Africa / Aristide R. Zolberg.
— Chicago: Rand McNally, 1966. vi, 168 p. 22 cm. — (Rand McNally studies
in political change) 1. Africa, West — Politics. 2. Africa, West — Politics and
government I. T.
DT471.Z6   320.966   LC 66-19458

Church, R. J. Harrison (Ronald James Harrison)   3.5321
West Africa: a study of the environment and of man's use of it / R. J. Harrison
Church; with a chapter on soils and soil management [by] P. R. Moss. — 8th ed.
— London; New York: Longman, 1980. xxxi, 526 p.: ill., maps; 24 cm.
(Geographies for advanced study) Includes index. 1. Africa, West —
Description and travel — 1951-1980 I. Moss, Rowland Percy. joint author.
II. T.
DT472.C44 1980   966   LC 79-41255   ISBN 0582300207

Curtin, Philip D.   3.5322
Africa & the West; intellectual responses to European culture [by] James W.
Fernandez [and others] Edited by Philip D. Curtin. — [Madison]: University of
Wisconsin Press, [1972] x, 259 p.: illus.; 23 cm. 1. Acculturation — Africa,
West — Addresses, essays, lectures. 2. Africa, West — Civilization —
European influences — Addresses, essays, lectures. I. Fernandez, James W.
II. T.
DT474.C87   301.29/6/01821   LC 77-176409   ISBN 0299061213

History of West Africa / edited by J. F. A. Ajayi and Michael   3.5323
Crowder.
3rd ed. — London: Longman, c1985-. v.: ill., facsim., geneal. tables, maps; 23
cm. 1. Africa, West — History I. Crowder, Michael, 1934- II. Ajayi, J. F.
Ade.
DT475.A77 1985   966   ISBN 0582646839

Fage, J. D.   • 3.5324
A history of West Africa: an introductory survey, by J. D. Fage. — 4th ed. —
London: Cambridge U.P., 1969. xii, 239 p.: maps; 23 cm. First-3d ed. published
under title: An introduction to the history of West Africa. 1. Africa, West —
History I. T.
DT475.F3 1969   966   LC 71-85742   ISBN 0521074061

Blake, John William.   3.5325
West Africa: quest for God and gold, 1454–1578: a survey of the first century of
white enterprise in West Africa, with particular reference to the Portuguese and
their rivalries with other European powers / John W. Blake.
— 2d ed., rev. and enl. — London: Curzon Press; Totowa, N.J.: Rowman and
Littlefield, 1977. xxi, 246 p.: maps.; 23 cm. 'Originally published in 1937 under
the title: European beginnings in West Africa, 1454-1578.' Includes index.
1. Africa, West — History I. T.
DT476.B55 1977   966   LC 77-373248   ISBN 0874719658

Davidson, Basil, 1914-.   3.5326
The African slave trade / Basil Davidson. — A rev. and expanded ed. —
Boston: Little, Brown, c1980. 304 p.: ill., maps; 22 cm. Previously published as:
Black mother. 'An Atlantic Monthly Press book.' Includes index. 1. Slave-
trade — Africa, West — History. 2. Slave-trade — Africa, Eastern — History.
3. Africa, West — History — To 1884 4. Africa, Eastern — History I. T.
DT476.D32 1980   967 19   LC 81-65588   ISBN 0316174394

Smith, Robert Sydney.   3.5327
Warfare and diplomacy in pre–colonial West Africa / Robert S. Smith.
[London]: Methuen; [New York]: distributed by Harper & Row, Barnes and
Noble Import Division, 1976. 240 p.; 19 cm. (Studies in African history; 15)
Includes index. 1. Africa, West — History 2. Africa, West — History,
Military. I. T.
DT476.S6   966   LC 77-358487   ISBN 0416550606

Crowder, Michael, 1934-.   • 3.5328
West Africa under colonial rule. Evanston [Ill.] Northwestern University Press,
1968. xv, 540 p. maps (1 fold.) 24 cm. 1. Africa, West — History — 1884-1960
I. T.
DT476.2.C76 1968b   966   LC 68-27618

Hargreaves, John D.   3.5329
The end of colonial rule in West Africa: essays in contemporary history / John
D. Hargreaves. — New York: Barnes & Noble Books, 1979. xvi, 141 p.; 23 cm.
The first essay was published separately in 1976 under title: The end of colonial
rule in West Africa. 1. Nationalism — Africa, West — Addresses, essays,
lectures. 2. Africa, West — Politics and government — 1884-1960 —
Addresses, essays, lectures. I. T.
DT476.2.H362 1979   966   LC 79-12129   ISBN 0064927059

Hargreaves, John D.   3.5330
West Africa partitioned / John D. Hargreaves. — Madison: University of
Wisconsin Press, 1974-1985. 2 v.: maps; 22 cm. 1. Africa, West —
Colonization. 2. Africa, West — History — 1884-1960 3. Africa, West —
Commerce — History. I. T.
DT476.2.H37 1974   325/.366/094   LC 74-10451   ISBN
0299067203

Langley, J. Ayodele.   3.5331
Pan–Africanism and nationalism in West Africa, 1900–1945: a study in
ideology and social classes / by J. Ayodele Langley. — Oxford: Clarendon
Press, 1973. x, 421 p.; 23 cm. (Oxford studies in African affairs.) 1. National
Congress of British West Africa. 2. Pan-Africanism 3. Nationalism — Africa,

West. 4. Africa, West — Politics and government — 1884-1960 I. T.
II. Series.
DT476.2.L36   320.5/4/0966   *LC* 74-155448   *ISBN* 0198216890

Adjaye, Joseph K., 1940-.   3.5332
Diplomacy and diplomats in nineteenth century Asante / Joseph K. Adjaye. —
Lanham, MD: University Press of America, c1984. viii, 309 p.; 22 cm. Includes
index. 1. Ashantis (African people) — Politics and government. 2. Ghana —
Foreign relations administration — History — 19th century. I. T.
DT507.A34 1984   966.7/01 19   *LC* 84-19533   *ISBN* 0819143022

Lewin, Thomas J., 1944-.   3.5333
Asante before the British: the Prempean years, 1875–1900 / Thomas J. Lewin.
— Lawrence: Regents Press of Kansas, c1978. xii, 312 p.: ill.; 24 cm. Includes
index. 1. Prempeh, King of Ashanti. 2. Ashanti — History. 3. Ghana —
Colonization. I. T.
DT507.L48   966.7   *LC* 78-8003   *ISBN* 0700601805

Wilks, Ivor.   3.5334
Asante in the nineteenth century: the structure and evolution of a political order
/ Ivor Wilks. — London; New York: Cambridge University Press, 1975. xvii,
800 p., [8] leaves of plates: ill.; 24 cm. — (African studies series. 13) Includes
index. 1. Ashantis (African people) 2. Ashanti — Politics and government.
I. T. II. Series.
DT507.W48   966.7   *LC* 74-77834   *ISBN* 0521204631

DT509 Gambia

Gailey, Harry A.   • 3.5335
A history of the Gambia, by Harry A. Gailey. New York, Praeger [1965] xi,
244 p. illus., fold. map. 23 cm. Bibliography: p. 218-222. 1. Gambia — History
I. T.
DT509.G3 1965   966.51   *LC* 65-11999

DT510–512 Ghana

Boateng, E. A.   • 3.5336
A geography of Ghana, by E. A. Boateng. — 2nd ed. — Cambridge: Cambridge
U.P., 1966. xv, 212 p.: 24 plates, maps, tables, diagrs.; 23 cm. 1. Ghana —
Description and travel. I. T.
DT510.B6 1966   916.67   *LC* 65-22922

Kaplan, Irving, 1923-.   3.5337
Area handbook for Ghana. Co–authors: Irving Kaplan [and others. Rev. 2d ed.
Washington; For sale by the Supt. of Docs., U.S. Govt. Print. Off.] 1971. xiv,
449 p. map. 24 cm. 'DA Pam 550-153.' 'One of a series of handbooks prepared
by Foreign Area Studies (FAS) of the American University.' Supersedes Special
warfare area handbook for Ghana, issued in 1962 by American University,
Foreign Areas Studies Division. 1. Ghana. I. American University
(Washington, D.C.). Foreign Area Studies. II. American University
(Washington, D.C.). Foreign Areas Studies Division. Special warfare area
handbook for Ghana. III. T.
DT510.K37 1971   916.67   *LC* 74-611338

Nkrumah, Kwame, 1909-1972.   • 3.5338
Ghana; the autobiography of Kwame Nkrumah. New York, International
Publishers [1971, c1957] xiii, 310 p. maps, port. 21 cm. 1. Nkrumah, Kwame,
1909-1972. 2. Ghana — Politics and government — To 1957 I. T.
DT510.6.N5 A33 1971   966.7/05/0924 B   *LC* 70-148514   *ISBN*
0717802930

Austin, Dennis, 1922-.   • 3.5339
Politics in Ghana, 1946–1960. Issued under the auspices of the Royal Institute
of International Affairs. — London, New York, Oxford University Press, 1964.
xiv, 459 p. maps. 22 cm. 'The Constitution of the Republic of Ghana': p.
[430]-446. Bibliography: p. [447]-451. 1. Ghana — Pol. & govt. I. Ghana.
Constitution. II. T.
DT511.A84   966.7   *LC* 64-55703

Kimble, David.   • 3.5340
A political history of Ghana; the rise of Gold Coast nationalism, 1850–1928. —
Oxford, Clarendon Press, 1963. xviii, 587 p. ports., maps, tables. 24 cm. 'In
substance ... the dissertation for which I was awarded the degree of Ph. D. in the
University of London.' Bibliographical footnotes. 1. Ghana — Pol. & govt.
I. T.
DT511.K42 1963   966.7   *LC* 63-4374

Nkrumah, Kwame, 1909-1972.   • 3.5341
I speak of freedom; a statement of African ideology. New York, Praeger [1961]
291 p. illus. 21 cm. (Books that matter) 1. Ghana — History 2. Africa —
Politics. I. T.
DT512.N55 1961   966.7   *LC* 61-14200

Nkrumah, Kwame, 1909-1972.   3.5342
Revolutionary path. [1st U.S. ed.] New York, International Publishers [1973]
532 p. 21 cm. 1. Nkrumah, Kwame, 1909-1972. I. T.
DT512.3.N57 A35 1973   966.7/05/0924   *LC* 73-78905   *ISBN*
0717804003 *ISBN* 0717804011

Davidson, Basil, 1914-.   3.5343
Black star; a view of the life and times of Kwame Nkrumah. New York, Praeger
[1974, c1973] 225 p. map. 21 cm. 1. Nkrumah, Kwame, 1909-1972. I. T.
DT512.3.N57 D38 1974   966.7/05/0924 B   *LC* 73-16035

DT513–515.9 Nigeria

Asiwaju, A. I., 1939-.   3.5344
Western Yorubaland under European rule, 1889–1945: a comparative analysis
of French and British colonialism / A. I. Asiwaju. — Atlantic Highlands, N.J.:
Humanities Press, 1977 (c1976). xvi, 303 p., [2] leaves of plates: ill.; 23 cm. —
(Ibadan history series) A revision of the author's thesis, University of Ibadan,
1971. Includes index. 1. Yoruba — Politics and government. 2. Yoruba —
Economic conditions. 3. Great Britain — Colonies — Administration
4. France — Colonies — Administration I. T. II. Series.
DT513.A78   301.45/19/63   *LC* 76-10146   *ISBN* 0391006053

Eades, J. S. (Jeremy Seymour), 1945-.   3.5345
The Yoruba today / J. S. Eades. — Cambridge [Eng.]; New York: Cambridge
University Press, 1980. 188 p.: ill., 5 maps. — (Changing cultures) Includes
index. 1. Yorubas I. T.
DT513.E23   DT513 E23.   301.29/669   *LC* 79-50236   *ISBN*
0521226562

Law, Robin.   3.5346
The Oyo Empire, c.1600–c.1836: a West African imperialism in the era of the
Atlantic slave trade / by Robin Law. — Oxford [Eng.]: Clarendon Press, 1977.
xiv, 340 p.: maps; 23 cm. — (Oxford studies in African affairs.) Originally
presented as the author's thesis, Birmingham, 1971. Includes index. 1. Yorubas
— History. 2. Slave-trade — Nigeria. 3. Slave-trade — Africa, West. I. T.
II. Series.
DT513.L38 1977   966.9/2/01   *LC* 77-6471   *ISBN* 0198227094

Hodgkin, Thomas Lionel, 1910-.   3.5347
Nigerian perspectives: an historical anthology / [compiled by] Thomas
Hodgkin. — 2d ed. — London; New York: Oxford University Press, 1975. xv,
432 p.: ill.; 23 cm. Includes index. 1. Nigeria — History — Sources. I. T.
DT515.A3 H6 1975   966.9   *LC* 75-323449   *ISBN* 0192154346

Coleman, James Smoot.   • 3.5348
Nigeria: background to nationalism. — Berkeley: University of California
Press, 1958. xiv, 510 p.: illus., ports., maps.; 24 cm. 1. Nationalism — Nigeria.
I. T.
DT515.C685   966.9   *LC* 58-10286

Shaw, Thurstan.   3.5349
Nigeria: its archaeology and early history / Thurstan Shaw; with 147
illustrations. — [London]: Thames and Hudson, 1978. 216 p.: ill.; 25 cm.
(Ancient peoples and places.) Includes index. 1. Nigeria — History I. T.
DT515.2.S43   *LC* 77-83799

Nigeria, a country study / Foreign Area Studies, the American   3.5350
University; edited by Harold D. Nelson.
4th ed. — Washington, D.C.: For sale by the Supt. of Docs., U.S. G.P.O.,
c1982. xxviii, 358 p.: ill.; 24 cm. — (Area handbook series.) (DA pam. 550-157)
Rev. ed. of: Area handbook for Nigeria / Harold D. Nelson. Rev. 3rd ed. 1972.
Includes index. 1. Nigeria. I. Nelson, Harold D. Area handbook for Nigeria.
II. American University (Washington, D.C.). Foreign Area Studies.
III. Series. IV. Series: DA pam. 550-157
DT515.22.N53 1982   966.9/03 19   *LC* 82-6795

Hill, Polly, 1914-.   3.5351
Population, prosperity, and poverty: rural Kano, 1900 and 1970 / Polly Hill. —
Cambridge; New York: Cambridge University Press, 1977. viii, 240 p.: ill.; 24
cm. Includes index. 1. Hausa (African people) 2. Kano State (Nigeria) —
Economic conditions. 3. Batagarawa, Nigeria — Economic conditions.
4. Kano State (Nigeria) — Social conditions. 5. Batagarawa, Nigeria — Social
conditions. I. T.
DT515.42.H53   309.1/669/5   *LC* 77-23167   *ISBN* 0521215110

Isichei, Elizabeth Allo.   **3.5352**
A history of the Igbo people / Elizabeth Isichei. — New York: St. Martin's
Press, 1976. xiv, 303 p., [4] leaves of plates: ill.; 23 cm. Includes index. 1. Igbo
(African people) — History. I. T.
DT515.42.I76 1976b   966.9/4/004963   *LC* 75-14713

Leis, Philip E.   **3.5353**
Enculturation and socialization in an Ijaw village [by] Philip E. Leis. New
York, Holt, Rinehart and Winston [1972] xiii, 112 p. illus. 24 cm. (Case studies
in education and culture.) 1. Ijo (African people) 2. Socialization — Case
studies. 3. Children — Nigeria I. T. II. Series.
DT515.42.L37   301.29/669   *LC* 76-179546   *ISBN* 0030911532

Berry, Sara.   **3.5354**
Fathers work for their sons: accumulation, mobility, and class formation in an
extended Yorùbá community / Sara Berry. — Berkeley: University of
California Press, c1985. x, 225 p.; 24 cm. Includes index. 1. Yorubas —
Economic conditions. 2. Yorubas — Social conditions. 3. Cocoa trade —
Nigeria. I. T.
DT515.45.Y67 B47 1985   306/.089963 19   *LC* 84-122   *ISBN*
0520051645

Drewal, Henry John.   **3.5355**
Gelede: art and female power among the Yoruba / Henry John Drewal and
Margaret Thompson Drewal. — Bloomington: Indiana University Press,
c1983. xxi, 306 p., [9] p. of plates: ill. (some col.); 27 cm. — (Traditional arts of
Africa.) Includes index. 1. Yorubas — Rites and ceremonies 2. Women,
Yoruba 3. Yorubas — Religion I. Drewal, Margaret Thompson. II. T.
III. Series.
DT515.45.Y67 D73 1983   306/.089963 19   *LC* 82-48388   *ISBN*
0253325692

Peel, J. D. Y. (John David Yeadon), 1941-.   **3.5356**
Ijeshas and Nigerians: the incorporation of a Yoruba kingdom, 1890s–1970s /
J.D.Y. Peel. — Cambridge [Cambridgeshire]; New York: Cambridge
University Press, 1983. xiii, 346 p.: ill.; 24 cm. — (African studies series. 39)
Includes index. 1. Yorubas — History. 2. Ilesha (Nigeria) — History. I. T.
II. Series.
DT515.45.Y67 P43 1983   966.9/5 19   *LC* 82-23660   *ISBN*
0521225450

Ayandele, Emmanuel Ayankanmi.   **3.5357**
Nigerian historical studies / E. A. Ayandele. — London; Totowa, N.J.: F. Cass,
1979. xi, 305 p.; 22 cm. 1. Nigeria — History — Addresses, essays, lectures.
2. Nigeria — Church history — Addresses, essays, lectures. I. T.
DT515.5.A93 1979   966.9/01   *LC* 79-312832   *ISBN* 0714631132

Crowder, Michael, 1934-.   • **3.5358**
A short history of Nigeria. — Rev. and enl. ed. — New York: F. A. Praeger,
[1966] 416 p.: illus., maps (1 fold.), ports.; 21 cm. 1. Nigeria — History I. T.
DT515.5.C68 1966   966.9   *LC* 66-13679

Flint, John E.   • **3.5359**
Nigeria and Ghana [by] John E. Flint. — Englewood Cliffs, N.J.: Prentice-Hall,
[1966] viii, 176 p.: maps.; 21 cm. — (A Spectrum book: The modern nations in
historical perspective) 1. Nigeria — History 2. Ghana — History I. T.
DT515.5.F5   966   *LC* 66-16343

Abubaker, Sa'ad, 1939-.   **3.5360**
The Lāmībe of Fombina: a political history of Adamawa, 1809–1901 / Sa'ad
Abubaker. — [Zaria, Nigeria]: Ahmadu Bello University Press: Oxford
University Press, 1979 (c1977). x, 190 p.: maps. — (Ahmadu Bello University
history series. [v. 1]) 1. Fulah Empire — History. 2. Adamawa (Emirate) —
History. I. T. II. Series.
DT515.6.A3 A26   966.9/5   *LC* 79-114835   *ISBN* 019575452

Awolowo, Obafemi, 1909-.   • **3.5361**
Awo; the autobiography of Chief Obafemi Awolowo. — Cambridge [Eng.]
University Press, 1960. 315 p. illus. 23 cm. I. T.
DT515.6.A9A3   923.2669   *LC* 60-50987

Azikiwe, Nnamdi, 1904-.   • **3.5362**
Zik, a selection from the speeches of Nnamdi Azikiwe. — Cambridge [Eng.]
University Press, 1961. 344 p. illus. 23 cm. 1. Nigeria — Pol. & govt. I. T.
DT515.6.A9A5   923.2669   *LC* 61-1177

Bello, Ahmadu, Sir, 1909-.   • **3.5363**
My life. — Cambridge [Eng.] University Press, 1962. 245 p. illus. 23 cm.
1. Nigeria — Pol. & govt. I. T.
DT515.6.B4A3   966.9   *LC* 63-6

Afigbo, A. E. (Adiele Eberechukwu)   **3.5364**
The Warrant Chiefs: indirect rule in southeastern Nigeria, 1891–1929, [by] A.
E. Afigbo. — New York: Humanities Press, 1972. xv, 338, [4] p.: facsim., maps,

ports.; 23 cm. — (Ibadan history series) 1. Ethnology — Nigeria 2. Nigeria —
Politics and government I. T. II. Series.
DT515.7.A43 1972b   325/.31/096694

Asiegbu, Johnson U. J.   **3.5365**
Nigeria and its British invaders, 1851–1920: a thematic documentary history /
by Johnson U.J. Asiegbu. — New York: Nok Publishers International, c1984.
xxxii, 377 p.: ill., [8] p. of plates, maps, port.; 24 cm. 1. Nigeria — History —
1851-1899 2. Great Britain — Foreign relations — Nigeria. 3. Nigeria —
History — 1900-1960 4. Nigeria — Relations — Great Britain I. T.
DT515.7.A8x   *LC* 83-62253   *ISBN* 0883571013

Leith-Ross, Sylvia.   **3.5366**
Stepping–stones: memoirs of colonial Nigeria 1907–1960 / Sylvia Leith–Ross;
edited and with an introduction by Michael Crowder. — London: Owen, 1983.
189 p., [8] p. of plates: ill., maps, ports.; 23 cm. 1. Nigeria — Social life and
customs. I. Crowder, Michael, 1934- II. T.
DT515.75.L44 1983   966.9/03/0924 19   *ISBN* 0720606004

Sklar, Richard L.   • **3.5367**
Nigerian political parties; power in an emergent African nation. — Princeton,
Princeton University Press, 1963. xi, 578 p. maps, tables. 25 cm.
Bibliography: p. 535-559. 1. Nigeria — Pol. & govt. 2. Political parties —
Nigeria. I. T.
DT515.8.S55   329.9669   *LC* 62-21107

Brenner, Louis.   **3.5368**
The Shehus of Kukawa; a history of the al–Kanemi dynasty of Bornu. Oxford,
Clarendon Press, 1973. 145 p. illus. map. 22 cm. (Oxford studies in African
affairs.) A revision of the author's thesis, Columbia University. 1. Bornu —
History. I. T. II. Series.
DT 515.9 B6 B83 1973   *LC* 73-160988   *ISBN* 0198216815

Adeleye, R. A.   **3.5369**
Power and diplomacy in Northern Nigeria, 1804–1906; the Sokoto Caliphate
and its enemies [by] R. A. Adeleye. — [New York]: Humanities Press, [1971]
xvi, 387 p.: illus., maps.; 23 cm. — (Ibadan history series) A revision of the
author's thesis, University of Ibadan. 1. Fulah Empire I. T. II. Series.
DT515.9.F8 A64 1971   966.9   *LC* 77-27825   *ISBN* 0391001698

Hiskett, M.   **3.5370**
The sword of truth; the life and times of the Shehu Usuman dan Fodio [by]
Mervyn Hiskett. — New York: Oxford University Press, 1973. xxii, 194 p.:
illus.; 21 cm. 1. Dan Fodio, Usuman, 1744-1817. 2. Fulah Empire I. T.
DT515.9.F8 H57   966.9/01/0924 B   *LC* 72-91010   *ISBN*
0195016483

DT516 Sierra Leone

Kaplan, Irving, 1923-.   **3.5371**
Area handbook for Sierra Leone / coauthors, Irving Kaplan ... [et al.]. — 1st ed.
— Washington: for sale by the Supt. of Docs., U.S. Govt. Print. Off., 1976. xiv,
400 p.: maps; 24 cm. 'DA Pam 550-180.' 'One of a series of handbooks prepared
by Foreign Area Studies (FAS) of the American University.' Includes index.
1. Sierra Leone. I. American University (Washington, D.C.). Foreign Area
Studies. II. T.
DT516.K36   966/.404   *LC* 76-49498

Fyfe, Christopher.   • **3.5372**
A history of Sierra Leone / by Christopher Fyfe. — London: Oxford University
Press, 1962. vii, 773 p.: fold. maps. 1. Sierra Leone — History I. T.
DT516.5.F85   *LC* 62-4324

Kup, Alexander Peter.   • **3.5373**
A history of Sierra Leone, 1400–1787. Cambridge [Eng.] University Press,
1961. 211 p. illus. 22 cm. 1. Sierra Leone — History I. T.
DT516.65.K85   *LC* 61-1075

Cox, Thomas S., 1944-.   **3.5374**
Civil–military relations in Sierra Leone: a case study of African soldiers in
politics / Thomas S. Cox. — Cambridge, Mass.: Harvard University Press,
1976. x, 271 p.; 24 cm. Includes index. 1. Sierra Leone. Army — Political
activity. 2. Civil-military relations — Sierra Leone. 3. Sierra Leone — Politics
and government — 1961- I. T.
DT516.8.C69   322/.5/09664   *LC* 75-17940   *ISBN* 0674132904

DT521–546 West Africa (Former French Areas, General). Guinea. Ivory Coast

Thompson, Virginia McLean, 1903-.   • 3.5375
French West Africa [by] Virginia Thompson and Richard Adloff. — Stanford, Calif.: Stanford University Press, [1957?] 626 p.: illus., maps, tables.; 23 cm. 1. Africa, French West. I. Adloff, Richard. joint author. II. T.
DT524.T5   966   *LC* 58-7722

Hargreaves, John D.   • 3.5376
West Africa: the former French states [by] John D. Hargreaves. Englewood Cliffs, N.J., Prentice-Hall [1967] viii, 183 p. maps. (A Spectrum book: The modern nations in historical perspective) 1. Africa, French West — History I. T.
DT532 H3   *LC* 67-14841

Morgenthau, Ruth Schachter.   • 3.5377
Political parties in French–speaking West Africa. — Oxford, Clarendon Press, 1964. xxii, 445 p. illus., maps. 23 cm. — (Oxford studies in African affairs.) Bibliography: p. [359]-376. 1. Africa, French West — Politics. 2. Political parties — Africa, French West. I. T. II. Series.
DT532.M6   320.966   *LC* 65-357

Levtzion, Nehemia.   3.5378
Ancient Ghana and Mali. — London: Methuen, 1973. x, 283 p.: 2 maps.; 19 cm. — (Studies in African history, 7) Distributed in the USA by Harper & Row Publishers, Barnes & Noble Import Division. 1. Ghana Empire 2. Mali empire I. T.
DT532.15.L48 1973   916.67   *LC* 73-160646   *ISBN* 0416758207

Thompson, Virginia McLean, 1903-.   3.5379
West Africa's Council of the Entente [by] Virginia Thompson. Ithaca, N.Y., Cornell University Press [1972] xxiii, 313 p. illus. 21 cm. (Africa in the modern world) 1. Houphouët-Boigny, Félix, 1905- 2. Council of the Entente. 3. Africa, French-speaking West — Politics and government — 1960- I. T.
DT534.T46   320.9/66   *LC* 70-171935   *ISBN* 0801406838 *ISBN* 0801491274

Nelson, Harold D.   3.5380
Area handbook for Guinea / coauthors, Harold D. Nelson ... [et al.]. — 2d ed. — Washington: For sale by the Supt., U.S. Govt. Print. Off., 1975. xii, 386 p.: maps; 24 cm. 'One of a series of handbooks prepared by Foreign Area Studies (FAS) of the American University.' 'DA Pam 550-174.' A revision of the 1961 ed. issued by Foreign Area Studies Division, American University. Includes index. 1. Guinea. I. American University (Washington, D.C.). Foreign Area Studies. II. American University (Washington, D.C.). Foreign Areas Studies Division. Area handbook for Guinea. III. T.
DT543.N44 1975   966/.5205   *LC* 75-26515

Camara, Laye.   3.5381
[Enfant noir. English] The dark child. With an introd. by Philippe Thoby-Marcellin. [Translated from the French by James Kirkup and Ernest Jones] New York, Farrar, Straus and Giroux [1969, c1954] 188 p. 21 cm. Translation of L'enfant noir. Autobiographical. 1. Camara, Laye. I. T.
DT543.4.C3513 1969   916.6/52/0330924 B   *LC* 73-5733

Rivière, Claude, fl. 1969-.   3.5382
Guinea: the mobilization of a people / Claude Rivière; translated from the French by Virginia Thompson and Richard Adloff. — Ithaca, N.Y.: Cornell University Press, 1977. 262 p.: ill.; 21 cm. (Africa in the modern world) Includes index. 1. Guinea — Politics and government — 1958-1984 I. T.
DT543.8.R5813   320.9/66/5205   *LC* 76-50262   *ISBN* 0801409047

Roberts, Thomas Duval, 1903-.   3.5383
Area handbook for Ivory Coast. Coauthors: T. D. Roberts [and others] 2d ed. [Washington; For sale by the Supt. of Docs., U.S. Govt. Print. Off.] 1973. lxvi, 449 p. illus. 25 cm. 'One of a series of handbooks prepared by Foreign Area Studies (FAS) of The American University.' First ed. (1962) prepared by the Foreign Area Studies Division of American University, Washington, D.C. Brought up to date by a new section entitled Summary of events: January 1963-December 1972, prepared by a team under the direction of B. Nimer. 1. Ivory Coast. I. Nimer, Benjamin. II. American University (Washington, D.C.). Foreign Area Studies. III. American University (Washington, D.C.). Foreign Areas Studies Division. Area handbook for Ivory Coast. IV. T.
DT545.R58 1973   916.66/8/035   *LC* 73-600169

Alland, Alexander, 1931-.   3.5384
When the spider danced: notes from an African Village / Alexander Alland, Jr. — 1st ed. — Garden City, N.Y.: Anchor Press, 1975. xii, 227 p., [8] leaves of plates: ill.; 22 cm. Includes index. 1. Abron (African people) I. T.
DT545.42.A43   966.6/8/05   *LC* 74-1521   *ISBN* 0385015933

Glaze, Anita J., 1940-.   3.5385
Art and death in a Senufo village / Anita J. Glaze. — Bloomington: Indiana University Press, c1981. xvi, 267 p., [2] leaves of plates: ill.; 24 cm. — (Traditional arts of Africa.) Includes index. 1. Senufo (African people) 2. Art, Senufo (African people) 3. Senufo (African people) — Funeral customs and rites I. T. II. Series.
DT545.42.G55   745/.09666/8 19   *LC* 79-2174   *ISBN* 0253171075

Thompson, Virginia McLean, 1903-.   • 3.5386
The emerging states of French Equatorial Africa [by] Virginia Thompson and Richard Adloff. — Stanford, Calif.: Stanford University Press, 1960. xii, 595 p.: illus., ports., maps.; 24 cm. 1. Africa, French-speaking Equatorial — Politics and government — 1884-1960 I. Adloff, Richard. joint author. II. T.
DT546.T48 1960   967.2   *LC* 60-13871

DT546.2–584 Congo (Brazzaville). Chad. Niger. Senegal. Mauritania. Cameroon

Gauze, René.   3.5387
The politics of Congo–Brazzaville. Translation, editing, and supplement by Virginia Thompson and Richard Adloff. Stanford, Calif., Hoover Institution Press [1973] xxvii, 283 p. illus. 29 cm. (Hoover Institution publications, 129) 'Supplement: the decade 1962 to 1972': p. [149]-238. 1. Youlou, Fulbert, 1917-1972. 2. Congo (Brazzaville) — Politics and government I. Thompson, Virginia McLean, 1903- II. Adloff, Richard. III. T.
DT546.275.G38   320.9/67/2405   *LC* 73-75886   *ISBN* 0817912916

Nelson, Harold D.   3.5388
Area handbook for Chad. Co–authors: Harold D. Nelson [and others]. 1st ed. Washington; For sale by the Supt. of Docs., U.S. Govt. Print. Off.] 1982, c1971. xiv, 261 p. illus. 24 cm. 'DA Pam 550-159.' 'One of a series of handbooks prepared by Foreign Area Studies (FAS) of the American University.' 1. Chad. I. American University (Washington, D.C.). Foreign Area Studies. II. T.
DT546.4.N44   916.7/43   *LC* 72-600075

Fuglestad, Finn, 1942-.   3.5389
A history of Niger, 1850–1960 / Finn Fuglestad. -- Cambridge [Cambridgeshire]; New York: Cambridge University Press, 1984 (c1983). vii, 275 p.: ill., maps; 24 cm. — (African studies series. 41) Revision of thesis (Ph. D.)—University of Birmingham, 1977. Includes index. 1. Niger — History — To 1960 I. T. II. Series.
DT547.65.F83   966/.2601 19   *LC* 83-1809   *ISBN* 0521252687

Nelson, Harold D.   3.5390
Area handbook for Senegal. Co–authors: Harold D. Nelson [and others]. 2d ed. [Washington, For sale by the Supt. of Docs., U.S. Govt. Print. Off.] 1974. xiv, 410 p. maps. 24 cm. 'DA pam 550-70.' 'One of a series of handbooks prepared by Foreign Area Studies (FAS) of the American University.' Edition of 1963 prepared by the Foreign Area Studies Division of American University. 1. Senegal. I. American University (Washington, D.C.). Foreign Area Studies. II. American University (Washington, D.C.). Foreign Areas Studies Division. Area handbook for Senegal. III. T.
DT549.N4 1974   916.6/3/035   *LC* 72-600061

Skurnik, W. A. E.   3.5391
The foreign policy of Senegal [by] W. A. E. Skurnik. — Evanston [Ill.]: Northwestern University Press, 1972. xx, 308 p.: illus.; 22 cm. 1. Senegal — Foreign relations. 2. Senegal — Foreign economic relations. I. T.
DT549.62.S58   327/.66/3   *LC* 70-176162   *ISBN* 0810103737

Johnson, G. Wesley.   3.5392
The emergence of Black politics in Senegal; the struggle for power in the four communes, 1900–1920 [by] G. Wesley Johnson, Jr. — Stanford, Calif.: Published for the Hoover Institution on War, Revolution, and Peace, by Stanford University Press, 1971. x, 260 p.: illus.; 24 cm. 1. Senegal — Politics and government I. T.
DT549.7.J64   320.9/66/303   *LC* 73-150326   *ISBN* 0804707839

Curran, Brian Dean.   3.5393
Area handbook for Mauritania. Co–authors: Brian Dean Curran [and] Joann Schrock. Prepared for the American University by the American Institutes for Research. Research and writing were completed March 1972. — [Washington,: For sale by the Supt. of Docs., U.S. Govt. Print. Off.], 1972. xiv, 185 p.: maps;

25 cm. 1. Mauritania. I. Schrock, Joann L. joint author. II. American Institute for Research in the Behavioral Sciences. III. T.
DT553.M2 C87　　916.61/03/5　　*LC* 72-600188

Gerteiny, Alfred G.　　　　　　　　　　　　• 3.5394
Mauritania [by] Alfred G. Gerteiny. — New York: Praeger, [1967] x, 243 p.: map; 22 cm. — (Praeger library of African affairs) 1. Mauritania. I. T.
DT553.M2 G4　　916.6/1　　*LC* 67-23574

Riesman, Paul.　　　　　　　　　　　　3.5395
[Société et liberté chez les Peul djelgôbé de Haute-Volta. English] Freedom in Fulani social life: an introspective ethnography / Paul Riesman; translated by Martha Fuller. — Chicago: University of Chicago Press, c1977. xiii, 297 p., [4] leaves of plates: ill.; 24 cm. Translation of Société et liberté chez les Peul djelgôbé de Haute-Volta. Includes index. 1. Riesman, Paul. 2. Ethnology — Field work. 3. Fulahs I. T.
DT553.U742 R5313　　966/.25/004963　　*LC* 76-25630　　*ISBN* 0226717410

Nelson, Harold D.　　　　　　　　　　　　3.5396
Area handbook for the United Republic of Cameroon. Co–authors: Harold D. Nelson [and others] 1st ed. [Washington; For sale by the Supt. of Docs., U.S. Govt. Print. Off.] 1974. xiv, 335 p. maps. 24 cm. 'DA Pam 550-166.' 'One of a series of handbooks prepared by Foreign Area Studies (FAS) of the American University.' 1. Cameroon. I. American University (Washington, D.C.). Foreign Area Studies. II. T.
DT564.N44　　916.7/11/034　　*LC* 73-600274

Brain, Robert.　　　　　　　　　　　　3.5397
Bangwa kinship and marriage. — Cambridge [Eng.]: University Press, 1972. ix, 195 p.: ill.; 24 cm. 1. Bangwa (African people) 2. Kinship I. T.
DT570.B69　　916.7/112　　*LC* 70-166945　　*ISBN* 0521083117

Le Vine, Victor T.　　　　　　　　　　　　• 3.5398
The Cameroons, from mandate to independence, by Victor T. Le Vine. — Berkeley, University of California Press, 1964. xi, 329 p. geneal. table, maps. 25 cm. Bibliography: p. 303-319. 1. Cameroun — Hist. 2. Cameroons — Hist. I. T.
DT572.L4 1964　　967.11　　*LC* 64-24585

Rudin, Harry Rudolph, 1898-.　　　　　　　　　　　　• 3.5399
Germans in the Cameroons, 1884–1914; a case study in modern imperialism, by Harry R. Rudin. [Hamden, Conn.] Archon Books, 1968. 456 p. fold. map. 22 cm. Reprint of the 1938 ed. 'This study ... originated in a doctoral dissertation at Yale University in 1931.' 1. Imperialism 2. Cameroon. 3. Germany — Colonies — Administration. I. T.
DT572.R8 1968　　325.3/43/096711　　*LC* 68-54380　　*ISBN* 020800680X

Rubin, Neville N.　　　　　　　　　　　　3.5400
Cameroun; an African federation [by] Neville Rubin. — New York: Praeger, [1971, i.e. 1972] x, 259 p.: maps.; 23 cm. — (Praeger library of African affairs) 1. Cameroon — Politics and government I. T.
DT572.R84 1972　　320.967/11 19　　*LC* 78-150705

An African experiment in nation building: the bilingual　　　3.5401
Cameroon Republic since reunification / edited by Ndiva
Kofele–Kale.
Boulder, Colo.: Westview Press, 1980. lii, 369 p.; 24 cm. (Westview special studies on Africa) 1. Cameroon — Politics and government — 1960-1982 2. Cameroon — Economic conditions — 1960- 3. Cameroon — Social conditions — 1960- I. Kofele-Kale, Ndiva.
DT576.A33　　967/.1104　　*LC* 79-5356　　*ISBN* 0891586857

DT591–617 Angola. Guinea-Bissau

Birmingham, David.　　　　　　　　　　　　• 3.5402
Trade and conflict in Angola: the Mbundu and their neighbours under the influence of the Portuguese, 1483–1790. — Oxford, Clarendon P., 1966. xvii, 178 p.: maps, tables; 22 1/2 cm. — (Oxford studies in African affairs.) Bibliography: p. [164]-168. 1. Angola — Hist. 2. Africa, West — Hist. 3. Slave-trade — Africa, West. 4. Mbundu (Bantu tribe) 5. Portuguese in West Africa. I. T. II. Series.
DT604.B5　　967.302　　*LC* 66-75626

American University (Washington, D.C.). Foreign Area Studies.　　3.5403
Angola, a country study / Foreign Area Studies, The American University; edited by Irving Kaplan. — 2d ed. — Washington; Foreign Area Studies, American University: for sale by the Supt. of Docs., U.S. Govt. Print. Off.,

c1979. xxiii, 286 p.: ill.; 24 cm. — (Area handbook series.) First ed., by A. B. Herrick and others, published in 1967 under title: Area handbook for Angola. 'Research completed October 1978.' 'DA pam 550-59.' Includes index. 1. Angola. I. Kaplan, Irving, 1923- II. Herrick, Allison Butler. Area handbook for Angola. III. American University (Washington, D.C.). Foreign Area Studies. IV. T. V. Series.
DT611.H47 1979　　967/.3　　*LC* 79-21789

Miller, Joseph Calder.　　　　　　　　　　　　3.5404
Kings and kinsmen: early Mbundu states in Angola / by Joseph C. Miller. Oxford [Eng.]: Clarendon Press, 1976. xviii, 312 p.: ill.; 23 cm. — (Oxford studies in African affairs.) Includes index. 1. Mbundu (Bantu tribe) — Politics and government. I. T. II. Series.
DT611.42.M56　　301.5/92/09673　　*LC* 76-366823　　*ISBN* 0198227043

Henderson, Lawrence W., 1921-.　　　　　　　　　　　　3.5405
Angola: five centuries of conflict / Lawrence W. Henderson. — Ithaca [N.Y.]: Cornell University Press, 1979. 272 p.: maps; 21 cm. — (Africa in the modern world) Includes index. 1. Angola — History I. T.
DT611.5.H46　　967/.3　　*LC* 79-5089　　*ISBN* 0801412471

Wheeler, Douglas L.　　　　　　　　　　　　• 3.5406
Angola [by] Douglas L. Wheeler and René Pélissier. — New York: Praeger Publishers, [1971] ix, 296 p.: illus., maps, port.; 23 cm. — (Praeger library of African affairs) 1. Angola — Politics and government I. Pélissier, René. II. T.
DT611.62.W54　　916.7/3/033　　*LC* 75-77309

Bender, Gerald J.　　　　　　　　　　　　3.5407
Angola under the Portuguese: the myth and the reality / Gerald J. Bender. — Berkeley: University of California Press, 1978. xxviii, 287 p.: ill.; 23 cm. (Perspectives on Southern Africa. 23) Includes index. 1. Race awareness — Angola. 2. Angola — Colonization. 3. Angola — Race relations. 4. Angola — Social conditions. 5. Angola — Economic conditions 6. Portugal — Colonies — Africa — Administration. I. T. II. Series.
DT611.7.B46　　967/.303　　*LC* 76-7751　　*ISBN* 0520032217

Davidson, Basil, 1914-.　　　　　　　　　　　　3.5408
In the eye of the storm; Angola's people. — [1st ed. in the U.S.A.]. — Garden City, N.Y.: Doubleday, 1972. xiv, 367 p.: maps.; 22 cm. 1. Nationalism — Angola. 2. Guerrillas — Angola. 3. Angola — History I. T.
DT611.7.D33　　967/.3　　*LC* 72-76710　　*ISBN* 0385031793

Marcum, John A.　　　　　　　　　　　　3.5409
The Angolan revolution. — Cambridge, Mass.: M.I.T. Press, [1969-78]. 2 v.: maps.; 24 cm. — ([Studies in communism, revisionism, and revolution, 15-22]) 1. Angola — History — Revolution, 1961-1975 I. T.
DT611.75.M37　　967/.303　　*LC* 69-11310

Chabal, Patrick, 1951-.　　　　　　　　　　　　3.5410
Amílcar Cabral: revolutionary leadership and people's war / Patrick Chabal. — Cambridge [Cambridgeshire]; New York: Cambridge University Press, 1983. xiii, 272 p.: maps; 24 cm. (African studies series. 37) Includes index. 1. Cabral, Amílcar, 1921-1973. 2. Partido Africano da Independência da Guiné e Cabo Verde. 3. National liberation movements — Guinea-Bissau. 4. Revolutionists — Guinea-Bissau — Biography. 5. Guinea-Bissau — Politics and government — To 1974 I. T. II. Series.
DT613.76.C3 C52 1983　　322.4/2/0924 B 19　　*LC* 82-14632　　*ISBN* 0521249449

DT621–637 Liberia

Liberia, a country study / Foreign Area Studies, the American　　3.5411
University; edited by Harold D. Nelson.
3rd ed. — Washington, D.C.: The Studies: For sale by the Supt. of Docs., U.S. G.P.O., 1984. xxxi, 340 p.: ill.; 24 cm. (Area handbook series) (DA pam. 550-38) Rev. ed. of: Area handbook for Liberia. 1972. 'Research completed September 1984.' Includes index. 1. Liberia. I. Nelson, Harold D. II. American University (Washington, D.C.). Foreign Area Studies. III. Area handbook for Liberia. IV. Series. V. Series: DA pam. 550-38
DT624.L54　　966.6/2 19　　*LC* 85-7393

Greene, Graham, 1904-.　　　　　　　　　　　　3.5412
Journey without maps. [2d ed.] New York, Viking Press, 1961. 310 p. illus. 21 cm. (Compass books, C75) 1. Liberia — Description and travel. 2. Guinea — Description and travel. I. T.
DT626.G7x　　916.66　　*LC* 61-66000

Buell, Raymond Leslie, 1896-1946.   • **3.5413**
Liberia: a century of survival, 1847–1947, by Raymond Leslie Buell. Philadelphia, University of Pennsylvania press, the University museum, 1947. 140 p. (African handbooks, ed. by H. A. Wieschhoff. 7) 1. Liberia. I. T.
DT632.B8   960   *LC* 47-1714

Shick, Tom W.   **3.5414**
Behold the promised land: a history of Afro–American settler society in nineteenth=century Liberia / Tom W. Shick. — Baltimore: Johns Hopkins University Press, c1980. xv, 208 p.: ill.; 24 cm. — (John[s] Hopkins studies in Atlantic history and culture) Includes index. 1. Afro-Americans — Liberia — History. 2. Afro-Americans — Colonization — Liberia. 3. Liberia — History — To 1847 4. Liberia — History — 1847-1944 I. T. II. Series.
DT633.S47   966.6/201 19   *LC* 79-22960   *ISBN* 0801823099

Blyden, Edward Wilmot, 1832-1912.   **3.5415**
Selected letters of Edward Wilmot Blyden / edited and with introductions by Hollis R. Lynch; foreword by Léopold Sédar Senghor. — Millwood, N.Y.: KTO Press, c1978. xxii, 530 p.: port. — (African diaspora) 1. Blyden, Edward Wilmot, 1832-1912. 2. Pan-Africanism — History — Sources. 3. Statesmen — Liberia — Correspondence. 4. Intellectuals — Liberia — Correspondence. 5. Intellectuals — Africa, West — Correspondence. 6. Liberia — History — 1847-1944 — Sources. 7. Africa, West — History — Sources. I. Lynch, Hollis Ralph. II. T.
DT634.3.B58 A4 1977   DT634.3B58 A4 1978.   966.6/202/0924
LC 77-56887   *ISBN* 0527588903

Tubman, William V. S., 1895-1971.   • **3.5416**
The official papers of William V. S. Tubman, President of the Republic of Liberia: covering addresses, messages, speeches and statements 1960–1967; edited by E. Reginald Townsend, assisted by Abeodu Bowen Jones. — London: published for the Department of Information and Cultural Affairs, Monrovia, Liberia, by Longmans, 1968. xxi, 687 p.: 9 plates, 17 illus., 2 maps.; 26 cm. 1. Tubman, William V. S., 1895-1971. I. Townsend, E. Reginald, ed. II. Jones, Abeodu Bowen, ed. III. Liberia. Dept. of Information and Cultural Affairs. IV. T.
DT636.T8 A5   966/.603/08   *LC* 68-115801

DT641–671 Zaire (Congo Kinhasa). Congo (Leopoldville). Cape Verde

American University (Washington, D.C.). Foreign Area Studies.   **3.5417**
Zaïre, a country study / Foreign Area Studies, The American University; edited by Irving Kaplan. — 3d ed. — Washington: FAS: for sale by the Supt. of Docs., c1979. xxi, 332 p.: ill.; 24 cm. — (Area handbook series.) Written by H. M. Roth and others. Supersedes the 1971 ed. prepared by G. C. McDonald and others, and issued under title: Area handbook for the Democratic Republic of the Congo (Congo Kinshasa) 'DA pam 550-67.' Includes index. 1. Zaire. I. Kaplan, Irving, 1923- II. Roth, H. Mark. III. McDonald, Gordon C. Area handbook for the Democratic Republic of the Congo (Congo Kinshasa) IV. T. V. Series.
DT644.A75 1979   967.5/103   *LC* 79-9987

Turnbull, Colin M.   • **3.5418**
The lonely African. — New York: Simon and Schuster, 1962. 251 p.: illus.; 22 cm. 1. Social change 2. Zaire — Social life and customs. I. T.
DT647.T8   916   *LC* 62-9611

Packard, Randall M., 1945-.   **3.5419**
Chiefship and cosmology: an historical study of political competition / Randall M. Packard. — Bloomington: Indiana University Press, c1981. xii, 243 p.: maps; 25 cm. — (African systems of thought.) Based of the author's thesis (Ph.D.) Includes index. 1. Bashi (African people) — Kings and rulers. 2. Bashi (African people) — Politics and government. I. T. II. Series.
DT650.B366 P3   967.5/17 19   *LC* 81-47013   *ISBN* 0253308313

Reefe, Thomas Q.   **3.5420**
The rainbow and the kings: a history of the Luba Empire to 1891 / Thomas Q. Reefe. — Berkeley: University of California Press, c1981. xx, 286 p.; 22 cm. Includes index. 1. Luba (African people) — History. 2. Zaire — History — To 1908 I. T.
DT650.L8 R43   967.5/101   *LC* 80-17627   *ISBN* 0520041402

Turnbull, Colin M.   • **3.5421**
The forest people. New York: Simon and Schuster, 1961. 288 p.: illus.; 25 cm. 1. Bambute 2. Ethnology — Zaire I. T.
DT650.T8   572.9675   *LC* 61-12850

Thornton, John Kelly, 1949-.   **3.5422**
The Kingdom of Kongo: civil war and transition, 1641–1718 / John K. Thornton. — Madison, Wis.: University of Wisconsin Press, 1983. xxi, 193 p.: map; 24 cm. Revision of thesis (Ph. D.)—University of California, Los Angeles, 1979. Includes index. 1. Kongo Kingdom — History. I. T.
DT654.T56 1983   967/.2401 19   *LC* 82-70549   *ISBN* 0299092909

Gann, Lewis H., 1924-.   **3.5423**
The rulers of Belgian Africa, 1884–1914 / L. H. Gann and Peter Duignan. — Princeton, N.J.: Princeton University Press, c1979. xv, 265 p.; 22 cm. Includes index. 1. Zaire — Politics and government — 1885-1908 2. Zaire — Politics and government — 1908-1960 I. Duignan, Peter. joint author. II. T.
DT655.G36   320.9/675/102   *LC* 79-83989   *ISBN* 0691052778

Slade, Ruth M.   • **3.5424**
King Leopold's Congo; aspects of the development of race relations in the Congo Independent State. — London, New York, Oxford University Press, 1962. xi, 230 p. illus., ports., maps (part fold.) 23 cm. 'Issued under the auspices of the Institute of Race Relations, London.' Bibliography: p. [215]-219. 1. Congo (Leopoldville) — Hist. — Early to 1908. I. T.
DT655.S55   967.5   *LC* 62-4981

Anstey, Roger.   • **3.5425**
King Leopold's legacy: the Congo under Belgian rule, 1908–1960. — London, Oxford U. P., issued under the auspices of the Institute of Race Relations, 1966. xv, 293 p. front. (map) 8 plates (incl. ports., facsim.) 22 1/2 cm. Bibliography: p. [265]-272. 1. Congo (Leopoldville) — Hist. — 1908-1960. I. T.
DT657.A6x   967.502   *LC* 66-70025

Lemarchand, René.   • **3.5426**
Political awakening in the Belgian Congo [by] René Lemarchand. — Berkeley, University of California Press, 1964. x, 357 p. illus., maps, ports. 25 cm. Bibliographical references included in 'Notes' (p. 312-347) 1. Congo (Leopoldville) — Pol. & govt. I. T.
DT657.L45   320.9675   *LC* 64-21774

Lumumba, Patrice, 1925-1961.   • **3.5427**
[Congo, terre d'avenir, est-il menacé? English] Congo, my country. With a foreword by Colin Legum. New York, Praeger [1962] 195 p. illus. 23 cm. (Books that matter) Translation of Le Congo, terre d'avenir, est-il menacé? 1. Zaire — Politics and government I. T.
DT657.L813 1962   967.5   *LC* 62-18269

Merriam, Alan P., 1923-.   • **3.5428**
Congo, background of conflict. — [Evanston, Ill.] Northwestern University Press, 1961. 368 p. illus. 23 cm. — (Northwestern University African studies, no. 6) Includes bibliography. 1. Congo, Belgian — Pol. & govt. I. T.
DT657.M4   967.5   *LC* 61-11381

Young, Crawford, 1931-.   • **3.5429**
Politics in the Congo; decolonization and independence by Crawford Young. Princeton, N.J., Princeton University Press, 1965. xii, 659 p. maps. 21 cm. 1. Decolonization — Zaire. 2. Zaire — Politics and government — 1960- I. T.
DT658.Y6   320.9/675/1   *LC* 65-10843

Lumumba, Patrice, 1925-1961.   **3.5430**
[Pensée politique de Patrice Lumumba. English] Lumumba speaks: the speeches and writings of Patrice Lumumba, 1958–1961. Edited by Jean van Lierde. Translated from the French by Helen R. Lane. Introd. by Jean–Paul Sartre. Boston, Little, Brown [1972] vi, 433 p. 22 cm. Translation of La pensée politique de Patrice Lumumba. 1. Zaire — Politics and government I. T.
DT663.L8 A2513   967.5/1/03   *LC* 72-3908   *ISBN* 0316536504

O'Brien, Conor Cruise, 1917-.   • **3.5431**
To Katanga and back: a UN case history / Conor Cruise O'Brien. — New York: Simon and Schuster, 1962. 370 p.: plates, ports; 21cm. 1. United Nations — Zaire — Case studies 2. Katanga, Zaire (Province) — Case studies I. T.
DT665.K3C7   *LC* 63-9271

Davidson, Basil, 1914-.   **3.5432**
No fist is big enough to hide the sky: the liberation of Guine-Bissau and Cape Verde: aspects of an African revolution / Basil Davidson; foreword by Amilcar Cabral; preface by Aristides Pereira. — London: Zed, 1982 (c1981). xiv, 187 p.; 23 cm. 1. Partido Africano da Independência da Guiné e Cabo Verde. 2. National liberation movements — Guinea-Bissau. 3. National liberation movements — Cape Verde. 4. Guinea-Bissau — Politics and government — To 1974 5. Cape Verde — Politics and government — To 1975 I. T.
DT671.C265 D38   966/.5702 19   *LC* 81-167706   *ISBN*
0905762932

DT701–720 Southwest Africa

Wellington, John H.   • 3.5433
South West Africa and its human issues, by John H. Wellington. — Oxford,
Clarendon P., 1967. xxiv, 461 p. front., 13 plates, maps, tables. 22 1/2 cm.
Bibliographical footnotes. 1. Africa, Southwest. 2. Africa, Southwest —
Native races. I. T.
DT703.W4   968/.8   *LC* 67-108668

Marshall, Lorna.   3.5434
The !Kung of Nyae Nyae / Lorna Marshall. Cambridge, Mass.: Harvard
University Press, 1976. xxiii, 433 p.: ill.; 25 cm. 1. !Kung (African people) I. T.
DT709.M37   301.45/19/61   *LC* 76-19152   *ISBN* 0674505697

Aydelotte, William Osgood.   • 3.5435
Bismarck and British colonial policy; the problem of South West Africa,
1883–1885. [2d ed., rev.] New York, Russell & Russell [1970] xvii, 207 p. ports.
23 cm. 1. Bismarck, Otto, Fürst von, 1815-1898. 2. Namibia — History
3. Germany — Foreign relations — Great Britain. 4. Great Britain — Foreign
relations — Germany I. T.
DT714.A85 1970   327.42/043   *LC* 73-113161

DT730–995 Southern Africa

Axelson, Eric, 1913- ed.   • 3.5436
South African explorers; selected and introduced by Eric Axelson. — London,
New York, Oxford University Press [1954] xxv, 346 p. fold. map. 16 cm. —
(The World's classics, 538) Bibliography: p. [xxiii]-xxv. 1. Africa, South —
Disc. & explor. I. T.
DT731.A79   968   *LC* A 56-643

Livingstone, David, 1813-1873.   • 3.5437
African journal, 1853–1856. Edited with an introd. by I. Schapera. Berkeley,
University of California Press, 1963. 2 v. (xxiii, 495) facims., maps. 23 cm.
1. Africa, Central — Description and travel 2. South Africa — Description
and travel I. T.
DT731.L732 1963   *LC* 63-5724

Jeal, Tim.   3.5438
Livingstone. — [1st American ed.]. — New York: Putnam, [1973] xiv, 427 p.:
illus.; 24 cm. 1. Livingstone, David, 1813-1873. I. T.
DT731.L8 J47 1973   916.7/04 B   *LC* 73-82030   *ISBN* 0399112154

Wellington, John H.   • 3.5439
Southern Africa; a geographical study. Cambridge [Eng.] University Press
1955. 1. Africa, South — Description and travel I. T.
DT732 W4   *LC* 55-4501

Cole, Monica M.   • 3.5440
South Africa, by Monica M. Cole. 2nd ed. London, Methuen; New York,
Dutton, 1966. xxx, 706 p. plates, maps, tables, diagrs. 24 cm. ([Methuen's
advanced geographies]) 1. South Africa — Description and travel — 1966-
2. South Africa — Industries. I. T.
DT733.C6 1966   916.8   *LC* 67-70598

Schreuder, D. M. (Deryck Marshall)   3.5441
The scramble for southern Africa, 1877–1895: the politics of partition
reappraised / D. M. Schreuder. — Cambridge; New York: Cambridge
University Press, 1980. xiii, 384 p.: map; 24 cm. (Cambridge Commonwealth
series) Includes index. 1. Africa, Southern — Colonization. 2. Africa,
Southern — History 3. South Africa — History — 1836-1909 I. T.
DT745.S36   325/.30968   *LC* 78-58800   *ISBN* 0521202795

Southern Africa: the continuing crisis / edited by Gwendolen M.   3.5442
Carter and Patrick O'Meara.
2nd ed., 1st Midland book ed. — Bloomington: Indiana University Press, 1982.
xii, 404 p.: maps; 24 cm. 'A Midland book.' 1. Africa, Southern — Politics and
government — 1975- — Addresses, essays, lectures. I. Carter, Gwendolen
Margaret, 1906- II. O'Meara, Patrick.
DT746.S63 1982   968.06 19   *LC* 81-48324   *ISBN* 0253354005

South Africa in southern Africa: the intensifying vortex of   3.5443
violence / edited by Thomas M. Callaghy.
New York, N.Y.: Praeger, 1983. viii, 420 p.: map; 25 cm. Include index.
1. Violence — Africa, Southern — Addresses, essays, lectures. 2. South Africa
— Relations — Africa, Southern — Addresses, essays, lectures. 3. Africa,

Southern — Politics and government — 1975- — Addresses, essays, lectures.
4. Africa, Southern — Economic conditions — 1975- — Addresses, essays,
lectures. 5. Africa, Southern — Relations — South Africa — Addresses,
essays, lectures. 6. South Africa — Politics and government — 1961-1978 —
Addresses, essays, lectures. 7. South Africa — Politics and government —
1978- — Addresses, essays, lectures. I. Callaghy, Thomas M.
DT747.S6 S68 1983   968.06/2 19   *LC* 83-4248   *ISBN* 0030603064

DT751–995 South Africa (Republic of South Africa)

Christopher, A. J.   3.5444
Southern Africa / A. J. Christopher. Folkestone, Eng.: Dawson; Hamden,
Conn.: Archon Books, 1977 (c1976). 292 p.: ill.; 23 cm. (Studies in historical
geography 0308-6607) Includes index. 1. Agriculture — Economic aspects —
Africa, Southern. 2. Africa, Southern — Historical geography. 3. Africa,
Southern — Industries. I. T.
DT753.C47   911/.68   *LC* 76-21207   *ISBN* 0208016201

South Africa, a country study / Foreign Area Studies, the   3.5445
American University; edited by Harold D. Nelson.
Rev. ed. Washington, D.C.: For sale by the Supt. of Docs., U.S. G.P.O., c1981.
xxix, 464 p.: ill.; 24 cm. — (Area handbook series.) (DA pam. 550-93)
'Supersedes 1971 edition.' 'Research completed December 1980.' Includes
index. 1. South Africa. I. Nelson, Harold D. II. American University
(Washington, D.C.). Foreign Area Studies. III. Series. IV. Series: DA pam.
550-93
DT753.S57 1981   968 19   *LC* 81-19155

DT759–764 Ethnography. Race Relations

Jabavu, Noni.   • 3.5446
Drawn in color: African contrasts. New York: St. Martin's Press [1962, c1960]
208 p.; 22 cm. 'A personal account of ... [the author's] experiences and
impressions of the differences between East and South Africa in their contact
with westernisation.' 1. South Africa — Social life and customs. 2. Uganda —
Social life and customs. I. T.
DT761.J25 1962   916.8   *LC* 62-8319

The Shaping of South African society, 1652–1820 / edited by   3.5447
Richard Elphick and Hermann Giliomee.
Cape Town: Longman, 1979. xvi, 415 p.: ill.; 22 cm. 1. Social structure —
Addresses, essays, lectures. 2. South Africa — Social life and customs —
Addresses, essays, lectures. 3. South Africa — Ethnic relations — Addresses,
essays, lectures. 4. South Africa — Race relations — Addresses, essays,
lectures. 5. South Africa — Social conditions — Addresses, essays, lectures.
6. South Africa — History — To 1836 — Addresses, essays, lectures.
I. Elphick, Richard. II. Giliomee, Hermann Buhr, 1938-
DT761.S5   968.03   *LC* 79-670377   *ISBN* 0582646448

Abrahams, Peter, 1919-.   • 3.5448
Return to Goli. London Faber and Faber [1953] 224p. 1. Africa, South —
Native races 2. Johannesburg — Description I. T.
DT763 A62 1953

Cornevin, Marianne.   3.5449
Apartheid: power and historical falsification / Marianne Cornevin. — Paris:
Unesco, 1980. 144 p.: maps; 24 cm. — (Insights) 1. Blacks — South Africa —
History. 2. Segregation — South Africa — History. 3. South Africa — Race
relations I. T.
DT763.C673   968/.004 19   *LC* 80-494168   *ISBN* 9231017691

De Gruchy, John W.   3.5450
The church struggle in South Africa / by John W. de Gruchy. — Grand
Rapids: W. B. Eerdmans Pub. Co., c1979. xv, 267 p.: map; 21 cm. 1. Race
relations — Religious aspects 2. South Africa — Race relations 3. South
Africa — Church history I. T.
DT763.D397   261.8/34/00968 19   *LC* 78-26761   *ISBN*
0802817866

From protest to challenge; a documentary history of African   3.5451
politics in South Africa, 1882–1964. Edited by Thomas Karis
and Gwendolen M. Carter.
Stanford, Calif., Hoover Institution Press 1977. 825 p. (Hoover Institution
publications, 89, 122-123, 161) 1. Blacks — South Africa — Politics and

government. 2. South Africa — Native races I. Karis, Thomas, 1919- ed. II. Carter, Gwendolen Margaret, 1906- ed.
DT763.F73   323.4/0968   *LC* 72-152423   *ISBN* 0817918914

Kuper, Leo.   • **3.5452**
Passive resistance in South Africa. New Haven, Yale University Press. New York, Kraus Reprint Co., 1971 [c1957] 256 p. illus. 23 cm. 1. Passive resistance — South Africa. 2. South Africa — Race question. I. T.
DT763.K8 1971   301.451/968   *LC* 73-148843

Macmillan, William M. (William Miller), 1885-1974.   • **3.5453**
Bantu, Boer, and Briton; the making of the South African native problem. — Rev. and enl. ed. — Oxford, Clarendon Press, 1963. xviii, 382 p. maps. 22 cm. 'Abbreviations, etc.' (Bibliographical): p. [XV] 'Bibliographical note': p. [372] 1. Africa, South — Hist. 2. Africa, South — Race question. 3. Bantus I. T.
DT763.M3 1963   968   *LC* 63-24832

Mandela, Nelson, 1918-.   **3.5454**
No easy walk to freedom: articles, speeches and trial addresses of Nelson Mandela / with a new foreword by Ruth First. — London: Heinemann Educational, 1973. xiv, 189 p.: ports.; 19 cm. — (African writers series) 1. South Africa — Race relations 2. South Africa — Politics and government — 1948-1961 3. South Africa — Politics and government — 1961-1978 I. T.
DT763.M35 1973   323.1/19/68   *LC* 77-373404   *ISBN* 0435901230

North, James.   **3.5455**
Freedom rising / James North. — New York: Macmillan Pub. Co., c1985. xi, 336 p., [8] p. of plates: ill.; 24 cm. Includes index. 1. National liberation movements — South Africa. 2. Civil rights — South Africa. 3. Guerrillas — South Africa. 4. South Africa — Race relations 5. Zimbabwe — Politics and government — 1979-1980 6. Zimbabwe — Politics and government — 1980- I. T.
DT763.N67 1985   305.8/00968 19   *LC* 84-21871   *ISBN* 0025899406

Representative South African speeches: the rhetoric of race and religion / edited by Alan L. McLeod and Marian B. McLeod; foreword by H.H. Anniah Gowda.   **3.5456**
Mysore: Centre for Commonwealth Literature and Research, University of Mysore, 1980. ix, 265 p.; 21 cm. (Powre above powres. 5) 1. Race relations — Religious aspects — Addresses, essays, lectures. 2. South Africa — Race relations — Addresses, essays, lectures. I. McLeod, A. L. (Alan Lindsey), 1928- II. McLeod, Marian B. III. Series.
DT763.R395   305.8/00968 19   *LC* 81-185877

Roux, Edward.   • **3.5457**
Time longer than rope; a history of the black man's struggle for freedom in South Africa. — [2d ed.]. — Madison, University of Wisconsin Press, 1964. xviii, 469 p. maps. 20 cm. Includes bibliographical references. 1. Africa, South — Native races. 2. Communism — Africa, South. I. T.
DT763.R6 1964   968   *LC* 64-12728

Shepherd, George W.   **3.5458**
Anti–apartheid: transnational conflict and Western policy in the liberation of South Africa / George W. Shepherd, Jr. — Westport, Conn.: Greenwood Press, 1977. xii, 246 p.; 22 cm. — (Studies in human rights. no. 3) 1. South Africa — Race relations I. T. II. Series.
DT763.S39   301.45/1/0968   *LC* 77-71868   *ISBN* 0837195373

Gerhart, Gail M.   **3.5459**
Black power in South Africa: the evolution of an ideology / Gail M. Gerhart. — Berkeley: University of California Press, c1978. xi, 364 p.: ill.; 23 cm. — (Perspectives on Southern Africa. 19) Includes index. 1. African National Congress. 2. Blacks — South Africa — Politics and government. 3. Blacks — South Africa — Race identity. 4. South Africa — Politics and government 5. South Africa — Race relations I. T. II. Series.
DT763.6.G47   301.45/19/6068   *LC* 75-13149   *ISBN* 0520030222

Schapera, Isaac, 1905- ed.   • **3.5460**
The Bantu–speaking tribes of South Africa; an ethnographical survey, edited for the (South African) Inter–university committee for African studies by I. Schapera. Contributors: Raymond A. Dart, Clement M. Doke and others ... London, G. Routledge & sons, ltd., 1937. xv, 453 p. illus. (music) XXIV pl. (incl. front.) double map. 24 1/2 cm. 1. Bantus 2. Ethnology — Africa, South. 3. Bantu languages 4. South Africa — Native races. I. Inter–university committee for African studies. II. T.
DT764.B2 S39   *LC* 38-90

Huttenback, Robert A.   • **3.5461**
Gandhi in South Africa; British imperialism and the Indian question, 1860–1914, by Robert A. Huttenback. Ithaca [N.Y.] Cornell University Press [1971] ix, 368 p. illus., map, ports. 22 cm. 1. Gandhi, Mahatma, 1869-1948. 2. East Indians in South Africa — History. 3. Great Britain — Colonies — Africa — Administration. I. T.
DT764.E3 H84   320.5   *LC* 73-124723   *ISBN* 0801405866

Pachai, Bridglal.   **3.5462**
The international aspects of the South African Indian question, 1860–1971 [by] B. Pachai. — Cape Town: C. Struik, 1971. xi, 318 p.; 25 cm. 1. United Nations — South Africa. 2. East Indians in South Africa. I. T.
DT764.E3 P3   301.451/91411/068   *LC* 76-871404   *ISBN* 086977008X

DT765–779 HISTORY

Galbraith, John S.   • **3.5463**
Reluctant empire; British policy on the South African frontier, 1834–1854. — Berkeley, University of California Press, 1963. 293 p. 25 cm. Includes bibliography. 1. Africa, South — Hist. I. T.
DT766.G3   968.04   *LC* 63-9801

Wilson, Monica Hunter.   • **3.5464**
The Oxford history of South Africa, edited by Monica Wilson and Leonard Thompson. — New York: Oxford University Press, 1969-71. 2 v.: illus.; 24 cm. 1. South Africa — History I. Thompson, Leonard Monteath. joint author. II. T.
DT766.W762   968   *LC* 74-77602

Barber, James P.   **3.5465**
South Africa's foreign policy, 1945–1970 [by] James Barber. — London; New York: Oxford University Press, 1973. 325 p.: ill.; 22 cm. 1. South Africa — Foreign relations — 1948-1961 I. T.
DT770.B3   327.68   *LC* 73-172971   *ISBN* 0192156519

Walker, Eric A. (Eric Anderson), 1886-.   • **3.5466**
The Great Trek. — 4th ed., rev. — London, A. & C. Black, [1960] viii, 377 p. illus. plates, maps 23 cm. (The Pioneer Histories, edited by V.T. Harlow and J.A. Williamson) 1. South Africa — History — Great Trek, 1836-1840. I. T.
DT773.W3 1960   968.2

De Kiewiet, C. W. (Cornelius William), 1902-.   • **3.5467**
The imperial factor in South Africa; a study in politics and economics. New York Russell & Russell 1966. 341p. 1. Africa, South — History 2. Africa, South — Race question 3. Africa, South — Economic condition I. T.
DT775 D4 1966

Lovell, Reginald Ivan.   **3.5468**
The struggle for South Africa, 1875–1899: a study in economic imperialism / by Reginald Ivan Lovell. — New York: Macmillan, 1934. xv, 438 p.: maps; 24 cm. Half-title: Bureau of International Research, Harvard University and Radcliffe College. 1. Rhodes, Cecil, 1853-1902. 2. South Africa — History 3. South Africa — Politics and government 4. Great Britain — Foreign relations — Germany 5. Germany — Foreign relations — Great Britain. I. Bureau of International Research of Harvard University and Radcliffe College. II. T.
DT775.L68   *LC* 34-2089

Carter, Gwendolen Margaret, 1906-.   • **3.5469**
The politics of inequality; South Africa since 1948 [by] Gwendolen M. Carter. — [3d] rev. ed. — London: Thames and Hudson, [1962, c1958] 541 p.: illus., maps.; 25 cm. 1. South Africa — Politics and government — 1948-1961 I. T.
DT779.7.C3 1962   *LC* 65-84528

Stultz, Newell Maynard.   **3.5470**
Afrikaner politics in South Africa, 1934–1948 / Newell M. Stultz. — Berkeley: University of California Press, 1975 (c1974) x, 200 p.; 22 cm. (Perspectives on Southern Africa. 13]) Includes index. 1. South Africa — Politics and government — 1909-1948 I. T. II. Series.
DT779.7.S76   320.9/68/05   *LC* 73-76116   *ISBN* 0520024524

Woods, Donald, 1933-.   **3.5471**
Biko / Donald Woods. — New York: Paddington Press, c1978. 288 p., [8] leaves of plates: ill.; 24 cm. Includes index. 1. Biko, Stephen, 1946-1977. 2. Woods, Donald, 1933- 3. Political prisoners — South Africa — Biography. 4. Journalists — South Africa — Biography. 5. South Africa — Race relations I. T.
DT779.8.B48 W66   322.4/4/0924 B   *LC* 78-1882   *ISBN* 0448231697

Luthuli, Albert John, 1898-.   • **3.5472**
Let my people go. New York, McGraw-Hill [1962] 255 p. illus. 22 cm. Autobiography. 1. Luthuli, Albert John, 1898- 2. South Africa — Race question. I. T.
DT779.8.L8 A3   323.168   *LC* 62-13819

Hancock, W. K. (William Keith), 1898-.   • **3.5473**
Smuts. Cambridge [Eng.] University Press, 1962-68. 2 v. ports., fold. maps (part col.), facsim. 24 cm. 1. Smuts, Jan Christiaan, 1870-1950. I. T.
DT779.8.S6 H28   968/.05/0924 B   *LC* 62-52102

Hepple, Alexander, 1904-. • 3.5474
Verwoerd. — Harmondsworth: Penguin, 1967. 253 p.; 18 cm. — (Political leaders of the twentieth century) (Pelican book A913.) 1. Verwoerd, Hendrik Frensch, 1901-1966. I. T.
DT779.8 V4H4   968/.05/0924 B   LC 67-108656

Change in contemporary South Africa / edited by Leonard 3.5475
Thompson and Jeffrey Butler.
Berkeley: University of California Press, c1975. xv, 447 p.; 25 cm. — (Perspectives on Southern Africa. 17) Based on a conference held at Seven Springs Farm Center, Mount Kisco, New York, from Apr. 7-12, 1974. Includes index. 1. South Africa — Politics and government — 1961-1978 — Addresses, essays, lectures. 2. South Africa — Social conditions — 1961- — Addresses, essays, lectures. 3. South Africa — Race relations — Addresses, essays, lectures. I. Thompson, Leonard Monteath. II. Butler, Jeffrey. III. Series.
DT779.9.C45   968.06   LC 74-82851   ISBN 0520028392

Hanf, Theodor. 3.5476
[Südafrika, friedlicher Wandel? English] South Africa, the prospects of peaceful change: an empirical enquiry into the possibility of democratic conflict regulation / Theodor Hanf, Heribert Weiland, and Gerda Vierdag; in collaboration with Lawrence Schlemmer, Rainer Hampel, and Burkhard Krupp; [translated by John Richardson; edited by Mark Orkin]. — London: R. Collings; Bloomington: Indiana University Press, c1981. xviii, 492 p.; ill.; 24 cm. Translation of Südafrika, friedlicher Wandel? Includes indexes. 1. South Africa — Politics and government — 1961-1978 2. South Africa — Race relations I. Weiland, Heribert, 1942- II. Vierdag, Gerda. III. Orkin, Mark. IV. T.
DT779.9.H3613 1981   960/.327 19   LC 81-47583   ISBN 0253353947

Van Zyl Slabbert, F. (Frederik) 3.5477
South Africa's options: strategies for sharing power / F. van Zyl Slabbert and David Welsh. — New York: St. Martin's Press, 1979. 196 p.; 22 cm. Includes index. 1. Blacks — South Africa — Politics and government. 2. South Africa — Politics and government — 1961- 3. South Africa — Race relations 4. South Africa — Ethnic relations. I. Welsh, David John. joint author. II. T.
DT779.9.V36 1979   320.9/68/06   LC 78-23291   ISBN 0312746962

DT781–848 Lesotho. Botswana

Ashton, E. H. (Edmund Hugh), 1911-. • 3.5478
The Basuto: a social study of traditional and modern Lesotho, by Hugh Ashton. 2nd ed. London, New York [etc.] published for the International African Institute by the Oxford U.P., 1967. xxxii, 359 p. front., 17 plates (incl. map), tables, diagrs. 22 1/2 cm. 1. Sotho (Bantu people) I. International African Institute. II. T.
DT782.A8 1967   916.8/6/03   LC 67-95012

Coates, Austin. • 3.5479
Basutoland. — London: H.M.S.O., 1966. xii, 135 p. col. front., illus., 17 plates (incl. col. map) 23 cm. — (Corona library) Bibliography: p. xiii. 1. Basutoland. I. T.
DT782.C6

Maylam, Paul. 3.5480
Rhodes, the Tswana, and the British: colonialism, collaboration, and conflict in the Bechuanaland Protectorate, 1885–1899 / Paul Maylam. — Westport, Conn.: Greenwood Press, 1980. x, 245 p.; ill.; 24 cm. (Contributions in comparative colonial studies. no. 4 0163 3813) Includes index. 1. British South Africa Company. 2. Tswana (African people) 3. Botswana — Colonization. I. T. II. Series.
DT791.M38   325/.341/09681   LC 79-8582   ISBN 0313208859

Sillery, A. • 3.5481
The Bechuanaland Protectorate. — Cape Town, New York, Oxford University Press, 1952. xii, 236 p. maps (1 fold.) tables. 22 cm. Bibliography: p. 219-222. 1. Bechuanaland. I. T.
DT791.S5   968.785   LC 52-12752

Young, Bertram Alfred, 1912-. • 3.5482
Bechuanaland. London H.M.S.O. 1966. 128p. (The Corona library) 1. Botswana. I. T. II. Series.
DT791 Y68

Howell, Nancy. 3.5483
Demography of the Dobe !Kung / Nancy Howell. — New York: Academic Press, 1979. xxi, 389 p.; ill.; 24 cm. — (Population and social structure.) 1. !Kung (African people) I. T. II. Series.
DT797.H68   306/.089961 19   LC 79-10147   ISBN 0123573505

Kalahari hunter–gatherers: studies of the !Kung San and their 3.5484
neighbors / edited by Richard B. Lee and Irven DeVore.
Cambridge, Mass.: Harvard University Press, 1976. xix, 408 p.; ill.; 25 cm. Includes index. 1. !Kung (African people) — Addresses, essays, lectures. 2. San (African people) — Addresses, essays, lectures. I. Lee, Richard B. II. DeVore, Irven.
DT797.K34   301.29/6   LC 75-28320   ISBN 0674499808

Lee, Richard B. 3.5485
The !Kung San: men, women, and work in a foraging society / Richard Borshay Lee. — Cambridge, [Eng.]; New York: Cambridge University Press, 1979. xxv, 526 p.; ill.; 24 cm. Includes index. 1. !Kung (African people) 2. San (African people) I. T.
DT797.L43   306/.089961 19   LC 78-25904   ISBN 0521225787

Shostak, Marjorie, 1945-. 3.5486
Nisa, the life and words of a !Kung woman / Marjorie Shostak. — Cambridge, Mass.: Harvard University Press, 1981. 402 p.: ill., ports.; 25 cm. 1. Nisa. 2. !Kung (African people) — Social life and customs. 3. !Kung (African people) — Biography. I. Nisa. II. T.
DT797.N57 S53   306/.08996106811 19   LC 81-4210   ISBN 0674624858

DT850–935 Central Africa (Former British Areas. Dutch Republics. Boer War)

Cairns, H. Alan C. • 3.5487
The clash of cultures; early race relations in Central Africa, by H. Alan C. Cairns. — New York, Praeger [1965] xvi, 330 p. 23 cm. Revision of thesis, Oxford University. Bibliography: p. 303-324. 1. Africa, Sub-Saharan — Race relations. 2. Africa, Sub-Saharan — History 3. British — Africa. I. T.
DT853.C36   301.2942067   LC 65-25487

Hanna, A. J. (Alexander John) • 3.5488
The story of the Rhodesias and Nyasaland [by] A. J. Hanna. — [2d ed.]. — London, Faber and Faber [1965] 331 p. illus., maps (part col.) 23 cm. Bibliography: p. 319-323. 1. Rhodesia, Northern — Hist. 2. Rhodesia, Southern — Hist. 3. Nyasaland — Hist. I. T.
DT853.5.H35 1965   LC 66-33124

Wills, A. J. (Alfred John) • 3.5489
An introduction to the history of Central Africa [by] A. J. Wills. 2nd ed. London, Oxford U.P., 1967. ix, 412 p. 10 maps, table. 22 1/2 cm. Map on endpaper. 1. Zimbabwe — History 2. Malawi — History 3. Zambia — History I. T. II. Title: The history of central Africa.
DT853.5.W5 1967   968.9   LC 67-77852

Hanna, A. J. (Alexander John) • 3.5490
The beginnings of Nyasaland and North–eastern Rhodesia, 1859–95. Oxford Clarendon Press 1956. 281p. 1. Nyasaland — History 2. Rhodesia, Northern — History I. T.
DT858 H3 1956

Nelson, Harold D. 3.5491
Area handbook for Malawi / coauthors, Harold D. Nelson ... [et al.]. — 1st ed. — Washington: For sale by the Supt. of Docs., U.S. Govt. Print. Off., 1975. xiv, 353 p.: ill.; 25 cm. 'DA Pam 550-172.' 'One of a series of handbooks prepared by Foreign Area Studies (FAS) of the American University.' Includes index. 1. Malawi. I. American University (Washington, D.C.). Foreign Area Studies. II. T.
DT858.N4   968.9/7/04   LC 75-619072

Pike, John G. • 3.5492
Malawi; a geographical study [by] J. G. Pike and G. T. Rimmington. — London, Oxford University Press, 1965. xiv, 229 p. illus., maps (part fold.) 26 cm. Includes bibliographies. 1. Malawi — Descr. & trav. I. Rimmington, Gerald T., joint author. II. T.
DT858.P5   LC 65-2172

Pachai, B. 3.5493
Malawi: the history of the nation / [by] B. Pachai. — New York: Longman, 1973. xi, 324 p.: ill.; 23 cm. 1. Malawi — History I. T.
DT859.P3   916.89/7/03   LC 73-173415   ISBN 0582645530

Shepperson, George. • 3.5494
Independent African; John Chilembwe and the origins, setting, and significance of the Nyasaland native rising of 1915, by George Shepperson and Thomas Price. — Edinburgh, University Press, 1958. x, 564 p. illus., ports., maps. 23 cm. — (Edinburgh University Publications; history, philosophy and economics

[no. 8]) 'Notes and references': p. 439-504. 'Sources': p. 505-526.
1. Chilembwe, John, d. 1915. 2. Booth, Joseph, 1851-1932. 3. Nyasaland —
Hist. 4. Missions — Nyasaland. I. Price, Thomas, 1907- joint author. II. T.
DT862.S4   968.97   *LC* 59-420

McMaster, Carolyn.   3.5495
Malawi, foreign policy and development / by Carolyn McMaster. — New
York: St. Martin's Press, 1974. x, 246 p.: ill., maps (on lining papers); 23 cm.
1. Malawi — Foreign relations 2. Malawi — Foreign economic relations.
3. Malawi — Foreign policy. I. T.
DT862.2.M33   327.68917   *LC* 74-80653

Williams, T. David.   3.5496
Malawi, the politics of despair / T. David Williams. — Ithaca [N.Y.]: Cornell
University Press, 1978. 339 p.: map. (Africa in the modern world) Includes
index. 1. Banda, H. Kamuzu (Hastings Kamuzu), 1905- 2. Malawi — Politics
and government 3. Malawi — Economic conditions. I. T.
DT862.2.W54   320.9/689/7   *LC* 77-90915   *ISBN* 0801411491

Kuper, Hilda.   • 3.5497
Indian people in Natal. — [Pietermaritzburg] Natal, University Press, 1960.
305 p. illus. 22 cm. 1. East Indians in Natal. I. T.
DT872.K8   301.45   *LC* 61-725

Krige, Eileen Jensen, 1904-.   3.5498
The social system of the Zulus. [4. ed.] Pietermaritzburg, Shuter & Shooter
[1962] xix, 420 p. illus., maps. 23 cm. 1. Zulus I. T.
DT878.Z9 K7x

Morris, Donald R.   • 3.5499
The washing of the spears; a history of the rise of the Zulu nation under Shaka
and its fall in the Zulu War of 1879 [by] Donald R. Morris. New York, Simon
and Schuster [1965] 655 p. illus., maps, ports. 24 cm. 1. Chaka, Zulu Chief,
1787?-1828. 2. Cetewayo, King of Zululand, ca. 1826-1884. 3. Zulu War, 1879
4. Zululand (South Africa) — History I. T.
DT878.Z9 M67   968.3   *LC* 65-12594

Ritter, E. A., 1890-.   • 3.5500
Shaka Zulu; the rise of the Zulu Empire. — London, New York, Longmans,
Green [1955] 383 p. illus. 23 cm. 1. Chaka, Zulu Chief, 1787?-1828. 2. Zulus
— Hist. I. T.
DT878.Z9R68   923.1683   *LC* 55-3983

Harrison, D. (David).   3.5501
The white tribe of Africa: South Africa in perspective / David Harrison. —
Berkeley: University of California Press, 1982. vii, 307 p.: ill.; 24 cm.
(Perspectives on Southern Africa. 31) Includes index. 1. Afrikaners — Ethnic
identity 2. Afrikaners — Psychology. 3. Afrikaners — Political activity.
4. South Africa — Race relations 5. South Africa — Politics and government
I. T. II. Series.
DT888.H37 1982   305.8/393606 19   *LC* 81-24057   *ISBN*
0520046900

Marais, Johannes Stephanus.   3.5502
The fall of Kruger's Republic. — Oxford, Clarendon Press, 1961. 345 p. 23 cm.
Includes bibliography. 1. Kruger, Paul, 1825-1904. 2. Transvaal — Hist. I. T.
DT929.M3   968.2   *LC* 61-3848

Van der Poel, Jean.   • 3.5503
The Jameson Raid. — Cape Town, New York, Oxford University Press, 1951.
271 p. map. 22 cm. Bibliography: p. 263-264. 1. Jameson's Raid, 1895-1896
I. T.
DT929.V3   968.2   *LC* 52-12756

Kruger, Rayne, 1922-.   • 3.5504
Good–bye Dolly Gray; the story of the Boer War. Philadelphia, Lippincott,
1960. 507 p. ill. 22 cm. 1. South African War, 1899-1902 I. T.
DT930.K8 1960   *LC* 60-7851

Pakenham, Thomas, 1933-.   3.5505
The Boer War / Thomas Pakenham. — 1st American ed. — New York:
Random House, c1979. xxix, 718 p., [16] leaves of plates: ill.; 25 cm. Includes
index. 1. South African War, 1899-1902 I. T.
DT930.P27 1979   968/.204   *LC* 79-4779   *ISBN* 0394427424

The South African War: the Anglo–Boer War, 1899–1902 /   3.5506
general editor, Peter Warwick; advisory editor, S.B. Spies.
Harlow, Essex: Longman, 1981 (c1980). 415 p.: ill.; 27 cm. Includes index.
1. South African War, 1899-1902 I. Warwick, Peter.
DT930.S68   968.04/8 19   *LC* 81-124692   *ISBN* 058278526X

DT946–963 Zimbabwe

Mason, Philip.   • 3.5507
The birth of a dilemma; the conquest and settlement of Rhodesia. Issued under
the auspices of the Institute of Race Relations. London, New York, Oxford
University Press, 1958. 366 p. ill. 23 cm. 1. Rhodesia — History. 2. Rhodesia
— Native races. I. T.
DT948.M28   *LC* 58-4475

Gann, Lewis H., 1924-.   • 3.5508
A history of Southern Rhodesia; early days to 1934, by L. H. Gann. — London,
Chatto & Windus, 1965. x, 354 p. fold. col. map. 25 cm. Imprint covered by
label: New York, Humanities Press. Bibliography: p. [341]-348. 1. Rhodesia,
Southern — Hist. I. T.
DT962.G33   968.9102   *LC* 66-1288

Zimbabwe, a country study / Foreign Area Studies, the   3.5509
American University; edited by Harold D. Nelson.
2nd ed. — Washington, D.C.: The Studies: For sale by the Supt. of Docs., U.S.
G.P.O., 1983. xxxiii, 360 p.: ill.; 24 cm. — (DA pam. 550-171) (Area handbook
series.) Rev. ed. of: Area handbook for Southern Rhodesia. 1975. 'Research
completed August 1982.' Includes index. 1. Zimbabwe. I. Nelson, Harold D.
II. Nelson, Harold D. Area handbook for Southern Rhodesia. III. American
University (Washington, D.C.). Foreign Area Studies. IV. Series. V. Series:
Area handbook series.
DT962.Z55 1983   968.91/04 19   *LC* 83-11946

Beach, D. N.   3.5510
The Shona & Zimbabwe, 900–1850: an outline of Shona history / D.N. Beach.
— New York: Africana Pub. Co., 1980. xiv, 432, 10 p.: ill.; 22 cm. Includes
index. 1. Mashona — History 2. Zimbabwe — History I. T. II. Title: Shona
and Zimbabwe, 900-1850.
DT962.42.B35 1980   968.91   *LC* 80-14116   *ISBN* 0841906246

Ranger, T. O. (Terence O.)   • 3.5511
The African voice in Southern Rhodesia, 1898–1930 [by] T. O. Ranger.
Evanston [Ill.] Northwestern University Press [1970] xii, 252 p. 23 cm. (The
African voice) 1. Zimbabwe — Native races. 2. Zimbabwe — Politics and
government — 1890-1965 I. T.
DT962.42.R35 1970b   325.3/42/096891   *LC* 71-135510   *ISBN*
0810103206

Blake, Robert, Baron of Braydeston, 1916-.   3.5512
A history of Rhodesia / Robert Blake. — 1st American ed. — New York:
Knopf, 1978, c1977. xxii, 435 p.: maps; 24 cm. Includes index. 1. Zimbabwe —
History 2. Africa, Southern — History I. T.
DT962.5.B55 1978   968.9/1   *LC* 77-20363   *ISBN* 0394480686

Davidow, Jeffrey.   3.5513
A peace in southern Africa: the Lancaster House Conference on Rhodesia, 1979
/ Jeffrey Davidow. — Boulder, Colo.: Westview Press, 1984. 143 p.; 23 cm. —
(Westview special studies on Africa.) 'Published under the auspices of the
Center for International Affairs, Harvard University.' Includes index.
1. Lancaster House Conference on Rhodesia (1979) 2. Zimbabwe — Politics
and government — 1979-1980 3. Zimbabwe — Constitutional history.
I. Harvard University. Center for International Affairs. II. T. III. Series.
DT962.75.D38 1984   968.91/04 19   *LC* 83-23393   *ISBN*
0865317038

Good, Robert C.   3.5514
U.D.I.; the international politics of the Rhodesian rebellion [by] Robert C.
Good. [Princeton, N.J.] Princeton University Press [1973] 368 p. illus. 23 cm.
1. Zimbabwe — Politics and government — 1965- I. T.
DT962.75.G66 1973b   327.689/1   *LC* 73-14082   *ISBN* 0691056471

Vambe, Lawrence, 1917-.   3.5515
From Rhodesia to Zimbabwe / by Lawrence Vambe; with a foreword by Judith
Acton. — Pittsburgh: University of Pittsburgh Press, 1976. xiv, 289 p.; 23 cm.
Includes index. 1. Vambe, Lawrence, 1917- 2. Missions — Zimbabwe.
3. Zimbabwe — History 4. Zimbabwe — Race relations. I. T.
DT962.75.V35 1976   968.9/1/02   *LC* 75-20354   *ISBN* 0822933179

DT963 Zambia

Gann, Lewis H., 1924-.   • 3.5516
The birth of a plural society; the development of Northern Rhodesia under the
British South Africa Company, 1894–1914. — [Manchester] Published on

behalf of the Rhodes-Livingstone Institute, Northern Rhodesia, by Manchester University Press [1958] xxi, 230 p. illus., fold. col. map. 23 cm. Bibliography: p. 192-210. 1. Rhodesia, Northern — Hist. I. T.
DT963.G3   968.94   *LC* 59-65059 rev

Hall, Richard Seymour, 1925-.   • 3.5517
Zambia [by] Richard Hall. — New York, Praeger [1966, c1965] viii, 357 p. maps. 22 cm. — (Praeger library of African affairs) Bibliography: p. [315]-320. 1. Zambia. I. T.
DT963.H3 1966   916.894   *LC* 65-18325

Zambia, a country study / edited by Irving Kaplan.   3.5518
3d ed. — Washington: American University, Foreign Area Studies: for sale by the Supt. of Docs., U.S. Govt. Print. Off., 1979. xxv, 308 p.: ill.; 25 cm. — (Area handbook series.) 'DA pam 550-75.' 'This volume is one of a continuing series of books written by Foreign Area Studies, the American University, under the Area Handbook Program.' Second ed., 1974, by I. Kaplan and others published under title: Area handbook for Zambia. 1. Zambia. I. Kaplan, Irving, 1923- II. Kaplan, Irving, 1923- Area handbook for Zambia. III. American University (Washington, D.C.). Foreign Area Studies. IV. Series.
DT963.K26 1979   968.9/4   *LC* 79-21324

Mainga, Mutumba.   3.5519
Bulozi under the Luyana kings; political evolution and state formation in pre-colonial Zambia. London, Longmans [1973] xvii, 278 p. illus., maps, ports. 22 cm. Based on the author's thesis, London, 1969. 1. Lozi (African people) I. T.
DT963.42.M3   968.9/4/01   *LC* 73-174757   *ISBN* 0582640733
ISBN 0582640881

Prins, Gwyn.   3.5520
The hidden hippopotamus: reappraisal in African history: the early colonial experience in western Zambia / Gwyn Prins. — Cambridge [Eng.]; New York: Cambridge University Press, 1980. xvi, 319 p.: ill.; 24 cm. (African studies series. 28 0065-406X) Includes index. 1. Lozi (African people) 2. Zambia — History — To 1890 3. Zambia — Colonization. 4. Zambia — History — 1890-1924 I. T. II. Series.
DT963.42.P74   968.94   *LC* 79-41658   *ISBN* 0521229154

Roberts, Andrew.   3.5521
A history of the Bemba; political growth and change in north–eastern Zambia before 1900 [by] Andrew D. Roberts. [Madison] University of Wisconsin Press [1973] xxxiv, 420 p. illus. 23 cm. A revision of the author's thesis, University of Wisconsin, 1966. 1. Bemba (African people) — History. I. T.
DT963.42.R62 1973   916.89/4/06963   *LC* 73-5813   *ISBN* 0299064506

Turner, Victor Witter.   3.5522
The forest of symbols: aspects of Ndembu ritual / [by] Victor Turner. — Ithaca, N.Y.: Cornell University Press, [1967] xii, 405 p.: ill.; 25 cm. 1. Ndembu (African people) I. T.
DT963.42.T8   392/.09689/4   *LC* 67-12308

Turner, Victor Witter.   3.5523
Revelation and divination in Ndembu ritual / Victor Turner. — Ithaca, N.Y.: Cornell University Press, 1975. 354 p.: ill.; 22 cm. (Symbol, myth, and ritual) Includes index. 1. Ndembu (African people) — Rites and ceremonies. 2. Ndembu (African people) — Religion. 3. Symbolism I. T.
DT963.42.T83   299/.6   *LC* 75-1623   *ISBN* 0801408636

Gann, Lewis H., 1924-.   • 3.5524
A history of Northern Rhodesia; early days to 1953, by L. H. Gann. — New York: Humanities Press, 1969 [c1963] xiv, 478 p.; 24 cm. 1. Zambia — History I. T.
DT963.5.G3 1969   968.94   *LC* 73-8132

Roberts, Andrew.   3.5525
A history of Zambia / Andrew Roberts. New York: Africana Pub. Co., 1976. xv, 288 p., [4] leaves of plates: ill.; 23 cm. Includes index. 1. Zambia — History I. T.
DT963.5.R62 1976   968.9/4   *LC* 76-40923   *ISBN* 0841902917

Hatch, John Charles.   3.5526
Two African statesmen: Kaunda of Zambia and Nyerere of Tanzania / John Hatch. — Chicago: Regnery, 1976. xv, 268 p., [4] leaves of plates: ill.; 25 cm. 1. Kaunda, Kenneth D. (Kenneth David), 1924- 2. Nyerere, Julius K. (Julius Kambarage), 1922- 3. Zambia — Presidents — Biography. 4. Tanzania — Presidents — Biography. I. T.
DT963.82.K39 H37 1976b   967.8/04/0924 B   *LC* 76-6268   *ISBN* 0809284057

DT964–995 Other Countries, Regions

Barker, Dudley.   • 3.5527
Swaziland. London H.M. Stationery Off. 1965. 145p. (The Corona library) 1. Swaziland. I. T. II. Series.
DT971 B3

Kuper, Hilda.   • 3.5528
The Swazi, a South African Kingdom. — New York: Holt, Rinehart and Winston, [c1963] vi, 87 p.: illus., map.; 24 cm. — (Case studies in cultural anthropology.) 1. Swazi (African people) I. T. II. Series.
DT971.K793   916.834   *LC* 63-22023

Kuper, Hilda.   • 3.5529
The uniform of colour; a study of white–black relationships in Swaziland. — New York: Negro Universities Press, [1969] xii, 160 p.: map, 32 plates.; 23 cm. Reprint of the 1947 ed. 1. Swaziland — Native races. I. T.
DT971.K8 1969   301.29/68/3   *LC* 70-97371   *ISBN* 0837124220

DU1–65 OCEANIA (GENERAL)

DU1–28 Description

Pacific islands year book.   **3.5530**
1st ed. Sydney: Pacific publications, 1932-. v. 1. Oceanica.
DU1.P15   919   *LC* 32-24429   *ISBN* 0858070499

Historical dictionary of Oceania / edited by Robert D. Craig   **3.5531**
and Frank P. King.
Westport, Conn.: Greenwood Press, 1981. xxxv, 392 p.: maps; 29 cm. Includes
indexes. 1. Oceania — History — Dictionaries. I. Craig, Robert D., 1934-
II. King, F. P.
DU10.H57   990/.03/21 19   *LC* 80-24779   *ISBN* 0313210608

Osborne, Charles, 1927-.   • **3.5532**
Australia, New Zealand, and the South Pacific: a handbook / edited by Charles
Osborne. — New York: Praeger, [1970] xi, 580 p.: ill., maps (part col.); 23 cm.
— (Handbooks to the modern world) 1. Oceania I. T.
DU15.O8 1970b   919.4   *LC* 69-12899

Oceania, a regional study / Foreign Area Studies, the American   **3.5533**
University; edited by Frederica M. Bunge and Melinda W.
Cooke.
2nd ed. — Washington, D.C.: For sale by the Supt. of Docs., U.S. G.P.O., 1985,
c1984. xv, 572 p.: ill.; 24 cm. (Area handbook series.) (DA pam. 550-94)
'Research completed June 1984.' Includes index. 1. Islands of the Pacific
I. Bunge, Frederica M. II. Cooke, Melinda W. III. American University
(Washington, D.C.). Foreign Area Studies. IV. Series. V. Series: DA pam.
550-94
DU17.O26 1985   990 19   *LC* 85-6043

Oliver, Douglas L.   • **3.5534**
The Pacific islands / Douglas L. Oliver; illustrations by Sheila Mitchell Oliver.
— Rev. ed. — Garden City, N.Y.: Doubleday, [1961] xxiii, 456 p.: ill., maps; 18
cm. (Natural history library. N14) (An Anchor Book.) 1. Islands of the Pacific
I. T. II. Series.
DU17.O56 1961   990   *LC* 61-19508

Beaglehole, J. C. (John Cawte)   • **3.5535**
Exploration of the Pacific. 3d ed. Stanford University Press, 1966.
346p.,fold.maps. 1. Oceania — Discovery and exploration. I. T.
DU19.B4 1966   919.9   *LC* 66-22429

Dunmore, John, 1923-.   **3.5536**
French explorers in the Pacific. Oxford: Clarendon Press, 1965-1969. 2 v.
1. Explorers — France. 2. Oceania — Discovery & exploration. I. T.
DU19.D8   *LC* 65-6800

Sharp, Andrew.   • **3.5537**
The discovery of the Pacific Islands. — Oxford, Clarendon Press, 1960. xiii,
259 p. maps. 23 cm. Bibliography: p. [225]-228. 1. Oceanica — Disc. & explor.
I. T.
DU19.S48   990   *LC* 60-50621

Cumberland, Kenneth Brailey.   • **3.5538**
Southwest Pacific; a geography of Australia, New Zealand, and their Pacific
island neighbors, by Kenneth B. Cumberland. [Rev. ed.] New York, Praeger
[1968] xviii, 423 p. illus., maps 23 cm. 1. Oceania — Description and travel —
1951-1980 I. T.
DU22.C85 1968   919   *LC* 68-14558

Keesing, Felix Maxwell, 1902-1961.   • **3.5539**
The South Seas in the modern world / by Felix M. Keesing; with a foreword by
J. B. Condliffe. — Rev. ed. — New York: J. Day, 1945. xxiv, 391 p.: ill., maps.
— (Institute of Pacific Relations. International research series) I. T.
DU22.K4   *LC* 45-9899

Friis, Herman Ralph, 1905-.   • **3.5540**
The Pacific basin; a history of its geographical exploration, edited by Herman
R. Friis. New York, American Geographical Society, 1967. xi, 457 p. illus.,

maps. 26 cm. (American Geographical Society. Special publication no. 38)
Some of the papers are revised and enlarged versions of papers presented at a
symposium held as part of the Tenth Pacific Science Congress meeting at the
University of Hawaii, Aug. 21-Sept. 6, 1961. 1. Pacific Area I. T.
DU23.F7   910.09/18/23   *LC* 67-12957

Robinson, Kenneth W.   • **3.5541**
Australia, New Zealand and the Southwest Pacific [by] K. W. Robinson. [2nd
ed. London] University of London Press [1968] xi, 344 p. maps, plates, tables.
22 cm. (A Systematic regional geography, v. 4) 1. Oceania — Description and
travel — 1951-1980 I. T.
DU23.R62 1968   919   *LC* 70-421067   *ISBN* 0340091355

DU28.3–65 History

Barclay, Glen St. John, 1930-.   **3.5542**
A history of the Pacific from the stone age to the present day / Glen Barclay. —
New York: Taplinger Pub. Co., 1978. 264 p., [8] leaves of plates: ill.; 25 cm.
Includes index. 1. Islands of the Pacific — History. I. T.
DU28.3.B37 1978b   990   *LC* 78-51996   *ISBN* 0800839021

Davidson, James Wightman, 1915-1973.   **3.5543**
Pacific Islands portraits. Editors: J. W. Davidson & Deryck Scarr. — Canberra:
Australian National University Press, 1970. xi, 346 p.: illus., maps, ports.; 25
cm. 1. Islands of the Pacific — History. 2. Islands of the Pacific — Biography.
I. Scarr, Deryck. joint author. II. T.
DU28.3.D28   920.09   *LC* 72-110412   *ISBN* 0708101666

Grattan, Clinton Hartley, 1902-.   • **3.5544**
The Southwest Pacific since 1900, a modern history; Australia, New Zealand,
the islands, Antarctica. — Ann Arbor: University of Michigan Press, [1963] x,
759, xxviii p.: maps; 24 cm. — (The University of Michigan history of the
modern world) 1. Oceania — History. 2. Antarctic regions — History. I. T.
DU28.3.G69   990   *LC* 63-14013

Grattan, Clinton Hartley, 1902-.   • **3.5545**
The Southwest Pacific to 1900; a modern history: Australia, New Zealand, the
islands, Antarctica. — Ann Arbor: University of Michigan Press, [1963] 558 p.:
illus.; 25 cm. — (The University of Michigan history of the modern world)
1. Oceania — History. I. T.
DU28.3.G7   990   *LC* 60-5670

Howe, K. R.   **3.5546**
Where the waves fall: a new South Sea Islands history from first settlement to
colonial rule / K.R. Howe. — Honolulu: University of Hawaii Press, c1984.
xix, 403 p.: ill., maps; 24 cm. — (Pacific islands monograph series. no. 2) Maps
on lining papers. Includes index. 1. Islands of the Pacific — History. 2. New
Zealand — History — To 1840 I. T. II. Series.
DU28.3.H68 1984   990 19   *LC* 83-18295   *ISBN* 0824809211

Maude, H. E. (Henry Evans), 1906-.   • **3.5547**
Of islands and men: studies in Pacific history / [by] H. E. Maude. —
Melbourne; New York [etc.]: Oxford University Press, 1968. xxii, 397 p.: ill.,
maps, tables; 23 cm. 1. Islands of the Pacific — History. I. T.
DU28.3.M38   990   *LC* 76-365876

Spate, O. H. K. (Oskar Hermann Khristian), 1911-.   **3.5548**
Monopolists and freebooters / O.H.K. Spate. — Minneapolis: University of
Minnesota Press, c1983. xxi, 426 p.: ill.; 26 cm. — (The Pacific since Magellan;
v. 2) 1. Pacific Area — History. 2. Pacific Area — Discovery and exploration.
I. T.
DU28.3.S67 1983   990 19   *LC* 83-181916   0816611210

Trumbull, Robert.   **3.5549**
Tin roofs and palm trees: a report on the new South Seas / Robert Trumbull. —
Seattle: University of Washington Press, c1977. x, 302 p., [8] leaves of plates:
ill.; 24 cm. Includes index. 1. Ethnology — Oceania 2. Oceania — History.
3. Oceania — Social conditions. I. T.
DU28.3.T78   990   *LC* 76-49164   *ISBN* 0295955449

Brookes, Jean Ingram.   • 3.5550
International rivalry in the Pacific islands, 1800–1875. — New York: Russell &
Russell, [1972, c1941] ix, 454 p.: fold. map.; 25 cm. 1. Competition,
International 2. Oceania — History. I. T.
DU29.B75 1972   327/.1/099   LC 77-173529

Oceania and beyond: essays on the Pacific since 1945 / F. P.   3.5551
King, editor.
Westport, Conn.: Greenwood Press, 1976. xxii, 265 p., [3] leaves of plates:
maps; 25 cm. 1. Oceania — Politics and government — Addresses, essays,
lectures. 2. Oceania — Economic conditions — Addresses, essays, lectures.
I. King, F. P.
DU29.O25 1976   990   LC 76-5261   *ISBN* 0837189047

Grattan, Clinton Hartley, 1902-.   • 3.5552
The United States and the Southwest Pacific / C. Hartley Grattan. —
Cambridge: Harvard University Press, 1961. 273 p.: ill.; 20 cm. (American
foreign policy library.) 1. United States — Foreign relations — Oceania.
2. Oceania — Politics. I. T.
DU30.G7   327.7309   LC 61-5583

Morrell, William Parker, 1899-.   • 3.5553
Britain in the Pacific Islands. — Oxford, Clarendon Press, 1960. xii, 454 p.
maps. 23 cm. Bibliographical footnotes. 1. Gt. Brit. — Colonies — Oceanica.
I. T.
DU40.M6   990   LC 60-3001

Scarr, Deryck.   • 3.5554
Fragments of empire: a history of the Western Pacific High Commission,
1877–1914. — Canberra: Australian National University Press [1967] xviii,
367 p.: ill., maps, ports.; 25 cm. 1. Great Britain. High Commission for
Western Pacific Islands. 2. Great Britain — Colonies — Oceania I. T.
DU40.S32   325.3/42/0996   LC 67-28349

Ward, John Manning, 1919-.   • 3.5555
British policy in the South Pacific, 1786–1893; a study in British policy towards
the South Pacific Islands prior to the establishment of governments by the great
powers. Sydney Australasian Pub. Co. [1948] 364p. 1. Oceanica — History
2. British in Oceanica I. T.
DU40 W3

Thompson, Virginia McLean, 1903-.   3.5556
The French Pacific Islands; French Polynesia and New Caledonia [by] Virginia
Thompson and Richard Adloff. — Berkeley: University of California Press,
1971. viii, 539 p.: illus.; 24 cm. 1. French Polynesia. 2. New Caledonia.
I. Adloff, Richard. joint author. II. T.
DU50.T47 1971   309.1/932   LC 71-138634   *ISBN* 0520018435

DU80–398 Australia

Clark, Charles Manning Hope, 1915- ed.   • 3.5557
Select documents in Australian history. Selected and edited by C. M. H. Clark
with the assistance of L. J. Pryor. Sydney: Angus and Robertson, 1950-55. 2 v.
22 cm. 1. Australia — History — Sources. I. T.
DU80.C58   LC 51-2907   *ISBN* 0207941432

Clark, C. M. H. (Charles Manning Hope), 1915- ed.   • 3.5558
Sources of Australian history. London, New York, Oxford University Press,
1957, reprinted 1963. 622 p. 16 cm. (The World's classics, 558) 1. Australia —
History — Sources. I. T.
DU80.C59   LC 58-1543

Australian dictionary of biography.   3.5559
[Melbourne] Melbourne University Press; London, New York, Cambridge
University Press [1966-< 1986 >. v. <1-10 > 26 cm. General editor, v. 1-6.
Douglas Pike; v. 7-10 Bede Nairn, Geoffrey Serle. 1. Australia — Biography —
Dictionaries. I. Pike, Douglas Henry, 1908- ed.
DU82.A9   920.094   LC 66-13723

The Australian encyclopaedia / [editor–in–chief, Bruce W.   3.5560
Pratt].
3rd ed. — Sydney: Grolier Society of Australia, 1977. 6 v.: ill. (part col.),
diagrs., maps; 27 cm. 1. Australia — Dictionaries and encyclopedias.
DU90.A82 1977   994/.003   LC 79-313911   *ISBN* 0959660402

Fitzpatrick, Kathleen, 1905- ed.   • 3.5561
Australian explorers: a selection from their writings / with an introduction by
Kathleen Fitzpatrick. — London; New York: Oxford University Press, 1958.
503 p.: ill.; 16 cm. — (The World's classics, 559) 1. Australia — Discovery and
exploration. I. Fitzpatrick, Kathleen, 1905- II. T.
DU97.F53   DU97.A9.   LC 58-3255

Moorehead, Alan.   • 3.5562
Cooper's Creek / by Alan Moorehead. — New York: Harper & Row, 1963. x,
222 p., 9 leaves of plates (1 col.): ill. maps, ports. — 1. Burke and Wills
Expedition, 1860-1861 2. Australia — Discovery and exploration. I. T.
DU102.M8 1963a   919.4   LC 63-20295

McKnight, Tom L. (Tom Lee), 1928-.   • 3.5563
Australia's corner of the world; a geographical summation [by] Thomas L.
McKnight. Englewood Cliffs, N.J., Prentice-Hall [1970] x, 116 p. maps. 23 cm.
(Foundations of world regional geography series) 1. Australia — Description
and travel — 1951- 2. Australia — History 3. New Zealand — Description
and travel — 1951-1980 I. T.
DU105.M26   919.4   LC 73-104897   *ISBN* 0130538019

O'Shaughnessy, Peter.   3.5564
The restless years; being some impressions of the origin of the Australian, by
Peter O'Shaughnessy, Graeme Inson [and] Russel Ward. — Rev. ed. —
Brisbane: Jacaranda, 1970. 138 p.: illus. (part col.) maps (facsims.); 31 x 38 cm.
1. National characteristics, Australian 2. Australia — History — Pictorial
works. I. Inson, Graeme, joint author. II. Ward, Russel Braddock. joint
author. III. T.
DU107.O8   LC 72-574327

King, Michael.   3.5565
Being Pakeha: an encounter with New Zealand and the Maori renaissance /
Michael King. — London: Hodder and Stoughton, 1985. 214 p., [1] leaf of
plates: ill.; 24 cm. 1. King, Michael. 2. Historians — New Zealand —
Biography. 3. Race relations — New Zealand. I. T.
DU109.K56 A3 1985   993.1/0072024 B 19   LC 86-182153   *ISBN*
0340387750

DU110–112 History (General)

Blainey, Geoffrey.   3.5566
The tyranny of distance: how distance shaped Australia's history / Geoffrey
Blainey. — Rev. ed. — [South Melbourne]: Macmillan, 1982. 366 p., [28] p. of
plates: ill.; 23 cm. 1. Transportation — Australia. 2. Anthropogeography —
Australia. 3. Australia — History I. T.
DU110.B54 1982   994 19   LC 82-213126   *ISBN* 0333338367

Clark, C. M. H. (Charles Manning Hope), 1915-.   • 3.5567
A history of Australia. [Carlton, Victoria] Melbourne University Press;
London, New York, Cambridge University Press [1962, i.e., 1963-< 81 >. v.
< 1-5 > illus. 24 cm. 1. Australia — History I. T.
DU110.C48   994   LC 63-5969   *ISBN* 052284054X

Crowley, F. K. (Francis Keble)   3.5568
A New history of Australia / edited by F. K. Crowley. — New York: Holmes &
Meier, 1974. xii, 639 p.; 25 cm. Includes index. 1. Australia — History I. T.
DU110.N38   994   LC 75-313618   *ISBN* 0855610352

Ward, John M.   • 3.5569
Earl Grey and the Australian colonies, 1846–1857: a study of self–government
and self–interest. Carlton, Victoria: Melbourne U.P., 1958. 496 p. 1. Grey,
Henry George Grey, 3d earl. 2. Australia — Politics and government I. T.
DU110 W3   LC 58-59633

Greenwood, Gordon, 1913-, ed.   • 3.5570
Australia; a social and political history. Sydney Angus and Robertson [1955]
445p. 1. Australia — History I. T.
DU112 G7

DU113 Diplomatic History

Australia in world affairs.   • 3.5571
1950/55-. Melbourne: F.W. Cheshire. v.: maps; 25 cm. 1. Australia — Foreign
relations — 1945- I. Australian Institute of International Affairs.
DU113.A7   LC 58-206

Rosecrance, Richard N.   • 3.5572
Australian diplomacy and Japan, 1945–1951. [Parkville] Melbourne University
Press [1962] 288p. 1. Australia — Foreign relations — Japan 2. Japan —
Foreign relations — Australia I. T.
DU113.5 J3 R6

DU114 BIOGRAPHY

La Nauze, John Andrew, 1911-.   • 3.5573
Alfred Deakin; a biography [by] J. A. La Nauze. [Melbourne] Melbourne University Press; New York, Cambridge University Press [1965] 2 v. (xiv, 695 p.). ports. 25 cm. 1. Deakin, Alfred, 1856-1919. I. T.
DU114.D35 L29 1965   994.040924 (B)   *LC* 65-25718

Tennant, Kylie, 1912-.   3.5574
Evatt; politics and justice. — [Sydney]: Angus and Robertson, 1971 (c1970). xii, 418 p.; illus., ports.; 25 cm. 1. Evatt, Herbert Vere, 1894-1965. I. T.
DU114.E88 T44   994/.05/0924 B   *LC* 76-22483   *ISBN* 020712051X

DU115–117 HISTORY, BY PERIOD

Hughes, Robert, 1936-.   3.5575
The fatal shore / Robert Hughes. — 1st American ed. — New York, N.Y.: Knopf; New York: Distributed by Random House, 1987, c1986. xvi, 688, [41] p. of plates: ill.; 24 cm. Includes index. 1. Penal colonies — Australia — History. 2. Australia — History — 1788-1900 3. Australia — Exiles — History. I. T.
DU115.H78 1987   994 19   *LC* 86-45272   *ISBN* 0394506685

Inglis, Kenneth Stanley.   3.5576
The Australian colonists: an exploration of social history, 1788–1870 / [by] K. S. Inglis. — Carlton, Vic.: Melbourne University Press, 1975 (c1974). xx, 316 p.: ill.; 25 cm. Includes index. 1. Australia — History — 1788-1900 2. Australia — Social conditions. 3. Australia — Social life and customs. I. T.
DU115.I53   994.02   *LC* 75-308305   *ISBN* 0522840728

Mills, Richard Charles, 1886-1952.   3.5577
The colonization of Australia (1829–42): the Wakefield experiment in empire building / by Richard Charles Mills; with an introd. by Graham Wallas. — Facsim. ed. / with a note by S. J. Butlin. — Sydney: Sydney University Press, 1975 (c1974). xx, 363 p.; 22 cm. — (Australian historical reprints) Photoreprint of the 1915 ed. published by Sidgwick and Jackson, London. Originally presented as the author's thesis, University of London. Includes index. 1. Wakefield, Edward Gibbon, 1796-1862. 2. Australia — Colonization. 3. Australia — History — 1788-1851 I. T.
DU115.M54   994.02/092/4   *LC* 74-84619   *ISBN* 0424000040

Australia, New Zealand, and the Pacific Islands since the First World War / edited by William S. Livingston and Wm. Roger Louis.   3.5578
Austin: University of Texas Press, c1979. x, 249 p.; 24 cm. 1. Australia — History — 20th century 2. New Zealand — History — 1876-1918 3. Islands of the Pacific — History. I. Livingston, William S. II. Louis, William Roger, 1936-
DU116.A9   990   *LC* 78-24094   *ISBN* 0292703449

Fitzpatrick, Brian.   • 3.5579
The Australian Commonwealth; a picture of the community, 1901–1955. Melbourne, F. W. Cheshire [1956] 337 p. 23 cm. 1. Australia — History I. T.
DU116.F5   994   *LC* 57-31383/L

Millar, T. B. (Thomas Bruce)   3.5580
Australia in peace and war: external relations 1788–1977 / T. B. Millar. — New York: St. Martin's Press, 1978. xxiii, 578 p.: ill.; 22 cm. Includes index. 1. Australia — Foreign relations — 1900-1945 2. Australia — Foreign relations — 1945- I. T.
DU116.M54 1978   327.94   *LC* 78-19211   *ISBN* 0312061188

Edwards, P. G.   3.5581
Prime ministers and diplomats: the making of Australian foreign policy, 1901–1949 / P.G. Edwards. — Melbourne; New York: Oxford University Press in association with the Australian Institute of International Affairs, 1983. x, 240 p.: ill.; 23 cm. Includes index. 1. Australia. Dept. of External Affairs — History. 2. Australia — Foreign relations — 1945- 3. Australia — Foreign relations administration. 4. Australia — Foreign relations — 1900-1945 I. T.
DU116.18.E38 1983   327.94 19   *LC* 83-132195   *ISBN* 0195543890

Hazlehurst, Cameron, 1941-.   3.5582
Menzies observed / [by] Cameron Hazlehurst. — Hornsby, N.S.W.: George Allen & Unwin Australia, 1979. 392 p.: ill.; 26 cm. 1. Menzies, Robert Gordon, Sir, 1894-1978. 2. Prime ministers — Australia — Biography. 3. Australia — Politics and government — 1901-1945 4. Australia — Politics and government — 1945- I. T.
DU116.2.M46 H39   994.05/092/4 B   *LC* 77-78556   *ISBN* 0868613207

DU120–122 ETHNOGRAPHY

Elkin, A. P. (Adolphus Peter), 1891-1979.   • 3.5583
The Australian aborigines, by A. P. Elkin. Garden City, N.Y., Anchor Books, 1964. xxvi, 369 p. map, plates. 19 cm. (Natural history library. N37) 1. Australian aborigines 2. Australia — Native races I. T. II. Series.
DU120.E4 1964   572.994   *LC* 64-19226

Stevens, Frank S. ed.   3.5584
Racism: the Australian experience; a study of race prejudice in Australia. New York, Taplinger [c1972.] 3 v. 25 cm. 1. Race discrimination — Australia. 2. Minorities — Australia. 3. Race relations 4. Australia — Social conditions. I. T.
DU 120 S84 1972   *LC* 70-179992   *ISBN* 0800865820

DU145–398 LOCAL HISTORY

Dodge, Ernest Stanley.   3.5585
New England and the South Seas / Ernest S. Dodge. — Cambridge, Mass.: Harvard University Press, 1965. xv, 216 p. ill., ports, 24 cm. 1. New Englanders — Oceania 2. Oceania — History. I. T.
DU28.3 D6   919   *LC* 65-19823

Pike, Douglas Henry, 1908-.   • 3.5586
Paradise of dissent; South Australia 1829–1857. — [2nd ed.]. — Melbourne: Melbourne University Press; London; New York: Cambridge University Press, [1967] xii, 580 p.: maps (on lining-papers); 25 cm. 1. South Australia — History. I. T.
DU320.P5 1967   994/.2/02   *LC* 67-29759

Powell, Alan, 1936-.   3.5587
Far country: a short history of the Northern Territory / Alan Powell. — Carlton, Vic.: Melbourne University Press; Beaverton, Or.: [Distributor] U.S.A. and Canada, International Scholarly Book Services, 1982. xii, 301 p.: ill.; 22 cm. Includes index. 1. Northern Territory — History. I. T.
DU396.P69 1982   994.29 19   *LC* 83-205460   *ISBN* 0522842267

DU400–430 New Zealand

The New Zealand official year–book.   3.5588
Wellington: Govt. Printer. v.: ill.; 21-25 cm. Annual. Began with: 1st (1893). Title varies slightly. Description based on: 1894. Vol. for 1947/49 and 1951/52 issued combined. 1. New Zealand — Politics and government — Yearbooks. 2. New Zealand — Statistics — Yearbooks. I. New Zealand. Registrar-General's Office. II. New Zealand. Census and Statistics Office. III. New Zealand. Census and Statistics Dept. IV. New Zealand. Dept. of Statistics.
DU400.A3   *LC* sn 85-62531

McNab, Robert, 1864-1917.   3.5589
Historical records of New Zealand. Wellington, J. Mackay, Govt. printer, 1908–14. — [Wellington: A. R. Shearer, Govt. printer, 1973] 2 v.; 22 cm. 1. New Zealand — History — Sources. I. T.
DU400.M3 1973   919.93/03   *LC* 74-162660

Taylor, Nancy M., ed.   • 3.5590
Early travellers in New Zealand. — Oxford, Clarendon Press, 1959. xxx, [ii], 594 p. maps (1 fold.) 23 cm. Bibliography: p. [xxxi] 1. New Zealand — Descr. & trav. — Collections. I. T.
DU400.T3   919.31   *LC* 60-502

Burdon, Randal Mathews, 1896-.   • 3.5591
New Zealand notables. [Christchurch, N.Z.] The Caxton press 1941-. 1. New Zealand — Biography I. T.
DU402 B8

An encyclopaedia of New Zealand. A. H. McLintock: editor.   3.5592
Wellington, N.Z.: R. E. Owen, Govt. printer, 1966. 3 v.: illus., maps.; 25 cm. 1. New Zealand — Dictionaries and encyclopedias. I. McLintock, Alexander H., ed.
DU405.E5   919.31/003   *LC* 67-4443

New Zealand encyclopedia / editor–in–chief, Gordon McLauchlan.   3.5593
Auckland, N.Z.: David Bateman, c1984. xv, 656 p.: ill. (some col.), maps; 25 cm. At head of title: Bateman. Includes index. Map on folded leaf. 1. New Zealand — Dictionaries and encyclopedias. I. McLauchlan, Gordon. II. Title: Bateman New Zealand encyclopedia.
DU405.N48   993.1003 19   *ISBN* 0908610211

Beaglehole, J. C. (John Cawte)   • 3.5594
The discovery of New Zealand. 2d ed. London Oxford University Press 1961.
102p. 1. New Zealand — Discovery and exploration I. T.
DU410 B4 1961

Dumont d'Urville, Jules-Sébastien-César, 1790-1842.   • 3.5595
The voyage of the Astrolabe, 1840; an English rendering of the journals of
Dumont d'Urville and his officers of their visit to New Zealand in 1840, together
with some account of Bishop Pompallier and Charles, Baron de Thierry, by
Olive Wright. Wellington, A. H. & A. W. Reed [1955] 180 p. illus. 25 cm.
1. Astrolabe Expedition, 1837-1840 2. New Zealand — Discovery and
exploration. I. Wright, Olive. II. T.
DU410.D815   LC 55-4069

Clark, Andrew Hill, 1911-1975.   • 3.5596
The invasion of New Zealand by people, plants and animals: the South Island.
New Brunswick Rutgers University Press 1949. 465p. (Rutgers University
studies in geography, no. 1) 1. South Island (N.Z.) — Population 2. Natural
history — South Island, N.Z. I. T.
DU411 C43

Cumberland, Kenneth Brailey.   3.5597
New Zealand [by] Kenneth B. Cumberland & James S. Whitelaw. — Harlow:
Longmans, 1970. xiii, 194 p.: illus., maps, plans.; 22 cm. — (The World's
landscapes, 5) 1. Anthropo-geography — New Zealand. 2. New Zealand —
Description and travel I. Whitelaw, James Sydney. joint author. II. T.
III. Series.
DU412.C79 1970   919.31   LC 71-549682   ISBN 0582311578

DU420–422 History. Biography

Adams, Peter, 1947-.   3.5598
Fatal necessity: British intervention in New Zealand, 1830–1847 / Peter
Adams. — [S.l.]: Oxford, 1977. 308 p.: ill.; 23 cm. Product of author's doctoral
thesis. Includes index. 1. Waitangi, Treaty of, 1840 2. New Zealand — History
— To 1840 3. New Zealand — History — 1840-1876 4. Great Britain —
Colonies I. T.
DU420.A6   993.101/9   LC 78-311292

Cowan, James, 1870-1943.   • 3.5599
The New Zealand wars: a history of the Maori campaigns and the pioneering
period. — New York: AMS Press, [1969] 2 v.: illus., maps, ports.; 23 cm.
Reprint of the 1922 ed. 1. New Zealand — History — 1840-1876 I. T.
DU420.C652   993.1/02   LC 76-100514   ISBN 0404006000

McClymont, William Graham.   • 3.5600
The exploration of New Zealand. 2d ed. London Oxford University Press 1959.
125p. 1. New Zealand — Discovery and exploration I. T.
DU420 M15 1959

Miller, John.   • 3.5601
Early Victorian New Zealand; a study of racial tension and social attitudes,
1839–1852. London, Oxford University Press, 1958. 217 p. ill. 1. New Zealand
— History — 1840-1876 2. New Zealand — Native races. 3. New Zealand —
Social conditions. I. T.
DU420.M56 1958   993.1   LC 58-3820

The Oxford history of New Zealand / edited by W.H. Oliver   3.5602
with B.R. Williams.
Oxford: Clarendon Press; Wellington; New York: Oxford University Press,
1981. xiii, 572 p.: ill.; 25 cm. Includes index. 1. New Zealand — History
I. Oliver, W. H. (William Hosking), 1925- II. Williams, B. R. (Bridget R.)
DU420.O9   993.1 19   LC 81-193391   ISBN 0195580621

Sinclair, Keith.   • 3.5603
A history of New Zealand. — London; New York: Oxford University Press,
1961. 305 p.: illus.; 23 cm. 1. New Zealand — History I. T.
DU420.S53 1961   993.1   LC 61-66687

Sinclair, Keith.   • 3.5604
The origins of the Maori wars. Wellington: New Zealand University Press,
1957. 297 p.: ill.; 23 cm. 1. New Zealand — History — 1840-1876 I. T.
DU420.S55   LC 61-35767

Sinclair, Keith.   3.5605
Walter Nash / Keith Sinclair. — [Auckland]: Auckland University Press; [New
York]: Oxford University Press, 1977 (c1976). vii, 439 p., [6] leaves of plates:
ill.; 25 cm. Includes index. 1. Nash, Walter, 1882-1968. 2. Prime ministers —
New Zealand — Biography. 3. New Zealand — Politics and government I. T.
DU422.N35 S56   993.103/092/4 B   LC 78-325231   ISBN
0196479495

Sinclair, Keith.   • 3.5606
William Pember Reeves, New Zealand Fabian / by Keith Sinclair. — Oxford:
Clarendon Press, 1965. x, 356 p.: ports. 1. Reeves, William Pember, 1857-1932
I. T.
DU422.R45 S5   LC 65-9091

Bloomfield, Paul, 1898-.   • 3.5607
Edward Gibbon Wakefield: builder of the British Commonwealth. [London]
Longmans [1961] 378p. 1. Wakefield, Edward Gibbon, 1796-1862. 2. Great
Britain — Colonies — History I. T.
DU422 W2 B4

DU423 Ethnography. Maoris

Best, Elsdon, 1856-1931.   3.5608
The Maori / by Elsdon Best. — 1st AMS ed. — New York: AMS Press, 1975. 2
v.: ill.; 22 cm. Reprint of the 1924 ed. published by the Board of Maori
Ethnological Research, Wellington, N.Z., which was issued as v. 5 of Memoirs
of the Polynesian Society. Includes index. 1. Maoris I. T.
DU423.A1 B45 1979   390/.09931   LC 75-35231   ISBN
0404143105

Metge, Alice Joan.   3.5609
The Maoris of New Zealand: Rautahi / Joan Metge. Rev. ed. — London;
Boston: Routledge & K. Paul, 1976. xv, 382 p., [8] leaves of plates: ill.; 23 cm.
Includes index. 1. Maoris I. T.
DU423.A1 M47 1976   993.101   LC 76-379263   ISBN 0710083521

Te Ao Hurihuri: the world moves on: aspects of Maoritanga /   3.5610
edited by Michael King; [photos. by John Miller].
Wellington: Hicks Smith, 1975. 233 p.: ill.; 21 cm. 1. Maoris — Addresses,
essays, lectures. I. King, Michael. II. Title: World moves on.
DU423.A1 T4   993.1/004/994   LC 76-458024   ISBN 0456018107

Buck, Peter Henry, 1880-1951.   • 3.5611
The coming of the Maori / by Te Rangi Hiroa, Sir Peter Buck. — [2d ed.]
Wellington: Maori Purposes Fund Board; [distributed by] Whitcombe and
Tombs, 1950. 551 p.: ill.; 26 cm. 1. Maoris I. T.
DU423.B83   LC 51-25987

Ward, Alan D.   3.5612
A show of justice; racial 'amalgamation' in nineteenth century New Zealand
[by] Alan Ward. — [Toronto; Buffalo]: University of Toronto Press, [1974] xv,
382 p.: illus.; 24 cm. Based on the author's thesis, Australian National
University. 1. Maoris — Government relations I. T.
DU423.G6 W37 1974   323.1/19/940931   LC 73-89847   ISBN
0802021174

Miller, Harold Gladstone, 1898-.   • 3.5613
Race conflict in New Zealand, 1814–1865 [by] Harold Miller. — Auckland:
Blackwood & J. Paul, 1966. xxvii, 238 p.: illus., maps, ports.; 23 cm. 'Tri-ocean
books.' 1. Maoris 2. New Zealand — Native races. I. T.
DU423.M5   993.101   LC 66-9283

King, Michael.   3.5614
Maori: a photographic and social history / Michael King. — [Auckland, N.Z.]:
Heinemann; Beaverton, OR: Exclusive distributor, ISBS, 1984, c1983. 287 p.:
ill.; 25 cm. Distributor from label on verso of t.p. Includes index. 1. Maoris —
Social conditions. 2. Maoris — Pictorial works. I. T.
DU423.S6 K56 1984   993.1/004994 19   LC 85-239844   ISBN
0868634034

Williams, John Adrian, 1935-.   • 3.5615
Politics of the New Zealand Maori; protest and cooperation, 1891–1909 [by]
John A. Williams. — Seattle: University of Washington Press, [1969] xi, 204 p.:
illus., maps, ports.; 22 cm. 1. New Zealand — Native races. 2. New Zealand —
Politics and government I. T.
DU423.W63   320.9/93/1   LC 69-14208

DU450–470 Tasmania

Robson, L. L. (Leslie Lloyd), 1931-.   3.5616
A history of Tasmania / Lloyd Robson. — Melbourne; New York: Oxford
University Press, 1983. v. <1 >: ill.; 24 cm. Includes index. 1. Tasmania —
History. I. T.
DU470.R6 1983   994.6 19   LC 83-204405   ISBN 0195543645

DU490–950 OCEANIA (ISLAND GROUPS)

Rivers, W. H. R. (William Halse Rivers), 1864-1922. ed. • 3.5617
Essays on the depopulation of Melanesia. With a pref. by Sir Everard im Thurn. Cambridge, At the University Press, 1922. [New York, AMS Press, 1972] xviii, 116 p. 19 cm. 1. Melanesia — Social conditions. I. T.
DU490.R5 1972   301.32/9/93   *LC* 74-96470   *ISBN* 0404053572

Elkin, A. P. (Adolphus Peter), 1891-1979. • 3.5618
Social anthropology in Melanesia: a review of research / A. P. Elkin; published under the auspices of the South Pacific Commission. — London: Oxford University Press, 1953. xiii, 166 p.: ill. 1. Melanesia 2. Melanesia — Bibliography. I. T.
DU500.E4   *LC* 53-3743

Wenkam, Robert, 1920-. 3.5619
Micronesia; the breadfruit revolution, by Robert Wenkham, with text by Byron Baker. [1st ed.] Honolulu, East-West Center Press [1971] 192 p. illus. (maps (on lining papers) 29 cm. 1. Micronesia (Federated States) I. Baker, Byron. II. T.
DU500.W44   919.65/03   *LC* 71-165399   *ISBN* 0824801024

Buck, Peter Henry, 1880-1951. • 3.5620
Vikings of the sunrise. Christchurch, N.Z.: Whitcombe and Tombs, 1954. 339 p.: ill. , 23 cm. 1. Polynesians 2. Ethnolgoy — Polynesia. I. T.
DU510.B77 1954   *LC* 55-24268

Goldman, Irving, 1911-. • 3.5621
Ancient Polynesian society. — Chicago: University of Chicago Press, [1970] xxviii, 625 p.: illus., maps.; 24 cm. Continued by The mouth of heaven. 1. Ethnology — Polynesia 2. Society, Primitive I. T.
DU510.G58 1970   301.29/96   *LC* 74-116028   *ISBN* 0226301141

Golson, Jack. ed. • 3.5622
Polynesian navigation; a symposium on Andrew Sharp's theory of accidental voyages. [Rev. ed.] Wellington Polynesian Society 1963. 153p. (Polynesian Society (N.Z.) Memoirs no. 34) 1. Polynesia — Discovery and exploration 2. Navigation, Primitive I. Polynesian Society, Wellington. Journal. Supplement II. T. III. Series.
DU510 G65 1963

Heyerdahl, Thor. • 3.5623
Sea routes to Polynesia / with editorial notes by Karl Jettmar and a foreword by Hans W:son Ahlman. — London: Allen & Unwin, 1968. 3-232 p.: 24 plates, ill., col. charts (on lining papers), maps, port.; 23 cm. 1. Polynesians 2. Polynesians — Origin. I. T.
DU510.H453 1968b   301.29/96   *LC* 68-143823

Keesing, Felix Maxwell, 1902-1961. • 3.5624
Social anthropology in Polynesia: a review of research / published under the auspcies of the South Pacific Commission. New York; London: Oxford University Press, 1953. x, 126 p.: ill.; 23 cm. 1. Polynesia 2. Polynesia — Bibliography. I. T.
DU510.K43   *LC* 53-3744

Sahlins, Marshall David, 1930-. • 3.5625
Social stratification in Polynesia / by Marshall D. Sahlins. — Seattle: University of Washington Press, 1958. xiii, 306 p. — (Monographs of the American Ethnological Society. 29]) 1. Social classes — Polynesia. I. T. II. Series.
DU510.S29   *LC* 58-10482   *ISBN* 0295740825

Sharp, Andrew. • 3.5626
Ancient voyagers in Polynesia. Berkeley University of California Press 1964. 159p. 1. Polynesia — Discovery and exploration 2. Navigation, Primitive I. T.
DU510 S5 1964

Mead, Margaret, 1901-1978. • 3.5627
New lives for old: cultural transformation —Manus, 1928–1953/ Margaret Mead; with a new preface, 1965. — New York: Morrow, 1966. xxvii, 548 p., [16] p. of plates: ill.; 22cm. 1. Manus tribe 2. Acculturation — Papua New Guinea — Admiralty Islands — Case studies. I. T.
DU520.M4   301.29/95   *LC* 65-28294

Romanucci-Ross, Lola. 3.5628
Mead's other Manus: phenomenology of the encounter / Lola Romanucci-Ross. — South Hadley, Mass.: Bergin and Garvey, 1985. xxi, 230 p.: ill.; 24 cm. Includes index. 1. Manus (Papua New Guinea people) I. T.
DU520.R66 1985   306/.0899912 19   *LC* 84-21592   *ISBN* 0897890647

Hezel, Francis X. 3.5629
The first taint of civilization: a history of the Caroline and Marshall Islands in pre–colonial days, 1521–1885 / Francis X. Hezel. — Honolulu: Pacific Islands Studies Program, Center for Pacific and Asian Studies, University of Hawaii Press, c1983. xvi, 365 p.: ill.; 24 cm. — (Pacific islands monograph series. no. 1) Includes index. 1. Caroline Islands — History. 2. Marshall Islands — History. I. T. II. Series.
DU565.H49 1983   996/.6 19   *LC* 83-10411   *ISBN* 0824808401

Goodenough, Ward Hunt. • 3.5630
Property, kin, and community on Truk [by] Ward H. Goodenough. Hamden, Conn., Archon Books [1967] 192 p. maps. 25 cm. Reprint of the 1951 ed. 1. Ethnology — Micronesia — Truk Islands. 2. Property — Micronesia — Truk Islands. 3. Kinship — Micronesia — Truk Islands. I. T.
DU568.T7 G6 1967   572.996/6   *LC* 66-30556

Fortune, Reo Franklin, 1903-. • 3.5631
Sorcerers of Dobu: the social anthropology of the Dobu Islanders of the western Pacific / by R. F. Fortune; introduction by Bronislaw Malinowski. — [Revised ed.]. — London: Routledge & Kegan Paul, 1963. — xxxii, 326 p.: ill., maps; 19 cm. 'Australasian National Research Council Expedition to New Guinea 1927-1928.' Chapter I issued also as thesis (Ph.D.) Columbia University under title: The social organization of Dobu. 1. Ethnology — Papua New Guinea — Dobu Island. 2. Magic — Papua New Guinea — Dobu Island. 3. Dobu Island (Papua New Guinea) — Social life and customs. I. T.
DU580.F6 1963   *LC* 66-646

Brown, Stanley. 3.5632
Men from under the sky; the arrival of Westerners in Fiji. With a foreword by Raymond Burr. — Rutland, Vt.: C. E. Tuttle Co., [1973] 327 p.: illus.; 20 cm. 1. Fiji — History. I. T.
DU600.B76   996/.11   *LC* 72-96774   *ISBN* 0804811032

Burns, Alan Cuthbert, Sir, 1887-. • 3.5633
Fiji / by Sir Alan Burns. — London: H.M. Stationery Office, 1963. xv, 255 p.: ill.; 22 cm. (Corona library; [8]) 1. Fiji Islands. I. T.
DU600.B78   919.611   *LC* 63-4125

Derrick, Ronald Albert, 1892-. • 3.5634
A history of Fiji. 2d ed. Suva: Print and Stationery Dept. [1942-] v.: ill., ports., maps (1 fold.); 26 cm. 1. Fiji Islands — History. I. T.
DU600.D45   996.1   *LC* 52-40961

Mayer, Adrian C. 3.5635
Peasants in the Pacific: a study of Fiji Indian rural society / by Adrian C. Mayer. — 2d ed. — Berkeley: University of California Press, [1973] xiv, 233 p.: ill.; 23 cm. 1. East Indians — Fiji. I. T.
DU600.M34 1973b   301.45/19/141109611   *LC* 72-91618   *ISBN* 0520023331

Scarr, Deryck. 3.5636
Fiji, a short history / Deryck Scarr. — Laie, Hawaii: Institute for Polynesian Studies, 1984. xvi, 202 p.: ill., map; 22 cm. Includes index. 1. Fiji — History. I. T.
DU600.S34   996/.11 19   *ISBN* 0939154366

DU620–629 Hawaii

Twain, Mark, 1835-1910. • 3.5637
Letters from the Sandwich Islands / written for the Sacramento Union by Mark Twain; introd. & conclusion by G. Ezra Dane; illus. by Dorothy Grover. Stanford University Press. — New York: Haskell House, 1972. xii, 224 p.: ill.; 23 cm. Reprint of the 1938 ed. 1. Hawaii — Description and travel — To 1950 2. Hawaii — Social life and customs. I. Sacramento Union. II. T.
DU623.C6 1972   919.69   *LC* 72-2113   *ISBN* 0838314716

Daws, Gavan. • 3.5638
Shoal of time: a history of the Hawaiian Islands. — New York: Macmillan [1968] xiii, 494 p.; 24 cm. 1. Hawaii — History I. T.
DU625.D28   996.9   *LC* 68-23630

Kuykendall, Ralph Simpson. • 3.5639
Hawaii: a history from Polynesian kingdom to American state / by Ralph S. Kuykendall and A. Grove Day. — Rev. ed. — Englewood Cliffs, N.J.: Prentice-

Hall, c1961. ix, 331 p., [4] leaves of plates: ill.; 21 cm. (Reward books) 1. Hawaii — History I. Day, A. Grove (Arthur Grove), 1904- II. Day, Arthur Grove. III. T.
DU625.K778 1961   996.9   *LC* 61-8894   *ISBN* 013384305X pbk

Bradley, Harold Whitman.   • 3.5640
The American frontier in Hawaii; the pioneers 1789–1843. — Gloucester, Mass.: P. Smith, 1968 [c1942] xi, 488 p.: map (on lining papers); 21 cm. 1. Hawaii — History — To 1893 I. T.
DU627.B7 1968   996.9/02   *LC* 70-3572

Kuykendall, Ralph Simpson, 1885-1963.   • 3.5641
The Hawaiian Kingdom. — Honolulu: University of Hawaii, 1938-67. 3 v.: illus., maps (on lining papers), ports.; 24 cm. Vol. 2-3 published by University of Hawaii Press. 1. Hawaii — History — To 1893 I. T.
DU627.K8   996.9   *LC* 38-28602

Russ, William Adam, 1903-.   • 3.5642
The Hawaiian Republic, 1894–98, and its struggle to win annexation. Selinsgrove, Pa., Susquehanna University Press, 1961. viii, 398 p. 24 cm. Sequel to The Hawaiian Pevolution, 1893-1898. 1. Hawaii — Politics and government — 1893-1898 I. T.
DU627.2.R79   *LC* 61-6689

Russ, William Adam, 1903-.   3.5643
The Hawaiian Revolution, 1893–94. Selinsgrove, Pa. Susquehanna University Press 1959. 372p. 1. Hawaii — History — Revolution of 1893 I. T.
DU627.2 R8

Tate, Merze, 1905-.   • 3.5644
Hawaii: reciprocity or annexation. — East Lansing: Michigan State University Press, 1968. xii, 303 p.: map.; 25 cm. 1. Hawaii — Annexation. I. T.
DU627.4.T27   996.9/02   *LC* 68-15011

Bell, Roger J. (Roger John), 1947-.   3.5645
Last among equals: Hawaiian statehood and American politics / Roger Bell. — Honolulu: University of Hawaii Press, c1984. x, 377 p.; 24 cm. Includes indexes. 1. Statehood (American politics) 2. United States — Politics and government — 1901-1953 3. United States — Politics and government — 1953-1961 4. Hawaii — Politics and government — 1900-1959 I. T.
DU627.5.B44 1984   996.9/03 19   *LC* 83-24330   *ISBN* 0824808479

DU647–720 Guam. Marquesas. Nauru

Carano, Paul.   • 3.5646
A complete history of Guam / by Paul Carano and Petro C. Sanchez. — [1st ed.] Rutland, Vt.: C. E. Tuttle [1964] xvii, 452 p.: ill., maps (1 fold.) ports.; 22 cm. 1. Guam — History. I. Sanchez, Pedro C., joint author. II. T.
DU647.C3   *LC* 64-21619

Suggs, Robert C. (Robert Carl), 1932-.   • 3.5647
The hidden worlds of Polynesia: the chronicle of an archaeological expedition to Nuku Hiva in the Marquesas Islands. — 1st ed. — New York: Harcourt, Brace, 1962. 247 p.: ill.; 22 cm. 1. Marquesas Islands I. T.
DU700.S83   996.3   *LC* 62-9445

Viviani, Nancy.   • 3.5648
Nauru, phosphate and political progress. — Canberra: Australian National University Press, 1970. xiv, 215 p.: illus., maps.; 23 cm. 1. Nauru. I. T.
DU715.V55   996/.85   *LC* 78-93784   *ISBN* 0708107656

DU740 Papua New Guinea

Bateson, Gregory.   3.5649
Naven: a survey of the problems suggested by a composite picture of the culture of a New Guinea tribe drawn from three points of view / by Gregory Bateson. — 2d ed. — Stanford, Calif.: Stanford University Press, 1958. -. xix, 312 p.: ill.; 23 cm. — 1. Rites and ceremonies — Papua New Guinea 2. Ethnology — Papua New Guinea 3. Iatmuls I. T.
DU740.B3 1958   572.995   *LC* 58-8720   *ISBN* 0804705208 pa

Encyclopaedia of Papua and New Guinea. [Edited by] Peter   3.5650
Ryan.
[Melbourne]: Melbourne University Press in association with the University of Papua and New Guinea, [1972] 3 v.: illus., diagrs., maps. (part fold.) (part col.) tables.; 27 cm. 1. Papua New Guinea — Dictionaries and encyclopedias. I. Ryan, Peter, 1923- ed.
DU740.E5   919.5/003   *LC* 72-188173   *ISBN* 0522840256

Fisk, E. K. (Ernest Kelvin) ed.   • 3.5651
New Guinea on the threshold: aspects of social, political, and economic development / edited by E. K. Fisk. — [Pittsburgh,]: University of Pittsburgh Press [1968] xii, 290 p.: ill., maps; 24 cm. 1. Papua New Guinea — Politics and government — To 1975 2. Papua New Guinea — Social life and customs. 3. Papua New Guinea — Economic conditions. I. T.
DU740.F55 1968   309.1/95   *LC* 68-21625

Hogbin, Herbert Ian, 1904-.   • 3.5652
Transformation scene: the changing culture of a New Guinea village. — London: Routledge & Paul [1951] xii, 326 p.: ill., maps; 23 cm. (International library of sociology and social reconstruction) 1. Ethnology — New Guinea 2. Busama (New Guinea Territory) I. T.
DU740.H55 1951   572.995   *LC* 51-8863

Lea, David A. M. (David Alexander Maclure)   3.5653
New Guinea, the territory and its people [by] D. A. M. Lea and P. G. Irwin. [2d ed.] Melbourne, New York, Oxford University Press [1971] 116 p. illus. 25 cm. 1. Papua New Guinea. I. Irwin, Peter George. joint author. II. T.
DU740.L427 1971   919.5/03   *LC* 72-186110   *ISBN* 0195501500

Mead, Margaret, 1901-1978.   3.5654
Sex and temperament in three primitive societies. New York: Morrow [c1963] xiv, 335 p.: ill.; 21 cm. (Morrow paperback editions) First published 1935. This 1963 edition contains new preface and preface to the 1950 edition. 1. Society, Primitive 2. New Guinea — Native races. I. T.
DU740.M39 1963   572.995   *LC* 50-11724

Rappaport, Roy A.   • 3.5655
Pigs for the ancestors; ritual in the ecology of a New Guinea people, by Roy A. Rappaport. New Haven, Yale University Press, 1967 [i.e. 1968] xx, 311 p. illus., map. 25 cm. 1. Tsembaga Maring 2. Agriculture, Primitive — Papua New Guinea. 3. Human ecology — Papua New Guinea. I. T.
DU740.R27   301.29/955   *LC* 68-13926

Rowley, C. D. (Charles Dunford)   • 3.5656
The New Guinea villager: the impact of colonial rule on primitive society and economy / C. D. Rowley. — New York: Praeger, 1966. 225 p.: maps on end papers; 21 cm. Includes index. 1. Australians — Papua New Guinea 2. New Guinea (Territory) — Politics and government. 3. New Guinea (Territory) — Economic conditions. I. T.
DU740.R77 1972

Souter, Gavin, 1929-.   • 3.5657
New Guinea: the last unknown. New York, Taplinger Pub. Co. [1966, c1963] 296 p. illus., maps (1 fold. col.) ports. 25 cm. Bibliography: p. 268-277. 1. New Guinea — History. I. T.
DU740.S67 1966   995   *LC* 66-10431

Feld, Steven.   3.5658
Sound and sentiment: birds, weeping, poetics, and song in Kaluli expression / Steven Feld. — Philadelphia: University of Pennsylvania Press, 1982. xii, 264 p., [2] p. of plates: ill. (some col.); 24 cm. (Publications of the American Folklore Society. new ser., v. 5) Based on the author's thesis (doctoral)—Indiana University, 1979. Includes index. 1. Kaluli (Papua New Guinea people) — Social life and customs. 2. Kaluli (Papua New Guinea people) — Rites and ceremonies. 3. Kaluli (Papua New Guinea people) — Music — History and criticism. 4. Folk music — Papua New Guinea — History and criticism. 5. Folk-songs, Bosavi — Papua New Guinea — History and criticism. 6. Birds — Papua New Guinea — Mythology. I. T. II. Series.
DU740.42.F44 1982   306/.0995/3 19   *LC* 81-43518   *ISBN* 0812278291

Gewertz, Deborah B., 1948-.   3.5659
Sepik River societies: a historical ethnography of the Chambri and their neighbors / Deborah B. Gewertz. — New Haven: Yale University Press, 1983. xii, 266 p., [6] p. of plates: ill.; 24 cm. Includes index. 1. Chambri (Papua New Guinea people) I. T.
DU740.42.G48 1983   306/.08999/2 19   *LC* 82-48902   *ISBN* 0300028725

Meggitt, Mervyn J., 1924-.   3.5660
Blood is their argument: warfare among the Mae Enga tribesmen of the New Guinea highlands / Mervyn Meggitt. — 1st ed. — Palo Alto, Calif.: Mayfield Pub. Co., 1977. xii, 223 p.: ill.; 22 cm. — (Explorations in world ethnology) Includes index. 1. Enga (New Guinea people) 2. Warfare, Primitive I. T. II. Series.
DU740.42.M4   301.6/33/09953   *LC* 76-28116   *ISBN* 0874843944

Ōtsuka, Ryūtarō.   **3.5661**
Oriomo Papuans: ecology of sago–eaters in lowland Papua / Ryutaro Ohtsuka. — [Tokyo]: University of Tokyo Press, c1983. xii, 197 p., [8] p. of plates: ill.; 23 cm. Includes index. 1. Gidra (Papua New Guinea people) — Economic conditions. 2. Human ecology — Papua New Guinea. I. T.
DU740.42.O88 1983   304.2/0899912 19   *LC* 83-167975   *ISBN* 0860083276

Schieffelin, Edward L.   **3.5662**
The sorrow of the lonely and the burning of the dancers / Edward L. Schieffelin. — New York: St. Martin's Press, c1976. viii, 243 p.: ill.; 21 cm. Includes index. 1. Bosavi (Papua New Guinea people) I. T.
DU740.42.S34   301.29/95/3   *LC* 75-10999

Sillitoe, Paul.   **3.5663**
Roots of the earth: crops in the highlands of Papua New Guinea / Paul Sillitoe. — Manchester [Greater Manchester]; Dover, N.H.: Manchester University Press, 1983. xvi, 285 p., 14 p. of plates: ill.; 24 cm. Includes index. 1. Wola (Papua New Guinea people) — Food 2. Ethnobotany — Papua New Guinea. 3. Food crops — Papua New Guinea. I. T.
DU740.42.S55 1983   338.1/0995/3 19   *LC* 82-62247   *ISBN* 0719008743

Strathern, Andrew.   **3.5664**
A line of power / Andrew Strathern. — London; New York: Tavistock, 1984. 170 p.: maps; 23 cm. Includes indexes. 1. Medlpa (Papua New Guinea people) 2. Wiru (Papua New Guinea people) 3. Social change — Case studies. I. T.
DU740.42.S77 1984   306/.0899912 19   *LC* 84-2521   *ISBN* 0422788902

Watson, James B. (James Bennett), 1918-.   **3.5665**
Tairora culture: contingency and pragmatism / James B. Watson. — Seattle: University of Washington Press, c1983. x, 346 p.: ill.; 25 cm. — (Anthropological studies in the eastern highlands of New Guinea. v. 5) Includes index. 1. Tairora (Papua New Guinea people) I. T. II. Series.
DU740.42.W37 1983   306/.0899912 19   *LC* 82-23776   *ISBN* 0295957999

Griffin, James.   **3.5666**
Papua New Guinea: a political history / James Griffin, Hank Nelson, Stewart Firth. — Richmond, Australia: Heinemann Educational Australia, 1980 (c1979). viii, 280 p.: maps; 22 cm. 1. Papua New Guinea — History I. Nelson, Hank. II. Firth, Stewart. III. T.
DU740.75.G74   995/.3   *LC* 80-474733   *ISBN* 0858591979

McSwain, Romola.   **3.5667**
The past and future people: tradition and change on a New Guinea island / Romola McSwain. — Melbourne; New York: Oxford University Press, 1977. xx, 213 p.: ill.; 23 cm. Revision of the author's thesis, University of Queensland. 1. Karkar Island, Papua New Guinea — History. 2. Karkar Island, Papua New Guinea — Native races. I. T.
DU740.9.K37 M33 1977   995.5   *LC* 77-374974   *ISBN* 0195505212

Howie-Willis, Ian, 1937-.   **3.5668**
Lae, village and city / [by] Ian Willis. — Carlton, Vic.: Melbourne University Press, 1975 (c1974). xvi, 173 p., [6] leaves of plates: ill.; 23 cm. Includes index. 1. Lae (Papua New Guinea) — History. I. T.
DU740.9.L33 W54   995/.5   *LC* 75-309136   *ISBN* 0522840760

DU744–950 Other Islands, A–Z

Matthiessen, Peter.   • **3.5669**
Under the mountain wall: a chronicle of two seasons in the stone age / Peter Matthiessen. — New York: Viking Press, 1962. xvi, 256, xvii-xxxii p., [32] p. of plates: ill., maps. 1. Ethnology — Indonesia — Irian Jaya. I. T.
DU744.M32   DU744 M32 1962.   919.51   *LC* 62-16796

Shapiro, Harry Lionel, 1902-.   • **3.5670**
The heritage of the Bounty / by Harry L. Shapiro; rev. with a new postscript. — Garden City, N.Y.: Doubleday, [1962] 301 p.: ill.; 19 cm. — (The Natural history library; N23) Includes index. Anchor books. 1. Pitcairn Island. I. T.
DU800.S53 1962   996/.18   *LC* 62-3006

Mead, Margaret, 1901-1978.   • **3.5671**
Coming of age in Samoa; a psychological study of primitive youth for western civilisation, by Margaret Mead ... foreword by Franz Boas ... New York, W.

Morrow & Company, 1928. xv p., 1 l., 297 p. front., plates. 21 cm. 1. Girls 2. Children — Samoan Islands 3. Women — Samoan Islands. 4. Adolescence 5. Samoan Islands — Social life and customs. I. T.
DU813.M4   *LC* 28-20670

Keesing, Felix Maxwell, 1902-1961.   • **3.5672**
Elite communication in Samoa; a study of leadership [by] Felix M. Keesing [and] Marie M. Keesing. — Stanford, Calif., Stanford University Press [1956] vii, 318 p. maps, diagrs. 23 cm. (Stanford anthropological series, no. 3) 1. Leadership 2. Acculturation 3. Samoan Islands — Civilization. I. Keesing, Marie M. (Marie Margaret) joint author. II. T. III. Series.
DU817.K36   572.9961   *LC* 56-10904

Masterman, Sylvia.   **3.5673**
The origins of international rivalry in Samoa, 1845–1884. London Allen & Unwin [1934] 233p. 1. Samoan Islands — History 2. Samoan question I. T.
DU817 M3 1934

Gray, J. A. C. (John Alexander Clinton)   **3.5674**
Amerika Samoa: a history of American Samoa and its United States Naval Administration. — Annapolis: United States Naval Institute [1960] 295 p.: ill.; 25 cm. 1. American Samoa — History. I. T.
DU819.A1 G7   *LC* 60-12080

Davidson, James Wightman, 1915-1973.   • **3.5675**
Samoa mo Samoa: the emergence of the independent state of Western Samoa / [by] J. W. Davidson. — Melbourne; New York [etc.]: Oxford University Press, 1967. xii, 467 p.: maps (on lining-papers); 23 cm. 1. Western Samoa — Politics and government. 2. Western Samoa — History. I. T.
DU819.A2 D3   996/.14   *LC* 68-79458

Oliver, Douglas L.   **3.5676**
Bougainville; a personal history [by] Douglas Oliver. Honolulu, University Press of Hawaii, 1973. ix, 231 p. illus. 22 cm. 1. Bougainville Island (Papua New Guinea) 2. Buka Island. I. T.
DU850.O38   919.3/5   *LC* 73-81594   *ISBN* 0824802896

Oliver, Douglas L.   • **3.5677**
A Solomon Island society: kinship and leadership among the Sinuai of Bougainville. — Cambridge: Harvard University Press, 1955. xxii, 533 p.: ill., ports., maps, music; 25 cm. 1. Siuai (Papuan people) 2. Leadership I. T.
DU850.O4   572.9935   *LC* 54-9776

Newbury, C. W. (Colin Walter), 1929-.   **3.5678**
Tahiti Nui: change and survival in French Polynesia, 1767–1945 / Colin Newbury. — Honolulu: University Press of Hawaii, c1980. xvi, 380 p.: ill.; 23 cm. Includes index. 1. Tahiti — History. 2. Tahiti — Colonization. I. T.
DU870.N48   996/.211   *LC* 79-23609   *ISBN* 0824806301

Oliver, Douglas L.   **3.5679**
Ancient Tahitian society / Douglas L. Oliver. — Honolulu: University Press of Hawaii, [1974] 3 v. (xv, 1419 p., [4] leaves of plates (1 fold.)): ill.; 24 cm. Includes indexes. 1. Ethnology — Tahiti. 2. Tahiti — History. 3. Tahiti — Antiquities. I. T.
DU870.O43   996/.211   *LC* 73-77010   *ISBN* 0824802675

Friendly Islands: a history of Tonga / edited by Noel   **3.5680**
Rutherford.
Melbourne; New York: Oxford University Press, 1977. xii, 297 p.: ill.; 22 cm. Includes index. 1. Tonga — History. I. Rutherford, Noel.
DU880.F74   996/.12   *LC* 78-322409   *ISBN* 0195505190

DX GYPSIES

Kenrick, Donald.   **3.5681**
The destiny of Europe's Gypsies, by Donald Kenrick and Grattan Puxon. — New York: Basic Books, [1973, c1972] 256 p.; 22 cm. — (The Columbus Centre series) 1. Gypsies — Europe. I. Puxon, Grattan. joint author. II. T.
DX145.K45 1973   301.45/19/149704   *LC* 72-76925   *ISBN* 0465016111

Wood, Manfri Frederick.   **3.5682**
In the life of a Romany gypsy / edited by John A. Brune; illustrated by Andrew Young. — London; Boston: Routledge & K. Paul, [1973] 130 p.: ill.; 22 cm. 1. Gypsies — Great Britain. I. T.
DX211.W66   301.45/19/1497042   *LC* 73-86581   *ISBN* 0710075952

E11–45 General Works. North America

(Mexico, Central America, South America: see F1201-3799)

Martí, José, 1853-1895.   **3.5683**
The America of José Martí; selected writings. Translated from the Spanish by Juan de Onís. With an introd. by Federico de Onís. — New York: Noonday Press, 1954. xiii, 335 p.: port.; 21 cm. 1. America 2. America — Biography I. T.
E13.M3 1968   970/.04

Eccles, W. J. (William John)   **3.5684**
France in America, by W. J. Eccles. [1st ed.] New York, Harper & Row [1972] xii, 297 p. illus. 22 cm. (The New American Nation series) 1. French in America. 2. France — Colonies — America. 3. America — History — To 1810 I. T.
E18.82.E25 1972   970.02   *LC* 72-79657   *ISBN* 0060111526

Gibson, Charles, 1920-.   **3.5685**
Spain in America. — [1st ed.]. — New York: Harper & Row, [1966] xiv, 239 p.: illus., maps, ports.; 22 cm. (The New American Nation series) 1. America — History — To 1810 2. Spain — Colonies — America. 3. America — Civilization — Spanish influences. I. T.
E18.82.G5   980.01   *LC* 66-21705

Gerbi, Antonello, 1904-.   **3.5686**
The dispute of the New World; the history of a polemic, 1750–1900. — Rev. and enl. ed. translated by Jeremy Moyle. — [Pittsburgh]: University of Pittsburgh Press, [1973] xviii, 700 p.; 25 cm. Published in 1955 under title: La disputa del Nuovo Mondo. 1. America in literature. 2. America — History — Errors, inventions, etc. I. T.
E19.G3713 1973   917.3/007/22   *LC* 70-181396   *ISBN* 0822932504

Douglass, William A.   **3.5687**
Amerikanuak: Basques in the New World / William A. Douglass and Jon Bilbao. — Reno: University of Nevada Press, 1975. xiv, 519 p., [24] leaves of plates: ill.; 22 cm. (The Basque series) Includes index. 1. Basques — America — History. I. Bilbao, Jon. joint author. II. T.
E29.B35 D68   970/.004/9992   *LC* 75-30830   *ISBN* 0874170435

Bastide, Roger, 1898-1974.   **3.5688**
[Amériques noires, les civilisations africaines dans le Nouveau monde. English] African civilisations in the New World. Translated from the French by Peter Green, with a foreword by Geoffrey Parrinder. New York, Harper & Row [1971] vi, 232 p. 23 cm. (A Torchbook library edition) Translation of Les Amériques noires, les civilisations africaines dans le Nouveau monde. 1. Blacks — America — Religion 2. Blacks — America 3. Africa — Religion I. T.
E29.N3 B4213 1971   200/.97   *LC* 75-158981   *ISBN* 0061360570

Thompson, Robert Farris.   **3.5689**
Flash of the spirit: African and Afro–American art and philosophy / Robert Farris Thompson. — 1st ed. — New York: Random House, c1983. xvii, 317 p.: ill. 1. Blacks — America — History 2. Afro-Americans — History 3. Arts, Black — America. 4. Afro-American arts I. T.
E29.N3 T48 1983   E29N3 T48 1983.   973/.0496 19   *LC* 79-5560
ISBN 0394505158

North America: the historical geography of a changing continent   **3.5690**
/ edited by Robert D. Mitchell & Paul A. Groves.
Totowa, N.J.: Rowman & Littlefield, c1987. xii, 468 p.: ill., maps; 28 cm. 1. North America — Historical geography. I. Mitchell, Robert D., 1940- II. Groves, Paul A.
E41.N68 1987   911/.7 19   *LC* 86-13918   *ISBN* 0847673472

E51–99 Pre-Columbian America

Driver, Harold Edson, 1907-.   **• 3.5691**
Indians of North America [by] Harold E. Driver. — 2d ed., rev. — Chicago: University of Chicago Press, [1969] xvii, 632 p.: illus., maps (1 fold. in pocket); 24 cm. 1. Indians of North America 2. Indians of Mexico 3. Indians of Central America 4. Indians of the West Indies I. T.
E58.D68 1969   970.1   *LC* 79-76207   *ISBN* 0226164667

Alcina Franch, José.   **3.5692**
[Art précolombien. English] Pre–Columbian art / José Alcina Franch; translated from the French by I. Mark Paris. — New York: H.N. Abrams, 1983, c1978. 614 p.: ill. (some col.); 32 cm. Translation of: L'art précolombien. Includes index. 1. Indians — Art 2. Indians — Antiquities 3. Latin America — Antiquities. I. T.
E59.A7 A413 1983   709/.01/1091812 19   *LC* 82-20626   *ISBN* 0810906457

Grieder, Terence.   **3.5693**
Origins of Pre–Columbian art / by Terence Grieder. — 1st ed. — Austin, Tex.: University of Texas Press, 1982. 241 p.: ill.; 23 cm. — (The Texas Pan American series) Includes index. 1. Indians — Art 2. Indians — Transpacific influences. 3. Culture diffusion 4. America — Discovery and exploration — Pre-Columbian I. T.
E59.A7 G74   709/.01/1097 19   *LC* 81-12966   *ISBN* 0292760213

Kubler, George, 1912-.   **3.5694**
The art and architecture of ancient America: the Mexican, Maya, and Andean peoples / George Kubler. — 3rd (integrated) ed. — Harmondsworth, Middlesex; New York: Penguin Books, c1984. 572 p.: ill., maps; 21 cm. — (Pelican history of art.) Includes index. 1. Indians — Art 2. Indians — Architecture 3. Indians — Antiquities 4. Latin America — Antiquities. I. T. II. Series.
E59.A7 K8 1984   709/.72 19   *LC* 81-10525   *ISBN* 0140561218

E61–74 Archaeology

Chronologies in New World archaeology / [edited by] R. E.   **3.5695**
Taylor, Clement W. Meighan.
New York: Academic Press, c1978. xiii, 587 p.: ill.; 24 cm. (Studies in archeology) 1. Indians — Antiquities — Addresses, essays, lectures. 2. Archaeological dating — America — Addresses, essays, lectures. 3. America — Antiquities — Addresses, essays, lectures. I. Taylor, R. E. (Royal Ervin), 1938- II. Meighan, Clement Woodward, 1925-
E61.C55   970.01   *LC* 78-2039   *ISBN* 0126857504

Wauchope, Robert, 1909-.   **• 3.5696**
Lost tribes & sunken continents: myth and method in the study of American Indians. — [Chicago]: University of Chicago Press [1962] 155 p.: ill.; 21 cm. Includes bibliography. 1. Indians — Origin I. T.
E61.W33   970.1   *LC* 62-18112

Willey, Gordon Randolph, 1913-.   **3.5697**
A history of American archaeology / Gordon R. Willey, Jeremy A. Sabloff. — 2d ed. — San Francisco: W. H. Freeman, c1980. xiii, 313 p.: ill.; 24 cm. Includes index. 1. Indians — Antiquities 2. America — Antiquities I. Sabloff, Jeremy A. joint author. II. T.
E61.W67 1980   970   *LC* 79-23114   *ISBN* 0716711222

Willey, Gordon Randolph, 1913-.   **• 3.5698**
An introduction to American archaeology. — Englewood Cliffs, N. J., Prentice-Hall, 1966-1971. 2 v. ill. (Prentice-Hall anthropology series) 1. Indians — Antiquities 2. America — Antiquities I. T.
E61.W68   *LC* 66-10096

Silverberg, Robert.   **• 3.5699**
Mound builders of ancient America: the archaeology of a myth / Robert Silverberg. — Greenwich, Conn.: New York Graphic Society, 1968. 369 p.:

illus., maps.; 22 cm. 1. Mound-builders 2. Mounds — US.. 3. United States — Antiquity. I. T.
E73.S58   970.4/3   *LC* 68-12370

E76–99 Indians of North America

Reference encyclopedia of the American Indian / Barry T. Klein.   **3.5700**
4th ed. — New York: Todd Publications, 1986. 2 v.; 26 cm. Vol. 2, 'Who's who.'
1. Indians of North America — Directories. 2. Indians of North America — Bibliography 3. Indians of North America — Biography I. Klein, Barry T. II. Title: Encyclopedia of the American Indian.
E76.2.R4 1986   973/.04/97   *LC* 86-50046

Handbook of North American Indians / William C. Sturtevant, general editor.   **3.5701**
Washington: Smithsonian Institution: for sale by the Supt. of Docs., U.S. Govt. Print. Off., 1978- <1984 >. v. <5-6, 8-10, 15 >: ill.; 29 cm. 1. Indians of North America 2. Eskimos I. Sturtevant, William C.
E77.H25   970/.004/97   *LC* 77-17162

Kehoe, Alice B., 1936-.   **3.5702**
North American Indians: a comprehensive account / Alice Beck Kehoe. — Englewood Cliffs, N.J.: Prentice-Hall, c1981. xii, 564 p.: ill.; 24 cm. 1. Indians of North America I. T.
E77.K43   970.004/97 19   *LC* 80-22335   *ISBN* 0136236529

Kroeber, A. L. (Alfred Louis), 1876-1960.   • **3.5703**
Cultural and natural areas of native North America / by A.L. Kroeber. — Berkeley, Calif.: University of California Press, 1939. — 242 p.: maps (some fold. in pocket); 26 cm.— (University of California publications in American archaeology and ethnology v.38.) 1. Indians of North America — Culture. 2. Anthropo-geography — North America. I. T. II. Series.
E77.K7   *LC* A40-56

Newberry Library. Center for the History of the American Indian.   **3.5704**
Bibliographical series. — Bloomington: Indiana University Press, 1976-1983. v.; 21 cm. Later volumes have imprint: Knoxville, Tn., University of Tennessee Press. Volumes have separate authors and titles. I. T.
E77.N4x

North American Indians in historical perspective. Edited by Eleanor Burke Leacock & Nancy Oestreich Lurie.   **3.5705**
[1st ed.]. — New York: Random House, [1971] xi, 498 p.: illus.; 25 cm. 1. Indians of North America — History 2. Indians of North America — Social conditions I. Leacock, Eleanor Burke, 1922- ed. II. Lurie, Nancy Oestreich. ed.
E77.N63   970.1   *LC* 70-130187   *ISBN* 0394468163

Oswalt, Wendell H.   **3.5706**
This land was theirs; a study of the North American Indian [by] Wendell H. Oswalt. — 2d ed. — New York: Wiley, [1973] xx, 617 p.: illus.; 23 cm. 1. Indians of North America I. T.
E77.O8 1973   970.1   *LC* 72-11973   *ISBN* 0471657174

Spencer, Robert F.   **3.5707**
The native Americans: ethnology and backgrounds of the North American Indians / Robert F. Spencer, Jesse D. Jennings, et al. — 2d ed. — New York: Harper & Row, c1977. xxi, 584 p.: ill.; 27 cm. Includes index. 1. Indians of North America 2. North America — Antiquities I. Jennings, Jesse David, 1909- joint author. II. T.
E77.S747 1977   970/.004/97   *LC* 76-46940   *ISBN* 0060463716

Swanton, John Reed, 1873-1958.   • **3.5708**
The Indian tribes of North America. Washington, U.S. Govt. Print. Off., 1952. Grosse Pointe, Mich., Scholarly Press, 1968. vi, 726 p. maps (part fold.) 24 cm. (Smithsonian Institution. Bureau of American Ethnology. Bulletin 145) 1. Indians of North America I. T.
E77.S94 1968   970.1   *LC* 71-9481

Turner, Frederick W., 1937- comp.   **3.5709**
The portable North American Indian reader, edited and with an introd. by Frederick W. Turner III. — New York: Viking Press, [1974] xi, 628 p.; 19 cm. — (The Viking portable library) Spine title: North American Indian reader. 1. Indians of North America 2. Indian literature 3. American literature — Indian authors I. T. II. Title: North American Indian reader.
E77.T937 1974   897   *LC* 72-12545   *ISBN* 0670119709

Waldman, Carl.   **3.5710**
Atlas of the North American Indian / Carl Waldman; maps and illustrations by Molly Braun. — New York, N.Y.: Facts on File, c1985. xi, 276 p.: ill. (some col.); 29 cm. Includes index. 1. Indians of North America 2. Indians of North America — Maps I. Braun, Molly. II. T.
E77.W195 1985   970.00497 19   *LC* 83-9020   *ISBN* 0871968509

Washburn, Wilcomb E.   **3.5711**
The Indian in America, by Wilcomb E. Washburn. — [1st ed.]. — New York: Harper & Row, [1975] xix, 296 p.: illus.; 22 cm. — (The New American Nation series) 1. Indians of North America I. T.
E77.W385 1975   970.1   *LC* 74-1870   *ISBN* 006014534X

The Elders wrote: an anthology of early prose by North American Indians, 1768–1931 / edited by Bernd Peyer.   **3.5712**
Berlin: Reimer, 1982. 196 p.: ports.; 24 cm. — (Beiträge zur Kulturanthropologie.) 1. Indians of North America — History — Sources. 2. Indian literature — United States 3. American literature — Indian authors 4. Indians of North America — Cultural assimilation I. Peyer, Bernd. II. Series.
E77.2.E43 1982   970.004/97 19   *LC* 83-100954   *ISBN* 3496005254

Fitting, James Edward.   **3.5713**
The development of North American archaeology: essays in the history of regional traditions / edited by James E. Fitting. — University Park: Pennsylvania State University Press, 1973. -. viii, 309 p.: maps; 19 cm. — 1. Indians of North America — Antiquities 2. Archaeology — History. I. T.
E77.9.F57 1973b   *LC* 73-5862   *ISBN* 0271011610

Jennings, Jesse David, 1909-.   • **3.5714**
Prehistory of North America / [by] Jesse D. Jennings. — New York: McGraw-Hill, [1968] xi, 391 p.: ill., maps.; 26 cm. 1. Indians of North America — Antiquities 2. North America — Antiquities I. T.
E77.9.J4   970.1   *LC* 68-13517

E78 BY REGION, A–Z

E78 A–C

Gumerman, George J.   **3.5715**
A view from Black Mesa: the changing face of archaeology / George J. Gumerman. — Tucson, Ariz.: University of Arizona Press, c1984. xiii, 184 p.: ill.; 23 cm. Includes index. 1. Indians of North America — Arizona — Black Mesa (Navajo County and Apache County) — Antiquities. 2. Excavations (Archaeology) — Arizona — Black Mesa (Navajo County and Apache County) 3. Black Mesa (Navajo County and Apache County, Ariz.) — Antiquities. 4. Arizona — Antiquities I. T.
E78.A7 G964 1984   979.1/35 19   *LC* 84-8581   *ISBN* 0816508488

Haury, Emil W. (Emil Walter), 1904-.   **3.5716**
The Hohokam, desert farmers & craftsmen: excavations at Snaketown, 1964–1965 / Emil W. Haury. — Tucson: University of Arizona Press, c1976. xii, 412 p.: ill. (some col.); 32 cm. Includes index. 1. Hohokam culture 2. Snaketown, Ariz. I. T.
E78.A7 H27   970/.004/97   *LC* 74-31610   *ISBN* 0816504458

Martin, Paul Sidney, 1899-.   **3.5717**
The archaeology of Arizona: a study of the southwest region / [by] Paul S. Martin [and] Fred Plog. — [1st ed.] Garden City, N.Y.: Published for the American Museum of Natural History [by] Natural History Press, 1973. xx, 422 p.: ill.; 27 cm. 1. Indians of North America — Arizona — Antiquities 2. Indians of North America — Southwest, New — Antiquities 3. Arizona — Antiquities 4. Southwest, New — Antiquities I. Plog, Fred. II. American Museum of Natural History. III. T.
E78.A7 M298   970.4/91   *LC* 72-76192   *ISBN* 0385070756

Fisher, Robin, 1946-.   **3.5718**
Contact and conflict: Indian–European relations in British Columbia, 1774–1890 / Robin Fisher. — Vancouver: University of British Columbia Press, c1977. xvi, 250 p., [6] leaves of plates: ill.; 24 cm. Includes index. 1. Indians of North America — British Columbia — History. 2. Indians of North America — Canada — Government relations I. T.
E78.B9 F57   301.45/19/709711   *LC* 77-367590   *ISBN* 0774800658

Gough, Barry M.   **3.5719**
Gunboat frontier: British maritime authority and Northwest Coast Indians, 1846–90 / Barry M. Gough. — Vancouver: University of British Columbia Press, 1984. xvii, 287 p., [16] p. of plates: ill.; 24 cm. (University of British Columbia Press Pacific maritime studies. 4) Includes index. 1. Indians of North America — British Columbia — History. 2. Indians of North America —

Canada — Government relations 3. British Columbia — History. I. T.
II. Series.
E78.B9 G68 1984   971.1/00497 19   *LC* 84-199366   *ISBN*
0774801751

Cook, Sherburne Friend, 1896-1974.   **3.5720**
The population of the California Indians, 1769–1970 / Sherburne F. Cook; with
a foreword by Woodrow Borah and Robert F. Heizer. Berkeley: University of
California Press, c1976. xvii, 222 p.: ill.; 24 cm. Includes index. 1. Indians of
North America — California — Population. I. T.
E78.C15 C698 1976   301.45/19/70794   *LC* 74-27287   *ISBN*
0520029232

Heizer, Robert Fleming, 1915-.   **3.5721**
The natural world of the California Indians / Robert F. Heizer and Albert B.
Elsasser. — Berkeley: University of California Press, c1980. 271 p., [4] leaves of
plates: ill.; 21 cm. — (California natural history guides. 46) Includes index.
1. Indians of North America — California I. Elsasser, Albert B. joint author.
II. T. III. Series.
E78.C15 H433   979.4/004/97   *LC* 79-65092   *ISBN* 0520038959

Kroeber, A. L. (Alfred Louis), 1876-1960.   **3.5722**
Handbook of the Indians of California / A. L. Kroeber. — New York: Dover
Publications, 1976. xviii, 995 p., [45] leaves of plates: ill.; 22 cm. Reprint of the
1925 ed. published by Govt. Print. Off., Washington, which was issued as no. 78
of the bulletin of the Bureau of American Ethnology, Smithsonian Institution.
Includes indexes. 1. Indians of North America — California I. T.
E78.C15 K78 1976   979.4/004/97   *LC* 76-19514   *ISBN*
0486233685

Moratto, Michael J.   **3.5723**
California archaeology / Michael J. Moratto with contributions by David A.
Fredrickson, Christopher Raven, Claude N. Warren; with a foreword by
Francis A. Riddell. — Orlando: Academic Press, 1984. xxxvii, 757 p.: ill.; 24
cm. — (New World archaeological record.) Includes indexes. 1. Indians of
North America — California — Antiquities 2. California — Antiquities
I. Fredrickson, David A. (David Allen) II. T. III. Series.
E78.C15 M665 1984   979.4/01 19   *LC* 83-7141   *ISBN*
012506182X

Bean, Lowell John.   **3.5724**
Native Californians: a theoretical retrospective / [edited] by Lowell J. Bean and
Thomas C. Blackburn. — Ramona, Calif.: Ballena Press, 1976. 452 p.: ill.; 24
cm. 1. Indians of North America — California — Addresses, essays, lectures.
I. Blackburn, Thomas C. II. T.
E78.C15 N37   301.45/19/70794   *LC* 76-355428

Crowe, Keith J.   **3.5725**
A history of the original peoples of northern Canada / Keith J. Crowe. —
Montreal: McGill-Queen's University Press [for the] Arctic Institute of North
America, 1974. xiii, 226 p.: ill. maps; 23 cm. 'A technical report from the Man
in the North Project' 1. Indians of North America — Canada, Northern.
2. Eskimos — Canada. I. Arctic Institute of North America. II. T.
E78.C2 C76   970.4/1   *LC* 73-93833   *ISBN* 0773502203 pa

Grant, John Webster, 1919-.   **3.5726**
Moon of wintertime: missionaries and the Indians of Canada in encounter since
1534 / John Webster Grant. — Toronto; Buffalo: University of Toronto Press,
c1984. viii, 315 p., [12] p. of plates: ill.; 24 cm. Includes index. 1. Indians of
North America — Canada — Missions — History. 2. Missions — Canada —
History. I. T.
E78.C2 G84 1984   266/.008997071 19   *LC* 84-217823   *ISBN*
0802056431

Jenness, Diamond, 1886-1969.   **3.5727**
The Indians of Canada / Diamond Jenness. — 7th ed. — Toronto; Buffalo:
University of Toronto Press, 1977. x, 432 p.: ill.; 24 cm. Originally published
in 1932 as Bulletin no. 65, Anthropological series no. 15 of the National
Museums of Canada. 1. Indians of North America — Canada I. T.
E78.C2 J28 1977   971/.004/97   *LC* 78-311022   *ISBN* 0802022863.
ISBN 0802063268 pbk

Martin, Calvin.   **3.5728**
Keepers of the game: Indian–animal relationships and the fur trade / Calvin
Martin. — Berkeley: University of California Press, c1978. xi, 226 p.: maps; 23
cm. 1. Indians of North America — Canada — Hunting. 2. Indians of North
America — Canada — Religion and mythology. 3. Micmac Indians —
Hunting. 4. Chippewa Indians — Hunting. 5. Fur trade — Canada. I. T.
E78.C2 M33   971/.004/97   *LC* 77-78381   *ISBN* 0520035194

Ray, Arthur J.   **3.5729**
Indians in the fur trade: their role as trappers, hunters, and middlemen in the
lands southwest of Hudson Bay, 1660–1870 / Arthur J. Ray. — Toronto;
Buffalo: University of Toronto Press, [1974] xii, 249 p.: ill.; 24 cm. Includes

index. 1. Indians of North America — Canada 2. Indians of North America —
Canada — Commerce. 3. Fur trade — Canada. I. T.
E78.C2 R35   380.1/439   *LC* 73-89848   *ISBN* 0802021182

Trigger, Bruce G.   **3.5730**
Natives and newcomers: Canada's 'Heroic Age' reconsidered / Bruce G.
Trigger. — Kingston: McGill-Queen's University Press, c1985. xiii, 430 p.: ill.;
24 cm. Includes index. 1. Indians of North America — History. 2. Iroquoian
Indians — History. 3. Indians of North America — First contact
with Occidental civilization 4. Canada — History — To 1763 (New France)
I. T.
E78.C2 T74 1985   971/.00497 19   *LC* 86-143857   *ISBN*
0773505946

Western Canadian Studies Conference, University of Calgary,   **3.5731**
1977.
One century later: Western Canadian reserve Indians since Treaty 7 / edited by
Ian A. L. Getty and Donald B. Smith. — Vancouver: University of British
Columbia Press, 1979 (c1978). xvi, 153 p., [8] leaves of plates: ill.; 23 cm.
1. Indians of North America — Canada — Congresses. 2. Indians of North
America — Canada — Government relations — Congresses. I. Getty, Ian A.
L., 1947- II. Smith, Donald B. III. T.
E78.C2 W53 1977   971/.004/97   *LC* 79-311050   *ISBN*
0774801034

E78 D–N

Custer, Jay F., 1955-.   **3.5732**
Delaware prehistoric archaeology: an ecological approach / Jay F. Custer. —
Newark: University of Delaware Press; London: Associated University Presses,
c1984. 224 p.: ill.; 24 cm. Includes index. 1. Indians of North America —
Delaware — Antiquities. 2. Delaware — Antiquities. I. T.
E78.D3 C97 1984   975.1/01 19   *LC* 83-40130   *ISBN* 0874132339

Brose, David S.   **3.5733**
Ancient art of the American Woodland Indians / text by David S. Brose, James
A. Brown, and David W. Penney; photographs by Dirk Bakker. — New York:
H.N. Abrams, in association with the Detroit Institute of Arts, c1985. 240 p.:
ill. (some col.); 29 cm. Catalogue of a traveling exhibition to be held at the
National Gallery of Art, Washington, D.C., the Detroit Institute of Arts, and
the Houston Museum of Fine Arts, Mar. 17, 1985-Mar. 2, 1986. 1. Woodland
Indians — Art — Exhibitions. 2. Indians of North America — Art —
Exhibitions I. Brown, James Allison, 1934- II. Penney, David W. III. Bakker,
Dirk. IV. Detroit Institute of Arts. V. National Gallery of Art (U.S.)
VI. Museum of Fine Arts, Houston. VII. T.
E78.E2 B76 1985   730/.0974/074013 19   *LC* 84-20462   *ISBN*
0810918277

Milanich, Jerald T.   **3.5734**
Florida archaeology / Jerald T. Milanich, Charles H. Fairbanks. — New York:
Academic Press, c1980. xvi, 290 p.: ill.; 24 cm. — (New World archaeological
record.) Includes index. 1. Indians of North America — Florida — Antiquities
2. Florida — Antiquities I. Fairbanks, Charles Herron, 1913- joint author.
II. T. III. Series.
E78.F6 M55   975.9/01   *LC* 80-524   *ISBN* 0124959601

Atlas of Great Lakes Indian history / Helen Hornbeck Tanner,   **3.5735**
editor–in–chief, Adele Hast, associate editor, Jacqueline
Peterson, Robert J. Surtees; Miklos Pinther, cartographer.
1st ed. — Norman: University of Oklahoma Press, c1987. xv, 224 p.: ill., col.
maps; 31 cm. — (The Civilizaton of the American Indian series; v. 174)
Includes index. 1. Indians of North America — Great Lakes Region —
History. 2. Great Lakes Region — History. I. Tanner, Helen Hornbeck.
II. Hast, Adele. III. Series.
E78.G7 A87 1986   977 19   *LC* 86-4353   *ISBN* 0806115157

Mason, Ronald J.   **3.5736**
Great Lakes archaeology / Ronald J. Mason. — New York: Academic Press,
c1981. xxiii, 426 p.: ill.; 24 cm. — (New World archaeological record.) Includes
index. 1. Indians of North America — Great Lakes region — Antiquities.
2. Indians of North America — Great Lakes region — History. 3. Great Lakes
region — Antiquities. I. T. II. Series.
E78.G7 M37   977/.01 19   *LC* 80-2340   *ISBN* 012477850X

Quimby, George Irving, 1913-.   **• 3.5737**
Indian life in the Upper Great Lakes, 11,000 B. C. to A. D. 1800. — [Chicago]
University of Chicago Press [1960] 182 p. illus. 25 cm. Includes bibliography.
1. Indians of North America — Great Lakes region. 2. Great Lakes region —
Antiq. 3. Indians of North America — Antiquities I. T.
E78.G7Q5   970.477   *LC* 60-11799

Anthropology on the Great Plains / edited by W. Raymond   **3.5738**
Wood and Margot Liberty.
Lincoln: University of Nebraska Press, c1980. vii, 306 p.: ill.; 27 cm. 1. Indians
of North America — Great Plains — Addresses, essays, lectures. I. Wood, W.
Raymond. II. Liberty, Margot.
E78.G73 A57   978/.00497   *LC* 79-28369   *ISBN* 0803247087

Frison, George C.   **3.5739**
Prehistoric hunters of the High Plains / George C. Frison. — New York:
Academic Press, c1978. xiv, 457 p.: ill.; 24 cm. — (New World archaeological
record.) Includes indexes. 1. Indians of North America — High Plains (U.S.)
— Hunting. I. T. II. Series.
E78.G73 F74   978   *LC* 77-75572   *ISBN* 0122685601

The Hidden half: studies of Plains Indian women / Patricia   **3.5740**
Albers, Beatrice Medicine.
Washington, D.C.: University Press of America, c1983. vi, 280 p.; 23 cm.
Consists chiefly of papers presented at a symposium entitled The Role and
status of women in Plains Indian cultures, held in 1977, at the Plains
Conference, Lincoln, Neb. 1. Indians of North America — Great Plains —
Women — Congresses. I. Albers, Patricia. II. Medicine, Beatrice.
E78.G73 H53 1983   305.4/8897/078 19   *LC* 82-23906   *ISBN*
0819129569

Agnew, Brad, 1939-.   **3.5741**
Fort Gibson, terminal on the trail of tears / Brad Agnew. — Norman:
University of Oklahoma Press, c1980. xi, 274 p.: ill.; 24 cm. Includes index.
1. Indians of North America — Government relations — 1789-1869
2. Indians of North America — Indian Territory 3. Indians of North America
— Removal 4. Fort Gibson (Okla.) — History. 5. Indian Territory. I. T.
E78.I5 A37   323.1/19/70766   *LC* 78-21391   *ISBN* 0806115211

Morse, Dan F.   **3.5742**
Archaeology of the central Mississippi Valley / Dan F. Morse, Phyllis A.
Morse. — New York: Academic Press, c1983. xviii, 345 p.: ill.; 24 cm. (New
World archaeological record.) 1. Indians of North America — Mississippi
River Valley — Antiquities. 2. Indians of North America — Mississippi River
Valley — History. 3. Mississippian culture 4. Mississippi River Valley —
Antiquities. 5. Mississippi River Valley — History I. Morse, Phyllis A. II. T.
III. Series.
E78.M75 M67 1983   977/.01 19   *LC* 82-22734   *ISBN* 0125081804

Salisbury, Neal.   **3.5743**
Manitou and providence: Indians, Europeans, and the making of New England,
1500–1643 / Neal Salisbury. — New York: Oxford University Press, 1982. xii,
316 p.: ill.; 22 cm. 1. Indians of North America — New England — History.
2. Indians of North America — New England — First contact with Occidental
civilization. 3. New England — History — Colonial period, ca. 1600-1775
I. T.
E78.N5 S24 1982   974/.02 19   *LC* 81-11238   *ISBN* 0195030257

Snow, Dean R., 1940-.   **3.5744**
The archaeology of New England / Dean R. Snow. — New York: Academic
Press, 1980. xiv, 379 p.: ill.; 24 cm. — (New World archaeological record.)
Includes index. 1. Indians of North America — New England — Antiquities.
2. Indians of North America — New England. 3. Excavations (Archaeology)
— New England. 4. New England — Antiquities. I. T. II. Series.
E78.N5 S58   974 19   *LC* 80-982   *ISBN* 0126539502

Lister, Robert Hill, 1915-.   **3.5745**
Chaco Canyon: archaeology and archaeologists / Robert H. Lister and
Florence C. Lister. — 1st ed. — Albuquerque: University of New Mexico Press,
c1981. xiv, 284 p.: ill.; 26 cm. 1. Indians of North America — New Mexico —
Chaco Canyon — Antiquities. 2. Archaeology — New Mexico — Chaco
Canyon — History. 3. Excavations (Archaeology) — New Mexico — Chaco
Canyon. 4. Chaco Canyon (N.M.) — Antiquities. 5. New Mexico —
Antiquities I. Lister, Florence Cline. II. T.
E78.N65 L57   978.9/82 19   *LC* 80-54566   *ISBN* 0826305741

Ritchie, William Augustus, 1903-.   • **3.5746**
The archaeology of New York State [by] William A. Ritchie. Rev. ed. Garden
City, N.Y., Published for the American Museum of Natural History [by] the
Natural History Press [1969] xxxiv, 357 p.: illus., maps. 27 cm. 1. Indians of
North America — New York (State) — Antiquities. 2. New York (State) —
Antiquities. I. American Museum of Natural History. II. T.
E78.N7 R476 1969   970.4/47   *LC* 68-22501

Ruby, Robert H.   **3.5747**
Indians of the Pacific Northwest: a history / Robert H. Ruby and John A.
Brown; with a foreword by Alvin M. Josephy, Jr. — 1st ed. — Norman:
University of Oklahoma Press, c1981. xviii, 294 p.: ill.; 29 cm. — (The Civilization of
the American Indian series; v. 158) Includes index. 1. Indians of North
America — Northwest, Pacific — History. I. Brown, John Arthur. II. T.
E78.N77 R8   979/.00497 19   *LC* 80-5946   *ISBN* 0806117311

Bancroft-Hunt, Norman.   **3.5748**
People of the totem: the Indians of the Pacific Northwest / text by Norman
Bancroft–Hunt; photos. by Werner Forman. — New York: Putnam, 1979.
128 p.: col. ill., map; 31 cm. — (Echoes of the ancient world) Includes index.
1. Indians of North America — Northwest coast of North America.
I. Forman, W. (Werner) II. T.
E78.N78 B36   E78N78 B36.   971.1/3/00497   *LC* 78-57977
    ISBN 0399119914

Drucker, Philip, 1911-.   • **3.5749**
Cultures of the north Pacific coast / Philip Drucker; with an introd. by Harry B.
Hawthorn. — New York: Chandler, 1965. xvi, 243 p.: ill.; maps. — (Chandler
publications in anthropology and sociology) Includes index. 1. Indians of
North America — Northwest coast of North America. I. T.
E78.N78 D67   *LC* 63-20546   *ISBN* 0810200872 pbk

Goddard, Pliny Earle, 1869-1928.   **3.5750**
Indians of the Northwest coast. — New York: Cooper Square Publishers, 1972.
175 p.: illus.; 23 cm. Reprint of the 1934 ed. 1. Indians of North America —
Northwest coast of North America. I. T.
E78.N78 G62 1972   970.4/7   *LC* 72-81191   *ISBN* 081540428X

Holm, Bill, 1925-.   **3.5751**
The box of daylight: northwest coast Indian art / Bill Holm; with contributions
by Peter L. Corey ... [et al.]. — Seattle, Wash.: Seattle Art Museum: University
of Washington Press, 1983. ix, 147 p.: ill.; 29 cm. Catalog of an exhibition held
at Seattle Art Museum, Sept. 15, 1983-Jan. 8, 1984. 1. Indians of North
America — Northwest coast of North America — Art — Exhibitions.
I. Corey, Peter L. II. Seattle Art Museum. III. T.
E78.N78 H587 1983   709/.01/109795074019777 19   *LC* 83-50231
    ISBN 0932216137

Lévi-Strauss, Claude.   **3.5752**
[Voie des masques. English] The way of the masks / Claude Lévi–Strauss;
translated from the French by Sylvia Modelski. — Seattle: University of
Washington Press, c1982. x, 249, [4] p. of plates: ill. (some col.); 22 cm.
Translation of: La voie des masques. Includes index. 1. Indians of North
America — Northwest coast of North America — Masks. 2. Indians of North
America — Northwest coast of North America — Art. 3. Indians of North
America — Northwest coast of North America — Religion and mythology.
I. T.
E78.N78 L4513 1982   732/.2 19   *LC* 82-2723   *ISBN* 0295959290

E78 O–Z

Hudson, Charles M.   **3.5753**
The Southeastern Indians / by Charles Hudson. — 1st ed. — Knoxville:
University of Tennessee Press, c1976. xviii, 573 p.: ill. Includes index.
1. Indians of North America — Southern States I. T.
E78.S65 H82   E78S65 H82.   975/.004/97   *LC* 75-30729   *ISBN*
0870491873

Southeastern Indians since the Removal Era / edited by Walter   **3.5754**
L. Williams.
Athens: University of Georgia Press, c1979. xvi, 253 p.: ill.; 24 cm. Includes
index. 1. Indians of North America — Southern States — History. 2. Indians
of North America — Southern States — Social conditions. 3. Southern States
— Race relations. I. Williams, Walter L., 1948-
E78.S65 S67   975/.004/97   *LC* 78-10490   *ISBN* 0820304646

Wright, J. Leitch (James Leitch), 1929-.   **3.5755**
The only land they knew: the tragic story of the American Indians in the Old
South / J. Leitch Wright, Jr. — New York: Free Press; London: Collier
Macmillan, c1981. xi, 372 p., [16] p. of plates: ill.; 25 cm. Includes index.
1. Indians of North America — Southern States — History. 2. Southern States
— History 3. Southern States — Race relations. I. T.
E78.S65 W74   975/.00497 19   *LC* 80-1854   *ISBN* 002935790X

Cordell, Linda S.   **3.5756**
Prehistory of the Southwest / Linda S. Cordell. — Orlando, Fla.: Academic
Press, 1984. xviii, 409 p.: ill.; 24 cm. (New World archaeological record.)
'A School of American Research book.' Includes index. 1. Indians of North
America — Southwest, New — Antiquities 2. Pueblo Indians — Antiquities
3. Indians of North America — Southwest, New — History. 4. Pueblo Indians
— History. 5. Southwest, New — Antiquities I. School of American Research
(Santa Fe, N.M.) II. T. III. Series.
E78.S7 C67 1984   979.01 19   *LC* 84-6387   *ISBN* 0121882209

Discovering past behavior: experiments in the archaeology of the   **3.5757**
American Southwest / edited by Paul Grebinger.
New York: Gordon and Breach, c1978. xvi, 279 p., [2] fold. leaves of plates: ill.;
24 cm. — (Library of anthropology.) 1. Indians of North America —
Southwest, New — Antiquities — Addresses, essays, lectures. 2. Southwest,

New — Antiquities — Addresses, essays, lectures. I. Grebinger, Paul.
II. Series.
E78.S7 D53   979   *LC* 76-53712   *ISBN* 0677160801

Dutton, Bertha Pauline, 1903-.   **3.5758**
Indians of the American Southwest / Bertha P. Dutton. — Englewood Cliffs,
N.J.: Prentice-Hall, [1975] xxix, 298 p.: ill.; 25 cm. Includes index. 1. Indians of
North America — Southwest, New I. T.
E78.S7 D79   301.45/19/7079   *LC* 74-30311   *ISBN* 0134568974

Hedrick, Basil Calvin, 1932- comp.   **3.5759**
The classic Southwest; readings in archaeology, ethnohistory, and ethnology,
edited by Basil C. Hedrick, J. Charles Kelley [and] Carroll L. Riley. —
Carbondale: Southern Illinois University Press, [1973] xii, 193 p.: illus.; 23 cm.
1. Indians of North America — Southwest, New 2. Indians of North America
— Southwest, New — Antiquities 3. Southwest, New — Antiquities I. Kelley,
J. Charles, 1913- joint comp. II. Riley, Carroll L. joint comp. III. T.
E78.S7 H43   970.4/9   *LC* 70-184966   *ISBN* 080930547X

John, Elizabeth Ann Harper, 1928-.   **3.5760**
Storms brewed in other men's worlds: the confrontation of Indians, Spanish,
and French in the Southwest, 1540–1795 / by Elizabeth A. H. John. — 1st ed.
— College Station: Texas A&M University Press, [1975] xvi, 805 p., [8] leaves
of plates: ill.; 23 cm. Includes index. 1. Indians of North America —
Southwest, New — History. 2. Indians of North America — Government
relations — To 1789 3. Southwest, New — History — To 1848 I. T.
E78.S7 J64   978/.004/97   *LC* 75-9996   *ISBN* 0890960003

Kent, Kate Peck.   **3.5761**
Prehistoric textiles of the Southwest / Kate Peck Kent. — 1st ed. — Santa Fe,
N.M.: School of American Research, c1983. xx, 315 p.: ill. (some col.); 27 cm.
— (Southwest Indian arts series.) Includes index. 1. Indians of North America
— Southwest, New — Textile industry and fabrics 2. Indians of North
America — Southwest, New — Antiquities 3. Southwest, New — Antiquities
I. T. II. Series.
E78.S7 K43 1983   746.1/4/0979 19   *LC* 82-20313   *ISBN*
0826305911

Kidder, Alfred Vincent.   • **3.5762**
An introduction to the study of Southwestern archaeology: with a preliminary
account of the excavations at Pecos, and a summary of Southwestern
archaeology today / by Rouse. Rev. ed. New Haven: Yale University Press,
1962. 377 p.: ill. 1. Pueblo Indians — Antiquities 2. Southwest, New —
Antiquities 3. Pecos, New Mexico. I. Rouse, Irving. II. T. III. Title:
Southwestern archaeology.
E78S7 K5 1962   978.9   *LC* 62-6993

McGregor, John C. (John Charles), 1905-.   **3.5763**
Southwestern archaeology, by John C. McGregor. 2d ed. Urbana: University of
Illinois Press, 1982. vii, 511 p.: ill.; 27 cm. 1. Indians of North America —
Southwest, New — Antiquities 2. Southwest, New — Antiquities I. T.
E78.S7 M15   970.491   *LC* 65-10079

Plog, Fred.   **3.5764**
The study of prehistoric change / [by] Fred T. Plog. — New York: Academic
Press, [1974] xii, 199 p.: ill.; 24 cm. — (Studies in archaeology) 1. Indians of
North America — Southwest, New — Antiquities 2. Archaeology —
Methodology 3. Social change 4. Southwest, New — Antiquities I. T.
E78.S7 P55   970.4/9   *LC* 73-17114   *ISBN* 0127856455

Southwestern Indian ritual drama / edited by Charlotte J.   **3.5765**
Frisbie.
1st ed. — Albuquerque: University of New Mexico Press, c1980. xii, 372 p.: ill.;
24 cm. (School of American Research advanced seminar series) 'A School of
American Research book.' Based on an advanced seminar sponsored by the
School of American Research, April 3-8, 1978. Includes index. 1. Indians of
North America — Southwest, New — Rites and ceremonies — Addresses,
essays, lectures. 2. Indians of North America — Southwest, New — Dances —
Addresses, essays, lectures. 3. Indians of North America — Southwest, New —
Drama — Addresses, essays, lectures. 4. Indians of North America —
Southwest, New — Music — Addresses, essays, lectures. I. Frisbie, Charlotte
Johnson.
E78.S7 S585   299/.74   *LC* 79-2308   *ISBN* 0826305210

Spicer, Edward Holland, 1906-.   • **3.5766**
Cycles of conquest; the impact of Spain, Mexico, and the United States on the
Indians of the Southwest, 1533–1960. Drawings by Hazel Fontana. — Tucson:
University of Arizona Press, [1962] xii, 609 p.: illus., maps.; 28 cm. 1. Indians
of North America — Southwest, New 2. Indians of North America — Cultural
assimilation 3. Southwest, New — History I. T.
E78.S7 S6   970.49   *LC* 61-14500

Tanner, Clara Lee.   **3.5767**
Indian baskets of the Southwest / Clara Lee Tanner. — Tucson, Ariz.:
University of Arizona Press, c1983. xi, 242 p.: ill. (some col.); 32 cm. Includes

index. 1. Indians of North America — Southwest, New — Basket making.
I. T.
E78.S7 T287 1983   746.41/2/08997078 19   *LC* 83-5000   *ISBN*
0816508119

Tanner, Clara Lee.   **3.5768**
Southwest Indian painting; a changing art. — 2d ed. — Tucson: University of
Arizona Press, [1973] xvii, 477 p.: illus. (part col.); 32 cm. 1. Indians of North
America — Southwest, New — Art. I. T.
E78.S7 T32 1973   759.979   *LC* 74-160812   *ISBN* 0816503095

Aikens, C. Melvin.   **3.5769**
Hogup Cave [by] C. Melvin Aikens. Chapters on textiles and wooden artifacts,
by J. M. Adovasio and G. F. Dalley. Ancillary studies, by K. T. Harper [and
others] Salt Lake City, University of Utah Press, 1970. xiii, 286 p. illus. 28 cm.
(Anthropological papers, (Salt Lake City) no. 93) Errata slip inserted.
1. Hogup Cave, Utah. I. T.
E78.U55 A78   917.92/43   *LC* 72-612762

Sheehan, Bernard W.   **3.5770**
Savagism and civility: Indians and Englishmen in Colonial Virginia / Bernard
W. Sheehan. — Cambridge; New York: Cambridge University Press, c1980. xi,
258 p.; 22 cm. Includes index. 1. Indians, Treatment of — Virginia. 2. Indians
of North America — Virginia — First contact with Occidental civilization.
3. Indians — Public opinion. 4. Public opinion — Great Britain. 5. Virginia
— History — Colonial period, ca. 1600-1775 I. T.
E78.V7 S53   975.5/02   *LC* 79-18189   *ISBN* 0521229278

Wright, Gary A.   **3.5771**
People of the high country: Jackson Hole before the settlers / Gary A. Wright.
— New York: P. Lang, c1984. ii, 181 p., [5] p. of plates: ill.; 23 cm. —
(American university studies. Anthropology/sociology. 0740-0489; v. 7)
1. Indians of North America — Wyoming — Jackson Hole Region —
Antiquities. 2. Jackson Hole Region (Wyo.) — Antiquities. 3. Wyoming —
Antiquities I. T. II. Series.
E78.W95 W75 1984   978.7/55 19   *LC* 83-49508   *ISBN*
082040103X

E81–87 INDIAN WARS

Brown, Dee Alexander.   • **3.5772**
Bury my heart at Wounded Knee: an Indian history of the American West / by
Dee Brown. — [1st ed.] New York: Holt, Rinehart & Winston [1971, c1970]
xvii, 487 p.: ill., music, ports.; 25 cm. 1. Indians of North America — West
(U.S.) — Wars. 2. Indians of North America — West (U.S.) 3. West (U.S.) —
History I. T.
E81.B75 1971   970.5   *LC* 70-121633   *ISBN* 0030853222

Utley, Robert Marshall, 1929-.   **3.5773**
The Indian frontier of the American West, 1846–1890 / Robert M. Utley. — 1st
ed. — Albuquerque: University of New Mexico Press, c1984. xxi, 325 p.: ill.; 25
cm. — (Histories of the American frontier.) Includes index. 1. Indians of North
America — Wars 2. Indians of North America — Government relations
3. West (U.S.) — History — 1848-1950 I. T. II. Series.
E81.U747 1984   978/.02 19   *LC* 83-12516   *ISBN* 0826307159

Downey, Fairfax Davis, 1893-.   **3.5774**
The red/bluecoats: the Indian scouts, U. S. Army / by Fairfax Downey &
Jacques Noel Jacobsen. Fort Collins, Colo.: The Old Army Press, c1973. 204 p.:
ill.; 23 cm. 1. United States. Army — Indian troops 2. Scouts and scouting
3. Indians of North America — Wars I. Jacobsen, Jacques Noel. II. T.
E82.D74 1973

Church, Benjamin, 1639-1718.   **3.5775**
Diary of King Philip's War, 1675–76 / by Benjamin Church; with an introd. by
Alan and Mary Simpson. — Tercentenary ed. — Chester, Conn.: Published for
the Little Compton Historical Society [by] Pequot Press, 1975. xxi, 226 p.: ill.;
24 cm. Original ed., 1716, published under title: Entertaining passages relating
to Philip's war. 'First edition.' Includes index. 1. King Philip's War, 1675-1676
I. Little Compton Historical Society. II. T.
E83.67.C54 1975   973.2/4   *LC* 74-27234   *ISBN* 0871060523

Parkman, Francis, 1823-1893.   • **3.5776**
The Conspiracy of Pontiac / with a new introduction by Samuel Eliot Morison.
— 10th ed. rev.: with additions. New York: Collier Books, 1962. 544 p.; 18 cm.
(Collier Books; BS93.) First published under title: History of the conspiracy of
Pontiac. 1. Pontiac's Conspiracy, 1763-1765 2. United States — History —
French and Indian War, 1755-1763 I. T.
E83.76.P279   971.02   *LC* 62-16980

Trafzer, Clifford E.   **3.5777**
The Kit Carson campaign: the last great Navajo war / Clifford E. Trafzer. —
1st ed. — Norman: University of Oklahoma Press, c1982. xviii, 277 p.: ill.,

ports.; 22 cm. Includes index. 1. Carson, Kit, 1809-1868. 2. Navajo Indians — Removal. 3. Navajo Indians — Wars. 4. Indians of North America — Southwest, New — Wars. 5. Indians of North America — Southwest, New — Removal. I. T.
E83.859.T7 1982   979/.02 19   *LC* 81-40283   *ISBN* 0806116838

Dunlay, Thomas W., 1944-.   **3.5778**
Wolves for the blue soldiers: Indian scouts and auxiliaries with the United States Army, 1860–90 / Thomas W. Dunlay. — Lincoln: University of Nebraska Press, 1982. 304 p., [12] p. of plates: ill.; 24 cm. Includes index. 1. United States. Army — Indians. 2. Indians of North America — Wars — 1866-1895 3. Indians of North America — Wars — 1862-1865 4. Indians of North America — West (U.S.) — Wars. 5. Scouts and scouting — West (U.S.) — History — 19th century. 6. West (U.S.) — History — 1848-1950 I. T.
E83.866.D86 1982   978/.02 19   *LC* 81-16326   *ISBN* 0803216580

Utley, Robert Marshall, 1929-.   **3.5779**
Frontier regulars; the United States Army and the Indian, 1866–1891, by Robert M. Utley. New York, Macmillan Pub. Co. [c1973] xi, 466 p. illus. 22 cm. (Wars of the United States.) 1. United States. Army — History 2. Indians of North America — Wars — 1866-1895 3. West (U.S.) — History I. T. II. Series.
E83.866.U87 1973   973.8   *LC* 74-164315

White, Lonnie J.   **3.5780**
Hostiles and horse soldiers; Indian battles and campaigns in the West, by Lonnie J. White. With contributions by Jerry Keenan [and others] With a foreword by Merrill J. Mattes. — Boulder, Colo.: Pruett Pub. Co., 1972. xix, 231 p.: illus.; 27 cm. 1. Indians of North America — Wars — 1866-1895 2. Sand Creek, Battle of, 1864 I. Keenan, Jerry. II. T.
E83.866.W52   973.8   *LC* 72-80262   *ISBN* 0871090613

Camp, Walter Mason, 1867-1925.   **3.5781**
Custer in '76: Walter Camp's notes on the Custer fight / edited by Kenneth Hammer. Provo, Utah: Brigham Young University Press, c1976. xiii, 303 p.: ill.; 24 cm. 1. Custer, George Armstrong, 1839-1876. 2. Little Big Horn, Battle of the, 1876 I. Hammer, Kenneth, 1918- II. T.
E83.876.C16   973.8/2   *LC* 75-28017   *ISBN* 0842503994

General Custer and the Battle of the Little Big Horn: the   **3.5782**
federal view / edited by John M. Carroll.
Centennial ed. — New Brunswick, N.J.: Garry Owen, 1976. xx, 177 p.: ill., map. — (Custeriana series) Includes reprints of U.S. federal documents originally issued 1876-1878. 1. Custer, George Armstrong, 1839-1876. 2. Little Big Horn, Battle of the, 1876 I. Carroll, John M. (John Melvin), 1928-
E83.876.G463 1976   *LC* 76-11331

Greene, Jerome A.   **3.5783**
Slim Buttes, 1876: an episode of the Great Sioux War / by Jerome A. Greene. — 1st ed. — Norman: University of Oklahoma Press, c1982. xvi, 192 p.: ill.; 22 cm. Includes index. 1. Slim Buttes (S.D.), Battle of, 1876 I. T.
E83.876.G74   973.8/2 19   *LC* 81-40291   *ISBN* 0806117125

Puritans among the Indians: accounts of captivity and   **3.5784**
redemption 1676–1724 / edited by Alden T. Vaughan & Edward
W. Clark.
Cambridge, Mass.: Belknap Press, 1981. x, 275 p.: ill., maps, facsims., 1 port; 24 cm. 1. Indians of North America — New England — Captivities. 2. New England — History — Colonial period, ca. 1600-1775 I. Vaughan, Alden T., 1929- II. Clark, Edward W., 1943-
E85.P87   974/.02/0922 18   974/.02/0922 19   *LC* 80-26033
ISBN 0674739019

E89–90 BIOGRAPHY

American Indian leaders: studies in diversity / edited by R.   **3.5785**
David Edmunds.
Lincoln: University of Nebraska Press, c1980. xiv, 257 p., [4] leaves of plates: ill.; 23 cm. 1. Indians of North America — Biography I. Edmunds, R. David (Russell David), 1939-
E89.A48   970.004/97 B   *LC* 80-431   *ISBN* 0803218001

Thatcher, Benjamin Bussey, 1809-1840.   **3.5786**
Indian biography; or, An historical account of those individuals who have been distinguished among the North American natives as orators, warriors, statemen, and other remarkable characters. — Glorieta, N.M.: Rio Grande Press, [1973] 2 v.: illus.; 24 cm. — (A Rio Grande classic) Reprint of the 1832 ed. published by A. L. Fowle, New York; with a new pref. by W. N. Fenton. 1. Indians of North America — Biography 2. Indians of North America — History I. T.
E89.T36 1973   970.1/092/2 B   *LC* 73-14660   *ISBN* 0873800893

Krupat, Arnold.   **3.5787**
For those who come after: a study of Native American autobiography / by Arnold Krupat. — Berkeley: University of California Press, c1985. xv, 167 p.: ill.; 22 cm. Includes index. 1. Indians of North America — Biography 2. Autobiography I. T.
E89.5.K78 1985   973/.0497022 B 19   *LC* 84-8688   *ISBN* 0520053079

Apes, William, b. 1798.   **3.5788**
A son of the forest. The experience of William Apes, a native of the forest. Comprising a notice of the Pequod tribe of Indians. Written by himself. New-York, The author, 1829. 216 p. 15 cm. 1. Indians of North America 2. Pequot Indians I. T.
E90.A5.A5   *LC* 11-9439

Black Elk, 1863-1950.   **3.5789**
Black Elk speaks; being the life story of a holy man of the Oglala Sioux, as told through John G. Neihardt (Flaming Rainbow) Illustrated by Standing Bear. Lincoln, University of Nebraska Press, 1961. 280 p. illus. 21 cm. (A Bison book, 119) 1. Black Elk, 1863-1950. 2. Oglala Indians I. Neihardt, John Gneisenau, 1881-1973. II. T.
E90.B82 A3 1961   970.2   *LC* 61-7236

Copway, George, Chippewa chief, 1818?-1863.   **3.5790**
Recollections of a forest life: or, The life and travels of Kah-ge-ga-gah-bowh, or, George Copway, chief of the Ojibway nation. — 2d ed. — [Toronto]: Canadian House, 1970. xii, 248 p. Facsimile reprint of the London, 1851 ed. published by C. Gilpin. 1. Copway, George, Chippewa chief, 1818?-1863 2. Chippewa Indians I. T. II. Title: The life and travels of Kah-ge-ga-gah-bowh
E90C7 C75   E90C76 A3 1851a.   *LC* 75-129275

Woodcock, George, 1912-.   **3.5791**
Gabriel Dumont: the Métis chief and his lost world / George Woodcock. — Edmonton: Hurtig, c1975. 256 p.: map (on lining paper); 23 cm. 1. Dumont, Gabriel, 1838-1906. 2. Riel Rebellion, 1885 I. T.
E90.D83 W66   970/.004/97 B   *LC* 76-357735   *ISBN* 0888300956

Kroeber, Theodora.   **• 3.5792**
Ishi in two worlds: a biography of the last wild Indian in North America / with a foreword by Lewis Gannett. — Berkeley: University of California Press, 1961. 255 p.: ill., ports., maps.; 24 cm. 1. Ishi, d. 1916. 2. Yana Indians I. T.
E90.I8 K7   970.3   *LC* 61-7530

Left Handed, 1868-.   **3.5793**
Son of Old Man Hat; a Navaho autobiography, recorded by Walter Dyk. With a foreword by Edward Sapir. Lincoln, University of Nebraska Press [1967, c1938] xiv, 378 p. 21 cm. (A Bison book) 1. Navajo Indians — Social life and customs. I. Dyk, Walter. II. T.
E90.L4L5 1967   970.3   *LC* 67-4921

Pokagon, Simon, 1830-1899.   **3.5794**
O–gi–maw–kwe mit–i–gwa–ki: (Queen of the Woods). — Hartford, Mi.: C. H. Engle, 1899. 255 p.: ill.; 19 cm. I. T. II. Title: Queen of the Woods.
E90.P7 P7   *LC* 99-2324/r

E91–97 GOVERNMENT RELATIONS. EDUCATION

Jacobs, Wilbur R.   **• 3.5795**
Dispossessing the American Indian; Indians and whites on the colonial frontier, by Wilbur R. Jacobs. — New York: Scribner, [1972] xiv, 240 p.: illus.; 24 cm. 1. Indians of North America — Government relations — To 1789 2. Indians, Treatment of — North America I. T.
E91.J3 1972   970.5   *LC* 72-37179   *ISBN* 0684128608

Jaenen, Cornelius J.   **3.5796**
Friend and foe: aspects of French–Amerindian cultural contact in the sixteenth and seventeenth centuries / Cornelius J. Jaenen. — New York: Columbia University Press, 1976. 207 p.: ill.; 24 cm. Includes index. 1. Indians of North America — Canada — Government relations 2. Canada — History — To 1763 (New France) I. T.
E92.J33 1976   323.1/197/071   *LC* 75-44212   *ISBN* 0231040881

The Aggressions of civilization: federal Indian policy since the   **3.5797**
1880s / edited by Sandra L. Cadwalader and Vine Deloria, Jr.
Philadelphia: Temple University Press, 1984. xvi, 258 p.; 22 cm. 1. Indians of North America — Government relations — 1869-1934 — Addresses, essays, lectures. 2. Indians of North America — Government relations — 1934- — Addresses, essays, lectures. 3. Indians of North America — Legal status, laws, etc. — Addresses, essays, lectures. I. Cadwalader, Sandra L. II. Deloria, Vine. E93.A34 1984   323.1/197 19   *LC* 84-94   *ISBN* 0877223491

Burt, Larry W., 1950-. 3.5798
Tribalism in crisis: federal Indian policy, 1953–1961 / Larry W. Burt. — 1st ed. — Albuquerque: University of New Mexico Press, c1982. x, 180 p.; 24 cm. Includes index. 1. Indians of North America — Government relations — 1934- 2. United States — Politics and government — 1953-1961 I. T.
E93.B975 1982   323.1/197/073 19   *LC* 82-11069   *ISBN* 0826306330

Deloria, Vine. • 3.5799
Custer died for your sins; an Indian manifesto. By Vine Deloria, Jr. [New York] Macmillan [1969] 279 p. 22 cm. 1. Indians of North America — Government relations — 1934- 2. Indians, Treatment of — United States I. T.
E93.D36 E467   970.1   *LC* 69-20405

Jahoda, Gloria. 3.5800
The trail of tears / Gloria Jahoda. — 1st ed. — New York: Holt, Rinehart and Winston, c1975. 356 p.: ill.; 24 cm. Includes index. 1. Indians of North America — Land transfers 2. Indians of North America — Government relations — 1789-1869 I. T.
E93.J2   813/.5/4   *LC* 75-5470   *ISBN* 0030148715

Jennings, Francis, 1918-. 3.5801
The ambiguous Iroquois empire: the Covenant Chain confederation of Indian tribes with English colonies from its beginnings to the Lancaster Treaty of 1744 / by Francis Jennings. — 1st ed. — New York: Norton, c1984. xxv, 438 p.: ill.; 24 cm. Continues: The invasion of America. 1976, c1975. Includes index. 1. Indians of North America — Government relations — To 1789 2. Iroquois Indians — Government relations 3. United States — History — Colonial period, ca. 1600-1775 I. T.
E93.J44 1984   974/.02 19   *LC* 82-22452   *ISBN* 0393017192

Jones, Dorothy V. 3.5802
License for empire: colonialism by treaty in early America / Dorothy V. Jones. — Chicago: University of Chicago Press, 1982. xiv, 256 p.; 23 cm. Includes index. 1. Indians of North America — Government relations — To 1789 2. Indians of North America — Treaties 3. Indians of North America — Government relations — 1789-1869 4. United States — Territorial expansion I. T. II. Title: Colonialism by treaty in early America.
E93.J63 1982   323.1/197/073 19   *LC* 81-19700   *ISBN* 0226407071

Viola, Herman J. 3.5803
Thomas L. McKenney: architect of America's early Indian policy, 1816–1830 / Herman J. Viola. — 1st ed. — Chicago: Sage Books, [1974] xii, 365 p., 10 leaves of plates: ill.; 24 cm. Includes index. 1. McKenney, Thomas Loraine, 1785-1859. 2. Indians of North America — Government relations — 1789-1869 I. T.
E93.M152 V56   353.008/48/4 B   *LC* 74-18075   *ISBN* 0804006687

Pearce, Roy Harvey. 3.5804
Savagism and civilization: a study of the Indian and the American mind / Roy Harvey Pearce. — Baltimore: Johns Hopkins Press, 1967, c1965. xi, 260 p.: ill.; 20 cm. First ed. published in 1953 under title: The savages of America. 1. Indians of North America — Cultural assimilation 2. Indians in literature I. T.
E93.P4 1967   970.00497   *LC* 67-5156   *ISBN* 0801805252

Prucha, Francis Paul. comp. 3.5805
Americanizing the American Indians; writings by the 'Friends of the Indian,' 1880–1900. Cambridge, Mass.: Harvard University Press, 1973. vii, 358 p.; 24 cm. 1. Indians of North America — Government relations — 1869-1934 — Addresses, essays, lectures. 2. Indians of North America — Cultural assimilation — Addresses, essays, lectures. I. T.
E93.P9652   970.5   *LC* 72-92132   *ISBN* 0674029755

Prucha, Francis Paul. 3.5806
The great father: the United States government and the American Indians / Francis Paul Prucha. — Lincoln: University of Nebraska Press, c1984. 2 v. (xxxii, 1302 p., [52] p. of plates): ill.; 24 cm. Includes index. 1. Indians of North America — Government relations I. T.
E93.P9654 1984   323.1/197073 19   *LC* 83-16837   *ISBN* 0803236689

Prucha, Francis Paul. 3.5807
Indian policy in the United States: historical essays / by Francis Paul Prucha. — Lincoln: University of Nebraska Press, c1981. ix, 272 p.; 24 cm. 1. Indians of North America — Government relations — Addresses, essays, lectures. I. T.
E93.P9664   323.1/197/073 19   *LC* 81-1667   *ISBN* 080323662X

Satz, Ronald N. 3.5808
American Indian policy in the Jacksonian era [by] Ronald N. Satz. — Lincoln: University of Nebraska Press, [1974, c1975] xii, 343 p.: illus.; 22 cm. 1. Indians of North America — Land transfers 2. Indians of North America — Government relations — 1789-1869 3. United States — Politics and government — 1829-1837 I. T.
E93.S27   970.5   *LC* 73-94119   *ISBN* 0803208235

Taylor, Graham D., 1944-. 3.5809
The New Deal and American Indian tribalism: the administration of the Indian reorganization act, 1934–45 / by Graham D. Taylor. — Lincoln: University of Nebraska Press, c1980. xiii, 203 p.; 24 cm. Includes index. 1. Indians of North America — Government relations — 1934- 2. Indians of North America — Legal status, laws, etc. 3. Indians of North America — Tribal government 4. New Deal, 1933-1939 I. T.
E93.T235   323.1/19/7073   *LC* 79-9178   *ISBN* 0803244037

Washburn, Wilcomb E. comp. 3.5810
The American Indian and the United States: a documentary history / [compiled by] Wilcomb E. Washburn. — Westport, Conn.: Greenwood Press, 1979, c1973. 4 v. (xiv, 3119 p.); 24 cm. Reprint of the 1st ed. published by Random House, New York. Includes index. 1. Indians of North America — Government relations — Sources. 2. Indians of North America — History — Sources. I. T.
E93.W27 1979   323.1/19/7073   *LC* 79-19895   *ISBN* 0313201366

Fuchs, Estelle. 3.5811
To live on this earth; American Indian education, by Estelle Fuchs and Robert J. Havighurst. [1st ed.] Garden City, N.Y., Doubleday, 1972. xiii, 390 p. illus. 22 cm. 1. Indians of North America — Education I. Havighurst, Robert James, 1900- joint author. II. T.
E97.F8   370/.8997 19   *LC* 73-172015

E98 SPECIAL TOPICS, A–Z

Dockstader, Frederick J. • 3.5812
Indian art in America: the arts and crafts of the North American Indian. — Greenwich, Conn.: New York Graphic Society, [1961] 224 p.: ill. (part mounted col.), map.; 29 cm. 1. Indians of North America — Art 2. Indians of North America — Industry. I. T.
E98.A7 D57   970.67   *LC* 60-8921

Dunn, Dorothy, 1903-. 3.5813
American Indian painting of the Southwest and Plains areas. — [1st ed. — Albuquerque]: University of New Mexico, 1968. xxvii, 429 p.: illus. (part col.); 29 cm. 1. Painting, Indian — Southwest, New. 2. Indians of North America — Great Plains — Art. 3. Indians of North America — Pictorial works I. T.
E98.A7 D8   759.01/1   *LC* 68-19736

Duff, Wilson, 1925-. 3.5814
Images, stone, B. C.; thirty centuries of Northwest coast Indian sculpture, photos. and drawings by Hilary Stewart. Saanichton, B. C., Hancock House, c1975. 191 p. ill. (some col.) 24 cm. 'An exhibition originating at the Art Gallery of Greater Victoria.' 1. Indians of North America — Northwest coast of North America — Art — Exhibitions. I. Art Gallery of Greater Victoria. II. T.
E 98 A7 D85 1975   *ISBN* 0919654274

Inverarity, Robert Bruce, 1909-. • 3.5815
Art of the Northwest Coast Indians. Berkeley, University of California Press, 1950. xiv, 243 p. illus. (part col.) map (on lining papers) 29 cm. Bibliography: p. 237-243. 1. Indians of North America — Art 2. Indians of North America — Northwest, Pacific. I. T.
E98.A7I5   970.67   *LC* 50-62872

Maurer, Evan M. 3.5816
The native American heritage: a survey of North American Indian art: the Art Institute of Chicago, July 16–October 30, 1977: [exhibition catalogue] / Evan M. Maurer. — Chicago: The Institute, c1977. 351 p., [6] leaves of plates: ill. (some col.); 28 cm. Label mounted on t. p.: Distributed by University of Nebraska Press, Lincoln, Nebraska. 1. Indians of North America — Art — Exhibitions I. Art Institute of Chicago. II. T.
E98.A7 M38   709/.01/1   *LC* 77-89620   *ISBN* 008328103X

Axtell, James. 3.5817
The European and the Indian: essays in the ethnohistory of colonial North America / James Axtell. — New York: Oxford University Press, 1981. xii, 402 p.: ill.; 22 cm. Includes index. 1. Indians of North America — Cultural assimilation — Addresses, essays, lectures. 2. Indians of North America — History — Addresses, essays, lectures. 3. North America — Civilization — Indian influences — Addresses, essays, lectures. 4. North America — History — Colonial period, ca. 1600-1775 — Addresses, essays, lectures. I. T.
E98.C89 A9   970.004/92 19   *LC* 80-25084   *ISBN* 0195029038

Hoxie, Frederick E., 1947-. 3.5818
A final promise: the campaign to assimilate the Indians, 1880–1920 / Frederick E. Hoxie. — Lincoln, Neb.: University of Nebraska Press, c1984. xvi, 350 p.; 24 cm. Includes index. 1. Indians of North America — Cultural assimilation 2. Indians of North America — Government relations — 1869-1934 I. T.
E98.C89 H68 1984   973/.0497 19   *LC* 83-6858   *ISBN* 0803223234

The Indians' book: an offering by the American Indians of Indian lore, musical and narrative, to form a record of the songs and legends of their race / recorded and edited by Natalie Curtis; ill. from photographs and from original drawings by Indians. **3.5819**
New York: Dover, 1968. xxxi, 584 p.: ill., music. Includes index. Reprint of 2d ed., 1923. 1. Folk-lore, Indian. 2. Indians of North America — Music I. Curtis, Doris M. (Doris Malkin) Natalie.
E98.F6 C8 1968   *LC* 68-19547   *ISBN* 0486219399 pbk

Schoolcraft, Henry Rowe, 1793-1864.   ● **3.5820**
Indian legends from Algic researches (The myth of Hiawatha, Oneota, the red race in America) and historical and statistical information respecting the Indian tribes of the United States; edited by Mentor L. Williams. [East Lansing] Michigan State University Press, 1956. xxii, 322 p. 24 cm. 1. Hiawatha, 15th cent. 2. Indians of North America — Legends 3. Indians of North America — Folklore I. Williams, Mentor Lee, 1901- , ed. II. T.
E98.F6 S32   *LC* 55-11688

Thompson, Stith, 1885- ed.   ● **3.5821**
Tales of the North American Indians, selected and annotated by Stith Thompson. — Bloomington, Indiana University Press [1966] xxiii, 386 p. fold. map. 22 cm. — (Midland books, MB-91) Reprint of the work first published in 1929. 1. Indians of North America — Legends 2. Folk-lore, Indian. I. T.
E98.F6T32 1966   398.2   *LC* 66-22898

Vanderwerth, W. C., comp.   **3.5822**
Indian oratory; famous speeches by noted Indian chieftains [by] W. C. Vanderwerth. Foreword by William R. Carmack. [1st ed. Norman, University of Oklahoma Press, 1971] xviii, 292 p. illus., ports. 20 cm. (Civilization of the American Indian series. v. 110) 1. Speeches, addresses, etc., American — Indian authors I. T. II. Series.
E98.O7 V33   970.4/3   *LC* 73-145502   *ISBN* 0806109483

Grant, Campbell, 1909-.   **3.5823**
The rock art of the North American Indians / Campbell Grant. — Cambridge [Cambridgeshire]; New York: Cambridge University Press, 1983. 62 p., [62] p. of plates: ill. (some col.); 25 cm. — (Imprint of man.) 'Published in Italian as L'arte rupestre degli Indiani nord-americani by Editoriale Jaca Book, Milan, 1983'—P. facing t.p. 1. Indians of North America — Painting 2. Rock paintings — North America. I. T. II. Series.
E98.P23 G73 1983   709/.01/130973 19   *LC* 82-23655   *ISBN* 0521254434

Berkhofer, Robert F.   **3.5824**
The white man's Indian: images of the American Indian from Columbus to the present / Robert F. Berkhofer, Jr. — 1st ed. — New York: Knopf: distributed by Random House, 1978. xvii, 261 p.; 25 cm. 1. Indians of North America — Public opinion 2. Public opinion — United States. 3. United States — Civilization — Indian influences I. T.
E98.P99 B47 1978   301.15/43/9700497   *LC* 77-15568   *ISBN* 0394484851

Drinnon, Richard.   **3.5825**
Facing west: the metaphysics of Indian–hating and empire building / by Richard Drinnon. — Minneapolis: University of Minnesota Press, c1980. xx, 571 p.: ill.; 22 cm. Includes index. 1. Indians of North America — Public opinion 2. Indians of North America — Civil rights 3. Race discrimination — United States 4. United States — Territorial expansion 5. United States — Race relations I. T.
E98.P99 D74   305.8/97/073 19   *LC* 80-10234   *ISBN* 0816609780

La Barre, Weston, 1911-.   **3.5826**
The peyote cult / Weston La Barre. — 4th ed. enl. — [Hamden, Conn.]: Archon Books, 1975. xix, 296 p.: ill.; 23 cm. 1. Peyotism 2. Indians of North America — Religion and mythology 3. Indians of North America — Rites and ceremonies I. T.
E98.R3 L3 1975   299/.7   *LC* 75-19425   *ISBN* 020801456X

Mooney, James, 1861-1921.   **3.5827**
[Ghost-dance religion and the Sioux outbreak of 1890] The ghost-dance religion and Wounded Knee. New York, Dover Publications [1973] 645-1136 p. illus. 24 cm. Reprint of the 1896 ed. published by the Govt. Print. Off., Washington, which was issued as pt. 2 of the fourteenth Annual report of the Bureau of Ethnology of the Smithsonian Institution, 1892-93, under title: The ghost-dance religion and the Sioux outbreak of 1890. 1. Ghost dance 2. Dakota Indians — Wars, 1890-1891 I. T.
E98.R3 M6 1973b   299/.7   *LC* 73-80557   *ISBN* 048620233X

Tedlock, Dennis, 1939- comp.   **3.5828**
Teachings from the American earth: Indian religion and philosophy / edited by Dennis Tedlock and Barbara Tedlock. — 1st ed. — New York: Liveright, [1975] p. cm. 1. Indians of North America — Religion and mythology — Addresses, essays, lectures. I. Tedlock, Barbara. joint author. II. T.
E98.R3 T42 1975   299/.7   *LC* 74-34146   *ISBN* 0871405597

Waddell, Jack O., 1933- comp.   ● **3.5829**
The American Indian in urban society. Edited by Jack O. Waddell [and] O. Michael Watson. — Boston: Little, Brown, [1971] xiv, 414 p.: maps.; 21 cm. — (The Little, Brown series in anthropology) 1. Indians of North America — Urban residence I. Watson, O. Michael. joint comp. II. T.
E98.S67 W3   301.3/6   *LC* 78-155318

Amsden, Charles Avery, 1899-1941.   **3.5830**
Navaho weaving, its technic and its history. Chicago, Rio Grande Press 1964. xviii, 261 p. illus. (part col.), fold. maps. 24 cm. (A Rio Grande classic) Reproduction of the 1st ed., Santa Ana, Calif., Fine Arts Press, 1934. 1. Indians of North America — Southwest, New — Textile industry and fabrics 2. Navajo Indians — Textile industry and fabrics I. T.
E98.T35 A5 1964   970.67461   *LC* 64-20401

Dockstader, Frederick J.   **3.5831**
Weaving arts of the North American Indian / Frederick J. Dockstader. — New York: Crowell, 1978. 223 p., [31] leaves of plates: ill. (some col.); 28 cm. Includes index. 1. Indians of North America — Textile industry and fabrics 2. Weaving I. T.
E98.T35 D62   746.1/4   *LC* 78-381   *ISBN* 0690017391

Deloria, Vine.   **3.5832**
The nations within: the past and future of American Indian sovereignty / Vine Deloria, Jr., Clifford M. Lytle. — 1st ed. — New York: Pantheon Books, c1984. 293 p.; 24 cm. Includes index. 1. Indians of North America — Tribal government 2. Indians of North America — Government relations — 1934- 3. Indians of North America — Civil rights I. Lytle, Clifford M. II. T.
E98.T77 D44 1984   323.1/197 19   *LC* 84-42663   *ISBN* 0394725662

Bataille, Gretchen M., 1944-.   **3.5833**
American Indian women, telling their lives / by Gretchen M. Bataille and Kathleen Mullen Sands. — Lincoln: University of Nebraska Press, c1984. ix, 209 p.; 24 cm. Includes index. 1. Indians of North America — Women — Biography. 2. Indians of North America — Women — Biography — History and criticism. 3. Indians of North America — Women — Biography — Bibliography. I. Sands, Kathleen M. II. T.
E98.W8 B37 1984   305.4/8897/073 B 19   *LC* 83-10234   *ISBN* 0803211597

Niethammer, Carolyn J.   **3.5834**
Daughters of the earth: the lives and legends of American Indian women / by Carolyn Niethammer. — New York: Collier books, 1977. xvii, 281 p.: ill.; 25 cm. Includes index. 1. Indians of North America — Women 2. Indians of North America — Social life and customs I. T.
E98.W8 N53   970/.004/97   *LC* 76-56103   *ISBN* 0025885804.
ISBN 0020961502 pbk

E99 Tribes, A–Z

E99 A–B

Morrison, Kenneth M.   **3.5835**
The embattled Northeast: the elusive ideal of alliance in Abenaki–Euramerican relations / Kenneth M. Morrison. — Berkeley: University of California Press, c1984. x, 256 p., [2] p. of plates: maps; 24 cm. 1. Abnaki Indians — Government relations — To 1789. 2. Indians of North America — Government relations — To 1789 3. Abnaki Indians — History — Colonial period, ca. 1600-1775. 4. New England — History — Colonial period, ca. 1600-1775 I. T.
E99.A13 M67 1984   305/.897 19   *LC* 83-18002   *ISBN* 0520051262

White, Leslie A., 1900-1975.   **3.5836**
The Acoma Indians, by Leslie A. White. With a new publisher's pref. [and] a new foreword by the author. — Glorieta, N.M.: Rio Grande Press, [1973] 17-192, 1087-1108 p.: illus. (part col.); 29 cm. — (A Rio Grande classic) On cover: The A'coma Indians, people of the sky city. Reprint of the 1932 ed. published by the U.S. Bureau of American Ethnology, Washington, as part of its 47th annual report, 1929-30. 1. Acoma Indians 2. Acoma Indians — Legends. I. T.
E99.A16 W45 1973   970.3   *LC* 72-13912   *ISBN* 0873801288

Apachean culture history and ethnology. Keith H. Basso and Morris E. Opler, editors. Collaborating authors: William Y. Adams [and others]   **3.5837**
Tucson, University of Arizona Press, 1971. viii, 168 p. illus. 27 cm. (Anthropological papers of the University of Arizona, no. 21) Based on the Apachean Symposium, held at the 69th annual meeting of the American Anthropological Association, Nov., 1969, New Orleans. 1. Apache Indians — Congresses. 2. Navajo Indians — Congresses. I. Basso, Keith H., 1940- ed.

II. Opler, Morris Edward, 1907- ed. III. Adams, William Yewdale, 1927-
IV. Apachean Symposium, New Orleans, 1969.
E99.A6 A63   970.3   *LC* 70-140453   *ISBN* 0816502951

Basso, Keith H., 1940-.   **3.5838**
Portraits of 'The Whiteman': linguistic play and cultural symbols among the western Apache / Keith H. Basso; ill. by Vincent Craig. — Cambridge [Eng.]; New York: Cambridge University Press, 1979. xxi, 120 p.: ill.; 22 cm. 1. Apache Indians — Joking. 2. Apache wit and humor — History and criticism. 3. Indians of North America — Arizona — Joking. I. T.
E99.A6 B2295   970/.004/97   *LC* 78-31535   *ISBN* 0521226406

Adams, Alexander B.   **3.5839**
Geronimo; a biography [by] Alexander B. Adams. — New York: Putnam, [1971] 381 p.; ill.; 22 cm. 1. Geronimo, Apache Chief, 1829-1909. 2. Apache Indians — History. I. T.
E99.A6G14 1971   970.3 B   *LC* 77-163402

Haley, James L.   **3.5840**
Apaches, a history and culture portrait / James L. Haley. — 1st ed. — Garden City, N.Y.: Doubleday, 1981. xxi, 453 p., [32] leaves of plates: ill.; 24 cm. Includes index. 1. Apache Indians — History. I. T.
E99.A6 H24   970.004/97 19   *LC* 76-42331   *ISBN* 0385121474

Tanner, Clara Lee.   **3.5841**
Apache Indian baskets / Clara Lee Tanner. — Tucson, Ariz.: University of Arizona Press, c1982. xi, 204 p.: ill.; 32 cm. Includes index. 1. Apache Indians — Basket making. 2. Indians of North America — Southwest, New — Basket making. I. T.
E99.A6 T25 1982   746.41/2/08997 19   *LC* 82-6920   *ISBN* 0816507783

Western Apache raiding and warfare, from the notes of   **3.5842**
Grenville Goodwin. Edited by Keith H. Basso, with the assistance of E. W. Jernigan and W. B. Kessell.
Tucson: University of Arizona Press, [1971] xii, 330 p.: illus.; 23 cm. 1. Apache Indians. 2. Indian warfare I. Goodwin, Grenville, 1907-1940. II. Basso, Keith H., 1940- ed.
E99.A6 W43   970.3   *LC* 73-142255   *ISBN* 0816502978

Fowler, Loretta, 1944-.   **3.5843**
Arapahoe politics, 1851–1978: symbols in crises of authority / Loretta Fowler; foreword by Fred Eggan. — Lincoln [Neb.]: University of Nebraska Press, c1982. xx, 373 p., [16] p. of plates: ill., ports.; 24 cm. Includes index. 1. Arapaho Indians — Tribal government. 2. Indians of North America — Wyoming — Tribal government. I. T.
E99.A7 F68 1982   323.1/197/0787 19   *LC* 81-10368   *ISBN* 0803219563

VanStone, James W.   **3.5844**
Athapaskan adaptations: hunters and fishermen of the subarctic forests [by] James W. VanStone. — Chicago: Aldine Pub. Co., [1974] x, 145 p.: illus.; 22 cm. — (Worlds of man: studies in cultural ecology) 1. Athapascan Indians I. T.
E99.A86 V36 1974   970.3   *LC* 73-89518   *ISBN* 0202011135

Winter, Keith John, 1935-.   **3.5845**
Shanandithi: the last of the Beothucks / by Keith Winter. North Pomfret, Vt.: David & Charles, 1976 (c1975). 160 p.: ill., map; 24 cm. 1. Shanandithi, 1801-1829. 2. Beothuk Indians — Biography. I. T.
E99.B4 W56   970/.004/97 B   *LC* 75-24546   *ISBN* 0888940866

Anderson, John Alvin.   **3.5846**
Crying for a vision: a Rosebud Sioux trilogy, 1886–1976 / photos. by John A. Anderson, Eugene Buechel, Don Doll; edited by Don Doll and Jim Alinder; foreword by Ben Black Bear, Jr.; introd. by Herman Viola. — Dobbs Ferry, N.Y.: Morgan & Morgan, 1976. ca. 150 p.: ill.; 23 x 27 cm. Exhibition catalogue based on a touring exhibition. 1. Brulé Indians — Pictorial works — Exhibitions. 2. Rosebud Indian Reservation (S.D.) — Pictorial works — Exhibitions. I. Anderson, John Alvin, 1869-1948. II. Buechel, Eugene. III. Doll, Don, 1937- IV. Alinder, James. V. T.
E99.B8 C79   970/.004/97   *LC* 77-371316   *ISBN* 0871001047

E99 C

Bean, Lowell John.   **3.5847**
Mukat's people; the Cahuilla Indians of southern California. — Berkeley: University of California Press, 1972. ix, 201 p.: illus.; 25 cm. 1. Cahuilla Indians 2. Human ecology — Case studies. I. T.
E99.C155 B4   970.3   *LC* 78-145782   *ISBN* 0520019121

Laird, Carobeth, 1895-.   **3.5848**
The Chemehuevis / Carobeth Laird. — 1st ed. — Banning, Calif.: Malki Museum, c1976. xxviii, 349 p.: ill., maps, port.; 25 cm. 1. Chemehuevi Indians

2. Indians of North America — California 3. Indians of North America — Culture. 4. Indians of North America — Arizona I. T.
E99.C493 L35   E99C493 L35.   *LC* 76-13780

Evarts, Jeremiah, 1781-1831.   **3.5849**
Cherokee removal: the 'William Penn' essays and other writings / by Jeremiah Evarts; edited and with an introd. by Francis Paul Prucha. — Knoxville: University of Tennessee Press, c1981. vii, 314 p.: port.; 23 cm. 1. Indians of North America — Southern States — Removal — Addresses, essays, lectures. 2. Cherokee Removal, 1838 — Addresses, essays, lectures. I. Prucha, Francis Paul. II. T.
E99.C5 E88 1981   323.1/197 19   *LC* 80-28449   *ISBN* 0870493132

Halliburton, R.   **3.5850**
Red over Black: Black slavery among the Cherokee Indians / R. Halliburton, Jr. Westport, Conn.: Greenwood Press, 1977. x, 218 p., [5] leaves of plates: ill.; 22 cm. (Contributions in Afro-American and African studies. no. 27) Includes index. 1. Cherokee Indians — Slaves, Ownership of. 2. Slavery in the United States. 3. Indians of North America — Southern States — Slaves, Ownership of. I. T. II. Series.
E99.C5 H223   301.44/93/0975   *LC* 76-15329   *ISBN* 0837190347

Perdue, Theda, 1949-.   **3.5851**
Slavery and the evolution of Cherokee society, 1540–1866 / Theda Perdue. — 1st ed. — Knoxville: University of Tennessee Press, c1979. xiv, 207 p.: ill.; 23 cm. Includes index. 1. Cherokee Indians — Slaves, Ownership of. 2. Indians of North America — Slaves, Ownership of 3. Afro-Americans — Relations with Indians 4. Slavery in the United States. I. T.
E99.C5 P394   301.45/19/7073   *LC* 78-16284   *ISBN* 0870492594

Franks, Kenny Arthur, 1945-.   **3.5852**
Stand Watie and the agony of the Cherokee Nation / by Kenny A. Franks. — Memphis: Memphis State University Press, c1979. viii, 257 p.: ill.; 24 cm. Based on the author's thesis, Oklahoma State University, 1973. Includes index. 1. Watie, Stand, 1806-1871. 2. Cherokee Indians — Tribal government. 3. Cherokee Indians — Biography. 4. United States — History — Civil War, 1861-1865 — Participation, Indian. I. T.
E99.C5 W433 1979   970.004/97 B   *LC* 79-124380   *ISBN* 0878700633

Grinnell, George Bird.   **3.5853**
The Cheyenne Indians: their history and ways of life / by George Bird Grinnell; photographs by Elizabeth C. Grinnell and Mrs. J. E. Tuell. — Lincoln: University of Nebraska Press, 1972. 2 v.: ill. 'A bison book.' 1. Cheyenne Indians I. T.
E99C53G77 1972   970.3   *LC* 72-195464   *ISBN* 0803257716 PB

Hoebel, E. Adamson (Edward Adamson), 1906-.   **3.5854**
The Cheyennes: Indians of the Great Plains / by E. Adamson Hoebel. — 2d ed. — New York: Holt, Rinehart and Winston, c1978. iv, 137 p.: ill.; 24 cm. — (Case studies in cultural anthropology.) 1. Cheyenne Indians I. T. II. Series.
E99.C53 H6 1978   970/.004/97   *LC* 77-25471   *ISBN* 0030226864

Broker, Ignatia.   **3.5855**
Night Flying Woman: an Ojibway narrative / by Ignatia Broker; illustrated by Steven Premo; with a foreword by Paulette Fairbanks Molin. — St. Paul: Minnesota Historical Society Press, 1983. xiv, 135 p.: ill.; 23 cm. 1. Chippewa Indians — Social life and customs — Juvenile literature. 2. Chippewa Indians — History — Juvenile literature. 3. Indians of North America — Minnesota — Social life and customs — Juvenile literature. 4. Indians of North America — Minnesota — History — Juvenile literature. I. Premo, Steven. ill. II. T.
E99.C6 B79 1983   306/.08997 19   *LC* 83-13360   *ISBN* 0873511646

Hickerson, Harold, 1923-.   **3.5856**
The Chippewa and their neighbors: a study in ethnohistory. — New York: Holt, Rinehart and Winston, [1970] x, 133 p.: illus., maps.; 24 cm. — (Studies in anthropological method) 1. Chippewa Indians — History. I. T.
E99.C6 H44   970.3   *LC* 79-118093   *ISBN* 0030844282

Vizenor, Gerald Robert, 1934-.   **3.5857**
The people named the Chippewa: narrative histories / Gerald Vizenor. — Minneapolis: University of Minnesota Press, c1984. 172 p.: ill.; 24 cm. Includes index. 1. Chippewa Indians — History. 2. Chippewa Indians — Biography. I. T.
E99.C6 V593 1984   970.004/97 19   *LC* 83-19800   *ISBN* 0816613052

Debo, Angie, 1890-.   • **3.5858**
The rise and fall of the Choctaw Republic. [2d ed.] Norman, University of Oklahoma Press [1961] xviii, 314 p. illus., ports., maps, facsim. 24 cm. (The Civilization of the American Indian [6]) 1. Choctaw Indians 2. Choctaw Indians — Government relations I. T.
E99.C8 D4 1961   970.3   *LC* 61-7973

Harrington, John Peabody. 3.5859
Tomol: Chumash watercraft as described in the ethnographic notes of John P. Harrington / edited and annotated by Travis Hudson, Janice Timbrook and Melissa Rempe; art work by Jane Jolley Howorth. — [Socorro, N.M.]: Ballena Press, c1978. 190 p., [5] leaves of plates: ill.; 28 cm. — (Ballena Press anthropological papers; no. 9) 1. Chumashan Indians — Boats. 2. Indians of North America — California — Boats. I. Hudson, Travis. II. Timbrook, Janice. III. Rempe, Melissa. IV. T.
E99.C815 H37   623.82/9   LC 78-102450   ISBN 0879190698

Hudson, Travis. 3.5860
The material culture of the Chumash interaction sphere / by Travis Hudson and Thomas C. Blackburn; with illustrations by Georgia Lee. — Los Altos, Calif.: Ballena Press; Santa Barbara, Calif.: Santa Barbara Museum of Natural History, c1985. 375 p.: ill.; 29 cm. — (BP-AP; no. 25, <27-28, 30 >) Includes indexes. 1. Chumashan Indians — Material culture — Catalogs. 2. Indians of North America — California — Material culture — Catalogs. 3. Chumashan Indians — Antiquities — Catalogs. 4. California — Industries — Catalogs. 5. California — Antiquities — Catalogs. I. Blackburn, Thomas C. II. T.
E99.C815 H83   306/.089970794 19   LC 82-13832   ISBN 087919099X

Jacobs, Melville, 1902-. 3.5861
The content and style of an oral literature; Clackamas Chinook myths and tales. [Chicago] University of Chicago Press [1959] viii, 285 p. 26 cm. 'This volume has also been issued ... as Viking Foundation publications in anthropology, number 26.' 1. Clackamas Indians — Legends. 2. Clackamas Indians 3. Indians of North America — Washington (State) — Legends. 4. Tales — Washington (State) I. T.
E99.C818 J3 1959   398.2   LC 58-5617

Hagan, William Thomas. 3.5862
United States–Comanche relations: the reservation years / William T. Hagan. New Haven: Yale University Press, 1976. xvi, 336 p.: ill.; 22 cm. (Yale Western Americana series. 28) Includes index. 1. Comanche Indians — Government relations. 2. Indians of North America — Government relations — 1869-1934 I. T. II. Series.
E99.C85 H26   323.1/19/7073   LC 75-43318   ISBN 0300019394

Jones, David E., 1942-. 3.5863
Sanapia, Comanche medicine woman, by David E. Jones. — New York: Holt, Rinehart and Winston, [1972] xvii, 107 p.: illus.; 24 cm. — (Case studies in cultural anthropology.) 1. Sanapia, 1895- 2. Comanche Indians 3. Indians of North America — Great Plains — Medicine. I. T. II. Series.
E99.C85 S25   615/.89 B   LC 73-179548   ISBN 003088456X

Andrews, Lynn V. 3.5864
Flight of the seventh moon: the teaching of the shields / Lynn V. Andrews; illustrations by N. Scott Momaday. — 1st ed. — San Francisco: Harper & Row, c1984. xii, 203 p.: ill.; 21 cm. Sequel to: Medicine woman. 1. Andrews, Lynn V. 2. Whistling Elk, Agnes. 3. Cree Indians — Religion and mythology. 4. Indians of North America — Great Plains — Religion and mythology. I. Andrews, Lynn V. Medicine woman. II. T. III. Title: Flight of the 7th moon.
E99.C88 A525 1984   299/.78 19   LC 83-18356   ISBN 0062500279

Andrews, Lynn V. 3.5865
Medicine woman / Lynn V. Andrews; illustrations by Daniel Reeves; frontispiece by Fritz Scholder. — 1st ed. — San Francisco: Harper & Row, c1981. 204 p., [1] p. of plates: ill. (some col.); 22 cm. 1. Andrews, Lynn V. 2. Whistling Elk, Agnes. 3. Cree Indians — Religion and mythology. 4. Indians of North America — Great Plains — Religion and mythology. I. T.
E99.C88 A53 1981   299/.78 19   LC 81-47546   ISBN 0062500252

Richardson, Boyce. 3.5866
Strangers devour the land: a chronicle of the assault upon the last coherent hunting culture in North America, the Cree Indians of northern Quebec, and their vast primeval homelands / Boyce Richardson. — 1st ed. — New York: Knopf:distributed by Random House, 1976. xix, 342, xiii p., [4] leaves of plates: ill.; 25 cm. 1. Cree Indians 2. Hydroelectric power plants — James Bay (Ont. and Québec) 3. James Bay Hydroelectric Project 4. James Bay region, Ont. and Que. I. T.
E99.C88 R52 1976   971.4/1/00497   LC 75-8222   ISBN 0394498380

Green, Michael D., 1941-. 3.5867
The politics of Indian removal: Creek government and society in crisis / Michael D. Green. — Lincoln: University of Nebraska Press, c1982. xiii, 237 p.; 24 cm. 1. Creek Indians — Removal. 2. Creek Indians — Tribal government 3. Indians of North America — Southern States — Removal. I. T.
E99.C9 G74 1982   970.004/97 19   LC 81-14670   ISBN 0803221096

Littlefield, Daniel F. 3.5868
Africans and Creeks: from the colonial period to the Civil War / Daniel F. Littlefield, Jr. — Westport, Conn.: Greenwood Press, 1979. xiii, 286 p.; 22 cm.

— (Contributions in Afro-American and African studies. no. 47 0069-9624) Includes index. 1. Creek Indians — Slaves, Ownership of. 2. Afro-Americans — Relations with Indians 3. Indians of North America — Slaves, Ownership of I. T. II. Series.
E99.C9 L57   301.44/93/0973   LC 78-75238   ISBN 0313207038

Blu, Karen I. 3.5869
The Lumbee problem: the making of an American Indian people/ Karen I. Blu. — Cambridge; New York: Cambridge University Press, 1980. xv, 276 p.; 24 cm. — (Cambridge studies in cultural systems. 5) Includes index. 1. Lumbee Indians 2. Ethnicity — North Carolina. I. T. II. Series.
E99.C91 B57   970/.004/97   LC 79-12908   ISBN 0521225256

Lowie, Robert Harry, 1883-1957. • 3.5870
The Crow Indians / by Robert H. Lowie. — New York: Farrar & Rinehart, incorporated, [c1935] xxii, 350 p.: front., ill., plates, ports.; 24 cm. 'Sources': p. 335-339. 1. Crow Indians 2. Indians of North America — Social life and customs I. T.
E99.C92 L913   970.3   LC 35-9409

E99 D–H

Bailey, John W., 1934-. 3.5871
Pacifying the plains: General Alfred Terry and the decline of the Sioux, 1866–1890 / John W. Bailey. — Westport, Conn.: Greenwood Press, c1979. xiv, 236 p.: ill.; 27 cm. (Contributions in military history. no. 17 0084-9251) Includes index. 1. Terry, Alfred Howe, 1827-1890. 2. United States. Army — Biography 3. Dakota Indians — Government relations — 1869-1934. 4. Dakota Indians — Wars, 1866-1895. 5. Indians of North America — West (U.S.) — Government relations — 1869-1934. 6. Generals — United States — Biography. I. T. II. Series.
E99.D1 B17   970/.004/97   LC 78-19300   ISBN 0313206252

Weslager, C. A. (Clinton Alfred), 1909-. 3.5872
The Delaware Indians; a history [by] C. A. Weslager. New Brunswick, N.J., Rutgers University Press [1972] xix, 546 p. illus. 25 cm. 1. Delaware Indians — History. I. T.
E99.D2 W39   970.3   LC 78-185397   ISBN 0813507022

Balikci, Asen, 1929-. • 3.5873
The Netsilik Eskimo. [1st ed.] Garden City, N.Y., Natural History Press, 1970. xxiv, 264 p. illus., col. map (on lining papers) 22 cm. Published for the American Museum of Natural History. 1. Eskimos — Northwest Territories, Can. I. American Museum of Natural History. II. T.
E99.E7 B16   970.4/12/2   LC 71-114660

Birket-Smith, Kaj, 1893-. 3.5874
[Eskimoerne. English] Eskimos. [American ed.] New York, Crown Publishers [1971] 277 p. illus. 28 cm. 1. Eskimos I. T.
E99.E7 B65 1971   919.8   LC 78-147326

Condon, Richard G. (Richard Guy) 3.5875
Inuit behavior and seasonal change in the Canadian Arctic / by Richard G. Condon. — Ann Arbor, Mich.: UMI Research Press, c1983. xvi, 228 p.: ill.; 24 cm. — (Studies in cultural anthropology. no. 2) Revision of thesis (Ph. D.)— University of Pittsburgh, 1981. Includes index. 1. Eskimos — Northwest Territories — Physical characteristics. 2. Man — Influence of environment — Northwest Territories. 3. Man — Influence of environment — Arctic Regions. 4. Eskimos — Northwest Territories — Psychology. 5. Arctic medicine 6. Diseases — Seasonal variations 7. Indians of North America — Northwest Territories — Physical characteristics. 8. Indians of North America — Northwest Territories — Psychology. I. T. II. Series.
E99.E7 C728 1983   306/.08997 19   LC 83-15556   ISBN 0835714721

The Far North: 2000 years of American Eskimo and Indian art 3.5876
/ Henry B. Collins ... [et al.].
Bloomington: Indiana University Press, 1977. xxx, 289 p.: ill. (some col.); 28 cm. Catalog of an exhibition held at the National Gallery of Art, March 7-May 15, 1973, and others. 1. Eskimos — Alaska — Art — Exhibitions. 2. Indians of North America — Alaska — Art — Exhibitions. I. Collins, Henry Bascom, 1899- II. National Gallery of Art (U.S.)
E99.E7 F28 1977   745   LC 77-3132   ISBN 0253321204. ISBN 0253281059 pbk

Mauss, Marcel, 1872-1950. 3.5877
[Essai sur les variations saisonnières des sociétés Eskimos. English.] Seasonal variations of the Eskimo: a study in social morphology / Marcel Mauss, in collaboration with Henri Beuchat; translated, with a foreword, by James J. Fox. — London; Boston: Routledge & Kegan Paul, 1979. 138 p.: ill.; 22 cm. Translation of Essai sur les variations saisonnières des sociétés Eskimos, which was originally published as pt. 7 of Sociologie et anthropologie. Includes index. 1. Eskimos — Social life and customs. I. Beuchat, Henri, joint author. II. T.
E99.E7 M45413   301.45/19/7   LC 79-40172   ISBN 071000205X

Maxwell, Moreau S. 3.5878
Prehistory of the eastern Arctic / Moreau Maxwell. — Orlando [Fla.]: Academic Press, 1985. xiii, 327 p.: ill.; 24 cm. (New World archaeological record.) Includes index. 1. Eskimos — Canada, Northern — Antiquities. 2. Eskimos — Greenland — Antiquities. 3. Indians of North America — Canada, Northern — Antiquities. 4. Canada, Northern — Antiquities. 5. Greenland — Antiquities. 6. Arctic regions — Antiquities I. T. II. Series.
E99.E7 M465 1985   971.901/11 19   LC 84-14488   ISBN 0124812708

Oswalt, Wendell H. 3.5879
Eskimos and explorers / Wendell H. Oswalt. — Novato, Calif.: Chandler & Sharp, c1979. xii, 349 p., [1] fold. leaf of plates: ill.; 24 cm. Includes indexes. 1. Eskimos 2. Explorers — Greenland. 3. Explorers — Canada. 4. Explorers — Alaska. I. T.
E99.E7 O79   970/.004/97   LC 78-10723   ISBN 0883165325

Pryde, Duncan, 1937-. 3.5880
Nunaga; ten years of Eskimo life. New York: Walker, [1972, c1971] 285 p.: col. illus.; 23 cm. 1. Eskimos — Northwest Territories, Can. — Franklin District. 2. Franklin District, Can. — Description and travel. I. T.
E99.E7 P77 1972b   970.1   LC 75-181349

Ray, Dorothy Jean. 3.5881
Aleut and Eskimo art: tradition and innovation in South Alaska / Dorothy Jean Ray. — Seattle: University of Washington Press, c1981. 251 p.: ill.; 29 cm. Includes index. 1. Eskimos — Alaska — Art. 2. Aleuts — Art. I. T.
E99.E7 R24   745/.08997   LC 79-56591   ISBN 0295957093

Ray, Dorothy Jean. 3.5882
Eskimo art: tradition and innovation in north Alaska / Dorothy Jean Ray. Seattle: Published for the Henry Art Gallery by the University of Washington Press, c1977. xi, 298 p.: ill.; 29 cm. (Index of art in the Pacific Northwest. no. 11) 'Published in connection with an exhibition shown at the Henry Art Gallery, University of Washington.' Includes index. 1. Eskimos — Alaska — Art. 2. Art — Alaska. I. Henry Art Gallery. II. T. III. Series.
E99.E7 R27   709/.01/1   LC 76-7797   ISBN 029595518X

Ray, Dorothy Jean. 3.5883
The Eskimos of Bering Strait, 1650–1898 / by Dorothy Jean Ray. — Seattle: University of Washington Press, c1975. xvi, 305 p., [8] leaves of plates: ill.; 25 cm. Includes index. 1. Eskimos — Alaska — Bering Strait region. 2. Bering Strait region — History. I. T.
E99.E7 R29   979.8/004/97   LC 75-17819   ISBN 0295954353

Spencer, Robert F. • 3.5884
The North Alaskan Eskimo; a study in ecology and society. — Washington, U.S. Govt. Print. Off., 1959. vi, 490 p. illus., maps (part fold.) 24 cm. — ([U.S.] Bureau of American Ethnology. Bulletin 171) Bibliography: p. 455-461. 1. Eskimos — Alaska I. T. II. Series.
E99.E7S6x   572.9798   LC 59-61386

Swinton, George. 3.5885
Sculpture of the Eskimo / George Swinton. — Boston: New York Graphic Society, [1972]. 255 p.: chiefly ill. (some col.); 32 cm. — Includes index. - 1. Eskimos — Sculpture. 2. Sculpture — Canada. 3. Eskimos — Art I. T.
E99.E7 S942 1972   E99E7 S96 1972b   732/.2/09701   LC 72-80420   ISBN 0821204041

Blackman, Margaret B. 3.5886
During my time: Florence Edenshaw Davidson, a Haida woman / Margaret B. Blackman. — Seattle: University of Washington Press; Vancouver: Douglas & McIntyre, c1982. xvii, 172 p.: ill.; 24 cm. Includes index. 1. Davidson, Florence Edenshaw, 1896- 2. Haida Indians — Biography. 3. Haida Indians — Women. 4. Indians of North America — Northwest coast of North America — Women. I. Davidson, Florence Edenshaw, 1896- II. T.
E99.H2 D383 1982   970.004/97 B 19   LC 82-8674   ISBN 0295959436

Colton, Harold Sellers, 1881-. 3.5887
Hopi kachina dolls: with a key to their identification / by Harold S. Colton; color photographs by Jack Breed. — Rev. ed. — Albuquerque: University of New Mexico Press, 1959, 1977 printing. 150 p.: ill. 1. Katcinas 2. Hopi Indians — Religion and mythology I. T.
E99.H7 C6 1959   LC 59-5480   ISBN 0826301800

Dockstader, Frederick J. • 3.5888
The kachina and the white man; a study of the influences of white culture on the Hopi kachina cult. Illustrated by the author. [Bloomfield Hills, Cranbrook Institute of Science, 1954] xiv, 185 p. illus. 24 cm. (Bulletin (Cranbrook Institute of Science) 35) An earlier version was published as the author's dissertation, Western Reserve University, under title: White influences on the Hopi kachina cult. 1. Katcinas 2. Hopi Indians — Religion and mythology 3. Acculturation I. T. II. Series.
E99.H7 D6x   970.62 [299.7] 970.1*   LC 54-6199

Hopi kachina: spirit of life: dedicated to the Hopi tricentennial, 1680–1980 / edited by Dorothy K. Washburn. 3.5889
[San Francisco]: California Academy of Sciences; Seattle: distributed by University of Washington Press, c1980. 158 p.: ill. (some col.); 28 cm. 'Published ... in conjunction with the exhibition Hopi kachina: spirit of life.' 1. Katcinas — Exhibitions. 2. Hopi Indians — Exhibitions. I. Washburn, Dorothy Koster. II. California Academy of Sciences, San Francisco.
E99.H7 H68   704/.0397 19   LC 79-54647   ISBN 0295957514

Thompson, Laura, 1905-. 3.5890
Culture in crisis; a study of the Hopi Indians. New York, Harper [1950] xxiv, 221 p. illus. col. map. 25 cm. 1. Hopi Indians. I. T.
E99.H7 T42   LC 50-10993

Trigger, Bruce G. 3.5891
The children of Aataentsic: a history of the Huron People to 1660 / Bruce G. Trigger. — Montreal: McGill-Queen's University Press, 1976. 2 v. (xxiii, 913 p.): ill.; 26 cm. Includes index. 1. Huron Indians — History. I. T.
E99.H9 T68   970/.004/97   LC 77-363367   ISBN 0773502394

E99 I–M

Pendergast, James F. 3.5892
Cartier's Hochelaga and the Dawson Site, by James F. Pendergast and Bruce G. Trigger, with additional papers contributed by James E. Anderson, Kenneth E. Kidd [and] Richard S. MacNeish. Foreword by William N. Fenton. — Montreal: McGill-Queen's University Press, 1972. xxvii, 388 p.: illus.; 26 cm. 1. Cartier, Jacques, 1491-1557. 2. Iroquoian Indians — Antiquities. 3. Montreal — Antiquities. I. Trigger, Bruce G. II. T.
E99.I69 P46   917.14/28   LC 78-184767   ISBN 0773500700

Kelsay, Isabel Thompson, 1905-. 3.5893
Joseph Brant, 1743–1807, man of two worlds / Isabel Thompson Kelsay. — 1st ed. — Syracuse, N.Y.: Syracuse University Press, 1984. xii, 775 p.: ill.; 24 cm. — (Iroquois book.) Includes index. 1. Brant, Joseph, 1742-1807. 2. Iroquois Indians — Biography. 3. Iroquois Indians — Government relations 4. Indians of North America — Government relations — To 1789 5. United States — History — Revolution, 1775-1783 — Participation, Indian. I. T. II. Series.
E99.I7 B784 1984   970.004/97 B 19   LC 83-4701   ISBN 0815601824

Graymont, Barbara. • 3.5894
The Iroquois in the American Revolution. — [1st ed.]. — [Syracuse, N.Y.]: Syracuse University Press, 1972. x, 359 p.: illus.; 23 cm. — (A New York State study) 1. Iroquois Indians — History. 2. New York (State) — History — Revolution, 1775-1783 I. T.
E99.I7 G67   973.3/43   LC 73-170096   ISBN 0815600836

Hauptman, Laurence M. 3.5895
The Iroquois and the New Deal / Laurence M. Hauptman. — 1st ed. — Syracuse, N.Y.: Syracuse University Press, 1981. xvi, 256 p., [1] leaf of plates: ill.; 24 cm. — (Iroquois book.) Includes index. 1. Iroquois Indians — Government relations 2. Indians of North America — Government relations — 1934- I. T. II. Series.
E99.I7 H33   323.1/197 19   LC 81-21198   ISBN 0815622473

The History and culture of Iroquois diplomacy: an interdisciplinary guide to the treaties of the Six Nations and their league / Francis Jennings, editor ... [et al.] for the D'Arcy McNickle Center for the History of the American Indian, the Newberry Library. 3.5896
1st ed. — Syracuse, N.Y.: Syracuse University Press, 1985. xviii, 278 p.: ill.; maps; 24 cm. (Iroquois book.) Series statement from jacket. Includes index. 1. Iroquois Indians — Government relations — To 1789 — Addresses, essays, lectures. 2. Indians of North America — Government relations — To 1789 — Addresses, essays, lectures. 3. Iroquois Indians — Treaties — History — Addresses, essays, lectures. 4. Indians of North America — Treaties — History — Addresses, essays, lectures. 5. Iroquois Indians — History. I. Jennings, Francis, 1918- II. D'Arcy McNickle Center for the History of the American Indian. III. Series.
E99.I7 H63 1985   973/.0497 19   LC 84-16234   ISBN 0815622716

Morgan, Lewis Henry, 1818-1881. 3.5897
League of the Ho-dé-no-sau-nee or Iroquois. — A new ed., with additional matter. Edited and annotated by Herbert M. Lloyd. — New York: B. Franklin, 1976. 2 v.: illus., fold. maps; 25 cm. — (Burt Franklin research source works series, #185) (American classics in history and social science, #28.) Reprint of the 1901 ed. 1. Iroquois Indians. 2. Iroquoian languages 3. Names, Geographical — New York (State) I. Lloyd, Herbert Marshall, 1862- II. T.
E99.I7 M8 1966   970.3   LC 74-6583

Gunnerson, Dolores A.   **3.5898**
The Jicarilla Apaches: a study in survival. — DeKalb: Northern Illinois University Press, c1974. xv, 326 p.: ill. 1. Jicarilla Indians I. T.
E99.J5G86   LC 72-2582   ISBN 0875800335 1312

Momaday, N. Scott, 1934-.   **3.5899**
The way to rainy mountain [by] N. Scott Momaday. Illustrated by Al Momaday. — [1st ed. — Albuquerque]: University of New Mexico Press, [1969] 88 p.: illus.; 25 cm. 1. Kiowa Indians — Legends. I. Momaday, Al, illus. II. T.
E99.K5 M64   970.3   LC 69-19154

Nelson, Richard K.   **3.5900**
Make prayers to the raven: a Koyukon view of the northern forest / Richard K. Nelson. — Chicago: University of Chicago Press, c1983. xvi, 292 p., [16] p. of plates: ill.; 24 cm. Includes index. 1. Koyukon Indians 2. Human ecology — Alaska. 3. Natural history — Alaska. I. T.
E99.K79 N44 1983   304.2/09798 19   LC 82-8441   ISBN 0226571629

Boas, Franz, 1858-1942.   • **3.5901**
Kwakiutl ethnography / Edited by Helen Codere. — Chicago: University of Chicago Press, [1966] xxxvii, 439 p.: ill., facsim., maps, ports.; 24 cm. — (Classics in anthropology) Contains a previously unpublished manuscript, together with selections from published materials. 1. Kwakiutl Indians I. Codere, Helen, ed. II. T.
E99.K9 B49   970.3   LC 66-13861

Hawthorn, Audrey.   **3.5902**
Kwakiutl art / Audrey Hawthorn. — Seattle: University of Washington Press, c1979. xx, 272 p., [16] leaves of plates: ill. (some col.). Includes much that was contained in Mrs. Hawthorn's Art of the Kwakiutl Indians and other Northwest coast tribes. Includes index. 1. University of British Columbia. Museum of Anthropology. 2. Kwakiutl Indians — Art. 3. Indians of North America — Northwest coast of North America — Art. I. T.
E99.K9 H3 1979   730   LC 79-4856   ISBN 0295956747

Meyer, Roy Willard, 1925-.   **3.5903**
The village Indians of the upper Missouri: the Mandans, Hidatsas, and Arikaras / by Roy W. Meyer. — Lincoln: University of Nebraska Press, c1977. xiv, 354 p., [8] leaves of plates: ill.; 24 cm. Includes index. 1. Mandan Indians — History. 2. Hidatsa Indians — History. 3. Arikara Indians — History. I. T.
E99.M2 M48   978.4/7/00497   LC 77-4202   ISBN 0803209134

Keesing, Felix Maxwell, 1902-1961.   **3.5904**
The Menomini Indians of Wisconsin: a study of three centuries of cultural contact and change / Felix M. Keesing; foreword by Robert E. Bieder. — Madison, Wis.: University of Wisconsin Press, 1987. p. cm. Reprint. Originally published: Philadelphia, Pa.: American Philosophical Society, 1939. Includes index. 1. Menominee Indians I. T.
E99.M44 K4 1987   977.5/00497 19   LC 86-24650   ISBN 0299109704

Guillemin, Jeanne, 1943-.   **3.5905**
Urban renegades: the cultural strategy of American Indians / Jeanne Guillemin. — New York: Columbia University Press, 1975. viii, 336 p.: maps; 21 cm. 1. Micmac Indians — Urban residence. 2. Indians of North America — Urban residence 3. Micmac Indians — Social conditions. 4. Indians of North America — Social conditions I. T.
E99.M6 G54   301.45/19/7074461   LC 74-30434   ISBN 0231038844

Upton, Leslie Francis Stokes.   **3.5906**
Micmacs and colonists: Indian–White relations in the Maritimes, 1713–1867 / L. F. S. Upton. — Vancouver: University of British Columbia Press, 1979. xvi, 243 p., [6] leaves of plates: ill.; 24 cm. Includes index. 1. Micmac Indians — History. 2. Micmac Indians — Government relations. 3. Indians of North America — Maritime Provinces, Can. — Government relations. 4. Maritime Provinces, Can. — History. I. T.
E99.M6 U67   971.5/00497   LC 80-462826   ISBN 077480114X

Mississippian settlement patterns / edited by Bruce D. Smith; with a foreword by James B. Griffin.   **3.5907**
New York: Academic Press, c1978. xxii, 512 p.: ill.; 24 cm. (Studies in archeology) 1. Mississippian culture I. Smith, Bruce D.
E99.M6815 M57   301.32/9762   LC 78-215   ISBN 012650640X

Anyon, Roger, 1952-.   **3.5908**
The Galaz ruin: a prehistoric Mimbres village in southwestern New Mexico / by Roger Anyon and Steven A. LeBlanc with contributions by Paul E. Minnis, Margaret C. Nelson, James Lancaster; edited by Paula L.W. Sabloff; foreword by J.J. Brody. — 1st ed. — Albuquerque: Maxwell Museum of Anthropology: University of New Mexico Press, 1985 (c1984). xi, 612 p.: ill.; 28 cm. (Maxwell Museum of Anthropology publication series.) 1. Galaz Site (N.M.) I. LeBlanc,

Steven A. II. Sabloff, Paula L. W. III. Maxwell Museum of Anthropology. IV. T. V. Series.
E99.M76 A6 1984   978.9/692 19   LC 83-27403   ISBN 0826307485

Brody, J. J.   **3.5909**
Mimbres painted pottery / J. J. Brody. — 1st ed. — Santa Fe [N.M.]: School of American Research, c1977. xxiii, 253 p., [4] leaves of plates: ill. (some col.); 27 cm. — (Southwest Indian arts series.) Includes index. 1. Mogollon culture 2. Indians of North America — Southwest, New — Pottery. I. T. II. Series.
E99.M76 B76   738.3/7   LC 76-57542   ISBN 0826304524

Brody, J. J.   **3.5910**
Mimbres pottery: ancient art of the American Southwest: essays / by J.J. Brody, Catherine J. Scott, Steven A. LeBlanc; introduction by Tony Berlant. — 1st ed. — New York: Published by Hudson Hills Press in association with The American Federation of Arts: Distributed in the U.S. by Viking Penguin, 1983. 128 p.: ill. (some col.); 27 cm. 'Published in conjunction with the exhibition ... organized by the American Federation of Arts ... AFA exhibition #81-1 circulated: January, 1984 — October, 1985'—T.p. verso. 1. Mogollon culture — Addresses, essays, lectures. 2. Indians of North America — New Mexico — Pottery — Addresses, essays, lectures. 3. Indians of North America — New Mexico — Art — Addresses, essays, lectures. 4. New Mexico — Antiquities — Addresses, essays, lectures. I. Scott, Catherine J., 1950- II. LeBlanc, Steven A. III. American Federation of Arts. IV. T.
E99.M76 B765 1983   738.3/7 19   LC 83-10812   ISBN 0933920466

E99 N–O

Williams, Roger, 1604?-1683.   **3.5911**
A key into the language of America. Edited with a critical introd., notes, and commentary by John J. Teunissen and Evelyn J. Hinz. — Detroit: Wayne State University Press, 1973. 322 p.; 24 cm. Definitive ed. of the author's work originally printed in 1643, by G. Dexter, London. 1. Narraganset Indians 2. Narraganset language I. T.
E99.N16 W67 1973   497/.3   LC 72-6590   ISBN 0814314902

Speck, Frank Gouldsmith, 1881-1950.   **3.5912**
Naskapi: the savage hunters of the Labrador peninsula / Frank G. Speck; foreword by J. E. Michael Kew. New ed. — Norman: University of Oklahoma Press, c1977. xii, 257 p.: ill.; 24 cm. (Civilization of the American Indian series. v. 10) 1. Nascapee Indians — Religion and mythology. 2. Indians of North America — Newfoundland — Labrador — Religion and mythology. 3. Nascapee Indians — Hunting. 4. Indians of North America — Newfoundland — Labrador — Hunting. I. T. II. Series.
E99.N18 S7 1977   299/.7   LC 77-365978   ISBN 0806114126

Berlant, Anthony.   **3.5913**
Walk in beauty: the Navajo and their blankets / Anthony Berlant and Mary Hunt Kahlenberg. — Boston: New York Graphic Society, c1977. 167 p., [24] leaves of plates: ill.; 29 cm. Includes index. 1. Navajo Indians — Textile industry and fabrics 2. Navajo Indians — History. 3. Indians of North America — Southwest, New — Textile industry and fabrics I. Kahlenberg, Mary Hunt. joint author. II. T.
E99.N3 B5   746.1/4   LC 76-30363   ISBN 0821206915

Boyce, George Arthur, 1898-.   **3.5914**
When Navajos had too many sheep: the 1940's, by George A. Boyce. [San Francisco] The Indian Historian Press [1974] xiii, 273 p. illus. 23 cm. 1. Navajo Indians I. T.
E99.N3 B62   970.3   LC 73-93691   ISBN 0913436127 ISBN 0913436135

Farella, John R.   **3.5915**
The main stalk: a synthesis of Navajo philosophy / John R. Farella. — Tucson, Ariz.: University of Arizona Press, c1984. x, 221 p.; 24 cm. Includes index. 1. Navajo Indians — Philosophy. 2. Navajo Indians — Religion and mythology. 3. Indians of North America — Southwest, New — Philosophy. 4. Indians of North America — Southwest, New — Religion and mythology. I. T.
E99.N3 F37 1984   191/.08997 19   LC 84-8803   ISBN 0816508593

Frisbie, Charlotte Johnson.   **3.5916**
Kinaaldá; a study of the Navaho girl's puberty ceremony. [1st ed.] Middletown, Conn., Wesleyan University Press [1967] xiii, 437 p. illus., map. 26 cm. Based on the author's master's thesis, Wesleyan University. Includes music. 1. Navajo Indians — Rites and ceremonies 2. Indians of North America — Southwest, New — Women. 3. Puberty rites 4. Navajo Indians — Women. 5. Indians of North America — Southwest, New — Rites and ceremonies. I. T. II. Title: Girl's puberty ceremony.
E99.N3 F84   970.3   LC 67-24106

Jett, Stephen C., 1938-.   **3.5917**
Navajo architecture: forms, history, distributions / Stephen C. Jett and Virginia E. Spencer. — Tucson, Ariz.: University of Arizona Press, c1981. xix, 289 p.:

ill.; 27 cm. Includes indexes. 1. Navajo Indians — Architecture. 2. Indians of North America — Arizona — Architecture. I. Spencer, Virginia E. joint author. II. T.
E99.N3 J39   722/.91/09791 19   *LC* 80-39684   *ISBN* 0816506884

Kahlenberg, Mary Hunt.   **3.5918**
The Navajo blanket [by] Mary Hunt Kahlenberg and Anthony Berlant. [New York] Praeger [1972] 112 p. illus. (part col.) 31 cm. Catalogue of an exhibition first held at Los Angeles County Museum of Art, June 27-Aug. 27, 1972, and subsequently at other museums. 1. Navajo Indians — Textile industry and fabrics — Exhibitions. 2. Indians of North America — Textile industry and fabrics — Exhibitions. I. Berlant, Anthony, joint author. II. Los Angeles County Museum of Art. III. T.
E99.N3 K3   746.9/2   *LC* 79-189549   *ISBN* 0875870503

Kluckhohn, Clyde, 1905-1960.   • **3.5919**
The Navaho [by] Clyde Kluckhohn and Dorothea Leighton. Rev. ed., by Lucy H. Wales and Richard Kluckhohn. Published in cooperation with the American Museum of Natural History. Garden City, N.Y., Natural History Library [1962] 355 p. illus. 18 cm. (Natural history library. N28) (A Doubleday anchor book) 1. Navajo Indians I. Leighton, Dorothea Cross, 1908- joint author. II. T. III. Series.
E99.N3 K54 1962   970.3   *LC* 62-6779

Left Handed, 1868-.   **3.5920**
Left Handed, a Navajo autobiography / [recorded and edited by] Walter and Ruth Dyk. — New York: Columbia University Press, 1980. xxv, 578 p.: port.; 24 cm. Translated from Navaho. Continues Son of Old Man Hat. Includes index. 1. Left Handed, 1868- 2. Navajo Indians — Biography. 3. Navajo Indians — Social life and customs. 4. Indians of North America — Southwest, New — Social life and customs. I. Dyk, Walter. II. Dyk, Ruth. III. T.
E99.N3 L545   970.004/97   *LC* 80-11954   *ISBN* 0231049463

McNitt, Frank.   **3.5921**
Navajo wars; military campaigns, slave raids, and reprisals. [1st ed. Albuquerque] University of New Mexico Press [1972] xii, 477 p. illus. 25 cm. 1. Navajo Indians — Wars. I. T.
E99.N3 M32   978.9   *LC* 72-86816   *ISBN* 0826302467

Matthews, Washington, 1843-1905.   **3.5922**
Navaho legends / collected and tr. by Washington Matthews... introduction, notes, illustrations texts, interlinear translations, and melodies. Boston and New York: Pub. for the American folk-lore society, by Houghton, Mifflin and company; etc., etc.: Reprinted by Kraus Reprint Co., 1976, 1897. viii, 299 p.: ill.; 25 cm. (Memoirs of the American folk-lore society, vol. V, 1897.) 'Melodies recorded on the phonograph by Washington Matthews, and noted from the cylinders by John C. Fillmore': p. 279-290. 1. Navaho Indians — Legends. 2. Indians of North America — Music I. T.
E99.N3M3x   *LC* 90-48

Mitchell, Frank, 1881-1967.   **3.5923**
Navajo Blessingway Singer: the autobiography of Frank Mitchell, 1881–1967 / edited by Charlotte J. Frisbie and David P. McAllester. — Tucson: University of Arizona Press, c1978. x, 446 p.: ill.; 24 cm. Includes index. 1. Mitchell, Frank, 1881-1967. 2. Navajo Indians — Biography. 3. Navajo Indians — Religion and mythology. 4. Indians of North America — Southwest, New — Religion and mythology. I. T.
E99.N3 M64 1978   784.7/51/0924 B   *LC* 77-75661   *ISBN* 0816506116. *ISBN* 0816505683 pbk

Newcomb, Franc Johnson.   **3.5924**
Hosteen Klah, Navaho medicine man and sand painter. [1st ed.] Norman, University of Oklahoma Press [1964] xxxiii, 227 p. illus., maps (1 fold.) ports. 23 cm. (Civilization of the American Indian series.) 1. Klah, Hasteen. 2. Navaho Indians. I. T. II. Series.
E99.N3 N37   970.2   *LC* 64-20759

Witherspoon, Gary.   **3.5925**
Language and art in the Navajo universe / Gary Witherspoon. — Ann Arbor: University of Michigan Press, c1977. xviii, 214 p., [2] leaves of plates: ill.; 24 cm. Includes index. 1. Navajo Indians — Philosophy. 2. Navajo language 3. Navajo Indians — Art 4. Indians of North America — Southwest, New — Philosophy. 5. Indians of North America — Southwest, New — Art. I. T.
E99.N3 W678 1977   970/.004/97   *LC* 77-3651   *ISBN* 047208965X

Witherspoon, Gary.   **3.5926**
Navajo kinship and marriage / Gary Witherspoon. — Chicago: University of Chicago Press, 1975. xii, 137 p.: ill.; 23 cm. Includes index. 1. Navajo Indians — Marriage customs and rites. 2. Indians of North America — Southwest, New — Marriage customs and rites. 3. Navajo Indians — Kinship. 4. Indians of North America — Southwest, New — Kinship. I. T.
E99.N3 W68   301.42/1/0979   *LC* 74-21340   *ISBN* 0226904199

Wyman, Leland Clifton, 1897-.   **3.5927**
Blessingway [by] Leland C. Wyman. With three versions of the myth recorded and translated from the Navajo by Berard Haile. Tucson, University of Arizona

Press 1975. xxviii, 660 p. illus., facsims., ports. 24 cm. 1. Navajo Indians — Rites and ceremonies I. Haile, Berard, 1874-1961. II. T.
E99.N3 W9323   299/.7   *LC* 66-28786   *ISBN* 0816501785

Olson, James C.   • **3.5928**
Red Cloud and the Sioux problem [by] James C. Olson. Lincoln, University of Nebraska Press [1965] xiii, 375 p. illus., map. (on lining papers) ports. 24 cm. 1. Red Cloud, 1822-1909. 2. Oglala Indians — History. 3. Indians of North America — Government relations I. T.
E99.O3 O4   970.50924   *LC* 65-10048

Walker, J. R. (James R.), b. 1849.   **3.5929**
Lakota society / James R. Walker; edited by Raymond J. DeMallie. — Lincoln: University of Nebraska Press, c1982. xvi, 207 p., [34] p. of plates: ill.; 23 cm. 'Published in cooperation with the Colorado Historical Society.' Includes index. 1. Oglala Indians — Social life and customs. 2. Indians of North America — Great Plains — Social life and customs. I. DeMallie, Raymond J., 1946- II. T.
E99.O3 W172 1982   978/.00497 19   *LC* 81-14676   *ISBN* 0803216564

Barnes, R. H. (Robert Harrison), 1944-.   **3.5930**
Two Crows denies it: a history of controversy in Omaha sociology / R.H. Barnes. — Lincoln: University of Nebraska Press, c1984. xiii, 272 p., [13] p. of plates (some folded); 24 cm. Includes indexes. 1. Omaha Indians — Kinship. 2. Omaha Indians — Social life and customs 3. Indians of North America — Nebraska — Kinship. 4. Indians of North America — Nebraska — Social life and customs. I. T.
E99.O4 B37 1984   306.8/008997 19   *LC* 84-2276   *ISBN* 0803211821

Welsch, Roger L.   **3.5931**
Omaha tribal myths and trickster tales / Roger L. Welsch. — Chicago: Sage Books, c1981. 285 p.: music; 24 cm. 1. Omaha Indians — Legends. 2. Indians of North America — Nebraska — Legends. 3. Trickster I. T.
E99.O4 W44   398.2/08997 19   *LC* 80-22636   *ISBN* 0804007004

Wilson, Dorothy Clarke.   **3.5932**
Bright Eyes; the story of Susette La Flesche, an Omaha Indian. — New York: McGraw-Hill, [1974] 396 p.; 24 cm. 1. La Flesche, Susette, 1854-1903. I. T.
E99.O4 W54   970.3 B   *LC* 73-15636   *ISBN* 0070707529

Din, Gilbert C.   **3.5933**
The imperial Osages: Spanish–Indian diplomacy in the Mississippi Valley / by Gilbert C. Din and A.P Nasatir. — 1st ed. — Norman, Okla.: University of Oklahoma Press, c1983. xv, 432 p.: ill.; 24 cm. — (Civilization of the American Indian series. [v. 161]) Includes index. 1. Osage Indians — History. 2. Spaniards — Mississippi River Valley — History — 18th century. 3. Mississippi River Valley — History — To 1803 I. Nasatir, Abraham Phineas, 1904- II. T. III. Series.
E99.O8 D5 1983   970.004/97 19   *LC* 82-40449   *ISBN* 0806118342

E99 P–S

Canfield, Gae Whitney, 1931-.   **3.5934**
Sarah Winnemucca of the Northern Paiutes / by Gae Whitney Canfield. — 1st ed. — Norman: University of Oklahoma Press, c1983. xiv, 306 p.: ill.; 22 cm. Includes index. 1. Hopkins, Sarah Winnemucca, 1844?-1891. 2. Paiute Indians — History. 3. Paiute Indians — Biography. I. T.
E99.P2 H722 1983   970.004/97 B 19   *LC* 82-40448   *ISBN* 0806118148

Underhill, Ruth Murray, 1884-.   **3.5935**
Papago woman / by Ruth M. Underhill. — New York: Holt, Rinehart and Winston, c1979. xiii, 98 p.; 24 cm. — (Case studies in cultural anthropology.) Part III originally published in 1936 as Memoir 46 of the American Anthropological Association. 1. Papago Indians — Women. 2. Indians of North America — Arizona — Women. I. T. II. Series.
E99.P25 U5194   301.45/19/70791 B   *LC* 79-318   *ISBN* 0030451213

Hyde, George E., 1882-1968.   **3.5936**
The Pawnee Indians. Foreword by Savoie Lottinville. — [New ed.]. — Norman: University of Oklahoma Press, [1974] xii, 372 p.: illus.; 24 cm. — (Civilization of the American Indian series.) 1. Pawnee Indians I. T. II. Series.
E99.P3 H93 1974   970.3   *LC* 72-9260   *ISBN* 0806110651

Anastas, Peter, 1937-.   **3.5937**
Glooskap's children; encounters with the Penobscot Indians of Maine. Photos. by Mark Power. — Boston: Beacon Press, [1973] 216 p.: illus.; 22 cm. 1. Penobscot Indians I. T.
E99.P5 A5   970.3/09741   *LC* 72-75534   *ISBN* 0807005185

Shaw, Anna Moore. 3.5938
A Pima past. — Tucson: University of Arizona Press, [1974] xv, 262 p.: illus.; 20 cm. 1. Shaw, Anna Moore. 2. Pima Indians — Social life and customs. I. T.
E99.P6 S52 970.3 B LC 73-87716 ISBN 0816504261

Edmunds, R. David (Russell David), 1939-. 3.5939
The Potawatomis, keepers of the fire / by R. David Edmunds. — 1st ed. — Norman: University of Oklahoma Press, c1978. xii, 367 p., [20] leaves of plates: ill.; 24 cm. — (Civilization of the American Indian series. v. 145.) Includes index. 1. Potawatomi Indians — History. I. T. II. Series.
E99.P8 E35 970/.004/97 LC 78-5628 ISBN 0806114789

Bunzel, Ruth Leah, 1898-. 3.5940
The Pueblo potter; a study of creative imagination in primitive art, by Ruth L. Bunzel. — New York: Dover Publications, [1972] 134 p.: illus.; 26 cm. Originally presented as the author's thesis, Columbia. Reprint of the 1929 ed. published by Columbia University Press, New York. 1. Pueblo Indians — Art. 2. Indians of North America — Arizona — Pottery. 3. Indians of North America — New Mexico — Pottery. I. T.
E99.P9 B88 1972 738 LC 72-79159 ISBN 0486228754

Frank, Lawrence Phillip. 3.5941
Historic pottery of the Pueblo Indians, 1600–1880 / by Larry Frank and Francis H. Harlow; photos. by Bernard Lopez. Boston: New York Graphic Society, 1974. xvi, 160 p., [18] leaves of plates: ill. (some col.); 28 cm. 1. Pueblo Indians — Pottery. 2. Indians of North America — Southwest, New — Pottery. I. Harlow, Francis Harvey, 1928- joint author. II. T.
E99.P9 F69 738.3/83 LC 73-89957 ISBN 0821205862

Kent, Kate Peck. 3.5942
Pueblo Indian textiles: a living tradition / Kate Peck Kent. — 1st ed. — Santa Fe, N.M.: School of American Research Press, c1983. xiv, 118 p.: ill. (some col.); 26 cm. — (Studies in American Indian art.) 'With a catalogue of the School of American Research collection.' Includes index. 1. School of American Research (Santa Fe, N.M.) — Catalogs. 2. Indians of North America — Southwest, New — Textile industry and fabrics 3. Pueblo Indians — Textile industry and fabrics — Catalogs. 4. Indians of North America — Southwest, New — Textile industry and fabrics — Catalogs. 5. Pueblo Indians — Textile industry and fabrics. I. School of American Research (Santa Fe, N.M.) II. T. III. Series.
E99.P9 K46 1983 746.1/4/08997 19 LC 83-3346 ISBN 093345208X

Ortiz, Alfonso, 1939- ed. 3.5943
New perspectives on the Pueblos / edited by Alfonso Ortiz. — [1st ed.] Albuquerque: University of New Mexico Press, [1972] xx, 340 p.: maps; 24 cm. (School of American Research. Advanced seminar series) 'A School of American Research book.' The work grew out of an advanced seminar at the School of American Research. 1. Pueblo Indians — Addresses, essays, lectures. I. T.
E99.P9 N48 970.3 LC 70-175505 ISBN 0826302289

Peterson, Susan (Susan Harnly) 3.5944
The living tradition of Mária Martínez / Susan Peterson. — 1st ed. — Tokyo: Kodansha International; New York: distributed through Harper & Row, 1977. 300 p.: ill. (some col.); 31 cm. Includes index. 1. Martínez, María Montoya. 2. Potters — New Mexico — San Ildefonso — Biography. 3. Tewa Indians — Pottery. 4. Tewa Indians — Biography. 5. Indians of North America — New Mexico — Pottery. 6. Indians of North America — New Mexico — Biography. 7. San Ildefonso (N.M.) — Biography. I. T.
E99.S213 M377 738.3/092/4 B LC 77-75373 ISBN 0870113194

Eastman, Charles Alexander, 1858-1939. 3.5945
From the deep woods to civilization: chapters in the autobiography of an Indian / by Charles A. Eastman (Ohiyesa); introd. by Raymond Wilson. — Lincoln: University of Nebraska Press, 1977, c1916. xxii, 206 p., [13] leaves of plates: ill.; 21 cm. Reprint of the 1936 ed. published by Little, Brown, Boston. Includes index. 1. Eastman, Charles Alexander, 1858-1939. 2. Santee Indians — Biography. I. T.
E99.S22 E183 1977 970/.004/97 B LC 77-7226 ISBN 0803209363

Garbarino, Merwyn S. 3.5946
Big Cypress: a changing Seminole community, by Merwyn S. Garbarino. — New York: Holt, Rinehart and Winston, [1972] x, 132 p.: illus.; 24 cm. — (Case studies in cultural anthropology.) 1. Seminole Indians 2. Acculturation — Florida. I. T. II. Series.
E99.S28 G3 970.3 LC 72-174774 ISBN 0030246723

Wallace, Anthony F. C., 1923-. • 3.5947
The death and rebirth of the Seneca, [by] Anthony F. C. Wallace, with the assistance of Sheila C. Steen. — [1st ed.]. — New York: Knopf, 1970 [c1969] xiii, 384, xi p.: illus.; 25 cm. 1. Handsome Lake, 1735-1815. 2. Seneca Indians I. Steen, Sheila C., joint author. II. T.
E99.S3 W3 1970 970.3 LC 79-88754

Howard, James Henri, 1925-. 3.5948
Shawnee!: The ceremonialism of a native Indian tribe and its cultural background / James H. Howard. — Athens, Ohio: Ohio University Press, c1981. xvi, 454 p.: ill.; 24 cm. Includes index. 1. Shawnee Indians 2. Shawnee Indians — Rites and ceremonies. 3. Indians of North America — Rites and ceremonies I. T.
E99.S35 H68 970.004/97 19 LC 80-23752 ISBN 0821404172

Edmunds, R. David (Russell David), 1939-. 3.5949
Tecumseh and the quest for Indian leadership / R. David Edmunds. — Boston: Little, Brown, c1984. viii, 246 p.: ill.; 20 cm. — (Library of American biography.) Includes index. 1. Tecumseh, Shawnee Chief, 1768-1813. 2. Shawnee Indians — Biography. 3. Indians of North America — Northwest, Old — Wars. 4. Indians of North America — Wars — 1812-1815 I. T. II. Series.
E99.S35 T136 1984 970.004/97 B 19 LC 83-19560 ISBN 0316211699

Ewers, John Canfield. • 3.5950
The Blackfeet; raiders on the Northwestern Plains. [1st ed.] Norman, University of Oklahoma Press [1958] xviii, 348 p. plates, ports., maps (1 fold.) plan. 24 cm. (The Civilization of the American Indian series, 49) 1. Siksika Indians 2. Piegan Indians 3. Kainah Indians I. T.
E99.S54 E78 970.3 LC 58-7778

Dempsey, Hugh Aylmer, 1929-. 3.5951
Red Crow, warrior chief / Hugh A. Dempsey. — Lincoln: University of Nebraska Press, c1980. 247 p., [7] leaves of plates: ill.; 24 cm. Includes index. 1. Red Crow. 2. Siksika Indians — History. 3. Siksika Indians — Biography. 4. Kainah Indians — History. 5. Kainah Indians — Biography. I. T.
E99.S54 R423 1980 970.004/97 B 19 LC 80-51872 ISBN 0803216572

E99 T–Z

Fire, John. 3.5952
Lame Deer, seeker of visions, by John Fire/Lame Deer and Richard Erdoes. — New York: Simon and Schuster, [1972] 288 p.: illus.; 22 cm. 1. Fire, John. 2. Teton Indians I. Erdoes, Richard. joint author. II. T.
E99.T34 F57 970.3 B LC 79-190730 ISBN 0671211978

Hill, W. W. (Willard Williams), 1902-1974. 3.5953
An ethnography of Santa Clara Pueblo, New Mexico / W.W. Hill; edited and annotated by Charles H. Lange. — 1st ed. — Albuquerque: University of New Mexico Press, c1982. xxxi, 400 p.: ill.; 26 cm. 'Constitution and Bylaws of the Pueblo of Santa Clara'—Appendix B. Includes index. 1. Tewa Indians — Social life and customs. 2. Indians of North America — New Mexico — Santa Clara Pueblo — Social life and customs. 3. Santa Clara Pueblo (N.M.) — Social life and customs. I. Lange, Charles H. II. T.
E99.T35 H5 1982 970.004/97 19 LC 80-52277 ISBN 0826305555

LeFree, Betty. 3.5954
Santa Clara pottery today / Betty LeFree. — 1st ed. — Albuquerque: University of New Mexico Press, c1975. xi, 114 p., [8] leaves of plates: ill. (some col.); 23 cm. (Monograph series - School of American Research; no. 29) 'Published for the School of American Research.' Includes index. 1. Tewa Indians — Pottery. 2. Indians of North America — Southwest, New — Pottery. 3. Santa Clara Pueblo (N.M.) I. School of American Research (Santa Fe, N.M.) II. T.
E99.T35 L43 738.3/7 LC 73-92996 ISBN 0826303218. ISBN 0826303226 pbk

Ortiz, Alfonso, 1939-. 3.5955
The Tewa world; space, time, being, and becoming in a Pueblo society. Chicago, University of Chicago Press [1969] xviii, 197 p. illus. 24 cm. A revision of the author's thesis, University of Chicago. 1. Tewa Indians 2. San Juan Pueblo (N.M.) I. T.
E99.T35 O7 1969 970.3 LC 72-94079 ISBN 0226633063

The Dene Nation, colony within / edited by Mel Watkins for 3.5956
the University League for Social Reform.
Toronto; Buffalo: University of Toronto Press, c1977. xii, 189 p.: maps; 23 cm. A revision and abridgement of material presented at the Mackenzie Valley Pipeline Inquiry (Berger Inquiry) by the Dene themselves and by others on their behalf. 1. Tinne Indians — Government relations — Addresses, essays, lectures. 2. Indians of North America — Canada — Government relations — Addresses, essays, lectures. 3. Mackenzie Valley Pipeline (N.W.T.) — Addresses, essays, lectures. I. Watkins, Mel. II. University League for Social Reform.
E99.T56 D46 323.1/19/707193 LC 76-54701 ISBN 0802022642

De Laguna, Frederica, 1906-.   • 3.5957
The story of a Tlingit community: a problem in the relationship between archeological, ethnological, and historical methods / by Frederica de Laguna. — Washington: U.S. Govt. Print. Off., 1960. x, 254 p.: ill., maps. — (U.S. Bureau of American Ethnology. Bulletin; 172) Bibliography: p.207-209. 1. Tlingit Indians 2. Angoon (Alaska) I. T.
E99.T6D4x   LC 60-60629

Oberg, Kalervo, 1901-1973.   3.5958
The social economy of the Tlingit Indians. Foreword by Wilson Duff. Seattle, University of Washington Press [1973] xvi, 146 p. illus. 23 cm. (American Ethnological Society. Monograph; 55) Originally presented as the author's thesis, University of Chicago, 1937. 1. Tlingit Indians — Economic conditions. I. T.
E99.T6 O3 1973   330.9/701   LC 73-16048   ISBN 0295952903

Radin, Paul, 1883-1959.   • 3.5959
The trickster; a study in American Indian mythology, by Paul Radin. With commentaries by Karl Kerényi and C. G. Jung. New York, Greenwood Press [1969, c1956] xi, 211 p. 23 cm. 1. Winnebago Indians — Religion and mythology. I. Kerényi, Karl, 1897-1973. II. Jung, C. G. (Carl Gustav), 1875-1961. III. T.
E99.W7 R142 1969   299/.7   LC 74-88986   ISBN 0837121124

Ishi, the last Yahi: a documentary history / edited by Robert F.   3.5960
Heizer and Theodora Kroeber.
Berkeley: University of California Press, c1979. viii, 242 p.: ill.; 21 cm. 1. Ishi, d. 1916 — Addresses, essays, lectures. 2. Yana Indians — Biography — Addresses, essays, lectures. 3. Yana Indians — Addresses, essays, lectures. I. Heizer, Robert Fleming, 1915- II. Kroeber, Theodora.
E99.Y23 I8   970/.004/97   LC 76-19966   ISBN 0520032969

Zitkala-Ša, 1876-1938.   3.5961
American Indian stories / by Zitkala-Ša; foreword by Dexter Fisher. — Lincoln: University of Nebraska Press, 1985, c1921. xx, 195 p.: port.; 21 cm. Reprint. Originally published: Washington, D.C.: Hayworth Pub. House, 1921. With new foreword. 1. Zitkala-Ša, 1876-1938. 2. Yankton Indians — Biography. 3. Indians of North America — Social conditions — Addresses, essays, lectures. I. T.
E99.Y25 Z57 1985   813/.52 19   LC 85-8699   ISBN 0803299028

Iverson, Peter.   3.5962
Carlos Montezuma and the changing world of American Indians / Peter Iverson. — 1st ed. — Albuquerque: University of New Mexico Press, c1982. xv, 222 p.: ill., maps.; 24 cm. Includes index. 1. Montezuma, Carlos, 1866-1923. 2. Yavapai Indians — Biography. 3. Indians of North America — Government relations — 1869-1934 I. T.
E99.Y5 M6534 1982   970.004/97 B 19   LC 82-13624   ISBN 0826306411

Crampton, C. Gregory (Charles Gregory), 1911-.   3.5963
The Zunis of Cubola / C. Gregory Crampton. — Salt Lake City: University of Utah Press, 1977. 201 p.: ill., maps. Includes index. 1. Zuñi Indians I. T.
E99.Z9 C7   E99Z9 C7.   LC 77-72586   ISBN 0874801206

Cushing, Frank Hamilton, 1857-1900.   3.5964
Zuñi: selected writings of Frank Hamilton Cushing / edited, with an introd. by Jesse Green; foreword by Fred Eggan. — Lincoln: University of Nebraska Press, c1979. xiv, 440 p.: ill.; 22 cm. 1. Zuñi Indians I. Green, Jesse, 1928- II. T.
E99.Z9 C93 1979   970/.004/97   LC 78-14295   ISBN 0803221002

Tedlock, Dennis, 1939-.   3.5965
The spoken word and the work of interpretation / Dennis Tedlock. — Philadelphia: University of Pennsylvania Press, 1983. ix, 365 p.: ill.; 24 cm. (University of Pennsylvania publications in conduct and communication.) Includes index. 1. Zuñi Indians — Legends. 2. Quichés — Legends. 3. Storytelling 4. Translating and interpreting 5. Language and languages — Phonetic transcriptions 6. Indians — Legends I. T. II. Series.
E99.Z9 T43 1983   398.2/08997 19   LC 82-40489   ISBN 0812278801

E101–135 Discovery of America. Early Exploration

Brebner, John Bartlet, 1895-1957.   • 3.5966
The explorers of North America, 1492–1806. New York Macmillan 1933. 502p. (The Pioneer histories) 1. America — Discovery and exploration 2. North America — History 3. Explorers I. T.
E101 B82 1933   LC 33-31647

First images of America: the impact of the New World on the   3.5967
Old / edited by Fredi Chiappelli, co–editors Michael J. B. Allen
& Robert L. Benson.
Berkeley: University of California Press, 1976. 2 v. (xxii, 957 p., [31] leaves of plates): ill. (some col.); 26 cm. Errata slip inserted. 1. America — Discovery and exploration — Congresses. 2. America — Civilization — Congresses. I. Chiappelli, Fredi, 1921- II. Allen, Michael J. B. III. Benson, Robert Louis, 1925-
E101.F53   970.01   LC 75-7191   ISBN 0520030109

Morison, Samuel Eliot, 1887-1976.   3.5968
The great explorers: the European discovery of America / Samuel Eliot Morison. — New York: Oxford University Press, 1978. xxv, 752 p.: ill., maps, ports.; 24 cm. 1. Voyages and travels 2. America — Discovery and exploration I. T.
E101.M852 1978   970.01   LC 77-21831   ISBN 0195023145

New American world: a documentary history of North America   3.5969
to 1612 / edited, with a commentary by David B. Quinn, with
the assistance of Alison M. Quinn and Susan Hillier.
New York: Arno Press, 1979 (c1978) 5 v.: ill. 1. America — Discovery and exploration — Sources 2. America — History — To 1810 — Sources. I. Quinn, David B. II. Quinn, Alison M. III. Hillier, Susan.
E101.N47   970.01   LC 77-20483   ISBN 0405107595

Quinn, David B.   3.5970
North America from earliest discovery to first settlements: the Norse voyages to 1612 / by David B. Quinn. — 1st ed. — New York: Harper & Row, c1977. xvii, 621 p., [8] leaves of plates: ill.; 22 cm. — (The New American Nation series) Includes index. 1. America — Discovery and exploration I. T.
E101.Q48 1977   970.01   LC 76-5525   ISBN 0060134585

Williams, Gwyn A.   3.5971
Madoc, the making of a myth / Gwyn A. Williams. — London: Eyre Methuen, 1979. 225 p., [4] leaves of plates: ill.; 24 cm. Includes index. 1. Madog ab Owain Gwynedd, 1150-1180? 2. America — Discovery and exploration — Welsh. I. T.
E109.W4 W544   398/.352   LC 80-477694   ISBN 0413394506

E111–120 Columbus

Colón, Fernando, 1488-1539.   • 3.5972
The life of the Admiral Christopher Columbus / by his son Ferdinand; translated and annotated by Benjamin Keen. — New Brunswick, N.J.: Rutgers University Press, 1959. xxxii, 316 p.: ill., maps; 25 cm. 1. Columbus, Christopher. 2. Indians of the West Indies I. Keen, Benjamin, 1913- II. T.
E111.C737   LC 58-6288//r

Madariaga, Salvador de, 1886-.   • 3.5973
Christopher Columbus; being the life of the very magnificent lord, Don Cristóbal Colón. [1st ed.] New York, F. Ungar Pub. Co. [1967] xviii, 524 p. port., maps (part fold.) 25 cm. 1. Columbus, Christopher. 2. Explorers — Spain — Biography. 3. Explorers — America — Biography. 4. America — Discovery and exploration — Spanish I. T.
E111.M172 1967   973.1/5/0924 B   LC 67-25588

Morison, Samuel Eliot, 1887-1976.   • 3.5974
Admiral of the ocean sea; a life of Christopher Columbus, by Samuel Eliot Morison. Maps by Erwin Raisz. Drawings by Bertram Greene. Boston, Little, Brown and Company, 1942. 2 v. fronts. (v. 2, port.) illus., plates, fold. maps, tables, diagrs. 24 cm. 'An Atlantic monthly press book.' 'Salve regina' (words and melody): v. 1, p. [235] Includes index. 1. Columbus, Christopher. I. T.
E111.M8614 1942   923.9   LC 42-5605

Morison, Samuel Eliot, 1887-1976.   • 3.5975
The Caribbean as Columbus saw it / by Samuel Eliot Morison and Mauricio Obregón. — 1st ed. — Boston: Little, Brown, 1964. xxxv, 256 p.: ill., maps, ports. (An Atlantic Monthly Press book) 1. Columbus, Christopher. 2. America — Discovery and exploration — Spanish 3. West Indies — Description and travel — 1951-1980 4. Central America — Description and travel — 1951- I. Obregón, Mauricio. II. T.
E112 M84   LC 64-17483

Columbus, Christopher.   • 3.5976
[Journal English] Journal. Translated by Cecil Jane [rev. and annotated by L. A. Vigneras] with an appendix by R. A. Skelton. 90 illus. from prints and maps of the period. New York, C. N. Potter [1960] xxiii, 227 p. illus. (part mounted, part col.) ports., maps (part col.) charts, coat of arms, facsims. 25 cm. Detail of French portulan chart from dust jacket inserted. 'Letter of Columbus, describing the results of his first voyage': p. [189]-202. 1. Columbus,

Christopher — Diaries. 2. Explorers — America — Diaries. 3. Explorers — Spain — Diaries. 4. America — Discovery and exploration — Spanish I. T.
E118.C725 1960   973.15   *LC* 60-14430

E121–143 Other Explorers

The Exploration of North America, 1630–1776 / W. P.   **3.5977**
Cumming ... [et al.].
New York: Putnam, 1974. 272 p.: ill.; 32 cm. Includes index. 1. America — Discovery and exploration 2. United States — Exploring expeditions 3. New France — Discovery and exploration. 4. North America — History — Sources. I. Cumming, William Patterson, 1900-
E121.E9   973.2   *LC* 74-81276   *ISBN* 0399114076

Parry, J. H. (John Horace), 1914-.   **3.5978**
The discovery of South America / J. H. Parry. — New York: Taplinger Pub. Co., 1979. 320 p.: ill.; 26 cm. Includes index. 1. America — Discovery and exploration 2. Latin America — History — To 1600 I. T.
E121.P37 1979b   980/.01   *LC* 78-57599   *ISBN* 0800822331

Sauer, Carl Ortwin, 1889-.   • **3.5979**
Sixteenth century North America; the land and the people as seen by the Europeans. — Berkeley: University of California Press, 1971. xii, 319 p.: illus.; 24 cm. 1. America — Discovery and exploration I. T.
E121.S26   973.1   *LC* 75-138635   *ISBN* 0520018540

McAlister, Lyle N.   **3.5980**
Spain and Portugal in the New World, 1492–1700 / by Lyle N. McAlister. — Minneapolis: University of Minnesota Press, c1984. xxvi, 585 p., [8] p. of plates: 7 maps; 24 cm. (Europe and the world in the Age of Expansion; v. 3) Cover title: Spain & Portugal in the New World, 1492-1700. Includes index. 1. America — Discovery and exploration — Spanish 2. America — Discovery and exploration — Portuguese. 3. Latin America — History — To 1830 4. Spain — Colonies — America — History. 5. Portugal — Colonies — America — History. I. T. II. Title: Spain & Portugal in the New World, 1492-1700.
E123.M38 1984   980/.01 19   *LC* 83-21745   *ISBN* 0816612161

Spanish explorers in the southern United States, 1528–1543.   • **3.5981**
New York, C. Scribner's sons, 1907. xx, 411 p. front. (facsim.) 2 fold. maps. 23 cm. 1. Vázquez de Coronado, Francisco, 1510-1549. 2. Soto, Hernando de, ca. 1500-1542. 3. Indians of North America 4. America — Discovery and exploration — Spanish 5. Florida — History — Colonial period, ca. 1600-1775 I. Núñez Cabeza de Vaca, Alvar, 16th cent. II. Castañeda de Nágera, Pedro de,$ III. Hodge, Frederick Webb, 1864-1956. ed. IV. Lewis, Theodore H., ed. V. Relaçam verdadeira dos trabalhos.
E123.S75   *LC* 07-10607

Todorov, Tzvetan, 1939-.   **3.5982**
[Conquête de l'Amérique. English] The conquest of America: the question of the other / Tzvetan Todorov; translated from the French by Richard Howard. — 1st ed. — New York: Harper & Row, c1984. x, 274 p.: ill.; 25 cm. Translation of: La conquête de l'Amérique. Includes index. 1. Indians of Central America — First contact with Occidental civilization. 2. Indians of the West Indies — First contact with Occidental civilization. 3. Indians of Mexico — First contact with Occidental civilization. 4. America — Discovery and exploration — Spanish I. T.
E123.T6313 1984   970.01/6 19   *LC* 83-47545   *ISBN* 0060151803

Hallenbeck, Cleve.   • **3.5983**
Álvar Núñez Cabeza de Vaca; the journey and route of the first European to cross the continent of North America, 1534–1536. — Port Washington, N.Y.: Kennikat Press, [1970] 326 p.: maps.; 22 cm. — (Kennikat Press scholarly reprints. Series in Latin-American history and culture) Pt. 1 is a paraphrase in

English of Núñez Cabeza de Vaca's La relación y comentarios. 1. Núñez Cabeza de Vaca, Alvar, 16th cent. 2. America — Discovery and exploration — Spanish I. Núñez Cabeza de Vaca, Alvar, 16th cent. La relación y comentarios. II. T.
E125.N9 H3 1970   973.1/6   *LC* 78-123490   *ISBN* 080461377X

Vega, Garcilaso de la, 1539-1616.   • **3.5984**
The Florida of the Inca; a history of adelantado, Hernando de Soto, Governor and Captain General of the kingdom of Florida, and of other heroic Spanish and Indian cavaliers, written by the Inca, Garcilaso de la Vega, an officer of His Majesty, and a native of the great city of Cuzco, capital of the realms and provinces of Peru. Translated and edited by John Grier Varner and Jeannette Johnson Varner. Austin, University of Texas Press, 1951. xiv, 655 p. port., map (on lining papers) 25 cm. 1. Soto, Hernando de, ca. 1500-1542. I. T.
E125.S7 G26   973.16   *LC* 51-10292

Hammond, George Peter, 1896- ed. and tr.   • **3.5985**
Narratives of the Coronado expedition, 1540–1542. Albuquerque, The University of New Mexico press, 1940. xii, 413 p. front. 28 cm. 1. Vázquez de Coronado, Francisco, 1510-1549. 2. Southwest, New — Discovery and exploration. I. Rey, Agapito, joint ed. and tr. II. T. III. Title: The Coronado expedition, 1540-1542, Narratives of.
E125.V3 H4   *LC* 40-12409

Vázquez de Espinosa, Antonio, d. 1630.   • **3.5986**
[Compendio y descripción de las Indias Occidentales. English] Description of the Indies, c. 1620. Translated by Charles Upson Clark. Washington, Smithsonian Institution Press [1968] xii, 862 p. 24 cm. (Smithsonian miscellaneous collections. v. 102) (Smithsonian publication 3646.) Reprint of the 1942 ed. published under title: Compendium and description of the West Indies. Translation of Compendio y descripción de las Indias Occidentales, from the Vatican Library manuscript Barberinianus Latinus 3584. 1. Indians 2. Latin America — Description and travel 3. Spain — Colonies — America. 4. Philippines — Description and travel I. T. II. Series.
E125.V35x   918   *LC* 68-25124

Arciniegas, Germán, 1900-.   • **3.5987**
[Amerigo el Neuvo Mundo English] Amerigo and the New World; the life & times of Amerigo Vespucci. [1st ed.] New York, Knopf, 1955. p. cm. 1. Vespucci, Amerigo, 1451-1512. I. T.
E125.V5 A65   *LC* 53-9487

Burrage, Henry Sweetser, 1837-1926.   **3.5988**
Early English and French voyages, chiefly from Hakluyt, 1534–1608, ed. by Henry S. Burrage. New York, Barnes & Noble [1952] xx, 451 p. 23 cm. (Original narratives of early American history) 1. America — Discovery and exploration — English 2. America — Discovery and exploration — French I. Hakluyt, Richard, 1552?-1616. II. T. III. Series.
E127.Bx   *LC* a 54-10008

McCann, Franklin Thresher, 1903-.   • **3.5989**
English discovery of America to 1585, by Franklin T. McCann. — New York: Octagon Books, 1969 [c1951] xiv, 246 p.: illus.; 23 cm. 1. America in literature. 2. English literature — History and criticism 3. Cosmography 4. America — Discovery and exploration — English. I. T.
E127.M15 1969   973.1/7   *LC* 73-86280

Quinn, David Beers, 1909- .   **3.5990**
England and the discovery of America, 1481–1620, from the Bristol voyages of the fifteenth century to the Pilgrim settlement at Plymouth: the exploration, exploitation, and trial–and–error colonization of North America by the English. — [1st ed.]. — New York: Knopf, 1974 [c1973] xxiv, 497, xviii p.: illus.; 25 cm. 1. America — Discovery and exploration — English. 2. Great Britain — Colonies — America 3. America — History — To 1810 I. T.
E127.Q49   973.1/7   *LC* 70-171123   *ISBN* 039446673X

Leonard, Irving Albert, 1896- comp.   **3.5991**
Colonial travelers in Latin America. Edited with an introduction by Irving A. Leonard. — [1st ed.]. — New York: Knopf, [1972] x, 235 p.; 19 cm. — (Borzoi books on Latin America) 1. Latin America — Description and travel — Collections. 2. America — Discovery and exploration — Collections. I. T.
E143.L4 1972   918/.04/1   *LC* 71-169694   *ISBN* 0394475577

E151–161 General Works. Social Life. Customs

Directory of American preservation commissions / National   **3.5992**
Trust for Historic Preservation; Stephen N. Dennis, ed., Andrea
Zizzi, comp.
[Washington, D.C.]: Preservation Press, [1981] iv, 123 p.; 26 cm. 1. Historic
sites — Conservation and restoration — Directories. 2. Historic buildings —
Conservation and restoration — Directories. I. Dennis, Stephen N. II. Zizzi,
Andrea. III. National Trust for Historic Preservation in the United States.
IV. Title: American preservation commissions.
E151 D57   *ISBN* 089133100X

Harder, Kelsie B.   **3.5993**
Illustrated dictionary of place names, United States and Canada / edited by
Kelsie B. Harder. — New York: Van Nostrand Reinhold Co., c1976. xiv,
631 p.: ill.; 24 cm. 'A Hudson group book.' 1. Names, Geographical — United
States. 2. Names, Geographical — Canada. 3. United States — History, Local
4. Canada — History, Local. I. T. II. Title: Dictionary of place names, United
States and Canada.
E155.H37   917.3/003   *LC* 75-26907   *ISBN* 0442230699

Stewart, George Rippey, 1895-.   • **3.5994**
American place–names: a concise and selective dictionary for the continental
United States of America / [by] George R. Stewart. — New York: Oxford
University Press, 1970. xl, 550 p.; 25 cm. 1. Names, Geographical — U.S. I. T.
E155.S79   917.3/003   *LC* 72-83018

Boatner, Mark Mayo, 1921-.   **3.5995**
Landmarks of the American Revolution; a guide to locating and knowing what
happened at the sites of independence [by] Mark M. Boatner III. [Harrisburg,
Pa.]: Stackpole Books, [1973] 608 p.: illus.; 24 cm. 1. Historic sites — United
States — Guide-books. 2. United States — History — Revolution, 1775-1783
I. T.
E159.B67   917.3/04/92   *LC* 73-6964   *ISBN* 0811709361

Eastman, John.   **3.5996**
Who lived where: a biographical guide to homes and museums / John Eastman.
— New York: Facts on File Publications, c1983. xxii, 513 p.; ill.; 29 cm.
Includes indexes. 1. Dwellings — United States — Directories. 2. Historic
buildings — United States — Directories. 3. Historical museums — United
States — Directories. 4. United States — Directories I. T.
E159.E23 1983   973 19   *LC* 82-7376   *ISBN* 0871965623

Greiff, Constance M.   **3.5997**
Lost America: from the Atlantic to the Mississippi. Edited by Constance M.
Greiff. With a foreword by James Biddle. [1st ed.] Princeton, N.J. Pyne Press
1971. 244p. 1. United States — Historic houses, etc. — Pictorial works I. T.
E159 G7   *LC* 75-162363   *ISBN* 0878610081

Greiff, Constance M.   **3.5998**
Lost America: from the Mississippi to the Pacific. Edited by Constance M.
Greiff. With a foreword by James Biddle. [1st ed.] Princeton [N.J.] Pyne Press
[1972] x, 243 p. illus. 29 cm. A companion volume to Lost America: from the
Atlantic to the Mississippi. 1. Historic buildings — United States — Pictorial
works. I. T.
E159.G72   917.8/04/3   *LC* 72-79151   *ISBN* 0878610332

Schlereth, Thomas J.   **3.5999**
Artifacts and the American past / Thomas J. Schlereth. — Nashville, Tenn.:
American Association for State and Local History, c1980. vii, 294 p.: ill.; 24 cm.
1. Historical museums — United States — Addresses, essays, lectures.
2. Photography in historiography — Addresses, essays, lectures. 3. United
States — Antiquities — Addresses, essays, lectures. 4. United States —
Civilization — Addresses, essays, lectures. I. T.
E159.5.S34   973 19   *LC* 80-19705   *ISBN* 0910050473

Sax, Joseph L.   **3.6000**
Mountains without handrails, reflections on the national parks / Joseph L. Sax.
— Ann Arbor: University of Michigan Press, c1980. 152 p.; 21 cm. Includes
index. 1. National parks and reserves — United States I. T.
E160.S29 1980   917.3   *LC* 80-36859   *ISBN* 047209324X

Tilden, Freeman, 1883-.   • **3.6001**
The national parks / foreword by George B. Hartzog, Jr. — [2d rev. ed.] New
York: Knopf, 1970 [c1951] xviii, 584, xx p.: ill., map; 23 cm. 'A revised &
enlarged edition ... with new information & evaluation on all of the national
parks, national monuments, & historic sites.' 1. National parks and reserves —
United States — Guide-books. 2. United States — Description and travel —
1981- — Guide-books. I. T.
E160.T5 1970   917.3   *LC* 79-16092

Tilden, Freeman, 1883-.   • **3.6002**
The State parks: their meaning in American life / foreword by Conrad L.
Wirth. — [1st ed.] New York: Knopf, 1962. 496 p., xi p.: ill.; 25 cm. 1. Parks —
United States. I. T.
E160.T53   917.3   *LC* 62-17547

Beard, Mary Ritter, 1876-1958. ed.   • **3.6003**
America through women's eyes. New York, Greenwood Press [1969, c1933]
558 p. 23 cm. 1. Women — United States — History. 2. United States —
Social conditions 3. United States — History I. T.
E161.B42 1969   301.41/2/0973   *LC* 68-54772

Blegen, Theodore Christian, 1891-1969.   • **3.6004**
Grass roots history [by] Theodore C. Blegen. — Port Washington, N.Y.:
Kennikat Press, [1969, c1947] x, 266 p.; 22 cm. 1. Frontier and pioneer life —
Minnesota. 2. Norwegians in the United States. 3. U.S. — Social life and
customs. I. T.
E161.B55 1969   917.3   *LC* 75-85987   *ISBN* 0804606021

Dulles, Foster Rhea, 1900-1970.   • **3.6005**
[America learns to play] A history of recreation; America learns to play. 2d ed.
New York, Appleton-Century-Crofts [1965] xvii, 446 p. illus., facsims. 21 cm.
Previously published under title: America learns to play; a history of popular
recreation. 1. Recreation — United States 2. United States — Social life and
customs I. T.
E161.D852 1965   790.0973   *LC* 65-25489

Handlin, Oscar, 1915- ed.   • **3.6006**
This was America: true accounts of people and places, manners and customs /
as recorded by European travelers to the western shore in the eighteenth,
nineteenth and twentieth centuries. — Cambridge: Harvard University Press,
1949. ix, 602 p.: ill., maps.; 25 cm. 1. United States — Description & travel.
2. United States — Social life & customs. I. T.
E161.H3   917.3   *LC* 49-7940

Schlesinger, Arthur Meier, 1888-1965.   • **3.6007**
Learning how to behave; a historical study of American etiquette books. —
New York: Cooper Square Publishers, 1968. ix, 95 p.; 21 cm. 'A Marandell
book.' Reprint of the 1946 ed. 1. Etiquette — United States. 2. Etiquette —
Bibliography. 3. United States — Social life and customs I. T.
E161.S25 1968   395   *LC* 68-28296

Wecter, Dixon, 1906-1950.   • **3.6008**
The saga of American society; a record of social aspiration, 1607–1937. New
York, Scribner [1970] xxii, 504 p. illus., ports. 25 cm. Reprint of the 1937 ed.,
with an introd. by Louis Auchincloss. 1. Portraits, American 2. Historic
buildings — United States. 3. United States — Social life and customs
4. Virginia — Social life and customs 5. New York (N.Y.) — Social life and
customs I. T.
E161.W43 1970   917.3/03   *LC* 78-103633

E162–169 Description. Travel, by Period

E162–163 1607–1783

Andrews, Charles McLean, 1863-1943.   • **3.6009**
Colonial folkways; a chronicle of American life in the reign of the Georges, by
Charles M. Andrews. — New Haven, Yale university press; [etc., etc.] 1921. ix,
255 p. col. front. 18 cm. — (Half-title: The chronicles of America series, Allen

Johnson, editor ... v. 9) 'Roosevelt edition.' 'Bibliographical note': p. 239-243. 1. United States — Soc. life & cust. — Colonial period. I. T.
E162.A57 E173.C56 vol. 9   *LC* 22-12131

Bridenbaugh, Carl.   • **3.6010**
Cities in revolt: urban life in America, 1743–1776. — [1st ed.]. — New York: Knopf, 1955. xiii, 433, [1], xxi p.: ill., ports., map, facsims.; 25 cm. 1. Cities and towns — United States. 2. United States — Social life and customs — Colonial period, ca. 1600-1775 I. T.
E162.B85   917.4   *LC* 55-7399

Demos, John. comp.   **3.6011**
Remarkable providences, 1600–1760 / Edited, with introd. and notes by John Demos. — New York: G. Braziller, [c1972] xiv, 382 p.; 24 cm. — (The American culture, 1) 1. United States — Civilization — To 1783 2. United States — Social conditions — To 1865 I. T. II. Series.
E162.D4 1972   917.3/03/208   *LC* 74-160130   *ISBN* 0807606170

Earle, Alice Morse.   • **3.6012**
Home life in colonial days / written by Alice Morse Earle in the year MDCCCXCVIII; illustrated by photographs, gathered by the author, of real things, works and happinings of olden times. — New York: Macmillan, 1913. xvi, 470 p.: ill. (The Macmilland standary library) 1. Home economics — History. 2. United States — Social life and customs — Colonial period. I. T.
E162.E18   917.3   *LC* 98-1504

Eggleston, Edward, 1837-1902.   • **3.6013**
The transit of civilization from England to America in the seventeenth century. With a new introd. by Arthur M. Schlesinger. Gloucester, Mass. P. Smith 1933. 344p. 1. United States — History — Colonial period 2. United States — Civilization I. T.
E162 E28

Gummere, Richard M. (Richard Mott), 1883-.   • **3.6014**
The American colonial mind and the classical tradition: essays in comparative culture. — Cambridge: Harvard University Press, 1963. xiii, 228 p.; 22 cm. 1. United States — Civilization — To 1783 2. United States — Civilization — Classical influences I. T.
E162.G88   917.3   *LC* 63-20767

Hamilton, Alexander, 1712-1756.   • **3.6015**
Gentleman's progress. Chapel Hill, Pub. by the Univ. of North Carolina Press, 1948. xxxii, 267 p. illus., maps (on lining-papers) 25 cm. 1. United States — Description and travel I. Bridenbaugh, Carl. ed. II. Institute of Early American History and Culture (Williamsburg, Va.) III. T.
E162.H21 1948   *LC* 48-28157

Kammen, Michael G.   • **3.6016**
People of paradox: an inquiry concerning the origins of American civilization. — [1st ed.]. — New York: Knopf, 1972. xvii, 316, xii p.: ill.; 22 cm. 1. National characteristics, American 2. United States — Civilization — To 1783 I. T.
E162.K2   917.3/03   *LC* 72-376   *ISBN* 0394460774

Rossiter, Clinton Lawrence, 1917-1970.   • **3.6017**
[Seedtime of the Republic] The first American Revolution; the American Colonies on the eve of independence. New York, Harcourt, Brace [c1956] 245 p. 19 cm. (A Harvest book, 17) 'Revised version of part I of Seedtime of the Republic.' 1. United States — History — Colonial period, ca. 1600-1775 2. United States — Civilization 3. United States — History — Revolution, 1775-1783 — Causes I. T.
E162.R7   973.2   *LC* 56-13741

Smith, James Morton. ed.   • **3.6018**
Seventeenth–century America; essays in colonial history. Chapel Hill, Published for the Institute of Early American History and Culture at Williamsburg, Va., by the University of North Carolina Press [1959] xv, 228 p. 24 cm. Based upon original papers presented at a symposium sponsored by the Institute of Early American History and Culture at Williamsburg, Va., in 1957. 1. United States — Social life and customs — Colonial period, ca. 1600-1775 — Addresses, essays, lectures. 2. United States — History — Colonial period, ca. 1600-1775 — Addresses, essays, lectures. 3. United States — Church history — Colonial period, ca. 1600-1775 — Addresses, essays, lectures. I. Institute of Early American History and Culture (Williamsburg, Va.) II. T.
E162.S66   973.2   *LC* 59-16299

Wertenbaker, Thomas Jefferson, 1879-1966.   • **3.6019**
The golden age of colonial culture / Thomas Jefferson Wertenbaker. — [2nd ed., rev.]. — New York: New York Univ. Press, [1949] 171 p.; 22 cm. (Anson G. Phelps lectureship on early American history.) Bibliographical footnotes. 1. United States — Civilization 2. United States — Social life and customs — Colonial period. I. T. II. Series.
E162.W48 1949   973.2   *LC* 49-4583 *

Wright, Louis B. (Louis Booker), 1899-.   • **3.6020**
The cultural life of the American Colonies, 1607–1763 / by Louis B. Wright. — New York: Harper & Row, [c1957] xiv, 292 p.: ill.,ports.,map; 22 cm. — (New

American nation series) 1. United States — Social life and customs — Colonial period, ca. 1600-1775 2. United States — Intellectual life I. T. II. Title: The cultural life of the American Colonies.
E162 W89 1962   917.303   *LC* 57-250

Chastellux, François Jean, marquis de, 1734-1788.   • **3.6021**
[Voyages dans l'Amerique septentrionale. English] Travels in North–America [in the years 1780, 1781, and 1782. Translated from the French by an English gentleman. New York] New York times [1968] 2 v. fold. illus., fold. maps. 23 cm. (Eyewitness accounts of the American Revolution) Translation of Voyages dans l'Amérique septentrionale. Reprint of the 1787 ed. 1. United States — Description and travel — To 1783 I. T. II. Series.
E163.C59 1968   917.4   *LC* 67-29046

Commager, Henry Steele, 1902-.   **3.6022**
The empire of reason: how Europe imagined and America realized the enlightenment / Henry Steele Commager. — Garden City, N.Y.: Anchor Press/Doubleday, 1977. xiv, 342 p., [8] leaves of plates: ill.; 22 cm. 1. Enlightenment 2. United States — Intellectual life — 18th century 3. United States — History — Revolution, 1775-1783 — Causes I. T.
E163.C7   973.2   *LC* 76-2837   *ISBN* 0385116721

St. John de Crèvecoeur, J. Hector, 1735-1813.   • **3.6023**
Letters from an American farmer, by J. Hector St. John de Crèvecoeur. — London & Toronto, J. M. Dent & sons, ltd.; New York, E. P. Dutton & co. [1912] xxiii, 256 p. 18 cm. — (Half-title: Everyman's library, edited by Ernest Rhys. Travel and topography. [no. 640]) 'First issue of this edition 1912. Reprinted 1926.' Title-page and page facing it (with quotation) have ornamental border. Includes reproduction of t.-p. of original edition, London, 1782. 'Introduction and notes by Warren Barton Blake.' Bibliography: p. xxi. 1. United States — Descr. & trav. 2. Nantucket (Mass.) I. Blake, Warren Barton, 1883-1918, ed. II. T.
E163.C826x   917.4   *LC* 36-37597

St. John de Crèvecoeur, J. Hector, 1735-1813.   • **3.6024**
Sketches of eighteenth century America: more 'Letters from an American farmer,' / by St. John de Crèvecoeur; edited by Henri L. Bourdin, Ralph H. Gabriel and Stanley T. Williams. — New Haven: Yale University Press; London: H. Milford, Oxford University Press, 1925. 6 p.l., 342 p.: front. (port.) facsim.; 24 cm. 1. Farm life 2. United States — Social life and customs — Colonial period. I. Bourdin, Henri Louis, ed. II. Gabriel, Ralph Henry, 1890-1987. ed. III. Williams, Stanley Thomas, 1888-1956. ed. IV. Philip Hamilton McMillan Memorial Publication Fund. V. T.
E163.C873   *LC* 25-23064

May, Henry Farnham, 1915-.   **3.6025**
The Enlightenment in America / Henry F. May. — New York: Oxford University Press, 1976. xix, 419 p.; 24 cm. 1. Enlightenment 2. United States — Intellectual life — 18th century I. T.
E163.M39   973   *LC* 75-32349   *ISBN* 0195020189

St. John de Crèvecoeur, J. Hector, 1735-1813.   **3.6026**
[Letters from an American farmer] Letters from an American farmer; and, Sketches of eighteenth–century America / by J. Hector St. John de Crèvecoeur; edited, with an introduction, by Albert E. Stone. — Harmondsworth, Middlesex, England; New York, N.Y., U.S.A.: Penguin Books, 1981. 491 p.; 18 cm. (Penguin American library.) Includes index. 1. St. John de Crèvecoeur, J. Hector, 1735-1813. 2. United States — Social life and customs — Revolution, 1775-1783 3. United States — Description and travel — To 1783 4. Nantucket Island (Mass.) — Social life and customs. I. Stone, Albert E. II. St. John de Crèvecoeur, J. Hector, 1735-1813. Sketches of eighteenth-century America. 1981. III. T. IV. Series.
E163.S73 1981   973.3 19   *LC* 81-12076   *ISBN* 0140390065

E164–166 1784–1860

Foster, Augustus John, Sir, bart, 1780-1848.   • **3.6027**
Jeffersonian America: notes on the United States of America, collected in the years 1805–6–7 and 11–12 / edited with an introd. by Richard Beale Davis. — San Marino, Calif.: Huntington Library, 1954. xx, 356 p.: port. (Huntington Library publications) 1. United States — Social life and customs 2. Washington (D.C.) — Social life and customs I. T.
E164.F76 1954

Moreau de Saint-Méry, M. L. E. (Médéric Louis Elie), 1750-1819.   • **3.6028**
[Voyage aux États-Unis de l'Am[a]erique, 1793-1798. English.] Moreau de St. Méry's American journey < 1793–1798 > / translated and edited by Kenneth Roberts [and] Anna M. Roberts; preface by Kenneth Roberts; introduction by Stewart L. Mims; frontispiece painting by James Bingham. — Garden City, N.Y.: Doubleday & Company, inc., 1947. xxi p., 1 l., 394 p.: col. front.; 24 cm.

'First edition.' 1. United States — Description and travel I. Roberts, Kenneth Lewis, 1885-1957. ed. and tr. II. Roberts, Anna S. (Mosser) joint ed. and tr. III. Mims, Stewart Lea, 1880- IV. T. V. Title: American journey.
E164.M832   *LC* 47-3941

Chevalier, Michel, 1806-1879.   • **3.6029**
Society, manners, and politics in the United States; being a series of letters on North America, by Michael Chevalier. — New York: B. Franklin, [1969] iv, 467 p.; 23 cm. — (Burt Franklin research and source works series, 352) (American classics in history and social science, 79.) Translation of Lettres sur l'Amérique du Nord. 1. U.S. — Description and travel — 1783-1848. 2. U.S. — Politics and government — 1829-1837. 3. U.S. — Social conditions — To 1865. I. T.
E165.C54 1969   309.1/73   *LC* 69-18620

Cobbett, William, 1763-1835.   • **3.6030**
A year's residence in the United States of America. — New York: A. M. Kelley, 1969. vii, 610 p.; 22 cm. — (America through European eyes) (Reprints of economic classics.) Reprint of the 1818-19 ed. 1. Agriculture — U.S. 2. U.S. — Description and travel — 1783-1848. 3. U.S. — Social life and customs — 1783-1865. I. T.
E165.C669   917.3   *LC* 70-85139   *ISBN* 0678005168

Wright, Frances, 1795-1852.   • **3.6031**
Views of society and manners in America. Edited by Paul R. Baker. — Cambridge, Mass., Belknap Press of Harvard University Press, 1963. xxiii, 292 p. 24 cm. — (John Harvard library.) 'Text ... used ... is that of the first London edition of 1821.' 1. U.S. — Descr. & trav. — 1783-1848. 2. U.S. — Soc. life & cust. I. T. II. Series.
E165.D2303   917.3   *LC* 63-10878

Dickens, Charles, 1812-1870.   • **3.6032**
American notes and Pictures from Italy / with 12 illus. by Marcus Stone, Samuel Palmer, and Clarkson Stanfield, and an introd. by Sacheverell Sitwell. London; New York: Oxford University Press, 1957. xiv, 433 p.: ill.; 19 cm. (The New Oxford illustrated Dickens) 1. United States — Description and travel — 1783-1848 2. United States — Social life and customs 3. Italy — Description and travel I. T. II. Title: Pictures from Italy. III. Series.
E165.D614   *LC* 57-4815

Fish, Carl Russell, 1876-1932.   • **3.6033**
The rise of the common man, 1830–1850 / by Carl Russell Fish. New York: The Macmillan company, 1937. xix p., 1 l., 391 p.: front., plates.; 22 cm. (History of American life. vol. VI.) 'Critical essay on authorities': p. 339-366. 1. United States — Social conditions 2. United States — Economic conditions 3. United States — Civilization I. T. II. Series.
E165.F52x   973.5   *LC* 38-34437

Grund, Francis Joseph, 1805-1863.   • **3.6034**
Aristocracy in America: from the sketch–book of a German nobleman / with an introd. by George E. Probst. — [1st American ed.]. — New York: Harper, [1959] xvii, 302 p.; 21 cm. — (Harper torchbooks, TB1001. The Academy library) 1. United States — Social life and customs — 1783-1865 I. T.
E165.G91 1959   917.3   *LC* 59-13839

Lyell, Charles, Sir, 1797-1875.   • **3.6035**
A second visit to the United States of North America. By Sir Charles Lyell. New York, Harper & brothers; London, J. Murray, 1850. 2 v. illus. 20 cm. 1. Geology — United States 2. United States — Description and travel I. T.
E165.L98   *LC* 01-26866

Martineau, Harriet, 1802-1876.   • **3.6036**
Society in America / Edited, abridged and with an introductory essay of Seymour Martin Lipset. — [1st ed.] Garden City, N.Y.: Anchor Books, 1962. 357 p.; 18 cm. (A Doubleday anchor original, A302) 1. Martineau, Harriet, 1802-1876. 2. United States — Economic conditions — To 1865 3. United States — Politics and government — 1815-1861 4. United States — Description and travel — 1783-1848 5. United States — Social life and customs — 1783-1865 I. T.
E165.M393 1962   917.3   *LC* 62-15241

Miller, Douglas T.   • **3.6037**
The birth of modern America, 1820–1850, by Douglas T. Miller. — New York: Pegasus, [1970] xvi, 192 p.: illus.; 21 cm. 1. U.S. — Civilization — 19th century. 2. U.S. — Social conditions — To 1865. I. T.
E165.M62   973.5   *LC* 79-114173

Sanford, Charles L., 1920-.   • **3.6038**
Quest for America, 1810–1824. [New York] New York University Press, 1964. xxxvii, 474 p. illus., ports. 24 cm. 1. United States — Civilization — 1783-1865 I. T.
E165.S25 1964a   *LC* 64-25921

Tocqueville, Alexis de, 1805-1859.   • **3.6039**
Journey to America. Translated by George Lawrence. Edited by J. P. Mayer. Rev. and augm. ed. in collaboration with A. P. Kerr. Garden City, N.Y.,

Doubleday, 1971. xvi, 424 p. 18 cm. 'Based on fourteen notebooks, details of which can be found in [the author's] Œuvres complètes, ed. J. P. Mayer, vol. V, 1, p. 57.' 1. United States — Description and travel — 1783-1848 I. T.
E165.T5433 1971   917.3/03/56   *LC* 78-157643

Pierson, George Wilson, 1904-.   • **3.6040**
Tocqueville in America / Abridged by Dudley C. Lunt from 'Tocqueville and Beaumont in America.'. — Garden City, N. Y.: Doubleday, 1959. 506 p.; 19 cm. — (Anchor books, A189) Includes bibliography. 1. Tocqueville, Alexis de, 1805-1859. 2. Beaumont, Gustave de, 1802-1866. 3. U.S. — Descr. & trav. — 1783-1848. I. T.
E165.T547 1959   917.3   *LC* 59-13981

Trollope, Frances Milton, 1780-1863.   • **3.6041**
Domestic manners of the Americans; edited, with a history of Mrs. Trollope's adventures in America, by Donald Smalley. [1st Borzoi ed.] New York, A. A. Knopf, 1949. lxxxiii, 454, xix p. illus., port. 25 cm. 1. United States — Social life and customs I. Smalley, Donald Arthur, 1907- ed. II. T.
E165.T84 1949   917.3   *LC* 49-11380

Trollope, Frances Milton, 1780-1863.   **3.6042**
Domestic manners of the Americans / by Frances Trollope; edited by Richard Mullen. — Oxford; New York: Oxford University Press, 1984. xxxi, 368 p.; 20 cm. Reprint. Originally published: 5th ed. London: G. Routledge, 1839. With new introd. 1. United States — Social life and customs — 1783-1865 I. Mullen, Richard. II. T.
E165.T84 1984   973 19   *LC* 84-7905   *ISBN* 0192814648

Welter, Rush.   **3.6043**
The mind of America, 1820–1860. — New York: Columbia University Press, 1975. xvi, 603 p.; 24 cm. 1. Public opinion — United States. 2. United States — Intellectual life — 1783-1865 I. T.
E165.W46   917.3/03/5   *LC* 74-14976   *ISBN* 0231029632

Busch, Moritz, 1821-1899.   **3.6044**
[Wanderungen zwischen Hudson und Mississippi, 1851 und 1852. English] Travels between the Hudson & the Mississippi, 1851–1852. Translated and edited by Norman H. Binger. [Lexington] University Press of Kentucky [1971] xix, 295 p. 24 cm. Translation of Wanderungen zwischen Hudson und Mississippi, 1851 und 1852. 1. United States — Description and travel — 1848-1865 2. United States — Social life and customs — 1783-1865 I. T.
E166.B9713 1971   917.3/03/64   *LC* 74-147857   *ISBN* 0813112516

Cobden, Richard, 1804-1865.   • **3.6045**
[American diaries] The American diaries of Richard Cobden. Edited, with an introd. and notes, by Elizabeth Hoon Cawley. New York, Greenwood Press [1969, c1952] xii, 233 p. illus., facsim., maps, ports. 23 cm. 1952 ed. published under title: American diaries. The mss. of the two diaries are in the British Museum (Add. mss. 43807 and 43808) 1. National characteristics, American 2. United States — Description and travel — 1848-1865 I. T.
E166.C6 1969   917.3/04/6   *LC* 75-90488   *ISBN* 0837122619

Nye, Russel Blaine, 1913-.   **3.6046**
Society and culture in America, 1830–1860. — [1st ed.]. — New York: Harper & Row, [1974] xiv, 432 p.: illus.; 22 cm. — (The New American nation series) 1. National characteristics, American 2. Reformers 3. United States — Civilization — 1783-1865 I. T.
E166.N93   917.3/03/5   *LC* 73-14277   *ISBN* 0060132299

E167–169.02 1861–

Russell, William Howard, Sir, 1820-1907.   • **3.6047**
My diary, North and South / edited and introduced by Fletcher Pratt. — Gloucester, Mass.: P. Smith, 1969 [c1954] xiii, 268 p.: port.; 21 cm. 1. Southern States — Description and travel 2. United States — History — Civil War, 1861-1865 I. T.
E167.R96 1969   917.3   *LC* 79-10920

Trollope, Anthony, 1815-1882.   • **3.6048**
North America. — New ed. [reprinted]. — London: Dawsons, 1968. 2 v.; 20 cm. — (Colonial history series) Facsimile reprint of new ed., 1869. 1. United States — Description and travel — 1848-1865 2. United States — Politics and government — Civil War, 1861-1865 3. Canada — Description and travel — 1763-1867 I. T.
E167.T8425 1869a   917   *LC* 79-350542   *ISBN* 0712903003

Ginger, Ray.   • **3.6049**
Age of excess; the United States from 1877 to 1914. — New York: Macmillan, [1965] x, 386 p.; 21 cm. 1. United States — Civilization — 1865-1918 I. T.
E168.G48   917.3   *LC* 65-12151

Morgan, H. Wayne (Howard Wayne) ed.   • **3.6050**
The gilded age, a reappraisal. [Syracuse, N.Y.] Syracuse University Press, 1963. 286 p. 24 cm. 1. United States — Civilization — 1856-1918 — Addresses, essays, lectures. I. T.
E168.M84   973.8   *LC* 63-13886

Offenbach, Jacques, 1819-1880.   • **3.6051**
[Offenbach en Amérique. English] Orpheus in America: Offenbach's diary of his journey to the New World / translated by Lander MacClintock; drawings by Alajálov. — New York: Greenwood Press [1969, c1957] 200 p.: ill.; 23 cm. Translation of Offenbach en Amérique. 1. Music — United States 2. United States — Social life and customs — 1865-1918 3. United States — Description and travel — 1865-1900 I. T.
E168.O332 1969   917.3/04/82   *LC* 69-14015

Sienkiewicz, Henryk, 1846-1916.   • **3.6052**
Portrait of America; letters. Edited & translated by Charles Morley. — New York: Columbia University Press, 1959. xix, 300 p.: illus.; 23 cm. Translation of selections from Listy z podrozy do Ameryki. 1. United States — Description and travel — 1865-1900 I. T.
E168.S5763   917.3   *LC* 59-7371

United States. National Archives and Records Service.   **3.6053**
The American image: photographs from the National Archives, 1860–1960 / Exhibitions staff, Office of Educational Programs, National Archives and Records Service. General Services Administration; with an introd. by Alan Trachtenberg. — 1st ed. — New York: Pantheon Books, c1979. xxxii, 191 p.: all ill.; 22 x 28 cm. 1. United States. National Archives — Photograph collections — Catalogs. 2. United States — Description and travel — Views — Catalogs. 3. United States — History — 1865- — Pictorial works — Catalogs. I. T.
E168.U565 1979   016.973/022/2   *LC* 79-1878   *ISBN* 0394507983

Webb, Beatrice Potter, 1858-1943.   • **3.6054**
Beatrice Webb's American diary, 1898 / edited by David A. Shannon. — Madison: University of Wisconsin Press, 1963. xv, 181 p.: ill. 1. Webb, Beatrice Potter, 1858-1943. 2. Webb, Beatrice Potter, 1858-1943. 3. Municipal goverment — United States 4. United States — Description and travel — 1865-1900 I. T. II. Title: American diary, 1898.
E168.W4   *LC* 63-8436

Cooke, Alistair, 1908-.   • **3.6055**
One man's America. [1st American ed.] New York, Knopf, 1952. 268 p. illus. 22 cm. Twenty—nine of a series of weekly talks to Britain called Letters from America, broadcast by the British Broadcasting Corp. and first published in London in 1951 under title: Letters from America. 1. United States. I. Letters from America (Radio program) II. T.
E169.C75 1952   917.3   *LC* 52-7542

Down & out in the Great Depression: letters from the 'forgotten   **3.6056**
man' / edited by Robert S. McElvaine.
Chapel Hill: University of North Carolina Press, c1983. xvii, 251 p.: ill.; 24 cm. 1. Depressions — 1929 — United States — Sources. 2. United States — Social life and customs — 1918-1945 — Sources. 3. United States — Social conditions — 1933-1945 — Sources. I. McElvaine, Robert S., 1947- II. Title: Down and Out in the Great Depression.
E169.D746 1983   973.91 19   *LC* 82-7022   *ISBN* 0807815349

First–person America / edited and with an introd. by Ann   **3.6057**
Banks.
1st ed. — New York: Knopf: distributed by Random House, 1980. xxv, 287 p.: ill.; 25 cm. Eighty narratives originally recorded by members of the Federal Writers' Project. Includes index. 1. Oral history 2. United States — Social life and customs — 1865-1918 3. United States — Biography 4. United States — Social life and customs — 1918-1945 I. Banks, Ann. II. Federal Writers' Project.
E169.F56   973.91   *LC* 80-7660   *ISBN* 0394413970

Gunther, John, 1901-1970.   • **3.6058**
Inside U.S.A. / by John Gunther. — Rev. ed. — New York: Harper, 1951. 1121 p.: ill. 1. United States — Description and travel — 1940-1960 I. T.
E169.G97 1951   917.3   *LC* 51-13816

Stearns, Harold, 1891-1943. ed.   • **3.6059**
Civilization in the United States: an inquiry by thirty Americans. Westport, Conn., Greenwood Press [1971] viii, 577 p. 23 cm. Reprint of the 1922 ed. 1. United States — Civilization — 1918-1945 I. T.
E169.S78 1971   917.3/03/913   *LC* 71-109977   *ISBN* 0837144833

White, C. Langdon (Charles Langdon), 1897-.   • **3.6060**
Regional geography of Anglo–America / [by] C. Langdon White, Edwin J. Foscue [and] Tom L. McKnight. — 3d ed. Englewood Cliffs, N.J.: Prentice-Hall [1964] xvii, 524 p.: ill., maps; 26 cm. 1. United States — Description and travel 2. Canada — Description and travel I. T.
E169.W54 1964   917   *LC* 64-10071

Wilson, Edmund, 1895-1972.   • **3.6061**
The American earthquake: a documentary of the twenties and thirties. — New York: Octagon Books, 1971 [c1958] 576 p.; 22 cm. 1. United States — Civilization — Addresses, essays, lectures. I. T.
E169.W658 1971   917.3/03/91   *LC* 78-139823

The American dimension: cultural myths and social realities /   **3.6062**
[edited by] W. Arens, Susan P. Montague.
Port Washington, N.Y.: Alfred Pub. Co., c1976. xvii, 221 p.; 23 cm. 1. Ethnology — United States — Addresses, essays, lectures. 2. United States — Social life and customs — 1971- — Addresses, essays, lectures. I. Arens, W., 1940- II. Montague, Susan P., 1942-
E169.02.A6483   301.29/73   *LC* 76-2411   *ISBN* 0882840304 pbk

12 photographers of the American social landscape / Bruce   • **3.6063**
Davidson ...[et al].
New York: October House, 1967. — [8] p., [48] p. of plates: ill.; 24 cm. 1. Photography, Artistic I. Davidson, Bruce, 1933- II. Rose Art Museum. III. Brandeis University. Poses Institute of Fine Arts. IV. Title: Twelve photographers of the American social landscape.
E169.02.B7   E169.02 B7.   917.3/03/921   *LC* 67-2298

Haas, Ernst, 1921-.   **3.6064**
In America / Ernst Haas. — New York: Viking Press, 1975. 144 p.: 105 col. ill.; 24 x 34 cm. — (A Studio book) 1. United States — Description and travel — 1960-1980 — Views. I. T.
E169.02.H28 1975   973.92/022/2   *LC* 75-9597   *ISBN* 0670394637

Life in rural America / [contributing authors: Clay Anderson   **3.6065**
and others]; prepared by the Special Publications Division,
National Geographic Society.
Washington: [National Geographic Society, 1974] 207 p.: ill.; 27 cm. A collection of essays by various authors. 1. United States — Social life and customs — 1945- 2. United States — Rural conditions I. Breeden, Robert, ed. II. National Geographic Society (U.S.). Special Publications Division.
E169.02.L43   917.3/03/92   *LC* 74-1562   *ISBN* 0870441469

Miller, Douglas T.   **3.6066**
The fifties: the way we really were / Douglas T. Miller and Marion Nowak. 1st ed. — Garden City, N.Y.: Doubleday, 1977. 444 p., [10] leaves of plates: ill.; 22 cm. Includes index. 1. United States — Social life and customs — 1945-1970 2. United States — Social conditions — 1945- I. Nowak, Marion, 1948- joint author. II. T.
E169.02.M485   973.92   *LC* 75-36602   *ISBN* 0385112483

Wolfe, Tom.   • **3.6067**
The pump house gang. — New York: Farrar, Straus & Giroux, [1968] x, 309 p.: illus.; 22 cm. 1. Social status 2. United States — Social life and customs — 1945- 3. England — Social life and customs — 20th century I. T.
E169.02.W6   917.3/03/923   *LC* 67-10922

E169.1 Civilization. Intellectual Life

E169.1 A–B

Adams, James Truslow, 1878-1949.   • **3.6068**
The American: the making of a new man / by James Truslow Adams. — New York: C. Scribner's sons, 1943. ix, 404 p. 1. National characteristics, American 2. United States — History I. T.
E169.1.A2   *LC* 43-51259

Adams, James Truslow, 1878-1949.   • **3.6069**
Our business civilization: some aspects of American culture. — New York: AMS Press, [1969] ix, 9-306 p.; 23 cm. Reprint of the 1929 ed. 1. National characteristics, American 2. U.S. — Civilization — 1918-1945. 3. U.S. — Social conditions — 1918-1932. I. T.
E169.1.A216 1969   917.3/03/16   *LC* 75-92608

Allen, Frederick Lewis, 1890-1954.   • **3.6070**
The big change: America transforms itself, 1900–1950. [1st ed.] New York, Harper [1952] 308 p. 22 cm. 1. United States — Civilization — 20th century 2. United States — Economic conditions — 1918-1945 3. United States — Social conditions — 1918-1932 4. United States — Social conditions — 1933-1945 I. T.
E169.1.A4717   973.91   *LC* 52-8455

American Academy of Arts and Sciences, Boston. Commission on the Year 2000. • 3.6071
Toward the year 2000; work in progress. Edited by Daniel Bell. — Boston: Houghton Mifflin Co., 1968. ix, 400 p.; 24 cm. — (The Dædalus library, v. 11) 'With the exception of 'Violence' by James Q. Wilson, which is published here for the first time, the essays in this book appeared in the summer 1967 issue of Dædalus, the journal of the American Academy of Arts and Sciences.' 1. Twenty-first century — Forecasts 2. United States — History — Prophecies — Addresses, essays, lectures. I. Bell, Daniel. ed. II. Dædalus. III. T.
E169.1.A47192   973   LC 68-17173

The American self: myth, ideology, and popular culture / edited by Sam B. Girgus. 3.6072
1st ed. — Albuquerque: University of New Mexico Press, c1981. x, 248 p.; 24 cm. 1. National characteristics, American — Addresses, essays, lectures. 2. United States — Civilization — Addresses, essays, lectures. 3. United States — Popular culture — Addresses, essays, lectures. I. Girgus, Sam B., 1941-
E169.1.A482   973 19   LC 80-52281   ISBN 0826305571

American Studies Association. • 3.6073
American perspectives: the national self–image in the twentieth century. / Edited by Robert E. Spiller and Eric Larrabee; associate editors: Ralph Henry Gabriel, Henry Nash Smith [and] Edward N. Waters. Cambridge: Harvard University Press, 1961. vii, 216 p. (Library of Congress series in American civilization) 1. National characteristics, American 2. United States — Intellectual life 3. United States — Economic policy I. Spiller, Robert Ernest, 1896- II. Larrabee, Eric. III. T. IV. Series.
E169.1.A49   LC 61-8841

Baritz, Loren, 1928-. • 3.6074
City on a hill; a history of ideas and myths in America. — New York: Wiley, [1964] xi, 367 p.: ports.; 24 cm. 1. Philosophy, American 2. United States — Intellectual life I. T.
E169.1.B225   917.3   LC 64-25896

Barker, Charles Albro, 1904-. • 3.6075
American convictions; cycles of public thought, 1600–1850, by Charles A. Barker. — [1st ed.]. — Philadelphia: Lippincott, [1970] xix, 632 p.: illus., ports.; 25 cm. 1. U.S. — Intellectual life. 2. U.S. — Religion. 3. U.S. — Civilization — To 1783. 4. U.S. — Civilization — 1783-1865. I. T.
E169.1.B228   917.3/03   LC 69-16960

Beard, Charles Austin, 1874-1948. • 3.6076
America in midpassage / by Charles A. Beard & Mary R. Beard. Drawings by Wilfred Jones. — Gloucester, Mass.: P. Smith, 1966, [c1939] 977 p.: ill.; 21 cm. Vol. 3 of the authors' The rise of American civilization. 1. United States — Civilization — 1918-1945 2. United States — History — 20th century I. Beard, Mary Ritter, 1876-1958. II. T.
E169.1.B282   LC 66-3464

Beard, Charles Austin, 1874-1948. • 3.6077
The American spirit, a study of the idea of civilization in the United States, by Charles A. Beard and Mary R. Beard. New York, The Macmillan company, 1942. vii p., 2 l., 696 p. 22 cm. Vol. 4 of the authors' The rise of American civilization. 1. Civilization — Philosophy 2. United States — Civilization I. Beard, Mary Ritter, 1876-1958. joint author. II. T.
E169.1.B285   LC 42-50003

Beard, Charles Austin, 1874-1948. 3.6078
The rise of American civilization. New York, The Macmillan company, 1927. 2 v. fronts., illus. 23 cm. 1. United States — Civilization 2. United States — History I. Beard, Mary Ritter, 1876-1958. joint author. II. T.
E169.1.B32   LC 27-9541

Bellah, Robert Neelly, 1927-. 3.6079
The broken covenant: American civil religion in a time of trial / Robert N. Bellah. — New York: Seabury Press, [1975] xvi, 172 p.; 21 cm. 'A Crossroad book.' 'The Weil lectures at Hebrew Union College/Jewish Institute of Religion in Cincinnati in the fall of 1971.' 1. Civil religion — United States — Addresses, essays, lectures. 2. United States — Religion — Addresses, essays, lectures. 3. United States — Moral conditions — Addresses, essays, lectures. 4. United States — Civilization — Addresses, essays, lectures. I. T.
E169.1.B435   917.3/03   LC 74-19479   ISBN 0816411611

Berman, Ronald. • 3.6080
America in the sixties: an intellectual history. — New York: Free Press, [1968] ix, 291 p.; 21 cm. 1. United States — Intellectual life I. T.
E169.1.B49   917.3/03/92   LC 68-10365

Bowers, David Freick, 1906- ed. • 3.6081
Foreign influences in American life; essays and critical bibliographies / edited for the Princeton program of study in American civilization. — New York: P. Smith, 1952 [c1944]. 254 p. (Princeton studies in American civilization) 1. Immigrants — United States 2. United States — Civilization 3. United States — Nationality. I. Princeton University. Program of Study in American Civilization. II. T. III. Series.
E169.1.B65

Bloom, Allan David, 1930-. 3.6082
The closing of the American mind / Allan Bloom. — New York: Simon and Schuster, c1987. 392 p. Includes index. Opposite t.p.: How higher education has failed democracy and impoverished the souls of today's students. 1. Education, Higher — United States — Philosophy. 2. United States — Intellectual life — 20th century I. T.
E169.1.B653 1987   973.92 19   LC 86-24768   ISBN 0671479903

Bode, Carl, 1911-. • 3.6083
The anatomy of American popular culture, 1840–1861. Berkeley, University of California Press, 1959. 292 p. illus. 24 cm. Includes bibliography. 1. United States — Civilization 2. United States — Intellectual life I. T.
E169.1.B657   917.3   LC 59-8759

Boorstin, Daniel J. (Daniel Joseph), 1914-. • 3.6084
America and the image of Europe: reflections on American thought. — New York: Meridian Books [1960] 192 p.; 19 cm. (Meridian books, M89) 1. National characteristics, American 2. United States — Civilization 3. United States — Relations — Foreign countries I. T.
E169.1.B75   917.3   LC 60-6769

Boorstin, Daniel J. (Daniel Joseph), 1914-. 3.6085
The Americans: the democratic experience [by] Daniel J. Boorstin. [1st ed.] New York, Random House [1973] xiv, 717 p. 25 cm. Final volume in a trilogy; the first of which is the author's The Americans: the colonial experience; and the second of which is his The Americans: the national experience. 1. United States — Civilization 2. United States — Economic conditions I. T.
E169.1.B7513   917.3/03/92   LC 73-3449   ISBN 0394487249

Boorstin, Daniel J. (Daniel Joseph), 1914-. • 3.6086
The image; or, What happened to the American dream. [1st ed.] New York, Atheneum, 1962 [c1961] 315 p. 22 cm. 1. National characteristics, American 2. United States — Civilization — 1945- I. T.
E169.1.B752   917.3   LC 62-7936

Brogan, Denis William. • 3.6087
America in the modern world / D.W. Brogan. — New Brunswick, N.J.: Rutgers University Press, 1960. 117 p.; 22 cm. 1. National characteristics, American 2. United States — Civilization 3. United States — Relations — Foreign countries I. T.
E169.1. B7968   LC 59-13541

Brogan, D. W. (Denis William), 1900-1974. • 3.6088
The American character, by D. W. Brogan. New York, A. A. Knopf, 1944. xxi, 168, [2] p. 22 cm. 'First edition.' 1. National characteristics, American I. T.
E169.1.B797   917.3   LC 44-8534

Bryce, James Bryce, Viscount, 1838-1922. • 3.6089
Reflections on American institutions: selections from the American Commonwealth / by James Bryce; with an introd. by Henry Steele Commager. — Greenwich, Conn.: Fawcett Publications, 1961. 272 p. 1. United States — Civilization — 1865-1918 I. T.
E169.1.B893   LC 61-66422

Burns, Edward McNall, 1897-. • 3.6090
The American idea of mission; concepts of national purpose and destiny. — New Brunswick, N. J., Rutgers University Press, 1957. 385 p. illus. 25 cm. Includes bibliography. 1. U.S. — Civilization. 2. National characteristics, American 3. U.S. — Hist. — Philosophy. I. T.
E169.1.B943   917.3   LC 57-10961

Bush, Clive. 3.6091
The dream of reason: American consciousness and cultural achievement from Independence to the Civil War / Clive Bush. — New York: St. Martin's Press, 1978, c1977. xi, 397 p.: ill.; 25 cm. Includes index. 1. Natural history — United States — History. 2. American literature — 1783-1850 — History and criticism. 3. United States in art. 4. United States — Intellectual life — 1783-1865 I. T.
E169.1.B975 1978   973 19   LC 77-93574   ISBN 0312219601

E169.1 C–F

Carter, Paul Allen, 1926-. 3.6092
Another part of the twenties / Paul A. Carter. — New York: Columbia University Press, 1977. xiii, 229 p.; 24 cm. Includes index. 1. United States — Civilization — 1918-1945 I. T.
E169.1.C284   973.91   LC 76-27679   ISBN 0231041349

Changing patterns in American civilization / by Dixon Wecter • 3.6093
[and others]; pref. by Robert E. Spiller.
Philadelphia: Univ. of Pennsylvania Press, 1949. xi, 176 p.; 23 cm. 1. United
States — Civilization I. Wecter, Dixon, 1906-1950.
E169.1.C445   *LC* 49-3802

Chase, Richard Volney, 1914-1962. • 3.6094
The democratic vista: a dialogue on life and letters in contemporary America /
by Richard Chase. — Garden City, N.Y.: Doubleday, 1958. x, 180 p. —
(Doubleday anchor books) 1. United States — Civilization I. T.
E169.1.C452   *LC* 58-7351

Commager, Henry Steele, 1902- ed. • 3.6095
America in perspective; the United States through foreign eyes. Ed., with an
introd. and notes, by Henry Steele Commager. — New York, Random House
[1947] xxiv, 389 p. 22 cm. Bibliography: p. [387]-389. 1. U.S. — Civilization.
2. National characteristics, American I. T.
E169.1.C67   917.3   *LC* 47-6240 *

Commager, Henry Steele, 1902-. • 3.6096
The American mind: an interpretation of American thought and character
since the 1880's. — New Haven: Yale University Press, 1950. ix, 476 p.: port.;
24 cm. 1. National characteristics, American 2. United States — Civilization
3. United States — Intellectual life — 1865-1918 4. United States —
Intellectual life — 20th century I. T.
E169.1.C673   917.3   *LC* 50-6338

Crunden, Robert Morse. 3.6097
From self to society, 1919–1941 [by] Robert M. Crunden. — Englewood Cliffs,
N.J.: Prentice-Hall, [1972] xii, 212 p.; 21 cm. — (Transitions in American
thought series) (A Spectrum book) 1. U.S. — Intellectual life. I. T.
E169.1.C836   309.1/73/091   *LC* 78-168740   *ISBN* 0133314219

The Cultural migration: the European scholar in America / by • 3.6098
Franz L. Neumann ... [et al.]; introd. by W. Rex Crawford.
Philadelphia: University of Pennsylvania Press, 1953. 156 p.; 23 cm. —
(University of Pennsylvania. Benjamin Franklin lectures; 1952.) 1. United
States — Intellectual life — 20th century — Addresses, essays, lectures.
2. Europe — Intellectual life — Addresses, essays, lectures. I. Neumann,
Franz.
E169.1.C84 1953   973.9   *LC* 53-6930

Curti, Merle Eugene, 1897-. • 3.6099
American paradox: the conflict of thought and action. — New Brunswick, N.J.:
Rutgers University Press, 1956. 116 p. 1. Intellectuals 2. United States —
Civilization I. T.
E169.1.C86

Curti, Merle. • 3.6100
The growth of American thought / by Merle Curti. — 3d ed. — New York:
Harper & Row, 1964. xx, 939p. [5] leaves of plates: ill., facsims., ports.; 22 cm.
1. United States — Intellectual life 2. United States — Civilization I. T.
E169.1.C87 1964   *LC* 64-12796

Curti, Merle Eugene, 1897-. 3.6101
Human nature in American thought: a history / Merle Curti. — Madison:
University of Wisconsin Press, 1980. xvii, 453 p.; 24 cm. 1. Man 2. United
States — Intellectual life I. T.
E169.1.C877   973   *LC* 79-3965   *ISBN* 0299079708

Curti, Merle Eugene, 1897-. • 3.6102
Probing our past. New York, Harper [c1955] 294 p. 22cm. Essays. 1. United
States — Intellectual life — Addresses, essays, lectures 2. United States —
Historiography 3. United States — Relations — Foreign countries I. T.
E169.1 C885   *LC* 54-11009

Curti, Merle Eugene, 1897-. • 3.6103
The roots of American loyalty, by Merle Curti. — New York: Atheneum, 1968
[c1946] xvi, 267 p.; 21 cm. — (Atheneum 115) 1. Patriotism — U.S. 2. U.S. —
History. I. T.
E169.1.C89 1968   973   *LC* 68-16409

Davidson, Donald, 1893-1968. • 3.6104
The attack on leviathan: regionalism and nationalism in the United States. —
Chapel Hill: The University of North Carolina press, 1938. x, 368 p.; 23 cm.
1. Sectionalism (United States) 2. United States — Nationality. 3. United
States — Civilization I. T. II. Title: Regionalism and nationalism in the
United States.
E169.1.D34   *LC* 38-9614

Dudden, Arthur Power, 1921-. • 3.6105
The United States of America, a syllabus of American studies. — Philadelphia:
University of Pennsylvania Press, 1963. 2 v.: ill. 1. United States — Civilization
— Outlines, syllabi, etc. I. T.
E169.1 D82   *LC* 63-5574

Echeverria, Durand. • 3.6106
Mirage in the West; a history of the French image of American society to 1815.
Foreword by Gilbert Chinard. New York, Octagon Books, 1966 [c1957] xvii,
300 p. 24 cm. 1. United States — Civilization 2. United States — Foreign
opinion, French. 3. United States — Relations — France 4. France —
Relations — United States I. T.
E169.1.E23 1966   917.3   *LC* 66-17509

Ekirch, Arthur Alphonse, 1915-. • 3.6107
The civilian and the military. — New York, Oxford University Press, 1956.
340 p. 24 cm. Includes bibliography. 1. Militarism — U.S. 2. Civil supremacy
over the military — U.S. I. T.
E169.1.E49   973   *LC* 56-5160

Fiedler, Leslie A. • 3.6108
An end to innocence: essays on culture and politics. — Boston: Beacon Press,
[1955] 214 p.; 21 cm. 1. United States — Civilization — Addresses, essays,
lectures. 2. United States — Politics and government — 1945- — Addresses,
essays, lectures. I. T.
E169.1.F5   973.9204*   *LC* 55-7798

Fishwick, Marshall William. 3.6109
Common culture and the great tradition: the case for renewal / Marshall W.
Fishwick. — Westport, Conn.: Greenwood Press, 1982. x, 230 p.: port.; 22 cm.
— (Contributions to the study of popular culture. 0198-9871; no. 2) Includes
index. 1. Popular culture 2. United States — Popular culture I. T. II. Series.
E169.1.F544 1982   973 19   *LC* 81-4232   *ISBN* 0313230420

Fleming, Donald, 1923-. • 3.6110
The intellectual migration; Europe and America, 1930–1960, edited by Donald
Fleming and Bernard Bailyn. Cambridge, Belknap Press of Harvard University
Press, 1969. 748 p. illus. 24 cm. 'An expansion of the second volume of
Perspectives in American history, an annual journal.'—book jacket.
1. Intellectuals — United States. 2. Refugees, Political — United States.
3. United States — Civilization — Foreign influences 4. Europe — Emigration
and immigration. I. Bailyn, Bernard. joint author. II. Perspectives in
American history. III. T.
E169.1.F6   001.2/0973   *LC* 78-75432

Frank, Waldo David, 1889-1967. • 3.6111
The re–discovery of America; an introduction to a philosophy of American life.
New York C. Scribner's sons 1929. 353p. 1. United States — Civilization I. T.
E169.1 F83

E169.1 G–L

Gabriel, Ralph Henry, 1890-1987. • 3.6112
The course of American democratic thought. — 2d ed. — New York: Ronald
Press Co., [1956] xiv, 508 p.; 24 cm. 1. Philosophy, American 2. Philosophy —
History — United States. 3. Democracy 4. United States — Civilization
5. United States — Intellectual life I. T.
E169.1.G23 1956   917.3   *LC* 56-6263

Greene, Theodore P., 1921-. • 3.6113
America's heroes: the changing models of success in American magazines / [by]
Theodore P. Greene. — New York: Oxford University Press, 1970. vi, 387 p.;
22 cm. The periodicals covered were published between 1757 and 1918
inclusive. 1. American periodicals — History. 2. Heroes in literature
3. United States — Social life and customs 4. United States — Intellectual life
I. T.
E169.1.G754   051   *LC* 70-117214

Guttmann, Allen. • 3.6114
The conservative tradition in America. — New York: Oxford University Press,
1967. viii, 214 p.; 22 cm. 1. Conservatism — United States. 2. United States —
Civilization I. T.
E169.1.G97   917.3/03   *LC* 67-25460

Handbook of American popular culture / edited by M. Thomas   3.6115
Inge.
Westport, Conn.: Greenwood Press, 1978-1981. 3 v.; 24 cm. 1. United States —
Popular culture 2. United States — Popular culture — Sources. 3. United
States — Popular culture — Bibliography. I. Inge, M. Thomas.
E169.1.H2643   301.2/1   *LC* 77-95357   *ISBN* 0313203253

Handlin, Oscar. • 3.6116
The American people in the twentieth century / by Oscar Handlin. — Boston:
Beacon Press, 1963. vi, 248 p.; 21 cm. Includes index. 1. Minorities — United
States 2. United States — Civilization — 20th century I. T.
E169.1.H265 1963   917.3   *LC* 63-2687

Hartshorne, Thomas L.   • **3.6117**
The distorted image; changing conceptions of the American character since
Turner [by] Thomas L. Hartshorne. — Cleveland: Press of Case Western
Reserve University, 1968. xiv, 226 p.; 24 cm. 1. National characteristics,
American I. T. II. Title: Changing conceptions of the American character
since Turner.
E169.1.H278   917.3/03/92   *LC* 68-9429   *ISBN* 082950141X

Hearn, Charles R.   **3.6118**
The American dream in the Great Depression / Charles R. Hearn. Westport,
Conn.: Greenwood Press, 1977. x, 222 p.; 22 cm. (Contributions in American
studies; no. 28) Includes index. 1. American literature — 20th century —
History and criticism. 2. Depressions — 1929 — United States 3. United
States — Civilization — 1918-1945 I. T.
E169.1.H32   973.9   *LC* 76-56623   *ISBN* 0837194784

Hofstadter, Richard, 1916-1970.   • **3.6119**
Anti–intellectualism in American life. — [1st ed.]. — New York: Knopf, 1963.
434, xiii p.; 25 cm. 1. Intellectuals — United States. 2. United States —
Civilization I. T.
E169.1.H74   917.3   *LC* 63-14086

Jones, Howard Mumford, 1892-.   • **3.6120**
The age of energy: varieties of American experience, 1865–1915. — New York:
Viking Press, [1971] xix, 545 p.: ill.; 23 cm. 1. U.S. — Civilization —
1865-1918. I. T.
E169.1.J6435 1971   917.3/03/8   *LC* 75-146599   *ISBN* 0670109665

Jones, Howard Mumford, 1892-.   • **3.6121**
O strange new world; American culture: the formative years. — New York:
Viking Press, [1964] xiv, 464 p.: illus., facsim.; 23 cm. 1. United States —
Civilization — To 1783 2. United States — Civilization — 1783-1865
3. United States — Civlization — European influences. I. T.
E169.1.J644 1964   917.3   *LC* 64-15062

Kaplan, Abraham, 1918-.   • **3.6122**
American ethics and public policy / with corrections. — New York: Oxford
University, 1963. 110 p. (Galaxy book) Originally published in The American
style:essays in value and performance,edited by Elting Morison." 'GB99.'
1. National characteristics, American 2. Political ethics I. T.
E169.1.K315   172   *LC* 63-5685

Ketcham, Ralph Louis, 1927-.   **3.6123**
From colony to country: the Revolution in American thought, 1750–1820 [by]
Ralph Ketcham. — New York: Macmillan, [1974] xiv, 318 p.; 24 cm. 1. United
States — Intellectual life I. T.
E169.1.K417   917.3/03/3   *LC* 73-18763   *ISBN* 0025629301

Kirk, Russell.   • **3.6124**
The American cause. -- Chicago: H. Regnery Co., 1957. 172 p.
1. Communism 2. United States — Civilization 3. United States —
Philosophy. I. T.
E169.1 K55

Knoles, George Harmon.   • **3.6125**
The jazz age revisited: British criticism of American civilization during the
1920's. — Stanford, Calif.: Stanford University Press, 1955. vii, 171 p.; 22 cm.
(Stanford University publications. University series: history, economics, and
political science, v. 11) 1. National characteristics, American 2. United States
— Civilization — 1918-1945 3. United States — Foreign opinion, British. I. T.
E169.1.K6 1955   917.3/03/91   *LC* 55-10016

Kohn, Hans, 1891-1971.   • **3.6126**
American nationalism; an interpretative essay. New York, Macmillan, 1957.
272 p. 22 cm. Includes bibliography. 1. National characteristics, American
2. Nationalism — United States. 3. Nationalism 4. United States —
Civilization — History. I. T.
E169.1.K63   917.3   *LC* 57-8101

Kraus, Michael, 1901-.   • **3.6127**
Intercolonial aspects of American culture on the eve of the Revolution: with
special reference to the northern towns. — New York: Octagon Books, 1964
[c1928] 251 p.; 24 cm. Bibliography: p. 227-244. 1. United States —
Civilization — To 1783 I. T. II. Title: American culture on the eve of the
Revolution.
E169.1.K688 1964   917.3   *LC* 64-24838

Laski, Harold Joseph, 1893-1950.   • **3.6128**
American democracy: a commentary and an interpretation. New York: Viking,
1948. x, 785 p.; 25 cm. 1. United States — Civilization 2. United States —
Politics and government 3. United States — Social conditions I. T.
E169.1.L38 1948   *LC* 48-2654

Lears, T. J. Jackson, 1947-.   **3.6129**
No place of grace: antimodernism and the transformation of American culture,
1880–1920 / T.J. Jackson Lears. — 1st ed. — New York: Pantheon Books,

c1981. xx, 375 p.; 24 cm. 1. United States — Civilization — 1865-1918
2. United States — Intellectual life I. T.
E169.1.L48 1981   973.8 19   *LC* 81-47200   *ISBN* 0394508165

Leighton, Isabel, ed.   • **3.6130**
The aspirin age, 1919–1941 / written by Samuel Hopkins Adams [and others].
— New York: Simon and Schuster, 1949. ix, 491 p.; 22 cm. 1. United States —
Civilization I. T.
E169.1.L526   917.3   *LC* 49-9336

Lerner, Max, 1902-.   • **3.6131**
America as a civilization: life and thought in the United States today. — New
York: Simon and Schuster, 1957. xiii, 1036 p.; 25 cm. 1. National
characteristics, American 2. United States — Civilization I. T.
E169.1.L532   917.3   *LC* 57-10979

Lipset, Seymour Martin.   • **3.6132**
The first new Nation; the United States in historical and comparative
perspective. — New York: Basic Books, [1963] xv, 366 p.; 25 cm. 1. National
characteristics, American 2. Comparative government 3. United States —
Civilization I. T.
E169.1.L546   917.3   *LC* 63-17345

Lukacs, John, 1924-.   **3.6133**
Outgrowing democracy: a history of the United States in the twentieth century
/ by John Lukacs. — 1st ed. — Garden City, N.Y.: Doubleday, 1984. viii,
423 p.; 24 cm. 1. United States — Civilization — 20th century 2. United States
— Civilization — 1865-1918 3. United States — Politics and government —
20th century 4. United States — Politics and government — 1865-1900 I. T.
E169.1.L855 1984   973.91 19   *LC* 81-43553   *ISBN* 0385175388

Lynes, Russell, 1910-.   • **3.6134**
The tastemakers. [1st ed. New York]: Harper, [1954] 362 p.: ill.; 25 cm.
1. Aesthetics 2. Art — United States. 3. United States — Civilization — 20th
century 4. United States — Social life and customs — 1945- I. T.
E169.1.L95   701/.03/0973 19   *LC* 54-8968

E169.1 M–N

Macdonald, Dwight.   • **3.6135**
Against the American grain. — New York: Random House, [1962] 427 p.; 22
cm. Essays. 1. United States — Popular culture I. T.
E169.1.M136   917.3   *LC* 62-17170

Marx, Leo, 1919-.   • **3.6136**
The machine in the garden; technology and the pastoral ideal in America. —
New York: Oxford University Press, 1964. 392 p.: illus.; 21 cm. 1. Nature
2. United States — Civilization I. T. II. Title: Technology and the pastoral
ideal in America.
E169.1.M35   917.3   *LC* 64-24864

Material culture studies in America / compiled and edited, with   **3.6137**
introductions and bibliography, by Thomas J. Schlereth.
Nashville, Tenn.: American Association for State and Local History, c1982.
xvi, 419 p.; 24 cm. Includes index. 1. Material culture — United States —
Study and teaching — Addresses, essays, lectures. 2. Material culture —
United States — Addresses, essays, lectures. 3. Archaeology and history —
United States — Addresses, essays, lectures. 4. United States — Civilization —
Study and teaching — Addresses, essays, lectures. 5. United States — Social
life and customs — Study and teaching — Addresses, essays, lectures.
6. United States — Civilization — Addresses, essays, lectures. 7. United States
— Social life and customs — Addresses, essays, lectures. 8. United States —
Industries — Addresses, essays, lectures. I. Schlereth, Thomas J.
E169.1.M416 1982   306/.0973 19   *LC* 82-8812   *ISBN* 0910050678

May, Henry Farnham, 1915-.   • **3.6138**
The end of American innocence: a study of the first years of our own time,
1912–1917. — [1st ed.] New York: Knopf, 1959. 412 p.; 22 cm. 1. United
States — Intellectual life — 20th century 2. United States — Civilization —
1865-1918 I. T.
E169.1.M496   917.3   *LC* 59-11236

Mead, Margaret, 1901-1978.   • **3.6139**
And keep your powder dry: an anthropologist looks at America. — Freeport,
N.Y.: Books for Libraries Press [1971, c1965] x, 274 p.; 23 cm. (Essay index
reprint series) 1. National characteristics, American I. T.
E169.1.M5 1971   917.3/03/917   *LC* 77-156694   *ISBN* 0836924169

Miller, Perry, 1905-1963.   • **3.6140**
The life of the mind in America: from the Revolution to the Civil War / Perry
Miller. — New York: Harcourt, Brace & World, [1965] xi, 338 p.; 24 cm. — (A

Harvest book) Contains books 1-2, and part of book 3, of a work intended to be complete in 9 books. The parts after book 3, chapter 1, were never completed. 1. United States — Intellectual life 2. United States — Civilization — 1783-1865 I. T.
E169.1.M6273   917.303   *LC* 65-19065

Miller, Perry, 1905-1963.   • **3.6141**
Errand into the wilderness. Cambridge, Belknap Press of Harvard University Press, 1956. x, 244 p. 24 cm. 1. Philosophy, American — 18th century 2. United States — Religion — To 1800 3. United States — Civilization I. T.
E169.1.M628   917.3   *LC* 56-11285

Miller, Perry, 1905-1963.   • **3.6142**
Nature's nation. Cambridge: Belknap Press of Harvard University Press, 1967. xvi, 298 p.; 24 cm. 1. Philosophy, American 2. United States — Intellectual life 3. United States — Religion I. T.
E169.1.M635   *LC* 67-17316

Miller, Raymond Curtis. ed.   • **3.6143**
Twentieth–century pessimism and the American dream. — Detroit: Wayne State University Press, 1961. 104 p.: ill. (The Leo M. Franklin memorial lectures; (1958) v.8) 1. Big business — United States. 2. United States — Civilization 3. United States — Economic conditions I. T. II. Series.
E169.1.M639x

Mills, C. Wright (Charles Wright), 1916-1962.   • **3.6144**
The power elite. New York: Oxford University Press, 1956. 423 p.; 22 cm. 1. Power (Social sciences) 2. Elite (Social sciences) — United States. 3. United States — Social conditions — 1945- I. T.
E169.1.M64   917.3   *LC* 56-5427

Morris, Clarence, 1903- ed.   • **3.6145**
Trends in modern American society / by John M Blum [and others]. — Philadelphia: University of Pennsylvania Press [1962] 191 p.; 22 cm. 1. United States — Civilization — 1945- I. T.
E169.1.M818   *LC* 62-11262

Mumford, Lewis, 1895-.   • **3.6146**
The golden day: a study in American literature and culture ... — Boston: Beacon press, [1957, c1953]. 144 p. (Beacon paperback; no. 38) 1. American literature — 19th century — History and criticism. 2. Culture 3. United States — Civilization 4. United States — Intellectual life I. T.
E169.1 M943   810

Nagel, Paul C.   • **3.6147**
This sacred trust; American nationality, 1798–1898 [by] Paul C. Nagel. — New York: Oxford University Press, 1971. xvi, 376 p.; 22 cm. 1. Nationalism — United States. 2. United States — Civilization — 19th century I. T.
E169.1.N25   973 19   *LC* 78-159648

Nash, Roderick.   **3.6148**
Wilderness and the American mind. — Rev. ed. — New Haven: Yale University Press, [1973] xvi, 300 p.; 21 cm. 1. Frontier and pioneer life — United States. 2. Nature conservation — United States. 3. United States — Civilization I. T.
E169.1.N37 1973   917.3/03   *LC* 72-91303   *ISBN* 0300016484

Niebuhr, Reinhold, 1892-1971.   • **3.6149**
Pious and secular America / Reinhold Niebuhr. — New York: Scribner's, 1958. viii, 150 p.; 23 cm. — Includes index. 1. United States — Civilization — Addresses, essays, lectures. I. T.
E169.1.N67 1977   973   *LC* 58-5721

Noble, David W.   • **3.6150**
The paradox of progressive thought. Minneapolis: University of Minnesota [1958] ix, 272 p.; 23 cm. 1. United States — Intellectual life 2. United States — Biography I. T.
E169.1.N7   917.3   *LC* 58-8765

Nye, Russel Blaine, 1913-.   • **3.6151**
The cultural life of the new Nation, 1776–1830. — [1st ed.]. — New York: Harper, [1960] xii, 324 p.: illus.; 22 cm. — (The New American Nation series) 1. United States — Intellectual life — 1783-1865 2. United States — History — 1783-1865 I. T.
E169.1.N9   973.3   *LC* 60-16496

E169.1 P–Z

Parkes, Henry Bamford, 1904-.   • **3.6152**
The American experience: an interpretation of the history and civilization of the American people. — 2d ed. rev. — New York: Knopf, 1955. 345, viii p.; 22 cm. 1. United States — Civilization I. T.
E169.1.P23 1955   917.3   *LC* 55-3076

Pells, Richard H.   **3.6153**
Radical visions and American dreams; culture and social thought in the Depression years [by] Richard H. Pells. [1st ed.] New York, Harper & Row [1973] xv, 424 p. 25 cm. 1. United States — Intellectual life — 20th century 2. United States — Civilization — 1918-1945 I. T.
E169.1.P42 1973   001.2/0973   *LC* 72-85471   *ISBN* 0060133317

Perry, Lewis, 1938-.   **3.6154**
Intellectual life in America: a history / Lewis Perry. — New York: F. Watts, c1984. xvii, 461 p.; 24 cm. 1. United States — Intellectual life I. T.
E169.1.P446 1984   306/.0973 19   *LC* 83-23544   *ISBN* 0531098265

Perry, Ralph Barton, 1876-1957.   • **3.6155**
Puritanism and democracy / [by] Ralph Barton Perry. — New York: The Vanguard press [1944] xvi, 688 p.; 22 cm. 'References': p. 643-678. 1. United States — Civilization 2. Puritans 3. Democracy I. T.
E169.1.P47   917.3   *LC* 44-41893

Persons, Stow, 1913-.   **3.6156**
The decline of American gentility. — New York: Columbia University Press, 1973. viii, 336 p.; 22 cm. 1. American literature — 19th century — History and criticism. 2. United States — Civilization — 19th century I. T.
E169.1.P476   917.3/03   *LC* 73-534   *ISBN* 0231030150

Perspectives on revolution and evolution / Henry S. Albinski ...   **3.6157**
[et al.]; edited by Richard A. Preston.
Durham, N.C.: Duke University Press, 1979. 300 p.; 24 cm. — (Publication - Duke University Center for Commonwealth and Comparative Studies; no. 46) 1. National characteristics, American — Addresses, essays, lectures. 2. National characteristics, Canadian — Addresses, essays, lectures. 3. United States — Civilization — Addresses, essays, lectures. 4. Canada — Civilization — Addresses, essays, lectures. 5. United States — History — Revolution, 1775-1783 — Influence — Addresses, essays, lectures. I. Albinski, Henry Stephen. II. Preston, Richard Arthur.
E169.1.P477   973   *LC* 78-74448   *ISBN* 0822304252

Peyre, Henri, 1901-.   • **3.6158**
Observations on life, literature, and learning in America. Carbondale: Southern Illinois University Press [1961] 253 p.; 23 cm. 1. Education — United States 2. United States — Civilization — Addresses, essays, lectures. 3. United States — Intellectual life 4. United States — Foreign opinion, French. I. T. II. Title: Life, literature, and learning in America.
E169.1.P5   917.3   *LC* 61-8218

Pierson, George Wilson, 1904-.   **3.6159**
The moving American / [by] George W. Pierson. — [1st ed.]. — New York: Knopf; [distributed by Random House], 1973 (c1972) xii, 290, xiii p.: ill.; 22 cm. 1. National characteristics, American 2. Migration, Internal — United States. I. T.
E169.1.P555   301.32/6/0973   *LC* 72-2259   *ISBN* 0394479343

Pochmann, Henry A. (Henry August), 1901-1973.   • **3.6160**
German culture in America: philosophical and literary influences, 1600–1900 / [by] Henry A. Pochmann; with the assistance of Arthur R. Schultz and others. — Madison: University of Wisconsin Press, 1957. xv, 865 p.; 26 cm. Bibliographical references included in 'Notes' (p. 495-799) 1. U.S. — Civilization — German influences. 2. Literature, Comparative — German and American 3. Literature, Comparative — American and German. I. T.
E169.1.P596   325.2430973   *LC* 55-6791

Potter, David Morris.   • **3.6161**
People of plenty: economic abundance and the American character. — [Chicago]: University of Chicago Press, [1954] xxvii, 219 p.: ill.; 22 cm. — (Charles R. Walgreen Foundation lectures) 1. National characteristics, American 2. United States — Economic conditions I. T.
E169.1.P6   917.3   *LC* 54-12797

Rourke, Constance, 1885-1941.   • **3.6162**
The roots of American culture and other essays / by Constance Rourke; edited, with a preface, by Van Wyck Brooks. — New York: Harcourt, Brace and company [1942] xii p., 1 l., 305 p.; 22 cm. 'First edition'. 1. United States — Civilization I. Brooks, Van Wyck, 1886-1963. ed. II. T.
E169.1.R78   917.3   *LC* 42-19827

Savelle, Max, 1896-. • 3.6163
Seeds of liberty: the genesis of the American mind / by Max Savelle. — Seattle: University of Washington Press, 1965. 618 p.: ill. 1. United States — Civilization — To 1783 I. T.
E169.1.S27 1965   *LC* 65-23913

Schmitt, Peter J. • 3.6164
Back to nature: the Arcadian myth in urban America / [by] Peter J. Schmitt. — New York: Oxford University Press, 1969. xxiii, 230 p.; 22 cm. — (The Urban life in America series) 1. Nature in literature 2. U.S. — Civilization — 1865-1918. I. T.
E169.1.S343   917.3/03/9   *LC* 70-83052

Shi, David E. 3.6165
The simple life: plain living and high thinking in American culture / David E. Shi. — New York: Oxford University Press, 1985. viii, 332 p.; 25 cm. Includes index. 1. National characteristics, American 2. Simplicity 3. United States — Civilization 4. United States — Social life and customs I. T.
E169.1.S556 1985   306/.0973 19   *LC* 84-12212   *ISBN* 0195034759

Siegfried, André, 1875-1959. • 3.6166
America at mid–century / Translated by Margaret Ledésert. — [1st American ed.] New York: Harcourt, Brace [1955] 357 p.: ill.; 22 cm. 1. United States — Civilization I. T.
E169.1.S568   917.3   *LC* 55-7422

Siegfried, André, 1875-1959. • 3.6167
[États-Unis d'aujourd'hui. English] America comes of age: a French analysis / translated by H. H. Hemming and Doris Hemming. — New York: Da Capo Press, 1974 [c1927] x, 358 p.: maps; 23 cm. (The American scene: comments and commentators) Translation of Les États-Unis d'aujourd'hui. Reprint of the ed. published by Harcourt, Brace, New York. 1. United States — Civilization — 1918-1945 2. United States — Race question. 3. United States — Economic conditions — 1918-1945 4. United States — Politics and government — 1901-1953 I. T.
E169.1.S58   917.3/03/91   *LC* 68-16244   *ISBN* 0306710250

Somkin, Fred. • 3.6168
Unquiet eagle; memory and desire in the idea of American freedom, 1815–1860. — Ithaca, N.Y.: Cornell University Press, [1967] xi, 233 p.: facsim.; 23 cm. 1. United States — Civilization — 1783-1865 I. T.
E169.1.S68   917.3/03/5   *LC* 67-23763

Susman, Warren, 1927- comp. 3.6169
Culture and commitment, 1929–1945 / edited with introd. and notes by Warren Susman. — New York: G. Braziller [1973] xi, 372 p.: ill.; 24 cm. (The American culture, 8) 1. United States — Civilization — 1918-1945 — Addresses, essays, lectures. I. T. II. Series.
E169.1.S973 1973   917.3/03/91   *LC* 77-188361   *ISBN* 0807606316
ISBN 0807606308

Torrielli, Andrew Joseph, 1912-. 3.6170
Italian opinion on America as revealed by Italian travelers: 1850–1900 / by Andrew J. Torrielli. — Cambridge, Mass.: Harvard University Press, 1941. vi, 330 p.; 24 cm. (Harvard studies in romance languages, vol. 15) Without thesis note. 1. Civilization, American 2. United States — History I. T. II. Series.
E169.1.T66 1941

Toynbee, Arnold Joseph, 1889-1975. • 3.6171
America and the world revolution and other lectures / Arnold J. Toynbee. — New York: Oxford University Press, 1962. 231 p.; 20 cm. 1. Civilization, Occidental 2. United States — Civilization 3. United States — Foreign relations 4. Latin America — Social conditions I. T.
E169.1.T69   327.73   *LC* 62-19209

Trachtenberg, Alan. 3.6172
The incorporation of America: culture and society in the gilded age / Alan Trachtenberg; consulting editor, Eric Foner. — 1st ed. — New York: Hill and Wang, 1982. viii, 260 p.; 22 cm. — (American century series.) Includes index. 1. United States — Civilization — 1865-1918 I. Foner, Eric. II. T. III. Series.
E169.1.T72 1982   973.8 19   *LC* 81-13339   *ISBN* 0809058278

Weyl, Nathaniel, 1910-. • 3.6173
The creative elite in America. — Washington: Public Affairs Press, 1966. vii, 236 p. 1. Intellectuals — United States. 2. Creation (Literary, artistic, etc.) 3. Jews in the United States — Intellectual life. I. T.
E169.1.W395   301.44   *LC* 66-23828

Wish, Harvey, 1909-. • 3.6174
Society and thought in America. 2d ed. New York, D. McKay Co. [19. v. illus. 22 cm. 1. United States — Civilization 2. United States — Intellectual life I. T.
E169.1.W652   917.3   *LC* 61-18349

Wolfe, Tom. • 3.6175
The kandy–kolored tangerine–flake streamline baby. [New York: Farrar, Straus and Giroux, 1965] xvii, 339 p.: ill.; 22 cm. 1. Social status — United States. 2. United States — Popular culture I. T.
E169.1.W685   309.173   *LC* 65-19050

Wylie, Philip, 1902-1971. • 3.6176
Generation of vipers, newly annotated by the author ... New York, Rinehart [1955] 331 p. 22 cm. 1. National characteristics, American 2. United States — Civilization — 1945- I. T.
E169.1.W9 1955   917.3   *LC* 55-6424

Zelomek, A. Wilbert, 1900-. • 3.6177
A changing America: at work and play. — New York: Wiley [1959] 181 p.; 22 cm. 1. United States — Civilization 2. United States — Social life and customs I. T.
E169.1.Z4   917.3   *LC* 59-6754

E169.12 CIVILIZATION, 1945-

Bell, Daniel. 3.6178
The cultural contradictions of capitalism / Daniel Bell. — New York: Basic Books, [1976] xvi, 301 p.; 25 cm. 1. Technology and civilization 2. United States — Civilization — 1945- 3. United States — Social conditions — 1945- I. T.
E169.12.B37   973.92 19   *LC* 75-7271   *ISBN* 0465015263

Carroll, Peter N. 3.6179
It seemed like nothing happened: the tragedy and promise of America in the 1970s / Peter N. Carroll. — 1st ed. — New York, N.Y.: Holt, Rinehart and Winston, c1982. ix, 421 p.; 24 cm. 'A William Abrahams book.' 1. United States — Civilization — 1970- I. T.
E169.12.C29 1982   973.92 19   *LC* 82-1047   *ISBN* 0030583195

Combs, James E. 3.6180
Polpop: politics and popular culture in America / James Combs. — Bowling Green, Ohio: Bowling Green University Popular Press, c1984. 172 p.; 24 cm. 1. United States — Popular culture — Political aspects. I. T.
E169.12.C576 1984   306/.2/0973 19   *LC* 83-73574   *ISBN* 0879722762

Fishwick, Marshall William. 3.6181
Parameters of popular culture [by] Marshall Fishwick. — Bowling Green, Ohio: Bowling Green University Popular Press, [1974] 175 p.; 23 cm. 1. United States — Popular culture — Addresses, essays, lectures. I. T.
E169.12.F64   917.3/03/9   *LC* 73-89531   *ISBN* 0879720646

Gans, Herbert J. 3.6182
Popular culture and high culture; an analysis and evaluation of taste [by] Herbert J. Gans. — New York: Basic Books, [1975, c1974] xii, 179 p.; 22 cm. 1. United States — Popular culture 2. United States — Intellectual life I. T.
E169.12.G36 1975   301.2/1   *LC* 74-79287   *ISBN* 0465060218

Gilbert, James Burkhart. 3.6183
Another chance: postwar America, 1945–1968 / James Gilbert. — Philadelphia: Temple University Press, 1982 (c1981). x, 307 p.: ill.; 22 cm. Includes index. 1. United States — Civilization — 1945- I. T.
E169.12.G54 1981b   973.92 19   *LC* 81-8916   *ISBN* 087722224X

Jewett, Robert. 3.6184
The American monomyth / by Robert Jewett and John Shelton Lawrence; foreword by Isaac Asimov. 1st ed. — Garden City, N.Y.: Anchor Press, 1977. xxi, 263 p., [12] leaves of plates: ill.; 22 cm. 1. United States — Popular culture I. Lawrence, John Shelton. joint author. II. T.
E169.12.J48   973   *LC* 76-18354   *ISBN* 0385122039

Pells, Richard H. 3.6185
The liberal mind in a conservative age: American intellectuals in the 1940s and 1950s / Richard H. Pells. — 1st ed. — New York: Harper & Row, c1985. xi, 468 p.; 22 cm. Includes index. 1. Intellectuals — United States — Attitudes — History — 20th century. 2. Liberalism — United States — History — 20th century. 3. United States — Intellectual life — 20th century I. T.
E169.12.P45 1985   973.91 19   *LC* 84-47594   *ISBN* 0060153512

Rosenberg, Bernard, 1923- comp. • 3.6186
Mass culture revisited / Edited by Bernard Rosenberg [and] David Manning White. — New York: Van Nostrand Reinhold, [1971] xii, 473 p.; 25 cm. 1. Mass media — U.S. 2. U.S. — Popular culture. I. White, David Manning. joint comp. II. T.
E169.12.R65   301.16/1/0973   *LC* 71-164986

Slater, Philip Elliot.   • 3.6187
The pursuit of loneliness: American culture at the breaking point / [by] Philip
E. Slater. — Boston: Beacon Press, [1970] xiii, 154 p.; 24 cm. 1. National
characteristics, American 2. U.S. — Civilization — 1945- I. T.
E169.12.S53 1970   917.3/03/92   LC 79-101327   ISBN 0807041807

Snowman, Daniel.   3.6188
Britain and America: an interpretation of their culture, 1945–1975 / Daniel
Snowman. — New York: New York University Press, 1977. 342 p.; 23 cm.
1. United States — Civilization — 1945- 2. United States — Civilization —
British influences. 3. Great Britain — Civilization — 1945- 4. Great Britain —
Civilization — American influences I. T.
E169.12 S62 1977b   941/.085   LC 76-56927   ISBN 0814777783

E169.5 AMERICANIZATION

Antin, Mary, 1881-1949.   • 3.6189
The promised land / with a foreword by Oscar Handlin. — 2d ed. Boston:
Houghton Mifflin, 1969 [c1912] xxii, 373 p.; 22 cm. Autobiographical.
1. Antin, Mary, 1881-1949. 2. Antin, Mary, 1881-1949. 3. Jews — United
States — Biography. 4. Jews — Soviet Union — Biography. 5. United States
— Emigration and immigration — Biography I. T.
E169.5.A66 1969   917.3/03/910924 B   LC 74-2734

E171–856 HISTORY

E171–172 Yearbooks. Societies

Directory of historical societies and agencies in the United   • 3.6190
States and Canada.
1956-1961. [Madison, Wis., etc.] American Association for State and Local
History. v. 26 cm. Biennial. 1. United States — History — Societies —
Directories. 2. Canada — History — Societies — Directories. I. American
Association for State and Local History.
E172.A538   970.62   LC 56-4164

Davies, Wallace Evan.   • 3.6191
Patriotism on parade; the story of veterans' and hereditary organizations in
America, 1783–1900. Cambridge, Harvard University Press, 1955. xiv, 388 p.
22 cm. (Harvard historical studies. v. 66) 'Bibliographical essay': p. [359]-367.
Bibliographical footnotes. 1. Patriotic societies I. T. II. Series.
E172.7.D3   369.1   LC 55-11951

E173 Sources. Documents

Bumgardner, Georgia B.   3.6192
American broadsides; sixty facsimiles dated 1680–1800, reproduced from
originals in the American Antiquarian Society. Selected & introduced by
Georgia B. Bumgardner. Barre, Mass., Imprint Society, 1971. 1 v. (unpaged)
facsims. 37 cm. 1. Broadsides — United States. 2. United States — History —
Sources I. American Antiquarian Society. II. T.
E173.B9   917.3/03/2   LC 75-142581   ISBN 0876360177

Commager, Henry Steele, 1902- ed.   3.6193
Documents of American history / edited by Henry Steele Commager. — 9th ed.
— Englewood Cliffs, N.J.: Prentice-Hall, c1973. 2 v.; 24 cm. 1. United States —
History — Sources I. T.
E173.C66 1973c   973   LC 78-113439   ISBN 0132169940

Commager, Henry Steele, 1902-.   • 3.6194
Living ideas in America. — New, enl. ed. New York: Harper & Row, 1964.
872 p. 1. United States — Civilization 2. United States — History — Sources
3. United States — Politics & government. I. T.
E173.C67 1964   LC 64-23898

Emery, Michael C. comp.   • 3.6195
America's front page news, 1690–1970. Edited by Michael C. Emery, R. Smith
Schuneman [and] Edwin Emery. . — Minneapolis: Vis-Com, inc.; trade
distribution: Doubleday, New York; educational multi-media distribution: 3M
IM/Press, St. Paul, [1970] 280 p.; 41 cm. Consists chiefly of facsim.

reproductions of over 300 newspaper front pages, each with an annotation.
1. American newspapers — Facsimiles. 2. U.S. — History — Sources.
I. Schuneman, R. Smith. joint comp. II. Emery, Edwin. joint comp. III. T.
E173.E53   917.3/03   LC 71-136211

Essays in American history dedicated to Frederick Jackson   • 3.6196
Turner.
New York: H. Holt and company, 1910. vii, 293 p.; 22 cm. Edited by Guy
Stanton Ford. 1. Turner, Frederick Jackson, 1861-1932. 2. Latin America —
History — Addresses, essays, lectures. 3. United States — History —
Addresses, essays, lectures. I. Ford, Guy Stanton, 1873-1962, ed.
E173.E78   Microfilm 37013 E.   LC 11-620

Historiography and urbanization: essays in American history in   • 3.6197
honor of W. Stull Holt / edited by Eric F. Goldman.
Baltimore: The Johns Hopkins press, 1941. 9, 220 p.; 21 cm. 1. Holt, W. Stull
(William Stull), 1896- 2. Historiography 3. United States — History
I. Goldman, Eric Frederick, 1915- ed. II. T.
E173.H67   973.04   LC 41-6878 revised

E174 Encyclopedias. Chronologies

Adams, James Truslow, 1878-1949. ed.   3.6198
Dictionary of American history / Louise Bilebof Ketz, Managing editor. —
Rev. ed. — New York: Scribner, 1976. 7 v. 1. United States — History —
Dictionaries I. Ketz, Louise Bilebof II. T.
E174 A43 1976   LC 76-6735   ISBN 0684138565

Dictionary of American history.   3.6199
Concise dictionary of American history. — New York: Scribner, c1983.
1140 p.; 29 cm. 'An abridgement of the eight-volume Dictionary of American
history, published in 1976'—Foreword. 1. United States — History —
Dictionaries I. T.
E174.D522 1983   973/.03/21 19   LC 82-42731   ISBN 0684173212

The Almanac of American history / general editor, Arthur M.   3.6200
Schlesinger, Jr.; executive editor, John S. Bowman.
New York: Putnam, c1983. 623 p.: ill; 24 cm. 'A Bison book'. Includes index.
1. United States — History — Chronology I. Schlesinger, Arthur Meier, 1917-
E174.5.A45 1983   973/.02/02 19   LC 83-3435   ISBN 0399128530

Carruth, Gorton.   3.6201
The encyclopedia of American facts and dates / by Gorton Carruth. — 8th ed.
— New York: Harper & Row, c1987. p. cm. Includes index. 1. United States —
History — Chronology I. T.
E174.5.C3 1987   973/.0202 19   LC 86-45645   ISBN 0061811432

Encyclopedia of American history / edited by Richard B.   3.6202
Morris; associate editor, Jeffrey B. Morris.
6th ed. — New York: Harper & Row, c1982. xiv, 1285 p.: ill.; 25 cm. Includes
index. 1. United States — History — Chronology 2. United States — History
— Dictionaries I. Morris, Richard Brandon, 1904- II. Morris, Jeffrey
Brandon, 1941-
E174.5.E52 1982   973/.03/21 19   LC 81-47668   ISBN 0061816051

E175 Historiography. Philosophy

Bellot, Hugh Hale, 1890-.   • 3.6203
American history and American historians; a review of recent contributions to
the interpretation of the history of the United States. [1st American ed.]
Norman, University of Oklahoma Press [1952] x, 336 p. fold. maps. 23 cm.
1. Historians — United States. 2. United States — History — Historiography.
3. United States — History — 1898- I. T.
E175.B44 1952   LC 52-12131

Bernstein, Barton J.   • 3.6204
Towards a new past: dissenting essays in American history, edited by Barton J.
Bernstein. — London: Chatto & Windus, 1970. xvi, 364 p.; 23 cm. 1. U.S. —
Historiography — Addresses, essays, lectures. I. T.
E175.B46 1970   973/.072   LC 77-852882   ISBN 0701114827

Billington, Ray Allen, 1903- ed.   • 3.6205
The reinterpretation of early American history; essays in honor of John Edwin
Pomfret. San Marino, Calif., Huntington Library [1966] viii, 264 p. port. 24 cm.
Includes bibliographical references. 1. Pomfret, John Edwin, 1898- 2. United

States — Historiography — Addresses, essays, lectures. I. Pomfret, John Edwin, 1898- II. T.
E175.B5   973.2/072   *LC* 66-31501

Callcott, George H., 1929-.   • **3.6206**
History in the United States, 1800–1860; its practice and purpose [by] George H. Callcott. — Baltimore: Johns Hopkins Press, [1970] viii, 239 p.; 22 cm. 1. U.S. — Historiography. 2. U.S. — History — Study and teaching. I. T.
E175.C3   907   *LC* 74-88115   *ISBN* 080181099X

Cartwright, William H. (William Holman), 1915-.   **3.6207**
The reinterpretation of American history and culture. William H. Cartwright and Richard L. Watson, Jr., editors. Washington, National Council for the Social Studies [1973] xix, 554 p. 24 cm. 1. United States — Historiography — Addresses, essays, lectures. I. Watson, Richard L. joint author. II. T.
E175.C36   973/.07/2   *LC* 73-84548

Craven, Wesley Frank, 1905-.   • **3.6208**
The legend of the Founding Fathers. New York: New York University Press, 1956. 191 p.; 24 cm. (New York University. Stokes Foundation. Anson G. Phelps lectureship on early American history) 1. National characteristics, American 2. United States — History — Colonial period. 3. United States — History — Historiography. I. T. II. Series.
E175.C7   973.2   *LC* 56-8593 rev

Davidson, James West.   **3.6209**
After the fact: the art of historical detection / James West Davidson, Mark Hamilton Lytle. — 1st ed. — New York: Knopf, c1982. xxxii, 388, xii p.: ill.; 23 cm. 1. United States — Historiography — Addresses, essays, lectures. 2. United States — History — Addresses, essays, lectures. I. Lytle, Mark H. II. T.
E175.D38 1982   973/.072 19   *LC* 81-13737   *ISBN* 0394523229

Higham, John. ed.   • **3.6210**
The reconstruction of American history. London, Hutchinson [1962] 244 p. 22 cm. Bibliographical footnotes. 1. United States — History — Historiography. I. T.
E175.H65 1962b   *LC* 62-66696

Higham, John.   • **3.6211**
Writing American history; essays on modern scholarship. — Bloomington, Indiana University Press [1970] x, 207 p. 22 cm. 1. United States — Historiography I. T.
E175.H654   973/.072   *LC* 70-108209   *ISBN* 0253197007 6.50

Jameson, J. Franklin (John Franklin), 1859-1937.   • **3.6212**
The history of historical writing in America. New York, Antiquarian Press, 1961. 160 p. 19 cm. 'First published 1891. Reprinted 1961.' 1. United States — History — Historiography. I. T.
E175.J3 1961   *LC* a 63-6001

Kraus, Michael, 1901-.   • **3.6213**
The writing of American history / by Michael Kraus. — Norman: University of Oklahoma Press, 1953. x, 387 p. 1. United States — Historiography I. T.
E175.K75   *LC* 53-8815

Loewenberg, Bert James, 1905-1974.   • **3.6214**
American history in American thought: Christopher Columbus to Henry Adams. — New York: Simon and Schuster, [1972] 731 p.; 22 cm. First 15 chapters previously published under title: Historical writing in American culture. 1. U.S. — Historiography. 2. America — Historiography. I. Loewenberg, Bert James, 1905- Historical writing in American culture. II. T.
E175.L6   973/.07/2073   *LC* 79-139641   *ISBN* 067120856X

McDermott, John Francis, 1902-.   • **3.6215**
Research opportunities in American cultural history. [Lexington] University of Kentucky Press [1961] viii, 205 p. 24 cm. A revision of papers delivered at a round table conference held at Washington University, St. Louis, Oct. 23-24, 1959. 1. History — Research 2. United States — History — Historiography. 3. United States — Civilization I. T.
E175.M3   *LC* 61-15623

Morton, Marian J., 1937-.   **3.6216**
The terrors of ideological politics; liberal historians in a conservative mood [by] Marian J. Morton. — Cleveland: Press of Case Western Reserve University, 1972. xi, 192 p.; 21 cm. 1. Historians — United States. 2. United States — Historiography I. T.
E175.M6   973/.07/2   *LC* 78-183309   *ISBN* 0829502297

Potter, David Morris.   **3.6217**
History and American society: essays of David M. Potter. Edited by Don E. Fehrenbacher. — New York: Oxford University Press, 1973. x, 422 p.; 22 cm. 1. National characteristics, American — Addresses, essays, lectures. 2. United States — Historiography — Addresses, essays, lectures. I. T.
E175.P64   917.3/03/92   *LC* 72-91008

Russo, David J.   **3.6218**
Families and communities: a new view of American history / [by] David J. Russo. — Nashville: American Association for State and Local History, [1974] x, 322 p.; 24 cm. 1. Local history 2. United States — Historiography I. T.
E175.R87   973/.07/2   *LC* 74-11389

Saveth, Edward Norman.   • **3.6219**
American historians and European immigrants, 1875–1925. New York, Columbia Univ. Press, 1948. 244 p. 23 cm. (Columbia University studies in the social sciences. no. 540) 1. Historians — United States. 2. United States — Emigration and immigration 3. United States — History — Historiography. I. T. II. Series.
H31.C7 no.540 E175.S35   *LC* 48-7605

Sheehan, Donald Henry, 1917- ed.   • **3.6220**
Essays in American historiography; papers presented in honor of Allan Nevins, edited by Donald Sheehan & Harold C. Syrett. New York, Columbia University Press, 1960. x, 320 p. port. 25 cm. Populism: its significance in American history, by E. Walters.—Imperialism and racism, by J. P. Shenton.—The muckrakers: in flower and in failure, by L. Filler.—A cycle of revisionism between two wars, by H. W. Baehr.—An interpretation of Franklin D. Roosevelt, by B. Bellush. 1. Nevins, Allan, 1890-1971. 2. United States — History — Historiography. I. Syrett, Harold Coffin, 1913- joint ed. II. Nevins, Allan, 1890-1971. III. T. IV. Title: American historiography.
E175.S48   *LC* 60-8187

The State of American history / edited with an introd. by   • **3.6221**
Herbert J. Bass.
Chicago: Quadrangle Books, 1970. xiv, 426 p.; 25 cm. A selection of essays originally presented at the 1969 meeting of the Organization of American Historians in Philadelphia. 1. U.S. — Historiography — Addresses, essays, lectures. I. Bass, Herbert J. ed. II. Organization of American Historians.
E175.S7 1970   973/.072   *LC* 77-101068

Sternsher, Bernard, 1925-.   **3.6222**
Consensus, conflict, and American historians. — Bloomington: Indiana University Press, [1975] ix, 432 p.; 24 cm. 1. Historians — United States. 2. United States — Historiography I. T.
E175.S74 1975   973/.07/2   *LC* 73-16531   *ISBN* 0253314100

Van Tassel, David D. (David Dirck), 1928-.   • **3.6223**
Recording America's past: an interpretation of the development of historical studies in America, 1607–1884. — Chicago: University of Chicago Press, [1960] 222 p. 1. United States — History — Historiography. 2. United States — History — Societies, etc. I. T.
E175.V3 1960   *LC* 60-14404

Wise, Gene.   **3.6224**
American historical explanations: a strategy for grounded inquiry / Gene Wise. — 2d ed., rev. — Minneapolis: University of Minnesota, c1980. xlvii, 381 p.; 24 cm. 1. Historiography 2. United States — Historiography I. T.
E175.W47 1980   973/.072   *LC* 80-17697   *ISBN* 0816609543

Wish, Harvey, 1909-.   • **3.6225**
The American historian: a social–intellectual history of the American past / Harvey Wish. — New York: Oxford University Press, 1960. viii, 366 p. 1. United States — Historiography I. T.
E175.W5   *LC* 60-13202

Lemisch, Jesse, 1936-.   **3.6226**
On active service in war and peace: politics and ideology in the American historical profession / by Jesse Lemisch; with an introd. by Thomas Schofield. Toronto: New Hogtown Press, 1975. vii, 150 p.; 20 cm. 'This essay was originally entitled 'Present-mindedness revisited: anti-radicalism as a goal of American historical writing since World War II.'' 1. United States — Historiography — Addresses, essays, lectures. I. T.
E175.1.L45   973.92/07/2   *LC* 75-18557   *ISBN* 0919940005

Mangione, Jerre Gerlando, 1909-.   • **3.6227**
The dream and the deal: the Federal Writers' Project, 1935–1943 / by Jerre Mangione. — [1st ed.] Boston: Little, Brown [1972] xvi, 416 p.: ill.; 24 cm. 1. Writers' Program (U.S.) — History. I. T.
E175.4.W9 M3   917.3/006/173   *LC* 75-187787   *ISBN* 0316545007

E175.45 HISTORIANS: COLLECTIVE
BIOGRAPHY

Cunliffe, Marcus.   • **3.6228**
Pastmasters; some essays on American historians. Edited by Marcus Cunliffe and Robin W. Winks. — [1st ed.]. — New York: Harper & Row, [1969] xv, 492 p.; 24 cm. 1. Historians — United States — Biography. I. Winks, Robin W. joint author. II. T.
E175.45.C8   973/.07/2022 B   *LC* 77-81380

Gay, Peter, 1923-. **3.6229**
A loss of mastery; Puritan historians in colonial America. — Berkeley, University of California Press [1966] viii, 164 p. 23 cm. — (Jefferson memorial lectures) 1. Historians — United States. 2. History — Philosophy 3. Church history — Philosophy 4. New England — History — Colonial period, ca. 1600-1775 — Historiography. I. T. II. Series.
E175.45.G3   974.02072   *LC* 67-10969

Hofstadter, Richard, 1916-1970. • **3.6230**
The progressive historians: Turner, Beard, Parrington. — [1st ed.]. — New York: Knopf, 1968. xvii, 498, xiii p.: ports.; 22 cm. — 1. Turner, Frederick Jackson, 1861-1932. 2. Beard, Charles Austin, 1874-1948. 3. Parrington, Vernon Louis, 1871-1929. 4. Historians — United States — Biography. 5. United States — Historiography I. T.
E175.45.H6   973/.072/022   *LC* 68-23944

Levin, David, 1924-. • **3.6231**
History as romantic art: Bancroft, Prescott, Motley, and Parkman. — Stanford, Calif.: Stanford University Press, 1959. 260 p.; 24 cm. — (Stanford studies in language and literature, 20) 1. Historiography 2. Historian — United States. I. T.
E175.45.L4   907.2   *LC* 59-10634

Skotheim, Robert Allen. • **3.6232**
American intellectual histories and historians. — Princeton, N.J.: Princeton University Press, 1966. xi, 326 p.; 21 cm. 1. Historians — United States. 2. United States — Historiography 3. United States — History — Philosophy I. T.
E175.45.S5   973.072   *LC* 66-11960

Twentieth–century American historians / edited by Clyde N. Wilson. **3.6233**
Detroit, Mich.: Gale Research Co., 1983. xi, 519 p.: ill., ports.; 29 cm. — (Dictionary of literary biography. v. 17) 'A Bruccoli Clark book.' Includes index. 1. Historians — United States — Biography. I. Wilson, Clyde Norman. II. Series.
E175.45.T85 1983   907/.2022 B 19   *LC* 82-24210   *ISBN* 0810311445

E175.5 HISTORIANS, A–Z

Adams, Henry, 1838-1918. • **3.6234**
The education of Henry Adams: an autobiography. — Boston; New York: Houghton Mifflin company, [1930] x, 517 p.; 22 cm. (The Riverside library) Privately printed 1907, first published in 1918 by the Massachusetts historical society, with editor's preface signed, Henry Cabot Lodge. I. Lodge, Henry Cabot, 1850-1924. ed. II. T.
E175.5.A17423   *LC* 32-23054

Adams, Henry, 1838-1918. • **3.6235**
Henry Adams and his friends: a collection of his unpublished letters, compiled, with a biographical introd., by Harold Dean Cater. — New York: Octagon Books, 1970 [c1947] cxix, 797 p.: ports.; 24 cm. I. Cater, Harold Dean, 1908- ed. II. T.
E175.5.A17428 1970   973/.072/024   *LC* 78-96175

Adams, Henry, 1838-1918. • **3.6236**
Letters of Henry Adams ... edited by Worthington Chauncey Ford. Boston and New York, Houghton Mifflin company, 1930-38. 2 v. fronts. (ports.) 24 1/2 cm. I. Ford, Worthington Chauncey, 1858-1941. ed. II. T.
E175.5.A1743   928.1   *LC* 30-25080

Baym, Max Isaac. • **3.6237**
The French education of Henry Adams. — New York: Columbia University Press, 1951. xiv, 358 p.; 23 cm. 1. Adams, Henry, 1838-1918. I. T.
E175.5.A1747   PS1004.A4 Z55.   *LC* 51-11489

Donovan, Timothy Paul. • **3.6238**
Henry Adams and Brooks Adams: the education of two American historians / by Timothy Paul Donovan. — 1st ed. — Norman: University of Oklahoma Press, [1961]. –. 220 p.: ill.; 23 cm. — 1. Adams, Henry, 1838-1918. 2. Adams, Brooks, 1848-1927. I. T.
E175.5.A1748   973.072   *LC* 61-6500

Jordy, William H. • **3.6239**
Henry Adams: scientific historian, by William H. Jordy. — [Hamden, Conn.]: Archon Books, 1970 [c1952] xv, 327 p.; 23 cm. 1. Adams, Henry, 1838-1918. I. T.
E175.5.A1755 1970   973/.072/024 B   *LC* 77-114423   *ISBN* 0208008284

Levenson, J. C. (Jacob Claver), 1922-. • **3.6240**
The mind and the art of Henry Adams, by J. C. Levenson. Stanford, Calif., Stanford University Press [1968, c1957] x, 430 p. illus., ports. 22 cm. 1. Adams, Henry, 1838-1918. I. T.
E175.5.A1765 1968   973/.072/024   *LC* 68-13745

Samuels, Ernest. • **3.6241**
Henry Adams: the major phase. — Cambridge, Mass.: Belknap Press of Harvard U.P., c1964. 687 p. The writings of Henry Adams from 1892: p.591-594. 1. Adams, Henry, 1838-1918. I. T.
E175.5 A1776   928.1   *LC* 64-21790

Samuels, Ernest, 1903-. • **3.6242**
Henry Adams, the middle years. Cambridge, Belknap Press of Harvard University Press, 1958. xiv, 514 p. 22 cm. 'The writings of Henry Adams, 1878-1891': p. [423]-426. Bibliography: p. [489]-497. 1. Adams, Henry, 1838-1918. I. T.
E175.5.A1777   928.1   *LC* 58-12975

Samuels, Ernest, 1903-. • **3.6243**
The young Henry Adams / by Ernest Samuels. — Cambridge, Mass.: Harvard University Press, 1948. xvi, 378 p. 1. Adams, Henry, 1838-1918. I. T.
E175.5 A178   *LC* 48-10525

Stevenson, Elizabeth, 1919-. • **3.6244**
Henry Adams: a biography. — New York: Macmillan, 1955. xiv, 425 p.: ill., ports.; 22 cm. 1. Adams, Henry, 1838-1918 — Biography. 2. Historians — United States — Biography. I. T.
E175.5.A1782   928.1   *LC* 55-13825

Wagner, Vern. • **3.6245**
The suspension of Henry Adams; a study of manner and matter. — Detroit: Wayne State University Press, 1969. 268 p.: front.; 24 cm. 1. Adams, Henry, 1838-1918. I. T.
E175.5.A1784   818/.4/08   *LC* 68-26875

Adams, Herbert Baxter, 1850-1901. • **3.6246**
Historical scholarship in the United States, 1876–1901: as revealed in the correspondence of Herbert B. Adams. Edited by W. Stull Holt. Westport, Conn., Greenwood Press [1970, c1938] 314 p. 23 cm. On spine: Historic scholarship in the United States, 1876-1901. 1. Adams, Herbert Baxter, 1850-1901 — Correspondence. 2. Historians — United States — Correspondence. 3. United States — Historiography I. T.
E175.5.A1797 1970   907/.2073 19   *LC* 71-113060   *ISBN* 083714695X

Nye, Russel Blaine, 1913-. • **3.6247**
George Bancroft, Brahmin rebel, by Russel B. Nye. — New York: Octagon Books, 1972 [c1944] x, 340, xii p.: illus.; 24 cm. 1. Bancroft, George, 1800-1891. I. T.
E175.5.B186 1972   973/.072/024 B   *LC* 72-4400   *ISBN* 0374961336

Canary, Robert H. **3.6248**
George Bancroft, by Robert H. Canary. — New York: Twayne Publishers, [1974] 142 p.; 21 cm. — (Twayne's United States authors series, TUSAS 266 [i.e. 226]) 1. Bancroft, George, 1800-1891. I. T.
E175.5.B1916   973/.072/024   *LC* 73-1668   *ISBN* 080570034X

Caughey, John Walton, 1902-. • **3.6249**
Hubert Howe Bancroft, historian of the West. New York, Russell & Russell [1970, c1946] 422 p. illus., facsims., ports. 23 cm. 1. Bancroft, Hubert Howe, 1832-1918. 2. Bancroft Library. I. T.
E175.5.B199 1970   978/.0072024   *LC* 77-102475

Beale, Howard K. (Howard Kennedy), 1899-1959. ed. • **3.6250**
Charles A. Beard: an appraisal, by Eric F. Goldman [and others. Lexington] University of Kentucky Press [1954] x, 312 p. port. 24 cm. 1. Beard, Charles Austin, 1874-1948. I. T.
E175.5.B38B4x   *LC* 53-5517

Borning, Bernard C. • **3.6251**
The political and social thought of Charles A. Beard / by Bernard C. Borning. — Seattle: University of Washington Press, 1962. xxv, 315 p. 1. Beard, Charles Austin, 1874-1948. I. T.
E175.5.B38B6x   *LC* 62-12129

Nore, Ellen, 1942-. **3.6252**
Charles A. Beard, an intellectual biography / Ellen Nore. — Carbondale: Southern Illinois University Press, c1983. xii, 322 p.: port.; 24 cm. Includes index. 1. Beard, Charles Austin, 1874-1948. 2. Historians — United States — Biography. I. T.
E175.5.B38 N67 1983   973/.072024 B 19   *LC* 82-19452   *ISBN* 0809310783

Berman, Milton. • 3.6253
John Fiske; the evolution of a popularizer. Cambridge, Harvard University Press, 1961. 297 p. illus. 21 cm. (Harvard historical monographs. 48) 1. Fiske, John, 1842-1901. I. T. II. Series.
E175.5.F49   *LC* 62-7334

The Marcus W. Jernegan essays in American historiography, by • 3.6254
his former students at the University of Chicago.
Chicago, Ill., The University of Chicago press [1937] x, 417 p. front. (port.) 24 cm. 1. Jernegan, Marcus Wilson, 1872-1949. 2. Historians, American. 3. United States — History — Historiography. I. Hutchinson, William Thomas, 1895-
E175.5.M37   *LC* 38-27

Parkman, Francis. • 3.6255
The journals of Francis Parkman / edited by Mason Wade. — 1st ed. — New York: Harper, 1947. 2 v. (xxv, 718 p.): ill., maps. Includes indexes. 1. United States — Description and travel 2. Canada — Description and travel — 1867-1950 I. Wade, Mason. II. T.
E175.5.P202   928.1   *LC* 47-11938

Parkman, Francis, 1823-1893. • 3.6256
Letters of Francis Parkman. Edited and with an introd. by Wilbur R. Jacobs. — [1st ed.]. — Norman, University of Oklahoma Press [1960] 2 v. illus., ports., map, facsims. 25 cm. 'Published in co-operation with the Massachusetts Historical Society.' Includes bibliographical references. I. T.
E175.5.P205   928.1   *LC* 60-8754

Doughty, Howard, 1904-. • 3.6257
Francis Parkman. New York, Macmillan, 1962. viii, 414 p. 23 cm. 1. Parkman, Francis, 1823-1893. I. T.
E175.5.P212   *LC* 61-12191

Gale, Robert L., 1919-. 3.6258
Francis Parkman, by Robert L. Gale. New York, Twayne Publishers, [c1973] 204 p. 21 cm. (Twayne's United States authors series, TUSAS 220) 1. Parkman, Francis, 1823-1893. I. T.
E175.5.P218   970/.0072/024 B   *LC* 72-9348   *ISBN* 0805705821

Pease, Otis A. • 3.6259
Parkman's history: the historian as literary artist / Otis A. Pease. — Hamden, Conn.: Archon Books, 1968, c1953. xi, 86 p. — (The Wallace Notestein essays; v. 1) 1. Parkman, Francis, 1823-1893. I. T. II. Series.
E175.5 P23 1968   E175.5 P25 1968.   973'072'024

Wade, Mason. • 3.6260
Francis Parkman, heroic historian / by Mason Wade. — New York: Viking Press, 1942. xiii, 466 p., [8] p. of plates: ill. Maps on lining papers. 1. Historians — United States — Biography. I. T.
E175.5P.28   928.1   *LC* 42-25856

Flower, Milton Embick. • 3.6261
James Parton, the father of modern biography [by] Milton E. Flower. — New York: Greenwood Press, 1968 [c1951] ix, 253 p.: illus., ports.; 24 cm. 1. Parton, James, 1822-1891. I. T.
E175.5.P3 F6 1968   920/.00924 B   *LC* 68-29742

Roper, John Herbert. 3.6262
U.B. Phillips, a southern mind / John Herbert Roper. — Macon, GA: Mercer, c1984. vi, 198 p.: ill.; 24 cm. Includes index. 1. Phillips, Ulrich Bonnell, 1877-1934. 2. Historians — United States — Biography. I. T.
E175.5.P47 R67 1984   973.8/092/4 B 19   *LC* 84-682   *ISBN* 0865540977

Cruden, Robert. • 3.6263
James Ford Rhodes: the man, the historian, and his work. With a complete bibliography of the writings of James Ford Rhodes. [Cleveland] Press of Western Reserve University, 1961. 290 p. 24 cm. 1. Rhodes, James Ford, 1848-1927. I. T.
E175.5.R436   *LC* 61-16743

Silver, James W. (James Wesley), 1907-. 3.6264
Running scared: Silver in Mississippi / by James W. Silver. — Jackson: University Press of Mississippi, c1984. xiii, 238 p.: ill.; 24 cm. Includes index. 1. Silver, James W. (James Wesley), 1907- 2. University of Mississippi — Faculty — Biography. 3. Historians — United States — Biography. 4. Mississippi — Social conditions. 5. Mississippi — Race relations. I. T.
E175.5.S49 A37 1984   976.2/0072024 B 19   *LC* 83-25921   *ISBN* 0878052097

Billington, Ray Allen, 1903-. 3.6265
Frederick Jackson Turner: historian, scholar, teacher. — New York: Oxford University Press, 1973. x, 599 p.: illus.; 24 cm. 1. Turner, Frederick Jackson, 1861-1932. I. T.
E175.5.T83 B49   973/.07/2024 B   *LC* 72-91005   *ISBN* 0195016092

Essays on Walter Prescott Webb / by Joe B. Frantz ... [et al.]; 3.6266
foreword by Jubal R. Parten; introd. by Ray Allen Billington;
edited by Kenneth R. Philp and Elliott West.
Austin: University of Texas Press, c1976. xxi, 123 p.; 23 cm. (Walter Prescott Webb memorial lectures. 10 0083-713X) 1. Webb, Walter Prescott, 1888-1963 — Addresses, essays, lectures. 2. Frontier thesis — Addresses, essays, lectures. I. Webb, Walter Prescott, 1888-1963. II. Frantz, Joe Bertram, 1917- III. Philp, Kenneth R., 1941- IV. West, Elliott, 1945- V. Series.
E175.5.W4 E77   907/.2/024   *LC* 75-37672   *ISBN* 0292720165

Furman, Necah Stewart. 3.6267
Walter Prescott Webb: his life and impact / Necah Stewart Furman. — 1st ed. — Albuquerque: University of New Mexico Press, c1976. xiv, 222 p., [4] leaves of plates: ill.; 24 cm. Includes index. 1. Webb, Walter Prescott, 1888-1963. I. T.
E175.5.W4 F87   907/.202/4 B   *LC* 75-40834   *ISBN* 0826304125

E175.7–175.8 METHODOLOGY. STUDY.
TEACHING

Benson, Lee. • 3.6268
Toward the scientific study of history; selected essays of Lee Benson. — Philadelphia: Lippincott, [1972] xi, 352 p.; 22 cm. 1. Historiography — Addresses, essays, lectures. 2. U.S. — Historiography — Addresses, essays, lectures. I. T.
E175.7.B4   907/.2   *LC* 73-161415   *ISBN* 039747265X

American studies: topics and sources / Robert H. Walker, 3.6269
editor.
Westport, Conn.: Greenwood Press, 1976. xi, 393 p.; 24 cm. (Contributions in American studies; no. 24) 'These essays have appeared or will appear in American studies international.' Includes indexes. 1. American studies — United States — Addresses, essays, lectures. I. Walker, Robert Harris, 1924- II. American studies international.
E175.8.A582   973/.07/2   *LC* 75-35675   *ISBN* 0837185599

Wyld, Lionel D. 3.6270
American civilization: introduction to research and bibliography / edited by Lionel D. Wyld. — 1st ed. — Deland, Fla.: Everett/Edwards, [1975] xv, 299 p.; 24 cm. 1. United States — Study and teaching — Addresses, essays, lectures. I. T.
E175.8.W9   917.3/03   *LC* 75-89568   *ISBN* 0912112034

FitzGerald, Frances, 1940-. 3.6271
America revised: history schoolbooks in the twentieth century / Frances FitzGerald. — 1st ed. — Boston: Little, Brown, c1979. 240 p.; 22 cm. 'Almost all of the book appeared initially in the New Yorker.' 'An Atlantic Monthly Press book.' 1. Textbook bias — United States. 2. United States — History — Text-books. 3. United States — Historiography 4. United States — History — Study and teaching I. T.
E175.85.F57   973/.07/1273   *LC* 79-16555   *ISBN* 0316284246

E175.9 PHILOSOPHY OF AMERICAN
HISTORY

Adams, Ephraim Douglass, 1865-1930. • 3.6272
The power of ideals in American history. — New York: AMS Press, [1969] xiii, 159 p.; 23 cm. — (Yale lectures on the responsibilities of citizenship) Reprint of the 1913 ed. 1. National characteristics, American 2. Idealism, American 3. U.S. — History — Philosophy. I. T. II. Series.
E175.9.A3 1969b   973/.01   *LC* 75-98025

Benson, Lee. • 3.6273
Turner and Beard: American historical writing reconsidered. — Glencoe, Ill.: Free Press, [1960] 241 p.; 22 cm. 1. Loria, Achille, 1857-1943. 2. Turner, Frederick Jackson, 1861-1932. 3. Beard, Charles Austin, 1874-1948. 4. United States — History — Philosophy 5. United States — Historiography I. T.
E175.9.B4   973.072   *LC* 60-10890

Fox, Dixon Ryan, 1887-1945. • 3.6274
Sources of culture in the Middle West; backgrounds versus frontier. New York, Russell & Russell, 1964 [c1961] 110 p. 22 cm. Three papers appraising F. J. Turner's historical theory relative to the influence of the frontier on American history, read at a special session of the 1933 annual meeting of the American Historical Association. 1. Turner, Frederick Jackson, 1861-1932. 2. United States — History — Philosophy 3. West (U.S.) — History 4. United States — Civilization — 1865-1918 I. T. II. Title: Culture in the Middle West.
E175.9.F69 1964   *LC* 64-15019

Handlin, Oscar, 1915-.   • **3.6275**
Chance or destiny; turning points in American history. — [1st ed.]. — Boston: Little, Brown, [1955] 220 p.; 22 cm. 1. United States — History — Philosophy I. T.
E175.9.H35   973.04   *LC* 55-7461

Hartz, Louis, 1919-.   • **3.6276**
The liberal tradition in America: an interpretation of American political thought since the Revolution. — [1st ed.]. — New York: Harcourt, Brace, [1955] 329 p.; 21 cm. 1. Liberalism — United States. 2. United States — History — Philosophy 3. United States — Politics and government I. T.
E175.9.H37   973   *LC* 55-5242

Koch, Adrienne, 1912-1971.   • **3.6277**
Power, morals, and the Founding Fathers; essays in the interpretation of the American enlightenment. Ithaca, N.Y.: Great Seal Books, [1961] 158 p.; 19 cm. 1. Statesmen — United States. 2. United States — History — Philosophy I. T.
E175.9.K6   973.01   *LC* 61-12995

Niebuhr, Reinhold, 1892-1971.   • **3.6278**
A Nation so conceived: reflections on the history of America from its early visions to its present power / by Reinhold Niebuhr and Alan Heimert. New York: Scribner, 1963. 155 p.; 21 cm. 1. United States — History — Philosophy 2. United States — Civilization I. Heimert, Alan. joint author. II. T.
E175.9.N5   973.01   *LC* 63-9458

Noble, David W.   **3.6279**
Historians against history; the frontier thesis and the national covenant in American historical writing since 1830 [by] David W. Noble. — Minneapolis, University of Minnesota Press [1965] 197 p. 24 cm. 1. United States — History — Philosophy I. T.
E175.9.N6 1965   973.01   *LC* 65-22811

Schlesinger, Arthur Meier, 1888-1965.   • **3.6280**
New viewpoints in American history, by Arthur Meier Schlesinger. New York, Macmillan, 1922. x, 299 p. 21 cm. Reprinted in part from various periodicals. 1. United States — History — Philosophy 2. United States — History 3. United States — Politics and government I. T.
E175.9.S34   *LC* 22-7401

Strout, Cushing.   • **3.6281**
The pragmatic revolt in American history: Carl Becker and Charles Beard. — New Haven: Yale University Press, 1958. ix, 182 p.; 23 cm. Bibliography: p. [163]-176. 1. Becker, Carl Lotus, 1873-1945. 2. Beard, Charles Austin, 1874-1948. 3. United States — History — Philosophy I. T.
E175.9.S8   973.01   *LC* 58-11262

Tuveson, Ernest Lee.   **3.6282**
Redeemer nation; the idea of America's millennial role. — Chicago: University of Chicago Press, [1968] xi, 238 p.; 22 cm. 1. Messianism, American. 2. Nationalism — Religious aspects — United States. I. T.
E175.9.T85 1968   973/.01   *LC* 68-14009

E176 Biography (General. Collective)

Aaron, Daniel, 1912-.   • **3.6283**
Men of good hope: a story of American progressives. — New York: Oxford University Press, 1951. xiv, 329 p.; 22 cm. 1. United States — Biography I. T.
E176.A2   920.073   *LC* 51-1402

Appleton's cyclopaedia of American biography. Edited by James   • **3.6284**
Grant Wilson and John Fiske. New York, Appleton, 1888.
Detroit: Gale Research Co., 1968. 7 v.: ports.; 24 cm. Vol. 7 edited by J. G. Wilson. 1. America — Biography — Dictionaries 2. U.S. — Biography — Dictionaries. I. Wilson, James Grant, 1832-1914. ed. II. Fiske, John, 1842-1901. joint ed.
E176.A666   920.07   *LC* 67-14061

Biographical directory of the governors of the United States,   **3.6285**
1789-1978 / edited by Robert Sobel and John Raimo.
Westport, Conn.: Meckler Books, 1978. 4 v. (xviii, 1785 p.); 24 cm. 1. Governors — United States — Biography — Dictionaries. 2. United States — Biography — Dictionaries. I. Sobel, Robert, 1931 Feb. 19- II. Raimo, John, 1946-
E176.B573   973/.0992 B   *LC* 77-10435   *ISBN* 0930466004

Bradford, Gamaliel, 1863-1932.   • **3.6286**
Damaged souls. — Port Washington, N.Y.: Kennikat Press, [1969, c1923] xi, 276 p.; 22 cm. — (Essay and general literature index reprint series) 1. U.S. — Biography. I. T.
E176.B8 1969   973   *LC* 77-85990   *ISBN* 0804605416

The Twentieth century biographical dictionary of notable   • **3.6287**
Americans. Editor-in-chief: Rossiter Johnson. Managing editor: John Howard Brown. Boston, Biographical Society, 1904.
Detroit: Gale Research Co., 1968. 10 v.: illus., ports.; 24 cm. 'Corrected edition of a work previously published under the titles: The Cyclopaedia of American biography, 1897-1903, and Lamb's biographical dictionary of the United States, 1900-1903.' 1. United States — Biography I. Johnson, Rossiter, 1840-1931. ed. II. Brown, John Howard, 1840-1917, ed. III. Title: The Cyclopaedia of American biography.
E176.C993   920.073   *LC* 68-19657

Dictionary of American biography, under the auspices of the   **3.6288**
American council of learned societies.
New York: C. Scribner's Sons, 1928-1958. 22 v.; 26 cm. Vol. 21 called Supplement one (to December 31, 1935); vol. 22 called Supplement two (to December 31, 1940). Editors: v. 1-3, A. Johnson; v. 4-7, A. Johnson and D. Malone; v. 8-20, D. Malone; v. 21, H.E. Starr; v. 22, R.L. Schuyler. Published under the auspices of the American Council of Learned Societies. 'No living persons have biographies in the Dictionary [and] no persons who [have] not lived in the territory now known as the United States.' —Introd., v. 1, p. vii. 1. United States — Biography — Dictionaries. I. Johnson, Allen, 1870-1931. II. Malone, Dumas, 1892- III. Starr, Harris Elwood, 1875- IV. Schuyler, Robert Livingston, 1883- V. American Council of Learned Societies.
E176.D56   920.073   *LC* 28-28500

Dictionary of American biography: complete index guide—   **3.6289**
volumes I–X, supplements 1–7.
New York: Published under the auspices of the American Council of Learned Societies [by] Scribner, c1981. 214 p.; 24 cm. 1. Dictionary of American biography — Indexes. 2. United States — Biography — Indexes. I. American Council of Learned Societies.
E176.D563 Index   920/.073 19   *LC* 81-9216   *ISBN* 068417152X

Dictionary of American biography: supplement three– < seven   **3.6290**
> : with an index guide to the supplements / John A. Garraty, editor.
New York: Scribner, [1973]- < c1981 >. v. < 3-7 >; 26 cm. Includes index. Supplements 1-2 comprise v. 11 of the main work. 1. United States — Biography I. Garraty, John Arthur, 1920-
E176.D563 Suppl   920/.073 19   *LC* 77-2942   *ISBN* 0684150549

Concise Dictionary of American biography.   **3.6291**
2d ed. — New York: Scribner, c1977. xii, 1229 p.; 29 cm. 'Joseph G. E. Hopkins, editor.' Edited under the sponsorship of the American Council of Learned Societies. 1. United States — Biography — Dictionaries. I. Hopkins, Joseph G. E. II. American Council of Learned Societies. III. Dictionary of American biography.
E176.D564 1977   920/.073   *LC* 76-49520   *ISBN* 0684146541

Fishwick, Marshall William, 1923-.   • **3.6292**
American heroes: myth and reality / introd. by Carl Carmer. — Washington: Public Affairs Press [1954] 242 p.; 24 cm. Errors in numbering of chapters: 4 and 5 numbered 1 and 4 respectively. 1. Heroes 2. United States — Biography I. T.
E176.F53   920.073   *LC* 54-12693

Kennedy, John F. (John Fitzgerald), 1917-1963.   • **3.6293**
Profiles in courage. [Memorial ed.] New York, Harper & Row [c1964] 287 p. port. 24 cm. 1. United States. Congress. Senate — Biography. 2. Courage I. T.
E176.K4 1964   923.273   *LC* 64-16194

Koenig, Louis William, 1916-.   • **3.6294**
The invisible presidency / Louis W. Koenig. — New York: Holt, Rinehart and Winston, 1960. viii, 438 p. 1. Executive power — United States 2. Presidents — United States 3. United States — Biography I. T.
E176.K6   *LC* 60-5341

McMullin, Thomas A.   **3.6295**
Biographical directory of American territorial governors / by Thomas A. McMullin and David Walker. — Westport, CT: Meckler, c1984. xxi, 353 p.; 24 cm. 1. Governors — United States — Territories and possessions — Biography. 2. United States — Biography 3. United States — Territories and possessions I. Walker, David Allan, 1941- II. T.
E176.M17 1984   973/.09/92 B 19   *LC* 84-9095   *ISBN* 093046611X

Madison, Charles Allan. • **3.6296**
Critics & crusaders: a century of American protest / Charles A. Madison. — 2d ed. — New York: Ungar, 1959. x, 662 p.: ill. 1. Liberty. 2. United States — Biography I. T.
E176.M22 1959   *LC* 58-14283

The National cyclopedia of American biography. • **3.6297**
v. 1-. Clifton, N.J. [etc.] J. T. White, 1893-. v. ill. 28 cm. Irregular. Title varies slightly. v.1-50 reprinted by University Microfilms in 1967-71. Vols. not issued consecutively. Some vols. issued in revised editions. Vol. 14 accompanied by a volume called Supplement 1. 1. United States — Biography
E176.N27   *LC* 21-21756

Nye, Russel Blaine, 1913-. • **3.6298**
A baker's dozen: thirteen unusual Americans. East Lansing, Michigan State University Press, 1956. 300 p. 22 cm. 1. United States — Biography I. T.
E176.N95   973.0922 920 920.073   *LC* 56-11739

Wecter, Dixon, 1906-1950. • **3.6299**
The hero in America: a chronicle of hero–worship / with headings by Woodi Ishmael. — [Ann Arbor]: University of Michigan Press [1963, c1941] 524 p.: ill., ports.; 21 cm. (Ann Arbor paperbacks) Bibliographical references included in 'Notes' (p. 493-513) 1. Heroes 2. United States — Biography I. T.
E176.W4   920.073   *LC* 64-9847

Who was who in America. • **3.6300**
1607/1896-. Chicago, Marquis-Who's Who [etc.] v. 27 cm. 'A companion biographical reference work to Who's who in America.' Vol. for 1607/1896 called Historical volume, published in 1963; vols. for 1897/1942-1951/60 called v. 1-3, were published prior to this volume. 1. United States — Biography I. Who's who in American history.
E176.W64   920.073   *LC* 43-3789

Who's who in America. • **3.6301**
v. [1]- 1899/1900-. Chicago, Marquis Who's Who [etc.] v. 20-31 cm. 'Who's Who in America and the Who Was Who comprise the 6 vol. set of Who's Who in American History.' Vols. 28-30 accompanied by separately published parts with title: Indices and necrology. 1. United States — Biography I. Leonard, John William, 1849- II. Marquis, Albert Nelson, d. 1943. III. Who's who in American history.
E176.W642   920.073   *LC* 04-16934

Who's who in American politics. • **3.6302**
1st- ed.; 1967/68-. [New York, Bowker] v. 29 cm. Biennial. 'A biographical directory of United States political leaders.' 1. United States — Biography I. Theis, Paul A., 1923- ed. II. Henshaw, Edmund Lee, ed.
E176.W6424   320/.0922   *LC* 67-25024

Who's who in the East and Eastern Canada. • **3.6303**
1st-11th ed.; 1942/43-1968/69. Chicago [etc.] A. N. Marquis [etc.] 11 v. 24-28 cm. Biennial. Title varies slightly. 'A biographical dictionary of noteworthy men and women of the Middle Atlantic and Northeastern States and Eastern Canada,' (varies). 1. Middle Atlantic States — Biography. 2. New England — Biography. 3. Canada, Eastern — Biography.
E176.W643   920.07   *LC* 43-18522

Who's who in the South and Southwest. • **3.6304**
1st- ed.; 1947-. Chicago, Marquis Who's Who [etc.] v. 24-27 cm. Biennial. 'A biographical dictionary of noteworthy men and women of the Southern and Southwestern States.' Vol. for 1947 published also under titles: Who's who in Alabama, Who's who in Arizona, Who's who in Florida, Who's who in Georgia, Who's who in Kentucky, Who's who in Louisiana, Who's who in Mississippi, Who's who in New Mexico, Who's who in North Carolina, Who's who in the Northwest, Who's who in the Pacific Coast, Who's who in South Carolina, Who's who in Tennessee, Who's who in Texas, and Who's who in Virginia. Includes names from the States of Alabama, Arkansas, the District of Columbia, Florida, Georgia, Kentucky, Louisiana, Mississippi, North Carolina, Oklahoma, South Carolina, Tennessee, Texas and Virginia, and Puerto Rico and the Virgin Islands. 1. Southern States — Biography — Dictionaries. 2. Southwest, New — Biography — Dictionaries.
E176.W645   920.073   *LC* 50-58231

Who's who in the West and Western Canada. • **3.6305**
1st ed. — Chicago: Marquis-Who's Who, 1947-. v. biennial (irregular) 1. Northwest, Canadian — Biography. 2. The West — Biography. I. Title: Who's who in the Pacific Coast.
E176 W646   *LC* 49-48186

E176.1 PRESIDENTS

Bailey, Thomas Andrew, 1902-. • **3.6306**
Presidential greatness: the image and the man from George Washington to the present / by Thomas A. Bailey. — 1st ed. — New York: Appleton-Century, 1966. xi, 368 p.; 23 cm. 1. Presidents — United States I. T.
E176.1.B17   973/.0992   *LC* 66-19996

Cooper, John Milton.   **3.6307**
The warrior and the priest: Woodrow Wilson and Theodore Roosevelt / John Milton Cooper, Jr. — Cambridge, Mass.: Belknap Press of Harvard University Press, 1983. xiv, 442 p., [18] p. of plates: ill.; 24 cm. 1. Wilson, Woodrow, 1856-1924. 2. Roosevelt, Theodore, 1858-1919. 3. Presidents — United States — Biography 4. United States — Politics and government — 1901-1909 5. United States — Politics and government — 1913-1921 I. T.
E176.1.C7919 1983   973.91/1 19   *LC* 83-6021   *ISBN* 0674947509

DeGregorio, William A., 1946-.   **3.6308**
The complete book of U.S. presidents / by William A. DeGregorio. — New York: Dembner Books: Distributed by W.W. Norton, c1984. xi, 691 p.: ill.; 24 cm. 1. Presidents — United States I. T. II. Title: Complete book of United States presidents. III. Title: Complete book of US presidents.
E176.1.D43 1984   973/.09/92 B 19   *LC* 83-23201   *ISBN* 0934878366

Kane, Joseph Nathan, 1899-.   **3.6309**
Facts about the presidents: a compilation of biographical and historical information / Joseph Nathan Kane. — 4th ed. — New York: Wilson, 1981. viii, 456 p.: ports.; 26 cm. Includes index. 1. Presidents — United States — Biography 2. Presidents — United States I. T.
E176.1.K3 1981   973/.09/92 B 19   *LC* 81-7537   *ISBN* 0824206126

Pollard, James Edward, 1894-. • **3.6310**
The Presidents and the press / James E. Pollard. — New York: The Macmillan Co., 1947. xiii, 866 p.; 22 cm. 'First printing'. 1. Presidents — United States 2. Government and the press — United States. I. T.
E176.1.P8 1973   323.44/5   *LC* 47-1213

The Presidents: a reference history / Henry F. Graff, editor.   **3.6311**
New York: Charles Scribner's Sons, c1984. xi, 700 p.; 29 cm. 1. Presidents — United States — History. 2. Presidents — United States — Biography 3. United States — Politics and government I. Graff, Henry F. (Henry Franklin), 1921-
E176.1.P918 1984   973/.09/92 B 19   *LC* 83-20225   *ISBN* 0684176076

Southwick, Leslie H., 1950-.   **3.6312**
Presidential also–rans and running mates, 1788–1980 / by Leslie H. Southwick. — Jefferson, N.C.: McFarland & Co., c1984. xiii, 722 p.; 24 cm. Includes index. 1. Presidents — United States — Election — History. 2. Presidential candidates — United States — Biography. 3. Vice-Presidential candidates — United States — Biography. 4. Vice-Presidents — United States — Election — History. 5. United States — Politics and government I. T.
E176.1.S695 1984   324.973 19   *LC* 83-25577   *ISBN* 0899501095

White, William Allen, 1868-1944. • **3.6313**
Masks in a pageant. — Westport, Conn.: Greenwood Press, [1971] xv, 507 p.: illus., ports.; 23 cm. Reprint of the 1928 ed. 1. Presidents — United States — Biography 2. Statesmen — United States. 3. United States — Politics and government I. T.
E176.1.W58 1971   973/.099   *LC* 73-110884   *ISBN* 0837145686

E178–179 American History: General Works

Bancroft, George, 1800-1891. • **3.6314**
History of the United States of America, from the discovery of the continent. New York, D. Appleton and company, 1891-92. 6 v. front. (port.) 23 cm. 1. United States — History — Colonial period, ca. 1600-1775 2. United States — History — Revolution, 1775-1783 3. United States — History — Confederation, 1783-1789 I. T.
E178.B2276   *LC* 18-8245

Beard, Charles Austin, 1874-1948. • **3.6315**
The rise of American civilization / by Charles A. Beard & Mary R. Beard; decorations by Wilfred Jones. — New ed., two volumes in one, rev. and enl. — New York: Macmillan, [1949] xi, 824, 903 p.: ill., col. maps; 21 cm. 1. United States — Civilization 2. United States — History I. Beard, Mary Ritter, 1876-1958. II. T.
E178.B4 1949

Burns, James MacGregor.   **3.6316**
The vineyard of liberty: the American experiment / by James MacGregor Burns. — 1st ed. — New York: Knopf: Distributed by Random House, 1982, c1981. xii, 741 p., [4] leaves of plates: maps; 24 cm. (The American experiment) 1. United States — History — 1783-1865 I. T.
E178.B96 1982   973 19   *LC* 81-47510   *ISBN* 0394505468

Channing, Edward, 1856-1931.   **• 3.6317**
A history of the United States / by Edward Channing. — New York: The Macmillan company, 1905-1925. 6 v.: ill. Vol. I dated 1928; vol. II-III, VI, 1927; vol. IV, 1929; vol. V, 1930. 1. United States — History I. Moore, Eva G. II. T.
E178.C442

Commager, Henry Steele, 1902- ed.   **• 3.6318**
The heritage of America / edited by Henry Steele Commager and Allan Nevins. — Rev. and enl. ed. — Boston: Little, Brown, 1949. xxiv, 1227 p.: ill.; 21 cm. 1. American literature 2. United States — History I. Nevins, Allan, 1890-1971. joint ed. II. T.
E178.C7274   973.082   *LC* 49-48565

Degler, Carl N.   **• 3.6319**
Out of our past: the forces that shaped modern America / [by] Carl N. Degler. — Rev. ed. — New York: Harper & Row, [1970] xx, 546 p.; 22 cm. 1. U.S. — History. I. T.
E178.D37 1970   973   *LC* 77-88637

Dulles, Foster Rhea, 1900-1970.   **• 3.6320**
The United States since 1865. — New ed. rev. and enl. — Ann Arbor: University of Michigan Press, [1969] ix, 562, xx p.: illus.; 25 cm. — (The University of Michigan history of the modern world) 1. U.S. — History — 1865- I. T.
E178.D87 1969   973   *LC* 69-15850

Hacker, Louis Morton, 1899-.   **• 3.6321**
The shaping of the American tradition / text by Louis M. Hacker, documents by Louis M. Hacker and Helene S. Zahler. — New York: Columbia University Press, 1947. 2 v. (xxiv, 1247 p.) 1. United States — History 2. United States — History — Sources 3. United States — Civilization — History. I. Zahler, Helene Sara, 1911- II. T.
E178.H14 1947a   *LC* 47-4680

Handlin, Oscar, 1915-.   **• 3.6322**
The Americans; a new history of the people of the United States. With illus. by Samuel H. Bryant. — [1st ed.]. — Boston: Little, Brown, [1963] 434 p.: illus.; 22 cm. 1. United States — History I. T.
E178.H24   973   *LC* 63-8951

Meinig, D. W. (Donald William), 1924-.   **3.6323**
The shaping of America: a geographical perspective on 500 years of history / D.W. Meinig. — New Haven: Yale University Press, c1986-. v. < 1 >: ill.; 26 cm. Includes index. 1. United States — History 2. United States — Historical geography I. T.
E178.M57 1986   973 19   *LC* 85-17962   *ISBN* 0300035489

Morison, Samuel Eliot, 1887-1976.   **• 3.6324**
The growth of the American Republic / [by] Samuel Eliot Morison, Henry Steele Commager, and William E. Leuchtenburg. — [6th ed., rev., and enl.]. — New York: Oxford University Press, 1969-. v.   : ill., maps, ports.; 24 cm. Abbreviated and newly rev. ed. published in 1977 under title: A Concise history of the American Republic. 1. United States — History I. Commager, Henry Steele, 1902- II. Leuchtenburg, William Edward, 1922- III. T.
E178.M852   973   *LC* 69-10494

Morison, Samuel Eliot, 1887-1976.   **• 3.6325**
The Oxford history of the American people. — New York: Oxford University Press, 1965. xxvii, 1150 p.: ill., coats of arms, facsims., maps, ports.; 24 cm. Includes unacc. melodies. 1. United States — History I. T.
E178.M855   973   *LC* 65-12468

Turner, Frederick Jackson, 1861-1932.   **3.6326**
The significance of sections in American history; with an introd. by Max Farrand. Gloucester, Mass., Smith, 1950 [c1932] ix, 347 p. maps. 21 cm. Essays, edited by Max Farrand and Avery Craven. 1. Sectionalism (United States) 2. United States — History I. T.
E178.T8   973

Wilson, Woodrow, 1856-1924.   **• 3.6327**
Division and reunion, 1829-1889. [11th ed.] New York: Collier Books [1961] xvii, 256 p.; 18 cm. 1. United States — History — Civil War, 1861-1865 2. United States — History 3. United States — Politics and government I. T.
E178.Wx   *LC* 63-22872

Bailey, Thomas Andrew, 1902-.   **• 3.6328**
The American pageant: a history of the Republic / [by] Thomas A. Bailey. — 3d ed. — Boston: Heath, [1965, c1966] xiv, 998, lx p.: ill., maps (part col.); 25 cm. 1. United States — History I. T.
E178.1.B15 1966   973   *LC* 66-11587

Hofstadter, Richard, 1916-1970.   **• 3.6329**
The United States [by] Richard Hofstadter, William Miller [and] Daniel Aaron. — 3d ed. — Englewood Cliffs, N.J.: Prentice-Hall, [1972] xvi, 879, xviia-lxiii p.: illus.; 25 cm. 1. United States — History I. Miller, William, 1912- joint author. II. Aaron, Daniel, 1912- joint author. III. T.
E178.1.H7 1972   973   *LC* 79-160528   *ISBN* 0139384235

E178.4–178.5 Humor. Pictorial Works

Armour, Richard Willard, 1906-.   **3.6330**
It all would have startled Columbus: a further mangling of American history that started with It all started with Columbus / Richard Armour; with ill. of the more unlikely events by Campbell Grant. — 2d ed. — New York: McGraw-Hill, c1976. 137 p.: ill.; 21 cm. First and rev. editions published under title: It all started with Columbus. 1. United States — History, Comic, satirical, etc. I. T.
E178.4.A7 1976   973/.02/07   *LC* 76-13203   *ISBN* 0070022720

Nevins, Allan, 1890-1971.   **• 3.6331**
A century of political cartoons: caricature in the United States from 1800 to 1900 / by Allan Nevins and Frank Weitenkampf; with 100 reproductions of cartoons. — New York: Scribner, 1944. 190, [1] p.: ill.; 26 cm. 1. Caricatures and cartoons — United States 2. United States — History, Comic, satirical, etc. I. Weitenkampf, Frank, 1866-1962. II. T.
E178.4.N47   973.5084   *LC* 44-3029

Album of American history / [by] James Truslow Adams, editor in chief [and others]   **• 3.6332**
New York: Scribner, 1944-[61] 6 v.: ill., ports., maps; 29 cm. 'The intent of the present work is to tell the history of America through pictures made at the time the history was being made.' 1. United States — History — Pictorial works I. Adams, James Truslow, 1878-1949. ed. II. Hopkins, Joseph G. E. ed.
E178.5.A48   973.022/2   *LC* 44-706

Davidson, Marshall.   **• 3.6333**
Life in America. — Boston: Houghton Mifflin, 1951. 2 v.: ill., ports., maps. "Published in association with the Metropolitan Museum of Art." 'Published in associaation with the Metropolitan Museum of Art.' 1. United States — History — Pictorial works 2. United States — Civilization — History. I. T.
E178.5.D3   973   *LC* 51-7084

E178.6–179 Essays

Aaron, Daniel, 1912- ed.   **• 3.6334**
America in crisis; fourteen crucial episodes in American history [by] Perry Miller [and others] Edited by Daniel Aaron. — Hamden, Conn.: Archon Books, 1971 [c1952] xiv, 363 p.; 22 cm. 1. U.S. — History — Addresses, essays, lectures. I. Miller, Perry, 1905-1963. II. T.
E178.6.A17 1971   973.08   *LC* 72-131372   *ISBN* 0208010432

Adams, Henry, 1838-1918.   **• 3.6335**
The great secession winter of 1860-61, and other essays / edited and with an introd. by George Hochfield. — New York: Sagamore Press [1958] xx, 428 p.; 24 cm. 1. United States — Politics and government — 1849-1877 — Addresses, essays, lectures. 2. United States — History — Addresses, essays, lectures I. T.
E178.6.A2   *LC* 58-9144

Bryce, James Bryce, Viscount, 1838-1922.   **• 3.6336**
The study of American history. With an appendix relating to the foundation. Westport, Conn., Greenwood Press [1971, c1922] 118 p. 17 cm. (Lecture of the Sir George Watson chair of American History, Literature and Institutions, 1921) 1. United States — History — Addresses, essays, lectures. I. T.
E178.6.B92 1971   973/.07   *LC* 72-136056   *ISBN* 0837152062

Fine, Sidney A., 1920- ed.   **• 3.6337**
The American past; conflicting interpretations of the great issues. Edited by Sidney Fine & Gerald S. Brown. — 2d ed. — New York: Macmillan, [1965] 2 v.; 24 cm. Vol. 1, edited by Gerald S. Brown. 1. United States — History — Addresses, essays, lectures. 2. United States — History — Philosophy — Addresses, essays, lectures. I. Brown, Gerald Saxon, ed. II. T.
E178.6.F522   973.082   *LC* 65-15184

Garraty, John Arthur, 1920-. • **3.6338**
Interpreting American history; conversations with historians [by] John A. Garraty. Drawings from life by Gail Garraty. — [New York]: Macmillan, [1970] 2 v. in 1: ports.; 24 cm. 1. United States — History — Addresses, essays, lectures. 2. United States — History — Philosophy — Addresses, essays, lectures. I. T.
E178.6.G27   973/.01   LC 70-97761

Williams, William Appleman. **3.6339**
History as a way of learning; articles, excerpts, and essays. — New York: New Viewpoints, 1973 [c1974] xvi, 430 p.; 22 cm. 1. United States — History — Addresses, essays, lectures. 2. United States — Historiography — Addresses, essays, lectures. I. T.
E178.6.W6 1974   973   LC 73-10469   ISBN 0531063623

Bailey, Thomas Andrew, 1902-. **3.6340**
Voices of America: the Nation's story in slogans, sayings, and songs / Thomas A. Bailey, with the assistance of Stephen M. Dobbs. — New York: Free Press, c1976. viii, 520 p.; 25 cm. Includes index. 1. Quotations, American 2. Slogans, American 3. Songs, English — United States — Texts. 4. United States — History I. T.
E179.B16   973   LC 76-8143   ISBN 0029012600

Hofstadter, Richard, 1916-1970. comp. • **3.6341**
American violence: a documentary history / edited by Richard Hofstadter and Michael Wallace. — [1st ed.]. — New York: Knopf, 1970. xiv, 478, xiii p.; 25 cm. 1. Violence — United States. 2. United States — History I. Wallace, Michael. joint comp. II. T.
E179.H8 1970   973   LC 73-111238   ISBN 0394414861

Shankle, George Earlie. • **3.6342**
American nicknames; their origin and significance. 2d ed. New York, Wilson, 1955. vii, 524 p. 26 cm. 1. Nicknames — United States. 2. Names, Geographical — United States. 3. Names, Personal I. T.
E179.S545 1955   929.4   LC 55-5038

E179.5–180 Historical Geography

Billington, Ray Allen, 1903-. • **3.6343**
America's frontier heritage. [1st ed.] New York: Holt, Rinehart and Winston [1966] xiv, 302 p.; 24 cm. (Histories of the American frontier.) 1. Frontier and pioneer life — United States. 2. National characteristics, American I. T. II. Series.
E 179.5 B57 1966   LC 66-13289

Billington, Ray Allen, 1903- ed. • **3.6344**
The frontier thesis: valid interpretation of American history?. — New York: Holt, Rinehart and Winston, [1966] 122 p.: port.; 24 cm. — (American problem studies) 1. Turner, Frederick Jackson, 1861-1932 The frontier in American history — Addresses, essays, lectures. 2. Frontier thesis — Addresses, essays, lectures. I. T.
E179.5.B625   973.01   LC 66-21640

Billington, Ray Allen, 1903-. **3.6345**
Westward expansion: a history of the American frontier / Ray Allen Billington, Martin Ridge. — 5th ed. — New York: Macmillan; London: Collier Macmillan Publishers, c1982. xv, 892 p.: maps; 25 cm. Includes index. 1. United States — Territorial expansion 2. United States — History 3. Mississippi River Valley — History — 1803-1865. 4. West (U.S.) — History I. Ridge, Martin. II. T.
E179.5.B63 1982   973 19   LC 81-8450   ISBN 0023098600

Brown, Ralph Hall, 1898-1948. • **3.6346**
Historical geography of the United States, by Ralph H. Brown, under the editorship of J. Russell Whitaker. — New York, Harcourt, Brace, [1948] viii, 596 p. illus., maps. 24 cm. Bibliography: p. [539]-571. 1. United States — Historical geography I. Whitaker, J. Russell (Joe Russell), 1900- ed. II. T.
E179.5.B9   973   LC 48-1500 *

Clark, Thomas Dionysius, 1903-. • **3.6347**
Frontier America: the story of the westward movement / [by] Thomas D. Clark. — 2d ed. — New York: Scribner, [1969] xii, 836 p.: ill., maps.; 25 cm. 1. Frontier and pioneer life — U.S. 2. U.S. — Territorial expansion. I. T.
E179.5.C48 1969   973   LC 69-11124

De Voto, Bernard Augustine, 1897-1955. • **3.6348**
The course of empire / with maps by Erwin Raisz. — Boston: Houghton, Mifflin, 1952. xvii, 647 p.: maps (part col.); 22 cm. 1. Indians of North America — History 2. North America — Discription and exploration. 3. United States — Territorial expansion I. T.
E179.5.D4   973.1   LC 52-5261

Graebner, Norman A. • **3.6349**
Empire on the Pacific; a study in American continental expansion. — New York, Ronald Press Co. [1955] ix, 278 p. maps. 21 cm. Bibliographical references included in 'Notes' (p. 229-257) 'Bibliographical essay': p. 258-265. 1. United States — Territorial expansion 2. Pacific States — Hist. 3. United States — Pol. & govt. — 1845-1849. I. T.
E179.5.G7   973.61   LC 55-10664

Hofstadter, Richard, 1916-1970. comp. • **3.6350**
Turner and the sociology of the frontier. Edited by Richard Hofstadter and Seymour Martin Lipset. — New York: Basic Books, [1968] vi, 232 p.: illus.; 22 cm. — (The Sociology of American history) 1. Turner, Frederick Jackson, 1861-1932. 2. Frontier and pioneer life — United States. 3. United States — Historiography I. Lipset, Seymour Martin. joint comp. II. T.
E179.5.H62   301.29/73   LC 68-22859

Kolodny, Annette, 1941-. **3.6351**
The land before her: fantasy and experience of the American frontiers, 1630–1860 / Annette Kolodny. — Chapel Hill: University of North Carolina Press, c1984. xix, 293 p.: ill.; 24 cm. Includes index. 1. Women pioneers — United States. 2. Frontier and pioneer life in literature — United States. 3. Women in popular culture — United States. 4. Women in literature 5. Frontier and pioneer life in literature. 6. United States — Territorial expansion I. T.
E179.5.K64 1984   973/.088042 19   LC 83-10629   ISBN 0807815713

Lewis, Kenneth E. **3.6352**
The American frontier: an archaeological study of settlement pattern and process / Kenneth E. Lewis. — Orlando: Academic Press, 1984. xxvi, 333 p.: ill.; 25 cm. — (Studies in historical archaeology) Includes index. 1. Frontier and pioneer life — United States. 2. Frontier and pioneer life — South Carolina. 3. Land settlement patterns — United States. 4. Land settlement patterns — South Carolina — Camden Region. 5. United States — Antiquities 6. South Carolina — Antiquities I. T.
E179.5.L49 1984   975.7/02 19   LC 83-19725   ISBN 0124465609

Merk, Frederick, 1887-. • **3.6353**
Manifest destiny and mission in American history: a reinterpretation / with the collaboration of Lois Bannister Merk. — [1st ed.]. — New York: Knopf, 1963. 265 p.; 25 cm. 1. Public opinion — United States. 2. Imperialism 3. United States — Territorial expansion I. T.
E179.5.M4   973.6   LC 63-8204

Odum, Howard Washington, 1884-1954. • **3.6354**
American regionalism: a cultural–historical approach to national integration / by Howard W. Odum and Harry Estill Moore. — New York: H. Holt, 1938. x, 696 p.: ill. 1. Regionalism — United States. I. Moore, Harry Estill. II. T.
E179.5.O43   LC 38-15648

Philbrick, Francis Samuel, 1876-. • **3.6355**
The rise of the West, 1754–1830 / by Francis S. Philbrick. — New York: Harper & Row, 1965. xvii, 398, [16] p.: ill., maps, ports. — (New American Nation series.) (New American Nation series.) 1. Northwest, Old — History — 1775-1865 2. Southwest, Old — History I. T. II. Series.
E179.5.P45   LC 65-21377

Pletcher, David M. **3.6356**
The diplomacy of annexation; Texas, Oregon, and the Mexican War [by] David M. Pletcher. — [Columbia]: University of Missouri Press, [1973] xiii, 656 p.: illus.; 25 cm. 1. Oregon question 2. United States — Territorial expansion 3. United States — Foreign relations — 1815-1861 4. United States — History — War with Mexico, 1845-1848 I. T.
E179.5.P57   973.6/1   LC 72-88573   ISBN 0826201350

Semple, Ellen Churchill, 1863-1932. **3.6357**
American history and its geographic conditions. Rev. in collaboration with the author by Clarence Fielden Jones. — New York: Russell & Russell, [1968, c1933] x, 541 p.: maps (part fold.); 22 cm. 1. Physical geography — United States. 2. Anthropo-geography — United States. 3. United States — Historical geography I. Jones, Clarence Fielden, 1893- II. T.
E179.5.S47 1968   911/.73   LC 68-25039

Slotkin, Richard, 1942-. **3.6358**
The fatal environment: the myth of the frontier in the age of industrialization, 1800–1890 / by Richard Slotkin. — 1st ed. — New York: Atheneum, 1985. xiii, 636 p.; 25 cm. Includes index. 1. Frontier and pioneer life — United States — Historiography. 2. Little Big Horn, Battle of the, 1876 — Historiography. 3. Frontier and pioneer life in literature. 4. American literature — 19th century — History and criticism. 5. Myth I. T.
E179.5.S6 1985   973/.072 19   LC 83-45084   ISBN 0689114109

Turner, Frederick Jackson, 1861-1932. • 3.6359
The frontier in American history / With a foreword by Ray Allen Billington. — New York: Holt, Rinehart and Winston, [1962] xx, 375 p.; 19 cm. 1. Frontier thesis 2. United States — History I. T.
E179.5.T956 1962   973   *LC* 62-12340

Taylor, George Rogers, 1895- ed. • 3.6360
The Turner thesis concerning the role of the frontier in American history. Rev. ed. — Boston: Heath, [1956] 109 p.; 24 cm. — (Problems in American civilization; readings selected by the Dept. of American Studies, Amherst College) 1. Turner, Frederick Jackson, 1861-1932. The frontier in American history. 2. Frontier thesis I. T.
E179.5.T96 T3 1956   973   *LC* 56-14601

Van Alstyne, Richard Warner, 1900-. 3.6361
The rising American empire. [1st ed.] New York: Oxford University Press, 1960. 215 p. illus. 23 cm. Includes bibliography. 1. Imperialism 2. United States — Territorial expansion 3. United States — Foreign relations I. T.
E179.5.V32   911.73   *LC* 60-52215

Weinberg, Albert Katz. • 3.6362
Manifest destiny: a study of nationalist expansionism in American history / [by] Albert K. Weinberg. — Baltimore: The Johns Hopkins Press, 1935. xiii, 559 p.; 24 cm. At head of title: The Walter Hines Page school of international relations, the Johns Hopkins university. 'Notes': p. 487-542. 1. Political science — History — United States. 2. Public opinion — United States. 3. Political ethics 4. United States — Nationality. 5. United States — Territorial expansion I. Walter Hines Page School of International Relations. II. T. III. Title: Expansionism in American history.
E179.5.W45   973   *LC* 35-9403

Winks, Robin W. • 3.6363
The myth of the American frontier; its relevance to America, Canada and Australia, by Robin W. Winks. — [Leicester, Eng.]: Leicester University Press, 1971. 39 p.; 22 cm. — (Sir George Watson lecture, 1971) 1. Frontier thesis 2. Frontier and pioneer life — United States. 3. Frontier and pioneer life — Canada. 4. Frontier and pioneer life — Australia. I. T. II. Series.
E179.5.W54 1971   917/.03   *LC* 72-185991   *ISBN* 0718511107

Kane, Joseph Nathan, 1899-. 3.6364
The American counties: origins of county names, dates of creation and organization, area, population including 1980 census figures, historical data, and published sources / by Joseph Nathan Kane. — 4th ed. — Metuchen, N.J.: Scarecrow Press, 1983. 546 p.; 23 cm. 1. United States — History, Local I. T.
E180.K3 1983   973 19   *LC* 82-5982   *ISBN* 0810815583

E181–182 Military and Naval History

Matloff, Maurice, 1915-. • 3.6365
American military history. Washington: Office of the Chief of Military History, U.S. Army; [for sale by the Supt. of Docs., U.S. Govt. Print. Off.] 1969. xvi, 701 p.: ill., maps, ports.; 26 cm. (Army historical series) Replaces earlier publications issued by the U.S. Dept. of the Army under the same title. 1. United States — History, Military I. United States. Dept. of the Army. American military history. II. T.
E181.A44 1969   355/.00973   *LC* 76-600410

Jacobs, James Ripley, 1886-. • 3.6366
The beginning of the U.S. Army, 1783–1812. — Princeton: Princeton Univ. Press, 1947. ix, 419 p.: ill., ports., maps, plans.; 23 cm. Bibliography: p. [387]-397. 1. United States. Army — Hist. 2. U.S. — History, Military. I. T.
E181.J2   973.4   *LC* 47-5140 *

Leonard, Thomas C., 1944-. 3.6367
Above the battle: war making in America from Appomattox to Versailles / Thomas C. Leonard. — New York: Oxford University Press, c1977. viii, 260 p.: ill.; 22 cm. 1. War — Public opinion. 2. Public opinion — United States. 3. War in literature 4. United States — History, Military I. T.
E181.L5   973

Millett, Allan Reed. 3.6368
For the common defense: a military history of the United States of America / Allan R. Millett, Peter Maslowski. — New York: Free Press; London: Collier Macmillan, c1984. xiv, 621 p., [16] p. of plates: ill.; 25 cm. Includes index. 1. United States — History, Military 2. United States — Armed Forces — History. I. Maslowski, Peter, 1944- II. T.
E181.M6986 1984   973 19   *LC* 84-13652   *ISBN* 0029215803

Millis, Walter, 1899-1968. • 3.6369
Arms and men: a study in American military history. — New York: Putnam, [1956] 382 p.; 22 cm. 1. United States — History, Military 2. United States — Armed Forces — History. 3. United States — Military policy I. T.
E181.M699   973   *LC* 56-10240

Palmer, Frederick, 1873-1958. • 3.6370
John J. Pershing, General of the Armies: a biography. — Westport, Conn.: Greenwood Press, [1970, c1948] xiii, 380 p.: ports.; 23 cm. 1. Pershing, John J. (John Joseph), 1860-1948. I. T.
E181.P512 1970   355.3/32/0924 B   *LC* 77-100253   *ISBN* 0837129869

Prucha, Francis Paul. • 3.6371
The sword of the Republic: the United States Army on the frontier, 1783–1846. — [New York]: Macmillan, [1968, c1969] xvii, 442 p.: ill., maps, ports.; 24 cm. — (Wars of the United States.) 1. U.S. Army — History. 2. U.S. — History, Military — To 1900. I. T. II. Series.
E181.P86   977/.02   *LC* 69-10292

Small, Melvin. 3.6372
Was war necessary?: National security and U.S. entry into war / Melvin Small. — Beverly Hills: Sage Publications, c1980. 311 p.; 23 cm. — (Sage library of social research; 105) 1. United States — History, Military 2. United States — National security I. T.
E181.S54   973   *LC* 80-13536   *ISBN* 0803914865

Williams, T. Harry (Thomas Harry), 1909-. 3.6373
The history of American wars from 1745 to 1918 / by T. Harry Williams. — 1st ed. — New York: Knopf: distributed by Random House, 1981. xviii, 435 p.; 24 cm. Includes index. 1. United States — History, Military I. T.
E181.W64 1981   973 19   *LC* 80-2717   *ISBN* 0394511670

Hagedorn, Hermann, 1882-1964. • 3.6374
Leonard Wood: a biography / by Hermann Hagedorn. — 1st ed. New York; London: Harper & brothers, 1931. 2 v.: ill., plates. ports.; 25 cm. 1. Wood, Leonard, 1860-1927. I. T.
E181.W83   *LC* 31-24003

Braisted, William Reynolds. • 3.6375
The United States Navy in the Pacific, 1897–1909. — New York: Greenwood Press, [1969, c1958] xii, 282 p.; 23 cm. 1. U.S. — History, Naval. 2. U.S. — Foreign relations — 1897-1901. 3. U.S. — Foreign relations — 1901-1909. I. T.
E182.B73 1969   327.73/018/23   *LC* 70-90473   *ISBN* 0837121329

King, Ernest Joseph, 1878-1956. • 3.6376
Fleet Admiral King: a naval record / by Ernest J. King and Walter Muir Whitehill. — [1st ed.] New York: W. W. Norton [1952] xv, 674 p. illus., ports., maps. 24 cm. 1. United States. Navy — History 2. World War, 1939-1945 — Naval operations, American I. Whitehill, Walter Muir, 1905- joint author. II. T.
E182.K53   *LC* 52-13493

Mahan, A. T. (Alfred Thayer), 1840-1914. 3.6377
Letters and papers of Alfred Thayer Mahan / edited by Robert Seager II and Doris D. Maguire. — Annapolis: Naval Institute Press, c1975. 3 v.: ports; 26 cm. (Naval letters series; 4) 1. Mahan, A. T. (Alfred Thayer), 1840-1914. 2. United States — History, Naval — Sources. I. T. II. Series.
E182.M24   359.3/32/0924   *LC* 73-91863   *ISBN* 0870213393

Livezey, William Edmund, 1903-. 3.6378
Mahan on sea power / by William E. Livezey. — Rev. ed. — Norman: University of Oklahoma Press, 1980, c1981. xvi, 427 p.: ill.; 22 cm. Includes index. 1. Mahan, A. T. (Alfred Thayer), 1840-1914. 2. Sea-power — United States. 3. Sea-power. 4. United States — History, Naval. I. T.
E182.M242 L58 1981   359.3/32/0924 B 19   *LC* 82-125808   *ISBN* 0806115696

Seager, Robert, 1924-. 3.6379
Alfred Thayer Mahan: the man and his letters / by Robert Seager II. — Annapolis, Md.: Naval Institute Press, c1977. xvii, 713 p.: ill.; 27 cm. 1. Mahan, A. T. (Alfred Thayer), 1840-1914. 2. United States. Navy — Biography 3. Historians — United States — Biography. 4. United States — History, Naval — To 1900 I. T.
E182.M242 S4   907/.2/024 B   *LC* 77-74158   *ISBN* 0870213598

O'Gara, Gordon Carpenter, 1920-. • 3.6380
Theodore Roosevelt and the rise of the modern Navy. New York: Greenwood Press [1969, c1943] x, 138 p.: ill.; 23 cm. 1. Roosevelt, Theodore, 1858-1919. 2. United States. Navy — History I. T.
E182.O34 1969   359/.00973   *LC* 69-14016   *ISBN* 0837114802

Drake, Frederick C., 1937-. 3.6381
The empire of the seas: a biography of Rear Admiral Robert Wilson Shufeldt, USN / by Frederick C. Drake. — Honolulu: University of Hawaii Press, c1984.

xv, 468 p., [16] p. of plates: ill., maps; 25 cm. Includes index. 1. Shufeldt, Robert Wilson, 1822-1895. 2. United States. Navy — Biography 3. Admirals — United States — Biography. 4. Diplomats — United States — Biography. 5. United States — Territorial expansion 6. United States — History, Naval — To 1900 I. T.
E182.S564 D7 1984   973.8/092/4 B 19   *LC* 84-66   *ISBN* 0824808460

Sprout, Harold Hance, 1901-.   • **3.6382**
The rise of American naval power, 1776–1918 / by Harold & Margaret Sprout. Princeton: Princeton University Press, 1939. vii, 398 p.: front., plates, map.; 24 cm. 'First edition.' 1. United States. Navy — History I. Sprout, Margaret (Tuttle) Mrs., joint author. II. T. III. Title: American naval power, The rise of.
E182.S78   *LC* 39-27471

Sprout, Harold Hance, 1901-.   • **3.6383**
Toward a new order of sea power: American naval policy and the world scene, 1918–1922 / by Harold and Margaret Sprout. — New York: Greenwood Press, [1969, c1943] xii, 336 p.: ill., maps.; 24 cm. Continuation of the author's The rise of American naval power. 1. U.S. Navy — History. 2. Sea-power 3. U.S. — History, Naval — 20th century. I. Sprout, Margaret Tuttle, 1903- joint author. II. T.
E182.S79 1969   359/.009   *LC* 69-14092

West, Richard Sedgewick, 1902-.   • **3.6384**
Admirals of American empire: the combined story of George Dewey, Alfred Thayer Mahan, Winfield Scott Schley, and William Thomas Sampson / by Richard S. West, Jr. — Westport, Conn.: Greenwood Press [1971, c1948] 354 p.: ill.; 23 cm. 1. Dewey, George, 1837-1917. 2. Mahan, A. T. (Alfred Thayer), 1840-1914. 3. Schley, Winfield Scott, 1839-1911. 4. Sampson, William Thomas, 1840-1902. 5. United States — History, Naval — To 1900 I. T.
E182.W45 1971   359/.00922 B   *LC* 73-156216   *ISBN* 0837161673

E183 Political History (General)

Burns, James MacGregor.   • **3.6385**
The deadlock of democracy: four–party politics in America. — Englewood Cliffs, N.J.: Prentice-Hall [1963] 388 p.; 24 cm. 1. Political parties — United States 2. United States — Politics and government I. T. II. Title: Four-party politics in America.
E183.B96   329   *LC* 63-8455

Ekirch, Arthur Alphonse, 1915-.   • **3.6386**
The decline of American Liberalism / [by] Arthur A. Ekirch. — New York: Atheneum, 1967. 401 p.; 19 cm. 1. Liberalism — United States. 2. United States — Politics and government I. T.
E183.E4 1967   *LC* 67-13171

Encyclopedia of American political history: studies of the   **3.6387**
principal movements and ideas / Jack P. Greene, editor.
New York: Scribner, c1984. 3 v. (viii, 1420 p.) Includes index. 1. Political science — United States — History — Dictionaries. 2. United States — Politics and government — Dictionaries. I. Greene, Jack P.
E183.E5 1984   320.973/03/21 19   *LC* 84-1355   *ISBN* 0684170035

Gregory, Dick.   **3.6388**
Dick Gregory's political primer / edited by James R. McGraw. — [1st ed.]. — New York: Harper & Row, [1972] ix, 335 p.: ill.; 22 cm. 1. U.S. — Politics and government. I. T. II. Title: Political primer.
E183.G7   329/.0973   *LC* 71-160648   *ISBN* 0060116013

Lipset, Seymour Martin.   • **3.6389**
The politics of unreason; right wing extremism in America, 1790–1970 [by] Seymour Martin Lipset and Earl Raab. — [1st ed.]. — New York: Harper & Row, [1970] xxiv, 547 p.; 25 cm. — (Patterns of American prejudice series, v. 5) 1. Right and left (Political science) 2. U.S. — Politics and government. I. Raab, Earl. joint author. II. T. III. Series.
E183.L56   320.5   *LC* 67-22529

Martin, Ralph G., 1920-.   • **3.6390**
The bosses. New York, Putman [1964] 349 p. 23 cm. 1. Corruption (in politics) — United States 2. United States — Politics and government I. T.
E183.M25   *LC* 64-18010

Rossiter, Clinton Lawrence, 1917-1970.   • **3.6391**
Parties and politics in America. — Ithaca, N.Y.: Cornell University Press, [1960] vii, 205 p.; 23 cm. 1. Political parties — United States I. T.
E183.R7   329   *LC* 60-16163

Schlesinger, Arthur Meier, 1917-.   **3.6392**
History of American presidential elections, 1789–1968 / Arthur M. Schlesinger, Jr., editor; Fred L. Israel, associate editor; William P. Hansen, managing editor. — New York: Chelsea House, [1971] 4 v. (xxxvii, 3959 p.); 24 cm. 1. Presidents — U.S. — Election — History. 2. U.S. — Politics and government. I. Israel, Fred L. joint author. II. T.
E183.S28   329/.023/73   *LC* 70-139269   *ISBN* 0070797862

Smith, William Raymond.   • **3.6393**
The rhetoric of American politics; a study of documents. — Westport, Conn.: Greenwood Pub. Corp., [c1969] xv, 464 p.; 22 cm. 1. Rhetoric — Political aspects — United States — Addresses, essays, lectures. 2. Debates and debating — Addresses, essays, lectures. 3. United States — Politics and government — Addresses, essays, lectures. I. T.
E183.S67   320.9/73   *LC* 71-95503   *ISBN* 0837114950

E183.7 Diplomatic History (General)

Bailey, Thomas Andrew, 1902-.   **3.6394**
A diplomatic history of the American people / Thomas A. Bailey. — 10th ed. — Englewood Cliffs, N.J.: Prentice-Hall, c1980. 1093, xxxix p.: ill.; 24 cm. 1. United States — Foreign relations I. T.
E183.7.B29 1980   327.73   *LC* 79-17620   *ISBN* 0132147262

Bailey, Thomas Andrew, 1902-.   • **3.6395**
The man in the street; the impact of American public opinion on foreign policy, by Thomas A. Bailey. — Gloucester, Mass., P. Smith, 1964 [c1948] v, 334 p. 21 cm. Bibliography: p. 321-323. 1. U.S. — For. rel. 2. Public opinion — U.S. I. T.
E183.7.B33 1964   327.73   *LC* 64-56381

Bemis, Samuel Flagg, 1891-1973.   • **3.6396**
The American secretaries of state and their diplomacy. New York, Cooper Square Publishers, 1963- < 1980 > [v. 1-10, c1928] < v.1-19; in 14 > ports. 22 cm. Vols. 11-< 19 > edited by Robert H. Ferrell. 1. Cabinet officers — United States. 2. Statesmen — United States. 3. United States — Foreign relations I. Ferrell, Robert H. II. T. III. Title: Secretaries of state.
E183.7.B462   327.73   *LC* 62-20139

Bemis, Samuel Flagg, 1891-1973.   • **3.6397**
A diplomatic history of the United States. 5th ed. New York: Holt, Rinehart and Winston, [1965] x, 1062 p.: ill., maps (part col.); 24 cm. 1. United States — Foreign relations I. T.
E183.7.B4682 1965   327.73   *LC* 65-11841

Brune, Lester H.   **3.6398**
Chronological history of United States foreign relations, 1776 to January 20, 1981 / Lester H. Brune. — New York: Garland, 1985. 2 v. (xviii, 1289 p.): maps; 27 cm. (Garland reference library of social science. v. 196) Includes index. 1. United States — Foreign relations — Chronology. I. T. II. Series.
E183.7.B745 1985   327.73 19   *LC* 83-48210   *ISBN* 082409056X

Combs, Jerald A.   **3.6399**
American diplomatic history: two centuries of changing interpretations / Jerald A. Combs. — Berkeley: University of California Press, c1983. xii, 413 p.; 24 cm. 1. United States — Foreign relations — Historiography I. T.
E183.7.C655 1983   327.73 19   *LC* 81-24067   *ISBN* 0520045904

Crabb, Cecil Van Meter, 1924-.   **3.6400**
The doctrines of American foreign policy: their meaning, role, and future / Cecil V. Crabb, Jr. — Baton Rouge: Louisiana State University Press, c1982. xii, 446 p.; 24 cm. 1. United States — Foreign relations I. T.
E183.7.C7 1982   327.73 19   *LC* 81-20846   *ISBN* 0807110167

De Conde, Alexander.   **3.6401**
A history of American foreign policy / Alexander DeConde. — 3d ed. — New York: Scribner, c1978. 2 v.; 23 cm. 1. United States — Foreign relations I. T.
E183.7.D4 1978   327.73   *LC* 78-7264   *ISBN* 0684152197

Dulles, Foster Rhea, 1900-1970.   • **3.6402**
The imperial years. New York, Crowell [1956] 340 p. illus. 22 cm. 1. United States — Foreign relations — 1865-1898 2. United States — Foreign relations — 1897-1901 3. United States — Foreign relations — 1901-1909 4. United States — Territorial expansion I. T.
E183.7.D78   *LC* 56-7790

Ferrell, Robert H.　　　　　　　　　　　　　　　**3.6403**
American diplomacy: a history / Robert H. Ferrell; [cartography by E. D. Weldon]. — 3d ed. — New York: Norton, [1975] xiv, 881 p.: ill.; 23 cm. 1. United States — Foreign relations I. T.
E183.7.F4 1975　　　327.73　　　*LC* 74-22220　　　*ISBN* 0393093093

Ferrell, Robert H. comp.　　　　　　　　　　　　**3.6404**
Foundations of American diplomacy, 1775–1872 / edited by Robert H. Ferrell. Cartography by Norman J. G. Pounds. — [1st ed.]. — Columbia: University of South Carolina Press, [1969] ix, 284 p.: maps.; 24 cm. — ([Documentary history of the United States]) Continued by America as a world power, 1872-1945. 1. United States — Foreign relations — Revolution, 1775-1783 — Sources. 2. United States — Foreign relations — 1783-1865 — Sources. I. T.
E183.7.F43 1969　　　327.73　　　*LC* 72-1652　　　*ISBN* 0872491226

Findling, John E.　　　　　　　　　　　　　　　**3.6405**
Dictionary of American diplomatic history / John E. Findling. — Westport, Conn.: Greenwood Press, 1980. xviii, 622 p.; 25 cm. 1. Ambassadors — United States — Biography. 2. Diplomats — United States — Biography. 3. United States — Foreign relations — Dictionaries. I. T.
E183.7.F5　　　327.73　　　*LC* 79-7730　　　*ISBN* 0313220395

Merli, Frank J., 1929-.　　　　　　　　　　　　　**3.6406**
Makers of American diplomacy: from Benjamin Franklin to Henry Kissinger / edited by Frank J. Merli and Theodore A. Wilson. — New York: Scribner, [1974] xix, 728 p.: ill.; 24 cm. 1. Diplomats — United States. 2. United States — Foreign relations I. Wilson, Theodore A., 1940- joint author. II. T.
E183.7.M472　　　327/.2/0922 B　　　*LC* 73-1321　　　*ISBN* 0684137860

Perkins, Dexter, 1889-.　　　　　　　　　　　• **3.6407**
The American approach to foreign policy / Dexter Perkins. — Rev. ed. — Cambridge: Harvard University Press, 1962. 247 p. 1. United States — Foreign relations I. T.
E183.7.P46 1962　　　*LC* 62-11400

Perkins, Dexter, 1889-.　　　　　　　　　　　• **3.6408**
The evolution of American foreign policy. 2d ed. New York: Oxford University Press, 1966. 168 p.; 21 cm. (A Galaxy book) 1. United States — Foreign relations I. T.
E183.7.P47 1966　　　327.73　　　*LC* 66-10824

Spykman, Nicholas John, 1893-1943.　　　　　　**3.6409**
America's strategy in world politics: the United States and the balance of power / maps by Richard Edes Harrison. — [Hamden, Conn.]: Archon Books, 1970 [c1942] 500 p.: maps.; 24 cm. 1. Pan-Americanism 2. World politics — 1933-1945 3. U.S. — Foreign relations. I. T.
E183.7.S7 1970　　　327.73　　　*LC* 75-103990

Williams, William Appleman.　　　　　　　　　• **3.6410**
From colony to empire; essays in the history of American foreign relations. Edited by William Appleman Williams. — New York: J. Wiley, [1972] viii, 506 p.: illus.; 23 cm. 1. United States — Foreign relations — Addresses, essays, lectures. 2. United States — Territorial expansion — Addresses, essays, lectures. I. T.
E183.7.W725　　　327.73　　　*LC* 72-545　　　*ISBN* 0471946850

E183.8 Relations with Particular Countries, A–Z

E183.8.A–.C AUSTRALIA. BRAZIL. CANADA. CHILE

Bartlett, Norman.　　　　　　　　　　　　　　　**3.6411**
Australia and America through 200 years; 1776–1976 / Norman Bartlett; foreword by Malcolm Fraser; introd. by Manning Clark. — 1st ed. — Sydney: published by S. U. Smith at the Fine Arts Press, 1976. xiv, 258 p., 8 leaves of plates: ill. (some col.); 26 cm. 1. United States — Relations — Australia 2. Australia — Relations — United States 3. Australia — History I. T.
E183.8.A8 B37　　　301.29/73/094　　　*LC* 77-354903　　　*ISBN* 0869170007

Hill, Lawrence F. (Lawrence Francis), 1890-.　　　• **3.6412**
Diplomatic relations between the United States and Brazil / by Lawrence F. Hill. — New York: AMS Press [1971] x, 322 p.; 23 cm. Reprint of the 1932 ed. 1. United States — Foreign relations — Brazil. 2. Brazil — Foreign relations — United States. I. T.
E183.8.B7 H56 1971　　　327.73/081　　　*LC* 76-169489　　　*ISBN* 0404032680

Atlantic Council Working Group on the United States and Canada.　　　　　　　　　　　　　　　　　　　　**3.6413**
Canada and the United States, dependence and divergence / the Atlantic Council Working Group on the United States and Canada; Willis C. Armstrong, chairman and rapporteur, Louise S. Armstrong, co-rapporteur; Francis O. Wilcox, project director; foreword by Kenneth Rush. — Cambridge, Mass.: Ballinger Pub. Co., c1982. xiv, 331 p.; 24 cm. 1. United States — Relations — Canada — Congresses. 2. Canada — Relations — United States — Congresses. I. Armstrong, Willis C. II. T.
E183.8.C2 A87 1982　　　327.71073 19　　　*LC* 81-20607　　　*ISBN* 0884108724

Cuff, Robert D., 1941-.　　　　　　　　　　　　　**3.6414**
Canadian–American relations in wartime: from the Great War to the cold war / R. D. Cuff, J. L. Granatstein. — Toronto: Hakkert, 1975. xiii, 205 p.; 22 cm. 1. United States — Foreign relations — Canada. 2. Canada — Foreign relations — United States I. Granatstein, J. L. joint author. II. T.
E183.8.C2 C87　　　327.71/073　　　*LC* 74-80412　　　*ISBN* 0888665563

Curtis, Kenneth M., 1931-.　　　　　　　　　　　**3.6415**
Canadian–American relations: the promise and the challenge / Kenneth M. Curtis, John E. Carroll. — Lexington, Mass.: Lexington Books, c1983. xi, 107 p.: map; 24 cm. Includes index. 1. United States — Relations — Canada 2. Canada — Relations — United States I. Carroll, John E. (John Edward), 1944- II. T.
E183.8.C2 C89 1983　　　327.73071 19　　　*LC* 83-47990　　　*ISBN* 0669067938

Doran, Charles F.　　　　　　　　　　　　　　　**3.6416**
Forgotten partnership: U.S.–Canada relations today / Charles F. Doran. — Baltimore: Johns Hopkins University Press, c1984. viii, 294 p.; 24 cm. 1. United States — Foreign relations — Canada. 2. Canada — Foreign relations — United States I. T.
E183.8.C2 D67 1984　　　327.73071 19　　　*LC* 83-48052　　　*ISBN* 0801830338

Preston, Richard Arthur. ed.　　　　　　　　　　**3.6417**
The Influence of the United States on Canadian development: eleven case studies [by] Irving M. Abella [and others] Edited by Richard A. Preston. Durham, N.C., Duke University Press, 1972. xii, 269 p. 24 cm. (Commonwealth-Studies Center. Publication 40) Papers presented at the inaugural seminar conference of the Association for Canadian Studies in the United States held at Duke University, April 1971. 1. United States — Relations — Canada — Addresses, essays, lectures. 2. Canada — Relations — United States — Addresses, essays, lectures. I. Abella, Irving M., 1940- II. Association for Canadian Studies in the United States. III. T.
E183.8.C2 I48　　　301.29/73/071　　　*LC* 72-81337　　　*ISBN* 0822302748

Pike, Fredrick B.　　　　　　　　　　　　　　　**3.6418**
Chile and the United States, 1880–1962; the emergence of Chile's social crisis and the challenge to United States diplomacy. [Notre Dame, Ind.] University of Notre Dame Press, 1963. 466 p. 24 cm. (International studies of the Committee on International Relations, University of Notre Dame) 1. United States — Relations — Chile 2. Chile — Relations — United States I. T.
E183.8.C4 P5　　　983.061　　　*LC* 63-9097

E183.8.C5 CHINA

Ch'ou pan i wu shih mo. English. Selections.　　　**3.6419**
China's management of the American barbarians; a study of Sino–American relations, 1841–1861, with documents. By Earl Swisher. — New York: Octagon Books, 1972 [c1953] xxi, 844 p.; 24 cm. — (Far Eastern Association. Monograph no. 2) An English translation of those sections of Ch'ou pan i wu shih mo which deal with the United States from 1841 to 1861. 1. United States — Foreign relations — China. 2. China — Foreign relations — United States. 3. United States — Foreign relations — 1815-1861 4. China — Foreign relations — To 1912. I. Swisher, Earl, 1902-1975. ed. and tr. II. T.
E183.8.C5 C555 1972　　　327.51/073　　　*LC* 70-38817　　　*ISBN* 0374976864

Congressional Quarterly, inc.　　　　　　　　　　**3.6420**
China: U.S. policy since 1945. — Washington, D.C.: Congressional Quarterly, [c1980] viii, 387 p.: ill.; 28 cm. Includes index. 1. United States — Foreign relations — China. 2. China — Foreign relations — United States. 3. China — History — 1945- 4. United States — Foreign relations — 1945- I. T.
E183.8.C5 C72 1980　　　327.51073　　　*LC* 79-27840　　　*ISBN* 0871871882

Dulles, Foster Rhea, 1900-1970.　　　　　　　　• **3.6421**
American policy toward Communist China, 1949–1969. Foreword by John K. Fairbank. — New York: Crowell, [1972] xiii, 273 p.: illus.; 25 cm. 1. United States — Foreign relations — China. 2. China — Foreign relations — United States. I. T.
E183.8.C5 D79 1972　　　327.73/052　　　*LC* 70-184974　　　*ISBN* 0690076126

Dulles, Foster Rhea, 1900-1970.   • **3.6422**
China and America; the story of their relations since 1784 [by] Foster Rhea Dulles. Princeton, N.J., Princeton university press, 1946. vii, 277 p. 21 cm. Bibliography: p. 263-267. 1. Eastern question (Far East) 2. China — Foreign relations — United States. 3. United States — Foreign relations — China. I. T.
E183.8.C5D8   *LC* A 46-14

Fairbank, John King, 1907-.   • **3.6423**
China: the people's middle kingdom and the U.S.A. / John K. Fairbank. — Cambridge: Belknap Press of Harvard University Press, 1967. xii, 145 p. 1. China — Relations — United States 2. United States — Relations — China I. T.
E183.8.C5 F28   *LC* 67-17307

Feis, Herbert, 1893-1972.   • **3.6424**
The China tangle: the American effort in China from Pearl Harbor to the Marshall mission. — Princeton: Princeton University Press, 1953. x, 445 p.: maps.; 25 cm. 1. United States — Foreign relations — China. 2. China — Foreign relations — United States. 3. United States — Foreign relations — 1933-1945 I. T.
E183.8.C5 F4   327.730951   *LC* 53-10142

The Future of US–China relations / edited by John Bryan   **3.6425**
Starr.
New York: New York University Press, 1981. xiii, 270 p.; 22 cm. — (UNA-USA policy studies book series.) 1. United States — Relations (general) with China — Addresses, essays, lectures. 2. China — Relations (general) with the United States — Addresses, essays, lectures. I. Starr, John Bryan. II. Series.
E183.8.C5 F85   327.73051 19   *LC* 81-9581   *ISBN* 0814778186

Hunt, Michael H.   **3.6426**
The making of a special relationship: the United States and China to 1914 / Michael H. Hunt. — New York: Columbia University Press, 1983. xii, 416 p.; 24 cm. 1. United States — Foreign relations — China. 2. China — Foreign relations — United States. I. T.
E183.8.C5 H86 1983   327.73051 19   *LC* 82-9753   *ISBN* 0231055161

Koen, Ross Y., 1918-.   **3.6427**
The China lobby in American politics [by] Ross Y. Koen. Edited with an introd. by Richard C. Kagan. — New York: Octagon Books, 1974. xxii, 279 p.; 23 cm. 'A publication of the Committee of Concerned Asian Scholars.' Reprint of the 1960 ed. published by Macmillan, New York. 1. United States — Foreign relations — China. 2. China — Foreign relations — United States. I. T.
E183.8.C5 K6 1974   327.73/051   *LC* 74-8960   *ISBN* 0374946027

Kusnitz, Leonard A.   **3.6428**
Public opinion and foreign policy: America's China policy, 1949–1979 / Leonard A. Kusnitz. — Westport, Conn.: Greenwood Press, c1984. xii, 191 p.: ill.; 25 cm. (Contributions in political science. 0147-1066; no. 114) Includes index. 1. Public opinion — United States — History — 20th century. 2. United States — Foreign relations — China. 3. China — Foreign relations — United States. 4. China — Foreign opinion, American. I. T. II. Series.
E183.8.C5 K87 1984   327.73051 19   *LC* 83-26508   *ISBN* 031324264X

MacFarquhar, Roderick. comp.   **3.6429**
Sino–American relations, 1949–1971 / documented and introduced by Roderick MacFarquhar. — New York: Praeger, 1972. xx, 267 p.; 22 cm. 1. United States — Foreign relations — China 2. China — Foreign relations — United States 3. United States — Foreign relations — Taiwan 4. Taiwan — Foreign relations — United States I. T.
E183.8.C5 M28   327.51/073   *LC* 70-189300

Pollack, Jonathan D.   **3.6430**
The Sino-Soviet rivalry and Chinese security debate / Jonathan D. Pollack; a Project Air Force report prepared for the United States Air Force. — Santa Monica, CA: Rand Corp., 1983. xi, 112 p.; 23 cm. 'R-2907-AF.' 'July 1982.' 1. United States — Foreign relations — China. 2. China — Foreign relations — United States. 3. China — Foreign relations — Soviet Union. 4. Soviet Union — Foreign relations — China. I. United States. Air Force. II. Rand Corporation. III. T.
E183.8.C5 P57 1983   327.73051 19   *LC* 82-11239   *ISBN* 0833004190

Schaller, Michael, 1947-.   **3.6431**
The U.S. crusade in China, 1938–1945 / Michael Schaller. — New York: Columbia University Press, 1979. xiii, 364 p.; 24 cm. Includes index. 1. World War, 1939-1945 — China. 2. United States — Foreign relations — China. 3. China — Foreign relations — United States. 4. China — Politics and government — 1937-1945 I. T.
E183.8.C5 S325   940.53/22/73   *LC* 78-15032   *ISBN* 0231044542

Sergeĭchuk, S.   **3.6432**
[SShA i Kitaĭ. English] Through Russian eyes: American–Chinese relations / by S. Sergeichuk; [authorized translation by Elizabeth Cody–Rutter; edited by Philip A. Garon]. — Arlington, Va.: International Library Book Publishers, 1975. xiii, 220 p.; 23 cm. Translation of SShA i Kitaĭ. 1. United States — Relations — China 2. China — Relations — United States I. T.
E183.8.C5 S4313   301.29/51/073   *LC* 74-75134   *ISBN* 0914250035

Sino–American normalization and its policy implications /   **3.6433**
edited by Gene T. Hsiao and Michael Witunski; foreword by Earl Lazerson.
New York, NY: Praeger, 1983. xliv, 515 p.; 25 cm. 1. United States — Foreign relations — China — Addresses, essays, lectures. 2. China — Foreign relations — United States — Addresses, essays, lectures. I. Hsiao, Gene T. II. Witunski, Michael.
E183.8.C5 S56 1983   327.73051 19   *LC* 82-16636   *ISBN* 0030580226

Stueck, William Whitney, 1945-.   **3.6434**
The Wedemeyer mission: American politics and foreign policy during the cold war / William Stueck. — Athens, Ga.: University of Georgia Press, c1984. x, 177 p.; 23 cm. Includes index. 1. Wedemeyer, Albert C. (Albert Coady), 1896-2. China — Foreign relations — United States. 3. United States — Foreign relations — Korea. 4. Korea — Foreign relations — United States. 5. United States — Foreign relations — 1945-1953 6. United States — Foreign relations — China. 7. China — History — Civil War, 1945-1949 8. Korea — Politics and government — 1945-1948 I. T.
E183.8.C5 S857 1984   327.73051 19   *LC* 83-27518   *ISBN* 0820307173

Tucker, Nancy Bernkopf.   **3.6435**
Patterns in the dust: Chinese–American relations and the recognition controversy, 1949–1950 / Nancy Bernkopf Tucker. — New York: Columbia University Press, 1983. x, 396 p.; 24 cm. — (Contemporary American history series.) Includes index. 1. United States — Foreign relations — China. 2. China — Foreign relations — United States. 3. United States — Foreign relations — 1945-1953 4. China — Foreign relations — 1949-1976 I. T. II. Series.
E183.8.C5 T836 1983   327.73051 19   *LC* 82-14724   *ISBN* 0231053622

U.S. Dept. of State.   • **3.6436**
United States relations with China, with special reference to the period 1944–1949. — New York: Greenwood Press, [1968] xli, 1054 p.; fold. map.; 24 cm. Reprint of the 1949 ed. 1. United States — Foreign relations — China. 2. China — Foreign relations — United States I. T.
E183.8.C5 U53 1968   327.73/051   *LC* 68-55123

E183.8.C8–D CUBA. DOMINICAN REPUBLIC

Bonsal, Philip Wilson, 1903-.   **3.6437**
Cuba, Castro, and the United States [by] Philip W. Bonsal. — [Pittsburgh]: University of Pittsburgh Press, [1971] xii, 318 p.: illus.; 24 cm. 1. Castro, Fidel, 1927- 2. U.S. — Foreign relations — Cuba. 3. Cuba — Foreign relations — U.S. I. T.
E183.8.C9 B6   327.7291/073   *LC* 72-151505   *ISBN* 0822932253

Gellman, Irwin F.   **3.6438**
Roosevelt and Batista; good neighbor diplomacy in Cuba, 1933–1945 [by] Irwin F. Gellman. [1st ed.] Albuquerque, University of New Mexico Press [1973] 303 p. illus. 23 cm. 1. Roosevelt, Franklin D. (Franklin Delano), 1882-1945. 2. Batista y Zaldívar, Fulgencio, 1901-1973. 3. United States — Foreign relations — Cuba. 4. Cuba — Foreign relations — United States. 5. Cuba — Politics and government — 1933-1959 I. T.
E183.8.C9 G44   327.73/07291   *LC* 73-77919   *ISBN* 082630284X

Jenks, Leland Hamilton, 1892-.   **3.6439**
Our Cuban colony; a study in sugar. New York, Vanguard Press. — St. Clair Shores, Mich.: Scholarly Press, 1972. xxi, 341 p.: illus.; 22 cm. Reprint of the 1928 ed., issued in series: American imperialism. 1. Sugar trade — Cuba. 2. United States — Foreign relations — Cuba. 3. Cuba — Foreign relations — United States. 4. Cuba — Economic conditions 5. Cuba — Industries. I. T.
E183.8.C9 J5 1972   330.9/7291   *LC* 74-145111   *ISBN* 0403010500

Welch, Richard E.   **3.6440**
Response to revolution: the United States and the Cuban revolution, 1959–1961 / Richard E. Welch, Jr. — Chapel Hill: University of North Carolina Press, c1985. ix, 243 p.; 24 cm. Includes index. 1. United States — Foreign relations — Cuba. 2. Cuba — Foreign relations — United States. 3. Cuba — History — Revolution, 1959 4. United States — Foreign relations — 1953-1961 I. T.
E183.8.C9 W34 1985   327.7307291 19   *LC* 84-25604   *ISBN* 0807816132

Atkins, G. Pope, 1934-.   **3.6441**
The United States and the Trujillo regime, by G. Pope Atkins and Larman C. Wilson. — New Brunswick, N.J.: Rutgers University Press, [c1972] viii, 245 p.: illus.; 22 cm. 1. U.S. — Foreign relations — Dominican Republic.

2. Dominican Republic — Foreign relations — U.S. I. Wilson, Larman Curtis, joint author. II. T.
E183.8.D6 A85   327.73/07293

E183.8.F–G7 France. Germany. Britain

Bowman, Albert Hall, 1921-.   **3.6442**
The struggle for neutrality: Franco–American diplomacy during the Federalist era. — [1st ed.]. — Knoxville: University of Tennessee Press, [1974] xvii, 460 p.; 23 cm. 1. United States — Foreign relations — France 2. France — Foreign relations — United States 3. United States — Foreign relations — Constitutional period, 1789-1809 I. T.
E183.8.F8 B65   327.73/044   *LC* 73-21917   *ISBN* 0870491520

Duroselle, Jean Baptiste, 1917-.   **3.6443**
[France et les États-Unis des origines à nos jours. English] France and the United States from the beginnings to the present / Jean–Baptiste Duroselle; translated by Derek Coltman. — Chicago: University of Chicago Press, 1978. viii, 276 p.; 22 cm. — (The United States in the world, foreign perspectives) Translation of La France et les États-Unis des origines à nos jours. Includes index. 1. United States — Foreign relations — France 2. France — Foreign relations — United States I. T.
E183.8.F8 D8713   327.73/044   *LC* 78-1467   *ISBN* 0226174085

Documents on Germany, 1944–1985 / United States Department   **3.6444**
of State.
[Washington, D.C.?]: U.S. Dept. of State, Office of the Historian, Bureau of Public Affairs, 1985. xxxviii, 1421 p.: 4 maps; 24 cm. — (Department of State publication; 9446) 4th ed., rev. Shipping list no.: 86-63-P. Item 876 S 1.2:G 31/5/944-85 1. Berlin question (1945-) — Sources. 2. United States — Foreign relations — Germany — Sources. 3. Germany — Foreign relations — United States — Sources. 4. Germany — History — Allied occupation, 1945- — Sources. I. United States. Dept. of State. Office of the Historian.
E183.8.G3 D62 1985   327.73043 19   *LC* 86-600826

Jonas, Manfred.   **3.6445**
The United States and Germany: a diplomatic history / Manfred Jonas. — Ithaca, N.Y.: Cornell University Press, 1984. 335 p.; 24 cm. Includes index. 1. United States — Foreign relations — Germany. 2. Germany — Foreign relations — United States. I. T.
E183.8.G3 J66 1984   327.73043 19   *LC* 83-15278   *ISBN*
0801416345

Kennedy, Paul M., 1945-.   **3.6446**
The Samoan tangle: a study in Anglo–German–American relations, 1878–1900 / Paul M. Kennedy. — New York: Barnes & Noble, 1974. xvi, 325 p.: maps; 23 cm. Includes index. 1. Samoan question 2. United States — Foreign relations — Germany. 3. Germany — Foreign relations — United States. 4. Samoan Islands — History. I. T.
E183.8.G3 K46 1974b   320.996/13   *LC* 74-188886   *ISBN*
006493635X

Neustadt, Richard E.   • **3.6447**
Alliance politics / [by] Richard E. Neustadt. — New York: Columbia University Press, 1970. xii, 167 p.; 22 cm. A reworked version of the author's Radner Lectures, delivered at Columbia University in 1966. 1. U.S. — Foreign relations — 1945- 2. U.S. — Foreign relations — Gt. Brit. 3. Gt. Brit. — Foreign relations — U.S. I. T.
E183.8.G7 N47 1970   327.73/042   *LC* 77-120855   *ISBN*
0231030665

Nicholas, H. G. (Herbert George), 1911-.   **3.6448**
The United States and Britain / H. G. Nicholas. — Chicago: University of Chicago Press, 1975. viii, 195 p.; 21 cm. (The United States in the world, foreign perspectives) Includes index. 1. United States — Foreign relations — Great Britain. 2. Great Britain — Foreign relations — United States. I. T.
E183.8.G7 N489   327.73/041   *LC* 74-16681   *ISBN* 0226580024

E183.8.H–I Hawaii. India. Indonesia. Israel. Italy

Tate, Merze, 1905-.   **3.6449**
The United States and the Hawaiian Kingdom: a political history. — New Haven: Yale University Press, 1965. 374p. INCLUDES INDEX. 1. United States — Foreign relations — Hawaii. 2. Hawaii — Foreign relations — United States. 3. Hawaii — Politics and government I. T.
E183.8.H3 T34   *LC* 65-22342

Palmer, Norman Dunbar.   **3.6450**
The United States and India: the dimensions of influence / Norman D. Palmer. — New York: Praeger, 1984. xiv, 302 p.; 25 cm. Includes index. 1. United States — Foreign relations — India. 2. India — Foreign relations — United States. I. T.
E183.8.I4 P35 1984   327.73054 19   *LC* 84-8272   *ISBN* 0030695562

Venkataramani, M. S., 1925-.   **3.6451**
Quit India: the American response to the 1942 struggle / M. S. Venkataramani, B. K. Shrivastava. — New Delhi: Vikas, c1979. x, 350 p.; 25 cm. 1. United States — Relations — India 2. India — Relations — United States 3. India — Politics and government — 1919-1947 4. United States — Foreign relations — 1933-1945 I. Shrivastava, B. K. joint author. II. T.
E183.8.I4 V46   327.73054 19   *LC* 79-900832   *ISBN* 0706906934

McMahon, Robert J., 1949-.   **3.6452**
Colonialism and cold war: The United States and the struggle for Indonesian independence, 1945–49 / Robert J. McMahon. — Ithaca, N.Y.: Cornell University Press, 1981. 338 p.; 22 cm. 1. United States — Foreign relations — Indonesia. 2. Indonesia — Foreign relations — United States. 3. Indonesia — Politics and government — 1942-1949 4. United States — Foreign relations — 1945-1953 I. T.
E183.8.I5 M35   327.730598 19   *LC* 81-66648   *ISBN* 0801413885

Bain, Kenneth Ray, 1942-.   **3.6453**
The march to Zion: United States policy and the founding of Israel / by Kenneth Ray Bain. — 1st ed. — College Station: Texas A&M University Press, 1980 (c1979). xviii, 235 p. 1. United States — Foreign relations — Palestine. 2. Palestine — Foreign relations — United States. 3. United States — Foreign relations — 1945-1953 I. T.
E183.8.I7 B34   E183.8I7 B34.   327.73/05694   *LC* 79-7413   *ISBN* 0890960763

Reich, Bernard.   **3.6454**
The United States and Israel: influence in the special relationship / Bernard Reich. — New York: Praeger, 1984. xiii, 236 p.; 25 cm. — (Studies of influence in international relations.) Includes index. 1. United States — Foreign relations — Israel. 2. Israel — Foreign relations — United States. I. T. II. Series.
E183.8.I7 R45 1984   327.7305694 19   *LC* 83-24795   *ISBN* 0030605660

Snetsinger, John.   **3.6455**
Truman, the Jewish vote, and the creation of Israel. Stanford, Calif.: Hoover Institution Press [1974] xv, 208 p.; 22 cm. (Hoover Institution studies, 39) 1. Truman, Harry S., 1884-1972 — Relations with Zionists. 2. United States — Foreign relations — Israel. 3. Israel — Foreign relations — United States. I. T. II. Series.
E183.8.I7 S63   327.73/05694   *LC* 70-187267   *ISBN* 0817933913

DeConde, Alexander.   **3.6456**
Half bitter, half sweet: an excursion into Italian–American history. — New York: Scribner, 1972 (c1971) vii, 466 p.; 24 cm. 1. Italian Americans 2. United States — Relations — Italy 3. Italy — Relations — United States I. T.
E183.8.I8 D4   301.29/73/045   *LC* 75-123851   *ISBN* 0684123665

E183.8.J–K Japan. Korea

Borg, Dorothy, 1902-.   **3.6457**
Pearl Harbor as history: Japanese–American relations, 1931–1941. Edited by Dorothy Borg and Shumpei Okamoto, with the assistance of Dale K. A. Finlayson. New York, Columbia University Press, 1973. xv, 801 p. 24 cm. (Studies of the East Asian Institute, Columbia University) 1. Pearl Harbor (Hawaii), Attack on, 1941 2. United States — Foreign relations — Japan 3. Japan — Foreign relations — United States I. Okamoto, Shumpei. joint author. II. T.
E183.8.J3 B67   327.73/052   *LC* 72-10996   *ISBN* 0231037341

United States–Japanese relations, the 1970's / edited by   **3.6458**
Priscilla Clapp and Morton H. Halperin.
Cambridge: Harvard University Press, 1974. 234 p.; 21 cm. 1. United States — Relations — Japan — Addresses, essays, lectures. 2. Japan — Relations — United States — Addresses, essays, lectures. I. Clapp, Priscilla, ed. II. Halperin, Morton H. ed.
E183.8.J3 C55   327.73/052   *LC* 74-80441   *ISBN* 0674925718

Encounter at Shimoda: search for a new Pacific partnership /   **3.6459**
edited by Herbert Passin and Akira Iriye.
Boulder, Colo.: Westview Press, 1979. xxii, 257 p.; 24 cm. (Westview special studies on China and East Asia) Papers presented at the 4th Shimoda Conference held in Sept. 1977 in Shimoda, Japan. 1. United States — Relations — Japan — Congresses. 2. Japan — Relations — United States — Congresses. 3. United States — Relations — East Asia — Congresses. 4. East Asia — Relations — United States — Congresses. 5. United States — Foreign relations — 1945- — Congresses. I. Passin, Herbert. II. Iriye, Akira.
E183.8.J3 E5   301.29/73/052   *LC* 79-4238   *ISBN* 0891584676

Harris, Townsend, 1804-1878.   • **3.6460**
The complete journal of Townsend Harris, first American consul and minister to Japan. Introd. and notes by Mario Emilio Cosenza. With a pref. by Douglas MacArthur, II. — Rev. [i. e. 2d] ed. — Rutland, Vt., C. E. Tuttle Co. [1959] xix, 616 p. plates, port., facsims. 23 cm. 1. U.S. — For. rel. — Japan. 2. Japan — For. rel. — U.S. 3. U.S. — For. rel. — Thailand. 4. Thailand — For. rel. —

U.S. 5. Japan — Descr. & trav. — 1801-1900. 6. Thailand — Descr. & trav. I. T.
E183.8.J3H3 1959   327.73052   *LC* 59-9397

Iriye, Akira.   **3.6461**
Pacific estrangement; Japanese and American expansion, 1897–1911. — Cambridge, Mass.: Harvard University Press, 1972. ix, 290 p.; 25 cm. — (Harvard studies in American-East Asian relations. 2) 1. United States — Foreign relations — Japan 2. Japan — Foreign relations — United States I. T. II. Series.
E183.8.J3 I74   327.52/073   *LC* 72-79307   *ISBN* 0674650751

Lee, Chae-Jin, 1936-.   **3.6462**
U.S. policy toward Japan and Korea: a changing influence relationship / Chae-Jin Lee and Hideo Sato. — New York, N.Y.: Praeger, 1982. 208 p.; 24 cm. — (Studies of influence in international relations.) Includes index. 1. United States — Foreign relations — Japan 2. Japan — Foreign relations — United States 3. United States — Foreign relations — Korea (South) 4. Korea (South) — Foreign relations — United States. I. Sato, Hideo, 1942- II. T. III. Series.
E183.8.J3 L43 1982   327.730519/5 19   *LC* 81-22656   *ISBN* 0030534712

Miyoshi, Masao.   **3.6463**
As we saw them: the first Japanese Embassy to the United States (1860) / Masao Miyoshi. — Berkeley: University of California Press, c1979. xi, 232 p., [7] leaves of plates: ill. (some col.); 25 cm. Includes index. 1. Man'en Gannen Kenbei Shisetsu (Japan) 2. United States — Relations — Japan 3. Japan — Relations — United States 4. Japan — Foreign relations — To 1868 I. T.
E183.8.J3 M57   973.6/8 19   *LC* 78-62851   *ISBN* 0520037677

Neu, Charles E.   **3.6464**
The troubled encounter: the United States and Japan [by] Charles E. Neu. — New York: Wiley, [1975] x, 257 p.; 22 cm. — (America and the world) 1. United States — Foreign relations — Japan 2. Japan — Foreign relations — United States I. T.
E183.8.J3 N367   327.73/052   *LC* 74-12426   *ISBN* 0471631906

Neumann, William Louis, 1915-.   • **3.6465**
America encounters Japan: from Perry to MacArthur. — Baltimore: Johns Hopkins Press, 1963. viii, 353 p.; 22 cm. — (The Goucher College series) 'Bibliographic essay': p. 315-343. 1. U.S. — Relations (general) with Japan. 2. Japan — Relations (general) with the U.S. I. T.
E183.8.J3N39   327.73052   *LC* 63-17667

Reischauer, Edwin O. (Edwin Oldfather), 1910-.   • **3.6466**
The United States and Japan, by Edwin O. Reischauer. 3d ed. Cambridge, Harvard University Press, 1965. xxv, 396 p. maps (1 col. on lining paper) 22 cm. (American foreign policy library.) 1. United States — Foreign relations — Japan 2. Japan — Foreign relations — United States I. T. II. Series.
E183.8.J3 R4 1965   327.73052   *LC* 64-8057

Schaller, Michael, 1947-.   **3.6467**
The American occupation of Japan: the origins of the Cold War in Asia / Michael Schaller. — New York: Oxford University Press, 1985. xii, 351 p.; 25 cm. Includes index. 1. United States — Foreign relations — Japan 2. Japan — Foreign relations — United States 3. United States — Foreign relations — Asia, Southeastern. 4. Asia, Southeastern — Foreign relations — United States. 5. Japan — History — Allied occupation, 1945-1952 6. United States — Foreign relations — 1945-1953 I. T.
E183.8.J3 S29 1985   327.73052 19   *LC* 85-8818   *ISBN* 0195036263

United States–Japanese political relations: the critical issues   • **3.6468**
affecting Asia's future.
Washington: Center for Strategic Studies, Georgetown University, 1968. ix, 104 p.; 22 cm. — (Center for Strategic Studies, Georgetown University. Special report series, no. 7) Report of a study by a panel convened by the Center for Strategic Studies under the chairmanship of R. E. Ward, with a background paper by D. F. Anthony. 1. United States — Foreign relations — Japan 2. Japan — Foreign relations — U.S.
E183.8.J3 U75   327.52/073   *LC* 68-31062

Buss, Claude Albert.   **3.6469**
The United States and the Republic of Korea: background for policy / Claude A. Buss. — Stanford, Calif.: Hoover Institution Press, Stanford University, c1982. xiii, 184 p.: ill.; 23 cm. (Hoover international studies.) (Hoover Press publication; 254) Includes index. 1. United States — Foreign relations — Korea (South) 2. Korea (South) — Foreign relations — United States. I. T. II. Series.
E183.8.K6 B87   327.730519/5 19   *LC* 81-82077   *ISBN* 081797542X

Child of conflict: the Korean–American relationship, 1943–1953   **3.6470**
/ edited by Bruce Cumings.
Seattle: University of Washington Press, 1983. xiv, 335 p.; 25 cm. — (Publications on Asia of the School of International Studies, University of Washington; no. 37) 1. United States — Foreign relations — Korea —

Addresses, essays, lectures. 2. Korea — Foreign relations — United States — Addresses, essays, lectures. I. Cumings, Bruce, 1943-
E183.8.K6 C45 1983   327.519073 19   *LC* 82-48871   *ISBN* 0295959959

Stueck, William Whitney, 1945-.   **3.6471**
The road to confrontation: American policy toward China and Korea, 1947–1950 / William Whitney Stueck, Jr. — Chapel Hill: University of North Carolina Press, c1981. 326 p.: maps; 24 cm. Includes index. 1. Truman, Harry S., 1884-1972. 2. United States — Foreign relations — Korea. 3. Korea — Foreign relations — United States. 4. United States — Foreign relations — China. 5. China — Foreign relations — United States. 6. United States — Foreign relations — 1945-1953 I. T.
E183.8.K7 S88   327.73051   *LC* 80-11818   *ISBN* 0807814458

E183.8.L LATIN AMERICA: GENERAL
(see: F1418)

E183.8.M–P MEXICO. NETHERLANDS. PAKISTAN. PANAMA. PHILIPPINES. POLAND. PUERTO RICO

Brack, Gene M.   **3.6472**
Mexico views manifest destiny, 1821–1846: an essay on the origins of the Mexican War / Gene M. Brack. — 1st ed. — Albuquerque: University of New Mexico Press, c1975. vii, 194 p.; 25 cm. Includes index. 1. United States — Foreign relations — Mexico. 2. Mexico — Foreign relations — United States. 3. United States — Territorial expansion 4. United States — History — War with Mexico, 1845-1848 — Causes. I. T.
E183.8.M6 B72   327.73/072   *LC* 75-17374   *ISBN* 0826303935

Schmitt, Karl Michael, 1922-.   **3.6473**
Mexico and the United States, 1821–1973: conflict and coexistence [by] Karl M. Schmitt. — New York: Wiley, [1974] xiii, 288 p.; 22 cm. — (America and the world) 1. United States — Foreign relations — Mexico. 2. Mexico — Foreign relations — United States. I. T.
E183.8.M6 S35 1974   327.72/073   *LC* 73-20327   *ISBN* 0471761982

A Bilateral bicentennial: a history of Dutch–American relations,   **3.6474**
1782–1982 / edited by J.W. Schulte Nordholt and Robert P.
Swierenga.
[New York]: Octagon Books; Amsterdam: Meulenhoff International, c1982. viii, 279 p.: ill.; 25 cm. 1. United States — Foreign relations — Netherlands — Addresses, essays, lectures. 2. Netherlands — Foreign relations — United States — Addresses, essays, lectures. I. Schulte Nordholt, J. W., 1920- II. Swierenga, Robert P.
E183.8.N4 B54 1982   327.730492 19   *LC* 82-8096   *ISBN* 0374961204

Shirin Tahir-Kheli.   **3.6475**
The United States and Pakistan: the evolution of an influence relationship / Shirin Tahir-Kheli. — New York: Praeger, 1982. xxi, 169 p.; 24 cm. — (Studies of influence in international relations.) Includes index. 1. United States — Foreign relations — Pakistan. 2. Pakistan — Foreign relations — United States. I. T. II. Series.
E183.8.P18 S5 1982   327.730549 19   *LC* 81-21160   *ISBN* 0030504716

Ealy, Lawrence O., 1915-.   **3.6476**
Yanqui politics and the Isthmian Canal [by] Lawrence O. Ealy. University Park, Pennsylvania State University Press [1971] 192 p. 24 cm. 'A Rider College publication.' 1. United States — Foreign relations — Panama. 2. Panama — Foreign relations — United States. 3. Panama Canal (Panama) I. T.
E183.8.P2 E15   327.73/0862   *LC* 74-127385   *ISBN* 0271011262

Shalom, Stephen Rosskamm, 1948-.   **3.6477**
The United States and the Philippines: a study of neocolonialism / Stephen Rosskamm Shalom. — Philadelphia, Penn.: Institute for the Study of Human Issues, c1981. xvii, 302 p.: maps; 24 cm. (Studies in political economy) Includes index. 1. United States — Foreign relations — Philippines. 2. Philippines — Foreign relations — United States. 3. Philippines — Politics and government 4. Philippines — Economic conditions I. T.
E183.8.P5 S5   327.730599 19   *LC* 80-29357   *ISBN* 0897270142

Wandycz, Piotr Stefan.   **3.6478**
The United States and Poland / Piotr. S. Wandycz. — Cambridge, Mass.: Harvard University Press, 1980. ix, 465 p.; 25 cm. — (American foreign policy library.) Includes index. 1. United States — Foreign relations — Poland. 2. Poland — Foreign relations — United States. I. T. II. Series.
E183.8.P7 W36   327.73/0438   *LC* 79-11998   *ISBN* 0674926854

Carr, Raymond.   3.6479
Puerto Rico, a colonial experiment / Raymond Carr. — New York: New York University Press, 1984. xxii, 477 p.; 22 cm. 'A Twentieth Century Fund study.' Includes index. 1. United States — Relations — Puerto Rico 2. Puerto Rico — Relations — United States 3. Puerto Rico — Politics and government — 1952- I. Twentieth Century Fund. II. T.
E183.8.P9 C37 1984   303.4/8273/07295 19   *LC* 83-23786   *ISBN* 0814713890

E183.8.R9 RUSSIA. SOVIET UNION
(see also: E183.8.S65)

Allison, Graham T.   3.6480
Essence of decision: explaining the Cuban missile crisis / [by] Graham T. Allison. — Boston: Little, Brown, [1971] xii, 338 p.; 21 cm. 'Written under the auspices of the Faculty Seminar on Bureaucracy, Politics, and Policy of the Institute of Politics, John Fitzgerald Kennedy School of Government, Harvard University.' 1. Cuban Missile Crisis, Oct. 1962 I. T.
E183.8.R9 A64   327.73/047   *LC* 70-168998

The American image of Russia, 1917–1977 / edited with an   3.6481
introd. and comments by Benson L. Grayson.
New York: Ungar, c1978. x, 388 p.: ill.; 22 cm. Includes index. 1. Public opinion — United States. 2. Soviet Union — Relations — United States 3. Soviet Union — Foreign opinion, American. 4. United States — Relations — Soviet Union I. Grayson, Benson Lee, 1932-
E183.8.R9 A74   301.29/73/047   *LC* 77-6972   *ISBN* 0804413088

Anschel, Eugene. comp.   3.6482
The American image of Russia, 1775–1917 / edited with an introd. and comments by Eugene Anschel. — New York: Ungar, [1974] xii, 259 p.; ill.; 22 cm. Includes index. 1. Soviet Union — Foreign opinion, American — Addresses, essays, lectures. I. T.
E183.8.R9 A84   301.15/43/0947   *LC* 73-91424   *ISBN* 0804410283

Bolkhovitinov, N. N. (Nikolaĭ Nikolaevich)   3.6483
[Stanovlenie russkoamerikanskikh otnosheniĭ. English] The beginnings of Russian–American relations,1775–1815 / Nikolai N. Bolkhovitinov; translated by Elena Levin. — Cambridge, Mass.: Harvard University Press, 1975. xviii, 484 p.; 25 cm. Translation of Stanovlenie russkoamerikanskikh otnosheniĭ. 1. United States — Foreign relations — Russia. 2. Russia — Foreign relations — United States. 3. United States — Foreign relations — Revolution, 1775-1783 4. United States — Foreign relations — 1783-1815 I. T.
E183.8.R9 B613   327.47/073   *LC* 75-5233   *ISBN* 0674064550

Gaddis, John Lewis.   3.6484
Russia, the Soviet Union, and the United States: an interpretive history / John Lewis Gaddis. — New York: Wiley, c1978. xiii, 309 p.; 22 cm. — (America and the world) 1. United States — Foreign relations — Russia. 2. Russia — Foreign relations — United States. 3. United States — Foreign relations — 20th century I. T.
E183.8.R9 G24   327.73/047   *LC* 77-12763   *ISBN* 0471289108

Hoff-Wilson, Joan, 1937-.   3.6485
Ideology and economics: U.S. relations with the Soviet Union, 1918–1933. — Columbia: University of Missouri Press, 1974. xv, 192 p.; 23 cm. 1. United States — Foreign relations — Soviet Union 2. Soviet Union — Foreign relations — United States 3. United States — Commerce — Soviet Union. 4. Soviet Union — Commerce — United States. I. T.
E183.8.R9 H68 1974   327.73/047   *LC* 73-89133   *ISBN* 0826201571

Kennan, George Frost, 1904-.   • 3.6486
Soviet-American relations, 1917–1920. Princeton, Princeton University Press, 1956-. v. illus., ports., maps, facsims. 25 cm. 1. United States — Foreign relations —Soviet Union 2. Soviet Union — Foreign relations — United States 3. Soviet Union — History — Revolution, 1917-1921 4. United States — Foreign relations — 1913-1921 I. T.
E183.8.R9 K4   327.730947   *LC* 56-8382

Kennedy, Robert F., 1925-1968.   • 3.6487
Thirteen days: a memoir of the Cuban missile crisis / with introductions by Robert S. McNamara and Harold Macmillan. — [1st ed.] New York: W. W. Norton [1969] 224 p.: ill., facsim. (on lining papers), ports.; 24 cm. 'Documents': p. 163-218. 1. Military bases, Soviet — Cuba. 2. United States — Foreign relations — Soviet Union 3. Soviet Union — Foreign relations — United States I. T.
E183.8.R9 K42   327.73/047   *LC* 69-15949

Rapoport, Anatol, 1911-.   • 3.6488
The big two: Soviet–American perceptions of foreign policy. — New York: Pegasus [1971] 249 p.; 21 cm. (American involvement in the world) 1. United States — Foreign relations — Soviet Union 2. Soviet Union — Foreign relations — United States I. T.
E183.8.R9 R23   327.47/073   *LC* 72-124676

Ulam, Adam Bruno, 1922-.   • 3.6489
The rivals: America and Russia since World War II / [by] Adam B. Ulam. — New York: Viking Press, [1971] vi, 405 p.; 25 cm. 1. U.S. — Foreign relations — Russia. 2. Russia — Foreign relations — U.S. I. T.
E183.8.R9 U4 1971   327.73/047   *LC* 75-160204   *ISBN* 067059959X

Williams, William Appleman.   • 3.6490
American–Russian relations, 1781–1947. New York: Octagon Books, 1971 [c1952] 367 p.; 24 cm. 1. Soviet Union — Foreign relations — United States 2. United States — Foreign relations — Soviet Union I. T.
E183.8.R9 W63 1971   327.73/047   *LC* 70-154671   *ISBN* 0374985812

E183.8.S6 SOUTH AFRICA

Bissell, Richard E.   3.6491
South Africa and the United States: the erosion of an influence relationship / Richard E. Bissell. — New York, N.Y.: Praeger, 1982. xx, 147 p.; 24 cm. — (Studies of influence in international relations.) Includes index. 1. United States — Foreign relations — South Africa. 2. South Africa — Foreign relations — United States. I. T. II. Series.
E183.8.S6 B57 1982   327.73068 19   *LC* 81-22663   *ISBN* 0030470269

Study Commission on U.S. Policy toward Southern Africa   3.6492
(U.S.)
South Africa: time running out: the report of the Study Commission on U.S. Policy Toward Southern Africa. — Berkeley: University of California Press, c1981. xxvii, 517 p., [26] p. of plates: ill., col. map; 24 cm. Map on lining papers. Includes index. 1. United States — Foreign relations — South Africa. 2. South Africa — Foreign relations — United States. I. T.
E183.8.S6 S78 1981   327.73068 19   *LC* 81-2742   *ISBN* 0520045475

E183.8.S65 SOVIET UNION
(see also: E183.8.R9)

Garthoff, Raymond L.   3.6493
Détente and confrontation: American–Soviet relations from Nixon to Reagan / Raymond L. Garthoff. — Washington, D.C.: Brookings Institution, c1985. xvi, 1147 p.; 24 cm. 1. United States — Foreign relations — Soviet Union 2. Soviet Union — Foreign relations — United States I. T.
E183.8.S65 G37 1985   327.73047 19   *LC* 84-45855   *ISBN* 0815730446

Taubman, William.   3.6494
Stalin's American policy: from entente to detente to cold war / William Taubman. — 1st ed. — New York: Norton, c1982. xii, 291 p.; 22 cm. 1. Stalin, Joseph, 1879-1953. 2. World War, 1939-1945 — Diplomatic history 3. United States — Foreign relations — Soviet Union 4. Soviet Union — Foreign relations — United States 5. United States — Foreign relations — 1945-1953 6. Soviet Union — Foreign relations — 1945- I. T.
E183.8.S65 T38 1982   327.73047 19   *LC* 81-38333   *ISBN* 0393014061

Whelan, Joseph G.   3.6495
Soviet diplomacy and negotiating behavior: the emerging new context for U.S. diplomacy / Joseph G. Whelan. — Boulder, Colo.: Westview Press, [1983] xxx, 573 p.; 23 cm. — (A Westview replica edition) Reprint. Originally published: Washington: Committee on Foreign Affairs, 1979? (Special studies series on foreign affairs issues; v. 1) 1. United States — Foreign relations — Soviet Union 2. Soviet Union — Foreign relations — United States 3. United States — Foreign relations administration 4. Soviet Union — Foreign relations — 1917- I. T.
E183.8.S65 W47 1983   327.47073 19   *LC* 82-83817   *ISBN* 0865319464

E183.8.S–Z SPAIN. VIETNAM. ZAIRE

Cortada, James W.   3.6496
Two nations over time: Spain and the United States, 1776–1977 / James W. Cortada. — Westport, Conn.: Greenwood Press, 1978. xi, 305 p.; 22 cm. — (Contributions in American history; no. 74 0084-9219) Includes index. 1. United States — Foreign relations — Spain. 2. Spain — Foreign relations — United States. I. T.
E183.8.S7 C67   327.73/046   *LC* 77-94752   *ISBN* 0313203199

Traina, Richard P.   • 3.6497
American diplomacy and the Spanish Civil War [by] Richard P. Traina. — Bloomington: Indiana University Press, [1968] xi, 301 p.; 25 cm. — (Indiana University international studies) 1. United States — Foreign relations —

Spain. 2. Spain — Foreign relations — United States. 3. Spain — History — Civil War, 1936-1939 — Participation, American. I. T.
E183.8.S7 T7   327.73/046   *LC* 68-27356

Gelb, Leslie H.   **3.6498**
The irony of Vietnam: the system worked / Leslie H. Gelb with Richard K. Betts. — Washington: Brookings Institution, c1979. xi, 387 p.; 24 cm. 1. Vietnamese Conflict, 1961-1975 2. United States — Foreign relations — Vietnam. 3. Vietnam — Foreign relations — United States. I. Betts, Richard K., 1947- joint author. II. T.
E183.8.V5 G4   327.73/0597   *LC* 78-26563   *ISBN* 0815730721

Kattenburg, Paul M.   **3.6499**
The Vietnam trauma in American foreign policy, 1945–75 / Paul M. Kattenburg. — New Brunswick, N.J.: Transaction Books, c1980. xvi, 354 p.; 24 cm. Includes index. 1. Vietnamese Conflict, 1961-1975 — United States 2. United States — Foreign relations — Vietnam. 3. Vietnam — Foreign relations — United States. I. T.
E183.8.V5 K36   327.73/0597   *LC* 79-66437   *ISBN* 0878553789

The Pentagon papers as published by the New York times / the   **• 3.6500**
Pentagon history was obtained by Neil Sheehan; written by Neil Sheehan [and others].
New York: Quadrangle Books, [1971] xix, 810 p.: ill.; 24 cm. 1. Vietnamese Conflict, 1961-1975 2. United States — Foreign relations — Vietnam. 3. Vietnam — Foreign relations — United States. 4. Vietnam — Politics and government I. Sheehan, Neil. II. New York times
E183.8.V5 P4   959.7/0432   *LC* 75-173846

The Pentagon papers: the Defense Department history of United   **3.6501**
States decisionmaking on Vietnam.
The Senator Gravel ed. — Boston: Beacon Press, [1971-72] 5 v.; 23 cm. Vol. 5: Critical essays, edited by N. Chomsky and H. Zinn, and an index to v. 1-4. 1. Vietnamese Conflict, 1961-1975 2. United States — Foreign relations — Vietnam. 3. Vietnam — Foreign relations — United States. 4. Vietnam — Politics and government — 1945-1975 I. United States. Dept. of Defense.
E183.8.V5 P42   959.7/0432   *LC* 75-178049   *ISBN* 0807005266

Weissman, Stephen R.   **3.6502**
American foreign policy in the Congo, 1960–1964 / [by] Stephen R. Weissman. Ithaca [N.Y.]: Cornell University Press [1974] 325 p.; 22 cm. 1. United States — Foreign relations — Zaire. 2. Zaire — Foreign relations — United States. 3. Zaire — Foreign relations — 1960- I. T.
E183.8.Z34 W44   327.73/0675/1   *LC* 73-14064   *ISBN* 0801408121

E184–185 Elements in the Population

E184 A1 GENERAL WORKS

Archdeacon, Thomas J.   **3.6503**
Becoming American: an ethnic history / Thomas J. Archdeacon. — New York: Free Press; London: Collier Macmillan, c1983. xviii, 297 p.; 25 cm. Includes index. 1. Minorities — United States — History. 2. United States — Emigration and immigration 3. Immigrants — United States I. T.
E184.A1 A75 1983   973/.04 19   *LC* 82-48691   *ISBN* 0029008301

Johns, Stephanie Bernardo.   **3.6504**
The ethnic almanac / Stephanie Bernardo. — Garden City, N.Y.: Doubleday, 1981. xv, 560 p. Includes index. 1. Minorities — United States — Miscellanea. 2. United States — Ethnic relations — Miscellanea. I. T.
E184.A1 B426   E184A1 B476.   973/.04 19   *LC* 80-18776   *ISBN* 0385141432

Blauner, Robert.   **3.6505**
Racial oppression in America. New York, Harper & Row [1972] x, 309 p. 21 cm. 1. Assimilation (Sociology) 2. Afro-Americans 3. United States — Race relations I. T.
E184.A1 B555   301.45/1/0973   *LC* 72-77484   *ISBN* 0060407719

Bodnar, John E., 1944-.   **3.6506**
The transplanted: a history of immigrants in urban America / John Bodnar. — Bloomington: Indiana University Press, c1985. xxi, 294 p.: ill.; 25 cm. (Interdisciplinary studies in history.) Includes index. 1. Minorities — United States — History. 2. City and town life — United States — History. 3. United States — Social conditions I. T. II. Series.
E184.A1 B59 1985   305.8/00973 19   *LC* 84-48041   *ISBN* 0253313473

Ethnic information sources of the United States: a guide to   **3.6507**
organizations, agencies, foundations, institutions, media, commercial and trade bodies, government programs, research institutes, libraries and museums, religious organizations, banking firms, festivals and fairs, travel and tourist offices, airlines and ship lines, bookdealers and publishers' representatives, and books, pamphlets, and audiovisuals on specific ethnic groups / Paul Wasserman, managing editor; Alice E. Kennington, associate editor.
2nd ed. — Detroit, Mich.: Gale Research Co., c1983. 2 v. (xix, 1380 p.); 29 cm. 1. Minorities — United States — Societies, etc. — Directories. 2. Minorities — United States — Information services — Directories. 3. Minorities — United States — Bibliography. I. Wasserman, Paul. II. Kennington, Alice E.
E184.A1 E836 1983   973/.04/025 19   *LC* 84-100771   *ISBN* 0810303671

Fermi, Laura.   **• 3.6508**
Illustrious immigrants: the intellectual migration from Europe, 1930–41. — Chicago: University of Chicago Press, [1968] xi, 440 p.: ports.; 24 cm. 1. Intellectuals — Europe. 2. Intellectuals — United States. 3. Immigrants — United States 4. United States — Civilization — Foreign influences I. T.
E184.A1 F47   917.3/03/917   *LC* 67-25512

Gossett, Thomas F.   **• 3.6509**
Race; the history of an idea in America. Dallas, Southern Methodist University Press, 1963. x, 512 p. 23 cm. 1. Race 2. Minorities — United States 3. United States — Race relations I. T.
E184.A1 G6   *LC* 63-21187

Greeley, Andrew M., 1928-.   **3.6510**
Ethnicity in the United States: a preliminary reconnaissance [by] Andrew M. Greeley. — New York: Wiley, [1974] ix, 347 p.; 23 cm. — (The Wiley series in urban research) 'A Wiley-Interscience publication.' 1. Minorities — United States I. T.
E184.A1 G827   301.45/0973   *LC* 74-11483   *ISBN* 0471324655

Greeley, Andrew M., 1928-.   **• 3.6511**
Why can't they be like us? America's white ethnic groups, by Andrew M. Greeley. — [1st ed.]. — New York: E. P. Dutton, 1971. 223 p.; 22 cm. Incorporates substantial portions of the author's Why can't they be like us? published in 1969 by the Institute of Human Relations Press of the American Jewish Committee. 1. Minorities — United States 2. Ethnicity — United States. 3. United States — Ethnic relations I. T.
E184.A1 G83 1971   301.45   *LC* 72-148473   *ISBN* 0525233709

Handlin, Oscar, 1915- ed.   **• 3.6512**
Immigration as a factor in American history. — Englewood Cliffs, N.J.: Prentice-Hall, 1959. 206 p.; 22 cm. 1. Immigrants — United States 2. United States — Emigration and immigration I. T.
E184.A1 H23   325.73   *LC* 59-9516

Handlin, Oscar, 1915-.   **• 3.6513**
Race and nationality in American life. — [1st ed.]. — Boston: Little, Brown, [1957] 300 p.; 21 cm. 1. Minorities — United States 2. United States — Race question. I. T.
E184.A1 H25   325.73 301.451*   *LC* 57-5827

Handlin, Oscar, 1915-.   **3.6514**
The uprooted. — 2d ed. enl. — Boston: Little, Brown, [1973] x, 333 p.; 22 cm. 'An Atlantic monthly press book.' 1. Acculturation — United States. 2. Immigrants — United States I. T.
E184.A1 H27 1973   325.73   *LC* 72-10280   *ISBN* 0316343013

Harvard encyclopedia of American ethnic groups / Stephan   **3.6515**
Thernstrom, editor; Ann Orlov, managing editor, Oscar Handlin, consulting editor.
Cambridge, Mass.: Belknap Press of Harvard University, 1980. xxv, 1076 p.: maps; 29 cm. 1. Minorities — United States — Dictionaries. 2. Ethnicity — United States — Dictionaries. 3. United States — Ethnic relations — Dictionaries. I. Thernstrom, Stephan.
E184.A1 H35   305.8/00973 19   *LC* 80-17756   *ISBN* 0674375122

Higham, John.   **3.6516**
Send these to me: immigrants in urban America / John Higham. — Rev. ed. — Baltimore: Johns Hopkins University Press, c1984. xiii, 261 p.; 21 cm. 1. Minorities — United States 2. Antisemitism — United States. 3. Nativism 4. United States — Emigration and immigration I. T.
E184.A1 H49 1984   305.8/00973 19   *LC* 84-47960   *ISBN* 0801824737

Higham, John.   **• 3.6517**
Strangers in the land; patterns of American nativism, 1860–1925. Corrected and with a new pref. New York, Atheneum, 1963. 431 p. illus. 19 cm. (Atheneum paperbacks, 32) 1. Minorities — United States 2. Prejudices —

United States. 3. Nativism 4. United States — Emigration and immigration
5. United States — Race relations 6. United States — Ethnic relations I. T.
E184.A1 H5 1963   301.45   LC 63-3476

Johnson, Harry Alleyn.   3.6518
Ethnic American minorities: a guide to media and materials / edited and
compiled by Harry A. Johnson. — New York: R. R. Bowker, 1976. xi, 304 p.;
24 cm. 1. Minorities — United States — Study and teaching — Audio-visual
aids — Catalogs. 2. Minorities — United States — Bibliography. I. T.
E184.A1 J58   016.30145/0973   LC 76-25038   *ISBN* 0835207668

Lieberson, Stanley, 1933-.   3.6519
A piece of the pie: Blacks and white immigrants since 1880 / Stanley Lieberson.
— Berkeley: University of California Press, 1981 (c1980). xiii, 419 p.: ill.; 24
cm. Includes indexes. 1. Minorities — United States 2. Afro-Americans —
Social conditions 3. Afro-Americans — Economic conditions 4. United States
— Ethnic relations 5. United States — Race relations I. T.
E184.A1 L49   305.8/00973   LC 80-12772   *ISBN* 0520041232

McLemore, S. Dale.   3.6520
Racial and ethnic relations in America / S. Dale McLemore. — Boston: Allyn
and Bacon, c1980. xv, 379 p.: ill.; 24 cm. Includes indexes. 1. Minorities —
United States 2. United States — Race relations 3. United States — Ethnic
relations I. T.
E184.A1 M16   301.45/1/0973   LC 79-16359   *ISBN* 0205068278

McWilliams, Carey, 1905-.   • 3.6521
Brothers under the skin. Rev. ed. Boston: Little, Brown, 1951. 364 p.; 21 cm.
1. Race relations 2. Minorities 3. United States — Race relations I. T.
E184.A1 M19 1951   LC 51-1031

Minority organizations: a national directory.   3.6522
1st- 1978-. [Garrett Park, Md., Garrett Park Press, c1978-. v. ill. 28 cm.
1. Minorities — United States — Directories.
E184.A1 M544   301.45/1/06173   LC 79-640122

Olson, James Stuart, 1946-.   3.6523
The ethnic dimension in American history / James Stuart Olson. — New York:
St. Martin's Press, c1979. xxv, 440, xiii p.: ill.; 24 cm. 1. Minorities — United
States — History. 2. United States — Ethnic relations 3. United States —
History I. T.
E184.A1 O45   301.45/1   LC 78-65208   *ISBN* 0312266111

Race relations in British North America, 1607–1783 / edited by   3.6524
Bruce A. Glasrud and Alan M. Smith.
Chicago: Nelson-Hall, c1982. xii, 355 p.; 23 cm. 1. Afro-Americans — History
— To 1863 — Addresses, essays, lectures. 2. Indians of North America —
Government relations — To 1789 — Addresses, essays, lectures. 3. Slavery —
United States — History — Colonial period, ca. 1600-1775 — Addresses,
essays, lectures. 4. United States — Race relations — Addresses, essays,
lectures. I. Glasrud, Bruce A. II. Smith, Alan M.
E184.A1 R315   973/.0496073 19   LC 81-18824   *ISBN* 0882293885

Refugees in the United States: a reference handbook / edited by   3.6525
David W. Haines.
Westport, Conn.: Greenwood Press, 1985. viii, 243 p.; 25 cm. Includes index.
1. Minorities — United States — Handbooks, manuals, etc. 2. Refugees —
United States — Handbooks, manuals, etc. 3. United States — Foreign
population — Handbooks, manuals, etc. I. Haines, David W.
E184.A1 R43 1985   305.8/00973 19   LC 84-12794   *ISBN*
031324068X

Ringer, Benjamin B. (Benjamin Bernard), 1920-.   3.6526
'We the people' and others: duality and America's treatment of its racial
minorities / Benjamin B. Ringer. — New York: Tavistock Publications, 1983.
xii, 1165 p.; 25 cm. 'In association with Methuen'—T.p. verso. Includes
indexes. 1. Racism — United States — History. 2. United States — Race
relations 3. United States — Colonial influence. I. T.
E184.A1 R49 1983   305.8/00973 19   LC 83-470   *ISBN*
0422781800

Joramo, Marjorie K.   3.6527
A directory of ethnic publishers and resource organizations / compiled by
Marjorie K. Joramo. — 2d ed. — Chicago: Office for Library Service to the
Disadvantaged, American Library Association, 1979. viii, 102 p.; 22 cm.
Edition of 1976 by B. J. Shapiro issued under title: Directory of ethnic
publishers and resource organizations, 1976. Includes index. 1. Minorities —
United States — Societies, etc. — Directories. 2. Publishers and publishing —
United States — Directories. I. Shapiro, Beth J. Directory of ethnic publishers
and resource organizations, 1976. II. T.
E184.A1 S57 1978   301.45/06/273   LC 78-31753   *ISBN*
0838932231

Sowell, Thomas, 1930-.   3.6528
Ethnic America: a history / Thomas Sowell. — New York: Basic Books, c1981.
353 p.; 24 cm. 1. Minorities — United States — History. 2. United States —
Ethnic relations I. T.
E184.A1 S688   973/.04 19   LC 80-68957   *ISBN* 0465020747

Sowell, Thomas, 1930-.   3.6529
Race and economics / Thomas Sowell. — New York: D. McKay Co., [1975] ix,
276 p.; 22 cm. 1. Minorities — United States — Economic conditions.
2. United States — Race question. I. T.
E184.A1 S69   330.9/73   LC 74-19982   *ISBN* 067950527X

Stein, Howard F.   3.6530
The ethnic imperative: examining the new white ethnic movement / Howard F.
Stein and Robert F. Hill. — University Park: Pennsylvania State University
Press, c1977. xii, 308 p.; 24 cm. 1. Minorities — United States 2. Ethnicity —
United States. 3. United States — Social conditions — 1960- I. Hill, Robert F.
joint author. II. T.
E184.A1 S79   301.451   LC 77-1694   *ISBN* 0271005084

Steinberg, Stephen.   3.6531
The ethnic myth: race, ethnicity, and class in America / Stephen Steinberg. —
1st ed. — New York: Atheneum, 1981. x, 277 p.: graph; 22 cm. 1. United States
— Ethnic relations — Addresses, essays, lectures. 2. Minorities — United
States — Addresses, essays, lectures. I. T.
E184.A1 S794 1981   305.8/00973 19   LC 80-69377   *ISBN*
0689111517

Takaki, Ronald T., 1939-.   3.6532
Iron cages: race and culture in nineteenth–century America / Ronald T.
Takaki. — 1st ed. — New York: Knopf; distributed by Random House, 1979.
xviii, 361 p. Includes index. 1. Minorities — United States — History.
2. United States — Race relations 3. United States — Civilization — 19th
century I. T.
E184.A1 T337 1979   E184.A1 T337 1979.   973/.04   LC 79-2213
    ISBN 0394483103

Williams, Robin Murphy.   3.6533
Mutual accommodation: ethnic conflict and cooperation / Robin M. Williams,
Jr., in collaboration with Madelyn B. Rhenisch. — Minneapolis: University of
Minnesota Press, c1977. xviii, 458 p.: graphs; 24 cm. Includes index.
1. Minorities — United States 2. Ethnicity — United States. 3. Intercultural
communication I. Rhenisch, Madelyn B. joint author. II. T.
E184.A1 W49 1977   301.45/1/0973   LC 77-90060   *ISBN*
0816608229

Wynar, Lubomyr Roman, 1932-.   3.6534
Encyclopedic directory of ethnic organizations in the United States / Lubomyr
R. Wynar, with the assistance of Lois Buttlar and Anna T. Wynar. — Littleton,
Colo.: Libraries Unlimited, 1975. xxiii, 414 p.; 24 cm. Includes index.
1. Minorities — United States — Societies, etc. — Directories. I. Buttlar, Lois,
1934- joint author. II. Wynar, Anna T., 1944- joint author. III. T.
E184.A1 W94   301.45/1/04206273   LC 75-28150   *ISBN*
0872871207

E184 ETHNIC GROUPS, A–Z

E184 A-H

Laxalt, Robert, 1923-.   3.6535
Sweet promised land / by Robert Laxalt; illustration by George Carlson;
foreword by William A. Douglass. — Reno: University of Nevada Press, [1986]
xix, 176 p.: ill.; 22 cm. — (Basque series.) Reprint. Originally published: New
York: Harper, c1957. 1. Laxalt, Dominique. 2. Laxalt, Robert, 1923- —
Family. 3. Basque Americans — Biography. I. Carlson, George, 1940- ill.
II. T. III. Series.
E184.B15 L3 1986   979.3/049992024 B 92 19   LC 86-13204
    ISBN 0874171148

Capek, Thomas, 1861-1950.   • 3.6536
The Čechs (Bohemians) in America: a study of their national, cultural, political,
social, economic, and religious life. — New York: AMS Press, [1969] xviii,
293 p.: maps, ports.; 23 cm. Reprint of the 1920 ed. 1. Czechs in the United
States. I. T.
E184.B67 C29 1969b   301.453/437/073   LC 79-90095

Berthoff, Rowland Tappan, 1921-.   • 3.6537
British immigrants in industrial America, 1790–1950. — New York: Russell &
Russell, [1968, c1953] ix, 296 p.: illus., maps.; 22 cm. 1. British Americans —
History. 2. United States — Emigration and immigration 3. Great Britain —
Emigration and immigration. I. T.
E184.B7 B4 1968   325.2/42/0973   LC 68-10901

Erickson, Charlotte.   3.6538
Invisible immigrants: the adaptation of English and Scottish immigrants in nineteenth–century America. — Coral Gables, Fla.: University of Miami Press, [1972] vi, 531 p.: ill.; 24 cm. 1. British Americans — History — Sources. 2. Scottish Americans — History — Sources. 3. United States — Emigration and immigration — History — Sources. I. T.
E184.B7 E74   917.3/06/21   *LC* 75-161437   *ISBN* 087024213X

The Asian in North America / [edited by] Stanford M. Lyman.   3.6539
Santa Barbara, Calif.: ABC-Clio Books, c1977. xiv, 299 p.; 25 cm. 1. Chinese Americans — Addresses, essays, lectures. 2. Japanese Americans — Addresses, essays, lectures. 3. United States — Race relations — Addresses, essays, lectures. I. Lyman, Stanford M.
E184.C5 A84   301.45/19/5073   *LC* 77-9095   *ISBN* 0894322547

Hsu, Francis L. K., 1909-.   3.6540
The challenge of the American dream: the Chinese in the United States / [by] Francis L. K. Hsu. — Belmont, Calif.: Wadsworth Pub. Co., [1971] 160 p.: ill.; 24 cm. — (Minorities in American life series) 1. Chinese Americans I. T. II. Series.
E184.C5 H8   301.451/951/073   *LC* 71-170311   *ISBN* 0534000436

Prpic, George J.   3.6541
The Croatian immigrants in America, by George J. Prpic. — New York: Philosophical Library, [1971] xiii, 519 p.: illus.; 22 cm. 1. Croatian Americans I. T.
E184.C93 P7   301.451/918/23073   *LC* 70-129066   *ISBN* 0802220355

Boswell, Thomas D.   3.6542
The Cuban–American experience: culture, images, and perspectives / Thomas D. Boswell, James R. Curtis. — Totowa, NJ: Rowman & Allanheld, 1984, c1983. xiii, 200 p.: ill.; 24 cm. 1. Cuban Americans I. Curtis, James R., 1947- II. T.
E184.C97 B67 1984   305.8/687291/073 19   *LC* 83-16042   *ISBN* 0865981167

Lucas, Henry Stephen, 1889-1961.   3.6543
Netherlanders in America; Dutch immigration to the United States and Canada, 1789–1950. — Ann Arbor: University of Michigan Press, 1955. xix, 744 p.: front., maps.; 24 cm. — (University of Michigan publications. History and political science, v. 21) 1. Dutch Americans — History. I. T.
E184.D9 L8   325.24920973   *LC* 55-8647

Lescott-Leszczynski, John, 1937-.   3.6544
The history of U.S. ethnic policy and its impact on European ethnics / John Lescott–Leszczynski. — Boulder, Colo.: Westview Press, c1984. xii, 237 p.; 22 cm. — John Lescott-Leszczynski.—uropean ethnics / — (A Westview replica edition) 1. European Americans — Government policy. 2. European Americans — Civil rights. 3. Civil rights — United States I. T.
E184.E95 L47 1984   323.1/73 19   *LC* 84-2305   *ISBN* 0865318255

Billigmeier, Robert Henry.   3.6545
Americans from Germany: a study in cultural diversity. — Belmont, Calif.: Wadsworth Pub. Co., [1974] 189 p.; 24 cm. — (Minorities in American life series) 1. German Americans — History. I. T. II. Series.
E184.G3 B38   917.3/06/31   *LC* 74-77331   *ISBN* 0534003559

Faust, Albert Bernhardt, 1870-1951.   • 3.6546
The German element in the United States. — New York: Arno Press, 1969 [c1927] 2 v.: illus., maps, ports.; 23 cm. — (The American immigration collection) 1. German Americans I. T.
E184.G3 F3 1969   973/.04/31   *LC* 69-18773

Saloutos, Theodore.   • 3.6547
The Greeks in the United States. — Cambridge: Harvard University Press, 1964. xiv, 445 p.: ill., ports.; 25 cm. 1. Greek Americans I. T.
E184.G7 S29   *LC* 64-13428

Butler, Jon, 1940-.   3.6548
The Huguenots in America: a refugee people in new world society / Jon Butler. — Cambridge, Mass.: Harvard University Press, 1983. viii, 264 p.: ill., ports.; 24 cm. — (Harvard historical monographs. v. 72) 1. Huguenots — United States — History. I. T. II. Series.
E184.H9 B87 1983   973/.088245 19   *LC* 83-8547   *ISBN* 0674413202

Széplaki, Joseph.   3.6549
The Hungarians in America, 1583–1974: a chronology & factbook / compiled and edited by Joseph Széplaki. — Dobbs Ferry, N.Y.: Oceana Publications, 1975. viii, 152 p.; 24 cm. — (Ethnic chronology series; no. 18) Includes index. 1. Hungarian Americans I. T. II. Series.
E184.H95 S86   973/.04/94511   *LC* 75-11505   *ISBN* 037900514X

E184 I IRISH. ITALIANS

Brown, Thomas N., 1920-.   • 3.6550
Irish–American nationalism, 1870–1890 / Thomas N. Brown. — Philadelphia: Lippincott, 1966. xvii, 206 p. — (Critical periods of history; P-18) 1. Irish Americans 2. Nationalism — Ireland. I. T.
E184.I6 B86   *LC* 66-14695

Diner, Hasia R.   3.6551
Erin's daughters in America: Irish immigrant women in the nineteenth century / Hasia R. Diner. — Baltimore: Johns Hopkins University Press, c1983. xvi, 192 p.: ill.; 24 cm. — (Johns Hopkins University studies in historical and political science; 101st ser., 2 (1983) 1. Irish American women — History — 19th century. I. T.
E184.I6 D56 1983   305.4/889162/073 19   *LC* 83-183   *ISBN* 0801828716

Fallows, Marjorie R., 1926-.   3.6552
Irish Americans: identity and assimilation / Marjorie R. Fallows. — Englewood Cliffs, N.J.: Prentice-Hall, c1979. xii, 158 p.; 24 cm. (Ethnic groups in American life series) 1. Irish Americans — Social conditions. 2. Irish Americans — Ethnic identity I. T.
E184.I6 F24   301.45/19/162073   *LC* 78-23323   *ISBN* 0135062616

Greeley, Andrew M., 1928-.   • 3.6553
That most distressful nation: the taming of the American Irish, by Andrew M. Greeley. Foreword by Daniel P. Moynihan. — Chicago: Quadrangle Books, 1972. xxviii, 281 p.; 22 cm. 1. Irish Americans I. T.
E184.I6 G73   301.45/19/162073   *LC* 74-182501   *ISBN* 8812902567

Potter, George W.   • 3.6554
To the golden door: the story of the Irish in Ireland and America. — [1st ed.] Boston: Little, Brown [1960] 631 p.: ill.; 22 cm. 1. Irish — United States 2. Ireland — Famine. 3. Ireland — Economic conditions 4. Ireland — Emigration and immigration. I. T.
E184.I6 P6   *LC* 60-5870

Shannon, William Vincent.   • 3.6555
The American Irish, by William V. Shannon. [rev. ed.] New York, Macmillan [1966] xiii, 484 p. illus., ports. 25 cm. 1. Irish — United States — History I. T.
E184.I6 S5 1966   301.4519162073   *LC* 66-2047

Cordasco, Francesco, 1920- comp.   3.6556
The Italians: social backgrounds of an American group / [by] Francesco Cordasco and Eugene Bucchioni. — Clifton [N.J.]: A. M. Kelley, 1974. xx, 598 p.; 24 cm. 1. Italians in the United States — Addresses, essays, lectures. 2. United States — Emigration and immigration — Addresses, essays, lectures. 3. Italy — Emigration and immigration — Addresses, essays, lectures. I. Bucchioni, Eugene. II. T.
E184.I8 C65   917.3/06/51   *LC* 74-3151   *ISBN* 0678013667

Gambino, Richard.   3.6557
Blood of my blood; the dilemma of the Italian–Americans. — [1st ed.]. — Garden City, N.Y.: Doubleday, 1974. viii, 350 p.; 22 cm. 1. Gambino, Richard. 2. Italian Americans I. T.
E184.I8 G35   917.3/06/51   *LC* 73-11705   *ISBN* 0385050585

Lopreato, Joseph.   • 3.6558
Italian Americans. — [1st ed.]. — New York: Random House, [1970] xiv, 204 p.; 21 cm. — (Ethnic groups in comparative perspective) 1. Italian Americans I. T.
E184.I8 L78   301.453/45/073   *LC* 71-105655

E184 J JAPANESE. JEWS

Conroy, Hilary, 1919-.   3.6559
East across the Pacific: historical & sociological studies of Japanese immigration & assimilation / edited by Hilary Conroy [and] T. Scott Miyakawa. — Santa Barbara, Calif.: American Bibliographical Center-Clio Press [1972] xvii, 322 p.: ill.; 23 cm. 1. Japanese in the United States. 2. United States — Emigration and immigration I. Miyakawa, Tetsuo Scott, joint author. II. T.
E184.J3 C66 1972   301.45/19/56073   *LC* 72-77825   *ISBN* 0874360862 *ISBN* 0874360870

Hosokawa, Bill.   • 3.6560
Nisei: the quiet Americans / by Bill Hosokawa. — New York: W. Morrow, 1969. xvii, 522 p.: ill., ports.; 25 cm. 1. Japanese Americans — History. I. T.
E184.J3 H6   301.453/52/073   *LC* 73-88356

American Jewish year book.   • 3.6561
v. 1- 1899/1900-.`Philadelphia [etc.] American Jewish Committee [etc.] v. ill. 22 cm. Annual. 1899/1900-1948/1949 also called 5660-5709. 1. Jews — Yearbooks. 2. Jews in the United States — Yearbooks. I. Adler, Cyrus,

1863-1940. ed. II. Szold, Henrietta, 1860-1945. ed. III. American Jewish Committee. IV. Jewish Publication Society of America.
E184.J5 A6   296 11   LC 99-4040

Blau, Joseph L. (Joseph Leon), 1909-1986. ed.   3.6562
The Jews of the United States, 1790–1840, a documentary history. Edited by Joseph L. Blau and Salo W. Baron. New York, Columbia University Press, 1963. 3 v. (xxxv, 1034 p.) 24 cm. (Jacob R. Schiff library of Jewish contributions to American democracy; no. 17-19.) 1. Jews — United States — History — Sources. I. Baron, Salo Wittmayer, 1895- joint ed. II. T. III. Series.
E184.J5 B5543   325.256930973   LC 64-10108

Borden, Morton.   3.6563
Jews, Turks, and infidels / Morton Borden. — Chapel Hill: University of North Carolina Press, c1984. x, 163 p.; 24 cm. Includes index. 1. Jews — Legal status, laws, etc. — United States. 2. Freedom of religion — United States. 3. Jews — United States — Politics and government. 4. United States — Politics and government — 19th century 5. United States — Ethnic relations I. T.
E184.J5 B68 1984   323.44/2/0973 19   LC 83-19863   ISBN 0807815926

A Coat of many colors: Jewish subcommunities in the United   3.6564
States / edited and compiled by Abraham D. Lavender.
Westport, Conn.: Greenwood Press, 1977. xiii, 324 p.; 25 cm. (Contributions in family studies. no. 1 0147-1023) 1. Jews — United States — Social conditions — Addresses, essays, lectures. 2. Jews — Southern States — Social conditions — Addresses, essays, lectures. 3. Women, Jewish — United States — Addresses, essays, lectures. 4. Sephardim — United States — Addresses, essays, lectures. 5. United States — Social conditions — 1960- — Addresses, essays, lectures. I. Lavender, Abraham D. II. Series.
E184.J5 C58   301.45/19/24073   LC 77-71865   ISBN 083719539X

Cohen, Naomi Wiener, 1927-.   3.6565
Encounter with emancipation: the German Jews in the United States, 1830–1914 / Naomi W. Cohen. — 1st ed. — Philadelphia, Pa.: Jewish Publication Society, 1984. xiv, 407, [10] p. of plates: ill.; 25 cm. 1. Jews, German — United States — History — 19th century. 2. Judaism — United States — History — 19th century. 3. United States — Ethnic relations I. T.
E184.J5 C618 1984   973/.04924 19   LC 83-26781   ISBN 0827602367

Coser, Lewis A., 1913-.   3.6566
Refugee scholars in America: their impact and their experiences / Lewis A. Coser. — New Haven: Yale University Press, c1984. xviii, 351 p.; 25 cm. 1. Jews — United States — Biography. 2. Refugees, Jewish — United States — Biography. 3. Refugees, Political — United States — Biography. 4. Scholars — United States — Biography. I. T.
E184.J5 C66 1984   973/.04924022 B 19   LC 84-40193   ISBN 0300031939

Elazar, Daniel Judah.   3.6567
Community and polity: the organizational dynamics of American Jewry / Daniel J. Elazar. — 1st ed. — Philadelphia: Jewish Publication Society of America, 1976. xv, 421 p.; 25 cm.. (Jewish communal and public affairs) Includes index. 1. Jews — United States — Politics and government. 2. United States — Politics and government I. T. II. Series.
E184.J5 E39   301.45/19/24073   LC 75-8167   ISBN 0827600682

Feingold, Henry L., 1931-.   3.6568
Zion in America: the Jewish experience from colonial times to the present / by Henry L. Feingold. — New York: Hippocrene Books, 1974. 357 p.; 23 cm. Includes index. 1. Jews — United States — History. 2. Judaism — United States. I. T.
E184.J5 F377 1974b   973/.04/924   LC 74-15754   ISBN 0882543075

Glanz, Rudolf.   3.6569
The Jewish woman in America: two female immigrant generations, 1820–1929 / by Rudolf Glanz. — New York: Ktav Pub. House, c1976. 213 p. Includes indexes. 1. Jews — United States 2. Women, Jewish — United States. 3. Jews — Migrations 4. Women immigrants — United States. 5. United States — Emigration and immigration I. T.
E184.J5 G493   973/.04/924   LC 75-29350   ISBN 0870684620

Karp, Abraham J.   3.6570
Haven and home: a history of the Jews in America / Abraham J. Karp. — New York: Schocken Books, 1985. xiii, 401 p.; 24 cm. Includes index. 1. Jews — United States — History. 2. United States — Ethnic relations I. T.
E184.J5 K168 1985   973/.04924 19   LC 84-5530   ISBN 0805239200

Karp, Abraham J. comp.   • 3.6571
The Jewish experience in America: selected studies from the publications of the American Jewish Historical Society / edited with introductions by Abraham J. Karp. — Waltham, Mass.: American Jewish Historical Society [1969] 5 v.: ill.,

facsims., ports.; 24 cm. 1. Jews — United States — History — Collections. I. American Jewish Historical Society. II. T.
E184.J5 K17   973/.09/74924   LC 72-77150

Marcus, Jacob Rader, 1896- ed.   3.6572
Memoirs of American Jews, 1775–1865. New York, Ktav Pub. House, 1974 [i.e. 1975, c1955] 3 v. in 2. illus. 24 cm. Reprint of the 1955-56 ed. published by the Jewish Publication Society of America, Philadelphia, in series: The Jacob R. Schiff library of Jewish contributions to American democracy. 1. Jews — United States I. T.
E184.J5 M233 1975   917.3/06/924 B   LC 73-16218   ISBN 0870682326

Schappes, Morris U. (Morris Urman), 1907- ed.   3.6573
A documentary history of the Jews in the United States, 1654–1875. Edited with notes and introductions by Morris U. Schappes. 3d ed.; [1st Schocken ed.] New York, Schocken Books [1971] xxiv, 766 p. 21 cm. 1. Jews — United States — History — Sources. I. T.
E184.J5 S35 1971   917.3/06/924   LC 72-122332

Sklare, Marshall, 1921- comp.   3.6574
The Jew in American society. Edited, with introductions and notes, by Marshall Sklare. New York, Behrman House [1974] ix, 404 p. 24 cm. (Library of Jewish studies) 1. Jews — United States — Political and social conditions — Addresses, essays, lectures. 2. Judaism — United States — Addresses, essays, lectures. I. T.
E184.J5 S5475   301.45/19/24073   LC 74-3051   ISBN 087441203X

Studies of the third wave: recent migration of Soviet Jews to   3.6575
the United States / edited by Dan N. Jacobs & Ellen Frankel
Paul.
Boulder, Colo.: Westview Press, 1981. ix, 176 p. — (A Westview replica edition) 1. Jews, Russian — United States — Addresses, essays, lectures. 2. Jews — Soviet Union — Politics and government — 1917- — Addresses, essays, lectures. 3. United States — Emigration and immigration — Addresses, essays, lectures. 4. Soviet Union — Ethnic relations — Addresses, essays, lectures. I. Jacobs, Dan N. (Daniel Norman), 1925- II. Paul, Ellen Frankel.
E184.J5 S873   E184J5 S873.   304.8/47/073 19   LC 80-29250   ISBN 0865311439

Waxman, Chaim Isaac.   3.6576
America's Jews in transition / Chaim I. Waxman. — Philadelphia: Temple University Press, 1983. xxv, 272 p.; 22 cm. Includes index. 1. Jews — United States — History. 2. Jews — Social conditions. 3. Judaism — United States — History. 4. United States — Ethnic relations I. T.
E184.J5 W285 1983   973/.04924 19   LC 83-9157   ISBN 0877223211

Whitfield, Stephen J., 1942-.   3.6577
Voices of Jacob, hands of Esau: Jews in American life and thought / Stephen J. Whitfield. — [S.l.]: Shoe String, 1984. 322 p.; 23 cm. Includes index. 1. Jews — United States — Intellectual life — Addresses, essays, lectures. 2. Jews — Southern States — Addresses, essays, lectures. 3. United States — Civilization — Jewish influences — Addresses, essays, lectures. 4. United States — Ethnic relations — Addresses, essays, lectures. 5. Southern States — Ethnic relations — Addresses, essays, lectures. I. T.
E184.J5 W5 1984   973/.04924 19   LC 83-25720   ISBN 0208020071

Who's who in American Jewry.   3.6578
1982 edition. Los Angeles, CA.: Standard Who's Who, 1980. 726 p.; 29 cm. Annual. 1. Jews — United States — Biography — Periodicals. 2. Jews — United States — Societies, etc. — Directories. 3. United States — Biography — Periodicals. I. Directory of American Jewish institutions.
E184.J5 W62   920/.0092924073 B   LC 80-645196

Zweigenhaft, Richard L.   3.6579
Jews in the Protestant establishment / Richard L. Zweigenhaft, G. William Domhoff. — New York, N.Y.: Praeger, 1982. viii, 133 p.; 24 cm. Includes index. 1. Jews — United States — Social conditions. 2. Elite (Social sciences) — United States. 3. Executives — United States. I. Domhoff, G. William. II. T.
E184.J5 Z826 1982   305.5/54/089924073 19   LC 82-13155   ISBN 0030626072

E184 K–O Koreans. Mennonites. Mexicans. Orientals (General)

The Korean diaspora: historical and sociological studies of   3.6580
Korean immigration and assimilation in North America /
Hyung–chan Kim, editor.
Santa Barbara, Calif.: ABC-Clio, c1977. xi, 268 p.; 24 cm. 1. Korean Americans — Addresses, essays, lectures. 2. Americanization — Addresses, essays, lectures. I. Kim, Hyung-chan.
E184.K6 K63   301.45/19/57073   LC 77-7080   ISBN 0874362504

Hostetler, John Andrew, 1918-. **3.6581**
Amish society / John A. Hostetler. — 3d ed. — Baltimore: Johns Hopkins University Press, 1980. xv, 414 p.: ill.; 24 cm. Includes index. 1. Amish — United States — Social life and customs. 2. Amish — Social life and customs I. T.
E184.M45 H63 1980   301.45/28/87   *LC* 79-23823   *ISBN* 0801823331

The Mexican American experience: an interdisciplinary **3.6582**
anthology / edited by Rodolfo O. de la Garza ... [et al.].
Austin, Tex.: University of Texas Press, Austin, c1985. p. cm. 1. Mexican Americans — Addresses, essays, lectures. 2. Mexicans — United States — Addresses, essays, lectures. I. De la Garza, Rodolfo O.
E184.M5 M5 1985   305.8/6872/073 19   *LC* 85-5317   *ISBN* 0292750889

Mirandé, Alfredo. **3.6583**
La Chicana: the Mexican–American woman / Alfredo Mirandé, Evangelina Enríquez. — Chicago: University of Chicago Press, 1979. x, 283 p.: ill.; 24 cm. Includes index. 1. Mexican American women I. Enríquez, Evangelina. joint author. II. T.
E184.M5 M55   301.41/2/0973   *LC* 79-13536   *ISBN* 0226531597

Weber, David J. comp. **3.6584**
Foreigners in their native land; historical roots of the Mexican Americans. Edited by David J. Weber. Foreword by Ramón Eduardo Ruiz. — [1st ed.]. — Albuquerque: University of New Mexico Press, [1973] xi, 288 p.: illus.; 24 cm. 1. Mexican Americans — History — Sources. I. T.
E184.M5 W42 1973   917.3/06/6872   *LC* 73-77858   *ISBN* 0826302785

Counterpoint: perspectives on Asian America / editor, Emma **3.6585**
Gee; associate editors, Bruce Iwasaki ... [et al.]; assistant editor, June Okida Kuramoto; art directors, Dean S. Toji, Glen Iwasaki.
Los Angeles: Asian American Studies Center, University of California, c1976. 595 p.; 29 cm. 1. Asian Americans — Addresses, essays, lectures. 2. United States — Race question — Addresses, essays, lectures. I. Gee, Emma.
E184.O6 C68   301.45/19/5073   *LC* 76-41528

E184 P POLES. PUERTO RICANS

Greene, Victor R. **3.6586**
For God and country: the rise of Polish and Lithuanian ethnic consciousness in America, 1860–1910 / Victor Greene. — Madison: State Historical Society of Wisconsin, 1975. x, 202 p., [4] leaves of plates: ill.; 23 cm. Includes index. 1. Polish Americans — History. 2. Lithuanian Americans — History. I. T.
E184.P7 G73   973/.04/9185   *LC* 75-19017   *ISBN* 0870201557

Lopata, Helena Znaniecka, 1925-. **3.6587**
Polish Americans: status competition in an ethnic community / Helena Znaniecki Lopata. — Englewood Cliffs, N.J.: Prentice-Hall, c1976. xvii, 174 p.: ill.; 23 cm. — (Ethnic groups in American life series) Includes index. 1. Polish Americans I. T.
E184.P7 L66   301.45/19/185073   *LC* 75-41401   *ISBN* 0136864449

Cordasco, Francesco, 1920- comp. **3.6588**
The Puerto Rican experience; a sociological sourcebook, by Francesco Cordasco [and] Eugene Bucchioni. — Totowa, N.J.: Rowman and Littlefield, [1973] xix, 370 p.: illus.; 22 cm. 1. Puerto Ricans in the United States. I. Bucchioni, Eugene. joint comp. II. T.
E184.P85 C67   301.45/16/87295073   *LC* 72-90922   *ISBN* 0874711622

Fitzpatrick, Joseph P. **3.6589**
Puerto Rican Americans; the meaning of migration to the mainland [by] Joseph P. Fitzpatrick. Englewood Cliffs, N.J., Prentice-Hall [1971] xvi, 192 p. illus., maps. 23 cm. (Ethnic groups in American life series) 1. Puerto Ricans in the United States. 2. Puerto Ricans in New York (City) 3. Puerto Rico — Social life and customs. I. T.
E184.P85 F5   305.8/687295/07471 19   *LC* 74-150712   *ISBN* 0137401000

Wagenheim, Kal. **3.6590**
A survey of Puerto Ricans on the U.S. mainland in the 1970s / Kal Wagenheim. — New York: Praeger, 1975. xv, 133 p.; 25 cm. (Praeger special studies in U.S. economic, social, and political issues) 1. Puerto Ricans in the United States — Economic conditions. 2. Puerto Ricans in the United States — Social conditions. I. T.
E184.P85 W33   301.45/16/87295073   *LC* 74-30712   *ISBN* 0275059804

E184 S–Z SCANDINAVIANS. SCOTS. WELSH

Nielsen, George R. **3.6591**
The Danish Americans / by George R. Nielsen. — Boston: Twayne Publishers, 1981. 237 p.; 21 cm. — (The Immigrant heritage of America series) Includes index. 1. Danish Americans I. T.
E184.S19 N53   973/.043981 19   *LC* 81-63   *ISBN* 0805784195

Blegen, Theodore Christian, 1891-1969. • **3.6592**
Norwegian migration to America, 1825–1860 [by] Theodore C. Blegen. — New York: Arno Press, 1969. xi, 413 p.: ill., facsims., maps; 24 cm. — (The American immigration collection) A reprint of the 1931 ed. 1. Norwegians in the United States. 2. Norway — Emigration and immigration. I. T.
E184.S2 B62   301.453/481/073   *LC* 69-18759

Lovoll, Odd Sverre. **3.6593**
[Løfterike landet. English] The promise of America: a history of the Norwegian–American people / Odd S. Lovoll. — Minneapolis: University of Minnesota Press in cooperation with the Norwegian-American Historical Association, c1984. 239 p.: ill.; 24 x 28 cm. Translation of: Det løfterike landet. Includes index. 1. Norwegian Americans — History. I. T.
E184.S2 L6913 1984   973/.043982 19   *LC* 83-27350   *ISBN* 0816613311

Benson, Adolph Burnett, 1881- ed. • **3.6594**
Swedes in America. London, H. Milford, Oxford university press, 1938. xvi, 614 p. front. plates, ports. 25 cm. Maps on lining-papers. 1. Swedes in the United states. 2. Swedes in the United States — Biography. I. Hedin, Naboth, 1884- joint ed. II. Swedish American tercentenary association. III. T.
E184.S23 B33   *LC* 38-27493

Ljungmark, Lars. **3.6595**
Swedish exodus / by Lars Ljungmark; translated by Kermit B. Westerberg. — Carbondale: Published for Swedish Pioneer Historical Society by Southern Illinois University Press, c1979. X, 165 p., [7] leaves of plates: ill.; 24 cm. Revised translation of the work published in 1965 under title: Den stora utvandringen. Includes index. 1. Swedish Americans 2. United States — Emigration and immigration I. Swedish Pioneer Historical Society. II. T.
E184.S23 L5313   304.8/73/0485 19   *LC* 79-10498   *ISBN* 080930905X

Graham, Ian Charles Cargill, 1919-. • **3.6596**
Colonists from Scotland: emigration to North America, 1707–1783. — Port Washington, N.Y.: Kennikat Press, [1972, c1956] x, 213 p.: map.; 23 cm. 1. Scottish Americans 2. Scotland — Emigration and immigration. I. T.
E184.S3 G7 1972   325.2/41/073   *LC* 70-153216   *ISBN* 0804615268

Leyburn, James Graham. • **3.6597**
The Scotch–Irish: a social history. — Chapel Hill: University of North Carolina Press [1962] xix, 377 p.: maps; 24 cm. Bibliography: p. [354]-372. 1. Scotch-Irish in the United States. 2. Scotland — Soc. condit. 3. Scotch in Ireland. I. T.
E184.S4L5   301.45   *LC* 62-16063

Ashton, E. T. (Elwyn Thomas) **3.6598**
The Welsh in the United States / by Elwyn T. Ashton. — Hove, Sussex: Caldra House, 1984. 182 p.: ill.; 22 cm. Includes indexes. 1. Welsh Americans — History. 2. Welsh Americans — Biography. I. T.
E184.W4 A84 1984   973/.049166 19   *LC* 85-125126

Conway, Alan, ed. **3.6599**
The Welsh in America; letters from the immigrants. Minneapolis, University of Minnesota Press [1961] 341 p. 24 cm. Bibliography: p. 330-332. 1. Welsh in the United States. 2. United States — Description and travel I. T.
E184.W4C6   325.24290973   *LC* 61-7724

Williams, David, 1900-. **3.6600**
Cymru ac America = Wales and America / David Williams. Cardiff: University of Wales Press, 1975. 89 p., leaf of plate, [4] p. of plates: ill., facsim., map, port.; 21 cm. First published 1946. English and Welsh. 1. Welsh Americans — History. I. T. II. Title: Wales and America.
E184.W4 W5 1975   973/.04/9166   *LC* 76-383488

E184.5 –185.97 Afro–Americans

Proceedings of the Black State conventions, 1840–1865 / edited **3.6601**
by Philip S. Foner and George E. Walker.
Philadelphia: Temple University Press, 1979- < 1980 >. v. < 1-2 >; 24 cm. 1. Afro-Americans — Congresses. 2. Afro-Americans — History — To 1863 — Sources. 3. Slavery in the United States — Anti-slavery movements —

Sources. 4. Afro-Americans — Colonization — Sources. I. Foner, Philip Sheldon, 1910- II. Walker, George E. (George Elizur), 1947-
E184.5.P75   973/.0496 19   *LC* 78-10841   *ISBN* 0877221456

Blassingame, John W., 1940- comp.   **3.6602**
New perspectives on Black studies / edited by John W. Blassingame. — Urbana: University of Illinois Press [1971] xx, 243 p.; 21 cm. 1. Afro-Americans — Study and teaching — Addresses, essays, lectures. I. T.
E184.7.B57   917.3/06/96073   *LC* 71-133942   *ISBN* 0252001354

Butler, Johnnella E.   **3.6603**
Black studies—pedagogy and revolution: a study of Afro–American studies and the liberal arts tradition through the discipline of Afro–American literature / Johnnella E. Butler. — Washington, D.C.: University Press of America, c1981. viii, 154 p.: ill.; 21 cm. 1. Afro-Americans — Study and teaching 2. American literature — Afro-American authors — History and criticism. I. T.
E184.7.B87   375.9730496073 19   *LC* 80-67213   *ISBN* 0819115681

Stanfield, John H.   **3.6604**
Philanthropy and Jim Crow in American social science / John H. Stanfield. — Westport, Conn.: Greenwood Press, 1985. xii, 216 p.; 24 cm. (Contributions in Afro-American and African studies. 0069-9624; no. 82) Includes index. 1. Afro-Americans — Research — United States — History. 2. Racism — United States — History. 3. Endowment of research — United States — History. 4. Endowments — United States — History. 5. Social sciences — Research — United States — History. 6. United States — Race relations — Research — United States — History. I. T. II. Series.
E184.7.S72 1985   305.8/96073 19   *LC* 84-8995   *ISBN* 0313238944

Aptheker, Herbert, 1915-.   • **3.6605**
A documentary history of the Negro people in the United States, edited by Herbert Aptheker. Pref. by W. E. B. Du Bois. [1st ed.] New York, Citadel Press [1951-1974] 3 v. illus. 22 cm. 1. Afro-Americans — History — Sources. I. T.
E185.A58   *LC* 51-14828   *ISBN* 0806503629

Bennett, Lerone, 1928-.   **3.6606**
Before the Mayflower: a history of black America / Lerone Bennett, Jr. — 5th ed. — New York: Penguin, 1984, c1982. xvi, 681 p.: ill.; 20 cm. Includes index. 1. Afro-Americans — History I. T.
E185.B4 1982   973/.00496073 19   *ISBN* 0140872144

Bennett, Lerone, 1928-.   **3.6607**
The shaping of Black America / Lerone Bennett, Jr.; illustrated by Charles White. — Chicago: Johnson Pub. Co., 1975. 356 p.: ill.; 25 cm. Includes index. 1. Afro-Americans — History I. T.
E185.B43   917.3/06/96   *LC* 74-20659   *ISBN* 0874850711

Black America: geographic perspectives / edited by Robert T.   **3.6608**
Ernst and Lawrence Hugg.
1st ed. — Garden City, N.Y.: Anchor Press, 1976. xiv, 438 p.: ill. Includes index. 1. Afro-Americans — Addresses, essays, lectures. 2. Anthropo-geography — United States — Addresses, essays, lectures. I. Ernst, Robert T. II. Hugg, Lawrence, 1949-
E185.B54   F185 B54.   301.32/973   *LC* 74-15783   *ISBN* 0385055366

Cruse, Harold.   • **3.6609**
Rebellion or revolution?. — New York, Morrow, 1968. 272 p. 22 cm. Bibliographical footnotes. 1. Negroes — Addresses, essays, lectures. I. T.
E185.C93   917.3/03/920917496   *LC* 68-29609

Davis, John P., 1905- ed.   • **3.6610**
The American Negro reference book. — Englewood Cliffs, N. J., Prentice-Hall [1969, c1966] xxi, 969 p. illus. Sponsored by the Phelps-Stokes Fund. I. Phelps-Stokes Fund. II. T.
E185.D25   *LC* 65-12919

Delany, Martin Robison, 1812-1885.   **3.6611**
The condition, elevation, emigration, and destiny of the colored people of the United States. — New York: Arno Press, 1968. 214 p.; 18 cm. — (American Negro, his history and literature.) Reprint of the 1852 ed., with a new introd. 1. Negroes. I. T. II. Series.
E185.D33 1968   301.451/96/073   *LC* 68-28993

Dormon, James H.   **3.6612**
The Afro–American experience: a cultural history through emancipation [by] James H. Dormon [and] Robert R. Jones. New York, Wiley [1974] viii, 274 p. maps. 22 cm. 1. Afro-Americans — History — To 1863 I. Jones, Robert Rivers, 1934- joint author. II. T.
E185.D65 1974   917.3/06/96073   *LC* 73-16475   *ISBN* 0471219134   *ISBN* 0471219142

Drimmer, Melvin, comp.   • **3.6613**
Black history; a reappraisal, edited with commentary by Melvin Drimmer. [1st ed.] Garden City, N.Y., Doubleday, 1968. xx, 553 p. 22 cm. Essays which present the Negro's role in American history, each prefaced by an analysis of

the historical events surrounding the period it covers. 1. Afro-Americans — History — Addresses, essays, lectures. I. T.
E185.D7   909/.09/7496   *LC* 67-19105

Encyclopedia of Black America / W. Augustus Low, editor,   **3.6614**
Virgil A. Clift, associate editor.
New York: McGraw-Hill, c1981. xx, 921 p.: ill.; 29 cm. Includes index. 1. Afro-Americans — Dictionaries and encyclopedias. I. Low, W. Augustus. II. Clift, Virgil A.
E185.E55   973/.0496073   *LC* 80-13247   *ISBN* 0070388342

Franklin, John Hope, 1915-.   **3.6615**
Racial equality in America / John Franklin. — Chicago: University of Chicago Press, c1976. ix, 113 p. — (Jefferson lecture in the humanities. 1976) 1. Afro-Americans — History — Addresses, essays, lectures. 2. Afro-Americans — Civil rights — Addresses, essays, lectures. I. T. II. Series.
E185.F72   E185 F826.   973/.04/96073   *LC* 76-26168   *ISBN* 0226260739

Franklin, John Hope, 1915-.   **3.6616**
From slavery to freedom: a history of Negro Americans / John Hope Franklin. — 5th ed. — New York: Knopf, 1980. xxvii, 554, xxxix: facsims., maps ports. Includes index. 1. Afro-Americans — History 2. Slavery in the United States — History. I. T.
E185.F825 1979   E185 F825 1980.   973/.04/96073   *LC* 79-9464   *ISBN* 0394507746

Frazier, Edward Franklin, 1894-1962.   • **3.6617**
The Negro in the United States. — Rev. ed. — New York, Macmillan [1957] xxxiii, 769 p. maps, diagrs., tables. 22 cm. Bibliography: p. 707-752. 1. Negroes. I. T.
E185.F833 1957   325.260973   *LC* 57-5224

Fredrickson, George M., 1934-.   • **3.6618**
The Black image in the white mind; the debate on Afro–American character and destiny, 1817–1914 [by] George M. Fredrickson. — [1st ed.]. — New York, Harper & Row [1971] xiii, 343 p. 22 cm. 1. Negroes — History. 2. Prejudices and antipathies — United States. 3. United States — Race relations I. T.
E185.F836   301.451/96/073   *LC* 71-138721   *ISBN* 006011343X

Jordan, Winthrop D.   • **3.6619**
White over black: American attitudes toward the Negro, 1550–1812 [by] Winthrop D. Jordan. Chapel Hill, Published for the Institute of Early American History and Culture at Williamsburg, Va., by the University of North Carolina Press [1968] xx, 651 p. map. 24 cm. 1. Slavery — United States — History 2. Afro-Americans — History — To 1863 3. United States — Race relations I. Institute of Early American History and Culture (Williamsburg, Va.) II. T.
E185.J69   973/.0974/96   *LC* 68-13295

Lynch, Hollis Ralph. comp.   **3.6620**
The black urban condition: a documentary history, 1866–1971, by Hollis R. Lynch. New York, Crowell [1973] xxiii, 469 p. 24 cm. 1. Afro-Americans — History — Addresses, essays, lectures. 2. Urbanization — United States — Addresses, essays, lectures. I. T.
E185.L96   301.45/19/6073   *LC* 72-13822   *ISBN* 0690146396

McKissick, Floyd, 1922-.   **3.6621**
Three–fifths of a man. [New York] Macmillan [1969] 223 p. 22 cm. 1. Afro-Americans — Civil rights — History. I. T.
E185.M3   323.1/19/6073   *LC* 69-12651

Meier, August, 1923-.   **3.6622**
From plantation to ghetto / by August Meier and Elliott Rudwick. — 3d ed. — New York: Hill and Wang, 1976. x, 406 p.; 21 cm. — (American century series) Includes index. 1. Afro-Americans — History I. Rudwick, Elliott M. joint author. II. T.
E185.M4 1976   973/.04/96073   *LC* 75-43729   *ISBN* 0809047926

Meier, August, 1923- comp.   • **3.6623**
The making of black America; essays in Negro life & history, edited by August Meier & Elliott Rudwick. [1st ed.] New York, Atheneum, 1969. xvi, 377, 507 p. 24 cm. (Studies in American Negro life) 1. Afro-Americans — History — Addresses, essays, lectures. I. Rudwick, Elliott M. joint comp. II. T.
E185.M43   301.451/96/073   *LC* 67-25486

Murray, Albert.   • **3.6624**
The omni–Americans: new perspectives on Black experience and American culture. — New York: Outerbridge & Dienstfrey: distributed by E. P. Dutton, [1970] 227 p.; 23 cm. 1. Negroes. I. T.
E185.M9 1970   *LC* 77-101313

Negotiating the mainstream: a survey of the Afro–American   3.6625
experience / Harry A. Johnson, editor.
Chicago: American Library Association, 1978. viii, 231 p. 1. Afro-Americans
— Addresses, essays, lectures. I. Johnson, Harry Alleyn.
E185.N38   E185 N38.   973/.04/96073   LC 77-29041   ISBN
0838902545

The Negro almanac: a reference work on the Afro–American /   3.6626
compiled and edited by Harry A. Ploski and James Williams.
4th ed. — New York: Wiley, c1983. xiii, 1550 p.; 29 cm. 'A Wiley-Interscience
publication.' Includes index. 1. Afro-Americans — Dictionaries and
encyclopedias. I. Ploski, Harry A. II. Williams, James D. (James De Bois),
1926-
E185.N385 1983   973/.0496073/00321 19   LC 82-17469   ISBN
0471877107

Philosophy born of struggle: anthology of Afro–American   3.6627
philosophy from 1917 / edited with an introduction and select
bibliography of Afro–American works in philosophy by Leonard
Harris.
Dubuque, Iowa: Kendall/Hunt Pub. Co., c1983. xxi, 316 p.: ill.; 24 cm.
1. Afro-Americans — Addresses, essays, lectures. 2. Afro-American
philosophy — Addresses, essays, lectures. I. Harris, Leonard, 1948-
E185.P46 1983   973/.0496 19   LC 82-83465   ISBN 0840328710

Redding, J. Saunders (Jay Saunders), 1906-.   3.6628
They came in chains; Americans from Africa [by] Saunders Redding. Rev. ed.
Philadelphia, Lippincott [1973] 340 p. 22 cm. 1. Afro-Americans — History
I. T.
E185.R4 1973   917.3/06/96   LC 73-401   ISBN 0397008120 ISBN
0397009747

Storing, Herbert J., 1928- comp.   3.6629
What country have I? Political writings by Black Americans. Herbert J.
Storing, editor. New York, St. Martin's Press [1970] x, 235 p. 24 cm. 1. Afro-
Americans — History — Sources. 2. Afro-Americans — Politics and
government — Addresses, essays, lectures. I. T.
E185.S87   301.451/96/073   LC 77-106206

Washington, Joseph R.   3.6630
Black and white power subreption, by Joseph R. Washington, Jr. Boston,
Beacon Press [1969] xi, 228 p. 21 cm. 1. Afro-Americans 2. United States —
Race relations I. T.
E185.W33   323.1/19/6073   LC 72-84799

Wilson, William J., 1935-.   3.6631
The declining significance of race: Blacks and changing American institutions /
William Julius Wilson. — 2d ed. — Chicago: University of Chicago Press, 1980.
xii, 243 p.; 22 cm. Includes index. 1. Afro-Americans — Economic conditions
2. Afro-Americans — Social conditions 3. United States — Race relations
I. T.
E185.W73 1980   305.8/00973   LC 80-18066   ISBN 0226901297

Woodson, Carter Godwin, 1875-1950.   • 3.6632
The mind of the Negro as reflected in letters written during the crisis,
1800–1860. New York, Russell & Russell [1969] xxxii, 672 p. 25 cm. Reprint of
the 1926 ed. 1. Afro-Americans — History — To 1863 2. Afro-Americans —
Social conditions 3. Slavery in the United States — Emancipation. I. T.
E185.W8877 1969   917.35   LC 69-14222

Woodson, Carter Godwin, 1875-1950.   • 3.6633
The Negro in our history, by Carter G. Woodson and Charles H. Wesley. 10th
ed., further rev. and enl. Washington, Associated Publishers [1962] 833 p. illus.
22 cm. 1. Afro-Americans — History 2. Slavery — United States I. Wesley,
Charles H. (Charles Harris), 1891-1987. joint author. II. T.
E185.W89 1962   326.973   LC 62-3979

Berlin, Ira, 1941-.   3.6634
Slaves without masters: the free Negro in the antebellum South. — [1st ed.]
New York: Pantheon Books [1975, c1974] xxi, 423 p.; 25 cm. 1. Afro-
Americans — History — To 1863 2. Freedmen in the Southern States. I. T.
E185.18.B47 1975   301.44/93/0975   LC 74-4761   ISBN
039449041X

Litwack, Leon F.   3.6635
Been in the storm so long: the aftermath of slavery / Leon F. Litwack. — 1st ed.
— New York: Knopf: distributed by Random House, 1979. xvi, 651 p.; 25 cm.
Includes index. 1. Afro-Americans — History — 1863-1877 2. Reconstruction
3. Afro-Americans — Southern States — History. 4. Southern States —
History — 1865-1877 5. Southern States — Social conditions I. T.
E185.2.L57 1979   973/.0496073 19   LC 78-24311   ISBN
0394500997

Rabinowitz, Howard N., 1942-.   3.6636
Race relations in the urban South, 1865–1890 / Howard N. Rabinowitz. —
New York: Oxford University Press, 1978. xxii, 441 p.: maps; 24 cm. — (The

Urban life in America series) Includes index. 1. Afro-Americans — Southern
States 2. Afro-Americans — Southern States — Segregation. 3. City and town
life — Southern States. 4. Afro-Americans — History — 1863-1877
5. Southern States — Race relations. I. T.
E185.2.R23   305.8/96073 19   LC 76-57260   ISBN 0195022831

E185.5–185.8 Social and Economic
Conditions

Moss, Alfred A., 1943-.   3.6637
The American Negro Academy: voice of the talented tenth / Alfred A. Moss,
Jr. — Baton Rouge: Louisiana State University Press, c1981. 327 p., [5] leaves
of plates: ports.; 24 cm. Includes index. 1. American Negro Academy —
History. 2. Afro-Americans — History I. T.
E185.5.A53 M67   975.3/00496073   LC 80-18026   ISBN
0807106992

Amistad (New York, N.Y.)   3.6638
Amistad / edited by Charles F. Harris and John A. Williams. — 1-2. — New
York: Vintage Books, 1970. 2 v.; 19 cm. Writings on black history and culture.
1. Afro-Americans — Collected works.
E185.5.A57   917.3/0496 19   LC 75-107196

Berry, Mary Frances.   3.6639
Long memory: the Black experience in America / Mary Frances Berry, John
W. Blassingame. — New York: Oxford University Press, 1982. xxi, 486 p.: ill.;
24 cm. Includes index. 1. Afro-Americans — History 2. Afro-Americans —
Civil rights 3. United States — Race relations I. Blassingame, John W., 1940-
joint author. II. T.
E185.5.B47   973/.0496073 19   LC 80-24748   ISBN 0195029097

The Black man: a monthly magazine of Negro thought and   3.6640
opinion / Marcus Garvey; compiled and with an introductory
essay by Robert A. Hill.
Millwood, N.Y.: Kraus-Thomson Organization, 1975. 476 p. in various
pagings: ill.; 29 cm. 1. Universal Negro Improvement Association. 2. Afro-
Americans — Periodicals. 3. Blacks — Periodicals. 4. Afro-Americans
5. Blacks I. Garvey, Marcus, 1887-1940.
E185.5.B533   301.45/19/6

Du Bois, W. E. B. (William Edward Burghardt), 1868-1963.   • 3.6641
Darkwater; voices from within the veil. — New York, Schocken Books [1969]
viii, 276 p. 21 cm. Reprint of the 1920 ed. 1. Negroes. I. T.
E185.5.D8 1969   910.03/174/96   LC 69-19627

Du Bois, W. E. B. (William Edward Burghardt), 1868-1963.   • 3.6642
The souls of black folk. With introductions by Nathan Hare and Alvin F.
Poussaint. New York, New American Library [1969] 280 p. music. 18 cm. (A
Signet classics) 1. Afro-Americans — Addresses, essays, lectures. I. T.
E185.5.D817 1969   301.451/96/073   LC 71-82444

Du Bois, W. E. B. (William Edward Burghardt), 1868-1963.   • 3.6643
W. E. B. Du Bois speaks; speeches and addresses. Edited by Philip S. Foner.
New York, Pathfinder Press, 1970. 2 v. 23 cm. 'A Merit book.' 1. Afro-
Americans — Collected works. I. T.
E185.5.D84   301.451/96/073   LC 78-108719

Madhubuti, Haki R.   3.6644
From plan to planet: life studies; the need for Afrikan minds and institutions, by
Don L. Lee. [Detroit] Broadside Press [1973] 159 p. illus. 23 cm. 1. Afro-
Americans — Race identity — Collected works. 2. Afro-Americans —
Education — Collected works. 3. Afro-American arts — Collected works.
I. T.
E185.5.M27   910/.039/6   LC 72-94350

Ovington, Mary White, 1865-1951.   3.6645
The walls came tumbling down. [1st ed.] New York, Harcourt, Brace [1947] x,
307 p. 21 cm. 'A history of the National Association for the Advancement of
Colored People.' Dust jacket. 1. National Association for the Advancement of
Colored People. I. T.
E185.5.N276 O9   LC 47-30961

Ross, Barbara Joyce.   • 3.6646
J. E. Spingarn and the rise of the NAACP, 1911–1939 [by] B. Joyce Ross. —
[1st ed.]. — New York: Atheneum, 1972. xii, 305 p.; 21 cm. — (Atheneum
[paperbacks] Studies in American Negro life, NL 32) Originally presented as
the author's thesis, American University. 1. Spingarn, Joel Elias, 1875-1939.
2. National Association for the Advancement of Colored People — History.
I. T.
E185.5.N276 R67 1972   301.45/19/6073062 B   LC 78-139326

Parris, Guichard. **3.6647**
Blacks in the city; a history of the National Urban League, by Guichard Parris and Lester Brooks. — [1st ed.]. — Boston: Little, Brown, [1971] xi, 534 p.: ports.; 24 cm. 1. National Urban League. I. Brooks, Lester. joint author. II. T.
E185.5.N33 P3 301.451/96073/01732 *LC 76-161866*

Bontemps, Arna Wendell, 1902-1973. • **3.6648**
100 years of Negro freedom. New York, Dodd, Mead, 1961. 276 p. illus. 22 cm. 1. Afro-Americans — History — 1877-1964 2. Afro-Americans — Biography. 3. Afro-Americans — History — 1863-1877 I. T.
E185.6.B74 325.2670973 *LC 61-11716*

Crockett, Norman L. **3.6649**
The Black towns / Norman L. Crockett. — Lawrence: Regents Press of Kansas, c1979. xv, 244 p.: ill.; 23 cm. Includes index. 1. Afro-Americans — History — 1877-1964 2. Black nationalism — United States — History. 3. Cities and towns — United States — History. 4. Afro-Americans — Segregation I. T.
E185.6.C93 973/.04/96073 *LC 78-15099* *ISBN* 0700601856

Daedalus. • **3.6650**
The Negro American. Edited and with introductions by Talcott Parsons and Kenneth B. Clark, and with a foreword by Lyndon B. Johnson. Illustrated with a 32 page portfolio of photos. by Bruce Davidson, selected and introduced by Arthur D. Trottenberg. — Boston, Houghton Mifflin, 1966. xxix, 781 p. illus. 24 cm. — (The Daedalus library [v. 7]) Most of the essays, some in slightly different form, appeared originally in the Fall 1965 and Winter 1966 issues of Daedalus. Includes bibliographical references. 1. Negroes — Addresses, essays, lectures. 2. Negroes — Civil rights — Addresses, essays, lectures. I. Parsons, Talcott, 1902- ed. II. Clark, Kenneth Bancroft, 1914- ed. III. T.
E185.6.D24 301.45196073 *LC 66-17174*

Frazier, Edward Franklin, 1894-1962. • **3.6651**
Negro youth at the crossways, their personality development in the Middle States. With an introd. by St. Clair Drake. Prepared for the American Youth Commission, American Council on Education. New York, Schocken Books [1967] xxxv, 299 p. maps. 21 cm. (Schocken paperbacks) 1. Afro-Americans — Psychology 2. Youth — Washington, D.C. 3. Youth — Louisville, Ky. 4. Personality I. American Council on Education. American Youth Commission. II. T.
E185.6.F74 1967 155.2/34/0917496 *LC 67-26987*

Johnson, Charles Spurgeon, 1893-1956. **3.6652**
The negro in American civilization. New York, H. Holt and company [c1930] xiv, 538 p. diagrs. 23 cm. 1. Negroes. 2. United States — Race question. I. National interracial conference, Washington, 1928. II. T.
E185.6.J665 *LC 30-15942*

Katz, William Loren. • **3.6653**
Eyewitness; the Negro in American history. Rev. ed. New York, Pitman [1971] xx, 603 p. illus., ports. 26 cm. 1. Afro-Americans — History — Sources. I. T.
E185.6.K3 1971 917.3/06/96073 *LC 71-24129*

Kirby, John B., 1938-. **3.6654**
Black Americans in the Roosevelt era: liberalism and race / John B. Kirby. — 1st ed. — Knoxville: University of Tennessee Press, c1980. xvii, 254 p.; 23 cm. — (Twentieth century America series) Includes index. 1. Afro-Americans — History — 1877-1964 2. Afro-Americans — Civil rights 3. United States — Politics and government — 1933-1945 4. United States — Race relations I. T.
E185.6.K548 973/.04/96073 *LC 79-10315* *ISBN* 0870492799

Meier, August, 1923-. • **3.6655**
Negro thought in America, 1880–1915; racial ideologies in the age of Booker T. Washington. — Ann Arbor, University of Michigan Press [1963] x, 336 p. 24 cm. 'Bibliographical note': p. 280-282. Bibliographical references included in 'Notes' (p. 283-316) 1. Washington, Booker Taliaferro, 1859?-1915. 2. Negroes — Hist. I. T.
E185.6.M5 301.451 *LC 63-14008*

Myrdal, Gunnar, 1898-. **3.6656**
An American dilemma: the Negro problem and modern democracy. With the assistance of Richard Sterner and Arnold Rose. 5th ed. New York, Harper & Row [1962] 1483 p. illus. 24 cm. 1. Afro-Americans I. T.
E185.6.M95 1962 301.451 *LC 62-19706*

Williams, Henry, 1951-. **3.6657**
Black response to the American left: 1917–1929. [Princeton, N.J.] History Dept., Princeton University [c1973] iii, 111 p. 22 cm. (Princeton undergraduate studies in history, 1) 1. Afro-Americans — Politics and government 2. Afro-Americans — Intellectual life. 3. Communism — United States — 1917- 4. Socialism — United States — History. 5. Afro-Americans — Economic conditions I. T. II. Series.
E185.6.W73 322.4/4/0973 *LC 73-22590*

E185.61 Race Relations

E185.61 A–G

Baker, Ray Stannard, 1870-1946. • **3.6658**
Following the color line; American Negro citizenship in the progressive era. Introd. and notes to the Torchbook ed. by Dewey W. Grantham, Jr. New York, Harper & Row [1964] xviii, 311, 8 p. illus., ports. 21 cm. (American perspectives) (Harper torchbooks. The University library.) 'TB 3053.' Chapters 1-8, 10-14, with slight revisions, originally appeared in the American magazine, Apr. 1907-Sept. 1908. 1. Afro-Americans 2. United States — Race relations I. T.
E185.61.B16 1964 301.451 *LC 64-2962*

Baldwin, James, 1924-. • **3.6659**
The fire next time. — New York: Dial Press, 1963. 120 p.; 21 cm. 1. Negroes 2. Mohammedans in the United States. 3. United States — Race question. I. T.
E185.61.B195 *LC 63-11713*

Baldwin, James, 1924-. • **3.6660**
Nobody knows my name: more notes of a native son. — New York: Dial Press, 1961. 241 p.; 22 cm. 1. Negroes. 2. United States — Race question. I. T.
E185.61.B197 *LC 61-11596*

Baldwin, James, 1924-. • **3.6661**
Notes of a native son. — New York: Dial Press, 1963,[c1955] 158 p.; 21 cm. Essays. 1. Negroes. 2. United States — Race question. I. T.
E185.61.B2 1963 *LC 64-115*

Barker, Lucius Jefferson, 1928-. **3.6662**
Black Americans and the political system / Lucius J. Barker, Jesse J. McCorry, Jr. — Cambridge, Mass.: Winthrop Publishers, c1976. ix, 383 p.: ill.; 23 cm. 1. Afro-Americans — Politics and government 2. United States — Politics and government — 1945- I. McCorry, Jesse J., 1935- joint author. II. T.
E185.61.B23 323.1/19/6073 *LC 75-33043* *ISBN* 0876260806. *ISBN* 0876260792 pbk

Bunche, Ralph J. (Ralph Johnson), 1904-1971. **3.6663**
The political status of the Negro in the age of FDR / Ralph J. Bunche; edited and with an introd. by Dewey W. Grantham. — Chicago: University of Chicago Press, 1973. xxxiii, 682 p.: ill.; 24 cm. Includes index. 1. Afro-Americans — Civil rights 2. Afro-Americans — Politics and government 3. United States — Race relations 4. United States — History — 1933-1945 I. T.
E185.61.B93 1973 323.1/196073/075 *LC 72-96327* *ISBN* 0226080285

Burk, Robert Fredrick, 1955-. **3.6664**
The Eisenhower administration and Black civil rights / Robert Fredrick Burk. — Knoxville: University of Tennessee Press, c1984. xi, 287 p.: ill.; 24 cm. (Twentieth-century America series.) Includes index. 1. Eisenhower, Dwight D. (Dwight David), 1890-1969. 2. Afro-Americans — Civil rights 3. United States — Politics and government — 1953-1961 I. T. II. Series.
E185.61.B955 1984 353.0081/496073 19 *LC 84-3212* *ISBN* 0870494317

Draper, Theodore, 1912-. • **3.6665**
The rediscovery of Black nationalism. New York, Viking Press [1970] x, 211 p. 21 cm. 1. Afro-Americans — Politics and government 2. United States — Race relations I. T.
E185.61.D77 1970 323.1/19/6073 *LC 70-104163* *ISBN* 0670591149

Essien-Udom, Essien Udosen. • **3.6666**
Black nationalism; a search for an identity in America. [Chicago] University of Chicago Press [1962] xiii, 367 p. illus., ports. 25 cm. 1. Black Muslims 2. United States — Race relations I. T.
E185.61.E75 297.0973 *LC 62-12632*

Frazier, Edward Franklin, 1894-1962. • **3.6667**
Black bourgeoisie. Glencoe, Ill., Free Press [1957] 264 p. 22 cm. 1. Afro-Americans 2. Middle classes — United States. 3. United States — Race relations I. T.
E185.61.F833 325.260973 *LC 56-11964*

E185.61 H–N

Handlin, Oscar, 1915-. • **3.6668**
Fire–bell in the night; the crisis in civil rights. [1st ed.] Boston, Little, Brown [1964] 110 p. 20 cm. 1. Afro-Americans — Civil rights I. T.
E185.61.H23 323.40973 *LC 64-17728*

Henderson, Lenneal J. comp.   **3.6669**
Black political life in the United States; a fist as the pendulum. Edited by Lenneal J. Henderson, Jr. San Francisco, Chandler Pub. Co. [1972] xiv, 273 p. 23 cm. (Chandler publications in political science) 1. Afro-Americans — Politics and government I. T.
E185.61.H488   323.1/1/96073   *LC* 77-37515   *ISBN* 0810204622

Hernton, Calvin C.   • **3.6670**
White papers for white Americans [by] Calvin C. Hernton. [1st ed.] Garden City, N. Y., Doubleday, 1966. 155 p. 22 cm. 1. Afro-Americans — Psychology 2. United States — Race question. I. T.
E185.61.H53   301.45196073   *LC* 66-12244

King, Martin Luther, Jr., 1929-1968.   • **3.6671**
Why we can't wait. [1st ed.] New York, Harper & Row [1964] xii, 178 p. illus., ports. 22 cm. 1. Afro-Americans — Civil rights I. T.
E185.61.K54   301.451/96/073   *LC* 64-19514

Lewis, Anthony, 1927-.   • **3.6672**
Portrait of a decade; the second American revolution [by] Anthony Lewis and the New York times. New York, Random House [1964] 322 p. illus. 25 cm. 1. Afro-Americans — Civil rights I. New York times II. T. III. Title: The second American revolution.
E185.61.L52 1964   323.40973   *LC* 64-14832

Lincoln, C. Eric (Charles Eric), 1924-.   **3.6673**
The Black Muslims in America [by] C. Eric Lincoln. [Rev. ed.] [Boston] Beacon Press [1973] xxxi, 302 p. 21 cm. Originally presented as the author's thesis, Boston University. 1. Black Muslims I. T.
E185.61.L56 1973   301.45/29/77073   *LC* 72-6234   *ISBN* 0807005126 *ISBN* 0807005134

Lincoln, C. Eric (Charles Eric), 1924-.   **3.6674**
Race, religion, and the continuing American dilemma / C. Eric Lincoln. — New York: Hill and Wang, c1984. xxi, 282 p.; 22 cm. Includes index. 1. Race relations — Religious aspects 2. Racism — United States. 3. Afro-Americans — Religion 4. United States — Race relations 5. United States — Church history I. T.
E185.61.L572 1984   305.8/00973 19   *LC* 84-15833   *ISBN* 0809080168

X, Malcolm, 1925-1965.   • **3.6675**
By any means necessary; speeches, interviews, and a letter, by Malcolm X. Edited by George Breitman. New York, Pathfinder Press, 1970. viii, 184 p. ports. 22 cm. 'A Merit book.' 1. Afro-Americans — Civil rights — Addresses, essays, lectures. 2. United States — Race relations — Addresses, essays, lectures. I. Breitman, George. ed. II. T.
E185.61.L577   301.451/96/073 B   *LC* 74-108718

Logan, Rayford Whittingham, 1897-.   • **3.6676**
[Negro in American life and thought: the nadir, 1877-1901] The betrayal of the Negro, from Rutherford B. Hayes to Woodrow Wilson, by Rayford W. Logan. New enl. ed. New York, Collier Books [1965] 447 p. 19 cm. 'Originally published as The Negro in American life and thought: the nadir, 1877-1901.' 1. Afro-Americans — Civil rights 2. Afro-Americans — History — 1877-1964 I. T.
E185.61.L64 1965   323.4   *LC* 65-23835

Lomax, Louis E., 1922-1970.   **3.6677**
The Negro revolt. [Rev. ed.] New York, Harper & Row [1971] xxi, 377 p. 19 cm. (Perennial Library, P 184) 1. Afro-Americans — Civil rights 2. United States — Race relations I. T.
E185.61.L668 1971   301.45/19/6073   *LC* 73-159460   *ISBN* 0060801840

McPherson, James M.   **3.6678**
The abolitionist legacy: from Reconstruction to the NAACP / James M. McPherson. — Princeton, N.J.: Princeton University Press, c1975. xiii, 438 p.: ill.; 25 cm. Includes index. 1. Afro-Americans — Civil rights — History. 2. Abolitionists — United States. I. T.
E185.61.M18   322.4/4/0973   *LC* 75-22101   *ISBN* 0691046379

Marable, Manning, 1950-.   **3.6679**
Race, reform and rebellion: the second Reconstruction in black America, 1945–1982 / by Manning Marable. — Jackson: University Press of Mississippi, 1984. xii, 249 p.; 22 cm. Includes index. 1. Afro-Americans — Politics and government 2. Afro-Americans — Civil rights 3. United States — Race relations I. T.
E185.61.M32 1984   305.8/96073 19   *LC* 84-7436   *ISBN* 0878052259

Meier, August, 1923-.   **3.6680**
CORE; a study in the civil rights movement, 1942–1968 [by] August Meier and Elliott Rudwick. New York, Oxford University Press, 1973. xii, 563 p. 24 cm.

1. Congress of Racial Equality. 2. Afro-Americans — Civil rights 3. Civil rights movements — United States. I. Rudwick, Elliott M. joint author. II. T.
E185.61.M516   322.4/4/0973   *LC* 72-92294   *ISBN* 0195016270

Moore, Jesse Thomas, 1936-.   **3.6681**
A search for equality: the National Urban League, 1910–1961 / Jesse Thomas Moore, Jr. — University Park: Pennsylvania State University Press, 1981. xiii, 252 p.; 24 cm. Includes index. 1. National Urban League. 2. Afro-Americans — Civil rights 3. Afro-Americans — History — 1877-1964 I. T.
E185.61.M784   322.4/4/06073 19   *LC* 80-24302   *ISBN* 0271003022

Morris, Aldon D.   **3.6682**
The origins of the civil rights movement: Black communities organizing for change / Aldon D. Morris. — New York: Free Press; London: Collier Macmillan, c1984. xiv, 354 p., [8] p. of plates: ill.; 25 cm. Includes index. 1. Afro-Americans — Civil rights 2. Afro-Americans — Southern States — History — 20th century. 3. United States — Race relations 4. Southern States — Race relations. I. T.
E185.61.M845 1984   305.8/96073/075 19   *LC* 84-10272   *ISBN* 002922120X

Moses, Wilson Jeremiah, 1942-.   **3.6683**
The golden age of Black nationalism, 1850–1925 / by Wilson Jeremiah Moses. — Hamden, Conn.: Archon Books, 1978. 345 p.; 23 cm. Includes index. 1. Black nationalism — United States — History. 2. Pan-Africanism — History. 3. Afro-Americans — History I. T.
E185.61.M886   320.9/73   *LC* 77-14566   *ISBN* 0208016902

Newby, Idus A.   • **3.6684**
Challenge to the Court; social scientists and the defense of segregation, 1954–1966 [by] I. A. Newby. Rev. ed. with commentaries by A. James Gregor [and others] Baton Rouge, Louisiana State University Press [1969] xii, 381 p. 24 cm. 1. Afro-Americans — Segregation 2. United States — Race relations I. Gregor, A. James (Anthony James), 1929- II. T.
E185.61.N46 1969   301.451/96/073   *LC* 69-17623   *ISBN* 0807106283

Newby, Idus A.   • **3.6685**
Jim Crow's defense; anti–Negro thought in America, 1900–1930 [by] I. A. Newby. Baton Rouge, Louisiana State University Press, 1965. xv, 230 p. 24 cm. 1. Race discrimination — United States 2. Black race 3. United States — Race relations I. T.
E185.61.N475   305.8/96073 19   *LC* 65-20297

E185.61 P–Z

Raines, Howell.   **3.6686**
My soul is rested: movement days in the Deep South remembered / Howell Raines. — New York: Putnam, c1977. 472 p.; 24 cm. 1. Afro-Americans — Civil rights — Southern States. 2. Civil rights workers — Southern States — Interviews. 3. Afro-Americans — Southern States — Interviews. I. T.
E185.61.R235 1977   323.4/0975   *LC* 76-51292   *ISBN* 0399118535

Record, Wilson, 1916-.   • **3.6687**
The Negro and the Communist Party. Chapel Hill, University of North Carolina Press [1951] x, 340 p. 21 cm. Bibliographical references included in 'Notes' (p. 317-331) 1. Negroes. 2. Communism — United States — 1917- I. T.
E185.61.R29   325.260973   *LC* 51-10538

Roman, Charles Victor, 1864-.   **3.6688**
American civilization and the Negro; the Afro–American in relation to national progress, by C. V. Roman. Northbrook, Ill., Metro Books, 1972. xii, 434 p. illus. 23 cm. Reprint of the 1916 ed. 1. Afro-Americans 2. United States — Race relations I. T.
E185.61.R75 1972   301.45/19/6073   *LC* 75-187910   *ISBN* 0841101000

Rustin, Bayard, 1910-.   **3.6689**
Down the line; the collected writings of Bayard Rustin. Introd. by C. Vann Woodward. Chicago, Quadrangle Books, 1971. xviii, 355 p. 25 cm. 1. Afro-Americans — Addresses, essays, lectures. 2. Afro-Americans — Civil rights — Addresses, essays, lectures. I. T.
E185.61.R965 1971   323.4   *LC* 70-143569   *ISBN* 0812901851

Samuels, Wilfred D.   **3.6690**
Five Afro–Caribbean voices in American culture, 1917–1929 / by Wilfred D. Samuels; with an introduction by John H. Clarke. Boulder, Colo.: Belmont Books, c1977. iv, 87 p.; 22 cm. 1. Afro-Americans — History — 1877-1964 2. Afro-Americans — Biography. 3. Afro-Americans — Civil rights 4. United States — Race relations I. T.
E185.61.S3x   *ISBN* 0899270018

Sitkoff, Harvard. 3.6691
A new deal for Blacks: the emergence of civil rights as a national issue / Harvard Sitkoff. — New York: Oxford University Press, 1978-. v.; 22 cm. 1. Afro-Americans — Civil rights 2. Afro-Americans — History — 1877-1964 3. New Deal, 1933-1939 I. T.
E185.61.S596   323.42/3/0973   *LC* 78-2633   *ISBN* 0195024184

Smith, Lillian Eugenia, 1897-1966. • 3.6692
Killers of the dream. Rev. and enl. — New York, Norton [1961] 253 p. 22 cm. 1. Afro-Americans — Southern States 2. Southern States — Soc. condit. I. T.
E185.61.S64 1961   917.5   *LC* 61-8781

Stalvey, Lois Mark. • 3.6693
The education of a WASP. — New York: Morrow, 1970. x, 327 p.; 22 cm. 1. Discrimination — United States. 2. WASPs (Persons) 3. United States — Race relations I. T.
E185.61.S77   301.45/0973   *LC* 79-107363

Williamson, Joel. 3.6694
The crucible of race: black/white relations in the American South since emancipation / Joel Williamson. — New York: Oxford University Press, 1984. xviii, 561 p.; 24 cm. Includes index. 1. Afro-Americans — Southern States — History. 2. Afro-Americans — Civil rights — Southern States. 3. Southern States — Race relations. I. T.
E185.61.W738 1984   305.8/96073/075 19   *LC* 83-24985   *ISBN* 0195033825

Woodward, C. Vann (Comer Vann), 1908-. • 3.6695
American counterpoint; slavery and racism in the North–South dialogue, by C. Vann Woodward. [1st ed.] Boston, Little, Brown [1971] 301 p. 22 cm. 1. United States — Race relations 2. Southern States — Social life and customs I. T.
E185.61.W85   301.451/96/073   *LC* 76-143715

Woodward, C. Vann (Comer Vann), 1908-. 3.6696
The strange career of Jim Crow [by] C. Vann Woodward. 3d rev. ed. New York, Oxford University Press, 1974. xvii, 233 p. 22 cm. 1. Afro-Americans — Segregation I. T.
E185.61.W86 1974   301.45/19/6073   *LC* 73-90370

Young, Whitney M. • 3.6697
To be equal [by] Whitney M. Young, Jr. [1st ed.] New York, McGraw-Hill [1964] 254 p. 22 cm. 1. Afro-Americans — Civil rights 2. Afro-Americans — Social conditions — To 1964 I. T.
E185.61.Y73   323.41   *LC* 64-23179

Zinn, Howard, 1922-. • 3.6698
SNCC; the new abolitionists. — [2d ed.]. — Boston, Beacon Press [1965] 286 p. 21 cm. 1. Student Nonviolent Coordinating Committee. 2. Negroes — Civil rights. 3. Civil rights — Southern States. I. T.
E185.61.Z49 1965   323.406273   *LC* 66-789

E185.615 1964–

The Black Panther leaders speak: Huey P. Newton, Bobby • 3.6699
Seale, Eldridge Cleaver and company speak out through the
Black Panther Party's official newspaper / edited by G. Louis
Heath.
Metuchen, N.J.: Scarecrow Press, 1976. xii, 165 p.; 22 cm. Includes index. 1. Black Panther Party — Addresses, essays, lectures. I. Newton, Huey P. II. Seale, Bobby, 1936- III. Cleaver, Eldridge, 1935- IV. Heath, G. Louis. V. The Black panther.
E185.615.B546   322.4/2/0973   *LC* 76-3585   *ISBN* 081080915X

Boxill, Bernard R. 3.6700
Blacks and social justice / Bernard R. Boxill. — Totowa, N.J.: Rowman & Allanheld, 1984. vi, 251 p.; 25 cm. Includes index. 1. Afro-Americans — Civil rights 2. Afro-Americans — Race identity 3. Social justice 4. Busing for school integration — United States. 5. Affirmative action programs — United States. I. T.
E185.615.B63 1984   323.4/08996073 19   *LC* 83-15983   *ISBN* 0847667553

Carmichael, Stokely. 3.6701
Black power; the politics of liberation in America [by] Stokely Carmichael & Charles V. Hamilton. New York, Random House [1967] xii, 198 p. 22 cm. 1. Black power 2. Afro-Americans — Politics and government I. Hamilton, Charles V. joint author. II. T.
E185.615.C32   323.4/0973   *LC* 67-22656

Cox, Oliver C. (Oliver Cromwell), 1901-1974. 3.6702
Race relations: elements and social dynamics / by Oliver C. Cox. — Detroit: Wayne State University Press, 1976. xv, 337 p.; 24 cm. Includes index. 1. Afro-

Americans — Social conditions — 1964- 2. Afro-Americans — Economic conditions 3. United States — Race relations I. T.
E185.615.C693 1976   301.45/19/6073   *LC* 75-38572   *ISBN* 0814315399

Gilliam, Reginald Earl. 3.6703
Black political development: an advocacy analysis / Reginald Earl Gilliam, Jr.; foreword by Arthur O. Eve. [s. l.]: Dunellen Pub. Co.; Port Washington, N. Y.: distributed by Kennikat Press, 1975. xvii, 334 p.; 22 cm. (University Press of Cambridge, Mass. series in the social sciences.) Includes index. 1. Afro-Americans — Politics and government 2. Afro-Americans — Social conditions — 1964- I. T.
E185.615.G54 1975   320.9/73/092   *LC* 73-88999   *ISBN* 0804670897

Harding, Vincent. 3.6704
There is a river: the Black struggle for freedom in America / by Vincent Harding. — 1st ed. — New York: Harcourt Brace Jovanovich, c1981. xxvi, 416 p., [24] p. of plates: ill.; 25 cm. Includes index. 1. Afro-Americans — Civil rights 2. Afro-Americans — History 3. United States — Race relations I. T. II. Title: Black struggle for freedom in America.
E185.615.H28   323.1/196073 19   *LC* 81-47304   *ISBN* 015189342X

Jackson, George, 1941-1971. 3.6705
Blood in my eye. — [1st ed.]. — New York: Random House, [1972] xix, 197 p.; 22 cm. 1. Jackson, George, 1941-1971. 2. Black power — United States 3. Revolutions — United States. 4. Fascism — United States. 5. United States — Social conditions — 1960- I. T.
E185.615.J28 1972   322/.42   *LC* 79-37423

King, Martin Luther. • 3.6706
Where do we go from here: chaos or community? [1st ed.] New York, Harper & Row [1967] 209 p. 1. Negroes — History — 1964- 2. Negroes — Civil rights I. T. II. Title: Chaos or community
E185.615 K5   *LC* 67-17072

Kochman, Thomas. 3.6707
Black and white styles in conflict / Thomas Kochman. — Chicago: University of Chicago Press, 1981. vi, 177 p.; 23 cm. Includes index. 1. Afro-Americans — Communication 2. Intercultural communication 3. United States — Race relations I. T.
E185.615.K57   305.8/00973 19   *LC* 81-3405   *ISBN* 0226449548

Marx, Gary T. • 3.6708
Protest and prejudice; a study of belief in the black community, by Gary T. Marx. [1st ed.] New York, Harper & Row [1967] xxviii, 228, 27 p. 24 cm. ([Patterns of American prejudice series, 3]) 1. Afro-Americans — Attitudes 2. Afro-Americans — Race identity 3. Afro-Americans — Civil rights 4. Afro-Americans — Relations with Jews 5. United States — Race relations I. California. University. Survey Research Center. II. T. III. Series.
E185.615.M32   301.451/96/073   *LC* 67-22531

Muse, Benjamin. • 3.6709
The American Negro revolution; from nonviolence to black power, 1963–1967. Bloomington, Indiana University Press [1968] xii, 345 p. 22 cm. 1. Afro-Americans — Civil rights 2. Afro-Americans — History — 1964- I. T.
E185.615.M83   301.451/96/073   *LC* 68-27350

Black elected officials: a national roster 1985 / Joint Center for 3.6710
Political Studies.
1984-   . — New York: UNIPUB, c1985. 1 v.; 22 cm. 1. Afro-American politicians — Directories. 2. Afro-Americans — Politics and government — Directories. 3. Afro-American leadership — Directories. 4. Afro-American legislators — Directories. 5. Afro-American mayors — Directories. 6. Afro-American government executives — Directories. 7. Afro-American judges — Directories. 8. Afro-Americans — Directories. I. Joint Center for Political Studies (U.S.)
E185.615.N29   353.002/22/08996073 19   *LC* 85-645982

The New black politics: the search for political power / edited 3.6711
by Michael B. Preston, Lenneal J. Henderson, Jr., Paul
Puryear.
New York: Longman, c1982. xx, 263 p.: ill.; 24 cm. 1. Afro-Americans — Politics and government — Addresses, essays, lectures. I. Preston, Michael B. II. Henderson, Lenneal J. III. Puryear, Paul Lionel, 1930-
E185.615.N38 1982   323.1/196073 19   *LC* 81-13734   *ISBN* 0582283515

The New Black vote: politics and power in four American cities 3.6712
/ edited by Rod Bush; foreword by Manning Marable.
San Francisco: Synthesis Publications, 1984. 381 p.; 21 cm. 'Chicago, Detroit, Boston, Oakland.' 1. Afro-Americans — Politics and government 2. Afro-Americans — Suffrage I. Bush, Rod.
E185.615.N383 1984   324/.08996073 19   *LC* 84-8850   *ISBN* 0899350380

Newton, Huey P.   **3.6713**
To die for the people; the writings of Huey P. Newton. Introd. by Franz Schurmann. — [1st ed.]. — New York: Random House, [1972] xxii, 232 p.: illus.; 22 cm. 1. Black Panther Party. I. T.
E185.615.N4 1972   322.4/2   *LC* 72-529   *ISBN* 0394480856

Thomas, Tony, 1949- comp.   **3.6714**
Black liberation & socialism. [1st ed. New York, Pathfinder Press, 1974] 207 p. illus. 21 cm. 1. Afro-Americans — Politics and government — Addresses, essays, lectures. 2. Black nationalism — United States — Addresses, essays, lectures. 3. Socialism — United States — Addresses, essays, lectures. I. T.
E185.615.T53   323.1/19/6073   *LC* 74-75358   *ISBN* 087348360X
ISBN 0873483596

Willie, Charles Vert, 1927-.   **3.6715**
Oreo: a perspective on race and marginal men and women / by Charles V. Willie. — Wakefield, Mass.: Parameter Press, [1975] 95 p.; 23 cm. 1. Marginality, Social — United States. 2. Social change 3. United States — Race relations I. T.
E185.615.W52   301.6/36   *LC* 74-24480   *ISBN* 088203006X

E185.625 Psychological and Social Conditions

The Black male in America: perspectives on his status in   **3.6716**
contemporary society / [compiled by] Doris Y. Wilkinson,
Ronald L. Taylor.
Chicago: Nelson-Hall, c1977. viii, 375 p.; 24 cm. Includes indexes. 1. Afro-Americans — Psychology 2. Afro-Americans — Families I. Wilkinson, Doris Yvonne. II. Taylor, Ronald Lewis, 1942-
E185.625.B56   301.45/19/6073   *LC* 76-44310   *ISBN* 0882292277

Grier, William H.   **3.6717**
Black rage, by William H. Grier and Price M. Cobbs. Foreword by Fred R. Harris. New York, Basic Books [1968] viii, 213 p. 22 cm. 1. Afro-Americans — Psychology I. Cobbs, Price M., joint author. II. T.
E185.625.G68   155.8/4/96   *LC* 68-29925

Jenkins, Adelbert H.   **3.6718**
The psychology of the Afro-American: a humanistic approach / Adelbert H. Jenkins. — New York: Pergamon Press, c1982. xix, 213 p.; 24 cm. — (Pergamon general psychology series. 103) Includes indexes. 1. Afro-Americans — Psychology 2. Afro-Americans — Race identity I. T. II. Series.
E185.625.J47 1982   155.8/496073 19   *LC* 81-10734   *ISBN* 0080272061

Kochman, Thomas. comp.   **3.6719**
Rappin' and stylin' out; communication in urban Black America. Urbana, University of Illinois Press [1972] xvii, 424 p. illus. 24 cm. 1. Afro-Americans — Psychology 2. Afro-Americans — Language. 3. Interpersonal relations 4. Social exchange I. T.
E185.625.K6   301.14   *LC* 75-177896   *ISBN* 0252002377

Moses, Wilson Jeremiah, 1942-.   **3.6720**
Black messiahs and Uncle Toms: social and literary manipulations of a religious myth / Wilson Jeremiah Moses. — University Park: Pennsylvania State University Press, c1982. xii, 278 p.; 24 cm. Includes index. 1. Messianism, Afro-American 2. Afro-Americans — Race identity 3. Black nationalism — United States 4. Afro-Americans — Religion I. T.
E185.625.M67   305.8/96073 19   *LC* 81-9645   *ISBN* 0271002948

Pettigrew, Thomas F.   • **3.6721**
A profile of the Negro American [by] Thomas F. Pettigrew. Princeton, N.J., Van Nostrand [1964] xiv, 250 p. illus. 21 cm. 1. Afro-Americans — Psychology 2. Afro-Americans — Social conditions — To 1964 3. United States — Race relations I. T.
E185.625.P4   301.451   *LC* 64-22340

White, Joseph L., 1932-.   **3.6722**
The psychology of Blacks: an Afro-American perspective / Joseph L. White. — Englewood-Cliffs, N.J.: Prentice-Hall, c1984. ix, 194 p.; 21 cm. 1. Afro-Americans — Psychology I. T.
E185.625.W47 1984   305.8/96073 19   *LC* 83-11203   *ISBN* 0137351348

E185.63 Afro-Americans in the Armed Forces

Blacks in the United States Armed Forces: basic documents /   **3.6723**
edited by Morris J. MacGregor and Bernard C. Nalty.
Wilmington, Del.: Scholarly Resources, 1977. 13 v.; 29 cm. 1. United States — Armed Forces — Afro-Americans — History — Sources. I. MacGregor, Morris J., 1931- II. Nalty, Bernard C.
E185.63.B55   355   *LC* 76-5603   *ISBN* 0842020985

Dalfiume, Richard M.   • **3.6724**
Desegregation of the U.S. Armed Forces; fighting on two fronts, 1939–1953, by Richard M. Dalfiume. Columbia, University of Missouri Press [1969] viii, 252 p. 23 cm. 1. Afro-Americans — Segregation 2. United States — Armed Forces — Afro-Americans I. T.
E185.63.D3   355.02/2   *LC* 68-54897   *ISBN* 0826283187

Foner, Jack D.   **3.6725**
Blacks and the military in American history; a new perspective [by] Jack Foner. Foreword by and conclusion by James P. Shenton. — New York: Praeger, [1974] x, 278 p.; 22 cm. — (New Perspectives in American history) 1. United States — Armed Forces — Afro-Americans I. T.
E185.63.F64 1974   355/.00973   *LC* 70-151952   *ISBN* 0275501808

Gropman, Alan L., 1938-.   **3.6726**
The Air Force integrates, 1945–1964 / by Alan L. Gropman. — Washington: Office of Air Force History, 1978. x, 384 p.: ill.; 24 cm. Includes index. 1. United States. Air Force — Afro-Americans — History. 2. Aeronautics, Military — United States — History. 3. Sociology, Military — United States — History. I. T.
E185.63.G76   358.4/008996073 19   *LC* 77-15569

Mandelbaum, David Goodman, 1911-.   **3.6727**
Soldier groups and Negro soldiers. Berkeley, University of California Press, 1952. viii, 142 p. 23 cm. 1. Negroes as soldiers. 2. United States — Armed forces — Negroes. I. T.
E185.63.M35   *LC* 52-10600

E185.7 Religion

Barrett, Leonard E.   **3.6728**
Soul-force: African heritage in Afro-American religion, by Leonard E. Barrett. [1st ed.] Garden City, N.Y., Anchor Press, 1974. viii, 251 p. 22 cm. (C. Eric Lincoln series on Black religion) 1. Afro-Americans — Religion I. T. II. Series.
E185.7.B33 1974   299/.6   *LC* 73-83612   *ISBN* 0385074107

Cleage, Albert B.   • **3.6729**
The black Messiah [by] Albert B. Cleage, Jr. New York, Sheed and Ward [1968] 278 p. 22 cm. 1. Jesus Christ — Afro-American interpretations 2. Afro-Americans — Race identity I. T.
E185.7.C59   200   *LC* 68-9370

E185.8 Economic Conditions. Employment

Bailey, Ronald W., comp.   **3.6730**
Black business enterprise: historical and contemporary perspectives / edited by Ronald W. Bailey. — New York: Basic Books [1971] xxi, 361 p.: ill.; 25 cm. 1. Afro-Americans in business — Addresses, essays, lectures. 2. Afro-Americans — Economic conditions — Addresses, essays, lectures. 3. Black power — United States — Addresses, essays, lectures. I. T.
E185.8.B145   338/.00973   *LC* 76-147008   *ISBN* 0465006906

The Black worker: a documentary history from colonial times to   **3.6731**
the present / edited by Philip S. Foner and Ronald L. Lewis.
Philadelphia: Temple University Press, 1978-. v. <1- >. 1. Afro-Americans — Employment 2. Afro-Americans — Economic conditions 3. United States — Race relations I. Foner, Philip Sheldon, 1910- II. Lewis, Ronald L., 1940-
E185.8.B553   331.6/3/96073   *LC* 78-2875   *ISBN* 0877221367

Cayton, Horace Roscoe, 1903-.   • **3.6732**
Black workers and the new unions, by Horace R. Cayton and George S. Mitchell. College Park, Md., McGrath Pub. Co. [1969, c1939] xviii, 473 p. 24 cm. 1. Afro-Americans — Employment 2. Trade-unions — United States — Afro-American membership I. Mitchell, George Sinclair, 1902-1962. joint author. II. T.
E185.8.C39 1969   331.6/3/96073   *LC* 69-17085

Cross, Theodore L., 1924-.   • 3.6733
Black capitalism; strategy for business in the ghetto [by] Theodore L. Cross. [1st
ed.] New York, Atheneum, 1969. xii, 274 p. 25 cm. 1. Afro-Americans —
Economic conditions 2. Afro-Americans in business 3. Economic assistance,
Domestic — United States I. T.
E185.8.C9   658.42   *LC* 72-80268

Farley, Reynolds, 1938-.   3.6734
Blacks and whites: narrowing the gap? / Reynolds Farley. — Cambridge,
Mass.: Harvard University Press, 1984. xii, 235 p.: ill.; 25 cm. (Social trends in
the United States.) Includes index. 1. Afro-Americans — Economic conditions
2. Afro-Americans — Social conditions 3. Afro-Americans — Economic
conditions — Statistics. 4. Afro-Americans — Social conditions — Statistics.
I. T. II. Series.
E185.8.F35 1984   305.8/96073 19   *LC* 84-638   *ISBN* 0674076311

Fusfeld, Daniel Roland, 1922-.   3.6735
The political economy of the urban ghetto / Daniel R. Fusfeld, Timothy Bates.
— Carbondale: Southern Illinois University Press, c1984. xv, 286 p.: ill.; 24 cm.
(Political and social economy series.) Includes index. 1. Afro-Americans —
Economic conditions 2. Afro-Americans — Segregation 3. Afro-Americans
— Employment — History — 20th century. 4. Cities and towns — United
States — History — 20th century. 5. United States — Economic conditions
6. United States — Race relations I. Bates, Timothy Mason. II. T. III. Series.
E185.8.F87 1984   330.973/00899607301732 19   *LC* 83-20424
        ISBN 0809311577

Higgs, Robert.   3.6736
Competition and coercion: Blacks in the American economy, 1865–1914 /
Robert Higgs. — Cambridge; New York: Cambridge University Press, 1977. x,
208 p.: ill.; 24 cm. (Hoover Institution publications; P163) Includes index.
1. Afro-Americans — Economic conditions I. T.
E185.8.H6   331.6/3/96073   *LC* 76-9178   *ISBN* 0521211204

Lee, Roy F.   3.6737
The setting for Black business development: a study in sociology and political
economy, by Roy F. Lee. Ithaca, New York State School of Industrial and
Labor Relations, Cornell University, 1973 [c1972] xvii, 249 p. 23 cm. A revision
of the author's thesis, New York University. 1. Afro-Americans in business
2. Afro-Americans — Economic conditions I. T.
E185.8.L4 1973   338/.04   *LC* 72-619630   *ISBN* 0875460399

Marshall, F. Ray.   3.6738
The Negro and organized labor [by] Ray Marshall. New York, Wiley [1965] ix,
327 p. 24 cm. 1. Afro-Americans — Employment 2. Discrimination in
employment — United States 3. Trade-unions — United States — Afro-
American membership I. T.
E185.8.M25   331.63   *LC* 65-15761

Northrup, Herbert Roof, 1918-.   • 3.6739
Organized labor and the Negro [by] Herbert R. Northrup. Foreword by
Sumner H. Slichter. [1st ed.] New York, Harper; New York, Kraus Reprint
Co., 1971 [c1944] xviii, 312 p. 23 cm. 1. Afro-Americans — Employment
2. Trade-unions — Afro-American membership 3. Labor and
laboring classes — United States I. T.
E185.8.N65 1971   331.88/0973   *LC* 74-157520

Perlo, Victor.   3.6740
Economics of racism U.S.A.: roots of Black inequality / Victor Perlo. — 1st ed.
— New York: International Publishers, 1975. xiii, 280 p.: ill.; 21 cm. 1. Afro-
Americans — Economic conditions 2. Afro-Americans — Employment
3. United States — Race relations I. T.
E185.8.P418   331.6/3/96073   *LC* 75-9911   *ISBN* 0717804186

Pinkney, Alphonso.   3.6741
The myth of Black progress / Alphonso Pinkney. — Cambridge,
[Cambridgeshire]; New York: Cambridge University Press, 1984. x, 198 p.; 22
cm. Includes index. 1. Afro-Americans — Economic conditions 2. Afro-
Americans — Social conditions — 1975- 3. Afro-Americans — Civil rights
4. Discrimination in education — United States. I. T.
E185.8.P56 1984   305.8/96073 19   *LC* 84-1912   *ISBN* 0521259835

Valentine, Bettylou, 1937-.   3.6742
Hustling and other hard work: life styles in the ghetto / by Bettylou Valentine.
— New York: Free Press, c1978. viii, 183 p.; 22 cm. Includes index. 1. Afro-
Americans — Economic conditions 2. Afro-Americans — Social conditions —
1975- I. T.
E185.8.V25   330.9/73   *LC* 78-427   *ISBN* 0029330602

Wesley, Charles H. (Charles Harris), 1891-1987.   • 3.6743
Negro labor in the United States, 1850–1925; a study in American economic
history. New York, Russell & Russell [1967, c1927] xiii, 343 p. map. 20 cm.
1. Negroes — Employment. I. T.
E185.8.W4 1967   *LC* 67-16001

E185.82 Higher Education. The Professions. The Arts

Cruse, Harold.   • 3.6744
The crisis of the Negro intellectual. — New York: Morrow, 1967. 594 p.; 24 cm.
1. Negroes — Intellectual life. I. T.
E185.82.C74   *LC* 67-25316

Locke, Alain LeRoy, 1886-1954. ed.   3.6745
The new Negro: an interpretation. — New York: Atheneum, 1968. xviii, 446 p.:
ill., facsims., music, ports.; 25 cm. (American Negro, his history and literature.)
Reprint of the 1925 ed. 1. Afro-Americans 2. American literature — Afro-
American authors I. T. II. Series.
E185.82.L75 1968b   700   *LC* 68-29008

E185.86 Social Conditions. Women. Family Life

The Afro–American woman: struggles and images / edited by   3.6746
Sharon Harley and Rosalyn Terborg–Penn.
Port Washington, N.Y.: Kennikat Press, 1978. xiii, 137 p.; 22 cm. — (Series in
American studies) (National university publications) 1. Afro-American
women — Addresses, essays, lectures. I. Harley, Sharon. II. Terborg-Penn,
Rosalyn.
E185.86.A34   301.41/2/0973   *LC* 78-9821   *ISBN* 0804692092

All the women are White, all the Blacks are men, but some of   3.6747
us are brave: Black women's studies / edited by Gloria T. Hull,
Patricia Bell Scott, and Barbara Smith.
Old Westbury, N.Y.: Feminist Press, c1982. xxxiv, 401 p.: ill.; 24 cm. Half title:
But some of us are brave. 1. Afro-American women — Addresses, essays,
lectures. 2. Feminism — United States — Addresses, essays, lectures. 3. Afro-
American women — Bibliography — Addresses, essays, lectures. 4. United
States — Race relations — Addresses, essays, lectures. I. Hull, Gloria T.
II. Scott, Patricia Bell. III. Smith, Barbara. IV. Title: But some of us are
brave.
E185.86.A4 1982   305.4/8896073 19   *LC* 81-68918   *ISBN*
0912670924

Beginnings: the social and affective development of Black   3.6748
children / edited by Margaret Beale Spencer, Geraldine Kearse
Brookins, Walter Recharde Allen.
Hillsdale, N.J.: L. Erlbaum, c1985. xx, 375 p.: ill.; 24 cm. — (Child
psychology.) Includes indexes. 1. Afro-American children — Psychology.
2. Afro-Americans — Families 3. Afro-Americans — Race identity
I. Spencer, Margaret Beale. II. Brookins, Geraldine Kearse. III. Allen,
Walter Recharde. IV. Series.
E185.86.B377 1985   155.4/5796073 19   *LC* 84-24742   *ISBN*
0898595207

Bell, Michael J. (Michael Joseph), 1947-.   3.6749
The world from Brown's Lounge: an ethnography of black middle–class play /
Michael J. Bell. — Urbana: University of Illinois Press, c1983. xii, 191 p.; 24
cm. 1. Afro-Americans — Social life and customs 2. Afro-Americans —
Folklore I. T.
E185.86.B378 1983   306/.48/0880622 19   *LC* 82-4732   *ISBN*
0252009568

Billingsley, Andrew.   • 3.6750
Black families in white America [by] Andrew Billingsley, with the assistance of
Amy Tate Billingsley. Englewood Cliffs, N.J., Prentice-Hall [1968] v, 218 p.
illus., map. 21 cm. (A Spectrum book) 1. Afro-Americans — Social conditions
— 1964- 2. Family — United States I. T.
E185.86.B5   301.44/7/0973   *LC* 68-54856

Black marriage and family therapy / edited by Constance E.   3.6751
Obudho.
Westport, Conn.: Greenwood Press, 1983. xiv, 269 p.; 25 cm. — (Contributions
in Afro-American and African studies 0069-9624; no. 72) 1. Afro-American
families — Addresses, essays, lectures. 2. Family psychotherapy — United
States — Addresses, essays, lectures. 3. Marriage — United States —
Addresses, essays, lectures. I. Obudho, Constance E. II. Series.
E185.86.B5257 1983   306.8/08996073 19   *LC* 82-20967   *ISBN*
0313221197

Black men / edited by Lawrence E. Gary.   3.6752
Beverly Hills, Calif.: Sage Publications, c1981. 295 p.: ill.; 23 cm. — (Sage focus
editions; 31) 1. Afro-American men — Addresses, essays, lectures. I. Gary,
Lawrence E.
E185.86.B526   305.3/08996073 19   *LC* 81-9021   *ISBN*
080391654X

Bambara, Toni Cade. comp. • 3.6753
The Black woman; an anthology. — [New York]: New American Library, [1970] 256 p.; 18 cm. — (A Signet book) 1. Afro-American women — Collections. I. T.
E185.86.C28   301.41/2   *LC* 70-121388

Chevigny, Paul, 1935-. 3.6754
Cops and rebels: a study of provocation. [1st ed.] New York, Pantheon Books [1972] xvii, 332 p. front. 22 cm. 1. Black Panther Party. 2. Afro-Americans — Social conditions — 1964- 3. Police — New York (N.Y.) 4. Trials (Conspiracy) — New York (City) I. T.
E185.86.C44   301.45/1/9607307471   *LC* 72-570   *ISBN* 0394472187

Davis, Allison. • 3.6755
Children of bondage; the personality development of Negro youth in the urban South, by Allison Davis and John Dollard, prepared for the American youth commission. Washington, D. C., American council on education, 1940. xxviii, 299, [1] p., 1 l. diagrs. 23.5 cm. Illustration mounted on cover. 1. Afro-Americans — Social conditions 2. Personality 3. Social psychology I. Dollard, John, joint author. II. American Council on Education. American Youth Commission. III. T.
E185.86.D38   325.260975   *LC* 40-13685

Davis, Angela Yvonne, 1944-. 3.6756
Women, race, & class / Angela Y. Davis. — 1st ed. — New York: Random House, c1981. 271 p.; 22 cm. 1. Afro-Americans — History 2. Sexism — United States. 3. Racism — United States. 4. United States — Race relations 5. United States — Economic conditions — 1961- I. T.
E185.86.D383 1981   305.4/2 19   *LC* 81-40243   *ISBN* 0394510399

Drylongso: a self–portrait of Black America / [edited by] John 3.6757
Langston Gwaltney.
1st ed. — New York: Random House, c1980. xxx, 287 p.; 25 cm. 1. Afro-Americans — Social conditions — 1975- — Addresses, essays, lectures. 2. Afro-Americans — Civil rights — Addresses, essays, lectures. 3. United States — Race relations — Addresses, essays, lectures. I. Gwaltney, John Langston.
E185.86.D77   305.8/96073   *LC* 79-5558   *ISBN* 0394510178

Du Bois, W. E. B. (William Edward Burghardt), 1868-1963. 3.6758
W. E. B. Du Bois on sociology and the Black community / edited and with an introd. by Dan S. Green and Edwin D. Driver. — Chicago: University of Chicago Press, 1978. viii, 320 p.; 21 cm. — (The Heritage of sociology) Includes index. 1. Afro-Americans — Social conditions — To 1964 — Collected works. I. Green, Dan S. II. Driver, Edwin D. III. T.
E185.86.D845 1978   301.45/19/6073   *LC* 78-770   *ISBN* 0226167593

Engram, Eleanor. 3.6759
Science, myth, reality: the Black family in one–half century of research / Eleanor Engram. — Westport, Conn.: Greenwood Press, 1982. xviii, 216 p.; 22 cm. — (Contributions in Afro-American and African studies. 0069-9624; no. 64) Includes index. 1. Afro-Americans — Families I. T. II. Series.
E185.86.E53 1982   306.8/08996073 19   *LC* 81-1262   *ISBN* 0313228353

The Extended family in black societies / editors, Demitri B. 3.6760
Shimkin, Edith M. Shimkin and Dennis A. Frate.
The Hague: Mouton, 1978. xxi, 526 p.: ill.; 24 cm. (World anthropology.) Papers prepared for the 9th International Congress of Anthropological and Ethnological Sciences, Chicago, 1973. 1. Afro-Americans — Families — Congresses. 2. Afro-Americans — Families — Mississippi — Holmes Co. — Congresses. 3. Blacks — Families — Congresses. 4. Holmes County (Miss.) — Social conditions — Congresses. I. Shimkin, Demitri Boris, 1916- II. Shimkin, Edith M. III. Frate, Dennis A., 1948- IV. International Congress of Anthropological and Ethnological Sciences. 9th, Chicago, 1973. V. Series.
E185.86.E9   301.42   *LC* 79-321340   *ISBN* 9027975906

Frazier, Edward Franklin, 1894-1962. • 3.6761
The Negro family in the United States. Rev. and abridged ed. Foreword by Nathan Glazer. Chicago, University of Chicago Press [1966] xxii, 372 p. 21 cm. Revised and abridged edition first published in 1948. 1. Afro-Americans — Social conditions — To 1964 2. Afro-American families — United States I. T.
E185.86.F74 1966   301.45196073   *LC* 66-13868

Giddings, Paula. 3.6762
When and where I enter: the impact of Black women on race and sex in America / Paula Giddings. — 1st ed. — New York: W. Morrow, 1984. 408 p.; 25 cm. Includes index. 1. Afro-American women — Political activity — History. 2. Feminism — United States — History. 3. Afro-Americans — Civil rights 4. United States — Race relations I. T.
E185.86.G49 1984   305.4/8896073 19   *LC* 84-164770   *ISBN* 0688019439

Glasgow, Douglas G. 3.6763
The Black underclass: poverty, unemployment, and entrapment of ghetto youth / Douglas G. Glasgow. — 1st ed. — San Francisco: Jossey-Bass Publishers, 1980. xv, 206 p.; 24 cm. — (The Jossey-Bass social and behavioral science series) Includes index. 1. Afro-American youth — Employment. 2. Afro-Americans — Economic conditions I. T.
E185.86.G54   331.3/46396073 19   *LC* 79-28310   *ISBN* 0875893929

Gutman, Herbert George, 1928-. 3.6764
The Black family in slavery and freedom, 1750–1925 / Herbert Gutman. — 1st ed. — New York: Pantheon Books, c1976. 664 p.: ill. 1. Afro-Americans — Families — History. 2. Afro-Americans — History 3. Afro-Americans — Social conditions I. T.
E185.86.G77 1976   301.42/0973   *LC* 76-7550   *ISBN* 0394471164

Johnson, Daniel M. 3.6765
Black migration in America: a social demographic history / Daniel M. Johnson and Rex R. Campbell. — Durham, N.C.: Duke University Press, 1981. viii, 190 p.: ill.; 24 cm. — (Studies in social and economic demography. [4]) 1. Afro-Americans — Population. 2. Migration, Internal — United States. 3. United States — Population I. Campbell, Rex R. II. T. III. Series.
E185.86.J63   305.8/96073   *LC* 80-16916   *ISBN* 0822304422

Ladner, Joyce A. 3.6766
The death of white sociology, edited by Joyce A. Ladner. [1st ed.] New York, Random House [1973] xxxiii, 476 p. 22 cm. 1. Afro-Americans — Social conditions — Research — United States. 2. Sociology — United States — History. I. T. II. Title: White sociology.
E185.86.L33 1973   309.1/73/092   *LC* 72-10450   *ISBN* 0394482085

Ladner, Joyce A. • 3.6767
Tomorrow's tomorrow: the Black woman [by] Joyce A. Ladner. [1st ed.] Garden City, N.Y., Doubleday, 1971. xxvi, 304 p. 22 cm. A revision of the author's thesis, Washington University. 1. Afro-American women 2. Afro-Americans — Families I. T.
E185.86.L34 1971   301.451/96/073   *LC* 78-139038

Lerner, Gerda, 1920- comp. 3.6768
Black women in white America: a documentary history. — [1st ed.]. — New York: Pantheon Books, [1972] xxxvi, 630 p.; 25 cm. 1. Afro-American women — Addresses, essays, lectures. I. T.
E185.86.L4   301.41/2/0973   *LC* 77-173892   *ISBN* 0394475402

Lewis, Jerry M., 1924-. 3.6769
The long struggle: well–functioning working–class Black families / Jerry M. Lewis and John G. Looney. — New York: Brunner/Mazel, c1983. x, 193 p.; 24 cm. 1. Afro-Americans — Families 2. Afro-Americans — Psychology I. Looney, John G., 1941- II. T.
E185.86.L48 1983   306.8/08996073 19   *LC* 83-14361   *ISBN* 0876303424

McKay, Claude, 1890-1948. 3.6770
The Negroes in America / Claude McKay; edited by Alan L. McLeod; translated from the Russian by Robert J. Winter. — Port Washington, N.Y.: Kennikat Press, 1979. xviii, 97 p.; 22 cm. — (National university publications) 1. Afro-Americans — Social conditions — To 1964 2. Afro-Americans — Race identity I. McLeod, A. L. (Alan Lindsey), 1928- II. T.
E185.86.M313   973/.04/96073   *LC* 79-11652   *ISBN* 0804692416

Martin, Elmer P. 3.6771
The black extended family / Elmer P. Martin, Joanne Mitchell Martin.. — Chicago: University of Chicago Press, 1978. 129 p.: ill.; 23 cm. Includes index. 1. Afro-Americans — Families I. Martin, Joanne Mitchell. joint author. II. T.
E185.86.M37   301.42/13   *LC* 77-17058   *ISBN* 0226507963

Rainwater, Lee. • 3.6772
Behind ghetto walls; Black families in a federal slum. Chicago, Aldine Pub. Co. [1970] xi, 446 p. 25 cm. 1. Afro-Americans — Social conditions — 1964- 2. Afro-Americans — Social life and customs 3. Afro-Americans — Missouri — Saint Louis I. T.
E185.86.R29   301.45/23   *LC* 77-113083   *ISBN* 0202301133

Reid, Inez Smith. 3.6773
'Together' Black women. Prepared for the Black Women's Community Development Foundation. — [1st ed.]. — New York: Emerson Hall Publishers; [distributed by Independent Publishers' Group, 1972] xiii, 383 p.; 22 cm. 1. Afro-American women — Interviews. I. Black Women's Community Development Foundation. II. T.
E185.86.R39   301.15/43/30917392   *LC* 73-188561   *ISBN* 0878290036

Stack, Carol B. 3.6774
All our kin: strategies for survival in a Black community [by] Carol B. Stack. [1st ed.] New York, Harper & Row [1974] xxi, 175 p. 22 cm. 1. Afro-

Americans — Families — Case studies. 2. Poor — United States — Case Studies. I. T.
E185.86.S697   301.45/19/6073   *LC* 73-4126   *ISBN* 0060139749

Staples, Robert.   **3.6775**
Black masculinity: the Black male's role in American society / Robert Staples. — San Francisco: Black Scholar Press, c1982. 181 p.; 22 cm. 1. Afro-American men 2. Masculinity (Psychology) I. T.
E185.86.S715   *LC* 81-69452   *ISBN* 0933296061

Staples, Robert.   **3.6776**
The Black woman in America: sex, marriage, and the family. — Chicago: Nelson-Hall Publishers, [1973] xv, 269 p.; 23 cm. — (Professional-technical series) 1. Afro-American women I. T.
E185.86.S72   301.41/2   *LC* 72-95280   *ISBN* 0911012559

Staples, Robert.   **3.6777**
Introduction to Black sociology / Robert Staples. — New York: McGraw-Hill, c1976. xi, 338 p.; 20 cm. 1. Afro-Americans — Social conditions — 1964- 2. Sociology I. T.
E185.86.S73   301.45/19/6073   *LC* 75-11571   *ISBN* 0070608407

Thompson, Daniel C. (Daniel Calbert)   **3.6778**
Sociology of the Black experience [by] Daniel C. Thompson. Westport, Conn., Greenwood Press [1974] x, 261 p. 21 cm. (Contributions in sociology, no. 14) 1. Afro-Americans — Social conditions 2. Afro-Americans — Families 3. Afro-Americans — Civil rights I. T.
E185.86.T44   301.45/19/6073   *LC* 73-20974   *ISBN* 0837173361

Rainwater, Lee.   • **3.6779**
The Moynihan report and the politics of controversy; a Trans–action social science and public policy report [by] Lee Rainwater [and] William L. Yancey. Including the full text of The Negro family: the case for national action by Daniel Patrick Moynihan. Cambridge, Mass., M. I. T. Press [1967] xviii, 493 p. illus. 25 cm. 1. United States. Dept. of Labor. Office of Policy Planning and Research. The Negro family, the case for national action. 2. Afro-American families — United States I. Yancey, William L., joint author. II. T.
E185.86.U54 R3   301.451/96/073   *LC* 67-15238

Willie, Charles Vert, 1927- comp.   • **3.6780**
The family life of Black people. Edited by Charles V. Willie. Columbus, Ohio, Merrill [1970] x, 341 p. 23 cm. (Merrill sociology series) 1. Afro-Americans — Families I. T.
E185.86.W54   301.42   *LC* 79-127082   *ISBN* 0675092973

Zollar, Ann Creighton.   **3.6781**
A member of the family: strategies for Black family continuity / Ann Creighton Zollar. — Chicago: Nelson-Hall, c1985. 174 p.: ill.; 23 cm. Includes index. 1. Afro-Americans — Families 2. Afro-Americans — Social conditions — 1975- I. T.
E185.86.Z65 1985   305.8/96073 19   *LC* 84-6849   *ISBN* 0830410317

E185.89.A5 Anthropological Studies

Herskovits, Melville J. (Melville Jean), 1895-1963.   • **3.6782**
The American negro; a study in racial crossing. New York, A. A. Knopf, 1928. 92 p.; 20 cm. 1. Negroes. I. T.
E185.89.A5 H5   *LC* 28-4908

E185.89.H6 Housing

Clark, Henry, 1930-.   • **3.6783**
The church and residential desegregation; a case study of an open housing covenant campaign. New Haven, College & University Press [1965] 254 p. 21 cm. 1. Afro-Americans — Housing 2. Discrimination in housing — United States 3. Race relations — Religious aspects — Christianity — United States. I. T.
E185.89.H6 C55   *LC* 64-20663

Clark, Thomas A., 1944-.   **3.6784**
Blacks in suburbs, a national perspective / Thomas A. Clark; with a foreword by George Sternlieb. — New Brunswick, N.J.: Rutgers University, Center for Urban Policy Research, c1979. xiii, 127 p.; 23 cm. Includes index. 1. Afro-Americans — Housing 2. Afro-Americans — Economic conditions 3. Afro-Americans — Social conditions — 1964-1975 4. Afro-Americans — Social conditions — 1975- 5. Suburbs — United States 6. Migration, Internal — United States. I. T.
E185.89.H6 C56   330.9/73   *LC* 79-12171   *ISBN* 088285061X

Laurenti, Luigi.   • **3.6785**
Property values and race; studies in seven cities. Berkeley, University of California Press, 1960. xix, 256 p. maps, diagrs., tables. 25 cm. 1. Afro-Americans — Housing 2. Housing — United States. I. Commission on Race and Housing. II. T.
E185.89.H6 L3   *LC* 59-13464

President's Conference on Home Building and Home Ownership, Washington, D.C., 1931.   • **3.6786**
Negro housing; report of the Committee on Negro Housing, Nannie H. Burroughs, chairman. Prepared for the committee, by Charles S. Johnson. Edited by John M. Gries and James Ford. New York, Negro Universities Press [1969] xiv, 282 p. illus. 23 cm. Reprint of the 1932 ed. 1. Afro-Americans — Housing 2. Afro-Americans — Social conditions I. Burroughs, Nannie Helen, 1879- II. Johnson, Charles Spurgeon, 1893-1956. III. Gries, John Matthew, 1877- ed. IV. Ford, James, 1884-1944, ed. V. T.
E185.89.H6 P7 1931c   301.5/4/0973   *LC* 79-89053   *ISBN* 0837119219

Rose, Harold M.   **3.6787**
Black suburbanization: access to improved quality of life or maintenance of the status quo? / Harold M. Rose. — Cambridge, Mass.: Ballinger Pub. Co., c1976. xiv, 288 p.: ill.; 24 cm. 1. Afro-Americans — Housing 2. Suburbs — United States 3. Residential mobility — United States. 4. Quality of life — United States. I. T.
E185.89.H6 R58   301.36/2/0973   *LC* 76-49004   *ISBN* 0884104451

E185.9–185.93 Special Regions. States

Litwack, Leon F.   • **3.6788**
North of slavery: the Negro in the free States, 1790–1860 / Leon F. Litwack. — Chicago: University of Chicago Press, 1961. 318 p. 23 cm. 1. Afro-Americans — History — To 1863 2. Freedmen 3. Afro-Americans — Segregation I. T.
E185.9.L5   326.973   *LC* 61-10869   *ISBN* 0226485862

Woodson, Carter Godwin, 1875-1950.   • **3.6789**
A century of Negro migration. New York, Russell & Russell [1969] 221 p. maps. 20 cm. Reprint of the 1918 ed. 1. Afro-Americans — History 2. Migration, Internal — United States. I. T. II. Title: Negro migration.
E185.9.W89 1969   301.3/2   *LC* 69-16770

Carson, Clayborne, 1944-.   **3.6790**
In struggle: SNCC and the Black awakening of the 1960s / Clayborne Carson. — Cambridge, Mass.: Harvard University Press, 1981. viii, 359 p., [4] leaves of plates: ill.; 24 cm. Revision of the author's thesis, University of California, 1975. 1. Student Nonviolent Coordinating Committee (U.S.) 2. Afro-Americans — Civil rights — Southern States. 3. Southern States — Race relations. I. T.
E185.92.C37 1981   323.1/196073/075   *LC* 80-16540   *ISBN* 0674447255

Lawson, Steven F., 1945-.   **3.6791**
In pursuit of power: southern Blacks and electoral politics, 1965–1982 / Steven F. Lawson. — New York: Columbia University Press, 1985. xix, 391 p.; 24 cm. (Contemporary American history series.) Includes index. 1. Afro-Americans — Southern States — Politics and government. 2. Afro-Americans — Southern States — Suffrage. 3. Voting — Southern States — History — 20th century. 4. Elections — Southern States — History — 20th century. 5. Southern States — Politics and government — 1951- I. T. II. Series.
E185.92.L37 1985   324.975/08996073 19   *LC* 84-17036   *ISBN* 023104626X

Mandle, Jay R.   **3.6792**
The roots of Black poverty: the Southern plantation economy after the Civil War / Jay R. Mandle. — Durham, N.C.: Duke University Press, 1978. xvi, 144 p.: graphs; 23 cm. Includes index. 1. Afro-Americans — Southern States — Economic conditions. 2. Plantation life — Southern States — History. 3. Southern States — Economic conditions I. T.
E185.92.M36   330.9/75/05   *LC* 78-52026   *ISBN* 0822304082

Southern businessmen and desegregation / edited by Elizabeth Jacoway & David R. Colburn.   **3.6793**
Baton Rouge: Louisiana State University Press, c1982. x, 324 p.; 24 cm. Includes index. 1. Afro-Americans — Civil rights — Southern States — Addresses, essays, lectures. 2. Industry — Social aspects — Southern States — Addresses, essays, lectures. 3. Southern States — Race relations — Addresses, essays, lectures. I. Jacoway, Elizabeth, 1944- II. Colburn, David R.
E185.92.S683 1982   323.4/08996073075 19   *LC* 81-19362   *ISBN* 0807108936

Savage, William Sherman.   **3.6794**
Blacks in the West / W. Sherman Savage. — Westport, Conn.: Greenwood Press, 1976. xvi, 230 p.; 22 cm. (Contributions in Afro-American and African studies. no. 23) Includes index. 1. Afro-Americans — West (U.S.) — History.

2. Frontier and pioneer life — West (U.S.) 3. West (U.S.) — History — 1848-1950 I. T. II. Series.
E185.925.S38   978/.004/96073   *LC* 75-44657   *ISBN* 0837187753

Browning, Rufus P.   **3.6795**
Protest is not enough: the struggle of blacks and Hispanics for equality in urban politics / by Rufus P. Browning, Dale Rogers Marshall, David H. Tabb. — Berkeley: University of California Press, c1984. xvi, 317 p.; 22 cm. Includes index. 1. Afro-Americans — California — Politics and government. 2. Hispanic Americans — California — Politics and government. 3. Political participation — California. 4. Municipal government — California. 5. California — Politics and government — 1951- I. Marshall, Dale Rogers. II. Tabb, David H. III. T.
E185.93.C2 B76 1984   323.1/196073/0794 19   *LC* 83-15552   *ISBN* 0520050339

Lapp, Rudolph M.   **3.6796**
Blacks in Gold Rush California / Rudolph M. Lapp. New Haven: Yale University Press, 1977. xiv, 321 p., [6] leaves of plates: ill.; 22 cm. (Yale Western Americana series. 29) Includes index. 1. Afro-Americans — California — History. 2. Slavery — California 3. Gold mines and mining — California — History. 4. California — Gold discoveries I. T. II. Series.
E185.93.C2L3x   979.4/004/96073   *LC* 76-30534   *ISBN* 0300019882

Borchert, James, 1941-.   **3.6797**
Alley life in Washington: family, community, religion, and folklife in the city, 1850–1970 / James Borchert. — Urbana: University of Illinois Press, c1980. xiv, 326 p.: ill.; 24 cm. (Blacks in the New World.) 1. Afro-Americans — Washington, D.C. — Social conditions. 2. Afro-Americans — Families — Washington, D.C. 3. Rural-urban migration — Washington, D.C. 4. Washington (D.C.) — Social conditions. I. T. II. Series.
E185.93.D6 B63   305.8/96073/0753   *LC* 80-12375   *ISBN* 0252006895

Brown, Letitia Woods.   **3.6798**
Free Negroes in the District of Columbia, 1790–1846. New York, Oxford University Press, 1972. ix, 226 p. 22 cm. (The Urban life in America series) 1. Afro-Americans — Washington (D.C.) I. T.
E185.93.D6 B69   917.53/06/96073   *LC* 77-186497   *ISBN* 0195015525

Painter, Nell Irvin.   **3.6799**
Exodusters: Black migration to Kansas after Reconstruction / Nell Irvin Painter. — 1st ed. — New York: Knopf, 1977, c1976. viii, 288 p., [4] leaves of plates: ill.; 22 cm. Includes index. 1. Afro-Americans — Kansas — History. 2. Afro-Americans — History — 1877-1964 3. Kansas — History I. T.
E185.93.K16 P34 1977   978.1/004/96073   *LC* 76-26858   *ISBN* 0394402537

Sterkx, H. E.   **3.6800**
The free Negro in ante–bellum Louisiana [by] H. E. Sterkx. Rutherford [N.J.] Fairleigh Dickinson University Press [1972] 346 p. illus. 22 cm. 1. Afro-Americans — Louisiana 2. Freedmen — Louisiana I. T.
E185.93.L6 S7   301.45/19/60730763   *LC* 76-146165   *ISBN* 0838678378

Field, Phyllis F.   **3.6801**
The politics of race in New York: the struggle for black suffrage in the Civil War era / Phyllis F. Field. — Ithaca, N.Y.: Cornell University Press, 1982. 264 p.: ill.; 24 cm. Includes index. 1. Afro-Americans — New York (State) — Suffrage. 2. Voting — New York (State) — History — 19th century. 3. New York (State) — Politics and government — 1865-1950. 4. New York (State) — Race relations. 5. New York (State) — Politics and government — 1775-1865 I. T.
E185.93.N56 F54 1982   323.1/196073/0747 19   *LC* 81-70717   *ISBN* 0801414083

Anderson, Eric, 1949-.   **3.6802**
Race and politics in North Carolina, 1872–1901: the Black Second / Eric Anderson. — Baton Rouge: Louisiana State University Press, c1981. xiv, 372 p., [3] leaves of plates: ill.; 24 cm. Includes index. 1. Afro-Americans — North Carolina — Politics and government. 2. North Carolina — Politics and government — 1865-1950 3. North Carolina — Race relations. I. T.
E185.93.N6 A5   305.8/96073/0756   *LC* 80-16342   *ISBN* 0807106852

Wilson, Emily Herring.   **3.6803**
Hope and dignity: older Black women of the South / text by Emily Herring Wilson; photographs by Susan Mullally; foreword by Maya Angelou. — Philadelphia: Temple University Press, 1983. xxii, 200 p.: ill.; ports.; 24 cm. 1. Afro-American women — North Carolina. 2. Afro-American women — Southern States. 3. Afro-American aged — North Carolina. 4. Afro-American aged — Southern States. 5. Oral biography 6. North Carolina — Biography.

7. Southern States — Social conditions 8. Southern States — Biography. 9. North Carolina — Social conditions. I. Mullally, Susan. II. T.
E185.93.N6 W54 1983   305.4/8896073/075 19   *LC* 82-19437   *ISBN* 0877222266

Gerber, David A., 1944-.   **3.6804**
Black Ohio and the color line, 1860–1915 / David A. Gerber. — Urbana: University of Illinois Press, c1976. xii, 500 p.; 24 cm. (Blacks in the New World.) 1. Afro-Americans — Ohio — History. 2. Ohio — Race relations. I. T. II. Series.
E185.93.O2 G47   977.1/004/96073   *LC* 76-27285   *ISBN* 0252005341

Holt, Thomas, 1942-.   **3.6805**
Black over white: Negro political leadership in South Carolina during Reconstruction / Thomas Holt. — Urbana: University of Illinois Press, c1977. 269 p.: graphs; 24 cm. — (Blacks in the New World.) Revised version of the author's thesis, Yale University. Includes index. 1. Republican Party. South Carolina. 2. Afro-American legislators — South Carolina. 3. Reconstruction — South Carolina. 4. South Carolina — Politics and government — 1865-1950 I. T. II. Series.
E185.93.S7 H64   975.7/004/96073   *LC* 77-7513   *ISBN* 0252005556

Williamson, Joel.   • **3.6806**
After slavery; the Negro in South Carolina during Reconstruction, 1861–1877. Chapel Hill, University of North Carolina Press [1965] ix, 442 p. 24 cm. 1. Afro-Americans — South Carolina 2. Reconstruction — South Carolina. I. T.
E185.93.S7 W73   301.451   *LC* 65-13671

Lamon, Lester C., 1942-.   **3.6807**
Black Tennesseans, 1900–1930 / Lester C. Lamon. — Knoxville: University of Tennessee Press, c1977. xi, 320 p.: ill.; 24 cm. — (Twentieth-century America series) Includes index. 1. Afro-Americans — Tennessee — History. 2. Afro-Americans — Social conditions — To 1964 3. Tennessee — Race relations. I. T.
E185.93.T3 L35   301.45/19/60730768   *LC* 76-49583   *ISBN* 0870492071

Hunt, Annie Mae, 1909-.   **3.6808**
I am Annie Mae: an extraordinary woman in her own words: the personal story of a Black Texas woman / collected and edited by Ruthe Winegarten; assistant editor, Frieda Werden. — Austin, Tex.: Rosegarden Press, c1983. xv, 151 p.: ill.; 23 cm. 1. Hunt, Annie Mae, 1909- 2. Afro-American women — Texas. 3. Afro-Americans — Texas — Biography. 4. Texas — Biography. I. Winegarten, Ruthe. II. Werden, Frieda. III. T.
E185.93.T4 H864 1983   976.4/00496073 B 19   *LC* 83-4473   *ISBN* 0961034009

E185.96 Collective Biography

Black leaders of the twentieth century / edited by John Hope   **3.6809**
Franklin and August Meier.
Urbana: University of Illinois Press, c1982. xi, 372 p.: ports.; 24 cm. — (Blacks in the New World.) 1. Afro-Americans — Biography. I. Franklin, John Hope, 1915- II. Meier, August, 1923- III. Series.
E185.96.B536 1982   920/.009296073 B 19   *LC* 81-11454   *ISBN* 0252008707

Boulware, Marcus H.   • **3.6810**
The oratory of Negro leaders, 1900–1968 [by] Marcus H. Boulware. Westport, Conn., Negro Universities Press [1969] xxii, 312 p. 22 cm. 1. Afro-American orators 2. Afro-Americans — History — 1877-1964 I. T.
E185.96.B66   808.5/0922   *LC* 72-90794   *ISBN* 0837118492

Brown, William Wells, 1815-1884.   **3.6811**
The black man; his antecedents, his genius, and his achievements. 4th ed. Miami, Fla., Mnemosyne Pub. Inc., 1969. 312 p. 23 cm. Reprint of the 1865 ed. 'Memoir of the author': p. 11-30. 1. Afro-Americans — Biography. I. T.
E185.96.B863 1969   970/.00974/96   *LC* 76-79018

Dictionary of American Negro biography / edited by Rayford   **3.6812**
W. Logan and Michael R. Winston.
1st ed. — New York: Norton, c1982. xxi, 680 p.; 26 cm. 1. Afro-Americans — Biography. I. Logan, Rayford Whittingham, 1897- II. Winston, Michael R.
E185.96.D53 1982   920/.009296073 B 19   *LC* 81-9629   *ISBN* 0393015130

Kaplan, Sidney, 1913-.   **3.6813**
The Black presence in the era of the American Revolution, 1770–1800. [Greenwich, Conn.] New York Graphic Society, 1973. xii, 241 p. illus., facsims., ports. 29 cm. Illustrations selected from the exhibition The Black presence in the era of the American Revolution, 1770-1800, held at the National

Portrait Gallery, July 1973. 1. Afro-Americans — Biography. 2. United States — History — Revolution, 1775-1783 — Afro-Americans I. T.
E185.96.K36 1973   973.3/092/2 B   *LC* 73-79335   *ISBN* 0821205412 *ISBN* 0821205415

Sterling, Dorothy, 1913-.   **3.6814**
Black foremothers: three lives / Dorothy Sterling; introd. by Margaret Walker; ill. by Judith Eloise Hooper. — Old Westbury, N.Y.: Feminist Press, c1979. xxiii, 167 p.: ill.; 23 cm. — (Women's lives, women's work.) Includes index. 1. Craft, Ellen. 2. Wells-Barnett, Ida B., 1862-1931. 3. Terrell, Mary Church, 1863-1954. 4. Afro-American women — Biography. I. T. II. Series.
E185.96.S75   973/.0992   *LC* 78-8094   *ISBN* 0070204330

Who's who in colored America.   • **3.6815**
Vol. 1 (1927)-   . — New York: Who's Who in Colored America Corp., [c1927-. v.: ill.; 22-27 cm. Publisher varies: 6th ed., 1941/44, by Thomas Yenser; 7th ed., 1950, by Christian E. Burckel & Associates. 'A biographical dictionary of notable living persons of Negro descent in America' (varies). 1. Afro-Americans — Biography — Periodicals.
E185.96.W54   *LC* sn 85-62500

E185.97 Individual Biography
(see also: E443-449)

Wells-Barnett, Ida B., 1862-1931.   **3.6816**
Crusade for justice; the autobiography of Ida B. Wells. Edited by Alfreda M. Duster. Chicago, University of Chicago Press [1970] xxxii, 434 p. ports. 23 cm. (Negro American biographies and autobiographies.) 1. Wells-Barnett, Ida B., 1862-1931. I. T.
E185.97.B26 A3 1970   323.4/0924 B   *LC* 73-108837   *ISBN* 0226893421

Williams, Roger M., 1934-.   **3.6817**
The Bonds; an American family [by] Roger M. Williams. — [1st ed.]. — New York: Atheneum, 1971. xvi, 301 p.; 25 cm. 1. Bond family 2. Bond, Julian, 1940- I. T.
E185.97.B75 W5 1971   917.3/03/80922 B   *LC* 74-165208

Brown, Claude, 1937-.   • **3.6818**
Manchild in the promised land. — New York: Macmillan, [1965] 415 p.; 22 cm. Autobiographical. 1. Harlem (New York, N.Y.) — Social conditions. I. T.
E185.97.B86 A3   309.17471   *LC* 65-16938

Brown, H. Rap, 1943-.   • **3.6819**
Die, nigger, die! By H. Rap Brown. — New York: Dial Press, 1969. 145 p.: illus.; 22 cm. — 1. Brown, H. Rap, 1943- I. T.
E185.97.B87 A3   323.2/0924 B   *LC* 77-76969

Harris, Sheldon H.   **3.6820**
Paul Cuffe: Black America and the African return / [by] Sheldon H. Harris. — New York: Simon and Schuster [1972] 288 p.: port.; 22 cm. 1. Cuffe, Paul, 1759-1817. I. T.
E185.97.C96 H36   973.4/092/4 B 19   *LC* 70-189039   *ISBN* 0671209795 *ISBN* 0671209809

Davis, Angela Yvonne, 1944-.   **3.6821**
Angela Davis—an autobiography [by] Angela Davis. — [1st ed.]. — New York: Random House, [1974] x, 400 p.; 22 cm. 'A Bernard Geis Associates book.' 1. Davis, Angela Yvonne, 1944- I. T.
E185.97.D23 A32   322.4/2/0924 B   *LC* 73-20580   *ISBN* 0394489780

Griffith, Cyril E.   **3.6822**
The African dream: Martin R. Delany and the emergence of pan–African thought / Cyril E. Griffith. University Park: Pennsylvania State University Press, c1975. xiv, 153 p.: ill.; 24 cm. Includes index. 1. Delany, Martin Robison, 1812-1885. 2. Afro-Americans — Colonization — Africa 3. Afro-Americans — Biography. I. T.
E185.97.D4 G74   973.7/092/4 B   *LC* 74-20559   *ISBN* 0271011815

Du Bois, W. E. B. (William Edward Burghardt), 1868-1963.   • **3.6823**
Dusk of dawn; an essay toward an autobiography of a race concept. New York, Schocken Books [1968] viii, 334 p. 21 cm. Reprint of the 1940 ed. 1. Du Bois, W. E. B. (William Edward Burghardt), 1868-1963. 2. Afro-Americans — Social conditions 3. Afro-Americans — Biography. 4. United States — Race relations I. T.
E185.97.D73 1968   305.8/96073 19   *LC* 65-14825

Du Bois, W. E. B. (William Edward Burghardt), 1868-1963.   **3.6824**
[Selections. 1982] Writings by W.E.B. Du Bois in non–periodical literature edited by others / compiled and edited by Herbert Aptheker. — Millwood, N.Y.: Kraus-Thomson, c1982. x, 302 p.; 24 cm. — (The complete published works of W.E.B. Du Bois) 1. Afro-Americans — Addresses, essays, lectures.

2. United States — Race relations — Addresses, essays, lectures. I. Aptheker, Herbert, 1915- II. T.
E185.97.D73 A2 1982   973/.0496073 19   *LC* 81-18607   *ISBN* 0527253448

Du Bois, W. E. B. (William Edward Burghardt), 1868-1963.   **3.6825**
A W. E. B. Du Bois reader. Edited by Andrew G. Paschal. Introd. by Arna Bontemps. New York, Macmillan [1971] xxix, 376 p. 21 cm. 1. Afro-Americans — Addresses, essays, lectures. 2. Africa — Addresses, essays, lectures. I. T.
E185.97.D73 A25 1971   370/.924 B   *LC* 70-150672

Du Bois, W. E. B. (William Edward Burghardt), 1868-1963.   **3.6826**
[Selections. 1982] Writings by W.E.B. Du Bois in periodicals edited by others / compiled and edited by Herbert Aptheker. — Millwood, N.Y.: Kraus-Thomson Organization, c1982. 4 v.; 25 cm. — (The Complete published works of W.E.B. Du Bois) On spine: Writings in periodical literature. 1. Afro-Americans — Addresses, essays, lectures. 2. United States — Race relations — Addresses, essays, lectures. I. Aptheker, Herbert, 1915- II. T. III. Title: Writings by WEB Du Bois in periodicals edited by others. IV. Title: Writings in periodical literature.
E185.97.D73 A25 1982   973/.0496073 19   *LC* 81-17186   *ISBN* 052725343X

Du Bois, W. E. B. (William Edward Burghardt), 1868-1963.   **3.6827**
Against racism: unpublished essays, papers, addresses, 1887–1961 / by W.E.B. Du Bois; edited by Herbert Aptheker. — Amherst: University of Massachusetts Press, 1985. xx, 325 p.: ports.; 25 cm. 1. Racism — United States — Addresses, essays, lectures. 2. Afro-Americans — Addresses, essays, lectures. 3. United States — Race relations — Addresses, essays, lectures. I. Aptheker, Herbert, 1915- II. T.
E185.97.D73 A25 1985   305.8/00973 19   *LC* 84-16173   *ISBN* 0870231340

Du Bois, W. E. B. (William Edward Burghardt), 1868-1963.   • **3.6828**
The autobiography of W. E. B. DuBois; a soliloquy on viewing my life from the last decade of its first century. [1st ed. New York] International Publishers [1968] 448 p. ports. 22 cm. 1. Du Bois, W. E. B. (William Edward Burghardt), 1868-1963. I. T.
E185.97.D73 A3   370/.924 B   *LC* 68-14103

Du Bois, W. E. B. (William Edward Burghardt), 1868-1963.   **3.6829**
The correspondence of W. E. B. Du Bois. Edited by Herbert Aptheker. [Amherst] University of Massachusetts Press, 1973-78. 3 v. illus. 25 cm. 1. Du Bois, W. E. B. (William Edward Burghardt), 1868-1963. 2. Afro-Americans — Correspondence. 3. Intellectuals — United States — Correspondence. I. Aptheker, Herbert, 1915- ed. II. T.
E185.97.D73 A4 1973   301.24/2/0924 B   *LC* 72-90496   *ISBN* 0870231324

Moore, Jack B.   **3.6830**
W.E.B. Du Bois / by Jack B. Moore. — Boston: Twayne Publishers, 1981. 185 p.: port.; 21 cm. — (Twayne's United States authors series. TUSAS 399) Includes index. 1. Du Bois, W. E. B. (William Edward Burghardt), 1868-1963. 2. Afro-Americans — Biography. I. T. II. Series.
E185.97.D73 M66 1981   303.4/84/0924 19   *LC* 81-2425   *ISBN* 0805773290

Edwards, Harry, 1942-.   **3.6831**
The struggle that must be: an autobiography / Harry Edwards. — New York: Macmillan, c1980. xiii, 350 p.; 24 cm. 1. Edwards, Harry, 1942- 2. Sports — Social aspects — United States. 3. Afro-Americans — Biography. I. T.
E185.97.E34 A37   973.92/092/4 B 19   *LC* 80-21034   *ISBN* 0025350404

Farmer, James, 1920-.   **3.6832**
Lay bare the heart: an autobiography of the civil rights movement / James Farmer. — New York: Arbor House, c1985. 370 p.; 24 cm. Includes index. 1. Farmer, James, 1920- 2. Afro-Americans — Biography. 3. Civil rights workers — United States — Biography. 4. Afro-Americans — Civil rights I. T.
E185.97.F37 A35 1985   323.4/092/4 B 19   *LC* 84-24297   *ISBN* 0877956243

Forman, James, 1928-.   **3.6833**
The making of Black revolutionaries; a personal account. New York, Macmillan [1972] xv, 568 p. 24 cm. 1. Forman, James, 1928- 2. Student Nonviolent Coordinating Committee (U.S.) 3. Afro-Americans — Civil rights I. T.
E185.97.F715 A3   322.4/2/0973   *LC* 72-158163

Clarke, John Henrik, 1915- comp.   **3.6834**
Marcus Garvey and the vision of Africa. Edited, with an introd. and commentaries by John Henrik Clarke, with the assistance of Amy Jaques [i.e.

Jacques] Garvey. — New York: Random House, [1974] xxxii, 496 p.; 19 cm.
1. Garvey, Marcus, 1887-1940. I. T.
E185.97.G3 C55 1974   301.45/19/6024 B   *LC* 73-4732   *ISBN*
0394718887

Cronon, Edmund David.   • 3.6835
Black Moses; the story of Marcus Garvey and the Universal Negro
Improvement Association. Madison, University of Wisconsin Press, 1955. xvii,
278 p. illus. 23 cm. Includes index. 1. Garvey, Marcus, 1887-1940.
2. Universal Negro Improvement Association. I. T.
E185.97.G3 C7   920.932526   *LC* 54-6931

The Marcus Garvey and Universal Negro Improvement   3.6836
Association papers / Robert A. Hill, editor.
Berkeley: University of California Press, c1983- < c1985 >. v. < 1-4 >: ill.; 26
cm. Vols. 3-4 Robert A. Hill, editor, Emory J. Tolbert, senior editor, Deborah
Forczek, assistant editor. 1. Garvey, Marcus, 1887-1940. 2. Universal Negro
Improvement Association — History — Sources. 3. Black power — United
States — History — Sources. 4. Afro-Americans — Race identity — History
— Sources. 5. Afro-Americans — Civil rights — History — Sources. 6. Afro-
Americans — Correspondence. I. Hill, Robert A., 1943- II. Tolbert, Emory J.,
1946- III. Forczek, Deborah. IV. Garvey, Marcus, 1887-1940. V. Universal
Negro Improvement Association.
E185.97.G3 M36 1983   305.8/96073 19   *LC* 82-13379   *ISBN*
0520044568

Haley, Alex.   3.6837
Roots / Alex Haley. — 1st ed. — Garden City, N.Y.: Doubleday, 1976. viii,
688 p.; 24 cm. 'A condensed version of a portion of this work first appeared in
Reader's digest.' 1. Haley, Alex. 2. Haley family 3. Kinte family 4. Afro-
Americans — Biography. I. T.
E185.97.H24 A33   929/.2/0973   *LC* 72-76164   *ISBN* 0385037872

Johnson, James Weldon, 1871-1938.   • 3.6838
Along this way: the autobiography of James Weldon Johnson. — New York:
Da Capo Press, 1973,[c1933] 418 p.: ill.; 23 cm. I. T.
E185.97.J692 A3 1973   *LC* 72-8404

Garrow, David J., 1953-.   3.6839
The FBI and Martin Luther King, Jr.: from 'Solo' to Memphis / David J.
Garrow. — 1st ed. — New York: W.W. Norton, c1981. 320 p.; 22 cm. 1. King,
Martin Luther, Jr., 1929-1968. 2. Hoover, J. Edgar (John Edgar), 1895-1972.
3. United States. Federal Bureau of Investigation. I. T. II. Title: F.B.I. and
Martin Luther King, Jr.
E185.97.K5 G37 1981   323.44/82/0924 19   *LC* 82-106389   *ISBN*
0393015092

Lewis, David L.   • 3.6840
King; a critical biography [by] David L. Lewis. New York, Praeger [1970] xii,
460 p. illus., ports. 22 cm. 2d ed. published in 1978 under title: King: a
biography of Martin Luther King, Jr. 1. King, Martin Luther, Jr., 1929-1968.
2. Afro-Americans — Biography. 3. Baptists — Clergy — Biography
4. Clergy — United States — Biography. I. T.
E185.97.K5 L45 1970   323.4/0924 B   *LC* 79-95678

Oates, Stephen B.   3.6841
Let the trumpet sound: the life of Martin Luther King, Jr. / Stephen B. Oates.
— 1st ed. — New York: Harper & Row, c1982. xiii, 560 p., [8] p. of plates: ill.;
24 cm. 1. King, Martin Luther, Jr., 1929-1968. 2. Afro-Americans — Civil
rights 3. Afro-Americans — Biography. 4. Baptists — United States — Clergy
— Biography. I. T.
E185.97.K5 O18 1982   323.4/092/4 B 19   *LC* 81-48046   *ISBN*
0060149930

Walton, Hanes, 1941-.   3.6842
The political philosophy of Martin Luther King, Jr. / introd. by Samuel DuBois
Cook. — Westport, Conn.: Greenwood Pub. Corp., [1971] xxxviii, 137 p.; 22
cm. — (Contributions in Afro-American and African studies. no. 10) 'A Negro
Universities Press publication.' A revision of the author's thesis, Howard
University, 1967. 1. King, Martin Luther, Jr., 1929-1968. I. T. II. Series.
E185.97.K5 W27   320/.01/0924   *LC* 76-111260   *ISBN*
0837146615

Tucker, David M., 1937-.   3.6843
Lieutenant Lee of Beale Street [by] David M. Tucker. Nashville, Vanderbilt
University Press, 1971. xi, 217 p. port. 21 cm. 1. Lee, George Washington,
1894- 2. Afro-Americans — Politics and government I. T.
E185.97.L43 T8   323.4/0924 B   *LC* 76-157743   *ISBN* 0826511724

X, Malcolm, 1925-1965.   • 3.6844
The autobiography of Malcolm X. With the assistance of Alex Haley. Introd. by
M. S. Handler. Epilogue by Alex Haley. — New York, Grove Press [1966]
c1965. xvi, 460 p. illus., ports. 24 cm. 1. Black Muslims I. Haley, Alex. II. T.
E185.97.L5A3   301.451960730924   *LC* 65-27331

Goldman, Peter Louis, 1933-.   3.6845
The death and life of Malcolm X [by] Peter Goldman. [1st ed.] New York:
Harper & Row [1972] xx, 438 p. illus. 22 cm. 1. X, Malcolm, 1925-1965.
2. Black Muslims — Biography. I. T.
E185.97.L5 G64 1973   320.5/4/0924 B   *LC* 70-138726   *ISBN*
0060115823

Moody, Anne, 1940-.   3.6846
Coming of age in Mississippi. — New York: Dial Press, 1968. 348 p.; 22 cm.
Autobiographical. 1. Moody, Anne, 1940- I. T.
E185.97.M65 A3   917.62/25/0360924 B   *LC* 68-55153

Murray, Pauli, 1910-.   3.6847
Song in a weary throat: an American pilgrimage / Pauli Murray. — 1st ed. —
New York: Harper & Row, c1987. xii, 451 p., [8] p. of plates: ill.; 24 cm.
Includes index. 1. Murray, Pauli, 1910- 2. Afro-Americans — Biography.
3. Feminists — United States — Biography. I. T.
E185.97.M95 A3 1987   973/.0496073024 B 19   *LC* 86-45674
    ISBN 0060157046

Anderson, Jervis.   • 3.6848
A. Philip Randolph; a biographical portrait. [1st ed.] New York, Harcourt
Brace Jovanovich [1973] xiv, 398 p. illus. 25 cm. 1. Randolph, A. Philip (Asa
Philip), 1889- I. T.
E185.97.R27 A82   323.4/092/4 B   *LC* 73-159449   *ISBN*
0151078300

Davis, Daniel S.   3.6849
Mr. Black labor; the story of A. Philip Randolph, father of the civil rights
movement, by Daniel S. Davis. Introd. by Bayard Rustin. [1st ed.] New York,
E. P. Dutton [1972] xii, 174 p. illus. 25 cm. 1. Randolph, A. Philip (Asa
Philip), 1889- 2. Afro-Americans — Civil rights 3. Civil rights movements —
United States — History. I. T.
E185.97.R27 D38 1972   323.4/092/4 B 19   *LC* 72-82599   *ISBN*
0525353259

Schweninger, Loren.   3.6850
James T. Rapier and Reconstruction / Loren Schweninger. — Chicago:
University of Chicago Press, c1978. xx, 248 p.; 23 cm. — (Negro American
biographies and autobiographies) Includes index. 1. Rapier, James T.,
1839-1883. 2. Reconstruction — Alabama. 3. Politicians — Alabama —
Biography. I. T. II. Series.
E185.97.R3 S38   328.73/092/4 B   *LC* 77-81734   *ISBN*
0226742407

Terrell, Mary Church, 1863-1954.   • 3.6851
A colored woman in a white world. Washington, D.C., Ransdell inc. [c1940]
7 p.l., 436, [1] p. front. (port.) 24 cm. I. T.
E185.97.T47   *LC* 40-34942

Fox, Stephen R.   • 3.6852
The guardian of Boston: William Monroe Trotter [by] Stephen R. Fox. [1st ed.]
New York, Atheneum, 1970. ix, 307 p. 23 cm. (Studies in American Negro life)
1. Trotter, William Monroe, 1872-1934. 2. Afro-Americans — History —
1877-1964 I. T.
E185.97.T75 F6 1970   323.1/19/6024 B   *LC* 78-108822

Washington, Booker T., 1856-1915.   3.6853
The Booker T. Washington papers. Louis R. Harlan, editor. Urbana, University
of Illinois Press [1972- < c1980 >. v. < 1-13 > illus. 25 cm. Vols. 8- < 13 >
edited by L.R. Harlan and R.W. Smock; v. 10, G. McTigue and N.E. Woodruff,
assistant editors; v. 11, G. McTigue, assistant editor; v. 13, Susan Valenza and
Sadie M. Harlan, assistant editors. 1. Washington, Booker T., 1856-1915.
2. Afro-Americans — History — 1863-1877 — Sources. 3. Afro-Americans —
History — 1877-1964 — Sources. 4. Afro-Americans — Correspondence.
I. Harlan, Louis R. II. Smock, Raymond. III. T.
E185.97.W274   301.45/19/6073024   *LC* 75-186345   *ISBN*
025201152X

Washington, Booker Taliaferro, 1859?-1915.   • 3.6854
Up from slavery; an autobiography. New York, Doubleday, Page & co., 1909.
xxiii p., 1 l., 330 p. front., plates, ports. 21 cm. 1. Tuskegee Institute. I. T.
E185.97.W314   *LC* 20-16686

Harlan, Louis R.   3.6855
Booker T. Washington; the making of a Black leader, 1856–1901 [by] Louis R.
Harlan. — New York: Oxford University Press, 1972. xi, 379 p.: illus.; 24 cm.
1. Washington, Booker T., 1856-1915. I. T.
E185.97.W4 H37   378.1/11/0924 B   *LC* 72-77499

Harlan, Louis R.   3.6856
Booker T. Washington: the wizard of Tuskegee, 1901–1915 / Louis R. Harlan.
— New York: Oxford University Press, 1983. xiv, 548 p.: port.; 24 cm.

1. Washington, Booker T., 1856-1915. 2. Afro-Americans — Biography. 3. Educators — United States — Biography. I. T.
E185.97.W4 H373 1983 378/.111 B 19 *LC* 82-14547 *ISBN* 0195032020

Cohen, Robert Carl.   **3.6857**
Black crusader; a biography of Robert Franklin Williams. — Secaucus, N. J., Lyle Stuart [c1972] 361 p. illus. 1. Race relations 2. Black power — United States I. T.
E185.97.W56 C6x *LC* 70-174654

White, Walter Francis, 1893-1955.   **3.6858**
A man called White, the autobiography of Walter White. New York, Viking Press, 1948. viii, 382 p. 22 cm. 1. Negroes. I. T.
E185.97.W6 A3 *LC* 48-8621

E186–879 AMERICAN HISTORY, BY PERIOD

E186–199 Colonial History (1607–1775)

Great Britain. Parliament.   **3.6859**
Proceedings and debates of the British Parliaments respecting North America, 1754–1783 / edited by R.C. Simmons and P.D.G. Thomas. — Millwood, N.Y.: Kraus International Publications, c1982- <c1986 >. v. <1-5 >; 26 cm. Vol. <5 > published in White Plains, N.Y. Vols. 4-<5 > printed on permanent paper. 1. United States — History — Colonial period, ca. 1600-1775 — Sources 2. United States — History — Revolution, 1775-1783 — Sources I. Simmons, R. C. (Richard C.), 1937- II. Thomas, Peter David Garner. III. T.
E187.G79 1982 973.3 19 *LC* 81-20814 *ISBN* 0527357235

Tracts and other papers relating principally to the origin, • **3.6860**
settlement, and progress of the colonies in North America from the discovery of the country to the year 1776 / collected by Peter Force.
New York: P. Smith, 1947. 4 v.: fold. plan. 1. United States — History — Colonial period, ca.1600-1775 — Sources. I. Force, Peter, 1790-1868.
E187.F E187.T73 1947. *LC* a 48-44

Raimo, John, 1946-.   **3.6861**
Biographical directory of American colonial and Revolutionary governors, 1607–1789 / by John W. Raimo. — Westport, Ct.: Meckler Books, c1980. xii, 521 p.; 24 cm. Includes index. 1. Governors — United States — Biography. 2. United States — Politics and government — Colonial period, ca. 1600-1775 3. United States — Politics and government — Revolution, 1775-1783 4. United States — Politics and government — 1783-1789 I. T.
E187.5.R34 E187.5 R34. 973/.09/92 B *LC* 80-13279 *ISBN* 0930466071

Andrews, Charles McLean, 1863-1943.   • **3.6862**
The colonial period of American history / by Charles M. Andrews; with a new foreword by Leonard W. Labaree. — New Haven: Yale University Press [1964] 4 v.; 21 cm. Includes bibliographical footnotes. 1. U.S. — Hist. — Colonial period. 2. Gt. Brit. — Colonies — America. I. T.
E188.A5745 973.2 *LC* 64-54917

Andrews, Charles McLean, 1863-1943.   • **3.6863**
Our earliest colonial settlements, their diversities of origin and later characteristics. New York, New York university press; London, H. Milford, Oxford university press, 1933. vi p., 1 l., 179 p. 24 cm. 1. Great Britain — Colonies — America 2. United States — History — Colonial period, ca. 1600-1775 3. Great Britain — Colonies — Administration 4. United States — Politics and government — Colonial period, ca. 1600-1775 I. T.
E188.A575 *LC* 33-28721

Boorstin, Daniel J. (Daniel Joseph), 1914-.   • **3.6864**
The Americans: the colonial experience. — New York: Random House [1958] 434 p.; 24 cm. First volume in a trilogy; the second of which is the author's The Americans: the national experience; and the third of which is his The Americans: the democratic experience. 1. National characteristics, American 2. United States — Civilization — To 1783 I. T.
E188.B72 917.3 *LC* 58-9884

Labaree, Leonard Woods, 1897-.   • **3.6865**
Conservatism in early American history. — New York: New York Univ. Press, 1948. xiii, 182 p.; 24 cm. — (Stokes Foundation. Anson G. Phelps lectureship on early American history) Bibliographical footnotes. 1. U.S. — Hist. — Colonial period. 2. U.S. — Civilization — Hist. I. T. II. Series.
E188.L3 973.2 *LC* 48-7475 *

Nash, Gary B.   **3.6866**
Red, white, and black: the peoples of early America [by] Gary B. Nash. — Englewood Cliffs, N.J.: Prentice-Hall, [1974] xvii, 350 p.: illus.; 24 cm. — (Prentice-Hall history of the American people series) 1. United States — History — Colonial period, ca. 1600-1775 2. America — Discovery and exploration I. T.
E188.N37 1974 917.3/03/2 *LC* 74-1003 *ISBN* 0137698100

Nash, Gary B.   **3.6867**
The urban crucible: social change, political consciousness, and the origins of the American Revolution / Gary B. Nash. — Cambridge, Mass.: Harvard University Press, 1979. xix, 548 p.; 25 cm. 1. United States — Politics and government — Colonial period, ca. 1600-1775 2. United States — Social conditions — To 1865 3. United States — Economic conditions — To 1865 4. United States — History — Revolution, 1775-1783 — Causes 5. Boston (Mass.) — History — Revolution, 1775-1783 — Causes. 6. New York (N.Y.) — History — Revolution, 1775-1783 — Causes. 7. Philadelphia (Pa.) — History — Revolution, 1775-1783 — Causes. I. T.
E188.N38 309.1/73/02 *LC* 79-12894 *ISBN* 0674930568

Rowse, A. L. (Alfred Leslie), 1903-.   • **3.6868**
The Elizabethans and America. New York, Harper [1959] 221 p. illus. 22 cm. 1. United States — History — Colonial period, ca. 1600-1775 2. United States — Civilization — English influences 3. Great Britain — History — Elizabeth, 1558-1603 I. T.
E188.R885 973.2 *LC* 59-10592

Wright, J. Leitch (James Leitch), 1929-.   **3.6869**
Anglo–Spanish rivalry in North America [by] J. Leitch Wright, Jr. — Athens: University of Georgia Press, [1971] xiii, 257 p.; 25 cm. 1. Great Britain — Colonies — America 2. Spain — Colonies — America. 3. Great Britain — Foreign relations — Spain. 4. Spain — Foreign relations — Great Britain. 5. North America — History — Colonial period, 1600-1775. I. T.
E188.W78 973.1 *LC* 72-156039 *ISBN* 0820303054

Wright, Louis B. (Louis Booker), 1899-.   • **3.6870**
The Atlantic Frontier: colonial American civilization, 1607–1763. Ithaca, N.Y., Cornell University Press [1959] xi, 354, xviii p. plates, maps. 22 cm. 1. United States — Civilization — To 1783 I. T.
E188.W8 1959 973.2 *LC* 59-16888

Bridenbaugh, Carl.   • **3.6871**
Cities in the wilderness: the first century of urban life in America, 1625–1742. — [2d ed.]. — New York: Knopf, 1955. xiv, 500 p.; 25 cm. 1. Cities and towns — United States. 2. United States — History — Colonial period, ca. 1600-1775 3. United States — Social life and customs — Colonial period, ca. 1600-1775 I. T.
E191.B75 1955 323.352 301.36* *LC* 55-8593

Lovejoy, David S. (David Sherman), 1919-.   • **3.6872**
The glorious Revolution in America [by] David S. Lovejoy. [1st ed.] New York, Harper & Row [1972] xvi, 396 p. 25 cm. 1. United States — History — Colonial period, ca. 1600-1775 2. Great Britain — History — Revolution of 1688 I. T.
E191.L68 1972 973.3 *LC* 71-156533 *ISBN* 006012721X

Osgood, Herbert Levi, 1855-1918.   • **3.6873**
The American colonies in the seventeenth century / by Herbert L. Osgood... New York: Columbia university press [c1930] v.; 23 cm. 'Published 1904, reprinted 1930.' 1. United States — Politics and government — Colonial period. 2. United States — History — Colonial period. I. T.
E191.O83 973.2 *LC* 30-26656

Pomfret, John Edwin, 1898-.   • **3.6874**
Founding the American colonies, 1583–1660 / by John E. Pomfret with Floyd M. Shumway. — [1st ed.] New York: Harper & Row, [1970] xvii, 380 p.: ill., maps, ports.; 22 cm. — (The New American Nation series) 1. United States — History — Colonial period. I. Shumway, Floyd Mallory. jt. author II. T.
E191.P64 1970 *LC* 68-15968

Wertenbaker, Thomas Jefferson, 1879-1966.   • **3.6875**
The first Americans, 1607–1690 / by Thomas Jefferson Wertenbaker. — New York: The Macmillan company, 1938. 358 p.: ill.; 22 cm. (A history of American life, vol. II) 1. United States — Social life and customs — Colonial period. 2. United States — Civilization I. T.
E191.W5x 973 *LC* 38-34436

Adams, James Truslow, 1878-1949.   • **3.6876**
Provincial society, 1690–1763, by James Truslow Adams. — New York: The Macmillan company, 1936. xvii p., 1 l., 374 p.: front., plates, ports., facsim.; 23 cm. — (A History of American life, vol. III) 'Critical essay on authorities': p. 324-356. 1. United States — Social life and customs — Colonial period, ca. 1600-1775 2. United States — Civilization I. T.
E195.A22x   LC 37-20159

Jensen, Merrill.   • **3.6877**
The founding of a nation; a history of the American Revolution, 1763–1776. — New York: Oxford University Press, 1968. xiii, 735 p.; 24 cm. 1. United States — History — Colonial period, ca. 1600-1775 2. United States — History — Revolution, 1775-1783 — Causes I. T.
E195.J4   973.31/1   LC 68-29720

Kammen, Michael G.   • **3.6878**
A rope of sand: the colonial agents, British politics, and the American Revolution / by Michael G. Kammen. — Ithaca, N.Y.: Cornell University Press, [1968] xviii, 349 p.: ill., ports.; 25 cm. 1. Colonial agents — United States. 2. Colonial agents — Great Britain. 3. United States — Politics and government — Colonial period, ca. 1600-1775 I. T.
E195.K28   325.3/42/0973   LC 68-16383

Osgood, Herbert Levi, 1855-1918.   • **3.6879**
The American Colonies in the eighteenth century. Gloucester, Mass., P. Smith, 1958. 4 v. 21 cm. 'The present volumes are a continuation of [the author's] The American Colonies in the seventeenth century.' 1. United States — Politics and government — Colonial period, ca. 1600-1775 2. United States — History — Colonial period, ca. 1600-1775 3. Great Britain — Colonies — America I. T.
E195.Ox   LC a 59-5015

Pole, J. R. (Jack Richon)   • **3.6880**
Foundations of American independence, 1763–1815 [by] J. R. Pole. Indianapolis, Bobbs-Merrill [1972] xix, 275 p. illus. 20 cm. (The History of American society) 1. United States — History — Colonial period, ca. 1600-1775 2. United States — History — 1783-1815 I. T. II. Series.
E195.P83   309.1/73   LC 71-173983

Parkman, Francis, 1823-1893.   • **3.6881**
Montcalm and Wolfe / by Francis Parkman; introd. by Allan Nevins. — New York: F. Ungar Pub. Co., [1965] 2 v.: ill.; 22 cm. (France & England in North America; v.8-9 American classics) 'Reprinted from the edition of 1884.' 1. Wolfe, James, 1727-1759. 2. Montcalm de Saint-Véran, Louis-Joseph, marquis de, 1712-1759. 3. United States — History — French and Indian War, 1755-1763 I. T.
E199.P255 1965   973.2/6   LC 72-186107

Rogers, Alan, 1936-.   **3.6882**
Empire and liberty: American resistance to British authority, 1755–1763 / Alan Rogers. — Berkeley: University of California Press, 1974. xiv, 205 p.; 24 cm. Includes index. 1. United States — History — French and Indian War, 1755-1763 I. T.
E199.R68   973.2/6   LC 72-82225   ISBN 0520022750

E201–298 American Revolution, 1775–1783

Bailyn, Bernard. ed.   • **3.6883**
Pamphlets of the American Revolution, 1750–1776 / edited by Bernard Bailyn; with the assistance of Jane N. Garrett. — Cambridge: Belknap Press of Harvard University Press, 1965-. v.   : facsims.; 25 cm. (John Harvard library.) 1. United States — History — Revolution, 1775-1783 — Pamphlets. I. T. II. Series.
E203.B3   973.3082   LC 64-21784

Commager, Henry Steele, 1902- ed.   • **3.6884**
The spirit of 'seventy-six: the story of the American Revolution as told by participants / edited by Henry Steele Commager and Richard B. Morris. — New York: Harper & Row, [1967] lii, 1348 p.: illus., facsims., maps, ports.; 25 cm. 1. United States — History — Revolution, 1775-1783 — Personal narratives 2. United States — History — Revolution, 1775-1783 — Sources I. Morris, Richard Brandon, 1904- joint ed. II. T.
E203.C69 1967   973.3/08   LC 67-11325

Great Britain. Colonial Office.   **3.6885**
Documents of the American Revolution, 1770–1783 / edited by K. G. Davies. — Shannon: Irish University Press, 1973 (c1972) 3 v. (Colonial Office series.) Documents selected from Colonial Office records in the Public Record Office. 1. United States — History — Revolution, 1775-1783 — Sources I. Davies, Kenneth Gordon, ed. II. Great Britain. Public Record Office. III. T.
E203.G68 1972   973.2/7   LC 74-156782   ISBN 0716520850

Morison, Samuel Eliot, 1887-1976. ed.   • **3.6886**
Sources and documents illustrating the American Revolution, 1764–1788: and the formation of the Federal Constitution / selected and edited by Samuel Eliot Morison. — 2d ed. — New York: Oxford University Press, 1965. xlii, 380 p.; 21 cm. — (A Galaxy book, GB135) 1. United States. Constitution 2. United States — History — Revolution, 1775-1783 — Sources 3. United States — History — Revolution, 1775-1783 — Causes I. T.
E203.M86 1965   973.3   LC 65-1330

Reconsiderations on the Revolutionary War: selected essays /   **3.6887**
edited by Don Higginbotham.
Westport, Conn.: Greenwood Press, 1978. x, 217 p.; 22 cm. — (Contributions in military history. no. 14 0084-9251) 'Papers presented at a symposium ... held at the United States Military Academy, West Point, New York, on April 22-23, 1976.' 1. Strategy — Congresses. 2. United States — History — Revolution, 1775-1783 — Congresses. I. Higginbotham, Don. II. Series.
E204.R4   973.3   LC 77-84757   ISBN 0837198461

E206–207 BIOGRAPHY

Billias, George Athan, 1919- ed.   • **3.6888**
George Washington's generals. New York: W. Morrow, 1964. xvii, 327 p.: ports., maps.; 22 cm. Essays. 1. United States. Army — Biography 2. Generals — United States. 3. United States — History — Revolution, 1775-1783 — Biography I. T.
E206.B5   LC 64-12038

Hoyt, Edwin Palmer.   **3.6889**
The damndest Yankees: Ethan Allen & his clan / by Edwin P. Hoyt. — Brattleboro, Vt.: S. Greene Press, c1976. viii, 262 p., [2] leaves of plates: ill.; 24 cm. Includes index. 1. Allen, Ethan, 1738-1789. 2. Allen, Ira, 1751-1814. 3. Allen family 4. Vermont — History — To 1791 I. T.
E207.A4 H65   974.3/02/0924 B   LC 74-27455   ISBN 0828902593

Alden, John Richard, 1908-.   • **3.6890**
General Gage in America: being principally a history of his role in the American Revolution. — New York: Greenwood Press, [1969, c1948] xi, 313 p.: map., ports.; 23 cm. 1. Gage, Thomas, 1721-1787. 2. United States — History — Revolution, 1775-1783 — British forces I. T.
E207.G23 A6 1969   973.33/0924 B   LC 77-90459   ISBN 0837122643

Nelson, Paul David, 1941-.   **3.6891**
General Horatio Gates: a biography / Paul David Nelson. — Baton Rouge: Louisiana State University Press, c1976. xiii, 319 p.: ill.; 24 cm. Includes index. 1. Gates, Horatio, 1728-1806. I. T.
E207.G3 N44   973.3/3/0924 B   LC 74-27191   ISBN 0807101591

Jones, John Paul, 1747-1792.   **3.6892**
Memoirs of Rear-Admiral Paul Jones, compiled from his original journals and correspondence. — New York: Da Capo Press, 1972. 2 v. in 1.: port.; 23 cm. — (The Era of the American Revolution) Reprint of the 1830 ed. 1. United States — History — Revolution, 1775-1783 — Naval operations I. T.
E207.J7 A3 1972   973.35/0924 B   LC 77-166333   ISBN 0306702479

Lafayette, Marie Joseph Paul Yves Roch Gilbert Du Motier,   **3.6893**
marquis de, 1757-1834.
Lafayette in the age of the American Revolution: selected letters and papers, 1776–1790 / Stanley J. Idzerda, editor, Roger E. Smith, associate editor, Linda J. Pike and Mary Anne Quinn, assistant editors. — Ithaca, N.Y.: Cornell University Press, 1977-. v. < 1-2,5 > : ill.; 25 cm. (The Papers of the Marquis de Lafayette) 'French texts': v. 1, p. [387]-464. v. 5, p. [361]-426. 1. Lafayette, Marie Joseph Paul Yves Roch Gilbert Du Motier, marquis de, 1757-1834. 2. Generals — United States — Correspondence. 3. Generals — France — Correspondence. 4. United States — History — Revolution, 1775-1783 — Sources 5. United States — History — Confederation, 1783-1789 — Sources. I. Idzerda, Stanley J. II. T.
E207.L2 A4 1977   944/.04/092/4 B   LC 76-50268   ISBN 0801410312

Olmsted, Gideon, 1749-1845.   **3.6894**
The journal of Gideon Olmstead: adventures of a sea captain during the American Revolution / introd. and reading text by Gerard W. Gawalt; coda, by Charles W. Kreidler. — Washington: Library of Congress, c1978. xvi, 129 p.: facsims.; 28 cm. The facsim. of the author's journal was made from a ms. located in the Frederick Law Olmsted papers in the Manuscript Division of the Library of Congress. 1. Olmsted, Gideon, 1749-1845. 2. Privateering 3. Shipmasters — United States — Biography. 4. United States — History — Revolution, 1775-1783 — Personal narratives 5. United States — History — Revolution, 1775-1783 — Naval operations I. Library of Congress. Manuscript Division. II. T.
E207.O5 A32   973.3/5 B   LC 77-608234   ISBN 0844402516

E208–209 General Works

Alden, John Richard, 1908-. • 3.6895
The American Revolution, 1775–1783. — [1st ed.]. — New York: Harper [1954] 294 p.: ill.; 22 cm. — (The New American nation series) Includes bibliography. 1. U.S. — Hist. — Revolution. I. T.
E208.A35   973.3   *LC* 53-11826

The American Revolution: explorations in the history of 3.6896
American radicalism / edited by Alfred F. Young.
Dekalb: Northern Illinois University Press, 1976. xv, 481 p.: ill.; 24 cm. (Explorations in the history of American radicalism.) 1. Radicalism — United States — Addresses, essays, lectures. 2. United States — History — Revolution, 1775-1783 — Addresses, essays, lectures. I. Young, Alfred Fabian, 1925- II. Series.
E208.A43   973.3   *LC* 75-45359   *ISBN* 0875800572

Essays on the American Revolution. Edited by Stephen G. 3.6897
Kurtz and James H. Hutson.
Chapel Hill, Published for the Institute of Early American History and Culture, Williamsburg, Va., by the University of North Carolina Press [1973] xi, 320 p. 22 cm. Papers originally presented at a symposium on the American Revolution held at the Institute of Early American History and Culture, Williamsburg, Mar. 8-12, 1971. 1. United States — History — Revolution, 1775-1783 — Addresses, essays, lectures. I. Kurtz, Stephen G., ed. II. Hutson, James H., ed. III. Institute of Early American History and Culture (Williamsburg, Va.)
E208.E83   973.3/08   *LC* 72-81329   *ISBN* 0807812048 *ISBN* 0393094197

Mackesy, Piers. • 3.6898
The war for America, 1775–1783. — Cambridge: Harvard University Press, 1964. xx, 565 p.: ill., ports., maps (1 fold. col.); 23 cm. Bibliography: p. [528]-535. 1. U.S. — Hist. — Revolution. 2. Gt. Brit. — Hist. — 1760–1789. I. T.
E208.M14   973.3   *LC* 64-2777

Main, Jackson Turner. 3.6899
The Sovereign States, 1775–1783. — New York: New Viewpoints, 1973. vii, 502 p.: maps; 22 cm. 1. United States — History — Revolution, 1775-1783 I. T.
E208.M33 1973   973.3   *LC* 75-190137   *ISBN* 0531063550

Middlekauff, Robert. 3.6900
The glorious cause: the American Revolution, 1763–1789 / Robert Middlekauff. — New York: Oxford University Press, 1982. xvi, 696 p., [8] leaves of plates: ports.; 25 cm. — (Oxford history of the United States. v. 2) Includes index. 1. United States — History — Revolution, 1775-1783 2. United States — History — Confederation, 1783-1789 I. T. II. Series.
E208.M45x   973 s 973.3 19   *LC* 81-9660   *ISBN* 0195029216

Miller, John Chester, 1907-. • 3.6901
Triumph of freedom, 1775–1783 / with maps by Van H. English. — [1st ed.]. — Boston: Little, Brown, 1948. xviii, 718 p.: maps.; 25 cm. 'An Atlantic Monthly Press book.' 1. United States — History — Revolution, 1775-1783 I. T.
E208.M5 1948   973.3   *LC* 48-6755

Morgan, Edmund Sears. • 3.6902
The birth of the Republic, 1763–89. — [Chicago]: University of Chicago Press, [1956] 176 p.; 21 cm. — (The Chicago history of American civilization) 1. United States — History — Revolution, 1775-1783 2. United States — History — Confederation, 1783-1789 I. T.
E208.M85   973.3   *LC* 56-11003

Morris, Richard Brandon, 1904-. • 3.6903
The American Revolution reconsidered / [by] Richard B. Morris. — [1st ed.]. — New York: Harper & Row [1967] xi, 178 p.; 22 cm. Includes bibliographies. 1. U.S. — Hist. — Revolution — Causes. 2. U.S. — Hist. — Revolution — Influences. I. T.
E208.M872   973.31/1   *LC* 67-13689

Robson, Eric, 1918-1954. • 3.6904
The American Revolution in its political and military aspects, 1763–1783. — New York: Da Capo Press, 1972. ix, [1], 254 p.; 22 cm. — (The Era of the American Revolution) Reprint of the 1955 ed. 1. United States — History — Revolution, 1775-1783 I. T.
E208.R6 1972   973.3   *LC* 74-171392   *ISBN* 030670417X

Smith, Page. 3.6905
A new age now begins: a people's history of the American Revolution / Page Smith. — New York: McGraw-Hill, c1976. 2 v. (xi, 1899 p., [24] leaves of plates): ill.; 25 cm. 'Volume[s] one[-two]' of the author's history of the United States. Includes index. 1. United States — History — Revolution, 1775-1783 2. United States — History — Revolution, 1775-1783 — Campaigns I. T. II. Title: People's history of the American Revolution.
E208.S67   973.3   *LC* 75-8656   *ISBN* 0070590974

Trevelyan, George Otto, Sir, 1838-1928. • 3.6906
The American Revolution / Edited, arr., and with an introd. and notes by Richard B. Morris. New York: D. McKay Co. [1964] xxiii, 580 p.; 22 cm. 1. United States — History — Revolution, 1775-1783 I. T.
E208.T836   973.3   *LC* 63-19340

Wright, Esmond. • 3.6907
Fabric of freedom, 1763–1800. — New York: Hill and Wang, [1961] 298 p.: illus.; 22 cm. — (The Making of America) 1. United States — History — Revolution, 1775-1783 2. United States — History — Constitutional period, 1789-1809 I. T.
E208.W9   973.3   *LC* 61-14479

Albanese, Catherine L. 3.6908
Sons of the fathers: the civil religion of the American Revolution / Catherine L. Albanese. — Philadelphia: Temple University Press, 1976. xiv, 274 p.; 23 cm. 1. Civil religion — United States. 2. United States — History — Revolution, 1775-1783 — Religious aspects I. T.
E209.A4   209/.73   *LC* 76-17712   *ISBN* 0877220735

Cohen, Lester H., 1944-. 3.6909
The Revolutionary histories: contemporary narratives of the American revolution / Lester H. Cohen. — Ithaca, N.Y.: Cornell University Press, 1980. 286 p.: 22 cm. 1. United States — History — Revolution, 1775-1783 — Historiography I. T.
E209.C63 1980   973.3/07/2   *LC* 80-11243   *ISBN* 0877541779

Gipson, Lawrence Henry, 1880-. • 3.6910
The coming of the Revolution, 1763–1775. — [1st ed.]. — New York: Harper, [1954] xiv, 287 p.: ill., ports., maps.; 22 cm. — (The New American nation series) 1. United States — History — Revolution, 1775-1783 — Causes I. T.
E209.G5   973.311   *LC* 54-8952

Jameson, J. Franklin (John Franklin), 1859-1937. • 3.6911
The American revolution considered as a social movement, by J. Franklin Jameson ... — Princeton, Princeton university press, 1926. 3 p. l., 157, [1] p. 20 cm. 'Lectures delivered in November 1925 on the Louis Clark Vanuxem foundation.' 1. United States — Hist. — Revolution. 2. United States — Soc. condit. I. T.
E209.J33   *LC* 26-10868

Noll, Mark A., 1946-. 3.6912
Christians in the American Revolution / by Mark A. Noll. — [Grand Rapids]: Christian University Press, c1977. 195 p.; 21 cm. 1. United States — History — Revolution, 1775-1783 — Religious aspects 2. United States — Church history — Colonial period, ca. 1600-1775 I. T.
E209.N64   277.3   *LC* 77-23354   *ISBN* 0802817068

Shaffer, Arthur H. 3.6913
The politics of history: writing the history of the American Revolution, 1783–1815 / by Arthur H. Shaffer. — Chicago: Precedent Pub., c1975. 228 p.; 24 cm. Includes index. 1. United States — History — Revolution, 1775-1783 — Historiography I. T.
E209.S5   973.3/07/2   *LC* 75-328809   *ISBN* 0913750093

Wright, Esmond. ed. • 3.6914
Causes and consequences of the American Revolution. — Chicago: Quadrangle Books, 1966. 316 p.; 22 cm. 1. United States — History — Revolution, 1775-1783 — Addresses, essays, lectures. 2. United States — History — Revolution, 1775-1783 — Causes 3. United States — History — Revolution, 1775-1783 — Influence I. T.
E209.W75   973.3   *LC* 66-11876

E210–221 Political History.
Declaration of Independence

Abernethy, Thomas Perkins, 1890-. • 3.6915
Western lands and the American Revolution. New York: Russell & Russell, 1959 [c1937] 410 p.: ill.; 24 cm. 1. Land tenure — United States — History. 2. United States — Public lands 3. United States — History — Revolution, 1775-1783 — Causes 4. Mississippi River Valley — History — To 1803 I. T.
E210.A15 1959   973.311   *LC* 59-63139

Andrews, Charles McLean, 1863-1943. • 3.6916
The colonial background of the American Revolution: four essays in American colonial history / Charles McLean Andrews. — New Haven: Yale University Press, 1961, c1958. xii, 220 p.; 21 cm. — (A Yale paperbound; Y-44) 1. United States — History — Colonial period, ca. 1600-1775 2. Great Britain — Colonies — America 3. United States — History — Revolution, 1775-1783 — Causes I. T.
E210.A55 1961   *LC* 61-19714

Baldwin, Alice Mary, 1879-. • **3.6917**
The New England clergy and the American Revolution. — New York: F. Ungar Pub. Co., [1958] xiii, 222 p.; 23 cm. 1. Clergy — United States. 2. United States — Politics and government — Revolution, 1775-1783 3. United States — Politics and government — Colonial period, ca. 1600-1775 I. T. II. Title: Clergy and the American Revolution.
E210.B18 1958   973.315   *LC 58-9335*

Becker, Carl Lotus, 1873-1945. • **3.6918**
The eve of the revolution: a chronicle of the breach with England / by Carl Becker. — New Haven: Yale University Press, 1920. xi, 267 p.: ill., col. front.; 18 cm. — (The chronicles of America series v.11) 'Textbook edition.' 1. United States — History — Revolution, 1775-1783 2. United States — Politics & government — Revolution, 1775-1783. I. T.
E210.B4x   E 18 C55 v.11.   *LC 22-12133*

Davidson, Philip Grant, 1902-. • **3.6919**
Propaganda and the American revolution, 1763–1783 [by] Philip Davidson. — Chapel Hill: The University of North Carolina press, 1941. xvi, 460 p.: front., pl., facsims.; 24 cm. 1. Propaganda, American 2. United States — History — Revolution, 1775-1783 — Causes I. T.
E210.D3   973.31   *LC 41-3098*

Higginbotham, Don. **3.6920**
The war of American independence; military attitudes, policies, and practice, 1763–1789. — New York: Macmillan, [1971] xvi, 509 p.: maps.; 24 cm. 1. United States — History — Revolution, 1775-1783 I. T.
E210.H63   973.3   *LC 74-132454*

Maier, Pauline, 1938-. • **3.6921**
From resistance to revolution: colonial radicals and the development of American opposition to Britain, 1765–1776. — [1st ed.]. — New York: Knopf, 1972. xviii, 318, xxvi p.; 22 cm. 1. United States — History — Revolution, 1775-1783 — Causes I. T.
E210.M27   973.3   *LC 74-154904*   *ISBN 0394461908*

Shy, John W. • **3.6922**
Toward Lexington; the role of the British Army in the coming of the American Revolution, by John Shy. — Princeton, N.J.: Princeton University Press, 1965. x, 463 p.: maps.; 21 cm. 1. Great Britain. Army — History. 2. United States — History — Revolution, 1775-1783 — Causes 3. United States — History, Military — To 1900 4. Great Britain — Colonies — America — Defenses. I. T.
E210.S5   973.3113   *LC 65-17160*

Paine, Thomas, 1737-1809. **3.6923**
[Common sense] Thomas Paine's Common sense: the call to independence / edited, with an introd., ill., and explanatory notes, by Thomas Wendel. — A Bicentennial ed. — Woodbury, N.Y.: Barron's Educational Series, inc., c1975. x, 163 p.: ill.; 21 cm. 1. Political science 2. Monarchy 3. United States — Politics and government — Revolution, 1775-1783 I. Wendel, Thomas. II. T. III. Title: Common sense.
E211.P1455 1975   973.3/11   *LC 75-28222*   *ISBN 0812006550*

Price, Richard, 1723-1791. **3.6924**
[Observations on the nature of civil liberty, the principles of government, and the justice and policy of the war with America] Two tracts on civil liberty, the war with America, the debts and finances of the kingdom. New York, Da Capo Press, 1972. xxvi, 112, xiv, 216 p. 22 cm. (The Era of the American Revolution) Reprint of the 1778 ed. 1. Finance, Public — Great Britain — 1688-1815 2. Finance, Public — France — To 1789 3. United States — Politics and government — Revolution, 1775-1783 4. United States — History — Revolution, 1775-1783 — Causes I. Price, Richard, 1723-1791. Additional observations on the nature and value of civil liberty, and the war with America. 1972. II. T.
E211.P9692   320.9/42/073   *LC 74-169641*   *ISBN 0306702339*

Morgan, Edmund Sears. • **3.6925**
The stamp act crisis: prologue to revolution / by Edmund S. Morgan and Helen M. Morgan. Chapel Hill: Published for the Institute of Early American History and Culture at Williamsburg, Va. by the University of North Carolina P., 1953. 310 p. 1. Stamp act, 1765 2. United States — History — Revolution — Causes. I. Morgan, Helen M. II. Institute of Early American History and Culture (Williamsburg, Va.) III. T.
E215.2 M58   973.3111   *LC 53-10190*

Weslager, C. A. (Clinton Alfred), 1909-. **3.6926**
The Stamp Act Congress: with an exact copy of the complete journal / C. A. Weslager. — Newark: University of Delaware Press, c1976. 279 p.: ports.; 22 cm. 'A University of Delaware bicentennial book.' Includes index. 1. Stamp Act Congress, New York, 1765. I. T.
E215.2.W47   973.3/111   *LC 75-21514*   *ISBN 0874131111*

Empire and nation: Letters from a farmer in Pennsylvania, John • **3.6927**
Dickinson. Letters from the Federal farmer, Richard Henry Lee. With an introd. by Forrest McDonald.
Englewood Cliffs, N.J., Prentice-Hall [1962] xvi, 173 p. 21 cm. (A Spectrum book; Classics in history series, S-CH-5) 1. United States. Constitution 2. United States. Constitutional Covention, 1787. 3. United States — History — Revolution, 1775-1783 — Causes I. Dickinson, John, 1732-1808. Letters from a farmer in Pennsylvania to the inhabitants of the British Colonies. II. Lee, Richard Henry, 1732-1794.
E215.5.E4   973.311   *LC 62-18084*

Stout, Neil R. **3.6928**
The Royal Navy in America, 1760–1775; a study of enforcement of British colonial policy in the era of the American Revolution, by Neil R. Stout. Annapolis, Md.: Naval Institute Press [1973] ix, 227 p. 24 cm. 1. Great Britain. Royal Navy. 2. United States — History — Revolution, 1775-1783 — Causes 3. Great Britain — History, Naval — 18th century I. T.
E216.S76   973.3/11   *LC 73-77771*   *ISBN 0870215531*

Wills, Garry, 1934-. **3.6929**
Inventing America: Jefferson's Declaration of Independence / Garry Wills. — 1st ed. — Garden City, N.Y.: Doubleday, 1978. xxvi, 398 p.; 22 cm. — (His America's political enlightenment) 'The Declarations of Jefferson and of the Congress': p. [374]-379. 1. Jefferson, Thomas, 1743-1826. 2. United States. Declaration of Independence. I. United States. Declaration of Independence. 1978. II. T. III. Series.
E221.W64   973.3/13   *LC 77-80922*   *ISBN 0385089767*

E230–275 MILITARY AND DIPLOMATIC HISTORY

Carrington, Henry Beebee, 1824-1912. **3.6930**
Battle maps and charts of the American Revolution: with explanatory notes and school history references / with a new introd. by George Athan Billias. — New York: Arno Press, 1974 [c1881] 88 p.: ill.; 44 cm. Reprint of the ed. published by A. S. Barnes, New York. 1. United States — History — Revolution, 1775-1783 — Campaigns 2. United States — History — Revolution, 1775-1783 — Maps I. T.
E230.C322 1974   912/.1/97333   *LC 74-8018*   *ISBN 0405055404*

Peckham, Howard Henry, 1910-. **3.6931**
The toll of independence: engagements & battle casualties of the American Revolution / edited by Howard H. Peckham. — Chicago: University of Chicago Press, 1974. xv, 176 p.; 24 cm. — (Clements Library bicentennial studies) Chiefly tables. Includes index. 1. United States — History — Revolution, 1775-1783 — Casualties (Statistics, etc.) 2. United States — History — Revolution, 1775-1783 — Campaigns I. T. II. Series.
E230.P35   973.3/3   *LC 74-75615*   *ISBN 0226653188*

Peckham, Howard Henry, 1910-. • **3.6932**
The War for Independence: a military history. — [Chicago]: University of Chicago Press [1958] 226 p.; 21 cm. — (The Chicago history of American civilization) Includes bibliography. 1. U.S. — Hist. — Revolution — Campaigns and battles. I. T.
E230.P36   973.34   *LC 58-5685*

Wallace, Willard Mosher, 1911-. • **3.6933**
Appeal to arms: a military history of the American Revolution. — [1st ed.] New York: Harper [1951] viii, 308 p.: ill., maps, facsims.; 22 cm. 1. United States — History — Revolution, 1775-1783 — Campaigns I. T.
E230.W3   *LC 51-348*

Bemis, Samuel Flagg, 1891-1973. • **3.6934**
The diplomacy of the American Revolution. Bloomington: Indiana University Press [1957] xii, 293 p.; 21 cm. (Midland books, MB6) 1. Treaty of Paris (1783) 2. United States — Foreign relations — Revolution, 1775-1783 3. Europe — Politics and government — 18th century I. T.
E249.B44 1957   973.32   *LC 57-7878*

Corwin, Edward Samuel, 1878-1963. • **3.6935**
French policy and the American alliance of 1778. — New York: B. Franklin, [1970] ix, 430 p.; 23 cm. — (Burt Franklin research & source works series, 476) (Selected essays in history, economics, & social science, 129.) Reprint of the 1916 ed. 1. United States — History — Revolution, 1775-1783 — Participation, French 2. United States — Foreign relations — Revolution, 1775-1783 3. United States — Foreign relations — France 4. France — Foreign relations — United States I. T.
E249.C83 1970   973.32/4   *LC 77-121599*

Dull, Jonathan R., 1942-.   3.6936
A diplomatic history of the American Revolution / Jonathan R. Dull. — New Haven: Yale University Press, c1985. xii, 229 p.; 21 cm. Includes index. 1. United States — Foreign relations — Revolution, 1775-1783 I. T.
E249.D859 1985   973.3/2 19   *LC* 85-5306   *ISBN* 0300034199

Hutson, James H.   3.6937
John Adams and the diplomacy of the American Revolution / James H. Hutson. — Lexington: University Press of Kentucky, c1980. vii, 199 p.; 23 cm. Includes index. 1. Adams, John, 1735-1826. 2. United States — Foreign relations — Revolution, 1775-1783 I. T.
E249.H87   973/.3/2/0924   *LC* 79-57575   *ISBN* 0813114047

Morris, Richard Brandon, 1904-.   • 3.6938
The peacemakers: the great powers and American independence / by Richard B. Morris. — [1st ed.]. — New York: Harper & Row [1965] xviii, 572 p.: ill., facsims., maps, ports.; 25 cm. Bibliographical references included in 'Notes' (p. 467-552) 1. Treaty of Paris (1783) 2. U.S. — For. rel. — Revolution. 3. Europe — Politics — 18th cent. I. T.
E249.M68   973.317   *LC* 65-20435

Clark, Dora Mae.   • 3.6939
British opinion and the American revolution / by Dora Mae Clark. — New Haven: Yale University Press; London: Milford, Oxford University Press, 1930. viii, 308 p.: diagr.; 23 cm. (Yale historical publications. Miscellany, 20) 1. United States — History — Revolution — Foreign public opinion 2. Public opinion — Gt. Brit. 3. Great Britain — Commerce — U.S. 4. United States — Commerce — Gt. Brit. 5. Great Britain — Colonies — North America — Financial questions 6. United States — History — Revolution — Causes I. T.
E249.3 C59

E251–273 ARMIES. NAVIES

Berg, Fred Anderson, 1948-.   3.6940
Encyclopedia of Continental Army units—battalions, regiments, and independent corps. [Harrisburg, Pa.] Stackpole Books [1972] 160 p. 24 cm. 1. United States. Continental Army — Directories. I. T.
E259.B47   973.3/4/025   *LC* 70-38505   *ISBN* 0811705447

Royster, Charles.   3.6941
A revolutionary people at war: the Continental Army and American character, 1775–1783 / Charles Royster. — Chapel Hill: Published for the Institute of Early American History and Culture, Williamsburg, Va., by the University of North Carolina Press, 1980 (c1979). xi, 452 p., [16] leaves of plates: 30 ill.; 25 cm. 1. United States. Continental Army. 2. National characteristics, American 3. United States — Civilization — To 1783 I. T.
E259.R69   973.3/4   *LC* 79-10152   *ISBN* 0807813850

The Sinews of independence: monthly strength reports of the   3.6942
Continental Army / edited by Charles H. Lesser.
Chicago: University of Chicago Press, c1976. xxxvii, 262 p.: ill.; 29 cm. (Clements Library bicentennial studies; v. 2) 1. United States. Continental Army — Registers. 2. United States — History — Revolution, 1775-1783 — Registers 3. United States — History — Revolution, 1775-1783 — Sources I. Lesser, Charles H. II. Series.
E259.S56   973.3/4   *LC* 75-12227   *ISBN* 0226473325

Wright, J. Leitch (James Leitch), 1929-.   3.6943
Florida in the American Revolution / J. Leitch Wright, Jr.; sponsored by the American Revolution Bicentennial Commission of Florida. — Gainesville: University Presses of Florida, [1975] xvi, 194 p., [4] leaves of plates: ill.; 23 cm. 'A University of Florida book.' Includes index. 1. Florida — History — Revolution, 1775-1783 I. Bicentennial Commission of Florida. II. T.
E263.F6 W74   975.9/02   *LC* 75-15923   *ISBN* 0813005248

Countryman, Edward.   3.6944
A people in revolution: the American Revolution and political society in New York, 1760–1790 / Edward Countryman. — Baltimore: Johns Hopkins University Press, c1981. xviii, 388 p.; 23 cm. — (Johns Hopkins University studies in historical and political science. 99th ser., 2) 1. New York (State) — Politics and government — Revolution, 1775-1783 2. New York (State) — Politics and government — 1775-1865 I. T. II. Series.
E263.N6 C68   974.7/03 19   *LC* 81-5993   *ISBN* 080182625X

Braeman, John.   • 3.6945
The road to independence: a documentary history of the causes of the American Revolution,1763–1776. — New York: Putnam, [1963] 314 p.; 23 cm. 1. United States — History — Revolution — Sources. 2. United States — History — Revolution — Causes. I. T.
E263.N6 M3   973.311   *LC* 63-8217

Nadelhaft, Jerome J.   3.6946
The disorders of war: the Revolution in South Carolina / by Jerome J. Nadelhaft. — 1st ed. — Orono, Me.: University of Maine at Orono Press, 1981. xi, 310 p.: ill.; 24 cm. Includes index. 1. South Carolina — History — Revolution, 1775-1783 I. T.
E263.S7 N33 1981   973.3/09757 19   *LC* 83-242647   *ISBN* 0891010491

Rice, Howard Crosby, 1904- comp.   3.6947
The American campaigns of Rochambeau's army, 1780, 1781, 1782, 1783. Translated and edited by Howard C. Rice, Jr. and Anne S. K. Brown. — Princeton, N.J.: Princeton University Press, 1972. 2 v.: illus.; 30 cm. 1. Rochambeau, Jean-Baptiste-Donatien de Vimeur, comte de, 1725-1807. 2. United States — History — Revolution, 1775-1783 — Participation, French 3. United States — History — Revolution, 1775-1783 — Campaigns I. Brown, Anne S. Kinsolving. joint comp. II. Clermont-Crèvecœur, Jean François Louis, comte de, 1752-ca. 1824. III. Verger, Jean Baptiste Antoine de, 1762-1851. IV. Berthier, Alexandre, prince de Neuchâtel et de Wagram, 1753-1815. V. T.
E265.R513   973.3/47   *LC* 71-166388   *ISBN* 0691046107

Gruber, Ira D.   • 3.6948
The Howe brothers and the American Revolution [by Ira D. Gruber. — [1st ed.]. — New York: Published for the Institute of Early American History and Culture at Williamsburg, Va. [by] Atheneum, 1972. ix, 396 p.: maps.; 25 cm. 1. Howe, Richard Howe, Earl, 1726-1799. 2. Howe, William Howe, Viscount, 1729-1814. 3. United States — History — Revolution, 1775-1783 — British forces I. T.
E267.G86   973.3/41   *LC* 71-183681

Kipping, Ernst.   3.6949
The Hessian view of America, 1776–1783. — Monmouth Beach, N.J.: Philip Freneau Press, 1971. 48 p.: illus.; 32 cm. — (Philip Freneau Press bicentennial series on the American Revolution) 1. United States — History — Revolution, 1775-1783 — German mercenaries 2. United States — Description and travel — To 1783 I. T. II. Series.
E268.K49   973.3/42   *LC* 72-161384   *ISBN* 0912480068

Schulte Nordholt, J. W. (Jan Willem), 1920-.   3.6950
[Voorbeeld in de verte. English] The Dutch Republic and American independence / by Jan Willem Schulte Nordholt; translated by Herbert H. Rowen. — Chapel Hill: University of North Carolina Press, c1982. xii, 351 p.: ill.; 24 cm. Translation of: Voorbeeld in de verte. Includes index. 1. United States — History — Revolution, 1775-1783 — Participation, Dutch 2. United States — Foreign relations — Revolution, 1775-1783 3. United States — History — Revolution, 1775-1783 — Influence I. T.
E269.D88 S3813 1982   973.3/46 19   *LC* 82-2563   *ISBN* 0807815306

Quarles, Benjamin.   • 3.6951
The Negro in the American Revolution. New York: Norton [1973, c1961] xiii, 231 p.: front.; 20 cm. (The Norton library) 1. United States — History — Revolution, 1775-1783 — Afro-Americans I. T.
E269.N3 Q3 1973   973.3/15/0396073   *LC* 72-10364   *ISBN* 0393006743

Allen, Gardner Weld, 1856-1944.   • 3.6952
A naval history of the American Revolution / Gardner W. Allen. — New York, N. Y.: Russell & Russell, 1962, c1940. 2 v. (xii, 752 p.): ill. Reprint of the 1913 ed. Includes index. 1. United States. Navy — History — Revolution, 1775-1783 2. United States — History — Revolution, 1775-1783 — Naval operations I. T.
E271 A42 1970   E271 A42 1962.   *LC* 61-17193

Fowler, William M., 1944-.   3.6953
Rebels under sail: the American Navy during the Revolution / William M. Fowler, Jr. — New York: Scribner, c1976. xi, 356 p., [8] leaves of plates: ill.; 24 cm. Includes index. 1. United States. Navy — History — Revolution, 1775-1783 2. United States — History — Revolution, 1775-1783 — Naval operations I. T.
E271.F68   973.3/5   *LC* 75-38556   *ISBN* 0684145839

United States. Naval History Division.   3.6954
Naval documents of the American Revolution / editor: William Bell Clark; with a foreword by President John F. Kennedy; and an introd. by Ernest McNeill Eller. — Washington: [For sale by the Supt. of Docs., U.S. Govt. Print. Off.], 1964. 12 v.: ill., facsims., maps, port.; 26 cm. Vols. 5- <8 > edited by W.J. Morgan. 1. United States. Navy — History — Revolution, 1775-1783 — Sources. 2. United States — History, Naval — Sources. 3. United States — History — Revolution, 1775-1783 — Naval operations I. Clark, William Bell, 1889-1968. ed. II. Morgan, William James. ed. III. T.
E271.U583   *LC* 64-60087

Rider, Hope S.   3.6955
Valour fore & aft, being the adventures of the continental sloop Providence, 1775–1779, formerly flagship Katy of Rhode Island's Navy / Hops S. Rider; [maps by Dorothy deFontaine]. Annapolis: Naval Institute Press, c1977. xiv,

259 p.: ill.; 24 cm. Includes index. 1. Providence (Sloop, U.S.) 2. United States — History — Revolution, 1775-1783 — Naval operations I. T. II. Title: Valour fore & aft ...
E273.P75 R5   973.3/5   *LC* 76-17516   *ISBN* 0870217445

E277–280 LOYALISTS

Calhoon, Robert M. (Robert McCluer)   3.6956
The loyalists in Revolutionary America, 1760–1781. — [1st ed.]. — New York: Harcourt Brace Jovanovich, [1973] xviii, 580 p.; 22 cm. — (The Founding of the American Republic) 1. American loyalists 2. United States — History — Revolution, 1775-1783 — Causes 3. United States — Politics and government — Colonial period, ca. 1600-1775 I. T.
E277.C24   973.3/14   *LC* 73-8835   *ISBN* 0151547459

Crary, Catherine S., comp.   3.6957
The price of loyalty: Tory writings from the Revolutionary era / narrative and editing by Catherine S. Crary; drawings by Cecile R. Johnson. — New York: McGraw-Hill, [1973] 481 p.: facsims.; 23 cm. — (Bicentennial of the American Revolution) 1. American loyalists 2. United States — History — Revolution, 1775-1783 — Sources I. T. II. Series.
E277.C72   973.3/14   *LC* 73-925   *ISBN* 007013460X

Hancock, Harold Bell, 1913-.   3.6958
The Loyalists of Revolutionary Delaware / Harold B. Hancock. — Newark: University of Delaware Press, c1977. 159 p.: ill.; 22 cm. 'A University of Delaware Bicentennial book.' Includes index. 1. American loyalists — Delaware. 2. Delaware — Politics and government — Revolution, 1775-1783 3. Delaware — Politics and government — 1775-1865 I. T.
E277.H26   973.3/14/09751   *LC* 76-14768   *ISBN* 0874131162

Palmer, Gregory.   3.6959
Biographical sketches of Loyalists of the American Revolution / by Gregory Palmer. — Westport, CT: Meckler, c1984. xxxvi, 959 p.; 24 cm. Rev. ed. of: Biographical sketches of Loyalists of the American Revolution / Lorenzo Sabine. 2nd ed. 1864. 1. American loyalists — Biography. I. Sabine, Lorenzo, 1803-1877. Biographical sketches of Loyalists of the American Revolution. II. T.
E277.P24 1984   973.3/14 19   *LC* 83-12137   *ISBN* 0930466144

Van Tyne, Claude Halstead, 1869-1930.   • 3.6960
The loyalists in the American revolution / by Claude Halstead Van Tyne. — New York: P. Smith, 1929. xii, 360 p.; 20 cm. 1. American loyalists 2. United States — History — Revolution, 1775-1883. I. T.
E277.V24 1929

Curwen, Samuel, 1715-1802.   3.6961
The journal of Samuel Curwen, loyalist. Edited by Andrew Oliver. — Cambridge, Mass.: Harvard University Press, for the Essex Institute, Salem, Mass., 1972. 2 v. (xxxiv, 1083 p.): illus.; 25 cm. — (The Loyalist papers) 1. Curwen, Samuel, 1715-1802. 2. American loyalists 3. United States — History — Revolution, 1775-1783 — Biography 4. England — Description and travel — 1701-1800 I. Oliver, Andrew, 1906- ed. II. T. III. Series.
E278.C9 A34 1972   *LC* 72-180150   *ISBN* 0674483804

Berkin, Carol.   3.6962
Jonathan Sewall: odyssey of an American loyalist. — New York: Columbia University Press, 1974. xi, 200 p.; 22 cm. Originally presented as the author's thesis, Columbia University. 1. De Coverly, Roger, Sir, 1728-1796. 2. American loyalists I. T.
E278.S48 B47 1974   973.3/14/0924 B   *LC* 74-10795   *ISBN* 0231038518

E301–453 Revolution to Civil War (1775/1783–1861)

Boorstin, Daniel J. (Daniel Joseph), 1914-.   3.6963
The Americans: the national experience / by Daniel J. Boorstin. — New York: Random House, c1965. 517 p. Continuation of the author's The Americans: the colonial experience. 1. National characteristics, American 2. United States — Civilization — 1783-1865 I. T.
E301.B6   *LC* 65-17440

Darling, Arthur B. (Arthur Burr), 1892-1971.   • 3.6964
Our rising empire, 1763–1803. — [Hamden, Conn.]: Archon Books, [1972, c1940] 595 p.; 24 cm. 1. United States — Politics and government — Colonial period, ca. 1600-1775 2. United States — Politics and government —

1783-1865 3. United States — Foreign relations 4. United States — Territorial expansion I. T.
E301.D23 1972   327.73   *LC* 72-183351   *ISBN* 0208003991

Greene, Evarts Boutell, 1870-1947.   • 3.6965
The revolutionary generation, 1763–1790, by Evarts Boutell Greene. — New York: The Macmillan company, 1943. xvii p., 1 l., 487 p.: front., plates, ports., maps (1 double), facsims. (1 double); 22 cm. — (History of American life. v. 4) 'Critical essay on authorities': p. 424-456. 1. United States — History — Colonial period, ca. 1600-1775 2. United States — History — Revolution, 1775-1783 3. United States — History — Confederation, 1783-1789 4. United States — Civilization — To 1783 I. T. II. Series.
E301.G75   973.27 973   *LC* 43-16080

E302 COLLECTED WORKS OF CONTEMPORARY STATESMEN

Adams, John, 1735-1826.   3.6966
Papers of John Adams / Robert J. Taylor, editor; Mary–Jo Kline, associate editor; Gregg L. Lint, assistant editor. — Cambridge, Mass.: Belknap Press of Harvard University Press, 1977. 2 v.; 26 cm. — (The Adams papers: Series III, General correspondence and other papers of the Adams statesmen) 1. Adams, John, 1735-1826. 2. Presidents — United States — Correspondence. 3. United States — Politics and government — Colonial period, ca. 1600-1775 — Sources. 4. Massachusetts — Politics and government — Colonial period, ca. 1600-1775 — Sources. 5. United States — Politics and government — Revolution, 1775-1783 — Sources. 6. United States — Politics and government — 1783-1809 — Sources. I. Taylor, Robert Joseph, 1917- II. T. III. Series.
E302.A275 1977   E302 A275 1977.   973.4/4/08   *LC* 77-4707   *ISBN* 0674654412

Franklin, Benjamin, 1706-1790.   • 3.6967
The papers of Benjamin Franklin / Leonard W. Labaree, editor; Whitfield J. Bell, Jr., associate editor. — New Haven: Yale University Press, 1959-. v.   : ill. (part fold., part col.), facsims., geneal. tables, ports.; 23 cm. Vols. 15- < 24 > edited by W.B. Willcox. 'Sponsored by the American Philosophical Society and Yale University.' 1. Franklin, Benjamin, 1706-1790. I. Labaree, Leonard Woods, 1897- ed. II. Willcox, William Bradford, 1907- ed. III. T.
E302.F82 1959   973.3/092/4   *LC* 59-12697   *ISBN* 0300016859

Greene, Nathanael, 1742-1786.   3.6968
The papers of General Nathanael Greene / Richard K. Showman, editor, Margaret Cobb and Robert E. McCarthy, assistant editors, assisted by Joyce Boulind, Noel P. Conlon, and Nathaniel N. Shipton. — Chapel Hill: Published for the Rhode Island Historical Society [by] University of North Carolina Press, c1976-<c1983 >. v. <1-3 >: ill.; 24 cm. 1. Greene, Nathanael, 1742-1786 — Correspondence. 2. United States. Army — Biography 3. United States. Continental Army — History — Sources. 4. Generals — United States — Correspondence. 5. United States — History — Revolution, 1775-1783 — Sources I. Showman, Richard K. II. Rhode Island Historical Society. III. T.
E302.G73 1976   973.3/3/0924 19

Hamilton, Alexander, 1757-1804.   • 3.6969
The papers of Alexander Hamilton. Harold C. Syrett, editor; Jacob E. Cooke, associate editor. — New York: Columbia University Press, 1961-79. 26 v.: illus., ports, maps.; 24 cm. Vols. 8-26 have various assistant and associate editors. 1. United States — History — Revolution, 1775-1783 — Sources 2. United States — History — Confederation, 1783-1789 — Sources. 3. United States — History — Constitutional period, 1789-1809 — Sources. I. Syrett, Harold Coffin, 1913- ed. II. Cooke, Jacob Ernest, 1924- ed. III. T.
E302.H2 1961   973 19   *LC* 61-15593

Jackson, Andrew, 1767-1845.   3.6970
The papers of Andrew Jackson / ed. by Harold D. Moser and Sharon Macpherson. — Knoxville: University of Tennessee Press, 1985 (c1984) 634 p.: ill.; 25 cm. 1. Jackson, Andrew, 1767-1845. 2. Presidents — United States — Correspondence. 3. United States — Politics and government — 1829-1837 — Sources. I. Smith, Sam B., 1929- II. Owsley, Harriet Fason Chappell. III. Moser, Harold D. IV. T.
E302.J35 1980   973.5/6/0924   *LC* 79-15078   *ISBN* 0870492195

Jay, John, 1745-1829.   3.6971
The correspondence and public papers of John Jay, 1763–1826. Edited by Henry P. Johnston. — New York: Da Capo Press, 1971. 4 v. in 1. Reprint of the 1890-1893 ed. 1. Jay, John, 1745-1829. 2. United States — Politics and government — 1783-1809 — Sources. 3. United States — Politics and government — Revolution, 1775-1783 — Sources. I. T.
E302.J423 1971   973.3/0924 B   *LC* 69-16639   *ISBN* 0306711249

Jefferson, Thomas, 1743-1826.   3.6972
The portable Thomas Jefferson / edited and with an introd. by Merrill D. Peterson. — New York: Viking Press, 1975. xlv, 589 p.; 19 cm. (The Viking

portable library; 80) 1. United States — Politics and government — Revolution, 1775-1783 — Collected works. 2. United States — Politics and government — 1783-1865 — Collected works. I. Peterson, Merrill D. ed. II. United States. President (1801-1809: Jefferson) III. T.
E302.J442 1975   973.4/6/0924   LC 74-5805   ISBN 0670703591.
ISBN 0670010804 pbk

Jefferson, Thomas, 1743-1826.   • **3.6973**
Papers / Julian P. Boyd, editor ... [et al.]. — Princeton, N.J.: Princeton University Press, 1950-. v.: ill., facsims. Editor, v. 21- Charles T. Cullen. I. Boyd, Julian P. (Julian Parks), 1903- II. Cullen, Charles T., 1940- III. T.
E302.J463   LC 50-7486 rev   ISBN 0691045828

Madison, James, 1751-1836.   **3.6974**
The mind of the founder: sources of the political thought of James Madison / edited with introd. and commentary by Marvin Meyers. — Indianapolis: Bobbs-Merrill [1973] liv, 581 p.; 21 cm. (The American heritage series, no. 39) 1. United States — History — 1783-1865 — Sources. I. Meyers, Marvin. ed. II. T.
E302.M185 1973   973.5/1   LC 72-158723   ISBN 0672517701
ISBN 067261183X

Madison, James, 1751-1836.   **3.6975**
The papers of James Madison / edited by R.A. Rutland. — [Chicago]: University of Chicago Press, 1973. 560 p.; ill., ports., maps; 25 cm. 1. Virginia — Politics and government — Revolution, 1775-1783 — Collected works. 2. United States — Politics and government — Revolution, 1775-1783 — Collected works. 3. United States — Politics and government — 1783-1865 — Collected works. I. Hutchinson, William Thomas, 1895- ed. II. Rachal, William M. E., ed. III. Rutland, Robert Allen, 1922- ed. IV. T.
E302.M19   973.5/1/0924   LC 62-9114

Mason, George, 1725-1792.   • **3.6976**
The papers of George Mason, 1725-1792. Robert A. Rutland, editor. — Chapel Hill: University of North Carolina Press, 1970. 3 v. (cxxvii, 1312 p.): illus., map, ports.; 25 cm. I. T.
E302.M38 1970   973.2/0924   LC 70-97016   ISBN 0807811343

Morris, Robert, 1734-1806.   **3.6977**
The papers of Robert Morris, 1781-1784 / E. James Ferguson, editor [and others]. — [Pittsburgh]: University of Pittsburgh Press, 1975. 400 p.: ill.; 25 cm. 1. Morris, Robert, 1734-1806. 2. United States — History — Revolution, 1775-1783 — Finance — Sources. I. Ferguson, E. James (Elmer James), 1917- II. Catanzariti, John, 1942- III. T.
E302.M82 1973   973.3/092/4   LC 72-91107   ISBN 082293485X

E302.1 POLITICAL HISTORY

Adams, Henry, 1838-1918.   • **3.6978**
History of the United States of America during the administration of Jefferson and Madison / Henry Adams; abridged and edited by Ernest Samuels. — Abridged ed. — Chicago: University of Chicago Press, c1967. xx, 425 p.: maps, ports; 21 cm. — (Classic American historians) 'The selection ... are taken from the nine volumes of the 1921 edition.' 1. United States — History — 1801-1809 2. United States — History — 1809-1817 I. Samuels, Ernest. II. T.
E302.1.A253   973.4   LC 67-21380

Banning, Lance, 1942-.   **3.6979**
The Jeffersonian persuasion: evolution of a party ideology / Lance Banning. — Ithaca, N.Y.: Cornell University Press, 1978. 307 p.; 22 cm. 1. Jefferson, Thomas, 1743-1826 — Political and social views. 2. Representative government and representation — United States — History. 3. Democracy 4. United States — Politics and government — 1783-1809 I. T.
E302.1.B2   320.5/0973   LC 77-14666   ISBN 0801411513

Lynd, Staughton.   • **3.6980**
Class conflict, slavery, and the United States Constitution; ten essays. Indianapolis, Bobbs-Merrill [1968, c1967] xiii, 288 p. geneal. table, maps. 22 cm. 1. United States Constitution — Addresses, essays, lectures. 2. Slavery in the United States — Addresses, essays, lectures. 3. United States — Politics and government — 1783-1809 — Addresses, essays, lectures. 4. United States — Politics and government — Revolution — Addresses, essays, lectures. I. T.
E302.1.L9   973   LC 67-21400

Maier, Pauline, 1938-.   **3.6981**
The old revolutionaries: political lives in the age of Samuel Adams / by Pauline Maier. — 1st ed. — New York: Knopf: distributed by Random House, 1980. xxii, 309 p.: facsim.; 22 cm. 1. Revolutionists — United States — Biography. 2. United States — History — Revolution, 1775-1783 — Biography 3. United States — Biography I. T.
E302.5.M23 1980   973.3/092/2 B   LC 80-7624   ISBN 0394510968

E302.6 BIOGRAPHY

E302.6 A–G

Davis, William C., 1946-.   **3.6982**
Breckinridge: statesman, soldier, symbol / William C. Davis. — Baton Rouge: Louisiana State University Press, [1974] xxii, 687 p., [7] leaves of plates: 18 ill.,; 24 cm. (Southern biography series.) Includes index. 1. Breckinridge, John Cabell, 1821-1875. I. T. II. Series.
E302.6.B84 D38   973.6/8/0924 B   LC 73-77658   ISBN 0807100684

Lomask, Milton.   **3.6983**
Aaron Burr: the conspiracy and years of exile, 1805–1836 / Milton Lomask. — New York: Farrar, Straus, Giroux, c1982. xviii, 475 p.; of plates: ill.; 24 cm. Includes index. 1. Burr, Aaron, 1756-1836. 2. Vice-Presidents — United States — Biography. 3. United States — Politics and government — 1783-1865 I. T.
E302.6.B9 L72   B   LC 78-31142   ISBN 0374100179

Malone, Dumas, 1892-.   • **3.6984**
The public life of Thomas Cooper, 1783–1839. Columbia, University of South Carolina Press, 1961. 434 p. illus. 23 cm. 1. Cooper, Thomas, 1759-1839. 2. United States — Politics and government — 1783-1865 I. T.
E302.6.C7 M2 1961   LC 61-18084

Franklin, Benjamin.   **3.6985**
The autobiography of Benjamin Franklin / edited by Leonard W. Labaree...[et al.]. — New Haven: Yale University Press, 1964. 351 p.: col. ill. 1. Franklin, Benjamin, 1706-1790. 2. Statesmen — United States — Biography. I. Labaree, Leonard Woods, 1897- II. Labaree, Leonard W. III. T.
E302.6F7A2 1964   923.273   LC 64-12653

Franklin, Benjamin, 1706-1790.   **3.6986**
The autobiography of Benjamin Franklin: a genetic text / edited by J. A. Leo Lemay and P. M. Zall. — Knoxville: University of Tennessee Press, c1981. lxiv, 288 p.: ill.; 24 cm. Includes bibliographical references and index. 1. Franklin, Benjamin, 1706-1790. 2. Statesmen — United States — Biography. I. Lemay, J. A. Leo (Joseph A. Leo), 1935- II. Zall, Paul M. III. T.
E302.6.F7 A2 1981b   973.3/092/4 B   LC 78-25907   ISBN 087049256X

Franklin, Benjamin, 1706-1790.   **3.6987**
Benjamin Franklin's autobiography: an authoritative text, backgrounds, criticism / edited by J.A. Leo Lemay and P.M. Zall. — 1st ed. — New York: Norton, c1986. xxi, 391 p.; 22 cm. — (A Norton critical edition) Includes index. 1. Franklin, Benjamin, 1706-1790. 2. Statesmen — United States — Biography. I. Lemay, J. A. Leo (Joseph A. Leo), 1935- II. Zall, Paul M. III. IV. Title: Autobiography.
E302.6.F7 A2 1986a   973.3/092/4 B 19   LC 84-3999   ISBN 0393017370

Aldridge, Alfred Owen, 1915-.   • **3.6988**
Franklin and his French contemporaries. — [New York] New York University Press, 1957. 260 p. 25 cm. Includes bibliography. 1. Franklin, Benjamin, 1706-1790. I. T.
E302.6.F8A47   923.273   LC 56-10778

Bowen, Catherine Drinker, 1897-1973.   **3.6989**
The most dangerous man in America: scenes from the life of Benjamin Franklin. — [1st ed.]. — Boston: Little, Brown, [1974] xiv, 274 p.: port.; 24 cm. 'An Atlantic Monthly Press book.' 1. Franklin, Benjamin, 1706-1790. I. T.
E302.6.F8 B79   973.3/2/0924 B   LC 74-10658   ISBN 0316103969

Clark, Ronald William.   **3.6990**
Benjamin Franklin: a biography / Ronald W. Clark. — New York: Random House, c1983. viii, 530 p., [16] leaves of plates: ill.; 24 cm. Includes index. 1. Franklin, Benjamin, 1706-1790. 2. Statesmen — United States — Biography. I. T.
E302.6.F8 C54 1983   973.3/092/4 B 19   LC 82-40115   ISBN 0394502221

Crane, Verner Winslow, 1889-.   • **3.6991**
Benjamin Franklin and a rising people. — [1st ed.]. — Boston: Little, Brown, [1954] 219 p.; 21 cm. — (The Library of American biography) I. T.
E302.6.F8 C77 1954   923.273   LC 54-5136

Lopez, Claude Anne.   **3.6992**
The private Franklin: the man and his family / by Claude–Anne Lopez and Eugenia W. Herbert. — 1st ed. — New York: Norton, [1975] xv, 361 p., [8]

leaves of plates: ill.; 24 cm. Includes index. 1. Franklin, Benjamin, 1706-1790. I. Herbert, Eugenia W. joint author. II. T.
E302.6.F8 L82 1975   973.3/092/4 B   *LC* 75-17530   *ISBN* 039307496X

Tourtellot, Arthur Bernon.   **3.6993**
Benjamin Franklin: the shaping of genius: the Boston Years / Arthur Bernon Tourtellot. 1st ed. — Garden City, N.Y.: Doubleday, 1977. xiii, 459 p., [12] leaves of plates: ill., map (on lining papers); 24 cm. Includes index. 1. Franklin, Benjamin, 1706-1790. 2. Statesmen — United States — Biography. I. T.
E302.6.F8 T7   973.3/092/4 B   *LC* 76-12054   *ISBN* 0385032307

Van Doren, Carl, 1885-1950.   • **3.6994**
Benjamin Franklin / by Carl Van Doren. — New York, The Viking press, 1938 [i. e. 1939] xix p., 2 l., [3]-845 p. ports. 24 cm. 1. Franklin, Benjamin, 1706-1790. I. T.
E302.6.F8 V36   *LC* 40-2537

Godbold, E. Stanly.   **3.6995**
Christopher Gadsden and the American Revolution / E. Stanly Godbold, Jr., Robert H. Woody. — 1st ed. — Knoxville: University of Tennessee Press, c1982. xi, 302 p.: ill.; 22 cm. Includes index. 1. Gadsden, Christopher, 1724-1805. 2. Statesmen — United States — Biography. 3. United States — Politics and government — Revolution, 1775-1783 4. South Carolina — Politics and government — Revolution, 1775-1783 I. Woody, Robert H. (Robert Hilliard), 1903- II. T.
E302.6.G15 G62 1982   973.3/092/4 19   *LC* 82-6915   *ISBN* 0870493620

Walters, Ray, 1912-.   • **3.6996**
Albert Gallatin: Jeffersonian financier and diplomat / Raymond Walters, Jr. — New York: Macmillan, 1957. viii, 461 p. Includes index. 1. Gallatin, Albert, 1761-1849. I. T.
E302.6.G16 W3   *LC* 57-8267

Billias, George Athan, 1919-.   **3.6997**
Elbridge Gerry, founding father and republican statesman / by George Athan Billias. — New York: McGraw-Hill, c1976. xviii, 442 p., [3] leaves of plates: ill.; 24 cm. Includes index. 1. Gerry, Elbridge, 1744-1814. I. T.
E302.6.G37 B54   973.3/092/4 B   *LC* 76-13481   *ISBN* 0070052697

E302.6 H–Z

Cooke, Jacob Ernest, 1924-.   **3.6998**
Alexander Hamilton / Jacob Ernest Cooke. — New York: Scribner's, c1982. vi, 277 p., [8] p. of plates: ill., ports.; 24 cm. 1. Hamilton, Alexander, 1757-1804. 2. Statesmen — United States — Biography. 3. United States — Politics and government — 1783-1809 I. T.
E302.6.H2 C73 1982   973.4/092/4 B 19   *LC* 81-18223   *ISBN* 0684173441

McDonald, Forrest.   **3.6999**
Alexander Hamilton: a biography / Forrest McDonald. — 1st ed. — New York: Norton, c1979. xiii, 464 p.; 24 cm. 1. Hamilton, Alexander, 1757-1804. 2. Statesmen — United States — Biography. 3. United States — Politics and government — 1783-1809 4. United States — Economic conditions — To 1865 I. T.
E302.6.H2 M32 1979   973.4/092/4 B   *LC* 78-26554   *ISBN* 0393012182

Hecht, Marie B.   **3.7000**
Odd destiny, the life of Alexander Hamilton / by Marie B. Hecht. — New York: Macmillan, c1982. xii, 464 p.; 25 cm. Includes index. 1. Hamilton, Alexander, 1757-1804. 2. Statesmen — United States — Biography. 3. United States — Politics and government — 1783-1809 I. T.
E302.6.H2 H42 1982   973.4/092/4 B 19   *LC* 81-18578   *ISBN* 0025501801

McCaughey, Elizabeth P., 1948-.   **3.7001**
From Loyalist to Founding Father: the political odyssey of William Samuel Johnson / Elizabeth P. McCaughey. — New York: Columbia University Press, 1980. xi, 362 p.: ports.; 24 cm. Includes index. 1. Johnson, William Samuel, 1727-1819. 2. United States. Congress. Senate — Biography. 3. Columbia University — Presidents — Biography. 4. Legislators — United States — Biography. 5. College presidents — United States — Biography. 6. Connecticut — Politics and government — Colonial period, ca. 1600-1775 7. United States — Politics and government — 1783-1789 I. T.
E302.6.J7 M3   973.3/092/4 B   *LC* 79-17042   *ISBN* 0231045069

Ernst, Robert, 1915-.   • **3.7002**
Rufus King: American federalist. — Chapel Hill, Published for the Institute of Early American History and Culture at Williamsburg, Va., by University of

North Carolina Press [1968] ix, 446 p. ports. 24 cm. 1. King, Rufus, 1755-1827. I. Institute of Early American History and Culture (Williamsburg, Va.) II. T.
E302.6.K5 E7   973.4/0924 B   *LC* 68-15747

Potts, Louis W., 1944-.   **3.7003**
Arthur Lee, a virtuous revolutionary / Louis W. Potts. — Baton Rouge: Louisiana State University Press, c1981. xiv, 315 p., [4] leaves of plates: ill.; 24 cm. — (Southern biography series.) Includes index. 1. Lee, Arthur, 1740-1792. 2. Diplomats — United States — Biography. 3. United States — Foreign relations — Revolution, 1775-1783 I. T. II. Series.
E302.6.L38 P67   973.3/2/0924 B 19   *LC* 80-21831   *ISBN* 0807107859

Beveridge, Albert Jeremiah, 1862-1927.   • **3.7004**
The life of John Marshall, by Albert J. Beveridge ... — Boston and New York, Houghton Mifflin company, 1919. 4 v. col. fronts., plates, ports, facsims. 23 cm. 'Works' cited at end of each volume. 1. Marshall, John, 1755-1835. I. T.
E302.6.M4B582   923.473   *LC* 33-29106

Rutland, Robert Allen, 1922-.   • **3.7005**
George Mason, reluctant statesman / foreword by Dumas Malone. — Williamsburg, Va., Colonial Williamsburg; [1961] xvi 123 p. illus. 21 cm. (Williamsburg in America series, 4) 1. Mason, George, 1725-1792. I. T. II. Series.
E302.6.M45Rx   *LC* 61-11480

Ver Steeg, Clarence Lester, 1922-.   • **3.7006**
Robert Morris: revolutionary financier. With an analysis of his earlier career. Philadelphia, University of Pennsylvania Press, 1954. 276 p. 24 cm. Issued also in microfilm form as thesis, Columbia University. 1. Morris, Robert, 1734-1806. I. T.
E302.6.M8 V4 1954   *LC* 54-7107

O'Connor, John E.   **3.7007**
William Paterson, lawyer and statesman, 1745-1806 / John E. O'Connor. — New Brunswick, N.J.: Rutgers University Press, c1979. xv, 351 p.; 24 cm. Includes index. 1. Paterson, William, 1745-1806. 2. United States. Congress. Senate — Biography. 3. Legislators — United States — Biography. 4. Judges — United States — Biography. 5. New Jersey — Politics and government — Revolution, 1775-1783 6. United States — Politics and government — 1783-1809 7. New Jersey — Governors — Biography. I. T.
E302.6.P3 O27   973.4/092/4 B   *LC* 79-15966   *ISBN* 0813508800

Clarfield, Gerard H.   **3.7008**
Timothy Pickering and the American Republic / Gerard H. Clarfield. — Pittsburgh, PA.: University of Pittsburgh Press, c1980. viii, 320 p.: port.; 24 cm. 1. Pickering, Timothy, 1745-1829. 2. Statesmen — United States — Biography. 3. United States — History — Revolution, 1775-1783 4. United States — Politics and government — 1783-1809 I. T.
E302.6.P5 C553   973.4/092/4 B   *LC* 79-24326   *ISBN* 0822934140

Zahniser, Marvin R.   • **3.7009**
Charles Cotesworth Pinckney, founding father, by Marvin R. Zahniser. Chapel Hill, Published for the Institute of Early American History and culture, Williamsburg, Va., by the University of North Carolina Press [1967] ix, 295 p. port. 24 cm. 1. Pinckney, Charles Cotesworth, 1746-1825. I. Institute of Early American History and Culture (Williamsburg, Va.) II. T.
E302.6.P55 Z3   973.4/0924 B   *LC* 67-28010

Turner, Lynn W.   • **3.7010**
William Plumer of New Hampshire, 1759–1850 / by Lynn W. Turner. — Chapel Hill, N.C.: Published for the Institute of Early American History and Culture at Williamsburg, Virginia by The University of North Carolina Press, 1962. 366 p.: port.; 24 cm. Based on thesis, Harvard University. 1. Plumer, William, 1759-1850. 2. Statesmen — United States — Biography I. T.
E302.6.P73 T8   *LC* 62-4988

Dawidoff, Robert.   **3.7011**
The education of John Randolph / Robert Dawidoff. — 1st ed. — New York: Norton, c1979. 346 p.: port.; 21 cm. Includes index. 1. Randolph, John, 1773-1833. 2. United States. Congress. House — Biography. 3. Legislators — United States — Biography. 4. United States — Politics and government — 1783-1865 I. T.
E302.6.R2 D28 1979   973.4/092/4 B   *LC* 79-16178   *ISBN* 0393012425

Mudge, Eugene Tenbroeck.   • **3.7012**
The social philosophy of John Taylor of Caroline; a study in Jeffersonian democracy [by] Eugene Tenbroeck Mudge. New York, Columbia University Press, 1939. xii, 227 p. 24 cm. (Columbia studies in American culture. no. 4) 1. Taylor, John, 1753-1824. 2. Political science I. T.
E302.6.T23 M8   *LC* 40-4266

Smith, Page.   • **3.7013**
James Wilson, Founding Father, 1742–1798. — Chapel Hill, N.C.: University of North Carolina Press for the Institute of Early American History and

Culture, [c1956] xii, 426 p.: port.; 24 cm. 1. Wilson, James, 1742-1798. 2. Statesmen — United States — Biography. I. T.
E302.6.W64 S6   973.3/092/4 B 19   *LC* a 56-2940

E303–440 BY PERIOD

E303–309 1775–1789. Confederation, 1783–1789

Burnett, Edmund Cody, 1864-.   • **3.7014**
The Continental congress. New York, The Macmillan company, 1941. xvii, 757 p. 25 cm. 1. United States. Continental Congress. 2. United States — Politics and government — Revolution, 1775-1783 I. T.
E303.B93   *LC* 41-20697

United States. Continental Congress.   **3.7015**
Index/Journals of the Continental Congress 1774–1789 / compiled by Kenneth E. Harris and Steven D. Tilley. — Washington: National Archives and Records Service, General Services Administration, 1976. xiv, 429 p. Consolidated index to the Library of Congress edition of Journals of the Continental Congress. 1. United States — History — Revolution, 1775-1783 — Sources I. Harris, Kenneth E., 1943-. II. Tilley, Steven D., 1947-. III. T.
E303.C6

Fiske, John, 1842-1901.   • **3.7016**
The critical period of American history, 1783–1789 / by John Fiske ... — Boston; New York: Houghton, Mifflin and company, 1888. xviii, 368 p.; 20 cm. 1. United States — History — Confederation, 1783-1789 I. T.
E303.F54   *LC* 01-670

Jensen, Merrill.   • **3.7017**
The New Nation; a history of the United States during the Confederation, 1781–1789. [1st ed.] New York, Knopf, 1950. xvii, 433, xi p. 24 cm. 'Essay on the sources': p. 429-432. 1. United States — History — Confederation, 1783-1789 I. T.
E303.J45 1950   973.318   *LC* 50-9344

E310–337 Constitutional Period (1789–1809)

Charles, Joseph, 1906-1952.   • **3.7018**
The origins of the American party system; three essays. Foreword by Frederick Merk. — Williamsburg, Va.: Institute of Early American History and Culture, 1956. 147 p.; 25 cm. 'A reprint from the William and Mary quarterly; a magazine of early American history, third series, volume XII, numbers 2, 3, and 4 (1955)' 1. Political parties — United States — History. 2. United States — Politics and government — Constitutional period, 1789-1809 I. T.
E310.C5   973.4   *LC* 57-1843

Circular letters of Congressmen to their constituents, 1789–1829   **3.7019**
/ edited, by Noble E. Cunningham, Jr.,; editorial assistant, Dorothy Hagberg Cappel.
Chapel Hill: Published for the Institute of Early American History and Culture, Williamsburg, Va., by the University of North Carolina Press, c1978. 3 v. (lxiii, 1634 p.); 24 cm. 1. United States — Politics and government — 1789-1815 — Sources. 2. United States — Politics and government — 1815-1861 — Sources. I. Cunningham, Noble E., 1926- II. Cappel, Dorothy Hagberg. III. Institute of Early American History and Culture (Williamsburg, Va.)
E310.C55   328.73/04   *LC* 76-29032   *ISBN* 0807812897

The Democratic–Republican societies, 1790–1800: a   **3.7020**
documentary sourcebook of constitutions, declarations,
addresses, resolutions, and toasts / edited, with an introd., by
Philip S. Foner; foreword by Richard B. Morris.
Westport, Conn.: Greenwood Press, 1977 (c1976). xiii, 484 p.; 25 cm. Includes index. 1. United States — Politics and government — Constitutional period, 1789-1809 — Sources. I. Foner, Philip Sheldon, 1910-
E310.D4   320.9/73/04   *LC* 76-5260   *ISBN* 0837189071

Link, Eugene Perry, 1908-.   • **3.7021**
Democratic–Republican societies, 1790–1800. — New York: Octagon Books, 1965 [c1942] xii, 256 p.: map; 24 cm. — (Columbia studies in American culture; no. 9) 1. Political clubs 2. United States — History — Constitutional period, 1789-1809 I. T. II. Series.
E310.L6 1965   973.4   *LC* 65-16776

Miller, John Chester, 1907-.   • **3.7022**
The Federalist era, 1789–1801 / by John C. Miller. — 1st Harper Torchbook ed. — New York: Harper, 1960. xv, 304 p.: ill. — (New American Nation Series) 1. United States — History — Constitutional period, 1789-1809 I. T.
E310.M5   *LC* 60-15321

Schachner, Nathan, 1895-.   • **3.7023**
The Founding Fathers. New York, Putnam [1954] 630 p. 22 cm. 1. United States — History — Constitutional period, 1789-1809 I. T.
E310.S4   *LC* 54-5497

Stewart, Donald Henderson, 1911-.   • **3.7024**
The opposition press of the Federalist period [by] Donald H. Stewart. — Albany: State University of New York Press, [1969] xiii, 957 p.; 24 cm. 1. American newspapers 2. Journalism — Political aspects — United States. 3. United States — Politics and government — Constitutional period, 1789-1809 I. T.
E310.S8   329/.2   *LC* 69-11319   *ISBN* 0873950429

Gilbert, Felix, 1905-.   • **3.7025**
To the Farewell address; ideas of early American foreign policy. — Princeton, N. J., Princeton University Press, 1961. 173 p. 23 cm. Includes bibliography. 1. Washington, George, Pres. U.S., 1732-1799. Farewell address. 2. U.S. — For. rel. I. T.
E310.7.G5   327.73   *LC* 61-7404

E311–337 BY PRESIDENTIAL ADMINISTRATION

E311–320 Washington, 1789–1797

De Conde, Alexander.   • **3.7026**
Entangling alliance: politics & diplomacy under George Washington / by Alexander DeConde. — Durham, N.C.: Duke University Press, 1958. xiv, 536 p. 1. United States — Foreign relations — 1789-1797 2. United States — Foreign relations — France 3. France — Foreign relations — United States I. T.
E311.D4   *LC* 58-8500

Cunliffe, Marcus.   • **3.7027**
George Washington, man and monument. [1st ed.] Boston, Little, Brown [1958] 234 p. illus. 22 cm. 1. Washington, George, 1732-1799. I. T.
E312.C88   923.173   *LC* 58-7859

Freeman, Douglas Southall, 1886-1953.   • **3.7028**
George Washington: a biography / by Douglas Southall Freeman. — New York: Scribner, 1948-1957. 7 v.: facsims, maps, ports.; 24 cm. 1. Washington, George, Pres. U.S., 1732-1799. I. Carroll, John Alexander. II. Ashworth, Mary Wells. III. T.
E312.F82   *LC* 48-8880

Jones, Robert Francis, 1935-.   **3.7029**
George Washington / by Robert F. Jones. — Boston: Twayne Publishers, 1979. 178 p.: port.; 21 cm. (Twayne's world leaders series; TWLS 80) Includes index. 1. Washington, George, 1732-1799. 2. Presidents — United States — Biography I. T.
E312.J79   973.4/1/0924 B   *LC* 79-16615   *ISBN* 0805777261

Flexner, James Thomas.   **3.7030**
George Washington / by James Thomas Flexner. — Boston: Little, Brown, 1965-1972. 4 v.: ill., facsim., map (on lining papers) ports.; 25 cm. 1. Washington, George, 1732-1799. 2. Presidents — United States — Biography I. T.
E312.2.F6   973.20924 B   *LC* 65-21361

Knollenberg, Bernhard, 1892-.   • **3.7031**
Washington and the Revolution, a reappraisal; Gates, Conway, and the Continental Congress. [Hamden, Conn.] Archon Books, 1968 [c1940] xvi, 269 p. port. 22 cm. 1. Washington, George, 1732-1799. 2. United States — History — Revolution, 1775-1783 I. T.
E312.25.K64 1968   973.4/1   *LC* 68-16331

Nettels, Curtis Putnam.   • **3.7032**
George Washington and American independence. — [1st ed.]. — Boston, Little, Brown, 1951. 338 p. ports., maps. 22 cm. Bibliography: p. [313]-324. 1. Washington, George, Pres. U.S., 1732-1799. 2. U.S. — Hist. — Revolution. I. T.
E312.25.N4   923.173   *LC* 51-6375

Flexner, James Thomas, 1908-.   **3.7033**
George Washington and the new nation, 1783–1793. [1st ed.] Boston, Little, Brown [1970] xi, 466 p. illus., facsims., fold. map, plan, ports. 25 cm. ([His George Washington, v. 3]) 1. Washington, George, 1732-1799. I. T.
E312.29.F55   973.4/1/0924   *LC* 78-117042

Wills, Garry, 1934-.   **3.7034**
Cincinnatus: George Washington and the Enlightenment / Garry Wills. — 1st ed. — Garden City, N.Y.: Doubleday, 1984. xxvi, 272 p., [4] p. of plates: ill.; 24 cm. Includes index. 1. Washington, George, 1732-1799 — Addresses, essays, lectures. 2. Enlightenment — Addresses, essays, lectures. 3. Heroes — United States — Addresses, essays, lectures. 4. United States — Intellectual life — 1783-1865 — Addresses, essays, lectures. I. T.
E312.62.W54 1984   973.4/1/0924 19   *LC* 81-43152   *ISBN* 0385175620

Washington, George, 1732-1799.   • **3.7035**
The writings of George Washington from the original manuscript sources 1745–1799 / prepared under the direction of the United States George Washington Bicentennial Commission and published by authority of Congress; John C. Fitzpatrick, editor. — Westport, Conn.: Greenwood Press [1970] 39 v.: ill., facsims., maps, plans, ports.; 22 cm. Reprint of the 1931-1944 ed. 'General index by David M. Matteson': v. 38-39. 1. Washington family 2. United States — History 3. United States — History — Revolution, 1775-1783 I. Fitzpatrick, John Clement, 1876-1940. II. Matteson, David Maydole, 1871-1949. III. George Washington Bicentennial Commission (U.S.) IV. T.
E312.7 1970   973.2/6   *LC* 68-31012   *ISBN* 0837131723

Washington, George, 1732-1799.   **3.7036**
The diaries of George Washington / Donald Jackson, editor, Dorothy Twohig, associate editor. Charlottesville: University Press of Virginia, 1978. 2 v.: ill.; 24 cm. Includes indexes. I. Jackson, Donald Dean, 1919- II. Twohig, Dorothy. III. T.
E312.8 1976   973.4/1/0924 B   *LC* 75-41365   *ISBN* 0813906431

Bemis, Samuel Flagg, 1891-1973.   • **3.7037**
Pinckney's treaty: America's advantage from Europe's distress, 1783–1800. Rev. ed. New Haven: Yale University Press, 1960. 372 p. 1. San Lorenzo treaty, 1795. 2. United States — Foreign relations — Spain. 3. Spain — Foreign relations — United States. 4. Mississippi River Valley — History — To 1803 I. T.
E313.B44 1960   *LC* 60-13681

Ritcheson, Charles R.   • **3.7038**
Aftermath of revolution; British policy toward the United States, 1783–1795 [by] Charles R. Ritcheson. — Dallas: Southern Methodist University Press, [1969] xiv, 505 p.; 24 cm. 1. Jay's treaty, 1794 2. U.S. — Foreign relations — Gt. Brit. 3. Gt. Brit. — Foreign relations — U.S. I. T.
E313.R5   327.42/073   *LC* 77-86328

Bemis, Samuel Flagg, 1891-1973.   • **3.7039**
Jay's treaty: a study in commerce and diplomacy / by Samuel Flagg Bemis. — Rev. ed. — New Haven: Yale University Press, 1962. xx, 526 p.: map; 21 cm. 1. United States. Treaties, etc., 1789-1797 (Washington) 2. Great Britain. Treaties, etc., 1760-1820 (George III) 3. Jay's treaty, 1794 4. United States — Foreign relations — Great Britain. 5. Great Britain — Foreign relations — United States. I. T.
E314.B453 1962a   *LC* 62-8233

Combs, Jerald A.   • **3.7040**
The Jay treaty; political battleground of the Founding Fathers [by] Jerald A. Combs. — Berkeley: University of California Press, 1970. xi, 254 p.; 24 cm. 1. Jay's treaty, 1794 2. U.S. — Foreign relations — Gt. Brit. 3. Gt. Brit. — Foreign relations — U.S. I. T.
E314.C6   327.73/042   *LC* 70-84044   *ISBN* 0520015738

Baldwin, Leland Dewitt, 1897-.   • **3.7041**
Whiskey rebels; the story of a frontier uprising. [Pittsburgh] University of Pittsburgh press, 1939. 6 p.l., 326 p., 1 l. illus. 24 cm. 1. Whisky insurrection, 1794. I. Western Pennsylvania historical survey. II. T.
E315.B25   *LC* 39-11763

E321–330 Adams, 1797–1801

Kurtz, Stephen G.   • **3.7042**
The Presidency of John Adams: the collapse of Federalism, 1795–1800. — Philadelphia: University of Pennsylvania Press [1957] 448 p.: ill.; 22 cm. 1. Adams, John, 1735-1826. 2. United States — Politics and government I. T.
E321.K8   973.44   *LC* 57-7764

Adams, John, 1735-1826.   • **3.7043**
Diary and autobiography / L. H. Butterfield, editor, Leonard C. Faber and Wendell D. Garrett, assistant editors. — Cambridge: Belknap Press of Harvard University Press, 1961. 4 v.: ill., facsims., maps, ports; 26 cm. — (Adams papers. Diaries.) I. Butterfield, L. H. (Lyman Henry), 1909- II. Faber, Leonard C. III. Garrett, Wendell D. IV. T. V. Series.
E322.A3   *LC* 60-5387

Adams, John, 1735-1826.   • **3.7044**
The Adams-Jefferson letters: the complete correspondence between Thomas Jefferson and Abigail and John Adams / ed. by Lester J. Cappon. — Chapel Hill: Published for the Institute of Early American History and Culture at Williamsburg, Va., by the University of North Carolina Press, c1959. 2 v. ([lix], 638 p., [2] leaves of plates): ports.; 24 cm. I. Adams, Abigail, 1744-1818. II. Jefferson, Thomas, 1743-1826. III. Cappon, Lester Jesse, 1900- IV. T.
E322.A516   *LC* 59-16475

Adams, Charles Francis, 1807-1886.   • **3.7045**
The life of John Adams / begun by John Quincy Adams; completed by Charles Francis Adams. — Rev. and corr. Philadelphia, Lippincott, 1871. St. Clair Shores, Mich.: Scholarly Press, 1971. 2 v.; 22 cm. 1. Adams, John, 1735-1826. 2. Presidents — United States — Biography I. Adams, John Quincy, 1767-1848. II. T.
E322.A52 1971   973.4/4/0924 B   *LC* 78-108455   *ISBN* 0403004705

Chinard, Gilbert, 1881-1972.   • **3.7046**
Honest John Adams. Boston, Little, Brown, and company, 1933. xii p., 3 l., [3]-359 p. front., plates, ports. 24 cm. 1. Adams, John, President, U. S. 1735-1826. I. T.
E322.C47   *LC* 33-32200

Morgan, Edmund Sears.   **3.7047**
The meaning of independence: John Adams, George Washington, Thomas Jefferson / by Edmund S. Morgan. — Charlottesville: University Press of Virginia, 1976. 85 p.: ports.; 24 cm. (Richard lectures for 1975, University of Virginia) 1. Adams, John, 1735-1826 — Addresses, essays, lectures. 2. Washington, George, 1732-1799 — Addresses, essays, lectures. 3. Jefferson, Thomas, 1743-1826 — Addresses, essays, lectures. I. T.
E322.M85   973.3/13/0922   *LC* 76-8438   *ISBN* 0813906946

Shaw, Peter, 1936-.   **3.7048**
The character of John Adams / by Peter Shaw. — Chapel Hill: Published for the Institute of Early American History and Culture, Williamsburg, Va., by the University of North Carolina Press, c1976. ix, 324 p., [3] leaves of plates: port.; 21 cm. 1. Adams, John, 1735-1826. 2. Presidents — United States — Biography I. Institute of Early American History and Culture (Williamsburg, Va.) II. T.
E322.S54   973.4/4/0924 B   *LC* 75-14306   *ISBN* 0807812544

Smith, Page.   • **3.7049**
John Adams / Page Smith. — 1st ed. — Garden City, N.Y.: Doubleday, 1962. 2 v. (xx, 1170 p., [16] leaves of plates): ill., ports. I. T.
E322.S64   *LC* 63-7188

Adams family. Archives.   • **3.7050**
Adams family correspondence. L. H. Butterfield, editor; Wendell D. Garrett, associate editor; Marjorie E. Sprague, assistant editor. Cambridge, Belknap Press of Harvard University Press, 1963-. v. illus., ports., maps, charts, facsims. 26 cm. (The Adams papers, ser., 2) Index. I. Butterfield, L. H. (Lyman Henry), 1909- ed. II. T. III. Series.
E322.1.A27   929.2   *LC* 63-14964   *ISBN*

Adams, Abigail, 1744-1818.   **3.7051**
The book of Abigail and John: selected letters of the Adams family, 1762–1784 / edited and with an introd. by L. H. Butterfield, Marc Friedlaender, and Mary–Jo Kline. — Cambridge, Mass.: Harvard University Press, 1975. ix, 411 p., [1] leaf of plates: ill.; 24 cm. Includes index. 1. Adams, Abigail, 1744-1818. 2. Adams, John, 1735-1826. I. Adams, John, 1735-1826. joint author. II. Butterfield, L. H. (Lyman Henry), 1909- III. Friedlaender, Marc, 1905- IV. Kline, Mary-Jo. V. T.
E322.1.A293   973.4/4/0924   *LC* 75-17509   *ISBN* 0674078551

Adams, Abigail, 1744-1818.   • **3.7052**
New letters of Abigail Adams, 1788–1801. Boston, Houghton Mifflin Co., 1947. xiii, 281 p. illus., ports., geneal. tables. 25 cm. I. Cranch, Mary (Smith), 1741-1811. II. Mitchell, Stewart, 1892- ed. III. T.
E322.1.A37   920.7   *LC* 47-11763

Akers, Charles W.   **3.7053**
Abigail Adams, an American woman / Charles W. Akers. — Boston: Little, Brown, c1980. x, 207 p., [1] leaf of plates: ill.; 20 cm. (Library of American biography.) Includes index. 1. Adams, Abigail, 1744-1818. 2. Adams, John, 1735-1826. 3. Presidents — United States — Wives — Biography. I. T. II. Series.
E322.1.A38 A35   973.4/4/0924 B 19   *LC* 79-2241   *ISBN* 0316020400

Withey, Lynne.   **3.7054**
Dearest friend: a life of Abigail Adams / Lynne Withey. — New York: Free Press; London: Collier Macmillan Publishers, c1981. xiv, 369 p., [8] p. of plates: ill.; 25 cm. Includes index. 1. Adams, Abigail, 1744-1818. 2. Adams, John, 1735-1826. 3. Presidents — United States — Wives — Biography. I. T.
E322.1.A38 W56   973.4/4/0924 B 19   *LC* 80-70694   *ISBN* 0029347602

De Conde, Alexander.   • 3.7055
The quasi–war: the politics and diplomacy of the undeclared war with France
1797–1801. — New York: Scribner, [1966] xiv, 498 p.: ill., map (on lining
papers) ports.; 24 cm. Sequel to Entangling alliance. 1. United States —
History — War with France, 1798-1800 2. United States — Foreign relations
— France 3. France — Foreign relations — United States 4. United States —
Politics and government — 1797-1801 I. T.
E323.D4   973.45   *LC* 66-24492

Miller, John Chester, 1907-.   • 3.7056
Crisis in freedom: the Alien and Sedition acts. — [1st ed.]. — Boston: Little,
Brown, 1951. 253 p.; 22 cm. 'An Atlantic Monthly Press book.' 1. Alien and
Sedition laws, 1798 2. United States — Politics and government — 1797-1801
I. T.
E327.M5   973.44   *LC* 51-14177

Smith, James Morton.   • 3.7057
Freedom's fetters: the Alien and Sedition laws and American civil liberties. —
Ithaca: Cornell University Press, [1956- v.   ; 24 cm. — (Cornell studies in
civil liberty) 1. Alien and Sedition laws, 1798 I. T.
E327.S59   973.44   *LC* 56-2434

E331–337 Jefferson, 1801–1809

Fischer, David Hackett, 1935-.   • 3.7058
The revolution of American conservatism: the Federalist party in the era of
Jeffersonian democracy. — [1st ed.] New York: Harper & Row [1965] xx,
455 p.; 25 cm. Bibliographical footnotes. 1. Federal Party (U.S.) 2. United
States — Politics and government — 1801-1815 I. T.
E331.F5   973.4   *LC* 65-14680

McDonald, Forrest.   3.7059
The Presidency of Thomas Jefferson / by Forrest McDonald. Lawrence:
University Press of Kansas, c1976. xi, 201 p., [1] leaf of plates: port.; 24 cm.
(American presidency series). Includes index. 1. United States — Politics and
government — 1801-1809 I. T. II. Series.
E331.M32   320.9/73/046   *LC* 76-803   *ISBN* 0700601473

Spivak, Burton.   3.7060
Jefferson's English crisis: commerce, embargo, and the republican revolution /
Burton Spivak. — Charlottesville: University Press of Virginia, 1979. xiii,
250 p.; 25 cm. Includes index. 1. Jefferson, Thomas, 1743-1826. 2. United
States — Politics and government — 1801-1809 3. United States — Foreign
relations — 1801-1809 I. T.
E331.S68   973.4/6/0924   *LC* 78-13110   *ISBN* 0813908051

Brodie, Fawn McKay, 1915-.   3.7061
Thomas Jefferson, an intimate history [by] Fawn M. Brodie. [1st ed.] New
York, Norton [1974] 591 p. illus. 23 cm. 1. Jefferson, Thomas, 1743-1826. I. T.
E332.B787   973.4/6/0924 B   *LC* 73-11348   *ISBN* 0393074803

Malone, Dumas, 1892-.   • 3.7062
Jefferson and his time. — [1st ed.]. — Boston: Little, Brown, 1948-<1981>. v.
<1-6> illus., ports., maps, 23 cm. 1. Jefferson, Thomas, 1743-1826.
2. Presidents — United States — Biography I. T.
E332.M25   973.4/6/0924 B 19   *LC* 48-5972

Peterson, Merrill D.   • 3.7063
Thomas Jefferson and the new nation; a biography [by] Merrill D. Peterson.
New York, Oxford University Press, 1970. ix, 1072 p. illus., ports. 24 cm.
1. Jefferson, Thomas, 1743-1826. I. T.
E332.P45   973.4/6/0924 B   *LC* 70-110394

Jackson, Donald Dean, 1919-.   3.7064
Thomas Jefferson & the Stony Mountains: exploring the West from Monticello
/ Donald Jackson. — Urbana: University of Illinois Press, c1981. xii, 339 p.:
maps; 24 cm. Includes index. 1. Jefferson, Thomas, 1743-1826 — Views on the
West. 2. Jefferson, Thomas, 1743-1826 — Books and reading. 3. West (U.S.)
— Description and travel — To 1848 I. T.
E332.2.J32   973.4/6/0924   *LC* 80-10546   *ISBN* 0252008235

Peterson, Merrill D.   • 3.7065
The Jefferson image in the American mind. New York: Oxford University
Press, 1960. 548 p.; 21 cm. 1. Jefferson, Thomas, 1743-1826 — Influence. I. T.
E332.2.P4   923.173   *LC* 60-6140

De Conde, Alexander.   3.7066
This affair of Louisiana / by Alexander DeConde. New York: Scribner, c1976.
x, 325 p., [6] leaves of plates: ill.; 24 cm. Includes index. 1. Louisiana Purchase
2. United States — Territorial expansion I. T.
E333.D42   973.4/6   *LC* 76-12468   *ISBN* 0684146878

McKee, Christopher.   3.7067
Edward Preble; a naval biography, 1761–1807. — Annapolis: Naval Institute
Press, 1972. x, 394 p.: illus.; 24 cm. 1. Preble, Edward, 1761-1807. I. T.
E335.P78 M32   359.3/31/0924   *LC* 76-151092   *ISBN* 0870215256

E337.5–400 Early 19th Century (1801/1809–1845)

E337.8 Collected Works of Contemporary Statesmen

Adams, John Quincy, 1767-1848.   • 3.7068
Writings of John Quincy, Adams. New York, The Macmillan company,
1913-17. 7 v. fronts. (v. 1-2, ports.) 23 cm. I. Ford, Worthington Chauncey,
1858-1941. ed. II. T.
E337.8.A21   *LC* 13-2027

Calhoun, John C. (John Caldwell), 1782-1850.   • 3.7069
[Works] The papers of John C. Calhoun / edited by Robert L. Meriwether. —
Columbia: Published by the University of South Carolina Press for the South
Caroliniana Society, 1959-<1984>. v. <1-16>: ports.; 24 cm. Vols. 2-9:
Edited by W. Edwin Hemphill; v. 10: Edited by Clyde N. Wilson and W. Edwin
Hemphill; v. 11-<16>: Edited by Clyde N. Wilson. Vols. 10-<15>:
Published by the University of South Carolina Press for the South Carolina
Dept. of Archives and History and the South Caroliniana Society. 1. Calhoun,
John C. (John Caldwell), 1782-1850. 2. Statesmen — South Carolina —
Biography. 3. United States — Politics and government — 1815-1861 —
Sources. 4. South Carolina — Politics and government — 1775-1865 —
Sources. I. Meriwether, Robert Lee, 1890-1958. II. Hemphill, William Edwin,
1912- III. Wilson, Clyde Norman. IV. South Caroliniana Society. V. South
Carolina. Dept. of Archives and History. VI. T.
E337.8.C148   973.5/092/4 B 19   *LC* 59-10351   *ISBN* 0872492478

Clay, Henry, 1777-1852.   • 3.7070
Papers / James F. Hopkins, editor; Mary W.M. Hargreaves, associate editor. —
[Lexington]: University of Kentucky Press, [c1959-. v.: ill., ports.; 25 cm.
Erratum slip inserted in v. 1. Vol. 6 edited jointly by Mary W.M. Hargreaves
and James F. Hopkins. Vol. 6-<8> published by University Press of
Kentucky. Vol. 7 edited jointly by Robert Seager, Richard E. Winslow, Melba
Porter Hay. Vol. 8 edited jointly by R. Seager and M.P. Hay. 1. Clay, Henry,
1777-1852 — Collected works. 2. United States — Politics and government —
1815-1861 — Collected works. I. Hopkins, James F. II. Seager, Robert, 1924-
III. T.
E337.8.C55 1959   973.5/092/4 B 19   *LC* 59-13605   *ISBN*
0813100569

Polk, James K. (James Knox), 1795-1849.   3.7071
Correspondence of James K. Polk. Herbert Weaver, editor. Paul H. Bergeron
associate editor. Nashville, Vanderbilt University Press, 1969-. v. <1-5> illus.,
maps, port. 25 cm. Vol. 5 edited by W. Cutler. 1. Polk, James K. (James Knox),
1795-1849. 2. Polk, James K. (James Knox), 1795-1849. 3. Presidents —
United States — Correspondence. I. Weaver, Herbert, ed. II. Cutler, Wayne,
1938- III. T.
E337.8.P63   973.6/1/0924   *LC* 75-84005   *ISBN* 0826511465

Webster, Daniel, 1782-1852.   3.7072
[Works. 1974] The papers of Daniel Webster / Charles M. Wiltse, editor,
Harold D. Moser, associate editor. — Hanover, N.H.: Published for Dartmouth
College by the University Press of New England, 1974-. 4 v. in 14; 25 cm.
Includes indexes. Ser. 2, v. 1- Alfred S. Konefsky, Andrew J. King, editors. Ser.
3, v. 1- Kenneth E. Shewmaker, editor; Kenneth R. Stevens and Anita
McGurn, assistant editors. Ser. 1, v.7, Charles M. Wiltse and Michael J.
Birkner, editors. 1. Webster, Daniel, 1782-1852. 2. Statesmen — United States
— Correspondence 3. United States — History — 1801-1809 — Sources.
4. United States — History — 1809-1817 — Sources. 5. United States —
History — 1815-1861 — Sources. I. Wiltse, Charles Maurice, 1907-
II. Konefsky, Alfred S. III. King, Andrew J., 1941- IV. Shewmaker, Kenneth
E., 1936- V. Birkner, Michael J., 1950- VI. Dartmouth College. VII. T.
E337.8.W373   973.5/092/4 B 19   *LC* 73-92705   *ISBN* 0874510961

E338 General Works

Blau, Joseph L. (Joseph Leon), 1909-1986. ed.   • 3.7073
Social theories of Jacksonian democracy; representative writings of the period
1825–1850. — New York, Liberal Arts Press [1954] 383 p. 21 cm. —
(American heritage series, no. 1) Includes bibliography. 1. United States —
Pol. & govt. — 1815-1861 — Sources. 2. United States — Econ. condit.
3. United States — Soc. condit. I. T. II. Title: Jacksonian democracy.
E338.B55 1954   973.56   *LC* 55-169

Craven, Avery Odelle, 1886-.   • **3.7074**
The coming of the Civil War. [2d ed. Chicago] University of Chicago Press [1957] 491 p. 24 cm. 1. Slavery — United States 2. United States — History — 1815-1861 3. United States — History — Civil War, 1861-1865 — Causes I. T.
E338.C92 1957   973.711   *LC* 57-8572

Dangerfield, George, 1904-1986.   • **3.7075**
The awakening of American nationalism, 1815–1828. — [1st ed.]. — New York, Harper & Row [c1965] xiii, 331 p. illus., facsims., ports. 22 cm. — (The New American Nation series) 'Bibliographical essay': p. 303-321. Bibliographical footnotes. 1. U.S. — Hist. — 1815-1861. 2. Nationalism — U.S. I. T.
E338.D3   973.5   *LC* 64-25112

Donald, David Herbert, 1920-.   **3.7076**
Liberty and Union / David Herbert Donald. — Boston: Little, Brown and Co., c1978. x, 318 p.: ill.; 24 cm. Includes index. 1. United States — History — 1783-1865 2. United States — History — 1865-1898 I. T.
E338.D58 1978   973   *LC* 78-54090   *ISBN* 0316189499

Livermore, Shaw, 1926-.   • **3.7077**
The twilight of federalism; the disintegration of the Federalist Party, 1815–1830, by Shaw Livermore, Jr. New York, Gordian Press, 1972 [c1962] ix, 292 p. 23 cm. Originally presented as the author's thesis, University of Wisconsin, 1959. 1. Federal Party (U.S.) 2. United States — Politics and government — 1815-1861 I. T.
E338.L5 1972   329/.1   *LC* 73-150413   *ISBN* 0877521379

Meyers, Marvin.   • **3.7078**
The Jacksonian persuasion: politics and belief. — Stanford: Stanford University Press, 1957. vi, 231 p.; 24 cm. Issued also (in microfilm form) with variations, as thesis, Columbia University. 1. Jackson, Andrew, 1767-1845. 2. United States — Politics and government — 1815-1861 3. United States — Civilization — 1785-1865. I. T.
E338.M53   973.5   *LC* 57-12515

Pessen, Edward, 1920-.   **3.7079**
Jacksonian America: society, personality, and politics / Edward Pessen. — Rev. ed. — Homewood, Ill.: Dorsey Press, 1978. xvi, 379 p.; 26 cm. — (The Dorsey series in American history) Includes index. 1. United States — History — 1815-1861 I. T.
E338.P4 1978   973.5   *LC* 77-88295   *ISBN* 0256016518

Risjord, Norman K.   • **3.7080**
The Old Republicans; southern conservatism in the age of Jefferson [by] Norman K. Risjord. — New York, Columbia University Press, 1965. 340 p. 25 cm. Bibliography: p. [315]-328. 1. U.S. — Pol. & govt. — 1783-1865. 2. Conservatism — Southern States. 3. Democratic Party — Hist. I. T.
E338.R57   320.52   *LC* 65-17642

Silbey, Joel H.   **3.7081**
The partisan imperative: the dynamics of American politics before the Civil War / Joel H. Silbey. — New York: Oxford University Press, 1985. xx, 234 p.; 25 cm. Includes index. 1. United States — Politics and government — 1815-1861 — Addresses, essays, lectures. I. T.
E338.S55 1985   320.973 19   *LC* 84-20691   *ISBN* 0195035518

Smelser, Marshall.   • **3.7082**
The Democratic Republic, 1801–1815. — [1st ed.]. — New York: Harper & Row, [1968] xiv, 369 p.: ill., facsims., maps, ports.; 22 cm. — (The New American Nation series) 1. United States — History — 1801-1809 2. United States — History — 1809-1817 I. T.
E338.S57   973.4   *LC* 68-28218

Turner, Frederick Jackson, 1861-1932.   • **3.7083**
The United States, 1830–1850; the Nation and its sections. With an introd. by Avery Craven. — New York, Norton [1965 c1935] ix, 602 p. maps (1 fold.) 20 cm. — (The Norton library, N308) The author's incomplete manuscript was edited by M. H. Crissey, Max Farrand, and Avery Craven. 'Chapter XIII 'Taylor administration and the compromise of 1850' ... was never written.' Bibliographical footnotes. 1. U.S. — Hist. — 1815-1861. I. Craven, Avery Odelle, 1886- ed. II. T.
E338.T92 1965   973.5   *LC* 65-5736

Wilson, Major L.   **3.7084**
Space, time, and freedom; the quest for nationality and the irrepressible conflict, 1815–1861 [by] Major L. Wilson. — Westport, Conn.: Greenwood Press, [1974] x, 309 p.; 22 cm. — (Contributions in American history, no. 35) 1. Nationalism — United States. 2. United States — Politics and government — 1815-1861 I. T.
E338.W684   320.9/73/05   *LC* 74-287   *ISBN* 0837173736

Young, James Sterling.   • **3.7085**
The Washington community 1800–1828 / James Sterling Young. — New York: Harcourt, Brace, and World Inc., 1966. xvi, 307 p. 1. Statesmen, American.

2. Politics, Practical 3. United States — Politics and government — 1783-1865 I. T.
E338.Y6   975.302   *LC* 66-14080

E340 BIOGRAPHY

Handlin, Lilian.   **3.7086**
George Bancroft, the intellectual as Democrat / Lilian Handlin. — 1st ed. — New York: Harper & Row, c1984. xvi, 415 p.; 25 cm. 'A Cornelia & Michael Bessie book.' 1. Bancroft, George, 1800-1891. 2. Diplomats — United States — Biography. 3. Historians — United States — Biography. 4. United States — History — 1815-1861 I. T.
E340.B2 H36 1984   973.8/092/4 19   *LC* 83-49057   *ISBN* 0060390336

Chambers, William Nisbet, 1916-.   • **3.7087**
Old Bullion Benton, Senator from the new West: Thomas Hart Benton, 1782–1858. — New York: Russell & Russell, [1970, c1956] xv, 517 p.: port.; 23 cm. 1. Benton, Thomas Hart, 1782-1858. I. T.
E340.B4 C5 1970   973.5/0924 B   *LC* 70-102476

Capers, Gerald Mortimer.   • **3.7088**
John C. Calhoun, opportunist: a reappraisal / Gerald M. Capers. — Gainesville: University of Florida Press, 1960. viii, 275 p. 1. Calhoun, John C. (John Caldwell), 1782-1850. I. T.
E340.C15 C25   *LC* 60-15788

Wiltse, Charles Maurice, 1907-.   • **3.7089**
John C. Calhoun, by Charles M. Wiltse. New York, Russell & Russell [1968, c1944-51] 3 v. illus., facsims., maps, ports. 24 cm. 1. Calhoun, John C. (John Caldwell), 1782-1850. I. T.
E340.C15W5x   973.6/0924 B   *LC* 68-11329

Eaton, Clement, 1898-.   • **3.7090**
Henry Clay and the art of American politics. — [1st ed.]. — Boston: Little, Brown, [1957] 209 p.; 22 cm. — (The Library of American biography) 1. Clay, Henry, 1777-1852. I. T.
E340.C6 E2   923.273   *LC* 57-5825

Van Deusen, Glyndon G. (Glyndon Garlock), 1897-.   • **3.7091**
The life of Henry Clay, by Glyndon G. Van Deusen. Boston, Little, Brown and company, 1937. xiii p., 4 l., [3]-448 p. front., plates (1 double), ports., facsims. 24 cm. 'First edition.' 1. Clay, Henry, 1777-1852. I. T.
E340.C6 V3   923.273   *LC* 37-24249

Kirwan, Albert Dennis.   • **3.7092**
John J. Crittenden; the struggle for the Union. [Lexington] University of Kentucky Press [1962] 514 p. illus. 24 cm. Includes bibliography. 1. Crittenden, John J. (John Jordan), 1787-1863. I. T.
E340.C9K5   923.273   *LC* 62-19380

Swisher, Carl Brent, 1897-1968.   • **3.7093**
Roger B. Taney. Hamden, Conn.: Archon Books, 1961 [c1935] 608 p.: ill.; 25 cm. 1. Taney, Roger Brooke, 1777-1864. I. T.
E340.T2S9 1961   923.473   *LC* 61-4990

Webster, Daniel, 1782-1852.   • **3.7094**
Speak for yourself, Daniel; a life of Webster in his own words. Edited and arr. by Walker Lewis. — Boston: Houghton Mifflin, 1969. xix, 505 p.: illus., facsims., ports.; 22 cm. I. Lewis, Walker. ed. II. T.
E340.W4 A13   973.5/0924 B   *LC* 69-12574

Bartlett, Irving H.   **3.7095**
Daniel Webster / Irving H. Bartlett. — 1st ed. — New York: Norton, c1978. xii, 333 p.: ill.; 24 cm. 1. Webster, Daniel, 1782-1852. 2. Legislators — United States — Biography. 3. United States — Politics and government — 1783-1865 I. T.
E340.W4 B26 1978   973.5/092/4 B   *LC* 77-27542   *ISBN* 0393075249

Baxter, Maurice G. (Maurice Glen), 1920-.   **3.7096**
One and inseparable: Daniel Webster and the Union / Maurice G. Baxter. — Cambridge, Mass.: Harvard University Press, 1984. x, 646 p.: ports.; 24 cm. 1. Webster, Daniel, 1782-1852. 2. United States. Congress. Senate — Biography. 3. Legislators — United States — Biography. 4. United States — Politics and government — 1815-1861 I. T.
E340.W4 B297 1984   973.5/092/4 B 19   *LC* 83-26597   *ISBN* 0674638212

Dalzell, Robert F.   **3.7097**
Daniel Webster and the trial of American nationalism, 1843–1852 / [by] Robert F. Dalzell, Jr. — Boston: Houghton Mifflin, 1973 [c1972] xv, 363 p.: port.; 24 cm. 1. Webster, Daniel, 1782-1852. 2. Nationalism — United States. 3. United States — Politics and government — 1815-1861 I. T.
E340.W4 D17   973.5/092/4 B   *LC* 72-2284   *ISBN* 0395139988

Fuess, Claude Moore, 1885-1963.   • 3.7098
Daniel Webster. — New York: Da Capo Press, 1968 [c1930] 2 v.: illus.,
facsims., ports.; 24 cm. — (The American scene) (A Da Capo Press reprint
edition.) 1. Webster, Daniel, 1782-1852. I. T.
E340.W4 F955 1968   973.5/0924 B   *LC* 68-8722

E341–400 BY PRESIDENTIAL ADMINISTRATION

E341–370 Madison, 1809–1817. War of 1812

Brant, Irving, 1885-.   • 3.7099
James Madison. Indianapolis: Bobbs-Merrill [1941-61] 6 v.: plates, ports.,
facsims.; 24 cm. Vols. 1-4: 1st ed. A condensed version of this work published in
1970 under title: The fourth President. 1. Madison, James, 1751-1836. I. T.
E342.B7   923.173   *LC* 41-19279

Ketcham, Ralph Louis, 1927-.   • 3.7100
James Madison; a biography, by Ralph Ketcham. New York, N.Y., Macmillan
[1971] xiv, 753 p. map (on lining papers) plates, ports. 24 cm. 1. Madison,
James, 1751-1836. I. T.
E342.K46 1971   973.5/1/0924 B   *LC* 79-85779

Long, David Foster, 1917-.   3.7101
Sailor–diplomat: a biography of Commodore James Biddle, 1783–1848 / David
F. Long. — Boston: Northeastern University Press, 1983. xvi, 312 p.: ill.; 24
cm. 1. Biddle, James, 1783-1848. 2. United States. Navy — Biography
3. Admirals — United States — Biography. 4. Diplomats — United States —
Biography. 5. United States — History — War of 1812 — Naval operations.
6. United States — History, Naval — To 1900 I. T.
E353.1.B5 L66 1983   973.5/092/4 B 19   *LC* 82-22236   *ISBN*
0930350391

Huff, Archie Vernon, 1937-.   3.7102
Langdon Cheves of South Carolina / Archie Vernon Huff, Jr. 1st ed. —
Columbia: Published for the South Carolina Tricentennial Commission by the
University of South Carolina Press, 1977. 276 p.: port.; 23 cm. (Tricentennial
studies; no. 11) Includes index. 1. Cheves, Langdon, 1776-1857. 2. Legislators
— United States — Biography. I. T.
E353.1.C45 H83   328.73/092/4 B   *LC* 76-49573   *ISBN*
0872492567

Coles, Harry L.   • 3.7103
The War of 1812 / by Harry L. Coles. — Chicago: University of Chicago Press,
1965. vii, 298 p.: ill., maps, port.; 21 cm. — (The Chicago history of American
civilization) 1. United States — History — War of 1812 I. T.
E354.C7   973.52   *LC* 65-17283

Mahan, A. T. (Alfred Thayer), 1840-1914.   • 3.7104
Sea power in its relations to the War of 1812. New York: Greenwood Press,
1968 [c1905] 2 v.: ill., maps, ports.; 22 cm. 'The present work concludes the
series of 'The influence of sea power upon history'.' 1. Sea-power 2. United
States — History — War of 1812 3. United States — History — War of 1812 —
Naval operations. 4. United States. Navy — History — War of 1812 I. T.
E354.M23   973.5/25   *LC* 69-10129

Berton, Pierre, 1920-.   3.7105
Flames across the border: the Canadian–American tragedy, 1813–1814 / Pierre
Berton; [maps by Geoffrey Matthews]. — 1st American ed. — Boston: Little,
Brown, 1982 (c1981). 492 p.: ill., maps; 25 cm. 'An Atlantic Monthly Press
book.' Includes index. 1. United States — History — War of 1812 —
Campaigns I. T.
E355.B46   973.5/2 19   *LC* 81-82541   *ISBN* 0316092177

Owsley, Frank Lawrence, 1928-.   3.7106
Struggle for the gulf borderlands: the Creek War and the Battle of New Orleans,
1812–1815 / Frank Lawrence Owsley, Jr. — Gainesville: University Presses of
Florida, c1981. vii, 255 p.: maps; 24 cm. 'A University of Florida book.'
Includes index. 1. Jackson, Andrew, 1767-1845. 2. New Orleans, Battle of,
1815 3. Creek War, 1813-1814 4. United States — History — War of 1812 —
Campaigns 5. Gulf States — History I. T.
E355.1.N5 O97   973.5/238   *LC* 80-11109   *ISBN* 0813006627

Brown, Roger Hamilton.   • 3.7107
The Republic in peril: 1812. — New York: Columbia University Press, 1964.
viii, 238 p.; 25 cm. Includes bibliographical references. 1. U.S. — Pol. & govt.
— War of 1812. 2. U.S. — Hist. — War of 1812 — Causes. I. T.
E357.B88   973.52   *LC* 64-12498

Horsman, Reginald.   • 3.7108
The causes of the War of 1812 / by Reginald Horsman. — Philadelphia:
University of Pennsylvania Press, 1962. 345 p.; 21 cm. Includes index.
1. United States — History — War of 1812 — Causes I. T.
E357 H7   *LC* 61-15201

Perkins, Bradford, 1925-.   • 3.7109
Prologue to war; England and the United States, 1805– 1812. — Berkeley:
University of California Press, 1961. x, 457 p.: ports.; 24 cm. Second vol. in a
trilogy, the first of which is the author's The first rapprochement; and the third
of which is his Castlereagh and Adams. 1. United States — History — War of
1812 — Causes. 2. United States — Foreign relations — Great Britain.
3. Great Britain — Foreign relations — United States. I. T.
E357.P66   973.521   *LC* 61-14018

Pratt, Julius William, 1888-.   • 3.7110
Expansionists of 1812. New York: P. Smith, 1949 [c1925] 309 p.; 21 cm.
1. United States — Politics and government — 1783-1865 2. United States —
Territorial expansion 3. United States — History — War of 1812 — Causes.
4. United States — Foreign relations — 1783-1865 I. T.
E357.P9 1949   *LC* 49-9879

Stagg, J. C. A. (John Charles Anderson), 1945-.   3.7111
Mr. Madison's war: politics, diplomacy, and warfare in the early American
republic, 1783–1830 / by J.C.A. Stagg. — Princeton, N.J.: Princeton University
Press, c1983. xviii, 538 p.; 25 cm. 1. Madison, James, 1751-1836. 2. United
States — History — War of 1812 — Causes. 3. United States — Politics and
government — War of 1812 4. United States — Politics and government —
1789-1815 I. T.
E357.S79 1983   973.5 19   *LC* 82-61386   *ISBN* 0691047022

Banner, James M., 1935-.   • 3.7112
To the Hartford Convention: the Federalists and the origins of party politics in
Massachusetts, 1789–1815 [by] James M. Banner, Jr. — [1st ed.] — New York:
Knopf, 1970 [c1969] xiii , 378, xii, p.: maps; 22 cm. 1. Hartford Convention,
1814. 2. Massachusetts — Politics and government I. T.
E357.7.B3   329/.009744   *LC* 75-88753

Perkins, Bradford, 1925-.   • 3.7113
Castlereagh and Adams; England and the United States, 1812–1823. —
Berkeley, University of California Press, 1964. viii, 364 p. ports. 24 cm.
Includes bibliographical references. 1. U.S. — For. rel. — War of 1812. 2. U.S.
— For. rel. — 1817-1825. 3. U.S. — For. rel. — Gt. Brit. 4. Gt. Brit. — For.
rel. — U.S. I. T.
E358.P4   327.73042   *LC* 64-19696

The Naval war of 1812: a documentary history / editor, William   3.7114
S. Dudley, associate editor, Michael J. Crawford with a
foreword by John D.H. Kane, Jr.
Washington, D.C.: Naval Historical Center; For sale by the Supt. of Docs., U.S.
G.P.O., 1985. 3 v.: ill.; 26 cm. 1. United States — History — War of 1812 —
Naval operations — Sources. 2. Canada — History — War of 1812 — Naval
operations — Sources. I. Dudley, William S. II. Crawford, Michael J.
III. Naval Historical Center (U.S.) IV. Title: 1812.
E360.N38   971.034   *LC* 85-600565

Roosevelt, Theodore, president of the United States, 1858-1919.   • 3.7115
The naval war of 1812: or, The history of the United States navy during the last
war with Great Britain, to which is appended an account of the battle of New
Orleans. — New library ed. — New York: G. P. Putnam [c1910] 2 v.: ill.
1. New Orleans, Battle of, 1815 2. Canada (History: War of 1812-1815)
3. United States — History — War of 1812-1815 — Naval operations.
4. United States (Naval history) I. T.
E360.R86 1910   973.525

E371–375 Monroe, 1817–1825

Dangerfield, George, 1904-1986.   • 3.7116
The era of good feelings. — [1st ed.]. — New York: Harcourt, Brace, [1952] xiv,
525 p.: maps.; 25 cm. 1. Ghent, Treaty of, 1814 2. Monroe doctrine 3. United
States — History — 1817-1825 4. United States — History — 1825-1829 I. T.
E371.D3   973.54   *LC* 51-14815

May, Ernest R.   3.7117
The making of the Monroe doctrine / Ernest R. May. — Cambridge, Mass.:
Belknap Press of Harvard University Press, 1975. xviii, 306 p.: ill.; 24 cm.
Includes index. 1. Presidents — United States — Election — 1824. 2. Monroe
doctrine 3. United States — Politics and government — 1817-1825 4. United
States — Foreign relations — 1817-1825 I. T.
E371.M38   327.73   *LC* 75-11619   *ISBN* 0674543408

Ammon, Harry.   • 3.7118
James Monroe: the quest for national identity. [1st ed.] New York, McGraw-
Hill [1971] xi, 706 p. 23 cm. 1. Monroe, James, 1758-1831. 2. United States —
Politics and government — 1817-1825 I. T.
E372.A65   973.5/4/0924   *LC* 78-141294   *ISBN* 0070015821

Moore, Glover, 1911-. • **3.7119**
The Missouri controversy, 1819–1821. — [Lexington]: University of Kentucky Press, [1953] viii, 383 p.: ports., map, facsim.; 24 cm. 1. Missouri compromise 2. United States — Politics and government — 1817-1825 I. T.
E373.M77   973.54   *LC* 53-5518

E376–380 Adams, 1825–1829

Adams, John Quincy, 1767-1848. **3.7120**
Diary of John Quincy Adams / David Grayson Allen, associate editor ... [et al.]. — Cambridge, Mass.: Belknap Press of Harvard University Press, 1982 (c1981). 2 v.: ill.; 26 cm. — (Adams papers. Diaries.) Includes index. 1. Adams, John Quincy, 1767-1848. 2. Presidents — United States — Biography 3. United States — History — 1783-1865 4. United States — Politics and government — 1783-1865 5. United States — Foreign relations — 1783-1865 I. T. II. Series.
E377.A185   973.5/5/0924 19   *LC* 81-6197   *ISBN* 0674204204

Adams, John Quincy, President. U. S., 1767-1848. • **3.7121**
[Memoirs of John Quincy Adams] Diary, 1794–1845: American diplomacy and political, social, and intellectual life from Washington to Polk / edited by Allan Nevins. — New York: Scribner, 1951. xxxv, 586 p.; 25 cm. 1. United States — History — 1783-1865 2. United States — Politics and government — 1783-1865 3. United States — Foreign relations — 1783-1865 I. Nevins, Allan, 1890-1971. ed. II. T.
E377.A213   *LC* 51-10345

Bemis, Samuel Flagg, 1891-1973. • **3.7122**
John Quincy Adams and the foundations of American foreign policy. New York: Knopf, 1949. 588, xv p.: ill., ports., maps (part fold., part col.) 1. Adams, John Quincy, President United States, 1767-1848. 2. United States — Foreign relations — 1783-1865 I. T.
E377 B45 1965   923.173   *LC* 49-10664

Bemis, Samuel Flagg, 1891-1973. • **3.7123**
John Quincy Adams and the Union. [1st ed.] New York, Knopf, 1956. xix, 546 p. illus., ports. 25 cm. 1. Adams, John Quincy, 1767-1848. 2. Presidents — United States — Biography 3. United States — Politics and government — 1815-1861 I. T.
E377.B46   923.173   *LC* 55-9271

E381–386 Jackson, 1829–1837

Schlesinger, Arthur Meier, 1917-. • **3.7124**
The age of Jackson / by Arthur M. Schlesinger, jr. — Boston: Little, Brown and company, 1945. xiv, 577 p.; 23 cm. 'First edition ... September 1945.' 'The outgrowth of a series of lectures entitled 'A reinterpretation of Jacksonian democracy' delivered at the Lowell institute in Boston in the fall of 1941.'— Acknowledgments. Bibliography: p. [529]-55. 1. Jackson, Andrew, 1767-1845. 2. United States — Pol. & govt. — 1829-1837. I. T.
E381.S38   973.56   *LC* 45-8340

Remini, Robert Vincent, 1921-. **3.7125**
Andrew Jackson and the course of American empire / Robert V. Remini. — 1st ed. — New York: Harper & Row, c1977-1984. 3 v.: ill.; 25 cm. Vol. 2 has title: Andrew Jackson and the course of American freedom; v. 3 has title: Andrew Jackson and the course of American democracy. 1. Jackson, Andrew, Pres. U.S., 1767-1845. 2. Presidents — United States — Biography 3. United States — Territorial expansion 4. United States — Politics and government — 1815-1861 I. T. II. Title: Andrew Jackson and the course of American freedom. III. Title: Andrew Jackson and the course of American democracy.
E382.R43 1977   973.5/6/0924 B   *LC* 77-3766 (v.1)   *ISBN* 0060135743

Ward, John William, 1922-. • **3.7126**
Andrew Jackson, symbol for an age. New York, Oxford University Press, 1955. xii, 274 p. plates, ports, facsim. 21 cm. Based on thesis, University of Minnesota. 1. Jackson, Andrew, 1767-1845. I. T.
E382.W24   973.56   *LC* 55-8125

Freehling, William W., 1935-. • **3.7127**
Prelude to Civil War; the nullification controversy in South Carolina, 1816-1836 [by] William W. Freehling. — [1st ed.]. — New York: Harper & Row, [1966] xiii, 395 p.: maps; 22 cm. Based on the author's thesis, University of California at Berkeley. 1. Nullification 2. South Carolina — Politics & government — 1775-1865. I. T.
E384.3.F7   973.561   *LC* 66-10629

Sharp, James Roger, 1936-. • **3.7128**
The Jacksonians versus the banks: politics in the States after the panic of 1837. — New York: Columbia University Press, 1970. xii, 392 p.: ill., maps.; 23 cm. 1. Banks and banking — U.S. — History. 2. U.S. — Politics and government — 1815-1861. I. T.
E386.S5   332.1/0973   *LC* 70-127783   *ISBN* 0231032609

E387–390 Van Buren, 1837–1841

Van Buren, Martin, 1782-1862. **3.7129**
The autobiography of Martin Van Buren. Edited by John C. Fitzpatrick. New York, Da Capo Press, 1973. 2 v. (808 p.) 23 cm. (The American scene: comments and commentators) Reprint of the 1920 ed., which was issued as v. 2 of the Annual report of the American Historical Association for the year 1918. 1. Van Buren, Martin, 1782-1862. I. Fitzpatrick, John Clement, 1876-1940. ed. II. T.
E387.A32 1973   973.5/7/0924 B   *LC* 72-75314   *ISBN* 030671275X

Niven, John. **3.7130**
Martin Van Buren: the romantic age of American politics / John Niven. — New York: Oxford University Press, 1983. xii, 715 p., [10] p. of plates: ill.; 24 cm. 1. Van Buren, Martin, 1782-1862. 2. Presidents — United States — Biography 3. United States — Politics and government — 1837-1841 I. T.
E387.N58 1983   973.5/7/0924 19   *LC* 82-14528   *ISBN* 0195032381

Wilson, Major L. **3.7131**
The presidency of Martin Van Buren / Major L. Wilson. — Lawrence, Kan.: University Press of Kansas, c1984. xiii, 252 p.; 24 cm. — (American presidency series.) Includes index. 1. Van Buren, Martin, 1782-1862. 2. United States — Politics and government — 1837-1841 I. T. II. Series.
E387.W54 1984   973/.5/7/0924 B 19   *LC* 83-17871   *ISBN* 0700602380

E396–400 Tyler, 1841–1845

Morgan, Robert J. • **3.7132**
A Whig embattled; the Presidency under John Tyler. Lincoln, University of Nebraska Press, 1954. xiii, 199 p. port. 24 cm. 1. Tyler, John, 1790-1862. 2. United States — Politics and government — 1841-1845 I. T.
E396.M6   973.58   *LC* 54-8442

Jones, Howard, 1940-. **3.7133**
To the Webster–Ashburton treaty: a study in Anglo–American relations, 1783–1843 / by Howard Jones. — Chapel Hill: University of North Carolina Press, c1977. xx, 251 p.: ill.; 23 cm. 'The Webster-Ashburton treaty': p. 181-187. Includes index. 1. Washington, Treaty of, 1842. 2. Northeast boundary of the United States 3. United States — Foreign relations — Great Britain. 4. Great Britain — Foreign relations — United States. I. United States. Treaties, etc., 1841-1845 (Tyler). Boundary, slave trade, and extradition. 1977. II. T.
E398.J66   327.73/041   *LC* 76-58341   *ISBN* 0807813060

Merk, Frederick, 1887-. • **3.7134**
Fruits of propaganda in the Tyler administration / [by] Frederick Merk; with the collaboration of Lois Bannister Merk. — Cambridge: Harvard University Press, 1971. x, 259 p.: facsims., map (on lining paper); 24 cm. 'Letter of Mr. Walker, of Mississippi, relative to the annexation of Texas': p. 221-252. 1. Tyler, John, 1790-1862. 2. Northeast boundary of the United States 3. United States — Politics and government — 1841-1845 I. Walker, Robert James, 1801-1869. Letter of Mr. Walker, of Mississippi, relative to the annexation of Texas. 1971. II. T.
E398.M55   973.5/8   *LC* 79-135547   *ISBN* 0674326768

E401–415.2 War with Mexico, 1845–1848

Bauer, K. Jack (Karl Jack), 1926-. **3.7135**
The Mexican War, 1846–1848, by K. Jack Bauer. — New York: Macmillan, [1974] 454 p.: ill. — (Wars of the United States.) 1. United States — History — War with Mexico, 1845-1848 I. T. II. Series.
E404.B37   973.6/2   *LC* 74-3489   *ISBN* 0025078908

Connor, Seymour V. **3.7136**
North America divided; the Mexican War, 1846–1848 [by] Seymour V. Connor and Odie B. Faulk. — New York: Oxford University Press, 1971. viii, 300 p.: maps.; 22 cm. 1. U.S. — History — War with Mexico, 1845-1848. I. Faulk, Odie B. joint author. II. T.
E404.C8   973.6/2   *LC* 77-161885   *ISBN* 0195014480

Johannsen, Robert Walter, 1925-. **3.7137**
To the halls of the Montezumas: the Mexican War in the American imagination / Robert W. Johannsen. — New York: Oxford University Press, 1985. xi, 363 p.: ill., map; 25 cm. Includes index. 1. United States — History — War with Mexico, 1845-1848 2. United States — History — War with Mexico, 1845-1848 — Influence. 3. United States — History — War with Mexico,

1845-1848 — Literature and the war. 4. United States — History — War with Mexico, 1845-1848 — Art and the war. I. T.
E404.J64 1985   973.6/2 19   *LC* 84-20696   *ISBN* 0195035186

Singletary, Otis A.   • **3.7138**
The Mexican War / by Otis A. Singletary. — Chicago: University of Chicago Press, 1960. xiii, 181 p.: ill., maps — (Chicago history of American civilization.) 1. United States — History — War with Mexico, 1845-1848 I. T. II. Series.
E404.S5   *LC* 60-7248

Smith, Justin Harvey, 1857-1930.   • **3.7139**
The war with Mexico. Gloucester, Mass., P. Smith, 1963 [c1919] 2 v. illus. 21 cm. Includes bibliography. 1. United States — History — War with Mexico, 1845-1848 I. T.
E404.S66 1963   973.62   *LC* 63-5089

Schroeder, John H., 1943-.   **3.7140**
Mr. Polk's war: American opposition and dissent, 1846–1848 [by] John H. Schroeder. — [Madison]: University of Wisconsin Press, [1973] xvi, 184 p.: illus.; 25 cm. 1. United States — History — War with Mexico, 1845-1848 — Public opinion I. T.
E415.2.S3   973.6/2   *LC* 73-2049   *ISBN* 0299061604

E415.6–440.5 Middle 19th Century (1845/48–1861)

Cole, Arthur Charles, 1886-.   • **3.7141**
The irrepressible conflict, 1850–1865. New York, Macmillan, 1938. — St. Clair Shores, Mich.: Scholarly Press, [1971?, c1934] xv, 468 p.: illus.; 22 cm. — (History of American life. v. 7) 'Critical essay on authorities': p. 408-450. 1. United States — History — 1849-1877 2. United States — History — Civil War, 1861-1865 — Causes 3. United States — History — Civil War, 1861-1865 I. T. II. Series.
E415.7.C69 1971   973.6   *LC* 71-144952   *ISBN* 0403009308

Essays on American Antebellum politics, 1840–1860 / by   **3.7142**
William E. Gienapp ... [et al.]; introduction by Thomas J.
Pressly; edited by Stephen E. Maizlish and John J. Kushma.
1st ed. — College Station: Published for the University of Texas at Arlington, by Texas A&M University Press, c1982. 229 p.; 24 cm. (The Walter Prescott Webb memorial lectures; no. 16) 1. United States — Politics and government — 1815-1861 — Addresses, essays, lectures. I. Gienapp, William E. II. Maizlish, Stephen E., 1945- III. Kushma, John J. (John James), 1949-
E415.7.E67 1982   973 19   *LC* 82-40314   *ISBN* 0890961360

Holt, Michael F. (Michael Fitzgibbon)   **3.7143**
The political crisis of the 1850s / Michael F. Holt. — New York: Wiley, c1978. xix, 330 p.; 22 cm. (Critical episodes in American politics) 1. Slavery in the United States — History. 2. Compromise of 1850 3. United States — Politics and government — 1845-1861 I. T. II. Series.
E415.7.H74   320.9/73/06   *LC* 77-13564   *ISBN* 0471408409. *ISBN* 0471408417 pbk

Leonard, Ira M., 1937-.   **3.7144**
American nativism, 1830–1860 [by] Ira M. Leonard [and] Robert D. Parmet. — New York: Van Nostrand Reinhold, [1971] vi, 185 p.; 20 cm. — (An Anvil original) 1. Nativism 2. Immigrants — United States 3. United States — Politics and government — 1815-1861 I. Parmet, Robert D., 1938- joint author. II. T.
E415.7.L46   301.29/73   *LC* 71-156750

Nevins, Allan, 1890-1971.   • **3.7145**
The emergence of Lincoln. — New York: Scribner, 1950. 2 v.: ill., ports., maps; 24 cm. Sequel to Ordeal of the Union. 1. Lincoln, Abraham, 1809-1865. 2. U.S. — Hist. — 1849-1877. 3. Slavery in the U.S. I. T.
E415.7.N38   973.68   *LC* 50-9920

Nevins, Allan, 1890-1971.   • **3.7146**
Ordeal of the Union. — New York: Scribner, 1947. 2 v.: illus., ports., maps.; 24 cm. 1. Slavery in the United States. 2. United States — History — 1849-1877 3. United States — History — Civil War, 1861-1865 — Causes I. T.
E415.7.N4   973.6   *LC* 47-11072

Rhodes, James Ford, 1848-1927.   • **3.7147**
History of the United States from the Compromise of 1850 to the McKinley-Bryan campaign of 1896. Port Washington, N.Y., Kennikat Press [1967, c1892-1919] 8 v. maps (part fold.), plans. 23 cm. 1. U.S. — History — 1849-1877. 2. U.S. — History — 1865-1898. I. T.
E415.7.R485   973

E415.9 BIOGRAPHY, A–Z

Chase, Salmon P. (Salmon Portland), 1808-1873.   • **3.7148**
Inside Lincoln's Cabinet: the Civil War diaries of Salmon P. Chase / edited by David Donald. — [1st ed.]. — New York: Longmans, Green, 1954. ix, 342 p.: port.; 24 cm. 1. United States — History — Civil War, 1861-1865 — Sources I. T.
E415.9.C4 A3   973.71   *LC* 54-7475

Dana, Richard Henry, 1815-1882.   • **3.7149**
The journal. Edited by Robert F. Lucid. — Cambridge: Belknap Press of Harvard University Press, 1968. 3 v. (xli, 1201 p.): illus., facsims., geneal. tables, ports.; 25 cm. 1. Lucid, Robert Francis, ed. II. T.
E415.9.D15 A16   818/.3/03   *LC* 68-14264

Douglas, Stephen Arnold, 1813-1861.   • **3.7150**
Letters. Urbana, University of Illinois Press, 1961. xxxi, 558 p. illus. 24 cm. 1. United States — Politics and government — 1815-1861 I. Johannsen, Robert Walter, 1925- ed. II. T.
E415.9.D73 A4   *LC* 61-62768

Capers, Gerald Mortimer.   • **3.7151**
Stephen A. Douglas: defender of the Union / edited by Oscar Handlin. — [1st ed.]. — Boston: Little, Brown, [1959] 239 p.; 21 cm. — (The Library of American biography) 1. Douglas, Stephen Arnold, 1813-1861. I. T.
E415.9.D73 C28   923.273   *LC* 59-5277

Johannsen, Robert Walter, 1925-.   **3.7152**
Stephen A. Douglas [by] Robert W. Johannsen. — New York: Oxford University Press, 1973. xii, 993 p.: illus.; 24 cm. 1. Douglas, Stephen Arnold, 1813-1861. I. T.
E415.9.D73 J55   973.6/8/0924 B   *LC* 72-92293   *ISBN* 0195016203

Egan, Ferol.   **3.7153**
Frémont, explorer for a restless nation / Ferol Egan. 1st ed. — Garden City, N.Y.: Doubleday, 1977. xv, 582 p., [16] leaves of plates: ill.; 24 cm. Includes index. 1. Frémont, John Charles, 1813-1890. I. T.
E415.9.F8 E33   979/.02/0924 B   *LC* 76-2770   *ISBN* 0385017758

Stewart, James Brewer.   • **3.7154**
Joshua R. Giddings and the tactics of radical politics. — Cleveland: Press of Case Western Reserve University, 1970. xiv, 318 p.; 24 cm. 1. Giddings, Joshua Reed, 1795-1864. 2. U.S. — Politics and government — 1815-1861. I. T.
E415.9.G4 S7   328.73/0924   *LC* 77-84496   *ISBN* 082950169X

Van Deusen, Glyndon G. (Glyndon Garlock), 1897-.   • **3.7155**
Horace Greeley: nineteenth–century crusader / by Glyndon G. Van Deusen. — New York: Hill & Wang, 1964, c1953. 444 p.: ill., ports.; 21 cm. — (American century series, AC72.) 1. Greeley, Horace, 1811-1872. I. T.
E415.9.G8 V3   *LC* 64-55560

Sewell, Richard H.   • **3.7156**
John P. Hale and the politics of abolition [by] Richard H. Sewell. — Cambridge, Harvard University Press, 1965. viii, 290 p. port. 22 cm. Includes bibliographies. 1. Hale, John Parker, 1806-1873. 2. Slavery in the U.S. — Anti-slavery movements. I. T.
E415.9.H15S4 1965   923.273   *LC* 65-13849

Durden, Robert Franklin.   • **3.7157**
James Shepherd Pike: Republicanism and the American Negro, 1850—1882 / Robert Franklin Durden. — Durham, N.C.: Duke University Press, 1957. 249 p.: ill.; 24 cm. 1. Pike, James Shepherd, 1811-1882. I. T.
E415.9.P53 D8   923.273   *LC* 57-6284   *ISBN* 0822303485

Van Deusen, Glyndon G. (Glyndon Garlock), 1897-.   • **3.7158**
William Henry Seward [by] Glyndon G. Van Deusen. New York, Oxford University Press, 1967. xi, 666 p. illus., ports. 24 cm. 1. Seward, William Henry, 1801-1872. I. T.
E415.9.S4 V3   973.7/0924 B   *LC* 67-28131

Current, Richard Nelson, 1912-.   • **3.7159**
Old Thad Stevens, a story of ambition, by Richard Nelson Current ... Madison, The University of Wisconsin Press, 1942. v, [1] p., 1 β., 344 p. front., illus. (map) plates, ports., facsim. 23 cm. I. Stevens, Thaddeus, 1792-1868. II. T.
E415.9.S84 C8   923.273   *LC* 43-52549

Strong, George Templeton, 1820-1875.   • **3.7160**
Diary / edited by Allan Nevins and Milton Halsey Thomas. — New York: Macmillan, 1952. 4 v.: ill., ports., facsims.; 25 cm. 1. Strong, George Templeton, 1820-1875. 2. Strong, George Templeton, 1820-1875. 3. United States — Politics and government — 19th century 4. New York (N.Y.) — Social life and customs 5. United States — History — Civil War, 1861-1865 — Personal narratives I. T.
E415.9.S86 A3   974.71   *LC* 52-11147

Donald, David Herbert, 1920-.   • **3.7161**
Charles Sumner and the coming of the Civil War. — [1st ed.]. — New York: Knopf, 1960. 392 p.: illus.; 25 cm. 1. Sumner, Charles, 1811-1874. I. T.
E415.9.S9 D6   923.273   *LC 60-9144*

Donald, David Herbert, 1920-.   • **3.7162**
Charles Sumner and the rights of man, by David Donald. — [1st ed.]. — New York: Knopf, 1970. xxiv, 595, xxxix p.: illus., ports.; 25 cm. 1. Sumner, Charles, 1811-1874. 2. United States — Politics and government — Civil War, 1861-1865 3. United States — Politics and government — 1865-1877 I. T.
E415.9.S9 D62 1970   973.7/0924   *LC 76-23393*

Flick, Alexander Clarence, 1869-1942.   • **3.7163**
Samuel Jones Tilden; a study in political sagacity, by Alexander Clarence Flick, assisted by Gustav S. Lobrano ... New York, Dodd, Mead, 1939. ix p. 1 l., 597 p. front., plates, ports. (American political leaders) 1. Tilden, Samuel J. (Samuel Jones), 1814-1886. 2. United States — Politics and government I. Lobrano, Gustav Stubbs, jt. author II. T. III. Series.
E415.9.T5 F5

Trefousse, Hans Louis.   • **3.7164**
Benjamin Franklin Wade, radical Republican from Ohio. — New York: Twayne Publishers, [1963] 404 p.: ill.; 22 cm. 1. Wade, B. F. (Benjamin Franklin), 1800-1878. I. T.
E415.9.W16 T7   923.273   *LC 63-11185*

Van Deusen, Glyndon G. (Glyndon Garlock), 1897-.   • **3.7165**
Thurlow Weed, wizard of the lobby, by Glyndon G. Van Deusen. New York, Da Capo Press, 1969 [c1947] xiv, 403 p. facsims., ports. 24 cm. (The American scene) (A Da Capo Press reprint series.) 1. Weed, Thurlow, 1797-1882. I. T.
E415.9.W39 V3 1969   329/.00924 B   *LC 73-87698*

Logsdon, Joseph.   **3.7166**
Horace White, nineteenth century liberal. — Westport, Conn.: Greenwood Pub. Corp., [1971] xiii, 418 p.; 22 cm. — (Contributions in American history, no. 10) 1. White, Horace, 1834-1916. I. T.
E415.9.W395 L6   973.8/0924 B   *LC 77-105982*   *ISBN 0837133092*

Abbott, Richard H.   **3.7167**
Cobbler in Congress; the life of Henry Wilson, 1812–1875 [by] Richard H. Abbott. [Lexington] University Press of Kentucky [c1972] xii, 289 p. ports. 1. Wilson, Henry, 1812-1875. I. T.
E415.9.W6 A64   *LC 70-147856*   *ISBN 0813112494*

E416–E440 BY PRESIDENTIAL ADMINISTRATION

E416–420 Polk, 1845–1849

Merk, Frederick, 1887-.   • **3.7168**
The Monroe doctrine and American expansionism, 1843–1849, by Frederick Merk with the collaboration of Lois Bannister Merk. — [1st ed.]. — New York: Knopf, 1966. xii, 289, ix p.: illus., map.; 25 cm. 1. Monroe doctrine 2. United States — Foreign relations — 1845-1849 3. United States — Territorial expansion I. T.
E416.M4   973.61   *LC 66-19390*

Polk, James K. (James Knox), 1795-1849.   • **3.7169**
Polk: the diary of a president, 1845–1849, covering the Mexican War, the acquisition of Oregon, and the conquest of California and the Southwest / edited by Allan Nevins. — London; New York: Longmans, Green, 1952. xxxi, 412, [1] p.; 24 cm. 'A selection from 'The diary of James K. Polk during his Presidency, 1845-1849,' edited and annotated by Milo Milton Quaife.' 1. United States — Politics and government — 1845-1849 2. United States — History — War with Mexico, 1845-1848 — Sources. I. Nevins, Allan, 1890-1971. ed. II. T.
E416.P77 1952   923.173   *LC 52-8933*

Sellers, Charles Grier.   • **3.7170**
James K. Polk, Jacksonian, 1795–1843. Princeton, N.J., Princeton University Press, 1957-. v. illus. 25 cm. Vol. 2 has title: James K. Polk, continentalist, 1843-1846. 1. Polk, James K. (James Knox), 1795-1849. I. T.
E417.S4   973.610924 B   *LC 57-5457*

E421–423 Taylor, 1849–1850

Hamilton, Holman.   • **3.7171**
Zachary Taylor. — Hamden, Conn.: Archon Books, 1966, [c1941-1951]. 2 v.: illus., ports., maps, facsim.; 24 cm. 1. Taylor, Zachary, 1784-1850. I. T.
E422.H3   923.173

Hamilton, Holman.   • **3.7172**
Prologue to conflict: the crisis and Compromise of 1850. — [Lexington]: University of Kentucky Press, [1964] viii, 236 p.: maps.; 23 cm. 1. Compromise of 1850. 2. United States — Politics and government — 1849-1861 I. T.
E423.H2   973.7113   *LC 64-13999*

E431–435 Pierce, 1853–1857

Malin, James Claude, 1893-.   • **3.7173**
The Nebraska question, 1852–1854. Lawrence, Kan. [1953] 455 p. 22 cm. 'This book, although designed to stand ... as a self-contained work, is, at the same time, an integral unit in the larger project of [the author's] Grassland historical studies.' 1. Kansas-Nebraska bill. I. T.
E433.M34   *LC 54-16070*

Rawley, James A.   • **3.7174**
Race & politics; 'bleeding Kansas' and the coming of the Civil War, by James A. Rawley. — [1st ed.]. — Philadelphia: Lippincott, [1969] xvi, 304 p.: map.; 21 cm. — (Critical periods of history) 1. Kansas — Nebraska bill. 2. United States — History — Civil War, 1861-1865 — Causes 3. Kansas — Politics and government — 1854-1861 4. United States — Race relations I. T.
E433.R25   973.7/113   *LC 73-85110*

E436–440 Buchanan, 1857–1861

Foner, Eric.   • **3.7175**
Free soil, free labor, free men: the ideology of the Republican Party before the Civil War. — New York: Oxford University Press, 1970. xii, 353 p.; 24 cm. A revision of the author's thesis, Columbia University. 1. Republican Party (U.S.: 1854-) 2. United States — Politics and government — 1849-1861 3. United States — History — Civil War, 1861-1865 — Causes I. T.
E436.F6 1970   329.6   *LC 70-97024*

Nichols, Roy F. (Roy Franklin), 1896-1973.   • **3.7176**
The disruption of American democracy. — New York, Macmillan Co., 1948. xviii, 612 p. illus., ports. 22 cm. 1. Democratic Party (U.S.) — History. 2. United States — Politics and government — 1857-1861 I. T.
E436.N56   973.66   *LC 48-6344*

Klein, Philip Shriver, 1909-.   • **3.7177**
President James Buchanan: a biography / Philip Shriver Klein. — University Park, Pa.: Pennsylvania State University Press, 1962. xviii, 506 p., [8] leaves of plates: ill., ports. 1. Buchanan, James, 1791-1868. I. T.
E437.K53   *LC 62-12623*

E440.5 1860–1861

Dumond, Dwight Lowell, 1895- ed.   • **3.7178**
Southern editorials on secession. Gloucester, Mass.: P. Smith, 1964 [c1931] xxxiii, 529 p.; 21 cm. At head of title: The American Historical Association. 1. Secession 2. United States — Politics and government — 1857-1861 I. American Historical Association. II. T. III. Title: Editorials on secession.
E440.5.D89 1964   *LC 64-3910*

Gunderson, Robert Gray.   • **3.7179**
Old gentlemen's convention: the Washington Peace Conference of 1861 / Robert Gray Gunderson. — Madison: University of Wisconsin Press, 1961. xiii, 168 p.: ill. 1. Conference Convention (1861: Washington, D.C.) 2. United States — Politics and government — 1857-1861 I. T.
E440.5.G965   *LC 61-10690*

Perkins, Howard Cecil, ed.   • **3.7180**
Northern editorials on secession, edited by Howard Cecil Perkins ... New York, London, D. Appleton-Century Company, Incorporated [c1942] 2 v. 23 cm. At head of title: The American Historical Association. Paged continuously. 'Prepared and published under the direction of the American Historical Association from the income of the Albert J. Beveridge Memorial Fund.' 'Materials used in a doctoral dissertation were ... greatly expanded, providing the basis of the present selection.'—Pref. 1. Secession 2. United States — Politics and government — 1857-1861 3. United States — History — Civil War, 1861-1865 — Causes I. American Historical Association. Albert J. Beveridge Memorial Fund. II. T.
E440.5.P45   973.68   *LC 42-2297*

Potter, David Morris.   • **3.7181**
Lincoln and his party in the secession crisis. New Haven: Yale University Press; London: H. Milford, Oxford Univ. Pr., 1942. x p., 1 l., 408 p.; 23 cm. (Yale historical publications...studies. XIII.) 'In an earlier form, this study was submitted as a doctoral dissertation at Yale [1940]'-p.x. 'Published under the direction of the Department of history from the income of the Frederick John Kingsbury memorial fund.' 1. Lincoln, Abraham, President United States,

1809-1865. 2. Republican Party 3. United States — Politics and government — 1857-1861 I. T. II. Series.
E440.5.P856   *LC* 42-4321

Stampp, Kenneth M. (Kenneth Milton)   • **3.7182**
And the war came; the North and the secession crisis, 1860–1861. [Baton Rouge] Louisiana State University Press [1950] viii, 331 p. illus., ports. 24 cm. 1. Secession 2. United States — Politics and government — 1857-1861 I. T.
E440.5.S78   973.713   *LC* 50-9835

Wooster, Ralph A.   • **3.7183**
The secession conventions of the South. Princeton, N. J., Princeton University Press, 1962. viii, 294 p. maps. 23 cm. 'Bibliographical note with selected bibliography': p. 267-274. 1. Secession 2. United States — Politics and government — 1857-1861 I. T.
E440.5.W9   973.713   *LC* 62-7046

E441–453 SLAVERY. ANTI-SLAVERY MOVEMENTS

American Negro slavery: a documentary history / edited by   **3.7184**
Michael Mullin.
Columbia: University of South Carolina Press, 1976. xii, 288 p.; 24 cm. 1. Slavery in the United States — History — Sources. 2. Afro-Americans — History — To 1863 — Sources. I. Mullin, Michael, 1938-
E441.A577 1976   301.44/93/0973   *LC* 74-7606   *ISBN* 0872493393

Barney, William L.   **3.7185**
The road to secession; a new perspective on the Old South. Foreword by James P. Shenton. — New York: Praeger, [1972] xv, 235 p.; 22 cm. — (New perspectives in American history) 1. Slavery in the United States — Economic aspects — Southern States. 2. United States — History — Civil War, 1861-1865 — Causes 3. Southern States — History — 1775-1865 I. T.
E441.B34   973.7/13 19   *LC* 77-189902

Boles, John B.   **3.7186**
Black southerners, 1619–1869 / John B. Boles. — Lexington, Ky.: University Press of Kentucky, c1983. xi, 244 p.; 23 cm. — (New perspectives on the South.) Includes index. 1. Slavery — Southern States — History. 2. Afro-Americans — Southern States — History. 3. Plantation life — Southern States — History. 4. Southern States — Race relations. 5. Southern States — History I. T. II. Series.
E441.B67 1983   975/.00496073 19   *LC* 83-10177   *ISBN* 0813103037

Davis, David Brion.   • **3.7187**
The slave power conspiracy and the paranoid style. Baton Rouge: Louisiana State University Press [1970, c1969] ix, 97 p.; 23 cm. (Walter Lynwood Fleming lectures in southern history.) 1. Abolitionists — United States. 2. United States — Politics and government — 1815-1861 3. Southern States — Politics and government — 1775-1865 I. T. II. Series.
E441.D25   322/.4   *LC* 79-96257   *ISBN* 0807109223

Donnan, Elizabeth, 1883-1955, ed.   • **3.7188**
Documents illustrative of the history of the slave trade to America. New York, Octagon Books, 1965. 4 v. fold. map. 27 cm. 1. Slave-trade — United States — History — Sources. 2. Slave-trade — History — Sources. I. T.
E441.D69   *LC* 65-15753

Du Bois, W. E. B. (William Edward Burghardt), 1868-1963.   • **3.7189**
The suppression of the African slave-trade to the United States of America, 1638–1870. New York, Schocken Books [1969] xxxvi, 335 p. 21 cm. (Sourcebooks in Negro history) A reprint of the 1896 ed. with a new introd. by A. Norman Klein, and the 'Apologia' of the author, dated 1954. 1. Slave-trade — United States. I. T.
E441.D81 1969   380.1/44/0973   *LC* 69-20337

Dumond, Dwight Lowell, 1895-.   • **3.7190**
Antislavery: the crusade for freedom in America. — Ann Arbor: University of Michigan Press [1961] x, 422 p.: ill., ports., maps, facsims.; 29 cm. Bibliographical references included in 'Notes' (p. [373]-413) 1. Slavery in the U.S. — Antislavery movements. I. T.
E441.D84   326.973   *LC* 61-5937

Huggins, Nathan Irvin, 1927-.   **3.7191**
Black odyssey: the Afro–American ordeal in slavery / by Nathan Irvin Huggins. — 1st ed. — New York: Pantheon Books, c1977. xvi, 250 p.; 22 cm. 1. Slavery in the United States — History. 2. Slavery in the United States — Condition of slaves. I. T.
E441.H89   301.44/93/0973   *LC* 77-5179   *ISBN* 0394416414

McManus, Edgar J.   **3.7192**
Black bondage in the North [by] Edgar J. McManus. — [1st ed. — Syracuse, N.Y.]: Syracuse University Press, 1973. xiii, 236 p.: illus.; 23 cm. 1. Slavery — New England 2. Slavery — Middle Atlantic States I. T.
E441.M16   301.44/93/0974   *LC* 72-12425   *ISBN* 0815600917

Perspectives and irony in American slavery: essays / by Carl N.   **3.7193**
Degler ... [et al.]; edited by Harry P. Owens.
Jackson: University Press of Mississippi, 1976. xii, 188 p.; 23 cm. Papers presented at a conference organized by the Dept. of History of the University of Mississippi and held Oct. 1975. 1. Slavery in the United States — Congresses. I. Degler, Carl N. II. Owens, Harry P. III. University of Mississippi. Dept. of History.
E441.P47   301.44/93/0973   *LC* 76-18283   *ISBN* 0878050744.
ISBN 0878050256 pbk

Phillips, Ulrich Bonnell, 1877-1934.   • **3.7194**
American Negro slavery; a survey of the supply, employment and control of Negro labor as determined by the plantation regime. [1st paperback ed.] Baton Rouge, Louisiana State University Press [1966] xxi, 529 p. 22 cm. (Louisiana paperbacks, L9) 1. Slavery in the United States — Economic aspects. 2. Slave labor 3. Plantation life — Southern States. 4. Southern States — Economic conditions I. T.
E441.P549 1966   301.45/22/0973   *LC* 66-31730

Rose, Willie Lee Nichols, 1927-.   **3.7195**
Slavery and freedom / Willie Lee Rose; edited by William W. Freehling. — New York: Oxford University Press, 1982. xiii, 224 p.; 22 cm. Includes index. 1. Slavery — United States — Addresses, essays, lectures. 2. Afro-Americans — History — To 1863 — Addresses, essays, lectures. 3. United States — Race relations — Addresses, essays, lectures. I. Freehling, William W., 1935- II. T.
E441.R79   973/.0496073 19   *LC* 81-3949   *ISBN* 0195029690

Stampp, Kenneth M. (Kenneth Milton)   • **3.7196**
The peculiar institution; slavery in the ante–bellum South, by Kenneth M. Stampp. New York, Vintage Books [1964, c1956] xi, 435, xiii p. 19 cm. 1. Slavery in the United States — Economic aspects — Southern States. I. T.
E441.S8 1956b   301.45/22/0975   *LC* 77-18363

Van Deburg, William L.   **3.7197**
Slavery & race in American popular culture / William L. Van Deburg. — Madison, Wis.: University of Wisconsin Press, 1984. xiii, 263 p.; 24 cm. Includes index. 1. Slavery — United States — Historiography. 2. Afro-Americans — Historiography. 3. Slavery and slaves in literature 4. Afro-Americans in literature 5. Afro-Americans in motion pictures 6. United States — Popular culture I. T. II. Title: Slavery and race in American popular culture.
E441.V23 1984   305.8/96073/072 19   *LC* 83-40272   *ISBN* 0299096300

Weinstein, Allen. comp.   **3.7198**
American Negro slavery: a modern reader / edited by Allen Weinstein, Frank Otto Gatell, and David Sarasohn. — 3d ed. — New York: Oxford University Press, 1979. ix, 317 p.; 21 cm. 1. Slavery in the United States — History — Addresses, essays, lectures. I. Gatell, Frank Otto. joint comp. II. Sarasohn, David. joint comp. III. T.
E441.W42 1979   326/.0973   *LC* 78-59690   *ISBN* 0195024702

Genovese, Eugene D., 1930-.   • **3.7199**
The political economy of slavery; studies in the economy & society of the slave South [by] Eugene D. Genovese. — New York: Pantheon Books, [1965] xiv, 304 p.; 21 cm. 1. Slavery in the United States — Economic aspects — Southern States. 2. Southern States — Economic conditions I. T.
E442.G45   326   *LC* 65-14583

E443–444 Slave Life. Biography

Beaumont de La Bonninière, Gustave Auguste de, 1802-1866.   • **3.7200**
Marie; or, Slavery in the United States: a novel of Jacksonian America. Translated from the French by Barbara Chapman. With an introd. by Alvis L. Tinnin. Stanford, Calif., Stanford University Press, 1958. xx, 252 p. 24 cm. 1. Slavery — United States — Condition of slaves. 2. United States — Social conditions I. T.
E443.B3713   326.973   *LC* 58-11693/L

Blassingame, John W., 1940-.   **3.7201**
The slave community: plantation life in the antebellum South / John W. Blassingame. — Rev. and enl. ed. — New York: Oxford University Press, 1979. xviii, 414 p.: ill.; 20 cm. Includes index. 1. Slavery — Southern States 2. Plantation life — Southern States. I. T.
E443.B55 1979   975/.004/96073   *LC* 78-26890   *ISBN* 0195025628

Elkins, Stanley M.   • 3.7202
Slavery; a problem in American institutional and intellectual life [by] Stanley
M. Elkins. 2d ed. Chicago, University of Chicago Press [1968] viii, 263 p. 21
cm. 1. Slavery in the United States. 2. Slavery in the United States —
Condition of slaves. 3. Afro-Americans — Social conditions — 1964- I. T.
E443.E4 1968   326/.0973   *LC* 68-7237

Lane, Ann J., 1931- comp.   • 3.7203
The debate over slavery: Stanley Elkins and his critics / edited by Ann J. Lane.
— Urbana: University of Illinois Press [1971] vi, 378 p.; 20 cm. (Illini books,
IB-73) 1. Elkins, Stanley M. Slavery. 2. Slavery in the United States —
Historiography. I. T.
E443.E42 L3   301.44/93   *LC* 79-141518   *ISBN* 0252001575

Fry, Gladys-Marie, 1931-.   3.7204
Night riders in Black folk history / by Gladys–Marie Fry. — 1st ed. —
[Knoxville, Tenn.]: University of Tennessee Press, [1975] xi, 251 p., [4] leaves of
plates: ill.; 24 cm. Based on the author's thesis, Indiana University. Includes
index. 1. Slavery — United States — Condition of slaves. 2. Afro-Americans
— Southern States 3. Afro-Americans — Folklore 4. Folklore and history —
Southern States. 5. Slavery — United States — Folklore. 6. Southern States —
Race relations. I. T.
E443.F89 1975   301.44/93/0973   *LC* 74-34268   *ISBN* 0870491636

Genovese, Eugene D., 1930-.   3.7205
Roll, Jordan, roll: the world the slaves made / [by] Eugene D. Genovese. — [1st
ed.]. — New York: Pantheon Books, [1974] xxii, 823 p.; 25 cm. 1. Slavery in
the United States — Condition of slaves. I. T.
E443.G46   975/.004/96073   *LC* 74-4760   *ISBN* 0394491319

Owens, Leslie Howard.   3.7206
This species of property: slave life and culture in the Old South / Leslie Howard
Owens. — Oxford; New York: Oxford University Press, 1977, c1976. 291 p.; 21
cm. 1. Slavery in the United States — Condition of slaves. 2. Slavery —
Southern States 3. Southern States — Social conditions I. T.
E443.O9 1977   301.44/93/0973   *LC* 77-2741   *ISBN* 0195022459

Bibb, Henry, b. 1815.   • 3.7207
Narrative of the life and adventures of Henry Bibb, an American slave. Written
by himself. With an introd. by Lucius C. Matlack. — 3d stereotype ed. — New
York: Negro Universities Press, [1969] xiv, 204 p.: illus., port.; 23 cm. Reprint
of the 1850 ed. 1. Slavery — Kentucky I. T.
E444.B58 1969b   301.45/22/0924 B   *LC* 76-84686   *ISBN*
0837112672

Bontemps, Arna Wendell, 1902-1973. comp.   3.7208
Great slave narratives / Selected and introduced by Arna Bontemps. — Boston:
Beacon Press, [1969] xix, 331 p.; 21 cm. 1. Slaves — United States —
Biography. I. T.
E444.B67   301.45/22/0922 B   *LC* 77-84792

'Dear Master': letters of a slave family / edited by Randall M.   3.7209
Miller.
Ithaca, N.Y.: Cornell University Press, c1978. 281 p.: ill.; 24 cm. Includes
index. 1. Skipwith family 2. Cocke, John Hartwell, 1780-1866. 3. Afro-
Americans — Colonization — Liberia — Sources. 4. Slavery in the United
States — History — Sources. I. Miller, Randall M.
E444.D42   976.1/004/96073   *LC* 77-90907   *ISBN* 0801411343

Federal Writers' Project.   • 3.7210
Lay my burden down; a folk history of slavery, edited by B. A. Botkin. Chicago,
Ill., University of Chicago press [1945] xxi, 285 p. front., plates. 24 cm. 'A
selection and integration of excerpts and complete narratives from the Slave
narrative collection of the Federal writers' project.' 1. Slavery — United States
— Condition of slaves 2. Afro-Americans — Biography I. Botkin, Benjamin
Albert, 1901- II. T.
E 444 F29   *LC* 45-5576

Brent, Linda, 1818-1896.   3.7211
Incidents in the life of a slave girl / written by herself; edited by L. Maria Child.
Boston, Published for the author, 1861. — [New York: AMS Press, 1973]
306 p.; 19 cm. 1. Brent, Linda, 1818-1896. 2. Slaves — United States —
Biography. I. T.
E444.J17 1973   301.44/93/0924 B   *LC* 79-170837   *ISBN*
0404002668

Osofsky, Gilbert, 1935- comp.   3.7212
Puttin' on ole massa; the slave narratives of Henry Bibb, William Wells Brown,
and Solomon Northup. [1st ed.] New York, Harper & Row [1969] 409 p. 22 cm.
1. Slaves — United States — Biography. I. Bibb, Henry, b. 1815. Narrative of
the life of Henry Bibb, an American slave. 1969. II. Brown, William Wells,
1815-1884. Narrative of William Wells Brown, a fugitive slave. 1969. III.
Northup, Solomon, b. 1808. Twelve years a slave: narrative of Solomon
Northup. 1969. IV. T.
E444.O8   301.45/22 B   *LC* 69-17285

Slave testimony: two centuries of letters, speeches, interviews,   3.7213
and autobiographies / edited by John W. Blassingame.
Baton Rouge: Louisiana State University Press, c1977. lxv, 777 p.: ill.; 24 cm.
1. Slavery in the United States — Personal narratives. 2. Slavery in the United
States — History — Sources. I. Blassingame, John W., 1940-
E444.S57   301.44/93/0973   *LC* 75-18040   *ISBN* 0807101842

Thomas, James P., 1827-1913.   3.7214
From Tennessee slave to St. Louis entrepreneur: the autobiography of James
Thomas / edited with an introduction by Loren Schweninger; with a foreword
by John Hope Franklin. — Columbia: University of Missouri Press, 1984. xi,
225 p.; 24 cm. Includes index. 1. Thomas, James P., 1827-1913. 2. Slaves —
Tennessee — Biography. 3. Slavery — Tennessee — Condition of slaves.
4. Tennessee — Biography. I. Schweninger, Loren. II. T.
E444.T46 A34 1984   976.8/00496073/0924 B 19   *LC* 83-16676
    ISBN 0826204317

Fields, Barbara Jeanne.   3.7215
Slavery and freedom on the middle ground: Maryland during the nineteenth
century / Barbara Jeanne Fields. — New Haven: Yale University Press, c1985.
xv, 268 p.: map; 24 cm. (Yale historical publications. Miscellany. 123) Includes
index. 1. Slavery — Maryland — History — 19th century. 2. Afro-Americans
— Maryland — Economic conditions. 3. Maryland — Race relations. I. T.
II. Series.
E445.M3 F54 1985   975.2/004962023 19   *LC* 84-20949   *ISBN*
0300023405

Lewis, Ronald L., 1940-.   3.7216
Coal, iron, and slaves: industrial slavery in Maryland and Virginia, 1715–1865 /
Ronald L. Lewis. — Westport, Conn.: Greenwood Press, 1979. 283 p.: ill.; 25
cm. — (Contributions in labor history. no. 6 0146-3608) Includes index.
1. Slave labor — Maryland. 2. Slave labor — Virginia. 3. Factory system —
Maryland — History. 4. Factory system — Virginia — History. 5. Mines and
mineral resources — Maryland — History. 6. Mines and mineral resources —
Virginia — History. 7. Maryland — History 8. Virginia — History I. T.
II. Series.
E445.M3 L48   331.1/1734/09752   *LC* 78-55333   *ISBN*
0313205221

Greene, Lorenzo Johnston, 1899-.   3.7217
The Negro in colonial New England. With a new pref. by Benjamin Quarles. —
New York: Atheneum, 1968 [c1942] 404 p.; 21 cm. — (Studies in American
Negro life) (Atheneum NL 1) 1. Slavery — New England 2. Afro-Americans
— New England 3. New England — History — Colonial period, ca. 1600-1775
I. T.
E445.N5 G7 1968   301.451/96073/074   *LC* 68-16413

Coughtry, Jay.   3.7218
The notorious triangle: Rhode Island and the African slave trade, 1700–1807 /
Jay Coughtry. — Philadelphia: Temple University Press, 1981. xiii, 361 p.: ill.;
24 cm. Includes index. 1. Slave-trade — Rhode Island. 2. Afro-Americans —
Rhode Island — History — 18th century. 3. Rhode Island — History I. T.
II. Title: Rhode Island and the African slave trade, 1700-1807.
E445.R4 C68   974.5/00496073 19   *LC* 81-4324   *ISBN* 0877222185

Wood, Peter H., 1943-.   3.7219
Black majority: Negroes in colonial South Carolina from 1670 through the
Stono Rebellion / [by] Peter H. Wood. — [1st ed.]. — New York: Knopf;
[distributed by Random House], 1974. xxiv, 346, viii p.; 25 cm. Based on the
author's thesis, Harvard, 1972. 1. Slavery — South Carolina 2. South Carolina
— History — Colonial period, ca. 1600-1775 I. T.
E445.S7 W66   301.44/93/09757   *LC* 73-20167   *ISBN* 0394483960

Morgan, Edmund Sears.   3.7220
American slavery, American freedom: the ordeal of colonial Virginia / Edmund
S. Morgan. — 1st ed. — New York: Norton, [1975] x, 454 p.: map; 24 cm.
Includes index. 1. Slavery — Virginia 2. Virginia — History — Colonial
period, ca. 1600-1775 I. T.
E445.V8 M67 1975   975.5/02   *LC* 75-17534   *ISBN* 039305554X

Mullin, Gerald W.   3.7221
Flight and rebellion; slave resistance in eighteenth–century Virginia [by] Gerald
W. Mullin. — New York: Oxford University Press, 1972. xii, 219 p.: illus.; 22
cm. 1. Slavery — Virginia I. T.
E445.V8 M8   301.44/93/09755   *LC* 73-173327   *ISBN* 0195015142

E446–448 History of Slavery to 1830

Dillon, Merton Lynn, 1924-.   • 3.7222
Benjamin Lundy and the struggle for Negro freedom [by] Merton L. Dillon. —
Urbana: University of Illinois Press, 1966. vi, 285 p.: port.; 24 cm. 1. Lundy,
Benjamin, 1789-1839. 2. Slavery in the United States — Anti-slavery
movements. I. T.
E446.D54   973.71140924 B   *LC* 66-15473

Jordan, Winthrop D.   3.7223
The white man's burden; historical origins of racism in the United States [by] Winthrop D. Jordan. New York, Oxford University Press, 1974. xvi, 229 p. 22 cm. 'Much of the material in this book has been derived from White over black: American attitudes toward the Negro, 1550-1812.' 1. Slavery in the United States — History. 2. Afro-Americans — History — To 1863 3. United States — Race question. I. Jordan, Winthrop D. White over black: American attitudes toward the Negro, 1550-1812. II. T.
E446.J67   301.45/19/6073   *LC* 73-86980   *ISBN* 0195017420

Noonan, John Thomas, 1926-.   3.7224
The Antelope: the ordeal of the recaptured Africans in the administrations of James Monroe and John Quincy Adams / John T. Noonan, Jr. — Berkeley: University of California Press, c1977. vii, 198 p.; 23 cm. 1. Antelope (Ship) 2. Slave-trade — United States — History. 3. United States — Politics and government — 1815-1861 I. T.
E446.N63   343/.73/08540264   *LC* 77-151642   *ISBN* 0520033191

Stewart, James Brewer.   3.7225
Holy warriors: the abolitionists and American slavery / James Brewer Stewart; consulting editor, Eric Foner. New York: Hill and Wang, c1976. 226 p.; 21 cm. (American century series) Includes index. 1. Slavery in the United States — Anti-slavery movements. I. T.
E446.S83 1976   322.4/4/0973   *LC* 76-22209   *ISBN* 0809055198

Windley, Lathan A.   3.7226
Runaway slave advertisements: a documentary history from the 1730s to 1790 / compiled by Lathan A. Windley. — Westport, Conn.: Greenwood Press, 1983. 4 v.; 25 cm. 1. Fugitive slaves — Southern States — History — 18th century — Sources. 2. Slavery — Southern States — History — 18th century — Sources. 3. Southern States — Social conditions — 18th century — Sources. I. T.
E446.W73 1983   975/.00496 19   *LC* 83-1486   *ISBN* 0313230250

Zilversmit, Arthur.   • 3.7227
The first emancipation: the abolition of slavery in the North / Arthur Zilversmit. — Chicago: University of Chicago Press, 1967. x, 262 p. 1. Slavery — United States — Anti-slavery movements. I. T.
E446.Z5   *LC* 67-15954

Aptheker, Herbert, 1915-.   • 3.7228
American Negro slave revolts. — New York: International Publishers, [1963] 409 p.; 21 cm. Issued also as thesis (PH.D.) Columbia University. 1. Slavery in the U.S. — Insurrections, etc. 2. Afro-Americans — History — To 1863 I. T.
E447.A67 1963   326.973   *LC* 63-19661

Miller, Floyd John, 1940-.   3.7229
The search for a black nationality: black emigration and colonization, 1787–1863 / Floyd J. Miller. — Urbana: University of Illinois Press, [1975] xiii, 295 p.; 24 cm. — (Blacks in the New World.) Includes index. 1. Afro-Americans — Colonization — Africa I. T. II. Series.
E448.M56   301.32/8/7306   *LC* 75-4650   *ISBN* 0252002636

Staudenraus, P. J.   • 3.7230
The African colonization movement, 1816–1865. — New York: Columbia University Press, 1961. ix, 323 p.; 25 cm. Bibliographical references included in 'Notes' (p. [252]-304) 'Bibliographical essay': p. [305]-310. 1. American Colonization Society. 2. Negroes — Colonization — Africa. I. T.
E448.S78   326.4   *LC* 61-8071

E449 1830–1863 General Works, A–Z

E449 A–G

Antislavery reconsidered: new perspectives on the abolitionists /   3.7231
edited by Lewis Perry and Michael Fellman.
Baton Rouge: Louisiana State University Press, c1979. xvi, 348 p.; 24 cm. 1. Slavery in the United States — Anti-slavery movements — Addresses, essays, lectures. 2. Slavery in Great Britain — Anti-slavery movements — Addresses, essays, lectures. I. Perry, Lewis, 1938- II. Fellman, Michael.
E449.A6237   322.4/4/0973   *LC* 78-10177   *ISBN* 0807104795

Birney, James Gillespie, 1792-1857.   • 3.7232
Letters of James Gillespie Birney, 1831–1857, edited by Dwight L. Dumond ... New York, London, D. Appleton-Century Company, Incorporated [c1938] 2 v. fronts. (ports.) 2 facsim. 23 cm. At head of title: The American Historical Association. Paged continuously. 'Prepared and published under the direction of the American Historical Association from the income of the Albert J. Beveridge Memorial Fund.' 'Published addresses, articles and monographs of James Gillespie Birney': vol. I, p. xxvii-xxviii. 1. Slavery — United States — Controversial literature. I. Dumond, Dwight Lowell, 1895- ed. II. American Historical Association. Albert J. Beveridge Memorial Fund. III. T.
E449.B6179   *LC* 38-24538

The Black abolitionist papers / C. Peter Ripley, editor; Jeffrey   3.7233
S. Rossbach, associate editor ... [et al.].
Chapel Hill: University of North Carolina Press, c1985- <c1986 >. v. <1-2 >: ill.; 24 cm. 1. Slavery — United States — Anti-slavery movements — Sources. 2. Abolitionists — United States — History — Sources. 3. Abolitionists — History — 19th century — Sources. 4. Afro-Americans — History — To 1863 — Sources. I. Ripley, C. Peter, 1941-
E449.B624 1985   973/.0496 19   *LC* 84-13131   *ISBN* 0807816256

Crusaders and compromisers: essays on the relationship of the   3.7234
antislavery struggle to the antebellum party system / edited by
Alan M. Kraut.
Westport, Conn.: Greenwood Press, 1983. xii, 286 p.; 25 cm. — (Contributions in American history. 0084-9219; no. 104) Includes index. 1. Slavery — United States — Anti-slavery movements — Addresses, essays, lectures. 2. Political parties — United States — History — 19th century — Addresses, essays, lectures. 3. United States — Politics and government — 1815-1861 — Addresses, essays, lectures. I. Kraut, Alan M. II. Series.
E449.C955 1983   324.275/09 19   *LC* 82-21085   *ISBN* 0313225370

Dick, Robert C.   3.7235
Black protest; issues and tactics [by] Robert C. Dick. Westport, Conn., Greenwood Press [1974] xiii, 338 p. ports. 21 cm. (Contributions in American studies, no. 14) 1. Slavery in the United States — Anti-slavery movements. 2. Afro-Americans — Colonization 3. Afro-Americans — History — To 1863 I. T.
E449.D53   322.4/4/0973   *LC* 72-794   *ISBN* 0837163668

Douglass, Frederick.   3.7236
The Frederick Douglass papers, Series 1: Speeches, debates, and interviews. Vol.1: 1841–46 / John W. Blassingame, editor .. — New Haven; London: Yale University Press, 1979. cii, 530 p., plate: col. port.; 24 cm. 1. Slavery in the United States — Anti-slavery movements. I. Blassingame, John W. II. T.
E449.D733   322.4/4/0973   *LC* 78-16687   *ISBN* 0300022468

Douglass, Frederick, 1817?-1895.   • 3.7237
The life and writings of Frederick Douglass [by] Philip S. Foner. — New York: International Publishers, [1950-55] 4 v.: ports.; 22 cm. 1. Slavery in the United States — Anti-slavery movements. I. Foner, Philip Sheldon, 1910- II. T.
E449.D736   322.4/4/0924   *LC* 50-7654

Douglass, Frederick, 1817?-1895.   • 3.7238
Narrative of the life of Frederick Douglass: an American slave / written by himself; edited by Benjamin Quarles. — Cambridge, Mass.: Belknap Press, 1960. xxvi, 163 p.: port., map; 22 cm. (John Harvard library.) 1. Douglass, Frederick, 1817?-1895. 2. Douglass, Frederick, 1817?-1895. 3. Slavery — Maryland I. T. II. Series.
E449.D74905   326.92 92   *LC* 59-11516

Huggins, Nathan Irvin, 1927-.   3.7239
Slave and citizen: the life of Frederick Douglass / Nathan Irvin Huggins; edited by Oscar Handlin. — Boston: Little, Brown, c1980. viii, 194 p.; 20 cm. — (Library of American biography.) 1. Douglass, Frederick, 1817?-1895. 2. Abolitionists — United States — Biography. 3. Afro-Americans — Biography. I. Handlin, Oscar, 1915- II. T. III. Series.
E449.D75 H83   326/.092/4 B   *LC* 79-89336   *ISBN* 0316380008

Martin, Waldo E., 1951-.   3.7240
The mind of Frederick Douglass / Waldo E. Martin, Jr. — Chapel Hill: University of North Carolina Press, c1984. xii, 333 p.; 24 cm. Includes index. 1. Douglass, Frederick, 1817?-1895. 2. Slavery — United States — Anti-slavery movements. 3. Abolitionists — United States — Biography. 4. Afro-Americans — Biography. 5. United States — Social conditions — To 1865 6. United States — Social conditions — 1865-1918 I. T.
E449.D75 M37 1984   973.8/092/4 B 19   *LC* 84-5140   *ISBN* 0807816167

Preston, Dickson J., 1914-.   3.7241
Young Frederick Douglass: the Maryland years / Dickson J. Preston. — Baltimore: Johns Hopkins University Press, c1980. xvii, 242 p.: ill.; 24 cm. Includes index. 1. Douglass, Frederick, 1817?-1895 — Childhood and youth. 2. Abolitionists — United States — Biography. 3. Slavery — Maryland I. T.
E449.D75 P74   973.8/092/4 B   *LC* 80-7992   *ISBN* 0801824397

Duberman, Martin B. ed.   • 3.7242
The antislavery vanguard; new essays on the abolitionists, edited by Martin Duberman. — Princeton, N.J.: Princeton University Press, 1965. x, 508 p.; 21 cm. Erratum slip inserted. 1. Abolitionists — United States. 2. Slavery in the United States — Anti-slavery movements. I. T.
E449.D84   973.7114   *LC* 65-10824

Filler, Louis, 1912-.   3.7243
Crusade against slavery: friends, foes, and reforms, 1820–1860 / Louis Filler. — Algonac, Mich.: Reference Publications, 1986. 389 p.: ill.; 22 cm. Rev. ed. of: The crusade against slavery, 1830-1860. [1st ed.]. 1960. Includes index.

1. Slavery — United States — Anti-slavery movements. I. Filler, Louis, 1912-
Crusade against slavery, 1830-1860. II. T.
E449.F493 1986   326/.0973 19   *LC* 85-30100   *ISBN* 0917256298

Fitzhugh, George, 1806-1881.   • 3.7244
Cannibals all! or, Slaves without masters. Edited by C. Vann Woodward. —
Cambridge: Belknap Press of Harvard University Press, 1960. 264 p.; 22 cm. —
(The John Harvard library) 1. Slavery in the United States. — Controversial
literature — 1857. 2. Slavery — Justification 3. Labor and laboring classes
I. T.
E449.F555 1960   326.973   *LC* 60-5400

Fogel, Robert William.   3.7245
Time on the cross; the economics of American Negro slavery, by Robert
William Fogel and Stanley L. Engerman. — [1st ed.]. — Boston: Little, Brown,
[1974] xviii, 286 p.: illus.; 22 cm. 1. Slavery in the United States — Economic
aspects. I. Engerman, Stanley L. joint author. II. T.
E449.F65   331.1/1734/0973   *LC* 73-18347   *ISBN* 0316287008

Reckoning with slavery: a critical study in the quantitative   3.7246
history of American Negro slavery / Paul A. David ... [et al.];
with an introd. by Kenneth M. Stampp.
New York: Oxford University Press, 1976. xvi, 398 p.; 21 cm. Includes index.
1. Fogel, Robert William. Time on the cross. 2. Slavery in the United States —
Economic aspects. I. David, Paul A.
E449.F653 R42   331.1/1734/0973   *LC* 75-38098   *ISBN*
0195020332 pbk

Foner, Philip Sheldon, 1910-.   3.7247
History of Black Americans: from the Compromise of 1850 to the end of the
Civil War / Philip S. Foner. — Westport, Conn.: Greenwood Press, c1983.
539 p. — (Contributions in American history; no. 103) Includes index. 1. Afro-
Americans — History — To 1863 2. Slavery — United States — History —
19th century. 3. Afro-Americans — History — 1863-1877 4. United States —
Race relations I. T.
E449.F68 1983   973/.0496073 19   *LC* 82-11702   *ISBN*
083717967X

Friedman, Lawrence Jacob, 1940-.   3.7248
Gregarious saints: self and community in American abolitionism, 1830–1870 /
Lawrence J. Friedman. — Cambridge [Cambridgeshire]; New York:
Cambridge University Press, 1982. xi, 344 p.; 24 cm. Includes index.
1. Abolitionists — United States. 2. Slavery — United States — Anti-slavery
movements. I. T.
E449.F86 1982   326/.0973 19   *LC* 81-15454   *ISBN* 0521244293

Thomas, John L.   • 3.7249
The liberator, William Lloyd Garrison: a biography. — [1st ed.]. — Boston:
Little, Brown, [1963] 502 p.: ill.; 22 cm. 1. Garrison, William Lloyd,
1805-1879. I. T.
E449.G26   923.673   *LC* 63-8310

Lerner, Gerda, 1920-.   • 3.7250
The Grimké sisters from South Carolina; rebels against slavery. Illustrated with
photos. — Boston: Houghton Mifflin, 1967. xiv, 479 p.: illus., facsim., ports.; 22
cm. 1. Grimké, Angelina Emily, 1805-1879. 2. Grimké, Sarah Moore,
1792-1873. I. T.
E449.G89   973.71/14/0922   *LC* 67-25218

E449 H–Z

Helper, Hinton Rowan, 1829-1909.   • 3.7251
The impending crisis of the South: how to meet it. — Westport, Conn.: Negro
Universities Press, [1970] 420 p.; 23 cm. Reprint of the 1857 ed. 1. Slavery in
the United States. 2. Slavery in the United States — Controversial literature —
1857. I. T.
E449.H483 1970   301.44/93   *LC* 73-107517   *ISBN* 0837137640

Kraditor, Aileen S.   • 3.7252
Means and ends in American abolitionism: Garrison and his critics on strategy
and tactics, 1834–1850 / by Aileen S. Kraditor. — [New York]: Pantheon
Books, [1969] xvi, 296 p.; 22 cm. 1. Garrison, William Lloyd, 1805-1879.
2. Slavery in the United States — Anti-slavery movements. I. T.
E449.K7   973.71/14   *LC* 68-26046

Dillon, Merton Lynn, 1924-.   • 3.7253
Elijah P. Lovejoy, abolitionist editor. Urbana, University of Illinois Press, 1961.
190 p. 23 cm. Includes bibliography. 1. Lovejoy, Elijah P. (Elijah Parish),
1802-1837. I. T.
E449.L889D5   923.673   *LC* 61-62765

McKitrick, Eric L., ed.   • 3.7254
Slavery defended: the views of the Old South. — Englewood Cliffs, N.J.:
Prentice-Hall, [1963] 180 p.; 21 cm. — (A Spectrum book) 1. Slavery in the
United States — Controversial literature. 2. Slavery — Southern States I. T.
E449.M16   326.7   *LC* 63-12270

McPherson, James M.   • 3.7255
The struggle for equality: abolitionists and the Negro in the Civil War and
Reconstruction / by James M. McPherson. — Princeton, N.J.: Princeton
University Press, 1964. ix, 474 p.: ill.; 25 cm. 1. Abolitionists 2. Slavery in the
United States — Emancipation. 3. Afro-Americans — History — 1863-1877
I. T.
E449.M176   973.7   *LC* 63-23411

McKivigan, John R., 1949-.   3.7256
The war against proslavery religion: abolitionism and the northern churches,
1830–1865 / John R. McKivigan. — Ithaca, N.Y.: Cornell University Press,
1984. 327 p.; 24 cm. Includes index. 1. Slavery — United States — Anti-slavery
movements. 2. Slavery and the church 3. Abolitionists — United States —
History — 19th century. I. T. II. Title: War against pro-slavery religion.
E449.M475 1984   973.6 19   *LC* 83-45933   *ISBN* 0801415896

Bartlett, Irving H.   • 3.7257
Wendell Phillips, Brahmin radical. — Boston: Beacon Press, [1961] 438 p.; 21
cm. 1. Phillips, Wendell, 1811-1884. I. T.
E449.P5594   923.673   *LC* 61-10570

Quarles, Benjamin.   • 3.7258
Black abolitionists. — New York: Oxford University Press, [1969] x, 310 p.; 22
cm. 1. Abolitionists 2. Slavery in the United States — Anti-slavery
movements. I. T.
E449.Q17   *LC* 69-17766

Schor, Joel.   3.7259
Henry Highland Garnet: a voice of Black radicalism in the nineteenth century /
Joel Schor. Westport, Conn.: Greenwood Press, 1977. xii, 250 p.; 22 cm.
(Contributions in American history; no. 54) Includes index. 1. Garnet, Henry
Highland, 1815-1882. 2. Slavery in the United States — Anti-slavery
movements. 3. Slavery in the United States — Emancipation. 4. Abolitionists
— United States — Biography. I. T.
E449.S294   322.4/4/0924 B   *LC* 76-8746   *ISBN* 0837189373

Sewell, Richard H.   3.7260
Ballots for freedom: antislavery politics in the United States, 1837–1860 /
Richard H. Sewell. — New York: Oxford University Press, 1976. xvi, 379 p.; 24
cm. 1. Slavery in the United States — Anti-slavery movements. 2. United
States — Politics and government — 1845-1861 I. T.
E449.S49   322.4/4/0973   *LC* 75-25464   *ISBN* 0195019970

Sorin, Gerald, 1940-.   • 3.7261
Abolitionism: a new perspective / foreword by James P. Shenton. — New York:
Praeger, [1972] 187 p.; 21 cm. — (New perspectives in American history)
1. Slavery in the United States — Anti-slavery movements. 2. Abolitionists —
United States. I. T.
E449.S697 1972   322.4/4/0973   *LC* 79-143981

Stowe, Harriet Beecher, 1811-1896.   • 3.7262
The key to Uncle Tom's cabin. New York, Arno Press, 1968. viii, 508 p. 22 cm.
(American Negro, his history and literature.) Reprint of the 1854 ed. 1. Stowe,
Harriet Beecher, 1811-1896. Uncle Tom's cabin. 2. Slavery in the United
States. — Condition of slaves. I. T. II. Series.
E449.S89592 1968b   813/.3   *LC* 69-19634

Stuckey, Sterling. comp.   3.7263
The ideological origins of Black nationalism. Boston, Beacon Press [1972]
265 p. 22 cm. 1. Slavery in the United States — History — Sources. 2. Afro-
Americans — History — Sources. I. T.
E449.S933 1972   301.45/19/6073   *LC* 72-75547   *ISBN* 0807054283

Wyatt-Brown, Bertram, 1932-.   • 3.7264
Lewis Tappan and the evangelical war against slavery. — Cleveland: Press of
Case Western Reserve University, 1969. xxi, 376 p.: port.; 24 cm. 1. Tappan,
Lewis, 1788-1873. 2. Slavery in the United States — Anti-slavery movements.
I. T.
E449.T18 W9   326/.0924   *LC* 68-19228   *ISBN* 0829501460

Ten Broek, Jacobus.   • 3.7265
[Antislavery origins of the Fourteenth amendment] Equal under law / [by]
Jacobus ten Broek. — New, enl. ed. New York: Collier Books [1965] 352 p.; 18
cm. First ed. published in 1951 under title: The antislavery origins of the
Fourteenth amendment. 1. Abolitionists 2. United States — Constitutional
law — Amendments — 14th I. T.
E449.T4 1965   342.7309   *LC* 64-24351

Trefousse, Hans Louis.   • 3.7266
The radical Republicans: Lincoln's vanguard for racial justice / [by] Hans L. Trefousse. — [1st ed.] New York: Knopf, 1969 [c1968] xiv, 492, xviii p.: ill., ports.; 22 cm. 1. Republican Party (U.S.: 1854-) 2. Slavery in the United States — Anti-slavery movements. 3. United States — Politics and government — 1849-1877 I. T.
E449.T79   973.71   LC 68-23937

Walters, Ronald G.   3.7267
The antislavery appeal: American abolitionism after 1830 / Ronald G. Walters. Baltimore: Johns Hopkins University Press, c1976. xvii, 196 p.: ill.; 24 cm. Includes index. 1. Slavery in the United States — Anti-slavery movements. I. T.
E449.W2   322.4/4/0973   LC 76-17229   ISBN 0801818613

Abzug, Robert H.   3.7268
Passionate liberator: Theodore Dwight Weld and the dilemma of reform / Robert H. Abzug. — New York: Oxford University Press, 1980. xi, 370 p.: port.; 22 cm. Includes index. 1. Weld, Theodore Dwight, 1803-1895. 2. Slavery — United States — Anti-slavery movements. 3. Abolitionists — United States — Biography. 4. Social reformers — United States. 5. United States — Social conditions — To 1865 I. T.
E449.W46 A29   326/.092/4 B   LC 80-11819   ISBN 019502771X

E450–453 Special Topics

Gara, Larry.   • 3.7269
The liberty line; the legend of the underground railroad. — Lexington: University of Kentucky Press, [1961] ix, 201 p.; 24 cm. 1. Underground railroad 2. Slavery in the United States — Fugitive slaves. I. T.
E450.G22   973.7115   LC 61-6552

Katz, Jonathan.   3.7270
Resistance at Christiana; the fugitive slave rebellion, Christiana, Pennsylvania, September 11, 1851: a documentary account. New York, Crowell [1974] viii, 359 p. illus. 24 cm. 1. Riots — Pennsylvania — Christiana. 2. Christiana (Pa.) — History. I. T.
E450.K28 1974   974.8/15/03   LC 73-21907   ISBN 0690003072

Ross, Alexander Milton, 1832-1897.   3.7271
Recollections and experiences of an abolitionist, from 1855 to 1865. New foreword by Donald Franklin Joyce. — Northbrook, Ill.: Metro Books, 1972. xv, 224 p.: illus.; 23 cm. Reprint of the 1875 ed. 1. Brown, John, 1800-1859. 2. Ross, Alexander Milton, 1832-1897. 3. Fugitive slaves — United States — Anti-slavery movements. 4. Fugitive slaves — United States I. T.
E450.R82 1972   322.4/4/0924 B   LC 77-99403   ISBN 0841100748

Boyer, Richard Owen, 1903-1973.   3.7272
The legend of John Brown: a biography and a history [by] Richard O. Boyer. — [1st ed.]. — New York: Knopf, 1973 [c1972] xxiii, 627, xvii p.: illus.; 27 cm. 1. Brown, John, 1800-1859. I. T.
E451.B77   973.6/8/0924 B   LC 69-10672   ISBN 039446124X

Oates, Stephen B.   • 3.7273
To purge this land with blood: a biography of John Brown / [by] Stephen B. Oates. — [1st ed.]. — New York: Harper & Row, [1970] xii, 434 p.: ill., maps, ports.; 25 cm. 1. Brown, John, 1800-1859. I. T.
E451.O17 1970   973.68/0924 B   LC 77-95979

Quarles, Benjamin. comp.   3.7274
Blacks on John Brown. — Urbana: University of Illinois Press, [1972] xv, 164 p.: illus.; 21 cm. 1. Brown, John, 1800-1859. I. T.
E451.Q37   973.6/8/0924 B   LC 72-188132   ISBN 0252002458

Villard, Oswald Garrison, 1872-1949.   • 3.7275
John Brown, 1800–1859; a biography fifty years after. Gloucester, Mass., P. Smith, 1965 [i.e. 1966. c1910] xiv, 738 p. facsims., map, plates, ports. 21 cm. 1. Brown, John, 1800-1859. I. T.
E451.V72 1966   LC 66-2893

Franklin, John Hope, 1915-.   • 3.7276
The Emancipation proclamation. [1st ed.] Garden City, N.Y., Doubleday, 1963. 181 p. illus. 22 cm. 1. United States. President (1861-1865: Lincoln). Emancipation Proclamation I. T.
E453.F8   973.714   LC 63-8296

E456–655 Civil War Period (1861–1865)

Hendrick, Burton Jesse, 1870-1949.   • 3.7277
Lincoln's war cabinet. — Garden City, N.Y.: Dolphin books, 1961 [c1946] 559 p. 1. Lincoln, Abraham, 1809-1865. 2. Cabinet officers — United States 3. United States — Politics and government — Civil War, 1861-1865 I. T.
E456.H4 1961

E457–457.92 LINCOLN. BIOGRAPHY. WRITINGS

Angle, Paul M. (Paul McClelland), 1900-1975. ed.   • 3.7278
The Lincoln reader / edited, with an introduction, by Paul M. Angle. — New Brunswick: Rutgers university press, 1947. vii, 564 p.: plates, ports., facsims.; 22.5 cm. 'A biography written by sixty—five authors.'—Foreword. Bibliography: p. [544]-547. 1. Lincoln, Abraham, 1809-1865. I. T.
E457.A58   923.173   LC 47-30067

Current, Richard Nelson.   • 3.7279
The Lincoln nobody knows. New York, Hill and Wang [1963, c1958] vi, 314 p. 21 cm. (American century series) 'AC59.' 'Bibliographical essay': p. 288-304. 1. Lincoln, Abraham, 1809-1865. I. T.
E457.C96 1963   LC 63-6069

Neely, Mark E.   3.7280
The Abraham Lincoln encyclopedia / Mark E. Neely, Jr. — New York: McGraw-Hill, c1982. xii, 356 p.: ill.; 29 cm. Includes index. 1. Lincoln, Abraham, 1809-1865 — Dictionaries, indexes, etc. 2. Presidents — United States — Biography 3. United States — History — 1815-1861 — Dictionaries. I. T.
E457.N48   973.7/092/4 B 19   LC 81-7296   ISBN 0070461457

Oates, Stephen B.   3.7281
Abraham Lincoln, the man behind the myths / by Stephen B. Oates. — 1st ed. — New York: Harper & Row, c1984. xiv, 224 p.; 22 cm. Includes index. 1. Lincoln, Abraham, 1809-1865. 2. Presidents — United States — Biography I. T.
E457.O16 1984   973.7/092/4 B 19   LC 83-48798   ISBN 0060153040

Oates, Stephen B.   3.7282
With malice toward none: the life of Abraham Lincoln / Stephen B. Oates. — 1st ed. — New York: Harper & Row, c1977. xvii, 492 p., [16] leaves of plates: ill.; 24 cm. 1. Lincoln, Abraham, 1809-1865. 2. Presidents — United States — Biography I. T.
E457.O17 1977   973.7/092/4 B   LC 76-12058   ISBN 0060132833

Randall, J. G. (James Garfield), 1881-1953.   • 3.7283
Lincoln, the president. New York: Dodd, Mead, 1945-55. 4 v.: ill.; 25 cm. (American political leaders.) Vol. 4 by J. G. Randall and R. N. Current. 1. Lincoln, Abraham, 1809-1865. I. T. II. Series.
E457.R2   LC 45-10041

Strozier, Charles B.   3.7284
Lincoln's quest for union: public and private meanings / Charles B. Strozier. — New York: Basic Books, c1982. xxiii, 271 p.: ports.; 24 cm. 1. Lincoln, Abraham, 1809-1865. 2. Presidents — United States — Biography I. T.
E457.S897 1982   973.7/092/4 B 19   LC 81-68406   ISBN 0465041191

Thomas, Benjamin Platt, 1902-1956.   • 3.7285
Abraham Lincoln: a biography / by Benjamin P. Thomas. — New York: Knopf 1952. xiv, 548, xii p.: ill., ports, maps.; 22 cm. 1. Lincoln, Abraham, 1809-1865. I. T.
E457.T427 1952

Mitgang, Herbert.   • 3.7286
Lincoln as they saw him / edited and narrated by Herbert Mitgang. — New York: Rinehart, 1956. xv, 519 p.: ill., ports.; 24 cm. 1. Lincoln, Abraham, President of the United States, 1809-1865. I. T.
E457.15.M5   973.7   LC 56-10181

Cox, LaWanda C. Fenlason.   3.7287
Lincoln and Black freedom: a study in presidential leadership / by LaWanda Cox. — 1st ed. — Columbia, S.C.: University of South Carolina Press, 1981. xiii, 254 p.; 24 cm. Includes index. 1. Lincoln, Abraham, 1809-1865 —

Relations with Afro-Americans. 2. Afro-Americans — History — To 1863 3. Afro-Americans — History — 1863-1877 I. T.
E457.2.C84   973.7/092/4 19   *LC* 81-3350   *ISBN* 0872494004

Quarles, Benjamin.   • 3.7288
Lincoln and the Negro / Benjamin Quarles. — New York: Oxford University Press, 1962. 275 p.: ill.; 21 cm. 1. Lincoln, Abraham, Pres. U.S., 1809-1865 — Relations with Afro-Americans. 2. Lincoln, Abraham, Pres. U.S., 1809-1865 — Views on slavery. I. T.
E457.2.Q3   *LC* 62-9829

Randall, Ruth (Painter)   • 3.7289
Mary Lincoln; biography of a marriage. — [1st ed.]. — Boston: Little, Brown, [c1953] xiv, 555 p.: illus., ports.; 23 cm. 1. Lincoln, Mary Todd, 1818-1882. I. T.
E457.25.R3   920.7   *LC* 52-12621

Turner, Justin G.   3.7290
Mary Todd Lincoln: her life and letters [by] Justin G. Turner [and] Linda Lovitt Turner. With an introd. by Fawn M. Brodie. — [1st ed.]. — New York: Knopf, 1972. xxv, 750, xxxvi p.: illus.; 25 cm. 1. Lincoln, Mary Todd, 1818-1882. I. Turner, Linda Lovitt, joint author. II. Lincoln, Mary (Todd) 1818-1882. Mary Todd Lincoln: her life and letters. 1972. III. T.
E457.25.T87 1972   973.7/092/4 B   *LC* 69-10700   *ISBN* 0394466438

Beveridge, Albert Jeremiah, 1862-1927.   • 3.7291
Abraham Lincoln, 1809-1858. Boston, Houghton Mifflin, 1928. St. Clair Shores, Mich., Scholarly Press, 1971. 2 v. illus., ports. 22 cm. 1. Lincoln, Abraham, 1809-1865. I. T.
E457.3.B576 1971   973.7/0924 B   *LC* 73-144879   *ISBN* 0403008654

Fehrenbacher, Don Edward.   • 3.7292
Prelude to greatness: Lincoln in the 1850's / Don E. Fehrenbacher. — Stanford, Calif.: Stanford University Press, 1962. 205 p. 1. Lincoln, Abraham, 1809-1865. I. T.
E457.3 F4   923.173   *LC* 62-8661   *ISBN* 0804701202

Sandburg, Carl, 1878-1967.   • 3.7293
Abraham Lincoln, the prairie years, by Carl Sandburg; with 105 illustrations from photographs, and many cartoons, sketches, maps, and letters. New York, Harcourt, Brace & company [1927] 2v. fronts., illus. (incl.maps) plates, ports., facsims. 24cm. 1. Lincoln, Abraham, 1809-1865. I. T.
E457.3.S226   *LC* 28-5762

Jaffa, Harry V.   • 3.7294
Crisis of the house divided: an interpretation of the issues in the Lincoln–Douglas debates. — [1st ed.]. — Garden City, N. Y.: Doubleday, 1959. 451 p.; 22 cm. 1. Douglas, Stephen Arnold, 1813-1861. 2. Lincoln-Douglas debates, 1858 3. Lincoln, Abraham, Pres. U.S. — Political career before 1861. I. T.
E457.4.J32   973.68   *LC* 59-10671

Lincoln, Abraham, 1809-1865.   • 3.7295
Created equal? The complete Lincoln–Douglas debates of 1858. Edited and with an introd. by Paul M. Angle. [Chicago] University of Chicago Press [1958] xxxiii, 421 p. ports., map (on lining papers) 24 cm. 1. United States — Politics and government — 1857-1861 I. Douglas, Stephen Arnold, 1813-1861. II. T.
E457.4.L77   973.68   *LC* 58-6885

Sandburg, Carl, 1878-1967.   • 3.7296
[Abraham Lincoln: the war years.] Abraham Lincoln; the war years, by Carl Sandburg. With 414 half–tones of photographs and 249 cuts of cartoons, letters, documents. New York, Harcourt, Brace & company [c1939] 4 v. fronts., illus. (incl. maps) plates, ports., facsims. 25 cm. 'First edition after printing 525 de luxe copies.' 1. Lincoln, Abraham, 1809-1865. 2. United States — History — Civil War, 1861-1865 I. T.
E457.4.S36   923.173   *LC* 39-27998

Turner, Thomas Reed, 1941-.   3.7297
Beware the people weeping: public opinion and the assassination of Abraham Lincoln / Thomas Reed Turner. — Baton Rouge: Louisiana State University Press, c1982. xvi, 265 p.: ill.; 24 cm. 1. Lincoln, Abraham, 1809-1865 — Assassination. 2. Public opinion — United States. I. T.
E457.5.T96 1982   973.7/092/4 19   *LC* 81-14252   *ISBN* 080710986X

Donald, David Herbert, 1920-.   • 3.7298
Lincoln reconsidered: essays on the Civil War era / by David Donald. — 1st ed. — New York: Knopf, 1956. xi, 200, xiv p. 1. Lincoln, Abraham, 1809-1865 — Addresses, essays, lectures. 2. United States — History — Civil War, 1861-1865 — Addresses, essays, lectures. I. T.
E457.8.D69   *LC* 56-5785

Lincoln, Abraham, 1809-1865.   • 3.7299
Collected works / The Abraham Lincoln Association, Springfield, Illinois; Roy P. Basler, editor; Marion Dolores Pratt and Lloyd A. Dunlap, assistant editors. — New Brunswick: N.J., Rutgers University Press, 1953-1955. 9 v.: ports., facsims.; 24 cm. I. Basler, Roy Prentice, 1906- II. Abraham Lincoln Association (Springfield, Ill.) III. T.
E457.91. 1953   *LC* 53-6293

Lincoln, Abraham, 1809-1865.   3.7300
The collected works of Abraham Lincoln; Supplement, 1832–1865 / Roy P. Basler, editor. — Westport, Conn.: Greenwood Press, 1974. xi, 320 p.: ill., facsim. — (Contributions in American studies; no. 7) 1. Lincoln, Abraham, 1809-1865. I. Basler, Roy Prentice, 1906- II. T.
E457.91.1953 Suppl   973.7/092/4

Lincoln, Abraham, 1809-1865.   • 3.7301
Abraham Lincoln, his speeches and writings / edited by Roy P. Basler; pref. by Carl Sandburg. — Cleveland: World Pub. Co., 1946. xxx, 843 p.: ports. Includes index. 1. Lincoln, Abraham, 1809-1865. 2. United States — Politics and government — 1815-1861 — Sources. 3. United States — History — Civil War, 1861-1865 — Sources I. Basler, Roy P. (Roy Prentice), 1906- II. T.
E457.92 1946   E457.92 1946.   *LC* 46-11909

Lincoln, Abraham, 1809-1865.   • 3.7302
The Lincoln encyclopedia: the spoken and written words of A. Lincoln arranged for ready reference / compiled and edited by Archer H. Shaw, with an introd. by David C. Mearns. — New York: Macmillan, 1950. xii, 395 p.; 26 cm. I. Shaw, Archer Hayes, 1876- ed. II. T.
E457.92 1950   308.1   *LC* 50-5351

E458–459 POLITICAL HISTORY, 1861–1865

Catton, William Bruce, 1926-.   • 3.7303
Two roads to Sumter, by William and Bruce Catton. New York, McGraw-Hill [1963] 285 p. 22 cm. 1. Lincoln, Abraham, 1809-1865. 2. Davis, Jefferson, 1808-1889. 3. United States — History — Civil War, 1861-1865 — Causes 4. United States — Politics and government — 1849-1861 I. Catton, Bruce, 1899- joint author. II. T.
E458.C3   973.711   *LC* 63-13930

Stampp, Kenneth M. (Kenneth Milton)   3.7304
The imperiled union: essays on the background of the Civil War / Kenneth M. Stampp. — New York: Oxford University Press, 1980. xv, 320 p.; 22 cm. 1. United States — History — Civil War, 1861-1865 — Causes — Addresses, essays, lectures. 2. United States — History — Civil War, 1861-1865 — Historiography — Addresses, essays, lectures. I. T.
E458.S825   973.7/1   *LC* 79-20276

Zornow, William Frank.   • 3.7305
Lincoln & the party divided. Westport, Conn.: Greenwood Press [1972, c1954] xi, 264 p.: ill.; 22 cm. 1. Lincoln, Abraham, 1809-1865. 2. Presidents — United States — Election — 1864. I. T.
E458.4.Z6 1972   973.7/1   *LC* 73-152619   *ISBN* 0837160545

Hyman, Harold Melvin, 1924-.   • 3.7306
Era of the oath: Northern loyalty tests during the Civil War and reconstruction. — Philadelphia: University of Pennsylvania Press, 1954. 229 p.: ill.; 24 cm. 1. Loyalty oaths — United States. 2. Reconstruction 3. United States — History — Civil War, 1861-1865 I. T.
E458.8.H9   *LC* 54-7108

Klement, Frank L.   3.7307
Dark lanterns: secret political societies, conspiracies, and treason trials in the Civil War / Frank L. Klement. — Baton Rouge: Louisiana State University Press, c1984. xiii, 263 p.: ill.; 24 cm. Includes index. 1. Secret societies — United States — History — 19th century. 2. Trials (Treason) — United States. 3. United States — History — Civil War, 1861-1865 — Societies, etc. 4. United States — Politics and government — Civil War, 1861-1865 5. United States — History — Civil War, 1861-1865 — Underground movements I. T.
E458.8.K673 1984   973.7 19   *LC* 84-834   *ISBN* 0807111740

Belz, Herman.   • 3.7308
Reconstructing the Union; theory and policy during the Civil War. — Ithaca, N.Y.: Published for the American Historical Association [by] Cornell University Press, [1969] ix, 336 p.; 24 cm. 1. Reconstruction 2. United States — Politics and government — Civil War, 1861-1865 I. American Historical Association. II. T.
E459.B4   973.71   *LC* 68-9747

Bogue, Allan G. 3.7309
The earnest men: Republicans of the Civil War Senate / Allan G. Bogue. — Ithaca: Cornell University Press, 1981. 369 p.: ill.; 25 cm. 1. Republican Party (U.S.: 1854-) — History — 19th century. 2. United States — Politics and government — Civil War, 1861-1865 I. T. II. Title: Republicans of the Civil War Senate.
E459.B723 973.7/1 19 *LC* 81-67176 *ISBN* 0801413575

Potter, David Morris. 3.7310
The impending crisis, 1848–1861 / by David M. Potter; completed and edited by Don E. Fehrenbacher. — 1st ed. — New York: Harper & Row, c1976. xv, 638 p., [12] leaves of plates: ill.; 21 cm. — (The New American Nation series) Includes index. 1. Sectionalism (United States) 2. United States — History — Civil War, 1861-1865 — Causes I. Fehrenbacher, Don Edward, 1920- II. T.
E459.P67 1976 973.7/11 *LC* 75-6354 *ISBN* 0060134038

E461–665 Civil War, 1861–1865

Commager, Henry Steele, 1902- ed. • 3.7311
The Blue and the Gray: the story of the Civil War as told by participants. — Indianapolis: Bobbs-Merrill [c1950] xxxviii, 1201 p.: ill., maps.; 24 cm. 1. United States — History — Civil War, 1861-1865 — Personal narratives I. T.
E464.C62 *LC* 56-16536

Hesseltine, William Best, 1902-1963. • 3.7312
The tragic conflict: the Civil War and reconstruction / selected and edited with introd. and notes by William B. Hesseltine. — New York: G. Braziller, 1962. 528 p. 25 cm. ([The American epochs series]) 1. Reconstruction 2. United States — History — Civil War, 1861-1865 — Sources I. T.
E464.H4 973.7 *LC* 62-9693

E467–467.1 Biography

Hesseltine, William Best, 1902-1963. • 3.7313
Confederate leaders in the New South. — Westport, Conn.: Greenwood Press, [1970, c1950] xi, 146 p.; 23 cm. 1. Confederate States of America — Biography 2. Southern States — History — 1865- I. T.
E467.H58 1970 973.71/3 *LC* 71-100230 *ISBN* 0837136865

Wakelyn, Jon L. 3.7314
Biographical dictionary of the Confederacy / Jon L. Wakelyn; Frank E. Vandiver, advisory editor. — Westport, Conn.: Greenwood Press, 1977. xii, 601 p.; 24 cm. Includes index. 1. Confederate States of America — Biography — Dictionaries. 2. United States — History — Civil War, 1861-1865 — Biography — Dictionaries. I. T.
E467.W2 973.7/13/03 *LC* 72-13870 *ISBN* 083716124X

Warner, Ezra J. 3.7315
Generals in blue: lives of the Union commanders / by Ezra J. Warner. — Baton Rouge: Louisiana State University Press, 1964. xxiv, 679 p. 1. Generals — United States — Biography. 2. United States. Army — Biography 3. United States — History — Civil War, 1861-1865 — Biography I. T.
E467.W29 973.741 *LC* 64-21593

Warner, Ezra J. 3.7316
Generals in gray: lives of the Confederate commanders / by Ezra J. Warner. — Baton Rouge: Louisiana State University Press, c1959. xxvii, 420 p.: ports.; 24 cm. 1. Generals — Confederate States of America. 2. United States — History — Civil War, 1861-1865 — Biography I. T. II. Title: Confederate commanders.
E467.W3 973.7 *LC* 58-7551 *ISBN* 0080710823

Williams, T. Harry (Thomas Harry), 1909-. • 3.7317
McClellan, Sherman, and Grant. New Brunswick, N.J.: Rutgers University Press [1962] 113 p.: ill.; 20 cm. (The Brown and Haley lectures, 1962) Includes bibliography. 1. McClellan, George Brinton, 1826-1885. 2. Sherman, William T. (William Tecumseh), 1820-1891. 3. Grant, Ulysses S. (Ulysses Simpson), 1822-1885. I. T. II. Series.
E467.W5 923.573 *LC* 62-21246

Duberman, Martin B. • 3.7318
Charles Francis Adams, 1807–1886, by Martin Duberman. — Stanford, Calif.: Stanford University Press, [1968, c1960] xvi, 525 p.: illus., ports.; 23 cm. 1. Adams, Charles Francis, 1807-1886. I. T.
E467.1.A2 D8 1968 973.7/0924 B *LC* 68-13742

Williams, T. Harry (Thomas Harry), 1909-. • 3.7319
P. G. T. Beauregard: Napoleon in gray. — Baton Rouge: Louisiana State University Press [1955, c1954] xiii, 345 p.: ill., ports., maps. 23 cm. 1. Beauregard, G. T. (Gustave Toutant), 1818-1893. I. T.
E467.1.B38 W5 *LC* 55-7362

Holzman, Richard S. • 3.7320
Stormy Ben Butler. New York: Macmillan, 1954. 297 p.: ill.; 22 cm. 1. Butler, Benjamin F. (Benjamin Franklin), 1818-1893. I. T.
E467.1.B87 H6 923.273 *LC* 54-12163

Davis, Jefferson, 1808-1889. 3.7321
The papers of Jefferson Davis. Baton Rouge, Louisiana State University Press, 1971- < 1985 > . v. < 1-5 > illus. 25 cm. 1. Davis, Jefferson, 1808-1889. I. T.
E467.1.D2596 973.7/13/0924 B *LC* 76-152704 *ISBN* 0807109436

Dodd, William Edward, 1869-1940. • 3.7322
Jefferson Davis. New York: Russell & Russell, 1966. 396 p.: port.; 23 cm. First published in 1907. 1. Davis, Jefferson, 1808-1889. I. T.
E467.1.D26 D8 1966 *LC* 65-17888

Eaton, Clement, 1898-. 3.7323
Jefferson Davis / Clement Eaton. — New York: Free Press, c1977. xii, 334 p., [4] leaves of plates: ill.; 25 cm. Includes index. 1. Davis, Jefferson, 1808-1889. 2. Confederate States of America — Presidents — Biography. 3. United States — History — Civil War, 1861-1865 4. Confederate States of America — History I. T.
E467.1.D26 E24 973.7/13 *LC* 77-2512 *ISBN* 0029087007

Strode, Hudson, 1892-1976. • 3.7324
Jefferson Davis. [1st ed.] New York, Harcourt, Brace [1955-64] 3 v. ports. 25 cm. 1. Davis, Jefferson, 1808-1889. I. T.
E467.1.D26 S73 973.7130924 B *LC* 64-18295

Lewis, Charles Lee, 1886-. • 3.7325
David Glasgow Farragut. Annapolis: United States Naval Institute [1941-43] 2 v.: fronts., ill. (facsim.) plates, ports., map.; 24 cm. 1. Farragut, David Glasgow, 1801-1870. I. United States Naval Institute, Annapolis. II. T.
E467.1.F23 L48 *LC* 41-10196

Jarrell, Hampton McNeely, 1904-. • 3.7326
Wade Hampton and the Negro: the road not taken. — Columbia: University of South Carolina Press, 1949. xi, 209 p.: port.; 24 cm. 1. Hampton, Wade, 1818-1902. 2. Afro-Americans — South Carolina 3. South Carolina — Politics and government — 1865-1950 I. T.
E467.1.H19 J3 *LC* 50-5796

Vandiver, Frank Everson, 1925-. • 3.7327
Mighty Stonewall. New York: McGraw-Hill [1957] xi, 547 p.: ill., ports., maps.; 24 cm. 1. Jackson, Stonewall, 1824-1863. I. T.
E467.1.J15 V3 923.573 *LC* 57-7247

Freeman, Douglas Southall, 1886-1953. • 3.7328
R. E. Lee: a biography / by Douglas Southall Freeman. — New York; London: C.Scribner's Sons, 1934-35. 4 v.: ill., plates, ports., maps, facsims.; 24 cm. 1. Lee, Robert E. (Robert Edward), 1807-1870. I. T.
E467.1.L4 F83 *LC* 34-33660

Hassler, Warren W. 3.7329
General George B. McClellan: shield of the Union. — 1st ed. Baton Rouge: Louisiana State University Press [1957] 350 p.: ill.; 24 cm. 1. McClellan, George Briton, 1826-1885. I. T.
E467.1.M2 H4 *LC* 57-7497

Lewis, Lloyd, 1891-1949. • 3.7330
Sherman, fighting prophet / illustrated with reproductions of maps, engravings, and photos; with a new appraisal by Bruce Catton. — New York: Harcourt, Brace 1958. xviii, 690 p.: ill., ports., maps; 25 cm. 1. Sherman, William T. (William Tecumseh), 1820-1891. I. T.
E467.1.S55 L48 1958 *LC* 58-14960

Merrill, James M. • 3.7331
William Tecumseh Sherman, by James M. Merrill. Chicago, Rand McNally [1971] 445 p. illus., ports. 24 cm. 1. Sherman, William T. (William Tecumseh), 1820-1891. I. T.
E467.1.S55 M4 355.3/31/0924 B *LC* 78-153112

Thomas, Benjamin Platt, 1902-1956. • 3.7332
Stanton; the life and times of Lincoln's Secretary of War [by] Benjamin P. Thomas and Harold M. Hyman. — [1st ed.]. — New York: Knopf, 1962. xvii, 642 p., xii p.: illus., ports., facsim.; 25 cm. 1. Stanton, Edwin McMasters, 1814-1869. 2. Statesmen — United States — Biography. 3. United States — History — Civil War, 1861-1865 I. Hyman, Harold Melvin, 1924- joint author. II. T.
E467.1.S8 T45 923.273 *LC* 61-17829

Von Abele, Rudolph Radama, 1922-. • **3.7333**
Alexander H. Stephens, a biography, by Rudolph von Abele. — Westport, Conn.: Negro Universities Press, [1971, c1946] xiii, 337, x p.: ports.; 23 cm. Originally presented as the author's thesis, Columbia, 1946. 1. Stephens, Alexander Hamilton, 1812-1883. I. T.
E467.1.S85 V6 1971   973.7/13/0924 B   *LC* 74-135614   *ISBN* 0837152011

McKinney, Francis F   1891-. • **3.7334**
Education in violence: the life of George H. Thomas and the history of the Army of the Cumberland / by Francis McKinney. — Detroit: Wayne State University Press, 1961. 530 p.: ill.; 25 cm. 1. Thomas, George Henry, 1816-1870. 2. United States. Army. Dept. of the Cumberland. 3. United States — History — Civil War, 1861-1865 — Regimental histories I. T.
E467.1.T4 M17   *LC* 61-6040

Niven, John.   **3.7335**
Gideon Welles: Lincoln's Secretary of the Navy. — New York: Oxford University Press, 1973. xii, 676 p.: ill.; 24 cm. 1. Welles, Gideon, 1802-1878. I. T.
E467.1.W46 N58   973.7/092/4 B   *LC* 73-82671   *ISBN* 0195016939

E468–468.9 General Histories

Barney, William L.   **3.7336**
Flawed victory: a new perspective on the Civil War / William L. Barney; foreword by James P. Shenton. — Lanham, Md.: University Press of America, c1980. xi, 215 p.: map; 22 cm. Includes index. 1. United States — History — Civil War, 1861-1865 I. T.
E468.B32 1980   973.7 19   *LC* 80-68972   *ISBN* 0819112739

Boatner, Mark Mayo, 1921-. • **3.7337**
The Civil War dictionary / by Mark Mayo Boatner III; maps and diagrs. by Allen C. Northrop and Lowell I. Miller. — New York: D. McKay Co., c1959. xvi, 974 p.: ill., maps.; 22 cm. 1. United States — History — Civil War, 1861-1865 — Dictionaries I. T.
E468.B7   *LC* 59-12267   *ISBN* 0679500138

Catton, Bruce, 1899-. • **3.7338**
America goes to war. — [1st ed.]. — Middletown, Conn.: Wesleyan University Press, [1958] 126 p.: illus.; 21 cm. 1. United States — History — Civil War, 1861-1865 I. T.
E468.C28   973.7   *LC* 58-13602

Catton, Bruce, 1899-. • **3.7339**
The centennial history of the Civil War / E. B. Long, director of research. — [1st ed.]. — Garden City, N.Y.: Doubleday, 1961-65. 3 v.: col. illus., col. maps.; 25 cm. 1. United States — History — Civil War, 1861-1865 I. T. II. Title: The coming fury. III. Title: Terrible swift sword. IV. Title: Never call retreat.
E468.C29   973.7   *LC* 61-12502

Catton, Bruce, 1899-. • **3.7340**
This hallowed ground: the story of the Union side of the Civil War. — [1st ed.]. — Garden City, N.Y.: Doubleday, 1956. ix, 437 p.: maps.; 25 cm. — (Mainstream of America series) 1. United States — History — Civil War, 1861-1865 I. T.
E468.C3   973.7   *LC* 56-5960

Donald, David Herbert, 1920- ed. • **3.7341**
Why the North won the Civil War / essays by Richard N. Current [and others. — Baton Rouge]: Louisiana State University Press, [1960] 128 p.; 23 cm. 1. United States — History — Civil War, 1861-1865 — Addresses, essays, lectures. 2. Confederate States of America — History — Addresses, essays, lectures. I. Current, Richard Nelson. II. T.
E468.D65   973.7   *LC* 60-13170

Fuller, J. F. C. (John Frederick Charles), 1878-1966. • **3.7342**
Grant & Lee, a study in personality and generalship. Bloomington: Indiana University Press, 1957. 323 p.: ill., maps. 21 cm. (Civil War centennial series) 1. Grant, Ulysses S. (Ulysses Simpson), 1822-1885. 2. Lee, Robert E. (Robert Edward), 1807-1870. 3. United States — History — Civil War, 1861-1865 4. United States — History — Civil War, 1861-1865 — Campaigns I. T. II. Series.
E468.F96 1957   973.7   *LC* 57-10723

Historical times illustrated encyclopedia of the Civil War /   **3.7343**
Patricia L. Faust, editor.
1st ed. — New York: Harper & Row, c1986. xxiv, 849 p.: ill.; 24 cm. 1. United States — History — Civil War, 1861-1865 — Dictionaries. 2. United States — History — Civil War, 1861-1865 — Pictorial works I. Faust, Patricia L.
E468.H57 1986   973.7 19   *LC* 86-45095   *ISBN* 0061812617

McPherson, James M.   **3.7344**
Ordeal by fire: the Civil War and Reconstruction / James M. McPherson. — 1st ed. — New York: Knopf: Distributed by Random House, c1982. xviii, 694, xxxii p.: ill.; 24 cm. Maps on lining papers. Includes index. 1. Reconstruction 2. United States — History — Civil War, 1861-1865 — Causes 3. United States — History — Civil War, 1861-1865 4. United States — History — 1865-1898 I. T.
E468.M23   973.7 19   *LC* 81-11832   *ISBN* 0394312066

Nevins, Allan, 1890-1971. • **3.7345**
The War for the Union. — New York: Scribner, [1959-71] 4 v.: illus., ports., maps; 24 cm. — (His The ordeal of the Union, v. 5-8) 1. United States — History — Civil War, 1861-1865 I. T.
E468.N43   973.7   *LC* 59-3690   *ISBN* 0684104296

Parish, Peter J.   **3.7346**
The American Civil War / Peter J. Parish. — New York: Holmes & Meier Publishers, 1975. 750 p.: ill.; 24 cm. Includes index. 1. United States — History — Civil War, 1861-1865 I. T.
E468.P27   973.7   *LC* 74-84660   *ISBN* 0841901767

Randall, J. G. (James Garfield), 1881-1953.   **3.7347**
The Civil War and Reconstruction [by] J. G. Randall [and] David Donald. 2d ed., rev. with enl. bibliography. Lexington, Mass., Heath [1969] xiv, 866 p. illus., maps, ports. 25 cm. 1. Reconstruction 2. United States — History — Civil War, 1861-1865 I. Donald, David Herbert, 1920- joint author. II. T.
E468.R26 1969   973.7   *LC* 74-76471

Divided we fought: a pictorial history of the War, 1861–1865 / • **3.7348**
picture editors: Hirst D. Milhollen and Milton Kaplan; caption editors: Hirst D. Milhollen, Milton Kaplan, and Hulen Stuart; author of the text and general editor: David Donald.
New York: Macmillan [c1956] viii, 454 p.: ill., ports.; 29 cm. 1. United States — History — Civil War, 1861-1865 — Pictorial works I. Milhollen, Hirst Dillon, 1906- ed. II. Kaplan, Milton, 1918- ed. III. Donald, David Herbert, 1920- ed.
E468.7.D5 1956   *LC* 56-58591

Gardner, Alexander, 1821-1882. • **3.7349**
Photographic sketch book of the Civil War. — New York, Dover Publications [1959] [8] p., reprint (2 v. 100 plates), [4] p. 23x28 cm. 'An unabridged and unaltered republication of the first edition published in 1866 ... titled Gardner's photographic sketch book of the war.' 1. U.S. — Hist. — Civil War — Pictorial works. 2. Virginia — Hist. — Civil War — Pictorial works. I. T.
E468.7.G19 1959   973.79   *LC* 58-13933

The Image of war, 1861–1865.   **3.7350**
Garden City N. Y.: Doubleday, 1981-1984. 6 v.: ill., map, ports. 'A project of the National Historical Society'. Includes index. Maps on lining paper. 1. United States — History — Civil War, 1861-1865 — Pictorial works I. National Historical Society.
E468.7.I43   *LC* 80-1659

Fredrickson, George M., 1934-. • **3.7351**
The inner Civil War: northern intelectuals and the crisis of the Union / [by] George M. Fredrickson. — [1st ed.]. — New York: Harper & Row, [1965] viii, 277 p.; 22 cm. 1. Intellectuals — United States. 2. United States — History — Civil War, 1861-1865 I. T.
E468.9.F83   973.715   *LC* 65-21013

E469 Diplomatic History

Adams, Ephraim Douglass, 1865-1930. • **3.7352**
Great Britain and the American Civil War. New York: Russell & Russell [1958?] 2 v. in 1: ill.; 22 cm. 1. United States — Foreign relations — 1861-1865 2. United States — History — Civil War, 1861-1865 — Foreign public opinion 3. Great Britain — Foreign relations — United States. 4. United States — Foreign relations — Great Britain. I. T.
E469.A25 1958   *LC* 58-5369

Crook, D. P. (David Paul)   **3.7353**
The North, the South, and the powers, 1861–1865 / by D. P. Crook. — New York: Wiley [1974] x, 405 p.: maps; 23 cm. 1. United States — Foreign relations — 1861-1865 2. Confederate States of America — Foreign relations I. T.
E469.C76   973.7/2   *LC* 73-16355   *ISBN* 0471188557

Monaghan, Jay, 1891-. • **3.7354**
Diplomat in carpet slippers; Abraham Lincoln deals with foreign affairs, by Jay Monaghan. Indianapolis: Charter Books [distributed by the Macfadden-Bartell Corp., New York], 1962. 505 p. illus. 23 cm. — (American history library) 1. Lincoln, Abraham, 1809-1865. 2. United States — Foreign relations — 1861-1865 I. T.
E469.M75 1962   973.7/2

Warren, Gordon H., 1944-.   **3.7355**
Fountain of discontent: the Trent Affair and freedom of the seas / Gordon H. Warren. — Boston: Northeastern University Press, 1981. xiv, 301 p.: ill.; 24 cm. Includes index. 1. Trent Affair, Nov. 8, 1861 2. United States — Foreign relations — 1861-1865 I. T.
E469.W3   973.7/2 19   *LC* 80-24499   *ISBN* 093035012X

Winks, Robin W.   **3.7356**
Canada and the United States: the Civil War years [by] Robin W. Winks. — [Rev. ed.]. — Montreal: Harvest House, [1971] xx, 432 p.; 20 cm. 1. U.S. — Foreign relations — 1861-1865. 2. U.S. — Foreign relations — Canada. 3. Canada — Foreign relations — U.S. I. T.
E469.W5 1971   973.72   *LC* 77-150658   *ISBN* 0887721176

Foner, Philip Sheldon, 1910-.   **3.7357**
British labor and the American Civil War / Philip S. Foner. — New York: Holmes & Meier, 1981. 135 p., [3] leaves of plates: ill.; 24 cm. 1. Public opinion — England. 2. Labor and laboring classes — England — History — 19th century. 3. United States — History — Civil War, 1861-1865 — Foreign public opinion, British. I. T.
E469.8.F66 1981   973.7 19   *LC* 80-26162   *ISBN* 0841906718

Jenkins, Brian (Brian A.)   **3.7358**
Britain & the war for the union / Brian Jenkins. — Montreal: McGill-Queen's University Press, 1974-1980. 2 v.; 24 cm. 1. Public opinion — Great Britain. 2. United States — History — Civil War, 1861-1865 — Foreign public opinion, British. 3. United States — Foreign relations — Great Britain. 4. Great Britain — Foreign relations — United States. 5. United States — Foreign relations — 1861-1865 I. T.
E469.8.J46   973.7/2 19   *LC* 74-77503   *ISBN* 0773501843

E470–480 Military Operations. Finance

Williams, T. Harry (Thomas Harry), 1909-.   • **3.7359**
Lincoln and his generals. [1st ed.] New York: Knopf, 1952. viii, 363, iv p.: ports., map.; 22 cm. 1. Lincoln, Abraham, 1809-1865 — Military leadership 2. Generals — United States. 3. United States — History — Civil War, 1861-1865 — Campaigns I. T.
E470.W78   973.741   *LC* 51-13211

Catton, Bruce, 1899-.   • **3.7360**
Glory Road: the bloody route from Fredericksburg to Gettysburg. — [1st ed.] Garden City, N.Y.: Doubleday, 1952. 416 p.: maps.; 22 cm. (His The Army of the Potomac; v. 2) 1. United States. Army of the Potomac. 2. United States — History — Civil War, 1861-1865 — Regimental histories 3. United States — History — Civil War, 1861-1865 — Campaigns I. T.
E470.2.C36   973.734   *LC* 52-5538

Catton, Bruce, 1899-.   • **3.7361**
Mr. Lincoln's Army / by Bruce Catton. — Garden City, N.Y.: Doubleday [1962] xii, 363 p.: maps; 22 cm. (His The Army of the Potomac; v. 1) 1. McClellan, George Brinton, 1826-1885. 2. United States. Army of the Potomac. 3. United States — History — Civil War, 1861-1865 — Regimental histories 4. United States — History — Civil War, 1861-1865 — Campaigns I. T.
E470.2.C37 1962   973.741   *LC* 62-1068

Catton, Bruce, 1899-.   • **3.7362**
A stillness at Appomattox. [1st ed.] Garden City, N.Y.: Doubleday, 1953. 438 p.: ill.; 22 cm. (His The Army of the Potomac; v. 3) 1. United States. Army of the Potomac. 2. Appomattox Campaign, 1865 3. United States — History — Civil War, 1861-1865 — Regimental histories 4. United States — History — Civil War, 1861-1865 — Campaigns I. T.
E470.2.C39   973.736   *LC* 53-9982

Freeman, Douglas Southall, 1886-1953.   • **3.7363**
Lee's lieutenants: a study in command / by Douglas Southall Freeman. — New York: C. Scribner's sons, 1942-44. 3 v.: ill. (ports.) maps (part fold.); 24 cm. 1. Confederate States of America. Army of Northern Virginia. 2. Confederate States of America — Biography 3. United States — History — Civil War, 1861-1865 — Biography 4. United States — History — Civil War, 1861-1865 — Regimental histories 5. United States — History — Civil War, 1861-1865 — Campaigns I. T.
E470.2.F7   973.73   *LC* 42-24582

Davis, William C., 1946-.   **3.7364**
Duel between the first ironclads / William C. Davis. — 1st ed. — Garden City, N.Y.: Doubleday, 1975. x, 201 p., [8] leaves of plates: ill.; 22 cm. Includes index. 1. Hampton Roads, Battle of, 1862 I. T.
E473.2.D36   973.7/52   *LC* 75-11071   *ISBN* 0385098685

Hoehling, A. A. (Adolph A.)   **3.7365**
Thunder at Hampton Roads / by A. A. Hoehling. — Englewood Cliffs, N.J.: Prentice-Hall, c1976. xvi, 231 p., [8] leaves of plates: ill.; 24 cm. Includes index.

1. Monitor (Ironclad) 2. Hampton Roads, Battle of, 1862 3. Shipwrecks — North Carolina — Hatteras, Cape. 4. Underwater archaeology 5. Hatteras, Cape — History. I. T.
E473.2.H57   973.7/52   *LC* 76-18261   *ISBN* 0139206523

Sears, Stephen W.   **3.7366**
Landscape turned red: the battle of Antietam / Stephen W. Sears. — New Haven: Ticknor & Fields, 1983. xii, 431 p., [16] p. of plates: ill.; 24 cm. Includes index. 1. Antietam, Battle of, 1862 I. T.
E474.65.S43 1983   973.7/336 19   *LC* 82-19519   *ISBN* 089919172X

E482–489 Confederate States of America

Chesnut, Mary Boykin Miller, 1823-1886.   **3.7367**
Mary Chesnut's Civil War / edited by C. Vann Woodward. — New Haven: Yale University Press, c1981. lviii, 886 p., [5] leaves of plates: ill.; 24 cm. Selections from this work were previously published under title: A diary from Dixie. 1. Chesnut, Mary Boykin Miller, 1823-1886. 2. United States — History — Civil War, 1861-1865 — Personal narratives, Confederate 3. Confederate States of America — History — Sources 4. Southern States — Biography. I. Woodward, C. Vann (Comer Vann), 1908- II. T.
E487.C5   973.7/82   *LC* 80-36661   *ISBN* 0300024592

Chesnut, Mary Boykin Miller, 1823-1886.   **3.7368**
The private Mary Chesnut: the unpublished Civil War diaries / [edited by] C. Vann Woodward, Elisabeth Muhlenfeld. — New York: Oxford University Press, 1984. xxix, 292 p.: 24 cm. 1. Chesnut, Mary Boykin Miller, 1823-1886. 2. United States — History — Civil War, 1861-1865 — Personal narratives, Confederate 3. Confederate States of America — History 4. Southern States — Biography. I. Woodward, C. Vann (Comer Vann), 1908- II. Muhlenfeld, Elisabeth, 1944- III. T.
E487.C525 1984   973.7/82 19   *LC* 84-12219   *ISBN* 0195035119

Connelly, Thomas Lawrence.   **3.7369**
The politics of command; factions and ideas in Confederate strategy [by] Thomas Lawrence Connelly [and] Archer Jones. Baton Rouge, Louisiana State University Press [1973] xv, 235 p. maps. 24 cm. 1. Confederate States of America — Military policy. 2. United States — History — Civil War, 1861-1865 — Campaigns I. Jones, Archer, 1926- joint author. II. T.
E487.C8   973.7/3013   *LC* 72-89113   *ISBN* 0807102288

Davis, Jefferson, 1808-1889.   • **3.7370**
The rise and fall of the Confederate Government. New York: T. Yoseloff [1958] 2 v.: ill., ports., maps.; 24 cm. 1. Confederate States of America — History 2. United States — Politics and government — Civil War, 1861-1865 3. United States — History — Civil War, 1861-1865 I. T.
E487.D263 1958   *LC* 58-12480

Degler, Carl N.   **3.7371**
The other South: Southern dissenters in the nineteenth century [by] Carl N. Degler. [1st ed.] New York, Harper & Row [1974] 392 p. 22 cm. 1. Slavery — United States — Anti-slavery movements. 2. Dissenters — Southern States — History — 19th century. 3. Abolitionists — Southern States — History — 19th century. 4. Confederate States of America — Politics and government 5. Southern States — Politics and government — 1865-1950 I. T.
E487.D327   320.9/75/04   *LC* 73-4076   *ISBN* 0060110228

Eaton, Clement.   • **3.7372**
A history of the Southern Confederacy / Clement Eaton. — New York: Macmillan, 1954. ix, 351 p.; 22 cm. 1. Confederate States of America — History 2. United States — History — Civil War, 1861-1865 I. T.
E487.E15   973.713   *LC* 54-8772

Holmes, Sarah Katherine (Stone) 1841-1907.   • **3.7373**
Brokenburn: the journal of Kate Stone, 1861–1868 / edited by John Q. Anderson. — Baton Rouge: Louisiana State University Press [1955] 400 p.: port., map (on lining papers); 22 cm. 1. United States — History — Civil War, 1861-1865 — Personal narratives, Confederate I. Anderson, John Q. ed. II. T.
E487.H74   *LC* 55-7363   *ISBN* 0807102318

Patrick, Rembert Wallace, 1909-.   • **3.7374**
Jefferson Davis and his cabinet / [by] Rembert W. Patrick. — Baton Rouge: Louisiana State University Press, 1944. x, 401 p.; 24 cm. 'Begun in 1936 as a doctoral dissertation at ... the University of North Carolina.'—Pref. 1. Davis, Jefferson, 1808-1889. 2. Cabinet officers — Confederate States of America. 3. Confederate States of America — Politics and government 4. Confederate States of America — Biography I. T.
E487.P3   973.716   *LC* 44-9637

Ramsdell, Charles William, 1877-1942.   • **3.7375**
Behind the lines in the Southern Confederacy. Edited with a foreword by Wendell H. Stephenson. — New York: Greenwood Press, [1969, c1944] xxi,

136 p.: port.; 23 cm. — (The Walter Lynwood Fleming lectures in Southern history, Louisiana State University) 1. Confederate States of America — Social conditions 2. Confederate States of America — Economic conditions I. Stephenson, Wendell Holmes, 1899-1970. ed. II. T.
E487.R2 1969　　973.71/3　　LC 73-88924　　ISBN 083712218X

Roland, Charles Pierce, 1918-.　　　　　　　　　　• 3.7376
The Confederacy. [Chicago]: University of Chicago Press, [1960] 218 p.: illus.; 21 cm. — (Chicago history of American civilization.) 1. Confederate States of America — History I. T. II. Series.
E487.R7　　973.713　　LC 60-12573

Tatum, Georgia Lee.　　　　　　　　　　　　• 3.7377
Disloyalty in the confederacy / by Georgia Lee Tatum. — Chapel Hill: The University of North Carolina press, 1934. xi, 176 p.; 24 cm. 1. Public opinion — Confederate States of America. 2. Confederate States of America — History 3. Confederate States of America — Social conditions 4. United States — History — Civil War, 1861-1865 — Peace I. T.
E487.T176　　LC 34-22569

Thomas, Emory M., 1939-.　　　　　　　　　　3.7378
The Confederate nation, 1861–1865 / by Emory M. Thomas. — 1st ed. — New York: Harper & Row, c1979. xvi, 384 p., [8] leaves of plates: ill.; 22 cm. — (The New American Nation series) Includes index. 1. Confederate States of America — History I. T.
E487.T483 1979　　973.7/13　　LC 76-26255　　ISBN 0060142529

Vandiver, Frank Everson, 1925-.　　　　　　　　3.7379
Their tattered flags: the epic of the Confederacy [by] Frank E. Vandiver. — [1st ed.]. — New York: Harper's Magazine Press, [1970] 362 p.: maps (1 fold. col.); 25 cm. 1. Confederate States of America — History I. T.
E487.V33 1970　　973.71/3　　LC 77-96018

Owsley, Frank Lawrence, 1890-1956.　　　　　　• 3.7380
King Cotton diplomacy: foreign relations of the Confederate States of America / by Frank Lawrence Owsley. — 2d ed. / rev. by Harriet Chappell Owsley. — Chicago: University of Chicago Press, 1959. xxiii, 614 p. 1. Cotton trade 2. Confederate States of America — Foreign relations I. T.
E488.O85 1959　　LC 58-11952

E491–586 Armies

Bruce, Robert V.　　　　　　　　　　　　• 3.7381
Lincoln and the tools of war. [1st ed.] Indianapolis: Bobbs-Merrill [1956] xi, 368 p.: ill., ports.; 23 cm. 1. Lincoln, Abraham, 1809-1865. 2. Ordnance 3. United States — History — Civil War, 1861-1865 — Equipment and supplies I. T.
E491.B7　　LC 56-6779

Murdock, Eugene Converse.　　　　　　　　　• 3.7382
One million men: the Civil War draft in the North / [by] Eugene C. Murdock. — Madison: State Historical Society of Wisconsin, 1971. xi, 366 p.: ill.; 24 cm. 1. United States. Army — Recruiting, enlistment, etc. — Civil War, 1861-1865 2. Draft — United States. I. T.
E491.M97　　973.7/41 19　　LC 72-168393　　ISBN 0870201166

Wiley, Bell Irvin, 1906-.　　　　　　　　　　• 3.7383
The life of Billy Yank, the common soldier of the Union. [1st ed.] Indianapolis: Bobbs-Merrill [1952] 454 p.: ill., ports.; 24 cm. 1. United States. Army — Military life 2. Soldiers — United States 3. United States — History — Civil War, 1861-1865 — Personal narratives I. T.
E491.W69　　973.7411　　LC 52-5809

Starr, Stephen Z.　　　　　　　　　　　　3.7384
The Union cavalry in the Civil War / Stephen Z. Starr. — Baton Rouge: Louisiana State University Press, 1980-1981. 2 v.: ill.; 24 cm. 1. United States. Army. Cavalry — History — Civil War, 1861-1865 2. United States — History — Civil War, 1861-1865 — Campaigns I. T.
E492.5.S7　　973.7/41　　LC 78-26751　　ISBN 0807104841

The Black military experience / Ira Berlin, editor; Joseph P.　　3.7385
Reidy, associate editor, Leslie S. Rowland, associate editor.
Cambridge [Cambridgeshire]; New York: Cambridge University Press, 1983 (c1982). xxxv, 852 p.: port.; 24 cm. — (Freedom, a documentary history of emancipation, 1861-1867. ser. II) 1. United States — History — Civil War, 1861-1865 — Afro-American troops — Sources. I. Berlin, Ira, 1941- II. Reidy, Joseph P. (Joseph Patrick), 1948- III. Rowland, Leslie S. IV. Series.
E492.9.B5x　　973.7/415 19　　LC 82-4446　　ISBN 0521229847

Higginson, Thomas Wentworth, 1823-1911.　　　　• 3.7386
Army life in a black regiment / with notes and a biographical introd. by John Hope Franklin; foreword by E. Franklin Frazier. — Boston: Beacon Press [1962] 300 p.; 21 cm. 1. United States. Army. South Carolina Volunteers, First. 2. United States — History — Civil War, 1861-1865 — Regimental histories

3. United States — History — Civil War, 1861-1865 — Personal narratives I. T.
E492.94 33d.H5 1962　　973.7415　　LC 62-9217

Leech, Margaret, 1893-1974.　　　　　　　　　• 3.7387
Reveille in Washington, 1860–1865. Westport, Conn.: Greenwood Press [1971, c1941] 483 p.: ill.; 24 cm. 1. Washington (D.C.) — History — Civil War, 1861-1865 I. T.
E501.L4 1971　　973.7/4/53　　LC 72-138121　　ISBN 0837156971

Cornish, Dudley Taylor.　　　　　　　　　　• 3.7388
The sable arm: Negro troops in the Union Army, 1861–1865. — New York: W. W. Norton [1966] 337 p.; 20 cm. (The Norton library, N334) 1. United States — History — Civil War, 1861-1865 — Participation, Afro-American. I. T. II. Title: Negro troops in the Union Army, 1861-1865.
E540.N3 C77 1966　　973.7415　　LC 66-14074

Quarles, Benjamin.　　　　　　　　　　　• 3.7389
The Negro in the Civil War. — Boston: Little, Brown, [1969] xvi, 379 p.; 20 cm. 1. United States — History — Civil War, 1861-1865 — Afro-Americans I. T.
E540.N3 Q3 1969　　973.71/5/30145196　　LC 71-11863

Vandiver, Frank Everson, 1925-.　　　　　　　• 3.7390
Rebel brass: the Confederate command system / by Frank E. Vandiver; introd. by T. Harry Williams. — New York: Greenwood Press, [1969, c1956] xvii, 142 p.: ill., ports.; 23 cm. 1. Confederate States of America — History, Military 2. Confederate States of America — Politics and government I. T.
E545.V3 1969　　973.7/42　　LC 79-88963　　ISBN 0837123216

E591–600 Naval Operations

Porter, David D. (David Dixon), 1813-1891.　　　　3.7391
The naval history of the civil war / by Admiral David D. Porter; illustrated from original sketches made by Rear Admiral Walke and others. — Secaucus, N.J.: Castle, 1984. 1 v. Includes index. 1. United States — History — Civil war — Naval operations. 2. United States — Navy — History — Civil war. I. T.
E591.P84　　973.75　　ISBN 0890095752

Spencer, Warren F., 1923-.　　　　　　　　　3.7392
The Confederate Navy in Europe / Warren F. Spencer. — University, Ala.: University of Alabama Press, c1983. xii, 268 p.; 25 cm. Includes index. 1. Confederate States of America. Navy — History 2. United States — History — Civil War, 1861-1865 — Naval operations 3. United States — Foreign relations — 1861-1865 4. Great Britain — Neutrality. 5. France — Neutrality. I. T.
E596.S7 1983　　973.7/57 19　　LC 81-23283　　ISBN 0817301151

E601–609 Personal Narratives

Holmes, Oliver Wendell, 1841-1935.　　　　　　• 3.7393
Touched with fire: civil war letters and diary of Oliver Wendel Holmes, Jr., 1861–1864 / edited by Mark De Wolfe Howe. — Cambridge, Mass.: Harvard University Press, 1946. — x p., 3 l., 3-158 p.: ill., plans, facsims., ports. I. Howe, Mark De Wolfe, 1906-1967. II. T.
E601.H73　　973.78　　LC 47-364

Strong, George Templeton, 1820-1875.　　　　　• 3.7394
Diary of the Civil War, 1860–1865. Edited by Allan Nevins. New York, Macmillan, 1962. liii, 664 p. illus. 25 cm. 'Originally appeared as volume III of The diary of George Templeton Strong ... edited by Allan Nevins and Milton Halsey Thomas.' 1. United States — History — Civil War, 1861-1865 — Personal narratives I. T.
E601.S888　　973.7　　LC 62-4535

Wiley, Bell Irvin, 1906-.　　　　　　　　　　• 3.7395
The life of Johnny Reb, the common soldier of the Confederacy / by Bell Irvin Wiley. 1st ed. Indianapolis; New York: Bobbs-Merrill [1943] 444 p.: plates, ports., facsims.; 25 cm. 1. Confederate States of America. Army — Military life. 2. United States — History — Civil War, 1861-1865 — Personal narratives, Confederate I. T.
E607.W5　　973.784　　LC 43-3253

Andrews, J. Cutler, 1908-.　　　　　　　　　• 3.7396
The North reports the Civil War. [Pittsburgh] University of Pittsburgh Press [1955] x, 813 p. illus., ports., maps (1 fold.) 24 cm. 1. United States — History — Civil War, 1861-1865 — Journalists I. T.
E609.A6　　LC 55-6873

Andrews, J. Cutler, 1908-.　　　　　　　　　• 3.7397
The South reports the Civil War, by J. Cutler Andrews. — Princeton, N.J.: Princeton University Press, 1970. xiii, 611 p.: illus., facsims., maps (1 fold.),

ports.; 25 cm. 1. United States — History — Civil War, 1861-1865 — Journalists I. T.
E609.A62   973.7   *LC* 75-90942   *ISBN* 0691045976

E611–655 Special Topics

Hesseltine, William Best, 1902-1963. comp.   • 3.7398
Civil War prisons: a study in war psychology / William Best Hesseltine. — Columbus: The Ohio State University Press, 1930. xi, 290 p.; 23 cm. — 1. United States — History — Civil War, 1861-1865 — Prisoners and prisons 2. United States — History — Civil War, 1861-1865 — Prisoners and prisons I. Civil War history. II. T.
E611.H453   973.7/7   *LC* 64-25556   *ISBN* 0804413827

Craven, Avery Odelle, 1886-.   • 3.7399
The repressible conflict, 1830–1861. [Baton Rouge] Louisiana State University Press 1939. 97p. (The Walter Lynwood Fleming lectures in Southern history, Louisiana State University, 1938) 1. United States — History — Civil War — Causes 2. United States — History — Civil War — Addresses, sermond, etc. I. T.
E649 C73

Rawley, James A.   • 3.7400
Turning points of the Civil War [by] James A. Rawley. — Lincoln: University of Nebraska Press, [1966] ix, 230 p.: map (on lining papers); 24 cm. 1. United States — History — Civil War, 1861-1865 — Addresses, essays, lectures. I. T.
E649.R28   973.7   *LC* 66-19266

Botkin, Benjamin Albert, 1901- ed.   • 3.7401
A Civil War treasury of tales, legends, and folklore; illustrated by Warren Chappell. — New York: Random House, [1960] 625 p.: illus.; 25 cm. 1. United States — History — Civil War, 1861-1865 — Anecdotes I. T.
E655.B65   973.7088   *LC* 60-5530

E660–738 Late 19th Century (1865–1900)

Garfield, James A. (James Abram), 1831-1881.   • 3.7402
The diary of James A. Garfield / Edited with an introd. by Harry James Brown [and] Frederick D. Williams. [East Lansing]: Michigan State University, 1967-. v.: ill., facsim., port.; 25 cm. I. Brown, Harry James, ed. II. Williams, Frederick D. ed. III. T.
E660.G223   973.8/4/0924 B   *LC* 67-12577   *ISBN* 0870131699

Grant, Ulysses S. (Ulysses Simpson), 1822-1885.   • 3.7403
The papers of Ulysses S. Grant. Edited by John Y. Simon. Carbondale, Southern Illinois University Press [1967- <c1985 >. v. <1-14 > illus., facsims., maps, ports. 26 cm. Prepared under the auspices of the Ulysses S. Grant Association. 1. Grant, Ulysses S. (Ulysses Simpson), 1822-1885. 2. Presidents — United States — Correspondence. 3. United States — History — Civil War, 1861-1865 — Campaigns 4. United States — Politics and government — 1869-1877 I. Simon, John Y. ed. II. Ulysses S. Grant Association. III. T.
E660.G756 1967   973.8/2/0924   *LC* 67-10725   *ISBN* 0809304716

Morgan, H. Wayne (Howard Wayne)   • 3.7404
From Hayes to McKinley; national party politics, 1877–1896 [by] H. Wayne Morgan. [1st ed.] Syracuse, N.Y., Syracuse University Press [1969] x, 618 p. illus., facsims., ports. 24 cm. 1. Political parties — United States — History. 2. United States — Politics and government — 1865-1900 I. T.
E660.M6   329/.02/0973   *LC* 69-17074

Cashman, Sean Dennis.   3.7405
America in the Gilded Age: from the death of Lincoln to the rise of Theodore Roosevelt / Sean Dennis Cashman. — New York: New York University Press, 1984. xiv, 370 p.: ill.; 24 cm. Includes index. 1. United States — History — 1865-1898 I. T.
E661.C38 1984   973.8 19   *LC* 83-14610   *ISBN* 0814713866

Crunden, Robert Morse.   3.7406
Ministers of reform: the Progressives' achievement in American civilization, 1889–1920 / Robert M. Crunden. — New York: Basic Books, c1982. xii, 307 p.; 24 cm. 1. Progressivism (United States politics) 2. United States — Politics and government — 1865-1933 I. T.
E661.C945 1982   973.91 19   *LC* 82-70848   *ISBN* 0465046312

Faulkner, Harold Underwood, 1890-1968.   • 3.7407
Politics, reform and expansion, 1890–1900 / by Harold U. Faulkner. — New York: Harper & Row, c1959. xiv, 312 p.: ill., maps. (The New American Nation series) 1. United States — History — 1865-1898 I. T.
E661.F3 1963   *LC* 56-6022

Garraty, John Arthur, 1920-.   • 3.7408
The new commonwealth, 1877–1890, by John A. Garraty. — New York: Harper & Row, [1968] xv, 364 p.: illus., ports.; 20 cm. — (The New American nation series) (Harper torchbooks, TB1410.) 1. U.S. — History — 1865-1898. I. T.
E661.G35x   973.8   *LC* 72-367

Goldman, Eric Frederick, 1915-.   • 3.7409
Rendezvous with destiny; a history of modern American reform. — [1st ed.]. — New York: Knopf, 1952. xiii, 503, xxxvii p.; 22 cm. 1. United States — Politics and government — 1865- I. T.
E661.G58   973.8   *LC* 52-6418

Goodwyn, Lawrence.   3.7410
Democratic promise: the Populist moment in America / Lawrence Goodwyn. New York: Oxford University Press, 1976. xxvii, 718 p.: ill.; 24 cm. 1. Populism — United States — History. 2. United States — Politics and government — 1865-1900 I. T.
E661.G67   329/.88/009   *LC* 75-25462   *ISBN* 0195019962

Hirshson, Stanley P., 1928-.   • 3.7411
Farewell to the bloody shirt: northern Republicans & the southern Negro, 1877–1893 / introd. by David Donald. — Bloomington: Indiana University Press [1962] 334 p.; 21 cm. 1. Afro-Americans — Southern States 2. United States — Politics and government — 1865-1900 3. Southern States — Race relations. I. T.
E 661 H66   *LC* 62-8975

Hollingsworth, J. Rogers (Joseph Rogers), 1932-.   • 3.7412
The whirligig of politics; the democracy of Cleveland and Bryan. Chicago, University of Chicago Press [1963] xii, 263 p. illus., ports. 23 cm. 1. Cleveland, Grover, 1837-1908. 2. Bryan, William Jennings, 1860-1925. 3. Democratic Party (U.S.) 4. United States — Politics and government I. T.
E661.H72   973.87   *LC* 63-18846

Josephson, Matthew, 1899-1978.   • 3.7413
The politicos, 1865–1896, by Matthew Josephson. — New York: Harcourt, Brace and company, [c1938] ix, 760 p.; 24 cm. 'First edition.' 1. Statesmen, American. 2. United States — History — 1865-1898 I. T.
E661.J85   973.8   *LC* 38-27301

Keller, Morton.   3.7414
Affairs of State: public life in late nineteenth century America / Morton Keller. Cambridge: Belknap Press of Harvard University Press, 1977. ix, 631 p.; 24 cm. 1. United States — History — 1865-1898 I. T.
E661.K27   973.8   *LC* 76-21676   *ISBN* 0674007212

Sproat, John G.   • 3.7415
The best men: liberal reformers in the gilded age / by John Sproat. — New York: Oxford University Press, 1968. ix, 356 p.; 22 cm. 1. United States — Politics and government — 1865-1900 I. T. II. Title: Liberal reformers in the gilded age.
E661.S65   320.9/73   *LC* 68-8413

Wiebe, Robert H.   • 3.7416
The search for order, 1877–1920, by Robert H. Wiebe. — [1st ed.]. — New York: Hill and Wang, [1967] xiv, 333 p.; 22 cm. — (The Making of America) 1. Middle classes — United States. 2. Progressivism (U.S. politics) 3. United States — Politics and government — 1865-1933 4. United States — Social conditions — 1865-1918 I. T.
E661.W58   973.8 19   *LC* 66-27609

E661.7 DIPLOMATIC HISTORY

Campbell, Charles Soutter, 1911-.   3.7417
The transformation of American foreign relations, 1865–1900 / by Charles S. Campbell. — 1st ed. — New York: Harper & Row, c1976. xviii, 393 p., [8] leaves of plates: ill.; 22 cm. (The New American nation series) Includes index. 1. United States — Foreign relations — 1865-1898 I. T.
E661.7.C36 1976   327.73   *LC* 75-23877   *ISBN* 0060106182

Dobson, John M.   3.7418
America's ascent: the United States becomes a great power, 1880–1914 / John M. Dobson. — DeKalb: Northern Illinois University Press, c1978. 251 p.; 24 cm. Includes index. 1. United States — Foreign relations — 1865-1921 I. T.
E661.7.D62   327.73   *LC* 77-90754   *ISBN* 087580070X

Dulles, Foster Rhea, 1900-1970.   • **3.7419**
Prelude to world power: American diplomatic history, 1860–1900. — New York: Macmillan, [1965] viii, 238 p.; 22 cm. — (History of American foreign policy series) 1. United States — Foreign relations — 1861-1865 2. United States — Foreign relations — 1865-1898 3. United States — Territorial expansion I. T.
E661.7.D8   327.73   *LC 65-11836*

LaFeber, Walter.   • **3.7420**
New empire: an interpretation of American expansion, 1860–1898. — Ithaca, N.Y.: Published for the American Historical Association, by Cornell U.P. 1963. xiii, 444 p.; 24 cm. 1. Imperialism 2. United States — Territorial expansion 3. United States — Foreign relations — 1865-1898 I. T.
E661.7.L2   973.8   *LC 63-20868*   *ISBN* 0801402417

May, Ernest R.   • **3.7421**
American imperialism; a speculative essay [by] Ernest R. May. — [1st ed.]. — New York: Atheneum, 1968. ix, 239 p.; 22 cm. 1. Imperialism 2. United States — Foreign relations — 1865-1921 3. United States — Territorial expansion I. T.
E661.7.M3 1968   327.73   *LC 68-12544*

Plesur, Milton.   • **3.7422**
America's outward thrust; approaches to foreign affairs, 1865–1890. DeKalb, Northern Illinois University Press [1971] vii, 276 p. 25 cm. 1. United States — Foreign relations — 1865-1898 2. United States — Relations — Foreign countries I. T.
E661.7.P55   327.73   *LC 76-137882*   *ISBN* 087580019X

E664 BIOGRAPHY

E664 A–H

Adams, Charles Francis, 1835-1915.   • **3.7423**
Charles Francis Adams, 1835–1915: an autobiography / with a Memorial address delivered November 17, 1915, by Henry Cabot Lodge. — Boston & New York: Houghton Mifflin company [c1916] lx, 224 p.: front. (port.); 25 cm. I. Lodge, Henry Cabot, 1850-1924. II. T.
E664.A19 A2   *LC 16-6471*

Brandeis, Louis Dembitz, 1856-1941.   • **3.7424**
Letters of Louis D. Brandeis. Edited by Melvin I. Urofsky and David M. Levy. — Albany: State University of New York Press, 1971-78. 5 v.: illus., ports.; 22 cm. Vol. 3-5: 1st ed. 1. Brandeis, Louis Dembitz, 1856-1941. 3. Statesmen — United States — Correspondence. 4. Judges — United States — Correspondence. I. T.
E664.B819 A4 1971   347/.73/2634   *LC 73-129640*   *ISBN* 087395078X

Urofsky, Melvin I.   • **3.7425**
A mind of one piece; Brandeis and American reform, by Melvin I. Urofsky. — New York: Scribner, [1971] xiii, 210 p.; 24 cm. 1. Brandeis, Louis Dembitz, 1856-1941. I. T.
E664.B819 U7   347/.7326/34 B   *LC 74-143945*   *ISBN* 0684123681

Parks, Joseph Howard.   **3.7426**
Joseph E. Brown of Georgia / Joseph H. Parks. — Baton Rouge: Louisiana State University Press, c1977. x, 612 p., [4] leaves of plates: ill.; 24 cm. — (Southern biography series.) Includes index. 1. Brown, Joseph Emerson, 1821-1894. 2. Legislators — United States — Biography. 3. Reconstruction 4. Georgia — Governors — Biography. 5. Georgia — Politics and government — 1775-1865 I. T. II. Series.
E664.B8613 P37   975.8/03/0924   *LC 74-27192*   *ISBN* 0807101893

Cherny, Robert W.   **3.7427**
A righteous cause: the life of William Jennings Bryan / Robert W. Cherny; edited by Oscar Handlin. — Boston: Little, Brown, c1985. x, 225 p.: ill.; 20 cm. (Library of American biography.) Includes index. 1. Bryan, William Jennings, 1860-1925. 2. Statesmen — United States — Biography. 3. United States — Politics and government — 1865-1933 I. Handlin, Oscar, 1915- II. T. III. Series.
E664.B87 C47 1985   973.91/092/4 B 19   *LC 84-19434*   *ISBN* 0316138568

Coletta, Paolo Enrico, 1916-.   • **3.7428**
William Jennings Bryan / by Paolo E. Coletta. — Lincoln: University of Nebraska Press, 1964-[69] 3 v.; 24 cm. 1. Bryan, William Jennings, 1860-1925. I. T.
E664.B87 C55   973.91/0924 B   *LC 64-11352*

Glad, Paul W., 1926-.   • **3.7429**
The trumpet soundeth; William Jennings Bryan and his democracy, 1896–1912. [Lincoln] University of Nebraska Press, 1960. xii, 242 p. illus., ports. 24 cm. 1. Bryan, William Jennings, 1860-1925. 2. Statesmen — United States — Biography. 3. Presidential candidates — United States — Biography. 4. Progressivism (United States politics) 5. Populism — United States — History. 6. United States — Politics and government — 1865-1933 I. T.
E664.B87 G55   923.273   *LC 60-12259*

Clark, Champ, 1850-1921.   • **3.7430**
My quarter century of American politics. New York, London, Harper & brothers [c1920] 2 v. fronts., plates, ports. 22 cm. 1. United States — Politics and government — 1865- I. T.
E664.C49 C4   *LC 20-4643*

Jordan, David M., 1935-.   • **3.7431**
Roscoe Conkling of New York: voice in the Senate, by David M. Jordan. — Ithaca [N.Y.]: Cornell University Press, [1971] xiii, 464 p.: ports.; 24 cm. 1. Conkling, Roscoe, 1829-1888. 2. U.S. — Politics and government — 1865-1900. I. T.
E664.C75 J6   328.73/0924 B   *LC 76-148021*   *ISBN* 0801406250

Ridge, Martin.   • **3.7432**
Ignatius Donnelly: the portrait of a politician. — [Chicago]: University of Chicago Press [1962] 427 p.: ill.; 25 cm. Includes bibliography. 1. Donnelly, Ignatius, 1831-1901. I. T.
E664.D68R5   928.1   *LC 62-19937*

Nevins, Allan, 1890-1971.   • **3.7433**
Hamilton Fish; the inner history of the Grant administration. With an introd. by John Bassett Moore. Rev. ed. New York, F. Ungar Pub. Co. [1957] 2 v. (xxi, 932 p.) illus., ports., coat of arms. 24 cm. (American classics) 1. Fish, Hamilton, 1808-1893. 2. Grant, Ulysses S. (Ulysses Simpson), 1822-1885. 3. United States — Foreign relations — 1869-1877 4. United States — Politics and government — 1869-1877 I. T.
E664.F52 N44   973.82   *LC 57-9967*

Nixon, Raymond Blalock, 1903-.   • **3.7434**
Henry W. Grady, spokesman of the New South, by Raymond B. Nixon. — New York: Russell & Russell, [1969, c1943] x, 360, xiv p.: illus., ports.; 23 cm. 1. Grady, Henry Woodfin, 1850-1889. I. T.
E664.G73 N5 1969   070.9/24 B   *LC 68-27076*

Hay, John, 1838-1905.   • **3.7435**
Lincoln and the Civil War in the diaries and letters of John Hay: selected and with an introd. by Tyler Dennett. — Westport, Conn.: Greenwood Press [1972, c1939] 1 v. 1. Lincoln, Abraham, 1809-1865. 2. Hay, John, 1838-1905. 3. United States — History — Civil War. I. Dennett, Tyler, 1883-1949. II. T.
E664.H41 A44 1972   973.7/0924 B   *LC 79-135598*   *ISBN* 0837151902

Welch, Richard E.   • **3.7436**
George Frisbie Hoar and the half–breed Republicans [by] Richard E. Welch, Jr. Cambridge, Harvard University Press, 1971. 364 p. illus., port. 25 cm. 1. Hoar, George Frisbie, 1826-1904. 2. Republican Party (U.S.: 1854-) — History. I. T.
E664.H65 W4   329.6/00924 B   *LC 70-133214*   *ISBN* 0674348761

Hughes, Charles Evans, 1862-1948.   **3.7437**
The autobiographical notes of Charles Evans Hughes. Edited by David J. Danelski and Joseph S. Tulchin. — Cambridge, Mass.: Harvard University Press, 1973. xxix, 363 p.: illus.; 24 cm. — (Studies in legal history.) 1. Hughes, Charles Evans, 1862-1948. I. Danelski, David Joseph, 1930- ed. II. Tulchin, Joseph S., 1939- ed. III. T. IV. Series.
E664.H86 A32   973.91/092/4 B   *LC 72-88130*   *ISBN* 0674053257

E664 L–Z

La Follette, Belle Case, 1859-1931.   • **3.7438**
Robert M. La Follette, June 14, 1855–June 18, 1925. New York: Macmillan, 1953. 2 v. (xx, 1305 p.): ill., ports., facsims.; 22 cm. Chapters I-XXVI by Belle Case La Follette and chapters XXVII-LXXII by Fola La Follette. 1. La Follette, Robert M. (Robert Marion), 1855-1925. I. La Follette, Fola. II. T.
E664.L16 L13   *LC 53-13106*

La Follette, Robert M. (Robert Marion), 1855-1925.   • **3.7439**
La Follette's autobiography; a personal narrative of political experiences. With a foreword by Allan Nevins. — Madison, University of Wisconsin Press, 1963. 349 p. illus. 22 cm. 1. United States — Pol. & govt. 2. Wisconsin — Pol. & govt. — 1848-1950. 3. Presidents — United States — Election — 1912. I. T.
E664.L16L16 1960   923.273   *LC 60-50989*

Maxwell, Robert S.   • **3.7440**
La Follette and the rise of the Progressives in Wisconsin [by] Robert S. Maxwell. New York, Russell & Russell [1973, c1956] viii, 271 p. illus. 23 cm. Reprint of the ed. published by the State Historical Society of Wisconsin,

Madison. 1. La Follette, Robert M. (Robert Marion), 1855-1925. 2. Progressivism (United States politics) 3. Wisconsin — Politics and government — 1848-1950 I. T.
E664.L16 M3 1973   973.91/092/4 B   *LC* 72-85000   *ISBN* 0846216965

Garraty, John Arthur, 1920-.   • 3.7441
Henry Cabot Lodge, a biography. — [1st ed.]. — New York: Knopf, 1953. xiii, 433, xvi p.: ports.; 25 cm. 1. Lodge, Henry Cabot, 1850-1924. I. T.
E664.L7 G3   923.273   *LC* 53-6852

Widenor, William C.   3.7442
Henry Cabot Lodge and the search for an American foreign policy / William C. Widenor. — Berkeley: University of California Press, c1980. xi, 389 p., [4] leaves of plates: ill.; 25 cm. Includes index. 1. Lodge, Henry Cabot, 1850-1924. I. T.
E664.L7 W45   327.73   *LC* 78-62863   *ISBN* 0520037782

Pinchot, Gifford, 1865-1946.   • 3.7443
Breaking new ground / introd. by James Penick, Jr. — Seattle: University of Washington Press, [1972, c1947] xxvi, 522 p.: ill.; 23 cm. — (Americana library, AL-22) Autobiography. 1. Pinchot, Gifford, 1865-1946. 2. Conservation of natural resources — United States I. T.
E664.P62 A3 1972   333.7/5/0924 B   *LC* 75-172901   *ISBN* 0295951818

McGeary, M. Nelson (Martin Nelson), 1906-.   • 3.7444
Gifford Pinchot, forester–politician. Princeton, N.J., Princeton University Press, 1960. 481 p. illus. 25 cm. 1. Pinchot, Gifford, 1865-1946. I. T.
E664.P62 M2   *LC* 60-12232

Robinson, William Alexander, 1884-.   • 3.7445
Thomas B. Reed, parliamentarian, by William A. Robinson. New York, Dodd, Mead & company, 1930. 423 p. illus. 24 cm. (American political leaders) 1. Reed, Thomas Brackett, 1839-1902. I. T.
E664.R3 R66   *LC* 30-30931

Jessup, Philip C. (Philip Caryl), 1897-.   • 3.7446
Elihu Root / by Philip C. Jessup. — [Unaltered and unabridged ed. Hamden, Conn.]: Archon Books, 1964 [c1938] 2 v.: ill., facsims., maps (part fold.) ports.; 23 cm. 1. Root, Elihu, 1845-1937. I. T.
E664.R7 J5 1964   *LC* 64-24716

Leopold, Richard William.   • 3.7447
Elihu Root and the conservative tradition. — [1st ed.]. — Boston: Little, Brown, [1954] 222 p.; 21 cm. — (The Library of American biography) 1. Root, Elihu, 1845-1937. I. T.
E664.R7 L4   923.273   *LC* 54-6870

Schurz, Carl, 1829-1906.   • 3.7448
The autobiography of Carl Schurz / an abridgment in one volume by Wayne Andrews; with an introduction by Allan Nevins. — New York: Scribner, 1961. — 331 p.; 24 cm. 'An abridgement ... of The reminiscences of Carl Schurz, originally published in three volumes, 1906-1908.' Includes index. 1. Schurz, Carl, 1829-1906. 2. Statesmen — United States — Biography 3. United States — Politics and government — 1857-1861 4. United States — Politics and government — Civil War, 1861-1865 I. Andrews, Wayne. II. T.
E664.S39A337   923.273 973.70924   *LC* 61-6900

Fuess, Claude Moore, 1855-1963.   • 3.7449
Carl Schurz: reformer; 1829–1906 / Claude M. Fuess. — Port Washington, N.Y.: Kennikat, 1963. 421 p.: ill., ports.; 22 cm. 1. Schurz, Carl, 1829-1906. I. T.
E664.S39 F92 1963   *LC* 63-20588

Trefousse, Hans Louis.   3.7450
Carl Schurz, a biography / by Hans L. Trefousse. — 1st ed. — Knoxville: University of Tennessee Press, c1982. viii, 386 p.: ill.; 24 cm. Includes index. 1. Schurz, Carl, 1829-1906. 2. United States. Congress. Senate — Biography. 3. Statesmen — United States — Biography. 4. Legislators — United States — Biography. I. T.
E664.S39 T7 1982   973.8/092/4 B 19   *LC* 81-3370   *ISBN* 0870493264

Simkins, Francis Butler, 1898-.   • 3.7451
Pitchfork Ben Tillman, South Carolinian. — Gloucester, Mass.: P. Smith, 1964 [c1944] xii, 577 p.: ill., facsim., ports.; 21 cm. — (Southern biography series.) 'Critical essay on authorities': p. [556]-566. 1. Tillman, Benjamin Ryan, 1847-1918. 2. South Carolina — Pol. & govt. — 1865-1950. I. T. II. Series.
E664.T57S5 1964   923.273   *LC* 65-1581

Cooling, B. Franklin.   3.7452
Benjamin Franklin Tracy: father of the modern American fighting Navy / by Benjamin Franklin Cooling. — [Hamden, Conn.]: Archon Books, 1973. xvi,

211 p.: ill.; 22 cm. 1. Tracy, Benjamin Franklin, 1830-1915. 2. United States. Navy — History I. T.
E664.T72 C66   353.7 B   *LC* 73-6645   *ISBN* 0208013369

Klingman, Peter D., 1945-.   3.7453
Josiah Walls: Florida's Black Congressman of Reconstruction / Peter D. Klingman. — Gainesville: University Presses of Florida, 1976. xi, 157 p.: port.; 24 cm. 'A University of Florida book.' Includes index. 1. Walls, Josiah T., 1842-1905. 2. Afro-Americans — History — 1863-1877 3. Afro-Americans — Politics and government I. T.
E664.W19 K54   975.9/06/0924 B   *LC* 75-45206   *ISBN* 0813003997

Woodward, C. Vann (Comer Vann), 1908-.   • 3.7454
Tom Watson, agrarian rebel. New York, The Macmillan company, 1938. xii p., 1 l., 518 p. pl., ports. 22 cm. 1. Watson, Thomas E. (Thomas Edward), 1856-1922. I. T.
E664.W337 W6   *LC* 38-8354

E666–738 BY PRESIDENTIAL ADMINISTRATION

E666–670 Johnson, 1865–1869

Benedict, Michael Les.   • 3.7455
The impeachment and trial of Andrew Johnson. [1st ed.] New York, Norton [1973] x, 212 p. 21 cm. (The Norton essays in American history) 1. Johnson, Andrew, 1808-1875 — Impeachment. I. T.
E666.B46 1973   973.8/1/0924 B   *LC* 72-10883   *ISBN* 039305473X
ISBN 0393094189

Castel, Albert E.   3.7456
The Presidency of Andrew Johnson / by Albert Castel. — Lawrence: Regents Press of Kansas, c1979. viii, 262 p.; 24 cm. — (American presidency series.) Includes index. 1. Johnson, Andrew, 1808-1875. 2. Reconstruction 3. Presidents — United States — Biography 4. United States — Politics and government — 1865-1869 I. T. II. Series.
E666.C23   973.8/1/0924 B   *LC* 79-11050   *ISBN* 0700601902

E668 Reconstruction, 1865–1877

Beale, Howard K. (Howard Kennedy), 1899-1959.   • 3.7457
The critical year: a study of Andrew Johnson and reconstruction. — New York: F. Ungar Pub. Co. [1958] 454 p.: ill.; 22 cm. (American classics) 1. Johnson, Andrew, 1808-1875. 2. Reconstruction 3. United States — Politics and government — 1865-1869 I. T.
E668.B354 1958   973.81   *LC* 58-9332

Benedict, Michael Les.   3.7458
A compromise of principle: Congressional Republicans and Reconstruction, 1863–1869. — [1st ed.] New York: Norton, 1975 (c1974) 493 p.: ill.; 24 cm. 1. Johnson, Andrew, 1808-1875. 2. Republican Party (U.S.: 1854-) — History. 3. Reconstruction 4. United States — Politics and government — 1865-1869 I. T.
E668.B46   973.8/1   *LC* 74-10645   *ISBN* 0393055248

Brock, William Ranulf.   • 3.7459
An American crisis: Congress and reconstruction, 1865–1867 / W. R. Brock. — New York: St. Martin's Press, 1963. xii, 312 p.; 23 cm. 1. United States. Congress — History. 2. Reconstruction 3. United States — Politics and government — 1865-1869 I. T.
E668.B85   *LC* 63-11348

Carter, Dan T.   3.7460
When the war was over: the failure of self–reconstruction in the South, 1865–1867 / Dan T. Carter. — Baton Rouge: Louisiana State University Press, c1985. xiv, 285 p.; 24 cm. 1. Reconstruction 2. Southern States — History — 1865-1877 I. T.
E668.C28 1985   975/.041 19   *LC* 84-21315   *ISBN* 0807111929

Dorris, Jonathan Truman, 1883-1972.   • 3.7461
Pardon and amnesty under Lincoln and Johnson; the restoration of the Confederates to their rights and privileges, 1961–1898. Chapel Hill, University of North Carolina Press [1953] xxi, 459 p. 24 cm. 1. Pardon — United States. 2. Amnesty — United States 3. Reconstruction 4. Political crimes and offenses — Southern States. I. T.
E668.D713   *LC* 53-13363

Du Bois, W. E. B. (William Edward Burghardt), 1868-1963.   • 3.7462
Black reconstruction in America: an essay toward a history of the part which black folk played in the attempt to reconstruct democracy in America,

1860–1880. — New York: Russell & Russell, [c1935] 746 p.; 22 cm. 1. Reconstruction 2. Afro-Americans — Politics and suffrage 3. Afro-Americans — Employment 4. Afro-Americans 5. United States — Politics and government — 1865-1877 I. T.
E668.D83 1935b   *LC* 35-8545

Dunning, William Archibald, 1857-1922.   • **3.7463**
Reconstruction, political & economic, 1865–1877. — New York: Harper, [1962, c1935] 378 p.: illus.; 21 cm. — (Harper torchbooks, TB1073. The Academy library) 'Originally published as volume 22 in the American Nation series.' 1. Reconstruction I. T.
E668.D927 1962   973.8   *LC* 62-5020

Fleming, Walter Lynwood, 1874-1932, ed.   • **3.7464**
Documentary history of Reconstruction. Gloucester, Mass., P. Smith, 1960 [c1935] 2 v. in 1. illus., facsims. 28 cm. 1. Reconstruction I. T.
E668.F58 1960   *LC* 60-52262

Franklin, John Hope, 1915-.   • **3.7465**
Reconstruction: after the Civil War. — [Chicago]: University of Chicago Press, [1961] 258 p.: illus.; 21 cm. — (The Chicago history of American civilization) 1. Reconstruction I. T.
E668.F7   973.8   *LC* 61-15931

Gillette, William.   **3.7466**
Retreat from Reconstruction, 1869–1879 / William Gillette. — Baton Rouge: Louisiana State University Press, c1979. xiv, 463 p.; 24 cm. Includes index. 1. Reconstruction 2. United States — Politics and government — 1865-1877 I. T.
E668.G45   973.8/2   *LC* 79-12450   *ISBN* 0807105694

McKitrick, Eric L.   • **3.7467**
Andrew Johnson and Reconstruction / by Eric L. McKitrick. — Chicago: University of Chicago Press, 1960. ix, 534 p. 1. Johnson, Andrew, 1808-1875. 2. Reconstruction 3. United States — History — 1865-1898 I. T.
E668.M156   973.81   *LC* 60-5467   *ISBN* 0226560457

Mantell, Martin E., 1936-.   **3.7468**
Johnson, Grant, and the politics of Reconstruction [by] Martin E. Mantell. New York, Columbia University Press, 1973. 209 p. 24 cm. Based on the author's thesis, Columbia University, with title: The election of 1868; the response to Congressional Reconstruction. 1. Johnson, Andrew, 1808-1875. 2. Grant, Ulysses S. (Ulysses Simpson), 1822-1885. 3. Reconstruction 4. United States — Politics and government — 1865-1869 I. T.
E668.M34   973.8   *LC* 72-13452   *ISBN* 0231035071

Perman, Michael.   **3.7469**
Reunion without compromise: the South and Reconstruction: 1865–1868. — Cambridge [Eng.]: University Press, 1973. 376 p.; 23 cm. 1. Reconstruction 2. Southern States — Politics and government — 1865-1950 I. T.
E668.P43 1973   973.8/1   *LC* 72-86418   *ISBN* 052120044X

Roark, James L.   **3.7470**
Masters without slaves: southern planters in the Civil War and Reconstruction / James L. Roark. 1st ed. — New York: Norton, c1977. xii, 273 p.; 22 cm. Includes index. 1. Reconstruction 2. Plantation life — Southern States. 3. Slavery — Southern States 4. Southern States — Social conditions I. T.
E668.R64 1977   976/.04   *LC* 76-47689   *ISBN* 0393055620

Sefton, James E.   • **3.7471**
The United States Army and Reconstruction, 1865–1877 / by James E. Sefton. — Baton Rouge: Louisiana State University Press, 1967. xx, 284 p.: ill. 1. Reconstruction 2. United States — History, Military — To 1900 I. T.
E668.S46   *LC* 67-21377

Singletary, Otis A.   • **3.7472**
Negro militia and Reconstruction. Austin, University of Texas Press [1957] 181 p. illus. 22 cm. 1. Reconstruction — Afro-American troops 2. Afro-Americans — Southern States — History — 19th century. I. T.
E668.S59   973.8   *LC* 57-7559

Stampp, Kenneth M. (Kenneth Milton)   **3.7473**
The era of Reconstruction, 1865–1877, by Kenneth M. Stampp. [1st ed.] New York, Knopf, 1965. ix, 228, [1] p. 22 cm. 1. Reconstruction I. T.
E668.S79   973.81   *LC* 64-13447

Trelease, Allen W.   • **3.7474**
White terror: the Ku Klux Klan conspiracy and Southern Reconstruction / by Allen W. Trelease. — [1st ed.]. — New York: Harper & Row, [1971] xlviii, 557 p.; 25 cm. 1. Ku-Klux Klan. 2. Reconstruction I. T.
E668.T7 1971   973.8   *LC* 79-123966

E669 Diplomatic History

Jensen, Ronald J., 1939-.   **3.7475**
The Alaska Purchase and Russian–American relations / Ronald J. Jensen. — Seattle: University of Washington Press, [1975] xx, 185 p., [2] leaves of plates: ill.; 23 cm. Includes index. 1. Alaska — Annexation. 2. United States — Foreign relations — Russia. 3. Russia — Foreign relations — United States. I. T.
E669.J46   327.73/047   *LC* 74-23716   *ISBN* 0295953764

E671–680 Grant, 1869–1877

Grant, Ulysses S. (Ulysses Simpson), 1822-1885.   • **3.7476**
Personal memoirs. Edited with notes and an introd. by E.B. Long. New York, Grosset & Dunlap [1962, c1952] xxv, 608 p. maps. 21 cm. (Universal library, UL129) 1. United States — History — Civil War, 1861-1865 — Campaigns and battles. 2. United States — History — War with Mexico, 1845-1848 — Personal narratives. I. T.
E672.Ax   *LC* 62-253

Catton, Bruce, 1899-.   • **3.7477**
Grant moves south. With maps by Samuel H. Bryant. [1st ed.] Boston, Little, Brown [1960] x, 564 p. port., maps. 22 cm. A continuation of Lloyd Lewis' Captain Sam Grant. 1. Grant, Ulysses S. (Ulysses Simpson), 1822-1885. 2. United States — History — Civil War, 1861-1865 — Campaigns I. Lewis, Lloyd, 1891-1949. Captain Sam Grant. II. T.
E672.C293   923.173   *LC* 60-5860

Catton, Bruce, 1899-.   • **3.7478**
Grant takes command / With maps by Samuel H. Bryant. [1st ed.] Boston: Little, Brown [1969] 556 p.: maps, plans, port.; 25 cm. 1. Grant, Ulysses S. (Ulysses Simpson), 1822-1885. 2. United States — History — Civil War, 1861-1865 — Campaigns I. T.
E672.C295   973.73/0924   *LC* 69-12632

Catton, Bruce, 1899-.   • **3.7479**
U.S. Grant and the American military tradition. [1st ed.] Boston, Little, Brown [1954] x, 201 p. 22 cm. (Library of American biography.) 'A note on the sources': p. [191]-193. 1. Grant, Ulysses S. (Ulysses Simpson), 1822-1885. I. T. II. Series.
E672.C3 1954   923.173   *LC* 54-6860

Lewis, Lloyd, 1891-1949.   **3.7480**
Captain Sam Grant. [1st ed.] Boston, Little, Brown, 1950. viii, 512 p. port. 23 cm. 1. Grant, Ulysses S. (Ulysses Simpson), 1822-1885. I. T.
E672.L48 1950   923.173   *LC* 50-7939

McFeely, William S.   **3.7481**
Grant: a biography / William S. McFeely. — 1st ed. — New York: Norton, c1981. xiii, 592 p.: ill.; 24 cm. Includes index. 1. Grant, Ulysses S. (Ulysses Simpson), 1822-1885. 2. Presidents — United States — Biography 3. United States — Politics and government — 1869-1877 4. United States — History — Civil War, 1861-1865 — Campaigns I. T.
E672.M15 1981   973.8/2/0924 B 19   *LC* 80-25279   *ISBN* 0393013723

Polakoff, Keith Ian.   **3.7482**
The politics of inertia: the election of 1876 and the end of Reconstruction. — Baton Rouge: Louisiana State University Press, [1973] xiv, 343 p.; 24 cm. 1. Presidents — United States — Election — 1876. 2. Reconstruction I. T.
E680.P73   329/.023/73082   *LC* 72-96400   *ISBN* 0807102105

E681–685 Hayes, 1877–1881

Woodward, C. Vann (Comer Vann), 1908-.   • **3.7483**
Reunion and reaction; the compromise of 1877 and the end of reconstruction, by C. Vann Woodward. Boston, Little, Brown [1966] xii, 263 p. map. 20 cm. 1. Reconstruction 2. United States — Politics and government — 1877-1881 I. T.
E681.W83 1966   973.83   *LC* 66-22490

Barnard, Harry, 1906-.   • **3.7484**
Rutherford B. Hayes and his America. — New York, Russell & Russell [1967, c1954] 606 p. illus., facsim., ports. 22 cm. Bibliographical references included in 'Notes' (p. 525-570) Bibliography: p. 571-588. 1. Hayes, Rutherford Birchard, 1822-1893. I. T.
E682.B3 1967   973.8/3/0924   *LC* 66-24667

Davison, Kenneth E.   • **3.7485**
The Presidency of Rutherford B. Hayes / [by] Kenneth E. Davison. — Westport, Conn.: Greenwood Press [1972] xvii, 266 p.: ill.; 25 cm. (Contributions in American studies, no. 3) 1. Hayes, Rutherford Birchard, 1822-1893. I. T.
E682.D38   973.8/3/0924 B   *LC* 79-176289   *ISBN* 0837162750

E686–695 Garfield, 1881. Arthur, 1881–1885

Doenecke, Justus D.   3.7486
The Presidencies of James A. Garfield & Chester A. Arthur / Justus D. Doenecke. — Lawrence: Regents Press of Kansas, c1981. xiii, 229 p.; 24 cm. (American presidency series.) Includes index. 1. Garfield, James A. (James Abram), 1831-1881. 2. Arthur, Chester Alan, 1829-1886. 3. United States — Politics and government — 1881-1885 I. T. II. Series.
E686.D63   973.8/4 19   *LC* 80-18957   *ISBN* 0700602089

Pletcher, David M.   • 3.7487
The awkward years; American foreign relations under Garfield and Arthur. — Columbia, University of Missouri Press [c1962] 381 p. 24 cm. Includes bibliography. 1. U.S. — For. rel. — 1881-1885. 2. U.S. — Pol. & govt. — 1881-1885. I. T.
E686.P5   973.84   *LC* 62-15589

Peskin, Allan.   3.7488
Garfield: a biography / by Allan Peskin. — Kent, Ohio: Kent State University Press, c1978. x, 716 p.: port.; 25 cm. Includes index. 1. Garfield, James A. (James Abram), 1831-1881. 2. Presidents — United States — Biography 3. United States — Politics and government — 1849-1877 4. United States — Politics and government — 1877-1881 I. T.
E687.P47   973.8/4/0924 B   *LC* 77-15630   *ISBN* 0873382102

Smith, Theodore Clarke, 1870-1960.   3.7489
The life and letters of James Abram Garfield. New Haven, Yale Univ. Press, 1925. 2 vol. port. 1. Garfield, James Abram I. T.
E687S66

Reeves, Thomas C., 1936-.   3.7490
Gentleman boss: the life of Chester Alan Arthur [by] Thomas C. Reeves. [1st ed.] New York, Knopf; [distributed by Random House] 1975. xvii, 500, xix p. illus. 25 cm. 1. Arthur, Chester Alan, 1829-1886. I. T.
E692.R43 1975   973.8/4/0924 B   *LC* 74-7760   *ISBN* 0394460952

E696–700 Cleveland, 1885–1889, 1893–1897

Cleveland, Grover, 1837-1908.   • 3.7491
Letters of Grover Cleveland, 1850–1908 / selected and edited by Allan Nevins. — Boston; New York: Houghton Mifflin Company, 1933. xix, 640 p.: front. (port.); 25 cm. I. Nevins, Allan, 1890-1971. II. T.
E697.C63   923.173   *LC* 33-35003

Nevins, Allan, 1890-1971.   • 3.7492
Grover Cleveland: a study in courage / by Allan Nevins. — New York: Dodd, Mead & company, 1934. xiii p., 1 l, 832 p.: front., plates, ports.; 24 cm. 1. Cleveland, Grover, 1837-1908. I. T.
E697.N468   *LC* 38-4611

E701–705 Harrison, 1889–1893

Williams, R. Hal.   3.7493
Years of decision: American politics in the 1890s / R. Hal Williams. — New York: Wiley, c1978. xi, 219 p.; 22 cm. (Critical episodes in American politics) Includes index. 1. Political parties — United States — History. 2. United States — Politics and government — 1889-1893 3. United States — Politics and government — 1893-1897 4. United States — Politics and government — 1897-1901 I. T. II. Series.
E701.W54   320.9/73/08   *LC* 78-6407   *ISBN* 0471948772. *ISBN* 0471948780 pbk

Sievers, Harry Joseph, 1920-.   • 3.7494
Benjamin Harrison. Introd. by Hilton U. Brown. [2d ed., rev.] New York, University Publishers [c1960-. v.: ill.; 24 cm. 1. Harrison, Benjamin, 1833-1901. I. T.
E702.S55   923.173   *LC* 60-12711

E711–738 McKinley, 1897–1901

Gould, Lewis L.   3.7495
The Presidency of William McKinley / by Lewis L. Gould. — Lawrence: Regents Press of Kansas, c1980. xi, 294 p.; 24 cm. (American presidency series.) Includes index. 1. McKinley, William, 1843-1901. 2. Presidents — United States — Biography 3. United States — Politics and government — 1897-1901 I. T. II. Series.
E711.G68   973.8/8/0924   *LC* 80-16022   *ISBN* 0700602062

Leech, Margaret, 1893-1974.   • 3.7496
In the days of McKinley. [1st ed.] New York, Harper [1959] viii, 686 p. illus., ports., facsims. 25 cm. 'Sources': p. 610-611. 'Notes and references': p. 612-669. 1. McKinley, William, 1843-1901. I. T.
E711.6.L4   923.173   *LC* 59-6310

Morgan, H. Wayne (Howard Wayne)   • 3.7497
William McKinley and his America / H. Wayne Morgan. — [Syracuse, N. Y.]: Syracuse University Press, 1963. xi, 595 p.: ill., ports. 24 cm. Bibliographical references included in 'Notes to chapters.' 1. McKinley, William, 1843-1901. I. T.
E711.6.M7   923.173   *LC* 63-19723

Beisner, Robert L.   3.7498
Twelve against empire: the anti–imperialists, 1898–1900 / by Robert L. Beisner. — New York: McGraw-Hill [1969] xvi, 310 p.; 22 cm. 1. Anti-imperialist movements — United States — History — 19th century. 2. United States — Foreign relations — 1897-1901 3. United States — Territorial expansion 4. United States — History — War of 1898 — Protest movements. I. T.
E713.B47   327.73   *LC* 68-13087

Pratt, Julius William, 1888-.   • 3.7499
Expansionists of 1898; the acquisition of Hawaii and the Spanish islands. — New York: P. Smith, 1951 [c1936] viii, 393 p.; 21 cm. — (The Albert Shaw lectures on diplomatic history, 1936) 1. United States — Territorial expansion 2. United States — Foreign relations 3. Hawaii — Annexation. I. T. II. Series.
E713.P895 1936a   973.88   *LC* 52-7706

E714–735 War of 1898

Croly, Herbert David, 1869-1930.   • 3.7500
Marcus Alonzo Hanna: his life and work. — Hamden, Connecticut: Archon, 1965, c1912. xiii, 495 p.: ill. 1. Hanna, Marcus Alonzo, 1837-1904. I. T.
E714.6.H35 C76   *LC* 65-15015

Millis, Walter, 1899-1968.   3.7501
The martial spirit: a study of our war with Spain / by Walter Millis ... — Boston and New York: Houghton Mifflin company, 1931. xii p., 1 l., 427 p.: front., plates, ports.; 23 cm. Maps on lining-papers. 'Bibliographical acknowledgment': p. [411]-417. 1. U.S. — Hist. — War of 1898. I. T.
E715.M76   973.89   *LC* 31-27021

Morgan, H. Wayne (Howard Wayne)   • 3.7502
America's road to empire; the war with Spain and overseas expansion [by] H. Wayne Morgan. New York, Wiley [1965] xii, 124 p. maps. 22 cm. (America in crisis.) 1. Imperialism 2. United States — History — War of 1898 3. United States — Territorial expansion I. T. II. Series.
E715.M85   973.891   *LC* 64-8714

Trask, David F.   3.7503
The war with Spain in 1898 / David F. Trask. — New York: Macmillan; London: Collier Macmillan, c1981. xiv, 654 p.: maps; 24 cm. — (Macmillan wars of the United States.) 1. United States — History — War of 1898 I. T. II. Series.
E715.T7   973.8/9 19   *LC* 80-2314   *ISBN* 0029329507

Welch, Richard E.   3.7504
Response to imperialism: the United States and the Philippine–American War, 1899–1902 / by Richard E. Welch, Jr. — Chapel Hill: University of North Carolina Press, c1979. xvi, 215 p.: ill.; 24 cm. Includes index. 1. United States — History — War of 1898 2. Philippines — History — Insurrection, 1899-1901 I. T.
E721.W4   959.9/031   *LC* 78-11403   *ISBN* 0807813486

Cosmas, Graham A.   3.7505
An army for empire; the United States Army in the Spanish–American War [by] Graham A. Cosmas. — [Columbia]: University of Missouri Press, [1971] 334 p.: illus.; 25 cm. 1. U.S. Army — History — War of 1898. I. T.
E725.3.C6   973.8/93   *LC* 76-149010   *ISBN* 0826201075

E740–879 20th Century

Allen, Frederick Lewis, 1890-1954.   • 3.7506
Only yesterday: an informal history of the nineteen–twenties / by Frederick Lewis Allen. — New York; London: Harper & brothers, 1931. xiv, p., 1 l., 370 p.: front., plates, ports., facsims.; 23 cm. 'Second printing.' 1. United States — History — 1919-1933 2. United States — Social conditions — 1933-1945 3. United States — Economic conditions — 1918-1945 I. T.
E741.A64   973.91   *LC* 31-28421

Allen, Frederick Lewis, 1890-1954.   • 3.7507
Since yesterday; the nineteen–thirties in America, September 3, 1929–September 3, 1939, by Frederick Lewis Allen. — New York; London: Harper & brothers, 1940. xiv, p., 1 l., 362 p.: front., plates, ports., facsims.; 23 cm. 'First edition.' 1. United States — History — 1919-1933 2. United States

— Social conditions — 1933-1945 3. United States — Economic conditions — 1918-1945 I. T.
E741.A66   973.916   *LC* 40-27130

Braeman, John. ed.   • **3.7508**
Change and continuity in twentieth–century America, edited by John Braeman, Robert H. Bremner [and] Everett Walters. [Columbus] Ohio State University Press [1965, c1964] x, 287 p. 22 cm. (Modern America, no. 1) Bibliographical footnotes. 1. United States — History — 20th cent. — Addresses, essays, lectures. I. Bremner, Robert Hamlett, 1917- joint ed. II. Walters, Everett, 1915- joint ed. III. T. IV. Series.
E741.B68   973.9082   *LC* 64-19380

Karl, Barry Dean.   **3.7509**
The uneasy state: the United States from 1915 to 1945 / Barry D. Karl. — Chicago: University of Chicago Press, 1984 (c1983). x, 257 p.; 24 cm. Includes index. 1. United States — History — 20th century I. T.
E741.K33 1983   973.91 19   *LC* 83-9134   *ISBN* 0226425193

Link, Arthur Stanley.   • **3.7510**
American epoch: a history of the United States since the 1890's / by Arthur S. Link; with the collaboration of William B. Catton and the assistance of William M. Leary, Jr. — 3d ed. — New York: Knopf, [1967] xxii, 926, xliv p.: ill., maps, ports.; 25 cm. 1. United States — History — 20th century I. T.
E741.L55 1967   973.91   *LC* 67-12258

Mowry, George Edwin, 1909-.   • **3.7511**
The urban nation, 1920–1960, by George E. Mowry. — [1st ed.]. — New York: Hill and Wang, [1965] x, 278 p.: maps.; 22 cm. — (The Making of America) Revised ed. (1981) published under title: The urban nation, 1920-1980. 1. Urbanization — United States. 2. United States — History — 20th century I. T.
E741.M7   973.9   *LC* 65-17423

Regier, Cornelius C., 1884-.   • **3.7512**
The era of the muckrakers. — Chapel Hill: The University of North Carolina press, 1932. xi, 254 p.: ports. 1. Corruption (in politics) — United States 2. Journalism — United States 3. United States — Politics and government — 20th century I. T.
E741.R34 1932   *LC* 32-30647

Rostow, W. W. (Walt Whitman), 1916-.   • **3.7513**
The United States in the world arena: an essay in recent history. — New York: Harper [1960] xxii, 568 p.: diagrs., tables; 24 cm. (Massachusetts Institute of Technology. Center for International Studies. American project series) 1. World politics — 20th century 2. United States — History — 20th century 3. United States — Foreign relations — 20th century I. T. II. Series.
E741.R67   327.73   *LC* 60-7568

Siegel, Frederick F., 1945-.   **3.7514**
Troubled journey: from Pearl Harbor to Ronald Reagan / Frederick F. Siegel. — New York: Hill and Wang, c1984. xiii, 289 p.; 24 cm. — (American century series.) Includes index. 1. World War, 1939-1945 — United States. 2. United States — History — 1945- I. T. II. Series.
E741.S48 1984   973.9 19   *LC* 83-26547   *ISBN* 0809094436

Sullivan, Mark, 1874-.   **3.7515**
Our times, 1900–1925. New York, Scribner, 1936 [c1927-35] 6 v. illus., ports., facsims., music. 25 cm. 1. World War, 1914-1918 — United States. 2. United States — History — 20th century 3. United States — Civilization I. T.
E741.S944   *LC* 51-4248

Mencken, H. L. (Henry Louis), 1880-1956.   • **3.7516**
A carnival of buncombe. Edited by Malcolm Moos. Baltimore, Johns Hopkins Press [1956] 370 p. 22 cm. 1. United States — Politics and government — 20th century I. T.
E742.M4   973.91504   *LC* 56-11658

Eisenhower, Dwight D. (Dwight David), 1890-1969.   • **3.7517**
The papers of Dwight David Eisenhower: the war years / Alfred D. Chandler, Jr., editor. Stephen E. Ambrose, associate editor [and others]. — Baltimore: Johns Hopkins Press, 1970. 5 v.: facsims., maps, ports.; 24 cm. 1. World War, 1939-1945 — Sources. I. Chandler, Alfred Dupont. II. T.
E742.5.E37 1970   940.54/012   *LC* 65-27672   *ISBN* 0801810787

Roosevelt, Franklin D. (Franklin Delano), 1882-1945.   • **3.7518**
Franklin D. Roosevelt and foreign affairs. Edited by Edgar B. Nixon. Cambridge, Belknap Press of Harvard University Press, 1969-. v. ports. 26 cm. 1. Roosevelt, Franklin D. (Franklin Delano), 1882-1945. 2. United States — Foreign relations — 1933-1945 — Sources. I. Nixon, Edgar Burkhardt, 1902- ed. II. T.
E742.5.R6 1969   327.73   *LC* 68-25617

Stevenson, Adlai E. (Adlai Ewing), 1900-1965.   • **3.7519**
The papers of Adlai E. Stevenson / Walter Johnson, editor; Carol Evans, assistant editor. — [1st ed.] Boston: Little, Brown, [1972-. v.: ill.; 24 cm.

1. Stevenson, Adlai E. (Adlai Ewing), 1900-1965. 2. Statesmen — United States — Correspondence. 3. United States — Politics and government — 1945- — Sources. 4. Illinois — Politics and government — Sources. I. Johnson, Walter, 1915- ed. II. T.
E742.5.S74 1972   973.921/092/4   *LC* 73-175478   *ISBN* 0316467510

E743 POLITICAL HISTORY

Blum, John Morton, 1921-.   **3.7520**
The progressive Presidents: Roosevelt, Wilson, Roosevelt, Johnson / John Morton Blum. — 1st ed. — New York: Norton, c1980. 221 p.; 22 cm. Includes index. 1. Executive power — United States 2. United States — Politics and government — 20th century I. T.
E743.B6135 1980   353.03/2 19   *LC* 79-22866   *ISBN* 0393013308

Chalmers, David Mark.   • **3.7521**
The social and political ideas of the muckrakers. — [1st ed.]. — New York: Citadel Press, [1964] 127 p.; 21 cm. 1. Journalists, American — Biography. 2. Journalism — Social aspects 3. Journalism — Political aspects I. T.
E743.C45   301.153   *LC* 64-15960

Chamberlain, John, 1903-.   • **3.7522**
Farewell to reform; the rise, life and decay of the progressive mind in America. — Chicago, Quadrangle Books [1965, c1932] xi, 333 p. 21 cm. — (Quadrangle paperbacks, QP19) 1. U.S. — Pol. & govt. — 1901-1953. 2. Progressivism (U.S. politics) 3. Social problems in literature I. T.
E743.C46 1965   973.91   *LC* 65-2646

Fulbright, J. William (James William), 1905-.   • **3.7523**
Fulbright of Arkansas: the public positions of a private thinker. Edited by Karl E. Meyer. With a pref. by Walter Lippmann. Washington, D.C.: R. B. Luce, [1963] 279 p. 21 cm. 1. World politics — 1945- — Addresses, essays, lectures 2. United States — Politics and government — 20th century — Addresses, essays, lectures. I. T.
E743.F8   *LC* 63-9331

Graham, Otis L.   • **3.7524**
An encore for reform: the old progressives and the New Deal / [by] Otis L. Graham, Jr. — New York: Oxford University Press, 1967. viii, 256 p.; 22 cm. 1. Progressivism (U.S. politics) 2. New Deal, 1933-1939 3. United States — Politics and government — 1901-1953 I. T.
E743.G7   973.91   *LC* 67-15126

Graham, Otis L.   • **3.7525**
The great campaigns: reform and war in America, 1900–1928 [by] Otis L. Graham, Jr. Englewood Cliffs, N.J., Prentice-Hall [1971] xiii, 386 p. illus., ports. 23 cm. (Prentice-Hall history of the American people series) 1. World War, 1914-1918 — United States. 2. Progressivism (United States politics) 3. United States — Foreign relations — 1865-1921 4. United States — Politics and government — 1901-1953 I. T.
E743.G72   973.91   *LC* 79-135756   *ISBN* 0133635724

Henry, Laurin L.   • **3.7526**
Presidential transitions. — Washington: Brookings Institution, [1960] xviii, 755 p.; 24 cm. 1. Presidents — United States — Transition periods 2. United States — Politics and government — 20th century I. T.
E743.H4   353.032   *LC* 60-53252

Hofstadter, Richard, 1916-1970.   • **3.7527**
The age of reform; from Bryan to F. D. R. [1st ed.] New York, Knopf, 1955. 328, xx p. 22 cm. 1. Progressivism (United States politics) 2. United States — Politics and government — 20th century I. T.
E743.H63   973.91   *LC* 54-7206

Hofstadter, Richard, 1916-1970.   • **3.7528**
The paranoid style in American politics: and other essays. — [1st ed.] New York: Knopf, 1965. xiv, 314 p.; 22 cm. 1. Right and left (Political science) — Addresses, essays, lectures. 2. Public opinion — United States — Addresses, essays, lectures. 3. United States — Territorial expansion — Addresses, essays, lectures. 4. United States — Politics and government — Addresses, essays, lectures. I. T.
E743.H632   320.973   *LC* 65-18758

Josephson, Matthew, 1899-1978.   • **3.7529**
The president makers; the culture of politics and leadership in an age of enlightenment, 1896–1919. With a new foreword by the author. — New York: F. Ungar Pub. Co., [1964] xii, 584 p.; 23 cm. — (American classics) 1. Statesmen — United States. 2. United States — Politics and government — 1865-1933 I. T.
E743.J65 1964   973.91   *LC* 64-8722

Krock, Arthur, 1886-. • 3.7530
Memoirs; sixty years on the firing line. — New York: Funk & Wagnalls, [1968]
xii, 508 p.; 24 cm. 1. Presidents — United States 2. United States — Politics
and government — 20th century I. T.
E743.K7   973.9/0924   *LC* 68-26106

Leuchtenburg, William Edward, 1922-. 3.7531
In the shadow of FDR: from Harry Truman to Ronald Reagan / William E.
Leuchtenburg. — Ithaca: Cornell University Press, 1983. xii, 346 p.; 24 cm.
1. Roosevelt, Franklin D. (Franklin Delano), 1882-1945 — Influence.
2. United States — Politics and government — 1945- I. T. II. Title: In the
shadow of F.D.R.
E743.L49 1983   973.92 19   *LC* 83-45147   *ISBN* 0801413877

Link, Arthur Stanley. 3.7532
Progressivism / Arthur S. Link and Richard L. McCormick. — Arlington
Heights, Ill.: Harlan Davidson, Inc., c1983. ix, 149 p.; 21 cm. — (The American
history series) Includes index. 1. Progressivism (United States politics)
2. United States — Politics and government — 1865-1933 I. McCormick,
Richard L. II. T.
E743.L56 1983   322.4/4/0973 19   *LC* 82-15857   *ISBN* 0882958143

Lubell, Samuel. • 3.7533
The future of American politics / by Samuel Lubell. — New York: Harper &
Brothers, 1952. viii, 285 p. 1. United States — Politics and government —
1945-1953 2. United States — Social conditions I. T.
E743.L85   *LC* 52-5462

Nash, George H., 1945-. 3.7534
The conservative intellectual movement in America, since 1945 / George H.
Nash. — New York: Basic Books, c1976. xv, 463 p.: ports.; 25 cm. Includes
index. 1. Conservatism — United States. 2. United States — Politics and
government — 1945- I. T.
E743.N37   320.5/2/0973   *LC* 75-7273   *ISBN* 0465014011

Roper, Elmo Burns, 1900-. • 3.7535
You and your leaders, their actions and your reactions, 1936–1956. New York,
Morrow, c1957. 288 p. 22 cm. 1. Public opinion — United States.
2. Statesmen, American. 3. Public opinion polls 4. United States — Politics
and government — 1933-1953 I. T.
E743.R67   973.917   *LC* 58-6672

Rovere, Richard Halworth, 1915-. • 3.7536
The American establishment and other reports, opinions, and speculations. —
[1st ed.] New York: Harcourt, Brace & World [1962] 308 p.; 21 cm. 1. United
States — Politics and government — 1945- — Addresses, essays, lectures. I. T.
E743.R68   973.92   *LC* 62-9438

Voorhis, Horace Jeremiah, 1901-. 3.7537
Confessions of a congressman, by Jerry Voorhis. — Garden City, N.Y.:
Doubleday, 1948. 365 p.; 23 cm. 1. Voorhis, Horace Jeremiah, 1901- 2. United
States. Congress. 3. United States — Politics and government — 1901-1953
I. T.
E743.V6 1970   328.73/09/24 B   *LC* 47-11412

Weinstein, James, 1926-. • 3.7538
The corporate ideal in the liberal state, 1900–1918. Boston: Beacon Press [1968]
xvii, 263 p.; 24 cm. 1. Progressivism (U.S. politics) 2. Business and politics —
United States. 3. United States — Politics and government — 1901-1953 I. T.
E743.W44   973.91 19   *LC* 68-12846

E743.5 "Un–American" Activities

United States. Congress. House. Committee on Un-American 3.7539
Activities.
Thirty years of treason; excerpts from hearings before the House Committee on
Un–American Activities, 1938–1968. Edited by Eric Bentley. New York,
Viking Press [1971] xxviii, 991 p. 25 cm. 1. Subversive activities — United
States. 2. Communism — United States — 1917- I. Bentley, Eric, 1916- ed.
II. T.
E743.5.A5 1971   322/.42/0973   *LC* 71-124318   *ISBN* 0670701653

Beyond the Hiss case: the FBI, Congress, and the Cold War / 3.7540
edited by Athan G. Theoharis.
Philadelphia: Temple University Press, 1982. xi, 423 p.; 22 cm. 1. Hiss, Alger
— Addresses, essays, lectures. 2. United States. Federal Bureau of
Investigation — Addresses, essays, lectures. 3. Internal security — United
States — History — 20th century — Addresses, essays, lectures. I. Theoharis,
Athan G.
E743.5.B43 1982   363.2/5 19   *LC* 82-3309   *ISBN* 087722241X

Buckley, William F. (William Frank), 1925-. • 3.7541
The committee and its critics; a calm review of the House Committee on Un–
American Activities, by William F. Buckley, Jr. and the editors of National

review. — New York, Putnam [1962] 352 p. 22 cm. 1. United States. Congress.
House. Committee on Un-American Activities. I. National review
(Washington, D.C.) II. T.
E743.5.B82   328.36   *LC* 62-7342

Carr, Robert Kenneth, 1908-. • 3.7542
The House Committee on Un–American Activities, 1945–1950. Ithaca, Cornell
University Press, 1952. xiii, 489 p. 24 cm. (Cornell studies in civil liberty.)
1. United States. Congress. House. Committee on Un-American Activities.
2. Communism — United States — 1917- I. T.
E743.5.C3   *LC* 52-14423

Chambers, Whittaker. • 3.7543
Witness. New York: Random House [1952] 808 p.; 22 cm. Autobiographical.
1. Hiss, Alger. 2. Chambers, Whittaker. 3. Communism — United States —
1917- 4. Spies — United States — Biography. I. T.
E743.5.C47   351.74 364.13*   *LC* 52-5149

Dies, Martin, 1901-. • 3.7544
Martin Dies' story. New York, Bookmailer [1963] 283 p. 22 cm. 1. United
States. Congress. House. Special Committee on un-American Activities.
2. Communism — United States — 1917- 3. Propaganda, Communist I. T.
E743.5.D52   328.36   *LC* 63-14765

Gellermann, William, 1897-. 3.7545
Martin Dies. — New York: Da Capo Press, 1972 [c1944] 310 p.; 22 cm. —
(Civil liberties in American history) 1. Dies, Martin, 1901- 2. U.S. Congress.
House. Special Committee on Un-American Activities (1938-1944) I. T.
II. Series.
E743.5.D55 G4 1972   328.73/0924 B   *LC* 77-151620   *ISBN*
0306702002

Hiss, Alger. 3.7546
In the court of public opinion / Alger Hiss. — New York: Knopf, 1957. 424 p.:
ill. — 1. Chambers, Whittaker. 2. Communism — United States — 1917-
I. T.
E743.5.H54   351.74   *LC* 57-7546   *ISBN* 0060902930

Cooke, Alistair, 1908-. • 3.7547
A generation on trial: U. S. A. v. Alger Hiss. [2d ed.] New York: Knopf, 1952.
356 p.; 22 cm. 1. Hiss, Alger. 2. Chambers, Whittaker. I. T.
E743.5.H55 C6 1952   *LC* 52-4255

Latham, Earl. • 3.7548
The communist controversy in Washington: from the New Deal to McCarthy.
Cambridge, Harvard University Press, 1966. viii, 446 p. 25 cm. (Communism in
American life) Bibliographical footnotes. 1. Communism in the United States
— 1917- 2. Internal security — United States 3. Subversive activities —
United States. I. T. II. Series.
E743.5.L35   335.430973   *LC* 66-14447

Lattimore, Owen, 1900-. • 3.7549
Ordeal by slander. Westport, Conn., Greenwood Press [1971, c1950] viii, 236 p.
23 cm. 1. McCarthy, Joseph, 1908-1957. I. T.
E743.5.L36 1971   973.91   *LC* 72-138156   *ISBN* 0837156130

Murray, Robert K. • 3.7550
Red scare: a study in national hysteria, 1919–1920. — Minneapolis: University
of Minnesota Press, [c1955] 337 p.: ill.; 23 cm. 1. Communism — United States
— 1917- 2. Subversive activities — United States. 3. Hysteria (Social
psychology) — Case studies. 4. United States — Economic conditions —
1918-1945 I. T.
E743.5.M8   973.91/3 19   *LC* 55-7034

Preston, William, 1924-. • 3.7551
Aliens and dissenters; Federal suppression of radicals, 1903–1933. —
Cambridge: Harvard University Press, 1963. 352 p.; 22 cm. 1. Industrial
Workers of the World. 2. Aliens — United States 3. Deportation — United
States. 4. Civil rights — United States I. T.
E743.5.P7   323.67   *LC* 63-10873

Ogden, August Raymond. • 3.7552
The Dies committee: a study of the special House committee for the
investigation of un–American activities, 1938–1944 / by August Raymond
Ogden. — [2d rev. ed.] Washington, D. C.: The Catholic University of America
Press, 1945. vi, 318 p.; 24 cm. 'This study appeared originally as a dissertation
submitted to the Faculty of the School of social science of the Catholic
university of America for the degree of doctor of philosophy.' - Pref. 1. Dies,
Martin, 1901- 2. Propaganda 3. United States. Congress. House. Special
Committee on Un-American Activities (1938-   ) I. T.
E743.5.U56 O3 1945   *LC* a 45-3189

Warren, Frank A. • 3.7553
Liberals and communism; the 'red decade' revisited, by Frank A. Warren, III.
Bloomington, Indiana University Press [1966] ix, 276 p. 22 cm. Includes

bibliographical references. 1. Intellectuals — United States. 2. Liberalism — United States. 3. Communism — United States — 1917- I. T.
E743.5.W28   320.510973   *LC* 66-12735

E744 DIPLOMATIC HISTORY

E744 A–F

Acheson, Dean, 1893-1971.   • **3.7554**
Present at the creation: my years in the State Department / [by] Dean Acheson. — [1st ed.] New York: Norton [1969] xiv, 798 p.: ill.; 25 cm. 1. Acheson, Dean, 1893-1971. 2. United States — Foreign relations — 1933-1945 3. United States — Foreign relations — 1945-1953 I. T.
E744.A2174   327.73   *LC* 69-14692   *ISBN* 039307448X

Agar, Herbert, 1897-.   • **3.7555**
The price of power: America since 1945. — [Chicago]: University of Chicago Press, [1957] 199 p.; 21 cm. — (The Chicago history of American civilization) 1. World politics — 1945- 2. United States — Foreign relations — 1945- 3. United States — Politics and government — 1945- I. T.
E744.A3   327.73   *LC* 57-8575

Almond, Gabriel Abraham, 1911-.   • **3.7556**
The American people and foreign policy / Gabriel A. Almond. — New York: Praeger, 1960. xxx, 269 p.; 20 cm. — (Praeger university series) 1. National characteristics, American 2. Public opinion — United States. 3. United States — Foreign relations — 1945- I. T.
E744.A47 1960   *LC* 60-16891

Aron, Raymond, 1905-.   **3.7557**
[République impériale. English] The imperial republic: the United States and the world, 1945–1973 / translated by Frank Jellinek. — Englewood Cliffs, N.J.: Prentice-Hall [1974] xxxviii, 339 p.; 24 cm. Translation of République impériale; les États-Unis dans le monde, 1945-1972. 1. United States — Foreign relations — 1945- 2. United States — Foreign economic relations I. T.
E744.A7613   327.73   *LC* 74-1389   *ISBN* 0134517814

Barnet, Richard J.   • **3.7558**
Roots of war / [by] Richard J. Barnet. — [1st ed.]. — New York: Atheneum, 1972. 350 p.; 25 cm. 1. United States — Foreign relations — 20th century 2. United States — Foreign relations administration 3. United States — Foreign economic relations 4. United States — Politics and government — 20th century I. T.
E744.B32   327.73   *LC* 71-184725

Bowie, Robert Richardson, 1909-.   • **3.7559**
Shaping the future; foreign policy in an age of transition. New York: Columbia University Press, 1964. viii, 118 p.; 21 cm. Contains the Radner lectures ... given by the author at Columbia University in April, 1963. 1. World politics — 1945- 2. United States — Foreign relations — 1945- I. T.
E744.B675   *LC* 64-15740

Brown, Seyom.   **3.7560**
The faces of power: constancy and change in United States foreign policy from Truman to Reagan / Seyom Brown. — New York: Columbia University Press, 1983. xvi, 672 p.; 24 cm. 1. United States — Foreign relations — 1945- I. T.
E744.B78 1983   327.73 19   *LC* 83-1861   *ISBN* 0231047363

Challener, Richard D.   **3.7561**
Admirals, generals, and American foreign policy, 1898–1914 [by] Richard D. Challener. — Princeton, N.J.: Princeton University Press, 1973. viii, 433 p.; 25 cm. 1. United States — Foreign relations — 1865-1921 2. United States — Armed Forces — Political activity 3. United States — Military policy I. T.
E744.C42   327.73   *LC* 72-732   *ISBN* 0691069166

Cottrell, Leonard Slater, 1899-.   • **3.7562**
American opinion on world affairs in the atomic age / by Leonard S. Cottrell, Jr. & Sylvia Eberhart; with a foreword by Frederick Osborn. — New York: Greenwood Press, [1969, c1948] xxi, 152 p.; 23 cm. 'Based on a report prepared for the Committee on the Social and Economic Aspects of Atomic Energy of the Social Science Research Council.' 1. Public opinion — U.S. 2. Atomic bomb 3. U.S. — Foreign relations — 1945-1953. I. Eberhart, Sylvia, joint author. II. Social Science Research Council. Committee on Social and Economic Aspects of Atomic Energy. Public reaction to the atomic bomb and world affairs. III. T.
E744.C77 1969   327.73   *LC* 69-13867

Davids, Jules.   • **3.7563**
America and the world of our time: United States diplomacy in the twentieth century. — 3d ed. — New York: Random House, [1970] viii, 722 p.; 25 cm. 1. U.S. — Foreign relations — 20th century. I. T.
E744.D25 1970   327.73   *LC* 76-97587

Isolation and security: ideas and interests in twentieth–century   • **3.7564**
American foreign policy / edited by Alexander DeConde; the contributors, William R. Allen ... [et al.].
Durham, N.C.: Duke University Press, 1957. xi, 204 p. 'Essays ... completed during an Interuniversity Summer Research Seminar held at Duke University from June 4 to July 28, 1956.' 1. United States — Foreign relations — 20th century I. De Conde, Alexander.
E744.D33   E744.I8.   327.73   *LC* 57-13022

Dulles, Foster Rhea, 1900-1970.   • **3.7565**
America's rise to world power, 1898–1954. — [1st ed.]. — New York: Harper, [1955] 314 p.: illus.; 22 cm. — (The New American nation series) 1. World politics — 20th century 2. United States — Foreign relations — 20th century I. T.
E744.D8   327.73

Ferrell, Robert H. comp.   **3.7566**
America as a world power, 1872–1945 / edited by Robert H. Ferrell. — Columbia: University of South Carolina Press, [1971] xxviii, 306 p.; 24 cm. — (Documentary history of the United States) The 2d of a 3 volume documentary history of American diplomacy from its beginning in 1775 to the present day. 1. U.S. — Foreign relations — 20th century — Sources. 2. U.S. — Foreign relations — 1865-1921 — Sources. I. T.
E744.F46 1971b   327.73   *LC* 70-171359   *ISBN* 0872492443

Ferrell, Robert H. comp.   **3.7567**
America in a divided world, 1945–1972 / edited by Robert H. Ferrell; cartography by John M. Hollingsworth. — Columbia, S.C.: University of South Carolina Press, 1975. xxxviii, 380 p.: maps; 24 cm. (Documentary history of the United States.) The last of a three-volume documentary history of American diplomacy from its beginning in 1775 to the present day, with collective title: History of American diplomacy. The 1st volume published in 1968 under title: Foundations of American diplomacy, 1775-1872, and the 2d, published in 1971 under title: America as a world power, 1872-1945. Includes composite index for entire three volumes. 1. United States — Foreign relations — 1945- — Sources. I. T. II. Title: History of American diplomacy.
E744.F47 1975   327.73   *LC* 75-22588   *ISBN* 0872493385

Foster, H. Schuyler (Harry Schuyler), 1905-.   **3.7568**
Activism replaces isolationism: U.S. public attitudes, 1940–1975 / by H. Schuyler Foster. — 1st ed. — Washington, D.C.: Foxhall Press, c1983. xi, 407 p.; 24 cm. 1. Public opinion — United States — History — 20th century. 2. United States — Foreign relations — 1933-1945 — Public opinion. 3. United States — Foreign relations — 1945- — Public opinion. I. T.
E744.F7698 1983   327.73 19   *LC* 83-81284   *ISBN* 0961112816

Fulbright, J. William (James William), 1905-.   • **3.7569**
The arrogance of power, by J. William Fulbright. New York, Random House [1967, c1966] xv, 264 p. Based on the Christian A. Herter lecture series, John Hopkins University, 1966. 1. World politics — 1945- — Addresses, essays, lectures 2. United States — Foreign relations — 1945- — Addresses, essays, lectures I. T.
E744 F82   *LC* 67-13859

E744 G–M

Gaddis, John Lewis.   **3.7570**
Strategies of containment: a critical appraisal of postwar American national security policy / John Lewis Gaddis. — New York: Oxford University Press, 1982. xi, 432 p. Includes index. 1. United States — Foreign relations — 1945- I. T.
E744.G24   E744 G24.   327.73 19   *LC* 81-772   *ISBN* 0195029445

Gaddis, John Lewis.   • **3.7571**
The United States and the origins of the cold war, 1941–1947. — New York: Columbia University Press, 1972. ix, 396 p.; 23 cm. — (Contemporary American history series) 1. United States — Foreign relations — 1945- I. T.
E744.G25   327.73   *LC* 75-186388   *ISBN* 0231032897

Gardner, Lloyd C., 1934-.   **3.7572**
A covenant with power: America and world order from Wilson to Reagan / Lloyd C. Gardner. — New York: Oxford University Press, 1984. xv, 251 p.; 22 cm. 1. Liberalism — United States — History — 20th century. 2. United States — Foreign relations — 20th century I. T.
E744.G3425 1984   327.73 19   *LC* 83-13149   *ISBN* 0195033574

Gibert, Stephen P. 3.7573
Soviet images of America / Stephen P. Gibert, contributing authors, Arthur A. Zuehlke, Jr., Richard Soll, Michael J. Deane. New York: Crane, Russak, c1977. viii, 167 p.; 24 cm. 'The research for this book was undertaken at the Stanford Research Institute's Strategic Studies Center.' Includes index. 1. Public opinion — Russia. 2. United States — Foreign relations — 1945- — Public opinion. 3. United States — Foreign relations — Russia — Public opinion. 4. Russia — Foreign relations — United States — Public opinion. 5. United States — Foreign opinion, Russian. I. Stanford Research Institute. Strategic Studies Center. II. T.
E744.G49 1977   301.15/43/32773047   LC 76-28569   ISBN 0844810185

Goldwater, Barry M. (Barry Morris), 1909-. • 3.7574
Why not victory?: A fresh look at American foreign policy. — [1st ed.] New York: McGraw-Hill [1962] 201 p.; 22 cm. 1. World politics — 1945- 2. United States — Foreign relations — 1945- I. T.
E744.G57   327.73   LC 62-14674

Graebner, Norman A. ed. • 3.7575
An uncertain tradition: American Secretaries of State in the twentieth century. — New York: McGraw-Hill, 1961. 341 p.; 24 cm. 1. United States. Dept. of State — Biography. 2. Cabinet officers — United States. 3. United States — Foreign relations — 20th century I. T.
E744.G7   LC 61-8654

Heilbroner, Robert L. • 3.7576
The future as history; the historic currents of our time and the direction in which they are taking America. [1st ed.] New York, Harper [1960] 217 p. 22 cm. 1. World politics — 1945- 2. United States — Relations — Foreign countries I. T.
E744.H45   327.73   LC 60-7527

Hoffmann, Stanley. 3.7577
Gulliver's troubles: or, The setting of American foreign policy. — [1st ed.]. — New York: Published for the Council on Foreign Relations by McGraw-Hill, [1968] xx, 556 p.; 21 cm. — (Atlantic policy studies.) Based on lectures entitled 'Restraints on American policy,' delivered at the Council on Foreign Relations April-May, 1965. 1. United States — Foreign relations — 1945- — Addresses, essays, lectures. I. Council on Foreign Relations. II. T. III. Title: The setting of American foreign policy. IV. Series.
E744.H632   327.73   LC 68-13516

Janis, Irving Lester, 1918-. 3.7578
Victims of groupthink: a psychological study of foreign-policy decisions and fiascoes / [by] Irving L. Janis. — Boston: Houghton, Mifflin [1972] viii, 277 p.; ill.; 23 cm. 1. Policy sciences — Case studies. 2. United States — Foreign relations — 1945- 3. United States — Foreign relations administration I. T.
E744.J29 1972   327.73   LC 72-4393   ISBN 0395140021 ISBN 0395140447

Kennan, George Frost, 1904-. • 3.7579
American diplomacy, 1900–1950. Chicago, University of Chicago Press [1951] ix, 154 p. 22 cm. (Charles R. Walgreen Foundation lectures) 1. United States — Foreign relations — 20th century — Addresses, essays, lectures. 2. United States — Foreign relations — Soviet Union — Addresses, essays, lectures. 3. Soviet Union — Foreign relations — United States — Addresses, essays, lectures. I. T.
E744.K3 1951a   327.73   LC 51-8841

Kolko, Joyce. • 3.7580
The limits of power: the world and United States foreign policy, 1945–1954 / [by] Joyce and Gabriel Kolko. — [1st ed.] — New York: Harper & Row, [c1972] xii, 820 p.; 24 cm. 1. U.S. — Foreign relations — 1945-1953. I. Kolko, Gabriel, 1932- joint author. II. T.
E744.K64 1972   327.73   LC 70-156530   ISBN 0060124474

Kolko, Gabriel. • 3.7581
The politics of war; the world and United States foreign policy, 1943–1945. — New York: Random House, [c1968] x, 685 p.; 25 cm. 1. World politics — 1933-1945 2. United States — Foreign relations — 1933-1945 I. T.
E744.K65   327.73   LC 68-28560

Langer, William L. (William Leonard), 1896-1977. • 3.7582
The challenge to isolation; the world crisis of 1937–1940 and American foreign policy, by William L. Langer and S. Everett Gleason. — Gloucester, Mass.: Peter Smith, 1970 [c1952] 2 v. (xiii, 794 p.); 22 cm. 1. World War, 1939-1945 — U.S. 2. World War, 1939-1945 — Diplomatic history 3. U.S. — Foreign relations — 1933-1945. I. Gleason, Sarell Everett, 1905- joint author. II. T.
E744.L3 1970   940.532/2/73   LC 76-17008

Levering, Ralph B. 3.7583
The cold war, 1945–1972 / Ralph B. Levering. — Arlington Heights, Ill.: H. Davidson, c1982. xi, 165 p.: ill.; 21 cm. — (The American history series) Includes index. 1. World politics — 1945- 2. United States — Foreign

relations — 1945- 3. United States — Foreign relations — Soviet Union 4. Soviet Union — Foreign relations — United States I. T.
E744.L494 1982   327.73 19   LC 81-13190   ISBN 0882958119

Lippmann, Walter, 1889-1974. 3.7584
U. S. foreign policy: shield of the republic. — [New York: Johnson Reprint Corp., 1972, c1971] xvii, 177 p. (Reprints in government and political science) 'An Atlantic Monthly Press book.' Reprint of the 1943 ed., published by Little, Brown, Boston. 1. United States — Foreign relations 2. United States — Foreign relations — 20th century I. T.
E744.L56 1972   LC 78-38862

May, Ernest R. • 3.7585
American intervention: 1917 and 1941 / by Ernest R. May. — Washington: Service Center for Teachers of History, 1960. 19 p. — (Service Center for Teachers of History.Publication; no.30) 1. World War, 1914-1918 — United States. 2. World War II, 1939-1945 — United States. I. T.
E744.M39   940.373   LC 60-12444

Millis, Walter, 1899-1968. • 3.7586
Arms and the state: civil–military elements in national policy / by Walter Millis; with Harvey C. Mansfield and Harold Stein. — New York: Twentieth Century Fund, 1958. 436 p.; 24 cm. 'A volume in the Twentieth Century Fund's project on civil- military relations.' 1. Civil supremacy over the military — United States. 2. United States — Foreign relations — 10th century. I. T.
E744.M56   327.73   LC 58-11837

Morgenthau, Hans Jonchim, 1904-. • 3.7587
In defense of the national interest; a critical examination of American foreign policy. — [1st ed.]. — New York, Knopf, 1951. xii, 283, viii p. 22 cm. 1. United States — For. rel. — 1945- I. T.
E744.M68   327.73   LC 51-11217

Morgenthau, Hans Joachim, 1904-. • 3.7588
The purpose of American politics. [1st ed.] New York: Knopf, 1960. 359 p.; 22 cm. 1. United States — Politics & government — 20th century. 2. United States — History — Philosophy 3. United States — Foreign relations — 20th century I. T.
E744.M69   973.91   LC 60-16504

E744 N–Z

Nevins, Allan, 1890-1971. • 3.7589
The New Deal and world affairs; a chronicle of international affairs, 1933–1945. New Haven, Yale University Press, 1950. ix, 332 p. ports. 21 cm. (Chronicles of America series. v. 56) 1. World politics — 1933-1945 2. New Deal, 1933-1939 3. United States — Foreign relations — 1933-1945 I. T. II. Series.
E744.N487 E173.C55 vol. 56   327.73   LC 50-8828

Nevins, Allan. • 3.7590
United States in a chaotic world: a chronicle of international affairs, 1918–1933. New Haven: Yale, 1950. 252 p. (Chronicles of America series. v.31) 1. World politics 2. United States — Foreign relations — 20th century I. T. II. Series.
E744.N493 1950   LC 52-4357

Niebuhr, Reinhold, 1892-1971. • 3.7591
The irony of American history. — New York: Scribner, 1952. 174 p.; 21 cm. 1. United States — Foreign relations — 1945-1953 2. United States — History — Philosophy 3. United States — Civilization I. T.
E744.N5   973   LC 52-8724

Niebuhr, Reinhold, 1892-1971. • 3.7592
The world crisis and American responsibility: nine essays / collected and edited by Ernest W. Lefever. — New York: Association Press [1958] 128 p.; 16 cm. — (A Reflection book) 1. World politics — 1945- 2. United States — Relations — Foreign countries I. T.
E744.N53   327.73   LC 58-11534

Offner, Arnold A. 3.7593
The origins of the Second World War: American foreign policy and world politics, 1917–1941 / Arnold A. Offner. — New York: Praeger, 1975. xvi, 268 p.; 25 cm. Includes index. 1. World War, 1939-1945 — Causes 2. United States — Foreign relations — 20th century I. T.
E744.O43   327.73   LC 72-82775   ISBN 0275502708

Osgood, Charles Egerton. 3.7594
An alternative to war or surrender. Urbana, University of Illinois Press, 1962. 183 p. 21 cm. (Illini books, IB-7) 1. International relations 2. United States — Foreign relations — 1961-1963 3. United States — Foreign relations — Soviet Union 4. Soviet Union — Foreign relations — United States I. T.
E744.O73   327.73047   LC 62-19089

Paterson, Thomas G., 1941-.   3.7595
On every front: the making of the Cold War / Thomas G. Paterson. — New York: Norton, c1979. xii, 210 p.; 20 cm. — (The Norton essays in American history) Includes index. 1. World politics — 1945- 2. United States — Foreign relations — 1945- 3. Russia — Foreign relations — 1945- 4. United States — Foreign relations — Russia. 5. Russia — Foreign relations — United States. I. T.
E744.P312 1979   327.73/047   *LC* 79-4509   *ISBN* 0393012387

Radosh, Ronald.   3.7596
Prophets on the right: profiles of conservative critics of American globalism / Ronald Radosh. — New York: Simon and Schuster, [1975] 351 p.: ports.; 22 cm. 1. Conservatism — United States. 2. United States — Foreign relations — 1933-1945 3. United States — Foreign relations — 1945-1953 I. T.
E744.R32   327.73   *LC* 74-20840   *ISBN* 0671219014

Miller, Lynn H. ed.   3.7597
Reflections on the cold war; a quarter century of American foreign policy. Edited by Lynn H. Miller and Ronald W. Pruessen. — Philadelphia: Temple University Press, [1974] viii, 207 p.; 23 cm. 1. World politics — 1945- — Addresses, essays, lectures. 2. United States — Foreign relations — 1945- — Addresses, essays, lectures. I. Pruessen, Ronald W. ed. II. T.
E744.R43   327.73   *LC* 73-88279   *ISBN* 087722028X

Roosevelt, James, 1907- ed.   • 3.7598
The liberal papers. — Chicago, Quadrangle Books [1962] 354 p. 22 cm. Includes bibliographical references. 1. United States — Foreign relations — 1945- — Addresses, essays, lectures. 2. United States — Defenses I. T.
E744.R79 1962a   327.73   *LC* 62-4538

Rosenberg, Emily S., 1944-.   3.7599
Spreading the American dream: American economic and cultural expansion, 1890–1945 / Emily S. Rosenberg; consulting editor, Eric Foner. — 1st ed. — New York: Hill and Wang, 1982. xi, 258 p.; 22 cm. — (American century series) Includes index. 1. United States — Foreign relations — 20th century 2. United States — Foreign relations — 1865-1921 3. United States — Foreign economic relations I. Foner, Eric. II. T.
E744.R82 1982   973.9 19   *LC* 81-13250   *ISBN* 0809087987

Schulzinger, Robert D., 1945-.   3.7600
American diplomacy in the twentieth century / Robert D. Schulzinger. — New York: Oxford University Press, 1984. viii, 390 p.: ill.; 24 cm. Includes index. 1. United States — Foreign relations — 20th century I. T. II. Title: American diplomacy in the 20th century.
E744.S399 1984   327.73 19   *LC* 83-6285   *ISBN* 0195033728

Schulzinger, Robert D., 1945-.   3.7601
The wise men of foreign affairs: the history of the Council on Foreign Relations / Robert D. Schulzinger. — New York: Columbia University Press, 1984. xiii, 342 p.; 24 cm. Includes index. 1. Council on Foreign Relations — History. 2. United States — Foreign relations — 20th century I. T.
E744.S3995 1984   327.73 19   *LC* 83-27321   *ISBN* 0231055285

Siracusa, Joseph M.   3.7602
New left diplomatic histories and historians: the American revisionists [by] Joseph M. Siracusa. Port Washington, N.Y., Kennikat Press, 1973. viii, 138 p. 24 cm. (Kennikat Press national university publications. Series in American studies) 1. United States — Foreign relations — Historiography I. T.
E744.S5367   327/.1/072073   *LC* 73-75575   *ISBN* 0804690375

Skolnikoff, Eugene B.   3.7603
Science, technology, and American foreign policy [by] Eugene B. Skolnikoff. — Cambridge: M.I.T. Press, [1967] xvi, 330 p.; 22 cm. 1. Science and state — United States. 2. Technology and state — United States 3. United States — Foreign relations — 1945- 4. United States — Foreign relations administration I. T.
E744.S57   327.73   *LC* 67-15239

Tompkins, E. Berkeley, 1935-.   3.7604
Anti–imperialism in the United States: the great debate, 1890–1920 / [by] E. Berkeley Tompkins. — Philadelphia: University of Pennsylvania Press [1970] 344 p.: ill.; 22 cm. 1. Anti-imperialist movements — United States. 2. United States — Foreign relations — 1865-1921 I. T.
E744.T6   327.73   *LC* 79-122382   *ISBN* 0812275950

Twentieth–century American foreign policy, edited by John Braeman, Robert H. Bremner [and] David Brody.   • 3.7605
[Columbus]: Ohio State University Press, [1971] ix, 567 p.; 22 cm. — (Modern America, no. 3) 1. U.S. — Foreign relations — 20th century — Addresses, essays, lectures. I. Braeman, John. ed. II. Bremner, Robert Hamlett, 1917- ed. III. Brody, David. ed. IV. Series.
E744.T9   327.73   *LC* 78-141495   *ISBN* 0814201512

The United States in world affairs.   • 3.7606
New York: Published for the Council on Foreign Relations by Harper & Brothers, 1932- v.: ill. (maps); 23 cm. Annual. 'An account of American

foreign relations.' 1. World politics 2. United States — Foreign relations 3. United States — Economic policy I. Royal Institute of International Affairs.
E744.U66   327.73   *LC* 32-26065

Westerfield, Bradford, 1928-.   • 3.7607
The instruments of America's foreign policy. New York, Crowell [c1963] 538 p. 24 cm. Includes bibliography. 1. United States — Foreign relations — 1945- 2. United States — Military policy 3. United States — Foreign economic relations I. T.
E744.W535   327.73   *LC* 63-7119

Williams, William Appleman.   • 3.7608
The tragedy of American diplomacy / [by] William Appleman Williams. — 2d rev. and enl. ed. — [New York: Dell Pub. Co., 1972] v, 312 p.; 21 cm. — (A Delta book) 1. United States — Foreign relations — 20th century I. T.
E744.W56 1972   327/.2/0973   *LC* 72-186145

Wolfers, Arnold, 1892- ed.   • 3.7609
Alliance policy in the cold war. Baltimore, Johns Hopkins Press, 1959. ix, 314 p. col. map (on lining papers) 23 cm. Bibliographical footnotes. 1. World politics — 1945- 2. Alliances 3. United States — Foreign relations — 1945- I. T.
E744.W58   327.73   *LC* 59-10764

E744.5 Cultural Relations

Elder, Robert Ellsworth, 1915-.   • 3.7610
The information machine: the United States Information Agency and American foreign policy / [by] Robert E. Elder. — [1st ed. Syracuse, N.Y.]: Syracuse University Press [1967] xvi, 356 p.; 24 cm. 1. United States Information Agency. I. T.
E744.5.U6 E4   327.73   *LC* 68-14105

E745 Military History

James, D. Clayton.   3.7611
The years of MacArthur [by] D. Clayton James. Boston, Houghton Mifflin, 1970-1985. 3 v. maps, ports. 22 cm. 1. MacArthur, Douglas, 1880-1964. 2. United States. Army — Biography 3. Generals — United States — Biography. 4. United States — History, Military — 20th century I. T.
E745.M3 J3   355.3/31/0924 B   *LC* 76-108685

Pogue, Forest C.   3.7612
George C. Marshall: organizer of victory, 1943–1945 / foreword by General Omar N. Bradley. New York: Viking Press, 1973. 683 p. 1. Marshall, George C. 2. World War, 1939-1945 I. T.
E745.M37 P6   *LC* 63-18373   *ISBN* 0670336947

Blumenson, Martin.   • 3.7613
The Patton papers / [by] Martin Blumenson; illustrated with photos. and with maps by Samuel H. Bryant. — Boston: Houghton Mifflin, 1972-. v.: ill.; 24 cm. 1. Patton, George Smith. I. Patton, George Smith, 1885-1945. The Patton papers. 1972- II. T.
E745.P3 B55   355.3/31/0924 B

Tuchman, Barbara Wertheim.   • 3.7614
Stilwell and the American experience in China, 1911–45 [by] Barbara W. Tuchman. — New York: Macmillan, [1970] xv, 621 p.: illus., maps, ports.; 24 cm. 1. Stilwell, Joseph Warren, 1883-1946. 2. World War, 1939-1945 — China. 3. U.S. — Foreign relations — China. 4. China — Foreign relations — U.S. I. T.
E745.S68 T8   951.04/2/0924 B   *LC* 77-135647

E747 Collective Biography

Anderson, Patrick, 1936-.   3.7615
The Presidents' men: White House assistants of Franklin D. Roosevelt, Harry S. Truman, Dwight D. Eisenhower, John F. Kennedy, and Lyndon B. Johnson. — [1st ed.]. — Garden City, N.Y.: Doubleday, 1968. viii, 420 p.; 25 cm. 1. Presidents — United States — Staff 2. United States — Biography I. T.
E747.A75   353/.03   *LC* 68-24832

Collier, Peter.   3.7616
The Rockefellers: an American dynasty / by Peter Collier and David Horowitz. — 1st ed. — New York: Holt, Rinehart and Winston, c1976. 746 p., [16] leaves

of plates: ill.; 24 cm. 1. Rockefeller family I. Horowitz, David, 1939- joint author. II. T.
E747.C64   973.9/092/2 B   *LC* 75-5465   *ISBN* 0030083710

Lippmann, Walter, 1889-.   • **3.7617**
Men of destiny / introd. by Richard Lowitt; drawings by Rollin Kirby. — Seattle: University of Washington Press, [1969, c1927] xxi, 244 p.: ill.; 23 cm. (Americana library) 1. U.S. — Biography — Addresses, essays, lectures. 2. U.S. — Politics and government — 1919-1933 — Addresses, essays, lectures. I. T.
E747.L76 1969   320.9/73   *LC* 71-9039

Luthin, Reinhard Henry, 1905-.   • **3.7618**
American demagogues: twentieth century. Gloucester, Mass., P. Smith, 1959 [c1954] 368 p. 1. United States — Biography 2. United States — Politics and government — 1901-1953 I. T. II. Title: Demagogues.
E747.L87 1959   *LC* 60-51507

Salter, John Thomas, ed.   • **3.7619**
The American politician / edited by J. T. Salter. — Chapel Hill: The University of North Carolina press, 1938. xvi, 412 p.: ports.; 24 cm. 1. Politics, Practical 2. Statesmen — United States. 3. United States — Politics and government — 20th century 4. United States — Biography I. T.
E747.S29   923.273   *LC* 38-36015

Steinberg, Alfred, 1917-.   **3.7620**
The bosses. — New York: Macmillan, [1972] 379 p.; 24 cm. 1. Corruption (in politics) — United States 2. United States — Politics and government — 1901-1953 3. United States — Biography I. T.
E747.S76   320.9/73/09   *LC* 73-190158

Who's who in the Midwest.   • **3.7621**
1st-   1947-. Chicago: A. N. Marquis Co. v. Biennial. Imprint varies. 1. United States — Biography — Dictionaries. 2. Canada — Biography — Dictionaries.
E747.W63   *LC* 50-289

E748 INDIVIDUAL BIOGRAPHY

E748 A–E

Acheson, Dean, 1893-1971.   **3.7622**
Fragments of my fleece / [by] Dean Acheson. — [1st ed.] New York: Norton [1971] 222 p.: port.; 22 cm. 1. Acheson, Dean, 1893-1971. I. T.
E748.A15 A29 1971   917.3/03   *LC* 73-152651   *ISBN* 0393086445

McLellan, David S.   **3.7623**
Dean Acheson: the State Department years / by David S. McLellan. — New York: Dodd, Mead & Co., c1976. xii, 466 p., [12] leaves of plates: ill.; 24 cm. 1. Acheson, Dean, 1893-1971. 2. United States — Foreign relations — 1945-1953 I. T.
E748.A15 M32   973.918/092/4 B   *LC* 76-8482   *ISBN* 0396073131

Baruch, Bernard M. (Bernard Mannes), 1870-1965.   • **3.7624**
Baruch. [1st ed.] New York: Holt [1957-60] 2 v.: ill.; 22 cm. Vol. 2 published by Holt, Rinehart and Winston. 1. Baruch, Bernard M. (Bernard Mannes), 1870-1965. I. T.
E748.B32 A3   923.273   *LC* 57-11982

Coit, Margaret L.   • **3.7625**
Mr. Baruch. Illustrated with photos. Boston, Houghton Mifflin, 1957. xiv, 784 p.: illus., ports. 22 cm. 1. Baruch, Bernard M. (Bernard Mannes), 1870-1965. I. T.
E748.B32 C6   923.273   *LC* 56-10289

Schwarz, Jordan A., 1937-.   **3.7626**
The speculator, Bernard M. Baruch in Washington, 1917-1965 / Jordan A. Schwarz; [frontispiece by Barry Moser]. — Chapel Hill: University of North Carolina Press, c1981. xvii, 679 p.: port.; 25 cm. Includes index. 1. Baruch, Bernard M. (Bernard Mannes), 1870-1965. 2. Statesmen — United States — Biography. 3. Capitalists and financiers — United States — Biography. 4. United States — Politics and government — 20th century I. T.
E748.B32 S3   973.9/092/4 B   *LC* 80-17386   *ISBN* 0807813966

Beam, Jacob D., 1908-.   **3.7627**
Multiple exposure: an American ambassador's unique perspective on East-West issues / Jacob D. Beam. — 1st ed. — New York: Norton, c1978. 317 p.; 22 cm. Includes index. 1. Beam, Jacob D., 1908-2. Ambassadors — United States — Biography. 3. United States — Foreign relations — Russia. 4. Russia — Foreign relations — United States. 5. United States — Foreign relations —

Europe, Eastern. 6. Europe, Eastern — Foreign relations — United States. I. T.
E748.B333 A34 1978   327.73/047   *LC* 78-4123   *ISBN* 0393075192

Hyman, Sidney.   • **3.7628**
The lives of William Benton. — Chicago: University of Chicago Press, [1969] xviii, 625 p.: illus., ports.; 24 cm. 1. Benton, William, 1900-1973. I. T.
E748.B337 H9   030.924 B   *LC* 72-88231   *ISBN* 0226365484

Braeman, John.   • **3.7629**
Albert J. Beveridge; American nationalist. — Chicago: University of Chicago Press, [1971] x, 370 p.; 23 cm. 1. Beveridge, Albert Jeremiah, 1862-1927. I. T.
E748.B48 B7   973.91/0924 B   *LC* 75-142041   *ISBN* 0226070603

Green, Adwin Wigfall, 1900-.   • **3.7630**
The man Bilbo. — Baton Rouge: Louisiana State University Press, 1963. xiii, 150 p.: ill., ports.; 23 cm. 'Critical essay on authorities': p. 139-145. 1. Bilbo, Theodore Gilmore, 1877-1947. I. T.
E748.B5G7   923.273   *LC* 63-16658

Bohlen, Charles E. (Charles Eustis), 1904-.   **3.7631**
Witness to history, 1929-1969 [by] Charles E. Bohlen. [1st ed.] New York, Norton [1973] xiv, 562 p. 24 cm. 1. United States — Foreign relations — Soviet Union 2. Soviet Union — Foreign relations — United States I. T.
E748.B64 A38   327/.2/0924 B   *LC* 72-13407   *ISBN* 0393074765

Byrnes, James Francis, 1879-1972.   • **3.7632**
All in one lifetime. [1st ed.] New York: Harper [1958] x, 432 p.: ill., ports.; 22 cm. 1. United States — Foreign relations — 20th century 2. United States — Politics and government — 20th century I. T.
E748.B975 A3   *LC* 58-11390

Creel, George, 1876-1953.   • **3.7633**
Rebel at large: recollections of fifty crowded years. — New York: G. P. Putnam's Sons, [1947] viii, 384 p.; 22 cm. — I. T.
E748.C937 A3   923.273   *LC* 47-11611

Smith, Richard Norton, 1953-.   **3.7634**
Thomas E. Dewey and his times / Richard Norton Smith. — New York: Simon and Schuster, c1982. 703 p., [16] p. of plates: ill., ports.; 25 cm. Includes index. 1. Dewey, Thomas E. (Thomas Edmund), 1902-1971. 2. Politicians — United States — Biography. 3. United States — Politics and government — 1945-1953 4. New York (State) — Politics and government — 1865-1950 5. New York (State) — Governors — Biography. I. T.
E748.D48 S65 1982   973.91/092/4 B 19   *LC* 82-370   *ISBN* 067141741X

Schapsmeier, Edward L.   **3.7635**
Dirksen of Illinois: senatorial statesman / Edward L. Schapsmeier and Frederick H. Schapsmeier. — Urbana: University of Illinois Press, c1985. xvi, 269 p.; 24 cm. Includes index. 1. Dirksen, Everett McKinley. 2. United States. Congress. Senate — Biography. 3. United States. Congress. Senate — Minority leader — History — 20th century. 4. Legislators — United States — Biography. 5. United States — Politics and government — 1945- I. Schapsmeier, Frederick H. II. T.
E748.D557 S33 1985   328.73/092/4 B 19   *LC* 83-21578   *ISBN* 0252011007

Douglas, Paul Howard, 1892-.   **3.7636**
In the fullness of time; the memoirs of Paul H. Douglas. — [1st ed.]. — New York: Harcourt Brace Jovanovich, [1972] xii, 642 p.: illus.; 24 cm. 1. United States — Politics and government — 1945- I. T.
E748.D68 A3   328.73/092/4 B   *LC* 74-182327   *ISBN* 0151443769

Pruessen, Ronald W.   **3.7637**
John Foster Dulles: the road to power / Ronald W. Pruessen. — New York: Free Press, c1982. xiv, 575 p., [8] p. of plates: ill. Includes index. 1. Dulles, John Foster. 2. Statesmen — United States — Biography. I. T.
E748.D868 P78 1982   973.921/092/4 B 19   *LC* 81-69264   *ISBN* 0029254604

Mosley, Leonard, 1913-.   **3.7638**
Dulles: a biography of Eleanor, Allen and John Foster Dulles and their family network / by Leonard Mosley. — New York: Dial Press, 1978. xii, 530 p., [16] leaves of plates: ill; 24 cm. Includes index. 1. Dulles family. 2. Dulles, John Foster, 1888-1959. 3. Dulles, Eleanor Lansing, 1895- 4. Dulles, Allen Welsh, 1893-1969. 5. Statesmen — United States — Biography. 6. Economists — United States — Biography. 7. United States Central Intelligence Agency — Officials and employees — Biography. 8. United States — Foreign relations — 20th century I. T.
E748.D87 M67   973.9/092/2 B   *LC* 77-19042   *ISBN* 080371744X

Dabney, Dick. 3.7639
A good man: the life of Sam J. Ervin / by Dick Dabney. — Boston: Houghton Mifflin, 1976. x, 356 p., [6] leaves of plates: ill.; 24 cm. 1. Ervin, Sam J. (Sam James), 1896-1985. I. T.
E748.E93 D32   973.924/092/4 B   *LC* 75-42421   *ISBN* 0395207150

E748 F–K

Farley, James Aloysius, 1888-. • 3.7640
Behind the ballots; the personal history of a politician [by] James A. Farley. — Westport, Conn.: Greenwood Press, [1972] 392 p.: port.; 23 cm. Reprint of the 1938 ed. 1. Politics, Practical 2. United States — Politics and government — 1933-1945 I. T.
E748.F24 A3 1972   320.9/73/0917 B   *LC* 78-114521   *ISBN* 0837147387

Albion, Robert Greenhalgh, 1896-. • 3.7641
Forrestal and the Navy / by Robert G. Albion and Robert H. Connery; with the collaboration of Jennie B. Pope; foreword by William T. R. Fox. — New York: Columbia University Press, 1962. 359 p.: ill.; 24 cm. 1. Forrestal, James, 1892-1949. 2. United States. Navy Dept — History. I. Connery, Robert Howe, 1907- joint author. II. T.
E748.F68 A6   *LC* 62-9974

Rogow, Arnold A. • 3.7642
James Forrestal, a study of personality, politics, and policy. New York, Macmillan [c1963] xv, 397 p. ports. 21 cm. 1. Forrestal, James, 1892-1949. I. T.
E748.F68 R6   923.273   *LC* 63-16126

Bell, Jack, 1904-. • 3.7643
Mr. Conservative: Barry Goldwater. [1st ed.] Garden City, N. Y., Doubleday, 1962. 312 p. 22 cm. 1. Goldwater, Barry M. (Barry Morris), 1909- I. T.
E748.G64 B4   923.273   *LC* 62-11443

Rovere, Richard Halworth, 1915-. • 3.7644
The Goldwater caper / Richard H. Rovere; with cartoons by Bill Mauldin. — [1st ed.]. — New York: Harcourt, Brace & World, 1965. x, 182 p.: ill. 1. Goldwater, Barry M. (Barry Morris), 1909- I. T.
E748.G64 R6 1965   *LC* 65-16951

George, Emily. 3.7645
Martha W. Griffiths / Emily George. — Washington, D.C.: University Press of America, c1982. vi, 295 p.; 22 cm. Includes index. 1. Griffiths, Martha Wright, 1912- 2. United States. Congress. House — Biography. 3. Legislators — United States — Biography. I. T.
E748.G876 G46 1982   328.73/092/4 B 19   *LC* 81-40922   *ISBN* 0819123471

Perkins, Dexter, 1889-. • 3.7646
Charles Evans Hughes and American democratic statesmanship / Dexter Perkins; edited by Oscar Handlin. — Boston: Little, Brown, 1956. xxiv, 200 p.; 23 cm. — (Library of American biography.) Includes index. 1. Hughes, Charles Evans, 1862-1948. 2. United States. Supreme Court — Biography. 3. Statesmen — United States — Biography. 4. Judges — United States — Biography. 5. United States — Foreign relations — 1921-1923 6. United States — Politics and government — 1901-1953 I. T. II. Series.
E748.H88 P4   973.91/092/4 B   *LC* 56-6767

Pusey, Merlo John, 1905-. • 3.7647
Charles Evans Hughes. New York, Macmillan, 1951. 2 v. (xvi, 829 p.) illus., ports. 24 cm. Bibliographical footnotes. 1. Hughes, Charles Evans, 1862-1948. I. T.
E748.H88P8   923.473   *LC* 51-7851

Wesser, Robert F. • 3.7648
Charles Evans Hughes; politics and reform in New York, 1905-1910, by Robert F. Wesser. — Ithaca, N.Y.: Cornell University Press, [1967] xvi, 366 p.: illus., ports.; 24 cm. 1. Hughes, Charles Evans, 1862-1948. 2. New York (State) — Politics and government — 1865-1950 I. T.
E748.H88 W4   974.7/04/0924   *LC* 67-19029

Hull, Cordell, 1871-1955. • 3.7649
The memoirs of Cordell Hull. — New York, Macmillan Co., 1948. 2 v. (xii, 1804 p.) port. 22 cm. I. Berding, Andrew Henry Thomas. II. T.
E748.H93A3   923.273   *LC* 48-6761 *

Humphrey, Hubert H. (Hubert Horatio), 1911-1978. 3.7650
The education of a public man: my life and politics / Hubert H. Humphrey; edited by Norman Sherman. — 1st ed. — Garden City, N.Y.: Doubleday, 1976. xiii, 513 p. [12] leaves of plates: ill.; 22 cm. Includes index. 1. Humphrey, Hubert H. (Hubert Horatio), 1911-1978. I. T.
E748.H945 A34   973.923/092/4 B   *LC* 75-36628   *ISBN* 0385056036

Eisele, Albert, 1936-. 3.7651
Almost to the Presidency; a biography of two American politicians. [1st ed.] Blue Earth, Minn., Piper Co. [1972] 460 p. 24 cm. 1. Humphrey, Hubert H. (Hubert Horatio), 1911-1978. 2. McCarthy, Eugene J., 1916- 3. United States — Politics and government — 1945- I. T.
E748.H945 E5   973.92/092/2 B   *LC* 76-187432   *ISBN* 0878320059

Solberg, Carl, 1915-. 3.7652
Hubert Humphrey: a biography / Carl Solberg. — 1st ed. — New York: Norton, c1984. 572 p.; 25 cm. Includes index. 1. Humphrey, Hubert H. (Hubert Horatio), 1911-1978. 2. Vice-Presidents — United States — Biography. 3. United States — Politics and government — 1945- I. T.
E748.H945 S65 1984   973.923/092/4 B 19   *LC* 84-1641   *ISBN* 0393018067

Ickes, Harold L. (Harold LeClair), 1874-1952. • 3.7653
The autobiography of a curmudgeon, by Harold L. Ickes. New York, Reynal & Hitchcock, [1943] xi, 350 p. front., plates, ports., facsims. 22 cm. 1. United States — Politics and government — 1901-1953 I. T.
E748.I28 A3   923.273   *LC* 43-51100

Gorman, Joseph Bruce. • 3.7654
Kefauver: a political biography. — New York: Oxford University Press, 1971. viii, 434 p.: ports.; 22 cm. 1. Kefauver, Estes, 1903-1963. I. T.
E748.K314 G6   973.9/0924 B   *LC* 77-159645   *ISBN* 0195014812

Kennan, George Frost, 1904-. • 3.7655
Memoirs / [by] George F. Kennan. — [1st ed.] Boston: Little, Brown [1967-72] 2 v.; 24 cm. 'An Atlantic Monthly Press book.' 1. Kennan, George Frost, 1904- 2. Ambassadors — United States — Biography. 3. Historians — United States — Biography. 4. United States — Foreign relations — Soviet Union 5. Soviet Union — Foreign relations — United States I. T.
E748.K374 A3   327/.73   *LC* 67-23834

Koskoff, David E., 1939-. 3.7656
Joseph P. Kennedy: a life and times / [by] David E. Koskoff. — Englewood Cliffs, N.J.: Prentice-Hall, [1974] x, 643 p.: ill.; 24 cm. 1. Kennedy, Joseph P. (Joseph Patrick), 1888-1969. I. T.
E748.K376 K67   973.9/092/4 B   *LC* 73-21578   *ISBN* 0135111544

E748 L–M

La Guardia, Fiorello H. (Fiorello Henry), 1882-1947. • 3.7657
The making of an insurgent, an autobiography, 1882–1919. New York, Capricorn Books [1961] 222 p. 19 cm. I. T.
E748.L23 A3 1961   *LC* 61-4089

Elliott, Lawrence. 3.7658
Little flower: the life and times of Fiorello La Guardia / Lawrence Elliott. — 1st ed. — New York: Morrow, 1983. 256 p.: ill.; 25 cm. Includes index. 1. La Guardia, Fiorello H. (Fiorello Henry), 1882-1947. 2. United States. Congress. House — Biography. 3. Legislators — United States — Biography. 4. Mayors — New York (N.Y.) — Biography. 5. New York (N.Y.) — Politics and government — 1898-1951 6. New York (N.Y.) — Biography. I. T.
E748.L23 E44 1983   974.7/104/0924 B 19   *LC* 82-23964   *ISBN* 0688020577

Mann, Arthur. • 3.7659
La Guardia, a fighter against his times. — 1st ed. — Philadelphia: Lippincott, 1959-1965. 2 v.: ill.; 22 cm. 1. La Guardia, Fiorello H. (Fiorello Henry), 1882-1947. I. T.
E748.L23 M3   *LC* 59-13077

Manners, William, 1907-. 3.7660
Patience and fortitude: Fiorello La Guardia: a biography / by William Manners. — 1st ed. — New York: Harcourt Brace Jovanovich, c1976. 290 p., [4] leaves of plates: ill.; 24 cm. Includes index. 1. La Guardia, Fiorello H. (Fiorello Henry), 1882-1947. I. T.
E748.L23 M33   974.7/1/040924 B   *LC* 76-895   *ISBN* 0151712905

Zinn, Howard, 1922-. • 3.7661
La Guardia in Congress. Ithaca, N. Y. Ithaca, N. Y., Published for the American Historical Association [by] Cornell University Press [1959] xi, 288 p. 24 cm. Issued also in microfilm form in 1958 as thesis, Columbia University. Bibliography: p. 275-284. 1. La Guardia, Fiorello H. (Fiorello Henry), 1882-1947. I. T.
E748.L23Z5 1959   923.273   *LC* 59-65375

Lilienthal, David Eli, 1899-1981. • 3.7662
The journals of David E. Lilienthal / Introd. by Henry Steele Commager. — [1st ed.] New York: Harper & Row [1964]- v.: ill., ports.; 25 cm. Vol. 7 edited by Helen M. Lilienthal. Vol. 7: A Cass Canfield book. 1. Lilienthal, David Eli,

1899-1981. 2. Statesmen — United States — Biography. I. Lilienthal, Helen M. II. T.
E748.L7 A33   973.9/0924   *LC* 64-18056

Williams, T. Harry (Thomas Harry), 1909-.   • **3.7663**
Huey Long [by] T. Harry Williams. [1st ed.] New York: Knopf, 1969. xiv, 884, xxii p.: ill., facsims., ports.; 25 cm. 1. Long, Huey Pierce, 1893-1935. I. T.
E748.L86 W48 1969   976.3/06/0924 B   *LC* 69-10692

Tarr, Joel Arthur.   **3.7664**
A study in boss politics: William Lorimer of Chicago. — Urbana: University of Illinois Press, [1971] xi, 376 p.: illus., facsim., map, ports.; 24 cm. 1. Lorimer, William, 1861-1934. 2. Illinois — Politics and government — 1865-1950 I. T.
E748.L892 T3   328.73/0924 B   *LC* 72-133945   *ISBN* 0252001397

McAdoo, William Gibbs, 1863-1941.   • **3.7665**
Crowded years: the reminiscences of William G. McAdoo. — Port Washington, N.Y.: Kennikat Press, [1971, c1931] x, 542 p.: illus., maps, ports.; 22 cm. — (Kennikat Press scholarly reprints. Series in American history and culture in the twentieth century) I. T.
E748.M14 M2 1971   973.91/3/0924   *LC* 74-137974   *ISBN* 080461430X

Buckley, William F. (William Frank), 1925-.   • **3.7666**
McCarthy and his enemies; the record and its meaning [by] Wm. F. Buckley, Jr. & L. Brent Bozell. Prologue by William Schlamm. New Rochelle, N.Y., Arlington House [1970, c1954] xix, 425 p. 22 cm. 1. McCarthy, Joseph, 1908-1957. 2. Subversive activities — United States. 3. Communism — United States — 1917- I. Bozell, L. Brent, joint author. II. T.
E748.M143 B8 1970   973.918   *LC* 70-18983   *ISBN* 0870001108

Fried, Richard M., 1941-.   **3.7667**
Men against McCarthy / Richard M. Fried. — New York: Columbia University Press, 1976. xii, 428 p.; 24 cm. (Contemporary American history series) Includes index. 1. McCarthy, Joseph, 1908-1957. 2. United States — Politics and government — 1945-1953 3. United States — Politics and government — 1953-1961 I. T.
E748.M143 F74   320.9/73/0918   *LC* 75-40447   *ISBN* 0231038720

Griffith, Robert, 1940-.   • **3.7668**
The politics of fear: Joseph R. McCarthy and the Senate. — Lexington: Published for the Organization of American Historians [by] University Press of Kentucky, 1970. xi, 362 p.; 23 cm. 1. McCarthy, Joseph, 1908-1957. I. Organization of American Historians. II. T.
E748.M143 G7   973.918/0924   *LC* 73-119812   *ISBN* 0813112273

Rogin, Michael Paul.   • **3.7669**
The intellectuals and McCarthy: the radical specter / Michael Paul Rogin. — Cambridge: M.I.T. Press, 1967. xi, 366 p.: ill., maps; 21 cm. 1. McCarthy, Joseph, 1908-1957. 2. Intellectuals — United States. 3. Right and left (Political science) I. T.
E748.M143.R57   973.90924   *LC* 67-16489

Rorty, James, 1890-1973.   • **3.7670**
McCarthy and the Communists / by James Rorty and Moshe Decter. — Boston: Beacon, [c]1954] viii, 163 p. 1. McCarthy, Joseph, 1908-1957. 2. Communism — United States — 1917- 3. Security, International — United States. I. Decter, Moshe. II. T.
E748.M143 R6   B   344.1   *LC* 54-11622

Rovere, Richard Halworth, 1915-.   **3.7671**
Senator Joe McCarthy. [1st ed.] New York, Harcourt, Brace [1959] 280 p. 21 cm. 1. McCarthy, Joseph, 1908-1957. I. T.
E748.M143 R62   923.273   *LC* 59-9464

Martin, Joseph William, 1884-1968.   **3.7672**
My first fifty years in politics, as told to Robert J. Donovan. New York, McGraw-Hill [1960] 261 p. illus. 22 cm. 1. United States — Politics and government — 20th century I. Donovan, Robert J. II. T.
E748.M375A3   923.273   *LC* 60-15002

Smith, Arthur Robert, 1925-.   **3.7673**
The tiger in the Senate; the biography of Wayne Morse. [1st ed.] Garden City, N.Y., Doubleday, 1962. 455 p. illus. 22 cm. 1. Morse, Wayne L. (Wayne Lyman), 1900-1974. I. T.
E748.M76 S55   *LC* 61-12583

E748 N–Z

Nixon, Richard M. (Richard Milhous), 1913-.   • **3.7674**
Six crises. [1st ed.] Garden City, N.Y., Doubleday, 1962. 460 p. 24 cm. 1. United States — History — 1945- I. T.
E748.N5 A3   973.92   *LC* 62-8074

Norris, George W. (George William), 1861-1944.   • **3.7675**
Fighting liberal: the autobiography of George W. Norris. — New York: The Macmillan company, 1945. xiv p., 2 l., 419 p.: front., ill. (incl. map) ports.; 22 cm. I. T.
E748.N65 A3   *LC* 45-3790

Lowitt, Richard, 1922-.   • **3.7676**
George W. Norris; the persistence of a progressive, 1913–1933. Urbana: University of Illinois Press [1971] xv, 590 p.: ill.; 24 cm. 1. Norris, George W. (George William), 1861-1944. I. T.
E748.N65 L62   328.73/0924 B   *LC* 76-147923   *ISBN* 0252001761

Cole, Wayne S.   • **3.7677**
Senator Gerald P. Nye and American foreign relations. Minneapolis, University of Minnesota Press [1962] 293 p. illus. 24 cm. Includes bibliography. 1. Nye, Gerald Prentice, 1892-1971. 2. United States — Foreign relations — 1933-1945 3. United States — Neutrality I. T.
E748.N9C6 1962   327.73   *LC* 62-21813

Coben, Stanley.   • **3.7678**
A. Mitchell Palmer: politician. — New York: Da Capo Press, 1972 [c1963] xii, 351 p.; 23 cm. — (Civil liberties in American history) 1. Palmer, Alexander Mitchell, 1872-1936. I. T. II. Series.
E748.P24 C6 1972   973.91/3/0924 B   *LC* 79-180787   *ISBN* 0306702088

Powell, Adam Clayton, 1908-1972.   **3.7679**
Adam by Adam; the autobiography of Adam Clayton Powell, Jr. — New York: Dial Press, 1971. x, 260 p.: ports.; 22 cm. — 1. Powell, Adam Clayton, 1908-1972. I. T.
E748.P86 A3   973.92/0924 B   *LC* 71-163587

Handlin, Oscar, 1915-.   • **3.7680**
Al Smith and his America. — [1st ed.]. — Boston: Little, Brown, [1958] 207 p.; 21 cm. — (The Library of American biography) 1. Smith, Alfred Emanuel, 1873-1944. I. T.
E748.S63 H16   923.273   *LC* 57-6446

Josephson, Matthew, 1899-1978.   • **3.7681**
Al Smith: hero of the cities: a political portrait drawing on the papers of Frances Perkins / [by] Matthew and Hannah Josephson. — Boston: Houghton Mifflin, 1969. xx, 505 p.: ports.; 22 cm. 1. Smith, Alfred Emanuel, 1873-1944. I. Josephson, Hannah (Geffen) joint author. II. Perkins, Frances, 1882-1965. III. T.
E748.S63 J6   973.91/5/0924 B   *LC* 73-79391

Smith, Alfred Emanuel, 1873-1944.   • **3.7682**
Up to now: an autobiography / by Alfred E. Smith. — New York: The Viking Press, 1929. 434 p.: front., plates, ports., facsims.; 25 cm. 1. New York (State) — Pol. & govt. — 1885- I. T.
E748.S63S6   *LC* 29-21291

Smith, Frank Ellis, 1918-.   • **3.7683**
Congressman from Mississippi / [by] Frank E. Smith. — New York: Pantheon Books [1964] ix, 338 p.; 22 cm. I. T.
E748.S656 A3   *LC* 64-18350

Martin, John Bartlow, 1915-1987.   **3.7684**
Adlai Stevenson and the world: the life of Adlai E. Stevenson / John Bartlow Martin. — 1st ed. — Garden City, N.Y.: Doubleday, 1977. 946 p., [12] leaves of plates: ill.; 24 cm. 1. Stevenson, Adlai E. (Adlai Ewing), 1900-1965. 2. Statesmen — United States — Biography. 3. United States — Politics and government — 1953-1961 4. United States — Foreign relations — 1961-1963 5. United States — Foreign relations — 1963-1969 I. T.
E748.S84 M36   973.921/092/4 B   *LC* 76-23781   *ISBN* 0385121792

Martin, John Bartlow, 1915-1987.   **3.7685**
Adlai Stevenson of Illinois: the life of Adlai E. Stevenson / John Bartlow Martin. — 1st ed. — Garden City, N.Y.: Doubleday, 1976. ix, 828 p., [12] leaves of plates: ill.; 25 cm. 1. Stevenson, Adlai E. (Adlai Ewing), 1900-1965. I. T.
E748.S84 M37   973.921/092/4 B   *LC* 75-21237   *ISBN* 0385070101

Sievers, Rodney M., 1943-.   **3.7686**
The last Puritan?: Adlai Stevenson in American politics / Rodney M. Sievers. — Port Washington, N.Y.: Associated Faculty Press, c1983. xiii, 154 p.; 24 cm. — (National university publications) 1. Stevenson, Adlai E. (Adlai Ewing), 1900-1965. 2. Statesmen — United States — Biography. 3. United States — Politics and government — 1953-1961 4. United States — Foreign relations — 1961-1963 5. United States — Foreign relations — 1963-1969 I. T.
E748.S84 S53 1983   973.921/092/4 19   *LC* 83-2826   *ISBN* 0804693188

Stimson, Henry Lewis, 1867-1950.   **3.7687**
On active service in peace and war / by Henry L. Stimson and McGeorge Bundy. — New York: Octagon Books, 1971 (c1948) xxii, 698 p.: port.; 24 cm.

'About one fifth of the material in this book was published serially [in the Ladies home journal] under the title of Time of peril.' 1. United States — Politics and government — 20th century 2. United States — Foreign relations — 20th century I. Bundy, McGeorge. II. T.
E748.S883A3   973.91   *LC* 48-6427 *

Morison, Elting Elmore.   • **3.7688**
Turmoil and tradition: a study of the life and times of Henry L. Stimson / Elting E. Morison. —. Boston: Houghton Mifflin, 1960. 686 p.: ill. 22 cm. 1. Stimson, Henry Lewis, 1867-1950. I. T.
E748.S883 M6   923.273   *LC* 60-10132

Patterson, James T.   • **3.7689**
Mr. Republican; a biography of Robert A. Taft [by] James T. Patterson. Boston, Houghton Mifflin, 1972. xvi, 749 p. illus. 24 cm. 1. Taft, Robert A. (Robert Alphonso), 1889-1953. I. T.
E748.T2 P37   328.73/092/4 B   *LC* 72-516   *ISBN* 0395139384

Blum, John Morton, 1921-.   • **3.7690**
Joe Tumulty and the Wilson era, by John M. Blum. With a new pref. [Hamden, Conn.] Archon Books, 1969 [c1951] xiii, 337 p. group port. 21 cm. 'Notes and bibliography': p. 271-324. 1. Tumulty, Joseph P. (Joseph Patrick), 1879-1954. 2. Wilson, Woodrow, 1856-1924. 3. United States — Politics and government — 1913-1921 I. T.
E748.T84 B6 1969   973.91/3/0924 B   *LC* 69-15787   *ISBN* 0208007369

May, Gary, 1944-.   **3.7691**
China scapegoat, the diplomatic ordeal of John Carter Vincent / Gary May; introd. by John K. Fairbank. — Washington: New Republic Books, 1979. 370 p., [12] leaves of plates: ill.; 24 cm. Includes index. 1. Vincent, John Carter, 1900- 2. Diplomats — United States — Biography. 3. China — History — Civil War, 1945-1949 4. United States — Foreign relations — China. 5. China — Foreign relations — United States. I. T.
E748.V564 M39   327/.2/0973 B   *LC* 79-4129   *ISBN* 0915220490

Markowitz, Norman D.   **3.7692**
The rise and fall of the people's century: Henry A. Wallace and American liberalism, 1941–1948 [by] Norman D. Markowitz. — New York: Free Press, [1973] xi, 369 p.: illus.; 22 cm. 1. Wallace, Henry Agard, 1888-1965. 2. United States — Politics and government — 1933-1945 3. United States — Politics and government — 1945- I. T.
E748.W23 M37   973.917/092/4 B   *LC* 72-86508

Wheeler, Burton Kendall, 1882-.   • **3.7693**
Yankee from the West: the candid, turbulent life story of the Yankee–born U.S. Senator from Montana / by Burton K. Wheeler with Paul F. Healy. Garden City, N.Y.: Doubleday, 1962. 436 p.: ill.; 22 cm. I. Healy, Paul F. II. T.
E748.W5 A3   *LC* 62-15909

Johnson, Donald Bruce, 1921-.   • **3.7694**
The Republican Party and Wendell Willkie. — Urbana, University of Illinois Press, 1960. ix, 354 p. 23 cm. — (Illinois studies in the social sciences, v. 46) Bibliography: p. 327-336. 1. Willkie, Wendell L. (Wendell Lewis), 1892-1944. 2. Republican Party I. T.
H31.I4 vol. 46 E748.W7 J6   923.373   *LC* 60-5352

Neal, Steve, 1949-.   **3.7695**
Dark horse: a biography of Wendell Willkie / Steve Neal. — 1st ed. — Garden City, N.Y.: Doubleday, 1984. ix, 371 p., [8] p. of plates: ill.; 22 cm. Includes index. 1. Willkie, Wendell L. (Wendell Lewis), 1892-1944. 2. Politicians — United States — Biography. 3. United States — Politics and government — 1933-1945 I. T.
E748.W7 N43 1984   973.917/092/4 B 19   *LC* 83-1977   *ISBN* 0385184395

E756–856 By Presidential Administration

E756–760 Roosevelt, 1901–1909

Gould, Lewis L.   **3.7696**
Reform and regulation: American politics, 1900–1916 / Lewis L. Gould. — New York: Wiley, c1978. ix, 197 p.; 22 cm. (Critical episodes in American politics) Includes index. 1. Progressivism (United States politics) 2. United States — Politics and government — 1901-1909 3. United States — Politics and government — 1909-1913 4. United States — Politics and government — 1913-1921 I. T. II. Series.
E756.G63   973.91 19   *LC* 77-21058   *ISBN* 0471319139. *ISBN* 0471319147 pbk

Marks, Frederick W.   **3.7697**
Velvet on iron: the diplomacy of Theodore Roosevelt / Frederick W. Marks III. — Lincoln: University of Nebraska Press, c1979. xiv, 247 p.; 22 cm. Includes index. 1. Roosevelt, Theodore, 1858-1919. 2. Presidents — United States — Biography 3. United States — Foreign relations — 1901-1909 I. T.
E756.M37   973.91/1/0924 B   *LC* 79-1216   *ISBN* 0803230575

Mowry, George Edwin, 1909-.   • **3.7698**
The era of Theodore Roosevelt, 1900–1912. [1st ed.] New York: Harper [1958] 330 p.: ill.; 22 cm. (The New American Nation series) 1. Roosevelt, Theodore, 1858-1919. 2. United States — Politics and government — 1901-1909 3. United States — Politics and government — 1909-1913 I. T.
E756.M85   973.911   *LC* 58-8835

Beale, Howard K. (Howard Kennedy), 1899-1959.   • **3.7699**
Theodore Roosevelt and the rise of America to world power. Baltimore: Johns Hopkins Press, 1956. 600 p.; 23 cm. (The Albert Shaw lectures on diplomatic history, 1953) 1. Roosevelt, Theodore, 1858-1919. 2. United States — Foreign relations — 1901-1909 I. T.
E757.B4   973.91/1/0924 19   *LC* 56-10255

Blum, John Morton, 1921-.   • **3.7700**
The Republican Roosevelt. Cambridge: Harvard University Press, 1954. 170 p.; 22 cm. 1. Roosevelt, Theodore, 1858-1919. 2. United States — Politics and government — 1901-1909 I. T.
E757.B65   823.173   *LC* 54-5182

Chessman, G. Wallace.   • **3.7701**
Theodore Roosevelt and the politics of power [by] G. Wallace Chessman. Edited by Oscar Handlin. Boston, Little, Brown [1969] viii, 214 p. 21 cm. (Library of American biography.) 'A note on the sources': p. [200]-204. 1. Roosevelt, Theodore, 1858-1919. I. T. II. Series.
E757.C55   973.91/1/0924 B   *LC* 68-20501

Gardner, Joseph Lawrence, 1933-.   • **3.7702**
Departing glory; Theodore Roosevelt as ex–President [by] Joseph L. Gardner. New York, Scribner [1973] xv, 432 p. illus. 24 cm. 1. Roosevelt, Theodore, 1858-1919. I. T.
E757.G29   973.91/1/0924 B   *LC* 72-11116   *ISBN* 0684133008

Harbaugh, William Henry, 1920-.   • **3.7703**
Power and responsibility; the life and times of Theodore Roosevelt. New York: Farrar, Straus and Cudahy [1961] 568 p.: ill.; 22 cm. Later ed. published under title: The life and times of Theodore Roosevelt. 1. Roosevelt, Theodore, 1858-1919. I. T.
E757.H28   973.911   *LC* 61-10128

Morris, Edmund.   **3.7704**
The rise of Theodore Roosevelt / Edmund Morris. — New York: Coward, McCann & Geoghegan, c1979. 886 p.: ill.; 24 cm. Includes index. 1. Roosevelt, Theodore, 1858-1919. 2. Presidents — United States — Biography 3. United States — Politics and government — 1901-1909 4. New York (State) — Politics and government — 1865-1950 I. T.
E757.M883 1979   973.91/1/0924 B   *LC* 78-23789   *ISBN* 0698107837

Pringle, Henry Fowles, 1897-1958.   • **3.7705**
Theodore Roosevelt, a biography. [Rev.] New York, Harcourt, Brace [c1956] 435 p. 19 cm. (A Harvest book, 15) 1. Roosevelt, Theodore, 1858-1919. I. T.
E757.P967   923.173   *LC* 56-13739

Roosevelt, Theodore, 1858-1919.   • **3.7706**
Autobiography. Condensed from the original ed., supplemented by letters, speeches, and other writings, and edited with an introd. by Wayne Andrews. Centennial ed. New York, Scribner [1958] xi, 372 p. 22 cm. I. T.
E757.R794   923.173   *LC* 58-11634

Roosevelt, Theodore, President, U. S., 1858-1919.   • **3.7707**
Letters / selected and edited by Elting E. Morison; John M. Blum, associate editor; John J. Buckley, copy editor. — Cambridge: Harvard University Press, 1951-54. 8 v.: ill., ports.; 25 cm. I. T.
E757.R7958   *LC* 51-10037

Roosevelt, Theodore, President, U. S., 1858-1919.   • **3.7708**
Selections from the correspondence of Theodore Roosevelt and Henry Cabot Lodge, 1884–1918 ... New York [etc.]: C. Scribner's sons, 1925. 2 v.: fronts. (ports.); 25 cm. 1. Lodge, Henry Cabot, 1850-1924. II. T.
E757.R799   *LC* 25-8869

E761–765 Taft, 1909–1913

Anderson, Donald F.   **3.7709**
William Howard Taft: a conservative's conception of the Presidency [by] Donald F. Anderson. Ithaca [N.Y.] Cornell University Press [1973] ix, 355 p. illus. 22 cm. 1. Taft, William H. (William Howard), 1857-1930. 2. Executive

power — United States 3. United States — Politics and government — 1909-1913 I. T.
E761.A83   353.03/13/0924   *LC* 73-8408   *ISBN* 0801407869

Coletta, Paolo Enrico, 1916-.   • **3.7710**
The Presidency of William Howard Taft, by Paolo E. Coletta. Lawrence, University Press of Kansas [1973] ix, 306 p. 24 cm. (American presidency series.) 1. Taft, William H. (William Howard), 1857-1930. 2. United States — Politics and government — 1909-1913 I. T. II. Series.
E761.C64   973.91/2/0924 B   *LC* 72-92564   *ISBN* 0700600965

Scholes, Walter Vinton, 1916-.   • **3.7711**
The foreign policies of the Taft administration, by Walter V. Scholes and Marie V. Scholes. Columbia, University of Missouri Press [c1970] 259 p. port. 25 cm. 1. Taft, William H. (William Howard), 1857-1930. 2. United States — Foreign relations — 1909-1913 I. Scholes, Marie V., joint author. II. T.
E761.S3   327.73   *LC* 70-122310   *ISBN* 082620094X

Pringle, Henry.   • **3.7712**
The life and times of William Howard Taft: a biography / by Henry F. Pringle. — Hamden, Conn.: Archon Books, 1964, c1939. 2 v. (1106 p.): ill., ports., facsim.; 24 cm. 1. Taft, William H. (William Howard), 1857-1930. I. T.
E 762 T12 1964

Wilson, Woodrow, 1856-1924.   • **3.7713**
A crossroads of freedom: the 1912 campaign speeches / edited by John Wells Davidson; with a pref. by Charles Seymour. — New Haven: Published [by] Yale University Press, 1956. xviii, 570 p.: ill., ports., facsims.; 25 cm. 1. Campaign literature, 1912 — Democratic. 2. United States — Politics and government — 1909-1913 I. Davidson, John Wells II. T.
E765.W5   *LC* 56-11796

E766–783 Wilson, 1913–1921

Buehrig, Edward H. (Edward Henry), 1910-.   • **3.7714**
Woodrow Wilson and the balance of power [by] Edward H. Buehrig. Gloucester, Mass., P. Smith, 1968 [c1955] x, 325 p. 21 cm. 1. Wilson, Woodrow, 1856-1924. 2. United States — Foreign relations — 1913-1921 I. T.
E766.B95 1968   327.73   *LC* 73-753

Houston, David Franklin, 1866-1940.   • **3.7715**
Eight years with Wilson's Cabinet, 1913 to 1920; with a personal estimate of the President. Garden City, N.Y., Doubleday, Page, 1926. St. Clair Shores, Mich.: Scholarly Press, 1970. 2 v.: ports.; 22 cm. 1. Wilson, Woodrow, 1856-1924. 2. United States — Politics and government — 1913-1921 I. T.
E766.H86 1970   973.91/3/0924   *LC* 79-145095   *ISBN* 0403007682

Link, Arthur Stanley.   • **3.7716**
Woodrow Wilson and the progressive era, 1910–1917. [1st ed.] New York, Harper, [c1954] xvii, 331 p. illus., ports., maps. 22 cm. (The New American nation series) 1. Wilson, Woodrow, 1856-1924. 2. United States — Politics and government — 1913-1921 I. T.
E766.L5   973.913   *LC* 53-11849

Lippmann, Walter, 1889-.   • **3.7717**
Early writings. Introd. and annotations by Arthur Schlesinger, Jr. — New York: Liveright, [1970] xii, 356 p.; 22 cm. 1. U.S. — Politics and government — 1913-1921 — Addresses, essays, lectures. 2. U.S. — Civilization — 20th century — Addresses, essays, lectures. I. T.
E766.L57   917.3/03/91308   *LC* 70-114385   *ISBN* 0871405032

Noggle, Burl.   **3.7718**
Into the twenties; the United States from armistice to normalcy. — Urbana: University of Illinois Press, [1974] ix, 233 p.; 23 cm. 1. United States — History — 1913-1921 I. T.
E766.N63   973.91/3   *LC* 74-1388   *ISBN* 0252004205

Baker, Ray Stannard, 1870-1946.   • **3.7719**
Woodrow Wilson; life and letters. — [1st ed.]. — New York: Greenwood Press, 1968 [c1927] 8 v.: facsims., ports.; 24 cm. 1. Wilson, Woodrow, 1856-1924. I. T.
E767.B16 1968   973.91/30924 B   *LC* 68-8332

Blum, John Morton, 1921-.   • **3.7720**
Woodrow Wilson and the politics of morality. [1st ed.] Boston, Little, Brown [1956] 215 p. 21 cm. (The Library of American biography) 1. Wilson, Woodrow, 1856-1924. I. T.
E767.B64   923.173   *LC* 56-10643

Garraty, John Arthur, 1920-.   • **3.7721**
Woodrow Wilson; a great life in brief. [1st ed.] New York: Knopf, 1956. 206 p.; 19 cm. (Great lives in brief; a new series of biographies) 1. Wilson, Woodrow, 1856-1924. 2. Presidents — United States — Biography I. T.
E767.G26   923.173   *LC* 56-5802

Hoover, Herbert, 1874-1964.   • **3.7722**
The ordeal of Woodrow Wilson. [1st ed.] New York, McGraw-Hill [1958] xiii, 318 p. illus., ports. 24 cm. 1. Wilson, Woodrow, 1856-1924. 2. United States — Foreign relations — 1913-1921 I. T.
E767.H78   973.913   *LC* 58-9257

Link, Arthur Stanley.   • **3.7723**
Wilson. Princeton: Princeton University Press, 1947-. v.: ill., plates, ports.; 24 cm. 1. Wilson, Woodrow, 1856-1924. I. T.
E767.L65   *LC* 47-3554

Mulder, John M., 1946-.   **3.7724**
Woodrow Wilson: the years of preparation / John M. Mulder. — Princeton, N.J.: Princeton University Press, c1978. xv, 304 p., [5] leaves of plates: ill.; 25 cm. (Supplementary volumes to The papers of Woodrow Wilson) Includes index. 1. Wilson, Woodrow, 1856-1924. 2. Princeton University — Presidents — Biography. 3. Presidents — United States — Biography 4. Historians — United States — Biography. I. T.
E767.M75   973.91/3/0924 B   *LC* 77-72128   *ISBN* 0691046476

Weinstein, Edwin A., 1909-.   **3.7725**
Woodrow Wilson, a medical and psychological biography / Edwin A. Weinstein. — Princeton, N.J.: Princeton University Press, c1981. xi, 399 p., [8] leaves of plates: ill.; 24 cm. — (Supplementary volumes to The papers of Woodrow Wilson.) Includes index. 1. Wilson, Woodrow, 1856-1924. 2. Presidents — United States — Biography I. T. II. Series.
E767.W42   973.91/3/0924 B 19   *LC* 81-47162   *ISBN* 0691046832

E768–780 *Period of World War I*

Cohen, Warren I.   • **3.7726**
The American revisionists: the lessons of intervention in World War I / [by] Warren I. Cohen. — Chicago: University of Chicago Press [1967] xv, 252 p.; 22 cm. 1. World War, 1914-1918 — United States. 2. United States — Foreign relations — 1913-1921 I. T. II. Title: Revisionists.
E768.C6   327.73   *LC* 66-20594

The Immigrants' influence on Wilson's peace policies / edited by   • **3.7727**
Joseph P. O'Grady.
[Lexington]: University of Kentucky Press, 1967. x, 329 p.; 23 cm. Developed from a lecture series at La Salle College, Philadelphia. 1. United States — Foreign relations — 1913-1921 — Addresses, essays, lectures. 2. United States — Foreign population — Addresses, essays, lectures. I. O'Grady, Joseph P., ed. II. La Salle College.
E768.I4   327.73   *LC* 67-23776

Levin, Norman Gordon.   • **3.7728**
Woodrow Wilson and world politics; America's response to war and revolution [by] N. Gordon Levin. London, New York, Oxford University Press [1970, c1968] xii, 340 p. 21 cm. (A Galaxy Book, 309) 1. Wilson, Woodrow, 1856-1924. 2. United States — Foreign relations — 1913-1921 I. T.
E768.L62 1970   327.73   *LC* 70-463170

Link, Arthur Stanley.   **3.7729**
Woodrow Wilson: revolution, war, and peace / Arthur S. Link. — Arlington Heights, Ill.: AHM Pub. Corp., c1979. viii, 138 p.; 22 cm. Based in part on the author's Wilson the diplomatist, first published in 1957. Includes index. 1. Wilson, Woodrow, 1856-1924 — Addresses, essays, lectures. 2. World War, 1914-1918 — Diplomatic history — Addresses, essays, lectures. 3. United States — Foreign relations — 1913-1921 — Addresses, essays, lectures. I. T.
E768.L67   973.91/3/0924   *LC* 79-50909   *ISBN* 0882957988

Smith, Daniel Malloy, 1922-.   • **3.7730**
The great departure; the United States and World War I, 1914–1920 [by] Daniel M. Smith. New York, J. Wiley [1965] xiii, 221 p. maps. 22 cm. (America in crisis) 1. World War, 1914-1918 — United States. 2. United States — Foreign relations — 1913-1921 I. T. II. Series.
E768.S62   940.373   *LC* 65-19813   *ISBN* 0471800066

Livermore, Seward W.   • **3.7731**
Politics is adjourned; Woodrow Wilson and the War Congress, 1916–1918 [by] Seward W. Livermore. [1st ed.] Middletown, Conn., Wesleyan University Press [1966] 324 p. 22 cm. 1. Wilson, Woodrow, 1856-1924. 2. United States — Politics and government — 1913-1921 I. T.
E780.L5   973.913   *LC* 66-14666

E784 1919–1933

Ellis, Lewis Ethan, 1898-.   • **3.7732**
Republican foreign policy, 1921–1933, by L. Ethan Ellis. — New Brunswick, N.J.: Rutgers University Press, [1968]. ix, 404 p.: illus., ports.; 25 cm. 1. United States — Foreign relations — 1921-1923 2. United States — Foreign relations — 1923-1929 3. United States — Foreign relations — 1929-1933 I. T.
E784.E4   327.73   *LC* 68-20886

Hicks, John Donald, 1890-. • 3.7733
Republican ascendancy, 1921–1933. — [1st ed.]. — New York: Harper, [1960] 318 p.: illus.; 22 cm. — (The New American nation series) 1. United States — History — 1919-1933 I. T.
E784.H5   973.914   LC 60-7528

E785–786 Harding, 1921–1923

Murray, Robert K. • 3.7734
The Harding era; Warren G. Harding and his administration, by Robert K. Murray. Minneapolis, University of Minnesota Press [1969] ix, 626 p. illus., ports. 25 cm. 1. Harding, Warren G. (Warren Gamaliel), 1865-1923. I. T.
E786.M8 1969   973.91/4/0924   LC 74-91797

Murray, Robert K. • 3.7735
The politics of normalcy: governmental theory and practice in the Harding–Coolidge era [by] Robert K. Murray. [1st ed.] New York: Norton [c1973] xii, 162 p.; 21 cm. (The Norton essays in American history) 1. Harding, Warren G. (Warren Gamaliel), 1865-1923. 2. Coolidge, Calvin, 1872-1933. 3. United States — Politics and government — 1921-1923 I. T.
E786.M83   973.91/4/0924   LC 72-8354   ISBN 0393054748 ISBN 0393094227

Sinclair, Andrew. • 3.7736
The available man; the life behind the masks of Warren Gamaliel Harding. New York, Macmillan [1965] viii, 344 p. illus., ports. 22 cm. 1. Harding, Warren G. (Warren Gamaliel), 1865-1923. I. T.
E786.S5   923.173   LC 65-14332

E791–796 Coolidge, 1923–1929

Fuess, Claude Moore, 1885-1963. • 3.7737
Calvin Coolidge, the man from Vermont, by Claude M. Fuess. Boston: Little, Brown and company, c1940. xii, 522 p.:bill.; 25 cm. 'First edition.' 1. Coolidge, Calvin, 1872-1933. I. T.
E792.F85   LC 40-27145

White, William Allen, 1868-1944. • 3.7738
A Puritan in Babylon, the story of Calvin Coolidge, by William Allen White. — New York: The Macmillan company, 1938. xvi p., 2 l., 460 p.: front. (port.); 24 cm. 'First printing.' 1. Coolidge, Calvin, 1872-1933. I. T.
E792.W577   923.173   LC 38-34760

Smith, Alfred Emanuel, 1873-1944. • 3.7739
Campaign addresses of Governor Alfred E. Smith, Democratic candidate for President, 1928. — New York: AMS Press, [1970] 322 p.: illus., ports.; 23 cm. Reprint of the 1929 ed. 1. Campaign literature, 1928 — Democratic. I. T.
E796.S64 1970   329/.01   LC 70-126683   ISBN 0404061176

E801–805 Hoover, 1929–1933

Fausold, Martin L., 1921-. 3.7740
The presidency of Herbert C. Hoover / Martin L. Fausold. — Lawrence, Kan.: University Press of Kansas, c1985. xii, 288 p.; 24 cm. (American presidency series.) Includes index. 1. Hoover, Herbert, 1874-1964. 2. United States — Politics and government — 1929-1933 I. T. II. Series.
E801.F25 1985   973.91/6/0924 B 19   LC 84-17252   ISBN 0700602593

Myers, William Starr, 1877-1956. • 3.7741
The Hoover administration; a documented narrative, by William Starr Myers and Walter H. Newton. New York, Charles Scribner's Sons, 1936. St. Clair Shores, Mich., Scholarly Press, 1971. viii, 553 p. port. 22 cm. 1. United States — Politics and government — 1929-1933 I. Hoover, Herbert, 1874-1964. II. Newton, Walter Hughes, 1880-1941, joint author. III. T.
E801.M94 1971   973.91/6/0924   LC 79-145202   ISBN 0403011264

Romasco, Albert U. • 3.7742
The poverty of abundance; Hoover, the Nation, the depression [by] Albert U. Romasco. New York: Oxford University Press, 1965. x, 282 p.; 22 cm. 1. Hoover, Herbert, 1874-1964. 2. Depressions — 1929 — United States 3. United States — Politics and government — 1929-1933 4. United States — Economic policy — To 1933 I. T. II. Title: Hoover, the Nation, the depression.
E801.R6   973.916   LC 65-26565

Rosen, Elliot A., 1928-. 3.7743
Hoover, Roosevelt, and the Brains Trust: from depression to New Deal / Elliot A. Rosen. — New York: Columbia University Press, 1977. x, 446 p., [8] leaves of plates: ill.; 24 cm. 1. Roosevelt, Franklin D. (Franklin Delano), 1882-1945. 2. Hoover, Herbert, 1874-1964. 3. Presidents — United States — Election — 1932. 4. New Deal, 1933-1939 5. United States — Politics and government — 1929-1933 I. T.
E801.R65   320.9/73/0916   LC 76-49976   ISBN 0231041721

Schwarz, Jordan A., 1937-. • 3.7744
The interregnum of despair: Hoover, Congress, and the depression [by] Jordan A. Schwarz. Urbana, University of Illinois Press [1970] ix, 281 p. 24 cm. 1. Hoover, Herbert, 1874-1964. 2. United States — Politics and government — 1929-1933 I. T.
E801.S3   973.91/6   LC 78-113768   ISBN 0252001125

Burner, David, 1937-. 3.7745
Herbert Hoover, a public life / David Burner. — 1st ed. — New York: Knopf, 1979, c1978. xii, 433 p., [8] leaves of plates: ill.; 24 cm. 1. Hoover, Herbert, 1874-1964. 2. Presidents — United States — Biography I. T.
E802.B87 1979   973.91/6/0924 B   LC 78-54912   ISBN 0394461347

Hoff-Wilson, Joan, 1937-. 3.7746
Herbert Hoover, forgotten progressive / Joan Hoff Wilson. — Boston: Little, Brown, [1975] viii, 307 p.; 20 cm. (Library of American biography.) 1. Hoover, Herbert, 1874-1964. I. T. II. Series.
E802.H67 1975   973.91/6/0924 B   LC 74-25676

Hoover, Herbert, 1874-1964. • 3.7747
Memoirs. New York, Macmillan, 1951-52. 3 v. illus., ports. 25 cm. 1. Hoover, Herbert, 1874-1964. 2. Presidents — United States — Biography 3. United States — Politics and government — 1919-1933 I. T.
E802.H7   973.91/6/0924 B   LC 51-13301

Smith, Richard Norton, 1953-. 3.7748
An uncommon man: the triumph of Herbert Hoover / Richard Norton Smith. — New York: Simon and Schuster, c1984. 488 p., [8] p. of plates: ill., ports.; 25 cm. Includes index. 1. Hoover, Herbert, 1874-1964. 2. Presidents — United States — Biography 3. United States — Politics and government — 20th century I. T.
E802.S68 1984   973.91/6/0924 B 19   LC 83-27175   ISBN 067146034X

Tugwell, Rexford G. (Rexford Guy), 1891-. • 3.7749
The Brains Trust, by R. G. Tugwell. New York, Viking Press [1968] xxxii, 538 p. 23 cm. 1. Roosevelt, Franklin D. (Franklin Delano), 1882-1945. 2. Presidents — United States — Election — 1932. I. T.
E805.T8   329/.023   LC 68-16079

E806–812 Roosevelt, 1933–1945

E806 A–M General Works

Beard, Charles Austin, 1874-1948. • 3.7750
American foreign policy in the making, 1932–1940; a study in responsibilities. — [Hamden, Conn.]: Archon Books, 1968 [c1946] 336 p.; 22 cm. Sequel: President Roosevelt and the coming of the war, 1941. 1. United States — Foreign relations — 1933-1945 2. United States — Foreign relations — 20th century 3. United States — Neutrality I. T.
E806.B42 1968   327.73   LC 68-8011   ISBN 0208006109

Beard, Charles Austin, 1874-1948. • 3.7751
President Roosevelt and the coming of the war, 1941; a study in appearances and realities. [Hamden, Conn.] Archon Books, 1968 [c1948] vi, 614 p. 22 cm. Sequel to American foreign policy in the making, 1932-1940. 1. Roosevelt, Franklin D. (Franklin Delano), 1882-1945. 2. World War, 1939-1945 — United States. 3. United States — Foreign relations — 1933-1945 I. T.
E806.B434 1968   327.73   LC 68-8012   ISBN 0208002650

Blum, John Morton, 1921-. 3.7752
V was for victory: politics and American culture during World War II / John Morton Blum. — 1st ed. — New York: Harcourt Brace Jovanovich, c1976. xii, 372 p.; 24 cm. 1. World War, 1939-1945 — United States. 2. United States — Politics and government — 1933-1945 3. United States — Social life and customs — 1918-1945 I. T.
E806.B58   973.917   LC 75-38730   ISBN 0151940800

Brinkley, Alan. 3.7753
Voices of protest: Huey Long, Father Coughlin, and the Great Depression / Alan Brinkley. — 1st ed. — New York: Knopf, 1982. xiii, 348 p., [8] p. of plates: ill.; 24 cm. 1. Long, Huey Pierce, 1893-1935. 2. Coughlin, Charles E. (Charles Edward), 1891-1979. 3. United States — Politics and government — 1933-1945 4. United States — Social conditions — 1933-1945 5. United States — Economic policy — 1933-1945 I. T.
E806.B75 1982   E806 B65 1982.   973.91/6 19   LC 81-48121   ISBN 0394522419

Brogan, D. W. (Denis William), 1900-1974.　　• **3.7754**
The era of Franklin D. Roosevelt; a chronicle of the New Deal and global war. — New Haven, Yale University Press, 1950. ix, 382 p. front. 18 cm. — (Chronicles of America series. v. 52) 'Bibliographical note': p. 365-372. 1. Roosevelt, Franklin D. (Franklin Delano), 1882-1945. 2. U.S. — Hist. — 1933-1945. I. T. II. Series.
E173.C56 vol. 52 E806.B78 1950a　　973.917　　*LC* 53-53

Cole, Wayne S.　　**3.7755**
Roosevelt & the isolationists, 1932–45 / Wayne S. Cole. — Lincoln: University of Nebraska Press, c1983. xii, 698 p.; 24 cm. Includes index. 1. Roosevelt, Franklin D. (Franklin Delano), 1882-1945. 2. United States — Neutrality 3. United States — Foreign relations — 1933-1945 I. T. II. Title: Roosevelt and the isolationists, 1932-45.
E806.C594 1983　　327.73 19　　*LC* 82-8624　　*ISBN* 0803214103

Conkin, Paul Keith.　　• **3.7756**
The New Deal / Paul K. Conkin. — New York: Crowell, 1967. vii, 118 p.; 21 cm. — (Crowell American history series) (Crowell publications in history) 1. Roosevelt, Franklin D. (Franklin Delano), 1882-1945. 2. United States — Politics and government — 1933-1945 3. United States — Social policy I. T.
E806.C6　　E806 C6.　　*LC* 67-14297

Dallek, Robert.　　**3.7757**
Franklin D. Roosevelt and American foreign policy, 1932–1945 / Robert Dallek. — New York: Oxford University Press, 1979. xii, 657 p.; 24 cm. Includes index. 1. Roosevelt, Franklin D. (Franklin Delano), 1882-1945. 2. United States — Foreign relations — 1933-1945 I. T.
E806.D33　　327.73　　*LC* 78-7910　　*ISBN* 0195024575

Daniels, Jonathan, 1902-.　　**3.7758**
White House witness, 1942–1945 / Jonathan Daniels. — 1st ed. — Garden City, N.Y.: Doubleday, 1975. xiv, 299 p., [8] leaves of plates: ill.; 22 cm. Includes index. 1. Daniels, Jonathan, 1902- 2. United States — Politics and government — 1933-1945 I. T.
E806.D34　　320.9/73/0917　　*LC* 74-9482　　*ISBN* 0385007620

Divine, Robert Alexander, 1929-.　　• **3.7759**
The illusion of neutrality. — [Chicago]: University of Chicago Press [1962] xi, 370 p.; 23 cm. 'Bibliographical essay': p. 336-351. 1. U.S. — For. rel. — 1933-1945. 2. U.S. — Neutrality. I. T.
E806.D58　　327.73　　*LC* 62-10993

Divine, Robert A.　　• **3.7760**
Second chance: the triumph of internationalism in America during World War II / [by] Robert A. Divine. — [1st ed.]. — New York: Atheneum, 1967. ix, 371 p. 1. International organization 2. United States — Foreign relations — 1933-1945 I. T.
E806.D59　　*LC* 67-14101

Leuchtenburg, William Edward, 1922-.　　• **3.7761**
Franklin D. Roosevelt and the New Deal, 1932–1940. [1st ed.] New York: Harper & Row [1963] 393 p.: ill.; 22 cm. (The New American Nation series) 1. New Deal, 1933-1939 2. United States — History — 1933-1945 I. T.
E806.L475　　973.917　　*LC* 63-12053

Manchester, William Raymond, 1922-.　　**3.7762**
The glory and the dream: a narrative history of America, 1932–1972, [by] William Manchester. — [1st ed.]. — Boston: Little, Brown, [1974] x, 1397 p.; 25 cm. 1. United States — History — 1933-1945 2. United States — History — 1945- I. T.
E806.M34　　917.3/03/92　　*LC* 74-10617　　*ISBN* 0316544965

McElvaine, Robert S., 1947-.　　**3.7763**
The Great Depression: America, 1929–1941 / Robert S. McElvaine. — [New York, N.Y.]: Times Books, c1984. xiv, 402 p.: ill.; 24 cm. 1. Depressions — 1929 — United States 2. New Deal, 1933-1939 3. United States — History — 1933-1945 4. United States — History — 1919-1933 5. United States — Social conditions — 1933-1945 6. United States — Economic conditions — 1918-1945 I. T.
E806.M43 1984　　973.91/6 19　　*LC* 82-40469　　*ISBN* 0812910613

Moley, Raymond, 1886-.　　• **3.7764**
After seven years. New York, Da Capo Press, 1972 [c1939] xii, 446 p. illus. 22 cm. (Franklin D. Roosevelt and the era of the New Deal.) 1. New Deal, 1933-1939 2. United States — Politics and government — 1933-1945 I. T. II. Series.
E806.M67 1972　　973.917　　*LC* 71-168390　　*ISBN* 0306703270

Moley, Raymond, 1886-.　　• **3.7765**
The first New Deal [by] Raymond Moley, with the assistance of Elliot A. Rosen. Foreword by Frank Freidel. — [1st ed.]. — New York, Harcourt, Brace & World [1966] xxiii, 577 p. 24 cm. Bibliographical footnotes. 1. U.S. — Pol. & govt. — 1933-1945. 2. U.S. — Economic policy. I. T.
E806.M68　　973.917　　*LC* 66-22282

E806 N–Z General Works

Ninkovich, Frank A., 1944-.　　**3.7766**
The diplomacy of ideas: U.S. foreign policy and cultural relations, 1938–1950 / Frank A. Ninkovich. — Cambridge [Eng.]; New York: Cambridge University Press, 1981. x, 253 p.; 24 cm. Includes index. 1. United States — Foreign relations — 1933-1945 2. United States — Foreign relations — 1945-1953 3. United States — Relations I. T.
E806.N56　　327.73　　*LC* 80-13388　　*ISBN* 0521232414

Patterson, James T.　　• **3.7767**
Congressional conservatism and the New Deal: the growth of the conservative coalition in Congress, 1933–1939 / by James T. Patterson. — [Lexington]: For the Organization of American Historians [by] University of Kentucky Press, 1967. ix, 369 p.: ill., ports.; 23 cm. 1. Conservatism — United States 2. United States — Politics & government — 1933-1945 3. United States — Social policy I. Organization of American Historians. II. T.
E806 P365　　*LC* 67-17845

Rauch, Basil, 1908-.　　• **3.7768**
The history of the new deal, 1933–1938, by Basil Rauch. New York, Creative age press, inc. [1944] xi p., 1 l., 368 p. 21 cm. 'Reference notes': p. 341-351. 1. New Deal, 1933-1939 2. United States — Economic policy 3. United States — Social policy 4. United States — Politics and government — 1933-1945 I. T.
E806.R3　　973.917　　*LC* 44-8426

Roosevelt, Franklin D. (Franklin Delano), 1882-1945.　　• **3.7769**
Complete presidential press conferences of Franklin D. Roosevelt. Introd. by Jonathan Daniels. New York: Da Capo Press, 1972-. v.: front.; 26 cm. 1. Presidents — United States — Press conferences 2. United States — Politics and government — 1933-1945 I. T.
E806.R7424 1972　　973.917　　*LC* 78-155953　　*ISBN* 030677500X

Rose, Lisle Abbott, 1936-.　　**3.7770**
After Yalta / [by] Lisle A. Rose. — New York: Scribner [1973] vi, 216 p.; 21 cm. 1. United States — Foreign relations — 1933-1945 2. United States — Foreign relations — 1945-1953 3. United States — Foreign relations — Soviet Union 4. Soviet Union — Foreign relations — United States I. T.
E806.R83 1973　　327.73　　*LC* 72-7866　　*ISBN* 0684131897

Schlesinger, Arthur Meier, 1917-.　　• **3.7771**
The age of Roosevelt / Arthur M. Schlesinger. — Boston: Houghton Mifflin, 1956-1960. 3 v. 1. Roosevelt, Franklin D. (Franklin Delano), 1882-1945. 2. United States — History — 1919-1933 3. United States — History — 1933-1945 I. T.
E806.S34　　*LC* 56-10293

Smith, Geoffrey S.　　**3.7772**
To save a nation; American countersubversives, the New Deal, and the coming of World War II [by] Geoffrey S. Smith. New York, Basic Books [1973] xii, 244 p. 24 cm. 1. Right and left (Political science) 2. New Deal, 1933-1939 3. United States — Politics and government — 1933-1945 I. T.
E806.S684　　320.9/73/0917　　*LC* 72-89181　　*ISBN* 046508625X

Terkel, Studs, 1912-.　　• **3.7773**
Hard times: an oral history of the great depression / [by] Studs Terkel. — New York: Pantheon Books [1970] xiii, 462 p.; 25 cm. 1. United States — Economic conditions — 1918-1945 — Addresses, essays, lectures. 2. United States — Social conditions — 1933-1945 — Addresses, essays, lectures. I. T.
E806.T45　　309.1/73　　*LC* 69-20195

Westerfield, H. Bradford, 1928-.　　• **3.7774**
Foreign policy and party politics: Pearl Harbor to Korea [by] H. Bradford Westerfield. — New York: Octagon Books, 1972 [c1955] x, 448 p.: ill.; 24 cm. 1. Political parties — U.S. 2. U.S. — Foreign relations — 1933-1945. 3. U.S. — Foreign relations — 1945-1953. I. T.
E806.W455 1972　　327.73　　*LC* 70-159236　　*ISBN* 0374983631

Young, Roland Arnold, 1910-.　　• **3.7775**
Congressional politics in the Second World War, by Roland Young. New York, Da Capo Press, 1972 [c1956] 281 p. illus. 22 cm. (Franklin D. Roosevelt and the era of the New Deal.) 1. United States. Congress — History. 2. World War, 1939-1945 — United States. 3. New Deal, 1933-1939 4. United States — Politics and government — 1933-1945 I. T. II. Series.
E806.Y69 1972　　320.9/73/0917　　*LC* 70-38757　　*ISBN* 0306704420

E807 Biography of Franklin Roosevelt

Roosevelt, Franklin D. (Franklin Delano), 1882-1945.　　**3.7776**
Roosevelt and Churchill, their secret wartime correspondence. Edited by Francis L. Loewenheim, Harold D. Langley [and] Manfred Jonas. [1st ed.] New York, Saturday Review Press, 1975. xvi, 805 p. illus. 24 cm. 1. Roosevelt, Franklin D. (Franklin Delano), 1882-1945. 2. Churchill, Winston, Sir, 1874-1965. I. Churchill, Winston, Sir, 1874-1965. joint author.

II. Loewenheim, Francis L. ed. III. Langley, Harold D. ed. IV. Jonas, Manfred. ed. V. T.
E807.A4 1975   940.53/22   *LC* 74-14854   *ISBN* 0841503311

Beschloss, Michael R.   **3.7777**
Kennedy and Roosevelt: the uneasy alliance / Michael R. Beschloss; foreword by James MacGregor Burns. — 1st ed. — New York: Norton, c1980. 318 p.: ill.; 24 cm. Includes index. 1. Roosevelt, Franklin D. (Franklin Delano), 1882-1945 — Friends and associates. 2. Kennedy, Joseph P. (Joseph Patrick), 1888-1969 — Friends and associates. 3. United States — Politics and government — 1933-1945 4. United States — Foreign relations — 1933-1945 I. T.
E807.B47 1980   973.917/092/2 19   *LC* 79-24548   *ISBN* 0393013359

Burns, James MacGregor.   ● **3.7778**
Roosevelt: the lion and the fox / James MacGregor Burns. — New York: Harcourt, Brace Jovanovich, 1956. xvi, 553 p., [8] leaves of plates: ill., ports. 'Vol. 1 of the first complete biography of F. D. R.' Includes index. 1. United States — Politics & government — 1933-1945 — Biography. I. T.
E807.B835   923.173   *LC* 56-7920   *ISBN* 0151788693

Burns, James MacGregor.   ● **3.7779**
Roosevelt: the soldier of freedom. [1st ed.] New York: Harcourt Brace Jovanovich [1970] xiv, 722 p.: ill., ports.; 22 cm. 1. Roosevelt, Franklin D. (Franklin Delano), 1882-1945. 2. World War, 1939-1945 — United States. I. T.
E807.B836   940.532/2/730924   *LC* 71-95877   *ISBN* 0151788715

Divine, Robert A.   ● **3.7780**
Roosevelt and World War II, by Robert A. Divine. Baltimore: Johns Hopkins Press [1969] x, 107 p.: ill.; 22 cm. (The Albert Shaw lectures in diplomatic history, 1968) 1. Roosevelt, Franklin D. (Franklin Delano), 1882-1945. 2. United States — Foreign relations — 1933-1945 — Addresses, essays, lectures. I. T.
E807.D57   940.532/2/730924   *LC* 69-13655

Freidel, Frank Burt.   ● **3.7781**
Franklin D. Roosevelt. [1st ed.] Boston, Little, Brown [1952-. v. ports. 23 cm. 1. Roosevelt, Franklin D. (Franklin Delano), 1882-1945. I. T.
E807.F74   973.917/092/4 B 19   *LC* 52-5521

Roosevelt, Elliott, 1910-.   ● **3.7782**
As he saw it, with a foreword by Eleanor Roosevelt. New York, Duell, Sloan and Pearce [1946] xviii, 270 p. 22 cm. 'First printing.' 1. Roosevelt, Franklin D. (Franklin Delano), 1882-1945. 2. World War, 1939-1945 — Congresses I. T.
E807.R64   973.917   *LC* 46-7078

Roosevelt, Franklin D. (Franklin Delano), 1882-1945.   ● **3.7783**
F. D. R.: his personal letters / foreword by Eleanor Roosevelt; edited by Elliott Roosevelt. — New York: Duell, Sloan and Pearce, 1947-1950. 4 v.: ill., facsims. Vol. 2 edited by Elliott Roosevelt, assisted by James N. Rosenau; vol. 3-4 edited by Elliott Roosevelt, assisted by Joseph P. Lash. 1. Roosevelt, Franklin D. (Franklin Delano), 1882-1945. I. Roosevelt, Elliott, 1910- ed. II. T.
E807.R649   *LC* 47-11935

Tugwell, Rexford G. (Rexford Guy), 1891-.   ● **3.7784**
The democratic Roosevelt; a biography of Franklin D. Roosevelt. — 1st ed. — Garden City, N.Y.: Doubleday, 1957. 712 p.: ill.; 25 cm. 1. Roosevelt, Franklin D. (Franklin Delano), 1882-1945. I. T.
E807.T76   *LC* 57-7290

Tugwell, Rexford G. (Rexford Guy), 1891-.   ● **3.7785**
In search of Roosevelt [by] Rexford G. Tugwell. Cambridge, Harvard University Press, 1972. ix, 313 p. 24 cm. 1. Roosevelt, Franklin D. (Franklin Delano), 1882-1945. I. T.
E807.T765   973.917/092/4   *LC* 72-76559   *ISBN* 0674446259

E807.1 Biography of Eleanor Roosevelt

Roosevelt, Eleanor.   ● **3.7786**
The autobiography of Eleanor Roosevelt. — New York: Harper, 1961. xix, 454 p., 12 leaves of plates: ill.; 25 cm. 1. Roosevelt, Eleanor, 1884-1962. 2. Presidents — United States — Wives — Biography. I. T.
E807.1R35   920.7   *LC* 61-12222

Roosevelt, Eleanor, 1884-1962.   ● **3.7787**
This I remember. [1st ed.] New York, Harper [1949] x, 387 p. illus., ports. 24 cm. 1. Roosevelt, Eleanor, 1884-1962. 2. Roosevelt, Franklin D. (Franklin Delano), 1882-1945. 3. United States — Politics and government — 1933-1945 I. T.
E807.1.R428   923.173   *LC* 49-48262

Lash, Joseph P., 1909-.   ● **3.7788**
Eleanor and Franklin: the story of their relationship, based on Eleanor Roosevelt's private papers, [by] Joseph P. Lash; foreword by Arthur M. Schlesinger, Jr.;introd. by Franklin D. Roosevelt, Jr. — New York: Norton, [1971] xviii, 765 p.: ill., geneal. table (on lining papers), ports.; 24 cm. 1. Roosevelt, Eleanor, 1884-1962. 2. Roosevelt, Franklin D. (Franklin Delano), 1882-1945. I. T.
E807.1.R572   973.917/0924 B   *LC* 72-152667   *ISBN* 0393074595

Lash, Joseph P., 1909-.   **3.7789**
Eleanor: the years alone [by] Joseph P. Lash. Foreword by Franklin D. Roosevelt, Jr. New York, Norton [1972] 368 p. 24 cm. Continues the biography of Mrs. Roosevelt which began in the author's Eleanor and Franklin. 1. Roosevelt, Eleanor, 1884-1962. I. T.
E807.1.R574   973.917/092/4 B   *LC* 72-2674   *ISBN* 0393073610

E813–816 Truman, 1945–1953

Alperovitz, Gar.   ● **3.7790**
Atomic diplomacy: Hiroshima and Potsdam: the use of the atomic bomb and the American confrontation with Soviet power. — New York: Simon and Schuster [1965] 317 p.; 25 cm. 1. United States — Foreign relations — 1945-1953 2. United States — Foreign relations — Soviet Union 3. Soviet Union — Foreign relations — United States I. T. II. Title: Hiroshima and Potsdam.
E813.A75   327.73047   *LC* 65-15029

Bernstein, Barton J. ed.   ● **3.7791**
The Truman administration; a documentary history, edited by Barton J. Bernstein and Allan J. Matusow. [1st ed.] New York, Harper & Row [1966] viii, 518 p.: ill., ports. 22 cm. 1. Truman, Harry S., 1884-1972. 2. United States — Politics and government — 1933-1953 — Sources. 3. United States — Foreign relations — 1945-1953 — Sources. I. Matusow, Allen J. joint ed. II. T.
E813.B45   973.918   *LC* 66-13938

Cohen, Bernard C.   **3.7792**
The political process and foreign policy: the making of the Japanese peace settlement. Princeton: Princeton University Press, 1957. 293 p. 'Part of a continuing inquiry ... on the part of the Center of International Studies.' 1. World War, 1939-1945 — Japan 2. United States — Foreign relations — 1945- I. Woodrow Wilson School of Public and International Affairs. Center of International Studies. II. T.
E813.C62   *LC* 57-8665

Donovan, Robert J.   **3.7793**
Conflict and crisis: the Presidency of Harry S. Truman, 1945–1948 / Robert J. Donovan. — 1st ed. — New York: Norton, c1977. xvii, 473 p., [8] leaves of plates: ill.; 24 cm. Includes index. 1. Truman, Harry S., 1884-1972. 2. World politics — 1945-1955 3. United States — Politics and government — 1945-1953 I. T.
E813.D6 1977   973.918/092/4   *LC* 77-9584   *ISBN* 0393056368

Donovan, Robert J.   **3.7794**
Tumultuous years: the presidency of Harry S. Truman, 1949–1953 / Robert J. Donovan. — 1st ed. — New York: Norton, c1982. 444 p.: ill., maps, ports.; 25 cm. 1. Truman, Harry S., 1884-1972. 2. Presidents — United States — Biography 3. United States — Politics and government — 1945-1953 4. United States — Foreign relations — 1945-1953 I. T.
E813.D63 1982   973.918 19   *LC* 82-6304   *ISBN* 0393016196

Freeland, Richard M., 1941-.   ● **3.7795**
The Truman Doctrine and the origins of McCarthyism: foreign policy, domestic politics, and internal security, 1946–1948 / [by] Richard M. Freeland. — [1st ed.] New York: Knopf, 1972 [c1971] xii, 419, xii p.; 22 cm. 1. Internal security — United States 2. Communism — United States — 1917- 3. United States — Politics and government — 1945-1953 4. United States — Foreign relations — 1945-1953 I. T.
E813.F74 1971   973.918 19   *LC* 71-142958   *ISBN* 0394465970

Gardner, Lloyd C., 1934-.   ● **3.7796**
Architects of illusion; men and ideas in American foreign policy, 1941–1949, by Lloyd C. Gardner. — Chicago: Quadrangle Books, 1970. xi, 365 p.; 22 cm. 1. United States — Foreign relations — 1933-1945 2. United States — Foreign relations — 1945-1953 I. T.
E813.G27   327.73   *LC* 69-20163

Goldman, Eric Frederick, 1915-.   ● **3.7797**
The crucial decade: America, 1945–1955 / Eric F. Goldman. — [1st ed.] — New York: Knopf, 1956. ix, 298 p. 22 cm. Includes index. 1. United States — History — 1945-1953 2. United States — History — 1953-1961 I. T.
E813.G6   973.918   *LC* 55-9285

Hamby, Alonzo L.   **3.7798**
Beyond the New Deal: Harry S. Truman and American liberalism / [by] Alonzo L. Hamby. — New York: Columbia University Press, 1973. xx, 635 p.;

24 cm. (Contemporary American history series) 1. Truman, Harry S., 1884-1972. 2. Liberalism — United States. 3. New Deal, 1933-1939 4. United States — Politics and government — 1945-1953 I. T.
E813.H26   973.918/092/4   LC 73-7593   ISBN 0231033354

Hersey, John, 1914-.   **3.7799**
Aspects of the presidency / John Hersey; introd. by Robert A. Dahl. — New Haven: Ticknor & Fields, 1980. xix, 247 p.; 22 cm. Contains 2 pts.: Harry S. Truman, first published in The New Yorker, 1950-1951; and Gerald R. Ford, which was originally published in 1975 under title: The President. 1. Truman, Harry S., 1884-1972 — Addresses, essays, lectures. 2. Ford, Gerald R., 1913- — Addresses, essays, lectures. 3. United States — Politics and government — 1945-1953 — Addresses, essays, lectures. 4. United States — Politics and government — 1974-1977 — Addresses, essays, lectures. I. Hersey, John, 1914- Harry S. Truman. 1980. II. Hersey, John, 1914- Gerald R. Ford. 1980. III. T.
E813.H45   353.03/1/0922 19   LC 79-27694   ISBN 089919012X

Jones, Joseph M. (Joseph Marion), 1908-.   • **3.7800**
Fifteen weeks (February 21–June 5, 1947) New York: Viking Press, c1955. 296 p. (Harbinger book.) 1. World politics — 1945- 2. United States — Foreign relations — 1945- I. T.
E813 J6 1955   327.73   LC 55-8923

Phillips, Cabell B. H.   • **3.7801**
The Truman Presidency: the history of a triumphant succession / [by] Cabell Phillips. — New York: Macmillan [1966] xiii, 463 p.; 24 cm. 1. Truman, Harry S., 1884-1972. 2. United States — Politics and government — 1945-1953 I. T.
E813.P5 1966   973.918   LC 66-16709

Politics and policies of the Truman Administration / Edited   • **3.7802**
with an introd. by Barton J. Bernstein.
Chicago: Quadrangle Books, 1970. 330 p.; 22 cm. 1. Truman, Harry S., 1884-1972 — Addresses, essays, lectures. 2. United States — Politics and government — 1945-1953 — Addresses, essays, lectures. 3. United States — Foreign relations — 1945-1953 — Addresses, essays, lectures. I. Bernstein, Barton J. ed.
E813.P6 1970   973.918   LC 70-78302

Theoharis, Athan G.   • **3.7803**
Seeds of repression; Harry S. Truman and the origins of McCarthyism, by Athan Theoharis. Chicago, Quadrangle Books, 1971. xi, 238 p. 22 cm. 1. McCarthy, Joseph, 1908-1957. 2. Internal security — United States 3. United States — Foreign relations — 1945-1953 4. United States — Politics and government — 1945-1953 I. T.
E813.T48   973.918   LC 71-116089   ISBN 081290169X

Truman, Harry S., 1884-1972.   • **3.7804**
The Truman administration, its principles and practice, edited by Louis W. Koenig. New York: New York University Press, 1956. xii, 394 p.; 25 cm. 1. Truman, Harry S., 1884-1972. 2. United States — Politics and government — 1945-1953 3. United States — Foreign relations — 1945-1953 I. Koenig, Louis William, 1916- ed. II. T.
E813.T68   973.918   LC 56-7425

Vandenberg, Arthur Hendrick, 1884-1951.   • **3.7805**
The private papers of Senator Vandenberg / edited by Arthur H. Vandenberg, Jr.; with the collaboration of Joe Alex Morris. — Boston: Houghton Mifflin, 1952. xxii, 599 p.: ill.; 23 cm. 1. United States — Politics and government — 1945- — Sources. 2. United States — Foreign relations — 1945- — Sources. I. Vandenberg, Arthur Hendrick, ed. II. Morris, Joe Alex. ed. III. T.
E813.V3   973.917   LC 52-5248

Truman, Harry S., 1884-1972.   **3.7806**
The autobiography of Harry S. Truman / edited by Robert H. Ferrell. — Boulder, Colo.: Colorado Associated University Press, c1980. xiii, 153 p.: ill., map, ports.; 23 cm. 1. Truman, Harry S., 1884-1972. 2. Presidents — United States — Biography 3. United States — Politics and government — 1901-1953 I. Ferrell, Robert H. II. T.
E814.A32   973.918/092/4 B 19   LC 80-66304   ISBN 0870810901

Truman, Harry S., 1884-1972.   **3.7807**
Strictly personal and confidential: the letters Harry Truman never mailed / edited by Monte M. Poen. — 1st ed. — Boston: Little, Brown, c1982. xiii, 210 p.; 21 cm. 1. Truman, Harry S., 1884-1972. 2. Presidents — United States — Correspondence. I. Poen, Monte M., 1930- II. T.
E814.A4 1982b   973.918/092/4 19   LC 81-20879   ISBN 0316712213

Burns, Richard Dean.   **3.7808**
Harry S. Truman: a bibliography of his times and presidency / compiled for the Harry S. Truman Library Institute by Richard Dean Burns. — Wilmington, Del.: Scholarly Resources Inc., 1984. xlviii, 297 p.: ill.; 27 cm. Includes indexes. 1. Truman, Harry S., 1884-1972 — Bibliography. 2. United States — Politics

and government — 1945-1953 — Bibliography. I. Harry S. Truman Library. Institute for National and International Affairs. II. T.
E814.B8x   016.973918/092/4 19   LC 84-20223   ISBN 0842022198

Daniels, Jonathan, 1902-.   • **3.7809**
The man of Independence. Port Washington, N.Y., Kennikat Press [1971, c1950] 384 p. 22 cm. (Kennikat Press scholarly reprints. Series in American history and culture in the twentieth century) 1. Truman, Harry S., 1884-1972. I. T.
E814.D3 1971   973.918/0924 B   LC 75-137969   ISBN 080461427X

Dunar, Andrew J.   **3.7810**
The Truman scandals and the politics of morality / Andrew J. Dunar. — Columbia: University of Missouri Press, 1984. viii, 213 p.; 23 cm. Includes index. 1. Truman, Harry S., 1884-1972 — Psychology. 2. Corruption (in politics) — United States — History — 20th century. 3. United States — Politics and government — 1945-1953 I. T.
E814.D86 1984   973.918/0924 19   LC 84-2205   ISBN 0826204430

McCoy, Donald R.   **3.7811**
The presidency of Harry S. Truman / Donald R. McCoy. — Lawrence, Kan.: University Press of Kansas, c1984. xii, 351 p.; 23 cm. — (American presidency series.) Includes index. 1. Truman, Harry S., 1884-1972. 2. United States — Politics and government — 1945-1953 I. T. II. Title: Harry S. Truman. III. Series.
E814.M38 1984   973.918/092/4 19   LC 84-3624   ISBN 0700602526

Miller, Merle, 1919-.   **3.7812**
Plain speaking; an oral biography of Harry S. Truman. New York, Berkley Pub. Corp.; distributed by Putnam [1974] 448 p. 24 cm. 1. Truman, Harry S., 1884-1972. 2. Presidents — United States — Biography 3. United States — Politics and government — 1945-1953 I. T.
E814.M54 1974   973.918/092/4 B   LC 73-87198   ISBN 0399112618

Truman, Harry S., 1884-1972.   • **3.7813**
Memoirs. [Kansas City ed.] Garden City, N.Y.: Doubleday, 1955-56. 2 v.: map (on lining paper, v. 1); 22 cm. 1. U.S. — Politics and government — 1945- - Sources. I. T. II. Title: Year of decisions.
E814.T76   973.917   LC 55-4830

Ross, Irwin.   • **3.7814**
The loneliest campaign; the Truman victory of 1948. [New York] New American Library [1968] viii, 304 p. illus., ports. 22 cm. 1. Truman, Harry S., 1884-1972. 2. Presidents — United States — Election — 1948. I. T.
E815.R6   329/.023   LC 68-18257

Walton, Richard J.   **3.7815**
Henry Wallace, Harry Truman, and the Cold War / Richard J. Walton. — New York: Viking, 1976. x, 388 p.; 22 cm. Includes index. 1. Wallace, Henry Agard, 1888-1965. 2. Truman, Harry S., 1884-1972. 3. Presidents — United States — Election — 1948. 4. United States — Foreign relations — 1945-1953 I. T.
E815.W34 1976   329/.023/730918   LC 76-17540   ISBN 0670368598

E835–837 Eisenhower, 1953–1961

Adams, Sherman, 1899-1986.   • **3.7816**
Firsthand report; the story of the Eisenhower administration. [1st ed.] New York: Harper [1961] 481 p.: ill.; 22 cm. 1. Eisenhower, Dwight D. (Dwight David), 1890-1969. 2. United States — Politics and government — 1953-1961 3. United States — Foreign relations — 1953-1961 I. T.
E835.A3   973.921   LC 61-6191

Alexander, Charles C.   **3.7817**
Holding the line: the Eisenhower era, 1952–1961 / Charles C. Alexander. — Bloomington: Indiana University Press, 1975. xviii, 326 p.: front.; 22 cm. (America since World War II) Includes index. 1. United States — Politics and government — 1953-1961 2. United States — Foreign relations — 1953-1961 I. T.
E835.A645 1975   320.9/73/0921   LC 74-11714   ISBN 0253328403

Bell, Daniel. ed.   • **3.7818**
The new American right. New York, Criterion Books [1955] xii, 239 p. 22 cm. Subsequently published under title: The radical right. 1. Conservatism 2. United States — Politics and government — 1953-1961 I. T.
E835.B4   LC 55-11024

Branyan, Robert L. comp.   • **3.7819**
The Eisenhower administration, 1953–1961: a documentary history / [by] Robert L. Branyan [and] Lawrence H. Larsen. — [1st ed.] New York: Random House [1971] 2 v. (1414 p.); 25 cm. 1. Eisenhower, Dwight D. (Dwight David),

1890-1969. 2. United States — Politics and government — 1953-1961 — Sources. I. Larsen, Lawrence Harold, 1931- joint comp. II. T.
E835.B685   973.921/.0924 B   LC 71-164935   ISBN 0394472411

Cook, Blanche Wiesen.   3.7820
The declassified Eisenhower: a divided legacy / Blanche Wiesen Cook. — 1st ed. — Garden City, N.Y.: Doubleday, 1981. xxiv, 432 p.: maps; 24 cm. Includes index. 1. Eisenhower, Dwight D. (Dwight David), 1890-1969. 2. Presidents — United States — Biography 3. United States — Foreign relations — 1953-1961 4. United States — Foreign relations — 1945-1953 I. T.
E835.C57   327.73/0092/4 19   LC 80-699   ISBN 0385054564

Divine, Robert A.   3.7821
Eisenhower and the cold war / Robert A. Divine. — New York: Oxford University Press, 1981. ix, 181 p.; 20 cm. 1. Eisenhower, Dwight D. (Dwight David), 1890-1969. 2. United States — Foreign relations — 1953-1961 I. T.
E835.D54   327.73/0092/4 19   LC 80-20600   ISBN 0195028236

Donovan, Robert J.   • 3.7822
Eisenhower: the inside story / by Robert J. Donovan. — New York: Harper, 1956. xviii, 423 p.: ill., ports. 1. Eisenhower, Dwight D. (Dwight David), 1890-1969. 2. United States — Politics and government — 1953-1961 3. United States — Foreign relations — 1945- I. T.
E835.D6   973.92   LC 56-9653

Hughes, Emmet John, 1920-.   • 3.7823
The ordeal of power: a political memoir of the Eisenhower years. — [1st ed.] New York: Atheneum, 1963. 372 p.; 22 cm. 1. Eisenhower, Dwight D. (Dwight David), 1890-1969. 2. United States — Politics and government — 1953-1961 I. T.
E835.H8 1963   973.921   LC 63-12783

Kennan, George Frost, 1904-.   3.7824
Realities of American foreign policy [by] George F. Kennan. — New York: Norton, [1966] ix, 119 p.; 20 cm. — (The Norton library, N320) First published in 1954. 1. World politics — 1945- 2. United States — Foreign relations — 1953-1961 I. T.
E835.K4 1966   327.73   LC 66-15309

Kissinger, Henry, 1923-.   • 3.7825
The necessity for choice; prospects of American foreign policy. [1st ed.] New York: Harper [1961] 370 p.; 22 cm. 1. World politics — 1955-1965 2. United States — Military policy 3. United States — Foreign relations — 1953-1961 I. T.
E835.K5   327.73   LC 61-6187

Larson, Arthur.   • 3.7826
A Republican looks at his party. [1st ed.] New York, Harper [1956] 210 p. 22 cm. 1. Republican Party (U.S.) 2. United States — Politics and government — 1953- I. T.
E835.L3   LC 56-9671

Lodge, Henry Cabot, 1902-.   3.7827
As it was: an inside view of politics and power in the '50s and '60s / Henry Cabot Lodge. — 1st ed. — New York: Norton, c1976. 224 p.; 22 cm. 1. Lodge, Henry Cabot, 1902- 2. United States — Politics and government — 1953-1961 3. United States — Foreign relations — 1953-1961 I. T.
E835.L57 1976   973.921/092/4 B   LC 76-17615   ISBN 0393055973

Lubell, Samuel.   • 3.7828
Revolt of the moderates. [1st ed.] New York: Harper [1956] 308 p.: ill.; 22 cm. 1. United States — Politics and government — 1953- I. T.
E 835 L92   LC 56-6118

Parmet, Herbert S.   • 3.7829
Eisenhower and the American crusades [by] Herbert S. Parmet. New York, Macmillan [1972] xi, 660 p. illus. 24 cm. 1. Eisenhower, Dwight D. (Dwight David), 1890-1969. 2. United States — Politics and government — 1953-1961 I. T.
E835.P3 1972   973.921/092/4   LC 73-189680

Richardson, Elmo R.   3.7830
The Presidency of Dwight D. Eisenhower / by Elmo Richardson. — Lawrence: Regents Press of Kansas, c1979. x, 218 p.; 24 cm. — (American presidency series.) Includes index. 1. Eisenhower, Dwight D. (Dwight David), 1890-1969. 2. Presidents — United States — Biography 3. United States — Politics and government — 1953-1961 I. T. II. Series.
E835.R53   973.921   LC 78-17923   ISBN 070060183X

Rovere, Richard Halworth, 1915-.   • 3.7831
The Eisenhower years; affairs of state / Richard H. Rovere. — New York: Farrar, Straus and Cudahy, 1956. xii, 390 p. 1. United States — Politics and government — 1953-1961 2. United States — Foreign relations — 1953-1961 I. T.
E835.R6   LC 56-6153

Eisenhower, Dwight D. (Dwight David), 1890-1969.   3.7832
The Eisenhower diaries / edited by Robert H. Ferrell. — 1st ed. — New York: Norton, c1981. xvii, 445 p.: ill.; 24 cm. Includes index. 1. Eisenhower, Dwight D. (Dwight David), 1890-1969. 2. Presidents — United States — Biography I. Ferrell, Robert H. II. T.
E836.A3155 1981   973.921/092/4 B 19   LC 80-27866   ISBN 0393014320

Ambrose, Stephen E.   3.7833
Eisenhower / Stephen E. Ambrose. — New York: Simon and Schuster, c1984. 2v.: ill.; 25 cm. 1. Eisenhower, Dwight D. (Dwight David), 1890-1969. 2. Presidents — United States — Biography I. T.
E836.A828 1983   973.921/092/4 B 19   LC 83-9892   ISBN 0671440691

Ambrose, Stephen E.   • 3.7834
The Supreme Commander: the war years of General Dwight D. Eisenhower / [by] Stephen E. Ambrose. — [1st ed.] Garden City, N.Y.: Doubleday, 1970. ix, 732 p.: col. maps, port.; 24 cm. 1. Eisenhower, Dwight D. (Dwight David), 1890-1969. 2. World War, 1939-1945 — Campaigns I. T.
E836.A83   940.54 B   LC 77-111141

Childs, Marquis William, 1903-.   3.7835
Eisenhower: captive hero; a critical study of the general and the President. [1st ed.] New York, Harcourt, Brace [1958] 310 p. illus. 21 cm. 1. Eisenhower, Dwight D. (Dwight David), 1890-1969. I. T.
E836.C5   923.173   LC 58-10905

Eisenhower, David, 1948-.   3.7836
Eisenhower at war, 1943–1945 / by David Eisenhower. — 1st ed. — New York: Random House, c1986-. xxvii, 977 p., [16] p. of plates: ill., maps. Includes index. 1. Eisenhower, Dwight D. (Dwight David), 1890-1969 — Military leadership. 2. United States. Army — Biography 3. Generals — United States — Biography. I. T.
E836.E38   973.921/092/4 B 19   LC 81-40212   ISBN 0394412370

Greenstein, Fred I.   3.7837
The hidden–hand presidency: Eisenhower as leader / Fred I. Greenstein. — New York: Basic Books, c1982. x, 286 p., [4] leaves of plates: ports.; 25 cm. 1. Eisenhower, Dwight D. (Dwight David), 1890-1969. 2. Leadership — Case studies. 3. United States — Politics and government — 1953-1961 I. T.
E836.G73 1982   353.03/1/0924 19   LC 82-70847   ISBN 0465029485

Larson, Arthur.   • 3.7838
Eisenhower: the President nobody knew. New York: Scribner [1968] xii, 210 p.: ill., ports.; 22 cm. 1. Eisenhower, Dwight D. (Dwight David), 1890-1969. I. T.
E836.L3   973.921/0924   LC 68-27778

E838–879 Later 20th Century (1961–

Hochman, Stanley.   3.7839
Yesterday and today: a dictionary of recent American history / Stanley Hochman. — New York: McGraw-Hill, c1979. viii, 407 p.: ill.; 24 cm. Includes index. 1. United States — History — 1945- — Dictionaries. I. T.
E838.6.H62   973.9   LC 79-12265   ISBN 0070291039

Brzezinski, Zbigniew K., 1928-.   • 3.7840
Between two ages: America's role in the technetronic era / [by] Zbigniew Brzezinski. — New York: Viking Press, [1970] xvii, 334 p.; 23 cm. 'Prepared under the auspices of the Research Institute on Communist Affairs, Columbia University.' 1. International relations 2. U.S. — Civilization — 1970- I. Columbia University. Research Institute on Communist Affairs. II. T.
E839.B7 1970   301.2/4   LC 76-104162   ISBN 0670160415

Heath, Jim F.   3.7841
Decade of disillusionment: the Kennedy–Johnson years / Jim F. Heath. — Bloomington: Indiana University Press, [1975] xvi, 332 p.; 22 cm. (America since World War II) Includes index. 1. United States — Politics and government — 1961-1963 2. United States — Politics and government — 1963-1969 I. T.
E839.H42 1975   973.922   LC 74-18871   ISBN 0253316701

O'Neill, William L.   • 3.7842
Coming apart; an informal history of America in the 1960's [by] William L. O'Neill. — Chicago: Quadrangle Books, 1971. ix, 442, xxvi p.: illus., ports.; 24 cm. 1. United States — History — 1961-1969 2. United States — Politics and government — 1945- I. T.
E839.O5 1971   973.921   LC 79-152098   ISBN 0812901908

Lubell, Samuel.   • **3.7843**
The hidden crisis in American politics. — [1st ed.]. — New York: Norton, [1970] 306 p.; 22 cm. 1. U.S. — Politics and government — 1945- I. T.
E839.5.L8 1970   320.9/73   *LC* 69-17630   *ISBN* 0393053709

Peirce, Neal R.   • **3.7844**
The megastates of America: people, politics, and power in the ten great States / [by] Neal R. Peirce. — [1st ed.] New York: Norton [1972] 745 p.; 24 cm. 1. State governments 2. United States — Politics and government — 1945- 3. United States — Economic conditions — 1971-1981 4. United States — Social conditions — 1960- I. T.
E839.5.P35   917.3/03/92   *LC* 70-163375   *ISBN* 0393054586

Rubin, Richard L.   **3.7845**
Press, party, and presidency / Richard L. Rubin. — 1st ed. — New York: Norton, c1981. x, 246 p.; 22 cm. Includes index. 1. Press and politics — United States. 2. Presidents — United States — Election 3. United States — Politics and government — 1945- I. T.
E839.5.R82 1981   320.973 19   *LC* 81-14108   *ISBN* 0393014975

Chomsky, Noam.   **3.7846**
Towards a new cold war: essays on the current crisis and how we got there / Noam Chomsky. — New York: Pantheon Books, c1982. 498 p.; 25 cm. 1. Kissinger, Henry, 1923- — Addresses, essays, lectures. 2. World politics — 1945- — Addresses, essays, lectures. 3. United States — Foreign relations — 1969-1974 — Addresses, essays, lectures. 4. United States — Foreign relations — 1945- — Addresses, essays, lectures. I. T.
E840.C49 1982   327.73 19   *LC* 81-47190   *ISBN* 039451873X

Gregg, Robert W., comp.   **3.7847**
After Vietnam: the future of American foreign policy / edited by Robert W. Gregg and Charles W. Kegley, Jr. — Garden City, N.Y.: Doubleday, 1971. ix, 343 p.; 18 cm. Includes 6 papers from a symposium held Feb., 1970 at the Maxwell Graduate School of Citizenship and Public Affairs, Syracuse University. 1. U.S. — Foreign relations — 1945- — Addresses, essays, lectures. I. Kegley, Charles W. joint comp. II. T.
E840.G73   327.73   *LC* 73-139077

Hilsman, Roger.   **3.7848**
To move a nation: the politics of foreign policy in the administration of John F. Kennedy. — [1st ed.] Garden City, N.Y.: Doubleday, 1967. xxii, 602 p.: maps; 24 cm. 1. Kennedy, John F. (John Fitzgerald), 1917-1963. 2. United States — Foreign relations — 1961-1963 I. T.
E840.H5   327.73   *LC* 67-10407

Lenczowski, John.   **3.7849**
Soviet perceptions of U.S. foreign policy: a study of ideology, power, and consensus / John Lenczowski. — Ithaca: Cornell University Press, 1982. 318 p.; 23 cm. 1. Public opinion — Soviet Union. 2. United States — Foreign relations — 1945- — Public opinion. I. T. II. Title: Soviet perceptions of US foreign policy. III. Title: Soviet perceptions of United States foreign policy.
E840.L42 1982   327.73 19   *LC* 81-70713   *ISBN* 0801414512

Lens, Sidney.   **3.7850**
The Maginot Line syndrome: America's hopeless foreign policy / Sidney Lens. — Cambridge, Mass.: Ballinger Pub. Co., 1983 (c1982). vii, 194 p.; 24 cm. 1. United States — Foreign relations — 1945- 2. United States — National security I. T.
E840.L43 1982   327.73 19   *LC* 82-20652   *ISBN* 0884108422

No more Vietnams? The war and the future of American foreign   • **3.7851**
policy. Contributors: Eqbal Ahmad [and others] Edited by
Richard M. Pfeffer.
[1st ed.]. — New York: Published for the Adlai Stevenson Institute of International Affairs by Harper & Row, [1968] x, 299 p.; 22 cm. 1. Vietnamese Conflict, 1961-1975 — United States 2. United States — Foreign relations — 1963-1969 I. Ahmad, Eqbal. II. Pfeffer, Richard M., ed. III. Adlai Stevenson Institute of International Affairs.
E840.N6   327.73   *LC* 68-58302

White, Theodore Harold, 1915-.   • **3.7852**
The making of the President, 1960. [1st ed.] New York, Atheneum Publishers, 1961. 400 p. 25 cm. 1. Nixon, Richard M. (Richard Milhous), 1913- 2. Kennedy, John F. (John Fitzgerald), 1917-1963. 3. Presidents — United States — Election — 1960. I. T.
E840.W5   329/.023/730921   *LC* 61-9259

E840.6–840.8 Biography

Parker, Thomas, 1947-.   **3.7853**
America's foreign policy, 1945–1976: its creators and critics / by Thomas Parker. — New York, N.Y.: Facts on File, c1980. xxvi, 246 p.; 26 cm. Includes index. 1. Statesmen — United States — Biography. 2. Legislators — United

States — Biography. 3. Politicians — United States — Biography. 4. Diplomats — United States — Biography. 5. United States — Foreign relations — 1945- I. T.
E840.6.P37   327.73/0092/2 B 19   *LC* 80-21192   *ISBN* 0871964562

Political profiles / editor, Nelson Lichtenstein, associate editor,   **3.7854**
Eleanora W. Schoenebaum.
New York: Facts on File, inc., c1976-. v.; 27 cm. Vol. [4]: associate editors: E. W. Schoenebaum and M. L. Levine. 1. United States — History — 1945- — Biography — Collected works. 2. United States — Biography — Collected works. I. Lichtenstein, Nelson. II. Schoenebaum, Eleanora W. III. Levine, Michael L. IV. Facts on File, Inc.
E840.6.P64   920/.073   *LC* 76-20897   *ISBN* 0871964503

Cohen, Richard M.   **3.7855**
A heartbeat away: the investigation and resignation of Vice President Spiro T. Agnew / [by] Richard M. Cohen [and] Jules Witcover. — New York: Viking Press, [1974] viii, 373 p.: ill.; 22 cm. 'A Washington Post book.' 1. Agnew, Spiro T., 1918- 2. Corruption (in politics) — Maryland. I. Witcover, Jules. joint author. II. T.
E840.8.A34 C56 1974   973.924/092/4 B   *LC* 74-28   *ISBN* 0670364738

Chisholm, Shirley, 1924-.   • **3.7856**
Unbought and unbossed. — Boston: Houghton Mifflin, 1970. xii, 177 p.; 22 cm. 1. United States — Politics and government — 1969-1974 I. T.
E840.8.C48 A3   328.73/0924   *LC* 79-120834

MacNeil, Neil, 1923-.   **3.7857**
Dirksen: portrait of a public man. — New York: World Pub. Co., [1970] xii, 402 p.: ports.; 24 cm. 1. Dirksen, Everett McKinley. I. T.
E840.8.D5 M3 1970   973.91/0924 B   *LC* 79-112432

Johnson, U. Alexis (Ural Alexis), 1908-.   **3.7858**
The right hand of power / U. Alexis Johnson with Jef Olivarius McAllister. — Englewood Cliffs, N.J.: Prentice-Hall, c1984. vi, 634 p.; 24 cm. Includes index. 1. Johnson, U. Alexis (Ural Alexis), 1908- 2. Diplomats — United States — Biography. 3. Vietnamese Conflict, 1961-1975 — Diplomatic history. 4. Korean War, 1950-1953 — Diplomatic history I. McAllister, Jef Olivarius. II. T.
E840.8.J59 A37 1984   327.2/092/4 B 19   *LC* 83-27067   *ISBN* 013781139X

Kissinger, Henry, 1923-.   **3.7859**
Years of upheaval / Henry Kissinger. — 1st ed. — Boston: Little, Brown, c1982. xxi, 1283 p., [40] p. of plates: ill.; 25 cm. 1. Kissinger, Henry, 1923- 2. Statesmen — United States — Biography. 3. United States — Foreign relations — 1969-1974 I. T.
E840.8.K58 A38   973.924/092/4 19   *LC* 81-86320   *ISBN* 0316285919

Kalb, Marvin L.   **3.7860**
Kissinger, by Marvin Kalb and Bernard Kalb. [1st ed.] Boston, Little, Brown [1974] xiii, 577 p. illus. 25 cm. 1. Kissinger, Henry, 1923- 2. United States — Foreign relations — 1969-1974 I. Kalb, Bernard. joint author. II. T.
E840.8.K58 K34   973.924/092/4 B   *LC* 74-5892

E841–879 By Presidential Administration

E841–843 Kennedy, 1961–1963

Chayes, Abram, 1922-.   **3.7861**
The Cuban missile crisis. — New York: Oxford University Press, 1974. viii, 157 p.; 22 cm. — (International crises and the role of law) 'Published under the auspices of the American Society of International Law.' 1. Cuban Missile Crisis, Oct. 1962 2. International law I. T. II. Series.
E841.C48 1974b   972.91/064   *LC* 74-75041   *ISBN* 0195197585

Dinerstein, Herbert Samuel, 1919-.   **3.7862**
The making of a missile crisis, October 1962 / Herbert S. Dinerstein. — Baltimore: Johns Hopkins Press, c1976. xii, 302 p.; 24 cm. 1. Cuban Missile Crisis, Oct. 1962 2. Russia — Foreign relations — Cuba. 3. Cuba — Foreign relations — Russia. I. T.
E841.D45   972.91/064   *LC* 75-36943   *ISBN* 0801817889

Fairlie, Henry, 1924-.   **3.7863**
The Kennedy promise; the politics of expectation. [1st ed.] Garden City, N.Y., Doubleday, 1973. 376 p. 22 cm. 1. Kennedy, John F. (John Fitzgerald), 1917-1963. 2. Kennedy, Robert F., 1925-1968. 3. United States — Politics and

government — 1945- 4. United States — Politics and government — 1961-1963 I. T.
E841.F34   320.9/73/0922   *LC* 70-186018   *ISBN* 0385005598

Halberstam, David.   3.7864
The best and the brightest. [1st ed.] New York: Random House [1972] 688 p.; 25 cm. 1. Vietnamese Conflict, 1961-1975 — United States 2. United States — Politics and government — 1963-1969 3. United States — Politics and government — 1961-1963 I. T.
E841.H25   973.922   *LC* 72-2728   *ISBN* 0394461630

Mailer, Norman.   • 3.7865
The presidential papers. — New York: Putnam, [1963] 310 p.; 22 cm. 1. United States — Civilization — 1945- — Miscellanea. I. T.
E841.M25   818.54   *LC* 63-20753

Miroff, Bruce.   3.7866
Pragmatic illusions: the Presidential politics of John F. Kennedy / Bruce Miroff. — New York: McKay, c1976. xvii, 334 p.; 22 cm. 1. Kennedy, John F. (John Fitzgerald), 1917-1963. 2. United States — Foreign relations — 1961-1963 3. United States — Politics and government — 1961-1963 I. T.
E841.M54   973.922/092/4   *LC* 76-7554   *ISBN* 0679302980

Paper, Lewis J.   3.7867
The promise and the performance: the leadership of John F. Kennedy / by Lewis J. Paper. — New York: Crown Publishers, [1975] xi, 408 p.; 24 cm. Published in 1980 under title: John F. Kennedy. 1. Kennedy, John F. (John Fitzgerald), 1917-1963. 2. United States — Politics and government — 1961-1963 I. T.
E841.P35 1975   973.922/092/4   *LC* 75-19456   *ISBN* 0517523426

Salinger, Pierre.   • 3.7868
With Kennedy. [1st ed.] Garden City, N.Y., Doubleday, 1966. xvi, 391 p. ports. 24 cm. 1. Kennedy, John F. (John Fitzgerald), 1917-1963. 2. United States — History — 1961-1969 I. T.
E841.S2   973.9220924   *LC* 66-17423

Schlesinger, Arthur Meier, 1917-.   • 3.7869
A thousand days; John F. Kennedy in the White House [by] Arthur M. Schlesinger, Jr. Boston, Houghton Mifflin, 1965. xiv, 1087 p. 22 cm. 1. Kennedy, John F. (John Fitzgerald), 1917-1963. 2. United States — Politics and government — 1961-1963 I. T.
E841.S3   973.922   *LC* 65-20218

Sorensen, Theodore C.   • 3.7870
Kennedy / [by] Theodore C. Sorensen. [1st ed.] New York: Harper & Row [1965] viii, 783 p.: port.; 25 cm. 1. Kennedy, John F. (John Fitzgerald), 1917-1963. 2. United States — History — 1961-1969 I. T.
E841.S6   973.922   *LC* 65-14660

Blair, Joan, 1929-.   3.7871
The search for JFK / by Joan and Clay Blair, Jr. — New York: Berkley Pub. Corp.: distributed by Putnam, c1976. 608 p., [16] leaves of plates: ill.; 24 cm. Includes index. 1. Kennedy, John F. (John Fitzgerald), 1917-1963. I. Blair, Clay, 1925- joint author. II. T.
E842.B58 1976   973.922/092/4 B   *LC* 76-8257   *ISBN* 0399114181

Bradlee, Benjamin.   3.7872
Conversations with Kennedy / Benjamin C. Bradlee. — New York: Norton, [1975] 251 p.: ill.; 22 cm. 1. Kennedy, John F. (John Fitzgerald), 1917-1963. 2. Bradlee, Benjamin. I. Kennedy, John F. (John Fitzgerald), 1917-1963. II. T.
E842.B69   973.922/092/4 B   *LC* 75-4736   *ISBN* 0393087220

Burns, James MacGregor.   • 3.7873
John Kennedy: a political profile. [1st ed.] New York, Harcourt, Brace [1960] 309 p. illus. 21 cm. 1. Kennedy, John F. (John Fitzgerald), 1917-1963. I. T.
E842.B8 1960   923.273   *LC* 60-5440

Manchester, William Raymond, 1922-.   • 3.7874
Portrait of a President: John F. Kennedy in profile / [by] William Manchester. — Rev. ed., with a new introd. and epilogue. Boston: Little, Brown [1967] xxii, 266 p.; 21 cm. 1. Kennedy, John F. (John Fitzgerald), 1917-1963. I. T.
E842.M3 1967   973.922/0924   *LC* 67-12910

Parmet, Herbert S.   3.7875
JFK, the presidency of John F. Kennedy / Herbert S. Parmet. — New York: Dial Press, c1983. viii, 407 p.; 24 cm. 1. Kennedy, John F. (John Fitzgerald), 1917-1963. 2. Presidents — United States — Biography 3. United States — Politics and government — 1961-1963 I. T. II. Title: J.F.K., the presidency of John F. Kennedy.
E842.P34 1983   973.922/092/4 B 19   *LC* 82-14575   *ISBN* 038527419X

Sidey, Hugh.   3.7876
John F. Kennedy, President. [1st ed.] New York: Atheneum, 1963. 400 p.; 24 cm. 1. Kennedy, John F. (John Fitzgerald), 1917-1963. 2. United States — Politics and government — 1961-1963 I. T.
E842.S5   923.173   *LC* 63-7800

United States. Warren Commission.   • 3.7877
Report of the Warren Commission on the Assassination of President Kennedy: introd. by Harrison E. Salisbury / with additional material prepared by the New York Times exclusively for this edition. — [1st ed.] New York: McGraw-Hill Book Co. [1964] xl, 726 p.: ill., ports.; 22 cm. 1. Kennedy, John F. (John Fitzgerald), 1917-1963 — Assassination. I. T.
E842.9.A55 1964b   364.152   *LC* 64-24803

Belin, David W.   3.7878
November 22, 1963; you are the jury [by] David W. Belin. [New York]: Quadrangle [1973] xiii, 521 p.; 25 cm. 1. Kennedy, John F. (John Fitzgerald), 1917-1963 — Assassination. I. T.
E842.9.B44   973.922/092/4 B   *LC* 73-82479   *ISBN* 0812903749

Epstein, Edward Jay, 1935-.   • 3.7879
Inquest: the Warren Commission and the establishment of truth / introd. by Richard H. Rovere. — New York: Viking Press [1966] xix, 224 p.: ill., map; 22 cm. 1. Kennedy, John F. (John Fitzgerald), 1917-1963 — Assassination. 2. Warren Commission. Report of the President's Commission on the Assassination of President John F. Kennedy. I. T.
E842.9.E6   364.15/24   *LC* 66-21197

Guth, DeLloyd J., 1938-.   3.7880
The assassination of John F. Kennedy: a comprehensive historical and legal bibliography, 1963–1979 / compiled by DeLloyd J. Guth and David R. Wrone. — Westport, Conn.: Greenwood Press, 1980. lvi, 442 p.: maps; 25 cm. Includes indexes. 1. Kennedy, John F. (John Fitzgerald), 1917-1963 — Assassination — Bibliography. I. Wrone, David R. joint author. II. T.
E842.9.G8x   016.973922/092/4   *LC* 79-6184   *ISBN* 0313212740

Meagher, Sylvia.   3.7881
Master index to the J. F. K. assassination investigations: the reports and supporting volumes of the House Select Committee on Assassinations and the Warren Commission / by Sylvia Meagher, in collaboration with Gary Owens. — Metuchen, N.J.: Scarecrow Press, 1980. xi, 435 p.; 23 cm. Includes indexes. Pt. 2 of this book is a slightly amended version of the author's Subject index to the Warren report and hearings & exhibits. 1. Kennedy, John F. (John Fitzgerald), 1917-1963 — Assassination — Indexes. 2. United States. Congress. House. Select Committee on Assassinations Investigation of the assassination of President John F. Kennedy — Indexes. 3. Warren Commission. Investigation of the assassination of President John F. Kennedy; hearings — Indexes. I. Owens, Gary, 1939- joint author. II. Meagher, Sylvia. Subject index to the Warren report and hearings & exhibits. III. T.
E842.9.M4x   364.1/524/0924   *LC* 80-17494   *ISBN* 0810813319

United States. Congress. House. Select Committee on Assassinations.   3.7882
Report of the Select Committee on Assassinations, U.S. House of Representatives, Ninety-fifth Congress, second session: findings and recommendations. — Washington: U.S. Govt. Print. Off.: for sale by the Supt. of Docs., U.S. Govt. Print. Off., 1979. xiii, 686 p.; 23 cm. (House report - 95th Congress, 2d session; no. 95-1828, pt. 2) At head of title: Union calendar no. 962. 'March 29, 1979.' 1. Kennedy, John F. (John Fitzgerald), 1917-1963 — Assassination. 2. King, Martin Luther, Jr., 1929-1968 — Assassination. I. T.
E842.9.U6x   364.1/524/0973 19   *LC* 79-603369

Wills, Garry, 1934-.   3.7883
The Kennedy imprisonment: a meditation on power / Garry Wills. — 1st ed. — Boston: Little, Brown, c1982. 310 p.; 25 cm. 'An Atlantic Monthly Press book.' Includes index. 1. Kennedy family 2. Power (Social sciences) I. T.
E843.W54   973.922/092/2 19   *LC* 81-18649   *ISBN* 0316943851

E846–848 Johnson, 1963–1969

Geyelin, Philip L.   3.7884
Lyndon B. Johnson and the world by Philip Geyelin. New York: F. A. Praeger, 1966. viii, 309 p.; 22 cm. 1. Johnson, Lyndon Baines, President United States, 1908- 2. United States — Foreign relations — 1963- I. T.
E846.G45   *LC* 66-13684

Johnson, Lyndon B. (Lyndon Baines), 1908-1973.   • 3.7885
The vantage point: perspectives of the Presidency, 1963–1969. — [1st ed.] New York: Holt, Rinehart and Winston [1971] x, 636 p.: ill.; 25 cm. 1. Johnson, Lyndon B. (Lyndon Baines), 1908-1973. 2. United States — Politics and government — 1963-1969 I. T.
E846.J58   973.923   *LC* 74-102146   *ISBN* 0030844924

Caro, Robert A.   **3.7886**
The years of Lyndon Johnson / Robert A. Caro. — 1st ed. — New York: Knopf, 1982. 882 p.: ill. Includes index. 1. Johnson, Lyndon B. (Lyndon Baines), 1908-1973. 2. Presidents — United States — Biography 3. United States — Politics and government — 1945- I. T.
E847.C34 1982   973.923/092/4 B 19   *LC* 82-47811   *ISBN* 0394499735

Dugger, Ronnie.   **3.7887**
The politician: the life and times of Lyndon Johnson: the drive for power, from the frontier to master of the Senate / by Ronnie Dugger. — New York: Norton, c1982. 514 p., [46] p. of plates: ill.; 24 cm. Includes index. 1. Johnson, Lyndon B. (Lyndon Baines), 1908-1973. 2. Presidents — United States — Biography 3. Texas — Politics and government — 1865-1950 4. United States — Politics and government — 1933-1945 5. United States — Politics and government — 1945- I. T.
E847.D78 1982   973.923/092/4 B 19   *LC* 81-22507   *ISBN* 039301598X

Evans, Rowland, 1921-.   • **3.7888**
Lyndon B. Johnson; the exercise of power; a political biography, by Rowland Evans & Robert Novak. [New York] New American Library [1966] viii, 597 p. 24 cm. 1. Johnson, Lyndon B. (Lyndon Baines), 1908-1973. 2. United States — Politics and government — 1933-1945 3. United States — Politics and government — 1945- I. Novak, Robert D. joint author. II. T.
E847.E9   973.9230924   *LC* 66-26040

Goldman, Eric Frederick, 1915-.   **3.7889**
The tragedy of Lyndon Johnson, by Eric F. Goldman. [1st ed.] New York: Knopf, 1969. xii, 531, xxi p.; 25 cm. 1. Johnson, Lyndon B. (Lyndon Baines), 1908-1973. 2. United States — Politics and government — 1963-1969 I. T.
E847.G6   973.923/0924   *LC* 67-22220

Goodwin, Doris Kearns.   **3.7890**
Lyndon Johnson and the American dream / Doris Kearns. — 1st ed. — New York: Harper & Row, c1976. xii, 432 p.; 24 cm. 1. Johnson, Lyndon B. (Lyndon Baines), 1908-1973. 2. Presidents — United States — Biography 3. United States — Politics and government — 1963-1969 I. T.
E847.K42 1976   973.923/092/4 B   *LC* 75-42831   *ISBN* 0060122846

Miller, Merle, 1919-.   **3.7891**
Lyndon, an oral biography / Merle Miller. — New York: Putnam, c1980. xix, 645 p.; 24 cm. Includes index. 1. Johnson, Lyndon B. (Lyndon Baines), 1908-1973. 2. Presidents — United States — Biography I. T.
E847.M54 1980   973.923/092/4 B   *LC* 80-273   *ISBN* 0399123571

E850–851 Presidential Campaigns of 1964, 1968

White, Theodore Harold, 1915-.   • **3.7892**
The making of the President, 1964 / Theodore H. White. — [1st ed.] — New York: Atheneum Publishers, 1965. xi, 431 p.; 25 cm. 1. Presidents — United States — Election — 1964. 2. United States — Politics and government — 1963-1969 I. T.
E850.W5   973.92   *LC* 65-18328

McCarthy, Eugene J., 1916-.   • **3.7893**
The year of the people [by] Eugene J. McCarthy. — [1st ed.]. — Garden City, N.Y.: Doubleday, 1969. viii, 323 p.; 22 cm. 1. Presidents — U.S. — Election — 1968. I. T.
E851.M28   329/.023/0973   *LC* 71-93229

McGinniss, Joe.   • **3.7894**
The selling of the President, 1968. New York, Trident Press [1969] 253 p. 22 cm. 1. Nixon, Richard M. (Richard Milhous), 1913- 2. Presidents — United States — Election — 1968. 3. Television in politics I. T.
E851.M3   329/.023/0973   *LC* 77-92157   *ISBN* 0671270435

White, Theodore Harold, 1915-.   **3.7895**
The making of the President, 1968 [by] Theodore H. White. — [1st ed.]. — New York: Atheneum Publishers, 1969. xii, 459 p.: maps (on lining papers); 25 cm. 1. Presidents — United States — Election — 1968. I. T.
E851.W5   329/.023/730923   *LC* 78-81935

E855–861 Nixon, 1969–1974

Brandon, Henry, 1916-.   • **3.7896**
The retreat of American power. [1st ed.] Garden City, N.Y., Doubleday, 1973. xiii, 368 p. 22 cm. 1. Nixon, Richard M. (Richard Milhous), 1913- 2. Kissinger, Henry, 1923- 3. United States — Foreign relations — 1969-1974 I. T.
E855.B67   327.73   *LC* 72-90969   *ISBN* 0385016557

Brown, Seyom.   **3.7897**
The crises of power: an interpretation of United States foreign policy during the Kissinger Years / by Seyom Brown. — New York: Columbia University Press, 1979. xi, 170 p.; 24 cm. 1. Kissinger, Henry, 1923- 2. United States — Foreign relations — 1974-1977 3. United States — Foreign relations — 1969-1974 I. T.
E855.B76   327.73   *LC* 79-15796   *ISBN* 0231042647

Drury, Allen.   **3.7898**
Courage and hesitation; notes and photographs of the Nixon administration. Notes by Allen Drury. Photos. by Fred Maroon. [1st ed.] Garden City, N.Y., Doubleday, 1971. 416 p. illus. 27 cm. 1. Nixon, Richard M. (Richard Milhous), 1913- 2. United States — Politics and government — 1969- I. Maroon, Fred J. II. T.
E855.D7   320.9/73/0924   *LC* 71-163205

Evans, Rowland, 1921-.   • **3.7899**
Nixon in the White House: the frustration of power [by] Rowland Evans, Jr., & Robert D. Novak. [1st ed.] New York: Random House [1971] viii, 431 p.; 25 cm. 1. Nixon, Richard M. (Richard Milhous), 1913- 2. United States — Politics and government — 1969-1974 I. Novak, Robert D. joint author. II. T.
E855.E9   973.924/0924 B   *LC* 75-140702   *ISBN* 0394462734

Kissinger, Henry, 1923-.   **3.7900**
White House years / Henry Kissinger. — 1st ed. — Boston: Little, Brown, c1979. xxiv, 1521 p., [24] leaves of plates: ill.; 25 cm. 1. Nixon, Richard M. (Richard Milhous), 1913- 2. Kissinger, Henry, 1923- 3. Statesmen — United States — Biography. 4. United States — Foreign relations — 1969-1974 I. T.
E855.K57   327.73   *LC* 79-90006   *ISBN* 0316496618

Macrae, Norman, 1923-.   • **3.7901**
The neurotic trillionaire; a survey of Mr. Nixon's America. — New York: Harcourt, Brace & World, [1970] xii, 112 p.; 20 cm. 'First appeared as a special supplement to the London economist on May 10, 1969.' 1. United States — Economic conditions — 1961-1971 2. United States — Social conditions — 1960- I. T.
E855.M3   309.1/73   *LC* 72-117929   *ISBN* 0155657216

Morris, Roger.   **3.7902**
Uncertain greatness: Henry Kissinger and American foreign policy / Roger Morris. — 1st ed. — New York: Harper & Row, c1977. viii, 312 p.; 25 cm. Includes index. 1. Kissinger, Henry, 1923- 2. Statesmen — United States — Biography. 3. United States — Foreign relations — 1969-1974 4. United States — Foreign relations — 1974-1977 I. T.
E855.M67 1977   327.73   *LC* 75-30339   *ISBN* 0060130970

Osborne, John, 1907-.   **3.7903**
[Nixon watch] The first two years of the Nixon watch. Illustrated by Robert Osborn and Bill Mauldin. Introductions by Tom Wicker and David Broder. New York, Liveright [1971] xv, 201, xiii, 218 p. illus. 22 cm. 'Liveright L-55.' Consists of articles which appeared in the New republic between Oct. 1968 and Jan. 1971. 1. Nixon, Richard M. (Richard Milhous), 1913- 2. United States — Politics and government — 1969-1974 I. Osborne, John, 1907- Second year of the Nixon watch. 1971. II. T. III. Title: Nixon watch. IV. Title: Second year of the Nixon watch.
E855.O813   973.924/0924   *LC* 70-177412   *ISBN* 087140060X

Osborne, John, 1907-.   **3.7904**
The third year of the Nixon watch. Illustrated by Pat Oliphant. New York, Liveright [1972] 216 p. illus. 22 cm. 1. Nixon, Richard M. (Richard Milhous), 1913- 2. United States — Politics and government — 1969-1974 I. Oliphant, Pat, 1935- illus. II. T.
E855.O83   973.924/092/4   *LC* 73-184101   *ISBN* 0871405512

Osborne, John, 1907-.   **3.7905**
The fourth year of the Nixon watch. Cartoons by Paul Conrad. New York, Liveright [1973] 218 p. illus. 22 cm. 'Consists of articles that appeared in the New republic between January 1972 and January 1973.' 1. Nixon, Richard M. (Richard Milhous), 1913- 2. United States — Politics and government — 1969-1974 I. T.
E855.O84   973.924/092/4   *LC* 72-97490   *ISBN* 0871405601

Osborne, John, 1907-.   **3.7906**
The fifth year of the Nixon watch. Caricatures by David Levine. New York, Liveright [1974] viii, 241 p. illus. 22 cm. Consists of articles that appeared in The New republic, Jan. 1973-Jan. 1974. 1. Nixon, Richard M. (Richard Milhous), 1913- 2. Watergate Affair, 1972-1974 3. United States — Politics and government — 1969- I. T.
E855.O85   320.9/73/0924   *LC* 73-93125   *ISBN* 0871405822

Reichley, James.   **3.7907**
Conservatives in an age of change: the Nixon and Ford administrations / A. James Reichley. — Washington, D.C.: Brookings Institution, c1981. xiv, 482 p.; 24 cm. 1. Nixon, Richard M. (Richard Milhous), 1913- 2. Ford, Gerald R., 1913- 3. United States — Politics and government — 1969-1974 4. United States — Politics and government — 1974-1977 I. T.
E855.R44   973.9 19   *LC* 81-1672   *ISBN* 0815773803

Safire, William, 1929-.   **3.7908**
Before the fall: an inside view of the pre–Watergate White House / William Safire. — 1st ed. — Garden City, N.Y.: Doubleday, 1975. xii, 704 p., [12] leaves of plates: ill.; 24 cm. Includes index. 1. Nixon, Richard M. (Richard Milhous), 1913- 2. United States — Politics and government — 1969-1974 I. T.
E855.S23   320.9/73/0924   LC 74-17771   ISBN 0385085958

Schell, Jonathan, 1943-.   **3.7909**
The time of illusion / Jonathan Schell. — 1st ed. — New York: Knopf: distributed by Random House, 1976, c1975. 392, xii p.; 22 cm. Includes index. 1. Watergate Affair, 1972-1974 2. United States — Politics and government — 1969-1974 I. T.
E855.S36 1976   320.9/73/0924   LC 75-35764   ISBN 0394402243

Ungar, Sanford J.   • **3.7910**
The papers & the papers: an account of the legal and political battle over the Pentagon papers / by Sanford J. Ungar. — [1st ed.] New York: Dutton, 1972. 319 p.; 25 cm. 1. The Pentagon papers. 2. Freedom of the press — United States. 3. United States — Politics and government — 1963-1969 4. United States — Politics and government — 1969-1974 I. T.
E855.U5 1972   323.44/5/0973   LC 77-190699   ISBN 0525174559

Nixon, Richard M. (Richard Milhous), 1913-.   **3.7911**
RN: the memoirs of Richard Nixon. — New York: Grosset & Dunlap, 1978. xi, 1120 p., [24] leaves of plates: ill.; 25 cm. 1. Nixon, Richard M. (Richard Milhous), 1913- 2. Presidents — United States — Biography 3. United States — Politics and government — 1945- I. T. II. Title: The memoirs of Richard Nixon.
E856.A35 1978   973.924/092/4   LC 77-87793   ISBN 0448143747

E859–860 Watergate Affair

Congressional Quarterly, inc.   **3.7912**
Watergate: chronology of a crisis / [compiled by editor William B. Dickinson, Jr.] Washington: Congressional Quarterly, inc., 1973. 291 p.: ill.; 28 cm. Based on material from CQ weekly report for the period covered. 1. Watergate Affair, 1972-1974 I. Dickinson, William B. ed. II. Goldstein, Janice L., ed. III. T.
E859.C62 1973   364.1/32/0973   LC 73-12792   ISBN 0871870592

United States. Congress. House. Comm. on the Judiciary.   **3.7913**
[Hearings on the impeachment of Richard M. Nixon]
Impeachment inquiry Books I–III: January 31–July 23, 1974. [S.l.]: U.S. Govt. Print. Off., 1974. 3 vols. (2258 p.) On spine: Committee on the Judiciary - Impeachment inquiry. 1. Watergate Affair, — 1972- 2. Presidents — United States — Election, 1972. 3. Corruption (in politics) — United States 4. Impeachment. I. T. II. Title: Impeachment inquiry.
E859.U6x

The Watergate hearings: break–in and cover–up; proceedings of   **3.7914**
the Senate Select Committee on Presidential Campaign
Activities as edited by the staff of the New York times.
Narrative by R. W. Apple, Jr. Chronology by Linda Amster.
General editor: Gerald Gold.
New York, Viking Press [c1973.] 886 p. illus. 23 cm. 1. Watergate Affair, 1972-1974 I. Apple, R. W. (Raymond Walter), 1934- II. United States. Congress. House. Select Committee on Presidential Campaign Activities. III. New York times
E 859 W32 1973   LC 73-14191   ISBN 0670751529

White, Theodore Harold, 1915-.   **3.7915**
The making of the President, 1972 [by] Theodore H. White. [1st ed.] New York, Atheneum Publishers, 1973. xix, 391 p. maps (on lining papers) 25 cm. 1. Nixon, Richard M. (Richard Milhous), 1913- 2. McGovern, George S. (George Stanley), 1922- 3. Presidents — United States — Election — 1972. I. T.
E859.W47 1973   329/.023/730924   LC 72-94252   ISBN 0689105533

Bernstein, Carl, 1944-.   **3.7916**
All the President's men [by] Carl Bernstein [and] Bob Woodward. New York, Simon and Schuster [1974] 349 p. ports. 24 cm. 'Portions of this book have appeared in Playboy magazine.' 1. Bernstein, Carl, 1944- 2. Woodward, Bob. 3. Washington post (1877) 4. Watergate Affair, 1972-1974 I. Woodward, Bob. joint author. II. T.
E860.B47   364.1/32/0973   LC 73-22334   ISBN 067121781X

Nixon, Richard M. (Richard Milhous), 1913-.   **3.7917**
Submission of recorded Presidential conversations to the Committee on the Judiciary of the House of Representatives, by Richard Nixon. [Washington, For sale by the Supt. of Docs., U.S. Govt. Print. Off.] 1974. 1308 p. 27 cm. 1. Nixon, Richard M. (Richard Milhous), 1913- 2. Watergate Affair, 1972-1974 — Sources. I. United States. Congress. House. Committee on the Judiciary. II. T.
E860.N58   364.1/32/0973   LC 74-601522

Congressional Quarterly, inc.   **3.7918**
Watergate: chronology of a crisis / [contributors, Marlyn Aycock ... et al.; editors, Mercer Cross, Elder Witt; art director, Howard Chapman]. — Washington: Congressional Quarterly, [1975] xxvii, 844, 195A p.: ill.; 29 cm. Includes index. 1. Watergate Affair, 1972-1974 I. Aycock, Marlyn. II. Cross, Mercer. III. Witt, Elder. IV. T.
E860.C64 1975   364.1/32/0973   LC 75-660   ISBN 0871870703

Dean, John W. (John Wesley), 1938-.   **3.7919**
Blind ambition: the White House years / by John W. Dean. — New York: Simon and Schuster, c1976. 415 p., [8] leaves of plates: ill.; 24 cm. Includes index. 1. Dean, John W. (John Wesley), 1938- 2. Watergate Affair, 1972-1974 — Personal narratives. 3. Lawyers — United States — Biography. 4. United States — Politics and government — 1969-1974 I. T.
E860.D38   364.1/32/0973   LC 76-26488   ISBN 0671224387

Drew, Elizabeth.   **3.7920**
Washington journal: the events of 1973–1974 / Elizabeth Drew. — 1st ed. — New York: Random House, [1975] xvii, 428 p.; 25 cm. 'Most of the material ... appeared originally in the New Yorker.' Includes index. 1. Nixon, Richard M. (Richard Milhous), 1913- — Impeachment 2. Nixon, Richard M. (Richard Milhous), 1913- — Resignation from office 3. Watergate Affair, 1972-1974 I. T.
E860.D73   973.924   LC 75-9803   ISBN 0394495756

Ervin, Sam J. (Sam James), 1896-1985.   **3.7921**
The whole truth: the Watergate conspiracy / Sam J. Ervin, Jr. — New York: Random House, c1980. xvi, 320 p.; 24 cm. Includes index. 1. Ervin, Sam J. (Sam James), 1896-1985. 2. Watergate Affair, 1972-1974 I. T.
E860.E78   364.1/32/0973   LC 78-21821   ISBN 0394480295

Lang, Gladys Engel.   **3.7922**
The battle for public opinion: the president, the press, and the polls during Watergate / Gladys Engel Lang and Kurt Lang. — New York: Columbia University Press, 1983. xiv, 353 p.; 24 cm. 1. Watergate Affair, 1972-1974 — Public opinion. 2. Public opinion — United States. 3. Press and politics — United States. I. Lang, Kurt, 1924- II. T.
E860.L36 1983   973.924 19   LC 82-12791   ISBN 023105548X

Lukas, J. Anthony, 1933-.   **3.7923**
Nightmare: the underside of the Nixon years / J. Anthony Lukas. — New York: Viking Press, 1976. x, 626 p.; 24 cm. Includes index. 1. Watergate Affair, 1972-1974 I. T.
E860.L84 1976   320.9/73/0924   LC 75-30667   ISBN 0670514152

White, Theodore Harold, 1915-.   **3.7924**
Breach of faith: the fall of Richard Nixon / Theodore H. White. — 1st ed. — New York: Atheneum Publishers, 1975. 373 p.; 25 cm. 1. Nixon, Richard M. (Richard Milhous), 1913- — Impeachment 2. Watergate Affair, 1972-1974 I. T.
E860.W48   364.1/32/0973   LC 74-20350   ISBN 0689106580

Woodward, Bob.   **3.7925**
The final days / Bob Woodward, Carl Bernstein. — New York: Simon and Schuster, c1976. 476 p., [8] leaves of plates: ill.; 24 cm. Includes index. 1. Nixon, Richard M. (Richard Milhous), 1913- — Impeachment 2. Nixon, Richard M. (Richard Milhous), 1913- — Resignation from office I. Bernstein, Carl, 1944- joint author. II. T.
E861.W66   973.924/092/4   LC 75-43719   ISBN 0671222988

E865–868 Ford, 1974–1977

Kennan, George Frost, 1904-.   **3.7926**
The cloud of danger: current realities of American foreign policy / George F. Kennan. — 1st ed. — Boston: Little, Brown, c1977. xiii, 234 p.; 22 cm. 'An Atlantic Monthly Press book.' 1. United States — Foreign relations — 1974-1977 2. United States — Foreign relations — 1977-1981 I. T.
E865.K46   327.73   LC 77-79616   ISBN 0316488445

Nessen, Ron, 1934-.   **3.7927**
It sure looks different from the inside / Ron Nessen. — 1st ed. — Chicago: Playboy Press; New York: trade distribution by Simon and Schuster, c1978. xv, 367 p., [4] leaves of plates: ill.; 24 cm. Includes index. 1. Ford, Gerald R., 1913- 2. Nessen, Ron, 1934- 3. Journalists — Washington, D.C. — Biography. 4. United States — Politics and government — 1974-1977 I. T.
E865.N47   973.925   LC 78-8185   ISBN 0872235009

Osborne, John, 1907-.   **3.7928**
White House watch: the Ford years / by John Osborne; cartoons by Ranan Lurie. — Washington: New Republic Book Co., 1977. xxxiii, 482 p.: ill.; 22 cm. 'Consists in part of articles that appeared in the New republic between September 1974 and January 1977.' Includes index. 1. United States — Politics and government — 1974-1977 — Collected works. I. T.
E865.O8   973.925   LC 77-5321   ISBN 0915220261

Reeves, Richard.   **3.7929**
A Ford, not a Lincoln / Richard Reeves. — 1st ed. — New York: Harcourt Brace Jovanovich, [1975] xi, 212 p.; 25 cm. Includes index. 1. Ford, Gerald R., 1913- I. T.
E866.R46   973.925/092/4 B   *LC* 75-22195   *ISBN* 015132302X

Ford, Betty, 1918-.   **3.7930**
The times of my life / Betty Ford, with Chris Chase. — 1st ed. — New York: Harper & Row, c1978. xi, 302 p., [12] leaves of plates: ill.; 24 cm. Includes index. 1. Ford, Betty, 1918- 2. Ford, Gerald R., 1913- 3. Presidents — United States — Wives — Biography. 4. Presidents — United States — Biography I. Chase, Chris. joint author. II. T.
E867.F66 1978   973.925/092/4 B   *LC* 78-2131   *ISBN* 0060112980

The Great debates: Carter vs. Ford, 1976 / edited by Sidney   **3.7931**
Kraus.
Bloomington: Indiana University Press, c1979. xi, 553 p., [4] leaves of plates: ill.; 25 cm. Includes the text of the 3 televised debates between J. Carter and G. R. Ford, and of the Vice-Presidential debate between R. J. Dole and W. F. Mondale, in the 1976 Presidential campaign. 1. Carter, Jimmy, 1924- 2. Ford, Gerald R., 1913- 3. Presidents — United States — Election — 1976. 4. Television in politics — United States 5. United States — Politics and government — 1974-1977 I. Kraus, Sidney. II. Carter, Jimmy, 1924- III. Ford, Gerald R., 1913-
E868.G73   329/.023/730925   *LC* 78-62422   *ISBN* 025330363X

E872–875 Carter, 1977–1981

Hill, Samuel S.   **3.7932**
The new religious–political right in America / Samuel S. Hill & Dennis E. Owen. — Nashville: Abingdon, c1982. 160 p.; 21 cm. 1. Conservatism — United States — History — 20th century. 2. Christianity and politics 3. Fundamentalism — History. 4. Evangelicalism — United States — History — 20th century. 5. United States — Politics and government — 1977-1981 6. United States — Politics and government — 1981- I. Owen, Dennis E. (Dennis Edward), 1944- II. T.
E872.H54 1982   261.7/0973 19   *LC* 81-20661   *ISBN* 0687278678

Johnson, Haynes Bonner, 1931-.   **3.7933**
In the absence of power: governing America / Haynes Johnson. — New York: Viking Press, 1980. 339 p.; 25 cm. Includes index. 1. Carter, Jimmy, 1924- 2. United States — Politics and government — 1977- I. T.
E872.J63   320.9/73/0926   *LC* 79-3625   *ISBN* 0670205486

Vance, Cyrus R. (Cyrus Roberts), 1917-.   **3.7934**
Hard choices: critical years in America's foreign policy / Cyrus R. Vance. — New York: Simon and Schuster, c1983. 541 p., [8] p. of plates: ill., maps; 25 cm. Includes index. 1. Vance, Cyrus R. (Cyrus Roberts), 1917- 2. United States — Foreign relations — 1977-1981 3. United States — Foreign relations administration I. T.
E872.V36 1983   327.73 19   *LC* 83-592   *ISBN* 0671443399

Glad, Betty.   **3.7935**
Jimmy Carter, in search of the great White House / by Betty Glad. — 1st ed. — New York: W. W. Norton, c1980. 546 p.; 24 cm. 1. Carter, Jimmy, 1924- 2. Presidents — United States — Biography 3. Georgia — Politics and government — 1951- 4. United States — Politics and government — 1977- I. T.
E873.G56 1980   973.926/092/4 B   *LC* 80-14744   *ISBN* 0393075273

The American elections of 1980 / edited by Austin Ranney.   **3.7936**
Washington, D.C.: American Enterprise Institute for Public Policy Research, c1981. xiii, 391 p.: graphs; 23 cm. — (AEI studies. 327) (Studies in political and social processes.) 1. Carter, Jimmy, 1924- — Addresses, essays, lectures. 2. Reagan, Ronald — Addresses, essays, lectures. 3. Presidents — United States — Election — 1980 — Addresses, essays, lectures. I. Ranney, Austin. II. Series. III. Series: Studies in political and social processes.
E875.A43   324.973/0926 19   *LC* 81-7907   *ISBN* 0844734470

E876–879 Reagan, 1981-

Barrett, Laurence I.   **3.7937**
Gambling with history: Ronald Reagan in the White House / Laurence I. Barrett. — 1st ed. — Garden City, N.Y.: Doubleday, 1983. xiv, 511 p.; 24 cm. 1. Reagan, Ronald. 2. United States — Politics and government — 1981- I. T.
E876.B37 1983   973.927/092/4 19   *LC* 82-46057   0385179381

Haig, Alexander Meigs, 1924-.   **3.7938**
Caveat: realism, Reagan, and foreign policy / Alexander M. Haig, Jr. — New York: Macmillan, c1984. xiii, 367 p., [16] p. of plates: ports.; 25 cm. Includes index. 1. Reagan, Ronald. 2. Haig, Alexander Meigs, 1924- 3. United States — Foreign relations — 1981- I. T.
E876.H34 1984   327.73 19   *LC* 84-936   *ISBN* 0025473700

McMahan, Jeff.   **3.7939**
Reagan and the world: imperial policy in the new Cold War / Jeff McMahan. — New York: Monthly Review Press, c1985. 300 p.; 21 cm. Includes index. 1. Reagan, Ronald. 2. United States — Foreign relations — 1981- I. T.
E876.M4 1985   327.73 19   *LC* 85-5028   *ISBN* 085345678X

Cannon, Lou.   **3.7940**
Reagan / Lou Cannon. — New York: Putnam, c1982. 464 p., [16] p. of plates: ill.; 24 cm. Includes index. 1. Reagan, Ronald. 2. Presidents — United States — Biography 3. California — Governors — Biography. I. T.
E877.C36 1982   973.927/092/4 B 19   *LC* 82-5370   *ISBN* 0399127569

F1–970 U.S. Local History

F1–105 New England

Shipton, Clifford Kenyon, 1902-.   • **3.7941**
New England life in the 18th century: representative biographies from Sibley's Harvard graduates. — Cambridge: Belknap Press of Harvard University Press, 1963. xxvii, 626 p.: ports., maps (on lining papers); 24 cm. A selection of biographies from the volumes written by Shipton. 1. Harvard University — Biography 2. New England — Biography. I. Sibley's Harvard graduates. II. T.
F3.S5   *LC* 63-9562

Warren, Austin, 1899-.   • **3.7942**
New England saints. Ann Arbor, University of Michigan Press [1956] v, 192 p. 22 cm. 1. Religious thought — New England. 2. American literature — New England — History and criticism. 3. New England — Biography. 4. New England — Intellectual life I. T.
F3.W3   *LC* 56-9721

Deetz, James.   **3.7943**
In small things forgotten: the archaeology of early American life / James Deetz; drawings by Charles Cann. — 1st ed. — Garden City, N.Y.: Anchor Press/ Doubleday, 1977. 184 p.: ill.; 18 cm. 1. New England — Antiquities. 2. New England — Social life and customs — Colonial period, ca. 1600-1775 I. T.
F6.D43   974/.02   *LC* 76-50760   *ISBN* 038508031X

Adair, John Eric, 1934-.   **3.7944**
Founding fathers: the Puritans in England and America / John Adair. — London: J.M. Dent, 1984 (c1982). xii, 302 p., [8] p. of plates: ill., ports.; 25 cm. Includes index. 1. Puritans — New England — History. 2. Puritans — England — History. 3. New England — History — Colonial period, ca. 1600-1775 I. T.
F7.A18   285/.9/0973 19   *LC* 82-194357   *ISBN* 0460044214

Bremer, Francis J.   **3.7945**
The puritan experiment: New England society from Bradford to Edwards / Francis J. Bremer; with an introd. by Alden T. Vaughan. New York: St. Martin's Press, c1976. xv, 255 p.: maps; 23 cm. Includes index. 1. Puritans — New England. 2. New England — History — Colonial period, ca. 1600-1775 I. T.
F7.B77   974/.02   *LC* 75-38013

Gura, Philip F., 1950-.   **3.7946**
A glimpse of Sion's glory: Puritan radicalism in New England, 1620–1660 / Philip F. Gura. — Middletown, Conn.: Wesleyan University Press, c1984. xv, 398 p.: ill.; 24 cm. Includes index. 1. Puritans — New England — History — 17th century. 2. Radicalism — New England — History — 17th century. 3. New England — Intellectual life 4. United States — Civilization — To 1783 I. T.
F7.G87 1984   974/.02 19   *LC* 83-21831   *ISBN* 0819550957

Haffenden, Philip S.   **3.7947**
New England in the English nation, 1689–1713 / by Philip S. Haffenden. — Oxford [Eng.]: Clarendon Press, 1974. xiii, 326 p., [1] leaf of plates: map; 22 cm. Includes index. 1. New England — History — Colonial period, ca. 1600-1775 2. Great Britain — Colonies — America I. T.
F7.H22   974/.02   *LC* 74-188338   *ISBN* 0198211244

Jennings, Francis, 1918-.   **3.7948**
The invasion of America: Indians, colonialism, and the cant of conquest / by Francis Jennings. — Chapel Hill: Published for the Institute of Early American History and Culture by the University of North Carolina Press, [1975] xvii, 369 p.: ill.; 24 cm. Includes index. 1. Indians of North America — New England. 2. Indians of North America — Government relations — To 1789

3. Iroquois Indians — Government relations 4. New England — History — Colonial period, ca. 1600-1775 I. T.
F7.J46   974/.02   *LC* 74-34275   *ISBN* 0807812455

Jones, James William, 1943-.   3.7949
The shattered synthesis; New England Puritanism before the Great Awakening [by] James W. Jones. — New Haven: Yale University Press, 1973. xi, 207 p.; 23 cm. 1. Puritans — New England. I. T.
F7.J66   974.4/02/0922   *LC* 73-77154   *ISBN* 0300016190

Mather, Cotton.   3.7950
Magnalia Christi Americana, Books 1 and 2 / [by] Cotton Mather. — [1st ed. reprinted] / edited by Kenneth B. Murdock with the assistance of Elizabeth W. Miller. — Cambridge, Mass.; London: Harvard University Press, 1977. xi, 500 p.: facsims., map, port.; 24 cm. — (John Harvard library.) Index. 1. New England — Church history. I. Murdock, Kenneth B. II. Miller, Elizabeth Williams. III. T. IV. Series.
F7.M4 1977   277/.4   *LC* 73-76383   *ISBN* 0674541553

Miller, Perry, 1905-1963.   • 3.7951
The New England mind: from colony to province. — Cambridge: Harvard University Press, 1953. xi, 513 p.: front.; 25 cm. 'Sequel to The New England mind: the seventeenth century.' 1. Puritans — New England. 2. American literature — New England. 3. New England theology 4. New England — Intellectual life 5. New England — History — Colonial period, ca. 1600-1775 I. T.
F7.M54   917.4   *LC* 53-5072

Miller, Perry, 1905-1963.   • 3.7952
The New England mind: the seventeenth century. Cambridge, Harvard University Press, 1954. xi, 528 p. 24 cm. 1. Puritans — New England. 2. Christian literature, American — New England. 3. American literature — Colonial period, ca. 1600-1775 — History and criticism. 4. American literature — New England — History and criticism. 5. New England — Intellectual life I. T.
F7.M56 1954   974/.02 19   *LC* 54-7507

Morgan, Edmund Sears.   • 3.7953
The Puritan family: religion & domestic relations in seventeenth–century New England / [by] Edmund S. Morgan. — New ed., rev. and enl. — New York: Harper & Row, [1966] x, 196 p.; 21 cm. — (Harper torchbooks. The Academy library, TB1227L) 1. Puritans — New England. 2. New England — Social life and customs I. T.
F7.M8 1966   309.174   *LC* 65-25695

Morison, Samuel Eliot, 1887-1976.   • 3.7954
The intellectual life of colonial New England. — [2d ed.]. — New York: New York University Press, 1956. 288 p.; 21 cm. First published in 1936 under title: The Puritan pronaos. 1. Education — New England — History. 2. Libraries — New England. 3. American literature — Colonial period, ca. 1600-1775 — History and criticism. 4. Puritans — New England. 5. New England — Intellectual life I. T.
F7.M82 1956   917.4   *LC* 56-8487

Saints & revolutionaries: essays on early American history /   3.7955
edited by David D. Hall, John M. Murrin, and Thad W. Tate.
1st ed. — New York: Norton, c1984. xv, 398 p.; 22 cm. Essays by students of Edmund S. Morgan, to whom the book is dedicated. 1. Morgan, Edmund Sears. 2. New England — History — Colonial period, ca. 1600-1775 — Addresses, essays, lectures. 3. United States — Civilization — To 1783 — Addresses, essays, lectures. I. Hall, David D. II. Murrin, John M. III. Tate, Thad W. IV. Title: Saints and revolutionaries.
F7.S24 1984   974/.02 19   *LC* 82-22439   *ISBN* 0393017516

Vaughan, Alden T., 1929-.   • 3.7956
New England frontier: Puritans and Indians, 1620–1675 / [by] Alden T. Vaughan. — [1st ed.] Boston: Little, Brown [1965] xvii, 430 p.: ill., facsim., map, ports.; 22 cm. 1. Indians of North America — New England — Government relations — To 1789. 2. Indians of North America — New England — History. 3. Indians, Treatment of — New England. 4. New England — History — Colonial period, ca. 1600-1775 I. T.
F7.V3   974.02   *LC* 65-20736

Vaughan, Alden T., 1929- comp.   3.7957
The Puritan tradition in America, 1620–1730. Edited by Alden T. Vaughan. — Columbia: University of South Carolina Press, [1972] xxviii, 348 p.; 24 cm. 1. Puritans — New England. 2. New England — History — Colonial period, ca. 1600-1775 — Sources. I. T.
F7.V32 1972b   974   *LC* 74-184660   *ISBN* 087249263X

Federal Writers' Project.   3.7958
Here's New England! A guide to vacationland, written and compiled by members of the Federal Writers' Project of the Works Progress Administration in the New England States; sponsored by the New England council, Boston. Boston, Houghton Mifflin, 1939. vi, 122 p. maps 21 cm. (American guide series.) The t.-p. is preceded by 31 unnumbered pages of illustrations and half-

title: Preview of New England. 1. New England — Description and travel — Guide-books. I. T.
F9.F44   *LC* 39-15700

F16–60 MAINE. NEW HAMPSHIRE. VERMONT

Clark, Charles E., 1929-.   3.7959
Maine: a Bicentennial history / Charles E. Clark. — New York: Norton, c1977. xv, 199 p., [8] leaves of plates: ill.; 22 cm. (The States and the Nation series) Includes index. 1. Maine — History I. T.
F19.C54   974.1   *LC* 77-22864   *ISBN* 0393056538

Maine: a guide to the Vacation State. Edited by Ray Bearse.   3.7960
2d ed. rev. — Boston: Houghton Mifflin, 1969. xii, 460 p.: illus., maps.; 21 cm. — (The New American guide series) First ed. written and compiled by the Federal Writers' Project, under title: Maine, a guide 'down east.' 1. Maine — Description and travel — Guide-books. I. Bearse, Ray, ed. II. Federal Writers' Project. Maine. Maine, a guide 'down east.'
F25.F44 1969   917.41   *LC* 69-12741

Horwitz, Richard P., 1949-.   3.7961
Anthropology toward history: culture and work in a 19th century Maine town / by Richard P. Horwitz. — Middletown, Conn.: Wesleyan University Press, c1978. xiii, 197 p.: maps; 24 cm. Includes index. 1. Winthrop (Me.: Town) — Civilization. 2. Winthrop (Me.: Town) — Occupations. I. T.
F29.W9 H67   974.1/6   *LC* 77-74560   *ISBN* 0819550140

Morison, Elizabeth Forbes.   3.7962
New Hampshire: a Bicentennial history / Elizabeth Forbes Morison, Elting E. Morison. — New York: Norton, c1976. ix, 209 p., [8] leaves of plates: ill.; 22 cm. (The States and the Nation series) Includes index. 1. New Hampshire — History I. Morison, Elting Elmore. joint author. II. T.
F34.M67   974.2   *LC* 76-4959   *ISBN* 0393055833

Daniell, Jere R.   3.7963
Colonial New Hampshire: a history / Jere R. Daniell. — Millwood, N.Y.: KTO Press, c1981. xvi, 279 p.: ill.; 24 cm. — (History of the American colonies.) Includes index. 1. New Hampshire — History — Colonial period, ca. 1600-1775 2. New Hampshire — History — Revolution, 1775-1783 I. T. II. Series.
F37.D25 1981   974.2/02 19   *LC* 81-6046   *ISBN* 0527187151

Turner, Lynn W.   3.7964
The ninth state: New Hampshire's formative years / Lynn Warren Turner. — Chapel Hill: University of North Carolina Press, c1983. xii, 479 p.: maps; 24 cm. 1. New Hampshire — Politics and government — 1775-1865 I. T.
F38.T87 1983   974.2/03 19   *LC* 82-13386   *ISBN* 0807815411

Federal writers' project. New Hampshire.   3.7965
New Hampshire, a guide to the Granite state. Boston, Houghton Mifflin company, 1938. xxix, 559 p. illus., plates, maps (1 fold. in pocket) 21 cm. 1. New Hampshire. 2. New Hampshire — Description and travel — Guide-books.
F39.F43   *LC* 38-6192

Drowned valley: the Piscataqua River basin / [compiled] by   3.7966
John P. Adams; with a foreword by Charles E. Clark.
Hanover: Published for the University of New Hampshire by University Press of New England, 1976. xix, 274 p.: ill.; 27 cm. Includes index. 1. Piscataqua River Valley (N.H. and Me.) — History — Miscellanea. 2. Great Bay region, N.H. — History — Miscellanea. I. Adams, John P. (John Phillip), 1932-
F42.P4 D76   779/.9/97426   *LC* 75-40868   *ISBN* 0874511232

Morrissey, Charles T.   3.7967
Vermont, a Bicentennial history / Charles T. Morrissey. — 1st ed. — New York: Norton; Nashville: American Association for State and Local History, c1981. xvi, 235 p., [8] leaves of plates: ill.; 22 cm. (The States and the Nation series) Includes index. 1. Vermont — History I. T.
F49.M67 1981   974.3 19   *LC* 80-21296

Vermont; a guide to the Green Mountain State.   3.7968
3d ed., rev., edited by Ray Bearse. — Boston: Houghton Mifflin, 1968. xix, 452 p.: illus., maps.; 21 cm. — (The New American guide series) First ed. written and compiled by the Federal Writers' Project. 1. Vermont — Description and travel — Guide-books. I. Bearse, Ray, ed. II. Federal Writers' Project. Vermont. Vermont.
F54.F45 1968   917.43   *LC* 68-14344

F61-75 MASSACHUSETTS

Brown, Richard D. 3.7969
Massachusetts: a Bicentennial history / Richard D. Brown. — New York: Norton, c1978. ix, 246 p., [8] leaves of plates: ill.; 22 cm. (The States and the Nation series) Includes index. 1. Massachusetts — History I. T.
F64.B86 974.4 *LC* 78-17525 *ISBN* 039305666X

Brown, Robert Eldon, 1907-. • 3.7970
Middle–class democracy and the Revolution in Massachusetts, 1691–1780 / by Robert E. Brown. — New York: Russell & Russell, [1968, c1955] ix, 458 p.; 24 cm. 1. Democracy 2. Massachusetts — Politics and government — Colonial period, ca. 1600-1775 3. Massachusetts — Politics and government — Revolution, 1775-1783 I. T.
F67.B86 1968 974.4 *LC* 68-10906

Battis, Emery John, 1915-. • 3.7971
Saints and sectaries; Anne Hutchinson and the Antinomian controversy in the Massachusetts Bay Colony. Chapel Hill, Published for the Institute of Early American History and Culture at Williamsburg, Va., by the University of North Carolina Press [1962] xv, 379 p. port., maps. 24 cm. 1. Hutchinson, Anne Marbury, 1591-1643. 2. Antinomianism I. Institute of Early American History and Culture (Williamsburg, Va.) II. T.
F67.H907 922 *LC* 63-8

Bailyn, Bernard. 3.7972
The ordeal of Thomas Hutchinson. — Cambridge, Mass.: Belknap Press of Harvard University Press, 1974. xx, 423 p.: ill.; 25 cm. 1. Hutchinson, Thomas, 1711-1780. I. T.
F67.H9805 973.3/14/0924 B *LC* 73-76379 *ISBN* 0674641604

Hutchinson, Thomas, 1711-1780. • 3.7973
The history of the colony and province of Massachusetts–bay, by Thomas Hutchinson. Edited from the author's own copies of volumes I and II and his manuscript of volume III, with a memoir and additional notes, by Lawrence Shaw Mayo. Cambridge, Mass., Harvard University Press, 1936. 3 v. 25 cm. With reproductions of original title-pages of vol. I and II, 2d ed., London, 1765-68. 'The text of the appendix has been carried over bodily ... from the edition of 1828. It does not appear in the author's manuscript, for it was compiled by his grandson, the Reverend John Hutchinson, the first editor of volume III.'—Editor's pref. to vol. III. 1. Massachusetts — History — Colonial period, ca. 1600-1775 I. Mayo, Lawrence Shaw, 1888-1947, ed. II. Hutchinson, John, 1793-1865, comp. III. T.
F67.H985 *LC* 36-12398

Labaree, Benjamin Woods. 3.7974
Colonial Massachusetts: a history / Benjamin W. Labaree. — Millwood, N.Y.: KTO Press, c1979. xvii, 349 p.: ill.; 24 cm. — (History of the American colonies.) Includes index. 1. Massachusetts — History — Colonial period, ca. 1600-1775 I. T. II. Series.
F67.L34 974.4/02 *LC* 79-33 *ISBN* 0527187143

Letters from New England: the Massachusetts Bay Colony, 1629–1638 / edited by Everett Emerson. 3.7975
Amherst: University of Massachusetts Press, 1976. xix, 263 p.: ill.; 24 cm. (The Commonwealth series; [v. 2]) 1. Massachusetts — History — Colonial period, ca. 1600-1775 — Sources. I. Emerson, Everett H., 1925-
F67.L663 974.4/02 *LC* 75-32484 *ISBN* 0870232096

Mather, Cotton, 1663-1728. • 3.7976
Diary of Cotton Mather. — New York: F. Ungar Pub. Co., [1957?] 2 v.: fold. map.; 25 cm. — (American classics) 1. Massachusetts — History — Colonial period, ca. 1600-1775 — Sources. I. T.
F67.M4213 974.4 *LC* 57-8651

Mather, Cotton, 1663-1728. 3.7977
Selected letters of Cotton Mather / compiled with commentary by Kenneth Silverman. — Baton Rouge: Louisiana State University Press, [1971] xxvi, 446 p.: port.; 24 cm. I. Silverman, Kenneth. II. T.
F67.M4215 917.3/03/25 *LC* 78-142338 *ISBN* 0807109207

Levin, David, 1924-. 3.7978
Cotton Mather: the young life of the Lord's Remembrancer, 1663–1703 / David Levin. — Cambridge, Mass.: Harvard University Press, 1978. xvi, 360 p.: ill.; 24 cm. 1. Mather, Cotton, 1663-1728. 2. Congregational churches — Clergy — Biography. 3. Clergy — Massachusetts — Biography. 4. Massachusetts — Biography. I. T.
F67.M43 L48 973.2/092/4 B *LC* 78-2355 *ISBN* 0674175077

Silverman, Kenneth. 3.7979
The life and times of Cotton Mather / Kenneth Silverman. — 1st ed. — New York: Harper & Row, c1984. x, 479 p., [8] p. of plates: ill.; 25 cm. 1. Mather, Cotton, 1663-1728. 2. Puritans — Massachusetts — Biography. 3. Massachusetts — History — Colonial period, ca. 1600-1775 I. T.
F67.M43 S57 1984 285.8/32/0924 B 19 *LC* 83-48385 *ISBN* 0060152311

Murdock, Kenneth Ballard, 1895-1975. • 3.7980
Increase Mather, the foremost American Puritan. — New York: Russell & Russell, 1966 [c1953] xv, 442 p.: illus., facsims., maps, ports.; 22 cm. 'Appendix C; list of books referred to': p. [407]-415. 'Appendix D; check list of Mather's writing': p. [416]-422. 1. Mather, Increase, 1639-1723. I. T.
F67.M477 1966 974.4/02/0924 *LC* 66-24736

Middlekauff, Robert. • 3.7981
The Mathers: three generations of Puritan intellectuals, 1596–1728. — New York: Oxford University Press, 1971. xii, 440 p.; 24 cm. 1. Mather, Richard, 1596-1669. 2. Mather, Increase, 1639-1723. 3. Mather, Cotton, 1663-1728. 4. Puritans — Massachusetts. I. T.
F67.M4865 285/.9/0922 *LC* 79-140912 *ISBN* 0195013050

Morison, Samuel Eliot, 1887-1976. • 3.7982
Builders of the Bay colony / by Samuel Eliot Morison. — Boston; New York: Houghton Mifflin Company, 1930. xiv, 365 p.: front., plates, ports., map, facsims.; 23 cm. Published also under title: Massachusettensis de conditoribus. Contains biographies of Richard Hakluyt, John Smith, Thomas Morton, John White, John Winthrop, Thomas Shepard, John Hull, Henry Dunster, Nathaniel Ward, Robert Child, John Winthrop, Jr., John Eliot and Anne Bradstreet. 1. Puritans 2. Massachusetts — History — Colonial period, ca. 1600-1775 3. Massachusetts — Biography. I. T. II. Title: Massachusettensis de conditoribus.
F67.M6 *LC* a 30-1055

Sewall, Samuel, 1652-1730. 3.7983
The diary of Samuel Sewall, 1674–1729. Newly edited from the ms. at the Massachusetts Historical Society by M. Halsey Thomas. — New York: Farrar, Straus and Giroux, [1973] 2 v. (xxxvii, 1254 p.): illus.; 25 cm. 1. Sewall, Samuel, 1652-1730. 2. Massachusetts — History — Colonial period, ca. 1600-1775 I. Thomas, Milton Halsey, 1903- II. T.
F67.S514 1973 917.44/03/20924 *LC* 73-81968 *ISBN* 0374139520

Winslow, Ola Elizabeth. • 3.7984
Samuel Sewall of Boston. New York, Macmillan c1964. 235 p. ill. 22 cm. 1. Sewall, Samuel, 1652-1730. 2. New Englanders — Biography. 3. New England — History — Colonial period. I. T.
F 67 S54 W77 1964 *LC* 63-16140

Dunn, Richard S. • 3.7985
Puritans and Yankees; the Winthrop dynasty of New England, 1630–1717. — Princeton, N.J.: Princeton University Press, 1962. xi, 379 p.: ports., map.; 25 cm. 1. Winthrop family 2. New England — History — Colonial period, ca. 1600-1775 I. T.
F67.W7957 974.402 *LC* 62-7400

Morgan, Edmund Sears. • 3.7986
The Puritan dilemma: the story of John Winthrop / edited by Oscar Handlin. — [1st ed.]. — Boston: Little, Brown, [1958] 224 p.; 21 cm. — (The Library of American biography) 1. Winthrop, John, 1588-1649. I. T.
F67.W798 923.273 *LC* 58-6029

Bradford, William, 1588-1657. • 3.7987
[History of Plymouth Plantation 1952] Of Plymouth Plantation, 1620–1647; the complete text, with notes and an introd. by Samuel Eliot Morison. New ed. New York, Knopf, 1952. xliii, 448, xv p. maps. 25 cm. First ed. published in 1856 under title: History of Plymouth Plantation. 1. Massachusetts — History — New Plymouth, 1620-1691 I. Morison, Samuel Eliot, 1887-1976. ed. II. T.
F68.B8073 974.4 *LC* 51-13222

Dillon, Francis. 3.7988
The Pilgrims / Francis Dillon. 1st ed in the U.S.A. — Garden City, N.Y.: Doubleday, 1975. x, 250 p.; 22 cm. Rev. ed. of the author's A place for habitation, first published in 1973. Includes index. 1. Pilgrims (New Plymouth Colony) I. T.
F68.D58 1975 973.2/2 *LC* 74-18792 *ISBN* 0385095945

Langdon, George D. • 3.7989
Pilgrim colony; a history of New Plymouth, 1620–1691, by George D. Langdon, Jr. — New Haven: Yale University Press, 1966. xi, 257 p.: map (on lining papers); 24 cm. — (Yale publications in American studies, 12) 1. Massachusetts — History — New Plymouth, 1620-1691 I. T. II. Series.
F68.L25 974.402 *LC* 66-21526

Massachusetts: a guide to the Pilgrim State. Edited by Ray Bearse. 3.7990
2d ed., rev. and enl. Boston, Houghton Mifflin, 1971. xiv, 525 p. illus., maps. 21 cm. (The New American guide series) First ed. compiled and written by the Federal Writers' Project, under title: Massachusetts: a guide to its places and people. 1. Massachusetts. 2. Massachusetts — Description and travel — Guide-books. I. Bearse, Ray, ed. II. Federal Writers' Project. Massachusetts. Massachusetts: a guide to its places and people.
F70.M425 1971 917.44/04/4 *LC* 68-16270 *ISBN* 0395120918

F72–74 Regions. Cities

Thoreau, Henry David, 1817-1862. • **3.7991**
A week on the Concord and Merrimack Rivers / edited with introd. and notes by Walter Harding. — New York: Holt, Rinehart & Winston [1963] xxiii, 340 p.; 19 cm. (Rinehart editions) 1. Concord River (Mass.) — Description and travel. 2. Merrimack River (N.H. and Mass.) — Description and travel. I. T.
F72.M7 T5 1963   *LC* 63-7886

Whitehill, Walter Muir, 1905-. **3.7992**
Boston; a topographical history. 2d ed., enl. Cambridge, Mass., Belknap Press of Harvard University Press, 1968. xl, 299 p. illus., maps. 25 cm. 1. Boston (Mass.) 2. Boston (Mass.) — Description I. T.
F73.3.W57 1968   974.4/61   *LC* 69-13769

Brown, Richard D. • **3.7993**
Revolutionary politics in Massachusetts; the Boston Committee of Correspondence and the towns, 1772–1774 [by] Richard D. Brown. Cambridge, Harvard University Press, 1970. xiv, 282 p. illus., facsim., maps, ports. 24 cm. 1. Boston Committee of Correspondence. 2. Massachusetts — Politics and government — Colonial period, ca. 1600-1775 3. Boston (Mass.) — Politics and government — Colonial period, ca. 1600-1775 I. T.
F73.4.B89   320.9/744   *LC* 71-119072   *ISBN* 0674767810

Rutman, Darrett Bruce. • **3.7994**
Winthrop's Boston; portrait of a puritan town, 1630–1649, by Darrett B. Rutman. New York, Norton [1972, c1965] x, 324 p. 20 cm. (The Norton library, N627) 1. Winthrop, John, 1588-1649. 2. Boston (Mass.) — History — Colonial period, ca. 1600-1775 I. T.
F73.4.R8 1972   974.4/61/02   *LC* 70-39159   *ISBN* 0393006271

Trout, Charles H. **3.7995**
Boston, the Great Depression, and the New Deal / Charles H. Trout. — New York: Oxford University Press, 1977. xx, 401 p.: ill.; 22 cm. — (The Urban life in America series) 1. Depressions — 1929 — United States 2. New Deal, 1933-1939 3. Boston (Mass.) — History — 1865- 4. Boston (Mass.) — Economic conditions. I. T.
F73.5.T76   974.4/61/04   *LC* 76-47439   *ISBN* 0195021908

Handlin, Oscar, 1915-. • **3.7996**
Boston's immigrants [1790–1880]: a study in acculturation. — Rev. and enl. ed. Cambridge, Mass.: Belknap Press of Harvard University Press, 1959. 382 p.: ill.; 22 cm. 'Originally published in 1941 as volume L of the Harvard historical studies.' 1. Irish Americans — Massachusetts — Boston. 2. Boston (Mass.) — Social conditions. 3. Boston (Mass.) — Foreign population. I. T.
F73.9.A1 H3 1959   305.8/009744/61 19   *LC* 59-7653

Lukas, J. Anthony, 1933-. **3.7997**
Common ground: a turbulent decade in the lives of three American families / J. Anthony Lukas. — 1st ed. — New York: Knopf: Distributed by Random House, 1985. x, 659 p.; 25 cm. 1. Diver family 2. Twyman family 3. Goff family 4. Busing for school integration — Massachusetts — Boston. 5. School integration — Massachusetts — Boston. 6. Boston (Mass.) — Race relations. I. T.
F73.9.A1 L85 1985   370.19/342 19   *LC* 85-127   *ISBN* 0394411501

Ikels, Charlotte. **3.7998**
Aging and adaptation: Chinese in Hong Kong and the United States / Charlotte Ikels. — Hamden, Conn.: Archon Books, 1983. xvii, 262 p.; 23 cm. Includes index. 1. Chinese American aged — Massachusetts — Boston Region. 2. Aged — Hong Kong. 3. Aging — Case studies. 4. Hong Kong — Social conditions. 5. Boston Region (Mass.) — Social conditions. I. T.
F73.9.C5 I36 1983   305.2/6/089951074461 19   *LC* 83-7130   *ISBN* 0208019995

Different strokes: pathways to maturity in the Boston ghetto: a **3.7999**
report to the Ford Foundation / Robert Rosenthal ... [et al.].
Boulder, Colo.: Westview Press, 1976. viii, 358 p.; 24 cm. 1. Afro-American youth — Massachusetts — Boston — Case studies. 2. Boston (Mass.) — Social conditions — Case studies. I. Rosenthal, Robert Alan. II. Ford Foundation.
F73.9.N4 D53   301.43/15/0974461   *LC* 76-7952   *ISBN* 0891580360

Horton, James Oliver. **3.8000**
Black Bostonians: family life and community struggle in the antebellum North / James Oliver Horton and Lois E. Horton. — New York: Holmes & Meier, 1979. xv, 175 p., [4] leaves of plates: ill.; 24 cm. Includes index. 1. Afro-Americans — Massachusetts — Boston — Economic conditions. 2. Afro-Americans — Massachusetts — Boston — Social conditions. 3. Afro-American families — Massachusetts — Boston 4. Boston (Mass.) — Economic conditions. 5. Boston (Mass.) — Social conditions. I. Horton, Lois E. joint author. II. T.
F73.9.N4 H67 1979   974.4/61/00496073   *LC* 78-24453   *ISBN* 0841904456

Greven, Philip J. • **3.8001**
Four generations: population, land, and family in colonial Andover, Massachusetts [by] Philip J. Greven, Jr. Ithaca, N.Y., Cornell University Press, 1970. xvi, 329 p. illus., fold. map. 23 cm. 1. Andover (Mass.) — Social life and customs. I. T.
F74.A6 G7   301.42/09744/5   *LC* 76-87018   *ISBN* 0801405394

Gross, Robert A., 1945-. **3.8002**
The minutemen and their world / Robert A. Gross. — 1st ed. — New York: Hill and Wang, 1976. xiii, 242 p.: maps; 21 cm. — (American century series) 1. Minutemen (Militia) — Massachusetts. 2. Concord, Battle of, 1775 3. Concord (Mass.) — Social conditions. 4. Concord (Mass.) — History — Revolution, 1775-1783. I. T.
F74.C8 G76 1976   974.2/72   *LC* 75-46595   *ISBN* 0809069334

Lockridge, Kenneth A. • **3.8003**
A New England town: the first hundred years, Dedham, Massachusetts, 1636–1736 [by] Kenneth A. Lockridge. [1st ed.] New York, Norton [1970] xv, 208 p. maps. 21 cm. (The Norton essays in American history) 1. Dedham (Mass.) — History — Colonial period, ca. 1600-1775. 2. New England — Civilization. I. T.
F74.D3 L83 1970   320.9/744/7   *LC* 69-14703

Hutchins, Francis G. . **3.8004**
Mashpee, the story of Cape Cod's Indian town / Francis G. Hutchins. — West Franklin, N.H.: Amarta Press, 1979. 202 p.: ill.; 22 cm. 1. Mashpee Indians 2. Mashpee (Mass.: Town) — History. I. T.
F74.M425 H87   974.4/92   *LC* 79-54890   *ISBN* 0935100008

Mancini, Janet K. **3.8005**
Strategic styles: coping in the inner city / Janet K. Mancini. — Hanover, N.H.: University Press of New England, 1980. xv, 330 p.; 24 cm. Includes index. 1. Afro-American youth — Massachusetts — Boston — Case studies. 2. Afro-American youth — Case studies. 3. Adjustment (Psychology) — Case studies. 4. Roxbury, Mass. — Social conditions. 5. Boston (Mass.) — Social conditions — Case studies. I. T.
F74.R9 M36   302 19   *LC* 79-56773   *ISBN* 0874511798

Young, Christine Alice, 1946-. **3.8006**
From 'good order' to glorious revolution: Salem, Massachusetts, 1628–1689 / by Christine Alice Young. — Ann Arbor, MI: UMI Research Press, c1980. vi, 263 p.: ill.; 24 cm. (Studies in American history and culture. no. 19) Includes indexes. 1. Salem (Mass.) — History — Colonial period, ca. 1600-1775 I. T. II. Series.
F74.S1 Y68   974.4/5 19   *LC* 80-20118   *ISBN* 0835711013

Frisch, Michael H. **3.8007**
Town into city: Springfield, Massachusetts, and the meaning of community, 1840–1880 / [by] Michael H. Frisch. — Cambridge, Mass.: Harvard University Press, 1972. ix, 301 p.: ill.; 24 cm. (Harvard studies in urban history.) Originated from the author's thesis, Princeton. 1. Springfield (Mass.) — History. I. T. II. Series.
F74.S8 F7 1972   301.36/3/0974426   *LC* 72-178075   *ISBN* 0674898206

Powell, Sumner Chilton, 1924-. • **3.8008**
Puritan village: the formation of a New England town. — [1st ed.] Middletown, Conn.: Wesleyan University Press [1963] xx, 215 p.: plates, maps, tables; 29 cm. 1. Municipal government — Great Britain. 2. Sudbury (Mass.) — Politics and government. 3. Sudbury (Mass.) — History — Colonial period, ca. 1600-1775. I. T.
F74.S94 P74   974.44   *LC* 63-8862

Parkman, Ebenezer, 1703-1782. **3.8009**
The diary of Ebenezer Parkman, 1703–1782. First Part. three volumes in one, 1719–1755 / ed. by Francis G. Walett. — Worcester, Mass.: American Antiquarian Society, 1974. 316 p.: map. 1. Parkman, Ebenezer, 1703-1782. 2. Westborough (Mass.) — Social life and customs. I. Walett, Francis G., ed. II. T.
F74.W65 P19   917.44/3/0320924

F76–105 RHODE ISLAND. CONNECTICUT

Federal writers' project. Rhode Island. • **3.8010**
Rhode Island, a guide to the smallest state. Boston, Houghton Mifflin company, 1937. xxvi, 500 p. plates, ports., maps (1 fold., in pocket) 21 cm. 1. Rhode Island. 2. Rhode Island — Description and travel — Guide-books.
F79.F38   *LC* 37-28463

McLoughlin, William Gerald. 3.8011
Rhode Island: a Bicentennial history / William G. McLoughlin. — New York: W. W. Norton, c1978. xiv, 240 p., [8] leaves of plates: ill.; 22 cm. (The States and the nation series) Includes index. 1. Rhode Island — History I. T.
F79.M32   974.5   *LC* 78-2911   *ISBN* 0393056759

Bridenbaugh, Carl. 3.8012
Fat mutton and liberty of conscience: society in Rhode Island, 1636–1690. — [Providence: Brown University Press, 1974] xxiv, 157 p.: ill.; 24 cm. 1. Rhode Island — History — Colonial period, ca. 1600-1775 2. Rhode Island — Commerce — History. I. T.
F82.B73   917.45/03/2   *LC* 74-6573   *ISBN* 0870571435

James, Mr. Sydney V. 3.8013
Colonial Rhode Island: a history / Sydney V. James. — New York: Scribner, [1975] xviii, 423 p.: ill.; 24 cm. (History of the American colonies.) Includes index. 1. Rhode Island — History — Colonial period, ca. 1600-1775 2. Rhode Island — History — Revolution, 1775-1783 I. T. II. Series.
F82.J35   974.5/02   *LC* 75-9685   *ISBN* 0684143593

Miller, Perry, 1905-1963. • 3.8014
Roger Williams: his contribution to the American tradition. [1st ed.] Indianapolis, Bobbs-Merrill [1953] 273 p. 23 cm. — (Makers of the American tradition series) 1. Williams, Roger, 1604?-1683. I. T.
F82.W788   *LC* 53-8874

Morgan, Edmund Sears. • 3.8015
Roger Williams: the church and the state / [by] Edmund S. Morgan. — [1st ed.]. — New York: Harcourt, Brace & World, [1967] 170 p.; 21 cm. 1. Williams, Roger, 1604?-1683. 2. Church and state I. T.
F82.W789   322.1   *LC* 67-25999

Winslow, Ola Elizabeth. • 3.8016
Master Roger Williams, a biography. — New York: Octagon Books, 1973 [c1957] xi, 328 p.: illus.; 23 cm. Original ed. published by Macmillan, New York. 1. Williams, Roger, 1604?-1683. I. T.
F82.W855 1973   974.5/02/0924 B   *LC* 73-8608   *ISBN* 0374986827

Gettleman, Marvin E. 3.8017
The Dorr Rebellion: a study in American radicalism, 1833–1849 [by] Marvin E. Gettleman. — [1st ed.]. — New York: Random House, [1973] xxii, 257 p.: illus.; 22 cm. 1. Dorr, Thomas Wilson, 1805-1854. 2. Dorr Rebellion, 1842 I. T.
F83.4.G47   974.5/03   *LC* 72-14312   *ISBN* 0394464702

Smith, Judith E., 1948-. 3.8018
Family connections: a history of Italian and Jewish immigrant lives in Providence, Rhode Island, 1900–1940 / Judith E. Smith. — Albany: State University of New York Press, c1985. xii, 228 p., [1] leaf of plates: ill.; 24 cm. (SUNY series in American social history.) Includes index. 1. Italian Americans — Families — Rhode Island — Providence — History — 20th century. 2. Jews — Families — Rhode Island — Providence — History — 20th century. 3. Italian Americans — Rhode Island — Providence — Social life and customs. 4. Jews — Rhode Island — Providence — Social life and customs. 5. Providence (R.I.) — Social life and customs. I. T. II. Series.
F89.P99 I87 1985   974.5/200451 19   *LC* 85-9855   *ISBN* 0873959647

Cottrol, Robert J. 3.8019
The Afro–Yankees: Providence's Black community in the antebellum era / Robert J. Cottrol. — Westport, Conn.: Greenwood Press, 1982. xviii, 200 p.; 22 cm. — (Contributions in Afro-American and African studies. 0069-9624; no. 68) Includes index. 1. Afro-Americans — Rhode Island — Providence — History. 2. Providence (R.I.) — History. 3. Providence (R.I.) — Race relations. I. T. II. Series.
F89.P99 N425 1982   974.5/200496073   *LC* 81-23717   *ISBN* 0313229368

Roth, David Morris, 1935-. 3.8020
Connecticut, a bicentennial history / David M. Roth. — 1st ed. — New York: Norton, c1979. xiv, 231 p., [8] leaves of plates: ill.; 22 cm. (The States and the Nation series) Includes index. 1. Connecticut — History I. T.
F94.R67   974.6   *LC* 79-16262   *ISBN* 0393056767

Bushman, Richard L. • 3.8021
From Puritan to Yankee: character and the social order in Connecticut, 1690–1765 / [by] Richard L. Bushman. — Cambridge: Harvard University Press, 1967. xiv, 343 p.: ill., maps.; 22 cm. — (A publication of the Center for the Study of the History of Liberty in America, Harvard University) 1. Connecticut — History — Colonial period, 1600-1775. 2. Connecticut — Social conditions. I. T.
F97.B89   917.46/03/2   *LC* 67-17304

Taylor, Robert Joseph, 1917-. 3.8022
Colonial Connecticut: a history / Robert J. Taylor. — Millwood, N.Y.: KTO Press, c1979. xvi, 285 p.; 24 cm. — (History of the American colonies.) Includes

index. 1. Connecticut — History — Colonial period, ca. 1600-1775 I. T. II. Series.
F97.T25   974.6/02   *LC* 79-1099   *ISBN* 0527187100

Federal writers' project. Connecticut. • 3.8023
Connecticut; a guide to its roads, lore, and people, written by workers of the Federal writers' project of the Works progress administration for the state of Connecticut; sponsored by Wilbur L. Cross ... — Boston: Houghton Mifflin company, 1938. xxxiii, 593 p.: plates, maps (1 fold., in pocket) diagr.; 21 cm. — (American guide series) Map on lining-paper. The plates are in eight groups, each preceded by half-title not included in paging. 1. Historic buildings — Connecticut. 2. Automobiles — Road guides — Connecticut. 3. Connecticut. 4. Connecticut — Description & travel — Guide-books.
F100.F45   917.46   *LC* 38-27339

Jeffries, John W., 1942-. 3.8024
Testing the Roosevelt coalition: Connecticut society and politics in the era of World War II / John W. Jeffries. — Knoxville: University of Tennessee Press, 1979 (c1978). xiv, 312 p. — (Twentieth-century America series) Includes index. 1. Political participation — Connecticut — History. 2. Connecticut — Politics and government — 1865-1950 I. T.
F100.J43   320.9/746/04   *LC* 78-14550   *ISBN* 0870492551

F106–205 Atlantic States

F116–130 NEW YORK

Bliven, Bruce, 1916-. 3.8025
New York, a Bicentennial history / Bruce Bliven, Jr. — New York: Norton; Nashville: American Association for State and Local History, c1981. xi, 195, [16] p. of plates: ill.; 22 cm. (The States and the Nation series) Includes index. 1. New York (State) — History. I. T.
F119.B69   974.7 19   *LC* 80-26246   *ISBN* 0393056651

Ellis, David Maldwyn. 3.8026
New York, state and city / David Maldwyn Ellis. — Ithaca, N.Y.: Cornell University Press, 1979. xi, 256 p.: ill.; 22 cm. 1. New York (State) — History 2. New York (N.Y.) — History I. T.
F119.E447   974.7   *LC* 78-15759   *ISBN* 0801411807

Bonomi, Patricia U. • 3.8027
A factious people; politics and society in colonial New York [by] Patricia U. Bonomi. — New York: Columbia University Press, 1971. xiii, 342 p.; 23 cm. 1. New York (State) — History — Colonial period, ca. 1600-1775 2. New York (State) — Politics and government — Colonial period, ca. 1600-1775 I. T.
F122.B65   917.47/03/2   *LC* 74-156803   *ISBN* 0231035098

Kammen, Michael G. 3.8028
Colonial New York: a history / Michael Kammen. — New York: Scribner, [1975] xix, 426 p.: ill.; 24 cm. (History of the American colonies.) Includes index. 1. New York (State) — History — Colonial period, ca. 1600-1775 I. T. II. Series.
F122.K27   974.7/02   *LC* 75-5693   *ISBN* 0684143259

Smith, William, 1728-1793. 3.8029
The history of the Province of New York / by William Smith, Jr.; edited by Michael Kammen. — Cambridge, Mass.: Belknap Press of Harvard University Press, 1972. 2 v.: ill.; 24 cm. — (John Harvard library.) '[The editor has] prepared a new volume one from the first edition (1757) and Smith's marginalia in his personal copy, and a new volume two from Smith's original manuscript of the Continuation.' 1. New York (State) — History — Colonial period, ca. 1600-1775 I. Kammen, Michael G. ed. II. T. III. Series.
F122.S64 1972   974.7/02   *LC* 78-160028   *ISBN* 0674403215

Zee, Henri A. van der. 3.8030
A sweet and alien land: the story of Dutch New York / by Henri and Barbara van der Zee. — New York: Viking Press, 1978. xx, 560 p., [13] leaves of plates: ill.; 25 cm. Includes index. 1. Dutch Americans — New York (State) — History. 2. New York (State) — History — Colonial period, ca. 1600-1775 I. Van der Zee, Barbara. joint author. II. T.
F122.1.V22   974.7/02   *LC* 76-50665   *ISBN* 067068628X

Benson, Lee. • 3.8031
The concept of Jacksonian democracy: New York as a test case. — Princeton, N.J.: Princeton University Press, 1961. xi, 351 p.; 25 cm. 1. Political parties — New York (State) 2. New York (State) — Politics and government — 1775-1865 I. T. II. Title: Jacksonian democracy.
F123.B49   974.703   *LC* 61-6286

Conklin, Henry, 1832-1915.   **3.8032**
Through 'Poverty's Vale': a hardscrabble boyhood in upstate New York, 1832–1862 / Edited with an introd. by Wendell Tripp. — [1st ed.]. — [Syracuse]: Syracuse University Press, 1974. xxiii, 262 p.: illus.; 23 cm. — (A York State book) 1. Conklin, Henry, 1832-1915 — Juvenile literature. 2. Frontier and pioneer life — New York (State) — Juvenile literature. 3. United States — History — Civil War, 1861-1865 — Personal narratives — Juvenile literature. I. T.
F123.C6917 1974   917.47/03/40924 B 92   *LC* 73-19980   *ISBN* 0815600984

Ingalls, Robert P., 1941-.   **3.8033**
Herbert H. Lehman and New York's Little New Deal / Robert P. Ingalls; with a foreword by George Meany. — New York: New York University Press, 1975. xx, 287 p.: ill.; 26 cm. Includes index. 1. Lehman, Herbert Henry, 1878-1963. 2. New Deal, 1933-1939 3. United States — Politics and government — 1933-1945 4. United States — Economic policy — 1933-1945 5. New York (State) — Politics and government — 1865-1950 I. T.
F124.I53   974.7/04/0924   *LC* 75-13744   *ISBN* 0814737501

McCormick, Richard L.   **3.8034**
From realignment to reform: political change in New York State 1893–1910 / Richard L. McCormick. — Ithaca, N.Y.: Cornell University Press, 1981. 352 p.; 24 cm. Includes index. 1. New York (State) — Politics and government — 1865-1950 I. T.
F124.M14   *LC* 80-69824   *ISBN* 0801413265

Writers' program. New York.   **3.8035**
New York; a guide to the Empire state, compiled by workers of the Writers' program of the Work projects administration in the state of New York ... New York, Oxford university press [1946] xxxi, 782 (i.e. 798) p. illus., plates (1 double) maps (3 on fold. l., in pocket) 21 cm. 1. New York (State) 2. New York (State) — Description and travel — Guide-books.
F124.W89 1946   *LC* 46-5765

F128 New York City

New York City guide.   **3.8036**
The WPA guide to New York City: the Federal Writers' Project guide to 1930s New York / prepared by the Federal Writers' Project of the Works Progress Administration in New York City; with a new introduction by William H. Whyte. — New York: Pantheon Books, c1982. xxxii, 680 p., [88] p. of plates: ill., maps; 22 cm. 'A comprehensive guide to the five boroughs of the metropolis—Manhattan, Brooklyn, the Bronx, Queens, and Richmond.' Reprint. Originally published: New York City guide. Rev. ed. New York: Random House, c1939. (American guide series) Includes index. 1. New York (N.Y.) — Description — Guide-books. I. Federal Writers' Project. II. T. III. Title: W.P.A. guide to New York City.
F128.18.N375 1982   917.47/10443 19   *LC* 82-47898   *ISBN* 0394527925

Cook, Adrian.   **3.8037**
The armies of the streets; the New York City draft riots of 1863. — [Lexington]: University Press of Kentucky, [1974] x, 323 p.; 25 cm. 1. Draft Riot, 1863 I. T.
F128.44.C76   974.7/1/03   *LC* 73-80463   *ISBN* 0813112982

Hammack, David C.   **3.8038**
Power and society: greater New York at the turn of the century / David C. Hammack. — New York: Russell Sage Foundation, c1982. xix, 422 p.: ill.; 24 cm. Includes index. 1. New York (N.Y.) — Politics and government — To 1898 2. New York (N.Y.) — Politics and government — 1898-1951 3. New York (N.Y.) — Economic conditions. 4. New York (N.Y.) — Social conditions. I. T.
F128.47.H2 1982   974.7/1041 19   *LC* 81-66977   *ISBN* 0871543486

Erenberg, Lewis A., 1944-.   **3.8039**
Steppin' out: New York nightlife and the transformation of American culture, 1890–1930 / Lewis A. Erenberg. — Westport, Conn.: Greenwood Press, 1981. xix, 291 p.: ill.; 22 cm. (Contributions in American studies; no. 50 0084-9227) Includes index. 1. Music-halls (Variety-theaters, cabarets, etc.) — New York (N.Y.) — History. 2. Restaurants, lunchrooms, etc. — New York (N.Y.) — History. 3. New York (N.Y.) — Popular culture. 4. New York (N.Y.) — Social life and customs I. T.
F128.5.E65   974.7/1041   *LC* 80-930   *ISBN* 0313213429

Heckscher, August, 1913-.   **3.8040**
When LaGuardia was mayor: New York's legendary years / August Heckscher; with Phyllis Robinson. — 1st ed. — New York: Norton, c1978. 448 p.: ill.; 24 cm. Includes index. 1. La Guardia, Fiorello H. (Fiorello Henry), 1882-1947. 2. Mayors — New York (N.Y.) — Biography. 3. New York (N.Y.) — Politics and government — 1898-1951 4. New York (N.Y.) — Biography. I. Robinson, Phyllis C. joint author. II. T.
F128.5.H44 1978   974.7/1/040924 B   *LC* 78-18203   *ISBN* 0393075346

Barrett, William, 1913-.   **3.8041**
The truants: adventures among the intellectuals / William Barrett. — 1st ed. — Garden City, N.Y.: Anchor Press/Doubleday, 1982. 270 p.; 24 cm. Includes index. 1. Barrett, William, 1913- 2. New York (N.Y.) — Intellectual life. I. T.
F128.52.B37   974.7/1043 19   *LC* 81-43141   *ISBN* 0385159668

Rieder, Jonathan.   **3.8042**
Canarsie: the Jews and Italians of Brooklyn against liberalism / Jonathan Rieder. — Cambridge, Mass.: Harvard University Press, 1985. viii, 290 p., [22] p. of plates: ill.; 25 cm. Include index. 1. Jews — New York (N.Y.) — Politics and government. 2. Jews — New York (N.Y.) — Attitudes. 3. Italian Americans — New York (N.Y.) — Politics and government. 4. Italian Americans — New York (N.Y.) — Attitudes. 5. Liberalism — New York (N.Y.) — Case studies. 6. Canarsie (New York, N.Y.) — Politics and government. 7. New York (N.Y.) — Politics and government — 1951- I. T.
F128.68.C36 R54 1985   974.7/23 19   *LC* 84-15660   *ISBN* 0674093607

Anderson, Jervis.   **3.8043**
This was Harlem: a cultural portrait, 1900–1950 / Jervis Anderson. — New York: Farrar Straus Giroux, c1982. x, 389 p.: ill.; 25 cm. 1. Afro-Americans — New York (N.Y.) — History. 2. Harlem (New York, N.Y.) — Civilization. 3. New York (N.Y.) — Civilization. I. T.
F128.68.H3 A65 1982   974.7/1 19   *LC* 81-17474   *ISBN* 0374276234

McKay, Claude, 1890-1948.   **3.8044**
Harlem: Negro metropolis. — New York: E. P. Dutton & company, inc, [c1940] xi p., 1 l., 15-262 p.: front., ill. (facsim.) plates, ports.; 23 cm. 1. Afro-Americans — New York (N.Y.) 2. Harlem (New York, N.Y.). I. T. II. Title: Negro metropolis.
F128.68.H3 M3   *LC* 40-32205

F128.9 FOREIGN POPULATION. MINORITIES

Glazer, Nathan.   **3.8045**
Beyond the melting pot: the Negroes, Puerto Ricans, Jews, Italians, and Irish of New York City / by Nathan Glazer and Daniel Patrick Moynihan. — 2d ed. — Cambridge: M.I.T. Press [1970] xcviii, 363 p.: map (on lining papers); 22 cm. (Publications of the Joint Center for Urban Studies) 1. Minorities — New York (City) 2. New York (N.Y.) — Foreign population. I. Moynihan, Daniel P. (Daniel Patrick), 1927- joint author. II. T.
F128.9.A1 G55 1970   301.451   *LC* 78-118346   *ISBN* 0262070391

Bayor, Ronald H., 1944-.   **3.8046**
Neighbors in conflict: the Irish, Germans, Jews, and Italians of New York City, 1929–1941 / Ronald H. Bayor. — Baltimore: Johns Hopkins University Press, c1978. xiiv, 232 p.: ill.; 24 cm. (The Johns Hopkins University studies in historical and political science; 96th ser., no. 1) 1. Irish Americans — New York (N.Y.) 2. German Americans — New York (N.Y.) 3. Jews — New York (N.Y.) 4. Italian Americans — New York (N.Y.) 5. New York (N.Y.) — Politics and government — 1898-1951 I. T.
F128.9.I6 B39   301.45/09747/1   *LC* 77-14260   *ISBN* 0801820243

Kessner, Thomas.   **3.8047**
The golden door: Italian and Jewish immigrant mobility in New York City, 1880–1915 / Thomas Kessner. — New York: Oxford University Press, 1977. xxvi, 224 p.; 23 cm. (The Urban life in America series) 1. Italian Americans — New York (N.Y.) — Social conditions. 2. Jews — New York (N.Y.) — Social conditions. 3. New York (N.Y.) — Social conditions. I. T.
F128.9.I8 K47   301.45/15/107471   *LC* 76-15872   *ISBN* 0195021169

How we lived: a documentary history of immigrant Jews in   **3.8048**
America, 1880–1930 / [edited by] Irving Howe and Kenneth Libo.
New York: R. Marek, c1979. 360 p.: ill.; 26 cm. Includes index. 1. Jews — New York (N.Y.) — Addresses, essays, lectures. 2. Lower East Side (New York, N.Y.) — Addresses, essays, lectures. 3. United States — Emigration and immigration — Addresses, essays, lectures. 4. New York (N.Y.) — Social conditions — Addresses, essays, lectures. 5. New York (N.Y.) — Intellectual life — Addresses, essays, lectures. I. Howe, Irving. II. Libo, Kenneth.
F128.9.J5 H58   974.7/1004924 19   *LC* 79-13391   *ISBN* 0399900519

Howe, Irving.   **3.8049**
World of our fathers / Irving Howe, with the assistance of Kenneth Libo. — 1st ed. — New York: Harcourt Brace Jovanovich, c1976. xx, 714 p., [24] leaves of plates: ill.; 25 cm. Includes index. 1. Jews — New York (N.Y.) 2. New York (N.Y.) — Social conditions. 3. New York (N.Y.) — Intellectual life. I. Libo, Kenneth. II. T.
F128.9.J5 H6   301.45/19/2407471   *LC* 75-16342   *ISBN* 0151463530

Mitchell, William E.   **3.8050**
Mishpokhe: a study of New York City Jewish family clubs / William Mitchell; foreword by Marshall Sklare. — The Hague: Mouton, c1978. 262 p.: ill.; 24 cm. — (New Babylon, studies in the social sciences: 30) Includes index. 1. Jews — Families — Societies, etc. 2. Jews in New York (City) — Societies, etc. 3. New York (N.Y.) — Social life and customs. I. T.
F128.9.J5 M5   301.45/19/2407471   LC 79-338997   ISBN 9027976953

Moore, Deborah Dash, 1946-.   **3.8051**
At home in America: second generation New York Jews / Deborah Dash Moore. — New York: Columbia University Press, 1981. xiii, 303 p.: ill.; 24 cm. — (Columbia history of urban life.) Includes index. 1. Jews — New York (N.Y.) 2. New York (N.Y.) — Ethnic relations. I. T. II. Series.
F128.9.J5 M66   974.7/1004924 19   LC 80-18777   ISBN 0231050623

Rischin, Moses, 1925-.   • **3.8052**
The promised city; New York's Jews, 1870–1914. Cambridge, Harvard University Press, 1962. 342 p. illus. 22 cm. 1. Jews — New York (N.Y.) — History. 2. New York (N.Y.) — History I. T.
F128.9.J5 R5   301.452   LC 62-11402

Weinberger, Moses, b. 1854.   **3.8053**
[Yehudim veha-Yahadut be-Nuyork. English] People walk on their heads: Moses Weinberger's Jews and Judaism in New York / translated from the Hebrew and edited by Jonathan D. Sarna. — New York: Holmes & Meier, 1982, c1981. 137 p.; 24 cm. Translation of: ha-Yehudim veha-Yahadut be-Nuyork. 1. Jews — New York (N.Y.) 2. Judaism — New York (N.Y.) 3. New York (N.Y.) — Ethnic relations. I. Sarna, Jonathan D. II. T. III. Title: Jews and Judaism in New York.
F128.9.J5 W413 1982   974.7/1004924 19   LC 81-6907   ISBN 0841907072

Kim, Illsoo, 1944-.   **3.8054**
New urban immigrants: the Korean community in New York / Illsoo Kim. — Princeton, N.J.: Princeton University Press, c1981. xvi, 329 p.; 24 cm. Includes index. 1. Korean Americans — New York (N.Y.) 2. New York (N.Y.) — Social conditions. 3. United States — Emigration and immigration 4. Korea (South) — Emigration and immigration. I. T. II. Title: Korean community in New York.
F128.9.K6 K55   305.8/957/0747 19   LC 80-8556   ISBN 0691093555

Johnson, James Weldon, 1871-1938.   **3.8055**
Black Manhattan. New York, Arno Press, 1968 [c1930] 284, xxxiv p. illus., plans, ports. 21 cm. (American Negro, his history and literature.) 1. Afro-Americans — New York (N.Y.) 2. Harlem (New York, N.Y.). I. T. II. Series.
F128.9.N3 J67 1968   974.71   LC 68-29003

Lewinson, Edwin R.   **3.8056**
Black politics in New York City / [by] Edwin R. Lewinson. — New York: Twayne Publishers, [1974] 232 p.; 22 cm. 1. Afro-Americans — New York (N.Y.) — Politics and government. 2. New York (N.Y.) — Politics and government I. T.
F128.9.N3 L48   320.9/747/104   LC 73-17445   ISBN 0805753265

Osofsky, Gilbert, 1935-.   • **3.8057**
Harlem; the making of a ghetto; Negro New York, 1890–1930. [1st ed.] New York, Harper & Row [1966] xi, 259 p. illus., facsims., ports. 22 cm. 1. Afro-Americans — New York (N.Y.) 2. Harlem (New York, N.Y.) — History. I. T.
F128.9.N3 O73   301.34   LC 66-10913

Lewis, Oscar, 1914-1970.   • **3.8058**
La vida: a Puerto Rican family in the culture of poverty—San Juan and New York. — New York: Random House [1966] lix, 669 p.; 25 cm. 1. Puerto Ricans — New York (N.Y.) — Social conditions. 2. Poor — New York (N.Y.) 3. Poor — Puerto Rico — San Juan. 4. New York (N.Y.) — Social conditions. 5. San Juan (P.R.) — Social conditions. I. T.
F128.9.P8 L4   301.451607471   LC 66-11983

F129–130 Other Cities

Brooklyn, 1976 Symposium (1976: Brooklyn College)   **3.8059**
Brooklyn USA: the fourth largest city in America / Rita Seiden Miller, editor. — [Brooklyn]: Brooklyn College Press; New York: distributed by Columbia University Press, 1979. xii, 371 p., [16] leaves of plates: ill.; 23 cm. (Studies on society in change; no. 7) 1. Brooklyn (New York, N.Y.) — Congresses. 2. New York (N.Y.) — Congresses. I. Miller, Rita Seiden. II. T. III. Series.
F129.B7 B74 1976   974.7/23   LC 78-62275   ISBN 0930888022

Yans-McLaughlin, Virginia, 1943-.   **3.8060**
Family and community: Italian immigrants in Buffalo, 1880–1930 / Virginia Yans–McLaughlin. — Ithaca: Cornell University Press, 1977. 286 p.: map; 22 cm. Includes index. 1. Italian Americans — Families — New York (State) — Buffalo — Economic conditions. 2. Buffalo (N.Y.) — Economic conditions. I. T.
F129.B819 I89   301.45/15/1074797   LC 77-3254   ISBN 0801410363

Kasson, John F., 1944-.   **3.8061**
Amusing the million: Coney Island at the turn of the century / John F. Kasson. — New York: Hill & Wang, c1978. 119 p.: ill.; 22 cm. (American century series) 1. Coney Island, N.Y. 2. New York (N.Y.) — Social life and customs I. T.
F129.C75 K37 1978   301.29/747/23   LC 78-6762   ISBN 0809026171

Briggs, John W., 1937-.   **3.8062**
An Italian passage: immigrants to three American cities, 1890–1930 / John W. Briggs. — New Haven: Yale University Press, 1978. xxii, 348 p., [4] leaves of plates: ill.; 22 cm. Includes index. 1. Italian Americans — New York (State) — History. 2. Italian Americans — Missouri — Kansas City — History. 3. Rochester (N.Y.) — History. 4. Utica (N.Y.) — History. 5. Kansas City (Mo.) — History. I. T.
F130.I8 B74   974.7/004/51   LC 77-22006   ISBN 0300020953

F131–145 New Jersey

Fleming, Thomas J.   **3.8063**
New Jersey: a Bicentennial history / Thomas Fleming. — New York: Norton, c1977. ix, 214 p., [8] leaves of plates: ill.; 22 cm. (The States and the Nation series) Includes index. 1. New Jersey — History I. T.
F134.F54   974.9   LC 77-22005   ISBN 0393056392

McCormick, Richard Patrick, 1916-.   **3.8064**
New Jersey from Colony to State, 1609–1789 / Richard P. McCormick. — Rev. ed. — Newark: New Jersey Historical Society, c1981. xv, 191 p.: ill.; 21 cm. — (New Jersey historical classics.) Includes index. 1. New Jersey — History — Colonial period, ca. 1600-1775 2. New Jersey — History — Revolution, 1775-1783 I. T. II. Series.
F137.M2 1981   974.9 19   LC 80-24780   ISBN 0911020020

Sheridan, Eugene R.   **3.8065**
Lewis Morris, 1671–1746: a study in early American politics / Eugene R. Sheridan. — 1st ed. — Syracuse, N.Y.: Syracuse University Press, 1981. xii, 257 p.: port.; 24 cm. — (New York State study.) Includes index. 1. Morris, Lewis, 1671-1746. 2. Judges — New York (State) — Biography. 3. New Jersey — Politics and government — Colonial period, ca. 1600-1775 4. New York (State) — Politics and government — Colonial period, ca. 1600-1775 5. New Jersey — Governors — Biography. I. T. II. Series.
F137.M63 S47   974.9/02/0924 B 19   LC 81-14531   ISBN 0815622430

Pomfret, John Edwin, 1898-.   **3.8066**
Colonial New Jersey; a history [by] John E. Pomfret. — New York: Scribner, [1973] xix, 327 p.: illus.; 24 cm. — (History of the American colonies.) 1. New Jersey — History — Colonial period, ca. 1600-1775 I. T. II. Series.
F137.P717 1973   974.9/02   LC 72-1228   ISBN 0684133717

Pomfret, John Edwin, 1898-.   • **3.8067**
The Province of East New Jersey, 1609–1702, the rebellious proprietary. Princeton, N.J., Princeton, University Press, 1962. x, 407 p. map. 25 cm. 1. New Jersey — History — Colonial period. I. T.
F137.P73   LC 62-7045

Federal writers' project. New Jersey.   **3.8068**
New Jersey, a guide to its present and past. New York, The Viking press, 1939. xxxii, 735 p. illus., maps (1 fold. in pocket) 21 cm. 1. Automobiles — Road-guides. 2. New Jersey — Description and travel — Guide-books.
F139.F45   LC 39-20654

Tice, George A.   **3.8069**
Paterson / [by] George A. Tice. — New Brunswick, N.J.: Rutgers University Press [1972] 1 v.: (chiefly ill.); 29 cm. 1. Paterson (N.J.) — Description — Views. I. T.
F144.P4 T5   917.49/24/00222   LC 79-163964   ISBN 0813507111
ISBN 0813507197

Landsman, Ned C., 1951-.   **3.8070**
Scotland and its first American colony, 1683–1765 / Ned C. Landsman. — Princeton, N.J.: Princeton University Press, c1985. xiv, 360 p.: maps; 22 cm. Includes index. 1. Scottish Americans — New Jersey — History. 2. Scottish Americans — History. 3. New Jersey — History — Colonial period, ca.

1600-1775 4. Scotland — History — 1660-1688 5. Scotland — History — 1689-1745 I. T.
F145.S3 L36 1985   974.9/0049163 19   *LC* 84-42891   *ISBN* 0691047243

F146–160 PENNSYLVANIA

Buck, Solon J. (Solon Justus), 1884-1962.   • **3.8071**
The planting of civilization in western Pennsylvania / by Solon J. Buck and Elizabeth Hawthorn Buck; illustrated from the drawings of Clarence McWilliams and from photographs, contemporary pictures and maps. — [Pittsburgh]: University of Pittsburgh Press [c1939] xiv, 565 p.: ill., plates, ports., maps, plans; 24 cm. Illustrated t.-p. 'This book is one of a series relating western Pennsylvania history, written under the direction of the Western Pennsylvania Historical Survey sponsored jointly by the Buhl foundation, the Historical society of western Pennsylvania and the University of Pittsburgh.' Illustrated t.-p. 1. Pennsylvania — History — Colonial period. 2. Pennsylvania. I. Buck, Elizabeth Hawthorn, Mrs., joint author. II. Western Pennsylvania historical survey. III. T.
F149.B83   *LC* 39-25307

Cochran, Thomas Childs, 1902-.   **3.8072**
Pennsylvania: a Bicentennial history / Thomas C. Cochran. — New York: Norton, c1978. xii, 207 p., [8] leaves of plates: ill.; 22 cm. (The States and the Nation series) Includes index. 1. Pennsylvania — History I. T.
F149.C7   974.8   *LC* 77-15017   *ISBN* 039305635X

Klein, Philip Shriver, 1909-.   **3.8073**
A history of Pennsylvania [by] Philip S. Klein [and] Ari Hoogenboom. — New York: McGraw-Hill, [1973] xiv, 559 p.: illus.; 24 cm. 1. Pennsylvania — History I. Hoogenboom, Ari Arthur, 1927- II. T.
F149.K55   917.48/03   *LC* 72-3991   *ISBN* 007035037X

Hanna, William S.   • **3.8074**
Benjamin Franklin and Pennsylvania politics / William S. Hanna. — Stanford, Calif.: Stanford University Press, 1964. x, 239 p. 1. Franklin, Benjamin, 1706-1790. 2. Pennsylvania — Politics and government — Colonial period, ca. 1600-1775 I. T.
F152.H37   *LC* 64-14557

Hutson, James H.   • **3.8075**
Pennsylvania politics, 1746–1770: the movement for royal government and its consequences / by James H. Hutson. — Princeton, N.J.: Princeton University Press, 1972. viii, 264 p.; 23 cm. 1. Pennsylvania — Politics and government — Colonial period, ca. 1600-1775 I. T.
F152.H86   320.9/748/02   *LC* 74-173756   *ISBN* 0691046115

Illick, Joseph E.   **3.8076**
Colonial Pennsylvania: a history / Joseph E. Illick. — New York: Scribner, c1976. xix, 359 p.: ill.; 24 cm. (History of the American colonies.) Includes index. 1. Pennsylvania — History — Colonial period, ca. 1600-1775 2. Pennsylvania — History — Revolution, 1775-1783 I. T. II. Series.
F152.I44   974.8/02   *LC* 75-37551   *ISBN* 0684145650

Tolles, Frederick Barnes, 1915-.   • **3.8077**
James Logan and the culture of provincial America. Boston, Little, Brown [1957] 228 p. 21 cm. (The Library of American biography) 1. Logan, James, 1674-1751. 2. Pennsylvania — History — Colonial period. I. T.
F152.L85   923.273   *LC* 57-6439

Nash, Gary B.   • **3.8078**
Quakers and politics; Pennsylvania, 1681–1726, by Gary B. Nash. — Princeton, N.J.: Princeton University Press, 1968. xii, 362 p.; 23 cm. 1. Friends, Society of. Pennsylvania — History. 2. Pennsylvania — History I. T.
F152.N25   974.8/02   *LC* 68-29386

Volwiler, Albert Tangeman.   • **3.8079**
George Croghan and the westward movement, 1741–1782 / by Albert T. Volwiler. — Cleveland: The Arthur H. Clark company, 1926. 370 p.: incl. front., maps (1 double) facsim.; 25 cm. 1. Croghan, George, d. 1782. 2. Frontier and pioneer life — Ohio valley. 3. Indians of North America Ohio valley. 4. Indians of North America — Commerce 5. Pennsylvania — History — Colonial period. I. T.
F152.V942   *LC* 26-7285

Endy, Melvin B.   **3.8080**
William Penn and early Quakerism [by] Melvin B. Endy, Jr. [Princeton, N.J.] Princeton University Press [1973] viii, 410 p. 24 cm. Based on the author's thesis. 1. Penn, William, 1644-1718. 2. Society of Friends — History. I. T.
F152.2.E52   289.6/092/4 B   *LC* 72-7798   *ISBN* 069107190X

Penn, William, 1644-1718.   **3.8081**
The papers of William Penn / editors, Mary Maples Dunn, Richard S. Dunn; associate editors, Richard A. Ryerson, Scott M. Wilds; assistant editor, Jean R. Soderlund. — Philadelphia, PA: University of Pennsylvania Press, 1981. 703 p.: ill. 1. Penn, William, 1644-1718. 2. Society of Friends — History — 17th century — Sources. 3. Society of Friends — History — 18th century — Sources. 4. Society of Friends — Biography. 5. Pioneers — Pennsylvania — Correspondence. 6. Pennsylvania — History — Colonial period, ca. 1600-1775 — Sources. I. Dunn, Mary Maples. II. Dunn, Richard S. III. T.
F152.2.P3956 1981   974.8/02/0924 B 19   *LC* 80-54052   *ISBN* 0812278003

William Penn and the founding of Pennsylvania, 1680–1684: a   **3.8082**
documentary history / editor, Jean R. Soderlund ... [et al.].
Philadelphia: University of Pennsylvania Press: Historical Society of Pennsylvania, 1983. viii, 416 p.: ill.; 25 cm. Includes index. 1. Penn, William, 1644-1718. 2. Pennsylvania — History — Colonial period, ca. 1600-1775 — Sources. I. Soderlund, Jean R., 1947-
F152.2.W53 1983   974.8/02 19   *LC* 82-60306   *ISBN* 0812278623

Writers' program. Pennsylvania.   **3.8083**
Pennsylvania; a guide to the Keystone state. New York, Oxford University Press [1940] xxxii, 660 p. illus., plates, maps (3 on 1 fold. l., in pocket) 21 cm. 1. Pennsylvania. 2. Pennsylvania — Description and travel — Guide-books.
F154.W94   *LC* 40-28760

Gudelunas, William A.   **3.8084**
Before the Molly Maguires: the emergence of the ethno–religious factor in the politics of the lower anthracite region, 1844–1872 / William A.Gudelunas, Jr. and William G. Shade. — New York: Arno Press, 1976. 165 p.: ill.; 24 cm. (The Irish-Americans) Based on W. A. Gudelunas' thesis, Lehigh University, 1973. 1. Schuylkill County (Pa.) — Politics and government. I. Shade, William G. joint author. II. T. III. Series.
F157.S3 G82 1976   301.5/92/0974817   *LC* 76-6344   *ISBN* 040509339X

F158 Philadelphia

Philadelphia: a 300 year history / editor, Russell F. Weigley,   **3.8085**
associate editors, Nicholas B. Wainwright, Edwin Wolf, 2nd.
1st ed. — New York: W.W. Norton, c1982. x, 842 p.: ill.; 25 cm. 'A Barra Foundation book.' 1. Philadelphia (Pa.) — History I. Weigley, Russell Frank. II. Wainwright, Nicholas B. III. Wolf, Edwin, 1911-
F158.3.P5664 1982   974.8/11 19   *LC* 82-8220   *ISBN* 0393016102

Warner, Sam Bass, 1928-.   **3.8086**
The private city: Philadelphia in three periods of its growth / Sam Bass Warner, Jr. — Rev. — Philadelphia: University of Pennsylvania Press, 1987, c1968. 1 v. Includes index. 1. Philadelphia (Pa.) — History I. T.
F158.3.W18 1987   974.8/11 19   *LC* 86-25124   *ISBN* 081228061X

Bridenbaugh, Carl.   • **3.8087**
Rebels and gentleman; Philadelphia in the age of Franklin, by Carl and Jessica Bridenbaugh. New York, Reynal & Hitchcock [c1942] xvii, 393 p. ill. 22 cm. 1. Philadelphia (Pa.) — History — Colonial period, ca. 1600-1775 2. Philadelphia (Pa.) — Social life and customs I. Bridenbaugh, Jessica, joint author. I. T.
F158.4.B6   *LC* 42-22812

Ryerson, Richard Alan, 1942-.   **3.8088**
The Revolution is now begun: the radical committees of Philadelphia, 1765–1776 / Richard Alan Ryerson. — Philadelphia: University of Pennsylvania Press, c1978. xv, 305 p.; 26 cm. Includes index. 1. Philadelphia (Pa.) — History — Colonial period, ca. 1600-1775 2. Philadelphia (Pa.) — History — Revolution, 1775-1783 3. Pennsylvania — History — Revolution, 1775-1783 I. T.
F158.4.R87   974.8/11/03   *LC* 77-81444   *ISBN* 0812277341

The Peoples of Philadelphia; a history of ethnic groups and   **3.8089**
lower–class life, 1790–1940. Edited by Allen F. Davis and Mark
H. Haller.
Philadelphia, Temple University Press [1973] ix, 301 p. illus. 23 cm. 'This book had its origin in a conference on the history of the peoples of Philadelphia held at Temple University April 1-2, 1971, and sponsored by the Committee for Urban Studies and the Center for the Study of Federalism [Temple University]' 1. Minorities — Pennsylvani — Philadelphia — Congresses. 2. Philadelphia (Pa.) — Social conditions — Congresses. 3. Philadelphia (Pa.) — History — Congresses. I. Davis, Allen Freeman, 1931- ed. II. Haller, Mark H., 1928- ed. III. Philadelphia. Temple University. Committee for Urban Studies. IV. Temple University. Center for the Study of Federalism.
F158.9.A1 P48   301.45/09748/11   *LC* 72-95879   *ISBN* 0877220530

Clark, Dennis, 1927-. 3.8090
The Irish in Philadelphia; ten generations of urban experience. — Philadelphia: Temple University Press, [1973] xvii, 246 p.; 22 cm. 1. Irish Americans — Pennsylvania — Philadelphia — History. I. T.
F158.9.I6 C55 917.48/11/069162 *LC* 72-95884 *ISBN* 0877220573

Ershkowitz, Miriam, comp. 3.8091
Black politics in Philadelphia / edited by Miriam Ershkowitz and Joseph Zikmund II. — New York: Basic Books [1973] xiv, 228 p.: ill.; 22 cm. 1. Afro-Americans — Pennsylvania — Philadelphia — Politics and government — Addresses, essays, lectures. I. Zikmund, Joseph, joint comp. II. T.
F158.9.N3 E77 320.9/748/11 *LC* 72-89284 *ISBN* 0465006981

F159 Other Cities, A–Z

Morawska, Ewa T. 3.8092
For bread with butter: the life–worlds of East Central Europeans in Johnstown, Pennsylvania, 1890–1940 / Ewa Morawska. — Cambridge [Cambridgeshire]; New York: Cambridge University Press, 1985. xvii, 429 p.: ill.; 24 cm. (Interdisciplinary perspectives on modern history.) Includes index. 1. East European Americans — Pennsylvania — Johnstown — History. 2. Johnstown (Pa.) — History. I. T. II. Series.
F159.J7 M83 1985 974.8/77 19 *LC* 85-12781 *ISBN* 0521306337

Baldwin, Leland Dewitt, 1897-. • 3.8093
Pittsburgh: the story of a city, 1750–1865, by Leland D. Baldwin. Illus. by Ward Hunter. [Pittsburgh] University of Pittsburgh Press [1970, c1937] xi, 341 p. illus., maps. 21 cm. (Pitt paperback, 56) 'This book is one of a series relating to Western Pennsylvania history written under the direction of the Western Pennsylvania Historical Survey sponsored jointly by the Buhl Foundation, the Historical Society of Western Pennsylvania, and the University of Pittsburgh.' 1. Pittsburgh (Pa.) — History I. Western Pennsylvania Historical Survey. II. Buhl Foundation. III. T.
F159.P6 B2 1970 917.48/86/034 *LC* 73-104172 *ISBN* 0822952165

Pittsburgh / edited by Roy Lubove. 3.8094
New York: New Viewpoints, 1976. 294 p.; 22 cm. (Documentary history of American cities) 1. Labor and laboring classes — Pittsburgh — History — Addresses, essays, lectures. 2. Pittsburgh (Pa.) — History — Addresses, essays, lectures. I. Lubove, Roy.
F159.P6 P49 974.8/86 *LC* 76-3119 *ISBN* 0531053849. *ISBN* 0531055906 pbk

Bodnar, John E., 1944-. 3.8095
Lives of their own: Blacks, Italians, and Poles in Pittsburgh, 1900–1960 / John Bodnar, Roger Simon, and Michael P. Weber. — Urbana: University of Illinois Press, c1982. 286 p.: ill.; 24 cm. — (Working class in American history.) 1. Minorities — Pennsylvania — Pittsburgh. 2. Afro-Americans — Pennsylvania — Pittsburgh 3. Italian Americans — Pennsylvania — Pittsburgh. 4. Polish Americans — Pennsylvania — Pittsburgh. 5. Pittsburgh (Pa.) — Social conditions. 6. Pittsburgh (Pa.) — Economic conditions. I. Simon, Roger D. II. Weber, Michael P. III. T. IV. Series.
F159.P69 A22 1982 974.8/86004 19 *LC* 81-3382 *ISBN* 0252008804

Bianco, Carla. 3.8096
The two Rosetos. Bloomington, Indiana University Press [1974] xv, 234 p. illus. 24 cm. 1. Italian Americans — Pennsylvania — Roseto. 2. Italian Americans — Pennsylvania — Roseto — Folklore. 3. Folklore — Italy — Roseto Valfortore. 4. Folklore — Pennsylvania — Roseto. 5. Roseto (Pa.) — Social life and customs. 6. Roseto Valfortore (Italy) — Social life and customs. I. T.
F159.R73 B52 917.48/22 *LC* 73-16523 *ISBN* 0253189926

F161–205 Delaware. Maryland.
District of Columbia

Delaware Federal Writers' Project. 3.8097
Delaware, a guide to the first state / compiled and written by the Federal Writers' Project of the Works Progress Administration for the State of Delaware. New and rev. ed. / by Jeanette Eckman; edited by Henry G. Alsberg. St. Clair Shores, Mich.: Scholarly Press, 1976. xxvi, 562 p.: ill., maps; 21 cm. Original ed. issued in series: American guide series. Includes index. 1. Delaware. 2. Delaware — Description and travel — Guide-books. I. T.
F164.D39 1973 917.51/04/4 *LC* 72-84465 *ISBN* 040302160X

Hoffecker, Carol E. 3.8098
Delaware: a Bicentennial history / Carol E. Hoffecker. — New York: Norton, c1977. xvi, 221 p., [8] leaves of plates: ill.; 22 cm. (The States and the Nation series) Includes index. 1. Delaware — History I. T.
F164.H62 975.1 *LC* 76-53844 *ISBN* 0393056201

Munroe, John A., 1914-. 3.8099
Colonial Delaware: a history / John A. Munroe. — Millwood, N.Y.: KTO Press, c1978. xvii, 292 p.: ill.; 24 cm. — (History of the American colonies.) Includes index. 1. Delaware — History — Colonial period, ca. 1600-1775 2. Delaware — History — Revolution, 1775-1783 I. T. II. Series.
F167.M84 975.1/02 *LC* 78-18738 *ISBN* 0527187119

Monroe, John A., 1914-. • 3.8100
Federalist Delaware, 1775–1815 / John A. Munroe. — New Brunswick, N.J.: Rutgers University Press, 1954. xiv, 286 p.: fold. map — (University of Delaware monograph series; no. 6) Includes index. 1. Delaware — History I. T. II. Series.
F168.M8 975.1 *LC* 54-11929

Maryland: a new guide to the Old Line State / compiled and 3.8100a
edited by Edward C. Papenfuse ... [et al.].
Baltimore: Johns Hopkins University Press, c1976. xx, 463 p.: ill.; 24 cm. (Studies in Maryland history and culture) Based on the 1940 ed. of Maryland, a guide to the Old Line State, compiled by the Writers' Program of the Work Projects Administration in the State of Maryland. Includes index. 1. Maryland — Description and travel — 1951-1980 — Tours. I. Papenfuse, Edward C. II. Writers' Program. Maryland. Maryland, a guide to the Old Line State. III. Series.
F179.3.M37 917.52/04/4 *LC* 76-17224 *ISBN* 0801818745. *ISBN* 0801818710 pbk

Bode, Carl, 1911-. 3.8101
Maryland: a Bicentennial history / Carl Bode. — New York: Norton, c1978. xvi. 204 p., [8] leaves of plates: ill.; 22 cm. (The States and the Nation series) Includes index. 1. Maryland — History I. T.
F181.B63 975.2 *LC* 77-17983 *ISBN* 0393056724

McDaniel, George W. 3.8102
Hearth & home, preserving a people's culture / George W. McDaniel. — Philadelphia: Temple University Press, 1982. xxiv, 297 p.: ill.; 24 cm. — (American civilization.) Includes index. 1. Historic buildings — Maryland. 2. Farmhouses — Maryland. 3. Afro-Americans — Housing — Maryland. 4. Maryland — Rural conditions. I. T. II. Title: Hearth and home preserving a people's culture. III. Series.
F182.M32 1982 975.2 19 *LC* 81-13627 *ISBN* 0877222339

Carr, Lois Green. 3.8103
Maryland's revolution of government, 1689–1692 [by] Lois Green Carr and David William Jordan. — Ithaca [N.Y.]: Cornell University Press, [1974] xviii, 321 p.: map.; 24 cm. — (St. Mary's City Commission publication no. 1) 1. Maryland — Politics and government — Colonial period, ca. 1600-1775 I. Jordan, David William, joint author. II. T.
F184.C29 320.9/752/02 *LC* 73-13055 *ISBN* 0801407931

Land, Aubrey C. • 3.8104
The Dulanys of Maryland; a biographical study of Daniel Dulany, the Elder (1685–1753) and Daniel Dulany, the Younger (1722–1797) by Aubrey C. Land. — Baltimore: Johns Hopkins Press, [1968, c1955] xiv, 390 p.; 24 cm. 'Originally published by the Maryland Historical Society.' 1. Dulany, Daniel, 1685-1753. 2. Dulany, Daniel, 1722-1797. I. T.
F184.D8 L3 1968 975.2/02/0922 *LC* 68-28873

Land, Aubrey C. 3.8105
Colonial Maryland, a history / Aubrey C. Land. — Millwood, N.Y.: KTO Press, c1981. xviii, 367 p.: ill.; 24 cm. — (A History of the American colonies) Includes index. 1. Maryland — History — Colonial period, ca. 1600-1775 2. Maryland — History — Revolution, 1775-1783 I. T.
F184.L34 975.2/02 19 *LC* 80-21732 *ISBN* 0527187135

Steiner, Bernard Christian, 1864-1926. • 3.8106
Maryland under the commonwealth: a chronicle of the years 1649–1658 / by Bernard C. Steiner. — Baltimore: Johns Hopkins Press, 1911. 178 p. — (Johns Hopkins University studies in historical and political science; ser. xxix, no. 1) Appendix: A summary of the Proceedings of the Provincial Courts, 1649 to 1658, chronologically arranged: p. 117-178. 1. Maryland — Politics and government — Colonial period, ca. 1600-1775 I. T.
F184.S813 *LC* 11-16268

The Chesapeake in the seventeenth century: essays on Anglo– 3.8107
American society / edited by Thad W. Tate and David L. Ammerman.
Chapel Hill: Published for the Institute of Early American History and Culture by the University of North Carolina Press, c1979. viii, 310 p.: ill.; 24 cm. 'Outgrowth of a conference ... held on November 1 and 2, 1974, at College Park and St. Mary's, Maryland.' 1. Chesapeake Bay region — History — Addresses,

essays, lectures. 2. Maryland — History — Colonial period, ca. 1600-1775 — Addresses, essays, lectures. 3. Virginia — History — Colonial period, ca. 1600-1775 — Addresses, essays, lectures. I. Tate, Thad W. II. Ammerman, David, 1938- III. Institute of Early American History and Culture (Williamsburg, Va.)
F187.C5 C46   975.5/18   LC 78-31720   ISBN 0807813605

Krech, Shepard, 1944-.   3.8108
Praise the bridge that carries you over: the life of Joseph L. Sutton / Shepard Krech III. — Boston, Mass.: G.K. Hall; Cambridge, Mass.: Schenkman Pub. Co., c1981. xxvii, 209 p., [1] p. of plates: ill.; 25 cm. 1. Sutton, Joseph L., 1885-1980. 2. Afro-Americans — Maryland — Talbot County — Social life and customs. 3. Afro-Americans — Maryland — Talbot County — Biography. 4. Talbot County (Md.) — Race relations. 5. Talbot County (Md.) — Biography. I. T.
F187.T2 S894   975.2/3204/0924 B 19   LC 81-1292   ISBN 0816190380

Washington information directory.   3.8109
[Washington]: Congressional Quarterly, Inc., 1975-. 863 p. Annual. 1. Washington Metropolitan Area — Directories. 2. Washington (D.C.) — Directories. 3. United States — Executive departments — Directories. I. Congressional Quarterly, inc.
F192.3.W33   975.3/0025   LC 75-646321

Green, Constance McLaughlin, 1897-.   • 3.8110
Washington. Princeton, N.J.: Princeton University Press, 1962-63. 2 v.: ill.; 25 cm. 1. Washington (D.C.) — History I. T.
F194.G7   LC 62-7402

Lewis, David L.   3.8111
District of Columbia: a bicentennial history / David L. Lewis. — New York: Norton, c1976. xiii, 208 p., [7] leaves of plates: ill.; 22 cm. (The States and the Nation series) Includes index. 1. Washington (D.C.) — History I. T.
F194.L48   975.3   LC 76-28397   ISBN 0393056015

Federal writers' project.   3.8112
Washington, city and capital. Washington, D.C., U. S. Govt. print. off. [1937] xxvi, 1140, [1] p. incl. front., illus., port., plans. maps (part fold.; part in pocket) 24 cm. 1. Washington, D.C. — Description — Guide-books. 2. Washington, D.C. — History. 3. Washington, D.C. — Intellectual life. 4. Washington, D.C. — Suburbs. I. T.
F199.F38   LC 37-26377

F206–220 Southern States: General

The Encyclopedia of Southern history / edited by David C.   3.8113
Roller and Robert W. Twyman; Avery O. Craven, Dewey W.
Grantham, Jr., general consultants; Paul V. Crawford,
consulting cartographer.
Baton Rouge: Louisiana State University Press, c1979. ix, 1421 p.: ill. (some col.); 27 cm. 1. Southern States — History — Dictionaries. I. Roller, David C., 1937- II. Twyman, Robert W., 1919-
F207.7.E52   975/.003   LC 79-12666   ISBN 0807105759

Link, Arthur Stanley. ed.   • 3.8114
Writing southern history; essays in historiography in honor of Fletcher M. Green, edited by Arthur S. Link & Rembert W. Patrick. — [Baton Rouge] Louisiana State University Press [1966, c1965] x, 502 p. port. 25 cm. Bibliographical footnotes. 1. Green, Fletcher Melvin, 1895- 2. Southern States — Hist. — Historiography — Addresses, essays, lectures. I. Green, Fletcher Melvin, 1895- II. Patrick, Rembert Wallace, 1909- joint ed. III. T.
F208.2.L5   975.07   LC 65-23761

The American South: a historical bibliography / Jessica S.   3.8115
Brown, editor; introduction by John B. Boles.
Santa Barbara, Calif.: ABC-Clio, c1986. 2 v.; 29 cm. (Clio bibliography series. no. 21-22) Includes indexes. 1. Southern States — History — Abstracts. 2. Southern States — History — Bibliography. I. Brown, Jessica S. II. Series.
F209.A45 1986   016.975 19   LC 85-19938   ISBN 0874364647

Bertelson, David.   • 3.8116
The lazy South. — New York: Oxford University Press, 1967. ix, 284 p.; 22 cm. 1. Work — Psychological aspects 2. Laziness 3. Southern States — Social life and customs. I. T.
F209.B42   917.5/03   LC 67-10854

Cash, Wilbur Joseph, 1901-1941.   • 3.8117
The mind of the South. — Garden City, N. Y., Doubleday, 1954 [c1941] 444 p. 19 cm. — (Doubleday anchor book, A 27) 1. Southern States — Civilization 2. Southern States — Soc. condit. I. T.
F209.C3 1954   975   LC 54-3719

Dabney, Virginius, 1901-.   • 3.8118
Liberalism in the South. — New York: AMS Press, [1970] xix, 456 p.; 23 cm. Reprint of the 1932 ed. 1. Liberalism — Southern States. 2. Southern States — Social conditions 3. Southern States — Politics and government I. T.
F209.D16 1970   309.1/75   LC 77-128983   ISBN 0404001467

Gaston, Paul M., 1928-.   • 3.8119
The new South creed: a study in southern mythmaking / [by] Paul M. Gaston. — [1st ed.]. — New York: Knopf, 1970. viii, 298, vi p.; 22 cm. 1. Southern States — Civilization 2. Southern States — Race relations. I. T.
F209.G3   917.5/03   LC 70-98640

A Band of prophets: the Vanderbilt Agrarians after fifty years /   3.8120
edited with an introduction by William C. Havard and Walter
Sullivan.
Baton Rouge: Louisiana State University Press, c1982. x, 190 p.: ill.; 23 cm. — (Southern literary studies.) 1. I'll take my stand — Addresses, essays, lectures. 2. Southern States — Civilization — Addresses, essays, lectures. I. Havard, William C. II. Sullivan, Walter, 1924- III. Series.
F209.I3732 1982   975 19   LC 81-19371   ISBN 0807110019

I'll take my stand; the South and the agrarian tradition.   • 3.8121
New York P. Smith 1951. 359p. 1. Southern States — Civilization — Addresses, essays, lectures I. Twelve southerners
F209 I44 1951

Phillips, Ulrich Bonnell, 1877-1934.   • 3.8122
Life and labor in the old South, by Ulrich Bonnell Phillips. — Boston: Little, Brown, and company, 1929. xix, 375 p.: front., illus., maps (1 fold.), diagr.; 23 cm. Awarded the prize of $2500 offered in 1928 by Little, Brown, and company for the best unpublished work on American history. 1. Slavery in the United States. 2. Southern States — Social conditions 3. Southern States — Economic conditions I. T.
F209.P56   LC 29-11204

Sellers, Charles Grier. ed.   • 3.8123
The southerner as American. [By] John Hope Franklin [and others]. — Chapel Hill, University of North Carolina Press [1960] 216 p. 24 cm. Includes bibliography. 1. National characteristics, American 2. Southern States — Civilization 3. Southern States — Hist. — Historiography. 4. Southern States — Race question. I. T.
F209.S44   917.5   LC 60-4104

Simkins, Francis Butler, 1898-.   • 3.8124
The everlasting South. [Baton Rouge]: Louisiana State University [1963] xv, 103 p.: front.; 22 cm. Five essays. 1. Southern States — Civilization I. T.
F209.S488   917.5   LC 63-20407

Taylor, William Robert, 1922-.   • 3.8125
Cavalier and Yankee; the Old South and American national character. — New York: G. Braziller, 1961. 384 p.; 22 cm. 1. National characteristics, American 2. Southern States — History — 1775-1865 — Philosophy. I. T.
F209.T3 1961   975   LC 61-15493

Wyatt-Brown, Bertram, 1932-.   3.8126
Southern honor: ethics and behavior in the old South / Bertram Wyatt-Brown. — New York: Oxford University Press, 1982. xxiv, 597 p.; 23 cm. 1. Honor 2. Southern States — Moral conditions. 3. Southern States — Civilization I. T.
F209.W9 1982   975 19   LC 81-22448   ISBN 0195031199

Young, Thomas Daniel, 1919-.   3.8127
Waking their neighbors up: the Nashville Agrarians rediscovered / Thomas Daniel Young. — Athens: University of Georgia Press, c1982. xii, 90 p.; 22 cm. — (Lamar memorial lectures. no. 24) Includes index. 1. I'll take my stand — Addresses, essays, lectures. 2. Authors, American — Southern States — Political and social views — Addresses, essays, lectures. 3. Southern States — Civilization — Addresses, essays, lectures. I. T. II. Series.
F209.Y68 1982   975 19   LC 81-14736   ISBN 0820306002

The American South: portrait of a culture / edited by Louis D.   3.8128
Rubin, Jr.
Baton Rouge: Louisiana State University Press, c1980. x, 379 p.; 24 cm. — (Southern literary studies.) 1. American literature — Southern States — History and criticism — Addresses, essays, lectures. 2. Southern States — Civilization — Addresses, essays, lectures. I. Rubin, Louis Decimus, 1923- II. Series.
F209.5.A47   975   LC 79-12316   ISBN 0807105627

Current, Richard Nelson. 3.8129
Northernizing the South / Richard N. Current. — Athens: University of Georgia Press, c1983. x, 147 p.; 23 cm. — (Lamar memorial lectures. no. 26) Includes index. 1. Regionalism — Southern States — Addresses, essays, lectures. 2. Southern States — Civilization — Addresses, essays, lectures. I. T. II. Series.
F209.5.C87 1983   974/.03 19   LC 82-23804   ISBN 0820306665

F212–214 EARLY TO 1865

Bridenbaugh, Carl. • 3.8130
Myths and realities; societies of the colonial South. Baton Rouge, Louisiana State University Press [1952] x, 208 p. 23 cm. (The Walter Lynwood Fleming lectures in southern history, Louisiana State University) Bibliographical footnotes. 'Bibliographical note': p. [197]-200. 1. Southern States — Social life and customs — Colonial period. 2. Southern States — Intellectual life I. T.
F212.B75   917.5   LC 52-13024

Craven, Wesley Frank, 1905-. • 3.8131
The southern colonies in the seventeenth century, 1607–1689. — [Baton Rouge]: Louisiana State Univ. Press, 1949. xv, 451 p.: ill., maps, facsims.; 24 cm. — (A History of the South, v. 1) 'Critical essay on authorities': p. 417-433. 1. Southern States — History — Colonial period, ca. 1600-1775 I. T. II. Series.
F212.C7   975   LC 49-3595

Davis, Richard Beale. 3.8132
Intellectual life in the Colonial South, 1585–1763 / by Richard Beale Davis. — Knoxville: University of Tennessee Press, c1978. 3 v. (xxxi, 1810 p.), 24 leaves of plates: ill.; 24 cm. 1. Southern States — Intellectual life — Colonial period, ca. 1600-1775 I. T.
F212.D28   975/.01   LC 77-1370   ISBN 0870492101

Robinson, Walter Stitt. 3.8133
The southern colonial frontier, 1607–1763 / W. Stitt Robinson. — 1st ed. — Albuquerque: University of New Mexico Press, c1979. xvii, 293 p.: ill.; 24 cm. — (Histories of the American frontier) Includes index. 1. Frontier and pioneer life — Southern States. 2. Southern States — History — Colonial period, ca. 1600-1775 I. T.
F212.R62   975/.02   LC 78-21432   ISBN 0826305024

Alden, John Richard, 1908-. • 3.8134
John Stuart and the Southern colonial frontier; a study of Indian relations, war, trade, and land problems in the Southern wilderness, 1754–1775. — New York: Gordian Press, 1966 [c1944] xiv, 384 p.: maps.; 24 cm. — (University of Michigan publications. History and political science, v. 15) 1. Stuart, John, 1718-1779. 2. Indians of North America — Southern States 3. Indians of North America — Government relations — To 1789 4. Southern States — History — Colonial period, ca. 1600-1775 I. T.
F212.S7 A6 1966   970.5   LC 66-29459

Abernethy, Thomas Perkins, 1890-. • 3.8135
The South in the new nation / by Thomas P. Abernethy. — Baton Rouge: Louisiana State University Press, 1961. xvi, 529 p.: maps. — (History of the South; v.4) 1. Southern States — History — 1775-1865 I. T. II. Series.
F213.A2   LC 61-15488

Alden, John Richard, 1908-. • 3.8136
The first South. Baton Rouge: Louisiana State University Press [1961] 144 p.; 21 cm. 1. Sectionalism (U. S.) 2. Southern States — History — Revolution. 3. United States — Constitutional history I. T.
F213.A39   LC 61-10831

Alden, John Richard, 1908-. • 3.8137
The South in the Revolution, 1763–1789 / by John Richard Alden. — Baton Rouge: Louisiana State University Press, 1957. xv, 442 p.: ill., map. — (History of the South; v.3) 1. Southern States — History — Revolution, 1775-1783 I. T. II. Series.
F213.A4   LC 57-12096

Cooper, William J. (William James), 1940-. 3.8138
Liberty and slavery: southern politics to 1860 / William J. Cooper, Jr. — 1st ed. — New York: Knopf, c1983. 309 p.: ill.; 22 cm. Includes index. 1. Southern States — Politics and government — 1775-1865 I. T.
F213.C68 1983   975/.02 19   LC 83-4311   ISBN 0394532899

Cooper, William J. (William James), 1940-. 3.8139
The South and the politics of slavery, 1828–1856 / William J. Cooper, Jr. — Baton Rouge: Louisiana State University Press, c1978. xv, 401 p.; 24 cm. Includes index. 1. Slavery in the United States — History. 2. Southern States — Politics and government — 1775-1865 I. T.
F213.C69   320.4/75/03   LC 78-751   ISBN 0807103853

Craven, Avery Odelle, 1886-. • 3.8140
The growth of Southern nationalism, 1848–1861. — [Baton Rouge] Louisiana State University Press [and] the Littlefield Fund for Southern History of the University of Texas [Austin] 1953. xi, 433 p. illus., group port. 24 cm. — (A History of the South, v. 6) 'Critical essay on authorities': p. 402-419. Bibliographical footnotes. 1. Sectionalism (U.S.) 2. Southern States — Pol. & govt. — 1775-1865. I. T. II. Series.
F213.C75   975   LC 53-11470

Dodd, William Edward, 1869-1940. • 3.8141
The cotton kingdom; a chronicle of the Old South, by William E. Dodd. — New Haven, Yale university press; [etc., etc.] 1921. ix, 161 p. col. front., fold. map. 18 cm. — (Half-title: The chronicles of America series, Allen Johnson, editor ... v. 27) 'Roosevelt edition.' 'Bibliographical note': p. 147-153. 1. Southern States I. T.
F213.D63 E173.C56 vol. 27   LC 22-12149

Eaton, Clement, 1898-. • 3.8142
The growth of Southern civilization, 1790–1860. [1st ed.] New York: Harper [1961] xvii, 357 p.: ill., ports.; 22 cm. (The New American Nation series) 1. Southern States — Civilization — 1775-1865 2. Southern States — History — 1775-1865 I. T.
F213.E18   975   LC 61-12219

Eaton, Clement, 1898-. • 3.8143
The mind of the Old South. — Rev. ed. — [Baton Rouge]: Louisiana State University Press, [1967] xi, 348 p.: ports.; 23 cm. 1. National characteristics, American 2. Southern States — Civilization 3. Southern States — Biography. I. T.
F213.E22 1967   917.5/04/3   LC 67-11684

Franklin, John Hope, 1915-. • 3.8144
The militant South, 1800–1861. — Cambridge: Belknap Press of Harvard University Press, 1956. 317 p.; 22 cm. 1. Militarism 2. Southern States — History — 1775-1865 I. T.
F213.F75   975   LC 56-10160

Franklin, John Hope, 1915-. 3.8145
A southern odyssey: travelers in the antebellum North / John Hope Franklin. — Baton Rouge: Louisiana State University Press, c1976. xvii, 299 p.: ill.; 24 cm. (The Walter Lynwood Fleming lectures in southern history) Includes index. 1. Travelers — Southern States. 2. Slavery in the United States. 3. Afro-Americans — History — To 1863 4. Southern States — History — 1775-1865 I. T.
F213.F76   917.4/04/3   LC 74-27190   ISBN 0807101613

Olmsted, Frederick Law, 1822-1903. • 3.8146
The Cotton Kingdom: a traveller's observations on cotton and slavery in the American slave States / based upon three former volumes of journeys and investigations by the same author; edited, with an introd., by Arthur M. Schlesinger. — New York: Knopf, 1953. lxiii, 626, xvi p.: facsim.; 25 cm. 1. Slaves — United States — Biography. 2. Cotton growing — Southern States. 3. Southern States — Description and travel 4. Southern States — Economic conditions I. T.
F213.O53 1953   917.5   LC 52-12193

Osterweis, Rollin G. (Rollin Gustav), 1907-. • 3.8147
Romanticism and nationalism in the Old South. Gloucester, Mass.,: P. Smith, 1964,c1949. 275p. (Yale historical publications. Miscellany, 49) 1. Southern States — Civilization 2. Romanticism 3. Southern States — History — 1775-1865 I. T.
F213 O8

Owsley, Frank Lawrence, 1890-1956. • 3.8148
Plain folk of the Old South. [Baton Rouge]: Louisiana State University Press, 1949. 235 p.: maps. (Louisiana State University and Agricultural and Mechanical College. Walter Lynwood Fleming lectures in Southern history.) "Quadrangle paperbacks." 1. Southern States — Social life and customs 2. Southern States — History — 1775-1865 I. T. II. Series.
F213.O94 1965   917.5   LC 49-11743

Rose, Lisle Abbott, 1936-. • 3.8149
Prologue to democracy: the Federalists in the South, 1789–1800 / [by] Lisle A. Rose. — Lexington: University of Kentucky Press, 1968. xvii, 326 p.; 23 cm. 1. Federal Party. Southern States. 2. Southern States — Politics and government — 1775-1865 I. T.
F213.R83   329/.1/009033   LC 67-29342

Schwaab, Eugene Lincoln, 1909- comp. 3.8150
Travels in the Old South, selected from periodicals of the times. Edited by Eugene L. Schwaab, with the collaboration of Jacqueline Bull. — [Lexington]: University Press of Kentucky, [1973] 2 v. (xiii, 579 p.): illus.; 22 x 28 cm. 1. Southern States — Description and travel — Addresses, essays, lectures. I. T.
F213.S38   917.5/04/3   LC 70-119814   ISBN 081311229X

Sydnor, Charles S. (Charles Sackett), 1898-. • **3.8151**
The development of Southern sectionalism, 1819–1848. — [Baton Rouge]
Louisiana State Univ. Press, 1948. xii, 400 p. illus., ports., maps. 25 cm. — (A
History of the South, v. 5) 'Critical essay on authorities': p. 346-381.
1. Southern States — Hist. — 1775-1865. 2. Sectionalism (U.S.) I. T.
II. Series.
F213.S92   975   *LC* 48-7627 *

Potter, David Morris. • **3.8152**
The South and the sectional conflict [by] David M. Potter. — Baton Rouge:
Louisiana State University Press, 1968. xi, 321 p.; 23 cm. Essays. 1. Southern
States — History — Addresses, essays, lectures. 2. United States — History —
Civil War, 1861-1865 — Historiography I. T.
F214.P6   975   *LC* 68-8941

Wiley, Bell Irvin, 1906-. • **3.8153**
The plain people of the Confederacy / [by] Bell Irvin Wiley. — Baton Rouge:
Louisiana State University Press, 1943. ix, 104 p.; 21 cm. 1. Confederate States
of America. Army. 2. Confederate States of America — Social life and customs
I. T.
F214 W56 1943

F215–216 1865-

Dykeman, Wilma. • **3.8154**
Seeds of Southern change: the life of Will Alexander / [by] Wilma Dykeman
and James Stokely. — [Chicago]: University of Chicago Press [1962] 343 p.: ill.;
23 cm. 1. Alexander, Will Winton, 1884-1956. 2. Southern States — Social
conditions 3. Southern States — Race question. I. Stokely, James, joint
author. II. T.
F215.A55 D9   *LC* 62-13923

Billington, Monroe Lee. **3.8155**
The political South in the twentieth century. New York, Scribner [1975] xiii,
205 p. illus. 24 cm. 1. Afro-Americans — Southern States 2. Southern States
— Politics and government — 1951- 3. Southern States — Politics and
government — 1865-1950 I. T.
F215.B56   320.9/75/04   *LC* 73-1312   *ISBN* 0684139839

Clark, Thomas Dionysius, 1903-. • **3.8156**
Pills, petticoats, and plows; the Southern country store. Norman, University of
Oklahoma Press [1964, c1944] xiv, 306 p. illus. 21 cm. 1. Retail trade —
Southern States. 2. Country life — Southern States. 3. Southern States —
Social life and customs — 1865- I. T.
F215.C6 1964   *LC* 64-11333

Daniels, Jonathan, 1902-. • **3.8157**
A southerner discovers the South / New introd. by the author. — New York:
Da Capo Press, 1970. xix, 346 p.: map.; 24 cm. — (A Da Capo Press reprint
series. The American scene) Originally published in 1938. 1. Southern States
2. Southern States — Social conditions I. T.
F215.D257   917.5   *LC* 68-16228   *ISBN* 0306710110

Dollard, John, 1900-. • **3.8158**
Caste and class in a southern town. 3d ed. Garden City, N.Y.: Doubleday, 1957
[c1949] xii, 466 p.; 18 cm. (Doubleday anchor books, A95) 1. Afro-Americans
— Southern States 2. Afro-Americans — Social conditions 3. Southern States
— Social conditions 4. Southern States — Civilization I. T.
F215.D65 1957   309.175   *LC* 57-505

Growing up southern: Southern exposure looks at childhood,   **3.8159**
then and now / edited by Chris Mayfield.
1st ed. — New York: Pantheon Books, c1981. xiv, 273 p.: ill.; 24 cm.
1. Children — Southern States — Addresses, essays, lectures. 2. Southern
States — Social life and customs — 1865- — Addresses, essays, lectures.
I. Mayfield, Chris. II. Southern exposure.
F215.G86 1981   975 19   *LC* 80-8658   *ISBN* 0394509137

Key, V. O. (Valdimer Orlando), 1908-1963. **3.8160**
Southern politics in state and nation / V.O. Key, Jr., with the assistance of
Alexander Heard. — New ed. — Knoxville: University of Tennessee Press,
1984, c1977. xlii, 675, xiv p., [16] p. of plates: ill.; 23 cm. Reprint. Originally
published: New York: Knopf, 1949. With a new introduction and profile.
1. Political parties — Southern States — History. 2. Southern States —
Politics and government — 1865-1950 I. Heard, Alexander. II. T.
F215.K45 1984   324.975/04 19   *LC* 84-3665   *ISBN* 0870494341

McGill, Ralph, 1898-1969. • **3.8161**
The South and the southerner. [1st ed.] Boston: Little, Brown [1963] 307 p.; 22
cm. 1. Southern States — Civilization 2. Southern States — Race question.
I. T.
F215.M16 1963   917.5   *LC* 63-8314

Odum, Howard Washington, 1884-1954. • **3.8162**
Southern regions of the United States. Chapel Hill, The University of North
Carolina press, 1936. xi, 664 p. incl. illus. (maps) tables, diagrs. 26 cm.
1. Southern States — Civilization 2. Southern States — Social conditions
I. Social science research council. Southern regional committee. II. T.
F215.O28   *LC* 36-10075

Potter, David Morris. • **3.8163**
The South and the concurrent majority [by] David M. Potter. Edited by Don E.
Fehrenbacher and Carl N. Degler. — Baton Rouge: Louisiana State University
Press, [1972] viii, 89 p.; 23 cm. — (The Walter Lynwood Fleming lectures in
southern history) 1. Southern States — Politics and government — 1865-1950
2. United States — Politics and government — 1865-1900 3. United States —
Politics and government — 1901-1953 I. T.
F215.P66   320.9/75/04   *LC* 72-84123   *ISBN* 0807102296

Region, race, and Reconstruction: essays in honor of C. Vann   **3.8164**
Woodward / edited by J. Morgan Kousser and James M.
McPherson.
New York: Oxford University Press, 1982. xxxvii, 463 p.: ill.; 24 cm.
1. Woodward, C. Vann (Comer Vann), 1908- 2. Reconstruction — Addresses,
essays, lectures. 3. Southern States — History — 1865- — Addresses, essays,
lectures. 4. United States — Race relations — Addresses, essays, lectures.
I. Woodward, C. Vann (Comer Vann), 1908- II. Kousser, J. Morgan.
III. McPherson, James M.
F215.R43 1982   975/.04 19   *LC* 81-16965   *ISBN* 0195030753

Sosna, Morton. **3.8165**
In search of the silent South: southern liberals and the race issue / Morton
Sosna. — New York: Columbia University Press, 1977. xvi, 275 p.; 24 cm. —
(Contemporary American history series) Includes index. 1. Odum, Howard
Washington, 1884-1954. 2. Dabney, Virginius, 1901- 3. Smith, Lillian
Eugenia, 1897-1966. 4. Liberalism — Southern States. 5. Southern States —
Race relations. 6. Southern States — Biography. I. T.
F215.S66   301.45/19/6073076   *LC* 77-4965   *ISBN* 0231038437

Tindall, George Brown. • **3.8166**
The emergence of the new South, 1913–1945. [Baton Rouge] Louisiana State
University Press, 1967. xv, 807 p. illus., ports. 24 cm. (A History of the South v.
10) 'Critical essay on authorities': p. 733-768. 1. Southern States — History —
1865-1951 I. T. II. Series.
F215.T59   975   *LC* 67-24551

Woodward, C. Vann (Comer Vann), 1908-. • **3.8167**
Origins of the new South, 1877–1913. [Baton Rouge] Louisiana State
University Press, 1951. xi, 542 p. illus. 24 cm. (A History of the South, v. 9)
1. Southern States — History — 1865-1951 2. Southern States — Social
conditions I. T. II. Series.
F215.W85   975   *LC* 51-14582

Grantham, Dewey W. **3.8168**
Southern progressivism: the reconciliation of progress and tradition / Dewey
W. Grantham. — 1st ed. — Knoxville: University of Tennessee Press, c1983.
xxii, 468 p.: ill.; 24 cm. — (Twentieth-century America series.) Includes index.
1. Progressivism (United States politics) 2. Southern States — Politics and
government — 1865-1950 I. T. II. Series.
F216.G73 1983   975/.04 19   *LC* 82-25918   *ISBN* 0870493892

Perman, Michael. **3.8169**
The road to redemption: Southern politics, 1869–1879 / by Michael Perman. —
Chapel Hill: University of North Carolina Press, c1984. xiv, 353 p.; 24 cm. —
(Fred W. Morrison series in Southern studies.) Includes index.
1. Reconstruction 2. Southern States — Politics and government — 1865-1950
I. T. II. Series.
F216.P47 1984   973.8 19   *LC* 83-12498   *ISBN* 0807815268

Bass, Jack. **3.8170**
The transformation of southern politics: social change and political
consequence since 1945 / Jack Bass & Walter De Vries. — New York: Basic
Books, c1976. xi, 527 p.: ill.; 25 cm. Erratum slip inserted. Includes index.
1. Afro-Americans — Southern States — Politics and government.
2. Southern States — Social conditions 3. Southern States — Politics and
government — 1951- I. De Vries, Walter. joint author. II. T.
F216.2.B39   320.9/75/04   *LC* 75-36375   *ISBN* 0465086950

Coles, Robert. **3.8171**
Farewell to the South. — [1st ed.]. — Boston: Little, Brown, [1972] viii, 408 p.:
illus.; 22 cm. 'An Atlantic Monthly Press book.' 1. Discrimination in education
— Southern States — Addresses, essays, lectures. 2. Southern States —
Addresses, essays, lectures. 3. Southern States — Race relations — Addresses,
essays, lectures. I. T.
F216.2.C58   917.5/03/4   *LC* 72-638   *ISBN* 0316151580

Lamis, Alexander P. **3.8172**
The two–party South / Alexander P. Lamis. — New York: Oxford University
Press, 1984. x, 317 p.: ill., maps; 25 cm. Includes index. 1. Political parties —

Southern States — History — 20th century. 2. Southern States — Politics and government — 1951- I. T.
F216.2.L35 1984   324/.0975 19   *LC* 84-9744   *ISBN* 0195034775

Murray, Albert.   **3.8173**
South to a very old place. [1st ed.] New York, McGraw-Hill [1971] 230 p. 22 cm. 1. Afro-Americans — Southern States 2. Southern States — Social life and customs — 1865- I. T.
F216.2.M87   917.5   *LC* 78-169023   *ISBN* 0070440735

Roland, Charles Pierce, 1918-.   **3.8174**
The improbable era: the South since World War II / Charles P. Roland. — Lexington: University Press of Kentucky, c1975. 228 p., [4] leaves of plates: ill.; 24 cm. Includes index. 1. Southern States — Politics and government — 1951- 2. Southern States — Economic conditions — 1945- 3. Southern States — Social life and customs I. T.
F216.2.R64   975/.04   *LC* 75-12082   *ISBN* 0813113350

Sherrill, Robert.   • **3.8175**
Gothic politics in the Deep South: stars of the new Confederacy. — New York: Grossman Publishers, 1968. 335 p.; 24 cm. 1. Southern States — Politics & government — 1951- I. T.
F216.2.S48   320.9/75   *LC* 67-21236

Sindler, Allan P. ed.   • **3.8176**
Change in the contemporary South. Durham: Duke University Press, 1963. 247 p.: diagrs.,tables. A revision of papers presented at a conference on 'The impact of political and legal change in the postwar South' sponsored by the Dept. of Political Science, Duke University, July 12-14, 1962. 1. Southern States — Civilization 2. Southern States — Politics and government — 1865- I. Duke University. II. T.
F216.2.S5   917.5   *LC* 63-21317

F217 REGIONS, A–Z

Our Appalachia: an oral history / edited by Laurel Shackelford   **3.8177**
and Bill Weinberg; photos. by Donald R. Anderson.
1st ed. — New York: Hill and Wang, 1977. ix, 397 p.: ill.; 22 cm. 1. Appalachian Region, Southern — Social life and customs. 2. Appalachian Region, Southern — Biography. I. Shackelford, Laurel, 1946- II. Weinberg, Bill, 1941- III. Anderson, Donald R.
F217.A65 O97 1977   975 B   *LC* 76-48625   *ISBN* 0809074621

Shapiro, Henry D.   • **3.8178**
Appalachia on our mind: the Southern mountains and mountaineers in the American consciousness, 1870–1920 / by Henry D. Shapiro. — Chapel Hill: University of North Carolina Press, 1978, c1977. xxi, 376 p.; 23 cm. Includes index. 1. Appalachian Mountains, Southern. I. T.
F217.A65 S52   301.29/74   *LC* 77-2301   *ISBN* 0807812935

Whisnant, David E., 1938-.   **3.8179**
All that is native & fine: the politics of culture in an American region / David E. Whisnant. — Chapel Hill: University of North Carolina Press, c1983. xv, 340 p.: ill.; 24 cm. — (Fred W. Morrison series in Southern studies.) 1. Social classes — Appalachian Region, Southern. 2. Appalachian Region, Southern — Popular culture. 3. Appalachian Region, Southern — Social life and customs. I. T. II. Title: All that is native and fine. III. Series.
F217.A65 W47 1983   306/.0974 19   *LC* 82-24851   *ISBN* 0807815616

F220 POPULATION

Evans, Eli N.   **3.8180**
The provincials: a personal history of Jews in the South / [by] Eli N. Evans. — [1st ed.] New York: Atheneum, 1973. xiv, 369 p.; 25 cm. 1. Evans, Eli N. 2. Jews — Southern States I. T.
F220.J5 E82 1973   917.5/06/924   *LC* 73-80747   *ISBN* 068910541X

F221–295 South Atlantic States

F221–235 VIRGINIA

Dabney, Virginius, 1901-.   **3.8181**
Virginia, the new dominion. — [1st ed.]. — Garden City, N.Y.: Doubleday, 1971. xvi, 629 p.: illus.; 25 cm. 1. Virginia — History I. T.
F226.D32   975.5   *LC* 78-157580

Rubin, Louis Decimus, 1923-.   **3.8182**
Virginia: a Bicentennial history / Louis D. Rubin, Jr. — New York: Norton, c1977. xii, 228 p., [8] leaves of plates: ill.; 22 cm. (The States and the Nation series) Includes index. 1. Virginia — History I. T.
F226.R7   975.5   *LC* 77-3250   *ISBN* 0393056309

Abernethy, Thomas Perkins, 1890-.   • **3.8183**
Three Virginia frontiers [by] Thomas Perkins Abernethy. University, La., Louisiana state university press, 1940. xiii, 96 p. 21 cm. (The Walter Lynwood Fleming lectures in southern history, Louisiana state university, 1940) 1. Frontier and pioneer life — Virginia. 2. Frontier and pioneer life — Kentucky. 3. Virginia — History — Colonial period, ca. 1600-1775 4. Kentucky — History I. T.
F229.A25   975.5   *LC* 41-3353

Beverley, Robert, ca. 1673-ca. 1722.   • **3.8184**
The history and present state of Virginia / ed., with an introd., by Louis B. Wright. — Chapel Hill.: Pub. for the Institute of Early American History and Culture at Williamsburg, Va., by the University of North Carolina press, 1947. xxxv, 366 p.: ill.;25 cm. 1. Indians of North America — Virginia. 2. Virginia — History — Colonial period, ca. 1600-1775 3. Virginia. I. Wright, Louis B. (Louis Booker), 1899- II. Institute of Early American History and Culture (Williamsburg, Va.) III. T.
F229.B593   975.5   *LC* 47-30522

Billings, Warren M., 1940-.   **3.8185**
Colonial Virginia: a history / Warren M. Billings, John E. Selby, Thad W. Tate. — White Plains, N.Y.: KTO Press, c1986. xvii, 420 p.: ill.; 24 cm. — (A History of the American colonies) Includes index. 1. Virginia — History — Colonial period, ca. 1600-1775. 2. Virginia — History — Revolution, 1775-1783. I. Selby, John E. II. Tate, Thad W. III. T. IV. Series.
F229.B613 1986   975.5/02 19   *LC* 86-139   *ISBN* 0527187224

Billings, Warren M., 1940- comp.   **3.8186**
The Old Dominion in the seventeenth century; a documentary history of Virginia, 1606–1689. Edited by Warren M. Billings. — Chapel Hill: Published for the Institute of Early American History and Culture at Williamsburg, Va., by the University of North Carolina Press, [1975] xxiv, 324 p.: maps.; 25 cm. — (Documentary problems in early American history) 1. Virginia — History — Colonial period, ca. 1600-1775 — Sources. I. T. II. Series.
F229.B615   975.5/02   *LC* 74-8302   *ISBN* 080781234X

Breen, T. H.   **3.8187**
Tobacco culture: the mentality of the great Tidewater planters on the eve of Revolution / T.H. Breen. — Princeton, N.J.: Princeton University Press, c1985. xvi, 216 p.: ill.; 23 cm. 1. Plantation owners — Virginia — History — 18th century. 2. Plantation life — Virginia — History — 18th century. 3. Tobacco industry — Virginia — History — 18th century. 4. Virginia — History — Colonial period, ca. 1600-1775 5. Virginia — History — Revolution, 1775-1783 — Causes — Case studies. 6. United States — History — Revolution, 1775-1783 — Causes — Case studies. I. T.
F229.B8 1985   975.5/03 19   *LC* 85-42676   *ISBN* 0691047294

Bruce, Philip Alexander, 1856-1933.   • **3.8188**
Economic history of Virginia in the seventeenth century: an inquiry into the material condition of the people, based upon original and contemporaneous records. — New York: Johnson Reprint Corp., [1966] 2 v.; 23 cm. Title page includes original imprint: New York, Macmillan, 1896. 1. Virginia — History — Colonial period, ca. 1600-1775 2. Virginia — Economic conditions. I. T.
F229.B882 1966   330.9755   *LC* 67-7008

Byrd, William, 1674-1744.   • **3.8189**
Histories of the dividing line betwixt Virginia and North Carolina. With introd. and notes by William K. Boyd, and a new introd. by Percy G. Adams. — New York: Dover Publications, [1967] xxxix, 340 p.: facsims., maps (1 fold.), port.; 22 cm. — (Dover Americana) Contains the author's 'The history of the dividing line betwixt Virginia and North Carolina' and 'The secret history of the line,' which is another version of the same subject matter, printed on opposite pagings. 'An unabridged republication of the work first published by the North Carolina Historical Commission in 1929 .. [with] a new introduction.'

1. Virginia — Boundaries — North Carolina. 2. North Carolina — Boundaries — Virginia. 3. Virginia — Description and travel 4. North Carolina — Description and travel I. Boyd, William Kenneth, 1879-1938. ed. II. T.
F229.B968 1967   917.55   LC 67-24220

Byrd, William, 1674-1744.   • 3.8190
The London diary, 1717–1721, and other writings. New York, Oxford University Press, 1958. vi, 647 p. illus., port. 24 cm. 1. London (England) — Social life and customs 2. Virginia — Social life and customs I. Wright, Louis B. (Louis Booker), 1899- ed. II. Tinling, Marion, 1904- ed. III. T.
F229.B9685   LC 57-10389

Byrd, William, 1674-1744.   • 3.8191
The secret diary of William Byrd of Westover, 1709–1712 / edited by Louis B. Wright and Marion Tinling. — Richmond, Va.: The Dietz press, 1941. xxviii p., 1 l., 622 p.: 2 facsim. (incl. front.); 23 1/2 cm. Title vignette (coat of arms) A transcription from the original shorthand of the first part of Byrd's diary now in the Henry E. Huntington library. Parts covering the period from December 13, 1717, to May 19, 1721, and from August 10, 1739, to August 31, 1741, are located in the Virginia historical society and the University of North Carolina library respectively. cf. Introd. 1. Virginia — Social life and customs I. Wright, Louis B. (Louis Booker), 1899- ed. II. Tinling, Marion, Mrs., joint ed. III. T.
F229.B9715   923.273   LC 41-21807

Byrd, William, 1674-1744.   • 3.8192
Another secret diary of William Byrd of Westover, 1739–1741: with letters & literary exercises, 1696–1726 / edited by Maude H. Woodfin; translated and collated by Marion Tinling. — Richmond, Va.: Dietz Press, 1942. xlv, 490 p.: facsims. Reproduced at the Henry E. Huntington Library from shorthand and holograph manuscripts owned by the University of North Carolina. 1. Virginia — Social life and customs I. Woodfin, Maude Howlett. II. Tinling, Marion, 1904- III. T. IV. Title: Secret diary of William Byrd of Westover.
F229.B9717   LC 43-1881 rev

Morton, Louis.   • 3.8193
Robert Carter of Nomini Hall, a Virginia tobacco planter of the eighteenth century. Williamsburgh, Va., Colonial Williamsburg, incorporated, 1941. xi p., 4 l., [3]-332 p. incl. illus., tables. front., plates, ports. 24 cm. 1. Carter, Robert, 1728-1804. I. T.
F229.C34 M6   LC 41-19439

Craven, Wesley Frank, 1905-.   • 3.8194
Dissolution of the Virginia Company; the failure of a colonial experiment. Gloucester, Mass., P. Smith, 1964 [c1932] vi, 350 p. 21 cm. 1. Virginia Company of London. 2. Virginia — History — Colonial period. I. T.
F229.C8951964   LC 65-1398

Isaac, Rhys.   3.8195
The transformation of Virginia, 1740–1790 / by Rhys Isaac. — Chapel Hill: Published for the Institute of Early American History and Culture, Williamsburg, VA., by University of North Carolina Press, c1982. xxxii, 451 p.: ill.; 22 cm. 1. Virginia — Social life and customs — Colonial period, ca. 1600-1775 2. Virginia — Civilization. I. T.
F229.I8 1982   975.5/02 19   LC 81-10393   ISBN 080781489X

Kupperman, Karen Ordahl, 1939-.   3.8196
Roanoke, the abandoned colony / Karen Ordahl Kupperman. — Totowa, N.J.: Rowman & Allanheld, 1984. viii, 182 p.; 22 cm. 1. Raleigh's Roanoke colonies, 1584-1590 2. Algonquian Indians — First contact with Occidental civilization. 3. Indians of North America — North Carolina — First contact with Occidental civilization. 4. Roanoke Island (N.C.) — History. I. T.
F229.K9 1984   975.6/175 19   LC 83-24419   ISBN 0847671275

Morton, Richard Lee, 1889-.   • 3.8197
Colonial Virginia. Chapel Hill, Published for the Virginia Historical Society by the University of North Carolina Press, 1960. 2 v. (xiv, 883 p.) illus., ports., maps, facsims. 25 cm. 1. Virginia — History — Colonial period. I. T.
F229.M75   975.502   LC 60-51846

Quinn, David B.   3.8198
Set fair for Roanoke: voyages and colonies, 1584–1606 / David Beers Quinn. — Chapel Hill; London: Published by America's Four Hundredth Anniversary Committee by the University of North Carolina Press, c1985. xxiv, 467 p.: ill.; maps; 24 cm. Includes index. 1. Raleigh's Roanoke colonies, 1584-1590 I. North Carolina. America's Four Hundredth Anniversary Committee. II. T.
F229.Q56 1985   973.1 19   LC 84-2345   ISBN 080781606X

Vaughan, Alden T., 1929-.   3.8199
American genesis: Captain John Smith and the founding of Virginia / Alden T. Vaughan; edited by Oscar Handlin. — Boston: Little, Brown, [1975] ix, 207 p.: ill.; 20 cm. (Library of American biography.) Includes index. 1. Smith, John, 1580-1631. 2. Virginia — History — Colonial period, ca. 1600-1775 I. T. II. Series.
F229.S7495   975.5/01/0924 B   LC 74-5914

Washburn, Wilcomb E.   • 3.8200
The Governor and the rebel: a history of Bacon's Rebellion in Virginia. — Chapel Hill: Published for the Institute of Early American History and Culture at Williamsburg by the University of North Carolina Press [1957] xv, 248 p.: port., maps, facsim.; 25 cm. 1. Bacon's Rebellion, 1676 I. Institute of Early American History and Culture (Williamsburg, Va.) II. T.
F229.W28   975.5   LC 58-97

Webb, Stephen Saunders, 1937-.   3.8201
1676, the end of American independence / Stephen Saunders Webb. — 1st ed. — New York: Knopf, 1984. xx, 440 p., [16] p. of plates: ill.; 25 cm. 1. Bacon's Rebellion, 1676 2. King Philip's War, 1675-1676 3. Indians of North America — Government relations — To 1789 4. United States — Politics and government — Colonial period, ca. 1600-1775 I. T.
F229.W36 1984   973.2/4 19   LC 83-48865   ISBN 0394414144

Wertenbaker, Thomas Jefferson, 1879-1966.   • 3.8202
Patrician and plebeian in Virginia: or, The origin and development of the social classes of the Old Dominion. — New York: Russell & Russell [1959] 239 p.; 22 cm. Thesis—University of Virginia. 1. Virginia — Social life and customs 2. Virginia — History — Colonial period. I. T.
F229.W49 1959   975.502   LC 59-11227

Wertenbaker, Thomas Jefferson.   • 3.8203
Planters of colonial Virginia / by Thomas J. Wertenbaker. — New York: Russell & Russell, c1959. iii, 260 p.; 22 cm. — 1. Slavery — Virginia 2. Virginia — History — Colonial Period. 3. Virginia — Economic conditions. I. T.
F229 W493 1959   975.502   LC 59-11228

Wright, Louis B. (Louis Booker), 1899-.   • 3.8204
The first gentlemen of Virginia: intellectual qualities of the early colonial ruling class / by Louis B. Wright. — San Marino, Calif.: Huntington Library, 1940. xi, 373 p. 1. Virginia — Social life and customs — Colonial period, ca. 1600-1775 2. Virginia — Intellectual life 3. Virginia — Biography I. T.
F229 W965   LC 40-8029

F230–231 1775–

Beeman, Richard R.   3.8205
The Old Dominion and the new nation, 1788–1801 / [by] Richard R. Beeman. — [Lexington]: University Press of Kentucky, [1972] xiv, 282 p.: maps; 24 cm. 1. Political parties — Virginia — History. 2. Virginia — Politics and government — 1775-1865 3. United States — Politics and government — 1783-1809 I. T.
F230.B43   320.9/755/03   LC 76-190531   ISBN 0813112699

Davis, Richard Beale.   • 3.8206
Intellectual life in Jefferson's Virginia, 1790–1830. — Chapel Hill: University of North Carolina Press, [1964] x, 507 p.: ill., ports.; 24 cm. 1. American literature — Virginia. 2. Virginia — Intellectual life. I. T.
F230.D3   917.55   LC 64-13548

Jefferson, Thomas, 1743-1826.   • 3.8207
Notes on the State of Virginia. Chapel Hill, Published for the Institute of Early American History and Culture, Williamsburg, Va., by the University of North Carolina Press, 1955 [c1954] xxv, 315 p. maps (1 fold.) 24 cm. 1. Virginia. I. Pede, William Harwood, 1913- ed. II. T.
F230.J5102 1955   LC 55-14659

Mays, David John, 1896-.   • 3.8208
Edmund Pendleton, 1721–1803; a biography. Cambridge, Harvard University Press, 1952. 2 v. illus., ports. maps. 25 cm. 1. Pendleton, Edmund, 1721-1803. 2. Robinson, John, 1704-1766. 3. Virginia — Politics and government — Colonial period, ca. 1600-1775 4. Virginia — Politics and government — 1775-1865 I. T.
F230.P425   923.273   LC 52-5036

Craven, Avery Odelle, 1886-.   • 3.8209
Edmund Ruffin, southerner; a study in secession, by Avery Craven ... New York, London, D. Appleton and Company, 1932. ix p., 283 p. front., plates, ports., facsims. 23 cm. 1. Ruffin, Edmund, 1794-1865. 2. Secession 3. Southern States — Politics and government — 1775-1865 I. T.
F230.R94   923.273   LC 32-8631

Sydnor, Charles S. (Charles Sackett), 1898-.   • 3.8210
Gentlemen freeholders: political practices in Washington's Virginia. — Chapel Hill: Published for the Institute of Early American History and Culture at Williamsburg, Va., by the University of North Carolina Press [1952] ix, 180 p.; 22 cm. 1. Virginia — Politics and government — Colonial period, ca. 1600-1775 2. Virginia — Politics and government — 1775-1865 I. Institute of Early American History and Culture (Williamsburg, Va.) II. T.
F230.S9   975.5   LC 52-3497

Maddex, Jack P., 1941-.   • **3.8211**
The Virginia conservatives, 1867–1879; a study in Reconstruction politics, by Jack P. Maddex, Jr. — Chapel Hill: University of North Carolina Press, [1970] xx, 328 p.: maps (on lining papers); 24 cm. 1. Reconstruction — Virginia 2. Virginia — Politics and government — 1865-1950 I. T.
F231.M2   320.9/755   LC 76-109465   ISBN 0807811408

Moger, Allen Wesley, 1905-.   • **3.8212**
Virginia: Bourbonism to Byrd, 1870–1925 [by] Allen W. Moger. — Charlottesville: University Press of Virginia, [1968] ix, 397 p.: ill., maps, ports.; 26 cm. 1. Virginia — History I. T.
F231.M66   975.5   LC 68-8538

Writers' Program. Virginia.   • **3.8213**
Virginia; a guide to the Old Dominion, compiled by workers of the Writers' Program of the Work Projects Administration in the state of Virginia ... Sponsored by James H. Price, governor of Virginia. New York, Oxford University Press [1946] xxix, 710 (i.e. 726) p. illus., plates, maps (2 on 1 fold. β., in pocket) 21 cm. (American guide series) 'First published in May 1940 ... Third printing, with corrections, 1946.' 1. Virginia. 2. Virginia. — Description and travel — Guide-books.
F231.W88 1946   917.55   LC 46-5684

Wilkinson, J. Harvie, 1944-.   • **3.8214**
Harry Byrd and the changing face of Virginia politics, 1945–1966 [by] J. Harvie Wilkinson III. — Charlottesville: University Press of Virginia, [1968] xvi, 403 p.: ill., maps, ports.; 25 cm. 1. Byrd, Harry Flood, 1887-1966. 2. Virginia — Politics and government — 1951- I. T.
F231.2.W5   320.9/755   LC 68-22731

F232–234 Regions. Cities

Breen, T. H.   3.8215
'Myne owne ground': race and freedom on Virginia's Eastern Shore, 1640–1676 / T. H. Breen, Stephen Innes. — New York: Oxford University Press, 1980. viii, 142 p.: ill.; 22 cm. 1. Afro-Americans — Eastern Shore (Md. and Va.) — History. 2. Afro-Americans — Virginia — History. 3. Eastern Shore (Md. and Va.) — Race relations. 4. Eastern Shore (Md. and Va.) — History. 5. Virginia — Race relations. I. Innes, Stephen. joint author. II. T.
F232.E2 B73   975.5/1   LC 80-12369   ISBN 0195027272

Beeman, Richard R.   3.8216
The evolution of the southern backcountry: a case study of Lunenburg County, Virginia, 1746–1832 / Richard R. Beeman. — Philadelphia: University of Pennsylvania Press, c1984. xvi, 272 p.: ill., maps; 24 cm. Includes index. 1. Lunenburg County (Va.) — Civilization. 2. Virginia — History — Colonial period, ca. 1600-1775 — Case studies. I. T.
F232.L9 B34 1984   975.5/643 19   LC 83-27397   ISBN 0812279263

Rutman, Darrett Bruce.   3.8217
A place in time: Middlesex County, Virginia, 1650–1750 / Darrett B. and Anita H. Rutman. — 1st ed. — New York: Norton, c1984. p. cm. Includes index. 1. Middlesex County (Va.) — History. 2. Middlesex County (Va.) — Social conditions. I. Rutman, Anita H. II. T.
F232.M6 R87 1984   975.5/33 19   LC 83-13378   ISBN 0393018016

Bridenbaugh, Carl.   3.8218
Jamestown, 1544–1699 / Carl Bridenbaugh. — New York: Oxford University Press, 1980. xiv, 199 p.: ill.; 22 cm. 1. Jamestown (Va.) — History. I. T.
F234.J3 B7   975.5/4251   LC 79-13989   ISBN 0195026500

Gavins, Raymond.   3.8219
The perils and prospects of Southern Black leadership: Gordon Blaine Hancock, 1884–1970 / by Raymond Gavins. — Durham, N.C.: Duke University Press, 1977. x, 221 p.; 23 cm. Includes index. 1. Hancock, Gordon Blaine, 1884-1970. 2. College teachers — Virginia — Biography. 3. Baptists — Clergy — Biography 4. Clergy — Virginia — Richmond — Biography. 5. Afro-Americans — Virginia — Richmond — Biography. 6. Afro-Americans — Civil Rights — Southern States. 7. Afro-American leadership — Virginia — Richmond. 8. Richmond (Va.) — Biography. I. T.
F234.R53 H363   301.45/19/6073075 B   LC 76-44090   ISBN 0822303817

Ward, Harry M.   3.8220
Richmond during the Revolution, 1775–83 / Harry M. Ward and Harold E. Greer, Jr. — Charlottesville: Published for the Richmond Independence Bicentennial Commission by the University Press of Virginia, 1977. xi, 205 p.: ill.; 24 cm. Includes index. 1. Richmond (Va.) — History — Revolution, 1775-1783 I. Greer, Harold E. joint author. II. Richmond Independence Bicentennial Commission. III. T.
F234.R557 W37   975.5/451/03   LC 77-22586   ISBN 0813907152

Bridenbaugh, Carl.   • **3.8221**
Seat of empire; the political role of eighteenth–century Williamsburg. New ed. Williamsburg, Va., Colonial Williamsburg; distributed by Holt, New York [1958] 85 p. illus. 21 cm. (Williamsburg in America series) 1. Williamsburg (Va.) — History 2. Virginia — Politics and government — Colonial period, ca. 1600-1775 I. T. II. Series.
F234.W7B8x   975.5425   LC 58-13522

Whiffen, Marcus.   • **3.8222**
The public buildings of Williamsburg, colonial capital of Virginia: an architectural history. — Williamsburg, Va.,: Colonial Williamsburg / [1958] xvi, 269 p. illus., ports., map, facsims., plans. (Williamsburg architectural studies. v. 1) 1. Williamsburg, Virginia I. T. II. Series.
F234.W7 W4   724   LC 57-13499

Morgan, Edmund Sears.   • **3.8223**
Virginians at home; family life in the eighteenth century. Williamsburg, Va., Colonial Williamsburg [1952] 99 p. illus. 21 cm. (Williamsburg in America series, 2) 1. Virginia — Social life and customs — Colonial period, ca. 1600-1775 I. T.
F234.W7 W7x   917.55   LC 52-14250

F236–250 WEST VIRGINIA

Alexander-Williams, John.   3.8224
West Virginia: a Bicentennial history / John Alexander Williams. — New York: Norton, c1976. xi, 212 p., [8] leaves of plates: ill.; 22 cm. (The States and the Nation series) Includes index. 1. West Virginia — History I. T.
F241.W72   975.4   LC 76-11797   ISBN 0393055906

Writers' Program. West Virginia.   3.8225
West Virginia, a guide to the Mountain State / compiled by workers of the Writer's Program of the Work Projects Administration in the State of West Virginia; edited by Jim Comstock. — Richwood, W. Va.: Comstock, 1974. 519 p.: ill.; 23 cm. — (The West Virginia heritage encyclopedia; v. 10-11) Reprint of the 1941 ed. published by Oxford University Press, New York, issued in series: American guide series. 1. West Virginia. 2. West Virginia — Description and travel — Tours. I. Comstock, Jim F. II. Series.
F241.W85 1974   975.4 s 917.54/04/4   LC 78-111751

F251–265 NORTH CAROLINA. SOUTH CAROLINA

Lefler, Hugh Talmage, 1901-.   • **3.8226**
North Carolina: the history of a Southern State, by Hugh Talmage Lefler and Albert Ray Newsome. Rev. ed. Chapel Hill: University of North Carolina Press [1963] 756 p.: maps; 25 cm. 1. North Carolina — History I. Newsome, Albert Ray, 1894-1951. joint author. II. T.
F254.L39 1963   LC 63-3932

Powell, William Stevens, 1919-.   3.8227
North Carolina: a Bicentennial history / William S. Powell. — New York: Norton, c1977. xviii, 221 p., [8] leaves of plates: ill.; 22 cm. (The States and the Nation series) Includes index. 1. North Carolina — History I. T.
F254.P59   975.6   LC 77-22440   ISBN 0393056384

Lefler, Hugh Talmage, 1901-.   3.8228
Colonial North Carolina; a history [by] Hugh T. Lefler [and] William S. Powell. — New York: Scribner, [1973] xvi, 318 p.: illus.; 24 cm. — (History of the American colonies.) 1. North Carolina — History — Colonial period, ca. 1600-1775 I. Powell, William Stevens, 1919- joint author. II. T. III. Series.
F257.L52   975.6/02   LC 73-5188   ISBN 0684135361

Federal Writers' Project. North Carolina.   • **3.8229**
The North Carolina guide; edited by Blackwell P. Robinson. Chapel Hill, University of North Carolina Press [1955] xxi, 649 p. illus., maps 21 cm. 1. North Carolina. 2. North Carolina — Description and travel — 1951-1980 — Guide-books. I. Robinson, Blackwell P. (Blackwell Pierce), ed.
F259.F44 1955   917.56   LC 55-2216

Watson, Harry L.   3.8230
Jacksonian politics and community conflict: the emergence of the second American party system in Cumberland County, North Carolina / Harry L. Watson. — Baton Rouge: Louisiana State University Press, c1981. xii, 354 p.: ill.; 24 cm. Includes index. 1. Jackson, Andrew, 1767-1845. 2. Cumberland County (N.C.) — Politics and government. 3. United States — Politics and government — 1815-1861 I. T.
F262.C9 W37   324/.09756/373 19   LC 81-2414   ISBN 080710857X

Durant, David N.   **3.8231**
Raleigh's lost colony / David N. Durant. — 1st American ed. — New York: Atheneum, 1981. xvii, 188 p. [4] leaves of plates : ill.; 23 cm. 1. Raleigh, Walter, Sir, 1552?-1618. 2. Raleigh's Roanoke colonies, 1584-1590 3. Roanoke Island — History. I. T.
F262.R4 D37 1981   975.6/175 19   *LC* 80-65992   *ISBN* 0689110987

Stick, David, 1919-.   **3.8232**
Roanoke Island, the beginnings of English America / David Stick. — Chapel Hill: Published for America's Four Hundredth Anniversary Committee by the University of North Carolina Press, c1983. xiii, 266 p.: ill.; 21 cm. Includes index. 1. Roanoke Island (N.C.) — History. 2. America — Discovery and exploration — English. I. North Carolina. America's Four Hundredth Anniversary Committee. II. T.
F262.R4 S74 1983   975.6/175 19   *LC* 83-7014   *ISBN* 0807815543

Chafe, William Henry.   **3.8233**
Civilities and civil rights: Greensboro, North Carolina, and the Black struggle for freedom / William H. Chafe. — New York: Oxford University Press, 1980. xii, 436 p.: ill.; 22 cm. 1. Afro-Americans — Civil rights — North Carolina — Greensboro. 2. Greensboro (N.C.) — Race relations. I. T.
F264.G8 C47   323.42/3/0975662   *LC* 79-12898   *ISBN* 019502625X

Prather, H. Leon, 1921-.   **3.8234**
We have taken a city: Wilmington racial massacre and coup of 1898 / H. Leon Prather, Sr. — Rutherford: Fairleigh Dickinson University Press, c1984. 214 p.: ill.; 25 cm. Includes index. 1. Afro-Americans — North Carolina — Wilmington — History — 19th century. 2. Riots — North Carolina — Wilmington. 3. Wilmington (N.C.) — History. 4. Wilmington (N.C.) — Race relations. I. T.
F264.W7 P72 1984   975.6/27 19   *LC* 82-49335   *ISBN* 0838631894

Ramsay, David, 1749-1815.   **3.8235**
The history of South–Carolina, from its first settlement in 1670, to the year 1808. By David Ramsay. Charleston: Published by David Longworth for the author. 1809. 2 v. fronts. (fold. map, fold. plan) 21 cm. 1. South Carolina — History I. T.
F269.R17   *LC* 01-10809

Wright, Louis B. (Louis Booker), 1899-.   **3.8236**
South Carolina: a bicentennial history / Louis B. Wright. — New York: Norton, c1976. xiv, 225 p., [8] leaves of plates: ill.; 22 cm. (The States and the Nation series) Includes index. 1. South Carolina — History I. T.
F269.W65 1976   975.7   *LC* 75-19031   *ISBN* 0393055604

Writers' program. South Carolina.   • **3.8237**
South Carolina; a guide to the Palmetto state. New York, Oxford University Press [1941] xxvii, 514 p. illus., plates, port., maps (1 fold. in pocket) 21 cm. 1. South Carolina — Description and travel — Guide-books.
F269.W7   *LC* 41-52304

Brown, Richard Maxwell.   • **3.8238**
The South Carolina Regulators / Richard Maxwell Brown. — Cambridge, Mass.: Belknap Press of Harvard University Press, 1963. xi, 230 p.: maps. (A publication of the center for the study of the History of Liberty in America, harvard University) 1. Vigilance committees — South Carolina. 2. Crime and criminals — South Carolina. 3. South Carolina — History — Colonial period. I. T.
F272 B75   974/.102   *LC* 63-7589

The Colonial South Carolina scene: contemporary views,   **3.8239**
1697–1774 / edited by H. Roy Merrens.
1st ed. — Columbia: University of South Carolina Press, 1977. xi, 295 p.; 23 cm. (Tricentennial edition; no. 7) 1. South Carolina — History — Colonial period, ca. 1600-1775 — Sources. I. Merrens, Harry Roy.
F272.C73   975.7/02/08   *LC* 76-54972   *ISBN* 0872492613

Crane, Verner Winslow, 1889-.   • **3.8240**
The southern frontier, 1670–1732. — [Ann Arbor] University of Michigan Press [1956, c1929] 359 p. 21 cm. — (Ann Arbor books, AA4) 1. Southern States — Colonial period. 2. South Carolina — Hist. — Colonial period. 3. Great Britain — Colonies — America 4. Indians of North America — Comm. I. T.
F272.C89 1956   975   *LC* 57-1007

Pinckney, Eliza Lucas, 1723-1793.   **3.8241**
The letterbook of Eliza Lucas Pinckney, 1739–1762. Edited by Elise Pinckney, with the editorial assistance of Marvin R. Zahniser, and an introd. by Walter Muir Whitehill. — Chapel Hill: University of North Carolina Press, [1972] xxix, 195 p.: illus.; 24 cm. I. Pinckney, Elise, ed. II. T.
F272.P6416   975.7/02/0924 B   *LC* 76-174783   *ISBN* 0807811823

Sirmans, Marion Eugene, 1934-1965.   • **3.8242**
Colonial South Carolina: a political history, 1663–1763 / by M. Eugene Sirmans; foreword by Wesley Frank Craven. — Chapel Hill: Published for the Institute of Early American History and Culture at Williamsburg, Va., by the University of North Carolina Press, 1966. — xiii, 394 p: map (on lining papers); 24 cm. 1. South Carolina — Politics and government — Colonial period, ca. 1600-1775 I. Institute of Early American History and Culture (Williamsburg, Va.) II. T.
F272.S5   975.702   *LC* 66-25363

Weir, Robert M.   **3.8243**
Colonial South Carolina: a history / Robert M. Weir. — Millwood, N.Y.: KTO Press, c1983. xix, 409 p.: ill.; 24 cm. — (A History of the American colonies) Includes index. 1. South Carolina — History — Colonial period, ca. 1600-1775. 2. South Carolina — History — Revolution, 1775-1783. I. T. II. Series.
F272.W46 1983   975.7/02 19   *LC* 82-48990   *ISBN* 0527187216

Woodmason, Charles, ca. 1720-ca. 1776.   • **3.8244**
[Journal] The Carolina Backcountry on the eve of the Revolution: the Journal and other writings of Charles Woodmason, Anglican itinerant / edited with an introd. by Richard J. Hooker. — Chapel Hill: Published for the Institute of Early American History and Culture at Williamsburg, Va., by the University of North Carolina Press, 1953. xxxix, 305 p.: map (on lining papers); 21 cm. 1. Church of England in South Carolina — Sermons. 2. Sermons, American 4. South Carolina — History — Colonial period, ca. 1600-1775 — Sources. I. Hooker, Richard James, 1913- ed. II. T.
F272.W77   975.7   *LC* 53-13218

Barnwell, John, 1947-.   **3.8245**
Love of order: South Carolina's first secession crisis / John Barnwell. — Chapel Hill: University of North Carolina Press, c1982. x, 258 p., [1] leaf of plates: map; 24 cm. Includes index. 1. Secession 2. South Carolina — Politics and government — 1775-1865 I. T.
F273.B28 1982   975.7/03 19   *LC* 81-11441   *ISBN* 0807814989

Channing, Steven A.   • **3.8246**
Crisis of fear: secession in South Carolina [by] Steven A. Channing. — New York: Simon and Schuster, [1970] 315 p.: map, ports.; 22 cm. 1. Secession 2. South Carolina — Politics and government — 1775-1865 3. South Carolina — History — Civil War, 1861-1865 I. T.
F273.C45   973.71/3   *LC* 72-116503   *ISBN* 0671205161

Faust, Drew Gilpin.   **3.8247**
James Henry Hammond and the Old South: a design for mastery / Drew Gilpin Faust. — Baton Rouge: Louisiana State University Press, c1982. xviii, 407 p.: ill.; 24 cm. — (Southern biography series.) Includes index. 1. Hammond, James Henry, 1807-1864. 2. Slavery — Southern States 3. Slaveholders — South Carolina — Biography. 4. South Carolina — Politics and government — 1775-1865 I. T. II. Series.
F273.H25 F38 1982   975.7/03/0924 B 19   *LC* 82-8939   *ISBN* 0807110485

The Hammonds of Redcliffe / edited by Carol Bleser.   **3.8248**
New York: Oxford University Press, 1981. xxii, 421 p., [8] leaves of plates: ill.; 24 cm. Includes index. 1. Hammond family 2. Hammond, James Henry, 1807-1864. 3. Family — South Carolina — History — Sources. 4. South Carolina — History — Sources. 5. Redcliffe, S.C. I. Bleser, Carol K. Rothrock.
F273.R33   975.7/04/0922 B 19   *LC* 80-26962   *ISBN* 0195029208

Rosengarten, Theodore.   **3.8249**
Tombee: portrait of a cotton planter / Theodore Rosengarten; with the journal of Thomas B. Chaplin (1822–1890) edited and annotated with the assistance of Susan W. Walker. — [s.l.]: Norton; 1986. 750 p.: geneal. tables, maps; 24 cm. Includes index. 1. Chaplin, Thomas Benjamin, 1822-1890 — Diaries. 2. Slaveholders — South Carolina — Saint Helena Island — Biography. 3. Plantation life — South Carolina — Saint Helena Island — History — 19th century. 4. Cotton trade — South Carolina — Saint Helena Island — History — 19th century. 5. Saint Helena Island (S.C.) — Biography. I. Chaplin, Thomas Benjamin, 1822-1890. II. Walker, Susan W. III. T.
F277.B3 C487 1986   975.7/9903/0924 B 19   *LC* 86-716   *ISBN* 0688054129

Rose, Willie Lee Nichols, 1927-.   • **3.8250**
Rehearsal for Reconstruction; the Port Royal experiment [by] Willie Lee Rose. With an introd. by C. Vann Woodward. Indianapolis, Bobbs-Merrill [1964] xviii, 442 p. illus., fold. map, ports. 24 cm. 1. Port Royal (S.C.) Expedition, 1861 2. Sea Islands — History. I. T.
F277.B3 R6   975.7995   *LC* 64-16720

Joyner, Charles W.   **3.8251**
Down by the riverside: a South Carolina slave community / Charles Joyner. — Urbana: University of Illinois Press, c1984. xxii, 345 p., [12] p. of plates: ill.; 24 cm. — (Blacks in the New World.) Includes index. 1. Slavery — South

Carolina — All Saints Parish — History. 2. Afro-Americans — South Carolina — All Saints Parish — Slaves — South Carolina — All Saints Parish — Folklore. 3. Slaves — South Carolina — All Saints Parish — Folklore. 4. Folklore — South Carolina — All Saints Parish. 5. Plantation life — South Carolina — All Saints Parish — History. 6. Gullah dialect 7. All Saints Parish (S.C.) — Social life and customs. I. T. II. Series.
F279.A43 J69 1984   975.7/89 19   LC 83-10369   ISBN 0252010582

No chariot let down: Charleston's free people of color on the   **3.8252**
eve of the Civil War / edited by Michael P. Johnson and James L. Roark.
Chapel Hill: University of North Carolina Press, c1984. xii, 174 p.: ill.; 24 cm. Includes index. 1. Ellison family 2. Johnson, James Marsh. 3. Afro-Americans — South Carolina — Charleston — Correspondence. 4. Afro-Americans — South Carolina — Charleston — History. 5. Charleston (S.C.) — Race relations. I. Johnson, Michael P., 1941- II. Roark, James L.
F279.C49 N46 1984   975.7/91500496073 19   LC 83-25897   ISBN 0807815969

Bethel, Elizabeth Rauh.   **3.8253**
Promiseland, a century of life in a Negro community / Elizabeth Rauh Bethel. — Philadelphia: Temple University Press, 1981. xvii, 329 p.; 24 cm. Includes index. 1. Afro-Americans — South Carolina — Promised Land — History. 2. Promised Land (S.C.) — History. I. T.
F279.P66 B47   975.7/33 19   LC 80-27732   ISBN 0877222118

F281–295 GEORGIA

Martin, Harold H.   **3.8254**
Georgia: a bicentennial history / Harold H. Martin. — New York: Norton, c1977. xii, 212 p., [8] leaves of plates: ill.; 22 cm. (The States and the Nation series) Includes index. 1. Georgia — History I. T.
F286.M42   975.8   LC 77-5736   ISBN 0393056066

Georgia. Dept. of Archives and History.   **3.8255**
Vanishing Georgia. — Athens: University of Georgia Press, c1982. 225 p.: chiefly ill.; 22 x 29 cm. 1. City and town life — Georgia — Pictorial works. 2. Georgia — Social life and customs — Pictorial works. 3. Georgia — Description and travel — Views. I. T.
F287.G27 1982   306/.09758 19   LC 82-4764   ISBN 0820306282

Abbot, W. W. (William Wright), 1922-.   • **3.8256**
The royal governors of Georgia, 1754–1775 / by W.W. Abbot. — Chapel Hill: Published for the Institute of Early American History and Culture at Williamsburg by the University of North Carolina Press, 1959. vii, 198 p.: maps. 1. Georgia — Politics and government — Colonial period, ca. 1600-1775 2. Georgia — Governors. I. T.
F289.A58   LC 59-9568

Coleman, Kenneth.   **3.8257**
Colonial Georgia: a history / Kenneth Coleman. — New York: Scribner, c1976. xviii, 331 p.: ill.; 24 cm. (History of the American colonies.) Includes index. 1. Georgia — History — Colonial period, ca. 1600-1775 2. Georgia — History — Revolution, 1775-1783 I. T. II. Series.
F289.C64   975.8/02   LC 75-37534   ISBN 0684145561

Davis, Harold E., 1927-.   **3.8258**
The fledgling province: social and cultural life in colonial Georgia, 1733–1776 / by Harold E. Davis. — Chapel Hill: Published for the Institute of Early American History and Culture, Williamsburg, Va., by the University of North Carolina Press, c1976. xi, 306 p., [1] leaf of plates: ill.; 24 cm. Includes index. 1. Slavery — Georgia 2. Georgia — Social life and customs — Colonial period, ca. 1600-1775 I. Institute of Early American History and Culture (Williamsburg, Va.) II. T.
F289.D24   975.8/02   LC 76-2570   ISBN 0807812676

Spalding, Phinizy.   **3.8259**
Oglethorpe in America / Phinizy Spalding. Chicago: University of Chicago Press, 1977. xi, 207 p., [2] leaves of plates: ill.; 22 cm. Includes index. 1. Oglethorpe, James Edward, 1696-1785. 2. Statesmen — Georgia — Biography. 3. Georgia — History — Colonial period, ca. 1600-1775 I. T.
F289.O367   975.8/02/0924 B   LC 76-8092   ISBN 0226768465

Coleman, Kenneth.   • **3.8260**
The American Revolution in Georgia, 1763–1789. — Athens: University of Georgia Press, [c1958] viii, 352 p.: maps.; 25 cm. 1. Georgia — History — Colonial period. 2. Georgia — History — 1775-1865 I. T.
F290.C55   975.802   LC 58-59848

McCash, William B., 1931-.   **3.8261**
Thomas R.R. Cobb (1823–1862): the making of a southern nationalist / by William B. McCash. — Macon, Ga.: Mercer University Press, c1983. 356 p.: ill.; 24 cm. Includes index. 1. Cobb, Thomas Read Rootes, 1823-1862. 2. Confederate States of America. Army — Biography. 3. Lawyers — Georgia

— Biography. 4. Generals — Southern States — Biography. 5. Politicians — Georgia — Biography. 6. Georgia — Politics and government — 1775-1865 I. T.
F290.C67 M37 1983   975.8/03/0924 B 19   LC 82-22925   ISBN 0865540497

Hahn, Steven, 1951-.   **3.8262**
The roots of southern populism: yeoman farmers and the transformation of the Georgia Upcountry, 1850–1890 / Steven Hahn. — New York: Oxford University Press, 1983. xvii, 340 p.; 22 cm. Includes index. 1. Populism — Georgia. 2. Cotton trade — Georgia — History — 19th century. 3. Georgia — Politics and government — 1775-1865 4. Georgia — Politics and government — 1865-1950 I. T.
F290.H33 1983   975.8/041 19   LC 82-12584   ISBN 0195032497

Johnson, Michael P., 1941-.   **3.8263**
Toward a patriarchal Republic: the secession of Georgia / Michael P. Johnson. — Baton Rouge: Louisiana State University Press, c1977. xxiv, 244 p.: ill.; 24 cm. Includes index. 1. Secession 2. Georgia — Politics and government — Civil War, 1861-1865 I. T.
F290.J65   973.7/13 19   LC 77-3029   ISBN 0807102709

Kemble, Fanny, 1809-1893.   • **3.8264**
Journal of a residence on a Georgian plantation in 1838–1839. Edited, with an introd., by John A. Scott. New York, Knopf, 1961. lxx, 415, viii p. port., maps, facsim. 22 cm. 1. Slavery — Georgia 2. Georgia — Social life and customs I. Scott, John Anthony, 1916- ed. II. T.
F290.K332 1961   975.8/03/0924 B   LC 60-53234

Myers, Robert Manson, 1921-.   • **3.8265**
The children of pride: a true story of Georgia and the Civil War / edited by Robert Manson Myers. — New Haven: Yale University Press, 1972. xxv, 1845 p.: maps (on lining papers); 26 cm. 'Who's who': p. [1449] - 1738. '[Selected] from the voluminous family papers of the Rev. Dr. Charles Colcock Jones (1804-1863), of Liberty County, Georgia.' 1. Georgia — History — Civil War — Sources. 2. United States — Biography I. Jones, Charles Colcock, 1804-1863. II. T.
F290.M9   917.58/03/3   LC 79-99835   ISBN 0300012144

Shryock, Richard Harrison.   **3.8266**
Georgia and the Union in 1850. Durham, North Carolina, Duke Univ. Press [1926] x, 406 p. maps. 1. Secession 2. Georgia — History I. T.
F290.S55

Bartley, Numan V.   **3.8267**
The creation of modern Georgia / Numan V. Bartley. — Athens: University of Georgia Press, c1983. viii, 245 p.: maps; 23 cm. 1. Georgia — Politics and government — 1865-1950 2. Georgia — Social conditions. I. T.
F291.B26 1983   975.8/04 19   LC 82-24791   ISBN 0820306681

Flynn, Charles L.   **3.8268**
White land, black labor: caste and class in late nineteenth–century Georgia / Charles L. Flynn, Jr. — Baton Rouge: Louisiana State University Press, c1983. xi, 196 p.: ill.; 24 cm. Includes index. 1. Reconstruction — Georgia. 2. Afro-Americans — Georgia — History — 19th century. 3. Afro-Americans — Georgia — Economic conditions. 4. Georgia — History — 1865- 5. Georgia — Economic conditions. I. T.
F291.F58 1983   975.8/00496073 19   LC 83-721   ISBN 0807110973

Anderson, William, 1941-.   **3.8269**
The wild man from Sugar Creek: the political career of Eugene Talmadge / William Anderson. — Baton Rouge: Louisiana State University Press, [1975] xviii, 268 p., [7] leaves of plates: ill.; 24 cm. Includes index. 1. Talmadge, Eugene, 1884-1946. I. T.
F291.T3 A52   975.8/04/0924 B   LC 74-82002   ISBN 0807100889

Georgia Writers' Project.   **3.8270**
Georgia, a guide to its towns and countryside. Rev. and extended by George G. Leckie. Foreword by Ralph McGill. Atlanta, Tupper & Love [1954] xxii, 457 p. illus., maps. 21 cm. (American guide series) 1. Georgia. 2. Georgia — Description and travel — Guide-books. I. Leckie, George Gaines, ed. II. Series.
F291.W94 1954   917.58   LC 54-10344

Hertzberg, Steven.   **3.8271**
Strangers within the Gate City: the Jews of Atlanta, 1845–1915 / Steven Hertzberg. — 1st ed. — Philadelphia: Jewish Publication Society of America, 1978. xiii, 325 p., [5] leaves of plates: ill.; 24 cm. Includes index. 1. Jews — Georgia — Atlanta — History. 2. Atlanta (Ga.) — History. I. T.
F294.A89 J54   301.4529/6/09758231   LC 78-1167   ISBN 0827601026

F296–395 Gulf States

F301–350 FLORIDA. ALABAMA. MISSISSIPPI

Jahoda, Gloria.   3.8272
Florida: a Bicentennial history / Gloria Jahoda. — New York: Norton, c1976. xi, 210 p., [8] leaves of plates; 22 cm. (The States and the Nation series) Includes index. 1. Florida — History I. T.
F311.J33   975.9   *LC* 76-6468   *ISBN* 039305585X

Lyon, Eugene, 1929-.   3.8273
[Adelantamiento of Florida, 1565-1568] The enterprise of Florida: Pedro Menéndez de Avilés and the Spanish conquest of 1565–1568 / Eugene Lyon. — Gainesville: University Presses of Florida, 1976. xxvi, 600 p. illus., maps (1 fold. in pocket) ill.; 24 cm. 'Originally published under the title The adelantamiento of Florida, 1565-1568'. 'A University of Florida book.' Includes index. 1. Menéndez de Avilés, Pedro, 1519-1574. 2. Florida — History — Spanish colony, 1565-1763 I. T.
F314.L98 1976   975.9/01   *LC* 76-29612   *ISBN* 0813005337

Federal writers' project. Florida.   • 3.8274
Florida; a guide to the southern-most state, compiled and written by the Federal writers' project of the Work projects administration for the state of Florida ... sponsored by state of Florida Department of Public Instruction. New York, Oxford University Press, 1939. xvi, 600 p. illus., maps (1 fold. in pocket) plates. 21 cm. (American guide series) 'First published in November 1939.' Map on lining-paper. 1. Florida. 2. Florida. — Description and travel — Guide-books. I. T.
F316.F44   *LC* 39-29497

Shofner, Jerrell H., 1929-.   3.8275
Nor is it over yet; Florida in the era of Reconstruction, 1863–1877 [by] Jerrell H. Shofner. — Gainesville: University Presses of Florida, 1974. x, 412 p.; 23 cm. 'A University of Florida book.' 1. Reconstruction — Florida. 2. Florida — Politics and government — 1865-1950 I. T.
F316.S56   975.9/06   *LC* 70-186325   *ISBN* 0813003539

Williamson, Edward C., 1916-.   3.8276
Florida politics in the gilded age, 1877–1893 / Edward C. Williamson. Gainesville: University Presses of Florida, 1976. x, 234 p.: maps; 24 cm. 'A University of Florida book.' Includes index. 1. Florida — Politics and government — 1865-1950 I. T.
F316.2.W54   320.9/759/06   *LC* 75-30634   *ISBN* 0813003652

Porter, Bruce D.   3.8277
The Miami riot of 1980: crossing the bounds / Bruce Porter, Marvin Dunn. — Lexington, Mass.: Lexington Books, c1984. xiv, 206 p., [1] p. of plates: ill.; 24 cm. 1. Riots — Florida — Miami. 2. Miami (Fla.) — History. 3. Miami (Fla.) — Race relations. I. Dunn, Marvin, 1940- II. T.
F319.M6 P67 1984   975.9/381063 19   *LC* 83-49201   *ISBN* 0669076635

Agee, James, 1909-1955.   • 3.8278
Let us now praise famous men: three tenant families / [by] James Agee [and] Walker Evans. — Boston: Houghton Mifflin [1960] xxii, 471 p.: ill.; 22 cm. 1. Agee, James, 1909-1955 — Journeys — Alabama. 2. Farm tenancy — Alabama — History. 3. Alabama — Rural conditions. 4. Alabama — Description. I. Evans, Walker, 1903-1975. joint author. II. T. III. Title: Three tenant families.
F326.A17 1960   917.61   *LC* 60-4027

Hackney, Sheldon.   • 3.8279
Populism to progressivism in Alabama. — Princeton, N.J.: Princeton University Press, 1969. xv, 390 p.: maps; 23 cm. 1. Alabama — Politics and government — 1865-1950 I. T.
F326.H14   320.9/761   *LC* 68-56311

Hamilton, Virginia Van der Veer.   3.8280
Alabama: a bicentennial history / Virginia Van der Veer Hamilton. — New York: Norton, c1977. xv, 189 p., [8] leaves of plates: ill.; 22 cm. (The States and the Nation series) Includes index. 1. Alabama — History I. T.
F326.H26   976.1   *LC* 76-54517   *ISBN* 039305621X

Rogers, William Warren.   • 3.8281
The one-gallused rebellion; agrarianism in Alabama, 1865–1896. — Baton Rouge: Louisiana State University Press, [1970] x, 354 p.; 24 cm. 1. People's

Party of the United States. Alabama. 2. Alabama — Politics and government — 1865-1950 I. T.
F326.R85   322/.44   *LC* 74-108202   *ISBN* 0807109355

Up before daylight: life histories from the Alabama Writers'   3.8282
Project, 1938–1939 / edited by James Seay Brown, Jr.
University, Ala.: University of Alabama Press, c1982. x, 261 p.: ill.; 24 cm. Includes index. 1. Oral history 2. Alabama — Social conditions — Addresses, essays, lectures. 3. Alabama — Biography — Addresses, essays, lectures. 4. Alabama — Social life and customs — Addresses, essays, lectures. I. Brown, James Seay, 1944- II. Alabama Writers' Project.
F326.U65 1982   976.1/062 19   *LC* 81-21988   *ISBN* 0817300996

Wiggins, Sarah Woolfolk, 1934-.   3.8283
The scalawag in Alabama politics, 1865–1881 / Sarah Woolfolk Wiggins. University: University of Alabama Press, c1977. 220 p., [3] leaves of plates: ill.; 22 cm. Includes index. 1. Republican Party. Alabama. 2. Reconstruction — Alabama. 3. Afro-Americans — Alabama 4. Alabama — Politics and government — 1865-1950 I. T.
F326.W53   320.9/761/06   *LC* 76-56833   *ISBN* 0817352333

Writers' Program (Ala.)   3.8284
Alabama, a guide to the deep South, compiled by workers of the Writers' Program of the Work Project Administration in the State of Alabama... Sponsored by the Alabama State Planning Commission. New York, R. R. Smith, 1941. xxii, 442 p. illus., plates, maps (2 on 1 fold. 1., in pocket) 21 cm. (American guide series.) Map on lining-paper. The plates are in eight groups each preceded by half-title not included in paging. 'First published in May, 1941.' 1. Alabama. 2. Alabama. — Description and travel — Guide-books. I. T. II. Series.
F326.W7   917.61   *LC* 41-52528

Howard, Gene L., 1940-.   3.8285
Death at Cross Plains: an Alabama Reconstruction tragedy / Gene L. Howard. — University, Ala.: University of Alabama Press, c1984. xiv, 151 p.: ill.; 23 cm. Includes index. 1. Luke, William C., d. 1870. 2. Lynching — Alabama — Cross Plains — History — 19th century. 3. Reconstruction — Alabama — Cross Plains. 4. Missionaries — Alabama — Cross Plains — Biography. 5. Civil rights workers — Alabama — Cross Plains — Biography. 6. Cross Plains (Ala.) — Race relations. 7. Cross Plains (Ala.) — Biography. I. T.
F334.C68 H68 1984   364.1/523/0976163 19   *LC* 83-5839   *ISBN* 0817301852

Fager, Charles (Charles Eugene), 1942-.   3.8286
Selma, 1965, by Charles E. Fager. New York, Scribner, 1974. 241 p. illus. 24 cm. 1. Civil rights — Selma, Ala. 2. Selma-Montgomery Rights March, 1965 3. Selma (Ala.) — Race question. 4. Selma (Ala.) — Politics and government. I. T.
F334.S4 F34   323.4/09761/45   *LC* 73-1110   *ISBN* 068413764X

Federal Writers' Project. Mississippi.   • 3.8287
Mississippi; a guide to the Magnolia State. New York, Hastings House [1949] xxiv, 545 p. illus., maps. 21 cm. 1. Automobiles — Road guides — Mississippi. 2. Mississippi. 3. Mississippi — Description and travel.
F341.F45 1949   *LC* 49-5823

Harris, William Charles, 1933-.   3.8288
The day of the carpetbagger: Republican Reconstruction in Mississippi / William C. Harris. — Baton Rouge: Louisiana State University Press, c1979. xiv, 760 p.; 24 cm. Continues the author's Presidential Reconstruction in Mississippi. Includes index. 1. Reconstruction — Mississippi. 2. Mississippi — Politics and government — 1865-1950 I. T.
F341.H298   976.2/06   *LC* 78-18779   *ISBN* 0807103667

Harris, William Charles, 1933-.   • 3.8289
Presidential Reconstruction in Mississippi [by] William C. Harris. — Baton Rouge: Louisiana State University, [1967] x, 279 p.: ill., maps, ports.; 24 cm. Continued by the author's The day of the carpetbagger. 1. Reconstruction — Mississippi. I. T.
F341.H3   917.62/03/6   *LC* 67-24418

Kirwan, Albert Dennis.   • 3.8290
Revolt of the rednecks; Mississippi politics: 1876–1925, by Albert D. Kirwan. — Gloucester, Mass., P. Smith, 1964 [c1951] x, 328 p. illus., maps, ports. 21 cm. Bibliography: p. [315]-320. 1. Mississippi — Pol. & govt. — 1865- I. T.
F341.K5 1964   976.206   *LC* 64-56715

Skates, John Ray.   3.8291
Mississippi, a Bicentennial history / John Ray Skates. — New York: Norton, c1979. xii, 188 p., [8] leaves of plates: ill.; 22 cm. (The States and the Nation series) Includes index. 1. Mississippi — History I. T.
F341.S65   976.2   *LC* 78-25931   *ISBN* 0393056783

Silver, James W. (James Wesley), 1907-.   • 3.8292
Mississippi: the closed society [by] James W. Silver. [1st ed.] New York, Harcourt, Brace & World [1964] xxii, 250 p. facsim., map. 21 cm.

1. Mississippi — Race question. 2. Mississippi — Politics and government — 1951- I. T.
F345.S5   301.451   *LC* 64-19939

Hermann, Janet Sharp.   3.8293
The pursuit of a dream / Janet Sharp Hermann. — New York: Oxford University Press, 1981. xi, 290 p., [2] leaves of plates: ill.; 22 cm. Includes index. 1. Davis, Joseph. 2. Montgomery, Benjamin. 3. Montgomery, Isiah. 4. Afro-Americans — Mississippi — Mound Bayou — History. 5. Afro-Americans — Mississippi — Mound Bayou — Economic conditions. 6. Slavery — Mississippi — Condition of slaves. 7. Plantation life — Mississippi. 8. Davis Bend (Miss.) — History. 9. Mound Bayou (Miss.) — History. I. T.
F349.D38 H47   976.2/00496073 19   *LC* 80-22539   *ISBN* 0195028872

Loewen, James W.   3.8294
The Mississippi Chinese: between Black and white / [by] James W. Loewen. — Cambridge, Mass.: Harvard University Press, 1971. 237 p.: ill.; 22 cm. — (Harvard East Asian series. 63) Originally presented as the author's thesis, Harvard University, 1968. 1. Chinese Americans — Mississippi. I. T. II. Series.
F350.C5 L6 1971   301.451/951/0762   *LC* 77-160025   *ISBN* 0674576608

F351–358.2 Mississippi Valley. Middle West

Dondore, Dorothy Anne, 1894-1946.   • 3.8295
The prairie and the making of middle America: four centuries of description. New York, Antiquarian Press, 1961. xiii, 472 p. illus., facsims. 21 cm. 1. American literature — History and criticism 2. Mississippi River Valley — Description and travel. I. T.
F351.D6   *LC* a 64-5982

Roosevelt, Theodore, 1858-1919.   • 3.8296
The winning of the West, by Theodore Roosevelt. New York, Current Literature Pub. Co., 1905 [c1889] 6 v. fronts. 19 cm. 1. Mississippi River Valley — History 2. Ohio River Valley — History 3. Northwest, Old — History 4. Louisiana — History 5. Kentucky — History 6. Tennessee — History I. T.
F351.R8x   *LC* a 13-1434

Alvord, Clarence Walworth, 1868-1928.   • 3.8297
The Mississippi Valley in British politics; a study of the trade, land speculation, and experiments in imperialism culminating in the American Revolution. — New York, Russell & Russell, 1959. 2 v. illus. 25 cm. 1. Mississippi River Valley — Hist. — To 1803. 2. Gt. Brit. — Colonies — America. I. T.
F352.A47 1959   977   *LC* 59-6233

Hennepin, Louis, 17th cent.   • 3.8298
Father Louis Hennepin's Description of Louisiana, newly discovered to the southwest of New France by order of the king; translated from the original edition by Marion E. Cross, with an introduction by Grace Lee Nute. [Minneapolis] Pub. for the Minnesota society of the Colonial dames of America, The University of Minnesota press, 1938. 3-190 p. ill. Includes reproduction of t.-p. of the original edition, 1683. 1. Indians of North America — Mississippi valley. 2. Louisiana — Description and travel 3. New France — Discovery and exploration. 4. Mississippi River — Discovery and exploration. 5. Mississippi River Valley — History — To 1803 I. Cross, Marion E. II. National Society of the Colonial Dames of America. Minnesota. III. T.
F352.H564   917.63   *LC* 38-38693

Weddle, Robert S.   3.8299
Wilderness manhunt: the Spanish search for La Salle [by] Robert S. Weddle. Austin, University of Texas Press [1973] xiv, 291 p. illus. 23 cm. 1. La Salle, Robert Cavelier, sieur de, 1643-1687. 2. Spaniards in North America. 3. French in the United States. 4. Mississippi River Valley — Discovery and exploration. 5. Texas — History — To 1846 I. T.
F352.W42   973.1/6   *LC* 72-1579   *ISBN* 0292790007

Whitaker, Arthur Preston, 1895-.   • 3.8300
The Mississippi question, 1795-1803: a study in trade, politics, and diplomacy / by Arthur Preston Whitaker. — New York; London: C. Appleton-Century Co., Inc. / [c1934] ix, 342 p.: fold. map; 23 cm. At head of title: The American historical association. 1. Mississippi River Valley — History — To 1803 2. Louisiana — History — To 1803 I. American Historical Association. II. T.
F352.W56   *LC* 34-13409

Twain, Mark, 1835-1910.   • 3.8301
Life on the Mississippi. New York, Harper [1950] xvi, 526 p. 21 cm. 1. Mississippi River — Description and travel. 2. Mississippi River Valley — Social life and customs. I. T.
F353.C6456 1950   *LC* 50-6261

Paul Wilhelm, Duke of Württemberg, 1797-1860.   3.8302
[Erste Reise nach dem nördlichen Amerika. English] Travels in North America, 1822–1824. Translated by W. Robert Nitske. Edited by Savoie Lottinville. [1st ed.] Norman: University of Oklahoma Press, 1974 (c1973) xxxiv, 456 p. illus. 24 cm. (American exploration and travel series. v. 63) Translation of Erste Reise nach dem nördlichen Amerika in den Jahren 1822 bis 1824. 1. Paul Wilhelm, Duke of Württemberg, 1797-1860. 2. Mississippi River Valley — Description and travel. 3. United States — Description and travel — 1783-1848 I. T. II. Series.
F353.P3213   917.7/04/2   *LC* 72-3596

Jensen, Richard J.   • 3.8303
The winning of the Midwest: social and political conflict, 1888–1896 [by] Richard Jensen. — Chicago: University of Chicago Press, [1971] xvii, 357 p.; 23 cm. 1. Middle West — Politics and government. I. T.
F354.J4   309.1/77/03   *LC* 71-149802   *ISBN* 0226398250

Kleppner, Paul.   • 3.8304
The cross of culture: a social analysis of midwestern politics, 1850–1900. — [2d ed.]. — New York: Free Press, [1970] x, 402 p.; 22 cm. 1. Middle West — Politics and government. 2. U.S. — Politics and government — 19th century. I. T.
F354.K55   320.9/77   *LC* 72-83365

Merrill, Horace Samuel.   • 3.8305
Bourbon democracy of the Middle West, 1865–1896. — Seattle: University of Washington Press, [1967] xiv, 300 p.: illus., ports.; 23 cm. — (Americana library, 2) Unabridged text of the 1953 ed., with a new introd. by the author. 1. Middle West — Politics and government. 2. United States — Politics and government — 1865-1900 I. T.
F354.M45 1967   329.3/0977   *LC* 68-1509

Selcraig, James Truett.   3.8306
The red scare in the Midwest, 1945–1955: a state and local study / by James Truett Selcraig. — Ann Arbor, Mich.: UMI Research Press, c1982. xviii, 208 p.; 24 cm. — (Studies in American history and culture. no. 36) Revision of thesis (Ph.D.)—University of Illinois at Urbana-Champaign, 1981. Includes index. 1. Anti-communist movements — Middle West — History — 20th century. 2. Middle West — Politics and government. I. T. II. Series.
F354.S44 1982   977/.033 19   *LC* 82-17545   *ISBN* 0835713806

Atherton, Lewis Eldon.   • 3.8307
Main street on the middle border / by Lewis Atherton. — Bloomington: Indiana University Press, 1954. xix, 423 p.: ill. 1. City and town life 2. Villages — Middle West. 3. Middle West — Social life and customs. I. T.
F355.A8   *LC* 54-7970

Gjerde, Jon, 1953-.   3.8308
From peasants to farmers: the migration from Balestrand, Norway to the upper Middle West / Jon Gjerde. — Cambridge [Cambridgeshire]; New York: Cambridge University Press, 1985. xiv, 319 p.: ill.; 24 cm. (Interdisciplinary perspectives on modern history.) 1. Norwegian Americans — Middle West — Economic conditions. 2. Norwegian Americans — Middle West — Social conditions. 3. Peasantry — Norway — Balestrand. 4. Farmers — Norway — Balestrand. 5. Balestrand (Norway) — Economic conditions. 6. Balestrand (Norway) — Social conditions. 7. Balestrand (Norway) — Emigration and immigration. 8. Middle West — Foreign population. I. T. II. Series.
F358.2.S2 G54 1985   304.8/77/0483 19   *LC* 84-21428   *ISBN* 052126068X

F366–380 Louisiana

Louisiana; a guide to the State. Harry Hansen editor.   3.8309
New rev. ed. — New York: Hastings House, [c1971] xxxiii, 711 p.: illus.; 21 cm. — (American guide series) 'Originally compiled by the Federal Writers' Program of the Works Projects Administration of the State of Louisiana.' 1. Louisiana — Description and travel — Guide-books. I. Hansen, Harry, 1884- ed. II. Writers' program. Louisiana. Louisiana. III. Series.
F367.3.L6 1971   917.63/04/6   *LC* 75-158007   *ISBN* 0803842724

Taylor, Joe Gray.   3.8310
Louisiana, a bicentennial history / Joe Gray Taylor. — New York: Norton, c1976. xi, 194 p., [8] leaves of plates: ill.; 22 cm. (The States and the Nation series) Includes index. 1. Louisiana — History I. T.
F369.T29   976.3   *LC* 76-24848   *ISBN* 0393056023

Giraud, Marcel, 1900-.   3.8311
[Histoire de la Louisiane française. English] A history of French Louisiana. Translation by Joseph C. Lambert. Rev. and corr. by the author. Baton Rouge, Louisiana State University Press [1974-. v. illus. 24 cm. Translation of Historie de la Louisiane française. 1. Louisiana — History — To 1803 I. T.
F372.G513   976.3   *LC* 71-181565   *ISBN* 0807100587

McCrary, Peyton, 1943-.　　　　　　　3.8312
Abraham Lincoln and Reconstruction: the Louisiana experiment / by Peyton McCrary. — Princeton, N.J.: Princeton University Press, c1978. xviii, 423 p.; 24 cm. Includes index. 1. Lincoln, Abraham, 1809-1865. 2. Reconstruction — Louisiana. 3. Louisiana — Politics and government — 1865-1950 I. T.
F374.M32　　976.3/06　　*LC* 78-51181　　*ISBN* 0691046603

Shugg, Roger W. (Roger Wallace)　　　• 3.8313
Origins of class struggle in Louisiana; a social history of white farmers and laborers during slavery and after, 1840–1875, by Roger W. Shugg. — [Baton Rouge]: Louisiana State University Press, [1968] xiv, 372 p.; 22 cm. — (Louisiana paperbacks, L-36) 1. Slavery in the United States — Economic aspects — Louisiana. 2. Plantations — Louisiana 3. Louisiana — Social conditions. I. T.
F374.S58 1968　　301.44/09763　　*LC* 74-1055

Sindler, Allan P.　　　　　　　　• 3.8314
Huey Long's Louisiana: State politics, 1920–1952. — Baltimore: Johns Hopkins Press, 1956. xv, 316 p.: maps, tables.; 23 cm. 1. Long, Huey Pierce, 1893-1935. 2. Louisiana — Politics and government — 1865-1950 I. T.
F375.L846　　976.3　　*LC* 56-11664

Taylor, Joe Gray.　　　　　　　3.8315
Louisiana reconstructed, 1863–1877 / Joe Gray Taylor. — Baton Rouge: Louisiana State University Press, c1974. xii, 552 p., [4] leaves of plates: ill.; 24 cm. Includes index. 1. Reconstruction — Louisiana. 2. Louisiana — Politics and government — 1865-1950 I. T.
F375.T23　　976.3/06　　*LC* 74-77327　　*ISBN* 0807100846

Hair, William Ivy.　　　　　　　3.8316
Carnival of fury: Robert Charles and the New Orleans race riot of 1900 / William Ivy Hair. — Baton Rouge: Louisiana State University Press, c1976. 216 p.: port.; 23 cm. Includes index. 1. Charles, Robert, 1865 or 6-1900. 2. Riots — Louisiana — New Orleans. 3. New Orleans (La.) — History I. T.
F379.N553 C424　　976.3/35/060924 B　　*LC* 75-34856　　*ISBN* 0807101788

Jackson, Joy J.　　　　　　　　• 3.8317
New Orleans in the gilded age: politics and urban progress, 1880–1896 / [by] Joy J. Jackson. — [Baton Rouge]: Published by Louisiana State University Press for the Louisiana Historical Association [1969] xi, 355 p.: ill.; 23 cm. 1. New Orleans (La.) — History I. Louisiana Historical Association. II. T.
F379.N557 J3　　309.1/763/355　　*LC* 70-89828　　*ISBN* 080710910X

Blassingame, John W., 1940-.　　　　3.8318
Black New Orleans, 1860–1880 [by] John W. Blassingame. Chicago, University of Chicago Press [1973] xvii, 301 p. illus. 23 cm. 1. Afro-Americans — Louisiana — New Orleans 2. New Orleans (La.) — History I. T.
F379.N59 B42　　917.63/35/0696073　　*LC* 72-97664　　*ISBN* 0226057070

F381–395 Texas

Frantz, Joe Bertram, 1917-.　　　　　3.8319
Texas: a Bicentennial history / Joe B. Frantz. New York: Norton, c1976. xiv, 222 p., [8] leaves of plates: ill.; 22 cm. (The States and the Nation series) Includes index. 1. Texas — History I. T.
F386.F72　　976.4　　*LC* 76-23132　　*ISBN* 0393055809

Meinig, D. W. (Donald William), 1924-.　　• 3.8320
Imperial Texas: an interpretive essay in cultural geography / by D. W. Meinig; introd. by Lorrin Kennamer. — Austin: University of Texas Press [1969] 145 p.: ill., maps; 25 cm. 1. Texas — Description and travel 2. Texas — Population. I. T.
F386.M35　　301.29/764　　*LC* 69-18807　　*ISBN* 0292783817

Ransom, Harry Huntt, 1908-.　　　　3.8321
The other Texas frontier / Harry Huntt Ransom; edited by Hazel H. Ransom; foreword by John Graves. — Austin: University of Texas Press, 1985 (c1984). 72 p.: ill.; 26 cm. 1. Frontier and pioneer life — Texas — Addresses, essays, lectures. 2. Pioneers — Texas — Biography — Addresses, essays, lectures. 3. Texas — Biography — Addresses, essays, lectures. I. Ransom, Hazel H. II. T.
F386.5.R36 1984　　976.4/009/92 19　　*LC* 84-10382　　*ISBN* 0292711018

Barker, Eugene Campbell, 1874-1956.　　• 3.8322
The life of Stephen F. Austin, founder of Texas, 1793–1836; a chapter of the Westward movement by the Anglo-American people. New introd. by Seymour V. Connor. New York, Da Capo Press, 1968. ix, xv, 551 p. maps, ports. 24 cm. (The American scene) (A Da Capo Press reprint edition.) 'An unabridged republication of the first edition published ... in 1925.' 1. Austin, Stephen F. (Stephen Fuller), 1793-1836. 2. Texas — History — To 1846 I. T.
F389.A936 1968　　976.4/03/0924 B　　*LC* 68-27723

Bolton, Herbert Eugene, 1879-1953.　　• 3.8323
Texas in the middle eighteenth century: studies in Spanish colonial history and administration. — New York: Russell & Russell, 1962. 501 p.: ill.; 23 cm. 1. Texas — History — To 1846 2. Spain — Colonies — Administration. 3. Spain — Colonies — North America. I. T.
F389.B75 1962　　*LC* 62-15151

Houston, Sam, 1793-1863.　　　　　• 3.8324
The autobiography of Sam Houston, edited by Donald Day & Harry Herbert Ullom. 1st ed. Norman, University of Oklahoma Press, 1954. xviii, 298 p. illus., ports., maps. 1. Texas — History — Sources. I. Day, Donald, 1899- II. Ullom, Harry Herbert, ed. III. T.
F390.H8474　　976.030924 B　　923.273　　*LC* 54-10051

James, Marquis, 1891-1955.　　　　　• 3.8325
The raven: a biography of Sam Houston. — Dunwoody, Ga.: N. S. Berg [1968, c1929] 489 p.: ill., maps, ports.; 23 cm. 1. Houston, Sam, 1793-1863. I. T.
F390.H8494　　976/.03/0924 B　　*LC* 68-2545

Merk, Frederick, 1887-.　　　　　　3.8326
Slavery and the annexation of Texas. With the collaboration of Lois Bannister Merk. — [1st ed.]. — New York: Knopf, 1972. xiii, 290, x p.; 25 cm. 1. Texas — History — Republic, 1836-1846 2. United States — Politics and government — 1841-1845 3. United States — Politics and government — 1845-1849 I. T.
F390.M55　　976.4/04　　*LC* 72-2229　　*ISBN* 0394481046

Olmsted, Frederick Law, 1822-1903.　　• 3.8327
A journey through Texas; or, A saddle–trip on the southwestern frontier, with a statistical appendix. — New York: B. Franklin, [1969] xxxiv, 516 p.; 19 cm. — (Burt Franklin research & source works series, 348. American classics in history & social science, 78) Reprint of the 1860 ed. 1. Olmsted, Frederick Law, 1822-1903. 2. Slavery — Texas 3. Texas — Description and travel I. T. II. Title: A saddle–trip on the southwestern frontier.
F391.O512 1969　　917.64/04/5　　*LC* 69-18606

Samora, Julian, 1920-.　　　　　　3.8328
Gunpowder justice: a reassessment of the Texas Rangers / Julian Samora, Joe Bernal, Albert Peña. — Notre Dame, Ind.: University of Notre Dame Press, c1979. 179 p.; 21 cm. Includes index. 1. Texas Rangers. 2. Police — Texas — Complaints against. 3. Mexican Americans — Texas — Social conditions. 4. Texas — Race relations. I. Bernal, Joe, 1927- joint author. II. Peña, Albert. joint author. III. T.
F391.S22　　363.2/09764　　*LC* 78-62969　　*ISBN* 0268010013

Webb, Walter Prescott, 1888-1963.　　• 3.8329
The Texas Rangers: a century of frontier defense / by Walter Prescott Webb; illustrated with drawings by Lonnie Rees and with photographs; foreword by Lyndon B. Johnson. — 2d ed. — Austin: University of Texas Press, 1965. xx, 583 p.: ill., facsims., ports. 1. Texas Rangers. 2. Frontier and pioneer life — Texas. 3. Texas — History I. T.
F391.W43 1965　　*LC* 65-23166

Writers' Program (Tex.)　　　　　• 3.8330
Texas: a guide to the Lone Star State / Harry Hansen, editor. — New rev. ed. New York: Hastings House [1969] xxxiv, 717 p.: ill., maps, ports.; 22 cm. (American guide series.) 'Originally compiled by the Federal Writers' Program of the Work Projects Administration in the State of Texas.' 1. Automobiles — Road guides — Texas. 2. Texas. 3. Texas — Description and travel — 1951-1980 — Guide-books. I. Hansen, Harry, 1884- ed. II. T. III. Series.
F391.W95 1969　　917.64/04/6　　*LC* 68-31690　　*ISBN* 0803870558

Rathjen, Frederick W., 1929-.　　　　3.8331
The Texas Panhandle frontier [by] Frederick W. Rathjen. — Austin: University of Texas Press, [1973] xii, 286 p.: illus.; 23 cm. — (The M. K. Brown range life series, no. 12) 1. Frontier and pioneer life — Texas. 2. Texas Panhandle (Tex.) — History. I. T.
F392.P168 R37　　917.64/8　　*LC* 73-7602　　*ISBN* 0292780079

Horgan, Paul, 1903-.　　　　　　• 3.8332
Great river: the Rio Grande in North American history. — New York: Holt, Rinehart and Winston, [c1954] 2 v. in 1.: illus.; 22 cm. 1. Rio Grande 2. Rio Grande Valley — History. I. T.
F392.R5 H65 1954a　　976.44　　*LC* 60-14369

García, Mario T.　　　　　　　3.8333
Desert immigrants: the Mexicans of El Paso, 1880–1920 / Mario T. García. — New Haven: Yale University Press, c1981. xii, 316 p., [7] leaves of plates: ill.; 25 cm. — (Yale Western Americana series. 32) Includes index. 1. Mexican Americans — Texas — El Paso — History. 2. El Paso (Tex.) — Ethnic relations. 3. El Paso (Tex.) — History. I. T. II. Series.
F394.E4 G36　　976.4/96　　*LC* 80-36862　　*ISBN* 0300025203

Davidson, Chandler.   3.8334
Biracial politics: conflict and coalition in the Metropolitan South. — Baton Rouge: Louisiana State University Press [1972] xviii, 301 p.; 24 cm. 1. Afro-Americans — Texas — Houston 2. Houston (Tex.) — Politics and government. I. T.
F394.H8 D33   320.9/764/141106   *LC* 76-185951   *ISBN* 0807102456

Haynes, Robert V.   3.8335
A night of violence: the Houston riot of 1917 / Robert V. Haynes. — Baton Rouge: Louisiana State University Press, c1976. xii, 338 p., [4] leaves of plates: maps; 24 cm. Includes index. 1. Riots — Texas — Houston. 2. Houston (Tex.) — History. I. T.
F394.H8 H39   976.4/1411/06   *LC* 75-18041   *ISBN* 0807101729

De León, Arnoldo, 1945-.   3.8336
The Tejano community, 1836–1900 / by Arnoldo De León; with a contribution by Kenneth L. Stewart. — 1st ed. — Albuquerque: University of New Mexico Press, c1982. xix, 277 p.: ill.; 25 cm. Includes index. 1. Mexican Americans — Texas — Social life and customs. 2. Mexican Americans — Texas — Social conditions. 3. Texas — Social life and customs. 4. Texas — Social conditions. I. T.
F395.M5 D4   976.4/0046872 19   *LC* 81-52053   *ISBN* 0826305865

De León, Arnoldo, 1945-.   3.8337
They called them greasers: Anglo attitudes toward Mexicans in Texas, 1821–1900 / by Arnoldo De León. — 1st ed. — Austin: University of Texas Press, 1983. xii, 153 p.: map; 24 cm. Includes index. 1. Mexican Americans — Texas — Public opinion — History — 19th century. 2. Public opinion — Texas — History — 19th century. 3. Texas — Race relations. I. T.
F395.M5 D43 1983   976.4/0046872 19   *LC* 82-24850   *ISBN* 0292703635

F396–475 Old Southwest. Lower Mississippi Valley

Dick, Everett Newfon, 1898-.   • 3.8338
The Dixie frontier a social history of the southern frontier from the first transmontane beginnings to the Civil War / E. Dick.—. [1st ed.] New York, A.A. Knopf, 1948. xix, 374, xxv p. illus. 22 cm. 1. Frontier and pioneer life — Southwest, Old. 2. Southwest, Old — History I. T.
F396.D5   975   *LC* 48-5379

New Spain and the Anglo–American west: historical   • 3.8339
contributions presented to Herbert Eugene Bolton.
[Los Angeles: Priv. Print., 1932] 2 v.: front. (port.); 27 cm. 1. Bolton, Herbert Eugene, 1870-1953. 2. Frontier and pioneer life — West (U.S.) 3. West (U.S.) — History — Sources. 4. Southwest, Old — History — Sources. 5. Southwest, New — History — Sources. 6. Mexico — History — Spanish colony, 1540-1810 — Sources. 7. Spain — Colonies — North America. 8. United States — Territorial expansion I. Hackett, Charles Wilson, 1888- ed. II. Hammond, George Peter, 1896- joint ed. III. Mecham, John Lloyd, joint ed. IV. Binkley, William Campbell, 1889- joint ed. V. Goodwin, Cardinal Leonidas, 1880- joint ed. VI. Rippy, James Fred, 1892- joint ed. VII. Ross, Mary. comp. VIII. Title: The Anglo-American west, New Spain and.
F396.N58   *LC* 33-3181

Whitaker, Arthur Preston, 1895-.   • 3.8340
The Spanish–American frontier, 1783–1795: the westward movement and the Spanish retreat in the Mississippi Valley / with an introd. by Samuel Eliot Morison. — Lincoln: University of Nebraska Press [1969, c1927] viii, 255 p.: maps; 21 cm. 'A Bison book.' 1. Southwest, Old — History 2. Mississippi River Valley — History 3. Spain — Colonies — America. I. T.
F396.W57 1969   976/.02   *LC* 75-2465

F406–445 Arkansas. Tennessee

Ashmore, Harry S.   3.8341
Arkansas: a Bicentennial history / Harry S. Ashmore. — New York: Norton, c1978. xxii, 202 p., [8] leaves of plates: ill.; 22 cm. (The States and the Nation series) Includes index. 1. Arkansas — History I. T.
F411.A85   976.7   *LC* 77-26622   *ISBN* 0393056694

Writers' program. Arkansas.   • 3.8342
Arkansas; a guide to the state. New York, Hastings House, 1941. xxvii, 447 p. illus. (incl. maps) plates. 21 cm. 1. Arkansas. 2. Arkansas — Description and travel — Guide-books.
F411.W8   *LC* 41-52931

Abernethy, Thomas Perkins, 1890-.   • 3.8343
From frontier to plantation in Tennessee; a study in frontier democracy. — University, Ala.: University of Alabama Press, [1967] xi, 392 p.: illus., maps; 21 cm. — (Southern historical publications, no. 12) Reprint of the 1932 ed. 1. Tennessee — History 2. Tennessee — Politics and government — To 1865 I. T. II. Series.
F436.A17 1967   976.8/03   *LC* 67-9183

Alexander, Thomas Benjamin, 1918-.   • 3.8344
Political reconstruction in Tennessee, by Thomas B. Alexander. — New York: Russell & Russell, [1968, c1950] 292 p.; 23 cm. 1. Reconstruction — Tennessee. 2. Tennessee — Politics and government — 1865-1950 I. T.
F436.A38 1968   976.8/05   *LC* 68-25026

Majors, William R., 1929-.   3.8345
The end of arcadia: Gordon Browning and Tennessee politics / William R. Majors. — Memphis, TN: Memphis State University Press, c1982. viii, 263 p.: port.; 24 cm. Includes index. 1. Browning, Gordon, 1889- 2. United States. Congress. House — Biography. 3. Legislators — United States — Biography. 4. Tennessee — Politics and government — 1865-1950 5. Tennessee — Governors — Biography. I. T.
F436.B86 M34 1982   976.8/05/0924 B 19   *LC* 82-3412   *ISBN* 0878700986

Corlew, Robert Ewing.   3.8346
Tennessee, a short history / by Robert E. Corlew; incorporating revisions developed by the late Stanley J. Folmsbee and the late Enoch Mitchell. — 2d ed. — Knoxville: University of Tennessee Press, 1981. xv, 634 p.: ill.; 24 cm. Edition for 1969 by S. J. Folmsbee, R. E. Corlew, and E. L. Mitchell. 1. Tennessee — History I. Folmsbee, Stanley John, 1899- Tennessee. II. Mitchell, Enoch L., 1903- III. T.
F436.C78 1981.   F436.C78 1981.   976.8   *LC* 80-13553   *ISBN* 0870492586

Crockett, Davy, 1786-1836.   3.8347
A narrative of the life of David Crockett of the State of Tennessee. A facsim. ed. with annotations and an introd. by James A. Shackford and Stanley J. Folmsbee. — Knoxville: University of Tennessee Press, [1973, c1834] xx, 211 p.: illus.; 20 x 22 cm. — (Tennesseana editions.) Original ed. published by E. L. Carey and A. Hart, Philadelphia. 1. Crockett, Davy, 1786-1836. 2. Creek War, 1813-1814 3. Tennessee — History I. Shackford, James Atkins. ed. II. Folmsbee, Stanley John, 1899- ed. III. T. IV. Series.
F436.C9395 1834aa   976.8/04/0924 B   *LC* 72-177358   *ISBN* 0870491199

Shackford, James Atkins.   • 3.8348
David Crockett, the man and the legend. Chapel Hill, University of North Carolina Press [1956] xiv, 338 p. port., map (on lining papers) 24 cm. 1. Crockett, Davy, 1786-1836. I. T.
F436.C9594   *LC* 56-13913

Dykeman, Wilma.   3.8349
Tennessee: a bicentennial history / Wilma Dykeman. — New York: Norton, c1975. xv, 206 p.: ill.; 22 cm. — (States and the nation.) Includes index. 1. Tennessee — History I. T. II. Series.
F436.D983 1975   976.8   *LC* 75-25873   *ISBN* 0393055558

Federal Writers' Project. Tennessee.   • 3.8350
Tennessee; a guide to the state. Comp. and written by the Federal Writers' Project of the Work Projects Administration for the State of Tennessee. New York, Hastings House, c1949. 558 p. ill. (American guide series) 1. Automobiles — Road guides — Tennessee. 2. Tennessee. 3. Tennessee — Description and travel — Guide-books. I. T.
F436.F45 1949   *LC* 49-5822

Arnow, Harriette Louisa Simpson, 1908-.   • 3.8351
Seedtime on the Cumberland. — New York: Macmillan, 1960. 449 p.: ill. 1. Frontier and pioneer life — Cumberland Valley, Ky. & Tenn. 2. Kentucky — History 3. Tennessee — History 4. Cumberland Valley, Ky. & Tenn. — History. I. T.
F442.2.A7   976.85   *LC* 60-7414

Capers, Gerald Mortimer, jr.   • 3.8352
The biography of a river town: Memphis: its heroic age / by Gerald M. Capers, jr. — Chapel Hill: The University of North Carolina Press, 1939. x, 292 p.: ill., maps, plates, diagrs.; 23 cm. This study was begun in the Graduate school of Yale University...and was submitted to that university in 1936 ... for the degree of doctor of philosophy. Foreword. I. T.
F444.M3 C3   976.8   *LC* 39-27481

Miller, William D.   • 3.8353
Mr. Crump of Memphis [by] William D. Miller. Baton Rouge, Louisiana State University Press, 1964. xiii, 373 p. illus., ports. 24 cm. (Southern biography series.) 'Critical essay on authorities': p. 353-359. 1. Crump, Edward Hull, 1874-1954. 2. Memphis (Tenn.) — Politics and government. I. T. II. Series.
F444.M5M66   923.273   *LC* 64-21594

Doyle, Don Harrison, 1946-.   **3.8354**
Nashville in the new South, 1880–1930 / Don H. Doyle. — Knoxville: University of Tennessee Press, c1985. xvii, 288 p.: ill.; 25 cm. Includes index. 1. Nashville (Tenn.) — History. I. T.
F444.N257 D69 1985   976.8/55 19   *LC* 84-11976   *ISBN* 0870494465

F446–460 KENTUCKY

Channing, Steven A.   **3.8355**
Kentucky: a Bicentennial history / Steven A. Channing. — New York: Norton, c1977. xv, 222 p., [8] leaves of plates: map. — (States and the nation.) Includes index. 1. Kentucky — History I. T. II. Series.
F451.C49   F451.C49.   976.9   *LC* 77-24635   *ISBN* 0393056546

Coward, Joan Wells, 1936-.   **3.8356**
Kentucky in the new republic: the process of constitution making / Joan Wells Coward. — Lexington: University Press of Kentucky, c1979. 220 p.: maps; 22 cm. Includes index. 1. Kentucky — Politics and government — To 1792 2. Kentucky — Politics and government — 1792-1865 I. T.
F454.C68   976.9/03 19   *LC* 77-92920   *ISBN* 0813113806

Watlington, Patricia.   • **3.8357**
The Partisan spirit: Kentucky politics, 1779–1792. — [1st ed.] New York: Atheneum, 1972. viii, 276 p.; 22 cm. 'Published for the Institute of Early American History and Culture at Williamsburg, Virginia.' 1. Kentucky — Politics and government — To 1792 I. Institute of Early American History and Culture (Williamsburg, Va.) II. T.
F454.W3 1972   976.9/02   *LC* 76-181463

Davenport, F. Garvin (Francis Garvin), 1905-.   • **3.8358**
Ante–bellum Kentucky. Oxford, Ohio, The Mississippi valley press, 1943. 238 p.: ill.; 24 cm. 1. Kentucky — History 2. Kentucky — Social life and custom. I. T.
F455.D36   *LC* 43-17548

Federal Writers' Project. Kentucky.   • **3.8359**
Kentucky; a guide to the Bluegrass State, compiled and written by the Federal Writers' Project of the Work Projects Administration for the State of Kentucky. Sponsored by the University of Kentucky. [Rev. ed.] New York, Hastings House [1954] xxix, 492 p. illus., maps. 22 cm. (American guide series.) 1. Kentucky. 2. Kentucky — Description and travel — Guide-books. I. T. II. Series.
F456.F44 1954   *LC* 54-1591

F461–475 MISSOURI

A History of Missouri. [William E. Parrish, general editor: the   • **3.8360**
Missouri sesquicentennial ed.
Columbia] University of Missouri Press [1971- < c1986 > . v. < 1-3, 5 > 25 cm. 1. Missouri — History I. Parrish, William Earl, 1931- ed. II. Foley, William E., 1938- III. McCandless, Perry, 1917-
F466.H58   977.8   *LC* 76-155844   *ISBN* 0826201083

McReynolds, Edwin C.   • **3.8361**
Missouri; a history of the Crossroads State. [1st ed.] Norman, University of Oklahoma Press [1962] xiv, 483 p. illus., ports., maps. 25 cm. 1. Missouri — History I. T.
F466.M2   *LC* 62-18052

Mitchell, Franklin D.   • **3.8362**
Embattled democracy; Missouri democratic politics, 1919–1932 [by] Franklin D. Mitchell. — Columbia: University of Missouri Press, [1968] 219 p.; 22 cm. — (University of Missouri studies, v. 47) 1. Missouri — Politics and government — 1865-1950 I. T.
F466.M69   320.9/778   *LC* 68-11347

Nagel, Paul C.   **3.8363**
Missouri, a Bicentennial history / Paul C. Nagel. — New York: Norton, c1977. xiv, 205 p., [8] leaves of plates: ill.; 22 cm. (The States and the Nation series) Includes index. 1. Missouri — History I. T.
F466.N3   977.8   *LC* 77-4395   *ISBN* 0393056333

Writers' Program of the Work Projects Administration in the   • **3.8364**
State of Missouri.
Missouri, a guide to the 'Show Me' State, compiled by workers of the Writers' Program of the Work Projects Administration in the State of Missouri. New York, Duell, Sloan and Pearce. St. Clair Shores, Mich., Somerset Publishers, 1973 [c1941] 652 p. illus. 22 cm. Original ed. issued in series: American guide

series. 1. Missouri. 2. Missouri — Description and travel — Guide-books. I. T.
F466.W85 1973   917.78/04/4   *LC* 72-84486   *ISBN* 0403021758

Gilmore, Robert K. (Robert Karl), 1927-.   **3.8365**
Ozark baptizings, hangings, and other diversions: theatrical folkways of rural Missouri, 1885–1910 / by Robert K. Gilmore; foreword by Robert Flanders. — Norman: University of Oklahoma Press, c1984. xxix, 264 p.: ill.; 22 cm. Includes index. 1. Amusements — Ozark Mountains Region — History. 2. Ozark Mountains Region — Social life and customs. I. T.
F472.O9 G55 1984   977.8/835 19   *LC* 83-40324   *ISBN* 0806118547

Dorsett, Lyle W.   **3.8366**
The Pendergast machine [by] Lyle W. Dorsett. New York, Oxford University Press, 1968. xiv, 163 p. maps. 22 cm. (The Urban life in America series) 1. Pendergast, Tom, 1870-1945. 2. Kansas City (Mo.) — Politics and government. I. T.
F474.K2 D6   352.0778/411   *LC* 68-15892

Brown, A. Theodore (Andrew Theodore), 1923-.   **3.8367**
K.C.: a history of Kansas City, Missouri / by A. Theodore Brown and Lyle W. Dorsett. — 1st ed. — Boulder, Colo.: Pruett Pub. Co., c1978. 303 p.: ill., ports.; 23 cm. — (Western urban history series. v. 2) 1. Kansas City (Mo.) — History. I. Dorsett, Lyle W. joint author. II. T. III. Series.
F474.K257 B76   F474K2 B76.   977.8/411   *LC* 78-14514   *ISBN* 0871085267

F476–485 Old Northwest. Northwest Territory

Bond, Beverley W. (Beverley Waugh), b. 1881.   • **3.8368**
The civilization of the Old Northwest; a study of political, social, and economic development, 1788–1812, by Beverley W. Bond, Jr. New York, Macmillan, 1934. St. Clair Shores, Mich., Scholarly Press, 1970. ix, 543 p. 22 cm. 1. Northwest, Old — Politics and government. 2. Northwest, Old — Economic conditions. 3. Northwest, Old — Social life and customs. I. T.
F479.B69 1970b   309.1/77/02   *LC* 77-144888   *ISBN* 0403008735

Ogg, Frederic Austin, 1878-1951.   • **3.8369**
The Old Northwest; a chronicle of the Ohio valley and beyond, by Frederic Austin Ogg. — New Haven, Yale university press; [etc., etc.] 1921. ix, 220 p. col. front., fold. map. 18 cm. — (Half-title: The Chronicles of America series, Allen Johnson, editor ... v. 19) 'Roosevelt edition.' 'Bibliographical note': p. 211-214. 1. Northwest, Old — Hist. 2. Ohio River Valley — Hist. I. T.
F479.O35   *LC* 22-12141

Kellogg, Louise Phelps, ed.   • **3.8370**
Early narratives of the Northwest, 1634–1699. New York, C. Scribner's sons, 1917. xiv, 382 p. 2 fold. maps, facsim. 23 cm. 1. America — Discovery and exploration — French. 2. Northwest, Old — Discovery and exploration. I. T.
F482.K29   *LC* 17-6235

Wainwright, Nicholas B.   • **3.8371**
George Croghan, wilderness diplomat / by Nicholas B. Wainwright. — Chapel Hill: Published for the Institute of Early American History and Culture (Williamsburg, Va.) by the University of North Carolina Press, 1959. viii, 334 p.: maps. 1. Croghan, George, d. 1782. I. T.
F483.C76 W3   *LC* 59-2353/L

Sosin, Jack M.   • **3.8372**
Whitehall and the wilderness; the Middle West in British colonial policy, 1760–1775. — Lincoln, University of Nebraska Press, 1961. xi, 307 p. maps. 24 cm. Bibliography: p. 269-292. 1. Northwest, Old — Hist. 2. Gt. Brit. — Colonies — America. 3. Indians of North America — Government relations — To 1789 I. T.
F483.S6   977   *LC* 61-10152

Buley, R. Carlyle (Roscoe Carlyle), 1893-1968.   • **3.8373**
The Old Northwest: pioneer period, 1815–1840 / by R. Carlyle Buley. — 2d printing. — Bloomington: Indiana University Press, 1951, c1950 (Scranton, Pa.: Haddon Craftsmen) 2 v. (v. 1 xiii, [1] p., [1] leaf, 632 p., [12] leaves of plates; v. 2 viii p., [1] leaf, 686 p., [10] leaves of plates): ill., maps; 23.4 x 15.2 cm. Reprint of the ed. published by the Indiana Historical Society. 1. Northwest, Old — History I. T.
F484.3.B94 1951   977   *LC* 52-6466

Hubbart, Henry Clyde, 1882-.   • **3.8374**
The older Middle West, 1840–1880; its social, economic, and political life, and sectional tendencies before, during and after the Civil War. Reprint of 1936

edition. New York, Russell & Russell, 1963 [c1936] ix, 305 p. illus. 23 cm. At head of title: The American Historical Association. 1. Northwest, Old — History 2. Northwest, Old — Social life and customs. I. American Historical Association. II. T. III. Title: Middle West.
F484.3.H885 1963   977   LC 63-8364

Kohlmeier, Albert Ludwig.   • 3.8375
The Old Northwest as the keystone of the arch of American federal union: a study in commerce and politics. Bloomington, Ind., The Principia press, inc., 1938. v, 257 p. 24 cm. 1. Northwest, Old — History 2. United States — History — 1815-1861 3. United States — Commerce — History 4. United States — Politics and govenent — 1815-1861. I. T.
F484.3.K798   LC 38-22330

Power, Richard Lyle, 1896-.   • 3.8376
Planting Corn Belt culture; the impress of the upland southerner and Yankee in the Old Northwest. Indianapolis, Indiana Historical Society, 1953. xvi, 196 p. illus., maps. 24 cm. (Indiana Historical Society publications. v. 17) 1. Northwest, Old — Civilization. I. T. II. Series.
F484.3.P6   LC 54-618

Rohrbough, Malcolm J.   3.8377
The trans–Appalachian frontier: people, societies, and institutions, 1775–1850 / Malcolm J. Rohrbough. — New York: Oxford University Press, 1978. xiv, 444 p.: maps; 24 cm. Includes index. 1. Frontier and pioneer life — Northwest, Old. 2. Frontier and pioneer life — Southwest, Old. 3. Frontier and pioneer life — Appalachian Region. 4. Northwest, Old — History — 1775-1865 5. Southwest, Old — History 6. Appalachian Region — History I. T.
F484.3.R64   977/.02   LC 77-28492   ISBN 0195022092

Schoolcraft, Henry Rowe, 1793-1864.   • 3.8378
Travels through the northwestern regions of the United States / Henry Rowe Schoolcraft. — Ann Arbor: University Microfilms, 1966. 419 p. [6] leaves of plates: ill., map. (March of America facsimile series; no. 66) Orig. t.p.: Narrative journal of travels from Detroit northwest through the great chain of American Lakes to the Sources of the Mississippi River in the year 1820. 1. Northwest, Old — Description and travel 2. Great Lakes — Description and travel 3. Mississippi River — Description and travel I. T. II. Series.
F484.3 S36 1821a   F484.3 S36 1821a.   917.704   LC 66-26336

F486–520 OHIO. OHIO VALLEY

Havighurst, Walter, 1901-.   3.8379
Ohio: a bicentennial history / Walter Havighurst. — New York: Norton, c1976. ix, 211 p., [8] leaves of plates: ill.; 22 cm. (The States and the Nation series) Includes index. 1. Ohio — History I. T.
F491.H4   977.1   LC 76-27764   ISBN 0393056139

Roseboom, Eugene Holloway, 1892-.   3.8380
A history of Ohio, by Eugene H. Roseboom and Francis P. Weisenburger. Edited and illustrated by James H. Rodabaugh. — [2d ed.]. — Columbus: Ohio Historical Society, 1969 [c1953] xiii, 443 p.: illus. (part col.); 30 cm. 1. Ohio — History I. Weisenburger, Francis Phelps, 1900- joint author. II. T.
F491.R76 1969   917.71   LC 78-636586

Wittke, Carl Frederick, 1892-1971. ed.   • 3.8381
The history of the state of Ohio. [Columbus, Ohio: [s.n.], 1941-44) 6 v. illus. (incl. ports., facsims.) maps (1 fold.) diagrs. (1 double) 24 cm. 1. Ohio — History I. Bond, Beverley Waugh, 1881- II. Utter, William Thomas, 1895- III. Weisenburger, Francis Phelps, 1900- IV. Roseboom, Eugene Holloway, 1892- V. Jordan, Philip Dillon, 1903- VI. Lindley, Harlow, 1875- VII. Ohio State Archaeological and Historical Society. VIII. T.
F491.W78   LC 41-7471

Cayton, Andrew R. L.   3.8382
The frontier republic: ideology and politics in the Ohio Country, 1780–1825 / Andrew R.L. Cayton. — Kent, Ohio: Kent State University Press, c1986. xii, 197 p.: map; 24 cm. Includes index. 1. Ohio — Politics and government — 1787-1865 I. T.
F495.C35 1986   977.1/03 19   LC 86-4706   ISBN 087338332X

Maizlish, Stephen E., 1945-.   3.8383
The triumph of sectionalism: the transformation of Ohio politics, 1844–1856 / Stephen E. Maizlish. — Kent, Ohio: Kent State University Press, c1983. xiv, 310 p.: map, ports.; 24 cm. Includes index. 1. Political parties — Ohio — History — 19th century. 2. Sectionalism (United States) — Case studies. 3. Ohio — Politics and government — 1787-1865 I. T.
F495.M34 1983   F495 M34 1983.   977.1/03 19   LC 83-11255   ISBN 0873382935

Warner, Hoyt Landon.   • 3.8384
Progressivism in Ohio, 1897–1917. — [Columbus] Ohio State University Press for the Ohio Historical Society [1964] xiii, 556 p. 24 cm. A completely revised

and rewritten version of the author's doctoral dissertation, Ohio's crusade for reform, 1897-1917, Harvard, 1950. Bibliography: p. 497-528. 1. Ohio — Pol. & govt. — 1865-1950. 2. Progressivism (U.S. politics) I. T.
F496.W3   977.104   LC 64-19164

Writers' Program. Ohio.   • 3.8385
The Ohio guide, compiled by workers of the Writers' Program of the Work Projects Administration in the State of Ohio. Sponsored by the Ohio State Archaeological and Historical Society. New York, Oxford University Press. — St. Clair Shores, Mich.: Somerset Publishers, 1973. p. Reprint of the 1940 ed., issued in series: American guide series. 1. Ohio. 2. Ohio — Description and travel — Guide-books. I. T.
F496.W96 1973   917.71/04/4   LC 72-84499   ISBN 0403021847

Stokes, Carl.   3.8386
Promises of power: a political autobiography / by Carl. B. Stokes. — New York: Simon and Schuster [1973] 288 p.; 22 cm. 1. Stokes, Carl. 2. Cleveland (Ohio) — Politics and government. I. T.
F499.C653 S86   320.9/771/3204 B   LC 73-3783   ISBN 0671216023

Barton, Josef J.   3.8387
Peasants and strangers: Italians, Rumanians, and Slovaks in an American City, 1890–1950 / Josef J. Barton. — Cambridge, Mass.: Harvard University Press, 1975. xii, 217 p.; 25 cm. — (Harvard studies in urban history.) 1. Italian Americans — Ohio — Cleveland. 2. Romanian Americans — Ohio — Cleveland. 3. Slovak Americans — Ohio — Cleveland. 4. Cleveland (Ohio) — History I. T. II. Series.
F499.C69 I83   301.45/09771/32   LC 74-14085   ISBN 0674659309

Kusmer, Kenneth L., 1945-.   3.8388
A ghetto takes shape: Black Cleveland, 1870–1930 / Kenneth L. Kusmer. — Urbana: University of Illinois Press, c1976. xiv, 305 p., [4] leaves of plates: ill.; 24 cm. (Blacks in the New World) Includes index. 1. Afro-Americans — Ohio — Cleveland — History 2. Cleveland — History. I. T. II. Series.
F499.C69 N34   F499C69 N34.   977.1/32/00496073   LC 75-40113   ISBN 025200289X

Barnhart, John Donald, 1895-.   • 3.8389
Valley of democracy: the frontier versus the plantation in Ohio Valley, 1775–1818. Bloomington, Indiana University Press, 1953. x, 338 p. fold. map. 25 cm. 1. Ohio River Valley — Politics and government. 2. Ohio River Valley — Economic conditions. I. T.
F517.B3   LC 53-10020

Jakle, John A.   3.8390
Images of the Ohio Valley: a historical geography of travel 1740–1860 / John A. Jakle; cartographer, Miklos Pinther. — New York: Oxford University Press, 1977. viii, 217 p.: ill., maps. — (The Anrew H. Clark series in historical geography of North America) Includes index. 1. Ohio River Valley — Historical geography. 2. Ohio River Valley — Description and travel. I. T.
F517.J28   F517 J28.   977/.02   LC 77-9570   ISBN 0195022408

Wade, Richard C.   • 3.8391
The urban frontier; the rise of western cities, 1790–1830. Cambridge, Harvard University Press, 1959. 362 p. 21 cm. (Harvard historical monographs. 41) 1. Cities and towns — Ohio River Valley. 2. City and town life I. T. II. Series.
F518.W15   977   LC 59-9285

F521–535 INDIANA

Barnhart, John Donald, 1895-1967.   3.8392
Indiana to 1816; the colonial period, by John D. Barnhart & Dorothy L. Riker. — Indianapolis: Indiana Historical Bureau, 1971. xvi, 520 p.: illus., maps, ports.; 24 cm. — (The History of Indiana, v. 1) 1. Indiana — History — To 1787 I. Riker, Dorothy Lois, 1904- joint author. II. T. III. Series.
F526.H55 vol. 1   977.2   LC 77-26828

Thornbrough, Emma Lou.   • 3.8393
Indiana in the Civil War era, 1850–1880. Indianapolis, Indiana Historical Bureau, 1965. xii, 758 p. illus., facsims., ports. 24 cm. (The History of Indiana, v. 3) 1. Indiana — History I. T. II. Series.
F526.H55 vol. 3   LC 66-63323

Phillips, Clifton Jackson.   • 3.8394
Indiana in transition; the emergence of an industrial commonwealth, 1880–1920, by Clifton J. Phillips. — Indianapolis: Indiana Historical Bureau, 1968. xiv, 674 p.: illus., ports, maps; 24 cm. — (The history of Indiana, v. 4) 1. Indiana — History I. T. II. Series.
F526.H55 vol. 4   917.72/03/4   LC 71-15507

Madison, James H.   **3.8395**
Indiana through tradition and change: a history of the Hoosier State and its people, 1920–1945 / by James H. Madison. — Indianapolis: Indiana Historical Society, 1982. xvii, 453 p., [16] p. of plates: ill.: 24 cm. — (The History of Indiana; v. 5) Includes index. 1. Indiana — History. I. T. II. Series.
F526.H55 vol. 5   977.2 s 977.2/042 19   *LC* 83-136811

Madison, James H.   **3.8396**
The Indiana way: a state history / James H. Madison. — Bloomington: Indiana University Press; Indianapolis: Indiana Historical Society, c1986. xvii, 361 p.: ill., maps, ports.; 24 cm. Includes index. 1. Indiana — History I. T.
F526.M22 1986   977.2 19   *LC* 85-45071   *ISBN* 025332999X

Peckham, Howard Henry, 1910-.   **3.8397**
Indiana: a bicentennial history / Howard H. Peckham. — New York: Norton, c1978. ix, 207 p., [8] leaves ofplates.: ill.; 22 cm. (The States and the Nation series) Includes index. 1. Indiana — History I. T.
F526.P43   977.2   *LC* 77-28308   *ISBN* 0393056708

Stampp, Kenneth M. (Kenneth Milton)   • **3.8398**
Indiana politics during the Civil War / by Kenneth M. Stampp. — Indianapolis: Indiana Historical Bureau, 1949. xiii, 300 p.; 24 cm. Includes index. 1. Indiana — Politics and government — Civil War, 1861-1865 I. T.
F526.S84   320.9/772/03   *LC* 77-23629   *ISBN* 0253370221

VanderMeer, Philip R., 1947-.   **3.8399**
The Hoosier politician: officeholding and political culture in Indiana, 1896–1920 / Philip R. VanderMeer. — Urbana: University of Illinois Press, c1985. xii, 256 p.: ill. Includes index. 1. Politicians — Indiana — History. 2. Indiana — Politics and government I. T.
F526.V26 1985   320.9772 19   *LC* 83-9260   *ISBN* 0252010418

Writers' program. Indiana.   • **3.8400**
Indiana, a guide to the Hoosier state. New York, Oxford university press [1945] xxvi, 548 (i.e. 564) p. illus., plates, ports., maps (3 on fold. 1. in pocket) 21 cm. 1. Indiana. 2. Indiana — Description and travel — Guide-books. I. T.
F526.W93 1945   *LC* 46-5683

Engel, J. Ronald.   **3.8401**
Sacred sands: the struggle for community in the Indiana Dunes / by J. Ronald Engel. — 1st ed. — Middletown, Conn.: Wesleyan University Press; Scranton, Pa.: Distributed by Harper & Row, c1983. xxii, 352 p., [16] p. of plates: ill. 1. Environmental policy — Indiana — History. 2. Indiana Dunes National Lakeshore (Ind.) — History. 3. Indiana Dunes State Park (Ind.) — History. I. T.
F532.I5 E53 1983   F532I48 E53 1983.   977.2/98 19   *LC* 82-20259   *ISBN* 0819550736

Esslinger, Dean R.   **3.8402**
Immigrants and the city: ethnicity and mobility in a nineteenth century midwestern community. — Port Washington, N.Y.: Kennikat Press, 1975. xii, 156 p.: maps; 23 cm. (Kennikat Press national university publications: Interdisciplinary urban series) 1. Urbanization — Indiana — South Bend. 2. Social mobility — South Bend, Ind. 3. South Bend (Ind.) — Foreign population. I. T.
F534.S7 E77   301.32/9/77289   *LC* 75-15947   *ISBN* 0804691088

Knox, George L., 1841-1927.   **3.8403**
Slave and freeman, the autobiography of George L. Knox / edited with an introd. by Willard B. Gatewood, Jr. — Lexington: University Press of Kentucky, c1979. 247 p.: port.; 23 cm. Includes index. 1. Knox, George L., 1841-1927. 2. Afro-Americans — Indiana — Biography. I. Gatewood, Willard B. II. T.
F535.N4 K554   977.2/004/96073 B   *LC* 78-21058   *ISBN* 0813113849

F536–550 ILLINOIS

Bogue, Margaret Beattie, 1924-.   • **3.8404**
Patterns from the sod: land use and tenure in the Grand Prairie, 1850–1900 / Margaret Beattie Bogue. — Springfield, Ill.: Illinois State Historical Library, 1959. 327 p.: charts, maps; 23 cm. — (Collections of the Illinois State Historical Library; v. 34. Land series; v. 1) 1. Land use — Illinois — History. 2. Land tenure — Illinois — History. I. T.
F 536 I29 v.34

Federal Writer's Project. Illinois.   • **3.8405**
Illinois; a descriptive and historical guide, compiled and written by the Federal Writer's Project of the Work Projects Administration for the State of Illinois. — St. Clair Shores, Mich.: Somerset Publishers, 1973. xxii, 687 p.: illus.; 22 cm. Original ed. issued in series: American guide series. 'Sponsored by Henry Horner, governor.' Reprint of the 1939 ed. published by A.C. McClurg &

Co.:Chicago. 1. Illinois — Description and travel — Guide-books. 2. Illinois — History I. T.
F539.3.F4 1973   917.73/04   *LC* 72-145010   *ISBN* 0403012929

Howard, Robert P.   **3.8406**
Illinois; a history of the Prairie State, by Robert P. Howard. — Grand Rapids, Mich.: W. B. Eerdmans Pub. Co., [1972] xxiv, 626 p.: illus.; 24 cm. 1. Illinois — History I. T.
F541.H68   977.3   *LC* 72-77179   *ISBN* 0802870252

Illinois. Centennial Commission.   • **3.8407**
The centennial history of Illinois. Springfield, Centennial Commission, 1918-1920. 5 v. 23 cm. (Illinois centennial publications) Edited by C. W. Alvord. 1. Illinois — History I. Alvord, Clarence Walworth, 1868-1928. ed. II. T.
F541.Ix   *LC* 85-64671

Jensen, Richard J.   **3.8408**
Illinois: a Bicentennial history / Richard J. Jensen. — New York: Norton, c1978. xix, 191 p., [8] leaves of plates: ill.; 22 cm. (The States and the Nation series) Includes index. 1. Illinois — History I. T.
F541.J46   977.3/04   *LC* 77-17626   *ISBN* 0393055965

Barnard, Harry, 1906-.   • **3.8409**
Eagle forgotten; the life of John Peter Altgeld. — New York: Duell, Sloan and Pearce, [1948] 484 p.; 21 cm. 1. Altgeld, John Peter, 1847-1902. I. T.
F546.Ax   923.273   *LC* a 50-9082

Brown, Stuart Gerry, 1912-.   • **3.8410**
Conscience in politics: Adlai E. Stevenson in the 1950's. — Syracuse, N.Y.: Syracuse University Press, 1961. 313 p.: ill.; 21 cm. (Men and movements series.) 1. Stevenson, Adlai E. (Adlai Ewing), 1900-1965. 2. United States — Politics and government — 1953-1961 I. T.
F546.S8 B72   973.920924 B   923.273   *LC* 61-17124

Faragher, John Mack, 1945-.   **3.8411**
Sugar Creek: life on the Illinois Prairie / John Mack Faragher. — New Haven: Yale University Press, c1986. xvii, 280 p.: ill., maps, ports. 1. Frontier and pioneer life — Illinois — Sugar Creek Valley (Macoupin County and Sangamon County) 2. Sugar Creek Valley (Macoupin County and Sangamon County, Ill.) — History. 3. Sugar Creek Valley (Macoupin County and Sangamon County, Ill.) — Social conditions. 4. Sugar Creek Valley (Macoupin County and Sangamon County, Ill.) — Economic conditions. I. T.
F547.S94 F37 1986   977.3/56 19   *LC* 86-5622   *ISBN* 0300035454

F548 Chicago

Mayer, Harold M. (Harold Melvin), 1916-.   • **3.8412**
Chicago: growth of a metropolis [by] Harold M. Mayer and Richard C. Wade. With the assistance of Glen E. Holt. Cartography by Gerald F. Pyle. Chicago, University of Chicago Press [1969] ix, 510 p. illus., facsims., maps, plans, ports. 25 cm. 1. Chicago — History — Pictorial works. I. Wade, Richard C. joint author. II. T.
F548.3.M37   917.73/11/03   *LC* 68-54054   *ISBN* 0226512738

Pierce, Bessie Louise, 1890-.   • **3.8413**
A history of Chicago ... New York, London, A. A. Knopf, 1937-57. 3 v. illus., plates, maps, diagrs. 25 cm. 1. Chicago — History. I. T.
F548.3.P54   *LC* 37-8801

Ginger, Ray.   • **3.8414**
Altgeld's America; the Lincoln ideal versus changing realities. — Chicago, Quadrangle Books [1965, c1958] 376 p. 21 cm. 'Sources and acknowledgments': p. 365-366. 1. Altgeld, John Peter, 1847-1902. 2. Chicago — Hist. I. T.
F548.5.G45 1965   *LC* 66-5630

Biles, Roger, 1950-.   **3.8415**
Big city boss in depression and war: Mayor Edward J. Kelly of Chicago / Roger Biles. — DeKalb: Northern Illinois University Press, 1984. 219 p.: ill.; 24 cm. Revision of thesis (Ph. D.)—University of Illinois. Includes index. 1. Kelly, Edward J. (Edward Joseph), 1876-1950. 2. Mayors — Illinois — Chicago — Biography. 3. Chicago (Ill.) — Politics and government — To 1950 4. Chicago (Ill.) — Biography. I. T.
F548.5.K44 B54 1984   977.3/11042/0924 B 19   *LC* 83-19391   *ISBN* 087580098X

Zorbaugh, Harvey Warren.   • **3.8416**
Gold coast and slum; a sociological study of Chicago's Near North side, by Harvey Warren Zorbaugh. Chicago, Ill., The University of Chicago press [c1929] xv, 287 p. maps, diagrs. 20 cm. (The University of Chicago sociological series) 1. Chicago (Ill.) — Social conditions. 2. Chicago (Ill.) — Description I. T.
F548.5.Z89   *LC* 29-12607

After Daley: Chicago politics in transition / edited by Samuel   **3.8417**
K. Gove and Louis H. Masotti.
Urbana: University of Illinois Press, c1982. xvii, 244 p.: ill.; 24 cm. 1. Daley, Richard J., 1902-1976. 2. Byrne, Jane, 1934- 3. Chicago (Ill.) — Politics and government — 1951- I. Gove, Samuel Kimball. II. Masotti, Louis H.
F548.52.A64 1982   F548.52 A36 1982.   320.8/09773/11 19   LC
81-10302   ISBN 0252009029

Rakove, Milton L.   **3.8418**
Don't make no waves—don't back no losers: an insider's analysis of the Daley machine / Milton L. Rakove. — Bloomington: Indiana University Press, [1975] xii, 296 p., [4] leaves of plates: ill.; 25 cm. Includes index. 1. Daley, Richard J., 1902-1976. 2. Chicago — Politics and government — 1951- I. T.
F548.52.R34 1975   320.9/773/1104   LC 75-1939   ISBN
0253117259

Walker, Daniel.   **• 3.8419**
Rights in conflict; the violent confrontation of demonstrators and police in the parks and streets of Chicago during the week of the Democratic National Convention of 1968. A report submitted by Daniel Walker, director of the Chicago Study Team, to the National Commission on the Causes and Prevention of Violence. [Chicago: [s.n.], 1968] xiii, 88, 233 p. illus. 28 cm. Commonly known as the Walker report. Cover title. 1. Democratic Party. National Convention, Chicago, 1968. 2. Police — Illinois — Chicago. 3. Chicago — Riot, Aug. 1968. I. United States. National Commission on the Causes and Prevention of Violence. II. T. III. Title: Walker report on the violent confrontation of demonstrators and police in the parks and streets of Chicago.
F548.52.W3   977.3/11/04   LC 68-67375

Kleppner, Paul.   **3.8420**
Chicago divided: the making of a Black mayor / Paul Kleppner. — DeKalb, Ill.: Northern Illinois University Press, c1985. xviii, 313 p.; ill.; 24 cm. Includes index. 1. Washington, Harold, 1922-1987. 2. Mayors — Illinois — Chicago — Election. 3. Chicago (Ill.) — Politics and government — 1951- 4. Chicago (Ill.) — Race relations. I. T.
F548.52.W36 K54 1985   324.9773/11043 19   LC 84-25531   ISBN
0875801064

The Ethnic frontier: essays in the history of group survival in   **3.8421**
Chicago and the Midwest / edited by Melvin G. Holli and Peter
d'A. Jones.
Grand Rapids: Eerdmans, c1977. 422 p.: ill.; 24 cm. 1. Minorities — Illinois — Chicago — History. 2. Minorities — Middle West — History. 3. Chicago — Race relations. 4. Middle West — Race relations. I. Holli, Melvin G. II. Jones, Peter d'Alroy.
F548.9.A1 E86   305.8/009773/11 19   LC 77-2746   ISBN
0802835058

Nelli, Humbert S., 1930-.   **• 3.8422**
Italians in Chicago, 1880–1930; a study in ethnic mobility [by] Humbert S. Nelli. — New York: Oxford University Press, 1970. xx, 300 p.: illus., maps.; 22 cm. — (The Urban life in America series) 1. Italian Americans — Chicago. I. T.
F548.9.I8 N4   301.453/45/077311   LC 76-123610

Drake, St. Clair.   **• 3.8423**
Black metropolis; a study of Negro life in a northern city [by] St. Clair Drake and Horace R. Cayton. Rev. and enl. ed. New York, Harcourt, Brace & World [1970] 2 v. (lxx, 814 p.) illus., maps. 21 cm. (A Harbinger book, H 078-H 079) 1. Afro-Americans — Chicago. 2. Afro-Americans — Social conditions — To 1964 3. Afro-Americans — Economic conditions — Chicago. I. Cayton, Horace Roscoe, 1903- joint author. II. T.
F548.9.N3 D68 1970   301.451/96/077311   LC 73-12271

Fry, John R.   **3.8424**
Locked–out Americans: a memoir / [by] John R. Fry. — [1st ed.]. — New York: Harper & Row, [1973] x, 174 p.; 22 cm. 1. Blackstone Rangers. 2. Negro youth — Chicago. 3. Chicago — Social conditions. I. T.
F548.9.N3 F78 1973   322.4/2/0977311   LC 72-11355   ISBN
0060630736

Philpott, Thomas Lee.   **3.8425**
The slum and the ghetto: neighborhood deterioration and middle–class reform, Chicago, 1880–1930 / Thomas Lee Philpott. — New York: Oxford University Press, 1978. xxiv, 428 p.: ill., maps. — (The Urban life in America series.) 1. Afro-Americans — Housing — Illinois — Chicago. 2. Minorities — Housing — Illinois — Chicago. 3. Housing policy — Illinois — Chicago. 4. Chicago — Race relations. I. T.
F548.9.N3 P48   F548.9N3 P48.   301.5/4   LC 77-9547   ISBN
0195022769

Spear, Allan H.   **• 3.8426**
Black Chicago; the making of a Negro ghetto, 1890–1920 [by] Allan H. Spear. — Chicago: University of Chicago Press, [1967] xvii, 254 p.: illus., col. maps, ports.; 23 cm. 1. Afro-Americans — Illinois — Chicago — History I. T.
F548.9.N3 S65   301.451/96/077311   LC 67-21381

Tuttle, William M., 1937-.   **• 3.8427**
Race riot; Chicago in the Red Summer of 1919 [by] William M. Tuttle, Jr. [1st ed.] New York, Atheneum, 1970. ix, 305 p. illus., maps. 22 cm. (Studies in American Negro life) 1. Riots — Illinois — Chicago. 2. Afro-Americans — Illinois — Chicago 3. Chicago (Ill.) — History I. T.
F548.9.N3 T8   977.3/11/04   LC 71-130983

Doyle, Don Harrison, 1946-.   **3.8428**
The social order of a frontier community: Jacksonville, Illinois, 1825–70 / Don Harrison Doyle. — Urbana: University of Illinois Press, c1978. xiii, 289 p., [8] leaves of plates: ill.; 24 cm. Includes index. 1. Frontier and pioneer life — Illinois — Jacksonville. 2. Jacksonville (Ill.) — History. I. T.
F549.J2 D68   977.3/463   LC 78-5287   ISBN 0252006852

F551–556 GREAT LAKES

Burns, Noel M.   **3.8429**
Erie: the lake that survived / Noel M. Burns. — Totowa, N.J.: Rowan & Allanheld, 1985. xviii, 320 p.: ill.; 25 cm. Includes index. 1. Natural history — Erie, Lake. 2. Pollution — Erie, Lake. 3. Erie, Lake — History. 4. Erie, Lake, Region — History. I. T.
F555.B87 1985   977.1/2 19   LC 84-29822   ISBN 0847673987

F561–575 MICHIGAN

Catton, Bruce, 1899-.   **3.8430**
Michigan: a Bicentennial history / Bruce Catton. — New York: Norton, c1976. xiii, 204 p., [8] leaves of plates: ill.; 22 cm. (The States and the Nation series) Includes index. 1. Michigan — History I. T.
F566.C3   977.4   LC 75-38691   ISBN 0393055728

Dunbar, Willis Frederick, 1902-.   **3.8431**
Michigan, a history of the Wolverine State / by Willis F. Dunbar; [ill. by Reynold Weidenaar]. — Rev. ed. / by George S. May. — Grand Rapids: Eerdman, 1980, c1979. xiii, 833 p.: ill.; 24 cm. Includes index. 1. Michigan — History I. May, George Smith, 1924- II. T.
F566.D84 1980   F566.D84 1980.   977.4   LC 79-17750   ISBN
0802870430

Russell, Nelson Vance, 1895-.   **• 3.8432**
The British régime in Michigan and the Old Northwest, 1760–1796, by Nelson Vance Russell. Northfield Minn., Carleton College [c1939] xi, 302 p. 23 cm. 1. Michigan — History 2. Northwest, Old — History I. T.
F566.R87   LC 40-6569

Writers' Program. Michigan.   **• 3.8433**
Michigan, a guide to the Wolverine State. Compiled by workers of the Writers' Program of the Work Projects Administration in the State of Michigan. New York, Oxford University Press. — St. Clair Shores, Mich.: Somerset Publishers, 1973 [c1941] xxxvi, 682 p.: illus.; 22 cm. Original ed. issued in series: American guide series. 1. Michigan. 2. Michigan — Description and travel — Guide-books. I. T.
F566.W9 1973   917.74/04/4   LC 72-84482   ISBN 0403021723

Henry, Alexander, 1739-1824.   **3.8434**
Attack at Michilimackinac; Alexander Henry's travels and adventures in Canada and the Indian territories between the years 1760 and 1764. Edited by David A. Armour. Illustrated by Dirk Gringhuis. Mackinac Island, Michigan, Mackinac Island State Park Commission, c1971. xii, 131 p. illus. 22 cm. Reprint; originally published New York, 1809, under title: Travels and adventures in Canada and the Indian territories. 1. Indians of North America — Canada 2. Canada — Description and travel — 1763-1867 I. Armour, David A. ed. II. T. III. Title: Travels and adventures in Canada and the Indian territories between the years 1760 and 1764.
F572.M16H47 1971   LC 79-625617//r853   ISBN 0911872310

Fragnoli, Raymond R., 1948-.   **3.8435**
The transformation of reform: progressivism in Detroit—and after, 1912–1933 / Raymond R. Fragnoli. — New York: Garland Pub., 1981. vii, 410 p.; 24 cm. — (Modern American history.) Errata slip inserted. Includes index. 1. Progressivism (United States politics) 2. Detroit (Mich.) — Politics and government. I. T. II. Series.
F574.D457 F73 1982   322.4/4/0977434 19   LC 80-8464   ISBN
0824048563

Vinyard, Jo Ellen.　　　　　　　　　　3.8436
The Irish on the urban frontier: Nineteenth century Detroit, 1850–1880 / JoEllen Vinyard. — New York: Arno Press, 1976, c1974. 446 p.: maps; 24 cm. — (The Irish-Americans) Originally presented as the author's thesis, University of Michigan, 1972. 1. Irish Americans — Michigan — Detroit — History. 2. Detroit (Mich.) — History. I. T. II. Series.
F574.D49 I78 1976　　301.45/19/162077434　　*LC* 76-6369　　*ISBN* 0405093616

Ezekiel, Raphael S., 1931-.　　　　　　　　　　3.8437
Voices from the corner: poverty and racism in the inner city / Raphael S. Ezekiel. — Philadelphia: Temple University Press, 1984. x, 220 p.; 24 cm. 1. Afro-Americans — Michigan — Detroit — Interviews. 2. Afro-Americans — Michigan — Detroit — Economic conditions. 3. Detroit (Mich.) — Race relations. 4. Detroit (Mich.) — Economic conditions. I. T.
F574.D49 N438 1984　　305.8/96073/077434 19　　*LC* 84-2637　　*ISBN* 0877223580

Katzman, David M.　　　　　　　　　　3.8438
Before the ghetto; black Detroit in the nineteenth century [by] David M. Katzman. Urbana, University of Illinois Press [1973] xii, 254 p. illus. 24 cm. (Blacks in the New World.) 1. Afro-Americans — Detroit — History. 2. Detroit (Mich.) — History. I. T. II. Series.
F574.D49 N448　　977.4/3400496073　　*LC* 72-76861　　*ISBN* 0252002792

Meier, August, 1923-.　　　　　　　　　　3.8439
Black Detroit and the rise of the UAW / August Meier and Elliott Rudwick. — New York: Oxford University Press, 1979. xii, 289 p.: ill.; 22 cm. Includes index. 1. International Union, United Automobile, Aerospace, and Agricultural Implement Workers of America. 2. Trade-unions — Michigan — Detroit — Afro-American participation. 3. Afro-Americans — Employment — Michigan — Detroit. 4. Detroit (Mich.) — Economic conditions. I. Rudwick, Elliott M. joint author. II. T.
F574.D49 N46　　331.88/12/920977434　　*LC* 78-26809　　*ISBN* 019502561X

Wrobel, Paul, 1942-.　　　　　　　　　　3.8440
Our way: family, parish, and neighborhood in a Polish–American community / Paul Wrobel. — Notre Dame, Ind.: University of Notre Dame Press, c1979. xv, 192 p.; 24 cm. 1. Polish Americans — Michigan — Detroit — Social conditions. 2. Catholics — Michigan — Detroit — Social conditions. 3. Detroit (Mich.) — Social conditions. I. T.
F574.D49 P78　　301.45/19/185077434　　*LC* 78-62967　　*ISBN* 0268014949

F576–590 WISCONSIN

Current, Richard Nelson.　　　　　　　　　　3.8441
Wisconsin: a Bicentennial history / Richard Nelson Current. — New York: Norton, c1977. xiv, 226 p., [8] leaves of plates: ill.; 22 cm. (The States and the Nation series) Includes index. 1. Wisconsin — History I. T.
F581.C87　　977.5　　*LC* 77-2176　　*ISBN* 0393056244

The History of Wisconsin. William Fletcher Thompson, general editor.　　　　　　　　　　3.8442
Madison, State Historical Society of Wisconsin, 1973- < 1985 > . v. < 1-3 > illus. 25 cm. 1. Wisconsin — History I. Thompson, William Fletcher, 1929-
F581.H68　　977.5　　*LC* 72-12941　　*ISBN* 0870201220

Nesbit, Robert Carrington, 1917-.　　　　　　　　　　3.8443
Wisconsin; a history [by] Robert C. Nesbit. — [Madison]: University of Wisconsin Press, [1973] xiv, 573 p.: illus.; 25 cm. 1. Wisconsin — History I. T.
F581.N47　　977.5　　*LC* 72-7990　　*ISBN* 0299063704

Kellogg, Louise Phelps, d. 1942.　　　　　　　　　　3.8444
The British régime in Wisconsin and the Northwest. — New York: Da Capo Press, 1971 [c1935] xvii, 361 p.: illus., facsims., maps, ports.; 23 cm. — (The American scene) (Publications of the State Historical Society of Wisconsin.) 1. British Americans — Wisconsin — History. 2. Wisconsin — History — To 1848 3. Northwest, Old — History 4. United States — History — Revolution, 1775-1783 5. United States — History — War of 1812 I. T.
F584.K26 1971　　977.5/02　　*LC* 74-124927　　*ISBN* 0306710471

Kellogg, Louise Phelps, d. 1942.　　　　　　　　　　• 3.8445
The French régime in Wisconsin and the Northwest. — New York: Cooper Square Publishers, 1968. 474 p.: illus., maps.; 24 cm. — (Publications of the State Historical Society of Wisconsin) Reprint of the 1925 ed. 1. French — Wisconsin 2. Wisconsin — History — To 1848 3. Northwest, Old — History — To 1775 4. America — Discovery and exploration — French. I. T.
F584.K27 1968　　977.5/01　　*LC* 68-31296

Miller, John E., 1945-.　　　　　　　　　　3.8446
Governor Philip F. La Follette, the Wisconsin Progressives, and the New Deal / John E. Miller. — Columbia: University of Missouri Press, 1982. 229 p., [1] leaf of plates: port.; 23 cm. 1. LaFollette, Philip Fox, 1897-1965. 2. Progressivism (United States politics) 3. Wisconsin — Politics and government — 1848-1950 I. T.
F586.L3 M54 1982　　F586.L3 M54 1982.　　977.5/042/0924 19　　*LC* 82-1982　　*ISBN* 082620371X

Margulies, Herbert F.　　　　　　　　　　• 3.8447
The decline of the progressive movement in Wisconsin, 1890–1920 / Herbert F. Margulies. — Madison: State Historical Society of Wisconsin, 1968. ix, 310 p.; 23 cm. 1. Progressivism (United States politics) 2. Wisconsin — Politics and government — 1848-1950 I. State Historical Society of Wisconsin. II. T.
F586.M35　　320.5/09775　　*LC* 68-63073

Marshall, James M., 1924-.　　　　　　　　　　3.8448
Land fever: dispossession and the frontier myth / James M. Marshall. — Lexington, KY: University Press of Kentucky, 1986. viii, 239 p. Includes index. 1. Morse, Omar, 1824-1901. 2. Pioneers — Wisconsin — Biography. 3. Pioneers — Minnesota — Biography. 4. Land tenure — Wisconsin — History — 19th century. 5. Land tenure — Minnesota — History — 19th century. 6. Frontier and pioneer life — Wisconsin. 7. Frontier and pioneer life — Minnesota. 8. Wisconsin — Rural conditions. 9. Minnesota — Rural conditions. I. T.
F586.M78 M37 1986　　977.5/04/0924 B 19　　*LC* 86-4030　　*ISBN* 081311568X

Thelen, David P. (David Paul)　　　　　　　　　　3.8449
The new citizenship: origins of progressivism in Wisconsin, 1885–1900 / [by] David P. Thelen. — [Columbia]: University of Missouri Press, [1972] 340 p.; 25 cm. 1. Progressivism (U.S. politics) 2. Wisconsin — Politics and government — 1848-1950 3. United States — Politics and government — 1865-1900 I. T.
F586.T47　　320.9/775/03　　*LC* 79-158075　　*ISBN* 0826201113

Writers' Program. Wisconsin.　　　　　　　　　　• 3.8450
Wisconsin, a guide to the Badger State. Compiled by workers of the Writers' Program of the Work Projects Administration in the State of Wisconsin. New York, Duell, Sloan and Pearce. — St. Clair Shores, Mich.: Somerset Publishers, 1973 [c1941] 651 p.: illus.; 22 cm. Original ed. issued in series: American guide series. 1. Wisconsin — Description and travel — Guide-books. I. T.
F586.W97 1973　　917.75/04/4　　*LC* 72-84517　　*ISBN* 0403021987

Still, Bayrd.　　　　　　　　　　• 3.8451
Milwaukee, the history of a city. Madison, State Historical Society of Wisconsin, 1948. xvi, 638 p. illus., ports., maps. 25 cm. 1. Milwaukee (Wis.) — History. I. T.
F589.M6 S8　　*LC* 49-7868

F591–598 The West: General

The American West, new perspectives, new dimensions / edited and with an introd. by Jerome O. Steffen.　　　　　　　　　　3.8452
1st ed. — Norman: University of Oklahoma Press, 1979. ix, 238 p.: ill.; 22 cm. 1. West (U.S.) — Civilization — Addresses, essays, lectures. I. Steffen, Jerome O., 1942-
F591.A415　　978　　*LC* 78-58097　　*ISBN* 0806114932

Billington, Ray Allen, 1903-.　　　　　　　　　　• 3.8453
The Far Western frontier, 1830–1860. [1st ed.] New York, Harper [1956] 324 p. illus. 22 cm. (The New American nation series) Includes bibliography. 1. Frontier and pioneer life — West (U.S.) 2. West (U.S.) — History 3. United States — Territorial expansion I. T.
F591.B55　　978　　*LC* 56-9665

Brown, Dee Alexander.　　　　　　　　　　3.8454
The Westerners [by] Dee Brown. New York, Holt, Rinehart and Winston [1974] 288 p. illus. 26 cm. 1. Indians of North America — West (U.S.) 2. West (U.S.) — Biography. 3. West (U.S.) — History I. T.
F591.B88　　917.8/03/0922　　*LC* 73-15456　　*ISBN* 0030883601

Dick, Everett Newfon, 1898-.　　　　　　　　　　• 3.8455
The sod-house frontier, 1854–1890: a social history of the northern plains from the creation of Kansas & Nebraska to the admission of the Dakotas / by Everett Dick. — New York; London: D. Appleton-Century Co., Inc., 1937. xviii, 550 p.: front., plates, port.; 23 cm. 1. Frontier and pioneer life — West (U.S.) 2. West (U.S.) — History I. T.
F591.D54　　*LC* 37-19335

Goetzmann, William H.   • **3.8456**
Exploration and empire; the explorer and the scientist in the winning of the American West, by William H. Goetzmann. [1st ed.] New York, Knopf, 1966. xxii, 656, xviii p. illus., maps. 24 cm. 1. West (U.S.) — Discovery and exploration. I. T.
F591.G62   917.8   *LC* 65-11123

Greever, William S.   • **3.8457**
The Bonanza West: the story of the Western mining rushes, 1848–1900. — [1st ed.] Norman: University of Oklahoma Press [1963] 430 p.: ill.; 24 cm. 1. Mines and mineral resources — West (U.S.) 2. Frontier and pioneer life — West (U.S.) 3. Klondike River Valley (Yukon) — Gold discoveries I. T.
F591.G79   978   *LC* 63-8991

Hafen, Le Roy Reuben, 1893-.   • **3.8458**
Western America: the exploration, settlement, and development of the region beyond the Mississippi / by Le Roy R. Hafen and Carl Coke Rister. — 2d ed. — Englewood Cliffs: Prentice-Hall, 1950. xviii, 695 p.: ill., maps (part col.) (Prentice-Hall history series) 1. The West — History. 2. The West — Discovery and exploration. I. Rister, Carl Coke, 1889-1955. II. T. III. Series.
F591.H2 1950   *LC* 50-8267

Hine, Robert V., 1921-.   • **3.8459**
The American West: an interpretive history / Robert V. Hine. — 2nd ed. — Boston: Little, Brown, c1984. xiii, 410 p.: ill.; 24 cm. Includes index. 1. West (U.S.) — History I. T.
F591.H663 1984   978 19   *LC* 84-962   *ISBN* 0316364452

Historians and the American West / edited by Michael P.   **3.8460**
Malone; foreword by Rodman W. Paul.
Lincoln: University of Nebraska Press, c1983. x, 449 p.; 24 cm. 1. West (U.S.) — Historiography — Addresses, essays, lectures. I. Malone, Michael P.
F591.H68 1983   978 19   *LC* 82-17550   *ISBN* 0803230710

Kraenzel, Carl Frederick, 1906-.   • **3.8461**
The Great Plains in transition. [1st ed.] Norman, University of Oklahoma Press [1955] xiv, 428 p. illus., maps (1 fold. col.) diagrs., tables. 25 cm. 1. Anthropo-geography — Great Plains. 2. Great Plains I. T.
F591.K7   978   *LC* 55-9628

McLoughlin, Denis.   **3.8462**
Wild and woolly: an encyclopedia of the Old West / by Denis McLoughlin. — 1st ed. — Garden City, N.Y.: Doubleday, 1975. 570 p.: ill.; 24 cm. 1. West (U.S.) — History — Dictionaries. 2. West (U.S.) — Biography. I. T.
F591.M155   978/.003   *LC* 73-83655   *ISBN* 0385002378

Malin, James Claude, 1893-.   • **3.8463**
The grassland of North America: prolegomena to its history, with addenda and postscript / by James C. Malin. — Gloucester, Mass.: P. Smith, 1967. viii, 490 p.; 21 cm. 1. Anthropo-geography — West (U.S.) 2. Physical geography — West (U.S.) 3. Grasslands — North America. I. T.
F591.M3 1967   917.8   *LC* 67-4595

Paul, Rodman Wilson, 1912-.   • **3.8464**
Mining frontiers of the Far West, 1848–1880. New York, Holt, Rinehart and Winston [1963] 236 p. illus. 24 cm. (Histories of the American frontier) 1. Mines and mineral resources — West (U.S.) 2. Frontier and pioneer life — West (U.S.) I. T.
F591.P3   978   *LC* 63-8818

The Reader's encyclopedia of the American West / edited by   **3.8465**
Howard R. Lamar.
1st ed. — New York: Crowell, c1977. x, 1306 p.: ill.; 24 cm. 1. West (U.S.) — Dictionaries and encyclopedias. I. Lamar, Howard Roberts.
F591.R38   978/.003   *LC* 78-17115   *ISBN* 0690000081

Riegel, Robert Edgar, 1897-.   • **3.8466**
America moves west [by] Robert E. Riegel [and] Robert G. Athearn. 5th ed. New York, Holt, Rinehart and Winston [1971] xiii, 599 p. illus., maps, ports. 25 cm. 1. West (U.S.) — History 2. Mississippi River Valley — History I. Athearn, Robert G. joint author. II. T.
F591.R53 1971   978   *LC* 72-113832   *ISBN* 0030843162

Smith, Henry Nash.   • **3.8467**
Virgin land: the American West as symbol and myth. — Cambridge: Harvard University Press [1971, c1950] xviii, 305 p.: ill.; 21 cm. (A Harvard paperback, HP 21) 1. West (U.S.) in literature. 2. American literature — 19th century — History and criticism. 3. West (U.S.) I. T.
F591.S65 1971   917.8/03/2   *LC* 75-30212   *ISBN* 0674939557

Sonnichsen, C. L. (Charles Leland), 1901-.   **3.8468**
The ambidextrous historian: historical writers and writing in the American West / by C.L. Sonnichsen. — 1st ed. — Norman: University of Oklahoma Press, c1981. 120 p.; 22 cm. Includes index. 1. Historiography — United States

— Addresses, essays, lectures. 2. West (U.S.) — Historiography — Addresses, essays, lectures. I. T.
F591.S67   978/.0072 19   *LC* 81-2786   *ISBN* 0806116900

Webb, Walter Prescott, 1888-1963.   • **3.8469**
The Great Plains. New York: Grosset & Dunlap [1957, c1931] 525 p.: ill.; 21 cm. (Grosset's universal library, UL-29) 1. Great Plains — History. 2. Mississippi River Valley — History I. T.
F591.W4x   978   *LC* 57-4356

F592–595 BY PERIOD

Steffen, Jerome O., 1942-.   3.8470
William Clark: Jeffersonian man on the frontier / by Jerome O. Steffen. 1st ed. — Norman: University of Oklahoma Press, c1977. xii, 196 p.: ill.; 22 cm. Includes index. 1. Clark, William, 1770-1838. 2. Indians of North America — Government relations — 1789-1869 I. T.
F592.C56 S74   917.8/04/20924 B   *LC* 76-15355   *ISBN* 0806113731

De Voto, Bernard Augustine, 1897-1955.   • **3.8471**
The year of decision, 1846. Boston, Houghton Mifflin, 1950 [c1943] xv, 538 p. maps. 22 cm. 1. United States — History — 1815-1861 2. United States — History — War with Mexico, 1845-1848 3. West (U.S.) — History I. T.
F592.D38 1950   *LC* 50-11676

DeVoto, Bernard Augustine, 1897-1955.   • **3.8472**
Across the wild Missouri / by Bernard DeVoto; illustrated with paintings by Alfred Jacob Miller, Charles Bodmer and George Catlin; with an account of the discovery of the Miller Collection by Mae Reed Porter. Boston: Houghton Mifflin, 1947. 483 p. 1. Fur trade — West (U.S.) 2. United States — History — 1815-1861 3. West (U.S.) — History I. Miller, Alfred Jacob, 1810-1874. II. T.
F592.D4 A3   *LC* 48-3175

Frémont, John Charles, 1813-1890.   3.8473
The expeditions of John Charles Frémont / edited by Donald Jackson and Mary Lee Spence. — Urbana: University of Illinois Press, 1973. 2 v.: ill., maps, ports.; 24 cm. 1. United States — Exploring expeditions 2. West (U.S.) — Description and travel — To 1848 I. Jackson, Donald Dean, 1919- II. Spence, Mary Lee. III. T.
F592.F73   *LC* 73-100374   *ISBN* 0252002490

Parkman, Francis, 1823-1893.   • **3.8474**
The Oregon Trail: sketches of Prairie and Rocky Mountain life / by Francis Parkman. — New York: Dodd, Mead, 1964. xi, 337 p.: ill., ports.; 23 cm. Includes index. 1. Indians of North America — West (U.S.) 2. Frontier and pioneer life — West (U.S.) 3. West (U.S.) — Description and travel 4. Oregon Trail I. T.
F592.P284 1964   917.8042

Hollon, W. Eugene (William Eugene), 1913-.   • **3.8475**
The lost pathfinder, Zebulon Montgomery Pike. [1st ed.] Norman, University of Oklahoma Press, 1949. xv, 240 p. illus., ports., map, facsim. 24 cm. 1. Pike, Zebulon Montgomery, 1779-1813. I. T.
F592.P657   *LC* 49-5390

Turner, Frederick Jackson, 1861-1932.   • **3.8476**
Rise of the new West, 1819–1829. Gloucester, Mass. . P. Smith, 1961, c1906. xviii, 366 p. . ill. , 21 cm. (The American nation: a history, v. 14) 'Critical essay on authorities': p. 333-352. 1. The West — History. 2. Mississippi River Valley — History. 3. Oregon — History — To 1859 4. United States — Politics and government — 1815-1861 I. T. II. Series.
F592.T87x E178.A555 vol. 14   *LC* 61-43184

Lewis, Meriwether, 1774-1809.   • **3.8477**
Original journals of the Lewis and Clark Expedition, 1804-1806; printed from the original manuscripts in the library of the American Philosophical Society and by direction of its Committee on Historical Documents, together with manuscript material of Lewis and Clark from other sources, including note-books, letters, maps, etc., and the journals of Charles Floyd and Joseph Whitehouse, now for the first time published in full and exactly as written / edited with introd., notes, and index, by Reuben Gold Thwaites. — New York: Antiquarian Press, 1959. 8 v.: ill. Vol. 8 has title: Atlas accompanying the original journals of the Lewis and Clark Expedition, 1804-1806, being facsimile reproductions of maps, chiefly by William Clark ... Now for the first time published, from the original manuscripts, together with a modern map of route ... First published in 1904-05. 1. Lewis and Clark Expedition. 2. West (U.S.) — Description and travel 3. Missouri River 4. Columbia River I. Clark, William, 1770-1838. II. Thwaites, Reuben Gold, 1853-1913. III. T.
F592.4.1959

Cutright, Paul Russell, 1897-.   • **3.8478**
Lewis and Clark, pioneering naturalists. Urbana: University of Illinois Press, 1969. xiii, 506 p.: ill., facsims., ports.; 23 cm. 1. Lewis and Clark Expedition (1804-1806) 2. Natural history — Great Plains. 3. Natural history — Northwest, Pacific. I. T.
F592.4 1969   917.8   *LC* 69-11043   *ISBN* 0252784227

The Journals of the Lewis and Clark Expedition / Gary E.   **3.8479**
Moulton, editor.
[Lincoln: University of Nebraska Press, c1983- <c1987 >. v. <1-3 >: ill., facsims., maps; 27-51 cm. Vol. 2- <3 >: Gary E. Moulton, editor; Thomas W. Dunlay, assistant editor. Vol. 2- <3 > has title: The Journals of the Lewis & Clark Expedition. 'Sponsored by the Center for Great Plains Studies, University of Nebraska—Lincoln, and the American Philosophical Society, Philadelphia'—Vol. 1, t.p. 1. Lewis, Meriwether, 1774-1809. 2. Clark, William, 1770-1838. 3. Lewis and Clark Expedition (1804-1806) (1804-1806) — Collected works. 4. West (U.S.) — Description and travel — To 1848 — Collected works. 5. United States — Exploring expeditions — Collected works. I. Lewis, Meriwether, 1774-1809. II. Clark, William, 1770-1838. III. Moulton, Gary E. IV. Dunlay, Thomas W., 1944- V. University of Nebraska—Lincoln. Center for Great Plains Studies. VI. American Philosophical Society. VII. Title: Journals of the Lewis & Clark Expedition.
F592.4 1983   917.8/042 19   *LC* 82-8510

Atlas of the Lewis & Clark expedition / Gary E. Moulton,   **3.8480**
editor.
Lincoln: University of Nebraska Press, c1983. 1 atlas (23 p., [151] p. of plates): facsims., maps; 51 cm. (Journals of the Lewis and Clark Expedition. v. 1) 'Sponsored by the Center for Great Plains Studies, University of Nebraska-Lincoln, and the American Philosophical Society, Philadelphia.' 1. Lewis and Clark Expedition (1804-1806) 2. Columbia River — Maps — To 1848. 3. Missouri River — Maps — To 1848. 4. Northwestern States — Maps. 5. West (U.S.) — Description and travel — To 1848 6. West (U.S.) — Maps. 7. United States — Exploring expeditions I. Lewis, Meriwether, 1774-1809. II. Clark, William, 1770-1838. III. Moulton, Gary E. IV. University of Nebraska—Lincoln. Center for Great Plains Studies. V. American Philosophical Society. VI. Title: Atlas of the Lewis and Clark expedition. VII. Series.
F592.4 1983 vol. 1 G1380   917.8/042 s 912/.78 19   *LC* 82-675167   *ISBN* 0803228619

Allen, John Logan, 1941-.   **3.8481**
Passage through the garden: Lewis and Clark and the image of the American Northwest. Urbana, University of Illinois Press, c1975. xxvi, 412 p. maps. 26 cm. 1. Lewis, Meriwether, 1774-1809. 2. Clark, William, 1770-1838. 3. Lewis and Clark Expedition 4. West (U.S.) — Description and travel — To 1848 I. T.
F 592.7 A418 1975   *LC* 74-14512   *ISBN* 0252003977

Bakeless, John Edwin, 1894-.   • **3.8482**
Lewis & Clark, partners in discovery. — New York, W. Morrow, 1947. xii, 498 p. illus., ports., maps (1 fold. col.) 22 cm. Bibliographical references included in 'Notes' (p. [467]-486) 1. Lewis, Meriwether, 1774-1809. 2. Clark, William, 1770-1838. 3. Lewis and Clark Expedition. I. T.
F592.7.B3   917.8   *LC* 47-12243 *

Betts, Robert B.   **3.8483**
In search of York: the slave who went to the Pacific with Lewis and Clark / by Robert B. Betts. — Boulder, Colo.: Colorado Associated University Press, c1985. x, 182 p., [8] p. of plates: ill. (some col.); 26 cm. Includes index. 1. York, ca. 1775-ca. 1815. 2. Lewis and Clark Expedition (1804-1806) 3. Slaves — West (U.S.) — Biography. 4. West (U.S.) — Biography. I. T.
F592.7.B48 1985   917.8/042/0924 B 19   *LC* 82-74150   *ISBN* 0870811444

Jackson, Donald Dean, 1919- ed.   • **3.8484**
Letters of the Lewis and Clark Expedition / with related documents, 1783–1854. Urbana: Univ. of Illinois Press, 1962.. xxi, 728 p.: ill., ports., maps, facsims. 24 cm. 1. Lewis and Clark Expedition (1804-1806) 2. West (U.S.) — History — Sources I. T.
F592.7.J14   *LC* 62-7119

Ronda, James P., 1943-.   **3.8485**
Lewis and Clark among the Indians / James P. Ronda. — Lincoln: University of Nebraska Press, c1984. xv, 310 p., [1] leaf of plates: ill., maps, ports.; 24 cm. Includes index. 1. Lewis, Meriwether, 1774-1809. 2. Clark, William, 1770-1838. 3. Lewis and Clark Expedition (1804-1806) 4. Indians of North America — West (U.S.) 5. Indians of North America — West (U.S.) — First contact with Occidental civilization. 6. West (U.S.) — Description and travel — To 1848 7. United States — Exploring expeditions I. T.
F592.7.R66 1984   978/.02/0922 19   *LC* 84-3544   *ISBN* 0803238703

Clark, Ella Elizabeth, 1896-.   • **3.8486**
Sacagawea of the Lewis and Clark expedition / Ella E. Clark and Margot Edmonds. — Berkeley, Calif.: University of California Press, 1980 (c1979). viii,
171 p., [1] leaf of plates: ill.; 22 cm. Includes index. 1. Sacagawea, 1786-1884. 2. Lewis and Clark Expedition (1804-1806) 3. Shoshoni Indians — Biography. I. Edmonds, Margot. joint author. II. T.
F592.7.S123 C55   970.004/97 B 19   *LC* 78-65466   *ISBN* 0520038223

Unruh, John David, 1937-1976.   **3.8487**
The plains across: the overland emigrants and the trans–Mississippi West, 1840–60 / John D. Unruh, Jr. — Urbana: University of Illinois Press, c1979. xviii, 565 p.: ill.; 26 cm. Includes index. 1. Overland journeys to the Pacific 2. Frontier and pioneer life — West (U.S.) 3. West (U.S.) — History — 1848-1860. 4. West (U.S.) — History — To 1848 I. T.
F593.U67 1979   978   *LC* 78-9781   *ISBN* 0252006984

Pomeroy, Earl Spencer, 1915-.   • **3.8488**
In search of the golden West: the tourist in western America. — [1st ed.] New York: Knopf, 1957. 233 p.: ill.; 22 cm. 1. Tourist trade — West (U.S.) 2. West (U.S.) — Description and travel I. T.
F595.P78   *LC* 57-5658

F596–597 FRONTIER AND PIONEER LIFE

Atherton, Lewis Eldon.   • **3.8489**
The cattle kings. Bloomington, Indiana University Press [1961] 308 p. illus. 25 cm. 1. Cattle trade — West (U.S.) 2. Cattle breeders — West (U.S.) — Biography. 3. Ranch life — West (U.S.) 4. West (U.S.) — Biography. I. T.
F596.A8   917.8   *LC* 61-13722

Billington, Ray Allen, 1903-.   **3.8490**
Land of savagery/land of promise: the European image of the American frontier in the nineteenth century / by Ray Allen Billington. — 1st ed. — New York: Norton, c1981. xv, 364 p.: ill.; 25 cm. Includes index. 1. Frontier and pioneer life — West (U.S.) — Public opinion — History — 19th century. 2. Public opinion — Europe — History — 19th century. 3. West (U.S.) — Foreign opinion, European — History — 19th century. I. T.
F596.B47 1981   978   *LC* 80-291   *ISBN* 0393012761

Dale, Edward Everett, 1879-1972.   • **3.8491**
Cow country / by Edward Dale. — Norman: University of Oklahoma press, 1942. ix p., 2 l., [3]-265, [1] p.: ill.; 21 cm. 1. Frontier and pioneer life — West (U.S.) 2. Cowboys 3. Cattle trade — West (U.S.) I. T.
F596.D25   *LC* 42-15483

Frantz, Joe Bertram, 1917-.   • **3.8492**
The American cowboy: the myth & the reality [by] Joe B. Frantz and Julian Ernest Choate, Jr. [1st ed.] Norman, University of Oklahoma Press [1955] 232 p. illus. 24 cm. 1. Cowboys — West (U.S.) 2. Frontier and pioneer life — West (U.S.) 3. Cowboys in literature I. Choate, Julian Ernest, 1916- joint author. II. T.
F596.F75   978   *LC* 55-9629

Ethnicity on the Great Plains / edited by Frederick C. Luebke.   **3.8493**
Lincoln: Published by the University of Nebraska Press for the Center for Great Plains Studies, University of Nebraska-Lincoln, c1980. xxxiii, 237 p. Papers originally presented at a symposium sponsored by the Center for Great Plains Studies, University of Nebraska-Lincoln. Includes bibliographical references and index. 1. Minorities — Great Plains — History — Congresses. 2. Great Plains — Civilization — Congresses. I. Luebke, Frederick C., 1927- II. University of Nebraska—Lincoln. Center for Great Plains Studies.
F596.2.E86   F596.2 E86.   978   *LC* 79-17743   *ISBN* 0803228554

Rochlin, Harriet, 1924-.   **3.8494**
Pioneer Jews: a new life in the Far West / Harriet and Fred Rochlin. — Boston: Houghton Mifflin, 1984. ix, 243 p.: ill.; 28 cm. Includes index. 1. Jews — West (U.S.) — History. 2. West (U.S.) — Ethnic relations. I. Rochlin, Fred, 1923- II. T.
F596.3.J5 R63 1984   978/.004924 19   *LC* 83-12647   *ISBN* 0395318327

F598 MISSOURI VALLEY

Briggs, Harold Edward, 1896-.   • **3.8495**
Frontiers of the Northwest. New York, London, D. Appleton-Century company, incorporated, 1940. xiv, 629 p. front., illus. (maps) plates, 4 port. on 1 pl. 23 cm. 1. Northwestern States — History 2. Frontier and pioneer life — Northwestern states. 3. Missouri valley — History. I. T.
F598.B84   *LC* 40-12572

F601–705 Northwestern States

F601–630 Minnesota. Iowa

Blegen, Theodore Christian, 1891-1969.   **3.8496**
Minnesota: a history of the State / Theodore C. Blegen; with a new concluding chapter, A State that works, by Russell W. Fridley. — 2d ed. — [Minneapolis]: University of Minnesota Press, c1975. xiv, 731 p., [8] leaves of plates: ill.; 24 cm. 1. Minnesota — History I. T.
F606.B668 1975   F606 B54 1975.   977.6   LC 75-6116   ISBN 0816607540

Bost, Théodore, 1834-1920.   **3.8497**
A frontier family in Minnesota: letters of Theodore and Sophie Bost, 1851–1920 / edited and translated by Ralph H. Bowen. — Minneapolis: University of Minnesota Press, c1981. xxv, 391 p., [4] leaves of plates: ill., ports. Includes index. Rev. and enl. translation of: Les derniers puritains, pionniers d'Amérique, 1851-1920. 1. Bost, Théodore, 1834-1920. 2. Bost, Sophie, 1835-1922. 3. Pioneers — Minnesota — Biography. 4. Swiss Americans — Minnesota — Biography. 5. Minnesota — Biography. I. Bost, Sophie, 1835-1922. II. Bowen, Ralph Henry, 1919- III. T.
F606.B75313   F606.B75313.   977.6/5 B 19   LC 81-10401
ISBN 0816610320

Chrislock, Carl Henry.   • **3.8498**
The progressive era in Minnesota, 1899–1918, by Carl H. Chrislock. — St. Paul: Minnesota Historical Society, 1971. xiii, 242 p.: illus.; 24 cm. — (Minnesota Historical Society. Public Affairs Center. Publications) 1. Progressivism (U.S. politics) 2. Minnesota — Politics and government — 1858-1950 I. T. II. Series.
F606.C477   320.9/776/05   LC 79-178677   ISBN 0873410674

Minnesota Federal Writers' Project.   • **3.8499**
Minnesota, a State guide. [Rev. ed.] New York, Hastings House [1954] xxx, 545 p. illus., maps. 21 cm. 1. Minnesota. 2. Minnesota — Description and travel — Guide-books. I. T.
F606.F44 1954   LC 54-589

Haynes, John Earl.   **3.8500**
Dubious alliance: the making of Minnesota's DFL Party / John Earl Haynes. — Minneapolis: University of Minnesota Press, c1984. viii, 264 p., [8] p. of plates: ill.; 24 cm. 1. Democratic-Farmer-Labor Party — History. 2. Communism — Minnesota — History — 20th century. 3. Political parties — Minnesota — History — 20th century. 4. Liberalism — Minnesota — History — 20th century. 5. Minnesota — Politics and government — 1858-1950 I. T.
F606.H28 1984   324.2776/02 19   LC 83-21786   ISBN 0816613117

Lass, William E.   **3.8501**
Minnesota: a bicentennial history / William E. Lass. — New York: Norton, c1977. xv, 224 p., [8] leaves of plates: ill.; 22 cm. (The States and the nation series) Includes index. 1. Minnesota — History I. T.
F606.L35   977.6   LC 77-8426   ISBN 0393056511

They chose Minnesota: a survey of the state's ethnic groups /   **3.8502**
June Drenning Holmquist, editor.
St. Paul: Minnesota Historical Society Press, 1981. xiii, 614 p.: ill., maps. — (Publications of the Minnesota Historical Society.) Includes index. 1. Minorities — Minnesota. 2. Minnesota — History 3. Minnesota — Ethnic relations. I. Holmquist, June Drenning. II. Series.
F615.A1 T45   F615A1 T45.   977.6/004 19   LC 81-14124
ISBN 0873511557

Federal Writers' Project. Iowa.   • **3.8503**
Iowa, a guide to the Hawkeye State. New York, Hastings House [1949] xxviii, 583 p. illus., port., maps. 21 cm. 1. Iowa — Description and travel — Guide-books. 2. Iowa. I. T.
F621.F45 1949   LC 49-5480

Richman, Irving B.   **3.8504**
Ioway to Iowa: the genesis of a corn and Bible commonwealth / by Irving Berdine Richman. — Iowa City: State Historical Society of Iowa, 1931. 479 p., [4] leaves of plates; col. ill.; 24 cm. — (Publications of The State Historical Society of Iowa) Each plate accompanied by guard sheet with descriptive letterpress. 1. Indians of North America — Iowa 2. Iowa — History I. T. II. Series.
F 621 R53 1931   LC 31-6477

Sage, Leland L. (Leland Livingston), 1899-.   **3.8505**
A history of Iowa [by] Leland L. Sage. [1st ed.] Ames, The Iowa State University Press, 1974. xii, 376 p. illus. 23 cm. 1. Iowa — History I. T.
F621.S15   977.7   LC 73-14984   ISBN 0813808405

Wall, Joseph Frazier.   **3.8506**
Iowa: a Bicentennial history / Joseph Frazier Wall. — New York: Norton, c1978. xviii, 212 p., [8] leaves of plates: ill.; 22 cm. (The States and the Nation series) Includes index. 1. Iowa — History I. T.
F621.W17   977.7   LC 77-17546   ISBN 0393056716

F631–660 North Dakota. South Dakota

Federal Writers' Project. North Dakota.   • **3.8507**
North Dakota, a guide to the northern prairie state / compiled by workers of the Federal Writers' Project of the Works Progress Administration for the State of North Dakota.— 2d ed. — New York: Oxford University Press, 1950. xix, 352 p.: ill., maps.; 21 cm. — (American guide series.) Sponsored by the State Historical Society of North Dakota. 1. North Dakota — Description and travel — Guide-books. I. T. II. Series.
F636.F45 1950   LC 50-9076

Robinson, Elwyn B.   • **3.8508**
History of North Dakota / by Elwyn B. Robinson; line drawings by Jack Brodie. — Lincoln: University of Nebraska Press, 1966. xi, 599 p.: ill. 1. North Dakota — History. I. T.
F636.R6

Wilkins, Robert P., 1914-.   **3.8509**
North Dakota: a Bicentennial history / Robert P. Wilkins, Wynona Huchette Wilkins. — New York: Norton, c1977. xii, 218 p., [8] leaves of plates: ill.; 22 cm. (The States and the Nation series) Includes index. 1. North Dakota — History. I. Wilkins, Wynona H., joint author. II. T.
F636.W49   978.4   LC 77-22102   ISBN 0393056554

Milton, John R.   **3.8510**
South Dakota: a bicentennial history / John Milton. — New York: Norton, c1977. xv, 200 p., [8] leaves of plates: ill.; 22 cm. (The States and the Nation series) Includes index. 1. South Dakota — History. I. T.
F651.M5   978.3   LC 76-57677   ISBN 0393056279

Schell, Herbert Samuel, 1899-.   • **3.8511**
History of South Dakota, by Herbert S. Schell. Line drawings by Jack Brodie. — 3d ed., rev. — Lincoln: University of Nebraska Press, 1975. xiii, 444 p.: illus.; 24 cm. 1. South Dakota — History. I. T.
F651.S29 1975   917.83/03   LC 74-18431   ISBN 0803208510

Lamar, Howard Roberts.   • **3.8512**
Dakota Territory, 1861–1889: a study of frontier politics / by Howard Roberts Lamar. — New Haven: Yale University Press, 1956- 304 p.: ports., maps, facsim.; 24 cm. — (Yale historical publications. Miscellany. 64) 'Originally prepared as a doctoral dissertation at Yale University.' 1. Dakota — Politics and government. I. T. II. Series.
F655.L25   LC 56-10098

South Dakota. Dakota Territory Centennial Commission.   **3.8513**
Dakota panorama. [Sioux, Falls.?] 1961. vii, 468 p. illus., ports., maps (part fold.) facsims. 27 cm. 1. Dakota Territory — History. I. Jennewein, John Leonard, 1910- ed. II. Boorman, Jane, joint ed. III. T.
F655.S74   LC 62-33623

Federal Writers' Project. South Dakota.   • **3.8514**
South Dakota, a guide to the State / compiled by the Federal Writers' Project of the Works Progress Administration. — 2d ed. / completely rev. by M. Lisle Reese. — New York: Hastings House, c1952. xxvii, 421 p., [28] leaves of plates: ill., maps; 21 cm. — (American guide series.) 1. South Dakota. 2. South Dakota — Description and travel — Guide-books. I. Reese, M. Lisle. II. T. III. Series.
F656.F45 1952   LC 52-7601

Fite, Gilbert Courtland, 1918-.   **3.8515**
Peter Norbeck: prairie statesman. Columbia, Univ. of Missouri, 1948. 217 p. illus., port. 27 cm. (The University of Missouri studies, v. 22, no. 2) Issued also, in microfilm form, as thesis, Univ. of Missouri. 1. Norbeck, Peter, 1870-1936. 2. South Dakota — Politics and government. 3. South Dakota — History. I. T. II. Series.
F656.N6 F5   LC a 48-9996

F661–690 NEBRASKA. KANSAS

Cherny, Robert W.   3.8516
Populism, progressivism, and the transformation of Nebraska politics, 1885–1915 / Robert W. Cherny. — Lincoln: Published by the University of Nebraska Press for the Center for Great Plains Studies, University of Nebraska—Lincoln, c1981. xviii, 227 p.: maps; 23 cm. Includes index. 1. Populism — Nebraska. 2. Progressivism (United States politics) 3. Voting — Nebraska. 4. Political parties — Nebraska. 5. Nebraska — Politics and government. I. University of Nebraska—Lincoln. Center for Great Plains Studies. II. T.
F666.C49   320.9782   *LC* 80-11151   *ISBN* 0803214073

Creigh, Dorothy Weyer.   3.8517
Nebraska: a Bicentennial history / Dorothy Weyer Creigh. — New York: Norton, c1977. xvi, 220 p., [8] leaves of plates: ill.; 22 cm. (The States and the Nation series) Includes index. 1. Nebraska — History I. T.
F666.C83   978.2   *LC* 77-5425   *ISBN* 0393055981

Nebraska. Federal Writers' Project.   • 3.8518
Nebraska, a guide to the Cornhusker State / compiled and written by the Federal Writers' Project of the Works Progress Administration for the State of Nebraska; sponsored by the Nebraska State Historical Society. — New York: Hastings House, 1947. xxiii, 424 p.: ill.; 21 cm. (American guide series.) 1. Nebraska — Description and travel — Guide-books. I. T. II. Series.
F666.F46 1947   917.82   *LC* 48-1227

Olson, James C.   • 3.8519
History of Nebraska, by James C. Olson. Line drawings by Franz Altschuler. Additional line drawings by Jack Brodie. — [2d ed.]. — Lincoln: University of Nebraska Press, 1966. xii, 387 p.: illus., maps, ports.; 24 cm. 1. Nebraska — History I. T.
F666.O48 1966   978.2   *LC* 67-8965

Sandoz, Mari, 1907-.   • 3.8520
Old Jules / by Mari Sandoz; with illustrations. — 20th Anniversary ed. New York: Hastings, 1955. 424 p.: ill. 1. Sandoz, Jules Ami, 1857?-1928. 2. Frontier and pioneer life — Nebraska. I. T.
F666.S345 1955   *LC* 55-7948

Davis, Kenneth Sydney, 1912-.   3.8521
Kansas: a bicentennial history / Kenneth S. Davis. — New York: Norton, c1976. xiii, 226 p., [8] leaves of plates: ill.; 22 cm. (The States and the Nation series) Includes index. 1. Kansas — History I. T.
F681.D37   978.1   *LC* 76-21674   *ISBN* 0393055930

Zornow, William Frank.   • 3.8522
Kansas; a history of the Jayhawk State. [1st ed.] Norman, University of Oklahoma [1957] 417 p. illus. 25 cm. 1. Kansas — History I. T.
F681.Z6   978.1   *LC* 57-7334

Malin, James Claude, 1893-.   • 3.8523
John Brown and the legend of fifty–six by James C. Malin. — New York: Haskell House, 1971. 2 v. (xii, 794 p.): facsims., maps.; 24 cm. 1. Brown, John, 1800-1859. 2. Kansas — History — 1854-1861 I. T.
F685.B877 M3 1971   973.6/8/0924   *LC* 70-117588   *ISBN* 0838310214

Johnson, Samuel A.   • 3.8524
The battle cry of freedom. Lawrence, University of Kansas Press, 1954. 357 p. illus., ports., maps. 24 cm. 1. New England Emigrant Aid Company, Boston. 2. Kansas — History — 1854-1861 I. T.
F685.J75   *LC* 54-11612

Farnsworth, Martha, 1867-1924.   3.8525
Plains woman: the diary of Martha Farnsworth, 1882–1922 / edited by Marlene Springer and Haskell Springer. — Bloomington: Indiana University Press, c1986. xxv, 322 p.: ill.; 24 cm. 1. Farnsworth, Martha, 1867-1924. 2. Pioneers — Kansas — Biography. 3. Women pioneers — Kansas — Biography. 4. Kansas — Biography. 5. Kansas — Social life and customs. I. Springer, Marlene. II. Springer, Haskell S. III. T.
F686.F37 A37 1986   978.1/031/0924 B 19   *LC* 84-43169   *ISBN* 0253345103

Kansas. Federal Writers' Project.   • 3.8526
Kansas, a guide to the Sunflower State / compiled and written by the Federal Writers' Project of the Work Projects Administration for the State of Kansas. — New York: Hastings House, [1949] xviii, 538 p.: ill., maps; 21 cm. — (American guide series) 'Sponsored by State Department of Education.' 1. Kansas — Description and travel — Guide-books. 2. Kansas. I. T.
F686.F45 1949   917.81/04/3

McCoy, Donald R.   • 3.8527
Landon of Kansas [by] Donald R. McCoy. — Lincoln: University of Nebraska Press, [1966] x, 607 p.: illus., ports.; 24 cm. 1. Landon, Alfred M. (Alfred Mossman) 1887-1987. I. T.
F686.L26   329.6/00924   *LC* 65-16190

Miner, H. Craig.   3.8528
West of Wichita: settling the high plains of Kansas, 1865–1890 / Craig Miner. — Lawrence, KS: University Press of Kansas, c1986. viii, 303 p.: ill.; 24 cm. Includes index. 1. Frontier and pioneer life — Kansas. 2. Kansas — History I. T.
F686.M56 1986   978.1/031 19   *LC* 85-26013   *ISBN* 0700602860

F691–705 OKLAHOMA

Dale, Edward Everett, 1879-1972.   • 3.8529
History of Oklahoma. New York, Prentice-Hall, 1948. x, 572 p. illus., maps (1 fold. col.) 21 cm. 1. Oklahoma — History I. Wardell, Morris L., 1889- joint author. II. T.
F694.D128   *LC* 48-7592

McReynolds, Edwin C.   • 3.8530
Oklahoma; the story of its past and present, by Edwin C. McReynolds, Alice Marriott [and] Estelle Faulconer. — Rev. ed. — Norman: University of Oklahoma Press, [1971] xx, 499 p.: illus.; 24 cm. 1. Oklahoma — History I. Marriott, Alice Lee, 1910- joint author. II. Faulconer, Estelle, joint author. III. T.
F694.M17 1971   976.6   *LC* 79-32120   *ISBN* 0806905097

Morgan, H. Wayne (Howard Wayne)   3.8531
Oklahoma: a Bicentennial history / H. Wayne Morgan, Anne Hodges Morgan. — New York: Norton, c1977. xv, 190 p., [8] leaves of plates: ill.; 22 cm. (The States and the Nation series) Includes index. 1. Oklahoma — History I. Morgan, Anne Hodges, 1940- joint author. II. T.
F694.M8175   976.6   *LC* 77-7052   *ISBN* 0393056422

Ruth, Kent. ed.   • 3.8532
Oklahoma; a guide to the Sooner State. [Rev. ed.] Norman, University of Oklahoma Press [1957] xxxv, 532 p.: illus., ports., maps (1 fold.) 21 cm. 1. Oklahoma. 2. Oklahoma — Description and travel — Guide-books. I. Oklahoma. University. Press. II. Writers' Program of the Work Projects Administration in the State of Oklahoma. Oklahoma; a guide to the Sooner State. III. T.
F694.R8   *LC* 57-7333

Scales, James R. (James Ralph), 1918-.   3.8533
Oklahoma politics: a history / by James R. Scales and Danney Goble. — Norman, Okla.: University of Oklahoma Press, c1982. xii, 372 p.: ill., ports. Includes index. 1. Oklahoma — Politics and government I. Goble, Danney, 1946- II. T.
F694.S28 1982   F694 S28 1982.   976.6/05 19   *LC* 82-40328   *ISBN* 0806118245

Oklahoma: new views of the forty–sixth state / edited by Anne Hodges Morgan and H. Wayne Morgan.   3.8534
Norman: University of Oklahoma Press, c1982. x, 308 p.; 24 cm. 1. Oklahoma — History — Addresses, essays, lectures. I. Morgan, Anne Hodges, 1940- II. Morgan, H. Wayne (Howard Wayne)
F694.5.O38 1982   976.6 19   *LC* 82-40327   *ISBN* 080611651X

Rister, Carl Coke, 1899-.   • 3.8535
Land hunger: David L. Payne and the Oklahoma boomers. Norman, University of Oklahoma press, 1942. xiii, 245 p. front., illus. (maps) plates, ports. facsims. 24 cm. 1. Payne, David Lewis, 1836-1884. 2. Oklahoma — History I. T.
F697.P35   *LC* 43-1028

Goble, Danney, 1946-.   3.8536
Progressive Oklahoma: the making of a new kind of state / by Danney Goble. — 1st ed. — Norman: University of Oklahoma Press, c1980. xi, 276 p.: ill.; 23 cm. Includes index. 1. Progressivism (United States politics) 2. Oklahoma — Politics and government — To 1907 I. T.
F699.G6   320.9/766   *LC* 79-4734   *ISBN* 0806115106

Thompson, John, 1953-.   3.8537
Closing the frontier: radical response in Oklahoma, 1889–1923 / by John Thompson. — 1st ed. — Norman: University of Oklahoma Press, c1986. xiii, 262 p.: ill.; 22 cm. Includes index. 1. Frontier and pioneer life — Oklahoma. 2. Radicalism — Oklahoma — History. 3. Oklahoma — History I. T.
F699.T49 1986   976.6 19   *LC* 86-1609   *ISBN* 0806119969

Bryant, Keith L.　　　　　　　　　　　　　　● 3.8538
Alfalfa Bill Murray, by Keith L. Bryant, Jr. [1st ed.] Norman, University of Oklahoma Press [1968] xiii, 287 p. illus., maps, ports. 24 cm. 1. Murray, William Henry, 1869-1956. I. T.
F700.M697　　976.6/05/924 B　　*LC* 68-10299

Ellsworth, Scott.　　　　　　　　　　　　　　3.8539
Death in a promised land: the Tulsa race riot of 1921 / Scott Ellsworth. — Baton Rouge: Louisiana State University Press, c1982. xvii, 159 p.: ill., maps, ports. Includes index. 1. Tulsa (Okla.) — Riot, 1921. 2. Tulsa (Okla.) — Race relations. I. T. II. Title: Tulsa race riot of 1921.
F704.T92 E44　　F704T92 E44.　　976.6/86 19　　*LC* 81-6017　　*ISBN* 0807108782

F721 Rocky Mountain States

Peirce, Neal R.　　　　　　　　　　　　　　● 3.8540
The Mountain States of America: people, politics, and power in the eight Rocky Mountain States / [by] Neal R. Peirce. — [1st ed.]. — New York: Norton, [1972] 317 p.: ill.; 24 cm. 1. Rocky Mountains region. I. T.
F721.P45 1972　　917.8/03/3　　*LC* 72-437　　*ISBN* 0393052559

West, Elliott, 1945-.　　　　　　　　　　　　3.8541
The saloon on the Rocky Mountain mining frontier / by Elliott West. — Lincoln: University of Nebraska Press, c1979. xvii, 197 p.: ill.; 23 cm. Includes index. 1. Frontier and pioneer life — Rocky Mountains Region. 2. Hotels, taverns, etc — Rocky Mountains Region — History. 3. Rocky Mountains Region — Social life and customs. I. T.
F721.W37　　978　　*LC* 78-24090　　*ISBN* 0803247044

F726–755 Montana. Idaho

Montana. Federal Writers' Project.　　　　　　● 3.8542
Montana, a state guide book / compiled and written by the Federal Writers' Project of the Work Projects Administration for the State of Montana. New York: Hastings House, 1949, 430 p.: ill., maps; 21 cm. — (American guide series.) Sponsored by Department of Agriculture, Labor and Industry, State of Montana. 1. Montana — Description and travel — Guide-books. I. T. II. Series.
F731.F44 1949

Howard, Joseph Kinsey.　　　　　　　　　　● 3.8543
Montana, high, wide and handsome / by Joseph Kinsey Howard; pref. by A. B. Guthrie; drawings by Peter Hurd. — New illustrated ed. — New Haven: Yale University Press, 1959. xiv, 347 p.: ill., map. 1. Montana — History. I. T.
F731.H86　　978.6　　*ISBN* 0030005768

Malone, Michael P.　　　　　　　　　　　　3.8544
Montana: a history of two centuries / by Michael P. Malone and Richard B. Roeder. Seattle: University of Washington Press, c1976. xiii, 352 p., [12] leaves of plates: ill.; 24 cm. Includes index. 1. Montana — History. I. Roeder, Richard B. joint author. II. T.
F731.M339　　978.6　　*LC* 76-7791　　*ISBN* 0295955201

Spence, Clark C.　　　　　　　　　　　　　3.8545
Montana: a bicentennial history / Clark C. Spence. — New York: Norton, c1978. xi, 211 p., [8] leaves of plates: ill.; 22 cm. (The States and the Nation series) Includes index. 1. Montana — History. I. T.
F731.S62 1978　　978.6　　*LC* 77-18829　　*ISBN* 0393056791

Spence, Clark C.　　　　　　　　　　　　　3.8546
Territorial politics and government in Montana, 1864–89 / Clark C. Spence. — Urbana: University of Illinois Press, c1975. x, 322 p., [4] leaves of plates: ports.; 24 cm. Includes index. 1. Montana — Politics and government. I. T.
F731.S63　　320.9/786/02　　*LC* 75-28343　　*ISBN* 0252004604

Toole, K. Ross (Kenneth Ross), 1920-1981.　　● 3.8547
Twentieth–century Montana: a State of extremes, by K. Ross Toole. — [1st ed.]. — Norman: University of Oklahoma Press, [1972] xix, 307 p.: illus.; 21 cm. 1. Montana — History. I. T.
F731.T66　　978.6/03　　*LC* 75-177348　　*ISBN* 0806109920

Writers' Program. Montana.　　　　　　　　● 3.8548
Copper camp; stories of the world's greatest mining town. New York, Hastings House [1943] x p., 1 1., 308 p. incl. front., illus. plates, ports. 21 cm. 1. Butte (Mont.) — History. I. T.
F739.B8 W7　　*LC* 43-12488

Idaho. Federal Writers' Project.　　　　　　　● 3.8549
Idaho, a guide in word and picture. [2d ed. rev.] New York, Oxford University Press, 1950. xiv, 300 p. illus., map (on lining paper) 21 cm. (American guide series.) 'Sponsored by the Secretary of State of Idaho.' 1. Idaho. 2. Idaho — Description and travel — Guide-books. I. T. II. Series.
F746.F453　　*LC* 50-13175

Malone, Michael P.　　　　　　　　　　　　● 3.8550
C. Ben Ross and the New Deal in Idaho, by Michael P. Malone. Seattle, University of Washington Press [1970] xxiii, 191 p. ports. 22 cm. 1. Ross, Charles Benjamin. 2. New Deal, 1933-1939 3. Idaho — Politics and government. I. T.
F746.M3　　320.9/796 B　　*LC* 69-14207

Peterson, Frank Ross.　　　　　　　　　　　3.8551
Idaho, a bicentennial history / F. Ross Peterson. — New York: Norton, c1976. xi, 203 p., [8] leaves of plates: ill.; 22 cm. (The States and the Nation series) Includes index. 1. Idaho — History. I. T.
F746.P47　　979.6　　*LC* 76-26873　　*ISBN* 0393056007

F756–785 Wyoming. Colorado

Larson, T. A. (Taft Alfred), 1910-.　　　　　　● 3.8552
History of Wyoming / T.A. Larson; line drawings by Jack Brodie. — Lincoln: University of Nebraska Press, 1965. xi, 619 p.: ill., maps. 1. Wyoming — History I. T.
F761.L3　　*LC* 65-15277

Larson, T. A. (Taft Alfred), 1910-.　　　　　　3.8553
Wyoming: a Bicentennial history / T. A. Larson. — New York: Norton, c1977. ix, 198 p., [8] leaves of plates: ill.; 22 cm. (The States and the Nation series) Includes index. 1. Wyoming — History I. T.
F761.L32 1977　　978.7　　*LC* 77-3592　　*ISBN* 0393056260

Writers' Program of the Work Projects Administration in the State of Wyoming.　　　　　　　　　　● 3.8554
Wyoming: a guide to its history, highways, and people / compiled by workers of the Writers' Program of the Work Projects Administration in the state of Wyoming; sponsored by Dr. Lester C. Hunt, secretary of state. — New York, Oxford University Press [c1941] xxvii, 490 p.: ill., plates, ports., maps (4 on fold. 1., in pocket); 21 cm. (American guide series) Map on lining-paper. The plates are in eight groups, each preceded by half-title not included in paging. 'First published in April, 1941.' 1. Wyoming. 2. Wyoming — Description and travel — Guide-books. I. T.
F761.W58　　*LC* 41-52444

Colorado. Writers' Program.　　　　　　　　● 3.8555
Colorado; a guide to the highest State. Compiled by workers of the Writers' Program of the Work Projects Administration in the State of Colorado. New York, Hastings House. — St. Clair Shores, Mich.: Somerset Publishers, 1973. xxxiii, 511 p.: illus.; 22 cm. Reprint of the 1948 ed. issued in series: American guide series. 1. Colorado — Description and travel — Guide-books. I. T.
F774.3.W74 1973　　917.88/04/3　　*LC* 72-84463　　*ISBN* 0403021588

Sprague, Marshall.　　　　　　　　　　　　3.8556
Colorado: a bicentennial history / Marshall Sprague. — New York: Norton, c1976. ix, 204 p., [8] leaves of plates: ill.; 22 cm. (The States and the Nation series) Includes index. 1. Colorado — History I. T.
F776.S76　　978.8　　*LC* 76-9800　　*ISBN* 039305599X

Ubbelohde, Carl.　　　　　　　　　　　　　● 3.8557
A Colorado history. — Boulder, Colo.: Pruett Pub. Co., [1965] x, 339 p.: ill., col. map; 24 cm. 1. Colorado — History I. T.
F776.U195 1965　　917.88/03　　*LC* 76-185174

F786–850 New Southwest. Colorado River

Tuska, Jon.　　　　　　　　　　　　　　　3.8558
Billy the Kid, a bio–bibliography / Jon Tuska. — Westport, Conn.: Greenwood Press, 1983. xvi, 235 p.: ill.; 25 cm. — (Popular culture bio-bibliographies. 0193-6891) 1. Billy, the Kid. 2. Billy, the Kid — Bibliography. 3. Outlaws — Southwest, New — Biography. 4. Southwest, New — Biography. I. T. II. Series.
F786.B54 T87 1983　　364.1/552/0924 B 19　　*LC* 83-5709　　*ISBN* 0313232660

Lamar, Howard Roberts.   • **3.8559**
Far Southwest, 1846–1912: a territorial history. New Haven: Yale University Press, 1966. 560p.,illus.,fold.map,ports. (Yale Western Americana series. 12.) 1. Southwest, New — History I. T. II. Series.
F786 L27   979.104   *LC* 66-12505

McWilliams, Carey, 1905-.   • **3.8560**
North from Mexico: the Spanish–speaking people of the United States / with an introd. to the Greenwood reprint ed. by the author. — New York: Greenwood Press, 1968 [c1948] 324 p.: map; 23 cm. 1. Mexican Americans 2. Southwest, New — History I. T.
F786.M215 1968   301.453/72/0791   *LC* 68-28595

Worster, Donald, 1941-.   **3.8561**
Dust Bowl: the southern plains in the 1930s / Donald Worster. — New York: Oxford University Press, 1979. x, 277 p.: ill.; 24 cm. 1. Agriculture — Southwestern States — History. 2. Agriculture — Great Plains — History. 3. Dust storms — Great Plains. 4. Dust storms — Southwestern States. 5. Depressions — 1929 — United States 6. Southwestern States — History. 7. Great Plains — History. I. T.
F786.W87   978   *LC* 78-27018   *ISBN* 0195025504

Powell, John Wesley, 1834-1902.   • **3.8562**
The exploration of the Colorado River / by John Wesley Powell. — Chicago: University of Chicago Press 1957. 138 p. ill.; 22 cm. — 'Based on the Smithsonian Institution text ... which appeared under the full title: Exploration of the Colorado River of the West and its tributaries.' 1. Colorado River. 2. United States — Exploring expeditions I. Smithsonian Institution. Exploration of the Colorado River of the West and its tributaries. II. T.
F788.P886   *LC* 57-6988   *ISBN* 0226677028

Chávez, John R., 1949-.   **3.8563**
The lost land: the Chicano image of the Southwest / John R. Chávez. — 1st ed. — Albuquerque: University of New Mexico Press, c1984. vii, 207 p.; 24 cm. Includes index. 1. Mexican Americans — Southwest, New — Attitudes. 2. Mexican Americans — Southwest, New — History. 3. Mexican Americans — Southwest, New — Ethnic identity. 4. Southwest, New — History 5. Southwest, New — Ethnic relations. I. T.
F790.M5 C49 1984   979/.0046872 19   *LC* 84-11950   *ISBN* 0826307493

Griswold del Castillo, Richard.   **3.8564**
La familia: Chicano families in the urban Southwest, 1848 to the present / Richard Griswold del Castillo. — Notre Dame, Ind.: University of Notre Dame Press, c1984. xv, 173 p.: ill.; 24 cm. Includes index. 1. Mexican Americans — Families — Southwest, New — History. 2. Southwest, New — Social conditions. I. T. II. Title: Chicano families in the urban Southwest, 1848 to the present.
F790.M5 G75 1984   306.8/50896872073 19   *LC* 84-40356   *ISBN* 0268012725

Rosenbaum, Robert J., 1943-.   **3.8565**
Mexicano resistance in the Southwest: 'the sacred right of self–preservation' / by Robert J. Rosenbaum. — Austin: University of Texas Press, c1981. xii, 241 p.: ill.; 24 cm. — (The Dan Danciger publication series) Based on the author's thesis, University of Texas at Austin. Includes index. 1. Mexican Americans — Southwest, New — History. 2. Southwest, New — History — 1848- 3. Southwest, New — Social conditions. I. T.
F790.M5 R67   979/.0046872 19   *LC* 80-18964   *ISBN* 0292775628

F791–820 New Mexico. Arizona

New Mexico. Writers' Program.   • **3.8566**
New Mexico, a guide to the colorful State / compiled by workers of the Writers' Program of the Work Projects Administration in the State of New Mexico. — New and completely rev. ed. / by Joseph Miller; edited by Henry G. Alsberg. — New York: Hastings House, 1962. xxxii, 472 p., [32] leaves of plates: ill.; 21 cm. — (American guide series.) 'Sponsored by the University of New Mexico.' 1. New Mexico. 2. New Mexico — Description and travel — 1951- — Guidebooks. I. Miller, Joseph, 1899- II. T. III. Series.
F794.3.W7 1962   917.89/04/5   *LC* 62-53065

Bancroft, Hubert Howe, 1832-1918.   • **3.8567**
History of Arizona and the New Mexico, 1530–1888. New Mexico foreword by Clinton P. Anderson. Arizona foreword byBarry Goldwater. A facsim. of the 1889 ed. published coinident to the 50th anniversary of New Mexico & Arizona statehood. Albuquerque, Horn & Wallace, 1962. 19 p., facsim.: xxxviii, 829 p. maps. 24 cm. 1. Arizona — History 2. New Mexico — History I. Oak, Henry Lebbeus, 1844-1905. II. T.
F796.B192   979   *LC* 62-13296

Simmons, Marc.   **3.8568**
New Mexico: a Bicentennial history / Marc Simmons. — New York: Norton, c1977. xiv, 207 p., [8] leaves of plates: ill.; 22 cm. (The States and the Nation series) Includes index. 1. New Mexico — History I. T.
F796.S54   978.9   *LC* 77-585   *ISBN* 0393056317

Bolton, Herbert Eugene, 1870-1953. ed.   • **3.8569**
Spanish exploration in the Southwest, 1542–1706. New York, C. Scribner's sons, 1916. xii p., 2 l., 3-487 p. 3 fold. maps (incl. front.) 23 cm. 1. America — Discovery and exploration — Spanish 2. Southwest, New — Discovery and exploration. I. T.
F799.B69   *LC* 16-6066

Hammond, George Peter, 1896- ed. and tr.   • **3.8570**
Don Juan de Oñate, colonizer of New Mexico, 1595–1628 [by] George P. Hammond [and] Agapito Rey. [Albuquerque] University of New Mexico Press, 1953. 2 v. (xvi, 1187 p.) fronts., fold. map. 28 cm. (Coronado Cuarto Centennial publications, 1540-1940, v. 5, 6) A translation of documentary sources chiefly from the Archives of the Indies in Seville. 1. Oñate, Juan de, fl. 1595-1622. 2. New Mexico — History — Sources. I. Rey, Agapito, 1892- joint ed. and tr. II. T. III. Series.
F799.H3   *LC* 53-12919

Jones, Oakah L.   **3.8571**
Los paisanos: Spanish settlers on the northern frontier of New Spain / Oakah L. Jones, Jr. — 1st ed. — Norman: University of Oklahoma Press, c1979. xv, 351 p.: ill.; 26 cm. Includes index. 1. Spaniards in the New Southwest — History. 2. Southwest, New — History — To 1848 3. Mexico — History — To 1810 I. T.
F799.J75   979   *LC* 78-58119   *ISBN* 0806114320

Bolton, Herbert Eugene, 1870-1953.   • **3.8572**
Rim of Christendom; a biography of Eusebio Francisco Kino, Pacific coast pioneer. — New York, Russell & Russell, 1960 [c1936] xiv, 644 p. illus., fold. maps, facsims. 25 cm. Bibliography: p. 597-627. 1. Kino, Eusebio Francisco, 1644-1711. I. T.
F799.K59 1960   922.273   *LC* 60-10705

Sauer, Carl Ortwin, 1889-.   • **3.8573**
The road to Cíbola / by Carl Sauer. — Berkeley, Calif.: University of California press, 1932. 3 p. l., 58 p.: fold. map.; 28 cm. (Published by the University of California Press, Berkeley, as no. 3 of Ibero-Americana.) 'Appendix of unpublished (early seventeenth century) documentary materials on the explorations into the Northwest': p. 51-58. 1. Cibola, Seven Cities of 2. Southwest, New — Discovery and exploration. 3. New Mexico — History — To 1848 I. T. II. Series.
F799.S27   973.16   *LC* A32-1971

Horgan, Paul, 1903-.   **3.8574**
Josiah Gregg and his vision of the early West / Paul Horgan. — New York: Farrar Strauss Giroux, c1979. 116 p.; 22 cm. Includes index. 1. Gregg, Josiah, 1806-1850. 2. Gregg, Josiah, 1806-1850. Commerce of the prairies. 3. Pioneers — Southwest, New — Biography. 4. Southwest, New — Description and travel 5. Mexico — Description and travel I. T.
F800.G74 H67 1979   976/.03/0924   *LC* 79-13081   *ISBN* 0374180172

Gregg, Josiah, 1806-1850.   • **3.8575**
Commerce of the prairies. Introd. by Archibald Hanna. [1st ed.] Philadelphia, Lippincott [1962] 2 v. (351 p.) illus., map, facsim. 21 cm. (Keystone Western Americana series, KB52-53) 'The 1844 edition, unabridged.' 1. Indians of North America — West (U.S.) 2. Southwest, New 3. New Mexico. 4. Mexico — Description and travel 5. Santa Fe Trail I. T.
F800.G844   979   *LC* 62-11339

Weber, David J.   **3.8576**
The Mexican frontier, 1821–1846: the American Southwest under Mexico / David J. Weber. — 1st ed. — Albuquerque: University of New Mexico Press, c1982. xxiv, 416 p.: ill.; 24 cm. — (Histories of the American frontier.) Includes index. 1. Southwest, New — History — To 1848 2. Mexico — History — 1821-1861 I. T. II. Series.
F800.W4 1982   979/.02 19   *LC* 82-2800   *ISBN* 0826306020

Traube, Alex, 1946-.   **3.8577**
Las Vegas, New Mexico: a portrait / photographs by Alex Traube; with a text by E.A. Mares. — 1st ed. — Albuquerque: University of New Mexico Press, [1984?] vii, 181 p.: ill.; 22 x 29 cm. 1. Photography, Artistic 2. Las Vegas (N.M.) — History. 3. Las Vegas (N.M.) — Description — Views. I. Mares, E. A., 1938- II. T.
F804.L3 T7 1984   978.9/55 19   *LC* 83-10179   *ISBN* 0826306705

Writers' Program (Arizona)   • **3.8578**
[Arizona; a state guide] Arizona, the Grand Canyon State; a State guide. Completely rev. by Joseph Miller; edited by Henry G. Alsberg and Harry Hansen. [4th completely rev. ed.] New York, Hastings House [1966] xxvi, 532 p. illus., maps, ports. 21 cm. (American guide series.) First published in

1940 under title: Arizona; a State guide. 'Originally compiled by the Federal Writers' Project of the Works Progress Administration in the State of Arizona.' 1. Arizona — Description and travel — Guide-books. I. Miller, Joseph, 1899- ed. II. T. III. Series.
F809.3.W7 1966   917.91045   LC 66-20364

Powell, Lawrence Clark, 1906-.   **3.8579**
Arizona: a bicentennial history / Lawrence Clark Powell. — New York: Norton, c1976. xviii, 154 p., [8] leaves of plates: ill.; 22 cm. (The States and the Nation series) Includes index. 1. Arizona — History I. T.
F811.P73   979.1   LC 76-2738   ISBN 0393055752

Sonnichsen, C. L. (Charles Leland), 1901-.   **3.8580**
Tucson, the life and times of an American city / by C.L. Sonnichsen; maps by Donald H. Bufkin. — Norman: University of Oklahoma Press, c1982. xiv, 369 p.: ill.; 27 cm. Includes index. 1. Tucson (Ariz.) — History. I. T.
F819.T957 S66 1982   979.1/77 19   LC 82-40329   ISBN 0806118237

F821–850 UTAH. NEVADA

Writers' Program (Utah)   • **3.8581**
Utah; a guide to the State. Compiled by workers of the Writers' Program of the Work Projects Administration for the State of Utah. New York, Hastings House, 1941. — St. Clair Shores, Mich.: Somerset Publishers, 1972. xxvi, 595 p.: illus.; 22 cm. 'Sponsored by the Utah State Institute of Fine Arts; co-sponsored by the Salt Lake County Commission.' Original ed. issued in series: American guide series. 1. Utah — Description and travel — Guide-books. I. T.
F824.3.W74 1972   917.92/04/3   LC 72-84510   ISBN 0403021936

Lee, John Doyle, 1812-1877.   **3.8582**
Journals of John D. Lee, 1846–47 and 1859 / edited by Charles Kelly; introduction by Charles S. Peterson. — Salt Lake City: University of Utah Press, 1984. xxviii, 244 p., [12] leaves of plates: ill.; 25 cm. Reprint. Originally published: Salt Lake City: Privately printed for R.B. Watt by Western Print. Co., 1938. 1. Lee, John Doyle, 1812-1877. 2. Mormons — Utah — Biography. 3. Mountain Meadows Massacre, 1857 — Personal narratives. 4. Utah — Biography. I. Kelly, Charles, 1889- II. T.
F826.L4715 1984   979.2/02/0924 19   LC 84-234912   ISBN 0874802423

Peterson, Charles S.   **3.8583**
Utah: a bicentennial history / Charles S. Peterson. — New York: Norton, c1977. ix, 213 p., [8] leaves of plates: ill.; 22 cm. (The States and the Nation series) Includes index. 1. Utah — History I. T.
F826.P48   979.2   LC 77-2726   ISBN 0393056295

Morgan, Dale Lowell, 1914-1971.   • **3.8584**
The Great Salt Lake / [by] Dale L. Morgan. Indianapolis: The Bobbs-Merrill Company [1947] 432 p.: ill. (maps) plates; 22 cm. (The American lake series) 1. Great Salt Lake (Utah) 2. Utah — History I. T.
F832.G7 M6   979.2   LC 47-2728

Provo, pioneer Mormon city / compiled by the workers of the   • **3.8585**
Workers' Program of the Work Projects Administration for the state of Utah; sponsored by the Utah State Institute of Fine Arts. Co-sponsored by the Provo City Commission, the Provo Board of Education, Brigham Young University, and Provo Chamber of Commerce.
Portland, Or.: Binfords & Mort, [c1942] 223 p.: plates; 21 cm. — (American guide series)
F834.P8W7   979.2   LC 43-1606

Laxalt, Robert, 1923-.   **3.8586**
Nevada: a Bicentennial history / Robert Laxalt. — New York: Norton, c1977. xi, 146 p., [8] leaves of plates: ill.; 22 cm. — (The States and the Nation series) Includes index. 1. Nevada — History. I. T.
F841.L39   979.3   LC 77-3885   ISBN 0393056287

Writers' program (Nevada)   • **3.8587**
Nevada: a guide to the Silver state / compiled by workers of the Writers' program of the Work projects administration in the state of Nevada; sponsored by Dr. Jeanne Elizabeth Wier, Nevada state historical society, inc. — Portland, Or.: Binfords & Mort, [1940] xviii, 315 p.: plates, maps (1 fold. in pocket); 21 cm. — (American guide series.) The plates are in eight groups each preceded by half-title not included in paging. 'First published in 1940.' 1. Nevada. 2. Nevada — Description and travel — Tours. I. T. II. Series.
F841.W77   917.93   LC 41-71

F851–951 Pacific States

Bancroft, Hubert Howe, 1832-1918.   • **3.8588**
The Works of Hubert Howe Bancroft. — New York: Arno Press, [196-?] 39 v.: ill., maps. — On spine: Bancroft's works. Vol. 2-8, 12, 14, 16-17, 19-26, 29-32, 34-39 have imprint: San Francisco, History Co. 1. Indians of North America 2. Pacific States — History. 3. Mexico — History 4. Central America — History 5. British Columbia — History. 6. The West — History. I. T. II. Title: Bancroft's works.
F851 B216   LC 67-29422

Experiences in a promised land: essays in Pacific Northwest   **3.8589**
history / edited by G. Thomas Edwards and Carlos A. Schwantes; foreword by Robert E. Burke.
Seattle: University of Washington Press, c1986. xvi, 397 p.; 24 cm. 1. Northwest, Pacific — History — Addresses, essays, lectures. I. Edwards, G. Thomas. II. Schwantes, Carlos A., 1945-
F851.E97 1986   979.5 19   LC 85-26470   ISBN 029596328X

Peirce, Neal R.   • **3.8590**
The Pacific States of America: people, politics, and power in the five Pacific Basin States / [by] Neal R. Peirce. — [1st ed.]. — New York: W. W. Norton, [1972] 387 p.: maps; 24 cm. 1. Pacific States 2. Alaska. 3. Hawaii. I. T.
F851.P43 1972   917.9/03   LC 72-2333   ISBN 0393052729

Pomeroy, Earl Spencer, 1915-.   • **3.8591**
The Pacific slope; a history of California, Oregon, Washington, Idaho, Utah, and Nevada. [1st ed.] New York, Knopf, 1965. xii, 403, [1], xvi p. illus., fold. map. 25 cm. 1. Northwest, Pacific — History. 2. Southwest, New — History I. T.
F851.P57   LC 65-11128

Cook, Warren L.   **3.8592**
Flood tide of empire; Spain and the Pacific Northwest, 1543–1819, by Warren L. Cook. — New Haven: Yale University Press, 1973. xiv, 620 p.: illus., 2 fold. maps (in pocket); 26 cm. — (Yale Western Americana series. 24) 1. Northwest Coast of North America — Discovery and exploration. 2. Northwest, Pacific — History. 3. Spain — Exploring expeditions I. T. II. Series.
F851.5.C83   979.5/01   LC 72-75187   ISBN 0300015771

Gough, Barry M.   **3.8593**
Distant dominion: Britain and the northwest coast of North America, 1579–1809 / Barry M. Gough. — Vancouver: University of British Columbia Press, c1980. 190 p., [12] p. of plates: ill., ports.; 24 cm. — (University of British Columbia Press Pacific maritime studies. 2) Includes index. 1. Northwest Coast of North America — History. 2. British Columbia — History. 3. Great Britain — History, Naval I. T. II. Series.
F851.5.G68   971.1/01 19   LC 81-142626   ISBN 0774801131

Pethick, Derek, 1920-.   **3.8594**
First approaches to the Northwest coast / by Derek Pethick. Vancouver: J. J. Douglas, c1976. xix, 232 p.: ill.; 24 cm. Includes index. 1. Fur trade — Northwest, Pacific. 2. Northwest, Pacific — Discovery and exploration. I. T.
F851.5.P47   970/.00964/3   LC 76-48398

Johannsen, Robert Walter, 1925-.   • **3.8595**
Frontier politics and the sectional conflict: the Pacific Northwest on the eve of the Civil War / by Robert W. Johannsen. — Seattle: University of Washington Press, c1955. xiii, 240 p.: ports., maps. 1. Northwest, Pacific — Politics and government. 2. United States — Politics and government — 1857-1861 I. T.
F852 J65   F852 J65.   LC 55-11915

Johansen, Dorothy O.   • **3.8596**
Empire of the Columbia: a history of the Pacific Northwest / by Dorothy O. Johansen and Charles M. Gates. — 2d ed. — New York: Harper & Row, [1967] xiii, 654 p.: ill., maps.; 24 cm. 1. Northwest, Pacific — History. I. Gates, Charles Marvin. II. T.
F852.J67 1967   979.5   LC 67-12548

Meinig, D. W. (Donald William), 1924-.   • **3.8597**
The Great Columbia Plain; a historical geography, 1805–1910, by D. W. Meinig. Seattle, University of Washington Press [1968] xxi, 576 p. illus., maps. (part fold.) 25 cm. (Emil and Kathleen Sick lecture-book series in western history and biography.) 1. Columbia River Valley. I. T. II. Series.
F853.M4   979.7   LC 68-11044

F856–870 CALIFORNIA

Hart, James David, 1911-.   **3.8598**
A companion to California / by James D. Hart. — New York: Oxford University Press, 1978. viii, 504 p., [3] leaves of plates: maps; 24 cm. 1. California — Dictionaries and encyclopedias. I. T.
F859.H33   979.4/003   LC 76-57286   ISBN 0195022564

Caughey, John Walton, 1902-.   • **3.8599**
California: a remarkable State's life history / [by] John W. Caughey. — 3d ed. Englewood Cliffs, N.J.: Prentice-Hall [1970] xxiv, 674 p.: ill., maps, ports.; 25 cm. (Prentice-Hall history series) Rev. ed. published as: California, history of a remarkable state. 4th ed. c1982. 1. California — History
F861.C34 1970   917.94/03   LC 73-118334   ISBN 013112482X

Cleland, Robert Glass, 1885-.   • **3.8600**
From wilderness to empire: a history of California. A combined and rev. ed. of From wilderness to empire, 1542–1900 & California in our time, 1900–1940 / edited and brought down to date by Glenn S. Dumke. [1st ed.] New York: Knopf, 1959. 445 p. ill. 1. California — History I. T.
F861.C598   979.4   LC 59-8037

Lavender, David Sievert, 1910-.   **3.8601**
California: a bicentennial history / David Lavender. — New York: Norton, c1976. ix, 243 p., [8] leaves of plates: ill.; 22 cm. (States and the nation.) Includes index. 1. California — History I. T. II. Series.
F861.L37   979.4   LC 75-45217   ISBN 0393055787

Chartkoff, Joseph L.   **3.8602**
The archaeology of California / Joseph L. Chartkoff and Kerry Kona Chartkoff. — Stanford, Calif.: Stanford University Press, 1984. xix, 456 p.: ill.; 25 cm. Includes index. 1. Indians of North America — California — Antiquities 2. California — Antiquities I. Chartkoff, Kerry Kona. II. T.
F863.C46 1984   979.4/01 19   LC 82-60182   ISBN 0804711577

Bolton, Herbert Eugene, 1870-1953.   • **3.8603**
Anza's California expeditions. New York, Russell Russell, 1966 [c1930] p. cm. 1. Anza, Juan Bautista de, 1735-1788. 2. San Francisco (Calif.) — History. 3. California — Description and travel I. Moraga, José Joaquin, 1741-1785. II. Eixarch, Thomas. III. Font, Pedro. IV. Palóu, Francisco, 1723-1789. V. Garcés, Francisco Tomás Hermenegildo, 1738-1781. VI. Diaz, Juan. VII. T. VIII. Title: California expeditions.
F864.B68 1966   LC 66-11364

Crespi, Juan.   • **3.8604**
Fray Juan Crespi, missionary explorer on the Pacific coast, 1769–1774. Berkeley, Calif., University of California press, 1927. 2 p.l., iii-ixiv p., 1 l., 402 p. front., plates, maps, facsim, 23 cm. 1. Portola's Expedition, 1769-1770 2. Missions — California. 3. Franciscans — California 4. Pacific coast — Discovery and exploration. I. Bolton, Herbert Eugene, 1870-1953. ed. II. T.
F864.C92   LC 28-6102

Harlow, Neal.   **3.8605**
California conquered: war and peace on the Pacific, 1846–1850 / Neal Harlow. — Berkeley: University of California Press, c1982. xvii, 499 p.: ill.; 24 cm. Includes index. 1. California — History — 1846-1850 I. T.
F864.H295 1982   979.4/03 19   LC 81-7588   ISBN 0520044304

F865–866 1848–

Caughey, John Walton, 1902-.   • **3.8606**
Gold is the cornerstone / with vignettes by W.R. Cameron. — Berkeley: Univ. of Calif. Press, 1948. 321 p.: ill.; 23 cm. (Chronicles of California) 1. Gold mines and mining — California 2. California — Gold discoveries I. T. II. Series.
F865.C33   LC 48-10984

Doten, Alfred, 1829-1903.   **3.8607**
The journals of Alfred Doten, 1849–1903 / edited by Walter Van Tilburg Clark. — Reno: University of Nevada Press, 1973. 3 v. (xx, 2381 p., [24] leaves of plates): ill.; 26 cm. Includes index. 1. Doten, Alfred, 1829-1903. 2. Silver mines and mining — Nevada — History. 3. California — Gold discoveries — History. 4. Nevada — History. I. T.
F865.D67 1973   979.4/04/0924   LC 72-76826   ISBN 087417032X

Holliday, J. S.   **3.8608**
The world rushed in: the California gold rush experience / J.S. Holliday. — New York: Simon and Schuster, c1981. 559 p.: ill., maps; 25 cm. Based on the diary of William Swain. Map on lining papers. Includes index. 1. Swain, William, 1821-1904. 2. Overland journeys to the Pacific 3. Pioneers — California — Biography. 4. California — History — 1846-1850 5. California — Gold discoveries 6. California — Biography. I. Swain, William, 1821-1904. II. T.
F865.H69   979.4/04 19   LC 81-9333   ISBN 0671255371

Paul, Rodman Wilson.   • **3.8609**
California gold. Cambridge, Harvard Univ, Press, 1947. xvi, 380 p. illus., maps. 23 cm. 1. Gold mines and mining — California 2. Frontier and pioneer life — California. 3. California — Gold discoveries I. T.
F865.P25   LC 47-5141

Mowry, George Edwin, 1909-.   • **3.8610**
The California progressives. Berkeley: University of California Press, 1951. xi, 349 p.: ill., ports.; 23 cm. 1. Progressivism (United States politics) 2. California — Politics and government I. T.
F866.M89   LC 51-63048

Olin, Spencer C.   • **3.8611**
California's prodigal sons; Hiram Johnson and the Progressives, 1911–1917, by Spencer C. Olin, Jr. Berkeley, University of California Press, 1968. ix, 253 p. ports. 23 cm. 1. Johnson, Hiram, 1866-1945. 2. Progressivism (U.S. politics) 3. California — Politics and government — 1850-1950 I. T.
F866.O47   979.4/05   LC 68-11968

Burke, Robert E. (Robert Eugene), 1921-.   • **3.8612**
Olson's new deal for California. Berkeley: University of California Press, 1953. 279 p. 1. Olson, Culbert Levy, 1876- 2. California — Politics and government I. T.
F866.O5 B8   LC 53-11244

Federal Writers' Project (California)   `   • **3.8613**
California, a guide to the Golden State. [Rev. ed.] New York, Hastings House [1955, c1954] xxxi, 716 p. illus., maps. 21 cm. 1. Automobiles — Road guides — California. 2. California. 3. California — Description and travel — Guidebooks. I. T.
F866.2.F4 1954   LC 55-4472

F867–868 Regions

Cleland, Robert Glass, 1885-.   • **3.8614**
The cattle on a thousand hills: Southern California, 1850–1880. — [2d ed.] San Marino: Huntington Library, 1951. xvi, 365 p.: ill., ports., maps; 24 cm. 1. California, Southern — History. I. T.
F867.C6 1951   LC 51-14546

Starr, Kevin.   **3.8615**
Inventing the dream: California through the Progressive Era / Kevin Starr. — New York: Oxford University Press, 1985. xi, 380 p., [22] p. of plates: ill.; 25 cm. Includes index. 1. California, Southern — History. 2. California, Southern — Social life and customs. I. T.
F867.S8 1985   979.4/9 19   LC 84-19093   ISBN 0195034899

Stewart, George Rippey, 1895-.   • **3.8616**
Ordeal by hunger; the story of the Donner Party. — New ed., with a suppl. and 3 accounts by survivors. — Boston: Houghton Mifflin, 1960. 394 p.: illus.; 22 cm. 1. Donner Party I. T.
F868.N5 S7 1960   978   LC 60-9361

Muir, John, 1838-1914.   • **3.8617**
Yosemite and the Sierra Nevada / photographs by Ansel Adams; selections from the works of John Muir; edited by Charlotte E. Mauk. — Boston: Houghton Mifflin, 1948. xix, 132 p.: ill.; 26 cm. 1. Yosemite Valley. 2. Sierra Nevada Mountains. I. Mauk, Charlotte E. II. T.
F868.Y6 M915   LC 49-7030

F869 Cities

Romo, Ricardo.   **3.8618**
East Los Angeles: history of a barrio / Ricardo Romo. — 1st ed. — Austin: University of Texas Press, 1983. xii, 220 p.; 24 cm. 1. Mexican Americans — California — East Los Angeles — Social conditions. 2. Mexican Americans — California — East Los Angeles — History. 3. East Los Angeles (Calif.) — Social conditions. 4. East Los Angeles (Calif.) — History. I. T.
F869.E18 R65 1983   305.8/6872/079494 19   LC 82-10891   ISBN 0292720408

Mann, Ralph.   **3.8619**
After the Gold Rush: society in Grass Valley and Nevada City, California, 1849–1870 / Ralph Mann. — Stanford, Calif.: Stanford University Press, 1982. xv, 302 p.: map; 23 cm. Includes index. 1. Grass Valley (Calif.) — History. 2. Nevada City (Calif.) — History. 3. California — Gold discoveries I. T.
F869.G76 M3 1982   979.4/37 19   LC 81-52825   ISBN 0804711364

Fogelson, Robert M.   • **3.8620**
The fragmented metropolis: Los Angeles, 1850–1930, by Robert M. Fogelson. Cambridge, Harvard University Press, 1967. xv, 362 p. illus., maps, plans, ports. 25 cm. (A publication of the Joint Center for Urban Studies of the

Massachusetts Institute of Technology and Harvard University) 1. Los Angeles (Calif.) — History I. T.
F869.L8 F6   917.94/93/034   *LC* 67-20876

Writers' Program (California)   • **3.8621**
Los Angeles: a guide to the city and its environs / compiled by workers of the Writers' Program of the Work Projects Administration in Southern California. — Completely revised. 2d ed. New York: Hastings House, c1951. liv, 441 p.: ill., maps; 21 cm. (American guide series) 'Sponsored by the Los Angeles County Board of Supervisors.' 1. Los Angeles (Calif.) — Description — Guide-books. I. T.
F869.L8 W85 1951   *LC* 51-11827

Modell, John.   **3.8622**
The economics and politics of racial accommodation: the Japanese of Los Angeles, 1900–1942 / John Modell. — Urbana: University of Illinois Press, c1977. xii, 201 p.; 24 cm. Based on the author's thesis, Columbia University, 1969. 1. Japanese Americans — California — Los Angeles — History. 2. Japanese Americans — California — Los Angeles — Social conditions. 3. Japanese Americans — California — Los Angeles — Economic conditions. 4. Los Angeles (Calif.) — Race relations. I. T.
F869.L89 J35   301.45/19/56079494   *LC* 77-6749   *ISBN* 0252006224

Tolbert, Emory J., 1946-.   **3.8623**
The UNIA and Black Los Angeles: ideology and community in the American Garvey movement / by Emory J. Tolbert. — Los Angeles: Center for Afro-American Studies, University of California, c1980. 138 p.: ill.; 24 cm. (Afro-American culture and society. v. 3) Includes index. 1. Garvey, Marcus, 1887-1940. 2. Universal Negro Improvement Association. 3. Afro-Americans — California — Los Angeles — Social conditions. 4. Afro-Americans — California — Los Angeles — Race identity. 5. Los Angeles (Calif.) — Race relations. I. T. II. Series.
F869.L89 N38   305.8/96073/079494   *LC* 80-18054   *ISBN* 0934934045

Twain, Mark, 1835-1910.   • **3.8624**
Mark Twain's San Francisco. Edited by Bernard Taper. New York, McGraw-Hill [1963] xxvi, 263 p. illus., port. 26 cm. Selections from his contributions to newspapers and journals, 1863-1866. 1. San Francisco (Calif.) — Social life and customs. I. Taper, Bernard. ed. II. T.
F869.S3C6   917.9461   *LC* 63-19737

Lotchin, Roger W.   **3.8625**
San Francisco, 1846-1856: from hamlet to city [by] Roger W. Lotchin. New York, Oxford University Press, 1974. xxii, 406 p. illus. 22 cm. (The Urban life in America series) 1. San Francisco (Calif.) — History. I. T.
F869.S3 L82   917.94/61/034   *LC* 73-90351   *ISBN* 0195017498

Nee, Victor, 1945-.   **3.8626**
Longtime Californ': a documentary study of an American Chinatown / by Victor G. and Brett de Bary Nee. — [1st ed.] — New York: Pantheon Books, [1973] xxvii, 410 p.; 22 cm. 1. Chinese Americans — California — San Francisco. 2. Chinatown (San Francisco, Calif.) I. Nee, Brett de Bary, 1943- joint author. II. T.
F869.S3 N27   301.45/19/51079461   *LC* 72-12389   *ISBN* 039446138X

Writers' Program. California.   • **3.8627**
San Francisco, the bay and its cities / comp. by workers of the Writers' Program of the Work Projects Administration in northern California. Sponsored by the City and County of San Francisco. [Rev. 2d ed.] New York: Hastings House, 1947. xvii, 531 p.: plates, maps; 21 cm. (American guide series.) 1. San Francisco (Calif.) — Description — Guide-books. 2. San Francisco Bay Area (Calif.) I. T. II. Series.
F869.S3 W95 1947   917.9461   *LC* 47-11536

Senkewicz, Robert M., 1947-.   **3.8628**
Vigilantes in gold rush San Francisco / Robert M. Senkewicz. — Stanford, Calif.: Stanford University Press, 1985. ix, 272 p.: ill.; 23 cm. Includes index. 1. Frontier and pioneer life — California — San Francisco. 2. Vigilance committees — California — History — 19th century. 3. San Francisco (Calif.) — History. 4. California — Gold discoveries I. T.
F869.S357 S46 1985   979.4/6104 19   *LC* 83-40284   *ISBN* 0804712301

Cinel, Dino.   **3.8629**
From Italy to San Francisco: the immigrant experience / Dino Cinel. — Stanford, Calif: Stanford University Press, 1982. viii, 347 p.: ill.; 23 cm. Includes index. 1. Italian Americans — California — San Francisco — History. 2. Italians — California — San Francisco — History. 3. San Francisco (Calif.) — History. I. T.
F869.S39 I82 1982   979.4/6100451 19   *LC* 80-53224   *ISBN* 0804711178

Daniels, Douglas Henry.   **3.8630**
Pioneer urbanites: a social and cultural history of Black San Francisco / Douglas Henry Daniels; foreword by Nathan Huggins. — Philadelphia: Temple University Press, 1980. 228 p. 1. Afro-Americans — California — San Francisco — History. 2. San Francisco (Calif.) — History. I. T.
F869.S39 N43   F869S39 N43.   979.4/6100496073   *LC* 79-25602   *ISBN* 0877221693

Camarillo, Albert.   **3.8631**
Chicanos in a changing society: from Mexican pueblos to American barrios in Santa Barbara and southern California, 1848–1930 / Albert Camarillo. — Cambridge, Mass.: Harvard University Press, 1979. xiii, 326 p.; 22 cm. Includes index. 1. Mexican Americans — California — Santa Barbara — History. 2. Mexican Americans — California, Southern — History. 3. Santa Barbara (Calif.) — History. 4. California, Southern — History. I. T.
F869.S45 C25   979.4/9/0046872   *LC* 79-10687   *ISBN* 0674113950

Writers' Program. California.   • **3.8632**
Santa Barbara; a guide to the Channel city and its environs. New York, Hastings House, 1941. xviii, 206 p. illus., plates. 21 cm. 1. Santa Barbara (Calif.) — Description. 2. Santa Barbara County (Calif.) — Description and travel — Guide-books. I. T.
F869.S45 W86   *LC* 41-46110

Myerhoff, Barbara G.   **3.8633**
Number our days / Barbara Myerhoff. — 1st ed. — New York: Dutton, c1978. xiii, 306 p.; 22 cm. Includes index. 1. Jews — California — Venice — Social life and customs. 2. Social work with the aged — California — Venice. 3. Aged — California — Venice. 4. Venice (Los Angeles, Calif.) — Social life and customs. I. T.
F869.V36 M9 1978   979.4/94   *LC* 78-8565   *ISBN* 0525169555

F870 Japanese Population

Daniels, Roger.   • **3.8634**
The politics of prejudice: the anti–Japanese movement in California, and the struggle for Japanese exclusion. — Berkeley: University of California Press, 1962. ix, 165 p.; 24 cm. (University of California Publications in history, v. 71) 1. Japanese Americans — California. 2. Race discrimination — California. I. T.
F870.J3D17 E173.C15 vol. 71   323.1/19/56073   *LC* 62-63248

F871–900 OREGON. WASHINGTON

Federal Writers' Project.   • **3.8635**
The Oregon trail; the Missouri River to the Pacific Ocean. Compiled and written by the Federal Writers' Project of the Works Progress Administration. New York, Hastings House. St. Clair Shores, Mich., Scholarly Press [1972? c1939] xii, 244 p. illus. 21 cm. (American guide series.) 'Sponsored by Oregon Trail Memorial Association, inc.' 1. Oregon Trail 2. West (U.S.) — Description and travel — Guide-books. I. T. II. Series.
F874.3.F4 1972   917.8/04   *LC* 70-145012   *ISBN* 0403012902

Dodds, Gordon B. (Gordon Barlow), 1932-.   **3.8636**
Oregon: a bicentennial history / Gordon B. Dodds. — New York: Norton, c1977. xiv, 240 p., [8] leaves of plates: ill.; 22 cm. (The States and the Nation series) Includes index. 1. Oregon — History I. T.
F876.D6   979.5   *LC* 77-9080   *ISBN* 0393056325

Merk, Frederick, 1887-.   • **3.8637**
The Oregon question: essays in Anglo–American diplomacy and politics. — Cambridge: Belknap Press of Harvard University Press, 1967. xiv, 427 p.: map; 25 cm. 1. Oregon question 2. Northwest boundary of the United States 3. United States — Foreign relations — Great Britain 4. Great Britain — Foreign relations — United States I. T.
F880 M537   *LC* 67-14345

Writers' Program (Oregon)   • **3.8638**
Oregon, end of the trail. Rev. ed. with added material by Howard McKinley Corning. Portland: Binfords & Mort [1951, c1940] xxxii, 549 p.: ill.; 22 cm. (American guide series.) Map on lining paper. 1. Oregon. 2. Oregon — Description and travel — Guide-books. I. Corning, Howard McKinley, 1896- II. T. III. Series.
F881.W76 1951   917.95   *LC* 52-11474

Toll, William.   **3.8639**
The making of an ethnic middle class: Portland Jewry over four generations / William Toll. — Albany: State University of New York Press, c1982. xii, 242 p.: ill.; 24 cm. 1. Jews — Oregon — Portland — History. 2. Middle classes — Oregon — Portland. 3. Portland (Or.) — Ethnic relations. I. T.
F884.P89 J57 1982   305.8/924/079549 19   *LC* 82-655   *ISBN* 0873956095

Avery, Mary Williamson, 1907-.   • **3.8640**
History and government of the State of Washington. Seattle, University of Washington Press, 1961. 583 p. illus. 23 cm. Part 2 previously published separately under title: Government of the State of Washington. 1. Washington (State) — History 2. Washington (State) — Politics and government I. T.
F891.A8   *LC* 61-8211

Clark, Norman H.   **3.8641**
Washington, a bicentennial history / Norman H. Clark. — New York: Norton, c1976. xix, 204 p., [8] leaves of plates: ill.; 22 cm. (The States and the Nation series) Includes index. 1. Washington (State) — History I. T.
F891.C57   979.7   *LC* 76-18284   *ISBN* 0393055876

Writers' Program (Wash.)   • **3.8642**
The New Washington: a guide to the Evergreen State / compiled by workers of the Writers' Program of the Work Projects Administration in the state of Washington; sponsored by the Washington State Historical Society. Rev. ed. / with added material by Howard McKinley Corning. Portland, Or.: Binfords & Mort, 1950, c1941. xxx, 687 p., [32] leaves of plates: ill., maps; 21 cm. (American guide series.) First ed. published in 1941 under title: Washington, a guide to the Evergreen State. 1. Washington (State). 2. Washington (State) — Description and travel — Guide-books. I. Corning, Howard McKinley, 1896- II. T. III. Series.
F891.W9 1950   *LC* 51-3893

Wood, Robert L.   **3.8643**
Men, mules, and mountains: Lieutenant O'Neil's Olympic expeditions / by Robert L. Wood. — Seattle: The Mountaineers, 1976. xx, 483 p., [11] leaves of plates: ill.; 21 cm. 1. O'Neil, Joseph Patrick, 1862-1938. 2. Mountaineering — Washington (State) — Olympic Mountains. 3. Olympic Mountains (Wash.) I. T.
F897.O5 W626 1976   917.97/94/0440924   *LC* 76-15458   *ISBN* 0916890430

F901–951 ALASKA

Bancroft, Hubert Howe, 1832-1918.   • **3.8644**
History of Alaska, 1730–1885; with a new introd. by Ernest Gruening. New York, Antiquarian Press, 1959. xxxviii, 755 p. maps (part fold.) 24 cm. 'Authorities quoted': p. xxii—xxxviii. 1. Alaska — History I. T.
F904.B3   *LC* A 62-8742

Hunt, William R.   **3.8645**
Alaska, a Bicentennial history / William R. Hunt. — New York: Norton, c1976. xiv, 200 p., [8] leaves of plates: ill.; 22 cm. (The States and the Nation series) Includes index. 1. Alaska — History I. T.
F904.H84   979.8   *LC* 76-44422   *ISBN* 039305604X

Gibson, James R.   **3.8646**
Imperial Russia in frontier America: the changing geography of supply of Russian America, 1784–1867 / James R. Gibson; cartographer, Miklos Pinther. — New York: Oxford University Press, 1976. x, 257 p.: ill.; 24 cm. (The Andrew H. Clark series in the historical geography of North America) Includes index. 1. Rossiĭsko-amerikanskaia kompaniia. 2. Food supply — Alaska. 3. Alaska — History — To 1867 I. T. II. Series.
F907.G52   F907 G52.   979.8/02   *LC* 74-21820

James, James Alton, 1864-1962.   **3.8647**
The first scientific exploration of Russian America and the purchase of Alaska / by James Alton James. — Evanston: Northwestern University, 1942. xii, 276 p.: ill., map. — (Northwestern University studies in the social sciences; no. 4) 1. Kennicott, Robert, 1835-1866. 2. Bannister, Henry M. (Henry Martyn), 1844-1920. 3. Alaska — Description and travel 4. United States — Exploring expeditions I. T. II. Series.
F907.J3   *LC* 42-50931

Federal Writers' Project.   • **3.8648**
A guide to Alaska, last American frontier / by Merle Colby, Federal writers' project .... New York: The Macmillan co., 1945. lxv, 427 p.: ill., plates, maps (part fold., 1 in pocket); 21 cm. (American guide series) Maps on lining-papers. The plates are in eight groups, each preceded by half-title not included in paging. 1. Alaska. 2. Alaska — Description and travel — Guide-books. I. Colby, Merle Estes, 1902-1969. II. T.
F909.F45   917.98   *LC* 39-27616

Green, Lewis, 1925-.   **3.8649**
The boundary hunters: surveying the 141st Meridian and the Alaska Panhandle / Lewis Green. — Vancouver: University of British Columbia Press, c1982. xii, 214 p., [24] p. of plates: ill.; 24 cm. Includes index. 1. Surveying — Yukon Territory — History. 2. Surveying — British Columbia — History. 3. Surveying — Alaska — History. 4. Canada — Boundaries — Alaska. 5. Alaska — Boundaries — Canada. I. T.
F912.B7 G79 1982   979.8/03 19   *LC* 82-183884   *ISBN* 0774801506

Berton, Pierre, 1920-.   • **3.8650**
The Klondike fever; the life and death of the last great gold rush. New York, Knopf, 1959. 457 p. illus. 22 cm. Rev. ed. published in 1972 under title: Klondike; the last great gold rush. 1. Klondike River Valley (Yukon) — Gold discoveries I. T.
F931.B49   971.21   *LC* 58-9666

F970 HAWAII: SEE DU620–629

F1001–1006 REFERENCE WORKS

Canadian annual review.   • **3.8651**
1960-. [Toronto] University of Toronto Press, 1960-. v.; 25 cm. 1. Canada — Yearbooks. 2. Canada — Politics and government — 1945- — Yearbooks. I. Saywell, John T., 1929- ed.
F1001.C215   *LC* 61-3380

Bissell, Claude Thomas ed.   • **3.8652**
Our living tradition: seven Canadians. Toronto: Published in association with Carleton University by University of Toronto P., 1957. 149p. "Given as public lectures at Carleton University." 1. Canada — Biography. I. T.
F1005.B586   920.071   *LC* A58-526

Dictionary of Canadian biography.   • **3.8653**
Toronto: University of Toronto Press, 1966-   . v.; 26 cm. Added t. p. in English and French. Issued also in French. To be complete in 24 v. 1. Canada — Biography.
F1005.D49   920/.071 19   *LC* 66-31909   *ISBN* 0802033199

The Macmillan dictionary of Canadian biography, by W.   • **3.8654**
Stewart Wallace.
3d ed., rev. and enl. London, Macmillan; New York, St. Martin's, 1963. 822 p. 25 cm. 'Canadians ... who died before 1961.' 1. Canada — Biography. I. Wallace, W. Stewart (William Stewart), 1884-1970. ed.
FC25.W17 1963   F1005.D5 1963.   *LC* 64-10158

Encyclopedia Canadiana. [Editor–in–chief; John E. Robbins]   **3.8655**
Ottawa, Canadiana co., [c1960] 10 v. illus. (part col.) ports., maps (part col.) 27 cm. 1. Canada — Dictionaries and encyclopedias. I. Title: Canadiana.
F1006.E625   917.1   *LC* 60-50632

Myers, Jay, 1949-.   **3.8656**
The Fitzhenry & Whiteside book of Canadian facts and dates / Jay Myers. — Markham, Ont.: Fitzhenry & Whiteside, c1986. 354 p.; 23 cm. Includes indexes. 1. Canada — History — Chronology. 2. Canada — History — Miscellanea. I. T.
F1006.M9x   971/.002/02 19   *ISBN* 0889025843

F1013–1021.2 DESCRIPTION. CIVILIZATION

Preston, Richard Arthur.   **3.8657**
For friends at home: a Scottish emigrant's letters from Canada, California, and the Cariboo, 1844–1864 / edited by Richard Arthur Preston. — Montreal: McGill-Queen's University Press, 1975 (c1974). xii, 338 p.: ill.; 20 cm. Consists primarily of a diary and letters written by J. Thomson; also includes letters written to him or about him. 1. Thomson, James, 1823-1895. 2. Canada — Description and travel — 1763-1867 3. California — Gold discoveries 4. Cariboo District — Gold discoveries. I. T.
F1013.T45   917.1/04/2   *LC* 73-79501   *ISBN* 0773501479

Berton, Pierre, 1920-.   • **3.8658**
The mysterious North / by Pierre Berton. — New York: Knopf, 1956. xiii, 245, xiv p.: ill.; 22 cm. Includes index. 1. Northwest Territories I. T.
F1015.B49   917.1   *LC* 55-9272

Hutchison, Bruce, 1901-.   • **3.8659**
The unknown country: Canada and her people / by Bruce Hutchison. — New York: Coward-McCann, c1942. x, 386 p.: ill., map; 22 cm. 1. National characteristics, Canadian 2. Canada — Description and travel I. T.
F1015.H9x   *LC* 42-3124

Notman, William.   • **3.8660**
Portrait of a period; a collection of Notman photographs, 1856-1915, edited by J. Russell Harper and Stanley Triggs, with an introduction by Edgar Andrew Collard. — Montreal: McGill University Press, 1967. 1 v.: illus.; 35 cm.

1. Canada — Description and travel — Views. I. Harper, J. Russell. ed. II. Triggs, Stanley. ed. III. T.
F1015.N6   779/.9/9171   *LC* 67-29772

Canadian Association of Geographers.   • **3.8661**
Canada: a geographical interpretation. Prepared under the auspices of the Canadian Association of Geographers and edited by John Warkentin. — Toronto; London [etc.]: Methuen, 1968. xvi, 608 p.: illus. (part col.), maps (part col.), port.; 25 cm. Part of illustrative matter in pocket. Updated French ed. published under title: Le Canada: une interprétation géographique. 1. Canada — Description and travel — 1951- I. Warkentin, John, 1928- ed. II. T.
F1016.C28   917.1   *LC* 68-82888

Canadian regions: a geography of Canada / editor, Donald F.   • **3.8662**
Putnam.
7th ed. — Toronto: Dent, 1965. ix, 601 p.: ill., maps. Includes index. 1. Canada — Description and travel — 1951- I. Putnam, Donald F., 1903-1977.
F1016.P8 1965   917.1   *LC* 67-95396

Bailey, Alfred Goldsworthy.   • **3.8663**
The conflict of European and Eastern Algonkian cultures 1504–1700: a study in Canadian civilization. — [2. ed. — Toronto]: University of Toronto Press, [1969] xxiii, 218 p.; 26 cm. 1. Indians of North America — Canada 2. Algonquian Indians 3. French-Canadians 4. Canada — Civilization I. T.
F1021.B25 1969   917.1/03/1   *LC* 78-434310   *ISBN* 0802015069

Lower, Arthur Reginald Marsden, 1889-.   • **3.8664**
Canadians in the making: a social history of Canada / by Arthur R. M. Lower. — Toronto: Longmans Canada, 1958. xxiv, 475 p. [4] leaves of plates: ill. graphs. 1. National characteristics, Canadian — History. 2. Canada — History I. T.
F1021.L67   *LC* 59-818

McKillop, A. B.   **3.8665**
A disciplined intelligence: critical inquiry and Canadian thought in the Victorian era / A. B. McKillop. — Montreal: McGill-Queen's University Press, c1979. xii, 287 p.; 24 cm. Includes index. 1. Philosophy — Canada — History — 19th century. 2. Religious thought — Canada. 3. Canada — Intellectual life. I. T.
F1021.M346   971.05   *LC* 80-458973   *ISBN* 0773503439

Frye, Northrop.   **3.8666**
Divisions on a ground: essays on Canadian culture / Northrop Frye; edited, with a preface, by James Polk. — Toronto: Anansi, c1982. 199 p.; 23 cm. 1. Canadian literature — History and criticism — Addresses, essays, lectures. 2. Education, Higher — Canada — Addresses, essays, lectures. 3. Canada — Civilization — 1945- — Addresses, essays, lectures. I. Polk, James. II. T.
F1021.2.F79 1982   971 19   *LC* 82-180003   *ISBN* 0887840930

F1024–1140 HISTORY

Berger, Carl.   **3.8667**
The writing of Canadian history: aspects of English–Canadian historical writing, 1900–1970 / Carl Berger. Toronto: Oxford University Press, 1976. x, 300 p.; 24 cm. Includes index. 1. Canada — Historiography. I. T.
F1024.B47   971/.007/2   *LC* 76-382537   *ISBN* 0195402529

Brebner, John Bartlet.   • **3.8668**
Canada, a modern history / by J. Bartlet Brebner. — New ed., rev. and enl. / by Donald C. Masters. — Ann Arbor: University of Michigan Press, 1970. xvii, 570, xviii p.: maps.; 25 cm. — (The University of Michigan history of the modern world) 1. Canada — History I. Masters, Donald Campbell, 1908- II. Masters, Donald C., 1908- III. T. IV. Series.
F1026.B84 1970   971   *LC* 72-107983   *ISBN* 0472070916

Careless, J. M. S. (James Maurice Stockford), 1919-.   • **3.8669**
Canada, a story of challenge, by J. M. S. Careless. — [Rev. and enl. ed.]. — New York: St. Martin's Press, [1964, c1963] xiii, 444 p.: illus., maps.; 20 cm. 1. Canada — History I. T.
F1026.C33 1964   971   *LC* 64-20638

Clark, S. D. (Samuel Delbert), 1910-.   • **3.8670**
Movements of political protest in Canada, 1640–1840. Toronto, University of Toronto Press, 1959. 518 p.; 24 cm. — (Social Credit in Alberta, 9) 1. Canada — Politics and government — To 1763 2. Canada — Politics and government — 1763-1867 I. T. II. Series.
F1026.C6   LC 60-29

Creighton, Donald Grant.   • **3.8671**
The empire of the St. Lawrence. Boston, Houghton Mifflin, 1958. 441 p. illus. 24 cm. First published in 1937 under title: The commercial empire of the St. Lawrence, 1760-1850 1. Canada — History 2. Canada — Commerce 3. Saint Lawrence River — Commerce. 4. Canada — Relations — United States 5. United States — Relations — Canada I. T.
F1026.C74 1958   971.4   LC 59-587

Creighton, Donald Grant.   • **3.8672**
A history of Canada, Dominion of the North. — Rev. and enl. ed. — Boston: Houghton Mifflin, 1958. 619 p.: ill., maps. First ed. and new Canadian ed. published in 1944 under title: Dominion of the North. 1. Canada — History I. T. II. Title: Dominion of the North.
F1026.C75 1958   LC 58-5741

Creighton, Donald Grant.   • **3.8673**
The story of Canada, by Donald Creighton. — [Rev. ed.]. — Toronto: Macmillan of Canada, [1971] 319 p.: maps.; 23 cm. 1. Canada — History I. T.
F1026.C76 1971   971   LC 72-178573

McInnis, Edgar, 1899-.   • **3.8674**
Canada; a political and social history. — 3d ed. — Toronto: Holt, Rinehart and Winston of Canada, [1969] xxii, 761 p.: illus., maps, ports.; 24 cm. 1. Canada — History I. T.
F1026.M15 1969   971   LC 73-453745

Martin, Chester Bailey, 1882-1958.   • **3.8675**
Foundations of Canadian nationhood. Toronto, University of Toronto Press, 1955. xx, 554 p. illus., maps. 1. Canada — History I. T.
FC163.M38   F1026.M38.

Morton, W. L. (William Lewis), 1908-.   • **3.8676**
The kingdom of Canada: a general history from earliest time / W.L. Morton. — Toronto: McClelland and Stewart, 1963. 556 p.: ill.; 24 cm. 1. Canada — History I. T.
F1026.M74   971   LC 65-73815

Underhill, Frank Hawkins, 1889-.   • **3.8677**
In search of Canadian liberalism. Toronto, Macmillan Co. of Canada, 1960 [i.e. 1961] xiv, 282 p. 23 cm. 'Articles written ... over the last thirty years.' Appendix (p. 271-274): A list of some other writings by Frank H. Underhill on various topics. 1. Liberalism 2. Canada — Politics and government — Addresses, essays, lectures. I. T.
F1026.U5   971.06   LC A 61-237

Winks, Robin W.   **3.8678**
The relevance of Canadian history: U.S. and imperial perspectives / by Robin W. Winks. — Toronto: Macmillan of Canada, c1979, vii, 99 p.; 24 cm. — (The Joanne Goodman lectures; 1977) 1. Canada — History — Addresses, essays, lectures. 2. United States — Territorial expansion — Addresses, essays, lectures. I. T.
F1026.6.W56   971   LC 79-315846   ISBN 0770517889

✓ **Armstrong, Elizabeth Howard, 1898-.**   • **3.8679**
The crisis of Quebec, 1914–18 / by Elizabeth H. Armstrong. — New York: Columbia University Press, 1937. xii, 270 p.; 24 cm. 1. French-Canadians 2. World War, 1914-1918 — Quebec (Province) 3. World War, 1914-1918 — Canada. 4. Nationalism — Canada. I. T.
F1027.A74   LC 37-22241

Le Canada français d'aujourd'hui: études rassemblées par la   • **3.8680**
société royale du Canada / Léopold Lamontagne, éd..
[Toronto]: Publié pour le compte de la société par University of Toronto Press et les Presses de l'Université Laval, 1970. viii, 161 p.; 24 cm. — (Société royale du Canada. Collection Studia varia; 14) 1. Canadian, French speaking. 2. Québec (Province) — Civilization. I. Lamontgne, Léopold. II. Royal Society of Canada.
F1027.C233   FC2919.C35.   LC 78-489431

Chaput, Marcel, 1918-.   • **3.8681**
Why I am a separatist. Translated by Robert A. Taylor. — Toronto, Ryerson Press [1962] 101 p. 21 cm. — (An encounter book, 3) 1. French-Canadians 2. Nationalism — Quebec (Province) I. T.
F1027.C443   LC 63-4553

Cook, Ramsay.   • **3.8682**
Canada and the French–Canadian question / Ramsay Cook. — Toronto: Macmillan of Canada, c1966. 219 p. Nine essays, most of which were previously published in various periodicals. 1. Canada — English-French relations

2. Québec (Province) — History — Autonomy and independence movements I. T.
F1027.C76   301.29/71   LC 67-79220   ISBN 0770500544

Finlay, John L., 1939-.   **3.8683**
Canada in the North Atlantic triangle: two centuries of social change / by John L. Finlay. — Toronto: Oxford University Press, 1975. 343 p.; 23 cm. Includes index. 1. Canada — History 2. United States — History 3. Great Britain — History — Modern period, 1485- I. T.
F1027.F5   971   LC 76-352800   ISBN 0195402375

Miller, J. R. (James Rodger), 1943-.   **3.8684**
Equal rights: the Jesuits' Estates Act controversy / J. R. Miller. — Montreal: McGill-Queen's University Press, c1979. xi, 223 p.: ill.; 24 cm. Includes index. 1. Jesuits — Québec (Province). 2. Church lands — Québec (Province) — History. 3. Canada — English-French relations 4. Canada — Politics and government — 1867-1914 I. T.
F1027.M57   971.05 19   LC 79-308004   ISBN 0773503021

Monet, Jacques.   • **3.8685**
The last cannon shot; a study of French–Canadian nationalism 1837–1850. — [Toronto]: University of Toronto Press, [c1969] x, 422 p.; 24 cm. 1. French-Canadians 2. Canada — English-French relations — History. 3. Canada — Politics and government — 19th century I. T.
F1027.M66   320.9/71   LC 70-455781   ISBN 0802052118

One country or two? Edited by R. M. Burns. With an introd.   **3.8686**
by John J. Deutsch.
Montreal: McGill-Queen's University Press, 1971. vii, 287 p.; 21 cm. 1. Canada — English-French relations — Addresses, essays, lectures. I. Burns, Ronald M. ed.
F1027.O5   301.29/71/0714   LC 76-174566   ISBN 0773501045

Quinn, Herbert Furlong, 1910-.   • **3.8687**
The Union nationale: a study in Quebec nationalism / Herbert F. Quinn. — [Toronto]: University of Toronto Press, [1963] ix, 249p.; 24cm. — (Canadian University paperbooks; 38) 1. Union nationale (Political party) 2. Nationalism — Québec (Province) 3. Québec (Province) — History — Autonomy and independence movements I. T. II. Series.
F 1027.Q86   FC2925.2.Q56 1963.   329.971   LC 63-5826   ISBN 0802060404

Rioux, Marcel. ed.   • **3.8688**
French–Canadian society, edited, and with an introd., by Marcel Rioux and Yves Martin. [Toronto] McClelland and Stewart [c1964-. v. 19 cm. (The Carleton library, no. 18-) Bibliographical footnotes. 1. French-Canadians 2. French in Canada. 3. Québec (Province) — Civilization. I. Martin, Yves, 1929- joint ed. II. T.
F1027.R53   309.1714   LC 66-265

Silver, A. I.   **3.8689**
The French–Canadian idea of Confederation, 1864–1900 / A.I. Silver. — Toronto; Buffalo: University of Toronto Press, c1982. ix, 257 p.; 24 cm. Includes index. 1. French-Canadians — Attitudes — History — 19th century. 2. Canada — English-French relations 3. Canada — History — 1867- I. T.
F1027.S562 1982   971/.004114 19   LC 82-147051   ISBN 0802055575

✓ **Vallières, Pierre.**   • **3.8690**
[Nègres blancs d'Amérique. English] White niggers of America. Translated by Joan Pinkham. Toronto, McClelland and Stewart [c1971] 278 p. 22 cm. Translation of Nègres blancs d'Amérique: autobiographie précoce d'un terroriste québécois. 1. French-Canadians 2. Québec (Province) — History — Autonomy and independence movements 3. Québec (Province) — Social conditions. I. T.
F1027.V313 1971b   322.4/2/0924 B   LC 72-180519   ISBN 0771086709

Wade, Mason, 1913-.   • **3.8691**
Canadian dualism: studies of French–English relations. — [Toronto]: University of Toronto Press, [1960]. xxv, 427 p.: diagrs., tables.; 24 cm. 'Edited ... for a committee of the Social Science Research Council of Canada under the chairmanship of Jean-C. Falardeau.' Added t.p. in French. English or French. 1. Nationalism — Canada. 2. French-Canadians 3. French in Canada. 4. Canada — Civilization — Addresses, essays, lectures. I. Social Science Research Council of Canada. Committee on Biculturalism. II. T. III. Title: La dualité canadienne.
F1027.W14   FC97.W24.   917.1   LC A61-3019

Wade, Mason, 1913-.   • **3.8692**
The French–Canadian outlook: a brief account of the unknown North Americans / by Mason Wade. — New York: Viking Press, 1946, t.p. 1947. 192 p. 1. French-Canadians 2. Canada — History I. T.
F1027.W15   LC 46-25235

Wade, Mason, 1913-.   • 3.8693
The French Canadians; 1760–1967. — Revised edition. — Toronto; London: Macmillan; New York: St. Martin's Press, 1968. 2 v.: illus.; 23 cm. 1. French-Canadians 2. Canada — History I. T.
F1027.W165   917.14/03   LC 68-16861

F1027.5 Nationalism. French Canadians

Nicholson, Norman L.   3.8694
The boundaries of the Canadian Confederation / Norman L. Nicholson. — Toronto: Macmillan of Canada; [Ottawa]: Institute of Canadian Studies, Carleton University, 1979. x, 252 p.: maps; 19 cm. — (The Carleton library; no. 115) Rev. and enl. ed. of the author's The boundaries of Canada, its provinces and territories, published in 1954. Includes index. 1. Canada — Boundaries. I. T.
F1027.5.N52 1979   911/.71   LC 80-450098   ISBN 0770517420

F1028–1029.5 Military and Diplomatic History

Morton, Desmond.   3.8695
Canada and war: a military and political history / Desmond Morton. — Toronto: Butterworths, 1981. vii, 228 p.; 23 cm. — (Political issues in their historical perspective.) Includes index. 1. Canada — History, Military. 2. Canada — Politics and government — 1867- I. T. II. Series.
F1028.M67   971.06 19   LC 81-173424   ISBN 0409852406

Canada in world affairs.   • 3.8696
[v.1]- 1941-. Toronto: Oxford University Press. v.; 23 cm. 1. Canada — Foreign relations — Yearbooks. I. Canadian Institute of Internatonal Affairs.
F1029.C3   LC 56-2289

Duke University. Commonwealth-Studies Center.   • 3.8697
The growth of Canadian policies in external affairs / Hugh L. Keenleyside [et al.]. — Durham, N.C.: Duke University Press, c1960. x, 174 p. — (Duke University Commonwealth Studies publications; no.14) 1. Canada — Foreign relations I. Keenleyside, Hugh Llewellyn, 1898- II. T.
F1029.D8   LC 60-13605

Glazebrook, G. P. de T. (George Parkin de Twenebroker), 1899-.   • 3.8698
A history of Canadian external relations / G.P. deT. Glazebrook. — Toronto: Oxford University Press, 1950. vii, 449 p. — part 1, is a reprinting of the author's Canadian external relations; an historical study to 1914. 1. Canada — Foreign relations 2. Canada — History I. T.
F1029.G55 1950   LC 50-4723 rev

Morton, W. L. (William Lewis), 1908-.   • 3.8699
The Canadian identity [by] W. L. Morton. 2d ed. [Madison] University of Wisconsin Press [1972] xi, 162 p. map. 22 cm. 1. Canada — Foreign relations — 1945- — Addresses, essays, lectures. 2. Canada — History — Addresses, essays, lectures. I. T.
F1029.M6 1972b   327.71   LC 72-194373   ISBN 0299061302 ISBN 0299061345

Stacey, C. P. (Charles Perry), 1906-.   3.8700
Canada and the age of conflict: a history of Canadian external policies / C. P. Stacey. — Toronto: Macmillan of Canada, c1981. 491 p.: ill. 1. Canada — Foreign relations I. T.
F1029.S73   327.71   LC 78-306832   ISBN 0770514286

Tennyson, Brian Douglas.   3.8701
Canadian relations with South Africa: a diplomatic history / Brian Douglas Tennyson. — Washington, D.C.: University Press of America, c1982. xvi, 238 p.; 22 cm. Revision of the author's thesis (Ph.D.)—University of London. Includes index. 1. Canada — Foreign relations — South Africa. 2. South Africa — Foreign relations — Canada. I. T.
F1029.5.S6 T46 1982   327.71068 19   LC 81-43774   ISBN 0819126330

F1030–1034 History, by Period

F1030–1030.9 NEW FRANCE (1603-1763)

Eccles, W. J. (William John)   • 3.8702
Canada under Louis XIV, 1663–1701 / W. J. Eccles. — Toronto: McClelland and Stewart, 1964. xii, 275 p.: ill., facisms, maps, ports. (Canadian centenary series.) 1. Canada — History — 1663-1713 (New France) I. T. II. Series.
F1030.E3   FC350.E25.   971.016   LC 64-56760

Eccles, W. J. (William John)   • 3.8703
The Canadian frontier, 1534–1760 [by] W. J. Eccles. New York, Holt, Rinehart and Winston [1969] xv, 234 p. illus., maps, ports. 24 cm. (Histories of the American frontier) 1. Canada — History — To 1763 (New France) I. T.
F1030.E312   971.01   LC 70-81783   ISBN 0030818346

Eccles, W. J. (William John)   • 3.8704
Frontenac, the courtier governor / W. J. Eccles. — Toronto: McClelland and Stewart, c1959. ix, 358 p.: map. — (Carleton library. no. 24) 1. Frontenac, Louis de Buade, comte de, 1620-1698 2. Canada — History — To 1763 (New France) I. T. II. Series.
F1030.F9276   LC 59-31011

Parkman, Francis, 1823-1893.   • 3.8705
[Works 1894] Francis Parkman's works. — New library ed. [Boston: Little, Brown, and Company, 1902-03] 12 v.: ill., maps; 21 cm. 1. Canada — History — To 1763 2. United States — History — Colonial period, ca. 1600-1775 3. New France — Discovery and exploration — French. 4. America — Discovery and exploration I. T.
F1030.P24 1902   LC 04-19149

Parkman, Francis, 1823-1893.   • 3.8706
[Selections] The Parkman reader; from the works of Francis Parkman. Selected and edited with an introd. and notes by Samuel Eliot Morison. [1st ed.] Boston, Little, Brown [1955] xv, 533 p. port., maps (1 fold.) 22 cm. 'Selections from ... France and England in North America.' 1. Canada — History — To 1763 (New France) 2. United States — History — Colonial period, ca. 1600-1775 I. T.
F1030.P246   971.01   LC 55-6535

Parkman, Francis, 1823-1893.   • 3.8707
Count Frontenac and New France under Louis XIV / Francis Parkman; with a prefatory note by Oscar Handlin. — Boston: Beacon Press, 1966. xiv, 463 p.: map. — (Beacon paperback; BP222) 1. Canada — History — To 1763 (New France) I. T.
F1030.P267 1966   LC 66-1981

Savelle, Max, 1896-.   • 3.8708
The diplomatic history of the Canadian boundary, 1749–1763. New York, Russell & Russell [1968, c1940] xiv, 172 p. maps. 25 cm. 1. Treaty of Paris (1763) 2. Canada — Boundary. 3. Canada — History — To 1763 (New France) 4. Great Britain — Foreign relations — France. 5. France — Foreign relations — Great Britain. 6. Great Britain — Foreign relations — Spain. 7. Spain — Foreign relations — Great Britain. 8. Great Britain — Colonies — America 9. France — Colonies — America. 10. Spain — Colonies — America. I. T.
F1030.S28 1968   327.71/073   LC 68-27084

Vachon, André, 1933-.   3.8709
[Rêves d'empire. English] Dreams of empire: Canada before 1700 / by André Vachon in collaboration with Victorin Chabot and André Desrosiers; [English translation by John F. Flinn]. — [Ottawa]: Canadian Government Publishing Centre, Supply & Services Canada, 1982. xi, 387 p.: ill. (some col.); 28 cm. — (Records of our history.) Translation of: Rêves d'empire. Includes index. 'Catalogue no. SA2-129/1-1982-1E'—T.p. verso. 1. Canada — History — To 1763 (New France) 2. Canada — History — To 1763 (New France) — Sources. I. Chabot, Victorin. II. Desrosiers, André. III. T. IV. Series.
F1030.V2813 1982   971.01 19   LC 82-202092   ISBN 0660110741

Bishop, Morris, 1893-1973.   • 3.8710
Champlain, the life of fortitude / Morris Bishop. — 1st ed. — New York: Knopf, 1948. 364 p.: ill., maps. 1. Champlain, Samuel de 2. Explorers — Canada — Biography. 3. Canada — History — To 1763 (New France) I. T.
Fl030.1B6   971.01130924   LC 48-8873

Champlain, Samuel de, 1567-1635.   • 3.8711
Voyages of Samuel de Champlain 1604–1618: with a map and two plans / edited by W.L. Grant. — New York: C. Scribner's Sons, 1907. xiii, 377 p., [3] leaves of plates (1 fold.): map, plans; 22 cm. — (Original narratives of early

American history) 1. Indians of North America — Canada 2. New France — Discovery and exploration. 3. America — Discovery and exploration — French. 4. Canada — History — To 1763 (New France) I. Grant, W. L. (William Lawson), 1872-1935 II. T. III. Series.
F1030.1.C494   *LC* 07-22899

Morison, Samuel Eliot, 1887-1976.   • 3.8712
Samuel de Champlain, Father of New France / Samuel Eliot Morison. — [1st ed.]. — Boston: Little, Brown, [1972] xix, 299 p.: illus.; 25 cm. 'An Atlantic Monthly Press book.' 1. Champlain, Samuel de, 1567-1635. 2. Indians of North America — Canada 3. New France — Discovery and exploration. 4. America — Discovery and exploration — French. I. T.
F1030.1.M6   971.01/13/0924   *LC* 71-186963

Parkman, Francis, 1823-1893.   • 3.8713
The discovery of the great West: La Salle / Francis Parkman; edited by William R. Taylor. — New York: Holt, Rinehart and Winston, 1956. xxiii, 354 p.: maps. — (Rinehart editions; 77) 1. La Salle, Robert Cavelier de, 1643-1687 2. New France — Discovery and exploration 3. Mississippi River — Discovery and exploration 4. Canada — History — To 1763 (New France) I. Taylor, William R. II. T.
F1030.5.P225 1956a   973.24   *LC* 56-59238

Jesuits.   • 3.8714
[Letters from missions (North America)] The Jesuit relations and allied documents: travels and explorations of the Jesuit missionaries in North America, 1610–1791 / with an introd. by Reuben Gold Thwaites; selected and edited by Edna Kenton; pref. by George N. Shuster. — New York: Vanguard Press, 1954. liv, 527 p.: ill.; maps; 23 cm. Includes index 1. Jesuits — Missions — North America. 2. New France — Discovery and exploration. 3. Indians of North America — Canada 4. Indians of North America — Missions I. Kenton, Edna. II. T.
F1030.7.Z8965   971.011   *LC* 54-11519

Stanley, George Francis Gilman.   • 3.8715
New France: the last phase, 1744–1760 [by] George F. G. Stanley. — [Toronto]: McClelland and Stewart, [1968] xvi, 320 p.: illus., maps.; 23 1/2 cm. — (Canadian centenary series. 5) 1. Canada — History — To 1763 (New France) I. T. II. Series.
F1030.9.S7   971.01/8   *LC* 68-143124

F1031–1032 1763–1867

Wilson, George Earl, 1891-.   • 3.8716
The life of Robert Baldwin: a study in the struggle for responsible government / by George E. Wilson. — Toronto: Ryerson Press, c1933. vii, 312 p. 'First undertaken as the thesis necessary for ... the degree of doctor of philosophy at Harvard university [1926]'.— Pref. 1. Baldwin, Robert, 1804-1858. 2. Canada — Politics and government — 1841-1867 I. T.
F1032.B22   *LC* 33-36988

Careless, J. M. S., 1919-.   • 3.8717
Brown of the Globe / J.M.S. Careless. — Toronto: Macmillan, 1959-1963. 2 v.: ill., maps, ports. 1. Brown, George. 2. Canada. Parliament. Legislative Assembly — Biography. 3. Globe and Mail (Firm) 4. Lesiglators — Canada — Biography. 5. Journalists — Canada — Biography. I. T.
F1032.B87   *LC* 60-30

Burroughs, Peter.   3.8718
British attitudes towards Canada, 1822–1849. — Scarborough, Ont.: Prentice-Hall of Canada, [1971] vii, 152 p.; 21 cm. — (Canadian historical controversies) 1. Canada — Politics and government — 1763-1867 2. Gt. Brit. — Colonies — Administration. I. T.
F1032.B928   325.3/42/0971   *LC* 70-134455   *ISBN* 0130831476

Burt, Alfred LeRoy, 1888-.   • 3.8719
The old province of Quebec. — New York: Russell & Russell, [1970, c1933] xiii, 551 p.: illus., maps, plans, ports.; 25 cm. 1. Canada — History — 1763-1791 2. Québec (Province) — History I. T.
F1032.B94 1970   971.02   *LC* 70-83856

Careless, J. M. S. (James Maurice Stockford), 1919-.   • 3.8720
Colonists & Canadiens, 1760–1867; edited by J. M. S. Careless. — Toronto: Macmillan of Canada, 1971. ix, 278 p.; 22 cm. 1. Canada — History — 1763-1867 — Addresses, essays, lectures. I. T.
F1032.C277   971.02   *LC* 70-155261

Careless, J. M. S. (James Maurice Stockford), 1919-.   • 3.8721
The union of the Canadas; the growth of Canadian Institutions, 1841–1857 [by] J. M. S. Careless. — Toronto: McClelland and Stewart, [1967] 256 p.: illus., facsims., maps, ports.; 24 cm. — (Canadian centenary series. [10]) 1. Canada — History — 1841-1867 I. T. II. Series.
F1032.C28   971.04   *LC* 68-70117

Confederation: essays by D.G. Creighton [et al.]; introduction by   • 3.8722
Ramsay Cook.
Toronto: University of Toronto Press, c1967. xiii, 118 p.; 23 cm. — (Canadian historical readings; 3) 1. Canada — History — 1841-1867 — Addresses, essays, lectures. 2. Canada — History — Confederation, 1867 I. Creighton, Donald, 1902-1979. II. Cook, Ramsay. III. Series.
F1032.C75   FC474.C65.   *LC* 67-113270   *ISBN* 0802014569

Corey, Albert Bickmore.   • 3.8723
The crisis of 1830–1842 in Canadian–American relations, by Albert B. Corey. — New York: Russell & Russell, [1970] x, 203 p.: maps.; 25 cm. — (Relations of Canada and the United States) 'First published in 1941.' 1. Hunter's Lodges (Secret societies) 2. U.S. — Foreign relations — Canada. 3. Canada — Foreign relations — U.S. 4. Canada — History — Rebellion, 1837-1838 5. U.S. — History — 1815-1861. 6. Northeast boundary of the United States I. T.
F1032.C77 1970   327.71/073   *LC* 77-102483

Coupland, Reginald, 1884-.   • 3.8724
The Quebec act; a study in statesmanship. Oxford, Clarendon press, 1925. 4 p.l., 224 p. 23 cm. 1. Quebec act, 1774. 2. Canada — Politics and government — 1763-1791 I. T.
F1032.C85   *LC* 26-3120

Creighton, Donald Grant.   • 3.8725
The road to Confederation: the emergence of Canada, 1863–1867 / Donald Creighton. — [1st American ed.] Boston: Macmillan, 1965 [c1964] 489 p.: ill.,maps,ports.; 23 cm. 1. Canada — Politics & government — 1841-1867. I. T.
F1032.C9 1965   971.04   *LC* 65-15162

Durham, John George Lambton, 1st Earl of.   • 3.8726
Lord Durham's report: an abridgement of Report on the affairs of British North America / by Lord Durham; edited and with an introd. by Gerald M. Craig. — Toronto: McClelland and Stewart, 1963. 179 p. — (Carleton library. no. 01) 1. Canada — History — Rebellion, 1837-1838 2. Canada — Politics and government — 1791-1841 I. Craig, Gerald M. II. T. III. Series.
F1032.D966   971.03   *LC* 67-6368   *ISBN* 0771097018

Skelton, Oscar Douglas.   • 3.8727
The life and times of Sir Alexander Tilloch Galt / Oscar Douglas Skelton. — Toronto: Oxford University Press, 1920. 586 p.: ill., maps, ports. 1. Galt, A. T. (Alexander Tilloch), Sir, 1817-1893. I. T.
F1032.G2   *LC* 21-8655

Guillet, Edwin Clarence, 1898-.   • 3.8728
The lives and times of the patriots; an account of the Rebellion in Upper Canada, 1837–1838, and of the patriot agitation in the United States, 1837–1842 [by] Edwin C. Guillet. — [Toronto]: University of Toronto Press, [1968] xiv, 304 p.: illus., maps, ports.; 24 cm. — (Canadian university paperbooks, 81) First published Toronto, T. Nelson, 1938. 1. Hunters' Lodges (Secret societies) 2. Canada — History — Rebellion, 1837-1838 3. United States — History — 1815-1861 I. T.
F1032.G89 1968   971.03/8   *LC* 68-115557

Phelan, Josephine.   • 3.8729
The ardent exile: the life and times of Thos. Darcy McGee. — Toronto: Macmillan, c1951. 317 p.: ill. facsim. — (on lining papers). 1. McGee, Thomas D'Arcy, 1825-1868. 2. Canada — Politics and government — 1841-1867 I. T.
F1032.M123   *LC* 52-19494

Kilbourn, William.   • 3.8730
The firebrand: William Lyon Mackenzie and the rebellion in Upper Canada / William Kilbourn; wood engraving by Rosemary Kilbourn . — Toronto: Clarke, Irwin, 1956. 283 p.: ill. Maps on lining papers. 1. Mackenzie, William Lyon, 1795-1861. 2. Statesmen — Canada — Biography. 3. Canada — History — 1763-1867 I. T.
F1032.M148   971.038   *LC* 57-249

Morton, W. L. (William Lewis), 1908-.   • 3.8731
The critical years: the union of British North America, 1857–1873 / W. L. Morton. — Toronto: McClelland and Stewart, 1964. xii, 322 p.: ill., maps. — (Canadian centenary series. v. 12) 1. Canada — History — 1841-1867 2. Canada — History — 1867-1914 3. Canada — Politics and government — 1841-1867 4. Canada — Politics and government — 1867-1896. I. T. II. Series.
F1032.M88   971.04   *LC* 65-3125

Neatby, Hilda, 1904-1975.   • 3.8732
Quebec: the revolutionary age, 1760–1791 [by] Hilda Neatby. [Toronto] McClelland and Stewart [c1966] xii, 300 p. illus., maps, ports. 24 cm. (Canadian centenary series. 6) 1. Québec (Province) — History 2. Canada — History — To 1763 (New France) 3. Canada — History — 1763-1791 I. T. II. Series.
F1032.N34   971.4/02   *LC* 67-81811

Read, Colin, 1943-.   **3.8733**
The rising in western upper Canada, 1837–8: the Duncombe revolt and after / Colin Read. — Toronto; Buffalo: University of Toronto Press, c1982. xii, 327 p.: maps; 24 cm. Based on the author's thesis (doctoral—University of Toronto) Includes index. 1. Duncombe, Charles. 2. Ontario — History 3. Canada — History — Rebellion, 1837-1838 I. T.
F1032.R27 1982   971.03/8 19   LC 82-168779   ISBN 0802054986

Stacey, C. P.   **• 3.8734**
Canada and the British army, 1846–1871: a study in the practice of responsible government / by C. P. Stacey. — Rev. ed. — Toronto: Published in association with the Royal Commonwealth Society by University of Toronto Press, 1963. xiv, 293 : ill. — (Scholarly Reprint series).) 1. Canada. Canadian Army. 2. Canada — History — 1763-1867 3. Canada — Defences. I. T.
F1032.S78 1963   971.04   LC 64-7285

Waite, Peter B.   **• 3.8735**
The life and times of Confederation, 1864–1867: politics, newspapers, and the union of British North America / P. B. Waite. — [Corr. ed.]. — Toronto: University of Toronto Press, c1962. vi, 379 p. 1. Canada — Politics and government — 1841-1867 I. T.
F1032.W16   LC 63-796

Whitelaw, William Menzies, 1890-.   **• 3.8736**
The Maritimes and Canada before confederation / by William Menzies Whitelaw; with a foreword by Sir Robert Laird Borden. — Toronto: Oxford University Press, 1934. x, 328 p. maps. 18 cm. 1. Canada — Politics and government — 1841-1867 2. Maritime Provinces I. T.
F1032.W437 1966   971.5   LC 34-25363

F1033 1867-1914

Berger, Carl Clinton, 1939-.   **• 3.8737**
The sense of power; studies in the ideas of Canadian imperialism, 1867–1914. [Toronto] University of Toronto Press [1971, c1970] 277 p. 23 cm. 18 mm. (Canadian university paperbooks) 1. Canada — Politics and government — 1867-1914 2. Canada — History — 1867-1914 I. T. II. Series.
F1033.B49 1970   LC 79-470040   ISBN 0802061133

Borden, Robert Laird, Sir, 1854-1937.   **• 3.8738**
Robert Laird Borden: his memoirs; edited and with a preface by Henry Borden; with an introd. by Arthur Meighen. — Toronto: Macmillan, 1938. 2 v.: ill., ports. — 1. Borden, Robert Laird, Sir, 1854-1937. 2. World War, 1914-1918 — Canada. 3. Canada — Politics and government — 1867- I. Borden, Henry, 1901- II. T.
FC556.B67 A3 1969   F1033.B76.   923/.271   LC 39-4233

English, John, 1945-.   **3.8739**
Borden: his life and world / John English. — Toronto; New York: McGraw-Hill Ryerson, c1977. 223 p.: ill.; 26 cm. — (Prime Ministers of Canada) Includes index. 1. Borden, Robert Laird, Sir, 1854-1937. 2. Prime ministers — Canada — Biography. 3. Canada — Politics and government — 1867-1914 4. Canada — Politics and government — 1914-1945 I. T. II. Series.
F1033.B76 E53   971.06/12/0924 B   LC 78-304660   ISBN 0070823030

Brown, Robert Craig.   **3.8740**
Canada, 1896–1921; a nation transformed [by] Robert Craig Brown and Ramsay Cook. — [Toronto]: McClelland and Stewart, [1974] xiv, 412 p.: illus.; 23 cm. — (Canadian centenary series. v. 14) 1. Canada — History — 1867-1914 I. Cook, Ramsay. joint author. II. T. III. Series.
F1033.B87   320.971/056   LC 74-174490   ISBN 0771022689

The Canadian who's who ... A handbook of Canadian biography   **3.8741**
of living characters.
v. 1 (1910)-. Toronto: Trans-Canada Press. c1910-. v. 20 cm. Triennial. Sub-title A handbook of Canadian biography of living characters (varies); With which is incorporated Canadian men and women of the time. Kept up to date by a semiannual supplement: Who's who biographical service, Canada. 1. Canada — Biography. I. Title: Canadian men and women of the time.
FC25.C255   F1033.C23.   LC 10-17752

Young, Brian J., 1940-.   **3.8742**
George–Etienne Cartier: Montreal bourgeois / Brian Young. — Kingston: McGill-Queen's University Press, 1981. xiv, 181 p.: ill.; 23 cm. Includes index. 1. Cartier, George-Etienne, Sir, 1814-1873. 2. Politicians — Canada — Biography. 3. Canada — Politics and government — 1841-1867 I. T.
F1033.C46 Y68 1981   971/.009/94 B 19   LC 82-188023   ISBN 0773503706

Creighton, Donald Grant.   **• 3.8743**
Canada's first century, 1867–1967. — New York: St. Martin's Press, [1970] 372 p.: illus., ports.; 24 cm. 1. Canada — History — 1867- I. T.
F1033.C83   971   LC 75-125604

Cook, Ramsay.   **• 3.8744**
The politics of John W. Dafoe and the Free press. — [Toronto, Buffalo] University of Toronto Press [c1963] xii, 305 p. illus. 24 cm. 1. Dafoe, John Wesley, 1866-1944. 2. Winnipeg Free Press. 3. Canada — Politics and government — 20th century I. T.
F1033.D2 C6   LC 64-1761

Dawson, Robert MacGregor, 1895-1958.   **• 3.8745**
William Lyon Mackenzie King: a political biography. — Toronto: University of Toronto Press, 1958-. v.: ill.; 24 cm. 1. King, William Lyon Mackenzie, 1874-1950. I. Neatby, H. Blair. The lonely heights. II. Neatby, H. Blair. The prism of unity. III. T.
F1033.K53 D3   923.271   LC 59-347   ISBN 0802053815

Ferns, Henry Stanley, 1913-.   **• 3.8746**
The age of Mackenzie King: the rise of the leader / by H.S. Ferns and B. Ostry. — London: Heinemann; Toronto: British Book, Service 1955. xii, 356 p., [4] f. de planches: ill., carte, portr.; 22 cm. 1. King, William Lyon Mackenzie, 1874-1950. 2. Industry and state — Canada — History. 3. Canada — History — 1867-1914 4. Canada — History — 1914-1918. I. Ostry, Bernard, 1927- II. T.
F1033.K53F4   FC581.K5F46.   LC A56-2307

Granatstein, J. L.   **3.8747**
Mackenzie King: his life and world / J. L. Granatstein; general editor, W. Kaye Lamb; picture editor, Paul Russell. — Toronto; New York: McGraw-Hill Ryerson, c1977. 202 p.: ill. (some col.); 26 cm. Includes index. 1. King, William Lyon Mackenzie, 1874-1950. 2. Prime ministers — Canada — Biography. 3. Canada — Politics and government — 1914-1945 I. Lamb, W. Kaye (William Kaye), 1904- II. T.
F1033.K53 G73   971.06/22/0924 B   LC 78-304849   ISBN 0070823049

Hutchison, Bruce, 1901-.   **• 3.8748**
The incredible Canadian: a candid portrait of Mackenzie King: his works, his times, and his nation / by Bruce Hutchison. — [1st American ed.] New York: Longmans, Green, 1953. 454 p./.: ill.; 22 cm. 1. King, William Lyon Mackenzie, 1874-1950. 2. Canada — History — 1914- I. T.
F1033.K53H8 1953   971.06/32/0924   LC 53-299

McGregor, F. A.   **• 3.8749**
The fall & rise of Mackenzie King: 1911–1919 / by F. A. McGregor. — Toronto: Macmillan of Canada, 1962. 358 p. 1. King, William Lyon Mackenzie, 1874-1950. 2. Prime ministers — Canada — Biography. 3. Canada — Politics and government — 20th century I. T.
F1033.K53.M2 1963   923.271   LC 63-3079

Mackenzie King: widening the debate / edited by John English,   **3.8750**
J. O. Stubbs.
Toronto: Macmillan of Canada, 1978 (c1977). ix, 253 p.; 23 cm. 1. King, William Lyon Mackenzie, 1874-1950. 2. Prime ministers — Canada — Biography. 3. Canada — Politics and government — 1914- I. King, William Lyon Mackenzie, 1874-1950. II. English, John, 1945- III. Stubbs, John O., 1943-
F1033.K53 M33   971.06/22/0924 B   LC 78-319629   ISBN 0770515290

Pickersgill, J. W., 1905-.   **• 3.8751**
The Mackenzie King record. — [Toronto]: University of Toronto Press, [1960-. v. : illus.; 24 cm. Continues the record begun in William Lyon Mackenzie King, a political biography by R. M. Dawson. 1. King, William Lyon Mackenzie, 1874-1950. 2. Canada — Politics and government — 1914-1945 3. Canada — Foreign relations I. Forster, Donald F., joint author. II. T.
F1033.K53 P5   923.271   LC 60-51004

Stacey, C. P. (Charles Perry), 1906-.   **3.8752**
A very double life: the private world of Mackenzie King / C. P. Stacey. — Toronto: Macmillan of Canada, c1976. 256 p., [8] leaves of plates: ill.; 24 cm. 1. King, William Lyon Mackenzie, 1874-1950. I. T.
F1033.K53 S72   971.06/22/0924 B   LC 76-366908   ISBN 0770513905

Dafoe, John Wesley, 1866-1944.   **• 3.8753**
Laurier, a study in Canadian politics / by J.W. Dafoe. — Toronto: T. Allen, c1922. 182 p. 19 cm. — 'Originally published in ... the Monthly book review of the Manitoba free press.' 1. Laurier, Wilfrid, Sir, 1841-1919. 2. Canada — Politics and government — 1867-1914 I. T.
F1033.L3595 1963   971.05/0924   LC 23-10112

Schull, Joseph.   • 3.8754
Laurier: the first Canadian / by Joseph Schull. — New York: St.Martin's Press, 1965,[i.e.1966]. 658 p.: ill., port.; 23cm. 1. Laurier, Wilfrid, Sir, 1841-1919. I. T.
F1033.L377S34   LC 65-26119

Skelton, Oscar Douglas, 1878-1941.   • 3.8755
Life and letters of Sir Wilfrid Laurier / by Oscar Douglas Skelton. — New York: The Century Co., 1922. 2 v.: ill., ports. 1. Laurier, Wilfrid, Sir, 1841-1919. 2. Canada — Politics and government — 1867-1914 I. T.
F1033.L386   LC 21-21755

Creighton, Donald Grant.   • 3.8756
John A. Macdonald. Boston, Houghton Mifflin, 1953-55. 2 v.: ill., ports., maps (on lining papers); 23 cm. 1. Macdonald, John Alexander, Sir, 1815-1891. 2. Canada — Politics and government — 1841-1867 3. Canada — Politics and government — 1867-1914 I. T.
F1033.M125 C72   LC 52-13914

Waite, Peter B.   3.8757
Macdonald: his life and world / P. B. Waite. — Toronto; New York: McGraw-Hill Ryerson, c1975. 224 p.: ill.; 26 cm. Includes index. 1. Macdonald, John Alexander, Sir, 1815-1891. 2. Canada — Politics and government — 19th century I. T.
F1033.M135   971.05/1/0924   LC 76-355909   ISBN 0070823014

Miller, Carman, 1940-.   3.8758
The Canadian career of the Fourth Earl of Minto: the education of a viceroy / Carman Miller. — Waterloo, Ont.: Wilfrid Laurier University Press, c1980. viii, 225 p., [3] leaves of plates: ill., ports.; 24 cm. Includes index. 1. Minto, Gilbert John Murray Kynynmond Elliot, Earl of, 1845-1914. 2. Heads of state — Canada — Biography. 3. Canada — Politics and government — 1867-1914 I. T.
F1033.M664 M54 1980   971.05/6/0924 B 19   LC 80-509641
ISBN 0889200785

Penlington, Norman.   • 3.8759
Canada and imperialism, 1896–1899 / Norman Penlington. — [Toronto]: University of Toronto Press, c1965. xiv, 288 p.: map. 1. Imperial federation 2. Canada — History — 1867-1914 3. Canada — Foreign relations — United States 4. United States — Foreign relations — Canada I. T.
F1033.P4   LC 65-1619   ISBN 0802051480

Siegfried, André, 1875-1959.   • 3.8760
Canada, by André Siegfried; translated from the French by H. H. Hemming & Doris Hemming. New York, Harcourt, Brace, c1937. 341 p. ill., maps. 21 cm. 1. Canada — Population. 2. Canada — Economic conditions — 1918- 3. Canada — Politics and government — 1867- I. T.
F1033.S562   LC 37-27316

Hall, D. J. (David John), 1943-.   3.8761
Clifford Sifton / D.J. Hall. — Vancouver: University of British Columbia Press, 1985. 437 p.: ill. 1. Sifton, Clifford, Sir, 1861-1929. 2. Canada — Politics and government — 1867-1914 4. Manitoba — Politics and government. I. T.
F1033.S59 H254   971.05/6/0924 B 19   LC 81-201998   ISBN 0774801352

Smith, Goldwin Albert.   • 3.8762
The Treaty of Washington, 1871; a study in imperial history, by Goldwin Smith. — New York: Russell & Russell, [1971, c1941] xiii, 134 p.; 23 cm. 1. Washington, Treaty of, 1871 2. Canada — Politics and government — 1867-1914 3. U.S. — Foreign relations — Gt. Brit. 4. Gt. Brit. — Foreign relations — U.S. 5. U.S. — Foreign relations — Canada. 6. Canada — Foreign relations — U.S. I. T.
F1033.S67 1971   971.05   LC 70-139940

Waite, Peter B.   3.8763
The man from Halifax: Sir John Thompson, prime minister / P.B. Waite. — Toronto; Buffalo: University of Toronto Press, c1985. ix, 547 p., [18] p. of plates: ill., ports.; 24 cm. Includes index. 1. Thompson, John S. D. (John Sparrow David), Sir, 1844-1894. 2. Prime ministers — Canada — Biography. 3. Cabinet officers — Canada — Biography. 4. Attorneys-general — Nova Scotia — Biography. 5. Judges — Nova Scotia — Biography. 6. Canada — Politics and government — 1867-1914 7. Nova Scotia — Politics and government — 1867- I. T.
F1033.T473 1985   971.05/5/0924 B 19   LC 85-183157   ISBN 0802056598

Saunders, Edward Manning, 1829-1916.   • 3.8764
The life and letters of the Rt. Hon. Sir Charles Tupper, bart. K. C. M. G. / edited by E. M. Saunders, D.D., with an introduction by the Rt. Hon. Sir R. L. Borden, K. C. M. G. — London; Toronto: Cassell, 1916. 2 v.: ports. 1. Tupper, Charles, Sir, 1821-1915. 2. Canada — Politics and government — 1867-1914 I. Tupper, Charles, Sir, 1821-1915. II. T.
FC526.T86 S37   F1033.T9.   LC 17-6541

Waite, Peter B.   • 3.8765
Canada 1874–1896: arduous destiny [by] Peter B. Waite. — Toronto: McClelland and Stewart, [1971] xii, 340 p.: illus., maps., ports.; 24 cm. — (Canadian centenary series. 13) 1. Canada — History — 1867-1914 I. T. II. Series.
F1033.W15   971.05   LC 76-597589   ISBN 0771088000

F1034–1034.3 1914–

Newman, Peter Charles.   • 3.8766
Renegade in power the Diefenbaker years. Indianapolis, Bobbs-Merrill [1964, c1963] 414p. 1. Diefenbaker, John G., 1895-1979. 2. Canada — Politics and government — 1914- I. T.
F1034.D5 N4   LC 64-4761

Eayrs, James George, 1926-.   • 3.8767
In defence of Canada [by] James Eayrs. [Toronto] University of Toronto Press [1965] < c1983 > . v. < 1-5 > illus., ports. 24 cm. (Studies in the structure of power, decision-making in Canada. 1, 3, 6, 8, 10) 1. Canada — Defenses. 2. Canada — History, Military. 3. Canada — Foreign relations I. T. II. Series.
F1034.E17   355/.033/071 19   LC 66-3834   ISBN 0802019072

Granatstein, J. L.   3.8768
Canada's war: the politics of the Mackenzie King government, 1939–1945 / J. L. Granatstein. — Toronto: Oxford University Press, 1975. xi, 436 p., [8] leaves of plates: ill.; 24 cm. 1. Nationalism — Canada. 2. World War, 1939-1945 — Canada. 3. Canada — Politics and government — 1914-1945 I. T.
F1034.G68   971.06/32   LC 75-306755   ISBN 0195402286

Graham, Roger.   • 3.8769
Arthur Meighen: a biography / by Roger Graham. — Toronto: Clarke, Irwin, 1960-1965. 3 v.: ill., ports. 1. Prime ministers — Canada — Biography. I. T.
F1034.M46 G7   971.060924 B

Morton, W. L. (William Lewis), 1908-.   • 3.8770
The Progressive Party in Canada / by W.L. Morton. — Reprinted with corrections. — Toronto: University of Toronto Press, 1967, c1950. xiii, 331 p. — (Social Credit in Alberta; v.1.) 1. Progressive Party (Canada) 2. Progressivism (Canadian politics) I. T. II. Series.
F1034.M6 1967   324.271096   LC 67-2778   ISBN 0802060625 PB

Neatby, H. Blair.   3.8771
The politics of chaos; Canada in the thirties [by] H. Blair Neatby. — Toronto: Macmillan of Canada, [1972] 196 p.: illus.; 20 cm. 1. Canada — Politics and government — 1914-1945 I. T.
F1034.N36   320.9/71/062   LC 70-187791   ISBN 0770508677

Documents on Canadian foreign policy, 1917–1939 / selected   • 3.8772
and edited by Walter A. Riddell.
Toronto: Oxford University Press, 1962. liii, 806 p. 1. Canada — Foreign relations 2. Canada — History — 1914-1945 — Sources I. Riddell, Walter Alexander, 1881-
F1034.R55   LC 62-5019

McNaught, Kenneth William Kirkpatrick, 1918-.   • 3.8773
A prophet in politics: a biography of J. S. Woodsworth / by Kenneth McNaught. — Toronto: University of Toronto Press, c1959. vi, 339 p.: ill. 1. Woodsworth, James Shaver, 1874-1942. I. T.
F1034.W6M23   LC 59-4879   ISBN 0802060188

Bothwell, Robert.   3.8774
Canada since 1945: power, politics, and provincialism / Robert Bothwell, Ian Drummond, John English. — Toronto; Buffalo: University of Toronto Press, c1981. xii, 489 p., [14] p. of plates: ill.; 24 cm. Includes index. 1. Canada — Politics and government — 1945-1980 2. Canada — Economic conditions — 1945- I. Drummond, Ian M. II. English, John, 1945- III. T.
F1034.2.B67   971.06 19   LC 81-152041   ISBN 0802024173

Canada and the Third World / edited by Peyton V. Lyon and   3.8775
Tareq Y. Ismael.
Toronto: Macmillan of Canada, c1976. l, 342 p.; 22 cm. 1. Economic assistance, Canadian — Developing countries. 2. Technical assistance, Canadian — Developing countries. 3. Canada — Foreign relations — 1945- 4. Developing countries — Foreign relations. I. Lyon, Peyton V., 1921- II. Ismael, Tareq Y.
F1034.2.C28   327.71/0172/4   LC 77-352444   ISBN 0770510396.
ISBN 077051040X pbk

Dobell, Peter C.   3.8776
Canada's search for new roles; foreign policy in the Trudeau era [by] Peter C. Dobell. London; New York: Published for Royal Institute of International

Affairs, by Oxford University Press, 1972. vi, 161 p. 21 cm. (Oxford paperbacks, 277) 1. Canada — Foreign relations — 1945- I. T.
F1034.2.D62   327.71   LC 72-169387   ISBN 0192850571

Fraser, Blair, 1909-1968.   • **3.8777**
The search for identity: Canada, 1945–1967. [1st ed.] Garden City, N.Y., Doubleday, 1967. viii, 325 p. map (on lining papers) 22 cm. (The Canadian history series v. 6) 1. Canada — Politics and government — 1945-1980 I. T. II. Series.
F1034.2.F7   320.9/71   LC 67-23823

Forum: Canadian life and letters, 1920–70: selections from the   **3.8778**
Canadian forum, edited by J. L. Granatstein and Peter Stevens.
Toronto: University of Toronto Press, c1972. xv, 431 p.: illus.; 21 x 27 cm. 1. Canadian literature — 20th century — Addresses, essays, lectures. 2. Canada — Politics and government — 20th century — Addresses, essays, lectures. I. Stevens, Peter, 1927- joint comp. II. Granatstein, J. L. III. Canadian forum.
F1034.2.G72 1972   917.1/03/6   LC 75-166930   ISBN 0802019099

Holmes, John Wendell, 1910-.   **3.8779**
The shaping of peace: Canada and the search for world order, 1943–1957 / John W. Holmes. — Toronto; Buffalo: University of Toronto Press, 1982. 443 p. 1. Canada — Foreign relations — 1945- I. T.
F1034.2.H63   327.71   LC 80-462171   ISBN 0802054617

Lyon, Peyton V., 1921-.   **3.8780**
Canada as an international actor / Peyton V. Lyon and Brian W. Tomlin. — Toronto: Macmillan of Canada, 1979. xiii, 209 p.: ill.; 22 cm. — (Canadian controversies series) Includes index. 1. Canada — Foreign relations — 1945- I. Tomlin, Brian W. joint author. II. T.
F1034.2.L93   327.71   LC 80-456016   ISBN 077050969X

✓ **Must Canada fail? / edited by Richard Simeon.**   **3.8781**
Montreal: McGill-Queen's University Press, 1977. x, 307 p.; 23 cm. 1. Federal government — Canada — Addresses, essays, lectures. 2. Nationalism — Canada — Addresses, essays, lectures. 3. Canada — Politics and government — 1945-1980 — Addresses, essays, lectures. 4. Québec (Province) — History — Autonomy and independence movements — Addresses, essays, lectures. I. Simeon, Richard.
F1034.2.M85   320.9/71/064   LC 78-307029   ISBN 0773503145. ISBN 0773503137 pbk

Schwartz, Mildred A.   • **3.8782**
Public opinion and Canadian identity / Mildred A. Schwartz; foreword by Seymour Martin Lipset. — Berkeley: University of California Press, 1967. xvii, 263 p.: ill. 1. Nationalism — Canada 2. Public opinion — Canada. 3. Canada — Politics and government — 1945- 4. Canada — Foreign relations I. T.
F1034.2.S3 1967   LC 67-17693

Simpson, Jeffrey, 1949-.   **3.8783**
Discipline of power: the Conservative interlude and the Liberal restoration / Jeffrey Simpson. — Toronto: Personal Library; Rexdale, Ont.: Distributed to the trade by J. Wiley, 1980. xiv, 369 p., [8] p. of plates: ports.; 25 cm. Includes index. 1. Canada — Politics and government — 1945-1980 I. T.
F1034.2.S53   971.064/5 19   LC 81-133616   ISBN 0920510248

Stewart, Walter.   **3.8784**
Trudeau in power. New York: Outerbridge & Dienstfrey, 1972 (c1971) 240 p. 24 cm. 1. Trudeau, Pierre Elliott. 2. Canada — Politics and government — 1945-1980 I. T.
F1034.2.S7   320.9/71/0644   LC 71-178904   ISBN 0876900481

Thordarson, Bruce.   **3.8785**
Trudeau and foreign policy: a study in decision–making. — Toronto: Oxford University Press, 1972. viii, 231 p.; 21 cm. 1. Trudeau, Pierre Elliott. 2. Canada — Foreign relations — 1945- I. T.
F1034.2.T47   327.71   LC 72-197796   ISBN 0195401972

Pearson, Lester B., 1897-1972.   **3.8786**
Mike: memoirs of the Right Honourable Lester B. Pearson. — New York: Quadrangle Books, 1972-1975. 2 v.: ill. ports.; 24 cm. 1. Pearson, Lester B., 1897-1972. 2. Canada — History I. T.
F1034.3.P4 Ax   LC cn75-6679

Bothwell, Robert.   **3.8787**
Pearson, his life and world / Robert Bothwell. — Toronto; New York: McGraw-Hill Ryerson, c1978. 223 p.: ill.; 26 cm. — (Prime Ministers of Canada) Includes index. 1. Pearson, Lester B. 2. Prime ministers — Canada — Biography. 3. Canada — Politics and government — 1945-1980 I. T. II. Series.
F1034.3.P4 B67   971.06/43/0924 B   LC 78-322388   ISBN 0070823057

Stursberg, Peter.   **3.8788**
Lester Pearson and the dream of unity / Peter Stursberg. — 1st ed. — Toronto: Doubleday Canada; Garden City, N.Y.: Doubleday, 1979 (c1978). xv, 456 p., [8] leaves of plates: ports.; 24 cm. Includes index. 1. Pearson, Lester B. 2. Federal government — Canada. 3. Prime ministers — Canada — Biography. 4. Québec (Province) — History — Autonomy and independence movements 5. Canada — Politics and government — 1945-1980 I. T.
F1034.3.P4 S86   971.064/3/0924 B   LC 77-16951   ISBN 0385134789

Pickersgill, J. W., 1905-.   **3.8789**
My years with Louis St. Laurent: a political memoir / J. W. Pickersgill. — Toronto; Buffalo: University of Toronto Press, c1975. viii, 334 p., [4] leaves of plates: ill.; 24 cm. Includes index. 1. Pickersgill, J. W., 1905- 2. St. Laurent, Louis S. (Louis Stephen), 1882-1973. I. T.
F1034.3.P52 A34   971.06/3/0924   LC 75-24675   ISBN 0802022154

Thomson, Dale C.   • **3.8790**
Louis St. Laurent, Canadian [by] Dale C. Thomson. New York, St. Martin's Press, 1968 [c1967] x, 564 p. illus., ports. 23 cm. 1. St. Laurent, Louis S. (Louis Stephen), 1882-1973. I. T.
F1034.3.S2 T48   971.06/3/0924 B   LC 68-11107

Smith, Arnold, 1915-.   **3.8791**
Stitches in time: the Commonwealth in world politics / Arnold Smith with Clyde Sanger. — Don Mills, Ont.: General Pub. Co., 1981. xix, 322 p.: maps; 24 cm. Maps on lining papers. 1. Smith, Arnold, 1915- 2. Commonwealth Secretariat — Biography. 3. Commonwealth Secretariat — History. 4. Diplomats — Canada — Biography. 5. Commonwealth of Nations — History — 20th century. I. Sanger, Clyde. II. T.
F1034.3.S63 A37 1981   327.2/092/4 B 19   LC 83-145340   ISBN 0773601007

Gwyn, Richard J., 1934-.   **3.8792**
The northern magus: Pierre Trudeau and Canadians / by Richard Gwyn; edited by Sandra Gwyn. — Toronto: McClelland and Stewart, c1980. 399 p.: ill., ports; 24 cm. Includes index. 1. Trudeau, Pierre Elliott. 2. Prime ministers — Canada — Biography. 3. Canada — Politics and government — 1945-1980 I. Gwyn, Sandra. II. T.
F1034.3.T7 G9   971.064/4/0924 B 19   LC 80-150399   ISBN 0771037325

Radwanski, George.   **3.8793**
Trudeau / George Radwanski. — New York: Taplinger Pub. Co., 1978. xii, 372 p.; 24 cm. Includes index. 1. Trudeau, Pierre Elliott. 2. Prime ministers — Canada — Biography. 3. Canada — Politics and government — 1945-1980 I. T.
F1034.3.T7 R32 1978b   971.06/44/0924 B   LC 78-67827   ISBN 0800878973

F1035 Elements in the Population

Two nations, many cultures: ethnic groups in Canada / edited   **3.8794**
by Jean Leonard Elliott.
Scarborough, Ont.: Prentice-Hall of Canada, 1978, c1979. xiii, 395 p.: ill.; 23 cm. 1. Minorities — Canada — Addresses, essays, lectures. 2. French-Canadians — Addresses, essays, lectures. 3. Indians of North America — Canada — Addresses, essays, lectures. 4. Canada — Race relations — Addresses, essays, lectures. I. Elliott, Jean Leonard.
F1035.A1 T85   301.45/1/0971   LC 79-311705   ISBN 0139352058

Woodsworth, James Shaver, 1874-1942.   **3.8795**
Strangers within our gates; or coming Canadians. Introd. by Marilyn Barber. — [Toronto; Buffalo]: University of Toronto Press, [c1972] xxiii, 279 p.: illus.; 23 cm. — (Social history of Canada.) 1. Missions — Canada. 2. Canada — Foreign population. 3. Canada — Emigration and immigration. I. T. II. Series.
F1035.A1 W6 1972   301.32/4/0971   LC 76-163836   ISBN 0802018912

✓ **Abella, Irving M., 1940-.**   **3.8796**
None is too many: Canada and the Jews of Europe, 1933–1948 / by Irving Abella and Harold Troper. — 1st American ed. — New York: Random House, c1983. x, 336 p., [8] p. of plates: ill.; 25 cm. 1. Jews — Canada — Politics and government. 2. Refugees, Jewish — Canada. 3. Holocaust, Jewish (1939-1945) 4. Canada — Emigration and immigration. 5. Canada — Ethnic relations. I. Troper, Harold Martin, 1942- II. T.
F1035.J5 A23 1983   971/.004924 19   LC 83-42864   ISBN 0394533283

Winks, Robin W.   • 3.8797
The Blacks in Canada; a history, by Robin W. Winks. Montreal, McGill-Queen's University Press; New Haven, Yale University Press, 1971. xvii, 546 p. maps. 24 cm. 1. Blacks — Canada — History I. T.
F1035.N3 W5   971/.04/96   LC 79-118740   ISBN 0300013612

F1035.8–1140 REGIONS.
PROVINCES

F1035.8–1049 Maritime Provinces

Forbes, Ernest R.   3.8798
The maritime rights movement, 1919–1927: a study in Canadian regionalism / Ernest R. Forbes. — Montreal: McGill-Queen's University, 1979. x, 246 p.: map; 24 cm. Includes index. 1. Federal government — Canada — History. 2. Maritime Provinces, Can. — Politics and government. I. T.
F1035.8.F59   320.9/71   LC 79-308545   ISBN 0773503218

MacNutt, William Stewart, 1908-.   • 3.8799
The Atlantic provinces: the emergence of colonial society, 1712–1857 / W.S. MacNutt. — Toronto: McClelland and Stewart, 1965. xii, 306 p.: ill.; 21 cm. — (Canadian centenary series. 9) 1. Maritime Provinces, Canada — History. 2. Newfoundland — History. I. T. II. Series.
F1035.8.M2 1972   971.501   LC 66-77421   ISBN 0771055870 Pbk

Brebner, John Bartlet, 1895-1957.   • 3.8800
The neutral Yankees of Nova Scotia; a marginal colony during the revolutionary years. New York, Russell & Russell [1970, c1937] xv, 388 p. fold. map. 25 cm. 1. New Englanders — Nova Scotia 2. Nova Scotia — History I. T.
F1038.B815 1970   971.6/02   LC 72-102471

Brebner, John Bartlet, 1895-1957.   • 3.8801
New England's outpost; Acadia before the conquest of Canada. Hamden, Conn., Archon Books, 1965 [c1927] 291 p. map. 22 cm. 1. Nova Scotia — History — To 1763 2. Acadia I. T.
F1038.B822 1965   971.6   LC 65-16895

Griffiths, Naomi Elizabeth Saundaus.   3.8802
The Acadians: creation of a people [by] Naomi Griffiths. — Toronto; New York: McGraw-Hill Ryerson, [1973] xiii, 94 p.: illus.; 22 cm. — (The Frontenac library, 6) 1. Acadians I. T.
F1038.G85 1973   971.6   LC 72-9529   ISBN 0070929661

Beck, J. Murray (James Murray), 1914-.   3.8803
Joseph Howe / J. Murray Beck. — Kingston: McGill-Queen's University Press, c1982. 389 p. 1. Howe, Joseph, 1804-1873. 2. Politicians — Nova Scotia — Biography. 3. Social reformers — Nova Scotia — Biography. 4. Nova Scotia — Politics and government I. T.
F1038.H82 B43 1982   971.6/02/0924 B 19   LC 83-185321   ISBN 0773503870

Pryke, Kenneth G., 1932-.   3.8804
Nova Scotia and Confederation, 1864–74 / Kenneth G. Pryke. — Toronto: University of Toronto Press, 1979. xi, 240 p.: map; 24 cm. — (Canadian studies in history and government; 15) Includes index. 1. Nova Scotia — Politics and government — 1763-1867 2. Canada — Politics and government — 1841-1867 I. T. II. Series.
F1038.P83   971.6/03   LC 79-322022   ISBN 0802053890

Rawlyk, George A.   3.8805
Nova Scotia's Massachusetts; a study of Massachusetts–Nova Scotia relations 1630 to 1784 [by] George A. Rawlyk. Montreal, McGill-Queen's University Press, 1973. xviii, 298 p. maps. 24 cm. 1. New Englanders — Nova Scotia 2. Nova Scotia — History — To 1763 3. Acadia 4. Massachusetts — History — Colonial period, ca. 1600-1775 I. T.
F1038.R38   971.6/01   LC 73-79091   ISBN 0773501428

MacNutt, W. S.   • 3.8806
New Brunswick: a history, 1784–1867 / W. S. MacNutt. — Toronto: Macmillan of Canada, 1963. xv, 496 p. [8] leaves of plates: ill., maps. 1. New Brunswick — History. I. T.
F1043.M29   971.5   LC 63-6068   ISBN 0770510159

Clark, Andrew Hill, 1911-1975.   • 3.8807
Three centuries and the island; a historical geography of settlement and agriculture in Prince Edward Island, Canada. [Toronto] University of Toronto Press [1959] xiii, 287 p. illus., maps. 26 cm. 1. Agriculture — Prince Edward Island. 2. Prince Edward Island — Historical geography. I. T.
F1047.C57   911.717   LC 59-2157

Harvey, Daniel Cobb, 1886-.   • 3.8808
The French régime in Prince Edward Island, by D. C. Harvey. — New York: AMS Press, [1970] xi, 265 p.: map.; 23 cm. 'Reprinted from the edition of 1926.' 1. French in Prince Edward Island. 2. Prince Edward Island — History. I. T.
F1048.H34 1970   971.7   LC 72-113193   ISBN 0404031536

F1050–1055 QUEBEC

Thoreau, Henry David, 1817-1862.   • 3.8809
[Selections. 1969] A Yankee in Canada, with Anti–slavery and reform papers. 12th ed. New York, Haskell House, 1969. 286 p. 23 cm. Reprint of the 1892 ed. 1. Brown, John, 1800-1859. 2. Slavery in the United States — Controversial literature — 1844-1860. 3. Québec (Province) — Description and travel I. T.
F1052.T48 1969   081   LC 68-25271   ISBN 0838302483

Basham, Richard Dalton.   3.8810
Crisis in blanc and white: urbanization and ethnic identity in French Canada / Richard Dalton Basham. — Boston: G. K. Hall, c1978. x, 287 p.: ill.; 24 cm. Includes index. 1. French-Canadians — History. 2. Urbanization — Québec (Province) 3. Biculturalism — Québec (Province) 4. Québec (Province) — History — Autonomy and independence movements 5. Canada — English-French relations I. T.
F1053.B29 1978   971/.004/41   LC 78-16950   ISBN 0816182515

Clift, Dominique.   3.8811
Quebec nationalism in crisis / Dominique Clift. — Kingston: McGill-Queen's University Press, 1982. viii, 155 p.; 21 cm. 1. Nationalism — Québec (Province) — History. 2. Québec (Province) — History — Autonomy and independence movements 3. Québec (Province) — Politics and government I. T.
F1053.C57 1982   971.4/04 19   LC 82-197673   ISBN 0773503811

Black, Conrad.   3.8812
Duplessis / Conrad Black. Toronto: McClelland and Stewart, c1977. 743 p., [8] leaves of plates: ill.; 24 cm. 1. Duplessis, Maurice LeNoblet, 1890-1959. 2. Union nationale (Canada) 3. Prime ministers — Québec (Province) — Biography. 4. Québec (Province) — Politics and government I. T.
F1053.D78 B55   971.4/03/0924   LC 77-357064   ISBN 0771015305

Manning, Helen (Taft), 1891-.   • 3.8813
The revolt of French Canada, 1800–1835; a chapter of the history of the British Commonwealth. [New York] St. Martins Press, 1962. 426 p. illus. 23 cm. Includes bibliography. 1. Nationalism — Quebec (Province) 2. Canada — Pol. & govt. — 1791-1841. 3. Gt. Brit. — Colonies — America. I. T.
F1053.M2   971.03   LC 62-1899

Reid, Malcolm, 1941-.   3.8814
The shouting signpainters; a literary and political account of Quebec revolutionary nationalism. — New York: [Monthly Review Press, 1972] 315 p.; 21 cm. 1. French-Canadians 2. French language in Canada. 3. Québec (Province) — History — Autonomy and independence movements I. T.
F1053.R4   323.1/1/410714   LC 75-158922   ISBN 0853451540

Saywell, John T., 1929-.   3.8815
Quebec 70; a documentary narrative [by] John Saywell. [Toronto] University of Toronto Press, [c1971] 152 p. illus. 24 cm. (Canadian University paperbooks, 113) 1. Cross, James Richard, 1921- 2. Laporte, Pierre, 1921-1970. 3. FLQ. 4. Kidnapping 5. Québec (Province) — Politics and government — 1960- I. T.
F1053.S29   320.9/714/04   LC 76-30964   ISBN 0802061346

Trofimenkoff, Susan Mann, 1941-.   3.8816
Action française: French Canadian nationalism in the twenties / Susan Mann Trofimenkoff. — Toronto: University of Toronto Press, [1975] x, 157 p.; 24 cm. Includes index. 1. Ligue d'action canadienne-française. 2. Nationalism — Quebec (Province) 3. French-Canadians 4. Québec (Province) — Politics and government I. T.
F1053.T84   322.4/4/09714   LC 74-79990   ISBN 0803053203

Coleman, William D. (William Donald), 1950-.   3.8817
The independence movement in Quebec, 1945–1980 / William D. Coleman. — Toronto; Buffalo: University of Toronto Press, c1984. xii, 274 p.; 23 cm. (Studies in the structure of power, decision-making in Canada. 0081-8690; 11) 1. Québec (Province) — History — Autonomy and independence movements 2. Québec (Province) — Social conditions. 3. Québec (Province) — Politics and government I. T. II. Series.
F1053.2.C65 1984   971.4/04 19   LC 84-228667   ISBN 0802065422

Lévesque, René, 1922-.   **3.8818**
[Passion du Québec. English] My Québec / René Lévesque; [English translation by Gaynor Fitzpatrick]. — Toronto; New York: Methuen, 1979. xiv, 191 p.; 24 cm. Translation of La passion du Québec. 1. Federal government — Canada. 2. Québec (Province) — Autonomy and independence movements 3. Québec (Province) — Politics and government — 1960- I. T.
F1053.2.L5813   320.9/714/04   LC 79-320865   *ISBN* 0458939803

Hughes, Everett Cherrington, 1897-.   • **3.8819**
French Canada in transition, by Everett Cherrington Hughes ... Chicago, Ill., The University of Chicago press; Toronto, W. J. Gage & co., limited [1943] ix, 227 p. front., illus. (maps) diagrs. 24 cm. Bibliography: p. 223-224. 1. French-Canadians 2. Québec (Province) — Social conditions. I. T.
F1053.5.H8   971.4   LC A 43-2759

Legget, Robert Ferguson.   **3.8820**
Ottawa Waterway: gateway to a continent / Robert Legget. — Toronto; Buffalo: University of Toronto Press, [1975] xi, 291 p.: ill.; 24 cm. Includes index. 1. Ottawa River (Québec and Ont.) — History. 2. Ottawa River Valley (Québec and Ont.) — History. I. T.
F1054.O9 L43   971.3/8   LC 75-6780   *ISBN* 0802021891

Miner, Horace Mitchell, 1912-.   • **3.8821**
St. Denis, a French-Canadian parish. — [Chicago]: University of Chicago Press, [1963, c1939] xix, 299 p.: illus., maps.; 21 cm. 1. St. Denis, Que. (Kamouraska County) — Social life and customs. 2. French-Canadians I. T.
F1054.S224 M5 1963   917.1475   LC 63-13068

Arnopoulos, Sheila McLead.   **3.8822**
[Fait anglais au Québec. English] The English fact in Quebec / by Sheila McLead Arnopoulos and Dominique Clift. — Montreal: McGill-Queen's University Press, 1980. xvi, 239 p.; 21 cm. French ed., by D. Clift and S.M. Arnopoulos, published in 1979 under title: Le fait anglais au Québec. 1. British — Québec (Province) 2. Québec (Province) — Ethnic relations. 3. Canada — English-French relations I. Arnopoulos, Sheila McLeod. joint author. II. T.
F1055.B7 C5713   305.8/112/0714 19   LC 81-464309   *ISBN* 0773503595

F1056–1059.5 ONTARIO

The Pre-Confederation premiers: Ontario government leaders, 1841–1867 / edited by J. M. S. Careless.   **3.8823**
Toronto; Buffalo: University of Toronto Press, 1980. xii, 340 p., [6] leaves of plates: ill.; 24 cm. — (Ontario historical studies series. 0380-9188) 1. Prime ministers — Ontario — Biography. 2. Ontario — Politics and government. I. Careless, J. M. S. (James Maurice Stockford), 1919- II. Series.
F1056.8.P73   971.3/02/0922 B 19   LC 80-501684   *ISBN* 0802033636

Craig, Gerald M.   • **3.8824**
Upper Canada: the formative years 1784–1841 / Gerald M. Craig. — Toronto: McClelland and Stewart, c1963. xiv, 317 p. — (Canadian centenary series. v. 7) 1. Ontario — History — 1791-1841 I. T. II. Series.
F1058.C68   LC 64-2294   *ISBN* 0771023111

Oliver, Peter, 1939-.   **3.8825**
G. Howard Ferguson: Ontario tory / Peter Oliver. — Toronto; Buffalo [N.Y.]: University of Toronto Press for the Ontario Historical Studies Series, c1977. xv, 501 p., [9] leaves of plates: ill.; 24 cm. (Ontario historical studies series. 0380-9188) Includes index. 1. Ferguson, George Howard, 1870-1946. 2. Prime ministers — Ontario — Biography. 3. Ontario — Politics and government. I. T. II. Series.
F1058.F466 O43   971.3/03/0924 B   LC 77-378936   *ISBN* 0802033466

Guillet, Edwin Clarence, 1898-.   • **3.8826**
Early life in Upper Canada / by Edwin C. Guillet. — Toronto: University of Toronto Press, 1963, c1933. xiiii, 782 p.: ill., maps. 1. Frontier and pioneer life — Ontario 2. Ontario — History I. T.
F1058.G87 1963   LC 64-4393   *ISBN* 0802012779

Landon, Fred, 1880-.   • **3.8827**
Western Ontario and the American frontier. New York, Russell & Russell [1970] xxiii, 295 p. maps. 25 cm. (The relations of Canada and the United States) 'First published in 1941.' 1. Canada — Relations — United States 2. United States — Relations — Canada 3. Ontario — History I. T.
F1058.L3 1970   301.29/713/073   LC 78-102514

Humphries, Charles W. (Charles Walter), 1932-.   **3.8828**
'Honest enough to be bold': the life and times of Sir James Pliny Whitney / Charles W. Humphries. — Toronto; Buffalo: Published by University of Toronto Press, c1985. xii, 276 p., [14] p. of plates: ill.; 24 cm. (Ontario historical studies series. 0380-9188) Includes index. 1. Whitney, James Pliny, Sir,

1843-1914. 2. Prime ministers — Ontario — Biography. 3. Ontario — Politics and government. I. T. II. Series.
F1058.W47 H86 1985   971.3/03/0924 B 19   LC 86-101367   *ISBN* 0802034209

Hamil, Frederick Coyne, 1903-.   • **3.8829**
The valley of the lower Thames, 1640 to 1850. [Toronto] University of Toronto Press, 1951. xi, 390 p. plates, maps (1 fold.) 24 cm. 1. Kent County (Ont.) — History. 2. Chatham (Ont.) — History. I. T.
F1059.K3 H3   971.333   LC 53-17557

Akenson, Donald H.   **3.8830**
The Irish in Ontario: a study in rural history / Donald Harman Akenson. — Kingston: McGill-Queen's University Press, c1984. ix, 404 p.: ill.; 24 cm. 1. Irish — Ontario — Leeds (County) — History. 2. Ontario — Leeds — Lansdowne — History. 3. Leeds (Ont.: County) — History. 4. Lansdowne (Ont.) — History. I. T.
F1059.L4 A38 1984   971.3/730049162 19   LC 85-101197   *ISBN* 0773504303

English, John, 1945-.   **3.8831**
Kitchener: an illustrated history / John English and Kenneth McLaughlin. — Waterloo, Ont.: Wilfrid Laurier University Press, c1983. xx, 259 p.: ill.; 26 cm. Includes index. 1. Kitchener (Ont.) — History. I. McLaughlin, Kenneth, 1943- II. T.
F1059.5.K6E5x   971.3/45 19   *ISBN* 0889201374

Gwyn, Sandra.   **3.8832**
The private capital: ambition and love in the age of Macdonald and Laurier / Sandra Gwyn. — Toronto, Ont.: McClelland & Stewart, c1984. 514 p.: ill.; 24 cm. Includes index. 1. Ottawa (Ont.) — Social life and customs. 2. Ottawa (Ont.) — History. 3. Canada — Officials and employees — Biography. I. T.
F1059.5.O9 G87 1984   971.3/84 19   LC 85-109051   *ISBN* 0771037368

Glazebrook, G. P. de T. (George Parkin de Twenebroker), 1899-.   **3.8833**
The story of Toronto [by] G. P. de T. Glazebrook. [Toronto] University of Toronto Press [1971] xi, 310 p. illus. 26 cm. 1. Toronto — History. I. T.
F1059.5.T6857 G55   971.3/541   LC 78-163815   *ISBN* 0802017916

Maxwell, Thomas R., 1911-.   **3.8834**
The invisible French: the French in metropolitan Toronto / Thomas R. Maxwell. — Waterloo, Ont.: Wilfrid Laurier University Press, c1977. xv, 174 p.; 23 cm. Originally presented as the author's thesis. University of Toronto. 1. French-Canadians — Ontario — Toronto region — Social conditions. 2. French — Ontario — Toronto region — Social conditions. 3. Toronto region (Ont.) — Social conditions. I. T.
F1059.5.T689 F85 1977   301.45/11/1140713541   LC 78-303931   *ISBN* 0889200297

F1060–1060.9 Canadian Northwest (General)

Campbell, Marjorie Wilkins, 1902-.   • **3.8835**
The North West Company / Marjorie Wilkins Campbell. — Toronto: Macmillan, 1957. xiv, 295 p., 3 leaves of plates: ill., maps. Includes index. 1. North West Company. I. T.
F1060.C18   LC 57-59416

Innis, Harold Adams, 1894-1952.   • **3.8836**
Fur trade in Canada: an introduction to Canadian economic history. / Harold Adams Innis. — Rev. ed. — [Toronto]: University of Toronto Press, 1956. xi, 463 p.; 24 cm. 1. Fur trade — Canada. 2. Canada — Economic conditions 3. Northwest, Canadian — History. 4. Canada — History — To 1763 (New France) I. T.
F1060.I58 1956   338.1791   LC 57-2937

Mackintosh, William Archibald, 1895-.   • **3.8837**
Prairie settlement, the geographical setting, by W. A. Mackintosh. — Toronto: The Macmillan company of Canada limited, 1934. xv, 242 p.: ill.; 28 cm. (Canadian frontiers of settlement; v. I) Cop.2 autographed. 1. Frontier and pioneer life — Prairie provinces. 2. Land settlement — Prairie provinces. I. T. II. Series.
F1060.M28   LC 34-23504

Morton, Arthur Silver, 1870-1945.   **3.8838**
A history of the Canadian west to 1870–71; being a history of Rupert's Land (the Hudson's Bay Company's territory) and of the North-West Territory (including the Pacific slope). Edited by Lewis G. Thomas. — 2d ed. —

[Toronto; Buffalo]: Published in co-operation with University of Saskatchewan by University of Toronto Press, [1973] xxviii, 1039 p.: 12 maps (in pocket); 23 cm. 1. Hudson's Bay Company. 2. Northwest, Canadian — History. 3. Northwest, Pacific — History. I. Thomas, Lewis Gwynne, 1914- ed. II. T.
F1060.M76 1973   917.12/2/03   LC 72-97150   ISBN 0802040330

The Prairie west to 1905: a Canadian sourcebook / general   3.8839
editor, Lewis G. Thomas; contributing editors, David H. Breen ... [et al.].
Toronto: Oxford University Press, 1976 (c1975). xiii, 360 p.: maps; 23 cm. 1. Prairie Provinces — History — Sources. I. Thomas, Lewis Gwynne, 1914- II. Breen, David.
F1060.P7   971.2   LC 76-375608   ISBN 0195402499

Van Kirk, Sylvia.   3.8840
Many tender ties: women in fur–trade society, 1670–1870 / by Sylvia Van Kirk. — 1st American ed. — Norman: University of Oklahoma Press, 1983. 301 p.: ill.; 24 cm. Includes index. 1. Fur traders' wives — Northwest, Canadian. 2. Fur trade — Northwest, Canadian — History. 3. Northwest, Canadian — Social conditions. 4. Northwest, Canadian — Social life and customs. 5. Northwest, Canadian — History. I. T.
F1060.V36 1983   305.4/09712 19   LC 82-40457   ISBN 0806118423

Wallace, W. Stewart (William Stewart), 1884-1970. ed.   • 3.8841
Documents relating to the North West Company [edited with introd., notes, and appendices, by W. Stewart Wallace] New York, Greenwood Press, 1968. xv, 527 p. illus., ports. 24 cm. (Champlain Society publication, 22) Title on spine: The North West Company. Reprint of the 1934 ed. Appendices (p. 425-513):—A. A biographical dictionary of the Nor'westers.—B. A select bibliography relating to the history of the North West Company. 1. North West Company (1967-) 2. Fur trade — Canada. 3. Northwest, Canadian — Biography. I. T.
F1060.W19 1968   338.7/63/911   LC 68-28610

Hearne, Samuel, 1745-1792.   3.8842
A journey from Prince of Wales's Fort in Hudson's Bay to the Northern Ocean, 1769, 1770, 1771, 1772 / by Samuel Hearne; edited with and introd. by Richard Glover. — Toronto: Macmillan, 1958. lxxii, 301 p.: ill., 1 fold map, port. 1. Hearne, Samuel, 1745-1792. 2. Hudson's Bay Company. 3. Indians of North America — Northwest, Canadian 4. Natural history — Northwest, Canadian. 5. Northwest, Canadian — Description and travel — To 1821 6. Northwest Passage 7. Northwest, Canadian — Description and travel I. T.
F1060.7 H42 1958   FC3205.1.H42 1958.   917.12   LC 59-3217

Crouse, Nellis Maynard, 1884-.   • 3.8843
La Verendrye, fur trader and explorer [by] Nellis M. Crouse. — Port Washington, N.Y.: Kennikat Press, [1972, c1956] ix, 247 p.: illus., maps (part fold.); 23 cm. 1. La Vérendrye, Pierre Gaultier de Varennes, sieur de, 1685-1749. 2. New France — Discovery and exploration. I. T.
F1060.7.L3914 1972   970/.03/0924 B   LC 79-153210   ISBN 0804615209

Mackenzie, Alexander, Sir, 1763-1820.   • 3.8844
First man West: Alexander Mackenzie's journal of his voyage to the Pacific coast of Canada in 1793 / edited by Walter Sheppe. — Berkeley: University of California Press, 1962. ix, 366 p.: maps; 24 cm. Includes index. 1. Indians of North America — Northwest, Canadian. 2. Fur trade — Northwest, Canadian. 3. Northwest, Canadian — Description and travel — To 1870. I. Sheppe, Walter. II. T.
F1060.7.M178 1976   917.11   LC 62-15084

Masson, L. R. (Louis Rodrigue), 1833-1903.   • 3.8845
Les bourgeois de la compagnie du Nord–Ouest: récits de voyages, lettres et rapports inédits relatifs au nord–ouest canadien / publiés avec une esquisse historique et des annotations par L. R. Masson. — Quebec: Impr. génnérale A. Coté et cie, 1889-1890. 2 v.: fold. map; 24 cm. 1. North West Company. 2. Northwest, Canadian — Description and travel I. T.
F1060.7.M42   LC 01-24515

Radisson, Pierre Esprit, ca. 1636-1710.   • 3.8846
Voyages of Peter Esprit Radisson, being an account of his travels and experiences among the North American Indians, from 1652 to 1684. Transcribed from original manuscripts in the Bodleian Library and the British Museum. With historical illus. and an introd. by Gideon D. Scull. New York, B. Franklin [1971?] vi, 385 p. 23 cm. (Burt Franklin research and source works series, 131. American classics in history and social science, 2) Reprint of the 1885 ed., which was issued as v. 16 of the Publications of the Prince Society. 1. Hudson's Bay Company. 2. Indians of North America — Canada 3. Iroquois Indians 4. Northwest, Canadian — History. 5. New France — Discovery and exploration. I. T.
F1060.7.R12 1971   917.1/04/16   LC 72-184164

Galbraith, John S.   • 3.8847
The Hudson's Bay Company as an imperial factor, 1821–1869 / by John S. Galbraith. — Berkeley: University of California Press, 1957. viii, 500 p.: cartes; 24 cm. 1. Hudson's Bay Company. I. T.
F1060.8.G3   FC3213.G24.   LC 57-12392

McMicking, Thomas, 1829-1866.   3.8848
Overland from Canada to British Columbia / by Thomas McMicking; edited by Joanne Leduc; with illustrations by William G. R. Hind. — Vancouver: University of British Columbia Press, c1981. xl, 121 p., [12] p. of plates: ill. (some col.); 23 cm. — (Recollections of the pioneers of British Columbia. 4th v.) Includes index. 1. McMicking, Thomas, 1829-1866. 2. Overland journeys to the Pacific 3. British Columbia — History. 4. Prairie Provinces — Description and travel. I. Leduc, Joanne. II. T. III. Series.
F1060.8.M39 1981   917.1/044 19   LC 82-108332   ISBN 0774801360

Spry, Irene Mary Biss.   • 3.8849
The Palliser expedition: an account of John Palliser's British North American expedition, 1857–1860 / Irene M. Spry. — Toronto: Macmillan Co. of Canada, 1963 [i.e. 1964]. vi, 310 p.: ill., maps, ports.; 23 cm. Includes index. 1. Palliser, John, 1807-1887. 2. Northwest, Canadian — Description and travel 3. Canada — Exploring expeditions. I. T.
F1060.8.P2 S6   FC3213.1.P2 S65.   LC 64-933

Simpson, George, Sir, 1786 or 7-1860.   • 3.8850
Fur trade and empire: George Simpson's journal entitled Remarks connected with the fur trade in the course of a voyage from York Factory to Fort George and back to York Factory 1824–25, with related documents / edited with a new introd. by Frederick Merk. — Rev. ed. — Cambridge, Mass.: Belknap Press of Harvard University Press, 1968. lxii, 370 p.: fold. map.; 24 cm. 1. Simpson, George, Sir, 1786 or 7-1860. 2. Hudson's Bay Company. 3. Fur trade — Northwest, Canadian — History. 4. Northwest, Canadian — Description and travel — 1821-1867 I. Merk, Frederick, 1887- ed. II. T.
F1060.8.S552 1968   917.12/04/1   LC 68-15646

Gray, James Henry, 1906-.   3.8851
The roar of the twenties / James H. Gray. — Toronto: Macmillan of Canada, c1975. 358 p., [16] leaves of plates: ill.; 24 cm. Includes index. 1. Prairie Provinces — History. 2. Prairie Provinces — Economic conditions. 3. Prairie Provinces — Social conditions. I. T.
F1060.9.G684   971.2/02   LC 75-324708   ISBN 0770512763

Howard, Joseph Kinsey, 1906-1951.   • 3.8852
Strange empire; a narrative of the Northwest. — New York: Morrow, 1952. xii, 601 p. maps. 22 cm. 1. Riel, Louis, 1844-1885. 2. Red River Rebellion, 1869-1870 3. Riel Rebellion, 1885 I. T.
F1060.9.H7 1974   971.05/1   LC 52-9705   *(1965)*

Owram, Doug, 1947-.   3.8853
Promise of Eden: the Canadian expansionist movement and the idea of the West, 1856–1900 / Doug Owram. — Toronto; Buffalo: University of Toronto Press, 1980. x, 264 p., [1] leaf of plates: map; 24 cm. 1. Northwest, Canadian — History. 2. Canada — Territorial expansion. I. T.
F1060.9.O94   971.2/01 19   LC 80-491231   ISBN 0802054838

Flanagan, Thomas.   3.8854
Louis 'David' Riel: prophet of the new world / Thomas Flanagan. — Toronto; Buffalo: University of Toronto Press, c1979. ix, 216 p.; 24 cm. 1. Riel, Louis, 1844-1885. 2. Revolutionists — Northwest Territories — Biography. I. T.
F1060.9.R5 F57   971.05/1/0924   LC 78-18497   ISBN 0802054307

Stanley, George Francis Gilman.   • 3.8855
Louis Riel. — Toronto: Ryerson Press, [1963] 433 p.: ill., maps, ports. 1. Riel, Louis, 1844-1885. I. T.
F1060.9.R5S8   LC 64-4396

Stanley, George Francis Gilman.   • 3.8856
The birth of western Canada: a history of the Riel Rebellions / by George F.G. Stanley; maps by C.C.J.Bond. — [2d ed.]. — Toronto: University of Toronto Press, 1961,c1960. xiv, 475 p., [18] leaves of plates: ill., maps; 21 cm. 1. Red River Rebellion, 1869-1870 2. Riel Rebellion, 1885 3. Northwest, Canadian — History. I. T.
F1060.9.S79 1961   LC 61-1393   ISBN 0802060102

F1061–1080 MANITOBA.
SASKATCHEWAN. ALBERTA

Friesen, Gerald.   3.8857
The Canadian prairies: a history / Gerald Friesen. — Lincoln: University of Nebraska Press, c1984. xv, 524 p., [35] p. of plates: ill.; 25 cm. Includes index. 1. Prairie Provinces — History. I. T.
F1062.F74 1984   971.2 19   LC 84-255837   ISBN 0803219725

Morton, W. L. (William Lewis), 1908-.   • 3.8858
Manitoba, a history [by] W. L. Morton. [2d ed. Toronto] University of Toronto Press [1967] xii, 547 p. illus., 7 maps. 24 cm. 1. Manitoba — History. I. T.
F1063.M88 1967   971.27   *LC* 67-4598

Pritchett, John Perry, 1902-.   • 3.8859
The Red River Valley, 1811–1849; a regional study. New York, Russell & Russell [1970, c1942] xvii, 295 p. map. 25 cm. (The Relations of Canada and the United States) 1. Selkirk, Thomas Douglas, Earl of, 1771-1820. 2. Red River Valley (Minn. and N.D.-Man.) — History. 3. Red River Settlement. I. T.
F1064.R3 P7 1970   971.27/4   *LC* 75-102532

Bennett, John William, 1915-.   • 3.8860
Northern plainsmen; adaptive strategy and agrarian life [by] John W. Bennett. Foreword by Walter R. Goldschmidt. — Chicago: Aldine Pub. Co., [1969] xvi, 352 p.: illus.; 22 cm. 1. Agriculture — Saskatchewan. 2. Saskatchewan — Civilization. I. T.
F1071.B45   301.29/7124   *LC* 76-75043

Stegner, Wallace Earle, 1909-.   3.8861
Wolf willow; a history, a story, and a memory of the last plains frontier. New York, Viking Press [1962] 306 p. 22 cm. 1. Stegner, Wallace Earle, 1909- — Biography — Youth. 2. Frontier and pioneer life — Cypress Hills region, Alta. and Sask. 3. Authors, American — 20th century — Biography. 4. Cypress Hills region, Alta. and Sask. — History. 5. Cypress Hills region, Alta. and Sask. — Fiction. I. T.
F1071.S7   917.124   *LC* 62-17939

Campbell, Marjorie Wilkins, 1902-.   • 3.8862
The Saskatchewan; illustrated by Illingworth H. Kerr. New York, Rinehart [1950] 400 p. illus., map. 21 cm. (Rivers of America.) 1. Saskatchewan River. 2. Northwest, Canadian — History. I. T. II. Series.
F1076.C18   971.23   *LC* 50-6401

F1088–1090.5 BRITISH COLUMBIA. NORTHWEST TERRITORIES. ARCTIC

Ormsby, Margaret Anchoretta, 1909-.   • 3.8863
British Columbia, a history / Margaret A. Ormsby. — [Toronto]: Macmillan, 1958. x, 558 p., [22] leaves of plates: ill. (some col.), col. maps; 24 cm. 1. British Columbia — History. I. T.
FC3811.O75   F1088.O7.   *LC* 59-23058

Hutchison, Bruce.   • 3.8864
The Fraser; illustrated by Richard Bennett. New York, Toronto, Rinehart [1950] 368 p. illus., map. 21 cm. (Rivers of America) Includes index. 1. Fraser River (B.C.) I. T.
F1089.F7 H8   971.1   *LC* 50-10549

Pethick, Derek, 1920-.   3.8865
The Nootka connection: Europe and the Northwest coast, 1790–1795 / Derek Pethick. — Seattle: University of Washington Press; Vancouver: Douglas & McIntyre, c1980. 281 p.: ill.; 24 cm. First published from label on t.p. Includes index. 1. Nootka Sound — History. 2. Northwest Coast of North America — History. 3. Northwest Coast of North America — Description and travel. I. T.
F1089.N8 P47 1980   979.5   *LC* 80-51074   *ISBN* 0295957549

Allison, Susan, 1845-1937.   3.8866
A pioneer gentlewoman in British Columbia: the recollections of Susan Allison / edited by Margaret A. Ormsby. — Vancouver, B.C.: University of British Columbia Press, c1976. xlix, 210 p., [6] leaves of plates: ill.; 24 cm. (Recollections of the pioneers of British Columbia; v. 2) Includes index. 1. Allison, Susan, 1845-1937. 2. Frontier and pioneer life — Okanagan River Valley (B.C. and Wash.) 3. Pioneers — Okanagan River Valley (B.C. and Wash.) — Biography. 4. Okanagan River Valley (B.C. and Wash.) — Biography. I. Ormsby, Margaret Anchoretta, 1909- II. T.
F1089.O5 A44 1976   971.1/4/030924 B   *LC* 77-354991   *ISBN* 0774800399

Cooke, Alan, 1933-.   3.8867
The exploration of northern Canada, 500 to 1920: a chronology / Alan Cooke and Clive Holland. — Toronto: Arctic History Press, c1978. 549, 25 p.: maps (1 fold. in pocket); 25 cm. Includes index. 1. Canada, Northern — Discovery and exploration — Chronology. 2. Canada, Northern — History — Chronology. I. Holland, Clive. joint author. II. T.
F1090.5.C67   917.1/04/0202   *LC* 80-457979   *ISBN* 0771022654

Diubaldo, Richard J.   3.8868
Stefansson and the Canadian Arctic / Richard J. Diubaldo. — Montreal: McGill-Queen's University Press, c1978. xii, 274 p., [4] leaves of plates: ill.; 25 cm. Includes index. 1. Stefansson, Vilhjalmur, 1879-1962. 2. Explorers — Canada — Biography. 3. Canada, Northern — Discovery and exploration. I. T.
F1090.5.D58   971.9/9/020924 B   *LC* 79-304078   *ISBN* 0773503242

Wallace, Hugh N.   3.8869
The Navy, the Company, and Richard King: British exploration in the Canadian Arctic, 1829–1860 / Hugh N. Wallace. — Montreal: McGill-Queen's University Press, c1980. xxix, 232 p., [6] leaves of plates: ill.; 25 cm. Includes index. 1. King, Richard, 1811?-1876. 2. Hudson's Bay Company. 3. Great Britain. Royal Navy — History — 19th century. 4. Canada, Northern — Description and travel. 5. Canada, Northern — Discovery and exploration. I. T.
F1090.5.W33   971.9/901 19   *LC* 80-496295   *ISBN* 0773503382

F1121–1139 Newfoundland. Labrador

Newfoundland in the nineteenth and twentieth centuries: essays in interpretation / edited by James Hiller and Peter Neary.   3.8870
Toronto: University of Toronto Press, 1980. viii, 289 p.: maps; 23 cm. Includes index. 1. Newfoundland — History. 2. Newfoundland — Politics and government. 3. Newfoundland — Economic conditions. I. Hiller, James K. II. Neary, Peter.
F1122.5.N4x   971.8   *LC* 80-506730   *ISBN* 0802054862 bd

Ingstad, Anne Stine, 1918-.   3.8871
The Discovery of a Norse settlement in America / by Anne Stine Ingstad; with contributions by Charles J. Bareis ... [et al.]; [translated by Elizabeth Seeberg]. — Oslo: Universitetsforlaget; Irvington-on-Hudson, N.Y.: Columbia University Press, c1977-. v. <1 >: ill.; 29 cm. Errata slip inserted in v. 1. 1. Excavations (Archaeology) — Newfoundland — L'Anse aux Meadows. 2. L'Anse aux Meadows (Nfld.) — Antiquities. 3. Newfoundland — Antiquities 4. America — Discovery and exploration — Norse I. T.
F1124.5.L36 D57 1977   971.8/01 19   *LC* 83-462228   *ISBN* 8200015130

Kerr, James Lennox, 1899-.   • 3.8872
Wilfred Grenfell, his life and work / by J. Lennox Kerr; with a foreword by Lord Grenfell of Kilvey. — London: Harrap, 1959. 272 p.: ill., port.; 23 cm. 1. Grenfell, Wilfred Thomason, Sir, 1865-1940. 2. Missionaries, Medical — Newfoundland — Biography. 3. Newfoundland — Description and travel. 4. Labrador — Description and travel. I. T.
F1137.G7K4 1959   266/.025/0924   *LC* 60-38934

F1201–1392 MEXICO

Cline, Howard Francis. • **3.8873**
Mexico; revolution to evolution, 1940–1960. London, New York, Oxford University Press, 1962. xiv, 375 p. maps. 21 cm. 1. Mexico — History — 1910-1946 2. Mexico — History — 1946-1970 3. Mexico — Civilization I. T.
F1208.C55   972.081   LC 62-4941

Mexico, a country study / Foreign Area Studies, the American   **3.8874**
University; edited by James D. Rudolph.
3rd ed. — Washington, D.C.: Headquarters, Dept. of the Army: For sale by the Supt. of Docs., U.S. G.P.O., 1985. xli, 472 p.: ill., maps; 25 cm. (Area handbook series.) (DA pam. 550-79) 'Research completed October 1984.' Includes index. 1. Mexico. I. Rudolph, James D., 1947- II. American University (Washington, D.C.). Foreign Area Studies. III. Series. IV. Series: DA pam. 550-79
F1208.M5828 1985   972 19   LC 85-15794

Lafaye, Jacques.   **3.8875**
[Quetzalcóatl et Guadalupe. English] Quetzalcóatl and Guadalupe: the formation of Mexican national consciousness, 1531–1813 / Jacques Lafaye; with a foreword by Octavio Paz; translated by Benjamin Keen. — Chicago: University of Chicago Press, 1976. xxx, 336 p.; 24 cm. Translation of: Quetzalcóatl et Guadalupe. 1. Guadalupe, Our Lady of 2. Quetzalcoatl 3. Mexico — Civilization — History. 4. Mexico — Religion. I. T.
F1210.L313   972   LC 75-20889   ISBN 0226467945

Leonard, Irving Albert, 1896-.   • **3.8876**
Baroque times in old Mexico: seventeenth–century persons, places, and practices / by Irving Leonard. — Ann Arbor: University of Michigan Press [1959] xi, 260 p.: ill., ports., map.; 24 cm. 1. Mexico — Social life and customs. 2. Mexico — History — Spanish colony, 1540-1810 I. T.
F1210.L4   LC 59-9734

Paz, Octavio, 1914-.   **3.8877**
[Laberinto de la soledad. English] The labyrinth of solitude: life and thought in Mexico. Translated by Lysander Kemp. New York, Grove Press [1962, c1961] 212 p. 21 cm. Essays. 1. National characteristics, Mexican 2. Mexico — Civilization I. T.
F1210.P313   917.2   LC 61-11777

Schmidt, Henry C., 1937-.   **3.8878**
The roots of lo mexicano: self and society in Mexican thought, 1900–1934 / by Henry C. Schmidt. — 1st ed. — College Station: Texas A&M University Press, c1978. xiii, 195 p.; 24 cm. Includes index. 1. Ramos, Samuel. 2. National characteristics, Mexican 3. Mexico — Intellectual life 4. Mexico — Civilization I. T.
F1210.S35   972.08   LC 77-99280   ISBN 0890960488

Humboldt, Alexander von, 1769-1859.   **3.8879**
[Essai politique sur le royaume de la Nouvelle-Espagne. English] Political essay on the kingdom of New Spain. The John Black translation (abridged) Edited with an introd. by Mary Maples Dunn. [1st ed.] New York, Knopf [1972] 242 p. 19 cm. (A Borzoi book on Latin America) Abridged translation of Essai politique sur le royaume de la Nouvelle-Espagne. 1. Mexico — Description and travel 2. Mexico — Economic conditions I. Dunn, Mary Maples. ed. II. T.
F1211.H925   917.2/03/2   LC 75-169695   ISBN 0394475569 ISBN 0394315103

F1219–1221 Antiquities. Indians

Bernal, Ignacio.   **3.8880**
A history of Mexican archaeology: the vanished civilizations of Middle America / Ignacio Bernal. — London; New York: Thames and Hudson, 1980. 208 p.: ill.; 25 cm. Includes index. 1. Indians of Mexico — Antiquities 2. Archaeological surveying — Mexico — History. 3. Mexico — Antiquities I. T.
F1219.B5162   972/.0072 19   LC 79-63882   ISBN 0500780080

Beyond the codices: the Nahua view of colonial Mexico /   **3.8881**
translated and edited by Arthur J. O. Anderson, Frances
Berdan, and James Lockhart; with a linguistic essay by Ronald
W. Langacker.
Berkeley: University of California Press, 1976. 235 p., [16] leaves of plates: facsims.; 24 cm. (UCLA Latin American studies series; v. 27) English and Aztec. 1. Nahuas — History — Sources. 2. Mexico — History — Sources. 3. Mexico — History — To 1810 — Sources. I. Anderson, Arthur J. O. II. Berdan, Frances. III. Lockhart, James.
F1219.B55   972/.02 19   LC 74-29801   ISBN 0520029747

Codex Nuttall.   **3.8882**
The Codex Nuttall: a picture manuscript from ancient Mexico: the Peabody Museum facsimile / edited by Zelia Nuttall; with new introductory text by Arthur G. Miller. — New York: Dover Publications, 1975. xxii, 84 p.: chiefly col. ill.; 22 x 29 cm. 1. Codex Nuttall. 2. Manuscripts, Mixtec — Facsimiles. 3. Mixtec Indians — Writing I. Nuttall, Zelia, 1858-1933. II. Peabody Museum of Archaeology and Ethnology. III. T.
F1219.C7 1975   745.6/7   LC 74-83057   ISBN 0486231682

Coe, Michael D.   • **3.8883**
America's first civilization, by Michael D. Coe. Consultant: Richard B. Woodbury. — [New York]: American Heritage; distribution by Van Nostrand [Princeton, N.J., 1968] 159 p.: illus. (part col.), col. maps, ports.; 27 cm. — (The Smithsonian library) 1. Olmecs I. T.
F1219.C7569   970.3   LC 68-55791

Davies, Nigel, 1920-.   **3.8884**
The Toltecs, until the fall of Tula / by Nigel Davies. 1st ed. — Norman: University of Oklahoma Press, c1977. xviii, 533 p.: ill.; 24 cm. (Civilization of the American Indian series.) Includes index. 1. Toltecs 2. Mexico — Antiquities I. T. II. Series.
F1219.D2783   972   LC 76-62513   ISBN 0806113944

Keen, Benjamin, 1913-.   **3.8885**
The Aztec image in Western thought. — New Brunswick, N.J.: Rutgers University Press, [1971] xviii, 667 p.: illus.; 25 cm. Running title: The Aztecs in Western thought. 1. Aztecs — Historiography. I. T. II. Title: The Aztecs in Western thought.
F1219.K43   972   LC 74-163952   ISBN 0813506980

Motolinía, Toribio, d. 1568.   • **3.8886**
History of the Indians of New Spain. Translated and edited by Elizabeth Andros Foster. [Berkeley, Calif.] Cortés Society, 1950. 294 p. ill. 27 cm. (Documents and narratives concerning the discovery & conquest of Latin America, new ser., 4) Cover title: The Indians of New Spain. 1. Franciscans — Mexico. 2. Indians of Mexico I. T. II. Title: The Indians of New Spain.
F 1219 M91 E5   LC 50-2863

Muser, Curt.   **3.8887**
Facts and artifacts of ancient Middle America: a glossary of terms and words used in the archaeology and art history of pre–Columbian Mexico and Central America / compiled by Curt Muser. — 1st ed. — New York: Dutton, c1978. xxviii, 212 p., [8] leaves of plates: ill. (some col.); 23 cm. 1. Indians of Mexico — Dictionaries and encyclopedias. 2. Indians of Central America — Dictionaries and encyclopedias. I. T.
F1219.M97 1978   972/.003   LC 77-79799   ISBN 0525102159

Sahagún, Bernardino de, d. 1590.   • **3.8888**
[Historia general de las cosas de Nueva España. English & Aztec] General history of the things of New Spain: Florentine codex / Bernardino de Sahagún. — Santa Fe, N.M.: School of American Research; Salt Lake City, Utah: University of Utah, 1950-. v.: ill.; 29 cm. (Monographs of the School of American Research. no. 14, pt. 1-13) English and Aztec. Translation of: Historia general de las cosas de Nueva España. Cover title: Florentine codex. Pts. 2-13, with notes and illustrations by Arthur J.O. Anderson and Charles E. Dibble. 1. Indians of Mexico — Antiquities 2. Aztecs 3. Natural history — Mexico. 4. Mexico — History — Conquest, 1519-1540 5. Mexico — Antiquities I. Anderson, Arthur J. O. II. Dibble, Charles E. III. T. IV. Title: Florentine codex. V. Series.
F1219.S1319   972/.02 19   LC 51-2409   ISBN 087480082X

Sahagún, Bernardino de, d. 1590.   **3.8889**
[Historia general de las cosas de Nueva España. English and Aztec] General history of the things of New Spain. Translated from the Aztec into English, with notes and illus., by Arthur J. O. Anderson [and] Charles E. Dibble. 2d ed., rev. Santa Fe, N.M., School of American Research, 19 < 70-81 > . v. < 1-4, 13 > illus. 29 cm. (Monographs of the School of American Research, no. 14, pt. < 1-4, 13 >) At head of title: Florentine codex. English and Aztec. Part 3, book

2: Order from University of Utah Press, Salt Lake City, Utah. 1. Indians of Mexico — Antiquities 2. Aztecs 3. Natural history — Mexico. 4. Mexico — History — Conquest, 1519-1540 5. Mexico — Antiquities I. T. II. Title: Florentine codex.
F1219.S13192   970.4/2   *LC* 71-29117   *ISBN* 087480194X

Weaver, Muriel Porter.   3.8890
The Aztecs, Maya, and their predecessors: archaeology of Mesoamerica / Muriel Porter Weaver. — 2nd ed. — New York: Academic Press, 1981. xxiii, 597 p: ill.; 24 cm. — (Studies in archaeology) Map and chart on lining papers. Includes indexes. 1. Indians of Mexico — Antiquities 2. Indians of Central America — Antiquities 3. Mexico — Antiquities 4. Central America — Antiquities. I. T.
F1219.W42 1981   972 19   *LC* 80-2344   *ISBN* 0127859365

1972

F1219.1 SPECIAL LOCALITIES, A–Z

Wasserstrom, Robert.   3.8891
Class and society in central Chiapas / Robert Wasserstrom. — Berkeley: University of California Press, c1983. x, 357 p., [8] p. of plates: ill.; 22 cm. Includes index. 1. Indians of Mexico — Chiapas — Social conditions. 2. Indians of Mexico — Chiapas — History. 3. Tzotzil Indians — Social conditions. 4. Chiapas (Mexico) — Social conditions. I. T.
F1219.1.C45 W37 1983   305.8/97/07275 19   *LC* 82-11126   *ISBN* 0520046706

Gibson, Charles, 1920-.   3.8892
The Aztecs under Spanish rule; a history of the Indians of the Valley of Mexico, 1519–1810. — Stanford, Calif., Stanford University Press, 1964. xii, 657 p. illus. (1 col.) maps. 24 cm. Bibliography: p. [607]-634. 1. Indians of Mexico — Mexico, Valley of. 2. Mexico — Hist. — To 1810. 3. Spain — Colonies — America — Administration. I. T.
F1219.1.M53G5   972.02   *LC* 64-12071

Sanders, William T.   3.8893
The basin of Mexico: ecological processes in the evolution of a civilization [by] William T. Sanders, Jeffrey R. Parsons [and] Robert S. Santley. — New York, Academic Press, 1979. 2 v. ill., maps.; 24 cm. (Studies in archaeology) Vol. 2 consists of 12 fold. maps in casing. Bibliography: p. 533-549. I. Parsons, Jeffrey R., jt. author II. Santley, Robert S., jt. author III. T.
F1219.1.M53 S23   *LC* 79-11697

Tehuacan Archaeological-Botanical Project.   3.8894
The prehistory of the Tehuacan Valley. — Austin: Published for the Robert S. Peabody Foundation, Phillips Academy, Andover [Mass., by the] University of Texas Press 1972. 290 p.: ill., maps; 29 cm. 1. Indians of Mexico — Mexico — Tehuacán River Valley — Antiquities. 2. Ethnobotany — Mexico — Tehuacán River Valley. 3. Indians of Mexico — Tehuacán Valley — Ethnobotany. 4. Tehuacán River Valley (Mexico) — Antiquities. I. Byers, Douglas S., 1903- ed. II. Robert S. Peabody Foundation for Archaeology. III. T.
F1219.1.T224 T4   970.4/2/4   *LC* 67-17873   *ISBN* 0292700687

Millon, René, 1921-.   3.8895
The Teotihuacán map / by René Millon. — Austin: University of Texas Press [1973] 2 v.: ill.; 28 cm. (His Urbanization at Teotihuacán, Mexico, v. 1) (v. 1 also in series: The Dan Danciger publication series.) Errata slips inserted. Part of illustrative matter in pocket. 1. Teotihuacán Site (San Juan Teotihuacán, Mexico) — Maps. I. T. II. Series.
F1219.1.T27 M83 vol. 1 GA485   301.36/0972/5 s 912/.72/5   *LC* 72-7588   *ISBN* 0292785011

Coe, Michael D.   3.8896
In the land of the Olmec / by Michael D. Coe and Richard A. Diehl. — Austin: University of Texas Press, c1980. 2 v.: ill. (some col.); 30 cm. Set includes folder containing 4 fold. col. maps. 1. San Lorenzo Tenochtitlán site. 2. Coatzacoalcos region, Mexico — Social life and customs. I. Diehl, Richard A. joint author. II. T.
F1219.1.V47 C63   972/.6   *LC* 79-17167   *ISBN* 0292775490

F1219.3 SPECIAL TOPICS, A–Z

Heyden, Doris.   3.8897
Pre–Columbian architecture of Mesoamerica / Doris Heyden and Paul Gendrop; translated by Judith Stanton. — New York: H. N. Abrams, [1973] 336 p. (History of world architecture) Translation of Architettura mesoamericana. 1. Indians of Mexico — Architecture 2. Indians of Central America — Architecture 3. Mexico — Antiquities 4. Central America — Antiquities. I. Gendrop, Paul. II. T. III. Series.
F1219.3.A6 H4913   720/.972   *LC* 75-8993   *ISBN* 0810910187

Marquina, Ignacio.   3.8898
Arquitectura prehispánica. [2. ed.] México: Instituto Nacional de Antropología e Historia, Secretaría de Educación Pública, 1964. xix, 1055 p.: ill., maps, plans, col. plates; 32 cm. (Memorias del I. N. A. H., 1) 1. Architecture — Mexico. 2. Indians of Mexico — Architecture 3. Mexico — Antiquities I. T.
F1219.3.A6 M37 1964   *LC* 64-53212

Covarrubias, Miguel, 1904-1957.   • 3.8899
Indian art of Mexico and Central America. Color plates and line drawings by the author. [1st ed.] New York, Knopf, 1957. 360, xvii p. 28 cm. Bibliography: p. 335-360. 1. Indians of Mexico — Art 2. Indians of Central America — Art 3. Mexico — Antiquities 4. Central America — Antiquities. I. T.
F1219.3.A7C58   970.65717   *LC* 57-59203

Dwyer, Jane Powell.   3.8900
Fire, earth, and water: sculpture from the Land Collection of Mesoamerican Art: [exhibited at the Fine Arts Museums of San Francisco, California Palace of the Legion of Honor, July 4, 1975–September 14, 1975, Honolulu Academy of Arts, January–March, 1976, Seattle Art Museum, April–June, 1976] / by Jane P. Dwyer and Edward B. Dwyer; [photos. by James Medley; ill. by Wendy Kitamata]. — [San Francisco]: Fine Arts Museums of San Francisco, c1975. 141 p.: ill. (some col.); 28 cm. 1. Land, Lewis K. — Art collections. 2. Indians of Central America — Sculpture — Exhibitions. 3. Indians of Mexico — Sculpture — Exhibitions. I. Dwyer, Edward Bridgman, joint author. II. California Palace of the Legion of Honor. III. Honolulu Academy of Arts. IV. Seattle Art Museum. V. T.
F1219.3.A7 D98   730   *LC* 75-14770   *ISBN* 0884010066

Stierlin, Henri.   3.8901
Art of the Aztecs and its origins / Henri Stierlin; [translated from the French. L'art aztèque et ses origines by Betty and Peter Ross]. — New York: Rizzoli, c1982. 228 p.: ill. (col.); 31 cm. Includes index. 1. Aztecs — Art 2. Indians of Mexico — Art I. T.
F1219.3.S8413 1982   F1219.3.A7 S7613 1982.   *LC* 82-50424   *ISBN* 0847804410

Aveni, Anthony F.   3.8902
Skywatchers of ancient Mexico / by Anthony F. Aveni; foreword by Owen Gingerich. — Austin: University of Texas Press, c1980. x, 355 p.: ill.; 26 cm. — (The Texas Pan American series) Includes index. 1. Indians of Mexico — Astronomy 2. Indians of Central America — Astronomy 3. Astronomy, Prehistoric 4. Mayas — Astronomy I. T.
F1219.3.A85 A9   520/.972   *LC* 79-27341   *ISBN* 0292775571

Caso, Alfonso, 1896-1970.   • 3.8903
[Pueblo del sol. English] The Aztecs; people of the sun / Illustrated by Miguel Covarrubias; translated by Lowell Dunham. [1st ed.] Norman: University of Oklahoma Press [1958] xvii, 125 p.: col. ill., 16 plates.; 28 cm. (The Civilization of the American Indian series, 50) Translation of El pueblo del sol. 1. Aztecs 2. Indians of Mexico — Religion and mythology I. T.
F1219.3.R38 C313   299/.792 19   *LC* 58-11603

F1219.7–.8 PRE-COLUMBIAN PEOPLES

Coe, Michael D.   3.8904
Mexico / Michael D. Coe. — 3rd ed., rev. and enl. — New York, N.Y.: Thames and Hudson, 1984. 180 p.: ill.; 24 cm. (Ancient peoples and places) Includes index. 1. Indians of Mexico — Antiquities 2. Indians of Mexico — History. 3. Mexico — History — To 1519 4. Mexico — Antiquities I. T.
F1219.7.C63 1984   972/.01 19   *LC* 83-72968   *ISBN* 0500273286

Conrad, Geoffrey W.   3.8905
Religion and empire: the dynamics of Aztec and Inca expansionism / Geoffrey W. Conrad, Arthur A. Demarest. — Cambridge [Cambridgeshire]; New York: Cambridge University Press, 1984. xii, 266 p.: ill.; 24 cm. — (New studies in archaeology.) Includes index. 1. Aztecs — History. 2. Aztecs — Religion and mythology 3. Aztecs — Politics and government. 4. Incas — History. 5. Incas — Religion and mythology 6. Incas — Politics and government. 7. Indians — Religion and mythology 8. Indians — Tribal government. I. Demarest, Arthur Andrew. II. T. III. Series.
F1219.73.C66 1984   972/.01 19   *LC* 83-14414   *ISBN* 0521243572

Pasztory, Esther.   3.8906
Aztec art / Esther Pasztory. — New York: H.N. Abrams, [1983] 335 p.: ill. (some col.); 31 cm. Includes index. 1. Aztecs — Art 2. Aztecs — History. 3. Indians of Mexico — Art I. T.
F1219.76.A78 P37 1983   709/.72 19   *LC* 82-11527   *ISBN* 0810906872

Zantwijk, R. A. M. van (Rudolf A. M.), 1932-.   3.8907
The Aztec arrangement: the social history of pre–Spanish Mexico / by Rudolph van Zantwijk; foreword by Miguel León–Portilla. — 1st ed. — Norman: University of Oklahoma Press, c1985. xxv, 345 p.: ill.; 25 cm. (Civilization of

the American Indian series. [v. 167]) 'Expanded and enlarged work based on Handel en wandel van de Azteken: de sociale geschiedenis van voor-Spaans Mexico, the original Dutch language edition, published 1977 by Van Gorcum Ltd., Assen, The Netherlands'—Verso of t.p. Includes index. 1. Aztecs — Social conditions. 2. Aztecs — History. 3. Indians of Mexico — Social conditions. I. Zantwijk, R. A. M. van (Rudolf A. M.), 1932- Handel en wandel van de Azteken. II. T. III. Series.
F1219.76.S63 Z36 1985   972/.01 19   *LC* 84-21927   *ISBN* 0806116773

F1221 MODERN INDIAN TRIBES

Perera, Victor, 1934-.   3.8908
The last lords of Palenque: the Lacandon Mayas of the Mexican rain forest / by Victor Perera and Robert D. Bruce. — 1st ed. — Boston: Little, Brown, c1982. 311 p.: ill.; 24 cm. 1. Lacandon Indians I. Bruce S., Roberto D. II. T.
F1221.L2 P47 1982   972/.00497 19   *LC* 82-32   *ISBN* 0316699160

Spores, Ronald.   3.8909
The Mixtecs in ancient and colonial times / by Ronald Spores. — Norman: University of Oklahoma Press, c1984. xiv, 263 p.: ill.; 24 cm. (Civilization of the American Indian series. [v. 168]) Includes index. 1. Mixtec Indians — History. 2. Indians of Mexico — Oaxaca (State) — History. 3. Mixtec Indians — Social life and customs. 4. Indians of Mexico — Oaxaca (State) — Social life and customs. I. T. II. Series.
F1221.M7 S66 1984   972/.74 19   *LC* 84-40279   *ISBN* 0806118849

Friedlander, Judith.   3.8910
Being Indian in Hueyapan: a study of forced identity in contemporary Mexico / Judith Friedlander. — New York: St. Martin's Press, [1975] xviii, 205 p.: ill.; 22 cm. Includes index. 1. Indians of Mexico — Race identity. 2. Nahuas — Social life and customs. 3. Hueyapan, Mexico. I. T.
F1221.N3 F74   301.45/19/70724   *LC* 74-23047

Pennington, Campbell W.   • 3.8911
The Tarahumar of Mexico: their environment and material culture. Salt Lake City, University of Utah Press [1963] 267 p. illus., 4 fold. maps (in pocket) 24 cm. 1. Tarahumare Indians 2. Indians of Mexico — Implements 3. Anthropogeography — Mexico — Chihuahua (State) I. T.
F1221.T25 P4   *LC* 64-1645

Foster, George McClelland, 1913-.   • 3.8912
Empire's children; the people of Tzintzuntzan, by George M. Foster, assisted by Gabriel Ospina. — Westport, Conn.: Greenwood Press, [1973] v, 297 p.: illus.; 29 cm. 'Prepared in cooperation with the United States Department of State as a project of the Interdepartmental Committee on Scientific and Cultural Cooperation.' Reprint of the 1948 ed., which was issued as Publication no. 6 of Smithsonian Institution Institute of Social Anthropology. 1. Tarasco Indians 2. Tzintzuntzan, Mexico. I. T.
F1221.T3 F67 1973   970.4/2/3   *LC* 73-118760   *ISBN* 0837150779

Gossen, Gary H.   3.8913
Chamulas in the world of the sun; time and space in a Maya oral tradition [by] Gary H. Gossen. Cambridge, Harvard University Press, 1974. xvii, 382 p. illus. 24 cm. 1. Tzotzil Indians 2. Tzotzil language 3. Tzotzil Indians — Folklore. 4. Indians of Mexico — Folklore. I. T.
F1221.T9 G67   970.3   *LC* 73-83424   *ISBN* 0674107268

Spicer, Edward Holland, 1906-.   3.8914
The Yaquis: a cultural history / Edward H. Spicer. — Tucson: University of Arizona Press, c1980. xiv, 393 p.: ill.; 27 cm. Includes index. 1. Yaqui Indians I. T.
F1221.Y3 S66   970.004/97   *LC* 79-27660   *ISBN* 0816505888

Whitecotton, Joseph W., 1937-.   3.8915
The Zapotecs: princes, priests, and peasants / by Joseph W. Whitecotton. — 1st ed. — Norman: University of Oklahoma Press, c1977. xiv, 338 p.: ill.; 24 cm. (Civilization of the American Indian series.) Includes index. 1. Zapotec Indians I. T. II. Series.
F1221.Z3 W48   970/.004/97   *LC* 76-62508   *ISBN* 080611374X

F1223–1235 History

Cline, Howard Francis.   • 3.8916
The United States and Mexico / by Howard F. Cline. Rev. ed., enl. Cambridge: Harvard University Press, c1963. 484 p.: maps; 20 cm. (American foreign policy library.) 1. Mexico — History 2. United States — Relations — Mexico 3. Mexico — Relations — United States I. T. II. Series.
F1226.C6 1963a   972.08   *LC* 63-25301

Meyer, Michael C.   3.8917
The course of Mexican history / Michael C. Meyer, William L. Sherman. — New York: Oxford University Press, 1979. xi, 696, xxxiii p.: ill.; 26 cm. Includes index. 1. Mexico — History I. Sherman, William L. joint author. II. T.
F1226.M54   972   *LC* 78-894   *ISBN* 0195024133

Parkes, Henry Bamford, 1904-.   • 3.8918
A history of Mexico. — 3d ed., rev. and enl. — Boston: Houghton Mifflin, 1960. 458 p.: illus.; 22 cm. 1. Mexico — History I. T.
F1226.P27 1960   972   *LC* 60-9360

Simpson, Lesley Byrd, 1891-.   • 3.8919
Many Mexicos. — 4th ed. rev. — Berkeley: University of California Press, 1966. xiii, 389 p.: illus., maps (part fold.); 24 cm. 1. Mexico — History 2. Mexico — Civilization I. T.
F1226.S63 1966   972   *LC* 66-19101

F1230 1519-1535

Braden, Charles Samuel, 1887-.   • 3.8920
Religious aspects of the conquest of Mexico. Durham, N.C., Duke university press, 1930. xv, 344 p. plates, 24 cm. 1. Cortés, Hernán, 1485-1547. 2. Indians of Mexico — Missions 3. Catholic Church — Mexico. 4. Catholic Church — Mexico. 5. Mexico — History — Conquest, 1519-1540 6. Mexico — Church history I. T.
F1230.B79   *LC* 30-31135

Cortés, Hernán, 1485-1547.   3.8921
[Cartas. English. 1977] Fernando Cortes, his five letters of relation to the Emperor Charles V [1519–1526] / Translated and edited, with a biographical introd. and notes compiled from original sources, by Francis Augustus MacNutt. — Glorieta, N.M.: Rio Grande Press, 1977,[c1908]. 2 v.: ill.; 24 cm. (A Rio Grande classic) On spine: Letters of Corte's to Emperor Charles V. Reprint of the ed. published by A. H. Clark Co., Cleveland. 'An introduction to an age of conquest, by John Greenway': v. 1, p. 1. Cortés, Hernán, 1485-1547. 2. Aztecs 3. Conquerors — Mexico — Biography. 4. Mexico — History — Conquest, 1519-1540 5. Mexico — Governors — Biography. I. Charles V, Holy Roman Emperor, 1500-1558. II. MacNutt, Francis Augustus, 1863-1927. III. Greenway, John. Introduction to an age of conquest. 1977. IV. T.
F1230.C856 1977   972/.02/0924   *LC* 77-1155   *ISBN* 0873801253

Díaz del Castillo, Bernal, 1496-1584.   • 3.8922
[Historia verdadera. English] The discovery and conquest of Mexico, 1517–1521. Edited from the only exact copy of the original MS. (and published in Mexico) by Genaro García. Translated with an introd. and notes by A. P. Maudslay. Introd. to the American ed. by Irving A. Leonard. [New York] Farrar, Straus, and Cudahy [c1956] xxxi, 478 p. illus., port., maps. 24 cm. Translation of Historia verdadera de la conquista de la Nueva España. 1. Mexico — History — Conquest, 1519-1540 I. T.
F1230.D5442 1956   972.02   *LC* 56-5758

Fuentes, Patricia de, ed. and tr.   • 3.8923
The conquistadors; first–person accounts of the conquest of Mexico. Pref. by Howard F. Cline. — New York: Orion Press, [1963] xxii, 250 p.: illus., ports., maps, plan.; 23 cm. 1. Mexico — History — Conquest, 1519-1540 2. America — Early accounts to 1600 I. T.
F1230.F9   972.01   *LC* 63-9525

León Portilla, Miguel, ed.   • 3.8924
The broken spears: the Aztec account of the conquest of Mexico / English translation by Lysander Kemp; illus., adapted from original codices paintings, by Alberto Beltran. — Boston: Beacon Press [1962] xxxi, 168 p.: ill., map.; 24 cm. Translation of Visión de los vencidos which was translated from Náhuatl by Angel Maria Garibay K. 1. Aztec literature — Translations into English. 2. English literature — Translations from Aztec. 3. Mexico — History — Conquest, 1519-1540 — Sources. I. Kemp, Lysander, 1920- tr. II. T.
F1230.L383   972.02   *LC* 62-7247

Prescott, William Hickling, 1796-1859.   • 3.8925
The conquest of Mexico, by W. H. Prescott. London & Toronto, J. M. Dent; New York, E. P. Dutton [1931-33] 2 v. double map. 18 cm. (Everyman's library. History. [no. 397-398]) 'First published in this edition, 1909: v. 1 reprinted, 1933; v. 2, 1931.' 'Introduction by Thomas Seccombe.' 'A list of the works of William Hickling Prescott': v. 1, p. xv. 1. Cortés, Hernán, 1485-1547. 2. Mexico — History — Conquest, 1519-1540 I. T.
F1230.P9692x   *LC* 36-37452

F1231–1232 1535–1849

Benítez, Fernando, 1911-.   • **3.8926**
The century after Cortés / by Fernando Benítez; translated by Joan MacLean. — Chicago: University of Chicago Press, c1965. 296 p.: ill. 1. Mexico — Social life and customs. 2. Mexico — History — Spanish colony, 1540-1810 I. T.
F1231.B4513   *LC* 65-25121

Israel, Jonathan Irvine.   **3.8927**
Race, class, and politics in colonial Mexico, 1610–1670 / by J. I. Israel. — London: Oxford University Press, 1975. xiii, 305 p.: map; 23 cm. — (Oxford historical monographs) Based on the author's thesis, Oxford. Includes index. 1. Social classes — Mexico. 2. Mexico — History — Spanish colony, 1540-1810 3. Mexico — Social conditions — To 1810 I. T.
F1231.I83   972/.02   *LC* 75-320631   *ISBN* 0198218605

MacLachlan, Colin M.   **3.8928**
The forging of the cosmic race: a reinterpretation of colonial Mexico / Colin M. MacLachlan, Jaime E. Rodríguez O. — Berkeley: University of California Press, c1980. xiv, 362 p., [6] leaves of plates: ill.; 24 cm. Includes index. 1. Mexico — History — Spanish colony, 1540-1810 I. Rodríguez O., Jaime E., 1940- joint author. II. T.
F1231.M32   972/.02   *LC* 78-68836   *ISBN* 0520038908

Calvert, Peter.   **3.8929**
Mexico. — New York: Praeger, [1973] 361 p.: illus.; 23 cm. — (Nations of the modern world.) 1. Mexico — History — 1810- I. T. II. Series.
F1231.5.C273   972   *LC* 70-76975

Anna, Timothy E., 1944-.   **3.8930**
The fall of the royal government in Mexico City / Timothy E. Anna. — Lincoln: University of Nebraska Press, c1978. xix, 289 p.; 22 cm. Includes index. 1. Mexico — Politics and government — 1810-1821 2. Mexico — Politics and government — 1540-1810 I. T.
F1232.A57   972/.03   *LC* 77-17790   *ISBN* 0803209576

Callcott, Wilfrid Hardy, 1895-.   • **3.8931**
Church and state in Mexico, 1822–1857 / by Wilfrid Hardy Callcott.— New York: Octagon Books, 1965. 357 p.; 24 cm. Includes index. 1. Mexico. Constitution. 2. Church and state — Mexico 3. Mexico — Politics and government — 1821-1861 I. T.
F1232.C142 1965   *LC* 65-16767

Hamill, Hugh M.   • **3.8932**
The Hidalgo revolt; prelude to Mexican independence [by] Hugh M. Hamill, Jr. — Gainesville: University of Florida Press, 1966. xi, 284 p.: facsims., ports.; 25 cm. 1. Hidalgo y Costilla, Miguel, 1753-1811. 2. Mexico — History — Wars of Independence, 1810-1821 I. T.
F1232.H6243   972.030924   *LC* 66-23070

Robertson, William Spence, 1872-.   • **3.8933**
Iturbide of Mexico. New York, Greenwood Press, 1968 [c1952] ix, 361 p. illus., coat of arms, map, ports. 24 cm. (Duke University publications) 1. Iturbide, Agustín de, 1783-1824. 2. Mexico — History — Wars of Independence, 1810-1821 3. Mexico — History — 1821-1861 I. T.
F1232.I925 1968   972/.03/0924 B   *LC* 68-23321

F1233–1233.5 1849/1861–191

Hanna, Alfred Jackson, 1893-.   **3.8934**
Napoleon III and Mexico; American triumph over monarchy, by Alfred Jackson Hanna and Kathryn Abbey Hanna. — Chapel Hill: University of North Carolina Press, [1971] xxii, 350 p.: illus.; 24 cm. 1. Mexico — History — European intervention, 1861-1867 2. Mexico — Foreign relations — 1861-1867 3. U.S. — Foreign relations — 1861-1865. I. Hanna, Kathryn Trimmer (Abbey) 1895- joint author. II. T.
F1233.H2   972/.07   *LC* 72-156761   *ISBN* 0807811718

Cadenhead, Ivie Edward, 1923-.   **3.8935**
Benito Juárez, by Ivie E. Cadenhead, Jr. New York, Twayne Publishers [c1973] 199 p. 21 cm. (Twayne's rulers and statesmen of the world series, TROW 23) 1. Juárez, Benito, 1806-1872. 2. Mexico — History — 1821-1867. 3. Mexico — History — 1867-1910 I. T.
F1233.J9342   972/.07/0924 B   *LC* 73-1761   *ISBN* 0805730540

Sinkin, Richard N.   **3.8936**
The Mexican reform, 1855–1876: a study in liberal nation–building / by Richard N. Sinkin. — Austin: Institute of Latin American Studies, University of Texas at Austin: distributed by University of Texas Press, c1979. 263 p.; 23 cm. (Latin American monographs; no. 49) Includes index. 1. Mexico — Politics and government — 1821-1861 2. Mexico — Politics and government — 1861-1867 3. Mexico — Politics and government — 1867-1910 I. T.
F1233.S56   972/.06 19   *LC* 78-620053   *ISBN* 0292750447

Smith, Gene.   **3.8937**
Maximilian and Carlota; a tale of romance and tragedy. New York, Morrow, 1973. 318 p. illus. 25 cm. 1. Maximilian, Emperor of Mexico, 1832-1867. 2. Carlota, Empress, consort of Maximilian, Emperor of Mexico, 1840-1927. I. T.
F1233.S66   972/.07/0924 B   *LC* 70-182969   *ISBN* 0688001734

Other Mexicos: essays on regional Mexican history, 1876–1911   **3.8938**
/ edited by Thomas Benjamin, William McNellie.
1st ed. — Albuquerque: University of New Mexico Press, c1984. xv, 319 p.: ill.; 24 cm. Includes index. 1. Mexico — Politics and government — 1867-1910 — Addresses, essays, lectures. 2. Mexico — Economic conditions — Addresses, essays, lectures. 3. Mexico — Social conditions — Addresses, essays, lectures. 4. Mexico — History, Local — Addresses, essays, lectures. I. Benjamin, Thomas, 1952- II. McNellie, William, 1949-
F1233.5.O84 1984   972.08/1 19   *LC* 84-5052   *ISBN* 082630754X

F1234 1910–1946

Brandenburg, Frank Ralph, 1926-.   • **3.8939**
The making of modern Mexico [by] Frank Brandenburg. Introd. by Frank Tannenbaum. — Englewood Cliffs, N.J.: Prentice-Hall, [1964] xv, 379 p.: map.; 24 cm. 1. Mexico — History — 1910-1946 2. Mexico — History — 1946-1970 I. T.*
F1234.B815   972.082   *LC* 63-16743

Calvert, Peter.   • **3.8940**
The Mexican Revolution, 1910–1914: the diplomacy of Anglo–American conflict. — Cambridge; London: Cambridge U.P., 1968. x, 331 p.: maps.; 22 cm. — (Cambridge Latin American studies. 3) 1. Mexico — History — 1910-1946 2. United States — Foreign relations — 1909-1913 3. Great Britain — Foreign relations — 1910-1936 I. T. II. Series.
F1234.C2125   972.08   *LC* 68-12056   *ISBN* 0521044235

Cumberland, Charles Curtis.   • **3.8941**
Mexican Revolution, genesis under Madero. New York, Greenwood Press [1969, c1952] ix, 298 p. illus., map, ports. 23 cm. 1. Madero, Francisco I., 1873-1913. 2. Mexico — History — 1910-1946 I. T.
F1234.C975 1969   972.08/1   *LC* 71-90495   *ISBN* 0837121264

Cumberland, Charles Curtis.   **3.8942**
Mexican Revolution: the constitutionalist years. With an introd. and additional material by David C. Bailey. — Austin: University of Texas Press, [1972] xix, 449 p.: illus.; 23 cm. — (The Texas Pan American series) 1. Mexico — History — 1910-1946 I. T.
F1234.C976   972.08/2   *LC* 74-38506   *ISBN* 0292750005

Hodges, Donald Clark, 1923-.   **3.8943**
Mexico, 1910–1982: reform or revolution? / Donald Hodges and Ross Gandy. — 2nd ed. — London: Zed Press; Westport, Conn.: U.S. distributor, L. Hill, 1983. 250 p.; 22 cm. Includes index. 1. Mexico — History — 1910-1946 2. Mexico — History — 1946-1970 3. Mexico — History — 1970- I. Gandy, Daniel Ross, 1935- II. T.
F1234.H797 1983   972.08 19   *LC* 83-113427   *ISBN* 0862321441

Meyer, Michael C.   **3.8944**
Huerta; a political portrait, by Michael C. Meyer. Lincoln: University of Nebraska Press [1972] xvi, 272 p.; 24 cm. 1. Huerta, Victoriano, 1854-1916. I. T.
F1234.H87 M48   972.08/1/0924 B   *LC* 70-162343   *ISBN* 0803208022

Levy, Daniel C.   **3.8945**
Mexico, paradoxes of stability and change / Daniel Levy and Gabriel Székely. — Boulder, Colo.: Westview Press, 1983. xiv, 287 p.: ill.; 24 cm. — (Westview profiles. Nations of contemporary Latin America.) Includes index. 1. Mexico — Politics and government — 20th century I. Székely, Gabriel, 1953- II. T. III. Series.
F1234.L65 1983   972.08 19   *LC* 82-16028   *ISBN* 0865310203

Ross, Stanley Robert, 1921-.   • **3.8946**
Francisco I. Madero: apostle of Mexican democracy / by Stanley R. Ross. — New York: AMS Press [1970, c1955] xii, 378 p. maps, port. 23 cm. Originally presented as author's thesis, Columbia University, 1955, under title: Mexican apostle; the life of Francisco I. Madero. 1. Madero, Francisco I., 1873-1913. 2. Díaz, Porfirio, 1830-1915. 3. Mexico — Politics and government — 1910-1946 I. T.
F1234.M244 1970   972.08/1/0924   *LC* 79-122591   *ISBN* 0404054099

Hall, Linda B. (Linda Biesele), 1939-.   **3.8947**
Álvaro Obregón: power and revolution in Mexico, 1911–1920 / by Linda B. Hall. — 1st ed. — College Station: Texas A&M University Press, c1981. xiv,

290 p., [20] p. of plates: ill.; 24 cm. Includes index. 1. Obregón, Alvaro, 1880–1928. 2. Mexico — Politics and government — 1910-1946 I. T.
F1234.O2 H34   972.08/22/0924 19   *LC* 80-6110   *ISBN* 0890961131

Quirk, Robert E.   **3.8948**
The Mexican Revolution and the Catholic Church, 1910–1929 / [by] Robert E. Quirk. Bloomington: Indiana University Press [1973] 276 p.: map; 24 cm. 1. Catholic Church — Mexico — History — 20th century. 2. Church and state — Mexico — History — 20th century 3. Mexico — History — Revolution, 1910-1920 — Religious aspects. 4. Mexico — History — Revolution, 1910-1920 I. T.
F1234.Q625 1973   972.08/2   *LC* 73-75399   *ISBN* 025333800X

Richmond, Douglas W., 1946-.   **3.8949**
Venustiano Carranza's nationalist struggle, 1893–1920 / Douglas W. Richmond. — Lincoln: University of Nebraska Press, c1983. xxi, 317 p., [8] p. of plates: ill.; 24 cm. Includes index. 1. Carranza, Venustiano, 1859-1920. 2. Nationalism — Mexico — History — 20th century. 3. Mexico — Politics and government — 1910-1946 I. T.
F1234.R554 1983   972.08/1 19   *LC* 83-3652   *ISBN* 0803238630

Ross, Stanley Robert, 1921- ed.   **3.8950**
Is the Mexican Revolution dead? / Edited with an introd. by Stanley R. Ross. — 2d ed. rev. and enl. — Philadelphia: Temple University Press, 1975. xxxviii, 339 p.; 19 cm. 1. Mexico — History — 1910-1946 — Addresses, essays, lectures. 2. Mexico — History — 1946-1970 — Addresses, essays, lectures. 3. Mexico — History — 1970- — Addresses, essays, lectures. I. T.
F1234.R85 1975   972.08   *LC* 75-14015   *ISBN* 0877220751

Ruiz, Ramón Eduardo.   **3.8951**
The great rebellion: Mexico, 1905–1924 / Ramón Eduardo Ruiz. — 1st ed. — New York: Norton, c1980. xii, 530 p.; 22 cm. Includes index. 1. Mexico — History — 1910-1946 I. T.
F1234.R9114 1980   972.08   *LC* 79-27659   *ISBN* 0393013235

Tannenbaum, Frank, 1893-1969.   • **3.8952**
Peace by revolution; an interpretation of Mexico Drawings by Miguel Covarrubias. — Freeport, N.Y.: Books for Libraries Press, [1971, c1933] 316 p.: illus.; 23 cm. 1. Mexico — History — 1910-1946 2. Mexico — History — 1810- 3. Mexico — Social conditions I. T.
F1234.T14 1971   917.2/03   *LC* 72-169776   *ISBN* 0836959965

Parkinson, Roger.   **3.8953**
Zapata: a biography / by Roger Parkinson. — New York: Stein and Day, 1975. 256 p., [4] leaves of plates: map; 24 cm. 1. Zapata, Emiliano, 1879-1919. I. T.
F1234.Z37 P37 1975   972.08/1/0924 B   *LC* 74-28202   *ISBN* 0812817761

F1241–1391 Regions. Cities

Warren, J. Benedict.   **3.8954**
The conquest of Michoacán: the Spanish domination of the Tarascan Kingdom in Western Mexico, 1521–1530 / by J. Benedict Warren. — 1st ed. — Norman: University of Oklahoma Press, c1985. xv, 352 p.: ill.; 24 cm. Includes index. 1. Tarasco Indians — History. 2. Indians of Mexico — Michoacán de Ocampo — History. 3. Michoacán de Ocampo (Mexico) — History. 4. Mexico — History — Conquest, 1519-1540 I. T. II. Title: Tarascan Kingdom in Western Mexico, 1521-1530.
F1306.W37 1985   972/.02/0924 19   *LC* 84-40280   *ISBN* 080611858X

Jiménez, Luz, d. 1965.   **3.8955**
[Porfirio Díaz a Zapata. English and Aztec] Life and death in Milpa Alta; a Nahuatl chronicle of Díaz and Zapata. Translated and edited by Luz Jiménez Horcasitas from the Nahuatl recollections of Luz Jiménez. Foreword by Miguel León-Portilla. Drawings by Alberto Beltrán. [1st ed.] Norman, University of Oklahoma Press [1972] xx, 187 p. illus. 21 cm. (Civilization of the American Indian series. v. 117) Contains the Aztec text from the original 1968 Aztec and Spanish ed. (De Porfirio Díaz a Zapata) with English translation. 1. Jiménez, Luz, d. 1965. 2. Milpa Alta. 3. Mexico — History — 1910-1946 I. Horcasitas, Fernando. ed. II. T. III. Series.
F1391.M55 J5 1972   917.2/5   *LC* 78-177338   *ISBN* 0806110015

Radfield, Robert, 1897-.   • **3.8956**
Tepoztlan, a Mexican village: a study of folk life / by Robert Redfield. Chicago, Ill.: The University of Chicago press, c1930. xi, 247 p.: ill., music, plates, double map, diagr.; 21 cm. (Ethnological series. .) Half-title: The University of Chicago publications in anthropology. 1. Ethnology — Mexico 2. Tepoztlán (Mexico) 3. Mexico — Social life and customs. I. T. II. Series.
F1391.T3 R31   917.24   *LC* 30-15556

F1401–1419 LATIN AMERICA: GENERAL

F1401–1407 Reference Works. Organization of American States

Latin America and Caribbean contemporary record.   **3.8957**
Vol. 1 (1981-1982)-   . — New York: Holmes & Meier, [c1983-. v.; 24 cm. Annual. 1. Latin America — Politics and government — 1980- — Yearbooks.
F1401.L3253   980/.03 19   *LC* 83-646058

The South American handbook.   • **3.8958**
[1st.- ed.] 1924-. Bath, Eng. [etc.] Trade & Travel Publications ltd. [etc.] [Chicago, Distributed in the United States of America by Rand McNally] v. ill., fold map. 19 cm. Annual. Includes the Caribbean, Mexico and Central America. 1. Latin America — Yearbooks. 2. Latin America — Statistics — Yearbooks. I. Hunter, J. A. II. Davies, Howell.
F1401.S71   *LC* 25-514

Encyclopedia of Latin America. Edited by Helen Delpar.   **3.8959**
New York: McGraw-Hill, [1974] ix, 651 p.: illus.; 29 cm. 1. Latin America — Dictionaries and encyclopedias. I. Delpar, Helen. ed.
F1406.E52   918/.03/03   *LC* 74-1036   *ISBN* 0070556458

Baily, Samuel L.   **3.8960**
Perspectives on Latin America, edited by Samuel L. Baily and Ronald T. Hyman. — New York: Macmillan, [1974] xix, 105 p.: illus.; 24 cm. — (Latin America series) 1. Latin America — Addresses, essays, lectures. I. Hyman, Ronald T. joint author. II. T.
F1406.7.B34   918/.03/308   *LC* 73-10689   *ISBN* 0025058304

Alexander, Robert Jackson, 1918-.   • **3.8961**
Prophets of the revolution, profiles of Latin American leaders. — New York: Macmillan, 1962. 322 p.; 22 cm. 1. Latin America — Biography. 2. Latin America — Politics and government I. T.
F1407.A38   923.28   *LC* 62-7363

F1408–1409.3 General Works. Description

James, Preston Everett, 1899-.   • **3.8962**
Latin America, by Preston E. James. Maps by Eileen W. James. — 4th ed. — New York: Odyssey Press, [1969] xx, 947 p.: illus., maps (part col.); 24 cm. 1. Latin America I. T.
F1408.J28 1969   918   *LC* 69-10222

West, Robert Cooper, 1913-.   • **3.8963**
Middle America; its lands and peoples [by] Robert C. West [and] John P. Augelli. — Englewood Cliffs, N.J.: Prentice-Hall, [1966] 482 p.: illus., maps.; 26 cm. 1. West Indies 2. Mexico. 3. Central America I. Augelli, John P. joint author. II. T.
F1408.W44   917.2   *LC* 66-14748

Wilgus, A. Curtis (Alva Curtis), 1897-1981.   **3.8964**
Latin America, a guide to illustrations / A. Curtis Wilgus. — Metuchen, N.J.: Scarecrow Press, 1981. xxviii, 250 p.; 23 cm. Includes index. 1. Latin America — History — Pictorial works — Catalogs. 2. Latin America — Biography — Portraits — Catalogs. I. T.
F1408.W667   980 19   *LC* 81-9070   *ISBN* 0810814595

Arciniegas, Germán, 1900-.   • **3.8965**
[Continente de siete colores. English] Latin America: a cultural history. Translated from the Spanish by Joan MacLean. [1st American ed.] New York, Knopf, 1967 [c1966] xxvii, 594 p. illus. 22 cm. Translation of El continente de siete colores. 1. Latin America — Civilization I. T.
F1408.3.A663   918/.03   *LC* 66-11342

Crawford, William Rex, 1898-.   **3.8966**
A century of Latin-American thought. Rev. ed. Cambridge, Mass., Harvard University Press, 1961. 322 p. 22 cm. Includes bibliography. 1. Philosophers,

Spanish-American. 2. Latin America — Civilization 3. Latin America — Intellectual life I. T.
F1408.3.C7 1961   918   *LC* 61-13749

Foster, George McClelland, 1913-.   • **3.8967**
Culture and conquest: America's Spanish heritage. — New York: Wenner-Gren Foundation for Anthropological Research, 1960. 272 p.: ill. (Viking Fund publications in anthropology. no. 27) 1. Acculturation 2. Spain — Civilization 3. Latin America — Civilization — Spanish influences. I. T. II. Series.
F1408.3.F6

Henríquez Ureña, Pedro, 1884-1946.   • **3.8968**
[Historia de la cultura en la América Hispánica. English] A concise history of Latin American culture. Translated and with a supplementary chapter by Gilbert Chase. New York, Praeger [1966] ix, 214 p. 21 cm. Translation of Historia de la cultura en la América Hispánica. 1. Latin America — Civilization I. Chase, Gilbert, 1906- ed. and tr. II. T.
F1408.3.H4513   918.03   *LC* 65-18079

Latin America and the enlightenment: essays / by Arthur P.   **3.8969**
Whitaker ... [et al.]; introduction by Federico de Onis; edited by
Arthur P. Whitaker.
2nd ed. — Ithaca: Cornell University Press, c1961. xv, 156 p.; 19 cm. 1. Enlightenment 2. Latin America — Intellectual life 3. Brazil — Intellectual life I. Whitaker, Arthur Preston, 1895-
F1408.3.L28 1961   *LC* 61-16668   *ISBN* 0801490545

Núñez, Benjamín, 1912-.   **3.8970**
Dictionary of Afro-Latin American civilization / Benjamin Nuñez, with the assistance of the African Bibliographic Center. — Westport, Conn.: Greenwood Press, 1980. xxxv, 525 p.: ill.; 24 cm. Includes indexes. 1. Latin America — Civilization — African influences — Dictionaries. 2. Caribbean Area — Civilization — African influences — Dictionaries. I. African Bibliographic Center. II. T.
F1408.3.N86   980/.003   *LC* 79-7731   *ISBN* 0313211388

Picón-Salas, Mariano, 1901-1965.   • **3.8971**
[De la conquista a la independencia. English] A cultural history of Spanish America, from conquest to independence. Translated by Irving A. Leonard. Berkeley, University of California Press, 1962. 192 p. 22 cm. Translation of De la conquista a la independencia. 1. Latin America — Civilization I. T.
F1408.3.P5213 1962   918   *LC* 62-15381

Schurz, William Lyttle, 1886-1962.   • **3.8972**
This New World: the civilization of Latin America / illus. by Carl Folke Sahlin. — [1st ed.]. — New York: Dutton, 1954. 429 p.: ill.; 22 cm. 1. Latin America — Civilization I. T.
F1408.3.S4   918   *LC* 54-5043

Platt, Robert S. (Robert Swanton), 1891-.   • **3.8973**
Latin America, countrysides and united regions. 1st ed. New York London, McGraw-Hill book company, inc., 1942. x, 564 p. incl. illus., tables, diagrs. 24 cm. 1. Latin America — Description and travel I. T.
F1409.P55   *LC* 43-74

Webb, Kempton Evans.   **3.8974**
Geography of Latin America; a regional analysis [by] Kempton E. Webb. Englewood Cliffs., N.J., Prentice-Hall [1972] xiv, 126 p. illus. 24 cm. (Foundations of world regional geography series) 1. Latin America — Description and travel — 1951-1980 I. T.
F1409.2.W4   918   *LC* 71-144096   *ISBN* 0133514528 *ISBN* 0133514455

F1409.6–1414 History

The Cambridge history of Latin America / edited by Leslie   **3.8975**
Bethell.
Cambridge [Cambridgeshire]; New York: Cambridge University Press, 1985 (c1984) v. < 1-3 >: ill.; 24 cm. 1. Latin America — History — Collected works. I. Bethell, Leslie.
F1410.C1834   980 19   *LC* 83-19036   *ISBN* 0521232236

Chapman, Charles Edward, 1880-1941.   • **3.8976**
Colonial Hispanic America: a history. — New York: Hafner Pub. Co., 1971 [c1933] xvii, 405 p.: maps, ports.; 22 cm. 'Facsimile of 1937 edition.' 1. Latin America — History — To 1830 2. Spain — Colonies — America. 3. Portugal — Colonies — America. I. T.
F1410.C433 1937a   980/.01   *LC* 72-152257

Collier, Simon.   **3.8977**
From Cortés to Castro; an introduction to the history of Latin America, 1492–1973 [by] Simon Collier. New York, Macmillan [1974] xii, 429 p. maps. 24 cm. 1. Latin America — History I. T.
F1410.C7   980   *LC* 74-3252   *ISBN* 0025271806

Diffie, Bailey W. (Bailey Wallys), 1902-1983.   • **3.8978**
Latin-American civilization, colonial period, by Bailey W. Diffie, with the assistance of Justine Whitfield Diffie. New York, Octagon Books, 1967. lxxxvi, 812 p. illus., facsim., maps, ports. 24 cm. 1. Latin America — Civilization 2. Latin America — History — To 1830 I. T.
F1410.D5 1967   918/.03/1   *LC* 67-18760

Gibson, Charles, 1920- comp.   **3.8979**
The Spanish tradition in America. [1st ed.] New York, Harper & Row [1968] vi, 257 p. 20 cm. (Harper torchbooks, TB1351) (Documentary history of the United States.) 1. Latin America — History — To 1830 — Sources. 2. America — Discovery and exploration — Spanish 3. Spain — Colonies — America — Administration. I. T.
F1410.G5   980/.01   *LC* 68-63011

Góngora, Mario.   **3.8980**
Studies in the colonial history of Spanish America / Mario Góngora; translated by Richard Southern. — Cambridge [Eng.]; New York: Cambridge University Press, 1975. xi, 293 p.; 23 cm. (Cambridge Latin American studies. 20) Includes index. 1. Latin America — History — To 1830 2. Spain — Colonies — America — Administration. I. T. II. Series.
F1410.G75   980/.03   *LC* 74-19524   *ISBN* 0521206863

Hamill, Hugh M. ed.   • **3.8981**
Dictatorship in Spanish America / edited with an introd. by Hugh M. Hamill, Jr. — [1st ed.]. — New York: Knopf, 1965. x, 242 p.; 19 cm. — (Borzoi books on Latin America) 1. Dictators — Latin America. 2. Latin America — Politics and government I. T.
F1410.H24   321.64098   *LC* 64-23731

Haring, Clarence Henry, 1885-1960.   • **3.8982**
The Spanish empire in America [by] C. H. Haring. — New York: Oxford university press, 1947. viii, 388 p.; 25 cm. Map on lining-papers. 'This book has its inception in a series of twelve lectures delivered in the spring of 1934 at the Instituto hispano-cubano of the University of Seville in Spain.'—Foreword. 1. Latin America — History — To 1830 2. Spain — Colonies — America — Administration. I. T.
F1410.H25   980   *LC* 47-1142

Hennessy, Alistair.   **3.8983**
The frontier in Latin American history / Alistair Hennessy. — Albuquerque: University of New Mexico Press, 1978. 202 p.; 25 cm. — (Histories of the American frontier) Glossary in Spanish and English. Includes index. 1. Frontier thesis 2. Frontier and pioneer life — Latin America. 3. Latin America — History I. T.
F1410.H45 1978   980   *LC* 78-58816   *ISBN* 0826304664

Herring, Hubert Clinton, 1889-.   • **3.8984**
A history of Latin America, from the beginnings to the present, by Hubert Herring with the assistance of Helen Baldwin Herring. — 3d ed. [rev., enl.]. — New York: Knopf, [1968] xxii, 1002, xxv p.: maps.; 24 cm. 1. Latin America — History I. Herring, Helen Baldwin, joint author. II. T.
F1410.H47 1968   980   *LC* 67-25977

Johnson, John J., 1912-.   • **3.8985**
The military and society in Latin America. — Stanford, Calif.: Stanford University Press, 1964. x, 308 p.; 23 cm. 1. Armed Forces — Political activity 2. Sociology, Military — Latin America. 3. Latin America — Armed Forces. I. T.
F1410.J7   980   *LC* 64-12073

Madariaga, Salvador de, 1886-.   • **3.8986**
The fall of the Spanish American empire. — New, rev. ed. — New York: Collier Books, [1963] 414 p.; 18 cm. 'BS176v.' A companion to The rise of the Spanish American empire. 1. Latin America — History — To 1830 2. Spain — Colonies — America. I. T.
F1410.M23 1963   980   *LC* 63-9893

Madariaga, Salvador de, 1886-.   • **3.8987**
The rise of the Spanish American empire. — New York, Macmillan Co., 1947. xix, 408 p. illus., port., maps (on lining-papers) 22 cm. 'This study ... is divided into two equal parts of which this book, 'The rise' is part one ... Part two, 'The fall,' will follow.' Bibliographical references included in 'Notes' (p. 336-380) Bibliography: p. 381-392. 1. Latin America — Hist. — To 1830. 2. Spain — Colonies — America. I. T.
F1410.M25 1947a   980   *LC* 47-12400 *

Parry, J. H. (John Horace), 1914-.   • **3.8988**
The Spanish seaborne empire, by J. H. Parry. [1st American ed.] New York, Knopf, 1966. 416 p. illus., facsim., maps. 22 cm. (The History of human society)

1. Latin America — History — To 1830 2. Spain — Colonies — America.
I. T.
F1410.P3 1966   325.346098   *LC* 66-10754

Silvert, Kalman H.   • 3.8989
The conflict society: reaction and revolution in Latin America [by] Kalman H. Silvert. — Rev. ed. — New York: American Universities Field Staff, [1966] xiv, 289 p.; 24 cm. 1. Latin America — Politics and government 2. Latin America — Social conditions — 1945- I. T.
F1410.S6 1966   320.98   *LC* 66-20311

F1411–1414.2 BY PERIOD

Casas, Bartolomé de las, 1474-1566.   3.8990
In defense of the Indians; the defense of the Most Reverend Lord, Don Fray Bartolomé de las Casas, of the Order of Preachers, late Bishop of Chiapa, against the persecutors and slanderers of the peoples of the New World discovered across the seas. Translated, edited, and annotated by Stafford Poole. DeKalb, Northern Illinois University Press [c1974] x, 385 p. illus. 25 cm. Translation of a ca. 1552 Latin ms. in the Bibliothèque nationale, Paris (Nouveaux fonds Latins, no. 12926) 1. Sepúlveda, Juan Ginés de, 1490-1573. 2. Catholic Church — America — Missions. 3. Indians, Treatment of 4. Spain — Colonies — Administration. I. Poole, Stafford. ed. II. T.
F1411.C425 1974   980/.01   *LC* 73-15094   *ISBN* 0875800424

Casas, Bartolomé de las, 1474-1566.   3.8991
[Selections. English] Bartolomé de las Casas; a selection of his writings. Translated and edited by George Sanderlin. [1st ed.] New York: Knopf [1971] x, 209 p. port. 19 cm. (Borzoi books on Latin America) 1. Indians, Treatment of — Latin America 2. America — Discovery and exploration — Spanish 3. Spain — Colonies — America. I. Sanderlin, George William, 1915- ed. II. T.
F1411.C4273 1971   973.1/6/08   *LC* 72-147886   *ISBN* 039446978X *ISBN* 0394315375

Hanke, Lewis.   • 3.8992
The Spanish struggle for justice in the conquest of America. — Philadelphia, Univ. of Pennsylvania Press, 1949. xi, 217 p. ports., maps (on lining-papers) facsim. 23 cm. At head of title: American Historical Association. 'Bibliographical appendices': p. 197-211. 1. Spain — Colonies — America. 2. Indians, Treatment of — Spanish America. 3. Latin America — Hist. — To 1830. I. T.
F1411.H37   970.5   *LC* 49-3817

New Iberian world: a documentary history of the discovery and   3.8993
settlement of Latin America to the early 17th century / edited,
wiii commentaries by John H. Parry and Robert G. Keith; with
the assistance of Michael Jimenez.
New York: Times Books: Hector & Rose, 1983. 5 v., 2912 p. Includes index. 1. Latin America — History — To 1600 — Sources. 2. America — Discovery and exploration — Sources I. Parry, John H. (John Horace), 1914- II. Keith, Robert G.
F1411.I18 1983   980/.01 19   *LC* 82-19664   *ISBN* 0812910702

Kirkpatrick, Frederick Alexander, 1861-1953.   • 3.8994
The Spanish conquistadores, by F. A. Kirkpatrick. — 2d ed. — New York: Barnes & Noble, [1967] xiii, 366 p.: maps.; 23 cm. — (The Pioneer histories) Reprint of the 1946 ed. 1. Latin America — History — To 1600 2. America — Discovery and exploration — Spanish I. T.
F1411.K57 1967   980/.01   *LC* 67-6852

Leonard, Irving Albert.   • 3.8995
Books of the brave: being an account of books and of men in the Spanish conquest and settlement of the sixteenth–century New World. New York: Gordian P., 1964. 381 p.: ill. Originally published 1949. 1. Spanish literature — Classical period, 1500-1700 — History and criticism. 2. Book industry and trade — Spanish America. 3. Spanish America — History — to 1600. 4. America — Discovery and exploration — Spanish 5. Spanish America — Intellectual life. I. T.
F1411 L57 1964   980.01   *LC* 64-8177

Letters and people of the Spanish Indies, sixteenth century /   3.8996
translated and edited by James Lockhart and Enrique Otte.
Cambridge; New York: Cambridge University Press, 1976. xiii, 267 p.: ill.; 22 cm. — (Cambridge Latin American studies. 22) Includes index. 1. Latin America — History — To 1600 — Sources. 2. Latin America — Social life and customs. I. Lockhart, James. II. Otte, Enrique. III. Series.
F1411.L58   980/.01   *LC* 75-6007   *ISBN* 0521208831

Lockhart, James.   3.8997
Early Latin America: a history of colonial Spanish America and Brazil / James Lockhart, Stuart B. Schwartz. — Cambridge [Cambridgeshire]; New York: Cambridge University Press, 1983. x, 480 p.: ill.; 24 cm. — (Cambridge Latin

American studies. 46) Includes index. 1. Latin America — History — To 1830 I. Schwartz, Stuart B. II. T. III. Series.
F1411.L792 1983   980 19   *LC* 82-23506   *ISBN* 0521233445

Simpson, Lesley Byrd, 1891-.   • 3.8998
The encomienda in New Spain; the beginning of Spanish Mexico. — [Rev. and enl. ed.]. — Berkeley, University of California Press, 1950. xv, 257 p. map, facsim. 21 cm. Bibliography: p. 245-251. 1. Encomiendas (Spanish America) 2. Mexico — Hist. — Spanish colony, 1540-1810. I. T.
F1411.S62 1950   972.02   *LC* 50-63487

Anna, Timothy E., 1944-.   3.8999
Spain & the loss of America / Timothy E. Anna. — Lincoln: University of Nebraska Press, c1983. xxiv, 343 p.; 23 cm. Includes index. 1. Latin America — History — Wars of Independence, 1806-1830 2. Spain — Politics and government — 1808-1814 3. Spain — Politics and government — 1813-1833 I. T. II. Title: Spain and the loss of America.
F1412.A6 1983   980/.02 19   *LC* 82-11118   *ISBN* 0803210140

Domínguez, Jorge I., 1945-.   3.9000
Insurrection or loyalty: the breakdown of the Spanish American Empire / Jorge I. Domínguez. — Cambridge, Mass.: Harvard University Press, 1980. ix, 307 p.; 24 cm. 'Written under the auspices of the Center for International Affairs, Harvard University.' 1. Revolutions — Latin America. 2. Royalists — Latin America — History — 19th century 3. Latin America — History — Wars of Independence, 1806-1830 I. Harvard University. Center for International Affairs. II. T.
F1412.D67   980/.02 19   *LC* 80-24095   *ISBN* 0674456351

Lynch, John, 1927-.   3.9001
The Spanish American revolutions, 1808–1826. — New York: Norton, [1973] xxvii, 433 p.: maps.; 21 cm. — (Revolutions in the modern world) 1. Latin America — History — Wars of Independence, 1806-1830 I. T.
F1412.L96 1973   980/.02   *LC* 73-4835   *ISBN* 0393053881

Halperín Donghi, Tulio.   3.9002
[Hispanoamérica después de la independencia. English] The aftermath of revolution in Latin America. Translated from the Spanish by Josephine de Bunsen. New York, Harper & Row [1973] viii, 149 p. 21 cm. (Harper Torchbooks, TB 1711) (Crosscurrents in Latin America) Translation of Hispanoamérica después de la independencia. 1. Latin America — History — 1830-1898 I. T.
F1413.H3413 1973   980/.03   *LC* 72-83822   *ISBN* 006136097X *ISBN* 006131711X

Skidmore, Thomas E.   3.9003
Modern Latin America / Thomas E. Skidmore, Peter H. Smith. — New York: Oxford University Press, 1984. xii, 419 p.: ill.; 24 cm. Includes index. 1. Latin America — History — 1830- I. Smith, Peter H. II. T.
F1413.S55 1984   980/.03 19   *LC* 83-8007   *ISBN* 0195033663

1989

Hodges, Donald Clark, 1923-.   3.9004
The Latin American revolution; politics and strategy from Apro–Marxism to Guevarism [by] Donald C. Hodges. — New York: W. Morrow, 1974. 287 p.: map.; 22 cm. 1. Communism — Latin America. 2. Revolutions — Latin America. 3. Communist strategy 4. Latin America — Politics and government 5. Latin America — History — 20th century I. T.
F1414.H62   335.43/098   *LC* 74-7085   *ISBN* 068800315X

Lieuwen, Edwin, 1923-.   • 3.9005
Generals vs. presidents; neomilitarism in Latin America. — New York: Praeger, [1964] vi, 136 p.; 22 cm. 1. Civil supremacy over the military — Latin America. 2. Militarism — Latin America. 3. Latin America — Politics and government — 1948- 4. United States — Foreign relations — Latin America I. T.
F1414.L5   320.98   *LC* 64-22492

Armies and politics in Latin America / edited by Abraham F.   3.9006
Lowenthal.
New York: Holmes & Meier, 1976. 356 p.: ill.; 24 cm. 1. Coups d'état — Latin America — History — 20th century. 2. Military government — Latin America — History — 20th century. 3. Civil-military relations — Latin America — History — 20th century. 4. Latin America — Politics and government — 1948- 5. Latin America — Armed Forces — Political activity — History — 20th century. I. Lowenthal, Abraham F.
F1414.2.A793   322/.5/098   *LC* 76-17832   *ISBN* 084190281X. *ISBN* 0841902828 pbk

Beyond Cuba: Latin America takes charge of its future / Edited   3.9007
by Luigi R. Einaudi. Contributors: Luigi R. Einaudi [and
others].
New York: Crane, Russak, [1974]. -. xiv, 250 p.; 24 cm. — Most of the papers were originally presented at a conference on 'Trends in Latin America,' organized by the Rand Corp., and held at Airlie House, Warrenton, Va., May 12-14, 1972. - Published in 1972 under title: Latin America in the 1970s. - 1. Latin America — Politics and government — 1948- 2. Latin America —

Economic conditions — 1945- I. Einaudi, Luigi R., 1936- ed. II. Rand Corporation.
F1414.2.B45 1974   309.1/8/003   *LC* 73-86440   *ISBN* 0844802247

F1415–1418 Diplomatic History

Davis, Harold Eugene, 1902-.   **3.9008**
Latin American foreign policies: an analysis / Harold Eugene Davis and Larman C. Wilson, with coauthors, Victor Alba ... [et al.]. — Baltimore: Johns Hopkins University Press, [1975] xiii, 470 p.; 23 cm. 1. Latin America — Foreign relations I. Wilson, Larman Curtis, joint author. II. T.
F1415.D34   327/.098   *LC* 74-24386   *ISBN* 0801816947

Robertson, William Spence, 1872-.   **• 3.9009**
France and Latin–American independence. — New York, Octagon Books, 1967 [c1939] xv, 626 p. 3 maps. 22 cm. — (The Albert Shaw lectures on diplomatic history, 1939) Bibliography: p. 587-606. 1. Latin America — For. rel. — France. 2. France — For. rel. — Latin America. 3. Latin America — Hist. — Wars of Independence, 1806-1830. I. T. II. Series.
F1416.F7R6 1967   980/.02   *LC* 67-18782

Kaufmann, William W.   **• 3.9010**
British policy and the independence of Latin America, 1804–1828. [Hamden, Conn.] Archon Books, 1967 [c1951] 238p. Reprint of the 1951 ed. 1. Latin America — Foreign relations — Great Britain. 2. Latin America — History — Wars of Independence, 1806-1830 3. Great Britain — Foreign relations — 1800-1837 4. Great Britain — Foreign relations — Latin America. I. T.
F1416.G7 K3 1967   *LC* 67-19547

Blasier, Cole, 1925-.   **3.9011**
The giant's rival: the USSR and Latin America / Cole Blasier. — Pittsburgh, Pa.: University of Pittsburgh Press, c1983. xvi, 213 p.; 21 cm. — (Pitt Latin American series.) 1. Latin America — Relations — Soviet Union 2. Soviet Union — Relations — Latin America I. T. II. Series.
F1416.S65 B57 1983   327.4708 19   *LC* 83-47826   *ISBN* 0822934868

F1418 RELATIONS WITH THE UNITED STATES

Bemis, Samuel Flagg, 1891-1973.   **• 3.9012**
The Latin American policy of the United States, an historical interpretation by Samuel Flagg Bemis ... New York, Harcourt, Brace and company [1943] xiv p., 1 l., 470 p. illus. (maps), diagrs. 24 cm. Half-title: Institute of international studies, Yale university. 'First edition.' 1. United States — Foreign relations — Latin America 2. Latin America — Foreign relations — United States I. Yale University. Institute of International Studies. II. T.
F1418.B4   327.73098   *LC* 43-51167

Blasier, Cole, 1925-.   **3.9013**
The hovering giant: U.S. responses to revolutionary change in Latin America / Cole Blasier. — [Pittsburgh]: University of Pittsburgh Press, c1976. xix, 315 p., [8] leaves of plates: ill.; 25 cm. (Pitt Latin American series) 1. Revolutions — Latin America. 2. United States — Foreign relations — Latin America 3. Latin America — Foreign relations — United States I. T.
F1418.B646   327.73/08   *LC* 75-9130   *ISBN* 0822933047

Callcott, Wilfrid Hardy, 1895-.   **• 3.9014**
The Caribbean policy of the United States, 1890–1920. New York, Octagon Books, 1966 [c1942] xiv, 524 p. 21 cm. (The Albert Shaw lectures on diplomatic history, 1942) 1. Caribbean Area 2. United States — Foreign relations — Latin America 3. Latin America — Foreign relations — United States I. T.
F1418.C22 1966   327.73/08   *LC* 66-28374

Connell-Smith, Gordon.   **3.9015**
The United States and Latin America: an historical analysis of inter-American relations / Gordon Connell-Smith. — New York: Wiley, [1974] xviii, 302 p.; 23 cm. 'A Halsted Press book.' 1. United States — Foreign relations — Latin America 2. Latin America — Foreign relations — United States I. T.
F1418.C8132   327.73/08   *LC* 74-11911   *ISBN* 0470168560

De Onís, José.   **• 3.9016**
The United States as seen by Spanish American writers, 1776–1890 / by José de Onís. — New York: Hispanic Institute in the United States, 1952. 226 p. 1. United States in literature. 2. Spanish American literature — History and criticism. 3. United States — Relations — Latin America 4. Latin America — Relations — United States I. T.
F1418.D45   *LC* 52-2725

Gantenbein, James Watson, 1900- ed.   **3.9017**
The evolution of our Latin–American policy; a documentary record. Compiled and edited by James W. Gantenbein. — New York: Octagon Books, 1971 [c1950] xxvii, 979 p.; 24 cm. 1. U.S. — Foreign relations — Latin America. 2. Latin America — Foreign relations — U.S. I. T.
F1418.G2 1971   327.73/08   *LC* 72-159187   *ISBN* 0374929874

Latin America and the United States: the changing political   **3.9018**
realities. Edited by Julio Cotler & Richard R. Fagen.
Contributors: Heraclio Bonilla [and others]
Stanford, Calif., Stanford University Press, 1974. x, 417 p. 24 cm. Papers prepared for a conference held at the Institute of Peruvian Studies in Lima, Nov. 1972. 1. Latin America — Relations — United States. 2. United States — Relations — Latin America — Congresses. I. Cotler, Julio. ed. II. Fagen, Richard R. ed. III. Bonilla, Heraclio. IV. Instituto de Estudios Peruanos.
F1418.L355   327.73/08   *LC* 73-94487   *ISBN* 0804708606 *ISBN* 0804708614

Manning, William Ray, 1871-.   **• 3.9019**
Diplomatic correspondence of the United States concerning the independence of the Latin–American nations / selected and arranged by William R. Manning. — New York: Oxford University Press, 1925. 3 v. — (Publications of the Carnegie Endowment for International Peace. Division of International Law) 1. United States — Foreign relations — Latin America 2. Latin America — Foreign relations — United States 3. Latin America — History — Wars of Independence, 1806-1830 — Sources I. United States. Dept. of State. II. T.
F1418.M27   *LC* 25-19089

Mecham, J. Lloyd (John Lloyd), 1893-.   **• 3.9020**
A survey of United States–Latin American relations [by] J. Lloyd Mecham. — Boston, Houghton Mifflin [1965] viii, 487 p. maps. 25 cm. Includes bibliographies. 1. U.S. — Relations (general) with Latin America. 2. Latin America — Relations (general) with the U.S. I. T. II. Title: United States-Latin American relations.
F1418.M373   327.7308   *LC* 65-9049

Whitaker, Arthur Preston, 1895-.   **• 3.9021**
The United States and the independence of Latin America, 1800–1830. New York, Russell & Russell, 1962 [c1941] 632 p. 22 cm. (The Albert Shaw lectures on diplomatic history, 1938) 1. Monroe doctrine 2. United States — Foreign relations — Latin America 3. Latin America — Politics — 1806-1830. 4. Latin America — History — Wars of Independence, 1806-1830 I. T. II. Series.
F1418.W6 1962   *LC* 61-13785

Wood, Bryce, 1909-.   **3.9022**
The dismantling of the good neighbor policy / by Bryce Wood. — 1st ed. — Austin: University of Texas Press, 1985. xiv, 290 p.; 24 cm. Includes index. 1. Latin America — Foreign relations — United States 2. United States — Foreign relations — Latin America I. T.
F1418.W682 1985   327.7308 19   *LC* 84-20950   *ISBN* 0292715471

Wood, Bryce, 1909-.   **• 3.9023**
The making of the good neighbor policy. — New York: Columbia University Press, 1961. x, 438 p.; 24 cm. 1. United States — Foreign relations — Latin America 2. Latin America — Foreign relations — United States I. T.
F1418.W683   327.7308   *LC* 61-15470

F1419 Ethnography

Harris, Marvin, 1927-.   **• 3.9024**
Patterns of race in the Americas. — New York: Walker, 1964. v, 154 p.: ill. — (The Walker summit library; no.1) 1. Ethnology — Latin America 2. Latin America — Race question. I. T.
F1419.A1 H3   301.45/1/042098   *LC* 64-23054

Levine, Robert M.   **3.9025**
Race and ethnic relations in Latin America and the Caribbean: an historical dictionary and bibliography / by Robert M. Levine. — Metuchen, N.J.: Scarecrow Press, 1980. viii, 252 p.; 23 cm. Includes index. 1. Latin America — Race relations — Dictionaries. 2. Latin America — Ethnic relations — Dictionaries. 3. Latin America — Race relations — Bibliography. 4. Latin America — Ethnic relations — Bibliography. I. T.
F1419.A1 L48   980/.004   *LC* 80-15179   *ISBN* 0810813246

Rout, Leslie B., 1936-.   **3.9026**
The African experience in Spanish America, 1502 to the present day / Leslie B. Rout, Jr. Cambridge; New York: Cambridge University Press, 1976. xv, 404 p.: maps; 22 cm. (Cambridge Latin American studies. 23) Includes index. 1. Blacks — Latin America — History. 2. Slavery — Latin America I. T. II. Series.
F1419.B55 R68   980/.004/96   *LC* 75-9280   *ISBN* 052120805X

Elkin, Judith Laikin, 1928-.   3.9027
Jews of the Latin American republics / Judith Laikin Elkin. — Chapel Hill: University of North Carolina Press, c1980. xv, 298 p.: ill.; 24 cm. Includes index. 1. Jews — Latin America — History. 2. Latin America — History I. T.
F1419.J4 E43   980/.004/924 19   LC 79-17394   ISBN 0807814083

F1421–1577 CENTRAL AMERICA: GENERAL

Adams, Richard Newbold, 1924-.   3.9028
Cultural surveys of Panama—Nicaragua—Guatemala—El Salvador—Honduras / by Richard N. Adams. — Detroit: B. Ethridge—Books, 1976. iii, 669 p.: ill.; 24 cm. Reprint of the 1957 ed. published by the Pan American Sanitary Bureau, Washington, which was issued as no. 33 of its Scientific publications. 1. Central America I. T.
F1428.A3 1976   301.29/728   LC 76-41776   ISBN 0879170565

Squier, E. G. (Ephraim George), 1821-1888.   3.9029
Notes on Central America; particularly the states of Honduras and San Salvador: their geography, topography, climate, population, resources, productions, etc., etc., and the proposed Honduras Inter–oceanic Railway. New York, AMS Press [1971] 397 p. illus. 23 cm. Reprint of the 1855 ed. 1. Honduras Interoceanic Railway. 2. Central America 3. Honduras. 4. El Salvador. I. T.
F1428.S75 1971   917.28   LC 70-172443   ISBN 0404062210

F1434–1435.3 Antiquities. Indians

The Archaeology of lower Central America / edited by   3.9030
Frederick W. Lange and Doris Z. Stone.
1st ed. — Albuquerque: University of New Mexico Press, c1984. xiv, 476 p.: ill.; 25 cm. — (School of American Research advanced seminar series.) 'A School of American Research book.' Papers presented at the Advanced Seminar on Lower Central American Archaeology, held Apr. 8-14, 1980, at the School of American Research, Santa Fe, N.M. Includes index. 1. Indians of Central America — Antiquities — Congresses. 2. Central America — Antiquities — Congresses. I. Lange, Frederick W., 1944- II. Stone, Doris, 1909- III. School of American Research (Santa Fe, N.M.) IV. Advanced Seminar on Lower Central American Archaeology (1980: School of American Research) V. Series.
F1434.A84 1984   972.8/01 19   LC 83-21747   ISBN 0826307175

Handbook of Middle American Indians. Robert Wauchope,   • 3.9031
general editor.
Austin: University of Texas Press, [1964-76] 16 v.: illus., maps, plans; 28 cm. 1. Indians of Central America — Collected works. 2. Indians of Mexico — Collected works. I. Wauchope, Robert, 1909- ed.
F1434.H3   970.4/2   LC 64-10316   ISBN 0292700148

Brunhouse, Robert Levere, 1908-.   3.9032
Pursuit of the ancient Maya: some archaeologists of yesterday / Robert L. Brunhouse. — 1st ed. — Albuquerque: University of New Mexico Press, [1975] viii, 252 p., [8] leaves of plates: ill.; 24 cm. Includes index. 1. Archaeologists — Biography. 2. Mayas — Antiquities 3. Mexico — Antiquities 4. Central America — Antiquities. I. T.
F1435.B875   930/.1/0922   LC 74-27443   ISBN 0826303633

The Classic Maya collapse. Edited by T. Patrick Culbert.   3.9033
[1st ed.]. — Albuquerque: University of New Mexico Press, [1973] xx, 549 p.: illus.; 25 cm. 'A School of American Research book.' 1. Mayas — Antiquities — Addresses, essays, lectures. 2. Central America — Antiquities — Addresses, essays, lectures. 3. Mexico — Antiquities — Addresses, essays, lectures. I. Culbert, T. Patrick, ed.
F1435.C6   970.3   LC 72-94657

Coe, Michael D.   • 3.9034
The Maya [by] Michael D. Coe. — New York: Praeger, [1966] 252 p.: illus., maps, plans.; 21 cm. — (Ancient peoples and places, v. 52) 1. Mayas — Antiquities 2. Mexico — Antiquities 3. Central America — Antiquities. I. T.
F1435.C72 1966a   970.3   LC 66-25117

Culbert, T. Patrick.   3.9035
The lost civilization: the story of the classic Maya / [by] T. Patrick Culbert. — New York: Harper & Row, [1974] xiii, 123 p.: ill.; 24 cm. (Harper's case studies

in archaeology) 1. Mayas — Antiquities 2. Mayas — History. 3. Central America — Antiquities. I. T.
F1435.C82   970.3   LC 73-10683   ISBN 0060414480

Farriss, Nancy M. (Nancy Marguerite), 1938-.   3.9036
Maya society under colonial rule: the collective enterprise of survival / by Nancy M. Farriss. — Princeton, N.J.: Princeton University Press, c1984. xii, 585 p.: ill.; 25 cm. Includes index. 1. Mayas — History. 2. Mayas — Social conditions. 3. Acculturation — Mexico. 4. Indians of Mexico — Yucatán — History. 5. Indians of Mexico — Yucatán — Social conditions. 6. Mexico — Social conditions — To 1810 I. T.
F1435.F28 1984   972/.6500497 19   LC 83-43071   ISBN 0691076685

Hammond, Norman.   3.9037
Ancient Maya civilization / Norman Hammond. — New Brunswick, N.J.: Rutgers University Press, c1982. xii, 337 p.: ill.; 26 cm. Includes index. 1. Mayas 2. Mayas — Antiquities 3. Mexico — Antiquities 4. Central America — Antiquities. I. T.
F1435.H35 1982   972/.01 19   LC 80-39819   ISBN 0813509041

Henderson, John S.   3.9038
The world of the ancient Maya / by John S. Henderson. — Ithaca N.Y.: Cornell University Press, 1981. 271 p., [8] leaves of plates: ill. (some col.); 25 cm. Includes index. 1. Mayas I. T.
F1435.H46   972/.01 19   LC 81-3148   ISBN 0801412323

Landa, Diego de, 1524-1579.   3.9039
[Relación de las cosas de Yucatán. English] The Maya: Diego de Landa's account of the affairs of Yucatán / edited and translated by A. R. Pagden. — Chicago: J. P. O'Hara, [1975] 191 p., [6] leaves of plates: ill.; 24 cm. Translation of Relación de las cosas de Yucatán. 'A Howard Greenfeld book.' Includes index. 1. Mayas 2. Yucatan (Mexico) — History. 3. Yucatan (Mexico) — Antiquities. I. T.
F1435.L3413 1975   972/.6/00497   LC 70-190752   ISBN 0879553030

Morley, Sylvanus Griswold, 1883-1948.   3.9040
The ancient Maya / Sylvanus G. Morley and George W. Brainerd. — 4th ed. / revised by Robert J. Sharer. — Stanford, Calif.: Stanford University Press, 1983. xviii, 708 p.: ill.; 24 cm. Includes index. 1. Mayas 2. Mayas — Antiquities 3. Indians of Mexico — Antiquities 4. Indians of Central America — Antiquities 5. Mexico — Antiquities 6. Central America — Antiquities. I. Brainerd, George W. (George Walton), 1909-1956. II. Sharer, Robert J. III. T.
F1435.M75 1983   972.81/01 19   LC 81-85451   ISBN 0804711372

Thompson, John Eric Sidney, Sir, 1898-1975.   3.9041
Maya history and religion [by] J. Eric S. Thompson. [1st ed.] Norman, University of Oklahoma Press [1970] xxx, 415 p. illus., maps. 24 cm. 1. Mayas I. T.
F1435.T496   970.3   LC 72-88144   ISBN 0806108843

Thompson, John Eric Sidney, Sir, 1898-1975.   • 3.9042
The rise and fall of Maya civilization / by J. Eric S. Thompson. — 2d ed. enl. — Norman: University of Oklahoma Press, [1966] xv, 328 p.: ill., maps.; 24 cm. — (The Civilization of the American Indian series [39]) 1. Mayas — Antiquities I. T.
F1435.T497 1966   970.3   LC 66-16530

Redfield, Robert.   • 3.9043
Chan Kom: a Maya village / Robert Redfield and Alfonso Villa R. Washington, D.C.: Carnegie Institution of Washington, 1934. viii, 387 p.: ill.; 31 cm. (Carnegie Institution of Washington; Publication no. 448) 1. Mayas — Religion and mythology 2. Maya language — Texts. 3. Chan Kom, Mexico. I. Villa R., Alfonso, joint author. II. T.
F1435.1.C47 R3   917.26   LC 34-32750

Redfield, Robert, 1897-.   • 3.9044
A village that chose progress: Chan Kom revisited. — [Chicago]: University of Chicago Press [1950] xiv, 187 p.: maps; 22 cm. 1. Mayas — Religion and mythology 2. Chan Kom, Mexico. 3. Mayas — Social life and customs. I. T.
F1435.1.C47 R32   LC 50-5750

Cenote of sacrifice: Maya treasures from the sacred well at   3.9045
Chichén Itzá / edited by Clemency Chase Coggins and Orrin C.
Shane III; catalogue by Clemency Chase Coggins; with
contributions by Gordon R. Willey and Linnea H. Wren;
forewords by C.C. Lamberg–Karlovsky and Wendell A. Mordy;
photographs by Hillel Burger.
Austin: University of Texas Press, c1984. 176 p.: ill. (some col.); 29 cm. Catalogue of an exhibition organized by the Science Museum of Minnesota in cooperation with the Peabody Museum of Archaeology and Ethnology, Harvard University. Includes index. 1. Peabody Museum of Archaeology and Ethnology — Exhibitions. 2. Indians of Mexico — Yucatán — Antiquities — Exhibitions. 3. Mayas — Antiquities — Exhibitions. 4. Chichén Itzá (Mexico)

— Exhibitions. I. Coggins, Clemency. II. Shane, Orrin C., 1939- III. Science Museum of Minnesota. IV. Peabody Museum of Archaeology and Ethnology.
F1435.1.C5 C46 1984   972/.01 19   *LC* 84-10458   *ISBN* 0292710976

Andrews, George F., 1918-.   **3.9046**
Maya cities: placemaking and urbanization [by] George F. Andrews. — [1st ed.]. — Norman: University of Oklahoma Press, [1975] xviii, 468 p.: illus.; 23 x 26 cm. — (Civilization of the American Indian series. v. 131) 1. Mayas — Architecture. 2. Cities and towns, Ruined, extinct, etc. — Mexico 3. Cities and towns, Ruined, extinct, etc — Central America. 4. Mexico — Antiquities 5. Central America — Antiquities. I. T. II. Series.
F1435.3.A6 A52   301.36/3/09701   *LC* 73-19390   *ISBN* 0806111879

Spinden, Herbert Joseph, 1879-.   • **3.9047**
Maya art and civilization / by Herbert Joseph Spinden. — Revised and enlarged with added illustration. — [Indian Hills, Colo.]: Falcon's Wing Press c1957. xliii, 432 p.: ill., maps. First published in 1913 under the title: A study of Maya art. On t.p.: Part I. A study of Maya Art. Part II. The nuclear civilization of the Maya and related cultures. 1. Mayas 2. Mayas — Art I. T. II. Title: A study of Maya art.
F1435.3.A7 S75 1957   *LC* 56-5124

Stierlin, Henri.   **3.9048**
[Art maya. English] Art of the Maya: from the Olmecs to the Toltec–Maya / Henri Stierlin; [translated from the French by Peter Graham]. — New York: Rizzoli, 1981. 211 p.: ill. (some col.); 32 cm. Translation of: L'art maya. Includes index. 1. Mayas — Art 2. Indians of Mexico — Art 3. Indians of Central America — Art I. T.
F1435.3.A7 S813 1981   709/.7281 19   *LC* 80-54674   *ISBN* 0847803686

Kelley, David H.   **3.9049**
Deciphering the Maya script / David Humiston Kelley. — Austin: University of Texas Press, c1976. xvii, p., [3] fold. leaves of plates; ill.; 32 cm. Includes indexes. 1. Mayas — Writing 2. Mayas — Antiquities 3. Mexico — Antiquities 4. Central America — Antiquities. I. T.
F1435.3.P6 K44   497/.4   *LC* 75-17989   *ISBN* 0292715048

F1435.4–1439 History

Woodward, Ralph Lee.   **3.9050**
Central America, a nation divided / Ralph Lee Woodward, Jr. — New York: Oxford University Press, 1976. 344 p.: maps; 22 cm. (Latin American histories) Includes index. 1. Central America — History I. T.
F1436.W66   972.8   *LC* 75-25467   *ISBN* 0195020146

The Central American crisis: sources of conflict and the failure   **3.9051**
of U.S. policy / edited by Kenneth M. Coleman and George C. Herring.
Wilmington, Del.: Scholarly Resources, c1985. xvii, 240 p.: map; 24 cm. 1. Central America — Foreign relations — United States — Addresses, essays, lectures. 2. United States — Foreign relations — Central America — Addresses, essays, lectures. 3. United States — Foreign relations — 1981- — Addresses, essays, lectures. 4. Central America — Economic conditions — 1979- — Addresses, essays, lectures. 5. Central America — Social conditions — 1979- — Addresses, essays, lectures. I. Coleman, Kenneth M. II. Herring, George C., 1936-
F1436.8.U6 C46 1985   327.730728 19   *LC* 84-27624   *ISBN* 0842022384

LaFeber, Walter.   **3.9052**
Inevitable revolutions: the United States in Central America / Walter LaFeber. — 1st ed. — New York: Norton, c1983. x, 357 p.: maps; 21 cm. Includes index. 1. Revolutions — Central America. 2. United States — Foreign relations — Central America. 3. Central America — Foreign relations — United States. I. T.
F1436.8.U6 L33 1983   327.730728 19   *LC* 83-4057   *ISBN* 0393017877

United States. National Bipartisan Commission on Central   **3.9053**
America.
Report of the National Bipartisan Commission on Central America. — Washington, D.C.: The Commission: For sale by the Supt. of Docs., U.S. G.P.O., 1984. 2 v.: ill.; 28 cm. Cover title. 'January 1984'—Report. 'March 1984'—Appendix. S/N 040-000-00477-7 (rpt.) S/N 040-000-00478-5 (app.) Item 851-J 1. Central America — Foreign relations — United States. 2. United States — Foreign relations — Central America. 3. Central America — Politics and government — 1951-1979 4. Central America — Politics and government — 1979- 5. Central America — Economic conditions — 1979-

6. Central America — Social conditions — 1979- 7. Central America — National security. I. T.
F1436.8.U6 U54 1984   972.8/052 19   *LC* 84-601568

Alvarado, Pedro de, 1485?-1541.   **3.9054**
[Relación hecha por Pedro de Alvarado a Hernando Cortés. English] An account of the conquest of Guatemala in 1524, edited by Sedley J. Mackie. With a facsim. of the Spanish original, 1525. Boston, Milford House [1972] 146 p. front., facsim. 22 cm. Translation of Relación hecha por Pedro de Alvarado a Hernando Cortés. Reprint of the 1924 ed., which was issued as no. 3 of Documents and narratives concerning the discovery and conquest of Latin America. 1. Central America — History — To 1821 2. Guatemala — History — To 1821 I. T.
F1437.A466 1972   972.8/02   *LC* 77-133338   *ISBN* 0878210768

Ireland, Gordon, 1880-1950.   **3.9055**
Boundaries, possessions, and conflicts in Central and North America and the Caribbean. — New York: Octagon Books, 1972, c1969. xiii, 432 p.: maps.; 27 cm. Orig. published by Harvard, 1941. 1. Central America — Boundaries. 2. North America — Boundaries. 3. America — Politics and government 4. West Indies — History I. T.
F1438.I7 1972   341.42

Central America: crisis and adaptation / edited by Steve C.   **3.9056**
Ropp and James A. Morris.
1st ed. — Albuquerque: University of New Mexico Press, c1984. xxii, 311 p.: ill.; 24 cm. Includes index. 1. Central America — Politics and government — 1979- — Addresses, essays, lectures. 2. Central America — History — Addresses, essays, lectures. I. Ropp, Steve C. II. Morris, James A., 1938-
F1439.5.C454 1984   972.8 19   *LC* 84-2273   *ISBN* 0826307450

Chace, James.   **3.9057**
Endless war: how we got involved in Central America and what can be done / James Chace. — 1st ed. — New York: Vintage Books, 1984. 144 p.; 18 cm. 'A Vintage original'—T.p. verso. 1. Central America — Politics and government — 1979- 2. Central America — Foreign relations — United States. 3. United States — Foreign relations — Central America. I. T.
F1439.5.C48 1984   972.8/052 19   *LC* 84-48004   *ISBN* 0394727797

F1441–1457 Belize

Dobson, Narda.   **3.9058**
A history of Belize. [Port of Spain, Trinidad and Tobago] Longman Caribbean [1973] xiv, 362 p. illus. 23 cm. 1. Belize — History. I. T.
F1446.D56 1973   972.82   *LC* 73-179191   *ISBN* 058276601X *ISBN* 058278512X

F1461–1477 Guatemala

Guatemala, a country study / Foreign Area Studies, the   **3.9059**
American University; edited by Richard F. Nyrop.
2nd ed. — Washington, D.C.: The Studies: For sale by the Supt. of Docs., U.S. G.P.O., c1983. xxvi, 261 p.: ill., maps; 24 cm. — (Area handbook series.) (DA pam. 550-78) 'Research completed May 1983.' Includes index. 1. Guatemala. I. Nyrop, Richard F. II. American University (Washington, D.C.). Foreign Area Studies. III. Series. IV. Series: DA pam. 550-78
F1463.G944   972.81 19   *LC* 84-413

Whetten, Nathan Laselle, 1900-.   • **3.9060**
Guatemala: the land and the people. — New Haven: Yale University Press, 1961. xvi, 399 p. ill., maps, diagrs. 25 cm. (Caribbean series, 4) 1. Guatemala — Rural conditions. 2. Guatemala — Social conditions. 3. Guatemala — Civilization. I. T.
F1463.5.W5   *LC* 61-7189

Popol vuh. English.   **3.9061**
Popol vuh: the definitive edition of the Mayan book of the dawn of life and the glories of gods and kings / translated by Dennis Tedlock, with commentary based on the ancient knowledge of the modern Quiché Maya. — New York: Simon and Schuster, c1985. 380 p.: ill.; 22 cm. Translated from the Quiché. 1. Quichés — Religion and mythology. 2. Indians of Central America — Guatemala — Religion and mythology. I. Tedlock, Dennis, 1939- II. T.
F1465.P813 1985   299/.79281 19   *LC* 84-23644   *ISBN* 067145241X *1976*

Tedlock, Barbara. 3.9062
Time and the highland Maya / Barbara Tedlock. — 1st ed. — Albuquerque: University of New Mexico Press, c1982. xii, 245 p.: ill.; 25 cm. Includes index. 1. Quichés — Calendar. 2. Quichés — Religion and mythology. 3. Indians of Central America — Guatemala — Calendar. 4. Indians of Central America — Guatemala — Religion and mythology. I. T.
F1465.2.Q5 T43 1982   299/.8 19   *LC* 80-54569   *ISBN* 0826305776

Bizarro Ujpán, Ignacio. 3.9063
Campesino: the diary of a Guatemalan Indian / translated and edited by James D. Sexton. — Tucson, Ariz.: University of Arizona Press, 1985. 448 p. Sequel to: Son of Tecún Umán. Includes index. 1. Bizarro Ujpán, Ignacio. 2. Tzutuhil Indians — Biography. 3. Tzutuhil Indians — Social conditions. 4. Indians of Central America — Guatemala — Social conditions. I. Sexton, James D. II. T.
F1465.2.T9 B588 1985   972.81/00497 B 19   *LC* 85-1115   *ISBN* 0816508143

Bizarro Ujpán, Ignacio. 3.9064
Son of Tecún Umán: a Maya Indian tells his life story / James D. Sexton, editor. — Tucson: University of Arizona Press, c1981. 250 p.; 24 cm. Includes index. 1. Bizarro Ujpán, Ignacio. 2. Tzutuhil Indians — Social conditions. 3. Indians of Central America — Guatemala — Social conditions. 4. Tzutuhil Indians — Biography. I. Sexton, James D. II. T.
F1465.2.T9 B59   972.81/00497 B 19   *LC* 81-11702   *ISBN* 0816507368

Tax, Sol, 1907-. • 3.9065
Penny capitalism: a Guatemalan Indian economy. — New York: Octagon Books, 1972. x, 230 p.: ill.; 28 cm. Reprint of the 1953 ed., which was issued as no. 16 of Smithsonian Institution. Institute of Social Anthropology. Publication. 1. Indians of Central America — Guatemala — Economic conditions. 2. Agriculture — Economic aspects — Guatemala — Panajachel. 3. Panajachel, Guatemala — Economic conditions. I. T.
F1465.3.E2 T3 1972   330.9/7281   *LC* 78-159254   *ISBN* 0374977852 *1963*

F1481–1537 El Salvador. Honduras. Nicaragua

Blutstein, Howard I. 3.9066
Area handbook for El Salvador. Co–authors: Howard I. Blutstein [and others]. Washington; For sale by the Supt. of Docs., U.S. Govt. Print. Off.] 1978. xii, 259 p. maps. 24 cm. 'DA pam 550-150.' 'One of a series of handbooks prepared by Foreign Area Studies (FAS) of the American University.' 1. El Salvador. I. American University (Washington, D.C.). Foreign Area Studies. II. T.
F1483.B55   309.1/7284/05   *LC* 78-609951

White, Alastair T. 3.9067
El Salvador. New York, Praeger [1973] 288 p. illus. 23 cm. (Nations of the modern world.) 1. El Salvador — History 2. El Salvador — Economic conditions. 3. El Salvador — Social conditions. I. T. II. Series.
F1483.W47 1973   972.84   *LC* 72-93302

Baloyra, Enrique A., 1942-. 3.9068
El Salvador in transition / Enrique A. Baloyra. — Chapel Hill [N.C.]: University of North Carolina Press, c1982. xviii, 236 p.: map; 24 cm. Includes indexes. 1. El Salvador — Politics and government — 1944-1979 2. El Salvador — Politics and government — 1979- 3. El Salvador — Foreign relations — United States. 4. United States — Foreign relations — El Salvador. 5. United States — Foreign relations — 1981- I. T.
F1488.B34 1982   972.84/05 19   *LC* 82-4815   *ISBN* 0807815322

Montgomery, Tommie Sue. 3.9069
Revolution in El Salvador: origins and evolution / Tommie Sue Montgomery; introduction by Román Mayorga Quiroz. — Boulder, Colo.: Westview Press, 1982. xiv, 252 p.: ill.; 23 cm. Includes index. 1. Catholic Church — El Salvador. 2. El Salvador — Politics and government 3. El Salvador — Economic conditions 4. El Salvador — History — Coup d'état, 1979. I. T.
F1488.3.M66 1982   972.84/052 19   *LC* 82-8367   *ISBN* 0865313865

Morris, James A., 1938-. 3.9070
Honduras: caudillo politics and military rulers / James A. Morris. — Boulder: Westview Press, 1984. xiv, 156 p.: ill.; 24 cm. (Westview profiles. Nations of contemporary Latin America.) Includes index. 1. Civil-military relations — Honduras. 2. Honduras — Politics and government — 1933-1982 3. Honduras — Armed Forces — Political activity. 4. Honduras — Economic policy. I. T. II. Series.
F1508.M67 1984   322/.5/097283 19   *LC* 83-21789   *ISBN* 0865311781

Nicaragua: a country study. 3.9071
2nd ed. / edited by James D. Rudolph. — Washington, D.C.: Foreign Area Studies, the American University: for sale by the Supt. of Docs., U.S. G.P.O., 1982. xxx, 278 p.: ill.; 24 cm. — (Area handbook series.) Previous ed. published as: Area handbook for Nicaragua. 1970. 'DA Pam 550-88'. Includes index. 1. Nicaragua. I. Rudolph, James D., 1947- II. Ryan, John Morris. Area handbook for Nicaragua. III. Series.
F1523.N569 1982   972.85 19   *LC* 82-13833

Walker, William, 1824-1860. 3.9072
The war in Nicaragua. Mobile, S. H. Goetzel, 1860. — Detroit: B. Ethridge—Books, 1971 [i.e. 1972] 431 p.: port.; 19 cm. 1. Nicaragua — History — Filibuster War, 1855-1860 I. T.
F1526.27.W28 1972   972.85/04   *LC* 72-165663   *ISBN* 0879170182

Gerson, Noel Bertram, 1914-. 3.9073
Sad swashbuckler: the life of William Walker / by Noel B. Gerson. — 1st ed. — Nashville: T. Nelson, c1976. 160 p.; 21 cm. Includes index. 1. Walker, William, 1824-1860. 2. Nicaragua — History — Filibuster War, 1855-1860 I. T.
F1526.27.W3 G47   972.85/04/0924 B   *LC* 76-2366   *ISBN* 0840764839

Nicaragua in revolution / edited by Thomas W. Walker. 3.9074
New York: Praeger, 1982. v, 410 p.: ill., 1 map; 25 cm. 1. Nicaragua — History — Revolution, 1979 I. Walker, Thomas W.
F1528.N498 1982   972.85/052 19   *LC* 81-17746   *ISBN* 0030579724

Nicaragua: the first five years / edited by Thomas W. Walker. 3.9075
New York: Praeger, 1985. vi, 561 p.: map. 1. Nicaragua — Politics and government — 1979- — Addresses, essays, lectures. 2. Nicaragua — Economic policy — Addresses, essays, lectures. 3. Nicaragua — Social policy — Addresses, essays, lectures. 4. Nicaragua — Foreign relations — 1979- — Addresses, essays, lectures. I. Walker, Thomas W.
F1528.N5176 1985   972.85/053 19   *LC* 85-3467   *ISBN* 0030695325

F1541–1577 Costa Rica. Panama

Biesanz, Richard. 3.9076
The Costa Ricans / Richard Biesanz, Karen Zubris Biesanz, Mavis Hiltunen Biesanz. — Englewood Cliffs, N.J.: Prentice-Hall, c1982. x, 246 p.: ill.; 23 cm. 1. Costa Rica. I. Biesanz, Karen Zubris. II. Biesanz, Mavis Hiltunen. III. T.
F1543.B57   972.86 19   *LC* 81-7380   *ISBN* 0131796062

Costa Rica, a country study / Foreign Area Studies, the 3.9077
American University; edited by Harold D. Nelson.
2nd ed. — Washington, D.C.: For sale by the Supt. of Docs., U.S. G.P.O., 1984. xxxi, 336 p.: ill.; 24 cm. (Area handbook series.) Rev. ed of: Area handbook for Costa Rica / co-authors, Howard I. Blutstein [and others]. 1970. 'Research completed November 1983.' Includes index. 'DA PAM 550-90'—T.p. verso. 1. Costa Rica. I. Nelson, Harold D. II. American University (Washington, D.C.). Foreign Area Studies. III. Title: Area handbook for Costa Rica. IV. Series.
F1543.C82 1984   972.86 19   *LC* 84-16888

Between continents/between seas: Precolumbian art of Costa 3.9078
Rica / text by Suzanne Abel–Vidor ... [et al.]; photographs by
Dirk Bakker
New York: H.N. Abrams; [Detroit]: Detroit Institute of Arts, 1982, [c1981]. 240 p.: ill. (some col.); 28 cm. 1. Indians of Central America — Costa Rica — Art — Exhibitions. 2. Indians of Central America — Costa Rica — Antiquities — Exhibitions. 3. Costa Rica — Antiquities — Exhibitions. I. Abel-Vidor, Suzanne. II. Bakker, Dirk. III. Detroit Institute of Arts. IV. Title: Precolumbian art of Costa Rica.
F1545.3.A7 B47   709/.7286/074013 19   *LC* 81-10862   *ISBN* 0810907291

Ameringer, Charles D., 1926-. 3.9079
Democracy in Costa Rica / Charles D. Ameringer. — New York, N.Y.: Praeger; Stanford, Calif.: Hoover Institution Press, 1982. xi, 138 p.: ill.; 25 cm. — (Politics in Latin America.) Includes index. 1. Costa Rica — Politics and government — 1948-1986 I. T. II. Series.
F1548.A43 1982   306/.097286 19   *LC* 82-9065   *ISBN* 0030621585

American University (Washington, D.C.). Foreign Area Studies. 3.9080
Panama: a country study / the American University, Foreign Area Studies; Richard F. Nyrop ... [et al.]. — Washington, D.C.: The University: for sale by the Supt. of Docs., U.S. Govt. Print. Off., 1981. xxiv, 276 p.: ill.; 24 cm. (Area handbook series.) 'DA pam 550-46; supersedes 1972 edition.' Edition for 1972, by T. E. Weil, published under title: Area handbook for Panama.

1. Panama. I. Nyrop, Richard F. II. Weil, Thomas E. Area handbook for Panama. III. T. IV. Series.
F1563.A63   972.87 19   *LC* 80-29255

Wafer, Lionel, 1660?-1705?   • 3.9081
A new voyage and description of the Isthmus of America. Edited by George Parker Winship. — New York: B. Franklin, [1970] 212 p.: illus., maps.; 23 cm. — (Literature of discovery, exploration & geography series, 5) (Burt Franklin research & source works series, 459) Reprint of the 1903 ed. 1. Indians of Central America — Panama 2. Natural history — Panama. 3. Panama — Description and travel I. Winship, George Parker, 1871-1952. ed. II. T.
F1564.W153   918.62/03/2   *LC* 79-114820

Perez-Venero, Alex.   3.9082
Before the five frontiers: Panama, from 1821–1903 / by Alex Perez-Venero. — New York: AMS Press, 1978. xi, 199 p.; 23 cm. Includes index. 1. Panama — History — To 1903 I. T.
F1566.45.P47   972.87   *LC* 77-78317   *ISBN* 0404160034

McCullough, David G.   3.9083
The path between the seas: the creation of the Panama Canal, 1870–1914 / David McCullough. — New York: Simon and Schuster, c1977. 698 p.: ill.; 24 cm. Includes index. 1. Panama Canal (Panama) — History. I. T.
F1569.C2 M33   972.875/04   *LC* 76-57967   *ISBN* 0671225634

F1601–2151 West Indies:
General

Fernández de Oviedo y Valdés, Gonzalo, 1478-1557.   • 3.9084
Natural history of the West Indies. Chapel Hill, University of North Carolina Press [1959] xvii, 140 p. illus., maps, facsim. 23 cm. 1. Indians of the West Indies 2. Indians of Central America 3. Natural history — West Indies. 4. Natural history — Central America. 5. America — Early accounts to 1600 I. T.
F1610.F4x   *LC* 59-63487

Blume, Helmut, 1920-.   3.9085
[Westindischen Inseln. English] The Caribbean islands. Translated by Johannes Maczewski and Ann Norton. [London]: Longman, [1974] 464 p. illus. 24 cm. Translation of Die Westindischen Inseln. 1. West Indies — Description and travel — 1951-1980 I. T.
F1612.B5513   917.29   *LC* 74-174848   *ISBN* 0582481643

Coke, Thomas, Bp., 1747-1814.   3.9086
A history of the West Indies, containing the natural, civil and ecclesiastical history of each island; with an ac- count of the missions instituted in those islands, from the commencement of their civilization; but more especially of the missions which have been established in that archipelago by the society late in connexion with the Rev. John Wesley. [Liverpool, Printed by Nuttall, Fisher, and Dixon, 1808]. London, F. Cass, 1971. 3 v. illus. 23 cm. (Cass Library of West Indian Studies, 21) 1. Wesleyan Methodist Church in the West Indies. 2. Missions — West Indies. 3. West Indies — History I. T.
F 1621 C68 1971   *ISBN* 0714619337

Newton, Arthur Percival, 1873-1942.   • 3.9087
The European nations in the West Indies, 1493–1688. — New York: Barnes & Noble, [1967] xviii, 356 p.: maps (part fold.); 23 cm. — (The Pioneer histories) Reprint of the 1933 ed. 1. Buccaneers 2. West Indies — History I. T.
F1621.N46 1967   972.902   *LC* 67-826

Parry, J. H. (John Horace), 1914-.   • 3.9088
A short history of the West Indies [by] J. H. Parry and P. M. Sherlock. 3d ed. London, Macmillan; New York, St. Martin's, 1971. xiii, 337 p., 14 plates. illus., map (on lining papers) 23 cm. 1. West Indies — History I. Sherlock, Philip Manderson, Sir. joint author. II. T.
F1621.P33 1971   972.9   *LC* 73-145588   *ISBN* 0333074572
    1968

Williams, Eric Eustace, 1911-.   • 3.9089
From Columbus to Castro: the history of the Caribbean, 1492–1969 [by] Eric Williams. — [1st U.S. ed.]. — New York: Harper & Row, [1971, c1970] 576 p.: illus., facsims., map (on lining papers), ports.; 23 cm. 1. West Indies — History I. T.
F1621.W68 1970b   972.9   *LC* 75-138773   *ISBN* 0060146680

Lowenthal, David.   3.9090
West Indian societies. — New York: Published for the Institute of Race Relations, London, in collaboration with the American Geographical Society [by] Oxford University Press, 1972. xvii, 385 p.: map.; 21 cm. — (American

Geographical Society research series, no. 26) 1. West Indies — Race relations. 2. West Indies — Social conditions. I. T.
F1629.A1 L6 1972b   301.45/09729   *LC* 72-186127   *ISBN* 0195015592

F1751–1849 Cuba

Cuba, a country study / Foreign Area Studies, the American   3.9091
University; edited by James D. Rudolph.
1st ed. — Washington, D.C.: Headquarters, Dept. of the Army: For sale by the Supt. of Docs., U.S. G.P.O., 1986. p. cm. (Area handbook series.) (DA pam. 550-152) 'Research completed March 1985.' Includes index. 1. Cuba. I. Rudolph, James D., 1947- II. American University (Washington, D.C.). Foreign Area Studies. III. Series. IV. Series: DA pam. 550-152
F1758.C957 1986   972.91 19   *LC* 86-3366

Smith, Robert Freeman, 1930- ed.   • 3.9092
Background to revolution; the development of modern Cuba. — [1st ed.]. — New York: Knopf, [c1966] xi, 224 p.; 19 cm. — (Borzoi books on Latin America) 1. Cuba — History — Addresses, essays, lectures. I. T.
F1776.S6   972.9106   *LC* 65-17485

Castro, Fidel, 1927-.   • 3.9093
[Selected works. English] Revolutionary struggle, 1947–1958. Edited and with an introd. by Rolando E. Bonachea and Nelson P. Valdés. Cambridge, MIT Press [1972] xx, 471 p. illus. 24 cm. (Selected works of Fidel Castro, v. 1) 1. Communism — Cuba — Addresses, essays, lectures. 2. Cuba — History — Revolution,1959 — Addresses, essays, lectures. 3. Cuba — History — 1933-1959 — Addresses, essays, lectures. I. Bonachea, Rolando E., ed. II. Valdés, Nelson P. ed. III. T.
F1788.C2713 1972   972.91/064/0924 B   *LC* 74-103892   *ISBN* 0262020653 *ISBN* 0262520273

Pérez, Louis A., 1943-.   3.9094
Cuba between empires, 1878–1902 / Louis A. Pérez, Jr. — Pittsburgh, Pa.: University of Pittsburgh Press, c1983. xx, 490 p.; 25 cm. — (Pitt Latin American series.) Includes index. 1. Cuba — History — 1878-1895 2. Cuba — History — Revolution, 1895-1898 3. Cuba — History — 1899-1906 I. T. II. Series.
F1785.P47 1983   972.91/06 19   *LC* 82-11059   *ISBN* 0822934728

Foner, Philip Sheldon, 1910-.   3.9095
The Spanish–Cuban–American war and the birth of American imperialism, 1895–1902 [by] Philip S. Foner. — New York: Monthly Review Press, [1972] 2 v. (xxxiv, 716 p.); 21 cm. — (Modern reader) 1. Cuba — History — Revolution, 1895-1898 2. United States — Foreign relations — Cuba. 3. Cuba — Foreign relations — United States. 4. United States — History — War of 1898 I. T.
F1786.F66   973.8/9   *LC* 79-187595   *ISBN* 0853452660

Bonachea, Ramón L.   3.9096
The Cuban insurrection, 1952–1959 [by] Ramón L. Bonachea [and] Marta San Martín. — New Brunswick, N.J.: Transaction Books, [1974] xxi, 451 p.: illus.; 24 cm. 1. Cuba — History — 1933-1959 I. San Martín, Marta, joint author. II. T.
F1787.5.B66 1974   972.91/063   *LC* 72-94546   *ISBN* 0878550747

Farber, Samuel, 1939-.   3.9097
Revolution and reaction in Cuba, 1933–1960: a political sociology from Machado to Castro / by Samuel Farber. — 1st ed. — Middletown, Conn.: Wesleyan University Press, c1976. xix, 283 p.; 22 cm. Includes index. 1. Communism — Cuba. 2. Cuba — Politics and government — 1933-1959 I. T.
F1787.5.F37   320.9/7291/063   *LC* 76-7190   *ISBN* 0819540994

Guevara, Ernesto, 1928-1967.   • 3.9098
[Pasajes de la Guerra Revolucionaria. English] Reminiscences of the Cuban Revolutionary War [by] Ernesto Che Guevara. Translated by Victoria Ortiz. New York, M[onthly] R[eview] Press; distributed by Grove Press [1968] 287 p. illus., map (on lining papers), ports. 22 cm. Revised and much enlarged translation of Pasajes de la Guerra Revolucionaria. 1. Cuba — History — 1933-1959 2. Cuba — History, Military. I. T.
F1787.5.G8253 1968d   972.91/06   *LC* 68-13655

Judson, C. Fred.   3.9099
Cuba and the revolutionary myth: the political education of the Cuban Rebel Army, 1953–1963 / C. Fred Judson. — Boulder, Colo.: Westview Press, c1984. ix, 294 p.: map; 23 cm. (A Westview replica edition) 1. Guerrillas — Education — Cuba — History — 20th century. 2. Guerrillas — Education — Political science — History — 20th century. 3. Political psychology 4. Cuba — Politics

and government — 1933-1959 5. Cuba — Politics and government — 1959-6. Cuba — History — Revolution, 1959 — Causes. I. T.
F1787.5.J83 1984   972.91/064 19   LC 84-50657   *ISBN* 0865318271

Calderío, Francisco, 1908-.   • **3.9100**
The Cuban revolution; report to the Eight[h] National Congress of the Popular Socialist Party of Cuba, by Blas Roca. New York, New Century Publishers, 1961. 127 p. 20 cm. Photocopy. Ann Arbor, University Microfilms, 1978. Translation of: La revolución cubana. 1. Partido Socialista Popular (Cuba) 2. Cuba — Politics and government — 1938-1959. 3. Cuba — Politics and government — 1959- I. T. II. Title: La revolución cubana.
F 1788 C14E5 1961   *LC* 61-2735

Castro, Fidel, 1927-.   • **3.9101**
[Historia me absolverá. English] History will absolve me. Translation from the Spanish of a defense plea by Fidel Castro. [New York, L. Stuart, 1961] 79 p. 23 cm. 1. Cuba — History — Moncada Barracks Attack, 1953 — Addresses, essays, lectures. I. T.
F1788.C27753 1961   972.91063   *LC* 61-11365

Del Aguila, Juan M.   **3.9102**
Cuba, dilemmas of a revolution / Juan M. Del Aguila. — Boulder, Colo.: Westview Press, 1984. xiii, 193 p.: ill.; 23 cm. (Westview profiles. Nations of contemporary Latin America.) 1. Cuba — Politics and government — 1959- I. T. II. Series.
F1788.D42 1984   972.91/064 19   *LC* 84-5178   *ISBN* 0865315639

Goodsell, James Nelson, comp.   **3.9103**
Fidel Castro's personal revolution in Cuba: 1959–1973. Edited with an introd. by James Nelson Goodsell. — [1st ed.] — New York: Knopf, [1975] xii, 349 p.; 19 cm. — (Borzoi books on Latin America) 1. Cuba — History — Revolution, 1959 — Addresses, essays, lectures. I. T.
F1788.G63   972.91/064   *LC* 74-17216   *ISBN* 0394488911

Halperin, Maurice, 1906-.   **3.9104**
The rise and decline of Fidel Castro; an essay in contemporary history. — Berkeley: University of California Press, [1972] x, 380 p.: illus.; 24 cm. Continued by author's The domestication of Fidel Castro. 1. Castro, Fidel, 1927- 2. Cuba — Foreign relations — 1959- 3. Cuba — History — 1959- I. T.
F1788.H27   972.91/064/0924   *LC* 77-182794   *ISBN* 0520021827

Huberman, Leo, 1903-1968.   • **3.9105**
Cuba: anatomy of a revolution [by] Leo Huberman [and] Paul M. Sweezy. — 2d ed., with new material added. — New York, Monthly Review Press, 1961 [c1960] 208 p. illus. 22 cm. Includes bibliography. 1. Castro, Fidel, 1927- 2. Cuba — Hist. — 1933-1959. 3. Cuba — Soc. condit. I. Sweezy, Paul Marlor, 1910- joint author. II. T.
F1788.H8 1961   972.91063   *LC* 61-3092

Meyer, Karl Ernest.   • **3.9106**
The Cuban Invasion: the chronicle of a disaster / by Karl E. Meyer and Tad Szulc. — New York: Praeger, [1962] 160 p.; 21 cm. — (Books that matter) 1. Cuba — History — Invasion, April, 1961. I. Szulc, Tad. joint author. II. T.
F1788.M45   972.91064   *LC* 62-15262

Cuba in the world / Cole Blasier, Carmelo Mesa–Lago, editors. • **3.9107**
Pittsburgh: University of Pittsburgh Press, c1979. vii, 343 p.; 24 cm. (Pitt Latin American series) 1. Cuba — Foreign relations — 1959- — Addresses, essays, lectures. I. Blasier, Cole, 1925- II. Mesa-Lago, Carmelo, 1934-
F1788.2.C82   327.7291   *LC* 78-53598   *ISBN* 0822933837. *ISBN* 082295298X pbk

Martin, Lionel.   **3.9108**
The early Fidel: roots of Castro's communism / by Lionel Martin. — 1st ed. — Secaucus, N.J.: L. Stuart, c1978. 272 p., [4] leaves of plates: ill.; 24 cm. 1. Castro, Fidel, 1927- 2. Heads of state — Cuba — Biography. I. T.
F1788.22.C3 M27 1978   972.91/064/0924 B   *LC* 77-12245   *ISBN* 0818402547

F1861–1941 Jamaica. Haiti. Dominican Republic

Kaplan, Irving, 1923-.   **3.9110**
Area handbook for Jamaica / coauthors, Irving Kaplan ... [et al.]. — 1st ed. — Washington: For sale by the Supt. of Docs., U.S. Govt. Print. Off., 1976. xiv, 332 p.: ill.; 24 cm. 'DA pam 550-177.' 'One of a series of handbooks prepared by Foreign Area Studies (FAS) of the American University.' Includes index. 1. Jamaica. I. American University (Washington, D.C.). Foreign Area Studies. II. T.
F1868.K36   972.92   *LC* 75-619401

Gardner, W. J. (William James), 1825-1874.   **3.9111**
A history of Jamaica from its discovery by Christopher Columbus to the year 1872, including an account of its trade and agriculture; sketches of the manners, habits, and customs of all classes of its inhabitants; and a narrative of the progress of religion and education in the island, by W.J. Gardner. [London] F. Cass, 1971. xvi, 510 p. illus. fold. map. 23 cm. (Cass library of West Indian studies. no. 17) 1. Jamaica — History I. T. II. Series.
F1881.G23 1971   917.292/03   *LC* 77-160139   *ISBN* 0714619388

Manley, Norman Washington, 1893-1969.   **3.9112**
Norman Washington Manley and the new Jamaica; selected speeches and writings, 1938–68. Edited with notes and introd. by Rex Nettleford. — Kingston: Longman Caribbean, 1971. cxii, 393 p.: illus.; 23 cm. 1. Jamaica — Politics and government — Addresses, essays, lectures. I. Nettleford, Rex M., 1933- ed. II. T. III. Title: Manley and the new Jamaica.
F1887.M3 1971   320.9/7292/05

St. John, Spenser Buckingham, Sir, 1825-1910.   **3.9113**
Hayti; or, The black republic. With a new pref. by Robert I. Rotberg. — [London]: F. Cass, [1971] xxiv, 389 p.: fold. map.; 23 cm. — (Source books on Haiti, no. 9) Reprint of 2d ed. published in 1889. 'Distributed in the United States by International Scholarly Book Services, Beaverton, Oregon.' 1. Haiti. I. T. II. Title: The black republic.
F1915.S2 1971   917.294/03/4   *LC* 70-171805   *ISBN* 0714627054

Weil, Thomas E.   **3.9114**
Area handbook for Haiti. Co–authors: Thomas E. Weil [and others] 1st ed., 5th printing. [Washington, For sale by the Supt. of Docs., U.S. Govt. Print. Off.] 1985, c1973. xiv, 189 p. maps. 25 cm. 'DA PAM 550-164.' 'Prepared by Foreign Area Studies (FAS) of the American University.' 1. Haiti. I. American University (Washington, D.C.). Foreign Area Studies. II. T.
F1915.W44   917.294/03/6   *LC* 73-600155

Weinstein, Brian.   **3.9115**
Haiti: political failures, cultural successes / Brian Weinstein and Aaron Segal. — New York: Praeger, 1984. xi, 175 p.: map; 25 cm. — (Politics in Latin America.) 'Copublished with Hoover Institution Press, Stanford University, Stanford, California.' Includes index. 1. Haiti. I. Segal, Aaron. II. T. III. Series.
F1915.W45 1984   972.94 19   *LC* 83-24501   *ISBN* 0030698693

Leyburn, James Graham.   • **3.9116**
The Haitian people, by James G. Leyburn. With a new introd. by Sidney W. Mintz. [Rev. ed.] New Haven, Yale University Press, 1966. xlviii, 342 p. fold. map. 21 cm. (Caribbean series, 9) 1. Social classes — Haiti. 2. Haiti — Social life and customs. 3. Haiti. I. T. II. Series.
F1921.L6 1966   972.94   *LC* 66-9411

Mackenzie, Charles, F.R.S.   **3.9117**
Notes on Haiti, made during a residence in that republic. With a new pref. by Robert I. Rotberg. — [London]: F. Cass [Distributed in the U.S. by International Scholarly Book Services, Beaverton, Or., 1971. 2 v.: ill., facsims., map; 23 cm. — (Source books on Haiti, no. 6) Reprint of the 1830 ed. published by H. Colburn and R. Bentley, London. 1. Haiti — History 2. Haiti — Description and travel I. T.
F1921.M152   917.294/03/4   *LC* 75-11412   *ISBN* 0714627100

Nicholls, David.   **3.9118**
From Dessalines to Duvalier: race colour, and national independence in Haiti / David Nicholls. — Cambridge [Eng.]; New York: Cambridge University Press, 1979. xi, 357 p.: map; 22 cm. (Cambridge Latin American studies. no. 34) Includes index. 1. Haiti — History 2. Haiti — Race relations. 3. Haiti — Politics and government I. T. II. Series.
F1921.N58   972.94/06   *LC* 78-27271   *ISBN* 0521221773

James, C. L. R. (Cyril Lionel Robert), 1901-.   • **3.9119**
The Black Jacobins; Toussaint L'Ouverture and the San Domingo Revolution. 2d ed., rev. New York, Vintage Books [1963] xi, 426 p. map. 19 cm. 'V242.' 1. Toussaint Louverture, 1743?-1803. 2. Haiti — History — Revolution, 1791-1804 I. T.
F1923.T85 1963   972.9403   *LC* 63-15043

Schmidt, Hans, 1938-.   **3.9120**
The United States occupation of Haiti, 1915–1934. — New Brunswick, N.J.: Rutgers University Press, [1971] x, 303 p.: illus., ports., map.; 24 cm. 1. Haiti — History — American occupation, 1915-1934 I. T.
F1927.S35   972.94/05   *LC* 70-152721   *ISBN* 0813506905

Weil, Thomas E.   **3.9121**
Area handbook for the Dominican Republic / coauthors, Thomas E. Weil ... [et al.]. — 2d ed. — Washington: For sale by the Supt. of Docs., U.S. Govt. Print. Off., 1982. xii, 261 p.: maps.; 24 cm. 'DA PAM 550-54.' 'This handbook supersedes DA Pam 550-54, December 1966' by T. D. Roberts et al. Includes index. 1. Dominican Republic. I. Roberts, Thomas Duval, 1903- Area handbook for

the Dominican Republic. II. American University (Washington, D.C.). Foreign Area Studies. III. T.
F1934.W44   917.293/03/54   *LC* 73-600179

Welles, Sumner, 1892-.   • 3.9122
Naboth's vineyard: the Dominican Republic, 1844–1924 / new foreword by Germán Arciniegas. — Mamaroneck, N.Y.: P. P. Appel, 1966. 2 v. (1058 p.): ill., fold. maps, ports.; 24 cm. 1. Dominican Republic — History — 1844-1930 2. Dominican Republic — Foreign relations — United States. 3. United States — Foreign relations — Dominican Republic. I. T.
F1938.4.W4 1966   972.93   *LC* 66-31307

Galíndez, Jesús de, 1915-.   3.9123
[Era de Trujillo. English] The era of Trujillo, Dominican dictator, by Jesús de Galíndez. Edited by Russell H. Fitzgibbon. Tucson, University of Arizona Press [1973] xxvii, 298 p. illus. 23 cm. Abridged and revised from the author's thesis, Columbia University, 1956, which was an English translation of a work originally written in Spanish and first published in 1956 under title: La era de Trujillo. 1. Trujillo Molina, Rafael Leónidas, 1891-1961. 2. Trujillo Molina, Hector Bienvenido, 1908- 3. Dominican Republic — Politics and government — 1930-1961 I. Fitzgibbon, Russell Humke, 1902- ed. II. T.
F1938.5.G313 1973   320.9/7293/053   *LC* 72-79292   *ISBN* 0816503931 *ISBN* 0816503591(pbk.)

Gutiérrez, Carlos María, 1926-.   3.9124
The Dominican Republic: rebellion and repression. Translated by Richard E. Edwards. — New York: Monthly Review Press, [1972] 172 p.; 21 cm. 1. Dominican Republic — Politics and government — 1961- — Addresses, essays, lectures. 2. United States — Foreign relations — Dominican Republic — Addresses, essays, lectures. 3. Dominican Republic — Foreign relations — United States — Addresses, essays, lectures. I. T.
F1938.55.G8713   320.9/7293/054   *LC* 72-81763

F1951–1983 Puerto Rico

Lewis, Gordon K.   • 3.9125
Puerto Rico; freedom and power in the Caribbean. — New York [Monthly Review Press] 1963. xii, 626 p. 24 cm. Bibliographical references included in 'Notes' (p. 575-613) 1. Puerto Rico. I. T. II. Title: Freedom and power in the Caribbean.
F1958.L4   917.295   *LC* 63-20065

Picó, Rafael.   • 3.9126
The geographic regions of Puerto Rico. Río Piedras, University of Puerto Rico Press, 1950. xiii, 256 p. illus., maps. 24 cm. 1. Puerto Rico. I. T.
F1958.P5   *LC* 51-26021

Hauberg, Clifford A.   3.9127
Puerto Rico and the Puerto Ricans, by Clifford A. Hauberg. — New York: Twayne Publishers, [1975, c1974] 211 p.; 21 cm. — (The Immigrant heritage of America series) 1. Puerto Ricans in the United States. 2. Puerto Rico — History I. T.
F1971.H38 1975   917.295/03/53   *LC* 74-8812   *ISBN* 0805732594

Williams, Byron, 1934-.   3.9128
Puerto Rico: commonwealth, state or nation? New York: Parents' Magazine Press [1972] vi, 249 p.; 22 cm. 1. Puerto Rico — History 2. Puerto Rico — Relations — United States 3. United States — Relations — Puerto Rico I. T.
F1971.W5   320.9/7295   *LC* 79-183127   *ISBN* 0819305731 *ISBN* 081930574X

Maldonado-Denis, Manuel, 1933-.   3.9129
Puerto Rico: a socio–historic interpretation. Translated by Elena Vialo. — [1st American ed.]. — New York: Random House, [1972] xiv, 336 p.; 22 cm. Translation of Puerto Rico: una interpretación histórico-social. 1. Nationalism — Puerto Rico. 2. Puerto Rico — History I. T.
F1975.M2713 1972   972.95   *LC* 71-37062   *ISBN* 0394473477

F2001–2151 Other Islands

Schomburgk, Robert H. (Robert Hermann), Sir, 1804-1865.   3.9130
The history of Barbados; comprising a geographical and statistical description of the island, a sketch of the historical events since the settlement, and an account of its geology and natural productions. [London] F. Cass, 1971. xx, 722 p. illus. 26 cm. (Cass library of West Indian studies. no. 19) Reprint of the ed. published in 1848 by Longman, Brown, Green & Longmans, London.

1. Natural history — Barbados. 2. Barbados — Description and travel. 3. Barbados — History. I. T. II. Series.
F2041.S36 1971   917.29/81   *LC* 77-171812   *ISBN* 0714619485

Atwood, Thomas, d. 1793.   3.9131
The history of the island of Dominica, containing a description of its situation, extent, climate, mountains, rivers, natural productions etc. etc., together with an account of the civil government, trade, laws, customs and manners of different inhabitants of that island, its conquest by the French and restoration to the British Dominions. [1st ed., new impression] London, Cass, 1971. viii, 285 p. 22 cm. (Cass library of West Indian studies. no. 27) Originally published London, 1791. 1. Dominica — Description and travel. I. T. II. Series.
F2051.A88 1971   972.93   *LC* 74-879415   *ISBN* 0714619299

Schoenhals, Kai P.   3.9132
Revolution and intervention in Grenada: the New Jewel Movement, the United States, and the Caribbean / Kai P. Schoenhals and Richard A. Melanson. — Boulder: Westview Press, 1985. xii, 211 p.; 23 cm. (Westview special studies on Latin America and the Caribbean.) Includes index. 1. Grenada — Politics and government 2. Caribbean Area — Foreign relations — United States. 3. United States — Foreign relations — Caribbean Area. 4. United States — Foreign relations — 1945- I. Melanson, Richard A. II. T. III. Series.
F2056.62.S36 1985   972.98/45 19   *LC* 85-3332   *ISBN* 0813302250

The Grenada papers / edited by Paul Seabury and Walter A.   3.9133
McDougall; with a foreword by Sidney Hook.
San Francisco, Calif.: Institute for Contemporary Studies, c1984. xvii, 346 p.: ill.; 24 cm. 1. Communism — Grenada — History — Sources. 2. Grenada — Politics and government — 1974- — Sources. 3. Grenada — History — American invasion, 1983 — Causes — Sources. I. Seabury, Paul. II. McDougall, Walter A., 1946-
F2056.8.G77 1984   972.98/45 19   *LC* 84-22356   *ISBN* 0917616685

Bishop, Maurice.   3.9134
Maurice Bishop speaks: the Grenada Revolution, 1979–83 / [edited by Bruce Marcus and Michael Taber]. — 1st ed. — New York: Pathfinder Press, 1983. xlvii, 352 p., [8] p. of plates: ill.; 22 cm. Includes index. 1. Grenada — Politics and government — 1974- — Addresses, essays, lectures. I. Marcus, Bruce, 1949- II. Taber, Michael. III. T.
F2056.83.B57 A5 1983   972.9/845 19   *LC* 83-63309   *ISBN* 0873486110

Shephard, Charles.   3.9135
An historical account of the Island of Saint Vincent. — [London]: F. Cass, 1971. xvi, 216, lxxvi p.: illus.; 23 cm. — (Cass library of West Indian studies. no. 23) Reprint of the 1831 ed. 1. Saint Vincent — History 2. Saint Vincent — History — Carib War, 1795-1796 I. T. II. Series.
F2106.S54 1971   972.9/844   *LC* 73-171811   *ISBN* 0714619515

Black, Jan Knippers, 1940-.   3.9136
Area handbook for Trinidad and Tobago / coauthors, Jan Knippers Black ... [et al.]. — 1st ed. — Washington: For sale by the Supt. of Docs., U.S. Govt. Print. Off., 1976. xiv, 304 p.: maps; 24 cm. 'DA Pam 550-178.' 'One of a series of handbooks prepared by Foreign Area Studies (FAS) of the American University.' Includes index. 1. Trinidad and Tobago. I. American University (Washington, D.C.). Foreign Area Studies. II. T.
F2119.B55   972.9/8304   *LC* 76-8513

Williams, Eric Eustace, 1911-.   3.9137
Forged from the love of liberty: selected speeches of Dr. Eric Williams / compiled by Paul K. Sutton. — [Port of Spain, Trinidad and Tobago]: Longman Caribbean, c1981. xxxvi, 473 p., [16] p. of plates: ill.; 22 cm. Includes index. 1. Trinidad and Tobago — Politics and government — Addresses, essays, lectures. I. Sutton, Paul K. II. T.
F2122.W497 1981   972.98/3 19   *LC* 85-167912   *ISBN* 0582643295

Burn, William Laurence.   • 3.9138
The British West Indies. London Hutchinson House 1951. 196p. (Hutchinson's university library: British Empire history) 1. West Indies, British — History I. T.
F2131 B87

Coombs, Orde. comp.   3.9139
Is Massa Day dead? Black moods in the Caribbean, edited, and with an introd., by Orde Coombs. [1st ed.] Garden City, N.Y., Anchor Books, 1974. xix, 260 p. 18 cm. 1. Blacks — West Indies, British 2. West Indies, British — Social conditions. I. T.
F2131.C73   917.29/06/96   *LC* 73-16501   *ISBN* 0385079478

Davy, John, 1790-1868.   3.9140
The West Indies before and since slave emancipation, comprising the Windward and Leeward Islands' military commend; founded on notes and observations collected during a three years' residence. — [London]: F. Cass, 1971. vii, viii 551 p.: map.; 23 cm. — (Cass library of West Indian studies. no. 22) Originally published London, W. & F. G. Cash, 1854. 1. Agriculture —

West Indies, British. 2. West Indies, British — Description and travel. I. T. II. Series.
F2131.D27 1971   917.29   *LC* 72-874141   *ISBN* 0714619353

✓ **Dunn, Richard S.**   **3.9141**
Sugar and slaves; the rise of the planter class in the English West Indies, 1624–1713, by Richard S. Dunn. Chapel Hill, Published for the Institute of Early American History and Culture at Williamsburg, Va., by the University of North Carolina Press [1972] xx, 359 p. illus. 24 cm. 1. Sugar — Manufacture and refining — West Indies, British. 2. West Indies — History — 17th century 3. West Indies, British — Social life and customs. I. Institute of Early American History and Culture (Williamsburg, Va.) II. T.
F2131.D8   917.29   *LC* 75-184229   *ISBN* 0807811920

F2161–2200 Caribbean Area. Caribbean Sea

Exquemelin, A. O. (Alexandre Olivier)   • **3.9142**
[Americaensche zee-roovers. English] The buccaneers of America. Translated from the Dutch by Alexis Brown, with an introd. by Jack Beeching. Baltimore, Penguin Books [1969] 232 p. maps. 18 cm. (The Penguin classics, L212) Translation of De Americaensche zee-roovers. 1. Buccaneers 2. Pirates 3. Spanish Main 4. West Indies — History I. T.
F2161.E8433 1969   917.29/03/3   *LC* 73-7683

Sauer, Carl Ortwin, 1889-.   • **3.9143**
The early Spanish Main. — Berkeley, University of California Press, 1966. xii, 306 p. illus., maps. 27 cm. Includes bibliographical references. 1. Spanish Main 2. America — Disc. & explor. — Spanish. 3. Indians of the West Indies I. T.
F2161.S25   972.902   *LC* 66-15004

West, Robert Cooper, 1913-.   **3.9144**
Middle America, its lands and peoples / Robert C. West, John P. Augelli. — 2d ed. — Englewood Cliffs, N.J.: Prentice-Hall, [1976] xvii, 494 p.: ill.; 24 cm. 1. West Indies 2. Mexico. 3. Central America I. Augelli, John P. joint author. II. T.
F2161.W42 1976   972   *LC* 75-14417   *ISBN* 0135815460

Lewis, Gordon K.   **3.9145**
Main currents in Caribbean thought: the historical evolution of Caribbean society in its ideological aspects, 1492–1900 / Gordon K. Lewis. — Baltimore: Johns Hopkins University Press, c1983. x, 375 p.; 24 cm. — (Johns Hopkins studies in Atlantic history and culture.) 1. Caribbean Area — Civilization I. T. II. Series.
F2169.L48 1983   972.9 19   *LC* 82-17128   *ISBN* 080182589X

Arciniegas, Germán, 1900-.   • **3.9146**
Caribbean: sea of the new world / [by] Germán Arciniegas; translated from the Spanish by Harriet de Onís. — New York: A.A. Knopf, 1946. xi, 464, xiv p.: plates, ports., fold. map.; 22 cm. 'First American edition.' 1. Caribbean Sea 2. Spanish Main 3. West Indies (Federation) — History. I. De Onís, Harriet, 1899- tr. II. T.
F2175.A7   *LC* 46-3862

Anderson, Thomas D.   **3.9147**
Geopolitics of the Caribbean: ministates in a wider world / by Thomas D. Anderson. — New York: Praeger, 1984. xiii, 175 p.: maps; 24 cm. — (Politics in Latin America.) 1. Geopolitics — Caribbean Area. I. T. II. Series.
F2176.A52 1984   327.1/01/109729 19   *LC* 83-21200   *ISBN* 0030705533

Langley, Lester D.   **3.9148**
The banana wars: an inner history of American empire, 1900–1934 / Lester D. Langley. — Lexington, Ky.: University Press of Kentucky, c1983. viii, 255 p.: ill., maps, ports.; 24 cm. Includes index. 1. Caribbean Area — Foreign relations — United States. 2. United States — Foreign relations — Caribbean Area. 3. Caribbean Area — Military relations — United States. 4. United States — Military relations — Caribbean Area. 5. Caribbean Area — History. 6. United States — Foreign relations — 20th century I. T.
F2178.U6 L34 1983   972.9/051 19   *LC* 83-10398   *ISBN* 0813114969

Confrontation in the Caribbean basin: international perspectives   **3.9149**
on security, sovereignty, and survival / Alan Adelman, Reid Reading, editors.
[Pittsburgh]: Published by the Center for Latin American Studies, University Center for International Studies, University of Pittsburgh with support from the Howard Heinz Endowment and the Rockefeller Foundation, [c1984] xi, 307 p.: map; 23 cm. — (Latin American monograph & document series; 8) Based on a conference held at the University of Pittsburgh, Oct. 1982. 1. Caribbean Area — Foreign relations — 1945- — Addresses, essays, lectures.

2. Caribbean Area — Politics and government — 1945- — Addresses, essays, lectures. I. Adelman, Alan, 1949- II. Reading, Reid, 1937-
F2183.C66 1984   327.729 19   *LC* 83-27435   *ISBN* 091600256X

F2201–2239 SOUTH AMERICA: GENERAL

Humboldt, Alexander von, 1769-1859.   **3.9150**
[Voyage aux régions équinoxiales. English] Personal narrative of travels to the equinoctial regions of America, during the years 1799–1804, by Alexander von Humboldt and Aimé Bonpland. Written in French by Alexander von Humboldt. Translated and edited by Thomasina Ross. New York, B. Blom, 1971. 3 v. 21 cm. (Bohn's scientific library) Abridged translation of Voyage aux régions équinoxiales du nouveau continent, which forms pt. 1 of Voyage de Humboldt et Bonpland. Reprint of the 1852-53 ed. 1. Natural history — South America. 2. Scientific expeditions 3. South America — Description and travel I. Bonpland, Aimé, 1773-1858. II. Ross, Thomasina, ed. III. T. IV. Series.
F2216.H928   918   *LC* 69-13241

F2221–2230.2 Description. Indians

Hanson, Earl Parker, 1899-.   • **3.9151**
South from the Spanish main; South American seen through the eyes of its discoverers, edited, annotated and introduced by Earl Parker Hanson. [New York] Delacorte Press [1967] xv, 463 p. maps. 24 cm. (The Great explorers series) 1. Explorers 2. South America — Description and travel 3. America — Discovery and exploration I. T.
F2221.H3   *LC* 67-19789

Ulloa, Antonio de, 1716-1795.   • **3.9152**
A voyage to South America [by] Jorge Juan and Antonio de Ulloa. The John Adams translation, abridged. Introd. by Irving A. Leonard. New York, Knopf, 1964. ix, 245 p. 19 cm. (Borzoi books on Latin America) 'LA—5.' Bibliography: p. [244]-245. A translation of Ulloa's Relación histórica del viage a la America Meridional ... Madrid, 1748. The account of the scientific work of the expedition, written by Jorge Juan y Santacilla, was published separately, Madrid, 1748, under title: 'Observaciones astronomicas, y phisicas hechas ... en los reynos del Perù ...' It is not included in this translation. 1. Scientific expeditions 2. South America — Social life and customs. 3. South America — Description and travel I. Juan y Santacilla, Jorge, 1713-1773. II. Adams, John, of Waltham Abbey. III. T.
F2221.U43   918   *LC* 64-13454

Von Hagen, Victor Wolfgang, 1908-.   **3.9153**
South America called them; explorations of the great naturalists: Charles-Marie de la Condamine, Alexander von Humboldt, Charles Darwin, Richard Spruce / Victor W. Von Hagen. — London: R. Hale, 1949. 401 p.: ill. 1. La Condamine, Charles-Marie de, 1701-1774. 2. Humboldt, Alexander von, 1769-1859. 3. Darwin, Charles, 1809-1882. 4. Spruce, Richard, 1817-1893. 5. South America — Description and travel I. T.
F 2221 V94 1949

Bryce, James Bryce, Viscount, 1838-1922.   • **3.9154**
South America: observations and impressions / by James Bryce. — New ed., corr. and rev. — New York: Macmillan, 1917, c1914. xxiv, 611 p.: maps. 1. South America 2. South America — Description and travel I. T.
F2223.B91 1914   *LC* 14-3120

Gross, Daniel R., comp.   **3.9155**
Peoples and cultures of native South America: an anthropological reader / edited with introd. by Daniel R. Gross. — [1st ed.]. — Garden City, N.Y.: Published for the American Museum of Natural History [by] Natural History Press, 1973. viii, 566 p.: ill.; 22 cm. 1. Indians of South America — Addresses, essays, lectures. I. T.
F2229.G76 1973   301.29/801   *LC* 77-171295   *ISBN* 0385057253

Steward, Julian Haynes, 1902-1972.   • **3.9156**
Native peoples of South America / [by] Julian H. Steward [and] Louis C. Faron. — New York: McGraw-Hill, 1959. xi, 481 p.: ill., maps.; 24 cm. 1. Indians of South America I. Faron, Louis C., 1923- joint author. II. T.
F2229.S77   980.1   *LC* 58-10010

Steward, Julian Haynes, 1902-1972. ed.   • **3.9157**
Handbook of South American Indians / Julian H. Steward, editor; prepared in cooperation with the U.S. Dept. of State as a project of the Indepartmental

Committee on Scientific and Cultural Cooperation. — New York: Cooper Square Publishers, 1963-. v.: ill., maps (some fold.); 24 cm. (Bulletin (Smithsonian Institution. Bureau of American Ethnology) 143) 1. Indians of South America I. United States. Interdepartmental Committee on Scientific and Cultural Cooperation. II. T. III. Series.
F2229.S7x   980.1   *LC* 63-17285

Bennett, Wendell Clark, 1905-1953.   • **3.9158**
Ancient arts of the Andes. With an introd. by René d'Harnoncourt. The Museum of Modern Art, New York, in collaboration with the California Palace of the Legion of Honor, San Francisco [and] the Minneapolis Institute of Arts. [New York: Museum of Modern Art, 1954] 186 p.: 209 illus. (part col.) maps.; 27 cm. 1. Indians of South America — Andes — Art. 2. Indians of South America — Antiquities 3. Indians of Central America — Art 4. Indians of Central America — Antiquities I. New York. Museum of Modern Art. II. T.
F2230.1.A7 B4   980.65715   *LC* 54-6135

Lapiner, Alan C.   **3.9159**
Pre–Columbian art of South America / Alan Lapiner. New York: H. N. Abrams, 1976. 460 p.; ill. (some col.); 34 cm. Includes index. 1. Indians of South America — Art I. T.
F2230.1.A7 L36   709/.01/1   *LC* 75-1016   *ISBN* 0810904217

Stierlin, Henri.   **3.9160**
[Art Inca et ses origines. English] Art of the Incas and its origins / Henri Stierlin. — New York: Rizzoli, 1984. 240 p.: ill. (some col.); 32 cm. 'Translation from the French, L'art Inca et ses origines: de Valdivia à Machu Picchu, by Betty and Peter Ross'— Verso t.p. Includes index. 1. Indians of South America — Andes Region — Art. 2. Incas — Art. I. T.
F2230.1.A7 S7513 1984   709/.85 19   *LC* 83-24693   *ISBN* 0847805298

Adaptive responses of native Amazonians / edited by Raymond   **3.9161**
B. Hames, William T. Vickers.
New York: Academic Press, 1983. xv, 516 p.: ill., map; 25 cm. — (Studies in anthropology) Includes index. 1. Indians of South America — Amazon River Valley — Social conditions — Addresses, essays, lectures. 2. Indians of South America — Amazon River Valley — Social life and customs — Addresses, essays, lectures. 3. Human ecology — Amazon River Valley — Addresses, essays, lectures. 4. Amazon River Valley — Social conditions — Addresses, essays, lectures. I. Hames, Raymond B. II. Vickers, William T.
F2230.1.S68 A3 1983   305.8/98/0811 19   *LC* 82-18399   *ISBN* 0123212502

F2231–2237 History

Wood, Bryce, 1909-.   • **3.9162**
The United States and Latin American wars, 1932–1942. New York, Columbia University Press, 1966. x, 519 p. 4 fold. maps. 24 cm. Bibliography: p. [486]-499. 1. United States — Foreign relations — South America. 2. South America — Foreign relations — United States. 3. South America — History — 20th century I. T.
F2231.5.W6   327.7308   *LC* 65-25493

Whitaker, Arthur Preston, 1895-.   **3.9163**
The United States and the southern cone: Argentina, Chile, and Uruguay / Arthur P. Whitaker. — Cambridge, Mass.: Harvard University Press, 1976. xiv, 464 p.; 25 cm. — (American foreign policy library.) Includes index. 1. Southern Cone of South America — Relations — United States. 2. United States — Relations — Southern Cone of South America. 3. Argentina — History 4. Chile — History 5. Uruguay — History I. T. II. Series.
F2232.2.U6 W47   301.29/8/073   *LC* 76-14400   *ISBN* 0674928415

Belaúnde, Víctor Andrés, 1883-.   • **3.9164**
Bolivar and the political thought of the Spanish American Revolution. — New York, Octagon Books, 1967 [c1938] xxiv, 451 p. 21 cm. — (The Albert Shaw lectures on diplomatic history, 1930) Bibliography: p. 407-427. 1. Bolívar, Simón, 1783-1830. 2. Latin America — Hist. — Wars of Independence, 1806-1830. 3. Latin America — Politics — 1806-1830. I. T. II. Series.
F2235.B673 1967   980/.02   *LC* 67-18750

O'Leary, Daniel Florencio, 1800-1854.   • **3.9165**
Bolívar and the war of independence. Translated and edited by Robert F. McNerney, Jr. — Austin: University of Texas Press, [1970] xvi, 386 p.: illus., maps, ports.; 24 cm. — (The Texas pan-American series) Abridged translation of Memorias del General Daniel Florencio O'Leary, v. 27-28: Narración. 1. Bolívar, Simón, 1783-1830. 2. South America — History — Wars of Independence, 1806-1830 3. Venezuela — History — War of Independence, 1810-1823 I. T.
F2235.O4   980.02/0924   *LC* 70-137997   *ISBN* 0292700474

Bolívar, Simón, 1783-1830.   • **3.9166**
Selected writings; compiled by Vincente Lecuna, edited by Harold A. Bierck, Jr., translation by Lewis Bertrand. Published by Banco de Venezuela. — New York, Colonial Press, 1951. 2 v. (lii, 822 p.) illus., ports., maps. 25 cm. 1. Latin America — Hist. — Wars of Independence, 1806-1830 — Sources. I. T.
F2235.3.A13   980   *LC* 51-3913

Masur, Gerhard, 1901-.   • **3.9167**
Simon Bolivar. — [Rev. ed.]. — Albuquerque: University of New Mexico Press, [1969] xiv, 572 p.: maps.; 25 cm. 1. Bolívar, Simón, 1783-1830. I. T.
F2235.3.M39 1969   980/.02/0924 B   *LC* 68-56230   *ISBN* 0826301312

Rojas, Ricardo, 1882-1957.   • **3.9168**
San Martín, knight of the Andes. Translated by Herschel Brickell and Carlos Videla. Introd. and notes by Herschel Brickell. New York, Cooper Square Publishers, 1967 [c1945] xiii, 370 p. port. 24 cm. (Library of Latin-American history and culture) Translation of El santo de la espada. 1. San Martín, José de, 1778-1850. I. T.
F2235.4.R852 1967   *LC* 66-30783

New military politics in Latin America / edited by Robert   **3.9169**
Wesson.
New York: Praeger, 1982. x, 230 p.; 25 cm. — (Politics in Latin America.) 1. Military government — South America — Congresses. 2. South America — Politics and government — 20th century — Congresses. I. Wesson, Robert G. II. Series.
F2237.N48 1982   322/.5/098 19   *LC* 82-9871   *ISBN* 0030618525

Petras, James F., 1937-.   **3.9170**
Latin America: from dependence to revolution / James Petras, editor. — New York: Wiley, 1974 (c1973) viii, 274 p.; 23 cm. 1. South America — Politics and government — 20th century — Addresses, essays, lectures. 2. South America — Economic conditions — 1918- — Addresses, essays, lectures. 3. South America — Relations — United States — Addresses, essays, lectures. 4. United States — Relations — South America — Addresses, essays, lectures. I. T.
F2237.P47   320.9/8/003   *LC* 72-13437   *ISBN* 0471684465

F2251–3799 INDIVIDUAL COUNTRIES

F2251–2299 Colombia

Galbraith, W. O.   • **3.9171**
Colombia: a general survey [by] W. O. Galbraith. — 2nd ed. — London; New York [etc.]: issued under the auspices of the Royal Institute of International Affairs by Oxford U.P., 1966. xii, 177 p.: maps, tables.; 21 cm. 1. Colombia. I. Royal Institute of International Affairs. II. T.
F2258.G3 1966   918.61   *LC* 67-72179

Colombia, a country study / coauthors Howard I. Blutstein, J.   **3.9172**
David Edwards, [et. al].
3d ed., 1976. Washington: For sale by the Supt. of Docs., U. S. Govt. Print. Off., c1983. xiv, 508 p.: ill. (Area handbook series.) (DA PAM 550-26) Limited cataloging. 'Stock no. 008-020-00647-5.' I. Blutstein, Howard I. II. American University (Washington, D.C.). Foreign Area Studies. III. Series.
F2258.W43   *LC* 77-60832

Reichel-Dolmatoff, Gerardo.   • **3.9173**
Colombia [by] G. Reichel–Dolmatoff. New York, Praeger [1965] 231 p. illus., maps, plates. 21 cm. (Ancient peoples and places, 44) Bibliography: p. 181-182. 1. Indians of South America — Colombia — Antiquities 2. Colombia — Antiquities I. T.
F2269.R4   980.461   *LC* 65-23078

Henao, Jesús María, 1870-.   • **3.9174**
[Historia de Colombia. English] History of Colombia, by Jesús María Henao and Gerardo Arrubla. Translated and edited by J. Fred Rippy. New York, Greenwood Press [1969, c1938] xii, 578 p. 23 cm. 1. Colombia — History I. Arrubla, Gerardo, 1872-1946. joint author. II. Rippy, James Fred, 1892- ed. III. T.
F2271.H4963 1969   986.1   *LC* 76-90527   *ISBN* 0837122945

Bergquist, Charles W.   **3.9175**
Coffee and conflict in Colombia, 1886–1910 / Charles W. Bergquist. — Durham, N.C.: Duke University Press, 1978. x, 277 p.: ill.; 25 cm. Includes

index. 1. Coffee trade — Colombia — History. 2. Colombia — Politics and government — 1886-1903 3. Colombia — Politics and government — 1903-1930 4. Colombia — Economic conditions I. T.
F2276.5.B47   320.9/861/061   *LC* 78-59581   *ISBN* 082230418X

Fluharty, Vernon Lee.   • 3.9176
Dance of the millions; military rule and the social revolution in Colombia, 1930–1956. — [Pittsburgh] University of Pittsburgh Press [1957] 336 p. illus., maps. 24 cm. Bibliography: p. 318-324. 1. Colombia — Pol. & govt. — 1930-1946. 2. Colombia — Pol. & govt. — 1946- 3. Colombia — Soc. condit. I. T.
F2277.F58   *986.1   *LC* 57-7360

Wilson, Peter J.   3.9177
Crab antics; the social anthropology of English–speaking Negro societies of the Caribbean [by] Peter J. Wilson. New Haven, Yale University Press, 1973. xvii, 258 p. illus. 23 cm. (Caribbean series, 14) 1. Blacks — West Indies 2. Blacks — Families 3. Old Providence Island, Colombia. I. T. II. Series.
F2281.S15 W54   301.29/729   *LC* 72-91319   *ISBN* 0300015364

F2301–2349 Venezuela

Blutstein, Howard I.   3.9178
Area handbook for Venezuela / coauthors, Howard I. Blutstein ... [et al.]. — 3d ed. — Washington: For sale by the Supt. of Docs., U.S. Govt. Print. Off., 1977. xiv, 354 p.: ill.; 24 cm. 'DA pam 550-71.' 'One of a series of handbooks prepared by Foreign Area Studies (FAS) of the American University.' 'Supersedes DA pam 550-71, 1971 [by T. E. Weil and others]' Includes index. 1. Venezuela. I. Weil, Thomas E. Area handbook for Venezuela. II. American University (Washington, D.C.). Foreign Area Studies. III. T.
F2308.W4 1977   309.1/87/063   *LC* 77-21735

Rouse, Irving, 1913-.   • 3.9179
Venezuelan archaeology. New Haven Yale University Press 1963. 179p. (Caribbean series, 6) 1. Venezuela — Antiquities 2. Indians of South America — Venezuela I. Cruxent, José María. jt. author II. T. III. Series.
F2319 R67

Wilbert, Johannes.   3.9180
Survivors of Eldorado: four Indian cultures of South America. — New York: Praeger Publishers, [1972] xi, 212 p.: ill.; 21 cm. 1. Indians of South America — Venezuela I. T.
F2319.W5   980.4/7   *LC* 71-173277

Lombardi, John V.   3.9181
Venezuela: the search for order, the dream of progress / John V. Lombardi. — New York: Oxford University Press, 1982. xv, 348 p.: ill.; 21 cm. — (Latin American histories.) Includes index. 1. Venezuela — History I. T. II. Series.
F2321.L58 1982   987 19   *LC* 81-9630   *ISBN* 0195030133

Robertson, William Spence, 1872-.   • 3.9182
The life of Miranda. — New York: Cooper Square Publishers, 1969. 2 v.: illus., maps, ports.; 24 cm. — (Library of Latin American history and culture) Reprint of the 1929 ed. I. Miranda, Francisco de, 1750-1816. II. T.
F2323.M6 R62 1969   987/.04/0924 B   *LC* 77-79203   *ISBN* 0815402910

Ewell, Judith, 1943-.   3.9183
Venezuela, a century of change / Judith Ewell. — Stanford, Calif.: Stanford University Press, 1984. xiii, 258 p.: ill.; 22 cm. Includes index. 1. Venezuela — History — 1830-1935 2. Venezuela — History — 1935- I. T.
F2325.E93 1984   987/.063 19   *LC* 83-40093   *ISBN* 0804712131

Alexander, Robert Jackson, 1918-.   3.9184
Rómulo Betancourt and the transformation of Venezuela / Robert J. Alexander. — New Brunswick, U.S.A.: Transaction Books, c1982. viii, 737 p.; 24 cm. Includes index. 1. Betancourt, Rómulo, 1908- 2. Venezuela — Politics and government — 20th century 3. Venezuela — Presidents — Biography. I. T.
F2326.B4 A73   987/.0633/0924 B 19   *LC* 81-14684   *ISBN* 0878554505

F2361–2471 Guyana

Johnson Research Associates.   3.9185
Area handbook for Guyana. [Co–authors: William B. Mitchell and others. Prepared for the American University. Washington, For sale by the Supt. of Docs., U.S. Govt. Print. Off.] 1981. xiv, 378 p. maps. 25 cm. Cover title. 'DA pam no. 550-82.' 1. Guyana. I. Mitchell, William Burton. II. American University (Washington, D.C.) III. T.
F2368.J6   918.8/1   *LC* 79-606159

Price, Richard, 1941-.   3.9186
First–time: the historical vision of an Afro–American people / Richard Price. — Baltimore: Johns Hopkins University Press, c1983. 189 p.: ill.; 27 cm. — (Johns Hopkins studies in Atlantic history and culture.) 1. Saramacca (Surinam people) — History. I. T. II. Series.
F2431.N3 P73 1983   988/.3 19   *LC* 83-29   *ISBN* 0801829844

F2501–2659 Brazil

Brazil, a country study / Foreign Area Studies, the American   • 3.9187
University; edited by Richard F. Nyrop.
4th ed. — Washington, D.C.: For sale by the Supt. of Docs., U.S. G.P.O., 1983. xxix, 410 p.: ill.; 24 cm. — (Area handbook series.) (DA pam. 550-20) 'Research completed December 1982.' Replaces: Area handbook for Brazil / Thomas E. Weil. 3rd ed. 1975. Includes index. 1. Brazil. I. Nyrop, Richard F. II. Weil, Thomas E. Area handbook for Brazil. III. American University (Washington, D.C.). Foreign Area Studies. IV. Series. V. Series: DA pam. 550-20
F2508.B855 1983   981/.06 19   *LC* 83-15847

Smith, T. Lynn (Thomas Lynn), 1903-.   • 3.9188
Brazil: people and institutions. [Rev. ed.] Baton Rouge, Louisiana State University Press, 1963. xx, 667 p. illus., maps, diagrs., tables. 25 cm. 1. Social institutions — Brazil. 2. Brazil — Social conditions — 1945-1964 3. Brazil — Population. I. T.
F2508.S6 1963   918.1   *LC* 63-13239

Azevedo, Fernando de, 1894-.   • 3.9189
[Culture brasileira. English] Brazilian culture; an introduction to the study of culture in Brazil. Translated by William Rex Crawford. New York, Hafner Pub. Co., 1971 [c1950] xxix, 562 p. illus., facsims., maps, ports. 27 cm. Translation of A culture brasileira. 1. Education — Brazil. 2. Brazil — Intellectual life 3. Brazil — Civilization I. T.
F2510.A933 1950a   918.1/03   *LC* 76-151829

Freyre, Gilberto, 1900-.   • 3.9190
New world in the Tropics; the culture of modern Brazil. — [1st ed.] — New York: Knopf, 1959. 285 p.; 22 cm. 'Expanded and completely rewritten version of [the author's] Brazil: an interpretation.' 1. Brazil — Civilization I. T.
F2510.F7519   918.1   *LC* 59-5488

Freyre, Gilberto, 1900-.   • 3.9191
[Casa-grande & senzala. English] The masters and the slaves (Casa–grande & senzala) A study in the development of Brazilian civilization; translated from the Portuguese by Samuel Putnam. 2d English language ed., rev. New York, Knopf, 1956. lxxi, 537, xliv p. plans. 25 cm. 1. Slavery — Brazil 2. Blacks — Brazil 3. Indians of South America — Brazil 4. Brazil — Social life and customs I. T.
F2510.F7522 1956   918.1   *LC* 56-5787

Freyre, Gilberto, 1900-.   • 3.9192
[Ordem e progresso. English] Order and progress; Brazil from monarchy to republic. Edited and translated from the Portuguese by Rod W. Horton. [1st American ed.] New York, Knopf, 1970. 1, 422, xxxiv p. illus., maps. 25 cm. In '... the English-language version of Ordem e progresso, cuts and condensations were made in the original text.' 1. Brazil — Civilization 2. Brazil — Social conditions I. T.
F2510.F754163 1970   918.1/03/5   *LC* 69-10713

Freyre, Gilberto, 1900-.   • 3.9193
[Sobrados e mucambos. English] The Mansions and the shanties (Sobrados e mucambos); the making of modern Brazil. Translated from the Portuguese and edited by Harriet de Onís. With an introd. by Frank Tannenbaum. [1st American ed.] New York, Knopf, 1963. 431 p. illus. 25 cm. 1. Brazil — Civilization 2. Brazil — Social conditions 3. Brazil — Race relations. I. T.
F2510.F7563   918.1   *LC* 62-15561

Graham, Richard. • **3.9194**
Britain and the onset of modernization in Brazil 1850–1914. — London,
Cambridge U. P., 1968. xvi, 385 p. 6 plates, 6 illus., 3 maps. 22 cm. —
(Cambridge Latin American studies. 4) Bibliography: p. 333-366. 1. Brazil —
Civilization — British influences. I. T. II. Series.
F2510.G7   301.29/81/042   LC 68-21393   ISBN 521070783

Moog, Clodomir Vianna, 1906-. • **3.9195**
Bandeirantes and pioneers. Translated from the Portuguese by L. L. Barrett. —
New York, G. Braziller [1964] 316 p. 25 cm. Bibliography: p. 295-301.
1. Brazil — Civilization 2. U.S. — Civilization. I. T.
F2510.M583   301.37   LC 62-19926

Wagley, Charles, 1913-. • **3.9196**
An introduction to Brazil. Rev. ed. New York, Columbia University Press,
1971. xv, 341 p. illus., maps. 22 cm. 1. Brazil — Civilization 2. Brazil — Social
conditions — 1945-1964 3. Brazil — Social conditions — 1964- I. T.
F2510.W26 1971   918.1/03/6   LC 71-146267   ISBN 0231035438

Maybury-Lewis, David. **3.9197**
The savage and the innocent. Cleveland, World Pub. Co. [1965] 270 p. illus.,
maps. 23 cm. 1. Indians of South America — Brazil — Motto Grosso (State)
2. Indians of South America — Brazil — Goyaz (State) 3. Brazil — Descr. and
travel — 1951- I. T.
F2516.M36 1965a   980.3   LC 65-23357

F2519–2520.1 INDIANS

Hemming, John, 1935-. **3.9198**
Red gold: the conquest of the Brazilian Indians / John Hemming. —
Cambridge, Mass.: Harvard University Press, 1978. xvii, 677 p., [8] leaves of
plates: ill.; 24 cm. Includes index. 1. Indians of South America — Brazil —
History. 2. Indians of South America — Brazil — Government relations.
3. Brazil — Discovery and exploration. I. T.
F2519.H45   981/.01   LC 77-22863   ISBN 0674751078

Lathrap, Donald Ward, 1927-. • **3.9199**
The upper Amazon, by Donald W. Lathrap. New York, Praeger Publishers,
1970. 256 p. illus., maps. 21 cm. (Ancient peoples and places, v. 70.) 1. Indians
of South America — Amazon Valley. I. T. II. Series.
F2519.1.A6 L3 1970   301/.29/801   LC 79-100031

Lévi-Strauss, Claude. • **3.9200**
[Cru et le cuit. English] The raw and the cooked. Translated from the French by
John and Doreen Weightman. [1st U.S. ed.] New York, Harper & Row [1969]
xiii, 387 p. illus., chart, maps, 25 cm. (His Introduction to a science of
mythology, 1) Translation of Le cru et le cuit. 1. Indians of South America —
Brazil — Religion and mythology. 2. Structural anthropology 3. Mythology
I. T.
F2519.3.R3 L4813 1969   299/.8   LC 67-22501

Lévi-Strauss, Claude. **3.9201**
[Tristes tropiques. English] Tristes tropiques. Translated from the French by
John and Doreen Weightman. [1st American ed.] New York, Atheneum, 1974
[c1973] 425 p. illus. 25 cm. 1. Indians of South America — Brazil 2. Brazil —
Description and travel — 1951-1980 I. T.
F2520.L4813 1974   918.1   LC 79-162975   ISBN 068910572X

F2520.3–2538 HISTORY

Burns, E. Bradford. **3.9202**
A history of Brazil / E. Bradford Burns. — 2d ed. — New York: Columbia
University Press, 1980. x, 579 p., [8] leaves of plates: ill.; 24 cm. Includes index.
1. Brazil — History I. T.
F2521.B89 1980   981   LC 79-27306   ISBN 0231047487

Poppino, Rollie E. **3.9203**
Brazil: the land and people [by] Rollie E. Poppino. — 2d ed. Illus. by Carybé
and Poty. — New York: Oxford University Press, 1973. viii, 385 p.: illus.; 22
cm. — (Latin American histories) 1. Brazil — History I. T.
F2521.P58 1973   918.1/03   LC 73-82626

Worcester, Donald Emmet, 1915-. **3.9204**
Brazil, from colony to world power [by] Donald E. Worcester. — New York:
Scribner, [1973] x, 277 p.: illus.; 24 cm. 1. Brazil — History I. T.
F2521.W67 1973   981   LC 73-1328   ISBN 0684133865

Marchant, Alexander Nelson de Armond, 1912-. • **3.9205**
From barter to slavery; the economic relations of Portuguese and Indians in the
settlement of Brazil, 1500–1580. Baltimore The Johns Hopkins Press 1942.

160p. (The Johns Hopkins university studies in historical and political
science.Ser. 60, no. 1) 1. Brazil — History — 1500-1548 2. Brazil — History
— 1549-1762 3. Portuguese in Brazil 4. Indians of South America — Brazil
I. T. II. Series.
F2524 M33 1942

Boxer, C. R. (Charles Ralph), 1904-. • **3.9206**
The golden age of Brazil, 1695–1750; growing pains of a colonial society.
Berkeley, Published in coöperation with the Sociedade de Estudos Históricos
Dom Pedro Segundo, Rio de Janeiro, by the University of California Press,
1962. xiii, 443 p. illus., ports., maps. 24 cm. 1. Brazil — History — 1549-1762
I. T.
F2528.B6 1962   981.03   LC 62-11583

Boxer, C. R. (Charles Ralph), 1904-. • **3.9207**
The Dutch in Brazil, 1624–1654. — Oxford, Clarendon Press, 1957. xiii, 327 p.
port., maps. 23 cm. 'Bibliographical note': p. 291-301. Bibliography: p. 302-309.
1. Brazil — Hist. — Dutch Conquest, 1624-1654. I. T.
F2532.B7   *981.03   LC 57-1712

Maxwell, Kenneth, 1941-. **3.9208**
Conflicts and conspiracies: Brazil and Portugal, 1750–1808 [by] Kenneth R.
Maxwell. Cambridge [Eng.] University Press, 1973. xix, 289 p. 22 cm.
(Cambridge Latin American studies. 16) 1. Brazil — History — 1763-1821
2. Minas Gerais (Brazil) — History — Revolution, 1789 3. Brazil —
Economic conditions 4. Portugal — Colonies — America. I. T. II. Series.
F2534.M29   309.1/81/03   LC 72-89813   ISBN 0521200539

Russell-Wood, A. J. R., 1939-. **3.9209**
From colony to nation: essays on the independence of Brazil / A. J. R. Russell-
Wood ... [et al.]; edited by A. J. R. Russell-Wood. — Baltimore: Johns Hopkins
University Press, [1975] xi, 267 p.; 23 cm. (Johns Hopkins symposia in
comparative history. 6th) 1. Brazil — History — 1763-1821 — Congresses.
I. T. II. Series.
F2534.R87   981/.03   LC 74-24381   ISBN 0801816653

Haring, Clarence Henry, 1885-1960. • **3.9210**
Empire in Brazil: a New World experiment with monarchy. — Cambridge,
Mass.: Harvard University Press, 1958. 182 p.: fold. map; 22 cm. 1. Brazil —
History — 1822-1889 I. T.
F2536.H3   LC 58-7250

Bernstein, Harry, 1909-. **3.9211**
Dom Pedro II. — New York: Twayne Publishers, 1974 (c1973). 267 p.; 21 cm.
— (Twayne's rulers and statesmen of the world series, TROW 20) 1. Pedro II,
Emperor of Brazil, 1825-1891. I. T.
F2536.P3619   981/.04/0924 B   LC 74-159827

Seckinger, Ron. **3.9212**
The Brazilian monarchy and the South American republics, 1822–1831:
diplomacy and state building / Ron Seckinger. — Baton Rouge: Louisiana State
University Press, c1984. xvi, 187 p.: ill.; 24 cm. Includes index. 1. Brazil —
Foreign relations — 1822-1889 2. Brazil — Foreign relations — South
America. 3. South America — Foreign relations — Brazil. I. T.
F2536.S42 1984   327.8108 19   LC 83-25588   ISBN 0807111562

F2537–2538.22 Republic, 1889–

Bello, José Maria, 1880-. **3.9213**
[História da República. English] A history of modern Brazil, 1889-1964.
Translated from the Portuguese by James L. Taylor. With a new concluding
chapter by Rollie E. Poppino. Stanford [Calif.] Stanford University Press, 1966.
xix, 362 p. maps. 24 cm. Translation of História da República. 1. Brazil —
History — 1889- I. T.
F2537.B4413   981.05   LC 65-21494

Cunha, Euclydes da, 1866-1909. • **3.9214**
Rebellion in the backlands (Os sertões) by Euclydes da Cunha, trans. by Samuel
Putnam. — [Chicago]: University of Chicago Press [1957, c1944] 532 p.; 21 cm.
(Phoenix books) 'Bibliography of the works of Euclides da Cunha': p. 485-487.
'A selected list of works, passages, and articles on Euclides da Cunha': p.
486-487. 1. Brazil — Hist. — Conselheiro insurrection, 1897. I. Putnam,
Samuel, 1892-1950. tr. II. T.
F2537.C9752   981   LC A 44-346

Skidmore, Thomas E. • **3.9215**
Politics in Brazil, 1930–1964; an experiment in democracy [by] Thomas E.
Skidmore. New York, Oxford University Press, 1967. xviii, 446 p. map. 22 cm.
1. Brazil — Politics and government — 1930-1954 2. Brazil — Politics and
government — 1954-1964 I. T.
F2538.S56   320.9/81   LC 67-20406

Flynn, Peter, 1936-.   3.9216
Brazil, a political analysis / Peter Flynn. — London: E. Benn; Boulder, Colo.: Westview Press, 1978. xii, 564 p., [8] leaves of plates: ill.; 23 cm. (Nations of the modern world.) (A Benn study: History) Includes index. 1. Brazil — Politics and government — 1954-1964 2. Brazil — Politics and government — 1964-1985 3. Brazil — Economic conditions — 1918- 4. Brazil — Politics and government — 1930-1954 I. T. II. Series.
F2538.2.F55   320.9/81/06   *LC* 77-16243   *ISBN* 0891587470

Page, Joseph A.   • 3.9217
The revolution that never was; Northeast Brazil, 1955–1964 [by] Joseph A. Page. New York, Grossman, 1972. xi, 273 p. map (on lining papers) 24 cm. 1. Brazil, Northeast — Politics and government. 2. Brazil, Northeast — Economic conditions. 3. Brazil — Politics and government — 1954-1964 I. T.
F2538.2.P26   322.4/2   *LC* 71-106293   *ISBN* 0670597066

Roett, Riordan, 1938-.   3.9218
Brazil: politics in a patrimonial society. Boston, Allyn and Bacon [1972] x, 197 p. 21 cm. (The Allyn and Bacon series in Latin American politics) 1. Brazil — Politics and government — 1954-1964 2. Brazil — Politics and government — 1930-1954 3. Brazil — Social conditions 4. Brazil — Armed Forces — Political activity 5. Brazil — Politics and government — 1964-1985 I. T.
F2538.2.R63   320.9/81/06   *LC* 77-190029

Wesson, Robert G.   3.9219
Brazil in transition / Robert Wesson, David V. Fleischer. — New York, N.Y., U.S.A.: Praeger, 1983. viii, 197 p.; 25 cm. (Politics in Latin America.) Includes index. 1. Brazil — Politics and government — 1964-1985 I. Fleischer, David V. II. T. III. Series.
F2538.2.W47 1983   981/.06 19   *LC* 82-16645   *ISBN* 0030630827

F2540-2651 REGIONS. CITIES

Wagley, Charles, 1913-.   • 3.9220
Amazon town; a study of man in the tropics. With a new epilogue by the author. Illus. by João José Rescála. New York, Knopf, 1964. xi, 315 p. illus., map. 19 cm. (Borzoi books on Latin America) 'LA-4.' 1. Human ecology — Brazil — Amazonas. 2. Amazonas (Brazil) — Social life and customs. 3. Amazonas (Brazil) — Description and travel. I. T.
F2546.W16 1964   *LC* 64-12068

Wallace, Alfred Russel, 1823-1913.   • 3.9221
A narrative of travels on the Amazon and Rio Negro, with an account of the native tribes, and observations on the climate, geology, and natural history of the Amazon Valley. With a biographical introd. by the editor. — New York: Greenwood Press, [1969] xiv, 363 p.: illus.; 23 cm. Reprint of the 1895 ed. 1. Natural history — Amazon Valley. 2. Indians of South America — Amazon Valley. 3. Amazon Valley — Description and travel. I. T.
F2546.W18 1969b   918/.11/044   *LC* 68-55226   *ISBN* 0837116414

Harris, Marvin, 1927-.   • 3.9222
Town and country in Brazil. [1st AMS ed.] New York, AMS Press [1969] x, 302 p. illus. 23 cm. Reprint of the 1956 ed., which was issued as no. 37 of Columbia University contributions to anthropology. 1. Cities and towns — Brazil — Case studies. 2. Minas Velhas, Brazil. I. T.
F2651.M5 H3x   301.29/81/4   *LC* 78-82364

Morse, Richard M. (Richard McGee), 1922-.   • 3.9223
From community to metropolis; a biography of São Paulo, Brazil. Gainesville University of Florida Press 1958. 341p. 1. São Paulo, Brazil (City) — History I. T.
F2651 S2 M6

F2659 AFRO-AMERICANS IN BRAZIL

Skidmore, Thomas E.   3.9224
Black into white; race and nationality in Brazilian thought [by] Thomas E. Skidmore. New York, Oxford University Press, 1974. xvi, 299 p. 22 cm. 1. Brazil — Race relations. I. T.
F2659.A1 S55   323.1/81   *LC* 73-90371   *ISBN* 0195017765

Degler, Carl N.   • 3.9225
Neither Black nor white; slavery and race relations in Brazil and the United States [by] Carl N. Degler. New York, Macmillan [1971] xvi, 302 p. 21 cm. 1. Blacks — Brazil — History. 2. Afro-Americans — Social conditions 3. Slavery — Brazil — History. 4. Slavery — United States — History 5. Brazil — Race relations. 6. United States — Race relations I. T.
F2659.N4 D42   301.451/96   *LC* 73-130946

Fernandes, Florestan.   • 3.9226
[Integração do negro na sociedade de classes. English] The Negro in Brazilian society. Translated by Jacqueline D. Skiles, A. Brunel, and Arthur Rothwell. Edited by Phyllis B. Eveleth. New York, Columbia University Press, 1969. xxv, 489 p. 23 cm. Translation of A integração do negro na sociedade de classes. 1. Blacks — Brazil 2. Brazil — Race relations. I. T.
F2659.N4 F413   301.451/96/081   *LC* 78-76247

Russell-Wood, A. J. R., 1939-.   3.9227
The Black man in slavery and freedom in colonial Brazil / A.J.R. Russell-Wood. — New York: St. Martin's Press, 1982. xiii, 295 p., [8] p. of plates: ill.; 25 cm. Includes index. 1. Blacks — Brazil 2. Slavery — Brazil 3. Brazil — Social conditions I. T.
F2659.N4 R86 1982   981/.00496 19   *LC* 81-18544   *ISBN* 0312083262

F2661-2799 Paraguay. Uruguay

Paraguay, a country study / Foreign Area Studies, the American University; coauthors, Thomas E. Weil ... [et al.].   3.9228
1st ed. — [Washington, D.C.]: Dept. of the Army: For sale by the Supt. of Docs., U.S. G.P.O., 1984 printing, c1972. xiv, 318 p.: maps; 24 cm. (Area handbook series.) (DA pam. 550-156) 'Research completed July 1971.' Includes index. 1. Paraguay. I. Weil, Thomas E. II. American University (Washington, D.C.). Foreign Area Studies. III. Series. IV. Series: DA pam. 550-156
F2668.P24 1972   989.2 19   *LC* 85-601648

Pendle, George.   • 3.9229
Paraguay: a riverside nation. — 3rd ed. — London, New York [etc.] issued under the auspices of the Royal Institute of International Affairs [by] Oxford U.P., 1967. ix, 96 p. maps, tables. 21 cm. 1. Paraguay. I. Royal Institute of International Affairs. II. T.
F2668.P4 1967   918.92/03   *LC* 67-76622

Warren, Harris Gaylord, 1906-.   • 3.9230
Paraguay: an informal history / by Harris Gaylord Warren. — 1st ed. — Norman: University of Oklahoma Press, 1949. xii, 393 p., [16] leaves of plates: ill., maps, ports.; 24 cm. 1. Paraguay — History I. T.
F2681.W3   *LC* 49-8903

Fitzgibbon, Russell Humke, 1902-.   • 3.9231
Uruguay; portrait of a democracy. New Brunswick, N.J., Rutgers University Press, 1954. 301p. illus. 22 cm. 1. Uruguay — Civilization I. T.
F2708.F5   918.1 *918.95   *LC* 54-6837

Weil, Thomas E.   • 3.9232
Area handbook for Uruguay. Co-authors: Thomas E. Weil [and others. Washington; For sale by the Supt. of Docs., U.S. Govt. Print. Off.] 1971. xiv, 439 p. map. 24 cm. 'DA pam 550-97.' 'One of a series of handbooks prepared by Foreign Area Studies (FAS) of the American University.' 1. Uruguay. I. American University (Washington, D.C.). Foreign Area Studies. II. T.
F2708.W44   309.1/895/06   *LC* 75-609527

Street, John.   • 3.9233
Artigas and the emancipation of Uruguay. Cambridge [Eng.] University Press, 1959. 406 p. illus. 23 cm. Includes bibliography. 1. Artigas, José Gervasio, 1764-1850. 2. Uruguay — History — 1810-1830 I. T.
F2725.A7S75   989.504   *LC* 59-65015

Vanger, Milton I.   3.9234
The model country: José Batlle y Ordóñez of Uruguay, 1907–1915 / Milton I. Vanger. — Hanover, N.H.: Published for Brandeis University Press by University Press of New England, 1980. xii, 436 p.: ill., port.; 24 cm. 1. Batlle y Ordóñez, José, 1856-1929. 2. Uruguay — Politics and government — 1904-1973 I. T.
F2728.V27   989.5/061/0924 19   *LC* 80-50489   *ISBN* 0874511844

Weinstein, Martin.   3.9235
Uruguay: the politics of failure / Martin Weinstein. — Westport, Conn.: Greenwood Press, 1975. xvii, 190 p.; 21 cm. Includes index. 1. Uruguay — Politics and government — 1904- 2. Uruguay — Social conditions 3. Uruguay — Economic conditions — 1918- I. T.
F2728.W44   309.1/895/06   *LC* 74-19809   *ISBN* 0837178452

Kaufman, Edy.   3.9236
Uruguay in transition: from civilian to military rule / Edy Kaufman. — New Brunswick, N.J.: Transaction Books, c1979. xv, 126 p.; 24 cm. Includes index. 1. Uruguay — Politics and government — 1973- 2. Uruguay — Politics and

government — 1904-1973 3. Uruguay — Armed Forces — Political activity. I. T.
F2729.K38   322/.5/09895   *LC* 78-55939   *ISBN* 0878552421

F2801–3021 Argentina

Argentina, a country study / Foreign Area Studies, the   3.9237
American University; edited by James D. Rudolph.
3rd ed. — Washington, D.C.: The Studies: For sale by the Supt. of Docs., U.S.G.P.O., 1985, 1986 printing. xxxiii, 404 p.: ill.; 24 cm. — (Area handbook series.) 'Research completed August 1985.' Maps on lining papers. Previous ed. published as: Area handbook for Argentina / Thomas E. Weil ... [et al.] Includes index. 1. Argentina. I. Rudolph, James D., 1947- II. Weil, Thomas E. Area handbook for Argentina III. American University (Washington, D.C.). Foreign Area Studies. IV. Series.
F2808.A6537 1986   982 19   *LC* 86-3616

Scobie, James R., 1929-.   • 3.9238
Argentina: a city and a nation [by] James R. Scobie. 2d ed. New York, Oxford University Press, 1971. 323 p. illus. 22 cm. (Latin American histories)
1. Argentina — History I. T.
F2808.S42 1971   982   *LC* 78-166005

Levene, Ricardo, 1885-1959.   • 3.9239
A history of Argentina / by Ricardo Levene; translated and edited by William Spence Robertson. — Chapel Hill: University of North Carolina Press, 1937. xii, 565 p., 22 leaves of plates: ill., maps. — (The Inter-American historical series) Translation of Lecciones de historia Argentina. Includes index. 1. Argentina — History. I. Robertson, William Spence, 1872-1955. II. T.
F2831.L653   *LC* 37-34878

Ferns, H. S. (Henry Stanley), 1913-.   • 3.9240
Britain and Argentina in the nineteenth century. — Oxford, Clarendon Press, 1960. x, 517 p. maps, tables. 23 cm. Bibliographical footnotes. 1. Argentine Republic — For. rel. — Gt. Brit. 2. Gt. Brit. — For. rel. — Argentine Republic. I. T.
F2833.5.G7F4   982.03   *LC* 60-50761

F2834–2849.2 HISTORY, BY PERIOD

Cunninghame Graham, R. B. (Robert Bontine), 1852-1936.   3.9241
The conquest of the River Plate. Boston, Milford House [1973] xi, 313 p. illus. 22 cm. Reprint of the 1924 ed. published by W. Heinemann, London. 1. Argentina — History — 1515-1535 2. Argentina — History — 1535-1617 3. Rio de la Plata region (Argentina and Uruguay) — History. I. T.
F2841.G74 1973   982/.02   *LC* 70-133344   *ISBN* 0878211144

Halperín Donghi, Tulio.   3.9242
Politics economics and society in Argentina in the revolutionary period / by Tulio Halperín–Donghi; translated by Richard Southern. — Cambridge [Eng.]; New York: Cambridge University Press, [1975] xii, 425 p.; 23 cm. — (Cambridge Latin American studies. 18) Includes index. 1. Argentina — History — War of Independence, 1810-1817 2. Argentina — History — 1817-1860 3. Rio de la Plata region (Argentina and Uruguay) — History. I. T. II. Series.
F2845.H33   982/.03   *LC* 74-79133   *ISBN* 0521204933

Rennie, Ysabel (Fisk) 1918-.   • 3.9243
The Argentina republic / by Ysabel F. Rennie. — New York: Macmillan, 1945. xvii, 431 p., 8 leaves of plates: ill. Includes index. 1. Argentina — History — 1817- I. T.
F2846.R394   *LC* 45-2874

Sarmiento, Domingo Faustino, 1811-1888.   3.9244
Life in the Argentine Republic in the days of the tyrants; or, Civilization and barbarism. From the Spanish. With a biographical sketch of the author by Mrs. Horace Mann. 1st American from the 3d Spanish ed. New York Hafner Pub. Co. [1960] 400p. (The Hafner library of classics, no. 21) 1. Quiroga, Juan Facundo, 1790-1835. 2. Aldao, José Félix, d. 1845 3. Argentine Republic — History — 1817-1860 4. Argentine Republic — Description and travel I. T.
F2846 S2472 1960

Bunkley, Allison Williams.   • 3.9245
The life of Sarmiento. New York, Greenwood Press [1969, c1952] xv, 566 p. illus., facsim., geneal. table, ports. 23 cm. 1. Sarmiento, Domingo Faustino, 1811-1888. I. T.
F2846.S26 B84 1969   982/.05/0924 B   *LC* 77-90475   *ISBN* 0837123925

Lynch, John, 1927-.   3.9246
Argentine dictator: Juan Manuel De Rosas, 1829–1852 / by John Lynch. — Oxford: Clarendon; New York: Oxford University Press, 1981. 414 p.: port., map; 23 cm. Includes index. 1. Rosas, Juan Manuel José Domingo Ortiz de, 1793-1877. 2. Heads of state — Argentina — Biography. 3. Argentina — Politics and government — 1817-1860 I. T.
F2846.3.R7 L93   982/.04/0924 B 19   *LC* 81-175574   *ISBN* 0198211295

Crawley, Eduardo.   3.9247
A house divided: Argentina, 1880–1980 / Eduardo Crawley. — New York: St. Martin's Press, 1984. xix, 472 p.: map; 23 cm. Includes index. 1. Argentina — History — 1860-1910 2. Argentina — History — 1910- I. T.
F2847.C7 1984   982/.05 19   *LC* 84-17697   *ISBN* 0312392540

McGann, Thomas Francis, 1920-.   • 3.9248
Argentina, the United states, and the Inter–American system 1880–1914. Cambridge, Harvard University Press, 1957. viii, 332 p. 22 cm. (Harvard historical studies. v. 70) 1. Argentina — History — 1860-1910 2. Argentina — History — 1910- 3. Argentina — Relations — United States 4. United States — Relations — Argentina I. T. II. Series.
F2847.Mx   *LC* a 57-8626

Rock, David, 1945-.   3.9249
Politics in Argentina, 1890–1930: the rise and fall of radicalism / David Rock. — Cambridge, Eng.: Cambridge University Press, 1975. ix, 315 p.; 23 cm. — (Cambridge Latin American studies. no. 19) Includes index. 1. Argentina — Politics and government — 1910-1943 2. Argentina — Politics and government — 1860-1910 I. T. II. Series.
F2848.R57   320.9/82/05   *LC* 74-12974   *ISBN* 0521206634

Smith, Peter H.   3.9250
Argentina and the failure of democracy; conflict among political elites, 1904–1955 [by] Peter H. Smith. [Madison] University of Wisconsin Press [1974] xx, 215 p. illus. 24 cm. 1. Argentina — Politics and government I. T.
F2848.S64   320.9/82/06   *LC* 74-5907   *ISBN* 0299066002

Perón, Eva, 1919-1952.   3.9251
Evita by Evita: Eva Duarte Perón tells her own story / by Evita. — London: Proteus; New York: Distributed by Two Continents, 1978. 235, [12] p., [4] leaves of plates: ill.; 23 cm. Translation of La razón de mi vida. 1. Perón, Eva, 1919-1952. 2. Perón, Juan Domingo, 1895-1974. 3. Argentina — Presidents — Wives — Biography. 4. Argentina — Social conditions I. T.
F2849.P313 1978   982/.06/0924 B   *LC* 78-395643   *ISBN* 0906071070

Fraser, Nicholas, 1948-.   3.9252
Eva Perón / Nicholas Fraser and Marysa Navarro. — 1st American ed. — New York: W. W. Norton, 1981, c1980. 192, [22] p., [12] p. of plates: ill.; 21 cm. Includes index. 1. Perón, Eva, 1919-1952. 2. Politicians — Argentine Republic — Biography. 3. Argentina — Presidents — Wives — Biography. I. Navarro, Marysa. joint author. II. T.
F2849.P37 F7 1981   982/.062/0924 B 19   *LC* 80-29148   *ISBN* 0393014576

Page, Joseph A.   3.9253
Perón, a biography / Joseph A. Page. — 1st ed. — New York: Random House, c1983. xiii, 594 p., [8] p. of plates: ill.; 25 cm. Includes index. 1. Perón, Juan Domingo, 1895-1974. 2. Argentina — Politics and government — 1955-1983 3. Argentina — Presidents — Biography. 4. Argentina — Politics and government — 1943-1955 I. T.
F2849.P48 P28 1983   982/.062/0924 B 19   *LC* 82-40136   *ISBN* 0394522974

F2850–3011 REGIONS

Slatta, Richard W., 1947-.   3.9254
Gauchos and the vanishing frontier / Richard W. Slatta. — Lincoln: University of Nebraska Press, c1983. 271 p., [4] p. of plates: ill.; 23 cm. Includes index. 1. Gauchos — Argentina — Buenos Aires (Province) 2. Buenos Aires (Argentina: Province) — History. I. T.
F2861.S53 1983   305.5/63/0982 19   *LC* 82-20014   *ISBN* 0803241348

Falkner, Thomas, 1707-1784.   • 3.9255
A description of Patagonia, and the adjoining parts of South America. With an introd. and notes by Arthur E.S. Neumann. Chicago Armann & Armann 1935. 168p. 1. Patagonia — Description and travel 2. Indians of South America — Patagonia 3. Falkland Islands. 4. Moluche language I. T.
F2936 F18 1774A

Hoffmann, Fritz L. (Fritz Leo), 1907-.   3.9256
Sovereignty in dispute: the Falklands/Malvinas, 1493–1982 / Fritz L. Hoffmann and Olga Mingo Hoffmann. — Boulder, Colo.: Westview Press, 1984. xiv, 194 p.: ill.; 24 cm. — (Westview special studies on Latin America and the Caribbean.) Includes index. 1. Falkland Islands — History. 2. Falkland Islands — International status. I. Hoffmann, Olga Mingo. II. T. III. Series.
F3031.H57 1984   997/.11 19   *LC* 83-23446   *ISBN* 0865316058

F3051–3285 Chile. Easter Island

Chile, a country study / Foreign Area Studies, the American   3.9257
University; edited by Andrea T. Merrill.
2nd ed. — Washington, D.C.: For sale by the Supt. of Docs., U.S. Govt. Print. Off., c1982. xix, 296 p.: ill.; 25 cm. — (Area handbook series.) (DA pam. 550-77) 'Research completed, May, 1982.' Rev. ed. of: Area handbook for Chile / Thomas E. Weil. 1st ed. 1969. Maps on lining papers. Includes index. 1. Chile. I. Merrill, Andrea T. II. Weil, Thomas E. Area handbook for Chile. 1969. III. American University (Washington, D.C.). Foreign Area Studies. IV. Series. V. Series: DA pam. 550-77
F3058.C5223 1982   983/.0647 19   *LC* 82-22610

Loveman, Brian.   3.9258
Chile: the legacy of Hispanic capitalism / Brian Loveman. — New York: Oxford University Press, 1979. xi, 429 p.: maps; 22 cm. — (Latin American histories) Includes index. 1. Chile — History I. T.
F3081.L68   983/.064   *LC* 78-13965   *ISBN* 0195025180

Barbier, Jacques A., 1944-.   3.9259
Reform and politics in Bourbon Chile, 1755–1796 / Jacques A. Barbier. — Ottawa, Canada: University of Ottawa Press, 1980. xiv, 218 p.; 23 cm. — (Cahiers d'histoire; no. 10) 1. Chile — Politics and government — 1565-1810 I. T.
F3091.B268   983/.03 19   *LC* 81-462702   *ISBN* 276035010X

Korth, Eugene H.   3.9260
Spanish policy in colonial Chile; the struggle for social justice, 1535–1700 [by] Eugene H. Korth. — Stanford, Calif.: Stanford University Press, 1968. xi, 320 p.: map (on lining papers); 24 cm. 1. Indians, Treatment of — Chile. 2. Chile — History — To 1810 3. Spain — Colonies — America — Administration. I. T.
F3091.K6   323.4/0983   *LC* 68-26779

Cunninghame Graham, R. B. (Robert Bontine), 1852-1936.   3.9261
Pedro de Valdivia, conqueror of Chile. Boston, Milford House [1973] xiii, 227 p. port. 22 cm. Reprint of the 1926 ed. published by W. Heinemann, London. 1. Valdivia, Pedro de, 1500?-1554? 2. Chile — History — To 1565 I. T.
F3091.V15 1973   983/.02/0924 B   *LC* 73-4895   *ISBN* 0878211349

Collier, Simon.   • 3.9262
Ideas and politics of Chilean independence 1808–1833 / by Simon Collier. — London: Cambridge University Press, c1967. xviii, 396 p. — (Cambridge Latin American studies. no. 1) 1. Chile — Politics & government — 1810-1824. 2. Chile — Politics & government — 1824-1920. I. T. II. Series.
F3094.C7   *LC* 67-15395

Clissold, Stephen.   • 3.9263
Bernardo O'Higgins and the independence of Chile. New York, Praeger [1969] 254 p. maps, ports. 23 cm. 1. O'Higgins, Bernardo, 1778-1842. 2. O'Higgins, Ambrosio, marqués de Osorno, 1720-1801. 3. Chile — History — War of Independence, 1810-1824 I. T.
F3094.O35517 1969   983/.04/0924 B   *LC* 69-11332

Burr, Robert Nathan, 1906-.   3.9264
By reason or force: Chile and the balancing of power in South America, 1830–1905 / by Robert N. Burr. — Berkeley: University of California Press, 1965. 322 p.: map. — (University of California publications in history; v.77) 1. Chile — History — 1824-1920 2. Chile — Foreign relations 3. South America — Politics and government — 1830- I. T.
F3095.B95 E173.C15 v.77

Zeitlin, Maurice, 1935-.   3.9265
The civil wars in Chile, or, The bourgeois revolutions that never were / by Maurice Zeitlin. — Princeton, N.J.: Princeton University Press, c1984. xiii, 265 p.; 22 cm. Includes index. 1. Middle classes — Chile — Political activity — History — 19th century. 2. Chile — History — Insurrection of 1851 — Causes. 3. Chile — History — Insurrection of 1851 — Influence. 4. Chile — History — Insurrection of 1859 — Causes. 5. Chile — History — Insurrection of 1859 — Influence. 6. Chile — History — Revolution, 1891 — Causes. 7. Chile — History — Revolution, 1891 — Influence. I. T.
F3095.Z43 1984   983/.06 19   *LC* 84-42551   *ISBN* 0691076650

Alexander, Robert Jackson, 1918-.   3.9266
The tragedy of Chile / Robert J. Alexander. — Westport, Conn.: Greenwood Press, 1978. xiii, 509 p.; 24 cm. (Contributions in political science. no. 8 0147-1066) Includes index. 1. Chile — Politics and government — 1920-1970 2. Chile — Politics and government — 1970-1973 3. Chile — Politics and government — 1973- I. T. II. Series.
F3100.A34   320.9/83/064   *LC* 77-91101   *ISBN* 0313200343

Davis, Nathaniel.   3.9267
The last two years of Salvador Allende / Nathaniel Davis. — Ithaca: Cornell University Press, 1985. xv, 480 p.: maps; 24 cm. Includes index. 1. Allende Gossens, Salvador, 1908-1973. 2. Chile — Politics and government — 1970-1973 I. T.
F3100.D36 1985   983/.0646 19   *LC* 84-23774   *ISBN* 0801417910

Roxborough, Ian.   3.9268
Chile: the state and revolution / Ian Roxborough, Philip O'Brien, Jackie Roddick, assisted by Michael Gonzalez. — New York: Holmes & Meier, 1977. x, 304 p.; 22 cm. Includes index. 1. Unidad Popular. 2. Chile — Politics and government — 1970-1973 3. Chile — History — Coup d'état, 1973 I. O'Brien, Philip J. joint author. II. Roddick, Jacqueline. joint author. III. T.
F3100.R68 1977   320.9/83/064   *LC* 75-35896   *ISBN* 0841902348

Bowman, Isaiah, 1878-1950.   3.9269
Desert trails of Atacama. New York American Geographical Society 1976. 362p. (Special publication (American Geographical Society of New York) no. 5) 1. Atacama (Chile) 2. Physical geography — Chile 3. Chile — Description and travel I. T. II. Series.
F3131 B68

Norwegian Archaeological Expedition to Easter Island and the   • 3.9270
East Pacific.
Reports / with contributions by Thor Heyerdahl and Edwin N. Ferdon, editors ... [et al.]. — [Stockholm: Forum Pub. House], 1961-1965. 2 v.: ill. (some col.), maps (some folded). — (Monographs of the School of American Research and the Museum of New Mexico; no.24, pt. 1-2) 1. Excavations (Archaeology) — Polynesia. 2. Easter Island — Antiquities. 3. Polynesia — Antiquities. I. Heyerdahl, Thor. II. Ferdon, Edwin N., 1913- III. T. IV. Series.
F3169.N6   *LC* 62-4648

F3301–3359 Bolivia

Osborne, Harold, 1905-.   • 3.9271
Bolivia, a land divided. — 3d ed. — London, New York, Oxford University Press, 1964. xii, 181 p. maps, diagrs., tables. 21 cm. 'Issued under the auspices of the Royal Institute of International Affairs.' Bibliography: p. 168-176. 1. Bolivia. I. T.
F3308.O8 1964   918.4   *LC* 64-1698

Weil, Thomas E.   3.9272
Area handbook for Bolivia. Coauthors: Thomas E. Weil [and others] Research completed July 1973. 2d ed. [Washington; For sale by the Supt. of Docs., U.S. Govt. Print. Off.] 1974. xiv, 417 p. maps. 24 cm. 'DA Pam 550-66.' 'One of a series of handbooks prepared by Foreign Area Studies (FAS) of the American University.' 'Supersedes DA Pam 550-66, August 1963.' Revision of 1963 ed. issued by the American University Foreign Area Studies Division. 1. Bolivia. I. American University (Washington, D.C.). Foreign Area Studies. II. American University (Washington, D.C.). Foreign Areas Studies Division. Area handbook for Bolivia. III. T.
F3308.W44 1974   918.4/03/5   *LC* 73-600327

Alexander, Robert Jackson, 1918-.   3.9273
Bolivia: past, present, and future of its politics / by Robert J. Alexander. — New York, N.Y.: Praeger; Stanford, Calif.: Hoover Institution Press, 1982. xix, 157 p.; 24 cm. — (Politics in Latin America.) Includes index. 1. Bolivia — Politics and government 2. Bolivia — History I. T. II. Series.
F3321.A43 1982   984 19   *LC* 81-22661   *ISBN* 0030617626

Klein, Herbert S.   3.9274
Bolivia, the evolution of a multi–ethnic society / Herbert S. Klein. — New York: Oxford University Press, 1982. xi, 318 p.: maps; 21 cm. — (Latin American histories.) Includes index. 1. Bolivia — History I. T. II. Series.
F3321.K54 1982   984 19   *LC* 81-9659   *ISBN* 0195030117

Arnade, Charles W.   • 3.9275
The emergence of the Republic of Bolivia [by] Charles W. Arnade. — New York, Russell & Russell [1970, c1957] xi, 269 p. maps. 23 cm. 1. Bolivia — History — Wars of Independence, 1809-1825 I. T.
F3323.A695 1970   984/.041   *LC* 70-102468

Klein, Herbert S.   • **3.9276**
Parties and political change in Bolivia, 1880–1952, by Herbert S. Klein. London, Cambridge U.P., 1969. xvi, 451 p. map. 23 cm. (Cambridge Latin American studies. 5) 1. Bolivia — History — 1879-1938 2. Bolivia — History — 1938-1982 I. T. II. Series.
F3325.K4   320.9/84   *LC* 77-85722   *ISBN* 0521076145

James, Daniel, comp.   • **3.9277**
The complete Bolivian diaries of Ché Guevara, and other captured documents. Edited and with an introd. by Daniel James. New York, Stein and Day [1968] 330 p. illus., facsims., maps, ports. 21 cm. 1. Guerrillas — Bolivia. 2. Subversive activities — Bolivia. 3. Bolivia — History — 1938-1982 I. Guevara, Ernesto, 1928-1967. II. T.
F3326.J3   984/.05/0922   *LC* 68-55642

Malloy, James M.   • **3.9278**
Bolivia: the uncompleted revolution [by] James M. Malloy. [Pittsburgh] University of Pittsburgh Press [1970] x, 396 p. map. 24 cm. 1. Bolivia — History — Revolution, 1952 2. Bolivia — Politics and government — 1952-1982 I. T.
F3326.M25   984/.05   *LC* 77-101486   *ISBN* 0822932032

Arzáns de Orsúa y Vela, Bartolomé, 1676-1736.   **3.9279**
[Historia de la villa imperial de Potosí. English. Selections] Tales of Potosí / Bartolomé Arzáns de Orsúa y Vela; edited, with an introd., by R.C. Padden; translated from the Spanish by Frances M. López–Morillas. — Providence: Brown University Press, [1975] xxxvi, 209 p.; 24 cm. Translated selections from Historia de la villa imperial de Potosí. 1. Potosí (Bolivia) — History. I. T.
F3351.P85 A8213 1975   984/.1/03   *LC* 74-6574   *ISBN* 0870571443

F3401–3619 Peru

Mariátegui, José Carlos, 1894-1930.   • **3.9280**
[7 [i.e. Siete] ensayos de interpretación de la realidad peruana. English] Seven interpretive essays on Peruvian reality. Translated by Marjory Urquidi. Introd. by Jorge Basadre. Austin, University of Texas Press [1971] xxxvi, 301 p. 23 cm. (Texas pan-American series) Translation of 7 [i.e. Siete] ensayos de interpretación de la realidad peruana. 1. Peru — Addresses, essays, lectures. I. T.
F3408.M3313   918/.5/03   *LC* 73-156346   *ISBN* 0292701152

Peru, a country study / Foreign Area Studies, the American   **3.9281**
University; edited by Richard F. Nyrop.
3rd ed. — Washington, D.C.: For sale by the Supt, of Docs., U.S. G.P.O., c1981. xvii, 302 p.: ill.; 24 cm. — (Area handbook series.) Revision of: Area handbook for Peru. 1972. 'Research completed July 1980.' 'DA Pam 550.42'- Verso t.p. Includes index. 1. Peru. I. Nyrop, Richard F. II. American University (Washington, D.C.). Foreign Area Studies. III. Area handbook for Peru. IV. Series.
F3408.P4647 1981   985/.063 19   *LC* 81-3456

F3429–3430.1 ANTIQUITIES. INDIANS

Bennett, Wendell Clark, 1905-1953.   • **3.9282**
Andean culture history, by Wendell C. Bennet and Junius B. Bird. New York, 1949. 319 p. illus., maps. 21 cm. 'Selected sources': p. 295-306. 1. Indians of South America — Antiquities 2. Peru — History — To 1548 3. Peru — Antiquities 4. Incas I. Bird, Junius Bouton, 1907- II. T.
F3429.B475   *LC* 49-2638

Bushnell, Geoffrey Hext Sutherland.   • **3.9283**
Peru. — Rev. ed. — New York: Praeger, [1963, c1956] 216 p.: illus., map; 21 cm. — (Ancient peoples and places) 1. Peru — Antiquities 2. Peru — History — To 1548 I. T.
F3429.B87 1963   985.01   *LC* 63-15849

Hemming, John, 1935-.   **3.9284**
Monuments of the Incas / text by John Hemming; photographs by Edward Ranney. — 1st ed. — Boston: Little, Brown, 1982. 228 p.: ill.; 25 x 27 cm. 'A New York Graphic Society book.' Includes index. 1. Incas 2. Incas — Architecture. 3. Indians of South America — Peru — Architecture. 4. Peru — Antiquities I. Ranney, Edward. II. T.
F3429.H38 1982   985/.01 19   *LC* 82-12668   *ISBN* 0821215213

Lanning, Edward P.   • **3.9285**
Peru before the Incas [by] Edward P. Lanning. — Englewood Cliffs, N.J.: Prentice-Hall, [1967] 216 p.: illus., maps.; 21 cm. — (A Spectrum book)
1. Indians of South America — Peru — Antiquities 2. Peru — Antiquities I. T.
F3429.L18   980.4/5   *LC* 67-28395

Lumbreras, Luis Guillermo.   **3.9286**
[De los pueblos, las culturas y las artes del antiguo Perú. English] The peoples and cultures of ancient Peru [by] Luis G. Lumbreras. Translated by Betty J. Meggers. Washington, Smithsonian Institution Press; [distributed by G. Braziller, New York] 1974. vii, 248 p. illus. 29 cm. Translation of De los pueblos, las culturas y las artes del antiguo Perú. 1. Indians of South America — Peru — Antiquities 2. Peru — Antiquities I. T.
F3429.L8813   980.4/5   *LC* 74-2104   *ISBN* 0874741467

Mason, John Alden, 1885-1967.   • **3.9287**
The ancient civilizations of Peru. — [Rev. ed. — Harmondsworth, Eng.]: Penguin Books, [1968] xvi, 335 p.: illus., map.; 19 cm. — (Pelican books, A395) 1. Indians of South America — Peru — Antiquities 2. Incas 3. Peru — Antiquities I. T.
F3429.M36 1968   *LC* 75-490842

Bingham, Hiram, 1875-1956.   • **3.9288**
Lost city of the Incas, the story of Machu Picchu and its builders. Duell, Sloan and Pearce [c1948] 263p. illus. Published also by Atheneum (240 p.) 1. Incas 2. Machu Picchu (Peru) 3. Peru — Antiquities I. T.
F3429.1.M3 P617   *LC* 48-9227

Bonavia, Duccio, 1935-.   **3.9289**
[Ricchata quellccani. English] Mural painting in ancient Peru / Duccio Bonavia; translated by Patricia J. Lyon. — Bloomington: Indiana University Press, c1985. xi, 224 p.: ill.; 29 cm. Translation of: Ricchata quellccani. Includes index. 1. Indians of South America — Peru — Painting. 2. Mural painting and decoration — Peru. 3. Indians of South America — Peru — Antiquities 4. Peru — Antiquities I. T.
F3429.3.A7 B6413 1985   751.7/3/0985 19   *LC* 84-47883   *ISBN* 0253339405

Ascher, Marcia, 1935-.   **3.9290**
Code of the quipu: a study in media, mathematics, and culture / Marcia Ascher and Robert Ascher. — Ann Arbor: University of Michigan Press, c1981. vii, 166 p.: ill.; 24 cm. 1. Quipu 2. Incas — Mathematics 3. Indians of South America — Andes Region — Mathematics. I. Ascher, Robert, 1931- joint author. II. T.
F3429.3.Q6 A82 1981   985/.01 19   *LC* 80-25409   *ISBN* 0472093258

Kubler, George, 1912-.   • **3.9291**
The Indian caste of Peru, 1795–1940; a population study based upon tax records and census reports. — Westport, Conn.: Greenwood Press, [1973] 71 p.: illus.; 29 cm. Reprint of the 1952 ed., which was issued as publication no. 14 of Smithsonian Institution, Institute of Social Anthropology. 1. Indians of South America — Peru 2. Peru — Population. I. T.
F3430.K82 1973   312/.93   *LC* 78-119552   *ISBN* 083715085X

F3430.3–3619 HISTORY

Dobyns, Henry F.   **3.9292**
Peru: a cultural history / Henry F. Dobyns and Paul L. Doughty. New York: Oxford University Press, 1976. 336 p.: maps; 22 cm. (Latin American histories) Includes index. 1. Peru — History I. Doughty, Paul L. joint author. II. T.
F3431.D6   985   *LC* 76-9224   *ISBN* 0195020898

Pike, Fredrick B.   • **3.9293**
The modern history of Peru / [by] Fredrick B. Pike. — London, Weidenfeld & Nicolson, [1967] xix, 386 p. 12 plates (incl. ports.), maps.; 23 cm. — (Latin America series) 'Bibliographical essay': p. 321-332. 1. Peru — History I. T.
F3431.P52 1967b   985   *LC* 67-101020

Cieza de León, Pedro de, 1518-1554.   • **3.9294**
[Chronica del Peru English] The Incas. Translated by Harriet de Onis. Edited, with an introd., by Victor Wolfgang von Hagen. [1st ed.] Norman, University of Oklahoma Press [1959] lxxx, 397 p. plates (part col.) fold. maps (1 col.) facsims. 24 cm. (Civilization of the American Indian series. v. 53) Translated from Chrónica del Perú. 1. Incas 2. Peru — Description and travel 3. Peru — History — To 1548 4. America — Early accounts to 1600 I. De Onís, Harriet, 1899- tr. II. Von Hagen, Victor Wolfgang, 1908- ed. III. T. IV. Series.
F3442.C5826   985/.01 19   *LC* 59-7955

Vega, Garcilaso de la, 1539-1616.   • **3.9295**
[Comentarios reales de los incas. English] Royal commentaries of the Incas, and general history of Peru. Translated with an introd. by Harold V. Livermore. Foreword by Arnold J. Toynbee. Austin, University of Texas Press [1966] 2 v. (xliv, 1530 p.) maps. 24 cm. (The Texas Pan-American series) Translation of Commentarios reales, pt. 1 of which was first published in 1609 under title:

Primera parte de los Commentarios reales, and pt. 2 of which was first published in 1617 under title: Historia general del Peru. 1. Incas 2. Peru — History — To 1548 3. Peru — History — 1548-1820 I. Livermore, H. V., 1914- ed. and tr. II. T.
F3442.G1823 1966   985.2   *LC* 65-13518

Hemming, John, 1935-.   • 3.9296
The conquest of the Incas. — [1st American ed.]. — New York: Harcourt, Brace, Jovanovich, [1970] 641 p.: illus., facsim., geneal. tables, maps, plates, ports.; 24 cm. 1. Incas 2. Peru — History — Conquest, 1522-1548 I. T.
F3442.H47   985/.02   *LC* 74-117573   *ISBN* 0151225605

Lockhart, James.   3.9297
The men of Cajamarca; a social and biographical study of the first conquerors of Peru, by James Lockhart. Austin, Published for the Institute of Latin American Studies by the University of Texas Press [1972] xvi, 496 p. map. 23 cm. (Latin American monographs, no. 27) 1. Peru — History — Conquest, 1522-1548 — Biography. I. T.
F3442.L77   985/.02/0922 B   *LC* 72-185236   *ISBN* 0292750013

Pizarro, Pedro, 16th cent.   • 3.9298
Relation of the discovery and conquest of the kingdoms of Peru. Translated into English and annotated by Philip Ainsworth Means. — Boston: Milford House, [1972] 2 v. in 1 (561 p.); 22 cm. Translation of Relación del descubrimiento y conquista de los reinos del Peru. Reprint of the 1921 ed., which was issued as no. 4 of Documents and narratives concerning the discovery and conquest of Latin America. 1. Peru — History — Conquest, 1522-1548 I. T.
F3442.P78 1972   985/.02   *LC* 73-133345   *ISBN* 0878210830

Prescott, William Hickling, 1796-1859.   • 3.9299
History of the conquest of Peru. Introd. by Samuel Eliot Morison. Illus. by Everett Gee Jackson. New York, Heritage Press [1957] lii, 504 p. col. illus., col. map. 24 cm. 1. Incas 2. Peru — History — Conquest, 1522-1548 I. T.
F3442.P933   *LC* 57-3308

Wachtel, Nathan.   3.9300
[Vision des vaincus. English] The vision of the vanquished: the Spanish conquest of Peru through Indian eyes, 1530–1570 / Nathan Wachtel; translated by Ben and Siân Reynolds. — New York: Barnes and Noble, 1977. v, 328 p., [12] leaves of plates: ill.; 23 cm. Translation of La vision des vaincus. Includes index. 1. Incas 2. Indians of South America — Peru — Government relations. 3. Peru — History — Conquest, 1522-1548 I. T.
F3442.W313 1977b   985/.02   *LC* 76-15792   *ISBN* 0064972607

Campbell, Leon G.   3.9301
The military and society in colonial Peru, 1750–1810 / Leon G. Campbell. — Philadelphia: American Philosophical Society, 1978. xviii, 254 p.: ill.; 24 cm. (Memoirs of the American Philosophical Society; v. 123 0065-9738) Includes index. 1. Peru. Ejército — History. 2. Sociology, Military — Peru — History. 3. Peru — History — 1548-1820 I. T.
F3444.C3x Q11.P612 vol. 123   081 s 985/.03   *LC* 77-91650   *ISBN* 087169123X

Juan, Jorge, 1713-1773.   3.9302
[Noticias secretas de América English] Discourse and political reflections on the Kingdoms of Peru, their government, special regimen of their inhabitants, and abuses which have been introduced into one and another, with special information on why they grew up and some means to avoid them / written by Jorge Juan and Antonio de Ulloa; edited with an introd. by John J. TePaske; translated by John J. TePaske and Besse A. Clement. — Norman: University of Oklahoma Press, 1979 (c1978). ix, 326 p.: map; 24 cm. (American exploration and travel series.) Translation of Noticias secretas de America. 1. Indians, Treatment of — Peru. 2. Peru — Social conditions 3. Peru — Politics and government — 1548-1820 4. South America — History — To 1806 I. Ulloa, Antonio de, 1716-1795. joint author. II. TePaske, John Jay. III. T. IV. Series.
F3444.J8213   985   *LC* 78-7135   *ISBN* 0806114827

Lockhart, James.   3.9303
Spanish Peru, 1532–1560; a colonial society. Madison, University of Wisconsin Press, 1968. xii, 285 p. illus., map. 24 cm. 1. Peru — History — Conquest, 1522-1548 2. Peru — History — 1548-1820 3. Peru — Social life and customs. I. T.
F3444.L83   918.5/03/2   *LC* 68-14032

Means, Philip Ainsworth, 1892-1944.   • 3.9304
Fall of the Inca empire and the Spanish rule in Peru, 1530–1780. Gordian Press [c1964] 351p. illus. Continues the author's Ancient civilizations of the Andes. Originally published 1931. 1. Incas 2. Peru — History — Conquest, 1522-1548 3. Peru — History — 1548-1820 4. Spain — Colonies — America — Administration. 5. Peru — Antiquities I. T. II. Title: The Spanish rules in Peru: 1530-1780.
F3444.M43 1964   *LC* 64-8176

Anna, Timothy E., 1944-.   3.9305
The fall of the royal government in Peru / Timothy E. Anna. — Lincoln: University of Nebraska Press, c1979. xi, 291 p.; 23 cm. Includes index. 1. Peru — History — War of Independence, 1820-1829 I. T.
F3446.A53   985/.04   *LC* 79-9142   *ISBN* 0803210043

Werlich, David P., 1941-.   3.9306
Peru: a short history / David P. Werlich. — Carbondale: Southern Illinois University Press, c1978. xii, 434 p.: maps; 24 cm. Includes index. 1. Peru — History — 1829- I. T.
F3446.5.W47   985/.06   *LC* 77-17107   *ISBN* 0809308304

Haya de la Torre, Víctor Raúl, 1895-.   3.9307
Aprismo; the ideas and doctrines of Victor Raúl Haya de la Torre. Selected, edited, and translated by Robert J. Alexander. — [Kent, Ohio]: Kent State University Press, [1973] xiii, 367 p.; 24 cm. 1. Haya de la Torre, Víctor Raúl, 1895- 2. Partido Aprista Peruano — Addresses, essays, lectures. 3. Latin America — Politics and government — 20th century — Addresses, essays, lectures. I. Alexander, Robert Jackson, 1918- ed. II. T.
F3448.H2912   320.5/092/4 B   *LC* 78-181083   *ISBN* 0873381254

Stein, Steve.   3.9308
Populism in Peru: the emergence of the masses and the politics of social control / Steve Stein. — Madison, Wis.: University of Wisconsin Press, 1980. xvi, 296 p.: ill.; 24 cm. Includes index. 1. Haya de la Torre, Víctor Raúl, 1895- 2. Sánchez Cerro, Luis M., 1889-1933. 3. Partido Aprista Peruano. 4. Populism — Peru. 5. Labor and laboring classes — Peru — Political activity. 6. Peru — Politics and government — 1919-1968 I. T.
F3448.S73   985/.063   *LC* 80-8315   *ISBN* 0299079902

The Peruvian experiment reconsidered / edited by Cynthia   3.9309
McClintock and Abraham F. Lowenthal.
Princeton, N.J.: Princeton University Press, c1983. xxi, 442 p.; 24 cm. 1. Peru — Politics and government — 1968- — Addresses, essays, lectures. 2. Peru — Economic conditions — 1968- — Addresses, essays, lectures. I. McClintock, Cynthia. II. Lowenthal, Abraham F.
F3448.2.P49 1983   320.985 19   *LC* 82-61377   *ISBN* 0691076480

F3701–3799 Ecuador

Linke, Lilo.   • 3.9310
Ecuador, country of contrasts. — 3d ed. Issued under the auspices of the Royal Institute of International Affairs. — London, New York, Oxford University Press, 1960. 193 p. illus. 22 cm. Includes bibliography. 1. Ecuador. I. T.
F3708.L5 1960   918.66   *LC* 60-4406

Weil, Thomas E.   3.9311
Area handbook for Ecuador. Co–authors: Thomas E. Weil [and others] [Washington, For sale by the Supt. of Docs., U.S. Govt. Print. Off.] 1973. xiii, 403 p. illus. 24 cm. 'DA pam 550-52.' Supersedes 1966 ed. by E. E. Erickson, and others. 'One of a series of handbooks prepared by Foreign Area Studies (FAS) of the American University.' 1. Ecuador. I. Erickson, Edwin E. Area handbook for Ecuador. II. American University (Washington, D.C.). Foreign Area Studies. III. T.
F3708.W44   918.66/03   *LC* 73-601644

Meggers, Betty Jane.   • 3.9312
Ecuador / Betty J. Meggers. — New York: Praeger 1966. 220 p.: ill. — (Ancient peoples and places; v.49) 1. Indians of South America — Ecuador — Antiquities 2. Ecuador — Antiquities I. T. II. Series.
F3721.M4   980.4   *LC* 66-18341

Whitten, Norman E.   3.9313
Sicuanga Runa: the other side of development in Amazonian Ecuador / Norman E. Whitten, Jr. — Urbana: University of Illinois Press, c1985. xi, 314 p.: ill.; 24 cm. Includes index. 1. Canelo Indians 2. Indians of South America — Ecuador — Ethnic identity. 3. Power (Social sciences) 4. Ecuador — Ethnic relations. 5. Amazon River Region — Ethnic relations. I. T.
F3722.1.C23 W48 1985   986.6/400498 19   *LC* 84-155   *ISBN* 0252011171

Phelan, John Leddy, 1924-.   • 3.9314
The Kingdom of Quito in the seventeenth century; bureaucratic politics in the Spanish Empire. Madison, University of Wisconsin Press, 1967. xvi, 432 p. maps. 25 cm. 1. Morga, Antonio de, 1559-1636. 2. Ecuador — Politics and government — To 1814. 3. Spain — Colonies — America — Administration. 4. Quito (Audiencia) I. T.
F3733.P48   918.66/03/2   *LC* 67-25940